D1266088

CURRENT
BIOGRAPHY

WHO'S NEWS AND WHY
1 9 4 1

EDITOR
Maxine Block

MANAGING EDITOR
E. Mary Trow

THE H. W. WILSON COMPANY
NEW YORK, N. Y.

FOREWORD TO THE 1971 REISSUE

Responding to widespread demand from librarians and other researchers, The H. W. Wilson Company has brought back into print the six early volumes of Current Biography Yearbook, 1940-45. Although their style and format depart considerably from present editorial policy, the volumes constitute a rich source of information on persons of the World War II period. They provide contemporary viewpoints on major world figures and furnish valuable leads to further research into the lives of a host of authors, organization heads, war correspondents, and women military leaders. And their reference value is enhanced by photographs that are difficult or impossible to come by elsewhere. The Company is pleased to make these volumes once again available to serve the research and reference needs of the scholarly community.

CHARLES MORITZ

Preface

With a world at war the task of bringing the information in the twelve monthly issues of CURRENT BIOGRAPHY up to date has been difficult. But it has occasionally been lightened by incidents such as our encounter with Franklin Pierce Adams of *Information Please,* former columnist for the New York *Post* and widely known as "F. P. A." Over the telephone we asked the person answering (presumed to be F. P. A.'s secretary): "What is Mr. Adams doing currently?" The voice replied: "Currently Mr. Adams is answering the telephone."

All biographies, including their accompanying lists of references, have been brought up to date so far as time and the printer's "deadline" have allowed. In nearly every case it has been possible to consult for this purpose published materials in newspapers, periodicals and books issued up to December 31, 1941.

This is the second annual volume of CURRENT BIOGRAPHY and is a cumulation of all the material in the twelve monthly numbers of CURRENT BIOGRAPHY for 1941. (These can now be discarded.) The total of 991 biographies in this volume includes: 1) long biographies of living persons; 2) short obituary notices. Many readers may wonder why only a brief mention is made of such important national figures as the late Associate Justice of the Supreme Court, Louis D. Brandeis, while lesser known living people are written up at length. This policy is the result of having questioned librarians, who tell us that the interest in persons no longer living can usually be satisfied by a brief description of their careers. To such description it is our practice to add full dates of birth and death, a bibliography of articles, books and newspaper stories, and, most important of all, references to longer obituary notices from generally available sources such as the New York *Times.* Photographs are included for living people only, except for a few photographs which accompanied obituary notices in our January 1941 issue.

Research for CURRENT BIOGRAPHY is an arduous undertaking. It entails constant search for biographical material through general catalogs and indexes of books and periodicals, through miscellaneous sources of biographical information, plus the reading and clipping of quantities of newspaper and magazine articles, supplemented by numerous telephone calls and letters to persons, publishers, agencies, special libraries and similar sources of information. The Editorial Staff includes, besides the Managing Editor, E. Mary Trow, the following writers: Frances Jennings, Lillian Price and Violet Smith. They, with the part-time contributors, Ruth Lechlitner, Charles E. Smith, Albert Friedman, Miriam Allen deFord and Herbert B. Grimsditch, share the responsibility of research and the writing of most of the sketches. A clerical staff assists with the correspondence, physical details of clipping, filing, etc., with the preparation of copy for the printer and with the preliminary proofreading.

Where it has been possible to get in touch with the biographees they have been approached for additional information and for the correction of any possible errors in fact. In no sense, however, are these official or "authorized" biographies.

A photograph of the subject accompanies each full sketch. Whenever these have been obtained from individual studios appropriate credit has been given. Of the remaining photographs, those not furnished by the biographees themselves were obtained from the Press Association, Inc., Rockefeller Plaza, New York City.

MAXINE BLOCK
Editor

Explanations

Authorities for forms of names are the Library of Congress and the Wilson Company bibliographical indexes. Exception is made to the authorized form when the shortened form of a name is better known: e.g., Monty Woolley instead of Edgar Montillion Woolley. If the full name is not given in the heading it will be found in the sketch itself.

Following the name at the beginning of each sketch is its pronunciation, if difficult, and dates of birth and death, so far as available. The person's occupation is next given. Following this information is the sketch proper, and after it a list of references to additional sources of information, including magazine and newspaper references (in one alphabet) and books. Space limitations require that these bibliographies be short, but an effort is made to include the most usable materials. For persons no longer living, references to obituaries in newspapers and magazines are added. The books chosen for listing are limited to those of a biographical or autobiographical nature, including such well known reference tools as *Who's Who, Who's Who in America,* etc. The absence of a date after the title of a publication which is issued annually indicates that the volume used is the latest published.

Magazine articles are listed under *References* in abbreviated form (see list "Periodicals and Newspapers Consulted" for complete title). The form of entry is as follows: *Mag Art* 32:78-9 S '39 por. This means that an article supplementing our sketch will be found in *Magazine of Art,* volume 32, pages 78-9, in the September 1939 number. The abbreviation *por* means that the article is accompanied by a portrait. In the case of newspapers, the name of the paper is followed by paging and date.

When a name is followed by "See sketch 1940 Annual" reference is made to the volume of CURRENT BIOGRAPHY published in December 1940.

Dr. W. Cabell Greet, professor of English at Barnard College, editor of *American Speech* and speech consultant to the Columbia Broadcasting System, and Mr. Jules Van Item of the National Broadcasting Company's Shortwave Listening Station have been consulted for CURRENT BIOGRAPHY's pronunciations.

At the end of this volume a complete index of all biographies published in 1940 and 1941 is given.

KEY TO PRONUNCIATION

āle, chăotic, câre, ădd, ăccount, ärm, ȧsk, sofȧ, saw; ēve, ĕvent, ĕnd, silĕnt, makĕr; īce, ill, charĭty; N=French nasal sound, as in boN; ōld, ŏbey, ôrb, ŏdd, cŏnnect; fōōd, fŏŏt; out, oil; cūbe, ŭnite, ûrn, ŭp, circŭs, menü; kh=ch in German ich, ach, zh=z in azure; " =secondary accent, ' =main accent

Contents

KEY TO ABBREVIATIONS

AAA	Agricultural Adjustment Administration
A.C.L.U.	American Civil Liberties Union
A. d. c.	Aide-de-camp
A. E. F.	American Expeditionary Force
A.F. of L.	American Federation of Labor
Ag	August
A. I. C. P.	New York Association for Improving the Condition of the Poor
A. M. A.	American Medical Association
Ap	April
A. P.	Associated Press
ASCAP	American Society of Composers, Authors and Publishers
assn	association
AYC	American Youth Congress
B. A.	Bachelor of Arts
BBC	British Broadcasting Corporation
B. D.	Bachelor of Divinity
B. E. F.	British Expeditionary Force
B. L.	Bachelor of Letters
blvd	boulevard
B. S.	Bachelor of Science
C. B.	Companion of the Bath
C. B. E.	Commander of (the Order of) the British Empire
CBS	Columbia Broadcasting System
C. I. O.	Congress of Industrial Organizations
C. M. G.	Companion of (the Order of) St. Michael and St. George
cond	condensed
C. P. A.	Certified Public Accountant
CROM	Confederación Regional Obrera Mexicano (Mexican Regional Confederation of Workers)
CTM	Confederación de Trabajadores Mexicanos (Confederation of Mexican Workers)
CWA	Civil Works Administration
D	December
DAR	Daughters of the American Revolution
D. C. L.	Doctor of Civil Law
D. D.	Doctor of Divinity
D. Eng.	Doctor of Engineering
D. Litt.	Doctor of Literature
Dr.	Doctor
D. Sc.	Doctor of Science
D. S. M.	Distinguished Service Medal
D. S. O.	Distinguished Service Order
ed	edited, edition, editor
F	February

FBI	Federal Bureau of Investigation
FCC	Federal Communications Commission
FERA	Federal Emergency Relief Administration
FHA	Federal Housing Administration
Four A's	American Association of Advertising Agencies
F. P. A.	Franklin Pierce Adams
G. B. E.	Knight or Dame Grand Cross Order of the British Empire
G. C. B.	Knight Grand Cross of the Bath
G.C.V.O.	Knight Grand Cross of Royal Victorian Order
G. H. A.	Group Health Association
G. H. Q.	General Headquarters
G. M.	General Motors
H. M.	His Majesty
il	illustration
I. L. A.	International Longshoremen's Association
I. L. G. W. U.	International Ladies' Garment Workers' Union
I. L. O.	International Labor Office
Inc	Incorporated
INS	International News Service
I. R. A.	Irish Republican Army
I. W. W.	Industrial Workers of the World
Ja	January
J. C. B.	Juris Canonici Bachelor
J. D.	Doctor of Jurisprudence
Je	June
Jl	July
K. C.	King's Council
K. C. B.	Knight Commander of the Bath
L. H. D.	Doctor of Letters of Humanity
Litt. D.	Doctor of Letters
LL. B.	Bachelor of Laws
LL. D.	Doctor of Laws
LL. M.	Master of Laws
M. A.	Master of Arts
mag	magazine
M. C.	Military Cross
M. D.	Doctor of Medicine
MGM	Metro-Goldwyn-Mayer
Mgr.	Monsignor, Monseigneur
M. Litt.	Master of Literature
M. P.	Member of Parliament
Mr	March
M. R. A.	Moral Rearmament
M. S. or M. Sc.	Master of Science
My	May
N	November
N. A. M.	National Association of Manufacturers
NBC	National Broadcasting System
nd	no date
NLRB	National Labor Relations Board

N. M. U.	National Maritime Union
no	number
ns	new series
NYA	National Youth Administration
O	October
o. p.	out of print
OPM	Office of Production Management
p	page
PAFA	Pennsylvania Academy of Fine Arts
pam	pamphlet
P. E. N.	Poets, Playwrights, Editors, Essayists and Novelists (International Association)
Ph. B.	Bachelor of Philosophy
Ph. D.	Doctor of Philosophy
pl-s	plate, -s
por-s	portrait, -s
P. R. M.	Party of the Mexican Revolution
pseud.	pseudonym
pt	part
PWA	Public Works Administration
R	Review
R. A.	Royal Academician
R. A. F.	Royal Air Force
RCA	Radio Corporation of America
RFC	Reconstruction Finance Corporation
R. H. A.	Royal Hibernian Academy; Royal Horse Artillery
RKO	Radio Keith Orpheum
S	September
SEC	Security Exchange Commission
ser	series
S. J. D.	Doctor Juristic Science
SPAB	Supply Priorities and Allocation Board
S. T. B.	Bachelor of Sacred Theology
S. T. D.	Doctor of Sacred Theology
sup	supplement
SWOC	Steel Workers' Organizing Committee
tab	tabulation
TNEC	Temporary National Economic Committee
tr	translated, translation, translator
T. U. C.	Trades Union Congress
TVA	Tennessee Valley Authority
U.A.W.A.	United Auto Workers of America
U. P.	United Press
U.S.S.R.	Union of Socialist Soviet Republics
v	volume
V. M. I.	Virginia Military Institute
w	weekly
WPA	Work Projects Administration
YMCA	Young Men's Christian Association

CURRENT BIOGRAPHY

1941

ABBOTT, BUD Oct. 2, 1900- Stage and screen comedian
Address: b. c/o Universal Pictures Corp, Universal City, Calif; h. Stony Brook, Long Island, N. Y.

COSTELLO, LOU Mar. 6, 1908- Stage and screen comedian
Address: b. c/o Universal Pictures Corp, Universal City, Calif; h. Paterson, N. J.

BUD ABBOTT and LOU COSTELLO

Since 1929 Bud Abbott has been knocking Lou Costello around. A lean and hawk-eyed wise guy, he has been getting his roly-poly and not-so-very-bright partner into trouble in vaudeville, on the stage, in night clubs, over the radio and most recently in the films. It is all old-fashioned farce, sometimes brought up to date by modern cracks, more often not. This team believes that people want to be entertained without mental effort and it has stuck to buffoonery and belly laughs throughout the years. "Ours is a talking act," says Abbott. "A loud talking act," adds Costello. "One might call it corn," they both admit, ". . . but we like it."

The straight man of the partnership was born William Abbott in Asbury Park, New Jersey, where his father, Harry Abbott, was at the time advance man for Ringling Brothers' Circus and his mother was performing as a bareback rider. By the time he was old enough to go to school his family had moved to Coney Island in New York, where Public School 100 had him as a pupil until he "could outrun the truant officers." He was in the fourth grade. From then on he helped his father a little, did odd jobs around and painted a lot of signs until at the age of 15 he ran afoul a Mickey Finn in a Brooklyn beer joint and was shanghaied onto a ship sailing for Norway.

Abbott jumped ship at Bergen and worked his way back to New York, where his father was now associated with one of the burlesque chains. He got Bud a job as assistant cashier in the Casino Theatre in Brooklyn. It wasn't long before Bud had saved enough money to form a show of his own which he called *Broadway Flashes*. From producing this, he went on, in partnership with his brother, to operate burlesque houses all over. First there was Abbott's Corinthian Theatre in Rochester; then houses in Buffalo, Toronto, Cleveland. And finally there came overexpansion. Abbott sold his interests and by 1929 was back in a Brooklyn box office, in the Empire Theatre. It was here that he met Costello.

Costello hadn't been idle either. His father ran a small silk mill in Paterson, New Jersey, where Lou was born in 1908 and christened Louis Francis Cristello. He wanted his son to be a doctor, but it was soon clear that schooling and Lou would never agree. He was the kind of boy in Public Schools 11 and 15 who pulled girls' pigtails, brought frogs to school in his pockets, hid coats and hats—"I was a perfect brute," he confesses. Night after night he had to stay after school and write on the blackboard 50 times: "I'm a bad boy." Since this later became his tag line, he feels his attempts at an education were worthwhile.

He quit high school to work in a local haberdashery and quit this position to become an actor. His first pilgrimage west ended in Pittsburgh, where he worked in a slaughter house for $8 a week. Back in Paterson he was "spoined" by a chorus girl and tried to end it all as a prize fighter. Fourteen fights and a number of broken ribs later, he was out on the West Coast being bounced over half the back lots of Hollywood as a studio stunt man. He was tossed from high

ABBOTT, BUD and COSTELLO, LOU
—Continued

places, bruised by whole football teams, chased by gorillas. "Yep," comments Costello, "I always was a very athletic fellow." "But," he adds, "my shape was different then."

Doubling for stars like Dolores Del Rio fired Lou with ambitions to become an actor. "When the talkies came in," he says, "I saw a lot of the actors was hotfooting it to New York for voice lessons. So I says if you gotta have voice lessons to be an actor, that's for me. So I decided to go to New York." On his way there he was stranded in St. Joseph, Missouri and hastened to answer a show's advertisement for a "Dutch" comedian. He got the job, changed his name to Costello and afterward stayed in burlesque and vaudeville, both in stock and on the circuit.

One of his engagements was for a week at the Empire Theatre in Brooklyn, New York. He had a straight man by then who was needed for the act. But the straight man fell ill, and Lou was at his wits' end looking for someone to replace him. Bud Abbott, in the box office, offered to fill in for a few nights—and never stopped. "Bud and I was right for each other," Lou knew from their first appearance together. They played most of the burlesque and many of the vaudeville circuits together, clowning, getting off old jokes, knocking each other around. Neither of them ever used a script. Abbott says it's because Costello "fumbles all over such things. He is one guy who gets lost when you give him directions."

Their first real break came in 1938 when a booker from the Loew's circuit caught their act in Washington. He signed them for a week at Loew's State in New York, and it was there that Ted Collins, Kate Smith's radio impresario, saw them. He gave them a 10-minute guest appearance spot on Kate Smith's program and from then on they appeared regularly on the program for a year and one-half. At first it was hard to tell over the air "who was asking and who was answering," but Lou fixed that up by adopting a thin falsetto which fitted in with his "I'm a bad boy" tag line. In the summer of 1940 they came on the radio again in Fred Allen's (see sketch this issue) place on NBC. There were critics, of course, who found their verbal slapstick "unoriginal and unfunny," but the public seemed to like their noisy, fast and foolish antics.

By the time they were filling in for Fred Allen, though, they had come up far from the early days of their partnership. As Abbott put it: "We have been partners 10 years— Minsky burlesque, vaudeville, presentation houses, lotsa hard times. Then we go over on the radio and we're sitting pretty." There was an engagement at Billy Rose's Casa Mañana and this brought an offer from the revue, *The Streets of Paris*, in 1939. The boys took it and with it got top billing, presenting on Broadway and at the New York World's Fair what was considered "some of the best music-hall clowning of our time."

They continued on Kate Smith's hour, too, and also managed to put on a talking act at the *Versailles* night club at supper.

But the success from this triple engagement was mild compared with what happened to Abbott and Costello when Hollywood got hold of them. Actually Hollywood had been blessed with their services before, in 1938, when they made *One Night in the Tropics*, "an indiscretion better overlooked." But it wasn't until *Buck Privates* burst upon an enraptured country that Hollywood remembered this. Called "the best and most promising clowns to hit the screen in 10 years," Abbott and Costello bowled over the country with their personal brand of foolishness, with Abbott's straight-man playing, with Costello's bumbling, lovable dopiness. It had cost only $180,000 to make *Buck Privates*. One of the biggest "sleepers" of all time, it returned more than a million dollars. Abbott and Costello were more surprised than anyone. "It's just the same old stuff we've always been doin'," they insisted.

Before this picture there had been some talk of having Abbott and Costello streamline their patter to some extent—having them use gags at least no older than 10 years. They fought this outrageous idea. And they won. *In the Navy*, which followed, stuck to the same pattern, with Costello magnificent as an admiral directing the mad maneuvering of a battleship in a desperate attempt to impress his girl, both of them startling in one of the wildest shell games of all time. There were criticisms of these two pictures, however, even from the fans. They felt that Abbott and Costello didn't need in their films the frequent services of the Andrews Sisters or even Dick Powell. As a result the boys were allowed to run most of the show in *Hold That Ghost*, a full-blown comedy thriller, and in *Keep 'Em Flying*, the saga of their encounter with the air corps.

These pictures are bringing in Abbott and Costello about $6,000 a week and they're enjoying success. They both have comfortable homes—Abbott's is in Stony Brook, Long Island; Costello's in Paterson, New Jersey— big cars and little swimming pools. They don't enjoy affluence together much, though. Abbott sticks close to Long Island, to his wife, Betty Smith Pratt, and to his five dogs; Costello likes Paterson, New Jersey, his wife, Ann Battler, and his two daughters, Patricia and Carol. But they keep close tabs on each other. "Everything I buy is in good taste," Abbott says. "Anything that Costello buys is just pure dog."

References

Collier's 108:42+ O 25 '41 pors
N Y Post p26 S 19 '41 pors
N Y Times IX p10 Ag 11 '40 pors; IX p5 Mr 23 '41; VII p8, 27 Ag 24 '41 pors
N Y World-Telegram p15 Mr 26 '40 por; p3 Je 14 '41 pors
New Yorker 15:16-17 Jl 8 '39
Newsweek 16:44 Jl 1 '40 pors
PM p24 Jl 3 '40 pors

ABBOTT, EDITH Sept. 26, 1876- Social worker; educator

Address: b. Faculty Exchange, University of Chicago, Chicago, Ill; h. 5544 Woodlawn Ave, Chicago, Ill.

Fernand De Gueldre

EDITH ABBOTT

The School of Social Service Administration at the University of Chicago in 1940 completed 20 years of its existence as one of the outstanding professional schools in a great University. It is Edith Abbott who, as dean of this school for the past 17 years, must be given credit for its remarkable history and excellent reputation. Miss Abbott came to her present position in 1924, after having been a member of the faculty of that University since 1913. During most of that time, from 1908 to 1920, she was a resident of Hull House, and later she assisted with the work of her sister, Grace Abbott, well known as former chief of the United States Children's Bureau. She has developed throughout her career her early interest, she says, "in the application of the use of social research methods in advancing the social reform program."

Nebraska born and bred, Edith Abbott comes of pioneer stock. She was born at Grand Island, Nebraska, September 26, 1876, the daughter of Othman A. and Elizabeth (Griffin) Abbott. On her father's side she represents the ninth generation of a family which came to this country in 1640 and was among the earliest settlers of Andover, Massachusetts. On her mother's side she comes from a colonial Quaker family which settled in DeKalb County, Illinois, the abolitionist section of the state. Her mother, born in a log house where the family kept a station on the "underground railroad," became noted for pioneer educational work in the West; in 1941, at the age of 96, she was still living in the Grand Island, Nebraska homestead.

Miss Abbott writes that in her childhood in this town on the old Overland Trail she experienced most of the difficulties of pioneer life. She saw the covered wagons moving West; she knew as a child the Pawnee Indians, gradually dispersed and disinherited through white encroachment on their lands. Her father became the first Lieutenant Governor of Nebraska and was a member of the first two constitutional conventions of that state.

For five years Edith Abbott attended an Episcopalian boarding school, Brownell Hall, in Omaha, and she was graduated from the University of Nebraska in 1901. She took an active part in college life, was author of the class play, and winner of Phi Beta Kappa honors.

Awarded a fellowship in economics at the University of Chicago, Miss Abbott received her Ph. D. degree there in 1905. She also took work in the Law School. The following year she held the European fellowship of the American Association of University Women and studied at the London School of Economics and Political Science of the University of London. She enjoyed her work there, but says that she counts as her greatest influence her contact with Mrs. Sydney Webb, who was then directing the research work for the Royal Commission on the Poor Laws and Relief of Distress.

Following her return to this country Miss Abbott taught economics for a year (1907-08) at Wellesley College. She was then offered the opportunity of joining the group of social reformers at Hull House who were "trying to set up a program of social investigation." In the research department of the Chicago School of Civics and Philanthropy (later the School of Social Service Administration) established by a grant of the Russell Sage Foundation, Miss Abbott began a series of studies that was afterward incorporated into a book, *The Tenements of Chicago, 1908-35* (1936). Her first book, however, published in 1910, was *Women in Industry*.

Becoming interested in the Juvenile Court of Chicago, she was co-author (with Sophonisba Breckinridge) of *The Delinquent Child and the Home* (1912). The year following, as statistician for the Chicago City Council Commission on Crime, she began a period of 10 years of work which led to various reports on the treatment of offenders in Chicago and particularly in the county jails of Illinois. Studies were also undertaken for the new United States Children's Bureau—in particular those of the early Mother's Aid experiment in Illinois. Her next publications were two large volumes on immigration problems. Appointed a consultant on the Wickersham Commission, she published in 1931 a series of studies on immigration and crime. When the depression led to great increases in relief and the organization of the new state relief administrations, Miss Abbott became a forceful advocate of the development of Federal aid for relief.

Meanwhile the School of Social Service Administration at the University of Chicago, of which she was dean, had expanded rapidly,

ABBOTT, EDITH—*Continued*
and for the next 10 years, from 1924 on, it registered more than 1,000 graduate students every year. Under her direction this school has been highly influential in public welfare administration and has published some three-score substantial volumes (many of them edited by Miss Abbott) as contributions to this field of work. Her most recently published book (1940), *Public Assistance,* is "a compilation of selected documents on public relief." Reading it, as one reviewer has written, "one gets a very good idea of the historical settings of our major welfare problems, and one is aware of the passion and insight of a great scholar and teacher whose influence extends beyond the walls of the classroom and whose message is timely for the intelligent layman as well as for the professional expert."

Miss Abbott was president of the American Association of Schools of Social Work for two terms and, in 1937, president of the National Conference of Social Work, the eighth woman in a period of sixty years to hold this office. She is currently the editor of the *Social Service Review,* a quarterly published by the University of Chicago Press. She has been a member of various boards and investigating committees of many social agencies, member of the Advisory Committee of the Cook County Bureau of Public Welfare since its organization in 1924, of the Advisory Committee of the Children's and Minors' Service of the Chicago Relief Administration since 1933, and president of the Illinois Conference of Social Work in 1939. She holds several honorary college degrees.

Despite her many scholarly publications, Edith Abbott prefers to be known simply as a social worker and as an educator of social workers. She is, she says, a pacifist, although she supports President Roosevelt because she believes in his social welfare program. A lifelong liberal with progressive ideas (she is proud that she comes from the home state of George Norris), she is not only a social worker, but a social reformer.

References

> Ind Woman 18:357 N '39 por
> Nat Conf Soc Work 1937:3-25 por
>   (front)
> Survey 73:190 Je '37 por
> Survey G 25:370-2 Je '36 il pors
> American Women
> Leaders in Education 1941
> Who's Who in America

ABBOTT, EDWIN MILTON June 4, 1877 —Nov. 8, 1940 Lawyer who was counsel for the late Smedley D. Butler; attorney to the Pennsylvania Department of Justice and secretary of the American Institute of Criminal Law and Criminology; as poet he wrote *Thoughts in Verse.*

References

> Who's Who Among North American Authors
> Who's Who in America
> Who's Who in Law

Obituaries

> N Y Herald Tribune p10 N 9 '40
> N Y Times p17 N 9 '40

ABETZ, OTTO (ä′bĕts)   Mar. 26, 1903-Ambassador of the Third Reich to the Vichy Government; High Commissioner of Occupied France

OTTO ABETZ

On July 4, 1939 Otto Abetz was expelled from France, suspected of being chief of the Nazi Fifth Column in that country. More than one Cabinet Minister and Cabinet Minister's wife must have grieved at his departure; and certain aristocratic and intellectual circles were desolated by the loss of such a charming and brilliant young man, so sincere, so peace-loving, so devoted to France —and with so much money to spend. In August 1940 the same people may or may not have been comforted: Otto Abetz came back to Paris in the uniform of Ambassador from the Third Reich, bearing the further rank of High Commissioner of Occupied France. Certainly no German better deserved the position.

Heinrich Otto Abetz, the son of a poor estate manager in Hanover, Germany, grew up around the time of the First World War. He lost his father when he was only 13. Idealistic, with artistic ambitions, he attended a fine arts school in the Grand Duchy of Baden and began his career as a drawing teacher during the difficult post-War period. With Briand in power in France and Stresemann in Germany, liberals were doing all they could to better relations between the two countries. There were international literary and scientific conventions; actors' companies were exchanged; a Franco-German Society was formed. Abetz, a Catholic working in the German Youth Movement, took an active part in all of this. He studied French literature, traveled in the French provinces, married a French girl from Lille (Suzanne de Brouckère, former secretary of his friend Jean Luchaire); from the industrial circles close to Stresemann he found patrons who helped to finance German-French youth congresses, supplemented by group tours of Germany and France, the publication of a Franco-German magazine at Stuttgart, the founding of a vacation camp in the Black Forest country of Sohlberg, where German and French youths lived together and swore eternal friendship. This movement, democratic and pacifistic, was discouraged by Stresemann's successors: youth congresses were canceled, the Franco-German Society dissolved.

Exactly what Abetz was doing just before Hitler's rise to power remains a little obscure. In any case, it is reported that it was 1932 when Von Ribbentrop (see sketch this issue) noticed him and suggested that he might be useful to the Nazis. Abetz hesitated at first, according to most versions of the story, and then was "simply drafted" to go to France to renew his old acquaintances and activities.

Jules Romains described him in 1934: "a healthy fellow, with reddish hair, an open, freckled face with frank, clear-cut features, a pleasant voice, often interrupted by laughter. . ." He spoke "impeccable French." He created an impression of "deepest sincerity." He represented himself as a western German who felt a bond of brotherhood with the Belgians, the northern French and the Swiss, nothing but aversion for the Prussians: as a "Man of Good Will" working "from the inside" in order to try to direct the Nazi movement (which had its regrettable features) into useful and pacific channels. Already, he confided, he had secured the confidence of one of Nazidom's rising men—Von Ribbentrop—who, though not yet in a position of great power, represented the more healthy and stable elements in Germany, and who promised to be very helpful. Romains, originator of a youth movement of his own—the July Ninth group—was charmed by the young German, inclined to believe him. He welcomed German speakers at a meeting of his group, accepted an invitation from Abetz to lecture in Germany in November 1934, let Abetz choose the subject of the lecture, was touched by a visit to Abetz's shabby apartment in Germany and the sight of his devoted French wife and the small son who symbolized Abetz's ideal of spiritual unity between the two countries.

M. Romains was by no means Herr Abetz's only success. His acquaintances broadened rapidly. He acquired honorary rank on the staff of Von Ribbentrop, later Germany's Foreign Minister. He became prosperous. (He is said to have disposed of 350,000 francs a month by himself.) He stayed at the Hôtel Irena in Paris and dined at Fouquet's on the Champs Élysées. He numbered among his dinner companions industrialists, statesmen, deputies, senators, aristocrats, intellectuals. He lectured to French clubs, veterans' associa-

tions, and also to organizations of German Nazis living in France. He was the guiding spirit of the *Comité France-Allemagne*. He could be depended upon to put Fascist parties and groups in touch with the press attaché of the German Embassy. He was always welcome at the Club Rive Gauche. It was through his efforts that the Franco-German Society and magazine were revived. He saw to it that papers whose policies Berlin approved received large advertising contracts. He was known as one always willing to lend money to hard up journalists or even bankers' wives. Authors were grateful to him for having helped sell their books to German publishers. They had received royalties in advance, even though the books themselves might gather dust in German files.

Many, too, were the distinguished Frenchmen who accepted invitations to tour Germany with all expenses paid and who came back thinking the Nazi evil had been slightly exaggerated. Herr Abetz was subtle: he didn't necessarily try to make Frenchmen into National Socialists; if he could create the impression that there was no reason why France and Germany should ever become enemies it was, very often, enough.

He found willing and efficient cooperation in high quarters as well. Among his close associates were Edouard Pfeiffer, former general secretary of the Radical Socialists and personal friend of Daladier; Count de Fels, who served as a liaison officer between Abetz and Flandin (see sketch this issue); Fernand de Brinon, editor of *L'Information,* who worked in the service of both Abetz and Georges Bonnet and who was vice-president of the *Comité France-Allemagne.* Georges Bonnet, Daladier's Foreign Minister, and Madame Bonnet were particularly dear friends. No one could have done more than this attractive young German to pave the way for Munich. Yet, after Munich, when Abetz accompanied Von Ribbentrop to Paris for the signature of the Franco-German accord of December 6, 1938 and proceeded to organize the official parties in celebration of the occasion, the guests found him as charming as ever. It was only after he had been repeatedly exposed in a very few such papers as Henri de Kérillis' *L'Époque* and after extensive Nazi espionage in France brought a number of arrests that French officialdom decided it could part with him. He went first to Belgium, then, in September 1939, returned to Berlin to direct the services of propaganda in France. Throughout the War he kept in close touch with his informers and agents in Paris.

In 1941 he is back in France, under slightly different circumstances. He has performed miracles in bringing about the fullest possible cooperation between Vichy and Germany's "new order." "And yet," Jules Romains mourns, "it is not certain that Abetz was a knave. It is not certain that he was not, in 1934, the man of good will, disinter-

ABETZ, OTTO—*Continued*

ested and fervent, of whom he gave me the picture. . ."

References

Cur Hist 52:17-19+ Ja 23 '41 por
Eur Nouv 22:737-8 Jl 8 '39; 22:817 Jl 29 '39
Liv Age 359:134-6 O '40
New Repub 100:72 Ag 23 '39
PM p5 Ag 20 '40
Sat Eve Post 213:27+ N 9 '40 por; 213:27+ N 16 '40
Pol, H. Suicide of a Democracy 1940

ACHESON, ALBERT R(OBERT) (ăch'-ĕ-sŭn) Oct. 12, 1882—Feb. 25, 1941 Mechanical engineer; head of the Department of Mechanical Engineering in the College of Applied Science at Syracuse University; notable as a consultant in the field of heating, ventilation and steam generation; and identified as consultant with the perfection of The Associated Press wire-photo.

References

Who's Who in America

Obituaries

N Y Times p21 F 26 '41

ACHESON, DEAN (GOODERHAM) (ăch'-ĕ-sŭn) Apr. 11, 1893- Assistant Secretary of State

Address: b. Department of State, Washington, D. C.; h. 2805 P St, N. W., Washington, D. C.

DEAN ACHESON

The appointment of Dean Acheson to the position of Assistant Secretary of State in January 1941 was considered a significant one by many commentators. For many months Mr. Acheson had been active in promoting American aid for Great Britain as a member of the Committee to Defend America by Aiding the Allies. He had stated firmly that "the defeat of Hitler is essential for the continuance of free government and free life in this country and for its security and independence"; he had been one of four lawyers who published an opinion that the destroyer-naval base deal with Britain was legal.

As a firm supporter of aid to Britain, as well as a prominent lawyer and former Under-Secretary of the Treasury, Dean Acheson was a logical choice to carry out the Administration's intentions in the Department of State. It was understood that he would "coordinate State Department activities in connection with the British purchasing and other agencies by serving as connecting link with the British Embassy and the Treasury," and would "also aid Secretary [of State] Hull in dealing with other important questions as they arise." One of the important questions which Acheson has dealt with since his appointment is aid to Russia. In July 1941 a Soviet military mission held consultations with him. And in October Secretary of State Hull issued orders creating a Board of Economic Operations with Acheson as its chairman—its duties to "assist in formulating policies and coordinate the activities of the various divisions of which the board is composed."

In 1940 and 1941 Dean Acheson was thoroughly in agreement with President Roosevelt's policies, a supporter of a third term ("in this time of crisis I believe that the safety of our country and all it stands for can best be assured by the election of President Roosevelt") and the head of one of the Administration's important committees. Such harmony did not always exist, however. In 1933 Mr. Acheson collided heavily with Roosevelt's policies in his first governmental position.

He came to this position with the reputation of a first-rate lawyer, a reputation he still has. He was born in Middletown, Connecticut, the son of Edward Campion and Eleanor (Gooderham) Acheson, and intended to be a lawyer almost from the start. First came a B. A. from Yale University in 1915 and then a Bachelor of Laws degree from Harvard University three years later. Before graduation he had married Alice Stanley of Detroit, Michigan in 1917 and served as an ensign in the United States Navy during the First World War. (They now have two daughters and one son.)

In 1919 Acheson got a position that almost every Harvard man of his generation wanted —he became secretary to Supreme Court Judge Louis D. Brandeis, who used to pick the star man of each class to assist him. With two years' experience with Brandeis behind him he entered the Washington law firm of Covington, Burling and Rublee in 1921 and remained there until 1933, when he was appointed Under-Secretary of the Treasury. It was thought at the time that Roosevelt made the appointment because of Acheson's association with Brandeis. But though Acheson had been affected by Brandeis' legal liberalism, his own economic ideology, it was generally felt, was less liberal.

Acheson remained at the Treasury for exactly six months, making a success of his job despite the fact that he was a lawyer rather than an economist or financial expert. Then the gold-purchase plan came up. Acheson's position was that it was illegal. He was emphatic in his view; it was impossible for him to carry out the policy; and Roosevelt asked for his resignation.

Acheson returned to his old firm, now Covington, Burling, Rublee, Acheson and Shorb, on January 1, 1934 and devoted himself to its large and prosperous practice. It was not until February 1939 that he again became associated with the government. It was at this time that he headed a committee appointed by the Attorney General which was set up to study the problem of administrative tribunals, "to suggest improvements to make the process more workable." At the end of January 1941 this committee made its report on "judicial fair play" in the New Deal reform agencies, a report which the New York *Times* hailed as "a landmark in the history of administrative reform."

The Assistant Secretary of State is a dark-haired, mustached, young-looking man who is a Fellow of the Yale Corporation, a trustee of the Brookings Institute and a member of Washington's Metropolitan Club and of the Century Club of New York.

References

> N Y Times p13 O 2 '40; p9 Ja 24 '41; p1, 9 Ja 25 '41; p20 F 1 '41
> Time 37:14 F 3 '41
> U S News 10:14 Ja 31 '41 por
> America's Young Men 1936-37
> Who's Who in America
> Who's Who in Law
> Who's Who in the Nation's Capital

ADAMS, FRANKLIN P(IERCE) Nov. 15, 1881- Author; member of the *Information Please* radio program

Address: h. Westport, Conn.

> Bulletin: Mr. Adams sends us the following information: "Fired from the New York *Post* on August 15, 1941, 5:02 Eastern D. S. T."

From July 1941 issue:

Franklin P. Adams, according to Frank Sullivan, "is not exactly handsome, yet he has élan. He is no Cesar Romero, yet he is not a Wallace Beery, either. Franklin has a certain electric dash and affects a kind of leer which seems to madden women." He affects other people other ways. His column, "The Conning Tower" in the New York *Post*, his grumpish, nimble comments on *Information Please*, his verse, comments, puns and rambling recollections of his weekly sorties, meetings, meals and reading have won for him what he calls "my adorers," a certain number of skeptics and even an occasional mild detractor.

> *For the purpose of record in history's book*
> *I was born in Illinois, County of Cook,*

Ray Lee Jackson

FRANKLIN P. ADAMS

he says. He was the son of Moses and Clara (Schlossman) Adams and was brought up in what, less poetically, is known as Chicago. F. P. A. (short for Franklin Pierce Adams) still remembers how

> *In our yard, near the drying shirts and socks*
> *I planted nasturtiums and four o'clocks.*

From 1889 to 1899 this occupation was interrupted by schooling at the Douglas School and at the Armour Institute of Technology, from which he was graduated in 1899. From there F. P. A. went to the University of Michigan "and almost completed my freshman year." Then he set out to earn his living. His first job was as an insurance supply clerk with Adolph Loeb & Son in Chicago; his next as an insurance solicitor. This job was an enlightening one. "Once," he recalls, "I asked George Ade to insure his household furniture and wearing apparel. This was on February 22, 1901. He was having breakfast at 11 o'clock in the morning, and strawberries—not a common breakfast for 1901, when we didn't have strawberries until June. So I thought: 'A writer's life for me.'"

By 1903 it had begun. For $25 a week he conducted a column in the Chicago *Journal* called "A Little About Everything" and wrote a daily weather story. One year later, despite an increase to $30, he came to New York and since then, he says: "I have done the same sort of work on the New York *Evening Mail, Tribune, World, Herald Tribune* [and *Post*]. If I had enough money I should do no work."

The *Evening Mail* column was called "Always in Good Humor," and the publisher insisted its name be lived up to. This was a strain, endured, however, until the end of 1913, when F. P. A. went over to the *Tribune,* his

ADAMS, FRANKLIN P.—*Continued*
farewell to the *Mail* being an Horatian ode,
Exegi monumentum aere perennius, which,
read acrostically, said "Read the *Tribune*."
His followers did, slightly relieved at the
new title, "The Conning Tower." They
were legion, for F. P. A.'s reputation as a wit
was, even then, no mean one. "Writers,
artists, dowagers and debs discussed his epigrams. Latin professors entertained their
classes with his versified translations of Horatian odes."

The daily stint, if not the wit, was interrupted for a while during the First World War,
in which F. P. A. served in the Intelligence
and wrote an occasional column, "The Listening Post," for the A. E. F. magazine, *The
Stars and Stripes.* He recalls his experiences
fondly:

> *I didn't fight and I didn't shoot
> But, General, how I did salute!*

After the War it was back to the *Tribune*
until 1923, when F. P. A. shifted over to the
World, and after the *World* expired in 1931 he
went back to the *Tribune,* now the *Herald
Tribune.*

For his "Conning Tower" in the *Herald Tribune,* syndicated in six newspapers, F. P. A.
received $25,000 a year at first and later $21,852.
But all was not sweetness and light between
him and Ogden Reid, the *Herald Tribune's* publisher. It has been whispered that Mr. Reid
didn't want F. P. A. on his newspaper in the
first place. And it is definitely known that
when F. P. A.'s contract ran out in 1934 he
missed a column for the first time in his history
until it was renewed. When it came up for
renewal again, sitting it out seemed no solution,
and in 1937 F. P. A. left the *Herald Tribune.*
He explained it easily: "They just wanted
me to work for less money, whereas I wanted
to work for more." He settled for a job with
the New York *Post* in May 1937.

"The Conning Tower" today differs little
from F. P. A.'s columns when he was but a
sprig of a boy. "His prose has been divided
between sane and salty comment on the current
United States scene, good humored corrections
of misquotations and bad grammar by other
journalists and the weekly 'Diary of Our Own
Samuel Pepys.'" Not infrequently his personal appreciation of the humor in situations
has got him into trouble. Once, back in 1921,
when P. F. Collier ran a full-page advertisement of Dr. Eliot's *Five-foot Shelf of Books,*
F. P. A. kidded it. He was rewarded by a
letter from the *Tribune's* business manager:
"I want to thank you for . . . yesterday's
column. It has cost us only about $12,000 in
the first 24 hours. My congratulations on your
effective work."

F. P. A.'s verse, despite the devastating twist
he usually manages to get into the last line
of a poem, has, on the whole, caused less
trouble. It is "mocking and impudent," written
in "rackety rhythms" and honest rhymes. Free
verse he scorns—he knows it is used because

> *The editors
> Buy it
> At
> So much
> A
> Line*

Many of the poems have been published in book
form, beginning with *Tobogganing on Parnassus* in 1910 (this venture was preceded by a
musical comedy, *Lo,* written with O. Henry)
and proceeding through 10 volumes until the
publication of *The Melancholy Lute,* his own
selection of the outpourings of 30 years, in
1936. Unimpressed by this, he still says his
favorite recreation is "not writing."

Once a week "The Conning Tower's" survey
of the general scene is interrupted by F. P. A.'s
survey of his own particular scene in "The
Diary of Our Own Samuel Pepys." He started
this back in 1911 "solely to get a day off." "At
the beginning," he confesses, "I tried to be fa-
cetious, using the old dodge of paraphrasing
modern slang in archaic words. I wince now
at reading it." Today in a mildly seventeenth
century form he tells the reader what he ate
during the week, the tennis and poker he
played, the books he read, the clothes he wore,
the teeth he had repaired, the plays he saw and,
particularly, the comings, goings and sayings of
his friends. They include most of Manhattan's
artists and writers, and a typical sentence
might run something like this: "At Neysa
[McMein's] and later to George and Beatrice
Kaufman's where I sat with Mrs. Dorothy
Parker who is deeply cherished by me; then
on to an evening with H. Swope, M. Van
Doren," etc., etc. The record of these excursions and activities has been preserved in two
volumes published in 1935 and dedicated to
F. P. A.'s children, Anthony, Timothy, Perse-
phone and Jonathan.

It is not his own writings alone that have
made "The Conning Tower" famous, however.
Frequently F. P. A. has been known as much
for his contributors as his contributions. Edna
St. Vincent Millay, Dorothy Parker, Arthur
Guiterman, Sinclair Lewis, John Erskine, Deems
Taylor, Groucho Marx are merely a few of the
now-famous who brightened the pages of the
Evening Mail, Tribune, et al.

Despite his many writings in his column
and elsewhere, and his equally numerous friends,
there were once some people in the United
States to whom the initials F. P. A. meant
little. This was remedied in May 1938. Mr.
Dan Golenpaul outlined the idea of *Information
Please* to F. P. A. and he jumped at it. "I
said I enjoyed that kind of stuff and would
be glad to do it for nothing. I still feel that
way and am glad that I don't have to do it
for nothing." On the program F. P. A. is
not only "a plinth of omniscience," but able
to "serve up his learning with a nice sprinkling
of Attic salt"—which means with startling
puns, informal quips and general deftness.
It is sheer modesty, listeners agree, that makes
him say he "can't remember a thing that's
happened in the last 10 years but remembers
everything before that."

Away from the mike and the *Post,* F. P. A.,
who has been accused of looking something like
a cross between the late King Alfonso of
Spain and Groucho Marx, loves to loll about
the Players Club, a large cigar in his mouth, a
loud necktie around his neck—he is "a pioneer
who has done more for the crimson cravat than
any other man living," according to Frank
Sullivan. He lives with his second wife, Esther
Sayles Root, whom he married in 1925 (he
was divorced from his first wife, Minna
Schwartze), and his four children in Weston,
Connecticut. He complains though, that "I
have to go to Redding to play tennis with
Stuart Chase."

References

Christian Sci Mon Mag p4 D 21 '38 il
    por
Lit Digest 118:12 O 6 '34; 123:35 Mr 13
    '37 por
Newsweek 9:32 Mr 13 '37 por; 18:46
Poetry 50:210-15 Jl '37
Scholastic 30:15 My 22 '37
Time 29:52+ Mr 15 '37 por; 38:51
    Ag 25 '41
    Ag 25 '41 por
Masson, T. L. Our American Humorists
    p21-5 1931
Variety Radio Directory
Who's Who Among North American
    Authors
Who's Who in America
Who's Who in American Jewry

ADAMS, JAMES TRUSLOW (trŭs′lō)
Oct. 18, 1878- Historian; writer

Address: b. c/o Charles Scribner's Sons, 597
Fifth Ave, New York City; h. Southport,
Conn.

James Truslow Adams, the eminent, readable
historian, believes that "there is a thread, a
movement to history." "There has been operative through the hundreds of thousands of
years of our mostly unrecorded history," he
says, "a gradual advance, call it progress or
what you will." This is the general philosophy
of history which has inspired his many books
and articles.

Unlike many other modern historians, Dr.
Adams doesn't believe in "the economic or any
other single theory of history." He believes it is
the historian's job to select facts "according to
their interest or importance," and then to "tell
the story as he honestly sees it, using the facts
as he determines them," seeing the scene as
a whole, impartially. And he believes, too, that
whatever he writes should be made "as readable
as possible." This, he says, "is not striving for
popularity but a duty owed to the reader. . ."
Critics have praised him for his "admirable
style—one of the best styles of the present
day," but there have been sterner ones in recent years to rebuke him for being an "amiable
popularizer of our marching destiny."

This man who feels "I have done the best
work I could in the way that pleased me best
and have had much fun out of it and some
profit by luck" tried his hand at a number of
things before he finally settled down as an

Harris & Ewing
JAMES TRUSLOW ADAMS

historian. His was an old family: the ancestors of his father, William Newton Adams,
settled in Virginia in 1658 and, during George
Washington's lifetime, owned the next-door
plantation at Mt. Vernon; his father's mother
could trace her ancestry back to Alejandro de
Ineypoy Rojas y Queypo, who was Spanish
Governor General in America in 1558. His
mother was the former Elizabeth Harper
Truslow. James Truslow Adams himself was
born in Brooklyn, New York, but "my memory," he says, "begins in France." After a
childhood spent much abroad, he attended
Brooklyn Polytechnic Institute with the intention of becoming an engineer.

Although he received a B. A. degree in 1898
from this institution, he never became an engineer. Instead he went on to Yale to take a
Master's Degree in 1900. During the period
he was studying there he intended to become
a professor of philosophy, but unfortunately
"the teaching discouraged me." He left Yale
for Wall Street, where for the next 13 years
"I was broker, banker, manufacturer and railroad man all on a small scale." One of the
few historians not associated with a university,
Dr. Adams (Doctor by virtue of seven honorary degrees) was to comment later that "too
long an academic training and career is rather
a detriment than a benefit to an historian and
it should at least be supplemented by some
years of an active career in affairs among men."
His 13 years were valuable for this reason, he
feels. "They taught me much of men and affairs
and incidentally took me into all but five states
of the Union."

But, Dr. Adams admits, "I got fed up and
quit on a small independent income to look for
something more interesting. I spent a year
studying Persian. Then I wrote a poor history
of the village where I lived." This "finger
exercise" for his later work was finished in

ADAMS, JAMES TRUSLOW—*Continued*
1916 and called *The Memorials of Old Bridge-hampton.* It was followed two years later by *The History of the Town of Southampton.* All these years, Dr. Adams insists, "I worked harder writing history than I had in Wall Street."

His interest in local history was superseded by an interest in world history during the years of America's participation in the First World War. He became a member of Colonel House's commission to prepare data for the Peace Conference and followed up this work with a position as captain in the Military Intelligence Division of the Army's General Staff. Then in 1919 he was detailed on special duty at the Paris Peace Conference. Dr. Adams got "immense stimulation from the group of specialists working for Colonel House"; "my experience in the War," he adds, "also taught me much as to how history is made."

As soon as the War was over, Dr. Adams settled down to an even closer consideration of historical problems and spent the next six years in solid work on a history of New England "without other occupation and without holidays." The first volume, published in 1921, was *The Founding of New England.* "In my innocence," Dr. Adams says, "I had expected to have to pay for it myself. It won the Pulitzer Prize." And it won instant, unanimous critical acclaim—was called by Samuel Eliot Morison "the best short history of early New England that has appeared for a generation." This volume on the origins of colonial life was followed in 1923 by *Revolutionary New England, 1691-1776* and in 1926 by *New England in the Republic, 1776-1850.* The trilogy as a whole was recognized as a work that would be "long indispensable to serious students," as a masterpiece of its kind.

In 1927 came *Provincial Society, 1690-1763,* a pathbreaking work of historical research, different from his later interpretive books. (Dr. Adams says, "I have deliberately tried my hand at different sorts of work.") This was the year, too, in which he was married to Kathryn M. Seely. Not long after their marriage the Adamses went abroad, where they lived most of the next nine years, commuting "between London, other capitals and the United States." Dr. Adams has always believed in living and traveling away from home. From it he has, he feels, gained "perspective and wider knowledge of human nature."

In 1928 Adams edited *Hamiltonian Principles* and *Jeffersonian Principles;* in 1929 he produced a work which diverged somewhat from those the public had come to expect of him. Its title was *Our Business Civilization* (it was published in 1930 in England as *A Searchlight on America*), and its main argument was a plea for a more contemplative and less material existence. In 1930 his *Adams Family* was published, an "eminently fair" book which one critic went so far as to call "perhaps his finest contribution to history."

By this time Dr. Adams, who had published many kinds of historical works on many subjects, had decided that "the ripest fruit of knowledge is to *interpret* facts, to try to find

out how they are related and how they influence one another." This he did in *The Epic of America* (1931), a book which sketched in our national history with broad strokes and interpreted the various elements and the qualities of character that have gone into its making. Called by Allan Nevins "the best single volume of American history in existence" and praised for its lucidity, geniality, intelligence and spirit by even those critics who found it not a great book and one marred by personal references, it soon topped the best-seller lists and was translated into French, German, Danish, Swedish, Italian, Hungarian, Spanish, Romanian and Portuguese.

In 1931 *The Tempo of Modern Life* was also published, a collection of Dr. Adams' magazine articles that provided a sampling of the work he contributed and continues to contribute to magazines as varied as the *Rotarian, Reader's Digest, Good Housekeeping, Current History* and the New York *Times Magazine.* The next year, the one in which he won the $1,000 prize given by the *Yale Review* for an article on public affairs of that year, saw the publication of the first volume of *The March of Democracy;* the second volume appeared in 1933, when both volumes were published in England under the title *History of the American People.* Considered by some "a popular yet scholarly account," the consensus of critical opinion, however, was that Dr. Adams had disappointed his public, that his latest work had a suggestion of the "commercialization of artistic and scientific effort." And critical comment on the book that followed, *Henry Adams* (1933), was little more enthusiastic.

America's Tragedy (1934) was called "a real contribution to a complex period in American history," and *The Record of America,* a high school text which he wrote the next year in collaboration with Charles G. Vannest, was praised for its understanding and "live treatment" of its complex subject. There was much more fuss and argument over *The Living Jefferson* (1936). Opinions on it varied from "shrewd and understanding, splendidly written, fair in its judgments, logical in its reasoning" to "an example of a very clever writer and historian at his worst." The book itself is generally conceded to be "an able though one-sided interpretation of Jeffersonian ideals and principles" in its first part; while its last two chapters comprise what has been called "a wholly gratuitous attack" on the New Deal. Those who remembered Dr. Adams' comment the year before—"There is only one certain thing ahead for me if I live some years more, and that is to pay for the New Deal"—and those who had followed his writings were not surprised. And it was not unexpected when the year following the publication of this book, he appeared before the Senate Judiciary Committee in opposition to Roosevelt's Supreme Court plan; when in 1940 he thundered against a third term, against the fact that "even in the United States the power of one man has become almost overwhelming"; when in 1941 he announced his indignation at "non-defense" expenditures, at "the groups and bureaus who like leeches are sucking the financial life blood of our nation."

In his writings Dr. Adams' next interest was Britain. *Building the British Empire,* the first volume of his work, appeared in 1938; the second volume, *Empire on the Seven Seas,* was published in 1940; and the whole was called "an eloquent tribute to the British world imperium, the overthrow of which, Mr. Adams feels, would constitute an almost inconceivable catastrophe." Critical opinion was divided on these books, too, and they were hailed as "a real contribution to the general reading public" and dismissed as "dull" and "too condensed."

There was no division, however, on the *Dictionary of American History,* edited by Dr. Adams and R. V. Coleman, which appeared in 1940, too. Containing 6,425 separate articles by more than 1,000 historians and experts, its volumes were immediately recognized as "indispensable," as "an important contribution to American historiography"; and the "care and learning of its editors" were praised.

Member of many societies, contributor to learned journals and encyclopedias, Dr. Adams, who is living quietly in Southport, Connecticut, indulging when he can his "simple tastes" (he merely prefers the best of everything in literature, food and friends), says he has discovered the ultimate object of his writing. It is, he says, "to make people think, and to relieve a certain pressure on my own mind. The latter is probably the real truth," he adds, "as I have no confidence in my ability to accomplish the first."

References

 Modern Mo p648-55 '33
 Pub W 131:40 Ja 2 '37 por
 Sat R Lit 10:777-8 Je 30 '34 por; 13:6
  Ap 4 '36 por; 18:11 O 1 '38 por
 Scholastic 26:7 Ap 13 '35 por; 36:8 Ap
  1 '40 por
 Time 36:13 S 16 '40 por
 Wilson Lib Bul 7:472 Ap '33 por
 International Who's Who
 Kraus, M. History of American History
  p492-545 1937
 Kunitz, S. J. ed. Authors Today and
  Yesterday 1933
 Leaders in Education 1941
 Millett, F. B. Contemporary American
  Authors 1940
 Schreiber, G. ed. Portraits and Self-
  portraits p1-4 1936
 Who's Who
 Who's Who Among North American
  Authors
 Who's Who in America

ADAMS, JOSEPH H(ENRY) 1867—Feb. 8, 1941 Inventor; author; civic leader and philanthropist who gave up medicine for research; perfected basic oil-cracking process which is used by leading oil companies in the manufacture of gasoline; between 1900 and 1910 wrote four books on handicrafts for boys; was frequent contributor to periodicals; was a benefactor of both Brooklyn, New York (a $50,000 church, auditorium and children's nursery) and Miami, Florida.

Obituaries

 N Y Times p17 F 10 '41 por

ADKINS, CHARLES Feb. 7, 1863—Mar. 31, 1941 Republican Congressman from Illinois from 1924 to 1932; former Speaker of the Illinois House of Representatives in 1911; served as Illinois Secretary of Agriculture from 1916 to 1920; was practical farmer and for many years farmed more than 500 acres in Platt County, Illinois.

References

 Who's Who in America 1934-35
 Who's Who in Government

Obituaries

 N Y Times p23 Ap 1 '41

ADLER, GUIDO Nov. 1, 1855—Feb.(?) 1941 Noted Viennese writer on music and professor of music at the University of Vienna from 1898 to 1937; authority on Wagner, Haydn and Mahler; was editor in chief of a monumental series of works on Austrian music of which he edited 16 of the 90 volumes published.

References

 Musical Q 21:484-6 O '35
 Baker's Biographical Dictionary of
  Musicians 1940
 Wer Ist Wer
 Wier, A. E. ed. Macmillan Encyclo-
  pedia of Music and Musicians 1938

Obituaries

 Musical Am 61:28 Ap 10 '41 por
 N Y Times p23 Ap 3 '41

ADRIAN, (GILBERT) (ā′drĭ-ăn) Mar. 3, 1903- Dress designer

Address: c/o Metro-Goldwyn-Mayer Studios, Culver City, Calif.

Gilbert Adrian, "Hollywood's highest-priced couturier," has probably been responsible for more fashion trends than any other designer in the United States. To him goes the credit for such international successes as the pill box hat, originated for Garbo in *As You Desire Me,* and the snood which he argued film executives into accepting for Hedy Lamarr in *I Take This Woman.*

Adrian is a New Englander by birth, having been born in Naugatuck, Connecticut, in 1903, the son of Mr. and Mrs. Gilbert Adrian, Sr. He left his home town to enter the School of Fine and Applied Arts in New York City and from there went on to Paris, where he studied, with intense interest, the creation of feminine fashions and modernistic designs.

It was as a student in Paris that Adrian first met Irving Berlin. The famous song composer saw one of Adrian's newly-designed gowns, was impressed and asked to see others. The result of the interview was a contract for

ADRIAN

special art work for the first *Music Box Revue* in 1921.

Two other *Music Box Revues* followed. When the series terminated Adrian handled special designing for the *Greenwich Village Follies* and George White's *Scandals*. It was Natacha Rambova who persuaded the young man to go to Hollywood for the first time to make Rudolph Valentino's clothes. Adrian remained with the famous picture star for some time.

His associations with Metro-Goldwyn-Mayer began in 1925, after Sid Grauman, Hollywood film theatre owner, had asked him to prepare a special prologue for Charlie Chaplin's *The Gold Rush*. So successful was his work that he received seven offers from motion picture corporations within twenty-four hours. By then he had practically discarded his first name, calling himself merely Adrian.

Greta Garbo is one of Adrian's best friends, and he has designed all her screen clothes for more than ten years. In 1936 she was included in his list of women who met his requirements for grace. Others in the select group were Elsa Maxwell, Lady Mendl, Joan Crawford, La Argentina, Katharine Cornell (see sketch this issue) and Mabel Strickland.

That was the year the couturier worked on costumes for Greta Garbo in *Camille*. This he particularly enjoyed, since it was the kind of story that gave him unusual opportunities to express his ideas. "Doing the costumes for *Camille*," he remarked, "was an exercise in charm. That charm could be expressed in everything from 40-yard crinolines to snoods, fringed parasols, bustles and pyramided skirts." Later that same year Adrian was invited to design an entire ballet for the *Monte Carlo Ballet Russe*.

Adrian studies every person for whom he designs clothes as a doctor studies a patient.

"I must know what an individual thinks about, what she likes and doesn't like, before I can get personality into her clothes," he declares. In his opinion, Garbo's glamour grows out of her "earthiness." Norma Shearer he describes as a typical, conservative young woman who looks her truest self in simple, tailored things. Joan Crawford typifies to the designer restless, active youth, and for this reason he expresses a great deal of freedom in her screen clothes.

He personally supervises the creation of all his costume designs for leading screen stars and often spends 15 or 18 hours a day on the set while a film is being made. Ordinarily Adrian works in a room whose walls and carpets are a soft shade of oyster white, flanked by sepia murals. At one end of the room is a dais where he keeps a dummy figure dressed in a costume from one of his current pictures.

In 1941 Adrian was beginning to turn his attention to mass production and custom-made costumes, making arrangements for a new shop in Beverly Hills. "No longer do I want to be associated only with glamor," he said. And despite the fact that he has created most of his fashions for Hollywood's most sophisticated stars, Adrian had chosen petite, unglamorous Janet Gaynor for his wife. The couple eloped to Yuma, Arizona, on August 14, 1939. They have a son, Robin Gaynor, born in late 1940. Miss Gaynor's signet ring was engraved, "Janet, I love you." It was Janet's second marriage; Adrian had previously been a bachelor.

In appearance, Adrian is wiry and small. His manner is reserved, yet intense. He has a thin, sensitive face, dark hair and eyes. His hobby is collecting antique furniture.

References

Am Mag 117:32 F '34 por
Cinema Arts Je '37 por
Ladies' H J 50:10-11+ F '33
Time 36:34 Jl 1 '40 pors
Vogue p70 N 15 '36
International Motion Picture Almanac

AGUIRRE CERDA, PEDRO (ä-gē'rä sĕr'dä pā'drō) Feb. 6, 1879—Nov. 25, 1941
Former President of Chile

Bulletin: On November 10, 1941, Aguirre Cerda turned over his Presidential authority to Chile's Vice-President, Geronimo Mendez, because of illness. On November 25 he died in Moneda Palace, Santiago, where he had been confined to bed for two weeks, suffering from acute bronchial and lung congestion. President Roosevelt personally apologized to the Chilean Government for an article on Aguirre which had appeared in *Time* shortly before and which, he said, spread lies about his drinking habits which were being used by Nazi propagandists.

From January 1941 issue:

Heading the Government of Chile is President Aguirre Cerda, a short, pock-marked man with a dark mustache and an attractive smile, sometimes known as "Don Tinto" because of the *tinto* or red wine pressed fom his vineyards. A millionaire landowner, a member of Santiago's most fashionable club, the Paperchase, by personal conviction a moderate rather than a radical (his Radical Party is primarily a party of the middle class), the accomplishments and objectives of his administration nevertheless express the common denominator which holds the ill-assorted parties of the Chilean Left together. He was elected in 1938 by a newly-formed coalition of Leftist parties called a Popular Front, although its program was fundamentally nationalistic and moderate. In 1940 the Popular Front was "officially" disbanded and President Aguirre made it clear that he had no obligation to the parties concerned—only to the program on which he had been elected. It remains a working combination, however.

Pedro Aguirre Cerda was born in Los Andes on February 6, 1879, the son of Juan Bautista Aguirre Campos and Clarisa Cerda Escuedero de Aguirre. He was educated at St. Felipe College, the Pedagogic Institute and the School of Law and Political Sciences of the University of Chile, received his diploma as professor of Spanish and philosophy in 1900 and his law degree in 1904, and was admitted to the Bar. He then not only took up the practice of law in Santiago but also taught in a school for non-commissioned army officers and instructed in civics, Spanish and philosophy in secondary schools. By 1930 he had become professor of political economy at the University of Chile, and at the time he became President in 1938 he was known both as a top-flight lawyer and as the dean of the University's School of Industry and Commerce which he had established in 1934.

In the meanwhile he had been making himself prominent in politics. As a member of the Commercial Education Council and of the Councils on University, Secondary and Primary Education, in 1910 he was commissioned by the government to study administrative and financial law in the University of Paris, and during his stay in Europe until 1912 represented Chile at a number of conferences, notably educational meetings in France, Italy and Belgium. In 1915 he was elected national deputy for Los Andes; in 1918 he represented Santiago and joined the Cabinet as Minister of Justice and Public Instruction; in 1920 he was appointed to the Ministry of the Interior for the first time; from 1921 to 1927 he was Senator for Concepción. In 1919 and 1926 he made journeys abroad to study industrial education in the United States and conditions in Europe, respectively, his 1926 trip resulting in two books on economics: *El Problema Agrario* (1929); and *El Problema Industrial* (1933). In 1930 he became president of the Council of Fiscal Defense. He was also Minister of State at various times, as well as president of the Radical Party.

Oddly enough, without the Chilean Nacistas (Fascists), Aguirre might never have come into power. In the election of 1938 his rivals for the Presidency were: the candidate of the Conservatives and Liberals, Gustavo Ross, backed by the outgoing Conservative government headed by President Allesandri, by most upper-class Chileans and by foreign business, including North American firms which helped finance his campaign; and General Carlos Ibáñez, the candidate of the Nacistas. The scholarly Aguirre was supported by the Popular Front, a Left coalition to which belonged the Confederación de Trabajadores (the labor organization), the Radicals, Radical Socialists, Socialists, Democraticos and Nacional Democraticos (Communists). The Leftist parties had never been able to attain a majority in the Chamber or Senate, which were controlled by the Rightists.

On September 5, 1938, a few weeks before the election, the Nacistas attempted a *putsch*. It was bloodily suppressed, 60 to 100 participants killed, and "most of them unnecessarily and in cold blood." Ibáñez and Gonzales von Marees, the Nacista chief, were jailed.

Chilean Consulate

PEDRO AGUIRRE CERDA

In a fury at President Alessandri some 15,000 Nacistas swung their votes to Aguirre in order to defeat the Administration's candidate, and in the election of October 25 Aguirre won by a majority of 4,111. (Most observers believe that the majority would have been greater if there had been no official intimidation.) Thus a liberal whose program stressed popular education, public health, social insurance, public housing and extended democracy for Chile was elected by the votes of the totalitarians who promptly organized into the Vanguardia Popular Socialista, which votes with the Conservatives and Liberals in its opposition to the Government and which faces dissolution. After the one-minute inaugural ceremonies on December 24 (Aguirre became President of Chile by the simple expedient of donning a tricolored sash), Aguirre

AGUIRRE CERDA, PEDRO—*Continued*
could hardly do less than pardon those Nacistas
who had been arrested in the abortive *putsch.*
Chilean politics are complicated.

He did other things, however. Almost
immediately he secured the routine resignations of fifteen ambassadors and of seven
top-ranking army leaders whom he suspected
of Rightist sympathies. He also ordered a
nationwide reduction in bread prices, raised
the hours of employment of Federal workers
to eight a day, decided that Cabinet ministers
must spend three hours each day receiving
the public in order "to keep in touch with the
masses," and gave his tacit approval to the
appointment of a Communist as Mayor of
Valparaiso (later replaced by a Radical).
The avowed aim of the Popular Front was
to take control away from the *haciendados*
and big businessmen and to befriend the
rotos ("ragged ones").

The new Government was to face many
difficulties in the months to come. There
were Cabinet crises; the Rightists still controlled Congress; huge sums of money were
expended for relief when an earthquake devastated the country; in August 1939 Aguirre
peacefully suppressed a revolutionary plot of
some generals, among whom was the ex-President of the republic; the Second World War
upset Chile's economy, European markets were
lost, and the trade balance with the United
States became increasingly unfavorable; the
prices of food and rent rose. Nevertheless
wages seemed to rise correspondingly, and
somehow business has been good. (Businessmen call it a "mild inflation.") There can
be no doubt that Aguirre is popular with the
working people of his country nor that he
has done as much as he can to develop new
industries and to diminish unemployment.

Most Rightists, however, fear Communist
participation in the Government more than
anything else—and although the Communists
are not actually represented in the Cabinet,
they are a power in the Popular Front.
Growing more and more restive, in November 1940 the Rightists called a mass meeting
of the Opposition, expecting 50,000 persons;
Aguirre let them meet, but only a fourth or
fifth of that number turned up. On the
other hand, a hastily organized Popular Front
meeting called for the same time brought a
far greater crowd, which marched to the
Presidential palace, the Moneda, to cheer
Aguirre. The next move on the part of the
Rightists was later in November, when one
of Aguirre's men was voted to victory in
a Senatorial by-election: they announced that
because of street disorders attendant upon
this election the Conservative and Liberal
Parties had decided not to participate in the
Congressional elections in March 1941, the
first since Aguirre came to power, in which
most observers had expected Popular Front
representation would be strengthened. *La
Hora,* a newspaper supporting Aguirre, wondered if this refusal were not a threat of a
Rightist revolution in the subtle language of
South American politics. The suspicion was

not removed when, over the opposition of the
parties of the Popular Front, the Rightist-
controlled Chamber passed a bill outlawing
the Communists which was later vetoed by
Aguirre on the grounds that it violated constitutional liberties.

No revolt materialized, however. And possibly the greatest danger to the Popular Front
program came from feuds between the parties
which made it up. The Socialists for a while
seemed about to withdraw support because of
their opposition to the Communists.

President Aguirre Cerda has much to worry
about. Perhaps it is just as well that he
owns a vineyard to which he can occasionally
retire, to drink his own wine (Conchali), ride
horseback, or go walking quietly with his
wife, Juana Rosa Aguirre Luco, in the Parque
Forestal.

References

Bul Pan Am Union 73:1-2 Ja '39 por
Nation 148:62-4 Ja 14 '39
N Y Herald Tribune II p5 Ag 11 '40;
  p37 N 17 '40; p11 N 27 '40
Newsweek 16:26 D 2 '40; 16:27-28 D
  16 '40 por
Scholastic 33:14S N 12 '38
Time 33:23 Ja 9 '39; 35:32+ F 19 '40
  por; 36:28 Jl 29 '40 por; 36:24 D 2
  '40; 37:28 Mr 17 '41; 38:32 O 20
  '41 por
Gunther, J. Inside Latin America p234-
  36 1941
International Who's Who
Who's Who in Latin America

Obituaries

N Y Times p10 N 26 '41 por

AKED, CHARLES F(REDERIC), REV.
(ā'kĭd) Aug. 27, 1864—Aug. 12, 1941 Pastor
and founder of All Souls Church of Los
Angeles; former pastor of the Fifth Avenue
Baptist Church of New York; career covered
more than 50 years as a theologian and church
leader, ranging from the pastorate of a village
chapel in England to the pulpits of some of
the largest and most influential churches in
the United States; in 1915 joined the Ford
Peace Expedition.

References

Who's Who
Who's Who Among North American
  Authors
Who's Who in America

Obituaries

N Y Times p17 Ag 13 '41 por

ALAIN, (DANIEL A.) (à-lăN') Sept.
11, 1904- Cartoonist; illustrator
Address: 31 E. 12th St, New York City

Alain's cartoons, which appear in magazines
like the *New Yorker, Collier's, Saturday Evening Post,* have been praised for their "fourfold
virtue of acute observation, clarity, humor and
pungency." His main characteristics as a
cartoonist are an economy and lightness of

line that give his drawings a peculiarly gay quality reminiscent of the line drawings of André Dunoyer de Segonzac.

Most of his cartoons are good-natured yet barbed comments on the earnest absurdities of human reactions. There is the lady bent on asking a question on what apparently is the *Town Meeting of the Air*, and she has had her hair done for the purpose. There are languid young men whose brief attempts at athletics end in mild disaster. And there are, most conspicuous of all, his favorite Mexicans and South Americans, whose capacity for utter and picturesque relaxation is a vivid comment on the activity of the visiting gringoes. ("I feel like a damned fool with that airplane luggage," says one of the gringoes crossly, sitting in an oxcart in the midst of a cactus-dotted landscape with a sleeping Mexican under every bush.)

Daniel A. Alain (he uses Alain for his signature) was born on September 11, 1904, in the disputed territory of Mulhouse, France and, until he became an American citizen in 1933, had a choice of three nationalities: French, German and Swiss. At the age of 14 he embarked on his career by publishing a little opus entitled *Petite Histoire de la Guerre en Caricatures.* He also had five years of schooling in Geneva's École des Beaux-Arts. After he had emerged as an interior decorator and printed-silk designer he went to Paris.

For a while he stayed there, and his drawings for printed silk brought him a certain amount of fame in the textile industry. Finally a New York silk firm engaged his services and imported him to the United States. "But," says Alain, "as soon as I could laugh in English I returned to cartooning." That is what he has been doing since, with Greenwich Village as his *pied-à-terre.* He also illustrated books, among them Lee Strout White's *Farewell to Model T* (1936) and Ernest Mortenson's *You Be The Judge* (1940), a thorough but humorous analysis of legal ways. Alain's sketches helped to set the mood of the book. "Along with the author's good-natured approach . . . they serve to rescue the law from mustiness and expose it to the sunshine of common-sense appraisal in terms of everyday living. . . With his intuitive touch, Alain could, I'm sure, illuminate all those court decisions which, presently clothed only in cold and cryptic type, even lawyers cannot understand. The profession of the law would be a simpler and a gayer pursuit if men like Alain . . . were engaged to decorate legal treatises."

Alain looks a little like the languid young men of his cartoons, blond, with a thoughtful little smile and a long wandering nose. He has made two yearly sketching trips to Mexico, and he returned with a wealth of cartoons about his beloved Latin Americans. He explains this aspect of his art: "My partiality for Mexicans and natives of Guatemala has been the source of many of my cartoons and occasionally my conscience has bothered me, in fear that they be misconstrued as slander. Actually it is difficult to sneer at Latin Americans, since when they are funniest they usually

ALAIN

manage to be most charming as well. Anyway I felt better on the subject after I had a certain reassuring experience.

"One day I had entered a small church in Guatemala, in a distant village rarely visited by white men. An old Indian shuffled from saint to saint, kneeling in front of each one. . . He finally came in front of me . . . put a knee on the ground, mumbled some incantation and gestured exactly as he had done in front of the holy images. . . I came out of the church with a glowing conviction that Christian love of my Pan-American brother was written on my visage. I have hoped ever since that something of it would transpire through my pictures."

References

Collier's 107:58 F 22 '41 il (p59) self por
N Y Herald Tribune My 5 '40
Vanity Fair 44:19 My '35
Who's Who in American Art

ALDRICH, CHESTER HOLMES June 4, 1871—Dec. 26, 1940 Architect; director of the American Academy in Rome since 1935; designed and planned many public buildings both in the United States and abroad.

References

Arts & Dec 31:59-62 O '29
American Art Annual 1924-25
Who's Who in America

Obituaries

N Y Times p19 D 27 '40 por

ALEGRÍA, CIRO (ä-lä-grē′ä thē′rô) 1909- South American writer

Address: c/o Farrar & Rinehart, Inc, 232 Madison Ave, New York City

Armed with but two useful English words, "Scotch highball," Ciro Alegría, young Peru-

CIRO ALEGRÍA

vian novelist whose book *El Mundo Es Ancho y Ajeno* (*Broad And Alien Is The World*) was the prize-winning entry in the 1941 Latin-American Novel Contest, has explored the American metropolis and capital and approves of both. He found especially democratic the fact that the Senators do not listen to their colleagues' speeches but read newspapers and talk to one another while history-making orations are under way.

Ciro was born in 1909 in Trujillo, the third largest city in Peru, of Spanish-Irish parents. His father and mother are cousins, and his great-grandfather on both sides was an Irishman named Diego (James) Lynch who amassed a fortune and settled down among his mines in the hills of Peru. He was known as a generous and convivial neighbor, and the Lynches lived in comfort until a flood destroyed the mines and ruined Diego Lynch. "He left his heirs a fine memory and a dozen silver spoons." Surrounded by Indian and *cholo* (part Indian, part Spanish) workers, Alegría and his brothers and sisters were attached to the peons, an attachment which worried his mother, who was still haunted by the family's former grandeur.

In 1928, at the age of 18, Alegría became a newspaper reporter in Trujillo and later joined the *Aprista* Party, now outlawed in Peru. He participated in the 1931 revolt and was taken to Lima as a political prisoner. During his prison term, until 1933, he read a great deal and wrote poetry. Exiled from Peru as a condition of his release, Alegría has lived since 1934 in Chile, where he spent a great deal of time recovering from a tubercular illness.

In 1935 he was awarded first prize for his novel *La Serpiente de Oro* (The Golden Serpent) in a contest held by the Chilean

publishers, Nacimiento. He is well known in literary circles throughout South America both for that novel and for another entitled *Los Perros Hambrientes* (The Starving Dogs).

In 1941 Alegría received the $2,000 award for *Broad And Alien Is The World* in the Latin-American Contest conducted by the Division of Intellectual Cooperation of the Pan American Union and sponsored jointly by the publishing house of Farrar & Rinehart and by *Redbook* Magazine. His prize-winning novel was submitted to the judges, Blair Niles, John Dos Passos and Ernesto Montenegro, by the Chilean Committee in spite of the fact that Alegría is a Peruvian. Of their choice Dos Passos said: "I can say without any hesitation that *El Mundo Es Ancho y Ajeno* is one of the most impressive novels I've ever read in Spanish."

The prize was awarded at a dinner at the Waldorf Astoria, April 14, 1941, Pan-American Day. A letter from Secretary of State Cordell Hull was read by Archibald MacLeish, Librarian of Congress, who presided. In the letter Mr. Hull hailed cultural interchange among the Americas as a "means of strengthening the friendship which prevails today." A dramatization of a scene from the book was written by Stephen Vincent Benét and produced for the assembled notables by Lowell Thomas and Henry Hull.

Broad And Alien Is The World is the story of a group of North Andeans who live in an isolated village. Their small civilization disintegrates and is finally destroyed by the pressure of powerful landowners who need man power to work their mines and estates. Using the small village in the Andes as a "focal point," Alegría has been able to describe the conditions existing in a larger section of South America.

Translated by Harriet de Onis, *Broad And Alien Is The World* was published in America on November 10, 1941. The critics, who felt that there was some justification for calling the book a "South American *Grapes of Wrath*," found it on the whole "loosely organized and none too astutely paced," though a novel of "real distinction." "Mr. Alegría sentimentalizes his story to some extent," the New York *Times* wrote, "but he gives an absorbing and richly detailed picture of the village, its dignity, tradition, superstitions and sorrows, and of the whole unstable complex of Peruvian Indian life."

Alegría writes vigorously and rapidly, as easily in New York as at home. His writing, moreover, takes little time. In four hours each day he writes thirty pages of longhand. The remaining time is left for sightseeing. In June 1941 he said he meant to stay here "as long as his money and passport are good."

Robert van Gelder, who interviewed Alegría in June 1941, reported that the Peruvian author was black-haired, stocky, and "healthy as a prize-fighter." In answer to his interviewer's query concerning the red hair of the Lynches which had figured so prominently in the publishers' press releases, the young author replied that when he lets his beard grow it comes in red.

References

    Bul Pan Am Union 75:366-8 Je '41 por
    N Y Times Book R p14 Mr 30 '41; p2, 12 Je 22 '41 por
    Pub W 139:1126 Mr 8 '41; 139:1658 Ap 19 '41 por
    Sat R Lit 23:21 Mr 29 '41

ALEXANDER, HARRY HELD 1867—Jan. 5, 1941 Metallurgist; supervised the building and operation of the first tin smelter in the United States; in 1940 was consulted on tin smelting by the National Defense Board.

Obituaries

    N Y Herald Tribune p10 Ja 6 '41

ALFONSO XIII, FORMER KING OF SPAIN May 17, 1886—Feb. 28, 1941 Last Bourbon monarch, born a king, died in Rome of heart disease; during forty-five years on the throne, eight attempts were made to assassinate him; lived through long series of tragedies both for Spain and his family; lost some of his popularity when he put his country in the hands of Dictator Miguel Primo de Rivera (1923), ousted him too late to divert his people's resentment against himself; Republicans sent him into exile in 1931; had six children of whom two sons died of hemophilia; renounced his claim to the throne in favor of his son Don Juan.

References

    Cath World 147:354-5 Je '38
    Collier's 104:64-5+ N 25 '39 por
    Illustration 201:544-5 D 24 '38 por
    Lit Digest 114:36 Jl 9 '32; 123:10-11 Ap 24 '37
    N Y Times p12 F 23 '41
    Newsweek 17:30 F 24 '41
    R Deux Mondes s8 27:794-823 Je 15 '35
    Time 37:34 F 24 '41
    Blasco Ibáñez, V. Alfonso XIII Unmasked 1924
    Churchill, W. L. S. Great Contemporaries p177-87 1937
    Erskine, B. Twenty-nine Years: the Reign of King Alfonso XIII of Spain 1931
    Graham, E. Life Story of King Alfonso XIII 1931
    International Who's Who
    Maria del Pilar, Princess of Bavaria and Chapman-Houston, D. Every Inch a King, Alfonso XIII 1931
    Sforza, C. European Dictatorships p210-25 1931
    Wells, W. B. Last King: Don Alfonso XIII of Spain 1934

Obituaries

    Commonweal 33:508 Mr 14 '41
    Life 10:28 Mr 10 '41 por
    N Y Times p16 Mr 1 '41 por
    Newsweek 17:26+ Mr 3 '41; 17:67 Mr 10 '41
    Time 37:27 Mr 3 '41 por

ALLEN, FLORENCE (ELLINWOOD) Mar. 23, 1884- Judge

Address: b. Federal Bldg, Cleveland, Ohio

Judge Florence Allen, of the United States Circuit Court of Appeals for the Sixth Circuit, is the first woman to have been assistant County Prosecutor of Ohio; the first woman to sit in a court of general jurisdiction (the Ohio Court of Common Pleas); the first woman to preside as a judge in a court of last resort (the Ohio Supreme Court); and the first woman appointed to a Federal Circuit Court of Appeals. Her recipe to women lawyers who would like a similar career is this: "Take one generous dose of persistency. Add one large measure of industry, the kind that takes no thought of dances, evening parties or prolonged vacations. Mix thoroughly and season with a good portion of humor and several ounces of tact—and don't be emotional. It's what the men expect us to be."

FLORENCE ALLEN

Blue-eyed, bobbed-haired Judge Allen has always led an ordered, purposeful life. She is never late for appointments and never scrambles to be on time. She gets up at 5:30 every morning and is in bed at 9:30 after a day in which there has been exercise, carefully chosen food and hard, concentrated work. The program, however, isn't actually a dull one. Judge Allen's walks, for instance, are great fun for her. Dressed in her walking costume of full knickers and stout shoes, her spaniel with her, she strides through the town, committing poetry to memory as she goes. And when she is with people she is "as old-fashioned and friendly and comfortable as last year's hat," with a fine sense of humor and a "chuckle that tumbles out and wreathes her kindly face in smiles."

Although Miss Allen seems and is a very feminine woman, she has no patience with the

ALLEN, FLORENCE—*Continued*

details of living that are supposed to be woman's chief interest. She lets others choose her clothes for her, and her milliner sighs over the way she jams a hat on her head. As she points out: "The other judges are not expected to be responsible for selecting the dining room draperies or entertaining at a luncheon. Why, just because I am a woman, should I? I don't cook or sew or shop for the simple reason that I haven't the time or energy for these things, any more than the men judges have."

Florence Allen comes of a family of Ohio pioneers who moved to Salt Lake City, Utah, where she was born. Her father, Clarence Emir Allen, was a professor of Latin and Greek at Western Reserve University until his health sent him to Utah, where he became the state's first Congressman. Her mother, Corinne Marie (Tuckerman) Allen, came from a long line of educators and was sent to Smith College by her father, one of the early advocates of higher education for women, the first year the school opened.

In Salt Lake City, Florence was brought up in a rambling house full of children, all of whom played musical instruments. When she was four she could read; when she was seven she studied Latin; and when she was eight she knew some Greek. And then when she was given a Sunday School prize it turned out to be a book of nursery tales! After having been tutored by her father, Florence Allen went to private school in Salt Lake City and at 14 was ready to go to college. But she waited two years before she entered Western Reserve University, spending those years studying music.

After being graduated in 1904 Miss Allen went with her family to Berlin to study music further and while there was music critic for the *Musical Courier.* For two years she attended concerts, practiced and studied, and returned to Cleveland, Ohio, determined on a musical career. But a nerve injury made that impossible, and Florence Allen accepted the turn of events calmly. "I don't believe I ever would have been satisfied with just the piano for a profession," she says. "I can't remember being too upset over the affair. There were ever so many other things I was interested in, too."

At first Miss Allen tried teaching and translating; then she became music critic for the Cleveland *Plain Dealer,* a position she held from 1906 to 1909. Her main concern, though, was with civic affairs; she enrolled at Western Reserve to study political science and got her M. A. in 1908, by this time certain that she really wanted to study law. For a year she studied at the University of Chicago, when Western Reserve wouldn't admit a woman into its law school, and then went to New York University. There she got her LL. B. in 1913, and, years later, the first LL. D. it ever gave a woman (just one of Judge Allen's seventeen honorary degrees).

Miss Allen returned to Cleveland and was admitted to the Bar in 1914. She tried to get a position with a law firm in town, but women weren't wanted. She opened her own office. The first year in it she made $800 and she didn't make much more the year after that; but she got valuable experience. She had volunteered as a counselor for the Legal Aid Society and did much work for them. She also handled the legal work of the Woman's Suffrage Party of Cleveland (and led suffrage parades as well).

In 1919 Miss Allen was appointed assistant prosecutor for Cuyahoga County, Ohio, and one year later was elected judge of the Court of Common Pleas by the greatest vote ever given any judicial candidate for that court in Cuyahoga County. In this position she brought about a number of reforms, one of them inspired by finding out that the prosecutor's principal witness in a theft case had spent the torrid summer in jail while the alleged thief was out on bail. In 1922 Miss Allen was elected to the Supreme Court of Ohio for a six-year term and was re-elected in 1928 by a 350,000 majority. On the Supreme Court bench she wrote some important decisions, including one upholding the constitutionality of the City Manager plan and another holding constitutional Cincinnati's zoning ordinance. In 1934 President Roosevelt appointed her to the United States Circuit Court of Appeals for the Sixth Circuit, where she still is.

The Circuit Court's cases deal with taxes, patents, civil suits, personal injuries, forgeries, stolen cars, narcotics, admiralty law, contracts, interstate commerce, interpretations of the Federal Constitution, and crime in all its branches under the Federal statutes. One day the lawyers' tables will be piled high with intricate parts of a mechanical device to argue a patent case; the next week a question like the TVA will be argued before it. But Judge Allen seems completely informed on every subject. She is said to be one of the few judges who come to court with the briefs of the case to be heard read in advance—accomplished by her ability to concentrate and her trick of extracting succinct points from a page almost at a glance.

Judge Allen's years of study and experience were combined in her book, *This Constitution of Ours,* published in 1940, in which, "in terms of vital significance today," she interprets the Constitution. The result, according to William Allen White, is "a splendid piece of work, illuminating, scholarly, at times eloquent, always interesting, and written from a new, fresh viewpoint."

In this book is seen Florence Allen's liberalism, a liberalism that in her writing and in her decisions is unprejudiced, unbiased. And in all Florence Allen's life is seen her belief in social justice. "That's why I'm in law," she says. "I am interested in its social significance. It is one of man's important tools to promote better living together."

References

Cleveland Plain Dealer O 6 '35
Ind Woman 17:45+ F '38 por; 18:385+
D '39

ALLEN, FRED May 31, 1894- Radio
comedian

Address: c/o Walter Batchelor, 1270 Sixth
Ave, New York City

Fred Allen, "king of the quick quip," is
in 1941 appearing with his troupe on CBS's
Texaco Star Theatre each Wednesday evening
at 9 p. m. "In his dry, unhappy, singsong
drawl" Allen is active in more than half of
the dialogue, gives his own news of the week,
interviews unexpected guests, presides over the
dramatic doings of the Texaco Workshop
and sprinkles the program with his famous
ad libs. His radio audience is estimated at
20,000,000 people.

These are much the same carryings-on the
rueful comedian presented for six years over
NBC for Ipana and Sal Hepatica. And he
still continues to write most of the show's
material himself, to the despair and amazement
of most of radio's other jokemen, whom he
calls "intellectual midgets living on borrowed
minds." What little he doesn't write, he
strenuously edits, doing his best to make
Wednesday night's quips Thursday morning's
by-words. He also finds time to turn out
occasional pieces like his hilarious introduction to H. Allen Smith's *Low Man on a Totem
Pole* (1941).

For about 25 years now Fred Allen has been
aiming toward becoming this century's Mark
Twain. And it all started in the Boston Public
Library. He was born John F. Sullivan in
Cambridge, Massachusetts and went to school
there, working after hours as a stack boy in
Boston's library. There he got hold of a book
on juggling (maybe to help him with his
work) and started practicing. When he felt
he could manage the balls and cues and dishes,
he entered one amateur contest after another,
getting nowhere. Then, he remembers, the
manager walked on one night in the middle
of his act. "Where did you learn to juggle?"
he coldly asked. Allen took a deep breath
and said: "I took a correspondence course
in baggage smashing." His career as a
funster was under way.

It staggered along for two more years, however, as Allen toured movie houses around
Boston as one of a troupe of amateurs, working at paying jobs at the same time. Then
he blossomed out as a small-time performer
under the name of Fred St. James, with a
patter added to his juggling act. "Several
people who knew me well intimated the 'Saint'
part of my name was superfluous," he says.
"Acceding to popular demand, I dropped it
and was known as 'Fred James.'"

As Fred James, Allen spent 14 months in
1915 and 1916 appearing in vaudeville theatres
throughout Australia, Tasmania, New Zealand
and Honolulu. Then he returned to America

FRED ALLEN

and "more years of vaudeville from California to Vermont and from Nova Scotia to
Louisiana." By this time he had changed
his name again. "So many theatre managers
had mistaken me for one of the James Boys
on salary days that I reluctantly changed my
professional name to Allen as a tribute to
Ethan Allen who had stopped using the name
shortly after the Revolution." His act had
become more of a monolog than a juggling
patter and Allen wasn't above using most of
the old vaudeville standbys. When a sally
met but a thin sound of applause, Allen would
work up laughs by turning to the audience with
a tender "Thank you, mother."

By the '20s Allen had graduated from vaudeville to revues. His first Broadway role
was in Hammerstein's ill-fated *Polly*, but despite the short run he was able to get roles
in other productions. There were the *Passing
Show* of 1922, with Willie and Eugene Howard; *The Greenwich Village Follies*; the first
Little Show, with Clifton Webb and Libby
Holman; *Three's A Crowd*; and others. There
were also assignments writing vaudeville acts,
sketches, articles and even film shorts.

It was during this theatrical pre-radio
period that Allen married Portland Hoffa
(named for her place of birth in Oregon)
in 1928. She had been with him in the
Little Show and *Three's A Crowd* and at the
time of their marriage was appearing in George
White's *Scandals*. "We had no extended
honeymoon," Allen recalls, "but spent a few
days in Waterbury, Connecticut to make it
seem longer."

In 1932 Allen entered radio, with a program
called *The Bath Club*. Then came the *Linit
Revue*, in 1933 the *Salad Bowl Revue* for
Hellman's Mayonnaise, and in 1934 the *Town
Hall Tonight* program for the Bristol-Meyers
Company. In this last program he continued

ALLEN, FRED—*Continued*

until late in 1940, when the sponsoring company insisted his hour show be cut to 30 minutes. The *Town Hall Tonight* shows presented the Mighty Allen Art Players, the Town Hall Quartet, Portland Hoffa and Peter Van Steeden and his Orchestra, and was one of the first network programs to introduce amateurs and other novelties. On the Texaco program, which began in October 1940, Allen's show includes the Texaco Workshop and Portland Hoffa, as well as tenor Kenny Baker and Al Goodman's Orchestra. The spurious feud with comedian Jack Benny (see sketch this issue) started back in 1936.

In 1935 Allen made his first full-length film, *Thanks a Million.* Three years later came *Sally, Irene and Mary,* and at the end of 1940 *Love Thy Neighbor,* with Jack Benny. All the movies have been hits, and Allen has made money from them all (he received $100,000 for *Love Thy Neighbor*), but he doesn't like Hollywood. He thinks it "phony," he rebels at having to dress up for garden parties, at showing off, running around. Besides, he says, "Hollywood is no place for a professional comedian. The amateur competition is too great."

Allen is a devout Catholic who "seldom drinks, has never gambled, and quietly gives away far more money than he spends on himself." He and his wife avoid social life—putting together an hour show every week leaves him little time for play. He lives in a four-room apartment in midtown Manhattan, which, "furnished in stiffish fashion, includes a well-stocked library equipped with everything from Joe Miller's Joke Book to the works of Schopenhauer." Allen describes his literary tastes by saying he likes "about three feet five inches of the Five Foot Shelf." Evenings Allen writes; mornings he sleeps; every Tuesday finds him taking boxing lessons to keep his tall, broad-shouldered frame in trim; every Friday finds him taking his wife to dinner and to the theatre. His voice, says a critic, "is not only dissonant, like a jarring string, but he [speaks] in sharp fourths, the most unpleasant sequence of sounds that can fall on the human ear." The late O. O. McIntyre once said that Allen "sounds like a man with false teeth chewing on slate pencils." Whether spending an evening out or talking before the microphone, his face retains its gloomy, parched expression, intensified by the slow motion of his jaws as they mull over a wad of tobacco. Allen thinks chewing tobacco is a safer habit than smoking cigarets: "When you smoke cigarets you're likely to burn yourself to death," he says. "With chewing tobacco the worst thing you can do is drown a midget."

References

N Y Post p6 S 2 '41 pors
Newsweek 15:420-3 Ap 29 '40 por
PM p15-19 N 13 '40 pors
Sat Eve Post 214:22-3+ O 4 '41 pors
Time 36:42 O 7 '40 il pors

International Motion Picture Almanac
Variety Radio Directory
Who's Who in America

ALLEN, JAY (COOKE, JR.) 1900- Journalist

Address: h. 21 Washington Sq, New York City

"The population of Occupied France is 95 per cent hostile to the Germans," said Jay Allen in August 1941. He had reason to know; he had just had a unique opportunity to study the situation. The Nazis arrested him March 13 and kept him in prison at Châlon-sur-Saône and Dijon for four months and seven days. They made one of the biggest mistakes of their lives. Not only did they fail to get any evidence whatever of espionage against him, but with the eye of an observant newspaperman he picked up much information, and on his return to America wrote a series of 10 articles, syndicated in newspapers throughout the United States, proving from direct experience the conclusion given here. These articles with added new material were to be published by Harpers in February 1942, in a book tentatively titled *My Trouble With Hitler.*

Jay Allen is, as the *New Republic* called him, "a crack American newspaperman." As Jay Cooke Allen, Jr., he was born in Seattle, Washington, the son of an attorney, Jay Cooke Allen, and Jeanne (Lynch) Allen. He attended Washington State College and Harvard University, but was graduated from neither. After brief service in a United States Naval unit and a trip as oiler on a Matson liner, he went to work as a reporter on the Eugene (Oregon) *Morning Register.* Next came a year as police reporter on the Portland *Oregonian.* Then, like so many young Americans of the time, he went in 1924 to Paris, and found work on the Paris edition of the Chicago *Tribune.*

The next year the *Tribune* made him correspondent of its foreign press service, covering France, Belgium, Spain, Italy, Austria, Poland, Germany and the Balkans. In 1935 he left the paper and for a while worked in Europe for the Chicago *Daily News.* When the Spanish Civil War broke out, he was not on any newspaper: he was living and writing in Malaga. He cabled the *Tribune* and asked for his old job back. He got it. But when he wanted the paper to send him to the danger zone, insuring his life for $50,000, they promptly refused, ordering him not to take risks. The next they heard was an account of the blowing up of the Alcazar at Toledo. He got his insurance! During this period he acted as correspondent also of the London *News-Chronicle.*

The *Tribune* should have known that nothing could scare Jay Allen. He had already been reported dead in the early days of the Civil War, in Madrid, when the car in which he was riding was shot at and his chauffeur was killed. "It does give you a kind of eerie feeling," he said, "to turn up and find all your friends mourning your death."

There was nothing new to Allen in securing adventurous "scoops." Although he does not like to talk about his exploits, the record shows that he secured the first newspaper interview ever given by General Francisco Franco, was the last reporter to see the Queen of Spain when she fled from the country with her children, covered the murder of Engelbert Dollfuss in Vienna and has interviewed Marshal Pilsudski, Ex-King Carol of Romania (and Madame Lupescu), Marshal Weygand, Marshal Pétain, Alfonso XIII of Spain, and Primo Rivera in his cell in Alicante Prison, just before his execution.

In December 1936 Allen came back to the United States, but by the next spring he was in Spain again, this time for Esquire Features Syndicate, with his headquarters in Bilbao. He returned home in January 1938 and stayed until October 1940, lecturing at the New School for Social Research in New York and collaborating with Elliot Paul in writing *All the Brave*, published in 1939, with drawings by Luis Quintanilla. In 1924 he had married Ruth Austin, an Oregon girl, and their son, Jay Cooke Michael, had been born in 1927. They took an apartment on the edge of Greenwich Village and settled down for a brief period.

By October 1940 Allen was once more on his way to Europe, however—this time to Vichy and North Africa to cover the Second World War for the North American Newspaper Alliance, serving also as war correspondent of *The Nation*. By March 1941 he was planning to come back to America, but decided to try to visit Paris first and gather some of the firsthand news which correspondents in Occupied France were not permitted to send out.

With Kenneth Downs of the International News Service, Allen, as he relates in his articles, succeeded in crossing the line and reaching Paris. He said later that this was done by thousands of persons daily, and that only one in a hundred got caught. Downs left for Syria, and Allen stayed for nine days. It was on his return journey, when on March 13 he was trying to cross the line at Montchanin, that he was arrested by a customs guard. The ostensible cause of his arrest was the lack of "proper credentials"—he did not know of a new regulation (perhaps invented for his special benefit) which required an extra stamp on his visa.

He was held in Châlon for two and a half months without trial and then sent to Dijon by the Gestapo. When the news of his imprisonment leaked out, it was generally rumored that the Nazis had locked him up to "kill" a news story he would otherwise have released. Actually he was in far more serious danger, as he was able to reveal after being held incommunicado in Châlon. By his own carelessness, as he afterward admitted, he was carrying a typewritten report which he had not even read, one which contained important information about German fortifications. His notebook and a list of addresses

JAY ALLEN

he had managed to destroy, however, and he had written a new fake notebook much more complimentary to his captors. He was fairly well treated, the Gestapo never forgetting that he was an American. "I met scores of German officers and soldiers who talked to me —their prisoner—as they never talked to civilians in the occupied areas," he said. It was from these conversations that he deduced a serious slump in German morale. But except for such encounters, he was held in virtual solitary confinement in Dijon, having only 15 minutes a day outside his cell, a period during which he was not allowed to talk or to smoke.

Finally Allen and another American newspaperman, Richard Hottelet of the United Press, were exchanged for three Germans held by American authorities. Even then, in Spain, on his way to Lisbon, Franco's police tried to take possession of him, but were prevented by the Nazis, who were fearful of trouble with the exchange arrangement.

Jay Allen was in the fall of 1941 again living in New York with his wife and son, lecturing on the European situation and working on a two-volume *History of Foreign Intervention in the Spanish War*. Tall, broadshouldered and handsome, with crisply waved brown hair and alert dark eyes, he is the very picture of the "foreign correspondent" of popular imagination. But he is more than that: he is, as *The Nation* said, "courageous, informative, and unprejudiced"—and he is, to quote George Seldes (see sketch this issue), "one of America's great journalists."

References

Nation 152:366 Mr 29 '41
New Repub 104:649 My 12 '41
(Continued next page)

ALLEN, JAY—*Continued*

N Y Herald Tribune p7 Mr 18 '41 por;
p11 My 8 '41; p7 Jl 8 '41; p1, 3 Ag 2
'41
N Y Times p6 Mr 18 '41 por; p24 Mr
23 '41; p1, 11 Jl 15 '41; p2 Jl 27 '41;
p8 Ag 6 '41; p6 Ag 11 '41
Newsweek 18:54 Ag 11 '41 por
PM p15 Jl 8 '41 por
Time 38:54-5 Ag 11 '41 por

Who's Who in America

ALLEN, ROBERT SHARON *See* Pearson, D. A. R. and Allen, R. S.

AMHERST, ALICIA-MARGARET, BARONESS ROCKLEY *See* Rockley, A.-M. A., Baroness

AMSDEN, CHARLES (AVERY) Aug.
18, 1899—Mar. 3, 1941 Archeologist; former
curator, secretary and treasurer of Southwest Museum in Los Angeles; took part in
archeological field work in nearly every state
in the Southwest; author of several technical
books; served as United States Vice-Consul
in cities in France, Switzerland and Mexico.

References

American Men of Science

Obituaries

N Y Times p21 Mr 6 '41

ANDERSEN, HENDRIK CHRISTIAN
Apr. 17, 1872—Dec. 19, 1940 Sculptor;
painter; Norwegian-born; lived in the
United States since infancy; best known for
his plans for an international city devoted to
peace and art, which he called a "World
Center of Communication"; plan took nine
years (1904-13) of his time, the assistance
of more than 40 experts, and the expenditure
of over $150,000.

References

Who's Who in America

Obituaries

N Y Times p25 D 20 '40

ANDERSON, SIR JOHN July 8, 1882-
Lord President of the British Council; member of the War Cabinet

Address: h. Picket Wood, Merstham, Surrey,
England

Few men in British public life have had to
stand up to more severe or continuous criticism than Sir John Anderson, today Lord President of the Council and a member of the
War Cabinet. A year before the Second World
War the London *Daily Herald* parodied Robert
Burns in a skeptical little ditty addressed to
him:

*John Anderson, my jo, John,
When we were first acquaint,
The cheering Tories hailed you
As superman plus saint.
The tasks they gave you then, John,*

*Larger and larger grow,
I wonder can you do them all,
John Anderson, my jo?*

Since that time his tasks have continued to
"larger and larger grow," and many British
voices have become even more skeptical. Before the War broke out his was the primary
responsibility for civil defense, including Air
Raid Precautions (A. R. P.). He took a skating holiday in Switzerland, and news photographs showed him skating on the ice when
(said his critics) he should have had his nose
to the grindstone, evolving schemes for the
protection of the public against imminent
danger. And when he did at last produce
his defense scheme in December 1938, it appeared to them that the mountains had been in
travail and had given birth to—the Anderson
shelter.

This celebrated contraption, consisting of
sheets of corrugated iron sunk a few feet into
the earth and forming a kind of cubbyhole, was
designed by an engineer friend of Sir John,
but has since become universally known as
"the Anderson." Protests against it arose
immediately; some ventured to ask why deep-dug shelters of reinforced concrete could not
be provided if war were not expected sooner
than the leisurely tempo of rearmament at
that time seemed to indicate. Plan after plan
was submitted by competent engineers and
architects, but Anderson turned them all down.
As late as June 1940 he was saying in Parliament: "In this war we must avoid at all costs
what I may call the deep-shelter mentality."
Yet as one Britisher put it, later events proved
that while the Anderson shelter was admirably
designed for growing mushrooms or celery, and
under certain circumstances would even stand
up to the blast of a bomb, it often gets full of
water and is no sort of a place to stay in for
more than a quarter of an hour or so.

Further criticism was aroused when Anderson became Home Secretary and Minister
of Home Security after Churchill took over in
May 1940. After the fall of Holland, Belgium
and France there was a widespread movement
in the popular press to intern all the aliens.
Anderson did just about that. He mixed up
Nazis and refugees who were among the most
bitter enemies of the Nazi regime, and in so
doing caused such widespread protest that some
of the "Class C" aliens later had to be released.
The "Silent Column" which he organized with
Duff Cooper was also abolished in July. But
Anderson's defense of the emergency regulation which allows the Home Secretary to suppress a newspaper "calculated to impede the
war effort" permitted the suppression of the
Daily Worker by Herbert Morrison some
months later, a suppression deplored by some
on the Voltairean principle: "I detest what you
say, but will defend to the death your right
to say it."

In spite of public opinion, when Winston
Churchill made Cabinet changes in October
1940 Sir John Anderson was not demoted,
but promoted to a seat in the War Cabinet.
According to the Prime Minister, although Anderson had been subjected to much irresponsible

criticism he had been "a tower of strength
to me." Since that time it has been frequently
rumored that he is favored by most Tories as
Churchill's possible successor.

This "lean, flint-like, tight-lipped Scotsman"
who has made so many enemies is the son of
an Edinburgh publisher, D. A. P. Anderson,
of Westland House, Eskbank, Midlothian. He
went to a well-known Edinburgh day school,
George Watson's College, and afterward to
Edinburgh University, where he was graduated
M. A., B. Sc. After study at the University
of Leipzig he entered the Colonial Office in
1905, and four years later was sent out to
Africa as secretary to the Northern Nigeria
Lands Committee.

After this any recital of Anderson's career
becomes a little dizzying. In 1911 he became
secretary to the West African Currency Committee. The next year he was principal clerk
in the office of the Insurance Commissioners;
the year following, secretary at the same office;
and from 1917 to 1919 he served as secretary to
the Ministry of Shipping. In 1918 he collected
the first of his distinguished orders, as Companion of the Bath. He was knighted as
K. C. B. the next year, and after service that
same year as additional secretary to the Local
Government Board and as second secretary to
the Ministry of Health he became chairman of
the Board of Inland Revenue. It was during
the Irish Rebellion in 1920, when Sir John was
joint Under-Secretary to the Lord Lieutenant of
Ireland, that he made himself at least partially
responsible for the formation of the Black
and Tans (auxiliary police). Among the Irish,
"every self-respecting assassin conceived it to
be his first duty to plug Sir John. But nobody
hit him."

Finally in 1922 Sir John became permanent
Under-Secretary of State at the Home Office.
As the *Daily Herald* put it: "At the Home
Office he must at last have found a room without a draught. At all events he stayed there
for 10 years." During that entire period he
was the civil servant responsible for the
guidance and support of successive Home Secretaries. In 1923 he advanced a grade in the
Order of the Bath to Knight Grand Cross.

In 1932, although it was decidedly unusual
for a civil servant to get such a post, Sir Samuel Hoare recommended Anderson's appointment as Governor of the Indian province of
Bengal during the most active period of Bengal terrorism. The talents he had shown in
crushing the general strikes in England in 1926
may have been a further recommendation.
"Well," Sir John is quoted as saying, "I
suppose that I have almost completed my career
in Whitehall, and being a Scot I am ready to
try another." In its course he was to collect
two more knighthoods—Grand Cross of the
Indian Empire when he started out and Grand
Cross of the Star of India after his term in
Bengal was finished. But his six years there
were stormy. At home a leader of the India
National Congress attending a Round Table
Conference had objected to his appointment
because he was "a gentleman connected with
the administration of the Black and Tans." And
in India he soon acquired the name "Iron Man,"

Pictures Inc.

SIR JOHN ANDERSON

his regime there being "hard-handed in the
extreme." Assassins blew up his train, shot
at him more than once; but he succeeded in
practically putting an end to civil disobedience.
The only inconsistently sentimental note was
his reprieve of one would-be assassin on the
grounds that "if he were given useful work
he would forget politics."

Shortly after his return to England, on
January 1, 1938, Anderson was appointed
to Chamberlain's Privy Council. On January
3 he became a director of Vickers, Limited, on
January 7 he joined the Board of the Midland
Bank, and within the next three months he
was elected to Parliament as a National Government member for the Scottish universities,
accepted the deputy chairmanship of the Rudyard Kipling Memorial Fund and was appointed
a director of the Imperial Chemical Industries.
He settled down in the rural Home County of
Surrey. In May he refused the chairmanship
of Imperial Airways but later accepted another
job: the chairmanship of a Parliamentary
Committee to consider civilian evacuation in
time of air raids. In November, Chamberlain
enlisted him to organize the whole business of
civilian defenses and anti-aircraft services, with
the portfolio of Lord Privy Seal. As has already been noted, he was one of those who survived the upset of May 1940, under Churchill,
becoming Home Secretary and Minister of
Home Security and in October of the same year
being appointed Lord President of the Council,
with a seat in the War Cabinet.

Despite criticism, one thing to Sir John's
credit is the organization of A. R. P. services
in general, which has been carried out with
great efficiency. If today wardens, firemen,
ambulance services, rescue squads and demoli-
tion parties are doing excellent work in the
British Isles, it is partly due to Sir John's
efficiency in the past. Yet, as one Englishman
sums up the situation: "He is a supremely

ANDERSON, SIR JOHN—*Continued*

efficient civil servant, a man of files and documents, rules and regulations and 'passed-to-you-please,' having all the virtues of that type and all the real and grave drawbacks attaching to the official mind. Give him a large-scale scheme to work out in detail, and he will do it splendidly. Every part will be in its place, every eventuality provided for. But if you want a man who can plan imaginatively and look a long way ahead, a man of humane sympathies who knows the lives and needs of the people, then don't ask him."

Anderson is a widower with one son and one daughter. He married, in 1907, Christina, third daughter of the late Andrew Mackenzie of Edinburgh. She died in 1920. One writer describes him: "To look at the long, rather broad face of this middle-aged widower, with its dour mouth and steadfast eyes, you might take Sir John for a Scottish cleric. He does not talk readily and he seems cold and rather hard in his manner. His habits of mind, one imagines, are inclined to be old-fashioned. He prefers mahogany furniture and has a low opinion of women in politics. Apropos of his humor, it has been said of him that 'he is a man who takes some time to laugh at his own jokes.' "

References

Asiatic R ns 31:37-40 Ja '35; 34:244-52 Ap '38
Gt Brit & East 49:682-3 N 18 '37 por
Liv Age 355:533-5 F '39
N Y Sun p10 Ag 20 '40; p29 S 19 '41
New Statesman & Nation 16:1112-13 D 31 '38
Penguin Hansard v3 1941
Picture Post 7:26-7 Je 1 '40
Scholastic 33:14S N 19 '38 por

Gunther, J. Inside Europe p345 1940
Who's Who

ANDERSON, JUDITH   Feb. 10, 1898-
Stage and screen actress
Address: b. c/o Metro-Goldwyn-Mayer Studios, Culver City, Calif; c/o National Theatre, W. 41st St, New York City; h. Pacific Palisades, Calif.

Near the end of the nineteenth century (February 10, 1898), Judith Anderson was born in Adelaide, South Australia, the daughter of James and Jessie Margaret (Saltmarsh) Anderson-Anderson. (She dropped half of the double-barreled name for stage purposes.) Her mother was English; her father, a Scotsman, had been wealthy but lost his money when this youngest of his four children was still quite small. He managed, however, to give the girl eight years of good schooling at two private institutions in South Australia, Rose Park and Norwood.

In 1915 Judith Anderson went on the stage, playing Stephanie in *A Royal Divorce*. She played in stock in various Australian cities for a few years, then in 1918, with her mother, set out for the greener fields of America. They landed in California and went to Hollywood, where the motion-picture industry was just beginning to toddle its first hesitant steps. But letters from Australian managers were no open sesame to the too-thin, awkward, wide-eyed girl in those pre-talkie days; and so Mrs. and Miss Anderson packed again and went on to New York.

There it was the same story. For a while Judith Anderson haunted booking agencies, while her mother (who was no seamstress) sewed for their living, and they lived somehow on next to nothing in a shabby room. Then came the big flu epidemic of the First World War period, and under-nourishment made Judith Anderson an easy victim. Barely able to be up again, she resumed her tramping from agency to agency. At last, one day, she felt so weak she was afraid she would faint on the street. Merely hoping for a chance to sit down, she dragged herself into another agency and fell into a chair. The manager of a 14th Street stock company, passing through, saw her. Without her even asking for it, he engaged her to play supporting parts at $40 a week—"and supply your own clothes."

She made good. The next year she was promoted to leads and to $50 a week. In 1920 she toured with William Gillette in *Dear Brutus*. Then, after leads in stock companies and other roles, came her first triumph on Broadway, as Elise Van Zile in *Cobra* (1924). She made this rather shoddy melodrama into a vibrant and unforgettable thing. Judith Anderson had arrived.

The plays in which she has starred since that time are many and varied. In 1925 she appeared in *The Dove* for two seasons for David Belasco. In 1927 she revisited her native Australia and played there in *Cobra, Tea for Three* and *The Green Hat,* returning to the United States that same year to appear in *Behold the Bridegroom*. In 1928, after appearing in *Anna*, she succeeded Lynn Fontanne (see sketch this issue) in the Theatre Guild production of Eugene O'Neill's *Strange Interlude*, playing the role of Nina to loud critical acclaim. She toured in *Strange Interlude* in 1929, and after a period from 1930 to 1931 during which she was the "Unknown One" of Pirandello's *As You Desire Me*, accepted the role of Lavinia in another O'Neill tragedy, *Mourning Becomes Electra*.

Appearances in a series of less spectacular successes followed: *Firebird* (1932); *Conquest,* the Theatre Guild production of *The Mask and the Face, The Drums Begin* (1933); *Come of Age, The Female of the Species* and *Divided by Three* (1934). In 1935 she played Delia in Zoë Akins' Pulitzer prize-winning *The Old Maid,* and the next year Gertrude in the John Gielgud production of *Hamlet*. In 1937 she made her first London appearance, as Lady Macbeth, and in the fall of 1941 (her only Broadway appearance during the interval having been as Mary, the mother of Jesus, in *Family Portrait* [1939]), returned to the same dark deeds and brooding thoughts in Maurice Evans' Broadway production of *Macbeth*.

Brooks Atkinson writing in the New York *Times* said of the performance: "Miss Anderson spreads a flame of acting over the highly wrought scenes. . . Her Lady Macbeth is her most distinguished work in our theatre. It has a sculptured beauty in the early scenes, and a resolution that seems to be fiercer than the body that contains it. It is strong without being inhuman. And she has translated the sleep-walking scene into something memorable; the nervous washing of the hands is almost too frightening to be watched. . . Magnificent acting." Many authorities consider her the finest emotional actress on the American stage. Her acting has been compared to "modern music with strange warm colors running through it." Her special field, however, is in tense, rich, meaty parts which are in essence glorified character roles and which give her a chance to show what she can do as an actress. This is as true on the screen as on the stage, and audiences will remember for a long time her magnificent playing of Mrs. Danvers, the malevolent housekeeper, in *Rebecca* (1940).

But those who identify Judith Anderson with roles like that of Mrs. Danvers don't know her real nature. She has, remarks Katharine Roberts, "a talent for gaiety and a genius for reticence." Immensely interested in other people—in what they are and what they think rather than in what they do—she is totally uninterested in herself, and "cannot be interviewed." When, soon after signing her seven-year MGM contract in 1940, she visited New York, newspaper interviewers were amazed to see a film star who came to New York for a week with only one suitcase and who wanted to talk only about her "baby"— which was her new house in Pacific Palisades.

"For years I lived in trunks, suitcases and railroad stations," she said, "and now I've bought a house. I'm a sleepy, lazy girl, and I love the earth. I love the space. I love the sunshine. I love the trees. Eucalyptus, mimosa, pepper trees, daphne, vegetables— marvelous! I've got to save my money to buy fertilizer and seeds. I've got no interest in clothes." A three-acre place can use up lots of seeds and fertilizer.

And she loves the movie life. She hated it in 1932, when she played a sort of "fuzzy gangster's moll" in a thing called *Blood Money* (1933). She felt that that first picture lived up to its title, and it took a very good offer to get her to try again in *Rebecca*. But then she went overboard entirely, agreed to play the schoolteacher in Eddie Cantor's (see sketch this issue) *Forty Little Mothers*, signed a seven-year contract—and bought her house. Even a role in another gangster picture, *Lady Scarface* (1941), couldn't make her quit the movies after that. She may be "sleepy" and "lazy," but she enjoys being up by dawn and in the studio from 6:45 a.m. to 7 p.m. She likes Southern California, appreciates the fact that "people don't wear hats, and nobody notices me because I'm bareheaded."

In 1937 Miss Anderson married Benjamin Harrison Lehman. They were divorced in

JUDITH ANDERSON   Vandamm

1939, and she has not remarried. Her constant companions are her two dachshunds. Once called "one of the best-dressed actresses," today she would far rather spend her money on her home than on clothes. One of her idiosyncrasies is to dress her dark hair in a different manner for every play in which she appears. Somehow she gives the appearance of being tall, though actually only five feet four inches. She has a brooding, wistful, arresting face, with haunting dark eyes. But there is nothing melancholy about her; she has a rich vein of humor, and her characteristic expression of interest is a low chuckle, as if she were communing with a highly sympathetic confidante inside her own mind.

References

Ind Woman 16:374 D '37 por
Lit Digest 119:12 Mr 2 '35 por
Photoplay 54:18-19 F '40 por
Theatre Arts Mo 20:834 N '36 por;
  23:276 Ap '39 por; 23:319 My '39 por
Time 33:61 Mr 20 '39 por

American Women
Sobel, B. ed. Theatre Handbook 1940
Who's Who in America
Who's Who in the Theatre

ANDERSON, SHERWOOD Sept. 13, 1876—Mar. 8, 1941 Noted American author; died at Cristobal, Canal Zone, while on a South American cruise; critics consider *Winesburg, Ohio* his best single work and the decade from 1919 to 1929 his most productive period; his name has been linked with such outstanding writers as Sinclair Lewis, Theodore Dreiser, Eugene O'Neill, Willa Cather and H. L. Mencken; his influence on novelists of his day was a great one; his theme was escape from reality and his locale the Midwest in which he had been

ANDERSON, SHERWOOD—*Continued*
bred; wrote two books of autobiography,
A Story Teller's Story (1924) ; and *Tar,
a Midwest Boyhood* (1926).

References

Lit Digest 115:15 My 13 '33; 119:26
  Ap 6 '35
Nation 135:454-6 N 9 '32
New Repub 89:103-5 N 25 '36
Scholastic 28:10-12+ F 1 '36
Anderson, S. A Story Teller's Story
  1924
Anderson, S. Tar, a Midwest Boyhood
  1926
Baldwin, C. C. Men Who Make Our
  Novels p26-33 1924
Boynton, P. H. More Contemporary
  Americans p157-77 1927
Chase, C. B. Sherwood Anderson 1927
Cowley, M. ed. After the Genteel
  Tradition p88-99 1937
Fagin, N. B. Phenomenon of Sher-
  wood Anderson 1927
Farrar, J. C. ed. Literary Spotlight
  p232-40 1924
Hansen, H. Mid-west Portraits p109-
  79 1923
Kunitz, S. J. ed. Living Authors 1937
Van Doren, C. C. American Novel,
  1789-1939 p294-302 1940
West, R. Strange Necessity p309-20
  1928
Whipple, T. K. Spokesmen: Modern
  Writers and American Life p115-38
  1928
Who's Who in America
Wickham, H. The Impuritans p235-90
  1929

Obituaries

N Y Times p41 Mr 9 '41 por

ANDREWS, ROY CHAPMAN Jan. 26,
1884- Explorer; former director of the American Museum of Natural History
Address: h. 11 E. 73rd St, New York City

Bulletin: In November 1941 Dr. Roy
Chapman Andrews resigned as director
of the American Museum of Natural
History. The world's political troubles,
he said, had curtailed "expeditionary" work
for which he was qualified and made
necessary a "financial" leadership for
which he did not believe himself equipped.

From January 1941 issue:

Roy Chapman Andrews is the executive
director of the American Museum of Natural
History, which contains $30,000,000 worth of
dinosaurs, birds, shells, insects, skulls and
artifacts, and is visited by about 1,700,000
persons every year. Under him is a staff of
some 800 curators, assistant curators, secretaries, technicians, guards and carpenters. He
is also the narrator on the "New Horizons"
geography and science program of Columbia's
American School of the Air, an author of
note and a famous explorer whose career "is

almost pure Alger, with a robust leavening of
Kipling, P. C. Wren and even a dash of Sax
Rohmer."

Until 1934 Dr. Andrews hadn't spent twelve
months in any one country for twenty-five
years. During this time he narrowly escaped
death from wild animals, typhoons, bandits,
bombing planes and poisonous reptiles. But
Dr. Andrews shrugs off these adventures,
telling those who approach him with admiring
wonder how he once nearly killed himself
in New York answering the telephone, and
quoting statistics on deaths from accidents in
the bathtub.

"Exploritis," says he, "is a congenital disease
and one is born an explorer." Roy Andrews
always knew he wanted to be one. He was
born in Beloit, Wisconsin, the son of Charles
E. Andrews, a druggist, and Cora M. (Chapman) Andrews. From the time he was nine
he owned a gun and loved to shoot and
mount the things he had shot. He went to
grammar and high school in Beloit, but hated
anything except nature study and spent more
time learning taxidermy than reading the
Idylls of the King or *The House of Seven
Gables*. And it was taxidermy that paid for
his four years at Beloit College.

Armed with his B. A., which he received
in 1906, Roy Andrews set out first for Chicago
and then for Pittsburgh. The museums of
both cities had no job for him. He arrived
in New York with about $30 and presented
himself at the American Museum of Natural
History. He would take any job, he said,
even a job washing floors. When the director
there suggested that a man of his education
wouldn't really want to wash floors, Andrews
replied: "Not *any* floors. But the museum
floors are different." The director took him
at his word, or almost, and gave him a job in
the preparations department, where he washed
the floor, mixed clay and did all sorts of
odds and ends.

Dr. Andrews' first important achievement in
the Museum was the construction of the
enormous model of a whale which hangs
between the second and third floors, to the
awe and amazement of school children and
their parents and teachers. He came to know
more and more about whales, and in 1908 was
sent on a whaling expedition to Alaska. It
was on this trip that his exploration of the
lives and loves and structure of these seagoing mammals really got under way. In
1909 and in 1910 he went on the cruise of the
U. S. S. Albatross to the Dutch Indies, Borneo
and Celebes. At one point during this cruise
he and two men Friday were left on an
island where they calmly ate monkey meat,
collected birds, mammals and reptiles before
going on to investigate whales in Japanese
coastal waters. In 1911 and in 1912 Dr.
Andrews was in Korea; in 1913 he was with
the Borden Alaska Expedition. Until 1914
Dr. Andrews continued to study whales, to
make collections for the Museum and to
write monographs on his discoveries. Before
he was 30 he was the leading authority on
whales, and Columbia University had given

him a Master's Degree (in 1913) for a thesis on the subject. Later, both Beloit College and Brown University conferred the degree of Doctor of Science on him.

From 1916 on Dr. Andrews was obsessed with the idea of exploring the deserts of outer Mongolia. In that year and the next he undertook two small reconnoitering expeditions in the surrounding region, and in 1919 his second expedition explored North China and outer Mongolia. The third expedition left for Central Asia in 1921, the first party ever manned by specialists drawn from so many fields. In 1922 it set out for the Gobi Desert with motor trucks and fought its way through sandstorms, bandits and overnight drops in temperature of 40 degrees, to carry out "the first phase of perhaps the most revelatory excavating work ever done in the science of paleontology."

When the series ended in 1930 the Gobi Desert had been mapped and opened to motor travel for commercial purposes. Many geological strata previously unknown had been discovered by it; and some of the richest fossil fields in the world had been opened; the first dinosaur eggs and skulls and parts of the skeleton of the Baluchitherium, the largest known mammal, had been found; and Central Asia had been established as one of the chief centers of the origin and distribution of the world's reptilian and mammalian life.

From these expeditions came many scientific papers, for Dr. Andrews believes that no expedition should ever be organized without provision for speedy publication of its field results. From these expeditions, too, came a number of books by Dr. Andrews, written in a terse, chatty, journalistic style. *On the Trail of Ancient Man* (1926); *Ends of the Earth* (1929); *The New Conquest of Central Asia* (1932); and *This Business of Exploring* (1935) are only a few of them. All of them have been popular, all of them fascinating reading. As one critic put it: "Roy Chapman Andrews has never written a dull book or an unscientific one." His latest book is *This Amazing Planet* (1940), into which he has packed miscellaneous knowledge from his explorations and his work at the Museum.

In his expeditions Dr. Andrews has always been a notable organizer of facts, material and men, and it is that talent combined with his scientific knowledge and experience which qualifies him so well for his present position, which he has held since 1935. Yet, in "his lean, scholarly face, softened by pince-nez glasses, there is little except the strong muscles of the jaw to suggest the character of a superb explorer."

Dr. Andrews has two children, George Borup and Roy Kevin, by his first marriage in 1914 to Yvette Borup of Paris, France. Since 1935 he has been married to Wilhelmina Christmas of New York City. Polo, fox hunting and shooting are his favorite sports, next to exploring. But whatever he does, whether it is work or play or both, Dr. Andrews is "all

ROY CHAPMAN ANDREWS

action. He was never content merely to see the world. He wanted to feel it—all of it—and wherever possible to wrench out whole chunks as scientifically priceless souvenirs."

References

Christian Sci Mon Mag p5+ O 16 '35 il pors
Nat Hist 45:118-21+ F '40 pors
New Yorker 5:22-5 Je 29 '29
Pop Sci 138:110-11 F '41 il por
Time 36:46-7 O 21 '40 por
American Men of Science
Andrews, R. C. Exploring with Andrews 1938
Andrews, R. C. This Business of Exploring 1935
Green, F. Roy Chapman Andrews, Dragon Hunter 1930
Hylander, C. J. American Scientists p174-6 1935
Tracy, H. C. American Naturists p164-72 1930
Who's Who Among North American Authors
Who's Who in America
Who's Who in American Education

ARCHBISHOP OF CANTERBURY *See* Lang, C. G., Archbishop of Canterbury

ARGESEANU, GEORGE (ăr-jä-shä'nü)
Died Nov. 27, 1940 Former Premier of Romania, executed by Iron Guardists before the open tomb of their martyred leader, Codreanu.

References

International Who's Who

Obituaries

N Y Herald Tribune p1, 4 N 28 '40 por
N Y Times p1, 6 N 28 '40 por

ARIAS, ARNULFO (ä'rĭ-äs är-nōōl'fô) Aug. 15, 1901- Former President of the Republic of Panama

DR. ARNULFO ARIAS

Bulletin: In October 1941, after a series of anti-United States actions climaxed by his refusal to let ships flying the Panama flag be armed, Arias fled secretly from Panama by plane. Immediately the second Vice-President of Panama, who had favored collaboration with the United States, was sworn in as acting head of the Government. When Arias returned, he was jailed, then forced to leave the country. In Nicaragua late that same month, it was reported that Canada would later admit him.

From May 1941 issue:

On March 5, 1941 Panama's dark and flaming President Arias proclaimed the solidarity of his nation with the United States in all matters pertaining to the defense of the Panama Canal. He announced an agreement permitting this country to use Panamanian territory for air bases and air defense stations during the duration of the War—a measure essential to adequate protection of the slim Canal Zone.

The news brought a measure of comfort to United States diplomats and citizens perturbed by the policy, pronouncements and acts which so far have characterized the "reign" of the world's youngest President. In December of 1940 editorial columns were buzzing about his obvious readiness to "embarrass" the United States by considering foreign claims to defense sites as valid as ours; in February of 1941 he declared our tenure of Rio Hato illegal, and seemed reluctant to grant six badly needed additional bases. For a brief time there seemed danger that consent might be refused entirely, either through sympathy with Nazi

aims and efforts or in an attempt to rally Latin-American support against "Yankee Imperialism." Now it appears that this serious crack in hemisphere solidarity has been averted, for the moment at least.

Jeremiahs are not lacking, however, to remind us that the dapper, compact President still has five years to go. On June 2, 1940 Arias was swept into office by the largest vote ever polled during Panama's 36 years as a republic. His opponent, Dr. Ricardo Alfaro, contributed to the victory by withdrawing the week before election day, charging that his party was denied the right of suffrage. Dr. Arias' own National Revolutionary Party had helped things along before that by clapping a number (2,000 according to Alfaro) of opposition supporters into jail on charges of revolutionary activity.

"I was not fighting a political party," Alfaro declared when he sought asylum in the United States, "I was fighting an army." How he managed to pile up as many as 3,022 votes against the steam roller's 107,759 remains a mystery.

On October 1, before 30,000 of his countrymen, Arnulfo Arias took office, swearing to uphold the constitution that had been adopted under the auspices of Theodore Roosevelt when Panama seceded from Colombia in 1904. Seventeen days later he presented to the unicameral legislature a Bill of Reforms which left the document as much like the original as a dictatorship is like a democracy. Among its provisions were: (1) a two-year increase of the Presidential term, from four to six years, applying retroactively to that of Arias; (2) disfranchisement of all non-Spanish-speaking Negroes, prohibition of further immigration by these, by Asiatics and by North Africans; (3) establishment of government monopolies and expropriation of private property at the discretion of the President; (4) declaration of a state of siege if and when the President deems necessary. The legislature approved these "reforms" and in November a plebiscite confirmed them by 100,000 affirmative votes to 537 in the negative. The zealous government saw that all votes were marked and all polls manned by watchers.

The new constitution leaves some 70,000 to 90,000 people without a country and—since three-quarters of the pay roll of any concern must go to Panamanians—perhaps also without a means of livelihood. Its provisions bear witness not only to the diligence with which Arias observed methods during his years in Fascist Italy, but also to his experience at home. His country has paid dearly for the privilege of being bisected by the most strategic waterway in the world. "He has seen most of its retail business taken over by Chinese, Eastern Europeans and East Indians. He has seen Jamaica Negroes, first imported to build the Canal, monopolize jobs on that waterway. He has seen the import business, utilities and banking taken over by Anglo-Saxon Americans, by the British and by Germans. He has heard English spoken on the streets as freely as Spanish. . . Finally, he has found that the wage scale for his own countrymen is lower than the scale for aliens."

The Arias family, long prominent politically, has become record-breaking in this generation, when for the first time two brothers have served as President of their country. Their sister Josefita is the first woman to hold office as Consul General, in which capacity she now represents Panama in New York. Arnulfo is the first man under 40 to be President of any country.

He was born on August 15, 1901, in the city of Penonomé, far in the beautiful interior of Panama. As a child his chief pleasures were swimming in the little river near the village and riding a white pony named Pisa Flora (walks on flowers). His father, Antonio Arias, died when Arnulfo was very young, and upon his mother, Carmen (Madrid) de Arias, fell the burden of educating five children. The tiny, black-eyed little woman devoted herself to the task, with spectacular results. After they were graduated from high school the three girls, Josefita, Eudoxia and Carmen, were sent to school in the United States. Harmodio, several years older than Arnulfo, went to the University of Cambridge in England. Arnulfo, like his sisters, came to the United States, where, after first attending Hartwick College in Oneonta, New York, he took his B. S. degree at the University of Chicago, and then went to Harvard for his M. D. This was followed by work at Boston City Hospital, where he was neurological assistant from 1924 to 1925. Returning to Panama, he became director of the clinics of surgery and gynecology in St. Thomas Hospital in Panama City, worked in the Students' Clinic and taught hygiene in the normal schools, besides carrying on a large private practice.

His medical interests survived through a good deal of his political career. This began with his membership in the patriotic society *Acción Communal*. Overnight his name became known, when his *coup d'état* on January 2, 1931 dislodged Dr. Florencio Harmodio Arosemena as President of Panama, replacing him with the recently defeated candidate, Dr. Alfaro, then First Vice-President. One reward for leading Panama's first and only revolution was an attempted assassination, which deposited two bullets in Dr. Arias' neck. Another was the position of secretary of the Department of Health and Charity, which he held from 1931 to 1936. He installed modern sewerage and water systems, built hospitals and dispensaries, contributed substantially to improving sanitary and hygienic conditions. At this time he was married to Señorita Ana Matilde Linares, described by his official biographer as "a lady distinguished for her culture, her wit, her beauty, and her illustrious lineage."

In 1932 he was largely responsible for his brother's election to the Presidency, and was soon given the post of Secretary of Agriculture and Public Works, organizing in 1933 Panama's first Health Congress. In August of the following year, before going to Italy as his brother's Envoy Extraordinary and Minister Plenipotentiary, he participated in founding the National Revolutionary Coalition, the nucleus of his present party. After his return from Italy in 1935 the political fireworks which led to the founding of the National Revolutionary Party and the forcible outlawing of all other parties began. Since that time Panama has been a one-party country and its small but vigorous military police force knows how to deal with competition.

When Harmodio's term ended in 1936, the capable Arias management secured the election for Dr. Juan Demóstenes Arosemena, who in the revolution of 1931 had been arrested and set to sweeping out a jail by order of Arias. During Arosemena's term, Arnulfo Arias returned to Italy as Minister, later moving on to France, Sweden, Denmark. At various times he served as delegate to the League of Nations and to European scientific congresses. In the capitals of Europe he made the most of opportunities to visit hospitals and clinics, keeping up with new medical technics. He also kept a studious eye on political technology and became convinced that what Panama needed was "State Socialism consonant with new social movements"—presumably those he had admired in Italy.

The outbreak of the present War found him in Paris. There he served in the hospitals until the end of 1939, returning home, with the Légion d'Honneur, to participate in the Presidential campaign. Brother Harmodio's paper, the *Panama American*, supported him staunchly. It had, in fact, been whispered that the ex-President, shrewd, able, and one of the wealthiest men in Panama, would probably try to establish a political dynasty by putting his brother in office while he remained the power behind the gavel.

Either the prophets or Harmodio's calculations missed fire. Almost at once the *Panama American* condemned Arnulfo's new constitution as fostering totalitarian trends. There are those who trace a connection between this stand and the fact that Harmodio legally represents large United States corporations, pointing out that despite the New-Dealish tone of its English section, the Spanish articles in the *Panama American* had been at least hospitable to Fascism. In any case, its present mood is definitely anti-totalitarian. In February 1941, Ted Scott, the pugilistic journalist who edited its English part, was ejected from Panama. He returned to America describing Arias as "a notorious Gringo-hater and anti-American."

Scott brought tales of a Panama controlled through a "vicious minority" due to the President's "rightabout-face on the issues of the election." He revived memories of Virginio Gayda's 1939 retort discourteous to President Roosevelt (that the Fascist frontier is now in Panama), and of Arias' own inaugural statement which appeared in the official version but was deleted from the address as delivered: that he believed the United States knew how to cooperate with Panama on a basis of good will, but that

ARIAS, ARNULFO—*Continued*

Panama, although too small to defend herself, could always make concessions to foreign countries who would defend her against demonstrations of ill will.

Yet, just as liberal journals were crying out that the core of the center of Western Hemisphere defense was rotten, came the manifesto and agreement of March 5, the first agreement on bases to be concluded in Latin America. Secretary of State Hull pronounced himself highly pleased and journalists held their pencils poised for the next move.

References

> Bul Pan Am Union 74:743-4 N '40 por
> Nation 152:279 Mr 8 '41
> N Y Herald Tribune p21 O 30 '41
> N Y Times IV p2 O 6 '40 por; IV p2
>   D 29 '40; p19 Ap 20 '41; p1+ O 10
>   '41 por; IV p5 O 12 '41 por
> PM p5 D 26 '40 por; p4 O 10 '41 il
> Read Digest 39:91-2 O '41
> Time 36:54 O 14 '40 por; 36:20+ D
>   30 '40 por 38:32 O 20 '41 por
>
> Gunther, J. Inside Latin America p147-
>   51 1941

ARMFIELD, ANNE CONSTANCE *See* Smedley, C.

ARMOUR, ALLISON V(INCENT) Mar. 18, 1863—Mar. 6, 1941 Noted specialist in plant research; yachtsman; had made eight voyages for plant research, some of them for the United States Department of Agriculture; was awarded the Frank M. Meyer Medal by the American Genetic Association for an 8,000-mile voyage in the Caribbean Sea in which he brought back 700 rare plant species for experimental cultivation in the Southern states; won the Edward VII Coronation Cup for yacht racing.

References

> Who's Who in America

Obituaries

> N Y Times p21 Mr 7 '41

ARSONVAL, JACQUES ARSÈNE D' (dàr'sôN'vȧl') June 8, 1851—Dec.(?) 1940 French physiologist; pioneer in electro-therapy; researches led to the discovery of high frequency currents and diathermy; won citation in the United States and many honors abroad.

References

> Illustration 200:253 Je 18 '38
> R Gén Sci 49:310-11 Je 30 '38
> Dictionnaire National des Contemporains 1936
> Qui Êtes-Vous?

Obituaries

> N Y Times p23 Ja 1 '41

ATTAWAY, WILLIAM (ALEXANDER) (ăt'ȧ-wā) Nov. 19, 1911- Novelist

Address: b. c/o Doubleday, Doran & Co, Inc, Garden City, N. Y.; h. 4636 S. Michigan Ave, Chicago, Ill.

WILLIAM ATTAWAY

When he was still a student at college, William Attaway decided to give up his scientific ambitions and become a writer. It seemed to him that the Negro had many competent professional men but few "good, honest" voices. He decided, therefore, to become a literary mouthpiece for his people. *Let Me Breathe Thunder* (1939), his first novel, revealed him as an "authentic young artist," but since it was not about Negroes, it represented for him a kind of literary groping, an effort to find his *genre*. In his second book, *Blood on the Forge* (1941), however, he sank his literary teeth deep into his chosen problem and emerged a more mature artist, closer to his goal of being a successful "voice" for his race.

William Alexander Attaway was born in Greenville, Mississippi, the son of Dr. William A. Attaway and Florence (Parry) Attaway. His father, he tells us, "was a doctor who did not want his children to grow up under the Southern caste system, so he packed up his family and followed the great migration North." In Chicago, Attaway attended a public elementary school and a technical high school, intending to become an automobile mechanic. Under the pressure of his family, who wanted him to have a profession rather than a trade, he changed to academic subjects and allowed himself to be sent to the University of Illinois, from which he was graduated in 1936 with a B. A. degree. Attaway's facility with his pen earned him much recognition there, and his play *Carnival* was produced at the University in 1935.

After spending his first year out of college traveling about the country to gather material for his first book, he came to New York City intending to earn his living as a free-lance writer. He did write his novel as planned, but he earned his living at a wide variety of jobs, including those of salesman in a ladies' dress shop and labor organizer.

The next two years Attaway spent as an actor. His sister Ruth, who had been on Broadway, succeeded in getting him a role in a road company of *You Can't Take It With You* which took him through almost every state in the Union. When he was traveling through Texas the news reached him that his book had been accepted for publication.

Let Me Breathe Thunder, his first book, is the tragic story of two young, hard-boiled, unscrupulous white hobos who pick up a little Mexican boy in the course of their wanderings and allow his charm to smooth down some of their roughness. Of the book his publisher said: "William Attaway has brought to his publishers a book as poised, as perceptive, as honest and tender as many an older writer with a solid list of books behind him would be proud to claim." The story has been criticized for its combination of sentimentality and "scatological, combative, alcoholic, and bawdy passages." Even those critics who did not praise Attaway's performance, however, were certain that it showed great promise.

In 1941, after the material had been collected on a Rosenwald Fellowship, Attaway's *Blood on the Forge* was published. It is the story of three Negro brothers who leave a farm in Kentucky to go to Western Pennsylvania to work in the steel mills just after the First World War, when a shortage of man power caused a mass migration of Southern agricultural labor to Northern industry. The story deals with the competition of Negro and White labor and the difficulties of agricultural labor to adjust itself to industrial conditions. In this book Attaway "writes of the suffering and frustrations of his people with crude power and naked intensity."

The *New Yorker* found that "Mr. Attaway writes of his people knowingly and with warm appreciation. . . Their speech sounds completely authentic. A fine sincere book." Milton Rugoff, writing in the *Herald Tribune Books,* said: "Mr. Attaway has a rich vein of human experience to explore and he has, I think, the equipment to do so. *Blood on the Forge* is only a beginning." According to Drake de Kay the book is a "faithful depiction of the primitive approach to life of a social group on whose laborious efforts the whole scheme of modern industrial life is based."

Attaway's prose style is largely monosyllabic, and he uses short, rapid dialogue to accelerate the momentum. His approach is naturalistic and his handling of detail is cumulative rather than selective. His characterizations are accomplished in gross, and he is especially capable in his handling of the earthier and more primitive aspects of human behavior.

William Attaway is unmarried. He is six feet tall, and weighs 185 pounds. His favorite sport is tennis.

ATWELL, WAYNE J(ASON) Oct. 19, 1889—Mar. 27, 1941 Head of the anatomy department at the University of Buffalo Medical School; outstanding biologist; listed in *American Men of Science* as one of the nation's 10 best anatomists; author of numerous biological articles; in 1938 received a grant of funds from the National Research Council for experimental work.

References

American Medical Directory
American Men of Science

Obituaries

N Y Herald Tribune p16 Mr 28 '41

AUGHINBAUGH, WILLIAM (ED-MUND) (ô-ĭn-bô) Oct. 12, 1871—Dec. 18, 1940 Physician; educator; lawyer; explorer; wrote and lectured on his worldwide travels; worked among lepers; studied the bubonic plague in India; made health survey for Egypt; wrote his autobiography, *I Swear by Apollo,* in 1938.

References

American Medical Directory
Aughinbaugh, W. E. I Swear By Apollo 1938
Who's Who Among North American Authors
Who's Who in America

Obituaries

N Y Times p25 D 19 '40 por

AUSTIN, F(REDERICK) BRITTEN May 8, 1885—Mar. 12, 1941 British author and playwright who contributed extensively to American magazines; in novels and articles predicted the coming of the Second World War and mechanized armies with remarkable accuracy; best known of his historical romances are *The Road to Glory* (1935), *In Action* (1913), and *The Red Flag* (1932); worked in Hollywood as scenarist; wrote *The Last Outpost* for the films.

References

Sat Eve Post 208:92 My 30 '36 por
Time 26:77 N 11 '35 por

Author's and Writer's Who's Who
Who's Who

Obituaries

N Y Times p21 Mr 13 '41
Newsweek 17:8 Mr 24 '41
Pub W 139:1467 Ap 5 '41
Time 37:67 Mr 24 '41

AUSTIN, HERBERT AUSTIN, 1ST BARON Nov. 8, 1866—May 23, 1941 British manufacturer of the Austin automobile; Lord Austin's name was associated, in the United States, with only one type of car he built, the Baby Austin, although in England the company builds standard-size cars; Baby Austin was introduced in the United States in 1929; Austin was knighted in 1917 and raised to the peerage in 1935; gave large sums to Cambridge University for scientific research.

(Continued next page)

AUSTIN, HERBERT AUSTIN, 1ST
BARON—*Continued*

References

Time 32:28 O 3 '38
Who's Who
Who's Who in Commerce and Industry
Obituaries
N Y Herald Tribune p10 My 24 '41 por

AYDELOTTE, FRANK (ā'dĕ-lŏt) Oct. 16,
1880- Educator
Address: b. Institute for Advanced Study,
Princeton, N. J.; h. 324 Cedar Lane, Swarthmore, Pa.

Bachrach

FRANK AYDELOTTE

"My life has been one of stirring adventure,"
said Dr. Frank Aydelotte in 1939. Some
people might consider that a queer phrase to
describe a career as teacher and college executive. But they do not know Dr. Aydelotte.
"He enjoys tight places for the fun of getting
out of them," remarked Brand Blanshard, professor of philosophy at the Quaker college,
Swarthmore, of which Dr. Aydelotte was
president for 19 years. "Enthusiasm for a
life of learning, zest for producing in the field
of scholarship"—these are his announced objectives.

Dr. Aydelotte was born in Sullivan, Indiana, the son of William E. and Matilda
(Brunger) Aydelotte, who were of French
Huguenot origin. He received his B. A. at
Indiana University in 1900, and his M. A.
at Harvard in 1903, his special field having
been English literature. From 1905 to 1907
he was Rhodes Scholar from Indiana, taking
a B. Litt. degree from Brasenose College,
Oxford, in 1908. He has honorary doctorates
from Allegheny College, Yale, Indiana, Oberlin, the Universities of Pennsylvania and of
Pittsburgh, and from Oxford, which made him
a D. C. L. in 1937. He is also an honorary

fellow of Brasenose. His connection with
Oxford has continued to be close: he has
been American secretary to the Rhodes Trustees since 1918. In this connection he performed one service which had been thought
impossible. Cecil Rhodes' will provided for
two scholarships from each of the United
States. But it did not seem fair to Dr.
Aydelotte that sparsely populated states should
have exactly the same number of Rhodes
Scholars as had those producing a far greater
number of potential scholars. He worked
until he got a law through Parliament, in
1929, providing for redistricting.

Dr. Aydelotte began teaching in the Southwestern State Normal School in California,
Pennsylvania in 1900. The following year he
was instructor in English at Indiana University, then for two years taught English in the
Louisville, Kentucky, Boys' High School. He
returned to Indiana as associate professor of
English from 1908 to 1915, for six years was
professor of English at Massachusetts Institute of Technology, and in 1921 became president of Swarthmore. During his tenure there
he not only secured $4,000,000 in additional
endowments, but inaugurated a system of
working for honors, "of teaching subjects for
content rather than courses for credits to
such of the undergraduates as were ready to
accept a stiffer intellectual discipline." He
had turned an average small college into one
of the best in the United States before, in
1939, he was appointed director of the Institute for Advanced Study. For a year he held
both positions; then he resigned from Swarthmore and became full-time director of this
unique institution.

The Institute for Advanced Study is not
to be confused with Princeton University, although it is in the same town, uses many of
the same facilities and works in close collaboration with Princeton. It was founded in
1939 by Louis Bamberger, a Newark merchant,
and his sister, Mrs. Felix Fuld, to provide a
place where a few highly qualified students
might engage in productive scholarship. It
confers no degrees, and its faculty of 17
world-renowned scholars (most famous of
whom is Albert Einstein [see sketch this issue]) and the 50-odd "members" (graduate
students or college teachers on leave) consider
themselves "all students together." At present
it has schools of mathematics, economics and
politics, and humanistics (with emphasis on archeology and Oriental art). Dr. Aydelotte succeeded the first director, Dr. Abraham Flexner
(see sketch this issue), whose lectures and
writings first suggested the idea of such an institute to Mr. Bamberger and Mrs. Fuld. No
better choice could have been made: as
Eleanor Kittredge has said, Dr. Aydelotte
"has a passion for excellence, and his life has
been spent in trying to release the superior
gifts of mind and character in the persons of
his associates." When he left Swarthmore
the faculty debated on a parting gift, and
finally, as most appropriate, wrote and published a volume, *An Adventure in Education,*
telling the story of their retiring president's
services to the college.

In Princeton Dr. Aydelotte, with his wife and son, lives in an elm-shaded house built in 1696. Here he has housed his fine sixteenth and seventeenth century library. In spite of the engrossing demands of his position as director, he still finds time for outside interests. He is a trustee of the Carnegie Foundation for Advancement of Teaching, chairman of the educational advisory board of the John Simon Guggenheim Memorial Foundation (it was he who organized the Guggenheim Fellowships), a member of the Senate of Phi Beta Kappa and of the Institute of International Education. In 1918 he was chairman of one of the divisions of the War Department's Committee on Education and Special Training. He has played a prominent part in the work of the American Philosophical Society, the World Peace Foundation and the National Research Council. Dr. Aydelotte writes occasional articles for the educational journals, and four of his books have been published: *Elizabethan Rogues and Vagabonds* (1913); *College English* (a textbook, 1913); *The Oxford Stamp, and Other Essays* (1917); and (with Laurence Alden Crosby) *Oxford of Today* (1922).

In 1907 he was married to Marie Jeannette Osgood of Cambridge, Massachusetts, and they have one son, William Osgood. Dr. Aydelotte is of medium height—five feet nine inches—and weighs one hundred-sixty pounds. Blue-eyed, he was once light-haired, but now is bald—which sets off still more than before his large, outstanding ears about which he has been teased all his life. But no one who observes his radiant, friendly smile or comes under the spell of his dynamic personality notices whether or not he is handsome. He works at top speed, bubbling over with enthusiasm, with "unquenchable and contagious gusto." But he is no extroverted "go-getter"; he is himself an austere and dedicated scholar. His salient qualities are modesty and profound integrity. In manifestation of the first, Dr. Aydelotte is a passionate golfer of more than average ability, but does not want the figures of his golf score published because he finds them "too hard to live up to." In evidence of the second characteristic, during his incumbency at Swarthmore he became a convert to the faith of the Society of Friends but did not formally join the Quakers until after he had resigned, so that no one could even suspect him of having had any ulterior motive.

It is natural that such a man should take the present chaotic situation of the world much to heart. Dr. Aydelotte is an advocate of some sort of international government after the War. But to succeed, he says, it must improve on the League of Nations in two respects: it must be joined by the strongest world powers, including the United States, and the states composing it must "definitely give up some part of their national sovereignty to the international government." Such a federal union, he believes, could follow only on defeat of the Axis powers. And when or if such a union is formed, there could be no wiser choice for an American member of its governing board than Dr. Frank Aydelotte.

References

Friends Intelligencer 97:671-3 O 19 '40
N Y Times VII p5+ Ja 5 '41 por; p12 Ap 6 '41; p17 Ag 26 '41
Newark Sunday Call p12 Mr 16 '41 por
Newsweek 11:34 Ja 3 '38 por
Sci ns 91:566 Je 14 '40
Time 23:47 Je 5 '33; 33:57 Je 12 '39; 35:42-3 Mr 4 '40 por
Leaders in Education 1941
Swarthmore College Faculty. An Adventure in Education; Swarthmore College under Frank Aydelotte 1941
Who's Who in America
Who's Who in the East

AYRES, AGNES 1898—Dec. 25, 1940 Star of silent films; once famous as the leading lady for Rudolph Valentino and Wallace Reid; lost out when sound came to films; attempted a recent unsuccessful comeback.

References

Motion Pict Classic 7:34-5 D '18 pors; 10:58-9+ Ag '20 pors; 13:34-5 N '21 pors
Motion Pict Mag 21:56-7+ My '21 pors; 24:72-3+ N '22 pors
Photoplay 17:44 Ap '20 pors; 20:21+ Ag '21 por
International Motion Picture Almanac 1937-38

Obituaries

N Y Times p19 D 26 '40 por

BACA-FLOR, CARLOS (bä-cä-flōr') 1869 —May (?) 1941 Peruvian portrait painter who became known as the "painter of millionaires" after he completed a series of portraits of the late J. Pierpont Morgan and other financiers; lived for many years in the United States; died near Paris; his work is exhibited in museums both in this country and in Europe; won many prizes and distinctions.

References

Who's Who in Latin America

Obituaries

N Y Herald Tribune p22 My 21 '41 por

BACH, REGINALD Sept. 3, 1886—Jan. 6, 1941 English actor and stage director who has been in the United States since 1927; acted in or staged nearly 150 plays in England and this country; produced *Love on the Dole* and acted in it in 1936; staged *Green Waters*; *The Holmes of Baker Street*; *And Now Goodbye*; *Antony and Cleopatra*; and *Foreigners*.

References

Who's Who in the Theatre

Obituaries

N Y Times p23 Ja 7 '41
Variety 141:54 Ja 15 '41

BACON, GEORGE P(RESTON) Aug. 24, 1866—Sept. 17, 1941 Professor emeritus and dean of the Tufts College Engineering School; after teaching physics at Simmons College and at Wooster, Beloit and Ripon Colleges in the Midwest, went to Tufts in 1919 as professor of physics; served as dean from 1929 to 1936.

References

Who's Who in America

Obituaries

N Y Times p17 S 20 '41

BACON, LEONARD May 26, 1887- Author; poet
Address: h. The Acorns, Peace Dale, R. I.

LEONARD BACON

The Pulitzer Prize in poetry for 1940 was awarded to Leonard Bacon, whom J. P. Marquand calls "a man of the world, of ideas and of letters," for his *Sunderland Capture, and Other Poems*. This collection of lyrics inspired one critic to write that "the author is a man who has dared to meet himself face to face" and another to comment that "Leonard Bacon is prolific, vigorous, tender, satirical, sometimes even savage, but in spite of some good work he has done in the ballad, he is really one of the best satirists of our time."

Sunderland Capture is Leonard Bacon's thirteenth published book of poetry and the seventeenth book to have his name on the title page. (Individual poems have frequently appeared under the pseudonym "Autolycus.") There have been critics who found him "without parallel in our contemporary American verse"; others who regretted his wordiness, his "lack of poetry," his lack of clarity. But even disagreeing critics agree that there are few satiric poets today who have his poetic equipment and knowledge and his ability to produce facile comments on the contemporary scene, political, literary or social.

This was decreed by superior powers
In a moment of wisdom sidereal
That those who dwell upon ivory towers
Shall have heads of the same material

is the sort of verse that hits quickly, lightly, successfully.

Much of the background and inspiration and knowledge and emotion that go into Leonard Bacon's poetry are revealed in his autobiography, *Semi-centennial* (1939), on which Stephen Vincent Benét comments: "It is a poet who has written this book." Leonard Bacon was born in Solvay, New York, into what he feels was the best of all possible families. "If it were possible to choose and I had been wise in the choice, I could not have done better," he says. There were famous men on both sides of the family, and to young Leonard his father, Nathaniel Terry Bacon, was a great man, too, a physical chemist who wrote essays on economics, was a remarkable linguist and an authority on Swiss history. His mother, Helen (Hazard) Bacon, was a lovely woman, her "mind finely cultivated." It was to her, Bacon remembers, that "I owe my permanent, early and intense interest in literature and specifically in poetry. Long before I could read I had, because of her tutelage, dozens of poems at my tongue's end." And, he questions: "What more could I ask than to be introduced as a child by a beautiful woman to divine beauty?"

"Up to my eleventh year," Bacon recalls, "I don't suppose there was a happier child on the planet than I. But I must have become a problem in some way, for the higher powers decided at that point that I ought to go to boarding school, and St. George's at Newport, then a tiny struggling affair with not more than 24 boarders, was my destined fate." The first year at school was "miserable," but from "wonderful" vacations Bacon returned annually to a school "that grew easier against the pull of the collar," and it was with some regret that he left it in 1905.

It was foreordained that he should go to Yale, for Yale was a Bacon tradition. There he met people he liked, teachers he liked and admired, and was immediately active on the Yale *Literary Magazine*. All this was interrupted in 1907, however, when an amiable Boston specialist decided that the "abominably scrawny" lad was suffering from a tubercular lesion ("I personally never believed it," Bacon says) and sent him abroad to the Alps. Bacon returned to Yale to become an editor of the *Literary Magazine* and class poet. He was graduated in 1909 and "went forth from the half-light of a world of learning and young mirth into the surrounding darkness of an America which seemed not to care particularly for poets, class or otherwise."

"My ambition was crystal clear," he says. "I knew I wanted to write poetry and nothing but poetry." Instead, he went that summer to a rubber plantation in Nicaragua with his father, "an exciting experience," and returned to the United States in the fall of 1909 to enroll at Yale for graduate work. This scholastic interlude was hardly a successful one— Bacon says it reminds him of Balfour's remark on the story of mankind: "a brief and discreditable episode in the history of a minor planet." But it was punctuated by the publication of his first book, "a privately printed volume of very immature verses called *The Scrannel Pipe.*" As the result of his graduate work or perhaps because of this publication, Bacon suffered a slight nervous collapse, gave up his studies and went to work on a cattle ranch in Montana, where he stayed until spring.

Next, in July 1910, Leonard Bacon settled down for 13 years of teaching English at the University of California. That first year was an exciting one: there was "the tigerish effort to keep half a jump ahead of three swollen divisions of freshmen"; he was writing verse "with a furious energy and little skill"; and he was falling rapidly in love with Martha Sherman Stringham, whom he married in 1912. (He still dogmatically affirms that no man has been more happily married.) Bacon also found a lot of fun in introducing to poetry "young ranchmen from the San Joaquin valley, or girls who know no delight beyond a Bakersfield drugstore"—particularly when not one of them had ever seen the *Oxford Book of English Verse.* But this joy was tempered when he found to his horror that he knew "hardly enough grammar to teach it. . . It was three mortal years before I even began to feel adequate, nor am I sure I ever was." Before then, though, Bacon had begun to teach the University of California's first course in verse composition—"I was as near happy with that class as a teacher ever gets"—and soon afterward his translations of *Heroic Ballads of Servia* (with G. R. Noyes, 1913) and of *The Song of Roland* (with Selden Rose, 1914) appeared.

In 1917 Bacon left literature and poetry to enlist as second lieutenant in the United States Air Service. There was a nightmare period of actual flying in Toronto, followed by a period at the radio school at Columbia University. It was January 1919 before Bacon sat down to teach English again and to write poetry. His translation of *The Lay of the Cid* appeared in that year and for a year and a half he was "'on fire" with the mock epic of *Ulug Beg* (1923), the book which "for better or worse shaped my fate and . . . got me more of what a man really desires than most of my other works." And then in 1923 he gave up teaching forever.

Everything would have been well except for the melancholia which descended upon him in the autumn of 1923. It was senseless, Bacon admits: "I was perfectly married, I had three lovely children, I had enough money for our modest necessities. *Ulug Beg* was out. A new book had been accepted, another was under way." But there it was, and for more than a year he suffered before finally, early in 1925, committing himself into the hands of Dr. Jung. By this time *Ph. D.s,*

Male and Female, Created He Them had been published; and while he was consulting Jung *Animula Vagula* (1926), "the record of my *saison en enfer,*" was written.

By 1926 Bacon was established poet enough to deliver the Phi Beta Kappa poem at Harvard ("it went off well"). And in that year, after the death of his parents, he and his family moved from California to Peace Dale, Rhode Island. "A new life began. *The Legend of Quincibald* (1928) was beginning to take a sort of shape. [1927 had seen the publication of *Guinea-fowl, and Other Poultry.*] And *Furioso* (1932), though only a couple of cantos along, was definitely on the way. Life was simple but intensely pleasant."

It was partly to prepare himself better for the writing of this last work, partly to finish up some loose ends with Jung, and partly because he had always wanted to live in Florence, that Leonard Bacon and his wife set sail for Europe in the spring of 1927. For three years they lived abroad, three full and happy years. During those three years the *Legend of Quincibald,* an attempt to deal symbolically with the stuff of personality, was published (1928). It was called "wordy" and "unclear" as well as praised for its "vigor, wit, brilliance, passion, energy." In 1930 *The Last Buffalo, and Other Poems* appeared. And in 1932 *Furioso* was finally published, a narrative poem in the Byronic manner and form, whose hero is Gabriele d'Annunzio. Bacon ruefully comments that it "created, if possible, even less excitement than is usually manifest when my volumes from time to time appear."

Back home in Rhode Island, Leonard Bacon continued to write poetry—*Dream and Action* (1934); *The Voyage of Autoleon* (1935); and *The Goose on the Capitol* (1936), satirical verses chiefly on contemporary political and social problems of which one critic wrote: "The verses seldom sting, instead they awkwardly bump and paw." Another, however, summed them up as "full of good witticisms." Of *Rhyme and Punishment* (1936), Irwin Edman commented: "It is never precise-edged light verse or, where lyrical in intent, genuinely lyrical in effect." Other volumes were *Bullinger Bound, and Other Poems* (1938), which included a title poem built on the Prometheus theme and, among other poems, a group of word portraits of people where "the satirist yields to the sound observer whose analysis of human behavior is keen and just, not without pity and sympathetic understanding"; and his Pulitzer Prize winner, *Sunderland Capture* (1940). He also judged poetry for earlier Pulitzer Prizes, worked on his autobiography and contributed articles on people and literary movements and material like his accounts of visits to Hawaii to magazines such as the *Saturday Review of Literature* and *Harper's.* These are often noteworthy for keen understanding and brisk phrasing (one familiar quip of his is "the end of the ultra-violet decade and the beginning of the infra-red").

Leonard Bacon continues to live in the lovely South County of Rhode Island, his

BACON, LEONARD—*Continued*

greatest interest outside poetry being fishing, particularly fly-casting for trout or salmon. This to him is "a sort of physical extension of poetry . . . a great deal more than a pastime." But poetry itself continues to be his life, "my blessing and my curse." As he says in the last paragraph of *Semi-centennial*: "In the event that a humanly great thought should burn across my brain and incarnate itself in inevitable and indestructible words that come home to men's businesses and bosoms, I should be happy indeed but only happier in degree than I have been, and still am, to be a part, no doubt inconspicuous, in a great effort to get people to seek true and essential pleasure. I may never think that thought or discover those words. But if you have had a better time than I have had trying, you've had a damned good one."

References

Harper 178:182-6 Ja '39; 178:249-52 F '39; 178:416-21 Mr '39
Pub W 139:1928-9 My 10 '41 por
Sat R Lit 24:7 My 10 '41 por
Bacon, L. Semi-centennial 1939
Who's Who Among North American Authors
Who's Who in America

BADA, ANGELO (bä′dä′) 1875—Mar. 24, 1941 Italian tenor who sang secondary and character roles at the Metropolitan Opera House from 1908 to 1938; died in Novara, Italy, where he had retired; possessed a repertoire of more than 150 operas; was dean of the singing personnel in length of continuous service at the Metropolitan Opera.

References

Who Is Who in Music
Wier, A. E. ed. Macmillan Encyclopedia of Music and Musicians 1938

Obituaries

N Y Times p23 Mr 27 '41
Opera News 5:23 Ap 14 '41 por

BADEN-POWELL OF GILWELL, ROBERT STEPHENSON SMYTH BADEN-POWELL, 1ST BARON (bä′děn-pō′ěl) Feb. 22, 1857—Jan. 8, 1941 Founder of the Boy Scout movement and one of Britain's most famous soldiers and military intelligence operatives; conceived movement in 1908 when he took a group of English boys on a camping trip; was hero of the Boer War; wrote his autobiography, *Lessons of a Lifetime*, in 1933 and many books on scouting and army tactics.

References

Rotarian 47:4 Ag '35 por
Sat R 157:538-38a My 12 '34 por
Author's and Writer's Who's Who
Baden-Powell, R. S. S. Lessons of a Lifetime 1933
Batchelder, W. J. and Balfour, D. Scout's Life of Baden-Powell 1929

Hathaway, E. V. Partners in Progress p275-92 1935
Kiernan, R. H. Baden-Powell 1939
Rowe, J. G. Boy's Life of Baden-Powell 1929
Wade, E. K. Boy's Life of the Chief Scout pam 1929
Wade, E. K. Piper of Pax 1931
Who's Who

Obituaries

Christian Cent 58:200 F 5 '41
N Y Times p10 Ja 9 '41 por
Pub W 139:440 Ja 25 '41
Survey 77:69 F '41
Time 37:36+ Ja 20 '41

BAER, WILLIAM J(ACOB) Jan. 29, 1860 —Sept. 21, 1941 Artist; started painting oil portraits but soon entered the miniature painting field; received many awards for his miniatures at exhibitions here and abroad, among the best known of which are *Aurora, Summer, Nymph* and *Primavera*; taught art at Princeton University and Cooper Institute; one of the founders of the American Society of Miniature Painters and served as its treasurer; in 1913 became an associate member of the National Academy.

References

Art Digest 8:22 F 15 '34 por
Who's Who in America
Who's Who in American Art

Obituaries

N Y Times p23 S 23 '41

BAIRD, JOHN LAWRENCE, 1ST VISCOUNT STONEHAVEN *See* Stonehaven, J. L. B., 1st Viscount

BAKER, CHARLES WHITING Jan. 17, 1865—June 5, 1941 Engineer and author; former editor of the old *Engineering News* and later of the *Engineering News-Record*; consultant on government engineering projects who advised General Goethals on the Panama Canal; author of *Monopolies and the People* and *Pathways Back to Prosperity*.

References

American Men of Science
Who's Who Among North American Authors
Who's Who in America
Who's Who in Engineering

Obituaries

N Y Herald Tribune p10 Je 7 '41

BANKHEAD, TALLULAH (BROCKMAN) Jan. 31, 1903(?)– Actress

Address: h. Gotham Hotel, New York City; Jasper, Ala.

In 1935, when Tallulah Bankhead was playing in a rather dreary comedy called *Something Gay*, John Mason Brown wrote: "She is so gorgeously endowed that it will be one of the tragedies of our time if before it is too late, and owing to faults in her own temperament or to deficiencies in her playwrights, she fails to take her place in our theatre as the really important performer she might so easily have become." In the role of Regina Giddens, a predatory Southern woman, in Lillian Hellman's (see sketch this issue) *The Little Foxes,* she finally supplied an answer to her friends' plaintive wail, sounded ever since she came back to the United States: "Tallulah, why don't you get a good play?" This role was a natural for Miss Bankhead, whose Southern background helped her make the characterization of Regina lifelike and convincing. Far from being discomfited by having to play an unsympathetic character, Miss Bankhead proclaimed publicly to all and sundry that she "loves Regina to death." She felt quite at home in the Giddens household. And audiences, accustomed to glimpsing her brilliance through the discouraging murk of mediocre plays, forgot the long row of sophisticated *femme fatale* portrayals and began to identify Tallulah with unscrupulous, money-loving but definitely fascinating Regina.

Tallulah Bankhead was born in Huntsville, Alabama, on January 31, 1903. Her father was William Brockman Bankhead (see sketch 1940 Annual), who was to become the Speaker of the House of Representatives. Her mother, Adalaide Eugenia (Sledge) Bankhead, one of Virginia's most beautiful women, died a few days after Tallulah's birth. Tallulah got her strange name from her grandmother, another Virginia belle. Her childhood pictures, however, show her as an extremely homely child: she was quite fat, had a deep voice and an "infectious laugh that already was slightly Rabelaisian." The deep, husky voice was the result of the bronchial ailment that plagued her as a child, but later Tallulah found it a considerable asset. She spent her childhood shuttling between seminaries and convents, both of which she loathed bitterly. Together with her sister Eugenia she attended the Convent of the Sacred Heart, Mary Baldwin Seminary, Convent of the Visitation, Convent of the Holy Cross in Virginia and the Fairmont Seminary in Washington, D. C. In-between she stayed at Montgomery with her aunt, Mrs. Thomas Owen, and when her father, then a rising politician, remarried, at his house in Virginia.

By 1917, when Tallulah's father was running for Congress, she had lost weight and become a beauty, with great blue eyes, tawny hair and a "vote-for-Daddy" smile. She had also discovered that she wanted to be an actress. There was no opposition from her family, it being tacitly assumed that the Bankheads were bound to be public characters of one sort or another. Her father, who himself narrowly missed being an actor in his youth, was frankly sympathetic. He was to see the name of Bankhead shine as brightly on the stage as it did in the halls of Congress, where his father, himself and his Senator brother John Hollis "represented Alabama for an aggregate of some threescore years." If Tallulah was often called "Speaker Bankhead's gal Tal," he himself was to be identified as "Tallulah's father." Her first

TALLULAH BANKHEAD

appearance was in the old Greenwich Theatre in New York City in a play called *Squab Farm,* in 1919. The next year she was appearing in "a somewhat footloose vehicle" entitled *Footloose* and in *39-East.* The next few years were occupied with run-of-the-mill roles in *Nice People* (1919); in 1922 in *Everyday Danger, Her Temporary Husband* and *The Exciters.*

In 1923 Tallulah was summoned to London to play in *The Dancers* with Sir Gerald du Maurier. The story is that at the last moment she got a cable canceling the engagement, ignored it and went to England anyway. She got the rather juicy role of Maxine in *The Dancers* and was immediately a tremendous success. For the next eight years she starred in fifteen London productions. Her husky intriguing drawl, her tawny hair, arched eyebrows and enigmatic smile endeared her to the hearts of the London audiences. Du Maurier called her "Swanface"; thousands of London flappers found her the epitome of glamor and besieged the stage door for a glimpse of her. They hailed her in 1924 in *Conchita, This Marriage,* and the *Creaking Chair* and in 1925 in *Fallen Angels.* Her greatest triumph, however, came with her performance as Iris March in Michael Arlen's *Green Hat* (1925), a part in which Katharine Cornell (see sketch this issue) also scored a hit in the United States. The audiences loved her sophistication, her brilliant humor, "that serious air of directness and simplicity which fitted in so strangely with certain decadent mannerisms." George Jean Nathan, it is true, numbered her (until her performance in *The Little Foxes*) as one of his histrionic skepticisms and remarked unkindly that her success seemed to be due largely to the fact that "with her wild and woolly ways and manner, she was a novelty to a stage whose women generally comport themselves as if they all had been written by Pinero, and that, further, in two of her exhibits she had taken her

BANKHEAD, TALLULAH—*Continued*

clothes off, which always gets the sedate London critics."

The sedate London critics had only unreserved praise for most of Tallulah Bankhead's performances, which ran through a pretty wide range, from that of Amy in *They Knew What They Wanted* (1926) to that of Marguerite Gautier in *The Lady of the Camellias* (1930). She was best liked, however, in sprightly parlor comedies such as *Her Cardboard Lover* (1928); *The Gold Diggers* (1926); and *Let Us Be Gay* (1930). Her social life reflected her performances in its brilliance. She belonged to the clever and elite Noel Coward (see sketch this issue) set. Her house on Farm Street, Mayfair, which she had reconditioned from a stable, was famed for the sensational parties given there and the important social figures that came visiting. Augustus John (see sketch this issue) painted her portrait. Her name was at one time coupled with that of Count Anthony de Bosdari, a prominent figure in the younger international set. But rumors of her engagements always subsided, after pleasurably exciting her admirers, with Tallulah's invariable statement that she preferred her "present bachelor state."

In 1931 Tallulah Bankhead came back to the United States after signing a long-term contract with Paramount. Her film career turned out to be a failure: somehow the elusive Bankhead personality failed to register on the screen except as a faint travesty of Marlene Dietrich. She was, besides, the victim of unfailingly bad pictures. In one of her first pictures, called *Tarnished Lady,* she flitted neurotically and to no purpose from luxurious penthouse to squalid dive. At one time she was co-starred with—and back-staged by—Charles Laughton in *Devil and the Deep.* Other pictures monosyllabically entitled *My Sin, The Cheat,* etc., exploited the Bankhead *femme fatale* reputation without ever suggesting her sophisticated stage personality. Her last film venture in 1933 was *Faithless.*

Disappointed, Tallulah Bankhead returned to the stage in *Forsaking All Others* (1933), a play which allowed her to be gay, pathetic, desperate and tragic all in one evening, and in 1934 she toured the United States in *The Snob,* a London success. In that same year she played Judith Traherne, the doomed heroine of *Dark Victory,* played it with the intensity and power that she possesses when her attention is turned to stark tragedy. Then in 1935 came the revival of *Rain* with Tallulah Bankhead as Sadie Thompson. Her characterization, hardboiled and raucous, was dismissed as merely an adequate impersonation of Jeanne Eagels. And critics felt that her sultry strength was wasted on negligible plays like *Something Gay* (1935) or *Reflected Glory* (1936). "Miss Bankhead," wrote one critic, "needs to be protected against that fretful energy of hers. It makes her wasteful of her gifts. . . It keeps her unsteady in her playing. Although her acting is enormously skillful it is sadly lacking in discipline. It tempts her into playing all

scenes with an equal drive instead of saving herself for her climaxes."

Probably what could be called the low of her acting career was her performance in 1937 in *Antony and Cleopatra.* Of this unlucky venture one critic wrote briefly: "Tallulah Bankhead barged down the Nile last night as Cleopatra—and sank. . . As the Serpent of the Nile she proves to be no more dangerous than a garter snake." This moment of deep darkness was followed by the first gleamings of the dawn. The revival of *The Circle* provided Tallulah Bankhead with a more suitable vehicle and found her giving a performance of poise and grace. Her personal life, too, had passed through a change: on August 31, 1937 she eloped with John Emery, an actor whom she married in Jasper, Alabama, where she had spent most of her childhood. "He is crazy as a hatter," she said cheerfully to excited interviewers, "but then so am I."

In 1939 she read the script of Lillian Hellman's *The Little Foxes* and knew at last that here was a role for her, something into which she could get her teeth. There was a little doubt at first about her getting the part: rumors circulated about the author's feeling that Tallulah looked too young and the actress' feeling that she need not sacrifice any of her beauty to bring reality to the part of Regina, who, in the play, has a grown-up daughter. Her performance was hailed as a "superb example of mature acting fully under control." After years of bad luck, bad casting and bad playing, Tallulah Bankhead seemed to have finally found the right vehicle for her "special brand of magic." She kept on playing Regina Giddens in New York and on the road for some time, stopping only to play the title role in *The Second Mrs. Tanqueray* in the summer of 1940 (a performance enriched by her experience in *The Little Foxes*) and to divorce her husband in Reno in June 1941 (reason: "that old debbil career"). In the fall of 1941, however, after touring cowbarns all summer with *Her Cardboard Lover,* she accepted a role in Clifford Odets' (see sketch this issue) *Clash By Night,* which Billy Rose was planning to produce.

Tallulah Bankhead, who has kept her cyclonic ways off as well as on the stage, is a complete rebuttal of the idea that Southern females are languorous. She has her share of activities outside of the stage. She has been voluble in various Equity rows: in 1939, a particularly busy year, she aided the adopt-a-Spanish-orphan movement, led the march on Washington in behalf of the Federal Theatre Project, which was to be cut, and publicly besought her father to "do something about it"; she has also taken up cudgels against fingerprinting aliens and, in 1940, proposed giving away her salary of $1,000 a week to the Finnish fund. The next year found her doing her bit for Fight for Freedom, Inc., and aid to Russia. She is a rabid baseball fan (a Giant rooter, because "I just couldn't root for a team named Yankees"); has given parties for her baseball heroes; and her dressing room decorations consist largely of various baseball souvenirs. When last heard from she had a

Pekinese named Annie, a golden marmoset called Senegas and a lion cub named Winston Churchill. She still thinks that "all you would need to do is to build a fourth wall and you could live right on the stage." She felt that way about *The Little Foxes* set; and of all her performances, her father, the late Speaker Bankhead, particularly enjoyed that of Regina Giddens, mostly because with her blonde hair up and dressed in the lush costumes of the 1900's she looks very much like her mother.

References

Delineator 130:11 Ja '37 por
Lit Digest 123:22 My 29 '37 por
N Y Times IX pl S '40; IX p2 Jl 27 '41
Spur 46:40 Jl-S '30
Theatre Arts Mo 23:718-19 O '39
Theatre World 26:231 N '36 por
Woman's H C 67:23+ Ag '40 il pors

Brown, J. M. Two on the Aisle p233-5 1938
International Motion Picture Almanac
Moses, M. J. and Brown, J. M. eds. American Theatre as Seen by its Critics p343-5 1934
Sobel, B. ed. Theatre Handbook 1940
Who's Who in America
Who's Who in the Theatre

BANTING, SIR FREDERICK GRANT

Nov. 4, 1891—Feb. 21, 1941 University of Toronto professor who won the Nobel Prize (1923) as co-discoverer of insulin; killed in crash in Newfoundland en route to Britain for research in medical problems of aviation; since the start of the Second World War had served as captain in the Canadian Army Medical Corps; called one of the great benefactors of mankind who lengthened the lives of untold numbers of diabetics the world over.

References

Canad Mag 81:47 F '34 por
Hygeia 16:497 Je '38 por; 16:1096 D '38 por
Ladies' H J 49:12+ N '32 por
Lit Digest 121:18-19 Je 6 '36 por
Time 34:27 S 18 '39 por

American Medical Directory
American Men of Science
Bruce, H. A. Our Heritage p70-1 1934
De Kruif, P. H. Men Against Death p59-87 1932
Law, F. H. Civilization Builders p344-6 1939
McCallum, J. D. ed. College Book of Essays p220-37 1939
McCallum, J. D. ed. College Omnibus p281-98 1936
Who's Who

Obituaries

N Y Times p25 F 25 '41
Newsweek 17:2 Mr 3 '41
Sci ns 93:202 F 28 '41
Time 37:50 Mr 3 '41

BARBER, MARY I(SABEL) Dietitian; food consultant

Address: b. War Department, Office of the Quartermaster General, Washington, D. C.; h. 74 Sherman Rd, Battle Creek, Mich.

MARY I. BARBER

Bulletin: Miss Barber writes us: "My appointment from the Office of Production Management terminated June 1, 1941. My title now is Expert Food Consultant to the Secretary of War and I am assigned to the Subsistence Branch of the Quartermaster Corps. My work is practically the same as it was under the Office of Production Management."

From July 1941 issue:

If he's "in the Army now," the young American male is getting five pounds of well-balanced rations daily, which make him considerably better fed than 60 per cent of the civilian population. Anxious mothers, wives and sweethearts who feel that their boys in training need to be fortified by extra boxes of home-cooked tidbits, may be thus reassured by Mary I. Barber, OPM food consultant, who helps prepare menus for the 4,200,000 meals a day fed to the Army's 1,400,000 men. Miss Barber, the first dollar-a-year woman in the defense program, is president of the American Dietetic Association. Prior to her present position in the Army's Quartermaster Corps she was head of the Home Economics Department of the Kellogg Company, Battle Creek, Michigan.

Food—its history, cost, preparation, conservation—has always been Mary I. Barber's career. Born in the country of the Pennsylvania Dutch (who know good food and enjoy it), she grew up in Titusville, Pennsylvania, the daughter of James Renwick and Emma Louisa (Michael) Barber. Following her graduation from the Titusville High School she entered Drexel Institute, later studied at the University of

BARBER, MARY I.—*Continued*

Pennsylvania, and received her B. S. in home economics at Columbia University in 1920. Miss Barber was a hospital dietitian and also taught cooking in a Philadelphia high school in pre-World War days. During the War, in the Government's drive to conserve food, she worked with the New York State Bureau of Conservation. After the War she became a member of the faculty of Teachers College, Columbia University.

Miss Barber was vice-president, 1937 to 1940, of the American Home Economics Association. She is currently president of the Michigan Home Economics Association and a member of the Business and Professional Women's Club and of the Altrusa Club. She was Pantry Editor of *Child Life* Magazine (1936-41); has contributed many articles on food to various periodicals; and is co-author, with M. B. Van Arsdale, of two books: *Our Candy Recipes* (1922) and *Some Reasons Why in Cookery* (1923). In connection with her work in cooking and dietetics she has traveled all over the United States, Central America and in three countries in Europe. Her chief hobby, she says, is old cookery books; for recreation she likes golf and swimming. In politics she is a Republican; her church affiliation is Episcopalian.

In an address on April 4, 1941 in New York City under the auspices of the Home Economics Women in Business, Miss Barber gave a report on how the United States is tackling the job of producing well-fed fighting men. In order to show how much better Army "chow" for the modern trainee is than that given our heroes who fought on rather lean stomachs in the country's past wars, Miss Barber arranged a demonstration. Soldiers from Fort Slocum, each in a uniform representing a different American war era, stepped forward, exhibiting on trays the food items allowed in other days. "Kitchen police" were universal in the Valley Forge era. Food (whatever could be mustered) was issued uncooked to each man, who prepared his own meals over a camp fire. More often—as during the Civil War—the men lived by foraging. When it could be supplied, Washington's men got each day a pound of beef, some flour and milk. They also were given 6.8 ounces of peas, 1.1 of rice and a quart of spruce beer daily. Extra luxuries (probably not for culinary purposes) were .06 ounces of candle and .18 of soap.

The above rations, Miss Barber said further, held pretty much through the Civil War, together with the heartily disliked "hardtack." Civil War days also brought mention of ʃeast powder" (baking powder), peas, dry beans, "green" coffee and sugar. An Act of Congress in 1812 provided each man also, besides his quota of beef and flour, with one gill each of vinegar and rum and .64 ounces of salt in addition to the allotted soap and candle. No stimulants were prescribed in the Civil War diet, nor in that of the Spanish-American War. In 1898 fresh potatoes were added to the diet, and field kitchens began to make their appearance.

According to Miss Barber, by 1917 the variety in the total of food items had been greatly increased over that established in 1913. Prunes, syrup and evaporated milk had arrived; coffee was roasted and ground; butter and lard were commonplace; cinnamon and even lemon extract appeared. In 1918 were added sweet potatoes and corn meal. The Army's World War food bill for one year, said Miss Barber, totaled $727,092,430, representing 3,777,500,000 pounds of food.

Although Miss Barber apparently itemized no typical menus for trainees in World War II, she assured her audience that a man could have no possible quarrel with his food except perhaps with its flavor. At home he might demand his roast beef rare; in camp he'd have to eat it well done, since that was majority preference, and Uncle Sam's chefs have not yet gotten around to catering to individual tastes. Modern army dietitians have set the stamp of approval on chocolate cake for dessert, and have made pie—the home variety—a specialty. But if mothers and sweethearts, still undismayed in the face of this drastic competition, want to send their men a bit of apple strudel, nut bread or just plain fudge, the Army (individually at least) probably won't object.

References

N Y Sun p27 Ap 2 '41
N Y Times p16 Ap 4 '41; IV p2 Ap 6 '41 por
American Women

BARKLEY, ALBEN W(ILLIAM) Nov. 24, 1877- Majority leader of the United States Senate

Address: b. Senate Office Bldg, Washington, D. C.; h. Paducah, Ky.

The majority leader in the Senate is Alben W. Barkley ("Dear Alben"), whom *Time* calls a "dependable, likable, old-dog sort of man," in politics "regular as a metronome." No Senator has been more consistently faithful to President Roosevelt than Alben Barkley, even though he once helped to override the President's veto of the Veterans' Bonus.

Alben William Barkley, Democratic Senator from Kentucky, was born there, in a Graves County log cabin, on November 24, 1877. The son of a tobacco farmer, John W. Barkley, and Electra A. (Smith) Barkley, he worked in the fields and attended county schools until old enough to enter Marvin College in Clinton. It was 1897 when he received his B. A., and he proceeded to put himself through Emory College, Oxford, Georgia, and the University of Virginia Law School at Charlottesville, Virginia by working as a janitor and a waiter. In 1901 he was admitted to the Bar and found his first law position in the office of Paducah's Judge W. S. Bishop (Irvin S. Cobb's "Judge Priest"). Two years later he married Dorothy Brower of Paducah, and in 1905 he conducted a "muleback campaign" that made him prosecuting attorney for McCracken County for a term of four years. At the expiration of his term he was elected judge of the McCracken

County Court, and he served in that capacity until elected to Congress on March 4, 1913, after covering the first Kentucky District with a horse and buggy.

In 1919 Barkley was chairman of the State Democratic Convention at Louisville, Kentucky. In the House his outstanding activity was to help foster the Prohibition Amendment and Volstead Act, even becoming a paid speaker for the Anti-Saloon League. In 1920 he was a delegate at large to the Democratic National Convention at San Francisco, where he voted to seat Franklin Delano Roosevelt. In 1923 he was an unsuccessful candidate for Governor of Kentucky. In 1924 he was once more chairman of the State Democratic Convention, this time at Lexington, Kentucky, and also a delegate at large to the Democratic National Convention in New York. And in 1926 he was a successful candidate for the United States Senate.

Barkley took his Senate seat on March 4, 1927. The next year, once again a delegate at large to the Democratic National Convention, he stumped for Al Smith. By 1932, the year he was for the first time temporary chairman of the Democratic National Convention at Chicago and delivered the keynote speech, he had come out openly for repeal of the Prohibition Amendment. His Republican opponents therefore promised to defeat four Barkleys: "the Free Trade Barkley, the Protectionist Barkley [before the New Deal he had voted for coal and oil tariffs], the Dry Barkley, the Wet Barkley." But the Republicans were unable to keep their promise, and after he returned to the Senate on March 4, 1933, Barkley was picked as lieutenant-leader by the late Joe Robinson.

Again in 1936 it was Barkley who was chosen, this time by President Roosevelt, to deliver the keynote speech at the Democratic National Convention in Philadelphia. The summer of 1937 found him once more honored by Roosevelt, who swung his election as Senate leader from Mississippi's Pat Harrison by the famous letter which began "Dear Alben." "Dear Alben" got it by one vote. Then in the Senatorial campaigns of 1938 Roosevelt backed Barkley's candidacy for the Senate against that of Governor Chandler, who was "still an avowed New Dealer." A letter by President Roosevelt which was made public announced: "Senator Barkley's long familiarity with national affairs, his integrity, his patriotic zeal, his courage and loyalty, and his eloquence . . . give him exceptional equipment as a legislator and a leader." There could be little question of Barkley's election after that, and his third term in the Senate began January 3, 1939.

In 1940 Barkley tried to halt the inquiry on the feasibility of a third Presidential term, although in 1928, in Coolidge's day, he himself had voted for a resolution to cut the Presidential tenure. He announced, dryly: "A wise man may change his mind, a fool never does." Appropriately enough, that summer he was permanent chairman of the Democratic National Convention in Chicago at which Roosevelt was nominated for the third time, and

ALBEN W. BARKLEY

he returned to head the Administration forces in the fight to put through the conscription bill. In 1941 it was he and Senator Byrnes (see sketch this issue) who nursed the Lend-Lease Bill through the Senate, holding the New Deal members firmly in line to vote against all restrictions. Barkley's critics, however, say that Byrnes, less plodding and more expert at handling people, did the most important part of this job.

In February 1941 Barkley's views on the Second World War were that a declaration of war was not yet necessary, but might later become so. "There is but one way to stop a conqueror," he proclaimed. "That way is to defeat him. The only way to stop Hitler is to defeat him, and if we do not help Great Britain and other nations now fighting him to defeat him over there we shall some day have to surrender to him or defeat him over here." He, with Tom Connally (see sketch this issue) sponsored the amendments to the Neutrality Act which passed the Senate in November 1941.

Hard-working Senator Barkley is chairman of the Committee on the Library of the United States Senate, and also serves on the following committees: Banking and Currency; Expenditure in Executive Departments; Finance; Foreign Relations; Interstate Commerce; Government Organization. He is a Methodist, an Elk, a member of the Delta Tau Delta Fraternity and of the Loyal Order of the Moose. With "heavy features . . . a chest like a keg" and a voice unrivaled by any hog-caller for "breath, depth and carrying power," he is the sort of earnest speaker who perspires and gesticulates, but impresses. He writes his own speeches, batting them out on a typewriter. A good-natured man, he "tries hard to turn a wisecrack" from time to time, will sing when requested, and, "as befits his plodding nature, his favorite song is *Wagon Wheels*." Senator and Mrs. Barkley have one son, David, and two daughters, Marion and Laura. In Wash-

BARKLEY, ALBEN W.—*Continued*

ington the Senator drives his own car, entertains "moderately but often." He is proud of his Senate record; he says: "If being loyal to the greatest President is hanging on his coat-tails, I'm proud to hang on."

References

Collier's 102:12-13+ Jl 16 '38 il por
Lit Digest 124(Digest 1):12 Jl 31 '37
Newsweek 11:15 Ja 31 '38 por
Time 30:9-11 Ag 23 '37 pors; 32:9-12 Ag 1 '38 il por
Who's Who in America
Who's Who in Government
Who's Who in Law
Who's Who in the Nation's Capital

BARNARD, JAMES LYNN Aug. 9, 1867—Aug. 10, 1941 Professor of political science at Ursinus College; taught at Columbia University, University of Pittsburgh, Harvard and Pennsylvania State College; was author of many books on political science.

References

Leaders in Education 1941
Who's Who Among North American Authors
Who's Who in America

Obituaries

N Y Times p13 Ag 11 '41

BARNETT, EUGENE E(PPERSON) Feb. 21, 1888- General Secretary of the National Council of the Young Men's Christian Association

Address: b. 347 Madison Ave, New York City; h. 45 Harvard Ct, White Plains, N. Y.

EUGENE E. BARNETT

The man considered the world's foremost leader of youth is Eugene E. Barnett, appointed

(January 1, 1941) General Secretary of the National Council of Y. M. C. A.'s and their World Service activities in 32 countries. The man who is director of more than two million American youth, as well as associated international groups, believes that youth itself—not buildings or equipment—is the primary concern of the Y. M. C. A. He is deeply convinced of the growing need for world cooperation and of the importance of the Y. M. C. A. in maintaining international good will and understanding. In his speech at the closing session of the annual meeting of the National Council in October 1940, Mr. Barnett said:

"We see mankind, notwithstanding all its conflicts and warfare, bound together by an amazing homogeneity of problems. We see mankind trying to assimilate science, technology and intercommunications, now suddenly become world-wide and instantaneous in its outreach. We see a revolution which, on the one hand, may be headed toward the abyss but one which, on the other hand, may lift humanity to a higher level of existence than we have ever dared to dream of. It goes without saying that America is inextricably involved in this world-wide revolution."

With years of extensive experience not only in this country but in Europe, the Orient, South America and other countries, few men know the problems of world youth so intimately as does Eugene Barnett. He believes that the primary importance of youth training is the development of leadership. "Leaders," he says, "are needed everywhere, men who will not only rebuild destroyed countries, replace outmoded equipment and develop new opportunities opened up by the events of the past three years, but who will meet the challenges of the century. One challenge is to achieve a democracy purged of selfish individualism and class barriers."

Since he entered Y. M. C. A. work in 1908 as student "Y" secretary at the University of North Carolina, Mr. Barnett has given his entire career to the building of the organization. He was born in Leesburg, Florida, February 21, 1888, the son of Robert H. and Sarah (Epperson) Barnett. After receiving his B. A. degree at Emory University in 1907, he did a year of postgraduate work at Vanderbilt University. From 1908 to 1910 he continued his studies at the University of North Carolina, and did further work at Columbia University from 1923 to 1930.

In 1910 he married Bertha Mae Smith of Jasper, Florida. The couple has three sons and a daughter: Robert Warren, former Rhodes scholar, now in China on a special project for the Institute of Pacific Relations; Eugenia Mae of Seattle, Washington; Henry DeWitt, a 1939 graduate of the University of North Carolina; and Arthur Doak, a student at Yale University. The Barnetts live modestly in White Plains, New York. Mr. Barnett is a member of several organizations, including the Masons. His religious affiliation is Methodist.

He was selected by the General Secretary of the Y. M. C. A. International Committee in 1910 to go to China. There Barnett began his work by founding the Hangchow Association. From 1921 to 1937 he served on the staff of the National Committee of the Chinese Y. M. C. A. as executive head of its City Division and concurrently as Associate National General Secretary. He pays special tribute to the work of Dr. David Z. T. Yui, China's national "Y" secretary, and his dream of democracy for China's young men. During this period Barnett's work took him all over China, where he made many friends among the country's civic, religious and educational leaders. He served as a member of the National Christian Council; as a college trustee of Methodist, Presbyterian and Baptist institutions; and as chairman of the Shanghai School for American children. Today he is regarded as one of the leading authorities on affairs and conditions in the Far East.

In 1937, while on furlough in the United States, Barnett was selected as executive of the World Service program, succeeding Francis S. Harmon. That summer he made extensive tours of Association work in Peru, Chile, Argentina, Uruguay, Brazil and Mexico, and during the following summer visited Y. M. C. A.'s in Europe. On both journeys he interviewed political, educational and youth leaders in each country, gathering a vast amount of information regarding youth conditions. During the summer of 1940 he returned to the Far East, spending some months in occupied and unoccupied regions of China, Japan, Korea, Manchuria and the Philippines. He had confidential talks with Baron Y. Sakatani of Japan, Baron Yun Chi-ho of Korea, Generalissimo Chiang Kai-shek and Dr. H. H. Kung of China, and President Manuel Quezon (see sketch this issue) of the Philippines.

After these conversations abroad and observations made also in the United States, Barnett expressed his keenly felt concern for the predicament of young people today, of "Youth —millions too many." These are "the youth of our cities—in factory, school, office and home. The youth of our colleges and universities. The youth who in increasing numbers will be making up our defense forces. The all but forgotten youth who comprise our neglected minorities—Negroes, North and South, Mexicans on our Southern borders, and Orientals in our great cities and across the continent. . . The youth of lands where the light of freedom has for the time been put out. The youth of lands where youth are so much cannon fodder for military machines. The youth of the world whose dreams no amount of frustration can quite extinguish. . . Youth out of which our new democratic collectivism, our new world order, youth out of which the Kingdom of God will yet be built."

A man of energy, care and insight with a capacity for quietly getting things done, in all parts of the world Eugene Barnett has made friends with whom he maintains a continuous correspondence. "Numerous executive problems seldom ruffle his Southern calm. There is always a sense of strength and sure-

ness in his quiet manner, no matter how great become the demands upon his time and energies." That a sense of humor goes with this organizing ability may be gathered from Mr. Barnett's quoting of a jingle he likes to remember:

The centipede was happy quite
Until a toad in fun
Said, "Pray, which leg goes after which?"
That worked her mind to such a pitch
She lay distracted in a ditch
Considering how to run.

References

N Y Herald Tribune p23 Ja 1 '41 por
Time 37:46 Ja 6 '41 por
Who's Who in America

BARRATT, SIR ARTHUR SHERIDAN

(băr'ăt) Feb. 25, 1891- British Air Marshal; head of the Army Cooperation Command

Address: Berkeley Square House, W. 1, London, England

Photographic News

SIR ARTHUR SHERIDAN BARRATT

Sir Arthur Sheridan Barratt, who learned to fly when aviation was in its elementary stages and who distinguished himself in the First World War as an intrepid pilot and a distinguished leader, was the man appointed to head the British Army Cooperation Command, established on December 1, 1940. This Royal Air Force command amounts to a special joint army command and works with the armies in the field. It is believed to be an important development for the time when Britain will take the offensive against Germany.

Barratt is an officer of the robust, sporting type, known as "one of the six best all-round athletes in the forces." He might easily have become a professional boxing champion,

BARRATT, SIR ARTHUR—*Continued*

and a story of his boyhood is still remembered in England. His school boxing instructor was having a bout with him and, being a professional, was able to keep the boy at arm's length. Barratt was laid flat three times, but he staggered up and put in a good left. The instructor lowered his guard, put an arm around Barratt's shoulders and said: "You've got guts. You can take it. And one day you'll be able to hand it out good and proper. Then I wouldn't like to be them as gets it."

Besides being a boxer, Barratt is an excellent angler, a crack shot, an outstanding steeple chaser and a winter sports expert. Billy Bishop, V. C. (see sketch this issue), in charge of the Canadian air training scheme, once said of him: "I know no one possessing such perfect coordination of mind and muscle. Nothing that Barratt really wants to do is beyond him." To his sporting tastes Barratt adds others, much more surprising in a fighting man. In peace time he can often be seen going round to the Bond Street galleries, indulging his real love for art which runs mainly to the extreme modernists. He is also something of a gourmet. In reading he is mainly interested in technical matter connected with his work, though nothing is better for relaxation than a good detective story, he thinks. Films are good, too, for entertainment; they are even better, he says, for use in training flyers.

Born at Peshawar, India, the son of Charles Henry Barratt of Clifton, Bristol, England, young Arthur was sent home at an early age (as is usual with children of parents stationed in hot climates) and at 14 went to Clifton College. From there he proceeded to the Royal Military Academy, Woolwich, took general and gunnery training and passed in 1910 into the Royal Artillery. Those were the days when to fly at all was an adventure, but Barratt, like Sir Cyril Newall, saw a great future for aviation and for its application to warfare. So, in 1914, he had himself trained at the Central Flying School, Upavon, and in July of that year was seconded to the Royal Flying Corps—as the army air arm, then separate from the naval, was called.

Very shortly after, Barratt was sent out to the 3rd squadron of the Royal Flying Corps to take part in the War in France. Most of his service was in the Ypres district. It was distinguished service, for he was mentioned in dispatches four times, won the Military Cross, the Belgian Croix de Guerre and the Croix de l'Ordre de la Couronne. At the beginning of 1916 he was promoted to the rank of squadron commander; in 1917 he became wing commander, in charge of the third and fourth wings; and in April 1918 he rose to lieutenant colonel. He went to the Rhineland with the Army of Occupation, was in charge of the second brigade of the R. A. F. for some time and finished his War service on the R. A. F. headquarters staff at Cologne.

The War over, Barratt decided to resign his army commission and throw in his lot with the Royal Air Force. He was given the rank of squadron leader, was raised to wing commander in November 1919 and was then posted to the directorate of training and organization. In 1924 he took a course at the army Staff College at Camberley, after which he became commandant of the School of Army Cooperation. In 1927 he was sent out to the Far East to serve under the general officer commanding the Shanghai Defence Forces and there worked alongside Lord Gort.

Barratt saw active service again in 1931 when he was posted to his birthplace, Peshawar, as air officer commanding the No. I (Indian) Group. But it wasn't too active to keep him from indulging in the region's sports: in polo, tentpegging and pigsticking. In 1932 he went up one step in rank, to air commodore, and acted as senior staff officer at the Indian headquarters until the end of 1934.

In 1935 Barratt was back in London, where he spent two years at the Air Ministry as director of staff duties. Then in 1936 he was promoted to the rank of air vice-marshal and made commandant of the R. A. F. Staff College at Andover, a position he kept until 1939, when he was again sent out to India as a commanding air officer. When the Second World War broke out he was immediately recalled and, since cooperation between airplanes and ground forces was his special study, was given liaison work with the French Air Force. Then, in January 1940, when a new British command called "British Air Forces in France" was formed to coordinate the work of the R. A. F. with the British and French Armies, he was made its air officer commanding in chief. On his return from France in July 1940 Barratt was again promoted, this time to air marshal, and knighted as Knight Commander of the Bath. He was already a Companion of the Bath and of the Order of St. Michael and St. George. From his return on, he was kept active in England on special duties until his appointment as head of the Army Cooperation Command was announced in November 1940.

This officer, now in one of England's most important positions, is in his late 40's, and his outlook is still as young as his years. Fellow officers like to tell the story of the wedding of his only child Suzanne (her mother is Norah Lilian Crew of Clifton). The ceremony had been scheduled early in 1940, and since Barratt was on duty in France there seemed no chance of his being able to attend it. But at the last moment he looked around, saw the front was quiet enough, stepped into a plane and was there right in time.

References

Christian Sci Mon p5 N 19 '40 por
Daily Express Ja 10 '40
Times [London] Ja 11 '40
Pollard, A. O. Leaders of the Royal Air Force 1940
Who's Who

BARRINGER, PAUL BRANDON Feb. 13, 1857—Jan. 9, 1941 Physician, educator and publicist who earned national distinction; head of Virginia Polytechnic Institute from 1907 to 1913; physician for 62 years.

References

American Medical Directory
Who's Who in America 1922-23
Who's Who in American Medicine

Obituaries

N Y Times p20 Ja 10 '41
Sch & Soc 53:80 Ja 18 '41

BARRYMORE, ETHEL Aug. 15, 1879-
Actress
Address: h. Mamaroneck, N. Y.

Vandamm

ETHEL BARRYMORE

On the evening of Tuesday, February 4, 1941 Ethel Barrymore, the undisputed First Lady of the American theatre, celebrated her fortieth anniversary as a star on the New York stage. First she played her usual role as Miss Moffat in Emlyn Williams' (see sketch this issue) *The Corn Is Green,* "the most heartwarming performance of her career"; next she listened to a broadcast over WJZ and the Blue Network in which Alexander Woollcott, Herman Shumlin (see sketches this issue), Helen Hayes, Arthur Hopkins, Louis B. Mayer, and her brothers Lionel and John paid tribute to her. Almost tearfully she thanked them all and the public. "If my years are to be lined up and counted off," she said, "I can think of no pleasanter way for it to happen. If I have little consciousness of the burden of years, it is because so many, known and unknown to me, have conspired to make those years light."

For 40 years Ethel Barrymore has been a star; for 40 years she has appeared on Broadway, in small towns from Maine to California; in stock, vaudeville, motion pictures. Audiences have seen her grow from a sprightly young thing into a mature woman, "gracious, imposing, regal." And always they have acclaimed her acting. As a Barrymore, she is used to that, for Barrymores have been figures on the American stage for many, many years. Maurice Barrymore, her father (his real name was Herbert Blythe), was acting long before she was born. Her mother, Georgiana (Drew) Barrymore, was the sister of the famous actor John Drew. And her brothers, Lionel and John, are familiar and important figures in the theatrical and film world.

Ethel herself began acting almost as soon as she could talk. She was born in Philadelphia and went to school there—to the Convent of Notre Dame. But it is not school books or school games that she and her brothers remember: it is rather the memory of tempestuous performances like that of *Camille* which the young Barrymores put on at the ages of 10, 12 and 14 in an old barn.

When she was only 12 Ethel got her first chance at a real performance, in a very minor role in her uncle John Drew's play, *The Bauble Shop.* And one night when Elsie de Wolfe, the leading lady, was ill, Ethel Barrymore stepped into her part, giving "a surprisingly good account of herself" in the role of a 32-year-old woman. People knew then that Maurice Barrymore had a clever daughter, and Uncle Drew advised producer Charles Frohman to keep an eye on the girl.

Frohman took the advice. In 1901, after Miss Barrymore had appeared in *That Imprudent Young Couple*; had made successful appearances in London in *Secret Service* (1897) and Sir Henry Irving's melodrama *The Bells* (there were reports then that she was engaged to Sir Henry's son Laurence); and had played at the Garrick Theatre with Annie Russell, he engaged her for the starring role of Madame Trentoni in *Captain Jinks of the Horse Marines.* The critics didn't like the play much, but they adored her. One week after the opening, Ethel Barrymore rounded the corner to the theatre to find her name in lights for the first time. She cried like a baby.

Other starring roles followed: in *Carrots, A Country Mouse, Cousin Kate* and *Sunday,* in which she spoke the famous line, "That's all there is, there isn't any more." She was Nora in Ibsen's *A Doll's House,* Mrs. Grey in Barrie's *Alice Sit-by-the-Fire,* the leading character in Galsworthy's *The Silver Box.* Ethel Barrymore became the nation's romantic idol. Young girls were solemn disciples of what they called the "Ethel Barrymore walk" and the "Ethel Barrymore voice." Some of them even talked about how they had "adopted" the "Ethel Barrymore neck."

Ethel Barrymore kept on appearing on the stage, year after year. With her beauty, glamor and fascinating voice which has always kept its plaintive, haunting quality (carpers call it monotonous), she was always sure of huge audiences when she played in drawing-room comedies, like Zoë Akins' *Déclassée,*

BARRYMORE, ETHEL—*Continued*

which gave her two profitable seasons in 1919 and 1920, and Somerset Maugham's *The Constant Wife*, which she first played in 1926 and frequently took around summer theatres later. But Miss Barrymore did not confine her roles to drawing room ones. She was the somber peasant in *Rose Bernd* in 1923; Sister Gracia in *The Kingdom of God* (she opened her own theatre, the Ethel Barrymore, with this play); she appeared in blackface in Julia Peterkin's *Scarlet Sister Mary*; she played frequent Shakespearean roles; she was often seen in Ibsen.

She appeared in one talking picture, too. There had been appearances in the silent films back in 1914 when she was seen on the screen in *The Awakening of Helena Ritchie,* in one of Edna Ferber's *Emma McChesney* stories and in other works, but it wasn't until 1933 that motion picture audiences saw her again. In that year she appeared in *Rasputin and the Empress* with her brothers, Lionel and John. She explains this solitary film appearance by saying: "I did it only to be with my brothers, whom I don't often see." And she confesses: "You know, I've never seen that picture. . . They tell me it was pretty good, too."

After a series of rather flimsy vehicles in recent years—in *Whiteoaks* (1938) and *Farm of Three Echoes* (1940) she played excessively aged if still vigorous characters, and in Vincent Sheean's (see sketch this issue) *An International Incident* she was a lady lecturer—Miss Barrymore was finally given in *The Corn Is Green* a drama of substance and an impressive part. As an English school mistress in a Welsh mining town she is triumphant, all critics have agreed. She herself says: "I like it better than anything I've ever had. It has everything in it that I care about." In May 1941 Mrs. Franklin D. Roosevelt presented her with the third annual Barter Theatre Award for the season's outstanding performance, and when in the fall of that year Ethel Barrymore gave her 300th performance in the play critics noted that she was having the longest run of her career.

In her 60's Ethel Barrymore is a mellowed, philosophical, witty and still occasionally imperious person who can and does quell an obstreperous stage hand with a withering glance. There was a report recently that she had hit one with a rolled-up piece of paper when he refused to obey her. She denied this. "I didn't need to hit him," said she. Miss Barrymore's personality and charm are as popular in the remotest touring towns as on Broadway. "I never know what some people mean when they complain about the rigors of the road," she says. "Lord, they must be very faded lilies indeed if they mind touring! Oh, I look forward to it—the drafty dressing rooms, the rats, everything! It's all part of it." She intends to get her chance at all this—and a good long chance—with *The Corn Is Green.* "I expect to fall into my grave playing it," she told a reporter, "which I hope will not be soon."

Ethel Barrymore's three children, Samuel Pomeroy Colt, John Drew Colt and Ethel Barrymore Colt, all feel about the theatre much the way their mother does. (She was divorced from their father, Russell Griswold Colt of Philadelphia, in 1923.) All three of them have appeared on the stage, and each of them has received the traditional Barrymore big red apple on opening night from their Uncle John. They spend a good deal of time with their mother, when they can, at her comfortable house in Mamaroneck, New York, where she has lived for the past 27 years.

When she is not acting, rehearsing, thinking about the stage or concerning herself with her children, Ethel Barrymore can whip up a lot of enthusiasm about sports. She has seen all of Joe Louis' and Henry Armstrong's fights and has a large collection of fight pictures. There's always a small radio in her dressing room to get prize fight and night baseball returns. Stage hands know, as one put it, "We never have to worry about getting the scores—we just listen outside her door." Miss Barrymore explains her interest by the fact that her father "was the amateur lightweight champion of England when he was in Oxford. He taught me to love sports from the time I was 12."

Music (she is an accomplished pianist), mystery stories and an occasional jaunt to the Stork Club also keep Miss Barrymore amused when she is off the stage. But it is the theatre she mostly thinks about and talks about. She doesn't worry about it, as so many other actors, actresses and playgoers do. "Four thousand years ago in Greece," she says, "they were saying the theatre was on the skids. Well, it never was and never will be. The theatre is perfectly wonderful. People always will want to go to it. It is the healthiest art there is."

References

Boston Transcript III p4 Mr 16 '40 pors
Ind Woman 20:1 Ja '41 por (cover)
N Y Herald Tribune VI p5 F 2 '41 pors; p15 F 5 '41 por
N Y Post p5 D '40 pors
N Y Sun p11 Jl 5 '41 por
N Y Times IX p1-2 D 22 '40; VII p11, 20 Ja 12 '41 por; p21 F 5 '41
N Y World-Telegram p6 F 3 '41 pors
Time 37:84-5 F 17 '41

American Women
Barrymore, J. Confessions of an Actor 1926
Le Gallienne, E. At 33 1934
Strange, M. pseud. Who Tells Me True 1940
Who's Who in America
Who's Who in the Theatre
Woollcott, A. Shouts and Murmurs 1922

BARUCH, BERNARD M(AN ES) (bà-rŏŏk') Aug. 19, 1870- Industri st

Address: b. 597 Madison Ave, New York City; h. 1055 Fifth Ave, New York City

One favorite quotation from Bernard Baruch is: "When God and the community have been so good to a man, isn't it natural that he should try to make some repayment?" Stock speculator and counselor to Presidents, Wall Street oracle and patriot, ever since the opening guns of the Second World War Baruch has been advocating for the United States "some plan along lines similar to the experience tested by the United States War Industries Board of 1917 and 1918," the Board which he headed. In June 1941 was published his *American Industry in the War*, a compilation of his most important current writings on industrial mobilization for war together with the report of the War Industries Board issued in 1921. And on July 10 Senate Republican Leader McNary, after conferring with Wendell Willkie, who urges a single defense head for the United States, praised Baruch as "a tower of strength deserving of every confidence."

Bernard Mannes Baruch was the son of a doctor, Simon B. Baruch, who left Poland in 1853 as "a refugee from attacks on freedom." In the United States the doctor married Belle Wolfe, the descendant of a Portuguese Jew who had settled in America in pre-Revolutionary days. Their son, Bernard, was born in South Carolina on August 19, 1870 and brought up on the Southern Lost Cause (he has been called "a South Carolinian first, a Democrat second, and an American third"), although his family moved to New York City when he was young. There he took his B. A. from the College of the City of New York in 1889, leaving behind him the reputation of an athlete and of a Phi Beta Kappa scholar. He soon found himself a job as a broker's boy on Wall Street at $3 a week. His father had wanted him to be a doctor, but one story says that when Bernard was small his mother took him to a phrenologist who examined his "bumps" and announced: "This young man has great gifts in finance and business. He might be a good lawyer. A doctor, no!"

Few phrenologists make such lucky hits. As a broker's boy young Baruch developed an almost photographic memory for financial reports—and at night school he studied law and bookkeeping. By the time he was 27 he had made himself so valuable that he felt he could ask for a salary of $50 a week. Instead he got a sixth interest in the business, but since 1897 was an unusually good year, he netted $6,000. He promptly married Annie Griffen of New York. (She died in 1938, leaving a son and two daughters.)

It wasn't long before Baruch himself, fortified by his studies of industrial geography and of the commodity and market situation, was investing money in the market. Ten thousand dollars borrowed from his father was soon lost, but he began to recoup—and by the time he was 30 he had made and lost a million. At the same time Baruch had lost his first reverence for certain minds on Wall Street: he

Blackstone

BERNARD M. BARUCH

found himself getting the better of the best of them. Legends grew up around the young speculator who made fortunes overnight and who seemed to operate by some infallible gambler's instinct.

"They called me a Robin Hood who took from the rich but did not give to the poor," Baruch once put it, contentedly. But the description was probably not entirely accurate. It was about 1905 when Baruch actually toyed with the idea (he had, by this time, sold his seat on the Stock Exchange) of becoming a voluntary, unpaid counselor in all cases involving the rights of the public, and although he didn't carry out the plan he did begin to contribute large sums to charitable causes.

His period of real public service came much later. When Woodrow Wilson ("the most Christlike man in America," Baruch called him later) became President, he offered Baruch the post of Secretary of the Treasury, but it was refused. In 1916, however, Baruch began making speeches urging the necessity for some prepared scheme of industrial mobilization, and soon Wilson appointed him to the Advisory Commission of the Council of National Defense. It was March 5, 1918 when Baruch was appointed chairman of the War Industries Board—he was chairman of the Commission on Raw Materials, Minerals and Metals, commissioner in charge of raw materials for the Board and member of the Commission in Charge of all Purchases for the Allies. Part of the country was shocked, for Baruch had been considered a mere speculator, but his abilities at unscrambling all sorts of messes and at choosing the right men to help him soon earned respect.

The War over, Baruch became connected with the American Commission to Negotiate Peace as a member of the Drafting Commission of the Economic Section, and he was also appointed a member of the Supreme Economic Council and chairman of its Raw Materials

BARUCH, BERNARD M.—*Continued*

Division, American delegate on the economics and reparations clauses and economic adviser for the American Peace Commission. According to one authority "his advice was so good that Wilson ignored it, for Baruch knew that it would be impossible to collect a huge indemnity from the Germans." In 1927, too, he predicted that the Dawes Plan would be scrapped within two years.

In October 1919 Baruch was a member of President Wilson's Conference for Capital and Labor and in 1922 a member of President Harding's Agricultural Conference. Known as the counselor of Presidents, often seen entering the White House "pince-nez on his nose, a broad smile on his face, and his tie askew," by this time Baruch had also resumed his market operations and was busy recouping losses entailed during the War years. (He had sold most of his stocks and bonds to put the money into Liberty bonds, and had once even paid for a government mission to England out of his own pocket.)

Yet a nostalgia for public service remained. One writer has said of Baruch: "He has an intuitive mind, but behind that and his tremendous pose of authority, there lurks what used to be known in the Hoover period as an inferiority complex. He wants so terribly to be known as something more than a speculator." It seems that he wanted to be known as the savior of the farmer, too; but three Republican Administrations turned down his farm plans, and he kept backing the wrong men for President. In 1924 it was William Gibbs McAdoo, in 1928 Al Smith. (He always backs the Democratic ticket.)

In the meanwhile things had been happening behind the stock market. It was the spring of 1929 when Baruch, whose least word on Wall Street received the attention due an oracle, wrote an article in which he foresaw not only a rosy future for American industry but the complete abolition of the "business cycle," basing his prediction on the settlement of the reparation question; exactly when he quietly withdrew his own investments and those of his friends from the market isn't certain. If not infallible, at least Baruch was one of the few Wall Street prophets who, after the crash, declined to look around nearby corners for prosperity. In March 1930 he announced for publication that a world-wide depression of several years' duration had arrived.

Hoover, like other Presidents, had consulted Baruch from time to time, both officially and unofficially. Baruch had given advice on the organization of the Reconstruction Finance Corporation, although he refused to accept a place on it; and in 1932 he was a member of the National Transportation Committee. Nevertheless, when stocks crashed again in the spring of 1932, Hoover decided that Baruch was one of the villains behind this "plot" to discredit his Administration. His files were searched, his income tax analyzed; nothing was found, and the matter went no further. But it was generally agreed that if Baruch had been subpoenaed, fear of his testimony on the inner

workings of some of the great banks would have resulted in a great wave of short selling.

If by 1932 Baruch was on bad terms with the outgoing President, it didn't seem likely that he would be much more friendly with the incoming one. It was rumored (though Baruch himself denies this) that he had called Franklin Roosevelt a "stuffed shirt" until New York's Governor got the nomination for which Baruch had quietly backed Governor Ritchie of Maryland. Yet when Roosevelt was nominated Baruch promptly made himself the heaviest single contributor to the Democratic cause—Hugh Johnson, his research assistant, was not the least of his contributions; he reassured Wall Street about Roosevelt; he prepared attacks on Hoover's "uncontrolled inflation."

By 1933 everyone expected that Baruch would be invited to enter Roosevelt's Cabinet, and even after the Cabinet was announced the press made much of the fact that although Baruch was not in it, AAA's George Peek and NRA's Hugh Johnson were Baruch's close associates; that the Farm Bill and NIRA were vaguely framed along lines once laid down by Baruch; that during Raymond Moley's absence at the London Conference, Baruch served as a relay between the President and the London delegation. The idea was that Baruch had become even more powerful than if he had been given a Cabinet post, actually a sort of "Assistant President." Bankers muttered that Baruch had sold Wall Street to Washington and Brain Trusters muttered that Baruch had sold Washington to Wall Street.

On the other hand, others pointed out that, far from being as influential either as his enemies suspected or as he would have liked to have been, Baruch found his farm program barely recognizable by the time the Brain Trust finished with it, and Roosevelt's financial policies made him deeply apprehensive. Certainly by February 1938, when Baruch testified before the Special Committee of the United States Senate to Investigate Unemployment and Relief, his testimony could with some justification be called "the heaviest gun . . . fired at the New Deal." This was precisely because he did not go in for wholesale condemnation of Administration policies ("I am . . . in sympathy with most of the great social objectives, for which I have myself argued for many years"), but rather created the impression of a socially-minded man who had reluctantly come to the conclusion that the traditional American profits system was being gravely endangered by some New Deal methods. In *The New Dealers* Baruch's "ingenuous effort to be all things to all men" is referred to; he is described as "a political amphibian, at home in both elements but unable to live permanently in either." The description seems apt. But he has also been described as a man who never holds grudges, political or otherwise.

In 1934 Baruch was given his first official post in Roosevelt's regime and made chairman of a committee to recommend legislation to take profits out of war, a step which he had advocated for nearly two decades. In February 1937 he presented to the Senate Committee on

Military Affairs his recommendations for legislation for war-time industrial mobilization. That same year, returning from abroad, he was quoted: "Europe is hopeless." He had been alarmed at the extent of German rearmament even before that and with "adamantine nationalism" had consistently urged rearmament, a war reserve of strategic materials, trained man power—and a careful neutrality in the war which he foresaw.

Yet although in 1937 Baruch spoke against selling munitions or lending money to belligerents, he is not found among the critics of Roosevelt's foreign policy today. In January 1941 he urged the centralization of the defense power in the President, also pleading for exemptions from the Sherman Act for committees of industrialists cooperating with the Government in the defense effort; for more labor representation; for increased taxes and a "pay-as-you-go" policy. And he has continued to make regular trips to Washington, to visit President Roosevelt (Raymond Clapper says he lunches with the President once a week) and defense chiefs, to preach the need for priorities and for placing a ceiling on prices, rents and wages. It is said that Leon Henderson is only one of the men who now consult him constantly, and in November 1941, after the House rejected the "over-all" plan of control of rents, prices and wages presented by Representative Gore and recommended by Baruch, Henderson still had other plans to present.

As a result of his experiences, Baruch is extremely critical of the way the present defense program has been carried out and of the "yes-men" who have been in charge of it. He wants one single defense chief. And in September 1941 he didn't believe the United States had yet begun to use its vast resources. "Don't forget that the Germans are using our plan," he was quoted. "The Germans said that they consciously followed the American plan of industrial mobilization and improved upon it. . . I think it's about time that we got ready and did some business."

Over six feet tall, with snowy white hair, aquiline features and blue-gray eyes, "fluent of gesture, perpetually smiling," Bernard Baruch "seems forever animated by some inner boyish pleasure." He would rather talk about himself than about anything else in the world, but few people mind that trait in him. He is a very careless dresser, and his mind is said to be unusually disorderly, too—more notable for astounding intuitions than for logic and sequence. The exact size of his fortune isn't known. Ferdinand Lundberg talked about $37,500,000; Baruch himself calls this figure "sheer nonsense." In 1934 he closed his offices in Wall Street and announced that he was going to write three books: an autobiography, a message to the youth of America, the story of man's conquest of nature. Since the publication of his *Making of Economic and Reparation Sections of the Peace Treaty* (1920) no books but economic treatises have yet appeared, however. Aside from writing, Baruch's hobbies are hunting, riding and golf; he hates

parties. It is true that he plays bridge, but (lesson to those who have never been known as Wall Street wizards) seldom for any but extremely small stakes!

References

Am Mag 116:36-8+ O '33 por
Life 10:22-3 Je 30 '41 por
Lit Digest 116:11 Jl 8 '33 il
New Repub 75:206-7 Jl 5 '33
New Yorker 2:15-16 Ap 7 '26
Newsweek 1:17-19 Jl 1 '33 por; 3:24-5 Je 30 '34 por; 4:15 D 22 '34 por; 5:7 Ap 6 '35 pors; 11:11 Mr 14 '38 pors
Time 31:13 Mr 14 '38 por; 35:20 My 27 '40; 37:16-19 My 12 '41 il por
Gilbert, C. W. Mirrors of Washington p145-60 1921
Mirrors of Wall Street p253-68 1933
Shumway, H. I. Famous Leaders of Industry 4th ser p55-72 1936
Unofficial Observer [pseud.] New Dealers p336-75 1934
Who's Who in America
Who's Who in American Jewry
Who's Who in Commerce and Industry

BEALS, CARLETON (bēlz) Nov. 13, 1893- Author; journalist
Address: h. 1943 Berkeley Way, Berkeley, Calif; Brockett's Point, Bramford, Conn.

Edward Mallory
CARLETON BEALS

Carleton Beals has lived what he calls a "life more changeful, colorful and disorderly than most." Today almost universally acknowledged as one of the major interpreters of Latin America, he has been a newsboy, grocery delivery boy, delicatessen clerk, carpenter, machinist, chauffeur, farm hand, bookseller, laboratory assistant, teamster, teacher, dishwasher, waiter, shoe clerk, ditchdigger, bookkeeper, cashier, professional chess player,

BEALS, CARLETON—*Continued*

porter, shipping clerk, advertising solicitor, principal of a high school, gold prospector. He has seen four Mexican revolutions. He has known personally or interviewed Premiers Data and Primo de Rivera and President Azaña of Spain, Mussolini, at least six Presidents of Mexico and three Presidents of Nicaragua. Indians and artists and revolutionaries and bums and politicians and ambassadors have been among his close friends —and enemies.

On the more conventional side, he has been lecturer at the University of California, the New School for Social Research and the National University of Mexico; he has been on the editorial or advisory board of at least half a dozen magazines, among them *Common Sense* and *Living Age*; he has written innumerable articles and perhaps 20 books. The year 1940 saw the publication of two: *The Great Circle,* the second autobiographical volume he has written; and *Pan America,* which gives Mr. Beals' own program for the Western hemisphere.

Carleton Beals was born on November 13, 1893, in Medicine Lodge, Kansas, the son of Leon Eli and Elvina Sybila (Blickensderfer) Beals. His grandmother was Carrie Nation— which may or may not account for a certain belligerently crusading spirit of which he has often been accused. "At the age of three years," he says, "I took my family to Pasadena, California." In what was then a "virgin empire," with mountains that were made for roaming, free from bungalows, concrete highways and monopoly, he lived until 1911. "The world was a symbol of hope." He was graduated from the Pasadena High School in 1911 and then went on to take his B. A. *cum laude* at the University of California in 1916. For the most part he studied mining and engineering.

With a scholarship Beals next set out for Columbia University to take his graduate degree. He wrote a thesis on the self-sufficient state, at the same time completing the work required for a Teachers College certificate and a book with which he hoped to get the Hart, Schaffner and Marx Economics Prize. And he worked in his non-existent spare time. The book ended up in the fire, but in 1917 he acquired his M. A. (later, Dr. Butler's signature was to be very useful when a Spanish gendarme demanded Beals' identification card) and then found a job punching an adding machine in the export department of California's Standard Oil Company.

It wasn't exactly his idea of living. In a year he was through, and with "that peculiar impulse" which, he says, "all my life had led me to reject easy solutions and try my powers in unusual situations," he set out through the California and Arizona deserts in a secondhand Ford. After the car broke down he hired burros. After his money ran out he walked and bummed rides on freight trains, working for almost nothing along the way. He kept going further south. He had troubles—he nearly starved, he got bitten by

a poisonous insect, he got lost, he got into mix-ups with soldiers (it was 1918)—and when he landed in Mexico City it was in a car of squealing pigs. There were 15 centavos in his pocket, the clothes he wore were worth something less than that, his feet were rubbed sore and he had no possessions but a blanket that was full of holes. He didn't know more than the Spanish he had picked up along the way, either, and he had no acquaintances in town. Yet Mexico City was probably the most fortunate place in which he could have found himself at that particular moment.

"Strange but providential things" happened to him there. Strangers—more than one— befriended him. He finally founded the English Institute with a couple of other Americans and in four months or so was making a modest living. He found a job teaching in the American High School, of which he shortly afterward became principal. He found another job teaching military English to the members of President Carranza's staff and also gave Shakespeare lectures once a week to the women of the American colony. In less than a year he was earning more than he ever had, and although his working day was already long he managed to find time for writing, too. Throughout his long journey across the country he had carried a little notebook with him, and that was full.

Then came another Mexican revolution. President Carranza fled; Beals lost first his position at the War Department, then at the American High School. But the first four articles he had ever written had been accepted by the first magazines to which he had sent them, and he had a book on Mexico completed. He decided to see Spain, since it seemed evident that a free-lance journalist could get along anywhere. It was 1920. He studied for a while at the University of Madrid, feasted on El Greco and Goya, and then went on to Italy. For nearly a year he read and talked only Italian, studied at the University of Rome, watched Mussolini's rise to power, wrote short stories, part of a novel, articles on Fascism and finally a book on Fascism (*Rome or Death,* published in 1923). Then, when he had an offer from a publisher to publish his book on Mexico if revised, he decided to return.

Said Beals of those European days: "Europe . . . was a closed-in world. For three years I had kept my hand on its palsied pulse, had felt the deathly fever rising." Already he foresaw a new war "to save the British empire," although he hardly foresaw the depression in the United States. Somehow he was glad to get back to the New World in 1923. In Mexico he revised his book, which was published the same year under the title *Mexico,* and attended the University of Mexico for a while. August 1924 found him in New York City—the first time he had been in his own country for more than six years. He was "again virtually penniless," and felt like a stranger.

In New York he worked on *Brimstone and Chili* (1927), the story of his personal experiences in the Southwest and in Mexico, and after plans to go to South America were frustrated he returned to Mexico. Those were the Mexican days of President Calles and Ambassador Morrow, of D. H. Lawrence and Colonel Lindbergh (see sketch this issue). Beals knew them all. He wrote articles for *The Nation* and the *New Republic,* among other publications, taught a couple of English classes, and in 1927, at the time of General Sandino's Nicaraguan "rebellion," made a dangerous journey through Honduras and Nicaragua and got an interview with the General when the entire American press and Army were convinced that the "rebel" had fled. *Banana Gold* (1932) tells the story of this adventure, and is filled with accounts of marine atrocities.

Early in 1929 Carleton Beals ventured into his own country again to lecture, and then it was abroad again—Spain, North Africa, Italy, Turkey, Russia, Germany—and back to Mexico. *Destroying Victor,* a novel, was published that year, too, but got a lukewarm reception from most critics. In 1930 he went on an anthropological and educational mission through the Oaxaca Mountains; in 1931 he published *Mexican Maze,* which added great prestige to his reputation not only as a journalist but also as a historian, travel writer and sociologist. From 1931 to 1932 he had a Guggenheim scholarship while completing *Porfirio Diaz, Dictator of Mexico* (1932). And from 1932 to 1933 he was in Cuba, gathering material for *The Crime of Cuba* (1933), which blasted at the bloody dictatorship of Machado and seriously questioned the unselfishness of the United States' role. The book was published almost simultaneously with Machado's overthrow, was "a mighty weapon on the side of the revolution," and made Carleton Beals the hero of the Cuban youth movement.

The year 1934, which Beals spent in Panama, Colombia, Ecuador and Peru, saw the publication of *Black River,* a fictionized history of American oil companies in Mexico, and *Fire on the Andes,* which told the story of Peru. He finally returned to the United States more or less permanently. He gathered material for *The Story of Huey P. Long* (1935), and in 1936 was a special correspondent for the New York *Post* at the Scottsboro trial in Alabama. The only other book by Beals which is concerned exclusively with the United States, however, is the bitter *American Earth* (1939). *Stones Awake* (1936) was a novel which carried a Mexican peasant girl from the time of the Diaz regime in 1910 to the present; the titles *America South* (1937); *The Coming Struggle for Latin America* (1938); and *Pan America* (1940) all speak more or less for themselves. *Glass Houses* (1938) and *The Great Circle* (1940) are autobiographical, the latter carrying on where the first left off.

Critics differ as to Carleton Beals' accuracy, although nearly everyone agrees that he is a "first-rate reporter." He is either full of prejudices, given to overstatement, "forever catching someone in a foul plot"—or a "refreshing debunker," his conclusions "ugly only because veracious." It depends almost en-

tirely on one's own point of view. Beals' sympathies, he says, are with the people, whether he is talking about Mexico or Nicaragua or Cuba, and he seldom likes the things that foreigners have been doing there even if the foreigners are American citizens. It is seldom that he has anything very good to say about the government of any country, either—except possibly that of Cárdenas in Mexico and the late Spanish Republic. He is little more sympathetic with Russia than with the Fascist countries, and he finds the democracy of the democracies pretty incomplete. As for the present War, his view in 1940 was that it is a struggle for essential raw materials, "a struggle bound to grow more bitter, whoever wins," that "the free market is gone anyway" and the United States had better see what it can do in the Western hemisphere without infringing on the rights of the South American countries instead of attempting to intervene in Europe. He is something of a cynic.

In 1931 Beals was married in the Palace of Cortés in Coyoacán to Elizabeth Wright Daniels. After a divorce he married Blanca Rosa Leyva y Arguedas in September 1934. Sandy-haired, blue-eyed, Beals is soft-spoken and mild-mannered but fond of a good fight. He likes even better horseback riding, "investigating social phenomena," the tropics, reading, outdoor travel, and almost all persons who have "interested themselves, in one way or another, in just causes." Writing he describes as "the shakeless point in my life."

References

Cur Hist 51:26 Ja '40
Wilson Lib Bul 7:150 N '32 por
America's Young Men 1936-37
Beals, C. Banana Gold 1932
Beals, C. Brimstone and Chili 1927
Beals, C. Glass Houses 1938
Beals, C. Great Circle 1940
Kunitz, S. J. ed. Authors Today and Yesterday 1933
Who's Who Among North American Authors
Who's Who in America

BEARD, CHARLES A(USTIN) Nov. 27, 1874- Professor; historian

BEARD, MARY Aug. 5, 1876- Author; historian

Address: b. Johns Hopkins University, Baltimore, Md.; h. New Milford, Conn.

"Tall, white-haired and angular in the Hoosier tradition," independent-minded Charles Beard has most of his life been provoking his fellow historians (and citizens) into either criticism or thought, and usually both. In the quarter of a century since his publication of the pioneering *An Economic Interpretation of the Constitution of the United States* his views have developed rather than changed, but in the meanwhile he has been spasmodically attacked and hailed as an ally by Right, Left and Center. Since the Second World War he has concentrated most of his forces in a battle

BEARD, CHARLES A. and BEARD, MARY—*Continued*

with United States interventionists; before that he was breaking lances with the internationalists. He calls his own foreign policy "continentalism." As for his books, they have been probably as thoroughly read and thoroughly dissected as those of any modern historian. A compound of history, economics, political science and salt, they have often been scoffed at by historians as "unreliable", "passionate", "impressionistic"; by economists as "pretty weak"; by political scientists as "muddy", "dogmatic." And yet, as one wistfully frank

CHARLES A. BEARD

rival said: "What he does may be, I think, probably vastly more important than the contributions of the more straight-laced of us. . ."

The son of William Henry and Mary (Payne) Beard, he was born on November 27, 1874 near Knightstown, Indiana. His great-grandfather had been a Federalist; his grandfather was a Whig and rebel Quaker who ran a "one-man church" with 600 volumes of comparative religion; his father was a "copper-riveted, rock-ribbed, Mark Hanna, true-blue" Republican—a building contractor who also ran a bank, read the classics and raised his family on a farm near Spiceland in order to develop its "backbone." Young Charles went to a nearby Quaker academy and outside of school hours ran a hand press. When he was graduated at 18 his grandfather bought him the weekly Knightstown *Sun* and for four years he and his brother ran it—even made it pay—before Charles went away to the Methodist DePauw University in Greencastle, Indiana. There, on the college team, he debated such subjects as the Federal income tax and the right of Labor to organize; in 1896 he spent a summer in Chicago, investigating Hull House, labor problems, the Demo-

cratic National Convention and the oratory of William Jennings Bryan; he reported for the Henry County *Republican*; joined Phi Gamma Delta, was awarded a Phi Beta Kappa key, and acquired his Ph. B. in 1898. After a youthfully patriotic attempt to mobilize a volunteer company for service in the Spanish War, he went abroad—to Oxford, to study English and European history. There he took part in the organization of Oxford's Labor College, now known as Ruskin.

Young Beard returned to America in 1899 to teach at Cornell University and to marry 23-year-old Mary Ritter of Indianapolis in March 1900. The daughter of Eli Foster and Narcissa (Lockwood) Ritter, she had taken her Ph. B. at DePauw the year before he had left college, and was a member of Kappa Alpha Theta and Phi Beta Kappa. The two of them went back to Oxford to lecture at Ruskin, to appear before labor groups and make friends with labor leaders. In England a daughter, Miriam, was born; and by 1902 they were again in the United States, studying economics, politics and the history of England and Europe at Columbia University. Beard acquired his M. A. in 1903, his Ph. D. in 1904 (the year Veblen published his *Theory of Business Enterprise*); then, with his wife and daughter, he settled on the edge of the University. In 1907 he became adjunct professor of politics, working with such colleagues as James Harvey Robinson and John Dewey.

He was then only a "tall, rangy young man . . . with a sharp aquiline profile, looking half farmer and half Roman philosopher," but, as one of his former students said: "When Beard strode into the classroom it was like a salty breeze blowing out the stuffiness from the room." He found history full of myths; he made it concrete, started giving his students a batch of Treasury statistics or pamphlets by John Taylor to analyze. In the meanwhile he was having rather startlingly unmythical studies published, some written in collaboration, and was promoted to an associate professorship of politics in 1910. His first collaboration with Mrs. Beard, who was active in both the women's and the labor movement, was *American Citizenship* (1914). And it was that same year when he leaped into fame or notoriety with the appearance of the eighth book carrying his name: *An Economic Interpretation of the Constitution of the United States.*

At that time the Founding Fathers were sacrosanct, perhaps because they had seldom been poked. Beard, with his "theory of economic determinism" which "had not been tried out in American history, and until it was tried out, could not be found wanting," suggested that they had not exactly ignored their own immediate economic interests when formulating the Constitution. Although his views were more Madisonian then Marxian, they were not docilely received. Taft and Elihu Root, the New York Bar Association and *The Nation* were among his more scathing critics, but 1915, the same year that saw the appearance of his wife's *Woman's Work in Municipalities*, brought forth his *Economic Origins of Jeffersonian Democracy.* He hadn't abandoned his thesis.

It was 1917 when Nicholas Murray Butler was supposed to have been asked: "Have you seen Beard's last book?" and to have replied, "I hope so." Beard was then still teaching at Columbia as a full-fledged professor. It was not for long. Although he supported America's entry into the First World War—with qualifications—he was quick to resent any attacks upon his fellow teachers and upon what he considered academic freedom. In October of that year he resigned, ostensibly as a protest against the dismissal of Professors Cattell and Dana, basically as a "protest against the business control of university educational policy" and the "doctrinal inquisition" of himself and others by trustees. The New York *Times* thereupon carried an editorial headed "Columbia's Deliverance."

It was several years before Beard returned to university life. Someone said: "Beard dabbles." From 1917 to 1922 he served as director of New York City's Training School for Public Service; in 1918 he organized the New School for Social Research with Dewey, Veblen and Robinson; in 1921 he was active with the Workers' Education Bureau. He was a "scorching critic" of the Lusk bills of 1921 and of post-War Red hunting. In 1922 **he was lecturing on war guilt** at Dartmouth College (he was the author of the first general study on the problem); later in the year he went with Mrs. Beard to Tokyo to become adviser to the Institute of Municipal Research there and to help plan the consolidation of a greater Tokyo; and after the 1923 earthquake he returned to advise Viscount Goto, Japanese Minister of Home Affairs, on the rebuilding of the city. From 1927 to 1928 he was adviser to the Yugoslavian Government, but found that the oppression of the Croats, Macedonians and Hungarians continued despite all his advice. He came home "cured"—convinced that all Europe was just a "big Balkans"—proceeded to start a dairy farm, eventually sold wholesale over 300,000 quarts of milk a year, and organized the milk producers. In September 1939 he finally rejoined the Columbia faculty as a visiting professor of government; and in the fall of 1940 he accepted his first regular academic appointment in 23 years and became professor of American history at Johns Hopkins University.

Along with all this "dabbling," Beard had managed to write a constant stream of articles for the *New Republic*, *Harper's*, *Scribner's* and *Current History*; to make himself active in the American Historical Association (president, 1933), the American Political Science Association (president, 1926) and the National Association for Adult Education; to engage in battles with J. P. Morgan and William Randolph Hearst; to have at least 20 books published after 1917—some written alone, some in collaboration; to edit numerous others. The *History of the United States* (1921, 1929) was the second product of his and his wife's collaboration (her *Short History of the American Labor Movement* [1920, 1925] had been published in the meanwhile), but it is

their two-volume *Rise of American Civilization* (1927) which has become a classic. One of its most memorable and disputatious feats is the picturing of the Civil War as a "second American Revolution" of the planting class against the capitalists, of the Fourteenth Amendment as a semi-conspiratorial method of protecting capitalist enterprise.

Their *America in Midpassage* (1939), actually the third volume of *Rise of American Civilization*, has been described by one critic as "not only history but a magnificent essay about history." "With the aloof amusement of two moralists who stayed sober while the rest of the world got tight, they investigate the causes of the crash, the closing of the banks, the New Deal and government by the Brain Trust." Before its appearance Mrs. Beard, "quick, incisive and camera-shy," had been writing *On Understanding Women* (1931) and editing and co-editing other books that might have been similarly titled, but she brought much more than a typically feministic viewpoint to its writing. In 1942 the Beards are working on a fourth volume of *The Rise of American Civilization*, titled *The Idea of Civilization in the United States*.

MARY BEARD

Today, Professor Beard would like to see America as "a workers' republic"—"worker" including "all those powers covered by the idea of 'management', 'artcraft' and 'statecraft,' in the broadest sense." He hates Imperialism above everything else, sees no natural or permanent advantages in free trade, sees our greatest problem as one of distribution. Therefore, although he wishes there were a "real internationalism" that would make world collaboration possible, he has consistently argued that America should cultivate her own garden in the world as it actually is. "Self-interest is not only a legitimate, but a funda-

BEARD, CHARLES A. and BEARD, MARY—*Continued*

mental cause for national policy; one which needs no cloak of hypocrisy"; and to his mind "the supreme interest of the United States is the creation and maintenance of a high standard of life for all its people and ways of industry conducive to the promotion of individual and social virtues within the frame of national security." To get it "there must be the utmost emancipation from dependence upon the course of international exchange." These are some of the ideas which he has expanded in such books as *The Idea of National Interest* and *The Open Door at Home* (1934); in *A Foreign Policy for America* (1940) and *Public Policy and the General Welfare* (1941). In 1939 he fought against revision of the neutrality law, calling it "An Act for Allowing the President of the United States to Enter Any War That Begins Abroad"; in April of that year he warned that "we're blundering into war," a war in which "civil liberty would perish" and which could not be held "to any alleged democratic purpose"; he has not changed his mind, although some were surprised to find his name listed in the "independent group" of 58 who in September 1941 united in a public condemnation of Roosevelt's "shoot on sight" order, a statement that was made public by General E. Wood (see sketch this issue) of the America First Committee.

Beard says: "Of the totality of things discussed knowingly by the Bright Boys, I am entirely ignorant." He doesn't make claim to any of the lordly objectivity usually appropriated by historians for themselves, but instead speaks scornfully of "the solemn and pompous deceptions of 'objective' history." The secret of successful collaboration, as far as his wife and he are concerned, is "division of argument." They probably have a lively, unacademic time of it, especially if their children, Miriam and William, should happen to be present. Miriam is married and is herself the author of *Realism in Romantic Japan* (1930) and *History of the Business Man* (1938). The Beards own a "dour, sprawling house, atop a Connecticut valley slope," and number among their good friends Senator George Norris and Vice-President Wallace.

References

Am R 4:297-309 Ja '35
Christian Sci Mon Mag p2+ Mr 9 '38 il; p5+ Jl 22 '39 il por
Harper 178:641-52 My '39
Nation 142:452-4 Ap 8 '36
New Repub 81:225-7 Ja 2 '35; 82:242 Ap 10 '35; 99:7-11 My 10 '39; 100: 228 O 4 '39
Newsweek 6:36-7 Ag 10 '35 por
Sch & Soc 52:27 Jl 13 '40; 52:362 O 19 '40
Time 33:91+ My 22 '39 por; 35:90+ My 20 '40 por
American Women
Blinkoff, M. Influence of Charles A. Beard Upon American Historiography 1936

Kraus, M. History of American History p453-91 1937
Leaders in Education [Charles Austin Beard] 1941
Lerner, M. Ideas Are Weapons p152-73 1939
Who's Who Among North American Authors [Mary Beard]
Who's Who in America

BEARD, DANIEL CARTER June 21, 1850—June 11, 1941 Founder of the first United States Boy Scout society on which others were modeled; National Scout Commissioner and honorary president of the Boy Scouts of America; interested in work for boys since 1878; author of *American Boys' Handy Book* (1882) and many other books of woodcraft, outdoor lore and camping; illustrated Mark Twain books and his own articles in *Recreation,* which he edited in 1905 and 1906, *St. Nicholas* Magazine and *Boys' Life,* of which he was associate editor.

References

Am Mercury 48:216-17 O '39
Good H 102:23 Je '36 por
Nature 29:327 Je '37
N Y Times VII p11 Je 16 '40 il por
New Yorker 8:17-20 Jl 23 '32
Newsweek 12:18 Jl 4 '38 por
Pub W 116:2061-4 O 26 '29
Time 34:68 S 25 '39 il

Clemens, C. and Sibley, C. Uncle Dan 1938
Kunitz, S. J. and Haycraft, H. eds. Junior Book of Authors 1935
Who's Who Among North American Authors
Who's Who in America
Who's Who in American Art

Obituaries

N Y Times p23 Je 12 '41 por
Newsweek 17:4 Je 23 '41 por
Pub W 139:2478 Je 21 '41
Time 37:18 Je 23 '41

BEARD, MARY See Beard, C. A. and Beard, M.

BEAUCHAMP, MARY ANNETTE *See* Russell, M. A. R., Countess

BECK, MARTIN 1869—Nov. 16, 1940 Theatrical producer, manager and actor who built the Palace and the Martin Beck Theatres and founded and headed the Orpheum Vaudeville Circuit.

References

Fortune 5:120 Je '32 por
Nat Mag 53:372-4 Mr '25 por
N Y Dramatic Mirror 72:17 Ag 19 '14
Newsweek 16:59 N 25 '40

International Motion Picture Almanac 1937-38
Who's Who in American Jewry

Obituaries

N Y Herald Tribune p40 N 17 '40 por
N Y Times p49 N 17 '40 por

BECKER, MAY LAMBERTON Aug. 26,
1873- Author; conductor of the Reader's
Guide, New York *Herald Tribune Books*

Address: b. New York Herald Tribune, 230
W. 41st St, New York City; h. 114 Morningside Drive, New York City

Few figures in the literary world are better
known to book lovers than May Lamberton
Becker, who, as conductor of the *Reader's
Guide*—first in the New York *Evening Post*,
then in the *Saturday Review of Literature*, and
since 1933 in the Sunday *Books* of the New
York *Herald Tribune*—has supplied invaluable
research service on books and authors to all
inquirers. Mrs. Becker has not only an encyclopedic knowledge of the field, aided by a
prodigious memory, but a truly human interest
in readers and a genuinely wholehearted desire
to serve them. As the *Publisher's Weekly* has
said: "Our book world would not be the same
without her." To further meet the needs of
readers she has published *A Reader's Guide
Book* (1924); *Adventures in Reading* (1927);
and *Books as Windows* (1929).

Besides her work as conductor of the
Reader's Guide and as a literary lecturer, Mrs.
Becker also edits a weekly *Books for Young
People* review section in the *Herald Tribune
Books*. Her unfailing good judgment and
lively estimates of what is best in children's
books have established her as an authority to
readers, writers and publishers of such books
for young people. She has found time also
to edit a series of tales for young readers—
the Golden Tales series covering the regional
output both in Canada and in this country:
Old South, New England, Prairie States, Far
West, Southwest, etc. In 1936 she published
First Adventures in Reading, and in 1937
Choosing Books for Children.

Mrs. Becker's latest book for young people,
Introducing Charles Dickens (1940), has exceptional interest and value because the author
has for many years been an enthusiastic
Dickensian. This knowledge and love for
the great English novelist she transfers to her
study of his life and writings. Not only his
characters, but Dickens himself comes alive in
her pages: "It is a book to put on like
spectacles and look through." According to
Anne Caroline Moore: "It brings Charles
Dickens to life in our own time, and she does
it without violating the confidence of the young
explorer of books bent on making his or her
choice." Other reviewers are impressed by its
special charm for grown-up readers, and com-
mend the prints, photographs and pen-sketch
illustrations. Still other reviewers were impressed by the success of her editing of *Growing Up With America,* an anthology published
in 1941.

May Lamberton Becker was born August 26,
1873 in New York City, in one of the huge
old Fourteenth Street "residences." Her

MAY LAMBERTON BECKER

father, Ellis Tinkham Lamberton, a Vermonter,
had the distinction of having been the "last
man to be mustered out of the Civil War."
Her mother, Emma Packard (Thurston)
Lamberton, Massachusetts-born, was a gifted
teacher. When the family moved to Jersey
City she established a special private school
there—one of the first schools for children
to employ modern "progressive" educational
methods. The mother herself taught her young
daughter (as she was later to teach Mrs.
Becker's own little daughter), and May
Lamberton was encouraged also to read anything she wanted to in the big family library.
Though she read enormously from the age of
four, she wasn't by any means an indoor
bookworm. She likes to recall the huge garden
back of the house where her family grew
vegetables, and where she and the neighborhood boys played and practically "lived." Mrs.
Becker says she owes to that hardy outdoor
life her "iron constitution and a digestion like
a horse," since she and the boys would cook
the garden vegetables in old tin cans and bake
potatoes black in their "camp" fires.

When she entered the Jersey City High
School she was determined to "get 100 in
everything," and she did, too—until she came
down with scarlet fever and had to be out of
school six months. Her record thus broken,
she decided not to be a "stuffy grind," but
to have a good time instead. In high school
she founded the Alpha Sigma Society, a
literary organization still in existence there.
When, at 16, she was graduated, she knew
exactly what she wanted to be: a newspaperwoman. Her father had died when she was 12,
and the family income was limited. Her Greek
teacher offered to send her to Barnard College,
all expenses paid. But the determined young
journalist didn't want either to become a
teacher or to be under financial obligation to
anyone. Accordingly she applied for a report-

BECKER, MAY LAMBERTON—*Cont.*

ing job on the Jersey City paper, and got it—"because of my good vocabulary." Her big chance came one day when the dramatic-and-baseball critic asked her to cover for him a matinee of Mansfield in *Beau Brummel.* Possibly because she had never read any drama criticism, she says, her piece on the play was so unusual and won so much attention that she became thereupon the regular drama critic, and later music critic also.

In 1894 May Lamberton married Gustav Louis Becker, pianist and composer, who came from Texas. Because she was the first in her family circle to marry outside New England, the family considered Gustav Becker a "foreigner." For their honeymoon the young couple went to Bayreuth to the Wagner Festival. On their return they settled in New York and took an active part in musical society: for years the "Becker Tuesdays," at which musicians and their friends met, were famous. A daughter, Beatrice, was born to them (the widow of Frederic Warde, typographer; and herself well known in the English typographical field as Paul Beaujon). The Becker marriage was dissolved in 1911.

Mrs. Becker began her own career as a lecturer on music; then, in 1907, substituted for a friend in delivering a series of talks on Victorian literature to women's clubs. As a lecturer in the book field she soon became widely known and in much demand. During the First World War she was chief of the Foreign News Bureau of the National Council of Defense. Afterward she served in editorial positions on magazines such as the *Pictorial Review, St. Nicholas* and *Scholastic.* It was in 1915 that she began the personal guidance, question-and-answer department called *Reader's Guide* for the New York *Evening Post,* a column which she now conducts for the New York *Herald Tribune Books.*

On her lecture tours Mrs. Becker has traveled extensively in this country and abroad. She used to spend summer vacations with her daughter in England where she was well known and popular in English literary circles. Her book, *Introducing Charles Dickens,* was later published in London. Its entire profits, including Mrs. Becker's royalties, go to war relief in London for rest centers for children whose homes have been bombed. In the United States the profits have paid for an ambulance, "the Charles Dickens," that has been operating in London. She is at present working on the American edition of *Tokens of Freedom*; and is under contract for "seven different books" which, she says, "I'll write when I can."

Tremendously energetic, with an energy constantly renewed not only by that "iron constitution" but by continuous fresh and happy interest in anything about books and people, Mrs. Becker is nonetheless always ready for a good chat with friends. She always enjoys a joke, and is the generous, keen, warm-hearted person her candid hazel eyes and hearty smile suggest. Cats are her chief

hobby; she loves talking about cats—hers or anyone's—more, perhaps, than anything else. Mrs. Becker's Siamese cats became famous in the book *Five Cats from Siam* (1935), in beautiful full-page photographs.

References

Pub W 120 :1683 O 10 '31
Scholastic 37 :18 O 14 '40 por
Wilson Lib Bul 7 :418 Mr '33
American Women
Kunitz, S. J. ed. Authors Today and Yesterday 1933
Who's Who Among North American Authors

BEEBE, WILLIAM July 29, 1877- Scientist; writer

Address: b. New York Zoological Park, The Bronx, New York City; h. 33 W. 67th St, New York City

Dr. William Beebe, director of tropical research of the New York Zoological Society and "the one professional zoologist of the first rank whose writings hold a high place in pure literature," sailed on May 16, 1941 for Bermuda. Before departing he said that United States Army defense preparations at Bermuda had probably ruined opportunities for him to continue his undersea studies at his six-acre laboratory and residence. Beebe had built a large house on this property, which he bought from the Bermuda Government. The laboratory-residence, "Nonsuch," figures in his book, *Nonsuch: Land of Water* (1932).

"There's nothing scientific about my journey," explained Beebe. "I'm just going to see if I can't rent my place to a general or an admiral." The Army had been extending its base near his property and the sand used had disturbed the waters, he went on to say. Beebe had also heard that gasoline from the army planes and their runway near his property had contaminated the Bermuda waters. In the event that he can no longer work at his Bermuda station, he is planning to establish a laboratory elsewhere, probably in South America.

Millions have seen Beebe's spherical steel diving chamber, or tank, a watertight ball with quartz windows which he christened the bathysphere—he had been writing about a deep-sea fish, Bathytroctes—when it was exhibited at the Chicago Century of Progress Exposition and later at the New York World's Fair. It was designed by Otis Barton, and Beebe were the first men to descend in it as far in the ocean's depths as 3,028 feet, and Beebe described the weird experience in *Half Mile Down* (1934). Usually accompanied by another observer, he would curl his lean length in the constricted chamber of the bathysphere and telephone his underwater observations to other members of his staff in the boat above. Occasionally language failed him temporarily, and he could only report: "Am writing at a depth of a quarter of a mile. A luminous fish is outside the window." But when he returned to the world of men, he wrote: "One thing we cannot escape—forever afterward, throughout all of life, the memory of the magic of water and its life, of the home which was once our own—this will never leave us."

William Beebe was born in Brooklyn, New York, the son of Charles and Henrietta Marie (Younglove) Beebe, and was christened Charles William. He received a B. S. degree from Columbia University in 1898, and then remained at Columbia another year to do postgraduate study. It was that same year (1899) that he became curator of ornithology at the New York Zoological Park, known in the city as The Bronx Zoo, and director of the Zoological Society's Department of Scientific Research. Honorary degrees have been conferred on him by Tufts College and Colgate University.

As a boy Beebe had been fond of reading the scientific romances of Jules Verne and the historical stories of G. A. Henty and had been "tremendously impressed" by Kipling. Later he read H. G. Wells and John Buchan. A taste for adventure and exploration so fostered must eventually find expression, and soon he made his first expedition into the heart of Mexico with his first wife, Mary Blair (who later divorced him, married Robert Niles, and became famous as Blair Niles, the novelist and writer of travel books). His *Two Bird-Lovers in Mexico* (1905) describes this trip. Later his wife collaborated with him in writing *Our Search for a Wilderness* (1910).

Next, Beebe's experiences at the Zoological Society's research station at Kartabo, British Guiana, yielded *Tropical Wild Life* (1917), written in collaboration with C. I. Hartley and P. G. Howes. There followed the beautiful series of monographs on pheasants. For his studies of pheasants, he lay for hours in the thick grass of Sarawak jungles to watch their mating dance, though tortured by an army of ants and in momentary danger of discovery by head-hunting Dyaks.

During the First World War, however, the scientist turned aviator. Theodore Roosevelt, whom Beebe regards as the greatest influence upon his life, was later to write: "Beebe, as bomber, has sailed in planes over the German lines; in company with a French officer he has listened to a wolf howl just back of the fighting front; he has gone with Iroquois Indians into the No Man's Land between the trenches of the mightiest armies the world has ever seen."

Much oppressed in mind as a result of his experiences, Beebe returned to Guiana after the War for peace and solace, and there he wrote the papers originally published in the *Atlantic Monthly* and elsewhere and collected in *Jungle Peace* (1918). He dedicated them to Colonel and Mrs. Roosevelt "with deepest friendship," and T. R. reciprocated with a book review in which he stated: "Mr. Beebe's volume is one of the rare books which represent a positive addition to the sum total of genuine literature. It is not merely a 'book of the season' or 'book of the year'; it will stand on the shelves of cultivated people, of people whose taste in reading is both wide and good, as long as men and women appreciate charm of form in the writings of men who also combine love of daring adventure with

WILLIAM BEEBE

the power to observe and vividly to record the things of strange interest which they have seen. Nothing like this type of book was written until within the last century and a half. Books of this kind can only be produced in a refined, cultivated, civilized society."

Walter Prichard Eaton and some other literary naturalists, on the other hand, have sometimes complained mildly that Beebe's style is a trifle too portentous and that he strives a little too obviously to create literature in everything he writes. The *Dial* termed his style "sonorous and imaginative rather than nervous."

Beebe's *Galápagos: World's End* (1924) was a fully illustrated account of those strange reptiles, sea-iguanas. Then in *Arcturus Adventure* (1926) he described the Zoological Society's first oceanographic expedition, naming his book after the vessel in which they had sailed. *Zaca Venture* (1938) recorded its thirty-fifth expedition, this time on the schooner *Zaca* in the Gulf of California, from March to May of 1936.

Beebe used to be conscious of the jangle and racket of New York only for a day after his return from jungle or sea; he claims to be able to work in a boiler factory. His idea of the perfect equalization of time is six months spent in the jungle or at sea and six months in the heart of New York City, within reach of the best operas, theatres and libraries. He does most of his reading at night, and is usually awake at dawn, finding five hours' sleep sufficient. He likes some intellectual games, but cannot abide bridge or poker. While clothes interest him little, he usually puts on a dinner coat in the evening. He dislikes thinking about food so long as it is well cooked, and has found the meat of the Mexican iguana particularly tasty. Beebe's wishes in regard to meals are to have a tabloid for breakfast, another for lunch, but a dinner of

BEEBE, WILLIAM—*Continued*

many courses, beautifully cooked and served, eaten slowly, with that rarest of things, real conversation. The cigarets he smokes are the mildest obtainable, and he never smokes when alone.

His writing and lecturing ability is still a mystery to him. He has an atrocious memory, yet when he sits down with a pen or stands in front of an audience words and sentences begin to materialize with almost no conscious effort on his part, and whether they are good or bad the conscious part of him reads or listens with interest to what is happening. Hence, he says, he can never become conceited because he always has the feeling of being a transmitting instrument for some impersonal source of supply.

Charles G. Shaw says Beebe "believes marriage the most wonderful thing in the world." The present Mrs. Beebe, whom he married in 1927, is also a writer: Elswyth Thane Ricker, author of *The Tudor Wench* and other books on British topics.

"Who can be bored for a moment in the short existence vouchsafed us here; with dramatic beginnings barely hidden in the dust, with the excitement of every moment of the present, and with all of cosmic possibility lying just concealed in the future, whether of Betelgeuze, of amoeba or—of ourselves?" inquires Beebe in *Edge of the Jungle*. "*Vogue la galère!*"

References

Bet Homes & Gard 15:36 S '36 il
Bookm 66:635-7 F '28 (Same cond. R of Rs 77:323 Mr '28)
Lit Digest 117:26 Ap 21 '34 il por; 123:18 My 22 '37 por
Nat Geog Mag 62:740-58 D '32 il pors; 66:661-704 D '34 il pors
St Nicholas 60:108-9 D '32 il
Scholastic 25:4 S 22 '34 il por; 28:7-8+ Mr 28 '36 il por
American Men of Science
Beebe, W. Arcturus Adventure 1926
Beebe, W. Half Mile Down 1934
Beebe, W. Jungle Days 1925
Gillis, A. and Ketchum, R. Our America p1-15 1936
Hylander, C. J. American Scientists p171-3 1935
Kunitz, S. J. ed. Living Authors 1937
Potter, G. R. Essays in Criticism p203-26 1929
Snyder, E. E. Biology in the Making p420-40 1940
Tracy, H. C. American Naturists p215-32 1930
Who's Who Among North American Authors
Who's Who in America

BEECHAM, SIR THOMAS, 2ND BARONET (bē-chǎm) Apr. 29, 1879- Conductor; composer

Address: b. c/o Columbia Broadcasting System, Inc, New York City

A pungent wit, a conducting skill accompanied by pyrotechnic displays of podium gymnastics, a prodigious memory and a viewpoint liberal and individualistic, fearlessly voiced in terms that have been quoted on both sides of the Atlantic, have made Sir Thomas Beecham a Shavian figure in the contemporary musical world. His background, too, adds a strong color note to the personality of the fiery, dapper little man with the tidy goatee.

Sir Thomas inherited his taste for music from his father, the late Sir Joseph Beecham, 1st Baronet, who collected old musical instruments, together with a fortune of some $150,000,000. Beecham, *père,* made this fortune in the world-famed Beecham pills. It is said that in one advertising campaign he issued a hymnal with paraphrased words that praised his product:

> *Hark! the herald angels sing,*
> *Beecham's pills are just the thing.*

And when Sir Thomas, like the herald angel, conducted his own orchestra in London, it was affectionately called "Beecham's P'ilharmonic."

Born April 29, 1879 in Lancashire, England, the son of Joseph and Josephine (Burnett) Beecham, young Godfrey Thomas, at the age of seven "scornful of staid convention and the usual childish music lessons, was learning Wagnerian and other scores in his home by listening again and again to a reed organ which could be played by perforated music rolls." With the financial assistance of his wealthy father, at the age of 10 he founded an amateur orchestra which was often conducted by the great Hans Richter and, at least once, "with considerable aplomb," by young Beecham himself.

His formal education at Rossall School and at Wadham College, Oxford, went on concurrently with his musical education. In 1903 he married Utica, daughter of Dr. Charles S. and Ella (Miles) Welles, of New York. Two sons were born of the marriage. It was in 1916, on the death of his father, that he became 2nd Baronet.

In 1902 Beecham toured with a traveling opera company, and in 1905 he made his first appearance in London, with the Queen's Hall Orchestra. At 27 he was rich enough to found his own orchestra, the New Symphony, and he served as its conductor until 1908, when he organized the Beecham Symphony Orchestra. Then, in 1910, he began producing operas at Covent Garden and later at Drury Lane. Season after season, including the four years of the First World War, he kept on giving such operas as *Pelléas et Mélisande, Elektra, Salomé* and Delius' *Village Romeo and Juliet.* All in all it cost him about a million pounds or so of his inheritance. When asked if he really did lose that much, he answered: "It wasn't quite that much. But someone added up the total for me. When I heard it I fainted and had to be revived with brandy." And he comments on the whole experience: "My most successful season [Drury Lane, 1913 to 1914] was in Russian. Nobody understood a word of it." In 1916 he was knighted for his services to music.

Beecham's first appearance in America was in 1928, when he was described as "the most athletic conductor America has seen for many a season." Called "a born evangel of action," when conducting "he leaps, ducks, weaves, lunges, skates and does everything but a back flip." When he was conducting the New York Philharmonic in January 1928, the audience still recalls that, following an unusual gymnastic workout, the maestro walked off the podium with stiff, mincing steps quite unlike his usual gait. "My braces snapped," he explained when he got off stage. Braces repaired, the athletic Sir Thomas resumed the concert. It is said that his violent conducting mannerisms are mostly put on as a show for the audience. In rehearsals "Tommy," as he is affectionately referred to by his men, conducts quietly, gets results by hard rehearsing and ironic British humor. At one time when the French horn came in too loud he said: "And now I'd like to hear the horn, too."

Fond of telling funny stories about his career, Sir Thomas recalls the night when a black cat made a shambles of a Covent Garden performance of *Tristan und Isolde* by going to sleep on the prompter's box in full view of the audience; and of the time an alcoholic harpist in the London Philharmonic so loudly improvised his cadenzas in *Lucia di Lammermoor* that Beecham and the orchestra had to interrupt "with a desperate, crashing chord in D major fortissimo."

Sir Thomas likes to talk of "my orchestra," the London Philharmonic, which he founded with socialite backing in 1932. This creation was his greatest achievement in the field of concert work. In the autumn of 1940 this famous orchestra was taken over by its members to play one-night stands throughout England. It missed one appearance when Liverpool was bombed, another when its busses were bogged in Lancashire snowdrifts; but it carries on in spite of war and has played to more than 150,000 persons. Many of its members have been called to the colors, but Sir Thomas says that the authorities have cooperated with him "by stationing the players near places where they will be available for concerts."

In the spring of 1940 Sir Thomas was on his way to Australia, admittedly as a lecturer-propagandist. At that time, on his stop-off in New York, he issued a scathing denunciation of the Chamberlain Government. "A firm hand would have avoided the terrible weakness, the shocking mistakes that the [British] Government has made before and during the present War," he said. This feeble Government, he felt, greatly endangered chances of an Allied victory, at least an early one. Sir Thomas says that democracy "represents the slow evolution of man's freedom and permits us to make fools of ourselves in our own way. The opposing philosophy forces us to make fools of ourselves in someone else's way." He is not worried about the searing effect of war on the artist, and he vigorously opposes those who would ban German music and who speak of Wagner as a prophet of Nazi philosophy. "Incidentally," he says, "*Die Meistersinger* is not Hitler's favorite opera, in spite of what Nazi propaganda bureaus say. His favorite

Cannon

SIR THOMAS BEECHAM

opera is *The Merry Widow*. I know because he told me so while we were both guests at the Wagner home in Bayreuth a few years ago." Of this meeting with Hitler in 1936 Sir Thomas said further: "I tried to persuade him to come to England. He said he was afraid that might 'put too much of a strain on your police force.' I pointed out that the King walked about with immunity. He said he did not think he could be sure of the same indifference and freedom from annoyance." As a postscript to this bit of Führer leg-pulling Sir Thomas added slyly: "Naturally, I made no comment on that."

Sir Thomas pulls no punches in stating his opinions, political or musical. California is still outraged over the remarks on cultural progress in America which he made there on tour in February 1941. These remarks included reference to an asserted lack of devotion to the better theatre in this country, absence of opera, deficiency in choral societies and even politics and statesmanship. He emphatically asserted that Hollywood musical directors did not produce music but only shocking noise. "No one with the slightest artistic refinement can listen to movie music without the utmost pain."

But the sardonic maestro is by no means severe in his criticism when it comes to orchestras. He likes an ensemble, he says, that "can play the notes." And because he likes also "to get in touch with the human side of orchestras" he was particularly delighted with Mayor La Guardia's invitation to him to conduct the orchestra of the New York City WPA Music Project. He feels that an orchestra represents "the most exact epitome of what a well-ordered social system should be. . . All are subordinated to one purpose, and there is variety within unity." He says proudly that "up to the present I have never

BEECHAM, SIR THOMAS—*Continued*
encountered an orchestra which failed to accomplish my purpose."

That the WPA Orchestra responded beautifully to Sir Thomas was enthusiastically admitted by music critics. Olin Downes called these concerts in 1941 among the most exciting given in New York. Pleased with the quality of his audience, plain men and women and numerous young people from all over town, Sir Thomas was in fine fettle. Conducting without score, he took the orchestra radiantly through the famed "Paris" Symphony of Mozart: "The music glowed and sang with a transfigural beauty and a veritable lust of life. No wonder that the audience resounded with an ovation." Other critics applauded his conducting of Haydn's Symphony in B-flat major, No. 102, especially for the "feeling of complete security with which the players of the orchestra moved under Sir Thomas' positive and knowing command." This particular program closed with a tone poem by Delius. Beecham, known for his unusually sensitive interpretations of Mozart, is universally recognized as the greatest exponent of the music of the late Frederick Delius, his close personal friend. It was he who organized the Delius Festival in October 1929, and it was with Delius' *Sea Drift* that he opened his concert series in the summer of 1941 over CBS. This concert series was followed by engagements in Montreal, Chicago, Mexico City and Seattle.

Soon after this series he was engaged to conduct opera performances for a six weeks' period during the New York Metropolitan Opera Company's 1941 to 1942 season. This engagement, which marks his first appearance as opera conductor in the United States, will begin with a four weeks' run in January 1942; after out-of-town appearances he will return for a fortnight in March. He is also scheduled to be guest conductor of symphony orchestras in New York, Philadelphia and Detroit, and with them he will feature works by contemporary American and British composers. Among the American compositions he plans to play are Aaron Copland's *El Salon Mexico*, Virgil Thomson's *Second Symphony*, Zoltan Kurthy's *Overture,* William Schuman's *American Festival Overture* and a new piano concerto by Courtlandt Palmer.

The Beecham musical memory is fabulous: he often conducts lengthy and difficult scores entirely from memory and without a mistake. The story is told of the time he arrived only a moment before curtain time in Manchester to conduct an opera troupe there. Beecham calmly lit a cigar while the manager nervously paced the floor and exclaimed: "But it's time to begin!" "Ah, yes," sighed Sir Thomas as he adjusted his tie, adding, as he paused at the door, "By the way, what opera are we playing tonight?"

Off the podium "the stormy petrel of British music" looks small (he is five feet five), relaxed and reserved. "Indeed, with his expressed desire for 'content and peace,' his kindly brown eyes, his neatly trimmed white goatee and his polished and beautiful speech,

he seems like a retired English schoolmaster, with just a hint every now and then of the gentleman who slipped when he came to dinner."

References

Etude 56:705 N '38 por; 58:588 S '40 por
Good H 113:11 S '41 por
Musician 40:9 D '35 por
New Statesman & Nation 9:42 Ja 12 '35; 15:611-12 Ap 9 '38
Newsweek 17:74 Ap 14 '41 il pors
Pict R 37:4+ Ja '36
Sat R 159:440 Ap 6 '35
Time 27:36+ Ja 13 '36; 29:49 My 3 '37 por; 31:50-1 My 16 '38; 37:94 Ap 21 '41

Baker's Biographical Dictionary of Musicians 1940
Ewen D. Man with the Baton p241-69 1936
Ewen, D. ed. Living Musicians 1940
Shore, B. Orchestra Speaks p31-46 1938
Smyth, E. M. Beecham and Pharaoh 1935
Thompson, O. ed. International Cyclopedia of Music and Musicians 1939
Who's Who

BEGG, COLIN LUKE 1873—Jan. 15, 1941
Physician; last surviving member of the group of seven doctors who founded the American Urological Association; spent 41 years in medical practice; consultant for many New York City hospitals; visiting professor at New York Post-Graduate School of Medicine for 25 years.

References

American Medical Directory
Directory of Medical Specialists 1939
Who's Who in American Medicine

Obituaries

N Y Herald Tribune p12 Ja 17 '41

BELL, THOMAS M(ONTGOMERY)
Mar. 17, 1861—Mar. 18, 1941 Democratic member of Congress from Georgia from 1904 until 1930; a leader in the movement to develop and maintain Federal highways; from 1905, when he first proposed the good roads issue, until 1914 he presented arguments for the measure during each session; in 1914 the House Committee on Roads was organized and his ideas adopted.

References

Who's Who in America 1932-33

Obituaries

N Y Times p21 Mr 19 '41

BEMELMANS, LUDWIG (bĕm'-ĕl-mĕns)
Apr. 27, 1898- Author; illustrator
Address: h. 20 Gramercy Park, New York City

Of Ludwig Bemelmans, William McFee comments: "Ludwig Bemelmans is one of those fortunate writers who have all the reviewers ranged on one side, rooting for him . . . one always wants to reread Bemelmans." *The Donkey Inside* (1941) was received with all the customary enthusiasm. This semi-fictional collection of 23 sketches, essays and anecdotes based on two trips to Ecuador, a country which Bemelmans calls "the quintessence of South America," inspires the following comment from one critic: "Mr. Bemelmans has a fine faculty for making *everything* seem strange and exciting, including tame headhunters, the servants on André Roosevelt's ranch, a cocktail party in Quito and the Indian lad whose bus-driving brother gets a bonus for calling his machine *Adolfo Hitler.*"

The author himself, however, is afraid that when Ecuador authorities receive copies of his book, which describes in story and picture the "beautful madness of this lovely land" from which he returned in October 1940, they won't permit him to revisit them. "I love the country," he says sadly, "and I say in the book how wonderful it is, but I also point out truthfully some things about it that the inhabitants are not pleased to see. You know the Spaniards. They are most eager to have you see what is good, but when you say: 'Yes, it is beautiful, but aren't there a great number of flies on it?' then they have no use for you."

Bemelmans' own country didn't have much use for him either. He was born in Meran in the Tirol on April 27, 1898, the son of Lambert and Frances (Fisher) Bemelmans. His father was a Belgian painter, his mother the daughter of a prosperous Bavarian brewer. After his parents were divorced Ludwig was brought up in Regensburg by his Grandfather Fisher, who looked upon all artists as *Lumpen*. Ludwig attended the Königliche Realschule at Regensburg, couldn't pass, and then was sent to a private academy for backward boys in Rothenburg until its rector wrote to take him away. After that there was nothing to do but become an apprentice for a Bavarian uncle who owned a string of hotels in the Austrian Tirol; Ludwig wanted to paint, but had been assured that painters were "hunger candidates." It took him a year to run through the string of hotels—every manager sent him back in despair—and at the last hotel he shot a vicious headwaiter who had struck him. It was then a choice between reform school and America, a land which, according to well-informed sources, would "sheer his pelt and clip his horns." He chose the latter.

So it was that in December 1914 Ludwig Bemelmans, age 16, sailed from Rotterdam for the United States, eager to see the Indians. In his pockets were letters of introduction to managers of several American hotels, and as soon as he reached New York he stopped at the employees' entrance to the Astor. The letter of introduction was effective, but only briefly so. As a bus boy he broke too many dishes. There were more letters, however, and the McAlpin manager was also impressed. There Ludwig stayed for a year, and then a hotel which he calls

LUDWIG BEMELMANS

the Splendide (critics think he refers to the Hotel Ritz) took him on as waiter's runner. This time it was his fondness for Belgian hothouse grapes as much as anything else that proved his undoing, but "Mr. Sigsag" of the Grill Room befriended him, and he was working there and studying painting in his spare time when the United States entered the First World War.

Young Bemelmans entered the First World War, too, shortly after his French had been gently corrected by Marshal Joffre, one of the Splendide's distinguished guests. The young man was variously stationed at Fort Ontario near Oswego, New York, at the Field Hospital, Unit N, and at the Officers' Training School at Camp Gordon near Atlanta, Georgia. His is perhaps the most unconventional war diary to be published in modern times, but it remained untranslated from the German until two decades later.

After the Armistice, Bemelmans, now a second lieutenant and a naturalized American citizen, planned to return to Munich to study painting. But "Mr. Sigsag," now assistant head of the banquet department of the Splendide, persuaded him that his was a better proposition, and until 1925 Bemelmans was associated with him. *Life Class,* published in 1938, might have been dedicated to this serious, kind, comic little man whose whole life centered in the Splendide and who finally perished in one of its elevator shafts. Bemelmans' own days at the Splendide are humorously and carefully recorded in the book's pages.

Next came the period when Bemelmans was himself part owner of the famous Hapsburg House on New York's East Side. At last he had an opportunity to satisfy his artistic aims. He joyously painted pictures on the walls of the restaurant—maybe an old coat, maybe a pair of open windows, a

BEMELMANS, LUDWIG—*Continued*

bird cage or a sprig of green vine—but pictures that were all, for some unknown reason, funny. Bemelmans, as a matter of fact, spent much of the Hapsburg profits in making the restaurant as interesting as he could. He spent some of them, too, in ordering the most expensive foods and the best dining room for himself; but apparently his partners didn't decide definitely to buy him out until they found him feeding their costliest imported wines to his pet dachshund. Now Bemelmans occasionally grows nostalgic about the life of a restaurateur who is also an epicure.

One day May Massee, editor of children's books for the Viking Press in New York City, was taken by a lithographer to see Bemelmans at his apartment on 8th Street. There he had painted Tyrolean landscapes on his window shades so that he could pull down the blinds when homesick or lonely and be comforted by the familiar scenes. Miss Massee, seeing them, immediately decided that here was a man who should be writing a book for children. She managed to persuade Bemelmans that she was right, and the first result of her persuasion was *Hansi* (1934), a story about Bemelmans' childhood in the Tirol, which he also illustrated.

In November 1935 Bemelmans married Madeline Freund, the daughter of a Westchester banker. They have one daughter, Barbara. *The Golden Basket* (1936), whose hero in real life was an old waiter in a hotel Bemelmans remembered, was his second book. More children's books followed: *Castle Number Nine* (1937) and *Quito Express* (1938), the story of a lost baby in Ecuador, to which Bemelmans had just made a four months' visit. Critics, nearly all critics, found them "enchanting", "delightful", "unexpected and lovable"—in other words, average Bemelmans.

The year 1937 also marked the appearance of *My War with the United States,* the war diary mentioned earlier. Naïve and wickedly apt, humorous and touching, full of war experiences that could never have happened to anyone else, the ravings of insane patients, homesickness, adventures with girls and odd little comparisons between Germany and the United States, critics had a difficult time describing it and deciding exactly what to say about it but apparently had little difficulty in admiring it. Bemelmans was by this time selling articles and illustrations to the *New Yorker, Town and Country, Vogue* and *Stage* with great regularity, and in 1938 made a trip to Europe for Condé Nast. *Life Class,* the story of his days at the Astor, McAlpin and Splendide, appeared the same year—"as perfect an equivalent of his ingenuously sophisticated drawings" as is James Thurber's prose of his. And in 1939 came *Madeline*—rhymed couplets about a little girl in a

Parisian school who made her schoolmates insanely jealous by having her appendix out. It had beautiful water-color reproductions of real scenes in Paris and no particular moral. "Humorous and delightful," said the *New Yorker.* That same year 10 of his short stories and sketches, illustrated by the author, were published under the title *Small Beer.* "I think no one in the informal-essay field today can equal it," said Otis Ferguson. *At Your Service; the Way of Life in a Hotel* was published in 1941. *Hotel Splendide,* a collection of sketches, mostly from the *New Yorker,* was published in December 1941 and hailed as "vintage Bemelmans . . . as mellow and fruity as ever."

When writing for children Bemelmans simply writes stories that he himself happens to like, although he does try them out on his young daughter Barbara. (She "loves much worse books much better," he says cheerfully.) Usually characters and illustrations are based on real people and real events: Bemelmans claims he has no imagination. Few would agree with him on that score, however; as one critic says: "[To Bemelmans] most of the world is slightly fantastic. In his pictures the most ordinary objects become, by some process in his mind, faintly ridiculous; and people walk, sit and talk in a fashion most disconcertingly ludicrous."

Bemelmans likes to draw really big pictures—he once tried to persuade Miss Massee that children's books should be three feet square. For the colored ones he uses water colors. He really likes painting much better than writing and probably would never write a word if he had plenty of money and no insomnia. As it is, writing serves as "occupational therapy," for Bemelmans seldom can get more than three or four hours sleep a night, and while lying awake makes a habit of writing in his mind, then putting the key phrases down and filling in between them. He rewrites four times or more. He still loves good food, good living and travel, but finds that all three are more readily available to a restaurateur than to a literary artist. Sighing philosophically, he says: "If a check bounces now and then—well, it is something I must accept."

References

N Y Times Book R p2, 23 Ja 26 '41 por
Newsweek 10:21 Jl 24 '37 por; 17:54 Ja 20 '41 por
Pub W 134:1508-10 O 22 '38 il por
Sat R Lit 19:7 N 12 '38 por; 23:16 Ja 18 '41
Stage 1:46-7 F '41 pors
Time 37:83 Ja 20 '41 por
Wilson Lib Bul 13:522 Ap '39 por
Bemelmans, L. Donkey Inside 1941
Bemelmans, L. Hotel Splendide 1941
Bemelmans, L. Life Class 1938
Who's Who in America

BENCHLEY, ROBERT (CHARLES)

Sept. 15, 1889- Humorist; writer; dramatic critic; actor

Address: b. c/o Metro-Goldwyn-Mayer, Hollywood, Calif; h. Scarsdale, N. Y.

One way to describe Robert Benchley is to say that he is all things to all men—and all of them funny. He is probably the most versatile humorist in America, and the most successful. He has written a score of brilliantly funny books; his articles and dramatic criticism in the *New Yorker* have been gospel to theatregoers; he has been the star of a popular radio program; his presence has enlivened many a motion picture; and he has produced and starred in one-reel films that have been considered the most profitable in that field outside of cartoons.

Perhaps it is through these one-reelers that the man in the street knows Benchley best, and with good reason; certainly Benchley, sprawled on his bed in picturesque disarray (in *How To Sleep*) or brightly adding national income for the year 1889 to two Irishmen and carrying one (in the immortal *Treasurer's Report*), is unforgettable. John O'Hara (see sketch this issue) says lyrically of him: "Robert Charles Benchley is like a summer sunset on Lake Louise. He is like India's coral strand. He's a Waldorf salad, a Berlin ballad, and, lately, he's Mickey Mouse." This last refers to Benchley's participation in the semi-documentary Disney fantasy called *The Reluctant Dragon*, in which he is shown happily wandering around the Disney studios, finding out what makes Donald Duck tick.

A modest little biography supplied by Benchley himself claims that he was born on the Isle of Wight, September 15, 1807, shipped as cabin boy on the *Florence J. Marble* in 1815, wrote *Tale of Two Cities* in 1820, married Princess Anastasie of Portugal in 1831 (children: Prince Rupprecht and several little girls) and was buried in Westminster Abbey in 1871. That is not strictly true. Mr. Benchley was born on September 15, 1889, in Worcester, Massachusetts, the son of Charles Henry and Jane (Moran) Benchley. He went to Phillips Exeter Academy, where he is still remembered as the author of a paper on "How to Embalm a Corpse," written after being given an assignment to write an exposition of how to do something practical. Then he drifted on to Harvard, from which he received his B. A. degree in 1912. Offspring of a plain, severe, devout New England family, he never drank, smoked or gambled throughout his whole college life, but merely exercised his more or less perverse sense of humor. He was president of the *Lampoon,* Harvard's comic magazine, participated in the Hasty Pudding show as a chorus girl (he recalls with pride that his waist then was a negligible 19 inches, far from today's comfortable girth) and delighted his friends with impromptu lectures. He received an excellent education in spite of the fact that his "courses were selected with a serious purpose in mind—no classes before 11 in the morning or after 2:30 in the afternoon

ROBERT BENCHLEY

and nothing on Saturdays." For a while he considered a diplomatic career—this project flopped when he had to write his term thesis on the Newfoundland Fisheries case. "His interpretation was scholarly, but his approach was from the point of view of the fish"—a point of view that he was to keep all his life.

Benchley's first position was as secretary to the director of the Boston Museum of Fine Arts. His next was in the New York advertising office of the Curtis Publishing Company, where he worked until 1914, when "Curtis stayed in Philadelphia in its small way and I went elsewhere." Back in Boston, Benchley married Gertrude Darling and got a position with the Russell Paper Company as a social service worker organizing clambakes and bowling matches for the employees. In 1915, a week after Benchley's first son, Nathaniel Goddard, was born, the directors decided "that the boys had had enough clams," and Benchley was fired.

His next association was more in his line. He worked under F. P. Adams (see sketch this issue) as associate editor of the New York *Tribune's* Sunday Magazine, writing weekly articles which steadily increased his reputation as a humorist and becoming a welcome after-dinner speaker at smokers and banquets. His best effort, perhaps, was his address on Prohibition and the Navy, when, in the character of Josephus Daniels' chief assistant, he disclosed to the Navy League the government's intention to drive "even the *memory* of vile spirits from our jolly jack tars."

The end of the association was an unhappy one. Benchley, who hates war violently, resigned in 1917 in protest against the *Tribune's* war policy. His next two years were rather desolately occupied with a job as press agent for William A. Brady and as publicity secretary to the Aircraft Board in Washington. Mean-

BENCHLEY, ROBERT—*Continued*

while, though, *Vanity Fair* was publishing his articles, and in 1919 he was hired as its managing editor. It was there that he met Robert Sherwood and Dorothy Parker, working respectively as photographic editor and dramatic editor. Although these three undoubtedly brought new wit and new life to the magazine, they were regarded with caution and even fear. For example, when a notice was posted forbidding employees to speculate about one another's salaries, the irrepressible trio took to wearing theirs on a placard around their necks. As a result of these high jinks—and a rather inconvenient sense of editorial independence—they left *Vanity Fair*. Benchley soon thereafter became *Life's* dramatic editor (1920) and kept that position—which he took with considerable misgivings, reiterating that he knew nothing about reviewing plays—until 1929.

Benchley and Sherwood, who had become *Life's* editors in 1924, helped to boost its circulation by their highly popular burlesque issues, taking off a dozen prominent magazines and even tabloids. (Benchley once posed for a newsphoto of an ax butcher, and Dorothy Parker was snapped as the murdered paramour.) Benchley's dramatic reviews were also getting him a steadily growing following of admirers. One of the high spots of his career as a dramatic critic was his *contretemps* with *Abie's Irish Rose*. Benchley panned it in 1922 and for five long years was faced with the task of describing the play in different terms every week in his "Confidential Guide." People bought *Life* merely to gloat over Benchley's plight and read such desperate paraphrases as "Just about as low as good clean fun can get"; "Showing that the Jews and the Irish crack equally old jokes"; "The kind of comedy you eat peanuts at"; and finally the mournful "Will the Marines *never* come?" During those years he also began to write books, each page of which was "riddled with pitfalls for sanity," among them *Love Conquers All* (1922); *The Early Worm* (1927); and *20,000 Leagues Under the Sea or David Copperfield* (1928). He also conducted a column called "Books and Other Things" in the New York *World* from 1920 to 1921.

In 1922 Benchley made his acting debut in a skit in *No, Sirree,* an amateur show produced and staged by eminent figures in the literary and art world (offstage music, the program note stated, was by Jascha Heifetz). The name of the skit was *The Treasurer's Report.* This little gem of mangled figures and metaphors, written by Benchley in a taxi on the way to the first rehearsal, was in 1930 incorporated into a book called *The Treasurer's Report, and Other Aspects of Community Singing,* which went into 12 editions and was translated into Swedish. Irving Berlin heard him and signed him up for his *Music Box Revue,* which ran nine months. Ten weeks in vaudeville followed, with his act obligingly scheduled early enough in the evening not to interfere with his duties as dramatic critic.

In 1929 Benchley resigned from *Life* Magazine to become dramatic critic of the *New Yorker,* for which he also wrote criticisms of the New York press under the signature of Guy Fawkes. He kept that position until more profitable Hollywood activities began to claim most of his time. He started in motion pictures in 1928 when, at the suggestion of Walter Wanger, then in Paramount, he dragged out his old stand-by, *The Treasurer's Report,* and went over it lightly at the Astoria studio. Audiences loved Mr. Benchley, loved his nightmare-like financial calculations, loved his apologetic chuckle—and he has since produced over 30 of these shorts for several studios.

Among his better short subjects are: *The Love Life of the Polyp; How To Vote; How To Sleep* (which gave MGM the Academy Award for the best short of the year); *An Evening Alone; Raising a Baby.* Aptly described as "Benchley humiliations recollected in tranquility," they all show him thwarted by the complexities of life around him. Although Benchley goes about producing them at his usual unhurried pace, the average shooting time is three days, the average cost around $8,000. Gross returns are five times that, and for this reason alone the portly Mr. Benchley is worth his weight in gold to Hollywood.

Nor is that all he has to offer. He is in 1941 under contract to MGM as actor, writer and director. Considered one of Hollywood's crack writers of light dialogue, he has been constantly called in to supply a light touch or to bolster up failing dialogue. After a while, when it became apparent that he could read his own lines with considerable effect, they put him to work as an actor in feature-length pictures. Benchley has played supporting roles such as the disillusioned newspaperman in *Foreign Correspondent,* the family lawyer in *Hired Wife,* the good-natured father in *Nice Girl,* the wayward husband in *You'll Never Get Rich,* with Fred Astaire and Rita Hayworth. The characters he portrays on the screen have a startling resemblance to himself and he occasionally gets a chance to play his mandolin, an accomplishment acquired during his Harvard days. Although Benchley has long fought off attractive radio offers (once when a tobacco firm questioned him about his favorite brand of cigaret, he wired back uncompromisingly: "Marijuana"), in 1938 his friends finally persuaded him to take part in an Old Gold program. He flourished like a green bay tree, rating sixth on a national popularity poll.

Benchley's friends often indulge in heated discussions about which of Benchley's manifestations are most expressive of him. Many of them agree that it is in such books as *My Ten Years in a Quandary, and How It Grew* (1936) or *After 1903—What?* (1938) that the true Benchley is to be found. Or even in his other books: *Of All Things* (1921); *Pluck and Luck* (1925); *No Poems; or, Around the World Backwards and Sideways* (1932); *From Bed to Worse* (1934); and *Why Does Nobody Collect Me?* (1935). Stephen Leacock it was who said: "None excels Robert Benchley in the ingenious nonsense of verbal humor." This humor is tinged with a sort of merry madness. He is the master of the dazzling *non sequitur* ("Is life made too easy for the youth of today? Are we raising a generation of pampered dawdlers? What is that on your necktie?"); his flights of extravagance threaten reason; yet his very lack of logic is implacably logical. And his nonsense is always couched in prose that is a model of clarity and elegance. There is, besides, something infectious about his style that forces all the critics to write like Benchley when reviewing his books.

"A bland punchinello," Benchley's private life is the stuff of which legends are made. His friends Ernest Hemingway and Donald Ogden Stewart (see sketch this issue) have put him in their books. Everybody has a favorite story about him: the time Benchley left a note to the milkman at Grant's tomb; the time a suite of offices directly below his office was devastated by fire while he sat tapping out a story in a fireman's helmet presented to him by his native Worcester; the time he telephoned the late ex-Kaiser at Doorn, on a sudden impulse to speak German. Through all these stories the Benchley personality emerges as an extremely likable one, a quality that carries over to the screen. Universally respected as a craftsman, his genuine kindness has won him legions of friends. "I cannot think of anyone," says John O'Hara, "who has not been advanced spiritually, culturally and even financially by association with Mr. B." Yet he is modest and has had to be lured into every step of his career by friends who thought more of his talents than he did. He has never done anything for himself but has merely been "tossed from pillar to post, augmenting his income at each rebound."

In life, as on the screen, Benchley carries on an indomitable if losing fight against the conspiracy of inanimate things. A confirmed foe of order, he tries to carry confusion wherever he goes, cunningly mixing up appointments, writing love letters to his bankers above his endorsement of checks. His rebellion against discipline is expressed in his favorite motto, plain above his desk: "The work can wait." He is a constant defier of the deadline, the creator of elaborate alibis. Yet, paradoxically, he has a phobia about unclean copy, and his typewritten manuscripts—he "cannot write more than three or four lines in longhand without fainting"—are models of tidiness. Hemingway used to call him "Garbage Bird" to describe his appearance "in the early morning light of Montparnasse on certain occasions." He himself says modestly that he is "handsome in an unusual sort of way." A grandfather, and the father of a second son, Robert Gale, Benchley has become resigned to a life of fervid activity and only occasionally remembers with a sigh his ancient ambition to write a history of the Queen Anne period.

References

Christian Sci Mon p6 Jl 26 '40 por
Group Discussion Guide 7:11 Je '41
N Y Times IX p5 F 9 '41
Newsweek 18:54 Jl 21 '41 pors
PM p54 O 13 '40 pors
Sat Eve Post 212:10-11+ S 23 '39 por;
    212:32+ O 7 '39 por
Sat R Lit 14:14 My 9 '36 por; 15:19
    D 26 '36; 17:22 Ja 8 '38
Time 32:48 S 19 '38 por
International Motion Picture Almanac
Masson, T. L. Our American Humorists
    p47-52 1931
Variety Radio Directory
Who's Who in America
Who's Who in the Theatre

BENEDICT, RUTH June 5, 1887- Anthropologist

Address: b. Department of Anthropology, Columbia University, New York City; h. 448 Central Park West, New York City

RUTH BENEDICT

If asked who is the foremost woman in anthropology today, most anthropologists would name Ruth Benedict either first or second. She is one of those who have contributed most to a stronger alliance among various branches of social science: anthropology, sociology, psychology. With others in this group of social-scientific pathfinders, she has gone a step further: having applied related technics to the materials of anthropology, she applies the findings of her science to fundamental problems of our day.

In her book, *Race: Science and Politics* (1940), she presented a popular account of what scientists have learned about race, and an analysis of what she calls "racism," examining and refuting the claims of racial superiority and analyzing the motivation of racial propagandists. "Dr. Benedict has put into her debt," wrote one reviewer, "all those who wish honestly to come to grips with the perennial race problem, whether in its Negro, Semitic,

BENEDICT, RUTH—*Continued*

Nordic, Oriental, or 100 per cent American guise." Most scholars agree with the fundamental thesis of her book although several take issue with specific items of fact.

Dr. Benedict writes not only as a scientist, but also as an Old American convinced "that all the arguments are on the side of the Founding Fathers who urged no discrimination on the basis of race, creed, or color." In 1799 "her ancestors 'went West' from Connecticut to New York on a bob-sled, with a cow tied on behind to give milk for the babies. Six of her ancestors fought in the Revolution. On the other side of her family, her great-great-grandfather in 1802 fled to the United States from his home in Nova Scotia because he dared to propose a toast to George Washington at a public banquet; only the influence of his relative Cornwallis had saved him from being shipped to Bombay as a political prisoner."

The descendant who was to pioneer in academic fields and fight for democracy with her pen was born in New York City on June 5, 1887. Her father, Dr. Frederick S. Fulton, a physician, died when she was two years old, and her mother, Bertrice J. (Shattuck) Fulton, supported her family by teaching. The first six years of Ruth Fulton's life were spent on the family farm in Norwich, New York. Then she and her sister followed the trail of their mother's teaching appointments through Missouri and Minnesota, keeping house for her and taking care of her. After taking her B. A. degree at Vassar in 1909 she taught English for a while in a girls' school, turned to anthropology only later. In 1914 she came East and was married to Dr. Stanley R. Benedict, a biochemist, who died in 1936.

Dr. Ruth Benedict was first known as a poet, though at the same time unknown, for she wrote under the name of Anne Singleton. Her verse became familiar to readers of *Poetry, The Nation* and other periodicals which published contemporary verse. In 1919, rather indifferently and chiefly because she wanted "busy work," she enrolled at Columbia University for some courses under Franz Boas (see sketch 1940 Annual), the grand old man of anthropology. Her interest was soon deeply serious and eventually she became, next to Dr. Boas himself, the key figure in the Department of Anthropology In 1923 she received her Ph. D. degree at Columbia and since that time she has been teaching there, the first eight years as lecturer, then as assistant professor, and since 1930 as associate professor. After the retirement of Dr. Boas in 1936 she was until 1939 acting head of the Department—a considerable distinction for a woman in any large university.

Her teaching career has been interspersed with periods in the field, where she studied the Pueblo Indians, the Mission Indians, the Apache, the Pima, the Blackfoot. Her students have gone on expeditions to New Guinea, Samoa, Fiji, Africa, South America and to many North American tribes. Dr. Benedict is in 1941 working on a book in which some of this widespread field work will be drawn together. Studying the manifold experiments in living represented by primitive peoples today has been exciting to her, she says, partly for the light it sheds on our own "tribal ways."

Dr. Benedict has made special studies of primitive religion, mythology and folklore, as well as what the profession calls "straight ethnology." Her *Tales of the Cochiti Indians* was published in 1931, and *Zuni Mythology* in 1935. In the '30s, when psychoanalysts began to appreciate the insight to be gained through direct collaboration with anthropologists, she was among the first to give active cooperation. Her *Patterns of Culture*, published in 1934, visualized culture as an integrated whole, applying to groups the psychiatric and psychological concepts usually employed in connection with individuals. Of this book, which aroused considerable controversy, the New York *Times* said: "By training, vocation and chief interest Dr. Benedict is an anthropologist, but a quartet of sciences, anthropology, sociology, psychology, and philosophy, is responsible for the volume, which is expertly conceived and brilliantly developed." A colleague, Dr. Melville Herskovits, commented that "quite aside from Dr. Benedict's argument her book represents a heartening return to the distinguished writing tradition of early anthropological literature."

The literary gift that determined her earlier choice of a career has proved an asset to Dr. Benedict's students and friends as well as to her readers. No matter how swamped she is with editorial and teaching duties, speeches to deliver, conferences to attend, "deadlines" to meet, she somehow always finds time to doctor the ailing manuscripts that are left on her doorstep.

Looking at Dr. Benedict, one would place her as poet rather than scientist. Tall, gray-eyed, with short, white hair smoothly outlining a finely shaped head, she habitually wears tones of grayed blue or green. She speaks in a soft, low voice, sometimes quite slowly, occasionally hesitating for a word. Although she no longer publishes poetry she still writes a little and reads a large part of what is being produced. For that matter, she finds time to read an amazing amount of contemporary prose. Aside from reading, her chief winter diversion is shifting from one task to another or traveling to attend some conference or make a speech. In summer, when she is not gathering data in the field or initiating a group of students into field methods on an Indian reservation, she usually retires to the old family farm in Norwich and works on her next book.

References

N Y Post p17 Je 6 '41 por
N Y Times p24 O 21 '34
American Men of Science
American Women
Who's Who in America 1938-39

BENNY, JACK Feb. 14, 1894- Radio and film actor

Address: b. c/o National Broadcasting Co, Sunset Blvd. and Vine St, Hollywood, Calif; h. 1002 N. Roxbury Dr, Beverly Hills, Calif.

Jack Benny has always been a worrier, and in Hollywood they say he lives on a diet of fingernails and black coffee. A hit ever since he entered radio in 1932, nobody has ever been able to understand why he should worry, and it was harder than ever to understand it in 1941. This was the year in which his eighth contract with the makers of Jell-O was better than any previous ones; the year in which more than 1,000 New York and Hollywood celebrities paid tribute to him in a coast-to-coast broadcast honoring the beginning of his tenth year in radio; the year in which he was cited for service to race relations "in terms of real democracy"; the year in which his salary from radio reached an estimated $350,000 and that from motion pictures $200,000; the year in which he was a guest on the *Quiz Kids* program. And still he worries!

Nobody else associated with him does, though. General Foods, his radio sponsor, considers him and his show important enough to get more than three-quarters of its advertising appropriation for Jell-O. His co-workers know they have a good thing. And millions of listeners forget their troubles for a half hour every Sunday night while he and his troupe make merry.

They have made merry in the same way ever since Benny has been on the air, for he hasn't varied his routine in all that time. Unlike other radio comedians, he doesn't depend on conventional question-and-gag routines, but instead builds up a clear picture of himself in a given situation and lets the audience follow him through the complications that develop out of it. The man who once said, "Gags die, humor doesn't," thinks up comic ideas that last a long time: he tries to sell his old Maxwell; he presents himself as a violin virtuoso; he palms himself off as a Western sheriff of the old school; he nurses along a feud with Fred Allen; he gets mixed up with the Navy. And no matter what the situation, the humor derives from it, rather than from independent gags.

No matter what the situation, too, Jack Benny gets it in the neck. Tenor Dennis Day, orchestra leader Phil Harris, announcer Don Wilson, sharp-tongued Mary Livingston, valet Rochester get their digs in every time. Benny explains that he tries to make his character "encompass about everything that is wrong with everybody. On the air I have everybody's faults." His fellow performers never let him forget it. Each one an individual with an established character, they toss back at him the fat lines for which Benny as straight man lays himself open.

Benny isn't the kind of comedian who can just throw these lines out. He's no ad libber, and probably the saddest and truest lines of his radio history came out when Fred Allen (see sketch this issue) had him on the ropes. "If I had my writers here," he moaned, "you

JACK BENNY

wouldn't talk to me like that and get away with it." But Benny works hard with his writers, and Sunday night's finished performance is the result of a week's hard work. Every Monday morning he and Bill Morrow and Eddie Beloin sit down to think out the next show. By Tuesday there is a rough draft, and anything from six to eighteen hours on Wednesday and Thursday are spent polishing, changing, building, cutting what they've thought up into a working rehearsal script. On Friday night there's a rehearsal and another on Saturday with the whole cast brought together. Often more revisions are made then, and it is not until Sunday, at final rehearsal, that the show is in its final form. By that time Benny and his co-workers have not only lined up a situation and written funny lines but they have also figured out ways in which to make the audience buy. The commercials, which Benny never figures as just necessary evils, have been trickily and neatly fitted into the program.

They buy a lot of Jell-O in Waukegan, Illinois, where Jack Benny was born, and they even planted a Jack Benny elm beside the city hall. There were few indications they would do so, however, back in the early 1900's when little Benny Kubelsky was practicing on his fiddle studying to be a concert violinist. He wasn't exactly a child genius, and Benny admits that his father, Mayer Kubelsky, gave him a monkey wrench at the same time he presented him with a violin. "He told me not to take chances. Plumbing isn't a bad business." His mother, Emma (Sachs) Kubelsky, agreed.

The family left Waukegan for a while to live in Chicago, but they were soon back, and their son went to high school in Waukegan and spent his summers there helping in his father's haberdashery store. He also kept practicing his violin, and became good enough to play with a small orchestra at school dances

BENNY, JACK—*Continued*

and firemen's balls but not quite good enough to get a job in the local theatre orchestra. He compromised with a job as doorman for the theatre and later with one as property man. Then, feeling he had had enough theatre training, he went on the stage himself.

He was 17, and his act was called "From Grand Opera to Ragtime." In it a vaudeville pianist named Cora Salisbury did her turn, and then Benny entered with his violin and sawed away with the little finger of his bow hand elegantly extended, pretending to be mesmerized by its motion back and forth. On the circuit around Waukegan he was a hit and sometimes made as much as $75 a week. For six years he did this until the Navy got his services, for much less, in 1918. But Benny never got to be a sailor. After his enlistment he was made a sort of juvenile lead in *Maritime Frolics,* a revue put on by the Great Lakes Naval Station, and with it toured the midlands. It was then that the Jack Benny of today was really born. He tried to raise money for the Navy by playing the violin, but discovered one day that joking with audiences was much more likely to bring forth contributions. Pretty soon he was really cutting loose with gags and thinking of himself as a monologuist rather than a musician.

He still called himself Benjamin Kubelsky, though. When the War was over, he decided Ben K. Benny was a neater name for a vaudeville performer. This eventually became Jack Benny when people began confusing him with a fiddler named Ben Bernie (see sketch this issue). It was easy to do this, for though Benny's act was a monologue, he always carried his violin on the stage and looked at it wistfully from time to time. He got along, and it wasn't long before he was able to walk on the stage of the Palace Theatre in New York, once the high temple of vaudeville, without any props and wow the audience. He was a success in the Shubert revues in which he appeared and the night clubs where he entertained.

At the end of one transcontinental vaudeville tour, Benny landed at the Orpheum Theatre in Los Angeles and played for eight straight weeks, establishing a new house record. MGM, just beginning to be interested in revues, promptly offered him a contract, and the *Hollywood Revue of 1929* was enlivened by his presence. Other feature pictures and shorts followed—for MGM, Vitaphone, United Artists —and Jack Benny pictures have continued through the years to be a Hollywood feature. It wasn't until 1936, however, after his performance in *Broadway Melody of 1936,* that he became a star. That was the year, too, in which he signed a contract with Paramount. Since then he has appeared in *College Holiday*; *Artists and Models*; *Artists and Models Abroad*; *Man About Town*; *Buck Benny Rides Again*; and *Love Thy Neighbor,* a continuation of his radio feud with Fred Allen. In 1941 he coyly convulsed audiences in a revival of *Charley's Aunt,* and then promptly reported to Warner Brothers for *The Widow Wouldn't*

Weep, a comedy of divorce by Dalton Trumbo (see sketch this issue).

But many wisecracks flowed over the stage between Benny's first film appearance and the time he became a star. Shortly after his first ventures, he went back to New York. He had a wife with him this time. Her name was Sadye Marks and she had been a stocking clerk in the May Company in Los Angeles before he married her on Valentine's Day (his birthday, too) in 1927. She is now Mary Livingstone, his highly vocal partner. The Bennys arrived in New York just as Earl Carroll was casting his annual edition of the *Vanities.* Benny got a part, became the show's star and for two years cashed in as a leading comedian and master of ceremonies.

It was in 1932 that Benny's voice first came over the air. On Ed Sullivan's broadcast there was an announcement: "Ladies and gentlemen, this is Jack Benny talking. There will be a slight pause while you say, 'Who cares?'" Canada Dry soon cared enough to sign him up for a year; Chevrolet followed suit in 1933 and 1934; and the General Tire and Rubber Company sponsored him in 1934. Then came Jell-O, which Benny still continues to sell, his program the "favorite program" five times and Benny the "favorite comedian" seven times in annual polls of radio editors; his Crossley rating consistently at the very top. Never has there been a lessening in his popularity. Even the fact that in April 1939 he pleaded guilty to cheating the Government of $700 in duty on trinkets which had been smuggled into the United States by Albert N. Chapereau, was fined $10,000 and given a suspended sentence of a year and a day, made no difference. Instead there were reports in the spring of 1941, when rumors of a rift with Jell-O were current, that he had been given a number of $25,000-a-week radio offers. He didn't take them but remained at his $17,500 salary and got three program lay-offs and an agreement to have the second show on Sunday night broadcast by recording.

Harrassed-looking, cigar-smoking Benny is no wit off the stage, and no playboy either. With Mary Livingstone and their adopted daughter, Joan Naomi, he lives quietly in their handsome Beverly Hills home, the silence broken only by occasional heckling from Mary, who takes their radio programs seriously but who does call him, sweetly, "Doll." (He calls her "Doll," too.) When he feels that he has to relax, he plays bridge or casino or even follows a golf ball for a mile or two.

References

    Liberty 18:16-17+ N 8 '41 por
    Motion·Pict 54:38+ Ag '37 por
    Newsweek 17:60 My 5 '41
    Photoplay 51:22+ N '37 il pors
    PM p21 O 6 '41 por
    Time 26:53 O 28 '35 por; 33:20 Ap 17
      '39 por; 36:48 D 23 '40 por

    International Motion Picture Almanac
    Variety Radio Directory
    Who's Who in America
    Who's Who in American Jewry

BENSON, FRANCIS COLGATE, JR.
1872(?)—Feb. 18, 1941 Surgeon and
radiologist; pioneer in treatment of cancer by
radium; associated with Hahnemann College
and Hospital for nearly 40 years and was
professor of radiology and surgery there at
the time of his death; author of books on
surgery and cancer treatment as well as
several volumes of verse.

References

American Medical Directory

Obituaries

N Y Times p21 F 19 '41

BENSON, SALLY Sept. 3, 1900- Author
Address: c/o Random House, Inc, 20 E. 57th
St, New York City; h. 151 E. 46th St, New
York City

Sally Benson's sister said to her once: "I
know you and I know just how smart you are.
You don't write your stories. You get them
through a Ouija board." If this is true, the
Ouija board is to be congratulated. Mrs.
Benson's latest collection of short stories,
Junior Miss, all dealing with the troubles,
trials and foibles of 12-year-old Judy Graves
and formerly published in the *New Yorker,* was
the Book-of-the-Month Club choice for June
1941. Writing in the New York *Times,* E. H.
Walton says: "Any one who is familiar with
Sally Benson's work will know how deft and
subtle and amusing *Junior Miss* is. Though she
has forsworn the sophisticated wit and irony
for which she is so noted, these seemingly
simple sketches still bear her hallmark and are
no less adroit than her earlier stories. In
writing of Judy Graves' minor adventures, Mrs.
Benson is as pithy and concise as ever, as much
a master of the perfect phrase, with an added
quality of warmth and gentleness which, until
now, she has rather conspicuously lacked."

Perhaps the talent for the "brilliantly malicious" phrase for which Mrs. Benson has
previously been most noted is a gift from her
mother, of whom she herself says: "Mother
is part Irish, but she always seems all Irish
to me. She never gives anybody a compliment.
She used to say, 'Go on to your party, you look
terrible but maybe somebody will dance with
you.'"

At the time when Sally was hearing those
words she was Sara Mahala Redway Smith,
who was born in St. Louis in 1900 and came
to New York City 11 years later. She was
the daughter of Alonzo Redway and Anna
(Prophater) Smith. She was graduated from
the Horace Mann School somehow ("I was
very dumb"), and since at 17 she had no desire
whatsoever to go to college she walked confidently into the National City Bank and
asked to see the president. She did, as a
matter of fact, succeed in seeing the vice-
president, who gave her a job "singing into
dictaphones" at $60 a month.

At 19 Sara Smith married Reynolds Benson,
now graduate manager of athletics at Columbia
University. A daughter, Barbara, was born
the next year. But she kept on with her

Robert McAfee

SALLY BENSON

career, next getting a job on the old *Morning
Telegraph* which entailed interviewing stray
authors, actors, actresses. After that she reviewed movies—32 a month—for a pulp-paper
house. Her salary was only $75 a month, but
she filled it in by continuing with her interviews. It was not until 1930 that Sally Benson
wrote her first piece of fiction. It was called
Apartment Hotel. She promptly sold it to the
New Yorker, and when she went to see the
fiction editor she was told that it was the best
story "of whatever its kind was" they had ever
published. Would she write more?

She would. But not right away. For three
months she simply gloried in the satisfaction
of having written and sold a story, for nine
months she couldn't get down to work. Getting
"broker and broker," she finally wrote another.
Since that time the magazine has refused only
one of her stories, *The Overcoat,* which was
later published in the *American Mercury* and
republished in O'Brien's collection of best short
stories. "It's true that I haven't had a rejection," Miss Benson once confided, "probably
because I haven't tried other markets. My style
fits here and it wouldn't most places. Every
once in a while editors of some of the national
magazines have asked for my stuff, but what
they really want are healthy, clean-limbed,
hearty young people on a raft, and that isn't
for me." Her stories have from time to time
appeared in other important magazines, however,
and she sees them in print just as they come
from her typewriter, first draft. She writes
with amazing speed—two or two-and-a-half
hours is average for a short story—and the *New
Yorker* provides her with an office to write
them in.

"I like stories that have rounded ends and
don't rise to climaxes; that aren't all wrapped
up in a package with plot," she says. "I like
them, that's why I write them." Most of them

BENSON, SALLY—*Continued*

are about women. Critics, however, have quarreled about her attitude toward her characters, who are not always entirely attractive. She has often been called a ruthless satirist, one who writes "with quiet malice and shrewd venom"; but of her first collection of short stories, *People Are Fascinating* (1936), William Rose Benét wrote: "I don't find, as the publishers aver, that Mrs. Benson is a cynic. In fact, she has an extraordinary sympathy for human beings. This usually involves seeing right through them and being unable to restrain oneself from exposing their weaknesses." Of *Emily* (1938), another collection, a second critic commented that the author was "ironic . . . . shrewd . . . too clear-eyed for comfort, but," he went on, "what she distills is not poison. And in the stories which deal with young girls she is compassionate in a way impossible to anyone except the very kind and the very wise."

The short stories in *Junior Miss* deal entirely with one young girl. Mrs. Benson got the idea for her first Judy story while riding on a Fifth Avenue bus and seeing a 13-year-old girl snubbed by her mother and her older sister when she dropped their fares. She began to tire of Judy very shortly, wanted to write about something else after one or two of the stories had appeared, but Harold Ross of the *New Yorker* told her to keep on, she couldn't do better. When in 1941 she heard that *Junior Miss* had been chosen as a Book-of-the-Month and 40,000 copies sold in advance, Mrs. Benson was grateful for the advice. She took a look at her check, swallowed, left her publisher's office, and in less than an hour a salesman was waiting for him to okay a bill for her new automobile. There has been some talk of the stories being used by Hollywood. She isn't too optimistic about that, however. "The poor things have no plot, no continuity as movie. . . What could be done with them I haven't the slightest idea." Two playwrights disagreed with Mrs. Benson, however. Jerome Chodorov and Joseph Fields have made *Junior Miss* into a play which opened on Broadway in the late fall of 1941 and charmed reviewers into recognizing it as a "new hit," as "a gay comedy about adolescence which should still be on Broadway a year from now." *Junior Miss* is also appearing as a coast-to-coast radio feature, with scripts written by Mrs. Benson herself.

Mrs. Benson has curly red bangs—wears her hair that way because her mother once told her her forehead was too high. Robert van Gelder says she is "as good company as you're likely to find and makes interview questions or work of any sort seem a bit drab." She is a person of violent likes and dislikes, and particularly detests "magazine women" of a certain type. That prejudice dates back from the time she went to visit Clare Boothe Luce at *Vanity Fair*. As Mrs. Benson tells it:

"There she sat, with her hat on, looking lovely. She told me how *Vanity Fair* had finally decided it might like to buy a story from me.

"So I said, crassly, how much?

"And she said $50.

"And I said, looking at her lovely clothes, because I don't go in for being smart, that I wouldn't write so much as a recipe for $50.

"And she smiled her beautiful smile and said so sweetly, 'But think of the prestige for you, my dear.'

"And I walked out."

No one in Mrs. Benson's immediate family seems to be particularly impressed with her success as an author. Her husband read one of her stories once, but only once. "Not bad," was the verdict. Her mother keeps saying that some day she will have to buy a copy of the *New Yorker*. Even her daughter, Barbara, who is five feet nine, quite thoroughly grown-up and "very pretty" ("She isn't Judy—at least she hasn't been for a long while"), remained uninterested until some Yale boys started asking about her mother. Only one of the stories is really about Barbara, Mrs. Benson says. "I remembered the era when she started reading all the cosmetic ads and nobody could get into the bathroom because she was always in the tub trying out some new kind of bubble stuff."

Writing about modern women is far from being all that Mrs. Benson does. In 1940 she published *Stories of the Gods and Heroes*, in which the stories of Greek and Roman mythology are simply and beautifully retold. "A book of rare distinction," wrote the *New Republic*. In 1941 she is finishing a book about home life in St. Louis, *Meet Me in St. Louis*, which is planned for publication in the spring of 1942. She also has a spare-time job reviewing mysteries for the *New Yorker*, averaging one a night. She spends so much time on mysteries, she says, because she prefers straight history to historical novels, "and then, too, I keep taking personal dislikes to authors. Why must all the men novelists get so damned virile, so chest-out, shoulders back, here-we-come girls, as soon as they hit a success? Why must they go trucking all over the world and slaver with delight at wars?"

References

N Y Post p3 My 6 '41 por
N Y Times Book R p2 My 18 '41 por
Scholastic 29:17 O 3 '36; 33:4 O 29
   '38 por; 37:22 N 4 '40 por

BERG, ERNST J(ULIUS) Jan. 9, 1871—Sept. 9, 1941 Mathematician and electrophysicist; came to the United States from Sweden in 1892 as assistant to the late Dr. Charles P. Steinmetz; consulting engineer with the General Electric Company 1904 to 1909; in 1910 made head of the Electrical Engineering Department at the University of Illinois; made professor of electrical engineering at Union College in 1913; dean of engineering there from 1932 until retirement in 1941; pioneer in radio development; assisted in preparation of some of Steinmetz' best-known works and himself won world recognition as the author of *Heaviside's Operational Calculus as Applied to Engineering and Physics* (1929).

References

N Y Times p27 D 6 '40
American Men of Science
Who's Who Among North American
   Authors
Who's Who in America
Who's Who in American Education
Who's Who in Engineering

Obituaries

N Y Times p23 S 10 '41 por
Sch & Soc 54:214 S 20 '41

BERG, GERTRUDE Oct. 3, 1899- Radio
actress; author-producer
Address: h. 115 Central Park West, New York
City

When *The Rise of the Goldbergs* in June
1941 added 30 new stations of the NBC's Red
Network to its list of 23 CBS stations and
MBS's WOR it obtained the "most thorough
airing" of any radio show ever heard in the
United States. Millions of listeners, most of
them American housewives preparing meals,
were reminded that this was the oldest of
soap-operas. It was in 1929 that Mrs. Gertrude Berg's Mollie Goldberg, acted by herself, shouted her familiar and neighborly
"Yoo-hoo! Mrs. Blo-om!" up the air shaft.
In all those years Mrs. Bloom has been
heard to speak only once, an exclamatory
"Oy" murmured when her back was being
rubbed with liniment. But the voice of Mollie
Goldberg, of her husband Jake, and of
their two children Sammy and Rosie, have been
heard several thousand times, by an estimated
10,000,000 listeners daily.

In 12 years, we learn, "the family has moved
to Park Avenue, to a Connecticut mill town,
to innumerable rural communities, all the while
solving multitudinous problems of unemployment, home training, budget, and social snobbery... [Mrs. Berg] decided while fictionally
ensconced on Park Avenue that perhaps her
'typical family' was getting out of touch with
'life.' Next week's scripts saw Papa Goldberg
lose a fortune, the family gain 'realism.'"

The highest paid triple-duty woman in radio,
Mrs. Berg's salary has been estimated at $7,500
weekly for writing, producing and starring in
her program. "Like her Goldbergs, whom 12
years have mellowed and enriched," observed
one writer, "Mrs. Berg's own family has grown
up and prospered. Her son Cherney Robert,
19 (of an age with Sammy), is studying music.
Harriet, 15 (two years younger than Rosie),
attends school. Mr. Berg, placid, bald, horn-
rimmed, very unlike the irascible Jake, is a
prosperous sugar technologist."

An only child, Mrs. Berg was born in the
Harlem section of New York City on October
3, 1899, the daughter of Jacob and Diana Netta
(Goldstein) Edelstein. She attended public
schools and at Columbia University, where she
studied writing and acting, she met Louis Berg,
a young chemical student. They were married
in 1918.

Up to the time of her radio debut, Mrs.
Berg's writing had found its chief outlet in the

GERTRUDE BERG

Jewish Art Theatre. The notion that her work
might have radio possibilities did not occur to
her until a friend suggested it. That was in
1929, a year in which her husband had suffered
business reverses and also, Mrs. Berg recalled,
"when my children were at school and housekeeping wasn't keeping me quite busy enough."

Her first radio script was *Effie and Laura*,
which was a flop. When she heard one of
Milt Gross' stories in dialect on the radio
she sat down and evolved *The Goldbergs*.

Radio bigwigs were skeptical, commenting,
that her idea had about as much entertainment
value as a telephone directory. But Mrs. Berg
persisted and finally the National Broadcasting
Company offered to try it out as a weekly
sustainer at $75 per week, out of which she
was to pay the cast. Thus on November 20,
1929 *The Rise of the Goldbergs* was first
heard on the air. Four weeks later its author
and leading actress had a throat infection and
a substitute played the part of Mollie. More
than 11,000 listeners wrote in demanding the
return of the original, and the station's switch-
board was jammed day and night.

Mrs. Berg's agent had "fallen in love" with
the script, Actor-Producer Hyman Brown became interested, and in 1931 a soap sponsor
was talking in terms of six programs a week.
The prospect of having to write that many
shows was frightening, but Mrs. Berg was
persuaded that she was capable of it. At a
memorable meeting of agent, sponsor, the advertising people and herself, she waited for someone to name a figure, not knowing enough about
it to suggest one herself. A spokesman for
the sponsor turned to her and said, "Mrs.
Berg, we can't pay a cent over $2,000 a week."
Said the creator of *The Goldbergs*: "I thought
they were kidding. When it sank in that they
were serious I fainted dead away."

Foresight and a belief in what she was doing
contributed to her success. She visualized the

BERG, GERTRUDE—*Continued*

importance of unseen drama and developed the idea that became the family serial script—*strip* in radio parlance—as we know it today. "People are most interested in each other," says Mrs. Berg, and her own people are real. As one listener put it: "The characters come out sharply as definite persons, people one could conceive running the nearby grocery store or boarding house." Listened to by millions irrespective of race or religion, *The Goldbergs* ("Rags to Riches" with a Yiddish accent) has been called "one of the most potent forces in the land for inter-racial understanding." Mrs. Berg helps this along by making some of the characters Irish.

Mrs. Berg's day begins at 6 a. m., when she locks herself in the library of her comfortably furnished 10-room duplex on Central Park West to work on scripts until 5:30. They are prepared three weeks in advance, and for a long time her husband was the only person who could transcribe her penciled scribblings to the typewritten page. A story is told of how, when she first brought her idea to the National Broadcasting Company, she offered to read the script aloud because of its undecipherable writing. They humored her in this, not realizing that her real purpose was to put across the Jewish-American characters whose individualities were conveyed in subtle inflections of speech rather than in broad dialect. Once she began reading it was obvious to her listeners that Mrs. Berg should act the leading role herself.

Mrs. Berg is five feet four inches tall, inclined to plumpness, has brown hair, sloe eyes and an olive complexion. "Playing the part of Mollie Goldberg for so many years," we learn, "the radio authoress has become so closely identified with the characters as to look like the listener's mental image of Jake's wife. Short, dark, homey, and matronly, on the buxom side, only her flashing eyes reveal the genius within her."

Her method of work has been described as follows: "First she decides on a character or incident around which she mentally builds a tentative story sequence. Plotted on paper, she blocks it off into weeks, each of which is divided into five days. Each day's episode points to the climax at the end of the week (five days now), which is also so planned as to leave the listener guessing." She has so perfected her technique that she is able to write a 15-minute script in something over an hour.

Mollie's philosophies and characteristics are said to be based on those of Mrs. Berg's grandmother, whom she adores. And Jake, fiery tempered and financially erratic, is said to be partly descriptive of her father. As to the children, no one doubts that her own have colored the delineations of Sammy and Rosie. As a family, the Goldbergs might be said to be familiarly matriarchal, for though Jake is the nominal head of the family Mollie Goldberg is the one who holds it together and guides its destinies.

She also has time to guide the destinies of another serial called *Kate Hopkins* which the station describes as "the exciting story of a visiting nurse."

Mrs. Berg is a conscientious observer of people on subways, at movies, in theatre lobbies, department stores and wherever else they gather. She knows intimately the crowded life of New York's East Side, the apartment-house panorama of Morningside Heights, and resort spots in the mountains. Occasionally in casting the 100 to 200 major characters *The Goldbergs* has presented, Mrs. Berg has used real people in their real-life roles—elevator operators, grocery clerks, and once a very famous singer. On the professional side, she has a keen sense of talent and has "graduated" such fine actors as John Garfield, Allan Jones and Martin Wolfson.

Precursor of soap-opera realism, *The Goldbergs* is less on the fantastic side than most similar programs. Its realism consists not merely in the deft handling of characterizations and plot, but extends to sound effects. "If the script calls for Rosie to answer a phone," Katherine Best tells us, "Rosie picks up a real phone. If eggs are to be fried, real eggs are broken into real frying pans before the microphone."

When *The Goldbergs* went off the air temporarily in 1934 it was chiefly to permit the cast to make a personal appearance tour in vaudeville and Mrs. Berg to write and produce *The House of Glass* (NBC Blue Network 1935). The latter script was based on memories of summer vacations spent at a Catskill resort hotel owned by her father. While successful, it did not approach the earlier program in popularity rating. In 1937 Mrs. Berg collaborated on the Bobby Breen film, *Make a Wish* (RKO). She liked screen work and believed it to be good practice for television, which, she anticipates, may utilize strips of film somewhat in the manner of radio transcriptions.

In 1937 Mrs. Berg's radio serial got a new sponsor and a long-term contract. This, and her family life, do not allow her much time for hobbies, but she does find time to relax during the summer at her impressive Candlewood Lake estate in Connecticut. She likes velvet gowns and collects copper kettles and pewter ware. Her main enjoyment is parodying various radio shows in which she casts her husband and daughter. "Her favorite is *The Good Will Hour,* for her own version of which she makes up some pretty startling problems."

References

Delineator 128:19 My '36 por
N Y Post My 3 '37
N Y Sun S 11 '37; Ja 7 '39
PM p57 D 1 '40 pors
Sat R Lit 21:11-12 Ap 20 '40 por
Time 37:55 Je 23 '41
Variety Radio Directory
Who's Who in American Jewry

BERG, IRVING H(USTED) Mar. 8, 1878 —Aug. 29, 1941 Dean of University College, New York University since 1936; chaplain of the University; ordained as minister 1904; served as pastor of various churches before he came to New York University as chaplain in 1919; instrumental in the establishment of the college-commerce curriculum and the college-education program which made it possible for students to train for careers in business and teaching.

References

Leaders in Education 1941
Who's Who in America
Who's Who in New York

Obituaries

N Y Times p13 Ag 30 '41 por
Sch & Soc 54:161 S 6 '41

BERGSON, HENRI (LOUIS) Oct. 18, 1859—Jan. 4, 1941 Famous French philosopher; writer; won Nobel Prize in literature (1927); lectured at the Collège de France, where his teaching had great influence on the trend of modern thought; was a member of the French Academy; in late 1940 renounced all his French posts and honors because of the recent discriminatory legislation against his fellow Jews.

References

Commonweal 17:14-17 N 2 '32
Contemp 136:205-12 Ag '29
Illustration 204:308 N 18 '39 por
J Philos 37:364 Je 20 '40
Lit Digest 116:18 Ag 19 '33 por
Nation 136:452 Ap 19 '33
Sat R Lit 6:720 F 8 '30
Alexander, H. B. Nature and Human Nature p301-18 1923
Alpern, H. March of Philosophy p348-55 1933
Bernstein, H. Celebrities of Our Time p143-53 1924
Chevalier, J. Henri Bergon 1928
Dictionnaire National des Contemporains 1936
Durant, W. J. Story of Philosophy p487-529 1926
Loomba, R. M. Bradley and Bergson 1937
Marble, A. R. Nobel Prize Winners in Literature, 1901-1931 p313-26 1932
Qui Êtes-Vous?
Routh, H. V. Towards the Twentieth Century p346-66 1937
Szathmary, A. Aesthetic Theory of Bergson 1937
Turquet-Milnes, G. R. Some Modern French Writers p51-78 1921
Who's Who

Obituaries

N Y Times p15 Ja 6 '41 por

BERNARD, ÉMILE 1868(?)—Apr. 19(?), 1941 One of the last of the French Impressionist painters; associate of Gauguin; fellow student of Van Gogh; art critic; wrote *Reflections of a Witness of the Decadence of the Beautiful, The Ashes of Glory, After the Fall,* and monographs on Tintoretto, El Greco, Magnasco and Manet.

Obituaries

N Y Times p44 Ap 20 '41
Time 37:71 Ap 28 '41

BERNIE, BEN May 30, 1891(?)- Orchestra leader
Address: b. c/o Station WBBM, Wrigley Bldg, Chicago, Ill; h. 50 E. 67th St, New York City

BEN BERNIE

For most orchestra leaders dialogue is the nexus between musical selections, but for Ben Bernie, "The Old Maestro," music is merely an interlude between snatches of talk. Bernie's suave and intimate patter has the pulse of the American public. His current trysts with the microphone rated first place in 1941 for daytime programs, according to the Crossley (see sketch this issue) popularity survey.

Bernie is five feet ten inches tall, weighs one hundred seventy-five pounds, has thinning hair and a bland face adorned with a cigar. (He smokes 25 of them a day.) His radio shows, like his person, reflect serenity and harmony, edged possibly by just a trace of condescension. Walter Winchell purports not to like him, but millions of other people do. One of radio's most effective virtuosos of patter, Bernie once seemed slated to become a second Kreisler.

Born Bernard Anzelevitz in New York City he was one of the 11 children of Julius and Anna (Melnick) Anzelevitz. Bernie attended Townsend Harris High School. After he had earned a local reputation as an infant wonder of the violin, his parents were convinced he was earmarked for immortality, and at the age of 14 his talents were displayed before a musically erudite audience at Carnegie Hall in a concert arranged by his mother.

One year later he was working as a "professor of the violin" at the short-lived Mozart

BERNIE, BEN—*Continued*

School of Music. When it closed its doors three months after opening them, Bernie, inexplicably, decided that he ought to be an engineer. He attended Cooper Union Institute and the College of the City of New York, but lavished more attention on collegiate theatricals and musicals than on his somewhat haphazardly selected profession. In these days he first used the genial "Yowsah," one of the inimitable ejaculations in the "Bible of Berniana."

Bernie's uninhibited chatter, his most useful commodity, was developed early. He used it to good effect when he was working as a violin salesman in a department store. One of the people who found him amusing was Joseph Schenck, the entertainment mogul. A conversation led to an offer of a 20-week contract at $35 per week on the Loew vaudeville circuit. Bernie appeared with another violinist named Charlie Klass; they were booked as the "Fiddle-Up Boys."

From 1910 to 1914 Bernie toured the country via the vaudeville route. His professional name was evolved, at the suggestion of a press agent, from his stage name of Bernard Berni. For a while Bernie played straight violin selections, reportedly discovering the value of his "gab" only during an exchange across the footlights with a heckling hillbilly.

Eventually his bookings became erratic, and Bernie had to content himself with "one-night hitches in the hinterlands" and impromptu solos for "throw money" in cheap cafes. Once he delivered some tunes on a train bound for Des Moines and passed the hat. On his return to the East he soloed for a time in the Haymarket Cafe, one of the Bowery's most dubious dives.

Bernie's first master-of-ceremonies job came with his appointment to the noted Reisenweber's Restaurant, rendezvous of many entertainment notables. He still liked vaudeville, however, and was soon planning a return. His decision led to an entertainment tie-up with Phil Baker, the accordion-and-chatter man. Bernie first met Baker, reportedly, when he was walking toward his parents' home in The Bronx in 1914. Hearing an accordionist playing in a nearby house, Bernie went over to introduce himself. This resulted in the Bernie-Baker team and the later independent radio careers of each. The partners first concentrated on straight music, but soon devised a better footlight formula in which repartee alternated with refrains. The routine gained considerable vogue until the First World War battered the vaudeville business.

Bernie then conceived the idea of starting his own band. Realizing that vaudeville was far on the down grade and that he would have to find another medium, Bernie thought of combining orchestra rhythms and his vaudeville gag technique. A visit to Paul Whiteman's band crystallized his determination, and in 1923 Ben Bernie started his band.

When the Roosevelt Hotel was first opened in New York, "Ben Bernie and All the Lads"

was the first orchestra hired by the management. Engaged for a mere six weeks, the band remained for nearly six years, as the chatty Bernian manner became tremendously popular. The band followed its stay at the Roosevelt with a year's engagement in Europe, where it played in the swank Kit Kat Club of London. Bernie returned amid the ominous rumble of crashing stocks. Virtually all his savings were lost in the crash.

After another short stay at the Roosevelt, Bernie decided to try to recoup his losses by a trip to Hollywood. In the film center Bernie's band appeared in the Montmartre Cafe, the Catalina Casino and other night clubs and was featured by Paramount Studios in *Shoot the Works* and *Stolen Harmony*. Then, following a brief vaudeville tour with Maurice Chevalier, the band parked at the College Inn in Chicago, an engagement that led to Bernie's first radio appearance.

Bernie was a radio "natural," and he was sought by sponsors. He was aired over WJZ for Mennen's Shaving Cream and in 1931 he broadcasted for Pabst Blue Ribbon Beer from a pavilion at the Chicago Century of Progress Exhibition. A radio engagement for Half 'n' Half tobacco terminated in 1940 because Bernie didn't think the quiz program he was compelled to conduct was particularly suited to his talents. His first real opportunity to display unadulterated Berniana came with the Wrigley's Gum program, for which he presented 15-minute variety shows five days a week over the Columbia network from 5:45 to 6 p.m. The program combines orchestra rhythms, songs by the Bailey Sisters and Bernie's unfailing chit-chat.

Bernie's appeal is solid and unmystifying: comfortable camaraderie enriched with gags. Delivery of music and voice form a smooth synthesis; there is perfect coordination. Not all of the "Old Maestro's" gags are original: some he buys in the open market and some are written for him. Despite his preoccupation with gags, however, Bernie is a dead serious musician. He is a ruthless perfectionist who insists on the ultimate in performance, a hard taskmaker in rehearsal. Many of his programs are without benefit of script, being fitted into the allotted radio time during the actual performance by the simple device of having new numbers added if time remains, or of having his program faded from the air if time runs short.

Bernie married his second wife, Dorothy Wesley, a Florida society girl, while he was filling a Miami engagement. He has one child, a boy, by his first wife, Rose Harris Anzelevitz, whom he married in 1915 and divorced on a charge of desertion in 1935.

Bernie's major musical passion is Mozart, and he has been known to listen for hours to the works of this master. His unmusical likes include horse races, police dogs and bridge, in which game he is unusually competent.

References

Motion Pict 47:59+ Je '34 pors
Movie Classic 7:38 S '34 por

N Y Times p4 Ja 21 '35; p8 F 16 '35;
p16 S 20 '35; p19 N 5 '35; p12 Ag
3 '39; p26 Ja 18 '40; p29 D 13 '40;
p18 D 24 '40
Newsweek 6:26 S 28 '35 por
Eichberg, R. Radio Stars of Today
1937
International Motion Picture Almanac
Variety Radio Directory
Who's Who in America
Who's Who in American Jewry
Who's Who in the East
Who's Who in New York 1929

**BERRY, WILLIAM EWERT, 1ST VIS-
COUNT CAMROSE** *See* Camrose, W. E.
B., 1st Viscount

BICKEL, GEORGE L. 1863(?)—June 5,
1941 Stage and film comedian; started
career at the age of 12 as super in a variety
show and later became a Dutch comedian and
star clown for the Donaldson and Gregory
circus; appeared first on stage in *Me, Him
and I,* which opened in 1904 and ran three
years; later was seen in *A Trip to Paris, Gypsy
Love* and other productions; in 1915 went to
Hollywood, where he made comedies for the
Edison Feature Film Company and later for
Fox Films; retired in 1930.

References

International Motion Picture Almanac
1936-37

Obituaries

N Y Times p17 Je 7 '41
Variety 143:46 Je 11 '41

**BIDDLE, ANTHONY J(OSEPH)
DREXEL, JR.** 1897- United States Ambassador to Polish and Belgian Governments
in Exile; Minister to Dutch and Norwegian
Refugee Governments in London
Address: American Embassy, London, England

In February 1941 lean, suave Anthony J.
Drexel Biddle, Jr., voted one of the 10 best-
dressed men in the world by tailors, and in
1937 appointed United States Ambassador to
Poland by President Roosevelt, was also appointed to serve in London as Ambassador to
Belgium and as Minister to The Netherlands
and Norway. He had been in the United
States since August 1940. In Stephen Early's
(see sketch this issue) words, this was an
"unprecedented step" in United States history,
and another precedent was broken when five
months later Biddle added to his posts that of
Minister to the Jugoslav Government in Exile.
He serves without any increase in pay, $17,500
annually being provided for an Ambassador
with a single responsibility.

Ambassador and Minister Biddle has not
been at this business of diplomacy for a long
time—only since 1935, when President Roosevelt appointed him Minister to Norway. Born
in Philadelphia, Pennsylvania in 1897, he
comes of the "internationally wealthy and

Wide World
ANTHONY J. DREXEL BIDDLE, JR.

honorable Drexel-Biddle banking family":
there are somewhere in the neighborhood of
70 Biddles listed in Philadelphia's *Social Register* today. Anthony Biddle, Jr.'s mother was
the former Cornelia Rundell Bradley; his
father, Anthony Joseph Drexel Biddle, Sr.,
was at one time known as "Tim O'Biddle," at
least in the ring. Among other distinctions,
he was one of the best amateur boxers of his
day, the founder of a movement known as
"Athletic Christianity" in which boxing and
Bible classes were somehow combined, and is
the author of books which range from travel
essays and boxing instructions to the *Froggy
Fairy Books.*

Young "Tony" Biddle, Jr., was educated at
Philadelphia schools and then at St. Paul's in
Concord, New Hampshire, from which he was
graduated. He was president of his senior
class, captain of crew and of football, and had
as his history master John C. Winant (see
sketch this issue), present Ambassador to
England. Biddle didn't attend college; instead,
at the age of 18, he married the Mary Duke
who was later to fall heir to the Duke tobacco
millions. It wasn't long afterward, when the
United States entered the First World War
that he joined the swank Squadron A cavalry.
By the time the War was over he had advanced to the rank of captain.

The post-War years found Tony Biddle, Jr.,
dividing his time between business (mainly
shipping), sports (mainly boxing, tennis and
polo) and international society (mainly in
France). Among other things, he bought a
Belgian middleweight boxer, René De Vos,
and introduced him at a hotel party at which
the pugilistic guests slipped away with the
silverware and wine and were ambitious
enough to try to steal the piano. In 1929, too,
he and some associates leased the Casino in the
middle of New York City's Central Park,
a project later abandoned because of protests
at public property's being used as a rendezvous
for the wealthy. Biddle was at home in
Newport and Palm Beach society, belonged to
the most exclusive and costly clubs in Europe
and America, was a member of the American

BIDDLE, ANTHONY J., Jr.—*Continued*
court tennis teams of 1932, 1933 and 1934, which competed for the Bathurst cup, and in 1934 was the winner of the court tennis championship of France. In 1931 his first wife divorced him; not long afterward he married the heiress to the Boyce Thompson mining millions, Mrs. Margaret (Thompson) Schulze (who in 1941 wrote *Women of England*).

As the director of the Sonora Products Corporation, before that known as the Acoustic Products Company, Biddle became involved in a lawsuit in 1931 when the firm went bankrupt. When sued by Sonora's receiver on the charge that he and associates had appropriated a contract, the Federal District Court judge acquitted the owners of the charge; in September 1934, however, the decision was reversed by the Circuit Court of Appeals in the case of Biddle and three others. Biddle was in Paris at the time, and the papers were full of rumors that he was about to be appointed to a diplomatic post. He returned to the United States, but denied that there was any truth in the rumors. What is more, he said that he had no assets with which to pay the stockholders, that most of his office furniture was his second wife's property.

It developed, however, that Biddle had recently donated $25,000 to the Roosevelt campaign, $25,000 to the campaign of George Earle, Democratic candidate for the Governorship of Pennsylvania, $5,000 to the Democratic National Committee. He explained that this was his wife's money. In July 1935 he sailed to take up the post of United States Minister to Norway, having finally settled the claims against him out of court. He held that post until April 1937, when Mrs. Harriman was sent to Oslo and Biddle shifted to Poland as Ambassador. At first his Polish experiences were comparatively uneventful: he returned to the United States for a vacation in 1938, was given an LL. D. by Temple University, was awarded the Meritorious Medal of the State of Pennsylvania for "services to the people of America" in cementing Polish-American relations.

In August 1940, however, when Ambassador and Mrs. Biddle returned once more to the United States, they had a harrowing tale to tell. The life of an American diplomat in Europe had turned out to be one of "real adventure," Biddle said. In September 1939 the Ambassador and his wife had fled Poland, where their country villa had been bombed and their furniture and art treasures lost in the destruction of Warsaw. With Polish officialdom they had reached Romania, finally France. Months later the German *Blitzkrieg* on the western front reached them at Angers. Still with the Polish refugee government, they fled to Tours, then to Bordeaux; Biddle served as the Deputy Ambassador to France while Bullitt stayed in Paris; and when France fell the Biddles followed the Polish Government to London. They didn't return to their own country until August 1940—for a visit during which both Mr. and Mrs. Biddle made an extended speaking tour on behalf

of the Democratic Party and President Roosevelt's candidacy. Mrs. Biddle said: "I am sincerely urging every one I address to get back of a larger and immediate defense program. . . I saw what could happen over there; I want to see that it doesn't happen over here."

Ambassador Biddle is described as "big, raw-boned, ugly," but lean and muscular, with a "superbly sloped pair of shoulders" that make him a tailor's delight. He has two children by his first wife.

References

Lit Digest 120:38 Jl 27 '35 por
Nation 141:149-51 Ag 7 '35
N Y Post p13 O 22 '40 por
N Y Sun p16 Je 24 '40
N Y Times p4 Je 25 '40; IV p2 Je 30 '40 por; p24 Ag 11 '40
N Y World-Telegram p10 F 22 '41 pors
Time 26:10 Ag 5 '35 por
Who's Who in America

BIDDLE, FRANCIS (BEVERLEY) May 9, 1886- Attorney General of the United States

Address: b. Dept. of Justice, Washington, D. C.; h. 1669 31st St, Washington, D. C.

Farm Security Administration
FRANCIS BIDDLE

"Fearless, brainy, freckle-browed" Francis Biddle is a Philadelphia lawyer who was once attorney for such great corporations as the Pennsylvania Railroad and the Atlantic & Pacific chain stores and who since 1934 has been a figure of considerable importance in the New Deal. Early in 1941, with Robert Jackson's elevation to the Supreme Court, he became Acting Attorney General of the United States and in August of that same year was nominated by President Roosevelt to succeed Mr. Jackson.

As one commentator put it: "Philadelphia plus law equals Biddle, and always has." One of Francis Biddle's ancestors was Edmund Randolph, America's first Attorney General. Biddle's only living son is named after him. His own paternal grandfather was George W. Biddle, who participated in the Hayes-Tilden controversy over the Presidency. His father, Algernon Sydney Biddle, who died when Francis was seven, was professor of law at the University of Pennsylvania. Francis Beverley Biddle was born in Paris on May 9, 1886 when his father and his mother, Frances (Robinson) Biddle, were spending some time in Europe. He was brought to the United States in his infancy.

His brother, George Biddle, the artist, has any number of anecdotes to tell about their childhood. He says: "I was the more prudent, he the more lively of the two. I had greater scruples and he a swifter imagination. I think of myself as the balance wheel and of him as the accelerator of this two-cylindered combination. His ardor often led him into crooked paths and consequently he was spanked more often." Francis was nine when he was sent to the Haverford School in Pennsylvania for four years. But that was not too young to be writing "poetry": a 34-verse epic of Sir Richard of Howeland, lyrics entitled *Spring* and *Fighting for Liberty*, an Odyssey of Olaf of Cedarwood which included these remarkable lines:

> *Remembreth thou the first Equarub,*
> *And thine horse Ibantinub?*
> *A! thou wert born in rough Balcinia,*
> *Not to befriend but fight the cub!*

Francis and George invented "new religions, monetary systems, maps, wars and Nordic aspirations for our heroes." According to George, they "were somewhat anticipating a similar but less innocent infantilism, which was to a great extent to engage the fantasy of Europe some 40 years later."

At Groton, which Francis Biddle attended from 1899 to 1905, he was champion boxer and captain of the gymnastic team. What is more, his scholastic record was excellent, and one Prize Day he took the prize for the best two-minute speech. During his six years at Harvard, where he received his B. A. *cum laude* in 1909 and his LL. D. *cum laude* two years later, he earned money tutoring and working on newspapers. From 1911 to 1912 he worked as private secretary to Justice Holmes of the United States Supreme Court, and then was admitted to the Pennsylvania Bar and became associated with the Philadelphia law firm of Biddle, Paul & Jayne. He remained with that firm for three years, until 1915; in 1917 he began to practice with Barnes, Biddle & Myers of the same city.

He was a highly successful lawyer. In 1922 he became a partner in his law firm and in that same year began a four-year term as special assistant to the United States attorney for the Eastern District of Pennsylvania. The next year found him a member of the Philadelphia County Board of Law Examiners, on which he was to serve until 1932, and of the committee of censors of the Philadelphia Bar Association (1923-25 and 1929-31). In 1927 he was admitted to practice before the Supreme Court of the United States.

Biddle was at this time a registered Republican, although he had voted for Theodore Roosevelt in 1912 and for Al Smith in 1928. In 1933, however, when a fellow Grotonian, Franklin Delano Roosevelt, became President of the United States, he changed to Democratic ranks. His tendencies had always been liberal, and now he became an ardent New Dealer. In 1934 a member of former Governor Pinchot's Commission on Special Policing in Industry, late that same year he also accepted the position of chairman of the National Labor Relations Board. To the job he brought "a lively sense" of the legal difficulties involved in investigating and adjusting controversies between employers and employees arising under the code-making section of the NIRA, Section 7a. By 1935 he was writing and speaking in favor of the Wagner collective bargaining proposal to abolish company unions, arguing that members of a company union are never in a position to bargain freely with an employer. His brother George painted his portrait into a labor scene in a Department of Justice mural, representing him as a champion of justice under the New Deal. He returned to Philadelphia after a year in Washington, however.

From 1938 to 1939 Biddle was a Class C director of the Federal Reserve Bank, and deputy chairman as well. In that same year, 1938, the Tennessee Valley Authority was being investigated by a committee, and he was hired as chief counsel. It was then that he uncovered the subsidizing of the *Free Press* by a subsidiary of Commonwealth and Southern— a discovery which brought about his claim in 1940 that Wendell Willkie had always been "on the side of the utilities, never on the side of the people," and which also brought about Senator Styles Bridges' charge that Biddle had abused his official position. It was then, too, that his inspection of the income and excess profits tax returns of the private utilities provoked Republican members of the committee into accusing him of conducting the investigation as if the utilities, and not TVA, were under fire.

In 1939 Biddle finally gave up his partnership in the firm of Barnes, Biddle & Myers to become a judge on the United States Circuit Court of Appeals, 3rd Circuit. But by January 1940 he was once more needed in Washington, and he left his life tenure post to accept that of Solicitor General of the United States at a salary of $10,000 a year, a cut in pay of $2,500. When in June 1940 immigration and naturalization activities were transferred to the Department of Justice, it was he who coordinated the work with the other services of the Department.

In charge of the Border Patrol, which seals United States borders against unwanted aliens,

BIDDLE, FRANCIS—*Continued*

Biddle proposed strengthening it and coordinating it with the Customs Patrol, the Coast Guard and the National Park Rangers. Alien registration he defended as a measure which actually protects loyal aliens, but he did urge a more tolerant attitude on the part of the American public toward alien groups, warned against amateur sleuthing. Other statements of his won the praise of laborites and the distrust of conservatives: he attacked the bill then before Congress to deport Harry Bridges as a "bill of attainder"; he criticized contractors who refused to accept defense work except at an "exorbitant profit"; he took a whack at critics of the NLRB by his statement before a convention of the American Bar Association that judicial review of the work of the administrative agencies of the government "could not possibly be a success."

The Nation and the *New Republic* were a little startled by some of Biddle's later activities, however. In June 1941, speaking before the National Conference of Social Work in Atlantic City, he proclaimed his disturbance over opposition to the Hobbs "concentration-camp" bill and the Model State Anti-Sabotage Bill, called it "flabby thinking." "Washington and Samuel Adams and the Minute Men at Lexington surely did not discuss their loss of civil liberties when they chose to fight," he explained. That same month one of his first orders as Acting Attorney General brought about charges of seditious conspiracy against Trotskyist union leaders in Minnesota whose union had recently seceded from Daniel Tobin's and joined the CIO. And in August friends of Harry Bridges attempted to prove that Biddle had been responsible for having his phone tapped by the FBI.

On August 25 Biddle was nominated by President Roosevelt as the fifty-eighth Attorney General of the United States, and on September 3rd the Senate Judiciary Committee unanimously voted to report his appointment. It was confirmed two days later by the Senate.

Dreamy-eyed Mrs. Biddle, whom he married in April 1918, is almost as well known as her husband—as Katherine Chapin, poet, author of the moving ballad-poems *Lament for the Stolen, And They Lynched Him on a Tree* and *Plain-Chant for America*. And Biddle himself, who was chairman of the Philadelphia branch of the Foreign Policy Association from 1924 to 1939, is the author of one published novel. *Llanfear Pattern* (1927) is described as a society novel, the story of a Philadelphian who "makes a stand for individuality, and carries his rebellion over into his business and political activities. But the family tradition is strong and he eventually conforms to it."

References

> Am Mag 119:57 My '35 por
> Life 8:23 F 19 '40
> Lit Digest 118:12 D 1 '34 por
> Nation 139:639-40 D 5 '34; 152:655 Je 7 '41; 152:66-7 Jl 26 '41
> N Y Times VII p8 S 21 '40 por

> Time 38:15 S 1 '41 por
> U S News 8:32 Ja 19 '40 por
> Biddle, G. American Artist's Story 1939
> Who's Who in America
> Who's Who in Law

BIGELOW, WILLIAM (PINGRY) Mar.(?), 1867—Mar. 16, 1941 Professor emeritus of music of Amherst College; served as head of the department for 20 years until his retirement in 1935; conducted oratorios at Amherst, Smith and Mount Holyoke Colleges; author of several musical compositions and compiler of the Amherst College *Songbook*.

References

> Who's Who Among North American Authors
> Wier, A. E. ed. Macmillan Encyclopedia of Music and Musicians 1938

Obituaries

> N Y Times p23 Mr 18 '41
> Sch & Soc 53:368 Mr 22 '41

BIGGERS, JOHN D(AVID) Dec. 19, 1888- Glass manufacturer

Address: b. Nicholas Bldg, Toledo, Ohio; h. 4365 Brookside Rd, Toledo, Ohio

At the beginning of 1941 John D. Biggers, president of the Libbey-Owens-Ford Glass Company, became head of the division of production of the OPM, Knudsen's "right-hand man" in the job of seeing that America produces for defense. Some months later, in July 1941, he was put in charge, too, of the newly set up commodity section, responsible for the steel, aluminum, magnesium, paper, pulp and chemicals vital to the defense program. The next month, in the rearrangement of powers of the defense administration, Biggers was given still another position: that of Special Minister to Britain, with the job of helping W. Averell Harriman (see sketch this issue) push lend-lease aid to Britain. After a month in England he returned to the United States, reported to the President and Mr. Hopkins and then set out, with the aid of lend-lease and OPM officials, to synchronize the facts he had ascertained with the American effort. In October 1941 he returned to private life on a leave of absence at his own request.

This tall, good-looking, carefully dressed industrialist who has been so active during the period of national emergency got his business start in Chamber of Commerce work. Even-tempered, always cordial, he is supposed to have still a little of the "Chamber of Commerce" manner. John David Biggers was born in St. Louis, Missouri, the son of William David and Emma Melvina (Fisse) Biggers, and received his preparatory education in St. Louis—at Smith Academy. In 1905 he went to Washington University in St. Louis but stayed there only a year before transferring to the University of Michigan, from which he was graduated in 1909.

Biggers' first position was that of advertising manager of Larned, Carter & Company in Detroit. One year later, in 1910, he became assistant secretary of the Detroit Chamber of Commerce. After a year's experience there he was made secretary of the Toledo, Ohio, Chamber of Commerce, and in 1912 he married Mary Isobel Kelsey. (They now have one son and two daughters.)

While still with the Chamber of Commerce Biggers came to the attention of Edward D. Libbey and Michael J. Owens, leaders in the glass industry, and in 1914 Libbey took Biggers from his position to make him assistant treasurer of his company. Biggers' rise from that point on was rapid. He was successively assistant treasurer, treasurer, assistant general manager and vice-president of the Owens Bottle Company until in 1926 he resigned to enter another field.

For five years Biggers was a member of the automobile industry, first as managing director of Dodge Brothers, Limited, in London for a year; then as vice-president of the Graham Brothers Corporation for six years, during one of which he was also vice-president of Graham-Paige International Corporation. In 1930, however, he returned to the glass industry as president of what had become the Libbey-Owens-Ford Glass Company, though he continued as vice-president of the Graham Brothers Corporation until 1933. This was a logical connection, for Biggers' glass company was a leader in the production of glass for motorcar windows and since 1931 has supplied practically all of General Motors' glass needs.

Biggers has long been an advocate of government and business teamwork. As he expressed his position back in 1937: if the government is to have an increasingly greater hand in business, business leaders should know more about government and take an active part in it. Nominally a Republican, he belonged to the Business Advisory Council of the Department of Commerce under Secretary Roper and he has aided President Roosevelt time and again, notably in 1937 when he directed the unemployment census.

To organize and manage this was a heavy assignment. Questionnaires were distributed by letter carrier and as the returns came in they were checked in various areas throughout the United States by a separate door-to-door census. The final number of unemployed was found to lie somewhere between the 7,845,016 who filled in blanks and the figure of 10,870,000 turned in by the supplementary door-to-door check. The census, it was felt, was not complete nor entirely accurate, but it was generally recognized that an important investigation had been accomplished efficiently under Biggers' direction.

Biggers first began to attack the defense problem in June 1940 when Knudsen drafted him to aid with the task of upping aircraft and aircraft engine production and overseeing and coordinating the letting of important contracts for Army and Navy equipment. As deputy commissioner of the National Advisory Defense Commission and later as production

O. E. M. Defense

JOHN D. BIGGERS

head of the Office of Production Management, he urged faster production and fuller cooperation before various groups throughout the country: before the National Association of Manufacturers, the Academy of Political Science, the Chamber of Commerce. I. F. Stone, however, called him "a shrewd and able man who represented the business point of view on every issue," and it has been said that he was sent to London because of the heavy artillery fire to which he had been subjected by New Dealers, some of whom felt that he was too strongly attached to the "business as usual" policy.

Biggers has worked hard and successfully as president of the Libbey-Owens-Ford Glass Company, but he has not devoted his time and energies exclusively to the company. Not only has he served the government in various dollar-a-year positions but he has been active in many civic betterment movements, in church work (he is a Congregationalist), in discussing with other businessmen the policies and economic problems before industry as a whole. His civic interests have led him to become a member of the executive committee of the Toledo Community Chest, a trustee of the Boys Club of Toledo and of the Toledo Museum of Art, and to give liberally of his time and money to important causes as they arise. There has seldom been much time left over for playing. Someday, though, Biggers expects to be able to spend more time with his family and friends or even to get out on the tennis court again.

References

Business Week p16 S 18 '37 por; p35 S 25 '37
N Y Sun p26 Je 7 '40
Newsweek 10:17 N 15 '37 por

(Continued next page)

BIGGERS, JOHN D.—*Continued*

Time 27:61 F 3 '36 por; 31:13 Ja 10
'38 por; 35:17 Je 17 '40 por; 37:23
F 24 '41 por

Who's Who in America
Who's Who in Commerce and Industry

BIRDSEYE, CLAUDE HALE   Feb. 13,
1878—May 30, 1941 Topographer; explorer;
geographer; chief of the United States Geological Survey's division of engraving and printing;
one of his better known achievements was the
mapping of the Kilauea volcano region in
Hawaii in 1912; in 1913 determined the elevation of Mount Rainier in a surveying and mapping expedition; in 1923, with an expedition of
10 men, he traveled 300 miles of the roughest
waters of the Colorado River through Marble
and Grand Canyons and led the men to safety
after they were reported lost.

References

American Men of Science
Who's Who in America
Who's Who in Engineering
Who's Who in the Nation's Capital

Obituaries

N Y Times p41 Je 1 '41

BISHOP, WILLIAM AVERY   Feb. 8,
1894- Air Marshal of Canada; in charge of
the Canadian Air Training Scheme

Address: b. Royal Canadian Air Force Head-
quarters, Jackson Bldg, Ottawa, Ontario,
Canada; h. 5 Blackburn Ave, Ottawa, Ontario,
Canada

Royal Canadian Air Force
WILLIAM AVERY BISHOP

Stocky, blue-eyed "Billy" Bishop is an air
ace of the First World War whose daring
exploits gave him every possible decoration
for valor and a reputation possibly more

dazzling than Richthofen's.   Eddie Ricken-
backer once said: "Bishop was the greatest.
None could compare with him."   It seemed
completely appropriate when the Second World
War found this "man absolutely without fear"
in charge of the Canadian Air Training Scheme
by which immense numbers of pilots were to
be trained on the broad flying fields of Canada,
far from any possibility of interference by the
enemy: British, Canadians, American volunteers,
Poles, Czechs and other Europeans who had
escaped the clutches of Fascism.

His popularity with these tyro pilots can be
easily accounted for by those who know his
story. The son of William Avery and Margaret
Louise (Greene) Bishop, born in Owen Sound,
Ontario on February 8, 1894, William Avery
Bishop had his early schooling at the Owen
Sound Collegiate School and then entered the
Royal Military College, Kingston, Ontario (the
Canadian equivalent of West Point) in 1912.
"A thin slip of a lad with blue eyes and a
shock of sandy hair" who could already ride
"any horse that could be saddled" and "knock
the ear off a gnat at 50 paces with a rifle,"
he was in his second year at college when war
broke out.   He enlisted in Toronto with the
4th Battalion, Canadian Mounted Rifles.

His unit was promptly shipped to England—
and arrived at a training camp during the
rainy season.   For days it was mud and rain—
mud and rain.   In his book *Winged Warfare*
Bishop tells us: "I had succeeded in getting
myself mired to the knees when suddenly,
from somewhere out of the storm, appeared
a trim little airplane.   It landed hesitatingly
in a nearby field as if scorning to brush its
wings against so sordid a landscape; then
away again up into the clean grey mists.
How long I stood there gazing into the
distance I do not know, but when I turned
to slog my way back through the mud, my
mind was made up.   I knew there was only
one place to be on such a day—up above the
clouds in the summer sunshine."

Bishop applied immediately for his transfer
to the Royal Flying Corps—and got it.   A
few months later he was in France.   There
he spent four months in action as an observer
before being sent back to England, late in
1916, to train as a fighting pilot.   During that
winter of training he went through the usual
steps from a ground school up to night flying
and served on the Zeppelin patrols.   Finally,
in March 1917, he received instructions to
report for a course at a special school where
he was to learn to fly one of the small and
extremely fast single-seater fighting planes.
He practiced by taking baskets of tin cans
up with him, tossing them over the sky, then
diving and shooting at them.   A few days
later Lieutenant William A. Bishop returned to
France to join the 60th Squadron.

It was March 25 when "Billy" Bishop shot
down his first enemy plane, and it was not
long after that when people began to realize
that here was no ordinary pilot.   In his first
few weeks he downed 20 enemy aircraft, and
on a single May day engaged 23 in combat.
Said King George V, awarding him the D. S. O.

in 1917: "His courage and determination have set a fine example to others."

What was probably Billy Bishop's most famous exploit, however, took place at dawn of June 2, 1917, when he decided to make a singlehanded attack on a German aerodrome in the hope of surprising the enemy as they were preparing to take off for the morning's work. There he found seven German machines ready to take off. Swooping down, he destroyed two of them on the ground; and when he was attacked in the air he shot down two more. This feat not only earned him his V. C., the greatest of all decorations for valor, but a substantial home leave in Canada. While in Toronto in October he took advantage of it by marrying Margaret Eaton (today the mother of a grown son who has enlisted in the Royal Canadian Air Force, and a daughter). It was during his honeymoon in Dayton, Ohio, where Bishop served as member of a British air mission, that he wrote his first book, *Winged Warfare* (1918). He then recruited in Canada and instructed in England until the spring of 1918.

Back in France, with a price on his head, Billy Bishop kept on flying his silver machine with its easily-recognized blue snout into and out of tight places. Once his squadron actually lost eleven planes out of eighteen in one day. In May 1918 he formed his own squadron, No. 85, picking the cream of the pilots from the English, the Canadian and the United States Air Forces. But the next month the General Staff decided he was too valuable to run further risks, and he was given 12 days in which to prepare to leave for London to do administrative work and help with recruiting.

Up to that time Bishop had shot down the startling total of 45 German planes. In the next twelve days he shot down twenty-five more—a larger number than the entire RAF had downed during the first month of the War—five of them in two hours on his last day as a pilot! When Billy Bishop finally signed on as a first grade staff officer (lieutenant colonel) on the Canadian General Staff his record showed 72 enemy aircraft destroyed, 170 battles fought in mid-air, 10 well-earned decorations. The King suggested this time: "There are no more letters we can put after your name, so I suggest we put some before it, and call you 'Archbishop.'"

In the period between the two Wars Bishop mingled business and flying. First he went to the United States and traveled through the country lecturing, but he soon returned to England, where he lived for 10 years, "prominent in financial and polo circles." In 1922 this skilled airman, who during the War had once fallen 4,000 feet in a burning plane and who had often limped back home in his plane with scores of bullet holes in its fuselage, came nearer to losing his life than he ever had before. Injured in a civil flying accident, he nearly lost his sight; the plastic surgeons had to go to work on him; and, once restored to health, he did not pilot a plane for 12 or 13 years.

In 1931 Bishop came back to Canada to become vice-president of the McColl-Frontenac Oil Company, Limited, Montreal, one of Canada's largest companies. (His business career has included successful operations in investment banking, and he is a director of the English Electric Company of Canada.) By this time he had also attained the honorary rank of group captain in the Royal Canadian Air Force, and soon he was wanting to fly again. He asked a friend to lend him a ship. As he tells it: "In 13 years they'd made new rules in my game—had made flying a science. There was only one thing to do—I had to learn flying all over again."

After a few lessons from an expert, Bishop was as confident as ever. In 1936 he was promoted to the rank of Air Vice-Marshal, in 1938 to Air Marshal—and in August 1938 he was made a member of the Honorary Air Advisory Committee to the Minister of National Defense. He had previously written that Canada's aviation policy was one of "drifting," and had urged training an extensive air personnel and building machines of the best quality. Now he was to take an active part in carrying out his own advice. After Canada joined Great Britain in declaring war against Germany, on September 8, 1939 Bishop was called up for active service with the Royal Canadian Air Force, and not long afterward he was given the office of Director of Air Force Recruiting.

Today Bishop is "a short man with very blue eyes and a closely cropped mustache" whose formerly sandy hair has thinned out and grizzled, while his earlier slimness has given place to some increase in girth. Quentin Reynolds (see sketch this issue) calls him "an intelligent, cultured gentleman, a *bon vivant*, an extraordinary host, one of the keenest businessmen in Canada." His wife collects china dogs; his own "collection" hangs on his library walls, and includes the bluesnouted propeller of 1918 days and the wing tip of Richthofen's plane. In his library might also be found another book he has written since that War, with Rothesay Stuart-Wortley: *The Flying Squad* (1927). Among his most treasured possessions is a book presented to him by the Berlin Aero Club at a banquet in 1928, when Bishop, as their guest, was photographed with Goering (see sketch this issue). In it Goering and others have inscribed "greetings to a competitor from the other side."

Riding, golf, polo and tennis are Billy Bishop's sports. Of the usual Canadian winter doings this amazing man says: "No. I can't skate. It hurts my shins. As for skiing —say, I don't know where those fellows get the courage. The falls you take. I shiver every time I see one of them go down. I'd be scared stiff to try it!"

References

Collier's 98:87-90 N 21 '36 por
Life 8:44 My 20 '40 il pors
Halstead, I. Wings of Victory p131-7 1941

(Continued next page)

BISHOP, WILLIAM AVERY—*Continued*

Kiernan, R. H. Captain Albert Ball
1933
Who's Who
Who's Who in Canada

BLACK, HUGO (LA FAYETTE) Feb.
27, 1886- Associate Justice of the United
States Supreme Court
Address: b. Supreme Court Bldg, Washington, D. C.; h. Birmingham, Ala.

The New York Public Library

HUGO BLACK

Hugo Black took his position as Associate
Justice of the United States Supreme Court
in August 1937 after one of the most bitter
and vigorous discussions of all time, after "an
orgy of vituperation." Today lawyers and
laymen alike are praising his "succinct, lawyer-
like and pointed opinions" on this court, the
"clarity, power and perspicacity of his dissents."

The man who holds one of the highest legal
positions in the land never finished secondary
school, never completed an undergraduate course
at college. Hugo La Fayette Black was born
in Harlan, Clay County, Alabama and spent
the first five years of his life on a farm there,
the next fifteen in the county's metropolis of
Ashland, where his father and mother, William
La Fayette and Martha Ardellah (Toland)
Black, ran a general store. Summers he
worked, winters he attended a "primitive sort
of academy" called Ashland College. When
his older brother, who was a doctor, decided
that Hugo should become a doctor, too, he
fell in with his wishes enough to complete a
two-year medical course in one year at the
University of Alabama. Then he decided to
become a lawyer, switched over to the University's law school and in 1906 received his
LL. B.

He went back to Ashland and opened a law
office over a grocery store. Since the town's
population of 500 didn't allow for much legal
business, it was rather a relief to Black when
the grocery store burned down and gave him
an incentive for moving on to Birmingham.
In Birmingham business was better. Black
made connections with the trade-unions, representing the miners' union in its first Alabama
strike and the carpenters' union in an important
suit, and built up a general practice as well.
Then, in 1910, he received his first judicial
experience. Elected a police court judge, for
18 months he spent his mornings in a hot
dingy courtroom disposing of defendants, mostly
Negro, "hauled in for shooting craps, loafing,
fighting and connubial incompatability." His
next public position was that of solicitor for
Jefferson County, Alabama and lasted from
1915 to 1917.

After the War, during which Black served
as a captain in the 81st Field Artillery and
as adjutant in the 19th Artillery Brigade, he
settled down to private law practice in
Birmingham and to home life with Josephine
Patterson Foster, whom he married in 1921.
Although Raymond Clapper has called him "a
failure as a country lawyer," others have
vouched for his ability in cross examination
technique (his was always "the soft question
which provokes the wrathful answer"), for his
uncanny knowledge of the law's loopholes, for
his success.

In 1926 Black decided to campaign in the
primaries for the Senate seat of Oscar Underwood, who had announced his retirement. John
Bankhead, since elected to the Senate, and
three others decided to do the same thing.
Undiscouraged, Black climbed into his Model T
Ford and stumped the State, dressed in a
wrinkled suit, sleeping at the home of any
farmer who would put him up, speaking at
every crossroads store "the right words to win
both Ku Klux Klan" and A F of L support.
This support won him the nomination and
eventually the election.

Black made news in his first year in the
Senate just once: he was "among those present"
at one of Coolidge's famous White House
breakfasts. The rest of the time he studied
routine, made himself familiar with legislative
business and kept discreetly silent. When he
had thoroughly prepared himself he began to
battle to restore Muscle Shoals to public
operation—his first Senate speech was on this.
He went on to fight with Senator Norris of
Nebraska against the utility interests.

It wasn't until Roosevelt was elected, however, that he came into his own. During
Roosevelt's first term Black voted for each
of the 24 major measures of the New Deal
program and consistently supported all labor
legislation. He himself presented a bill in
the Senate for a 30-hour week and got it
passed, although it never became law in its
original form. Instead it was incorporated
in part into the NRA, which Black, incidentally,
denounced, one of the few men in the Senate
"who had the acumen and vision to perceive

precisely what the NRA was and what it would be."

From the 30-hour-week fight, Black threw himself into the problem of merchant marine subsidies. He had been working on this ever since 1928, when he had held up an appropriation bill carrying Coolidge's salary in an attempt to force into it an amendment to limit the salaries of Shipping Board officials to $10,000 a year. In 1930 he again investigated the whole question of subsidies and by 1933 was conducting a full-fledged investigation. Sensational headlines resulted from his hearings. He wrung out testimony "by convincing those who take the stand that he already has the facts but merely wishes them confirmed for the record out of the mouths of the witnesses."

As Raymond Clapper described it then, "armed with stacks of letters and documents, Senator Black sits back easily in his chair, puffs slowly on his cigar, rolls his large open eyes quite innocently and with a wise smile undertakes to refresh the memory of a squirming witness." The disclosures of the Black committee were startling. Contributions from taxes, it was proved, "in great part found their way into the pockets of profiteers, stock manipulators, political and powerful financial groups, who never flew a plane, who never invented an engine, who never improved an airplane part. Huge subsidies paid by the government to build up a merchant marine have been diverted from that channel and have been largely spent in high salaries, extravagant expense accounts, highly paid lobbyists and huge dividends."

After "almost singlehandedly saving the Administration from defeat" in the Utility Holding Company fight of 1935, Black went on to stir up even larger headlines as head of the Senate Lobby Investigating Committee. This work wasn't new to him, for the late Senator Caraway of Arkansas had asked him to become a guest on his lobby committee back in 1929. Black plunged in with enthusiasm; not long afterward he was accused of violating the Fourth Amendment and severely taken to task by the District of Columbia Court of Appeals. He had ordered the Postal Telegraph and Western Union Companies to comb their files for all wires which smacked of high pressure lobbying methods and later had subpoenaed the complete telegraphic correspondence of more than 1,000 specified persons and groups. More than 5,000,000 wires were piled up, and with them the wrath of the newspapers, those being investigated, the public and the courts. Black's rejoinder was to call it all "a gross and malicious campaign of misrepresentation."

During Black's last year in Congress he drove the Wage and Hour Bill through the Senate at great risk to his own political neck, for his sponsorship aroused violent reactions among Alabama employers who would have made a determined effort to defeat him if he had run for a third term. Every weekday, in office hours from 10 to 2 and on Saturdays from 10 to 1, he met his constituents. Between sessions he rented a house in Birmingham and traveled around his own and neighboring states on speaking tours. But all this came to an end on August 12, 1937 when President Roosevelt nominated him for the position of Associate Justice of the Supreme Court.

Senator Ashurst asked for the Senate's unanimous consent. Senator Johnson objected, and a senatorial precedent to confirm the nomination of any member to office without reference to committee was shattered. Objections flew. Emphasis was placed on the fact that he was a partisan litigant rather than a calm, impartial weigher of opposing arguments; on his lack of judicial experience. Senator Henry Cabot Lodge, Jr., found him insufficiently "tolerant, liberal and judicial in his view of the religious faiths and racial equality of his fellow citizens"; *Commonweal* called the President's choice "an unfortunate impulse of the moment"; fellow Senators brought up legal technicalities against his appointment. Only the liberals and liberal magazines like *The Nation*, which once called him "a passionately sincere humanist guided throughout by his understanding of the fundamental truth of the new militant liberalism," applauded the choice. Yet Black received his commission and, unknown to the public, on the same day took his oath as Associate Justice. Then he sailed for Europe.

Less than a month later Ray Sprigle, a reporter for the Pittsburgh *Post-Gazette,* wrote a series of six articles for that paper and the North American Newspaper Alliance in which he showed that Black had joined the Robert E. Lee Klan Number One, Invisible Empire, Knights of the Ku Klux Klan on September 11, 1923 and resigned on July 9, 1925 on the eve of his campaign for the Democratic nomination for United States Senator; that he had been welcomed back and made a life member on September 2, 1926 and given a gold "grand passport." The outcry was almost unanimous. Black had "betrayed" Roosevelt, it was said; the whole was "a deplorable episode without precedent or parallel in the history of this Republic"; and Hugh Johnson asked: "What difference does it make if Hugo Black is a uniformed Kluxer? . . . It was plain from his record that he is a born witch burner—narrow, prejudiced and class conscious." Black had his defenders, however. The *New Republic* explained Black's joining of the Klan as the error of years back, unimportant today; Max Lerner called it "simply a piece of political behavior," necessary for his election, and stated firmly: "Hugo Black is no Klansman. Everything that he has stood for in his 11 years in the Senate runs counter to what the Klan has stood for."

Black himself said nothing from abroad, and Roosevelt told the press: "I know only what I have read in the papers." Black returned to explain his actions in a radio speech. It began with a discourse on religious liberty and continued: "I did join the Klan. I later resigned. I never rejoined. . . I have never considered and do not now consider the unsolicited card given to me shortly after my nomination to the Senate as a membership

BLACK, HUGO—*Continued*

of any kind in the Ku Klux Klan. I never used it. I did not even keep it."

Black took his seat on the Supreme Court, his first official act to hear two separate but similar motions which challenged his right to the office. It was expected that from then on Black would go slowly, give himself a chance to mellow. He didn't. Although the cases assigned to him in his first year on the Court were small in number and narrow in issue, he managed to distinguish himself as a loud, lusty and lone dissenter. In less than eight months on the bench he had given out thirteen dissents. This was hailed by the *New Republic* as a sign of liberalism; by the late Paul Y. Anderson as revealing an attitude that "may well guide the Court out of the metaphysical wilderness into which it has wandered."

Marquis Childs, however, stated in magazine articles that Black's dissents were notable less for their liberalism than for their technical incompetence and went on further to say that Black's legal training and experience had been revealed as painfully unequal to his position on the nation's highest tribunal. His opinions, he stated, often had to be rephrased by colleagues to conform to Court standards. He himself had been unable to carry his share of routine work; his presence had been "an acute discomfort and embarrassment" to the other justices. Raymond Clapper corroborated this in his newspaper column, and the *Daily News* went so far as to say that Supreme Court members "had hitched up their judicial robes and in dignified fashion were in the process of putting the slug on their colleague." Denials then flooded the pages of newspapers, magazines, law periodicals. Walton Hamilton, professor of law at Yale, said Black had "courage almost to the point of audacity," praised his "eminently lawyer-like opinions" and prophesied that Black would be "an outstanding figure in the history of the court," for he "brings a breath of fresh air into a rather musty courtroom." Harold C. Havighurst of Northwestern University supported Hamilton, insisting with him that the dominant distinction between Black and his fellow jurists was his "insistence upon reality."

The controversy died down in the course of time, even though in 1941 Justice Black is still a frequent dissenter. Some of his decisions have been notable: in February 1940 he delivered a decision, freeing four Negroes who under torture had confessed to crimes, which was called "far and away the most direct, sweeping and brilliantly written application of the 14th Amendment to human rights that has come from our highest Court"; for this and for another denouncing the exclusion of Negroes from trial jury panels Black's name was added to the Honor Roll of Race Relations by the Schomburg Collection of Negro Literature in the New York Public Library in 1941. Later, in April 1941, he voted that Negroes had a right to receive equal train accommodations with whites.

In February 1941 Black had the triumph of participating in a Supreme Court decision certifying the constitutionality of the child labor provisions of the Wage and Hour Law which he had helped to get passed. In that same month he vigorously protested a Felix Frankfurter (see sketch this issue) decision upholding the right of state courts to issue injunctions against picketing "set in a background of violence." Somewhat removed from these cases was his opinion in March 1941 outlawing agreements by which manufacturers of hats and dresses sought to eliminate style "piracy" by registering new creations and penalizing anyone copying the designs.

There are many today who believe that Black is a "legislator among judges"; many who now agree with Walton Hamilton's summing up of his decisions: "There is no verbal display of priestcraft, no strutting of the higher pyrotechnics, no triumphant victory over difficulties of the jurist's own creation. Instead a recitation of the facts, a sharp definition of the issue, an argument that turns not to right or left but marches straight to its goal—and the trick is done. All the cases are disposed of deftly, simply, certainly, in accordance with justice and common sense."

Black, who was once a great joiner, former Grand Chancellor of the Knights of Pythias of Alabama and member (to his later sorrow) of almost every organization that asked him to join, doesn't go out much now except on family jaunts with Mrs. Black and their three children or to spend an occasional evening with a fellow justice or an Administration friend. He dislikes games and drinking and is reported to be happiest when reading works on history and economics at home.

References

  Atlan 163:667-74 My '39
  Newsweek 2:17 N 11 '33 por; 7:21 Mr
    14 '36 por; 10:7-9 Ag 21 '37 pors
  R of Rs 89:18-20+ Ap '34 por
  Scholastic 24:19 My 5 '34 por; 27:25
    S 21 '35 por
  Time 26:14-17 Ag 26 '35 por (cover);
    30:10-11 S 27 '37 por
  Univ Chicago Law R 8:20-41 D '40
  Lerner, M. Ideas Are Weapons p254-66
    1939
  Who's Who in America
  Who's Who in Government
  Who's Who in Law
  Who's Who in the Nation's Capital

BLACKTON, J(AMES) STUART

Jan. 5, 1875—Aug. 13, 1941 One of the outstanding pioneers of the motion picture field, which he entered in 1896; founder of the old Vitagraph Company, the first company to produce film plays; at one time was associate of the late Thomas A. Edison; was producer of such widely known early pictures as *The Christian* and *The Battle Cry to Peace;* was discoverer of a host of early motion picture stars.

References

Blue Book 19:243-7 Jl '14 il pors
Dramatic Mirror 77:3 Jl 21 '17 por; 77:
10 O 13 '17 por
Motion Pict Classic 7:16-17 S '18 por
Motion Pict Mag 10:85 O '15 por; 16:85
O '18 por
Sch Arts 31:sup 9-12 D '31
International Motion Picture Almanac
Who's Who
Who's Who in America 1930-31

Obituaries

N Y Times p17 Ag 14 '41 por

BLAKE, DORIS Journalist

Address: c/o New York Daily News, 220 E. 42nd St, New York City

If it is a broken heart that ails you, there are many remedies you can seek, from the conclusive one of suicide to the sterner one of absorbing your ache in a new charity or hobby. What you are more likely to do, as 200,000 of your contemporaries do annually, is to write to Doris Blake in care of any one of the forty-five papers served by the New York *Daily News*-Chicago *Tribune* syndicate.

According to the nature of your problem, you will be advised to be less free with your kisses, to stay away from married men in the future, or to learn to flatter men's egos. Doris Blake also will help you to make decisions. "Should I tell her I was married and have a girl 1½ years old?" "You should certainly enlighten her as to your status."

If your problem is that of excess avoirdupois, acne or an inability to apply make-up properly, you will find the same lady a willing guide and mentor, this time under her real name, Antoinette Donnelly. "Beauty Answers" as well as the feature articles in the beauty column appear under her name in the papers of the same syndicate.

Antoinette Donnelly, of Irish-Catholic ancestry, was born a half century or so ago in Mount Forest, Ontario, one of nine children. Her father was Michael Donnelly, a station agent, and her mother was Maria (Furey) Donnelly, an avid reader of French novels, whence the "Antoinette." When Antoinette's father died her mother took the family to Buffalo, New York, where Antoinette managed to teach herself typewriting and shorthand and secure a position as a stenographer.

Her first newspaper work was writing obituaries for the *American Lumberman*. Her next job was that of assistant to the woman's editor of the Chicago *Tribune*. She was subsequently given the beauty column to write, and her skill inspired the editors to revive an advice-to-the lovelorn column which had previously been dropped. The name, Doris Blake, was selected for this project because it was "pure American and not too flossy."

During the First World War, as beauty editor of the *Tribune*, Antoinette Donnelly was active in the anti-hoarding-fat campaign. In competition with her colleague, Dr. William Evans, the health editor, she took a class of fat men to Grant Park everyday for reducing

DORIS BLAKE

exercises. The doctor had a class of women. The men got thin first.

When Antoinette Donnelly-Doris Blake came to work in the New York office of the *Tribune-News* syndicate, her department was described as an "island of love, beauty and cosmetics amid the hurly-burly of one of America's most rowdy newspapers." She is more popular as Doris Blake than Antoinette Donnelly and besides answering questions individually, provides her readers with any one of a set of booklets which fit some of the more common difficulties. For a self-addressed, stamped envelope the reader may be edified by *Growing Up, For That Winning Personality, Getting and Keeping Boys Interested, Why Not Be Popular?, Don't Be Lonely, Love Quiz, The Technique That Wins Men, What About Petting?* and *How To Be Happy Though Married.*

Antoinette Donnelly's day is supposed to begin at 6:45 and end at 7 in the evening. Most of the letters are answered by her staff under her personal supervision. She keeps abreast, however, of the latest developments in her field, and her library contains many such titles as: *The Questions Girls Ask, How To Live Without a Woman, The Genteel Female, Ain't Love Gland?, Love Letters of Great Men and Women, Why We Love and Hate, No Nice Girl Swears, Live Alone and Like It, Wisdom for Widows, The Fruit of the Family Tree, Why Men Like Us* and *The Art of the Body.*

As Doris Blake, Miss Donnelly's advice to the perplexed is based on a series of fundamental beliefs: any young person can be popular; young people should not indulge in too much kissing and petting; newly-married couples should never live with their in-laws; women should not smoke (Miss Donnelly is a "chain" smoker); girls should not telephone boys; couples should not elope; and a woman's place is in the home fulfilling her natural functions of wife and mother. Among her descriptive

BLAKE, DORIS—*Continued*

headlines, many of which are nearly as long as the articles themselves, can be found: "DARK FUTURE SEEN FOR BACHELOR TOO SELFISH TO MARRY", "LAD IS TURNED DOWN BECAUSE OF PIMPLES BUT HE CAN YET WIN", "HE'D WED, THEN LIVE IN HER HOME, TOTING A BOTTLE WITH HIM," etc.

Antoinette Donnelly is also co-editor of the *Woman's Almanac* and a contributor to Catholic magazines. Her hobbies include piano study and interior decoration, and she is fond of swimming. Her husband, from whom she is separated, is a Canadian. His name is now "taboo in her presence." She lives with two adopted daughters, Mary and Josephine.

She has "dry bushy hair" and has been described as a "frowsy, gentle, jittery, earnest and overworked woman of some 50 years." The fact that she is not a good advertisement for her beauty column has proved a handicap in her few public lectures.

Her social world is largely composed of newspaper people who enjoy her company and her piano playing. Both her friends in the newspaper world and her daughters' friends not infrequently come to her for advice and comfort about their own love difficulties. They, like her readers, no doubt, take her suggestions when they happen to coincide with their inclinations.

References

Life 11:65-6+ S 15 '41 il pors
American Women

BLAKESLEE, A(LBERT) F(RANCIS)
Nov. 9, 1874- Botanist; geneticist
Address: b. Carnegie Institution, Cold Spring Harbor, Long Island, N. Y.

A. F. BLAKESLEE

In December of 1940 Dr. Albert F. Blakeslee, director of the Department of Genetics of the Carnegie Institution of Washington and one of the nation's great biologists, completed his one-year term as president of the American Association for the Advancement of Science. He himself has contributed to that advancement by indulging his natural penchant for pioneering experiments in botany and genetics. In 1937 he discovered that colchicine, long used as a remedy for gout, could change the nature of plant heredity, thereby "prodding evolution." This discovery provides the first experimental evidence that "genes, the factors inside all living cells controlling heredity, and viruses, organisms which produce some diseases in plants and animals, can produce similar effects in plants. The discovery promises to open up new horizons in virus disease, which in man include the common cold, influenza, yellow fever and infantile paralysis. It also provides for the first time a link between heredity and environment, showing how environmental factors may produce the same effect as hereditary factors."

At Cold Spring Harbor, on the north shore of Long Island, New York, there are greenhouses and fields belonging to the Carnegie Institution's Department of Genetics. In them Dr. Blakeslee and his associates care for more than 150,000 rank-smelling jimson weeds. Using these plants as basic material, an effort is being made to find out how evolution occurs. The weed produces two generations a year and can be forced to produce four. As part of his experiments, Dr. Blakeslee soaked some of the weeds in colchicine solution. Almost immediately changes showed that something important had happened. The leaves roughened, the grains of pollen became larger, and a count of the chromosomes showed that the number had doubled.

From the viewpoint of economics, Dr. Blakeslee says, the process of soaking plants in the solution "offers the hope of making fertile hybrid plants which are often sterile" because of difficulty in proper pairing of the chromosomes. Doubling of the chromosomes (induced by the drug) naturally provides twice as many chromosomes to form pairs. From these chromosomes it is possible for the plant to breed a new race. In the past "such spontaneously doubled chromosome plants have produced some of the most desirable economic varieties in tobacco, wheat, cotton and timothy."

Sixty-five different kinds of plants have been shown to mutate by treatment with colchicine. Such plants as black-eyed Susan, phlox, portulaca, violets and many others have increased the size of their flowers. Independent breeders were quick to realize that such commercially important blossoms as giant-sized zinnias and marigolds find a ready sale. Fruits have developed healthier and stronger characteristics when their trees have been treated with the drug, although they have shown no size increase.

The Cold Spring Harbor laboratory workers believe that the speeding up of the evolution-ary process has caused laymen to expect too much magic. Many people, reading in the papers of the drug, have written in to say: "If it will grow better plants, is it good for hair on the head?" Dr. Blakeslee says that the only answer is: "No results have yet been obtained in mammals."

Before these experiments the genial blazer of laboratory trails was already known in physiology and horticulture as well as genetics for his work on inheritance in jimson weeds, "a turning point in modern genetics." Before this he had "revolutionized our understanding of reproduction in all the lower plants" by discovering sexuality in some of the fungi. More recently, he has been probing at human inheritance with his "taste tests."

Dr. Blakeslee's mother was Augusta Mirenda (Hubbard) Blakeslee. His father, Francis Durbin Blakeslee, was at various times pastor, educator, lecturer, newspaper correspondent, university president. When his second son, Albert Francis, was born in Geneseo, New York on November 9, 1874, he was principal of the East Greenwich Academy, East Greenwich, Rhode Island. There Albert went to school until he was ready to enter Wesleyan University at Middletown, Connecticut. After receiving his Bachelor's Degree there in 1896 he taught science for four years, both at his father's school and at Montpelier Seminary in Montpelier, Vermont. In 1900 he entered Harvard for graduate work. While studying for the Doctor's Degree which he received in 1904 he continued to teach, as instructor of botany at Radcliffe College and as teaching fellow in botany at Harvard.

His first research work was sponsored by the Carnegie Institution where he is now department director. On a research grant he was able to spend two years in Germany with his fungi. After his return to the United States he became instructor of botany for a year at Harvard and at Radcliffe, then for eight years served as professor of botany (later of botany and genetics) at Connecticut Agricultural College, Storrs. During these years, in addition to becoming known as a "born teacher," he worked out a scheme of tree identification described in his book, *Trees in Winter* (1926); he produced one of the first hybrid pines achieved in this country; and he developed a "live museum" of growing trees.

On leave from the Connecticut Agricultural College during the year 1912 to 1913, he worked at the Department of Genetics of the Carnegie Institution, and in the fall of 1915 he returned there as investigator in plant genetics. In June of 1919 he was married to Margaret Dickson Bridges. He kept planning to get back to teaching because he liked it, but the Carnegie liking won, and he is still there—since 1936 as head of the department. He indulges his love of explaining and interpreting experimental results by conducting a large seminar every summer, and in 1938 Dr. Blakeslee and Dr. A. G. Avery, a co-worker in the Carnegie laboratory, wrote *Methods of Inducing Doubling of Chromosomes in Plants.*

Among Dr. Blakeslee's outstanding characteristics are a gray goatee, a genial twinkle and a well known readiness to help all scientific workers. His horticultural activities have raised for him a large crop of scientific honors here and abroad.

References

Nature 145:341 Mr 2 '40
N Y Times IV p2 F 4 '40 por; p34 Ja 1 '41
N Y World-Telegram p8 Mr 24 '41 por; p21 Je 26 '41 il por
Newsweek 15:26 Ja 8 '40 por
Sci ns 91:103-4 F 2 '40
Sci N L 35:51 Ja 28 '39 por; 37:4 Ja 6 '40 il por (pl)
Sci Mo 50:182-5 F '40 por
American Men of Science
Who's Who in America

BLATCH, HARRIOT STANTON Jan. 20, 1856—Nov. 20, 1940 Famous suffragette who was associated in England with Sylvia Pankhurst and led the radical wing of the movement in the United States.

References

Blatch, H. S. and Lutz, A. Challenging Years 1940
Who's Who Among North American Authors 1931-32
Who's Who in America 1928-29

Obituaries

N Y Herald Tribune p32 N 21 '40 por
N Y Times p29 N 21 '40 por

BLISS, A(NDREW) RICHARD, JR. Nov. 10, 1887—Aug. 12, 1941 Dean of the College of Medicine of the University of Alabama; recognized as one of the leading educators in the field of medicine; served on the faculties of six colleges and universities; author of numerous books on medicine and many articles in technical periodicals.

References

American Men of Science
Leaders in Education 1941
Who's Who in America
Who's Who in American Medicine

Obituaries

N Y Herald Tribune p8 Ag 16 '41

BLIVEN, BRUCE (blĭv'ĕn) July 27, 1889- Magazine editor

Address: b. 40 E. 49th St, New York City; h. 133 W. 11th St, New York City

Described both as a "progressive journalist with a rangy feel for the value and tempo of news" and as a "liberal who never knows his own mind," Bruce Bliven has been president and editor since 1930 of the *New Republic,* a weekly magazine. In the skyscraper editorial offices which he shares with three other magazines, offices designed by Lescaze in chrome steel and blue, streamlined and modern, Bliven does most of the editorial writing for the

BRUCE BLIVEN

New Republic and acts as the New York correspondent for the *Manchester Guardian.*

Bruce Bliven was born in Emmetsburg, Iowa, July 27, 1889, the son of Charles F. and Lilla C. (Ormsby) Bliven. He was graduated from Stanford University in 1911 with the degree of B. A. From 1909 until 1912, while he was still an undergraduate, young Bliven was a member of the editorial staff of the San Francisco *Bulletin*. During the next two years he was employed at intervals as an advertising writer. His name, meanwhile, was becoming known in American journalism through his contributions to various periodicals.

In 1914 Bliven combined pedagogy with journalism when he accepted the position of director of the Department of Journalism of the University of Southern California, a position which he held for two years, moving in 1916 to the editorial staff of *Printer's Ink*. From there he went to the editorial offices of the liberal daily, the New York *Globe,* where from 1919 to 1923 he was successively chief editorial writer, managing editor and associate editor.

He was connected with the *New Republic* in 1923 as managing editor, and seven years later he became president and editor. Under his direction the editorial policy of the *New Republic* has been consistently liberal. One of his colleagues on the *New Republic*, George Soule, said of him: "Bruce Bliven knows his United States from side to side and from top to bottom. . . There are few who can observe more closely what goes on in America, interpret it more accurately, or write about it more cogently." Although labeled "pinko" by *Time*, Bliven supported Roosevelt's policy of military preparedness and aid to Britain when those on the Left, before the German invasion of Russia, were shouting that this was an "imperialist war."

During the First World War the *New Republic,* founded in 1914 by Willard D. Straight and Herbert Croly, supported Great Britain and the policies of Woodrow Wilson, but after the Armistice the magazine turned against the League of Nations in support of Borah and Hiram Johnson and, disillusioned with the Versailles Treaty, took the position that America's entry had been a mistake. In 1924 it supported Robert M. La Follette, the elder, and the Third Party. After the death of Willard Straight, the controlling financial interest in the publication passed to his widow, now Mrs. Leonard K. Elmhirst, who has retained financial control without interfering with the weekly's editorial policies.

When the editorial policy came directly under the guidance of Bruce Bliven, it moved noticeably to the Left. In 1932 the *New Republic* supported Norman Thomas for the Presidency. The next year, however, it endorsed Roosevelt's policies and the NRA, and it has continued for the most part to support both his foreign and domestic policies. Before the present War, although it published articles by both isolationists and internationalists, its editorial position on foreign policy was that of opposing appeasement and attacking Chamberlain but at the same time expressing fear that full-fledged American participation in any collective security bloc would draw the United States into another war for which she was not responsible. After September 1939 it shifted gradually to the position of all-out aid to Great Britain without the reservation "short of war," but by August 25, 1941 was going a little further than Roosevelt in its leading editorial, which advocated immediate declaration of war on the Axis powers.

On the whole the *New Republic* appeals to the serious-minded reader. Its articles on economic, social and political questions and its reviews of literature and the arts are written by individuals well known in the field of liberal letters. Besides Bruce Bliven and George Soule, its editorial staff includes Malcolm Cowley and Stark Young. Its table of contents has listed names like Charles A. Beard (see sketch this issue), Heywood Broun, Harold Laski (see sketch this issue), Edmund Wilson and others.

Besides his arduous editorial duties for the *New Republic* and his correspondence for the *Manchester Guardian,* Bliven finds time to contribute articles to other magazines and to maintain an active directorship on the boards of the Twentieth Century Fund, the Consumers' League of New York and the Foreign Policy Association of the United States.

In the same 24-hour day Bliven is available for public lectures. Always current, some of his lecture topics are: "The Press and Public Opinion", "Politics and Democracy", "The Future of Liberty," and "Who Will Win the War?"

In February 1942 *Men Who Make the Future*, by Bruce Bliven, is expected to appear. Bliven has just signed a contract with Duell,

Sloan & Pearce, Inc., for the book, in which he will survey new achievements in various fields of science, basing his studies on interviews with prominent men in each field. These interviews have been published in various issues of the *New Republic.*

Bliven's essay, *Public Opinion, the Case of Citizen Jones,* appeared in a volume edited by Harold Stearns, *America Now, an Inquiry into Civilization in the United States by Thirty-Six Americans,* published in 1938. In this essay Bliven discusses the effects of anti-democratic pressure groups on public opinion and comes to the conclusion that it would be "folly" to attempt to suppress them. "The cure for propaganda," he writes, "is more propaganda." Rather than attempt the futile task of silencing those who would undermine democracy, he feels that through education we should build in the individual a resistance to the wrong influences.

In 1913 Bruce Bliven married Rose Emery of San Jose, California. They have one son, Bruce Bliven, Jr., who writes timely articles for the *New Republic* as well as other magazines.

Of himself, Bliven writes: "I am five feet nine, and try not very successfully to keep my weight down to 180. My hair and eyes are brown. My favorite recreations are walking, swimming, very bad golf, driving a car, the theatre, movies, music, and reading."

References

> Sat Eve Post 213:92 F 15 '41
> Survey G 29:21 Ja '40
> Time 34:21 N 13 '39 por
> Who's Who in America
> Who's Who in Journalism
> Who's Who in the East

BLOCK, PAUL Nov. 2, 1877—June 22, 1941 Newspaper publisher and president of Paul Block and Associates, newspaper advertising agency; at one time or another owned a number of newspapers all over the country, but at the time of his death published only the Pittsburgh *Post-Gazette,* the Toledo *Blade* and the Toledo *Times;* frequently wrote editorials patterned in style and typography on those of William Randolph Hearst and the late Arthur Brisbane which he published on the front pages of his own newspapers and sometimes reprinted in space bought in other newspapers; benefactor of Yale University and the Hotchkiss School and of Jewish philanthropic societies.

References

> Newsweek 6:8 D 21 '35 por
> R of Rs 76:313 S '27 por
> Who's Who in America
> Who's Who in American Jewry

Obituaries

> N Y Times p17 Je 23 '41 por
> Newsweek 17:4 Je 30 '41 por
> Time 37:78 Je 30 '41

BLUMENTHAL, GEORGE Apr. 7, 1858— June 26, 1941 President of the Metropolitan Museum of Art and president emeritus of Mount Sinai Hospital in New York City; one of the ablest financiers on Wall Street, he gave up banking in 1925 to devote his life to art and medicine; donated millions of dollars to these causes.

References

> Art Digest 8:8 Ja 15 '34
> Art N 32:5 Ja 13 '34 por
> Chicago Art Inst Bul 28:30 Mr '34
> Lit Digest 117:20 Ja 27 '34 por
> Museum News 11:1 Ja 15 '34
> Newsweek 6:38 D 28 '35 por
> Who's Who in America
> Who's Who in American Jewry
> Who's Who in Commerce and Industry

Obituaries

> N Y Times p17 Je 27 '41 por

BODANSKY, MEYER (bŭ-dăns'kê) Aug. 30, 1896—June 14, 1941 Biochemist and pathologist; taught at Stanford University and the American University at Beirut, Syria, and since 1930 had been professor of pathological chemistry at the University of Texas; author of textbooks on physiological chemistry and contributor to scientific journals; member of the editorial board of the *American Journal of Clinical Pathology.*

References

> American Men of Science
> America's Young Men 1936-37
> Who's Who in America
> Who's Who in American Jewry

Obituaries

> N Y Herald Tribune p10 Je 16 '41

BOLLES, STEPHEN (bōlz) June 25, 1872 —July 8, 1941 Republican Representative in Congress from Wisconsin; foe of New Deal and the La Follettes; veteran newspaper editor who had been a journalist since 1890.

References

> Who's Who in America
> Who's Who in Journalism

Obituaries

> N Y Times p21 Jl 9 '41 por

BONHAM, MILLEDGE LOUIS, JR. Feb. 21, 1880—Jan. 22, 1941 Head of the Hamilton College History Department since 1919; began to teach in 1900; an authority on Canadian-American relations and on Civil War history.

References

> Leaders in Education 1941
> Who's Who Among North American Authors
> Who's Who in America

Obituaries

> N Y Times p22 Ja 23 '41

BONINE, FREDERICK N. (bŏ-nēn')
Oct. 21, 1863—Aug. 22, 1941 Noted eye
specialist; unpretentious office in Niles, Michigan became a mecca for thousands who
suffered from cataracts on their eyes; once
estimated that in 38 years he had treated
1,500,000 patients from the United States,
Canada and foreign countries; had treated
500 people in a single day; was star runner
in his youth; held the 100-meter dash record
for 36 years; had served as Mayor of Niles
and as alderman.

References

American Medical Directory

Obituaries

N Y Times p35 Ag 24 '41

BOOTH, EVANGELINE (CORY) Dec.
25, 1865- Former head of the Salvation Army
Address: h. Hartsdale, N. Y.

EVANGELINE BOOTH

Evangeline Booth, fourth daughter of General William Booth, the founder of the Salvation Army, and Catherine (Mumford)
Booth, was born in London, England, on Christmas Day 1865. From her earliest days the
spirit of militant religion was bred in her;
childhood games consisted of leading meetings
and making speeches. By the time most girls
begin to think about clothes and beaux, Evangeline Booth was assisting her father in his
work among the poor of London's East End.

With the expansion of the Salvation Army,
she was given large responsibility and when
still in her teens was appointed by her father
captain of a Salvation Army Corps in the
worst part of the East End of London. Opposition from the neighborhood toughs was
fierce and brutal. Evangeline Booth devoted
herself all the more to the slum and its
people, and before long had won them over

to the Army's message. The toughs even
banded themselves into a bodyguard for her
protection.

The same thing happened time and time
again, perhaps most spectacularly in Torquay,
the exclusive English seaside resort on the
coast of Devon. There was a section of
Torquay that definitely did not want the Sal-
valtion Army around; it set about fighting
the Salvation Army's right to preach the
gospel. A long legal battle followed with
Evangeline Booth fighting it through to the
Houses of Parliament and getting the repeal
of the by-law forbidding preaching. As a
special mark of the General's appreciation and
the Army's gratitude, the rank of commissioner
was given her.

For two years the new commissioner traveled
through Europe, making speeches, leading
songs and getting huge crowds to hear her.
Then in 1888, at 23, she was appointed to the
command of all Salvation Army operations in
London, with the oversight of the International Training College thrown in. The immense gatherings she was able to address in
this period are still quoted as peaks in Salvation Army achievement.

When changes in the higher commands left
the leadership of Canada vacant, General Booth
asked his daughter to take the position. Beginning in 1893 she worked there for nine
years, expanding every branch of the Army's
work. During the gold rush of 1898 she
organized a mission and nursing corps, taking
it herself to the Klondike and sharing the
hardships of the pioneers.

In 1904 Miss Booth was appointed to the
national leadership of the Salvation Army in
the United States, a post which she held for
30 years. During those years hers was a
single-minded devotion to her work. Faced,
at the beginning, with problems of money and
personnel, she revolutionized the financial
system of the Army and strengthened its resources. The old hand-to-mouth system of
"panhandling" was discarded and in its place
was set up a dignified system of appeal to the
public through Community Chests and special
campaigns. She herself went around the
country speaking to many groups of people,
winning numbers of them over.

During the First World War, Evangeline
Booth placed the resources of the Army at the
disposal of the Government, and, at home and
in France, Army women ministered day and
night to the soldiers. As a mark of his appreciation President Wilson gave Miss Booth
the Distinguished Service Medal. When the
Armenian atrocities broke out, Miss Booth
herself hurried there to shepherd whole companies to safety and peace. When famine
ravaged India, she led the Army in sending
thousands of dollars for relief. When the
Japanese earthquake occurred, she raised
money on a large scale.

During the latter years of her command in
America, the members of the Salvation Army
in other parts of the world insisted that
General Booth visit them. Strenuous cam-
paigns were made in Japan, England, Norway,
Sweden, Denmark, France, Germany—cam-

paigns in which she impressed large audiences with her eloquence as she gave such lectures as *The World's Greatest Romance, Rags, The Hand of God* and led in the singing of songs she had composed for the Army.

In November 1934 Evangeline Booth was elected general of the international forces of the Salvation Army and set sail for England. Her farewell to America was held in New York City's Madison Square Garden, where 20,000 people gathered to honor her for her 30 years of work. From then until her retirement in October 1939, General Booth was active at international headquarters in London and found time, too, to conduct services throughout the British Isles.

When she retired, it was to her home at Hartsdale, New York. There she plays the harp and continues to compose hymns and band music. A collection of her Army songs was published in 1927 and she is the author of a number of books as well: *The War Romance of the Salvation Army*, written with Grace Livingston Hill (1919); *Love is All* (1925); *Toward a Better World* (1928); and *Woman* (1930).

Evangeline Booth has been awarded honorary degrees by Columbia University and Tufts College; she has received the Distinguished Service Medal and the Eleanor Van Rensselaer Fairfax Gold Medal for "eminent patriotic services"; she has been awarded the Vasa Gold Medal by the King of Sweden and the Gold Medal of the National Institute of Social Sciences.

References

> Christian Sci Mon Mag p7 Ag 19 '39
> pors
> Illustration 189:37 S 8 '34 por
> R Deux Mondes s8 38:353-65 Mr 15 '37
> Spec 153:867 D 7 '34
> American Women
> Mackenzie, F. A. Clash of the Cymbals 1929
> Salvation Army. Around New York with the Salvation Army pam nd
> Who's Who in America
> Wilson, P. W. General Evangeline Booth 1935

BORGLUM, GUTZON (bôr'glŭm gōōt'sŭn) Mar. 25, 1871—Mar. 6, 1941 Internationally known sculptor who achieved fame with the mammoth figures of Washington, Jefferson, Lincoln and Theodore Roosevelt, hewn in granite into the cliffs of Mount Rushmore in the Black Hills of South Dakota; this work, begun in 1927 and not yet completed, has been called the grandest sculptural project conceived and executed by man; he also achieved fame for his Stone Mountain sculpture begun in 1916 for the DAR, abandoned during the First World War and then again interrupted by temperamental outbursts on the part of the sculptor, who was dismissed from the project; his Lincoln head in the rotunda of the Capitol in Washington is an outstanding conception; sculptor was christened John Gutzon de la Mothe Borglum and was a student under Rodin in France.

References

> Nation 135:617-18 D 21 '32
> N Y Herald Tribune p20 S 24 '40
> N Y Times VII p8-9+ Ag 25 '40 il por
> Newsweek 14:23 Jl 10 '39 il
> Read Digest 36:113-15 My '40
> Sci Am 148:7-9 Ja '33 por
> Johnson, G. W. Undefeated 1927
> McSpadden, J. W. Famous Sculptors of America p213-44 1924
> Who's Who in America
> Who's Who in American Art

Obituaries

> N Y Times p21 Mr 7 '41 por

BORIS III, KING OF BULGARIA (bō'rĭs) Jan. 30, 1894-
Address: Royal Palace, Sofia, Bulgaria

In March 1941, when Nazi troops began marching into the Bulgarian capital, King Boris III was in his Sofian palace thinking his own thoughts. They must have been depressing. He had seen uprisings and insurrections, revolutions and counter-revolutions since the day he ascended the throne in 1918, but this was the first time he could no longer, except euphemistically, call his crown his own.

King Boris is only the second of his line to occupy the throne of Bulgaria. His father, Ferdinand of Coburg, was the fifth son of Prince Augustus of Saxe-Coburg and Gotha, a lieutenant in the Austrian hussars when a Bulgarian delegation, touring Europe in search of a monarch, offered him the throne. He ascended it in 1887. Boris' mother was Princess Marie Louise of Bourbon, the eldest daughter of Duke Robert of Parma. She died in 1899 when Boris was only five years old, and nine years later Ferdinand married Princess Eleanor of the House of Reuss. It was in this same year that Ferdinand, taking advantage of a Turkish crisis, raised his principality to a kingdom and proclaimed himself Tsar of the Bulgars.

Boris was born on January 30, 1894 and baptized in the Orthodox Church, of which he is still a devout member, in order to win Russian approval. He attended Sofia's military academy and university and was taught French, Italian, German and English by his tutors—so well that he later read newspapers in each of these languages, and in Bulgarian, in bed every morning. During these years Boris became passionately devoted to railroad engines: he became a member of the Bulgarian Railroad Engineers Union and is supposed to have begged King Ferdinand to allow him to go to America to become a railroad engineer. This devotion never diminished. A few years ago, when the royal train caught fire, King Boris dashed from carriage to carriage of the moving train, took the throttle from the injured engineer and piloted the train for the rest of the journey. Another time, dressed in grease-covered overalls, with his face

BORIS III, KING OF BULGARIA

smeared, he brought the express into Sofia two minutes late. The superintendent, who didn't recognize him, took him sharply to task, and Boris, the good engineer, apologized.

It was 1918 when Boris ascended the Bulgarian throne. The military defeat of Bulgaria in the First World War had brought the immediate abdication and flight of King Ferdinand, who had been largely responsible for his country's joining the Central Powers.

Boris was in a precarious position—the last member of a defeated dynasty. October 1919 found Stambuliski, the leader and founder of the Agrarian League, who had once been condemned to death by his father, in power. As Boris' Prime Minister he earned the enmity of conservatives by setting up a severe dictatorship of the "Green Left" and enforcing sweeping agricultural reforms and a labor service system. His foreign policy made enemies, too. Bulgaria had been the only Balkan loser in the First World War. The Peace Treaty of Neuilly, far from restoring the large sections of Macedonia and of Dobrudja which had been lost to her in 1913, had thrown her back from the Aegean and cut off a million Bulgarians from their homeland, and its disarmament portions had placed her at the mercy of her neighbors. The groundwork was thereby laid for a strong revisionist movement. Stambuliski nevertheless encouraged a policy of friendship with the other Balkan countries and worked for a union of South Slavs under peasant leadership, a policy which particularly antagonized the Macedonian revolutionaries.

Boris bided his time. Finally, on June 9, 1923, conservative elements, plus the discontented Macedonians and the Military League, overthrew Stambuliski by a *coup d'état* and murdered him. The man who now came to power as Boris' Prime Minister was

Professor Alexander Tsankov, a Social-Democrat turned Fascist. Something resembling civil war followed, Agrarians, Socialists and Communists all participating in the ensuing riots. They were rigorously suppressed, especially after an episode in April 1925 when a bomb exploded in the Charles Cathedral of Sofia where government officials were attending a service. According to one source, during the two years of Tsankov's regime 10,000 peasants and workers were killed without trial.

How responsible Boris was for Tsankov's terroristic policies—or, for that matter, for later events—is uncertain. One story has it that when Tsankov reported to his King he was asked: "Why so few dead? You must give them a blood-letting they will never forget." This hardly accords with more familiar descriptions of Boris as a simple, mild man who once boasted that "there is no man in this country to whom I cannot talk as an equal," who spent one morning in the palace grounds netting butterflies because he was receiving an entomologist for lunch that day, and who commonly roamed the streets of Sofia alone, without fear because of his great popularity with his people. But there are many versions of Boris' character and true position. One has it that during most of his rule he was an amiable figurehead, and quotes him as having said: "It would not frighten me if I were to lose my throne. If that were to happen, I would go right to America and get a job as a mechanic." André Simone in *Men of Europe* insists that after 1923 he was an absolute autocrat, though an autocrat who was disarmingly clever at creating the impression that others were doing the ruling. And to Douglas Reed he was, "in kingship, what Cinquevalli was in juggling and Blondin on a tight-rope." Reed believed that by skill and guile Boris "outwitted all enemies, revolutionary plotters and military conspirators alike."

Whatever the truth, in January 1926 a more democratic form of government was restored under Liapchev. Although Macedonian terroristic activity continued unchecked in Bulgaria and in raids on Jugoslavia and Greece, the Agrarians were allowed to reconstruct their party, Parliament was permitted to complete a full term, and the May 1927 elections were "relatively free." But this period of relative political stability was not long. In 1930 the Cabinet was reconstructed for the second time, in 1931 for the third time, and the elections of June 1931 gave Liapchev the final blow. By this time, moreover, Bulgaria was facing a grave economic crisis. In September 1932 the Communist Party (which had been dissolved in 1924 and 1925, but which had since reappeared under various guises) won 19 of the 35 seats in the municipal council of Sofia, and in June 1933 the Government proclaimed a state of siege. Fascist activity also increased. Finally, on May 19, 1934, there was another *coup* by the Military League (outlawed but reconstructed as a secret organization) in collaboration with a nationalist-fascist group, the Zveno. At four a. m. on that day

Boris was forced to sign a manifesto overthrowing "the system": political parties and Parliament were once more dissolved, the constitution suspended.

The new military dictatorship promised certain reforms, and it is true that it brought about debt reductions and the temporary suppression of the Macedonian revolutionary organization, which had so jeopardized Jugoslavian-Bulgarian relations. But Boris could not be dislodged from power. He gradually divided the Military League, and upon the discovery of a conspiracy by the challenged leader, Colonel Veltchev, liquidated both the League and the Zveno. In November 1935 another Cabinet fell without having fulfilled its promise to promulgate a new constitution. The victorious King was now apparently determined to steer the country along a middle course. Although free speech, the right of assembly and the freedom of the press remained non-existent, in March 1937 the royal dictatorship granted suffrage to certain classes of women, and a decree of October 1937 called for parliamentary elections and extended the right to vote to all men over 21 and to women who had been married. The new Parliament then occupied itself with approving the authoritarian decrees which had been already enacted, but it did seem that Bulgaria might be moving hesitantly toward a revival of constitutionalism.

Foreign policy, however, indicated that the fate of this Balkan kingdom was inextricably tied up with the authoritarian powers. After the First World War, British bankers had invested in the reconstruction in the country, and before 1933 only about one quarter of Bulgaria's trade had been with Germany. But even that early Bulgaria's hope of recovering Aegean Sea outlets had placed her on the side of the revisionist bloc of Austria, Hungary, Germany and Italy. What is more, in 1930 Boris had married Princess Giovanna, the daughter of Italy's King Vittorio Emanuele III, and the Balkan powers had begun to suspect him of a secret alliance with Italy. He refused to join the Balkan Entente of Turkey, Greece, Yugoslavia and Romania, for that would have meant giving up all revisionist aims. Finally, when Hitler began rearming Germany, thus establishing a precedent for the defeated powers, and Bulgaria got permission to rearm, Bulgaria negotiated a barter agreement with Germany by which German arms deliveries could be paid for with Bulgarian products other than tobacco, and it was the German General Staff which drew up the plans for Bulgarian rearmaments and fortifications.

By 1938 Germany was the biggest buyer of Bulgarian exports, taking from 60 to 70 percent of her products, and only a slightly smaller percentage of Bulgarian imports came from Germany. German capital also got control of textile and sugar industries and several key banks. According to André Simone, the Western democracies gave tacit consent to this situation, and "since 1937 King Boris has known that even if he wanted to become an ally of the Western democracies, he would not be welcome." The king had few illusions about Chamberlain and Daladier. In August 1938, talking to a Czech envoy to Sofia about Lord Runciman's mission, he told him: "You will have to give in." Shortly afterward, about to set out on a farewell trip to Great Britain, he announced: "There will be no war." This visit, just before Munich, was played up by the British and French press as showing his sympathy for the democracies; only the perspicacious Pertinax revealed, in *L'Ordre,* that he was suspected of secret dealings with Hitler.

This pro-Axis policy was hardly agreeable to the majority of his people, for their historic, social and linguistic sympathies had always been for Russia. Boris had once asked a French envoy: "Don't you know that my peasants love Russia more than they do me? Are you going to protect me against them when they rise again? They nearly got me in 1923." The Soviet Union had broken off relations with the Bulgarian Government after the *putsch* of 1923, and until 1934 Italy had discouraged every attempt on the part of Bulgaria to resume negotiations, but that year the U. S. S. R. was recognized again. The popular demand was for an alliance with her.

This demand became stronger during the first part of the Second World War, when the airline Sofia-Moscow was constructed and Soviet sports teams and cultural delegations visited Bulgaria. In the summer of 1940 official thanks were extended to Russia for her support of Bulgarian claims on Southern Dobrudja, at that time ceded by Romania. Boris was in an impossible position, between the devil and the deep. For a long while Hitler's attempts to make Bulgaria an Axis adjunct were avoided by neat diplomatic sidestepping on his part and on the part of his Premier, Bogdan Philoff (see sketch this issue), who was, however, generally considered pro-Nazi. Both kept affirming and reaffirming their desire for both freedom and peace, as mass meetings demanded a "policy of neutrality in close collaboration with the Soviet Union."

But the conclusion was foregone. Finally, in March 1941, after more than one conference with Hitler, Philoff's signature to the Berlin-Rome-Tokio alliance was obtained in Vienna, and two hours later Nazi columns began rolling into Sofia. A Soviet protest came too late. Next, while Moscow and Belgrade were negotiating a non-aggression pact, Bulgarian territory was granted to Germany and Italy as a base for the victorious attack on Yugoslavia and on Greece, and after the German invasion of the Soviet Union, Bulgarian press attacks on the latter became vitriolic. On September 11, 1941 Moscow formally accused Bulgaria of acting as a full-scale base for the German-Italian attacks on the Soviet Union and of preparing to participate in them herself, and on September 20 a state of emergency was declared in Bulgaria. It was reported that thousands of Bulgarians were herded into

BORIS III—*Continued*

concentration camps to prevent open anti-Nazi outbreaks.

In the meanwhile, in his yellow palace—the long, unpretentious building where Boris lives with his wife, his children (Prince Simeon, born in 1937, is his heir), his unmarried sister Princess Eudoxies and his brother Cyril—Boris entertained Nazi officials. What these visitors saw was a man with a pale complexion, blue, appealing eyes with a kind of "doe-like softness," an auburn mustache, a high forehead made higher by receding hair, a long hooked Bourbon nose and a bold profile. What they found was an "expert handshaker and a good quiet listener." But what went on behind the charm of Boris' manners remained as mysterious as ever. And it seemed doubtful that Boris III, King of Bulgaria, would ever dare again to roam the streets of Sofia alone.

References

> Ann Pol et Litt 103:90-1 Jl 27 '34 il
> pors
> Eur Nouv 20:117-18 Ja 30 '37
> Friday 1:9 D 27 '40 pors
> Liv Age 336:174-6 My '29 pors; 351:
> 318-21 D '36
> Newsweek 4:13 D 8 '34 por
> R Deux Mondes s8 35:165-70 S 1 '36
> Scholastic 30:16 Mr 6 '37 por; 38:5+
> F 24 '41 il
> Time 36:22 D 2 '40 por; 37:23-5 Ja 20
> '41 por
> Gunther, J. Inside Europe p471-2 1940
> International Who's Who
> Kovacs, F. W. L. The Untamed Balkans p97-104 1941
> Reed, D. Insanity Fair p279 1938
> Roucek, J. S. The Politics of the Balkans p118-37 1939
> Simone, A. Men of Europe p192-96 1941

BOWERS, CLAUDE G(ERNADE) (bou'-ĕrz) Nov. 20, 1878(?)- United States Ambassador to Chile; historian

Address: Department of State, Washington, D. C.; United States Embassy, Santiago, Chile

In the fall of 1939, when Claude G. Bowers sailed for Chile to become United States Ambassador there, it was with the hope that he would "be able further to contribute toward the mutual understanding and growing feeling of our friendship not only with Chile but all South American republics." Ambassador Bowers is far from being the usual career diplomat. Until 1933, when he was appointed Ambassador to the Spanish Republic, he had been known as a "newspaperman, editorial writer, historian and speech maker." An authority on Jefferson and on Jackson, he has also been called "the greatest living practitioner of what for want of a better term may be called personal history." He has not lost this reputation, but it is his record in Spain which particularly qualified him to represent the United States before the Popular Front Government of Chile.

Claude Gernade Bowers was born in Hamilton County, Indiana, the son of Lewis and Juliet (Tipton) Bowers. His lifelong interest in Jefferson he acquired, ironically enough, when he was a high school lad preparing a eulogy on Hamilton for a state oratorical contest. Just to be well informed he read Jefferson's side, too, and found that he agreed with him; but he went on and won the contest. His first newspaper position was acquired almost as accidentally: a friend writing editorials for the Indianapolis *Sentinel* wanted to go on a fishing trip, and asked Bowers, who was then studying law, to take his place. That was in 1901, and Bowers was to remain in newspaper work for a long time.

Until 1903 Bowers was with the *Sentinel;* then he found a position with the Terre Haute *Star* and stayed with that newspaper for three years. In the meanwhile he continued to be sought after as a speaker and by 1904 had been nominated for Congress from the Terre Haute District. A general Republican landslide prevented him from being the youngest man in the United States House of Representatives, but he contented himself with joining the Terre Haute Board of Public Improvements. In 1911 he spoke so convincingly to Sybil McCaslin that she was persuaded to marry him (they now have one daughter, Patricia), and in the same year he talked himself into a position as secretary to United States Senator John W. Kern.

It was 1917, the year after the publication of Bowers' first book, *Irish Orators,* when Senator Kern died, and Claude Bowers became editor of the Fort Wayne *Journal Gazette.* While editing that paper he also managed to find time for research and for the writing of his *Life of John Worth Kern* (1918) and *The Party Battles of the Jackson Period* (1922), and for attending more than one Democratic national and state convention. In 1920 he delivered his first keynote speech—at the Democratic State Convention. In the meanwhile several men had been instructed to keep on the watch for a good editorial writer for the New York *World.* Independently but unanimously they selected Claude Bowers after reading his leaders in the *Journal Gazette,* and in 1923 he went to New York City to accept the *World's* offer.

Bowers was with the *World* until 1931. That period saw the publication of *Jefferson and Hamilton* (1925), for which he received the Jefferson Medal at the formal dedication of Monticello to the nation on July 4, 1926. Bowers is convinced that it is his best book. After almost 20 years it is still selling and is used as supplementary reading in most universities. It was widely reviewed by leaders in Government, including Franklin D. Roosevelt.

In 1927 the Governor of Tennessee appointed him member of a commission "to determine the true historical value of Jackson's triumph at New Orleans," and he was not only made honorary president of the Andrew Jackson Society, created "to foster more just treatment of Jackson in school histories," but also invited to give a Jackson Day dinner speech in Washington. (The next year found him delivering the keynote address at the National Democratic Jackson Day banquet.) Then, in the summer of 1928, Bowers gave the keynote address at the Democratic National Convention, proclaiming that "we [Democrats] battle for the honor of the nation besmirched and bedraggled by the most brazen and shameless carnival of corruption that ever blackened the reputation of a decent and self-respecting people" and crying: "To your tents, O Israel!"

The Tragic Era (1929), a Literary Guild selection, is no doubt Bowers' most famous work of "personal history." For three and a half years, while working for the *World*, he spent his lunch hours in The New York Public Library, since the newspapers of the period from 1865 to 1877 about which he was writing were available to readers only between nine in the morning and five in the afternoon. In this time he also managed to digest some 800 books, including diaries of the period, and on September 1, 1928 he was finally ready to begin the writing. *The Tragic Era* was completed nine months later, and Bowers could stop eating sandwiches for lunch. Critics called this book, subtitled The Revolution After Lincoln, "an unforgettable record of an unforgivable period in American history", "a vigorous, denunciatory, often entrancing book", "one of the most distinguished books of the year." It was criticized by some for its iconoclasm and even called reactionary in its viewpoint, but what seemed to a few critics prejudice and political bias appealed to others as "fire and feeling" and a desire to call spades spades. Its sale was "tremendous."

In 1930 *Civil and Religious Liberty*, a collection of Bowers' speeches, was published; in 1931 he began writing a daily political column for Hearst's New York *Journal*; the year 1932 saw the publication of his *Beveridge and the Progressive Era*. Then, in 1933 President Roosevelt appointed him Ambassador to Spain, where it seemed that he might find "relative quiet" as well as an opportunity to study the early days of a sister Republic. It was true that Bowers wrote his *Jefferson in Power* (1936) in his book-lined study on the second floor of the Madrid Embassy, but even foregoing afternoon siestas and most of the usual social life of an Ambassador didn't provide either much leisure or appetite for scholarly research after his first days in Spain.

During the Spanish War, Bowers was chairman of the Society for the Relief of Spanish Children, acted as an intermediary for the exchange of prisoners, and, when four Americans in Majorca managed to create an international incident, he won praise for his handling of the situation. In 1939 he returned to the United States. Surprisingly enough, *The Spanish Adventures of Washington Irving* (1940), "an engaging if not important book" that "recaptured the flavor of the past and restored a Spain that has gone," was the fruit of those tragic years. Mr. Bowers tells us:

"It was finished just before the Spanish War and was intended solely for publication in Spanish in Spain as a gesture. The War ended reading in Spain, so I let my publisher here [in the United States] have it on his request." Bowers was later said to be at work on another book with the tentative title *Spanish Memories*.

When in 1939 Claude G. Bowers was appointed Ambassador to Chile, Freda Kirchwey

Harris & Ewing

CLAUDE G. BOWERS

of *The Nation* announced that he represented "the best of the New Deal expressed in terms of diplomacy." She said further: "By nature Mr. Bowers is no diplomat. He is a lot of other things, such as historian and newspaperman and Jeffersonian, old-style. He is plainspoken, sharp-witted, and, I should think, completely irreverent." She mentioned the fact that in October 1939 he had been the United States' delegate to a Pan-American housing convention, and there had spoken in behalf of all the Republics at the opening meeting. Together with the delegates from Chile, Mexico, Colombia, Panama and Cuba he had agreed that the best solution of the housing problem was to pay a decent living wage.

This diplomat-historian smokes thick black cigars, and "his conversation, judiciously phrased and impressive in its dignity, is punctuated frequently by expressions of vigor for which his listeners are unprepared." He is physically rather unimpressive, however: a "thin man with mournful eyes." Bowers himself tells the story of an Irish politician who was waxing enthusiastic in his praise of a speech on Irish patriots that Bowers had made. "But," the Irishman finished ruefully, "he shurre is no *looker!*"

(Continued next page)

BOWERS, CLAUDE G.—Continued

References

Bul Pan Am Union 74:164 Mr '40 por
Christian Sci Mon Mag p6 O 16 '35
    por; p5+ Jl 15 '39 il por
Lit Digest 115:8 Je 24 '33 por
Nation 149:569-70 N 25 '39
New Outlook 163:37 My '34
Newsweek 1:8 Ap 15 '33; 14:9 Ag
    21 '39 por; 15:40 Mr 4 '40 por; 17:63
    F 24 '41
Wilson Lib Bul 11:86 O '36
Who's Who in America
Who's Who in Journalism

BOWES, EDWARD (bōz) 1874- Radio
program director; corporation executive
Address: b. 1697 Broadway, New York City;
h. Rumson, N. J.

To a radio audience estimated variously at
from 15 to 37 million listeners, the mention of
fate suggests *Major Bowes' Original Amateur
Hour* and the "genial, slightly unctuous voice"
of its master of ceremonies, Major Edward
Bowes. His "Around and around she goes
and where she stops nobody knows," might

EDWARD BOWES

well be a paraphrase of Confucius' statement,
"The Wheel of Fortune turns round incessantly, and who can say to himself, 'I shall
today be uppermost'?"

The Wheel of Fortune has been kind to the
Major. In 1939 radio gossip placed his net
income at no less than $15,000 weekly. Other
estimates brought it nearer $10,000. United
States Treasury reports disclosed that the
Major's income in 1937 as executive director
of Edmar Enterprises was $427,817. In real
estate and other business ventures for more
than half a century, this phase of his career

has been obscured by the figure of Major
Bowes, radio impresario.

Edward Bowes was born in 1874 in
San Francisco, the son of John M. and Caroline Amelia (Ford) Bowes. His earliest memory is of his father, a public official, weighing
cargoes of spice, cotton and rubber on the
San Francisco water front. His father died
when Edward was six, leaving the support
of himself and his three sisters in the hands
of their mother. Formal education ended for
him at 13 when he was graduated from Lincoln Grammar School. It was not long before young Edward got his first job, and
from that time on enterprise marked his career
in business, as it was to distinguish his rapid
rise in radio. He quickly turned to advantage
his job as usher at a National Education Association Convention by writing calling cards in
flowing Spencerian script, decorated with fan-
ciful birds, which he sold to visitors for 25
cents a dozen. His next job as office boy in a
real estate concern at $3 a week catapulted
him right into the real estate business and by
1900 he was a successful businessman. In
1903 he married an actress, Margaret Illington,
and they enjoyed a happy, almost idyllic marriage until her death in 1934.

Major Bowes served on the grand jury
which exposed local corruption in San Francisco in 1904, and was active in the successful
anti-vice crusade which created such a stir
nationally that Theodore Roosevelt sent William J. Burns, private detective, out to the
coast to lend his assistance. With the subsequent trials over, Bowes made a pilgrimage to his ancestral home in the North of
Ireland, where his grandfather had been a
Methodist minister. He returned home just
in time for the great earthquake of 1906. The
fire that followed this destructive quake turned
to ashes much of Edward Bowes' investments
in real estate. It was a time to act fast or
not at all. His reaction was to draw up
plans for a new office building, choosing a location that he believed had a future. This
decision turned out to be correct, and with
business running smoothly, Bowes came to
New York.

In the Eastern metropolis he went into
business with John Cort and Peter McCourt.
Jointly they owned and operated the Cort
Theatre in New York and the Park Square
Theatre in Boston. In 1918 he joined with
Messmore Kendall in building the Capitol
Theatre, a venture that led indirectly to the
famous *Amateur Hour*—in 1922, when radio
was young, a weekly broadcast called *Roxy
and His Gang* was used to promote the theatre,
and when Roxy left in 1925 the program continued as *Major Bowes' Capitol Family*. Into
this program he injected bits of homely philosophy and an occasional poem that was highly
sentimental and moral in tone. These verses
were published in 1937 in a volume called
Verses I Like. The concert orchestra featured at the Capitol is said to have influenced
motion picture theatres all over the country.

During the 1920's Major Bowes was associated with the Selwyn Company in the

production of plays, was manager of radio station WHN (owned by Loew's, Incorporated) and was also vice-president of Goldwyn Pictures Corporation. Thus until 1935 his business interests were far more important than his radio career. But in 1934 things had already begun to change, for in that year the Major quietly inaugurated an amateur hour over WHN. In 1935 he resigned as vice-president of Goldwyn Pictures Corporation and on March 24th of that year *Major Bowes' Original Amateur Hour,* sponsored by Standard Brands for Chase & Sanborn, had its debut over the 60 stations of NBC's Red Network.

Since that historic date more than 300 performances of the *Amateur Hour* have been given, presenting more than 8,000 hopeful amateurs out of an estimated 117,000 auditions (CBS figures). Of the 8,000 and more who have signed the Major's "amateur's oath"— bell ringers, toothbrush players, musical sawyers, jug players, tap dancers and vocalists—most went back home, taking with them the memory of one shining moment in show business. Twice as many men apply for auditions as women. Of those selected the majority are singers, then instrumentalists, mimics, vocal and instrumental combinations. A successful applicant usually receives $10 for his appearance, plus all that he or she can eat the night of the broadcast.

The program actually gets under way with the auditions. To these Major Bowes listens through a loud-speaker in his pretentiously Victorian office as the applicants are auditioned in various studios. When the program goes into rehearsal all visitors are barred from the studio. On one occasion NBC's vice-president in charge of production was almost forcibly ejected by the Major's chauffeur and bodyguard from the studio where the Major was at work.

During and after each broadcast telephone operators in New York and in the "honor city" of that particular week receive and record the votes for performers. Sometimes as many as 16 units of 20 to 25 amateur graduates are on tour at a time. Salaries for the performers range from $50 to $100 weekly. In addition to the road units and the managerial and travel expenses for them, a staff of 65 is maintained in New York. Overhead for the *Bowes' Hour* also includes bills for musicians, producers, coaches and unit booking.

When Bowes changed sponsors in 1936, going to the Chrysler Corporation on the CBS network, it was rumored that his new sponsor had enticed him with an offer of $15,000 weekly. To these rumors Major Bowes' office let it be known that the Major and the late Walter Chrysler were old friends and that his relations with his sponsor were "of the happiest." Speculation persisted, naturally enough, and in 1939 radio business covertly estimated his weekly (gross) income at $20,000 plus another $10,000 to $15,000 from theatres for his road company units. The reputation for being a shrewd executive this shift in sponsors gave him is borne out by

the profitable sidelines that have mushroomed from his *Amateur Hour*—games, a magazine, two monthly film shorts (RKO), a Major Bowes alarm clock.

Many amateurs have graduated from the *Amateur Hour* to the professional world of theatre, radio and films. Among those who have since become famous are Clyde Barrie, talented Negro baritone, Doris Weston, who went into motion pictures, and Lucielle Browning, whose voice has been heard at the Metropolitan Opera House. Many, also, are the hopefuls who have been encouraged to develop their talents further, like thirteen-year-old Winfield Cook, Jr., who flunked the program three years ago but came back in 1941 with a set of imitations of sounds that easily won him first place.

Major Bowes is heavy-jowled but by no means flabby, dresses stylishly without being Broadwayish. "He still has most of his finely spun orange-blond hair," said *Time* in describing him, "and skin that seems to have been massaged, steamed and lotioned for days. From any angle his nose is mightier than Jimmy Durante's."

His offices and living quarters, a 14-room apartment in the Capitol Theatre building, are so cluttered with mementos that one writer compared them to a series of Atlantic City auction parlors. Here, or at his estate in Rumson, New Jersey, the Major admires his hundreds of paintings, his fine old silver, his numerous antiques, his collection of colored diamonds set in rings; and he occasionally entertains friends with the contents of a baronial wine cellar.

In his youth the Major's hobbies included yachting, a training stable and automobile racing. He won a 50-mile non-stop race in the days when every racing driver was a daredevil. Yachting remained a hobby until 1940, when he gave his yacht, *Edmar,* to the United States Navy. His interest in books is reflected in the fact that he is vice-president of the Shakespeare Association of America. Many churches and public-spirited organizations have benefited from his gifts. In 1939 he presented to St. Patrick's Cathedral in New York City 15 trees for the sidewalks around it and also an Andrea Del Sarto painting, and during the same year gave an entire estate to the Lutheran Church.

The *Major Bowes' Amateur Hour* is listed among the 10 most popular programs on the air and in this achievement Major Bowes' prestige is recognized to be a big drawing card. People still ask for "that good Major Bowes coffee" even though he left Chase & Sanborn back in 1936. From 210 honor cities, to one of which the program is dedicated each week, he has an array of more than 1,000 honorary titles to go with his Major (which comes from an obsolete Reserve commission of the United States Army).

References
Delineator 127:70 D '35 il por
Etude 57:773-4+ D '39 il por
Lit Digest 120:30 O 5 '35 por
(Continued next page)

BOWES, EDWARD—*Continued*

N Y Sun p19 Ap 22 '41
N Y Times p7 Ap 8 '39; p12 O 20 '39;
  p2 O 21 '39; p9 O 29 '39
Pub W 129:993 F 29 '36
Time 27:63 Je 22 '36 por; 33:30 Ap 3
  '39 por
American Catholic Who's Who
Eichberg, R. Radio Stars of Today p47-
  51 1937
International Motion Picture Almanac
Variety Radio Directory
Who's Who in America

BOWES, MAJOR *See* Bowes, E.

BOWMAN, GEORGE E(RNEST) Jan. 5,
1860—Sept. 6, 1941 Historian; editor; founder,
1896, of the Massachusetts Society of Mayflower Descendants; compiler of historical records and considered authority on the genealogies
of the Mayflower passengers; member of numerous historical, patriotic and Colonial organizations.

References
Who's Who in America
Obituaries
N Y Times p49 S 7 '41

BRACKEN, BRENDAN 1901-   British
Minister of Information
Address: h. 8 Lord North St, London, S. W. 1,
England

BRENDAN BRACKEN

The fourth man since the opening guns of
the Second World War to take over the job
of Britain's Minister of Information, in the
ministry which has been called "the graveyard
of ministerial reputations," was "jerky, be-

spectacled, carrot-haired" Brendan Bracken. In
July 1941 he replaced Alfred Duff Cooper (see
sketch 1940 Annual) in that position. He had
for many months been Parliamentary Private
Secretary to Prime Minister Churchill, and in
1940 became a Privy Councillor.

Of Irish descent, Brendan Bracken was born
in 1901, the son of the late J. K. A. Bracken
of Ardvullen House, Kilmallock. He was educated at Sydney and at Sedbergh. Although
he had admired and worked with Churchill
politically since 1923, it was not until 1929
that he himself was elected a member of
Parliament from North Paddington, running
at that time as a candidate of the Unionist
Party. (He is now a Conservative.) His
name is even better known in journalism than
in the political world. He has been editor,
director or chairman of *Financial News*,
The Banker and *The Economist* as well as
director of a firm that prints Bibles. He has
always taken a great interest in news, particularly as it affects the United States, and *The
Nation* says of him: "As a publisher he understands news and newspapermen. Under his
direction the London *Financial News* was
resurrected to become a model of financial
journalism—critical, courageous and objective.
It was one of the first British newspapers to
grasp and explain the military nature of Nazi
economics."

As Churchill's disciple, Bracken had long
been a scathing critic of appeasement. Conservative Party whips used to call him "the
Red-Headed Beast" during the days when
Churchill led an anti-Chamberlain Conservative
group in Parliament known as "Winston's
Glamour Boys." During the Second World
War he continued to criticize; his *Financial
News* was used "to harass Sir John Simon
for not spending fast enough on British
armament." It is said that he often expressed
distaste for the Ministry of Information position, and it was at one time rumored that if
he took it some head man would be transferred
to that organization.

"Outspoken and direct in manner," Bracken
"shares Churchill's taste for black cigars,
voluminous reading, vigorous talk." And since
he has been in office there has been a new
dash of showmanship in British news and
pictures. His words have also made headlines.
In September 1941 he invited United States
Congressmen to come over and see how lend-
lease materials were being used. "We want
the independents and the critics to come," he
said. "But no peace mongers."

References
Life 11:16 Ag 4 '41 por
N Y Times p4 Jl 18 '41
Newsweek 18:25-6 Jl 28 '41 por
Time 35:30 Je 3 '40 por
Author's and Writer's Who's Who
Who's Who

BRAINERD, NORMAN, pseud. *See* Fuller, S. R., Jr.

BRANDEIS, LOUIS D(EMBITZ)
(brăn'dīs) Nov. 13, 1856—Oct. 5, 1941 Retired
Associate Justice of the Supreme Court;
after graduation from Harvard Law School
practiced law in Boston; engaged in memorable
legal battles, as counsel for a policy holders'
protective committee in the Equitable Insurance
scandal in 1905, as counsel for the National
Consumers League in its endeavor to prove
constitutional an Oregon law limiting the hours
of women workers to 10 a day and in many
other cases involving social legislation; appointment to Supreme Court in 1916 opposed by
leading corporation lawyers because of the
causes in which he had distinguished himself;
on the court often linked in dissents with the
late Justice Holmes and until nearly the end of
his career maintained a position of judicial
liberalism; sided with the Administration 10
times out of 16 in the consideration of major
New Deal laws; resigned from the Supreme
Court in 1939; during most of his early career
intensely interested in Zionism, and interest in
this cause was reawakened in 1938 by the
plight of the German Jews.

WALTER BRENNAN

References

Fortune 13:184+ My '36 por (p84)
Lit Digest 117:9+ Ap 7 '34 pors
Nation 125:330-1 O 5 '27; 132:156-7 F
    11 '31; 133:513-14 N 11 '31; 143:422
    O 10 '36; 143:565-6 N 14 '36; 148:222
    F 25 '39
New Repub 69:4-6 N 18 '31; 72:50 Ag
    24 '32; 89:150 D 2 '36; 92:61-2 Ag
    25 '37
Scrib Mag 87:11-19 Ja '30
Survey G 25:596-7 N '36 por
Time 30:14-15 N 15 '37; 33:11 F 20 '39
U S Law R 70:599-607 N '36; 72:624,
    72:632-6 N '38
Bartlett, R. M. They Did Something
    About It p61-72 1939
De Haas, J. Louis D. Brandeis 1929
Frankfurter, F. Law and Politics p108-
    26 1939
Frankfurter, F. ed. Mr. Justice Bran-
    deis 1932
Lerner, M. Ideas Are Weapons p70-
    112 1939
Lief, A. Brandeis 1936
Mason, A. T. Brandeis: Lawyer and
    Judge in the Modern State 1933
Pearson, D. and Allen, R. S. Nine Old
    Men p163-85 1936
Who's Who in America
Who's Who in American Jewry

Obituaries

N Y Times p1, 9 O 6 '41 por
Time 38:16+ O 13 '41 por

BRENNAN, WALTER (ANDREW)
July 25, 1894- Film actor
Address: b. Samuel Goldwyn Studios, 1041
N. Formosa Ave, Hollywood, Calif; h. North
Hollywood, Calif.

At least one film actor who is a consistent
winner of "Oscars," as Academy Award cups
are affectionately known in Hollywood, has

no reason to fear the march of time. In
fact, another decade or so will probably serve
only to perfect Walter Brennan's virtuosity
in playing various old reprobates and lovable
though spunky old gentlemen in a succession
of other hits.

And he has no desire for stellar billing.
"I'll take second and third billing any week,"
he told Maxine Cook of the New York *World-
Telegram* in June 1940. "Besides, my role in
Come and Get It got me the Academy Award
for a best supporting performance, the first
one given to a supporting player. Next year
Joseph Schildkraut got it. Then I got it the
second time for *Kentucky*. This year it went
to Thomas Mitchell. I figure my role of
Judge Bean in *The Westerner* might get it
for me again, and I'd be the first to have
three Oscars. Say, I'd spoil my chance by
being a star." Brennan got the third Oscar,
at the Academy dinner in March 1941.

Walter Brennan was born in Lynn, Massachusetts, July 25, 1894, the son of William
John and Margaret Elizabeth (Flanagan)
Brennan. From 16 to 20 he studied at the
Swampscott (Massachusetts) High School,
after a period spent roaming the states with
"turkey shows," small-time comedies that tour
the sticks, and working in Maine lumber
camps. He was graduated from Rindge Technical School at nearby Cambridge in 1915, and
when the United States entered the First
World War spent 19 months (1917-1919) in
France with the American Expeditionary Force
in the 101st Field Artillery. In France he
alternated stints at the front line with performances in a vaudeville act at soldiers'
gatherings behind the front. According to
Theodore Strauss, writing in the New York
Times: "Mr. Brennan still respects the doughboys as the world's toughest audience. 'They
defied you to be good.'"

BRENNAN, WALTER—*Continued*

Before the War Brennan had worked a while as messenger in the local bank, and his father, an engineer with numerous inventions registered at the Patent Office in Washington, had hoped that Walter would either follow in his own footsteps or continue working in a bank. Brennan did work for a time as an investment broker. He toyed with the idea of going to Guatemala until he learned of the sanitary accommodations there. Relinquishing any dreams of going into the pineapple business, he collected Mrs. Brennan, who as Ruth Caroline Wells had sat behind him all through grade school, and set out for Los Angeles. "As a salesman of suburban lots he chaperoned busloads of customers to the site of the proposed subdevelopments and there harangued them on the beauties of the countryside."

"I made $69 the first week, $79 the second and $89 the third," Brennan told Strauss. "And then for four weeks I didn't make a dime. Later on, in 1921 and 1922, I made a lot of money, until I decided in 1923 that I could make it a lot faster and lost my last nickel. For the next 10 years I was on my uppers. I sold stapling machines, insurance, anything. Now and then I'd make a try at the studios, but I hadn't thought of pictures as a career. No class or respectability."

According to Donald Hough of the New York *Herald Tribune*, Brennan's first break came when he brayed like a donkey for a harassed director, after the latter's real animal actor had been seized by a fit of temperament and refused to perform. The relieved director offered Brennan a bit part at $25 the next day.

"For some time after that he played small character roles until finally the part of Old Atrocity in *Barbary Coast* made him the most sought-after character actor in Hollywood. Parts came thick and fast after that. He made another hit as one of the principals in *The Three Godfathers*; then, in *Come and Get It*, in 1936, he won the Academy Award for the best supporting performance of the year. Then came *Banjo on my Knee*, *Buccaneer*, *The Texans*; and just two years after he had won the first supporting award, he won another for outstanding work as Uncle Peter Goodwin in *Kentucky*."

Continues Hough: "When Brennan was walking the streets, back in his braying days, he got acquainted with a chap who was just coming into fame. A fellow from Montana, Gary Cooper [see sketch this issue]. They became friends—have been ever since; and it is more than accidental that they played in a number of pictures together. First there was *The Wedding Night*, later *The Cowboy and the Lady*, and [then] *The Westerner*. Brennan played a minor role for all it was worth in *Northwest Passage*, then carried the film *Maryland* on his own bent old shoulders." His last two pictures with Gary Cooper were *Meet John Doe*, and *Sergeant York*. In the three years prior to June 1940, Brennan appeared in seventeen films.

At home on his ranch, he told Maxine Cook, he has one of the finest wives a man can have, and three children: a daughter named Ruth Caroline and two sons, Arthur Wells and Walter Andrew Brennan, Jr. "I don't go out nights. I get through with one picture, start on another, and with a wife and children and a nice home I don't need anything else. Besides, the man who saves his money out there doesn't have to worry about slipping back. I watch these fellows make a few dollars, get all puffed up and first thing they know they're out in the cold. I work for it, save it, and, I tell them, that's why I've got it. I could stick a pin in some of these stuffed shirts."

An important reason for Brennan's success is that he is always in character when on the lot. With Alexander Kahn, a United Press writer, he went to lunch one day while working on *Maryland*. "He walked to the cafe with the labored walk of a man [of 70], eased his apparently creaking bones into a chair and ordered his meal in a semi-senile voice. 'If you knew what a job it is to assume an aged character like this,' he explained, 'you would understand why I don't dare step out of it during the day. If I stepped out of character during the lunch hour, I would have a heck of a time getting back into it during the first few scenes after lunch.' "

Though Brennan is well over six feet tall, he can appear as short as five feet four, especially when dumped down into one of the assortment of old pants which he keeps hanging in his garage. By removing all or parts of his set of artificial teeth (his own went when he was gassed in the War; what were left were accidentally knocked out by an extra man's boot) he can push his face into varying shapes. "I wear misfits in all my pictures. Have a hard time getting past the gatemen at any stage I'm working on without my make-up because I wait until I get dressed up to stand up straight. Why, I've never played myself in a film."

Standing up straight, however, Walter Brennan is a pleasant-looking man with light blue eyes and few gray hairs in his head. "Good parts, that's what I want. I'm satisfied with second or third billing," he told Theodore Strauss, adding with a wink: "After all, there isn't any romance for the public in a guy with a pan like mine."

In February 1941 Brennan's unmistakable voice was heard over the air in *Destry Rides Again*, on the Columbia Network's *Screen Guild Theatre*. He played Washington Disdale, the town drunk who is elected sheriff and appoints Destry his deputy.

References

Motion Pict 54:50+ Ag '37 pors
N Y Herald Tribune X p13 O 20 '40 pors
N Y Times IX p4 Je 9 '40
N Y World-Telegram p7 Je 8 '40 pors
Photoplay 53:31 Jl '39 por; 18:100-1 Mr '41 por (p46)

International Motion Picture Almanac
Who's Who in America

BREUER, MARCEL (broi'yĕr) May 21,
1902- Architect; educator
Address: b. 1430 Massachusetts Ave, Cambridge, Mass; h. Woods End Road, Lincoln,
Mass.

Although perhaps best known as the inventor of tubular steel furniture in 1925 and
more recently (1935) of furniture in plywood,
Marcel Breuer has won a reputation among
architects in America equal to that of Walter
Gropius and Frank Lloyd Wright (see sketches this issue). Born in Hungary, trained
in Germany, Breuer has lived in the United
States since 1937, when he became an associate
professor in the Department of Architecture
at Harvard University, where he works in
partnership with Gropius. He is particularly
interested in the adaptation of modern architecture to American needs and technical possibilities.

Internationally educated in the living tradition of modern architecture from its beginning, Marcel Breuer was born in Pécs, a
Hungarian provincial capital, May 21, 1902,
the son of Jacques and Franciska (Kan)
Breuer. He was graduated from the local
Gymnasium in 1920. His father was a middle-
class doctor; but at 18 young Breuer had ambitions to be a sculptor. He went first to
the Art Academy in Vienna, and soon found
the teaching there inadequate. Later, while
working in the office of an architect, he heard
about the newly established school of arts,
the Bauhaus, at Weimar, Germany.

Architect Walter Gropius, reorganizer of
the Bauhaus, held a concept of the crafts as
technics in his theory of education; besides
"experimental" artists, like Klee and Kandin-
sky, he welcomed the cooperation of students
such as Bayer, Albers and Breuer. As a student Breuer advanced so rapidly (he received
his Master of Architecture degree in 1924)
that he soon became qualified as a professor
(1925) in the newly founded Bauhaus at
Dessau. His earliest published work was in
the Bauhaus yearbook for 1923. His chief
work at this time was in the carpenter shop
at Dessau.

In 1925 Breuer's analysis of the modern
furniture problem led to his invention of the
tubular steel chair in its original form. An
essentially new idea in furniture design, it
was an important contribution toward the
adaptation of modern technics to human needs.
This steel furniture by Breuer was executed
in the Dessau shop; it did not go into commercial production until 1928.

Breuer was in private architectural practice
in Berlin in 1928, at which time he began his
studies on pre-fabricated, low-cost housing.
His aim was low cost plus a high quality of
design in color, form and materials. His
first published architectural project was for
a small, pre-fabricated steel house, *Klein-
metallhaus Typ 1926*, having as constructive
principle a light metal skeleton, window and
other units set in, to be erected in two or
three weeks.

In Berlin, however, times were difficult for
an ambitious young architect. Breuer's metal

MARCEL BREUER

furniture began to bring him in a fairly good
income, but the political and economic crisis
in Germany forced him to leave the country.
From 1931 to 1935 he traveled—in Spain,
North Africa, Greece, England and the middle
of continental Europe—working now and
again at various jobs and on various publications. He took part also in the organization
of the International Congress of Modern
Architecture.

He had entered designs for private interiors
at the Paris Exhibition at the Grand Palais
in 1930, and in the Berlin Bauhaustellung of
1931. But more important in his development
had been his larger, purely architectural projects, notably one for rebuilding the Potsdam-
erplatz in Berlin in 1928. In this he made
independent use of the clover-leaf intersection
which was to become, in later years, the
major technic of advanced highway design.
Other projects of this period (1929-30) had
been for a large hospital, a factory and the
Kharkov Theatre. The hospital "took startling advantage of skeleton construction to
produce a thin-terraced building of which the
rising stories projected at the rear as they
receded at the front. This ingenious device
for hospitals has since been introduced by
other architects."

From his travels in Spain and Morocco in
1931 Breuer gained, architecturally, what one
of his critics, Mr. Henry-Russell Hitchcock,
Jr., calls "greater suavity" and "more Latin
clarity" of form, in contrast to the "extreme
articulation" of the Russian Kharkov Theatre
and other earlier achievements. Hence his
first important executed work, the Harnisch-
macher house in Wiesbaden in 1932, shows
differences: the creation of a markedly independent architectural personality, making original use of varying levels. "This first house
of Breuer's justly took rank at once as one
of the finest modern houses in the world."

BREUER, MARCEL—*Continued*

Photographs of it were widely published in the periodicals of many different countries.

The next year saw Breuer's construction of the blocks of flats in the Dolderthal, Zurich. Studies of these, published in the *Architectural Record* (October 1936) and in the *Architectural Review* (February 1937), show "an ingenious and agreeable use of oblique forms" that vary and enhance the main rectangular forms; a structural expression "combining in a wholly personal synthesis the articulation of the North and the unbroken surfaces of the South." Like the Wiesbaden house, these flats were also accepted as a "classic of contemporary architecture." Breuer is said to be most pleased, however, by the fact that they were soon 100 per cent rented, while others nearby were only 70 per cent occupied.

Two new types of furniture, following his steel tube furniture, were produced by Breuer: aluminum, first designed in 1933, and plywood, initiated in 1935. The latter, together with the work of Aalto in the same medium, constitutes an important contemporary achievement. It has as many or more structural advantages as steel, and represents a return to the use of traditional, more acceptable, material.

In 1935 Breuer went to England, where he entered into partnership with F. R. S. Yorke in London. Notable among his British commissions was his project for a "Garden City of the Future," exhibited at Olympia, of which the most original unit was the Shopping Center, "consisting of a continuous spiral ramp, with the individual lines of shops along the ramp projecting out at the rear so that all may be approached from the open front terraces as from a street." The Ganes Pavilion at the Royal Horticultural Exhibit was also largely the work of Breuer. In this he employed glass screens of wall height and internal screen partitions of plywood.

The work that now engages Breuer in this country has commanded much interest. That interest on the part not only of architectural experts but of the general public was aroused by his exhibition at Harvard's Robinson Hall in July 1938, where many models and photographs of his designs were shown. According to a report in *Time* (August 1, 1938), "visitors were impressed most by the variety and ingenuity of architect Breuer's projects. They range from a great 'Garden City of the Future' to chairs made of plywood. They include his multiplying glass window—a group of small round windows, each curved like a camera lens, so that the same scene appears in a different focus, or from a different angle, in each panel. Associated with Gropius in designing houses as well as in teaching, Breuer is considered the more imaginative and intuitive of the two architects, Gropius the more logical and precise."

Breuer's work has appeared in three books published in London: *The Modern Flat* (1937); *Circle;* and *The Flat* (1939). As Gropius' partner, buildings and interiors designed by him include: in Massachusetts, the Gropius house in Lincoln, the Hagerty house in Cohasset, the Chamberlain house in Wayland; furnishings for a dormitory at Bryn Mawr College, Pennsylvania; project for the Black Mountain College in North Carolina; the Pennsylvania exhibition at the New York World's Fair; and the New Kensington, Pennsylvania, defense housing project consisting of 250 units, built in 1941.

With short-clipped brown hair, keen blue eyes and the figure of an athlete—not always a physical characteristic of architects—it is not surprising that Breuer's outdoor hobbies are skiing and tennis. When not busy at his desk with plans for building, Breuer paints. He was married in 1940 to Constance Crocker Leighton. The Breuers live in a house of his own design in Lincoln, Massachusetts.

References

> Arch Forum 67:sup 12 N '37 por (sup 10) ; 74:145 Mr '41 por
> Arch Rec 80:243 O '36 por; 84:57-9 S '38 il
> Art Digest 15:16 Ja 1 '41
> House & Gard 77:46-7+ Ap '40 por
> Time 32:19 Ag 1 '38 il por

BREWSTER, BENJAMIN, BISHOP Nov. 25, 1860—Feb. 2, 1941 Episcopal Bishop who entered the ministry in 1887 and was head of Maine Diocese since 1916; a vigorous exponent of "militant Christianity" and a noted liberal in religion, politics and economics.

References

> Who's Who in America

Obituaries

> N Y Times p17 F 3 '41

BREWSTER, CHAUNCEY BUNCE, BISHOP Sept. 5, 1848—Apr. 9, 1941 Protestant Episcopal bishop of the Connecticut Diocese for 29 years until 1928 and oldest living alumnus of Berkeley Divinity School, now Yale University; descendant of Elder William Brewster of Plymouth, Massachusetts; noted liberal leader who was an ardent advocate of the League of Nations after the First World War and a foe of prohibition.

References

> Stowe's Clerical Directory of the American Church 1932
> Who's Who Among North American Authors
> Who's Who in America

Obituaries

> N Y Times p24 Ap 10 '41 por

BRIDGE, FRANK Feb. 26, 1879—Jan. 11, 1941 British composer of chamber music who was regarded as one of the better modern composers and whose works were especially used by string quartets; had been guest conductor of the Rochester, New York Symphony

Orchestra; was also violist with several ensemble groups.

References

Baker's Biographical Dictionary of Musicians 1940
Ewen, D. ed. Composers of Today 1936
Pierre Key's Musical Who's Who
Thompson, O. ed. International Cyclopedia of Music and Musicians 1939
Who's Who

Obituaries

Christian Cent 58:200 F 5 '41
N Y Herald Tribune p36 Ja 12 '41
Variety 141:54 Ja 15 '41

BRIDGES, ROBERT July 13, 1858—Sept. 2, 1941 Editor and writer; started his career as a journalist and poet; joined *Scribner's Magazine* at the time of its founding in 1887 and became editor in 1914; retired in 1930; author of *Bramble Brae,* a collection of poems, *Overheard in Arcady* and *Suppressed Chapters;* pen name "Droch."

References

Scrib Mag 101:23 Ja '37 por
Survey 57:430 Ja 1 '27 por

Leaders in Education 1941
Who's Who Among North American Authors
Who's Who in America
Who's Who in Journalism

Obituaries

N Y Herald Tribune p16 S 3 '41 por
Pub W 140:926 S 13 '41

BROOK, ALEXANDER July 14, 1898- Artist

Address: c/o Rehn Galleries, 683 Fifth Ave, New York City; h. 14 Factors Walk, Savannah, Ga.

To most minds the Odyssey of success in art, as in other fields, is marked with struggle and drama. The career of Alexander Brook appears to have little of either. In Hollywood in 1940 he did a full-length portrait of Katharine Hepburn. Thoroughly modern, it also suggested traditional figure portraiture, and it was widely hailed as another triumph in the career of this artist.

Recent successes have revived the concept of Brook as "the unstruggling artist." In the surface flow of events there has been much to support this contradictory appellation. Brook himself has said: "I haven't jumped any freight cars, I haven't had any desire to go roaming about. I have had no adventures. I find that my life, like my painting, can be realized on the back porch." A person of tremendous vitality, he looks upon life, as one writer put it, "with the gusto of a hungry man about to eat a large dinner." His blunt attitudes are the opposite of those of a professional portrait painter, and through his career runs an undercurrent of determination. Of portraiture he says quite characteristically: "If I don't like it I'll destroy it.

ALEXANDER BROOK

If you don't like it I'll keep it and sell it as a painting."

Alexander Brook was born in Brooklyn, New York, of long-lived antecedents. His great-grandmother died at the age of 113, while dancing at a wedding, and one of her daughters lived to be almost 100! His father was O. Gregory and his mother Eudoxia (Gelescu) Brook. Alexander had five older sisters. When he was nine his family moved to Manhattan. At the age of 12 he was stricken with infantile paralysis, as a consequence of which he still has a slight limp. Bedridden for months, he asked for a set of paints with which to occupy himself. These were brought to him, along with the palette he uses today, by a Van Dycked and frock-coated neighbor who made his living painting portraits in oil from photographs. Under the old man's direction young Alex did his first oil on canvas, a picture of a battleship and a spot of land. His career was decided upon. He would be an artist.

His teacher, he wrote, "came two or three times a week and sketched for me, in the twinkling of an eye and with the assurance of a statistician, a sunset, a turgid sea or some poetic autumnal scene, all flourishingly signed, which I in turn copied as accurately as possible." Nor was faith hard to come by. "Every child who chooses to paint at the age of 12," he put it, "invariably shows a great aptitude and remarkable ability. I was no exception. At that time, and in the vernacular, painting was a cinch."

Apart from a short stay at the Pratt Institute in Brooklyn, New York, Alexander Brook's training in art got under way when he went to the Art Students League in 1915. At the League he won a scholarship and almost every prize within reach of a student. His principal teacher was Kenneth Hayes Miller, whom one critic calls the "tutorial father of modern American art." One sees the erstwhile pupil of this teacher in the statement of Brook that a working credo might be: "To add more to the quality of a picture

BROOK, ALEXANDER—*Continued*

and produce more," and: "A picture should represent a surprising experience completed; the more succinctly it is realized, the greater pleasure it will give to the sympathetic beholder."

A sensitive, long-haired art student, Brook did a self-portrait that contrasts strikingly with the Neroesque person who went to Hollywood in the summer of 1940 to paint Dick Powell's two children. He pointed to this change himself when a critic contrasted the robust quality of his mature painting with the pale figures of his youthful work. "I guess it's because I used to be thin and pale myself. Now I'm fatter and more robust, so things naturally look fatter to me."

Halfway through the League in 1917, Brook made his first sale. At an auction at the Penguin Club, a painting called *The Widow* fetched $12.50, and its buyer was Jules Pascin, a gratifying detail to an art student. His second sale, two years later, was a landscape. This went for $50 to an anonymous purchaser who later turned out to be one of America's leading painters. In 1920 he married Peggy Bacon (see sketch 1940 Annual) and took to the uncertain business of trying to make a living at his vocation. Here again was a period of illness and suffering, about which Brook doesn't talk much.

When his health improved Brook resumed painting. One of his canvases at an Independents' exhibit caught the attention of Brummer, connoisseur and art dealer, and in 1923 a joint exhibit was arranged for Brook and Peggy Bacon. Since then he has exhibited constantly. Harry Salpeter estimated that in museums throughout the country Brook had had more one-man shows than any other living American, and that many of his single paintings had been shown five and six times apiece. In 1923 Forbes Watson, editor of *The Arts,* asked to do an article about him. Brook countered with the proposal that he himself do an article—at space rates. That first article was on Toulouse-Lautrec and contained an attack against studio preciosity. Today he himself has to look back upon a period when he was regarded as a studio painter. "I think it's true," he once admitted. "But I can't help it. A painter can be a good painter if he's true to himself. Then it doesn't matter whether he's a studio painter, an outdoor painter, or a social painter."

A valuable contact was his meeting with Juliana Force (see sketch this issue), now the director of the Whitney Museum of American Art. Under her, he was assistant director of the Whitney Studio Club from 1924 to 1927. And if, in this capacity, his enterprise, interest and friendliness toward the work of other artists put them in his debt, it also placed him squarely in the front ranks of young Americans. He had background and creative vigor. But often these virtues never make themselves known. In this sense, perhaps, Brook was better placed than many artists. It was he who could help Raphael

Soyer (see sketch this issue), from this practical point of view, and not vice versa.

A successful artist at 30, it was nevertheless possible for Brook to say in 1936—when he was 38—that in his entire career he had sold only 100 paintings. (Of course, this is by no means extreme. Van Gogh could count his lifetime sales on his fingers.) For some years he supplemented this uncertain income with teaching jobs, principally at the Art Students League. But beginning in 1929 economic need was no longer foremost. In that year he won a $2,500 prize at the Chicago Art Institute—which also honored him with a one-man show. In 1930 at the Carnegie International (Pittsburgh) show he won second prize as well as the Albert C. Lehman Award, a total of $3,500 in addition to the purchase price of the painting. In 1931 he was given the Temple Gold Medal (PAFA) and went to Europe on a Guggenheim Fellowship. His only other trip abroad was a holiday jaunt. But he has been up and down and around America, painting the lush landscapes of Woodstock, New York, the sardonic loneliness of a pasture north of San Francisco and the mute human poverty of a Georgia jungle.

In his approach to subject matter Brook has always had three distinct phases in his work. First, there is the studio phase, whether of still life or of posed models. Second, there are the portraits. He first got into this field by doing studies of friends, such as his portrait of George Biddle, and charmingly informal canvases of his growing children, Sandy and Belinda. He also did several portraits of Peggy Bacon, from whom he was divorced in the year 1940. A third phase of his work consists of landscapes. These are brighter today, less somber in tone, but he still sees a mood in a landscape.

In the 1930's, particularly under the influence of Miller—who had taught many of them—a number of American artists adapted the technique of under-painting. (The revival of this technique is credited generally to the European theoretician, Max Doerner.) Brook describes his method of painting as follows: "My method or technique is a simple one. On a canvas prepared with a white ground, I apply a thin, transparent warm tone or veil; I then make my drawing in charcoal on the toned canvas. Then I paint with either an egg or casein emulsion, using only white, depending on the tone for shadows and form. The completed under-painting is complete in every way but for the color. When it is thoroughly dry I paint as thinly and as directly as I can with oil paints, using to advantage whatever happy accident the under-painting offers."

In recent years critics speak of the increased richness of his palette, its complexity, its gradations of tone and refinements of color. To this might be added the more commonplace observation that in the late 1930's Brook got away from the studio, looking at life with renewed freshness, putting into practice his own words: "We are becoming interested in ourselves and our surroundings, in our own particular brand of civilization."

On the negative side, critics have suspected Brook now and again of being "fluent rather than explorative" (New York *Sun*), and Jewell once pointed out that certain pictures —*Children's Luncheon,* for example—"expose themselves to the criticism that opulence has lured the artist into over-diffused, insufficiently disciplined statement."

Although Brook recently completed a mural for a Washington, D. C. postoffice and has done some graphic work, he is best known as an easel painter. He lives in Savannah, Georgia, with his second wife Libby (Berger) Brook, whom he married in California in 1940. Normal social interests and a zest for living characterize him, but if you asked Brook his favorite hobby it would probably be that of many artists—throw an easel and a box of paints in the back of the car and just drive off aimlessly until something new and interesting in the landscape induces one to stop.

In his early 40's Alexander Brook is vigorously youthful, a little Roman in appearance, with clear blue eyes and closely cropped sandy hair. In her incisive prose Peggy Bacon spoke of him as: "Big hooked nose like a weapon. Fierce blue eyes beneath a cliff of brow, with the black look of an animal glaring from its lair, a violent stare compound of rage and gaiety, slightly berserk. Bull neck, broad shoulders and an air of force and energy. Mercurial, overbearing and intense. A stiff proposition."

Widely exhibited, Alexander Brook is also represented in the permanent collections of 21 museums throughout the country, including the Metropolitan Museum of Art, Museum of Modern Art and Brooklyn Museum in New York City; Art Institute, Chicago; Corcoran Gallery of Art, Washington, D. C.; Museum of Fine Arts, Boston; and the San Francisco Museum, San Francisco. He is affiliated with the Modern Artists of America and with the Society of Independent Artists.

References

Am Mag Art 27:520-9 O '34 il por; 29:112 F '36 il
Art Digest 11:23 Je '37
Creative Art 5:713-18 O '29 il
Esquire 6:105-7+ O '36 il
Life 10:50-2 Ja 13 '41 il pors
Living Am Art Bul p1-2 Ap '39
London Studio 18 (Studio 118):19-21 Jl '39 il
Mag Art 32:248 Ap '40 por
Jewell, E. A. Alexander Brook 1931
Murrell, W. Alexander Brook 1922
New Standard Encyclopedia of Art
Who's Who in American Art

BROOKE, SIR ALAN (FRANCIS) July 23, 1883- Commander in chief of the British Home Forces

Address: Government House, Salisbury, England

Whether or not the Germans will ever attempt an invasion of England is known only to the gods and Hitler—and perhaps only to the gods.

SIR ALAN BROOKE

But if they ever do, the British Army will immediately spring into action under the command of Sir Alan Francis Brooke, since July 1940 commander in chief of the Home Forces. He is an officer whose chief reputation rests on his skill in artillery, but has served in cavalry, commanded infantry and had the kind of experience which makes him "the best all-round officer in Britain."

In his years in the Army, Brooke, whom the soldiers call "Wizard," has taken what the Liverpool *Daily Post* calls "the most modern and scientific view of warfare." He has been responsible for many advances in artillery practice and in large part for the mechanization of the British Army. In action, he won a knighthood for his efficiency in carrying out the retreat from Dunkirk—"it was due to his rapid decision and energetic action that a defensive flank was formed to meet the situation created when the Belgian Army ceased fighting." And the "job he did in one week, of whipping together the Southern command out of tens of thousands of exhausted men who were landed back in England, scattered at different ports when Germany was expected to follow them across the Channel at any moment, was called 'the major feat of organization in British Army history.'"

Like many another important British soldier, Brooke comes from Ireland, from the Ulster Protestant county of Fermanagh, where there is a family seat at Colebrook belonging to his nephew, Sir Basil Brooke, Minister of Agriculture in the Government of Northern Ireland.

BROOKE, SIR ALAN—*Continued*

His father, the late Sir Victor Brooke, baronet, was an Irish landowner who couldn't live in the damp Irish climate because of a lung infection and moved to Pau in France. Here, for many years, he was master of the local hounds, a pack supposed to be descendants of hounds hunted by the Duke of Wellington's officers in the Peninsular War.

Alan Francis Brooke was born at Baguères de Bigorre, France, and sent to a private school in Pau. However, he spent his holidays in Ireland, where he learned to be an excellent angler and one of the ten best shots in Great Britain. He received his elementary soldiering education at the Royal Military Academy in Woolwich, from which, in 1902, he passed as a subaltern into the Royal Field Artillery. After four years' service in Ireland, Brooke went to India, was transferred to the Royal Horse Artillery in 1909 and stayed there until the outbreak of the First World War. In India he reveled in sports, especially pigsticking, and he is "one of the few men who can claim to have ridden down and speared a wolf from horseback."

In September 1914 Brooke, then a captain, landed at Marseille with the Secunderabad Cavalry Brigade, in command of an ammunition column. By February 1915 he was adjutant of the second Indian Brigade, R. H. A.; in November of that year he became brigade major of the 18th division of artillery; and by February 1917 he was a major with "red tabs"—on the staff of the Royal Artillery Canadian Corps. In July 1918 he rose to be general staff officer of the first grade and he served with the Royal Artillery of the First Army until March 1919. During the War, Brooke invented a barrage map for directing artillery fire which came into wide use. Seven times he was mentioned in dispatches, and he won the D. S. O. with bar and the Belgian Croix de Guerre.

Home again in England in April 1919 Brooke was sent to take an instruction course at the Staff College at Camberley. From 1920 to 1923 he was general staff officer, second grade, to the Northumbrian division of the territorial army and from 1923 to 1927 he was at the Staff College with the same rank. Then, in 1927, he went to the Imperial Defence College as army instructor and for the next seven years he was engaged entirely in the study and exposition of modern strategy and tactics and artillery work, first at the School of Artillery and later at the Imperial Defence College again. He was a first-rate teacher— "he has a supple mind; his views are broad and he puts a premium on the ability to think for oneself."

Since January 1923 Brooke had been a full colonel and in June 1935, when he was in command of the 8th Infantry Brigade, he was raised to the rank of major general and transferred to the War Office as inspector of the Royal Artillery. It wasn't long before his teaching ability got him promoted to the position of director of Military Training at the War Office. Then, in 1937, an entirely new Mobile Division was formed, and because of

his specialization in mechanical warfare Brooke was an obvious choice for its first commander.

The international situation was already becoming blacker and blacker, and one of Britain's main concerns was anti-aircraft protection. In June 1938 Brooke was made a lieutenant general and placed in charge of the Territorial Anti-Aircraft Corps. A year later he was for a short time general officer commanding the Anti-Aircraft Command; in 1940 he was made general officer in charge of the Southern Command.

As soon as the Second World War broke out and until the evacuation from Dunkirk in which he figured so brilliantly, Brooke was on service in Belgium. Before his command went out he told his staff: "You have all read your military text books, and don't ever forget what's in them; but you must think for yourselves, for this is a war of new methods." During the first months of comparative stagnation he wasn't merely a military-minded officer—he used to require one of his staff officers to give a talk on the world situation each week. After Dunkirk, after days of sharing perils with his men, he was given the post he now holds.

The London *Daily Telegraph* describes Brooke as having "a firm lip and far-seeing eye," and according to the London *Daily Mail* "he looks like a businessman. He has a clipped mustache and horn-rimmed glasses and a sense of humor. And that's just what he is—a soldier who still believes in the methods of business." He is married to Benita Pelly Lees and has four children, one son and daughter being the children of his first marriage to Jane Mary Richardson.

On December 25, 1941 he will succeed Sir John Dill (see sketch this issue) as chief of the British Imperial General Staff.

References

Britain Today 32:5-7 Ag 23 '40 por
Manchester Guardian Jl 22 '40
Time 36:18 Jl 29 '40 por (p16); 36:32-3 Ag 5 '40 por (cover)
Who's Who

BROOKE-POPHAM, SIR ROBERT (MOORE) (brŏŏk-pŏp'-ăm) Sept. 18, 1878- Air Chief Marshal of the R. A. F.; British commander in chief in the Far East

Address: General Headquarters, Singapore, India

Sir Robert Brooke-Popham arrived in Singapore on November 14, 1940 to take command of all the British forces in the Far East. After transferring Singapore to a military powerhouse, after consulting informally with American Army and Navy chiefs at Manila and defense leaders in Australia and the Netherlands East Indies, he was able to announce firmly: "We're ready for anything and anyone." In December 1941 Brooke-Popham and the forces under him were better prepared than ever when Japan declared war on Great Britain and the United States.

When he took over this command at the age of 62, Brooke-Popham had a longer

record of service with the R. A. F. than
any other man engaged in the Second World
War. One of the earliest of all British pilots,
his royal Aero Club certificate No. 108, he was
one of the first pilots to cross the German
lines in the First World War. He has been
a fighting pilot, instructor, production expert, staff college commandant, officer commanding air regions both at home and abroad
and member of air missions to Canada and to
South Africa.

Born at Mendlesham, Suffolk, Robert
Brooke is the son of the late Henry Brooke
of Wetheringsett Manor, Suffolk, and his
wife Dulcibella, daughter of the late Reverend
Robert Moore. (He assumed the additional
name of Popham by Royal Licence in 1904,
only to find himself christened "Brookham"
by his colleagues.) Brooke-Popham was educated at Haileybury, a well known public
school, and went from there to Sandhurst,
the military college, from which in 1898 he
entered the Oxfordshire Light Infantry as
a subaltern. By the outbreak of the First
World War he had reached the rank of
captain.

Before then, in 1912, he had combined with
other adventurous young officers to form an
Air Battalion of the Royal Engineers, this
at a time when airplanes were rickety contraptions of wire and canvas, liable to crash
on the slightest provocation. The War Department, which felt, and rightly, that flying
was a desperate adventure, refused any official
recognition to these men, but did smile
tolerantly at them. Despite gentle tolerance,
before long the Royal Flying Corps had
been formed from this nucleus, its function
to look after land operations while the Royal
Naval Air Service dealt with operators over
the sea. Brooke-Popham was made an instructor in the R. F. C. and when the War
broke out was sent to France.

As early as November 1914 Brooke-Popham
had won the Legion of Honor for gallantry,
and early in 1915 he won his majority and
the D. S. O. Throughout the War he continued flying with great daring, accumulating
further decorations, including the Order of
St. Stanislaus and the Air Force Cross. In
the great 1918 retreat he managed to get
cut off at headquarters and was forced to
hide for days in a place singularly ill-adapted
for normal human habitation. He managed
to get out and rejoin the British at Amiens
only after great trials.

Brooke-Popham emerged from this earlier
War with a reputation for being "the best
administrative brain of all our airmen." He
was made a Companion of the Order of St.
Michael and St. George in 1918 and a Companion of the Bath the following year, and
was immediately put to building up the new
R. A. F. First he acted as controller of the
technical department, which was responsible
for aircraft production; then, after a short
time, he became director of research at the
Air Ministry. In 1921 he became commandant
of the R. A. F. Staff College at Cranwell.
There he remained for five years, and it has

SIR ROBERT BROOKE-POPHAM

been said that "like a great headmaster he
left an indelible stamp upon the rising generation of airmen."

In 1926 Brooke-Popham took over the air
command of the fighting area of Great Britain
and remained in charge of it for two years.
Since that time much has been done by other
hands, but to Brooke-Popham belongs much
of the credit for the organization which has
proved its worth in the War. He was knighted
as K. C. B. in 1927 and from 1928 to 1930
was air officer commanding in the Iraq area.
From 1931 to 1933 he returned to the supervision of instruction, as commandant at the
Imperial Defence College, and then from 1933
until 1935 took over the British defence areas
again. He was principal air A. D. C. to the
King from 1933 to 1937.

Brooke-Popham acquired an additional order
of knighthood, the G. C. V. O., in 1935.
In 1935 and 1936 he acted as Inspector General
of the R. A. F., and then in 1937 he was
put on the retired list. He didn't withdraw to private life, however, but took on
the job of Governor of Kenya and distinguished himself as the most successful Governor this province ever had. The day the
Second World War was declared he rounded
up every German in the country, commandeered every plane and worked out a plan for
keeping the farms of this agricultural country
running.

But he was needed in England and brought
home for duty. Less than a month after the
War began he was in Canada on a special
mission which established the Empire Air
Training scheme. This was followed by a
similar mission to South Africa before he
returned to the Air Ministry in June 1940.
Here he established a useful and unconventional "ideas pool" to make the best use of
"wrinkles" evolved by all ranks of flying personnel out of actual air fighting experience.

BROOKE-POPHAM, SIR ROBERT—
Continued

He presided personally at round-table meetings where flying officers, radio operators, gunners, mechanics, navigators and maintenance men met to put forward their ideas.

It was in mid-November 1940 that Brooke-Popham was made the first British commander in chief of the Far Eastern Station, his duties "to consult and cooperate with the Navy in Far Eastern waters, to keep in touch with the commander in chief of India, and to communicate with the Commonwealth and Dominion Governments of Australia and New Zealand." This command marked the first time that an air force office had been given seniority over the other two services and constituted, some commentators felt, a formal recognition of the vital part that air operations now play in warfare.

Brooke-Popham is a lean, hard man with "sandy hair, a rugged face and a penetrating voice" who speaks in "clipped, astringent" accents. He is very methodical, exacting the utmost from his subordinates while still managing to be a good mixer, and is personally popular. He is an excellent horseman. In 1926 he was married to Opal Mary, second daughter of Mr. Edgar Hugonin, and the couple have one son and one daughter.

References

Army Q 42:256-67 Jl '41
Christian Sci Mon p1, 4 N 14 '40 por; p26 N 23 '40 por
N Y Sun p24 F 15 '41
N Y Times p1, 4 Ap 5 '41
Who's Who

BROOKS, MATILDA M(OLDEN-HAUER) Physiologist

Address: b. University of California, Berkeley, Calif; h. 630 Woodmont Ave, Berkeley, Calif.

In 1933 a young man in San Francisco took cyanide of potassium with suicidal intent. This is the swiftest and most deadly of poisons—as any detective story reader knows. Hitherto there had been no effective antidote. But this young man was promptly given an injection of methylene blue—and he recovered. (Later he went away and took cyanide again where nobody could find him, and died; but that was not the fault of the treatment!)

The discoverer of the methylene blue treatment in both cyanide and carbon monoxide poisoning is Dr. Matilda M. Brooks, research associate in biology at the University of California. Her findings were first published in 1932, and ever since then other research workers have been trying to claim the credit for them. The theory had been known since 1919, but no one before Dr. Brooks saw the application to human poisoning cases; there is not the slightest doubt that she was the first to publish the suggestion. She is working now, and has been for several years, on the mechanism of the action—that is, it has been proved that methylene blue does act as an antidote to cyanide and carbon monoxide, but it has not yet been established *how* it acts.

Dr. Brooks was born Matilda Moldenhauer in Pittsburgh, Pennsylvania, toward the end of the nineteenth century. Her parents were both of German descent; she speaks German fluently, has spent much time in Germany, and has had scientific articles published there. She is nevertheless as authentically American as corn on the cob. Her father, Rudolph Moldenhauer, died when she was a child, and her early years were spent struggling to obtain an education. When she was about 15 she moved with her mother, Selma (Neuffer) Moldenhauer, and brothers to Philadelphia, where she was graduated from the Girls' High School. At this time she was a painfully shy, spectacled, almost inarticulate girl with light hair strained back from her forehead, who led her classes in spite of the fact that it was agony for her to recite her lessons in public. Those were hard, dull years; after school she taught music to children at 25 cents an hour, or served in small stores as a salesgirl.

After her graduation the family returned to Pittsburgh, where she received her B. A. and her M. S. degrees at the University of Pittsburgh. Then she went to Harvard University, which gave her a Ph. D. in 1920. Before that, however, in 1917, she had worked as bacteriologist at the Research Institute of the National Dental Association, and that same year had been married to Dr. Sumner Cushing Brooks, a New Englander born in Sapporo, Japan, the son of an agriculturist who helped found the first agricultural college in Nippon. He is now professor of zoology at the University of California.

Ever since their marriage both have worked in close association, though independently. From 1920 to 1924 Dr. Matilda Brooks was assistant biologist in the hygienic laboratory of the United States Public Health Service, and for two years after that associate biologist. Her appointment at the University of California followed, in the same year as her husband's, 1927. From 1927 to 1932 she held a Bache Grant of the National Academy of Sciences, and did research in Bermuda and in the South Seas. In 1930 and 1931 she held the grant of the National Research Council at Naples, also holding the Naples Woman's Table in 1931. She has, besides, made several long tours with her husband—once around the world—and there are very few portions of the planet with which she is not familiar. During 1934 and again in 1936 Dr. Sumner Brooks was very ill, and his wife closed her laboratory and took over his entire course of lectures at the University. The University has a ruling which forbids both husband and wife to hold salaried positions on the faculty; therefore, though all her expenses are provided and her assistants paid, her work as research biologist is purely a gift to science.

Dr. and Mrs. Brooks spend nearly every summer at Woods Hole, where they have long owned a cottage, and where Mrs. Brooks is a member of the corporation of the Marine Biological Laboratory of which her husband is a trustee. During the autumn, winter and spring they live in a house situated in North Berkeley, just on the dividing line between Alameda and Contra Costa Counties. They were their own architects, with very successful results: the heart of the house is a huge living room, with a large fireplace at one end, and flanked by two bedroom wings. Over the garage, which forms an ell, is a large study. Both husband and wife are ardent gardeners, and there is always at least one cat, usually an extremely pampered one. At least one of these was a refugee from the laboratory, where its engaging ways saved it from becoming an experimental animal.

DR. MATILDA M. BROOKS

The animals used by Dr. Brooks in her own experiments are white rats. She tells one story about the time when she returned from a research trip to the South Seas to find that the assistant left in charge had suddenly gone insane and released all the animals, mixing infected and control rats, so that the work had to be done all over again. Before she began her present line of research she did much work in problems of respiration, the antagonism of salts, the effects of arsenic on cells, the permeability of cells and oxidation reduction. In fact, she says, "my work in general is on oxidation reductions in living cells."

In 1940 the Radcliffe chapter of Phi Beta Kappa elected Dr. Brooks to honorary membership. She is also a member of the scientific fraternity, Sigma Xi, and of the Bermuda Biological Corporation, the American Physiological Society, the Society of Experimental Biology and Medicine, and the American Association for the Advancement of Science. She was vice-president of the Western Society of Naturalists in 1929.

This all sounds very formidable, but actually Matilda Brooks is anything but a dry, professorial person. She is tall and robust, with wavy light hair, looks much younger than her age, and in spite of a markedly forthright and direct nature has a touch of childlike naïveté which endears her to her friends. She is very musical, plays the piano well, but her chief

avocation is painting, and she is a not-at-all-bad landscapist. Her hobby is attending furniture auctions, where she is a passionate and shrewd bargainer. She is also an unusually good tennis player and demon car driver, is a member of the Sierra Club, a California mountain-climbing society, and is keenly interested in political and economic questions. Somehow she finds the energy to spend all day in the laboratory, do her own housework and cooking, hold open house on Sunday at tea time for faculty acquaintances, and yet get in all these other things that interest her. An hour and a half every evening, for instance, are sacred to a concert of classical music broadcast by a Berkeley radio station. The Brookses lead a very quiet life between work and home. Very early in life, Mrs. Brooks learned the industry, organization, patience and quiet perseverance which in the old days were basic parts of the German character.

References

American Men of Science
American Women
Who's Who Among North American Authors
Who's Who in the East

BROOKS, ROBERT C(LARKSON) Feb. 7, 1874—Feb. 2, 1941 Educator and author who was nationally known in the field of political and social science; for 33 years served as professor of social sciences at Swarthmore College; during 1940 was elected president of the American Political Science Association, the first professor from a small college ever to be elected to that position; author of many books on politics and education.

References

Leaders in Education 1932
Who's Who in America

Obituaries

N Y Times p21 F 4 '41 por
Sch & Soc 53:177 F 8 '41

BROOKS, VAN WYCK (văn wĭk) Feb. 16, 1886- Author; critic

Address: h. Westport, Conn.

Known today as America's most distinguished literary critic and historian, with *New England: Indian Summer, 1865-1915* (1940) Van Wyck Brooks continues the classic study of the American cultural scene which he began in 1936 with *The Flowering of New England, 1815-1865.* This further assessment and analysis of the American cultural cycle has been called "the richest, most penetrating and significant of his books." The two books are merely the beginning of "a 16-year job of examining the writers of all America," however. Brooks plans to fill four books, giving himself four years for each, and at present is at work upon *The Age of Washington Irving,* which will precede *The Flowering* as the first of the series. Before its publication, in November 1941, however, *The Opinions of Oliver Allston,* first printed in the *New Republic,* appeared and was hailed by Hendrik

BROOKS, VAN WYCK—*Continued*

Willem Van Loon as "the wisest book that has been written on this side of the ocean for many a year." *Indian Summer* was a strong contender for the Pulitzer Prize in 1941, and if chosen would have repeated the record of *The Flowering of New England* in 1937. It was, in fact, the first choice, in the history category of the book reviewers who were asked by the *Saturday Review of Literature* to state their nominations for the Pulitzer Prize.

Van Wyck Brooks was born in Plainfield, New Jersey, February 16, 1886, the son of Charles Edward and Sarah (Ames) Brooks. "I am not myself a New Englander, except in

V. Semler

VAN WYCK BROOKS

part by heredity and in part by adoption," he says in an introduction to *Indian Summer*. His forefathers were an interesting mixture: both grandfathers were Vermonters, both grandmothers were New Yorkers. He says he has never actually felt at home in New England as he has in New York State and in the Hudson Valley. He began writing, however, about Emerson, and one New Englander led to another. With his book on Washington Irving, he feels that he will be on more native ground.

At the age of 12 he went abroad for a year with his parents. This trip awakened his interest in France, an interest continued throughout his life, and its influences are discernible in his numerous translations from the French and in his own literary style. Upon his graduation from Harvard in 1908 with Phi

Beta Kappa honors, he joined the editorial staff of Doubleday, Page & Company, where he remained for a year.

In 1909 he wrote his first book, *The Wine of the Puritans*. It was important because therein he first examined the issues upon which his life's study was to be based. Beginning his search for the "usable past," he stated the concept which he later illustrated in his well-known biographical critiques: that all great art must have roots in a receptive native soil. Almost immediately his contemporaries recognized a fresh and lucid mind at work on significant cultural problems. It continued at work. In 1911 Brooks began teaching at Leland Stanford University, and in the following years came his studies of *John Addington Symonds* (1914); *The World of H. G. Wells* (1915); and *The Malady of the Ideal* (1913), "a collection of essays on European writers . . . in which he dwelt upon figures who were products of a richer, older civilization than ours, yet whose lives illuminated the problems we faced." Finally, when in *America's Coming of Age* (1915) Brooks returned to explore American civilization, he spoke his thesis with an authority and maturity that put him at the head of a new school of criticism.

Called by Stephen Vincent Benét a literary *J'Accuse,* this last work made profound inquiries into the American cultural past and future, both of which had been somewhat fatuously taken for granted. Brooks found that somehow his country had failed as a fertile soil for the seeds of genius, "that in American literature something has always been wanting, that a certain density, weight and richness, a certain poignancy, a something far more deeply interfused, is simply not there." This thesis was further pursued in his *Letters and Leadership* (1918), a study of the hollowness of our culture, the unsatisfying grossness of our life, the deceptiveness of our pursuit of the false goddess Success. Brooks, moreover, followed his reasoning to its logical conclusion: self-fulfillment as an ideal had to be substituted for self-assertion. "On the economic plane," he wrote, "this implies socialism; on every other plane it implies something which a majority of Americans in our day certainly do not possess." He berated the over-extended adolescence of the American mind.

These statements of austere pessimism and rebellion became the platform of a school of liberal and radical writers and critics of the '20s, and their author won a leading position in modern criticism. The young men who read him found him exciting and stimulating, admired the lofty standards he set. "For good or bad," as Bernard Smith said in 1937, "something of Van Wyck Brooks seeped into almost every American critic under fifty." Curiously sensitive to every tendency in literature, he predicted the restless crosscurrents of the '20s. Yet for the past 20 years his main project has been the writing of a synthesis of American culture.

Most of the critical studies of nineteenth century personalities that Brooks wrote during that time applied his familiar thesis to single writers. *The Ordeal of Mark Twain* (1920) and *The Pilgrimage of Henry James* (1925) probed the shadowy sense of unfulfillment sensed in their writing and illustrated the moral that an American artist is inevitably thwarted by American life—directly thwarted if he stays here (as did Mark Twain, who compromised with success), indirectly if he is uprooted from his native soil, as was the expatriate Henry James. But by 1932, when his *Life of Emerson* was published, Brooks had found a solution in the complete and creative life of the transcendentalist sage.

Like many another writer who began as an opposition critic, with his *Life of Emerson* (1932) Van Wyck Brooks had lived to become a popular author (to the great disappointment of many admirers who liked to feel themselves a small eclectic group who understood Brooks). In the meanwhile he had gone also into the editorial field. He held a position with the Century Company from 1915 to 1918; he was assistant editor of the brilliant but short-lived *Seven Arts* in 1917; he collaborated on *The Freeman* from 1920 to 1924. Criticism was still his forte: in 1923 he had won the Dial Prize of $2,000 for distinguished critical work. But to understand Brooks it is necessary to regard him as more than a literary critic. Though his works are literary masterpieces in themselves, he stems from an older line of artist historians. He has always regarded literature as rooted in social and communal factors, and his probings of the American mind have been aptly described as "a history of New England society as reflected in its cultural activities."

Published in 1936, *The Flowering of New England* won the 1937 Pulitzer Prize and the Limited Editions Gold Medal Award in 1938. Carl Van Doren, expressing the consensus of critical opinion, described it as "not only the best history of American literature, but one of the best literary histories in any language." Malcolm Cowley wrote of it: "More than any other writer, Brooks makes us feel the strength and richness . . . of American literature during its one great period." Almost the sole deprecating statement came from Bernard Smith, who apparently preferred the rebellious to the mellowed Brooks: "In many ways it is the finest portrayal ever made of the artistic and intellectual life of New England's 'golden age.' But it is wholly lacking in analysis. It explains nothing, neither causes nor consequences, and therefore it truly estimates neither the significance of the 'flowering' nor its ultimate value."

The zenith of New England's glory—when "there is a springtime in the air . . . a moment of equipoise . . . a widespread flowering of the imagination"—was brilliantly captured in *The Flowering of New England*. In contrast, the mood of the *Indian Summer* is somber and autumnal. Ghosts walk across its austere landscape fitfully lighted by the flaming goldenrod. The book opens with William Dean Howells coming to Boston to re- ceive the "apostolic succession" of Lowell and Holmes. Together with Henry James and Henry Adams, he dominates the host of countless minor littérateurs who attend New England's waning glory; and there is a promise of the resurgence of spring only with the coming of Robert Frost, Amy Lowell, Edwin Arlington Robinson, Edna St. Vincent Millay and others. Rootlessness, colonialism, pedantry, temporary feminine monopoly of literature—those were some of the characteristics of the twilight of New England. In contrast to the New England of *The Flowering* it evinces centripetal tendencies, a taint of disintegration and of decay. Van Wyck Brooks shows himself still a master of the telling phrase (he describes Emily Dickinson as "always in the act of disappearing," condemns Horatio Alger for making "virtue and purity odious"). Polished and gracious to the smallest footnote, his book "is one of the key books of our period, which places us in time and space and tells us what to think of ourselves."

Van Wyck Brooks lives quietly in Westport, Connecticut, with his wife (the former Eleanor Kenyon Stimson, whom he married in 1911) and his two sons, Charles Van Wyck and Oliver Kenyon. He remains a strangely reticent and mysterious personality even to those who know him best. John Hall Wheelock, the poet who has been his lifelong friend (the two published a book of undergraduate poems jointly), says that the first impression one gets of Brooks is "a feeling of extreme sensitivity, of something fastidious, holding in check an extraordinary vehemence of thought and feeling." Wheelock further describes him as gentle, genial, with a fine sense of humor, an amazing memory and talk that is individual, gay and exciting. He cares more than most people about books, ideas and the rightness and wrongness of things. In politics he has always been a Socialist—is perhaps the only member of the American Academy of Arts and Letters to have belonged to that party. He is strongly anti-Hitler, and in September 1941 was one of the 1,100 signers of a telegram asking President Roosevelt to urge upon Congress the immediate declaration of war against Nazi Germany.

"In appearance," writes Stephen Benét, "Mr. Brooks is a trifle difficult to describe. He looks a little like a reasonable and unterrifying dean—a little like a reassuring consultant who is going to make sure that you are comfortable, even if you do have the operation. Of medium height, gray-mustached, thick-haired, he is neat without being precise and wears good clothes easily."

Robert Van Gelder, writing of Brooks' method of work, says that he reads six hours a day, goes through about nine hundred books in preparation for each of his New England histories. Of his writing method: "As he reads he makes notes on the margins of the pages. . . He then copies these notes. Browsing through them when the reading is finished, he comes to a few that fit together and makes this the basis for the sketch of an incident."

BROOKS, VAN WYCK—*Continued*

After some 50 of these sketches he plans his book, starts writing, very slowly, "only about a page a day." He goes on rewriting, cutting, polishing, with the result that his finished style has been called one of the most perfect in contemporary literature. He is also a distinguished and polished translator from the French, having translated 31 books in his lifetime, among them works by André Chamson, Romain Rolland and H. F. Amiel.

Van Wyck Brooks' opinions of present-day literature and its chances of survival can be found in *On Literature Today,* an address delivered at Hunter College in October 1940 and published in 1941. In it he analyzes the pessimism of the American writers today as a sort of "inverted idealism" and sees "on all sides a hunger for affirmations, for a world without confusion, waste or groping, a world that is full of order and purpose, and for ourselves, in America, a chance to build it." He himself has made a journey similar to the one he describes—from rebelliousness to faith in the American destiny.

References

> Cath World 140:412-21 Ja '35
> New Repub 88:69-72 Ag 26 '36; 103: 452-4 S 30 '40
> N Y Herald Tribune Books p9 O 6 '40 por
> N Y Times Book R p2, 18 O 6 '40 por
> Scholastic 32:19E Mr 12 '38 por; 38:19 Mr 10 '41 por
> Cowley, M. ed. After the Genteel Tradition p64-78 1937
> Kunitz, S. J. ed. Living Authors 1937
> Rosenfeld, P. Port of New York p19-63 1924
> Smith, B. Forces in American Criticism p302-59 1939
> Who's Who Among North American Authors
> Who's Who in America

BROWN, CARLETON (FAIRCHILD)
July 15, 1869—June 25, 1941 Philologist and educator; taught at Harvard, Bryn Mawr, the University of Minnesota and New York University; scholar of medieval English who compiled several volumes of religious and English lyrics of the thirteenth, fourteenth and fifteenth centuries; secretary of the Modern Language Association of America from 1920 to 1934 and its president in 1936.

References

> PMLA 50:iii-iv D '35 por (front)
> Essays and Studies in Honor of Carleton Brown, by various authors p330-2 1940
> Leaders in Education 1932
> Who's Who Among North American Authors
> Who's Who in America

Obituaries

> N Y Times p23 Je 26 '41 por

BROWN, CHARLES H(ARVEY) Dec. 23, 1875- Librarian
Address: b. Iowa State College, Ames, Iowa; h. 317 Lynn Ave, Ames, Iowa

"The failure of the world today, the failure of civilization, is to a large extent the failure of the book; the failure of our populations to read and to think; the failure to learn from past events," said Charles H. Brown at the annual meeting of the American Library Association in Boston on June 24, 1941. Addressing the Association as president-elect, he asserted that the colleges and universities of America are isolated from life and from each other. America, he believes, cannot have a coordinated system of education while its colleges and universities continue to duplicate services and engage in rivalry and competition for students. He proposed "Education for Defense" for the A. L. A. program for 1942, suggesting that librarians make a special study of the place of libraries in the educational system with stress on the library as a medium for cooperation with other educational organizations. For the past year he has been chairman of an A. L. A. committee to conduct a cooperative study, "The Use of Books in Specific Courses of Instruction," which is part of a movement to bring about a closer relationship between school faculties and libraries.

Dr. Brown—"who objects to being called Dr.," and who writes: "How about a plain Mister?"—has been studying the problems of "learning through reading (for those who know how to read)" for many years. His father, the Reverend James H. Brown, was a Methodist clergyman who had married a Methodist clergyman's daughter, Mary E. Smith, and Charles Harvey was born in Albany, New York, on December 23, 1875. After being graduated from Wesleyan University in Connecticut in 1897 he continued with his studies and took a Master's Degree in mathematics in 1899. He received his Doctor of Letters from the same institution in 1937, and was elected an honorary fellow by Stanford University in 1941.

While studying for his graduate degree at Wesleyan (1897-99), Mr. Brown worked as assistant librarian at the University library, and after leaving school he enrolled in the New York State Library School. After two years as a student of library science he worked as an assistant in the Library of Congress; in 1903 he joined the John Crerar Library staff in Chicago, first as classifier, and then, in 1904, as reference librarian. In 1909 he became assistant librarian at the Brooklyn Public Library, where, for a period of 10 years, he was active in New York State and New York City library affairs.

Mr. Brown combined his duties at the Brooklyn Library during the First World War with work in the Army and Navy posts on Long Island in the Library War Service of the A. L. A. "So distinguished was his work in this field" that he was called by the United States Navy to serve as library specialist. He served as adviser to the Department on Naval Libraries for three years; then became librarian of Iowa State College in

November 1922. In the 20 years he has been there the library has increased from 80,000 to 315,000 volumes; the appropriations have more than doubled; the use of the library, as measured by outgoing loans, has increased more than 400 per cent; he has built up an "outstanding staff" equipped to render exceptional services to the faculty, including translations from all European languages. During the period from 1933 to 1938 he taught summer courses in college libraries at the Columbia University School of Library Service.

While carrying on his administrative duties with distinction, Mr. Brown has done important committee and organization work for the A. L. A. as a council member from 1923 to 1926; for various state associations; and for college and research libraries. He was consulting expert for the *Land Grant College Survey* (1928-30) for the United States Bureau of Education; from 1928 to 1929 he was president of the Iowa Library Association; and he has been chairman of many A. L. A. committees (Reorganization Committee College and Reference Section 1937, Periodicals Committee 1938, Committee on Boards and Committees 1941, etc.).

In 1933 *Circulation Work in College and University Libraries*, written in collaboration with H. G. Bousfield, was published. This "exhaustive analysis of the problems connected with circulation work in the institutions of higher learning" is a "real contribution to library science" into which has gone "much thought, investigation and hard work." Other publications include a report to the Iowa State Planning Board on *Library Service in Iowa* (1935) and numerous articles in leading library, educational and scientific periodicals.

Mr. Brown has long been active on periodicals committees. In 1935, as chairman of the A. L. A. Committee on German Periodicals, he made a trip to Europe. Ten days in Germany conferring with a committee of the Börsenverein and the various officials and publishers resulted (with the aid of a Government subsidy) in a 25 per cent reduction in the export prices of German books and periodicals.

Mr. Brown was also chairman of the A. L. A. Third Activities Committee out of which grew the revised constitution of the Association. This Committee was responsible for remodeling a constitution which had originally met the needs of a membership of 1,500 but which was hardly geared to meet the needs of an organization of 15,000 nor the needs of the 12 library organizations which had sprung up since the formation of the A. L. A. The Committee worked on a plan to revise the structure of "our national library association, its constitution and by-laws; its organization into boards and committees; its relation to other national organizations of librarians, affiliated and independent."

Dynamic, balding Mr. Brown is six feet tall, weighs one hundred sixty pounds, is blond and has blue eyes. Mr. Spaulding wrote

CHARLES H. BROWN

in 1937: "When asked what his hobby was, he [Mr. Brown] replied that it was the development of college and university libraries from the standpoint of use and in an attempt to obtain the point of view of both faculty and students in their instruction and research." But, Mr. Spaulding is inclined to think, Mr. Brown's chief hobbies are actually much less academic—"his wife [Julia W. Heath of Chicago, whom he married in 1909], his son Robert Heath [associate professor at Clark University], and his son Charles Howard [until recently a practicing physician at Los Angeles and now a lieutenant (medical) in the Air Corps of the United States Army]." Mr. Brown himself says his hobbies are "tennis [he belonged to the now defunct Sterling Tennis Club in New York City from 1910 to 1917] and mountain hiking—not climbing." There is a fourth opinion, held by many fellow librarians and educators, that his hobby is a "search for frankness and discussion ... that to find the truth it is necessary to argue passionately on both sides of all questions ... and that one must face facts, however disagreeable."

References

Bul Bibliog 16:21-2 Ja-Ap '37 por (front)
Leaders in Education 1941
Who's Who in America
Who's Who in Library Service

BROWN, HELEN DAWES May 15, 1857— Sept. 5, 1941 Author of books for girls; taught English at Vassar College for four years and at the Brearley School in New York for thirteen years; one of the founders of the Women's University Club in New York; author of twelve books for girls, the latest of which was *Snapshots of Nancy and Brothers* (1939).

(Continued next page)

BROWN, HELEN DAWES—*Continued*

References

> Who's Who Among North American Authors
> Who's Who in America

Obituaries

> N Y Times p51 S 7 '41
> Sch & Soc 54:190 S 13 '41

BROWNE, DAME SIDNEY JANE Jan. 5, 1850—Aug. 13, 1941 British nurse; known as "the modern Florence Nightingale"; devoted herself to nursing soldiers and in the course of a long life had served in four campaigns, including the Egyptian War, the Sudan campaign, the Boer War and the First World War; received many honors; was mentioned in dispatches; served as first president of the Royal College of Nursing.

References

> Author's and Writer's Who's Who
> Who's Who

Obituaries

> N Y Times p17 Ag 14 '41

BRUSH, GEORGE DE FOREST Sept. 28, 1855—Apr. 24, 1941 American portrait painter whose fine draftsmanship and classical portraits of his family won for him a wide reputation as an academician and painter of the Italian Renaissance school; paintings appear in the important museums of the country and have won many prizes.

References

> Caffin, C. H. American Masters of Painting p129-40 1902
> New Standard Encyclopedia of Art
> Who's Who in America
> Who's Who in American Art

Obituaries

> N Y Herald Tribune p16 Ap 25 '41 por
> Time 37:64 My 5 '41

BUCK, GENE Aug. 8, 1885- President of the American Society of Composers, Authors and Publishers

Address: b. American Society of Composers, Authors and Publishers, 30 Rockefeller Plaza, New York City; h. Kensington, Great Neck, N. Y.

> Bulletin: On October 29, 1941 the dispute which had kept ASCAP songs from being broadcast over NBC and CBS for ten months was ended with the signing of new contracts, making 1,250,000 tunes available to the networks. (MBS had returned ASCAP tunes to the air in May.) According to Gene Buck, the ten-month fight had "cost ASCAP something over $4,000,-000 in lost revenue which we did not collect this year."

From February 1941 issue:

"I care not who writes the nation's songs, so long as I can get the boys some money for it." Maybe Gene Buck said that and maybe he didn't; at any rate, they seem like appropriate words to put into the mouth of the president of the American Society of Composers, Authors and Publishers (ASCAP). It was New Year's Day of 1941 when the battle between ASCAP and the recently-formed Broadcast Music, Incorporated (BMI), a subsidiary of the National Association of Broadcasters, culminated in an air-boycott by the broadcasting chains of all ASCAP music.

The networks claim that ASCAP is a monopoly which asks an undue amount of money for its members in return for the privilege of playing their music over the air, that their own BMI has acquired 250,000 or more tunes and "is prepared to supply every type of music the public demands," and that listeners don't miss the music of Mr. Buck's boys, anyway. ASCAP claims that it merely submitted a contract which would reduce the fees to individual stations and require the chains, who had never paid anything for music before, "to assume their just proportion of the cost"—that the chains "want to control music, not pay for it." In the meanwhile the United States Department of Justice, with sublime impartiality, proposes to start an antitrust suit against everybody— ASCAP, BMI, NBC, CBS—and ASCAP has a plan for licensing radio advertisers directly for use of its music.

Eugene Edward Buck, who calls for a "fight to the finish," is used to fighting. He was born in Detroit, Michigan on August 8, 1885, the son of George William and Katherine (McCarthy) Buck. He started early as an artist, song writer and playwright, a producer of school shows (among them *John's Myth—Pretty Pocahontas* and *Bing, Bang, Boom—Dewey Did It!*) and then went on to the University of Detroit. His father had died when he was a youngster and he couldn't afford to complete college, but after he left he found himself a job as messenger for Detroit's Dime Savings Bank (salary $2 a week) and in the evenings studied at the Detroit Art Academy.

He soon put to practical use a talent for improving on the "Gibson Girl," and became a designer of scrolls and borders for the publishers of sheet music. The illustrated cover was his invention, as a matter of fact, and he had designed several thousand of them before he was "fired for going blind through overwork." He spent several months in a dark room before he recovered. Then, in 1907, he packed up and went to New York, ambitious to become a great artist. He spent four years at it before, one day in 1911, he gazed at one of his most ambitious paintings and muttered his lifetime motto: "Don't kid yourself." He didn't. He decided to become a great song writer instead.

Gene Buck's first song began, "Daddy has a sweetheart," worked up suspense, and finally ended, with surprising morality, "and mother is her name." After it was thrown out of Ziegfeld's *Follies* along with the actress who was going to sing it, Buck brought both to

Oscar Hammerstein's theatre in an act which he directed and whose setting he designed. They made a hit; Ziegfeld called and apologized; and in 1912 Buck became principal librettist for the Ziegfeld *Follies*, eventually writer of themes and songs for more than 30 of Ziegfeld's productions.

A particularly successful year was 1914. Buck organized the *Midnight Frolic* for Ziegfeld on the New Amsterdam Roof, invented the cabaret-with-stage show, the use of exploding colored balloons for decoration, the mingling of the chorus with the audience. Only prohibition could close the *Midnight Frolic,* and it did, in 1922, after Buck had written 16 editions of it. But in the meanwhile it was there that Buck introduced Will Rogers to New York night life (persuading him to liven up his rope-twirling act with a running fire of comment on the news), and Ziegfeld finally left to Buck the problem of finding male talent for most of his shows. The song writer "helped to thrust fame upon" Ed Wynn, Eddie Cantor (see sketch this issue) and many others. He brought Joseph Urban, painter of stage settings, to the popular theatre. (Urban showed his gratitude by doing the interior decorating for the $100,000 estate at Great Neck, Long Island, which Buck bought after his marriage to Helen Falconer, Fred Stone's prima donna, in 1919.) He kept peace between Ziegfeld's actors "thirsty for each other's heart blood"—among them the late Frank Tinney and Leon Errol. He wrote hundreds of songs, among them *Hello Frisco, Tulip Time, 'Neath the South Sea Moon.* And it was as Ziegfeld's right-hand man that he helped to launch the battle against the song pirates.

In the days before ASCAP, no one paid the writer or composer simply for playing his music in public. It was, in fact, considered a favor to the song writer: his song was getting free advertising. "The result of receiving favors from everybody was that the song writer was in danger of death by starvation. It is true that the pirates popularized the song, but they popularized them chiefly with other pirates." One day, before the First World War, Victor Herbert walked into Shanley's restaurant and heard the orchestra playing one of his copyrighted pieces. He wondered why they shouldn't be paying him something. He sued, and while the suit was still pending he proposed founding a society which would protect the interests of authors and composers. Buck was one of the group who thought it a good idea, and from 1914 to 1924 he served as its president without compensation. Nathan Burkan donated his legal services and represented ASCAP in the courts; but it was 1921 before the income from royalties that legal battles won for ASCAP's members amounted to more than the cost of collecting them. The friendship between Gene Buck and Victor Herbert was a close one: later Buck was to be the executor of Herbert's will and to have erected the monument to the composer which today stands in Central Park, New York City.

Harris & Ewing

GENE BUCK

In 1922 Buck heard a radio for the first time —and what he heard was someone playing his own *Tulip Time* and *'Neath the South Sea Moon.* He sent word to his fellow-members that here was new work to be done. As the radio industry became bigger, ASCAP brought one suit after another for royalties. They weren't too successful at first. A national association of broadcasters was formed to fight them, and the courts kept deciding against ASCAP. One Federal judge even held that broadcasting was strictly private.

In 1926 Buck left Ziegfeld to become an independent producer. He produced *Yours Truly* (1926) and *Ringside* (1927), and kept right on writing songs. As a matter of fact, between his ASCAP duties, his song writing, and commuting from his Great Neck home, he was so busy that he tried to retire from the presidency of ASCAP in 1929. They wouldn't let him, and after that he received a regular salary for his services. Since 1931 Buck has confined his activities almost entirely to ASCAP, although he returned to Ziegfeld temporarily for the *Follies* of 1931.

Not until September 1932 did ASCAP force the radio business to come to terms by threatening to order jazz and popular music off the air after its contract had been declined. When the contract was actually signed with the broadcasters' association it provided $960,000 for ASCAP, plus three per cent of the gross income from advertising in 1933, four per cent in 1934, five per cent in 1935. By 1939 ASCAP had made five appearances before the Supreme Court, listed around a thousand top-flight composers and song writers among its members, and collected five or six million a year from hotels, motion picture theatres, showboats, ocean liners, night clubs, restaurants—and, of course, the radio. Members were divided into eight

BUCK, GENE—*Continued*

classifications according to the "quality, vogue and popularity" of their compositions (there were quarterly promotions and demotions), and received shares of ASCAP's income proportionately. Radio stations applied at the daily licensing bureau at ASCAP's offices for permission to play songs, and if an application for a certain song was rejected, the song simply wasn't played. By 1940, however, the chains were so rebellious that they refused to negotiate with ASCAP for licenses. There were also composers who, like Aaron Copland (see sketch this issue), resented ASCAP's attitude toward serious music—others who, having been refused admission, called ASCAP a "closed corporation."

The president of ASCAP is a man with graying hair, eyes that are pale blue and usually smiling, and lean, bony hands. He is voluble, profane and sentimental—sentimental about the disappearance of the parlor piano, among other things. He has been "confidant and counselor, oracle and guide, to thousands" of Broadwayites. The speaker at a Lambs' Club dinner once became more than a little sentimental about *him* and described him as possessing "the soul of a Sister of Charity and the efficiency of a Schwab."

Gene Buck has two sons: Eugene Falconer and George William. He is a Democrat and a Catholic; a clubman (New York's Dutch Treat, Players, Lambs') who has never tasted liquor in his life; a member of the board of American Dramatists and of the council and executive committee of the Authors' League of America. His motto, as mentioned before, is, "Don't kid yourself." As for his definition of a good song, it's "a perfect marriage between words and music, so perfect that you can't think of one without the other." He thinks ASCAP members have written far too many of those for the radio public to accept tamely their disappearance from the air.

References

Am Mag 128 :96 O '39 por
Collier's 85 :32+ F 15 '30 il por
Etude 59 :152-53+ Mr '41 por
Lit Digest 118 :32 Jl 28 '34
N Y Times VII p9+ O 20 '40 por
New Yorker 8 :22-5 D 17 '32 ; 8 :19-22
  D 24 '32
Time 36 :66 O 7 '40 por
Who's Who in America

BUCKNER, EMORY R(OY) Aug. 7, 1877—Mar. 11, 1941 Lawyer; former United States Attorney for the Southern District of New York during the days of prohibition when he won wide publicity for his padlock campaign against 1,000 speak-easies and night clubs, and for his prosecution of Harry M. Daugherty, Thomas W. Miller and Maurice Connolly; was considered one of the greatest American trial lawyers of his generation.

References

New Yorker 8 :21-3 Mr 12 '32 ; 8 :24-7
  Mr 19 '32

Who's Who in America
Who's Who in Law

Obituaries

N Y Times p21 Mr 12 '41 por
Time 37 :67 Mr 24 '41

BUDENNY, SEMYON M(IKHAILO-VICH) (boo'yô'nê sê-mjôn' mê-khĭ-lô-vĭch) Apr. 25, 1883- First vice-commissar of defense of the USSR

Address: Moscow, Ul. Granovskovo 3, Ap. 78, Russia

Marshal Semyon M. Budenny, whom *Time* called in one issue the "toughest and ablest military man in Russia" and in a later issue characterized as "a cavalry noncom of incredible dash and dumbness," was in July 1941 put in command of the Southern sector of the Soviet forces then protecting Kiev and the Ukraine, where some of the most stubbornly fought battles between the Soviet and German Armies have since taken place. Nearly every German victory in that region while it was under his command was followed by a Nazi report that he had been executed at Stalin's order, captured or shot; and his armies were almost daily disorganized, surrounded and even annihilated in DNB dispatches. Early November found both Budenny and his armies still very much in existence, however, although the Ukraine defenders had by this time been pushed back to the gates of Rostov. It was only then that Marshal Timoshenko (see sketch this issue) was sent to replace Budenny, while the latter was reported assigned to the creation of new reserve armies as the Nazis pressed on in the great offensive designed to break the back of Russian resistance before winter. Before long the Russians were on the offensive, at least temporarily.

"Rather short and stocky, of muscular build, with big, blazing black eyes and an air of command, augmented by his untamed mustache—about eight inches on the beam," Budenny not only looks but fights like a Cossack. He was, however, born of non-Cossack parents in a Cossack district, the settlement of Koziurin in the Salsk District of the Don Oblast which Sholokhov's novels have made famous. His mother and father were poor peasants, and Semyon began to work as a cattle herdsman and peasant-laborer at the age of nine. He taught himself to read before being conscripted into the Czar's Army in 1903, fought as a private in the Russo-Japanese War (1905-07) and eventually became a non-commissioned officer in his Cossack cavalry regiment, living on starvation pay and almost literally starving in intervals between feasts. (He had, and still has, a voracious appetite.)

The First World War found Budenny still with the Army. During the February Revolution of 1917 elected a member of the squadron's Soldiers' Committee which voiced the opinions of the common soldiers, and then chairman of his Regimental Committee, he was in conflict with the old regime but not yet a member of the Bolshevik Party of Lenin. He took an active part in the October Revolution, however, and, having left his regiment without bothering about its being demobilized, started back to his native village from Minsk. Along the way (according to one story) he and six deserters, two of them his brothers, encountered a detachment of Denikin's troops sleeping in a wood. The deserters' arms were an old rifle with 4 cartridges, a revolver with 7 bullets, and a sword, but, whooping through the woods, they frightened the sleeping men into flight and captured 275 horses, 360 rifles, 16,000 bullets and 8 men, who joined them. Back home with their spoils, Budenny joyously cried: "Proletarians, to horse!"

This was the beginning of the spectacular role during the civil war which made Budenny the hero of countless Soviet folk tales and songs and which made the mere mention of his name throw terror into the Whites. He and his guerrillas, living in the forest and emerging at night to fall on Denikin's men, formed the nucleus of the Bolshevik cavalry army. They grew to 100 in the first real attack against counter-revolutionaries in August 1918; they became a regiment; they became a division. When Budenny first asked to form that division into a cavalry army the Bolsheviks told him that cavalry was "outdated" and "of no military importance." But he soon proved that they were wrong. In the second half of 1918 his men took part in the defense of Tsaritsyn against the Whites and won a series of victories over Krasnov's infantry and cavalry. At the end of 1919, the year when Budenny joined the Communist Party, they took part in Stalin's plan for the defeat of Denikin and were finally allowed to become the 1st Cavalry Army. They then rode to the sea of Azov, mopping up the remnants of Denikin's forces, and by the end of March 1920 the entire Northern Caucasus was cleared of White Guards. Red Marshals Timoshenko and Voroshilov (see sketch this issue) were both among Budenny's lieutenants at the time.

But the fighting was by no means over. In May 1920 Polish troops invaded Russia from the Baltic almost to the Black Sea. Rushing to the relief of Kiev, within a month Budenny had driven them back to the neighborhood of Pinsk, in east Poland. At the same time the Soviet Armies in the north were preparing a drive. They broke through the Polish lines and with Budenny's forces advanced to the gates of Warsaw, where, however, they met defeat at the hands of Weygand. Then it was east and south to the Crimea to wipe out General Wrangel, who had tried to take up where Denikin left off the year before.

There are many stories about the fierce, hard-riding, uneducated Budenny of this period. Trotsky praised him for his frankness and openness, but mourned to Lenin: "I see right into Budenny's soul, and I wish it were not so rough and rude." He was noted not so much as a commander of thought and careful decision but as an intuitive and daring fighter who never kowtowed to anyone—not to Trotsky or Stalin or Lenin himself—and to whom the capture of a city always meant a raid on its supply of liquor.

Sovfoto

SEMYON M. BUDENNY

Four times the press of the world reported that he and the 1st Cavalry Army had been wiped out; four times the report was contradicted by their miraculous appearance in some other sector. Lenin said: "I don't understand him, but he fights." Once he sent Budenny a short summary of what Marx had said so that he would know exactly why he was risking his life so recklessly. It was never read. Inquired the puzzled Lenin: "Comrade, suppose you were asked what you were fighting for—what would you say?" Replied Budenny: "Comrade, I would say that Lenin knows." Another time Trotsky scolded him for not having sent in a written report about a certain battle. "But I won it!" Budenny protested. "How am I to know that?" asked Trotsky. "I brought my army back! Whenever I go out to battle and fail to bring my army back you will know that I lost."

Budenny's recreations were wild races on horseback, fencing without guards, revolver shooting (he could put out a lighted candle with his revolver at 40 paces). It is said that his wife was one of the best rifle shots in Russia, too, and that she rode and fought with him. But it is also said that she was one of the best cooks in Russia, and that the otherwise untamed commander was so much under her thumb that at home he would shave, put on respectable clothes, attend church and spend most of his time tending his flower garden and his apple orchard quite contentedly. He maintained a horse-breeding farm after the civil war, and encouraged others to do the same.

With the Soviet Republics at last free from the invaders, Budenny's rise in the Army was rapid. In 1920 he was elected to the Russian Central Committee, in 1923 to the Central Committee of the Soviet Union, and the next year he became inspector of cavalry of the Red

BUDENNY, SEMYON M.—*Continued*

Army. Finally, in 1928, at the age of 46, the untutored peasant who had once said, "I never read—it gives me a headache" was sent to the Moscow Military Academy to get his first formal education. Three years later he became a member of the Commissariat of Agriculture, and in 1932 he was graduated from the Military Academy with honors. In 1935 he became one of the five marshals of the Soviet Union; surviving the army purge of 1937, he was made commander in chief of the Moscow District; in 1938 he joined the Presidium of the Supreme Council, in 1939 the Central Committee of the Communist Party; and since August 1940 he has been first vice-commissar of defense. He played an outstanding role in the final victory over the Finns in 1940.

The "fierce, outspoken, dare-devil, vodka-loving, horse-smelling, barrel-chested, mustache-proud" Soviet Marshal is now married to a famous actress of the Mali Theatre in Moscow. In 1925 he mourned the death of his first wife, killed accidentally while cleaning a rifle.

References

Am R Soviet Union 4:54-6 Ag '41
China W R 97:208-9 Jl 19 '41 por
Cur Opinion 70:185-6 F '21
Life 11:18 Jl 21 '41 por
N Y Sun p19 Ja 30 '40; p19 Jl 18 '41
Newsweek 6:26 N 16 '35 por; 9:14 Je 19 '37 por
PM p4 Jl 7 '41
Time 35:32 F 26 '40 por; 38:21-3 N 13 '41 pors

International Who's Who

BUDGE, DONALD June 13, 1915- Former professional tennis player

Address: b. Budge-Wood Service Launderers, 1160 Madison Ave, New York City

In June 1941 tennis lost its most popular figure. Redheaded, lanky, likeable Davis Cup champion Donald Budge, after a Forest Hills professional tournament for British War Relief, gave up barnstorming to devote his time and energy to Sidney Wood's laundry business in Manhattan. Once the property of Wood and Frank Shields, it is known as the Budge-Wood Service.

Walter L. Pate, captain of the United States Davis Cup team, considers Budge the supreme player of all time, though admirers of "Big Bill" Tilden dissent. But Budge didn't always like tennis. He had to be coaxed to play and went to the courts only to please his older brother, Lloyd. Baseball, football, basketball, hockey, bicycle riding, roller skating and marbles appealed much more to him. In fact, he was frequently scolded by his father, who had once suffered a serious injury playing soccer in Glasgow, for spending so much time in the streets with football.

Donald Budge's parents, John and Pearl (Kincaid) Budge, were Scotch-Irish and in modest circumstances when he was born in Oakland, California on June 13, 1915. Besides being an athletic boy, Donald was handy with tools and liked to make things out of wood for himself and his sister, Jean. For four years, from the ages of 11 to 15, he would not go near a tennis court, and his elder brother Lloyd reconciled himself to being the only tennis player in the family. Ironically, Lloyd never became a great player, although he has made a name for himself as a coach.

One night in June 1930, at the Budge family dinner table, Lloyd asked Donald, with mild sarcasm, why he did not brush up on his tennis and enter the California state boys' championship, a week away. Donald failed to join in the general laugh at his expense, but on the following day was out on the courts practicing. "The succeeding week he was in the field that started out in the California state boys' championship, and he went straight through to the finals—in corduroy pants. On the day of the finals, he appeared in new white ducks, as spotless as though they had just come from the laundry which his father managed in Oakland. He played Paul Newton and defeated him by a score of 6-0, 6-4. He had won the first tournament in which he had ever competed." His success came to him as a fifteenth-birthday present.

Don decided then and there that he would keep on playing tennis and that he would become a champion. In 1933 he became the first player in years to win both the state junior and senior championships in the same season. Encouraged and helped by his amazed but gratified brother Lloyd, Don made further strides, and was sent by the Northern California Association to play in the national junior championships at Culver, Indiana. "For the first time now they were beginning to visualize in this serious-minded, rapidly growing youngster another California Comet," for although "he was not a volleyer, nor was he an abnormally hard hitter," he was playing a steady, back-court game. He had, in fact, a dread of going to the net, quite different from the later smashing style of attack which ran his opponents ragged. (His backhand, however, has not changed: he still hits with both hands on the handle, exactly as if he were using a baseball bat. Originally the shot was a slice, but he now hits into the ball instead of down.)

Budge won the national junior title at Culver, and the player he defeated in the finals was Gene Mako of Los Angeles, later his Davis Cup partner, who was to share with him the winning of the national and Wimbledon championships. It was 1934 when Budge joined forces with Mako in doubles to carry off the Pacific coast sectional championship at Santa Barbara, then set off for the East, stopping off at Chicago for the national clay court championship. At his Eastern "unveiling" at the Seabright Lawn Tennis and Cricket Club in New Jersey, onlookers were impressed by his similarity to Ellsworth Vines, who had created a sensation there in 1930, but Budge's only notable conquest of the season in the

East was his victory over Bryan ("Bitsy") Grant in the championship at Forest Hills.

Returning to California, rather dissatisfied, Budge corresponded with Sidney Wood, Wimbledon champion in 1931, who had played there with both Lloyd and Donald, and decided to change his grip. (The so-called Western grip was the one he had been using.) Tom Stow, coach of the University of California tennis team and the Claremont Country Club, thereupon taught him a grip that was halfway between the Eastern and the Continental, and in the spring of 1935, while he was with the Davis Cup team in Mexico, Walter Pate advised Budge to use the flat Eastern. He has used it ever since, until by 1937 he felt the same confidence in his forehand as in his backhand.

In 1935, only a year after he had played on Eastern turf for the first time, Budge gained the stature of an international player. The Davis Cup had been lost to France in 1927, and all efforts to bring it back had failed. The committee which selected the Davis Cup team decided that new blood was needed to bring back the cup established by Dwight Davis in 1900. Budge, although he ranked ninth, was chosen with Wilmer Allison, No. 1 player, for the singles.

By this time his partner Mako's "affable, breezy manner and irrepressible good nature" had helped Budge to overcome his shyness when meeting people, especially girls, to such an extent that there are some who swear, no doubt falsely, that at Wimbledon that year he waved his racket at Queen Mary when she entered the Royal Box and received an amused wave of the hand in return. (By that same year he could follow Mako's example in taking over the traps of Benny Goodman's or Tommy Dorsey's band.) As for his tennis, in the Davis Cup challenge with Great Britain Budge lost both of his matches to the English stalwarts, Fred Perry and "Bunny" Austin, but he defeated the German baron, Gottfried von Cramm, by taking three straight sets after losing the first at love.

Back home again, Budge proceeded to win an unusually fine Newport, Rhode Island tournament from Frank Shields, and he was also a finalist with Mako in the national doubles championship. In the national singles, however, Bitsy Grant defeated him again at White Sulphur Springs in the spring of 1936. By the summer of 1936 Budge had improved his short-court attack so much that Perry was the only player who could defeat him on turf all season. His fatigue and evident physical distress during some of the games were later revealed to be the result of an over-indulgence in drinking malted milks late at night! (Budge is still fond of them, although wary of over-indulgence before a big match.)

On July 27, 1937 the Davis Cup was regained for the United States at Wimbledon after an absence of ten long years, six of which had been spent in France and four in England. Writes Fenno: "America's victory was carved out primarily by the devastating racket of Donald Budge. In him the United States had not only a representative who took his place as the world's foremost singles player of that year by winning all his Davis Cup matches against Japan, Australia, Germany and England, as well as the Wimbledon, American and Australian singles champion-

DONALD BUDGE

ships, but she had also a strong doubles player who was the vital cog in the Budge-Mako combination which won all its Davis Cup doubles contests." Budge participated in 12 winning cup matches that year and lost none. And "not only his prowess with the racket but his flaming red hair, his ingratiating smile and his thorough sportsmanship and lack of affectation on and off the court won him a lasting place in the hearts of sports followers at home and abroad."

In England Budge had won over Baron von Cramm in an unbelievably brilliant game. If the latter had won the Davis Cup would have gone to Germany for the first time, and his defeat reportedly had something to do with his later imprisonment by the Nazi Government on a morals charge! In protest, Budge refused to play in Germany in 1938, although he went to France, England and Yugoslavia. In that same year, besides other triumphs, Budge led the United States in the successful defense of the Davis Cup against Australia at the Germantown Cricket Club, Philadelphia. And in October of that year he had the privilege of refusing an offer of $75,000 annually to turn professional, asking $100,000. But terms were finally arrived at amicably, and, with the blessing of the United States Lawn Tennis Association, Donald Budge left the amateur ranks. "Amateur officialdom showed how it felt toward him in turning out *en masse*, along with some 16,000 others, for his professional debut at Madison Square Garden the night of January 3, 1939." Con-

BUDGE, DONALD—*Continued*

trary to predictions, he readily adapted his game to the conditions of indoor play and won handsomely, as he did against Perry in March.

Since then Budge has toured all over the country; his two books on tennis, *How Lawn Tennis Is Played,* written with others (1937), and *On Tennis* (1939), are best sellers in the field; he had a business connection with Wilson's Sporting Goods Company in San Francisco; and now he has the Budge-Wood Service.

Among Budge's proudest possessions is the James E. Sullivan Memorial Trophy which he received as the outstanding amateur athlete of the United States in 1937, presented to him in August 1938. He is a Protestant and a Republican, and his favorite recreations are swing music and basketball. He is no longer an eligible young bachelor, however: on May 26, 1941 Budge was married to Deirdre Conselman, a sophomore at Stanford University and daughter of the late Bill Conselman, creator of the "Ella Cinders" comic strip.

References

> Collier's 100:18+ S 11 '37 il por; 105: 18+ My 4 '40 por
> Lit Digest 120:35 Jl 13 '35 il por
> PM p30 Jl 30 '40 pors
> Sat Eve Post 211:8-9+ N 19 '38 pors
> Scholastic 30:24 My 22 '37 pors
> Time 26:26-8 S 2 '35; 30:40 Jl 12 '37 por; 30:20-1 S 13 '37 por; 37:63 Ap 14 '41; 37:74 My 26 '41

America's Young Men
Atkinson, L. and others Famous American Athletes of Today 5th ser. p29-63 1937
Budge, D. On Tennis 1939
Kaese, H. and others Famous American Athletes of Today 6th ser. p39-67 1938
Who's Who in America

BUFFUM, CHARLES A(LBERT) 1853(?)
—July 19, 1941 Educator who taught Latin as a living language for 44 years at Williston Academy, Massachusetts; known to thousands of Williston alumni, many of whom went on to teach Latin in schools and colleges; called "Old Buff" or "Mr. Chips of Williston."

Obituaries

> N Y Times p31 Jl 20 '41

BURKE, EDMUND J., FATHER 1859
—Jan. 1, 1941 Educator; author; taught political economy and biology at Fordham University, New York City; author of many books on those subjects; member of the Society of Jesus.

Obituaries

> N Y Herald Tribune p14 Ja 2 '41

BURLEIGH,   HARRY   T(HACKER)
(bûr'lê) Dec. 2, 1866- Singer; composer
Address: h. 823 E. 166th St, New York City

"The first time a Negro song became a major theme in a great symphonic work" was in 1893, when Antonin Dvořák's *New World Symphony* was played. Part of the credit, though he denies it, for that inspiration must go to Harry T. Burleigh, who impressed upon Dvořák the beauty of the Negro songs. During the course of a full life he has continued to spread their beauty.

The grandson of a blind slave discarded by his Maryland owners when his usefulness had ceased, Harry Thacker Burleigh was born in Erie, Pennsylvania. His mother, Elizabeth (Waters) Burleigh, a college graduate, became janitress of a public school after the death of her husband, Henry T. Burleigh. Young Burleigh worked as a lamplighter, as desk steward and at many other jobs. He also sang in various church choirs in Erie, and sang so well that later it was suggested that he try for a scholarship at the National Conservatory of Music, New York. Mrs. MacDowell, mother of the composer, Edward MacDowell, and a member of the staff of the Conservatory, learned of Burleigh's interest in music and helped him to get the scholarship. He spent four years at the Conservatory, for two years assisting in the teaching of piano and solfeggio. He studied harmony with Rubin Goldmark and counterpoint with Max Spicker. He joined the Conservatory Orchestra, playing double bass and, later, timpani; and he was also librarian of the Orchestra. One summer while he was at the Conservatory he worked as a waiter in a hotel at Saratoga, New York. The next summer he returned to Saratoga, but as baritone soloist in the Episcopal Church.

In 1900 Burleigh joined the choir at Temple Emanu-El, New York City. He held that post for 25 years, the only Negro ever to have sung in this synagogue, one of the largest in the country. He has also sung on the concert stage, here and abroad, having appeared in a command performance before King Edward VII as well as before many other notables, including Theodore Roosevelt, the Archbishop of Canterbury (see sketch this issue), Prince Henry of Prussia, Paderewski and Anton Seidl. He was a pioneer in introducing Spirituals on the concert stage and also a pioneer in setting down on paper Negro folk songs that had been preserved only orally. He made arrangements of these songs so that they could be sung with accompaniment. Alain Locke, in his *The Negro and His Music,* says that "more than any other single person, Mr. Burleigh as arranger, composer and baritone soloist played the role of a pathbreaking ambassador of Negro music to the musically elect." The contribution that he made in the preservation of these songs was invaluable, for he came along at a time when there was danger they would be lost because many of the Negroes wanted to forget them and the conditions out of which they had grown.

Burleigh has arranged more than 100 Spirituals, among the best known *Deep River;* *Nobody Knows the Trouble I've Seen;*

Couldn't Hear Nobody Pray; Let Us Cheer the Weary Traveler; Were You There? He has also composed more than 250 original songs, mostly semi-classical ballads, for some of which he wrote the words as well as the music, and several anthems and pieces for the violin. Among the well known songs which he has set to music are: Walter Brown's *Little Mother of Mine;* Rupert Brooke's *The Soldier;* Walt Whitman's *Ethiopia Saluting the Colors;* and *The Young Warrior,* by James Weldon Johnson, the last made popular during the First World War by Pasquale Amato of the Metropolitan Opera. His arrangement of *Little Mother of Mine* was included in John McCormack's repertoire for many years, and McCormack became such a close friend that he once quit his rooms at the Ritz-Carlton because Burleigh was asked to use the freight elevator.

In the meanwhile Burleigh had been singing at St. George's Church, where in 1894 he had applied for a position as baritone soloist and in competition with 60 candidates won out. Although not all the people of the Church welcomed a Negro in the choir, the rector disregarded objections—he was interested only in Burleigh's magnificent voice. Later the elder J. P. Morgan, for 28 years senior warden of St. George's, requested that Burleigh sing *Calvary* at his funeral. And today, although Burleigh has retired from concert work, he is still singing in the choir of St. George's. In addition to the regular services he sings at an annual service of Spirituals, which has been held at the Church each year since 1923 and which is made up for the most part of many of his own arrangements. The first solo that he sang in the choir was Fauré's *The Palms,* in 1895, and he has sung it on every Palm Sunday since then. The choirmaster, George W. Kemmer, said three or four years ago that he expects that on Burleigh's fiftieth anniversary at St. George's he will sing *The Palms,* and as richly as ever. When and if he does give up his choir duties the veteran musicologist plans to roam through the South to salvage old folk melodies that are dying off. "If they'd only *let* me retire," he pleads. For a number of years he has been musical editor for G. Ricordi and Sons, New York City music publishers, once an ASCAP firm but now a BMI affiliate.

A. Walter Kramer, the music critic, in an appraisal of Burleigh's life and work said: "This man is a composer by divine right, and what is more, he is a thinker, a man who writes music not because he enjoys seeing his name on the program of some singer, but because he feels deeply, profoundly in the language of tone... Burleigh is contributing to American art-songs examples of creative music that deserve world-wide attention and respect."

In 1917 Burleigh received the Spingarn Medal (awarded each year for an outstanding contribution to Negro life) for distinguished achievement in music. Atlanta University has conferred upon him the honorary degree of Master of Arts, Howard University

that of Doctor of Music, and he is a charter member of the American Society of Composers, Authors and Publishers, for whose board of directors he was nominated in August 1941, the first Negro to be so honored. He married Louise Alston in 1898; they have one son, Captain Alston Waters Burleigh.

HARRY T. BURLEIGH

References

Mis R 59:297 Je '36 por
N Y Age p7 O 29 '38 il
N Y Herald Tribune p13 My 22 '33; p7 Mr 26 '34; p10 Ag 7 '41 por
PM p20 Ag 6 '41 por
Time 33:49 My 29 '39 por
Baker's Biographical Dictionary of Musicians 1940
Brawley, B. G. Negro Genius p171-89 1937
Bullock, R. W. In Spite of Handicaps p35-43 1927
Hare, M. C. Negro Musicians and Their Music p321-51 1936
Johnson, J. W. Along This Way 1933
Johnson, J. W. Black Manhattan 1930
Locke, A. Negro and His Music p119-20 1936

BURNETT, WHIT *See* Foley, M. and Burnett, W.

BURNHAM, JAMES Nov. 22, 1905- Author; educator

Address: b. New York University, Washington Sq, New York City; h. 137 E. 73rd St, New York City

Critics reading James Burnham's *The Managerial Revolution* (1941) couldn't decide exactly what they had there. To Lewis Corey it was "the Olympian defeatism of a doc-

JAMES BURNHAM

trinaire radical gone sour," to Peter Drucker "one of the best recent books on political and social trends" and probably "the Bible of the next generation of neo-Marxists," to Ordway Tead a book "worth reading . . . not for the conclusions it imparts but for the disturbance to habitual thought patterns which it will engender." No one at all found the predictions in this book anything but gloomy, but most found it absorbing, and with masochistic thoroughness Ralph Thomson of the New York *Times* devoted two separate days to reviewing it. His estimate of its importance was apparently shared by others.

Burnham says he has excluded "all moral and emotional considerations" when he writes that the trend of the times is toward an economy ruled by the technical and managerial middle classes, more efficient but far more ruthless than capitalism, and just as much an exploiting economy. He sees its fullest development in the Soviet Union; he sees it in Germany, which to him is a "young, new, rising social order"; he sees it foreshadowed in the New Deal, whose "historical direction . . . as a whole runs entirely counter to the ideals and aims of liberalism." He is equally clairvoyant about the War. The United States will enter it in 1941, too late to save Britain but in time to seize much of the British Empire, will be gradually transformed by the crisis into one of the managerial states described, and will swallow most of the rest of the western hemisphere. By this time the rest of the world will consist of two super-states, with their centers of industry in western Europe and eastern Asia, respectively. There can follow only a series of endless wars between the three superstates in their bids for world power.

Ralph Thomson comments that some of Mr. Burnham's ideas sound like Hitler's, but that Hitler didn't invent them any more than Mr.

Burnham did, "and it is proved every time an acorn sprouts or an oak falls of its own weight in a forest." Burnham's ideas are related to those of Robert Michels, Gaetano Mosca, Vilfredo Pareto and Max Nomad.

James Burnham was born in Chicago, Illinois on November 22, 1905, the son of Claude George Burnham, British-born executive vice-president of the Burlington Railroad at the time of his death in 1928, and of Mary May (Gillis) Burnham. When he took his B. A. at Princeton in 1927 he was the Latin Salutatorian (the equivalent of "first scholar") of his class. He continued his education at Oxford University in England, where he received a B. A. in 1929. Since that time he has been a member of the Department of Philosophy at Washington Square College of New York University, where he is now an assistant professor.

For four years, from 1930 to the end of 1933, he was co-editor with Philip E. Wheelwright of *The Symposium,* a critical review published quarterly. In 1932, the year he received his M. A. from Oxford, he and Wheelwright published *Introduction to Philosophical Analysis,* a textbook for college students which, according to S. K. Langer, writing in the *Journal of Philosophy,* was a book "written in the spirit of modernity—a book with an unacademic metropolitan atmosphere: alive, rapid, colloquial. . . On the whole, the *Introduction to Philosophical Analysis,* despite many shortcomings due to the extreme difficulty of its task, is a full and right-minded book; could the detailed elaboration of the work only have equalled in excellence the general conception, it would have been a pedagogical masterpiece."

It was in 1933 that Burnham first became associated with the political group known as "Trotskyists" or "Fourth Internationalists." As he himself puts it: "The official names of the group changed frequently; and the changes would hardly be intelligible without a supplementary history of radical politics during those years." Between 1933 and 1940 he was a frequent contributor to the *Partisan Review* and to "labor and radical" publications; at one time he was co-editor of *The New International,* the theoretical magazine of the United States Trotskyists; and in 1937 he was author of a pamphlet entitled *Peoples' Front; the New Betrayal,* attacking the Communist conception of a "peoples' front against Fascism."

But his quarrels with Trotsky himself soon became almost as bitter. In 1939 he was carrying on a bitter polemical struggle with Trotsky, then still alive and in Mexico, and early in 1940 he broke definitively with the Trotskyists. "The basic reason for the break," he says, "was my conclusion that Marxism is false, and that Marxist politics in practice lead not to their alleged goal of democratic socialism but to one or another form of totalitarian despotism." (In his book, however, he expresses his certainty that socialism is impossible "of achievement or even of approximation," and that in any case the particular form of totalitarian despotism which he calls the managerial society is more than probable.) Since the break with Trotsky, he says, "I have had no politics."

Mr. Burnham contributed one of the ten essays which comprise the book, *Whose Revolution?*, published in 1941, and in November of that year an article by him called *The Coming Rulers of the United States* appeared in *Fortune*. Away from the classroom, writing does not occupy all of his spare time, however. He and his wife, the former Marcia Lightner, whom he married in March 1934, and their children, Marcia and James Bernard, spend as much time as they possibly can in the country, where they raise flowers and vegetables. His brother, David, is the author of four novels, and another brother, Philip, is an editor of the Catholic weekly *Commonweal*.

References

    Sat R Lit 24:9 My 10 '41 por
    Time 37:98 My 19 '41 por

BURR, HENRY Jan. 15, 1885—Apr. 6, 1941 American singer called "dean of ballad singers"; heard by millions on air, concert stage and phonograph; more than 10,000,000 phonograph records were made of such favorites as *Goodnight Little Girl, Goodnight, In the Shade of the Old Apple Tree, Always, Just a Baby's Prayer at Twilight,* and *When You and I Were Young, Maggie*; credited with making the first "transcontinental broadcast"; real name was Harry H. McClaskey.

References

    Variety Radio Directory

Obituaries

    N Y Times p17 Ap 7 '41 por

BURWASH, LACHLIN TAYLOR Sept. 5, 1874—Dec. 21, 1940 Veteran Canadian explorer; explored the Arctic for 40 years; flew to the magnetic pole in 1929; from 1925 to 1926 and in 1930 made trips to trace the route of the ill-fated Franklin Expedition of 1845.

References

    Canad Mag 84:8-9+ Jl '35 il por
    Who's Who
    Who's Who in Canada

Obituaries

    N Y Times p30 D 22 '40 por

BUSH, WENDELL T. Sept. 25, 1866— Feb. 10, 1941 Professor emeritus of philosophy at Columbia University and for 33 years an active member of the teaching staff; co-founder of *The Journal of Philosophy*; presented to the University a unique collection of religious objects to furnish a social science laboratory.

References

    Who's Who in America 1938-39

Obituaries

    N Y Times p23 F 11 '41 por

BUTLER, NEVILE (MONTAGU) Dec. 20, 1893- Junior British Minister to the United States

Address: British Embassy, 3100 Massachusetts Ave, Washington, D. C.

Allied News

NEVILE BUTLER

When in 1939 the late Lord Lothian came to the United States as Ambassador, efficient, publicity-shunning Nevile Butler was selected to be his assistant as the Counselor of the British Embassy. A few weeks before Lord Lothian's death Mr. Butler received the rank of Minister; it was he who was sent to read Lothian's last speech at the Farm Bureau Federation in Baltimore the night before his chief's death; and until the appointment of Lord Halifax as new British Ambassador he served as chargé d'affaires in Washington. Since Halifax has taken up his duties, Nevile Butler has been junior British Minister to the United States.

Nevile Montagu Butler is the son of a scholar—Henry Montagu Butler, D. D., late Master of Trinity College, Cambridge—and of Agnata Frances (Ramsay) Butler. The "old school tie" which he wears is that of Harrow, and he received his university education at Trinity. Then came the First World War. From 1916 to 1918 young Butler was to be found variously in the Scottish Horse, the Household Battalion and finally in the British Intelligence Corps; and in May 1920 he entered the Foreign Office.

After serving his apprenticeship there, Nevile Butler acted as private secretary to the successive parliamentary under-secretaries of state for foreign affairs from February 1924 to June 1927, and then for two months acted as private secretary to Viscount Cecil of Chelwood, at that time Chancellor of the Duchy of Lancaster. From October 1927 to June 1929 he was private secretary to the

BUTLER, NEVILE—*Continued*

late Lord Cushendun, and from 1930 to 1935 to the late Prime Minister Ramsay Mac-Donald. During that period he was appointed Commander of the Royal Victorian Order, in 1933, and after MacDonald's fall from power was sent to Persia to serve as Counselor at the British Legation at Teheran. It was from Persia that he was called to the United States in 1939.

In 1923 Mr. Butler married Oonah Rose McNeile, and they have two daughters. The new Minister enjoys walking, riding, lawn tennis and golf—when his duties at the Embassy permit any recreation at all.

References

Who's Who

BYERS, MARGARETTA Dec. 2, 1901-
Fashion designer; author

Address: b. c/o Simon & Schuster, Inc, 1230 Sixth Ave, New York City; h. Pukka Purchase, Shackamaxon Drive Extension, Westfield, N. J.

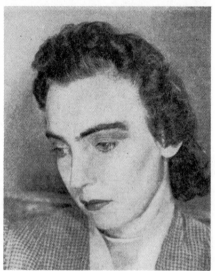

Harlen Byers

MARGARETTA BYERS

Fashion may be spinach, but "spinach" may also take the form of palatable advice on careers in the lucrative realms of women's wear. Margaretta Byers' *Help Wanted—Female* (1941), on the business of making good in the fashion industry, is written from the author's own practical experience. It seems that there are hundreds of varied and interesting positions open to attractive, intelligent young women in the how-to-be-beautiful field. Mrs. Byers tells the aspiring fashion expert in workaday terms just what and what not to do. She helps the novice analyze her own personality through concrete tests and self-quizzes, so that she can find the position best suited to her individual talent and ability.

As one who came up "the hard way" to her top-flight position in the fashion world, Margaretta Byers says: "My new book, *Help Wanted—Female*, turned out to be more autobiographical than I should like, since, of necessity, in telling job-hunters what not to do, it related many of my more egregious blunders. Aside from the incidents related therein, I'm afraid my life has not made very good reading. Born [December 2, 1901] under the sign of Sagittarius, I seem always to have been shooting hopefully at pretty unattainable goals. I suppose I shot so many arrows into the air that some of them were bound to be bull's-eyes. And in such cases, I was always the last to believe that there hadn't been some mistake."

Margaretta Manning Byers was born in Albany, New York, the daughter of Samuel and Mary Kellogg (Seymour) Manning. "In my early teens I did win a contest for composing a school theme on some patriotic subject. This was during the late War. The school telephoned the unbelievable news and summoned me to meet the photographers pronto. Not being as grownup as my theme must have sounded, I was discovered building a bridge over a brook. Always over-enthusiastic, I had just fallen in! Even then, clothes were a great source of concern to me. Of course, I had to borrow a complete costume—which, to my unspeakable satisfaction, was infinitely more grown-up, sophisticated and altogether glamorous than anything afforded by my adolescent wardrobe."

She attended Radcliffe College, where she received her B. A. degree in 1923. "At Radcliffe I took a shot at the Sargent Prize, offered to Harvard and Radcliffe students for a metrical translation of a Horatian ode. Confidentially, I took *two* shots. The second came close—won honorable mention. To my disgust, a Harvard man walked off with the money!"

After graduation she secured a position on the woman's page of *Today in New York*, where she remained until it folded in 1929. Then came fashions and gossip for "The Sportsman Pilot," a shopping column for *Holiday*. In between times she wrote verses, too. Her poetic flight began when, early in her career, she was "a brow-beaten secretary. . . My boss, who fancied herself as somewhat of an efficiency expert, had just perpetuated mayhem upon me for using an unnecessary flip of the wrist in tying the knot of one of her parcel-post packages. The things she said to me sent me dashing into the stockroom, muttering:

> *I'd rather be a dentist*
> *psychoanalyst or thug*
> *than an energetic woman*
> *with the organizing bug!*

"I sent it to the *New Yorker* a few days later, and they took it, seeming to like the genuine viciousness of this and other similar verses of mine later printed by them."

Thus, like Margaret Fishback (see sketch this issue), with whom she was to work as assistant in institutional advertising at Macy's in New York (1930), she found an outlet also for her talents in light verse. But it seems that Mrs. Byers soon concluded that her particular forte in authorship was prose, and began writing articles about clothes and fashions for various national magazines. Meantime she was busy gathering further advertising experience at Lord & Taylor's, Gimbels, Saks Fifth Avenue, and in the special beauty shops of Elizabeth Arden and Margery Wilson.

Designing Women (1938), her first book, written with Consuelo Kamholz, tackled the fine points of the art and technique of being beautiful at little cost. Of this advice on how to be economically attractive most reviewers approved. Elizabeth (*Fashion Is Spinach*) Hawes (see sketch 1940 Annual), however, rather frostily commented that while some readers might pick up valuable hints, "most of them will emerge just where they started or maybe a little more balled up."

But *Designing Women* bids fair to gain immortality. As Mrs. Byers says: "The publishers very cleverly got it buried in the Westinghouse Time Capsule [at the New York World's Fair] on the grounds that it would serve as 'a record of the aims of contemporary women with regard to fashion and beauty.' Before the capsule was sealed we went and squinted down into the hole in the ground and wondered if anyone would ever dig up my brainchild, though Mr. Schuster [see sketch this issue] assured me 'posterity is just around the corner.' Later, in his comic strip, Buck Rogers proceeded to dig up the capsule. We read that episode eagerly. But Buck seemed to take no interest whatsoever in that musty little volume on feminine foibles, dimly entitled *Designing Women*. Or perhaps he thought the title risqué."

A slim, attractive young woman who has made the most of her brown hair and green eyes in practicing what she preaches, Margaretta Byers is known as one of the best-dressed women in a city of best-dressed women. She is no parlor socialite, however. She is devoted to the theatre, having been an active worker in Professor Baker's "47" Workshop while at college. Married in 1929 to Harlen Hatch Byers, a photographer, she likes best to go with him on his picture-taking trips. On these junkets "we both take a busman's holiday—he photographing, I writing the captions. That would be the ideal job, we think, making travelogues of out-of-the-way places, delving deep into the woods stalking small game with a camera, or nosing out stories like the one about that inn in the mountains so reminiscent of the Tyrol which we discovered had been a spy rendezvous, with documentary evidence to prove it." In 1941, however, Mrs. Byers was not as busy discovering the haunts of spies as she was conducting her fashion column for the Des Moines *Register and Tribune* Syndicate.

References

American Women
Byers, M. Help Wanted—Female 1941

BYRNES, JAMES F(RANCIS) (bûrns) May 2, 1879- Associate Justice of the United States Supreme Court

Address: b. United States Supreme Court, Washington, D. C.; h. Spartanburg, S. C.

JAMES F. BYRNES

Bulletin: On June 12, 1941 James F. Byrnes' nomination to the United States Supreme Court was unanimously confirmed by his fellow Senators. On July 8 he took the oath of office.

From June 1941 issue:

There have been only eight justices on the United States Supreme Court since Justice James McReynolds resigned on January 31, 1941. If President Roosevelt has been slow about naming McReynolds' successor, most people believe it is because he plans to name South Carolina's James F. Byrnes—and these days Byrnes is a hard man to spare from the Senate, invaluable there as a Democratic leader and liner-up of votes. Southern Senators and Republicans are alike unanimous in supporting Byrnes' claims, and as late as April 29 the President cheered a South Carolina reporter by his announcement that when the ninth justice is finally named he hoped there would be no disappointment in South Carolina.

James Francis Byrnes is described by Joseph Alsop and Robert Kintner as "a small, wiry, neatly made man, with an odd, sharply angular face from which his sharp eyes peer out with an expression of quizzical geniality." They say his enemies call him the slyest, his friends the ablest, member of the Senate. Not a great speechmaker, "to see him at his best, he must be watched getting McNary's promise not to object, conciliating the prideful House leaders and craftily waiting his chance on the Senate floor to drive one of the great defense bills to immediate passage." He knows the political

BYRNES, JAMES F.—*Continued*

situation in every state; he knows the prejudices, the weaknesses, the enmities of all the Senators, by what margin and by what groups they were elected, who are their chief opponents. His knowledge and his ability to use it make him and Pat Harrison a smoothly working team when it comes to taking a poll. There are greater scholars and more profound thinkers in the Senate, but it is still true that almost never has President Roosevelt "lost in the Senate on an important bill when Senator Byrnes was with him; almost never has he won when Senator Byrnes was against him." For Byrnes, in *Time's* words, is "a politician's politician as other men are poet's poets or engineer's engineers."

The Senator from South Carolina is very quotable. "Most big issues are partly political, and where there's politics there's got to be compromise. . ." "You've got to sacrifice your opinion to your party on minor questions, or you'll lose all your influence on big issues. But if you start giving in too much on the big issues you may as well go home." And he is as energetic as he is shrewd. Yet, according to Alsop and Kintner, "he is a man of nervous constitution, ill-fitted to carry the double burden of public business and the endless petty tasks of politics. . . All South Carolina batters daily at his doors, demanding everything from postmasterships and free seeds to housing projects, more CCC camps and $50,000,000 dams." And at present he is in a position where he is "doing many of the jobs of leadership without an official leader's authority."

Byrnes was born in a "little, sagging-galleried frame house in King Street in old Charleston" on May 2, 1879, the son of James Francis and Elizabeth E. Byrnes. His father had died a few months before, and his mother was left penniless with a large household to support. She managed by going into the dressmaking business. Her children delivered dresses almost as soon as they could walk, and learned shorthand almost before they had conquered the three R's.

James was a brilliant student who won scholarships, but he had to leave school at the age of 14. He found a position as office boy in a law firm, did stenography after closing hours, and before he was out of his teens was making enough money with these two jobs for his mother to quit working. In 1900 he entered a competition for official reporter which he won; he moved with his mother to Aiken, South Carolina to take up the position. In the meanwhile he had been studying law under the supervision of a friendly judge and was soon ready for his Bar examination. After being admitted to the Bar in 1903 he continued as court reporter, however, and also bought the Aiken *Journal and Review*, which he paid for in two years and edited for four.

In 1908 Byrnes resigned his court reporter's job to run for solicitor of the Second South Carolina Circuit, a position equivalent to district attorney. He was elected, and after having cleaned up Barnwell County decided to run for Congress in 1910. "I campaigned on nothing but gall," he said later, "and gall won by 57 votes."

In Washington, where he arrived in 1911 for the winter session, Byrnes lived in an old hotel near the Capitol, a hangout for Congressmen. There he made friends, "learned there was more to the United States than the Second South Carolina District." One of the first things he did was to force the formation of the House Committee on Roads, from which grew the present Federal road-aid system. ("We fellows in Congress have mostly got to promise our people something from the Treasury, and in the old days in the South and West we generally used to promise Federal roads," he explained.) Later he was appointed to the Banking and Currency Committee, and went enthusiastically after the "money trust" during the Pujo Investigation.

Nevertheless Byrnes, who learned fast, soon learned that preoccupation with money trusts was no way to hold his constituents, who were incidentally charging him with endangering "white supremacy" by supporting a constitutional amendment for direct Senatorial primaries. When he returned for his second term he therefore began doing jobs for Democratic leaders instead of trying to be a statesman right away, and before long he had his reward: an appointment to the House Appropriations Committee. He handled his first bill long before the First World War, and by the time the United States entered it he was a member of the deficiency subcommittee of the Appropriations Committee, one of three men who had the chief power of the purse over the nation. The principal government officials appeared before them, publicly or privately, to ask for billions for one purpose or another; President Wilson himself consulted them. It was at this time that Byrnes made the acquaintance of Franklin D. Roosevelt and of Bernard Baruch (see sketch this issue).

Toward the end of the War, Byrnes went abroad with Representative Richard S. Whaley and Senator Carter Glass (see sketch this issue), celebrating the Armistice in Edinburgh; after he returned his first act was to present a bill repealing seven billion dollars in contracts appropriated for, and seven billions in cash authorizations. But the Republicans had captured the House. Byrnes, who didn't particularly enjoy being in opposition, by 1924 was willing to risk an attempt to get himself elected to the Senate. Defeated, he went back to practicing law in South Carolina not too reluctantly, for there was no year of law practice in which he didn't take in several times his Congressional salary. By 1930, when the Republican tide had ebbed, he was ready to return to the Senatorial race. This time he won, and his rise in the Senate was rapid. He lined up South Carolina's delegates for Roosevelt, and in the 1932 Presidential campaign moved into "brain-trust headquarters" at the Hotel Roosevelt to advise on budgetary matters.

Immediately after he came into office Roosevelt began using Byrnes for jobs that the late Senate chieftain Joe Robinson didn't want to handle. Byrnes' efficiency at them made him Senate spokesman for the White House, and in his campaign for re-election he stuck to the proposition: "Roosevelt will be elected and so will Jimmy Byrnes." (He had opened the campaign with the pithy comment: "What South Carolina needs is not a good political campaign but a good rain.") In any case, his record was consistently pro-New Deal. He had fought for legislation to abolish the abuses of the stretch-out system in the cotton mills of the South; he had put through Congress a resolution making it a felony to transport strike breakers in interstate commerce.

It was not until Roosevelt's second term that Byrnes formed an active alliance with some of the "moderates" in the Senate who opposed many New Deal measures. Conservative by nature, he undoubtedly regretted having managed the $4,800,000,000 relief bill of 1936, was disillusioned by its results. And the political wind was changing. In 1937 he gave the first indications of his new orientation when he attempted to cut appropriations for the La Follette Civil Liberties Committee and authored the anti-sit-down strike amendment to the Guffey Coal Bill. By 1938 he was insisting that the budget be balanced, fighting the anti-lynch bill, asking for the immediate repeal of the undistributed-profits tax and modification of the capital-gains levy, trying to force the House to defeat the wage-hour bill which he had opposed in the Senate the year before; and he also helped his colleague, "Cotton Ed" Smith, when Roosevelt wanted to "purge" him in the 1938 primaries. In 1939 he battled for reductions in WPA appropriations.

Byrnes had no quarrel with Roosevelt's foreign policy, however, and he and the President speedily made up. Since that time he has captained the Senate Democrats in many difficult fights: over the repeal of the arms embargo, the extension of the trade agreements, the emergency defense appropriations and most of the subsequent features of the defense program. (In matters of national defense Byrnes has no "economy" psychosis.) In the spring and summer of 1940 he was being frequently mentioned for the Democratic Vice-Presidential nomination, with Bob La Follette commenting, dryly: "I like Byrnes, but I must say I hope to God he doesn't get it. We have a hard enough time now, but with the President in the White House again and Byrnes running the Senate, bills will go through here so fast we won't even have a chance to offer an amendment."

Though Wallace got the Vice-Presidential nomination, Byrnes fought hard for Roosevelt's re-election, speaking over the radio to endorse the third term, replying to Willkie's "campaign oratory." Since that time he has more than once delivered vigorous public speeches in favor of aid to Britain, and "it is now established that the lease-lend law came through the Senate so well as it did chiefly because of the able management of Byrnes . . .

who made the checks, talked to the waverers, soothed the grumblers and shepherded the doubters into line . . . who deftly arranged the remarkable compromise on the Ellender Amendment." His next job was to be one of the floor managers for the seven billion dollar appropriations bill. It is not surprising if the President hates to lose him.

Mrs. Byrnes is the former Maude Perkins Busch, of Aiken, South Carolina, whom he married in 1908, joining the Presbyterian church that same year. Her husband's favorite recreations are "good fellowship, the study of human nature," telling long, "saltily humorous" anecdotes. Outside of politics, his wants are satisfied by "two tailor-made suits a year, three meals a day, and a reasonable amount of good liquor." And he "needs only two or three to make a quorum for *Carolina Moon, Keep Shinin'.*" Maybe he will find them in the Supreme Court; maybe he won't.

References
Bus Week p8 Je 1 '40
Christian Sci Mon Mag p5 Ap 26 '41 pors
Collier's 91:13 Mr 25 '33
N Y Herald Tribune p10 F 4 '41; II p2 Mr 30 '41
Newsweek 14:16 Jl 24 '39 por; 17:18 Je 23 '41 por
PM p9 Je 13 '41
Sat Eve Post 213:18-19+ Jl 20 '40 il il pors
Time 28:17-22 Ag 24 '36 il por; 36:15 O 28 '40 por; 37:15 Je 23 '41 por
Michie, A. A. and Ryhlick, F. Dixie Demagogues p68-86 1939
Who's Who in America
Who's Who in Government
Who's Who in the Nation's Capital

BYRON, WILLIAM D(EVEREUX) May 15, 1895—Feb. 27, 1941 Democratic member of the House of Representatives from Maryland; killed in plane crash while on way to Mexico City; had been a member of Congress since his election in November 1938; in 1940 defeated the Republican candidate, Walter Johnson, noted baseball pitcher, to return to the House of Representatives.

References
Who's Who in America

Obituaries
N Y Times p1, 12+ F 28 '41

CALFEE, JOHN EDWARD (căl′fē) Feb. 7, 1875—Nov. 28, 1940 Retired president of Asheville, North Carolina Normal and Teachers College; was well known for his work in education of mountain boys and girls; author of a number of books.

References
Leaders in Education 1941
Who's Who Among North American Authors

(Continued next page)

CALFEE, JOHN EDWARD—*Continued*
Who's Who in America
Who's Who in American Education
Obituaries
N Y Times p17 N 30 '40

CALVERTON, V(ICTOR) F(RANCIS)
June 25, 1900—Nov. 20, 1940 Author of books
on sociology and literature, best known for
his *Sex in Civilization*; lectured widely
throughout the country; real name George
Goetz.
References
Author's and Writer's Who's Who
Who's Who in America
Obituaries
N Y Herald Tribune p32 N 21 '40
N Y Times p29 N 21 '40 por

CAMMERER, ARNO B(ERTHOLD)
(kăm'mĕr-rēr) July 31, 1883—Apr. 30, 1941
Former director of the United States National
Park Service from 1933 until 1940 when he
resigned because of overwork; headed the
Service during one of the periods of greatest
expansion and improvement in its history; had
jurisdiction over 21,930,000 acres and appor-
tioned more than $200,000,000 in park funds
allotted through emergency relief appropria-
tions.
References
Recreation 34:333 Ag '40
Who's Who in America
Who's Who in Government
Who's Who in the Nation's Capital
Obituaries
N Y Herald Tribune p18 My 1 '41 por

CAMPBELL, E. SIMMS Jan. 2, 1906-
Cartoonist; artist
Address: Saw Mill River Rd, White Plains,
N. Y.

Readers of *Esquire* are no doubt familiar
with the signature of E. Simms Campbell,
for each issue of that magazine contains 10 or
12 full-page cartoons by him. Campbell is the
first Negro artist to work for national publications and national advertisers. He has
contributed to the following periodicals: *Cosmopolitan, Red Book, New Yorker, Collier's,
Saturday Evening Post, College Humor,
Judge, Life, Delineator, Opportunity* (organ
of the National Urban League). He has done
full pages of cartoons for the New York
Sunday *Mirror*, the black and white illustrations for Jack Kofoed's *Great Dramas in
Sports* in *Life* Magazine, the cover called
Into the Light for the brochure in honor of
and promoting the fiftieth anniversary of the
Y. M. C. A., and is in 1941 under contract
with *Esquire*, for which he has done pages
and pages of drawings ever since that periodical first came out in 1933. His women
approximate a Yale junior's ideal of female
desirability in the moments when the "Petty

Philadelphia Society for
Negro Records & Research

E. SIMMS CAMPBELL

Girl" begins to pall, and probably only the
pink-pated magnates and Eastern potentates
who usually lurk somewhere in the background
make Campbell's water colors less popular
than Petty's for college walls.

Campbell was born in St. Louis, Missouri.
His father was a chemistry teacher and assistant principal in a high school there; his
mother did water colors for her own satisfaction. He went to Chicago, and there attended the Englewood High School, where
he drew cartoons for the school paper. In
1923 he won a nationwide contest for the
best cartoon in a high school paper, an
Armistice Day cartoon. For a year he attended Chicago University, and then went to
the Art Institute of Chicago for three years,
meantime starting work for a humorous
magazine.

When the magazine failed Campbell returned to St. Louis. Unable to find work
there as an artist, he took a job as a waiter
on a dining car. About this part of his experience he has said: "I was a good waiter."
But between times he drew caricatures of
the people on the train—the passengers, the
other waiters and the train officials. On one
of his return trips to St. Louis he succeeded
in showing these drawings to J. P. Sauer-
wein, manager of the Triad Studios, one of
the largest commercial art studios in the
Midwest. The Triad Studios hired him, and
he worked with them for a year and a half,
until he left of his own free will to go to
New York City to try his luck there.

It was Elmer Carter, editor of *Opportunity*,
who had challenged Campbell to come to
New York. Campbell by request had sent
Carter a cover for *Opportunity* and had re-

marked that he did not like the covers on that magazine. Carter thought that the young artist was good, but wrote that if he were really good he ought to be able to meet the competition in New York, where it was "hot," and be able to draw for any of the magazines, not just for *Opportunity*, which is a Negro publication. In New York, Campbell did not find it easy to get established. For a while he worked for an advertising agency at one-eighth the salary he had been getting in St. Louis. He also sold "gags" to other artists, sometimes 50 a week. Then one day he met Ed Graham, a former school friend of his, who had become one of America's outstanding cartoonists. Graham took him to the editors of some of the humorous magazines, and soon Campbell was receiving plenty of commissions. Shortly thereafter *Esquire* was started and with it his assignments from that magazine.

Campbell is a hard worker. He draws about 300 full-page cartoons a year for magazines, at least one each day in transparent water colors, in addition to cartoons for advertising agencies. He also does drawings for other publications—in 1936 he won a $1,000 prize offered by a large Chicago newspaper for the best cartoon depicting the tax grabber. Unlike many other artists, he writes his own "gags." He sits up all night drawing under a strong light, drinking coffee to keep awake. He said that he seldom drinks liquor because anything he can do drunk he can do much better sober. A great deal of fan mail comes to him, much of it from aspiring artists, often very young, or from parents who are eager to know whether their children possess talent. All of this mail Campbell answers. He is very generous in giving his time to young artists, inviting them to his home for criticism and advice, making connections for them in the commercial art world, encouraging them as once he needed encouragement.

References

Esquire 9 :62-5+ Ap '38 por
N Y Age p6 My 14 '38
N Y World-Telegram p17 Ja 12 '37
Opportunity 10 :82-5 Mr '32 il por

CAMPBELL, SIR GERALD Oct. 30, 1879- Director general of British Information Services

Address: British Information Services, 30 Rockefeller Plaza, New York City

On January 15, 1941 the British Foreign Office announced that Sir Gerald Campbell, at that time in Ottawa as High Commissioner for Great Britain, had been appointed British Minister to the United States. Five months later, on June 3, 1941, it was announced in London that he would in the future act as director general of British Information Services in the United States. According to the official statement, the new appointment was "in response to the increasing demand in the United States for fuller and more complete information concerning Britain's war effort and

for the improvement of the supply of news from British sources."

Gray-haired, ruddy, genial Sir Gerald had already lived 19 years in the United States as consul general in Philadelphia, San Francisco and New York until 1938, and is supposed to have considerable knowledge of American economy. At his first press conference after a three weeks' visit to England in July, his

SIR GERALD CAMPBELL

first since the War began, he defined the chief function of his office as the provision of interpretation "against the British background" of news and pictures obtained by correspondents to American editors, columnists and radio commentators. One of the principal things he wanted to accomplish was to show American working men the great effect their work was having in a grateful Britain.

Sir Gerald was born on October 30, 1879, the son of the late Reverend Colin Campbell of Weston-super-Mare. He was educated at Repton and at Trinity College, Cambridge, where he received his B. A.; he entered the British diplomatic service in 1907 as vice-consul at Rio de Janeiro. From 1908 to 1913 he was in the Belgian Congo, from 1913 to 1915 in Venice and from 1915 to 1919 served as consul at Addis Ababa.

It was not until 1920 that he came to the United States to be consul general at Philadelphia; a year later he was appointed to the same duties at San Francisco. In 1923 he was made a Companion of St. Michael and St. George. He came to New York City in 1931 as consul general and in 1934 was knighted as Commander of St. Michael and St. George. It was in 1938 that he became High Commissioner for the United Kingdom in Canada.

CAMPBELL, SIR GERALD—*Continued*

When Sir Gerald left the United States he left behind him "an indelible impression compounded of friendliness, intelligence and a most engaging humor." Nearly a thousand people attended a farewell dinner arranged to do him honor, for he had been rated as New York City's busiest public speaker.

In 1911 Sir Gerald married Margaret C. Juler, and they have three daughters, one of whom was born in Addis Ababa. He has received numerous honors: possesses an honorary LL. D. from Queens, McGill and Toronto Universities in Canada, Rutgers University, Union College and New York University in the United States. He is also an officer of the Order of St. John of Jerusalem, a fellow of the Royal Geographical Society, and wears the Star of Ethiopia. On May 28, 1940 he received the first award of the Canadian Club of New York "because of accomplishment in the line of duty over a long and honorable career." His recreations are hockey, golf, tennis—and telling funny stories to an appreciative audience. He is very quotable. What is more, he can be witty in more than one language: he knows "Portuguese, Spanish, French, Italian and, in a pinch, Kiswahili and Amharic."

References

> N Y Herald Tribune p1 Ja 16 '41 por
> N Y Times p6 Ap 24 '40 por; p7 Ja 16
> '41 por; IV p2 Ja 19 '41 por
> Time 37:21 Ja 27 '41 por
> Who's Who

CAMPBELL, PHILIP P(ITT) Apr. 25, 1862—May 26, 1941 Former Representative who served in the House of Representatives for 20 years, becoming Speaker just before his final term ended; was head of Rules Committee; fought against allowing President Wilson to go to Versailles; was a noted isolationist; since 1922 when he was defeated for re-election he had practiced law in Washington, D. C.

References

> Who's Who in America
> Who's Who in the Nation's Capital

Obituaries

> N Y Times p23 My 27 '41

CAMPBELL, WILLIS C(OHOON) Dec. 18, 1880—May 4, 1941 Internationally known orthopedic surgeon and head of the Campbell Clinic of Memphis, Tennessee; acted as consultant in orthopedic surgery in many hospitals; was professor in his field at the College of Medicine of the University of Tennessee since 1910; had studied in Vienna as a pupil of the celebrated Adolph Lorenz.

References

> American Medical Directory
> American Men of Science
> Directory of Medical Specialists   1939
> Who's Who in America

Obituaries

> N Y Times p17 My 5 '41

CAMPINCHI, CÉSAR (käN-päN-shē) May 4, 1882—Feb. 23, 1941 Former Minister of the French Navy and Deputy from Corsica, who belonged to the group in the Daladier Cabinet which consistently opposed the Munich policy; served as Navy Minister until the capitulation of France; named by the Pétain Government as one of those responsible for "throwing our country into war, although they knew we were not ready to fight"; was not brought to trial on the charges.

References

> Dictionnaire National des Contemporains 1936
> International Who's Who
> Qui Êtes-Vous?
> Who's Who

Obituaries

> N Y Times p15 F 24 '41 por

CAMROSE, WILLIAM EWERT BERRY, 1ST VISCOUNT June 23, 1879- British newspaper publisher

Address: b. Daily Telegraph Offices, Fleet St, London, E. C. 4; h. 25 St. James's Pl, London, S. W. 1, England

Lord Camrose has never been so spectacular a Fleet Street personality as the late Lord Northcliffe, but his holdings in British newspapers have probably been just as great. Northcliffe was an innovator who made news sensational, ran stunts, awarded prizes. Camrose, though he took over financial control of a large part of the great organization Northcliffe built up, is associated in British public opinion chiefly with the *Sunday Times* and the *Daily Telegraph*, both dignified and non-sensational organs of opinion. And throughout the years he has almost consistently refused to change the established policy of the papers he has acquired.

Lord Camrose spent all his working life up to 1937 in close association with his brother Lord Kemsley (Gomer Berry), and the history of the one man is in large part the history of both. These brothers who control an $80,000,000 publishing empire owe their huge wealth, their prestige and their titles to sheer ability and hard work, coupled, perhaps, with some good luck. William Ewert Berry was born in Gwaelodygarth, Merthyr Tydfil, Wales, the son of the late Alderman John Mathias Berry, a realtor. He was brought up in modest comfort, which did not include a public school education, and quit school altogether at the age of 14 to work on the Merthyr *Times*.

For five years William Berry stayed in South Wales, as office boy and reporter on various local papers, until in 1898 he went to London as a reporter on the *Investor's Guardian*, at $7 a week. He had a hard time, punctuated by periods of unemployment, one of which lasted three months, and not much relieved by the low salaries he earned when he had newspaper positions. Tired of working, or not working, for others, in 1901 he started his own weekly paper, the *Advertising World*.

Berry wrote most of the paper himself, canvassed for advertisements and laid out the paper himself. He made a profit from the start. Before long he brought up his younger brother, Gomer, from Wales, and from that time on the fortunes of the brothers ran together. William looked after the policy and contents of their papers while Gomer supervised the finance and management. In 1905 they sold the *Advertising World,* bought a publishing business and founded the journal *Boxing.* Other papers were soon founded or acquired by them, and they began to make money.

The acquisition of the *Sunday Times* in 1915, however, was the first time the Berrys became first-class publishers. This paper has no connection with *The Times* itself, but resembles that august organ in its dignity of news presentation, its chastity of format and its highly expert treatment of literature, art and music. Berry took it over almost by accident. He was lunching with the financier, Jimmy White, when, in the words of Bernard Falk, "West de Went Fenton, traveler and journalist, sauntered up to the table. Having secured an option on the *Sunday Times,* he wanted White to come in and help find the money. He was told that the man he should address was the guest—William Berry."

Fenton was bought out and the principal owner, Herman Schmidt, ratified the option. Then Berry had to deal with the actual holders, who included Sir Basil Zaharoff, the Greek armaments magnate, and Sir Arthur Steel-Maitland, one of the Conservative Party chiefs. Neither of these men wanted Berry to take the paper over, and it was only after a tussle that he won out. The Berry brothers quickly followed up their success here by purchasing the printing works at which the paper was set up, St. Clement's Press, and this purchase gave them control, too, of the *Financial Times,* the leading investors' paper.

During the next 10 years the Berrys went on from success to success, buying up publishing, newspaper, printing and paper concerns right and left. A big buy was that of the fashion house of Weldons, which ran about 20 dress magazines for women. Another was that of Kelly's Directories, which publishes most of the local directories in England. Still another was that of the *Graphic* group, consisting of the *Sunday Graphic* and the *Bystander.* Then the Berrys launched out into the provinces and in 1924 took over the Hulton group of Manchester; in 1925 they bought the Newcastle group, the Glasgow group and papers in South Wales, Sheffield and Aberdeen. All over Britain were Berry papers, weeklies, dailies, monthlies. William Berry was made a baronet in 1921; in 1929 he was raised to the peerage as Baron Camrose of Long Cross; and in 1941 he was made a Viscount, his name leading the King's honors list.

Meanwhile, in 1926, a further Napoleonic deal had taken place. William and Gomer bought the whole business of the Amal-

LORD CAMROSE

gamated Press from the executors of Lord Northcliffe, a business which comprises more than 100 daily, weekly and monthly papers, ranging from boys' comics through technical journals, women's papers and general journals to encyclopedias. Then, on January 2, 1928, the Berry brothers took control of the *Daily Telegraph.*

This old established morning paper belonged to shareholders, chief of whom was Lord Burnham. It had solid traditions and a price of four cents a copy, as opposed to the standard price of two cents. Burnham saw that the concern was losing money and was hopelessly out of date, but saw, too, that it was impossible to modernize it and make it profitable without foregoing dividends over a long period, a sacrifice which his fellow shareholders could hardly afford So he sold out to Lord Camrose, who took over not only as proprietor but as editor in chief. Lord Camrose carried out the necessary modernization, reduced the price to two cents, built palatial offices in Fleet Street and trebled the circulation in five years.

In the control of the *Daily Telegraph,* Lord Camrose was associated with his brother and Lord Iliffe, but early in 1937 the three split up because the high joint holdings were cumbersome. Lord Camrose's chief interest remained with the *Daily Telegraph,* the Amalgamated Press and the *Financial Times.* In the summer of that same year another old and famous paper fell to Lord Camrose, the *Morning Post,* the last stronghold of die-hard Toryism in the country. Since die-hard Toryism had sunk in popularity until it had a very small following indeed, the *Morning Post* was sick and ailing. Lord Camrose amalgamated it with the *Telegraph* within two months. His latest venture was *War Illustrated,* which

CAMROSE, WILLIAM, 1ST VISCOUNT
—Continued

came out as soon as the Second World War was declared. (For a time in this War he also assisted the Government at the Ministry of Information.)

Lord Camrose has always believed in playing a major part in the direction of his principal papers, and he has fine offices in the Telegraph building itself. "Attached to his suite of rooms is a luncheon apartment, where he often entertains a few friends. . . His punctilious habits call into being a picturesque ritual. The lift is at his floor the moment he signifies his departure. On entering it, he is helped on with his overcoat. By the time the ground floor is reached, his motor car has drawn up opposite the main entrance and the door is open ready to receive him— all so much clockwork."

This newspaper magnate is a healthy, happy man who dresses quietly, avoids "society" and is liked by his employees. He has been responsible for a number of generous philanthropic gestures and takes a lively interest in the fine arts. His hobby is yachting, and he is a member of the Royal Yacht Squadron. In 1905 he married Mary Agnes, eldest daughter of the late Thomas Corns of London, and the couple have four sons and four daughters, the heir being the Hon. John Seymour Berry, born in 1909.

References

Liv Age 357:17-21 S '39
Newsweek 10:18 Ag 7 '37 por; 10:39 O 25 '37
So Atlan Q 34:419-43 O '35
Time 30:53+ Ag 9 '37; 34-48 S 25 '39 por
Author's and Writer's Who's Who
Camrose, W. E. B. London Newspapers: Their Owners and Controllers 1939
Falk, B. Five Years Dead 1937
Who's Who
Who's Who in Commerce and Industry

CANDLER, WARREN A(KIN), BISHOP

Aug. 23, 1857—Sept. 25, 1941 Leader of the Southern Methodist Church for more than half a century; in 1888 was elected president of Emory College and held this position until he became a bishop in 1898; drew national attention many times during his career.

References

Lit Digest 98:8 S 15 '28 por; 114:20 Jl 16 '32 por; 117:21 My 19 '34
Who's Who Among North American Authors
Who's Who in America

Obituaries

N Y Times p23 S 26 '41 por

CANNON, ANNIE J(UMP)

Dec. 11, 1863—Apr. 13, 1941 Most famous woman astronomer in the world; called the "Census Taker of the Sky" because during her lifelong researches at Harvard University since 1897 she had classified almost 400,000 stellar bodies; honored as the first woman ever to receive an honorary Doctor's Degree from Oxford University and the first woman ever elected an officer of the American Astronomical Society; listed in 1929 among 12 "greatest living American women" chosen by the National League of Women Voters.

References

Sci N L 36:121 Ag 19 '39
American Men of Science
American Women
Who's Who in America

Obituaries

N Y Times p17 Ap 14 '41 por
Sch & Soc 53:507 Ap 19 '41
Time 37:90 Ap 21 '41

CANTERBURY, ARCHBISHOP OF
See Lang, C. G., Archbishop of Canterbury

CANTOR, EDDIE

Jan. 31, 1892(?)- Radio, stage and screen actor

Address: b. Station WEAF, 30 Rockefeller Plaza, New York City; h. Beverly Hills, Calif.

"Gentlemen," Eddie Cantor told his radio sponsors who begged him to avoid controversial topics, "long after I'm through as a comedian, I'll still be a man." "After that," he told John T. McManus, "I was court-martialed, only in my case they stood me up against a wall and took my contract away from me."

Radio sponsors, for obvious reasons, prefer that their actors refrain from offending any possible purchaser of cigarets, toothpaste, coffee and the like, and not many radio performers are willing to jeopardize their careers even to preserve their personal integrity. Eddie Cantor, however, has apparently never weighed speaking his mind or espousing a cause against its possible effect on his pocketbook. At times his philanthropic gestures may seem so covered with bathos and his devotion to democracy so steeped in sentimentality that the over-critical listener fails for the moment to be swayed. Cantor's sincerity and wholeheartedness, however, have never been questioned.

Eddie Cantor was born Edward Israel Iskowitz, the son of Russian immigrant parents, Michael and Minnie Iskowitz, on Eldridge Street in New York City's lower East Side. Orphaned at the age of two, he was raised by a maternal grandmother known to her family and friends as "Esther." Esther managed a none-too-prosperous domestic employment agency and tried to provide as well as she could for her grandson. Eddie attended a public school and Wood's Business School in the Williamsburg section of Brooklyn.

At home and at the Surprise Lake Camp to which his grandmother had petitioned the Welfare Board to send him, Eddie was popular for his mimicry and impersonations. His talents were used also "to hold the attention of street corner crowds with political orations while his confederates picked the spectators' pockets."

When Eddie was fourteen he met Ida Tobias, "the belle of Henry Street," and eight years later they were married despite the objections of her family, who felt that Eddie would never amount to anything. Their honeymoon trip to Europe was interrupted by America's entry into the First World War, and Cantor returned to participate in the sale of Liberty Bonds and the entertainment of the A. E. F.

Although Eddie Cantor has still to reach the half-century mark, his has been a long and varied career. His first stage appearance was made at the notorious Miner's Bowery Theatre, where amateurs rose and fell at the whim of one of the severest audiences of all time. Eddie did not get the "hook": he won applause and five dollars.

Heartened by this dramatic success, Cantor got a job as a singing waiter at Coney Island, where he formed a lasting friendship with the saloon's pianist, Jimmy Durante. In 1912 he played a black-faced butler in Gus Edwards' *Kid Kabaret*. From then until 1916 he played in vaudeville and burlesque. His first real opportunity was in the 1916 *Midnight Frolic* at the Amsterdam Roof. Included in the *Ziegfeld Follies* of 1917, 1918 and 1919, he toured as Sam Beverly Moon in *Canary Cottage* and, in 1920, made his first starring appearance in *The Midnight Rounders*. In the same year he appeared in *Broadway Brevities* and, in 1922, in *Make It Snappy*.

From 1923 to 1926 he starred in *Kid Boots* and in 1929 in the record-breaking *Whoopee*. The screen version of *Kid Boots,* made in 1926, was his first screen appearance. He has since played in such films as *Special Delivery;* the 1927 *Follies; Glorifying the American Girl* (1929); *Whoopee* (1930); *Palmy Days* (1932); *The Kid From Spain* (1932); *Roman Scandals* (1933); *Kid Millions* (1934); *Strike Me Pink* (1936); *Ali Baba Goes to Town* (1937); and *Forty Little Mothers* (1940).

As a radio comedian, Cantor has been active since 1931. His first National Broadcasting Company network appearance was made in February 1931 on Rudy Vallee's program, and in September of the same year he starred in a program of his own for Chase and Sanborn coffee. After five years on the same program he moved to the Columbia Broadcasting System in 1935, where he starred on the Pebeco, Texaco and Camel programs. He then left radio for a season, returning for Sal Hepatica and Ipana, on whose programs in 1941 he is heard Wednesday at nine.

Eddie Cantor's comedy is known for its combination tear-and-smile approach and for its use of his protruding eyeballs as well as his ad libbing talents. (It is safe to say that many of the best lines in everything in which he appears are due to his impromptu wit.) He claims to be an innovator in several fields of his varied activities. For one thing, he introduced the "announcer-stooge," using the sponsor's representative in the script. He was the first to bring the studio reaction into the home: in the early history of variety programs, studio audiences had been told to maintain a rigid silence. Furthermore, as one of the few performers to preview programs, Cantor treats a preview audience to

EDDIE CANTOR

a double script two days before the program is scheduled to go on the air. The reaction to the jokes is carefully checked and items which fail to get laughs are eliminated. Experience has given him an unshakable conviction that insults are the very backbone of humor, and Eddie has been waiting for a long time to spring one of his own, now filed away in his Hit Parade of Insult Classics. When chubby Alexander Woollcott (see sketch this issue) finally tells him that things are not going well with him, Eddie will look him straight in the eye and say, quick as a flash: "Chins up, old boy!"

Exceptionally active in discovering new talent for the screen and radio, Cantor counts among his "finds" Burns and Allen, Deanna Durbin (see sketch this issue), Bobby Breen and Parkyakarkus.

In 1928 Cantor dictated his autobiography to David Freedman, and the homely sentimental tale of the trip from Eldridge Street to Broadway and Hollywood called *My Life Is In Your Hands* was serialized in the *Saturday Evening Post* and published in book form. Other articles written by Eddie Cantor include *Yoo Hoo Prosperity!; The Eddie Cantor Five Year Plan; Caught Short; Your Next President; Does Hollywood Make Bad Pictures on Purpose?;* and *Dear Ida, A Wedding Anniversary Letter to the Mother of My Five Daughters.*

As a philanthropist and generally public-spirited citizen Cantor's reputation is second only to his reputation as a comedian. In 1936 he originated the successful scheme of the March of Dimes, based on the notion that people are thrilled to send money to the President; he is the founder of the Eddie Cantor Camp Committee which sends poor and undernourished boys to the country; and he is active in both Jewish and Christian

CANTOR, EDDIE—*Continued*

charities, frequently appearing in more than 100 benefit performances in a single season.

He also performs for draftees, broadcasts comedy by short wave to Britain, and is otherwise active in national and patriotic movements, although his efforts are not always successful. In January 1936 a $5,000 scholarship which he offered for an essay on *How America Can Stay Out of War* was won by a boy who submitted a plagiarized article and resulted in publicity more unfavorable than otherwise.

Eddie Cantor is president of the Jewish Theatrical Guild of America and of the American Federation of Radio Artists. He is a Mason and a member of the board of directors of Surprise Lake Camp, where he spent part of his own underprivileged youth.

Besides his busy activities on the radio and his patriotic and charitable pursuits, Eddie Cantor returned to the stage late in 1941 in a musical comedy, *Banjo Eyes,* a musical version of *Three Men on a Horse* and "the biggest show of the season." Its two dozen scenes were played on two turntables, and in the finale Mr. Cantor returned to the blackfaced role with which he was associated in his early vaudeville days. The expenses of the production, estimated at about $100,000, were to be divided between Cantor and Warner Brothers, who expect to convert the show into a film in 1942.

Eddie Cantor stands five feet, seven and one-half inches tall. His hair is black and his "taw" eyes, a pair of characteristics on which he has capitalized throughout his career, are brown.

His five daughters, whom he has never allowed his audiences to forget, are: Marjorie, Natalie, Edna J., Marilyn and Janet. He has one grandchild, a son, born to Natalie and Joseph Metzger in the fall of 1939. Eddie was on a personal appearance tour when the news of his grandfatherhood reached him in Boston. "Boy, oh boy, am I happy!" he shouted to an audience of 5,000 persons. "Is that perfection!"

References

Am Mag 121:47+ Ja '36 il; 123:43+ Ja '37 por
Cue 10:3 S 27 '41 por
Delineator 130:46 Mr '37 por
Etude 58:804+ D '40
Good H 104:34-5+ Ap '37 il pors
N Y Post p9 N 23 '40 por
N Y Times IX p10 Ag 31 '41 por
Time 26:43 Jl 15 '35 por
Cantor, E. My Life Is in Your Hands; as Told to David Freedman 1928
International Motion Picture Almanac
Sobel, B. ed. Theatre Handbook 1940
Variety Radio Directory
Who's Who in America
Who's Who in American Jewry
Who's Who in the Theatre

CAREY, CHARLES HENRY Oct. 27, 1857—Aug. 26, 1941 Former vice-president of the American Bar Association; once president of the Oregon Bar Association; member of the Institute of Pacific Relations; an active career included corporation law practice, judicial procedure, reform work, international peace efforts and writing histories of his state and other historical works.

References

Who's Who Among North American Authors
Who's Who in America
Who's Who in Law

Obituaries

N Y Times p19 Ag 28 '41

CAREY, JAMES B(ARRON) Aug. 12, 1911- National secretary of the Congress of Industrial Organizations

Address: b. 261 Fifth Ave, New York City; 1106 Connecticut Ave, N. W., Washington, D. C.; h. 5924 Worthington Dr, Lee Boulevard Heights, Falls Church, Va.

When James B. Carey and six other men at the radio factory in Philadelphia where he worked began to organize a "fishing club" no one, least of all Carey himself, could have known that this was the first step that would bring him to the national secretaryship of the CIO at the age of 27. For one thing, there wasn't any CIO. For another thing, Carey was merely an exceedingly youthful electrical worker without any union experience.

James Barron Carey was born in Philadelphia on August 12, 1911, one of the eleven children of John C. and Margaret (Loughery) Carey. His father was a paymaster at the United States mint and a friend and admirer of the conservative Sam Gompers, first president of the American Federation of Labor. Young Carey attended St. Theresa's Parochial School and was graduated from high school in Glassboro, New Jersey in 1929 before getting his job in the radio laboratory of the Philco Radio Corporation in Philadelphia. In the evenings he studied electrical engineering at the Drexel Institute. Then the Phil-Rod Fishing Club was started, with seven members. In 1931 Carey dropped his studies at the Drexel Institute and enrolled at the Wharton Evening School of the University of Pennsylvania for courses in the management of industrial enterprises, business forecasting and finance. These subjects, he thought, would help him in handling the problems of the growing organization of sports lovers, for the Phil-Rod Fishing Club was really a union.

In 1933 the National Industrial Recovery Act was enacted, stimulating a move in many places toward collective bargaining agreements between employers and employees. Carey's company set up a "Company Congress" for this purpose, and the "fishermen" elected their members to it. Soon the Philadelphia Storage Battery Company found itself with a strike on its hands. At one strike meeting Carey called upon the men to insist on a single plant-wide union—an independent union, if the A F of L wouldn't take them on those terms. He was thrown off the platform, but the strikers voted for his program, and he helped negotiate a settlement with the company for them.

In October of that same year he was sent as a delegate from his local to the A F of L convention in Washington. There the decision as to what was to be done with the workers all over the country who were felt to want organization was postponed until January 1934. In December 1933, in preparation for that January meeting, representatives of 12 Federal and independent unions in the electrical industry met in New York and formed the Radio and Allied Trades National Labor Council. Twenty-two-year-old James Carey was elected president, and given the hopeless job of convincing the A F of L leaders that the Council should be chartered as a separate international union for the radio and electrical manufacturing industries—an industrial, not a craft, union. In July 1934 he left his job as a radio worker when appointed general organizer for the United States by the A F of L, but a year later he quit this job in order to take the presidency of his local union at a salary of $40 a week. By this time he and the other officers of the Council were persuaded that they could not make the A F of L see things their way, but they were determined to make a last stand at the A F of L convention in Atlantic City that year.

It was an historical convention. The Radio and Allied Trades National Labor Council opened headquarters in Atlantic City for all delegates who were "friends of industrial unionism." Carey spoke, charging that the A F of L leaders were more interested in holding down comfortable jobs than in organizing the unorganized. "For a while we had them worried," he said later. "We had a considerable number of delegates and we made a lot of noise. It took the Old Guard a couple of days to realize that while we might make the noise, they had the votes." John L. Lewis, of course, was the leader of the insurgents; he congratulated Carey on the work he was doing. When, the day after the convention, the Committee for Industrial Organization was set up by Lewis and associates, Carey was kept in touch with all developments and advised on his own course of action.

When the A F of L would not allow the Radio and Allied Trades to have an international industrial union charter, 28 locals finally set themselves up as an international industrial independent union: the United Electrical and Radio Machine Workers of America. Carey was elected president. Only six months later the UERMWA came into the CIO, of whose governing committee Carey was already a member. He had also been elected vice-chairman of the American Youth Congress.

JAMES B. CAREY

Two years later, in November 1938, came the constitutional convention in Pittsburgh at which the Committee for Industrial Organization became the Congress of Industrial Organizations. There was talk of peace with the A F of L, on terms which would split the UERMWA into fragments. Carey spoke. "The CIO wants peace—without pieces," he said. With the support of Lewis he was chosen national secretary of the CIO at that convention, and then he hurried home to Long Island, where his wife, the former Margaret McCormick (they had been married in January), was expecting a baby. It was a son, James Barron, Jr.

Before September 1939 there were none of the serious battles within CIO ranks over national foreign policy that were to come later. James Carey was known as a follower of John L. Lewis. He addressed American Student Union conventions, assailed the Dies Committee before the American Congress for Peace and Democracy, explained resolutions of the American Youth Congress. Late in 1939, when he acted as an International Labor Office Regional American Conference delegate, he was himself assailed by Luigi Antonini of the American Labor Party's Right wing for not having defended the "good neighbor" policy from Conference attack. As late as July 1940 he ridiculed Gene Tunney's attacks on the American Youth Congress and opposed the Kramer totalitarian governments' resolution there. In September 1940 he was elected general president of the UERMWA with the support of all factions.

Inter-union struggles grew more intense, however. In the 1940 election Carey supported Roosevelt and Roosevelt's foreign policy, and relations between Carey and Lewis and Lewis' supporters grew increasingly cool. Early in 1941 Carey was appointed a member of the nine-man Production Planning Board

CAREY, JAMES B.—*Continued*

of the Office of Production Management and an alternate member of the National Defense Mediation Board, but remained critical of the defense setup. He backed Philip Murray's (see sketch this issue) plan for industrial councils of labor, management and government; in speeches he placed most of the blame for strikes on the greed and the law violations of great corporations, most of the responsibility for delay in defense production on "business refusal to plan for expansion." Later he was to concur with other officers of the UERMWA in a report which condemned the OPM as a "super-government" dominated by "big business" and announced that labor representatives in the OPM had been relegated to the function of "glorified office boys, given a few errands to run from time to time." And even later, in November 1941, he was to join other CIO members in resigning as a NDMB alternate in protest at the Board's decision refusing the union shop to the captive miners. In September 1941, however, when the convention of the UERMWA met, finally united on foreign policy, and passed a resolution calling for all-out aid to Great Britain and Russia, Carey was not ready to make his peace with John L. Lewis' former supporters. His effort to push through the resolutions committee a resolution specifically condemning Communism was repudiated by a majority of the delegates, and in the ensuing battle Carey failed to be re-elected as president. It was said that his defeat came from a coalition of those who thought his job as national secretary of the CIO occupied too much of his time, those with unpleasant recollections of Martin Dies (who had once called Carey a Communist), and some out-and-out Left wingers. Carey himself was quoted: "I've been arbitrary as hell—that had a lot to do with it." He said he would, however, continue to fight for a constitutional change giving local unions autonomy to ban Communists as officers. Even opponents of his resolution praised his leadership of their union, which had, during his regime, gained more than 100,000 members, doubled its dues collections, established itself as one of the five largest unions in the CIO, and yet engaged in fewer strikes than many old-line A F of L unions.

At the annual convention of the CIO in November 1941 Carey was re-elected national secretary, and since then he has frequently been the spokesman of the CIO in matters involving labor as a whole. It was he who, with Philip Murray and William Green, protested against the passage of any legislation banning strikes; he who accused Secretary of the Navy Knox of backing "mob violence" against "lawful union activity."

Slight, tense, with hazel eyes and "abundant, dark, tousled hair" which is seldom covered by a hat, James Carey looks even younger than he is. *Time* once described him as "a short-sleeve union boss, a good swing maestro or trap drummer in a different setting, juggling telephones and barking out orders through a 16-hour work day." He smokes a short-stemmed black pipe, which he clenches in his teeth when nervous. Besides being national secretary of the CIO, he is an executive officer of the United Construction Workers and of the Utility Workers Organizing Committee, chairman of the CIO's committee on unemployment, a contributor to labor journals, and has had the singular honors of having spoken as official representative of the CIO on a Labor Day broadcast with President Roosevelt, of having delivered talks on union aspects of industrial management at Princeton University, and of having received the 1940 award of *Parents'* Magazine for service to youth. Away from a union office, though, he is happiest when boxing, playing basketball or tennis—or trying to get a candid camera shot of James, Junior's, young sister, Patricia Ann.

References

N Y Herald Tribune p38 S 4 '41 por
PM p19 S 22 '40 il pors; p8 Ap 6 '41
 por; p19 S 3 '41 por; p15 S 5 '41
Scrib Com 9:39-44 Ja '41; 10:83-7 Jl '41
Time 32:12 N 28 '38; 37:16 Ja 27 '41
 por

CARLE, RICHARD July 7, 1871—June 28, 1941 Stage and screen actor; theatrical career began with *Niobe* in 1891 and included successful roles in *The Tenderfoot, The Spring Chicken* and *Jumping Jupiter,* vehicles of which he was also producer-author-composer; his songs, *I Picked a Lemon in the Garden of Love* and *Peculiar Julia,* are still remembered; film career began in 1916 and was mainly devoted to the portrayal of mock-solemn butlers and crotchety old millionaires; most recent appearance was in *That Uncertain Feeling;* real name Charles Nicholas Carleton.

References

Dramatic Mirror 61:6 Ap 10 '15 por;
 74:26 S 15 '15 por
N Y Dramatic News 64:8 O 27 '17 por
Photoplay 36:149 Je '29 por

International Motion Picture Almanac
Who's Who in America
Who's Who in the Theatre

Obituaries

N Y Times p33 Je 29 '41
Variety 143:54 Jl 2 '41

CARMICHAEL, HOAGY (kär'mĭ-kl)
Nov. 22, 1899- Song writer

Address: c/o Elie Leslie, 9441 Wilshire Blvd, Hollywood, Calif; h. 626 N. Foothill Dr, Beverly Hills, Calif.

One of America's leading jazz song writers, Hoagy Carmichael and his compositions are known wherever jazz music is played. In the United States numbers such as *Stardust* are known to the trade as "swing standards" and in England "hot" music fans refer to them as "Evergreens." Hoagy has been a prominent ASCAP member since 1931. In the midst of the BMI-ASCAP controversy that barred music of ASCAP publishers from the air, Hoagy's *Rockin' Chair* and *Georgia On My Mind* were played almost as often as Jeanie-of-the-public-domain. The mystery was cleared up when it was discovered that these two numbers were published by a firm not affiliated with ASCAP.

Hoagy's first compositional efforts were inspired by a piano player of the "strictly barrelhouse" school, and some of his best-known tunes were created on the player piano of a Greek candy store just off the Indiana University campus. Since it was completely unliterary, students dubbed this place The Book Nook. "There was a player piano in the back room," said Hoagy, "where we used to feed ice cream to our best girls. I had composed several pieces on that old hurdy-gurdy— *Washboard Blues, Riverboat Shuffle,* and *Rockin' Chair* among them." From jazz and jazz bands he went on to the popular music field, first to Broadway and then to Hollywood, where he has been writing music for pictures since 1935.

Hoagy didn't start out to be a song writer. There was a long period when he was sure he was going to be a lawyer, perhaps one with a strong liking for and interest in jazz, but a lawyer nonetheless. Hoagland Howard Carmichael was born in Bloomington, Indiana, the son of Howard and Lida (Robison) Carmichael, and grew up there. His mother taught him to play the piano, but he first became interested in jazz when he heard a Negro piano player named Reggy Duval. "He showed me the art of improvising," said Hoagy—"using the third and sixth of the chord as a basis for arpeggios." With his solid bass, complex rhythms and stress of the afterbeat, the playing of this pianist fascinated young Hoagy, whose musical training up to that point had been along thoroughly conventional lines.

Hoagy also recalls a crude and raucous jazz band: "It was disjointed music, unorganized, but full of screaming notes and a solid rhythm." But while he liked it he was not sure that he could play it. Then, up at Northwestern at a party, he heard Bix Beiderbecke playing with musicians of his acquaintance. His enthusiasm brought Bix and The Wolverines to the Indiana University campus, to play for the spring (1924) dances at the Kappa Sigma fraternity house. "Hoagy went nuts," a fraternity brother recollected. "He and Moenkhause began the Bix cult that had the band back on the campus 10 week ends in a row."

Hoagy confirms this story himself: "When they [The Wolverines] started off with *Tiger Rag,* I froze to a spot in front of the band. . . Bix's breaks were 'hot,' and he selected each note with musical care. Then I realized that jazz could be musical." The *"break"* in jazz is similar to the cadenza in classical music, though it is always brief—at most eight bars—and usually permits of solo improvisation against the rhythm. Hoagy had written a number that "offered the possibility of four 'breaks' in the main theme." He called it *Free Wheeling* and offered it to Bix

McClelland Barclay

HOAGY CARMICHAEL

and The Wolverines to record out at the old Gennett studio in Richmond, Indiana. The boys liked everything but the title, which Bix changed to *Riverboat Shuffle.*

Hoagy formed his first band, The Collegians, in the fall of 1923. He later forsook the study of law temporarily to organize another band. In that period he recorded his *Washboard Blues* for Gennett. Those were the days of acoustical recording, and the disc now sounds both sadly waxed and somewhat dated as to performance. But in the middle of it there is a piano passage by Hoagy, and out of it, startlingly, emerges the phrase that later inspired his song hit *Lazybones.* However, the music business didn't work out and Hoagy went back to college, staying there until 1926, when he got his LL. B.

His first step toward becoming a lawyer was to work for The Equitable Trust Company in New York City. He followed this up with a trip to Florida, where he tried unsuccessfully to start a law practice. Then he returned to Indiana to work for Bingham-Mendenhall, Attorneys. His progress in law was again cut short by an offer to join Jean Goldkette's Orchestra. A few months later he organized another band of his own in Indianapolis. Then with completed manuscripts of *Stardust* and other songs he set out for Hollywood; he found the film industry cold to beginning song writers, and turned eastward again.

In New York he got a job in a publishing house as an arranger. By this time his songs were becoming known. When Paul Whiteman heard the old Gennett record of *Washboard Blues* he kidded Hoagy about it but asked him to sing the number on a 12-inch disc. This was the first time the verses were recorded. They have something

CARMICHAEL, HOAGY—*Continued*

of a folk quality, and were written by a stone-cutter in an Indiana quarry.

The musical idea for *Stardust* came to him while he was on a visit to Bloomington in 1928, and the first rough outline was worked out on the player piano of The Book Nook. The title was suggested by a friend. "I had no idea what it meant," said Hoagy, "but I thought it would make a gorgeous title." Lyrics were supplied by a writer on the staff of the publisher, and the number, brought out in 1931, has sold close to 1,000,000 copies—three times the present number of a hit tune. *Lazybones* came out in 1933, with Johnny Mercer contributing the lyrics. From then on Hoagy continued to write numerous successful songs and worked on piano scores in classical forms as well, convinced that jazz lore might be crystallized in such a medium.

Hoagy Carmichael has written Broadway show music, having contributed *Little Old Lady* to *The Show Is On*, a revue that starred Beatrice Lillie. More recently he did the score for *Walk With Music* (1940). In Hollywood he has attained the kind of success that the undergraduate might have sometimes dreamed about over the yellowed keys of that old piano in The Book Nook. His contributions to films included music for: *Anything Goes* (1936); *Topper* and *Every Day's A Holiday* (1937); *Sing, You Sinners, College Swing* and *Thanks For The Memory* (1938); and *St. Louis Blues* (1939). He appeared in the role of pianist-composer in the short film *Paramount Presents Hoagy Carmichael*. Jack Teagarden, who has worked on many record dates with Hoagy, also appeared in the film.

When he was at Indiana University a classmate once handed Hoagy some verses with the remark that they'd make a good song. Hoagy worked on the idea and years later when he dug it out of his trunk he decided it was worth publishing. But he had no idea who the author was. He read the lyrics over the radio and, he tells us: "The plot thickened. Forty-eight people claimed to have written the thing." The author was finally located, however, and the fact established that the poem had appeared years before in *Life* Magazine, signed *J. B.* Its author was Mrs. Jane Brown Thompson of Philadelphia. But she never heard the music. She died January 18, 1940, the day before the tune, *I Get Along Without You Very Well*, was sung over the air for the first time, by Dick Powell.

Five feet seven and one-half inches tall, Hoagy has been described by Michel Mok as "a dark-haired, brown-eyed fellow with foxy features, a dry, business-like manner and a nasal Indiana drawl." When reminiscing about jazz, however, Hoagy's manner is anything but dry. He is a most enthusiastic partisan. On March 14, 1936 he married Ruth M. Meinardi. They have two children, Randy Bob, "named after nobody," and Hoagy Bix, "after the great Bix Beiderbecke." Through the 1920's Hoagy and Bix remained close friends. In 1931, shortly before Bix's death, Hoagy got together a recording band that featured Bix and other jazzmen. Hoagy had

been in the studio when the youthful Bix recorded at Richmond, Indiana, with The Wolverines. And it was with Hoagy's recording band in an RCA-Victor studio on East 24th Street, New York, that Bix blew the last recorded note from his silver cornet. When he died, Hoagy says: "My interest in music dropped 50 per cent."

Hoagy likes to play tennis and confesses that "carrying baggage across the country seems to be one of my hobbies."

References

Etude 59:13 Ja '41 il
Metronome 49:18-19+ Jl '33 por; 49:16-18 Ag '33
N Y Post Ap 3 '39
N Y World-Telegram F 16 '39
America's Young Men
International Motion Picture Almanac
Ramsey, F. and Smith, C. E. eds. Jazzmen 1939

CARNEGIE, DALE　Nov. 24, 1888-

Author and public speaking instructor

Address: b. 50 E. 42nd St, New York City; h. 27 Wendover Rd, Forest Hills, Long Island, N. Y.

Sometimes Dale Carnegie bewails the fact that in his youth he was denied the benefit of a book such as his own ubiquitous *How To Win Friends and Influence People*, but it seems to have done him no harm. America's leading apostle of self-help is a household word in the country today; his books, radio talks and newspaper columns have reached millions, and his classes are a cross section of national frustration. Among thousands of bewildered salesmen, aging executives and hapless housewives as well as among the public at large Carnegie has certainly won friends and influenced people.

Dale Carnegie, a small, bouncing man with erect posture and alert eyes behind rimless specs, probably never dreamed during his boyhood in Maryville, Missouri, where he was born on a farm on November 24, 1888, that he would become so eminent. Neither, probably, did his father, James William Carnegie, who had to wage a losing battle with the One Hundred and Two River—a stream which, year after year, inundated his farm land and kept the family in a state of chronic poverty. Mrs. Carnegie (Amanda Elizabeth Harbison), a devout Methodist, wanted her two sons, Dale and Cliff, to become missionaries.

Dale liked to recite. And he was by no means backward about displaying his oratorical wares at Sunday-school recitals and local festivals. Later he was further encouraged by Nicholas M. Souder, a schoolteacher who boarded with the family and who liked using fancy words like "psychology" and "philosophy" in his conversations with Dale.

Getting an education at the State Teachers College at Warrensburg, Missouri was a hard struggle for young Carnegie. He was one of the four students in the school who couldn't afford to board in town, and he had to ride to and from school on horseback. This had its compensations, however, because Carnegie could try out his recitations on the horse. Carnegie is remembered as a slight and insignificant youth in ill-fitting clothes who joined the debating team because his physique barred him from sports. Notwithstanding his experience, Carnegie was a flop as a debater until he happened to hear a Chautauqua lecturer. The talk on that particular day was a lachrymose personal testimony describing how the speaker had pulled himself up from his humble beginnings by his own bootstraps. He studied carefully the speaker's gestures and his colloquial vocabulary; then, with practice, he adapted them for use in his own debates.

After graduation from college in 1908 Carnegie had to earn his keep. Quite naturally he turned to salesmanship, traveling to Nebraska as a representative of the International Correspondence Schools. To a telephone company lineman who was unable to leave his post on the top of a telephone pole, Carnegie sold his first and last correspondence course. Then he got a job managing a hinterlands route in South Dakota for Armour and Company, and was successful in building one of the most backward sectors into one of the most profitable.

At this period he undoubtedly began to apply the technique that he eventually exalted into a formula of success. One slight indication of this is that he had acquired the habit of signing his name without removing his pen from the paper. This was a peculiarity of his boss, Rufus E. Harris. In Carnegie's eyes anything a man of importance said or did was important, even if it was only the way he signed his name.

But salesmanship failed to assuage Carnegie's irresistible desire for recognition, despite the fact that his achievement resulted in the offer of an executive post. With $500 he had managed to save from his earnings, he decided to realize a long-standing ambition to become a Chautauqua lecturer. Then a casual conversation with a minister on a train convinced him he would make a better actor than speaker, and Carnegie detoured to New York to attend the American Academy of Dramatic Arts in 1911. His record as an actor was not outstanding; he played the role of Dr. Hartley in a road show of *Polly and the Circus,* and that terminated his career before the footlights.

In 1912 Carnegie found himself in New York, jobless and without prospects. Somewhere in his voluminous writings he says that at one time he contemplated suicide, but whether this was the time or not is unrevealed. At any rate, Carnegie decided, with the sort of resoluteness that he now teaches in his classes, to take an unprecedented step: he would teach public speaking. When he carried his proposal to the YMCA on 125th Street the manager was more than skeptical, but told Carnegie that if he insisted on exercising his talents he was welcome to do so at a party planned for the following week. Much to the manager's surprise Carnegie accepted with alacrity; he appeared at the party

DALE CARNEGIE

and his recitations were an instant hit. Then the manager became more interested. He allowed Carnegie to conduct the first night classes in public speaking ever held in the YMCA, and after a preliminary argument over Carnegie's demand for a $2-per-night fee it was agreed that the instructor would get 80 per cent of the net proceeds of the classes.

Pioneering at 24 in a field that has since become a major American industry, Carnegie had to learn as he went along. Even in his first session he accidently made some important discoveries. For example, after a lengthy introductory survey, Carnegie suddenly found himself destitute of things to say and in his desperation urged the students to get up and deliver impromptu talks. When they complained that they didn't know what to talk about, Carnegie told them to think about something that made them angry. The results were gratifying, for the students actually found themselves able to speak before an audience.

In essential outlines the Carnegie method hasn't deviated from this maiden session, although, of course, the founder has since learned a good deal more about the art of teaching. Gradually, too, he came to discover the tremendous desire of most American people to express themselves and to gain self-confidence. Carnegie had a commodity of incalculable appeal. So successful did his courses become that soon he was drawing $25 a session, and by 1914 his earnings mounted to $500 weekly.

He was lecturing to packed houses, and in 1916 he hired, for the first time, Carnegie Hall. His choice of this particular hall was no accident: Carnegie was not unaware of the publicity value of names. His own name had been spelled Carnegey, as a matter of fact, when he lived in Missouri, despite his father's claim to distant kinship with the millionaire Andrew

CARNEGIE, DALE—*Continued*

Carnegie. The son changed it because, he said, it was foolish to confuse the public with divergent spellings of the same name.

As business increased Carnegie was physically unable to handle it all himself. He opened an office near Times Square and hired substitute instructors to take care of his widely scattered classes. Meanwhile, in order to standardize his methods in each of the classes, he began publishing pamphlets, never dreaming his literary effusions would one day wind up on the best-seller lists. Eventually he collected his writings into book form, and the volume that resulted was called *Public Speaking; a Practical Course for Business Men* (1926), later published as *Public Speaking and Influencing Men in Business* (1932). This soon became a standard text for many public-speaking classes and sold quite well.

In the midst of his manifold enterprises the dynamic ex-salesman somehow managed to find time to take courses at Columbia and New York Universities and at the Baltimore School of Commerce and Finance. He thus garnered a trailer of formidable degrees and titles to follow his name on the title pages of his books. They include B. Pd, B. C. S., Litt. D. and F. R. G. S., the latter bestowed on him by the Royal Geographic Society as the result of his extensive travel throughout Europe, Africa and Asia while lecturing on various topics.

It was at the behest of Lowell Thomas (see 1940 Annual), the radio commentator (then a college teacher of English), that Carnegie first took to travel abroad. Carnegie's admiration for Thomas verges on reverence, and although the latter reciprocates with no small measure of regard, he has had occasion to refute the widely held idea of a teacher-pupil relationship. The future news analyst first got in touch with Carnegie because he wanted some help on a talk he was scheduled to deliver at the Smithsonian Institute. Pleased with the speech instructor's suggestions, Thomas once again sought out Carnegie when he needed a business manager to direct a lecture tour which he planned to conduct in Great Britain. The two men thus began a business relationship that proved highly successful for a number of years. Thomas lectured on "With Lawrence in Arabia and Allenby in Jerusalem" with the use of colored slides and was such a sensation that he assigned Carnegie to preside over a second company to present the lecture simultaneously in other parts of the country.

There had been a hiatus in Carnegie's breakneck rise to success when the nation's entry into the First World War interrupted his career, but after a period at Camp Upton, Carnegie returned to post-War New York, and reassembled his classes. With characteristic energy he began the new phase of his career. After his lectures in Great Britain, he hired an assistant to do research work on famous men; he traveled throughout the country interviewing the nation's prominent. Out of this emerged two collective biographies written in the breezy, slam-bang sentences characteristic of his lectures and rather reminiscent of newspaper and bill-poster headlines. They are *Five Minute Biographies* (1937) and *Little Known Facts About Well Known People* (1934). He also wrote a book about his favorite hero called *Lincoln, the Unknown* (1932), which, a critic says, "will never rank as a major contribution to Lincolniana."

How To Win Friends And Influence People first appeared in 1937 and within a few months had gone through 17 editions. It was a more popular version of his earlier text on the same subject. The sales were fabulous: the book was soon being described as the most popular work of non-fiction in modern times, although it was not too favorably hailed by critics, and sales demand continued to exceed supply in bookstores. Eventually it was printed in mass quantity in a 25-cent paper-covered form, and bids were even solicited from the publisher for supplying copies to the inmates of Leavenworth, Atlanta and Alcatraz Federal Prisons. Concurrently, Carnegie's fame and fortune increased, for the book helped to publicize Carnegie's classes, while his classes, in turn, brought the attention of additional thousands to the book.

Never loath to seize an opportunity, Carnegie began inserting full-page ads in the metropolitan newspapers inviting the public to free demonstrations of the Carnegie method in huge halls; and new classes mushroomed throughout the East. In the meantime his services were in demand by the radio networks and by newspapers. His weekly programs over the air were question-and-answer periods devoted to solving domestic as well as business problems of the public. The application of Carnegianism to domestic problems was a new and extremely profitable facet of his career, since it increased by tenfold his potential audience. It was foreshadowed by the chapter in *How To Win Friends And Influence People* called "Seven Rules For Making Your Family Happy." To stabilize his enterprises Carnegie established the Carnegie Institute of Effective Speech and Human Relations. Carnegie himself is unmarried and prefers to be regarded as a bachelor lest his divorce of his wife several years ago reflect on his integrity as a dispenser of connubial advice.

Carnegie's newspaper column has been called "a growth rather than a column." It has appeared through syndication in 71 daily newspapers. The columns are capsule preachments on success illustrated with anecdotes from Carnegie's fabulous collection of trivia about great men.

With all his success Carnegie is said to retain a pristine faith in his own formulae, which, according to Sinclair Lewis, can best be summed up as "'yessing' the boss, and making Big Business right with God." He retains his devout affection for men of standing, even for Sinclair Lewis, whose satirical hammer has pulverized many a Carnegian platitude. Carnegie is ready to prescribe the famous Carnegie formulae for virtually all the world's ills, from wars to dental decay. In an article a few years ago, for instance, Carnegie provided an engagingly simple solution to a problem that has long baffled world economists. Depressions, he said, can be overcome by confidence.

Carnegie is a man with simple tastes who still responds with intermittent wonder to the extent of his own success. He likes to point out his lowly beginnings and to demonstrate that his own career, no less than that of many another public figure, proves the possibility of success for even the humblest.

References

> Lit Digest 122 :28+ N 21 '36 por
> Nation 146 :325+ Mr 1 '38
> Newsweek 10 :31 N 15 '37 por
> Sat Eve Post 210 :88 Ag 7 '37 por; 210 : 12-13+ Ag 14 '37 il pors
> Sat R Lit 15 :6 Ja 30 '37 por
> Time 31 :13 Jl 3 '38 por
> Who's Who in America

CARTER, JOHN FRANKLIN, JR. *See* Franklin, J., pseud.

CASTILLO, RAMÓN S. (käs-tē'lyō rä-mōn') Nov. 20, 1873- Acting President of Argentina

Address: Casa Rosada, Buenos Aires, Argentina

Since the day when illness forced President Roberto Ortiz to retire temporarily from his duties, Argentina has been in a state of tension. The key to this lies in the fact that ever since their accession to office in 1938, the President and the Vice-President of Argentina have been "on the opposite sides of the political fence." President Ortiz is a Radical, a member of a political group credited with vaguely New Dealish tendencies; Vice-President Castillo is a Conservative, is supposed to be supported by the once all-powerful ex-President (or, as some put it, ex-dictator) General Augustín Justo, and to believe in government by the privileged. But it is Señor Castillo who is in 1941 the man in Argentina's Casa Rosada (its White House, which is really pink) and who, in spite of having promised to follow the policies of the incapacitated President, has some very strong ideas of his own.

Ramón S. Castillo was born on November 20, 1873, in Catamarca, Argentina, the son of Rafael and Mariá (Barrionueva) Castillo. He attended elementary and secondary schools in his native town but went to study law in the National University of Buenos Aires, and was graduated in 1894 with the degree of Doctor of Jurisprudence. Soon after that he became secretary of the Commercial Court of Buenos Aires and in 1903 he got the judgeship of the city's Criminal Court. In 1905 he was appointed to the Civil and Commercial Board of the province of Buenos Aires and in 1907 occupied the bench of the Commercial Court. Throughout his career he seems constantly to have divided his activities between the civil and the criminal branches of the law. He was on the Criminal Court of Appeals from 1910 to 1913

Argentine Information Bureau
RAMÓN S. CASTILLO

and on the Commercial Court of Appeals from 1913 to 1918.

Señor Castillo became well known as an authority on commercial law. He contributed articles to many magazines and was the author of two books on bankruptcy: *Procedimiento Preventivo de la Quiebra* (1910) and *Proyecto de Ley de Quiebras* (1917). He taught law at his Alma Mater from 1907 to 1912 and at the University of La Plata during summer sessions. On the advisory board of the Buenos Aires University from 1915 to 1928, he taught law and social sciences and from 1923 to 1928 was the dean of the law school. Throughout his academic career he wrote numerous monographs on law, commerce and various cultural subjects, and his lectures were subsequently published in textbook form. He has an honorary degree from the Universities of Heidelberg and Rio de Janeiro, is a member of the Spanish Academy and vice-president of the Argentine Commission for Pan-American Commercial Arbitration.

In 1929 depression hit Argentina. The restrictive measures taken by the Irigoyen Administration in order to combat it brought on an uprising of conservative elements, led by General José F. Uriburu. The constitutional government was overthrown by force. Ramón Castillo and Roberto Ortiz found themselves in the same camp. When Augustín Justo was put into power in a steam-roller election of the kind that was to prevail in Argentina thereafter, Ortiz was his Minister of Public Works. Castillo was a member of the Constituent Assembly in 1931. The next year his native district of Catamarca sent him to Congress.

Castillo began forging his way to the top. The Justo Administration appointed him Minister of Justice and Public Instruction in 1936. That same year, while temporarily the Acting

CASTILLO, RAMÓN, S.—*Continued*

Foreign Minister, he made headlines by urging the Madrid Government to spare the life of José Antonio Primo de Rivera, the captive pro-Fascist son of the former Spanish dictator. In 1937 he was Minister of the Interior, a post which he gave up to participate in the Presidential elections. A shrewd, canny politician, he was by that time considered one of the most trusted conservative leaders, nicknamed *El Zorro*, the Fox. It was only natural to put him on Roberto Ortiz's ticket to represent the Conservative element of the Conservative-Radical coalition that put the present Administration into power. Among the pledges put forward by Ortiz were promises to build up the armed forces of Argentina, to preserve democracy by insuring honest elections—a pledge which the Conservatives disregarded, since the 1937 elections were conducted in the usual style, with such devices as quarantining entire districts, jailing political opponents and incapacitating opposition poll watchers by liberal libations of the Argentine variety of "Mickey Finn."

It was nevertheless on the rock of honest elections that the Ortiz-Castillo harmony ship finally split. Argentine politicians soon found President Ortiz no pliable tool, found him favoring democratic decentralized government and eager to cooperate with the United States. Señor Castillo, on the other hand, was always for strong central authority and was a loyal party man. The ultimate test came in February and March of 1940 when Ortiz re-ran questionable provincial elections in Catamarca and Buenos Aires and ousted the Conservative candidates supported by the Vice-President. Castillo objected, openly expressing sympathy with the ousted candidates, and the result was a quarrel which almost ended in his own resignation as Vice-President.

Ortiz's plans, however, were prevented by illness. Stricken by diabetes, half blind, on the advice of physicians he turned over the executive power to Castillo for an indefinite period. The question with which Argentina was now faced was how much President Ortiz's policies would be modified by the Acting President. Castillo himself underwent some extremely tense moments after his induction into office. In August the Ortiz Administration, as represented by the Cabinet, was put into a rather ticklish situation by an investigation into a doubtful land deal which was traced to the doors of the War Ministry. A deputy shot himself, and Ortiz, though admittedly having nothing to do with the scandal, offered his resignation to the Congress. The latter's unanimous refusal to accept it was said to have foiled a Fascist plot to take over the Government. It was after this that Castillo voiced his decision to follow internal and foreign policies initiated by Ortiz. His appointments to the reorganized Cabinet seemed to bear out the promise. For a while it looked as if Ortiz were coming back and, at any rate, was keeping his hand on the executive reins.

This impression faded gradually as Ortiz's health showed few signs of improvement.

Castillo, solidly backed by the Conservatives, consolidated his position. Ortiz's friend Julio Roca resigned from his post as Minister of Foreign Affairs, and Ortiz publicly voiced his disapproval of Cabinet changes made by Castillo, who on his part claimed that he was under no obligation to follow undeviatingly in his predecessor's footsteps. The crisis deepened when the Radicals in the Congress charged fraud in the provincial elections of Santa Fe and Mendoza, won against all expectations by the Conservatives, and clamored for an official investigation. Señor Castillo, for whom victory in these provinces meant 130 electoral votes in the 1944 elections, turned a deaf ear to their pleas. As a result, in January he was faced in the Chamber of Deputies with a legislative boycott that left Argentina without legislation for the next five months. By April 1941 only six out of some forty bills had been voted on, and the Castillo Administration was unable to win even the Chamber's approval of the budget. On April 26 President Castillo announced that he would govern Argentina by decree for the time being. On May 7, the Radical Party, having abandoned its original hope that Ortiz would recover his health sufficiently to return to his post, voted to put an end to the legislative boycott, thus removing the reason for Castillo's rule by decree.

Señor Castillo is a lean man with a lined ascetic face and silvery-white hair. He gives the impression of being a scholar rather than a politician, but this fools no one; he is recognized as an astute and tough fighter. He is married to Mariá Delia Luzuriaga, has five children and one of his sons is now working for him as a secretary. Castillo has at least followed Ortiz's policy of building up an army. At the end of 1940 he opened a campaign to train 5,000 civilian fliers in three years and also proposed to spend a lot of money on military aviation to make Argentina supreme in the air over South America. It is not known, however, whether his intention is to attempt to pursue an independent imperialist policy designed to dominate the rest of South America or to continue the policy of solidarity with the United States. American observers found him reluctant to move from his position of strict neutrality and not too enthusiastic about the need for naval collaboration that President Roosevelt and the United States Navy think desirable.

In June 1941, in his Annual Message to Congress, Castillo merely reaffirmed Argentina's "firm and loyal neutrality," announcing that Argentina was "foreign to" the causes of the War. He refused to support a Congressional investigation of fifth-column activities and disassociated his Administration from a vote of censure passed by the Chamber of Deputies against German Ambassador Von Thermann, in spite of a growing popular demand that the Nazi political and economic machine in Argentina be broken up. As a result of his apparent Nazi sympathies, when in September 1941 word of a seditious plot participated in by Argentinian Army officers began to leak out in the press, many wondered about Castillo's role in it. He, however, minimized its importance,

announced that everything was under control—
and continued to ignore popular opposition to
his policies. In October he was responsible
for what was generally condemned as a "dictatorial" and "unconstitutional" act when his
Cabinet dissolved a democratically elected
Municipal Council and replaced it with a
board of Government appointees, and the next
month his ban on some 3,000 scheduled meetings of the pro-Ally Accion Argentina resulted
in the heaviest storm of indignation and criticism in years. An earlier refusal of haven
for 86 anti-Hitler refugees was also widely
condemned.

References

> Christian Sci Mon p2 Je 16 '41
> N Y Times p1 Jl 4 '40 por (p4) ; p8 Ag
> 29 '40; p6 Ap 26 '41 por; p9 My 30
> '41 ; p16 Je 15 '41
> Newsweek 18 :27 O 6 '41 por
> Time 36 :24 Jl 15 '40; 37 :27 Ja 6 '41 por;
> 37 :36+ My 5 '41 pors
> Gunther, J. Inside Latin America p287-
> 92 1941
> International Who's Who
> Who's Who in Latin America

CAULDWELL, LESLIE GIFFEN   Oct.
18, 1861—Apr. 9, 1941   American portrait
painter and interior decorator who passed most
of his life in Paris as a leader of the American
art colony in France; died in Paris; works have
been hung in many galleries and public buildings in France, England, the United States and
Germany; in his art work he complied strictly
with academic rules and not only disregarded
but loathed the painting of modernistic schools.

References

> Who's Who in America 1912-13
> Who's Who in American Art

Obituaries

> N Y Herald Tribune p22 Je 4 '41 por
> N Y Times p23 Je 4 '41

CECIL, MARY (sē'sĭl) 1885—Dec. 21,
1940   Stage, screen and radio actress; appeared in stage and screen versions of Clare
Boothe's *The Women* and in MGM's *Dr. Kil-
dare* films; newspaper contributor and author
of a book of monologues.

Obituaries

> Variety 141 :54 D 25 '40

**CECIL OF ESSENDON, ROBERT AR-
THUR JAMES CECIL, 1ST BARON** (sĭs'-
il") Aug. 27, 1893-   British Secretary of
State for the Dominions
Address: 25 Charles St, Berkeley Sq, Lon-
don, W. 1, England

From the days of Queen Elizabeth and
William Cecil, Lord Burleigh, the Cecil fam-
ily has been one of the most famous in Great
Britain and its members have often taken a
prominent part in public affairs. The third
Marquess of Salisbury was for long Prime
Minister in late Victorian days, and Lord

LORD CECIL OF ESSENDON

Cecil of Chelwood has since the First World
War been the chief upholder of the League
of Nations. Lord Cranborne (as Baron Cecil
of Essendon is usually called, since his peerage dates only from January 1941) has not
as yet shown quite the statesmanship of the
latter, who is his uncle, but his interests have
been similar. Best known as the faithful friend
and lieutenant of Anthony Eden, he was appointed Dominions Secretary in October 1940.

Lord Cranborne is the eldest son and heir
of the fourth Marquess of Salisbury. He
was educated at Eton and at Christ Church,
Oxford, and at the beginning of the First
World War took a commission in the Guards.
He fought in France, winning the Croix de
Guerre, was invalided home in September
1915, and that same year married Elizabeth
Vere, eldest daughter of Lord Richard Caven-
dish (brother of the Duke of Devonshire). He
took no part in public life until 1929. After the
War he went into bill-broking in the City of
London, with the firm of King and Foa, and
early in 1933 he was made a director of the
Westminster Bank.

Meanwhile, at the election of 1929, he had
been returned to the House of Commons as
Conservative member for South Dorset. (He
was to be re-elected by the same constituency
in 1931 and 1935, and to remain in the Commons until December 1940, when he was
elevated to the peerage.) It was 1934 when
he was first picked out for minor office. Eden
was at that time Lord Privy Seal and later
Minister without Portfolio, his main duty the
supervision of all matters connected with the
League of Nations. Cranborne was appointed
his parliamentary private secretary, went with
him to Berlin and Moscow, and apparently
saw eye to eye with him in all he did. His
own oral and written work at Geneva was
said to have been "masterly," and when, in
October 1935, Eden succeeded Sir Samuel

CECIL OF ESSENDON, ROBERT, 1ST BARON—*Continued*

Hoare at the Foreign Office, Cranborne became Parliamentary Under-Secretary of State for Foreign Affairs. There were some murmurings of "Tory nepotism" and of favoritism toward a hitherto rather undistinguished member of the Cecil clan, but Stanley Baldwin, speaking at the time, explained that "Mr. Eden and Lord Cranborne had worked together with great sympathy and success in Europe for a long time, and they would be an extremely strong pair for the work that lay before them."

This proved to be true. But although a staunch Tory (in 1934 he said of the National Government that no government of modern times could show such a record of success), Cranborne, like Eden, was soon at odds with the more violent advocates of appeasement within his own party. In February 1936 he had a talk with the Cambridge University branch of the League of Nations Union. "For many years I have gone about preaching disarmament," he said, "but in the existing situation the League nations have to arm against the others." Two years later, on February 20, with Chamberlain urging immediate negotiations with both Germany and Italy and with the other apostles of an entente with Berlin pressing the Foreign Minister to the wall, Eden resigned, and Cranborne with him. And on February 21 the latter followed Eden's speech of "personal explanation" to the House of Commons with a bolder one of his own. Although the differences that had caused the two men to resign were not merely over the issue of the Anglo-Italian talks, it was that issue that was emphasized.

"I have found myself forced to resign," Lord Cranborne said, "because I am in the very fullest agreement with my right honorable friend. I am bound to him, not only by those natural ties of affection which will be felt by anybody who has had the privilege of working with him, but also because I believe him to be absolutely right." It was a matter of principle, the principle of good faith in international affairs. If the Italians really had such good faith they could have shown it by stopping anti-British propaganda in the Near East and withdrawing some of their troops from Libya and Spain—neither of which they had done. "I am afraid," he went on, "that for his Majesty's Government to enter on official conversations would be regarded not as a contribution to peace, but as a surrender to blackmail." At the end of February he also explained his resignation to his constituents, who fully endorsed his action.

For the next two and a half years (except for a brief period in the minor office of paymaster general) Cranborne was an ordinary Member of Parliament, still maintaining a critical attitude toward the policy of appeasement and urging the vital necessity of rearmament. His views of the totalitarian countries were at no time flattering. At a Canford School speech-day in July 1938 he referred to them as places where men "are driven along like cattle with whips, and . . . do not exist as individuals. They do what they are told, not because they think it right but because they are not allowed to think at all."

His most memorable speech, however, came two months later. It was immediately after Munich, in the House of Commons. Speaking of Chamberlain's talk of "peace with honor," Cranborne was bitter: "Peace he certainly brought back to us, and there is not one of us who will not wish to thank him with a full heart for that priceless gift . . . but where is honor? I have looked and looked but I cannot see it. It seems to me a wicked mockery to describe by so noble a name the agreement which has been reached." These were again far bolder words than Eden's. Nevertheless the implication was not that England should have declared war. When shortly after, Cranborne was put on the carpet by his South Dorset constituents and asked to explain a reference to Czechoslovakia as "a country thrown to the wolves," he explained that he had intended no reflection on the honor of Neville Chamberlain, that in his opinion Great Britain ought to have dissociated itself from the Czech question altogether. But that same month, speaking of policy, he announced: "It is a very simple thing—rearm, rearm and rearm."

Early in October 1940 Cranborne took office as Secretary of State for the Dominions, and at that time expressed his satisfaction that all the Dominions (with the exception of Eire) were finally playing their part in the British struggle against Hitler. In a world-wide broadcast delivered on December 10 he had bitter and apposite words to say about the latter's vaunted "new order." "It represents not a step forward in the history of the world," he said, "but a very long step back. It is naked tyranny, the triumph of force over liberty, of cruelty over kindness, of deceit over good faith."

In debate Cranborne has "many of the mannerisms and gestures of the Cecils, but speaks less jerkily than his father." Since he is a young man as statesmen go and has shown a capacity for public affairs unsuspected for a long time, it is possible that he may yet do as much in the political sphere as the most distinguished of his ancestors. He himself has two sons, who have not as yet followed him into the political arena.

References

Eugenics R 28:82 Ap '36
Illustrated London News 198:3 Ja 4 '41 por
Liverpool Daily Post Ag 28 '33 por
Times [London] Ag 7 '35; F 22 '38; F 28 '38; Je 27 '38; O 13 '38; O 8 '40
Who's Who

CERDA, PEDRO AGUIRRE See Aguirre Cerda, P.

CERF, BENNETT A(LFRED) (sûrf)
May 25, 1898-   Publisher

Address: b. 20 E. 57th St, New York City;
h. 132 E. 62nd St, New York City

Bennett A. Cerf has been called "the reader's unknown benefactor." His 95 cent Modern Library reprints, started with Donald Klopfer in 1925, had sold 10,000,000 copies by the fall of 1941. The list averages about 200 titles, besides the double-size "Giants," and Cerf keeps weeding out those which don't sell well and adding new titles, trying always to keep a small, active list of books that sell at least 1,000 copies a year. Just now, he says, the trend is toward the classics—the real classics, Plato, Aristotle and Homer. "We like it," he told an interviewer. "These are the authors who never kick about new jacket designs or cause any trouble at all. Yes, you may say we are very well pleased with Aristotle!"

Bennett Alfred Cerf is a born New Yorker, the son of the late Gustave and of Fredericka (Wise) Cerf, of French-Jewish descent. He was educated at Columbia, from which he received his B. A. in 1919 and in 1920 his Litt. B. from the School of Journalism. College was followed by a short period as a reporter on the New York *Herald Tribune* and this in turn by a stretch in a Wall Street brokerage house. But by 1923 he was through with stockbroking and became a member of the staff and one of the many vice-presidents of Boni & Liveright, the publishing house.

It was not until 1925 that he started out in the publishing business for himself. "Fairly well-heeled, heir to some wholesale tobacco money," he and Donald Klopfer, his friend of many years, bought from Boni & Liveright for a whopping sum the Modern Library, a series of staple books that hadn't been a particularly lucrative sideline for his old firm. Immediately the two young publishers got to work, and by the time three years had passed had earned back their original investment. They had the books redesigned by Elmer Adler and Rockwell Kent, they got a new printer, they started a new selling and advertising policy. Modern Library books rolled off the presses and into people's homes all over the country. Then, in 1931, Cerf and Klopfer began issuing the Modern Library Giants, at a slightly higher price, but still, according to the New York *Times*, "the greatest book bargain in the United States today."

Random House, the other venture of the two partners, was started in 1927, soon after it was clear that the Modern Library was going to be a profitable venture. Cerf and Klopfer, as their first move, got the exclusive American agency for the Nonesuch Press, an English firm specializing in beautiful limited editions. Then they proceeded to work on beautiful editions of their own. The first Random House book was issued in 1928, a limited edition of Voltaire's *Candide* illustrated by Rockwell Kent, and other elegant books followed. Cerf himself was a collector

Ray Platnick

BENNETT A. CERF

of "firsts" and fine editions in those days and has continued to be.

But this was luxury trade, and with hard times it dwindled. The firm began to pay more attention to its infant trade publishing department and in 1933 began publishing trade books on a broad scale with the signing of contracts with Eugene O'Neill and Robinson Jeffers. In 1936 the firm of Harrison Smith and Robert Haas, Incorporated, was made a part of Random House. Today Bennett Cerf is president of Random House and Modern Library, as he has always been; Robert Haas is vice-president and Donald Klopfer is treasurer. Cerf leans toward the literary side of their publishing and Klopfer toward the business side, but the two men collaborate closely on every problem. They've worked at adjoining desks, face to face, for many years now, and Cerf says they've never had a fight in all that time. And that, he adds, is quite a record among publishers.

Cerf, particularly, is concerned with Random House's authors, who include Vincent Sheean (see sketch this issue), William McFee, André Malraux, Mignon Eberhart, John Strachey, Margaret Kennedy and many other important writers here and abroad. But he recognizes that they are a problem sometimes. "When I first entered the publishing business," he once said, "it was my childish belief that publishers and authors were one happy family together, living as one in a beautiful world of literature and dreams, but that illusion was shattered at the very outset by my employer the day I went to work for him. 'The first thing that you will have to remember in this business,' he told me, 'is that authors must be treated differently from all other human beings. The fact is, you see, that they are all slightly batty.'" Bennett Cerf admits he has found this out

CERF, BENNETT A.—*Continued*

for himself occasionally, that authors can often be a severe trial to a publisher trying to make money for himself and them, but he nevertheless insists that he likes them, enjoys knowing and working with them. And, he says, "in my years of publishing, I am proud to say that my house has never lost an author that it really wanted to keep."

The president of Random House, which is the American publisher of James Joyce, which has presented the complete works of Havelock Ellis and Marcel Proust to the country, which publishes (besides novels, fiction, biography, travel books and books of every other kind read in America) plays and juveniles, is an authoritative spokesman on other topics than authors. Very frequently he speaks for the book trade as a whole on problems of selling, distribution and on the many questions that concern him and his fellow publishers in journals like *Publishers' Weekly* and the *Saturday Review of Literature*. He is, too, an editor who has a number of books to his credit, including *Great German Short Novels and Stories* (1933); *The Bedside Book of Famous American Stories*, with John Angus Burrell (1936); *The Bedside Book of Famous British Stories*, with Henry Curran Moriarty (1940); *Three Famous Murder Novels* (1941); *Arabian Nights, or, The Book of a Thousand and One Nights* (1941); and *Sixteen Famous American Plays*, with Van H. Cartmell (1941). With Cartmell he has also collaborated in editing *Sixteen Famous British Plays*, to be published in 1942. He is especially interested in the short story form and was formerly a director of *Story* Magazine, which he was instrumental in bringing to America.

On October 1, 1935, Cerf and Sylvia Sidney, the motion-picture star, eloped from Hollywood in an airplane and were married in Phoenix, Arizona. But the marriage did not last long; the following April Miss Sidney sued for divorce, charging that her husband objected to her career and that he "did not understand motion-picture people." On September 17, 1940, he was married for the second time, to Phyllis Fraser, a cousin of Ginger Rogers, the screen star. Miss Fraser had formerly been a radio actress and at the time of her marriage was radio story editor for a large advertising agency. The ceremony was performed by Mayor Fiorello H. LaGuardia in the "Summer City Hall" at the New York World's Fair. They have one son, born in late 1941.

Brown-eyed, tall, dark, bespectacled, with smooth dark hair, a frank, friendly face and what has been described as a "prep-school-teacherish" manner, Bennett Cerf for the most part lives and breathes publishing—he calls it his "favorite vocation and avocation." Still, he does get away from authors and manuscripts and the presidency of his firm occasionally for a game of tennis and even more occasionally for a whirl at New York's social life. There's no doubt that he is the most frequently mentioned publisher in

columns like Leonard Lyons', but undoubtedly many would not entirely agree with this description of him: "Bennett Cerf, the socially conscious-minded publisher at Random House, is never seen at anything but the most de luxe and snobbish cocktail levées and house parties."

Most people who know Cerf, however, would agree that he is socially conscious: his struggle against censorship benefited all publishers and established a principle of freedom of writing; recently he has been very active in securing relief for anti-Nazi writers who face the difficulties of exile; and his own firm has long been considered one of the most progressive and liberal-minded in the country.

References

N Y Herald Tribune O 2 '35 por; Ap 10 '36 por
N Y World-Telegram p13 My 27 '41 por
Newsweek 14:36 O 16 '39 por
Pub W 138:2244 D 21 '40 por; 139:2368 Je 14 '41
America's Young Men
Who's Who in America
Who's Who in American Jewry
Who's Who in Commerce and Industry

CHADOURNE, MARC (shä-dŏŏrn') May 23, 1895—Jan. (?), 1941 French writer; won the Gringoire Prize with his essay, *China*, in 1931; won the Paul Flat Prize for his novel, *Vasco*, in 1927 and the Femina Prize for his *Cecile la Follie* in 1930; wrote scripts for films produced by Alexander Korda.

References

Dictionnaire National des Contemporains 1936
International Who's Who

Obituaries

N Y Times p45 Ja 5 '41

CHAPIN, CHARLES VALUE (chā'pĭn) Jan. 17, 1856—Jan. 31, 1941 Health officer retired in 1932 after 48 years spent as Superintendent of Health in Providence, Rhode Island; authority on sanitation and methods of infection, he received three medals for his services; author of numerous texts in his field.

References

Am J Pub Health 22:732-3 Jl '32; 25: 83-4 Ja '35
American Medical Directory
American Men of Science
Who's Who in America
Who's Who in American Medicine

Obituaries

N Y Herald Tribune p10 F 1 '41

CHAPMAN, BLANCHE 1850(?)—June 7, 1941 Retired actress, former member of the Chapman Sisters team, who appeared in practically every medium of the drama from pantomime to light operas opposite such famous players as Edwin Booth and Dion Bouccicault; played in silent and talking pictures and in a radio drama over WOR, New York; the widow of Henry Clay Ford, manager of Ford's Theatre in which Lincoln was assassinated, she was an authority on Lincolniana.

Obituaries

N Y Times p48 Je 8 '41 por
Variety 143:46 Je 11 '41

CHEN CHENG 1900- Chinese military leader

Address: Chungking, China

General Chen Cheng, in command of China's Sixth War Area, is one of the most important military leaders in the fight against Japan, and has been considered by many as the probable successor to Chiang Kai-shek (see sketch 1940 Annual). Chiang Kai-shek himself has done much to bolster up that opinion: he introduced Chen Cheng to his second wife, Miss Tan Chang, daughter of the late President Tan Yen-kai of the Executive Yuan; he addresses Chen Cheng, as he addresses no other generals, by the Chinese diminutive *ti*, "little brother"; and Chen Cheng and General Hu Tsung-nan, also considered a candidate for the succession, are the only two generals in China permitted to receive orders direct from the Generalissimo without the counter-signature of Ho Ying-chin, Minister for War.

This dapper little General has been associated with Chiang Kai-shek ever since 1924. He was born in Ching-Tien, Chekiang in 1900 and received his military training at the Paoting Military Officers' College, the school which turned out eight classes of men to implement the Revolution of Sun Yat-sen. From Paoting, Chen Cheng went to the Whampoa Military Cadets' Academy, under the direction of Chiang Kai-shek, in 1924, as an instructor to the first class enrolled there. This period of teaching, according to *Time,* was when Chen Cheng "hitched his wagon to Chiang's star." Their reporter adds that he "has been riding high ever since."

From Whampoa, Chen Cheng went into the army as company commander and later field commander of the Nationalist Revolutionary Forces and rose to fame in Chiang Kai-shek's northern campaign of 1926. He left field activity not long afterward to become chief of the military education bureau of the Military Council and then departmental director in the Canton Military Government.

In 1930 Chen Cheng returned to active fighting again as commander of the 18th Nationalist Army and within a short time was shifted to the position of commander of the Fourth Nationalist Division with headquarters at Nanchang, Kiangsi. In 1932 he married his present wife, after having obtained a divorce from his first wife. Then, in 1934, he became field commander of the Northern Route of the Communist Suppression Forces for the

China Institute in America

CHEN CHENG

provinces of Kiangsi, Kwangtung, Fukien, Hunan and Hupeh.

After participating in almost all the battles of the northern punitive and anti-rebel expeditions, Chen Cheng in 1936 became director of the Military Readjustment Committee of the Wuchang Provisional Headquarters of the President of the Military Affairs Commission. Later, with China united against Japan, he continued in a supervisory position—political minister of the National Military Council and right-hand man to Chiang Kai-shek. As such he announced, in 1939: "Before 1941 Japan will be begging for peace."

Long before that peace seemed possible, however, Chen Cheng was back in the field. In the summer of 1939 Ichang fell to the Japanese, and Chen Cheng was blamed by some for the bad strategy which lost that key city. He gave up his job in Chungking as chief of the Army's Political Training Department and went to the front, publicly vowing not to return until he had retaken Ichang. At the front he has proved himself a skillful soldier, personally able to lead divisions up mountainsides, well aware of tactics of silent deployment, timely retreat, ambuscade, and a master of China's most important technique: the skillful use of great superiority in numbers to compensate for shortages of equipment. It was in recognition of his ability that Chiang Kai-shek chose him to defend the Gorges, which meant defending Chungking, which, in turn, meant defending Chiang Kai-shek.

References

Time 34:21 Jl 17 '39 por; 37:25 Je 16 '41 por (cover)
Who's Who in China

CHESTER, EDMUND 1897- CBS Director of Foreign Broadcasting
Address: Columbia Broadcasting System, Inc, 485 Madison Ave, New York City

EDMUND CHESTER

Since November 1940 Edmund Chester, veteran foreign correspondent, has been CBS's director of broadcasting to foreign countries. As head of CBS's greatly expanded Latin-American operations, it is his job to bring the daily life of the United States more sharply to the attention of its southern neighbors, as well as to Europe.

Chester has eight years of South American experience to aid him, and many more years of press training. Born in Louisville, Kentucky, his first newspaper position was that of reporter on the Louisville *Courier-Journal*. He left his home in 1915 to join the Army for the Mexican border expedition under General Pershing, returned to Louisville after his military experience but stayed there only a short time before he was called to service overseas in the artillery.

Back from the First World War, he continued in Louisville, doing general reporting and writing special stories. By 1930 he was covering the Harlan coal strikes for the Associated Press. His work there, and the fact that he knew Spanish, led to his transfer and promotion to Latin-American editor of the Associated Press in the New York office. Two years later, on six hours' notice, he was off to Cuba for the revolution. This marked the beginning of eight years of traveling in which he covered 250,000 miles. By 1937 he was head of the Associated Press' Latin-American Division, a position he held until he took up his duties at CBS.

Chester covered South America, Central America and Cuba. He was the first newspaperman on the scene to report the horror and tragedy of the Chilean earthquake in January 1939 which brought death to 35,000 people, and among his other assignments were the Lima Pan-American Conference in 1938 and the Havana Pan-American Conference in 1940.

Chester is wiry and short, with curly gray hair and bushy black eyebrows. He was honeymooning in the States when he joined CBS after having just been married to Enna Rogers Moreño of Chile.

CHEVROLET, LOUIS 1879(?)—June 6, 1941 Pioneer motorcar designer and auto racer; in first race in 1905 defeated Barney Oldfield; experimented on racing cars and drove them on various tracks throughout the country; associated with motorcar company bearing his name from 1911 to 1915; later associated for a short time with the Stutz Automobile Company and then organized the Chevrolet Aircraft Company.

Obituaries

N Y Times p17 Je 7 '41
Time 37:82 Je 16 '41

CHIAPPE, JEAN (shē-äp') May 3, 1878— Nov. 27, 1940 High Commissioner in Syria for the Vichy Government, Chiappe met his death when his plane was machine-gunned on its way to Beirut; was police chief of Paris for seven years, then president of the Paris Municipal Council; was supporter of the extreme Right and considered a Fascist.

References

Newsweek 6:13 Jl 6 '35
R of Rs 94:58 Jl '36 por
Scholastic 24:23 F 24 '34 por
Time 26:20 Jl 8 '35 por
Dictionnaire National des Contemporains 1936
Gunther, J. Inside Europe p200-12 1940
International Who's Who

Obituaries

N Y Times p38 D 1 '40 por
Newsweek 16:27-8 D 9 '40

CITRINE, SIR WALTER (MCLENNAN) (sĭ-trēn') Aug. 22, 1887- General secretary of the British Trades Union Congress
Address: b. Transport House, Smith Sq, Westminster, S. W. 1, London, England

In November 1940 the general secretary of the British Trades Union Congress, "hulking, grizzled" Sir Walter Citrine, arrived in the United States to participate, among other things, in the New Orleans convention of the American Federation of Labor. He was kept busy. He told reporters that if England wins "Labor will be stronger than ever," that in Great Britain "much of the restrictions upon Labor are voluntary and have been made for the good of the country," and that "in the course of this War, Labor has enhanced its position in the community." He asked the A F of L Convention for American and British Labor solidarity in bringing about a British victory. He told a Columbia network audience about the "major issues of the War and achievements of British workers during the emergency." And in general he found enthusiastic and sympathetic audiences everywhere, although he failed to make contact with CIO leaders. In *My American Diary* (1941) he tells of his three months in the United States and Canada, describing not only "the busy round of a travelling speaker" but also American production, labor and social problems.

John Gunther (see sketch this issue) begins a sketch of Sir Walter Citrine by quoting from A. J. Cummings, writing a few years before: "For my part, I would rather rely on Sir Walter Citrine, archpriest of British trade unionism, than on Mr. Baldwin, the Conservative Prime Minister, to keep the present system intact. There is today no Toryism more fearful and immovable than that which is enshrined in the ideals and practice of the trade-union leadership."

The general secretary of the Trades Union Congress, says another writer, "is in a position to censor virtually any program the Labor Party brings forward. . . Like all trade-union officials, he has a substantial stake in the existing order." There are between five and six million British workers in the Congress, whose president is elected for only a year but whose general secretary holds a permanent position, and although it is the general rule that Congress chieftains should stay outside active politics, they control Labor Party policies because of their control over the Party's funds. Sir Walter Citrine is, therefore, one of the most influential men in Great Britain today. Ernest Bevin, who as Minister of Labor cooperates closely with Churchill, has often been called "Citrine's mouthpiece." At the annual Trades Union Congress in Britain in 1940 it was Sir Walter's duty to reply on behalf of the General Council to the innumerable resolutions of the 650 delegates. He is known for the "skill, knowledge and good humor" with which he performs this responsibility, only one of the many which fall on his shoulders.

They are very capable shoulders. "During the past decade he has turned British trade unionism into Big Business. He is the granddaddy of all organizers—a man who habitually travels with two brief cases, a secretary and a card index. From his desk in Transport House he runs his allied unions exactly as he might direct the regiments of a well-drilled army." John Gunther even calls him a "filing Robot," and tells a story about his being invited to an informal discussion of Party business among some Labor intellectuals. Sir Walter took along his files and a secretary that time, too, and the secretary took down everything he said—presumably so that he couldn't be misquoted!

SIR WALTER CITRINE

Born in Liverpool on August 22, 1887, Walter Citrine hardly achieved his present position through influential family connections. He came of a working-class family, and after attending elementary schools found himself a job as an electrician in Lancashire, earning £1 18s a week. In his spare time he was active in the electricians' union, and in 1914, the year after he married Doris Slade, he became Mersey District secretary of the Electrical Trades Union. He held that position until 1920, but in the meanwhile found himself also a member of the Liverpool Trades Council (1915); president of the Federation of Engineering and Shipbuilding Trades for his district (1917-18), and from 1918 to 1920 its secretary; parliamentary candidate for Wallasey in the 1918 election; in 1919, chairman of the Wallasey Labor Party. It was 1920 when he became assistant general secretary of the Electrical Trades Union; in 1924 he was appointed assistant secretary of the Trades Union Congress; and in October of the following year his efficiency was rewarded with an appointment to the position of acting secretary. He brought with him long experience with the problems of the shipbuilding, ship repairing and general engineering trades as well as a genius for organization. And one of his followers in 1940 could still claim proudly: "Walter could do a bit o' wiring as well as any lad today—that 'e could!"

The years during which Sir Walter Citrine (he was plain "Mr." until 1935, when the National Government "shrewdly" knighted him) has guided Labor policy have been among the most difficult and dangerous years in history. Although he had visited Russia in 1925 and his comments had not been entirely unsympathetic, he made himself "the chief opponent of the Party radicals," rejecting for the Labor Party any united front with the Communists against either the Na-

CITRINE, SIR WALTER—*Continued*

tional Government or foreign Fascism. In 1933 he introduced into the Trades Union Congress a document called *Dictatorships and the Trade-Union Movement,* the gist of which was: "We must oppose equally all dictatorships whether of the Right or of the Left." In 1934, however, he raised a fund to help the Austrian workers, and, with his colleagues, tried to arrange for a supply of arms for the Austrian Socialists. "When your constitutional right is taken away from you, when you are proceeding along the path of democratic procedure and the Government blocks that way to you, then you would be less than men if you did not take what remedies were open to you," he stated, firmly—a policy which the radicals also approved. After a second visit to the Soviet Union in the fall of 1935, which resulted in a book, *I Search for Truth in Russia* (English edition 1936; American edition 1937), he returned to the Congress more convinced than ever that there could be no collaboration with the extreme Left, and the Congress followed his advice in voting.

At that same session of the Congress in 1935, Sir Walter pointed out the necessity of opposing Italian aggression in Abyssinia by the application of sanctions (at this time nearly everyone assumed that this was also the policy of the National Government); the Labor leaders berated the pacifists in the Labor movement and dismissed the late George Lansbury from the leadership of the Labor Party for not following the same line. Nevertheless, when the Government abandoned sanctions, Labor was quiescent, and in 1936 at the meeting of the Congress shortly after Franco had struck in Spain, Sir Walter, in the name of the General Council, persuaded his organization to support the British Government's adherence to the non-intervention pact.

Sir Walter has continued to battle with the Communists. In June 1939 he became a member of the Privy Council. He threw the support of British Labor wholeheartedly into the War, and in December 1939, after a flying visit to the French Minister of Labor, agreed to a proposal by the then Chancellor of the Exchequer Sir John Simon that pay increases in Britain be stopped. The London *Daily Worker* thereupon published a series of articles accusing him and his colleagues of "plotting with the French Citrines to bring millions of Anglo-French Trade Unionists behind the Anglo-French imperialist war machine." Sir Walter sued for libel, and in court accused the *Daily Worker* of taking orders and money from Moscow. He was awarded damages of £300. In all, he has won three actions against the *Daily Worker.* And in September 1941, when the Trades Union Congress approved the organization of an Anglo-Russian Trade Union Council, he made a speech in which he announced: "We are not prepared to collaborate in any measure or in any degree with the British Communist Party."

In addition to leadership of the Trades Union Congress, Sir Walter holds office in the International Federation of Trade Unions (president since 1928); from 1930 to 1933 was a member of the Government Economic Advisory Council; is a member of the British Broadcasting Company's General Advisory Committee; and was an original member and governor of the National Institute for Economic and Social Research. These are merely a few of his varied responsibilities. He is the author of several books and booklets: *The Labour Chairman*; *The Trade-Union Movement of Great Britain* (1926); *Labour and the Community* (1928); *I Search for Truth in Russia* (1937); *My Finnish Diary*; and *ABC of Chairmanship.* He keeps careful journals, which he often brightens up with pencil sketches of persons and scenes; he is an excellent stenographer; he has been an expert swimmer since boyhood; and the Japanese remember him for a bit of verse he directed their way in 1938:

> *Yankee talks a lot of bunk*
> *When his ships are bombed and sunk;*
> *Jap knows Yank is in a funk*
> *Afraid of war in China.*
> *John Bull, he is sitting tight,*
> *Can't decide which side is right;*
> *A little scared of Jappy's might;*
> *Afraid of war in China.*
> *Far away in Tokyo*
> *Cafe lights are all aglow,*
> *Geisha girls sing soft and low;*
> *There ain't no war in China.*
> *From each busy city street*
> *Comes the sound of marching feet.*
> *Why do war drums loudly beat?*
> *There ain't no war in China.*

John Gunther characterizes this British Labor chieftain rather unflatteringly: "He is cold, precise and incredibly efficient; he never had a live idea in his life; and his speeches are 'like a drizzle of incessant rain.'" There are many others, however, who find him better described in the terms of the *Christian Science Monitor's* correspondent: "A fine sense of realities, moderation, calm wisdom and courageous resolution." He has two sons, and is greatly helped in his work by his wife, who usually accompanies him on trips, although she was not with him during this latest visit to the United States. Her chief interest is not trade unionism, however, but music.

References

Christian Sci Mon p15 N 20 '40; p4 Ja 13 '41 por
Harper 170:499 Mr '35
Time 35:38+ My 13 '40 por
U S News 9:17 N 22 '40
Author's and Writer's Who's Who
Citrine, W. M. I Search for Truth in Russia 1937
Gunther, J. Inside Europe p359-60 1940
Strachey, E. J. St. L. What Are We To Do? 1938
Who's Who

CLAIR, RENÉ Nov. 11, 1898(?)- Film director

Address: c/o Universal Pictures Corp, Universal City, Hollywood, Calif.

For many years René Clair, the French film director, has been decidedly lukewarm in his enthusiasm for Hollywood. He has admired the speed, precision and scene per scene economy of its best films, but has at the same time deplored its tawdriness, type casting, its hasty adaptations of stage plays, its wanton spending of money. Yet, impelled by the Nazi invasion of France, he has been in Hollywood since August 1940 and he has been making films under the Hollywood conditions he once scorned.

His first presentation was *The Flame of New Orleans* (1941), and to Clair admirers it was a sad disappointment. What had become, they asked, of his Gallic wink, his verve, his inventive humor? And what had happened to all those tenets of film making he had held by ever since he started directing? For years René Clair had worked alone; he had written the stories of his films, constructed the scenarios, directed the production and supervised the cutting, undisturbed by story conferences, by producers' relatives or the opinions of women's clubs. The result had been singularly personal work, combining satire and slapstick with occasional flashes of sentiment.

Unlike Hollywood producers Clair had been able to ignore the pleas of the writers who sometimes work for him—"they can't know a story nor its correct treatment as a director does"; he had avoided complicated plot material; he had avoided using "stars" and had succeeded always in making his actors' portrayals and appearance as natural as possible; he had been content with the cheapest and simplest sets; he had never depended on camera angles to express particular moods. "I prefer," he once said, "to combine box office with artistic values." So far, Clair fans believe, Hollywood hasn't allowed him to follow the style, the patterns, the methods for which he became famous, but they are hopeful that he will be able to work out some kind of a compromise between his ideas and Hollywood's that will give the American public the sustained pleasure his European films have so long given.

This most famous of French directors was born René Chomette in Paris and brought up there by his parents, Marius and Marie Chomette. He attended the Lycée and would have gone to the university if it hadn't been for the War. At the age of 18 he enlisted, but he served for only a few months until an attack of illness laid him low for more than a year. When he was well he joined the staff of the Paris newspaper *L'Intransigeant*. By 1921 he was a well known and contented journalist on this paper's staff and would have remained such if one of those accidents that change careers and men hadn't occurred. It happened one night when René Chomette was dining with convivial friends at a cafe on the Champs Élysées and learned

RENÉ CLAIR

that they were going out the next day to act bit parts in a film just for the fun of it. He had the day free and went along. Almost overnight, René Chomette, the journalist, became René Clair, the actor.

He appeared as an extra in *Parisette*, played in the Loie Fuller *Le Lys de la vie*, in some of Protazanov's films, in some of the pictures the Gaumont film studios were making. The producers, conscious of his interest in films, offered him a writing assignment on the strength of his reputation as a journalist, but René Clair turned it down to take, instead, a position as assistant director. For many months he was assistant to Baroncelli, the veteran French director, months in which he learned screen technique, and then he was asked to direct a picture of his own. There was no money to work with, little technical equipment, no staff. Clair didn't mind; he had a story he had written, he gathered actors and he made a picture.

It was a short experimental film, produced in 1923, called *Paris Qui Dort*. Fantastic, satirical, it appealed to the Parisian public and was followed the next year by *Le Fantôme du Moulin Rouge*, a less fascinating film which told the story of a soul which separates itself from its body. That same year, however, came *Entr'acte*, with music by Erik Satie and a scenario by Picabia, the whole a sort of dream without subject or plot in which incongruous images freely succeed one another. A great *succès de scandale*, by its fantasy it prepared the way for *Le Voyage Imaginaire* in 1925, a fairy tale with wonderful glimpses of Paris and some Mack Sennett chases.

Already with this picture Clair was emerging as the portrayer of his city, already he was showing a sophisticated charm, an ability to create a "delicate softness of contour with which he endows Paris—the roof tops, squares and even people, who become generalized into

CLAIR, RENÉ—*Continued*

something like timeless abstractions." Already he was showing his feeling that everything there was enormously amusing, wonderfully good. This film was followed in 1926 by *La Proie du Vent*, where that technical ability which distinguishes Clair's work was apparent even through a mess of intricate plots. This was the year, incidentally, in which his only novel, *Adams*, published in England as *Star Turn*, appeared.

All these films made before 1927 were experimental, training grounds for discovering the uses of the camera. While making them Clair studied other directors' work, other films. Chaplin was his idol, and every aspect of his pictures was carefully studied; from the speed of Mack Sennett comedies Clair learned much, too. He was ready to produce a full-length film. Since 1925 he had had a contract with Albatross-Sequana and it was for them that he completed in 1927 *Le Chapeau de Paille d'Italie* (*The Italian Straw Hat*), a delightful farce taken from Labiche's work which enraged all of comfortable middle-class France with its social satire. Clair had to wait a whole year, until the rancor against this film subsided, before Albatross-Sequana would allow him to make another picture. On his own he made *La Tour*, a poetic documentary film, and then, restored to grace, produced *Les Deux Timides*. It was with this picture, distinguished by trick photography, by clever montage, especially of the "contrast" type, that the critics began to speak of the "Clair touch."

By this time sound pictures had come in, and René Clair sadly commented: "Sound is the death of film." He himself, nevertheless made a sound picture, *Sous les Toits de Paris* (1930), which established his reputation internationally. Here was a new talking picture technique which startled the world by its simplicity and its brilliant blending of sight and sound, which exploited impressively the idea of making music the binding continuity of the visual action, making it clear that "the film as a form of art must not be confused with the necessarily static stage play."

The plot itself was simple; dialogue was used sparingly; the effect was achieved through stylized realism, achieved through the constant variation of perspective, composition and light, through the use of motion itself— motion of facial expression and body. Here René Clair attained what has been considered characteristic of his work, "the finest kind of balance maintained between the ridiculous and the delicate, between the false and the true, between exaggeration and exquisiteness," so well that in the words of Mark Van Doren *Sous les Toits de Paris* "came as near to perfection as any conceivable film of its kind."

Its successor was *Le Million* (1931), the first speaking vehicle of Annabella, and the picture on which her stardom was founded. The "gayest of Clair's pictures, rich in minor characters, conceived without a trace of exaggeration and seeming . . . as fresh and unruffled as dolls in a shop window," it is the story of a chase after an old coat containing a lottery ticket. With beautiful fluidity it moves forward through fantasy, achieved not through tricks of setting or photography but by the mobile use of the camera, toward an ending rich in irony. Like its predecessor it is rich in fresh twists of continuity devices that employ sound as well as the visual image.

Le Million caused Clair to be attacked as a Communist by the extreme Right and as a Fascist by the extreme Left. He shrugged the epithets away. "I have no political opinion. I am just French," he said then, and later. That he did have a social point of view, however, was demonstrated in his next picture, *À Nous la Liberté* (1932). Called "one of the rare European masterpieces of the comic cinema" and "the most complete expression of Clair's genius," this film tells the story of two friends in prison who plan to escape; the one of them that does get out sets up a large phonograph factory. In portraying the factory, Clair's satire plays sharply on rationalization and factory methods, delicately and ironically on the characters he creates. Here are the stylized realism of *Sous les Toits de Paris* and the fantasy of *Le Million*, with implications as well as events allowed to assume dramatic and convincing shape. And here, according to Margaret Marshall, is a technique "closer to the technique of music than of any other art."

It was after the production of this picture that critical praise was richly lavished on Clair. His work, according to the New York *Sun* critic in 1932, is "something that takes the best features of silent picture technique, the best features of talkie technique, the best features of sound, the best features of music, the best features of words. It somehow merges them into what I feel is the ideal talkie." And *Vanity Fair* commented: "René Clair is one of the few motion picture directors whose adult and civilized influence is gradually beginning to leaven the soggy lump which has hitherto been the cinema industry." Clair himself was skeptical of the extent of this influence, and while praises continued to pour in delivered himself of a stinging indictment of the film industry, where innovators weren't allowed a free hand, where directors seldom had ability, where the ruling powers were guided by mere crochets, where routine standardization and mass production combined to kill the goose that lays the golden egg. Four years later, in 1936, he didn't feel much improvement had taken place. "So much talk as there now is on the screen puts me to sleep," he complained.

In 1933 he followed up the great success of *À Nous la Liberté* with *Quatorze Juillet*. Until this picture, he said, his work was "too cerebral"; with this film he eschewed all technical tricks and told a simple story of a pretty little flower girl and a handsome taxi driver, smoothly developed—yet, audiences felt, mannered like a Clair pattern. By some it was called "utterly delightful", "slyly intelligent", "the best of his films to date"; by others it was considered "primarily an item for Clair collectors."

There was little critical argument about its successor, *Le Dernier Milliardaire*; Clair's admirers were disappointed. "A tremendous failure," Clair called it, but hastened to explain why. It opened in Paris at the time of the Stavisky affair and since there was a similarity between the film's material and current events, disapproval was inevitable. In some places where it was shown there were riots, even, and it had to be re-called. Where it was allowed on the screen, box-office returns were painfully light. Nevertheless, it won second prize at the First Soviet Cinema Festival.

It was in 1936 that René Clair for the first time really aimed at a mass audience, for the first time made a film in English (for Alexander Korda), for the first time let someone else do his screen story (Robert Sherwood). Made in England, this story of the Glourie Spook who has to haunt his castle until he can tweak the nose of a MacLaggan and compel him to admit that one Glourie can thrash fifty MacLaggans gave the critics a hard job. Most of them thought *The Ghost Goes West* brilliantly funny, gayly urbane, sly, adroit and darn good fun, but they felt it important to state, at the same time, that it wasn't "pure Clair." Mark Van Doren went even further than that. "There is no lack of nice things here and there along the way," he admitted, "and there is always the reminder that this man once held a precious secret in his hands. But," he sadly added, "he has lost it."

Those who saw a Hollywood touch in *The Ghost Goes West* hastened to say "I told you so" when Clair came to the United States for the first time, shortly after it was released. But he disappointed them greatly by not going near Hollywood and by stating that he was in America for three simple reasons: to meet an American "reportaire" in the flesh and blood; to see an American "gangstaire" in real life; to watch American audiences react to his film. He also didn't hesitate to inform the public that there had been no improvement in motion pictures in the past five years, no experimentation, no going forward. He softened his censure, however, by saying, "I would go to Hollywood if it would give me the same facilities Europe does. I mean I don't want to work by order. . . If I do not find a story which interests me as an author I am afraid I cannot make a good picture." It was four years and some pictures later, after his filming of *Air Pur* had been half completed and then abandoned, that Clair arrived in the United States with his wife and 14-year-old son, two steamer trunks and a few suitcases. He reached Hollywood just as Universal acquired the script of *The Flame of New Orleans* and was offered the directorship of it by Joe Pasternak. He accepted, and not many months later his own dicta were tossed back at him.

Sober looking, yet with a quick spasmodic smile, René Clair is fairly tall and frail. His face is thin, his features serious and ascetic, his manner shy, and even in tweeds he is elegant. Like many Frenchmen he is a seasoned gourmet, but one who indulges in no nonsense about wines. "If he wants red wine with the fish," his friend Robert Sherwood says, "he will damn well take it."

References

Life and Letters Today 13:200 S '35
Lit Digest 121:28 Ja 25 '36
Liv Age 342:181-2 Ap '32
Nation 134:659-60 Je 8 '32; 142:138+ Ja 29 '36
New Theatre 3:12-13+ F '36
N Y Post p7 Ja 28 '41
N Y Times p8 Mr 4 '41; IX p3 My 11 '41
New Yorker 11:13 S 14 '40
Bardèche, M. and Brasillach, R. History of Motion Pictures p242-51, 327-34 1938
International Motion Picture Almanac
Rotha, P. Celluloid, the Film Today p181-95 1931
Who's Who

CLARK, BENNETT CHAMP Jan. 8, 1890-   United States Senator

Address: b. Senate Office Bldg, Washington, D. C.; Paul Brown Bldg, St. Louis, Mo; h. Ladue Village, Mo.

BENNETT CHAMP CLARK

To understand Bennett Champ Clark, one of the leaders of the "peace bloc" in Congress until the Japanese attack on Pearl Harbor, it is necessary to go more in detail into his family history than into that of most men. The keynote of Senator Clark's temperament and career is his clannishness and his adoration of his father, the late Speaker Champ Clark, the "Little American."

The first Clarks came to Connecticut in 1639. As far back as they can be traced they were stubborn, independent individuals. The Senator's paternal grandfather was known in Kentucky, where he eventually settled, as "the

CLARK, BENNETT CHAMP—*Continued*

Contrary Old Gentleman," and he lived up to the name from the time when, at 14, he ran away from his home in New Jersey rather than be apprenticed to anyone and lose his freedom. His grandson has inherited many of his tendencies. He worships the memory of his father, and has never forgotten or forgiven the Democratic Convention of 1912, when Champ Clark had a majority of votes for nomination as President, but was defeated by the two-thirds majority rule and by the defection of William Jennings Bryan, who switched over to Woodrow Wilson. In 1936 Champ Clark's son was to lead the fight for abolition of the two-thirds rule.

Bennett Champ Clark practically grew up in the Capitol at Washington, where his father had become a Representative when the boy was only three. (Incidentally, he was christened Joe Bennett Clark, but changed his name when he was a college student, since a brother named Champ had died in infancy and he thought the ancestral name should be perpetuated. His oldest son is also named Champ.) At that time Congressmen's children were given the freedom of the House floor, and he and his sister Genevieve (who as Mrs. James M. Thomson, wife of the publisher of the New Orleans *Tribune* and *Star,* has been one of his chief political aides) were, to quote Raymond Moley, "educated as much in the Capitol as at school and college." He started campaigning for his father when he was little more than a child, and was a precinct captain at 14. Politics and the Democratic Party are part of his lifeblood.

Bennett Champ Clark was born in Bowling Green, Missouri, and received his B. A. at the University of Missouri in 1913. He then studied law at George Washington University in Washington, D. C., got his LL. B. in 1914, and was admitted to the Missouri Bar. He has since had honorary doctorates from Missouri, Washington and Lee, Marshall, and Bethany. After practicing for a short time in Bowling Green, he became a member of a law firm in St. Louis which specialized in corporation law. He was never very active as an attorney, however, his interests from the beginning being primarily in politics. Nevertheless, when he was appointed to the United States Senate in 1933, his only previous experience in office had been as parliamentarian in the House of Representatives, from 1913 to 1917, when his father was Speaker.

Clark, like his father, was opposed to America's entry into the First World War. But when war was declared, he was one of the first to enlist. He entered the Army as a captain in the United States Reserve, was sent to Fort Myer, in Virginia, and then overseas as a lieutenant colonel in the infantry. A characteristic story comes from his days at Fort Myer. The first night he knelt by his bed to say his prayers. (He is a devout Presbyterian.) Somebody gave a catcall. The praying officer rose to his feet, offered, with suitable profanity, to "bust

the ———'s head in," and having thus mastered the situation finished his prayers without further interruption. In 1919 he was promoted to a colonelcy and transferred to the General Staff. He raised heaven and earth to try to stay in active service, enlisting the help of his father, but to no avail. After the War he was one of the 17 charter members of the American Legion, and he is its past national commander; but when the Legion at its 1941 convention came out for abandonment of the neutrality law, Clark called its present attitude a "disgrace" and said it had repudiated all it originally stood for.

In 1933, when Harry B. Hawes resigned as Senator from Missouri, Clark was appointed to fill his unexpired term. He has since been twice elected to that office, though at his first election the betting against his nomination was three to one. He was opposed both by a dry candidate (he was a Wet) and by a representative of the then powerful Pendergast machine. Thanks to his early rearing, he did not have to undergo the tongue-tied period which afflicts most new Congressmen. In July 1933 he headed a group of Missouri admirers who presented a horse to President Roosevelt as a symbol of the New Deal; but from the beginning he showed his independence from it. He backed Roosevelt's monetary policy, but opposed his economy act of 1933, fought the NRA, the AAA, the government and Supreme Court reorganization bills, and in January 1939 backed the WPA fund cut.

What is more, he was a consistent isolationist. Soon after beginning to serve on Senator Nye's (see sketch this issue) Senate Munitions Committee in 1934 he drafted a plan for the elimination of war profits; and he has always urged the invoking of the Neutrality Act in the Sino-Japanese War, denounced munitions sales for use in civilian bombings, favored the war referendum. In April 1939 he was appointed to the Senate Foreign Relations Committee, and with the deepening of the European crisis and the outbreak of the Second World War he became even more closely affiliated with the group of aggressive self-styled anti-interventionists in the Senate. Having opposed repeal of the arms embargo in September 1939, he soon began to quote Charles Lindbergh (see sketch this issue) on the floor of the Senate, to attack aid to Britain, the draft bill, the lend-lease bill and subsequent measures. (In May 1941, however, his suggestion that the United States take over by force French possessions in the Western Hemisphere outdid a few "interventionists.")

Three things actuated him in his stand, according to a friendly commentator: hatred of war, hatred of Communism and a burning belief that Congress, not the President, should make the laws and create the policies of the United States. He is also by nature a conservative, with a dubious eye for any fundamental economic changes. In 1940 he was prominently mentioned among possible Democratic Presidential nominees; but he was a close friend of Vice-President Garner, and when the Convention sheered away from Garner and the conservative Garner group, Clark also lost out. He repeatedly declared his opposition to a third term for President Roosevelt, although he came out for him at the last moment. He was, however, one of the few isolationists who has not been personally on bad terms with the President, and he was not one of those named in the Roosevelt "purge" in 1938. In 1936 he favored a six-year term for United States Presidents— but that suggestion may have been in the class with his bill, introduced in 1934, proposing a two and one-half cent coin.

In the fall of 1941 Senator Clark was much in the public eye as co-sponsor of the resolution calling for an investigation of the movies which resulted in the appointment of a Senate subcommittee to determine if the investigation should be held. The entrance of Russia into the War had made him even more firmly isolationist than before. "I hereby charge," he thundered at one of the hearings, "that a handful of men have gotten possession of both the radio microphone and the moving picture screen. . . Dozens of pictures . . . are used to infect the minds of their audiences with hatred, to inflame them, to arouse their emotions and make them clamor for war. And not one word on the side of the argument against war is heard." Fight for Freedom, Inc., described the investigation as "the most barefaced attempt at censorship and racial persecution."

Mrs. Clark shared her husband's ideas. She is the former Miriam Marsh, a tall, auburn-haired Iowa girl whom he married in 1922. She is a talented musician who had studied architecture as well, but whose heart, like her husband's, was in politics. (Her father had been treasurer of the Democratic National Committee.) Mrs. Clark was even more of an isolationist than is her husband, and was active in the America First Committee. She was once quoted: "Politics is the most fascinating of all games. I love it!" They have three boys, the two younger being twins. They still keep their house in Ladue Village, Missouri, but have also bought one in Washington, where Mrs. Clark has indulged her talent for interior decorating. The heart of the house is the library, which is large and well-selected. It is the Senator's own special study, but since he is devoted to his family and likes to have them around him, usually all of them gather about the big fireplace in the evening.

Senator Clark is really a scholar. He is perhaps the only Congressman who before his election had read the entire file of the *Congressional Record!* He has "a capacity for working hard at any task that tickles his fancy," and in 1932 he produced a very creditable biography of John Quincy Adams: *Old Man Eloquent*. He also compiled the *Constitution Manual and Digest of Practice of the House of Representatives* from 1913 to 1916, inclusive, and he was co-author of *Social Studies* (1934).

A large man, over six feet tall and more than two hundred pounds in weight, Clark has been described as "bulgy, hearty, eupeptic." Robert McCormick remarked that he

inherited from his father his "barrel chest, broad shoulders, rectangular jaw, and thin mouth," though in general he does not much resemble his father physically. He has what McCormick calls "a magnificent set of vocal cords"; but it has also been said that in argument he sometimes uses them "almost like a schoolboy." His boyish grin and penchant for "kidding" his opponents somewhat abandoned in these grim times, there remains "a genius for public rudeness" that is almost as useful. Jack Alexander once called him an "impolitic politician" who was "born without tact," and in 1941 Frank Sullivan nominated him for an All-American Stuffed Shirt Team; but there are others who think of him quite differently. In 1932 a commentator thought him "incapable of making and keeping enemies," and outside of politics he is still amiable and easy-going—a man who enjoys his friends, goes fishing with them and sleeps while they fish, is a passionate baseball fan and an authority on baseball history.

References

Business Week p61 My 29 '37 por; p7 Ag 17 '40 por
Christian Sci Mon Mag p4 S 11 '35 por; p2 Mr 11 '39 por; p13 My 29 '40
Collier's 102:22+ O 22 '38 por
Lit Digest 120:19 D 7 '35 por; 121:33 Ja 18 '36
Newsweek 6:6 Ag 17 '35 por; 7:9 Ja 18 '36 por; 7:14 Ja 25 '36 por; 13:52 Ap 24 '39
PM p10 F 23 '41 por
Sat Eve Post 211:5-7+ O 8 '38 pors
Time 27:14 Ja 20 '36 por; 34:17 Jl 17 '39 por
Who's Who in America
Who's Who in the Nation's Capital

CLAUSSEN, JULIA (klô'sn) June 11, 1879 —May 1, 1941 Opera singer with the Metropolitan Opera Company from 1917 to 1932; died at her home in Stockholm, Sweden; sang with the Chicago Opera Company and made guest appearances in London, Paris, Stockholm and Mexico City; while with the Metropolitan she sang roles in many operas, among them *Tannhäuser, Die Walküre, Lohengrin, The Flying Dutchman* and *La Gioconda*.

References

Baker's Biographical Dictionary of Musicians 1940
Thompson, O. ed. International Cyclopedia of Music and Musicians 1939
Who's Who in America
Wier, A. E. ed. Macmillan Encyclopedia of Music and Musicians 1938

Obituaries

Musical Am 61:28 My 10 '41 por
N Y Times p15 My 3 '41 por

CLAY, LAURA Feb. 9, 1849—June 29, 1941 Pioneer in the woman's suffrage movement who at the 1920 Democratic Convention

CLAY, LAURA—*Continued*

was the first woman to receive a vote for the Presidential nomination; first president of the Kentucky Equal Rights Association and took the fight for suffrage into other states throughout the country.

References

Leonard, J. W. ed. Women's Who's Who of America 1914-15
Who's Who in America 1930-31

Obituaries

N Y Times p17 Je 30 '41 por

CLEMENSEN, ERIK CHRISTIAN
1876(?)—May 19, 1941 Internationally known chemist; had developed formulas for manufacture of canned meat and soup preservatives, saccharin (a substitute for sugar used by diabetics), and coumerin (a crystalline compound used for flavoring and in perfumes); recently developed a process for tanning leather which has been in wide demand in South America.

Obituaries

N Y Herald Tribune p22 My 22 '41 por

CLINCHY, EVERETT R(OSS), REV.
Dec. 16, 1896- Clergyman
Address: b. 300 Fourth Ave, New York City; h. 46 Prospect St, Madison, N. J.

Bachrach

THE REV. EVERETT R. CLINCHY

To the Reverend Everett Ross Clinchy religious liberty is the "keystone of democracy." The director of the National Conference of Christians and Jews believes that today, more than ever before, "we must be on our guard. . . At this particular time a better understanding among the people of all religions becomes of the utmost importance.

All are threatened and all must live together as friends, working together for the welfare of a common country."

There are few men in America who have fought more fiercely against religious intolerance than this "tall, rangy man with the fire of belief in his deep-set eyes"; few Americans who are better informed about relations among the various racial and religious groups in our population. And yet, by his own admission, Dr. Clinchy was brought up to look on people of religions other than his own with suspicion. He was born in New York City, the son of James Hugh and Lydie (Stagg) Clinchy, both staunch Scotch Presbyterians. "I was brought up," he remembers, "with the idea that Catholics were different from us. I would not have ventured into the Catholic cathedral for anything. My father was a fine, God-fearing man who would have willingly harmed no one. . . Yet I was imbued with a distrust of other worthy citizens. The result was that I mingled only with my own group. The world, as far as I was concerned, was a small back yard enclosed by a high fence which I did not dare to climb." When he heard, for instance, that a Mormon missionary had visited his grandmother, he was shocked.

This feeling persisted during high school and even in his first years of college. It was in 1916 that he entered Wesleyan University in Middletown, Connecticut, earning his way by selling sandwiches through the dormitories in the evenings. A year and one-half later he was a member of a field artillery unit. Two years later he was in France. Before he left, however, he had sent a wire to Winifred Mead in Denver, Colorado asking her to marry him and she, a bishop's daughter, had wired back the words of Ruth to Naomi: "Whither thou goest, I will go, and where thou lodgest I will lodge." On September 21, 1918 they were married, and a short time afterward Everett Clinchy went abroad.

Dr. Clinchy went from a buck private to commissioned officer in the United States Field Artillery. More important, he came out of the War believing that all men, regardless of their religious beliefs, are brothers. He had seen Protestants, Catholics and Jews working, playing, firing and fighting together, "a basic human and divine unity among them." The Scotch Presbyterian had lost his narrow outlook and developed tolerance. It was with this new outlook that he returned to college—this time to Lafayette College in Easton, Pennsylvania, which awarded him a Bachelor of Science degree in 1920.

The next year Dr. Clinchy spent studying at the Union Theological Seminary and at Columbia University in New York City. With a Master's Degree from Columbia, which he received in 1921, the year he was ordained, he took up his first pastoral duties at the Fairmount (New Jersey) Presbyterian Church. For two years Dr. Clinchy was associated with this church, while at the same time continuing his graduate studies at Yale University (later graduate work won him his Ph. D. in 1934 from Drew University). Then in 1923 he was called to the Church of Christ at Wesleyan University.

At Wesleyan his home was a place where the students used to gather to play with his son and daughter (there has been another daughter since then), to eat waffles and to discuss their life problems. For five years Dr. Clinchy stayed in Middletown, and one of his great accomplishments there was the building up of round-table discussions among students of different faiths. Other religious men had begun to see the importance of this sort of activity, and a Good-Will Committee of the Federal Council of Churches of Christ in America was establishing contact with a similar committee of the Conference of American Rabbis. The kind of work Clinchy was doing became known to the Federal Council of Churches of Christ in America, and in 1928 he became its secretary.

Dr. Clinchy stayed with this organization until 1933, and it was at the beginning of his association with it that the National Conference of Christians and Jews was formed, with the Council's blessing. Behind the new movement were important men like Charles Evans Hughes (see sketch this issue) (given the Conference's Inter-Faith Award in 1940) and Dr. S. Parkes Cadman, but the "active living force," most clergymen agree, "has always been Dr. Clinchy." It was to give his full time to this organization that he left the Federal Council.

The National Conference of Christians and Jews holds community meetings all over the country, maintains organizations in many cities, supervises discussions on college campuses, broadcasts programs, sends out news releases, all in the interest of creating tolerance among Catholics, Protestants and Jews. It also sponsors the Williamstown Institute of Human Relations conferences. And Dr. Clinchy's part of its work is that of organization, of giving leadership. He himself travels widely over America and has made frequent trips abroad—thousands of miles to spread his gospel of good will. (In September 1941, for instance, Dr. Clinchy, along with a Roman Catholic priest and a Jewish rabbi, made a trip to London to study and to report on the religious and social trends among the organized religious groups in the British Isles. On his return he proposed a peace expeditionary force to spread the doctrine of Americanism in Europe following the War.) He has also written many articles for both religious and secular periodicals, a book, *All in the Name of God* (1934), and "Prejudice and Minority Groups," a chapter in *Our Racial and National Minorities* (1937).

In Dr. Clinchy's writings there are warnings to the American people, warnings that intolerance is growing, that "the religious people of America must translate their faith in the fatherhood of God and the brotherhood of man into a working, democratic economy." There is also hope and faith in "a love for America so great that no one will be able to hate any group in the American neighborhood." What Dr. Clinchy writes is not

academic; it is based on what he has known and seen and sought out. When he enters a town he doesn't visit only the ministers and rabbis, the schools and churches; he tries to get the reactions of taxi drivers, waitresses, clerks, gas station attendants, laborers. Once, it is told, his investigations along these lines were a little less successful than usual. As told in the Lafayette College *Alumnus* of May 1938, Dr. Clinchy and Rabbi Morris Lazaron were once returning from an evening meeting in New York and it was about 11:30 when they stopped at the Commodore Hotel to have something to eat. Interested in learning something about working conditions there, Dr. Clinchy asked the attractive hat-check girl: "What time tonight do you stop work?" The girl looked him over and replied: "At midnight; what have you got in mind?"

References

> Christian Cent 55:749 Je 15 '38
> N Y Post p6 S 29 '41 por
> N Y Times VII p11 D 22 '40 por
> Time 31:55 Je 13 '38 por
> America's Young Men
> Who's Who in America

COATES, JOHN June 29, 1865—Aug. 16, 1941 Famous English grand opera tenor; had given recitals in the United States and Canada; was considered the supreme interpreter of tenor roles in the works of Sir Edward Elgar; made public debut at the age of 12; for 50 years sang in opera and light opera in all parts of the world.

References

> Baker's Biographical Dictionary of Musicians 1940
> Ewen, D. ed. Living Musicians 1940
> Who's Who

Obituaries

> N Y Times p39 Ag 17 '41

COFFIN, HASKELL 1878(?)—May 12, 1941 Magazine illustrator; portrait painter; died a suicide after undergoing treatment for melancholia; until some 15 years ago he was recognized as one of the nation's most successful commercial artists; a terrific worker, he managed to draw a pretty girl's head a day and once painted a portrait of the late David Belasco in three hours; full name William Haskell Coffin.

Obituaries

> N Y Times p12 My 13 '41

COHEN, BENJAMIN V(ICTOR) Sept. 23, 1894- Counselor to the American Embassy in London; lawyer

Address: b. American Embassy, London, England; h. 119 E. 47th St, New York City

The famous law team of Corcoran (see sketch 1940 Annual) and Cohen, considered by many the Administration's real "Brain Trust," has finally split up. Thomas Corcoran was, in 1941, still in Washington, D. C., and

BENJAMIN V. COHEN

Benjamin V. Cohen was with Ambassador Winant (see sketch this issue) in London, Counselor to the Embassy there. But many who knew these two lawyers and their work feel that this split is probably only a temporary one—they have complemented each other too long and too well to end it all.

Since 1933 they have been working together, drafting legislation for the New Deal, attacked as a "menace to American Government," praised as "patriotic citizens who have worked unremittingly over long years to try to make this country a better place for its people." They have written speeches for Congressmen, conferred long and privately with the President, helped drive measures through Congress. Their exact duties have been called everything from those of "shock troopers who go where the fighting is hottest" to those of the "Führer's tutors." They themselves said they were merely catalysts, agents who cause reactions to occur without themselves being altered.

The less conspicuous member of this "conjunction of dreamy intellectual Jew and effervescent Irishman" has been Benjamin Cohen, a "naturally shy and retiring man" who has been content to do the actual drafting of that legislation for which he and his partner are responsible while Corcoran buzzed around seeing people, putting ideas across, getting ideas. Cohen was born in Muncie, Indiana, the son of Moses and Sarah (Ringold) Cohen. His was a comfortable middle class home: his father was an ore dealer who had fled from Poland in 1868 and settled down in the Midwest. Benjamin's youth was uneventful—he is said to have been a serious child who "neglected marbles for Descartes and Spencer."

From high school in Muncie, Cohen went to the University of Chicago and was called by Professor Harold Moulton, later head of the Brookings Institution, "the most brilliant student I ever taught." He received his Ph. B. in 1914 and a year later a Doctor of Jurisprudence degree, after making the highest marks ever recorded in the law school. Cohen then decided on graduate work at the Harvard Law School. For one year he studied there, coming under the influence of Professor Felix Frankfurter (see sketch this issue), and was graduated with the degree of Doctor of Juridical Science in 1916. Immediately afterward he was admitted to the Illinois Bar.

Cohen's first position, after law school, was that of secretary to Judge Julian William Mack of the Federal Circuit Court in New York City. Almost every important receivership case came up at one time or another before Judge Mack, and Cohen learned much about the complexities of the law on corporate reorganization. Mack was pleased with Cohen's work—"I never had a better secretary," he used to say. After a year Cohen resigned to act as an attorney for the United States Shipping Board during the War, when his weak eyes kept him out of active army service.

When the War was over, Cohen spent two years, from 1919 to 1921, as counsel for the American Zionists negotiating the terms of the Palestine mandate at the Peace Conferences. It was while he was abroad that he met the economist John Maynard Keynes (see sketch this issue), who interested him in the theory that a national depression could be combated by priming private industry through a public works program. It was abroad, too, that he is supposed to have developed concretely a theory of securities control.

Back in New York, Cohen entered into law practice, his clients mostly lawyers who brought him their knottiest problems. Corporate reorganization was his specialty, and many of New York's corporations sought him out for advice. At the same time Cohen, who has always had a sincere feeling for the oppressed, was the unpaid counsel of the National Consumers League and for them drafted a model minimum wage law for New York State. He was also speculating in Wall Street during the '20s and is supposed to have done well for himself, though part of what he made disappeared in the crash of 1929.

It was in 1933 that Cohen first went to Washington. This was the year when the bill designed to regulate the selling of securities was being put together. There were hitches all along the way until, after a hurry call for advice, Frankfurter sent James Landis, later head of the SEC, and Ben Cohen to Washington. These two rewrote the first "Truth in Securities" Act and Congress passed it. So carefully drafted was it that years later lawyers were looking for loopholes without success.

In 1933 Cohen was made general counsel to the Public Works Administration in charge of railroad loans; he held this position until 1934, when he became counsel to the National

Power Policy Commission, a job he kept until his appointment to England. Corcoran at this time was counsel to the Reconstruction Finance Corporation. But both lawyers were active in drawing up legislation for the New Deal. They had met over the Securities Act of 1933, and together they wrote the Securities Exchange Act of 1934. The Public Utility Holding Company Act of 1935 was "their baby from start to finish." They drafted it, helped enact it and, as special assistants to the attorney general, defended it against 81 suits brought by holding companies.

Together Corcoran and Cohen were responsible for plans for the Federal Housing Administration, for the TVA, for the Wage and Hour Law, for extensions of the RFC, for plans for the Electric Farm and Home Authority, for regional conservation bills and some say, for the court packing plan. And Cohen by himself, in his position as counsel to the National Power Policy Commission, largely conceived most of the Commission's plans. "Every bill but one that Cohen and Corcoran drafted is now the law of the land," due mostly, it is agreed, to Cohen's skill as a legislative draftsman—the most skillful one in the country, many lawyers think.

The two men worked wonderfully well together. Bachelors, they even took an apartment together so that they would be able to spend 16 or 18 hours a day working. For a while they lived with several other young government lawyers in Georgetown and then in 1938 they moved into an apartment on K Street, an arrangement that lasted until Corcoran was married in March 1940. At work and away from it they were entirely different: Cohen pessimistic where Corcoran was optimistic, Cohen interested in detail, slow working, thorough, Corcoran more mercurial. And Cohen, tall, slouched, with spectacles perched on a long nose, with his high forehead under receding dark hair, was physically very unlike his out-of-doors-loving collaborator.

It was generally known in Washington that Cohen and Corcoran were in the very inner circle of the circle around Roosevelt, that they were responsible for much of his legislation, that they provided the ideas, facts and figures for much of his activities. In Washington they used to call them "The Gold Dust Twins" ("Let the Gold Dust Twins do your work"), Frankfurter's "two chief little hot dogs", "the Brain Twins." Yet outside of Washington their names weren't much known, for they were content to stay in the background. They didn't talk much in public, write books or try to get their names in print.

Extremely important in 1936, 1937 and 1938, there were rumors in the summer of 1940 that Corcoran and Cohen were on their way out, rumors that grew as the months passed. Their supporters denied this, pointing out that since the Administration had taken the emphasis off new reforms to place it on national defense, actually Cohen's special talents as a draftsman and Corcoran's as a pusher-through-of-legislation were less needed in Washington than they had been. These rumors died down, to be replaced by one that Corcoran was slated to be Assistant Secretary of the Navy in charge of Air (as yet unconfirmed) and another that Cohen was slated to go to England in a legal capacity (which has been confirmed).

His task there is to design legal machinery for closer British-American operations during the War, and his major assignment has been reported to be the drafting of a plan that will enable the British to pledge their assets in foreign lands as security for loans to be made under the Lend-Lease Bill. "Whatever he does, Mr. Cohen's influence is certain to be great," and undoubtedly his slouching figure, his drawl, his habits of dressing like a tramp, gobbling food absentmindedly and sleeping in the office when work presses will become as well known abroad as they have been for eight years in Washington.

References

Am Mag 124:22-3+ Ag '37 por
Am Mercury 43:38-45 Ja '38
Lit Digest 123:7-8 My 22 '37 por
Nation's Bus 25:25-6+ Jl '37 por
New Repub 92:46 Ag 18 '37 (Same abr. Lit Digest 124[Digest 1]:24-5 S 11 '37) ; 104:40 Ja 13 '41
Newsweek 6:24-5 Jl 13 '35 por; 11:13-14 F 21 '38 pors
Time 32:22-4 S 12 '38 por (cover); 36:10 Ag 5 '40
U S News 10:41 Mr 14 '41 por
America's Young Men
Who's Who in America
Who's Who in American Jewry
Who's Who in the Nation's Capital

COLBY, CHARLES DEWITT Oct. 23, 1865—Sept. 23, 1941 Physician; specialist in the treatment of tuberculosis; after Army career and wide practice became chief of staff at the Nose and Throat Clinic at the University of Michigan; practiced in Asheville, North Carolina for almost 30 years before his death and was active in the development of Asheville as a health center.

References

American Medical Directory

Obituaries

N Y Times p23 S 24 '41

COLLIER, JOHN May 4, 1884- Commissioner of Indian Affairs

Address: b. 4160 Interior Bldg, Washington, D. C.; h. Janney's Lane, Route 2, Alexandria, Va.

In 1933 John Collier took office as Commissioner of Indian Affairs with an aim unique among political appointees: the gradual diminution of his own power and authority. The appointment itself was unusual in its selection of the person who up to that time had been the most caustic and effective critic of government policy and practice.

U. S. Indian Service

JOHN COLLIER

For the previous decade, as executive secretary of the American Indian Defense Association, Incorporated, Collier had been conducting an ardent crusade on behalf of the vanishing red man, whose property and rights were also vanishing. From 133,000,000 acres in 1887 the land holdings of Indians had decreased to 47,000,000 in 1933; and the Allotment Act of 1887 continued to implement those interests intent upon acquiring whatever natural resources they still retained. The Institute of Government Research described the reservations as "islands surrounded completely by sharks"; and the Defense Association in its report declared the situation "so bad as to be spectacular, so spectacular as to be incredible."

Collier's purpose was to increase the self-sufficiency of the Indians and eventually the degree of self-government granted to them. In 1934 a tremendous step toward this goal was achieved with the passage of the Wheeler-Howard Bill (Indian Reorganization Act), designed to establish their political and economic home rule, to bulwark them against the encroachments of unscrupulous whites, to improve their educational opportunities.

This Indian Reorganization Act, which forms the legal basis of his program, was to a large extent Collier's own work, framed with the aid of two Interior Department attorneys. It marked the first time in history that the associations chiefly active in defense of Indian interests had agreed on a policy; nevertheless it was highly controversial. Ardent advocates hailed it as our nation's greatest Indian reform. Opponents argued that it marked a regression for the Indian to a less civilized state and paved the way for a renaissance of Indian culture and race pride that might lead to a rebirth of paganism and a weakening of Christian influence. Adversaries in Congress

tried to discredit it by pointing out that Collier was on speaking terms with officers of the Civil Liberties Union and that among the many poems he had published was one about a dancing woman named "Eyesadore" Duncan.

Despite these obstacles the Reorganization Act and a number of sustaining bills were passed which by 1935 had enabled 258 individuals to enter college and 141 to be placed in vocational schools. Among the most ardent supporters was Tony Luhan, Indian husband of Mabel Dodge Luhan; he went about among the Indians urging them to accept the optional arrangement provided by the bill, explaining that Commissioner Collier was their friend and would help them gain political freedom and economic security. Seventy-six tribes rejected it, convinced—the proponents claimed through misrepresentation and misunderstanding—that it would deprive them of their rights as American citizens. The only large tribe among the dissenters, however, was the Navaho. One hundred and seventy-six adopted the new scheme of tribal ownership, tribal council, local constitution. By 1940, as one indication of progress, half the employees under the Department of Indian Affairs were Indians, in contrast to the negligible fraction formerly employed; and the caliber of the white employees and agents was very different from what had formerly been the rule.

The New Deal emancipator stems from the land of slavery. He was born on May 4, 1884, in Atlanta, Georgia, a city of which his father, Charles A. Collier, was at one time Mayor. His mother was Susie (Rawson) Collier. Probably Collier's earliest knowledge of Indians came through stories of the grandfather who once fought against them. His feeling for the underprivileged is hardly based on personal experience, for he grew up in an environment of prosperity. His college education began at Columbia University, which he attended from 1902 to 1905, and continued for a year at the Collège de France, in Paris. In the fall of that year, 1906, he was married to Lucy Wood of Philadelphia. Their children are Charles Wood, Donald and John, Jr.

Before he had finished his schooling, in 1905, Collier was doing social work with immigrants in Atlanta, Georgia; and since graduation his work has always been in behalf of some group or groups. In 1907 he became a staff member of the People's Institute in New York, and from 1909 to 1919 he served that organization as civic secretary. While holding this position he helped to organize the National Board of Review of Motion Pictures in 1910, acting as secretary until 1914; he served as director of the National Training School for Community Centers from 1915 to 1919; and he helped to establish, and served on the board of, the Child Health Organization, later called the American Child Health Organization.

In 1919 he moved to California, where he directed community organization under the State government. The following year he began extensive traveling throughout the Southwest, where he studied the Indians and their conditions, piling up the knowledge and the indignation which made him their foremost defender. In 1923 he became executive secretary of the American Indian Defense Association, Incorporated, a position he held until he entered the Federal Government.

These were the years in which he became familiar to liberal weeklies as a crusader, and to certain business and political circles as "that dangerous lobbyist." He waged a bitter fight for religious liberty when the attempt was made to forbid the performance of ancient Indian rituals and ceremonies. More acclaim and more enemies were won by his vigorous part in defeating the Bursum Bill which would have opened the way for further preying on Indian properties. The point of view he developed in the Southwest and pounded home in Washington, D. C., found further expression in the magazine, *American Indian Life*, which he edited and to a large extent wrote during his last seven years with the Association.

Collier still fathers a publication devoted to the Indian—*Indians at Work*, published monthly by the Indian Affairs Office. It is circulated on reservations, at Indian schools, among libraries and various institutions throughout the country, and goes to many individual anthropologists. Collier, in fact, is the first Commissioner of Indian Affairs to regard the anthropologist as more than a bookworm armed with a shovel. Although the Bureau of Ethnology had been studying the Indian since 1870, formerly there was little systematic effort on the part of the administrative branch to make practical use of its researches. Collier has also gone outside the Bureau proper, sending out anthropologists who had worked on Indian reservations a questionnaire asking for observations and suggestions based on their experience, and inviting their cooperation.

The great prerequisite to Indian home rule is education, and on this the Commissioner from the first has centered serious effort. He has eliminated most of the boarding schools which were a scandal to liberty loving Americans and has substituted day schools where small children could begin their education without being torn from their often protesting parents, subjected to shocking conditions, and so forcibly wrenched from their native roots that in many cases they were forbidden to talk their own language even on the playground.

In contrast to the former Government policy of "civilizing" the Indian by trying to make him forget his background, Collier has stimulated interest in Indian art and music, folklore and custom. The formation in 1936 of the Indian Arts and Crafts Board, headed by René d'Harnoncourt, has resulted in new life and considerable publicity for this phase of Indian culture. Museums throughout the country begin to realize that Indian paintings are art as well as specimens; and popular interest in their songs and folklore begins to awaken.

The Indian's most militant defender is a "soft-spoken" man, blond, spare, quiet, slightly stooped; with eyes "so blue they make you gasp." He is the author of six volumes of verse, privately printed, and has contributed articles to many magazines, among them *The Nation, New Republic, Survey Graphic*. Like most men in public office he has weathered blasts of criticism, but unlike most he has yet to experience aspersions on his sincerity or integrity. Many feel that his program has to a degree sentimentalized the Indian; that its methods, even its aims, are not always realistic. Some say it attempts to move too fast. Yet those who have studied the situation are overwhelmingly of the opinion that Collier's administration has at long last begun to win the rights of citizenship for the first Americans. "Since Collier came in," declared a man who has known the Indians under several regimes, "you can at least go on a reservation without feeling ashamed to be a white man."

References

Am Mag 116:52 Ag '33 por
Christian Cent 50:549 Ap 26 '33; 52:767 Je 5 '35
Good H 98:50+ Ap '34
Lit Digest 116:9 Jl 29 '33 por; 117:21 Ap 7 '34 il por; 121:20 Ap 18 '36 por
Nation 136:459 Ap 26 '33; 140:479-80 Ap 24 '35
Scholastic 24:19 Ap 14 '34 por; 28:23 F 29 '36 por; 29:27 O 24 '36 por
Survey G 29:168-74 Mr '40 il por
Time 31:49 My 2 '38 por; 35:15 Je 24 '40 por
Report of the Commissioner of Indian Affairs 1940
Who's Who in America
Who's Who in the Nation's Capital

COLLISON, WILSON Nov. 5, 1893(?)— May 24, 1941 Motion picture writer and playwright; for past 13 years had been writing for films; wrote the "Maisie" series of films starring Ann Sothern; co-author with Otto Harbach of *Up in Mabel's Room* and with Avery Hopwood of *Getting Gertie's Garter*, popular farces of two decades ago; used pseudonym Willis Kent for some of his writings.

References

International Motion Picture Almanac
Who's Who in the Theatre

Obituaries

N Y Herald Tribune p10 My 26 '41

COMPTON, KARL T(AYLOR) Sept. 14, 1887- Physicist; president of the Massachusetts Institute of Technology

Address: b. Massachusetts Institute of Technology, Cambridge, Mass; h. 111 Charles River Rd, Cambridge, Mass.

In November 1940 Columbia University awarded Dr. Karl T. Compton a Doctor of Science degree for his contributions to the physical sciences and his successful administration of the Massachusetts Institute of Technology. In doing so it merely underlined

KARL T. COMPTON

facts that have been well known for many years.

Dr. Compton belongs to that famous Compton family whose members include his father, Elias Compton, a Presbyterian clergyman and professor of philosophy and psychology at the College of Wooster; his brother, Arthur Holly Compton, worker in cosmic rays and professor at the University of Chicago; his brother, Wilson Compton, lawyer, manager of the National Lumber Manufacturers' Association, economics adviser to the United States Department of Commerce and a professor of economics at George Washington University; and his mother, Otelia (Augspurger) Compton, who received an LL. D. from Western College at Oxford, Ohio "for outstanding achievement as a wife and mother." Mrs. Compton says she raised her children "on the Bible and common sense."

Karl Taylor Compton was born in Wooster, Ohio, spent his boyhood there and did his undergraduate and part of his graduate work at the College of Wooster, from which he received a B. A. degree in 1908 and an M. S. in 1909. Immediately he was given an appointment at his Alma Mater to teach chemistry. For one year he was an instructor and then left to attend the graduate school of Princeton University. There he studied under Professor O. W. Richardson, the pioneer investigator of thermionics, and was awarded a Ph. D. in 1912.

In 1912 Dr. Compton began a two-year period as instructor in physics at Reed College, Portland, Oregon, at the end of which he returned to Princeton as assistant professor of physics. He proceeded not only to teach but to engage in researches "which have contributed greatly to our understanding of the great variety of complex processes which occur in electrical discharge through gases."

These researches into atomic physics were interrupted by the First World War, in which Dr. Compton was first an aeronautical engineer for the Signal Corps and then a scientific attaché at the American Embassy at Paris.

When the War ended Dr. Compton returned to Princeton as full professor and remained there until 1930, becoming Cyrus Fogg Bracket Professor of Physics and, in 1929, head of his department. Under his guidance was gradually assembled a large group of experimental research workers engaged in the study of many problems in fundamental atomic physics. He himself made important contributions to our "knowledge of the photo-electric effect, investigation of the structure of crystals by X-rays, fluorescence and dissociation of gases and thermionic emission." From 1927 to 1929 he served as president of the American Physical Society and was associated with the work of the National Research Council and the National Academy of Sciences.

While he was contributing to pure science Dr. Compton was always interested in the fundamental scientific problems of technology. In 1930, when M. I. T. was looking for a president, he was a "natural" for this college, "which is a rigorous training school for science as the handmaiden of industry to produce men whose combination of technical background and point of view will steer them toward the administration desks of high industrial affairs."

In his years at M. I. T., Dr. Compton "has brought the Institute's prestige to a new high." He has greatly broadened the curriculum, adding many new courses and rearranging others to meet the needs of industry in a changing world. He fostered the formation of a well-developed Division of Humanities and introduced a five-year plan of study combined with industrial cooperation which is designed to give students some idea of the social and economic implications of their professions. Under Dr. Compton, too, there has been brought about at the Institute a close integration between fundamental science and technological studies, realized most recently in several research projects for United States' defense that M. I. T. is undertaking.

Dr. Compton's interest in his school has not been entirely scientific—he has been concerned with the students' social welfare as well as with their academic opportunities. Under him the Graduate House was built and new facilities for extra-curricular activities were started. The Institute's system of student government which administers undergraduate affairs flourished under his guidance.

Despite his administrative duties Dr. Compton has found time to keep in close touch with the work of the physics laboratory, to explain the achievements of atom smashers in public lectures and to supervise his own program of experimental work in spectroscopy. And he has continued to be active in the scientific field as a whole. From 1931 to 1933 Dr. Compton was consulting physicist for the Department of Agriculture and the General

Electric Company. From 1931 to 1936 he was chairman of the governing board of the American Institute of Physics. In 1937 he was elected president of the American Association for the Advancement of Science. He was president of the American Academy of Arts and Sciences in 1935 and 1936 (in 1931 he was awarded the Academy's Rumford Medal), and has long been an active member of most of this country's scientific societies.

Dr. Compton has also contributed a good deal of time to public activities, convinced that the municipal, state and federal governments offer technically trained men broad opportunities for raising the standards of public service. As chairman of the Science Advisory Board, appointed by President Roosevelt in 1933 to consider the relation of science to the activities of the Federal Government, he was charged with working out a scientific program for the New Deal. As a member of a joint civilian and army commission appointed in 1934 he also gave much time to a study of the United States Army Air Corps, and during that same year served on the visiting committee of the United States Bureau of Standards and as a member of the Business Advisory and Planning Council of the Department of Commerce. In Massachusetts, Dr. Compton has taken an active interest in the establishment of a compulsory system of unemployment insurance and has served as chairman of the New Products Committee of the New England Council.

Dr. Compton was married to Margaret Hutchinson in 1920 and they have three children. After many years of service to science, M. I. T. and the public, Dr. Compton is still broad-shouldered, of average height and weight and able to beat most of his faculty at tennis. And despite years of research into higher mathematics he is still able to understand the simple arithmetic of balance sheets and the simple rule of psychology that make it easy to run a large institution. As one colleague said: "He's awfully good at drawing teeth." Or as another put it: "When I talk to Compton I come closest to telling the truth."

References
Fortune 14:132+ N '36 por (p108)
J Eng Ed 29:3-6 S '38 por
Sci Mo 40:188-91 F '35 il por
American Men of Science
Leaders in Education 1941
Who's Who in America
Who's Who in Engineering

CONANT, JAMES B(RYANT) (kō′nănt) Mar. 26, 1893- President of Harvard University; chemist

Address: b. Harvard University, Cambridge, Mass; h. 17 Quincy St, Cambridge, Mass.

Since 1933 the president of Harvard University has been an unassuming man who looks like a professor in a New England university (which is exactly what he was). James B. Conant is a gangling six-footer with a permanent stoop to his shoulders, blond hair with an inclination to hang down over his forehead, confident blue eyes behind pedagogic steel-rimmed spectacles. In February 1941 Harvard's lanky president was among those who testified in the Senate for the Lend-Lease bill, H. R. 1776; and on February 15 he sailed for Lisbon on his way to England as head of a three-man commission created by President Roosevelt to confer with British scientists and transmit directly to Washington recent scientific developments of importance to national defense. He returned two months later. The duty of the National Defense Research Committee, of which Dr. Conant is a member, is to "correlate and support scientific research on the mechanisms and devices of warfare," and other scientists from this committee may be sent to England in the future.

Conant was born in Dorchester, Massachusetts, a rather unfashionable suburb of Boston, on March 26, 1893. His mother was Jennett Orr (Bryant) Conant; his father, James Scott Conant, was a photoengraver. Even as a

Bachrach

JAMES B. CONANT

youngster he showed an interest in chemistry, and his father built him a small lean-to to use as a laboratory. Later, "a towhead with a Dutch cut and a broad collar," he studied chemistry under the guidance of Professor Henry Black at the Roxbury Latin School while preparing for Harvard.

Young Conant entered Harvard in the fall of 1910, more interested in chemistry than ever. He acquired his B. A. in only three years, and also membership in Phi Beta Kappa, Sigma Xi and Alpha Chi Sigma. During the next summer he worked in the laboratories of a steel company and seriously contemplated entering business, but returned to Harvard, and in 1916 received his Ph. D. for chemical research. He was an instructor in the Chemistry Department when the First World War

CONANT, JAMES B.—*Continued*

interrupted his teaching career. In 1917 he was doing research for the Chemical Warfare Service in Washington, D. C., with the rank of lieutenant; by the end of the War he was engaged in establishing a large-scale gas production unit in Cleveland, Ohio, with the rank of major. Earlier in 1918 he had discovered that G 34, or lewisite, the most deadly gas in existence, could be manufactured in a laboratory, and he had been sent immediately to this factory for its manufacture—a factory that was called "The Mousetrap" because no one who entered was allowed to leave until the War was over.

After the War, Dr. Conant left The Mousetrap for Harvard—this time as an assistant professor of chemistry. In 1924 he was a visiting lecturer at the summer school of the University of California in Berkeley. In 1925 he spent nearly eight months in Germany studying methods of research and instruction, and upon his return to Harvard became an associate professor. In 1927 there were a few months as research associate at the California Institute of Technology at Pasadena and a promotion to full professorship at Harvard. In 1929 he was elected to the Sheldon Emery Professorship of Organic Chemistry, and in 1931 to the chairmanship of the department. *Organic Chemistry* (1928); *The Chemistry of Organic Compounds* (1933, revised edition 1939); and *Practical Chemistry* (written with N. H. Black, and published in 1920) are among his publications.

In the meanwhile he had been doing extremely important work in his field—work that doubtless would have eventually earned him the Nobel Prize if he had been able to complete it. He had made significant discoveries in the field of "free radicals" and hemoglobin; he had become a world authority on the substance and chemical structure of chlorophyll. His work on chlorophyll, published in 1932, revolutionized the subject of photosynthesis in plants and brought him the William H. Nichols Medal of the American Chemical Society, and Columbia University's Chandler Medal. Other recognition had come with his election to the American Academy of Arts and Sciences and to the Board of Scientific Directors of the Rockefeller Institute. Dr. Conant was still almost unknown outside his own scientific world, however—not considered important enough even for a trusteeship of his own Roxbury Latin School—when in June 1933 the choice of the Harvard Corporation for Harvard's new president was announced. The quiet and retiring professor of chemistry was the choice of its members.

So it was that Dr. Conant "abdicated from chemistry" at the age of 40 to become one of Harvard's youngest presidents, and the only president, with the exception of Dr. Eliot, who had been a scientist. A few wondered about his qualifications for a position that required a man who was not only an educator but also a super-salesman, financial expert, super-executive, administrator. Others were afraid he would prove to be more interested in the laboratory than in the present-day world. Since that time there has of course been a certain amount of criticism of President Conant, as of every man in his position, but hardly for the reasons anticipated.

His first words of acceptance were stirring: "I promise to govern according to the statutes of the University and in conformity with that spirit of freedom which has marked our past and must guarantee our future." And Conant continued to speak out for the preservation of free inquiry, for greater flexibility in the college curriculum, for greater interdepartmental cooperation—against narrow specialization. He created the Harvard Council of the Faculty of Arts and Sciences, with 60 representative professors, and became chairman of the Council. He introduced new University professorships which enabled their holders to move freely from one department to another as their research inclined them. He established the Harvard National Scholarships, awarded on merit rather than financial need. He established a program for the extracurricular study of American history. He made changes which gave students greater freedom of choice in courses; he established new schools; he revolutionized teaching methods in certain departments. Without any previous experience in public speaking, he managed to gain and hold the attention of both the academic and non-academic worlds through the vigor and liberalism of his ideas. In 1934 and 1935 he was bold enough to turn down Nazi scholarships and to criticize the "teacher's oath." He proved that he had a sense of humor, too —students liked that. And his capabilities as a "super-salesman, financial expert, super-executive, administrator" must have amazed even himself.

At the 1936 Harvard Tercentenary, President Conant fearlessly demanded that we "build an educational basis for a unified, coherent culture suited to a democratic country in a scientific age." Later, an undergraduate wrote in the *Harvard Advocate*: "Many must remember the sigh that rolled over the Tercentenary theatre when President Conant, with a slightly raised voice, declared that scholarship must probe the innards of the economic structure as well as the innards of the atom. That sigh represented much more than frightened selfishness." The implications aren't quite clear, but the writer was apparently among those who feel that President Conant's liberalism has grown somewhat less ardent since that time. Another critic went so far as to say that Conant, "enthusiastic in 1935, became cautious in 1937, fearful in 1938, despairing in 1939, tyranically jittery in 1940." He gave as one example the dismissal of two active members of the Cambridge Union of University Teachers in April 1937, the recommendation of a committee of nine senior professors that they be reinstated after a year's investigation, and President Conant's subsequent announcement that the recommendation be ignored.

Other concrete examples are not numerous, however, and it seems certain that the most bitter criticism of Conant has come from students and others who oppose his views on the present War. He was a very early, very active member of the Committee to Defend America by Aiding the Allies, and testified before the Senate Military Affairs Committee in favor of the Burke-Wadsworth Bill. He has never made any proviso that aid to Britain must be "short of war." All Harvard students are not of like mind, and as early as the fall of 1939 the undergraduate daily, the *Harvard Crimson,* denounced him as among those "earning an unenviable place in the road-gang that is trying to build for the United States a super-highway straight to Armageddon. . . The lofty positions of these men give their words weight beyond their worth." In January 1941 Conant himself inquired: "How can we give all possible aid to the country in this hour of peril without jeopardizing unduly our fundamental mission, which by its very nature requires long-range planning?" But he also believes that "to assume that under the stress of war we shall destroy our form of government or plunge our land into social chaos is to deny the virility of our birthright." In May 1941 he joined the Fight for Freedom Committee.

President Conant was married in April 1921 to Grace Thayer Richards, the daughter of his old chemistry professor, and they have two children: James Richards and Theodore Richards. He is far better versed in literature, history and economics than the average scientist; he enjoys tennis, sailing, mountain climbing; he isn't very fond of the movies. Cigarets he smokes only occasionally, and he never drinks anything stronger than beer. His well-tailored appearance is probably the result of a strong sense of responsibility toward his position, since it is a definite change from his comfortable chemistry days. He has a nice wit. One story about him tells of the time when he was a guest at the Signet Club. A professor began scolding him (in Latin) for having recommended the elimination of that language as a B. A. requirement. Retorted Conant: "I thought we had come to praise the Signet, not to bury Caesar."

References

Am Mag 116:20-1+ O '33 por
N Y Times VII p11+ Jl 20 '41 il por
Nation 136:571 My 24 '33
New Repub 95:145 Je 15 '38
New Yorker 12:20-4 S 12 '36; 12:23-7
    S 19 '36
Read Digest 29:81-4 N '36
Scholastic 29:29 O 3 '36 por
Time 28:26 S 28 '36 por (cover)
American Men of Science
America's Young Men 1936-37
Leaders in Education 1941
Sargent, P. What Makes Lives p181-
    212 1940
Who's Who in America

CONDON, FRANK 1882—Dec. 19, 1940
Short story writer; scenarist; humorist; was best known for his stories in the *Saturday Evening Post* and *Collier's* magazine where he was a regular contributor under contract.

Obituaries

N Y Times p25 D 20 '40
Variety 141:54 D 25 '40

CONN, BILLY Oct. 8, 1917- Former light-heavyweight champion of the world; referee

Address: c/o Twentieth Century Sporting Club, 1619 Broadway, New York City

"I lost my head and a million bucks," said Billy Conn in his dressing room at the Polo Grounds in New York City on the night of June 18, 1941. It was just 10 minutes after Joe Louis (see sketch 1940 Annual), heavyweight champion of the world, had sent a depth-bomb into the challenger in round 13 of their scheduled 15-round battle before a crowd of 54,487 wildly excited fight fans who had paid $450,000 for the privilege of watching the heavyweight championship bout. Conn's share of the gate was $77,202.40.

The famed Brown Bomber came close to being toppled from his throne in his eighteenth defense of the title he had won from Jim Braddock in 1937 in Chicago. For the first two rounds, The Kid jabbed and danced away like an elusive shadow. In the third round, after Louis had nailed him but failed to knock him down, Conn began to grin scornfully at the Champ. In the fourth, Billy began to tattoo him with lightning-quick pokes. By the end of the twelfth, Conn's sustained attack had the crowd on its feet, yelling. "The fleet-fisted Kid had confounded, dumbfounded and dazed the title holder," and most observers believed that the title would change hands. Swaggering, Conn came out for the thirteenth. "I got you, Joe," he taunted. Then he did just what he had been warned not to do: he sailed into Shufflin' Joe and began exchanging punches. That was what the Dark Destroyer had been waiting for, and before the over-confident youngster knew what had struck him he was staggering under a bombardment of rights and lefts. Two seconds before the bell he curled up on the canvas for the count. Ironically, Louis, who is four years older and twenty-five and one-half pounds heavier, had called the turn before the fight when he said: "If Conn will keep his head he will give me one of my toughest fights."

William David Conn became a contender for the heavyweight crown by climbing the lightweight, welterweight, middleweight and light-heavyweight rungs of the boxing ladder. He was born in East Liberty, a suburb of Pittsburgh, Pennsylvania, and attended the Sacred Heart Parochial School. There are a number of legends about his beginnings in the fight game. According to one, Johnny Ray was running a tumble-down gymnasium for fighters when he was asked by William Robert Conn, an Irish plumber, to give his son a few boxing lessons. "He's having a

Cosmopolitan

BILLY CONN

lot of trouble with some of the tough kids on our block. I want him to be able to take care of himself." Another story has it that Billy used to hang around the gymnasium and ridicule the fighters until challenged by Ray to put on the gloves. He did! "When Billy got off into a corner by himself and started shadow boxing," writes Ray, "so help me, I fell in love with him." Ray became his trainer, manager, friend; calls him "My boy Billy", "Junior."

After two years of sparring in the gymnasium Billy's career began with trooping through nearby coal towns; he was fighting for money by the time he was fifteen. He got $2.50 for his first professional fight; lost his first decision to Dick Woodwer in 1935. Milton Jaffee, a Pittsburgh sportsman, became interested and provided backing.

Since that time Billy has had 65 fights: 13 knockout victories, 44 won decisions and 8 lost decisions. In 1935 he won nine matches and lost four. In 1936 he won 19 and lost none. In 1937 victories were scored over Babe Risko, Vince Dundee, Teddy Yarosz, Oscar Rankins, Young Corbett, III, and Ralph Chong. That year he lost to Young Corbett, III; then to Solly Krieger of Brooklyn. It is said that Conn got very little recognition in New York for that last fight, which went 12 rounds. But in 1938 he got a 12-round return match in New York for which his backer had to pay $50, and which he won. In 1938 there were six other fights: one knockout (Ray Actis), four won decisions and one lost. After July 25, 1938, the date when he dropped a 12-round decision to Teddy Yarosz, Conn remained unbeaten in the ring, however. In 1939 he beat Fred Apostoli, recognized by the New York Athletic Commission as the world's middleweight champion, and he repeated the victory a month

later. Then he drubbed Krieger again, but was unable to claim the championship because he was growing fast and was a few pounds over the limit.

Next, in the light-heavyweight class, Conn won eight victories. He acquired the championship on July 13, 1939, when he whipped Melio Bettina, the southpaw from Beacon, New York, in Madison Square Garden, and he defended it against Melio's challenge two months later in Pittsburgh. A knockout decision over Gus Dorazio in Philadelphia followed. On January 10, 1940 he engaged Henry Cooper, whom reporters say he outclassed, in Madison Square Garden. In September came Bob Pastor to challenge him; Bob was flattened in 13 rounds. Decisions over Al McCoy in Boston and Lee Savold in Madison Square Garden also came in 1940.

After successfully defending the lightheavyweight title in a 15-round match against Gus Lesnevich in Detroit in the fall of 1940, Conn voluntarily gave up the title in order to challenge Louis.

The 1941 record shows four victories: all knockouts, all non-title bouts, all in the heavyweight class. Ira Hughes in Clarksburgh, West Virginia in the fourth round on February 27; Dan Hassett in Washington, D. C. in the fifth round on March 6; Gunnar Barlund of Finland in Chicago in the eighth round on April 4; Buddy Knox in Pittsburgh in the eighth round on May 26. Then, on June 18, Billy joined Al McCoy, Red Burman, Gus Dorazio, Abe Simon, Tony Musto and Buddy Baer as a member of Louis' "Bum of the Month Club." Later in the fall he acted as referee for several fights.

Billy has won one decision over Joe Louis, however. William Taub, arbiter of men's fashions, has crowned Conn the No. 1 dude among the nation's 10 best-dressed men, with Max Baer holding second place and Louis third. "Conn is terrific," says Taub, "with the accent on light shades, sports stuff, and armhole vests." Another title, "Fighter of the Year," was awarded Conn in 1940 by sports editor Nat Fleisher in his rating of the 40 leading athletes. "My boy" is the title crotchety, crusty, childless promoter Mike Jacobs has assigned to Conn. "He is Uncle Mike's crown prince," reports Jack Miley. "A father-son relationship developed. . . Billy spent his spare time at the Jacobs' country show place on the Shrewsbury River at Rumson, New Jersey. He vacationed at Uncle Mike's Miami Beach estate. He shared the promotor's Central Park West duplex. He was chauffeured about in Mike's town car. He wore expensive suits built by Mike's tailor, silk shirts and $5 cravats that his benefactor bought him. He drove a flashy cream-colored roadster that was also a gift from Uncle Mike."

The curly-haired, broad-shouldered young man with the toothpaste-ad grin who is "Hollywood's idea of what a prize fighter should look like and Tenth Avenue's notion of how one should act" starred in a Republic film, *The Pittsburgh Kid,* with Jean Parker, released in late 1941.

Billy is the eldest of five children. (His mother, Margaret [McFarland] Conn, died June 27, 1941.) And although the family now lives in a home purchased by Billy in the Shadyside district of Pittsburgh, on the right side of the tracks, there were objections to his proposed marriage to Mary Lou Smith. Her father, Greenfield Jimmy Smith, retired National League infielder and now a well-to-do Pittsburgh night club owner, is reported to have said: "If that fellow don't stay away from my daughter, I'll punch hell out of him." Billy and Mary Lou were married July 1, 1941, in Philadelphia.

References

Collier's 103:22+ Je 3 '39 por; 107:15+ My 24 '41 por
Newsweek 14:34 Jl 24 '39; 17:55 Ap 27 '40 por; 17:49 Je 9 '41 por
Sat Eve Post 213:37+ Je 7 '41 il pors
Time 37:56 Je 30 '41 por

CONNAH, DOUGLAS JOHN (kô-nä') Apr. 20, 1871—Aug. 23, 1941 Artist; since 1925 co-director of the American School of Design; had exhibited in the Paris Salon, the Royal Academy in London and in many cities in the United States; was intimate friend of the late John Singer Sargent and of James McNeill Whistler; during more than 40 years of teaching had been instrumental in developing such artists as George Bellows, Guy Pène duBois, Rockwell Kent and Nicholas Vachel Lindsay.

References

Who's Who in America

Obituaries

N Y Times p15 Ag 25 '41 por

CONNALLY, THOMAS TERRY *See* Connally T.

CONNALLY, TOM Aug. 19, 1877- United States Senator from Texas; chairman of the Senate Foreign Relations Committee

Address: b. Senate Office Bldg, Washington, D. C.; h. Marlin, Falls Co, Texas

Tom Connally, newly appointed head of the Senate Foreign Relations Committee, claims that he has "been in more wars and done less shooting than anyone else in the Senate." In 1898 he volunteered for the infantry and was on his way to Puerto Rico when the Spanish-American War ended. In 1917, when he was elected to the House of Representatives, his first act was to vote for a declaration of war against Germany and his second to join the Army. When the First World War ended, however, he was still at Camp Meade.

"I'm not an especially religious man," Connally said of that first vote for declaration of war on Germany, "but I sure did pray over that." When the Second World War was

Bachrach

TOM CONNALLY

declared in September 1939 he remarked that "the first and most important thing . . . is that the United States must not get into this frightful and brutal War." More recently, however, he modified that first pronouncement. "We don't desire war," he said in 1941, "but the world might as well know that we have rights and possessions for which we are ready to fight if it's necessary for their security."

Thomas Terry Connally was born in McLennan County, Texas, on August 19, 1877, the son of Jones and Mary Ellen (Terry) Connally, both originally from Georgia. He was educated in the public schools of Eddy, Texas, and received his B. A. in 1896 from Baylor University in Waco, Texas. Before beginning his law studies he worked for a few months as a reporter for the Waco *Telephone,* then attended the University of Texas, which gave him his LL. B. degree in 1898. He was admitted to the Texas Bar that same year.

After he took his law degree Connally volunteered for service in the 2nd Texas Infantry Volunteers, but was soon mustered out of the Army. Entering early into Democratic Party politics, his experience in the private practice of law was brief. In 1901 he was elected to the Texas House of Representatives, an office which he held for two terms, until 1904. In 1906 he became prosecuting attorney for Falls County, Texas, a position which he held until 1910. He was a member of the 65th to 70th Congresses, 1917 to 1929, as Representative from the 11th Texas District, and he has been United States Senator from Texas since 1929.

During his many years of Congressional experience Connally has deviated from "orthodox Democracy" just once on a major issue. In 1937 he joined Senator Burton Wheeler in his fight against President Roosevelt's plans for reform of the Supreme Court and, as

CONNALLY, TOM—*Continued*

a member of the Senate Judiciary Committee, helped to kill it. That same year he also led the filibuster against the anti-lynching bill, and he fought hard for Southern differentials in the Wage-Hour Law. He has served on many committees, and as chairman of the Senate Committee on House and Grounds he has been instrumental in improving the appearance of the nation's Capital. He promoted legislation favoring reduction of the gold content of the dollar, earmarking 30 per cent of customs receipts for export bounties on agricultural exports, and regulating income tax schedules. He is also responsible for the Connally Hot Oil Act and, with Senator Barkley (see sketch this issue) framed the Barkley-Connally Amendments to the Neutrality Act which would permit United States ships to be armed, to enter belligerent ports and to cross combat zones and which was passed in November 1941.

Connally has been an ardent supporter of all phases of Roosevelt's foreign policy. He fought for the repeal of the arms embargo and for the enactment of the Lend-Lease and Selective Service Acts. He defended Roosevelt's course in sending troops to Iceland and has been active in the movement for "hemisphere defense." In July 1941 he was designated chairman of the Foreign Relations Committee, although remaining an important member of the Finance and Judicial Committees, on which he has served for a long time.

When Connally was informed of his appointment to this important post, he said: "I'll have to buy some spats now, and maybe a cane and swallow-tailed coat." In a less frivolous vein he told reporters that he felt that "a vigorous and firm foreign policy is essential to secure respect for our rights abroad and the security of our people at home." On June 7, 1941 Connally introduced an amendment to the Selective Service Act to permit President Roosevelt to take over and operate any defense plant where production is delayed because of labor disputes or other causes. In August 1941 he suggested a billion dollar increase in the House-approved Tax Bill, and in a radio broadcast that same month declared that Hitler's desire to rule the world was the only "reason why this peaceful nation" is arming itself at unprecedented speed. "Modern aircraft and modern warfare," he declared, "can span the Atlantic in far less time than it took Columbus to reach the shores of the New World. . . We arm to resist the enthronement of the sword as the ruler of the world."

Besides attending to his legislative duties Connally served as delegate to the Democratic National Convention in 1920, 1932 and 1936. He was a delegate to the Inter-Parliamentary Union when it met in Geneva in 1924, in Washington, D. C., in 1925, in London in 1930 and in Istanbul in 1934. He is a member of the Knights of Pythias, having acted as the grand chancellor of Texas in 1913 and 1914, and a member of the Freemasons, Shriners and Odd Fellows.

In 1904 he married Louise Clarkson of Marlin, Texas, who died in 1935. Their son, Ben Clarkson, born December 28, 1909, is now an attorney in Houston, Texas. In 1936 Connally's Alma Mater, Baylor University, awarded him an LL. D. degree, and in that same year he received an LL. D. degree from Howard Payne University.

Connally is tall, dynamic and "physically striking in the Bryanesque mode." He is known as the "best rough and tumble debater in the Senate." A picturesque figure, well known in Washington, he wears his graying black hair long in the back, gold studs in his shirt front, a string tie around his neck and a black sombrero on his head. Walking, fishing and hunting are his favorite sports, but he also enjoys watching baseball and football games. He is known to be fond of dancing and "he shakes," as they say in Texas, "a smart hoof."

References

> N Y Herald Tribune p9 Jl 31 '41 por;
>   X p7+ N 2 '41 pors
> N Y Sun p19 Ag 1 '41
> N Y World-Telegram p15 Jl 31 '41 por
> Newsweek 10:10 N 29 '37 por; 11:9 Je
>   20 '38 por; 18:18 Ag 11 '41 il por
> Time 33:76 My 22 '39; por; 34:15 N
>   6 '39 por; 38:14 Ag 11 '41 por
> U S News 11:18 O 17 '41 por
>
> Who's Who in America
> Who's Who in Government
> Who's Who in Law
> Who's Who in the Nation's Capital

CONNELL, KARL 1879(?)—Oct. 18, 1941 Surgeon; inventor; as designer of the first all-American gas mask to be used by the American Army in the First World War, received the D. S. M.; held 10 patents in the development of anesthetic apparatus; served as surgeon with the United States Army, and at the Presbyterian Hospital in Omaha, Nebraska until his retirement in 1925; devoted himself to anesthetic apparatus.

References

> American Medical Directory
> Who's Who in America

Obituaries

> N Y Times p45 O 19 '41

CONNERY, LAWRENCE J(OSEPH) (kŏn'ẽr-ĭ) Oct. 17, 1895—Oct. 19, 1941 United States Representative from Massachusetts; succeeded his brother, the late William P. Connery, to 75th Congress in 1937 and was re-elected in 1939 and 1941; worked for the passage of the Black-Connery Bill, of which his brother was co-author, and sponsored legislation protecting native textile products against foreign competition.

References

> Newsweek 10:14 O 11 '37
> Time 30:9 D 27 '37 por

Who's Who in America
Who's Who in the Nation's Capital

Obituaries

N Y Times p17 O 20 '41

CONNESS, ROBERT (kō-nĕs') 1867(?)
—Jan. 15, 1941 American actor who was
known to theatre-goers on two continents for
forty-six years; appeared in several pictures
during silent film days.

References

N Y Dram 76:23 N 11 '16 por

Obituaries

N Y Times p17 Ja 17 '41

COOLIDGE, ELIZABETH SPRAGUE
Oct. 30, 1864- Music patron
Address: h. 2400 16th St, Washington, D. C.

Elizabeth Sprague Coolidge is without doubt
the "fairy godmother of music and musicians."
Throughout this country and throughout the
world there are orchestras, chamber music
groups, composers and performers who have
been able to present important new and old
music because of her generosity. But Mrs.
Coolidge hasn't just given money. She has
"entered directly into the musically creative
life of her time, has had an influence in
directing the stream of contemporary musical
composition and has brought significant works
into being."

Mrs. Coolidge has been interested in music
all her life. She was born in Chicago, Illinois,
the daughter of Albert Arnold and Nancy Ann
(Atwood) Sprague, and began to study the
piano at quite an early age. She never went
to college—the lack of a degree has since been
remedied by honorary ones from half a dozen
—and shortly after she left private school was
married, in 1891, to Dr. Frederic Shurtleff
Coolidge of Boston. She has one son, Albert
Sprague.

Mrs. Coolidge began early to exercise "the
fine art of paying the bill." Among her gifts
was one to establish a pension fund for the
Chicago Symphony Orchestra and a contribution to construct the Sprague music building
at Yale University. Then, in 1918, came her
interest in chamber music, an interest which
was to support this art for many years. It
was in that year that, at the suggestion of
Frederick Stock of the Chicago Symphony,
she engaged a house quartet to help her during
days over which sickness, the death of her
husband, grief and loneliness had cast shadows.

From this house quartet the Berkshire Festivals were born, and until 1924 a series of
public concerts was given at her estate on
South Mountain outside Pittsfield, Massachusetts. The performers at the Festivals included her own quartets and others, some
brought over from Europe especially for the
Festivals, and Mrs. Coolidge herself, who
occasionally played the piano in ensembles.
The programs were made up of the classics
of chamber music and of modern compositions, many of them played for the first time,

ELIZABETH SPRAGUE COOLIDGE

many of them commissioned by her. There
were prizes offered for new chamber music
in competitions open to composers of all nationalities. In November 1941 a string quartet by Mrs. Coolidge was performed in Washington. The concensus of critical opinion was
that it was not an outstanding composition.

By 1924 the Festivals had attracted a good
deal of attention, and Mrs. Coolidge moved
them to Washington, built a chamber music
hall adjoining the Library of Congress and
endowed the Elizabeth Sprague Coolidge
Foundation which is administered by the Music Division of the Library. This move "inaugurated a new era for America's national
library—it engaged the Federal Government,
at last, directly and definitely in the affairs
of music and musicology." Mrs. Coolidge
at that time explained her gift and the creed
by which her donations have been made: "I
have wished to make possible through the
Library of Congress the composition and performance of music in ways which might
otherwise be considered too unique or too
expensive to be ordinarily undertaken. Not
this alone, of course, nor with a view to
extravagance for its own sake; but as an occasional possibility of giving precedence to
considerations of quality over those of quantity, to artistic rather than to economic values
and to opportunity rather than to expediency."

At the Coolidge Foundation festivals are
given, international prize competitions are
sponsored, there are occasional concerts given
in the library and elsewhere. And the festivals there have become the most important
chamber music event in America. "They
have come to serve as a sort of musical
weather vane. They show us how the mind
is set in contemporary music as well as any
single set of concerts can do."

During her long life as a music patron
this "portly, good-natured, partly deaf widow"

COOLIDGE, ELIZABETH SPRAGUE—
Continued

has presented many of the world's best-known chamber music players—Roth, Gordon, Kolisch, to mention only a few. She has commissioned works by Hindemith, Prokofiev (see sketches this issue), Bartók, Respighi, Schoenberg, Stravinsky, Bloch and others, and in giving commissions has attached no strings. The composer has been and is free to write what he pleases, "provided the result comes under the elastic category of chamber music." Only once or twice has she stipulated the form or instrumentation—as in the case of Arthur Bliss, whom she commissioned to write an oboe quintet because she wanted something for the oboist Leon Goossens to play.

Although Mrs. Coolidge is not connected with the Coolidge Foundation, she has, since she presented it to the Library of Congress, continued to hold festivals, prize competitions and concerts on her own, and there are few cities in the United States which haven't at one time or another heard concerts which she has sponsored. For her services to music France has awarded her the Légion d'Honneur; Belgium has given her the Order of Leopold and the Order of the Crown; Frankfort has made her an honorary citizen; and the Cobbett Medal "for services to chamber music" was awarded her by the Worshipful Company of Musicians of London.

References

> Am Mercury 22:115-9 Ja '31
> Etude 50:697+ O '32
> Time 32:28 O 3 '38 por
>
> Baker's Biographical Dictionary of Musicians 1940
> Kinscella, H. G.   Music on the Air p116-20 1934
> Who's Who in America

COOPER, GARY May 7, 1901- Film actor
Address: h. 7511 Franklin Ave, Brentwood, Calif.

There are all sorts of legends current about Gary Cooper, chief of which is that he came to the screen from the range, that he is a transformed cowboy. As a matter of fact, though he was born in Helena, Montana, and though his father did own a small cattle ranch where he learned to ride, shoot and punch cows, that was the most incidental part of his boyhood. His father, Charles Henry Cooper, was a lawyer from Bedfordshire, England, who came to Helena and married a Montana girl, Alice Louise. Besides managing his ranch, Charles Cooper continued to practice law and eventually became a justice of the Montana Supreme Court. The son (christened Frank James Cooper) went to high school for a while in Bozeman, Montana. Then the Coopers moved to England, and the boy attended Dunstable School there for two years. It was not one of the more important "public" schools, but it had plenty of snobbery in it. Young Cooper was sent to Coventry for degrading himself by having a fight with a newsboy! Upon his return to the United

States he attended Wesleyan College in Helena, and also studied at Grinnell College, in Iowa, for three years, from the fall of 1920 to the spring of 1924. He had wanted to be a surgeon, but this was not a very serious ambition; actually his chief interest was in cartooning, and while in high school he had taken four hours of drawing lessons every day.

It was at Grinnell that he tried out for the dramatic club and was unhesitatingly turned down. He had stage fright so badly that he stuttered—and did that in a whisper! As a matter of fact he has never had any dramatic training, and still stands in awe of the technical tricks of experienced actors. He says his only concern is to try *not* to play himself. But it is the fact that he does play himself, that he underplays and is completely natural, which has brought him to the outstanding position he now occupies in the films.

He was not graduated from Grinnell, but went back to Helena and tried to make a living drawing cartoons for a local paper. The paper took them and let him sign them, but didn't consider them worth paying for. The rest of the time he punched cattle for his father. But he soon grew dissatisfied with that sort of existence and went to Chicago to try his hand at commercial art. He failed completely. Almost broke, he made his way to Los Angeles, not because he had the movies in mind but because he had decided that he would rather starve where it was warm than starve and freeze, too. He got a job selling electric advertising signs but was fired because he sold exactly none. Then he did turn to the motion pictures, and for a while lived a precarious life as a cowboy extra. Two-bit dinners were a luxury, and Cooper is a big man—six feet two and three-quarter inches, weighing one hundred eighty-one pounds—who likes plenty to eat.

From extra work he progressed to bits in "horse operas" produced by Samuel Goldwyn. His first real chance came when he was engaged as the second male lead with Ronald Colman in *Winning of Barbara Worth*, at $75 a week. He seemed doomed to being "typed" as a cowboy before he finally broke the spell, in Paramount's production of *Wings*. It was finally discovered that, trained or not, Gary Cooper was an actor. For more than 10 years now he has been one of the most dependable of motion-picture stars. Among the pictures in which he has taken the lead are: *A Farewell to Arms* and *Design for Living* (1934); *Lives of a Bengal Lancer* and *Peter Ibbetson* (1935); *Desire* and *The General Died at Dawn* (1936); *Mr. Deeds Goes to Town* (1937); *The Adventures of Marco Polo* and *Bluebeard's Eighth Wife* (1938); *Beau Geste* (1939); *Northwest Mounted Police* (1940); *Meet John Doe* and *Sergeant York* (1941), which the real York permitted to be filmed only if Cooper portrayed him. He was prominently mentioned for the film version of *For Whom the Bell Tolls*—in fact it was he who sold the film rights for Ernest Hemingway, a personal friend.

But to the average picture fan, Gary Cooper is Longfellow Deeds and John Doe. In two pictures, *Mr. Deeds Goes to Town* (1937) and *Meet John Doe* (1941), Cooper played the sort of role which is peculiarly his own—that of the "little man" (socially, not physically) pitted against the more deplorable aspects of society. They are roles particularly dear to his heart; he himself is socially-minded, strongly democratic and anti-Fascist. It is not for nothing that the Veterans of Foreign Wars bestowed on him in 1941 its Distinguished Citizenship Medal. Yet he is anything but a "pink"; he is not even a New Dealer, having voted for Wendell Willkie in 1940, though unalterably opposed to the Old Guard and the reactionary wing of the Republican Party. Many people think he resembles Lincoln in appearance, and Lincoln is his ideal as a citizen.

The Gary Coopers are among the movie couples who never provide columnists with scandal. In the late 1920's he played around a bit with Clara Bow, with Lupe Velez, with the American Countess Dorothy diFrasso (he traveled to Europe and Africa with gay parties she organized); but in 1933 he met and married Veronica Balfe, Social Register debutante, and settled down for keeps. Miss Balfe, known on the screen as Sandra Shaw (her husband calls her "Rocky"), was the stepdaughter of Paul Shields, governor of the New York Stock Exchange. After their marriage she retired from pictures. In 1938 their daughter Maria was born. The three of them live in a white Georgian house with three and a half acres around it, with a swimming pool, tennis courts, dogs, ducks, chickens, vegetables and a citrus grove. Their summers they spend on a Long Island estate where their friends are members of the social set.

Cooper is a hearty eater, but drinks very little and smokes denicotinized cigarets. He likes to play tennis, bridge and backgammon, but most of all he likes to sleep: he is always taking naps both at home and on the lot. He is crazy about guns and knows a great deal about them in a technical way. He likes to get into comfortable old clothes on every possible occasion. His wife, a striking brunette, enjoys the same things he does, and they are constant companions. He is not yet used to being famous and rich; there is still a touch of naïve surprise in his attitude. "You can't take anything for granted," he says. "It's fatal." He detests and avoids premières and has done so ever since the opening of *Design for Living,* when his clothes were torn off his back and he had to be rescued by a squad of policemen.

With his rangy height, his brilliantly blue eyes, his one-sided smile, he is at heart, as someone has remarked, "an extremely good-natured Montana sportsman." His celebrated taciturnity is more of a defense against intrusion than anything else: he can talk readily enough among his friends, to whom he is "Coop," a swell guy with a touch of seriousness about him. To the picture-going

GARY COOPER

public, he is something more—"the cinema's epitome of a natural American."

References

Arts & Dec 43:15-17+ N '35 il
Motion Pict 49:7 il pors; 49:28-9 F '35 por; 49:34-5 Jl '35 por; 51:32+ Je '36 il por; 53:44+ Mr '37
Movie Classic 9:25+ O '35 por; 10:42+ Ap '36 por; 10:33+ Je '36 il por; 11:28-9+ Ja '37
Photoplay 50:30-1+ Ag '36 il pors; 52:18-19+ Ap '38; 53:20-1+ O '39 il pors
Pict R 38:12-13+ O '36 pors
Time 30:50 Ag 23 '37 por; 37:78+ Mr 3 '41 il pors
America's Young Men
Hughes, E. Famous Stars of Filmdom p154-73 1932
International Motion Picture Almanac
Who's Who in America

COPELAND, BENJAMIN, REV. 1855— Dec. 1, 1940   Methodist minister and poet of Buffalo, New York; served as minister for 42 years; wrote additional stanza for *America.*

References

Lit Digest 123:22 My 15 '37 por

Obituaries

N Y Times p23 D 2 '40

CORNELL, KATHARINE   Feb. 16, 1898- Actress

Address: b. 1270 Sixth Ave, Rockefeller Center, New York City; h. 23 Beekman Pl, New York City

"He is a very great man," Katharine Cornell said recently of George Bernard Shaw. "I suppose no dramatist has drawn women more

Vandamm

KATHARINE CORNELL

sympathetically or more humanly—but he always gives them a hint of mystery. That is the Shavian touch; it saves him from admitting how much he likes them." The First Lady of the American theatre has been notably successful in depicting three of Shaw's women: Candida, Saint Joan, and Jennifer Dubedat in *The Doctor's Dilemma*, a role which she played as recently as 1941.

When she assumed the leading role in Shaw's *Candida* in 1924, the famous Irish dramatist wrote her: "I don't think I was ever so astonished by a picture as I was by your photograph. Your success as Candida, and something blonde and expansive about your name, had created an ideal suburban British Candida in my imagination. Fancy my feeling on seeing in the photograph a gorgeous dark lady from the cradle of the human race! . . If you look like that, it doesn't matter a rap whether you can act or not. Can you? Yours, breath-bereaved, G. Bernard Shaw."

That she could act was attested to at that time by leading American savants of the theatre. Hammond found her the "most promising of the younger actresses." In 1926 the museum of her native city, Buffalo, commissioned home-town artist Eugene Speicher to do a full-length portrait of her, posed in the warm red gown that had been designed for her role as Candida. Hand-on-hip gesture and eyebrows arched in surprise recall an old family photograph of the star as a beribboned child, aged four, with an overly large mouth and brooding dark eyes.

In 1918, when family friend Jessie Bonstelle wrote to Dr. Cornell that his daughter had been signed for the Bonstelle stock company, he replied, "Are you crazy?" While "Kit" had had a few small parts with the Wash-

ington Square Players, her father did not, at that time, take her acting seriously. To him she was still the lanky girl roller-skating through the lobby of his theatre, getting in the way of people who wanted to buy tickets for Sothern & Marlowe. But "Kit" had been won over to the stage when she saw Maude Adams in *Peter Pan*. "If I could just walk out on the stage," was her memory of how it began.

A three-pound baby, Katharine Cornell was born of American parents on February 16, 1898, in Berlin, Germany, where her father was doing postgraduate work in medicine. Her parents were Dr. Peter Cortelyou and Alice Gardner (Plimpton) Cornell. A few years after returning to Buffalo the doctor became "Doc," as Miss Cornell's father became part owner and manager of the Star Theatre. Aside from kindergarten plays, however, little Katharine's first stage appearance was strictly a walk-on. She had wanted to feed an elephant, but balked at the real thing—having in mind the picture-book variety. Her father insisted, as a matter of discipline, and she threw a bun in the general direction of the elephant's trunk, then ran screaming from the stage.

Her first press notice was in a handwritten paper prepared by a member of the cast. She and a friend had written an "A-1 play," and it was forthwith produced at the summer home of her parents in Canada. The review of *The Hidden Treasure* concluded with the practical note: "We made 20 cents on the whole thing." As a little girl she had less interest in serious dramatics than in what are generally termed "dumb acts." A trouper-friend of her father's taught her the slack wire, and she installed a trapeze in her room. Perhaps, to her, such activity was a release for a personality that was more than normally sensitive.

"Kit" Cornell thought of herself as "a terribly ugly" child. "I knew I wasn't popular. I was timid even with children of my own age. I suppose I had an instinctive fear of being hurt. . . I had been hurt so often. . . Some nights before the performance I find myself caught by a foolish dread that it takes all my strength to control. . . You see, I can remember so many occasions when fear has had the best of me." And her husband, thinking along the same lines, wrote: "She still suffers from a supersensitive and frightened childhood. She has not outgrown the peculiar and psychic sensitiveness which has always been her principal asset as an artist and her principal liability as a person."

At Miss Merrill's school, Oaksmere, Mamaroneck, New York, she studied dramatics and returned there to teach from 1915 to 1916. Edward Goodman of the Washington Square Players came up to the school to help coach a play that Miss Cornell had written. He suggested that she try out, some time, for the Players. She acted on it at the first possible moment, appearing at a rehearsal to read some lines. But fear choked her. In an almost inaudible voice she mouthed the lines, all the rich deep inflections we associate with her vocal technique missing—and when it was over she didn't have to be told she had failed. She knew it in the hollow way that failure sinks home. Nor was it just the part. Her mother's death a short time before had left a blank. Seeking the cool, dim recesses of a nearby cathedral, she gave way to loneliness and tears.

In November, Miss Cornell appeared with the Washington Square Players, speaking four words, "My son, my son," in *Bushido*. She was with the Washington Square Players two years and made only $40 the whole time; fortunately she had an income from her mother's estate. A part in *Plots and Playwrights* (1917) won the comment: "There is a new face that stands out—Katharine Cornell. . . A tall girl with a fine strong head, broadly spread eyes and full mouth—mentality, physical control and simplicity." And a young talent scout for Winthrop Ames, Guthrie McClintic, wrote opposite her name on the program: "Interesting. Monotonous. Watch."

In 1918 Miss Cornell joined the Jessie Bonstelle stock company, doing 10 performances a week and learning a new play as well. In Buffalo, on the stage of her father's theatre, she played what she considered her first professional role, a part in *Cheating Cheaters*. Next, through Miss Bonstelle, the young actress was given a good part in the Brady road company of *The Man Who Came Back*, at a salary of $100 a week (1918-19). Then came her first London appearance, November 1919, in *Little Women*, a part that created almost as much of a stir in New York as in London. Returning to New York, she took a part in Bonstelle stock (Detroit) rather than tackle Broadway, and was there from 1920 to 1921, directed by her future husband, Guthrie McClintic. By the time of her marriage to Mr. McClintic on September 8, 1921, she was getting leading parts in New York productions and was regarded as one of the most capable of the younger actresses.

The McClintic production of *The Way Things Happen* (1924) was a flop, nor did *The Outsider*, her next vehicle, run much longer. There was still time for the Belasco production of *Tiger Cats*, and the successful run in Shaw's *Candida* that had to be cut short because of contractual obligations for *The Green Hat* (1925). The Arlen play, like all of Miss Cornell's since, was directed by Guthrie McClintic. It marked the first time Miss Cornell, who puts play above star, allowed her name up in lights—and then only on the road, after her husband had persuaded her that it was an essential part of theatre exploitation. Alexander Woollcott (see sketch this issue) didn't like her "reeling, writhing and fainting in coils" in *The Letter* (1927), but to Miss Cornell the unsympathetic role of the woman who murdered her lover "without a single decent motive" presented an intriguing acting problem.

Good notices were by this time commonplace. In 1931 a great part came with Rudolf Besier's *The Barretts of Wimpole Street*. The first of the plays bought for the new Cornell-McClintic firm of which she was manager, it had been turned down by 27 producers. Of Miss Cornell in the part of Elizabeth, Arthur Ruhl wrote: "Her pale beauty, the strength of her weakness, the fire and longing of her spirit reaching through the moral miasmas which enveloped her—all this was brought out with fine truth, with a poetry no less poetic for being unexpressed, with fine authority, with glamor."

The Barretts opened at the Empire on a rainy night in February 1931, with only 52 people in the orchestra when the curtain went up. The orchestra gradually filled, as did the balcony, and they kept coming for a long run. "Doc" Cornell saw it first from the wings, just as he had witnessed his daughter's initial professional appearance. Turning to a friend, he said: "She's come into her own." And Miss Cornell liked the play, perhaps more than any other in which she had appeared.

The Barretts of Wimpole Street was played more than 700 times, and the long road trek was chronicled by Woollcott and others. Once in Seattle on Christmas night, a performance was given long after midnight, the train having been delayed, and the stage preparations went on in full view of the audience. Miss Cornell likes the "road," believes in giving it the best; and, according to Woollcott, some movie theatre owners refuse to rent their stages to her, so fearful are they of the public's hankering for the legitimate theatre when embodied in the person of Katharine Cornell.

Since *The Barretts*, Miss Cornell has successfully undertaken no less than 10 productions, new plays as well as occasional revivals. Of these, *Romeo and Juliet, Saint Joan, The Wingless Victory*, and *No Time For Comedy* brought new depth and power to her acting. To her, "a new part is like Kipling's ship that found itself. After three weeks of rehearsals you know a good deal about the person you want to be and you know the play. Yet until you have given a good many performances, your part doesn't live and breathe. The moment always comes, though, when the things you have thought and felt and planned begin working together. When that happens, the part is like that ship—it has found itself."

Miss Cornell's reluctance to tackle a part until ready for it has long been a matter of common knowledge. A long succession of exotic and emotionally beset characterizations caused her critics to fidget now and again, but they stayed for the play to unfold. Ellery Rand has observed: "She is driven by her desire for perfection." And, again, a critic has expressed it: "That sense of destiny, that inward, driving force is a rare gift which may lead her to greatness." Something of this force is revealed in her autobiography, *I Wanted To Be An Actress* (1939), simply written, candid—"the stuff that makes a person and not a myth."

CORNELL, KATHARINE—*Continued*

Hollywood offers have not thus far tempted Katharine Cornell, though she recently relented sufficiently to say that she might take a part—if she honestly felt she could play it better than any other person in the world! "Nothing at all could compensate me for the direct contact with my audience, the direct audience-reaction—the most precious, the most vital thing the theatre has to give." Radio has fared better, for Miss Cornell consented in November 1940 to do an excerpt from *The Barretts* for a Red Cross benefit broadcast. At the first test play-back she was surprised at the rich, low tones of her voice, and at its tragic implications—wondered how she managed comedy!

Guthrie McClintic and Katharine Cornell have been happily married for many years. They have lived almost all of that time in a high-ceilinged old-fashioned house on Beekman Place, and now that they cannot go abroad for vacations they usually spend part of the summer at Martha's Vineyard, where they have a house. "Guthrie is my greatest inspiration," said Miss Cornell. "I was born old, old as sand. Guthrie is younger. He has impeccable taste. I never know about clothes and furniture. . . Our ideals are fundamentally the same, but we have that saving grace to marriage—different methods of approach."

Regarded individually, Katharine Cornell's features are still overly large. High cheekbones, dark brown eyes set wide apart, and a large mouth create a total effect that is deeply moving, like the elements in an impressionist painting. "Kit embodies and projects beauty," wrote her husband. "She can be old or young, radiant or dull, splendid, drab, inspired, buoyant, harsh, grief-stricken—whatever she chooses to be."

Katharine Cornell likes sports, plays a fair game of tennis and golf, and likes trapshooting, but when busy in a play she seldom indulges these tastes, preferring to rest during her leisure time. She and Mr. McClintic have amassed an almost complete collection of original drawings, paintings and sculptures with her as their subject, and it overflows a room of the Beekman Place house. She has a private charity, the Katharine Cornell Foundation, incorporated in 1935, and has honorary literary degrees from a number of colleges, among them Smith College, the University of Wisconsin and Elmira College for Women. In 1935 she was awarded the Drama League's Medal for her performance as Juliet.

Curtain speeches are not easy for Miss Cornell. The first time she attempted one, during the Buffalo playing of *The Green Hat,* she came out before the audience, began, "For years I have planned what I would say if ever I was asked to make a speech. . ." Her words trailed off, stopped. Miss Cornell looked helplessly at the audience, bowed and left the stage.

References

Am Mag 120:22-3+ N '35 por
Christian Sci Mon Mag p3 Ap 20 '38 pors

Ladies' H J 53:9+ Jl '36 por
New Yorker 6:23-5 F 14 '31
Scholastic 36:17-19+ Ap 8 '40 pors
Theatre Arts Mo 21:36-51 Ja '37 pors
Time 33:23 Ap 3 '39
Woman's H C 63:12-13+ D '36 pors; 64:20-1+ Ja '37 pors
American Women
Bower, W. ed. New Directions p436-42 1937
Brown, J. M. Upstage p124-8 1930
Cornell, K. I Wanted To Be An Actress 1939
Eustis, M. Players at Work p59-73 1937
Nathan, G. J. Passing Judgments p66-73 1935
Ormsbee, H. Backstage With Actors p230-65 1938
Who's Who in America
Who's Who in the Theatre

COSTELLO, LOU *See* Abbott, B. and Costello, L.

COUDERT, FREDERIC RENÉ, JR.

(kōō'dâr') May 7, 1898- New York State Senator

Address: b. c/o Coudert Bros, 2 Rector St, New York City; h. 988 Fifth Ave, New York City

Hearty praise and bitter censure have attended every step of the investigations of the Rapp-Coudert Committee of the New York State Legislature. Set up in 1940 to look into the problems of both school costs and "subversive activities" in New York City's public schools, with Assemblyman Herbert A. Rapp in charge of the costs problem and Senator Frederic René Coudert heading the subcommittee ferreting out "un-American" teachers, the doings of Coudert's section of the inquiry have far overshadowed those of his colleague's.

Senator Coudert's Committee first burst into the headlines at the end of 1940, when it began to expose Communist activities at Brooklyn College. Teachers and students were subpoenaed to testify and from their testimony five professors, who later denied the charge, were accused of being Communists. Not long after, the Committee turned its guns on New York's City College and charged through the testimony of William Martin Canning, instructor of history, that 54 members of the faculty there were Communists. Since that time hearings have been held, teachers have been suspended from their positions, and the response to the whole inquiry has been overwhelming.

Three large New York and Philadelphia locals of the American Federation of Teachers, which were accused by Coudert in a suit to get their records of being "under the influence if not the domination of the Communist Party," raised their voice. Through the Committee for the Defense of Public Education they have called the hearings undemocratic, objected to the fact that testimony has often been taken in secret sessions and that testimony for the defense has often been limited. They have described the whole investigation as an attempt to pare educational expenditure and terrorize liberal teachers. With this point of view liberal magazines like *The Nation* and *New Republic* have largely agreed: the *New Republic* condemned the Committee's "capacity for digging up unpleasant things in unpleasant ways." In August 1941 the annual American Federation of Teachers Convention denounced it as "playing into the hands of the enemies" of education, although the same Convention approved the expulsion of the three locals criticized by Coudert. And there have been individuals, like Edwin S. Smith, who have not hesitated to call the inquiry "an inquisition." Critics of the Committee have pointed out that its activities have been confined to the exposure of Communism to the exclusion of fascism, fascist organizations, and other subversive and un-American activities.

The Committee's supporters have been equally vocal and equally convinced. Various groups of teachers at City College adopted a resolution supporting the Rapp-Coudert Committee, announcing: "We welcome whatever assistance may come from the investigation in freeing us" from the "destructive activities of relatively very small numbers of teachers and students." Acting President Harry N. Wright of the college has affirmed that the Committee is entirely within its rights and deserving of support; the New York *Times* feels that the Committee "has consistently gone about its work in a fair and liberal spirit."

Senator Coudert himself, in his report to the Legislature in March 1941, while not minimizing the "insidious" activities of Party members in the schools, still hastened to reassure the public that the "great majority" of city teachers "are loyal and devoted supporters of the democratic system of government." And to a direct accusation by a Brooklyn high school principal that he was an "outstanding foe of public education," he replied: "This is simply silly."

As evidence Senator Coudert points to his legislative record since he has been in Albany. During his first term, which began in 1938, he sponsored legislation to provide tenure for members of the city colleges' faculties. In 1939 he introduced the anti-dual job bill, supported by the Teachers' Union, which forbids multiple jobs in the schools and so helps spread employment. He sponsored legislation to implement the exchange of students between the city colleges and Latin-American countries. And he sponsored a bill, which later became law, to permit the New York City Board of Education to weed out unstable teachers, a bill praised by James Marshall, the Board's head, as "a great progressive step," though received by teachers with mixed feelings.

Senator Coudert's opponents concede the time and energy he spends on educational problems, but at the same time object occasionally to the form this interest takes. His proposal to change the retirement age of teachers from 70 to 65 (defeated by the Assembly) was opposed by many teachers and organizations, as was his proposed amendment to simplify legislative procedure on school legislation and the Coudert-McLaughlin bill to permit religious education on public school time which became law in 1940. The Teachers' Union points out, too, that he voted for cuts in the educational budget in 1939 and 1940 and introduced teacher pay cut bills in those same years.

Even his decriers will admit that Senator Coudert knows his law. If legal ability is inheritable, Frederic René Coudert, Jr., had a good start. The first Coudert, an officer in Napoleon's Guard of Honor, arrived in

FREDERIC RENÉ COUDERT, JR.

America after escaping "with a false name and a horse pistol" from a death sentence for conspiracy to overthrow the Bourbons after Napoleon's fall. His sons, one of them the Senator's grandfather, founded the law firm of Coudert Brothers in 1853. It prospered, representing many crowned heads in Europe and many important interests both there and in America.

Frederic René Coudert, Sr., the Senator's father, joined the firm and during the years of his association with it became an authority on international law, representing the British Government in this country during the last War. He was suggested for the post of American Ambassador to France in 1914 and mentioned for Secretary of State in the early 1930's. He still guides the firm today. In 1897 he married Alice Tracy Wilmerding, a member of one of Manhattan's wealthiest families, granddaughter of General Benjamin F. Tracy, Secretary of the Navy under President Benjamin Harrison. Of his sons, Mr. Coudert, Sr., says: "Fred, Jr., is the politician, Ferd is the lawyer and linguist, and Alexis is the fencer."

COUDERT, FREDERIC RENÉ, JR.—
Continued

The politician's son was born on East 15th Street in New York and has lived all his life in the district he now represents—the 17th (or "silk stocking"), running from Harlem down Park Avenue past Union Square. He attended Columbia University, with time out to serve in the War as first lieutenant in the 27th Division of the 105th United States Infantry. After his graduation in 1918 he entered Columbia's law school, was awarded the Kent scholarship for proficiency in the study of law and received his LL. B. in 1922. One year later he was admitted to the New York Bar and one year after that became a member of Coudert Brothers.

Senator Coudert's government activities began in 1924 when he served for a year as Assistant United States Attorney for the Southern District of New York; his political activities in 1929, when he was Republican candidate for District Attorney of New York County. One year later he was a delegate to the New York State Republican Convention and continued as a delegate in 1932, 1934 and 1936; in that year and in 1940 he was a delegate to the Republican National Convention.

In 1938 Coudert was elected to the New York State Senate and in 1940 he was re-elected with the support of the Citizens' Union, which reported his voting record as "the best in the city Senate delegation." During the years he has been in the Senate, Coudert has served as chairman of the Military Affairs Committee, as a member of the Joint Legislative Committee for Recodification of the Insurance Laws and, in his second term, as chairman of the Committee on General Laws.

His record of bills sponsored is large. Besides the various educational bills, he presented a bill to eliminate the notarization of income tax returns; another to repeal the one-cent city cigaret tax; still another to reorganize the old New York City Health Department pension fund so that excess revenues may be retained by the city—all these became law. He was less successful with his bills to curb the illegal use of evidence obtained by wire tapping, to remove double taxation on odd lots of stock, to exempt from taxation the Metropolitan Opera House, to change voting hours. When the Teachers' Union asserted that his voting record showed him in favor of "crippling labor unions" he replied, in November 1940: "I'll let my voting record answer that false charge. I didn't oppose a single labor bill last session." They insist, however, that this is disproved by the fact that he voted for the Bewley Bill and against the Teamsters' Union in 1939, for the Wicks Bill calling for an open shop in the New York City transit system in 1940 and for the new Wicks Bill in 1941, and for the Ives Bill requesting a "waiting period" before strikes in 1941.

Senator Coudert's main interest for the past year, however, has been in the subcommittee investigating "subversive" activities which he now heads. And it was because of this interest that he declined an invitation from his Party to run for the United States Congressman's post of the late Kenneth Simpson. That the inquiry was supported by his fellow legislators was evidenced in January 1941 when further funds were voted the Rapp-Coudert Committee and again in April when it was given $247,000 to continue its work—$100,000 for the New York City part of the inquiry, $47,000 for counsel fees. Governor Lehman, however, vetoed the $47,000 part of this appropriation, intended to pay counsel and associate counsel of the Committee, on the grounds that lawyers' fees were excessive. Senator Coudert protested: "I cannot understand why the Governor should want to hamstring if not fatally cripple the subcommittee," he said. "The Committee has won the approval of . . . authorities and of citizens of the City and State generally and now it is sabotaged by our own Governor."

In June 1941, speaking of the kind of teachers who, to his way of thinking, made the investigation necessary, he told members of the Republican Business Women: "Now if your dog had rabies you wouldn't clap him into jail after he had bitten a number of persons— you'd put a bullet in his head, if you had that kind of iron in your soul. It is going to require brutal treatment to handle these teachers. . . Two things are sure. They simply cannot live under the American flag and the Constitution. Either they or the flag and the Constitution must go."

On November 27 it was disclosed that Coudert's subcommittee would go out of existence on December 31 and that the Legislature would probably not appropriate any more money for the Rapp-Coudert Committee as a whole because it had neglected to make the sweeping survey of State educational problems (other than Communism) that it had set out to do.

The subject of all this controversy is an unusually handsome politician, with blue eyes and curly hair, "Fritz" to his friends and "the Junior" to members of Coudert Brothers. During sessions he doesn't see much of his wife, Paula (Murray) Coudert, whom he married in 1931, or of their three children. When legislative matters are put aside for a while, though, he spends a good deal of time with his family and a good deal of time, too, boating. He is a member of clubs like the Piping Rock, Racquet and Tennis, Pilgrims, but reports have it that he infinitely prefers foul smelling pipes and old clothes and days on the water to any other activities they offer.

References

N Y World-Telegram p10 N 1 '40 por; My 3 '41 por

Who's Who in America

COUNTS, GEORGE S(YLVESTER) Dec. 9, 1889-   Educator; author; trade unionist

Address: b. Teachers College, Columbia University, New York City; h. 440 Riverside Drive, New York City

Called a Fascist by Communists and labeled a Communist by some of his opponents on the Right, Professor Counts considers himself a "cross between a Jeffersonian Democrat and a Lincoln Republican, struggling with the old problem of human freedom in an age of science and technology."

Professor Counts, educator, labor organizer and author, opened his campaign in 1941 as American Labor Party candidate for the City Council in Manhattan. When in October 1941 the board of elections rejected the ALP petition for his candidacy on the grounds of an insufficient number of valid signatures, his name was restored to the ballot under the emblem of the Citizen's Non-Partisan League.

"If elected," he said, "I shall work unceasingly in the Council for clean, efficient government, for protecting and advancing the interest of working people and all underprivileged groups, for guarding and improving the educational opportunities of children, for cultivating tolerance, understanding and sympathy among all races, nationalities and religions, for the elimination of every totalitarian tendency and movement, for the strengthening of the democratic process and the entire democratic heritage." Although he made a good showing he was defeated.

Born on a farm near Baldwin City, Kansas, December 9, 1889, George Sylvester Counts was the third of six children of James Wilson Counts and Mertie Florella (Gamble) Counts. He claims to be a direct descendant of William Bradford, Pilgrim leader and 30 times elected Governor of Plymouth Colony.

As a boy Counts spent most of his spare time doing chores on the farm. He did find the opportunity, however, to swim, skate, ride, and make collections of birds' eggs and arrow heads. During his teens he found hunting and trapping a lucrative sport and planned to "pioneer" in northern Canada. He even went so far as to estimate the cost of such an expedition, using the Montgomery Ward catalog for prices of arms, axes, beans, rice, dried beef, shoes, etc.

Counts' education began in a one-room schoolhouse. After two years, having completed the fourth grade, he attended the public schools of Baldwin City until 1907, when he was graduated from high school. It was a "dry and formal high school course in botany" that destroyed his desire to become a naturalist and "later challenged him to work to vitalize the subject matter of the schools."

In 1911 Counts received the B. A. degree from Baker University, a Methodist College in Baldwin City, and started his teaching career in the Sumner County High School in Wellington, Kansas. In 1913 he entered the graduate school of the University of Chicago, specializing in psychology, sociology and education, and paying his way with scholarships and odd jobs. He received the Ph. D. degree with honors in 1916 and in that year became head of the Department of Education and director of the summer school of Delaware College, Newark, Delaware. In 1918 he went to Harris Teachers' College, St. Louis, as

Blackstone

GEORGE S. COUNTS

an instructor; in 1919 to the University of Washington at Seattle; in 1920 to Yale University; in 1926 to the University of Chicago; and in 1927 to Teachers College, Columbia University, where he has remained. He has lectured at Harvard, Stanford, Ohio, Michigan, Iowa, Illinois, Minnesota, Virginia, Alabama and many other universities. "In all of these posts his studies and lectures were directed primarily toward the problem of adjusting the program of education to the conditions and purposes of American democracy."

Even before he came to Columbia he had served on educational commissions. In 1925 he assisted in the study of the educational system of the Philippine Islands as a member of the Philippine Educational Survey Commission. Among his writings in the field of education were: *The Selective Character of American Secondary Education* (1922), an inquiry into the relation of educational opportunity to economic condition and social status; *The Principles of Education* (1924), with Professor James Crosby Chapman of Yale, a textbook widely used in teacher-training institutions; *The Senior High School Curriculum* (1926); and *The Social Composition of Boards of Education* (1927), which showed that the various boards governing public education were composed of persons drawn from a narrow section of the population. His writings already frankly expressed the belief that effective educational theory must be intimately related to social life and institutions and should stimulate thinking on the problems which they offer. But this belief was strengthened when, from 1927 to 1932, he served as an associate director of the International Institute, making a number of trips abroad in order to study the social institutions of the Slavic countries.

COUNTS, GEORGE S.—*Continued*

"In 1927," he wrote later, "I spent approximately three months in Soviet Russia, traveling extensively by railroad, visiting institutions of many kinds and engaging citizens from all walks of life in conversation. Two years later I returned to Russia and remained seven months. On this occasion I took a Ford car into the country and during July, August, September and October drove approximately 6,000 miles through the European parts of the Union from Leningrad across the Caucasus Mountains and from Odessa to Nizhnii Novgorod and regions beyond. I shaped the route myself and motored alone for about 1,000 miles. . . It was an illuminating and thrilling experience." He said that these visits, particularly, challenged his thinking "on both educational and social questions."

His next books, following the publication of *School and Society in Chicago* (1928), showed the effects of his combined experiences. *The American Road to Culture* (1930), a dispassionate survey of education in the United States, was concerned not with "the theories of professors but with the practices of American schools," and was called by Jerome Davis "one of the best brief social interpretations" of the subject then available. *Soviet Challenge to America,* published the same year, was especially recommended by Louis Fischer "to those who may believe that planned economy is possible under capitalism." In *The Social Foundations of Education* (1934) Counts, as a "collectivist," pictured the economic system developed over three centuries as breaking down, and insisted that education should shift its role to meet the new day—a thesis similar to that of a speech delivered two years earlier and later published in pamphlet form, *Dare the School Build a New Social Order?* In this he had said of the classroom teacher: "Neutrality with respect to the great issues that agitate society, while perhaps theoretically possible, is practically tantamount to giving support to the forces of conservatism. . . Capitalism is proving itself weak at the very point where its champions have thought it impregnable . . . it no longer works; it is unable to organize and maintain production . . . it is not only cruel and inhuman; it is also wasteful and inefficient. . . This situation gives to teachers an opportunity and a responsibility unique in the annals of education."

Counts was at the same time active in the National Education Association (he served on its Educational Policies Commission at one time) and the Progressive Education Association. In 1934 he was one of the founders and the first editor of *Social Frontier,* a magazine intended "to arouse teachers and others to the magnitude and gravity of the crisis facing American democracy." Their role, as he stated it in the first issue, was to "make clear the fundamental conflict of interests which today divide society into opposing groups and make impossible the fulfillment of the democratic tradition." In 1935, at the convention of the Progressive Education Association, he

declared that "the teaching profession should unionize from kindergarten to college," and he was himself an early and active member of the New York Teachers Union, at one time serving with Reinhold Niebuhr (see sketch this issue), and with his good friend John Dewey on a "United Committee to Save the Union" during a period of great factional strife. He supported President Roosevelt, attacked the American Legion, the Teachers' Oath, the Liberty League and William Randolph Hearst (who, in turn, called him "Red Russia's Apostle").

The Prospects of American Democracy (1938), however, showed Counts in fundamental disagreement with the extreme Left, not only in a new disillusionment with the working-out of the Russian system but in other matters. In this book he was emphatic in his opposition to all forms of totalitarianism, both Left and Right. He asserted his conviction that American democracy, though in great danger, had an opportunity of salvation greater than that of any other capitalist country, and put forward a nine-point program for democratic action which included government monopoly of military and police power, guaranteeing of civil liberties, exposure of political propaganda, and avoidance of war through a program of international cooperation. (The United States, however, should at no time "permit itself to be drawn into an alliance intended to maintain the *status quo.* Certain of the aggressive nations have just grievances which can be disregarded only at the peril of war" and the destruction of free institutions.)

Throughout the War, Counts has been a strong supporter of President Roosevelt's policies. In 1939 elected to the presidency of the American Federation of Teachers, and re-elected in 1940 and 1941, he has fought for "academic freedom" from interference by such bodies as the Rapp-Coudert Committee, and at the same time has urged the expulsion from the American Federation of Teachers of those locals which the Federation considered Communist-dominated. He has engaged in political activity as a member of the right wing of the American Labor Party, the only political party to which he has ever belonged. He has continued to write on current problems; in 1941 *The Education of Free Men in American Democracy* was published. And he remains an active member of the executive committee of the nationwide Committee on Education and National Defense.

Dr. Counts is approximately five feet eleven inches tall and weighs close to two hundred pounds. Reddish-haired and blue-eyed, with a small mustache and sharp features, his "faint resemblance to Leon Trotsky" has been remarked by *Time* Magazine. He is, however, described by those who have worked with him as a "mild, kindly gentleman" whom it is hard to anger "even at times when one would like to have a mild display of temper." In 1913 he married Lois Hazel Bailey, the daughter of a Methodist minister of Fort

Scott, Kansas. They have two daughters, Esther Mae and Martha.

Since he no longer has time to go hunting and fishing, Professor Counts finds his major source of recreation in a small farm in New Hope, Pennsylvania, where he devotes an occasional holiday to the care of shrubs and trees. During the course of his globe-trotting he has collected seeds of shrubs and trees that interested him and has had such good success in growing them on his farm that he is now supplying his neighbors with exotic plants.

References

> Am Mercury 40:462-72 Ap '37
> Fortune 14:74 Jl '36 por
> Lit Digest 121:34 Mr 7 '36 por
> N Y Times p17 Ag 23 '40; p12 S 15 '41
> Time 28:66+ Jl 20 '36 por
> Leaders in Education 1941
> Who's Who Among North American Authors
> Who's Who in America
> Who's Who in the East

COWARD, NOEL (PIERCE) Dec. 16, 1899- Playwright; actor

Address: b. c/o John C. Wilson, 10 Rockefeller Plaza, New York City; h. Folkstone, Kent, England

On April 29, 1940 Noel Coward arrived in New York, via Paris, on a "confidential" government mission. He spoke vaguely to reporters of his activity in Paris (pursued in a simple double-breasted suit), but wouldn't say whether it had anything to do with propaganda work. His first "government activity" in this country was to act as master of ceremonies at the Allied Relief Ball at the Hotel Astor May 10, 1940. Further activities included a night at the New York World's Fair (Noel Coward Night), a trip to Washington ("to see the Lincoln Memorial," though incidentally he spoke with the President) and a visit to Hollywood, with a Chicago stopover, to chat with actor friends.

Meanwhile members of Parliament wanted to know just what Noel Coward was doing in the United States. Harold Nicolson, secretary to the Ministry of Information, said he was, among other things, "expected to call on President Roosevelt." Said the London *Daily Mirror*: "Mr. Coward, with his stilted mannerisms, his clipped accents and his vast experience with the useless froth of society may be making contacts with the American equivalents . . . but as a representative for democracy he's like a plate of caviar in a carman's pull-up."

It was not until July that Coward revealed his mission here: to see "whether the United States was isolationist or would become interventionist on humanitarian grounds." Further, he told reporters, he was here to find homes "for 58 British children, sons and daughters of destitute actors and actresses." He also expressed a desire to be back home and get into actual fighting (in the last World War he saw

NOEL COWARD

no fighting but spent the time mostly ill in the hospital). When a friend suggested to him that the infantry was safest, since in a combat division only one man in five gets killed, Coward had a quick comeback: "But you know how I am. Whenever I'm with a crowd, I always pick up the check."

This particular visit to the United States later cost the playwright a fine of $800 for violation of Britain's wartime finance regulations. Having gone abroad with the Government's consent but with only $40 in his pocket, he made use of assets in the United States which should have been offered to his Government.

Coward's next mission for the British Government brought him to Australia and New Zealand, where he wrung approximately 1,400 hands daily and raised some £10,000 for the Red Cross. Then, after another brief visit in New York, he sailed for London—but apparently not in order to get into any fighting. In August 1941 a new Noel Coward comedy, *Blithe Spirit*, written blithely between and during the earlier air raids over London, had a brilliant opening at the Piccadilly. A "fourth dimensional farce," it concerned the unhappy lot of a man with two wives who had both turned into ghosts, and delighted Londoners, whose problems were quite, quite different. *Blithe Spirit* had an equally brilliant opening in New York on November 5, 1941. In the same period Coward found time to write a book, *Australia Visited, 1940*.

COWARD, NOEL—*Continued*

Although he says he is happiest when "packing up his bag to go somewhere else," Noel Coward likes New York, and has been a perennial favorite in the City's social and theatrical circles. The brilliant playwright, actor and play-producer (his profits once ran in New York alone to some $6,000 weekly), who has been and probably will continue to be "for years and years a member of the Younger Generation," was born in Teddington, London, England December 16, 1899. He was educated privately and at Croydon, and is the first of his family to turn to the stage. He made his initial stage appearance at the age of 12 (he was a choirboy before that) to augment the family income. Of his father, Arthur Sabin Coward, who died in 1937, Noel Coward said in his autobiography, *Present Indicative* (1937): "He made small model yachts for his own amusement" while his mother, Violet (Veitch) Coward, "worked like a slave." "Master Noel" became a member of Charles Hawtrey's provincial repertory players, with two other juveniles, "Gertie" Lawrence and Estelle Winwood. He was a precocious child who discovered early that "conversation with casual strangers was stimulating to the imagination. I shocked many kindly, interfering old ladies with picturesque descriptions of my appalling life at home." He received some formal dramatic training at the Italia Conti Academy, the foremost dramatic school in England. His budding professional career was interrupted by the War, though he never saw active army service. In 1916 he had toured the Provinces in *Charley's Aunt*; at the end of the War he appeared in Cosmo Hamilton's *Scandal*. After this came *London Calling*. All he did in the latter was to write the book, lyrics and music, and play the lead song-and-dance role himself. But he had always been more interested in writing plays than in acting: his first play, *The Rat Trap*, was written at the age of 18. *I'll Leave it to You* (1920) was a failure; *The Young Idea* (1924) was scarcely more successful.

Feeling unappreciated in England, Coward dreamed of New York. "There were apparently two very attractive brothers called Shubert. . . There was also a kindly old boy named Al Woods, who produced the best melodramas in the world, outside of David Belasco, who was of course a species of divinity. In addition to these brilliant philanthropists, there was the Flatiron Building, the Woolworth Building . . . and most exciting of all, Broadway by night. . . Its splendors and its noise and its crowds haunted my imagination. Its gigantic sky signs dazzled my dreams, flashing in a myriad of lights, with unfailing regularity, the two words, 'Noel Coward.'"

His New York opportunity came when Gilbert Miller offered him by cable a first year's option on his play, *The Vortex* (1925). *The Vortex* was a success in both London and in New York; in New York he made friends with George Kaufman, Alexander Woollcott (see sketches this issue), George Jean Nathan, and—particularly—Alfred Lunt and Lynn Fontanne (see sketches this issue). The latter were to help make his play, *Hay Fever* (1924), a success. His first full-charge revue, *On With the Dance,* was also well received in England. Then a nervous breakdown took him for a rest to Hawaii, where he wrote *Bitter Sweet* (1929), and he returned to New York to direct its production, with Evelyn Laye in the leading role (1929-30).

Not always, however, did Coward meet with success. When *Sirocco* (1927) opened, Arnold Bennett observed that "every Noel Coward opening provided two shows, one on each side of the footlights." *Cavalcade* (1932), one of his most spectacular productions, was not received without controversy: its author was accused of writing "nationalistic propaganda." *Home Chat,* on its London production, was greeted with catcalls and boos. In the midst of the turmoil a galleryite rose and shouted to Coward, "Look 'ere, we expected something better." "So did I," coolly replied Mr. Coward. But such plays as *Private Lives* (1931), in which he himself played the leading role, brought him in New York, at least, an enviable dramatic reputation.

Coward has been described as "tall and slim, not handsome, yet strikingly attractive, with neatly parted black hair, clear blue eyes, sensitive hands and an engaging smile. His clothes are unobtrusive, but chosen with a nice discrimination. His accent is 'standard Southern English,' his conversation easy and sometimes witty. He moves and thinks quickly, and enjoys acting. He is able to work practically anywhere. He is unmarried." Coward writes his plays at terrific speed, first in longhand, then on the typewriter. He considers *Hay Fever* (which took him three days to write) his best comedy; *The Vortex* his best drama. "I like traveling," he writes, "better than anything else. Travel rests me and gives me the only time I really have to myself—to think and especially to read. And I always do a great deal of writing aboard ship. I am never seasick." He has been around the world more than once; his companion on these trips has been his friend Jeffrey Holmesdale. Traveling light and stopping at only the best hotels, they have touched many ports. Coward once acted in Singapore and got influenza in Shanghai, where he wrote *Private Lives*. But he says he likes South America best of all.

He owns an apartment in New York City on the East River and 52nd Street, but usually sublets it. His real home is a farm in Kent, England. "I have remodeled the barn into a studio that looks out over the Channel." There he doesn't "loll in bed until noon," but gets up at eight and begins work, usually by strumming on the piano. He gets in a working day of about seven hours.

References

    Arts & Dec 47:12-14+ S '37 il
    N Y Herald Tribune p5 Ap 30 '40 por
    N Y Post p4 Ap 29 '40; p11 My 15 '40
    N Y Sun p3 Jl 31 '40; p9 Ag 6 '40
    New Yorker 4:21-5 Ja 19 '29; 16:12-13
    Je 8 '40

PM p10 O 6 '40 por
Sat R Lit 9:445-6 F 25 '33 por; 15:16
  Ap 17 '37
Time 36:67 S 9 '40 por
Braybrooke, P. Amazing Mr. Noel
  Coward 1933
Brown, J. M. Letters from Greenroom
  Ghosts p117-68 1934
Coward, N. P. Present Indicative 1937
Cunliffe, J. W. Modern English Play-
  wrights p208-51 1927
Hamilton, C. People Worth Talking
  About p167-74 1933
Kunitz, S. J. ed. Living Authors 1937
Swinnerton, F. A. Georgian Scene p433-
  59 1934
Who's Who
Who's Who in America
Who's Who in the Theatre

COXE, HOWARD (CLEVELAND) Nov.
9, 1898—Nov. 23, 1940 Novelist and newspaperman who served on the New York
Herald Tribune, the *New Republic* and other
publications.

HOWARD COXE

References
  America's Young Men
Obituaries
  N Y Herald Tribune p42 N 24 '40
  N Y Times p17 N 25 '40

**CRAIGAVON, JAMES CRAIG, 1ST VIS-
COUNT** (krăg-ăv'ŏn) Jan. 8, 1871—Nov.
24, 1940 Prime Minister of Northern Ireland since the establishment of the Ulster
Government in 1920; known as strong foe
of Irish independence.

References
  Who's Who

Obituaries
  N Y Herald Tribune p10 N 25 '40 por
  N Y Times p17 N 25 '40 por
  Time 36:53 D 2 '40

Underwood & Underwood
VISCOUNT CRAIGAVON

**CRANBORNE, ROBERT ARTHUR
JAMES CECIL, VISCOUNT** *See* Cecil
of Essendon, R. A. J. C., 1st Baron

**CRIPPS, CHARLES ALFRED, 1ST
BARON PARMOOR** *See* Parmoor, C.
A. C., 1st Baron

CROSBY, BING May 2, 1904(?)- Radio
and film star
Address: h. 10500 Camarillo St, North Hollywood, Calif.

Bing Crosby's "dulcet, broken-toned" voice
has made him the highest-paid singer in the
world. There are other men in the United
States who earn $700,000 annually, but most
of them at least make a pretense of having
struggled for it. It is rather refreshing to
learn that "hard work, attention to detail,
and the other story-book maxims" have played
little part in "The Groaner's" success. "I've
just been a very lucky guy," Bing says. "A
crooner gets his quota of sentimentality with
half his natural voice. That's a great saving.
I don't like to work."

The parents of problem children may also
be encouraged to learn that Bing started life
as the bad boy of Tacoma, Washington, where
he was one of the seven children of Harry
Lowe and Catherine Helen (Harrigan)
Crosby, devout Catholics. He was christened Harry Lillis Crosby, and the truant
officers were always taking that name down
for one reason or another. Bing was promi-

BING CROSBY

nent in other fields than mischief, however. He sang, as did all his family. He acted: his first appearance on the stage, in a school production of *Julius Caesar*, gave him a reputation as a comedian when the heavy curtain began to descend on him. He played par golf. An expert swimmer, he worked one summer as lifeguard in a municipal pool, and once brought away from a swimming meet nine first-place medals and two seconds. The only time he ran away from home it was with the idea of becoming a baseball player. He might, as a matter of fact, be with the Dodgers today if he hadn't worked in a lumber camp one summer and come home with gashes above both knees. This accident prevented him from playing shortstop on the baseball team when he started back to Gonzaga, a Catholic university in Spokane, but he did win his letter later playing infield.

Bing had been sent to Gonzaga to study law. One part of his law training was a course in elocution in which he learned "phrasing"—separating a speech into its various thought-patterns before delivering it— and he still insists that he learned everything he knows about singing in that course. "If I am not a singer, I am a phraser. Diseur is the word. I owe all to elocution." He owes something, though, to the fact that he and a friend of his, Al Rinker, organized a seven-piece band while still in college. Bing played the traps, Rinker played the piano, they both sang—and soon there were as many party engagements as they could handle. One triumphant engagement in a local theatre at $40 a week gave them a mercenary idea. Said Bing, afterward: "I knew a great many young lawyers in town, and I found that very few of them were making as much as $40 a week. And they had to work hard. I said to Al Rinker: 'Let's hit for Los Angeles. Maybe

there's some more of this easy dough down there.'"

With Mrs. Crosby providing a battered car, in 1924 the two boys quit school and set out to see Rinker's sister, Mildred Bailey, today the "swing-style" vocalist of radio. They had to walk the last two miles, but she got them an engagement at the Tent Cafe at $65 a week for the team, booked as "Two Boys and a Piano." It was one Pacific coast night club or vaudeville stand after another until in 1927 they wound up at Los Angeles' Metropolitan Theatre at a salary of $65 a week apiece. Paul Whiteman heard them, offered $150, and signed them up immediately. They went to New York with him, where Harry Barris joined them—and that was the beginning of Paul Whiteman's Rhythm Boys, who were a sensation in Broadway night clubs of the late '20s.

They were three years with Paul Whiteman. Then, in 1930, they all landed in California again, where Whiteman was making *The King of Jazz*. When Whiteman returned East, they stayed on, singing under the artificial palms of the Cocoanut Grove. Bing's "Bay-bub-do-ee-do-dee-do" made him a hit as a soloist. He did not, however, make a hit with Dixie Lee (Wilma W. Wyatt of Memphis, Tennessee), an attractive young actress whom he wooed to the tune of *I Surrender, Dear*. "I'd never marry a playboy," she told him, observing with disapproval that he was spending twice what he made.

In September she reconsidered and married him, and it was shortly after that that Bing's affairs took a turn for the better financially. His brother Everett sent *I Surrender, Dear* recordings to both NBC and CBS in New York. They both wanted an audition, and some time in 1931 Bing departed for New York, leaving behind him a "trail of broken bottles and unpaid bills." CBS signed him up; Everett induced him to form "Bing Crosby, Ltd., Inc." to keep his hands off his own property and separated him from his agents and night club contracts for $35,000. The morning of the day he was to have his première over a national hookup Bing lost his voice, and the doctor, examining him, found nodules on his vocal chords. He hadn't lost his voice permanently, however, and, as it developed, these nodules (now insured for $100,000) produced "the effect of a lad with his voice changing singing into a rain-barrel" which has made Bing famous. Soon, with his radio contract and personal appearances and best-selling records, he was averaging some $7,000 a week.

He had already made a few radio shorts for Mack Sennett as well as a "campus comedy" for Pathe tastefully called *Two Plus Fours*. He wasn't very hopeful about motion pictures, though; the first producer he propositioned told him his ears stuck out too much. Besides, as one critic put it: "His first short subjects were quite as broken-winded and spavined as the ordinary run of things and also made the conventional error . . . of playing him up as if he were making a personal appearance instead of giving him something to do." But when Paramount made their first *Big Broadcast* they naturally put him in it along with other radio personalities, and his singing in that seemed to warrant their giving him a contract for feature-length pictures and putting him in *College Humor* and *Too Much Harmony* in 1933. That same year MGM borrowed him for *Going Hollywood,* and it turned out that Bing, unlike most other radio stars, actually had box-office appeal.

At this time Bing's acting was not all it might have been, perhaps because he was invariably cast in the role of a romantic collegian (wide pants, sweaters, saxophones, snappy roadsters, snappy chatter). His voice had given him the title "the Romeo of radio," and he was automatically expected to provide love interest. Even then a natural talent for comedy began to show itself, though; he was, surprisingly, "innocuous to his own sex" (according to one male critic, this was because he never seemed to be trying to be charming); and by 1934, when *We're Not Dressing* was produced, he was turning in what most critics considered very finished performances. *She Loves Me Not*, in which he starred for the first time, followed that same year, and soon J. C. Furnas was writing about his acting: "He borrows something from the deadpan school of slapstick comic and something from the insouciant ogle of the professional masher to produce an effect of being congenitally at home and sure of himself anywhere."

In *Mississippi* (1935), *Rhythm on the Range* (1936), *Pennies from Heaven* (1936), *Waikiki Wedding* (1937), *Double or Nothing* (1937) and *Doctor Rhythm* (1938) Bing made further successes—particularly in *Pennies from Heaven,* which was the first production he made for himself, with Columbia paying half the cost. But it was in *Sing You Sinners* (1938) that Bing really found himself—or, more accurately, that his audience discovered him. Here he played a "rough sketch of himself"—a lazy, happy-go-lucky, undependable but goodhearted fellow who is mad about horses. There wasn't a love scene for him in it, and his brother got the girl—but as far as Bing was concerned that was all to the good, and the audience liked the real Crosby even better than the Crosby they had seen before. Later pictures, *Road to Singapore* and *Road to Zanzibar,* both with Dorothy Lamour and Bob Hope (see sketch this issue), brought him a well-deserved reputation as a mad comedian to whom love and Lamour are purely incidental. *Birth of the Blues* released late in 1941 was acclaimed by the critics who also have high hopes for *Holiday Inn* on which, in late 1941, he is working with Fred Astaire. Bing from the start "has insisted on having important stars around him, while his contemporaries were fighting for single billing," and this may account to some degree for 10 years of consistent Hollywood success.

In radio, too, he has outlasted nearly everyone who started with him. NBC's Kraft Music Hall, on the air since 1936, has turned him from a mere singer to a master of ceremonies. On his first few programs as master of ceremonies his talk sounded stilted ("I told you I am a man who should just sing"), but then a plot was hatched. On every program some questions not in the script were sprung on him, and, forced to ad lib, he would answer in his own easy drawl. Gradually he learned to talk to visiting celebrities (Leopold Stokowski, Lotte Lehmann [see sketches this issue], José Iturbi, Pat O'Brien, Dorothy Lamour) over the air as easily as he would in his own home, and since that time what has made the program so popular has been as much its atmosphere of relaxed informality and of leisureliness as it has been Bob Burns' wit or Bing's crooning. One rival producer called the show "a disgrace, ragged, unfinished, fumbling"; commentators point out that it is precisely its "small details, snatches of saucy dialog, and other tricks and trappings, none of them remarkable or even bright alone, but in the assembled show producing a mood and tempo that make for popularity" that are its chief charm. Bing's radio scripters have been commended for the remarkable vocabulary which Bing uses with comical effect on the show.

And if Bing's radio program is one of the most informal on the air, Bing himself is probably radio's most informal star. He goes around looking, for the most part, even more untidy than in the days before he was a conspicuous success. Hawaiian shirts, open at the collar; a battered felt which is seldom removed, outdoors or in; ancient slacks that have never felt an iron; a generous mouthful of gum—these are distinguishing characteristics. He is five feet nine, has light blue eyes and light brown hair, getting scanty, an altogether engaging grin and a picturesque way of talking.

He still likes sports better than almost anything else. Mornings, when he's not working, he often goes to the race-track for the workouts, drops over to the golf course for a couple of dozen holes, then returns to the track for the afternoon racing. He himself owns the popular race track at Del Mar, a 100-acre breeding ranch nearby, and some 75 horses, mainly Argentine and American thoroughbreds. He is, in fact, a "minor business octopus" whose ventures have included an employment agency, a gold mine, a real estate project, a music publishing company, an office building, the management of two prize fighters and a girls' baseball team. There are, besides, substantial royalties on records ($77,000 in 1940); on the radio his voice is worth $7,500 a week for an hour's broadcast; and he gets $175,000 for the three pictures which he makes every year. His income tax for 1940 was $377,000.

Bing's quietly-furnished semi-Colonial home has 14 rooms with an adjoining tennis court and swimming pool, and there he spends a good deal of time with Dixie and with the four young male Crosbys: Gary Evan, the eldest; Philip Lang and Dennis Michael, twins; and Howard Lindsay, the youngest. Every few months or so he asks his old musician friends to come over for a jam session. Among his favorite conductors, though,

CROSBY, BING—*Continued*

are Toscanini and Damrosch. He was presented with the degree of Doctor of Philosophy in Music by Gonzaga in October 1937. A devout Catholic, he often sings in the church choir on Sundays; he reads a lot— likes detective stories. especially those by Dashiell Hammett, and enjoys the novels of Somerset Maugham, William McFee and Joseph Conrad; he has tried writing a novel himself, tells his boys bedtime stories "in Crosbyesque slang," and would like to settle down and write short stories some day. In that far-off day when he realizes *all* his ambitions he will be a tap dancer like Astaire and a tennis tournament player, too. Sometimes his friends wonder: is it possible that this fabulously lazy guy Crosby is really not a lazy guy at all?

References

Arts & Dec 49:3-6 D '38 il por
Collier's 95:20+ Ap 27 '35 por
Life 5:54-5 S 5 '38 il por
Motion Pict Mag 51:36+ F '36 por; 52:32-3+ S '36 pors
Newsweek 16:62 S 16 '40
Photoplay 50:21+ S '36 por; 52:38-9 My '38 il por; 53:22-3+ F '39 il pors
Sch & Soc 46:760 D 11 '37
Time 37:92+ Ap 7 '41 pors
Crosby, E. J. and Crosby, L. E. Bing 1937
International Motion Picture Almanac
Variety Radio Directory
Who's Who in America

CROSS, RONALD H(IBBERT), 1ST BARONET May 9, 1896- British High Commissioner to Australia

Address: Canberra, Australia

In the sudden reshuffle of May 1, 1941, Ronald Hibbert Cross, Privy Councillor and United Kingdom Minister of Shipping, was appointed United Kingdom High Commissioner to Australia. The New York *Times'* correspondent commented that he is "well known in Australia, is liked by [former] Premier Robert G. Menzies (see sketch this issue) and is being sent there because of the critical necessity of keeping the Empire happy." The opinion of a Labor M.P., that he "was sent off to Australia by Churchill because he was noisy in his opposition to some understanding with Stalin" was not generally shared. On the King's birthday honors list issued in June 1941 the British High Commissioner was raised to a newly created baronetcy.

Sir Ronald is "a merchant-banker of the conservative Eton-Army-business pattern." Born on May 9, 1896, the son of James Carlton Cross, he went from Eton straight into the Duke of Lancaster's Own Yeomanry and later into the Royal Flying Corps as a fighter-pilot. After the First World War ended he went into business, and in 1925 married Louise Marion, daughter of the late Walter Emmott of Emmott Hall, Colne, Lancashire. It was

Harris & Ewing

SIR RONALD H. CROSS

not until 1931 that he was elected to Parliament as a Unionist from Rosendale, Lancashire, but the year 1935 found him Government Whip. For two years he held voters in the House of Commons in line.

By this time considered one of the most promising younger men in Parliament, in 1937 Cross became a Lord of the Treasury and later Vice-Chamberlain of His Majesty's Household. The latter post he held until 1938, when he was appointed Parliamentary Secretary of the Board of Trade; and in 1939, after Britain declared war on Germany, he took over the important post of Minister of Economic Warfare. His was the responsibility for marshaling England's "credit and trade battalions" in the War.

In Nazi eyes Minister of Economic Warfare meant "Minister of Starvation." Londoners, more jokingly, called Cross' Ministry MEW, also pointing out that his cable address was WHISKERS, LONDON. Cross himself, working in great obscurity with his staff of 800 in the gloomy building where the London School of Economics had formerly been housed, announced that Britain's objective was not primarily to starve Germany of food but of industrial resources. This meant an attempt to break Germany's economic strength by cutting off German trade both by means of a naval blockade and by trying to undersell and overbid Germany in markets that couldn't be cut off by the British blockade —at that time The Netherlands, Belgium, Scandinavia, the Balkans, etc.

The first report of the Minister of Economic Warfare to Parliament on January 17, 1940 was extremely optimistic—over-optimistic, as later events proved. He reported that after only four and one-half months of economic warfare Germany had been reduced to the economic straits of 1916, and that although there were still gaps in the British blockade Germany was suffering from shortages of many vital commodities as well as lack of clothing, soap, food. "We look forward," he predicted, "to the day when we shall have so strangled Germany's economic life that she can no longer sustain her war effort." The first result of that speech was to intensify the growing movement to put the Minister of Economic Warfare in the British Cabinet.

In the general upset of May 1940, on the same day that Lord Beaverbrook became Minister of Aircraft Production, Ronald H. Cross was appointed Shipping Minister, with the job of making sure that there would be ships for British supplies. It is generally believed that in that position he did a good job under great difficulties. Although British shipping losses grew heavier and heavier after the fall of France, shipyards worked at full capacity both to replace losses of cargo ships and to reduce losses by building more warships to protect convoys.

On January 25, 1941, in a transatlantic broadcast to the United States, Britain's Shipping Minister assured Americans that Britain can beat "the U-boat threat," but "we must have your industrial support." On April 30 he defended the pinch of the blockade. "Americans should realize Britain is fighting for her life," he said. "By waging economic warfare to the utmost we believe we shall shorten the War by many months and this weapon can thus be the means of saving innumerable lives and of hastening the time when the world again will be free from the curse that now lies upon it." And even after having resigned as Minister of Shipping he remained hardly less concerned about the problems of that office. In June 1941 asked about England's greatest need from the United States, he replied: "Ships, ships, ships."

Slender, six-foot-three, "fair-haired, direct, pleasant, incisive," Cross is well known for his tact. In April 1940, when the Italian press was making exceedingly nasty statements about Great Britain, he announced that "we have no quarrel with Italy and we have every wish to be friends." He and his wife have three daughters, Angela, Diana and Susanna, and up to the time of the War led a simple and quiet home life.

References

N Y Sun p24 Ap 19 '40; p14 Je 13 '41
N Y Times p7 Je 14 '41
Newsweek 15:24 Ja 29 '40 por; 17:27
  My 12 '41
Time 35:25-6 Ja 29 '40 por
Who's Who

CROSSLEY, ARCHIBALD M(ADDOCK) Dec. 7, 1896- Research director
Address: b. Crossley, Inc, Princeton, N. J.; 330 W. 42nd St, New York City; h. 21 Battle Rd, Princeton, N. J.

One of America's important new industries is public opinion analysis. It's new only in

ARCHIBALD M. CROSSLEY

the sense that it now boasts a scientific method, for actually there were "straw polls" in the days of Andrew Jackson, when newspapers first attempted to predict elections by "the straws in the wind." Currently, disgruntled legislators complain that opinion polls are making Congressmen a useless luxury, and they speak none too cheerfully of "Government by Gallup." But no one can deny the increasing accuracy of the opinion polls.

All of which is a far cry from the immortal boner of 1936 made by the late *Literary Digest,* which many predicted would be the poll to end all polls. Actually, however, it ended only the magazine, while the opinion-takers went merrily on their way to bigger and better predictions. Among these was shrewd, spectacled Archibald M. Crossley, president and treasurer of Crossley, Incorporated, with offices in Princeton, New Jersey and New York City. Today America's three major opinion agencies are the Gallup (see sketch 1940 Annual) poll, the *Fortune* Magazine surveys and the Crossley surveys.

Crossley was born in Fieldsboro, New Jersey and is the son of Martha Jane (Bullock) and Joseph Crossley, both of England. He attended New Jersey schools and Princeton University, from which he was graduated in 1917. That year he inauspiciously launched his career by selling vacuum cleaners. Later he sold classified ads for a Philadelphia advertising agency and eventually found a niche in the purchasing department of the Day & Zimmerman Company.

Sometime during his various occupations Crossley discovered that he had a knack for research work, for the year 1918 found him already installed as research manager of the J. H. Cross advertising agency in Philadelphia. Here he served with distinction, and the *Literary Digest* acquired him in 1922 to serve as assistant director of research. Later he

CROSSLEY, ARCHIBALD M.—*Cont.*

was appointed chief of the research department.

Despite its electoral error of some years later, the *Digest* was a trail-blazer in the field of promotion and research and contributed a great deal to the science of the public survey. Its predictions from 1920 to 1932 gained it a reputation for infallibility. Crossley learned much, and probably contributed to the magazine just as much as he learned. In 1926 he was finally ready to go out on his own. Meanwhile, in 1920, he had married Dorothy Fox of Lexington, Massachusetts, and had settled down in Princeton. (There are three children: Helen Martha, a Radcliffe college student; Joseph, 2nd, a Princeton undergraduate; and Dorothy Irving, who won't be attending college for a few years yet.)

Crossley soon became a big name in the survey field. His studies were recognized as almost indispensable business aids for newspapers, advertising agencies and corporations producing commodities. He was one of the first to sample public reaction to brand names of breakfast foods, toothpastes, soap and other widely advertised products. More important, however, was his research in connection with radio advertising, listening habits and audience participation; here he is acknowledged to be preeminent. And his ratings of radio stars have made Crossley a byword among the listening public.

Polling election opinion was a sort of sideline to Crossley's business of analyzing markets, but he has proved no amateur in political prediction. In 1936 he predicted President Roosevelt would defeat Landon by a wide margin. But ex-Postmaster General Jim Farley's intuition that year proved more accurate than even the most painstaking poll. It was Farley alone who said the Republicans could confidently count on only Maine and Vermont; Crossley picked six certain and seven potential Landon states. When the votes were counted they showed Crossley had underestimated the President's strength by seven per cent, while Farley had hit the bull's eye.

Still, Crossley was considerably more accurate than the *Digest,* which had insisted Roosevelt would get only 43 per cent of the votes. Incidentally, Crossley has since analyzed the reason for the magazine's fiasco; he said it had failed to take into account the political effect of economics and was relying on the pre-depression basis of numerical votes received, rather than on a qualitative analysis of the economic status of the straw voters. In other words, the big vote for Landon might have come from people who weren't impoverished by recent events; but to get a true picture, it was necessary to sample opinion with regard to all income levels, including those which had suffered under a Republican regime.

Crossley's Presidential poll of 1940 was remarkably accurate: it was within 1.8 percentage points of the actual outcome of the elections. Like its predecessor, the poll was published in leading newspapers and attracted considerable attention.

It is his marketing research for which Crossley is chiefly known, however. His private surveys for advertisers provide a reliable means of checking on how a given amount of advertising will go, which media are the most effective for a particular product, how a given audience will be apt to react to a given type of advertising. As a means of getting the maximum out of each advertising dollar, of preventing waste and of planning a campaign along definite lines, the Crossley surveys are probably one of the greatest single influences in current advertising trends.

Crossley's radio work has been particularly outstanding. His famous Cooperative Analysis of Broadcasting, a continuous measurement of audience reaction to various programs, is the undisputed authority in the field today. Advertisers use it to help them slant their programs toward a particular income level, to help them pick the most appropriate talent and to choose the stations apt to give them the best service in relation to their specialized needs. Thousands of telephone calls, house-to-house canvassing and other devices are employed. Begun in March 1930, the survey is now operated on a non-profit basis for the governing committee of advertisers and advertising agencies. Crossley ratings of stars decide many a radio career, since a high rating usually means a star can command a higher salary for his services, while a low rating means a star's virtual oblivion. Non-commercial events as well as advertising programs are rated by the survey, and this makes it an invaluable service for government agencies as well as business groups. It was awarded the Final Harvard Advertising Reward for outstanding research.

Another important Crossley enterprise is the Continuing Study of Magazine Audiences, begun in 1938 under the sponsorship of *Life* Magazine and now operated by the Magazine Audience group. It is a useful link between magazine management and the reading public. It helps periodicals achieve maximum effectiveness as advertising media.

Research is Crossley's only hobby, as well as his life work. He has delivered many lectures before business groups and colleges on public opinion and kindred topics and he is a voluminous writer of articles on business who has contributed to *Public Opinion Quarterly, Advertising and Selling* and other periodicals, and, in addition is the author of a book called *Watch Your Selling Dollar!* (1930), published by B. C. Forbes. His high forehead, white hair, and spectacles, give him a professorial air. He has traveled in every state of the Union, in Canada, Mexico and throughout Europe.

References

Am Mag 130:31+ N '40 por
J of Marketing Ap '41

CROUSE, RUSSEL (krous) Feb. 20, 1893-
Author; playwright; producer
Address: b. 1430 Broadway, New York City;
h. 159 E. 78th St, New York City

The dramatization of Clarence Day's *Life
With Father* was the first non-musical venture
of the writing team of Howard Lindsay and
Russel Crouse. It opened at Skowhegan,
Maine on August 14, 1939, "a simple nostalgic
comedy" (New York *Times*) staged by Mel
Burke's Lakewood Players. When the play
came into New York for its sellout opening,
Lucius Beebe, commenting on Crouse the
dramatist, said that it "partakes less of his
talent for musical shows than of his talent
for wistful souvenirs of departed Americana
. . . there is more kinship between the spirit
of *Life With Father* and *Mr. Currier and Mr.
Ives* than between the play and, say, *Red, Hot
and Blue*."

According to Mr. Crouse himself, *Life With
Father* represents "the first time my passion
for Americana in general and New York
memorabilia in particular met up with
the theatre in my professional economy."
In dramatizing the book Lindsay and Crouse
had to be extremely selective in the use
of such material, so as not to clutter up
the atmosphere: "We allowed topical references to intrude themselves into the action
only when they were essential to or had some
direct bearing on the progress of the drama."

Before *Life With Father* tagged Crouse as
a dramatist and *Arsenic and Old Lace* established him as co-producer, he had high professional ratings in the newspaper, book and
press agentry fields. In *Mr. Currier and Mr.
Ives* (1930) he chronicled the lives and times
of the two famous print-makers. Until that
year his writing had been confined largely to
newspaper work; from 1924 to 1929 his humorous column *Left At The Post* was a feature of the New York *Evening Post*. In 1931
Crouse published *It Seems Like Yesterday*
and in 1932, the year he became press agent
for the Theatre Guild, he published two books,
Murder Won't Out and *The American Keep-
sake*. That he should be drawn to *Arsenic
and Old Lace* was natural. Here was a play
that combined in one theatre piece a distinctly American flavor, deft comedy and enough
murder to satisfy the most insatiable homicide
fan.

Crouse's explanation of how and why he
and Lindsay produced *Arsenic and Old Lace,*
their first job as a producing unit, begins:
"During the past few weeks I have been
asked by the New York *World-Telegram,*
the Brooklyn Chamber of Commerce, my aunt,
Mrs. A. C. Crouse of Washington, D. C., the
Morris Plan Bank, which has perhaps the most
complete collection of my autographs, and a
large swarm of little people who keep coming out from under my rug and making faces
at me, why Howard Lindsay and I produced
Arsenic and Old Lace." In the process of
dismissing reasons why, he blandly lists the
benefits that have accrued to the collaborators as a result of this experiment, but
triumphantly concludes that the real reason

for the venture was that they were "both
nuts. I don't want to take much of the credit
on that score because I'm not very nuts. Just
a little bit. You'd hardly notice it. But that
Lindsay! He's good and crazy."

Russel Crouse was born in good mental
health on February 20, 1893, in Findlay, Ohio,
the son of Hiram Powers and Sarah (Schu-
macher) Crouse. Educated in the public
and high schools of Toledo, he began his
writing career at the age of 17 as a reporter

Vandamm

RUSSEL CROUSE

on the Cincinnati (Ohio) *Commercial-Trib-
une*. From 1911 to 1916 he worked as news
and sports reporter on the Kansas City (Missouri) *Star,* and in 1917 was political reporter
for the Cincinnati (Ohio) *Post*. He left
newspaper work to join the Navy during the
First World War, serving as yeoman 2nd
class from 1917 to 1919. At the end of his
enlistment Crouse broke into the New York
newsrooms, working in turn for the New
York *Globe,* New York *Evening Mail* and,
finally, the New York *Evening Post*.

With the production of Ward Morehouse's
play, *Gentlemen of the Press*, the newspaperman had an eight-line acting debut. It was
duly chronicled by Brooks Atkinson in an un-
subtle play upon words: "One R. Crouse,
who has been picked from the *Evening Post*
staff to bring a touch of verisimilitude to a
newspaper play, spoke his lines gently last
evening. His performance was muted as
Duse."

That was in 1928. During his brief appearance in the play Crouse continued to write his
column for the *Evening Post*, and in 1929,
another actor having taken the part in the
road company, he began writing scenarios for
short films on newspaper life. Later, when
the play was filmed, Crouse had a two-line
part to which he sometimes refers as the

CROUSE, RUSSEL—*Continued*

height of his career. "I took Marc Connelly to see the movie," he says, "and at the psychological moment Marc dropped his glasses, stooped to pick them up, and missed the entire performance."

Crouse's first attempt to do a libretto for a musical comedy was *The Gang's All Here* (1931). It had, as he put it, a run of "two consecutive weeks." But in 1933 he collaborated with Corey Ford on the book for the far more successful Joe Cook show, *Hold Your Horses.* And in addition to his sorties into the theatrical field and his books he was at this time press agent for the Theatre Guild, a job that most people would have conceded to be full time in itself.

Yet his versatility had only begun to assert itself. In 1934 Lindsay and Crouse got together for the first time, on the book of *Anything Goes,* adapted by them from the story by Guy Bolton and P. G. Wodehouse. A dream was responsible. A worried producer confided to Neysa McMein, the illustrator (see sketch this issue), that he couldn't think of a collaborator for Lindsay. Miss McMein admitted that she couldn't, either, but that night she dreamed of one, and it was Russel Crouse. Within a few days the deal was on. Percy Hammond called it "a big show." It proved a loosely plotted but properly pointed and irreverent vehicle for such talents as Ethel Merman (see sketch this issue), Victor Moore and William Gaxton, and was the first of a series of Lindsay-Crouse box-office bonanzas. In 1936 they completed *Red, Hot and Blue;* this was followed by the Ed Wynn show, *Hooray for What,* on which they teamed up with E. Y. Harburg.

In 1937 Crouse finally resigned from his press agent's job with the Guild. It was during the run of *Idiot's Delight,* and the company drew up a testimonial to the effect that, having won his spurs, Crouse was "now hereby entitled to full program credit as a qualified A No. 1 playwright, and, moreover, we, the undersigned members of the *Idiot's Delight* company, do hereby swear our love and gratitude to him to have and to hold from this day forth and forevermore, most especially because we know he's the dearest friend we've had—flood or no flood." The flood referred to occurred in Pittsburgh when the company played there in March 1937. At the time there was just the shade of a suspicion that the whole thing had been engineered by Crouse in the interests of publicity.

Then, after more dinners and farewell parties than had ever been tendered any one individual on Broadway, Crouse set out for one of his annual visits to Hollywood—his first had been in 1934. In 1937 he began his work for Paramount by co-authoring the screen play *Mountain Music;* subsequently he collaborated on *The Big Broadcast of 1938; Artists and Models Abroad* (1938); and *The Great Victor Herbert* (1939). In 1940 he and Lindsay reaped their Broadway triumph: they were given the Drama League's Roi Cooper Megrue Prize of $500 for their play, *Life*

With Father, and in the same year the Theatre Club, Incorporated, struck two medals to honor them.

Russel Crouse is agile, his bushy hair is thinning out toward the front, and he has dark eyes and a small mustache. Known to his friends as "Buck" because of his amateur buck-and-wing dancing, he is an ardent poker fan. Known also for his light touch in the usually blatant field of press-agentry, he is suspected of having had a hand in the following description of himself from an old playbill: "He has curly hair, likes huckleberry pie, makes his own clothes, and says that when he grows up he wants to be a streetcar conductor."

Crouse, who belongs to the Dutch Treat Club and is active in the Dramatists' Guild of the Authors' League, is married to Alison Smith, onetime dramatic editor of the old New York *World.* Their marriage took place on June 17, 1923. They have a house in New York and four cats, three of them moderately Persian and the fourth altogether so. On the walls are many more cats, in chromos, lithographs, prints and photographs. Usually the collaborators work in the less feline study of Lindsay's house on West 11th Street, however, Crouse sitting at the typewriter and Lindsay pacing the floor. They used to write at the latter's farm in Hunterdon County, but Crouse claimed he could not stand the noise the birds made.

Up to the time of *Arsenic and Old Lace* Lindsay had seldom attended his own openings (with the exception of *Life With Father,* in which he plays the lead), and neither member of the team had pretended to possess any backstage talent. In 1941, with two hits on their hands, they are, as it were, resting on their laurels—Lindsay busy as an actor and Crouse making the rounds of the theatres with a greater sense of ease than he could have experienced in the days when he was doing three jobs at once. "We're just lying fallow," said Lindsay between shows, "and you can imagine what a difficult jumping-off-place we're in with two such terrific hits on our hands. It's a setup that's going to be awfully hard to improve upon, even if we get up the energy to try."

References

N Y Post p11 Ap 15 '40
N Y World-Telegram p6 Mr 1 '41
Stage 15:43-6 Ag '38 il por

America's Young Men 1936-37
International Motion Picture Almanac
Who's Who in America

CROW, CARL (krō) Sept. 26, 1883- Author

Address: 969 Highland Ave, Pelham Manor, N. Y.

A "hard-headed and practical American businessman" who knows China better than most people know their own home state, for the past few years Carl Crow has been communicating what he knows to American audiences in a series of books marked by understanding and wit and a generous sympathy for the Chinese people. When *Four Hundred Million Customers* was published in 1937 in English, French, German, Swedish, Danish and Polish, it became an immediate best seller, and he has followed that success with six other books, one of which, *Meet the South Americans* (1941), turns from the Orient to look at our neighbors to the South.

Born in Highland, Missouri on September 26, 1883, the son of George Washington and Elvira Jane (Sharrock) Crow, Herbert Carl Crow was the eldest of four children. His father was a country schoolteacher, and most of his ancestors, who were all living in America during Colonial days, had been pioneer schoolteachers or preachers. None ever made money, and his father was no exception.

Carl was 16 when his father died and he had to begin making a living for himself. For a while he served as a printer's apprentice; then as a journeyman printer; and at 19 he borrowed some money and founded a weekly newspaper. It was not very successful, but he sold it at a profit, and in 1906 decided to go to the University of Missouri, having previously studied at Carleton College in Farmington, Missouri for a year. He landed in Columbia with only $7 because the friend who was taking care of his savings had spent the money!

He remained at the University until 1907, however, for a time working as a printer at 15 cents an hour, later as reporter for the *Columbian Missourian,* a paper founded by the late Dean Walter Williams and then famous as America's "Model Country Weekly." While carrying full courses at the University he acted as local editor of this paper and also as correspondent for the Chicago *Tribune,* St. Louis *Post-Dispatch,* St. Louis *Republic* and Kansas City *Star.* Instead of completing his college course he quit to become the partner of Dean Williams in the publication of the *Missourian;* then, until 1911, he served on the editorial staff of the Fort Worth *Star-Telegram.*

In 1911 he was offered a post as associate city editor of the *China Press* in Shanghai, the first American daily in China. While there he compiled and wrote *Travelers' Handbook for China* (1912), which has been a steady seller ever since. After 18 months he returned to New York, and a book written en route, *America and the Philippines,* was published in 1914. It dealt with Japanese imperialism in the Far East, particularly in relation to the United States' promise to give the Philippines their independence some day. Mr. Crow then resumed his writing for such magazines as *World's Work, Collier's, Review of Reviews* and *Outlook.*

In 1913 Crow went to Tokyo as business manager and—for a few months—as acting editor of the *Japan Advertiser.* He also acted as Tokyo correspondent for the United Press, and was credited with scooping the world on Japan's famous "21 Demands on China."

CARL CROW

In 1914 he returned to New York once more, continued his magazine writing, saw the publication of *Japan and America: a Contrast* (1916), and then went on to San Francisco. He bought a small fruit ranch which he ran very profitably until America's entry into the First World War brought him back to China as Far Eastern representative of the Committee on Public Information (1916-18). Still in China after the Armistice, he founded and edited the Shanghai *Evening Post* (with which he is no longer connected), became the proprietor of an advertising agency in Shanghai (1919-37), published two small magazines about travel in China and directed an anti-Communist campaign financed by foreign businessmen in Shanghai.

In 1925 he married Helen Marie Hanniger. (She died November 23, 1941.) It was August 1937 when they returned to America, where Crow has since divided his time between free-lance writing and his business as an advertising agent. He revisited China in 1938, however, and in the autumn of 1940 was in South America.

His first best seller, *Four Hundred Million Customers,* was largely a digest of letters written over a period of about 20 years in answer to inquiries from clients about the possibility of selling goods to the Chinese. These inquiries showed so much widespread ignorance and misinformation about the Chinese market that Crow thought it worthwhile writing a book which would discuss these problems in non-technical language but from the point of view of practical experience. Lin Yutang says: "There isn't a dull page in it. . . It trips lightly along on the surface of everyday business facts in the tenor of pleasant after-dinner shop talk. One never loses the sense of reality or of the living medium." Most critics were delighted by its humor, "as

CROW, CARL—*Continued*

often at the expense of the author and his clients as of the Chinese."

This book, for most readers Carl Crow's introduction to the American public, was followed in 1937 by *I Speak for the Chinese,* dealing with the war in China, and by *Master Kung; the Story of Confucius* (1938). In 1939 came *He Opened the Door of Japan,* also published in London as *Harris of Japan,* a life of Townsend Harris; and *The Chinese Are Like That,* published in London under the title *My Friends, the Chinese,* which described aspects of Chinese life little known here with the humor and informality which his readers had grown to expect. *Foreign Devils in the Flowery Kingdom* (1940) was described by one reviewer as a "rich and eventful story of the foreigner in China, from Marco Polo's discovery of macaroni to what Crow calls the end of 'the era of the foreign devils' in 1937." And *Meet the South Americans,* published in the fall of 1941, was written with the hope that "this book will help to arouse more interest in South America; will cause more books to be written and read; will cause more people to visit this long-neglected area which is destined to be the continent of the future."

Mr. Crow has known Chinese war lords and businessmen and bandits, men in the streets of the great harbor cities and men in the tiny villages of the interior (though he has apparently come into contact with few Chinese scholars). He has known them and liked them and been willing to learn from them, and he discusses them with a "peculiarly American philosophy that is reminiscent of the late Will Rogers at his best." He has always been firmly opposed to appeasing Japan—so much so that in 1938 one critic wondered (*I Speak for the Chinese*) "why Mr. Crow has nowhere reminded us that imperialism in China has not been exclusively a Japanese and German phenomenon . . . why the Chinese currency reform of 1935 is described without reference to the American silver purchase policy which made it necessary—a course which would involve untoward reflection on the conduct of the United States—although Japan is justly pilloried for its attempt to sabotage that reform"; and regretted Mr. Crow's tacit advocacy of intervention when speaking of "the peace-at-any-price Americans who virtuously sidestep present problems for future generations to settle." Apparently most Americans have now come to agree with Mr. Crow, however. Since Japan joined the Axis Carl Crow has written several articles on her plans and the possibilities of their success.

Carl Crow's hobbies are gardening, raising chickens, collecting old books and exploring new places in China, in all of which Mrs. Crow was an enthusiastic collaborator.

References

> Newsweek 11:31 My 16 '38 por
> Pub W 133:1106 Mr 5 '38 por
> Sat R Lit 17:8 D 4 '37 por; 17:18 D 18 '37

Scholastic 32:12 F 26 '38 por
Time 31:75 My 16 '38 por
Who's Who Among North American Authors
Who's Who in America

CSÁKY, ISTVÁN, COUNT *See* Csáky, S., Count

CSÁKY, STEPHEN, COUNT (chô′kĭ) 1894(?)—Jan. 27, 1941 Hungarian Foreign Minister since 1938; diplomat and statesman; was firm believer in close friendship between Hungary and the Axis; threw his country's lot in with Central Powers by signing anti-Comintern pact in 1939.

References

> Life 8:18 Ja 22 '40 por; 10:72-3 Je 9 '41 por
> N Y Herald Tribune p4 D 12 '40
> PM p4 S 1 '40
>
> International Who's Who

Obituaries

> N Y Times p1, 6 Ja 27 '41 por
> Time 37:21 F 3 '41

CUBBERLEY, ELLWOOD P(ATTERSON) (kŭb′ẽr-lĭ) June 6, 1868—Sept. 14, 1941 Dean emeritus of the School of Education of Stanford University since 1933; began his association with Stanford in 1898; made professor in 1906 and dean of the School of Education in 1917; retired from active teaching in 1933; donor of the $535,000 School of Education Building; author or editor of many books.

References

> Am Mag 122:109 D '36 por
> El Sch J 33:249-50 D '32
> Harvard Ed R 9:43-62 Ja '39
> Lit Digest 123:22 Ja 9 '37 il por
> Nat Educ Assn J 22:44 F '33 por; 28:95 Mr '39 por
> Sch & Soc 17:687 Je 23 '23; 37:714-15 Je 3 '33; 37:738-40 Je 10 '33; 37:783-5 Je 17 '33
> Sierra Ed News 35:11 Ja '39 il por
> Time 32:32+ N 21 '38
>
> Almack, J. C. ed. Modern School Administration p349-77 1933
> American Men of Science
> Leaders in Education 1941
> Who's Who Among North American Authors
> Who's Who in America

Obituaries

> N Y Times p17 S 15 '41 por
> Sch & Soc 54:214 S 20 '41
> Time 38:42 S 22 '41

CUNNINGHAM, SIR ANDREW BROWNE 1883- British commander in chief in the Mediterranean

Address: The Palace House, Bishop's Waltham, Hants, England

The outstanding British admiral in the Second World War is Sir Andrew Browne

Cunningham, who as commander in chief of the fleet in the Mediterranean scored two great successes and continues to aim for more. It was he who headed the fleet that crippled the Italians at Taranto in November 1940 and he who brought the Battle of the Ionian Sea to an apparently successful conclusion in March 1941. Later disasters—at Greece and at Crete—in which a tremendous amount of tonnage was lost, were blamed on lack of heavy equipment. It was he, too, who, after British attacks on Libya in the fall of 1941, made the Army job easier by his sudden swoops on Axis convoys bound for the African front.

The man who mopped up the Italians in the Eastern Mediterranean and is trying in 1941 to keep the Mediterranean clear is supposed to know this sea so well that his men used to insist that when Mussolini referred to "mare nostrum" (our sea) he really meant "mine and Cunningham's." Brusque and taciturn even in relaxation, while on duty Admiral Cunningham is "short, tight-mouthed, efficient as a gyro-compass and untiring as the Mediterranean sun." According to one report this expert seaman "has such a loud voice for commands that his underlings say that inter-ship signals in battle are just a waste of effort; and he is such an expert navigator that his crews say he could cut an egg in half with a battleship."

He has been sailing the seas since he was a young boy. The son of the late D. J. Cunningham, professor of anatomy at Dublin and Edinburgh, and Elizabeth Cumming (Browne) Cunningham, he was sent first to Edinburgh Academy and then to Stubbington House, Fareham. He left school to train on *H. M. S. Britannia*, and in 1898, at the age of 15, entered the Royal Navy. Cunningham's first active duty was on the South Africa station, and during the Boer War he was a midshipman on the cruiser *Doris*. He continued to serve in the Navy, mostly on small ships, and was rapidly promoted.

Before he was 30 Cunningham was in command of the 900-ton *Scorpion* and when England entered the First World War proceeded to establish a reputation for dash and bravery. With this ship he harried many enemy ships during the Gallipoli campaign; with it he whipped into the Sea of Marmora to sink a disabled enemy submarine. In return the Government in 1915 awarded him a D. S. O. and gave him command of the destroyer *Termagent* and a place in the famous Dover Patrol. This Patrol, which kept the channel clear for Britain and raided enemy harbors on the nearby Belgian coast, offered its members one of the most hazardous jobs in the Navy. Cunningham did his job well and in 1919, after the War ended, was made a captain and awarded a bar to his D. S. O. A year later he received a second bar.

His assignments from then on were mostly in the Mediterranean, mostly aboard destroyers. By 1932 he had become a Naval A. D. C. to the King and the next year he was made

SIR ANDREW BROWNE CUNNINGHAM

a rear admiral and given command of the destroyer flotillas of the Mediterranean fleet. In 1937 he was promoted again, this time to vice-admiral. His command was shifted to the Battle-Cruiser Squadron and broadened to include the position of second in command of the whole Mediterranean fleet.

Then in 1938 came Cunningham's first period of duty ashore, as Lord Commissioner of the Admiralty and Deputy Chief of the Naval Staff. This assignment lasted only a year— Admiral Cunningham, always a foe of red tape, makes no secret of his dislike of work ashore. Made a knight (K. C. B.) in 1939, he left the Admiralty in that year, promoted to the position of commander in chief of the Mediterranean. This was just in time for the Second World War, and his flagship, the reconditioned *Warspite*, was soon smashing through heavy German fire to storm Narvik Fjord. From Narvik it sailed to the Mediterranean.

At the same time that Admiral Sir Andrew Browne Cunningham (referred to as "A. B. C.") was chalking up his initial successes in the Second World War on the sea, his younger brother, Lieutenant General Alan Gordon Cunningham, was doing important work in East Africa. It was he who commanded the "spectacular" British assault which in March 1941 resulted in the capture of Magadiscio, the capital of Italian Somaliland, and he was at the head of the British advance into Libya in November 1941. Later he was relieved of his command because of ill health. The friendly rivalry between the army and navy branches of the Cunningham family is carried on into their life on leave. Andrew Browne and Alan Gordon vie in growing the best flowers on their Hampshire estate, in catching the biggest fish, in telling the tallest tales, in extolling the virtues of their dogs (Andrew's is a Scotty; Alan's an Airedale). Sir Andrew's

CUNNINGHAM, SIR ANDREW—*Cont.*

hope, once the fighting is over, is to retire to this estate, to his wife, Nona Christine (Byatt) Cunningham, whom he married in 1929, and to gardening competitions with his brother.

References

Christian Sci Mon p5 N 14 '40 por
Cur Hist 52:33-4 My '41
Newsweek 17:27 F 17 '41 por
Scholastic 38:5 Ap 14 '41 por
Time 37:34 F 17 '41 por (cover); 37:24
　Mr 10 '41 por; 37:27-8 Ap 7 '41 por;
　37:38+ Je 9 '41
Chatterton, E. K.　Leaders of the Royal
　Navy pam　1940
Who's Who

CUNNINGHAM, WILLIAM FRANCIS

May 18, 1885—Nov. 19, 1940　Pathologist who was early investigator of Hodgkins disease; associated with the Department of Experimental Pathology at the College of Physicians and Surgeons, Columbia University.

References

American Medical Directory
Leaders in Education 1941

Obituaries

N Y Herald Tribune p24 N 20 '40

CURRAN, PEARL GILDERSLEEVE

(kûr'răn)　1876(?)—Apr. 16, 1941　Composer of popular and concert ballads and religious songs; two of her songs were introduced to the public by Enrico Caruso and John Charles Thomas; wrote *Life, Nocturne, The Best Is Yet To Be, Rain, The Lord's Prayer, The Lord Is My Shepherd,* and *The Crucifixion and Resurrection.*

References

American Women
Wier, A. E. ed.　Macmillan Encyclo-
　pedia of Music and Musicians 1938

Obituaries

N Y Herald Tribune p22 Ap 17 '41

CURRIE, LAUCHLIN (BERNARD)　Oct. 8, 1902-　Administrative assistant to President Roosevelt

Address: b. The White House, Washington, D. C.; h. 3132 P St, N. W., Washington, D. C.

Lauchlin Currie is one of President Roosevelt's six administrative assistants, probably the most anonymous of these men who are chosen, according to the President, because of their "passion for anonymity." "Polite, diplomatic and unassuming," it is his job to keep "ideas flowing smoothly back and forth between Roosevelt and Administration officials, big and little."

In the beginning of 1941 these duties were extended, and much of his anonymity dispensed with, when Lauchlin Currie was sent to China on a special mission, similar to Harry Hopkins' (see sketch this issue) mission to England.

He returned in March of the same year to make his report. Although it has not been made public, most commentators agree that Currie, while in the East, studied China's economic structure in general and its special problems of currency and transportation in order to determine the best way for the United States to help the Chungking Government. This interpretation of his mission was given weight by Currie's own remarks while there. After conferring with Chinese leaders, he called China an "outpost of the world's present struggle for democracy" and talked of his country's responsibility to aid it.

Time (April 14, 1941) states that back of the reforms of the Kuomintang in April, "letter and spirit, one of the strongest influences was the United States, represented by the bespectacled face of Lauchlin Currie." It also states that Currie helped clear up the Communist problem by suggesting that Chiang Kai-shek's Government "raise needed revenue and undercut Communist influence by taxing the landlords while feeding and pleasing the peasants."

This short, Scotch, graying economist, sometimes called the No. 1 United States disciple of John Maynard Keynes (see sketch this issue), has been working for the United States Government since 1934. He was born in West Dublin, Nova Scotia, the son of Lauchlin and Alice (Eisenhauer) Currie, and was educated at the London School of Economics, which awarded him a B. S. degree in 1925. He immediately came to the United States (he was naturalized in 1934) and settled down at Harvard. In 1927, the year he was married to Dorothy York Bacon (they have two sons), he became an instructor at the University and for seven years taught Harvard boys "that the purpose of business is profit." At the same time he was working for his Ph. D., which Harvard gave him in 1931, and acting as professor of international economics (in 1933 and 1934) at the Fletcher Graduate School of Law and Diplomacy in West Medford, Massachusetts. He was busy outside the academic world as consultant to the Kendall Company of Boston, producer of cotton products.

Currie's reputation spread far beyond Boston. His classes were well known; his articles on monetary policy, credit, loans, income were widely read; his book, *The Supply and Control of Money in the United States* (1934) became a standard work on the subject. It was not an unexpected move when Secretary of the Treasury Morgenthau persuaded him to come to Washington in 1934 as senior analyst. His appointment later in the same year to the position of assistant director of research and statistics for the Federal Reserve Board was even less unexpected.

In this position Currie won enthusiastic recognition inside "political brain-picking circles," but his highly technical duties were not such as to make him known to Washington and the public at large. It was in 1938 that he began to give evidences of his growing importance. In that year he put forward a plan to solve railroad troubles by a lend-lease procedure by which the roads would get equip-

LAUCHLIN CURRIE

ment in much the same way that Britain gets war goods under the Lend-Lease Bill. In that year, too, he wrote an "influential memo" on the causes of the recession, in which, among other things, he discussed social security taxes and pointed out that compensatory Federal spending to stimulate heavy industry might be more flexible if concentrated "in large part outside the regular budget."

A year later, in May 1939, the nation at large began to take notice of him when he gave his testimony, heavily authenticated by charts, before the Temporary National Economic Committee. In this testimony he showed that investment still follows production, not the editorial page; that since 1932 State and local governments have been piling up savings and that the net Federal investment has to be at least $1,000,000,000 to provide equivalent purchasing power. Then, in July 1939, he was made Roosevelt's personal economic adviser and administrative assistant.

In Washington, Currie is known as the man who had never in his life been in an airplane until his recent flight to China, as "an inflexible unenthusiast, and as the man who dictated his abstruse economic drafts while lying on a sofa, preferably with his eyes closed."

References

Business Week p7 O 14 '39 por; p52 F 1 '41
Life 10:100-3 My 5 '41 por
Nation's Bus 29:48+ Ag '41 por
N Y Sun p20 Ja 21 '41
PM p6 F 24 '41 pors; p12 Mr 24 '41 pors
Time 34:52 Jl 24 '39 por; 37:15 Mr 3 '41 por; 37:16 Mr 24 '41 por; 37:37+ Ap 14 '41
Who's Who in America

CURRY, JOHN STEUART Nov. 14, 1897- Artist

Address: b. University of Wisconsin, Madison, Wis; h. 432 Lorch St, Madison, Wis.

"The theme I have chosen," John Steuart Curry said when discussing his sketches for the murals at the Kansas Capitol, "is the struggle of man with nature. This struggle has been a determining factor in my art expression." Along with Grant Wood and Thomas Hart Benton, Curry is a painter of the Midwest, "his work as American as a Kansas wheat field." In it are recorded the tremendous sweep of thunderstorms over the prairie, the cataclysms of flood and cyclone, the expanse of fields ripe with grain.

Often Curry's conception is big—in *The Line Storm*, a presentation of destructive forces "done from the memory of many such storms before which we fled"; in *Mississippi*, a strong study of natural forces on a rampage; in *Kansas Wheat Ranch*, a painting "heavy with a feeling of the tremendous acreage of the desert of wheat." Often it is vigorous and robust—in animal studies like *Hogs Fighting* or *Hen and Hawk*. There are times, too, when it is precise and even delicate, as in *Osage Orange* or *Kansas Cornfield*. But no matter what the conception, no matter what the subject, Curry's work is painted with "veracious intensity." It is real, free from symbols, romanticism, propaganda, irony. "I am not the painter for people who want pretty pictures," Curry says.

Most critics—with the possible exception of Ralph Pearson, who feels that Curry's work lacks "visual music," that with all its virtues it is still illustration—agree more or less with Grant Wood that "when Curry is right he is the most moving painter alive," and that when he is not right he is completely undistinguished. His work is uneven, "ranging from the most majestic landscapes in contemporary art to commissioned portraits of surprising mediocrity." In actual technique there are, according to Royal Cortissoz, "roughnesses, moments when the drawing is a trifle too casual," and yet these "cannot counterbalance the essential directness and force of what he does."

This painter of the Midwest was born in Kansas, brought up there and first painted there. His birthplace was Dunavant, a tiny town that no longer exists, and his heritage was a farming one. His father, Smith Curry, lived and worked on a farm for most of his life, as had his father and grandfather before him. But unlike many other farmers Smith Curry managed to travel around a bit, and when he married Margaret Steuart in 1895 he took her to Scotland for a wedding trip.

John was the first-born of five children. "I was raised," he recalls, "on hard work and the shorter catechism. . . We were up at four o'clock the year round, feeding the steers, planting and plowing corn, cutting hay and wheat; and in the school months doing half a day's work before we rode to town on horseback to our lessons. But we didn't mind. It

Peter A. Juley & Son

JOHN STEUART CURRY

was the only life we knew—and I had a good constitution." Young John did more than farm work. He had begun to draw, his mother says, "when he wore skirts and curls." He "was always at it. He drew the things he saw on the farm and the old Northwestern express that roared by at dusk. And one winter, after the corn had been laid by, we went to Arizona, where John's pictures of cowboys, bucking bronchos and long horned cattle were much prized by the pupils of the country school."

At the county high school Curry, with his powerful shoulders and firm build, was an outstanding athlete, a mediocre student and a devoted artist. He left there in 1916 to study at the Kansas City Art Institute, fortified by money earned working as a section hand on the railroad, a suit of city clothes and art knowledge gained from studying reproductions of the Old Masters which his mother had gathered on her wedding trip. He stayed in Kansas City only a month and then moved on to the Chicago Art Institute, where he studied for two years, earning his way as a bus boy in a cafeteria. From Chicago he went into the Army as a private during the War and then in 1919 entered Geneva College in Pennsylvania as a special student of art. Here he distinguished himself rather more, it is reported, as a star halfback.

From Geneva College, Curry went to Tenafly, New Jersey to work in the studio of Harvey Dunn, an important magazine artist. Eventually he was offered a commission by the *Saturday Evening Post*. "I had no idea of the way in which illustrations were manufactured," he confesses. "The subject was a passenger train and I just went ahead and made a picture of the old Northwestern express." For this, his first published work, Curry received $25.

For the next five years or so Curry supported himself and his wife, Clara H. (Derrick) Curry, whom he married in 1923, by doing illustrations for the *Saturday Evening Post*, *St. Nicholas* and other magazines. "Never a shining light in the field of popular illustration," commissions began to drop off about 1925. Curry had been doing independent pictures during these years and when he saw he wasn't going to be able to get along with his magazine work he borrowed $1,000 and went to Paris with his wife in 1926. He stayed there a year, studying at the Russian Academy, and returned in 1927 a vastly improved draughtsman, uninfluenced by cubism or impressionism. Then came some time studying at the Art Students League in New York, where he not only painted but began, under the tutelage of Charles Locke, to make lithographs, a medium in which he has worked on and off ever since. In fact, it has been said that "the precision of his line, his concentration on design, his economy of means are better realized in these graphic works than in his paintings."

But lithographs were only a side line then to Curry. In 1928 he borrowed money from his brother to buy a small house near Westport, Connecticut and retired there, determined that he would paint something good. On his first trial he created *Baptism in Kansas*, which was "instantly acclaimed as the work of a new master of American genre" and bought by Gertrude Whitney (see sketch this issue) for her museum. She also subsidized him for the next two years, years in which he produced important work.

By 1931 Curry was holding his first Kansas exhibition, sponsored by William Allen White, and creating a furor in his home state. They called his *Baptism in Kansas* "drab," his *Hogs Killing Rattlesnake* "unnecessary," his *Tornado* "uncivic." But the East was more impressed. *Tornado* won second prize in the Carnegie International Exhibition of 1933; *Spring Shower* was acquired by the Metropolitan Museum; and other works like *The Gospel Train* and *the Return of Private Davis* won critical acclaim. Museums all over began to buy his work and by 1935 even the Kansas State College had acquired a Curry. Curry shrugged this purchase off as he had shrugged off the reception to his 1931 exhibition. "Why should Kansas want any of my work?" he asked. "It has Kansas."

Before this, however, Curry had forsaken scenes of his home state to paint circus pictures, "the finest thus far done in America," according to one critic. In 1932 he had accompanied the Ringling Brothers, Barnum and Bailey Circus on its New England tour and produced from it paintings of acrobats and animals and one of his most effective canvases, *The Flying Codonas*. He had also married Kathleen Muriel Gould of London in 1934 after the death of his first wife in 1932, decorated the auditorium of the Westport High School, and become a teacher at the Art Students League.

By 1935 Curry's position was established, and in that year the Federal Government ordered two large murals for the Department of Justice Building in Washington. It took Curry two years to complete these studies of *Western Migration,* portrayals of the pioneers on a grand scale. Then in 1936 the University of Wisconsin, "undertaking to give added impetus to regional art as a force for rural as well as urban culture in this Middle West area," appointed him "artist in residence" and gave him a four-year contract at $4,000 a year. In the fall of 1937 Curry moved to Wisconsin, promptly painted "Professor Curry" on his garbage can and proceeded to invest the college with a feeling for art. He has done paintings of current agricultural topics, given informal instruction to the students, lectured on art. With his "face-cracking, cherubic grin and piping voice," he is popular among the students. Curry has continued with his own work, too, doing oils of football players, of farm stock and of rural scenes that are considered by some critics to be somewhat weaker than his Kansas paintings.

He has also continued to paint murals. Shortly after he came to Wisconsin, Curry was commissioned by the State of Kansas to paint murals for the Capitol which would depict Kansas "in a sane and sensible manner." He began work on these in 1938, and in 1939 also did murals for the General Land Office in the Interior Building in Washington—murals called *Oklahoma Land Rush* and *The Homestead and the Building of the Barbed Wire Fences,* painted in the standard Curry colors of reds for dust and soil, gold for sunlight, green for fields of grain. In the summer of 1941 his Kansas murals, by that time partially completed, caused considerable controversy ("hideous things," one State legislator called them) because of his depiction of John Brown. But harsh words didn't keep the legislature from voting him money enough to finish them. In these murals, as in all the work he is doing now and plans to do, Curry has demonstrated that whether he is painting of the past or of the present, direct from the scene or from imagination or memory, "it is everyday human material that lends my brush its fill of inspiration."

References

Art Digest 9:29 S '35; 11:18 O 1 '36 il; 11:13 Ag '37; 13:21 Ap 1 '39 il
Demcourier 11:1-24 il por Ap '41
Life 7:34 D 25 '39 por; 8:61 My 6 '40 por
Lit Digest 122:22+ O 17 '36 il
London Studio 13(Studio 113):326-30 Je '37 il
Newsweek 5:24-5 F 16 '35 il; 18:58 Jl 7 '41 il
Scrib Mag 103:36-41+ Ja '38 il self por
Time 31:32-3 Ja 24 '38 self por; 34:36+ Ag 28 '39 il
Bower, W. ed. New Directions p303-20 1937
Who's Who in America
Who's Who in American Art

CURTIN, JOHN (kûr'tĭn) Jan. 8, 1885- Prime Minister of Australia

Address: b. Parliament House, Canberra, Australian Capitol Territory; h. 24 Jarrad St, Cottesloe, Western Australia

Australian News & Information Bureau
JOHN CURTIN

Bulletin: On October 2, 1941 John Curtin accepted a commission to form a new Australian Government and four days later organized his Cabinet, with himself as Minister for Defense Coordination as well as Prime Minister. It was the first Labor Government in Australia since 1932. The Cabinet of Arthur W. Fadden, which followed that of Robert G. Menzies (see sketch this issue) after the latter's resignation on August 28, had fallen after having been defeated on a motion regarded as a vote of confidence, 36 to 33.

From July 1941 issue:

John Curtin, leader of Australia's Federal Parliamentary Opposition since October 1935, has repeatedly refused to form a National Government with Australia's two conservative parties, the United Australia and the United Country parties. Instead he has chosen to preserve Labor's political independence and to use his party's strong Parliamentary position (the War Government has a majority of only two votes) to get more social legislation.

Yet under his leadership both Parliamentary Labor and the Australian Council of Trades Unions have declared unqualified support in the War against the Axis, and Curtin himself has entered the War Advisory Council. When, after the Allied defeat in Greece, "much of the Australian press, a majority of Australians and almost all of the continent's vociferous Laborites wanted to know why the Anzacs had been sent into the hopeless Greek campaign in the first

CURTIN, JOHN—*Continued*

place," it was Curtin who answered them and answered the enemy propagandists who wrote of the apparent defection of Australia in headlines like "British Empire Crumbling to Pieces."

To his own countrymen he said that many of their statements were "mischievous and unwarranted." To the world at large he announced: "As leader of Australian Labor, I say to Germany and Japan: Australia and the workers of Australia unite in determination to give their all in the War. We are pledged to devote the nation's entire resources to this and bear willingly any burden imposed upon us to preserve our security and to demonstrate to the Empire and our Allies that we shall not be found wanting in this crucial struggle for human liberty."

John Curtin was born at Creswick, Victoria, in the Ballarat gold fields, the son of John and Katherine (Bourke) Curtin. After receiving his education at State schools, he quickly engaged in labor journalism. In 1911 he became secretary of the powerful Victorian Timber Workers' Union and joined the political theorists who grouped around the *Labor Call*, the State's leading Labor newspaper, published at Melbourne. In 1917 he moved to Perth, West Australia to edit the Westralian *Worker*, and he remained the guiding spirit of this paper until 1928. He had seen the Labor movement split on the issue of conscription in 1917 (he had been one of the leaders of the anti-conscription fight), and his aim now was to give Labor a theoretical structure that would survive similar issues. To this end he published a long series of pamphlets, the most important of which were *The Heritage* (1927), and a booklet, *Australia's Economic Crisis* (1931). And always he remained the articulate exponent of the Australian Labor Party's dual traditions of nationalism and theoretical socialism.

Curtin left the *Worker* to take his first full-time political position, as member of the House of Representatives. He had represented his country before that—in 1924, when he was a delegate to the League's International Labor Conference, and in 1927 and 1928, when he was a member of the Royal Commission on Family Allowances. He stayed in Parliament until 1931, and during that time was a member of the Joint Committee on Public Works (1929-39). From 1933 to 1935 he was State Advocate for Government of Western Australia to the Commonwealth Grants Commission; in 1934 he re-entered the House of Representatives. One year later Curtin became the leader of the Opposition, and in that position has maintained a certain detachment from the rough and ready politics of industrial labor which led many to accept him as the Labor Party's philosopher. Since 1940 he has been a member of the Australian War Council.

Mr. Curtin was married to Elsie Needham in 1917 and has one son and one daughter. Once an ardent cricket player and footballer, today his recreations, when he has time for any, are swimming and walking. He is a member of the Australian Workers Union and of the Australian Journalists Association.

References

> N Y Herald Tribune p3 O 4 '41 por
> Who's Who
> Who's Who in Australia

CUSHING, CHARLES C(YPRIAN) S(TRONG) Oct. 27, 1879—Mar. 6, 1941 American playwright; known professionally as Tom Cushing; first represented on Broadway as the author of *Sari*, a musical comedy, in 1912; was co-author with Winchell Smith of *Thank You* and with David Belasco of *Laugh, Clown, Laugh;* himself wrote the adaptation of Blasco Ibañez's novel, *Blood and Sand*, and many other plays; was scenarist in Hollywood.

References

> Mantle, B. Contemporary American Playwrights 1938
> Who's Who in America
> Who's Who in the Theatre

Obituaries

> N Y Times p21 Mr 7 '41
> Variety 142:54 Mr 12 '41

CUSHING, TOM *See* Cushing, C. C. S.

CZETTEL, LADISLAS (chĕt'tĕl lä'dĭs-läs) Costume and fashion designer

Address: b. c/o Constance Hope Associates, Inc, 29 W. 57th St, New York City; h. 168 E. 63rd St, New York City

"I create subconsciously out of my soul," explains Ladislas Czettel, designer of costumes for the Metropolitan Opera House and a well known creator of modern gowns in the United States, when asked where he gets his ideas. But if it is costumes for the Metropolitan that he is designing, a great deal of study of the history of the period, the country, the people and the customs precedes the creation.

Mr. Czettel designed the 570 costumes used in Verdi's *The Masked Ball*, which opened the 1940 to 1941 Metropolitan Opera season. Since he had received the assignment only five weeks in advance he had to work day and night in order to complete the costumes in time. And before he could begin designing it was necessary for him to do some research, for every item in the production had to be entirely new. This was the first time *The Masked Ball*, which had not been done at the Metropolitan for twenty-four years, was being given in its original setting, the eighteenth century Swedish court of King Gustavus III, instead of in the usual Puritan Boston.

Before Mr. Czettel could begin on his assignment it was necessary for him to find out what was being worn in Sweden during the latter part of the eighteenth century. "The fashion of today," he has said, "becomes the costume of tomorrow." And so it was the fashion of the eighteenth century Swedish court and the history and customs of the people of that country that he had to study, in order to design the costumes for "tomorrow's" opera.

But he had some help. "In designing the costumes for *The Masked Ball,* I must confess," he said, "that I have enjoyed the assistance of a distinguished collaborator—no less a personage than the late Gustavus III of Sweden!" When Czettel went to the New York Public Library to do research on the period he found that the Swedish King had been a designer and had left original sketches of the dress of his day, both that of the court and of the peasants, and copies of these sketches were at the 42nd Street Library.

Mr. Czettel's work was not finished when he had completed his designs for the 570 costumes. He has to be on hand during the production of an opera to see that the costumes are all right and that the performers have make-up and hairdresses according to instruction. Every change of costume must have his approval before the actor goes on the stage. "Not until the last change has been made do I breathe freely," the designer has confided.

Born in Budapest, Hungary, Ladislas Czettel had had a successful career before coming to this country in 1936. When he was only three years old he began sketching. When he was five he designed a wedding dress for his grandfather's cook. By the time he was 12 he was designing clothes for his mother, and when he was 15 he did costumes for Sári Fedák, the second Mrs. Molnár, the great Hungarian operetta star. "I always wanted to be a designer," Mr. Czettel explains, "and I never had a 'second choice.'" As a little boy he dressed many dolls in all kinds of fantastic costumes. Today in the Vienna State Library there are other dolls, 20,000 of them, each about a foot high, which are dressed in exact replicas, accurate in every detail, of costumes and dresses that he has designed.

He studied first at the Academy of Art in Munich. Then at the age of 16 he went to Paris, where he became the only pupil of Leon Bakst, the famed designer for the Russian Ballet. Bakst introduced him to Poiret, who launched him on his career. For 12 years he was head designer of the Vienna State Opera, and during that time he created costumes for hundreds of glamorous divas. He designed also for the Moss-Empire Theatrical Corporation, the Gaumont-British Film Company and Max Reinhardt's Theatres in Berlin, Vienna, Salzburg. The first designs by him widely shown in the United States were in the film version of Bernard Shaw's *Pygmalion.*

In 1941 Mr. Czettel is designing for the Metropolitan Opera Company for the third season, and by February 1941 had done costumes for *The Daughter of the Regiment* as well as for *The Masked Ball.* In order to work in this country he had to join the stage designers' union, and to qualify for that had to pass an eight-hour examination. Prior to

LADISLAS CZETTEL

this season he did, among other costumes, those for *Falstaff, Thaïs, The Wedding of Figaro,* and costumes for Lotte Lehmann (see sketch this issue) in *Der Rosenkavalier,* Kerstin Thorborg in *Tannhäuser,* Grace Moore in *Faust,* Jan Kiepura in *Manon.* For the Allied Relief Ball of 1940 he designed costumes for Mrs. Edward Warburg, Mrs. Howard Dietz, Mrs. Irving Berlin, Mrs. George Kaufman and others. For the Beaux Arts Ball (1940) one of his creations was a dress for a five-and-ten-cent store salesgirl, at a cost of $7.28.

But costume designing is only one of his activities. He is also an "ace-high designer of *haute couture,*" and has created clothes for many prominent women here and abroad, including Countess Esterhazy, Princess Elizabeth Bourbon, Lady Dorothy Meynell, Mrs. Herbert Lehman, Marlene Dietrich, Lady Chichester, Mrs. Wood Halifax and a number of others. Late in 1940 he designed a group of day and evening clothes for Henri Bendel's exclusive 57th Street specialty shop in New York, and he is now working on another collection for that shop. In addition he lectures on these two separate and distinct phases of designing at the New School for Social Research, where he had a one-man show. He holds the honorary degree of Doctor of Arts from the Berlin State Art Academy.

Though none of Mr. Czettel's 20,000 Viennese dolls has been shown in this country designs of both his costumes and his modern gowns have been exhibited at the Museum of Modern Art (New York City), he has shown sketches at the Museum of the City of New York and in two Scenic Artists shows, and the American Federation of Arts has exhibited his designs from coast to coast.

(Continued next page)

CZETTEL, LADISLAS—*Continued*

References

Cue 9 :22 N 30 '40 il por
Harper's Bazaar 74 :98 D '40 il
N Y Times p21 N 2 '39; p14-15 D 1
'40 il
Opera News 5 :8-9 D 9 '40 il
Vehanen, K. Marian Anderson 1941

DACHÉ, LILLY (dä'shä') Hat designer
Address: b. 78 E. 56th St, New York City;
h. Bedford Village, N. Y.

LILLY DACHÉ

As Lilly Daché puts it: "A hat that is
well designed never goes out of fashion. . ;
I wear some of mine three and four years."
Perhaps that accounts for the number of
customers who are willing to pay $25 and
more for an original Lilly Daché creation.
This hard-working, quick-tempered Frenchwoman designs some 9,000 hats a year—hats
that go into 47 department stores as well as
into her own 56th Street shop. And if she
has begun to think of millinery as art rather
than as merely an unusually profitable business, she has some excuse: on April 29, 1941
she was one of the recipients of an American Design Award of $1,000 (sponsored by
Lord & Taylor and inaugurated in 1937) for
her creation of the half-hat, "which counter-
acted the hatless craze." At that time she
was also praised for having originated the
turban fashion of the last few years and for
conspicuous bravery in adoption of new materials, even those which she has difficulty in
pronouncing. (She introduced plastic viny-
lite in January, although she still calls hats
"'ots.")

Lilly Daché has been displaying a flair for
original hats ever since the ripe age of 10, when
her mother ordered a traveling suit for her:
black and white checked skirt, bright red
jacket. Lilly promptly stopped in at a shop
where men's bicycle caps were made and ordered
a red one to go with the suit. It was an
unheard-of idea in her native town of Beigles,
France, and one that was never consummated
because the incredulous shop owner went to
Mme. Daché for confirmation. But to this
day the visored cap is her idea of a smart and
correct travel hat, and no collection of hers
is ever launched that doesn't include one in
some variation or another.

Her talents for design probably came from
her mother, who had married a middling prosperous farmer of Beigles. "She was the most
extravagant woman," says Lilly. "Very pretty
and very proud of it, she loved clothes passionately and designed her own—rather startling
ones, but lovely. She used to send to Paris
for handwoven linens and all kinds of special
materials for her clothes." Lilly would save the
scraps and sew them into doll's dresses and
hats. (She is left-handed, by the way.) There
were trips to Paris, too, when two exceptionally good crop years swelled the coffers, for
Mère Daché was never particularly intrigued
with being merely the wife of a farmer.

Lilly hated school bitterly and played hooky
so constantly that when she was 14 her parents
refused to waste money on books for her any
more. (Now she studies something all the
time—at present she has three art lessons a
week.) She wanted to be an actress, and would
put on the usual backyard plays—hers always
were tear-jerking tragedies about a woman
whose husband deserted her. But she wanted
most of all to be independent, and took the
first opportunity to get herself apprenticed to
an aunt in Bordeaux who was a milliner.
Next she begged until the aunt arranged an
apprenticeship for her at Réboux's in Paris,
and was a midinette there for four years.
Before coming to the United States she also
worked briefly for another famous milliner
whom Mme. Daché will not name because
she was so cruel to her apprentices.

Lilly Daché arrived in New York on September 13, 1924 with $15 and the names of two
stores—R. H. Macy and Henri Bendel. At
Macy's she was promptly hired as a salesgirl in millinery. There she sold a lot of hats,
but couldn't understand the intricacies of writing sales slips, and was finally fired after getting
into an argument with a floorwalker over her
mistakes. Next she worked for a hole-in-the-
wall milliner at 77th Street and Broadway.
She earned $25 a week, saved $15, and after
10 weeks bought the place for $100. She had
no capital, no stock, no "collection," but she
had her methods. When a woman came in for
a hat and asked to see models, Miss Daché
went into a Gallic rage and said: "But Madame!
I wouldn't think of letting you wear a hat
that someone else has. I weel design something special for you!" With the $2 deposit
she rushed out and bought material and did
acutally cut and fit that hat on the woman's
head the next day. The first day she made
$80. Soon 40 to 50 hats a day became an
average turnout. Although she never displayed a hat in the window (she doesn't believe

in it to this day), sometimes there would be such a crowd waiting that the police would come to see whether there was a fire.

In those days the smartest section of New York was around 82nd Street and Broadway. The Ansonia Hotel was the chic gathering place. Hattie Carnegie's was at 85th Street, Milgrim at 74th Street. Daché's 77th Street establishment having become far too small after six months, she moved to 82nd Street, too. But she was not there long. Convinced that her customers would follow her anywhere, after another six months she moved to an office building, the first milliner to do so. They did follow her—in such numbers that she later became the first milliner to have her own building.

The cornerstone of this "nine-story modern building with glass brick front, ultra luxurious mirrored interior" contains the first Daché hat sensation—a black cloche trimmed with black and white checkered ribbon, red cherries and pink cherry blossoms. It was made for Marion Davies, then a Follies beauty. Mère Daché also sent her daughter a "good luck" package to go in the cornerstone. It is bad luck to look inside, so Lilly doesn't know exactly what it contains, but imagines it holds "the necessities of life" dictated by French folklore—bread, salt and light (represented by a candle).

In the meanwhile, in 1932, Lilly Daché had married Jean Despres. Three years before they had been introduced by a mutual friend, who made a "blind date" for them, and since that day they have never missed a day lunching and dining together. It is a typically French marriage. "Unconsciously, he's my boss," is the way she expresses it. A typical day finds her waking up to a breakfast of *café au lait* and *croissants*. By 8:30 she is dictating to her secretary, looking at sales reports, supervising purchases from samples. Next she goes to the designing room and stock room, working in a little office with wholesale customers climbing over her, pinning hats on a disreputable looking stockingette head with painted eyes, no other features. At 12:30 her entire establishment closes for an hour so that she can lunch with her husband without being disturbed, and then it is back to the showroom, where she usually spends the afternoon with customers. Important clients—Marlene Dietrich, Carmen Miranda (see sketch this issue), Carole Lombard, Brenda Frazier, Joan Crawford, Sonja Henie and Mrs. Orson Munn—are closeted with Mme. Daché in a private design sanctum upholstered from floor to ceiling in changeable green faille like the inside of a Victorian jewel box.

In her workrooms Lilly Daché is an empress, very excitable and quick-tempered. She works harder than anybody in the place and expects the maximum effort from everyone there. She would come to work herself in a rush season even when ill, and has little patience with "self-pamperers." She is not opposed to organized labor, she says, although in March 1941 the United Hatters, Cap and Millinery Workers' Union (A F of

L) called a strike in her establishment after negotiating unsuccessfully for wage increases of $5 weekly and a 35-hour week for manufacturing employees. Union leaders announced that this was a drive "to close the gap between the low wages paid to milliners who turn out hats for the wealthy and the relatively high wages of milliners producing styles for the masses," and that wages of Mme. Daché's workers were between $16 and $30, with an average of $22 for a 40-hour week. Lilly Daché's spokesmen retorted that the agents of the union did not represent the workers—besides, the company was paying the highest wages in the industry. And the *New Yorker* later found its favorite picket on the picket line outside Lilly Daché, Incorporated—pleading: "Please Do Not Patronize America's Foremost Milliner!"

Entirely apart from her business, Lilly Daché has the French worship of the soil and the French belief that you do not belong to a country until you own earth in it. With the first money she earned she bought a house in the country, at Bedford Village, New York. It is 125 years old and is surrounded by woods and brooks, with a three-acre lake. She has horses, and rides a great deal. She also plays some golf, but doesn't swim. She paints, and perhaps some day will let one of her paintings be seen. Her garden is her pride, particularly her delphiniums and roses. She is mad about clothes and not only collects hats but owns quantities of dresses, most of which hang unworn in her closets from one season to the next while she wears the same simple black every day. Sometimes she buys one that she has no intention of wearing, simply because it is a work of art. (She hopes to design dresses some day, too.) She used to be careless about her appearance, but has made herself into a fashion plate with conscious effort, and sometimes when she is wearing something particularly exciting will ask her husband to take her out. Then they "do the town"; otherwise they don't go out much. Her likes, she says, are rough textures, rich colors and long hot baths. She hates flattery, lobster and runover heels.

References

Collier's 107:13 Mr 1 '41 pors
N Y Herald Tribune p15 Ap 30 '41 il por
N Y Times p15 Ap 30 '41 por
PM p10 My 8 '41 il; p15 Jl 5 '41 por

DALY, THOMAS A., FATHER (dā'lĭ) 1864(?)—Jan. 8, 1941 Catholic missionary; member for many years of the Paulist Mission Band; established the Good Shepherd parish in New York; former secretary-treasurer of the Catholic Missionary Union of America; First Consultor of the Paulist Community in the United States since 1934.

Obituaries

Cath World 152:619-20 F '41
N Y Times p20 Ja 9 '41 por

DAMEREL, DONNA (dăm'ĕr-ĕl) July 8, 1912—Feb. 15, 1941 Radio actress, known as "Marge" in radio serial *Myrt and Marge*; died in childbirth; mother was Myrtle Damerel, who appeared with her on the radio, and her husband was Peter J. Fick, champion swimmer; radio program was begun nine years ago and recounted the adventures of a mother and daughter intent upon getting into the theatre; called "one of the most popular of the daytime serials, its estimated audience was 2,750,000 five times a week, twice a day, over CBS."

References

Variety Radio Directory

Obituaries

N Y Times p39 F 16 '41
Newsweek 17:10 F 24 '41 por
Time 37:55 F 24 '41 por

DANFORTH, WILLIAM May 13, 1867— Apr. 16, 1941 One of the country's most able and celebrated performers of Gilbert and Sullivan operettas; had appeared in more than 5,000 performances of the satirical operas and had portrayed the title role of *The Mikado* 1,000 times; started his career at the age of 11 and for the next 57 years played almost every important role in the Gilbert and Sullivan catalog; original name William Daniels.

References

Stage 14:65 Ap '37 por
Theatre Arts Mo 9:321-2 My '25
Who's Who in the Theatre

Obituaries

N Y Times p23 Ap 17 '41 por
Variety 142:54 Ap 23 '41

DANVIN, MME. CHARLES *See* Radziwill, C., Princess

DARGAN, E(DWIN) PRESTON Sept. 7, 1879—Dec. 13, 1940 Professor of French literature at the University of Chicago since 1911; was considered a leading American authority on the work of Honoré de Balzac; wrote many books on French literature.

References

Leaders in Education 1941
Who's Who Among North American Authors
Who's Who in America
Who's Who in American Education

Obituaries

N Y Times p17 D 14 '40

DARLAN, JEAN (LOUIS XAVIER FRANÇOIS) (dàr-län zhäɴ) Aug. 7, 1881- Vice-Premier of France; National Defense Minister in charge of the Ministries of War, Navy and Aviation; Minister of Foreign Affairs; Minister for Information Services

Address: Vichy, France

On February 9, 1941 Jean Darlan, "the Admiral of the Fleet," became a directing member of the French Cabinet. His double appointment by Marshal Pétain gave him even more power than Laval had under the Vichy Government, for he not only retained his post as Minister of Marine but also succeeded Flandin (see sketch this issue) as Foreign Minister and took Laval's old post as Vice-President of the Cabinet, charged with the coordination of all ministerial activities. Shortly afterward Darlan was named Pétain's successor, and on February 16, after the resignation of Marcel Peyrouton as Minister of the Interior, it was announced that he would also take over M. Peyrouton's post and head all departments connected with information, propaganda, radio and the cinema.

Thus came to power in France Jean Louis Xavier François Darlan, who in August 1941 became National Defense Minister in charge of the Ministries of War, Navy and Aviation under the Vichy regime—a position perhaps more important than Pétain's. Generally known in France by the last of his four given names, he was born at Nérac in the Department of Lot et Garonne on August 7, 1881, the son of Jean Baptiste and Marie Marguerite (Espagnac) Darlan. His father had been a French Minister of Justice and at one time Vice-Mayor of Nérac; his grandfather had been a sea captain and the owner of a dozen sailing ships; his great-grandfather had also been a sea captain, the commander of a French warship at Trafalgar. In this Gascon, seafaring, rather stiff-necked family François grew up, under the protection of Georges Leygues and President Fallières, both of whom were from his home district. It was October 1, 1899 when he himself entered the French Naval Academy after being graduated from the Lycée St. Louis in Paris; and it was 1902 when he entered the French Navy.

From 1902 to 1904 young Darlan took part in the Chinese campaign, in 1904 was promoted to ensign, and until the First World War divided his time between participation in campaigns in Western waters and attending schools for training naval pilots. He specialized in naval gunnery; after promotion to the rank of lieutenant in 1912 he himself became an instructor on the training-ship *Jeanne d'Arc*. There he distinguished himself for his emergency service when a fire broke out.

War came. Darlan was given command of a battery of naval guns on the Western front, took part in the battle of Verdun, was on the Balkan front for a time and was cited three times. Although much of this service had been on land, in July 1918 he was promoted to the captaincy of a warship (first grade), and after the War he commanded a flotilla on the Rhine. In 1920, after promotion to the captaincy of a frigate (second grade), he went to the Far East. For a year he commanded the *Altaïr* in China, won high praise from his superiors there and in 1922 returned to France to take over a school for naval pilots.

In 1926, after service as chief of staff of a naval division, Darlan was promoted to a senior grade captaincy and called by the Minister of Marine, Georges Leygues, to head his military cabinet. Two years later he left this post to command the *Jeanne d'Arc*. He attended the School of Advanced Naval Studies, passed out first with special mention, and in November 1929 was promoted to rear admiral. At 48 he was the youngest man in Europe to hold this rank. Darlan immediately returned to his post in the Ministry of Marine, however, and for five years didn't leave it except for brief commands. In 1930 he was cited by his Minister for "exceptional services" at the London Conference; on December 4, 1932 he was made vice-admiral and commander of the Légion d'Honneur.

It was October 4, 1934 when Admiral Darlan assumed command of the second (Atlantic) squadron. He conducted a cruise from the Azores to Dakar in the French West Indies, greatly distinguished himself in the maneuvres of 1935, and on December 31, 1935 was made grand officer of the Légion d'Honneur. In July 1936 he once more returned to the Ministry of Marine, this time as director of M. Gasnier-Duparc's military cabinet, and only two months later was appointed chief of the French Naval Staff. He did not take up his new duties until December 31, 1936, however.

According to the French journalist, Pertinax, Admiral Darlan's chief ambition during these years was to be named chief of staff of national defense, the same position held by General Keitel in Germany. And although on June 6, 1939 Admiral Darlan became commander in chief of the French Naval Forces, Pertinax says that he resented Gamelin's holding the powers he had coveted and did all he could to limit and weaken them. In turn, French advocates of a vigorous policy toward Germany resented Darlan's own appointment and denounced it as political, for during the period of appeasement there had been indications that his diplomatic weight had been thrown on the side of the Bonnets and the Lavals. His political sympathies were also thought to be royalist.

Admiral Darlan's words, however, had always been vigorous. In 1938, writing on the role of the fleet in national defense, he began with a quotation from Richelieu: "Without a fleet it is impossible either to wage war or to profit from peace." And after the long-expected war with Germany finally came in September 1939 there were no hints that he lacked confidence in the ultimate triumph of the Allies. His Christmas message in 1939 was: "We know we are invincible and that victory is assured." As for his navy, fourth among the great fleets of the world, Pertinax says "he pretended to think that everything was easy for it, that no enterprise was beyond the forces at his command, and that he could readily dispense with British assistance."

According to Pertinax, though, Darlan "flattered the English, but underneath was jealous of them and detested them." True or not, on

French Information Center

JEAN DARLAN

June 16, 1940, after the French disaster, Darlan met the British Navy chiefs and promised them that the French fleet would disarm rather than fall into Axis hands. At another meeting he argued with Admiral Sir Dudley Pound, his good friend for many years, about the most practical method of preventing the Axis from seizing the French warships; and at the next meeting of the French Cabinet he is supposed to have pleaded that the French fleet must not be allowed to fight against the British—that it should be disarmed by the French.

Many observers believe that his resentment of the British actually dates from later events: the treatment of French soldiers and naval officers in Britain after the break with France and the British attacks on the French Navy at Dakar and Mers-el-Kebir; even more important, the opportunistic realization that to disagree with the men of Vichy would have been fatal to his career. In any case, after the removal of Pierre Laval from office it was Admiral Darlan, Minister of the Navy and the Merchant Marine under Pétain, who took his place as negotiator between France and Germany. After his Cabinet appointments many observers expected Darlan to follow Laval's policy of cooperation with Germany without meeting so much antagonism from the French people, since he did not have Laval's reputation for being pro-German. He soon showed the Germans that he could outdo even Laval, however, and especially when in May 1941 he threatened to defy the British blockade in order to feed France. So "cooperative" was his attitude, in fact, that in August he was rewarded with his new position as generalissimo of the French land, sea and air forces and the overseas colonies. As such he could give orders to Weygand in North Africa, and it is probably he who

DARLAN, JEAN—*Continued*

forced Weygand's resignation in November 1941.

Admiral Darlan is "small but husky, with a square, jutting chin." His profile has been described as Roman, although the pipe which is nearly always in his mouth doubtless spoils the classical effect a little. His friends say he is a man of simple tastes, always cheerful, always completely natural; Pertinax, more critical, complains that "he affected the rough language of a sea dog, which had the advantage of concealing his natural vulgarity." Ambition is clearly his dominant characteristic. Admiral Darlan was married in 1910 to Berthe Morgan, has one son, and possesses not only the Grand Cross of the French Légion d'Honneur, bestowed on him in 1937, but also the decoration of a British order of chivalry: he is, ironically enough, a Knight Grand Cross of the Royal Victorian Order.

References

Christian Sci Mon Mag p5 N 18 '39 il por
Cur Hist & Forum 52:10 F 13 '41; 52: 41-3+ Mr '41 il
Foreign Affairs 19:320-1 Ja '41
Liv Age 358:52 Mr '40
Newsweek 17:19-20 Ja 13 '41 por
PM p4 Ja 5 '41 por
R Deux Mondes s8 56:532-8 Ap 1 '40
Time 33:23 Ap 24 '39 por; 37:31 My 26 '41 por (cover); 37:26+ Je 16 '41
Who's Who

DARRÉ, R(ICHARD) WALTHER (OSKAR) (dà-rā′) July 14, 1895- German peasant leader and Reichsminister for Agriculture

Address: b. Berlin, W. 8, Wilhelmstrasse 72, Germany

R. WALTHER DARRÉ

In 1933, just a few months after he became virtual agricultural dictator of Germany, Walther Darré caused a monument to be erected at Weisbaden in his own honor, financed by "voluntary" donations of the peasantry. The monument was marked "Blood and Soil," and Darré himself made the dedicatory speech. Although even his own adherents and his superiors felt that the event showed him a little deficient in modesty, he has proved himself eminently successful in "selling" Hitler's racial theories to the German peasantry and in whipping into Hitler-approved shape agrarian sentiment in Germany.

An *Auslandsdeutscher* (German living abroad) like a number of Hitler's other advisers, Richard Walther Oskar Darré was born on July 14, 1895 in Buenos Aires. His father, Richard Oskar Darré, Huguenot in ancestry, was the head of an Argentine firm which imported German goods. His mother, Emilia Berta Eleonora Lagergren, was a Swede. Young Walther studied at the German School in Belgrano and the Evangelical Lutheran Normal School in Gödesburg. He was sent to England to study at King's College at Wimbeldon and then to Germany to take specialized courses in overseas methods of farming at the German Colonial School at Witzenhausen, later attending the universities at Halle and Giessen. After the interval of the First World War, when he served as a reserve officer, Darré returned to his agricultural studies. His entry into the Nazi movement, therefore, was not so much as a politician or soldier as it was as an agrarian expert.

Before his connection with the National Socialist Party, Darré had been a civil servant in the East Prussian Chamber of Agriculture and had held a position as manager of a model farm. He was fired by the Ministry of Agriculture because of "financial irregularities" in his books. He turned, therefore, to the Hitler group to afford him an opportunity to rise in his chosen field, and joined the Party in 1928.

During his activities as a civil servant in the agriculture ministry, Darré had studied farming conditions in far eastern Germany and Finland. On the basis of his research he evolved the theory that the rehabilitation of Germany could best be effected through an agricultural and racial revival. His motto became "Race and Agriculture" and he published several books expounding various aspects of his thesis.

At a meeting of Nazi Party leaders in Munich, 1930, Darré finally summarized his theories. Hitler was impressed, and after several further consultations during which the Führer was fascinated by Darré's plans for human breeding and purifying the Nordic stock, he was given the role of Peasant Leader, ordered to "tickle the peasants' racial pride" and "induce them to swallow the Nazi nostrums." It is said that Hitler's early meetings with Darré were among the rare occasions during which the German leader did the listening.

The farmers at first were not particularly concerned with Darré's agricultural theories nor with his anti-Semitism. It was his anti-capitalism, his repeated insistence on the necessity for according agriculture a greater role in the national economy, which won the peasantry. They were also flattered by his doctrine of the Nordic racial superiority of the German peasants, who were to form the new German aristocracy.

Darré's success was so marked that in 1933, when he received the office of Reichsminister for Agriculture, he became agricultural dictator of Germany. He arranged a price-fixing system for grain and originated the Hereditary Farms Act which prevents the peasant from selling or mortgaging his holdings, which must pass in entail to the owner's descendants.

Counted from the beginning among the more radical elements of the Party, Darré enjoys the personal favor of Hitler. As Minister of the Food Supply he has been responsible since the capitulation of France for the underfeeding of all Europe west of Russia. According to André Simone, Darré does not enjoy Goering's (see sketch this issue) good opinion. Goering calls him the "Minister of Malnutrition," and it is from Goering's circle that scandalous rumors emanate about Darré's personal activities in his race-breeding experiments.

Darré's theories have always been a little more radical than was expedient for practical purposes. His plans for purifying the race have centered about the idea of the *Hegehöfe* (human ranches) where young girls and men of the "highest race" would be placed to breed German thoroughbreds. Rumor has it that such ranches already exist in secluded spots of East Prussia, but there is no actual evidence of their establishment.

It is with the peasantry, Darré maintains, that racial purity must begin, and he has classified German women into four categories: those who are urged to marry and breed Nordics, those who may marry and breed if they wish, those who may marry but may not have children, and those who are forbidden either to marry or to have children. The peasant's ancestry is traced back at least to 1800, and Darré is supposed to have a "stud book," one of the largest card indexes in the world, with all racial blemishes recorded.

According to Darré, (*A New Nobility From Blood And Soil*, Munich, 1930), it was the ascendancy of Roman culture which brought about the rise of Christianity, capitalism and bolshevism, all basically Jewish products, as well as the "incredibly stupid doctrine of the equality of all men before God." His anti-Semitism is based largely on the Jewish dietary laws which exclude the pig. In *The Pig as Criterion of Nordic and Semite* (Munich, 1933) he wrote: "The Semites do not understand the pig, they do not accept the pig, they reject the pig, whereas this animal occupies the first place in the cult of the Nordic People." Darré is also supposed to

advocate a kind of slavery in which people of inferior race will be the slaves of a German master folk.

Darré has been married twice. By his first wife, Alma Staadt, he had one daughter. He is married at present to Margaret Charlotte von Vietinghoff.

A Grand Commander in the Storm Troopers' organization, Reich leader of the National Socialist German Workers' Party, head of the Reich Agricultural Organization, and member of the Reich Hunting Board, Darré, obstinate and set in his theories, has a great deal of power, but he lacks the personal magnetism of Goering and Goebbels (see sketch this issue). A slight foreign accent is noticeable in his speech. He is tall, but not especially Nordic in appearance. The black uniform of the Élite Guards is his usual costume, and he is known to be an intimate friend of Gestapo Chief Heinrich Himmler (see sketch this issue).

References

Life 9:43-4 D 9 '40 por
Lit Digest 116:13 O 21 '33 por
R of Rs (London) 86:10 F '35
Gunther, J. Inside Europe p77 1940
International Who's Who
Roberts, S. H. House That Hitler Built p189-92 1938
Simone, A. Men of Europe p126-37 1941
Wer ist's?

D'ARSONVAL, JACQUES ARSÈNE
See Arsonval, J. A. d'

DARWELL, JANE   Film actress
Address: b. c/o 20th Century-Fox Film Corp, Beverly Hills, Calif.; h. 5450 Ethel Ave, Van Nuys, Calif.

"Plump, middle-aged, blue-eyed," reads a description of Jane Darwell, "she comes nearest to filling the place left vacant by the death of Marie Dressler." Jane Darwell herself denies this, for she considers Miss Dressler's place unique. And today, with an Academy "Oscar" for the best feminine supporting role of the year 1940—for her characterization of Ma Joad in *The Grapes of Wrath*—it is evident that Miss Darwell's talents need no qualitative standards of measurement.

20th Century-Fox gave Jane Darwell a screen test for the role of Ma Joad mainly out of politeness. It wasn't merely that she lacked the proportions of a gaunt Okie. It was, even more than that, the weight of her previous Hollywood experience. In 10 years of more than 65 characterizations, few had departed from a standardized sameness. They had begun to pall on the actress, since she herself, at least, had some idea of what she was capable. "I was so tired of the parts they gave me," she said. "Those mealy-mouthed women, how I hated them. I played so many of them—those genial small-town wives. I was getting awfully tired of them,

JANE DARWELL

and the studio didn't have anything else for me, so we were preparing regretfully to part."

Fifty-three actresses took screen tests for the role of Ma Joad. The one who took her test before Miss Darwell made such an impression on studio executives that they were about to leave the projection room—all in favor of signing her up—when Director John Ford (see sketch this issue) asked if they were not going to look at the Darwell test. They apologized and went back to their seats, watching the test in silence and in growing amazement. With her hair skinned back and a wan look on her face she had managed to effect a remarkable characterization. After the test had been run through it was agreed that the other actress had given a fine performance but that Jane Darwell *was* Ma Joad.

Jane Darwell was born in Palmyra, Missouri, close to half a century ago. Her given name was Patti Woodard and her father, W. R. Woodard, was a railroad tycoon of the 1880's, at one time president of the Louisville Southern Railroad. She spent her childhood in Chicago, St. Louis and Louisville, where her father had business interests, and at the family ranch near Iron Mountain, Missouri. On the ranch she indulged her liking for animals (she has 14 dogs and 17 cats on her estate outside Hollywood) and also practiced to fulfill a secret ambition—to become a bareback rider!

She was educated at Miss Loring's private school, Chicago, at a girls' school in Louisville, Kentucky, and at Dana Hall, Boston. At school her wish to be a trouper took a more dignified turn and she decided to be an actress. Her parents objected but were willing to compromise enough to let her study

voice and dramatics in order to qualify for roles in light opera. Right out of finishing school, Miss Darwell found her way to the stage entrance of the old Chicago Opera House, where Bessie Barriscale and Howard Hickman, matinee idols of their time, were playing stock. After two years' apprenticeship with the company, Miss Darwell went to London and Paris, to study and to add to her experience by minor acting roles. Her father's death cut short her European stay.

Miss Darwell is a pioneer in films, for she was a member of the Lasky Film Company that made *Rose of the Rancho* in 1914. Other early films in which she appeared were *The Master Mind* and *Brewster's Millions.* Except for two seasons on Broadway and a summer in the Keith-Albee stock company at Providence, Rhode Island, she has remained on the West Coast. While on Broadway she had a role in Sidney Howard's first play, *Swords,* which opened in September 1921.

On the Coast she alternated between work on the legitimate stage and picture work. Unlike most veterans of silent films, she didn't have to learn how to use her voice in order to qualify for sound. She appeared in a series of plays at the Alcazar in San Francisco when Henry Duffy took it over in 1924. She also did repertoire in Henry Duffy's company in Portland, Seattle and other Coast cities. And in stock, as well as in pictures, she played character roles.

"Jane Darwell," we learn, "was never an ingenue who aged into character roles, a star who slipped back to supporting roles. She's been playing character parts from the very start, and playing them in preference to leads. . . For 25 years she has been plodding along in pictures, one of that little army of dependable character actors and actresses who supply the unspectacular background against which are silhouetted in bold relief the more richly rewarded performances of the stars. Their names seldom reach the headlines. . . A line among the screen credits, an occasional mention in a buried phrase in a review, are their only recognition."

Miss Darwell, who chose her stage name from a fictional character, has acted in numerous pictures, from *Rose of the Rancho* to *Gone With the Wind* and *The Grapes of Wrath.* In the early 1930's her acting added to such pictures as *Huckleberry Finn; Jennie Gerhardt; One Sunday Afternoon;* and *Design for Living.* After *The White Parade* (20th Century-Fox 1934), it became the usual thing for critics to point out the contribution of Miss Darwell to the films in which she appeared. Among the parts for which she has won praise are her roles in *McFadden's Flats* (Paramount 1935); *Captain January* (20th Century-Fox 1936); *Craig's Wife* (Columbia 1936); *Nancy Steel Is Missing* (20th Century-Fox 1937); *Jesse James* (20th Century-Fox 1939); *The Rains Came* (20th Century-Fox 1939) and *Gone With the Wind* (Selznick-MGM 1940).

From the moment Jane Darwell began to read John Steinbeck's novel, she wanted to play the character of Ma Joad. She liked it because there was so much to admire in Ma Joad. "She is such a fine strong character," the actress said, "able to endure anything. All these terrible things happen to her. She still manages to go on. . . Oh, it's a grand part."

Miss Darwell praised highly the work of Director John Ford, and described to an interviewer his working methods. After the preliminaries Ford would say: "Go ahead," leaving the rest to the players. "He never comes over and tells anyone he's been good or the scene is great. If it's all right he says: 'That's the way we'll take it.' But if he swears, then it's good. One day Henry Fonda and I made a particularly difficult scene and after one take John Ford stood back and looked at us and said: 'Well, I'll be—!' That was the nicest compliment I've ever had."

The nearest to comedy that she came in her role of Ma Joad, she recalled, was the scene "in which Henry Fonda insists I dance, and whirls me around and around until I'm dizzy." She likes comedy and feels that in many respects it demands more of an actress than straight parts do. But her Ma Joad was no conventional straight part. It had depth and humanity and will stand as one of the finest character portrayals out of Hollywood.

Jane Darwell is five feet six inches tall, her weight has been estimated at 165 pounds, and her dark brown hair is streaked with gray. She lives within easy commuting distance of the studios, with two girls to whom she is Aunt Pat. She calls them her nieces but actually they are her brother's grand-nieces. The estate she calls her ranch, though it is only a few acres. There she putters around in the garden, sees to her cats and dogs, and relaxes. She claims she never had much luck until she stopped dieting and got plump.

"Jane Darwell will tell you that she is no longer young," says a well-known movie critic, "and that she really is glad of it. She's at a comfortable age now. Over caviar and *escalopes de veau* and *mocha parfait,* she said happily that it was very pleasant to be able to eat just what one wanted to eat, to worry no longer about keeping a figure slim or falling in and out of love."

After more than a quarter of a century in films, she looks forward to years of acting. And Hollywood agrees that she deserves them, for, like Ma Joad, she has "kept a-comin'." No one who has seen the film is likely to forget her expression or the tone of her voice as she said, in the film: "Rich fellas come up an' they die. An' their kids ain't no good an' they die out. But we keep a-comin'. We're the people that live. Can't nobody wipe us out. Can't nobody lick us. We'll go on forever. We're the people."

References

N Y Sun p15 Ja 23 '40
Photoplay 47:11 F '35; 54:89-90 Ap '40
International Motion Picture Almanac

DAUGHERTY, HARRY M(ICAJAH) (dŏ′ĕr-tĭ) Jan. 26, 1860—Oct. 12, 1941 Attorney General of the United States during Harding's and Coolidge's Administrations; during his term was several times accused of misconduct in office and though never convicted was driven to political obscurity after his resignation in 1924 over the Teapot Dome scandal; attacked many of his enemies in *The Inside Story of the Harding Tragedy* (1932).

References

Collier's 73:7 Ap 19 '24 por; 77:24 Je 19 '26
Cur Opinion 76:396 Ap '24
Lit Digest 73:13 Je 10 '22; 76:16 F 10 '23; 81:5-8 Ap 12 '24; 92:11 Mr 19 '27 por
Nation 115:243 S 13 '22; 118:333-4 Mr 26 '24; 122:551-3 My 19 '26; 123:423-4 O 27 '26
New Repub 48:267-9 O 27 '26
Who's Who in America
Who's Who in Law

Obituaries

N Y Times p17 O 13 '41 por
Time 38:81 O 20 '41

DAVENPORT, EUGENE June 20, 1856—Mar. 31, 1941 Outstanding contributor to the agricultural development of Illinois and dean emeritus of the College of Agriculture, University of Illinois; connected with the University for 27 years; recognized authority on farm economics; organized farm associations and was a leader in the development of crop rotation.

References

Leaders in Education 1941
Who's Who Among North American Authors
Who's Who in America

Obituaries

N Y Times p23 Ap 1 '41 por
Sch & Soc 53:440 Ap 5 '41

DAVIES, SIR (HENRY) WALFORD Sept. 6, 1869—Mar. 11, 1941 British composer of oratorios and cantatas; organist; choirmaster; credited with exerting a major influence on the church music of his generation; since 1924 noted for his radio talks on music in England and for his "perfect radio voice"; wrote more than a hundred songs and compositions of which his cantata, *Everyman,* the most important, was produced in 1904; received the highest honor a British musician can receive in 1934 when he succeeded Sir Edward Elgar, the composer, as Master of the King's Musick; also received knighthood in 1922 for his musical work.

References

Newsweek 3:16+ Ap 14 '34
Author's and Writer's Who's Who
Baker's Biographical Dictionary of Musicians 1940

(Continued next page)

DAVIES, SIR WALFORD—*Continued*

Ewen, D. ed. Composers of Today 1936
Who's Who

Obituaries

N Y Times p21 Mr 12 '41

DAVIS, BETTE (bĕt′ê) Apr. 5, 1908- Film actress

Address: b. c/o Warner Brothers Pictures, Inc, Burbank, Calif; h. Glendale, Calif.

BETTE DAVIS

Bette Davis has become famous in motion pictures by taking roles that would send most Hollywood beauties protesting to their agents. She has played spitfires and hard-boiled hussies, women with dark and jealously guarded secrets, women gallantly facing some dreadful doom. And she has played them with tremendous distinction. For the good of a part, beauty, sympathy, flattering angle shots can all go hang. "I'm no Pollyanna," she admits. "I love parts you can sink your teeth into."

"Tempestuous, intense, compact and case-hardened . . . her big eyes lit with a cold blue glitter" on the screen, with "as wide a dramatic range as any actress in the business," Bette Davis personally is "singularly bright and likable." She is the kind of person who likes to sleep late and lounge around her unpretentious Hollywood house in slacks, who likes to read and mix with people and buy herself uncompromisingly feminine lingerie; who likes horseback riding and swimming in the ocean.

Bette to movie-goers, Bess to her friends, she was born Ruth Elizabeth Davis in the city of Lowell, Massachusetts, and proceeded to grow up into the kind of small girl who at four snipped off her sister's curls, at six

threw dolls out the window. Mostly she was brought up by her mother, Ruth Elizabeth (Favor) Davis, who was divorced from her father, Harlow Morrell Davis, when Bette was eight. "My life was shaped by my mother," she says. One of the things her mother did after the divorce was to send Bette and her sister Barbara to a 200-acre farm school in the Berkshires. Here, Bette confesses, she never had any desire to act. "We had school plays but the fact that I tried to run the productions, build the sets and design the costumes had no professional significance. I directed because I wanted to order the other children about." In fact, it wasn't until after she had entered Cushing Academy in Ashburnham, Massachusetts, after more schooling in New York City; East Orange, New Jersey; Newton, Massachusetts and elsewhere, that she began to think of acting.

It all happened one summer when Bette's mother was at Peterboro, New Hampshire making photographs of the Mariarden School of Dancing and the stock company there. She enrolled her daughter in the dancing school; Frank Conroy, the actor, came to know them and told her to let Bette act. "She has," he said, "something you can't buy and something you can't imitate. Even if she doesn't open her mouth she has the quality that draws the audience to her. I think that someday, if she works hard, she will be a fine actress." Inspired, Bette returned to Cushing to take part in all the school plays and to star in the senior play, in which Harmon Nelson, later her husband, also had a part.

In 1927, after Bette's graduation, Mrs. Davis decided she had to have real dramatic training and took her to see Eva Le Gallienne, whose school was famous. Miss Le Gallienne gave Bette the part of a Dutch woman of 70 to read and then asked her questions about her attitude toward the theatre. At the end of the interview she fixed the applicant with a frigid eye and said: "I can see that your attitude toward the theatre is not sincere enough to warrant taking you as a pupil. You are a frivolous little girl." Undaunted, Mrs. Davis took Bette to John Murray Anderson's dramatic school, informed him she would pay the tuition as she could and left her daughter there for study. Bette won a scholarship soon, but she never completed the course. She got a job.

The job consisted of a single line in a play called *Broadway*, which George Cukor was producing during his stock season in Rochester, New York. On her mother's advice, Bette also learned one of the important parts and later acted it. This acting experience was followed by a summer at the Cape Playhouse in Dennis, Massachusetts, where she thought she had been offered a position and found, after she got there, that she hadn't. After working as an usher most of the season, she finally got one part. The next two summers she returned there, but not as an usher.

Back from the first summer, though, things looked dark, and there was a long, fruitless period of searching for a part until George Cukor took her on again in Rochester as ingénue. She finally hit Broadway's fringe in *The Earth Between,* given at the Provincetown Playhouse in Greenwich Village, New York, and even got a critical comment from Brooks Atkinson. He said she was "an interesting creature who plays in a soft unassertive style." Her next appearance, held up by an attack of the measles, was with Blanche Yurka on the road in *The Wild Duck.* Her next, after a summer on Cape Cod, was in *Broken Dishes,* which opened in November 1929, ran for 178 performances in New York and more on the road.

With this play, Bette Davis says, "at last I was accepted as a bona fide actress." She was even asked by Samuel Goldwyn to make a screen test. When she looked at the results, she remembers, she "ran from the projection room screaming"; when Goldwyn saw them he merely asked: "Who wasted my time with that one?" Nevertheless she was given another test, this time by Universal, after her appearance with Richard Bennett in *The Solid South.* And this time a contract resulted. In December 1930 Bette and her mother left for Hollywood.

That first contract was for a year, but it stated that at the end of three, six and nine months, the studio could change its mind. After the first three, in which Bette did nothing and took many not so favorable tests, it looked as though the studio would do just that. But Bette was kept on and given a part in *Bad Sister.* Nobody paid much attention to her, and she made up for the part exactly as she would have for the stage. "As a result she looked not only like a wallflower [she was the good sister] but like something that had been set out on the front porch for the Salvation Army." It was that picture, Bette insists "that gave me a horror of nobility. Ever since I have fought against portraying saccharine characters."

Although she felt she had been terrible in this film, her option was renewed again and she was given a part in *Seed.* But Universal felt they had made a mistake and proceeded to loan her out to other studios until the year was up—to Columbia for *Menace,* a "dilly" of a picture—"every time a door opened, out tumbled Davis"; to another studio for *Hell's House;* to RKO for *Way Back Home,* the best film of the lot. Then her option was dropped with comments like: "No more sex appeal than a stringbean" or "Junior" Laemmle's: "I can't imagine any guy giving her a tumble." Bette Davis got ready to leave Hollywood as a failure.

Instead, she played opposite George Arliss in *The Man Who Played God,* and when the picture was finished found herself with a long-term contract with Warner Brothers. Her light brown hair rinsed to an ash blond, for a while she tried to justify the studio's idea that she was "a schoolgirl Constance Bennett"—in *The Rich Are Always With Us,*

with Ruth Chatterton and George Brent, for instance. And in 1932 she married Harmon Nelson, by that time a bandleader, later a Hollywood agent. In December 1938 they were divorced.

Bette Davis' next film after her marriage was *Cabin in the Cotton,* with Richard Barthelmess. It was the first time she had a chance to develop what *Time* calls "her stripe of cinemeanness," but it was followed by *20,000 Years in Sing Sing* and four "impossible" pictures. The first of her prolonged and colorful feuds with Warner Brothers soon opened. She said she was an actress; the studio said she was an upstart they had lifted to prominence who thought herself the modern Duse. It wasn't until 1934 that a few people began to think that maybe she really was what she thought herself. It began with a picture called *Fog Over Frisco* (First National), in which she played a psychopathic case and "gave the first indication of the talent which was later to be given full rein"; it was followed by *Of Human Bondage* (RKO). Bette had worked and fought to get the role of Mildred in that picture. She got it and with it established as a first-rate actress. As one critic put it: "In the book Mildred's skin was supposed to have a greenish cast. Well, this girl *looked* green!" It was expected that she would receive an Academy Award for this performance, but it wasn't until 1936 that she received her first one, for her performance in *Dangerous* (1935).

But *Dangerous* was preceded and followed by a series of "unbelievably bad films," and Bette Davis decided she had had enough. With her husband she went to London to act with an English company, in violation of her contract. Warners slapped down an injunction, and a battle royal followed. The press said it was over her "inadequate" $3,000-a-week salary; she said the fight had little to do with money (and besides she was making only $1,700 a week) but was centered on whether she could make a limited number of pictures a year, have vacations, be given suitable stories. She lost, after spending $18,000, and returned in December 1936 "to serve five years in the Warner jail." Later she admitted that Warners had treated her decently—waiving a judgment for the court costs, increasing her salary—and that the atmosphere had been cleared. Since then, however, she has been suspended from salary several times for refusing to do pictures and has gone on a couple of "one-woman strikes." She herself doesn't hesitate to admit that she's probably "a very disagreeable person" and that her mother calls her "willful." And critics admit that among their fellowship there are some who feel that not only has her screen work developed her as an actress, but also brought out a "shrewish" streak. Personally, they hasten to add, she's a pleasant, forthright young woman.

After her return from London her parts were better in *Marked Woman, Kid Galahad, That Certain Woman, It's Love I'm After.* She was the proud Southern belle in *Jezebel,*

DAVIS, BETTE—*Continued*

able "by force of personal intensity and able acting" to give "her emotional crises a convincing importance"; able to win for this portrayal a second Academy Award in 1938. But even a good part like this couldn't compensate for some of the stories Warners offered her, and a suspension followed her refusal to accept assignments. When she returned to the studio it was in *The Sisters,* and this film was followed by *Dark Victory,* which Bette feels is "one of the finest films I have made."

Juarez, The Old Maid ("I cared little for it," she says) and *Elizabeth and Essex,* which she hated, followed, and after this last film a state of nervous exhaustion came. Bette Davis, weighing less than 100 pounds, went off to "Butternut," her New Hampshire farm in which she has installed early American furniture and modern American plumbing. She returned rested enough to play the French governess of *All This and Heaven, Too* (1940), and then to return to modernity in *The Letter* and *The Great Lie,* the latter a "weak story", according to the critics, in which she was, nevertheless, "believable and moving."

The première of *The Great Lie* was held on Bette's birthday in Littleton, New Hampshire, where she and her second husband, Arthur Farnsworth, were staying. Even the studio press agents had been taken by surprise by Bette's marriage on New Years' Eve 1941 to the former manager of Peckett's Inn at Sugar Hill, a White Mountain lodge where she had spent several vacations. Soon after her marriage she announced that the way to keep a marriage going was never to have breakfast with one's husband.

There was probably no relation between the two events, but shortly after her marriage Miss Davis decided that she ought to get away from heavy melodramatic roles occasionally. After a slight disagreement with her studio over the vehicle, Miss Davis was then seen in *The Bride Came C. O. D.,* in which with James Cagney she took the bit in her teeth and "flung her breathless way through a rough and tumble comedy with no gags barred." It was followed by another dramatic and shrewish role, that of Regina Giddens in Lillian Hellman's (see sketch this issue) *The Little Foxes,* "a magnificent performance," according to the unanimously enthusiastic critics. Her next assignment was that of Maggie Cutler, the secretary in *The Man Who Came to Dinner,* a much coveted role in one of Hollywood's most discussed films, followed by a role in the film of Ellen Glasgow's *In This Our Life.* In November 1941 she succeeded producer Walter Wanger as president of the Academy of Motion Picture Arts and Sciences, the first actress to be thus honored.

This actress, who is often called "the First Lady of Cinema," has achieved that pinnacle not only through innate talent, but through hard work. There are long and thorough rehearsals, long and thorough preparations for every role. Once she was considered for the role of a German girl who spoke with an accent. She hired a teacher and took German lessons, "because I didn't think I could speak with a German accent without first knowing how to speak German." Another time, when slated for the part of a professional horsewoman, she worked with a riding master two hours a day for several weeks. She didn't get either of these roles, but she wanted to be prepared. When she does get one she's ready for it. As her stand-in wrote in a *Good Housekeeping* article: "Bette's never late. I've never seen her muff a line. She's a quick study, learns easily but always memorizes her scenes the night before." And when she plays it, it's without all the tricky make-up so many other stars feel necessary. "It's impossible to give a decent performance with junk on you," she says.

Despite the fact that she is a leading screen figure, Bette Davis makes no bones about the fact that she doesn't like Hollywood and never did. "I shiver each time I see an auction of a star's personal belongings advertised in the papers. I don't want that to happen to me. I don't want to own anything here I can't pack in a trunk," she says. If and when she ever does pack that trunk she's going off to "run a small theatre in which youngsters with genuine ability would be given a chance." She confesses: "I see myself as an old lady running around the country seeking out unknowns and helping them equip themselves for a career. Probably I'll be a great nuisance. I'll find kids with talent and cuss my way past casting directors and make life miserable for producers until they give my protégés a chance."

References

Am Mag 127:91 Mr '39 il por; 132:52 O '41 por
Collier's 94:18+ N 17 '34 pors
Good H 106:40-1+ Ap '38 pors; 108: 38-9+ Je '39 il por
Ladies' H J 58:16-17+ Jl '41 pors
Life 5:62-5 S 5 '38 il pors; 6:52-8 Ja 23 '39 il pors; 10:126-9 Ap 28 '41 il pors
Movie Classic 8:25+ Ag '35 por; 9:47+ F '36 por; 10:38-9+ S '36 pors; 11: 58-9+ N '36 il por
Photoplay 47:26-7+ My '35 pors; 48: 48+ S '35 il pors; 50:54+ Ag '36 por; 51:54-6+ Ag '37 pors; 52:10-11+ Ag '38 pors; 52:24-5+ D '38 il pors; 53:18-19+ Ap '39 il pors
Stage 15:12-13 Ap '38 pors; 15:20 Je '38 por
Theatre Arts 25:632-9 S '41 pors
Time 31:33-4+ Mr 28 '38 il pors
American Women
International Motion Picture Almanac
Who's Who in America
Who's Who in American Jewry

DAVIS, WILLIAM H(AMMATT) Aug.
29, 1879- Chairman of the National Defense
Mediation Board; lawyer
Address: b. 165 Broadway, New York City;
h. 130 E. 74th St, New York City

The life and activities of William H. Davis,
the wild-haired, mild-spoken chairman of
the National Defense Mediation Board, present an apt illustration of his own favorite
saying: "The democratic principle is rooted in
persuasion." Mr. Davis' powers of persuasion
have been heavily taxed ever since President
Roosevelt created the Board "to afford means
for voluntary arbitration and to try to negotiate
agreements." Since it was conceded that its
best chance of working depended mostly on
the calibre of the men selected, the choice of
Davis as vice-chairman of the Board was
applauded by most critics—even by those who
branded the Board as either a clumsy compromise or an unwarranted intrusion into a
situation fraught with danger.

William Davis' record on the willing but
overburdened Mediation Board justifies their
confidence. To him belongs the credit for
settling the Allis-Chalmers strike, which had
lasted 75 days, held up $45,000,000 worth of
defense contracts, produced explosions in Congress and resisted all efforts of the Labor
Department, Sidney Hillman, William Knudsen
and Secretary of the Navy Knox. His
handling of this case, which has been called a
model for mediators, earned him a unanimous
resolution from both management and labor
thanking him for his "able, patient and impartial work." Davis is often commended in
this way. The stormy New York bus strike
of March 1941 ended on a similar note with
the union's assurance that, with his appointment as arbitrator, "busmen could rely on
getting a fair break." The settlement of the
General Motors strike on May 16, 1941, was
another victory to his credit, as was the
settling of the disagreement between John L.
Lewis' United Mine Workers Association and
the Southern coal operators the next month.
When on June 21, 1941 President Roosevelt
selected Davis to succeed Clarence A. Dykstra
(see sketch this issue) as chairman of the
Board, very few commentators expressed surprise.

Ranking among the top dozen of practicing
labor experts in America, William Hammatt
Davis has for years given the best part of his
time to representing the public interest in labor
relations. For that reason his calm voice
coming through the clamor of indignation in
Washington was listened to with respect as he
testified before the House Military Affairs
Committee on April 8, 1941. He called on
the industry "to accept and recognize without
reservation the spirit of the NLRA and collective bargaining," and on labor "to use their
legal remedy and not the remedy of force."
He warned that compulsory legislation would
make "the working man a slave and there is no
use in America's producing defense materials
if it is a nation of slaves."

Wide World

WILLIAM H. DAVIS

The use of arbitration (voluntary, for
"compulsory arbitration so distorts the processes
of persuasion that they become practically useless") has long been Mr. Davis' favorite principle. In an article written in 1939 he suggested that the Government "may properly provide agencies for voluntary mediation and
conciliation with established panels of trained
arbitrators who may be brought into a dispute
at the joint request of the contending parties."
His presence on the Mediation Board is the
logical conclusion of his ideas on the subject.

After watching Davis' activities, it is hard
to believe that labor relations are merely his
avocation. Actually William H. Davis is a
brilliant patent attorney, the senior partner
in the firm of Pennie, Davis, Marvin and
Edmonds. He was born in Bangor, Maine, on
August 29, 1879, the son of Owen Warren
and Abigail (Gould) Davis. He was educated
at the Corcoran Scientific School in Washington, D. C., and was graduated in 1901 from
the Washington University Law School. He
became an examiner in the United States
Patent Office in 1902, but left this position
in 1903 to join the law firm of Betts, Betts,
Sheffield and Betts of New York City. In
1906 he married Grace Greenwood Colyer of
Baltimore and changed over into the firm of
Pennie and Goldsborough (now Pennie, Davis,
Marvin and Edmonds), where he has remained
since. In 1911 he joined the firm as a partner
and since 1920 he has been its senior member.

When the First World War came, the War
Department borrowed him to make use of
his administrative abilities. In 1917 he was
the head of the contract section of the Planning
Division of Purchase, Storage and Traffic.
In 1918 he became ordnance member and legal
adviser to the War Department's Claims Board
and in 1919 he handled appeals from the War
Department Board of Contract Adjustments.

DAVIS, WILLIAM H.—*Continued*

His positions provided him with an opportunity for complex legal work, for handling a mass of administrative detail, and for furthering good public relations.

After the War, Davis was allowed to practice law in peace until with the New Deal there came new demands for his experience and tact. From 1933 to 1934 he was in Washington as administrator and national compliance director of the NRA until its demise; in 1936 he was appointed a member of the Federal Commission of Industrial Analysis. As a member of the three-man Emergency Board set up to enact the Railway Labor Act, he came in close contact with labor relations functioning under a prearranged structure of agreement. And out of his experience in that connection came his conviction that best relations are achieved under a body of agreement between management and labor with provisions for mediation made in advance—always providing that there is equality of strength between the two groups.

In 1937, too, he became the chairman of the New York State Mediation Board. In that capacity he has often sat at the bargaining table between labor and industry, has helped to settle many hundreds of threatened labor disputes and has prevented an even greater number. One of the important strikes later settled through his mediation was the food strike that tied up 22 warehouses in 1939.

In 1938 he was appointed to the President's Committee of Industrial Relations, a study group of nine men representing business, industry, labor, the general public and the law, who were sent abroad to investigate industrial labor conditions in Great Britain and Sweden. The report the group submitted to the Secretary of Labor upon their return included a valuable body of material upon which the Administration intended to base its wage and labor policies. It also provided the basis for a survey of labor relations in the United States which was started by the labor committee of the Twentieth Century Fund. Mr. Davis was the chairman of that committee and was often invited to air the opinions he had formed as a result of his trip. On several occasions he pointed out that legislation like the Wagner Act is unnecessary in either Great Britain or Sweden, which have developed a mature method of establishing workable industrial conditions.

Davis was for a period in 1939 a member of the New York City Housing Authority. Then in December 1940, he found himself too involved in activities and submitted his resignation from the State Mediation Board because of the pressure of his private law practice. But the year 1941 found him back in harness again, giving the benefit of his experience and tact to the Government.

A short, sloppily dressed man with a wild mop of sandy hair, William H. Davis looks something like a kindly but determined bulldog. He is pleasantly, reassuringly homely. He has a son, and two married daughters. His outstanding characteristics are his capacity for calm in the midst of turbulent situations and his all-pervading, obstinate optimism. He doggedly believes that with honest good will and willingness to cooperate, any dispute can be settled. After a session with him the harassed disputants begin to believe it, too. It is for this reason that his services as a mediator have been so widely sought throughout his career.

Then, too, he has a tremendous capacity for work: the day after the exhausting week end during which the Allis-Chalmers strike was settled he appeared before the United States Supreme Court to argue a patent-infringement case. He has apparently been given all the administrative work of the board: at least he has taken over the task of appointing panels to arbitrate the strikes that have been certified to the National Mediation Board by Secretary Perkins. He played a leading role in the Air Associates and "captive mines" disputes, and surprised many CIO members by voting against the union shop in the latter. CIO representatives resigned from the Board in protest, but most union leaders still retained enough faith in his fair-mindedness to approve his chairmanship of the conference of industry and labor which met in December 1941 to draft a policy for war-time labor relations.

References

N Y Times p20 Ap 9 '41; p28 Je 22 '41
PM p19 My 23 '41 por
Time 37:14 Mr 31 '41; 37:24-5 Ap 21
'41 por
U S News 10:43 My 16 '41 por
Who's Who in America
Who's Who in Law

DAVIS, WILLIAM RHODES Feb. 10, 1889—Aug. 1, 1941 Late oil operator

> Bulletin: On August 1, 1941 William Rhodes Davis died of a heart attack in Houston, Texas.

From March 1941 issue:

William Rhodes Davis is the oil operator whom Verne Marshall (see sketch this issue) named on December 30, 1940 as having offered to underwrite his No Foreign War Committee. According to Mr. Marshall, Mr. Davis was the man who brought a German "agenda" for peace from Berlin to the United States State Department in the fall of 1939. And according to many newspaper sources, Mr. Davis has not only sold Mexican oil to Germany and Italy but has been associated with Dr. Hertslet, Hitler's ace war economist. Mr. Davis has not been enjoying his recent publicity, and on January 5, 1941 gave a press conference in which he made public a letter to Senator Wheeler asking if he could appear before a Senate committee to explain his activities and refute the charges against him.

At the press conference Mr. Davis swiftly denied that he was the financial backer of the No Foreign War Committee, although he said that he was in sympathy with the aims of all organizations which held ideas of world tranquillity similar to his own. He also asserted that he had not been in Germany since September 1939, shortly after war broke out, and that since that time no oil had been shipped to either Germany or Italy, "only a few cargoes" before; that he was "just an oil operator," with no plan of his own for peace; that he wanted the War to end, "but not on Hitler's terms." Most questions, however, he parried with the explanation that their answers touched upon matters of state and that it would therefore be "unethical and even unlawful for me to lay them before the public."

Davis, according to the autobiographical sketch which accompanied his letter to Senator Wheeler, is a direct descendant of both Jefferson Davis and of the British empire-builder, Cecil Rhodes. (*The Nation* points out that standard biographies of Rhodes fail to mention either marriage or children, however.) Davis was born in Montgomery, Alabama on February 10, 1889, attended Stark College there, and left before graduation in order to work for the Union News Company on Southern railroads. Later he became a train butcher, a fireman, and eventually a locomotive engineer, working for the M. O. & G. Railroad of Muskogee, Oklahoma from 1910 to 1918.

In the meanwhile he was already organizing his own companies: in 1913 it was the Best Test Oil and Gas Company of Muskogee, in 1915 the Gotham Mining and Milling Company at Joplin, Missouri and then the Malcona Zinc Corporation at Joplin. After the United States entered the First World War he enlisted in the Army at Muskogee in June 1918, and was discharged as a second lieutenant in 1920 after having seen active service in the 21st Engineers Light Railway Detachment.

Upon his discharge Davis set up offices in Tulsa, Oklahoma as a lease broker. He organized scores of oil companies, on the side dabbled in cheese and rubber, was engaged in scores of lawsuits; in 1929 he was one of several financiers who took over a large concession in Peru with plans to build a railroad to the coast and to import 50,000 colonists. The Peruvian Revolution deposed the dictator who had granted him this concession, and nothing came of it. But always his plans were incredibly bold. He thought in large terms: millions of dollars, millions of Reichsmarks, millions of pounds sterling.

After the Nazis came to power in Germany their restrictions on foreign exchange induced Davis to build one of the largest oil refineries in the world at Hamburg. This was so that a Boston bank might "unfreeze" some of its German investment. But the project lost money, and Davis set up an English company to finance it. This later resulted in Davis' being sued on charges of attempting to defraud a Danish oil company. He was found guilty in a lower court, but was unanimously cleared of the charges in the London court of appeals.

It was Davis' need for further supplies of crude oil for his refineries that brought him to Mexico in 1938. Even earlier than that, in May 1936, Davis said that he had met President Roosevelt in order to try to work out some kind of a three-cornered trade arrangement between the United States, Germany and

WILLIAM RHODES DAVIS

Mexico. Nothing had come of this effort, but by the end of 1938 Davis had cut loose from his English connections and had obtained a virtual monopoly of expropriated oil from Mexico, which he himself began to barter to the Axis in return for tankers and oil machinery. He is said to have sold $10,000,000 worth until the War and the British blockade stopped him. His willingness to deal in Mexican expropriated oil (rather than his willingness to deal with the Axis) made him unpopular in the State Department and in oil circles at this time. Plans to extend the barter agreement even further were rejected by Germany, however.

Nor were his barter arrangements completely successful. Before the present War Davis proposed to deliver 17 German Junkers airplanes to Mexico in payment for oil, airplanes which he said he had originally bought from Germany for sale to the Spanish Loyalists; a protest by the American Ambassador to Mexico stopped their delivery. And after the War began two of his chartered ships carrying oil—consigned to the Scandinavian countries, according to Davis—were captured by the British. Now he could not sell oil to Germany and Italy on account of the blockade; he could not sell it to American and English oil companies because they considered it their own; his luck with South America was negligible. It was apparently about at this time that he hopefully visited Germany and brought back the much-discussed peace "agenda."

It seems likely, however, that the War can continue indefinitely and Mr. Davis still remain a rich man. He collected more than $400,000 from the Germans in 1940. And although his holdings include a terminal at Malmo, Sweden and distributing facilities in Sweden, Norway, Denmark and Finland as well as a great investment in Mexican

DAVIS, WILLIAM RHODES—*Cont.*

oil reserves, his main source of revenue consists of properties in Texas and Louisiana. He is responsible for the recent development of the largest oil reserve in Southern Texas, and in November 1940 he reportedly sold a half-interest in it for several million dollars.

Davis is described as a man of rather less than average height, "impeccably dressed, gray-haired, ruddy-faced," with an Alabama drawl—"affable but nervous, a man anxious to talk, but not on all subjects." He married May Tankin of Boston in 1909, and they have two living sons: Joe Graham and Currie Boyd Davis. There is also a granddaughter by another son who was killed in an airplane accident in Nicaragua in 1933. Mr. Davis takes a lively interest in politics, reportedly made large contributions to President Roosevelt's campaign funds in 1932 and 1936, and his office mantelpiece boasts a photograph of the President which is signed: "To Major W. R. Davis from his friend, Franklin Delano Roosevelt." (In 1940 Davis is said to have switched to the Republican camp, however.) He is a Protestant, a Mason and a Colonel in the New Mexico National Guard.

References

Life 10:20 Ja 13 '41 por; 10:26 Ja 20 '41

Nation 152:30 Ja 11 '41

N Y Herald Tribune p1, 9 Ja 2 '41; p1, 6 Ja 6 '41 pors; p12 Jl 15 '41

N Y Sun p3 D 31 '40 por

N Y Times p6 D 31 '40 por; p8 Ja 6 '41

Newsweek 17:15-16 Ja 13 '41 por; 17:12 Ja 20 '41

PM p10 Ja 6 '41; p20 Ap 25 '41 por; p18 Ap 27 '41 pors; p22 Ap 28 '41 por; p22 Ap 29 '41 por; p22 Ap 30 '41; p9 My 2 '41 il; p19 My 4 '41 pors; p22 My 5 '41 por; p11 My 6 '41 pors; p14 Jl 27 '41

Time 37:12 Ja 6 '41

Obituaries

N Y Times p15 Ag 2 '41 por

DAWSON, WILLIAM Aug. 11, 1885- United States Ambassador to Uruguay

Address: Department of State, Washington, D. C.

A tactful move in the direction of Hemisphere Solidarity is to raise a Latin American nation from ministerial to ambassadorial status. Colombia, Venezuela and Panama have all been promoted in the past few years, and in February 1941 President Roosevelt appointed the United States' first Ambassador to Uruguay. "Precise, perspicacious" William Dawson, a seasoned diplomat with more than a decade's Latin-American experience, received the appointment.

William Dawson was born in St. Paul, Minnesota on August 11, 1885, the son of William and Maria (Rice) Dawson. He acquired his B. A. at the University of Minnesota in 1906,

Wide World

WILLIAM DAWSON

and then went on to the École Libre des Sciences Politiques in Paris, where so many career diplomats have received their training. On March 28, 1908 he received his first appointment in the United States Foreign Service —as vice and deputy consul general in St. Petersburg, Russia. Three months later he was given the post of vice and deputy consul. That same year brought him an assignment in Barcelona, Spain; in 1910 he went to Frankfort, Germany; and in 1913 he received his first South American assignment—as consul at Rosario, Argentina. He was there until 1917, spent two years as consul at Montevideo, Uruguay, and then returned to Europe to act as consul in Danzig from 1919 to 1921 and at Munich from 1921 to 1922.

More important assignments followed. From 1922 to 1924 Mr. Dawson acted as consul general at large, and from 1925 to 1928 was chief instructor in the Foreign Service School of the Department of State. The Mexican Embassy claimed him next, and he served as consul general in Mexico City from 1928 to 1930 before receiving his first ministerial appointment as envoy extraordinary and minister plenipotentiary to Ecuador in 1930.

In 1935, the year after Dawson left Ecuador to take up the same post in Colombia, a reciprocal trade agreement was signed between Colombia and the United States. During Dawson's period of service in Colombia the United States State Department was doing its best to break down a sudden attitude of independence toward foreign capital, and the problem has been similar in other Latin American countries—often complicated by German and Italian economic penetration. The year 1937 found Dawson in the same post in Uruguay, where he had been a consul 20 years before. March 1939 brought Dawson an assignment as first United States Ambassador to Panama, four months before the United States Senate ratified the General Treaty (signed at Washington in 1936) whereby the United States renounces the right to acquire additional lands and waters and the right to intervene to keep order in that Republic. Then he returned to an Uruguay that is firmly committed to a policy of intercontinental cooperation.

On June 8, 1926 Ambassador Dawson married Agnes Balloch Bready of Washington, D. C. He is a member of Chi Psi, an Episcopalian, and belongs to the Metropolitan and Cosmos Clubs in Washington.

References

Newsweek 17:20 F 17 '41 por
Who's Who in America
Who's Who in Government
Who's Who in the Nation's Capital

DEANE, MARTHA, pseud. *See* McBride, M. M.

DE FOREST, LEE Aug. 26, 1873- Inventor; research engineer

Address: b. 5106 Wilshire Blvd, Los Angeles, Calif; h. 8190 Hollywood Blvd, Los Angeles, Calif.

Lee de Forest is the holder of over 300 invention patents, and because of them "we telephone over half the world, speech is broadcast over the whole world, the movies talk, television has come, cosmic rays tell their story and atomic energies are revealed." His latest efforts are being turned toward the development of a pilotless "television torpedo plane" which he believes will provide the United States military forces with an inexpensive means of getting information by aerial surveys and which can be used also as a robot bomber.

Ever since he was a boy Lee de Forest has been inventing. The first products of his inventiveness were made in Talladega, Alabama, where his parents had moved six years after Lee was born in Council Bluffs, Iowa. His father, the Reverend Henry Swift de Forest, was head of Talladega College there, founded to educate and uplift Negroes. His mother, Anna Margaret (Robbins) de Forest, had been a choir leader in the Reverend De Forest's church back in Iowa before her marriage. It took Lee's parents quite a while to get used to the fact that they had a scientifically-minded son.

Lee spent his childhood trying to build locomotives; he constructed his own electric motor; and when he was 15 he proudly announced that he had discovered the secret of perpetual motion. Nevertheless, his father still wanted him to study the classics in preparation for the ministry. Lee put an end to these hopes after he entered Mt. Hermon Preparatory School in 1891. He wrote to his father: "Dear Sir: I intend to be a machinist and inventor because I have great talent in that direction." That was the end of the con-

LEE DE FOREST

troversy, and Lee went on to the Sheffield Scientific School at Yale in 1893.

At Yale, De Forest had very little to do with his classmates. He spent his time studying, reading works on electricity and inventing—one of his brain-children was the design for an underground trolley. After he received his Ph. B. in 1896 he stayed on at Yale for graduate work, burying himself in the electrical laboratory and completing the research on "Reflection of Short Hertzian Waves from the Ends of Parallel Wires" which won him his Ph. D. in 1899. (Yale, Syracuse and Lewis have since given him honorary degrees.)

Then he started looking for a job. He wandered west to Chicago, where he began working as a laborer in the dynamo factory of the Western Electric Company. A little later he was promoted to the telephone laboratory. Every spare moment he could find he spent developing a device for detecting wireless signals, and early in his research discovered that he could use a telephone receiver as an indicating device in receiving wireless signals. After his discovery in 1900 he left Chicago and settled down in a shack in Milwaukee with Professor Johnson, who was doing some experiments of his own on wireless sets. De Forest refused to give him his own anti-coherer idea (detector)—and found himself fired.

De Forest returned to Chicago, where he obtained a position on the staff of an electrical magazine, and another teaching at the Armour Institute. He continued working on his detector, which he called a "Sponder," until 1901, when he gave it its first long-distance test—and discovered that it worked! Immediately he and his partner, E. W. Smythe, decided to go ahead with the patenting and marketing of the device, only to discover that money and publicity were necessary. To get publicity De Forest persuaded the Publishers'

DE FOREST, LEE—Continued

Press to let him report the International Yacht Races with his wireless in competition with Marconi operators, who were doing this for the Associated Press. De Forest's broadcast was a complete failure. But so was that of his rivals, and the publicity was successful.

Encouraged by it, De Forest set up a machine shop on the Jersey City water front and erected the first wireless station of its kind in that vicinity. Eventually he was able to interest Wall Street sufficiently to form the De Forest Wireless Telegraph Company and with the money from the capitalization bought equipment and set up transmitting rooms. In 1903 he went to England to demonstrate his invention and while there communicated by wireless from Wales to Ireland. From a third voyage in 1906 he returned to find his company in financial difficulties and the other directors anxious for him to resign. Business matters had always weighed heavily, and it was with a feeling of relief that he took the few hundred dollars offered him and set out on his own again.

He improvised a laboratory in the loft of the Parker Building in New York City and began making tests. "I'll build a better detector for wireless reception," he announced. "I'll try to send the human voice through the air instead of messages by dots and dashes." Shortly after he was awarded gold medals at the St. Louis World's Fair in 1904 (the first of many) he began to give up the wireless field—partly because his electrolytic detector had been declared to interfere with the patents of another inventor, mostly because he was particularly interested in transmitting the human voice. He started work on his audion tube.

Using an arc light surrounded by a ceramic chimney into which a hydrocarbon vapor was pumped, De Forest generated from this crude device wireless waves and with it spanned space with messages and music. This was in 1907. Immediately he formed the De Forest Radio Telephone Company to promote his idea and by the end of the year, after a public trial of radio-telephone apparatus, the Navy Department had ordered enough radiophone sets to equip the fleet.

De Forest celebrated by marrying Nora Stanton Blatch in 1908 and going with his bride to Paris to install one of his radio telephone transmitters on top of the Eiffel Tower. Back from his honeymoon, he built an aerial on top of the Metropolitan Life Insurance Building and shortly afterward installed microphones in the Metropolitan Opera House. It was through these, on January 2, 1910, that the voice of Caruso was transmitted in the first radio broadcast of its kind.

De Forest became short of funds again—he has never been a success as a businessman—and went out to San Francisco to take a position as research engineer for the Federal Telegraph Company, while his own company slowly died. In 1914 it came to life again for a while when he refinanced it with the $50,000

he had received from the sale of his audion tubes to the American Telephone and Telegraph Company. De Forest had already been working in New York—his San Francisco position lasted only two years—and he set up another laboratory at Highbridge, New York City and later a transmitter at the World Tower Building, from which regular radio broadcasts of vaudeville were given for the first time.

In 1917 De Forest sold further rights to his audion tubes to the American Telephone and Telegraph Company and used the money for more experimental machinery. As radio developed he was manufacturing radio tubes for this new industry, but his heart wasn't in this work. He was seeing ahead even further—toward the development of talking motion pictures. By 1923 he had shown for the first time a sound-on-film program in a theatre (the Rivoli in New York) and had invented his "noiseless recording" positive prints and "glow-light" recording of sound on films. The motion picture producers weren't interested until 1927, when Warner Brothers plunged into the field.

From talking pictures De Forest turned his interest, later, to television and from television in general to the problem of "television torpedo planes." Meanwhile, in 1934, after years of litigation with Edwin H. Armstrong, his claim to the invention of the "feed-back" and oscillating vacuum tube circuits had been upheld by the Supreme Court of the United States. Yet despite recognition from learned societies, manufacturers and scientists, De Forest failed in these years to make money. By 1937 he had filed a bankruptcy petition listing assets of $390 and liabilities of $104,000.

In 1934 he founded the Lee De Forest Laboratories devoted chiefly to research and manufacture in the new field of short wave, or radio, diathermy, the application of high frequency currents to heating of the human tissues, found highly beneficial in all cases where congestion is involved. The United States Army and Navy are today using large numbers of De Forest Dynatherms in their numerous hospitals and on all battleships.

Still active in his work after almost 50 years of inventing, the "father of radio" lives quietly in California with his third wife, Marie Mosquini, whom he married in 1930 (his second marriage, to Mary Mayo, took place in 1912). He gets up each morning at seven, does setting-up exercises and then eats exactly the same breakfast every day—two poached eggs, corn muffins and a glass of milk. Never does he use cigarets or drink coffee. Those, he feels, dull the perceptions, and an inventor, he knows, must always keep his keenly alert. He is ardently fond of fine music and mountain climbing.

References

N Y Times IX p12 F 16 '41 il; IX p12 Mr 30 '41
Radio News 24:8+ D '40 por
American Men of Science
Carneal, G. Conqueror of Space 1930

(Continued next page)

Hylander, C. J. American Inventors
p185-98 1934
International Motion Picture Almanac
Who's Who in America
Who's Who in Commerce and Industry
Who's Who in Engineering

DEHN, ADOLF (ARTHUR) (dän) Nov. 22, 1895- Artist
Address: 230 E. 15th St, New York City

Exhibitions of graphic work by Adolf Dehn have come to be annual events in the art world. Those of 1941, scheduled for May as usual, were held at the Associated American Artists Gallery and comprised another prolific crop of water colors, lithographs and drawings. Five years ago, when Dehn took up water colors at the age of forty, he did one a day. In 1940 he had two shows of new work simultaneously, one in Chicago at the International Water Color Show, where his works had a special room, and one at the Weyhe Gallery in New York. "The new pictures," said Edward Alden Jewell, "betoken a new robustness, a deepened sense of the realities that lie behind appearances. Adolf Dehn, unless in some of the piquant caricatures, makes no bid for facile réclame."

A Guggenheim Fellow in 1939 and winner of honors and awards in the print division at the Philadelphia Art Alliance from 1933 to 1934, Dehn is no ivory tower resident. "Half straight, half comic," said *Time*, "his squirming, salty lithographs were prized by art connoisseurs as well as magazine readers, made the grade of leading United States and European museums." His sharp, subtle commentaries on the contemporary scene first saw the light of day in *The Liberator* and have since been published in numerous magazines ranging from the famous European satirical publication, *Simplicissimus,* to *Harper's Bazaar* and *The New Yorker*.

Chubby-faced, black-browed, with unruly gray hair parted vaguely in the middle and an expression at once youthful and worldly-wise—Dehn is a complex of his works. In him there is a little of the Friar out of Rabelais, of the sharp sophisticate, and of the serious artist intent upon the American scene.

Adolf Dehn was born November 22, 1895, on a farm in Waterville, Minnesota. His great-grandparents were among the first land-hungry nineteenth century pioneers to settle in that part of the state. His parents, Arthur and Emilie (Haase) Dehn, were farmers. Along with a sturdy verisimilitude, Dehn's studies of farm life, particularly in his native Minnesota, have a lyrical sensitiveness that speaks of such simple things as love for the soil and the dignity of those who make their living from it.

At the age of 19 he went to Minneapolis to attend classes at the Art Institute, where he had as fellow students such artists as Arnold Blanch, Wanda Gág and Harry Gottlieb. "Traditional instruction," said Alan Burroughs, "did not cover the Carl Sand-

Peter A. Juley & Son
ADOLF DEHN

burg-Spoon River spirit which forms his background. When he came to New York he still felt 'Main Street' about him. He made drawings of the waterfront; he lingered over the details of ugly shacks, warehouses and docks. He drew *The Harvest*, showing three frightened women going through ash cans for garbage or saleable junk."

Dehn came from the Minneapolis Art Institute to New York's Art Students League on a scholarship in 1917. Sent to teach art in a Reconstruction Camp in the South during the World War years, he found time to sketch landscapes as well. An early influence on his work was Boardman Robinson (see sketch this issue), though he did not study with this famous instructor. He was hard up a good deal of the time and did odd jobs to keep going. He managed a year of study with Kenneth Hayes Miller, wanted to work with Sloan as well but didn't get in many lessons. In 1921 he went to Europe, studying and visiting galleries, and finally settled in Vienna, where jobs, including some magazine work, enabled him to meet his $30 monthly living expenses.

Before going abroad Dehn had followed the trend of the times by paying tribute in some of his work to Oriental art, particularly that of China and Japan. In Europe more contemporary influences made themselves felt, those of Picasso, George Grosz and Pascin. The assimilation of these, and of the great graphic work of Daumier, was an almost obvious learning process with Dehn. His own style was so integrated with what he wanted to say that it had little trouble in emerging from the chrysalis of these influences.

While some of the early work of Dehn's stay in Vienna shows the influence of Grosz, he could not subscribe wholeheartedly to the disillusionment and cynicism that dominated

DEHN, ADOLF—*Continued*

the art of post-War Europe. His zest for life is present even in the most incisive of his lithographs. "With Dehn," said Guy Pène du Bois, "there is a depth of laughter which can be made of nothing short of pure good nature." Also speaking of his satirical work, Ernest Brace writes that he seems always "to focus upon some manifestation of the ingrowing: greed in all its aspects from the carnal to the pecuniary, pomposity and the like."

Although he remained in Europe for almost 10 years, returning to the United States in 1929 to stay put for a while, Dehn's work can hardly be called that of the expatriate artist. Some of the subject matter deals with his travels, but the majority of lithographs, drawings and water colors depicts his native land. In lithography, as in magazine work, Dehn has been best known for his satire. In the water colors he carries into a new medium the study of landscape begun in lithography. His subtle and lyric color, as well as his penetrating handling of subject, have brought him within the short space of five years into the front ranks of American water colorists. In lithography, which he began in 1920, he has also been unusually prolific, completing at least 250 from 1927 to 1936.

His satirical lithograph, *Sunday Painters*, is typical of this phase of his work. It shows two well-dressed gentlemen in a mad struggle to put on canvas the placid lyricism of a river scene, obviously working against time. *Art Lovers* depicts a group of "art lovers" taking in an exhibit or, as Brace put it, "pointing their sharp noses on the scent of culture." Speaking of his gift for satire Brace said: "There is nothing unreal in his landscapes, they are not merely sentimental; but when man, or, more often, woman, enters the picture, we are suddenly confronted with all the grim perversity of reality. We feel as if we had been on a long vacation at the mountains or the seashore and were back in the city again taking our first ride on the subway."

"Both as an artist and as a person," this writer tells us, "he shows an unusual lack of reticence. . . He seems to have little need for either reserve or evasion." To most critics, who praise his work without stint, this tendency is a welcome relief from the currents of informed innocence that dominate so much of our native satirical art. "Graciousness and soft beguilement," McBride once commented philosophically, "are not the specialties of Mr. Dehn. He has a northern and severe point of view."

Within the range of graphic work Adolf Dehn shows a rare versatility both in the variety of his subject matter and in his knowledge of technique. He might use a number of black and white mediums in one drawing, merging them easily, and again he might choose to depict his subject in delicate line. In lithography, Brace points out: "He has lavished upon hundreds of stones his feeling for the form and texture of objects. The invariable mark of his work is his sure understanding of the tactile qualities of his subject. . . The richness of his tones, their precision, and their infinite range are the result of his synthesis of skill and creative imagination."

Despite wide representation in museums and a fame enjoyed by few men in his field, Dehn never won a prize, as he put it, "until the Philadelphia Art Alliance came along and spoiled everything with a first prize in 1934." The winning lithograph was one of his sturdy characterizations of common folk and was called *Native of Woodstock, New York*. (His sister, Olivia Dehn, who studied in Vienna, won the Scribner $250 book cover prize in 1932.) He likes the country, and his Guggenheim Fellowship took him all over the Southwest and the West, with a long stay among the lakes, rolling hills and farmlands of his native Minnesota.

Many of his water colors in the exhibition at the Associated American Artists Galleries in the spring of 1941 were landscapes, although others, like *Homage to Mr. Mellon's Millions*, were wicked satires. But nearly all of them were appreciated in a solid sort of way: four museums and dozens of private collectors carried off original Dehns.

While not long enough on the government art project to be identified with it, Dehn was for a time on a Public Works Art Project. He has been too busy as an artist to find much time to teach, but his two experiences in this field found him popular with students. One was a short period recently at Stevens College. Another was his stay in the summer of 1940 at the Colorado Springs Fine Arts Center.

No hobbyist, Dehn likes to play tennis, plays a fair game of ping-pong and has a little place in the country where he tries to coax along a garden when he is not busy doing sketches of the surrounding landscape. Similarly, when he goes to an opera or a concert he is as much interested in the audience as in the program.

Dehn is represented in numerous museums here and abroad. These include the Metropolitan Museum of Art, the Whitney Museum of American Art and Brooklyn Museum (New York City); Minneapolis (Minnesota) Institute of Fine Arts; British Museum (London); and many more. He is a member of the American Society of Painters, Sculptors and Engravers; Associated American Artists (Gallery); American Print Makers; American Artists Congress.

References

Am Mag Art 29:92-9 F '36 il
Art Digest 14:19 My 15 '40 il
Creative Art 5:15 My 15 '31; 9:32-6 Jl '31 il
Life 11:40-4 Ag 11 '41 il por
Minneapolis Inst Bul 21:138-9 O 29 '32
N Y World-Telegram p15 My 23 '41 por
Time 35:59 My 13 '40
Who's Who in American Art

DEKLEINE, WILLIAM (dê-klīn') Nov. 28, 1877- Medical director of the American Red Cross

Address: b. American Red Cross, Washington, D. C.; h. 3000 Tilden St, Washington, D. C.

Under the supervision of Dr. William DeKleine, medical director of the American Red Cross, a drive for 10,000 donated pints of blood plasma for the United States Navy began in New York City February 1, 1941. The organization planned to seek an "unlimited supply" of the plasma for the United States Army as well. In a speech (January 13, 1941) before the New York branch of the American Pharmaceutical Association, Dr. DeKleine said he was "wary about discussing the plan" lest the public get the idea that, because of the urgent requests of the Navy for this plasma so vital in transfusion emergencies, the United States was "going to get into the War." He explained that Navy vessels were, by their very nature, exposed to unpredictable dangers in peace-time line of duty.

Dr. DeKleine said further that the Red Cross was terminating its collection (made jointly with the Blood Transfusion Betterment Association of New York) of 5,000 litres of plasma to be sent to England. He indicated that the immediate supply of plasma for the Navy would come mainly from the 17,000 registered donors who had already "offered their blood to Great Britain in its hour of need." As in the case of its shipment to England, the plasma, more durable than whole blood, would be prepared in a dried form that could be utilized at need with a distilled water solvent.

The blood plasma research studies that were being made by a committee of famous physicians under the direction of the National Research Council of Washington were described by Dr. DeKleine in a recent issue of the *Red Cross Courier* (September 1940). "Plasma is obtained by centrifuging whole blood. It works on the same principle as a cream-separator. Centrifugal force causes the cells to settle at the bottom of the container, leaving an upper layer of golden colored plasma. This is drawn off, placed in sterile containers, and stored in a refrigerator until ready for use." Plasma has several advantages over whole blood: "Not only can it be kept much longer and transported any distance without damage, but it does not require typing like whole blood. It can be pooled in large containers to simplify storage and can be administered anywhere." It is for this important reason that plasma is ideally suited for the emergency treatment of the wounded in military as well as civilian practice.

A pioneer in the public health field, Dr. DeKleine's special interests during his medical career have been the combating of tuberculosis (he was director of the Michigan Tuberculosis Survey Campaign) and the pellagra problem of the South. He was born on a farm in Jamestown, Ottawa County, Michigan on November 28, 1877. Of his

DR. WILLIAM DEKLEINE

parents Dr. DeKleine writes us: "My father, Hilbert, was born in The Netherlands in 1845, youngest of seven children of Derk DeKleine, who came to the United States in 1848 with a group of Dutch immigrants under the leadership of Albertus Christiaan Van Raalte, a minister of the Dutch Reformed Church. This group trekked to Ottawa County, Michigan and founded a Dutch Colony known as Holland on the shores of Lake Michigan. Derk DeKleine settled his family near Holland on a tract of land purchased from the Government, and became a prosperous farmer. Hilbert also became a farmer and had six children, of whom I am the fourth. My mother, Alice Kremers, was born in Michigan in 1852, the daughter of Willem Kremers, also a member of this Colony. He also became a prosperous farmer."

William DeKleine went to Hope College, Holland, Michigan, where he received his B. A. in 1902, and was graduated from Northwestern University Medical School in 1906. He began his medical practice in Grand Haven, Michigan, remaining there until 1914, when he went to the University of Michigan to study public health under the direction of the late Dr. V. C. Vaughan, dean of the Medical School. The following year he received a degree of Master of Science in public health.

In 1915 Dr. DeKleine was appointed director of a tuberculosis survey campaign conducted by the Michigan State Board of Health. "This was a two-year state-wide educational campaign; the first one of its kind ever conducted in this country," he writes. "We traveled from county to county with a group of specialists, offering free examinations to anyone suspected of having tuberculosis. This campaign reached thou-

DEKLEINE, WILLIAM—*Continued*

sands of people and started a wave of interest throughout the state in early diagnosis and treatment. Mobile units of all kinds have since been introduced in every part of the country."

In 1917 he was appointed first full-time health officer of Flint, Michigan, and he served in the same capacity in Saginaw from 1922 to 1924. For four years thereafter he was associated with private agencies in New York City engaged in promoting nationwide interest in child health work. It was while directing the medical relief work for the Red Cross in connection with the Mississippi Flood Disaster of 1927 that Dr. DeKleine became interested in the South's pellagra problem. He inaugurated there a yeast distribution program, since "pure yeast contains more of the pellagra preventive than any food known, and is therefore an important emergency measure in the absence of an adequate diet. The distribution of large quantities of this product, coupled with the promotion of gardening, has contributed largely to the recent marked reduction in deaths from this disease." Red Cross chapters under Dr. DeKleine's direction are still distributing large quantities of yeast in the South. The present pellagra death rate is said to be 70 per cent below the rate in 1927, when the work was started.

Dr. DeKleine has "participated in all the major disasters in this country since 1927, including floods, hurricanes, tornadoes, fires, epidemics, explosions, droughts, etc." His work in public health has taken him to all parts of the United States, supervising the organization of health departments, of "traveling tuberculosis clinics," and directing the rehabilitation of disaster-victims who are unable to help themselves. He is a member of the Board of Directors of the National Health Council, Fellow of the American Medical and the American Public Health Associations, and a member of the D. C. Medical Society and of the Southern Medical Association.

In connection with these many activities Dr. DeKleine has found time to write a number of monographs on his surveys. These include "Community Clinics and Public Health" (*Journal Michigan State Medical Society*, October 1921); "Recent Trends in Pellagra" (*American Journal of Public Health*, June 1937); "Red Cross Blood Transfusion Projects" (*Journal American Medical Association*, December 3, 1938); and "Cerebrospinal Meningitis in a Flood Refugee Center" (*Southern Medical Journal*, January 1938).

A strong physique—Dr. DeKleine is six feet two inches tall, weighs nearly two hundred pounds—has given him energy and endurance for the long, hard hours of emergency work he has supervised during major disasters. He is married (in 1906 to Lottie M. Hoyt of Holland, Michigan) and has one son, Dr. Edwin H. DeKleine, who is a plastic surgeon in Buffalo. A young grandson is one of Dr. William DeKleine's major interests.

Besides his work on the supervision of the blood plasma drive, Dr. DeKleine says

that his "present special interest is in the subject of health nutrition; believing that the next important contribution to the public health and the prolongation of life will come through the general application of the newer knowledge of nutrition. Other things being equal, individuals and families who observe correct dietary habits and practices will be less subject to illness and live longer than those who do not. I hope to devote the remainder of my life mostly to promoting interest in that subject and to helping make it possible for people to have access to the foods they need."

References

> Am J Pub Health 7:182-6 F '17
> Country Gentleman 107:10-11+ Ag '37
> J Am Medical Assn 111:2101-3 D 3 '38
> N Y Herald Tribune Ja 14 '41
> Red Cross Courier S '40
> So Medical J 31:75-8 Ja '38
> American Medical Directory
> Who's Who in America
> Who's Who in the Nation's Capital

DE LONG, EMMA J. WOTTON Mar. 11, 1851—Nov. 24, 1940 Widow of Lieutenant Commander George Washington De Long, naval officer and Arctic explorer; edited his journal and wrote *Explorer's Wife.*

References

> American Women
> De Long, E. J. W. Explorer's Wife 1938
> Who's Who Among North American Authors

Obituaries

> N Y Herald Tribune p22 N 26 '40
> N Y Times p23 N 26 '40

DENNIS, LAWRENCE Dec. 25, 1893-
Journalist

Address: b. Weekly Foreign Letter, 205 East 42nd St, New York City; h. 420 Warwick Ave, West Englewood, N. J.

Lawrence Dennis, publisher of *The Weekly Foreign Letter,* has been called by *Barron's Weekly* "this country's leading intellectual Fascist"; by the *New Republic* "our first American National Socialist philosopher"; by Dorothy Thompson "braintruster extraordinary to the forces of democratic defeat." In December 1940 United States Secretary of the Interior Ickes (see sketch this issue) named him among the leading native Fascists in America in a speech at Columbia University, and Mr. Dennis countered with a letter to the New York *Times* in which he said: "The reality in America which comes nearest to Fascism is Mr. Ickes and the reality which comes next nearest to Fascism is Mr. Roosevelt's third term. . . I wrote a book about The Coming American Fascism and predicted it would come through a war against Fascism. I have since repeatedly said that Mr. Roosevelt and his New Deal were the only significant Fascist trends in America. I have never belonged to or been connected with any movement or organization of a political character in my entire life."

Dorothy Thompson points out that "Mrs. Lindbergh's phrase, 'The Wave of the Future' and the whole argument she marshals to support her 'Faith' that Communism, Fascism and Nazism are riding this wave . . . was first advanced by Mr. Dennis in almost identical words." *The Nation* notes that a student recently visited the New York office of the No Foreign War Committee and, upon asking a member of the office staff "what form of democracy" the committee wanted to preserve, received the reply that he might read Lawrence Dennis to get the answer.

Dennis himself, however, is not exactly an isolationist—or at least not an isolationist of the garden variety. He has announced that although he believes the present war futile for the purposes for which it is being fought, he will "try to help it along once it becomes clear that the majority have been inveigled into wanting it." Nevertheless in the fall of 1941 he was still favoring America First meetings with his encouraging presence.

Lawrence Dennis was born in Atlanta, Georgia on Christmas Day 1893, the son of George and Mary (Smith) Dennis. He attended Philips Exeter Academy (1913-15) and Harvard, where his studies were interrupted by the First World War. After having paid his expenses to attend Plattsburg during the summer of 1915 and again in 1917, he volunteered and went overseas as a lieutenant of infantry with the First Army Headquarters Regiment. He said later that he considered American participation in the War "wholly unjustified and wrong at the time," but that "if he is not too old, he will similarly volunteer to fight in the next war," which he also "feels fairly certain he will not approve of." If too old for that, "I shall be delighted to serve my country with its war propaganda. I am just as ready to lie as to kill for my country. Any ethic which does not put a man's country above all else is a stench in my nostrils." In 1919 he received his honorable discharge as a first lieutenant.

Following demobilization, for three months Dennis wandered around Europe, playing the foreign exchange markets "on a shoe string." He returned to Massachusetts in September 1919 and received his B. A. from Harvard a year later. In September 1920 he entered the United States diplomatic service, and served as American chargé d'affaires in Romania and Honduras before being sent to Nicaragua in the same capacity in 1926. All during the Revolution and the American intervention he was there, and finally in June 1927 he criticized the policy of the United States and resigned. It was his opinion that warfare on General Sandino at the cost of "100 American and 3,000 Nicaraguan lives" served "no useful purpose." Dennis does not believe in permitting such acts as the Mexican oil expropriation on the part of Latin American Governments any more than he believes in open military intervention, however. He thinks that "our only hope in Latin America lies in

Continental

LAWRENCE DENNIS

developing native governments more respectful of our rights and more amenable to our demands"—Sumner Welles' "good neighbor" policy.

After his resignation from the diplomatic service, Dennis joined J. W. Seligman and Company, an international banking firm, and represented them in Peru until 1930. While engaged in this work, he said later, he had doubts concerning the "magic" of Kreuger, Insull, Mitchell and others. He began wondering how foreign loans could be repaid if a favorable balance of commodity trade was needed, how investment trusts could make millions by trading with one another in common stocks, how industry could go on expanding in a world of falling prices, declining birth rates and stagnant migration. He was adviser to the bankers who floated the Peruvian and other South American loans, and testified in 1932 before the Johnson Committee that he had advised against making these loans.

By 1930, however, he had retired to his farm near Becket, Massachusetts, and had begun to write and lecture on "current social change." His first book, *Is Capitalism Doomed,* appeared in 1932. Dealing with finance, agriculture, free trade, international cooperation and foreign investments in a decidedly critical spirit, insisting that "business needs to receive orders—not to give them," Dennis pointed out the necessity for government planning. At that time the Left took this Right-wing economist comfortably to its bosom: Norman Thomas said "the convinced Socialist will find more ammunition in it than in most radical books."

Actually, however, the ideas expressed in this book do not seem to be inconsistent with those in Dennis' later writings which have

DENNIS, LAWRENCE—*Continued*

furnished arguments for the extreme Right. Convinced that capitalism was in its "old age," Dennis was here presenting "suggestions of moderation or restraint" which might prolong and render its declining years more pleasant rather than definitely prophesying or advocating any other system. Among his suggestions were high taxation, a self-sufficient national economy, high tariffs and the abandonment of international cooperation, a "mischievous fallacy" which led inevitably to war. It was after the publication of his book that he spoke before a Senate Committee on "Spending Our Way Out of Depression."

In 1933, writing in *The Nation*, Dennis announced that the banks could not be safe without the "substitution of some form of state capitalism"; in 1934, criticizing the planlessness of the "Roosevelt revolution," he spoke of need for a single authority, a single theory, since the day of "the liberal American state" was over in any case. By 1935 he was already painting the portrait of what he called American Fascism (although, he said, its party exponents of the future would probably deny it was Fascism at all). It would come most easily, he said, if there were another world war to defend the British Empire, and the President were allowed "to exercise virtually unlimited powers within the Constitution." This was not the only way it might come, however. In April 1935 he was quoted as saying that if Huey Long "could get up before 500 of our big industrialists in a secret meeting" the Kingfish could give them a "proposition" to their liking.

Dennis' second book, *The Coming American Fascism* (1936), expanded his first theory, predicted that the war would take place within five years, and attempted to give "one man's picture of what a desirable Fascism... would be like." It was not received so well as his first: most reviewers found it a mixture of "keen, incisive thinking" and "reckless generalization," of "common sense" and "cheap cynicism"—even "patent self-contradiction." Some, however, said in effect that it "should be made required reading for capitalists and reformers at this juncture."

From April 1936 to October 1939 Dennis held a position at E. A. Pierce & Company as consultant and economist. During that time he contributed a great many articles to the *American Mercury*, edited a magazine called *The Awakener*, and eventually started his own mimeographed *Foreign News Letter*. He consistently opposed all attempts at collective security as unrealistic, announced that "whether anyone likes it or not, that is what we are in for, the rule of naked force." In the United States he was one of the half dozen private customers of Manfred Zapp's Transocean News Service, a Nazi news service.

Since the Second World War Dennis has been devoting his time entirely to writing and lecturing again, and his name has been linked with that of many prominent isolationists. In 1940 he published his *Dynamics of War and Revolution*. Addressed to "the elite or the ruling groups, actual and potential" (Dennis does not believe in "democracy or the intelligence of the masses as my critics will generally use these terms"), in this book the Fascism-through-war thesis of *The Coming American Fascism* is developed even further. Here, however, Dennis begins to use the terms "Fascism" and "Socialism" almost interchangeably; in the past he had made a distinction. One critic summed up *The Dynamics of War and Revolution* by saying: "A high state of literacy in economic literature plus a mind uninhibited by moral enthusiasms . . . has made a sharper analysis of democratic capitalism than has been produced in many a year." Liberals were disapproving—and, many of them, admiring. Quincy Howe placed the book in a list of 10 recommended books ("Required Reading for Liberals Only"). In February 1941 Dennis was one of the members of the Eighth Fortune Round Table, discussing the subject "Peace Aims."

"Tall, dark, broad-shouldered," Lawrence Dennis has been married since 1933 (his wife's name is Eleanor) and has two children, Emily and Laura. His hobbies are "anything except sport." He announces: "I am much too intellectual to be a good demagogue."

References

Life 10:26-7 Ja 20 '41 por
Lit Digest 121:24 Ja 4 '36 por
Nation 152:101 Ja 25 '41
N Y Sun p16 My 25 '40
N Y Times p22 D 19 '40
Newsweek 7:40 Ja 4 '36 por
Time 26:84 D 16 '35

America's Young Men 1936-37

DENNIS, OLIVE WETZEL   Nov. 20, 1885- Service engineer

Address: b. Baltimore and Ohio Railroad, Baltimore, Md; h. 710 Walnut Ave, Rognel Heights, Baltimore, Md.

Olive Wetzel Dennis is a "service engineer" with the Baltimore and Ohio Railroad, probably the only woman in the country with that title. As such she travels about 50,000 miles a year looking for ways and means to improve railroad service. From her travels and from her observations, always based on a solid foundation of engineering knowledge, have come suggestions for many of those things which have transformed the modern railroad from a "nightmare of red plush, straight-backed seats and smoke-filled cars" to a comfortable, pleasant way of getting from one place to another.

Miss Dennis likes to emphasize the fact that her work is advisory. "I do not claim credit for doing definite things on the railroad," she says. "I only make suggestions." From these suggestions, however, have come plans leading to the first air-conditioned train; the first reclining-back seats with foot and head rests in coaches for night travel; the first large dressing rooms for women with free paper towels, liquid soap and drinking cups;

car ceiling lights that can be dimmed at night and individual wall lights; lunch counters; new designs for train interiors; designs for the china service for the B. & O. and changes in its menus. Her latest interest is in the newly designed low-rate, triple-decked Pullmans, devised as another step between de luxe day and night coaches and the more expensive sleepers, and she is now trying to find out the advantages and defects of this equipment her company rents.

She is doing this mostly by actual testing, for whenever new devices are being tried out, Miss Dennis is the guinea pig. Once she took a trip to Chicago just to sleep both ways in order to discover the relative merits of two different mattresses. (She slept fine on both.) On other occasions she has sat up all night traveling across the country, or eaten most of the way across, in order to test, check up on or figure out angles in railroad travel.

Other woman have tried to do this sort of thing, and few of them have been successful at it. This, Miss Dennis thinks, is "because they lack a technical background and the civil engineer's knowledge of railroads." She confesses that she herself is more interested in the mechanical and engineering problems her job presents than in those little touches which appeal to women passengers. "She would rather puzzle over the arrangement of doors and cabinets to avoid blocked passages or detect flaws in the construction of a Pullman berth than compose a color scheme for the club car."

Another reason why so many women fail at Miss Dennis' kind of job is that the men who have been running the railroads for years tend to resent criticism or even suggestions from a woman. "Probably the most important phase of a job like mine," she says, "is developing tact. . . Problems must be handled diplomatically." And she has discovered that "if one can present casual ideas for service improvement and refrain from chirping 'I told you so' when a feminine idea works out in practical application, the rest is easy."

This kindly, soft-spoken, retiring little woman with graying hair and a friendly smile has been making "suggestions" and getting them carried through on the B. & O. (and then taken up by other railroads) since 1921. She was born in Thurlow, Pennsylvania, the daughter of Charles Edwin and Annie (Wetzel) Dennis, and brought up in Baltimore. In Baltimore she went to public school and first began to practice engineering principles. While all the other little girls were playing with dolls, she was building doll furniture with her father's tools—not for the dolls' sake but for the sake of her own interest in mechanics.

From public school and the Peabody Conservatory of Music, Olive Dennis went to Goucher College, which gave her a Phi Beta Kappa key and a B. A. in 1908, and from there to Columbia, to get her M. A. in mathematics in 1909 on a Goucher alumnae fellowship. Then she started teaching mathematics, first in Washington, D. C., and then elsewhere.

It was while she was imparting mathematics to students at the University of Wisconsin one summer that she took some survey courses and immediately decided to study civil engineering. She went to Cornell University to do this and received her Civil Engineer's degree in 1920, the second woman to be graduated from the college's Civil Engineering Department.

It was shortly after graduation that Olive Dennis joined the Baltimore and Ohio Railroad. "I always wanted to build bridges," she recalls, "and was delighted to have a job

Bachrach

OLIVE WETZEL DENNIS

as draughtsman with the B. & O. when I left college." This was the time when the railroads were beginning to feel the effects of competition with automobiles and buses, and also beginning to realize the necessity for doing something about it. Within a year Miss Dennis had been appointed to the newly created post of Engineer of Service with the assignment of offering constructive ideas for technical and general improvements. She has been offering them ever since.

When she is not traveling around the country testing berths and meals or figuring out construction problems, Miss Dennis figures out cryptograms and puzzles. She is a member of the American Cryptogram Association and former president of the National Puzzlers' League. And when she wants really to relax she listens to music or works in her garden.

References

N Y Times II p4 D 22 '40 por
American Women
Who's Who in Engineering

DE PALENCIA, ISABEL *See* Palencia, I. de

DE PONCINS, GONTRAN JEAN-PIERRE DE MONTAIGNE, VICOMTE *See* Poncins, G. J.-P. de M., Vicomte de

DE POURTALÈS, GUY, COUNT *See* Pourtalès, G., Count de

DE SEVERSKY, ALEXANDER P(RO-COFIEFF) (sâ-věr'skê) June 7, 1894- Airplane designer
Address: h. Asharoken Beach, Northport, Long Island, N. Y.

Wide World

ALEXANDER P. DE SEVERSKY

Alexander de Seversky is a slim, well-built, kinky-haired, energetic Russian who has designed many speed planes, amphibians and pursuit planes; who has invented a good many of the modern refinements and advances in airplanes; and has himself broken a number of the world's speed records. For his contributions to aviation for over 25 years he was awarded the 1939 Harmon Trophy in December 1940.

The character of the Second World War has inspired him to see a future of planes more powerful and effective than those we now have, and within the next five years, he prophesies, there will be air battleships capable of 22,000-mile nonstop flights. Toward this future he contributed in November 1940 a new pursuit plane which gives the pilot greater visibility and more firing power because of its engine in the rear and its four propellers. He is also working in 1941 on plans for a completely new type of military plane and a novel kind of helicopter. Believing that America's choice is between air power second to none and the danger of humiliating defeat, he has written numerous articles with this thesis in order to wake up the public. One article in the *American Mercury*, "Why Lindbergh Is Wrong," has been widely quoted.

Seversky has been interested in aviation all his life. He was born Alexander Nicolaiovitch Procofieff-Seversky in Tifflis, Russia, the son of Nicholas and Vera (Vasilieff) Procofieff-Seversky. His parents sent him to the Imperial Naval Academy of Russia and while there he spent most of his free time hanging around a factory for which Sikorsky was then designing planes. Once in a while he was allowed to sneak a ride in them as ballast. After he was graduated from the Naval Academy in 1914, he took postgraduate work at the Russian Military School of Aeronautics. It was in Russia that he invented a combination pontoon and ski which allowed Russian naval planes to continue in service during the winter.

When Russia entered the First World War Seversky became an aviator. In July 1915 his plane was shot down and his right leg was blown off by the last of his own bombs. It looked as though his military career was over, and perhaps his career as an aviator. But only one year later he was back at the front with an artificial leg and a special decree from the Czar, and before the Revolution had downed 13 German planes and "won every kind of decoration in Russia."

Just as the Revolution started Seversky was appointed to an aviation commission visiting the United States and on the way over got the present form of his name. His Russian passport was issued in French, and the "de" was a French gesture. Seversky liked it and kept it.

In 1918 De Seversky, as he now called himself, saw no reason for returning to his homeland and settled down in America, first as a test pilot and then as a consulting engineer to the United States Air Service. It was in 1921 that General Mitchell asked him whether he could perfect a bomb sight. De Seversky was sure he could, and though he wasn't a citizen General Mitchell got the engineering appointment for him as his special assistant. For three years De Seversky devoted all his time to this work and developed a bomb sight which tested with 100 per cent accuracy. Mitchell arranged for the United States Government to buy De Seversky's 364 patent claims for $50,000, and with the money De Seversky founded the Seversky Aero Corporation in 1922.

Immediately he became busy on a long list of inventions: retractable landing gears for use on land, water and ice; new methods of structural design, wing flaps, etc. But his company didn't do well financially, and in 1931 he started another. By this time De Seversky was a real American. He had married an American girl, Evelyn Olliphant, in 1925; he had become a naturalized citizen in 1927; and he had joined the United States Army Air Corps Reserve, in which he rose to be a major.

The new company which De Seversky organized in 1931 with Wall Street backing specialized in long-range pursuit planes, and

De Seversky was its founder, president, chief designer and test pilot. During its first three years he did nothing but experiment—a mechanism generally used for mid-air refueling and an amphibian which set a world speed record for its type plane were among the results. When this same amphibian, stripped of its pontoons, was entered in a competition for army trainers, De Seversky won a Government contract for 35 planes. Next he made a pursuit model, the *P35*, which incorporated every modern efficiency device airplane designers had perfected, and the Government bought 85 of these.

Despite Government purchases and planes which set one world's record after another, the Seversky Aircraft Corporation was losing money. At the end of 1938 its backlog was nonexistent and its losses, including "experimental costs," averaged about $1,000,000 a year. De Seversky suggested that W. Wallace Kellett, a director of the corporation, be made vice-president. Five months later, in the spring of 1939, the directors made Kellett president and demoted De Seversky to director. In October 1939 they changed the company's name to the Republic Aviation Corporation and in May 1940 took De Seversky off the board altogether. Finances improved —the company made its first profits—in the first half of 1940 it earned $842,000.

De Seversky, though, resented having been eased out. In August 1940 he filed a stockholders' suit for damages totaling $23,000,000 against the Republic Aviation Corporation, claiming that in ousting him the stockholders lost their biggest asset—his talents as a designer—and that the management of the corporation deprived the stockholders of profits on orders of $50,000,000 by preventing him from selling planes to England. He is also suing for the right to use his own name in business.

References

> N Y Times p29 D 20 '40 por
> New Yorker 16:14 O 5 '40
> Newsweek 7:31 Je 27 '36 il
> Time 28:32 Ag 31; 36:56-7 S 2 '40 por
> Blue Book of American Aviation
> Who's Who in America
> Who's Who in Commerce and Industry

DEVANEY, JOHN PATRICK (dĕ-vă′nĭ) June 30, 1883—Sept. 21, 1941 Former Chief Justice of the Minnesota Supreme Court; practiced law all his career except when judge from 1933 to 1937; chairman of the Minnesota Crime Commission since 1934; appointed by President Roosevelt to a special emergency board to settle labor disputes on several occasions; recently announced his candidacy for United States Senator on the Democratic ticket.

References

> Lit Digest 123:8 Mr 27 '37 por
> American Catholic Who's Who
> Who's Who in America
> Who's Who in Law

Obituaries

> N Y Times p15 S 22 '41 por

DEVEREAUX, WILLIAM CHARLES (dĕv′ĕr-ō) 1874(?)—July 6, 1941 Senior meteorologist of the United States Weather Bureau at Abbe Observatory in Cincinnati since 1911; veteran weatherman was regarded as the nation's leading flood forecaster; in 1937 worked day and night predicting the expected rise of the water in the Ohio River Valley flood as well as in the famous 1913 Miami Valley flood at Cincinnati; had worked in weather stations in Havana (Cuba), Atlantic City (New Jersey) and Ithaca (New York).

Obituaries

> N Y Times p19 Jl 8 '41

DE VRY, HERMAN A. Nov. 26, 1877— Mar. 23, 1941 Pioneer in the use of motion pictures for educational purposes; inventor or manufacturer of a number of devices which developed the motion-picture industry; founder and president of the De Vry Corporation, which manufactures motion-picture equipment; credited with making the first talking movie equipment with plans drawn by Lee de Forest (see sketch this issue) and the first sound pictures for use in the home.

References

> International Motion Picture Almanac 1937-38

Obituaries

> N Y Times p17 Mr 24 '41

DILL, SIR JOHN G(REER) Dec. 25, 1881- Governor of Bombay; former chief of the British Imperial General Staff

Address: Government House, Bombay, India

> Bulletin: General Sir John G. Dill retired as chief of the British Imperial General Army when he reached his sixtieth birthday, December 25, 1941. He was succeeded by Sir Alan Brooke (see sketch this issue). General Dill, who was a field marshal, became Governor of Bombay, which is one of the most important jobs in the Indian Government and second only to that of the Viceroy.

From February 1941 issue:

The chief of the British Imperial General Staff is the practical soldier who works hand in hand with the Secretary of State for War, representing the Army at the chief of staff's committees and at meetings of the War Cabinet. He must possess not only the widest practical and theoretical view of strategy and tactics, but a full understanding of office routine and administration. He is called on to make quick decisions which may affect the whole course of a war; he must think far ahead, ponder carefully and act resolutely.

It is a good thing, the British think, that Sir John Dill now occupies this responsible post, for he has been called "our best general since Marlborough" and has been described

Wlde World

SIR JOHN G. DILL

by the Germans themselves as "the only British general worthy of our steel." And Dill is not only admired for his military brilliance, he is liked for being an officer who rules by winning the affection and respect of his troops rather than by jack boot methods. When in active command he has always gone among his men and has always shown a warm humanity. Once, when he was in charge of the Aldershot Command, the case of a youth of 17 who had been sentenced by a district court martial for desertion came before him. Dill learned that the boy's father was dead, that his mother had died recently, that his grandmother was now trying to exist on her old-age pension of $2 a week and that the boy had deserted to get work to support the old lady. Dill quashed the sentence. Another time, when Dill was investing a young private with the Military Medal, he asked him: "Have you ever seen your comrades march past? No? Then come over here and you shall." The private and general stood side by side at the saluting base as the troops went by.

John Greer Dill is an Irishman from the Protestant stronghold of Belfast in Ulster, and comes from a family which traces its descent back to a Dutch soldier who went over with William of Orange. His grandfather was a Presbyterian minister and his father, John Dill, a bank official; his mother was the former Jane Greer. Young John was sent first to Cheltenham College and then to the Military College at Sandhurst. In 1901 he became a subaltern in the Leinster Regiment, served in South Africa for what remained of the Boer War and won the Queen's Medal with five clasps. Back in England he found peacetime soldiering as a junior officer very boring, so boring that at one point he almost gave it up.

He decided to stick it out, however, and in 1911 was made a captain. When the War broke out three years later he was taking a course at the Staff College, Camberley. He went straight to France as a brigade major and remained there throughout the War, most of the time on the General Staff. In 1915 he was awarded the D. S. O., in 1918 the C. M. G., and during the War France gave him the Croix de Guerre and the rank of Officier de la Légion d'Honneur, and Belgium presented him with the Croix de Guerre and the Croix de la Couronne.

After the Armistice Dill's temporary rank of brigadier in the Operations Branch, which he achieved in 1918, had to be relinquished, but in 1920, before he was 40, he became a colonel. From 1923 to 1926 Dill commanded the 2nd Infantry Brigade and then spent two years at the Imperial Defence College as army instructor. In 1929 he was sent to India as brigadier on the General Staff and stationed at Quetta. The following year he was raised to the rank of major general, and in 1931, after being promoted over the heads of six seniors, became commandant of the Staff College at Camberley. Another big jump over older men came in 1934, when he was transferred to the War Office as director of Military Operations and Intelligence. Here he made a point of seeing how other armies work. In September 1935 he attended the German maneuvers in East Prussia, went over the battlefield of Tannenberg and made the personal acquaintance of Keitel, Von Brauchitsch, Von Reichenau and other generals. Later, too, he established contact with high officers in the French Army and surveyed the Maginot Line.

By 1936 events in Palestine and Trans-Jordan had reached a serious pass, and it was felt that the presence of a really original-minded and experienced officer was required. Dill was raised to lieutenant general and sent out. "He was an unqualified success as a commander in the field. The pacification of the troublesome protectorate was due very largely to his tact and firmness in dealing with both Arab and Jew, and also, it may be said, with the civil administration of the time." His instructions to his troops were: "Don't trail the coat. Fire only if fired upon"; but when he was forced to take drastic action he used, on a minor scale, the new German technique of airplanes and tanks. In retaliation Fawzi Kawakji, the Arab rebel leader, offered £500 for "that devil Dill, dead or alive."

The Palestine job well done, Dill was brought home and placed in charge of Britain's huge infantry base at Aldershot in 1937 and later promoted to full general. In 1937, also, he was knighted as K. C. B. While in England he took part in the General Staff talks with France and Belgium that followed Germany's remilitarization of the Rhineland and was active in drawing up plans for Britain's rearmament.

At the outbreak of the Second World War in September 1939, Dill went to France as a corps commander. A month later he was appointed A. D. C. to the King and in April 1940 he became vice-chief of the Imperial General Staff. One month later he succeeded General Sir Edmund Ironside as chief of the Imperial Staff. In the first months of 1941 he and Anthony Eden headed a British delegation which visited Ankara, Egypt and Athens in order to examine the situation in the Middle East and in the Balkans.

With all these years of experience behind him and all the military tasks before him, General Dill still doesn't look much like a soldier. He is tall, slight and fair-haired, and has "keen, sharp eyes, with little wrinkles at the corners, showing shrewdness and the ability to smile; a spruce mustache; a firm, determined mouth with a humorous twist at the corners." He has one son by his first marriage to Ada Maud Le Mottee. In October 1941 he was married for the second time, to Mrs. Nancy Furlong, the widow of a brigadier general killed in action the year before.

A good deal of his success as a leader of men has come through his conciliatory attitude and quick practicality in emergency. This ability to think and act fast, yet pleasantly, has been demonstrated probably hundreds of times, but an incident of October 1914 illustrates it as well as any other. A great body of recruits from South Wales had arrived in the Sussex town of Lewes, burning to begin their training to fight the Kaiser's men, only to find themselves without uniforms, warm overcoats or canteen facilities. It was a menacing situation, with thousands of tough industrial Welshmen getting disgruntled, and one which demanded the presence of a senior officer. Such an officer was sent, but when he arrived he found that a certain young Captain Dill had fixed the whole thing up—he had rung up Lyons, the caterers in London, to send down a complete canteen installation, and had requested one of the largest tailoring firms to provide civilian overcoats.

References

Britain To-day No. 34 Ag 23 '40 por
London Daily Herald My 27 '40
London Evening News My 27 '40
London Times p6 My 27 '40
Ministry of Information Clip-Sheet No. 9 Mr 6 '40
N Y Herald Tribune p2 My 27 '40
N Y Times p1, p5 My 27 '40 por
Who's Who

DIMAGGIO, JOE (dĭ-mäj'ē-ō) Nov. 25, 1914- Baseball player

Address: c/o New York Yankees, 55 W. 42nd St, New York City

"It's by far the worst slump of my life," Joe DiMaggio confessed in the spring of 1941 as the New York Yankees moved northeastward for their first series of the season in Boston. In 10 games in the Midwest DiMaggio had wangled only a half-dozen hits—a tour average of .177—and not until the middle of May did his batting look like a comeback. "Off the figures, I look terrible," he himself admitted at the time. "But I have belted a good many hard balls, only to have them caught. Mind, I am offering no excuses."

From the boy who came off the San Francisco sand lots to become in 1936 "the American League's most sensational recruit since Ty Cobb," this situation needed, and got, an explanation. "It's my timing," said Joe. "It's 'way off. I was going fine until I ran into McCrabb of the Athletics. He wasn't fast. He wasn't tricky. He had only a dinky curve and a little sinker. But he could put the ball places. Did he start me on the slump? No.

JOE DIMAGGIO

It just happened he was the pitcher that afternoon. When it hits, you do some lunging. You hit some on the handle. You start pressing and it gets worse than ever. Then you decide to concentrate on your timing, and the harder you try the tougher the going. There is no remedy. Time and confidence in yourself are about all you can look to."

In spite of this pessimistic approach, the situation was rather sensationally remedied in a very short time. During the summer of 1941 Joe DiMaggio set a new modern record by a hitting streak of 56 games which began on May 15 and ended on July 17 and was named athlete of the year by the Associated Press poll of the sports experts. "I just keep swinging," he said.

Joseph Paul DiMaggio, Jr., was born in Martinez, California on November 25, 1914, next to the youngest of nine children. There were four girls and five boys. Two of the boys, like the father, became crab fishermen. The other three went into baseball, all graduating into the Major Leagues. Vince was the first to begin, and although Joe got ahead of him in the race he, too, is now out of the bushes and with the Pittsburgh Pirates. Dominic, the bespectacled baby of the family, nicknamed by sports writers "the little Pro-

DIMAGGIO, JOE—*Continued*

fessor," came along with the handicap of an old taunt that he was riding on Joe's reputation. But he closed his first season batting .306, and his second was a point higher, which placed him first in runs scored, first in total hits (on the Coast). What is more, he was voted the most valuable player of his league (1939) and in 1940 was sold to the Boston Red Sox for $40,000 and a couple of players.

As a boy, Joe DiMaggio sold newspapers to help support his family. When he played baseball in junior high school he was the one without the uniform: his father, with nine children to support, couldn't afford any extras. But around the North Beach section of San Francisco where DiMaggio grew up he didn't have his fill of baseball. He wanted more. High school was a chore, but he got through his freshman year. Then, when his brother Vince went to the San Francisco Seals, Joe watched them work out through a knothole in the fence surrounding the field. During the season of 1932 Francis "Lefty" O'Doul, manager of the Seals, let Joe practice with them occasionally, and when toward the end of that season a player left the team he was allowed to finish out the three remaining games. He played shortstop.

His batting was excellent, his work at shortstop merely satisfactory. Finally in 1933 he got his first real break, when a shoulder injury put Vince out of the game and Joe was substituted in the outfield. For it has been as an outfielder that DiMaggio has made his reputation. His outfielding, plus his batting talent, added up to something for the home town to cheer about. "From the very first day," we learn, "he covered the outfield like a tent. By 1934, he was acknowledged the greatest player the Coast League had ever produced."

Even at the outset of his career, scouts from the big leagues had him spotted as promising talent. In 1934 the bidding began. The New York Yankees got him the following year (1935), reputedly for $75,000 and five players. Meanwhile a knee injury delayed delivery, but the Yankees kept their option, and in 1936 Joe reported for spring training at their Florida camp. Next he hurt his instep, then burned it under a diathermic lamp, and he missed the early games. But he came in for 138 of them, and his batting stood at .323 at the close of his first season in the Majors.

Joe DiMaggio has been described as an essentially modest fellow with a sense of family responsibility typical of his Sicilian-American upbringing. In his early big-league years his attempts to be breezy and casual were much commented upon. "Everyone in San Francisco knew what he was doing," observed a sympathetic commentator. "They giggled a bit, but they sympathized. But the boys in the East saw only the brashness, and were unkind enough to make him say for publication that everything would be all right with the Yankees once he was in the line-up. . . It was the simple truth, of course."

"In his career so far," this writer continued, "he has made only one serious mistake: his holdout in 1937. Fans thought that this young man ought to be satisfied with the $25,000 Colonel Ruppert offered him. But Joe answered by turning in one of his best years, and topping it with a phenomenal 1939 which won him the Sporting News' annual award as the most valuable player in his league." In the holdout year (1937), 259 leading sports writers, voting in an annual poll for an All-Star team, gave Joe 258 of their votes for his outfield position! He was one of only two players to be so honored in the first year with a big-league team.

That was also the year when DiMaggio's batting average was .347, when he hit 46 home runs, and when he won the home-run championship of the American League. But he had tacked up a few other records, too, even before his phenomenal hitting in 1941. He is one of the three players in his league to hit two home runs in a single inning, and he is the only player in the more than 100 years of the national game to play on four pennant-winning and world's championship teams in his first four years in the Major Leagues. He has however, never played a complete season. In August 1941, after 121 games for the Yanks, he went to the hospital with a sprained ankle.

His dark eyes, dark hair and prominent nose suggest his Southern Italian antecedents. He has a large mouth and a slow, friendly smile. Rangy in build, his height—six feet one and a half inches—takes care of his one hundred ninety-five pounds. He is one of those rare baseball players—Babe Ruth was that way in the outfield—who never seem to be in a hurry except when speed is indicated; that is, his timing is so good that most catches seem to be easy and effortless. He is a remarkable judge of line drives and in 1940 at the Yankee Stadium (New York City) raced far back to the flagpole in center field to catch Hank Greenberg's tremendous drive. All in all, when he works in the outfield his grace and ease suggest that he is able to judge a play by a split second, and this is quite true.

At bat, DiMaggio has always been one of the "greats" of big leagues—no one regarded the late-spring falling off as more than a lull. He uses a heavy 40-ounce bat and, as *Time* describes it, "hits with a loose easy swing, flicking power into the bat with his wrists at the last possible moment." Perfect co-ordination has helped him to success as a big-league batter, and he had already won the American League crown in this category for two seasons (1939 and 1940).

DiMaggio has a tremendous following, and his fan mail is said to exceed that of the great Babe's at its peak. He is, understandably, the idol of Italian-Americans. Some 30,000 San Franciscans tried to crowd into the Cathedral of Sts. Peter and Paul on the occasion of his marriage to lovely Dorothy Arnold, an actress. With their new baby, they live in a West End Avenue penthouse in New York City.

Joe DiMaggio's $100,000 grotto, a highly modernistic restaurant with a large bar, a dance floor and band, is famous for its sea food. It is located at Fisherman's Wharf, San Francisco Bay, and is managed by Tom DiMaggio. This venture is the nearest Joe ever came to being a fisherman. His yearning for the sea is said to be the work of imaginative writers: since childhood, Joe DiMaggio has had one important yearning, to be a great baseball player, and he was a natural for that.

Joe has been praised by Taub (haberdasher to America's famous athletes) as a smooth dresser. His first trip with the Seals, as reported by a sports writer, sounds like something out of Ring Lardner. "Admiring the *sang-froid* of Trainer Johnson and the Seals' first baseman, Jack Fenton, who was his roommate on road trips, he did the best he could to copy their mannerisms, dress and replies to wisecracks." To the question of where he had been he had a stock reply: "I've been meandering nonchalantly down the pike." And that pike, it hardly need be stressed, led nonchalantly to the Yankee Stadium.

References

Collier's 97:22+ Je 13 '36 por; 104:17+ Jl 29 '49 por
Liberty 17:53-5 Mr 2 '40 por
Life 11:65-7 S 29 '41 por
N Y Times VII p9+ Jl 13 '41 il pors
N Y World-Telegram p17 My 10 '41
Newsweek 17:48 Mr 3 '41
Time 28:42-4 Jl 13 '36 por (cover); 38:44 Jl 14 '41 por

Atkinson, L. and others. Famous American Athletes of Today 5th ser. p137-60 1937

DINSMORE, CHARLES ALLEN, REV.
Aug. 4, 1860—Aug. 14, 1941 Professor emeritus of spiritual literature at the Yale Divinity School; had been on faculty since 1920; was pastor at several churches and visiting professor at many universities; was author of many theological works and of critiques in which he demonstrated the spiritual messages of great poets; an authority on the works and life of the Italian poet, Dante; author of five books on that poet.

References

Who's Who Among North American Authors
Who's Who in America

Obituaries

N Y Times p17 Ag 15 '41

DIRKSEN, EVERETT M(CKINLEY)
Jan. 4, 1896- United States Representative from Illinois

Address: b. House Office Bldg, Washington, D. C.; h. Pekin, Ill; Mayflower Hotel, Washington, D. C.

"Hailed as Republican coup-of-the-week when it was voted in while 65 Democrats went

EVERETT M. DIRKSEN

to lunch in one afternoon," the amendment to the Lend-Lease Bill giving Congress authority to rescind the Lend-Lease authority by concurrent resolution of both Houses was the work of Representative Everett McKinley Dirksen of Illinois, generally known as an isolationist and critic of the Administration until his switch to support of Roosevelt's foreign policy in September 1941. At that time he announced: "To disavow or oppose that policy now could only weaken the President's position, impair our prestige and imperil the nation." In domestic affairs he remained anti-New Deal, however, and late in 1941 voted for the Smith Bill.

Everett Dirksen was born on January 4, 1896 in Pekin, Illinois, the son of Johann Frederick and Antje (Conrady) Dirksen. It was the year of McKinley's election, and 11 months after Everett was born a devoted Republican father conferred upon him the middle name of McKinley. He tells us that his childhood years were "uneventful except that they were filled with the usual amount of mischief," and after being graduated from Pekin High School with salutatorial honors he found employment working from 11 to 13 hours each night for the lucrative sum of $55 a month. It was the summer of 1914 when he visited a half brother in Minneapolis and became interested in attending the University of Minnesota. The advertising department of the Minneapolis *Tribune* gave him a job, and he managed to borrow enough money to pay the matriculation fee.

Young Dirksen's college career continued through two years in the College of Arts and a year and a half in the College of Law before "Uncle Sam selected a nice fresh . . . suit in olive drab color." He entered the United States Army on January 4, 1918 and after completing the prescribed course of the 3rd Officers' Training Camp at Camp Custer,

DIRKSEN, EVERETT M.—*Continued*

Michigan, was invested with the rank of sergeant and sent overseas. Another course at the French Artillery School at Saumur followed, after which the rank of second lieutenant was conferred on him and he rejoined the 328th Field Artillery as a full-fledged training officer.

A shortage in balloon observers developed in the A. E. F., and Dirksen was assigned for duty in that capacity. He soon found himself in the St. Mihiel sector as a member of the Observers' Corps of the 69th Balloon Company attached to the 4th Army Corps. His military service consisted of balloon observations at the front and a subsequent assignment to the 2nd Section of the general staff. There he served for eight months in the occupied area of Germany, doing various kinds of intelligence duties.

He was mustered out of the service in September 1919 and proceeded to engage in a number of lines of business. They included the manufacture of household equipment, a position as general manager of the Cook Dredging Company (1922-25) and a part proprietorship in a wholesale bakery establishment. It was not until 1927, the year he married Luella Carver of Pekin, that he was elected City Commissioner of Pekin. Until 1931 he served as Commissioner of Finance. The April 1930 primaries found him a candidate for the Republican nomination for Congress in the 16th Illinois District, and although at that time he was defeated by 1,100 votes, his nomination in 1932 was more successful. In "rough and tumble" campaigning he has won every successive election, and in 1941 is serving his fifth continuous term in the House.

Dirksen's first committee assignments in Congress consisted of membership on the Committee on Territories, the Committee on the District of Columbia and the Committee on Immigration and Naturalization. Subsequently he was assigned to the Committee on Banking and Currency, the Special Committee on Reorganization of the Executive Branch, the Special Committee to Investigate Real Estate Bondholder Reorganizations, the Special Committee to Investigate Crime in the District of Columbia and the Appropriations Committee. He became known as one of the most effective debaters on the floor of the House, a "good political showman," and generally popular with his colleagues.

The Republican from Illinois has also been one of the most consistent critics of New Deal fiscal and monetary policies—particularly of New Deal spending policies—and during his years in Congress associated himself closely with Representative Joseph W. Martin, who in 1940 became chairman of the Republican National Committee and minority leader of the House. For six years Dirksen served as a member of the Republican Congressional Campaign Committee; in 1941 he served his fourth year as vice-chairman in charge of the Midwestern area; and in 1940 he was a vigorous campaigner for Dwight H.

Green, who was elected Governor of Illinois. In January 1941 there was a campaign in Illinois and other central states for Dirksen's own election as chairman of the Republican National Committee to succeed Martin when he retires. He is in 1941 a member of the Appropriations Committee, an assignment which is exclusive.

By attending evening school in Washington, D. C., Mr. Dirksen completed the unfinished law course begun at the University of Minnesota, and has been admitted to the Bar in both the District of Columbia and the State of Illinois. He is a member of the American Legion and of the Veterans of Foreign Wars, a Mason, an Elk and an Eagle. Mr. and Mrs. Dirksen have one daughter, Danice Joy.

References:

> N Y Herald Tribune p12 Ja 5 '41 por
> N Y Times p8 Mr 8 '41
> Time 37:16-17 F 17 '41 il
> America's Young Men 1936-37
> Who's Who in America
> Who's Who in the Nation's Capital

DIVINE, FRANK H(ENRY), REV. Mar. 19, 1865—Apr. 1, 1941 Baptist clergyman who had raised an estimated $35,000,000 for Protestant churches of all denominations since 1921, when he resigned from other ministerial work to found the Big Brother Financial Agency; helped churches which planned new buildings or wanted to wipe out debts; his method was to conduct evangelistic campaigns in which he would endeavor to show how much the community owed the church for its service.

References

> Who's Who in America

Obituaries

> N Y Herald Tribune p22 Ap 2 '41

DOLLY, JENNY Oct. 25, 1892—June 1, 1941 Dancer, who with her twin sister, Roszika, formed the once internationally famous dance team, the Dolly Sisters; committed suicide in Hollywood; started in vaudeville in 1909, appeared in the *Ziegfeld Follies* in 1911 and then starred in a long list of musical comedies.

References

> Photoplay 24:30 N '23 por
> Vanity Fair 39:26 F '33 por
> Who's Who in the Theatre

Obituaries

> N Y Times p19 Je 2 '41 por

DONNELLY, ANTOINETTE *See* Blake, D. pseud.

DONOVAN, WILLIAM J(OSEPH) Jan. 1, 1883- Lawyer; United States coordinator of information

Address: b. 2 Wall St, New York City; Department of State Bldg, Washington, D. C.; h. 742 Delaware Ave, Buffalo, N. Y.

Colonel William J. Donovan, in the First World War known as "Wild Bill" of the Fighting 69th, seems likely to go down in history as one of the mystery men of this War. During 1940 and 1941 he shuttled back and forth from country to country without any diplomatic title but obviously with the blessing of President Roosevelt, and wherever he went rumors followed. His itinerary for February 1941 included Jerusalem, Cairo, Malta, Gibraltar and Spain; and the New York *Times,* discussing his previous tour of the Balkans, said: "His resolute presentation of the position of the United States in the struggle of the free nations against dictatorships is everywhere remarked to have had tremendous effect, stiffening resistance to Germany in the Balkans." It was shortly after this comment that Germany sprang her Balkan *coup,* however.

William Joseph Donovan was born in Buffalo, New York on New Year's Day 1883, the son of Timothy P. and Anna (Lennon) Donovan. (His father was the Republican leader in an Irish ward.) Donovan attended the preparatory department of Niagara University and then went on to Columbia to take his B. A. in 1905, also acquiring a reputation as a football star, the rather unsuitable nickname of "Wild Bill," and membership in Phi Kappa Psi and Phi Delta Phi. He earned enough money by tutoring to take his law degree in 1907, and then went back to Buffalo to hang out his shingle.

Donovan's career as a lawyer was uneventful—although highly successful—until the First World War. It was July 1914 when he married Ruth Rumsey, daughter of one of the oldest and wealthiest families in Erie County, New York (the Donovans had two children, David Rumsey and Patricia); and it was only two years later when he organized a National Guard cavalry troop and served on the Mexican border as its captain. He also saw service in Poland when he was sent there by the Rockefeller Institute to obtain and distribute milk for children, and it was in Poland that he met Herbert Hoover for the first time.

When the United States entered the First World War Donovan went as a major with the 165th Infantry (the old Irish 69th, New York) to the front. He was soon promoted to lieutenant colonel and then colonel, and his coolness under fire and his daring exploits made him almost a legendary figure among the men of the A. E. F. "By Armistice Day Bill was the most famous man in the A. E. F., even including General Pershing." He was wounded three times, received the Congressional Medal of Honor, the Distinguished Service Cross, the Distinguished Service Medal, the Légion d'Honneur, the Croix de Guerre with a palm and silver star, the Croci de Guerra—became "one of the best decorated heroes of the World War." In 1919 he was exploring China on his own, then was sent to Siberia to observe the Kolchak Government, and, once back in Europe, wound up as special counsel for the Fuel Commission.

WILLIAM J. DONOVAN

Not wishing to capitalize on his fame, after these experiences Donovan went quickly back to the practice of law, however. It was 1922 before he entered politics: in that year he ran for Lieutenant Governor of New York State on the Republican ticket. The victory went to the Democrats, but Donovan ran well ahead of his ticket, and a few months later he was appointed United States District Attorney for the Western District of New York. He promptly made himself obnoxious to the Wets by his attempts to enforce the new prohibition law, and after a raid on his own club some of his best friends stopped speaking to him and his senior law partner severed all connections. But he had received much valuable newspaper publicity, he formed another law firm, and in 1924 he was called to Washington by United States Attorney General Harlan F. Stone (see sketch this issue) to become Assistant Attorney General. Stone had once had Donovan as his law pupil at Columbia.

In Washington Donovan's awesome reputation had preceded him. But fears that he would turn out to be a trust-buster were soon calmed. He was "never prominent among those who . . . denounced Messrs. Fall, Doheny and Sinclair"; he endorsed the evidence against Senator Wheeler, who had broken the Daugherty machine; and when he campaigned for Theodore Roosevelt, Jr., for the Governorship of New York in 1924 he said nothing about Roosevelt's connection with the oil scandals.

March 1925 found Donovan in the post of first assistant to the new United States Attorney General, John G. Sargent, a position which he held under President Coolidge until 1929. It was while in charge of antitrust investigations that he inaugurated the practice of giving opinions in advance upon proposed mergers. All in all, his theory that business

DONOVAN, WILLIAM J.—*Continued*

needed "a traffic policeman rather than a detective" and that American businessmen "should not be treated as though they were narcotic peddlers" met with general approval. It is true that one writer said of Donovan in 1929 that he was "essentially Tory," and at one investigation the late Senator Walsh insinuated that he was "less than diligent" in pushing a certain inquiry into the Aluminum Company of America because the late Andrew Mellon had once been a large stockholder in the concern; but it is also true that John T. Flynn praised his methods, and Oswald Garrison Villard, writing somewhat later, called him "a man of great charm, of unquestioned courage and unusual ability."

Donovan had been one of Herbert Hoover's closest advisers long before the Kansas City convention in 1928. When Hoover became the Republican Presidential nominee he assisted Hoover with his public statements and speeches, even though Donovan himself didn't make speeches, on behalf of his candidacy; and it was generally understood that when Hoover became President, Donovan would become United States Attorney General. According to most stories Hoover broke his word, saying that since there was already one New Yorker in his Cabinet he couldn't include a second New York man who was also a Catholic.

After 1929 Donovan therefore busied himself with his private law practice as a member of the firm of Donovan, Leisure, Newton and Lumbard, and took on further duties as United States commissioner and chairman of the Colorado River Commission. Among other things, he worked on the reorganization of the bankruptcy laws of the United States; he served as a member of the Board of Arbitration under the National Mediation Board; and in 1932 he was the Republican nominee for the Governorship of New York. He was an articulate opponent of the New Deal, and when in October 1937 the Federal Government brought 57 ranking oilmen to trial under the Sherman Antitrust Act he headed the attorneys for the defense.

When the Second World War broke out Donovan was not slow in expressing his opinions, either. His curiosity had brought him to Ethiopia during the Italian conquest, and to Spain during the war there. In 1938 he had watched Germany's military maneuvers, and he was concerned over the state of American preparedness. Nevertheless he wrote (in November 1939): "I do not think that America is in danger of invasion; current talk of a victorious Hitler invading the United States or South America tomorrow or following the War, to me is so much nonsense." Early in 1940, when there was talk of conscription, he suggested that we stop sending our young men to war first—in mechanical warfare older men could do just as well, he said, and "we would face disaster greater than any we might fight to avert, if victory has been achieved by squandering the youth upon which we must rely for greatness in the future." In May

1940 he stated emphatically that "the United States is the one nation on earth which enjoys complete freedom to remain neutral with impunity," that essentially Great Britain and France were "fighting not for democracy but for survival as great powers," and he predicted impoverishment and dictatorship if the United States should enter the War. What he recommended was simply military preparedness and "concentration" on the Western hemisphere.

Dissimilar to President Roosevelt's as these opinions were, they were of such short duration that they did not prevent Donovan from carrying out certain missions for him. On July 14, 1940 the Colonel boarded a clipper for Lisbon, ostensibly on private business, but carrying a special passport which allowed him to travel in a British plane. When he returned in August he announced that he had been abroad on a confidential mission for Secretary of the Navy Knox and reported both to Knox and to the President. Not long afterward he released a series of articles, prepared with Edgar Mowrer, which described the workings of the German Fifth Column; and soon after that the "destroyer deal" with England took place. All this led some observers to believe that actually Donovan had negotiated the deal while abroad.

After his return from Europe Donovan spent a short time in Hawaii with Knox, reportedly gathering material for another exposé; on December 14 he once more left for Lisbon by clipper. The Army and the Navy Departments professed ignorance of any official complexion to this trip, too, but guesses were plentiful: Donovan was going to the Near East to inspect the British forces and to try to swing Weygand around to the Allied cause; he was going to England to counteract the impressions left by Kennedy; he was going to carry out any number of missions, all of them highly important, all of them highly confidential.

When in March 1941 the quiet-spoken, discreet Republican lawyer returned from having dined and talked with important men in nearly all the capitals of Europe and the Balkans, from London to Istanbul, his mission remained almost as mysterious to the public. But his radio report that same month and subsequent speeches on what he had learned abroad left no doubt that he believed Hitler a direct menace to the United States and its economy, and did much to convince Americans that speedier and bolder action was necessary. It was not, however, until July 1941 that President Roosevelt gave him an official title and an office without precedent in United States history: that of coordinator of information. In 1941 he and Edgar Ansel Mowrer (see sketch this issue) wrote *Fifth Column Lessons for America*.

Donovan is "forthright, friendly and energetic"—adventurous, but the kind of man who never lets his clothes get rumpled. Mrs. Donovan can be described in almost the same words. A few years ago she sailed around the world in a 90-foot schooner with their daughter (who was later killed in an automobile accident) and their son, now a Virginia farmer.

References

Business Week p31 Ap 2 '30; p61 D 14 '40 por
Collier's 82:8 D 15 '28 por; 83:8-9 F 23 '29; 83:8-9 Mr 2 '29 por; 86:10 Ag 2 '30 por
Cur Hist & Forum 52:23-5+ Ap '41 il por
N Y Times IV p2 Ag 11 '40 por; p49 D 8 '40; p3 F 3 '41; VII p8+ My 4 '41 por
Newsweek 16:9 Ag 19 '40; 16:29 Ag 26 '40; 16:10 S 23 '40; 18:15-16 Jl 21 '41 por
Outlook 151:47-50 Ja 9 '29 por
R of Rs 79:120-2 F '29; 86:23 N '32 por
Time 26:84 D 16 '35; 30:63 O 18 '37 por; 31:51 Ja 31 '38 por; 36:17-18 S 2 '40; 36:75-6 S 9 '40 por; 37:19-20 Mr 31 '41 por; 38:12 Ag 4 '41
American Catholic Who's Who
Who's Who in America
Who's Who in Law
Who's Who in the Nation's Capital

Lawrence Kronquist

DONALD W. DOUGLAS

DOUGLAS, DONALD W(ILLS) Apr. 6, 1892- Aircraft manufacturer

Address: b. Douglas Aircraft Co, Santa Monica, Calif; h. 1433 San Vicente Blvd, Santa Monica, Calif.

In 1941 Donald W. Douglas announced that "the planes being produced for America's defense and for aid to Britain are, on the whole, second to none, and in some categories, vastly superior to anything in the world." As the airplane designer and producer who since 1915 "has done more than any other individual to give man mastery of space," who won the Collier Award in 1936 for "the outstanding twin-engined commercial transport plane" and the Guggenheim Gold Medal in 1940 for his contribution to the development of commercial and military airplanes, Donald Douglas' words carried weight. His factories in Southern California, employing more than 28,000 persons, were even then busy night and day filling orders for medium bombers, for attack ships, for dive bombers, for troop and cargo transports, both for the United States Army and Navy and foreign governments.

Douglas has become the outstanding plane manufacturer he is, one associate says, because he is a man "who dips into the future with the mind of a poet and the slide rule of an engineer." And airplanes have always been the great interest of his life. He was born in Brooklyn, New York, and went to Trinity Chapel School in New York City. His father, William Edward Douglas, then a banker and now assistant treasurer of his son's company, planned a naval career for young Donald, and urged him to apply for admission to the United States Naval Academy. His application was accepted and in 1909 Donald left his father and his mother, Dorothy (Locker) Douglas, to start his career as a midshipman at Annapolis.

Not long afterward he was among the small group that saw the Wright brothers demonstrate their frail little biplane at Fort Myer, Virginia. He saw it leave the ground, circle the course and return to its starting point. After that, training cruises, navigation and mathematics seemed important to him only insofar as they related to wings and skies. When he should have been studying seafaring problems, he was experimenting with model airplanes and gliders, building small workable models. It was one of these models that ended his naval career. It was a beautiful job and it sailed smoothly through the air after Douglas had launched it from the roof of his dormitory. It made a beautiful three-point landing, too, but on an admiral's head. Donald Douglas resigned from Annapolis in 1912.

He immediately entered Massachusetts Institute of Technology to study aeronautics and in 1914 he was graduated with a B. S. in engineering. His first job was an appointment at M. I. T. as assistant in aeronautical engineering at a salary of $500 a year. For one year he worked with Commander J. C. Hunsacker on the first wind tunnel, a development that helped take the guesswork out of airplane performance and laid the foundation for aviation's development in the next quarter of a century.

In 1915 Douglas joined the Connecticut Aircraft Company in New Haven as consultant, working there on the *D-1*, the Navy's pioneer dirigible. After a short time he went to the Glenn L. Martin Company's plant in Los Angeles as chief engineer, but he left this position in 1916 to become chief civilian aeronautical engineer for the United States Signal Corps. In 1917 he was back with the Glenn L. Martin Company, again as chief engineer,

DOUGLAS, DONALD W.—*Continued*

but this time at their new Cleveland factory. He stayed there until 1920.

It was in that year that he launched out for himself and came to Southern California, a young man who had little more than a pleasing personality, a good technical background, a roll of blueprints, an abiding faith in the future of aviation and the hope of finding someone with money who wanted an airplane. He found David R. Davis, a wealthy Los Angeles sportsman who was anxious to be the first man to make a nonstop flight across the North American continent, and persuaded him to give him the necessary financial assistance. With an office at the rear of a Santa Monica barbershop and space rented on the second floor of a planing mill, he started work on the Douglas *Cloudster*. The *Cloudster* didn't make the first trans-continental flight—another plane did—but it did introduce startling and important innovations in plane manufacture. It was the first airplane to attain material increase in speed by streamlining; the first plane with gas dump valves; the first plane with a truly effective instrument panel.

Douglas went to the United States Navy with the plans of his *Cloudster* and officials there were interested enough to give him a contract to build three planes. But Douglas hadn't the money to get going. Day after day he went around trying to induce bankers and businessmen to put up the funds, and times were hard for his wife, Charlotte Ogg, whom he had married in 1916, and for his growing family (he now has four sons and one daughter). Finally, through a reporter on the Los Angeles *Times,* he was introduced to the *Times'* publisher, Harry Chandler, and managed to interest him in supporting his project. Chandler sent a note around to 10 other local businessmen, and through these men the money was secured.

This government contract was finished in 1921, and the Davis Douglas Company which had built the first *Cloudster* became the Douglas Company. Other government contracts followed, and in 1923 there came the most important one of Douglas' career up to that time. The Army had been looking for a plane to fly around the world and after talking the matter over with a number of other manufacturers came to Douglas to get the job done. On April 6, 1924 specially designed Douglas planes took off from Seattle, Washington on the first successful round-the-world flight.

As a result of this flight Douglas planes got a good deal of publicity, and orders began coming in both from the United States Government and from foreign governments. By 1928 the firm was ready for a reorganization and expansion program, and its name was changed to the Douglas Aircraft Company. Before this time Douglas had turned back every penny earned into his company, which had shown a consistent profit almost from the first. Today it is probably the most prosperous of the nation's plane manufacturers,

and even in 1937, a pre-War year, it showed a profit of $1,081,513.

Throughout the '20s Douglas' company developed and built advanced military aircraft of every type, but in 1932 it branched out into another field. In that year a contract was signed with Transcontinental and Western Airlines for the development of a new modern, twin-motored, all metal commercial transport. The *DC-1,* the result of the Douglas Aircraft Company's designs, took to the air in 1933, was later modified and named the *DC-2* and in its new form superseded almost every commercial model then being used. Its basic design was further developed into a sleeper transport plane, the *DC-3.* The *DC-4,* the biggest and almost the fastest land transport in the United States, was developed by Douglas at the request of the four largest domestic airlines and Pan American Airways, and in 1938 took to the air. Douglas hadn't driven a single one of the 1,300,000 rivets in this plane, but he knew "exactly where each one is, and why it is there, knew how many hours and minutes it would take to replace it." All these DC planes (DC stands for Douglas Commercial) brought to air travel new standards of safety, speed and comfort. Today they are serving airline routes covering 57 countries, and in the United States itself they now carry the vast majority of all air passengers, airmail and express.

During this same period new military models also continued to be developed and sold to the United States and foreign governments, including Germany, quite impartially. This caused the Senate committee investigating munitions to list Douglas Aircraft along with Curtiss-Wright and Pratt and Whitney as one of the American aircraft companies "helping to build an air fleet for Germany." Business with all foreign governments except the Allies ceased, of course, after the outbreak of the Second World War, and since the fall of 1940, contracts awarded earlier having been finally signed, the main business of the Douglas plants has been national defense.

One of the biggest jobs they have turned out is the *B-19,* the Douglas super-bomber, the largest airplane ever built, with a wingspread of 212 feet, a cruising range of 7,500 miles and room for 125 people. For government projects like this and others, Douglas pushed construction of a huge new "blackout" factory at Long Beach, California and another assembly plant at Tulsa, Oklahoma. Plans called for the employment of more than 50,000 men and women with an annual payroll of about $90,000,000 when completed. Douglas insists, however, that all this business and a backlog in 1941 of orders amounting to $350,000,000 haven't meant tremendous profits for his company: according to his testimony before a Senate committee investigating the national defense program, he has actually been losing money on government contracts.

According to a number of commentators, it is "thoroughness, determination and a desire to be his own boss" that have made Douglas one of the leading aircraft manufacturers in the world. Douglas said once: "It would be impossible for any banker to tell me how to run this business. If any persons tried I should certainly get out. It just wouldn't work." He feels, too, that it isn't possible for his workers to dictate to him. Possibly as a result of this attitude, Douglas Aircraft had two serious strikes in 1937. The outcome of one of them was an agreement which the employees had to sign as a pledge that they wouldn't strike, damage property or sabotage planes. There have been National Labor Relations Cases against Douglas, too. Since the strikes Douglas has showered his men with pamphlets on their relationship. A typical one is entitled *Your Job and Mine, a Heart to Heart Talk with the Boss.*

Whether he is beset by labor trouble or the rush of national emergency production, Douglas is never hurried, never harried. He gets to work at nine, leaves at four and always manages to get enough time for yachting, fishing and even quiet evenings at home with a few friends. "Lean, athletic, with a finely chiseled face, bronzed from the sun and sea breezes," it has been said that he built his tremendous plant near Santa Monica because he wanted to live near the smooth sailing waters there.

References

China W R 91 :384-6 F 10 '41 il por
Collier's 98 :20+ Jl 4 '36 il por
Forbes Mag 47 :20+ Je 15 '41
Nation's Bus 25 :26-9+ Mr '37 il por
N Y Herald Tribune X p4+ Je 8 '41 il pors
Pop Sci 137 :126-7 D '40 il por
Sci Am 163 :3 Jl '40 por
Time 27 :46 Je 29 '36 por; 30 :14-15 N 8 '37; 31 :33-4+ My 23 '38 il por (cover)
America's Young Men 1936-37
Blue Book of American Aviation
Who's Who in America
Who's Who in Commerce and Industry

DOUGLAS, WALTER J. 1873(?)—July 2, 1941 Consultant engineer; served as engineer of maintenance of the Panama Canal, chief engineer of the Cape Cod Canal, consultant on the La Guardia Airport in New York City; among the well known bridges designed by him are the Arlington Memorial and Pennsylvania Avenue Bridges in Washington and the Jamestown Bridge in Rhode Island; also designed a vehicular tunnel in Canada and one in Belgium; in 1912 was awarded the Thomas Fitch Rowland Prize.

Obituaries

N Y Times p19 Jl 3 '41

DOUGLAS, WILLIAM O(RVILLE) Oct. 16, 1898- Associate Justice of the United States Supreme Court

Address: b. United States Supreme Court Bldg, Washington, D. C.; h. Eastern Ave, Silver Spring, Md.; 1778 Pennsylvania Ave, Washington, D. C.

WILLIAM O. DOUGLAS

When William O. Douglas took his seat on the United States Supreme Court in April 1939 he was the youngest man to fill that position in 125 years. And with his unruly sandy hair hanging over his forehead, his lean figure, boyish look and usually disheveled clothes, he looked even younger than his 41 years. Nevertheless he had a distinguished career behind him, as professor and as chairman of the Securities and Exchange Commission.

This career was achieved the hard way; everything William Douglas ever got he worked and fought for. He was born on October 16, 1898 in Maine, Minnesota, where his father, William Douglas, was a Presbyterian "home missionary." Five years later, worn out by traveling on horseback in all kinds of weather, by the hard life of an itinerant preacher, William's father died, and his mother, Julia Bickford (Fiske) Douglas, was left with three small children and about $2,000 in insurance. After wandering over much of the West, Mrs. Douglas and the children finally settled down in Yakima, Washington.

Keeping the family going was a struggle, and William did everything to earn money— ran errands, mowed lawns, worked in stores. As he grew up, it looked as though there would be no money for a college education for him, but in his last year in high school he won a tuition scholarship to Whitman College in Walla Walla, Washington. He started out for college with no other resources than that, but soon picked up jobs in a jewelry store, waiting on tables, acting as janitor. Summers he picked cherries, made fruit boxes, worked in the wheat fields. When he was graduated in 1920, he had behind him not only four years in which he had supported himself and contributed to his family, but a school record that included the presidency of the

DOUGLAS, WILLIAM O.—*Continued*

student body, membership on the debating team, and election to Phi Beta Kappa.

Without trouble, Douglas found a position teaching English and Latin in the Yakima High School and found his duties augmented by coaching the debating team and teaching public speaking. He had taken the position to try to save enough money to attend law school, but with the effort involved in keeping himself going and helping out at home, it looked as though he would never get to be a lawyer. "Finally," he says, "I decided it was impossible to save enough money by teaching and I said to hell with it." With a train of Chicago-bound sheep to nurse, he started for New York and Columbia Law School.

Douglas arrived in New York in September 1922 looking like a tramp and with about 12 cents in his pocket. At the Beta Theta Pi clubhouse he found a fraternity brother from Washington to stake him to $75, and with it he enrolled in the law school. But the money lasted only a short time, debts piled up, and it began to look as though William Douglas' ambition to become a lawyer would never be fulfilled. Just when things were worst, he learned from the appointments office at Columbia that some one was wanted by a firm to lay out a correspondence course in law. There were only six months of law school behind William Douglas, but he took the job and earned $600. Other openings followed, and by the end of his first year he had $1,000 in cash.

He took it and went back to LaGrande, Oregon to Mildred Riddle, whom he had known in his schoolteaching period. In August 1923 they were married and, Douglas recalls, "blew in my thousand bucks." But it wasn't hard to replace them, and the Douglases managed well until William Douglas was graduated from law school in 1925, second in his class and one of the editors of the *Law Review*. And then he found a position in the law firm of Cravath, De Gersdorff, Swaine and Wood.

In law school Douglas had been particularly interested in the study of the relation between law and business, and, according to one commentator, he went into his Wall Street firm "like an anthropologist" to "study the facts of law and life among the natives." Under Robert R. Swaine, one of the best corporation lawyers in the country (who years later was to be hammered away at by his former assistant in the course of an SEC investigation), Douglas mastered the intricacies of corporation finance. It was the time of a boom market and there was a bright future before him as a corporation lawyer.

But Douglas was never part of Wall Street and its maneuverings. He made one plunge into the market, saw his stock triple within a week, sold it and saw it dip back again to where he had bought it. This was enough for him, and he never speculated again. At the same time, too, he was building up a curious feeling of detachment toward the whole business, his attitude influenced by works like Veblen's *Absentee Ownership* and Brandeis' *Other People's Money*.

In 1927 he resigned his position and went back to Yakima to hang out his shingle. Within ten days he had started back to New York, for he had found himself one of sixty-five lawyers in a town of twenty thousand. He didn't return to his old firm, however, but instead devoted himself to teaching. Columbia Law School, at which he had been lecturing during his two years with Cravath, De Gersdorff, Swaine and Wood, offered him a full-time position as assistant professor, and he accepted it. One year later he resigned, after President Butler appointed a dean for the Law School without consulting his faculty.

Douglas wasn't out of a position long. Robert Maynard Hutchins, then dean of law at Yale University, offered him a position at Yale, and in 1928 Douglas started in there as an assistant professor; within a year he had been raised to associate professor; in 1931 he was made a professor; and in 1932 he was made Sterling Professor of Law. Hutchins, who tried unsuccessfully to inveigle him to the University of Chicago with an offer of $20,000 a year, called him "the outstanding professor of law in the nation." And at Yale Douglas was indeed revolutionizing the teaching of corporation law. He insisted that the students be taught exactly what happens, rather than sterile legal concepts; he insisted that they learn how corporations really work and what lawyers' problems really are. And he himself did important work on corporation law and especially on bankruptcy, part of which was published in the bankruptcy studies of the Yale Institute of Human Relations from 1929 to 1932, part of which appeared in articles in law journals and in his books, the first four written with C. M. Shanks: *Cases and Materials on the Law of Management of Business Units; Cases and Materials on the Law of Financing Business Units; Cases and Materials on the Law of Corporate Reorganization* (all three published in 1931); *Cases and Materials on Business Units, Losses, Liabilities, and Assets* (1932); *Cases on the Law of Partnership, Joint Stock Associations, Business Trusts, and Other Non-Corporate Business Organizations,* with Charles Edward Clark (1932).

While teaching at Yale, Douglas entered the service of the Government, at the request of President Hoover, to direct bankruptcy studies in collaboration with the Department of Commerce. It was partly as a result of these studies that he was asked to direct the study of protective committees carried out by the Securities and Exchange Commission. From 1934 to 1936 Douglas held hearings, examined records, investigated these committees which spring up whenever a business fails, and his report, released in sections over a year and one-half, criticized the performance of bankers as bond trustees and pointed out glaring abuses on the part of protective and reorganization committees. Many of its suggestions recommending reforms have since been put into effect.

In January 1936 Douglas was made a member of the Securities and Exchange Commission set up in 1934 to police Wall Street, and before long Wall Street got its first savoring of the kind of man he was. Before the New York Bond Club, he spoke on "Democracy in Industry and Finance," and the terms he used were terms like "corporate kidnapping," the proposals he made were for the complete remaking of investment banking with management responsible to the will of the "real owners of the business." There was little jubilation in Wall Street in the fall of 1937 when he was made chairman of the SEC to replace Joseph P. Kennedy. Charles R. Gay, president of the New York Stock Exchange, did call the promotion "gratifying," Fred Moffat, president of the New York Curb Exchange did say it was an "excellent choice," but the mutterings were loud, and the phrases most often heard were "inconsistent meddler" and "impractical reformer."

Douglas hastened to answer one question for Wall Street: "What kind of a bird am I?" In his first press conference he said: "To tell you the truth I think I am really a pretty conservative sort of fellow from the old school, perhaps a school too old to be remembered. . . I am the kind of conservative who can't get away from the idea that simple honesty ought to prevail in the financial world. I am the kind of a fellow who can't see why stockholders shouldn't get the same kind of fair treatment they would if they were big partners instead of little partners in industry. . . I think that the SEC in the role of investors' advocate can do a great deal to preserve and revitalize the capitalistic system upon truly conservative standards."

Still looking like a Western college boy who had come East and made good, in Max Lerner's words "a slow moving fellow, lowvoiced and deliberate in speech—a simple sort of fellow with slouching ways and carelessly chosen clothes," a man who during investigations would "twist himself in knots, sit on tables or drape his legs over the side of his chair," William Douglas got under way. Now, he felt, was the time for action, and he told the Stock Exchange so. "The job of regulation has got to be done. It isn't being done and, damn it, you're going to do it or we are. All you've been giving us is the run-around. If you'll produce a program of reorganization I'll let you run the Exchange. But if you just go on horse trading, I'll step in and run it myself." For months the Exchange produced proposals which Douglas rejected as ambiguous and vague, but finally a report was produced by an Exchange committee recommending everything Douglas was asking for. In March 1938 the Stock Exchange voted for reorganization.

Douglas continued to get things done— "partly through a blend of toughness, shrewdness and reasonableness which Wall Streeters could recognize and appreciate." He kept a sharp eye on reorganizations, he was alert for all the kinds of maneuvering which can go on behind the respectable façade of cor-

poration law, he didn't hesitate to call suggestions "phoney" and he was able to establish an amicable working truce while doing it. By organizing round-table conferences, he helped the Stock Exchange govern itself without using many of the SEC's drastic police powers. William Douglas, it has been said, "found the New York Stock Exchange a private club and left it a public institution, collecting the scalp of Dick Whitney and the magic symbols of the Street's Elder Bankers in transit." His *Democracy and Finance* (1940) was written during this period.

In March 1939 President Roosevelt nominated him an Associate Justice of the Supreme Court in an appointment that pleased Congress, the inner White House circle and the public. Since then Justice Douglas has "brought to the Court something it could well use—an intimate knowledge of corporate finance and familiarity with the complexities of sound business finance as distinct from the complexities of financial finagling." A man who, according to Max Lerner, has one of the sharpest and deftest minds in Washington, he has shown himself on the court to be a liberal and a reformer. He is not a reformer just for reform's sake, but a man who believes that reforms have been and are needed to revitalize both our economy and our national morale.

Away from the Court he spends his spare time with his wife and his two children, Mildred, and William, known as "Bumble"; plays a little bridge, poker or golf; reads the biographies of great and little men and women.

References
   Am Mag 127:20-1+ My '39 por
   Collier's 97:9+ My 9 '36 por; 101:12-13+ Ja 29 '38
   Lit Digest 125:12-13 Ja 29 '38 por
   Nation 145:429-32 O 23 '37; 152:48-50 Ja 11 '41
   Newsweek 13:13 Mr 27 '39 por
   Read Digest 34:58-60 Je '39
   Time 27:50 Ja 27 '36 por; 29:71 Ap 5 '37 por; 30:61-2+ O 11 '37 pors; 33:12-13 Mr 27 '39 por

   America's Young Men
   Lerner, M. Ideas Are Weapons p267-74 1939
   Who's Who in America
   Who's Who in Law
   Who's Who in the Nation's Capital

DOWNS, ROBERT B(INGHAM) May 25, 1903- Librarian
Address: Library, New York University, New York City

As part of the national defense program, a commission of librarians has been created to survey the emergency research facilities of 700 of the nation's chief libraries. This commission, known as the Joint Committee on Library Research Facilities for National Emergency, was organized at the suggestion of Archibald MacLeish in cooperation with the

ROBERT B. DOWNS

Library Service Division of the United States Office of Education, the Special Libraries Association and the American Library Association. Its activities were made possible by funds from the latter and from the Carnegie Corporation, although much of the actual work has been done by volunteers from 200 general and 500 special libraries.

Descriptions of collections numbering millions of volumes and other library data needed in the work of the National Defense Council have been assembled in the Library of Congress by the Joint Committee. A summary of this material was published by the American Library Association under the title *Guide to Library Facilities for National Defense*, for distribution to Government officials and research libraries of the United States. The survey of library resources covers widely spread fields of technology and science: aeronautics, bridges, copper, fortifications, gas, hydrography, irrigation, lighthouses, mineralogy, phosphates, sulphur, timber, zinc; war contracts; financing of plant expansion for defense purposes.

This is the first time in the history of American libraries that such a survey has been undertaken. Robert B. Downs, chairman of the committee, believes that its value will not be limited to the present emergency period, but that it will prove equally important in normal times. He says that it may be the springboard for the establishment of a centralized source of information of the nation's technical research resources. The present committee's efforts may lead to a similar but even larger study of the 150,000,000 books now in the research libraries throughout the country.

Robert Downs has had much experience in surveying the resources of libraries. In 1938 he edited *Resources of Southern Libraries*. This study started with the organization of the committee on resources of Southern libraries by the American Library Association. "As a reference book, this guide," says one reviewer, "will be consulted frequently and profitably. As a book to be read through at successive sittings, it offers most interesting if somewhat disconnected information and suggests the possibility of a regional bibliographical tour filled with delightful surprises."

Robert Bingham Downs has an understanding of the South. He was born in Lenoir, North Carolina, where his Scotch-Irish father, John McLeod Downs, was a merchant, a postmaster and a member of the State Legislature. His mother, Clara Catherine (Hartley) Downs, was of Dutch-English descent. He had his first library experience at the University of North Carolina, where he worked as an assistant while attending the University. He was graduated in 1926 and then entered the School of Library Service at Columbia University, from which he received a B. S. in 1927 and an M. S. in 1929. In the meantime he worked as a reference assistant at the New York City Public Library. In 1923 he published a pamphlet, *American Humor*, written in collaboration with Elizabeth Crooks, a classmate from Newark, Delaware, whom he married in 1929. They have two children, Clara Breckenridge and Mary Roberta.

From 1929 to 1931 Robert Downs was librarian and assistant professor of bibliography at Colby College, Waterville, Maine. Then he returned to the University of North Carolina to serve as assistant to Dr. Louis Round Wilson, the librarian. After one year, following Dr. Wilson's appointment to the University of Chicago Graduate Library School, Downs was made acting librarian and a year later librarian and professor of library science. With Dr. Wilson he wrote *Special Collections for the Study of History and Literature in the Southeast* (1934). Along with his administrative work he conducted courses in reference, bibliography and the history of books and libraries; and to the graduate students of the University he gave a special series of bibliographical lectures. To encourage recreational reading he had a book store installed in the library building and arranged for weekly talks by authors and critics.

At the time of Downs' appointment to the directorship of the New York University Libraries (1938) it was written: "Considering Mr. Downs' professional activities in the direction of library coordination and cooperation, it is apparent that he has had a fertile field in the South and has worked it well. As a member of the American Library Association's board on resources of American libraries, and as chairman of the Association's Committee on Resources of Southern libraries, he conducted a survey, the results of which are of extraordinary potential value to American scholars. As librarian of the University of North Carolina he aided the integration of regional resources, cooperating closely with Duke University." In other directions as well, says this same commentator, "his work has been notable. Strong collections in such fields as Negro history and State documents have been built up; passage of a law requiring a deposit of 25 copies of all State documents in the University library was obtained; and a system of extensive duplicate exchange was developed."

He has contributed many papers to library and other periodicals and has published *The Story of Books* (1935), a pamphlet popularizing the history of printing, and a *Guide for the Description and Evaluation of Research Materials* (1939), a list of classified headings to use in estimating the strength of a library.

Robert M. Downs is at present also working on a survey of the library resources of New York City for the American Library Association, and under his direction a study of union catalogs will be undertaken as a Carnegie project for 1941. He is president of the Association of College and Reference Librarians and a member of many professional associations as well as of the Grolier and Salmagundi clubs. He is a Democrat; golf and travel are his hobbies.

References

Lib Service News 7:25-6 Ap '38 por
N Y Times p19 Mr 17 '38
Leaders in Education 1941
Who's Who in America
Who's Who in Library Service

DRAPER, DOROTHY (TUCKERMAN)
Nov. 22, 1889- Decorator; real estate stylist
Address: b. 38 E. 57th St, New York City

"All that anyone needs to become a good decorator is a sense of beauty, a sense of fun, and some common sense," says Dorothy Draper, America's foremost woman decorator and real estate stylist. Her achievements include the redesigning and furnishing of New York's famous Hampshire House (the biggest decorating job ever awarded to a woman), the Terrace Club of the World's Fair, the Hotel Carlyle, Hollywood's Arrowhead Springs Hotel, Camillia House at the Drake Hotel in Chicago, the Delnor Hospital, St. Charles, Illinois, New York's new Maison Coty and the Mayflower Hotel, Washington, D. C. Mrs. Draper has not only done face-lifting operations on old buildings and pulled many an anemic property out of the red, but has smartened up the apartments—and lives—of "Top Drawer Society." Among decorating circles the term "Draperized" is used to indicate her particular and individual technique. In April 1941 she was appointed director of the Studio of Architecture Building and Furnishing of *Good Housekeeping* Magazine, and assumed her new duties on June 1.

To thousands of homemaking women throughout the United States, Dorothy Draper is already known through her articles in magazines such as *Vogue* and *House and Garden*. Her extension course, "Learn to Live," grew

DOROTHY DRAPER

out of the countless letters on decorating and entertaining problems she received from women in many countries. Early questions ranged from "I have red hair, but do you think I can do my bedroom in pink?" to "Will a new dining room rug help me hold my husband?" It soon became apparent to Mrs. Draper that women's whole lives often needed refurbishing: the course became as much concerned with such matters as Understanding Yourself and How To Love And Be Loved as with formal versus informal home styling.

Two well-received books by Mrs. Draper have recently been published: *Decorating Is Fun! How To Be Your Own Decorator* (1939) and *Entertaining Is Fun! How To Be a Popular Hostess* (1941). In the former she showed how women can decorate their homes, expressing their own tastes, at little expense: what to do about awkwardly shaped rooms, how to economize on floor coverings, how to reupholster furniture, etc. It is a practical book answering "a huge variety of questions with a blithe spirit as well as with professional competence." In her new book, *Entertaining Is Fun*, Mrs. Draper emphasizes the art of enjoying oneself as hostess. Her advice on how to make guests want to come again includes "intelligent planning, daring and originality." The book covers everything from a buffet supper to a week end, and includes a chapter on how to entertain one's husband.

The success story behind Dorothy Draper, Inc., is not at all the feminine version of the Horatio Alger pattern. Dorothy Tuckerman was born into a family long regarded as one of New England's most aristocratic, has always been listed in the *Social Register*, started her career from the ballrooms of Newport and Tuxedo Park, belongs to the River and Tuxedo Clubs (two of New York's most exclusive), and entertains the best people in her beautiful tower apartment in Hampshire House. She

DRAPER, DOROTHY—*Continued*

was born in New York City of Colonial ancestry. Her paternal great-great-great grandfather was Oliver Wolcott, one of the signers of the Declaration of Independence. Her parents were Paul and Susan (Minturn) Tuckerman. She grew up in New York and Newport, and had "no schooling to speak of, except that I was brought up where I had the privilege of being constantly in touch with surroundings of pleasant good taste." She didn't study art or decorating in school, and lays claim to no special talents; but extensive travels in Europe augmented and enriched her own background and natural good taste.

Following her marriage in 1912 to Dr. George Draper, she lived as a glamorous young society matron. "Tall, statuesque, always beautifully dressed and meticulously groomed," she wrought such magic in her own houses that friends and acquaintances began urging her to "do" their houses or apartments for them. News of what she was able to do in decorative matters got around to architects and real estate men. Her professional career began in earnest when Douglas Elliman, one of New York's best-known realtors, gave her the Hotel Carlyle to decorate. She achieved the Hall of Fame (1933) for the decorating of the River Club, for work brimful of originality, and for her latest venture—remodeling of tenements. In 1934 she was chosen as sole representative in decoration by the National Federation of Business and Professional Women.

"She is slender and vibrant, dark-haired and dark-eyed, this Mrs. Draper who has three children and a grandchild three months old. [This was written before she became twice a grandmother.] She thinks a great deal of superfluous nonsense is talked about women combining careers with normal home life. The way to combine the two, she thinks, is to combine the two and not dramatize them." But she says, too, that "American women are divided into two classes, the happily married and the decorators." She herself has been divorced for years.

Mrs. Draper, who calls herself a "stylist and designer," lands orders by presenting to hardboiled realty owners instances where "lowcost but intelligently-applied cheerfulness has boosted rentals." She combats drabness in buildings by selling principally "imagination and paint-and-color jobs." Once she did no more with an old building than paint the outside shiny black with white trim, and the doors in different striking colors. Within three months it was 100 per cent rented. "Her prize exhibit is a block of once disconsolate New York tenements belonging to the Henry Phipps Estates. Under the Draper rejuvenation an average of $15,000 was spent on each of the 11 buildings. Results: 100 per cent occupancy with a comforting waiting list of high-type tenants; increase of rentals from $25 to an average $100; return of property to an income-paying basis in addition to amortization of improvement costs; general betterment of neighborhood."

She has decorated the homes of many society leaders, including those of Mrs. Frank Vanderlip, Mrs. Owen Young and Mrs. Preston Davies. The only valid test of a successfully decorated room, she asserts, is the reaction of a person standing in the doorway—whether he or she exclaims: "What a lovely room!" Visitors to Mrs. Draper's own tower apartment are said to enter with exactly that exclamation. "A small but conveniently arranged foyer is hung with brilliantly colored wallpaper and eighteenth century engravings which are family heirlooms. There is a generous mirror above a handsome black lacquer commode designed by Mrs. Draper, and side chairs in green leather. Her spacious drawing room manages to achieve an elegance and a dramatic quality without infringing upon the general atmosphere of restfulness and comfort. It combines furniture of many periods, mostly eighteenth century, but with a few modern notes, including small tables of black mirror, white plaster lamps and white damask curtains heavily fringed in wool. The walls are dark and the chairs slip-covered in quilted chintz in a brilliant pattern. A fireplace with shining brass and, when the weather is cool, a glowing fire, is the room's focal point."

References

Business Week p34+ S 5 '36 il
Cue 10:16 Jl 5 '41 por
Christian Sci Mon Mag p6 Ag 25 '37 il por
Harper's Bazaar 74:84+ Ja '41
American Women 1937-38

DRIDZO, SOLOMON ABRAMOVICH *See* Lozovsky, S. A., pseud.

DRIESCH, HANS (ADOLF EDUARD) (drēsh) Oct. 28, 1867—Apr. 17, 1941 Internationally known philosopher; died in Leipzig; had lectured in the United States and was a close friend of Professor John Dewey of Columbia University; had been a biologist before he became one of the outstanding philosophers of Europe; published many philosophical works; in 1934, the year after Hitler's rise to power, Dr. Driesch put forward the ideas of National Socialism as his principal plank in a platform of modern philosophy at the International Philosophical Congress at Prague.

References

Wer ist's?
Who's Who

Obituaries

N Y Times p21 Ap 18 '41

DROCH, pseud. *See* Bridges, R.

DRUM, HUGH A(LOYSIUS) Sept. 19, 1879- Commander of the First Army, United States of America

Address: Headquarters, First Army, Governors Island, N. Y.

Lieutenant General Hugh A. Drum, the only United States officer now on active service who was chief of staff of a combat army in action during the First World War, believes now as he did in 1917 that "mechanical devices in war are inferior to the human element." Though modern equipment is needed, he says, "back of it all must be men, well trained, well versed in the profession of arms and patriotic in the finest sense." As commander of the First Army, which comprises the 1st, 2nd and 6th Army Corps, including eight divisions, numerous corps and Army troops, an Air Defense Command and Harbor Defense Commands along the North Atlantic Coast, he is working day and night to build the kind of army in which he believes.

He has more than 40 years' army experience to guide him, and a military family background before that. Many Drums distinguished themselves in the United States Army, and General Drum's father, Captain John Drum, was one of the volunteer officers of the Civil War who obtained a commission in the regular Army and kept it. His mother, Margaret (Desmond) Drum, gave birth to Hugh at the army post of Fort Brady, Michigan. His early life was spent in a succession of army posts, and it wasn't until 1894, when his father was detailed as instructor at the College of St. Francis Xavier in New York City, that he stayed in any one place for any length of time. He studied at this college for a while and later at Boston College, which gave him a B. A.

From Boston College, Hugh A. Drum went to the Philippine Islands in 1898. He was already a second lieutenant in the Army, made one at 19 by President McKinley after his father had been killed in the assault on San Juan Hill in Cuba. In the Philippines, Drum spent two years fighting malaria, flies and bad water as well as insurgents. In 1901 he was in Mindanao fighting the Moros, winning his brevet as captain and a Silver Star. Colonel Frank D. Baldwin, the expedition commander, liked his work and took him along as aide de camp when he was promoted brigadier general and assigned to command the Department of the Visayas, and later when he was sent home to command the Department of Colorado.

Captain Drum was assigned to the Southwestern Division until 1906, and two years later was shifted back to the Philippines. He returned to the United States to attend the Army School of the Line at Fort Leavenworth, from which he was graduated with honors in 1911, and the Army Staff College, from which he was graduated in 1912. Immediately afterward he went on duty on the Mexican border and spent two years there.

During these years of service and study Drum was busy writing on tactical subjects; he did work in improving small arms practice; he made plans for attacking cities built of stone. This last project came to the attention of Major General Fred Funston, and as a result Drum was taken along as aide de camp when the General was detailed to command the 1914 expedition to Vera Cruz. Later Captain Drum worked out plans for the defense of the Rio Grande frontier and for the concen-

U. S. Signal Corps

HUGH A. DRUM

tration there of the regular Army and the National Guard, made a reality in 1916. General Pershing was as impressed as General Funston had been and retained Drum on his staff. And when Pershing sailed with his original general headquarters staff of the A. E. F. in May 1917, Captain Drum was with him.

Captain Drum was soon given the temporary rank of lieutenant colonel and the job of studying the problem of which ports the French Government was to turn over to the A. E. F. for receiving and forwarding troops and supplies. His next position was in the Operations Section of Pershing's general staff, his problem, with others, to decide how American troops were to be organized for battle. He was at the front lines discovering this, first with the British in Flanders, then with the French, finally with the American 42nd Division. There he was described as a "square-shouldered, beautifully turned out little hawk-nosed" soldier.

On July 4, 1918 Colonel Drum was made chief of staff of the First Army, A. E. F. He found himself organizing headquarters to handle an army which had swelled to a million and one-quarter and helping to forge the victories at Saint-Mihiel and Meuse-Argonne. By the time the Armistice was signed, he had advanced through colonel to brigadier general, both ranks temporary, and had served as chief of staff of Service Supply.

During the post-War decade General Drum (his brigadier general's commission was made permanent in December 1922) moved around a good deal. In 1919 he was director of the Army School of the Line; in 1920 and 1921 commandant of the General Service Schools. In 1922 he left teaching for a while to take the command of the coast and air defenses of the 2nd Corps Area and in 1923 he became

DRUM, HUGH A.—*Continued*

assistant chief of staff for Operations and Trainings. His three years in Washington in this position, under General Pershing, came at a time when the Army was going through the throes of reorganization; his own job was heading a board to consider the Army's aerial requirements and later acting as executive chairman of the Baker Board which made a broad survey of the problem. Clashes with General "Billy" Mitchell, later court-martialed, and others resulted from his activities here, for General Drum never agreed with those who insisted that the airplane was the be-all and end-all of modern warfare. He insisted on this in the general staff report submitted to the President in 1925, and he has continued to insist on it. Successful modern war, he believes, can be achieved only through a balanced plan in which the Navy and Army, each with its proper air component, bears its proper part.

General Drum left Washington in 1926 to take over the command of the First Division. In 1930 he was made inspector general of the Army. As such he investigated athletic activities at West Point, then under fire from Hamilton Fish (see sketch this issue), and gave the Academy a fairly clean bill of health. There followed two years as commander of the 5th Corps Area, from 1931, when he was made general, to 1933, when he was made deputy chief of staff under Douglas MacArthur (see sketch this issue). In this position he studied the problem of army aviation, helped to modernize the Army and build the Civilian Conservation Corps. Also, as a member of the Army and Navy Joint Board, he studied plans for the cooperation of the two services.

His studies here were given a practical application when in 1935 he was appointed commander of the Army's largest peacetime command, the Hawaiian Department. In his two years in Hawaii, General Drum directed the building of more than 50 miles of military roads and a bombproof ammunition depot, saw a bombing base completed, started the Hawaiian Service Command to help make Hawaii self-sufficient in food. He returned to the United States in 1937 to take command of the 6th Corps Area and the Second Army, with headquarters in Chicago, and in the fall of 1938 moved from Chicago to New York, where he was given command of the premier Corps Area of them all, the 2nd, with headquarters on Governors Island.

Made a lieutenant general in 1939, General Drum is now in command of the First Army, one of the four armies into which the whole United States area is being divided. Always a firm supporter of national preparedness, a believer, before the present Selective Service Act, in universal military service, he now has an opportunity to change those "haphazard methods we have followed in the past." The intensive training of troops is his job now, and it was he who directed the maneuvers of the First Army in northern New York in 1940; he who in March 1941 set competitive

tests with unit and individual awards for the First Army; he who planned the comprehensive and exacting maneuvers for the First Army in the summer and fall of 1941. His job, he feels, is to prepare the "military man who insures our peace," not to commit himself on whether this military man will go to war. His answer when asked in April 1941 was: "I don't know about that. You'll have to ask a higher authority—perhaps God."

In his career General Drum has received almost all the honors a soldier can win: the Silver Star, the Distinguished Service Medal, the Croix de Guerre with two palms; he is a commander of the French Légion d'Honneur, of the Belgian and Italian Orders of the Crown. He is also an honorary member of the West Point Society of New York and the possessor of perpetual membership in the New York Society of Military and Naval Officers of the World War, and in September 1941 Fordham University gave him an honorary LL. D. None of these honors means so much to him, however, as the Laetare Medal which he received in 1940—"to me, from the spiritual viewpoint, [this] is the pinnacle of all I desire." Awarded annually by the University of Notre Dame to an outstanding member of the Catholic laity, it was presented to General Drum with the citation: "His genius in war is equalled only by his brilliant leadership in peace." His name, the *Catholic World* commented, "has long been associated with the highest standards of religious and civic endeavor. . . . The simplicity of his religious life has always endeared him to the rank and file of his military associates."

These associates have long been impressed, too, by General Drum's abilities as a hard driver and a hard worker. A short, stocky, shrewdminded man who looks younger than his years, he is always smartly turned out, whether in uniform or civilian clothes. For relaxation the General, "Drummie" to his wife, Mary Reaume, whom he married in 1903, rides, plays golf and badminton. Their daughter, Anna Carroll Drum, lives with her father and mother in a 100-year-old house on Governors Island, New York. Called by Major George Fielding Eliot a man whose "mind is still elastic, still eagerly seeking for new ideas," he once sent his entire staff to see *Hellzapoppin* "because," said he, "that show is a great display of rhythm, precision and deliberate maneuver-timing."

References

Cath World 151:108 Ap '40
Cue 10:42 Ap 5 '41 por
Life 9:95 D 2 '40 por; 10:82-4+ Je 16 '41 il pors
Lit Digest 117:7 Mr 24 '34 por
N Y World-Telegram p21 My 27 '41 pors
Scrib Mag 105:5-9+ F '39 por
American Catholic Who's Who
Who's Who in America
Who's Who in Government
Who's Who in the Nation's Capital 1934-35
Who's Who in the Regular Army

DUBOIS, EUGÈNE Jan. 28, 1858—
Feb. (?), 1941 Internationally known anthropologist and discoverer (1891) of the Java
ape-man, Pithecanthropus erectus; died in
Holland; professor of anthropology at the
University of Amsterdam from 1898 to 1928;
his discovery of the Java man started a fierce
controversy between the followers of evolution
theories and those who opposed the doctrine
for religious reasons and was, in a sense, a
forerunner of the famous Tennessee "monkey
trials."

Obituaries

> N Y Times p23 Mr 27 '41
> Newsweek 17:8 Ap 7 '41
> Time 37:88 Ap 7 '41

**DU BOSE, HORACE MELLARD, BISH-
OP** (dōō-bōz') Nov. 7, 1858—Jan. 15, 1941
Retired Bishop of the Southern Methodist
Church; advocate of unification of the various
branches of Methodism; former editor of *The
Epworth Era, The Pacific Methodist Advocate*
and *The Methodist Quarterly Review;* served
as pastor in Atlanta, Georgia until elected a
Bishop in 1918; author of many volumes of
theology, verse and adventure stories for
boys; the best known of his books is *The
Bible and the Ages* (1930).

References

> Du Bose, H. M. Through Two Genera-
>   tions: A Study in Retrospect 1934
> Murray, J. O. F. Du Bose as a
>   Prophet of Unity 1924
> Who's Who in America

Obituaries

> N Y Herald Tribune p16 Ja 16 '41 por
> Time 37:55 Ja 27 '41

DUKE, VERNON Oct. 10, 1903- Composer
Address: b. 799 7th Ave, New York City; h.
41 E. 61st St, New York City

For many years the dual musical personality
of Vladimir Dukelsky held the fascinated attention of music critics. Would Dukelsky, the
classicist, retain his hold in that field while
making a name for himself as Vernon Duke in
popular music? Or would Vernon supersede
Vladimir? By 1941 there could no longer
be any doubt—Dukelsky was as active in
classical music as he had been at any time in
his long and varied career. He had completed
a violin concerto at the request of Jascha
Heifitz and had it accepted for performance by
the Boston Symphony Orchestra, and a suite
from his ballet *Entre'acte,* for which Balanchine
wrote the scenario, was given its première by
Leon Barzin and the National Orchestral Association. To some extent the outlooks of
Dukelsky and Duke have merged, bringing the
ballet to Broadway. In the process his music
has tended toward a more American, and a
more popular, idiom. Torch songs (*I Can't
Get Started With You*), show music (*April
in Paris*) and ballet music such as that created
for Zorina (see sketch this issue) in *Goldwyn

Follies (1937), have made the name of Vernon
Duke familiar to the public. With *Cabin in
the Sky* (1940) he completed his most successful theatre job to date, in the musical comedy
story form that he prefers to the revue, then
began working with John Latouche, his collaborator on *Cabin in the Sky,* on a song and
dance show with a Scotch flavor to be produced by George Abbott, on songs for a George
Marion, Jr.-Fred Thompson show and on songs

VERNON DUKE

for Eddie Cantor's (see sketch this issue)
musical *Banjo Eyes.* At the same time he
was completing a musical setting for playwright Behrman's *Serena Blandish.*

Vladimir Dukelsky was born October 10,
1903, in Pskov, Russia, the son of Alexander
and Anna (Kopylov) Dukelsky. His mother
was part Spanish, his father Georgian (South
Russian). Of his background he says: "My
parents were well-to-do people in the sugar
business. My uncle, Prince Toumanov, was
Governor of the Caucasus. I was slated for
a diplomatic career, so at four I started the
study of languages. But before I was seven
I was trying to compose." At the age of
eight he completed a heroically long (fourteen-
act) ballet, and a few years later he forsook
the Imperial Naval Academy for the Kiev
Conservatory. He also studied for a time in
Moscow. His early instructors were Glière
and B. Javorsky.

Living in Russia at the time of the First
World War and the Revolution, he recalls
himself as "an extremely pale young man unsuccessfully imitating Debussy." The first
public performance of his work occurred at
Kiev in 1918, when *Intermezzo* was played;
and in 1919 a students' orchestra gave two
movements of a string sextet. During his
last days in Russia the Red Cross discovered
that he knew a little English and appointed

DUKE, VERNON—*Continued*

him a guard, with an old rifle that wouldn't shoot. Then, with his parents, he left Russia for Constantinople in January 1920, arriving "after all sorts of usual adventures that were quite unpleasant in those days but seem monotonous now, as they are the inevitable 'repertoire' of every Russian."

Although it was to be fully seven years before jazz became a part of his own musical outlook (during the Revolution he had been immersed in the study of fugues and of such composers as Bach, Scarlatti and Mozart), even in 1921 jazz interested him when he heard it in the incongruous setting of post-War Constantinople. While in Turkey he began working in the popular field, harmonizing three Turkish folk songs for a musical show; and in collaboration with the Russian painter Paul Tchelitchev he wrote an *Oriental Ballet* that was produced in 1921 at the Théâtre des Petits-Champs, Constantinople. His own music was, in fact, distinctly modern, and an overture, *Gondola,* played at Carnegie Hall soon after his arrival in America in 1922, was called by Krehbiel "a farrago of atrocious noises." With the doors of Carnegie Hall all but closed to him as a result, the young Russian branched out into a many-sided career during which he appeared in vaudeville, wrote Dada poetry, wrote incidental music for a variety act of sawing a woman in half and wrote a musical thriller to an Edgar Wallace mystery, *The Yellow Mask.*

That wasn't all, though. During this first American stay Dukelsky also met the late George Gershwin, his greatest inspiration in the popular music field and the one who later suggested the name Vernon Duke. According to the impressionable young composer, Gershwin was "leading the American popular composers away from the light operatic genre and into a field accentuated by new rhythms. He was also discrediting the old theory that a score should contain two hits and so much incidental music."

Nevertheless in 1924 the bulk of Dukelsky's music was still cast in a classical mold. Included were a piano concerto, two orchestral scores and a vocal suite. Late in 1924, while living in Monte Carlo, he completed the ballet *Zéphyr et Flore,* which had its première there in 1925 and opened in London in November 1925. Produced by Diaghilev, its choreography was by Massine and settings were designed by the French artist Georges Braque. In London the composer became popular and something of a public figure—a tall, top-hatted, romantic-looking youth with brown eyes and jet-black hair. "He became so entranced with 'la vie artistique,'" said Benjamin Welles, "that he donned purple shirts, orange cravats, pinned a baby orchid to his lapel and went strolling with the better ballet types, shepherd's crook in hand. A little near-sighted even then, he adopted a monocle—this ornament he discarded years later after some Broadway acquaintances had pleaded with him all night at a New York restaurant. . . Duke's color sense, one feels sure, must

take a high place in any inventory of his personal capabilities."

It was not until after a few songs of his had found their way into Cochran revues in London that Vladimir Dukelsky's career as Vernon Duke finally got off to a slow start with a musical play, *Yvonne* (1926)—promptly dubbed by Noel Coward (see sketch this issue) "Yvonne the terrible." Some of his revue numbers fared better, as did the works under his real name: a sonata for piano and orchestra was conducted by Koussevitzky in Paris in 1926, with Dukelsky at the piano, and his *First Symphony* was conducted by Koussevitzky in Paris and in Boston in 1927. "Thus," Vernon Duke recalls, "began a dual life, which, according to my perhaps unduly dogmatic critics, has so far been notable for its two sharply contrasted phases: (1) when I wrote 'promising' serious music and bad jazz; (2) productive of bad serious music and jazz laden with promise. . . I await eagerly the symptoms of a third period when the two sides of my musical nature will go hand in hand and be of equally good quality."

Late in the 1920's Duke returned to America. In 1930 Aaron Copland introduced him to the producer of the *Garrick Gaieties,* for which he wrote several numbers that year, teaming up with lyricist "Yip" Harburg. Dukelsky's *Second Symphony,* together with Gershwin's *An American In Paris,* represented the United States at the London and Oxford festivals of the I. S. C. M. It has been performed by the Boston, Chicago, Paris and Warsaw Symphony Orchestras. From 1931 to 1932 he did an operatic work and an *Epitaph,* both under his real name and both dedicated to Diaghilev, and in 1932 Duke's *Walk a Little Faster* had its Broadway debut while Dukelsky's *Second Symphony* was given a performance by the Chicago Symphony Orchestra.

"Duke and Dukelsky," Isaac Goldberg wrote in 1933, "dwell in perfect, if at times modernistic, harmony." But Duke was definitely in the ascendancy. In 1930 this versatile Broadway composer was at Paramount's Long Island studio, doing incidental music for films. He had access to a library "containing the most fabulous catalog imaginable, listing every existing emotion—'fury', 'jealousy', 'lust', 'indifference', etc., and hundreds of fragments to express the emotion in musical terms." In 1933 he contributed music to *Shoot the Works* and to the *Ziegfeld Follies* of that year. He did the score for the *Ziegfeld Follies* of 1935 and in 1936 was called in to complete the score begun by Gershwin for the *Goldwyn Follies.* He was the first composer to write a ballet expressly for the screen—the famous water ballet for Zorina (see sketch this issue) in the last-named film. For the Beatrice Lillie revue, *The Show Is On,* Duke wrote two ballet sequences, one of which was cut from the final show. Other Broadway shows to which he contributed music were *Three's A Crowd* and *Americana.* An interesting judgment on Duke's popular compositions in those days was that of Isaac Goldberg, who wrote: "He can become capricious and petulant. . .

It may be significant that his music is not as rich as it might be in the humor, the bubbling spirits and fun that make Gershwin's songs and dances such a tonic." But that was in the early 1930's.

At about the same time works by Dukelsky included a ballet taken from Gide's *The Counterfeiters* and *The End of St. Petersburg*—the latter a musical treatment of the works of several Russian poets. *The End of St. Petersburg* enjoyed a fair reception at the hands of the critics, though Gilman found much of the score "a threshing of old straw."

In 1938, discussing the field in which Vernon Duke excels, this critic remarked: "The modern composer of music for the theatre must be a combination of musician, technician, artist and long-suffering diplomat. . . [He] is obliged to alter his attitude toward the music he wishes to write and think almost entirely in terms of the market." Yet as Vernon Duke, Dukelsky has been able to maintain a high technical level. His ballet *Raffles*, written in 1940 for Ray Bolger, was a feature of *Keep Off the Grass*. In 1941, while Balanchine's production of *Entre'acte* (Dukelsky) was getting under way, Vernon Duke wrote the music for the Eddie Cantor show, *Banjo Eyes*, as well as the score for an American production starring England's Jessie Matthews.

An artist who likes good clothes and still has a flair for color, Vernon Duke has nevertheless toned down some since the 1920's. His favorite hobby is writing on musical subjects for newspapers and magazines. He is a member of ASCAP and also has a card in Local 802, A F of M. As for his musical ideas, many of them come to him while traveling. Although he finds trains most conducive to imaginative work, he has also thought up ideas while en route on ferryboats, ocean liners, in taxicabs and in automobiles. But not in airplanes. He has what amounts to a phobia of high places, and fainted once while sight-seeing atop a Mexico City cathedral.

References

Musical Rec 1:180-3 '33
N Y Times XI p5 N 14 '37; IX p3 D 29 '40; p11 F 22 '41
N Y World-Telegram p6 Ag 31 '40 por
Newsweek 11:30 Ja 10 '38 por
Theatre Arts Mo 21:209-15 Mr '37
Baker's Biographical Dictionary of Musicians 1940
Thompson, O. ed. International Cyclopedia of Music and Musicians 1939
Who's Who in the Theatre

DUKELSKY, VLADIMIR *See* Duke, V.

DUNCAN, SIR ANDREW RAE 1884-
President of the British Board of Trade

Address: b. Board of Trade, London, England; h. Dunure, Foxgrove Rd, Beckenham, Kent, England

On January 6, 1941 it was officially announced from the office of the British Prime Minister that several new executive com-

SIR ANDREW RAE DUNCAN

mittees had been set up to obtain "more rapid and decisive action" in the prosecution of the War. The first of these was the Import Executive, consisting of the five ministers who are the chief importers; the second was the Production Executive, to allocate raw materials, productive capacity and labor; the third was the Lord President's Committee, which was to coordinate the work of all the other committees and advise the War Cabinet as to how they are working. Sir Andrew Rae Duncan, Minister of Supply since October 3, 1940, was chairman of the first of these committees and a member of the other two. One of the more important executives in the British Cabinet, he had the task of seeing that the three British forces get the guns, the tanks, the lorries, shells, rifles and machine guns that are England's need. On June 29, 1941 his duties were taken over by Lord Beaverbrook and he was returned to his former position as President of the Board of Trade.

"Square-faced, burly, dourly Scottish, he has withstood the hurricane of Government change. . . He has proved himself a capable speaker, loyal to his 'rr's'; and even those who see in him the traditional figure of Big Business admit his undoubted capacity as an administrator." Duncan is a typical Scotsman, determined, tenacious, full of "go." He attends kirk regularly on Sundays and is a member of the Caledonian Club and the London Ayrshire Society, where he used to foot an eightsome reel with the best of them. There aren't eightsome reels for him now: the grim needs of the War are paramount, and for Duncan their grimness has had a bitter personal emphasis in the loss of his elder son in action in June 1940.

Duncan began life without any of the "advantages" and might have remained an ordinary schoolmaster in an ordinary school all his life. Instead he studied law, made contacts with large business interests on the Clyde and made spectacular progress in business, the Civil Service and politics. His father was a social worker at Irvine, Ayr-

DUNCAN, SIR ANDREW RAE—*Cont.*

shire, Scotland, where Andrew Rae was born. He was educated there, too, at the Irvine Academy ("academy" is the usual Scottish term for a good secondary school) and then went on to the University of Glasgow, from which he was graduated with a composite M. A., LL. B. degree.

Duncan started to teach English at Ayr Academy, but with true Scotch industry and thrift he saved enough from his small salary to take a law course. Passing out as a solicitor, he succeeded at a very early age in becoming a partner in one of Glasgow's best legal firms, Biggart, Lumsden and Company, which had many industrial connections. Duncan got to know many of the Clyde shipbuilders and engineers; his chief, Sir Thomas Biggart, was honorary secretary to the Shipbuilding Employers' Federation; and when, at the beginning of the First World War, that organization moved to London, Duncan became its full-time paid secretary there.

At the same time he was given a Civil Service war job, as secretary to the Merchant Shipbuilding Advisory Committee. Sir Eric Geddes, then First Lord of the Admiralty, next made him joint secretary to the Admiralty Shipping Council. By the time he was 34 Duncan was already known as an important man, considered one of Lloyd George's "discoveries." And when others of these "discoveries" went back into private industry after the War, Duncan stayed on with the Government. He was appointed coal controller and given his first chance to mediate industrial disputes, a type of work in which he always has shone. His task was to bring the mines back from State control to private ownership. When this work was successfully concluded in 1921, he received a knighthood.

In the 1918 election Duncan had put up for the Cathcart Parliamentary Division of Glasgow as a Coalition Liberal, but failed by 33 votes in a three-cornered contest. In 1920 he was called to the Bar by Gray's Inn and in that same year, when the Advisory Committee of the Coal Mines Department was formed, he was appointed its chairman, a position he held until 1929. It was in 1920, too, that he became permanent vice-president of the Shipbuilding Employers' Federation (he gave this up in 1927). In 1921 he became a Knight Bachelor. In 1922 he made a further attempt at Parliament, but was again beaten, this time in Dundee, by the late E. D. Morel, the pacifist.

Though he didn't win a seat in Parliament, Sir Andrew's talents were much used in the next few years. In February 1924 he was appointed to serve on the Dock Strike Inquiry and in July on the Royal Commission on National Health Insurance. October 1925 brought a visit to Nova Scotia, where he investigated the bitter grievances of the miners who were burning the pits. Here, in a Scottish colonial community, this Scotsman made himself *persona grata*, was given an honorary degree by Dalhousie University,

and succeeded in settling the quarrel. As a result of his success, in the following April he was asked by the Canadian Government to deal with the long-standing differences between the Maritime Provinces and the Midwest. These, too, he settled.

In January 1927 Sir Andrew got his biggest job yet, at a salary of £7,000 a year. An enormous electrical setup known as the Grid was being arranged to take current into every part of England. To control it, the Minister of Transport established a Central Electricity Board and made Duncan its chairman. (He served in that capacity until 1935, and he remained a member of the Board until recently.) Again his duties were of a conciliatory nature, his task the settlement of the varied and often conflicting interests of all the parties within the industry. In that same year, too, he became a member of the Civil Service Arbitration Tribunal and technical assessor of the Permanent Court of International Justice at The Hague (labor section). In January 1929 he became a director of the Bank of England; from 1931 to 1932 he was a member of the Industrial Court, representing the Chancellor of the Exchequer for Civil Service arbitrations; from 1933 to 1935 he was chairman of the Sea-Fish Commission.

In November 1934 the Government took Sir Andrew from his work on the Grid, made him the independent chairman of the executive committee of the Iron and Steel Federation, with a salary of £8,000. With the outbreak of the present War this body became merged in the Ministry of Supply, and Duncan, as a result, automatically became a civil servant. In January 1940 the late Neville Chamberlain took him into the Cabinet as president of the Board of Trade, and a seat in Parliament was found for him in the solid Tory City of London. When Churchill took over in May 1940, Duncan was one of the few men he retained, and five months later he appointed him Minister of Supply. After eight months, however, he was returned to his previous position.

His success, it is said, according to the *Picture Post*, "is due to the teacher in him. He is usually on good terms with the Head. He picks the bright boys. He does not force them along, but encourages them to think for themselves and have the courage of their own judgment. In resolving difficulties he is a catalyst. A catalyst is a chemical which makes other chemicals combine, but remains, itself, unchanged."

In 1938 Duncan was advanced a grade in knighthood to G. B. E., and before the entry of Italy into the War he held the Order of St. Maurice and St. Lazarus from that country. In 1916 he was married to Annie, daughter of the late Andrew Jordan. There were two sons before the War; there is one, now.

References

Gt Brit & East 54:30 Ja 11 '40 por
Picture Post p20 Je 1 '40 por
Who's Who

DUNHAM, KATHERINE 1910- Dancer; choregrapher

Address: 43 W. 66th St, New York City

The New York daily papers of January 17, 1941 carried a piquant notice to the effect that the chief dancer in one of Broadway's current musical hits would lecture to the Anthropology Club of the Yale University Graduate School on the practical application of primitive materials to the theatre, demonstrating her discourse with the aid of 10 performers. The notice was no more striking than the combination of talents in this gifted Negro choregrapher, and the career they have shaped for her. Katherine Dunham has danced her way from the pews of a Methodist Church, through the torrid mysteries of Haitian voodoo and primitive ceremonials in Jamaica, Martinique, Trinidad, to recherché Sunday night concerts in New York ("Tropics and le Jazz Hot" she called her programs) and Broadway stardom.

That meant incidentally dancing her way through hardship, discouragement, indefatigable labor, to success. From one point of view she has "arrived"; yet she feels herself still definitely on the way. Her goal is suggested by the dictum of the New York *Herald Tribune's* critic, Walter Terry: "Katherine Dunham is laying the groundwork for a great Negro dance."

She has mastered the steps and contortions that characterize Negro dances from the plantation to the Harlem "joint"; has studied and reproduced the juba, the rumba, the *danse du ventre*, as well as the cakewalk and the shimmy. These become, however, not her performance but her raw material: elements to be fused and developed into an idiom of her own. It is never an "arty" idiom, and always expresses the vitality we associate with the dance and with the Negro. The same critic remarked that one feels "as if the performers (of her troupe) were dancing because they felt an overpowering urge for rhythmic movement and not merely because they were scheduled to give a show."

Miss Dunham's background contributed a number of elements to her diverse career. Her family was a pillar of the church in Joliet, Illinois, where she was born in 1910. Her mother, Annette Poindexter Dunham, was a schoolteacher. Her father, Albert Millard Dunham, descended from Madagascar via Tennessee, kept a cleaning and dyeing establishment by day. At night he indulged a fondness for playing the mandolin and guitar, somewhat to the distress of Katherine and her brother Albert, who were commandeered to form a trio until Katherine openly revolted and Albert fled to the University of Chicago. Here he became one of the most brilliant students ever graduated from that institution. After taking his Master's Degree at Harvard he returned to Chicago for his Ph. D. and then went to teach at Howard University.

His little sister's education carried her to more distant and more exotic places. Her interest in the dance was evident even in Joliet, where at the age of eight she split

KATHERINE DUNHAM

the congregation wide open by staging a "cabaret party" to raise funds for the church. She cleared $32, which at the time seemed almost as much as the $2,000 her 1941 troupe takes in weekly. Her parents did not worry too much about her twinkling feet, since she stood very well in her studies, was class poet and occasionally a paid contributor to *Child Life Magazine*. But by the time she entered the University of Chicago she knew that choreography was her field, and had determined to earn her way through college by forming a dancing school. The school was in a cold, drafty barn, and it took rather violent instruction to save teacher and pupils from pneumonia. They shivered and sneezed through it without fatal results, and the teacher managed at the same time to win distinction as a student in her college courses. More important, for present purposes, she discovered the study of anthropology, which made it legitimate—and feasible—to study primitive dances.

Through a staunch friend, who is now one of the *Easy Aces* radio performers, she met Mark Turbyfill, a ballet dancer with the Chicago Opera Company, and they developed the idea of a Negro ballet. Earl Delamarter, assistant director of the Chicago Symphony Orchestra, was enlisted, and the three established a Negro school of the dance which staged its first public appearance in 1931, with a *Negro Rhapsody* at the Chicago Beaux Arts Ball.

The Katherine Dunham Dance Group made its way slowly, until a performance in an abandoned loft resulted in a Julius Rosenwald Foundation Fellowship which enabled Miss Dunham to study native dance, ritual and folklore in the Caribbean and in Brazil. The steps she had to master were no more intricate than her social role in communities where

DUNHAM, KATHERINE—*Continued*

both Negro and white elements eyed with suspicion a young woman who "frequently disappeared into the bush for days on end" and sometimes came back with the eggs and feathers of a voodoo ceremony sticking to her hair. In Port au Prince she was actually warned to leave. Instead she rented the biggest theatre the town afforded and announced a concert. Her audience came armed with epithets and ripe fruit; but all that was flung at her was a shower of "Lovely, lovely!", "How artistic!" and a pitter-patter of applause. For she appeared in a long tulle dress sprinkled with rosebuds, pranced daintily through a bit of Debussy, followed it with a respectable though castanet-clicking Spanish number and ended with a Fire Dance, at the close of which she released a flock of doves into the audience. In comparison to that dual feat of penetrating the inner circles of local aristocracy and native priesthood, her recent conquest of Broadway seems almost a minor achievement. She returned from her travels with a large repertoire of dances, quantities of authentic and illuminating films, and a store of inside information on primitive cults and customs that commands the respect of anthropologists.

Although critics and audiences have been glowing in their praise of Miss Dunham's own performance she rather prides herself on a realization that she is not a great dancer. She feels her forte to be choregraphy, the planning and directing of dances, the training of dancers. Those who rhapsodize over her own prowess may be to some extent confused between pleasure in the dance and in the dancer, for not the least of Katherine Dunham's gifts is beauty. Moreover she has the ability—partly executive—to achieve settings and costumes which further her choregraphic and dramatic effects. She is less a singer than a dancer, yet her low voice, half singing, half speaking, greatly enhances certain of her numbers.

Off stage her voice is also low, and unusually pleasing. Always quiet and reserved, she has an unusual ability to express herself in words, written or spoken. Two of her articles on dancing in Martinique were published in *Esquire* in 1939, and she is now working on more. An exhaustive analysis of dances in Haiti is waiting for final revision, and she hopes, Broadway willing, soon to finish her book on the Maroon peoples of Jamaica.

Asked about her role in *Cabin in the Sky,* Miss Dunham confesses that she looks forward to a different type of performance. Her ambition is to be an actress on the legitimate stage and to combine choregraphy with this, in a new type of vehicle. Her troupe meanwhile is being held together and developed technically, while in Chicago new recruits are training. She is directing a group of children there in the study of classic ballet, and looks forward to adding them to her company. During her absence classes are directed by Olga Rostova, formerly of the Russian Ballet.

The agent who first dubbed Katherine Dunham "the Marian Anderson of the dance" was not too happily inspired, for they are far more different than similar. Critics feel that Miss Dunham's own name is quite enough to characterize an artist whose talent, intelligence and abounding vitality put it in her power to rank as a major figure in the American dance.

References

> Collier's 107:22-3+ Ja 11 '41 il pors
> N Y Herald Tribune VI p10 Ap 28 '40 il
> N Y Post p12 Ja 17 '41 por
> N Y Sun p21 Mr 11 '40
> New Yorker 17:14-15 F 22 '41
> PM p53 F 16 '41 pors
> Theater 9:63 D 9 '40 pors

DUNKERLEY, WILLIAM ARTHUR *See* Oxenham, J.

DUNN, J(OSEPH) ALLAN (ELPHINSTONE) Jan. 21, 1872—Mar. 25, 1941 Author; journalist; explorer; death resulted from a complication of ailments which his friends trace to a tropical disease contracted in the South Pacific years ago; acted as correspondent in the Spanish-American War and the Russo-Japanese War; edited *Sunset Magazine*; for a number of years devoted himself largely to the writing of books and magazine stories, principally tales of adventures taking place in faraway lands or in the American West of an earlier day.

References

> Who's Who in America

Obituaries

> N Y Times p23 Mr 26 '41

DU PUY, WILLIAM ATHERTON (dū-pwē') Jan. 6, 1876—Aug. 11, 1941 Journalist and author; worked on newspapers in many cities; ex-head of the National Press Club; in 1923 became editor for the International Labor Office of the League of Nations at Geneva; an inveterate traveler, Mr. Du Puy was an expert on the international situation in the post-War years; also wrote many books about nature.

References

> Who's Who Among North American Authors
> Who's Who in America
> Who's Who in Journalism

Obituaries

> N Y Times p19 Ag 12 '41

DURBIN, DEANNA Dec. 4, 1922- Film actress

Address: b. c/o Universal Pictures Corp, Universal City, Calif; h. Brentwood, Calif.

The girl who made the awkward age look graceful on the screen has really grown up. On her eighteenth birthday, December 4, 1940, her parents announced her engagement to her first beau, Vaughn Paul, a fellow worker on the Universal lot, who was assistant to the assistant director on her first film and later was made associate producer. The wedding took place in Hollywood on April 18, 1941 before 900 guests in the church and a crowd of about 2,000 fans waiting outside.

The public she numbers in tens of millions finds it hard to believe that little Deanna Durbin has graduated from child actress to *ingenue*. It was only in 1936 that she first adolesced onto the screen in *Three Smart Girls*. Since then, in 10 successive box-office hits, she has "singlehandedly lifted Universal out of the red," has won the hearts of America's film audience with her famous smile, their ears with her "perfect blue-white diamond of a voice"; has developed into an actress who received the small "Oscar" of the Academy of Motion Picture Arts and Sciences for the best junior screen performance in 1938; and signed a contract that calls for $1,750 a week, a $50,000 bonus for each film and an annual increase of $250 weekly until 1943. This, in addition to the annual fortune she reaps from "commercial interests" such as the use of her name for clothing and accessories, put her well up in the $200,000 salary bracket in 1940. It has been said, however, that her greatest achievement has been to stay just a simple, buoyant young girl who finds the limelight as healthy and invigorating as sunshine.

Deanna was christened Edna Mae in Winnipeg, Canada, where she was born December 4, 1922. Her mother, Ada (Read) Durbin, and her father, James Durbin, had both come from England, where her sister Edith was born in 1912. When Edna Mae was a year old Mr. Durbin's health forced them to move to Southern California, where he went into the real-estate business. The Durbins were simple, sturdy folk, with no musical careers in the family, although Uncle Arthur sang in a church choir and all of them liked to gather around the piano.

The Durbin girls lived a normal go-to-school life in Los Angeles. Edith completed high school with honors, took a Master's Degree at the University of California, and now as Mrs. Clarence Heckman teaches dramatics in a Los Angeles junior high school. The less studious Edna Mae detested arithmetic, liked history and English, was very fond of school dramatics and singing in church socials. It was Edith who first insisted that her little sister must have singing lessons and used part of her earnings as a schoolteacher to provide them. The Durbins were not thinking of Hollywood at the time, nor had any of them entered its studios only a few miles away.

But Hollywood came to Edna Mae, plucked her from her classes at the Bret Harte Junior High School, changed her name to Deanna, and thrust her into a fame that seldom happens in one's early teens—and if it does, seldom lasts into maturity. In 1935 the Metro-Goldwyn-Mayer officials had almost given up hope of finding a girl to portray Madame Schumann-Heink as a child, and asked an

actors' agent to help them. Through a friend he heard about Deanna Durbin's singing at some neighborhood party and arranged for an audition. He was startled at the loveliness of her voice, and presently the Durbins were startled by a contract.

At this point Madame Schumann-Heink fell ill, the proposed picture was called off and the contract canceled. Meanwhile Deanna, once "discovered," had made a number of public appearances, sung over the radio and begun to develop a local following. She had also made such an impression on Rufus LeMaire that when he transferred from Metro-Goldwyn-Mayer to Universal he remembered "the blue-eyed youngster with the golden voice," sent for her and placed her under contract at $300 a week.

DEANNA DURBIN

After the usual exasperating wait for just the right picture, *Three Smart Girls* was decided upon, to be directed and produced by the then unrecognized and now almost unrivaled twosome, Koster and Pasternak. While it was still in production Eddie Cantor (see sketch this issue) signed Deanna as prima donna of his air show, and by the time the film was released she had an enthusiastic radio audience to be surprised by the unexpected acting ability she displayed. Next came *100 Men and a Girl*, in which she appeared with Leopold Stokowski (see sketch this issue), followed by *Mad About Music* in the spring of 1938. The next fall *That Certain Age* added the fourth sensational success and won her the critics' vote for the best performance of the month by a cinema actress. *Three Smart Girls Grow Up* reunited the trio of Pasternak, Koster and Durbin, who had been the open secret of each other's success. It also marked the beginning of Deanna's own growing up, which became more apparent in *First Love* and in *It's a Date*. At the end of February 1941,

DURBIN, DEANNA—*Continued*

her ninth picture, *Nice Girl?*, came in like a lion—complete with Franchot Tone, serious love scenes and loud acclaim. And the next picture, *It Started With Eve*, in which she co-starred with Charles Laughton, showed a genuine talent for sophisticated comedy.

Stars do not shine without polishing, and Deanna Durbin's sparkle represents years of intensive work and regular living, getting up at 6:30 or 7 every morning except Sunday and following through her exacting regime until 5; then a quiet evening, usually at home with her parents, and early to bed. The private tutor assigned by the school board of Los Angeles worked with her on the studio lot three hours of every school day in the year until in 1940 she proudly received her high school diploma. Then there was voice study, under Andres de Segurola, former baritone of the Metropolitan Opera Company, who has been her teacher and coach since her first radio success at 13, when he pronounced her vocal apparatus as fully developed as that of a mature soprano. But the chief work, of course, was the making of pictures, which for Deanna involves dual rehearsals and performances—her songs are recorded separately and then synchronized with the motions of her mouth in the unrecorded singing she does while the picture is being taken. An ingenious mathematician estimated that the average Durbin song gave 3 minutes of melody and consumed 12 cups of coffee, 48 cigarets (not hers, for she doesn't smoke), 5 pieces of chalk, 550 feet of celluloid, 776 working hours of 97 specialists, male and female.

To find the best environment for this busy life her parents moved to a large, cozily formal house in the exclusive suburb Laughlin Park, where homes are large, quiet and covered with vines. Mrs. Durbin keeps the household running as smoothly as she did in their humbler homes, and before Deanna was married both parents collaborated in seeing that their daughter remained the model of a well-brought-up young girl. When she drove her own gray roadster she was expected to phone every morning and report her safe arrival at the studio—usually by 8 a. m.

In some ways fame has meant a cloistered life, with study, rehearsal and rest so closely fitted that there has been little time for random "living." Consequently Deanna seems younger than many of her contemporaries. Her promptness and feeling for perfection are as unusual among stars and as much appreciated by her colleagues as her even disposition. Her strongest cuss words are "fuzz", "bats" and "phooey." One of her favorite diversions is going to the movies, but mostly she is too busy making them. The one entertainment she has always found time for is concerts. Among her large collection of recorded classics she treasures the complete recordings of Stokowski, which he presented to her during the making of *100 Men and a Girl*. Recently she has also collected air-mail stamps, particularly from first flights,

Her favorite pets are "Tippy," a dog of dubious pedigree, Ferdinand the parakeet and three miniature turtles: Penny, Kay, and Eddie Cantor. Her favorite sport is swimming, but autograph hounds bar her from public beaches, so before her marriage she had to swim in the great pool among the Durbins' terraced gardens. Horseback riding and badminton she likes; also roller skating, but the studio has a prejudice against that prolific breeder of bruises. Ping-pong is a recent and safer enthusiasm. It is said that her interest in sports increased with her interest in Vaughn Paul. Another bond they share is the ability to laugh at the same things—"zany humor or sophisticated humor, but no sophomore puns."

In October 1941, however, it seemed possible that her marriage might also mean her retirement from picture-making, for she was suspended by her studio for refusing to work. The studio maintained that she demanded working conditions and supervision of her films not in her contract. She insisted that her husband was a Universal producer in "name only," and when he left the studio after demands to produce an important film she hoped to follow him. Later in the year, however, she patched up her difficulties with her studio.

References

Collier's 101:19 My 21 '38 por; 108:14+ S 27 '41 por
Etude 58:76+ F '40 por; 59:84 F '41 por
Fortune 20:66-9+ O '39 il pors
Good H 106:35+ Ja '38 pors; 113:4+ S '41 il pors
Ladies' H J 57:19+ S '40 pors
N Y Times p29 D 6 '40 por; IX p4 Mr 23 '41; p17 Ap 19 '41 por
Parents' Mag 15:29+ N '40 il pors
Photoplay 8:21-2+ Ag '40 pors

American Women
International Motion Picture Almanac
Who's Who in America

DYKSTRA, CLARENCE A(DDISON) (dĭk'strŭ) Feb. 25, 1883- President of the University of Wisconsin

Address: b. University of Wisconsin, Madison, Wis; h. 130 N. Prospect Ave, Madison, Wis.

Bulletin: On March 19, 1941 President Roosevelt named Dr. Dykstra chairman of the newly-formed Defense Mediation Board, as one of the public's representatives. Two days later it was announced that Dr. Dykstra had resigned as Director of Selective Service in order to devote all of his time to his new duties. On June 19, however, his resignation from the Defense Mediation Board was also accepted; Dr. Dykstra wished to give more time to his university than he had found possible. He remains on call for panel service in defense labor controversies, and is still an advisory member of the joint Army-Navy Board.

From January 1941 issue:

Public opinion is unanimous that the choice of Clarence A. Dykstra to head Selective Service was a "singularly fortunate" one. The position needs an expert administrator, and as city manager for Cincinnati and president of the University of Wisconsin Dr. Dykstra has shown himself to be just that.

His nomination approved unanimously by the Senate, Clarence Dykstra took the oath of office on October 17, 1940 and told the American people: "Those who have thought we were supine or soft or that a democracy could not move with effectiveness may be disappointed." Immediately he took hold of the organization that had already been built up, "authorized and empowered to appoint necessary members of local boards, local board physicians, government appeal agents and members of appeal boards."

This large, six-feet-three and almost 200-pound civilian who is now in charge of drafting young men into the Army was born in Cleveland, Ohio, where his father, Lawrence Dykstra, was pastor of the Dutch Reformed Church. He was the second of six children, and Cleveland was just one of the many pastorates in which his father and mother, Margaret (Barr) Dykstra served. Most of Clarence's early education was received in the public schools of Chicago. His college was the State University of Iowa, where his principal study was the science of municipal government.

After he was graduated in 1903, Dr. Dykstra spent a year at the University of Chicago as a fellow in history and an assistant in political science. The next two years he spent as a teacher in private schools in Pensacola, Florida. Between 1906 and 1908 he was back at the University of Chicago. Then came one year as an instructor in history and government at Ohio State University and nine years, from 1909 to 1918, as professor of political science and head of the department at the University of Kansas.

During all these years of teaching Dr. Dykstra had been building up a good deal of theory about state and municipal government. His first real experience in governmental affairs came in 1918 when he became executive secretary of the Cleveland (Ohio) Civic League. He stayed there eighteen months and then spent two years as secretary to the Chicago City Club. From Chicago he went to Los Angeles, where until 1926 he was secretary to the City Club and commissioner of the Department of Water and Power. As commissioner he was a member of the board which built a $300,000,000 aqueduct and which constructed hydroelectric plants for Los Angeles. In 1926 he became the director of personnel and efficiency for the Department of Water and Power, after qualifying for the position by passing a competitive Civil Service examination. During these years he was also a professor of municipal administration at the University of California.

From 1930 to 1937 Dr. Dykstra was city manager of Cincinnati, where, after years of

Wide World

CLARENCE A. DYKSTRA

political mismanagement, the citizens were anxious to keep their new charter and clean government. Dr. Dykstra proceeded to expand and improve city services. Zoning, waste-collecting, hiring, purchasing were all carried out efficiently and without political bias. Yet during these years of expanding municipal service, Cincinnati's tax rate was not raised—in fact it was kept the lowest in the country for a city of its size. Dr. Dykstra was as approachable as he was efficient, and story has it that it wasn't unusual for a housewife to phone him if the garbage truck wasn't on time.

Dr. Dykstra expressed his own idea of city government like this: "We live in communities and a community is the sum of our lives. This is an age of cities, of ever expanding growth and multiplication of functions. The proper carrying out of these functions with the least possible expense with the most efficient personnel and the most appropriate appliances is the task of municipal statesmanship."

During these years Dr. Dykstra received many academic honors and many important related positions. He was president of the International Association of City Managers, a member of the Technical Advisory Board of the National Emergency Public Works Administration, a member of the Ohio State Advisory Committee of the United States Employment Service and chairman of the National Resources Board's committee to survey "The Role of the Urban Community in the National Economy." It was in 1937, however, that his greatest popular fame came—during the disastrous flood.

During the flood crisis Dr. Dykstra was granted unprecedented dictatorial powers by

DYKSTRA, CLARENCE A.—_Continued_

Cincinnati's City Council. He organized flood relief and flood control coolly, ably and efficiently. For 36 hours at a stretch he stayed at his desk; for hours he waded about the city. When everything had been brought into order in eight days, Dr. Dykstra was a national hero.

In 1937, perhaps because he felt that he had already proved his ability to translate academic theory into practical political achievement, Dr. Dykstra accepted the post of president of the University of Wisconsin, even though it meant a cut of $10,000 from the $25,000 salary he was receiving. The job at that time was a tough one, "under the handicap imposed by the national hullabaloo stirred up when Dr. Glenn Frank was summarily dropped." The choice was hailed as "wholly admirable," and soon after he took office Dr. Dykstra proceeded to organize the University on the same lines of efficiency he had established in Cincinnati.

His "at homes" became a regular feature of college life and he has been consistently looked up to and admired in the years he has been there, although, according to _Time_, he has "so far kindled no fire among the faculty or students." Dr. Dykstra didn't want to leave the University to take over his present position, and it was only because of a good deal of persuasion on the President's part and his own belief that "we should all do our bit" that he was induced to accept the position he now holds. However, he is officially merely on leave of absence, with permission to spend necessary time on university work. Wisconsin, which is receiving his $10,000 draft salary, has appointed an administrative committee of three to handle routine and policy details in his absence.

Dr. Dykstra was married in 1909 to Ada M. Hartley, who died in 1926. Dr. Dykstra's second marriage, to Lillian K. Rickaby, who was dean of women of the Riverside School in California when he met her, took place in 1927. He now has a daughter, Elizabeth Sylvester, a stepson, Franz Lee, and a young grandson named Stephen Dykstra Posey.

As professor, city manager, college president and as head of the draft, Dr. Dykstra is "unemotional, unspectacular and wholly interested in efficiency." As one observer put it, "In reasoning and movement he is as impetuous as the town clock." His speeches seem to reflect his personality. In them he is "terse and direct; his speech deliberate, his voice resonant. He never makes use of a humorous anecdote. Much to be said, little time in which to say it, no time to be wasted." His work has always been his main interest; music his only hobby. It has been said "he would walk an earthquake to hear Bauer, Iturbi or Rachmaninoff play the piano." But the same biographer reminds us that Dykstra is the kind of man who after playing a better than average performance of Debussy's _Clair de Lune_, in his Cincinnati days, would get up from the piano saying: "The man we need for that police job is Bumblenunger."

References

Am Mag 131:69 F '41
Christian Cent 54:373-4 Mr 24 '37
Collier's 19:13+ Ap 10 '37 il (Same abr. Read Digest 30:87-9 Je '37)
Cur Hist 52:11 N 7 '40
Nation 144:309 Mr 20 '37
N Y Times p18 O 15 '40; p10 O 16 '40; p8 O 18 '40 por; VII p9+ N 10 '40 por
Survey G 26:204-6 Ap '37 por
Time 29:28 Mr 22 '37; 33:57 Je 12 '39; 36:23 O 21 '40 por
Who's Who in America

EARLY, STEPHEN T. Aug. 27, 1889- Secretary to President Roosevelt

Address: b. The White House, Washington, D. C.; h. 7704 Morningside Dr, N. W., Washington, D. C.

Stephen T. Early, secretary to President Roosevelt, is the kind of secretary whose secretaries have secretaries. The White House is one of the greatest news sources in the world, and it is he who directs its public and press relations. Every morning at 9:20 Early is in the President's bedroom, conferring with him on daily business, storing up in his head the plans and thoughts of the President which he will interpret to the press at his daily conference.

The conference comes every morning at 10:30. To the scores of newspapermen gathered around, Early is straightforward and usually reasonable. There are times, of course, when he blows up (_Time_ calls him "occasionally liverish"), but on the whole he maintains "an innate objective approach to his job." His attitude, appreciated by the press, is that reporters are entitled to forthright replies to important questions, and he gives them.

When he isn't holding his own conferences, he is often taking care of the problems which arise during the day, able to answer reporters' queries because he has the President's complete confidence, because he is in and out of the White House executive offices nine or ten times a day. At the President's own press conferences, "Steve" is by his elbow, now and again asking the President to clear up a remark he thinks might be misunderstood, offering suggestions.

Considered "the most expert press officer the White House has ever known," Early got that way through long newspaper experience. His own years as reporter and news writer gave him his "understanding of the active reporter's problems and of the pressure for quick action that lies behind the dozens of questions" asked. Stephen T. Early was born in Crozet, Virginia, the son of Thomas Joseph and Ida Virginia (Wood) Early. From private schools in Virginia and high school in Washington, D. C., he went directly into newspaper work in 1908.

His position was on the Washington staff of the United Press, and he kept it until 1913 when he went over to the Associated Press. When Roosevelt was Assistant Secretary of the Navy,

Early was covering the State-War-Navy beat. He managed to teach Roosevelt some of the ropes of Washington publicity. His activities along these lines were cut short when, after nearly a decade of newspaper work, he went overseas with a machine gun company. In France he served as a captain of infantry and as a staff member of the A. E. F. official newspaper, *The Stars and Stripes,* and returned to the United States with a Silver Star citation "for meritorious service."

Early didn't return to newspaper work immediately. For a while in 1920 he acted as advance man for Roosevelt's Vice-Presidential campaign and then became publicity director for the United States Chamber of Commerce. After a year of this he joined the Associated Press again and soon was its "fast, crack, spot-news man." He was assigned to cover President Harding on his Western tour and scored a six-minute "beat" on his death by slipping down the fire stairs of a San Francisco hotel and telephoning the news to the AP before the official announcement. In 1924 he covered the Presidential campaign of John W. Davis. And in every year of his association with the AP he could be depended on to turn in important, readable stories.

This association ended in 1927 when Early became the Washington representative of the Paramount-Publix Corporation and Paramount News, a position he held until March 1933, when Roosevelt appointed him an assistant secretary in the White House, in charge of press relations. Early took the job with the firm conviction that the most popular thing the Roosevelt Administration could do would be to throw the doors wide open to the press and keep them open. It was his decision, with Roosevelt's approval, to banish "the White House spokesman" forever and no longer require correspondents to submit written questions to the President in advance of his conferences. He insisted that he be permitted to break in on the President at all times to check up between press conferences on the questions put to him by reporters. And he insisted that this same policy be followed by other press representatives in other government departments and agencies. As another innovation he had a news ticker installed in his office in order to keep tabs on the news breaking on all fronts.

These new policies were appreciated by hard-working reporters who had found press relations a perpetual source of difficulty under President Hoover. Newspapers praised Early's efficiency and understanding, made allowances for his being "hard-boiled and short-tempered at times." They have continued to do so, and even Hugh Johnson, newspaperman now, was inspired to write in 1940: "Never have I included Mr. Early among those who recklessly plan our future from positions of official irresponsibility but close personal relation with an overburdened President. . . Steve is one of the fairest and most fearless of the President's associates and, at least among those I know personally, the most dependable." When in the fall of 1941 the reporters covering the President felt that they were getting less out

STEPHEN T. EARLY

of press conferences than before, it was Early whom they asked to intercede for them.

Of course there have been rifts between Early and the press in these years, and especially after July 1937, when Early was raised from assistant secretary to secretary. No one denies that Early's "hot temper" has occasionally got him into trouble; that occasionally he has been less well-informed than he might have been. A number of years back he took the "rap" for rebuking Lindbergh (see sketch this issue), after the cancellation of air-mail contracts, for publishing a telegram in the press before the President had been given the courtesy of reading it. As it happened the "publicity motives" which he attacked were not Lindbergh's at all. Again he got into trouble when he delivered what sounded like a Presidential rebuke to Henry Wallace for urging the third term; once again when he relayed the President's views on the Monroe Doctrine in terms "so confusing that neither State Department papers, editorials or his own cryptic statements later could clear them up."

But all this trouble was mild compared with the jam Early found himself in during the 1940 Presidential campaign. It was in November, and Early was trying to get to the President's train which was leaving the station. Policemen prevented him from doing so, and the report went out that he had kicked a Negro policeman so hard that he had to be taken home in an ambulance and put to bed. The papers immediately got to work; Joe Louis paid a call of condolence on the cop; and Early sadly wondered "why Republican politicians are attempting to find political significance in this incident." Perhaps the kindest criticism then came from *Time,* which stated: "Besides committing a first-rate political blunder, he had misbehaved in a way no decent citizen should. But for once newsmen were sorry for him, blaming it all on his hot temper."

(Continued next page)

EARLY, STEPHEN T.—*Continued*

Some of them were sufficiently sorry, and interested, to get the facts, which, as published later in *Editor and Publisher* and backed by many Washington correspondents, were these: when Early tried to get to the train, the police shoved him back so violently that he had to be caught, and as he fell his leg was flung into the air and struck a Negro policeman. Since this policeman had recently had an abdominal operation, his wound was injured.

Roosevelt was elected, in any case, and Early continued his job of informing the press and the world of the President's position on significant issues. During the passage of the Lease-Lend Bill he was frequently the White House spokesman; he insisted that "the President is keeping his hands strictly off"; he warned of the forces opposed to the President who were deliberately seeking to confuse the country and undermine confidence in the administration of the defense program. Later he revealed the President's views on weeding out all senior Army reserve officers incapable of active service. In April 1941 he definitely informed the country that the Government had no intention of establishing a domestic press censorship; one month later he denied that the President or Harry L. Hopkins (see sketch this issue) knew anything about a report from Vichy that 26 American ships with war supplies for the British had arrived at Suez accompanied by United States warships. And it was Early who, in June 1941, announced to the press that Roosevelt would commandeer the strike-bound North American Aviation Company. Since that time hardly a day passes in which Early doesn't inform the press and the country of some event, decision, plan. In November 1941, for instance, he warned that Hitler was planning an "economic peace conference" of puppet nations. On December 7th he confirmed the report that Japan had bombed Hawaii.

This is the kind of information he gives out, and always he is vigilant to kill what he called in a *Saturday Evening Post* article in June 1939 the "slanderous, grossly untrue and unfair reports . . . manufactured, passed on by word of mouth, printed and otherwise given currency." Early works hard at this—as he works hard at the hundreds of tasks his position involves. And he works almost as hard when he plays. He is a good golfer, he guns for ducks; he goes deep-sea and fly-fishing; he plays poker occasionally; he follows the races. Once in a while, however, he settles down for a quiet evening with Mrs. Early, the former Helen Wrenn, whom he married in 1921, and their three children in his comfortable home on the edge of Washington. But there is no guarantee it will remain quiet. Reporters stay up all hours of the night, the presses must be fed, and Early is the man who knows the answers.

References

Lit Digest 117:12 Mr 17 '34 por
Look 5:12-15 Mr 11 '41 pors
Nation 141:348-9 S 25 '35
New Outlook 164:26 Jl '34
N Y Times VII p11+ Jl 27 '40
R of Rs 91:47-50+ Ap '35 pors
U S News 9:39 D 6 '40 il
Who's Who in America
Who's Who in the Nation's Capital

ECCLES, MARRINER S(TODDARD) (ĕk'lz) Sept. 9, 1890- Chairman of the Federal Reserve Board

Address: b. Board of Governors, Federal Reserve System, Washington, D. C.; h. 2541 Van Buren Ave, Ogden, Utah; Shoreham Hotel, Washington, D. C.

In January 1941 the Federal Reserve Board, headed by Marriner S. Eccles, came out openly for specific fiscal legislation for the first time in its history. Intended to protect the country against the inflationary tendencies of the defense program, the Board's plan suggested repeal of Roosevelt's power to devaluate the dollar, the Administration's authority to issue new currency and the Treasury's right to issue $1.29 worth of silver coins for each ounce of foreign silver it buys. It also recommended that the Board be given power to double the amount of reserve funds which member banks have to keep on deposit at Federal Reserve Banks, that the Treasury find a way to "insulate" the foreign gold it buys, and suggested a method of financing defenses as well. *Time* called this plan "succinct and vigorous"; the National City Bank of New York found "little reasonable basis for difference of opinion on it"; and Ralph Robey called it the only plan that could offer the promise of success.

To a good many people these measures looked like a reversal of those policies Eccles had been advocating publicly ever since 1934. His fiscal theory has been one of bold Government spending, of "easy money"—Senator Byrd of Virginia blamed the debts of the New Deal on his "crackpot" ideas. Today, however, Eccles feels that circumstances are different from what they were during the depression and recession; that the Government should spend its way out of depressions, but adopt a pay as you go policy when the national income warrants.

When Eccles first went to Washington he had a reputation for success and for having original ideas, a reputation he still has. He won it as a practical banker and corporation director and president. He had a good start toward becoming these. His father, David Eccles, was a Scotsman who was taken to Utah by his immigrant family after its conversion to the faith of the Church of Jesus Christ of Latter Day Saints. David Eccles dug coal in Wyoming, ox-carted logs through the South Pass, got hold of a lumber business in Oregon, founded banks, sugar beet companies, insurance enterprises.

Marriner Stoddard Eccles was the eldest son of David Eccles' second wife, Ellen (Stoddard) Eccles, and one of 22 children. He went to the district schools of Logan, Utah, where he was born, and spent the years between 1905 and 1909 at Brigham Young College. Summers he worked with his father, tending stores, working in logging camps, learning to boss men. Then in 1909 his father asked him to accept a "call" from the head of the Mormon Church, and for two years Marriner toured Scotland in the frock coat and silk hat of a Mormon missionary. His chief convert was May Campbell Young, who followed him back to Utah to become Mrs. Eccles in 1913. (They have three children—one of their daughters died some years ago.)

By this time David Eccles had died and left a fortune of seven millions to his family. Marriner began to take over his business interests and by 1916 had organized the Eccles Investment Company, a holding company for his family's widespread enterprises. Through it he acquired a number of banks and by 1927 was president of the First Security Corporation, which operated 26 banks in Utah, Idaho and Wyoming. He was also president of the Sego Milk Products Company, the Stoddard Lumber Company, the Utah Construction Company (one of the six that built Boulder Dam), the Amalgamated Sugar Company and director of many other corporations. And all these banks and companies were successful—not one depositor in an Eccles bank lost a dollar in the crash of 1929 or its aftermath.

Nevertheless Marriner Eccles felt that there was something wrong with the way things were being run in this country. In the early days of the depression he wanted an answer to the problems of unemployment and insecurity. In characteristic fashion he pondered them, read long and hard on economic questions, thought even longer and harder. It was the results of this thinking that he expressed one night in 1933 in an impromptu speech. Stuart Chase, the economist, was delayed by a blizzard from a lecture engagement in Ogden, and Eccles pinch-hit for him. Chase got there just in time to hear the closing part of Eccles' speech and was impressed enough to suggest Eccles get in touch with Tugwell (see sketch this issue), who was then working out New Deal plans.

Eccles didn't get in touch with Tugwell right away, but he did ask to testify before the "depression clinic" conducted by the Senate Finance Committee. To the committee a "slight young man with dark bright eyes darting out of a thin, rather nervous face" gave his ideas on the causes and cure of the depression. A few days before Roosevelt took office he, a capitalist and banker who had voted Republican until 1932, declared boldly for "reflation" and Government spending, for higher income and inheritance taxes, for Federal grants for the unemployed, Federal control of securities and the stock exchanges, for child labor laws, national planning for security, cancellation of the war debts, unification of the banking system, further transportation regulation. Actually his proposals were "nothing less than a detailed blue print of the New Deal"; all of them, except that on war debts, were adopted in principle by the Roosevelt Administration.

After giving his testimony he stopped in with a letter from Stuart Chase to see Rexford Tugwell, who at that time, according to Raymond Clapper, was planning to bring key

Underwood & Underwood

MARRINER S. ECCLES

figures into the Administration. Whether Tugwell was instrumental or not, it is certain that within a few months Eccles was made an assistant to the Secretary of the Treasury and that six months afterward, in November 1934, he was named head of the Federal Reserve Board. "They tell me he has had a string of banks for a long time and none of them has failed," said President Roosevelt of his choice.

Eccles' confirmation took a long time, with objections raised because of his many financial interests. Actually the reason for the delay lay in Eastern bankers' distrust of his Western background and extreme youth and in the general feeling in banking circles that a man who believed in a strong banking authority and the need for the country's spending its way out of the depression was not quite the right person to head the Federal Reserve Board.

The big bankers found little reason in the next few years after his appointment to take him any more warmly to their bosoms. Among his significant statements were: "We need to recognize that the principle of the flexible budget is a necessary safeguard of private capitalism"; and "it is absolutely essential to develop agencies which by conscious and deliberate compensatory action will obviate the necessity of drastic downward or upward adjustments of cost and prices, wages and capital structures. If we do not develop such agencies our present economy and perhaps our present form of government cannot long survive."

Eccles promulgated the theory, as summed up in *Fortune*, that money and credit are not ends in themselves but tools which can be used to realize the desired social ends. He started on its way the Banking Act of 1935, providing for strengthening of the Reserve

ECCLES, MARRINER S.—*Continued*
Board's control over monetary and credit policy and opposed in many of its sections by the American Bankers' Association. In early 1936 he upped the margin requirements on stock from 45 per cent to 55 per cent. By 1940, when he was reappointed for another four-year term, Ralph Robey (see sketch this issue) was expressing the viewpoint of a number of conservative people when he called the reappointment "just one more item in that constant stream of little things coming out of Washington that keeps business confidence on tenterhooks and thereby hinders continued recovery." Those who support Eccles countered, in the words of one of his friends: "He talks loose but he banks hard."

During these years, however, Eccles was not entirely supported by labor and all those workers who, he felt, should have a greater share of the national income. There were reasons for this, too. In 1937, at a time when he was called "one of the closest White House advisers," he said in a discussion of Roosevelt's housing program that one of the chief obstacles to building was the high wages paid labor. Later that same year he managed to antagonize the CIO.

In 1941, however, there is less controversy about Eccles than there was in the days when he advocated easy money. Particularly in financial circles it is felt that he is offering well-thought-out plans for this period of national defense and that the new Federal Reserve Board suggestions are practical. Among Eccles' own suggestions has been a plan for taxation that recommended high "selective" sales taxes on commodities like autos and refrigerators and low or no taxes on middle income necessities, though at the same time he suggested broadening the individual income tax base. The choice, he said, was not between guns and butter, but between guns and autos. And he announced the Board's regulations restricting installment credit. "Get out of debt," he warned wage earners. People are recognizing even more than before, too, his ability to carry out all the duties of his position as head of the Board—to act as liaison officer with Congress on the subject of banking laws, to maintain contact with Reserve Banks, to take charge of matters of policy affecting changes in open-market operations and reserve requirements.

It is usually what Eccles has to say rather than the way he says it that has impressed legislative bodies and the public since his first speech in Ogden, Utah back in 1933. A number of his public addresses, statements, reports and testimonies have been collected into a volume (called *Economic Balance and a Balanced Budget* [1940] and edited by Rudolph L. Weissman) which the *Wall Street Journal* calls "required reading." Eccles is lean, smallish and nervous in appearance; dry and intense in his speech; impersonal in his manner. Outside of legislative halls he seems much the same. He eats sparingly, smokes little, drinks very little and lets himself go only when he is out shooting ducks or is given a bag of peanuts.

References

Am Mag 119:56 Ap '35 por
Collier's 95:13 Je 29 '35 por
Fortune 11:62-5 F '35 pors
Nation 141:184 Ag 14 '35
New Repub 93:196 D 22 '37
Newsweek 4:34 N 17 '34 por; 5:32 Mr
    30 '35 por; 6:17 Jl 20 '35 por; 15:50
    F 12 '40 por; 17:42 Ja 13 '41; 17:68
    Mr 3 '41
R of Rs 92:22-5 Jl '35 pors
Time 27:60+ F 10 '36 por (cover);
    28:47 S 7 '36; 29:57 Mr 29 '37; 33:9
    Ja 2 '39; 37:15 Ja 13 '41 por
Who's Who in America
Who's Who in Commerce and Industry
Who's Who in the Nation's Capital

EDDINGTON, SIR ARTHUR (STANLEY) Dec. 28, 1882- Astronomer; author
Address: The Observatory, Cambridge, England

Among scientists Sir Arthur Stanley Eddington is known for his outstanding contributions to astrophysics and the study of relativity. To the public he became important first for reconciling the average man to relativity and later for reconciling religion with science. Today most people think of him as "a kind of senior member of the firm of Eddington and Jeans, Interpreters of the Universe." The seniority is in popular publication only, for he is five years younger than Sir James Jeans (see sketch this issue) whose career in many respects runs parallel to his.

The son of a Quaker schoolmaster, Eddington was born on December 28, 1882, in the little Westmorland town of Kendal in England. He began his studies at the Sammongate School, where his father was headmaster and where more than a hundred years ago the great scientist John Dalton also taught. Later he took his Master's Degree at Owens College (now Manchester University) and then proceeded to Trinity College, Cambridge, where he piled up an impressive array of honors. In 1907 he was Smith's Prizeman, like Jeans before him, and became a Fellow of Trinity College.

His real initiation into astronomy began in 1906 when he was appointed chief assistant at the Royal Observatory, Greenwich. Seven years later he returned to Cambridge as Plumian Professor of Astronomy and director of the Cambridge Observatory, positions which he still holds in 1941. This has not interfered with temporary lectureships elsewhere, notably the important Gifford Lectures which he delivered in Edinburgh in 1927. The Messenger Lectures delivered at Cornell in 1934 formed the basis for *New Pathways in Science* (1935).

Eddington's first important work was on the streaming of the stars. Later he turned his attention to the mysteries of their internal structure, and has done perhaps more than any astronomer to solve them. The fascinating story of his explorations is told for the lay reader in his *Stars and Atoms* (1927). He is also not only the most popular expounder of relativity but one of the few original workers in this field of research. He was "Einstein's [see sketch this issue] chief field-marshal in the battle for relativity" and led the expedition which went to West Africa to test the theory by observing the total eclipse of the sun on May 28, 1919. His *Space, Time, and Gravitation,* published in 1920, is an accepted classic.

It was only after 25 years of struggle with problems beyond the public view that he began to translate the abstractions of science into popular terms. Immediately he revealed a gift for lucid exposition and graceful prose which won him the response and also the gratitude of the common reader. His *Nature of the Physical World* (1928) probably did more than any other single publication to let the public know what relativity was about. It went further, and ventured a word concerning the implications of scientific knowledge for human problems and for speculations about man's place and his probable future.

Science and the Unseen World followed in 1929, and from then on Eddington became increasingly familiar as a public lecturer and radio speaker. His *Expanding Universe* of 1933 was based on a series of radio broadcasts delivered over a national network the preceding year. Meanwhile, maintaining a sort of intellectual double life, he continued his researches and more technical writing. In 1936 he was busy trying to link up relativity and the quantum theory. That year he presented to the conference on cosmogony at the Harvard Tercentenary celebration a paper on the Cosmical Constant and Recession of the Nebulae, and to another group a discussion on the structure of stars. That year also was published his *Relativity Theory of Protons and Electrons,* in which he sought "a harmonization, rather than a unification, of relativity and quantum theory." This book, according to the London *Times,* "in the elegance of its treatment and the importance of its results . . . ranks with the greatest works of science. . . It is a book . . . of which British science may justly feel proud."

His exposition of scientific material—whether popular or technical—has met with unanimous applause. When he begins to interpret it, however, opinion divides. Eddington calls his own philosophy "selective subjectivism," although it has been suggested that a more accurate name might be "monistic, spiritual, selective, relativistic, epistemological subjectivism." One of his most quoted statements is that "matter may eventually turn out to be thought," yet he repudiates the "all mind" postulate of matter.

In philosophizing and even theologizing about science, like his colleagues Jeans and Millikan, he has won sardonic comment as well as fame and popularity. H. L. Mencken declares that Eddington's deity, being made in his own image, is "a Quaker imperfectly denaturized at Cambridge, and now a don there." The *Manchester Guardian* wistfully remarks that "intellectuals of the status of Eddington and Jeans might be

SIR ARTHUR EDDINGTON

expected to complete their philosophical education in private." Yet, writing about *The Nature of the Physical World,* the *Saturday Review* declared that "to any intelligent and thoughtful reader who would know something of . . . the bearings of the new [scientific] theories . . . on the eternal problems of philosophy and theology, it would be difficult to suggest a better or nobler introduction than this brilliant book."

Neither the majority of scientists nor of philosophers accepts him as the spokesman of science with regard to its philosophical implications, nor for that matter does Sir Arthur so regard himself. As an individual he reserves the Quaker's full freedom to speculate and to share his speculations. But as a scientist he declares that officially: "There is no approach of science to religion, and science has nothing to say about religion."

With a dozen honorary degrees, memberships and offices in at least as many honorary societies, two successful careers and a number of special awards, Sir Arthur remains a modest English bachelor who sparkles quietly —a skilled dialectician, a man of profound culture, a pretty wit. The suavity, humor and imagination that swing his readers through his books are equally evident in his manner and conversation. His friends say that being created a Knight in 1930 touched him less than the honor shown him that same year by his home town. With pomp and ceremony Kendal accorded him the Honorary Freedom of the City, the Mayor presented a scroll on which their decision was recorded, after which Eddington lectured at the Friends' School, where his father had taught. In 1938 he was awarded the Order of Merit, one of the highest distinctions in the King's gift, the membership being limited to 24.

(Continued next page)

EDDINGTON, SIR ARTHUR—*Continued*

References

> Am Scholar 6 no 1 :71-84 '37
> N Y Herald Tribune II p12 My 19 '40
>   por
> N Y Times Book R p1 D 24 '39
> Sci Mo 43 :385-95 N '36 por (p485)
> Times [London] Lit Sup p940 N 21
>   '36
> Author's and Writer's Who's Who
> Leavis, F. R. ed. Determinations p281-
>   312 1934
> Macpherson, H. C. Makers of Astron-
>   omy p212-40 1933
> Phillpotts, E. Essays in Little p79-90
>   1931
> Wallace, A. Religious Faith of Great
>   Men p139-73 1934
> Who's Who

EGGLESTON, EDWARD MASON
1883(?)—Jan. 14, 1941 Illustrator and portrait painter who illustrated the magazine
stories of Arnold Bennett, Zona Gale and
other authors; created the "Time to Retire"
trade-mark of the Fiske Tire Company; his
last work was a portrait of Lowell Thomas.

Obituaries

> N Y Herald Tribune p16 Ja 15 '41

EICHER, EDWARD C(LAYTON) (ī'kẽr)
Dec. 16, 1878- Chairman of the Securities and
Exchange Commission

Address· b. Securities and Exchange Commission, Washington, D. C.; h. Washington, Iowa

EDWARD C. EICHER

A "100 per cent New Dealer from a
normally Republican District," Edward C.
Eicher was on April 9, 1941 unanimously

elected to succeed Jerome Frank (see sketch
this issue) as chairman of the Securities and
Exchange Commission.

Edward Clayton Eicher was born on a farm
near Noble, Washington County, Iowa, on
December 16, 1878, the son of Benjamin
Eicher, founder of a Mennonite congregation
there, and Lydia (Sommer) Eicher. After
attending private academies in Washington,
Iowa, and Illinois, he went to the University
of Chicago, where his brother Alpha Delts
knew him as "Schlitz" and he took his Ph. B.
in 1904. In 1903 he had begun the study of
law there; he completed his law course in
1905; and a year later he was admitted to the
Iowa Bar.

He did not begin law practice immediately,
however, but from 1907 to 1909 worked as
assistant registrar at the University of Chicago. In 1909 he became assistant attorney of
the Iowa district of the Chicago, Burlington
& Quincy Railroad Company, and not until
1918 did he leave the firm. Then he practiced
law privately at Washington, Iowa until in
1933 he was elected to Congress from the
first Iowa district on the Democratic ticket.
One of his campaign planks was that government expenses should be reduced.

Mr. Eicher served as a member of the
House of Representatives during the 73rd,
74th and 75th Congresses (1933-39). In 1935
he presented a "cost of production" bill to
solve the farm problem which Secretary of
Agriculture Wallace called impractical. Actually, though, antitrust legislation proved to
be his field. He was an early defender of
the constitutionality of the holding company
act. He was the sponsor of a bill to tighten
up the Clayton antitrust act to prohibit the
acquisition of control of one corporation by
another through the purchase of stock and
assets. During the 75th Congress he was
chairman of the securities subcommittee of
the Committee on Interstate and Foreign
Commerce. In the summer of 1938 he was
one of fifteen antitrust investigators, and that
same year was appointed one of the three
Congressional members of the Temporary National Economic Committee. During his term
he supported Roosevelt absolutely. When on
January 1, 1939 his term as Representative
expired he did not stand for re-election, however, having already accepted an appointment
as SEC commissioner for the balance of the
term of John W. Hanes. And early in 1940
he was reappointed to the Commission for
the term ending June 5, 1945.

On August 19, 1908 Mr. Eicher married
Hazel Mount of Washington, Iowa. (They
have one daughter, Elizabeth, a foster child.)
Mr. Eicher is a member of the Bars of Illinois
and of the United States Supreme Court, as
well as that of Iowa, a member of the National Lawyers' Guild, of Alpha Delta Phi and
Phi Delta Phi.

References

> Business Week p18+ Ap 19 '41
> N Y Sun p18 F 26 '41
> N Y Times p35 Ap 10 '41 por
> Time 37 :86-7 Ap 21 '41

Who's Who in America
Who's Who in Law
Who's Who in the Nation's Capital

EIDMANN, FRANK LEWIS (īd'măn)
Dec. 20, 1887—Sept. 4, 1941 Professor of
mechanical engineering at Columbia University
since 1930; associated with the Olds Gas
Power Company of Michigan from 1903 to
1913 and designed parts for some of the
earliest farm tractors; supervised development
of manufacturing processes and served as engineer for a number of companies until he
became associate professor at Princeton University in 1923.

References

American Men of Science
Who's Who in America
Who's Who in Engineering

Obituaries

N Y Times p21 S 5 '41 por

EINSTEIN, ALBERT (īn'stīn) Mar. 14,
1879- Theoretical and mathematical physicist
Address: b. Institute for Advanced Study,
Princeton, N. J.; h. 112 Mercer St, Princeton,
N. J.

"What I have done personally is much
exaggerated. What is really beautiful is
science! It is a great gift if one is permitted
to work in science for his whole life."

That is one aspect of the man whose work
has been called "the greatest single stride
science has ever made," and the 30-page paper
in which it was first suggested, "the most
important document of the century." Here is
another aspect: "As long as I have any choice,
I will stay only in a country where political
liberty, toleration, and equality of all citizens
before the law is the rule."

"America's No. 1 refugee" was born in
Ulm, a. d. Donau, Germany, the son of
Hermann and Pauline (Koch) Einstein. In
1881 his father moved his family to Munich,
where he opened a business dealing in technical electrical materials. Though the family
was Jewish, both parents were freethinkers,
and Jewish customs and rites were not observed in the household. For 14 years
Einstein's electrical business had been prosperous and the family enjoyed a measure of ease
and modest luxury. Then their fortunes began to decline until, on the verge of bankruptcy, they decided to give up their Munich
home and moved to Milan, Italy, where
cousins of the family were doing well.

Although the boy was slow to learn to
talk, and in early childhood was considered
backward, his mother was convinced from the
beginning that he would grow up to be a "great
professor." He never had any gift for languages and when he first came to America
was unable to make a speech in English. At
14, however, he taught himself integral and
differential calculus and analytical geometry
from textbooks! He wanted from the beginning to devote his life to abstract study,
but his parents' poverty compelled him to find

ALBERT EINSTEIN

a means of making a living. Music and study
made up his world. Like so many others, he
fixed on teaching as the profession least likely
to interfere with his real life.

When his parents went to Milan, they left
the boy behind at school. He managed to
secure a certificate stating that he was suffering from nervous exhaustion, and succeeded
in joining them. His half year in Italy was
pure heaven. In an impulsive gesture he
abandoned his German citizenship and resolved
never to return. Where he did go was to
Switzerland, where he studied in a technical
school in Aarau and then at the Zurich Technical Academy. He became a Swiss subject, and
it was in this school that he met a Serbian
fellow-student, a gifted mathematician named
Mileva Marec, whom he married in 1901 and
by whom he had two sons, Albert, Jr., and
Edward. They were divorced 15 years later.

In this same year, 1901, he began teaching,
first in the Technical School in Winterthur,
then as a private tutor in Schaffhausen. In
1902 he went to work as a patent office examiner in Berne. This was the period when
he first began the research and studies which
culminated in the formulation of the Relativity Theory, the first paper being *On the
Electrodynamics of Moving Bodies,* published
in 1905. He also took his Ph. D. degree from
the University of Zurich. In 1909 he was
appointed a professor at the University of
Zurich. He lectured on theoretical physics,
principally on the science of heat. His only
regular attendants were two personal friends!
At this time he received a position at Berne
University as lecturer.

Already, in 1908, he had been invited to
lecture on relativity and the constitution of
light before the congress of scientists, meeting in Salzburg. It was his first appearance
at such an official gathering, and the first rec-

EINSTEIN, ALBERT—*Continued*

ognition of his work. It led indirectly to his appointment as ordinary professor of physics at the German University in Prague (1911-12). He hated to leave Switzerland to go to what was then Austro-Hungary, but once there he found his position much pleasanter than it had been in the larger university in Zurich. When, a year and a half later, he was called back to Zurich, this time to the Confederate Polytechnic Academy, where he had once been a student, he was reluctant to go. He had a wife and two small boys to support, however, and had no choice. This time his lectures were well attended and enthusiastically received.

In 1914, already a figure of world prominence, an opportunity was offered him that he did not dare refuse. Through the efforts of Max Planck, the famous physicist, a professorship was offered him by the Prussian Academy of Sciences in Berlin, with no official duties, little teaching, but unlimited opportunity for study. A separate Physical Institute was to be established for him but he declined this, since his work was by now almost entirely theoretical. He went to Berlin in 1914, retaining his Swiss citizenship, and remained there until the Nazis forced him to leave.

From 1912 to 1928 Albert Einstein was professor of physics at the University of Leyden, "commuting" for that purpose from Berlin and continuing right through the First World War. His avowed pacifism in that war made no difference in the Germany of that day. He suffered no inconvenience because of it, and it helped to make him the first German to appear publicly in the Allied countries after the Armistice. In 1928 his heart became affected. He had to take a long rest and he resigned the Leyden position. (His health was later completely recovered.)

It is impossible to explain briefly to lay readers just what the Theory of Relativity implies, or what its significance is. Put as simply as possible, it regards time as the fourth dimension, thus making all physical phenomena (from our point of view as three-dimensional beings) relative, not absolute. It explains mass, gravity, inertia, space and time. It is mathematical in origin, though most of its proofs and demonstrations come from astronomy and astro-physics. Einstein is devoting the remainder of his life to a search for a "unified field theory" which will bridge relativity and quantum mechanics (the mathematics of the atom and its parts), and thus embrace all phenomena from the electron to the universe. Over 4,000 books and pamphlets and uncountable numbers of articles have been written commenting on, modifying, opposing or upholding the special and general Relativity Theory. Bitterly fought in some scientific circles, it is now accepted, as a whole, by most physicists and mathematicians. But either expositions or attacks involve a technical background which limits profitable discussion to the world of professional science.

Einstein received the Nobel Prize in physics in 1921 and gave all the prize money to charity.

He himself does not know how many honorary degrees he has received or to how many learned societies he belongs. With characteristic modesty, he lists among all his various medals and decorations only the Copley Medal of the Royal Society, received in 1925, and the Franklin Institute Medal, received in 1935. He was a research student of Christ Church, Oxford, until 1931, when he was Rhodes Memorial Lecturer and received an honorary D. Sc. degree there. The same year he was Rouse Ball Lecturer at Cambridge. During his years in Berlin he traveled frequently to give lectures abroad and in 1931 he spent several months at the California Institute of Technology. He also made at least one long trip around the world.

It is impossible to exaggerate Albert Einstein's fame and acclaim in Berlin during the years of the Weimar Republic. Though he had rejected the establishment of a Physical Institute, he was persuaded to become director of Theoretical Physics in the Kaiser Wilhelm Institute. Prussia made him an honorary citizen. Potsdam erected an Einstein Tower in its Astro-Physical Institute. On his fiftieth birthday, in 1929, though he fled the city to avoid a celebration, it required several washbaskets to hold all the cards, letters and telegrams of congratulation, and the gifts would have filled a freight car. Four years after his citizenship was revoked, he was expelled from the Academy of Sciences, his house was searched for arms, he was removed both as professor and director, all his property (including the suburban house which had originally been intended as a birthday gift from the city of Berlin, and which, because of a series of mishaps, he finally bought himself) was confiscated, and he was an exile with a price of 20,000 marks (about $6,800) on his head.

During all these years he had lived with the same simplicity which has always characterized him. In 1917 he married again, this time his cousin, Elsa Einstein, who was doubly his first cousin, their fathers being brothers and their mothers, sisters. She was the buffer between him and the world, especially after they came to America, until her death in 1936. She, too, had been married and divorced, and had two daughters, one of whom lives now with her stepfather (who is also her second cousin) in Princeton.

When Einstein left Germany, he went first to France, then to Belgium, then to England. Then the Institute for Advanced Study offered him a life professorship. He accepted, but asked so small a salary that to keep up its own standards the Institute had to raise it! (Einstein is literally without concern for money. Once for weeks he used as a bookmark a check for $1,500 from the Rockefeller Foundation and then lost the book!) He came to Princeton in 1933 and has been there ever since. In October 1940 he became an American citizen.

"In his humility, his shyness, his lack of desire for controversy, his generosity and simplicity," says Henry Hazlitt, "he reminds one strikingly of other great scientists, particularly

Charles Darwin." He is "profoundly pacifistic, profoundly democratic." Sympathetic to Zionism, he is still, as he has always been, religiously an agnostic. He does not believe in a personal God or in personal immortality, and approaches near to the pantheism of that other great Jew, Spinoza. In the present crisis, war hater though he is, he is ardently for active aid to the democratic nations against Hitler. He has never been a milk-and-water "peace at any price" pacifist, but in 1933 headed the committee which issued the *Brown Book of the Hitler Terror*.

Einstein's appearance, his halo of wildly waving white hair, his wonderful, deep-set dark eyes under bushy brows, his sturdy, stocky body are familiar to everyone. He hates formal clothes, and dresses in loosely fitting garments of the sports variety. Unless he is watched, he is likely to go out of doors in his carpet slippers. He never wears a hat. His house, a modest two-storied gray frame building, is on a narrow street shaded by tall oak and elm trees. He works in a small study, writing on a pad on his knee, rising frequently to pace the room in thought. He wanders about the streets of Princeton, lost in a maze of abstraction, with a beaming smile for those who accost him, but his mind is far away. His shyness and his hatred of publicity are proverbial. Once a crowd gathered outside a Princeton drugstore. The great man was within, and what was he doing? He was standing at a counter, licking an ice-cream cone!

He is a better than average violinist whose favorite composers are Bach and Mozart. Once a critic who had never heard of him as a physicist wrote that he did not understand his world-wide fame, since many violinists were better than he! He improvises constantly on the piano—he calls it "a necessity of his life"—but only to himself, never for listeners. He does not read much general literature. He says "any man who reads too much and uses his own brain too little falls into lazy habits of thinking." He is devoted, however, to Shakespeare, Sophocles, and above all to Dostoevsky, who, he says (ultimate praise!) gives him "more pleasure than Gauss" (the great mathematician).

Dr. Einstein's chief recreations are sailing and walking. He enjoys writing doggerel verse or playing simple parlor games. He enjoys a good joke. He cares little for paintings, but is interested in sculpture and architecture. He writes a clear, fine hand, and although he has little manual dexterity except as a violinist, pianist and sailor, that he is not all theoretician was proved when in 1936 he patented an automatic electric-eye camera. Many of his characteristics classed as eccentricities are merely a conscious attempt to simplify his life, down to such details as going without socks, or using the same soap for washing and shaving. Though he seldom knows what he eats, he is boyishly fond of a dish of his childhood, pike served with mushrooms. He drinks no alcohol, but smokes three pipes of tobacco a day.

Most of Einstein's books are in German. But in 1923 English translations were published: *The Meaning of Relativity* and *Side-Lights on Relativity*; and in 1926 the earlier *Investigation of the Theory of the Brownian Movement*. *On the Method of Theoretical Physics* appeared in 1933. In 1938, with Dr. Leopold Infeld (see sketch this issue), a Polish-Jewish refugee physicist whom Einstein brought to the Institute for Advanced Study and who is now at the University of Toronto, he published *The Evolution of Physics*. His non-scientific books include *About Zionism* (1931); *Builders of the Universe* (1932); *Why War?* (with the late great Sigmund Freud, 1933); and *The World As I See It* (1934). He was also one of the contributors to the anthology *Living Philosophies,* and has published numerous scientific articles and brochures.

This man who "changed the concept of the universe" has, as Edwin Muller remarked, "the look of a man at peace with himself." And, to quote Archibald Henderson, "he fulfills one's expectation of a genius."

References

Christian Cent 57:1268 O 16 '40
Forum 95:174-6 Mr '36 por
Jewish Frontier 6:33-50 Je '39 pors
N Y Times VII p6 Ja 5 '41
Read Digest 33:37-40 O '38 (Same abr. Nation 147:267-8 S 17 '38)
Sci Am 143:466 D '30 il; 160:275 My '39; 160:358-9 Je '39 por; 161:22-4 Jl '39 por
Time 27:72+ Mr 16 '36; 35:44 My 27 '40 por; 36:46 S 23 '40 por; 37:45 F 3 '41 il por
Wilson Lib Bul 7:435 Mr '33

American Men of Science
Bridges, T. C. and Tiltman, H. H. Master Minds of Modern Science p95-103 1931
Garbedian, H. G. Albert Einstein, Maker of Universes 1939
Henderson, A. Contemporary Immortals p1-23 1930
Infeld, L. Quest 1941
Moszkowski, A. Einstein, the Searcher 1922
Reichinstein, D. Albert Einstein 1934
Reiser, A. Albert Einstein 1930
Schreiber, G. ed. Portraits and Self-Portraits p25-7 1936
Weil, E. comp. Albert Einstein 1937
Who's Who
Who's Who Among North American Authors
Who's Who in America
Who's Who in American Jewry
Woolf, S. J. Drawn from Life p30-41 1932

ELDRIDGE, EDWARD H(ENRY) Feb. 8, 1870—Apr. 20, 1941 Director-emeritus of Simmons College Secretarial School and author of several shorthand and secretarial textbooks of which *Shorthand Dictation Exercises* (1922); *Essentials of Expert Typewriting* (co-

ELDRIDGE, EDWARD H.—*Continued*
author, 1919); *Business Speller and Vocabulary* (1913); and *New Shorthand Dictation Exercises* (1922) are well known.

References

Leaders in Education 1941
Who's Who Among North American Authors
Who's Who in America

Obituaries

N Y Times p19 Ap 21 '41

ELIZABETH, pseud. *See* Russell, M. A. R., Countess

ELLINGTON, DUKE Apr. 29, 1899-
Conductor; composer

Address: b. c/o Hansen & Williams, Inc, Room 801, RKO Bldg, 1270 Sixth Ave, New York City

William Morris

DUKE ELLINGTON

One of the first swing concerts ever held in an institution of higher learning was given by Duke Ellington's Orchestra at Colgate University, Hamilton, New York, December 11, 1940, as part of the regular concert series. The audience responded enthusiastically to a program of twenty-two numbers, twelve of which were Ellington's own compositions and four other works on which he and some of his musicians had collaborated.

Ellington, variously called "The Aristocrat of Swing", "The King of Swing", "The King of Jazz", "the most inventive and resourceful composer that jazz has produced," has an orchestra that for the last decade and more has consistently been up among the 10 most popular orchestras of the country, and by some critics and fans has even been rated the leader of them all.

"Mr. Ellington and his Orchestra," says a *Fortune* article (August 1933), "offer rich, original music, music stemming out of the lyricism of the Negro and played with great virtuosity. Ellington's music is jazz. It is the best jazz." According to a writer in *Melody Maker*, a leading British music journal, he "stands alone in jazz as the one artist who has something to say that is not only personal but also universal, not only down-to-earth but also indicative of a fine and dignified mind. Dignity. That's what Ellington has that no other artist in jazz has had consistently."

For more than 10 years Duke Ellington and his Orchestra have been stellar attractions in motion picture and vaudeville houses, having by now appeared in almost every large theatre in the country. They have also "played dance engagements from Bowdoin College, Maine, to Frank Sebastian's Cotton Club in Los Angeles," and, at the invitation of the instructor, Percy Grainger, have performed for a music appreciation class at New York University. They are familiar to every collector of jazz or swing records and every listener of popular bands on the radio.

Though it is "jazz" or "swing" with which Duke Ellington's name is associated, his music differs from that of other conductors whose names are associated with these terms. In the first place he composes his tunes, contributes the harmony, makes his own arrangements, and as pianist-conductor interprets the music; whereas in the usual band the tune is written by one person, harmonized by another, arranged by a third, interpreted by a fourth. Even when Ellington uses the work of another composer he takes only the melody—the harmony, scoring and interpretation are his own. In the second place, more consistently than any other group, his orchestra plays true jazz or swing—music which is "built around passages in which the musicians improvise, or exercise their own fancy." C. E. Smith says that Ellington was one of the first, if not actually the first, to build a style on the basis of jazz, "utilizing its somewhat contrapuntal method of ensemble, its off-beat rhythm, and the instrumental intonation and accent that derive from blues."

Duke Ellington was born April 29, 1899, in Washington, D. C., where his father, familiarly called "Uncle Ed," was a blueprint tracer in the Navy Yard. He was christened Edward Kennedy, but in high school acquired the nickname "Duke" because of his care for his appearance. When he was seven years old his parents "attached" him, as he describes it, to a piano keyboard. "Though I liked music I never got on with practicing lessons," he confesses. "Before I knew it I would be fashioning a new melody and accompaniment instead of following the score."

However, in spite of this tendency to "fashion new melodies," Duke did not plan to be a composer, but an artist, and during his last year in high school he even won a scholarship for the Pratt Institute of Fine Arts, Brooklyn. A job as "soda jerker" in a Washington ice cream parlor and poolroom called The Poodle Dog, where there was a piano which he was often called on to play, and an opportunity to play in a band changed his mind about the art course. What he calls his "first break" came when he was 17. The leader of a society band offered him a place in his third band if by evening he could play *Siren Song*. He spent all day learning the tune. When he arrived on the job he found that the band was "legitimate" and that he would have to know about correct chords. On the spur of the moment he decided to copy a trick that he had seen Lucky Roberts use—throwing his hands away from the piano. "Before I knew it the kids around the stand were screaming with delight and clapping for more," he has said. "In two minutes the flashy hands had earned me a reputation, and after that I was all set."

Soon Ellington was experimenting with his own band, and for several years he "jobbed around" in Washington. He and the men who played with him called themselves The Washingtonians, or The Wildcats, and many Washingtonians and Wildcats are still with him. Ellington's success was hardly spectacular, however. Once he was asked to play one of the five pianos in Russell Wooding's 60-piece orchestra, but he lasted only halfway through his first concert—he couldn't resist getting in a "hot lick" (his own improvisation) where the score called for a pause, and Wooding promptly fired him.

It was 1923 when Duke Ellington went to New York to try his luck. There he found little more than split-week theatre engagements with Wilbur Sweatman and occasional engagements to play at Harlem "Parlor Socials" or "Rent Parties" (unpromising but entertaining). He hadn't been in New York long before he made a trip home to Washington, but he returned later in the year and, after experiencing "some mighty hot nights and a few hungry dawns," a five-piece band that he had assembled was hired by the Kentucky Club.

Before long music publishers, song pluggers, newspapermen, band leaders (when their own clubs closed) and celebrities were crowding into the Kentucky Club to hear the five-piece combination that Ellington had built around his piano. One of the music publishers who eventually came was Irving Mills. Almost immediately he placed Ellington under contract, and assisted him in enlarging his band to 12 pieces. He was particularly interested in the conductor as a composer and in making his orchestra available for recordings. "Naturally I agreed," recalls Ellington, "and we got together four originals."

During the decade and more that has since elapsed, Duke Ellington's Orchestra has made a surprising number of recordings, including many transcriptions for the radio. Of twenty-eight records given top rating in *Swing* during 1940, seventeen are Ellington's. Two recent records by the full band, *Cotton Tail* and *Never No Lament*, and *Portrait of Bert Williams* and *Bojangles*, elicited this remark from Geoffry Marne (*Swing*, September 1940): "If these two new Ellington records aren't perfection they will do until the next Ellington record comes along."

After the orchestra had been at the Kentucky Club for over four years Mills was instrumental in placing it in the Cotton Club, a cabaret which was at the time in Harlem but which later moved downtown. They opened there on December 4, 1927. The orchestra was already broadcasting over WHN every day.

"Then we really got a break," said Duke. The Columbia Broadcasting Company put them on the air. At the same time the orchestra began to appear on the stage of the leading theatres. They played for Florenz Ziegfeld's *Show Girl* and were billed with Maurice Chevalier. They also were featured in several films, including *Check and Double Check* with "Amos 'n' Andy," *She Got Her Man* with Mae West, and Earl Carroll's *Murder at the Vanities*.

Through his recordings and his tours Duke Ellington is almost as well known in Europe as in the United States. During the orchestra's first European tour, in 1933, at some of its London appearances one of its most enthusiastic listeners was the Duke of Windsor, then Prince of Wales, who had one of the best collections of Ellington records in Europe and who had a standing order in this country for each new record of his. In 1938, though it was five years since the conductor-composer had been in Europe, it was reported that his fan mail from England was almost as extensive as from the United States. During 1939 he again toured Europe, playing 28 concerts in as many evenings in France, Holland, Norway, Denmark and Sweden. In Paris, where he played twice to a full house at the bombproof underground Théâtre National de Chaillot, the audience was particularly enthusiastic over his *Mood Indigo*, his arrangement of Rachmaninoff's *Prelude in C Sharp Minor*, *Rocking in Rhythm*, *Solitude*, *Harmony in Harlem*, *Riding a Blue Note*.

As composer, arranger and conductor for a group that is more or less a unit, Ellington is able to get the rare effects for which he is noted. He never uses a baton. From the piano he controls his men with movements of his head, shoulders, elbows and even eyebrows—not to mention his hands. Since he constructs his arrangements around individual players, no other band is able to play his music exactly as he conceived it. Paul Whiteman says that he took his arranger, Ferde Grofé, to listen to Ellington for six consecutive nights, and that they were unable to "borrow" as much as eight bars.

The master of swing, who is working on an opera which will present the history of the Negro in five episodes, says: "My men and my race are the inspiration of my work. I try to catch the character and mood and feeling of my people. The music of my race is something more than the American idiom. It is the result of our transplantation to American soil and was our reaction, in plantation days, to the life we lived. What we could not say openly we expressed in music.

(*Continued next page*)

ELLINGTON, DUKE—*Continued*

The characteristic, melancholic music of my race has been forged from the very white heat of our sorrows and from our gropings. I think the music of my race is something that is going to live, something which posterity will honor in a higher sense than merely that of the music of the ballroom."

Ellington has shown that jazz compositions may be skillful portraits—of a mood, of a period, of a man. His first, *Soda Fountain Rag*, belongs to the days of "jerking" sodas at The Poodle Dog. *Bojangles* creates Bill Robinson (see sketch this issue) for the listener; *A Portrait of Bert Williams* somehow manages to describe the burnt-cork artist; *Sophisticated Lady* was inspired by a worldly schoolteacher in Washington, D. C.; *Breakfast Dance and Flaming Youth* recalls life in ·the late '20s. Not one of them is without meaning. For *Solitude* Ellington received the $2,500 ASCAP Prize.

Ellington has one son, Mercer, who is also interested in music—he is a student at the Juilliard School of Music, New York, and has a band of his own. He writes music, too, but his father tries not to influence him. "Duke, the man" has been described by his secretary in these words: "The Duke loves everybody. I've never seen him lose his temper. I've never heard him say he disliked a person. There's a lot of fine philosophy in him. He's deeply religious. He's one man who not only reads his Bible, but lives it. He's not a boss to his men, he's a father. They come to him with their problems—just like kids."

References

> Detroit Free Press Mag p26-7 Mr 3 '40;
> p29 Mr 10 '40 por
> Fortune 8:47-9 Ag '33 il por
> Life 5:58 O 3 '38 por
> N Y Age p8 My 14 '38; p6 O 1 '38
> N Y Times X p10 D 8 '40
> Swing 2:10+ F '40; 2:9+ Mr '40 il;
> 2:10+ My '40 por; 2:11+ Je '40 il;
> 3:10+ Jl '40 pors; 3:10 Ag '40; 3:8-
> 9+ S '40 pors
> Time 21:26-7 Je 12 '33 por
> Victor Record R 3:13+ O '40; 3:11+
> N '40 por; 3:13+ Ap '40 por
> International Motion Picture Almanac
> Miller, P. E. ed. Down Beat's Yearbook
> of Swing, 1939 1939
> Panassié, H. Hot Jazz 1936
> Ramsey, F. and Smith, C. E. eds. Jazzmen 1939
> Wier, A. E. ed. Macmillan Encyclopedia of Music and Musicians 1938

ELLIS, CARLETON Sept. 20, 1876—Jan. 13, 1941 Chemist, and holder of 750 patents; helped develop paint improvements, plastics, anti-knock gasoline; consultant for many large firms and author of books on scientific subjects.

References

> Fortune 13:73 Mr '36
> Pop Sci 128:11-13+ Ja '36 por

Chemical Who's Who
Who's Who in America

Obituaries

> N Y Herald Tribune p16 Ja 14 '41 por
> Time 37:55 Ja 27 '41

ELTINGE, JULIAN (ĕl'ting) May 14, 1883—Mar. 7, 1941 Actor and female impersonator who achieved international fame in vaudeville and in such plays as *The Crinoline Girl* and *The Fascinating Widow*; was said to have made $3,000,000 as an actor and lost three fortunes; had theatre named for him; in 1907 gave a command performance for King Edward VII; had recently tried a comeback after long retirement from stage; real name was William Dalton.

References

> Am Mag 85:36-7 My '18 por
> N Y World-Telegram p8 Je 24 '40 por
> PM p20 Ag 1 '40
> Who's Who in America 1930-31
> Who's Who in the Theatre

Obituaries

> N Y Times p19 Mr 8 '41 por

EMERSON, VICTOR LEE 1863(?)—May 6, 1941 Inventor of the universal joint used on automobiles and of more than 100 other mechanical devices; was known widely as "the Philadelphia Edison" because of the number and importance of his inventions, many of which helped develop the automobile from its "horseless carriage" era.

Obituaries

> N Y Times p25 My 7 '41

EMMERSON, LOUIS LINCOLN Dec. 27, 1863—Feb. 4, 1941 Governor of Illinois from 1929 to 1933; for many years was Illinois Republican Secretary of State and active in Republican politics; retired from politics and became president of the Third National Bank of Mt. Vernon after term as Governor.

References

> Who's Who in America
> Who's Who in Government

Obituaries

> N Y Times p20 F 5 '41

EMMET, WILLIAM L(EROY) July 10, 1858—Sept. 26, 1941 Electrical engineer; inventor; associated with the General Electric Company from 1892 until his retirement a few years before his death; held 122 patents and was associated with the development of important innovations in power production; recipient of many honors and awards for his work.

References

> Lit Digest 79:20 D 29 '23 por
> Sci Am 123:424 O 23 '20 por; 130:80
> F '24 por
> World's Work 47:350 F '24 por

American Men of Science
Emmet, W. L. Autobiography of an
Engineer 1931
Who's Who Among North American
Authors
Who's Who in America
Who's Who in Engineering

Obituaries

N Y Times p17 S 27 '41 por

ESCH, JOHN J(ACOB) (ĕsh) Mar. 20,
1861—Apr. 27, 1941 United States Representative from the 7th Congressional District
from 1899 to 1921 and former member of the
Interstate Commerce Commission; appointed
a member of the Commission by President
Harding and served as chairman of that body
in 1927; attained national prominence as a co-
author of the Transportation Act of 1920.

References

Who's Who in America
Who's Who in Law
Who's Who in the Nation's Capital

Obituaries

N Y Times p15 Ap 28 '41

ESTES, HARLOW (ĕs'tēz) Dec. 11,
1900- Author

Address: b. c/o Dodd, Mead and Co, 449
Fourth Ave, New York City; h. 60 Pinckney
St, Boston, Mass.

Winner of the 1940 novel contest prize of
$10,000, offered jointly by Dodd, Mead and
Redbook Magazine, is a "thin, pleasant, thirty-
ish and not-too-overwhelmed Back Bay housewife." Harlow Estes' book, *Hildreth*—her
first venture into the novel field—was the
last but three of some 640 manuscripts submitted in the contest. It is, she explains, an
expansion of a short story she had long tried
to sell; for some 10 years she had been writing
short stories, most of them being returned to
her with the editorial comment that they had
"too many characters." She finally decided
to write a novel instead, "with this astonishing result."

First published serially in *Redbook Magazine,* then in book form (November 1940),
Hildreth is a character novel full of true-to-
life people psychologically but sympathetically
dissected. It is the story of an intense, unhappy girl of 19 who "looks after" her divorced, complacent, almost childish 38-year-old
mother. While they are summering on the
Maine coast the mother's young widowed sister, Laura, with her four sons, comes visiting.
During the summer Hildreth falls in love
with a personable young man, Geoffrey—who
in turn falls violently for the attractive aunt
Laura. This jolt to Hildreth is only the
climax to many happenings that cause her to
rearrange her ideas of people, to "grow up."

"The theme might be called the contrast
between the emotional immaturity of a young
girl and the stability of an experienced woman," the author says of her story. "I chose
it because contrast helps to reveal character.

HARLOW ESTES

The two women highlight each other by their
difference. My chief interest in writing fiction
is to reveal character." Critics in general have
praised highly this first novel. One has said
that it shows "exceptional balance and breadth
of perspective," another that it is "too mature,
too sure and subtle to be called merely promising."

Harlow Estes—her unusual given name was
the family name of her mother—was born in
Seattle, Washington, daughter of Dr. Henry
Robert Wilson, a physician who became a
Unitarian minister. Her mother, Gertrude
Burt (Harlow) Wilson, was "a Yankee of
English stock, one of the New England Har-
lows." Mrs. Estes says she "grew up in
various places: Santa Barbara, California, a
year in Kansas, two years in New York
State, three years in Berkeley, California."
She was educated in a small-town high school
in Monrovia, California and spent three years
at the University of California (taking no
degree), majoring in English and studying
short-story writing from 1919 to 1922. She
spent one year at Cornell, too. "Writing appears to be an inherited disease in my family,"
she says. "Father, mother, uncles, cousins all
write, or did. They were all bookish people."
She claims "a very distant relationship on my
father's side with Sir Walter Scott, and am
naturally glad to claim it, however far removed; also a first cousinship with the late
Violet Wilson, author of *Queen Elizabeth's
Maids of Honor* and other books of the his-
torical-research type."

Mrs. Estes has seen much of this country,
except the far South, but beyond a few brief
trips to Canada has not done a great deal
of traveling. "I like to stay long enough in
one place to get the 'feel' of it and know
some of the people." Since her marriage in
1928 to Stanley Goddard Estes, a professor

ESTES, HARLOW—*Continued*

of psychology at Northeastern University, Boston, she has lived in the East, mostly in Boston. The Esteses have no children.

Mr. Estes is said to be both amazed and proud of his prize-winning wife, whose manuscript he had not read before it received the $10,000 award. "She never showed a line of her writings to me," he said, "nor, so far as I know, to anyone else. She doesn't play bridge, she belongs to no clubs, and she is a neat, indeed, an excellent housewife and an amazingly good cook. She does all her housework." Mr. Estes is quite convinced he has married a wonderful woman.

Concerning her pastimes and hobbies besides writing, Harlow Estes admits that she likes to cook: "Am an incurable experimentalist in cookery but haven't made anyone ill as yet." She also does some painting in water color, landscape and flowers, and portraits in pencil. "But I am hampered by the medium; I have better luck with words." Apparently, however, her writing success is not a mere matter of luck. She has strict writing hours, from nine to three, five days a week. "It took me five months of actual writing to complete my novel," she confesses. "I'd had the characters in mind, however, for four or five years and I'd tried them in numerous short stories, but without any luck. I did the first chapter at least 100 times."

Among modern novelists Mrs. Estes names as her favorites Joseph Hergesheimer, Somerset Maugham, Robert Nathan, Oliver La Farge, Edith Wharton, Ellen Glasgow, May Sinclair, Selma Lagerlöf, Walter Edmonds. "I have a special passion for Thomas Hardy, Jane Austen, *The Constant Nymph, Main Street* and *Nocturne.* Yes, and some Proust, and Joseph Conrad. . . I like best the character analysis and stream-of-consciousness types of writing; I am infinitely grateful for any humor that is offered; and I thoroughly enjoy sports and mystery stories, though I dislike both mystery and sports intensely in real life." Mrs. Estes' second novel, *Long Week End* (1941), has been called "an extraordinarily civilized and an extraordinarily agreeable tale," and "a witty and cleverly told story."

References

> N Y Herald Tribune Books p5 N 10 '40 por
> N Y Sun p26 Ap 26 '40
> N Y Times Book R p16, 28 N 10 '40
> N Y World-Telegram p23 Ap 26 '40 por
> Pub W 137:1659 Ap 27 '40 por

ETTL, JOHN Aug. 1, 1872—Dec. 22, 1940 Sculptor, born in Budapest, came to the United States in 1898; noted as art teacher; inventor of the Ettl machine to enlarge sculptures.

References

> Who's Who in American Art

Obituaries

> N Y Times p15 D 24 '40

EVANS, ANNE 1869—Jan. 6, 1941 Civic leader; sponsor of many art projects; member of one of Colorado's pioneer families; best known project was the institution of a dramatic festival in the old Opera House in Central City, Colorado, a ghost town of the early mining days to which she brought noted stars of stage and opera.

Obituaries

> N Y Times p23 Ja 7 '41
> Variety 141:54 Ja 15 '41

EVANS, SIR ARTHUR (JOHN) July 8, 1851—July 11(?), 1941 Famous British archeologist who engaged in excavations in Crete from 1893 onward; rediscovered and restored the palace of King Minos of Crete; expert on Greece who gave the world a new conception of that ancient civilization; was a member of a family greatly interested in past civilizations, and was fifth successive member of the family to be elected to the Royal Society.

References

> Atlan 158:233-41 Ag '36
> Nature 138:979 D 5 '36
> Travel 65:18-22+ O '35 il
> Who's Who

Obituaries

> N Y Times p13 Jl 12 '41
> Time 38:72 Jl 21 '41

EVANS, SIR EDWARD R(ATCLIFFE) G(ARTH) R(USSELL) Oct. 28, 1881- A regional commissioner for London

Address: b. London Regional Organization, Romney House, London, S. W. 1; h. 76, Cadogan Sq, London, S. W. 1, England

"Hats off to the present; coats off to the future!" is the slogan advanced for this War by Admiral Sir Edward R. G. R. Evans, "a short and sturdy man with an energetic step and a Welsh-Irish lilt in his voice." Too old to take an active part at sea, he has been employed since the opening of the conflict on the London Regional Organization, and until recently was active solving the problem of warm and adequate shelter for London's people. Each night, in this job, he went around inspecting refuges in subways, tunnels, basements, sheet-steel huts; each morning he was at his desk in London Civil Defence headquarters keeping his staff and the telephones busy. Today he is doing purely administrative work for the London region.

Evans has been a man of action all his life, with a reputation for getting things done and done well. A real blue-sea admiral, he must be chafing at the fact that his post, important though it is, does not allow him to have a crack at the enemy. He is the son of Frank Evans, a barrister, and was educated at the Merchant Taylors' School and aboard the training ship *Worcester,* from which he passed into the Navy in 1897.

His first promotion, to sublieutenant, came in 1900. Two years later, as lieutenant, he had his first taste of Antarctic exploration when he sailed on the steam yacht *Morning*, the relief ship of Captain Robert Falcon Scott's *Discovery* expedition to the South. By 1907 he had distinguished himself sufficiently to win the Shadwell Testimonial Prize awarded by the Admiralty. Then, in 1909, he set out on the first great adventure of his career, as second in command to Scott on his South Pole expedition.

The gallant story of that expedition has often been told. It is well known that Scott reached the Pole only to find that he had been forestalled by Amundsen—and the heroism of Oates and the death of Scott have passed into history. It was Edward Evans (he had had a cape named after him by Scott) who took charge of the expedition after the leader died and who brought the survivors back. He returned home to a promotion to the rank of commander, invested with the C. B., and to the discovery that his wife, Hilda Beatrice Russell, had died in his absence. In 1914 he came to the United States to tell the story of the Scott expedition.

Back in England he plunged into war duties, and before 1914 was over had been mentioned in dispatches for his work in *H. M. S. Mohawk*, which bombarded the right wing of the German Army on the Belgian coast. Another mention came the following year when he was on the *Viking*. A further major event of his war years occurred in 1916, when at a Christiania Legation dinner in Norway he met Elsa Andvord and proposed to her 10 minutes later. They now have two sons. (Evans has no children by his first marriage.)

Early in 1917 Evans was appointed to the command of the old destroyer *Broke*, on the Dover Patrol. On the night of April 20 six German destroyers came in near to Dover, fired several rounds into a ploughed field and began to attack shipping. But the *Swift* and the *Broke* located them at 12:40 a. m. and "as the *Swift* turned to ram the leader, the *Broke* got home a torpedo on the second and then steamed full speed against the third."

As Evans tells it: "Those in the destroyer we intended to run down had gathered what our intention was, but for them it was too late. A cloud of smoke and sparks belched forth from their funnels and we got a momentary whiff of this as we tore toward her; it all happened in a few seconds, and the feeling of exhilaration as we were about to strike her can never be repeated. At the moment we crashed into her port side, abreast of the after funnel, my enthusiasm overcame me and I shouted out: 'That means two months' leave.'" A bloody, old-fashioned fight followed, and the *Broke* eventually got free carrying a number of prisoners. She was disabled by a shell in the boiler room; her compass, wireless and searchlight had all been knocked out by small ammunition; and her bridge had been hit in 32 places. But though she had to be towed into Dover, she and the *Swift* had sunk two German destroyers and put the other four to flight. Both commanders received the D. S. O. and special

SIR EDWARD R. G. R. EVANS

promotion to the rank of captain, and Evans won for himself the title "Evans of the Broke," by which most of England knows him.

Evans, who already possessed the Edward VI and George V medals for Antarctic Exploration, came out of the War with the United States Navy Cross, the Croix de Guerre and the orders of Officer of the Légion d'Honneur and Commander of the Crown of Belgium. He won a First Class medal for saving life at sea in 1919 and in 1921 the Board of Trade silver medal for the same feat. In 1921, too, he received a special gold medal from Lloyd's for saving life in the Hung Moh disaster in the China Seas. He was in command of *H. M. S. Carlisle* from 1921 to 1922, and from 1923 to 1926 was with the Patrol Mine-Sweeping and Fishery Protection Flotilla. From 1926 to 1927 he was on the battle cruiser *Repulse*.

At the same time that he was sailing the seas and indulging in bold adventures, Evans had been writing books of naval life intended mainly for the boys' market. *Keeping the Seas* (1920) related his experiences during the World War, and *South With Scott* (1921) told of the Antarctic expedition. There were many others, all written in a breezy, forthright style.

In 1929 Evans was made a rear admiral, and until 1931 was in command of the Royal Australian Navy. He became Companion of the Bath (military division) in 1932 and in 1935 was made Knight Commander of the same order. From 1933 to 1935 he was in command of the Africa Station, and in 1934 undertook a scientific survey in the Antarctic, during which he located and charted Bouvet Island. He had the home command of the Nore from 1935 to 1939.

At the beginning of the Second World War, Evans was made one of the three

EVANS, SIR EDWARD R. G. R.—*Cont.*

regional commissioners for London and during the long period in which the Capital was free from air raids worked ceaselessly to build up an A. R. P. organization. In April 1940, since his wife is Norwegian and he speaks Norwegian fluently, he was made an additional naval attaché in Norway. "If anyone had told me," he commented a month later, "that as Civil Defence Commissioner for the London Region I should find myself acting as a machine-gunner in a Norwegian aeroplane, hedge-hopping, tree-hopping and mountain-hopping before dropping out of the clouds into my Norwegian mountain home, I should have said they were dreaming." After the Norwegian collapse Evans was appointed by Lord Beaverbrook to take charge of the local protection and security of the organization of all aircraft factories and aerodromes.

Evans has been honored by universities, geographical societies and governments for his expeditionary work, as well as for his naval feats. He was Lord Rector of Aberdeen University from 1937 to 1939 and was reappointed for a second term, to extend until 1942. He is a Freeman of Calgary, of Dover and of Chatham and a Knight of the Order of St. John of Jerusalem.

References

> N Y Herald Tribune X p12+ N 17 '40 por
> N Y Times p1+ O 2 '40
> Times [London] p6 Ap 19 '40; p9 My 11 '40; p6 My 29 '40
> Evans, E. R. G. R. Keeping the Seas 1920
> Evans, E. R. G. R. South With Scott 1921
> O'Neill, H. C. History of the British Navy During the War (adapted from John Buchan's History of the War) p309-12 1918
> Times [London]. History of the War v16 p155-6 1918
> Who's Who

EVES, REGINALD GRENVILLE 1876—June 14, 1941 English portrait painter; among greatest successes were studies of Thomas Hardy, Sir Frank Benson and many of the leading figures of England including royalty; caused a sensation in 1931 when three paintings submitted to the Royal Academy were discovered to be photographs painted over; elected to the Royal Academy in 1939 and at time of his death was an official war artist.

References

> Who's Who

Obituaries

> N Y Times p37 Je 15 '41 por

FADIMAN, CLIFTON May 15, 1904-Literary critic; radio master of ceremonies

Address: b. 40 W. 57th St, New York City; h. 930 Fifth Ave, New York City

Every Friday 9,000,000 listeners tune in on *Information Please* to listen to Clifton Fadiman urging his four experts along their intellectual race track with the ease of a Ben Hur handling his spirited steeds. His is the perfect mixture of bright interest and delicate malice that spurs the experts to do their desperate best. Whenever Deems Taylor or F. P. Adams (see sketch this issue), both brilliant wits in their own right, has taken over on the rare occasions when Fadiman was unable to preside, something has gone out of the program. No one else can so well snub an irrepressible Levant, point up Kieran's uncanny accuracy, wring the last drop of wry erudition out of F. P. A. or encourage a stage-struck guest.

Fadiman's ingratiating personality, with its intriguing dash of affable arrogance, is the key to his success in a varied career as soda jerker, office boy, clerk, student, teacher, librarian, tutor, mail sorter, writer, editor, lecturer and master of ceremonies on one of the most popular programs on the air. Like many other strange and wondrous phenomena in American life, he sprang from Brooklyn, born there on May 15, 1904. His father, a Russian immigrant called Isidore M. Fadiman, was a druggist; his mother, Grace Fadiman, a nurse. Even as a child young Clifton showed the tremendous curiosity and retentive memory that have ever since contributed to his erudition. At five, his brother Ed trained his memory by making him memorize elaborate geographic data. At 10 Clifton (onomatopoeically nicknamed "Kip" after an attack of hiccoughs) had read Homer, Sophocles, Dante and Milton.

Clifton Fadiman's was a busy and enterprising boyhood and youth. In Brooklyn he jerked sodas in his father's drugstore and ran numerous errands all over town. He worked as a ship chandler and as an office boy for the French-American line. He helped his brother Edwin to run a paper called the Forest Hills *Reporter*. When he went to Columbia University he paid his way with a series of strange and unconnected jobs, among them running a bookshop in the Pennsylvania Terminal, doing translations, lecturing on French symbolist poetry, helping out in amusement parks, writing book reviews for *The Nation*. Altogether he claims he never made less than $1,000 a year as an undergraduate. He also edited Columbia's undergraduate publication, *Morningside*. He took time off in his junior year to work in the stock room of the publishing firm of Alfred A. Knopf but came back to Columbia a year later after making sure that he would probably never better his microscopic salary. He was graduated from Columbia in 1925 with Phi Beta Kappa honors, a slim, supercilious, golden-haired stripling.

After being graduated from Columbia, Fadiman taught English in the Ethical Culture High School. Possibly those years added the charmingly pedantic air that tinges his *Information Please* manner. In 1925 he lectured for Everett Dean Martin's People's Institute, talking on great literary classics. In 1927 he became associated with Simon & Schuster as assistant editor, still teaching on the side, and in 1929 he became a full-fledged editor. His first best-seller hunch was *Trader Horn*, which he recommended to the firm in 1927. By the time his connection with Simon & Schuster dwindled to that of editorial adviser in 1935, Fadiman was well known in literary circles as one of the country's leading editors. As editor in chief of Simon & Schuster, according to his own estimate, he examined more than 25,000 manuscripts and interviewed some 2,000 authors.

Fadiman's theory has ever been—and still is—that the taste of the American people is steadily improving. He has considered himself a sort of intellectual middleman, a purveyor of culture to the masses, be it in books, lectures or radio. He has added distinction to the "Essandess" fiction list: he was responsible for such novels as Hans Fallada's *Little Man, What Now?*, for Leonard Ehrlich's *God's Angry Man*, for Josephine Johnson's *Now in November*, a Pulitzer Prize winner in 1934. He also persuaded his firm to publish Ernest Dimnet's *Art of Thinking*.

In 1933 Fadiman, now well known as a lecturer and author whose articles were published in *The Nation, Stage, Harper's Bazaar* and other important publications, was engaged to review books for the *New Yorker*. Since then the *New Yorker's* book pages have become a power in the literary world. Their lucid, elegant style has brought Fadiman a formidable following; the impeccable judgment beneath the often flippant pose has made them a citadel of literary criticism. His reviews have evinced a merciless perception that enables him to put his finger on a writer's weak spot with an elegant but unerring touch. His tags stick because of their inherent justice. He coolly dismissed Dr. Cronin's *The Citadel* as second-rate *Arrowsmith*, and remarked acidly about Faulkner's *The Wild Palms*: "The reader will detect no soft alteration in Mr. Faulkner's Gorgon's eye view of human existence." His comment on *Kitty Foyle* was: "Those who have been afraid of Mr. Morley because they figure his whimsy will come off on them should not on that account steer clear of *Kitty Foyle*."

In 1934 Fadiman reviewed books on the radio for six months. He was not over-successful. The next time he came on the air it was in 1938, on the program that made his name a byword in every household. It was a result of an idea by a radio producer named Dan Golenpaul; he thought "stumping the experts" would be a welcome change from other quiz programs whose purpose was to expose the ignorance of the average man. The program was sustaining until Canada Dry took it over with its present panel of experts. It is now sponsored by Lucky Strike.

Soon *Information Please* was listed as one of the five best programs on the air. Its appeal is universal: in 1940 it was awarded the *Saturday Review of Literature* yearly prize for having done most to elevate American taste, and in the same week given a medal by the Hoboes of America. Being invited as a visiting expert to *Information*

CLIFTON FADIMAN

Please is a badge of honor for which the recipient works hard before Mr. Fadiman gets through with him. In his capacity as master of ceremonies he has wheedled and bullied such guests of varied talents and reputations as Wendell Willkie, Elsa Lanchester, J. P. Marquand, Harpo Marx—who whistled his answers—Alice Duer Miller, John Gunther and Warden Lawes (see sketches this issue).

Today Fadiman looks like a highly successful businessman. His main characteristics are still an unbounded capacity for work and a good craftsman's delight in putting out a polished job. He reads something like 10 or 15 books a week, but his 150-page-per-hour reading speed makes this easy: he can put away a mammoth-sized novel like *Gone With The Wind* or *Musa Dagh* in less than a day. Simon & Schuster still expect him to write a great book, and he has numerous ambitious outlines. He himself doubts that he will ever do anything with them, self-deprecatingly calling himself "an amiable hack." In 1939 he edited a book called *I Believe,* including credos of men like Jules Romains, Lin Yutang, Harold Laski (see sketch this issue), George Santayana and James Thurber. His next undertaking was sponsoring the Readers Club, an organization to distribute books reprinted on the advice of himself, with Sinclair Lewis, Carl Van Doren and Alexander Woollcott (see sketch this issue). The club has now 80,000 readers. Then in the fall of 1941 was published his *Reading I've Liked*, a personal anthology of widely assorted authors, prefaced by a 64-page foreword.

Fadiman married Pauline Elizabeth Rush in 1927 and has a young son called Jonathan Rush, who thinks his father is a fascinating person. Fadiman is an ardent cyclist and tennis player. He is sociable in general: at

FADIMAN, CLIFTON—*Continued*

his caustic best in front of an audience, but witty under any circumstances. He has a morbid passion for atrocious puns, to which he gives way shamelessly during *Information Please*: once while quizzing the experts upon Othello's words as he murdered Desdemona, he murmured irrepressibly: "A good example of smother love, eh?"

References

> Christian Sci Mon Mag p4 D 21 '38 il por
> Sat Eve Post 213:27+ Ja 11 '41 por
> America's Young Men
> Variety Radio Directory
> Who's Who in America

FAGNANI, CHARLES P(ROSPERO), REV. (fän-yä'nĕ) Oct. 29, 1854—Nov. 25, 1940 Theologian; professor emeritus of Old Testament literature at the Union Theological Seminary, New York; during the First World War aligned himself with the Allies and was expelled from Bavaria in 1921 because of his "enmity for Germany ever since 1914"; death took place in occupied France "under circumstances that have not been clarified"; author of theological books.

References

> Leaders in Education 1941
> Who's Who Among North American Authors
> Who's Who in America

Obituaries

> N Y Times p25 Ja 7 '41 por
> Sch & Soc 53:50 Ja 11 '41

FAIRBANKS, DOUGLAS (ELTON), JR. Dec. 9, 1909- Film and stage actor
Address: h. Westridge, Pacific Palisades, Calif.; Boxwood Farm, Hot Springs, Va.

A perhaps apocryphal story tells of a Hollywood director who was giving instructions to a nameless actor on how his part should be played. "Now," he announced, "I want you to be as English as Basil Rathbone, but only half as English as Douglas Fairbanks, Jr."

One of the most genuinely cosmopolitan of Hollywood's actors, Douglas Fairbanks, Jr., is as much at home in London as in New York, and his French accent is as good as his British. He was educated at the Harvard Military School in Los Angeles, the Polytechnic Preparatory School in Pasadena, the Bovée Art School, New York's Collegiate Military Academy and Paris art schools. The son of the late Douglas Fairbanks and of his first wife, Anna Beth Sully, Douglas Fairbanks, Jr., was born in New York City on December 9, 1909 and made his first visit to Europe at the age of six months, returning soon afterward to his grandfather's estate at Watch Hill, Rhode Island. His introduction

to the stage and to Hollywood was also early: he was taken on road junkets with his famous father, and when in 1915 Douglas, Sr., entered screen work, his young son made his acquaintance with motion pictures.

At that age art interested the boy most. He was nine when he painted a caricature of Raymond Hitchcock which the latter used on billboards for years. In 1918 his parents were divorced, and not long afterward his mother remarried and took him abroad to study art. When he returned to a private school in Pasadena, he was unhappy and begged his mother to take him abroad again. By that time her divorce settlement was almost wiped out, but they managed to live in interesting poverty in the Latin Quarter for a while.

It was 1923 when the precocious boy (he was 13) first decided to act. "There was an urgent need of making money on a big scale, and motion pictures presented the best opportunity," as he puts it. Paramount offered him a four-week contract at a salary of $2,000 a week and a part in *Stephen Steps Out*. "The echo of that flop still resounds," he confessed later. Dropped by the studio, he returned to Paris to resume his art studies and to do some writing. But it was not for long: Paramount reconsidered and gave him another chance in a Western and fast action picture.

Not until 1925, however, did the son of Douglas Fairbanks (determined not to make capital out of his father's fame), play in a real movie success, in *Stella Dallas*, with Ronald Colman and Belle Bennett. Other movie roles followed, and he also appeared on the legitimate stage in Los Angeles. Among the plays in which he has acted are *Romeo and Juliet, The Jest, Saturday's Children, Toward the Light, The Ambush* and the memorable *Young Woodley*. In 1926 he worked with his father on the technical end of *The Black Pirate*, being engaged to write the subtitles. In 1927 he wrote the titles for *The Gaucho*, in which Douglas, Sr., appeared, and for *Two Lovers*, as well as appearing in comedies which are better forgotten: *Women Love Diamonds, Iz Zat So?, The Texas Steer*. That year, too, he met and became engaged to Joan Crawford, although he was to appear opposite her only once, in *Our Modern Maidens*. They were married on June 3, 1929 at St. Malachi's Roman Catholic Church in New York City, with his mother present at the wedding.

By this time young Doug was working as a free-lance actor. In Hollywood, at least, there was a boom in the "live-while-you-may" youth who spent his nights dancing and emptying glasses expertly but with a slightly crooked smile. Barely 20, Fairbanks, Jr., was still not too young to carry miscellaneous neuroses and a lost-generation expression of varied intensity through picture after picture, their titles indicative of their content: in 1929 *A Woman of Affairs* (with the great Garbo), *The Jazz Age, Fast Life, The Forward Pass,*

The Careless Age; in 1930 *Loose Ankles* and *Party Girl.* It was perhaps one of these that inspired a critic to comment, rather lyrically: "While by no means handsome, he has so mobile a face and such expressive eyes that the observer considers only what he is feeling, not how he looks. In much of his playing there is the impression of strain—whether this is because he works under high tension or merely because he feels the character in question requires it, cannot be said."

In 1930 he appeared in a different sort of picture—*Dawn Patrol,* in which his part was as important as that of the star, Richard Barthelmess. As a result of his performance he was starred by his studio, First National. But his luck didn't hold. He was presently loaned to Universal for the lead in a comedy, *Little Accident,* which was a hit, but then proceeded to play in First National's *One Night at Susie's.* *Outward Bound* was a better picture, but with such an excellent cast that his really good performance didn't stand out, and *The Way of All Men* sent no sane critic into ecstasies. *Little Caesar,* in which he co-starred with Edward G. Robinson, broke the chain temporarily, and *It's Tough To Be Famous* and *Union Depot* were also successes, but they were followed by two pictures which "emphatically were *not*": *Love Is a Racket* and *Scarlet Dawn.*

During all this time Doug had been taking regular vacations in Europe and also doing some writing—he had begun to publish rather precious poetry and to contribute to *Vanity Fair* caricatures of movie stars accompanied by original character sketches. After he made *Morning Glory* (1933) with Katharine Hepburn his American public saw him no more for a while. He was in England early in 1933; in May, when he returned to make *Design for Living,* he was prevented by pneumonia; and although in August it was reported that he was planning joint films with his father, the plans did not go through. Soon he was back in England, appearing with Elizabeth Bergner in one of the best performances of his career, as the mad Peter in *Catherine the Great* (1934). He also played on the stage in *Moonlight Is Silver* with Gertrude Lawrence, and in *Winding Journey.* By this time it was apparent that his infinitely sophisticated hairline mustache (in no way reminiscent of his father's) was as permanent as his accent.

The next two years were a period of intense interest in British films. In 1935 he was seen in *Mimi,* in 1936 in *The Amateur Gentleman, Accused* and *Jump for Glory,* all British made. He then played Rupert of Hentzau in Selznick's *The Prisoner of Zenda* (1937). This was a solid success, and his salary jumped from a reported $25,000 a picture to $100,000.

There followed more financial, artistic and social triumphs. In 1938 he returned, apparently permanently, to American films in the joyous *Having Wonderful Time,* and then followed his success with three mad but far from naïve comedies: *Joy of Living, The Young in Heart* and *The Rage of Paris.*

In December he was seeing Anthony Eden off for the United States and being himself entertained by Lord Tweedsmuir, President Roosevelt, Cordell Hull, Sumner Welles and other figures of international importance. The following year *Gunga Din* and *The Sun Never Sets* set Anglophobes' teeth on edge, although empire-building was forgotten in *Rulers of the Sea.*

Joan Crawford had filed suit for divorce in April 1933, and had acquired her final decree sometime later. Married in April 1939 to the socialite Mary Lee Epling of Bluefield, Virginia, the former Mrs. G. Huntington Hartford, Douglas Fairbanks, Jr., soon proceeded to settle down in elaborately comfortable style in a 12-room home in the Pacific Palisades, "English and a little French and Spanish on the outside." The next year found him wandering through South American and African jungles, white-helmeted, in *Green Hell* and *Safari,* and he was also star and co-producer with Ben Hecht of the less exotic *Angels Over Broadway.* In 1941

DOUGLAS FAIRBANKS, JR.

his activities were more exclusively public-spirited. As vice-president of the Southern California branch of the Committee to Defend America by Aiding the Allies he had frequent conferences with public officials, and in April accepted a mission from President Roosevelt to make a tour of South America—Argentine, Brazil, Peru, Uruguay, Panama. He was asked to "ascertain the views and suggestions of the governments and peoples . . . with respect to improving the role of the theatrical arts as a possible vehicle for bringing about improved inter-American understanding." His Spanish "not so good" but his French fluent, he was apparently one of the more successful of the United States' would-be ambassadors of good will. The *Nación* was flattering: "He talks of books, of the theatre and painting like a man accustomed to move in

FAIRBANKS, DOUGLAS, JR.—*Cont.*

cultured circles. He is genuinely curious about us." *Noticias Graficas* informed its readers: "The truth is that he doesn't say anything new but says it with a smile and easily, and with no commercial intent." These were impressions denied only by the Nazi press. Fairbanks, Jr., was "spy extraordinary" to Buenos Aires' *Pampero,* and, after an episode when heckling youths exploded firecrackers in front of him, that paper's headline crowed, quite falsely: "Hero of a Hundred Films Almost Dies of Fright!"

In October 1941 the actor became an active service naval lieutenant, junior grade, and in the late fall was on a warship bound for Iceland. He had temporarily given up the screen.

Douglas Fairbanks, Jr., (he refuses to take the "Jr." off his name) is a little over six feet tall, weighs one hundred-seventy pounds, has light brown hair and mustache, blue eyes and a face that has frequently been called faun-shaped—livened by a smile as flashing as his father's, but less bold. Lean, athletic, he rarely misses a daily workout of tennis, swimming, wrestling or boxing. He used to be good at track, too. His reading tastes run to history, biography, political economics, and he also enjoys detective stories and metaphysical philosophy. His musical tastes run to concerts rather than opera. A more tenacious and recently acquired taste than any of these is a daughter, Daphne, who narrowly escaped being named Penelope. The young man who used to be Hollywood's "most active playboy and most ardent practical joker" has responsibilities now.

References

    Christian Sci Mon Mag p2 Ag 9 '41
      por
    Life 10:24 Je 2 '41 il pors
    N Y Times IV p2 Ap 27 '41 por
    Photoplay 50:14-16+ Jl '36 il pors; 52:
      22+ O '38 por
    PM p22 Je 4 '41 por
    Scholastic 38:8 Ap 28 '41 por
    Springfield Repub p24 F 16 '40
    Time 37:24 My 12 '41 por
    America's Young Men
    Hughes, E. Famous Stars of Today
      (Men) p197-218 1932
    International Motion Picture Almanac
    Who's Who in America
    Who's Who in the Theatre

FALKNER, ROLAND POST (fôk'nẽr) Apr. 14, 1866—Nov. 27, 1940 Statistician, economist and educator, associated with the National Industrial Conference Board for past 15 years; previously held a number of Government posts: chief of Division of Documents, Library of Congress; Commissioner of Education, Puerto Rico; assistant director of the Census Bureau.

ROLAND POST FALKNER

References

    Who's Who in America
Obituaries
    N Y Times p21 N 29 '40 por

FARNY, GEORGE W(IMBOR) Mar. 21, 1872—Sept. 1, 1941 Consulting mining engineer; leader in state planning in New Jersey; born in Russia and educated in France, Belgium and Germany before coming to the United States when he was 23 years old; acted as consulting engineer for public improvements and for mining companies in Russia and China; employed by Turkey to report on a national system of highways.

References

    Who's Who in Engineering
Obituaries
    N Y Herald Tribune p14 S 2 '41

FELLER, BOB Nov. 3, 1918- Baseball pitcher

Address: b. c/o Cleveland Indians, Cleveland, Ohio; h. Van Meter, Iowa

Sometime in 1941 the big, good-natured, prize pitcher of the Cleveland Indians, Bob Feller, allowed a sculptor to pour plaster over his mighty pitching arm to make a cast. It was to be displayed at the Cleveland Health Museum along with models of the arms of Bobby Jones, golfer; the Mayo Brothers, doctors; and Rachmaninoff, famous pianist.

Feller regards this right arm, which earns him around $40,000 a year, with proper respect. "In explaining how he throws a certain kind of ball, Feller will gladly demonstrate in slow motion the subtle and graceful movements of shoulder, elbow, wrist and fingers," writes St. Clair McKelway in *Life.* "He does this with the enthusiasm of a jeweler showing off the inside of a precious timepiece which he did not make but passionately admires. 'Look at it!' Feller will exclaim delightedly. 'Notice that little twist there just as its fingers let go the ball?' He is a modest, good-natured, self-effacing young man and is awed by the arm rather than proud of it."

Going through a crowd at the entrance to a ball park, he instinctively uses his left arm for pushing, according to McKelway. "Feeling his way through a dark room, he puts out his left hand to find the light switch; if he stumbles, it is his left arm that goes up in a reflex motion to break his fall. If he ever swings on an umpire, the chances are a hundred to one that he will try a left hook." He held Number 7,846 in the draft, and with no dependents (except his fellow-players, someone facetiously said), found himself putting "It," as he reverently calls this mighty member, to novel uses. The sports world lost by enlistment in December 1941 a young Feller whom the *Sporting News* in the winter of 1940-41 named the No. 1 major league baseball player. In 1940 he pitched 31 complete games, and led the American League in strike-outs (263).

Born on the edge of an Iowa village named Van Meter eight days before the beginning of the Long Armistice, Robert William Andrew Feller had a Swiss-French father, William A. Feller, who was a comparatively well-to-do farmer, and a French-German mother, Lena (Forret) Feller. The elder Feller had played baseball as a youth, as had Mrs. Feller's father, and as Bob grew up he bought him the best gloves obtainable and helped him organize neighborhood teams. They became great companions; Mrs. Feller became used to having the males of the family late to dinner because they lost track of time playing catch behind the barn, or had gone off to a nearby sand-lot game.

By the time Bob was in high school he was making from $35 to $50 a Sunday playing semi-professional baseball in Iowa towns within a 100-mile radius of his home, and he decided that he might as well make the game his lifework. "I knew I was going to make it my career," he has said, "and, anyway, I liked to play baseball better than I liked to do anything else, and I still do." When he was only 16 the Cleveland Indians signed him up, after, says Henry McLemore, they had heard about a rustic fireball who thought nothing of striking out 18 batsmen in a seven-inning game. This feat was accomplished in the National semi-pro tournament at Dayton, Ohio, in the summer of 1935. He was then signed with the New Orleans Pelicans, but decided to finish high school. On July 6, 1936, Bob struck out eight of nine St. Louis Cardinals he faced in an exhibition at League Park, and a week later was bought by the Indians. The authorities of the Adel (Iowa) High School gave him permission to remain with the Indians until September 27, the date of their last game, before returning to resume his senior year in high school. In August he had struck out 17 Athletics and broken Rube Waddell's 27-year-old mark.

In 1937 and 1938 Feller, who hadn't learned the fine points of pitching, "had about as much control as a drunken swallow," writes McLemore. He spent his time on the mound either striking them out or walking them, breaking records in both departments—and fracturing Hank Leiber's skull with one cannon ball smash, according to Jack Chance in *Friday* Magazine. He relied too much on his superhuman fast ball and youthful energy. Feller himself says of those days: "I didn't know much. I just reared back and let them go. Where the ball went was up to Heaven. Sometimes I threw the ball clean up into the stands."

In 1937 he won 9 games and lost 7; in 1938 he made it 17 and 11; in 1939 it was 24 and 9; in 1940, 27 and 11 and in 1941, 25 and 13. The number of his strikeouts has risen to much over 1,000. And his popularity with the fans has risen in proportion. Although the schedule usually calls for Feller to pitch about every fourth day, he is required to be on the field at every game, mostly for promotional purposes.

BOB FELLER

It is Feller's fast ball that fascinates the crowd. Bill Dickey, the Yankee catcher, says that it looks just like an aspirin tablet coming up to the plate, only not quite as large. It travels about 100 miles per hour, and has a peculiar upward hopping motion known as the "hop" in addition to its great forward velocity. In the course of a game Feller makes between one hundred fifteen and one hundred thirty pitches, and on a hot day may lose as much as four pounds in weight. Sometimes he sniffs ammonia or douses his wrists with ice water to pull himself together.

After a hot day's game he gets an alcohol rubdown from Lefty Weismann, the Indians' trainer, who has no medical degree but is an intuitional diagnostician; drinks a glass of hot salt water at his hotel to counteract

FELLER, BOB—*Continued*

the heavy perspiration; has a nap and a shower; and stokes up at dinner time on roast beef, steak or sea food. In Cleveland, Feller lives at the Tudor Arms, a residential club, sharing a suite of two bedrooms and parlor with an outfielder named "Soup" Campbell, with whom he also rooms on road trips. He spends most of his time with his teammates, occasionally going with them to a quiet party, a dance, the movies, or the Municipal Opera at Forest Park in St. Louis.

When not playing ball, Feller lives luxuriously with his parents in a new, nine-room brick house which he built for them at a cost of $25,000. It is equipped with two bathrooms, three bedrooms, a recreation· room and shooting gallery, a two-car garage, a flood-lit skating rink and a tennis court. Feller's parents spend winters in Florida at his expense. On the long summer evenings his younger sister, Marguerite, pastes newspaper stories about her brother in one scrapbook and photographs in another. An electric eye in the garage opens the doors when Bob wheels his Buick up the driveway. He has a weakness for fast driving and has added to it a passion for flying, which he took up in 1941.

Bob Feller, says McKelway, is solidly built, a fraction under six feet tall, and weighs on a year-round average about one hundred eighty-five pounds. He has "a longish face with a generous mouth and clear, intelligent eyes." He laughs easily at jokes and at funny situations, and enjoys himself "in a restrained, agricultural way." He has never smoked; chews gum, not tobacco; will take a glass of wine or beer if feeling in good condition. Besides baseball, he plays table tennis, golf and billiards, and enjoys skating and trap and target shooting in the off season. "He likes girls well enough but has thus far escaped being identified with any particular girl by the gossip writers, which is a neat feat in itself."

References

Collier's 99:22+ Mr 6 '37 pors
Friday 1:25 My 24 '40 por
Life 10:51-4+ My 12 '41 il pors
Look 5:20+ Ap 22 '41 pors
N Y Times VII p12+ Ag 17 '41 il pors
Sat Eve Post 209:12-13+ F 20 '37 pors
Scholastic 30:24-5 My 29 '37 il pors
Time 34:22 Jl 24 '39 pors; 37:49 F 3 '41 por

Nason, J. and others Famous American Athletes of Today 7th ser p177-207 1940
Who's Who in the Major Leagues

FIELD, MARSHALL, III Sept. 28, 1893-
Industrialist; philanthropist
Address: b. 250 Park Ave, New York City; h. 740 Park Ave, New York City

Since October 1940 the largest single stockholder in the New York City newspaper *PM* has been Marshall Field, III. At that time the stockholders in The Newspaper *PM*, Incorporated voted to accept his offer of $300,000 and a 15 per cent interest in a new corporation in return for all the assets of the old corporation, which had run through some $1,500,000 cash in three months. Although Mr. Field's business and philanthropic ventures have been numerous, probably more curiosity has been aroused by his financial backing of this newspaper than by any of the others. His total investment in *PM* has been reported as several millions. Robert Ingersoll, *PM's* editor, explained Field's attitude toward the paper: "Mr. Field," he said, "compares *PM* in some ways with the Philharmonic Orchestra. No one thinks of disbanding the Philharmonic merely because it doesn't now support itself nor never has."

It was not much later when Field announced, to the consternation of other capitalists: "I happen to have been left a great deal of money. I don't know what is going to happen to it and I don't give a damn. If I can't make myself worthy of the three square meals I eat a day, I don't deserve them."

And losses didn't deter Marshall Field from another newspaper venture. In September 1941 he announced that he and "a group of friends" had decided to launch a new newspaper to break the Chicago morning paper monopoly of the isolationist Chicago *Tribune*. He himself was to be the paper's owner, and its policy, he said, was to be one of unequivocal opposition to isolationism. On December 4th the first issue of the Chicago *Sun* appeared, to the accompaniment of congratulatory telegrams from prominent people all over the United States, including President Roosevelt himself.

Marshall Field, III is listed in *Who's Who in America* as Republican and Catholic. He was born in Chicago, Illinois (the home of the department store, Marshall Field & Company) on September 28, 1893, the son of Marshall Field, Jr., who in 1905 committed suicide in his Chicago home, and Albertine (Huck) Field. He was reared and educated in England—he attended Eton College and Cambridge University—and, returning to the United States around the time of the First World War, he enlisted as a private in the 1st Illinois Cavalry in 1917. He was promoted through the grades to a captaincy, arrived in France in March 1918, participated in the St. Mihiel and Meuse-Argonne operations and was honorably discharged on February 20, 1919.

Marshall Field, III returned from the Army to occupy himself with hunting, horses, dogs (mainly retrievers), and the varied responsibilities that go with the inheritance of a fortune of hundreds of millions. But that was by no means all. Settled in Chicago with his wife, the former Evelyn Marshall of New York whom he had married in 1915, he insisted on working for a time as an apprentice in the office of Lee Higginson & Company, brokers. Asked why he worked, he replied: "I would consider it criminal if I did not take advantage of my opportunity to assist in the development of American industry." As a sideline he found jobs for ex-service men.

In 1921 the Fields moved to New York, where Marshall Field, III, built a town house and a Georgian mansion on Lloyds Neck, "Caumsett," and organized the investment-banking firm of Field, Glore, Ward & Company. Nine years later he was divorced from his first wife (there were a son and two daughters by this marriage), and in the same month he married Mrs. Audrey James Coats. It was at about this time that he took up flying and speedboat racing.

In 1934 divorced from his second wife, Field apparently found himself at loose ends—though hardly from lack of responsibilities: a trustee of the estate of Marshall Field, Marshall Field, III, has also been a director of the Continental Insurance Company, the Continental-Illinois National Bank & Trust Company, the Westinghouse Electric and Manufacturing Company and, of course, Marshall Field & Company. He was already vaguely interested in social problems. In 1932 he had voted for Hoover, but by 1934, as he put it: "I got rather disgusted with the Republican Party and I got interested in Roosevelt and what he was trying to do." *Time* says that in 1935 he was "well psycho-analyzed and emerged with a desire to do good in the world"—and that his first act was to donate the next earnings of one of his race horses to Dr. Zilboorg (see sketch this issue), his psychoanalyst. (They reportedly totaled some $500,000, and became the foundation for Dr. Zilboorg's famous study of suicide.)

A few years ago Mr. Field organized a New York committee on child welfare and through it gave new buildings, new equipment and increased personnel to 10 different children's societies. In 1936 he retired from investment banking. Since the Second World War he has acted as chairman of the United States Committee for the Care of European Children, and he himself took five British refugee children into his luxurious home, which already held five of his own. It was September 1940 when he announced that a new diplomatic agreement between the United States and Great Britain would enable non-British refugee children in England, too, to come to the United States without quota restriction. Unfortunately, however, the child removal scheme was suspended the month after this announcement as too hazardous, and Mr. Field's committee was forced to reduce its activities at about the same time Mr. Field became *PM's* principal stockholder. Since that time the main function of the United States Committee for the Care of European Children has been to guarantee proper care for those already here. Mr. Field has also donated generously to the USO and to British and Russian relief organizations, in all of which he is active; he is chairman of the Defense Council of Public Relief Administration; and he heads Mayor LaGuardia's organization for dispensing hospitality to servicemen on leave. With all his activities and philanthropies, in 1941 he was so busy that he not only worked a full eight-hour day in his

Ira L. Hill

MARSHALL FIELD, III

Park Avenue office without vacation, but often spent his evenings in conferences.

Mr. Field has been described as "sturdily handsome, with a grayish pompadour and a biggish, sharp nose." He dresses conservatively and well. On January 15, 1936 he was married for the third time—to Mrs. Ruth Pruyn Phipps. The couple have two small daughters. Field is a member of New York's Knickerbocker Club and of various tennis, golf, hunting and yacht clubs, and in Chicago holds membership in the Chicago, University, Union League, and Saddle and Cycle Clubs. He has also been president of the Philharmonic Symphony Society of New York and treasurer of The Metropolitan Museum. In November 1940, before the choice of John Winant (see sketch this issue) as Ambassador to Great Britain, he was mentioned as a possible successor to Joseph P. Kennedy. It was reported that there was "no doubt here that Mr. Field would be *persona grata* to the British court and foreign office."

References

Am Mag 131:71 Ja '41 il por
Cue 10:34 O 4 '41 por
N Y Herald Tribune p9 S 25 '40; p11 O 8 '40; p1, 14 N 20 '40 por
N Y Sun p24 S 6 '40
Newsweek 16:51 O 28 '40 por
Sat Eve Post 214:14-15+ D 6 '41 pors
Time 36:56 O 7 '40 por

Who's Who in America
Who's Who in Commerce and Industry
Who's Who in Finance, Banking and Insurance

FIELDING, MANTLE Sept. 20, 1865—Mar. 27, 1941 American architect; authority on paintings and engravings of the early American era; expert on early American

FIELDING, MANTLE—*Continued*

artists, particularly those who had done portraits of George Washington; wrote many volumes on early painting and engraving.

References

> American Art Annual 1924-25
> Who's Who in America

Obituaries

> N Y Times p23 Mr 28 '41

FIELDS, GRACIE Jan. 9, 1898- British comedienne

Address: h. 22 Charing Cross, Rd, London, W. C. 2, England; Peacehaven, Sussex, England

GRACIE FIELDS

The War, which has spoiled so many things, has even cast a cloud on Gracie Fields, as much England's sweetheart as Mary Pickford was ever America's. In the British Parliament on July 26, 1940 a Labor member got up and asked some awkward questions. Why had Gracie and her new husband, "the well-known Fascist," Mario Bianchi (better known as Monty Banks) been allowed to take out of the country valuable jewels and sums of money far in excess of the amounts permitted by the defence regulations? Was it true that Gracie had left "practically no assets" in England?

In reply the Financial Secretary to the Treasury said that nothing irregular had been done; that the dollars Gracie would earn in the United States would eventually be assets on the British side; and that although Banks' nationality was dubious, it had been decided to treat him as a British subject who would also have to account for his dollars. A little later Gracie's accountants denied that she had left no assets in England, and the firm of George Music and Sons, from whom she

was supposed to have made heavy purchases of jewels, said it had never seen either her or her husband. Protestations were capped by an announcement by the Navy League that Gracie was giving her services free at 32 concerts from Vancouver, British Columbia to Halifax, Nova Scotia to aid in getting war comforts for the Navy and in training youth. And Gracie herself said: "Everything I have is the Government's whenever they want it."

The situation stirred up quite a row, but then, anything that affects the "Lancashire Lass" comes close to the hearts of most of England's people. It has been that way for over 20 years now, which means that Gracie Fields has come a long way from the small cotton town of Rochdale, Lancashire, where she was born and where she first worked. Her father and mother, Fred and Sarah Jane (Bamford) Stansfield, were poor working people. Gracie was born in a standardized street and wore clogs; a public primary schooling was all she got in the way of education.

At school Gracie was described as one of the shyest girls there, very reserved and very particular about making friends, but generous and intelligent. It was acting, not school, that really counted for her. "I started when I was seven—singing from the gallery to a woman on the stage," she once said. "I'd made up my mind to be an actress." So schooling became an off-and-on affair when Gracie got a job acting with a troupe at 25 cents a week. At 12 she was allowed to do a comic number on her own account and at 14 reached the dizzy heights of $25 a week. But it wasn't for long.

Gracie's mother by this time had decided that her daughter had better get all this acting nonsense out of her head and go into the mill like the rest of her schoolmates. So Gracie spent two years in a cotton mill, in a shop and in a paper bag factory. It was no use, Mrs. Stansfield found, for in April 1915, when Gracie was 17, she got herself a job in a revue called *Yes, I Think So* at Hulme, Manchester. In the company the principal comedian was Archibald Selinger (he acted as Archie Pitt), whom Gracie married some years later and divorced in 1939.

From Manchester, Gracie went on to make her first London appearance. It was at the old Middlesex Music Hall, on July 5, 1915, in the same revue. From then on her career was well under way, though it was not until after the end of the First World War that she reached real fame. For a while she played mainly in the provinces. In February 1916 she was playing in *It's a Bargain* at the Tivoli in Manchester and she then toured with this revue for two years. In 1918 she got the part of Sally Perkins in the phenomenally successful light show, *Mr. Tower of London*, which ran for seven years, and she appeared in it on July 30, 1923 in the West End of London. Her success was immediate and striking. Gracie was in the big money from then on.

"In the old days," Gracie once told an interviewer, "my ambition was to earn a hundred pounds a week at the Coliseum, and when eventually I got it I wanted to frame the note —make a picture of it to look at—but they wouldn't let me. Since then I've often earned £750 a week, but I hate to get that much as salary; it worries me; I feel I can't be worth it. I don't mind if I draw it on a sharing basis." Since she made that statement Gracie's income has gone up and up until it has been computed at about $1,000,000 a year.

It comes from her stage appearances, from films and from victrola records. In 1931 she appeared in the film *Sally in Our Alley,* in 1932 in *Looking on the Bright Side,* and from then on in a number of pictures. In 1935 she signed a contract with Associated Talking Pictures which brought her about $600,000 over a period of two years. Then she made three pictures for Twentieth Century-Fox in England, *We're Going To Be Rich, Smiling Along* and *Shipyard Sally,* pictures which were shown widely in America and brought forth comments as varied as: "The production offers nothing to ingratiate Miss Fields in the eyes of the average American"; and "[she is] the most refreshing comedy personality to hit the American screen" in many a year. On the basis of the more favorable reviews, Darryl Zanuck (see sketch this issue) imported Gracie to America in 1937 and then kept her under contract for eight months. Nothing came of it, however.

Gracie made her first record in 1928. By 1933 she was able to entertain her father and mother, the Mayor of Rochdale and others at a Lancashire luncheon celebrating the pressing of her four-millionth record. The *Manchester Guardian* commented a little later: "The only singer who may have exceeded Gracie Fields in the number of recordings was Caruso." When people comment to Gracie on the amount of her income she tells them that most of it goes in taxes. "I'm paying for rearmament," she says. "They'll probably name a battleship after me."

Gracie Fields' popularity is due to her combination of talents as a vocalist and comedienne, coupled with a delightful, informal personality. She is the essence of Lancashire, with its quick humor and forthright speech and its broad accent. She "expresses on the stage the triumph of the common girl who won't be put on." The London *Times* writes of "her large friendliness, cheerful common sense and persistent joy in what is ridiculous"; *Time,* on the other hand, describes her "sheer animal vulgarity, including flea-scratching and grimaces." It is probably all these things, together with a really excellent voice, which improved the morale of the British troops in France in the winter of 1939 to 1940 and of the civilians in Canada and the United States in 1940 and 1941 when she entertained them.

Gracie's London home is on Charing Cross Road. Lately, however, she has lived mostly at Peacehaven, Sussex, and before that spent some time on her estate on the island of Capri. Gracie is still modest about all this prosperity. Her elderly parents are still her first care; and she is an indefatigable performer for charity,

especially for charities of her native town, Rochdale, which made her an honorary Freeman in 1937. In return she entertained 9,000 natives of Rochdale in Windsor and London with tea and her own special kind of fun.

References

Collier's 108 :15+ Ag 9 '41 il
Manchester Guardian F 15 '33; My 20 '37; My 22 '37
N Y Herald Tribune p19 Mr 19 '40; p3 Ag 14 '40
N Y Sun p3 F 17 '41 por
Time 31 :22 F 28 '38 por; 36 :61 Ag 19 '40 por
Times [London] Ap 9 '36; Je 18 '37; O 28 '38; S 1 '39
Hodson, J. L. No Phantoms Here 1932
International Motion Picture Almanac
Who's Who
Who's Who in the Theatre

FIELDS, LEW Jan. 1, 1867—July 20, 1941 American vaudeville comedian who, with his partner Joe Weber, combined slapstick and German dialect for sixty years on the stage as the nation's outstanding comedy duo; they began career together on the Bowery at the age of nine; appeared all over the country, split up their act, appeared in plays and motion pictures, but always came back together again; owned Weber and Fields Music Hall, an enormously successful theatre in which they gathered around themselves the greatest number of stars ever assembled; Fields' real name Lewis Maurice Fields.

References

Collier's 86 :10+ Jl 19 '30
Lit Digest 85 :42-8 Ap 25 '25 pors
Sat Eve Post 196 :3-4 My 31 '24; 196: 24-5 Je 14 '24; 196 :20-1 Je 28 '24; 197 :20-1 Jl 12 '24; 197 :18-19 Jl 26 '24; 197 :20-1 Ag 9 '24; 197 :28-31 Ag 23 '24; 197 :18 O 4 '24; 197 :44-7 O 11 '24; 197 :22 O 18 '24 pors
Stage 14 :84-5 Ag '37 il pors
Theatre 49 :30 Ap '29 por
International Motion Picture Almanac 1937-38
Isman, F. Weber and Fields 1924
Moses, M. J. and Brown, J. M. eds. American Theatre As Seen By Its Critics, 1752-1934 p332-5 1934
Who's Who in America 1934-35
Who's Who in American Jewry 1928
Who's Who in the Theatre

Obituaries

N Y Times p19 Jl 22 '41 pors
Time 38 :53 Jl 28 '41 por

FIELDS, STANLEY 1884(?)—Apr. 23, 1941 Motion picture, vaudeville and stage actor; turned to pictures 12 years ago; among his film appearances were parts in *The Lady from Cheyenne, Cimarron, Little Caesar, Mu-*

FIELDS, STANLEY—*Continued*
tiny on the Bounty, and *O'Malley of the Mounted;* real name was Walter Agnew.

References

Motion Pict 41:66 Jl '31 por
Motion Pict Classic 31:26 Ag '30 por
International Motion Picture Almanac

Obituaries

Variety 142:70 Ap 30 '41

FIENE, ERNEST (fē'nê) Nov. 2, 1894-
Artist
Address: b. Studio 908, Carnegie Hall, New York City; h. Southbury, Conn.

Associated American Artists' Galleries

ERNEST FIENE

Ernest Fiene is a versatile artist, and, as Hermon More says: "It is not surprising that his vitality and his interest in all manifestations of life should demand the use of many mediums for his expression." He works in oil, water color, *gouache,* aquatint; he has painted frescoes; he is the author of 45 editions of lithographs and etchings; he has illustrated advertisements, designed book jackets; he has illustrated books, two of them included in the "Fifty Best Books of the Year." Fiene himself says he believes in a broad scope in the expression of art, akin to the work and conception of the Old Masters.

From his many years of painting have come resonant water colors of the Adirondacks and effective, haunting but starker oils like *Yard Engine, Newtown Church* and *Spring.* There have come flower paintings, straightforward portraits, stimulating still lifes, landscapes of much of America, and many, many pictures of New York. In these city pictures, "without ever illustrating or stooping to sentimental narrative Fiene imparts a poignancy to the

rapid change and reconstruction of the life of the city." Fantastic skyline, river-vaulting bridges, towering steel structures, brownstone houses, downtown, Union Square, uptown—they are all there. In his capturing of New York as in many other paintings, Fiene shows himself socially conscious, aware of current problems. Yet never is there a morbid quality or a sense of false brooding; always, even in a deeply poetic canvas like *Nocturne,* a picture of Union Square in winter, there is an impression of detachment.

In many of his works Fiene has demonstrated his belief that paint must have a rich body to resist the effects of aging. He seeks an enameled quality, believing that paint must have its own beauty in body and that a freshly painted picture should have the brilliance of new pigment and not be forcefully aged on the palette. The colors the paints show have been called "almost a study in instrumentation. What has sometimes been regarded as harshness or crudity is actually the change of accent and beat, the variation of tonal resonance and withal the refusal to allow a passage to die on the retina of the eye."

But Fiene never depends on color alone for his compositions. He has a keen sense of design, "governed more often by the subject and the form than by a purely decorative scheme." He has a keen realization of the importance of line and the effectiveness of an occasional bold stylization of detail. Always, though, "one feels in his work the desire to capture by plastic means the spirit of the scene or arrangement that stimulated him to put it on canvas."

Ernest Fiene, who has at various times been accused of being a Primitive, an Impressionist, an Abstractionist, a painter's painter, has nevertheless managed at every stage of his artistic development to imbue his work with something of his personality—"his vitality and intensity of emotion." And he has been painting "ever since I can remember." He was born in Elberfeld, Germany on November 2, 1894, the son of Henry William and Maria (Egger) Fiene, and came to the United States in 1912. For a while he worked at an engineering career, "developed some bulging muscles from it," and then turned to art.

He got himself a job in a decorator's shop and enrolled in the National Academy of Design in 1914. For four years he studied there and never finished a picture. At the same time, though, from 1916 to 1918, he was studying at the Beaux Arts, and in 1923 he spent a year at the Art Students League. Before then, in 1920, he had made his first exhibition appearance with the Society of Independent Artists, and in 1921, the year he was married to Jeanette Ettarre of New York, had begun to concentrate almost full-time on his work.

From 1921 to 1928 his work consisted mainly of landscapes, figure compositions and portraits. Particularly he loved winterscapes and the ironclad appearance of the snowy New England fields, but there were, too, pictures of the Catskill Valley of the Hudson River, of Maine, New Hampshire and Vermont at every season of the year. His work was well received. In 1922 William Murrell called him "a romantic with a strong unaffected faith in his own vision of the world, untainted by any intellectual or esthetic theories." His 1924 exhibition drew critical praise, as did his 1927 exhibition of paintings, water colors, lithographs and drawings.

In 1928 and 1929, after becoming an American citizen, Fiene was in Paris and Brittany, doing a series of water colors of Brittany and a group of figure paintings. He returned to the United States to work especially on his series of paintings of New York, most of which were made after 1930. Two years later, in 1932, he received a Guggenheim fellowship and spent a year in Italy studying the early Renaissance masters and, in Florence, the technique of fresco painting. But, one critic commented, his European excursion was only "an interlude between two periods of painting the American scene."

His return from abroad was marked with an exhibition at the Downtown Galleries in 1934, his first one-man show in several years. Edward Alden Jewell rejoiced that a "former harsh and acidulous quality has been to a large extent replaced by a palette much more various and flexible"; that his "color has warmed and mellowed. It is less brittle and flat." And there were many who agreed with Henry McBride of the New York *Sun*: "Ernest Fiene as painter of the American scene in its broad scope has made a foremost place for himself. . . His great research in technic has given him an easy means of expression, particularly in recent years. Today there is a spontaneous quality and a complete unity in his paintings. . . The commonplace scene under Fiene's brush develops into a dramatic experience in the spectator's life."

A year later Fiene, "an excellent teacher," was spending the summer teaching painting at the Fine Arts Center in Colorado Springs. In that same year he showed water colors of New Mexico, works in which the use of selection and compression makes *Sacred Mountain, Taos* and *Rain Over Mountain, New Mexico* "vibrant pictures, restrained yet rich in color and alive with curving motion." He also showed oils of Wyoming and New England, "pictures that glow . . . as though from a steady internal combustion, the coil being electrified to red-hot heat. Through the brick-red of this earth, or at its sides, peeps out chromium yellow, while overhead the blue finishes off the palette." This was the year, one critic stated, in which Fiene "found himself." "Possessed of an interesting style, he has at last mastered it, has ceased being rather self-conscious over it as in the days when he painted stiff churches against the snow or even those able nocturnes of New York City, and has broadened out into a powerful artist."

Late in this same year, Fiene left the Connecticut farm he had had since 1933 to make a trip through Pennsylvania and West Virginia. "It was a winter of continued blizzards and snow," he says. "I traveled by car and although it was hazardous my enthusiasm for the strange visual beauty of the industrial regions blanketed in snow led me on." In 1937, through the medium of the Pittsburgh Commission for Industrial Expansion, an exhibition of the work done on this trip was held. There were industrial themes—*Night Shift, Old Coke Ovens;* there were paintings of Negro slums—*Coming Home, The Red House;* and the show was a success.

In that same year Fiene was given a commission to do four murals in the Department of the Interior Building in Washington, D. C., and not long after that he started two murals for the Central High School of Needle Trades in New York. These two murals were finished after two and one-half years' work. Allegorical in treatment, they present in over 2,000 square feet more than 200 figures—labor leaders, progressive manufacturers, legislators and social workers who have contributed to the progress of the industry and helped bring about reforms in working conditions. The first, called *Victory of Light Over Darkness,* showing sweatshops, the Triangle Fire, etc., has been said to surge with movement and vitality. The second, *Harmony and Achievement,* showing the members of the five needle trades working together and all the improvements in their lives, has been called, in comparison, static. Fiene explained that: "Heaven," he said, "is harder to paint than hell. It ought to be painted statically. It represents an end in aspiration."

Before he started these murals, Fiene had been honored with the Harris Silver Medal and a prize of $500 at the Chicago Art Institute for his *Frosty Morning.* Other prizes include the Clark Prize at the Corcoran Gallery for *Spring Evening;* honorable mention in the Carnegie International for *Razing the Old Post Office;* and the Ada S. Garrett Prize of $750 at the Chicago Art Institute for the same painting. He is represented at the Denver Art Museum, the Whitney Museum, the Phillips Memorial Gallery, the Newark Art Museum, the Boston Museum, the Mia Collection in Japan and at many other museums and private and public collections of art.

The most recent, as well as the largest and most comprehensive exhibition of the work of this large, solid-framed, blond artist was held in January 1940 after he returned from Hollywood, where he had painted a scene of the film *The Long Voyage Home.* In this exhibition were shown a series of water colors, pictures in the genre tradition, a *tour de force* called *Kitchen Table,* painted with his left hand after he broke his right arm, and many examples of the diversified subjects and forms that distinguish Fiene's art. Of them William Murrell wrote: "His sympathies have widened, his experience has deepened, his technique has grown supple and sure. There is more power, control and restraint. . . Fiene's superb orchestration of abstract color spaces within the framework of Nature is a most significant contribution to the art of our time. . . Life and a prodigious amount of work have tempered his realism from its earlier romantic leanings to its present-day clarity and flexibility. Nothing can apparently temper his robust exuberance."

(Continued next page)

FIENE, ERNEST—*Continued*

References

> Am Mag Art 27:121 Mr '34 self por
> Art Digest 9:29 S '35
> Mag Art 30:95-9 F '37 il self por; 33:111
>   F '40 il; 33:482-3 Ag '40 il por
> Murrell, W. Ernest Fiene 1922
> Who's Who in America
> Who's Who in American Art

FILOV, BOGDAN DIMITROV   *See* Philoff, B. D.

FINGER, CHARLES JOSEPH Dec. 25, 1869—Jan. 7, 1941 Author and editor, best known for his tales of adventurous life in wild regions and his autobiography, *Seven Horizons;* won the Newbery Medal in 1924 for his *Tales from Silver Lands* and the Longmans Green juvenile fiction prize in 1929 for his *Courageous Companions;* edited *Reedy's Mirror* for a while and was managing editor for the Bellows-Reeve Company; reviewed adventure and travel books for New York *Herald Tribune Books.*

References

> Scholastic 33:8 D 17 '38 por
> Wilson Lib Bul 4:51 O '29
> Cooper, A. P. Authors and Others
>   p61-4 1927
> Finger, C. J. Seven Horizons 1930
> Gillis, A. and Ketchum, R. Our America p185-201 1936
> Kunitz, S. J. and Haycraft, H. eds. Junior Book of Authors 1935
> Kunitz, S. J. ed. Living Authors 1937
> Who's Who Among North American Authors
> Who's Who in America

Obituaries

> N Y Times p19 Ja 8 '41 por
> Pub W 139:440 Ja 25 '41
> Wilson Lib Bul 15:454 F '41

FISH, HAMILTON Dec. 7, 1888- United States Representative from New York

Address: b. House Office Bldg, Washington, D. C.; h. 2319 Ashmead Pl, N. W., Washington, D. C.

Hamilton Fish, for a long time one of the most vocal of American isolationists, was born in Garrison, Putnam County, New York on December 7, 1888. His father was Hamilton Fish, Congressman and Speaker of the New York Assembly; his grandfather had been a Senator, Governor and Secretary of State. Like the rest of his family, he went to Harvard, and there the name Fish became temporarily synonymous with football rather than statesmanship: he captained the varsity eleven and was Walter Camp's All-American tackle. In 1910 he received his B. A., *cum laude,* and remained at Harvard for another year, studying law. It was 1912 when he made his first trip to Czarist Russia, and he was more favorably impressed than when

he re-visited the country in 1923. In 1914, following the family tradition, he was elected to the New York Assembly for two years on the Republican ticket.

Even Mr. Fish's opponents can find little fault with his record in the First World War. He led the 15th New York Volunteers of the Colored Infantry, later known as the 369th Infantry, took part in the Battle of Champagne, received the Croix de Guerre for bravery, had his horse blown up behind the lines, wrote home to his father excoriating "the maggots of pacifism," and ended up as a major of infantry of the 4th Division of the Army of Occupation. Today he is a colonel in the Officers Reserve Corps—a graduate of the Army and General Staff College of the American Expeditionary Force—and in July 1941 he reported to Fort Bragg, North Carolina, for a "refresher hitch" of four weeks.

In 1919 Hamilton Fish was elected to the 66th Congress to represent the inhabitants of Orange, Putnam and Dutchess counties in New York for a two-year term; he has been re-elected to the House of Representatives from the 26th New York District ever since. In his first five minutes in the House he displayed the patriotism that has distinguished him to date, and introduced a resolution providing for the Tomb of the Unknown Soldier. He then saw to it that nine towns near his home received captured cannons, and it was not long afterward that he helped to organize the American Legion. In 1921 he married Grace Chapin, daughter of a former Mayor of Brooklyn, New York.

During his first decade in the House, Representative Fish was distinguished for his championship of Negro rights, prison relief, an appropriation of $100,000,000 for the starving Germans, and the recommendation that Doheny, Sinclair and Fall be jailed. Perhaps unfortunately for Mr. Fish, he is even better remembered for bills to make *The Star-Spangled Banner* our national anthem; to jail all Americans who abuse the Administration's (then Coolidge's) foreign policy while abroad; to restore the Army-Navy football game by having President Hoover call a conference of the Secretaries of the Army and the Navy and the superintendents of the two academies, and force the schools to play by law.

In 1930 Mr. Fish decided to do in a small way what Mr. Dies some years later decided to do in a large way. At that time he introduced a resolution for the appointment of a special committee to investigate Communistic activity in the United States, and became its chairman. The Fish Committee was not very successful. During the Red-hunt it raided a Baltimore warehouse and discovered a few crates of lettuce, and the public was amused rather than alarmed. Its chairman filed a report in January 1931 recommending, among other things, that alien Communists be deported, that the postal law be amended so that their literature could not be mailed and that the Communist Party be outlawed, but although he continued to introduce such bills no action was taken on any of them. Although someone else might have had his spirit of rivalry aroused by such a spectacular successor as Mr. Dies, Hamilton Fish has consistently praised his work. "I love the Dies Committee for the enemies it has made," he says now.

In 1931 Mr. Fish addressed the American Legion, calling every man to his post. He announced: "It is the manifest duty of the Legion, the largest veterans' organization in the United States, to take the leadership on most of the non-political and non-partisan issues affecting the interests of the American people, and help in shaping the destinies of our country and making it a better place to live in for oncoming generations." He was also one of the most ardent defenders of the veterans' bonus.

Soon the voluble Congressman was dividing his attention between the Bolshevik danger and the foreign war threat with more emphasis on the latter. As senior Republican member of both the House Rules Committee and Foreign Affairs Committee, he was in a position to do so. In March 1938 he testified before the Naval Affairs Committee, asking for naval parity with Japan, but voted against the bill for naval expansion. In October 1938, speaking at a German Day rally in Madison Square Garden from a swastika-decorated platform, he decided that it was unfortunate that the policies of our Administration had "embittered our relations with Japan, Italy and Germany." In the spring of 1939 he proposed a National Committee to Keep America Out of Foreign Wars; it was formed, and in May the Committee offered prizes on "Why America Should Keep Out of Foreign Wars." As for the foreign War itself, he did all that one man could do to stop it: traveling in Europe in the summer of 1939, he talked with Von Ribbentrop (see sketch this issue), decided that Germany's claims on Danzig were "just," and in August arrived in Von Ribbentrop's airplane at the Interparliamentary Union in Oslo, Norway and offered to arbitrate the Danzig dispute if someone would extend an invitation. He also proposed a 30-day moratorium during which Great Britain, France, Germany and Italy would talk things over; if failure resulted, the case was to be referred to the Kings of Norway and Belgium and the President of Switzerland. The Union didn't pay much attention to his suggestions; Mr. Fish sadly announced: "I wash my hands of the whole thing," and came home.

He remained active in the United States, however. In October 1939 Virginia's Clifton Woodrum announced that thirty-seven Republicans and one Democrat, led by Fish, had organized a "propaganda racket that makes the utility outfit and that of Dr. Townsend look like pikers." His Committee to Keep America Out of Foreign Wars, with headquarters in Fish's Washington office, was allegedly using government facilities and employees and appealing for campaign funds on official stationery. "There is no member of this body or any other body who has so unfailingly, so persistently, so regularly, so systematically and

HAMILTON FISH

so ineffectively opposed the present Administration," it was charged.

In November 1939 Representative Fish voted against repeal of the arms embargo, and in the summer of 1940 against conscription. Mr. Willkie's views being different, some Republicans began to worry, and in October 1940 a move began to defeat Hamilton Fish for re-election to the House—prompted by the fact that a Republican victory would automatically give him the leadership of either the Rules or Foreign Affairs Committee. The move was not successful, but Republican hopes and fears both proved unjustified.

Until Japan's attack on Hawaii he opposed the Lend-Lease Bill, the extension of selective service and major revision of the Neutrality Act, delivering fiery isolationist speeches before America First meetings and in the House. (He voted for the arming of American merchant ships, however.) He has also been accused of having permitted anti-Semitic, anti-British material to be mailed under his Congressional frank, a charge which he called a "frame-up, a smear." His franked envelopes disappeared from an office just before Federal investigators swooped down upon it; one of his secretaries was indicted for "corrupt perjury" by a federal grand jury investigating Nazi propaganda; and finally, in November 1941, the grand jury served a subpoena upon Fish himself, after he had failed to respond to an invitation to appear voluntarily. The House called this an infringement upon his immunities, but "authorized" him to testify.

The outbreak of Japanese-American hostilities changed all this. Fish announced that the American people "should present a united front in support of the President of the United States," and suggested that he would like to lead Negro troops, as he had in the First World War.

(Continued next page)

FISH, HAMILTON—*Continued*

"Loud, big-boned," rather handsome, six-feet-three when he takes off his size-twelve shoes, Representative Fish is noted for his "windmilling arms, roof-raising voice and not-quite-legal logic." He has made a habit of speaking of himself in the third person to interviewers, thus displaying an objectivity rare in the world of politics. One story gives him credit for making a two-minute call on President Hoover and then gravely offering the waiting reporters a 1,500-word release containing his remarks!

References

Am Mercury 52:440-7 Ap '41
Lit Digest 120:35 N 16 '35 por
Liv Age 340:31-3 Mr '31
Nation 151:476 N 16 '40
New Repub 65:158-62 D 24 '30; 94:99 Mr 2 '38
Outlook 155:490 Jl 30 '30 por
Time 34:21-2 Ag 28 '39 por
Who's Who in America
Who's Who in the Nation's Capital
Wilson, E. American Jitters p10-27 1932

FISH, MARIE POLAND May 22, 1902-
Ichthyologist

Address: b. Narragansett Marine Laboratory, Kingston, R. I.

Van Dale

MARIE POLAND FISH

Mrs. Fish, like her husband, must get very tired of having jokes made about her name and her profession. But the fact remains that she and he *are* both ichthyologists (students of fish). Indeed, Mrs. Fish is the first person to discover the eggs of the eel. The breeding habits of eels were for more than two thousand years one of the greatest mysteries of science, since these elongated fish lay their eggs and have their young far out in the ocean.

Marie Poland's career began almost by accident. She was born in Paterson, New Jersey, and went to Smith College with every intention of becoming a physician. At college she took a pre-medical course, earning membership in Phi Beta Kappa, and for a year after acquiring her B. A. in 1921 was a research assistant in cancer problems in the Department of Medical Research of the Carnegie Institution. She had entered the College of Physicians and Surgeons when, in February 1923, she abandoned the idea of securing an M. D. degree to marry Dr. Charles John Fish, one of the earliest American oceanographers. Her scientific bent still remained, however, and soon she was looking around for some way to satisfy it.

She found it when she discovered that the United States Bureau of Fisheries, with which her husband was associated, had very little information on the life histories of Atlantic fish, and urgently needed some. Embryology had always interested her, and the embryology of fish or human beings is fundamentally the same—in fact, every human embryo at some time recapitulates the fish stage of its ancestry.

Like many scientists, the Fishes have a summer home and laboratory at the Woods Hole Marine Biological Station in Massachusetts. There Mrs. Fish began studying the development of local marine species and passing on her findings to the Bureau. The work thus done on a voluntary basis was soon recognized as valuable, and led to her becoming a field assistant in the Bureau of Fisheries a few months later. She remained with the Bureau until 1927. In the meanwhile, in 1925, she was elected to the New York Zoological Society as an assistant in the Department of Tropical Research, an honorary position which she kept until 1932.

She accompanied Dr. Fish on numerous oceanographic expeditions, and was often called upon to take complete charge of them. Her husband enjoys telling of an episode during one of the Massachusetts surveys, when he was called to Labrador and turned over command of the survey to her. The research vessel, being under control of the Bureau of Fisheries, was manned by a regular Navy crew. When Dr. Fish returned he went to sea on this vessel, and found that his wife had trained her crew so thoroughly that when she barked out commands in the style of an admiral the hard-boiled sailors snapped to attention and ran to obey her without a smile. Neither she nor they saw any incongruity in their being commanded by a girl in her early 20's, just a trifle over five feet tall!

It was in 1923, with William Beebe (see sketch this issue) and her husband on the "Arcturus" Oceanographic Expedition to the Sargasso Sea, the Galapagos and Cocos Islands, that Mrs. Fish, in charge of all young specimens, put into a finger bowl on her desk four little eggs which had come up in a net from five hundred fathoms below the surface. A week later one of these hatched into a young American eel. These four eggs are still the only eggs of the American eel known to science.

From 1928 to 1931 Mrs. Fish was curator of ichthyology at the Buffalo Museum of Science, of which her husband had become director in 1927. She was a member of the Bermuda Oceanographical Expedition in 1929, of the Cooperative Survey of Lake Erie from 1928 to 1930, of the survey of the Gulf of Maine from 1929 to 1930, and of the International Expedition to the Bahamas in 1930. With her husband she made several oceanographic trips into northern waters as well as into the South Atlantic, studying ocean life in a diving helmet, taking underwater pictures and preparing museum exhibits. In 1931 Dr. Fish requested a leave of absence from the Buffalo Museum to accept the post of executive secretary and director of the International Passamaquoddy Bay investigation, and in 1934 he and his wife accepted the invitation of Rhode Island to come to Kingston to develop a laboratory that would do for fishing, the second most important industry in the state, what agricultural experiment stations do for farming.

It was 1937 when Dr. Fish built and became director of the first Narragansett Marine Laboratory, and Mrs. Fish was a research associate from its beginning. In the fall of 1938 the great New England hurricane caused a tidal wave which swept away the entire laboratory—buildings, equipment, records and the newly built research vessel *Judeth*. But by 1940 a new and much finer laboratory took its place. In it Mrs. Fish has conducted research in the embryology and early life history of fresh-water fish, with a special interest in the embryology and development of the American eel. In 1941 she holds the title of Ichthyologist for the State of Rhode Island.

Mrs. Fish leads one of the busiest lives on record. She is a tiny woman, only five feet one inch, weighs one hundred eighteen pounds and has dark hair and blue eyes. But she has plenty of energy in spite of her frail appearance. Beside her regular laboratory research, she lectures frequently; writes popular science articles often for the magazines and technical papers for the United States Bureau of Fisheries, the New York State Conservation Department, and other scientific bodies; and for three years ran a regular column called "Science for Everybody," which appeared in the Providence *Evening Bulletin*.

She takes time also to be a devoted mother to her daughter, Marilyn Poland Fish, who was born in 1931. Marilyn, who is always called the "Minnow" by her parents' scientific associates, never had a real home until they settled in Kingston, Rhode Island when she was six.

In Kingston the Fishes have bought a large old colonial house and stocked it with seventeenth and eighteenth century furniture, the collection of which is one of their hobbies. There are many family heirlooms in the house

as well, for both the Fish and the Poland ancestors came to America before 1630. Here, in her scant leisure hours, Mrs. Fish leads the life of any other young American matron. She swims and sails, she plays bridge and she enjoys amateur dramatics with the Kingston Players, whose president she was in 1936 and 1937. In Buffalo she belonged to the Junior League, in Kingston she belongs to the Junior League of Providence, Dunes Club, Triangle Club and the Smith College Club of Rhode Island. She is a Presbyterian and a Republican. No one would think on casually meeting her that she is one of the foremost scientists of America, or that her life has been and still is full of hard intellectual work spiced with scientific adventure.

She has received many honors. She is a member of the Society of Ichthyologists and Herpetologists, of the Society of Women Geographers and of the Buffalo Society of Natural Science. In November 1940 she was selected as one of the "hundred outstanding career women of the world" to be honored by the Women's Centennial Congress, in New York.

Naturally, Mrs. Fish has had little leisure for writing of greater length than would be required for a magazine or newspaper article, though she would like some day to write a book. She has material enough to prepare more than one, and if she gets around to it they should be as popular as those by her friend and ex-associate, William Beebe. So far, her only publication in book form has been a technical monograph called *Contributions to the Early Life-History of Fishes From Lake Erie and Its Tributary Waters*.

Looking back on the achievements of the past 20 years, Mrs. Fish might be forgiven if she felt some complacent self-congratulation. Quite to the contrary, however, she is modesty itself, and has "a complete horror" of self-praise or first-person biography. She is as vitally interested in her husband's work as she is in her own (his special fields are the distribution of plankton organisms—the minute animal life of the ocean surface, physical oceanography and the ecology of ocean fish), and she feels that with all that she has accomplished she has still only touched the surface of her subject and has much work still to do.

References

American Men of Science
American Women

FISHBACK, MARGARET Mar. 10, 1904- Author

Address: b. R. H. Macy & Co, Inc, New York City; h. 5 Riverside Drive, New York City

Poetess-laureate of Manhattan—champion, in verse, of the 9 to 5 white-collar Kitty Foyles, foe of suburban life and matrimony (until she married the swellest man in the world, with whom she now spends her summers on a Maine farm)—Margaret Fishback has combined a successful light-verse career with an equally successful one as advertising copy-

MARGARET FISHBACK

writer for R. H. Macy & Company, New York. *Time for a Quick One* (December 1940) is Miss Fishback's fifth volume of light verse. Like her representative best in a previously published omnibus collection, *One to a Customer* (1937), these lyrics chant, from the feminine viewpoint, the praises of New York life.

As a reviewer says of them: "If a selection of Margaret Fishback's verse could have appeared on the marble and ormolu table of a Victorian parlor, the young lady in mutton-leg sleeves and whalebone stays would have decided from the titles that the poems were written either in code or some jargon faintly resembling English. . . But if she studied the poems beneath the cryptic labels, she would have discovered that they dealt with fashions, husbands, food, gardens and the weather. Those were a woman's inexhaustible topics of discussion in her day. They still are. Margaret Fishback has changed the lyrics without changing the tune; she is Victorian without the petticoats, with lipstick instead of rice powder. That's why she clicks."

The girl whose wit has clicked as readily in advertising copy as in the more sophisticated pages of such periodicals as the *New Yorker*, *Harper's Bazaar* and *Mademoiselle* came to New York City in the '20s, determined on a career and fame. She was born in Washington, D. C., March 10, 1904, daughter of Frederick Lewis and Mabel (Coleman) Fishback. Soon after she received her B. A. degree at Goucher College, Baltimore (she was a member of Gamma Phi Beta and won Phi Beta Kappa honors), Miss Fishback—a pretty blonde girl with poise, wit and real determination—came to Manhattan. At that time, it seems, she had ideas of becoming a dean of women, so she took genteel rooms in a club run by the Ladies' Christian Temperance Union and spent a year on further college

courses to fit her for such a position. Just for a little contrast, she also took an evening course in ballet dancing. She and other ballet students were glad to "crawl into red tights and yellow wigs" to earn $1 a performance as walk-ons in Metropolitan operas.

Finding the atmosphere of the Temperance Union boarding house a bit stifling, Margaret Fishback and two girl friends rented a basement apartment of their own and began to live what they considered the proper Bohemian life. "This consisted mainly in having At Home evenings every Tuesday and serving the swarms of guests with strawberry ice-cream dunked in ginger ale." In 1927 Miss Fishback landed a job as an assistant copywriter at Macy's. In just two weeks' time she got a break: a sudden vacancy gave her an immediate rise in the Macy world; and the fact that her institutional copy was no less than brilliant kept her there.

Her first verse was a couplet scribbled on the back of an old envelope during a dull train ride—and it brought $3 from a magazine. Knowing what attracts customers, Miss Fishback was shrewd enough to stick to the kind of light verse women readers enjoy. In couplet, quatrain and triolet she voiced the perennial problems of the New York working girl, the one-room-and-kitchenette denizen who, Lux box in hand, muses:

> *"I wonder where, I wonder where*
> *I can hang up my underwear.*

Miss Fishback knew well the trials of the bachelor girl in pursuit of a worthy career. Macy's kept her busy and self-sufficient:

> *To be a mother and a wife*
> *I'm often urged by all my kith*
> *And kin—but as for husbands, life*
> *Is easier without than with.*

Then, one day, she chanced to go down to Macy's seventh floor, where she fell in love: first, with a handsome Algerian rug; second, with Mr. Alberto Antolini, the rug buyer himself, who assured her that he would be only too delighted to come and supervise the rug's installation in her living room. As an astonished sales clerk said later, this was "the first time a rug buyer was given away free with the purchase of a Macy rug." On June 14, 1935, she and Alberto Antolini were married, and the Algerian magic carpet went to grace the home of the newlyweds. The Fishback reading public was soon amazed to find the cynical, independent career-girl penning such lines as:

> *His wash-cloth is a humid wad,*
> *His Turkish towels hang out of line,*
> *But do they make me squawk, 'Oh God'?*
> *No, ma'am. They just proclaim he's mine.*

And the scorner of the little home in the country soon became the proud joint possessor of an 86-acre farm on the St. George River near Portland on the coast of Maine. There, during blissful summer vacations, the confirmed Manhattanite muse may be found digging in her garden, shingling the barn roof, or reading up on farm plumbing.

Husband Alberto is said to be wholeheartedly proud of his wife's fame, and to get as great a kick out of her fan mail as she does. This mail "ranges from frenzied blank verse sent by would-be poets to an interesting proposition from a combination chiropodist and Justice of the Peace, who offered to barter his services for autographed copies of her books. Her public also includes the versatile-minded youth who requested poems about 'Women's Short Skirts or Women's Brief Bathing Suits, and have you written any poems about Cows?'"

Besides her five books of light verse, Miss Fishback has produced a volume of Etiquette, called *Safe Conduct* (1939), illustrated by Helen Hokinson. She also wrote a rhymed primer, illustrated by Russell Patterson, which was given free to children who visited Macy's 1940 Santa Claus. In addition to her work for Macy's she has done freelance advertising for a number of non-competitive accounts, including steamship lines and automobiles. But, counting fame and fortune and all, Margaret Fishback still thinks that her marriage is the best thing that ever happened to her. It is reported that she once went to a luncheon given for a group of big-name women. When she got home she said to her husband thoughtfully: "Alberto, if I ever act like a career woman, will you please sock me in the jaw?"

References

N Y Herald Tribune Books p10 D 22 '40
N Y Journal & American Home Mag Je 29 '40 il por
N Y Post p15 N 11 '40 por
American Women

FISHER, CLARENCE S(TANLEY) Aug. 17, 1876—July 20, 1941 Distinguished American archeologist; acting director of the American School of Oriental Research; died in Jerusalem; had directed archeological expeditions to Egypt and Palestine since 1900; was associated with the Carswell Institute of Philadelphia, Harvard University, the Boston Museum of Fine Arts, Princeton University, Haverford College, Yale University, the University of Chicago and the University of Pennsylvania; directed the excavation of the ancient city of Ur, the throne room of the palace of Meneptah and the mound of the battle of Armageddon at Megiddo in Palestine.

References

Who's Who in America 1912-13

Obituaries

N Y Times p19 Jl 22 '41 por
Sch & Soc 54:59 Jl 26 '41

FISKE, JAMES PORTER Nov. 22, 1866—Oct. 24, 1941 Orthopedic surgeon; manager of the New York State Hospital for Crippled and Deformed Children since 1908; introduced into the United States the ambulatory treatment of fractures of the leg; founded schools for crippled children: his specialty was deformities and errors of development, on which he wrote many papers and monographs.

References

American Medical Directory
Who's Who in America
Who's Who in American Medicine 1925

Obituaries

N Y Times p34 O 25 '41

FITZGERALD, CISSY 1873(?)—May 5, 1941 Stage and screen actress who claimed distinction as the first woman to appear in film dramas; won fame in the 1890's on the New York stage; appeared in many films and starred in two-reel comedies; at one time operated her own motion-picture production companies; used her married name, Mrs. Cissy Tucker, in later life.

References

Motion Pict Classic 29:46 Je '29 por
Photoplay 31:67+ Ap '27 pors
International Motion Picture Almanac 1937-38

Obituaries

N Y Herald Tribune p38 My 11 '41 pors

FITZGERALD, F(RANCIS) SCOTT (KEY) Sept. 24, 1896—Dec. 21, 1940 American novelist, short story writer and scenarist; in his writings epitomized "all the sad young men" of the post-War decade and interpreted the "lost generation" of the jazz era; critics considered *The Great Gatsby* (1925) his best novel, but *The Last Tycoon* (1941), an unfinished novel of Hollywood, published post-humously, was called by Edmund Wilson his most mature work.

F. SCOTT FITZGERALD
(Continued next page)

FITZGERALD, F. SCOTT—*Continued*

References

New Yorker 11:20-1 Ap 17 '26
Sat R Lit 16:4 Je 12 '37 por
Scholastic 27:5+ O 12 '35 por
Va Q R 13:107-21 Ja '37

Baldwin, C. C. Men Who Make Our
  Novels p166-73 1924
Boyd, E. A. Portraits p217-26 1924
Farrar, J. C. ed. Literary Spotlight
  p125-34 1924
Kunitz, S. J. ed. Living Authors 1937
Rosenfeld, P. Men Seen p215-24 1925
Who's Who in America

Obituaries

N Y Times p19 D 23 '40 por
Newsweek 16:43 D 30 '40

FITZGIBBONS, JOHN July 10, 1868—
Aug. 4, ·1941 Former Representative at Large
from New York State; three times Mayor of
Oswego; for 30 years was considered one of
labor's leading spokesmen at the State Capitol
in Albany; as legislative counsel for the
Brotherhood of Railroad Trainmen of New
York he figured in events which led to the
impeachment of Governor William Sulzer.

References

American Catholic Who's Who
Who's Who in America 1938-39
Who's Who in the Nation's Capital
  1934-35

Obituaries

N Y Times p17 Ag 6 '41

FITZPATRICK, D(ANIEL) R(OBERT)
Mar. 5, 1891- Cartoonist

Address: b. St. Louis Post-Dispatch, St.
Louis, Mo; h. 501 Clara Ave, St. Louis, Mo.

SELF PORTRAIT OF   Colten
D. R. FITZPATRICK À LA PICASSO

D. R. Fitzpatrick is a slight, sandy-haired,
red-faced Irishman who is constantly jabbing
"a satirical needle into politicians, racketeers,
war-crazy dictators or 'anybody who sticks
his neck out' in this mad world." The most
outspoken cartoonist in America and one of
the most widely reproduced, his drawings
are syndicated in 35 American newspapers
and have been greeted with vituperation, argument or praise in every country of the world
where newspapers and magazines are printed.

A cross-section of his daily stint was presented in New York City in April and May
1941 at the Associated American Artists Galleries, his first political cartoon show in New
York. It ranged from "bulge-jawed Mus-
solinis and neurasthenic Hitlers to war-racked
skeletons, the bums and shady politicians of
St. Louis' own legendary Rat Alley." There
were *The Road Ahead* with thousands of
refugees pouring past a sign pointing to
"blood, sweat and tears"; a huge iron swastika in the form of a grindstone grinding
scores of human bodies into rivers of blood
labeled *Liberty, Equality, Fraternity;* John
L. Lewis and a fat industrialist picketing the
White House simultaneously over the caption,
Fancy Meeting You Here. And as a concession to "Art" there were two oil paintings
among the cartoons, "one a Daumier-brown
picture of a group of card players; the other
a dour, Picassoesque self-portrait. Of the
latter he said sadly: 'It was done in one of
my blue periods, during a hangover.'"

There are many who believe that Fitzpatrick, winner of the John Frederick Lewis
Prize of the Philadelphia Academy of Fine
Arts in 1924 and the Pulitzer Prize in 1926,
need make no concessions to "Art." Museums, libraries and collectors (including
Franklin D. Roosevelt) all over the world
treasure their Fitzpatricks, and in Moscow
the Museum of Western Art has eight of
his works hanging among its Renoirs and
Gauguins. Even fellow cartoonists take off
their hats to him, to his slick technique of
getting his points over without capsizing his
cartoons with explanatory captions. As one
commentator puts it: "Fitzpatrick's muscular
draftsmanship and Doré-like spaciousness are,
if not art, something very close to it."

This artist who was "kicked out of high
school at 16 because he spent his time draw-
ing instead of studying algebra and history,"
always knew he wanted to be a cartoonist.
Daniel Robert Fitzpatrick was born in Superior,
Wisconsin, the son of Patrick and Delia Ann
(Clark) Fitzpatrick, and it was the Superior
High School he left for the sake of art.
For a while he studied at the Chicago Art
Institute (his only other training consisted
of a summer spent studying with Henry
Varnum Poor) and then, in 1911, he got
his first job, doing comic-page drawings for
the Chicago *Daily News.* This lasted less
than a year, for when the editorial cartoonist
became ill Fitzpatrick took his place, and
before he was 21 he was doing front-page
cartoons.

His work was good, good enough to get
him the position of editorial cartoonist on

the St. Louis *Post-Dispatch* in 1913. He set out for St. Louis with his bride, Lee Anna Dressen, and immediately drew his first cartoon there—an attack on the old wooden railroad coaches, showing a coffin on wheels on railroad tracks passing a crossing sign of skull and crossbones. Since then his career has unfolded in a tiny office in the *Post-Dispatch's* Olive Street Building, punctuated occasionally by clashes of editorial opinion between him and the paper's editor and its publisher, Joseph Pulitzer.

In more than 10,000 cartoons in his paper and in *Collier's* Magazine Fitzpatrick has "whittled down the most complicated economic, political or social issues into a few simple strokes of his black crayon." The day Prohibition began he produced his most startling sketch, the Statue of Liberty diving into the Atlantic, and for years he campaigned violently against the dry laws. During the depression his cartoons were particularly striking. Under the title of *Our Great Machine Produces—an Apple* he showed a tremendous industrial mechanism letting down a great chain with a hook, on the end of which was a little apple and a very little man looking at it. *Strange Bedfellows* showed "Wheat Surplus" and "Hunger" side by side on a park bench. Always in these cartoons there were added to his skill as an artist a "grasp of the causes of involuntary idleness and a poignant feeling for the man who asks for work and is set at the peddler's semi-begging trade."

During Fitzpatrick's years on the *Post-Dispatch* there have been crusades against Hitler, war, war-profiteering, rackets, "foul-smelling politicians," holding companies, anti-unionists. A bold liberal, he was finally jailed for contempt of court in 1940 for his attacks on lawlessness and injustice in Missouri. Libel suits against him and his paper, carried through several courts of the State, started reform movements through Missouri and particularly St. Louis to clean up the rackets he exposed. Hated and feared by many, he once complained: "The trouble with my job is I have no friends."

Nevertheless, he manages to get together a few of them now and again for a game of poker or a round of golf, or even to go off with him on a duck-hunting or fishing trip. These trips, or his excursions into oil painting, don't happen often, however. There are too many of the world's and man's failings to be exposed; too much rottenness to be raked up; too many events to be interpreted.

References

Lit Digest 117:11 Ja 13 '34 self por
Newsweek 5:37 Ap 6 '35; 17:60 Ap 28 '41 il por
Time 37:48 My 5 '41 il self por
Who's Who in America
Who's Who in American Art

FITZPATRICK, GEORGE L., MONSIGNOR 1868(?)—Apr. 26, 1941 Pastor of the Holy Cross Roman Catholic Church of Harrison, New Jersey for the last 27 years;

leader in civic betterment for the community; was opposed to the erection of motion picture theatres in the town; attacked drunkeness and the holding of the Dempsey-Fulton fight; had charge of constructing a $250,000 parochial school and day nursery; reduced the church debt.

Obituaries

N Y Times p39 Ap 27 '41 por

FLANAGAN, E(DWARD) J(OSEPH), MGR. July 13, 1886- Director of Father Flanagan's Boys Home
Address: Boys Town, Nebraska

Walter S. Craig

RT. REV. MGR. FLANAGAN

"Boys are better capable of governing themselves than of submitting to government by adults. Don't repress a boy, give him outlets for his energies. Don't preach at him, give him the example you want him to follow. Make him responsible. Remember, *there are no bad boys.*"

It is by following these principles that a tall, rangy, Irish priest has built up one of the most interesting and successful social experiment stations in America. In 1917 a parish priest in Omaha, whose interest in the welfare of the poor had already led him to organize and operate a Workingmen's Hotel, decided to do something about the underprivileged boys he saw playing in slum streets or read about when they got into trouble with the police. He had no money, but he borrowed $90 and rented a house, and into this Home for Homeless Boys he introduced five youngsters, three of them referred to him by the Juvenile Court. Three months later there were thirty.

The next year he moved 11 miles outside of Omaha, and Boys Town, as millions of people now know it, began. Today it has

FLANAGAN, E. J., MGR.—*Continued*

a capacity of 525, and a long waiting list. When a boy leaves, rehabilitated, he goes back to his home if he has a home fit to go back to; if not, to a foster home selected and supervised by the state. Once the majority of Father Flanagan's boys came to him from the Juvenile Court; now only 10 per cent are delinquents. Father Flanagan, director and secretary-treasurer of Boys Town, never despairs of a boy. He once worked for four years to make a decent human being of an eight-year-old boy with a criminal record longer than his height. It was two years before that child ever let a smile crack his grim, sullen little face. But today he is one of the most valued citizens of Boys Town, on the way to becoming a real man. Father Flanagan never scolds, never punishes; he would rather rely on a man-to-man approach, sweetened by the box of candy always in the upper right-hand drawer of his desk. "It costs $5,000 to put a boy in prison," he says, "and $2,000 to make him a good citizen. Which is the better investment?"

Boys Town is a real town, incorporated, with its boy Mayor and six boy councilmen regular members of the Nebraska League of Municipalities. Its Chamber of Commerce is affiliated with the Junior Chamber of Commerce of Omaha, its football team is a member of the Nebraska High School Athletic Association. Its police chief, its fire chief, its parks and grounds commissioner, and its two commissioners of sanitation are all boys. Elections are held twice a year, and are hotly contested. A boy who shirks his duties loses his vote—and mighty few will take a chance on that. The boys make up their own punishments for "delinquents" and enforce them, with trimmings. A boy may be condemned to stay out of the swimming pool for a certain period— but he has to put on his swimming trunks, take a shower, and then watch the other boys enjoy themselves in the pool. "Capital punishment," the worst of all, obliges a boy to go to the movies with the others—and stand with his back to the screen! Tender-hearted Father Flanagan protested against this as too severe, but the boys shouted him down.

By now Father Flanagan has welcomed more than 4,000 citizens to Boys Town, and has still to see a single one go wrong after leaving it. There are no distinctions of race, nationality or creed; Protestant or Jewish boys are just as welcome as Catholic boys. All that is demanded is that a boy need the opportunity, and that there be room for him. These boys were all once homeless, neglected, abandoned—many of them from broken homes or homes which were a travesty on the name.

There is a *Life at Boys Town* series broadcast over station WLW, and in 1937 Metro-Goldwyn-Mayer made a picture about Boys Town which was a smash hit, with Spencer Tracy and Mickey Rooney in the principal roles. In 1941 appeared its sequel, *Men of Boys Town*. The first picture was filmed in Boys Town itself, the second in a reproduction of it in Hollywood. So popular have these pictures been that probably thousands of persons, when they hear the name "Father Flanagan," think of Spencer Tracy. Actually, however, Father Edward J. Flanagan has no physical resemblance to Tracy. He is six feet one inch tall, and though he weighs 187 pounds there is no fat on his bones and he appears thin. His dark hair is very thin on top, and his spectacles conceal heavy eyebrows. He looks like a kindly schoolteacher—which in essence is what he really is.

Edward Joseph Flanagan was born in Roscommon, Ireland, the son of John and Honora (Larkin) Flanagan, and since he did not come to the United States until he was 18, his speech still retains a perceptible brogue. He was naturalized as an American citizen in 1919. He had an extensive education for the priesthood: received his B. A. from Mt. St. Mary's College, Emmitsburg, Maryland, in 1906, his M. A. in 1908; studied at St. Joseph's Seminary, Dunwoodie, New York, in 1906 and 1907; then spent a year at the Gregorian University in Rome and three years more at the Jesuit University at Innsbruck, Austria. He has an honorary LL. D. from Mt. St. Mary's, bestowed in 1938, and others from St. Benedict's College, Atchison, Kansas, and Creighton University, Omaha, Nebraska.

He was ordained a priest at Innsbruck in 1912. Returning to America, he was for a year assistant pastor of St. Patrick's Parish, O'Neill, Nebraska. He then spent three years as assistant pastor of St. Patrick's Parish in Omaha. In 1914 he started his Workingmen's Hotel, while still continuing his parochial duties. Since 1918 all his time has been given to Boys Town. He has written many articles and pamphlets on juvenile delinquency, and acted as "technical adviser" when the first film about Boys Town was made. Officially, in the Church, he is the Right Reverend Monsignor Flanagan, but to the boys he is not "Monsignor" but "Father."

In 1941 he went to California to talk to the boys at the Whittier Reform School. Whittier had been badly managed in the past, having had its share of scandals, but Father Flanagan by no means despairs of it. He believes that no matter how tough the problem—or the boys—the methods he uses in Boys Town will eventually rehabilitate any boy, whatever his resistance or his record. Often when he reads of a boy who is to be sentenced to a reform school or even a penitentiary he pleads with the authorities to send the boy to him instead. Whenever that has been done, he has been able to save the boy from a life of crime.

Boys are Father Flanagan's hobby and recreation as well as his business. Everything he does in the way of work or play, aside from his office as a Roman Catholic priest, is somehow connected with them. But, as his establishment of the Workingmen's Hotel shows, general social welfare is also dear to his heart. He was for 10 years president of the Omaha Welfare Board, and is a member of the children's committee of the National

Conference of Catholic Charities. He is by nature a sociable man, active in the Knights of Columbus and a member of the Omaha Athletic Club.

The value and uniqueness of Father Flanagan's work were recognized long ago by the general public as well as by his co-religionists. In the former category, in 1930 Post No. 1 of the American Legion in Omaha announced him as Omaha's First Citizen. And in the latter category, it was a recognition of what he has done for boys that led in 1937 to his being named by Pope Pius XI as a domestic prelate, with the title of Right Reverend Monsignor.

References

Bet Homes & Gard 18:42-3+ Mr '40 il pors

Who's Who in America

FLANDIN, PIERRE-ÉTIENNE (fläN-däN) Apr. 12, 1889- Former Foreign Minister of Vichy Government

Address: b. Vichy, France; h. 139 Boulevard Malesherbes, Paris, 17e, France

On December 14, 1940 Pierre Laval was suddenly removed from the posts of Vice-Premier and Foreign Minister which he had held in the Vichy Government; Pierre-Étienne Flandin, it was announced, would take over the office of Foreign Minister under Premier Pétain. The exact significance of this upset for the future foreign relations of France was, for the moment, anybody's guess. To De Gaulle, it was a "palace revolution," a bluff, symptomatic only of growing discontent among the French people; some rejoiced that henceforth France's foreign policy would be steered by a man who had once been known as pro-British (at any rate M. Flandin is on the tweedy side, likes to hunt, fish and shoot, and his "connections with Big Business, banks and the Stock Exchange in London have been close and cordial"); others remembered his telegram of congratulations to Hitler after Munich, and wondered if he might not be even more acceptable to the Nazis than Mussolini-admirer Laval. Speculation was soon ended; in February 1941 Flandin was dropped from the Cabinet and his portfolio given to Admiral Darlan (see sketch this issue).

Called the "Giant of Avallon," the "skyscraper of the French Parliament," the "unfinished one," M. Flandin's height has been estimated at everything between six-feet-four and six-feet-seven, his political inclinations as everything from Right Center to Fascist. He is Parisian-born but blond, a Norman descended from the Norwegian Vikings. His father was a French resident-general of Tunisia in northern Africa who left a fortune to his children. Pierre learned English at an early age, received what the French call a "British education," then attended Paris University, where he received his diploma from the school of political sciences in 1909. He took his law degree in 1913, the year after his marriage

PIERRE-ÉTIENNE FLANDIN

to Mlle. Léon-Barbier (he and his wife are known as "one of the tallest couples in Europe"). They have four children.

Immediately after beginning his career as a corporation lawyer M. Flandin entered the French Chamber of Deputies from the rural district of the Yonne. He was the "baby deputy," only 25; a member of the Left Republicans (who are more often Right than not); and the First World War soon brought him opportunities for advancement. One of the first French military aviators, by 1917 he had become director of the Inter-Allied Aeronautical Service; he was a delegate to the Versailles Peace Conference in 1919; and in both the Millerand and Leygues Cabinets he was included as Under Secretary of State for Air.

The French Left has always accused Flandin of being "little more than a shrewd businessman who has always confused the interests of the State with those of the firms which he represents more or less openly," has named among those firms Schneider-Creusot, the Crédit Lyonnais, the Banque de l'Union Parisienne, the Comité des Forges, De Wendel. If all the charges of his enemies are true, he started early; for they have claimed that from January 1920 to January 1921, while in charge of liquidating war materials, he sold them at low prices to a consortium of contractors who then resold them to the French War Ministries at a profit of a billion francs—and thus acquired some grateful clients who could count on continued benefits from his political influence.

In 1924 he was Minister of Commerce in the Marsal Cabinet; in 1928 he was Vice-President of the Chamber of Deputies; from 1929 to 1930 he was Minister of Commerce in Tardieu's Cabinet; in 1931 he stepped into Laval's Cabinet as Minister of Finance. It is held against him, justly or not, that in this

FLANDIN, PIERRE-ÉTIENNE—*Cont.*

last office he publicly proclaimed his faith in the stability of the pound sterling two days before the Bank of England went off the gold standard, thus enabling some speculators to make handsome profits; and the Aéropostale financial scandal that was exposed that same year (Flandin had been on the company's payroll as legal adviser) did not add to his reputation. Nevertheless in 1932, when he served as Minister of Finance in Tardieu's Cabinet from February to May, the Chamber officially cleared him of any guilt.

For some time Tardieu and Flandin contended for the command of the Center in the Chamber. Tardieu thought of the Radical Socialists, the Socialists and the Communists as equal "enemies of France"; Flandin, on the other hand, was all for a coalition with the Radical Socialists after he became president of the Left Republicans in 1933. His moment finally came. In February 1934 Doumergue became Premier, and there followed months during which parliamentary rule in France seemed finished. Doumergue obeyed the Bank of France in every particular, while in the streets the rioting Fascist Ligues were a continual threat to Parliament if it did not fall into line. The Premier's "constitutional reform" plan would have introduced practical dictatorship, and in addition a *putsch* seemed imminent. Although Flandin previously had served only in Rightists' Cabinets and was at the time Doumergue's Minister of Public Works, he saw his chance in a quick turn to the Left and offered to join forces with Herriot's Radical Socialists in the formation of a new Ministry which would not include Doumergue. Thus in November 1934, at the age of 45, he became France's youngest Prime Minister.

The Left had not forgiven him: on his first day he was greeted in the Chamber with cries of "Aéropostale!" But on the whole France was probably much relieved. As Premier, Flandin announced that he would put constitutional controversies aside and concentrate on economic problems: the fight against poverty and unemployment, the restoration of the national economy, the maintenance of strong public finances, the rejuvenation and reform of the State. Herriot became his Minister of State, Laval was retained as Minister of Foreign Affairs. All might have gone well, but it took only six months for the Bank of France to smash Flandin. He had decided that, unlike his predecessor, he would avoid anything that might suggest "government from above." He therefore refused to ask for full powers in order to devaluate or deflate the franc and proposed instead a policy of easier money. In retaliation, the Bank refused to rediscount government short-term loans; the French began to buy gold and ship capital abroad; there was a financial "crisis"; and when, desperate, Flandin finally appealed to the Chamber for full powers in June 1934, he was overthrown.

Flandin's next office was as Minister without Portfolio in Laval's Cabinet from 1935 to January 1936, followed by a period as Minister of Foreign Affairs in Sarraut's Cabinet until June 1936. It is evident that he had not yet definitely committed himself to a policy of appeasement, for in February 1936 he asked for the ratification of the Franco-Soviet pact which had been signed by Laval, criticizing those who preferred the policy of encouraging war between Germany and the Soviet Union. And although he opposed mobilization when Hitler made his first move to reoccupy the Rhineland (he had already conferred with Baldwin and Eden on the situation), at the League of Nations meeting which followed the Nazi march in March 1936 he grew outraged and almost hysterical at the League's complacent attitude toward Hitler's breach of Locarno. His views on Laval's handling of the earlier Ethiopian crisis were more than a little ambiguous, however.

It was probably only after Flandin's visit to Germany in 1937, when he made friends with Goering and Von Ribbentrop (see sketches this issue), that he was won over wholeheartedly to the idea of a Franco-German alliance. Henri de Kérillis, editor in chief of *L'Époque*, once said of Flandin: "Every one of his individual actions has been dictated by a desire to help Germany achieve its objectives." Flandin, however, went further than even the British appeasers. According to Heinz Pol, it was he who collected funds to enable the French Fascist Doriot to buy the paper *Liberté*, and he himself made use of its columns to discourage French rearmament, to fight the Popular Front, to warn that it was the Communists who were trying to lead France into an unnecessary war, to try to break the Franco-Soviet pact, to point out the advantages of friendship with Germany and Italy. He and Laval apparently saw eye to eye. In February 1938, before Hitler absorbed Austria, Flandin sneered to the Chamber: "A policy based on the League of Nations, collective security and mutual assistance is outdated and old-fashioned." During the Czechoslovakian crisis he tried to make it apparent that France had no intention of coming to the aid of her ally; an interview in the *Revue de France* suggested that France accept or encourage the expansion of Germany toward the East; and posters signed with his name protested French mobilization if Czechoslovakia should be attacked. Flandin's telegram of congratulations to Hitler after Munich is well remembered, and also Hitler's reply: "I have constantly followed your activity in the past year with great interest and sympathy."

On March 12, 1939 Flandin was still calming fears: "Echoes reaching us from London these last days are much more optimistic concerning the international situation. It is a fact that the prophets who worked so hard and are still working to alarm public opinion in France now see their sinister predictions given the lie one by one." On March 15 Hitler entered Prague.

Naturally Flandin and his clique opposed the declaration of war in September 1939. On March 20, 1940, even before the Nazi *blitz,* he gave an off-the-record interview which may or may not completely explain his reasons for opposing it. He affirmed that years ago England and France had already lost the opportunity to establish permanent military, political and economic domination of Europe after the Treaty of Versailles, which is exactly what Hitler did do. Since that was unfortunately the case, the sensible thing to do was to acknowledge it and let Hitler control France's foreign policy and Army and Navy ("France's preeminently agricultural economy would complement Germany's industrial economy"), though insisting on an "independent spiritual, cultural and racial existence." He was already intriguing, with Laval, for an opportunity to lead France to this dependent independence. However, after the fall of France and before his succession to Laval's post, Flandin spent most of his time away from Vichy, in Paris and the provinces. It is reported that Laval barred him from entering the Cabinet on his terms: as Minister of Economics and Finance answerable only to Pétain. He himself remained Foreign Minister of the Vichy regime only until February 1941 when he resigned under apparent German pressure.

Erect, athletic, with gray-blue eyes, "a long head, partly bald, towering over extremely broad shoulders," Flandin is an impressive figure. His clothes are made by a London tailor but, unlike many Englishmen, he prefers British cooking to French. One of his hobbies is collecting tickets for speeding. (He has often expressed admiration for American institutions.) He is the author of a book, *Paix et Liberté* (1939), a collection of speeches to the members of his *Alliance Démocratique* in which he expressed more love for the former than the latter. He has also been a frequent contributor to the *Revue de Paris* and the *Revue de France.*

References

Christian Sci Mon Mag p3 Ja 11 '41 il pors
Eur Nouv 21:899-902 Ag 20 '38
Lit Digest 118:15 N 17 '34; 119:14 F 2 '35; 119:13+ Ap 13 '35
Liv Age 354:332-5 Je '38
New Statesman & Nation 9:373-4 Mr 16 '35
N Y Herald Tribune p2 D 16 '40
N Y Times p3 D 15 '40 por
Gunther, J. Inside Europe 1940
Pol, H. Suicide of a Democracy 1940
Qui Êtes-Vous?
Simone, A. J'Accuse 1940
Who's Who

FLEXNER, ABRAHAM Nov. 13, 1866- Educator

Address: b. 20 Nassau St, Princeton, N. J.; h. 150 E. 72nd St, New York City

"Oh, Abraham Flexner!" wrote the late Hans Zinsser. "We have fought with you on minor points, have alternately admired and disliked you, have applauded you for wisdom and detested you for opinionatedness. But in just retrospect, layman as you are, we hail you as the father—or, better, the uncle of modern medical education in America."

Teacher, annalist of educational problems, administrator of philanthropies, educational pioneer and author, Abraham Flexner has received innumerable such tributes. According to the New York *Times* "it is no exaggeration to say that many a patient today owes his life or his health to Abraham Flexner's fearlessness and his passion for what he calls 'excellence.'" He has been the "guiding spirit behind the philanthropies of such men as John D. Rockefeller, Andrew Carnegie, George Eastman, J. P. Morgan, Julius Rosenwald and Louis Bamberger." His

ABRAHAM FLEXNER

peculiar gift of "extraction" caused George Eastman to write: "Flexner is the worst highwayman that ever flitted in and out of Rochester. He put up a job on me and cleaned me out of a thundering lot of my hard-earned savings." And when Flexner's autobiography, *I Remember,* appeared in 1940, Charles A. Beard (see sketch this issue) wrote: "A delightful human document which, at the same time, gives an illuminating insight into the course of the highest learning in America for more than 50 years."

Abraham Flexner was born in Louisville, Kentucky on November 13, 1866, the sixth of nine children of Morris and Esther (Abraham) Flexner, both "pious Hebrews." His father had been a teacher in Bohemia before emigrating to the United States in 1853, went into the wholesale hat business and was ruined in the panic of 1873. There was never much money. But there were ways of managing. Fifteen-year-old Abraham, while attending the Louisville High School, found a

FLEXNER, ABRAHAM—*Continued*

part-time post in a private library, the Louis-ville Library, at $16 a month, which he held for two years; after that a younger brother took it over. Shortly after he was graduated from high school his oldest brother sent him to Johns Hopkins University, "the nation's first genuine university."

Flexner took his B. A. from Johns Hopkins in 1886, having finished the three-year course in two years. After college he flirted with law and political economy for a brief period, then, at the age of 19, settled down to a high school assistantship. Those being the days when such things were possible, at the end of his first term he was promoted to a "full professorship," and for four years he not only acquired teaching experience but read Greek and studied the educational classics more fully. He came to the conclusion that the ideal school was not a large one with a restricted curriculum and large classes, and by 1890 was ready to prove this thesis by starting his own school.

At first Flexner confined himself to preparing a small group of boys for passing college entrance examinations, but his methods were radical: there were no rules, no examinations, records or reports, and each student was allowed to go at his own pace. Results were so successful that both his school and his fame grew astonishingly. President Eliot of Harvard noticed that the pupils of "Mr. Flexner's School" were entering college at an earlier age, being graduated more quickly, and wrote: "What are you doing?" Flexner visited Eliot in order to answer him, and at his suggestion wrote his first article on an educational topic, *A Freshman at Nineteen,* published in 1899. Previously he had contributed only occasional letters to newspapers and to *The Nation.*

In the meanwhile, in 1898, Flexner had married Anne Laziere Crawford, who had been his first female student some six years before. In his autobiography he quotes her as asking: "What is your idea of the future? I think that we will grow old, be comfortably well-to-do, and lead dull lives." They decided to break loose from such a future. In 1905 "Mr. Flexner's School" was closed forever, and the next autumn found Flexner at Harvard. Observing teaching methods all the time, he studied psychology, philosophy, visited the leading private schools in New York, acquired his M. A., and in the summer of 1906 left for Europe. A year at the University of Berlin came next. And the following summer Flexner settled down in Heidelberg to write his first book, *The American College: a Criticism* (1908), "a workmanlike, unbiased exposure of the shortcomings of our educational institutions." He criticized particularly the elective system, the lecture system, the system of assistantships as he had observed them functioning at Harvard. After his return to America in 1908 the book was published, created no great sensation—but Dr. H. S. Pritchett, president of the Carnegie Foundation for the Advancement of Teaching, heard of Flexner and asked him to make a similar survey

of medical schools from the point of view of the intelligent layman.

In December of 1908 Flexner therefore set to work. He read all he could find on his subject; he talked to the faculty at Johns Hopkins, which he took more or less as his model; he visited all of the medical schools in the United States and Canada. Even he had not dreamed that he would find conditions so depressing. The publication of his *Medical Education in the United States and Canada* (1910), Bulletin Number Four of the Carnegie Foundation, which gave his observations and recommendations, threw a bombshell into the medical world. It also marked the beginning of reform. A study of the medical schools of Great Britain, Germany and France followed, published as *Medical Education in Europe* (1912), Bulletin Number Six of the Carnegie Foundation. And these bulletins were only the first of a long series of studies in professional education conducted by investigators under the Division of Educational Inquiry of the Carnegie Fund for the Advancement of Teaching. In 1912 Flexner visited Europe once more, investigating prostitution for the Bureau of Social Hygiene. His subsequent report was translated into many foreign languages.

After joining the General Education Board of the Rockefeller Foundation in 1913 as assistant secretary, Flexner continued his work in the Division of Medical Studies. Then, in July 1915, he was asked to frame a project of another kind—a plan for a model school. His pamphlet, *A Modern School* (1916), was the immediate result, and in 1917 came the carrying-out of his recommendations by the establishment of the Lincoln Experimental School of Teachers College, under an endowment from the General Education Board.

In 1917, too, Flexner became secretary of the General Education Board, and it was at his suggestion that John D. Rockefeller, Sr., gave $50,000,000 to be spent, principal and interest, for the reorganization of American medical education. This sum was entirely spent in the next 10 years. What is more, between 1919 and 1928 the General Education Board "directly and indirectly added half a billion dollars or more to the resources and endowments of American medical education." In 1920, for example, Flexner wangled $5,000,000 from George Eastman for the creation of the medical school of the University of Rochester. The Whitneys gave him $8,000,000 for Cornell, J. P. Morgan $2,000,000. In the process of reform the number of American medical schools decreased from 155 to a well-equipped 60 or 70.

In 1928 Flexner retired as director of the division of studies and medical education of the Board, a position which he had held since 1925. In 1927 he had been invited to Oxford to give the Rhodes Trust Memorial Lectures. It was the spring term of 1928 when he went there, and his lectures were later expanded into his much-discussed *Universities—American, English, German* (1930). In this book he criticized the universities of all three countries, especially those of America, and proposed as a partial solution the creation of a small institute for advanced study.

Nearly everything Flexner wrote turned out to be more fruitful than anyone could have dreamed. This was no exception. When his recommendations came to the attention of Louis Bamberger, who had just sold his department store in Newark to R. H. Macy & Company, he and his sister, Mrs. Felix Fuld, approached Flexner. The result of the interview was an $8,000,000-endowment for the founding of the Institute for Advanced Study at Princeton, with Flexner as director. Opened in 1930, a year after Flexner received an honorary M. D. from the University of Berlin, the plan was for the Institute to develop gradually. (The success of the Rockefeller Institute for Medical Research, which Dr. Flexner's brother Simon had directed since its inception, seemed to prove the soundness of this plan.) Staff and students were to be few, teachers were not to be involved in administrative work, and all subjects were to be "fundamental" in character. Mathematics was the first, and when Einstein joined the faculty in 1933 he exclaimed: "This is heaven!"

In October 1939, when newspapers announced Dr. Flexner's retirement as director of the Institute of Advanced Study, carrying with it a pension of full salary for the remainder of his life, the New York *Times* wrote: "A great company of those who know and respect his work will wish that the future years of the founder of the Institute for Advanced Study may be spent in illustrating to us the noble employment of leisure in a land of free human beings." Since that time Dr. Flexner has chosen to illustrate it by his continued interest in domestic and international politics (he is firmly anti-Nazi), art, literature and music, and by delivering lectures on various phases of his experience all over the country.

Dr. Flexner has always believed that the true concern of a university is study, not training, and that proper subjects of study are "the constitution of the stars, the constitution of the atom, the constitution of Oklahoma, Danzig, or Kenya." (He calls domestic science, journalism, etc., the "make-believe professions," ridicules masters' theses on dishwashing, labels correspondence schools "service stations.") To him "a genuine university is an organism characterized by definiteness of aim," and with the exception of his Institute he finds none in the United States.

Dr. and Mrs. Flexner have two daughters: Jean Atherton (Mrs. Paul Lewinson) and Eleanor. Several years ago a *New Yorker* sketch described Dr. Flexner as "a lean gentleman with no hair on his head to speak of, but with features that may vaguely be described as spiritual: a very delicate mouth; a fine, long aquiline nose that flowers into spirited nostrils; a large, placid forehead that hints at the quality of the intellect behind it; and eyes whose constant expression is a concern for the welfare of what they behold." In his 70's now, he can still say: "The deepest joy in life is to be creative."

References

Assn Am Col Bul 26:587-90 D '40
Bookm 73:225-40 My '31
Cath World 135:669-73 S '32
Commonweal 32:513-14 O 11 '40
N Y Times Book R p4 O 6 '40 por
New Yorker 6:29-32 N 22 '30
Newsweek 16:54 S 30 '40
Time 36:48+ O 7 '40 por

Flexner, A. I Remember 1940
Leaders in Education 1941
Who's Who in America
Who's Who in American Jewry

FLORINSKY, MICHAEL T. Dec. 27, 1894- Educator

Address: b. Columbia University, New York City; h. 270 W. 11th St, New York City

MICHAEL T. FLORINSKY

Lecturer in economics at Columbia University and author of several books on the economic and political scene in Europe and in the U. S. S. R., Michael T. Florinsky's most recent works include a section on Soviet Russia in *Governments of Continental Europe*, edited by James T. Shotwell (1940), first published in a separate volume as *Toward an Understanding of the U. S. S. R.* (1939). This is an evaluation of the politico-economic history of Russia with special emphasis on conditions under the Soviet regime. According to the late Ernest Sutherland Bates, writing in the New York *Herald Tribune Books:* "It soon becomes evident that Dr. Florinsky is out to damn the whole Communist system both in its theory and in its practice. . .

FLORINSKY, MICHAEL T.—*Continued*

What promised to be a very useful work thus turns out in the end to be only 'another book on Russia' in the *con*-class." The London *Times Literary Supplement* said, however: "Hostile in spirit, the book is nevertheless judicial in manner, the work of a trained historian with a firm grasp of jurisprudence and of economics who has based his study almost exclusively upon official Soviet sources." And there were other reviews that stressed his impartiality and objectivity.

Nevertheless Dr. Florinsky does not deny his critical attitude toward Russia, an attitude which the German attack on the Soviet Union did not diminish. On June 26, 1941 he told the University of Virginia's Institute of Public Affairs that "the predatory policies of both Germany and the Soviet Union would seem to reap their deserved reward in this titanic struggle for mutual destruction between the totalitarian states."

Michael T. Florinsky (Mikhail Timofeevich Florinskiï) writes us: "I was born on December 27, 1894, in Kiev, Russia. My father, Timothy D. Florinsky was professor of Slavonic history and language at the University of Kiev. He was an eminent authority on Slavonic language, ethnography, history and literature. My mother was Vera Kremkov, daughter of General Ivan Kremkov, chairman of the board of the Government-owned armament works in St. Petersburg.

"I entered the Law School of the University of Kiev [1913] and at the outbreak of war volunteered for service. I went to the Michael Military Academy at St. Petersburg whence, in June 1915, I received a commission of second lieutenant in the Imperial Field Artillery. I served through the War in the Russian Army, being wounded in action in 1916, and was decorated four times. After the Revolution [he returned to the Law School of the University of Kiev in 1918] I left Russia and lived in France and Italy, going finally to England. From 1920 to 1921 I studied at the London School of Economics and from 1922 to 1923 did work at King's College in London. In 1927 I received my M. A. degree from Columbia University, from which institution I received my Ph. D. degree in 1931.

"In England in 1920 I became associated with one of the most distinguished historians and jurists, Sir Paul Vinogradov, F. B. A., corpus professor of jurisprudence in the University of Oxford. In that year Professor James T. Shotwell, of Columbia University, was organizing the *Economic and Social History of the World War*, published by the Carnegie Endowment for International Peace. Sir Paul was chosen as the editor of the Russian series of this work, and I became his assistant. Upon Sir Paul's death in December 1925 I came to the United States and edited 12 volumes of the Russian series for the Carnegie Foundation, which were published between 1928 and 1932. Since 1931 I have been at Columbia University in the Department of Economics, in the faculty of political science (graduate school), from 1931 through 1936 as an asso-

ciate in economics and since 1937 as a lecturer in economics."

Besides the works already mentioned, Dr. Florinsky is the author of several other political studies. *The End of the Russian Empire* (1931), which treated conditions in Russia during the First World War, was called by the *American Historical Review* "the best and most scholarly work on the causes of the Russian Revolution that has thus far appeared in any language." *World Revolution and the U. S. S. R.* (1933), given favorable reviews for the most part, piqued the *New Republic's* critic into commenting: "Dr. Florinsky is interested in the reappearance of Russia as a Great Power, not in socialism. He belongs to a Russian generation condemned to guess at Russian significances from documents read in exile, offering to foreign interests such gleanings as will be acceptable. Sometimes a certain wistfulness escapes him at Russian phenomena viewed across a gulf." But Louis Fischer reported that "the changing Bolshevik ideas are presented in orderly, academic, faithful fashion," and the *American Economic Review* recommended it to "all students of the Russian scene." It was translated into Chinese and published in Shanghai in 1935.

Next a summer's visit to the Saar region in 1934 and a great deal of research resulted in Dr. Florinsky's *The Saar Struggle* (1934), a history of that region since 1920, published shortly before the plebiscite in January 1935. It was also generally well received, as was *Fascism and National Socialism* (1936), the result of Dr. Florinsky's visit to Italy and Germany late in 1935. Many of the statements in the latter book were based upon what Italian and German officials had told him about their regimes. "It has been said that the democratic form of government is the best but also the most difficult," Dr. Florinsky says somewhere in this book. "After surveying the ways of the totalitarian states, one feels more convinced than ever that the effort to overcome the difficulties is distinctly worth continuing."

Dr. Florinsky has also contributed a chapter to *Contemporary Europe* (1941), and for the Carnegie Endowment for International Peace has edited and written prefaces for two volumes of *Commercial and Tariff History of the Principal European Countries* published in 1941: Frederic Benham, *Great Britain Under Protection*, and F. A. Haight, *A History of French Commercial Policies*. Volumes on Germany and Italy in the same series are being prepared, but may be delayed by the War.

"I consider myself a man of liberal views," writes Dr. Florinsky. "In commenting on *Fascism and National Socialism* the *Survey Graphic* said: 'Mr. Florinsky is objective and fair, disapproving as a liberal of many Fascist phases, yet ever showing tolerance and understanding that denote true liberalism.' Writing as I do on controversial subjects, I have been called at times, according to the reviewer's own opinions, either a horrid reactionary or a flaming Communist. As to more personal matters, I frequently go to Europe and have a strong affection for English clothes and usually wear a carnation. I am unmarried, I enjoy music, but do not play any instrument. Am also very fond of outdoor life and never go to the movies or listen to the radio."

Michael Florinsky is a member of the American Economic Association, of the Institute of Pacific Relations, of the Academy of Political Science, and of the Council on Foreign Relations. His church is the Russian Greek Orthodox Church; his clubs are the Columbia (New York) and the Author's (London).

References

Who's Who in America
Who's Who in American Education

FOLEY, MARTHA (fō'lĕ) Editor; writer
BURNETT, WHIT Aug. 14, 1899- Editor; writer

Address: b. 432 Fourth Ave, New York City; h. 136 Old Post Rd, Croton-on-Hudson, N. Y.

For 26 years, while he was editing the yearly American and British anthologies of *Best Short Stories,* Edward J. O'Brien used to read eight American and eight British magazines through every day just as part of his routine. For 10 years, as co-editor of *Story* Magazine with her husband, Whit Burnett, Martha Foley has been helping to tackle from 100 to 150 short-story manuscripts a day. When O'Brien died in England on March 1, 1941 it was Miss Foley who was asked to take over his job, and she accepted because O'Brien was one of the people "I loved best in the world." Her resignation from the editorial staff of *Story* in order to edit *The O'Brien Memorial Best Short Story Yearly Anthology,* which appeared in June 1941 with an introduction by her, she said, made her husband as hurt as if she had just divorced him.

The attitude is understandable. The history of Martha Foley and Whit Burnett is that of *Story*—at least after their marriage on June 6, 1930. Martha Foley was born in Boston, Massachusetts, the daughter of Walter and Margaret Millicent (McCarthy) Foley; Whit Burnett was born in Salt Lake City, Utah on August 14, 1899, the son of Benjamin James and Anna Marian (Christensen) Burnett. She attended the Girls' Latin School in Boston from 1909 to 1915 and then, for two years, Boston University; at about the time she was leaving college Burnett was starting at the University of Southern California (he also attended the University of Utah and the University of California) and getting himself the first of a series of jobs on California newspapers. It was 1922 before Martha Foley found herself in San Francisco as a member of the editorial staff of the *Journal;* by that time Burnett was editor of the Associated Press there. Whether they met then or not, from that time on their lives coincided rather nicely.

In 1925, after two years as feature editor of the Los Angeles *Illustrated Daily News,* Martha Foley went to New York to become a

MARTHA FOLEY and WHIT BURNETT

caption writer first for the New York *Daily News* and then for the *Mirror.* By 1926 Whit Burnett was in New York, too, where he finally found a job as an assistant city editor. The year 1927 found both of them working for the Paris edition of the New York *Herald*—she as a reporter, he as city editor. And after he organized the Balkan news service for the New York *Sun* Foreign Service and the Consolidated Press in Vienna in 1929, she became Central European correspondent for it. In the meantime, in 1930, they had been married.

Burnett describes his travels: "From Paris to Moscow, from London to Ankara, from Vienna and Prague to Majorca and Cadiz." In the spring of 1931 he was in Vienna with his wife; it was there that their son David was born, and it was there that Whit Burnett and Martha Foley decided to do something for literature. *Story* began merely as a mimeographed job which the Burnetts planned to send around to publishers who might be interested in its contents. Mimeographing didn't prove to be practical, though: after endless labor the editors emerged with 67 or 68 copies which had cost them nearly $1 apiece! (The fact that the Duke of Kent, some years later, paid $400 for one of those first copies didn't help matters at all.) After that *Story* was printed in Vienna—as a magazine, since publishers hadn't understood its original purpose—and finally in the Balearic Islands. The Burnetts had started for Romania to interview King Carol and had somehow landed in Majorca; there they stayed, with their four months' old infant and their Project.

Story was already famous. One year O'Brien had gone to Vienna to ask for permission to reprint four *Story* pieces in his anthology, and another year there were eight of them represented. As Martha Foley says: "We believed in the same things: freshness, characterization, feeling. We hated the too slick, the mechanical,

FOLEY, MARTHA and **BURNETT, WHIT**—*Continued*

the trick ending—the pseudo O. Henry school of writing." And although it was daring for the Burnetts to return to New York in 1933, completely without funds, even in the heart of the depression they found people who were interested enough in their magazine to back them financially. Their first real offices were at 57th Street and Madison Avenue, and they were thrilled. But the first day their magazine appeared on newsstands in the United States was the day Roosevelt selected to shut down the banks.

Since that time writers like William Saroyan, Jesse Stuart, Tess Slesinger and Richard Wright have first been published in *Story's* pages. Perhaps the Burnetts' most famous discovery is William Saroyan; after the publication of *The Daring Young Man on the Flying Trapeze* the editors received one short story a day for 30 days from him. Some of their best stories, according to Martha Foley, have been written by men in prison. And even some of their rejection slips have had interesting results. Once they received a large package from the author of a story they had rejected. Inside was a stout rope with a noose and a request that they use it to hang themselves at once.

Besides reading a terrifyingly large number of manuscripts every day, the Burnetts edited *A Story Anthology, 1931-1933* (1933); *Story in America, 1931-1934* (1934), the second anthology; and *The Flying Yorkshireman* (1938), a book of novellas. Martha Foley continued to publish short stories of her own in magazines and lectured on the short story at summer sessions of the University of Colorado in 1935 and 1936, at Columbia University in 1936 and at New York University in 1937. Whit Burnett has for several years been an instructor in the advanced short story at Columbia University, and is also the author of two books, *The Maker of Signs* (1934), a collection of short stories, and *The Literary Life and the Hell With It* (1939), informal autobiographical essays. After they moved to Croton-on-Hudson, New York, Martha Foley appeared only four days a week in *Story's* office, on those days commuting by train: her husband would neither let her drive "his precious car" nor tolerate her back-seat driving.

Martha Foley is described as "a little woman who wears tailored suits and horn-rimmed spectacles and looks like a pleasant young housewife." Whit Burnett is noted for his small, neatly trimmed, pinkish beard. He is a "passionate fisherman and a great teller of funny stories, which he delivers in a dry, dead-pan manner."

As for Martha Foley's present job, she said when she took it over: "If I do one-tenth as well as he [O'Brien] did I'll be perfectly satisfied." She is far from being hopeless about the future of the short story in the next few years "War always seems to be a spur to great writing, with its emotional ordeal and its jolt to any sensitive persons," she says.

"This war hasn't had quite enough time to sink in yet, but when it does we should see something."

References

N Y Post p3 Mr 11 '41 por
N Y World-Telegram p9 Mr 11 '41 por
Newsweek 13:31-2 Ja 23 '39 por; 17:50 Mr 24 '41 por
Sat R Lit 19:11 Ja 28 '39 por; 23:11 F 8 '41 por
Scholastic 27:5 Ja 25 '36 por; 32:4 My 7 '38 por; 33:10 O 22 '38; 36:18 My 6 '40 por; 38:28 Mr 24 '41
American Women
America's Young Men
Burnett, W. The Literary Life and the Hell With It 1939
Who's Who in America

FOLGER,   A(LONZO)   D(ILLARD) (fōl'jẽr) July 9, 1888—Apr. 30, 1941 Democratic Representative of North Carolina who was elected in 1938 and re-elected in 1940; died of injuries suffered in an automobile accident at Mount Airy, North Carolina near his home.

References

Who's Who in America
Who's Who in Law

Obituaries

N Y Herald Tribune p18 My 1 '41

FONTANNE, LYNN   See Lunt, A. and Fontanne, L.

FORCE, JULIANA   1888(?)-   Museum director

Address: 10 W. 8th St, New York City

One of the foremost museum directors in America is the woman in charge of the Whitney Museum of American Art, Juliana Force. "In her slim, beautifully fitted clothes, in her effectively tailored gray dresses, with her odd heavy jewelry," wrote Adlene Talmey, "Mrs. Force runs this feminized museum with the bluntness, the directness, that practically no men possess."

The story of how the museum came into being is characteristic, however apocryphal it may be in detail. In 1928 the Whitney collection of American art, comprising some three hundred paintings accumulated during the two decades during which the Whitney Studio Club and the Whitney Gallery had helped to support young American art, was offered to an uptown New York museum. Mrs. Force was authorized to make the offer by the wealthy and socially prominent Gertrude Whitney (see sketch this issue) and to suggest that funds might be forthcoming for a wing to house them. In conference with the museum's director, Mrs. Force indicated the scope of the collection. Tactfully the director pointed to a refusal. He had, as he put it, enough Americans already. And as Mrs. Force departed, with the offer of the new wing unmentioned, the director said, "And give my love to Gertrude." By this time Mrs. Force was in a fury. As one writer put it: "She jumped into a taxi, her pale eyes mad as a hornet's nest, and said to herself, 'We'll build our own museum.'"

Juliana Force was born not far from New York City. After her formal education had been completed she taught in a private school in New England. When barely a girl out of her teens she left this position to become secretary to Gertrude Vanderbilt Whitney, her first task to edit a novel Mrs. Whitney had written. The novel, however, was soon put aside to make way for a career that could with difficulty be crowded into one book. In 1908 the Whitney Studio Gallery had its opening at 8 West 8th Street. In Mrs. Force's cluttered, amusing office she poured tea for Sloan, Henri, Bellows, and many another luminary of American art. "I didn't learn anything," she explains, "but I just grew more and more astonished."

The policy of the Whitney Studio Gallery was substantially that of the Whitney Club that followed it. Emphasis was upon native art and artists. Even in those days, as her championship of Luks and Sloan shows, she was regarded as daring and modern in her tastes. Without neglecting tradition, the Whitney Museum, since its establishment in 1931, has maintained that reputation. Aside from its annual showings of oil paintings, of sculpture, water colors and graphic work, it features historically significant exhibits such as one of a few years back that brought forcefully to the art-conscious public the importance of Eakins and his colleagues.

The Whitney Studio Club, which opened in 1914 in a brownstone front on West 4th Street, formulated openly what had been the tacit policy of the Whitney Studio Gallery. It exacted small dues and gave its members large shows. Hopper, Schnackenberg and many more of today's prominent artists had their first exhibits sponsored there. The Whitney collection was purchased as art and never by way of disguised charity. If such outstanding artists as John Steuart Curry (see sketch this issue) received monthly stipends it was because, as investments in American art, they seemed worth the expenditure.

By 1928 it was felt that the Club had outgrown its usefulness. The period between the end of the Club and the opening of the museum was bridged over by an exhibit gallery at 14 West 8th Street, of which Mrs. Force appointed Alexander Brook (see sketch this issue) director. Meanwhile, plans for an entirely new type of museum began to take shape in earnest. Three houses on West 8th Street were renovated to make up the salmon-pink facade of The Whitney Museum of American Art that had its formal opening November 1931. It was then, as it is today, the only museum in New York devoted in its entirety to American achievement in the field of painting, sculpture and the graphic arts. Its opening exhibit consisted of the 300 or so paintings then in its collection.

JULIANA FORCE

Sole control of the Whitney Museum is in the hands of Mrs. Whitney and Mrs. Force. There are no juries and no prizes, though around $20,000 yearly is spent for the purchase of works of art to be added to its permanent collection. Anyone may submit work to the Whitney, subject to the procedure governing submission. Mrs. Force and the museum's curators look at five examples of work by each new artist, grade them as follows: (A) invite, (B) possibility, (C) ask to submit again, and (D) never want to see again.

In 1933 and 1934 the Whitney Museum found itself the geographical center of a controversy over governmental relief policies—and art. Picket lines formed by the Artists' Committee of Action, predecessor of United American Artists (CIO) of which Rockwell Kent is now president, marched back and forth in front of the Whitney (which was also Mrs. Force's address), and influential groups of conservative artists raised a dignified hullabaloo in the press—all because Mrs. Force had been appointed regional head of the newly created Public Works of Art Project. Behind this opposition was no personal animosity but the belief, on the one hand, that PWAP lacked a clearly enunciated policy based upon economic need—such was more or less the stand of the ACA—and the belief on the part of the conservatives that Mrs. Force favored modern art to the extent that the use of governmental wall space would be denied all but a small clique.

Before the winter was out the *Art Digest* (Peyton Boswell) had outdone itself in strongly worded editorials, and hints of the dangers of sabotage had impelled Mrs. Force to close the Whitney exhibit six weeks earlier than had been planned. In the thick of the controversy Mrs. Force was authorized to

FORCE, JULIANA—*Continued*

eliminate from her work use of the words "needy" and "relief," but eventually, when the Federal Art Project was created under Holger J. Cahill, it was based not upon the need for the art but upon the artist in need.

Mrs. Force is a discerning collector, but this hobby, like her famous parties, seems merely an extension of her role in the field of art. At one time she had three homes, a thatched cottage near Oxford, England, an apartment above the museum of which she was director, and an old gray stone house in Bucks County, Pennsylvania, the gift of her husband, Dr. W. B. Force. She was in England in 1936 when she sold the Bucks County estate to George S. Kaufman (see sketch this issue), completing the transaction by transatlantic telephone.

The apartment above the museum is reached by an elevator of red lacquer. Furnishings include blue satin curtains that sweep the floor, a fabulous white stove, black oilcloth curtains with tiny scattered bouquets of opals embroidered on with gold thread, an antique Aubusson rug, a small modern sitting room with bakelite table and white couch, and a bedroom with a curlicued brass and iron bed with flowered panel inset and a canopy with pink mull curtains. Few decorators could hope to bring esthetic order out of such a bewildering conglomeration of objects, yet in these rooms good taste is the essence of arrangement. "Even if you have never seen Mrs. Force," said Mary Fanton Roberts, "these rooms give you an impression of her varied interests, her dramatic temperament, her artistic integrity and the force of character which have made her one of the foremost women of her generation."

Mrs. Force is dynamic, capable, controlled. A look of preoccupation in her gray-blue eyes suggests hidden depths of personality, as though the real person were somewhere behind them. She has been sculptured by Lachaise, who did a head of her, and an early Sloan portrait emphasizes thin face, heavy gold hair. Peggy Bacon wrote a satirical description of her that she included in *Off With Their Heads*. It reads: "Dependably indiscreet, brutally witty, she talks effectively, constantly, sparing no feelings, letting people know exactly where they stand. . . Handsome auburn *chevelure,* cream-coloured skin, and small menacing eyes that miss nothing. Nose of Cyrano de Bergerac, mouth like a circumflex accent. Figure erect, trim, magnetic, packed with audacity and challenge."

Mrs. Force is said to have a fear of cats, dating from a childhood episode when her brother asked her to touch one, and she did so without looking. Much to her horror it was a furry animal, and alive. It is said that cat-owning friends put their pets away when Mrs. Force calls. The story is told of one occasion when a hostess, unaware of Mrs. Force's dislike for them, left her pet cat asleep in the drawing room during her visit. Mrs. Force sat down some distance from the cat but it awakened precipitately when a

pianist opened a number with a crashing chord, and leaped—so the story goes—right into Mrs. Force's lap.

The Whitney Museum has been compared to an elegant private home with the furniture removed. This would hardly apply today, for domestic touches have been eliminated, and even the deep red carpets that save one from "museum feet" emphasize its functional character. As director of this museum and as director in turn of each of the galleries and clubs that led up to it and of the various exhibitions the Museum presents—in 1941 there was "This Is Our City" and a show of children's work—critics inevitably pay tribute to Mrs. Force when they praise the museum. And their praise has been given without stint. Forbes Watson referred to it as "our most influential museum of American art," and Peyton Boswell summed it up with: "The Whitney idea helped American art to speak its own language. While others talked American art, the Whitney bought and supported it."

References

Arts & Dec 41:42-4 Je '34 il
Mag Art 32:558-67+ O '39 il
N Y Times II p1 Mr 11 '34
Vogue 95:94 F 1 '40 il pors

FORD, BLANCHE CHAPMAN *See* Chapman, B.

FORD, JOHN Feb. 1, 1895- Motion-picture director
Address: b. c/o 20th Century-Fox Film Corp, Beverly Hills, Calif; United States Navy Dept, Washington, D. C.; h. 6860 Odin St, Hollywood, Calif.

In the fall of 1941 John Ford directed *How Green Was My Valley* and then left Hollywood to head a newly formed photographic unit for the United States Navy. The Navy Department gained a man who in 1940 was chosen as the best director of the year by the New York Film Critics and by the Hollywood Academy for his work in *The Grapes of Wrath* and *The Long Voyage Home*, and *The Grapes of Wrath* was honored as the year's outstanding film by both the Film Critics and the National Board of Review of Motion Pictures. After 25 years of constant activity in Hollywood, Ford figures his percentage of hits at about 90, but points out that some films he thought "junk" were great successes and others which he liked just didn't take.

In these 20 years Ford has directed scores of pictures, some historical, some action; some about murder, some about love; some humorous, some sad. Almost all of them have shown his "distinct flair in the use of the camera, care in composition, a feeling for mood, a deft cutting style, an appreciation of movement as the prime element of the movies, an eye for colorful characterization and a great ease in the manipulation of all these elements." And most of them are distinguished by a certain vital realism that Ford has made his own. He dislikes make-up, camera tricks and theatricalism. He is not afraid to shift the camera viewpoint from the eye level, to move into a scene and around characters and to light a set for mood and realism.

Most important to Ford is the real quality of the story he is filming; a good story to him is one that tells of real people and real problems, a story that has social meaning, a story that can be presented with bold strokes and with sympathy, too. In other words, a story like *The Grapes of Wrath.*

John Ford always knows exactly what he wants to do before he even starts on a picture. He doesn't get on a set until he has approved every detail of a finished script and by the time filming begins has memorized every camera angle, every "bit" action and much of the dialogue. "Most directors," he says, "like to 'shoot around' the script so that they can eliminate later, but I try to manage with an absolute minimum of retakes." He did this in *The Long Voyage Home,* and in *Stagecoach* dropped out only one two-minute scene in the cutting room. This means that Ford works on a strict production schedule and usually is able to finish a day or two ahead of it.

"I rehearse the cast carefully on all scenes," he explains, "and use a minimum of dialogue. I believe movies are primarily pictures, so I play them that way. Let the pictures do the talking for you." Actors like to work under him. When a scene pleases him he says: "That's fine." When it doesn't he mildly suggests: "We'll have to do better." When a player muffs a line or miscues, Ford points out the error without raising his voice, makes a few corrective gestures and hurries to get the retake. All the time, dressed in shabby clothes, his feet in sneakers with holes in the toes, he keeps smoking his pipe—and to many the way the smoke comes out is indicative of what he is thinking.

"Six-foot-two and as Irish as Paddy's pig," John Ford was born Sean O'Feeney in Cape Elizabeth, Maine, the son of Sean and Barbara (Curran) O'Feeney. When he was an infant his family moved to Portland, Maine and there Sean attended grade school and high school until he was graduated in 1914. He tried to get an appointment to Annapolis, but did not succeed. Instead he enrolled at the University of Maine, but stayed there only a short while. His brother, Francis, had gone out to Hollywood and become successful and John decided to join him.

In Hollywood in 1914 he got his first film job as property man at Universal City, changed his name to John Ford and proceeded to learn about motion pictures. He filled in as Indian, soldier, horseback rider, carried props, tended the camera and watched the direction carefully. By the end of the year he had become an assistant director. Then he was assigned to direct short films and Westerns, some of them starring Tom Mix. From these he learned to think and act quickly, to estimate footage and develop

Gene Kornman

JOHN FORD

thrills. By 1919 he had a contract with Fox to direct feature films.

Ford's first important screen work was *Cameo Kirby,* which introduced John Gilbert to the screen public. It was followed by many others, including one of the biggest historical silent films, *The Iron Horse,* and the great hit, *Four Sons.* With the talking pictures Ford's ability became even more apparent—many hits appeared under his direction. There were *Men Without Women* (he wrote the story of this, too); and *Up the River,* in which Spencer Tracy gave his first important performance. In 1931 came *Arrowsmith* and in 1932, *Flesh.*

Then, in 1934, came *The Lost Patrol,* the first picture of note made by Ford and Dudley Nichols (see sketch this issue), the screen writer, together. It was an indication of what these two, who have worked in close collaboration during the past years, could do. Essentially, *The Lost Patrol* was merely a pulp adventure story. Yet Ford and Nichols were able to make it an exciting movie, one which one reviewer went so far as to call "a virile poem, a short impressive saga of man's courage." In it were seen many qualities of Ford's later work—"a single strong situation, unity of time, place, mood, vivid characterization, colorful locale, suspense."

Because of the success of *The Lost Patrol,* Ford and Nichols set about making Liam O'Flaherty's *The Informer,* which they had been trying to get the studios to make for years. It took only three weeks to film and was, Ford says, the easiest picture he ever directed. No wonder, he adds: "I had been dreaming of it for five years." Under "Ford's compact direction the film was the tragedy of a stool pigeon told in somber key, dark shadows, muffled voices, carousing, night

FORD, JOHN—*Continued*

sounds. Mood, pace, character and sound are blended in it into a fluid unity which . . . holds the spectator taut."

Until *The Informer,* Ford was hardly known outside the trade, although he had been directing for almost 21 years and making a number of successes. With this picture, which has become the outstanding American film classic, his reputation was established. It won the 1935 Academy Award for best direction and was a tremendous critical, as well as popular, success. Then followed other important pictures: *Mary of Scotland* and *The Plough and the Stars* (both written by Dudley Nichols); *The Hurricane*; *Young Mr. Lincoln*; *Drums Along the Mohawk*; *The Grapes of Wrath*; and *The Long Voyage Home,* of which he was also producer with Walter Wanger. In 1941 Ford was working for Twentieth Century-Fox with a contract that allowed him to make one outside picture a year, and for them he directed *Tobacco Road* and the highly acclaimed *How Green Was My Valley.*

All in all John Ford has made over 80 pictures, for a number of companies, and has received the Photoplay Gold Medal (1928), the New York Critics Award, the Foreign Press Club Award and three Academy Awards, Hollywood's highest accolade—first for *The Informer;* second for *Stagecoach;* and third for the direction of two films, *The Long Voyage Home* and *The Grapes of Wrath.* And all these years he has fought a constant battle to "do something fresh. First they want you to repeat your last picture. . . Then they want you to continue whatever vein you succeeded in with the last picture." Ford will have none of this. "I've got a whole lot of respect for the people who go to see motion pictures," he says.

In all these years in Hollywood, Ford has made hundreds of friends—actors whom he has given a new lease on life, new stars he has brought forward. But he has never really become a part of the glamorous Hollywood the motion picture magazines and the press agents tell about. He has had only one wife in all these years—Mary McBryde Smith whom he married in 1920—and his son and daughter so far seem to have no movie aspirations. He has kept the nine-room house in Hollywood he had fifteen years ago; when in Hollywood he avoids night life, interviews and idle chatter.

When a picture was finished, he used to board his 110-foot yacht *Araner* and travel over the South Seas, Central America, the Pacific, often sailing the ship himself, reading all the biographies and autobiographies he could get hold of. "Characters," he explains it. "Characters. I love characters."

References

Christian Sci Mon Mag p5 Je 21 '41 il pors
Motion Pict 52:62 O '36 il pors
N Y Times IX p5 O 26 '41
Photoplay 50:14-15+ O '36 il pors

International Motion Picture Almanac
Jacobs, L. Rise of the American Film p479-86 1939
Who's Who in America

FORD, W(ILLIAM) W(EBBER) Dec. 15, 1871—Feb. 10, 1941 Professor emeritus of bacteriology of Johns Hopkins University; taught at University since 1917; noted for researches on early anesthesia; served on Maryland State Board of Health.

References

American Medical Directory
American Men of Science
Leaders in Education 1932
Who's Who in America
Who's Who in American Medicine
Who's Who in Government

Obituaries

N Y Times p23 F 11 '41

FORD, WORTHINGTON C(HAUNCEY) Feb. 16, 1858—Mar. 7, 1941 Author, economist and historian; in 1928 was sent to Europe by the Library of Congress to collect Americana; lived in France since, except for periodic visits to America; died at sea on way to United States; from 1903 to 1909 was chief of the manuscript division of the Library of Congress; former editor of the Massachusetts Historical Society; editor of the *Letters of Henry Adams* and author of numerous historical volumes.

References

Leaders in Education 1941
Who's Who
Who's Who in America
Who's Who in Government

Obituaries

N Y Times p19 Mr 8 '41

FOREST, LEE DE *See* De Forest, L.

FORREST, ALLAN Sept. 1, 1889—July 25, 1941 Motion-picture star of silent film days who played opposite such famous leading stars as Mary Miles Minter, Norma and Constance Talmadge, Mary and Lottie Pickford from 1915 to 1929, then was connected with a commercial film studio in Detroit; real name Allan Forrest Fisher.

References

Motion Pict Mag 19:46 Mr '30 por
Photoplay 17:24 Ja '20 por; 19:23 Mr '21; 27:44 F '25 por
International Motion Picture Almanac 1936-37

Obituaries

N Y Times p30 Jl 27 '41

FORSYTHE, ROBERT S(TANLEY) (fôr-sīth') Oct. 6, 1886—June 5, 1941 Bibliographer; head of the department of book selection for the Newberry Library in Chicago since 1933; served before then as instructor in English at the University of Kansas, Western Reserve University and Northwestern University; author of articles and reviews and member of advisory board of several publications.

References

Leaders in Education 1941
Who's Who Among North American Authors
Who's Who in America

Obituaries

N Y Times p17 Je 7 '41
Sch & Soc 53 :754 Je 14 '41

FOUGNER, G. SELMER (fōōg-nâr') Aug. 24, 1884—Apr. 2, 1941 New York newspaperman and publicist who conducted the column "Along the Wine Trail" in the New York *Sun*; started his career in 1906 working in Paris and New York for the New York *Herald*; was war correspondent; his column on food and wine brought him recognition as an authority on wines, liquors and food in the United States and abroad.

References

N Y Herald Tribune p14 Ap 6 '40 por
Scrib Mag 102 :6+ S '37
Who's Who Among North American Authors
Who's Who in America

Obituaries

N Y Times p23 Ap 3 '41 por

FRANK, HANS May 23, 1900- Governor General of Nazi-occupied Poland

During the last days of 1939 Dr. Hans Frank, Governor General of the occupied districts of Poland, had a conference with General Blaskowitz, military commander, about the task of pacifying the conquered Polish territory. This discussion was mainly an argument about the methods to be used. Herr Frank came out victorious; he succeeded in convincing the General that it was the aim of the German National Socialists to make the Polish people understand that "a master-race is reigning over them." With this declaration he took the historic responsibility for the brutal policy that has since been described in documents issued by the Vatican. Although for many months there was a fairly effective veil of silence over what goes on in Poland, it was generally admitted that shortly after the Nazi occupation executions took place, some million men and women were sent to forced labor in Germany, and both private and public property was confiscated. And gradually even more shocking revelations reached the outside world—revelations which caused some commentators to describe Nazi policy as "aimed at eventual extermination of the entire Polish people."

This man who today rules with almost unlimited power over the life and death of a population of 14 or 15 million people was at one time a lawyer. An early biographer, never dreaming that Frank would one day occupy

HANS FRANK

one of the most important administrative posts in present-day Europe, described him as a man "loaded with energy . . . .a very good fighter in the courtroom," a man "clever in finding the opponent's weakness . . . always ready to jump, and immune to bluffing."

Hans Frank was born on May 23, 1900, the son of Karl F. and Magdalena (Buchmeier) Frank. His childhood days were not very happy ones, for his father, also a lawyer, was disbarred after having been exposed for swindling, and his family circumstances seemed to have fluctuated between actual poverty and middle-class prosperity. During the First World War he was more fortunate than some, however. He ended his Gymnasium days by passing an emergency examination and then did not volunteer for war service, but waited until he was drafted through the regular channels. He served in the infantry regiment *Koenig,* and in 1918, at the outbreak of the German Revolution, was in a hospital.

Any signs of nationalist sentiment in Hans Frank were indiscernible until April 1919, when he realized that the Republic showed hardly any resistance to its opponents. At that time many "Free Corps" (private military organizations) came into existence. Frank joined the "Free Corps Epp" (in 1941 Epp is a Bavarian Cabinet Minister) and later the mounted "Free Corps Seefried 21"; he served with them until October. It was in these circles that he came into contact with members of the Reichswehr (the regular German Army). During the summer and fall of 1920, after beginning in 1919 to study law and national economy at Munich, Kiel and Vienna, he served illegally as a temporary voluntary private in the Reichswehr.

In Munich, during his student days, Frank was also induced to become a member of the

FRANK, HANS—*Continued*

Thule Society, a sort of religious order for the perpetuation of old German paganism; he became acquainted with Adolf Hitler; he joined the "German Workers Party." Because of his experience he served with the military organization of the Party, and after the creation of the Storm Troops was made one of its higher leaders. In the famous Munich beer-hall *putsch* of 1923 he served as a member of the mounted "Corps Wrede" and helped to proclaim the Hitler Government, but fled with all the others when the police and Army opposed the "revolutionists." In spite of the minor role he had played he then became afraid and left the country for a while.

Back in Germany once more, after an investigation Frank was even permitted to retain his official title of "Referendar." Now his difficulties were mainly financial. His family had originally lived in the Rhenish Palatinate. One of his grandfathers had been a baker, another had owned an oil mill, but the family had never been prosperous. Hans' father, Karl Frank, known officially in customary German bureaucratic style as Frank I, had made few friends even before having been disbarred as a lawyer, and had no well-disposed connections. Hans himself, in order to continue his studies, had been forced to take a job as bookkeeper in a law office. But in 1924 he finally received his LL. D., in 1927 passed his examination for "assessor," and the same year became a member of the Reich Leadership of the National Socialist Party and head of its legal department. In 1925 he married Brigitte Herbst. (A son, Norman, and two daughters, Sigrid and Brigitha Maria, were born to them.)

Frank began to practice as an attorney in 1928 and immediately tried to rescue the remnants of his father's former circle of clients. He had not yet been officially admitted to the Bar but, with the help of some obliging Jewish colleagues who gave him permission to act as their substitute, he succeeded in making a bare living. By the end of the same year he managed to open an office of his own and become an attorney for his Party, and during the following year he actually became quite active as a lawyer. He found time for an extensive tour through Italy and appeared in a great many trials in the courts of the Republic, where he soon attracted attention by his extremely smart appearance and aggressive behavior. He even lectured at the Seminary of Jurisprudence of the Technical College in Munich—a feat of which he loves to boast. The man who had made it possible for him to give those lectures—Privy Councillor Calker, an old friend from the Thule Society—lived to regret his complacence when he heard that Frank later bolstered his Nazi theories in an argument with an experienced lawyer by the remark: "What? You dare to doubt a German teacher of law?"

As attorney for members of the Nazi Party, Frank always resorted to a most provocative attitude and way of speaking during court trials: one Nazi biographer called his eloquence "brilliant," his personal behavior "passionate," his intelligence "daring." At one trial concerning the legality of the Nazi Party in Republican Germany the representative of the Department of the Interior actually left the courtroom in protest against Frank's language and behavior. By the end of 1930 Frank had become the infant prodigy of the Reichstag when he entered it as one of its 107 elected Nazi members, and by parliamentary procedure he soon became chairman of its law committee. This committee, however, never did any practical work.

Frank's great hour finally came. Hitler took over power, and on March 10, 1933, after the conquest of Bavaria, made him acting Minister of Justice for Bavaria. A month later he became the full-fledged Minister of Justice. This last nomination enabled Frank to accomplish two otherwise impossible feats: he forced the Bar Association to reinstate his father and permit him to wear the lawyer's robe again; he obtained permission to continue his own private law office. The results fully justified this last venture: his own private office, managed by assistants, was beseiged by clients who wanted expert professional advice on how to petition Hans Frank, the Bavarian Minister of Justice! True, his professional colleagues in Munich protested vociferously, and one fine day his shingle even disappeared; but lawyer Frank II did not close his private law office until 1934—then only after an unmistakable hint from higher up, and after he had amassed a nice little fortune for himself. His father did not have equal success, however. Shortly after being readmitted to the Bar he committed new embezzlements, and even his son finally refused to come to his rescue.

Despite these peculiar events, Hitler continued to express his approval of favorite Hans Frank. New posts were thrown into his lap: he became Reich Commissioner for Justice (April 1933) and, in December 1934, after the abolishment of all formerly independent law administrations of the different German states, took over the office of Minister without Portfolio in the Reich Government. At the same time he obtained many Party jobs—among them membership in the Reich Investigation and Arbitration Committee, which played an important role during the investigation of the bloody events of June 30, 1934. Frank was also made Führer of the Bund of National Socialist Lawyers and president of the Academy of German Law, founded by Hitler in 1934 and given legal status in the same year.

The publications of the Academy of German Law, necessary after all parliamentary activity in Germany had ceased and the theoretic will to action of the lawyers had to find some kind of an outlet, are indeed voluminous. Among Frank's contributions are *The National Socialist Handbook for Jurisprudence and Law,* which appeared toward the end of 1934 and was published under his name, and a pamphlet entitled *The Juridical Foundation of the National Socialist Führer State* (1938). His talents as a theoretician may be judged by such quotations as this one, from the second edition of the first book: "The state built up by Adolf Hitler is the medium for the realization of National Socialism. . . And so, in utter deviation from the juridical literature of former days, this handbook is a juridico-political confessional, as it were, with the character of a Party and legal law-code." His pamphlet contains this equally remarkable sentence: "Adolf Hitler's victory in the battle for the equality of the German people constitutes the magnificent confirmation of his fitness to be the highest representative of the German people's law."

Since March 1933 Dr. Frank has undertaken many an extravagant little excursion in the interest of this "representative," Hitler. At that time he made a speech against the Dollfuss Government, and in May he followed up his first speech by making speeches all over Austria, ridiculing the "Little Metternich." The police had originally informed him that he was unwelcome, and he had ignored them; only after they had grown more aggressive and after political interventions had taken place in Berlin did Frank consent to leave. Tauschitz, Austrian Ambassador in Berlin, made a personal appeal to Hitler, but the Führer declared that it was impossible to chase after every public speaker.

This, then, is the man whom in 1939 Hitler made Governor General of Poland. Scarcely 40 years of age, he immediately began to govern the Poles according to his theory about the treatment of criminals. ("In the National Socialist state the criminal must shiveringly fear the inexorable moral severity of the people.") Herr Frank teaches a whole people how to shiver. "The swastika will fly over this land forever," he says.

References

    International Who's Who
    Von Schmidt-Pauli, E. Die Maenner
      um Hitler nd
    Wer ist's?

FRANK, JEROME N(EW) Sept. 10, 1889- Judge of the United States Circuit Court of Appeals

Address: United States Circuit Court of Appeals, 2nd District, New York City

Corporation lawyer, member of the original New Deal "brain trust," author of *Save America First*, chairman of the Securities and Exchange Commission—these are among the titles that have come Jerome N. Frank's way in the course of his varied and brilliant career. In February 1941 he was nominated by President Roosevelt as judge of the United States Circuit Court of Appeals in the 2nd District, which embraces New York, Vermont and Connecticut.

Jerome New Frank was born on September 10, 1889 in New York City, the son of lawyer Herman Frank and Clara (New) Frank.

JEROME N. FRANK

His family moved to Chicago not long afterward, and he attended Hyde Park High School before going on to the University of Chicago. There he received his Ph. B. in 1909 and then went on to the University's law school. "One of the two brightest students of pre-War generations," he was graduated in 1912 with Phi Beta Kappa honors and the degree of Doctor of Jurisprudence. That same year he was admitted to the Illinois Bar, and until 1929 practiced law in Chicago as a member of the firm of Levinson, Becker, Schwartz and Frank, corporation specialists.

In Chicago, Frank was a member of the "kitchen cabinet" of William E. Dever, the city's Progressive Democratic Mayor. From 1921 to 1925 he helped to negotiate the traction settlement for the city that was defeated by Samuel Insull. He did corporate reorganization work, particularly for the First National Bank in Chicago, and his technique took better care of the small security holder than was customary. He was, in short, a highly successful corporation lawyer of liberal tendencies, with a reputation for hard work, absent-mindedness and a habit of writing novels that never reached a publisher's office.

It was 1929 when Jerome Frank came to New York to become a member of the firm of Chadbourne, Stanchfield and Levy, who often said: "It's worth $50,000 a year to us to have Jerry around just to hear him talk." He had met Felix Frankfurter (see sketch this issue) before, and he saw a great deal of him now. Benjamin Cardozo and Morris Cohen were also among his friends. In 1930 was published Frank's first book, *Law and the Modern Mind*, written on trains in his spare time and dealing with the psychology of individual judges in interpreting the "sup-

FRANK, JEROME N.—*Continued*

posedly unchangeable rules of law." There followed articles in law journals (including one plaintively titled *Are Judges Human?*), lectures at the New School for Social Research and an appointment in 1932 as research associate of the Yale Law School.

Then, after Roosevelt's victory, Felix Frankfurter recommended Jerome Frank (a "lawyer who watches the bread-lines more closely than the price-quotations") to handle the Department of Agriculture's legal business. Although Farley blocked the appointment, in May 1933 Secretary of Agriculture Henry Wallace made Frank general counsel to the AAA, and he also became general counsel to the Federal Surplus Relief Corporation.

It was Frank's first entrance into public life. Until that time he had moved for the most part in literary circles both in Chicago and in New York: his wife, the former Florence Kiper, whom he married in July 1914 and by whom he has one daughter, Barbara, had been a well known poet and playwright at the time of her marriage; the late Harriet Monroe, Carl Sandburg, Rebecca West, the late Sherwood Anderson, Floyd Dell, Max Eastman and Harry Hansen had been his friends. And all was not sweetness and light in Washington. George Peek, whose Moline Plow Works in Chicago had been very competently liquidated by Frank, joined the staff of the AAA, thus creating an uncomfortable situation. Warfare between Peek and consumer-minded New Dealers led by Frank, plus occasional threats of resignation on Frank's part, brought about Peek's shift to the job of looking after exports in the fall of 1933. But (according to Drew Pearson and Robert Allen [see sketches this issue]) Frank's "meditative exercises" finally threw Frank himself into "cross purposes with Henry Wallace and Wallace's chief associate of the day, Chester Davis. They considered him a stratosphere thinker, far from reality, and he was 'purged.' "

In February 1935 Frank resigned, although serving for a short time in Washington that year as special counsel to the RFC and then going to PWA to win the Alabama Power case against the late Newton D. Baker. Back in private practice in 1937, he earned $38,000 helping in the reorganization of Union Pacific. He remained highly influential with President Roosevelt, however, and in December 1937 was offered a commissionership in the Securities and Exchange Commission. The salary of $10,000 a year could have been no inducement; he knew he was "temperamentally unsuited to trench warfare"; but he accepted the appointment reluctantly.

In the meanwhile *Save America First* had been begun, back in 1932, as a criticism of much current economic writing. Its writing had been interrupted by Frank's governmental activity, but a first draft had nevertheless been completed by 1935. In 1937 Whit Burnett (see sketch under Foley this issue) saw it, insisted that he finish it, and several months before

Frank returned to Washington the manuscript was completed. It was published in 1938.

Save America First insisted that America's continental unity made her problems totally unlike those of Europe's, that "a depression in America is a mental, not an economic, phenomenon," and that the greater purchasing power for the general consumer necessary to maintain the profit system could here be brought about by an enlightened capitalism. The Reverend Reinhold Niebuhr (see sketch this issue) decided that the "two major themes . . . partially contradict each other," and Stuart Chase announced that although it was the "kind of a book this age needs," that although he agreed in large part with Frank's analysis of the depression, "when it comes . . . to reforming the Big Shots and asking them to act at right angles to the way they have been conditioned to act," he had his fingers crossed. Raymond Moley, however, was confident that a rereading of the National Association of Manufacturers' latest statement of principles revealed little that could not be harmonized with Frank's major thesis, and John Chamberlain called *Save America First* "the most beautifully open-minded book that has come this way in years."

In May 1939 Jerome Frank became chairman of the "split, faction-ridden" Securities and Exchange Commission. Charged with enforcing the Securities Act of 1933, the Securities Exchange Act of 1934 and the Public Utility Act of the security market, Frank engaged in occasional bouts with Wall Street and the Investment Bankers Association. (The SEC is one of the governmental agencies which would have been most vitally affected had the Walter-Logan Bill become law.)

Ralph Robey (see sketch this issue) of *Newsweek* called Frank "arrogant, nervous, argumentative, unreasonable, even insulting at times" in his attitude toward certain businessmen, and the *Saturday Evening Post* was no more complimentary; but on taking office Frank proclaimed that the major function of the SEC and its laws is essentially conservative: "To aid the conservation of our American profit system under our American form of government." And before the Kiwanis Club of Cleveland he announced on April 25, 1940: "You are probably thinking, at once, in terms of further government control over business. If that worries you, let me say that it also worries me." His was a delicate job, but he believes that the SEC's "unscrambling" of utilities provides new outlets for investment as much as it protects the "10,000,000-odd trusting United States investors."

As for Frank's views on the United States' role in the world today, they have changed since he wrote, in *Save America First*: "There might be some point in America's fighting, or threatening to fight, in order to unify Europe; such a consummation might be worth great sacrifices on our part, for it would probably ensure peace in Europe. But in such an enterprise, England will not be our friend or ally but our enemy. For she does not want peace in Europe by means of European integration; that is a price she has always refused to pay... If we want to forestall and defeat American

Fascism, let us do so in America and not in Europe." Today he believes that if Great Britain is defeated it will be necessary for the United States to fight Hitler, and that we should aid England to the hilt. He says: "I was one of those who believed Western Hemispheric isolation was not only desirable but achievable, but the harsh realities of violent change have compelled me long since to admit the futility of my hopes." As early as May 1940 he was making notes on a plan to finance the United States' possible participation in the War, modeled on that of Britain's John Maynard Keynes (see sketch this issue).

Frank is a member of the Association of the Bar of the City of New York, of the New York State Bar Association and of the Order of the Coif. *Time* describes him as a "warm-blooded, quick-witted, supersensitive, argument-loving man . . . with a bald sloping brow, bulging eyes, and the slightly travel-worn air of a shambling, sub-leonine cat." He is sometimes too busy to have a haircut, and "often lets his graying mane hide his ears." Fond of parties, fond of involved word games, "subtle, learned, mentally insatiable, he combs arcane source books for cosmic ideas, wholesales them in brilliant conversation to friends." He is "largely responsible for the semantics fad." His memory is phenomenal. He is skeptical, impatient, pragmatic. With all that, he is sensitive to criticism, wants to be liked and makes a habit of writing letters to newspapers defending his views. Perhaps from a Federal bench such communications will be less necessary.

References

Business Week p18+ D 18 '37 por; p24 My 27 '39 por
N Y Times p38 F 14 '41 por
Newsweek 12:40 Jl 4 '38; 15:52 Ap 1 '40 por
Sat R Lit 21:3-4+ Mr 30 '40
Time 30:53 D 20 '37 por; 35:71-7 Mr 11 '40 pors
U S News 8:34 My 17 '40 por
Unofficial Observer, [pseud.] New Dealers p96-102 1934
Who's Who in America
Who's Who in American Jewry
Who's Who in Law
Who's Who in the Nation's Capital

FRANK, LOUIS 1867(?)—Mar. 22, 1941 Ex-professor of surgery at the University of Louisville Medical School; had practiced medicine for 53 years and had been a surgeon for 40 years; noted for research work and contributions to medical journals.

References

American Medical Directory
Directory of Medical Specialists 1939

Obituaries

N Y Times p45 Mr 23 '41

FRANKEN, ROSE Dec. 18, 1895- Playwright; author

Address: b. c/o Farrar & Rinehart, Inc, 232 Madison Ave, New York City; h. Longmeadow Farm, Old Lyme, Conn.

ROSE FRANKEN

After confining herself almost solely to non-theatrical fiction for nine years, in 1941 Rose Franken came back to the stage with a tender little play called *Claudia,* based on her book of the same name. The play proved a most pleasant and profitable venture to all concerned, from young Dorothy McGuire (see sketch this issue), a talented newcomer to the theatre whose performance in the title role was enthusiastically hailed, to the author herself, for whom it landed a fat Hollywood contract and has made, to date, more than half a million dollars.

Claudia's popularity is mostly due to the fact that it is very easy to take, in a charming, almost Barrie-like, sunny-smile-through-tears manner. It deals with a young girl who is happily married but unable to grow up, intellectually or emotionally, because of an abnormal attachment to her mother. She remains a child-wife to her indulgent husband until the dreadful news of her mother's imminent death (she is dying of cancer) matures her. Claudia learns to face life, "to make friends with pain," and to let go of people she loves— "to hold close with open hands," as her mother puts it. The last act of the play is devoted to the gallantry of affectionate banter, "desperately carried on above the surface of impending calamity."

Essentially *Claudia* is a woman's play. John O'Hara (see sketch this issue) remarked, after a benevolent review, "I know no man who read the Claudia stories. . . But a great many women seem to have known about Claudia all along." "It is the sort of play," said another critic, " that is more palatable in the afternoon

FRANKEN, ROSE—*Continued*

than in the evening, when theatregoers are suspected of being more censorious." One sour soul commented with asperity that "Claudia's unhealthy immaturity remains masked for three acts behind a screen of tedious, relentless *Ladies' Home Journal* cuteness." But most critics, while agreeing that the pathos she injects into the last act softens the fiber of a play that had begun as a skillful comedy, also agreed that Rose Franken's dialogue is buoyantly expert in its brilliantly casual way, and that she handles a difficult problem with a light and sure hand. And all of them had a good word for Rose Franken's direction of her play.

There was a strong possibility that *Claudia* would never be produced because of the difficulty of finding the right person to play the title role—an actress in her early 20's "who could look 19 and has had about 25 years of experience in show business." "Diogenes," recalls Rose Franken, "never searched so relentlessly for an honest man as we did for an actress for the title part of my play." This went on for 16 weeks, and the author and John Golden had almost lost all hope before they found Dorothy McGuire, having previously interviewed something like 800 actresses. It was Rose Franken who took Dorothy McGuire out to her home in Connecticut for a week end and "built her up" for her success. The results definitely paid.

It is possible that Rose Franken drew on her own life's experience for her portrait of Claudia. She was born in Gainesville, Texas, the daughter of Michael and Hannah (Younker) Lewin, but came to New York when she was still a child. She attended the Ethical Culture School. Like her heroine, she chose marriage in preference to a college career when she was 18. Her husband, Dr. Sigmund Walter Anthony Franken, was a famous oral surgeon. She bore him three sons, Paul, John and Peter. This steadily accumulating family notwithstanding, Rose Franken found time to write and achieved considerable success in that profession. At first she wrote only short stories which appeared in many magazines, but by 1925, when her second son John was born (Paul came in 1920 and Peter in 1929), her first novel, *Pattern* (1925), had been published. The other novels she has written since, *Twice Born* (1935) and *Of Great Riches* (1937), published a year later as *Gold Pennies*, were cordially received, and of course the Claudia books which came much later were a phenomenal success.

In the meanwhile, she had decided to try her hand at playwriting. Her first play, *Fortnight,* was given the usual run-around. When it failed to get a production that was promised it in a suburban theatre, Rose Franken grimly ploughed into another one. This was called *Hallam Wives* (1929) and dealt with the problem of a sensitive and talented woman marrying into a stolidly bourgeois family, with values completely divergent from hers, and dominated by a brutally selfish mother. The conflict precipitated when the woman desperately tried to teach her husband "her language"

and to keep him from reverting to the Hallam pattern was at last happily resolved. The play was produced in Connecticut over the summer, and was so well received that a New York production seemed in order. In 1932 this play appeared in New York under the title *Another Language.*

Another Language put Rose Franken in the forefront of American playwrights. With Dorothy Stickney and Glenn Anders in the main roles, it rolled up an impressive total of 433 performances—a record for a first play. Critics described it as an intelligent and rather therapeutic study of family life, delighted in its portrayal of the clannish Hallam family, "with its violent little feuds, its chicken salad, its tight shoes, its corseted fat, its rather mean practical jokes and its self-righteous mutual bullying." The screen version of the play was able to recapture much of the original feeling. Helen Hayes contributed a delicate performance as Stella Hallam. Since then the only other play Rose Franken had written until she decided to work on *Claudia* was *Mr. Dooley, Jr.,* a play for children which was produced at the Heckscher Theatre and elsewhere, written with Jane Lewin.

After her husband's death Rose Franken continued to write under her married name. She produced more than 130 short stories and innumerable radio sketches. She went to Hollywood to write motion picture scripts. She also married again—her husband is William Brown Meloney, journalist and writer of fiction. The two of them became a successful literary team, writing woman's magazine serials and novels, including *Strange Victory* (1939) and *American Bred* (1941), under the pseudonym of Franken Meloney. The last book deals with raising Great Danes, a subject on which the Meloneys are experts, this being one of the hobbies of the household.

Rose Franken also wrote her Claudia stories, stories about a young married couple called David and Claudia Naughton. Sprightly and tender chronicles of a marriage, 20 of these stories appeared in the *Red Book* at $2,500 each. Later they were published in book form as *Claudia* (1938) and *Claudia and David* (1940), and in the fall of 1941 an omnibus volume containing both, *The Book of Claudia,* was published after the play had made Rose Franken's happy couple almost a national institution. Film rights were bought for $135,000 and Rose Franken was engaged to write the screen continuity. Its radio serialization was by that time being heard on Friday nights over station WABC, supplementing the Kate Smith program.

With the help of *Claudia,* Rose Franken is maintaining a farm called Longmeadow at Old Lyme, Connecticut. There she and her husband have herds of purebred cattle, sheep and hogs. "We haven't yet brought ourselves to eat a goose or a pig or a duck," she writes, "but otherwise we're pleased to believe we are farming." Rose Franken often brings fresh country eggs and cream to John Golden, her producer, to his great discomfiture. He usually takes them up to Sardi's to be "fixed up for lunch."

The house is a wonderful remodeled old farmhouse, painted pale yellow with white shutters and surrounded by immaculate lawns. A pair of Great Danes and a troupe of Irish wolfhounds and shepherds rush in and out of the house; there is also a cat and a monkey.

A pretty, slim woman, with an elfin face and short dark hair, Rose Franken is an indefatigable and efficient worker. She does everything fast, "from furnishing apartments to writing plays." Reportedly she did *Claudia* in three days, bettering the record she made when she wrote *Another Language* in six. She finds it easy to write her brilliant, delicately humorous dialogue. Perhaps that is why she has never taken herself overseriously as a writer. Being the mother of a family takes all self-importance out of a woman, she claims. "Your family keeps you in your place and prevents you from becoming fatuous."

She is not particularly feminist or defiant about being a woman playwright. "You can't tell a woman's play from a man's, usually because the best people have strains of both the feminine and the masculine within them." But she does admit that "in a love story it is always the woman's relation to the man that is the more interesting, that makes the story. Naturally, a woman writer ought to understand that particularly well."

References

House B 80:40-2+ N '38
N Y Times VII p10-11+ My 4 '41 il
    por
Time 10:42 Mr 22 '41 por
American Women
International Motion Picture Almanac
    1937-38

FRANKFURTER, FELIX Nov. 15, 1882-
Associate Justice of the United States Supreme Court
Address: United States Supreme Court Bldg., Washington, D. C.

Felix Frankfurter, Associate Justice of the United States Supreme Court, is a "stocky, tense, five-foot-five-inch figure of a man, with a finely rounded, graying head and a keen face, which usually [has] a lively, birdlike expression." Born in Vienna, Austria, the son of Leopold and Emma (Winter) Frankfurter, he is a descendant of three centuries of rabbis. His father, however, quit the theological seminary for trade, and in 1893, on a business trip to the United States, "fell in love with this country." He stayed, after some months persuaded his family to follow him, and on New York's East Side became not only a retail fur merchant but also "the Unofficial Perpetual Charity Commissioner of New York."

Since his father's habits did not make for material success, Felix, who attended Public School No. 25 with his three brothers, did odd jobs after school while his mother put his earnings away in order to send him to college. When only 19 he was graduated with a B. A. degree from the College of the City of New York, the third highest in his class, and after taking a civil service examination worked for a brief period as a clerk in the city's Tenement House Commission. He quit that for Harvard's Law School, which gave him his LL. B. in 1906.

Equipped with a letter from Dean Ames, the young lawyer immediately found a job with the law firm of Hornblower, Byrne, Miller and Potter. At about the same time Henry Stimson was appointed United States Attorney for the Southern District of New

Bachrach

FELIX FRANKFURTER

York, with "trust-busting" orders from Theodore Roosevelt. Stimson applied to Harvard for an assistant, was told about Felix Frankfurter, and until 1910 the two men worked together. According to Frankfurter, this experience under Stimson inculcated in him "a high and fastidious regard for the administration of criminal justice"—and this period also marked the beginning of his practice of helping both Democratic and Republican Administrations find youngsters for legal jobs in New York and in Washington.

It was 1911 when Stimson became Secretary of War and took Felix Frankfurter with him as law officer for the War Department's Bureau of Insular Affairs. Frankfurter quit this post when appointed a professor at the Harvard Law School in 1914, but he spent most of the time between 1917 and 1919 in various administrative and legal posts in Washington, where Justice Holmes named his bachelor lodgings "The House of Truth" because of the earnest discussions on good government that went on in them.

During the First World War Frankfurter was assistant to Secretary of War Newton D. Baker, secretary and counsel to President Wilson's Mediation Commission, assistant to the Secretary of Labor. In 1917 he was sent

FRANKFURTER, FELIX—*Continued*

abroad on a war mission, in 1918 on a confidential mission to England, and early in 1918, too, as secretary and counsel of the President's Mediation Commission he investigated Tom Mooney's San Francisco trial and the Arizona mine strikes. (Theodore Roosevelt condemned the attitude shown by his reports on both as "fundamentally that of Trotsky and the other Bolshevik leaders in Russia.") Finally, in the spring of 1918, Frankfurter became chairman of the War Labor Policies Board, with general supervision of all labor troubles of the nation at war. Franklin Delano Roosevelt, Assistant Secretary of the Navy, whom Frankfurter had met before when he was Stimson's assistant, was also a board member.

It was 1919 when Frankfurter went to the Peace Conference at Paris, where he was occasionally consulted by President Wilson and Colonel House. Although himself not an orthodox Jew, he represented the Zionist cause there. Then in December of that year he married Marion A. Denman, of Longmeadow, Massachusetts, and returned to Harvard to teach the government regulation of private business as Byrne Professor of Administrative Law. Ever since 1914 he had been collaborating with former Justice Brandeis in securing legal sanction before the Supreme Court for state minimum hours laws challenged in the courts, and outside his classroom he continued to advise on public cases without a fee and to do appellate work on behalf of labor legislation, social welfare and civil liberties. (He was one of the original stockholders of the *New Republic,* and one of the founding members of the American Civil Liberties Union.) Among the civil rights cases on which he argued or gave advice were the famous Scopes case, involving the right to teach evolution in the public schools in Dayton, Tennessee; the case of the silk strikers in Passaic, New Jersey, in 1926; the case of the suppression of the *American Mercury* in Boston, which culminated in H. L. Mencken's arrest.

Perhaps, however, Frankfurter is best remembered for his connection with the case of Sacco-Vanzetti, which by 1926 he was convinced was "one of the most glaring cases of a prejudiced trial in American history." He said so, in an article in the *Atlantic Monthly* in March 1927; the article was quoted in the press all over the country, creating a storm in Boston. According to a friend, "Felix always believed in the good, cultured people of Massachusetts; he believed that when the Better Element knew the truth they would cause the verdict to be set aside." He was wrong. And in the meanwhile efforts were being made to have him expelled from Harvard. Yet when it was suggested that he might resign Frankfurter inquired: "Why should I resign? Let Lowell resign."

Gradually criticism died down. By this time Frankfurter's intensive law course was known as the Case-a-Month Club. A caustic tongue, a talent for heckling and intensive use of the Socratic method made him a little

hard on his less brilliant students, but the proportion of bright young men turned out of his seminars who later rose to legal fame testifies to the effectiveness of his methods. One student has said: "He brought to the individual a sense of his own active, continuous participation in the real world outside. With Frankfurter, one had a finger in the affairs of Washington, Paris and London." Frankfurter also continually preached the ideal of serving as lawyers "for the community." Absorbed in his pupils, he continued to keep in touch with them after graduation; and in Washington, Administration after Administration continued to ask him to recommend especially promising graduates. (Thomas Corcoran, for instance, was Frankfurter's gift to Hoover's Reconstruction Finance Corporation, and continued his brilliant work under Roosevelt.)

Frankfurter was soon to take a more direct part in the life of the Government. Having helped actively in his friend Franklin Delano Roosevelt's first campaign for President, "in the period of 1933 and 1939, Frankfurter, as one of President Roosevelt's advisers, probably had between a third and a fourth of the Presidential ear." He was a sort of "Jiminy Cricket to President Roosevelt's Pinocchio," but would take no official position. In June 1932 he had declined Governor Ely's nomination to the Massachusetts Supreme Judicial Court; and in 1933 he refused the post of United States Solicitor General.

Obviously, Frankfurter preferred to teach— from 1933 to 1934 he was George Eastman visiting professor at Oxford—and it was probably true that no Court or Cabinet member could have wielded his influence. "A letter from this professor in the Harvard Law School carried as much weight in its own way as a letter from the Morgan office at 23 Wall Street." Frankfurter's correspondence was "as voluminous as Voltaire's"—nearly every day dozens of notes went out to Governors, Senators, leading members of the Bar, bankers, social workers, labor leaders, newspaper editors, former pupils "who had become assistant President or assistant Senator." They might be notes of appeal, of praise or of blame— but they were most likely to contain advice. Furthermore his young men in Washington— among them Corcoran (see sketch 1940 Annual), Cohen, Dean Acheson (see sketches this issue)—were now writing some of the New Deal's most important laws, and New Deal measures with which he himself was known to have been associated were the Securities Act and the Public Utility Act.

In anti-New Deal circles, of course, rumors of Frankfurter's "sinister" influence were current. Hugh Johnson spread a good many of them; Hearst and Father Coughlin took up the theme, calling him "the Iago of the Administration"; and Frankfurter's so-called "100 Happy Hot Dogs", "borers from within" who were seeking "a short cut to collectivism," became famous. When Johnson said that Frankfurter had advised Roosevelt to kill the NRA he was undoubtedly right: Frankfurter had warned that the NRA probably wouldn't withstand a Supreme Court test. But most observers who knew the situation well believed that Frankfurter, a representative of the "old-fashioned Woodrow Wilson liberalism," actually exercised a cautionary influence on Roosevelt. Someone described him as "not . . . a liberal or a conservative but . . . a realist, sometimes a powerfully cautious one." He had no fixed economic beliefs, "least of all Marxian ones." And certainly he was unhappy, if silent, during the fight over the 1938 court-packing bill. Three years before he had written: "There is no magic in the number nine, but . . . experience is conclusive that to enlarge the size of the Supreme Court would be self-defeating."

It was January 5, 1939 when Frankfurter himself was nominated Associate Justice of the Supreme Court of the United States by President Roosevelt. In a not very usual step, the Senate Judiciary Committee held open hearings on a man's "fitness" for this office. Elizabeth Dilling of "Red Network" fame, among others, appeared to call him a Red, a Jew, an alien. Said Frankfurter: "I can express with very limited adequacy the passionate devotion to this land that possesses millions of our people, born, like myself, under other skies, for the privilege that this country has bestowed in allowing them to partake of its fellowship." It was January 17 when the appointment was confirmed without a dissenting vote, and January 30 when Frankfurter took office.

The Nation had previously written of Frankfurter that he had "the concrete economic grasp and passion for justice of Brandeis, the technical legal knowledge and the long perspectives of Cardozo, and something of Holmes's humanity and his gift for seeing life as a battle." Now it editorialized: "We believe that in the perspective of history the appointment of Felix Frankfurter to the Supreme Court will not seem the least of Franklin Roosevelt's accomplishments." But on the eve of Frankfurter's departure a friend found him packing. "Do you know, I'm scared," he said.

Since that time Frankfurter has plugged big loopholes in the tax laws; he has found license for new government commissions in a new interpretation of the Constitution; he has been praised by liberals for such decisions as his annulment of the sentence of Jehovah's Witnesses convicted for playing records in public attacking a religious denomination. Other decisions have puzzled his friends on *The Nation* and the *New Republic*. While the Battle of Flanders was going on he upheld the expulsion of two Jehovah's Witnesses from a Pennsylvania public school for refusing to salute the American flag, and a Yale law authority announced that he was engaged in "heroically saving America from a couple of school children." His opinion restricting the Federal Trade Commission's police powers and his decision in the Chicago milk vendors' case that peaceful picketing might be enjoined when it is "set in a background of violence" have also created controversy. It has been explained, however, that "legal experts regard Justice Frankfurter as being particularly sensitive to preserving states' rights." According to the *United States News,* in the session ending in June 1941 he established himself as the Supreme Court's most dominant member.

Justice and Mrs. Frankfurter live in a rented house on a "not-too-quiet" street in Georgetown. Every morning he rides across Washington in his own chauffeur-driven Pontiac, usually arriving at the Supreme Court Building the earliest of the nine justices. He works hard, his only exercise is walking, and he seldom gets more than four or five hours' sleep a night. But although the Frankfurters pretend to avoid an active social life, that doesn't mean avoiding gatherings with their friends, among whom are Secretaries Stimson and Knox, Eugene Meyer (see sketch this issue), Hugo Black (see sketch this issue), Archibald MacLeish (whose appointment as Librarian of Congress Frankfurter was influential in arranging). The late Lord Lothian was also a good friend of Frankfurter. Frankfurter has, in fact, the reputation of an Anglophile, having fallen in love with Oxford even before the First World War. He has taken three English refugee children into his home—children of a former student—and is astonished at how little noise they make.

Frankfurter is generally said to talk much better than he writes, being particularly fond of unusual words like palimpsest, gallimaufry, expertise. Of his writings one critic says there is "nothing profoundly original or in wide use among law students. . . [His] literary style is part commonplace, part lush, and runs to the excessive use of elegant quotations. . ." Another critic, however, speaking of his "fugitive pieces" collected by two of his students into *Law and Politics* (1939), applies Frankfurter's estimate of Charles Beard (see sketch this issue) to Frankfurter himself: "[He] has helped to make the times, thus achieving the ultimate success of every thinker in politics, namely, to rob his ideas of novelty." In addition to articles, many of them unsigned, in the *New Republic,* the *Atlantic Monthly,* the *Harvard Law Review* (of which he was an editor) and other magazines, Frankfurter's published works include: *The Case of Sacco and Vanzetti* (1927); *The Public and Its Government* (1930); *The Commerce Clause Under Marshall, Taney and Waite* (1937); *Mr. Justice Holmes and the Supreme Court* (1938). He is the co-author of other books, and editor and co-editor of numerous volumes. His wife, herself co-editor with Gardner Jackson of *The Letters of Sacco and Vanzetti,* reads and criticizes most of what her husband writes.

Frankfurter's enemies, who do exist, call him brusque, full of self-importance and an "irritating inner conviction of his own righteousness," a man who has "only half mastered the old Boston art of being rude graciously." His innumerable friends claim: "Wherever Frankfurter is, there is no boredom. He brings with him the sweep of national affairs and the human interest of personal gossip." They call him "brilliant, talkative, vain, warm-hearted, preoccupied, effervescent, learned,

FRANKFURTER, FELIX—*Continued*

naive, wise, and exasperating." And the late Gutzon Borglum is quoted as saying: "Felix is so much nicer than he used to be. He even lets other people talk occasionally!"

References

Am Mag 117:51 Mr '34 por; 127:20-1+ F '39 por
Fortune 13:63+ Ja '36
Harper 183:449-59 O '41
Life 8:53-6+ F 12 '40 il pors
   (Same abr. Read Digest 36:33-6 Ap '40)
Nation 135:67 Jl 27 '32; 147:196-7 Ag 27 '38; 148:52-3 Ja 14 '39; 148:94 Ja 21 '39; 152:203-4 F 22 '41 il
New Repub 71:191 Jl 6 '32; 97:297 Ja 18 '39; 101:145-6 N 22 '39
New Yorker 16:24-8+ N 30 '40 por; 16:36-40+ D 7 '40 por; 16:32-6+ D 14 '40 por
Scrib Mag 105:67 Ap '39
Unofficial Observer [pseud.] New Dealers p307-35 1934
Who's Who Among North American Authors
Who's Who in America
Who's Who in American Jewry
Who's Who in Law

FRANKLIN, IRENE June 12, 1876(?)— June 16, 1941 Stage and film actress; toured the British Empire and the United States in child dramatic parts; featured in the *Passing Shows* of 1917 and 1918 and in *Hands Up*, and played her biggest role in *Sweet Adeline* from 1929 to 1930; made her last stage appearance in 1935, in *Merrily We Roll Along*; played many supporting roles in the films; died an inmate of the Actors' Fund Home.

References

Cosmopolitan 56:120-1 D '13 pors
Green Bk Mag 8:692-9 O '12 pors
N Y Drama 72:19 D 16 '14 pors
Sat Eve Post 209:16-17+ O 24 '36 por (p104)

International Motion Picture Almanac
Who's Who in the Theatre

Obituaries

N Y Times p21 Je 17 '41 por
Time 37:69 Je 23 '41
Variety 143:43-4 Je 18 '41

FRANKLIN, JAY Apr. 27, 1897- Author; columnist; radio commentator .

Address: b. National Press Bldg, Washington, D. C.; h. 2130 LeRoy Pl, N. W., Washington, **D. C.**

Jay Franklin is the pseudonym for the prolific author of 18 works of fiction and non-fiction under various pen names including the Unofficial Observer, Innocent Bystander, Diplomat, Jay Franklin, John Carter as well as his own name, John Franklin Carter. He has written mystery stories, social commentaries, novels, biographies, articles; he con-

tributes a daily Washington column, "We, The People," to the newspapers; he broadcasts for NBC. Probably the most generally accepted summation of all his activity is the comment a reviewer once made: "Mr. Franklin is brilliant, cynical, occasionally cock-eyed and always exciting."

Jay Franklin's latest book is *1940* (1940), in which he discusses the men, measures and tendencies of today and forecasts the political outline of tomorrow. Called both tremendously telling and "provocative but not always accurate," it is one of a number of books which have analyzed the current scene. His first came in 1926, *Man Is War*. Two years later appeared *Conquest*, a "remarkably keen criticism of American political life and of our foreign policies." *What This Country Needs* was published in 1931 and *What We Are About To Receive* in 1932. In 1939 *The Future Is Ours*, a survey of Federal power activities as represented by the TVA, Bonneville and other projects, came out. In all of these books, Franklin draws upon "a rich store of economic and social understanding."

He has approached the contemporary political scene from the personal angle, too. *The New Dealers* (1934), which he wrote with others, is the story of the men in and behind the Government which came into being in 1932. It was called superficial and prejudiced, but even unsympathetic reviewers had to credit it with being entertaining reading matter. This book was followed by *American Messiahs* (1935) and *Our Lords and Masters* (1935). In 1937 appeared a study of a single man, *La Guardia*, which told of the career of New York's Mayor "with sparkle and dash born of the enthusiasm of an ardent New Dealer."

Much of what Jay Franklin learned in Washington has gone into his mystery stories as well as into his social studies. Their very titles are significant: *Murder in the Embassy* (1930); *Murder in the State Department* (1930); *Scandal in the Chancery* (1931); *The Corpse on the White House Lawn* (1932); *Death in the Senate* (1933); and *The Brain Trust Murder* (1935). All these stories star Dennis Tyler, the diplomatic detective; all are "delightfully dizzy" and "larkish." In 1937 Jay Franklin departed somewhat from his usual lines of creativeness to write *The Rectory Family*, a reminiscent novel of life in a Massachusetts college town in the early 1900's.

Franklin's name appears frequently as a contributor to *Liberty, Atlantic Monthly, Forum, Reader's Digest* and other magazines. It appears every day over his syndicated column; it is heard over the radio in an electrically transcribed series, *The Week in Washington*. Today he is sticking to "Jay Franklin," but explains the multiplicity of his pseudonyms by the fact that he spent so many years in the government service that he couldn't use his own name—it might have embarrassed his superiors or confused his readers.

This pro-New Deal author and commentator was born John Franklin Carter, Jr., in Fall River, Massachusetts, the son of the Reverend John Franklin and Alice Schermerhorn (Henry) Carter. His father moved later to

JAY FRANKLIN

Williamstown, Massachusetts, where he was rector of St. John's Episcopal Church. Young John was educated at St. Mark's School in Southboro, Massachusetts and at Yale University. At Yale he specialized in European history under Dr. Charles Seymour (see sketch this issue), Yale's president since 1937, and received his Bachelor's Degree in 1920.

During the closing years of the First World War, Franklin was serving at the State Department and at the United States' embassies at Rome and at Constantinople. In 1920 he enrolled at the École des Sciences Politiques in Paris but left shortly after to become private secretary to the American Ambassador to Rome. He kept this position a year and then returned to the United States. But 1922 saw him back in Rome, this time as Rome correspondent for the London *Daily Chronicle*. After a year at this the New York *Times* hired him and kept him working until 1928 as general reporter, ship news reporter and in the Sunday department.

In 1928 he re-entered the State Department as economics specialist in the Division of Western Europe and remained there until 1932 when, after a tour of special duty in the Far Eastern Division, he resigned to support himself by independent writing, mostly by acting as Washington correspondent of *Liberty* Magazine. In 1934 he returned to government service as special adviser to Rexford Tugwell (see sketch this issue) in the Department of Agriculture, organized the information program for the Rural Resettlement (now Farm Security) Administration and then resigned in March 1936 to write his daily column, "We, The People."

From August 1938 to August 1939 Jay Franklin toured the country, reporting en route on the "State of the Nation" twice each week for the National Broadcasting Company. Then, at the opening of the 1939 winter session of

Congress, he debated the news of the week in Washington with Mark Sullivan in a program called *Public Interest in Democracy*. His latest radio series is the transcribed *The Week in Washington*.

Jay Franklin was married in 1927 to Sheila Sutherland. They have one daughter, Sonia.

References

Newsweek 5:36 Je 15 '35 por
Time 37:63-4 Ap 7 '41
Who's Who in America
Who's Who in Journalism

FRAZER, SIR JAMES (GEORGE) Jan. 1, 1854—May 7, 1941 Anthropologist; folklore authority; in 1890 appeared his small volume which was the first version of his great work, *The Golden Bough;* by 1915 it filled 12 large volumes; this work, a vast collection of savage and civilized beliefs and customs, is considered among the greatest works of anthropology; the second of his major works, *Totemism and Exogamy,* was issued in 1910; his third major study was *The Belief in Immortality and the Worship of the Dead* which appeared between 1913 and 1924; in his opinion his outstanding work was *Totemica,* which appeared in 1937; his wife, the former Lilly Grove, a writer whom he married in 1896, worked with him on much of his research; she died 12 hours after his death on May 7.

References

Liv Age 348:135-9 Ap '35
Author's and Writer's Who's Who
Dawson, W. R. ed. Frazer Lectures p172-89 1922-32
Downie, R. A. James George Frazer 1941
Gosse, Sir E. W. More Books on the Table p27-35 1923
Hind, C. L. More Authors and I p107-12 1922
Men of Turmoil p337-45 1935
Who's Who

Obituaries

Christian Cent 58:766 Je 4 '41
N Y Times p23 My 8 '41 por
Pub W 139:2014 My 17 '41
Time 37:72+ My 19 '41 por

FREDERICK, JOHN T(OWNER) Feb. 1, 1893- Radio book critic; author; educator
Address: b. Northwestern University, Evanston, Ill; h. Glennie, Alcona County, Mich.

Since 1937 John T. Frederick, literary critic, editor and educator, has conducted a weekly book review program, *Of Men and Books,* sponsored by Northwestern University, on the Columbia Broadcasting System. This broadcast, currently scheduled on Saturdays around noontime, originates in Chicago (where Professor Frederick teaches modern letters at Northwestern's Medill School of Journalism) and is heard over more than 50 CBS stations.

So popular has this purely cultural broadcast become that when Mr. Frederick offered

FREDERICK, JOHN T.—*Continued*

his listeners a list of 50 books recommended for Christmas 1940, more than 2,000 requests for copies came in. It is said that the radio public sends in about a thousand letters a month in response to the program. Not only are book readers interested in Professor Frederick's excellent talks, but booksellers as well, who report an increase in book sales because of them. And in several cities where the program is heard local literary clubs meet especially to hear it.

Of Men and Books owes its increasing popularity in large part to the fact that Professor Frederick is a remarkably good speaker who talks of books simply and informally,

JOHN T. FREDERICK

from a warmly sympathetic viewpoint, with both understanding and humor. His manner of quiet sincerity and convincing enthusiasms for what is good in the current output makes listeners want to read the books themselves. Moreover, the program is unusual: often Mr. Frederick invites famous "guest" authors to talk informally about their writings with him. Among those who have spoken on the program are Dr. Lin Yutang, Archibald MacLeish, Marquis Childs and Robert Nathan. Another distinguishing feature is that at least half the books discussed never find their way into best-seller lists.

"That doesn't mean they aren't worth reading," Professor Frederick says. "On the contrary, they frequently are of greater literary merit than works that sell by the hundreds of thousands. But they aren't written by popular authors, or as well publicized. The American reading public consequently is quite unaware of their existence. And that's why I review them. I want my listeners to become acquainted with authors of really important books."

John Towner Frederick's own life and accomplishments are as interesting as some of the biographies he has discussed on *Of Men and Books*. He was born on a farm two miles from Corning, Iowa, February 1, 1893, only child of Oliver Roberts and May E. (Towner) Frederick. From the day he was big enough to handle a hoe he worked on his father's farm. He rode a pony to the town's grade school, and was graduated from the Corning High School in 1909. While still a boy he was tutored in Greek and German to earn advance credit for the University. Determined to get a college education, he entered the State University of Iowa, where he washed dishs and scrubbed floors during the first year to pay his expenses. He then stayed out two years and taught school: at $75 a month he was principal, athletic coach and sole high school teacher at Prescott, Iowa from 1911 to 1913. Then he returned to the University and finished his course in two years, taking an active part in literary affairs. He was president of the senior class; and it was during his senior year, too, that he founded *The Midland,* a magazine which later under his editorship was to acquire a national reputation.

Soon after his graduation in 1915, Frederick married Esther Paulus of Iowa City. They have two children, John Joseph and James Oliver. He taught in the English Department at the University of Iowa for two years, receiving his M. A. in 1917. For the next two years he was head of the English Department at the State Teachers College, Moorhead, Minnesota; taught again at the University of Iowa; and after a year at the University of Pittsburgh, returned to Iowa as full professor, teaching there until 1930.

Besides teaching, Frederick found time to write two excellently received novels of Midwestern farm life: *Druida* (1923) and *Green Bush* (1925). He published also four college textbooks: *A Handbook of Short Story Writing* (1924), and, with Leo L. Ward, *Good Writing* (1932), *Reading for Writing* (1935), second edition, (1941) and *Present-Day Stories* (1941). It was during the years at Iowa City that *The Midland,* originally conceived as a regional magazine, won a national circulation and reputation, rated highly by the late Edward J. O'Brien and other critics for the high standard of its contents. Under Frederick's editorship, and later his coeditorship with Professor Frank Luther Mott, *The Midland* first printed the work of many writers who have since become well known, such as Albert Halper, James T. Farrell, Paul Engle, Ruth Suckow, Paul Corey, Marquis Childs, MacKinley Kantor, Phil Stong and August Derleth.

To widen the scope of *The Midland,* Professor Frederick moved to Chicago in 1930 and took part-time teaching positions at Northwestern University and the University of Notre Dame. He was compelled to suspend the magazine in 1933, however, for lack of money. In 1936 he became full professor at Northwestern's Medill School of Journalism.

He served also, 1937 to 1940, as regional director of the WPA Writers' Project.

Professor Frederick has continued to be interested in farming as well as books. In 1919 he bought a tract of wild land near Glennie, Alcona County, Michigan. It consists of 1,400 acres, including two lakes, woodland, pasture and 200 acres of farm land. In partnership with his father, and with the aid of his two sons, John and James (the latter now in the University of Michigan law school), Frederick raises cattle, sheep and alfalfa. They have built a large stone house, laid with their own hands. Mr. and Mrs. Frederick both like gardening and now spend as much of the year as possible at Glennie. If he ever retires, Frederick says, this farm will be his year-round home.

References

Pub W 136 :2186 D 16 '39

Who's Who in America 1928-29

FREDMAN, SAMUEL, RABBI (frĕd'-màn) Mar. 7, 1886—Apr. 14, 1941 Nationally known leader of Philadelphia's conservative Jewish clergy; had been rabbi for nearly 28 years; president of the Philadelphia Board of Jewish Ministers; active in many civic and charitable groups.

References

Who's Who in American Jewry

Obituaries

N Y Times p23 Ap 15 '41 por

FREEMAN-THOMAS, FREEMAN, 1ST MARQUESS OF WILLINGDON See Willingdon, F. F.-T., 1st Marquess of

HOLLIS FRENCH

FRENCH, HOLLIS June 26, 1868—Nov. 21, 1940 Consulting engineer and president of the Robert Breck Brigham Hospital in Boston; was authority on early American silver and author of works on it.

References

Who's Who in Engineering

Obituaries

N Y Herald Tribune p18 N 22 '40

N Y Times p23 N 22 '40

Pub W 138 :2128 D 7 '40

FREUNDLICH, HERBERT (MAX FINLAY) (froind'lĭk) Jan. 28, 1880—Mar. 30, 1941 Chemist; held post of distinguished service professor of colloidal chemistry at the University of Minnesota since 1938; served as professor at the University of Berlin, the Kaiser Wilhelm Institute in Berlin and University College in London; author of a number of authoritative books on chemistry.

References

Who's Who

Obituaries

N Y Times p23 Ap 1 '41

FROHMAN, DANIEL Aug. 22, 1851— Dec. 26, 1940 Dean of American theatrical producers; began his career in the middle '80s; introduced many noted stars; retired about 1912; was active as president (1903-

DANIEL FROHMAN

1940) of the Actor's Fund of America; wrote his autobiography, *Daniel Frohman Presents,* in 1935.

References

Lit Digest 116 :9 S 2 '33 por

Musical Courier 76 :18+ Je 20 '18

(Continued next page)

FROHMAN, DANIEL—*Continued*

New Yorker 9:21-4 O 28 '33; 9:21-4
N 4 '33

Photoplay Mag 25:59 Ap '24 por

Frohman, D. Daniel Frohman Presents
1935

Marcosson, I. F. Adventures in Interviewing p290-309 1919

Sobel, B. ed. Theatre Handbook 1940

Who's Who in America

Who's Who in American Jewry

Who's Who in the Theatre

Obituaries

N Y Times p14 D 27 '40 por
Newsweek 17:4 Ja 6 '41

FULLER, S(AMUEL) R(ICHARD), JR.
Feb. 19, 1879- Former chief of the Materials
Branch, the United States Office of Production
Management; rayon manufacturer; author

Address: b. 261 Fifth Ave, New York City

Randolph Macdonald

S. R. FULLER, JR.

Chief of the Materials Branch of the Office
of Production Management until June 23, 1941
was S. R. Fuller, Jr., according to *Time* a
"chubby, good-natured" man who "looks like
Cinemactor Eugene Pallette with spectacles."
Mr. Fuller is known to business colleagues as a
rayon manufacturer and may still be remembered by boys now out of their teens as the
author of a series of books for ambitious young
heroes, beginning with *Winning His Shoulder-
straps* (1909) and culminating with *The Cadet
Sergeant* (1930). (His pen name was Norman
Brainerd.)

Samuel Richard Fuller, Jr., was born in
Corning, New York, the son of Samuel
Richard and Leora Campbell (Brainerd)
Fuller. After studying at the De Veaux
School in Niagara Falls from 1890 to 1896 he

spent two years as a student at Trinity College, Hartford, Connecticut, where he joined
Alpha Beta Phi fraternity. For some time
he was employed in an iron-casting company.
It was 1905 when he married Lillian Alice
Russell (they now have one son and three
married daughters), and four years later he
emerged as the author of the first book in
the series mentioned, obviously both moral and
manly in tone. *Winning the Eagle Prize*
(1910); *Winning the Junior Cup* (1911); and
Winning His Army Blue (1917) followed,
but it was the Navy that Mr. Fuller joined
when the United States entered the First
World War.

A commander in the United States Naval
Reserve Force, Mr. Fuller was soon working
under Franklin Delano Roosevelt, then Assistant Secretary of the Navy, as boss of the
Navy Department's steel and machine-tool
procurement. In this position his previous
experience in the steel and malleable iron-
casting industry and his reputation as a trouble
shooter were possibly even more helpful than
his talents for making everything come out
all right in the end.

From 1919 to 1921 Mr. Fuller was president
of the Stafford Company of Readville, Massachusetts. Then in 1921 he went to Sherbrooke,
Quebec to the Canadian Connecticut Cotton
Mills, Limited, as chairman of the board and
treasurer of the company. Tire-fabric mills
were suffering from the post-War slump; Fuller decided that the trouble was overtooling.
While putting the company's plants into shape
he also managed to find time to breed
thoroughbred Jersey cattle on his Grayburn
Farms in Waterville, Quebec, and it was 1929
before he returned to the United States. In
that year he was sent to the North American
Rayon plants in Tennessee, then having labor
troubles, according to *Business Week* "to
straighten out a situation which appeared tense
to the state militia posted around the factories."
He stayed as the president of the North
American Rayon Corporation (then the American Glanzstoff Corporation) and of the American Bemberg Corporation of New York City,
and changed what had been a steady run of
deficits into a steady run of profits.

It was the middle of 1935 when trouble
once more arose—this time at the Alaskan
settlement project at Matanuska. With
luggage packed for a trip to Europe, Mr.
Fuller received an emergency call from
the United States Government, which remembered his talents. He canceled his
sailing, went to Alaska, and there was given
a free hand to straighten things out as
special administrative assistant to the
Alaska Rural Rehabilitation Corporation.
After only a short period in Matanuska he
returned to his New York office, and there
he remained until in 1940 he began commuting
to Washington in an advisory capacity, later
taking up residence there and devoting most of
his time to his new duties.

As head of the Production Planning Board
which advised the Office of Production Management before his appointment to the Materials Branch itself in April 1941, it **was**

Mr. Fuller's responsibility "to get a hilltop perspective of the present and future, advise the United States how to avoid crooked paths and hopelessly blocked roads . . . [to do] centralized planning of the defense program, long-range planning for the sag that must inevitably come when the United States has more swords than ploughshares." The Board's first move after its creation in February 1941 was to start a study of defense production both in the First World War and the present emergency, with special emphasis on M-Day plans.

Having completed his service in governmental work, Mr. Fuller returned to New York to govern the affairs of his two firms as a full-time job again. Occasionally, too, he has spoken on national problems, his approach typified by his remarks at the Economic Club of New York in December 1941. At that time he insisted that demand for price control represented a governmental "reaching for power": prices couldn't be controlled unless wages were. Besides, "If Uncle Sam isn't able to lick John L. Lewis, he'd better think twice before tackling Adolf Hitler."

References

Business Week p14 Mr 1 '41 por
N Y Sun p12 F 22 '41
Time 37:20 Mr 3 '41 por
Who's Who in America
Who's Who in Commerce and Industry

WALTER DEANE FULLER

FULLER, WALTER DEANE June 5, 1882- Former president of the National Association of Manufacturers; president of the Curtis Publishing Company

Address: b. Curtis Publishing Co, Independence Sq, Philadelphia, Pa; h. Penn Valley, Narberth, Pa.

In December 1940 Walter Deane Fuller of the Curtis Publishing Company was elected president of the National Association of Manufacturers for 1941. Like his predecessor, Henning W. Prentis, Jr., Mr. Fuller saw as the main task of the N. A. M. the achievement of total preparedness. "We must make doubly sure," he said at the N. A. M.'s convention, "that everything within the power of management is done to meet the public's expectancy in armament." Shortly afterward he announced over the radio that industry recognized as its three major problems for 1941 "first, swift and efficient production for national defense, its supreme task; second, maintenance of as high a scale of living as the defense program will permit; and third, preparation now to make adjustments after the emergency is over." Because of Mr. Fuller's past record and present activities, industry and the public were agreed that he would be able to "mobilize the N. A. M.'s growing membership in all sections of the country enthusiastically behind the defense speed-up."

As N. A. M. head until December 1941 Fuller has urged a longer work week, a ceiling on wages, a revision of the Wagner Act to end mass picketing and the suspension of antitrust prosecutions against industries collaborating to heighten preparedness efficiency—all in the interests of national defense. He has called strikes the "major bottleneck" in defense production. He has asserted (July 1941) that the "production and delivery of vital armament equipment has not been delayed to date by a shortage of aluminum." Many of these statements have been made at the "defense clinics" which the N. A. M. set up all over the country.

It was while he was making such pronouncements that he revealed, on May 16, 1941, that the *Saturday Evening Post*, major publication of the Curtis Publishing Company and isolationist up to that time, was going to do an "about face" in its attitude toward the international situation. Fuller explained by saying: "We are in an undeclared war now, and the best thing we can do is face it and get behind it as fast as possible."

Walter Deane Fuller, who has held one of the most important positions an American businessman can have, started his career on a very low rung of the ladder. He was born in Corning, Iowa, the son of Walter and Nellie Elizabeth (Deane) Fuller, and spent his boyhood in Norwich, Connecticut. Here he attended grammar and high school, later took courses at evening school and by correspondence, and supported himself by summertime jobs. Here, too, he worked at his first full-time job—as clerk in the Dime Savings Bank, from 1899 to 1903. Four years' experience in Norwich were followed by another clerical banking position, this time in the Bank of Metropolis in New York City.

It was in 1904 that Mr. Fuller started out in the publishing field, as salesman for the Butterick Publishing Company. Within a year he had become junior office manager. Shortly after, however, he shifted to the Crowell Publishing Company and stayed there

FULLER, WALTER DEANE—*Continued*
until 1906, as junior office manager. Then
came two years as manager of the subscription division of the S. S. McClure Company
and finally, in 1908, his first position at the
Curtis Publishing Company.

At the Curtis Publishing Company, Mr.
Fuller was made manager of the circulation
sales office force. By 1911 he was manager
of the accounting department and by 1916
comptroller of the firm. One year later he
was made secretary and acted in that capacity
for 10 years, during one of the most profitable periods in the firm's history. His next
step up was to second vice-president in 1927;
his next after that to first vice-president and
secretary, in 1932. Since November 30, 1934
he has been president of the company, head
of its 12-story building at Independence
Square in Philadelphia and of its four magazines (*Saturday Evening Post, Ladies' Home
Journal, Country Gentleman* and *Jack and
Jill*), which have a combined circulation of
over eight million.

It was because of his business record and
his position as president of this large company that Fuller was drafted by Governor
James of Pennsylvania in 1938 to direct a
huge and hurried job-mobilization drive. In
November 1939 he and a committee of Pennsylvania businessmen started a whirlwind campaign. They enlisted business, religious and
civic groups; they urged every trader, every
retailer, every plant to develop new outlets,
to increase production, to start construction
and alteration projects. In March 1940 Fuller
announced that his committee had created at
least 30,000 new jobs and decreased the number of Pennsylvania citizens on relief. The
first fact has been disputed; the second has
not.

Mr. Fuller has had other positions of civic
importance: he is chairman of the Planning Commission of Lower Merion Township in Pennsylvania and of the Penn Valley
Civic Association. He has, of course, been
active in businessmen's associations, too, even
before he was elected to the N. A. M. presidency. He has been a vice-president of the Pennsylvania Chamber of Commerce and of the
National Publishers Association, a director of
the Society for the Advancement of Management, and was, before becoming president of
the N. A. M., a vice-president and head of
its 1940 Congress Platform Committee.

Despite all his business and civic commitments, Mr. Fuller occasionally finds time
for his four clubs (Union League, Poor Richard, Bala Gold, Seaside Park Yacht). He
has three children by his first marriage and
was married a second time, in 1931, to Mae
Schaeffer.

References

Newsweek 15:53 Mr 11 '40 por; 16:31-
3+ D 23 '40 por
Time 34:78 D 4 '39 por
Who's Who in America
Who's Who in Commerce and Industry

GABIN, JEAN (gä-băN') May 17, 1904-
Film actor
Address: b. 20th Century-Fox Film Corp,
Hollywood, Calif.

In the spring of 1941, New York City,
which has received so many visitors from
war-torn Europe, experienced a slight flurry
at the arrival of "the most glamorous refugee of them all." Jean Gabin, the leading
motion-picture actor of France, a muscular
gentleman with a moody, Gallic grace all
his own, came to New York right after
the première of his film, *Pepe le Moko*.
Then he flew to the Coast to start working
for 20th Century-Fox, for which he is expected to make his American debut in *Moon
Tide* in the spring of 1942.

Pepe le Moko, shown here four years
after its production in France, gave the
American public an opportunity to compare Gabin's performance with that of
another French actor, Charles Boyer, who
played the same role in *Algiers*, a Walter
Wanger picture based on *Pepe le Moko*.
It was felt by at least one or two of the
critics that "Jean Gabin's tough unsentimental performance of the title role was
much more credible and revealing than
Charles Boyer's sad-eyed mooning in *Algiers*."

Gabin has never hesitated to play humble or dubious characters: he made his
fame in France by playing the *salopard*,
the average tough artisan or mechanic.
It has been said, for that reason, that Gabin
has put the forgotten man into French
films. He has always taken the part of a
strong individualist, a social outcast, a
man in the toils of a secret tragedy to
which he finally succumbs. "He never sub-
stitutes mere charm for an honest and
subtle characterization, constantly related
to the other portrayals in the motion picture." For that reason, perhaps, he has
been called "the French Spencer Tracy,"
and he modestly acknowledges the resemblance—"not physically, but there is a
mental relationship." Perhaps the resemblance lies in the realism and integrity of
their interpretations.

Ever since Gabin was brought to the
attention of the American public (particularly after *Grand Illusion* was shown here
in 1938) Hollywood has been trying to
get him. But Gabin was content to stay
where he was; besides, he suspected, with
some justification, that pictures of the
type he preferred would be subject to censorship in the United States. Accordingly
he remained in France, humorously pleading a gourmet's attachment to his native
land's wines and foods. It took war and
German occupation to uproot him. He saw
no future in making German propaganda
films, the only possible occupation left him
today.

Jean Gabin was born in Paris in 1904.
His family name was Monçorge. Both of
his parents were theatrical people, his
father, Joseph Monçorge, performing under the

name of Jean Gabin, which his son later adopted. His mother, who was professionally known as Hélène Petit, died when Jean was 13. Jean, the youngest of six children, spent his boyhood in the village of Meriel, where he was brought up by his sister. He was a young incorrigible in school, particularly when he was taken away from his beloved Meriel, where he had studied under the gentle tutelage of "père Dervelloy," and sent to a Paris lycée.

Young Gabin, whose sole ambition in those days was to be independent, ran away from the lycée and at 16 became a cement mixer at 12 francs a day. Later he worked in an automobile factory. He had a passion for mechanics and in those days wanted above all to run a loco-motive. This dream of independence lasted only a year. Gabin's father, an ardent actor, who loved the stage above everything, had different ambitions for his son's career. He wanted to see him become a comedian. That was how it happened that when Jean was only 17 his father took him to see his friend, the impressario Fréjol, who gave him a job at the *Folies Bergère*. Young Gabin, who at that time did not share his father's love for the stage, went about carrying the inevitable spear in a daze of misery. Repeatedly he brought to the frivolous roles he played some-thing of the heavy tragic quality that later made him an outstanding dramatic actor. His apprenticeship was interrupted by a year of military service at Lorient. (Gabin is a seaman of second rank.)

Then it was back to vaudeville, to playing at Bouffes Parisiens in operettas with frivo-lous titles like *La Dame en Décolleté* and *Trois Jeunes Filles Nues*. An enchanting in-terlude was a tour in South America, with Gabin singing cabaret songs of the Chevalier type. When he came back he played in shows starring Mistinguette and Elsie Janis. It was while playing with Meg Lemonnier in *Arsène Lupin* that he got an offer to play a small role in a film called *Chacun La Chance* (1933). He agreed and was never seen on the stage again. He played in a multitude of pictures, some of them made in Germany, including films like *La Foule Hurle, Coeur de Lilas, Étoiles de Valencia, La Belle Marinière,* Pabst's *De Haut en Bas.* He became rather well known, married an actress called Do-riane in 1932 (they are divorced now) and certainly made a much better living in films than in the theatre. But real fame came when he met Julien Duvivier, a director known for his ability to discover promising actors, who sensed the latent dramatic quality in Gabin and utilized it in *Maria Chapdelaine* (1934).

The picture was shot on the spot in Can-ada, and after it was shown, Gabin was made. *Maria Chapdelaine* won the Grand Prix and Gabin's performance was loudly acclaimed by the critics. When it was shown in the United States in 1935, it was adjudged one of the 10 best pictures of the year. After this, there followed the period of collaboration with Duvi-vier in which Gabin's popularity as an actor soared. He became the unchallenged box-

office champion of France. Except for a pic-ture like *Golgotha,* in which Gabin played Pontius Pilate, he specialized in parts in which he had a chance to produce the simple hard-bitten characterizations that made him famous. With Duvivier he made *Bandera, Belle Équipe,* (produced in the United States in 1938 under the title *We Were Five*), *Pepe le Moko.*

JEAN GABIN

Never a "contract slave," Gabin made it a rule never to begin a film without insisting on his right to choose his own scenario and di-rector. Most of his scripts were written by Spaak, who was responsible for the delightful *La Kermesse Héroïque.* After Julien Du-vivier left France, Gabin teamed up with a director of equal genius, Jean Renoir. This collaboration had equally successful results: *Les Bas Fonds* (released as *Lower Depths* in the United States), *Grand Illusion, Le Mes-sager, Gueule d'Amour* were among them. He also played in *Quai des Brumes* (called *The Port of Shadows* here), with Marcel Carne di-recting, and his gripping performance as an engineer with a homicidal mania in *La Bête Humaine* will long be remembered. The last picture in which he played was *Daybreak,* "the last major product of an industry that was as long on brains as it was short on budget."

When the War came, Gabin, with many other film stars, was fighting for his country, serving as a second rank seaman on a mine sweeper. When the German Army broke through in June 1940, he was on furlough in Drieux. He left the city 15 minutes before the invaders came and rejoined his naval unit in the West Channel ports. After the arm-istice he was demobilized at Toulon, lived in Nice for a while and then went on to the United States via Lisbon. The next step was to learn English.

Reporters who interviewed Gabin on his ar-rival agreed unanimously that the Gabin

GABIN, JEAN—*Continued*

charm carries over from the screen. No pretty boy, Gabin is wide-shouldered, tall, muscular, with rugged features. His hair, which photographs blond, is really "a shining silver gray," and his eyes are a startling blue in a sun-bronzed face. Gabin has retained from his childhood a love of the land, had a farm of his own in France. He still is mechanically inclined and has a warm spot in his heart for locomotives. He is somewhat of a gourmet, likes to hunt, is rather moody and taciturn, sometimes quick-tempered, but has been described by fellow actors as a good *copain.*

References

N Y Herald Tribune VI p3 Jl 28 '40;
   p7 Mr 5 '41 por; VI p3 Ap 13 '41
N Y Post p5 Mr 1 '41 por; p5 Mr 8 '41
N Y Sun p12 Mr 3 '41
N Y Times IX p5 Mr 9 '41
PM p56 Mr 16 '41 pors
Theatre Arts Mo 23:433 Je '39 por
Visages et Contes du Cinema 21:3-43
   '39

International Motion Picture Almanac

GANNETT, LEWIS (STILES) Oct. 3, 1891- Journalist; book critic

Address: b. New York Herald Tribune, 230 W. 41st St, New York City; h. West Cornwall, Conn.

Ben Pinchot

LEWIS GANNETT

The New York *Herald Tribune's* daily book-review column, "Books and Things," has since 1931 been one of the paper's outstanding features. In that year Lewis Gannett, well known journalist and author, became its conductor. Gannett's wide experience as a newspaper-

man in this country and abroad, as well as his keen interest in the current output of fiction and non-fiction, have given him unusual qualifications for the book critic's exacting job. Readers find his estimates dependable, his taste discriminating, his style informal but sure, and always readable. To vary the column and to provide a cross section of opinion, Gannett has for the past year or two turned over "Books and Things" on Mondays to alternating young critics of fiction.

Lewis Stiles Gannett was born in Rochester, New York on October 3, 1891, the son of William Channing and Mary Thorn (Lewis) Gannett. He had one older sister, Charlotte Katharine MacDowell, who died October 23, 1940. His father was a Unitarian minister, his mother a Quaker. Young Lewis went to the public schools in Rochester. He grew up in a "house full of books," and from an early age loved reading. But his boyhood ambition was to be a naturalist: he took long hikes through the countryside around Rochester, learned a great deal about the local trees and plants and became especially interested in birds. At the age of 10, he says, he carefully compiled a bird book. The budding young naturalist-author was pretty badly disillusioned when it failed to find a publisher, but that didn't stop him from going on with his chosen career. He had a side line, however. When he was 12 he was elected Class Poet. This honor, it seems, came to him on the strength of one poem, the subject matter of which aroused the lively admiration of his classmates when it was surreptitiously circulated. But the school principal somehow failed to appreciate young Gannett's *tour de force* when it fell into her hands.

Destined for Harvard (his father, grandfather, and great-grandfather before him had been Harvard graduates), Lewis Gannett entered the University to study natural science. For three summers he worked in the Marine Biological Laboratory at Woods Hole, Massachusetts; but late in his college course he "shifted to philosophy," then did graduate work in economics. He received his B. A. in 1913, his M. A. in 1915, after studying for a year at the Universities of Berlin and Freiburg.

After his graduate year at Harvard he decided he wanted to see the world and came to New York City intending to learn about life as a taxi or truck driver. Fate took him in hand and made him a reporter for the New York *World* (1916-17). Then came the War; and Gannett, an ardent pacifist, joined the American Friends' Service Committee in France (1917-19). He acted as correspondent for *The Survey* and other papers at the Paris Peace Conference. On his return he joined the staff of *The Nation,* a position he held until 1928. He was also (1922-23) American correspondent for the *Manchester Guardian.* During his first year on *The Nation* he visited Western Europe and Russia; and his observations on a survey trip (1925-26) to Japan, China, Mongolia, etc., were published in his book, *Young China* (1926).

Having seen a good deal of Europe and Asia, but never having traveled extensively in his own country, Gannett in 1933 took the first of his cross-continent trips by automobile. He made a leisurely, informal, firsthand study of places and people in the great Middle States, and in the West and Northwest. What he saw, and what he learned from talking with persons of varied occupations and interests, he set down in the book *Sweet Land* (1934). This trip, Gannett says, gave him more solid pleasure than all his years of book reviewing. Three years later he made another such cross-country trek behind the wheel; and in 1939 he followed still a third route from coast to coast.

"Driving across America," he wrote, "gives one at least a sense of the magnificent distances that separate the sections of this continental America. It gives one also a realization that the twin gods of modern America, the idols to which we pay tithes from Calais, Maine to San Diego, are roads and schools." On this trip, talking with all types of people, he found that Americans weren't "the same" all over, just as "the countryside behind the signs is never twice the same."

In 1917 he married the author, Mary Ross; two children were born to them, Michael Ross and Ruth Stiles. The couple separated in 1929; in 1931 he married Ruth Chrisman Arens, artist, who has illustrated several books for young people, and who did the drawings for Gannett's own book about America.

Mr. Gannett's reviews and articles have appeared in other publications besides the *Herald Tribune*. He has also taken part in various progressive activities, and is a member of the American Newspaper Guild. He has never lost his love for plant and animal life and is an enthusiastic gardener on his farm at West Cornwall, Connecticut. There he and Mrs. Gannett take pride in their young fruit trees and vegetable garden, and in canning their own produce. Gannett's own specialty and favorite is his Golden Bantam corn.

References

N Y Herald Tribune p1, 4 Je 17 '35 por
Pub W 134:2049 D 10 '38 por; 137:1734
    My 4 '40 por; 139:1818-19 My 3 '41
America's Young Men 1936-37
Who's Who in America

GANSO, EMIL (găn'sō) Apr. 14, 1895— Apr. 18, 1941 Internationally known artist and lithographer; joined the University of Iowa faculty in September 1940; in 1926 he was a night worker in a bakery in Manhattan when he first won recognition for exceptional talent; his paintings are represented in collections of America's leading museums.

References

Art Digest 10:12 Ap 1 '36 il; 14:27 Ja 1
    '40; 15:16 Ja 1 '41
Milwaukee Inst Bul 14:3 My '40
Time 27:48 Mr 30 '36
Who's Who in American Art

Obituaries

N Y Times p15 Ap 19 '41
Time 37:71 Ap 28 '41

GARLAND, JUDY June 10, 1922(?)- Film actress

Address: c/o Metro-Goldwyn-Mayer Studios, Culver City, Calif.

JUDY GARLAND

Of the multitude of babies who sing *Jingle Bells* on the stages of local theatres at Christmas time, extremely few become stage or screen stars. As a matter of fact, when Francis, Jr., at 30 months sang in the Christmas program at her father's theatre, it is probable that the audience discovered neither the sex nor the latent talent. Those who saw and heard the performance of Judy Garland in *The Wizard of Oz* 15 years later, however, doubted neither her femininity nor her competence.

Francis, Jr., was really Frances Gumm, third daughter of Frank and Ethel (Milne) Gumm. During a vacation in Wisconsin, Frank Gumm, a graduate of Sewanee University, got a job as singer in a movie house. There he met and married the theatre's pianist and the two toured in vaudeville as "Jack and Virginia Lee, Sweet Southern Singers," until their first child was born. Since it was necessary to settle down in order to raise their family properly, the Gumms bought a movie theatre in Grand Rapids, Minnesota, where Frances was born and where she made her debut. In 1927 they moved to Los Angeles, where the children went to school. They had expected to buy another movie house in some nearby town, but Mr. Gumm's health failed until finally he was no longer able to work.

The three Gumm sisters, then twelve, seven and five, had long been a "natural" dancing and singing team. Their mother made them costumes and trained them in a routine, with herself at the piano. Their first appearance was at a civic banquet, where the three girls together earned $1.50. After years of dis-

GARLAND, JUDY—*Continued*

couragement, the team "clicked" at the Oriental Theatre in Chicago, where they had been
billed as "The Glum Sisters." The master of
ceremonies, George Jessel, suggested that they
change their name, and at the age of 12
Frances Gumm became Judy Garland.

The next year the "Three Garlands" had a
season engagement at Lake Tahoe. A movie
agent heard Judy sing and wanted her to
try out for the moving pictures. The legend
has it that Mrs. Gumm demurred because
she didn't think Judy was "pretty enough."
Three days after they returned to Los Angeles,
however, the agent turned up and took Judy
and her father to MGM, where he secured
for her a seven-year contract, reputedly the
only one given on the lot without either screen
or sound tests.

At first Judy was not given major parts.
She appeared in *Pigskin Parade* in 1936,
Broadway Melody of 1938 and *Thoroughbreds
Don't Cry* in 1937, and in *Everybody Sing,
Love Finds Andy Hardy* and *Listen Darling*
in 1938. Her first big part came in *The
Wizard of Oz*, in which she proved herself
capable of maintaining a sustained role with
even excellence and convinced Hollywood that
she possessed one of the best voices of its
kind in the film capital. In 1939 she received the Academy Award for the best
juvenile performance of the previous year
and was promoted out of juvenile roles by
her studio. In *Ziegfeld Girl* (1941), although
the romance given her was of the "puppy love"
variety, her part called for more adult characterization than had her previous roles, and
her costumes were designed by Adrian, a
distinction that lifted her definitely out of
the juvenile class. In *Life Begins for Andy
Hardy* and *Babes on Broadway*, (both 1941),
she had lead roles.

In July 1941 Judy was married to David
Rose at Las Vegas, Nevada. Rose, a composer and arranger for radio, is more than
10 years Judy's senior; but they had been
friends for a number of years. Rumors of
their impending marriage began soon after
Rose's divorce from Martha Raye in 1940.
They live in a rented house in Beverly Hills
while their own is being built.

Judy has appeared as guest star on a number of radio programs and in January 1941
she appeared in *Love's New Sweet Song* for
the Silver Theatre program. She wrote the
original script, which was adapted by True
Boardman.

Judy is snub-nosed and red-haired. Three
years ago Sophie Tucker said of her that she
would become "America's next red-hot mam-
ma." Judy has expressed the desire, however,
to become a great dramatic actress and push
the singing and dancing gradually into the
background.

References

Am Mag 125:114 My '38 por
Ladies' H J 57:19+ S '40 pors
Life 4:66-8 Mr 28 '38 il pors
Look 5:39-41 My 6 '41 pors
N Y Post p15 S 12 '41

N Y Times p9 Jl 29 '41 por
Photoplay 54:32-3+ My '40 pors; 54:
14-15+ D '40 il pors; 18:27-8+ Mr
'41 pors; 19:6 S '41 pors
Time 37:68 Je 9 '41 por; 38:47 Ag 4
'41

International Motion Picture Almanac
Variety Radio Directory

GAUSS, CLARENCE E(DWARD) (gŏs)
Jan. 12, 1887- United States Ambassador to
China

Bulletin: In February 1941 Clarence E.
Gauss was appointed United States Ambassador to China, an indication to Japanese commentators that the United States
was preparing to follow a more active
policy in China. He arrived in Chungking
to take up his duties in May 1941 and told
China's President Lin Sen: "I bring you
from America a message of conviction that
the principles in which your people and my
people believe will prevail."

From January 1941 issue:

Clarence Edward Gauss, "regarded by many
an admiring American as the ablest United
States diplomat in the Orient," has a delicate

CLARENCE E. GAUSS

and important task as our first Minister to
Australia. The Far Eastern situation is
touchy, what with Japan looking with covetous
eyes on the Netherlands East Indies only 300
miles to the southeast of Australia, and England's fleet occupied in the Western Hemisphere. Mr. Gauss, who as consul general at
Shanghai has since July 1937 been in the
East's most conspicuous trouble spot and who
has been one of the State Department's "ace
trouble shooters" for years, is eminently well
qualified to represent his country in Australia.

Since 1907 he has roamed around China, serving in several different cities: all of his service, except for brief stays in Washington and in Paris, has been in the Far East. Clarence Gauss' first government positions, however, were undistinguished ones. Born in Washington, D. C., the son of Herman and Emilie J. (Eisenman) Gauss, he received his education in Washington's public high schools and under private tutors. It was in 1903 that he entered the government service as a stenographer in the House of Representatives. After three years in this position and as a worker on the Invalid Pensions Committee, he entered the Department of State in 1906 as a clerk.

After a year's service in Washington Mr. Gauss was sent to Shanghai as Deputy Consul General. In 1909 he returned to Washington on duty, to study for the foreign service and to take charge of the consular school in the Department of State, but in 1912, after passing the career consular examinations, he was back in Shanghai again as Deputy and Vice-Consul General. By 1915 he was in full charge of the American Consulate there, but shortly afterward began his wider service in the Far East. In 1916 he went to Tientsin, where he was in charge of the Consulate; the next four years he spent at Amoy. In 1917 he married Rebecca Louise Barker of Los Angeles. They have one son, Charles Barker Gauss.

From Amoy Mr. Gauss went to Tsinan, Shantung; from there, in 1923, to Mukden, Manchuria; then back in Tientsin in 1924, to Shanghai in 1926 and Tientsin in 1927. In 1931 he was assigned to the Department of State, but it was only two years before he was back in China, at Peiping, as Counselor of the Legation. In 1935 he was in Paris as Counselor of the Embassy and Consul General, but stayed there only a few months before he became Consul General at Shanghai, a position he continued to hold until his promotion to the position of Minister to Australia in January 1940.

In Shanghai, as the Chinese-Japanese War grew fiercer, Mr. Gauss, "hardboiled and short-spoken," sharp-faced, medium-tall and so constant a smoker "that he seems naked without a cigar," worked his regular six-day week and Sundays, too, unperturbed by bomb explosions outside his office or endless arguments with Japanese officers over violations of American rights. Frequently he had to act on his own without consulting Washington and every time he did so he seemed to show "a genius for being right." It was his reports from Shanghai that kept the Department of State up to the minute on Far Eastern affairs. This same "genius for being right" and ability to keep his superiors completely informed is already well in evidence in his Australian activities.

References

Life 8:18 Ja 22 '40 por
Scholastic 36:10 F 5 '40 por
Time 37:18 My 5 '41 por
Who's Who in America
Who's Who in Government

GEER, ALPHEUS 1863(?)—Aug. 17, 1941 Founder of the Marshall Stillman Movement for the rehabilitation of criminals; organization later became the Association for Better Citizenship with Mr. Geer as head; organized clubs for under-privileged boys; aided many ex-felons in finding jobs.

References

Collier's 74:15 Jl 26 '24 por
Lit Digest 80:34 Mr 29 '24 por
New Yorker 5:23-6 My 11 '29
World's Work 48:133 Je '24 por

Obituaries

N Y Herald Tribune p8 Ag 18 '41 por

GEHRIG, LOU (gĕr'ĭg) June 19, 1903—June 2, 1941 Former baseball star; parole commissioner in New York City; one of the outstanding batsmen baseball has known; died of a rare disease which caused hardening of the spinal cord (see sketch 1940 Annual).

Obituaries

N Y Times pl, 26 Je 3 '41 pors

GILDERSLEEVE, VIRGINIA C(ROCH-ERON) Oct. 3, 1877- Dean of Barnard College, Columbia University

Address: Barnard College, Columbia University, New York City

Pach Bros.

VIRGINIA C. GILDERSLEEVE

Doctor of Philosophy, Doctor of Literature, Doctor of Laws, recipient of many honorary degrees and medals, Dean Gildersleeve was described in an article in *Literary Digest* as having "enough caps and gowns to fill an ordinary New York apartment closet." She is undoubtedly one of the foremost women in American education.

Virginia Crocheron Gildersleeve was born in New York City in 1877, the daughter of a

GILDERSLEEVE, VIRGINIA C.—*Cont.*

Supreme Court Justice, Henry Alger, and Virginia (Crocheron) Gildersleeve. A vital, dark-eyed, dark-haired figure, she is tall and erect and has the poise and dignity becoming to her position. Dean of a women's college for 30 years, she has always emphasized the great value of that training of the mind and character offered by the good "colleges of liberal arts." The combination of such a "liberal" education with some technical or professional training which gives tools with which to work —with which to express one's personality and serve the community—seems to her the essence of education.

Although she has a strong interest in the youthful worries of her charges, she has never yielded to the desire to be called "The Dear Dean" and to pry into their private affairs. She calls students by their last names and herself prefers to be a stern "older sister" rather than a "mother" to her girls.

"Everyone knows that the Dean is a good executive, a magnificent speaker, a wise woman, an intellectual," Alice Duer Miller has written of her, "but not everyone knows she can lose her temper over examples of stupidity and spite, and that, therefore, her tact and calm are the more to be admired, since they are achieved and not wholly innate."

Dean Gildersleeve is inclined to deprecate her own accomplishments. She once said to an interviewer: "I never had to try for anything in my life. My mother sent me to college and after that everything fell into my lap." However, she has a passion for perfection. As a student she was dissatisfied unless she received an "A" rating on every paper. In 1899 she was awarded her first degree, B. A., from the college where she is now dean, and received her M. A. from Columbia University. Before being appointed dean, she was instructor in English at Barnard College.

Archeology is one of her hobbies. On summer vacations she used to look for old stones on the traces of early Roman roads near the cottage of a friend who lives in Sussex, England, and always hoped some day to find a Carthaginian penny. She plays deck tennis for relaxation. Occasionally she smokes a cigaret and enjoys a glass of claret with her meals. She is fond of dogs, and of books on polar exploration. The "Deanery," her home in the college, is a comfortable apartment with the living room filled with many soft chairs and lamps, and lined with books.

Dean Gildersleeve feels that in war time it is particularly important that the women's colleges should continue to keep their students at their usual studies and turn out college graduates, so that the nation may not lack a supply of citizens trained to think: of doctors, social workers, teachers and other highly trained professional workers whose professional education must be based on a foundation of college studies.

Although she is a gifted scholar in English literature, Dean Gildersleeve has always taken an active interest in current national and international affairs. In politics she is a vigorous Independent Democrat. International relations are her specialty. To the cause of understanding and cooperation between nations she has devoted most of the time she could spare from her deanship. One of the founders of the International Federation of University Women, she has twice served as its president, from 1924 to 1926, and again from 1936 to 1939. She was an early advocate of the idea of a League of Nations and still believes in the absolute necessity of some form of international world organization to insure order and justice. She is a member of the Commission to Study the Organization of Peace; and she has also worked with the Committee to Defend America.

References

Assn Am Col Bul 25:258-67 My '39
Lit Digest 121:35 F 29 '36 por
Newsweek 7:46 F 22 '36 por; 9:34 Mr 27 '37
American Women
Gildersleeve, W. H. Gildersleeve Pioneers 1941
Leaders in Education 1941
Who's Who Among North American Authors
Who's Who in America

GILL, ERIC (gĭl) Feb. 22, 1882—Nov. 18, 1940 Internationally known sculptor and engraver who created war memorials and is particularly known for his illustrations for the *Songs of Solomon*; author and typographer who cut one of the most famous types, the Gill Sans, and many others.

Leighton—Studio Publications
ERIC GILL

References

Casson, S. Some Modern Sculptors p88-110 1928

Catholic Who's Who

Jackson, H. Printing of Books p140-54 1939

Rutherston, A. D. comp. Eric Gill 1924

Thorp, J. P. Eric Gill 1929

Who's Who

Who's Who in Art

Obituaries

N Y Herald Tribune p26 N 19 '40

N Y Times p24 N 19 '40

Pub W 138:2133-5 D 7 '40 il por

GILLESPIE, LOUIS JOHN June 10, 1886—Jan. 24, 1941 Professor of physical chemistry at Massachusetts Institute of Technology; former bacteriologist of New York City Board of Health and biochemist in the Bureau of Plant Industry of the United States Department of Agriculture; widely known for his contributions to bacteriology, biochemistry and the chemistry of soils; had also done research in thermodynamics and the mass action law for compressed gases.

References

American Men of Science

Chemical Who's Who

Obituaries

N Y Times p36 Ja 26 '41

GINSBERG, SAMUEL *See* Krivitsky, W. G.

GLASS, CARTER Jan. 4, 1858- United States Senator from Virginia

Address: b. Senate Office Bldg, Washington, D. C.; h. Mayflower Hotel, Washington, D. C; Lynchburg, Va.

"I've lived too long," said five-foot-four, 100-pound, bellicose Senator Carter Glass in 1938. The sharp-voiced Virginia legislator had of late appeared increasingly reflective and melancholic. A changing world with newfangled theories of government still drew sparks from his oratorical anvil, but now the Senator was perturbed. He had come to doubt the direction of progress; he had accumulated fears concerning the national economy; and he had grown nostalgic. "Today we no longer have democracy. We have mobocracy," he mourned. And the elections of Senators by the electorate at large rather than by the State legislatures had been, to his way of thinking, one of the first symptoms of this new "mob rule."

Perhaps this attitude is partly due to the fact that Carter Glass, who was born in Lynchburg, Virginia on January 4, 1858, was brought up during the Civil War. He remembers gray-clad soldiers marching through his native town and he remembers Lee's surrender at Appomattox Court House less than 25 miles from his home. Carter Glass is "a red, rolling ball of fury" both by reason of his rebel traditions and his personal temperament. His father, Major Robert Henry Glass, was a rambunctious newspaper editor who distinguished himself in the war by fighting two enemies who

CARTER GLASS

had opened fire from opposite sides. As a result of the encounter the elder Glass lost an eye. From his father Carter inherited utter fearlessness and a blazing temper still much in evidence.

In post-War Virginia, rife with the bitterness of the South's defeat, Glass launched a career marked by wrath, determination and single-mindedness. As a boy he had earned the nickname of "Pluck." Later he became the terror of the Senate because of his fighting words and his readiness to augment them, if necessary, with his fists. His favorite boyhood sport was cockfighting, and many have since compared the diminutive Senator to a fighting bantam because of the white hair shooting up from his head like a rooster's comb and his willingness to face an adversary at the drop of a hat.

When Glass was 15 years old he had to leave school and find work to bolster a family income badly depleted during the post-War depression. He traveled down the river to Petersburg and became a printer's devil at $1.50 a week. His fellow employees recall him as a studious and resolute redhead who spurned recreation and devoted himself to learning his trade and to reading the classics. His perseverance bore fruit; he was made a full-fledged journeyman printer in two years instead of the customary four. Glass held many jobs in the mechanical departments of country newspapers, serving variously as compositor and pressman and, as was usual at the time, turning his hand occasionally to news and editorial writing. During his journeys his baggage totaled "an extra shirt, a fighting rooster and a 'library,'" the latter consisting of second-hand classics which Glass purchased whenever possible. He was later able to augment his self-education by attending William and Mary College, where he was a member of Phi Beta Kappa; an honorary LL. D. was given him by Lafayette College and other colleges.

GLASS, CARTER—*Continued*

Drifting back to Lynchburg, Glass became editor of the Lynchburg *Daily News*. When the owner, wishing to retire, offered to sell the paper, Glass sought frantically for backers. Unexpectedly a relative came through with a loan and, at 30, Glass was a publisher and editor. He made a down payment of $100 in cash on the $13,000 proposition and then struck out audaciously. His policy was to write sizzling editorials such as the South had never before seen and to roast the opposition press with masterful invective. The paper grew, and it was not long before Glass was also able to buy the afternoon paper, the *Daily Advance*, which he consolidated with the *Daily News*. Glass still owns the *News-Advance*, which his son, Carter, Jr., now edits, and whenever he returns to his home town he heads straight for the brick structure on Main Street that houses the editorial and publishing offices.

In his efforts to pulverize the rival press Glass at one time was the object of an attack by a paper called *The Earth*. A correspondent known as "The Lion Tamer" cast reflections on a relative for whom Glass was named. Glass lashed out, calling "The Lion Tamer" "an unmitigated liar," whereupon his rival challenged him to a duel for which he never showed up. The next day Glass gave his opponent one of the most brutal editorial drubbings in the history of local journalism. Humiliated by this ridicule, "The Lion Tamer's" wife strode into Glass' office and aimed a horse pistol at his heart, saying: "My husband's a coward, but I am not." Glass faced the woman calmly. "I cannot defend myself against a lady," he said; "please get it over in a hurry." The astounded intruder could only stare and flee. Shortly after, "The Lion Tamer" and his wife departed from Lynchburg and were never heard from again.

The Virginian's political life began almost as a matter of course. His journalistic ventures attracted widespread attention; since he espoused the cause of the Democratic Party, he soon came to be recognized as a political force. In 1894 he was persuaded to run for Mayor of Lynchburg, but although he was sufficiently popular to have won had he decided to stay in the contest, he withdrew before election day. He was given a small job as clerk of the local council and in 1898 was elected to the Virginia State Senate without having waged a campaign. Glass, at the time, had been ill; periodic sickness has interrupted his activity almost from infancy, and doctors have frequently despaired of his life. His tremendous energy has always pulled him through, however, and at least one physician has become reconciled to the Southerner's outbursts of irascibility. "They're good for him," the doctor explains. "He gets rid of the poisons inside him."

In 1901, returning from New York, where he had been recuperating from another illness, Glass attended the State Constitutional Convention held primarily for the purpose of changing the liberal but seldom observed voting laws that had been the product of Reconstruction. At the meeting Glass gained considerable attention by his bold proposals to delimit the franchise. A $1.50 poll tax and the establishment of investigation boards for literacy tests, measures sponsored by him, were adopted. When asked whether this had not been accomplished by "fraud and discrimination" he replied, according to the authors of *Dixie Demagogues*: "By fraud, no; by discrimination, yes . . . that is exactly what this convention was elected for—to discriminate to the very extremity possible under the limitations of the Federal Constitution with a view to the elimination of every Negro voter who can be gotten rid of, legally, without materially impairing the numerical strength of the white electorate."

After the Convention, Glass was appointed to fill the unexpired term of P. J. Otey, Representative from the Sixth Congressional District. In 1902, when election day rolled around again, Glass campaigned vigorously and successfully against the powerful Swanson-Martin machine. It was one of the few times when he actually took to the stump to seek re-election, for since that time Glass has usually been returned to office like clockwork. There followed 10 years in Congress during which Glass delivered few important speeches and sponsored little or no major legislation; but it was he who, at the National Convention of the Democratic Party in Baltimore in 1912, delivered the entire Virginia delegation to Woodrow Wilson despite factional opposition from Senator T. S. Martin, backed by financier Thomas Fortune Ryan. Wilson's election and the seniority rules of the House resulted in the Virginian's appointment as chairman of the Committee on Banking and Currency.

With the economist H. Parker Willis, Glass next fashioned the famous Federal Reserve Bank Act which has been called the greatest achievement in financial banking since the Civil War. Five months of debate against disheartening opposition featured Glass' struggle to gain passage of the bill. President Wilson, in referring to the legislator's odd habit of talking from the side of his mouth, said: "Carter snarled the Federal Reserve Act through Congress out of one side of his mouth. Think what he would have done with both sides." In recognition of his services, the President appointed him Secretary of the Treasury; but later, when Senator Martin died in office, Glass resigned from the Cabinet to serve out the unexpired term. There he became chairman of the Senate Committee on Banking and Currency.

In 1928 Glass took to the stump for the second time. This was when the South repudiated its traditional adherence to the Democratic Party because the Democratic candidate, Alfred E. Smith, was both a Catholic and an enemy of Prohibition. Glass, a Methodist and a Dry, in speech after speech castigated religious intolerance; defied 30,000 hooded members of the Ku Klux Klan assembled in Lynchburg to impress him with their strength; and urged his state to vote for Smith. But the tide was against Smith, and Glass returned to Congress a vehement opponent of President

Herbert Hoover. He was soon excoriating Hoover's policy of granting loans to industry, insisting on holding to a balanced budget and rigid enforcement of the Federal Reserve Act.

In the Democratic Convention of 1932 Glass contributed the "sound money" plank to the Party platform. He looked forward to the election of Franklin D. Roosevelt to carry on the policies which Glass had long advocated. But Glass was doomed to disappointment. When Roosevelt later called him the "Unreconstructed Rebel," Glass said proudly: "I shall remain the 'Unreconstructed Rebel' until the policies of this Government are changed." Even more than the philosophy of Hoover did the philosophy of the New Deal run counter to the Virginian's traditions and temperament. Nothing in his long years of government service so incensed him as the "spendthrift policies of the New Deal." When the President offered him the post of Secretary of the Treasury, Glass refused. He regarded the New Deal as "dishonest and dishonorable," the "Administration of Insanity", "a disasterbound socialistic experiment." Calling himself a "Jeffersonian Democrat," he plunged into bold denunciations of relief spending, the Public Works Administration, and, later, the President's Supreme Court reform program. Twice, too, in committee investigations of 1933 and 1936, he came chivalrously forward to protect J. P. Morgan against his questioners.

It was the New Deal's fiscal policies, though, which made the Virginian's temperature reach boiling point. For years Glass had been the watchdog of the Federal Reserve Act; encroachments on its spirit and intent touched a particularly sensitive spot. Once the talkative Huey Long held up the passage of one of the Senator's banking measures for days with a filibuster that included the Declaration of Independence and the Lord's Prayer. When the measure was passed Long walked up to Glass and genially addressed him as "Carter." Glass immediately burst into a stream of profanity that left Long flabbergasted; then he offered to fight Long in the cloakroom. Glass later said, "I used words I did not even dream were in my vocabulary."

Yet, despite the Senator's distrust of the New Deal, even the most ardent members of the Administration appreciated his contribution to financial reform. In December 23, 1938 a bas-relief of the Senator was unveiled in the Federal Reserve Building in Washington at ceremonies marking the twenty-fifth anniversary of the signing of the Federal Reserve Banking Act. High Administration leaders paid tribute to the Senator's long fight for the passage of the bill. Much moved, Glass said: "I think a man's funeral ought to be held before he dies." An additional honor came to Glass on July 10, 1941 when he was elected president *pro tempore* of the Senate, succeeding the late Senator Harrison.

And eventually Glass found himself in complete harmony with Roosevelt's aims in foreign policy, at least. An early interventionist, he more than once vigorously denounced Charles A. Lindbergh (see sketch this issue). He was one of the original sponsors of the Fight for Freedom Committee. In February 1941 he said he would like to "shoot hell" out of the Nazis. And when a peace group of mothers led by Mrs. Elizabeth Dilling of *Red Network* fame conducted a sit-down strike before the Virginia Senator's office, Glass said it was "a noisy disorder of which any self-respecting fishwife would be ashamed. It is pertinent for the Federal Bureau of Investigation to inquire into whether they are mothers—for the sake of the race I devoutly hope not."

On June 23, 1940, at the age of 82, Glass was married to the 50-year-old Mrs. Mary Scott Meade of Amherst, Virginia, a widow. His first wife, Aurelia Caldwell Glass, had died on June 5, 1937, leaving four children— Powell, Carter, Mary Archer and Augusta Christian.

Among his friends Carter Glass is known as a cultured, warm-hearted, sensitive man. He likes to argue that Bacon wrote Shakespeare's plays, to tell jokes, attend baseball games and prize fights. Rarely does he miss his favorite team, the Philadelphia Athletics, when they play a visiting game against the Washington Senators. Once, in his home town, when he was displeased with the umpire of a local game, he chased him with a bat and then routed the visiting team from the field in the same manner.

The "fireball" of the Senate is rarely challenged directly on the floor today, for his fellow legislators dread serving as target for his deadly wit. On one occasion when a supporter cheered his attack on another Senator by shouting, "Blast him, Carter; dynamite him!" Carter replied: "Why use dynamite when insect powder will do just as well?"

References
Collier's 87:38 Ap 18 '31; 89:16 Ap 2 '32; 93:14+ F 10 '34 pors; 96:19+ N 30 '35 por

Fortune 17:82 Je '38 por

New Repub 85:368 F 5 '36

Newsweek 6:20-1 Ag 17 '35 por; 12:11 S 5 '38 por; 13:40-2 My 15 '39 pors; 15:44 Ja 15 '40 por

No Am 235:420-6 My '33

Sat Eve Post 208:22 Ag 3 '35; 210:16-17+ Ag 28 '37 pors

Michie, A. A. and Ryhlick, F. Dixie Demagogues p159-81 1939

Palmer, J. E. Carter Glass, Unreconstructed Rebel 1938

Smith, R. and Beasley, N. Carter Glass 1939

Who's Who in America

Who's Who in Government

Who's Who in the East

GOEBBELS, JOSEPH (gûb'ĕls) Oct. 29, 1897- Reichsminister of Propaganda and Public Enlightenment

Address: Berlin, W. 8, Wilhelmplatz 8-9, Germany

Joseph Goebbels is the "lame, lop-eared, loose-mouthed" little man who since 1933 has been Germany's Minister of Propaganda and

The New York Public Library

JOSEPH GOEBBELS

Public Enlightenment. As perhaps the world's outstanding authority on the subject, he has said: 'Propaganda has only one object, to conquer the masses. Every means that furthers this aim is good; every means that hinders it is bad." It is in order that no publicly unenlightened facts may reach those masses with bad effect that everything published in the Reich is published with the consent of his Ministry, which employs thousands of officials.

No journalist may be employed in Germany until his acceptability and political reliability have been certified by Dr. Goebbels. Even the words of fellow Cabinet members may not be printed unless he approves of them. He can order anything he wishes published in any newspaper in the country, can command the page and the column in which he would like to see it. And his authority over German "cultural" life as a whole goes so far that he can decide when flags shall be flown at half mast, can forbid public entertainment and dances for the day, can, if he wishes, decide that traffic all over Germany shall stand still at a certain moment and all work cease while everyone in the Reich sneezes in unison. One awed foreign observer wrote: "From an anthropological viewpoint the publicity legislation of the Propaganda Ministry appears as the official organization of the ritualistic side of magic."

This practitioner of modern sorcery is the author of innumerable books and pamphlets devoted to Nazi theory, among them *The Unknown S. A. Man*; *Lenin or Hitler*; *The Second Revolution* (1926); *Buch Isidor* (1929); *Knorke*, a second Isidor book (1929); *The Damned Nazis* (1929); *Battle for Berlin* (1934); *My Part in Germany's Fight* (1935). His mind is "keen as steel, cold and calculat-

ing," remarkable for its "mixture of cynicism and guile." His energy is inexhaustible, his power of concentration unusual—he once spent three days thinking out two words for a new poster.

But if these gifts make the Goebbels touch on Nazi war communiqués, for instance, worth any number of *panzer* divisions, they do not make him any more popular with the German people, who call him "the malicious dwarf" and "the latest reincarnation of the devil." One year he ordered a motion picture made showing him among his loved ones, and titled, with brilliant bad taste, *It's Daddy's Birthday;* boos and whistles forced it out of German theatres after three performances. Even the circulation of his paper, *Der Angriff* (The Attack) has dropped phenomenally since Hitler came to power.

Yet perhaps this lack of popular applause actually sharpens the genius for venom expressed in such confessions as: "A Jew is for me an object of disgust. I vomit when I see one. Christ cannot possibly have been a Jew. I don't have to prove that scientifically. It is a fact. . . I treasure an ordinary prostitute above a married Jewess." Goebbels says: "That's my trade. Hatred. It takes you a long way further than any other emotion." And it is true that this intellectual who is famed for his rantings against intellectualism, this apostle of Nordic superiority whose exceedingly un-Aryan appearance has brought about the invention of a special classification in Aryan ethnology—*Nachgedunkelter Schrumpfgermane*, "a dwarflike German who grew dark"—has come a long way in the worldly sense of the word.

Younger than either Hitler or Goering (see sketch this issue), Paul Joseph Goebbels was born in the industrial town of Rheydt in the Lower Rhineland on October 29, 1897, the son of Fritz and Maria (Oldenhausen) Goebbels. His father's occupation has been variously reported as factory clerk, farmer, teacher; at any rate, he came of peasant stock, was none too wealthy, and his wife was the daughter of a blacksmith. Paul Joseph was lame from birth, but he was an intelligent lad. After completing his studies in the Catholic Volkschule at Rheydt and in the Gymnasium and after being rejected for military service during the First World War, he visited one university after another, helped by Catholic scholarships. (He is, however, extremely anti-Catholic today.) He studied history, philology and the history of art and literature at the universities of Bonn, Freiburg, Wünzburg, Munich, Cologne and Berlin, then finished at Heidelberg, where he took his Ph. D. in 1921.

In those days Paul Joseph, shut out from strenuous physical activity, dreamed of becoming a great writer. But the world refused to recognize him, just as it refused to recognize the creative efforts of a certain Vienna housepainter. *Michael*, written when he was 24, was described as "probably as bad a book as has ever been published." Berlin theatre managers refused to be tactful about his two plays, *Blutsaat* and *Der Wanderer.* Nor would the *Berliner Tageblatt* accept him as a reporter. Goebbels said later: "When I think of the humiliations of my youth, I see no reason to shrink from applying any treatment to our adversaries." In the light of this statement, the fact that the editor and owners of the *Berliner Tageblatt* were Jews, as were many Berlin theatre managers, may have some significance.

It was by pure chance that Goebbels, in 1922, entered a meeting hall in Munich and heard Hitler speak. Although F. L. Schuman says that he did not actually join the Nazi Party until 1924, it seems to be established that he went to the Rhineland to organize party groups even before that and, next to Hitler, became the most valuable orator in the movement. His appearance at Nazi meetings is dramatically described: "A flat brow with straight black hair brushed back and flanked by pointed, protruding ears. Piercing dark eyes in an angular, cadaverous face, deeply lined about the large, mobile mouth. Diminutive, emaciated, almost insignificant as he limped into meetings completely surrounded by S. A. or S. S. bodyguards. But on the platform he was a wizard of demagoguery, with his resonant, penetrating voice, his keen cynical intelligence, his satire and irony, his utter unscrupulousness in attack, and his restless hands with their fascinatingly delicate yet powerful gestures." Even then he was inventing catch phrases: "Heads will roll!" "Out with the Jews!" "Germany, awake!"

In 1924 expelled from the Rhineland by the French authorities, Goebbels went to live in Elberfeld. He became an organizer and agitator in the Ruhr and that same year founded and edited the *Völkische Freiheit.* This particular Nazi organ achieved little influence, but the following year he and Gregor Strasser created a secret news organ for Party members, the *Nationalsozialistischen Briefe,* and set out to bring the entire Nazi Party under their influence by attacks on what they considered the suspiciously conservative policies of Streicher and Feder and indirect attacks on Hitler himself. What little proletarian following the Nazis got is supposed to have been due to Strasser and to Goebbels; but their association was not to last long. In 1926 Strasser went to the Bamberg conference of Party delegates, taking Goebbels with him as his secretary. There, when delegates split on the issue of how much genuine socialism there should be in National Socialism, Goebbels opportunistically sided against Strasser. In October of that year he was rewarded by Hitler with the post of *Gauleiter* for Berlin, later for the entire province of Brandenburg.

During four years in Berlin, Goebbels, known as "The Doctor," built up a powerful defense squad, made Berlin the chief stronghold of the Hitlerites next to Munich itself. In 1927 he founded the weekly, *Der Angriff,* which in 1929 became a biweekly and in 1930 a daily. In his paper he reviled the "gutter press" (non-Nazi journalism), and was so

reckless in his assaults on certain individuals that at one time there were 126 libel suits pending against him. But vitriol was profitable even then: in 1928 he was elected to the Reichstag; in 1929 he became town councilor and was appointed Reich propaganda leader of the Nazi Party; in 1930 he was re-elected to the Reichstag.

His split with Strasser was complete by this time. In June, at a meeting of the General Assembly, he attacked his former associate bitterly for his dangerous ideas and disruptive influence, and Strasser was ejected. Two months later a group of rebels of Strasser's faction stormed Goebbels' offices, doing much damage, and then scattered a leaflet headlined AWAKENING GERMANY BETRAYED BY GOEBBELS! This did not mean that Goebbels had ceased to talk in revolutionary terms, however. In 1931, in the pages of *Der Angriff,* he was still offering to the German worker "the fight for freedom and bread," reassuring him that "we are today a labor party in the best sense of the word," even promising that dictatorship would not be permanent.

During the years 1931 and 1932 Goebbels kept a diary, which was later published. On December 8, 1932 he was writing: "Treason! Treason! Severe depression prevails. . . Financial troubles make all organized work impossible. . . The danger now exists of the whole Party's going to pieces. . . For hours on end Der Führer walks up and down the hotel room. . . Once he stops and says: 'If the Party should ever break up, I'll make an end of things in three minutes with a revolver.'" But barely a month later Hitler was Chancellor, and although Goebbels was not made a member of that first Cabinet he wrote that the whole thing was "like a dream." In March 1933 he himself was appointed "Minister of Folk Enlightenment" in order to prevent a "political lethargy" among the German people.

It was not, however, until June 30 of that year that the Ministry of Propaganda and Public Enlightenment was officially set up, with Goebbels at its head. A decree made him "responsible for all factors influencing the mental life of the nation . . . responsible for winning allegiance to the State, its culture and its economy; for the conduct of internal and external publicity, and for the administration of all institutions contributing to these ends." It made him ruler of the press, the radio, the theatre, the cinema and most musical, cultural and even scientific activities. How this power would be used was indicated at his first meeting with German newspapermen, when he said that the press would remain relatively free—"But do not imagine that we shall allow you to swindle the people out of our hands. We know only too well how this can be done." There were, at first, clashes with Goering over the control of the Prussian theatre, clashes with Goering, Rosenberg (see sketch this issue), Rust and Frick over the control of art (was or was not

GOEBBELS, JOSEPH—*Continued*
all art propaganda?)—but Goebbels was eventually victorious in most of them.

Since that time the scope of the activities of his Ministry has been extraordinary. A Reich Culture Chamber was set up, with Goebbels as president of its central body; anyone wishing to participate in any sort of creative activity in the Third Reich must be a member of the proper chamber. The man who, as "stage manager to the Nazi Party," had invented the dramatic technique of the great mass meetings, also became stage manager of the book burnings, the May Day and Harvest Festivals and the *Winterhilfe* relief campaign, introduced in September 1933. The fabrication of stories of oppression and attacks against Germany and against Germans in other countries was an even more important part of his job. And his talents in inventing Jewish atrocities were so far-famed by 1933 that when he made his first appearance as Germany's official representative at a session of the League of Nations that year, a local paper published a caricature of him with the caption: "And who may this man be? Why, to be sure, it is the representative of the well-built, healthy, blond and blue-eyed Nordic race!" The Press Law of October 1933 and the Cinema Law of February 1934 gave that representative even greater power.

Goebbels' Ministry also got all subsidies and grants of assistance for influencing the foreign press, for foreign publications and for the construction of propaganda organizations abroad. From 1933 to 1937 the propaganda fund was said to amount to £20,000,000 sterling annually, and since 1937 it has probably been even larger. Goebbels once told Goering: "You wouldn't have to fight at all if I had my way. I could win any number of wars for you with no losses but suicides on the other side." In 1938 he became a member of the Cabinet Council.

The theory of Germany's Minister of Propaganda is that "you can make a man believe anything if you tell it to him in the right way," and he also relies on the conviction that all news is so short-lived that the memory of the masses doesn't count. That is why the author of tirades against German capitalists could write, in December 1933: "Our socialism . . . is the legacy of the Prussian Army. . . It is that kind of socialism which enabled Frederick the Great to carry on a war for seven years." That is why he could announce, straight-faced, after "Bloody Saturday" in June 1934 (he had been with Hitler at the time): "Morality, decency and purity have been restored." That is why the man who as early as May 1931 had written that "the only instrument with which one can conduct foreign policy is alone and exclusively the sword" and whose glorifications of war verge on the hysteric can still speak unblushingly of Nazi Germany's deep and abiding love for peace. And that is, finally, why a frankly pagan war against "democracy", "plutocracy", "capitalism" can turn swiftly

and neatly into a religious crusade against "Bolshevism" in Nazi press releases—or back again. But there are indications that even Goebbels cannot make all the Germans believe that they are happy and well-fed. One was his warning, in November 1941, that they must resign themselves to a "hard, relentless war" which, if lost, will leave them facing an "inferno."

Oddly enough, Goebbels seems to have a certain fascination for women. His wife is Magda (Ritschel) Quandt, whom he married December 19, 1931. She had been married previously to one of Germany's greatest industrialists. She was more than 25 years younger than Herr Quandt, by whom she had a son, Harald. Still called the First Lady of the Reich, she helped Goebbels a great deal in his earlier career, giving brilliant and extravagant evening parties which were often attended by Hitler himself. They live in great luxury: Goebbels owns a great estate and a sumptuous villa in Germany, and there are rumors of millions deposited in foreign lands. He has other advantages, too. In his library at home this embittered intellectual, it is whispered, keeps thousands of books which are now *verboten* in Germany—and enjoys nothing more than reading them over and over again. His attentions to various prominent actresses are the subject of scandal all over Germany, too: at one time it was rather reliably reported that he had been beaten within an inch of his life in the apartment of one young actress and that as a result his wife had asked Hitler to let her divorce him. Shortly afterward, photographs showing Hitler with the smiling couple and their children enlightened the public to the contrary in newspapers throughout the Reich.

References

Am Mercury 36:306-7 N '35; 49:135-42 F '40
Contemp 159:295-9 Mr '41
Cur Hist 51:48+ My '40
Eur Nouv 17:446-7 Ap 28 '34; 17:497-8 My 12 '34; 22:103-4 Ja 28 '39
Liv Age 346:504-6 Ag '34; 354:76-7 Mr '38
New Repub 79:316-17 Ag 1 '34
Newsweek 13:20-1 Ja 9 '39 il por
Time 33:20 Ja 9 '39; 34:25-6 S 18 '39 por
Bayles, W. D. Caesars in Goose Step p114-31 1940
Dutch, O. pseud. Hitler's 12 Apostles p64-80 1940
Forbes, R. T. These Men I Knew p47-59 1940
Goebbels, J. My Part in Germany's Fight 1935
Gunther, J. Inside Europe p66-70 1940
International Who's Who
Reichenau, J. This Man Goebbels pam 1940
Simone, A. Men of Europe p92-8 1941
Wer ist's?

GOERING, HERMANN (WILHELM)

Jan. 12, 1893- Marshal of the Reich; head of the German Council of Economic Warfare and of the German Air Force

Address: h. Berlin, W. 8, Leipziger Str. 3, Germany

A "mixture of Falstaff, Murat and Bismarck," Hermann Goering, the god Thor of modern German mythology, is the man who built the German Air Force, who diverted 50 per cent of the national income to war preparations, who helped to build the Army, to organize the Secret Police and concentration camps. He has been Prime Minister of Prussia, Commandant of the Prussian Police, Head of the State Secret Police, President of the Reichstag, Air Minister, Commander in Chief of the German Air Force, Chief Forester of the Reich, Reich Commissioner for the Four-Year Plan—and has held more than 20 other special offices in Nazi Germany, from Supreme Head of the National Weather Bureau and Chief Liquidator of Sequestrated Estates to Chief Huntsman and Game Warden. He has become one of the world's most powerful industrialists. The Führer himself named him as his successor.

In mid-July 1941, a report coming over the Moscow radio announced that Marshal Goering was in disgrace with Adolf Hitler because he argued that the German Air Force which he commands could not undertake the campaign against the Soviet Union without substantial reinforcements. According to this report, Hitler called his Marshal a coward, himself took over direction of the Air Force; and Heinrich Himmler (see sketch this issue), chief of the Gestapo, was said to be insisting that he be sent to a concentration camp. Later, stories appeared that both his legs had been blown off; still later, that he had been placed in supreme command of the German armies on the Eastern front.

There have been stories of Goering's friction with his Führer before, their reliability hardly enhanced by the fact that Goering has been called a "moderate" and an extreme "Rightist"; one of Hess' (see sketch this issue) best friends and one of his most bitter enemies; the man who has continually urged caution on Hitler and the man who, put in charge of Germany's destiny, would place even greater emphasis on militarism, blood and conquest. But one thing nearly all writers seem to have agreed on: Heinrich Himmler is the only man who can make the lionhearted Hermann tremble. If the Moscow report had been true, it would have indicated that dissension within the Nazi hierarchy was even more serious than the outside world had suspected. Photographs coming out of Germany, however, show Goering and Hitler together and characterize the whole story as "Russian propaganda." And on November 30, 1941 a meeting between Goering and Pétain was reported at St. Florentin-Vergigny.

One of the very few Nazi leaders who come of a distinguished family, Hermann Goering was born at Rosenheim, Bavaria on January 12, 1893, the son of Dr. Heinrich Ernst Goering, who had been the first Governor of the German Protectorate of South West Africa and Elizabeth (Lohe) Goering. He grew up in the mountains and forests of South Germany and Austria, spending much of his childhood in a medieval castle in Franconia. "School bored and irritated me," he said later. "I hated lessons. . . All I wanted was to be a soldier." He was finally sent to the cadet college of Karlsruhe.

When the First World War broke out, Goering was a mere lieutenant, a slender young man with burning eyes, in the 112th Prinz

German Railroads Information Office

HERMANN GOERING

Wilhelm Infantry Regiment in Alsace-Lorraine. Later joining the Air Force, he became an aerial observer, a pilot and combat flier, eventually the ace who is reported to have shot down from 23 to 36 planes during the War. In 1917 he himself was shot down, a bullet in his hip. This war wound was to trouble him throughout his life, and some say that it accounts for his present obesity. Returning to the front, by June 1918 he had become commander of the "Flying Circus" made famous by Von Richthofen, and he received Germany's highest decoration for valor, the Pour le Mérite.

There can be no doubt of his fantastic bravery. After the Armistice, when ordered to surrender his machines to the advancing Americans, he defiantly flew them back to Germany, and they were finally destroyed only after a series of remarkable exploits. At a farewell celebration he and his officers then toasted the 56 dead Circus pilots and pledged to work for Germany's "liberation."

When Goering returned to Berlin, a group of Socialists, seeing him in uniform, tore his officer's insignia from his coat lapels. His indignation and resentment at this may account to some small degree for his later con-

GOERING, HERMANN—*Continued*

version to National Socialism, but there were more important factors. After the War there was no place for him in Germany; he was penniless except for a small captain's pension; he was untrained for anything but war. The year 1920 found him in Sweden, where, after working as a commercial pilot and mechanic, he achieved the position of official in the Svenska Lufttrafik in Stockholm. There he met and fell in love with the unhappily married Baroness Karin von Fock, who divorced her husband and returned to Germany with him.

Goering already thought of his country as the "Jew Republic." He had no more prospects there than before, but his wife had money, and there were friends who could help him, among them the late Ernst Roehm, who was already working for Hitler. In 1922, when Goering went with Karin to Munich and enrolled in the University for an economics course, he was seldom found at the lectures: he himself was busy organizing the S. A. (the "Storm Troops"), whose leader he became in December of that year. The failure of the Nazi beer-hall *putsch* in 1923 temporarily upset all his hopes. Karin's jewels had been sold; they were living on borrowed money; he had been wounded again in the *putsch*. Despairing, they made a trip back to Sweden, where in September 1925 he was admitted to an asylum as an "extremely dangerous asocial hysteric," a morphine addict. Karin was ill, too, with epilepsy—too ill to travel when he was released from the asylum. Anxious to return to Germany after the amnesty of 1926, he left behind him not only Karin but Karin's child, for they had been deprived of its custody.

During the next year Goering reorganized the S. A., and was elected to the Reichstag as one of its first Nazi deputies. He also became head of the motor-works in Munich, and tried with some success to persuade aircraft and motor industrialists that when Nazism came into power it would revive the industry through air rearmament. In 1930, safely re-elected to the Reichstag, where the number of Nazi deputies had now increased from 12 to 107, he became the Nazi Party's political agent in Berlin. August of that year found him elected President of the Reichstag, where he and Hitler fought together against what they called Von Papen's (see sketch this issue) "dictatorship." Then, in October, came sad news from Stockholm: Karin was dying. He hurried back; Hitler telegraphed him to return; and it was in Berlin that he received word of his wife's death.

Goering was corpulent now, "a great, rotund man with a ruddy face, thin lips, steely eyes," and an all-consuming ambition. In 1932, with Nazi strength in the Reichstag increased to 230 deputies, he was re-elected its President. In January 1933 he informed the credulous Von Hindenburg that Von Schleicher meant to march in with troops and arrest him—and thus secured the signature of the decree appointing Hitler Chancellor. He became Minister with-

out Portfolio, one of the three Nazis in Hitler's first Cabinet. His first step was to take over the offices of the Prussian Minister of the Interior, which gave him control of the police. Dismissing leading police officials, he replaced them with S. A. men, persuaded Hindenburg to give special powers to the police, and by his orders incited the murder of dissenters from the regime, the breaking up of opposition meetings, the plundering of Jewish business houses. As he put it: "You must all become accustomed to the idea that I am not in office to dispense justice but to destroy and exterminate." It was several months before his position was weakened by the abolition of the S. A. auxiliary police; 10 days after Himmler consolidated the control of all the state political police into his own hands, in April 1934, Goering resigned as Prussian Minister of the Interior, and shortly after that he yielded control of the administrative and criminal police.

Another act of Goering's, according to many accounts, was the plotting of the Reichstag fire of February 1933. Although he may have taken a "moral whipping" at Dimitrov's hands during the trial that followed, Goering remained urbane. Shortly afterward he saw a new ministry formed, composed almost exclusively of Nazis; he himself promptly stepped into Von Papen's shoes as Premier of Prussia. In June 1934 it is said that the voice at Hitler's ear, hinting at a plot against him, was Goering's; that the ill-fated Roehm and Gregor Strasser would have made peace with Hitler if he had not interfered; that it was Goering who made out the longest list of proscribed persons. Whatever the facts in the matter, while Hitler was superintending the executions in South Germany on "Bloody Saturday" Goering was settling accounts in North Germany, and it was he who announced the shooting of Frau von Schleicher for "resisting" her husband's arrest.

He had already begun what was to be his most important service to the Nazi Party, too. When Hitler came into power Germany had been permitted only 100,000 soldiers and a little artillery—no tanks, no planes. Hitler promptly ordered Goering to build the greatest air force the world had ever seen. In the spring of 1933 the *Reichsluftschutzbund* had therefore been founded, and the Ministry of Aviation formed with Goering at its head. Thousands of young men began learning to fly in what were presumably air sports clubs; to foreign diplomats Goering announced: "Germany has no air force yet." The construction of aviation factories went on underground and in sparsely settled regions, and if the commercial aviation industry was being reorganized in order to build transports which could easily be converted to military uses, that was a secret, too. Not until March 1935 did the young men take off their plus fours and pullovers, don uniforms and reveal themselves as the German Air Force.

The very next year, in March 1936, when Hitler proclaimed Germany's "unshackled sovereignty" and reoccupied the Rhineland, Goering handed over to the Army 56,000 soldiers quietly trained as special police. In April of that year he was put in charge of controlling and coordinating the activities of the ministries and departments concerned with questions of raw materials and foreign exchange; and in October he was made commissioner for the Four-Year Plan, previously approved by the bankers and industrialists whose foremost spokesman he was, which he introduced to the world at the Nuremberg Party Congress that year. "Guns are better than butter," he announced, and he acted on his announcement. Given powers "to subordinate to the party all banks, industrial concerns, foreign trading associations, finance and note-issuing houses," he concentrated on making Germany not only bristling with armed might but self-supporting, independent of foreign raw-material imports, with gold and foreign exchange carefully husbanded. He was now officially the Reich's second-in-command.

It was while in this position that Goering himself became one of the world's great industrialists. Under a decree of July 1937 he took over certain low-grade iron deposits, and with $2,000,000 of the Reichsbank's money formed the Hermann Goering Works. Gradually he acquired coal fields, gravel pits, quarries, lignite mines, lime deposits, refractory materials, oil fields, commercial houses and shipping companies in other countries as well as in Germany. When in 1939 Fritz Thyssen left Germany, Goering took over his holdings, the largest steel mills in Germany. By 1941 his trust's capital account amounted to $800,000,000, according to *Time's* figures; what percentage of its profits goes to Goering himself is not certain, but he is said to have $1,250,000 in a Brazil bank, large investments in stock in American railroad and steel companies, and other substantial sums tucked away in Switzerland and in Italy.

In the meanwhile Goering was also becoming well known as the genial host to distinguished visiting foreigners, among them Colonel Lindbergh (see sketch this issue), the Marquess of Londonderry, Lord Halifax, Lord Lothian, other gentlemen of the Anglo-German Fellowship, and Hungary's Admiral Horthy. They usually came away charmed and convinced that Germany's case had been much misrepresented by her enemies—or, at least, that Goering was one of the Reich's "responsible" elements. Sir Nevile Henderson, British Ambassador to Germany, was particularly impressed—called him "a typical and brutal buccaneer," but one who "had certain attractive qualities." He admired his "loyalty to Hitler, administrative ability, physical courage, sportsmanship, above all his frankness, which does not stoop to devious deceits." He wrote to the late Neville Chamberlain suggesting that for diplomatic reasons *unser Hermann* would be more acceptable than Hitler to Britain.

In February 1938 Goering was given the highest German military rank, that of Field Marshal, and in that same year became a member of the Cabinet Council. Henderson credited him with intervening decisively for

"peace" in September 1938, and in August 1939 he was again conferring with the jovial Hermann. Goering promised him that if Germany and Britain went to war the German Air Force would bomb only military objectives. Henderson replied that bombs might easily fall on residential London, and that he, personally, would object to being struck by such a "present." Goering, smiling as always, retorted that if such a thing should happen he would send a special plane to drop a wreath at his friend's funeral.

Just before the Polish invasion, Hitler appointed a "Cabinet Council for the Defense of the Reich" and made Goering chairman, with authority to issue decrees without his signature. He also announced: "If anything should happen to me, my successor will be Field Marshal Goering." This, however, did not prevent rumors during the first months of the War that Goering was "in disgrace, biding his time in the country, and intriguing with the Allies." They stopped only after a decree of January 4, 1940, when a new Council of Economic Warfare, uniting all the chief offices of Germany having to do with war economy policy, was created under his leadership. In July 1940 he received the newly-created title Marshal of the Reich, and the Grand Cross of the Iron Cross was bestowed upon him. The fact that surprisingly little news of him had come out of Germany since June 1941, when he paid tribute to the activities of the German air force in Crete, may have lent credence to the Moscow report.

Goering has never forgotten his first wife. Two years after her death he built a huge memorial for her, and all Germany was required to go into mourning when it was unveiled. This, however, did not prevent him from making his second marriage (April 1935), to Emmy Johanna (Sonnemann) Henny, of the Prussian State Theatre, an occasion for national jubilation. They have one daughter, Edda, named after Mussolini's daughter; she is an adopted child, if rumors are true. The fabulous luxury of the Goering establishments is known all over Germany, and even Goering's air ministry in Berlin has 2,500 rooms. Their Berlin home is a large structure, almost a palace, in Leipziger Strasse; and in Bavaria they can boast of a castle, Karinhall, set in the middle of a 100,000-acre game preserve. Museums and private collections have been plundered for Goering's El Grecos, Raphaels, Titians and Rembrandts. Some of Karinhall's other features are Roman sarcophagi, a Byzantine room with a fountain, a Viking Hall, a Louis Quinze dining hall, a private gymnasium—and one room with an artificial mountain landscape and a miniature electric railway!

Equally famous is Goering's collection of uniforms. "Public Clothes-Horse No. 1," he is supposed to own at least 50, and all different. They include a mailed costume of the ancient Teutonic knights, and Goering once went on a hunting expedition carrying a spear and wearing bearskins and Wagnerian headgear. A

GOERING, HERMANN—*Continued*

passion for medals makes his costumes even more astonishing. It was once whispered that he donned an admiral's uniform when he took a bath, with rubber duplicates of all of them. Photographed at all sports except swimming, Germans also joke that he "sits down on his stomach" and wears corsets on his thighs—but his is "fat atop an immensity of muscle." Besides, he went from 270 to 230 pounds in 1939, and then proceeded to address citizens of the Reich: "Look at me! I have lost pounds in the service of the country. Why do you complain at cutting down your meals a little?"

Goering likes to be referred to as "Iron Hermann," and his emblem is a fist clutching an iron ring. Douglas Reed says his philosophy is: "Live, but don't let live." His conversation is "crude vernacular," seasoned with "brutal epithets of the street"; his fun is grim fun. A medieval hangman's ax hangs on the wall of one of his rooms, and he used to wrestle on the lawn with a pet lion cub, Caesar. He is said to have no regard whatsoever for life—his own or others—and in November 1938 it was he who signed the most drastic anti-Semitic decrees ever issued in Germany, although it has been said that he is personally no anti-Semite. One of the many jokes that have gone the rounds (Goering is one of the few Nazi higher-ups who always delighted in hearing jokes about himself, no matter how rude) is the tale of the time when Goering was late in meeting an English friend at a Berlin luncheon. He apologized, explaining that he had been out shooting. "Ah," replied the poker-faced Englishman. "Animals, I presume?"

References

Cur Hist 51:27+ F '40 il
Life 7:53+ S 11 '39 pors (Same abr. Read Digest 35:52-5 N '39)
Liv Age 348:338-40 Je '35; 354:300-1 Je '38
Nation 150:360-4 Mr 16 '40
New Yorker 16:42+ Mr 23 '40
Time 28:19-20 N 2 '36 por; 35:33 Ja 22 '40; 35:24+ Ap 1 '40 il pors; 37:79 F 24 '41 il
Bayles, W. D. Caesars in Goose Step p67-93 1940
Blood-Ryan, H. W. Göring, the Iron Man of Germany 1938
Dutch, O. pseud. Hitler's 12 Apostles p44-63 1940
Forbes, R. T. These Men I Knew p47-59 1940
Gritzbach, E. Hermann Goering: the Man and his Work 1939
Gunther, J. Inside Europe p61-6 1940
International Who's Who
Muhlens, P. R. W. Field Marshal Goering 1938
Singer, K. Göring: the Most Dangerous Man in Europe 1940
Wer ist's?

GOETZ, GEORGE *See* Calverton, V. F.

GOGARTY, OLIVER (ST. JOHN) (gō'-gĕr-tĭ) Aug. 17, 1878- Author; poet; physician

Address: h. 15 Ely Place, Dublin, Ireland

Oliver Gogarty is the witty, Casanovian Irishman whose semi-autobiography, *As I Was Going Down Sackville Street* (1937), first brought him wide attention in American literary circles. A later book, *Going Native* (1940), continues his autobiographical reminiscences together with sketches and episodes that are perhaps purely imaginary. One Gideon Ouseley (Gogarty himself) is the narrator: an Irishman who goes native in England. Beginning with a description of Yeats in old age, he proceeds to a visit with the vicar of Mea Culpa and a meeting with the vicar's beautiful niece. Gogarty's mixture of blarney, wit and scandalous asides is enjoyed by many readers and critics, heartily disliked by others. Some condemn his attempts to be risqué; others say of the book that it represents once again "the witty, gay and mischievous Gogarty contributing once more to the gayety of nations." He has been called "at once sensitive and savage, poet and ghoul, hero and knave." His most recent book is *Mad Grandeur* (1941), a novel of eighteenth century Dublin, a book which sparkles with "audacity, incisiveness, originality."

Beyond what may be gathered about him from reading his books, little is actually known of Gogarty. He is, in fact, a distinguished physician, a throat specialist who works in an up-to-date hospital and is a Fellow of the Royal College of Surgeons of Ireland. And although he pretends to be a carefree bachelor in his writings, he was married in 1906 and is the father of two sons and a daughter. Oliver St. John Gogarty was born in Dublin on August 17, 1878 and was formally educated at Stonyhurst, at Trinity College, Dublin and at Oxford. He became active in Irish politics and was elected a Senator of the Irish Free State, an office which he held from 1922 to 1936. Early one night in 1921 he was routed out of his Dublin house by his political enemies and "taken for a ride." He escaped only by jumping into the icy waters of the Liffey. To the Liffey he promised (should she return him home safely) an offering of two swans. She did, and although his country house was burned down and he and his family had to flee to England for safety, later he got the two swans and set them ceremoniously asail on the Liffey. Hence the title of his first book of poems, *An Offering of Swans* (1924).

In England after his fracas with the enemies of the Irish Free State, Gogarty spent some time with Talbot Clifton, English sportsman and explorer. Although opposed to the Government in Ireland he returned in 1937 and took no active part in politics. In that year his first full-length prose work, *As I Was Going Down Sackville Street*, appeared. It was a tour of Dublin and Dublin personalities, real and fictitious. Shortly after its publication a Dublin art dealer won a suit against Gogarty for "libelous verse and prose passages" in the book. In 1938 appeared *I*

OLIVER GOGARTY

Follow St. Patrick, and in 1939 *Tumbling in the Hay,* an autobiographical novel of his own medical student days in Dublin which one critic says "defies every convention of decency and reticence" and another calls "incoherent." Gogarty is also the author of further books of poetry: *Wild Apples* (1929) and *Elbow Room* (1939). His poems are noted for their use of epigram, their precision and clarity, revealing a talent "authentic within narrow dimensions." They have been called "as cool and fresh as a fountain, and delicate as a beautiful change of light."

In the winter of 1939 Gogarty came to America on an extensive lecture tour while he was completing his *Going Native.* He likes Americans; they like him. An interviewer wrote of the Dublin doctor: "With his erect stature, ecclesiastic countenance, lively blue eyes and stiffly brushed gray hair, he looks like a jolly Irish army chaplain in mufti."

Of his Buck Mulligan role in *Ulysses* Gogarty said: "I'm the only figure in *Ulysses* who swims, shaves, washes his neck and brushes his teeth. There is not another person in the work who has the slightest contact with soap and water." His feeling for the late Joyce, his fellow student, was one of sharp distaste because of Joyce's habit of keeping notes on every bit of conversation.

Gogarty has been further described as a man of fierce loyalties and fierce hates. Among literary figures he admires William Butler Yeats and George Moore. He loathes Eamon de Valera; he exalts Michael Collins and Arthur Griffith. Yeats was a frequent visitor to Gogarty's country house, which boasted an extremely active ghost. On one visit Yeats proceeded to "lay" it by sending

it an itemized manifesto of "don'ts." Gogarty says it worked.

Among his many interests Gogarty lists archery, which he practices when he is at his country home in Renvyle, County Galway; and aviation: he pilots his own plane. When he was younger he was a motorcycle racing enthusiast. His personality is dynamic, many-sided, his wit as ready and keen in conversation as it is in his books. He is a devout Catholic.

References

N Y Post p11 Ja 18 '40 por
Sat R Lit 10:373 D 23 '33; 10:438 Ja 27 '34 por
Time 29:83 Ap 5 '37 por
Wilson Lib Bul 11:654 Je '37 por
Catholic Who's Who
Gogarty, O. As I Was Going Down Sackville Street 1937
Gogarty, O. Going Native 1940
Gogarty, O. Tumbling in the Hay 1939
Griffin, G. Wild Geese p196-205 1938
Who's Who

GOLDMARK, HENRY June 15, 1857— Jan. 15, 1941 Civil engineer who designed and supervised the construction of lock gates for the Panama Canal; designed and built bridges for a number of railroads and was one of the first to use steel in bridge construction; had been consulting engineer to New York City and supervisor of important projects throughout the world.

References

American Men of Science
Who's Who in American Jewry
Who's Who in Engineering

Obituaries

N Y Times p22 Ja 16 '41

GOODRICH, ARTHUR (FREDERICK) Feb. 18, 1878—June 26, 1941 Novelist and playwright; started career in publishing firm and then held editorial posts on *World's Work, Outing Magazine* and the *American Magazine*; first play *Yes or No* (1917) was followed by a number of successful productions, the most outstanding of which was *Caponsacchi,* produced at the Metropolitan in 1936; author of novels, the most recent of which was *The Sound of Wings* (1941).

References

Cur Opinion 73:626 N '22 por
Theatre 27:75 Mr '18 por
Mantle, B. Contemporary American Playwrights p269 1938
Who's Who in America
Who's Who in the Theatre

Obituaries

N Y Times p18 Je 27 '41
Variety 143:54 Jl 2 '41

GOODRICH, MARCUS (AURELIUS)
Nov. 28, 1897- Author; scenarist
Address: b. c/o Farrar & Rinehart, Inc, 232
Madison Ave, New York City

Paul Woolf

MARCUS GOODRICH

Late in the '20s, a young man, doing odd
writing jobs for the newspapers and the screen,
used to fascinate his friends by telling them
stories of violent action, colored by passionate
and rich imagination, and mostly having to do
with a ship. Clifton Fadiman (see sketch this
issue), who had listened to those stories, writes
about the young man: "Above all things he
wanted to be a writer, but none of us was
convinced he would ever be. He was, we
thought, too good a talker. He saved nothing
for the writing desk. I knew vaguely that he
was at work on a long novel. As the years
passed . . . my conviction was, with regret,
reinforced, that Marcus Goodrich would never
finish that book."

Fadiman was wrong. Marcus Goodrich did
finish that book, though it took him more than
15 years to do it. Called *Delilah*, it was enthusiastically greeted by most of the reviewers
when Farrar & Rinehart brought it out on
January 29, 1941, and reached the best-
seller list. On March 20, 1941, its author
flew to Chicago from the coast to receive the
$1,000 1941 award from the Friends of
American Writers.

The story charts Goodrich's own experiences on a destroyer during the last War,
"heightened by his study of Melville's
towering symbolism, Conrad's profuse style
and James' snakelike character analysis."
Add to this long-drawn-out Proustian dissec-
tion of impressions and actions, as applied to
the simple seaman, and you will see that
Delilah is no mere adventure story. It is
really an impassioned and highly personal
study of the complicated organism that is a

destroyer; the plot is a progression of increasingly brutal episodes, starting with the
ship's race across the Sula Sea and ending
in a "crescendo of riot, bloodshed and insanity
that coincides with the declaration of war."
During that time the author has been able to
transmit to the reader the personalities of the
violent yet sturdy people who man the ship:
the Old Man, with his almost superhuman
responsibility; O'Connel, the huge Irishman
whose spell of bloody madness ends the book;
the dapper Bidot; the bully Feenan; the old
monk whose conflict with the drunken trader
makes some of the best pages in the book.

Marcus Aurelius Goodrich was born November 28, 1897 in San Antonio, Texas, son
of Briggs Benjamin and his cousin Helene
(Goodrich) Goodrich. The Goodrich family
was a well known one. Benjamin Briggs
Goodrich, the author's great-grandfather,
signed the Texas Declaration of Independence
and helped draft the Texas Constitution;
another Goodrich was killed in the Battle of
the Alamo, an historical occurrence that means
a great deal to Marcus Goodrich, who
digresses for many pages in his book to write
a vivid description of it. He received his
education in the public schools of San Antonio
(Stephen F. Austin Grammar School, Breck-
enbridge Junior High School, San Antonio
High School). During that time he also acquired a passion for literature. His mother,
"a blonde who read Elinor Glyn" but who
"knew what I wanted and wanted to help me,"
fed him volume after volume of Everyman's
Library. After high school Marcus served
with the Texas National Guard on the Mexican border through part of the 1914 crisis
there.

Shortly afterward he ran away to sea and
joined the Navy as an apprentice seaman.
He stayed there all through the War years,
serving on cruisers, a battleship, a gunboat,
a submarine and a torpedo-boat destroyer,
which was lost in action. During his service
he took copious notes which were very useful to him later when he wrote *Delilah*. It
is probable that Warrington, the bookish
Texan lad in his story, was a picture of himself in those days. He served on a tiny anti-
quated destroyer, the *U. S. S. Chauncey*,
which was one of the first to take action
against the enemy submarines after a spectacular dash from Manila to Gibraltar. He
left the Navy in 1920 as a commissioned officer and naval aviator.

His Navy days over (although he had to
return as reserve flying officer for a few
weeks every year until 1925), he finished his
education, which had been interrupted by the
War, at Columbia University. He had decided
to become a writer. He found employment on
various newspapers here and abroad. He
worked for the New York *Tribune*, the New
York *World*, the New York *Evening Post*.
He was for a while dramatic editor and
second dramatic critic on the New York
Tribune and also used to write special features for the New York *Times Magazine*.
His essay on Maugham's *Of Human Bondage*
was supposed to have renewed interest in

that classic. Periodically he traveled to Europe, where he would work for the Paris *Herald*, send back stories to the *Times* and spend his time sitting around cafes with the Ernest Hemingway group and killing what seemed to be a great thirst. Goodrich himself says cheerfully of those days: "I was drunk most of the time. My father had been a drunk and my grandfather. I didn't see how I could avoid it. People told me that drinking was nothing to worry about, that great art came from liquor and that without its help imagination was not free. . . I've been pulled out of gutters in many of the best cities in the world." (What home life he had he shared with Caroline Sleeth whom he married in 1927 and from whom he was divorced some years later after the birth of a daughter Helene.)

Mr. Goodrich thought the situation over and found that drinking interfered with his writing. "I compared my writings in sobriety with my drunken efforts," he says gravely. "The sober work was better." Henceforth he devoted his time solely to writing the traditional "great novel," which in his case was *Delilah*. Since writing one book for fourteen years is not a paying proposition, Goodrich kept himself going by odd writing jobs. He wrote advertising copy for N. W. Ayer & Son of Philadelphia. He drifted into the movies, where his good "story mind" served to good purpose. His first experience was working as a scenarist with Vitaphone. Later he worked as writer and technical adviser for MGM, United Artists, RKO (*Night Waitress*, 1936), Republic (*Navy Born*, 1936) and Paramount (*The Trumpet Blows,* 1934). During that time he had been "keeping his soul alive" by talking *Delilah* to anybody who would listen.

In 1932 he signed a contract with John Farrar, who was enthralled with the book just from hearing Goodrich tell his stories about it. The publishers have helped him generously, and he took jobs only when he absolutely had to, spending his time mostly in Mexico or Central America, where living is cheap. In 1937 he collaborated on a play called *The Mighty Treve*. But his main activity was writing and rewriting his book.

Goodrich is an ardent and deliberate stylist, a man who is enthralled with the sound of words. And he prefers 25-dollar words. As a matter of fact, one of *Delilah's* failings is that in many parts they get the better of him and in his intoxication he loses the sight of their meaning. In one of the few detractory reviews of *Delilah*, Otis Ferguson of the *New Republic* remarks on that. He also says sourly that the "ear appeal of this book is apparently strong to armchair navigators but I hardly think it will go down as literature." Yet Goodrich, a tall rugged Texan with craggy features and blue eyes, is rather pleased with the style he evolved—a style which is a sort of Melville-out-of-Hemingway creation with a dash of Proust. He is frankly scornful of the "fetish of short sentences and short words", "the insistence that all Ameri-

cans . . . write like backwoodsmen." He is pleased with the book as a whole. Its failure —a failure of 15 years' steady work—would have meant that his whole life was a failure. As it is, he has regained a complete sense of personal integrity and is ready to go on with a sequel, *Delilah in War*, which will take about a year to write.

References

> N Y Herald Tribune Books p1 F 2 '41 por
> N Y Times Book R p2, 14 F 16 '41 por
> New Yorker 16:53 F 1 '41
> Pub W 139:241 Ja 18 '41 il
> International Motion Picture Almanac

GORDON, C(HARLES) HENRY June 17, 1884—Dec. 3, 1940 Screen villain, seen most recently in *Kit Carson*; name originally was Henry Racke.

References

> Motion Pict 216:22 O '33 por
> Photoplay 45:72, 100 D '33 por
> International Motion Picture Almanac 1937-38

Obituaries

> N Y Times p27 D 4 '40 por

GÖRING, HERMANN WILHELM *See* Goering, H. W.

GOUDY, FREDERIC W(ILLIAM) (gou'dĭ) Mar. 8, 1865- Typographer *Address:* h. Marlborough-on-Hudson, N. Y.

FREDERIC W. GOUDY

Most of the popular type faces of today were designed years ago: Caslon, Baskerville, Jenson, Bodoni, to name the best-known. But not all. Frederic William Goudy, who cele-

GOUDY, FREDERIC W.—*Continued*

brated his seventy-sixth birthday on March 8, 1941, is the creator of over a hundred type faces, "outstanding for their simple strength and beauty." These types have been widely used in fine books; they have been widely seen in advertisements and are, indeed, supposed to "have transformed the advertising pages of every magazine in America." It is easy to understand why *"Goudiamus igitur* has been the motto of printers for some years."

Goudy came to his position of eminence in the typographical world only after a career that was dogged by misfortune—a career marked by unprofitable work as an accountant, thin spells of free-lancing and two fires which destroyed a good part of his work. He was born in Bloomington, Illinois, the son of John Fleming Goudy, a schoolmaster, and Amanda M. (Truesdell) Goudy. When his parents moved to Shelbyville, Illinois, young Goudy attended school there and was graduated from high school in 1883. He had earned part of his living by acting as janitor and copying drawings, and when he left school he started to earn his living in earnest as assistant to Shelbyville's leading paper hanger.

Goudy was a paper hanger for only a short while. His father soon moved to South Dakota, where he became a Federal probate judge and a real-estate operator, and took Frederic with him as his bookkeeper. Frederic worked for his father for three years and then spent a number of years wandering through the Midwest, getting jobs here and there as an accountant, learning practical printing in small-town shops. He was becoming, during these years, more and more interested in typography and lettering; and in 1895, together with an English teacher named C. Lauren Hooper, he set up his Camelot Press in Chicago. It was here that he drew his first type face. He sent it off to the Dickinson Type Foundry in Boston with a note saying that if they could use it, it was worth $5. The company sent back a check for $10, and since this face, Camelot, is still selling today, has probably never regretted its generosity.

The Camelot Press printed a rather precious artistic journal called the *Chap-Book* which soon faded out, and the Press with it. Goudy was thrown back on bookkeeping and got himself a job as cashier for a journal called the *Michigan Farmer.* He soon lost it—before him he saw a future of a dreary succession of dreary small-town accounting jobs. Anything was better than that. He decided to strike out in another direction, and went with his wife, Bertha M. Sprinks, whom he had married in 1897, to Chicago to set himself up as a free-lance designer of book jackets, advertising layouts, initial letters. He survived, but only just.

Then things began to improve. In 1903, the year he evolved an alphabet which was used for advertisements for Kuppenheimer clothes, he acquired a partner, some 150 pounds of type and a small hand press. He and his wife set themselves up in an old barn at Park Ridge, Illinois and together ran the modest Village Press, its first book an essay on printing by William Morris. In 1904 they moved the Village Press to Hingham, Massachusetts, a little later to New York. Then in 1908 the Village Press burned. There was little insurance, and Goudy found himself back where he had been five years before.

He had to start all over again. He took desk space in an advertising agency in return for odd drawing jobs and turned his designing once more to commercial ends. Within a year he had scraped together enough to visit Europe to study old types, and he returned from his trip determined to be almost exclusively a type designer. Soon afterward he was asked by Mitchell Kennerley, the New York publisher, to design a book face and font of display capitals. The result was Kennerley, "the most beautiful type put within the reach of English printers since the first Caslon began casting about the year 1724." Kennerley, Forum Titling and other faces were taken up by such solid concerns as the British firm of Caslon, and the American Type Founders' Corporation bought his Goudy, Goudy Bold and Goudy Old Style. Other firms bought other faces—they became immensely popular, widely used for both book work and display. The Lanston Monotype Company in 1920 made him its consultant and he still holds this position.

A few years after the War, Goudy had re-established his Village Press, and in 1924, with the profits from his many commissions and from a lucky real-estate deal, bought a house and workshop (Deepdene) at Marlborough-on-Hudson. Here his wife (he dedicated his one-hundredth original font to her) composed for him until she died in 1935; his son, Frederic T. Goudy, ran the machines; and Goudy himself learned to cut matrices. Every process of book making, from design to printing, was carried out there by the family. And then, after 15 years, this workshop, too, was gutted by fire, on January 26, 1939. The old mill in which everything was housed was burned to the ground and with it type patterns, drawings, foundry matrices and machinery for cutting matrices, much of these irreplaceable. But Goudy didn't give up. "I still have my right hand," he said, "and can always buy a pencil." He started work almost immediately on drawing and pattern making and began working even harder on his autobiography. His friends and fellow artists and the general public as well rallied around and presented him with a testimonial fund at a dinner in his honor—a fund that has been used to build and equip a one-room studio addition to the Goudy home at Marlborough.

Goudy's types are, according to one critic, "beautiful because they are simple; they are dignified, they are sturdy and honest and strong." They stand up well whether they are displayed in an advertisement or grouped on a book page. "I have never permitted myself to allow my craft to become an end in itself instead of a means only to a desirable and useful end," he once said. In recognition of what he has done for American graphic arts he has been awarded the gold medals of the American Institute of Architects, the Architectural League of New York and the American Institute of Graphic Arts, as well as medals from the Ulster-Irish Society of New York and Syracuse University's School of Journalism.

Goudy has been author and editor as well as type designer. His *The Alphabet* was published in 1918, and *Elements of Lettering* followed in 1922. In 1936 *Capitals from the Trajan Column at Rome* was published and in 1940 *Typologia* appeared. Goudy has also been the editor of *Ars Typographica*, a quarterly magazine, and he has lectured in many schools and universities. It was while this genial, bespectacled typographer "who looks like a Sunday-school superintendent" was giving a course in lettering at New York University years ago that he made one of his more famous characteristic remarks. As told in the *New Yorker*, a sweet bright young thing in his class raised her hand and asked: "Professor, how do you design type?" Goudy turned to her: "You think of a letter, and then you mark around it," he easily replied.

References

Art Digest 13:11 F 15 '39
Christian Sci Mon Mag p5 Ap 14 '37 il por
Lit Digest 116:11 N 11 '33 por
New Yorker 8:20-5 Ja 14 '33
Newsweek 1:28 Jl 8 '33; 13:30 F 6 '39 pors
Pub W 127:1067 Mr 9 '35; 134:378-9 Ag 6 '38 por; 135:593 F 4 '39; 135:1140 Mr 18 '39
Sat R Lit 17:14+ Mr 5 '38; 24:12 My 24 '41

Beilenson, P.   Story of Frederic W. Goudy 1939
Bower, W. ed. New Directions p427-35 1937
Lewis, B. Behind the Type 1941
Mackaye, M. Glorifier of the Alphabet: Frederic W. Goudy 1933
Orton, V. Goudy 1939
Who's Who Among North American Authors
Who's Who in America
Who's Who in American Art

GRACE, EUGENE GIFFORD Aug. 27, 1876- Steel manufacturer

Address: b. Bethlehem Steel Corp, 25 Broadway, New York City; h. 12th and Prospect Aves, Bethlehem, Pa.

One of the firms most important to national defense is the Bethlehem Steel Corporation, whose president is tall, slender, placid-faced Eugene Gifford Grace. Since the First World War the Pennsylvania town which claims Mr. Grace as first citizen has not presented such a picture of frenzied industry. There is a boom in steel; in February 1941 the Bethlehem Steel Company had over a billion dollars in defense contracts. And since the death of Charles Schwab in 1939 the name of Eugene

Grace has been synonymous with that of Bethlehem Steel.

Eugene Gifford Grace was born on August 27, 1876, the son of John W. and Rebecca (Morris) Grace. Even as a boy he was interested in mechanical and electrical matters, and fond of performing experiments in order to work out some of his theories. When he went to Lehigh University in 1895 he used to wander about the steel mills, and would sometimes get permission to work in them in order to perform further experiments for his laboratory courses. His scholastic record was excellent, and he acquired his "L" as captain of the varsity baseball team before taking his degree in Electrical Engineering in 1899. (Three decades later the University gave him an honorary degree of Doctor of Engineering.) June 29, 1899 was his first day at Bethlehem as operator of an electric crane—a laborer's job which paid less than $2 a day. But Grace was determined to forge his career in steel.

He rose quickly. By 1902 Eugene Grace was superintendent of yards and transportation, by 1905 general superintendent of the Juragua Iron Company, a subsidiary company of Bethlehem. Charles Schwab, "the American Krupp," already had his eye on him. The following year he was promoted to the general superintendency of Bethlehem, and two years later he was elected its general manager and a member of the board of directors. It was 1911 when he was appointed both vice-president and general manager of Bethlehem and a director of the Bethlehem Steel Corporation, and it was April 1, 1913 when he became president of Bethlehem Steel Company.

At that time Schwab's company was mainly a munitions and ship firm, but even in 1914, when many other companies were losing money, its earnings were $9,600,000. With the coming of the First World War the Allies signed contracts for its full munitions capacity, and in two years $300,000,000 in munitions were sold to Great Britain. "Bethlehem became War Bride No. 1 on the New York stock exchange," rising from an average of 30 in the years from 1913 to 1914, to 600 in 1915. In 1916 Schwab bought the Pennsylvania Steel Company, doubling Bethlehem's capitalization and transforming it into a general steel organization matching United States Steel. Grace became president of the Bethlehem Steel Corporation on February 17 of that year, and he proceeded to acquire a staff of experts and metallurgical specialists to undertake research and experimentation on a vast scale and also to introduce new methods of mining, smelting, refining and manufacturing.

In October 1917 Grace also acquired the presidency of the Bethlehem Shipbuilding Corporation, which got huge Government contracts for transports, cruisers and ships of all kinds, and which became known for its success in getting the boats from the "keel-laying stage" to the water in record time. Cannon, ammunition and armor plate were also supplied to the United States Government, and "Schwab's organization emerged from the War as the

EUGENE GIFFORD GRACE

world's most prosperous and second largest steel firm."

During April and May of 1918 there was a series of swift strikes among Bethlehem employees. The National War Labor Board begged the company to bargain collectively with them. As a result, in 1918 a plan providing for the election of employees' representatives was installed in Bethlehem—a plan which also offered a program of group health, plant safety and sports. It was called the Employee Representation Plan and was considered forward-looking by Bethlehem officials, but after the fierce repulsion of the 1919 steel strikes and the adoption of ERP by such companies as United States Steel, Labor began to think of it as synonymous with company unionism.

Bethlehem continued to expand. Schwab, as chairman of the Board, acquired the Cambria Plant at Johnstown, Pennsylvania, the Lackawanna Steel Company near Buffalo, the Maryland Steel Company at Sparrows Point, the Pacific Coast Steel Company, the McClintic-Marshall Corporation. From 1917 to 1931 Grace collected from Bethlehem $12,282,000 in bonuses alone. (In 1938 the stockholders sued to check what they termed a "present" of $16,000,000 to Schwab, Grace and other officers, but they lost the suit.)

Then, in 1933, came the NIRA. The board of the American Iron and Steel Institute, which represented 95 per cent of the total steel producing capacity of the United States and numbered among its members the president of Bethlehem, organized itself as the code authority for steel. Grace was on the administrative committee. His views were that the NIRA constituted a "charter of liberties" under which "our business structure is being put on a firmer basis, which will be helpful to our national economy. . . The Government, through the Industrial Recovery Act, aims to

make possible recurring profits and dividends, which cannot be accomplished by robbing the capital which makes the output possible." And, although "certain groups of labor agitators" were trying to "chisel special advantages under the Recovery Act," Bethlehem's representation plan actually represented the "democratization of industry in its highest form." In accordance with this understanding the board of the American Iron and Steel Institute set about to fix prices and labor policies in the steel industry. Grace was to serve as its president from 1935 to 1936, and later to become director.

In 1934, the year in which he was awarded the Gary Medal, Grace announced at the open banquet of the Institute: "I believe I voice the opinion of everyone within my hearing when I say that we shall continue to maintain the open shop in the steel industry and by so doing insure to the employees the recognition and reward for industrial effort as against the closed union shop where all men are equal."

Nevertheless NIRA died, and the open shop was not maintained throughout the steel industry. After 1937 the Steel Workers Organizing Committee of the CIO got contracts in Big Steel and other plants. And after an appeal to the National Labor Relations Board by the CIO, following the 1937 strike in Bethlehem's Cambria plant, Bethlehem itself was ordered to withdraw recognition from and disestablish ERP at its 10 most important plants. This order Bethlehem officials are still fighting in 1941, on the grounds that ERP is not company unionism. (For months they also refused to heed the Government's order to pay ·a 62½-cent hourly minimum as provided by the Walsh-Healey Act, but eventually agreed to this.) Strikes have broken out as the CIO has gained strength in Bethlehem plants; minority stockholders have protested against the corporation's labor policies.

Even in 1939 Bethlehem's big Eastern shipyards were running at full capacity, and in October of that year President Grace announced the first dividend for Bethlehem's stockholders since 1937. "We are," he said, "in a position to be War Baby No. 1, as in the last War, but I can tell you that our directors and associates don't want that kind of business." This does not mean that Grace is opposed to war profits, however. On February 25, 1935, testifying before the Senate Committee investigating munitions industries, he stated that "private industry should be aided and encouraged in time of war and in my opinion should not be subjected to conscription the same as man power," for "nothing has ever been invented, in war-time or peace-time, that would make men work as hard as the lure of money and profit" In 1940 Bethlehem profits reached an all-time peak of $48,677,524; orders on hand also set a new record. Net profit for the first half of 1941 was $16,087,485, the decrease due to a higher rate of taxation. And in 1940 Grace's salary was listed as $478,144.

Mr. Grace is a trustee of St. Luke's Hospital and president of the board of trustees of Lehigh University in Bethlehem, a member of the Iron and Steel Institute of Great Britain, of the American Institute of Mining and Metallurgical Engineers, of the Society of Arts and Sciences in New York. He is a Presbyterian. He is a champion golfer. In 1917 he won the Hay Cup in the Northampton County Country Club Tournament; in 1919 he won the cup in the Shawnee Fall Tournament; and as recently as 1928 he acquired the Saucon Valley Country Club championship. On June 12, 1902 he married Marion Brown of Bethlehem, and they have a daughter and two sons: Emmeline Marion, Charles Brown and Eugene Gifford Grace, Jr., now all grown. His house is a regal structure on what has become known as "Bonus Hill."

References

Fortune 23:60-5+ Ap '41 por
Nation 143:236-7 Ag 29 '36
New Repub 95:102 Je 1 '38
N Y Times p16 F 25 '41
Newsweek 16:50-1 Ag 5 '40
PM p19-21 F 10 '41 pors; p18-19 F 14 '41 il pors; p18 F 16 '41 il pors; p21 F 27 '41 pors; p19 Mr 2 '41 por
Time 29:11 Je 28 '37 por; 33:18 Ja 9 '39 por; 33:67 My 15 '39 por; 34:67 N 6 '39 por; 37:16 Mr 10 '41 por
O'Connor, H. Steel—Dictator 1935
White, T. M. Famous Leaders of Industry 3d ser. p81-90 1931
Who's Who in America
Who's Who in Commerce and Industry

GRAHAM, FRANK P(ORTER) Oct. 14, 1886- Member of the National Defense Mediation Board; president of the University of North Carolina

Address: b. University of North Carolina, Chapel Hill, N. C.

Frank Porter Graham, president of the University of North Carolina and a "fiery and apostolic liberal," was made a member of the National Defense Mediation Board when it was set up in March 1941. As a representative of the public (rather than of industry or labor) he is helping to negotiate agreements in industrial disputes which don't seem likely to be settled by ordinary means.

Dr. Graham had to recommend him for this position a long career devoted to the achievement of social justice. Back in 1929, when the textile strikes in Gastonia and Marion were turning North Carolina into a battleground, he addressed to the people of the State a statement of principles which in substance asked that the constitutional and legal rights of person, property and lawful freedom of speech and assembly be guaranteed equally to all persons in North Carolina without regard to birthplace, race, ownership or labor status, unionism or non-unionism, religion, politics or economic views. This statement, signed by more than 400 people, also called for a nationwide, non-partisan economic and social survey of the textile industry in America.

FRANK P. GRAHAM

Since then, whenever industrial conflicts have started, he has written, lectured, argued as the "flaming apostle of a better social order." As president of the North Carolina Conference of Social Service he helped prepare and sponsor the first workmen's compensation act in North Carolina, still considered the best in the Southern states. And in this position he constantly pleaded for a commonwealth "where individualism will not mean the freedom of any individual to impair the lives of other men . . . where machines shall not . . . tyrannize over the bodies and spirits of men; where children in factories shall become children in school; where there shall be no industrial night work for women."

In his fight for social justice, too, Dr. Graham founded the Citizen's Liberation Movement and in 1941 is a member of the general board of the Southern Electoral Reform League, which aims at a "direct frontal attack on the voter poll tax and the politicians who defend it."

Besides his liberalism and knowledge of the industrial problems of the South, Dr. Graham had his record of government service to recommend him for his position on the Mediation Board. During the days of the National Recovery Administration he was vice-chairman of the Consumers' Board, and in the fall of 1934 was made chairman of the National Advisory Council to the Cabinet Committee on Economic Security. He is also chairman of the Industries Committee of American Railroads and a member of the President's Committee on Education.

Dr. Graham comes of a family of teachers. His cousin, Dr. Edward Kidder Graham, was president of the University of North Carolina from 1914 to 1918; his father, Alexander Graham, who founded the public schools of

GRAHAM, FRANK P.—*Continued*

Fayetteville, North Carolina and was head of the schools at Charlotte from 1888 to 1913, is called the father of the graded schools system in North Carolina. His mother was Katherine Bryan (Sloan) Graham. Frank Porter Graham was born in Fayetteville and brought up in Charlotte, where he attended high school. In 1905 he entered the University of North Carolina as a freshman, four years later received his B. A., and then studied law at the University's law school (he has a license to practice from the Supreme Court).

After a period teaching English in the Raleigh High School, Dr. Graham (he is Doctor by virtue of six honorary degrees) returned to the University of North Carolina as secretary of the Y. M. C. A. In 1914 he was appointed an instructor in history there, and the following year studied at Columbia University, which awarded him an M. A. in 1915. His next leave of absence from the University took place in 1917, when the United States entered the First World War. Dr. Graham enlisted as a private in the marine corps and rose to first lieutenant before he was mustered out in July 1919.

He returned to the University of North Carolina as assistant professor of history and for one year held the position of dean of students. It was during this year and the next that largely through his inspiration and leadership a bond issue of $20,000,000 was provided by the Legislature for the educational and charitable institutions of the State. In 1921 Dr. Graham was made an associate professor and the following year went to the University of Chicago for graduate study. Here he won the two-year Amherst Memorial fellowship. A year in Washington, D. C., studying at the Brookings Institute and the Library of Congress, came next, followed by a period of research and study at the British Museum, the London School of Economics and the League of Nations in Geneva. In 1925 Dr. Graham returned to North Carolina and two years later became a full professor.

During the years he taught, Dr. Graham did more than just his class work: he went to football rallies, gave Phi Beta Kappa addresses, attended meetings of the local post of the American Legion, led the movement to improve North Carolina's library facilities ("We mean to hew to the line and cut through ignorance, indifference, inertia and inequality," he said, "until every person has equal public access to books in every county in North Carolina"). And the last year he taught he was voted by the senior class one of the best teachers in the University.

That was in 1930, for in June of that year, "over his protests," he was elected to the presidency of his Alma Mater. He took over the position "with wider approval than could have been given any other man." Since then, "generally rated the ablest United States state university president, he has helped make North Carolina tops in the South." Shortly after he took over, North Carolina found itself "enmeshed by the depression in one of the worst educational tangles in the country."

Graham was given responsibility by the board of trustees for writing the plan for consolidating the three institutions of higher learning (State College of Agriculture, North Carolina College for Women and University of North Carolina) which now constitute the University of North Carolina.

It was not long after his inauguration, too, that he became involved in one of the many fights for freedom of thought and speech which have distinguished his career. One of the first of these fights had taken place back in 1925 when the Fundamentalists tried to restrict teaching in North Carolina. Graham, who was in Europe at the time, sent a statement to the press on "Evolution, the University and the People," which urged the people of his state to fight against the "false fear of the foes of freedom" and to hold "the first line trench against bigotry." When the Fundamentalists revived their effort two years later, Graham helped stop it dead in its tracks.

His next big fight came in 1932 when a petition was sent to the Governor of North Carolina protesting the fact that Bertrand Russell and Langston Hughes were being allowed to speak on the campus. Graham in answer told a class of students that the University would never shut its windows to outside light and never close the book of knowledge. Today, when various interests and the Legislature try to silence his liberal professors, he fights back; and in speeches and in articles he fights for the cause of academic freedom and democracy in education all over the United States. Dr. Graham still holds fast to the words of his inaugural address: "Freedom of the University means freedom of the scholar to find and report the truth honestly without interference by the University, the State or any interests whatever."

Dr. Graham, after many years of bachelorhood, was married in 1932 to Marian Drane of Edenton, North Carolina. Today she shares his reputation for being "favorably known in every nook and corner of North Carolina. He calls by their first names more people than any other man in the state and is addressed by more people in the same intimate manner." And most of these people will agree that the eulogies written of him when he became the University's president still hold good today. "He combines in his astounding personality," *The Nation* wrote, "high intellectual ability, convictions that are firm but free from intolerance, an unbounded patience, limitless energy, an enthusiasm almost apostolic in its fervor, an extraordinary capacity and natural felicity for finding a direct way into personal and public confidence and above all a quiet willingness to be forgotten."

References

Nation 131:240-1 S 3 '30
New Outlook 164:28 S '34

Leaders in Education 1941
Who's Who in America

GRANGER, WALTER Nov. 7, 1872—Sept. 7, 1941 Noted explorer and paleontologist; member of the staff of the American Museum of National History in New York for more than a half century; veteran of 28 expeditions which took him, among other places, to the deserts of Egypt and Mongolia; author of several books on paleontology; well known as a college lecturer; was largely responsible for the towering skeletons of dinosaurs in the American Museum of Natural History which have given visitors a popular interest in paleontology.

References

Nat Hist 47:172-6 Mr '41 por

American Men of Science
Who's Who in America

Obituaries

N Y Times p15 S 8 '41 por

GRANT, CARY Jan. 18, 1904- Film actor
Address: h. Santa Monica, Calif.

In his years in Hollywood, Cary Grant, six-foot-one, black-haired, dark-eyed, has played in more than 40 films—parts that include everything from the mock turtle in *Alice in Wonderland*, Pinkerton in *Madame Butterfly* and Mae West's "warm, dark and handsome" young man to Katharine Hepburn's sophisticated comedy lead. And in 1941 he was even being announced for the role of Sheridan Whiteside in *The Man Who Came to Dinner*. He went to work on other films instead, among them Alfred Hitchcock's (see sketch this issue) atmospheric psychological thriller, *Suspicion*, in which critics applauded him in a new kind of role. But his reputation for versatility wasn't hurt. Cary Grant likes it. He still ruefully remembers the days when he was a stock player at Paramount, a period when "I was just the nice young man who knew how to put his hands in his pockets and smile broadly at the girl."

Now one of the highest priced actors on the screen, in constant demand by glamorous stars like Carole Lombard, Irene Dunne, Rosalind Russell and Katharine Hepburn, his performances consistently praised by the critics, Cary Grant started his acting career as a knockdown comic, clown, eccentric dancer and stiltwalker. He was about 13 at the time. He was born in Bristol, England, christened Alexander Archibald Leach by his parents, Elias and Lillian (Kingdom) Leach, and sent to Fairfield Academy in Somerset. He ran away from school to join Bog Pender's Acrobats, but his father, a clothing manufacturer who was not influenced by the fact that his own father, Percival Leach, had played Shakespearean roles with Forbes-Robertson, caught up with Archie in about four weeks.

Archie submitted to education for about two years and then, at the age of fifteen, ran off again. This time he stuck with the Pender troupe and for five years lived the hard life of an acrobatic comic trouper in training. With the troupe he came to New York in 1921 to do an act in a Fred Stone show. Pender's acrobats then moved over to the

CARY GRANT

Hippodrome, and from there went back to England. But not Archie. He stayed.

There were times when he wished he hadn't. He played in honky-tonks, walked stilts in a carnival show at Coney Island and at one time is reputed to have sunk to painting neckties with Orry-Kelly. After two years of not much better than this Archie Leach returned to England, where without much trouble he landed small parts in musical comedies. An Arthur Hammerstein scout saw him and signed him to sing the juvenile lead in New York in *Golden Dawn*. After this came other parts: roles in *Polly* and in *Boom Boom*, the lead in *Wonderful Night* and a romantic role opposite Queenie Smith in *Street Singer*. The summer of 1931 was spent in St. Louis, playing the lead in 12 operettas at the St. Louis Municipal Opera in Forest Park. In the fall he was back on Broadway playing with Fay Wray and Kent Douglass in *Nikki*. This was his last Broadway appearance. For five years, altogether, Archie Leach had been working in Hammerstein musicals and for the Shuberts, and though he had hardly set the world, or even much of Broadway, afire.

He set out for Hollywood in a secondhand car, lived for a while in cheap hotels and finally found himself a job in motion pictures and the name of Cary Grant. His debut was in *This Is The Night* in 1932, his part that of Thelma Todd's gesturing, javelin-throwing husband. Other parts followed fast—in *Hot Saturday*, *Merrily We Go To Hell*, in *Blonde Venus* with Marlene Dietrich, in *She Done Him Wrong* with Mae West. Cary Grant still thinks fondly of his two pictures with Mae West. "I learned everything from her," he says. "Well, no—not quite everything, but almost everything. She knows so much. Her instinct is so true, her timing so perfect, her grasp of the situation so right."

GRANT, CARY—*Continued*

Grant was under contract to Paramount during these years, though he was occasionally lent out to other studios. And after his sessions with Mae West his assignments were mostly run-of-the-mill ones. He admitted "they had a lot of leading men over there with dark hair and a set of teeth like mine and they couldn't be buying stories for each of us." Then in 1936 he was borrowed by RKO for *Sylvia Scarlett*, playing opposite Katharine Hepburn. This picture did nothing to endear its female lead to the public, but it helped make its male lead a success. He liked his part of a dastardly fellow: "For once they didn't see me as a nice young man with regular features and a heart of gold," and when favorable comments began rolling in Cary Grant decided to become a free lance after his contract with Paramount expired in 1937.

Along came *Topper*, *The Awful Truth* and *Bringing Up Baby*, and within 12 months after he went on his own Cary Grant was accepted as the screen's leading light comedian, on top of the Hollywood heap. But he didn't stick only to comedy: there were serious pictures like *Gunga Din*, *Only Angels Have Wings* and *The Howards of Virginia*. And Grant was satisfied with his free-lance status. "Working for more than one company has its advantages," he commented. "You are able to get staple assignments and often a studio will buy a story with you in mind." The studios paid him well, too, reputedly $125,000 for his role in *Philadelphia Story*, for instance.

This last money he donated to British War Relief. Other money he has spent in the usual Hollywood manner. His suits are London tailored, usually worn with a scarf instead of a tie, and seldom topped off with a hat—"I never can get a hat that looks good. I have that kind of a face." His house on the beach at Santa Monica has 12 rooms, a secretary who runs it and enough servants to keep it going smoothly. Its location is perfect, he thinks. "I like the ocean because no one can build a house in front of me or plant a high hedge or put up a billboard." And its interior is distinctive among Hollywood houses because there aren't any photos of him around, no more than in his studio dressing room. All pictures of Cary Grant are kept in his bathroom, which, he feels, is the correct place for them.

Some of his earnings, of course, go to entertain his friends and especially girls, and rumors about his love-life are always current. A long time ago he was seen frequently with Mary Brian, and tales of this romance were followed by pictures of Cary with various society girls. Later Mary Carlisle was reported his main interest, then Ginger Rogers (see sketch this issue). In February 1934 he temporarily stopped speculation with his marriage to blonde Virginia Cherrill, who played the poverty-stricken flower girl in Chaplin's *City Lights*. He announced that he and his wife were going to "live a simple, quiet life." Eight months later Cary Grant was being treated in a sanatorium after what was hardly a simple, quiet separation, and finally in March 1935 they were divorced. Since then Cary Grant has remained one of Hollywood's most eligible bachelors, his name linked with Phyllis Brooks for a while and then with Barbara Hutton, but he himself noncommittal.

He gets around Hollywood a lot and likes gay parties. At them, as often as not, he gravitates to the piano to play favorites like *Nola* or *Kitten on the Keys* or even his own jazz improvisations. He doesn't need an audience, either, and the same sort of thing goes on at home. Much of the time at home, though, he studies his scripts carefully, for he's canny about his career. And he also spends happy moments reading current novels, just lying on the beach, playing backgammon or sporting with his two Sealyhams, Cholmondeley and Archie Leach, whose names (like the kippers and tea he has for breakfast) are fond heritages of old England and his own past.

References

Motion Pict Mag 50:38-9+ Ja '36 il por; 52:35+ D '36 por
Photoplay 49:48-9+ Jl '36 il pors; 51: 4 Je '37 por; 52:22+ My '38 il pors; 53:26-7+ Ap '39 il pors; 54:22+ F '40 il pors; 54:20-2+ S '40 il pors; 54:14-15 N '40 il pors
Stage 16:34-6 Ap 15 '39 por
Time 35:86+ My 20 '40 por
Woman's H C 66:7 O '39 por

International Motion Picture Almanac
Who's Who in America

GRASER, EARLE W. (grā'zer) 1909(?)—Apr. 8, 1941

Radio performer who as the voice of the "Lone Ranger" was a hero to countless thousands of radio listeners not only in the United States but in many foreign countries as well; killed in an automobile accident; for the last nine years had played the radio role of the crusading "Lone Ranger," whose familiar call, "Hi-yo, Silver!" was echoed as a sort of "battle cry" by thousands of children on playgrounds throughout the land; program broadcast over 150 network radio stations and scores of independent stations; Graser was a lawyer and holder of three college degrees.

References

Sat Eve Post 212:20-1+ O 14 '39 il por

Obituaries

N Y Times p27 Ap 9 '41 por
Time 37:54+ Ap 21 '41
Variety 142:22 Ap 9 '41

GRAUER, BEN(NETT FRANKLIN) (grou'er) June 2, 1908-

Radio commentator; announcer

Address: b. c/o National Broadcasting Co, Rockefeller Center, New York City; h. 1 W. 67th St, New York City

Ben Grauer is the announcer of some of radio's best-known commercial programs— *Walter Winchell for Jergen's Lotion*, Lucky

Strike's *Kay Kyser's* (see sketch this issue) *Kollege*, Molle's *Battle of the Sexes* are only a few of them—as well as commentator, master of ceremonies and quiz master. He has covered sporting events at the Olympic Games, football classics, golf matches; he has described the opening of the opera and Mayor Walker's Beer Parade; he has been quiz master of Tum's *Pot o' Gold* and of his own programs, *Name the Place* and *What Would You Have Done?*; and now he is adding to all these activities a wide schedule of NBC sustaining programs, including his own news commentary (sponsored by the American Chicle Company) titled *Drama Behind the News* and roundups of spot news in conjunction with NBC's staff of overseas commentators. Of all the things he does Grauer prefers ad lib, special events and commentating work; straight announcing, he feels, doesn't have the future these do, and these are what he intends to concentrate on.

Ben Grauer came to the microphone straight out of college. But there was a long and varied theatre career behind him. He was born on Staten Island, New York on June 2, 1908, the son of Adolph Grauer, a civil engineer, and Ida K. (Goldberg) Grauer. Six years later his family moved permanently to the Morningside Heights section of Manhattan, and young Ben went to Public School No. 10. His schooling was soon interrupted by his professional career, which started at one of those Saturday afternoon dancing schools where little boys learn how to be polite to little girls. A motion picture scout one Saturday afternoon chose several of the youngsters to take part in a film production, Ben among them. By the time he was eight he was playing in pictures at the old Fort Lee studios with stars of the "silent" days like Theda Bara, Carlyle Blackwell, Madge Evans and Pauline Frederick.

Grauer created the original role of Georgie Bassett in *Penrod* in the theatre in 1918 in a cast that included a new ingenue named Helen Hayes. Then he proceeded to do his bit during the First World War. Dressed as an army officer, he appeared at army camps throughout the East in entertainments and rallies for the doughboys. (Strangely enough today, some 23 years later, he is touring various service posts as master of ceremonies of the Clark Candy Company radio program, *Service With a Smile*.) Other stage and film parts followed—a starring part in *The Town that Forgot God*, roles in *Betty at Bay, Maytime*, and the revival of *Floradora;* the leading part of Tyltyl in Maeterlinck's *The Blue Bird* in 1923 and a role in the Theatre Guild's production of *Processional* in 1925. There was also, after the success of the picture *The Town that Forgot God*, an extensive personal tour of the East.

Schooling of a sort had gone on during these years, but his family felt it was time that Ben settled down and got some education. He went to Townsend Harris High School in New York and then to City College, from which he was graduated in 1930 after a career that included being dramatic critic of the school paper, editor in chief of its literary magazine and the winner of the Sandham Prize for Extemporaneous Speaking.

In college Grauer had majored in English and in his senior year had become interested in rare books and first editions. For a very short while after graduation he ran a little

BEN GRAUER

shop on Sixth Avenue, New York City, where he conducted a highly hazardous mail-order business. It was clear to Grauer almost from the start that he would never make his fortune as a bookseller. He decided to return to the theatre and through old friends got a job playing radio juveniles. Shortly after that he was referred to Pat Kelly, NBC's supervisor of announcers; an audition was held; and two hours later he was signed up as an announcer. This was in October 1930, and Grauer has been with NBC ever since.

This young bachelor still keeps his interest in book collecting, particularly books on typography and the graphic arts, and has even developed new interests: golf, which he plays with relish and harrowing results, riding, tennis, and especially archeology. Recent vacations have been spent in Mexico and Central America, and if all he does on the radio and wants to do ever gives him the time, he intends to do a little serious field work in Yucatan.

References

PM p21 F 18 '41 por

America's Young Men
Variety Radio Directory

GRAZIANI, RODOLFO (gräts-iä'ni) Aug. 11, 1882- Former commander of Italian troops in Africa

Marshal Rodolfo Graziani, self-made marquis and Italy's "best desert fighter," was until

RODOLFO GRAZIANI

March 25, 1941 commanding all the Italian troops in Africa. He has a reputation as "the cruelest and one of the most efficient of Italian generals"; a family motto—"An enemy forgiven is more dangerous than a thousand foes"; and a nickname, "Lucky." Up to quite recently all have been quite appropriate. Early in 1941, however, the encirclement tactics of Britain's General Wavell (see sketch this issue) had brought about one Italian defeat after another; and after the siege of Bardia and the fall of Sidi Barrani it seemed unlikely that Graziani would ever use his nickname again.

Furthermore, cut off from drastically needed supplies—infantry, mechanized forces, armored power, motor transport, guns, local aviation—and faced with hints of defection from his native troops, it was doubtful that even help from the Nazis could restore the former luster to Marshal Graziani's military reputation. On the home front in February 1941, Italians were apparently being prepared for the worst. They were told that it didn't matter how much territory Italy lost in Africa and Albania—provided the Axis won the War. They were assured that an Axis victory was certain if Italy could keep fighting through the spring or summer, thus using up large British land, naval and air forces in the Mediterranean and in Africa. Late the next month the "resignation" of Graziani from his African command (and from his positions as chief of the army staff and Governor of Libya) could not have been any great surprise to them. At the same time it was reported that Nazi troops occupied El Agheila in Italian Libya, and that Nazi armored divisions in Eastern Libya had been greatly reenforced.

Rodolfo Graziani was born August 11, 1882 in Frosinone, a town in central Italy close to Rome. He was the son of Filipo and Adelia (Clementi) Graziani, and first began his military career in Eritrea in 1908, soon after having been commissioned as a sub-lieutenant. He was sent from there to Libya in 1914, and the First World War found him there. A year later he was serving as commander of the 131st Brigade. He participated in hard fighting on the Italian front, was twice wounded and won the rank of major for distinguished service. In 1919 he became commander of the 61st Infantry in Macedonia.

In 1921, not very long after the Armistice, Italy went back to Libya to reassert its sovereignty over the territory which native forces had been unsporting enough to reoccupy during the diversion of the World War. Graziani took part in the occupation of Fezzan; in 1923 he became a brigadier general and, with De Bono, finally drove back the Senussi Arabs from the outskirts of Libya's Mediterranean seaports in a series of campaigns distinguished for their military brilliancy. They were distinguished for their "pitiless severity and cruelty," too. At one time the Senussi were obtaining help from the inhabitants of the Cyrenaican desert; Graziani transported the entire population of 80,000 men, women and children to the Mediterranean seaboard and put them into concentration camps with all their worldly possessions. At the end the last fighting sheik was captured, and asked for the status of defeated warrior; Graziani had him shot as a brigand. The Italian conqueror then finished the job of mopping up by sending "flying tribunals" winging from the seacoast to the inland towns and desert villages of Cyrenaica to try—and execute—prisoners.

From 1930 to 1934 Graziani commanded the Libyan forces, in 1932 being made commanding general of an army corps for his exceptionally meritorious work as soldier and administrator; he conducted the operations leading to the occupation of the oasis of Kufra and the final pacification of the colony; and from 1934 to 1935 he commanded the Udine Corps.

At the start of the Ethiopian War, Graziani was placed in command of the mixed Italian and native armies in Somaliland, and with General De Bono he led the murderous southern campaign in Ethiopia. In 1935 he had been appointed Governor of Italian Somaliland in recognition of his ability; in 1936 he was made Viceroy of Ethiopia, charged with "consolidation" of the Italian victory. The next year, at Addis Ababa, an attempt on his life resulted in his being wounded by a would-be assassin's hand grenade. In revenge he had at least 1,600 natives slaughtered—all those who happened to be found in possession of fire arms at the time! Even Mussolini remonstrated a little; Graziani's answer was: "Mild measures never retained conquered soil." Nevertheless it was not long before another Viceroy succeeded him and he returned to Italy, ostensibly for reasons of health. In 1938 he was made Honorary Governor of Italian East Africa. The title Marchese di

Neghelli was conferred on him during the
Ethiopian War.

In November 1939 Graziani became chief
of staff of the Italian Army and commander
of the Army of the Po—the Army's No. 2
man and field chief, commanding the divisions
along the French frontier when Italy entered
the Second World War in 1940. After the
French armistice he was no longer needed in
that position, and the mysterious death of
Italo Balbo brought him (in July 1940) the
appointment as Governor-General of Libya
and commander of all the Italian troops in
Africa. It was not until almost the end of
1940 that the series of spectacular, if short-
lived, British victories began.

Marshal Graziani has been rather roman-
tically described as a man with "clean-cut
features, reminding one of pictures of the
leaders of the Ancient Roman legions, a firm
jaw, straight-lipped mouth and typically Roman nose. His eyes are piercing, like those
of an eagle; and the wrinkles gathering in
their corners are the only sign on Graziani's
face that he is more than 50 years old. He
is over six feet tall, tough as steel and hard
as nails."

References

Collier's 96:21+ N 23 '35 por
Eur Nouv 21:409 Ap 23 '38
Life 10:24 F 17 '41 por
Liv Age 359:541-4 F '41 por
New Repub 90:236-7 Mr 31 '37
N Y Times p6 Mr 26 '41 por
Newsweek 17:22 Ja 27 '41
Time 26:23 O 14 '35 por; 34:31 N 13
    '39; 37:20 Ja 6 '41

Chi è?
International Who's Who

GREENBIE, SYDNEY June 28, 1889-
Author; lecturer
Address: h. Penobscot, Me.

In common with many another American
author, Sydney Greenbie's recent writing interests have centered in the American scene and
in the American character—the character that
developed the virtues of "rugged individualism"
largely in the pioneer territory west of the
Mississippi. Unlike other writers, however,
Greenbie started "seeing America whole" only
after an extended period of travel, and the
writing of books about his experiences and
observations in foreign countries—*Japan, Real
and Imaginary* (1920); *Gold of Ophir: the
China Trade in the Making of America* (1925);
etc. In 1941, by way of completing the cycle
of his own education through travel and
return, Greenbie became interested in furthering the inter-cultural relations of the American
nations and began work on a series of books,
"Good Neighbor Series," on the Latin American world. They are designed to "acquaint
America with the wonderful stories of the
aspiration and achievements of our neighbors."
There are eight titles, and they are to be used
in schools, high schools and colleges.

Franco

SYDNEY GREENBIE

Greenbie's convictions about the educational
values of travel have found expression, in
the past, through his special work in progressive education. He was the president of an
original educational experiment, the Floating
University (1928-29), which endeavored to
work out a college course for students to
pursue while traveling around the world, and
he conducted a similar experiment of his own
called "Traversity" (1928-32).

Sydney Greenbie was born in Dakota Territory on June 28, 1889, the son of Benjamin
and Eva (Helford) Greenbie. Growing up
on a lonely pioneer farm, the highly imaginative boy dreamed of adventure and travel in
far countries. He read all that he could find
to read; but he was not a boy content to
travel vicariously. He wanted to see for himself what the world beyond a Dakota prairie
was like. The family had little money; and
anyhow college in the conventional sense did
not appeal to a young person who wanted more
than anything else to "go, look, see." Accordingly he devised a system of college education
for himself which would include not only
travel and study, but long periods of residence
in countries of his own choosing.

From 1910 to 1919 young Greenbie saw not
only quite a bit of America, but of Europe;
and he lived for two years in New Zealand
and Australia, nearly three in China and
Japan. After his trip to Europe (where he
covered many countries on foot) he concluded
that, with the outbreak of War in 1914, the
"Atlantic Era of world civilization" was ending, that civilization would rebuild itself around
the Pacific shores. Consequently he spent
some six years living and studying near the
Pacific, starting a progressive school in California and ending with teaching in Japan.
He was also on the staff of the *Japan Chronicle*, a British paper, and for a time taught in

GREENBIE, SYDNEY—_Continued_

the Kobe Higher Commercial School (Japanese Government College). Meanwhile he had visited the islands of the South Seas.

It was while in Japan that he met and married (1919) a young American writer, Marjorie Latta Barstow (author of _American Saga_ and other books)). The couple have two children, Barstow and Alison.

On his return from Japan, Greenbie took his notes on his impressions and experiences there to a publisher, Douglas Z. Doty of Harpers. Because of several books on Japan then appearing, at first he encountered some delay in getting a contract; but Doty was interested in the young author, and in 1920 his first book, _Japan, Real and Imaginary_, was published. This was followed by _The Pacific Triangle_ (1921), and _Gold of Ophir: the China Trade in the Making of America_ (1925), written with Mrs. Greenbie. A further book on the Orient, _The Romantic East_, appeared in 1930.

Nearer to his heart than these publications, however, was the idea of a travel university. In 1928 Greenbie was asked to head the Floating University. He devised a curriculum based on travel and observation as he felt it should be. He himself was convinced of the feasibility of this new kind of college education—provided that a suitable faculty could be assigned to carry it out. But he found that "the inability of the academic mind to function properly in the living world" was the greatest stumbling block to the project. Greenbie solved some of these initial problems in his own Traversity (1928-32), but depression, the Second World War and other disrupting conditions put an end to his efforts for the time being.

He observed, coincidentally, the failure of "liberal efforts" to introduce any practical understanding of world affairs. Instead there was only "mouthing about social, economic and political forces" which brought about the total collapse of world peace. International good will, he thought, must be brought about by practical technics. These ideas Greenbie voiced in a series of lectures when the United States Office of Education under Dr. John W. Studebaker started the public forum movement. Greenbie became one of the first forum leaders, and from 1936 to 1940 was a forum demonstrator stationed in various centers throughout the country. At these he conducted a regular series of discussions on world affairs. He is now a lecturer for the lecture bureau of CBS, and for several years has been a feature writer for the _Christian Science Monitor_.

His picturesque, epic stories of the early fur traders, _Frontiers and the Fur Trade_ (1929) and _Furs to Furrows_ (1939), received excellent critical notice not only for the accuracy of the presentation of frontier life, but for the "search for a key to some of our national characteristics." R. L. Duffus wrote in his review of _Furs to Furrows_: "The theme is fascinating, the writing (apart from a few flights whose wings might well be clipped) eloquent. No one could read this rich narrative without a better understanding of America."

Entertaining the notion that modern Americans can enjoy more leisure than they think they have, Greenbie turned his attention in 1935 to leisure as a public problem. He started the magazine, _Leisure_, which he edited for some 15 months; and in 1940 his book, _Leisure for Living_, appeared. In this he advanced the idea of "creative using" as a better basis for practical education than the current businessman's demand for "skills with which to make things." He advocated fun, love and other vital factors of full living as a means "to big dividends." Greenbie's current interests in furthering inter-cultural relations between the American nations devolved from a trip to South America a few years ago, and a residence (1940-41) in Mexico. But his was no superficial acquaintance. He has spent the last 10 years studying Latin America, and he plans to return to Mexico again in the winter of 1941-42.

For several years the Greenbies have owned a farm in the Penobscot hills of Maine, which Greenbie calls "the most wonderful spot in the world." Among these woods and hills he finds what he calls "the essence of self-surrender and self-discovery . . . the soul's greatest affirmation." He finds, too (building upon the old adage, "As Maine goes —"), the complete representation, in Maine, of a national trait, an individualism that is "one of the greatest treasures in our modern world."

Of his further interests, Sydney Greenbie has written: "I love to read the repetitious rise and fall of dictators in ancient Rome and to replace the names Gibbon gives us with the names in the newspapers. I love to watch people and think of how they act in the same circumstances in the South Sea Islands, where I have also been. I like to think of myself as a naturalist of men. . . I love to raise fruit trees, to cook, music of all kinds, dancing, and picking blueberries in the depths of my creeping juniper fields. During eight or nine months, until winter drives me out, we remain on the farm; then it is the city, or wherever fate decides.

"People are frequently curious as to how an author works. It would make them dizzy to watch this specimen circling round his typewriter. There is not a distant noise that does not justify his going to see what it's about; there is not a pedestrian task that does not put life into his heels. He writes a sentence and measures a fireplace; he adds another word, and lets the cat in. The only time he actually completes one sentence at one sitting is when he is anchored with a favored black cat in his lap."

References

N Y Times Book R D 24 '30
Portland [Maine] Sunday Telegram Sec D N 1 '36 por
Who's Who Among North American Authors
Who's Who in America

GREENFIELD, ABRAHAM LINCOLN
Feb. 15, 1898—July 25, 1941 Professor and
head of the Department of Radiography at
the New York University College of Dentistry;
was international authority on the interpretation of dental X rays and was often a lecturer
on this subject here and in Europe; author of
many books and papers, some of which have
been published in several languages.

Obituaries

N Y Times p15 Jl 26 '41 por

GREENOUGH, CARROLL (grēn'ō)
1883(?)—Aug. 18, 1941 American architect
known especially for his work in France during
a long residence there; designed many American hospitals in France; was associated with
Whitney Warren, architect of the restored
Louvain Library; designed the American
Church of Paris; in this country since 1934, he
had worked on various projects of the United
States Housing Program.

Obituaries

N Y Times p17 Ag 21 '41

**GREENWAY, WALTER BURTON,
REV.** Aug. 18, 1876—Dec. 21, 1940 Presbyterian clergyman and president of Beaver College for Women from 1928 to 1939; ordained
in 1900; held various pastorates; wrote many
religious books.

References

Leaders in Education 1932

Obituaries

N Y Times p31 D 22 '40

GRESLEY, SIR (HERBERT) NIGEL
(grĕz'lĭ) June 19, 1876—Apr. 5, 1941 British
engineer; noted for his work in developing
modern high-powered streamlined British
railroad engines; was designer of the *Flying
Scotsman*, *Silver Jubilee* and *Coronation*
expresses; some of his engines set world
speed records; knighted for his work in
1936.

References

Who's Who

Obituaries

N Y Times p17 Ap 7 '41

GREW, JOSEPH CLARK May 27, 1880-
Former United States Ambassador to Japan

Address: b. United States Department of State,
Washington, D. C.

Joseph Grew, the United States Ambassador
to Japan since 1932, was for a long time sure
that there were "no questions between Japan
and America which cannot be negotiated." But
by December 1941 the issues between the two
countries were more complicated than they had
ever been before, and even while Secretary of
State Hull continued to "negotiate" with
Japan's envoy to the United States the shrewd,
tactful, seasoned American Ambassador must
have been wondering how much longer he

JOSEPH CLARK GREW

would be staying in Japan. By December 7
he knew the answer.

He "has always been the foremost advocate of befriending Japan." For eight years,
according to *Life*, Grew has been practicing
"an honorable appeasement that was alert for
moral aims and economic interests alike; an
appeasement that has consisted of alternate
protestations of affection and protests against
outrageous behavior." According to the Grew
concept, diplomacy is reduced to simple human
terms: "I want to like you." He strongly
dislikes the "ill-used and often misinterpreted"
term "appeasement." He much prefers the
phrase "constructive conciliation." There have
been times when this attitude and that of
Roosevelt's have differed. "You know, Joe,
the only trouble with you is you're too darn
nice," commented the President once.

Grew's post in Tokyo, one of the most
important in the diplomatic service, was the culmination of long years of service. But young
Joseph Grew was never intended for diplomacy. Born in Boston, the son of Edward
Sturgis and Annie Crawford (Clark) Grew,
he was the third son of a solid banking family which expected him to become a banker,
too. His childhood was spent doing the right
things—summers on the North Shore, bird
stalking on his grandfather's estate, taking
piano lessons, collecting stamps, attending teas
at his family's large house on Marlborough
Street. He went to the right schools—Groton
and Harvard (where he was two years ahead
of Franklin D. Roosevelt)—and distinguished
himself at the University by becoming a champion miler, president of the Advocate and an
editor of the *Crimson*.

After he was graduated from Harvard in
1902, Joseph Grew wangled a modern grand
tour out of his father, planning to enter the
banking business after he had got a good look
at the world. Mostly he traveled over the

GREW, JOSEPH CLARK—*Continued*

East—Malaya, India, Southern Asia—and in the East was stricken with an attack of malaria that nearly killed him and left him partially deaf. It was while he was recovering in India that Grew first began to consider the diplomatic service as a career, for the American Consul there in long conversations impressed him with the importance and advantages of the diplomatic life.

Back in the United States, Grew managed to get a clerk's job in the Consulate at Cairo, Egypt, checking invoices and inspecting hides, and went out there in 1904. Very shortly after, his career really started. President Theodore Roosevelt read Grew's book on his trip, *Sport and Travel in the Far East,* and was impressed particularly by a chapter in which Grew reported a duel with a cave-tiger and a "half nelson" on an angry bear. He decided Grew would make a good diplomat and gave him a regular position in the service, as deputy consul general in Cairo.

It was while he was serving at Cairo that Grew married Alice de Vermandois Perry, granddaughter of Commodore Matthew Calbraith Perry whose American warships opened Japan to the West in 1853, and daughter of an American teacher in Japan. He had courted her before he left for Egypt; after he had been there a year he cabled a proposal; he was accepted and hurried to Boston to be married on October 7, 1905. All three of the Grew daughters have carried on the family tradition by marrying into the foreign service.

After Cairo there were short terms as third secretary in Mexico City, third secretary in St. Petersburg, second secretary in Berlin, secretary in Vienna. Then, from 1912 to 1916 were four years as secretary to the Embassy in Berlin, two of which he spent trying to keep us out of the War, as aide-de-camp to Ambassador Gerard. When relations with Germany were broken off early in 1917, Grew went to Vienna as chargé d'affairs and counselor of the Embassy, and stayed there until diplomatic relations ended.

The last winter of the War, Grew spent in Washington in the State Department, and in 1918 was made chief of the Division of Western European Affairs. Then he was chosen to go to Europe with Colonel House as secretary to the American delegation in the pre-Armistice negotiations, and after the Armistice was raised to Envoy Extraordinary and Minister Plenipotentiary and made secretary general of the American Committee to Negotiate Peace. The following year he acted as American secretary on the International Secretariat of the Peace Conference; in 1920 he was Envoy Extraordinary to Denmark; in 1921 Envoy Extraordinary to Switzerland.

In 1922 and 1923 Grew was the American representative to the Conference on Near Eastern Affairs at Lausanne, and his "energy and persuasiveness are credited with helping to prevent a recrudescence of the war between Turkey and Greece." In 1923 he negotiated and signed a treaty with Turkey, and in 1924 he was an unofficial representative for the United States with the League of Nations' Committee for Control of Traffic in Arms.

Grew became Under-Secretary of State in 1924. His appointment coincided with the passage of the Rogers Act, which took the diplomatic service out of politics, and it was Grew's job to administer the new setup. Because of this work and his work as chairman of the board of examiners for the foreign service, people began to call him the "Father of the Foreign Service." After three years' service in the State Department, Grew was appointed Ambassador to Turkey, in 1927.

In his five years as Ambassador to Turkey Grew did "a monumental job of promoting American interests there." He negotiated and signed a treaty of commerce and navigation in 1929 and a treaty of residence and sojourn in 1931. He also superbly accomplished his main task—making friends with Mustafa Kemal, which some observers say he did mainly by losing to his host in all-night poker games. Then, in 1932, Hoover offered him the post of Ambassador to Japan. As he once told it: "Mrs. Grew and I hesitated about accepting. We were very happy in Turkey. . . Finally I told Mrs. Grew it was possible that, if we took the post in Tokyo, some day we might be in a position to sway the issue of peace or war between Japan and the United States. I cabled my agreement to the assignment. We have never regretted the decision."

Once there Grew's personal qualities endeared him to the Japanese. They liked his appearance—his six-foot height, his gray hair, dark mustache and horn-rimmed glasses, which add up to the picture of a storybook diplomat. They were awed by his sporting ability—his shooting, skiing, swimming and golf. They admired his gentlemanly capacity for hard work and saki (rice wine), his good clothes, his beautiful house filled with Oriental antiques. They were impressed by the way he and Mrs. Grew fitted themselves into the Japanese scene; by Mrs. Grew's Japanese flower arrangements, her patronage of Japanese musicians, by their membership in scores of clubs and societies, by their ability to "make the touchiest Japanese patriot feel at home."

In 1932 Tokyo was already an uneasy seat. Japanese troops were in Manchuria, Secretary of State Stimson had announced a "non-recognition" policy and there was talk of boycotts and retaliation. The mortality among Ambassadors there had been high, with five in a decade and two within the past two years. Grew said he intended to do a good job and wanted a chance to do it. "If an Ambassador is to interpret the underlying aims, character and ideals of the people among whom he is living to his own country, time is important. . . I sincerely hope that I am going to be allowed to stay for a long time to come."

During his years in Japan, Ambassador Grew was outspoken when necessary: over the *Panay* incident, over Japan's interference with American rights in the East, over Japanese bombings of American property in Chungking, over obstacles put in the way of Americans who wished to leave Japan. His speech in October 1939, which warned the Japanese of "the increasing extent to which the people of the United States resent methods which Japanese armed forces are employing in China and what appear to be their objectives," was shockingly frank. He has also been a delicate negotiator who believes war is the greatest humiliation a diplomat can have in his career. He has been aided in his negotiations by one deaf ear which he knows how to turn at the right moment. There was the time in 1934 when a welcoming speech to him after a furlough in the United States said war between the United States and Japan was remote "unless the United States ever . . . prevented Japan from her pacific and natural expansion in this part of the world." Grew rose, in turn, to speak. He said he was sorry that because of his deafness he had missed parts of the speech, but he had taken notes on what he had been able to hear. Consulting them, he gave a "pleasant little talk."

It is not only deafness, but natural skill and shrewdness which have guided Grew through many ticklish situations. In November 1940, for instance, when the Burma Road situation, Axis action and Japan's turning toward the Netherland Indies had made tension higher than ever before, Grew found himself obliged to deliver felicitations to the Japanese Emperor. Yet he was able in his message to please *both* Japan and the United States by his tactful hope that Japan "would increasingly contribute to the well-being of mankind."

References

Christian Sci Mon Mag p2+ Jl 20 '40 il por
Life 9:76-83 Jl 15 '40 il pors
Newsweek 10:11 D 27 '37 por
Scholastic 37:10 O 21 '40 por
Time 33:15-16 My 29 '39 por; 34:21 O 30 '39 por
U S News 9:56-7 O 18 '40 por
Who's Who Among North American Authors
Who's Who in America
Who's Who in the Nation's Capital

GREY, CLIFFORD Jan. 5, 1887—Sept. 26, 1941 Lyric and film writer: wrote the words of *If You Were the Only Girl in the World* and other popular songs; author of lyrics of *Artists and Models, Hit the Deck, The Three Musketeers* and of many other productions in England and on Broadway; best-known film *Rome Express.*

References

International Motion Picture Almanac
Who's Who
Who's Who in the Theatre

Obituaries

N Y Times p17 S 27 '41
Variety 144:94 O 1 '41

GRIEFF, JOSEPH NICHOLAS, MGR. Jan. 12, 1855—June 8, 1941 Founder of the American Passion Play which he wrote and produced for the first time in 1915; pastor of the Holy Family Church, Union City, New Jersey at the time of his death; active in the Franciscan Order.

Obituaries

N Y Times p10 Je 9 '41 por
Time 37:82 Je 16 '41

GRIFFITH, J(OHN) P(RICE) CROZER Jan. 5, 1856—July 28, 1941 Noted pediatrician; president of the board of trustees of Crozer Theological Seminary; regarded as one of the country's foremost specialists in the field of children's diseases; had been a member of the faculty of the School of Medicine of the University of Pennsylvania since 1889.

References

American Medical Directory
American Men of Science
Who's Who Among North American Authors
Who's Who in America

Obituaries

N Y Times p17 Jl 30 '41

GRIMSHAW, ROBERT Jan. 25, 1850— Apr. 9, 1941 Internationally known consulting engineer and inventor; devoted the last 10 years of his life to preparing and distributing Braille literature for the blind; spent 60 years in industrial engineering during which he perfected many technical improvements for railroads, foundries and other metal-working plants, petroleum and vegetable oil refineries, newspapers and many other industries; served the United States Departments of War, Navy and Treasury as consultant; wrote many technical books and articles.

References

Who's Who Among North American Authors
Who's Who in America
Who's Who in Engineering

Obituaries

N Y Times p23 Ap 10 '41

GRIZODUBOVA, VALENTINA (STEPANOVNA) (grĕ-zô-dōō'bô-vä vä-lân-tē'nä) 1910(?)- Soviet aviatrix; head of women's aviation in the U. S. S. R.

In 1908 Valentina Grizodubova's father, a poor mechanic of Kharkov, saw a motion picture showing the Wright Brothers' plane. Filled with dreams of emulating the birds, he went home and built himself a plane. In 1910 he built and flew one of the first Russian airplanes, sometimes taking his daughter with him. A picture of Valentina at the age of three crawling over its crude wings is in existence.

Fired by her father's interest in aviation, Valentina became a pilot at the age of 19, and won early recognition for her skill and endurance. She was a member of the famous Maxim Gorky Squadron which flew to remote sections of the U. S. S. R. on educational mis-

Sovfoto

VALENTINA GRIZODUBOVA

sions, and she has won many awards for long-distance flights and broken numerous records.

On September 24, 1938, as commander of the plane *Rodina* (The Motherland), Valentina Grizodubova, with two assistants, Captain Paulina Ossipenko, the second pilot, and Senior Lieutenant Marina Raskova, took off from Shcholkovo, a flying field near Moscow, in an effort to break the international women's long-distance record. The three young women ate a hearty breakfast and then set off in their well-stocked plane. When they had flown some 4,000 miles, their gasoline was running out, so a forced landing had to be made. Knowing that the plane might plunge nose first into the marsh, endangering the life of Marina Raskova, who was acting as navigator, Grizodubova ordered her to jump to save her life. Ossipenko fired a revolver as they flew on to give Marina their direction. The other two brought the plane down into a marsh. When they crawled out of their half-sunken plane, they could not find Marina. Attracted by the smell of food, bears visited them and were driven off with difficulty. A large cat which ensconced itself in the cockpit turned out to be a lynx. For three days a heavy storm threatened to submerge the plane. Their radio worked, but no one seemed to pick up their signals; passing planes ignored their flares. The Russian Government had waited until it seemed time for their fuel to give out, then a rescue mission was organized. After considerable search, they were sighted on October 3rd.

In the meantime, Marina, who had parachuted to the ground alone, had freed herself of her parachute and set out to find her comrades in the direction the plane had taken. They had food to last for two months, but she had nothing but a few chocolate bars. She managed, however, to subsist on the clear spring waters and birch leaves, caterpillars, Rowan berries and mushrooms. She was found not far from the plane at about the same time as the others.

When the young fliers and the rescue party reached Moscow, they were given a rapturous welcome. The whole city turned out in the excitement, which wound up in a great reception at the Kremlin on October 27, 1938. Government leaders, party leaders, aviators, scientists, artists, writers and workers appeared to congratulate them and make speeches. The bravery of the young trio and the glory of Soviet womanhood were in turn extolled. One speaker, expressing the tenor of the speeches, said: "Women in our socialist land have long ago shattered the chains of their age-old slavery and the old perverted theories of their inequality and lack of ability to do great deeds. . . You have demonstrated for what great things Soviet women are fitted. You have opened a fresh page in the history of the development of one-half of mankind—womankind."

Grizodubova and her party had shattered the international women's long-distance record. Their route from Moscow to the Far East, although interrupted, covered 4,000 miles in a broken line and 3,687 miles in a straight line. Added to her previous decorations, Grizodubova received the title of Hero of the Soviet Union, and the order of Lenin. She is a deputy to the Supreme Soviet of the U. S. S. R., and on March 9, 1939 was appointed to a new post as head of women's aviation.

Valentina Grizodubova is a plump young woman of medium height. When she is not engaged in aviation activities, she enjoys a cheerful domesticity with her husband and their young son, Valerik.

References

Soviet Russia Today 7:16 D '38
Soviet Women Moscow 1939

GROPIUS, WALTER (ADOLF GEORG) (grō'pě-ŏŏs väl'tēr) May 18, 1883- Architect; educator

Address: b. Harvard University, Cambridge, Mass; h. Baker Bridge Rd, Lincoln, Mass.

Walter Gropius has more than once been described in such terms as "one of the founders of the concrete-pipe-and-plate-glass school of architectural modernism known as the 'International style.'" The founder of the world-famous Bauhaus in Germany is horrified at any such suggestion of "the multiplication of a fixed idea of 'Gropius architecture.'" "I have sometimes felt a certain disappointment," he once wrote, "at being asked only for the facts and tricks in my work when my interest was in handing on my basic experiences and underlying methods."

It is his basic experiences and underlying methods that Gropius is today engaged in handing on to his young architectural students at Harvard University. Today not all of them seem shockingly revolutionary. There are many to agree with him, for instance, when he writes: "I want a young architect to be able to find his way in whatever circumstances; I want him independently to create true, genuine forms out of the technical, economic and social conditions in which he finds himself instead of imposing a learned formula onto surroundings which may call for an entirely different solution." And his early dream of developing an architecture "immediately and ideally fitted to the industrial age" has become the aim of most modern designers.

It was not always a dream that was shared. When Walter Adolf Georg Gropius was born in Berlin on May 18, 1883, the son of Walter Adolf Gropius, privy surveyor of government at the Policy Presidency in that city, and of Manon (Scharnweber) Gropius, it was an age when architecture and decoration were thought of as almost synonymous, when the theory of "l'art pour l'art" had many staunch supporters.

There were early indications that young Gropius, the great-nephew of an architect, was to be one of the pioneer exponents of an entirely different concept. He attended the "Humanistic Gymnasium" in Berlin, was graduated in February 1903, did volunteer work in the studio of Professors Solf and Wichards from 1903 to 1904, and in 1903 also began studying architecture at the Institute of Technology in Munich. From 1904 to 1905 his studies were interrupted while he served as a volunteer in a regiment of hussars (he became a corporal in 1905, a vice-sergeant major the next year), but he returned to them in 1905 as a student at Berlin's Institute of Technology. While still there he executed his first independent buildings: country houses and agricultural buildings in Pommern. Already interested in experimental low-cost housing, he also designed several workmen's dwellings in Janikow while acting as head assistant to Professor Peter Behrens of the Institute from 1908 to 1910. Then he went into practice for himself.

Even before the First World War his buildings, astonishingly "advanced" in style (a factory at Alfeld, settlements in Wittenberge and in Frankfurt, factories and residences), began to attract attention because of their clean, functional lines, their freedom from the decoration characteristic of the period, the unusual materials in which they were executed. Nor did the young designer confine himself to architecture: he designed furniture, interiors, even benzol-driven locomotives. In 1913 he was awarded a Gold Medal at the World Exhibition in Ghent, Belgium.

The First World War interrupted a promising career. For four years Gropius served in a reserve regiment of hussars, and by the time he was dismissed from the Army in November 1918 he had added several war medals to his Gold Medal. Almost immediately he was called to Weimar as director of the Grand Ducal Saxon Academy of Art and Grand Ducal Saxon Institute for Applied Arts. Here was his opportunity to introduce a new functional, all-embracing conception of art and with it a new educational method. The first Bauhaus ("building house")

WALTER GROPIUS

was founded by uniting the two schools under the name "Staatliches Bauhaus, Weimar," and its slogan was: "Let us conceive and create the new building of the future, which will embrace architecture *and* sculpture *and* painting in one unity. . . The complete building is the final aim of the visual arts." Students were set to work not merely at the drawing board but in workshops, learning as skilled artisans to create out of stone, wood, clay or whatever the suitable material might be the conceptions that were in their minds. In Gropius' own words, it was necessary "to help the formal artist to recover the fine old sense of design and execution being one, and make him feel that the drawing board is merely a prelude to the joy of fashioning."

Both Gropius' own work during this period —a town theatre at Jena, various residences in middle Germany, a paper factory and warehouse at Alfeld, several tombs, a scheme for the Chicago *Tribune* Tower, an exhibition building in Leipzig—and the results of Bauhaus instruction were soon having a profound effect on techniques of art production and education in other parts of Germany and in foreign countries. His Bauhaus, however, lacked funds, and politicians accused him of teaching "architectural socialism." Finally, in 1925, when the opposition in Weimar grew too strong, the city of Dessau (a factory town in the heart of the coal belt) offered funds and a site, and a new Bauhaus building was presently being executed by Gropius. On December 4, 1926, a day after the title of professor had been conferred on him by the Government of Anhalt, 2,000 people danced at a Bauhaus ball to dedicate the new $230,000 schoolhouse, "architecturally the most important structure of its decade." "Friends of the Bauhaus" included Albert Einstein (see sketch this issue), Arnold

GROPIUS, WALTER—*Continued*

Schönberg, Franz Werfel and Gerhardt Hauptmann.

It was this new Bauhaus in Dessau that Herbert Read later called "the greatest experiment in esthetic education yet undertaken." It was here that Walter Gropius and his associates, among them his chief disciple, Lázló Moholy-Nagy, and artists Paul Klee and Lyonel Feininger, had for a brief period perfect freedom in their attempt to "fuse art with technique and reintegrate the artist into the daily work of the nation," to turn out a new type of worker who would have "an intimate knowledge of biological, sociological, technical and artistic problems" and would therefore be "able to combine the qualities of an artist, a technician and a businessman." Here the workshop method was further developed. During its lifetime the Bauhaus did as much for city planning, furniture design and painting as it did for architecture Students designed and fashioned things as prosaic as advertising display models, as practical as streamlined pottery and metalware and early tubular chairs and tables, as ambitious as models of the city of the future. And when on April 1, 1928 Gropius resigned his directorship in order to devote all his time to his own architectural practice (which he had, however, never discontinued), his associates were quite capable of carrying on without him.

Between the years 1926 and 1933 Gropius was responsible for an astonishing variety of projects, among them not only private residences but a research settlement for the Reich and a Labor Exchange Building in Dessau, settlements in Berlin, Siemenstadt, Frankfurt; a Werkbund exhibition in Paris, two building exhibitions and a metal exhibition in Berlin; prefabricated copper houses for Hirsch Kupfer, Finow; bodies for Adler cars, standard stoves for the Frank Factory and standard furniture for workmen. In 1931 he was elected vice-president and German delegate of the International Congresses for New Building.

Hitler's rise to power marked the beginning of his voluntary exile from Germany. His Bauhaus was one of the first things scrapped by the Nazis—Hitler denounced its style as "Oriental"—and in its place a *Landschule* was opened to teach domestic science to country girls. By 1934 Gropius was engaged in private practice in London, where he did much to bring contemporary British architecture abreast of the building practices of the Continent, and in partnership with Maxwell Fry he executed school buildings in Cambridge and several residences in London and in Kent. He also became vice-president of London's Institute of Sociology and added to his numerous memberships in German and foreign architectural associations an honorary membership in the Royal Institute of British Architects.

Finally, in 1937, Gropius accepted a professorship at the Harvard Graduate School of Design. He had already visited the United States in 1928 in order to study its "extraordinary building organization." Now, he said, he came once more as much to learn as to teach. It seemed, too, that there would be a resumption of his Bauhaus experiment with the opening in Chicago that same year of a school of architectural and industrial design called the New Bauhaus and headed by Moholy-Nagy, with Gropius as its adviser. It still goes on, under the name of Chicago School of Design. And students in Harvard's Department of Architecture, of which Gropius became chairman in 1938, are given a certain grounding in Bauhaus methods. Before being graduated they must have a thorough knowledge of building materials, training in three-dimensional rather than "paper" thinking and actual work under a contractor.

Bauhaus methods have also been publicized by the exhibit which was taken on a nation-wide tour in 1939, sponsored by New York City's Museum of Modern Art, as well as by Gropius' book, *The Bauhaus, 1919-1928* (1939), put out by the Museum as a catalog for the exhibit. Perhaps the only actual architectural work of Gropius which had been seen by a wide public in the United States was the Pennsylvania State Exhibition Building at the New York World's Fair, executed in partnership with Marcel Breuer (see sketch this issue). Other buildings built together with Breuer include the Gropius, Breuer and Ford houses in Lincoln, Massachusetts; the Hagerty house in Cohasset and the Abele house in Framingham; a large residence in Pittsburgh, Pennsylvania; projects for Black Mountain College in North Carolina and Wheaton College in Massachusetts; Aluminum City Terrace in New Kensington, Pennsylvania, a defense housing project consisting of 250 units. But those interested in his theories will find them in many magazine articles both in German and in English, and in books other than the one already named: *Staatliches Bauhaus, Weimar, 1919-23* (1923); *Internationale Architektur* (1925); *Bauhausbauten in Dessau* (1930); and *The New Architecture and the Bauhaus* (1937).

Married in 1916 to Alma (Schindler) Mahler, by whom he had one daughter, Alma Manon, Gropius was married in 1923 for the second time to Ise Frank. Walter and Ise Gropius now live with their daughter, Beate Eveline, in their own home in Lincoln, Massachusetts, a home which Gropius designed in collaboration with Marcel Breuer. Every room has an attractive view and is turned so as to receive the greatest possible benefit from the sun; there are vast windows, protected from the summer sun, and glass doors; there is a super-heating system. One visitor with preconceived ideas of modern architecture was curious to know why it also included a fireplace. To that question Mrs. Gropius replied (and it could not have been said better by her husband): "We want to keep all that is beautiful and useful and only discard the superfluous and the awkward."

References

Arch Rec 81:sup34b Mr '37 por (p35);
  81:8-11 My '37 por
Arch R 76:42 Ag '34 il; 78:44-6 Ag
  '35
Cur Hist 47:90-2 D '37 il
House & Gard 77:46 Ap '40 por
Mag Art 30:186 Mr '37
Newsweek 12:21 D 12 '38
Pencil Points 17:422-32 Ag '36 il
Time 29:32+ F 8 '37 por; 31:39-40 Ap
  11 '38

Barr, A. H. and others Modern Archi-
  tects p57-61 1932
Crowther, J. G. Osiris and the Atom
  p152-7 1932
Giedion, S. Space, Time and Architec-
  ture p390-406 1941
Giedion, S. Walter Gropius 1931
Leaders in Education 1941
New Standard Encyclopedia of Art
New York City. Museum of Modern
  Art. The Bauhaus, 1919-1928 1939
Who's Who
Who's Who in America

CHAIM GROSS

GROSS, CHAIM (grōs khĭ'm) Mar. 17,
1904- Sculptor

Address: h. 63 E. 9th St, New York City

Chaim Gross is a sculptor who works
mostly in wood, his work saved from softness by the lusty forms and the nature of
the woods he prefers: ebony, snakewood,
boxwood and above all lignum vitae, which
he has "exploited like a virtuoso." "I am
essentially a carver," he says of his own
work, "and the harder the wood the more
pleasure I get from chipping away and exposing the forms that I want."

Usually the form he wants is dictated by
the particular block of wood on which he is
working, and his is the ability to exploit
its grain and texture to the maximum degree.
To be guided by the wood is only natural,
he says. "Suppose several different materials
—a dark wood, a light wood with colorful
grain, marble or granite—were given to me
with an order to make a figure from each,"
he once said. "The result would not be the
same figure. In each case I would be concerned not only with synthesizing in a pleasing manner the forms of the figure but also
with the character of the material—its texture,
grain, color and hardness."

"I believe that subject matter, as such, is
of little importance," this sculptor says. "It
is merely an avenue through which to express
the medium. The important thing is to get
an esthetic response from the arrangement
of forms." Yet he has consistently explored
the properties of muscular acrobats in active
groups, frequently with one figure poised in
the air. In doing this "by a perfect weighing
of mass against mass and figure against
figure, tense and solid, a beautiful equilibrium
and rhythmic interplay of concave and con-
vex surfaces are achieved."

Gross explains his use of acrobats, in
works like *Balancing, Basketball Players,*

High Jump, Circus Girls and *Handlebar
Riders,* by saying that he isn't interested "in
acrobats *per se,* but I use these subjects because I find in them many possibilities of
variations in form and movement. As a matter
of fact I do not consider a work of mine
successful unless it can be turned upside
down and still evoke an esthetic response.
My acrobats allow me to combine and inter-
lock forms and permit a flow of one form
into another. In addition, this subject matter
lends itself to spiraling which aids me in
achieving a three dimensional effect."

Because of Gross' predilections for linear
rhythms and for making the most of the
various grains of wood to enhance the beauty
of his figures, there have been critics who
have found his work primarily decorative,
lacking a "human quality," leaving the admirer "rather cold." But even those critics
who agree that it "seldom strikes the deep
human chords" insist on its other exceedingly
appealing qualities, and E. M. Benson says
sharply to detractors: "Call Gross' work genre
pieces if you are unable to control your passion for pigeonholes, but they are no less
beautiful for the names you call them."

This sculptor who hasn't lost, despite
academic training, the intimate appeal and
rugged quality found in the work of Old
World wood carvers was born on March 17,
1904, the son of Moses and Leah (Sperber)
Gross, in a little mountain shack in the dense
woods of the Carpathian Mountains in East
Austria, where his father was a lumber merchant. "When I was seven years old," he
says, "we moved to the city of Kolomyja.
Three years later the World War broke out
and our city was occupied by Russian Cossacks. The usual wartime hardships of home-
lessness, hunger, invasion by army after army
and evacuation from one city to another

GROSS, CHAIM—*Continued*

marked my childhood and early adolescence."
He saw his mother attacked by Cossacks and
both his father and mother killed before his
eyes. Completely alone, he made his way for
two wretched years, taken by the Austrian
Army to dig trenches and graves, trying time
after time to escape, caught time after time.

In 1916, when part of the Russian Army
settled down in his city and started a reign
of terror, he made his escape. For months
he marched with other refugees across the
country, trying to find a place of refuge.
Finally he landed in a refugee camp in what
was later Czechoslovakia and from there escaped with a friend and made his way to
Budapest. Once in Budapest, Gross supported
himself for the next two years by a wide
assortment of jobs in wine cellars, factories
and stores. "I wandered haphazardly from
job to job," he says, "and finally apprenticed
myself to a jeweler. It was at this time
that my interest in drawing began to manifest
itself."

After the Hungarian revolution of 1918
Gross won a scholarship to one of Budapest's
art schools, and made his first contact with
the formal study of art. But it lasted only
a short time; the revolution was suppressed
and all foreigners deported to Austria. In
1921 Gross finally left Europe and at the
age of 17 arrived in America. Immediately
he got a position as a delivery boy in a grocery store and began spending his evenings
studying at the Educational Alliance Art
School in New York. He stayed there a
year (he was later to teach there and at the
New School of Art), and met and became
friends with the Soyer brothers (see sketch
this issue), Peter Blume and Louis Riback.
Then he attended the Beaux-Arts Institute of
Design for four years.

After this period of study was over, Gross
rented a small studio and gave all his time
and energy to sculpture. "My existence," he
remembers, "was typical of the conscientious
artist with little income. I lived from hand
to mouth and often went for days without
a decent meal." Finally, he confesses, "I got
fed up with this haphazard existence and left
New York City to obtain a dishwasher's job
in an upstate hotel. Before leaving, I left
a vague note on my door about being tired
of life." His friends became alarmed and
thought he had committed suicide; they
searched for his body in the morgues and
rivers. And by reporting his death they were
able to make the first sale of his work, for
a wealthy collector hastened to atone for his
neglect of the living Gross. Then Gross returned from his dishwashing job, and, he
comments grimly: "The market value of my
work took a drop."

Until 1933, he says, "I had a very difficult
time getting along because of economic problems." E. M. Benson thinks that the reason
why the public was slow to recognize Gross'
work was partly the fact that it was neither
sufficiently academic to invite the interest of
a *Prix de Rome* audience nor faddist enough

to excite the sophisticated palates of those
weaned on the more experimental types of
European sculpture. Whatever the reason, it
wasn't until the Public Works of Art Project
was organized that Gross was able to support
himself at his work. This project he believes has "produced some of the most important works created to date."

Under the Treasury Department art program ("one of the finest things that has ever
happened to art in America") Gross won a
national competition with his *Alaskan Mail
Carrier*, which is now placed in the Post Office Department Building in Washington. The
following year he earned competitively a
commission to do an over-door panel, *Steel
Worker*, on the exterior of the Federal Trade
Commission Building and won, too, the Silver
Medal at the Paris International Exposition.
Meanwhile he was exhibiting his works in
Philadelphia in 1935; in 1936 in a joint show
with Ahron Ben-Shmuel at the Guild Art
Gallery in New York; in 1937 in a large solo
show chiefly of wood sculpture at the Boyer
Galleries in New York. And collectors and
museums were beginning to buy his work.

When the New York World's Fair was
being planned, Gross was asked to do sculptures for the France Overseas Building
and for the Switzerland Building. In 1940
at the Fair, in view of 100,000 pairs of eyes,
he carved a statue, *Ballerina*, out of imbuya,
as a demonstration of how an artist works.
And at the same time he listened to hundreds
of inquiries. "I would look the people over,"
he says, "and if they looked intelligent I
would answer their questions, but if not I
would keep on working." When the completed figure was bought by the Brooklyn
Museum, Gross achieved a unique distinction
—100 per cent coverage of the New York art
museums. He is represented, too, in many
museums and private collections throughout
the country.

In December 1932 Chaim Gross was married to Renee Nechin, and they have one
son, Yehudi Zachary.

References

Am Mag Art 29:39-41 Ja '36 il
Art Digest 15:14 O 1 '40 il
Mag Art 30:176 Mr '37 il; 31:694-8 D
'38 il
Parnassus 9:12-14+ F '37 il
Who's Who in American Art
Who's Who in American Jewry

GRUBER, FRANK (grōō'bēr) Feb. 2,
1904- Author

Address: h. 60 Church Lane, Scarsdale, N. Y.

The mystery writer, Frank Gruber tells
us, "has no social security card and is not
eligible for the WPA." There are few
writers, however, who have found the field
more lucrative than he, and there are even
fewer, if any, who are capable of an output
as large and as rapid as his. Frank Gruber
writes a complete mystery novel in 16 days
and then "uses the other 14 days of the month

to knock out a historical serial for a magazine." Four mystery novels and one historical novel appeared under his name in 1941 and in the "other eight months," he explains, "I wrote two serials for *Adventure Magazine* and a quantity of shorter fiction for several pulp magazines." He plans to duplicate this feat in 1942.

Frank Gruber was born on a farm near Elmer, Minnesota, February 2, 1904, the son of Joseph Gruber and Susan (Reisinger) Gruber. The Gruber family, he tells us, "shuttled between Minnesota and Chicago until 1920, when they finally sold the farm." In that year he ran away to enlist in the Army, serving one year in the 32nd Infantry, where he "learned how to manipulate the dice and at one time could throw thirty-five straight sevens. He has lost this skill through lack of practice."

From 1921, when he was discharged from the Army, until 1934, when he came to New York City to try his luck as a free-lance writer, Gruber worked at a remarkable succession of jobs. He was an elevator operator, bellboy, order picker, office clerk, employee of a leather factory, a paper box company, a wholesale grocery. For two months he was a hobo.

In 1927 he got a job in the Middle West on a trade journal, *The Turkey World,* and he continued to edit poultry journals for five years. He edited journals in other fields, among them *Roadstand Management* and *How To Sell.* His earlier efforts in the free-lance field were confined to money-making hints for juvenile papers, short stories for Sunday School papers, and an article on *How To Eradicate Worms From Poultry.*

All would-be writers who quit steady if uninspiring jobs to come to New York for the purpose of "crashing down editorial doors" are gamblers in a game where the odds are all against the young and ambitious. After six months of being locked out of hotel rooms for non-payment of rent, eating one meal a day on the days when he did not skip eating entirely, and riding the subways all night in inclement weather, Gruber's stories began to "click" with the pulp magazines.

He has sold over 200 magazine stories, 11 books, and has written a number of stories for Paramount Studios in Hollywood. His books include *The French Key,* "rated the best mystery novel for 1940," *The Laughing Fox* (1940), chosen by the Brentano Book Stores as their mystery selection for the month, and the four published in 1941: *The Talking Clock, Simon Lash: Private Detective, The Hungry Dog,* and *The Navy Colt.* The magazines to which Gruber contributes are: *Black Mark, Adventure, Short Stories, Argosy, Detective Fiction Weekly, Esquire, Liberty* and more than 30 others. In writing his mystery stories Gruber uses only two rules: "I always make the murderer one of the principal characters. You can't have a fellow killed by a chauffeur or butler. And I don't cheat the reader. Everything should be in the story so the reader can figure it out if he wants to."

FRANK GRUBER

Frank Gruber is a writer of what Howard Haycraft (see sketch this issue) has called "the hard-boiled tale of detection," using the "justly famous American wisecrack" to good effect. Linked with the school of Dashiell Hammett by those who consider this *genre* worthy of literary notice and classification, Gruber himself has no patience with those "literati" who raise eyebrows at pulp fiction.

Gruber was employed as a scenario writer by Paramount and Republic Studios in 1939. His Oliver Quade series was sold to Paramount, and *Death of a Champion,* starring Lynne Overman, was made from his stories.

Despite the bulk of his literary output in the crime fiction field, Gruber has had time to acquire a reputation as an authority on the Civil War period and the outlaws and gunfighters of the post-Civil War period in Missouri. He has written many articles in this field and two historical novels, *Peace Marshal* (1939) and *Outlaw* (1941). His hobby is collecting western Americana, and he owns what is perhaps the finest library of rare books on outlaws and gunfighters of the frontier.

Gruber is five feet eleven inches tall and weighs one hundred seventy-five pounds. His hair is dark brown and his coloring, in his own words, is "fair to ruddy." He was married to Lois Mahood on May 23, 1931, and has one son, Robert James, born August 11, 1940.

References

N Y Times Book R p14 Ap 13 '41
N Y World-Telegram p30 Jl 15 '41
    por
Pub W 139:1450-4 Ap 5 '41
Writers' Digest Ja '40; Ja '41
Haycraft, H. Murder for Pleasure
    p266 1941

GUERTNER, FRANZ (gürt'nûr) Aug. 26, 1881—Jan. 28, 1941 German Minister of Justice since 1932; was Minister of Justice in Bavaria from 1922 to 1932, when appointed to his latest post; as Reich Minster of Justice promulgated the sterilization law, inaugurated the People's Court to deal with cases of high treason and espionage, urged decrees intended to destroy the economic position of Jews in the Reich, and as Hitler's chief legal officer (he joined the Nazi Party in 1937) was the official interpreter of German law.

References

> Newsweek 6:14 Ag 31 '35 por
> Time 26:17 S 2 '35 por
> International Who's Who
> Wer ist's?

Obituaries

> N Y Times p21 Ja 30 '41 por
> Time 37:68 F 10 '41

GUEST, EDGAR A(LBERT) Aug. 20, 1881- Author

Address: 17471 Hamilton Dr, Detroit, Mich.

Maurice Seymour

EDGAR A. GUEST

"I just take simple everyday things that happen to me and figure that they probably happen to a lot of other people, and I make simple rhymes out of 'em, and people seem to like 'em."

That is Edgar A. Guest's (he stopped being "Eddie" Guest a long time ago) own judgment of his work. He is the most popular and the best paid verse writer in the world, though no one with any pretension to critical judgment has ever called him a poet. He deals in the things ordinary people love and believe in—home, mother, a simple religious faith, hard work, the common everyday doings of common everyday men and women.

For years he has been the stock butt of the intellectuals, but their gibes simply roll off his back. John Bakeless called him "inventor of the mass-production lyric," Benjamin DeCasseres said he was "the epiphany of the qualities without which no real home is complete." He is a master of cliché. His verses are all "a wooden succession of monotonous iambics." Deliberately employing some of Guest's own clichés, J. P. McEvoy, who has been his friend for many years, said he was "simple as a child, common as an old shoe, friendly as a puppy, foolish like a fox."

This small, pale, wiry man with graying black hair that won't stay combed, with a homely smile-wrinkled face, with his old-fashioned bow tie and the spectacles he uses for reading and then forgets to take off, gives the impression of shyness and embarrassment—until one sees his keen, twinkling eyes. He is a master of crowd psychology. When he lectures, as McEvoy says, "you never hear anything that you haven't known since childhood, but it all sounds new when 'Eddie' tells it." The answer is that he himself believes all that he says and writes—that he lives just as do the people whom he writes about and who read his verses.

This apotheosis of old-fashioned Americanism was actually born in Birmingham, England, and didn't see America until he was 10. But he has no trace of "English accent"—he drawls like a Hoosier. His parents, Edwin and Julia (Wayne) Guest, were poor; they left England in a financial panic, went to Detroit, and found themselves in the midst of another panic. Eddie left high school after the first year and became a soda jerker in a drugstore at 13. To a bookkeeper on the *Free Press* he confided his longing to be a newspaperman. A $1.50 a week office-boy job followed.

In 1896 he was promoted to be editorial office boy, then he became exchange editor (which really meant handling the clippings from other papers), next a police reporter. The most he ever made in these positions on the paper was $50 a week and in the depression he was cut to $37.50. Once his reporter son got his check by mistake and was so insulted he almost quit. But Edgar Guest was getting along in another way. One day he wrote four lines of verse. He was encouraged to do some more. Soon he had a weekly column, at first called "Chaff," then "Blue Monday." For many years his column, now called "Edgar A. Guest's Breakfast Table Chat" (the *Free Press* is a morning paper), has appeared daily and has been syndicated in about 300 papers. For it he writes a "poem" every day—he figures he has written some 10,000 in all. In 1931, when he was 50, he decided to retire. He went to bed and spent a year being ill, with no apparent cause except lack of occupation. Then he got up and went back to work, and now he says he'll never retire.

In 1902 he was naturalized; in 1906 he married Nellie Crossman, a Detroit girl; in 1912 his son, "Bud" (Edgar A. Guest, Jr.), was born, and in 1922 his daughter Janet. All these events were chronicled in his verses. McEvoy remarks: "I've never heard so many things that aren't so said about anybody, [yet] an oyster on the half-shell is a closed book compared to Eddie Guest." In early days his reticent English mother, shocked by his exposure of his private life, exclaimed: "Eddie, have you no shame?" Yet this private life is so blameless and genial that there is no reason why he should not share it with the world—as he does.

It centers about his home. He hates to leave Detroit. Once he went with Charles F. Kettering on his yacht to Yucatan. He wirelessed his wife every hour on the yacht, and telephoned her so frequently when he landed that she cabled him to come home—to save expenses! He can't write unless she is in the house; when he strikes a snag in his work he wanders around looking for her, and when he finds her he goes peaceably back to his typewriter. His house is on the edge of the fairway of the Detroit Golf Club; he can tee off from his back porch and play the twelfth hole. He plays a good game of golf—usually goes around in the low 80's. He is a masterly poker player—all the better because his meek and deprecating air deceives his opponents.

He never speculates. A close friend of Henry Ford's from that industrialist's earliest days, he declined to buy any stock in so fantastic an enterprise as an automobile. But on the other hand, his refusal ever to speculate in the boom days left him thoroughly solvent when the crash came in 1929. In 1935 he was induced to go to Hollywood to star in a picture built around his verses. He stayed for a number of weeks, drawing a large salary for doing nothing. Then he went back to Detroit, disgusted at such a waste of the producer's money.

He has everything he wants (his income from books, radio talks, greeting cards, calendars and odds and ends of all kinds is more than $100,000 a year)—his big house with the white columned portico and the garden in back, his summer home at Pointe Aux Barques, Michigan, his family, and the love and praise of countless thousands of strangers who write him huge quantities of fan mail and feel he is their friend. He is a genuinely friendly person—the kind of man who always has the same waiter, the same bellboy, the same porter. Once when he heard that "his" porter was ill in a Chicago hospital he went up immediately to see him. These trips to Chicago he has taken weekly, with a short interval, since 1932, to give a half-hour radio broadcast. In 1941 the program is being given three times weekly, and he stays in Chicago for the three days, very homesick for Detroit.

"The dread of poverty has kept me trying," he said once. His first book, *Home Rhymes*, was printed by his brother on a press in the attic in 1910; there were 800 copies. Two years later his brother printed *Just Glad Things*. In 1914, when a similar small edition of *Breakfast Table Chat* was in prospect, the Detroit Rotary Club heard of it and ordered

3,500 copies. His first commercially published book, *A Heap o' Livin'*, came out in 1916. Since then he has published 13 books of verse: *Just Folks* (1917); *Over Here* (1918); *When Day Is Done* (1921); *All That Matters* (1922); *The Passing Throng* (1923); *Rhymes of Childhood* (1924); *The Light of Faith* (1926); *Harbor Lights of Home* (1928); *The Friendly Way* (1931); *Life's Highway* (1933); *Collected Verse* (1934); *All in a Lifetime* (1938). In 1938 he also published two prose books: *Between You and Me*, subtitled My Philosophy of Life, and *Edgar A. Guest Says It Can Be Done*.

In 1925 the Michigan legislature voted him the State's poet laureate. Governor Alex I. Groesbeck vetoed the bill on the ground that such an office was inappropriate in a republic. But February 14, 1936 was declared by gubernatorial proclamation to be Eddie Guest Day in Michigan. It was climaxed by a banquet at which W. J. Cameron, Ford's publicity director, was the speaker; they had been reporters on the *Free Press* together. A commentator in *Time* remarked on this occasion that Guest was "one of the most valuable newspaper properties in the United States." He is an ex-president of the American Press Humorists and a thirty-third degree Mason. Aside from this, he is not a joiner.

As has been said, Edgar Guest really believes the things he writes about; no cynic writing with his tongue in his cheek could appeal for so long to so enormous a public—a public which has bought some 3,000,000 copies of his books. But intellectually his tastes are not so simple: he reads the modern poets, (who seldom return the compliment), and his favorites among the classical poets are Browning and Whitman. He loves music, though he is tone deaf and cannot carry a tune. There is nothing flamboyant or vulgar about his taste in any direction. He simply likes simple people and simple things and knows how to say so in uninspired but competent verse. He belongs to an American tradition which has long been moribund and is not likely to survive the present world crisis; socially, politically, religiously, he is thoroughly nineteenth century in his views. He likes to think of himself as doing "the same kind of jingles that James Whitcomb Riley used to write," and this is a shrewd comparison. He is hardly a literary figure, but no one can doubt that his is a friendly and engaging personality.

References

Am Home 14:177-9+ Ag '35 il por
Am Mercury 6:322-7 N '25; 10:146 F '27
Outlook 155:527-9 Ag 6 '30 pors
Rotarian 44:22-4+ Je '34 por; 57:22-4 S '40 il pors
Sat Eve Post 210:8-9+ Ap 30 '38 il pors
Sat R Lit 19:4 Mr 4 '39 por
Time 26:66 S 9 '35 por; 27:51-2 F 24 '36 por

Guest, E. A. Between You and Me 1938

(Continued next page)

GUEST, EDGAR A.—*Continued*

Reilly & Lee Company. Edgar A.
Guest, Man and His Work pam 1927
Who's Who Among North American
Authors
Who's Who in America

GUNTHER, JOHN (gŭn'thĕr) Aug. 30,
1901- Journalist; author
Address: c/o Harper & Bros, 49 E. 33rd
St, New York City

JOHN GUNTHER

"A good reporter," John Gunther once
wrote, "has to be something like Dr. Freud,
since he must be a psychologist; he must be
something like Gibbon, since he is necessarily an historian; he ought to be like Max
Planck, a scientist; he is like Dr. Gallup, a
sounder-out of opinion; he certainly must be
a politician; he may even have to be a prophet." Gunther himself doesn't claim to be
all of these things, but no one has yet disputed
the fact that the author of *Inside Europe*
(1936); *Inside Asia* (1939); and *Inside South
America* (1941) is, as a reporter, one of the
best. *Current History* calls him the "most
valuable non-fiction property in the world."
Like Vincent Sheean (see sketch this
issue), tall, fair-haired John Gunther is a
Chicago product. He was born there on
August 30, 1901, the son of Eugene McClellan
and Lisette (Schoeninger) Gunther, and took
his Ph. B. at the University of Chicago in
1922. Long before that, however, he had become interested in writing; at 10 he wrote 200
pages of an encyclopedia. "It sounds childish
—of course it is childish," he says. "There
were five sections, Great Dates of History,
Battleships, Animals, Greek Mythology, I don't
remember the other. I spent a lot of my time
reading and working at stuff like that. Never
took much interest in games. As I grew

older I developed a split personality—if you
don't take that too technically I was schizo-
phrenic. I was interested in the world around
me, in who ran it and how, but the main thing
I wanted to do was write literature, stories,
novels. And I was hungry for travel."
He satisfied his desire for travel by making
a trip to Europe on a cattle boat, and his very
first job was a newspaper job—as a reporter
on the Chicago *Daily News*. In two years he
was in England, working as assistant London
correspondent for the same paper. He hadn't
been sent there, but had simply quit his job
in Chicago, gone to London, and called at the
Daily News office there for his mail. A kind
editor told him to report to work, setting a
bad precedent for other members of the Chicago staff who might also like to travel.
After a few weeks Gunther therefore "went
over to the United Press, saved three of the
ten pounds I was paid each week, and when I
had enough went to Southern France and lived
in a police station on a little island," where
he worked on a "lousy novel" until the *News*
relented and hired him back. After that he
had fine experience during vacations at the
various bureaus all over Europe as "the
emergency man sent out to where the stuff
was breaking." It was 1925 when he started
his private morgue, which now contains some
75,000 clippings.
In that "neolithic yesterday that preceded
Hitler and Mussolini," Gunther says, only
half nostalgically, "facts were facts, names
were names, wars were wars." From 1926 to
1929 correspondent for the *Daily News* in
Paris, Moscow, Berlin, Rome, Scandinavia,
Geneva, Spain and the Near East, he covered
such definite events as the French war in
Syria in 1926 and the Palestine riots of 1929.
During that same period, in March 1927, he
participated in another event with a happier
outcome: his marriage to Frances Fineman
of New York. Then, in 1930, he became
Central European and Balkan correspondent
for the *News*, with chief headquarters in
Vienna.
The Gunthers, both connoisseurs of good
food, liquor and conversation, were happy
for five years in Vienna, where Gunther, in
addition to his newspaper work, began sending home to *The Nation* articles about "petty
revolutionary movements in Romania," about
"changes in the political picture in Austria
which no one but an Austrian metaphysician
could understand"—descriptions of "what was
almost a comic-opera world." But the comedy
soon turned into melodrama. During those
years Gunther covered the evacuation of the
Rhineland and the return of King Carol to
Romania in 1930; the Sino-Japanese "crisis" at
Geneva, the Austro-German customs union
crisis and the crash of the Vienna Credit-
Anstalt in 1931; the Spanish revolution of
1932; the Reichstag fire trial and Germany's
departure from the League of Nations in
1933; and civil warfare in Austria itself in
1934.
By the time Gunther left Vienna for London in the summer of 1935, sent there once

more as the *News'* correspondent, he was not only a well known foreign correspondent and the author of material in *The Nation,* the *New Republic, Esquire, Vanity Fair, Harpers,* the *Atlantic Monthly,* the *Saturday Evening Post* and various European publications, but the author of several novels on which apparently no two critics ever agreed and which few biographers ever mention. *Red Pavilion* (1926), a study of the younger generation in Chicago with emphasis on the sex problem, was the first, and a Boston *Transcript* reviewer wrote: "Armed apparently with the *Encyclopedia Britannica,* the University of Chicago study courses and a copy of *The Green Hat,* Mr. Gunther has sat himself down to write the Great American Novel. He has not succeeded. The result of his efforts is more like *The Century Book of Facts,* with supplementary notes on the use of the finger bowl by Emily Post." Even the assurance of the London *Spectator* that *Red Pavilion* was "one of the best, most cultivated and human of recent American books" could not make up for that.

Eden For One (1927), the next, a story of a small boy's encounter with magic, was generally dismissed as the sort of thing that is "fun to write, but . . ." Gunther tried no more juveniles. *Golden Fleece* (1929) was read by Shaemas O'Sheel, who reported, in the New York *World:* "We know of no novel in which the whole close-woven fabric of life is more fully and honestly presented," but in the New York *Herald Tribune Books* there was a murmuring of "distinctly unpleasant . . . dull people." Even on *Bright Nemesis* (London, 1932), a mystery, the critics failed to see eye to eye. Summed up by the *Spectator,* it was a story of "murder in the Balkans, described as if the crime report, the gossip paragraphs and the foreign news of a go-ahead paper had got badly mixed in proof"; but, according to the London *Times Literary Supplement,* "since the days when Sidney Grier wrote about Balkan thrones and plots, no one has made any part of that picturesque but uncomfortable area live so vividly and realistically."

In London, where even an account of Gunther's dinner engagements reads like a catalog of British notables ("nine-tenths of European journalism from Europe is a combination of private ingenuity and public friendship"), he was busy putting the finishing touches on another kind of book. A little before Christmas 1934 he had walked into Harpers' New York office at the invitation of Cass Canfield, president of the firm, and *Inside Europe* had been planned at lunch that day. It was written with astonishing speed, after working hours, on week ends, "holidays." Based on two decades of experience and research during which Gunther had himself interviewed or made the acquaintance of many of the characters who appear in it—among them Flandin, Litvinov (see sketches this issue), Lloyd George, De Valera, Masaryk, Beneš, King Carol, Trotsky, Dollfuss—and had been present when much of its history was being made, it was written, Gunther

says, "out of the conviction that Europe was the prisoner of three men."

Published in 1936, the colorful, gossipy, eminently readable but remarkably erudite modern history called *Inside Europe* was immediately acclaimed. Dorothy Thompson called it "indispensable. . . The book to date has no rival." The *Manchester Guardian* insisted that it had "probably the highest proportion of popularity combined with the lowest proportion of misstatement that can be achieved." Malcolm Cowley criticized the point of view "that accidents of personality play a great role in history," was sure that it couldn't always be right, but, like everyone else, agreed that it was an excellent job. It went through several revised editions, the 1940 war edition finally containing 90,000 more words than the original; it was translated into French, Spanish, Dutch, German, Norwegian, Swedish, Hungarian and Finnish; it was published in 14 countries, banned in Germany, Italy and Jugoslavia, "pirated" in Chile. It was, in other words, read.

For his second book of the same kind, *Inside Asia* (1939), Gunther's young son John, Jr., gave him the idea. Gunther had already been to the Far East four times for the *Daily News* and in 1937 and 1938 he covered 30,000 miles of territory—China, Japan, the Philippines, Siam, Persia, India, the East Indies, Palestine—as correspondent of the North American Newspaper Alliance. This book (which he really wanted to call *Outside Asia,* since he was "outside, looking in") also centered around personalities. He asks: "What would contemporary China be without Chiang Kai-shek, India without Gandhi, the Philippines without Quezon [see sketch this issue], Arabia without Ibn Saud?" *Inside Asia,* if New York *Herald Tribune Books* is to be believed, was the "biggest one-man reportorial job that has ever been undertaken, and . . . one of the most competently done jobs for a half dozen widely separated parts of Asia of which this reviewer has some knowledge." John Chamberlain credits it with "all the charm, humor, balance, factual richness and ultimate theoretical weakness that are inseparable from Mr. Gunther's character as a person." Over a million copies of *Inside Europe* and *Inside Asia* have been sold.

When Gunther left the *Daily News* as a regular correspondent, he returned to the United States, set up his home in Connecticut and for a while tried to write there. But soon he decided that he and his wife were "losing touch with things," and they moved to New York City. There he began doing most of his work, 12 to 15 hours daily, in a small midtown office. But he couldn't stay in New York. In June 1939 he sailed for Europe; in July he was quoted as doubting that war would break out that summer; in August, proving himself an incurable newspaperman, he was sending back dispatches on an interview with Poland's Minister Beck during the Danzig crisis. The next year found him in South America, gathering material for *Inside Latin America* (1941), which

GUNTHER, JOHN—Continued

was presently selected by the Book-of-the-Month Club as its November choice. Its reviews were almost uniformly laudatory (Harry Hansen called it "a good, balanced and exciting job"), and its sale was phenomenal. In March 1941, back from five months in South America, its author began a new series of broadcasts over the NBC-Blue Network.

A movie executive once told Norman Cousins that Gunther was Hollywood's idea of a perfect type to play the role of foreign correspondent because he had "intelligent features" and was "witty, clever, with a proper balance between sophistication and boyishness." Gunther himself, though, seems to be less confident. His English diary was full of side remarks like these: "As a rule I can never say anything satisfactory in a discussion of this kind until the next day, when it is too late." "Whenever I am with a group like this, I want to crawl away for six weeks or six years and read all the books in the world, from Plato down."

Perhaps both his chief charm and his chief weakness as a writer and as a person is liking nearly everyone. He once mourned: "I suppose I am a bad newspaperman because I instinctively tend to believe people rather than disbelieve them." That is perhaps why, a month before the massacre of February 1934, he was writing of Austria's "little Metternich," Dollfuss, as "Europe's first bulwark against Hitler" and praising his modesty and sincerity and simplicity; why, in 1936, it was to him inconceivable that Baldwin could stand for the betrayal of Ethiopia after all he had been saying for months; why, in January 1940, he was praising Daladier for having at last "united France."

Attractive Frances Gunther is also a writer and an authority on world affairs; she edits her husband's work and does much of his research for him. But it is as a maker of epigrams that she is most appreciated by their friends. Sample: "Remove liberty from Germany and you unite the country; remove liberty from France, and you have a revolution." And, speaking of Chiang Kai-shek: "There is Methodism in his madness." It speaks well for Gunther's honorable restraint that he has never appropriated them as his own for a bright chapter on Germany or China.

References

> Atlan 159:266-78 Mr '37; 159:389-96 Ap '37
> Cur Hist 50:1-4 Jl '39; 51:20 Ja '40 por
> N Y Times Book R p2 O 26 '41 por
> Newsweek 13:40 Je 12 '39 por; 14:43 S 11 '39 por
> Pub W 130:1406 O 3 '36 por
> Sat Eve Post 209:92 Ja 23 '37 por
> Time 33:26 Je 12 '39 por
> Wilson Lib Bul 11:660 Je '37 por
> America's Young Men
> Who's Who in America

HAAS, ARTHUR E(RICH) (häs) Apr. 30, 1884—Feb. 20, 1941 Professor of physics at Notre Dame University and an authority on the atomic theory of matter and the source of the sun's energy; joined faculty of Notre Dame in 1936 after having taught physics at the Universities of Vienna, Leipzig and London; widely known as a writer on physics and author of a standard work on theoretical physics which has been translated into 10 languages.

References

> American Catholic Who's Who
> American Men of Science

Obituaries

> N Y Times p19 F 21 '41

HACKETT, HORATIO B(ALCH) May 8, 1880—Sept. 8, 1941 Architect; associated with many private companies and in 1934 general manager of the Federal Public Works Emergency Housing Corporation, from which post he went to the PWA as assistant administrator; was graduated from West Point where he was a football star; as colonel during the First World War won many decorations.

References

> Am Arch 146:56 F '35 por
> Arch Forum 62:579 Je '35 por
> Business Week p20 F 24 '34 por; p16 My 18 '35 por
> Newsweek 6:8 O 26 '35 por
> Who's Who in America
> Who's Who in Commerce and Industry
> Who's Who in Government

Obituaries

> N Y Times p23 S 9 '41 por

HAILE SELASSIE I, EMPEROR OF ETHIOPIA (hī'lĕ sĕ-làs'ĕ) July 24, 1891(?)-

In July 1940, shortly after Italy declared war, a mild, scholarly man known in Britain as Mr. Tafari alighted from a plane in Alexandria, Egypt. It was there, in the men's washroom of a former Italian Yacht Club, that he exchanged his civilian clothes for the uniform of an Ethiopian Generalissimo, drank a toast in wine left behind by the Italians, and proceeded on to the Anglo-Egyptian Sudan to try to rally some of his 10 million former subjects around him. The man was King of Kings, the Lion of Judah, Defender of the Christian Faith, Haile Selassie, Emperor of the Ancient Kingdom of Ethiopia, The Chosen of God.

On January 15, 1941, Haile Selassie arrived in Ethiopia from his Sudan headquarters, once more by plane. There a unit of his gradually expanding Ethiopian Army awaited his arrival at the secret landing ground prepared by his troops. He unfurled his red, green and yellow flag; "royal war drums sounded on the crags, summoning black warriors to turn on their Italian conquerors"; and Emperor Haile Selassie urged his subjects to raise their arms against the enemy "and wipe him from the face of Ethiopia!" Plans were for the Emperor's forces to support British troops against Italy in a lunge into the Northwest provinces of his former kingdom. On May 5, 1941, five years after the Italians drove him into exile, he returned to his throne, and in November 1941 the last Italian stronghold in Ethiopia surrendered.

The "Black Napoleon" was born Tafari Makonnen on July 24, 1891. He was the second son of Ras Makonnen, the accepted heir of Emperor Menelek. (Legend says that the Imperial Family is descended from the seduction by King Solomon of Sheba's Virgin Queen, and members of the Amhara or ruling race call themselves white people, Aryans. They were Christianized in the Third Century A. D.) Tafari Makonnen was a sickly child, but studious. He was only seven when he started to learn French from imported tutors, and in 1906, after his father died, he went to a French Roman Catholic Mission to complete his education. At 14 he was Governor of Garamollata; he became Dejazinatch Tafari of Sellalie Province; in 1909 he took on the duties of Governor of Sidamo; and a year later he was governing his home province, Harar. But it was his more vivacious and popular cousin, Lidj Yassu, who was chosen heir by the Emperor in 1909.

In 1911 Tafari Makonnen married Princess Woyzero Menen, now a "portly, olive-complexioned, heavy-lidded woman" who has been content to bear him five children (two sons and three daughters) and remain in the background. Soon the Emperor Menelek died. Lidj Yassu ascended the throne. Came the First World War—and German and British intrigue in Ethiopia. Lidj Yassu fell under German influences, and under the protection of Turkey began to show Mohammedan sympathies. The party of Coptic priests was shocked, and British agents began looking around for a rival Emperor. They found Tafari Makonnen willing and ready. In 1916 a revolt was engineered and in September of that year "the Crafty Fox of Harar" was appointed heir apparent. The Empress Zawditu, Menelek's favorite daughter, became regent.

But the deposed Lidj Yassu was not reconciled. For nearly five years there was guerrilla warfare, until in 1921 a direct attempt by Yassu to regain the throne was frustrated. He was captured and, some say, interned luxuriously at Harar until he died. Now the Empress Zawditu became a rallying point for the opponents of Tafari Makonnen. He did not have the support of all the Ethiopian chiefs, some of whom looked upon him with contempt because he was no warrior. Some criticized his attempts at reform as too radical, some as too mild. Nevertheless on October 7, 1928 he was crowned King of Ethiopia, and when the Empress died early in 1930 his coronation as Emperor finally took place. It was after 20 years of almost continuous bloodshed.

HAILE SELASSIE I

At the coronation Tafari Makonnen changed his name to Haile Selassie, which means The Power of the Trinity. (When an American was told its meaning, he announced: "He'll need all that—and more.") His wife became Queen Etega Menen, Queen of Queens of Ethiopia. Among coronation presents he received an electric refrigerator, a typewriter, a combination radio-phonograph, a bound set of American magazines and an airplane. These gifts give some indication of his admiration for Western civilization and his desire to bring some of its benefits to his backward kingdom, both judicially and scientifically.

In 1931, for instance, he proclaimed by his own free will a constitution with two legislative chambers. He tried to start a police system on European lines. He imported an American financial expert who put Ethiopia on the gold standard—at about the same time the United States went off! And he tried to bring into Ethiopia not only electric lights, films and improved roads but also new schools and research clinics in hospitals. Haile Selassie, moreover, was shrewd, and a linguist: he understood how Western civilization often dealt with civilization less advanced, he stayed on his guard and sometimes even did them one better. Once the Italians supplied him with a powerful radio station at cut rates; as soon as it was in working order he had the entire Italian staff of technicians fired.

Haile Selassie's efforts did not mean, of course, that Ethiopia was beginning to approach Western civilization by the time Mussolini approached it with bombs and tear gas. But his country was slowly advancing from the jungle to the comforts of, say, the Middle Ages. Slavery persisted, although under his laws it would eventually have disappeared as

HAILE SELASSIE I, EMPEROR OF ETHIOPIA—*Continued*

an institution; and Ethiopia remained a feudal state, ruled by feudal chiefs.

As for the country's place in world affairs, one might go back to the First World War in order to understand it. At that time Great Britain had let Italy understand that Abyssinia was reserved for her to "expand" in. Italy felt betrayed by Britain's less generous post-War attitude, but Haile Selassie (then Prince Tafari) remained uneasy. He wanted to get Ethiopia into the League for safety's sake. Shrewdly, after his request for admission had been refused, he started yielding deceptively to French and Italian efforts to obtain important concessions in his empire. By 1923 both France and Italy were insisting that their apparently cooperative friend Ethiopia be admitted.

Tafari Makonnen's first complaint after admission to the League was in 1926; he had caught Britain and Italy exchanging notes with a view to recognizing "spheres of influence" for each other in Ethiopia. It was toward the end of 1934 when he turned once more toward the League for help—an "incident" had occurred, and Italy and Ethiopia were shrieking "Aggression!" at one another. Months later a League commission decided that no one had been to blame, but in the meanwhile Italy was insisting that Ethiopia be ousted from the League and Italian mobilization was already going on. Great Britain counseled "moderation," said she would not give arms to either power, a decision which naturally caused more sorrow in Ethiopia than in Italy; diplomatic efforts to make Mussolini back down merely stiffened his attitude.

On October 2, 1935 Italian troops crossed the Ethiopian border and Haile Selassie ordered mobilization. The half-hearted application of sanctions at last began; the Hoare-Laval plan was revealed and Sir Samuel Hoare resigned as British Foreign Minister in December 1935; and by January 1936 *Time* was talking of the dangers of world war and giving Haile Selassie a backhanded compliment for "dexterously pitching the issue of the war on such grounds that the white race in general feels the future of the League of Nations to be at stake in the future of a Museum of Peoples in Africa."

It was in May 1936 that Haile Selassie announced that further defense of Addis Ababa was impossible. He, his Empress and children fled the country. Gassed, his health weakened, he boarded the British *Enterprise* at Djibouti. With him he took possessions that some claim were worth several million dollars; others say his fabulous wealth was "pure myth." In England he found many sympathizers, but not much financial support for a proposed $10,000,000 "war chest." He was offered a role in a film and the Texas Centennial Exposition made wistful advances, but diplomats snubbed him, George VI wouldn't receive him, and in June 1936 Anthony Eden told him that sanctions against Italy would be dropped.

In July 1936 Emperor Haile Selassie himself appeared before the League of Nations to make his plea against the final dropping of sanctions—an unprecedented move which, Eden warned, would "compromise his imperial dignity." There was dignity in his speech: "Apart from the Kingdom of the Lord, there is not on this earth any nation superior to any other. . . Are the States going to set up the terrible precedent of bowing before force? . . It is international morality which is at stake!" Nevertheless, in accordance with the spirit of "candid realism" in which Eden announced Geneva must act, his words went unheeded. Sanctions were officially and universally dropped. Ethiopia was "finished."

The Emperor of Ethiopia retired with his family to a 14-room Georgian house at Fairfield, Bath. Now he wore a black coat and trilby hat and kept the imperial crown locked in a London safe. He never went to restaurants or the theatre; he busied himself with a 90,000-word story of his life, written in Amharic and translated into English; he listened to his beloved Beethoven; he read his diplomatic, ecclesiastical and medical histories; he continued to keep the Coptic fasts. He looked less than ever like a warrior as he busied himself with his books: five feet four, slight and fragile, with an "olive complexion, a thin hooked nose, tiny fluttering hands, a ruff of coarse black hair brushed over a high forehead," lips thin and sensitive, chin unobtrusive "behind the dignity of mustache and beard." Yet it seems certain that Mr. Tafari Makonnen, alias Haile Selassie, was preparing for what was to come. On May 12, 1938, he made what everyone thought was his last stand before the League of Nations council table. Then, faced with the cold eyes of Lord Halifax and Georges Bonnet, who had decided to recognize Mussolini's conquest, he announced: "Whatever the world will do, my people will fight on until they have forced Italy from the country or are themselves exterminated!" Once more they fought—and this time, with England's help, they won.

References

Harper 162:574-84 Ap '31
Life 10:22 F 3 '41 por; 11:31-4 Jl 21 '41 il pors
Liv Age 335:355-9 Ja '29 il pors; 348: 38-40 Mr '35; 349:318-24 D '35
N Y Times VII p5, 23 Mr 9 '41 pors
Newsweek 5:25 F 23 '35 por; 11:15-16 My 23 '38 por; 17:25-6 Ja 27 '41; 17:19-20 F 3 '41 il
Sat Eve Post 208:8-9+ S 21 '35 il
Survey G 26:267-9 My '37 por
Time 27:13-17 Ja 6 '36 il pors; 27:21-2 My 11 '36 il; 27:22 My 18 '36 por; 27:20 Je 15 '36; 28:18 Jl 6 '36; 28:17-19 Jl 13 '36 por; 30:23-4 N 15 '37; 37: 24 Mr 3 '41

Asfa Yilma, Princess Haile Selassie, Emperor of Ethiopia 1936

(Continued next page)

Dunckley, F. C. Eight Years in Abyssinia 1935
Hindle, W. H. ed. We Were There p209-32 1939
Jacoby, C. On Special Mission to Abyssinia 1934
Lyons, E. ed. We Cover the World p11-48 1937
MacLean, R. John Hoy of Ethiopia 1936
Who's Who

HALL, FRANK O(LIVER), REV. Mar. 19, 1860—Oct. 18, 1941 Pastor emeritus of the Universalist Church of the Divine Paternity in New York City which he served for 35 years; professor emeritus of homiletics and philosophy at the Crane Theological School; well known as author and orator (among his published books are *The Common People* and *Soul and Body*); was trustee and chairman of the executive committee of the Church Peace Union.

References

Who's Who Among North American Authors
Who's Who in America

Obituaries

N Y Times p44 O 19 '41 por

HALL, GEORGE A(LBERT) 1890—Oct. 5, 1941 General secretary of the New York State Child Labor Committee since 1905; secretary of a commission appointed by the New York Legislature to study child welfare legislation from 1921 to 1925; active worker in the Boy Scout movement.

Obituaries

N Y Times p17 O 6 '41

HALL, GEORGE W(ASHINGTON) June 18, 1869—Oct. 25, 1941 Neurologist; for many years was head of the Department of Nervous and Mental Diseases at Rush Medical College, and was senior neuropsychiatrist at St. Luke's Hospital in Chicago.

References

American Medical Directory
Directory of Medical Specialists 1939
Who's Who in America

Obituaries

N Y Times p42 O 26 '41

HANDY, WILLIAM C(HRISTOPHER) Nov. 16, 1873- Composer; music publisher
Address: Handy Brothers Music Co, Inc, 1587 Broadway, New York City; h. 400 Convent Ave, New York City

For more than a third of a century William C. Handy, "father of the blues," has been writing down melodies, arranging spirituals, composing and publishing songs. He is an old man now, but the tunes still come to him.

He is blind now but he has them written down by others.

The type of song known as "blues" was being sung and played by illiterate Negroes— "bar-room pianists, nomadic laborers, watchers of incoming trains and steamboats, street corner guitar players"—long before any of them were written down. Where the name originated no one knows, but by 1910 it was being used by Negroes from Missouri and Kentucky to the Mississippi Delta. The

WILLIAM C. HANDY

original blues song had a three-line verse, with a definite musical pattern, and usually expressed a lament of some kind, often ending in "ironical self-ridicule, fatalistic resignation" or "absurd incongruous laughter." There was no author or composer—as with all folk music, someone started a song, others took it up, added to it, changed it; eventually it was being sung by many people and in many different versions, and all trace of the originator was lost. Handy collected some of these songs and was the first to write them down. That is why he is called "father of the blues." He has also composed blues, these composed songs being known as "artificial blues"—in contradistinction to "folk blues," which "just grew."

The story of his musical career, "which has affected as many lives as that of Bach, Brahms or Wagner," was published under the title *Father of the Blues* in June 1941. In this book the "Beethoven of Beale Street" tells with dignity and integrity, in rambling and entertaining fashion, all the events of his full life, all its ups and downs.

Handy was born in Florence, Alabama. In the public school there he had a teacher who introduced him to choruses from Wagner and

HANDY, WILLIAM C.—*Continued*

Bizet. He heard itinerant bands in the barber shops. He heard spirituals in the African Methodist Church built by his grandfather, in which his father was minister. Every time a band or a group of singers came nearby he tried to go listen to it. Though his mother, Elizabeth (Brewer) Handy, and father, Charles Bernard Handy, had planned for him to be a minister, he early decided that he wanted to be a musician. His father looked upon a professional musician as a "sinner," and Handy had to leave home in order to carry out his ambition. He walked all the way to Birmingham, Alabama. There he taught school for two years and then went into the Bessemer iron works, where he was better paid. At the iron works he heard songs which 30 years later he put into his *Harlem Blues*.

When the depression of 1893 (it was called a "panic" then) resulted in general unemployment, Handy organized a quartet which traveled to the World's Fair in Chicago. He did not stay there long, however, for the quartet was not well received. For several years thereafter he wandered around, working as a bricklayer, teaching music in a school in Alabama, traveling as band leader and solo cornetist for Mahara's Colored Minstrels, and finally forming his own band. At a white subscription dance in Mississippi where his type of band playing was not what the people wanted he noticed the enthusiasm with which they responded to a band consisting of a mandolin, bass violin and guitar. He had not realized that the kind of music he had heard all around him among the Negroes in the South would be acceptable elsewhere. He left Mississippi then for Memphis, Tennessee, to begin collecting these tunes and experimenting with them. As George Lee says in *Beale Street: Where the Blues Began*: "He returned to Beale Street and set his pen to music paper. Memphis woke up one morning with the blues."

During a Mayoralty election campaign in Memphis in 1909, in which there were three candidates, each with his own band, Handy had been hired by Edward Crump, later a Congressman. For the campaign song, *Mr. Crump*, which Handy wrote, he used a blues tune. Crump was elected, and Handy's band became so popular that soon he had a chain of bands, sending out as many as 90 men in a single night. His song, *Mr. Crump*, he changed somewhat and called *Memphis Blues*. When he failed to find a publisher for it he issued a thousand copies himself. Later he sold it to a white arranger for $100, and when in 1926 he published an anthology of his compositions he was not permitted to include it.

After *Memphis Blues* other blues followed: *St. Louis Blues* (the best known), *Beale Street Blues, Mississippi Blues, Joe Turner Blues*—more than 60 in the last 20 years. Some of these Handy recalled from having heard them sung around him; others he composed. In order to get them published Handy, in partnership with Harry Pace, a song writer, founded a music publishing house in New York City, "commencing a revolution in the popular tunes of this land comparable only to that brought about by the introduction of ragtime." *St. Louis Blues* became one of the most popular tunes in the history of song writing. Even today it is said to bring in $25,000 a year in royalties. In the publishing business Handy has made and lost more than one fortune, and his company has gone through various changes, the present one being a family affair, The Handy Brothers Music Company, Incorporated.

Handy's work has not been confined to blues. He has written other secular songs, made arrangements of many spirituals, and has also done orchestral work both as a composer and a leader. His evolution of the blues was used in 1924 by Vincent Lopez in the latter's first jazz concert at the Metropolitan Opera House in New York City. In 1925 Handy presented a band of his own, consisting of 30 pieces and a large chorus, in a Carnegie Hall concert which traced music from Africa to spirituals and jazz. During the summer of 1940 he appeared as guest conductor of the New York World's Fair Band, leading the Band in a presentation of *St. Louis Blues*.

Among other means of giving recognition to Handy a park in Memphis, Tennessee, once a part of the famous Beale Street, "where the blues began," has been named in his honor. One of the most colorful tributes paid to him was a series of celebrations commemorating his sixty-fifth birthday: a testimonial dinner at the Cotton Club (New York City's famous night club); a reception at the Delphic Studio, New York; the playing of *St. Louis Blues* 15 times by as many bands at a musical jamboree of the American Federation of Musicians in Hollywood; and, as a culmination, a concert in Carnegie Hall, with many of the "name bands" on the program, Maxine Sullivan among the soloists, and *St. Louis Blues* rendered in a variety of arrangements.

Handy was married to Elizabeth Virginia Price in 1898. Five of their six children are living.

References

Etude 58:152+ Mr '40 por
N Y Age p7 O 1 '38; p7 D 3 '38; p4 N 16 '40 por
N Y Times p24 Ag 24 '37; IV p2 Ag 29 '37; p15 N 5 '38; p28 N 22 '38; p21 My 5 '40; VI p7 N 17 '40
Time 27:54 My 25 '36 por
Handy, W. C. ed. Blues 1926
Handy, W. C. Father of the Blues 1941
Lee, G. W. Beale Street 1934
Locke, A. The Negro and His Music p74-80 1936
Who's Who in Colored America

HANSON, HOWARD (HAROLD) Oct. 28, 1896- Composer; conductor; educator

Address: b. Eastman School of Music, Rochester, N. Y.; h. 362 Oakdale Dr, Rochester, N. Y.

Composer, scholar, conductor and educator, Howard Hanson has probably done more than any musician "to foster an appreciation of native music." Through his own compositions, through his guest conducting of most of America's great orchestras, through his leadership of the Eastman School of Music, through his work in many musical and music-teaching organizations, this accomplished musician has wielded a tremendous influence on the musical life of our times.

Howard Harold Hanson was born in a little town in Nebraska called Wahoo, where his grandparents had come from Sweden in the '70s. His father and mother, Hans and Hilma Christina (Eckstrom) Hanson, were, like their parents, good Swedes, good Americans and good Lutherans. And Mrs. Hanson was, besides, a musician who taught her son whatever she knew.

Howard Hanson remembers Wahoo well. "The principal assets of this little city—aside from its name, which was an immense help to us in making up high school yells for the football games—were a small but excellent Swedish college, a very good public school system and a population rather above the average for a town of its size in culture." Howard went to the public schools and later to the Swedish Luther College, "where I received, among other things, a rather solid musical grounding." "My early musical fare," he recalls, "consisted of Swedish folk songs and Lutheran chorales on the one hand and the usual public school music diet of that period on the other. My earliest musical memories are a mixture of *Sweet Adeline, Down by the Old Mill Stream, Neckens Polska* . . . Lutheran chorales, the *Messiah* and something by Grieg."

In Wahoo, Hanson learned to play first the piano and then the cello and at the age of 15 left home to study further at the University of Nebraska. From there he went on to the Institute of Musical Art and then on to Northwestern University on a teaching fellowship to study composition, acoustics and the piano and to receive his Bachelor of Music degree in 1916. (Six colleges have since made him a Doctor of Music.) Next he attended the Institute of Musical Art in New York City, where Dr. Percy Goetschius encouraged him to become a composer instead of a concert pianist.

In 1919 Hanson was in California, acting as dean of the College of the Pacific at San Jose and professor of theory and composition. It was while he was here that his first compositions began to be known. He wrote the score of the *California Forest Play of 1920* and a symphonic poem, *Before the Dawn*, compositions which won him the *Prix de Rome* in 1921. He went abroad to study and spent three productive years in Italy. From them came the *Nordic Symphony*, the première of

HOWARD HANSON

which he conducted in 1922 in Rome; a symphonic poem, *North and West* ("All of my best music," he says, "has been the result of an acknowledgement of these two sources, the North and the West"); *Lux Aeterna*, a work for chorus and orchestra; *The Lament for Beowulf*, called "pathetic, thrilling and immensely powerful . . . inexorable, granitic"; and a string quartet commissioned by Mrs. Elizabeth Sprague Coolidge (see sketch this issue).

As a result of his conducting of the premières of the *Nordic Symphony* and *Lux Aeterna*, Walter Damrosch invited Hanson early in 1924 to direct the New York Symphony in a first performance of *North and West*. He accepted and accepted, too, an invitation to visit Rochester to conduct the *Nordic Symphony* with the Rochester Philharmonic Orchestra. Here he met George Eastman, who had founded and endowed the Eastman School of Music at the University of Rochester, and President Rush Rhees of the University. Not long after he returned to Rome to complete his stay there they asked him to become the director of the Eastman School of Music. In 1924 he took this position.

At Rochester, Dr. Hanson has been active as teacher, conductor and composer. Here he "teaches in one of the most significant all-American composition departments in our land." His desire as a teacher, he says, "is to make good teachers rather than to hunt for genius. Genius declares itself." As director he has built the school up into "one of the liveliest centers of interest in American music." In his school "the instrumental departments have become outstanding, the student orchestra is a splendid ensemble and the ear-training is actually taught, not merely printed in the catalog. . . . All the major theory teachers are

HANSON, HOWARD—*Continued*

themselves composers, many of them graduates of the school."

There are concerts at Rochester by the School Symphony, with the Rochester Philharmonic and the Rochester Civic Orchestra. Most important for American music is the series of American Composers' Orchestral Concerts, started by the Eastman School of Music in May 1925. Begun originally as "a sort of composers' laboratory to give beginners and amateurs a chance to experiment and hear their works," this series has developed into annual festivals of American chamber, choral, symphonic and stage music which "surpass in the number of American works given those in the entire country elsewhere combined." Their purpose, Dr. Hanson sums up, is "to make them the means of enabling young composers to hear the first performance of their works." These concerts "have given performances of both new and old works of established composers, enabling the hearers to form some estimate of the directions in which American music is moving"; and they have "made it possible to test and retest the value of certain manuscript works which for commercial reasons have never achieved publication."

Apart from these concerts, Dr. Hanson spends much time trying to convince conductors to play American music. "There exists in the United States," he tells other conductors, "a large number of gifted creators of music, well-equipped technically and seeking to express through their art the life of our time and of our nation." These composers should be supported: there should be "intense concentration upon our own composers," he believes.

Hanson has done much to disseminate these beliefs in articles, as president of the Music Teachers National Association and of the Commission on Graduate Study of the National Association of Schools of Music, and as a member of the Oberlaender Trust and of the National Advisory Committee of the Federal Music Project. He has probably done most to convince the public of the importance of American music through his own compositions.

Hanson's style, it was said by John Tasker Howard, "is best classified by that much-used term 'conservatively modern.' He believes in the constant expansion of harmonic, melodic and rhythmic idioms, but his innovations have their roots firmly planted in the classics." His "harmonic innovations have seldom offended concert-goers' ears, and when a juicy melody comes to mind he uses it unhesitatingly." ("I believe in melody," he said of his opera *Merry Mount*.) Busy in the late 1920's with works like *Pan and the Priest,* the *Heroic Elegy* and *Beat! Beat! Drums!,* in 1930 Hanson inaugurated "what at that time appeared to be a one-man movement in behalf of romanticism in music," with the performance of his *Romantic Symphony* by the Boston Symphony Orchestra. This work, he said, "represents my escape from the rather bitter type of modern musical realism which occupies so large a place in contemporary thought." And he added that though he recognized that "romanticism is . . . the poor stepchild without the social standing of her elder sister, neo-classicism . . . nevertheless I embrace her all the more fervently, believing as I do that romanticism will find in this country rich soil for a new, young and vigorous growth."

In this symphony and in others of his works, Dr. Hanson demonstrated his own belief that "the composer must always remain untrammeled and unhindered by theories . . . free to express himself according to the dictates of his own artistic conscience." He demonstrated it again in *Merry Mount,* his opera commissioned by the Metropolitan Opera and first performed on February 10, 1934 with Lawrence Tibbett and Gladys Swarthout in the leading roles. Most critics found it uneven ("Hanson's work at its best is manly and imposing. . . At its worst it is effect and content with mere tonal wise-cracking," said one), but there were fifty curtain calls, and though only three performances had been guaranteed, twelve were given before the season ended.

The latest work of this tall, lanky, stooped-shouldered composer, whose rather boyish face is adorned by a goatee and whose straight straw hair straggles above, is the *Symphony No. 3,* which had its first performance with its composer conducting in 1939. He has conducted much of the work of others, too, at the Composers' Concerts and in guest appearances all over the United States. Called "one of the most brilliant conductors of modern music," Hanson has an uncanny sense of contrast and climax. "Characteristic of him is the spontaneous smile of commendation he bestows on an orchestral section or soloist that has nicely turned a phrase. Careful as a rehearser, he nevertheless gets his results quickly by drawing out the performers themselves rather than by seeming to impose his will upon them."

In his conducting, as in his composing, it has been suggested that "perhaps there are too many high points, too much of horns and trumpets striving, or an over-beating of drums." But behind these "is a vigorous personality, full of the joy of living and above all thoroughly sincere."

References

Musical Q 22:140-53 Ap '36 por
Musician 39:4 D '34 por; 40:8-9 Ap '35; 40:10 My '35; 41:17+ Ja '36 por; 43: 36 F '38
Newsweek 15:44 My 6 '40 por
Top Notes 1:9 F 1 '30

America's Young Men 1936-37
Armsby, L. W. Musicians Talk p175-84 1935
Baker's Biographical Dictionary of Musicians 1940
Cowell, H. ed. American Composers on American Music p97-100 1933
Ewen, D. ed. Composers of Today 1936
Howard, J. T. Our American Music p462-579 1939
Leaders in Education 1941
Who's Who in America

HARMSWORTH, HAROLD SIDNEY, 1ST VISCOUNT ROTHERMERE *See* Rothermere, H. S. H., 1st Viscount

HARRIMAN, W(ILLIAM) AVERELL
Nov. 15, 1891- American "defense expediter" in London; industrialist

Address: b. American Embassy, London, England; 59 Wall St, New York City; h. Harriman, N. Y.

In March 1941 W. Averell Harriman left for England to coordinate aid to Britain from the British end and to carry through the details of the Lease-Lend Bill after it passed Congress. President Roosevelt called him a "defense expediter" for lack of a better title, and indicated that Mr. Harriman would not have diplomatic rank.

As liaison officer Harriman has kept this Government informed of British needs and the British Government informed of production situations in the United States. He has coped with special problems of transportation, purchasing and financing which affect United States' help to all the Allies. He has gone to the Middle East to discuss the receipt of America's equipment there. And in September 1941 John Biggers (see sketch this issue) temporarily took over his duties in London while he headed the American delegation to Moscow to consider aid to Russia.

In this last capacity Harriman informed Soviet leaders that the flow of tanks and planes from his country would be "constantly increased and eventually . . . limited only by problems of transport." Back in London, he delivered a statement for both the American and British delegations, then made a flying visit to the United States to consult with President Roosevelt and other defense heads in which he pronounced himself greatly impressed with Russia's ability to withstand the Nazi onslaught, with Russian morale and leadership. He was soon back in England, however. And, as Alexander Woollcott (see sketch this issue) put it during his own British visit: "There'll always be an England, now that Averell's here."

The second Mrs. Harriman, the former Mrs. Marie Norton Whitney, whom he married in 1930, and Mr. Harriman's two children by his first marriage in 1915 to Kitty Lanier Lawrance, have remained here. Mrs. Harriman explains that her inability to be on time for appointments, and to get things done when she hopes to, disqualify her for any pretensions toward being an "expediter."

Mr. Harriman, however, seems to have all the necessary qualifications. He is familiar with London ("I have been there off and on ever since I was a boy"); he has been around Washington enough to know how to cut through organizational and personal intricacies; he has served on the defense program since its beginning in half a dozen capacities and at the time of his appointment was chief of the Industrial Materials Division of the Office of Production Management; and he has had special experience in the fields of transportation, purchasing and finance.

W. AVERELL HARRIMAN

Mr. Harriman, who is chairman of the board of the Union Pacific Railroad, chairman of the executive committee of the Illinois Central Railroad, a partner in the investment house of Brown Brothers, Harriman and Company, a director of the Guaranty Trust Company and of the Western Union Telegraph Company, is one of America's outstanding business leaders and one of its richest men. He became a business leader through his own efforts; he became wealthy less through them than through the head start of a $100,000,000 fortune left by his father, the late Edward H. Harriman.

E. H. Harriman was "one of the most dynamic men who ever raided Wall Street: he feared neither God nor Morgan." He won control of the Union Pacific Railroad and brought it back to health. He engineered interlocking controls of other roads, won control over still others, and when he died in 1909 was the country's outstanding railroad man. W. Averell Harriman's mother was Mary (Averell) Harriman, famous for her charities and her donations to cultural activities, a woman who "tapped the resources that have enriched the life of our country." Their son was brought up to meet their standards.

After preparatory school William Averell entered Yale and was graduated from the University in 1913, a dark, lanky, broad-shouldered young man who had been elected to Skull and Bones and had rowed for the Yale crew. He had also been interesting himself in the family business, spending summer vacations in the shops and offices of the Union Pacific Railroad. With college over he went to the railroad's headquarters in Omaha as a member of the rail inspection gang and later worked as a surveyor, fireman on locomotives and workman in the shops. After a year of this he was made vice-presi-

HARRIMAN, W. AVERELL—*Continued*
dent in charge of purchases and elected a
director to represent his family's dominant interest.

Harriman wasn't content to follow his
father's footsteps and stick to railroading. He
branched out for himself and in the next
years proceeded to make and lose millions in
shipbuilding, foreign mines, investment banking, aviation. Nevertheless he managed at
the same time to concentrate hard on railroads
and by 1931 had become chairman of the
board of the Illinois Central and by 1932
chairman of the board of the Union Pacific.

When he headed the Union Pacific things
began to happen. This road had not been
doing well: gross revenue had dropped and
passenger traffic had been especially hard hit.
Harriman proceeded to do a smart merchandising job. While other railroads were retrenching in 1933, he instituted a $5,000,000
modernization program. He ordered a streamlined lightweight Diesel-driven train which
saved much time and also speeded up freight
traffic in other trains; he had the coaches
redecorated, rates lowered, meals served more
cheaply. And he built up Sun Valley, Idaho
as a real and exclusive attraction. Here in
the Sawtooth Mountains, on a branch of the
Union Pacific, he created and advertised a
skier's paradise (he's no skier himself) which
has since developed into a popular vacation
resort for all four seasons of the year.

At the same time that he was building up
the profits of this railroad, Harriman was
concerning himself with labor problems and
the conditions of work for the many Union
Pacific employees. As he once said: "In the
railroad industry, management and labor are
closer to an understanding, perhaps, than in
any great industry in the country. Although
the U. P. has been a leader in the railroad
industry in the improvement of facilities and
improvement in service, I put this human
accomplishment as the greatest contribution to
progress that the Union Pacific has made to
the country."

This sort of attitude, which is consistent in
Harriman, has won him a reputation as one
of the most liberal of the big industrialists.
Even in the most hectic days of the New Deal
he continued to believe "that a compromise
can and may be worked out between Wall
Street and Pennsylvania Avenue." An old
friend of the President, he was advising him
on railroad policy during the 1932 Presidential
campaign, and when Roosevelt was elected he
was given a number of special jobs to do,
among them the drafting of legislation for
the relief of bankrupt municipalities.

When the NRA was started, Harriman was
made a member of Secretary of Commerce
Roper's Business Advisory Council and later
its chairman. He was in charge of the NRA
for the state of New York and later in 1933
placed on the Industrial Advisory Board.
After Malcolm Muir left the NRA, Harriman
became Divisional Administrator in charge
of heavy industry. (At the same time his
sister, Mrs. Charles Cary Rumsey, was chair-

man of the NRA's Consumers Advisory
Board.) From NRA days on into defense
program days, Harriman has frequently been
consulted by the Government, which recognizes him as a financial leader who is willing
to listen to all points of view.

One of the results, though perhaps not the
most important, of this activity and Harriman's energy in his various businesses is that
America has lost an outstanding polo player.
At one time Harriman had an eight goal rating and in 1928 played in the international
matches between the United States and Argentina. He still breeds ponies—"the fastest
in the world"—at his Genesee Valley farm,
and is known to be a right smart horse trader. He is also known as a collector of French
art.

Harriman is a modest, quiet man, tall, dark-
haired and sufficiently impressive in appearance
to have once been placed by Madeleine Carroll
on her list of America's 10 most handsome men.

References

> Cue 10:6 Mr 29 '41 por
> Fortune 19:64-5+ Ja '39 il (Same cond.
>   Read Digest 34:55-8 F '39)
> N Y Herald Tribune p1, 12 F 19 '41
>   por
> N Y Times p6 F 19 '41 por; p12 Mr 11
>   '41
> Newsweek 8:34-6 D 5 '36 por
> Time 27:74+ My 11 '36 por; 37:13 Mr
>   3 '41
> U S News 10:16 F 28 '41 por; 10:40-1
>   Mr 7 '41 por
> Who's Who in America
> Who's Who in Commerce and Industry

HARRIS, JAMES RENDEL 1852—Mar.
1, 1941 British archeologist, theologian and
authority on the writings of antiquity; taught
at several European universities and at Johns
Hopkins University and Haverford College
in this country; traveled extensively in the
Orient in search of old manuscripts; owned
cup believed to have been used at The Last
Supper; his writings fill a column in the
British *Who's Who,* making his sketch one
of the longest in the book.

References

> Who's Who

Obituaries

> N Y Times p42 Mr 2 '41
> Sch & Soc 53:309 Mr 8 '41

HARRIS, SAM H(ENRY) Feb. 3, 1872—
July 3, 1941 Theatrical producer; started career as a prize fight promoter and went from
promoting into horse racing before he started
producing melodramas; in 1904 went into
partnership with George M. Cohan with *Little
Johnnie Jones* and in the next 15 years these
two produced many successful shows; after
1919, as an independent producer, was responsible for 28 hit plays, among them *Rain,
The Jazz Singer, June Moon, Dinner at Eight,
As Thousands Cheer, Of Mice and Men* and

most recently *The Man Who Came to Dinner, George Washington Slept Here* and *Lady in the Dark*; only independent producer to present three Pulitzer Prize winners; unofficial partner in recent years was the playwright George S. Kaufman (see sketch this issue).

References

Am Mag 93:24-5+ My '22 por
Dramatic Mirror 77:5 My 26 '17 por
Green Book Mag 11:140-8 Ja '14 il pors
Lit Digest 118:23 Ag 4 '34 por
Stage 12:24-6 D '34 il
Theatre 47:34+ F '38
Theatre Arts Mo 22:745-55 O '38 por
Who's Who in America
Who's Who in American Jewry
Who's Who in the Theatre

Obituaries

N Y Times p13 Jl 4 '41 por

HARRISON, PAT Aug. 29, 1881—June 22, 1941 United States Senator from Mississippi; president pro-tem of the Senate; chairman of the Senate Finance Committee; helped engineer early New Deal legislation through Congress and was active in putting through the Lend-Lease Bill; nevertheless, frequently clashed with Administration officials over Treasury tax theories and was credited with an important part in stopping the "wealth sharing" tax bill in 1936 and undoing the undistributed profits tax measure in 1937; began career as lawyer in 1902 and soon went into politics; member of the House of Representatives from 1910 to 1919, when he entered the Senate; given name Byron Patton Harrison.

References

Cur Opinion 77:26-8 Jl '24
N Y Herald Tribune X p6+ Mr 30 '41 por
Newsweek 5:20 My 11 '35 por; 8:9-10 S 5 '36 por; 10:14 D 13 '37 pors
Outlook 158:430-2+ Ag 5 '31 pors
Sat Eve Post 195:27 Ap 21 '23
Michie, A. A. and Ryhlick, F. Dixie Demagogues p68-86 1939
Who's Who in America
Who's Who in Law
Who's Who in the Nation's Capital

Obituaries

Nation 152:739 Je 28 '41
N Y Times p1+ Je 23 '41 por
Newsweek 17:25 Je 30 '41
Time 37:15 Je 30 '41 por

HART, MERWIN K(IMBALL) June 25, 1881- President of the New York State Economic Council

Address: b. 505 Fifth Ave, New York City; h. Winship Rd, New Hartford, N Y.

In 1941 the name of Merwin K. Hart, founder and president of the New York State Economic Council, began appearing in the news, consistently linked with the names of Charles

MERWIN K. HART

A. Lindbergh, (see sketch this issue), Father Coughlin (see sketch 1940 Annual), and Lawrence Dennis (see sketch this issue). Harold Ickes, United States Secretary of the Interior (see sketch this issue), publicly denounced him more than once as belonging to the same group of the "Fascist-minded," and in April 1941 a member of the United States House of Representatives, speaking at a Council luncheon, announced that he would not have been there if he had known in advance of the views "on our American democracy and its defense" held by "certain sponsors" of the Council. Mr. Hart was kept busy demanding retractions, denying allegations that he was "anti-Semitic, anti-Negro or anti-sharecropper," denying that he has even met any of the men with whom he has been linked except Lindbergh, with whom, he said, he frequently conferred.

Merwin Kimball Hart has had a varied career. Born in Utica, New York on June 25, 1881, the son of Henry Gilbert and Lucy Lord (Kimball) Hart, he was educated at St. Paul's School in Concord, New Hampshire and at Harvard University, where he received his B. A. in 1904. He entered politics three years later when he was elected a member of the New York Assembly, 1907 to 1909, and during the last year of his term he married Katherine Margaret Crouse of Utica, New York. After studying law he was admitted to the Bar in 1911, and became a member of the firm of Hart, Senior & Nichols. Three years later he founded the Utica Mutual Insurance Company, and he later became president of the Genesee-Hopper Corporation, vice-president of the Allied Fire Insurance Company, director of the Utica Mutual Insurance Company and of other firms.

In the meanwhile, during the First World War, Hart had trained at Plattsburg in Aug-

HART, MERWIN K.—*Continued*

ust 1915 and at Fort Niagara, New York from August to November 1917. Appointed to the rank of captain of infantry, from January 1918 to February 1919 he had served in France. He had not been very active in public affairs since 1912, when he was chairman of the Progressive County Committee in Oneida County, New York. From 1926 to 1929, however, he acted as a member of the New York State Industrial Survey Commission (representing employers); later he was chairman of the Committee of 25 of the New York State-wide Economic Congress. And in 1931, perhaps as an outgrowth of that experience, he organized and became president of the New York State Economic Council.

An announcement sent out from the Council set, forth its objectives: "to curb public spending and to prevent legislation harmful to those who live by private enterprise." One commentator interpreted this as meaning that "the Council's perennial mission is to combat social legislation"; and it is true that during the heyday of the New Deal the Council's bi-monthly *Letter,* sent out under Hart's name to approximately 17,000 persons in the state of New York, usually contained tirades against "pump-priming," against such measures as WPA and unemployment insurance. In 1941 the Council had around 2,000 members, according to Mr. Hart. It is supported by contributions, and when asked from whom it received its chief support Mr. Hart replied that James H. Rand, Jr., president of Remington Rand, "contributed off and on."

Although Mr. Hart gave up his law practice in order to devote all of his time to the work of his Council, his activities were by no means confined to the one organization. He was chairman of the short-lived Committee for American Private Enterprise, chairman of the Church Layman's Association (he is an Episcopalian) and from 1932 to 1933 he was a member of the New York State Budget-Advisory Commission. The author of *America, Look at Spain* (1939), from 1938 to 1940 he was also chairman of the American Union for Nationalist Spain. During the Spanish War he went to investigate what went on in Franco's territory and over the Spanish national hookup he broadcasted an address in which he attempted to correct the impression that if Franco won he would have to depend on the Germans and Italians in order to govern. Then, upon his return to the United States, in a number of speeches before various organizations he confided that the bombing of Guernica and the massacre of Badajoz had never actually occurred, that there had been "no Nationalist atrocities beyond individual crimes (and little evidence of these)." "I have not changed my views about Spain," Mr. Hart said in a 1941 interview. He stated his belief that the United States should cultivate a much closer relationship with Franco's Government.

Hart has denied any connection with either Father Coughlin or the Christian Front. It seems to be well established, however, that an article under his name appeared in *Social Jus-tice* and that in December 1938, at a Council-sponsored luncheon where Martin Dies was guest speaker and where Fritz Kuhn and James Wheeler-Hill, secretary of the German-American Bund, were guests, members of the Christian Front distributed leaflets announcing a mass meeting of their own. In February 1939 Hart ran a "pro-American" mass meeting at the 7th Regiment Armory in New York for which the Christian Front was one of the chief agencies of ticket distribution and at which his chief aides were Allen Zoll and Bernard D'Arcy, the latter "chief distributor of *Social Justice.*" At a Madison Square Garden meeting in honor of Martin Dies in November 1939, whose proceedings Hart was chosen to direct, members of the Christian Front were admitted to the balconies on free tickets. According to the New York *Times,* at that meeting "references by speakers to General Franco, Premier Mussolini and Chancellor Hitler were applauded."

Communism never had a stauncher foe than Mr. Hart. In January 1938 he asserted that just as Communism was spreading all over the face of Europe "until the Nazis overwhelmed it," so President Roosevelt was bringing it into the United States. The undistributed profits tax, the Wagner Act and La Follette's Civil Liberties Committee seemed equally dangerous to him. His pamphlet, *Is Your Town Red?,* has been widely distributed, and he highly recommends the similar work of Harry Jung (generally considered pro-Nazi) and of Mrs. Elizabeth Dilling.

Mr. Hart believes, too, that "if you find any organization containing the word 'democracy' it is probably directly or indirectly affiliated with the Communist Party." The United States was founded as a republic, not a democracy, he assured a Union League Club audience in New York in February 1940. His views on the Second World War were also rather uncompromising even at that date. In the same speech he explained that he thought the United States was in danger of getting into it because the country was flooded by from 200,000 to 500,000 refugees, here "lawfully or unlawfully," and, "blinded by fury at the prosecution of minorities in Germany, this force would be as willing to engulf us in this [War] . . . as it was willing to engulf Britain and France a year ago." A week after the German attack on Russia he told the Senate Military Affairs Committee that the Soviet Union should be excluded from any benefit under pending legislation to permit the President to requisition private property.

One of the most active figures in the campaign against the books of Harold Rugg (see sketch this issue), in a speech entitled "Are There Subversive Activities In Our Schools?" delivered before the Exchange Club of Binghamton, New York, Hart suggested that "if the per pupil cost in New York were reduced to the per pupil cost in Indiana, which has an excellent school system, it would save $142,-000,000 a year for the people of New York State." A few months later he announced the formation of the American Parents Council on Education, with the object of "rooting out the subversive teachings which are taking place in many public schools."

Hart, who has three sons (a daughter Margaret is deceased), is described as an "angular, square-jawed man, solidly built, gray-haired, his face deeply lined. He wears glasses." To a *PM* reporter he gave the impression of "graciousness and studied nonchalance. Mr. Hart is obviously a gentleman." He is a Mason and a member of the University, Harvard and Uptown Clubs in New York. He is particularly disturbed by suggestions that he and his Council are anti-Semitic. "Most of the people with whom we do business are Jews," he was quoted. "Why, we have Jewish members on our board of directors." Besides, he added, "all men are my friends—in a sense."

References

Frontiers of Democracy 7:45-7 N '40
Nation 151:260-1 S 28 '40
N Y Post p7 Ap 10 '41
N Y Times p9 F 27 '41
PM p10-11 Ja 5 '41 por
Who's Who in America
Who's Who in Law

HARTWELL, JOHN A(UGUSTUS) Sept. 27, 1869—Nov. 30, 1940 Former director and president of the New York Academy of Medicine; clinical professor at Cornell Medical College and associate director of the American Society for the Control of Cancer.

DR. JOHN A. HARTWELL

References

Sci Mo 35:284 S '32 por
American Medical Directory
American Men of Science
Who's Who in America
Who's Who in American Medicine

Obituaries

N Y Times p62 D 1 '40 por

HARTWIG, WALTER (härt'wĭk) 1880(?) —Jan. 17, 1941 Leader of the little theatre movement who originated the annual Little Theatre Tournament in 1923 and was general manager of the competitions until they ended in 1931; after being associated with Daniel Frohman and David Belasco he directed his own little theatre group in New York, Connecticut and then in Ogonquit, Maine; worked in Hollywood and directed on Broadway.

References

International Motion Picture Almanac 1936-37

Obituaries

N Y Herald Tribune p10 Ja 18 '41 por

HARTY, SIR (HERBERT) HAMILTON Dec. 4, 1880—Feb. 19, 1941 British composer and conductor; from 1920 to 1933 conductor of the Halle Orchestra in Manchester, England; guest conductor of orchestras both in England and the United States; composer of orchestral and vocal works, he was knighted in 1925 for his contributions to English and Irish music.

References

Armsby, Mrs. L. W. Musicians Talk p144-8 1935
Baker's Biographical Dictionary of Musicians 1940
Ewen, D. ed. Living Musicians 1940
Shore, B. Orchestra Speaks p93-100 1938
Thompson, O. ed. International Cyclopedia of Music and Musicians 1939
Who's Who

Obituaries

Musical Am 61:28 F 25 '41 por
N Y Herald Tribune p18 F 20 '41
Variety 141:54 F 26 '41

HAWKINS, ERSKINE July 26, 1914-
Band leader

Address: c/o Gale, Inc, 48 W. 48th St, New York City

Erskine Hawkins, leader of one of the most popular Negro orchestras in the country (he is billed as "Erskine Hawkins and His Orchestra") claims allegiance to what one veteran called "the real old jazz." The solid swinging jazz born in the Midwest, where Bennie Moten's Orchestra, McKinney's Cotton Pickers and Andy Kirk's Clouds of Joy Negro dance bands stomped away from conventional dance music, is the music on which Erskine Hawkins' is based. He has taken on polish in the years, but from this vigorous quasi-folk music he has assimilated a core of rich vitality. This is true not only of his conducting but of his compositions like *Tuxedo Junction* and *Dolemite*.

Erskine Hawkins was born July 26, 1914, in Birmingham, Alabama. His mother was a schoolteacher. His father was with the A. E. F. in France during the First World War, and was killed in action. Hawkins has three brothers and a sister, all musically

ERSKINE HAWKINS

inclined. His own musical career began inauspiciously at home, and with school chums he organized a neighborhood band. At State Teachers College, Montgomery, Alabama, he brought together the nucleus of his present orchestra. Most of the musicians in it are under 30, and most of them are from Hawkins' native Birmingham.

He was graduated from State Teachers College in 1934 but taught music and dramatics for a year before putting his orchestra on a professional basis. The band, with substantially the personnel it had comprised at State Teachers College, barnstormed for a year or so before it came into New York. Billed as The 'Bama State Collegians, they made their debut in 1936 at the Harlem Opera House and soon after that went into Harlem's Savoy Ballroom. At the Savoy they were given a radio wire three times a week, got a recording contract and began to acquire a national reputation. Columnists and reviewers have been friendly to the band almost since its New York debut.

The 'Bama State Collegians could pull together with real swing, and their musical performance was refreshing to listeners. They had what more sophisticated bands sometimes lacked, the freshness of music that sounded as though the musicians were enjoying it. If they acquired a fault it was that they took on polish too soon, before they had the music to back it up. That, at any rate, was how it sounded to some critics when they played at the Harlem Uproar House on New York's 52nd Street early in 1937. They were yet to learn fully the welding of effort to inspiration —the lesson that Duke Ellington's (see sketch this issue) men had learned so well through the years.

Hawkins himself played and plays several instruments in his band, but the trumpet has always been his favorite, and he plays it with tremendous facility and brilliance of tone. They bill him as the "Twentieth Century Gabriel" and wait for him to produce high tones—which he does with the aid of a special mouthpiece he developed. Publicity stories in the late '30s used to emphasize that he blew from his stomach, instead of his lungs, and therefore could triple-tongue high C's at his leisure. Whether he did or not, he was able to win polls as an outstanding trumpet player (as an orchestra leader as well). He's seldom seen without his trumpet, which he uses even while conducting instead of a baton.

As a composer he is probably best known for his *Tuxedo Junction* (1939). Tuxedo Junction is the nickname of a suburb of Birmingham near the great steel mills of that city, a transfer point for trolleys, busses and trains. As a boy, Hawkins was intrigued by its many roundhouses, turntables and switches. He also got to know the little "juke box joint" where railroad men and workers from the steel mills often stopped to change into street clothes and, more rarely, into tuxedos, preparatory to stepping out for the evening. When the roar of the mills had died down and before the night shift had begun, through the open door there came the myriad sounds of trains switching, bells clanging and engines puffing. Within the little room the men kidded with each other as they poured nickels into the "juke box" to hear the latest records. The place seemed alive with good fellowship and gaiety. That was the inspiration for his piece, though according to Artie Atlas in *Down Beat* the musical phrase that opens *Tuxedo Junction* was for years a sign-off phrase of bands at the Savoy Ballroom in Harlem. He says that one night when the late Chick Webb was due to come on and didn't show up on time, for a joke, Hawkins and his men improvised on the phrase. In any case, Hawkins worked it into an extraordinarily effective train piece that has been used by modern dance groups as well as by dance bands.

The critics felt that with *Tuxedo Junction* it was at last possible to hear what the band could really do. The arrangement was unconventional, but without tricks; where brilliance entered into the music, it was properly a fillip and not the show itself. The orchestra was just as good in his *Norfolk Ferry* (1940), a work similar in inspiration, based on the ferry from Cape Charles to Norfolk, Virginia which bands often take when motoring to or from the South. On the boat they sometimes get out their instruments and hold impromptu jam sessions while the ferry plods up Hampton Roads past Old Point Comfort and past ships from every port in the world, anchored in the roadstead.

When he first began to write music Hawkins worked only at night. He confesses that when he was younger this seemed the proper way to go about it. "Most of the really important song-writers I knew about worked only at night," he said, "and I thought it necessary to write songs while burning the midnight oil." But he found it didn't work out, possibly because playing dance dates that ran into the small hours of the morning didn't leave one with energy to compose. Now he works at his music mostly when the sun is pouring into his window, leaving the hour or so after the night's work for relaxation. One of his first "daytime" compositions was the successful *After Hours.*

Hawkins believes that "you've got to have perseverance and fortitude in addition to talent if you want to write song hits." He decries alike the attitude that a song is something "dashed off in a leisure moment, dreamed up during a peaceful slumber," or "that there is a soul-stirring melodramatic story behind each song." Patience and industry, he believes, should be harnessed to imagination before the latter can get anywhere. Mr. Hawkins uses this method diligently and his works are both inspired and thought out. He composes usually at the piano.

Hawkins' favorite hobby is collecting old phonograph records. For recreation he spends part of his time learning to pilot an airplane, and hopes some day to make a good-will tour of South America. Erskine Hawkins married Florence Browning, a schoolteacher, in 1935. He is of average height with even features and dark brown eyes. His suave appearance is enhanced by a thin line of mustache and the double-breasted pin-stripe suits he likes to wear.

References

Down Beat 7:17 Ap 1 '40
Swing 3:22-3 F '41 por
Miller, P. E. Down Beat's Yearbook of Swing 1939

HAWLEY, H. DUDLEY 1879(?)—Mar. 29, 1941 Actor; born in England and came to the United States as an infant; appeared last in the road company of *The Man Who Came to Dinner;* spent nearly 50 years on the stage; appeared in many highly successful plays.

References

International Motion Picture Almanac 1935-36

Obituaries

N Y Times p15 Mr 31 '41
Variety 142:46 Ap 2 '41

HAWLEY, WILLIS C(HATMAN) May 5, 1864—July 24, 1941 Former Republican Representative from Oregon and ex-head of the Ways and Means Committee; co-author of the controversial Smoot-Hawley Tariff Act; from 1906 to 1932, when he represented the First Oregon Congressional District, he was leading advocate of the protective tariff policy and was also known as a financial expert.

References

Cur Hist 30:614 Jl '29 por
Lit Digest 100:5 Mr 9 '29 por
Outlook 152:133 My 22 '29 por
Sunset 60:49 Je '28 por
Who's Who in America
Who's Who in Government

Who's Who in the Nation's Capital 1934-35

Obituaries

N Y Times p15 Jl 25 '41 por
Sch & Soc 54:77 Ag 2 '41

HAYCRAFT, HOWARD July 24, 1905-
Editor; author; publisher
Address: b. 950 University Ave, New York City

Howard Haycraft's *Murder for Pleasure: The Life and Times of the Detective Story* was published in September 1941 and within two weeks went into its second printing. Writing in the New York *Times Book Review,* Katherine Woods declared that this book (the first full-length history and survey of police fiction) "makes an encyclopedic appeal to real students of this genre and that not merely in

Oggiano

HOWARD HAYCRAFT

the comprehensiveness of its main historical text, but also in its bibliography and lists of authors and characters, in its detective story quiz, and in its chapters on the rules and the democratic alliances of detective fiction. But the general excellence of Howard Haycraft's work rests upon an even broader basis—he understands the detective story and presents it with fairness and balance, and his writing has the lively intellectual interest of a good detective story itself." Other critics were equally favorable.

Mr. Haycraft tells us in an autobiographical account written especially for *Current Biography:*

"There really isn't much to tell. I was born in Madelia, Southern Minnesota where my father [Julius Everette Haycraft] was a lawyer and at the time the local postmaster; he is now a judge. His ancestry included English, Welsh, Dutch, and Huguenot French,

HAYCRAFT, HOWARD—*Continued*

all plain people, going back to the 1660's. His father was a Kentuckian who had followed the Lincoln trail to Illinois, served in the Union Army, and then homesteaded in Minnesota. My mother [Marie (Stelzer) Haycraft] had been a schoolteacher; at one time, in fact, she was the first teacher in one of the 'boom' iron-mining towns in Northern Minnesota, when it was only six months old. Her parents both came from Germany, arriving in Minnesota just in time for the Indian outbreaks during the Civil War. No more loyal Americans ever lived than my German-born grandparents. My father was born on a farm and his formal education did not go beyond grammar school. He taught himself after that, and learned his law the old-fashioned way, by 'reading' in the office of a member of the Bar. I have been proud of my father and mother from the time I can remember, and feel that by contrast with theirs, my life has been soft and sheltered. But at least I had a small town, Middle Western boyhood, which I would not trade for a good deal.

"After finishing high school I went to the state university, in Minneapolis. The idea was that I was to follow in my father's footsteps and become a lawyer. But it wasn't to be. I had got the smell of printer's ink in my nostrils, working on the local daily paper after school and during vacations, and I started writing for the Minneapolis newspapers and for the student daily newspaper, of which I eventually became chief editor in my senior year. I did most of the things young people did and thought exciting at college age back in those distant 1920's, but I think probably the most important and lasting thing that happened was the attempt of a local Fundamentalist preacher to force an anti-evolution bill through the state legislature (this was in the days of the Scopes foolishness). The 'professional' press did not seem at all anxious to take a stand on the issue, so it fell to the student newspaper to lead the fight against the bill—which, I am glad to say, went down to overwhelming defeat and has never been revived since. This experience first gave me the strong convictions which I hold today against all forms of censorship, suppression, intolerance, special pleading, or pressure, which I feel to be the greatest internal threats to our democratic way of life. I believe passionately in the latter—for all its imperfections—as a creed and faith.

"After college I spent a short time with the University of Minnesota Press and then set out for New York, where, in January 1929, I was fortunate enough to join the staff of The H. W. Wilson Company, library and bibliographical publishers. Here I am still, having become a director in 1934 and vice-president in 1940. One of my jobs has been the editing, in collaboration with Stanley J. Kunitz, of the Wilson 'Authors' series of biographical literary dictionaries. On my own, I have edited for Harper & Brothers a series of detective story anthologies for younger readers; I should perhaps explain that reading detective stories has been a hobby of many years' standing, and I felt that these anthologies were a good way of turning a hobby into something profitable and, I hoped, useful to others. Presumably they have had some usefulness, or they wouldn't be still in print. Another idea grew out of the same thing. One day I wanted some information in a hurry about some detective story or its author—I'm not sure now what the exact question was. I went to The New York Public Library and asked for a factual history and analysis of detective story writing. To my surprise, there was no book that filled the bill, so I began to think of writing one myself. I took the idea to the D. Appleton-Century Company and they liked it. After three years of research and writing, nights, week ends, and holidays (for I continued to hold down a full-time job) the book finally was published under the title *Murder for Pleasure: The Life and Times of the Detective Story*; and at present writing it is doing quite nicely, thank you, both with the critics and the public, and is shortly to be published in war-time England. The fact that the book was issued just 100 years after Poe wrote the first detective story, and that a good deal has been made of this anniversary in the public prints, hasn't been exactly harmful to sales.

"Following the pleasant reception of *Murder for Pleasure*, I was asked to contribute a monthly department of detective story criticisms to *Harper's Magazine*, beginning in the December 1941 issue.

"I am unmarried and for several years have lived in a bachelor apartment overlooking the East River in New York City. I spend week ends on the South Shore of Long Island, where I have a small sailboat and have recently built a modest year-round cottage on a high point of woodland on an arm of Great South Bay. My hobbies are sailing, music, and—still!—reading and collecting detective fiction. I like most people I meet, but have little taste for formal 'society.' In politics I am an independent. In world affairs I was anti-totalitarian and anti-isolationist long before the brutal awakening at Pearl Harbor. I believe strongly that American isolationists of the past 20 years—however sincere and well-intentioned—must share the blame with European reactionaries for having made the hideous crime of Hitlerism possible; and I feel that the cure, for this tragic mess cannot lie in *more* of the same blind ostrich-ism that helped bring it about, but in *less*. I hope that we Americans have at last learned our lesson—that we shall never again have real peace the easy or negative way, by merely wishing for it, or prating that we are 'against' war, or talking of 'truces' with criminals and gangsters. We've got to do a lot better than we have. This time we've got to win the *peace*."

References

Harper 183:unpaged Ja '42
Sat R Lit 24:6-7+ O '41 por

HAZARD, PAUL Apr. 20, 1878- Professor of French history and literature
Address: b. The Sorbonne, Paris, France

Bulletin: In January 1941 Dr. Paul Hazard was summoned from his teaching duties at Columbia University to take over the presidency of the Sorbonne in Paris. However, his appointment was rejected by the German officials, and Dr. Hazard went to Lyon where he found some of his colleagues from the Collège de France. Together they tried to conduct the Collège de France. In December 1941 he was back in Paris teaching at the Sorbonne.

From March 1941 issue:

The year 1940 brought two high distinctions to Professor Paul Hazard: in January he was elected to the French Academy, to the seat left vacant by the death of Georges Goyau; in November of the same year Columbia University conferred on him a Doctor of Letters Degree.

Dr. Hazard, who is visiting professor at Columbia during the session of 1940 to 1941, has been lecturing on "Literary Portraits of the Eighteenth Century," and it is probably for his work on the eighteenth century that he is best known. His *The Crisis of the European Conscience, 1685-1715*, completed in 1935, is considered one of the most important works of the past decade, and he has done studies of Lamartine, Chateaubriand and others. But there are many other books, articles and studies to his credit, some of them the result of his years as co-editor of the *Revue de Littérature Comparée*.

Paul-Gustave-Marie-Camille Hazard was born in the small village of Nordpeene near the Belgian border in 1878. He was admitted to the École Normale Supérieure in Paris in 1899, to the *agrégation des lettres* in 1903, and received his doctoral degree from the Sorbonne in 1910. Immediately he began to teach comparative literature at Lyon University. His reputation spread, and after the first World War he was asked to come to the Sorbonne, where he remained until, in 1925, he was appointed to the chair of Modern Comparative Literature in the Collège de France.

In 1914 Dr. Hazard was appointed visiting professor of French at Columbia University, but the outbreak of the First World War prevented him from accepting the appointment. In 1923 Columbia invited him to America again, and this time he was able to come for the academic year of 1923 to 1924. Then, from 1932 on, Dr. Hazard was made visiting lecturer at Columbia during the winter session in alternate years, directing studies of the eighteenth century and training students in the preparation of doctors' theses.

Professor Hazard, who is an officer of the Légion d'Honneur and who has received the Croix de Guerre, was made a lieutenant colonel at the outbreak of the Second World

PAUL HAZARD

War, his duties the direction of "the more intellectual phases of French propaganda abroad." With France's armistice he was able to return to his consideration of problems of comparative literature and France's great literary figures, a consideration he is continuing in America.

References

Illustration 205:70 Ja 20 '40 por
N Y Times p28 N 26 '40 por
New Yorker 15:44 Ja 20 '40
R Litt Comp 20:5-12 Ja '40
International Who's Who
Qui Êtes-Vous?

HAZEN, CHARLES D(OWNER) Mar. 17, 1868—Sept. 18, 1941 Historian; professor emeritus of European history at Columbia University; began his academic career as professor of history at Smith College and in 1916 joined the history faculty at Columbia, where he remained, except for periods as guest professor at the University of Strasbourg, until his retirement in 1937; special field was the period of the French Revolution and Napoleon Bonaparte; author of many books, some of which are used as school textbooks.

References

Leaders in Education 1941
Who's Who in America

Obituaries

N Y Times p23 S 19 '41 por

HEATTER, GABRIEL (hĕt'ẽr) 1890-
Radio commentator
Address: b. c/o WOR, Newark, N. J.

In January 1941 Gabriel Heatter, who has been sponsored by "everything from a brewery to a personal loan company," added Forhan's toothpaste to his current list, which included *Liberty* Magazine and Kreml. Five times a week he presents the news over the Mutual Broadcasting System.

As a news commentator, Heatter has broadcast from a caisson below the Hudson River, from the roof edge of a Manhattan skyscraper, from a coal mine, from an airplane (he frankly admits he prefers clean, quiet studio broadcasts). He has talked about national,

GABRIEL HEATTER

international and local affairs, and once said: "Facts should be presented unbiased by personal beliefs and editorial interpretations should be eliminated." But at the same time he has been able to make them really alive. In recognition of this the Women's National Committee in Radio chose him as one of the two outstanding radio reporters, citing especially his colorful presentation, his high standard of English and his excellent diction.

Heatter's *We, the People* programs, which were on the air 1937 to 1941 aroused just as much enthusiasm. As director he introduced a half dozen or so representatives of the American public—a deep sea diver, a lady wrestler, a farm girl, an Arctic explorer, for instance—and let them tell about themselves. It was a fascinating job and inspired him to start on a book about the 50 to 75 most important people who turned up among hundreds of others on the program. Finally, though, he gave it up in order to devote all his efforts to his newscasts.

Heatter came to radio and newsreel commentating with newspaper and author train-

ing. Born on Manhattan's lower East Side in 1890, he was a reporter by the time he was 13 and in school there. Two years later he was covering Brooklyn, and acting as messenger as well, for Hearst's New York *American.* At that time Hearst was running for Governor and thought it might be a good idea to have a boy orator precede his orations. Heatter got the job and went all over New York "trumpeting the virtues of candidate Hearst."

From the *American,* Heatter went to a full-time job on the old Brooklyn *Times,* reporting crime stories. There was a short period then when he felt he wanted to be a lawyer and matriculated in the New York University Law School. This ambition lasted only until he got a real "scoop," startling the journalistic world by unearthing the hideout of a prominent, embezzling banker. From the *Times,* Heatter went to Hearst's New York *Journal,* where he mostly reported activities in New York's slums and won that day's equivalent of a Pulitzer Prize for his article *Children of the Crucible.* And from the *Journal,* Heatter went to the New York *Herald,* working as a political correspondent in Albany.

Heatter's success in Albany got him a chance to go abroad as the Paris representative for the Foreign Language Publishers' Association shortly after the War, doing articles on conditions abroad. At this time and later he was also active writing stories and articles under his own name and ghostwriting material for many prominent Americans. It was Heatter's writing, in fact, that actually got him into radio. In 1932 he wrote a series of articles for *The Nation,* debating socialism with Norman Thomas, which created quite a stir. Donald Flamm was so excited by them that he signed him up as news commentator on Station WMCA in New York City.

It was in 1936 that Heatter first appeared on the "big time" when he covered the trial of Bruno Hauptmann for MBS and distinguished himself for his impartial observations. When Hauptmann was executed Heatter unexpectedly found himself in the position of setting a record for ad libbing. The execution had been scheduled for 8:05 p. m. but it was close to 9 when Hauptmann actually died, and for 50 minutes Heatter had to keep talk going over the microphone. From then on he was one of the nation's foremost broadcasters—heard over MBS, CBS and NBC.

Heatter is a large man, six feet tall, with dark brown eyes, and is usually dressed in tweedy tweeds and blue oxford shirts. He is married and has a daughter, Nada, who is a fashion designer, and a son, Basil, who is the author of a number of radio shows. The family keeps pretty much together, especially in the country, where Heatter is an expert on dogs and a popular judge at dog shows. But all of them are aware that their country home, like their New York penthouse, is wired for the latest radio and news bulletins and that Gabriel Heatter may have to dash off any moment either to write a news story or broadcast it.

References

Pict R 37:66 Ag '36
Time 37:57-8 Ja 13 '41
International Motion Picture Almanac
Variety Radio Directory
Who's Who in American Jewry 1928

HECKSCHER, AUGUST (hĕk'shĕr) Aug. 27(?), 1848—Apr. 26, 1941 Philanthropist; real-estate operator; mine executive; financier; came to America as a German immigrant boy, started as a coal-mine laborer and became one of the nation's foremost capitalists; donated $5,000,000 in 1922 for construction of a social service building in New York City; endowed many parks and summer camps for the benefit of tenement dwellers in New York City.

References

Forbes, B. C. Men Who Are Making America p191-6 1917
Leaders in Education 1941
Who's Who in America
Who's Who in Commerce and Industry

Obituaries

N Y Times pl, 41 Ap 27 '41 por
Newsweek 17:8 My 5 '41 por

HELLMAN, LILLIAN June 20, 1905-
Playwright

Address: Hardscrabble Farm, Pleasantville, N. Y.

"The theatre found its voice last night," Louis Kronenberger wrote on April 2, 1941, the day after Lillian Hellman's *Watch on the Rhine* opened in New York City. "It found its voice and gave us a play that shrivels anything else produced on Broadway this season." It was in recognition of this that three weeks later on April 23, its author was given the annual award of the New York Drama Critics Circle.

The play's core is the belief that "the death of Fascism is more desirable than the lives and well-being of the people who hate it." It tells the story of an American woman who has returned from Europe to her parents' home in Washington, D. C., with the German engineer she married years before. He is an underground fighter against Hitler, about to sneak back into Germany with funds for the movement. When his secret is discovered by another guest who threatens to inform the Nazi Embassy, the German kills the blackmailer, says farewell to his wife and children and leaves on his fearful mission which has by this time been complicated by the arrest of two of his comrades whom he must rescue from Nazi prisons.

Watch on the Rhine is, in the words of Richard Watts, Jr., "a moving and beautiful play filled with eloquence and a heroic spirit." It is, nevertheless, most critics agree, an uneven play whose first two acts are mostly talk in comparison with the last act in which "the stage takes fire," in which Paul Lukas

Vandamm

LILLIAN HELLMAN

as the German gives "one of the great performances of recent years."

This play is Lillian Hellman's fourth, and the fourth to be directed and produced by Herman Shumlin (see sketch this issue), in whose office she was working when her first play, *The Children's Hour*, appeared on Broadway. Before that time hers had been rather an unsettled career, mostly connected with the stage but not actually of it. She was born in New Orleans, Louisiana, the only daughter of Max Bernard and Julia (Newhouse) Hellman, and brought up on New York's Riverside Drive, where she used to hunt spies during wartime. She attended New York's public schools (except for the short period when she became bored with home life and set out on her own at the age of 14) and eventually landed at New York University. Three years here were enough for her, though in an ambitious moment she enrolled later for courses in Dante at Columbia, and in 1924 she started earning her living.

This living consisted of the $17.50 a week paid her by Horace Liveright, Incorporated, publishers, for being a general factotum around the office. After a year of it she married Arthur Kober, playwright and author (*Having Wonderful Time, Thunder Over The Bronx*, etc.), and decided to make writing her life-work. What actually happened was that Lillian Hellman found herself in 1925 and later reviewing books for the New York *Herald Tribune*, helping her husband with his publicity work, reading plays, promoting a Rochester, New York stock company. Her own creative work appeared in one place only, the Paris *Comet*, and was called *Introspective Writing*.

By 1927 this welter of activities had narrowed down to the field of play-reading, for Harry Moses, Leo Bulgakov (she discovered

HELLMAN, LILLIAN—*Continued*

Vicki Baum's *Grand Hotel* while working for him), for Anne Nichols. Then in 1930 she went with her husband to Hollywood and found herself a position reading scenarios for Metro-Goldwyn-Mayer. The next two years were discouraging ones: she was divorced from Arthur Kober, and her own writing was getting no place. "I was selling practically nothing," she says, "living on less."

In 1932 she returned to New York and began reading plays for Herman Shumlin. She also worked on plays of her own, and in 1934 her *Children's Hour* was finally finished. (She had written another play before that, *Dear Queen,* in collaboration with Louis Kronenberger, but it never reached the stage, though at least one producer thought well enough of it to pay advance royalties.) She had worked and worked on *The Children's Hour,* written and rewritten the characters, tested and retested the motivations and each fragment of dialogue. Some of the scenes had been done over twenty times and the whole play at least six.

Based on the Great Drumsheugh Case included by William Roughead in his collection of Scotch historical trials, this story of a baseless charge against two schoolteachers by a willful student, with its dark hints of abnormality, was enough to dismay any producer. Yet actors were finally secured, Shumlin directed and produced the play, and it proceeded to last 691 performances on Broadway, to be taken on tour, to be mentioned seriously for the Pulitzer Prize and to be adapted by Miss Hellman into a successful film, *These Three.*

For a while she went out to Hollywood to adapt her play for the films, and to work on *Dark Angel* (1935) and others. (In 1937 she adapted *Dead End.*) Then she returned to New York, to finish work on her second play, *Days to Come,* and to see it fail in 1936 after only one week on the stage. No critic liked this play on the cruelty and stupidity of strikebreaking, and there was variety only in the amount of dissatisfaction.

That was the year, too, when Miss Hellman went to Europe. She saw the theatre in Russia, she explored Paris and she went to Spain, where for a month in 1937 she was under bombardment by the Franco forces. She returned to America a militant anti-Fascist, to champion actively the cause of Loyalist Spain. Since then she has continued to fight Fascism with all her heart and strength. As she once said: "I am a writer. I am also a Jew. I want to be quite sure that I can continue to be a writer and that if I want to say that greed is bad or persecution is worse, I can do so without being branded by the malice of people who make a living by that malice. I also want to go on saying that I am a Jew without being afraid that I will be called names or end in a prison camp or be forbidden to walk down the street at night." This is the feeling that inspired *Watch on the Rhine.*

Back in America, too, Miss Hellman soon started working on her third play, *The Little Foxes,* which opened in New York in February 1939 with Tallulah Bankhead (see sketch this issue) in the leading role. Called "the season's most tense and biting drama," this candid and cruel play of life in the deep South at the turn of the century ran over a year in New York and then went on tour. It is the story of the two Hubbard brothers and their sister Regina, clever, voracious and unscrupulous, who are on the eve of putting through a big business deal and who turn on each other through rapacity and lust. Written with "sound dramaturgy and an exceptional economy of style," it is the sort of play that "offers keen interest but not much pleasure."

Miss Hellman adapted this play, too, for the screen in a version that had Bette Davis (see sketch this issue) in the lead and she continued to work in Hollywood after *Watch on the Rhine* got under way. Her contract with Samuel Goldwyn is an unusual one, permitting her to write two films a year of her own choosing. If she doesn't wish to carry out an assignment, the contract is automatically extended for an additional half year.

With the money she made from her successes Lillian Hellman bought a country place and indulged in much good living. She even began to complain that success was making her fat, though her friends assured her "it had improved her disposition, smoothed down sharpish nerves."

Blond-haired, brown-eyed Miss Hellman's life between Broadway and Hollywood is a busy one, and one she likes to leave behind her occasionally just to loaf in her country place and forget that she is "the United States' Number One Woman Playwright," and a witty and sociable member of the theatre world. But she can't escape her career long: ideas take hold of her and have to be worked out. The one that is keeping her most interested these days is a plan to dramatize Zola's *Germinal.* That would be a play, she thinks!

References

Lit Digest 120:33 S 14 '35
Mademoiselle 11:123 My '40 por
N Y Times IX p1 Ap 13 '41; IX p1+
   Ap 20 '41; VII p10-11+ My 4 '41 il
   por
New Yorker 18:22-35 N 8 '41 por
Stage 12:34 Ja '35; 16:46 Mr 15 '39 por
Theatre Arts Mo 19:270-1 Ap '35
Wilson Lib Bul 13:632 My '39 por

American Women
International Motion Picture Almanac
Who's Who in America
Who's Who in American Jewry
Who's Who in the Theatre

HENRY, JULES 1889(?)—June 10, 1941 French Ambassador to Turkey; entered diplomacy in 1919 as third secretary at the French Embassy in Washington, D. C., and by 1930 had advanced to the rank of counselor; called back to France in 1938 when his Government sent him to Spain as Ambassador to the

Republican Government; in 1939 appointed Ambassador to Brazil and in 1940 was transferred to Turkey where he defended the Pétain Government against all charges.

References

Who's Who in the Nation's Capital 1934-35

Obituaries

N Y Times p10 Je 11 '41 por

HEPBURN, MITCHELL F(REDERICK)

Aug. 12, 1896-   Premier and Provincial Treasurer of Ontario, Canada

Address: b. Parliament Bldgs, Toronto, Canada; h. R. R. No. 5, St. Thomas, Ontario, Canada

Ever since, as a boy, he was accused of pelting with an apple the august head of a gentleman named Sir Thomas Beck, controversy has been ganging up on the dark, round-faced, heavy-set Mitchell F. Hepburn of Canada. "Mitch," as his friends call him, denied that he threw the apple, but many were the occasions in subsequent years when he hurled mightier missiles. His favorite targets have been John L. Lewis and W. L. Mackenzie King, Prime Minister of Canada (see sketch 1940 Annual).

According to reports the apple incident ended Mitchell Frederick Hepburn's hopes for attending college; and he had to quit St. Thomas Collegiate Institute, located in his home town of St. Thomas, Ontario, where he was born in 1896, the son of William Frederick and Margaret (Fulton) Hepburn. He subsequently got a job with the Canadian Bank of Commerce and in the three years of his employment armed himself with a practical knowledge of accounting, to which he added some courses at the La Salle Extension University. Thus equipped, Hepburn turned from banking to dairy farming and eventually became one of the best informed farmers in his district. He also began to participate in politics.

After returning in 1918 from service abroad, where he had been an infantry lieutenant and a member of the Royal Air Force, Hepburn married Eva Burton in Finegal, Ontario. Joining the United Farmers' Movement, he campaigned vigorously for better farm conditions. Gifted with an inordinate share of boldness and a gusty, flamboyant vocabulary as well as an innate appreciation of dramatic appeal that has since earned him the title of the "Huey Long of Canada," Hepburn was elected to the House of Commons. This was in 1926. Hepburn was 30 years old, the youngest member of the ruling body and a Liberal in a district that had always been Conservative.

Big Business interests quailed as Hepburn unleashed his deadly oratory; he was regarded as a rabble rouser, a Red, for he fulminated against political extravagance, high taxes and "the interests." Throughout all his extraordinary adventures, "Happy" Hepburn, as some have dubbed him, promised to make the Dominion into "Happy" Canada. Pleased with

MITCHELL F. HEPBURN

his popular appeal, Liberal Party chiefs called him from Commons in 1930, just after he had been elected for a second term, so that he could assume leadership of the Ontario branch of the Party. He was everywhere proclaimed as "The Moses of the Liberal Party" and "a rampant champion of the people"; and, true to his role, Hepburn promised to crack down on the power companies, to cut the salaries of public officials and to place their "official" cars on public auction.

After a breath-taking campaign in which he covered over 7,000 miles in a month and gave an average of five speeches a day, Hepburn was swept into the Ontario Legislature. In 1934 he was overwhelmingly elected Premier of Ontario, the wealthiest, most industrialized and most populated Province in Canada. Then he proceeded for a time to carry out his widely publicized program. He canceled power company contracts made by previous Administrations, but was defeated in the higher courts; he passed legislation forcing the lumber barons to put their idle lands to use, thus alleviating unemployment; he passed a minimum-wage and a new tax law. Then he cut his own salary from $12,000 to $10,000 annually and those of his associates from $10,000 to $8,000. In addition, he actually did auction off the publicly-purchased cars of the Conservative ex-Ministers. To protect himself against the powers-that-be, Hepburn ostentatiously traveled with a group of bodyguards and drove through Ontario streets in an armored car.

One of the greatest publicity opportunities ever to befall a public official came with the birth of the famous Dionne quintuplets, and Hepburn wasn't slow to take advantage of it. As the babies became a world attraction, Hepburn's name regularly appeared in the newspapers, now in connection with a vitriolic attack on the "Stork

HEPBURN, MITCHELL F.—*Continued*

Derby" of the wealthy eccentric Charles Vance Millar whereby the Toronto mother who raised the most children in 10 years would receive $750,000; now in reference to the establishment of a special department called the Dionne Quintuplet Guardianship, whereby the babies would become wards of the King; and now in connection with the launching of a fund campaign for orphan babies. Incidentally, it was at this time that Hepburn announced that he and his wife were adopting two orphan children, their own two children having died in infancy.

But the quintuplets were not the only reason that the national spotlight was focused on the Administration of Premier Mitchell Hepburn. First, there was a financial crisis in many Ontario cities resulting, in part, from a business recession in the United States in 1937 that caused a dwindling demand for wood pulp, one of Ontario's major products. As relief payments declined, desperate families descended on town halls. The crisis also precipitated Hepburn's split from the Dominion Administration, although his relations had never been especially cordial with Ottawa. He blamed the Mackenzie King Government for having failed to provide its equitable share of relief funds.

When members of the General Workers Union entered the municipal building in Lakeview in Toronto Township, imprisoning the relief administrator for several hours, Hepburn saw this as evidence of Communist agitation and he took vigorous steps to suppress the uprising. Later, when the union members organized a "hunger march" on Queen's Park and demanded a hearing from the Premier, Hepburn had a number of them arrested, accepted the report of the relief administrator that the townspeople had been adequately provided with food and refused to increase their relief payments, saying: "There is going to be no mob-rule in the Province." When a group of prominent United Church clergymen passed a resolution condemning his handling of the marchers, Hepburn referred to them as "psalm-singing, sanctimonious preachers in Toronto" who had "lost touch with public sentiment." A further sequel was Hepburn's demand for the resignation of his Attorney General Arthur Roebuck, who had termed the action "provocative" and "highhanded."

Meanwhile Hepburn's speeches before business groups and luncheon clubs became increasingly violent. He spoke of a "Red tide" which must be beaten back with every means; of "outside agitators" who had, he said, "reduced the U. S. A. to a state of anarchy." Canadian labor was aroused. Some said Hepburn's seeming solicitude for the corporations was actually motivated by his desire to stem the sweep of the CIO before it reached the gold-mining industry, which employed many natives of Ontario. The first test of strength between Hepburn and the CIO occurred at a strike at the B. F. Goodrich plant at Kitchener. Hepburn vowed Ontario would tolerate no sit-down strikes.

His stand turned a projected sit-down into a walkout at the General Motors plants at Oshawa and Windsor, organized by the United Automobile Workers Association, a CIO affiliate. Then the Premier delivered broadsides against the CIO as a "racketeering" outfit dominated by Communists. He refused to deal with the organizers from Michigan, consented to hold meetings only with local union leaders. In addition, he challenged John L. Lewis to cross the border. The CIO leader, he said, would be arrested at once and sentenced by a Canadian judge. According to many, Hepburn's intercession helped to prolong the deadlock.

Members of the Toronto District Council accused the Premier of taking sides with the company in the conflict. An embarrassed Dominion Administration signaled its disapproval, but outside criticism Hepburn countered only by references to the "vacillating, weak-kneed" King Government. Before Hepburn had finally withdrawn the mounted police he sent, there occurred a split in both the Liberal and the Conservative Parties, as members of both organizations crossed political lines to condemn or to approve of Hepburn's policies. There was even talk of a Conservative-Liberal Hepburn re-alignment after the leader of the Conservatives quit in protest against a Party resolution favoring collective bargaining.

As the result of Dominion coolness to Hepburn's labor stand and to his policy on hydroelectric power, Hepburn proclaimed at a banquet in 1937, "I am a reformer, but I am no longer a Mackenzie King Liberal." At the end of the year he campaigned for re-election on his demonstrated policies, giving his windup speech in Oshawa to an indignant, catcalling audience of laborites. Nevertheless Hepburn's party lost only three seats—these from strong centers of union organization—and Hepburn himself was returned to office.

The most consistent cause for verbal exchanges between Hepburn and Prime Minister Mackenzie King was the proposed St. Lawrence waterway project. Hepburn opposed the plan and in the course of his opposition criticized President Roosevelt, who, along with the Prime Minister, was one of the most ardent supporters of the project. It was this issue which initially brought Hepburn in contact with Prime Minister M. Maurice Duplessis of Montreal, leader of the Union Nationale and friend of the Fascist Armand Arcand. Duplessis was the proponent of a vaguely clerical-Fascist corporate state and author of the notorious Padlock Law, which was dubbed by liberals and laborites as a most flagrant violation of civil rights. Hepburn said of Duplessis: "He is a great national character," and proceeded to gain his cooperation in a titanic effort to oust the King Government. Rallying cry for the opposition move was a Provincial version of State's rights.

Hepburn's effort to supplant King was not rewarded at the national Liberal Party caucus when delegates overwhelmingly upheld their leader, whose position had been bolstered by his conclusion of the very popular trade pact with the United States. Moreover, with the outbreak of War, Hepburn lost his main prop through the defeat of Duplessis, when the latter made a test of his opposition to conscription at the polls. At the same time Hepburn gained a measure of additional support from some sections of the population by his sponsorship of legislation liberalizing state fund appropriations for parochial schools. His position, however, was not unaccompanied by conflict; he placed a rarely-invoked closure rule on the opposition and ousted one of the more vociferous opponents from the legislative hall.

At first Hepburn's attitude toward the War effort was rather wary, though he inferentially rebuked one of his Ministers for advocating full participation in the conflict and, even when he conceded the rightness of the British cause, qualified it by citing the possibility that foreign trade interests might have had their part in the military action. Later, however, he tried a new tack. Accusing the King Government of inexcusable laxity and incompetence in organizing for defense, he cited the danger of a Hitler invasion.

In many speeches Hepburn advocated interning labor "agitators" for the duration of the War and making illegal all defense strikes. Forgetting his earlier opposition to President Roosevelt, he became an outspoken admirer of the American President, calling him, along with Prime Minister Winston Churchill, one of the greatest men of all times. Climaxing his fervent support of the War, Hepburn said in August 1941 that he planned to resign as Premier of Ontario and leader of the Provincial Liberal Party to go to Britain to engage in war work. But at the same time he continued to wage his internecine struggle against the Dominion Government as he announced the banning of the March of Time film called *Canada at War* because, he claimed, it glorified the King Administration.

Hepburn is a bold, vigorous yet unpredictable leader, who because of his faultless dress has been called the "Jimmie Walker of Canada."

References

Canad Forum 19:40-1 My '39
Collier's 101:13-14+ Ja 15 '38
Lit Digest 124 (Digest 1):9 O 23 '37
Liv Age 353:44-7 S '37
Newsweek 9:12-13 Ap 17 '37; 11:21 Mr 14 '38 por
PM p19 N 14 '41 pors
Sat R 159:538 Ap 27 '35 por
Scholastic 31:28S O 30 '37 por
Time 30:16-18 S 20 '37 por (cover); 35:24 Mr 18 '40 por
Who's Who
Who's Who in Canada

HERSHEY, LEWIS B(LAINE) Sept. 12, 1893- Director of Selective Service

Address: b. Selective Service System, 21st and C Sts, N. W., Washington, D. C.; h. 5425 31st St, N. W., Washington, D. C.

Ever since the Selective Service Act went into effect in October 1940, Brigadier General Lewis B. Hershey has been an extraordinarily busy man. He has prescribed supplementary regulations, issued public notices, orders and instructions, appointed assistants. As part of his activities in the spring of 1941, he urged local draft boards to be careful about drafting needed scientists and technicians and warned them that they must "not only select those who

Harris & Ewing

LEWIS B. HERSHEY

are needed by the armed forces, but must also defer those who are necessary in the production of defense materials." He has successfully proposed the narrowing of draft limits—men over 30 are "too settled," he says. He has told local draft boards to reclassify registrants deferred because of defense work when they "cease to perform the jobs"; he has suggested the induction of the unfit and their salvaging in the Army; he has set up a program to insure the re-employment of men released from the Army. He has discussed deferment for various groups and made pronouncements on this. One which caused a stir was directed toward college students. "I do not think there is anything sacred about a college education," he said. . . "The thing that frightens me is the 'business as usual' cry. . . Going to school because you have nothing else to do is last year's hat." His activities and his duties were tremendously increased when the United States declared war in December 1941.

This "big redheaded stoop-shouldered Hoosier" who is continually explaining the laws' workings to local boards and the public and is running the whole complicated process of Selective Service is a soldier who reached the top without the academic, social or military advantages of West Point training. His father,

HERSHEY, LEWIS B.—*Continued*

L. F. Hershey, was a backwoods farmer and rural sheriff and with his mother, Rosetta (Richardson) Hershey, who died when Lewis was four, did his best to make a living from the farm near Angola, Indiana on which Lewis Blaine Hershey was born.

He attended a one-room school at a place called Hell's Point and then went on to high school in Fremont, Indiana. Before he was 17 he had been graduated and was teaching a country school near Fremont. At the same time he was attending Tri-State College, which gave him a B. S., a B. Pd., and a B. A. by the time he stopped taking courses in 1914. By then Hershey had progressed from school-teacher to rural school superintendent, but after two years of this work resigned to serve with the National Guard, which he had joined in 1911, on the Mexican border. He was a second lieutenant before he started his service, through the simple process of having been elected one by his regiment, and was promoted to first lieutenant while serving.

When Mexican border fighting was over, Hershey entered the University of Indiana to study for his Ph. D., but his academic career was cut short by the entrance of the United States into the First World War. Shortly after he was married to his childhood sweetheart, Ellen Dygert, in November 1917 (they now have two sons and two daughters), Hershey began to train at Fort Sill. Not long before the Armistice he went to France and stayed there for more than a year, attending a French artillery school and arranging for the return of American troops.

When he returned to America in 1919, Hershey was a captain and had decided to quit teaching to join the regular Army. He passed the examinations and then was ordered to the field artillery school at Fort Sill, Oklahoma. Since then he has spent four years as assistant professor of Military Science and Tactics at Ohio State University, four years in active service and teaching at Fort Bliss, Texas, two years as a member of the General Staff School at Fort Leavenworth, Kansas. In 1934 he was graduated from the Army War College and then proceeded to Hawaii, where he was stationed until the spring of 1936. He was then called to Washington. During all these years of service Hershey's colleagues have considered him one of the outstanding army officers of his rank—one officer called him "the best battery commander I ever saw."

In Washington, Hershey, a major in the Army since 1935, became executive officer of the Joint Army-Navy Selective Service Commission, which spent the next four years shaping specific plans for a modern system of selective service. Day and night Hershey worked over the problems; day and night he tried to push home his ideas about it: that there should be local civilian control of registration, selection, review, no fingerprinting, no red tape. "Let's keep this thing so simple," he said, "that even the crooks will say, 'I'll be patriotic and register just like all the other guys.'"

While the Selective Service Act in its present form was being formulated, Hershey, now a lieutenant colonel, was much in demand at the hearings. Opponents and supporters asked him for information, and Hershey gave it—all sorts of data in his head and at his finger tips. Then in October 1940, after the Act was passed, Colonel Hershey, considered its "father" by many, was appointed acting director of the Selective Service system and continued to function as such even after Dykstra (see sketch this issue) had been appointed the civilian director of the draft. In the spring of 1941, after Dykstra's resignation, he was made its deputy director and on June 31, 1941 its director. He probably knows more about its workings both in general and in particular than any other one man. That is why a number of people were impressed in May 1941 when, in response to a question as to whether drafted men would be out of service in a year, he replied: "I'm no prophet. I couldn't tell for sure if it would rain today, but if I was a farmer and it looked like this I'd get my hay in." That is why, too, reporters eagerly sought his comments after war was declared. He told them that the future policy of the selective service system "depends entirely on what the Army believes it needs in the way of men."

In conversations like this and in his supervision of the carrying out of the Selective Service Act, General Hershey (he was made a brigadier general in October 1940) has shown himself very different from the brass hat kind of officer, "still a good civilian at heart," with a fine sense of humor that crops out now and again in the tall stories which he tells with gusto. He doesn't look or act like an officer either, with his Midwest accent and homespun manner—more like a country schoolteacher or a dirt farmer. Nor is his hobby a usual one among military men. It is the study of psychology, and his library has most of the standard works on the subject. "I want to know what makes the human animal tick," General Hershey says.

References

N Y Herald Tribune X p15, 22 O 13 '40 por
N Y Times p9 S 30 '40 por
Scholastic 37:13 O 14 '40 por
U S News 9:36-7 O 11 '40 por

Who's Who in the Nation's Capital
Who's Who in the Regular Army

HESS, RUDOLF Apr. 26, 1894- Former Reichsminister without Portfolio

Bulletin: On the night of May 10, 1941 a twin-engined Messerschmitt 110 crashed to earth in Scotland. Its passenger, who had parachuted to safety nearby, was Rudolf Hess. The excitement and uproar of the fantastic happening spread all over the world. Rumor had it that his flight was caused by inner dissension within Germany, that Hess had broken with his Führer especially over German-Russian relations; that he had come to England with peace proposals on his personal initiative; that he had brought peace proposals from Hitler. Month after month passed, with Hess interned in England, without any solution of the mystery of his flight being given out. It was felt in some quarters in England that Churchill and a few other leaders there knew the answer, but questionings in Parliament, the press and elsewhere brought forth no information. The most commonly accepted explanation, however, seemed to be that he had come to England in hopes of contacting certain Tory appeasers who might consider a bargain by which Hitler would attack the Soviet Union while Great Britain would make peace with Germany.

From March 1941 issue:

The name of Rudolf Hess is not so familiar abroad as others among the men who run Germany. Since the beginning of World War II, he has publicly issued a few proclamations and summonses, made a few speeches, and that is about all. In Germany itself, however, it is a different matter. At the annual Nazi Congresses he gets more applause than anyone except Hitler. His office is continually so filled with office-seekers and people wanting to see the Führer that some call it the "Wailing Wall of the Third Reich." He is Hitler's private secretary, the deputy leader of the Nazi Party, and Reichsminister without Portfolio. Besides all these responsibilities, he is the man whom the Führer has named to become his successor after Goering (see sketch this issue)

Actually it doesn't seem likely that Rudolf Hess will ever become Germany's dictator, for a man with a nickname like "the brown mouse" would seem out of place at the head of the blustering Third Reich. Herr Hess doesn't talk much and has a reputation for being modest and retiring except when execution of Hitler's orders requires him to be otherwise; then he is quite ready to get into any kind of a brawl. Oswald Dutch calls him "one of the few inborn decent personalities of the party, merely induced to infamous actions by bad company." Others find little in his career, though perhaps much in his manner, to back up this judgment. But whatever his hidden motives or ambitions, it does seem to be true that almost his entire life has been devoted to Hitler. He is Hitler's shadow, watchdog of the Reich.

Many of the most enthusiastic Nazis have been born outside of Germany. Walter Richard Rudolf Hess, one of them, was born in Alexandria, Egypt. His mother, the former Klara Münch, came of a Swiss farming family, and his father, Fritz H. Hess, was in the export business. Until Rudolf was 14 he was educated in Alexandria, and there came very much under the influence of the Arabs. Already an ardent German nationalist, however, he went to Germany to finish his education. For two years he attended high school

German Railroads Information Office
RUDOLF HESS

in Godesburg on the Rhine, for the most part studying physics, and then when he was 17 began a commercial course in preparation for entering his father's business. He spent a short time in French Switzerland, a short time in Hamburg, and he was in Hamburg when the First World War broke out. He immediately enlisted on the German side.

In 1916 Hess was wounded at Verdun (he later wrote a poem with the title Verdun). Six months later he returned to the field and fought in Romania as a lieutenant in the infantry; just before the end of the War he joined the German Air Force and flew with the scouting Flight "35." Aviation has been his hobby ever since. He had already had a chance encounter with the man who was later to influence him so much—it was in the late autumn of 1917, on the Western Front—but Hess barely noticed Hitler at this time. According to one source, in politics he had grown to think he was a Socialist, and November 1918 found him fighting in the Independent Socialist Revolution in Bavaria. According to another, he volunteered in the Munich Leibregiment against the Bavarian Soviet Republic.

In either case, it was not long before Hess became a member of the nationalist and anti-Semitic Thulesgesellschaft. He was out distributing anti-Semitic pamphlets in Munich one day in the spring of 1919 when he barely escaped arrest and subsequent execution at the hands of the Reds, who had chosen that same hour to raid the place where he worked. On May 1 he was fighting against the Social Democrats and escaped death once more when his friends dragged him away after he had been wounded in the leg. He decided to rejoin the mercantile profession—it was at least less dangerous—but his attempt wasn't successful. And then, in May 1921, he heard

HESS, RUDOLF—*Continued*

Hitler speak for the first time, and his career was decided. He belonged to the Leader for life. "If anyone can put Germany on its feet again, it will be this fellow Hitler," were his reported words. From that time on, Hitler's only known rival for Hess' loyalty was Ilse Proehl, whom Hess married in July 1927—and it has been said that this marriage was merely designed to kill rumors of abnormality.

During this time Hess has been reported as earning his living as private secretary to his former brigade commander, now Professor Dr. Karl Haushofer, director of the "Institute of Geo-Politics," whose theories are supposed to have formed the basis of the Nazi scheme for world conquest.

Hess was the first "gentleman" to join the Nazi Party. He also became Hitler's first bodyguard: he is the "brave Maurice" of Hitler's *Mein Kampf*. On November 8, 1923 he was in charge of the brutal kidnapping of the Bavarian Premier and the Minister of Home Affairs. At the same time Hitler's "beer-hall" *putsch* was taking place. Both Hitler and his trusted bodyguard ended up in prison at Landsberg, and it was there that Hess began setting *Mein Kampf* down on paper from his Leader's dictation. After they were freed it was back to plotting, more fights, and increasingly successful attempts to raise money from German industrialists. By 1925 the future Führer was able to afford a private secretary, and the secretary was Hess. Not until seven years later, however, did "the brown mouse" rise to any official prominence in the Nazi Party. On December 9, 1932, after Gregor Strasser's disgrace, Hitler gave him *carte blanche* authority over the Party machine, made him head of its political section. He it was who forced Strasser's followers to put their signatures to a document vowing unquestioning submission to both Hitler and himself. Unlike Strasser, as Deputy Leader he fought anti-capitalist ideas.

Not much over a year later, on February 4, 1934, with the National Socialist Party the only legal party in Germany and Hitler the Reichschancellor, Hitler created a new cabinet council—the "inner citadel of German power." It included Von Ribbentrop, Goering, Goebbels (see sketches this issue), Dr. Hans Lammers, Von Brauchitsch, General Keitel, Admiral Raeder—and Hess. Hess actually was given no government department, but became a cabinet minister who acted as coordinator among the other ministries. He excelled particularly at certain branches of "public relations." It was he who made the first public apologia for the murders of June 30, 1934—in which, according to at least one source, he had been Hitler's main executioner next to Goering. It was he who ruled that same year that a committee would henceforth watch and pass on all publications by Party writers. And, second in command of the Storm Troops, it was he who instructed them not to beat up foreign visitors

to Germany or expect them to give the Nazi salute, not to wear uniforms outside Germany nor accept decorations from foreign governments.

Hess is also credited with the responsibility for having placed Germans living outside of the Reich at the service of the Nazi Government and, as superintendent of the Nazi *Auslandsdeutsche Bewegung,* to have signed his name to Dollfuss' death-warrant. On numerous official occasions he appeared for Hitler and took over some of his business and receptions; and at the Moscow treason trial of January 1937 he was named as the German official who collaborated with Trotsky for the overthrow of the Soviet Union. Still Hitler's private secretary, too, he was so close to the Führer that many thought he would be named as Hitler's successor. Apparently Hess himself had no other ambition.

It is quite possible that Hitler really would have liked to have named him before Goering. Goering is considered much the stronger man, however, and on September 1, 1939, after the Polish campaign had begun, Hitler at last made the official announcement as to his chosen successors—in case anything "happened to him." And it was Hess, his second choice, who on February 9, 1941 delivered the Breslau speech in which he boasted that "the largest war machine of all times is ready for a decisive battle," and promised that what the English had felt until then was nothing more than "a foretaste" of what they would experience in the future.

Hess is described as being "built somewhat along the lines of the prize fighter, Max Baer," large-framed, "primitively strong," his mouth "as uncompromising as the slot in a letter box," his heavy eyebrows "as woolly as a chow dog's back," a "restrained fanaticism" in his gray-green eyes. On the back of his head is a scar which, it is reported, he acquired in a barroom brawl. One interest outside of his Führer is faith-healing, and he has founded a Dresden hospital devoted to "cures" by means unrecognized by scientific medicine. He is reportedly a Buchmanite.

References

Contemp 159:616-19 645-50 Je '41
Foreign Affairs 20:73-86 O '41
J Débats 41 pt1:1096-7 Jl 13 '34
Lit Digest 118:14 Jl 14 '34 por
Newsweek 4:14 Jl 21 '34 por
R of Rs (London) 85:65-7 Jl '34 por
Scholastic 25:18 O 13 '34 por
Time 37:24 My 19 '41; 37:24-7 My 26 '41; 37:28 Je 2 '41; 37:25 Je 23 '41
Bayles, W. D. Caesars in Goose Step p94-113 1940
Dutch, O. pseud. Hitler's 12 Apostles p97-108 1940
Gunther, J. Inside Europe p72-3 1940
Murphy, J. Who Sent Rudolf Hess? pam 1941
Simone, A. Men of Europe p114-21 1941
Wer ist's?

HESSELGREN, KERSTIN (hĕs'sĕl-grĕn)
Apr. 1, 1872- Swedish sociologist
Address: Stockholm, Bergsgatan 16, Sweden

The general election in Sweden on September 15 and 16 (1940) returned to the Second Chamber of the Riksdag for a second four-year term Kerstin Hesselgren, Liberal, one of the country's outstanding women, the first woman to be a member of the Riksdag (she served in the First Chamber from 1921 to 1934), and the only woman ever to have held this latter office.

Miss Hesselgren is often called the "Jane Addams of Sweden." For more than 30 years she has been taking a leading part in various types of social work in her country, initiating as well as directing many programs for social betterment. For her work the Swedish Government has presented her with a medal. When the tercentenary of the founding of New Sweden was being celebrated in this country in the spring of 1938, her Government sent her as an official delegate to represent the social workers of Sweden. At a luncheon held during that celebration, in New York July 27, 1938, where 500 women representing 28 national and local organizations met to honor her for her more than 20 years of work in behalf of women everywhere, Mrs. Franklin D. Roosevelt introduced her as a "woman who has participated so richly in the life of her times that it would be impossible to do justice to all her activities without staying here all afternoon."

One of her activities she herself reported on at this luncheon. She was one of four experts on a League of Nations Committee on the Legal Status of Women, and with her American colleague, Miss Dorothy Kenyon, made an initial report of what the Committee was doing. When in 1931 the topic was first introduced into the League it caused no little amusement among the men, she said, but she felt that their attitude had changed: various scientific institutions did the actual work of the investigation, which had begun in 1937 and took three years. The investigation, she reported, embraced three divisions: public law, concerning such questions as women's right to vote, to hold office, to obtain an education and to practice a profession; private law, dealing with marriage, right to separate names, right to earnings, right to make contracts, relations of parents and children, etc.; criminal law—that is, respects in which women's criminal responsibility differs from that of men.

Since she had pioneered as a woman in many activities and had worked in the interests of women in her native country and elsewhere, Miss Hesselgren was admirably suited to be one of the experts in this field. She studied at Cassel Women Teachers Training College and at Bedford College, London. She had wanted to be a doctor, but her health was not good enough; therefore she had trained as a district nurse. When household economics was introduced as a school subject she took up the study of this, and for seven years (1897-1903) taught cooking, later becoming supervisor of the teaching of domestic science.

KERSTIN HESSELGREN

In 1906 she was made inspector of housing in Stockholm, the first woman to hold this position. From 1913 to 1914 she worked as a factory inspector, the first woman to hold this position also. During the First World War she was one of the women councilors of the government food commission, and she has organized and conducted courses on the care of infants and on training for charitable and social work.

Miss Hesselgren has been called in as an expert by the League on other occasions. She has also been a delegate to the League of Nations Assemblies. Often she has attended conferences of the International Labor Office as a delegate. In 1919 she was a delegate to the International Labor Conference in Washington. A rather ironical story is told of her encountering labor trouble when she arrived for the Washington conference: at the dock she had to carry her own luggage; at the hotel where she registered a strike was in progress. From 1926 to 1929 she was chairman of an international society called Human Relations in Industry. In 1939 she was chairman of a committee appointed by the Swedish Government to make a thorough investigation of the problem of married women in the labor market.

As a result of all her experience in industrial and international affairs Kerstin Hesselgren has come to this conclusion: "Labor peace is the way to world peace."

References

Am Scand R 10:41 Ja '22 por; 17:287-8 My '29 por; 26:267 S '38; 27:168 Mr '39

(Continued next page)

HESSELGREN, KERSTIN—*Continued*

    Am Swedish Mo 32:23 Je '38
    N Y Times VI p5 My 29 '38; IV p2
    Jl 10 '38 por
    International Who's Who
    Vem är det?

HEWLETT, J(AMES) MONROE Aug. 1, 1868—Oct. 18, 1941 Architect; mural painter; scenic designer; as architect designed many structures including the Brooklyn, New York, Hospital; painted murals for clubs, banks, office buildings, schools; designed stage sets for Maude Adams; former president of the Architectural League of New York, director of the Fontainebleau School in Paris and resident director (1932-35) of the American Academy in Rome.

    References

        Am Arch 142:30 N '32 por
        House & Gard 49:128-9 Ap '26 il plans
        American Art Annual 1924-25
        Who's Who in American Art

    Obituaries

        N Y Times p44 O 19 '41 por

HEYDT, HERMAN A(UGUST) (hīt) Dec. 5, 1868—Aug. 4, 1941 Lawyer; poet; author; teacher; musician; world-traveler; wrote more than 30 volumes on his travels throughout the world; 300 poems of his were collected in a volume.

    References

        Who's Who in America
        Who's Who in Law

    Obituaries

        N Y Times p19 Ag 5 '41 por

HICKEY, THOMAS F., ARCHBISHOP Feb. 4, 1861—Dec. 10, 1940 Roman Catholic Archbishop; served for 56 years in the diocese of Rochester, New York; was former chaplain of the New York State Industrial School.

    References

        American Catholic Who's Who

    Obituaries

        N Y Times p27 D 11 '40

HIGGINS, FREDERICK ROBERT Apr. 24, 1896—Jan. 8, 1941 Irish poet and manager of the Abbey Theatre; books of verse include *Salt Air* (1924) which received the Aonach Tailteann Award, *Arable Holdings* (1933) which received the Casement Award of the Irish Academy of Letters, and *The Gap of Brightness;* since 1935 managed Abbey Theatre in Dublin and visited the United States with the Abbey Company in 1937; author of the play, *A Deuce of Jacks,* and editor with William Butler Yeats of *The Broadsides.*

    References

        New Statesman & Nation 10:848-50 D
        7 '35
        Scholastic 32:20E Ap 23 '38 por

    Author's and Writer's Who's Who
    Who's Who

    Obituaries

        N Y Times p20 Ja 9 '41
        Time 37:76 Ja 20 '41

HILL, BILLY July 14, 1899—Dec. 24, 1940 American song writer who wrote many hit songs, including *The Last Roundup,* a best seller which was credited with introducing a new tempo into dance music; among his other hits were *They Cut Down the Old Pine Tree, Wagon Wheels* and *In a Chapel in the Moonlight;* real name William Joseph Hill.

    Obituaries

        N Y Times p27 D 25 '40 por

HILL, FRANK PIERCE Aug. 22, 1855—Aug. 24, 1941 Librarian of the Brooklyn Public Library from 1901 to 1930; founder of the first free public library in New Jersey, at Paterson, in 1885; had been a librarian since 1881; author of four books; president of the American Library Association in 1906; in 1917 was chairman of the Association's committee which raised $1,700,000 to erect library buildings at Army camps and provide reading material for soldiers and sailors.

    References

        Libraries 35:52 F '30
        Library J 51:279-80 Mr 15 '26; 55:113
        F 1 '30; 55:282 Mr 15 '30 por; 58:
        540-3 Je 15 '33; 58:842 O 15 '33 por;
        59:693-7 S 15 '34; 61:486 Je 15 '36
        por; 63:664 S 15 '38
        Leaders in Education 1941
        Who's Who in America
        Who's Who in Library Service

    Obituaries

        Library J 66:738 S 1 '41
        N Y Herald Tribune p12 Ag 26 '41

HILL, J(OHN) B(OYNTON) P(HILIP) CLAYTON May 2, 1879—May 23, 1941 Represented the 3rd Maryland District in Congress from 1921 to 1927; led the anti-prohibition fight in Congress in the early '20s; joined the National Guard in 1904 and rose through the ranks to major; served in the First World War and received many medals for his heroism.

    References

        Who's Who in America
        Who's Who in Law
        Who's Who in the Nation's Capital

    Obituaries

        N Y Herald Tribune p10 My 24 '41 por

HILL, JUSTINA HAMILTON Oct. 1, 1893- Bacteriologist

Address: b. Johns Hopkins Hospital, Baltimore, Md; h. Calvert Court, Baltimore, Md.

Justina Hill, who is head of the bacteriological laboratory of the Brady Institute of the Johns Hopkins Medical School and Associate in Urology in the same school, admits there may be another female associate in urology. But if so, she adds, we have never crossed swords. For many years her work has been recognized among scientists, and now in 1941 the layman has been given a chance to appreciate it, with the publication of her book, *Germs and the Man*. Called by Karl Menninger "the best popular presentation of an important field of biological science that has appeared," it is a conscientious and accurate, yet informal and witty, account of the war against infection. There are sections on the healing of wounds, on germicides, antiseptics and disinfectants; descriptions of how the body fights infection and the worst enemies it has to fight; and a conclusion that looks toward the future.

Miss Hill says it was "undertaken originally in fun, partly also because the information seems to me to be of vital importance to everyone. . . The story of our own defenses against infection is one of the least known, more important and most interesting aspects of human behavior." The book, she adds now that it is finished and published, "is intended for the intelligent lay reader possessed of scientific curiosity, concerned with his or her own health and that of children. The subject matter here treated concerns every civilian who may be in an automobile accident or even remotely in danger of an air raid."

Many, many years of research and practical experience have equipped Justina Hamilton Hill to write *Germs and the Man*. She was born on October 1, 1893 in Washington, D. C., the daughter of Robert T. and Jennie Justina (Robinson) Hill, and grew up in Washington. After a short time in high school there she went to Miss Capen's School for Girls in Northampton, Massachusetts for three years, next to Smith College, which gave her a B. A. in 1916, and then to Michigan University, from which she received an M. S. in 1917. (In June 1941 Smith College gave her an honorary Doctor of Science degree.) The First World War was raging when Miss Hill left college, and she was anxious to donate overseas the scientific knowledge she had accumulated, but the Red Cross decided she was too young. She did serve with that organization in this country, however, for 15 months, mostly at Spartanburg, South Carolina. There she ran a bacteriological laboratory with the Extra Cantonment Zone Sanitary Service, "a hybrid of the Red Cross and the United States Public Health Service." As she puts it: "Went from one epidemic into another and in between times cultured pop bottles, prostitutes, drinking water and mill hands."

From Spartanburg, Miss Hill went with the Smith College Unit to the Near East with the Near East Relief and "summered in Aleppo at a temperature of 110, running a laboratory for 5,000 refugees trying to get back through the Syrian bottleneck into Turkey and sorting medical supplies, also trying to prevent all of the quinine from being sent to one place, with an infinite amount of malaria and dysentery." "At mountains with no communication with the outside world, except by occasional trucks

JUSTINA HAMILTON HILL

or camels. More dysentery, more malaria, plenty of typhus and one oilstove for the operating room, the delivery room and the laboratory. Fine way to develop chillblains and a philosophy of simplicity."

Back in the United States, Justina Hill found herself in the comparative calm of Johns Hopkins Hospital. In 1920 she was made an associate in bacteriology in the Brady Urological Institute and in 1922 an instructor in urology in the Johns Hopkins School of Medicine. Later she was made an associate in urology. These are the positions she holds today, and this is her work. She wants it emphasized, however, that: "I am a bacteriologist, not a urologist," and offers as evidence the efforts she is making now to try to find out more about how sulfanilamide works. "The interesting thing to me," says this scientist, whose highly technical articles have been appearing for years in scientific journals and whom *Time* calls "one of the most colorful of . . . medical women," is "doing experiments."

References

Time 37:54 Ja 13 '41

American Men of Science

HILL, ROBERT (THOMAS) Aug. 11, 1858—July 28, 1941 Chief geologist of the United States Geological Survey from 1886 to 1930; studied the geology of Mexico, Central America and the Panama Canal; in association with Alexander Agassiz of Harvard University explored the American-Caribbean region; discovered many Texas oil fields; headed many expeditions for various institutions; was a founding member of 14 scientific societies,

(Continued next page)

HILL, ROBERT—*Continued*

References

American Men of Science
Who's Who in America 1924-25

Obituaries

N Y Times p15 Jl 29 '41

HILL, WILLIAM JOSEPH *See* Hill, B.

HILLER, WENDY Aug. 15, 1912- Stage
and screen actress
Address: "Spindles," The Grove, Radlett,
Herts, England

After some six months of intense and nerve-
racking work—dodging the shots of the Luftwaffe and RAF planes, facing the "klieg"
lights and directorial exactions of both Shaw
and Pascal while on the set in Denham, England—Wendy Hiller completed another leading
role in a Pascal-directed screen adaptation of
one of George Bernard Shaw's plays. Quite

WENDY HILLER

different from *Pygmalion,* the first Shaw-
Pascal-Hiller triumph of 1938, *Major Barbara*
(which had its United States première in the
Astor Theatre at New York City in June 1941)
had much more to it than the usual "boy gets
girl" movie formula. It was a film about
"humanitarianism versus power," about "religious hypocrisy," about a soul-saving Salvation Army lass who had become thoroughly
disillusioned by and far wiser from the material
alliance of her co-workers with her millionaire,
munitions-making father from whom she had
become estranged. Preceded by an eight-minute
prologue in which the inimitable Shaw personally addressed his United States audience, the
screen version of his play (he wrote its scenario and dialogue) was a "cinema treat." The
film had an ever timely message to impart

("35 years after its first appearance it comes
to one fresh as a daisy, a daisy, moreover,
which, planted in one world, has grown into
another") and dialogue which was "brilliant,
provocative, richly comic," to say nothing of
the directing of Gabriel Pascal and the good
work of the supporting cast. According to
critics Wendy Hiller gave a "superb acting
performance."

It would seem that fine performances have
been only the usual thing for Wendy. While
in attendance at the Winceby House School,
Bexhill, she won several elocution contests and
participated in several school plays, thereby
reaffirming her early childhood decision to become an actress. To this decision she found no
family objections. On the contrary, in early
childhood she frequently induced the whole
family to take part in her plays; and as often
as not she was staging and/or acting in the
impromptu theatre which her mother, Marie
Elizabeth (Stone) Hiller, helped her build in
the Hiller nursery. It is not unlikely that her
mother fostered in Wendy this liking for the
theatre. For Mrs. Hiller's fondness for the
drama and particularly her deep admiration for
Sir James Barrie's plays were even reflected in
the naming of her other children—René,
Michael and John. Apparently Wendy's father,
Frank Watkin Hiller, did not have much to
say in the naming of his daughter, born at
Bramhall, Cheshire on August 15, 1912.

Having completed her formal education at
the Winceby School, Wendy managed to join
the Manchester Repertory Company in September 1930 at the age of 18. Once in this
company Wendy plodded and at times paced
through the various stages from non-salaried
apprentice to actor-manager. She had her share
of "walk-on" parts and understudied for a
whole year. Then in 1931 she became assistant
stage manager, continuing to act in anything
and everything—from Ibsen's tragedies to Ald-
wych's comedies.

Of her busy life and work with this group
Miss Hiller has said: "For marvelous experience in the theatre there's nothing to beat a
repertory company. For three years without a
break this was my life: Get to the theatre at
10; rehearse all morning; stay in theatre over
lunch hour to work with staff and music and
lighting. Rehearse all afternoon (or play a
matinee); plan next week's wardrobe, or stage
sets, or lighting; make up for evening show,
play my part, prompt and work the operating
cues for the play. In bed by about half-past
midnight with next week's play propped on my
knees, either learning my own part or planning
out stage directions, lighting, props, music cues.
Lights out at two o'clock, with luck, and up
again at eight next morning."

Before Wendy Hiller in her best Lancashire
accent "spoke" her way into the part of Sally
Hardcastle in *Love on the Dole* (1935), she
had reached an impasse in her acting career.
Aside from a job as extra in a Gaumont-
British film, an understudy's job in *Evensong,*
and a bit of radio broadcasting on a children's
hour in London, she had little chance to make
use of the excellent training she had received

with the Manchester Repertory Company, which she had decided to leave in order to "crash" London's West End. Nevertheless, with that "inner vibrancy" and "outer glow," that "deeply felt characterization" and that "clear voice" which Miss Hiller brought to her first important role, in *Love on the Dole,* she rapidly made up for lost acting time.

With her success in that play both in London (1935) and New York (1936), and her engagement to its author, Ronald Gow (they were married in 1937), Miss Hiller went on to scale new acting heights in Shaw's *Saint Joan* (1936). Mr. Shaw had been so favorably impressed with her performance in *Love on the Dole* (he saw the play in New York) that he chose her for the part of Joan of Arc in his *Saint Joan.* It was during one of these performances at a theatre in Malvern (July 1936) that Gabriel Pascal thought she could qualify for the screen role of the Cockney lass, Eliza Doolittle, in *Pygmalion.* After a satisfactory screen test in which she competed with "five other Elizas" Wendy received the role in which she "justified the phonetics expert's prophecy, 'I'll pass this unpolished Cockney flower girl off as a Duchess!'" And, of course, Professor Higgins (Leslie Howard) brought about the transformation with corrective courses—in speech, posture, diet and dress. Her superb acting during these long, grueling, often comic pupil-teacher sessions soon won the admiration and sympathy of a new audience, and in her first movie role Wendy Hiller displayed a "brilliance of wit" and a "warmth of humanity" that is unmatched so far. The immediate success of this first Shaw-Pascal-Hiller dramatic venture is legend by now, *Pygmalion* having won the Hollywood Academy Award in 1937.

Under contract to Pascal for five years, Wendy assiduously avoided the lucrative bids of the Hollywood movie moguls who had been trying to sign her up since her film debut in *Pygmalion.* Though for two years she did not appear in any films, she preferred this arrangement to work under another director. Miss Hiller, who in 1941 was helping out at an air raid precaution post and undoubtedly concerned over her husband and three brothers (all on active duty), nevertheless had a "great ambition to come to America, drive over the country by car and see the Rockies!"

Five feet, seven inches tall, Wendy Hiller, who has "thick chestnut brown hair, hazel eyes and broad cheek bones" and is called by some "tall and scraggly," by others "graceful and lithe," has a strange and singular beauty. Her clear fresh complexion, gleaming curly hair and clear eyes reflect the wholesomeness, the vigor and beauty of her native Lancashire countryside. She is a quiet and unassuming person who does not seek publicity. Little is known of her personal life, which she prefers to keep completely apart from her screen work. She and Ronald Gow have one daughter, Anne. Miss Hiller likes to "cook, play golf, attend the theatre and every Garbo film." She "adores ballet music and goes low-brow on hillbilly songs."

References

Christian Sci Mon Mag p4 My 11 '40 il pors
Life 5:31-2 D 12 '38 pors
Photoplay 19:68+ Je '41 pors
Theatre Arts 20:442-3 Je '36 por
Theatre World 23:179 Ap '35 por; 26: 34 Jl '36 por

International Motion Picture Almanac
Who's Who in the Theatre

HIMMLER, HEINRICH (hĭm'lĕr) Nov. 7, 1900- Reich Commander of the Elite Guard (SS); head of the German police
Address: Berlin, S. W. 11, Prinz Albrecht Str, 8, Germany

German Railroads Information Office
HEINRICH HIMMLER

As Hitler's *Wehrmacht* overruns one land after another, it is followed by a terror that to some is worse than the German invasion. In its wake come the SS-men and Gestapo agents, whose business it is to consolidate Army gains, to mop up the remnants of resistance and make sure that Hitler's triumphant path is clear and safe. These people act with dispatch and efficiency; they are armed with lists of names covering all the dangerous elements. They are feared more than the Army; and indeed there is continuous friction between the Army men and the chief of the German police, Heinrich Himmler, because of the latter's constant interference with Army efforts to placate the population. Himmler is not interested in placating the populace, but rather in the "destruction of the old order whenever we can get our hands on it." For that reason his appearances in Holland or in Norway (he revisited Norway in February 1941 to advise the Quislingists on how to control recalcitrant Norwegians) are always followed by a wave of terror and repression.

HIMMLER, HEINRICH—*Continued*

Himmler is not as well known outside of Germany as the more flamboyant Goering or Von Ribbentrop (see sketches this issue). He is nevertheless considered Hitler's eyes and ears and one of the few irreplaceable men in Nazi Germany. In the possession of his Gestapo are dossiers on every National Socialist dignitary—complete to the last detail, for Herr Himmler is an efficient and orderly man (it has even been said that he keeps a dossier on himself). As a result, if certain reports are true, even the all-powerful Goering walks softly before the meeklooking, nearsighted Police Reichsführer, whose appearance is paradoxically far from sinister. His pudgy face with the pince-nez looks singularly unmilitary beneath the steel helmet. He is quiet and retiring by disposition and could easily be mistaken for a scoutmaster. Yet, as the dread Reichsführer of the notorious Schutzstaffel and the inspector of the state secret police, he has helped Hitler keep his position by balancing powerful groups against each other in order to maintain the supremacy of the Nazi Party. He has created the greatest police system in history.

Like many other Nazi chieftains, Himmler's early career was far from brilliant. He was born on November 7, 1900 in Munich, the son of Gebhard and Anna (Heyder) Himmler. His father was a pious Catholic and a school supervisor. Heinrich got a thorough classical education in the town of Landshut, but was never too enthusiastic about it. At 17 he became an ensign-bearer in the 11th Bavarian Regiment, but saw no active service because his superiors made use of his administrative abilities behind a desk, where he dealt with requisitions and reports. In 1919, after the War was over and he found himself at loose ends, he joined the National Socialist German Workers' Party led by Adolf Hitler. At that time he worked in a fertilizer factory but spent most of his days in beerhall meetings. When the abortive *Putsch* that landed Hitler in prison took place in 1923, Himmler was too insignificant a figure to be punished. He remained at large and attended classes in experimental agriculture at the University of Munich.

During the early '20s the National Socialists lived on a fairly modest scale. Storm troops (SA) were forming slowly, and there was not much money in the treasury. Himmler lived modestly, too, operating a chicken farm with indifferent success. In 1925 his exceptional organizing talents were given some scope and he was appointed business manager of the Bavarian branch of the Nazi Party. There he did a masterly job of organization. Having acted as Gregor Strasser's secretary also, it was on Strasser's recommendation that in 1929 he was finally given a chance at the leadership of the SS—he was the fourth to try the job, and was found completely satisfactory. Under his leadership the Schutzstaffel Corps was to become a considerable weapon in Hitler's hands.

The idea of the Schutzstaffel was conceived by Hitler when he realized that the unwieldy sprawling body of the storm troopers was weak and unreliable. He decided to form a carefully chosen elite group of men upon whom he could rely implicitly. Himmler's genius for organization came in handy. By the time Hitler became Chancellor, he had at his command over a hundred thousand well-armed trained men, the toughest and most intelligent in the Party. Himmler, who in 1930 had become a member of the Reichstag, soon showed that this army could function on a national scale. In 1933, when the last vestiges of the Weimar Republic went up in the Reichstag fire, Himmler had in his possession carefully compiled lists of the opposition and was able to liquidate it at a moment's notice. No wonder then that when the late Ernst Roehm came back to Germany from Bolivia in 1930 he found the Führer's affections transferred to the SS.

Fierce internal strife ensued between the SA, of which Roehm was leader, and the SS. It culminated in the "Night of the Long Knives"—June 30, 1934, at which 1,000 or more followers of Roehm were rounded up and killed, after nearly "48 hours of uninterrupted work." Among the butchered dissidents was Himmler's erstwhile employer, Gregor Strasser. But of course by this time Himmler's only loyalty was to Hitler, to whom he was directly responsible for his actions. With Roehm dead and the SA shattered, Himmler's SS Guards and his Gestapo became the mainstay of the Nazi regime.

According to more than one source, Himmler had already added to his prestige and to the efficiency of his organization by creating the dreaded *Geheim Staats Polizei*, better known as the Gestapo. According to another source, however, others originally created the Gestapo under Goering's supervision—and Himmler started merely as Police President of Munich, first building up the Bavarian Secret Police, in imitation of the Gestapo, later heading similiar organizations in other small German provinces. In either case, he rose rapidly until he was named police commissioner of all the German states except Prussia, where Goering still held sovereignty. Goering was inimical to Himmler, who, he felt, was forging ahead too fast and was too close to Hitler. Nevertheless Himmler managed to creep into the Prussian stronghold. On April 20, 1934 he became the head of the Prussian Secret Police—though, according to one source, only on condition that certain of Goering's followers be given positions of influence under him. Goering was finally prevailed upon to surrender his Prussian Home Ministry, and in 1936 Himmler was proclaimed police commissioner and supreme director of law and order in Germany.

The Gestapo worked hand in hand with the Schutzstaffel, from whose ranks many of its agents were recruited. By means of this organization the whole of Germany was swathed in a network of espionage. It was the business of the Gestapo to ferret out and put down the slightest symptom of dissatisfaction in Germany. The SS-men completed the work of the Gestapo by arresting, trying and executing the victims.

The foreign section of the Gestapo, the UA-1, has, in Himmler's hands, become an important part of Hitler's expansion policy and has done outstanding work in that field. During the years of preparation for the Second World War, Herr Himmler's agents were awaiting *Der Tag* wherever German interests existed. His bright young men were serving as elevator operators in French newspaper buildings and frequenting French salons; they were compiling the data that enabled them later to lay their hands on every important anti-Nazi and fill the jails overnight in Austria, Poland and The Netherlands.

Naturally Himmler's influence has been growing apace. He has time and again proved his absolute devotion to the Führer as well as his complete ruthlessness and unscrupulousness. "With the Schutzstaffel for his arm and the Gestapo for his eyes," he is politically unassailable. The SS uniform has been worn by several members of the Cabinet. The only rival to his expanding ambitions, the Army, has resented strongly the divided authority which is created by his activities in the occupied countries. And Goering is said to side with the Army. It was Otto Strasser, the brother of Gregor Strasser whom Himmler had murdered, who said that "within one hour of the accession of Goering to power, Goebbels (see sketch this issue) and Himmler would be shot dead."

So far, however, these protests have not served to impair Hitler's faith in his police inspector. It is the information Himmler submits to the Führer out of Gestapo files that enables Hitler to deal with any spark of revolt in the Army. Dossiers on Von Blomberg and Von Fritsch, who deplored Hitler's reckless foreign policies, brought about their downfall in 1938. In order to persuade the reluctant members of the *Wehrmacht* of the wisdom of Hitler's plans, Himmler has since been put in charge of several purges that took place in the Army. He does not need to assure Hitler of his usefulness. Nevertheless it has been said that he is not above staging a demonstration occasionally. It was claimed, for example, that the Bürgerbräu Keller explosion which occurred on November 9, 1940, a few minutes after the Führer had left the place, was engineered by Himmler's men as a reminder to Hitler of the need for their existence.

Himmler's pet project is the Schutzstaffel, the "National Socialist Soldierly Order of Nordic Men." It now boasts a membership of about 250,000 and is "the most exotic body of cops the world has ever known." Not a mere police service but a cult, membership in the Schutzstaffel is considered a privilege. Himmler has created tradition by making this band of praetorians a "blood aristocracy" of Germany and by building up a semi-pagan, semichivalric ritual around it. To belong, the SS-men must prove unstained Aryan pedigree back to 1750. They must comply with the physical standards of Frederick the First's bodyguard. They celebrate the Solstice, a pagan festival, and on their belt buckles is inscribed the motto "True Until Death." The fact that a group of SS-men (the *Leibstandarte*) is entrusted with the task of guarding Hitler, and does so day and night, is also helpful to Himmler, who in that way knows everything that goes on around the Führer. (Another and less known regiment, the Death's Head Brigade, is given the less attractive job of guarding the concentration camps.)

It is also Himmler's idea to use the powerful young giants of the SS to build a race of supermen. Himmler does not allow his SS-men to marry without a thorough investigation of their mates; they are, however, encouraged to produce as many illegitimate children as possible. This breeding project is doubtless a carry-over from Himmler's farming days. He has recently put out a magazine called *Victory of Arms—Victory of Children,* in which he claims that "two weapons are available to every people fighting for its existence: its power to defend itself and its natural fertility." He himself is married (his wife is the former Marga Boden) and is completely devoted to his little daughter Gudrun.

A consistent man, Himmler is completely absorbed in his work. One constantly hears of his traveling to one place or another to learn more and better police methods. Only recently he appeared in Spain to study the methods of the Falange. He has read all the books on the subject and has great reverence for the notorious Colonel Nicholai of the First World War and even more for Fouché, whom he hopes to surpass. Unlike other Nazi leaders, he lives simply and unostentatiously in a modest but well-guarded house in a Berlin suburb and, when not otherwise occupied, likes to putter around his chicken farm.

References

Collier's 101:43 My 14 '38
Commonweal 23:372-4 Ja 31 '36
Contemp 158:641-5 D '40
Cur Hist 51:28-31 Je '40 il por (Same abr. Read Digest 37:92-6 Jl '40)
Liv Age 352:515-17 Ag '37; 357:303 D '39
Sat Eve Post 212:12-13+ Ap 6 '40 il por
Sat R 162:298-9 S 5 '36 il por
Time 33:24-6 Ap 24 '39 por
Bayles, W. D. Caesars in Goose Step p150-72 1940
Dutch, O. pseud. Hitler's 12 Apostles p109-22 1940
Gunther, J. Inside Europe p73-4 1940
International Who's Who
Lennhoff, E. Agents of Hell pam 1940
Simone, A. Men of Europe 1941
Wer ist's?

HINCKLEY, ROBERT Apr. 3, 1853— June 1, 1941 Distinguished American portrait painter; worked with John Singer Sargent in Paris; was a descendant of John Cotton

HINCKLEY, ROBERT—*Continued*

and of Governors Simon Bradstreet, Thomas Dudley and Thomas Hinckley of Plymouth Colony; painted the portraits of some 350 prominent Americans; many of his portraits are hung at West Point and Annapolis.

References

Who's Who in America

Obituaries

N Y Times p21 Je 3 '41

HINDEMITH, PAUL (hĭn'dĕ-mĭth) Nov. 16, 1895- Composer; musician
Address: b. Yale University School of Music, New Haven, Conn.

Rudolf Hindemith

PAUL HINDEMITH

"Play this piece wildly, but always in very strict time, like a machine. Consider the piano here as an interesting kind of percussion instrument." So ran Paul Hindemith's instructions for playing the last movement of his piano suite entitled *1922.* In 1933 the Nazi Government issued instructions even more emphatic about *not* playing suites or any other music written by the acknowledged leader of the young German polyphonists. Their decree included the words "degenerate" and "culturally Bolshevistic."

"You can search me why they called my music degenerate," Hindemith told American reporters who greeted him at the dock in February of 1939. "I suppose because it is modernistic."

So non-Bolshevist an institution as Yale University apparently disagrees with Herr Hitler's official critic, for in 1940 Hindemith became a visiting member of the faculty of the Yale University School of Music, and in 1941 he was made a regular member of the faculty. Here he gives courses in advanced composition and theory, chamber music and medieval composition, no doubt indoctrinating the sons of Eli with the subversive principles of Bach and Handel, whose mastery of musical forms he admires and emulates. He is conceded to be probably the most expert contrapuntist of our day. When his appointment to Yale was announced in May 1940, it was also disclosed that he had been awarded the Howland Memorial Prize, given to a citizen of any country for distinguished achievement in literature, the arts or government.

It is ironic that Hindemith has so often been called the playboy of modern music, since he is the avowed champion of "workaday" or utilitarian music—*Gebrauchsmusik,* in the language of the fatherland that disowned him. "A composer should never write," he once declared, "unless he is acquainted with the demand for his work. The times of consistent composing for one's own satisfaction are probably gone forever." His application of his theories won him recognition as "the unrivaled leader of that section of the young generation which believes in carrying to its limit the idea that art-music should be adapted to the demands of its time." It also has gained him a piquant array of epithets and an exile tempered by honor in several countries not his own.

Hindemith was born in the mathematical middle of the decade famous for everything he grew up to condemn—in 1895, in the town of Hanau, Germany. From earliest infancy he breathed in the musical tradition of Germany—breathing it out again, the Nazi authorities believed, into smoke and flame. He came of a musical but very poor family of Silesian craftsmen and almost from childhood had to earn his living; but from the first there was no doubt about his vocation. At six he began to receive lessons. By the time he was 13 he had acquired command of the violin. From then on he played wherever opportunity offered: in movie houses, for musical comedies, at theatres, in dance bands. It all went toward making him "undoubtedly one of the most proficient musicians alive." His chief skill is on the viola, but it has been said that he could probably play on some instruments, with at least reasonable competence, any part of any composition he has written.

In his late teens he studied composition with Arnold Mendelssohn and later with Bernard Sekles, and at 19 became concertmaster of the orchestra of the Frankfurt Opera, a position which he kept until 1924. Then came a year of military service. After that he left to tour Europe with the enormously successful Amar-Hindemith String Quartet, which he and his friend Licco Amar had organized in 1921. He remained with them until 1929, as violist; and later his brother Rudolf joined the group as cellist.

During the '20s he was active in directing the Donaueschingen Festivals and it was through these that his chamber music became internationally known. The Amar Quartet played his *String Quartet No. 2* with great success at the first of these festivals in 1921. A few years later, in 1925, his *Concerto for Orchestra,* played at the Venice Festival of the International Society for Contemporary Music, "first presented its composer as a fiery protagonist of modernism."

Like many of our moderns, Hindemith has been especially interested in chamber music and works for small orchestras, feeling that for many purposes the full orchestra is uneconomical, unsuitable, unwieldy. His works for small groups often employed rather startling combinations of instruments, especially in his second phase, when he was leaning toward experiments in mechanical effects. This was the period in which he gave freest rein to a sense of fun which is characteristic of him and far from common among his compatriots. The earlier phase was formative and eclectic, groping toward an individual idiom. The third, or latest, is marked by a neo-classical strain, a more sympathetic and "humanized" outlook and a tendency to reconcile linear counterpoint with tonal harmony.

The much discussed *Gebrauchsmusik,* a product of the second period, is friendly to the machine which shapes present-day needs, tastes and pursuits. Some of Hindemith's works were actually composed for the pianola and mechanical organ—some of them to accompany the *Felix the Cat* films. He was among the first to take film music seriously and during the years 1927 to 1937, when he taught a master class at the Berlin Hochschule für Musik, he conducted a Film-Music Studio where his most gifted pupils studied "the mechanical processes of film production and the synchronizing of musical measures with sections of film, and for practice . . . [composed] music to old films cut and fitted for the purpose."

Another expression of *Gebrauchsmusik* was the notorious *Lehrstück* (Lesson Piece), once described as "an effort to carry artistic composition into the sphere of the community sing." The musical world responded to it with every emotion except indifference and even some of his ardent disciples found it too stiff a dose. Its performance in 1929 caused an outbreak of hostility, but later the British Broadcasting Company, which has performed a great deal of Hindemith's music, played it successfully.

Hindemith's works for the stage include a number of operas which were performed in Europe before enthusiastic audiences. The best known is *Cardillac* (1926), the story of the goldsmith who was so enamored of his own masterpieces that every time one of them was purchased he murdered the buyer. It was remarked that the real hero of the opera was not Cardillac but counterpoint, and that treating the 40 members of the orchestra as soloists was not strictly in the neo-classical spirit.

Even more unusual was that "engaging trifle" *Hin und Zurück,* a chamber opera which lasts only a few minutes, has five characters in the cast and eight in the orchestra. It consists of a prelude, aria, duet and trio, leading to a monologue after which the previous trio, duet and aria are repeated, but with all the stage action and the musical phrases in reverse order. The moral is that to the powers above it makes little or no difference whether man is born and dies, or dies and is born again. A more recent opera on the grand scale, *Mathis der Maler,* had its première in 1938, in Zurich.

It was his works and not the composer on which the Nazis placed their first ban—which was hotly and vainly protested by the spirited conductor, Dr. Wilhelm Furtwängler. Hindemith himself was treated with great personal consideration, and spent part of his time in Germany until 1938. He was never exiled. Four months of each year he spent in Turkey, where he served the Government as director of musical education and musical adviser, commissioned to organize all branches of music study and research in accordance with European standards. This involved, among other things, building up a state symphony of 80 men and organizing government schools of music that are already said to be turning out promising musicians and composers. He banned his own music in Turkey, declaring: "I won't have anyone say that I used my position here to get my music performed."

In 1936, just when the German Propaganda Minister ordered the press not to mention this representative of "spiritual non-Aryanism" who was destroying the musical ear of German youth, Hindemith was invited to the United States, and the following year appeared in concerts of his own works at the Coolidge Festival in Washington, D. C., with the New York Philharmonic Society, in Chicago, and throughout the country. His performance in his viola concerto *Der Schwanendreher* (turner of a barbecued swan in the kitchen), introduced at Washington, aroused more unanimous delight than the composition itself.

Since his return to America in 1939, Hindemith has appeared in a number of cities, both as performer and as guest conductor. The Philadelphia Orchestra in 1939 introduced his *Nobilissima Visione* from the ballet *St. Francis* at Carnegie Hall in New York. The ballet itself, with choregraphy by Massine, representing the conversion of St. Francis, had been performed the previous year at the Drury Lane Theatre in London. This example of Hindemith's more recent style was well received, as were the symphonic excerpts from *Mathis der Maler* played in New York by the Boston Symphony in 1940. But it was his Symphony in E Flat, which had its world première in Minneapolis in November 1941, that drew the greatest number of "bravos" from its audience. John K. Sherman commented on its "logic and urgency of message," its "close weft of pattern," and the "directness and superb unity of the work as a whole."

A stocky man with blue eyes, sensitive mouth and less hair than the old-fashioned romantic artist might require, Hindemith has been described as a connoisseur of wines and of European walking possibilities, an amateur artist in black and white, and a grief to many

HINDEMITH, PAUL—*Continued*

critics. "How can a man who has written so much excellent music write so much dull music?" wailed one. Another lamented: "If only heaven had bestowed on this composer warmth of heart and a lyrical faculty when it dowered him so plentifully with brains, systems, and counterpoint!" He has also been described as "an influence on modern musical thought second only to Stravinsky, if not by now the more potent of the two."

References

Etude 57:629 O '39 por
Neue Rundsch 45 pt 1:590-2 My '34
New Statesman & Nation 11:262-3 F 22 '36
Newsweek 9:30 Ap 24 '37 pors; 13:26 My 1 '39
Time 29:41-2 Ap 19 '37 por; 31:47-8 Mr 14 '38 por
Baker's Biographical Dictionary of Musicians 1940
Ewen, D. Twentieth Century Composers p203-11 1937
Ewen, D. ed. Composers of Today 1936
Fraser, A. A. Essays on Music p91-111 1930
International Who's Who
Lambert, C. Music Ho! p246-56; p268-74 1934
Pannain, G. Modern Composers p75-94 1933
Rosenfeld, P. Discoveries of a Music Critic p217-29 1936
Strobel, H. Paul Hindemith 1928
Tovey, Sir D. F. Essays in Musical Analysis v4 p172-6 nd

HIRST, HUGO HIRST, 1ST BARON
Nov. 26, 1863- British industrialist

Address: b. General Electric Co, Magnet House, Kingsway, London, W. C. 2, England; h. Fox Hill, Earley, near Reading, Berkshire, England

"When I was very young," Lord Hirst said a few years ago, "I chose the words 'I will' for my motto, and it remains the same today. My aim is constantly to advance and to consolidate. Hard work done intelligently is always repaid. Young people are apt to look at big organizations as institutions which have been there forever; they should realize that everything has been started and built up by a man's striving and determination."

Hirst has always been an individualist and has always believed in what the individual can do. At the 25th Individualist Luncheon in 1929 he said: "After the War individualism seemed to be dead. Today we hear too much about democracy and communism, and too much about nationalization and combined efforts, without realizing that we need individualists in the interests of progress." Nevertheless this typical old-fashioned capitalist who rose from nothing to the chairmanship of the world's largest electrical organization differs from the usual pattern in a number of ways. First, his is a highly inventive mind and his

part in the building up of the General Electric Company was never confined to financial wizardry. Secondly, he has never forgotten his early working years and lays great stress on the importance of good working conditions. In his factories, write Bridges and Tiltman, "the heating, lighting and ventilation are as perfect as care and forethought can make them. Dining halls and canteens have been instituted where good food is provided at a low price. Rooms are available for concerts, dances and the like, and every facility is given for cricket, football, tennis and all sorts of sports. The management is in every case left to the workers themselves."

Hirst's name was originally Hirsch, and he was born of German parents. His father was a distiller and gave his son two years' training in chemistry to prepare him to enter that business. But Hugo went off on his own and joined a firm that was making the first accumulators. In those days he was quite an athlete, and when the firm produced an electrically-propelled vehicle, he was asked to run in front of it with a red flag. At this and at his other tasks he worked long and hard, he studied languages and eventually his ability and knowledge brought him up from a routine job into the head office.

As early as 1884 Hirst was offered a post by a Manchester firm which planned to send him to Australia to trade with $50,000 worth of goods. When a collapse of land values prevented the journey, Hirst proposed opening a London shop to sell the material, and when the store was opened Hirst managed it. He earned a fair share of the profits and gained valuable experience.

Shortly afterward he set out to master the business of electric lighting which was at that time in an embryonic state. One of his first successes was in securing some measure of standardization and centralization in accessories, and by 1887 he was able to produce the first catalog of electrical equipment. In 1893, when public power stations were started, he set up the Robertson Lamp Works at Witton, Manchester, and this venture was followed by the acquisition of a glass works at Lemington-on-Tyne for the manufacture of bulbs. These were set up in a crucial year, for it was in 1893 that Edison and Swan's patents for carbon filaments expired. Hirst was able to proceed with a much superior filament invented by C. J. Robertson.

Experimentation continued, however, for Hirst felt that an even tougher fibre had to be found. Eventually he arrived at tungsten, and it was from tungsten that the first stronger filaments were made. The factory for the Osram lamps, known all over Great Britain, was built by Hirst at Hammersmith, London. Then he went on to work on the gas-filled lamp. In September 1900 the General Electric Company was registered, its works at Witton the only ones in the Kingdom producing lamp-carbon. The Admiralty saw the vital importance of this material and helped on the work of Hirst and his collaborators. Through all the quiet but uneasy years preceding the First World War expan-

LORD HUGO HIRST

though, he insists that tariffs must not be used as an excuse for slackness in industry. In 1936 Hirst was appointed president of the Federation of British Industries and of late he has been particularly interested in fuel research. He has been president of the Institute of Fuel and as such has frequently deplored the British coal-mining industry's lack of imagination in research.

In 1925 Hirst was created a baronet and in 1934 was raised to the peerage as first Baron Hirst of Witton. In 1892 he married Leontine, daughter of Herman Hirsch. At the time of her death in 1938 she was described as "the devoted wife of her versatile and super-energetic husband . . . generous in charity, a gracious and charming personality." Two daughters were born to this marriage, and now Hirst's heir is a grandson, Harold Hugh, born in 1911.

References

Gt Brit & East 47:865-6 D 10 '36 por
Times [London] Mr 22 '29; My 23 '29
Bridges, T. C. and Tiltman, H. H.
   Kings of Commerce p125-37 1928
Who's Who
Who's Who in Commerce and Industry

sion continued. Factory after factory was built or acquired; more and more types of electrical equipment were brought into the orbit of the company. In 1913, with Pirelli of Milan, Hirst established a big electric cable factory at Southampton.

After that earlier War the G. E. C. set up a big research organization at Wembley, near London. Radio was now becoming important, and the firm added radio research to its activities, producing a set which became known as the Gecophone. Another product of the company's laboratories was the mechanically controlled lighthouse which needs no keeper. Hirst watched over the expansion of his company, whose capital investment rose from £85,000 in 1900 to £9,600,000 in the most recent listing, and at the same time was ready to build a gadget himself whenever one was needed.

His interests as an industrialist have extended beyond his own company. From 1923 to 1925 he was a member of the Board of Trade Advisory Council. He has been a member of the Prime Minister's Trade and Employment Panel, economic adviser to the Cabinet Research Committee and scientific representative of H. M. Government on the League of Nations. When in 1928 Sir Alfred Mond (later Lord Melchett) embarked on a series of conversations directed toward peace in industry with the trade-union leader, Ben Turner, Hirst was among the big employers who took part. In that same year he went to Australia as a member of the Federal Government's committee to inquire into developments in that continent and returned convinced of the great potentialities there not fully realized because of an over-rigid tariff system. However, Hirst is no free trader: he has always been a Conservative and a convinced upholder of tariffs. At the same time,

HITCHCOCK, ALFRED (JOSEPH)
Aug. 13, 1899- Film director

Address: c/o RKO Radio Studios, Inc, 780 Gower St, Los Angeles, Calif.

The great popular success of Frank Capra's *Mr. Deeds Goes to Town* and John Ford's (see sketch this issue) *The Informer* made millions of movie-goers acquainted with the fact that a fine picture necessarily has a good, even a fine director behind it. The great crowds who flocked to see *Rebecca,* after reading Daphne Du Maurier's best selling novel of that name, and who later had their spines chilled by *Foreign Correspondent,* will be likely to respond automatically to the announcement of another picture made by Alfred Hitchcock. The smaller but more fanatic cult which never misses a reshowing of *The Thirty-Nine Steps, The Lady Vanishes* and *The Woman Alone* are gratified but not surprised to have their judgment confirmed. They knew all that time that Hitchcock was master of screen melodrama of a particularly convincing, thrilling and atmospheric kind. He has established a school of directing whose imitators are perfectly frank in acknowledging that he is their master. *Blackout* and *Night Train,* which use some of Hitchcock's own actors, are examples of this sincerest form of flattery.

The master of suspense is "an affable man-mountain with bright black eyes who is given to noonday steaks and lemonade," according to Lupton A. Wilkinson. Born in London, the son of William Hitchcock, a poultry dealer and fruit importer, and Emma Hitchcock, he soon acquired an urge to travel. (Trains, buses, ships and planes figure largely in his films.) "The bright and varied goods in his father's shop set him longing for far places. By the

ALFRED HITCHCOCK

time he reached his eighth birthday he had ridden to the end of every bus line—which amounted to almost a life career in London. Those terminals included the London docks, accelerating his dreams. For a hobby he kept a huge wall map of the world. Each afternoon he asked a newsdealer to let him see Lloyd's bulletin; then he hurried home to mark with flag-pins the positions of British ships throughout the world."

After attending St. Ignatius College, a Catholic school in London, Hitchcock intended to be an electrical engineer, but was obliged to give up his courses at the University of London to help support his family by working as a technical clerk in a London cable manufacturing company. He rose from a clerkship to the advertising department, where he applied a natural talent for drawing to the making of advertising layouts. (In preparing to shoot *Rebecca* he indicated the facial expression of key characters by rough but unmistakably indicative sketches.) His friend, the newsdealer, had also lent him British film trade magazines, which he read.

Learning one day that the Famous Players Company was to open London studios, Hitchcock "went to work on a pet idea," according to Walter Wanger, producer of *Foreign Correspondent.* "He thought film titles atrocious and decided to design some to show the new producers that Englishmen too had good ideas. He spent five days and nights lettering art title cards, using the announced title of the first Famous Players London film and names of friends to fill out the customary list of credits." After running the gamut of secretaries and assistants Hitchcock reached the "head man," interested him in his work and shortly thereafter, in 1920, shifted his activities from the cable advertising department to the Famous Players title department.

Later he joined another studio (Gainsborough Pictures) as art director, script writer, assistant director and production manager. He had no thought of becoming a real director until a friend offered him a chance to direct a picture to be made in Munich. Hitchcock took a film company over most of Europe on a $50,000 total budget. During the ninth shooting his employers cabled: "Come home; use sets," and Hitchcock persuaded Alma Reville, a hazel-eyed girl who became his co-writer and general assistant, to marry him in 1926. (They now have a daughter, Patricia, and live in Carole Lombard's former home—a well-hidden, hill-side house in the Bel Air district beyond Beverly Hills and Hollywood in California.) The director reads a great deal, avoiding novels, likes hock and abhors Scotch.

Alfred Hitchcock received his first credit as a director in *Woman to Woman.* Soon after he was credited with the full direction of *Blackmail,* a picture which, in the words of the Boston *Transcript,* "made America conscious of the occasional excellence of British talkies." For several years he worked for British International, turning out *Murder, The Ring, Juno and the Paycock,* Hall Caine's *The Manxman, The Farmer's Wife, Rich and Strange, The Lodger* and *The Case of Lady Chamber. The Thirty-Nine Steps,* starring Robert Donat in an adaptation of the first story of the late John Buchan's Richard Hannay trilogy, won critical acclaim, attracted the notice of Hollywood and is still shown repeatedly in film houses which specialize in superior pictures.

In 1938, says Wanger, Hitchcock first came to Hollywood to size up the place and sign a contract with Selznick-International ($800,000 for five pictures). "He returned the next year," says Wanger, "to direct the sensational *Rebecca,* although it was not his usual type of material. When *Rebecca* was completed, Hitchcock came to us for *Foreign Correspondent* and wrote the original story from which he later directed a picture I was very proud to produce. During the filming 'Hitch' lost 30 pounds, but he has more than 200 left." In February 1941 *Rebecca* was voted the best picture of the year in the annual Academy Award.

None of the effects in *Foreign Correspondent,* as in *Rebecca,* was accidentally achieved, writes Duncan Underhill in the New York *World-Telegram.* "Hitchcock, the rotund engineer who plays Coal Oil Johnny to the Hollywood taverniers in the six or eight fleeting hours a day that he can spare away from his constructive labors, is the foremost living user of the 'gimmick,' or suspense-building device. Suspense, shock and depression are rampant on his cosmic negative, and he will gladly explain how he achieves any or all of them. 'Mrs. Danvers in *Rebecca,*' he will confess to you on a moment's acquaintance, 'upsets you because she comes suddenly from nowhere right into your consciousness. Had I built her one of those stately pedestrian entrances your reaction would have been at once, 'Oh, here comes the menace. I'm not scared a bit.'"

More than any other director in motion pictures, Alfred Hitchcock has staked his career on suspense and has made it work for him in every foot of every reel: *The Girl Was Young, The Man Who Knew Too Much, The Thirty-Nine Steps, The Lady Vanishes.* Writes Lupton Wilkinson: "Each of these British-made thrillers that built up his tremendous reputation was a separate and unique study in suspense. (Incidentally, it is interesting to note that he never resorts to horror devices.)" Another major part of Hitchcock's technique is the accentuation of the terrifying by contrast with the commonplace, the little trifles of life. "Pain, your own pain, is amusing—till it hurts," Hitchcock once said smilingly. "If someone tickles the soles of your feet, you laugh. The same act, carried a trifle farther, becomes a Chinese torture. I apply the pain gently." Hitchcock feels that the camera is really a participating actor in every action and that, representing the audience as it does, it should mingle with the actors and share their adventures with them, not merely stand aloof as an observer or, as a mechanical recording device, be jerkily shifted from one vantage to another.

In Hitchcock's picture released in the spring of 1941, *Mr. and Mrs. Smith,* he fulfilled "an often voiced ambition to direct a typical American comedy about typical Americans." "The striking thing about this film," said the motion picture critic of *Look* Magazine, "is that Hitchcock has employed the same strategy that marks his blood-chilling melodramas. Here again are his unmistakable touches—the same casual approach, the same pell-mell finish, the same corner-of-the-eye viewpoint, the same direction by indirection. The net effect is the same, too: another Alfred Hitchcock hit." His picture, *Suspicion,* with Cary Grant and Joan Fontaine (the lady of *Rebecca*), returned to "blood-chilling melodrama," but this was "a melodrama of the mind" in which he thrust aside his usual suspense-creating tricks and relied on the emotions of the characters themselves to hold the audience. He was completely successful; more than one reviewer called it a cinema masterpiece.

The famous director is "fat, 40 and full of fire," according to Walter Wanger. "I've seen him climb a ladder with unbelievable agility, and I've seen him doze off to sleep looking at pictures. Twenty-seven spotlights wouldn't faze Hitchcock if he became drowsy, and what he can do to a double-thick steak is no Hollywood secret. On the set it's different. He arrives in the morning, is punctual on the stage, makes a careful check of his script scenes before he starts and, while he drinks a cup of black coffee, directs the set-up for the first scene of the day in the minutest detail. His script is an historical document." In addition to having art directors prepare many sketches showing lights, shades and suggested composition, Hitchcock will make as many as 300 quick pencil sketches of his own to show his crew just how he wants scenes to look. When

the cameras begin to turn his actors find Hitchcock a most responsive audience. At least once in each picture he plays a small character-part.

The most important task the director has to perform, Hitchcock told Cecelia Ager of *PM,* is to keep his audience awake. "You ask them to look at a square frame for an hour and a half at a time. You've got to put something in there to keep 'em looking." The hard thing, he says, is to take a dramatic moment and put in comedy. "To make of the whole, entertainment. To employ an art form satisfactorily: that is, to please the rank and file too." Yet he also told Duncan Underhill that "movies are delightfully simple. What you do is take a given piece of time, add color and pattern and you have a movie. Quite."

References

Arts & Dec 51:24 D '39
Collier's 104:22 Ag 5 '39 por
Cur Hist & Forum 52:13-14 D 24 '40 por
Life 7:33-4 N 20 '39 pors
Nation 144:305-6 Mr 13 '37
New Yorker 14:28-32 S 10 '38
Newsweek 12:28-9 O 17 '38 il por
Theatre Arts 25:40-3 Ja '41 il por (p45)
International Motion Picture Almanac Who's Who

HODGES, COURTNEY H. Jan. 5, 1887-
Chief of infantry of the United States Army
Address: War Department, Washington, D. C.

A popular promotion was that of Major General Courtney H. Hodges, who on May 23, 1941 took over the job of Major General George Arthur Lynch as chief of infantry of the United States Army. General Hodges left the post of commandant of Fort Benning, Georgia, the world's largest infantry school.

He is one of the few Army leaders who is not a West Point graduate. Born in Georgia on January 5, 1887, he obtained an appointment to West Point when he was 17, and after a year was found "deficient in mathematics" and flunked out. But he was a born Army man. Once back in Georgia, he wasn't satisfied to enter his father's newspaper business in Perry: he wanted to be a soldier. Finally, in 1906, he enlisted at Fort McPherson, Atlanta, as the humblest of the privates in the 17th Infantry. For two and a half years he was a sergeant there before he got his commission in 1909 as a second lieutenant of infantry—and after that life was more adventurous.

Young Hodges served successively at Fort Leavenworth, Kansas, at San Antonio, Texas and in the Philippine Islands before being sent to Mexico as an officer of the 6th Infantry with General Pershing's Punitive Expedition. When the United States entered the First World War he served with the 6th Infantry in France, and although he saw action in St. Mihiel and other offensives, the most remarkable thing that happened to him during the War, he says, was remaining with

COURTNEY H. HODGES

his outfit under fire for 20 hours before the Meuse-Argonne offensive. He was awarded the Distinguished Service Cross and the Silver Star for valor in action.

After the World War, Hodges served at Fort Sill, Oklahoma and at the United States Military Academy, West Point, New York. In 1920 he was graduated from the Field Artillery School; in 1925 he was graduated from the Command and General Staff School; from 1929 to 1933 he was a member of the Infantry Board. After 1933 he served at the Vancouver, Washington, Barracks and as a member of the general staff of the Philippines Department, having been graduated from the Army War College in 1934. By 1938 he was an assistant commandant of the Infantry School at Fort Benning, Georgia, with the rank of lieutenant colonel; and on October 8, 1940 he was named commandant of the school after the retirement of Brigadier General Asa L. Singleton. He himself acquired the rank of brigadier general, and later with the new appointment he was made a major general.

Hodges is a slender, shy man of medium height. At Fort Benning his favorite recreation was skeet shooting: he is an excellent marksman who has won more than one distinction for his shooting ability, as well as being one of the Army's ablest leaders in the field of military tactics.

References

Newsweek 17:40 My 12 '41
Time 37:18 Mr 3 '41
Who's Who in the Regular Army

HOGBEN, LANCELOT (THOMAS)
(hŏg'bĕn) Dec. 9, 1895- Scientist; author; teacher

Address: b. c/o W. W. Norton, 1 Lexington Ave, New York City

Lancelot Hogben has a considerable reputation among scientists as a biologist, and among ordinary people as a popularizer of the mysteries of science and mathematics. In setting himself up as a combination iconoclast and Messiah of what he calls "scientific humanism," however, some critics feel that he may be in danger of letting the notoriety of his uncurbed sarcasm and indiscriminate wit rob his name of the dignity and repute to which his more constructive efforts have entitled him.

Professor Hogben, who is addressed by his Aberdeen students as "Lancelot" and "Uncle," is reported by those who have known him to be a humanist in the basic sense of the word. His *Mathematics for the Million,* which sold over 70,000 copies in the United States alone, and his *Science for the Citizen* were genuine attempts to bring these subjects within the scope of all literate persons. In *Author in Transit,* however, he indulged himself by criticizing the Russians because they don't read English and are dirty, in praising the Japanese because they have English newspapers and are clean, in indicting all students of the social sciences because they do not reason scientifically, and in coating the concept of "science" with so much of his personal idiosyncrasy that it becomes "just another philosophical abstraction, another metaphysical myth and word of power of the kind which Mr. Hogben scorns so wittily when he finds them in the mouths of economists or conventional educators."

Lancelot Thomas Hogben was born in Southsea, near Portsmouth, England, on December 9, 1895, the son of Thomas Hogben, a seaman's parson. His mother, Margaret (Prescott) Hogben, named him Lancelot, not for Tennyson's gallant hero, but for a missionary in whose steps she expected her son to follow. Many years later, when Hogben broke with those of his friends who belonged to the group of British intellectuals turned Communist, he explained that his childhood had been "largely devoted to a reluctant religion," and that he "had no intention of giving his adulthood to Communism, a dogma and faith in which he could not believe." Although Hogben became a biologist instead of a missionary, in the opinion of some critics he "retains a hereditary impulse to convert the heathen. The heathen at whom he preaches, however, are chiefly the Tories and Communists in his own country."

At Trinity College, Cambridge, Hogben was a Senior Scholar and Frank Smart Prizeman. As a college professor his career led him into widely different localities and types of work. He was a lecturer in zoology at the Imperial College of Science (1919-22), a director of animal breeding research (1923), a lecturer at Edinburgh for two years, assistant professor of zoology at McGill University, professor at the University of Cape Town (1927-30) and professor of social biology at the University of London (1930-37). He has been research professor of human biology at the University of London and served from 1937 to 1940 as Regius Professor of natural history at the University of Aberdeen. In 1941 he accepted the chair of the zoology at the University of Birmingham. In 1936 he was elected a Fellow of the Royal Society for his research work on the pituitary gland and won the Gold Medal of the Royal Society of Edinburgh for his published works on the mathematical theory of genetics, particularly human inbreeding. In 1936 he gave the Moncure Conway Lectures, which were published under the title of *Retreat from Reason* (1937), in which he expounds his doctrine of "scientific humanism," which, he claims, is based on Thomas Huxley's aphorism that "the great end of life is not knowledge but action." Although this was his first sociological work, Hogben's earliest books foreshadowed to some extent his later sociological interests. *The Nature of Living Matter* (1931) was well written, showed wide scientific knowledge and attacked the ideas of such classical scientific thinkers as Haldane, Eddington (see sketch this issue) and Darwin. *Nature and Nurture* (1933) was a brilliant study of genetics.

Mathematics for the Million (1937) was his first great success in making scientific knowledge popular. He says he wrote the book for his own amusement while recovering from an illness, in his "capacity as a private citizen." A firm believer in the popularization of scientific knowledge, Hogben believes this work is being done better in the United States than elsewhere. The American, he says, "works without the medieval hangovers that still obsess and obstruct a Europe full of young men who know all about the glory that was Greece and have no idea of how the internal combustion engine works." His specific aim in writing the book was to stimulate the interest and remove the inferiority complex of "some of the million or so who have given up hope of learning through the usual channels." Its incredible success can be accounted for because it told "what mathematics was about, not as a series of particularly baffling and useless cross-word puzzles, but by showing what it was, how it arose, and what it did." H. G. Wells declared that it was a great book, one that should be read by "every intelligent youth from 15 to 90 who is trying to get the hang of things in this universe." Because he used as illustrative material iconoclastic social criticism, and because his manner of presentation can best be described as "arrogant," he inspired some criticism, too. One American reviewer wrote: "The author knows more things that are not so in more fields, with more 'half-baked' theories, than any of the most famous extravagantists."

Hogben's second attempt in the field of popularizing difficult subjects for the layman was *Science for the Citizen* (1938). Written to obtain tuition for his daughter's university course, it, too, brought contradictory reactions from the press. Some critics regarded it as a "magnificent achievement in the line of progress and courageous social thinking"; others found it lacking in "an instinctive wisdom about human beings," and full of errors and prejudices.

In the introduction to *Retreat from Reason* (1937) Julian Huxley states that Hogben is "one of the rare few who can claim to talk with authority on the subject of scientific humanism." In this book Hogben proceeds from such statements as "reason is everywhere in retreat," and "democracy is becoming a farce," to a criticism of the educational system which he feels has brought about this condition, and a very general outline of the ways in which scientific planning for human needs can better the situation. "The supremacy of reason," he states, "can be maintained only by emphasizing the reasonable grounds for hope in the future of the human experiment." He finds that political leaders "have too little knowledge of technological resources," which makes it impossible for them to plan intelligently. "An arrogant and rather humorless tirade against practically everything extant which has any connection with public affairs," according to one critic, *Retreat from Reason* offers "little constructive except a mild restatement of the ideals of the Technocrats." The book was not without its admirers, however. Horace Kallen called it "forthright, witty, ironical," and placed its author in the front rank of the army of pamphleteers.

LANCELOT HOGBEN

Hogben's book after *Science for the Citizen* was a readable text book, *Principles of Animal Biology* (1940). It was followed the same year by a collection of essays and addresses under the title *Dangerous Thoughts* (1940), dealing with "the state of society and what ought to be done about it." The thesis of the book was still "scientific humanism," and it still, in the opinion of some, sounded very much like Technocracy. The title of the book was chosen, Hogben says, "because no church endorses my views." In it he expressed his belief that "capitalism is no longer a creative force," chiefly because it is "drab." "The

HOGBEN, LANCELOT—*Continued*

straphanging multitudes of our great cities need circuses as well as bread."

When the Germans entered Norway, Hogben and his daughter, Sylvia, were in Oslo. Hogben could have returned to England by diplomatic plane but he could not secure a place for his daughter. They took the hard way, therefore, via Sweden, Russia, Siberia, Japan and the United States. In 1940, when he reached New York after completing the first 12,000 miles out of 20,000 to get to Aberdeen, just a few miles from Oslo by the Western route, Hogben wrote *Author in Transit,* "a kind of documentary film produced in the brains of a highly receptive observer."

In Sweden Hogben found the architecture and the intellectual caste system so displeasing that the excellent food could not compensate for it. In Russia he found that the industrial system had broken down, that few people outside of scientific conferences could do simple arithmetic, that Russians did not read and that living conditions were so disgraceful that "for the next century Russian Marxism will be kept busy by the unromantic task of slum clearance." He denied that Japan is Fascist and expressed the opinion that when it recovered from its present "Boer War" politics it would have a great deal to teach the Western countries, because Japan, "perhaps more than any in the world, comes closest to practising his beliefs on the theory of living in a beautiful environment." As a matter of fact Hogben sums up his attitude towards the use of the word Fascist in these words: "Of late years the word Fascist has been used by liberals and Communists to signify dislike for a person or a system of government, as commercial pinheads, hayseed Senators, and British press lords use the word 'Bolshevik' for anyone who has a higher I. Q. than they have." For the United States, Hogben has great hopes so long as the nation is willing to adapt itself to new conditions and "peaceful planning by piecemeal persuasion" can be maintained.

Hogben's wife, to whom he was married in 1918, is Dr. Enid Charles, a scientist in her own right. They have two sons and two daughters. His daughter, Sylvia, who was the reason for his long journey home, entered the University of Wisconsin in the fall of 1940. Her father accompanied her to Madison, Wisconsin, where he delivered a series of lectures at the University on the "History and Significance of Science."

Professor Hogben's style has been described as "reminiscent of that of Bertrand Russell or of J. B. S. Haldane. He falls somewhat short of them in wit and lucidity, though not in sheer vigor." The character of his wit is exemplified by a reference he makes to the Hegelian dialectic taken over by Marx: "Authors who use a language which allows them to put the nouns on the first page of their works and collect the verbs in the final chapter of the last volume have an unfair disadvantage over the rest of us."

Although he was 45 when he visited the United States, Hogben gave observers an impression of extraordinary youth and freshness. He is small and slight, with auburn hair that hangs attractively over his forehead, dark eyes and a look of "youthful disorder." His voice is quiet and he smiles frequently. Of his personal appearance he himself says: "The surprising state of preservation which the *Evening Standard* described as my boyish appearance is due to the fact that I systematically refuse invitations to dinner parties at which people overeat and underthink in costumes to inhibit excessive cerebration." He does, however, oversmoke. He knows several languages; Russian is not among them. His hobbies are building furniture and designing gardens and he is vehement about his preference for living away from the noise of large cities. "Conventional chatter" about the Oriental virtue of contemplation, however, means nothing to him. "If the choice lies between plumbing and daydreams," he says he is "on the side of the plumbers every time."

References

> Demcourier 10:3-6 D '40 por
> Nation 147:506-9 N 12 '38
> N Y Herald Tribune Books p1-2 F 25 '40 por
> 19th Cent 127:324-32 Mr '40
> Pub W 138:235-6 Jl 27 '40 por (p247)
> Sat R Lit 18:7 O 8 '38 por; 19:3 D 3 '38 por; 19:8 Ja 14 '39; 20:13 Ag 26 '39 por; 23:16 N 9 '40 por
> Sch & Soc 48:338-40 S 19 '38
> Wilson Lib Bul 14:492 Mr '40 por
> Author's and Writer's Who's Who
> Hogben, L. Author in Transit 1940
> Who's Who in America

HOHENZOLLERN, FRIEDRICH WILHELM VICTOR ALBERT *See* Wilhelm II, Former German Kaiser

HOLLAND, CHARLES THURSTAN Died Jan. 16, 1941 English radiologist who first experimented with the X ray a few months after Roentgen and was among the first Englishmen to realize its potentialities; during the First World War perfected methods of detecting bullets and shell fragments in patients' bodies; member of leading X-ray societies throughout the world; lectured at Liverpool University.

References

> Author's and Writer's Who's Who
> Who's Who

Obituaries

> N Y Times p17 Ja 17 '41

HOLMES, JOHN HAYNES, REV. Nov. 29, 1879- Minister of Community Church, New York City

Address: b. 10 Park Ave, New York City; h. 26 Sidney Pl, Brooklyn, N. Y.

Speaking in November 1939 as a "pacifist minister to his brethren," John Haynes Holmes, pastor of the famed Community Church in New York City, warned: "We will be accused of using our pulpits for subversive

purposes. . . Especially will we be denounced
for dismembering the church—for spreading
confusion before its altars, at the very time
when the unity of the spirit should be the bond
of war." Since that time he has been busy
preaching against the growing spirit of militarism in the United States, warning against
violation of civil liberties through Fifth Column hysteria, denouncing conscription as a
Fascist measure, heading the Citizens Peace
Petition Committee, making his church New
York's unofficial center for conscientious objectors.

One of America's most unconventional and
courageously vocal preachers, Holmes was
born in Philadelphia on November 29, 1879,
the son of Marcus Morton and Alice F.
(Haynes) Holmes. His was a family that had
settled in Plymouth back in 1630; his grandparents and parents were "respectable and
even influential citizens of the city of Boston,"
Unitarians and conservative. His maternal
grandfather, John C. Haynes, for 50 years
head of the Ditson music publishing firm in
Boston, provided a tradition of liberalism.

Young Holmes attended public schools, Mal-
den High School, then went on to Harvard.
There he majored in philosophy and history,
joined the debating team and Delta Upsilon,
and as yet showed no symptoms of social conscience. In fact, at that time he was denouncing trade unions along with most of the
other students—cheering when President Eliot
proclaimed the "scab" the great American
hero. In 1902 he was graduated *summa cum
laude* and went on to Harvard's divinity
school with his Phi Beta Kappa key. He was
graduated in 1904, S. T. B., already ordained
and installed as minister of the Third Religious
Society (Unitarian) of Dorchester, Massachusetts. Three days after graduation he married
Madeleine H. Baker of Brooklyn, New York.

It was not long before he was reading
Henry George's *Progress and Poverty*, Ida
Tarbell's history of Standard Oil, Lloyd's
Wealth Against Commonwealth and other similar books and finding his conservatism wearing
a bit thin. After he came to The Church of
the Messiah in New York ("one of the finest
plums in the denomination") in 1907 Dr.
Collyer, the minister emeritus, was heard
asking: "What's this socialism you are talking? I don't understand it. I don't like it.
But if you believe it, preach it for all you are
worth." From 1908 to 1911 he acted as president of the Unitarian Fellowship for Social
Justice; in 1909 as vice-president of the National Association for the Advancement of
Colored People. In one sermon he revised
the Ten Commandments to make them more
applicable to modern times, and the late Heywood Broun, then reporter for the *Tribune*,
wrote a flippant story about it. Sent by his
city editor to see Holmes, Broun learned about
the importance of being earnest. (A quarter
of a century later, Holmes was praying for
the restoration of Broun's geniality.) Broun
described the young minister at the time:
". . . a consecrated young man. I thought
then, as I still think, that it is a lovely head.
But the expression was not warm. On the

THE REV. JOHN HAYNES HOLMES

contrary, it was a little weary. Possibly
John Haynes Holmes had some premonition of
the quarter of a century that lay ahead of him
and of the service that he would give along
the front fighting for righteous and decidedly
unpopular causes."

John Haynes Holmes discovered one of his
most "unpopular" causes when, not long before America's entrance into the First World
War, he made himself one of the moving
spirits in the organization of the American
Civil Liberties Union, which in 1917 emerged
from the Committee Against Preparedness and
the Committee Against Militarism. And the
day before Congress declared war on Germany Holmes' sermon was entitled: "A
Message to My People on the Eve of War."
He told his parishioners: "I am opposed to
war in general and this war in particular. . .
In this church, if nowhere else in America,
the Germans will still be included in the family
of God's children." He was denounced as a
traitor in pulpit and press; members of a
Midwestern religious sect who incorporated
sections of his sermon into their literature were
sent to Federal prisons; later in the War his
sermon was scattered behind the Allied lines
by German aviators. But although Holmes
continued to preach against the War his
resignation was not demanded by the board
of trustees of his church, and he himself was
not threatened with arrest until late in the
War, when Civil Liberties' headquarters were
raided and its leaders got bail ready and prepared for the worst. The Armistice saved
them from prison. Holmes did, however, have
the post-War honor of being condemned by the
Lusk Committee investigating "seditious activi-

HOLMES, JOHN HAYNES, REV.—*Cont.*
ties," charged with responsibility for an "insidious anti-religious campaign." When Japanese-American hostilities began in December 1941 Holmes offered his undated resignation as minister of the Community Church after telling members of the congregation that he could not "bless, sanction or support" war and must remain a pacifist. The resignation was not accepted. In the First World War the same thing happened.

In 1921 John Haynes Holmes left the Unitarian ministry, changed the name of his church to The Community Church, removed all Unitarian and Christian implications from its covenant so that it might express "the unity of all men in the spirit" and welcome Indians, Chinese, Jews, Roman Catholics and Hindus as well as Protestants. A ceremony at the tenth anniversary of the founding of the League of Nations symbolized something of the spirit and cosmopolitanism of the Church. Thirty-one members, born in thirty-one different countries, were asked to come to the pulpit. There they lit candles at a common altar, each in celebration of the country of his birth. At the end of the ceremony both participants and congregation joined in a pledge of service to humanity and the cause of human brotherhood.

John Haynes Holmes has been described as "newsboy, student, clergyman, journalist, magazine editor, author, book lover and collector, enthusiastic theatregoer, musician, husband, father, student of social and political history, courageous pacifist, ardent democrat and social reformer." He is the editor of *Unity*, published in Chicago, and a contributing editor to *Opinion.* He has reviewed books for the New York *Herald Tribune.* He has been a contributor to the *American Dictionary of National Biography.* He is the author of innumerable hymns, pamphlets and magazine articles and of books which range from *The Revolutionary Function of the Modern Church* (1912) and *New Wars for Old* (1916) to *The Heart of Scott's Poetry* (1932) and *Rethinking Religion* (1938). He "has probably established an international record for the number of other people's books to which he has written introductions." As an exponent of non-violence, he became president of the All World Gandhi Fellowship in 1929, and in the same year acting chairman of the War Resisters League, of which he is now honorary chairman. His only play, written with Reginald Lawrence, *If This Be Treason,* was produced by the Theatre Guild in 1935 and was written around the theme of pacifism. (Oswald Garrison Villard approved, but another reviewer found "a strong whiff of the parsonage in *If This be Treason's* incorrigible unreality.")

From 1914 to 1938 he traveled extensively in England, Europe, Russia and the Near East. In 1929 he was on a special mission to Palestine for the Jews, staying there several weeks as a guest of the late Nathan Straus; in 1933 he won the annual Gottheil Medal for service to Jews. From 1929 to 1938 he was chairman of the City Affairs Committee of New York, active in the ousting of Mayor Walker from office. And all this time he has championed nearly every liberal cause extant, although no longer considered a radical. In February 1940 he was elected chairman of the board of directors of the American Civil Liberties Union—chosen unanimously when the Rev. Harry F. Ward declined to seek re-election.

Tall and energetic, he has been alternately accused of extravagance in his judgment and utterances and praised for his facility in dramatizing any appeal—with "all the fervor and prophetic thundering of a Savonarola." He may denounce the evils of liquor as fervently as the evils of war or Fascism. Sometimes called a humanist, he has been perhaps more accurately described as a modernist and theist. He respects the early days of Christianity; warns, "Put not your trust in institutions." In 1934 he suggested a code for the churches: abandonment of denominationalism; fidelity to truth and to science; a pledge to democracy; a pledge to fight nationalism, war, poverty, prejudice, and to reconcile man to his "fated life on this planet."

For years Holmes has been an enthusiastic book collector. His library contains thousands of volumes, and among them are numerous first editions of Sir Walter Scott—his favorite novelist since boyhood. He has one son and a daughter: Roger Wellington and Frances Adria Holmes.

References

Christian Cent 52:1546-9 D 4 '35; 54:1322-4 O 27 '37; 54:1554-6 D 15 '37; 55:234-7 F 23 '38; 56:1374-7 N 8 '39; 57:248-9 F 21 '40; 57:698 My 29 '40; 57:896-8 Jl 17 '40
Nation 123:562-3 D 1 '26; 141:399, 420 O 9 '37
New Repub 92:369 N 3 '37
Time 26:38 O 7 '35 il
World Tomorrow 13:119-22 Mr '30 por; 14:189-91 Je '31; 17:86-7 F 15 '34; 17:330-1 Je 28 '34
Jones, E. D. American Preachers of To-day p311-17 1933
Rusterholtz, W. P. American Heretics and Saints p290-301 1938
Who's Who in America

HONEGGER, ARTHUR (hŏn'ĕg-ēr) Mar. 10, 1892- Composer

Honegger says that his model is Bach, that he believes music should be constructed as solidly, accurately and ingeniously as an automobile, and that he makes his living chiefly by writing for films. Critics say that his music is wholly atonal, based on counterpoint, that its dissonances are painful, its harshness sometimes cruel but never useless, and their only real reproach is for its occasional tendency toward pedantry. What the public remembers is that this composer, who looks like a cross between a classic poet and an ex-football hero, has written music about engines and football games, and that his *Le Roi David* became a "musical best seller" in the '20s. With somewhat less publicity in America than in France, his name has steadily continued to appear on concert and opera programs, among his more recent compositions being the Quartet for piano and strings sponsored by Elizabeth Sprague Coolidge (see sketch this issue) and played at the Coolidge Festival in Washington in 1938 and *Nicholas de Flue*, presented for the first time in America in New York in May 1941. Movie-goers have heard his music with 30 or more films, of which the best known are *Mayerling, Pygmalion* and *Harvest*.

Although a Swiss citizen, Honegger was born in Le Havre, France, where business had taken his family long before his birth on March 10, 1892. One type of critic sees a connection between the city's wharves, steamers, engines and the type of music he later produced. He grew up among art lovers, though not artists, and by the time he was 13 he had crowded his classroom notebooks with two operas, some chamber music, lieder, sonatas and piano pieces—all written with one staff, since as a violin student he did not know about the F clef.

He studied composition first in Le Havre, later in Zurich, and finally in Paris under Gédalge, Capet, Widor and d'Indy; and in 1916 his work began to attract attention. That year, with a number of fellow students, he formed a group known as *Les Nouveaux Jeunes* (The New Youths) under the leadership of Erik Satie, and with Jean Cocteau as literary spokesman. They gave concerts in the Théâtre du Vieux-Colombier, where, on December 2, 1918, Honegger's first large-scale work was performed: incidental music to Paul Méral's *Le Dit des Jeux du Monde*.

Another member was the "exquisite, poetic" Andrée Vaurabourg, a highly accomplished pianist-composer. The two were married during the group's first year and from then on she merged her career with his, giving up her own composition and frequently being the first to perform his works for piano. The number of works he has dedicated to her implies his recognition of her help. One of these was the Concertino for piano and small orchestra (1925), of which the conductor Ansermet exclaimed: "This is the Mozart of today!"

In 1920 Honegger's *Pastorale d'Eté* (Summer Pastoral) won the Prix Verley, annually awarded to the best work for small orchestras. This was the year the "Group of Six" began to enjoy world-wide notoriety. It included, besides Honegger, Milhaud, Poulenc, Auric, Durey and Germaine Tailleferre; and for about six years it represented what was most novel, most daring, most artfully arty in music. After about 1926 "The Six" was heard of chiefly in the past tense, although certain of its members, notably Honegger and Milhaud (see sketch this issue), commanded increasing attention.

Honegger loves sports almost as much as locomotives, in his adolescent years was enthusiastic about football and bicycle races, and as a mature musician never misses an important match. His *Rugby* (1928) might be called a "tour de force of circumstances," for it grew out of his idle comment to a reporter

ARTHUR HONEGGER

that he could conceive of a symphonic poem picturing the musical equivalent of a football game. Immediately the story spread that he was writing such a composition, and comment buzzed on both sides of the Atlantic. Honegger at first was amused, then interested; and in 1928 *Rugby* had its Paris première. More recent works for orchestra are the Cello Concerto performed in Boston in 1930, and the symphony written in honor of the fiftieth anniversary of the Boston Symphony Orchestra, performed there by Koussevitzky in 1931.

Although Honegger has remarked that "one can hardly afford to write an opera today," his *l'Aiglon* (1937), in collaboration with Jacques Ibert, was the only opera since *Der Rosenkavalier* to have twenty-one performances the first year it was put on by the Paris Grand Opera. This, Honegger asserts, was due to the popularity of the leading lady, Fanny Helden. His many other works for the stage include the opera, *Antigone* (1924), to a text by Cocteau; one operetta; seven ballets; and incidental music to thirteen dramatic works. Some of these are André Gide's *Saul* (1922); Romain Rolland's *Liluli* (1923); René Morax's *Judith* (1925)—Mary Garden sang the Chicago première in 1926; d'Annunzio's *Phaedra* (1926); Paul Valéry's *Amphion*, a ballet melodrama produced by Ida Rubenstein at the Paris Opera in 1931; Paul Claudel's mystery play, *Jeanne d'Arc au Bûcher* (1938); and his four-part cycle, *La Danse des Morts* (1940). The Swiss city of Neuchâtel commissioned him to do music for a large-scale popular spectacle at the 1940 Zurich Exposition, and it was this work, redone, which was heard as *Nicholas de Flue* in New York. He has also written numerous works for the piano and for voice.

The work hailed as marking "the complete emancipation of Honegger's talent" was

HONEGGER, ARTHUR—*Continued*

Horace Victorieux (1920-21), a "mimed symphony" based on the narrative by Livy. A more sensational reception was met by the oratorio *Le Roi David*, given dramatic performance at Mézières, Switzerland in 1923. One critic claimed that this "dramatic psalm" owed its great popularity to the fact that, as it had been commissioned for immediate use, it had to be written in great haste. It had orchestral performances in Paris and various American cities, and in 1926 was played in the Coliseum at Rome and at the Zurich festival of the International Society for Contemporary Music.

Those who know Honegger only by one work are familiar with his *Pacific 231,* played so often that Olin Downes felt it was "in danger of disaster caused by over-popularity." Some critics shrugged it aside as "mere onomatopeia," a mechanical and unimaginative transcription of a locomotive rather than a musical re-creation of one. But in 1923, when this "most provocative" of Honegger's works was first performed, machinery in music was news. Audiences twittered no less over the realistic hoots and chuggings of the orchestra than over the composer's much quoted declaration that: "I love locomotives the way other men love women or animals." When he came to America in 1929 the "bob-haired composer" gave color to his statement by riding on a locomotive of the New Haven line clad in beret and white overalls.

There is a dramatic quality in the appearance of this composer, whose greatest claim is that his music represents the "honest work of an honest workman." Of majestic build, with Roman nose, square jaw, tremendous sweep of brow and "penetratingly electric" eyes, he is given to dark green corduroy suits, sports togs and a vast collection of pipes. In 1926, a public debate was staged in Paris: Has Honegger genius? Somewhat to the surprise of the well-bred Parisian audience, the subject himself attended with his publisher, sitting in a conspicuous box. The question was argued pro and con until an admirer who had just published a dithyrambic book about Honegger clinched the argument. This musician of 35, he announced, was undoubtedly a man of genius, since at that age Beethoven had not surpassed the *Heroic Symphony,* Wagner was still at the phase of *Tannhäuser* and *Lohengrin,* and Debussy at *L'Après-Midi d'un Faune* and *Pelléas et Mélisande.*

Opinions differ, sometimes gruffly, about the precise musical evaluation of his compositions. We hear of his "scholastic pedantry" and also that "the best of his many aspects is his lyrical one . . . sometimes touched with a melancholy that expresses itself in songs of winged sweetness." One critic inveighs against his music as "mechanical romanticism" more appropriate to the cinema than the concert hall. Olin Downes, on the other hand, recovering from his earlier apathy, in 1929 declared Honegger the "most lively, full-blooded, cosmopolitan and generally contemporaneous figure among young French composers," adding: "There is speed for you. There is wow—in terms of masterful, entertaining music."

References

Christian Sci Mon Ja 27 '26
Liv Age 356:49-50 Mr '39
London Mercury 39:532-3 Mr '39
Musical Am F 10 '39
Pro Musica Q p4-7 Je '28
Time 35:77 Ap 15 '40 por
Baker's Biographical Dictionary of Musicians 1940
Ewen, D. ed. Composers of Today 1936
George, A. Arthur Honegger 1926
Hill, E. B. Modern French Music p374-9 1924
International Motion Picture Almanac
Lambert, C. Music Ho! p239-46 1934
Pannain, G. Modern Composers p221-35 1933
Rosenfeld, P. By Way of Art p174-85 1928
Taylor, D. Of Men and Music p182-6 1937
Thompson, O. ed. International Cyclopedia of Music and Musicians 1939
Who's Who

HOPE, BOB May 29, 1903-   Radio entertainer; film actor

Address: c/o Paramount Pictures, 5451 Marathon St, Hollywood, Calif.

Bob Hope, one of the most ingratiating zanies in motion pictures and radio. was born in Eltham, Kent, England, the son of a stone contractor and a Welsh concert singer, Agnes Townes Hope. He started life as Leslie Townes Hope, but quickly shifted to "Bob" when the boys in school began to call him "Hope-less." By this time he had settled in Cleveland with his family (the Hopes came over in 1907 when Bob was four) and had started a busy boyhood. There were six children in his not-too-prosperous family, and Bob sold papers, collected money prizes in Cleveland's racing events (he was the best sprinter in school), won prizes for Charlie Chaplin imitations, saved carfare by singing for his fare on streetcars (his was a lovely soprano voice before it changed) and worked as a helper in his older brother's butcher shop.

After he was graduated from high school, Bob Hope started looking around for a trade for a bright young man. He tried boxing and got to the semi-finals of the Ohio novice championship under the name of "Packy East." There his boxing career was cut short, and Hope began giving lessons in Sojack's Dancing Academy. For a short while he held a job with the Chandler Motor Company, keeping it, he claims, only because of his ready wit which shone brightly during conventions and picnics. Finally he decided to go on the stage. With a partner, another stage-struck lad called George Byrne, he toured Midwest towns hoofing and singing in blackface until he discovered, or was told by show business colleagues, that he was much funnier without blackface and a better monologuist than dancer. (This was after he and Byrne joined the act of a pair of Siamese twins.)

For a while Hope starved in Chicago, living in a Southside theatrical boarding house where "the maid came in once a day to change the rats." Little by little, however, he worked his way into the larger Midwest circuits and was able, finally, to form his own Chicago company. Edgar Bergen and Charlie McCarthy were in it, and it was quite successful. Hope moved on to New York. Here again his steady flow of superior wisecracks took him into the hearts of large and sophisticated audiences. For a while he tapped the RKO vaudeville circuit, then in 1927 was given a small part in *The Sidewalks of New York* and in 1928 a larger one in *Smiles*.

His first big stage part came in the *Bally-hoo of 1932* and it was followed in 1933 by *Roberta*, in which he played Huckleberry Haines, a fast-talking, piano-playing, singing, dancing part that established him in the theatre. It was during the run of *Roberta*, too, that Hope met and married Dolores Reade, then a singer at the Vogue Club. In 1936 he was capering on the stage with Fannie Brice in *Ziegfeld Follies*; from that show he was snatched to play with Ethel Merman (see sketch this issue) and Jimmie Durante in Cole Porter's *Red, Hot and Blue*.

His reputation as a successful comedian with a swift, crackling style of patter securely established, radio claimed him. Hope had once declined a radio offer because he felt "radio would never amount to anything" and so lost five years of ether bonanza. He now began making up for those five years, his first appearance being on the *Atlantic Family* program in 1935. Then he starred for the Jergens-Woodbury Sales Corporation in the *Rippling Rhythm Review*, where he left an indelible mark on the radio, and doubtless on his own history, by inventing a stooge called "Honeychile" Wilder, possessor of a syrupy Southern drawl and a minimum of brains. Hope is generally fond of surrounding himself with stooges of weird and marvelous personality, like Jerry Colonna of the eerie mustache, Brenda and Cobina, and an attenuated character called Skinnay Ennis. He became well known in Hollywood for his program *Music for Hollywood*, and in 1941 boosted Pepsodent. His Crossley rating is third highest, which means 22,000,000 listeners for the Pepsodent Company.

Bob Hope's film career began in 1938 when he was put into the *Broadcast of 1938* to sing a sentimental song called *Thanks for the Memory* with Shirley Ross. The song survived the picture and resulted in a screen venture of the same name, in which Hope played the lead. For the next year he appeared in lively but not too distinguished comedies for Paramount, and then, with *The Cat and the Canary*, which starred him and Paulette Goddard, a successful formula for him was found. It consisted of building up a

sinister situation and then injecting Hope into it. In *The Cat and the Canary* (1939) his long, curious nose pursued mystery along dark, damp Florida bayous. In his next picture, *The Ghost Breakers*, he pursued it in a forsaken castle in Cuba, complete with ghosts, skeletons, zombies and other ghastly effects. He was no hero, but a frank and shameless coward who found himself in

BOB HOPE

ticklish situations merely from sheer good nature and curiosity.

In the tenth film of his career, *The Road to Zanzibar* (1941), shovel-chinned, wise-cracking Bob Hope played Fearless Frazier and with Bing Crosby managed to present one of the best musical comedy successes of the year. The scene was darkest Africa; the plot just "one darn gag after another."

Hope fans had hardly stopped laughing in it when they were given *Caught in the Draft*, a "lively package of nonsense" in which Hope tears himself to pieces all because of the Selective Service Act. Its successor, just as beautifully abundant in gags and also blessed with Hope's dry, off-hand delivery, was *Nothing But the Truth*, an ancient farce kicked around blithely, with Hope trying ($100,000 was at stake) to tell the truth for 24 hours.

All these parts together combined to get Hope a new term contract at a reported $150,000 a picture. Other comedians undoubtedly envy him his contract, but many of them turn greener at his ad libbing prowess and his irresistible facility in producing gags. Some of his quips, indeed, have become a part of everyday conversation: "You and your education", "That's what I keep on telling them down at the office", "How do you like that traffic cop?" and the ingenuous query of "Who's Yehudi?" Hope doesn't write all of his own gags, but he is admitted to be the

HOPE, BOB—*Continued*

best radio gag editor in the business. And he does all right on his own, as his performance at the Annual Film Award banquet proved. He was unexpectedly given a medal "in recognition of his unselfish services to motion pictures" (in the form of 258 benefit appearances) and made a knockout impromptu speech. In the fall of 1941 his autobiography, *They Got Me Covered*, appeared.

Bob Hope has been described as a "portrait of a young man in a hurry." He is unhappy in repose, but is fortunately kept busy—and prosperous—what with peddling Pepsodent on the radio, making pictures for Paramount, endorsing testimonials and occasionally issuing from Hollywood to make incursions on local purses in the form of tremendously successful personal appearance tours. Bob Hope at home is very like Bob Hope on the screen or radio. A genial, brawny six-footer, with gimlet-like brown eyes and chin and nose profiled like ski-slides, he loves playing golf, driving fast, funnies, detective stories, billiards. He collects bad notices, carefully frames them and hangs them in his bar. He is fairly superstitious, believes in hunches, will never miss a boxing match. His favorite occupation is being a comedian, and you can depend on him for a Hope-ism almost any time.

References

> N Y Times IX p11 F 25 '40; IX p3 Je 2 '40
> Photoplay 53:30 Ap '39 por; 54:19+ Ap '40; 54:22-3+ O '40 pors; 54:70-1+ N '40 pors
> Time 38:64+ Jl 7 '41
>
> Hope, B. They Got Me Covered 1941
> International Motion Picture Almanac
> Variety Radio Directory
> Who's Who in the Theatre

HOPKINS, ALFRED Mar. 14, 1870—May 3, 1941 Architect; best known as the architect of Federal penitentiaries at Lewisburg, Pennsylvania and Terre Haute, Indiana and many other corrective institutions throughout the country; became known as an authority on the construction of prisons; author of several books on architecture; was amateur musician, composer and student of bookbinding.

References

> House & Gard 64:23-5+ N '33

Obituaries

> N Y Times p21 My 6 '41 por

HOPKINS, HARRY L(LOYD) 1890- Executive Secretary of the United States War Cabinet to Administer the Lend-Lease Act

Address: c/o The White House, Washington, D. C.

Harry Hopkins, most commentators agree, is "uniquely the President's friend, counselor and confidant." Since the day Germany invaded Belgium and Holland he had slept in the White House, one of Roosevelt's key aids on national defense. In January 1941

he was sent to London as Roosevelt's personal representative, without diplomatic standing. He returned to this country five weeks later after conferring with England's leaders to inform the United States that Great Britain needed our help "desperately" and needed it "now" and to present the Administration with details of how that aid should be given. Not long afterward he was given the responsibility of administering the Lend-Lease Bill. In his capacity of administrator he flew back to England in July 1941 and from there hopped over to Moscow to offer Stalin an immediate flow of United States war supplies to aid Russia's fight against the German armies. Then he returned to Washington.

Facts about all that Harry Hopkins observed abroad and all that he has the responsibility of observing here are relayed directly to the President. For many years now these two men have been exceedingly close, and since 1933, when Hopkins came to Washington as head of the Federal Emergency Relief Administration, he has been considered one of the strongest personal influences on the President. It was he, opinion has it, who sold the President the idea that the unemployed must be fed and given work; he who, according to Raymond Clapper, led Roosevelt to dramatize the one-third of our population which he described as ill-fed, ill-housed and ill-clothed. As Secretary of Commerce, Hopkins' relationship with the President continued exceedingly close, and it was he who in 1940 handled the draft-Roosevelt movement at the Democratic Convention, performing "like a commanding general in the field."

This "rangy, slangy Iowan" and the President see eye to eye on social, economic and political questions, despite innumerable differences of background, upbringing and training. Hopkins' interest in social questions is the interest of a lifetime spent working with poverty, of a lifetime "deeply devoted to the cause of human welfare." Virtually every position he has held since college has been devoted to making better the condition of that unhappy "one-third of a nation."

Harry Hopkins was born in Sioux City, Iowa, where his father was a harness maker. Later his father became a traveling salesman in leather goods, and the family moved to a small town in Nebraska, then to Chicago and finally to Grinnell, Iowa, where Hopkins senior opened another harness shop. Mrs. Hopkins was a pious Methodist who gave her five children a thorough Methodist training, taught them hymns and saw that they attended church regularly.

Harry was 11 when his family moved to Grinnell, a homely, big-eared youngster who was continually getting himself into hot water. Like others in his family he went to the college there (Grinnell) and was the "big man of the class of 1912," business manager of the college paper, a member of the varsity basketball and tennis teams, and a politician of note. His majors were history and political economy, and he was graduated *cum laude*.

Out of college, he was about to take a job on a Montana weekly newspaper when one of his professors urged him to spend the summer as director of a boys' camp in New York State, run by Christadora House, a settlement house on the lower East Side of New York City. After a summer at camp he began work for the settlement house in New York. After a year there he went to the New York Association for Improving the Condition of the Poor, in charge of fresh air work and unemployment relief. While working for this organization he was married to Ethel Gross, secretary to the head of Christadora House. (There are three sons of this marriage, which was ended by divorce in 1930.)

From 1915 to 1917 Hopkins was handling widows' pensions for the New York City Board of Child Welfare. Then came the First World War. Rejected from the Army because of defective eyesight, Hopkins became chairman of the Southern Division of the Red Cross with headquarters in New Orleans. After taking this Division through the War and the depression of 1921, Hopkins returned to New York and the A. I. C. P. (now Community Service Society of New York) as assistant director. Two years later, in 1924, he became head of the New York Tuberculosis Association (now the New York Tuberculosis and Health Association) and proceeded to build up an organization which has become "one of the most potent forces in the country for research in preventive medicine and the encouragement of local action."

It was in 1928 that Hopkins first met Roosevelt—during the Al Smith campaign. The two men instantly liked each other, and when in 1931, as Governor of New York, Roosevelt wanted somebody to head his Temporary Relief Administration, he remembered Hopkins and his experience. While still keeping part of his Tuberculosis Association position, Hopkins became working director of the Relief Administration and in 1932 its chairman. In two years he spent $140,000,000 in public relief funds. Swimming pools were built, day schools for practical training of the unemployed were opened, forestry camps were set up and few new methods of relief were left untried.

Hopkins worked hard and efficiently at his administrator's job and at the same time was generally "indefatigable in promoting sound living." He wrote hundreds of letters to editors of papers on safety rules for swimmers, exterminating flies, tuberculosis, letters praising girls who led healthy outdoor lives, condemning women who spent more on cosmetics than toothbrushes. And he managed at the same time to lead a fairly regular suburban life which included golf, poker and playing with his sons. He had been married again in 1931, too—to Barbara Duncan, whom he met while he was working with the Tuberculosis Association. She died in 1937, and the one daughter by this marriage spends much of her time at the White House.

Then came Washington. When Roosevelt transplanted New York's Temporary Emergency Relief Administration on a national scale, he transplanted Hopkins with it. He had never had any other man in mind for the job, he said. Hopkins immediately took

Associated Press

HARRY L. HOPKINS

over the job of Administrator of the Federal Emergency Relief Act and from that date, May 20, 1933, until July 1, 1938, spent almost $8,500,000,000 for unemployment relief. As one columnist put it: "Hopkins is history's greatest spender. Beside him Solomon was a miser . . . the Caesars a bunch of small town boys on a Saturday night spree at the local tavern."

With a "wild slicing of red tape," Hopkins got under way. Shortly after, in November 1933, the President set up the Civil Works Administration to put men to work on simple activities that needed arms and legs rather than complicated plans and machinery. Paul Ward says the CWA was Hopkins' own idea. Whether it was or not, he headed it with the firm belief that the necessary thing for the Government to do in those days of unemployment and relief was to "get projects that have dignity and are useful." The CWA fixed up rural schools, repaired courthouses, brought school records up to date, did health research and many more things. Its life was brief but many felt when it was ended in 1934 that it stood out "as the most successful of New Deal endeavors."

By the time of its demise Hopkins was a well known figure in Washington. His plain speaking had become famous even before his tilt with Al Smith, who called the CWA "a grapefruit halfway between the lemon of public works and the orange of relief." Hopkins talked right back: "If putting 4,000,000 men back to work means going into the grapefruit business then I am delighted to be in it. Al Smith taught me the word 'baloney' and now he has taught me sour grapefruit juice." Hopkins told state Governors: "You're getting in my hair"; he urged Senators to "quit lousing up my office with protests." He informed General Johnson that his NRA codes were

HOPKINS, HARRY L.—*Continued*

"lousy" and Secretary of the Interior Ickes (see sketch this issue) that his public works program was "all haywire." The critics of his projects were just "too . . . dumb to understand." Harry Hopkins has never been one to mince words.

When the CWA was terminated, the FERA took over the work of relief and Hopkins inaugurated its Rural Rehabilitation Program in 1934. In 1935 he was put in charge of the Works Progress Administration, which was created to carry out constructive work. Roads were drained, bridges built, storage dams improved, roads built. There was an Emergency Educational Program which taught 2,000,000 adults to read and write; and there was the NYA, under the WPA, which helped boys and girls to get an education. "The fastest, hardest worker in the Federal service," Hopkins was active during these years not only in his own job but on the President's Drought Committee and on the Committee on Economic Security; he handled the Federal Surplus Relief Corporation, too, and became a member of the National Emergency Council and the National Resources Board.

In his four and one-half years as head of Federal relief, Hopkins was the subject of "more criticism and controversy than all other New Dealers combined." People appreciated his determination "that no one shall go hungry," the humanity behind his hard-boiled briskness, his vision of a better time when the "people in America are going to live in decent homes, the fear of unemployment will be abolished in America, the economic losses due to illness will be abolished, old age will be made secure, and above all, people will have through their days an opportunity to live in an environment from which fear of economic insecurity is banished." People, too, recognized that he was an administrator and organizer of the first class—"he thinks faster than any one working for, against or with him. He remembers everything. He thinks in chunks of detail, smashes systems and gets things done."

At the same time there were many who accused him of playing Santa Claus, of building up a huge political machine to keep him and his friends in power. (There was the report of his saying before an election: "Spend and spend, tax and tax, elect and elect.") His "ribbing of businessmen in public and private" was resented, and he was believed to have designs on the capitalistic system because he stated that he had no faith in any relief program that did not remedy the underlying causes of destitution.

To these critics his appointment as Secretary of Commerce in December 1938 came as a shock. To others it came as a sign that the President intended, by the appointment of his "closest counselor," to crack down on business; to still others as a sign that he was offering business an olive branch. And some were sure it was a sign that Roosevelt was grooming him for the 1940 Presidential nomination. Unperturbed by the fuss, to the Senate Committee Hopkins affirmed his belief that, despite lack of business experience, he could do the job. "I have bought and sold millions and millions worth of goods. I have negotiated with businessmen on hundreds and thousands of deals." He also said he would mostly "just listen to what businessmen have to say." His job, he knew, was to study every aspect of the problems he would have to solve —labor, taxation, the utilities, the railroads, trade with Latin-America, the improvement of business conditions.

High-strung, hard-driven, hit by the death of his second wife at the end of 1937, it was not very long before Secretary Hopkins' health began to fail. Finally, in August 1940, he resigned his position, and Roosevelt wrote him: "Dear Harry. . . You may resign the office—only the office—and nothing else. Our friendship will and must go on as always." The friendship has continued, with Hopkins living in the White House, "one of the family, friend and counselor." And Harry Hopkins wasn't without an office long.

Even before he came to live at the White House or became Lend-Lease Administrator, Harry Hopkins never had much time for social life. When he did get a free evening he spent it at home playing poker—"an infrequent but frenzied player." George Creel once accused this long, loose-jointed, mildly lantern-jawed government worker of having something "of the weary, melancholy look of an ill-fed horse at the end of a hard day," a verdict that may or may not be generally acceptable. Probably the one written in *Fortune* in 1935 hits a little closer to most people's reaction to Harry Hopkins: "He gives off a suggestion of quick cigarets, thinning hair, brief sarcasm, fraying suits of clothes and wholly understandable preoccupation."

References

Collier's 96:37+ N 9 '35 por; 103:13+
My 13 '39 por
Fortune 12:58-64+ Jl '35 pors; 19:53-
9+ Je '39 il por tab
Forum 98:283-7 D '37
Life 11:88-90+ S 22 '41 pors
Newsweek 2:17-18 D 9 '33 por; 13:52
Ja 9 '39; 13:13-14 Ja 30 '39 por
(cover)
R of Rs 89:14-17+ Ja '34 il por
Sat Eve Post 213:9-11+ Ap 19; 29+ Ap
26 '41 il pors
Time 32:9-11 Jl 18 '38 por (cover); 32:
22-4 S 12 '38 por; 33:11-12 Mr 6 '39
por; 36:14 S 2 '40; 37:13 Ap 28 '41
Unofficial Observer [pseud.] New Dealers p172-202 1934
Who's Who in America
Who's Who in Commerce and Industry
Who's Who in the Nation's Capital

HORE-BELISHA, LESLIE (hōr-běl-lē-shá) Sept. 7, 1893- British member of Parliament; former Secretary of State for War

For a short while after Leslie Hore-Belisha had resigned from the Chamberlain Government on

January 4, 1940 there were few signs of life from him. But soon he was back in the limelight making public speeches that became increasingly stormy as Britain's military forces suffered reverses. By the time the "military disaster" of Crete was over, he was saying: "We suffer defeat after defeat and always for the same reasons—lack of appreciation, lack of preparation and the imperfect execution of the project. Each reverse is glossed over by the same series of incompatible explanations and the narcotic of false confidence in the future is invariably applied." Repeatedly he has warned Parliament, the Government and the people that "you cannot win a 1941 war at a 1914 pace." He has criticized the British information service; he has demanded that Britain invade the German-held coastline as a means of helping the Russians. A daring suggestion in the typical Hore-Belisha style was his proposal of a common citizenship for the British Empire and the United States.

Because of his energetic work as Minister of Transport, his efforts in building the first "National" Government, his whirlwind activity at the War Office, Hore-Belisha's words carry weight, especially among those English who for many years have seen him as an energetic, unconventional, original-minded man, constantly being hindered by stuffy formalists. But there are some in England who have never quite trusted him or his judgment—to them he is a go-getter, a careerist with too much of an eye on the main chance, a playboy seeking publicity and meddling with matters he doesn't know anything about.

Hore-Belisha is a Sephardic Jew whose ancestors came to Portugal from Morocco. His father, Captain Jacob Isaac Belisha, emigrated from Portugal to England and became a successful real-estate trader and financier. Leslie Belisha was born in a tall brick house in Kilburn, a London suburb, and was sent at 17 to Clifton College, in Bristol. His father had died, and while Leslie was in school his mother was remarried, to Sir Adair Hore, permanent secretary to the Ministry of Pensions. As was not unusual, Leslie hyphenated his new name to his old one and became Hore-Belisha.

At Clifton, Hore-Belisha was a sprinter who won the 100-yard dash two years in succession, and he was the school's "show-boy" on speech day. Already he showed "definite leanings to law and oratory"; he developed a feeling for words and periods which he never lost, and spent a good deal of time learning and declaiming famous speeches. Just before the First World War he took his first trip abroad, visiting Paris and Heidelberg. Then, in the autumn of 1913, he went up to St. John's College, Oxford.

His stay there was interrupted by the War and in October 1914 he joined the Public Schools Battalion as a private. Later he got his commission, in the Royal Army Service Corps, and served throughout the War, in France, Salonika and Cyprus. He was mentioned in dispatches and promoted to major. In 1919 he returned to Oxford and there played rugby, lived in luxurious rooms,

LESLIE HORE-BELISHA

staged a good many parties, and still found time to become the first post-War president of the Union (the University Debating Club), that "famed springboard to Parliament," and to be graduated with honors in history.

Out of college, Hore-Belisha began to read law and to write articles on politics for the *Daily Express* and *Sunday Express.* Then, in 1922, his stepfather suggested that he stand for Parliament. He entered the contest in the dockyard town of Devonport, as a Liberal, since the incumbent was a Conservative, and was beaten. He tried again in 1923, won the seat and has held it easily ever since. All the time he was in Parliament, particularly in 1928 and 1929, he was associated with the formation of various companies to sell or exploit one thing or another. His record here was one of general failure, and at the time of his resignation the weekly *Truth* pointed out examples of his financial incompetence.

In Parliament he made little impression until 1931, at the time of the British financial crisis, when he began to ask embarrassing questions. Then he helped bring about the mutiny against Lloyd George in the Liberal Party, leading a good number of its members out of Lloyd George's camp. In the National Government then formed he was rewarded with the minor post of Parliamentary Secretary to the Board of Trade and later, from 1932 to 1934, acted as Financial Secretary to the Treasury.

Hore-Belisha got his first big job in 1934, when he was made Minister of Transport. Immediately he announced that he was going to stop "mass murder" on the roads and began flooding the country with pamphlets, rules and safety hints. Among other measures, he installed the "Belisha Beacon," a yellow globe on a black and white post to mark pedestrian crossings all over England—they

HORE-BELISHA, LESLIE—*Continued*
used to call him "the archbeacon" for this.
His picture, for one effort or another, appeared in the papers almost every day. He was a success as Transport Minister and in October 1935 was appointed Privy Councillor and taken into the Cabinet.

It was May 1937 when Hore-Belisha took Duff Cooper's place as head of the War Office and proceeded to turn everything upside down. He retired old generals and appointed young ones. He raised the pay, improved the uniform, gave the soldiers better food, granted them leaves more freely. He made promotions from the ranks and "vigorously democratized" the Army. (Later, in his resignation speech, he was to remark: "It did not occur to me that we were making the Army too democratic to fight for democracy.") Hore-Belisha went to Paris, Alsace, Rome, Malta and Gibraltar, interviewing high officers and statesmen and attending maneuvers. He provided more guns and personnel for anti-aircraft work. And he even started a national fitness campaign, with the "people doing physical jerks and nip-ups all over the place and children getting free milk." When, in December 1938, he survived what was known as a "revolt of the under-secretaries," there were some who went so far as to talk about "a second Disraeli."

Yet at the beginning of 1940 Hore-Belisha resigned. Hundreds of reasons were advanced: he was a victim of anti-Semitism and snobbishness; he had had a "quarrel with the brass-hats"; he had disagreed with the Army over the kind and amount of aid to be given Finland; he split with the Government over English policy toward Russia; there was objection to his tactic of staying on the defensive in the War. According to the London *Times,* however, the cause was "a cumulative series of minor personal frictions," and this seemed confirmed by Chamberlain's explanation to Parliament: "I had become aware of difficulties—perhaps I might describe them as arising out of the very great qualities of my right honorable friend—which, in my view, made it desirable that a change should occur."

There was some fear of a domestic crisis as newspapers of all persuasions and the public in general demanded to know the reason for the ouster of a Minister "with Mr. Hore-Belisha's energy and imaginative grasp." The man in the street, according to one commentator, had come to think of Hore-Belisha as being a good deal like his own bull terrier —"no beauty, but a dandy fighter snapping energetically at festoons of dusty red tape and through it all remaining the comedian who never forgot to grin broadly, usually toward the cameras, before nipping another august shin." The crisis was averted by Hore-Belisha's graceful acceptance of Chamberlain's wish. He refused a position as head of the Board of Trade which was offered him, and contented himself with being a private, if far from retiring, member of Parliament. He also resigned the chairmanship of the Liberal National group, obtaining

thereby, it was said, greater freedom to assist those elements which through public criticism hoped to infuse a greater vigor into the direction of the War.

When speaking Hore-Belisha is ready and resourceful. "From the standpoint of abstract elocution he is perfect. He articulates every syllable; he 'gets across' his matter superbly well, but to him 'getting across' has no relation to sympathy," J. Johnston says. He also comments that Hore-Belisha "is ambitious. Probably however, he suffers from the divided mind which is hostile to political success. He has interests other than politics and he is too attached to them and too doubtful of the political prospect to pledge his time and his abilities entirely to politics."

Among his "other interests" are dining out, playing golf and generally leading the life of a bachelor around town. His home in London was designed by Sir Edwin Lutyens, president of the Royal Academy, and is supposed to be a good example of Hore-Belisha's rich, flamboyant tastes. It is hung with heavy gold curtains, filled with heavy, rococo furniture and surmounted by innumerable gilded cupids. There is another piece of architecture associated with Hore-Belisha—the Belisha Hall—erected in his honor in 1931 by his constituents of Devonport, a tribute which has been accorded to no other living member of Parliament.

References

Christian Sci Mon Mag p4 S 18 '35; p3
        D 9 '36 por
Collier's 102:21+ Ag 20 '38 por
New Repub 102:68 Ja 15 '40
Newsweek 15:17-19 Ja 15 '40 por; 15:
        21-2 Ja 29 '40
R Deux Mondes s8 45:442-6 My 15 '38
Scholastic 32:18S My 7 '38 por; 35:11
        Ja 15 '40
Spec 162:41-2 Ja 13 '39
Time 30:16-17 Ag 23 '37 por; 35:19-20
        Ja 14 '40 por; 35:27 Ja 29 '40

Audax, pseud. Men in Our Time p144-
        57 1940
Johnston, J. A Hundred Commoners
        1939
Who's Who
Who's Who in American Jewry

HORGAN, STEPHEN H(ENRY) Feb. 2, 1854—Aug. 30, 1941 Inventor of the halftone engraving process, first used in the New York *Daily Graphic* in 1880, later adapted to the fast press; as art director of New York *Herald* was fired by James Gordon Bennett, Jr., for his "idiotic" idea of a halftone; was honored in England in 1930 on the fiftieth anniversary of the perfection of the halftone process.

References

N Y Herald Tribune II p7 Mr 3 '40 il
        por
Pub W 136:1454+ O 7 '39 il por

Obituaries

N Y Times p23 Ag 31 '41 por
Newsweek 18:8 S 8 '41
Pub W 140:825 S 6 '41

HORNEY, KAREN (hôrn-ī') Sept. 16, 1885- Psychiatrist
Address: 240 Central Park South, New York City

In psychoanalytic circles 1941 will probably be remembered as the year in which the Association for Advancement of Psychoanalysis was formed. Among its members are some of the most eminent names in the field and on its Executive Council is Dr. Karen Horney, prominent European analyst and teacher. Formation of the new group took place after a meeting of the New York Psychoanalytic Institute disqualified Dr. Horney as training analyst and instructor. No official reason was given, and it was estimated that almost 50 per cent of the members present refrained from voting.

One of the first concrete steps taken by the new group was the promulgation of a training center, the American Institute for Psychoanalysis, of which Dr. Horney was elected dean. The constitution of the Association is so designed that no one individual's or group's theories may control it; the democratic principles of its foundation are enunciated in its Statement of Principles that reads, in part: "To advance the science of psychoanalysis in a spirit of free inquiry, tolerance and open-mindedness upon the foundation laid by the basic discoveries of Freud. . . We believe that mankind is inherently constructive and capable of creating an environment in which the potentialities of each individual may be encouraged to unfold." Through the fall and winter of 1941 to 1942 the New School for Social Research (New York) was sponsoring a series of lectures and seminars in which members of the Association participated.

"Dr. Horney," we learn from an interview with the magazine writer, Evelyn Seeley, "is white-haired, vital, strong and direct in appearance and manner. There is a trace of German in her speech; for years she was secretary of the Berlin Psychoanalytic Institute before coming to the United States as associate director of the Chicago Institute for Psychoanalysis and then to New York as practicing analyst and lecturer at the New School for Social Research.

"Her apartment, high up in a modern apartment house, is like her—warm, strong colors; furniture luxuriously comfortable but austere in design; no gadgets to distract you or make you ill at ease, and the view of Central Park undramatic and comprehensible."

Dr. Karen Horney was born September 16, 1885 in Hamburg, Germany, the daughter of a Norwegian father and a Dutch mother, Berndt and Clotilde (van Ronzelen) Danielsen. It was while studying at medical school at the University of Berlin that she first became interested in psychoanalysis. She took her examinations in 1911, began to practice in 1913, and from then until 1915 studied with Dr. Karl Abraham.

After her intern year Dr. Horney was a resident physician at a psychiatric hospital in Berlin for four years, 1915 through 1918, and for a further year was on the staff of the Neu-

DR. KAREN HORNEY

rological Out-Patient Clinic in the same city. Besides working as a practicing analyst she gave courses in the technique of analysis from 1920 to 1932 at the Berlin Psychoanalytic Institute.

One day in 1932, as she sat working at her desk, the phone rang. It was a transatlantic call from Dr. Franz Alexander, head of the Institute for Psychoanalysis in Chicago, inviting her to go there to be assistant director of the Institute, a post she held until 1934. In that year Dr. Horney moved to New York, where, since that time, she has given lectures at the New School for Social Research, trained analysts at the New York Psychoanalytic Institute, written extensively and worked as a practicing analyst.

She has also published two books: *The Neurotic Personality of Our Time* (1937) and *New Ways in Psychoanalysis* (1939). The first is a thorough description of her theory of the neurotic's "attempt to cope with life under difficult internal conditions"; Dr. Bernard S. Robins found it "a genuine contribution to the study of interpersonal relationships." *New Ways in Psychoanalysis* clarifies the various concepts in psychoanalytic theory, explains both her own attitude and wherein she disagrees with others, and is said to have provided great impetus to the scientific advance of psychoanalysis.

Her views and those of an increasing number of psychoanalysts represent, in the words of Leonard S. Cottrell, Jr., a "decided trend toward a restatement of Freudian theory that is at the same time more useful to and in line with sociological and anthropological theory and research. Dr. Horney's work is to date the most explicit and complete statement of the shift in orientation."

Dr. Horney first studied with a well known pupil of Freud's, Dr. Karl Abraham, and she has remarked that "I could not have made a

HORNEY, KAREN—*Continued*

step without Freud." But though she considers that her interpretation rests on Freudian grounds she is unwilling to accept without question all the tenets of the founder of modern psychoanalysis. In the introduction to her first book she states: "I believe that deference for Freud's gigantic achievements should show itself in building on the foundations that he has laid, and that in this way we can help to fulfill the possibilities which psychoanalysis has for the future, as a theory as well as a therapy."

"My desire to make a critical re-evaluation of psychoanalytical theories," wrote Dr. Horney in her second book, "had its origin in a dissatisfaction with therapeutic results." Her first important difference with Freudian concepts was formulated almost two decades ago and dealt with the concept of feminine psychology. She has written many papers on this subject, both in German and in English, and a chapter devoted to it in *New Ways in Psychoanalysis* shows in what way her approach differs from that of Freud and also reveals her emphasis on the impact of cultural factors on the personality structure.

Dr. Horney's attitude is positive, and in her lectures she stresses that human beings are essentially constructive, that we want happiness, that we want to develop, to unfold. Significantly, her second departure from strictly Freudian principles consisted in a refutation of his explanation of the so-called "destructive drives." Dr. Horney's insistence also that "every neurosis is essentially a character disorder," and that "this view introduces social viewpoints into a field claimed by medical psychiatry," has resulted in much controversy. At one discussion on theory, the chairman, a prominent psychoanalyst, remarked: "Well, we have *our* differences, to be sure, but at least we don't mix psychoanalysis with cultural anthropology."

"The relevant factor in the genesis of a neurosis," Dr. Horney writes, "is neither the Oedipus complex nor any kind of infantile pleasure strivings but all those adverse influences which make a child feel helpless and defenseless and which make him conceive the world as potentially menacing. Because of his dread of potential dangers the child must develop certain 'neurotic trends' permitting him to cope with the world with some measure of safety. Narcissistic, masochistic, perfectionistic trends seen in this light are not derivatives of instinctual forces, but represent primarily an individual's attempt to find paths through a wilderness of unknown dangers. The manifest anxiety in neuroses is then not the expression of the 'ego's' fear of being overwhelmed by the onslaught of instinctual drives or of being punished by a hypothetical 'super-ego,' but is the result of the specific safety devices' failure to operate."

Concluding a series of lectures on Self-Analysis at the New School for Social Research in the spring of 1941, Dr. Horney commented: "I must leave it entirely open, because I simply don't know how many people can analyze themselves, and to what extent, whether it is possible without the previous experience with an expert. But the experiences I have had with it have encouraged me, and have made it an obligation to me to start a ball rolling, to encourage people to make the attempt to do something with their own problems, at any rate to give up that paralyzing attitude of helplessness, as if one couldn't do anything about one's problems oneself, and as if one were entirely dependent on the help of a specialist." In the spring of 1942 her publishers plan to issue her third book, which will discuss the possibilities and limitations in self-analysis.

Of medium height, Dr. Horney has light brown eyes set wide apart. Prominent cheekbones lend angularity to her features. Her hair is white, her forehead high and rounded. A student's remark: "She smiles with her whole face," is descriptive and perhaps indicative of her personal charm. On the lecture platform she is completely informal, her affirmative attitude suggesting an unusually well-balanced personality.

She was married, in Berlin in 1909, to Oscar Horney, a lawyer, and has three daughters. The eldest is Brigitte Horney, the actress. Of the other two, one is a practicing psychoanalyst in New York City and the other, the youngest, is married and living in Mexico. Dr. Horney does a seemingly incredible amount of work, is a member of the Association for the Advancement of Psychoanalysis, of the American Institute for Psychoanalysis and of the American Psychiatric Association, and will now have additional duties thrust upon her in connection with the new Association, whose membership is growing rapidly. Yet she finds time to spend week ends in the country, driving to her place on the Hudson, where she paints and putters about the garden.

She is outspokenly anti-Fascist. She believes that democratic principles, "in sharp contrast to Fascist ideology", "uphold the independence and strength of the individual and assert his right to happiness."

References

Am J Soc 45:426-32 N '39
Ind Woman 19:113+ Ap '40
American Medical Directory

HORSFALL, FRANK L(APPIN), JR.

(hôrs'făl) Dec. 14, 1906- Physician; medical research worker

Address: b. Rockefeller Institute for Medical Research, York Ave. & 66th St, New York City; h. 400 E. 59th St, New York City

If the vaccine discovered in the spring of 1940 by Dr. Horsfall and Dr. E. H. Lennette proves successful, it will mean protection against the most fatal epidemic mankind has suffered. The last worldwide wave of influenza swept from the South Seas to the Arctic Circle and carried off 20 million people, dwarfing the toll of the First World War and the great plagues of history. For years medical research workers have been seeking an effective way to cope with this elusive and complex disease.

Like many important discoveries, Dr. Horsfall's climaxed a succession of studies carried on in a number of countries. Since 1933 it had been established that influenza is caused by a virus too minute to be detected by a microscope, and not nourished by the usual broths used for breeding bacteria. Presently it developed that a number of different viruses were responsible for various types of flu.

The actual discovery of a vaccine which may be effective against what Dr. Horsfall calls "Virus A" resulted from an accident that occurred shortly after he took charge of influenza research at the Rockefeller Institute in New York. An epidemic of distemper attacked the hundred ferrets being used for test purposes, and those which had been inoculated for distemper apparently became immune to the influenza virus. This was the first step that led to a vaccine combining the flu virus from human beings and the distemper virus from dogs, cultured in an egg deposited in an incubator which is kept at 100° F.

The results on ferrets have been highly satisfactory, but the human response has yet to be determined definitely. A hundred laboratory volunteers in New York were inoculated, and a check indicated that they are one-eighth as likely to get the disease as those who have not been inoculated. But fortunately for that city, no real epidemic has put this to the test.

In the summer of 1940 vaccine was rushed to Puerto Rico where an epidemic had broken out, but the disease left before the cure arrived. The following December inoculations were given during an outbreak of flu on the West Coast, but results are not yet definite. Meanwhile, there has been much foreboding that conditions in England will make for an influenza epidemic there, which might develop into a pandemic comparable to that of the First World War; and plans are under way to combat such a possibility with the new vaccine. British health authorities are interested in cooperating, and technicians at the Rockefeller Institute are working overtime to prepare a million doses for immediate use—with the hope that the "Virus A" of Dr. Horsfall's vaccine would prove to be the required type.

When Dr. Horsfall announced his discovery to the American Public Health Association in the fall of 1940, he was 34 years old. Born in Seattle, Washington, on December 14, 1906, he shares his father's profession and Alma Mater as well as his name. Dr. Frank Lappin Horsfall, Sr. was graduated from the medical division of McGill University in Montreal, Canada, in 1903; twenty-nine years later his son took a medical degree there. In 1937, after completing his internship at the Rockefeller Hospital, he received his official license.

From the hospital Dr. Horsfall, Jr., went to the Rockefeller Foundation, where he is

DR. FRANK L. HORSFALL, JR.

now a staff member of the International Health Division, in charge of their work on influenza. Two other things he has done since that transfer were to be married and to become, in 1939, the father of a son. To the layman his dark good looks and mellow voice may suggest a bedside manner somewhat wasted on a swarm of ferrets and an incubator full of eggs. If the threatened epidemic comes, however, he will be ready to administer by proxy to a host of human patients.

References

Collier's 107:18+ Ja 18 '41 il
N Y Times p16 O 11 '40; p25 O 22 '40
Sci ns 87:80 Ja 28 '38
American Medical Directory

HOUGHTON, ALANSON B(IGELOW) (hō't'n)　Oct. 10, 1863—Sept. 16, 1941 Former Ambassador to Germany and Great Britain; president of the Corning Glass Works before he entered the diplomatic service in 1922 and unsuccessful Republican candidate for the United States Senate from New York after leaving the Ambassadorship in 1928; regarded his missions in Germany and England through the eyes of a businessman rather than a diplomat.

References

Collier's 77:9 Mr 13 '26 por
Lit Digest 94:8-9 Jl 16 '27
Liv Age 329:306-8 My 8 '26
Nation 125:32 Jl 13 '27; 127:389 O 17 '28
Outlook 139:128-9 Ja 28 '25 por; 159:389 N 25 '31 por
Woman's H C 53:15 Ja '26 por
World's Work 49:467 Mr '25

(Continued next page)

HOUGHTON, ALANSON B.—*Continued*
Who's Who in America
Who's Who in the Nation's Capital
Wilson, B. America's Ambassadors to
    England (1785-1929) p481-85 1929

Obituaries
N Y Times p23 S 17 '41 por

HOUSTON, ANDREW JACKSON (hūs'-
tŭn) June 21, 1854—June 26, 1941 United
States Senator from Texas; the oldest man
ever to enter the Senate, he was appointed to
his position on April 22, 1941 by Governor
Lee O'Daniel to fill out the unexpired term
of the late Morris Sheppard; appointed United
States Marshal by President Theodore Roosevelt and served from 1902 to 1910; candidate
of the Prohibition Party for Governor in 1910
and 1912, after which withdrew into private
life; appointed custodian of the San Jacinto
battleground where his father General Sam
Houston crushed the Mexican Army.

References
Business Week p34 My 3 '41 por
Newsweek 17:19 My 5 '41
Time 37:20-1 My 5 '41

Obituaries
N Y Times p17 Je 27 '41
Time 38:40 Jl 7 '41

HOVEY, OTIS ELLIS (hŭv'ê) Apr. 9,
1864—Apr. 15, 1941 Civil engineer and director of the Engineering Foundation; regarded as an authority on movable types of
bridges; for 24 years was assistant chief
engineer of the American Bridge Company;
taught at Washington University in St. Louis,
Missouri, and at both Yale and Princeton Universities; his *Movable Bridges* (1927) received
critical praise.

References
Who's Who in America
Who's Who in Engineering

Obituaries
N Y Herald Tribune p18 Ap 16 '41

HOWARD, BART B. May 13, 1871—Feb.
12, 1941 Editorial writer and winner in 1940
of the Pulitzer Prize for distinguished writing; (see sketch 1940 Annual).

References
St. Louis Post-Dispatch p1C My 7 '40
    por

Obituaries
N Y Times p19 F 13 '41

HOWARD, CORDELIA *See* MacDonald,
C. H.

HOWE, SAMUEL B(URNETT) July
15, 1879—Feb. 16, 1941 Educator, publisher
and author; retired head of the Social Science
Department of the South Side High School,

Newark, New Jersey, where he taught from
1914 until 1940; also taught in summer session
in a New Jersey state normal school and
Hunter College; was publisher of the New
Jersey *Journal of Education* and co-author of
many books of history.

References
Who's Who Among North American
    Authors
Who's Who in America

Obituaries
N Y Times p23 F 18 '41 por
Sch & Soc 53:243 F 22 '41

HOXIE, CHARLES A. 1867(?)—Oct. 13,
1941 Inventor in the fields of talking pictures
and radio communication; often called "the
father of the present-day talking picture"; first
devised process of turning sound into light
and recording it on a transparent film; had
worked for the General Electric Company
from 1912 until 1932, when he retired on a
pension.

References
Lit Digest 75:26-7 D 9 '22 por

Obituaries
N Y Times p23 O 14 '41
Variety 144:54 O 15 '41

HRDLIČKA, ALEŠ (hûr'dlĭch-kà) Mar. 29,
1869- Anthropologist
Address: b. United States National Museum,
Washington, D. C.; h. 2900 Tilden St, N. W.,
Washington, D. C.

Called "the Grand Old Man of American
anthropology," Dr. Aleš Hrdlička, since 1910
director of the United States National Museum, has staunchly defended from that date
to the present his convictions, based on numerous surveys of fossil sites, that America's
first settlers were migrants from Asia. Willing to concede the existence of man in North
America some 8,000, perhaps even 10,000
years, to all anthropological proponents of
greater antiquity Dr. Hrdlička says no. As
Harvard's anthropologist, Earnest Albert
Hooton, remarks: "Dr. Aleš Hrdlička has
stood like Horatius at the land bridge between Asia and North America, mowing
down with deadly precision all would-be geo-
logically ancient invaders of the New World."

But the problem of keeping America young
has in recent years (according to *Time*, February 19, 1940) "got tougher for Horatius
Hrdlička." Chief challengers to the Hrdlička
stand are the "Folsom" men, whose skeletons
have never been found, but whose weapons
have been turned up in abundance near Folsom, New Mexico—some of them imbedded
in fossil bison said by other anthropologists
to be as old as 20,000 years. Early in 1940
two Harvard geologists studied a "Folsom"
site in Lindemeier, Colorado and concluded
that the bison bones found there (with tool
points in the vertebrae) were quite possibly
25,000 years old. Said Dr. Hrdlička: "It's

a delusion. . . The geology of the earth is
not like writing or even hieroglyphics—it is
vague and indecisive. I have stopped arguing."

It was in 1939, after several years of digging in fossil sites in Alaska, Kodiak Island
and the Aleutians, that Dr. Hrdlička's theories received substantial bolstering through
a remarkable discovery by a young Soviet
scientist who found a fossilized Neanderthal
child's skeleton on a high cliff in Middle
Asia. Hrdlička pronounced it a genuine Neanderthal specimen—"one of the most precious
children in anthropology's bare nursery." The
skull of this child, together with the measurements of a large series of important neolithic
crania, showed close affinities with certain
types of American skulls. "We had been
hoping," Dr. Hrdlička said, "but hardly daring
to hope, for some such discovery, and now
this young Soviet archeologist has done it.
It shows that Neanderthal man was widely
spread over the Old World. For the first
time it gives us evidence of a culture extending clear across Europe to the Far East."
Hrdlička is convinced that prehistoric Siberian
skulls "may now be definitely connected with
Siberia, and Alaska with the rest of America."

It is almost literally true that Dr. Hrdlička's
scientific activities are his whole life. He was
born on March 29, 1869, the first of seven
children in a middle-class family in Hum-
polec, Bohemia. His father, Maxmilian, was
a master cabinetmaker; his mother, Karolina,
the daughter of a cabinetmaker. Young Aleš,
who learned rapidly, was taught reading and
writing at the age of four by his mother,
and once in school his ability to learn drew
the attention of a Jesuit priest, who tutored
him for two years in Latin and Greek.

In 1882, when Aleš was 13, his father decided to come to New York to make a new
home to which in due time the rest of the
family would come. The boy brought with
him a recommendation from his Jesuit friend
to an American college. But when he arrived
in New York he learned that the college was
in the Middle West and that knowledge of
English was necessary for admission. Accordingly Aleš went to work in a tobacco
factory in order to help his father earn money
and studied English at evening schools. In
1886 he suffered a severe attack of typhoid
fever. His physician, Dr. M. Rosenbleuth,
formerly a rabbi, took an interest in him and
suggested a medical course instead of the
proposed business career which he found so
distasteful. Since the Doctor was a trustee
in the Eclectic Medical College of New York,
he acted as preceptor for the boy's entrance
there.

The young student had so little money
left after his tuition was paid that he walked
daily to and from his home on 71st Street
to the college on East 14th Street, three
miles away. Later, when he could afford to
take the streetcar, he studied languages as he
rode. In the meantime Dr. Rosenbleuth would
take him along to visit his cases; he had
his own pharmacy where Aleš learned to

ALEŠ HRDLIČKA

identify drugs and how to use them. By the
third year of his medical course Hrdlička
was given charge of the college dispensary
one day a week. At this time, too, he began
taking cases in the Margaret Strachan Home
for Wayward Girls. He also lectured to a
group of medical students. Attending these lectures was Marie S. Dieudonnée, a girl of
French descent, who in 1896 became Mrs.
Hrdlička.

After his graduation from medical school
in 1892 at the head of his class, he set up
practice and became almost immediately physician to some six organizations on the East
Side. But he soon realized it would be advantageous to have a degree from schools
specializing in homeopathic and allopathic
medicine; therefore he entered the New
York Homeopathic Medical College, going
to classes and clinics in the daytime and
attending to his own practice at night. Following his graduation in 1894 from this college, he went to Baltimore and took the
State Board Examination in order to enter
Johns Hopkins Hospital. The same year,
however, he was offered and accepted a research position at the new State Homeopathic
Hospital for the Insane at Middletown, New
York.

Dr. Hrdlička's earliest publications were
concerned with his studies of the insane,
and there was early evidence of his anthropological interests. In 1895 he published a
study of the measurements of 1,000 individuals arranged according to sex and types of
insanity. These researches led to an invitation to join the staff of the Institute of New
York State Hospitals as associate in anthropology. On Dr. Hrdlička's request, however,
he was permitted to go first to Europe for
further studies which he considered necessary.

(Continued next page)

HRDLIČKA, ALEŠ—*Continued*

In 1896 he left for Paris. There he studied anthropology, physiology and medico-legal problems under famed specialists and attended numerous clinics. He also visited institutions in several European countries, including his native Bohemia. On his return to New York he devised a far-reaching program for the Pathological Institute, a detailed study of some 40,000 abnormals of all classes cared for in state institutions. He had lined up 22 collaborators for the work when he encountered a major obstacle: there was no comparable data on normal people. While searching for normal subjects to furnish the comparison with the abnormal, Hrdlička made a number of contacts that were to influence his later career. One was Professor George S. Huntington, an anatomist who was assembling a vast skeletal collection; another, Professor Frederick W. Putnam, in charge of the American Museum of Natural History in New York. Through the latter he learned of Lumholtz's work in Mexico. Hrdlička believed that among the primitive Mexican tribes he might find the "normal" population for which he was looking. His first visit there was in 1898. The following year he was given charge of physical and medical anthropological research on one of the Hyde Expeditions for the American Museum: thus began his systematic trips to the Southwest and Mexico yearly until the end of 1902.

When it was decided to establish a National Museum to house the Huntington and other skeletal collections, Dr. Hrdlička was put in charge of the division. At the beginning his entire equipment consisted of an old kitchen table, chair, inkwell, pen and pencil. But he proceeded to build up his division until it has come to rival in size and importance the oldest and best collections in the world.

Between 1905 and 1910 Hrdlička continued his investigations and field studies. He published his observations on the tribes of the Southwest and Mexico; he investigated fossil remains in Florida; he spent some time investigating tuberculosis among various Indian tribes; and in 1909 he went to Egypt, where he measured the pre-dynastic remains stored in Cairo and secured for the National Museum a large collection of skeletal remains. The results of his various expeditions are included in the publications of the American Museum of History, the reports of the Smithsonian Institute and journals dealing chiefly with anthropological and archeological findings.

In connection with his work on the antiquity of man in North America, Dr. Hrdlička in 1910 found it possible to extend similar studies to South America, where he examined remains attributed to ancient man in Brazil, Argentina and Peru. In 1912 he was asked to prepare an exhibit in anthropology for the forthcoming Panama-California Exposition. On his $30,000 grant for this job Hrdlička arranged for seven expeditions to obtain data

and materials, and a number of publications were made on the findings from these.

Several important studies of the status of blood mixture with Whites among the Chippewa and Sioux Indians were made in 1915. In that year also Dr. Hrdlička was named general secretary of the Nineteenth International Congress of Americanists. Continued studies of the American Indians and of the "normal" American population were undertaken. In 1918, following the death of his wife, Dr. Hrdlička was urged to make a short trip to Florida; and this trip served to round out his anthropological survey of the state.

An invitation to give a series of lectures before the Peking Union Medical College resulted in extensive work in the Far East in 1920. During the early '20s he made further expeditions to sites relating to early man in England and on the Continent, in Australia and South Africa. In the last-named region he investigated the site of Rhodesian Man; and the trip also furnished him with new examples of a phenomenon that he had been observing since his first visit to Mexico: quadruped progression in the human child. A book on this, *Children Who Run on All Fours,* was published in 1931. In 1927 Hrdlička gave the Huxley Lecture before the Royal Anthropological Society, and his findings on early man in Europe were published in 1930 as *The Skeletal Remains of Early Man.* His other publications include *Physical Anthropology* (1919); *Anthropometry* (1920); *Old Americans* (1925); and *Anthropology of the American Indian* (1927).

Besides publications already mentioned, Dr. Hrdlička has done considerable writing as editor of the *American Journal of Physical Anthropology* which he founded in 1918. He was also for some years associate editor of the *American Naturalist,* and in 1929 he became the first president of the American Association of Physical Anthropologists. Two of the important books in his field are his account of the scope, aims and history of physical anthropology and a book on anthropometry. For many years Hrdlička contributed funds for anthropological work in Czechoslovakia, and for the establishment of various foundations there, notably at the Charles University in Prague. His efforts in these and other lines have won for him a number of honors. Important among his works of recent years has been the laying of foundations for a future "Museum of Man" under the Smithsonian Institution.

Dr. Hrdlička was married for the second time in 1920. "It is his firm belief that woman's place is in the home; women are the chief pivots of human relationships, he says, and their first duty is to their homes and their families. He hints that past civilizations have fallen out of joint when their women obtained too many privileges." He is a "square-built, stocky man, speaks with a trace of foreign accent, likes baseball and sports generally, also music. He used to get most of his clothes abroad, doesn't believe in wearing an overcoat, and recommends heavy woolen underwear, two suits if necessary."

References

Am J Physical Anthropology 26:3-40 Mr '40

Am Mag 121:62 F '36 por; 121:11 Mr '36 por

Lit Digest 120:15 D 14 '35 por

Nature 143:631 Ap 15 '39

New Outlook p44-5 Mr '35

Newsweek 8:31 O 17 '36 por; 9:46 Ap 17 '37 por

Sci N L 36:155 S 2 '39

Time 30:28 D 27 '37 por; 34:34 Jl 17 '39 por; 35:48-9 F 19 '40 por

American Medical Directory

American Men of Science

Jaffe, B. Outposts of Science p47-80 1935

Who's Who Among North American Authors

Who's Who in America

Who's Who in Central and East-Europe

Who's Who in the Nation's Capital

HUBERMAN, BRONISLAW   Dec. 19, 1882-   Violinist

Address: Plaza Hotel, New York City

"The story of the Palestine Symphony Orchestra," Ross Parmenter observed, "is largely the story of Bronislaw Huberman." Huberman, world-famous violinist, went to Palestine some years ago for a concert tour and was much impressed with the enthusiastic manner in which audiences participated in musical experiences. "Here," said Mr. Parmenter, "were audiences to whom music seemed to mean more than to any audiences in the world. His third visit was in 1933. Hitler had come to power. This time Mr. Huberman discussed the idea of an orchestra with representatives of the people. Steps were taken to organize it. 'I had a great helper in Mr. Hitler,' Huberman said with a smile. 'He furnished me with the cream of Central Europe's orchestras.'"

Huberman undertook the difficult task of forming an orchestra and assuring its support first of all because he had faith in the people. "I would never have given so much of my life to an orchestra that would be just a wonderful orchestra," he said afterward.

This faith was justified. The Federation of Labor contributed an unsolicited gift of $5,000. Workmen agreed to work at night so that the orchestra might give its first scheduled concert, waiving the overtime pay but asking for seats for the concert. Huberman raised $80,000, auditioned musicians (several hundred of them) and found halls in which the orchestra might play. Among the exiles were both Jews and non-Jews, a circumstance gratifying to Mr. Huberman. Of Polish-Jewish parentage, he has always thought of himself as a European and an internationalist. In 1925 and again in 1932 he published books on the Pan-European idea (for a United States of Europe).

When Toscanini consented to open the series of concerts by the Palestine Symphony Orchestra December 26, 1936, Mr. Huberman had not dared to ask him to sacrifice the time for a second visit. "But after the final concert—for workers—he had the saddest expression on his wonderful face. . . He said: 'I am so sad to leave this wonderful audience.' There was a silence. Then he said, 'I must come back.

Suse Byk

BRONISLAW HUBERMAN

I feel I must come back.'" That, Huberman felt, was the greatest possible tribute to the orchestra he had organized, and to its audiences. And Toscanini did return for a second season, despite Mr. Huberman's plea that he needn't attempt the trip because of unsettled world conditions.

At the start of the fourth season in 1939 war broke out. Felix Weingartner was able to fulfill his engagement as guest conductor, but Eugen Szenkar, Malcolm Sargent and Issay Dobrowen all had to cancel theirs. Huberman felt personally responsible, and left his Switzerland home for appearances with the orchestra in order to make up for the absence of the conductors the subscribers had been promised. There followed a tour to South Africa during which France was conquered, and the violinist found himself cut off from the orchestra as well as from his former associates on the continent. Meanwhile the orchestra carries on. Cut off from the choice of guest conductors it has had in the past, it manages with local conductors. In 1941 it went on several Egyptian tours and more concerts than ever in Palestine, where audiences include increasing numbers of the Arabian, as well as the Jewish, population.

Born in Czestochowa, near Warsaw, December 19, 1882, Bronislaw Huberman is the son of Jacob and Alexandra (Goldman) Huberman. His father was a lawyer. When

HUBERMAN, BRONISLAW—*Continued*
he showed an aptitude for music, at the
age of six, his parents brought him to the
Warsaw Conservatory to study with Michael-
ovitch, Rosen, and Isidor Lotto. At seven
he performed a Spohr concerto and participated in a concert with a string quartet. He next studied in Berlin with Gregoro-
vitch, under the supervision of Joseph
Joachim, the famous teacher, and in 1892 gave
his first recital at the International Exhibition of Music in Vienna, after which he was
commanded to play before Emperor Franz
Joseph of Austria. This was the first of
many command performances, and Huberman recalls it with pleasure, for Franz Joseph
presented him with a valuable violin.

At 11 his concert career got under way
with recitals in Holland, Belgium, France,
England and Germany. Hearing him in London, Adelina Patti engaged him to appear
with her at her farewell concert in Vienna,
January 12, 1895. This led to a series of 12
concerts, climaxed by one at which Brahms
put in a surprise appearance in order to listen
to the playing of his own D Major violin
concerto. The appearance of Brahms caused
a flutter backstage as well as in the auditorium, for the aged composer was supposed
to have a chip on his shoulder. He didn't
believe in immature children playing mature
works. But to the young violinist his presence
was merely a challenge to do his best. Recalling the incident later, he remarked that
perhaps his own youthfulness helped him to
go through with it: he could think of Brahms
as being great without being perturbed by
his actual presence. And after the concert
the great man, his tears not dry on his cheeks,
came down to the musicians' room and embraced the young violinist, saying: "My heavens,
what an interpretation!"

In 1896 Huberman made the first of many
concert tours to the United States. Wearing
a dark velvet or white silk suit with a sailor-
style blouse, he faced his audiences with
solemn gray-blue eyes, dark wavy hair, and
the underlip prominent, as it is today. After
commenting on his fine technique the critic
of *Harper's Weekly* wrote: "An interesting
lad in looks, too, with his grave unchildish
eyes, the spiritual upper half of his face
and thick dark hair like a heavy silk fringe
falling about his cheeks."

"The youthful artist achieved a success so
brilliant," wrote another critic on that occasion, "as could not be exceeded by the
brightest star in the galaxy of artists," and
he possessed "a phenomenal endowment of
musical inspiration and musicianly capacity."
But his parents and tutors did not wish him
to burn himself out, and after the American
tour there was a period of six years during
which the violinist gave few concerts. He
had, however, been appointed Court Violinist
to the Queen of Romania in 1896. In 1902
he resumed his concert career, giving a recital in Budapest, Hungary, and in 1903 he
was invited by the municipality of Genoa to
play a recital on Paganini's violin (a rare
Guarnerius). A special law was passed to

permit the temporary removal of the instrument from municipal museum to concert hall.
Today Huberman has his own 1754 Guarnerius, which he almost always uses for concerts. He keeps it together with his rare
Stradivarius in a double violin case, pneumatic-
lined.

He gave a series of eight concerts in St.
Petersburg, Russia, in 1911, fourteen in Paris
in 1920, ten in Vienna in 1924, and eight in
Berlin in 1926, in each city establishing records. Huberman has worked steadily at
his profession since childhood and has toured
most countries not once, but many times.
In 1926 the city of Vienna offered him the
use of Hetzendorf Palace, former residence
of Emperor Karl. For years he was on the
staff of the Vienna State Academy, leaving
it in August 1936 to devote his full time to
the organization of the Palestine Symphony
Orchestra.

After the Nazis came to power in 1933
Huberman was invited by Dr. Wilhelm Furtwängler to play in concerts with the Berlin
Philharmonic—as he had for many years
prior to that year when President Hindenburg
invited Hitler to form a Cabinet. Mr. Huberman refused in a powerful indictment that
called to task the apathy of certain German
intellectuals as well as the barbarism of
Fascism itself. In it he said: "In reality it
is not a question of violin concertos nor
even merely of the Jews: the issue is the
retention of those things that our fathers
achieved by blood and sacrifice, of the elementary pre-conditions of our European culture, the freedom of personality and its
unconditional self-responsibility unhampered
by fetters of caste or race."

In reporting a concert given by Mr. Huberman in 1934 a critic wrote: "Mr. Huberman's
popularity has grown of late, not just because he plays Beethoven and Mozart better
than formerly, but for one reason because
he is a true humanitarian, and because, for
another, he so handsomely threw down the
argumentative glove to Furtwängler and reduced the worthy State Councilor to a helpless splutter of Nazi platitudes."

Typical of the superlatives heaped upon
Huberman as a violinist is the statement by
Olin Downes: "He is an artist of the experience and authority which equip him to
interpret a work of the dimensions of the
Brahms D Major concerto with an authoritative grasp of the composition as a whole, and
to deliver certain passages with the sweep
and breadth of line of a greatly gifted artist."
His accurate sense of tempo, his sensitive
bowing, and his virtuoso gifts have often been
commented upon.

Huberman today is a stocky man, a little
less than medium in height, with gray-brown
hair thinning back from a broad forehead.
He married once, was divorced 25 years ago,
and has a son, John. He came to New York
in the spring of 1941 after completing a successful tour of Canadian cities in the winter.
He went on a concert tour of the United
States in the fall of that year. Meanwhile he

intends to rest and, as he expressed it, "pray for England, Poland, and humanity."

References

Manchester Guardian Mr 7 '36; Jl 31 '37

N Y Times S 14 '33; F 9 '36; IX p7 Mr 30 '41

Newsweek 4:22 N 3 '34

Picture Post Mr 11 '39

Baker's Biographical Dictionary of Musicians 1940

Ewen, D. ed. Living Musicians 1940

Saleski, G. Famous Musicians of a Wandering Race 1927

Who's Who in Central and East-Europe

HUGHES, CHARLES EVANS Apr. 11, 1862- Former Chief Justice of the United States Supreme Court

Address: h. 2223 R St, Washington, D. C.

On June 2, 1941 Chief Justice of the United States Supreme Court, Charles Evans Hughes, retired from active service under the provisions of the Act of Congress of March 1, 1937. "Considerations of health and age," he wrote President Roosevelt, "make it necessary that I should be relieved of the duties which I have been discharging with increasing difficulty." President Roosevelt acknowledged his letter— "My every inclination is to beg you to remain; but my deep concern for your health and strength must be paramount," he wired— and at the age of 79 the justice who has been hailed as "a great liberal" and a "deadly conservative" stepped down from the highest judicial position in the world.

Charles Evans Hughes was born in Glens Falls, New York, where his father, the Reverend David Charles Hughes, a preacher who had come over from Wales in 1855, headed a Baptist congregation. He was educated at first by his mother, Mary Catherine (Connelly) Hughes, and then in the public schools of Newark, New Jersey and New York City. The minute he set foot in school he was recognized as a prodigious young man, and he himself acknowledged this by evolving at a very early age what he called "The Charles Evans Hughes Plan of Study," a curriculum which added new and ambitious subjects to regular studies and allowed no time for review of lessons already covered. Unfortunately, or perhaps fortunately for his classmates, this was never adopted. Undaunted, Charles studied enough in orthodox fashion to write a high school essay on "The Limitations of the Human Mind," and another on "The Evils of Light Literature."

Once out of high school, at the age of 13 or so, Charles' parents kept him at home, reading, playing, exercising until he was 14, and then sent him to Colgate University. He stayed there the two years from 1876 to 1878 and then transferred to Brown University. He went there intending to become a preacher but soon gave up this ambition, and reports that "I spent my time playing cards when I was an undergraduate." Despite this convivial occupation, he made Phi Beta Kappa

Harris & Ewing

CHARLES EVANS HUGHES

and was graduated third in his class with a B. A. in 1881.

Hughes decided to teach school for a while to earn enough to get through law school. But he was 19 and looked younger. No school would have him, until he hit upon the idea of conducting his entire application for a position by mail. Even so, there were difficult moments when he showed up at the Delaware Academy in Delhi, New York and was accused of having "no more beard than an egg." As soon as he could he remedied this. (His retirement, incidentally, left the Supreme Court whiskerless for the first time in at least 80 years.)

From teaching, Hughes entered Columbia University's Law School and in 1884 received his LL. B. with highest honors, plus an annual fellowship of $500 for three years. In that same year he was admitted to the Bar and without difficulty got himself a position with the firm of Chamberlain, Carter and Hornblower. He plunged into work which gradually became more responsible, and distinguished himself by an aptitude for cross examination and for rapid mastery of involved problems. He also, four years after he was hired, married Antoinette Carter, the senior partner's daughter.

Hughes never spared himself at his work, and by 1891 his health had given way. As a partial rest he accepted a law professorship at Cornell University and for two years taught there, known to his students for both his understanding and his preciseness. He was the kind of teacher who always used to take the same number of steps from door to desk, and always demanded, above all, accuracy.

Back from Cornell, Hughes resumed practice with the reorganized firm of Carter, Hughes and Dwight, while still acting as special lecturer on the Cornell faculty for the next two years

HUGHES, CHARLES EVANS—*Continued*

and later on that of the New York Law School. He lived quietly on West End Avenue in New York City, taking long and fairly frequent vacations in Europe, Bermuda and Maine. Occasionally he played golf or went fishing or rode in a motor car or went to the theatre; many evenings he spent at home reading aloud to his children from *Uncle Remus* and *Mr. Dooley* in dialect. He had no interest in politics and his only outside activity was the organization of the Bible class in the Fifth Avenue Baptist Church which John D. Rockefeller, Jr., (see sketch this issue) later taught.

In 1905 this retirement ended. The Stevens Committee of the New York Legislature, about to start an investigation into gas rates, was looking for a bright attorney for counsel. Hughes got the job, did exceptional work, and as a result $800,000 annually was saved in the lighting of the city's streets and the gas rate for consumers was reduced from $1 to 80c. Impressed, the Armstrong Committee of the New York Legislature, in that same year, asked him to direct its investigation of the insurance companies. Hughes went to work, and most of the financial figures of New York squirmed under his probing questions as he proceeded to establish a link between corrupt politics and corrupt finance. The public hailed him as the man who changed the insurance business "from a public swindle into a public trust," and the newspapers called him a wizard of the Bar. This annoyed Hughes. "There is no wizardry about it," he said. "It is work."

While the insurance investigation was under way Hughes had been offered the Republican nomination for Mayor of New York but turned it down to finish what he was doing. His work completed, in 1906, he accepted the Republican nomination for Governor of New York to campaign against William Randolph Hearst. He won the election, the only one on his ticket to do so, and on January 1, 1907 took office. On January 1, 1909 he entered the Governor's mansion for a second term.

Even before he became Governor, Hughes had a reputation for austerity—when asked to lighten his sensible campaign speeches, he had replied that he would not "make any appeal to the passions of the populace"—and he did nothing to change it. He lived and worked efficiently, restricting himself to a rigid half hour for lunch, working in a room littered with papers, not politicians. There were some mutterings when he refused with chilly contempt to appoint political friends to office; there were loud cries of "Charles the Baptist" when he attacked race track gambling and had it banned from the State.

In many ways his was a reform Administration: Hughes secured legislation to set up a system of commission regulation for utility rates; he recommended passage of a child labor law, urged the passage of a workmen's compensation act, sponsored and put through reforms in insurance company regulations, fought and lost a battle for a direct primary. At the same time, it has been pointed out, he vetoed a two-cent railroad-rate bill and opposed a constitutional amendment for an income tax.

On October 6, 1910 Governor Hughes resigned to become an Associate Justice of the Supreme Court with the understanding, some historians say, that he would be elevated to the position of Chief Justice should a vacancy occur. (A vacancy did occur, but he did not fill it.) On the Supreme Court, Justice Hughes was no flaming liberal or great dissenter, but a judge whose opinions were solid, analytical, carefully prepared and usually a little to the left of center. Significant are his decisions championing the right of Federal and State governments to regulate industry, railroads and utilities; his opinions upholding an Illinois statute prohibiting the employment of children under 16, upholding a California statute forbidding the employment of women for more than an eight-hour day or forty-eight-hour week, upholding an act of Congress limiting the hours of work on interstate railroads. Significant, too, was his vote that an Alabama law which held Negro farm laborers criminally liable for violations of wage contracts was unconstitutional and his dissent in the Coppage *vs.* Kansas case which upheld the "yellow-dog" contract. When the score is added up for his six years there, he voted with the liberals 51 times, with the conservatives only 10 times.

It was only after long consideration that he stepped down from the Supreme Court, and only because an even higher office than that of Associate Justice seemed possible for him. He accepted the Republican Party's nomination for President in 1916 and in his acceptance speech called for a firmer diplomatic policy, for the maintenance of America's rights as a neutral, for preparedness. Then, despite advice from the politicians, he made a tour of the country. His speeches were earnest, careful, honest, well thought out. But they were not the speeches of a practicing politician, and the epithets "animated feather duster" and "the human icicle" followed him from coast to coast. According to many, however, he still might have become President had he supported Hiram Johnson of California (see sketch this issue) openly and not snubbed him (actually he didn't, but the impression was the same) when he visited California. He went to bed on the evening of November 6, 1917 thinking himself President; he woke on the morning of November 7 to discover he had lost to Wilson by merely the margin of California's electoral votes.

Hughes retired to practice with the law firm of Hughes, Rounds, Schurman and Dwight (his clients included the New York Life Insurance Company, the Beech-Nut Packing Company, the Interborough Rapid Transit Company, the Wabash Railroad and the United Mine Workers), to the presidency of the Union League Club, the presidency of the New York State Bar Association, to membership in many societies and foundations. Yet, when asked to, he helped Wilson's Administration, first as chairman of the district board of appeals, then as special Federal investigator of the wartime aviation industry, heavily subsidized by the Government.

He continued a staunch Republican, nevertheless, and in 1920 strongly supported Harding. On the day Harding took office as President, Hughes became Secretary of State. Immediately reporters began to write about the "new Hughes" who, it seems, was no longer cold and reserved but a warm and jovial sort of fellow, witty, pleasant, almost a backslapper. The man who had been remote from Washington's social life as Associate Justice began attending social functions nearly six nights a week as Secretary of State, distinguishing himself as a raconteur— in practically every dialect—as a charming guest and equally charming host.

Confronted with many problems left over from the First World War, in the State Department he became what Pearson and Allen (see sketch this issue), no great admirers of his, call "one of the most outstanding and forthright Secretaries of State in recent years." During his term of office he was able to conclude more than 50 treaties with foreign nations; he was able to reestablish friendly relations with South America; he was able successfully to negotiate the treaties made at the 1921 Washington Disarmament Conference which he headed. Yet, though praise for his activities as Secretary of State is almost unanimous, those who hesitate to call Hughes a liberal, or even a great statesman—the *New Republic,* for instance—point out that he was active "in defending the interests of American capitalists in Mexico," that he was conservative enough to refuse to recommend recognition of Soviet Russia, that he was consistently and acutely aware of property rights and their maintenance all over.

This latter group found confirmation of their opinion when Hughes resigned in 1925 to recoup his private fortune. Although he continued to work for Pan-American friendship (he spent two months at the sixth Pan-American Conference in Havana in 1928 and in 1929 served on the Pan-American Arbitration Conference); although he served well as a member of the Permanent Court of Arbitration at The Hague from 1926 to 1930; although he was chairman of the New York State Reorganization Commission in 1926, still his major interest was in his practice with Hughes, Rounds, Schurman and Dwight.

His was a lucrative practice, and Hughes himself was one of the most expensive and successful of corporation lawyers. As in his previous period of practice Hughes' clients were powerful ones, and their interests, for which he fought, weren't always the interests of the public. He attempted to free public utilities and large business concerns from the burdens of taxation and regulation; he defended Truman Newberry, the Michigan Senator-elect whom the Senate refused to seat because of the excessive money spent in his successful campaign. A powerful pleader with a persuasive voice and appearance, he won many cases. He lost some, too, partly because they were already lost when

turned over to him; partly, some say, because of the large number he had to handle.

His effective service in his clients' interests was remembered by the Senate when Herbert Hoover in 1930 sent in his name for the position of Chief Justice of the Supreme Court. The Senate growled. "No man in public life so exemplified the influence of powerful combinations in the financial and political world," it was pointed out by Norris of Nebraska, Borah of Idaho, Coleman Blease of South Carolina. And other Senators, less worried than they about Hughes' taking "the most perfect care of their [the corporations'] interests" challenged, in the words of Carter Glass (see sketch this issue), his "lack of sensibility" in leaving the bench in 1916. For four days the fight raged, fuel for the opposition heaped up by the liberal papers such as *The Nation,* which held forth on Hughes' "fixed, set, intolerant mentality, closed on various issues and deadly conservative"; support coming from those who held him to be "the country's greatest advocate." Finally, on February 14, 1930, his appointment was confirmed, with 26 Senators voting against it. Charles Evans Hughes, "looking like a Victorian child's image of Almighty God," became Chief Justice of the Supreme Court, and his son, Charles Evans Hughes, Jr., resigned his position as solicitor general.

One year later, after his first term on the Bench, Senators, President Hoover and Justice Hughes' fellow justices were pleased or annoyed to find that his decisions lined him up with the liberals on the Court. He upheld a New Jersey act regulating insurance rates and an Indiana tax on chain stores. He wrote an opinion about a Minnesota "gag" law which was a forthright defense of the freedom of the press; another in a California case in which a woman was convicted for waving a red flag stating that free political discussion was essential if the Government was to remain responsive to the will of the people; and he upheld the rights of the railway clerks to form their own labor union. With the liberals he dissented in the famous MacIntosh case, in which a Canadian-born Yale professor was denied citizenship for refusing to take the oath to bear arms in case of war.

In fact, until New Deal days, the case for Hughes as a liberal seemed clinched. And then discussion rose again, discussion that continued past his resignation in 1941. There are those who say that as Chief Justice he combined "vision with the practical talents of a constitutional arbiter"; others who with Pearson and Allen call him an "acrobatic liberal"; still others who agree with the analysis of his liberalism in a 1937 *New Republic* article which pointed out that when the Court was liberal and Hughes one of the liberals he wrote more than his share of opinions, while when the Court was reactionary and Mr. Hughes one of the reactionaries he practically never wrote the opinion. In other words, he is a "combination of voluble liberalism and silent conservatism."

The record shows that in twenty-seven measures covering a wide range of social legislation

HUGHES, CHARLES EVANS—*Continued*
he voted for Administration measures eighteen times and in five of them his vote was the deciding one. With the liberals he wrote the opinion upholding the constitutionality of municipal bankruptcy acts; with them he wrote the opinion upholding the Government of the gold clause decisions. He furthered the rights of Negroes in the Scottsboro case and in the decision of April 1941 which ruled that Negroes were entitled to railroad accommodations equal to Whites'. He sustained the National Labor Relations Act, the TVA, the social security laws; and in his last term on the Bench he upheld the Federal Wages and Hours Act, the Government's power of regulation over navigable streams and the Government's power to regulate State primaries and upheld the National Labor Relations Board and the unions in several cases.

On the other hand, he voted against the AAA, limited the power of the Securities and Exchange Commission to protect the investing public, declared the Guffey Coal Act unconstitutional, and was on the conservative side in the cases of Rogers *vs.* the Guaranty Trust Company and the United States *vs.* the Elgin Railway. Actually, a summation shows that in his 10 years as head of the Supreme Court, Justice Hughes carefully avoided permanent alignment with any side. When asked once whether he regarded himself as a liberal or a conservative, he replied: "These labels do not interest me."

As Chief Justice, Mr. Hughes developed a mania for speed and was able to keep the docket fairly clear—it was on the basis of efficiency that he argued against Roosevelt's attempt to pack the Court. Court sessions, under his leadership, moved briskly. (He was ruthless in holding attorneys to their time allowance, stern in keeping them to the point. And at the same time he was rarely caustic in asking them questions, almost always gracious.) His decisions were written quickly—sometimes as many as thirty in an eight months' session—and about them, as about the man, critics disagree. To some they are vigorous, vital and pointed; to others "dull and ponderous, wading through reams of ambiguous language before coming to the conclusions."

To keep the court up-to-date on its business and to get his own decisions written, Justice Hughes drafted and kept to a rigid schedule of living, which he adhered to from 6:30 a.m. to 10 p.m. At 6:30 he got up and not long afterward breakfasted with Mrs. Hughes. Then at 8:00 came his morning walk and at 9:00 he was in his study on the ground floor of his house reading or dictating until 11:30 when, during the time Court sat, he was driven to the Capitol. Back at 5:00, he would work for an hour or so before dinner. After dinner he read for a while—newspapers, magazines, fiction, biographies—and by 10:00 he would be in bed. Social life was sternly restricted and limited mainly to Saturday nights, for which he was dated up months ahead. "I'm to see you

at a dinner in May," a friend once told Mrs. Hughes in January. In retirement, life will probably be less rigidly scheduled: there will be more reading, more travel with Mrs. Hughes, and perhaps more time spent with their children: Charles Evans Hughes, Jr., head of a New York law firm; Mrs. William T. Gossett, whose husband is a member of Charles, Jr.'s legal firm; Mrs. Chauncey L. Waddell, who is in 1941 chairman of the drive to raise $50,000 for the Polish Medical Center in Edinburgh. (There was another daughter, Helen, who died.)

Mr. Hughes, whose long and active life has been honored by countless college degrees, by countless medals and awards (the latest was given him in December 1940 by the National Conference of Christians and Jews for his contribution toward the improvement of human relations) retires from the highest judicial position in America while still considered "something of a paradox." "His life is an example to the nation of that virtue of disinterested service of which he has long been an earnest advocate," says one commentator, and many agree with him. Still Pearson and Allen and some others suggest that occasionally Hughes was less public minded than he might have been. Perhaps the judgment with which most agree, however, is that of J. P. Pollard. As a lawyer, he points out, Mr. Hughes was retained by powerful clients; as a judge he was retained by the American people. In both positions he served his clients well.

References

Am Bar Assn J 27:407-19 Jl '41 por (cover)
Am Mag 121:22-3+ Ap '36 por
Christian Sci Mon p11, 16 Je 5 '41 pors
Fortune 13:172+ My '36 por (p82)
N Y Herald Tribune p14 Je 3 '41 pors
New Repub 87:232-3 Jl 1 '36; 91:295-8 Jl 21 '37; 91:329-32 Jl 28 '31; 104:776 Je 9 '41
New Yorker 11:20-4 Je 29 '35; 11:18-22 Jl 6 '35; 11:18-23 Jl 13 '35
No Am 229:444-8 Ap '30; 237:351-8 Ap '34
Outlook 159:171-3+ O 7 '31 por
R of Rs 81:36-9 Mr '30
Babson, R. W. Washington and the Revolutionists p119-37 1934
Gillis, A. and Ketchum, R. Our America p17-33 1936
Lowry, E. G. Washington Close-Ups p168-79 1921
Pearson, D. and Allen, R. S. Nine Old Men p74-97 1936
Umbreit, K. B. Our Eleven Chief Justices p451-500 1938
Walter, E. A. ed. Essay Annual, 1936 p121-50 1936
Who's Who in America
Who's Who in Government
Who's Who in Law
Who's Who in the Nation's Capital
Woolf, S. J. Drawn from Life p214-22 1932

HUGHES, HOWARD (ROBARD) Dec. 24, 1905- Motion-picture producer; aviator
Address: b. Hughes Tool Co, Houston, Texas; c/o 20th Century-Fox Film Corp, Beverly Hills, Calif; h. 3921 Yoakum Blvd, Houston, Texas

Howard Hughes had just broken the transcontinental flying record in 1936. Reporters crowded around him asking for his comments. "I haven't anything to say," he answered. "I didn't do anything sensational." In 1938 he broke the round-the-world record. On his return he had to make the second public speech of his life. He confessed that he was a great deal more nervous over the speech than he had been over the flight.

That is typical of this remarkable young man, who at 20 had an income of $2,000,000 a year, yet has remained "simple in manners, careless in dress, unconscious of social distinctions." He was born December 24, 1905 in Houston, Texas. His father, Howard Hughes, Sr., had invented important oil-well drilling machinery, and headed the Hughes Tool Company. The boy and his father (who was a brother of Rupert Hughes, the writer) were great friends, and the son inherited mechanical ability and scientific curiosity. At 12 he made a radio transmitter out of a doorbell and a self-starting motor for his bicycle. He was a member of the Radio Relay League, and he made his first airplane flight at 14. He was educated at the Fessenden School, West Newton, Massachusetts, the Thatcher School, Ojai, California and Rice Institute of Technology in Houston. He was a freshman there when his father died; his mother, Alene (Gano) Hughes, had died when he was 16.

He left college (though afterward he took some courses at the California Institute of Technology) and took over direction of his father's huge business. When he was offered $7,500,000 for it, he refused, and he still controls it. But he wanted something else to do that would require more personal attention. He came to Hollywood before he was twenty-one, and in six years there he produced many prize-winning pictures, as well as a few of lesser caliber. *Hell's Angels,* the first and only $4,000,000 picture in Hollywood's history, was one of the big box-office hits of all time. It was really made twice, for just as the silent version was finished, the talkies arrived. For the sound version, Hughes selected an unknown girl to play the star feminine role. Her name was Jean Harlow; that was the beginning of her fame.

He has, indeed, a flair for making unknowns into celebrities. He did the same thing with Paul Muni in *Scarface,* one of the first, and one of the most successful, of the gangster pictures. *The Front Page* (recently remade by another producer as *My Girl Friday,* with a girl in the reporter's role) was another smash hit—which, incidentally, fixed in the public mind a conception of newspaper editors and reporters and how they act, which newspapermen deplore! Among his other successful pictures were *The Sky Devils, The*

HOWARD HUGHES

Racket and *Two Arabian Knights.* Some critics felt dubious before *Scarface* was shown, especially as the name inevitably suggested Al Capone; but the picture (like other gangster films which followed it) provided a strong moral lesson as well as an exciting story, and it started a new fashion in pictures— as well as giving Muni his start as a character actor.

While he was in Hollywood, Hughes lived simply, in apartments or rented houses, and took little part in the social life of the film world. He had been married, very young, to Ella Rice, of Houston, but they were divorced by 1929, and he has not remarried though he has been frequently engaged.

It was natural that the boy who had led all his classes in science should be irresistibly drawn back to his early love, aviation. He established an experimental aviation company, and in 1935 he set a record for land flying speed of 352 miles per hour. In January 1936 he broke all records for transcontinental flight by flying from Burbank, California to Newark, New Jersey in nine hours, twenty-five minutes, ten seconds, and he won the Harmon Trophy. Exactly a year later he flew the same course again and broke his own record, cutting his time down to seven hours, twenty-eight minutes, twenty-five seconds. Then, in July 1938, he flew around the world in a Lockheed monoplane, *New York World's Fair 1939,* again breaking all records. His time for 14,716 miles was three days, nineteen hours, eight minutes, ten seconds. He made six stops: at Paris, Moscow, Omsk, Yakutsk, Fairbanks and Minneapolis. To him these flights were not stunts, but scientific experiments; he has plenty of daring but no bravado whatever. He made the most careful preparations for every eventuality, testing and retesting even to the kind of bread which would keep fresh longest for sandwiches. His plane was equipped

HUGHES, HOWARD—*Continued*

with a Sperry Gyro-pilot and a Line of Position Computer, and proved the worth of both these inventions. Once more he received the Harmon Trophy, and the Collier Trophy as well.

Then he gave up aviation and went back to Houston, where for three years he devoted all his time to his tool business. But in 1940 he came back to Hollywood and to films. In 1941 he produced a picture called *The Outlaw,* based on the life of the bandit, Billy the Kid. It has been held up by censorship trouble. The leading roles were given to a boy and girl utterly unknown to the screen and without film experience of any kind—Jack Buetel and Jane Russell.

The same swift, methodical and thorough workmanship which distinguished Mr. Hughes' flying exploits marks his motion picture work as well. One man, watching his decisiveness and energy on the set, was heard to exclaim: "Holy cats! He's still flying!" In spite of his forcefulness he is shy and reticent—people who are less discreet have called him secretive—but when he feels at ease he is a friendly young man with an infectious grin, a young man who looks strikingly like Gary Cooper, six feet three inches tall, lanky and dark. At school he played baseball and football, and he still plays golf. He is one boy who started from the top and made good!

References

Am Mag 113:34-5+ Ap '32 il pors
Collier's 89:25+ Mr 19 '32 il por; 104:
    78 N 25 '39 il
New Repub 95:289 Jl 20 '38
N Y World-Telegram p6 Ja 27 '40
Scholastic 33:11 S 17 '38 por
Time 27:31+ Ja 27 '36 por; 29:62 F 1
    '37 por
America's Young Men
Blue Book of American Aviation
Who's Who in America
Who's Who in Commerce and Industry

HUGHES, MARTHA GROOMES   *See* Hughes, T.

HUGHES, TONI   Artist

Address: c/o Willard Gallery, 32 E. 57th St, New York City

Toni Hughes calls herself a "chicken wire sculptor" and proves it by cutting caricatures from bits of tin and wire netting. She considers her work "perfectly sound modern art"; others consider it a unique form of fantasy in hardware materials. The Willard Gallery in New York City gave her her first one-man New York show, *Hardware Arabesques,* in January 1941. "Though some serious art critics sniffed a little at the unorthodox figures," many people came, blinked, gaped and found much to admire.

Among those who admired was the critic of *Art News,* who found the arabesques "only more expressive and modeled mobiles." He called it an "intriguing and blithe new art

Fred Hamilton

TONI HUGHES

form" of "cut-out silhouettes made to sway ever so slightly," and, he continued: "Just when you might consider stopping to marvel at the expressiveness of line and economy of delineation—electric-light bulbs for heads, birthday-cake rosettes for bouquets, etc.—you will discover that music boxes can be wound underneath the figures. All of Miss Hughes' concoctions are great good fun."

Before Miss Hughes took hardware shears in hand, she had tried various activities, mostly in the art field. Born Martha Groomes Hughes in Portland, Oregon, she is the daughter of Sterling Worth Hughes and Maude (Gilliland) Hughes, descendants of New England and Oregon covered-wagon pioneers. After study at the Los Angeles Art Institute, she began her career as a photo retoucher on the Los Angeles *Examiner.* While using the black and white retouching inks, she began experimenting with display cartoons and sold enough of them to finance a trip to New York, where she conducted an illustrated column in the New York *Mirror* in 1929. The next year found her in Paris, where she painted "acres of nudes" at the Julian Academy on an exchange scholarship from the Los Angeles Institute. Modern art forms seemed too static as a means of expression and she found a job as "handyman" to a French motion-picture company, working as script girl, scenarist and cutter with Alberto Cavalcanti from 1932 to 1934.

Returning to New York then, she began to experiment with the creative possibilities of the short film as a vehicle for the expression of abstraction and fantasy. Though at the time she was not very successful, in 1941 she plans to animate her figures for film production in short subjects. By 1936 she had returned to her native West Coast and settled down in Hollywood. Here she made her first metal figure, inspired by her childhood tinkering with an Erector Set. When this first figure, constructed from scraps of wire and metal found in an airplane factory, was exhibited it brought her orders for window displays of football and baseball players made of hardware. Miss Hughes felt that she had finally found her art medium. In early 1940 she had a first one-man show at the Walker Galleries in Hollywood. MGM ordered some of the figures for decoration for the film *Susan and God.*

Miss Hughes' studio does not look like a sculptor's. Her sources for material to work with "may be the dime store, a junk yard, or a hardware shop. She creates best with wire screening, all kinds of perforated metal (especially the lacework pattern variety), plumber's tape (the kind which braces pipes), chicken wire, nuts, bolts, screws, rubber balls, tin globes, wheels from kids' toys, and even Christmas-tree ornaments. Her tools are whopping metal shears, a screw driver, a hammer, pliers, and a hacksaw." It all adds up to a small boy's dream workshop.

This "Thurber in sheet metal" does both window exhibits (such as the series of decorative functional figures made for Macy's in New York City) and abstractions (like the 20 shown in her one-man show). All belong in the realm of fantasy. Most of them have no faces but all of them have wit and spirit, such as the "buxom body of an elegantly attired female known as 'Miss Columbia the Gem of the Ocean.'" The figure called "The Extrovert" beats his own drum and blows his own horn; a trio of chorus girls is "mostly plumbers' tape, with shreds of copper scouring pads for bodices, and bells on their toes." "Gibson Girl" is an empty Chianti bottle, topped with coiled wire for hair.

The humor in Miss Hughes' work is reflected in her person. "Addicted to sticky caramels," says one observer, "with tousled hair and casual clothes, mostly a turtle-necked sweater, green slacks and sneakers, she stands on no ceremony—which is probably one reason why her 'art' is so much fun and why Toni always seemed a better name than Martha."

Miss Hughes likes her work. She says she is "tired of neurotic art," and is all for the healthy kind that makes people happy. "To me a surrealist is a guy being sick in public."

References

Art N 39:17+ Ja 25 '41
Cue 10:20 Ja 11 '41 il por
Friday 2:24 My 2 '41 il pors
Newsweek 17:60 Ja 27 '41 il por

HUNTLY, FRANCES E., pseud. *See* Mayne, E. C.

HUNTZIGER, CHARLES (LÉON CLÉMENT) (hŭn'tzĭg-ēr) June 25, 1880— Nov. 12, 1941 Late Minister of War of the Vichy Government and commander in chief of the French land forces

CHARLES HUNTZIGER

Bulletin: General Charles Léon Clément Huntziger was killed on November 12, 1941 in an airplane accident as he was returning from a tour of inspection of the defenses of France's African colonies. The crash occurred at Le Vigan, not far from Nîmes, in the south of France.

When Vice-Premier Darlan (see sketch March issue) took over the post of War Minister in the Vichy Government, General Charles Huntziger was transferred from his position as national defense head to Algiers, with authority over General Weygand (see sketch 1940 Annual), commander of French-African forces. Most London observers interpreted this move of August 1941 as further evidence of Darlan's determination to hand over the French-African colonies to the Germans, since it was believed that Weygand stood in the way of certain measures of "collaboration" which the Nazi Government demanded. The transfer was also believed to be linked with efforts to undermine American influence in French North Africa.

A blond, sharp-featured Breton, General Huntziger was one of the French Army's most distinguished officers, having attained his distinction chiefly through his colonial administrative career. The son of an Alsatian who was given his choice of citizenship in 1871 and chose French citizenship, Charles Léon Clément Huntziger grew up in Lesnevan, "fervently patriotic and fervently anti-German." He was graduated from St. Cyr when he was not quite 20, and left immediately for the colonies with the 2nd Colonial Infantry Regiment in search of adventure and battle. He found both in Madagascar, the Senegal and the Sudan. He took brief time out to attend L'École Supérieure de Guerre; then, with the rank of captain, went on to Tankin.

(Continued next page)

HUNTZIGER, CHARLES—*Continued*

With the outbreak of the First World War he returned to France in 1914. In a brilliant two-day and two-night battle near Mantez (December 1914) he victoriously withstood with two companies a vastly superior German force. For this he won his Croix de Guerre. A major in 1916, he was called to the general staff of the 2nd Colonial Army Corps, then to the general staff of the Armies of the Orient. There, as second in command, he rendered noteworthy service, mapping under the most difficult conditions the great victory of Skra di Legeor, which brought about the capitulation of Bulgaria.

As lieutenant colonel he was, in 1922, with the Ministry of War, and he attended classes in high military training. In 1924 he became a colonel and took command of the Army of Occupation in China. In 1928 he was made a brigadier general, the youngest general in France. He first headed General Claudel's general staff, then became inspector general of colonial troops, and afterward served as head of the French military mission to Brazil. In 1934, as major general, he was called to the high command of the French troops in the Near East.

When the Germans attacked in the Second World War, Huntziger became commander of the 2nd Army during the Battle of France. Following the collapse of France, Huntziger attained world-wide notice on June 22, 1940 when he headed the French Armistice delegation that signed the peace terms with Germany at Compiègne Forest. At that time he announced that he had been ordered to sign the terms, and in a tense voice cried: "I would like to make a personal statement. France is forced to accept conditions whose severity must be emphasized. I appeal to the soldiers' spirit in the hope that the French will never have cause to regret the step we are now taking."

Close to Pétain in all French military maneuvers, the "lean, unsmiling, poker-faced" Huntziger was known to have a strong distaste for the British Empire and as a colonial administrator had often tangled with the British. By decree of the Pétain Government, in September 1940 he was named generalissimo and commander in chief of the French land forces, thus succeeding General Weygand. In the "Vichy Triumvirate" to aid Pétain, Huntziger was appointed Minister of War in charge of defense.

The recent transfer of Huntziger to Algiers completed the cycle of France's outstanding colonial careerist, the "cold, inscrutable and ambitious" leader of her "manifest destiny" group. In view of British plans for offensive moves in the Mediterranean area, Huntziger was given a highly important key position in Axis defense.

References

Christian Sci Mon p5 Ja 3 '41 por
Cur Hist & Forum 52:9 F 13 '41
Illustration 205:404 Ap 27 '40 por (p407)
N Y Post p8 Ap 28 '41

N Y Sun p26 D 21 '40
N Y Times p8 S 27 '40 por
Newsweek 16:13 Jl 1 '40 por

Obituaries

N Y Times N 13 '41 por

HUROK, S(OLOMON)   Apr. 9, 1888-
Theatrical impresario

Address: b. Hurok Attractions, Inc, Rockefeller Plaza, Radio City, New York City; h. 145 W. 58th St, New York City

S. Hurok, whose name appears on the programs of scores of music and dance recitals, is a "thickset, moon-faced Russian" who, according to the New York *Times*, "has done more for music in America than the invention of the phonograph." Marian Anderson, Rudolph Serkin and the Kolisch String Quartet made their first United States tours under his management; Anna Pavlowa, Feodor Chaliapin, Tetrazzini, Mischa Elman, Mary Wigman are only a few of the world's gifted who have appeared under his aegis; and he has presented entertainment as varied as the Monte Carlo Ballet Russe, the Moscow Cathedral Choir, the German Grand Opera Company and the Habima Players.

This "most irrepressible of music managers" is today the fountain head of personal information about most famous singers, dancers and instrumentalists. He can and will reminisce about Chaliapin tantrums and his ability to handle them. He tells of Richard Strauss' inveterate poker playing, of Isadora Duncan's habit of signing checks that bounced, of Pavlowa's eating habits. He can describe at length the dressing, shaving, marital and artistic habits of almost any artist the world is curious about. And there is nothing he doesn't know about artistic temperament.

He believes temperament to be the sole property of genius, however; impresarios can't afford to be anything but calm and collected. And it is probably this trait of always knowing exactly what he is about, together with a real flair for recognizing attraction, which has brought him, through ups and downs, to a position of real importance in the cultural entertainment world.

Solomon Hurok was born in Pogar, Russia, the son of Israel Hurok, a hardware merchant, and Anna (Schream) Hurok. In his early teens he was sent with 1,500 rubles to the big city to learn the hardware business. He didn't even inquire into its workings but ran away to America and arrived there in 1903 knowing no English and with less than three rubles in his pockets. He decided to make his way in Philadelphia—"I wanted to start where Benjamin Franklin started, in the city where the Declaration of Independence was signed." It was an inauspicious start. First he peddled needles, but found his job complicated by the fact that he couldn't explain to housewives what he was selling and why.

From selling needles Hurok went on to running a streetcar. This didn't last long. either, after the company discovered he was letting people off at the wrong corners. Then came jobs washing soda pop bottles for $1 a day, working in a mattress factory, bundling newspapers for the midnight edition of the Philadelphia *Press*. Finally, Hurok decided that he had done his duty by Philadelphia and set out for New York, where his first job, thanks to early training, was in a hardware store.

During these months of unprofitable jobs Hurok heard music whenever he could, standing for hours at the box office of the old Hammerstein Theatre and spending scraped-together pennies for the privilege of standing for five hours to listen to *Parsifal*. He began to see a career in music, and at 18 organized the Van Hugo Musical Society and arranged concerts for clubs and labor organizations. Pretty soon, whenever a Brooklyn charity wanted to give a concert, Hurok was the one who engaged the artists and made all the arrangements. By the time he was 21 he was renting huge Madison Square Garden and offering concerts there. And he had already presented top-notch artists at popular prices at the Hippodrome.

From the time he started, long-established managers looked upon him as an upstart, and they have continued to be astonished by the lavish amount of talent he has steadily produced. In 1925 Hurok seemed to justify the other managers' opinion of him: he went into bankruptcy. But during the depression, when they were retrenching, his presentations were more lavish than ever. In 1934 he opened the *Continental Varieties* at the Little Theatre in New York, presenting Lucienne Boyer, Vicente Escudero and others. And in that same year he spent $75,000 to import the Monte Carlo Ballet Russe. Great names continued to appear under his management and in the 1941 season he was presenting Artur Rubinstein, the Don Cossack Chorus, Argentinita, Marian Anderson—to name only a few.

Before the Second World War, Hurok used to travel every year to Europe looking for talent, "signing more new big contracts than any one man in his risky profession." Today he is spending most of his time going around the country, finding out the likes and dislikes of every sizable town in the Postal Guide. His spare time he spends listening to music (he still can't read it) and devouring all the political and international news he can get hold of. A good many important artists have discovered by now that if Hurok is not in his Radio City offices, Carnegie Hall, Town Hall or the Opera House they're pretty sure of catching him up in the NBC radio room with his ear glued to the amplifier. Hurok is married to Emma Rifkin and has one daughter, Ruth, who is Mrs. Barry Hyams.

References

Cue 10:34 O 18 '41 por
Etude 59:443+ Jl '41 por
Time 26:50+ N 4 '35 por; 35:58 Ap 22 '40 por
Who's Who in American Jewry

S. HUROK

HYMANS, PAUL (hĭ'măns) 1865—Mar. 8, 1941 Former Foreign Minister of Belgium who served for four terms; former president of the League of Nations Assembly; Belgian representative at the Peace Conference; with Woodrow Wilson he had the task of preparing the draft of the Covenant of the League; served as professor of international law at the University of Brussels; Ambassador to Great Britain from 1914 to 1917; one of three Belgian Ministers who drafted the reply to the German ultimatum at the beginning of the First World War; author of legal texts and considered one of the foremost scholars of his country.

References

Asia 32:406 Jl '32 por
Who's Who

Obituaries

N Y Times p40 Mr 9 '41

HYVERNAT, HENRY, MGR. (ē-vĕr-nä') June 30, 1858—May 29, 1941 A member of the faculty of Catholic University of America since its establishment in 1889; at first he taught Oriental languages at the University, and subsequently was professor of Biblical Archeology and head of the Department of Semitic and Egyptian Languages and Literature; his greatest achievement was the editing of the Coptic version of the Bible; wrote and collaborated on many books and papers related to the study of the Bible; raised to the rank of Prothonotary Apostolic in 1939 during the Golden Jubilee year of Catholic University by the late Pope Pius XI; full name Eugene-Xavier Louis Henry Hyvernat.

(Continued next page)

HYVERNAT, HENRY, MGR.—*Continued*

References

American Catholic Who's Who
Who's Who in America

Obituaries

N Y Times p11 My 31 '41

ICKES, HAROLD L(E CLAIRE) (ĭk'ĭs)
Mar. 15, 1874- Secretary of the Interior;
Petroleum and Solid Fuels Coordinator for
National Defense

Address: b. Interior Bldg, Washington, D. C.;
h. Headwaters Farm, Olney, Md.

One of the most forceful and colorful
personalities in Washington is Harold L.
Ickes, who, in his capacity as Secretary of
the Interior and "the custodian of National
resources," carries perhaps wider responsibilities than any other Cabinet member. He administers, among others, the General Land
Office, Office of Indian Affairs, Geological
Survey, Fish and Wildlife Service, Bureau of
Reclamation, National Park Service and the
National Power Policy Committee. This full
slate, however, has never prevented him from
periodically declaring his readiness to take on
other duties For over a year he had been
issuing warnings about the oil shortage in
the East. On May 28, 1941, President Roosevelt named him as Petroleum Coordinator
for National Defense, making him the virtual
czar of the American oil industry and establishing what came close to government control of oil. Mr. Ickes, who has always
advocated strict conservation of petroleum
resources, served as head of the Federal Oil
Administration during the NRA days and had
many clashes with private oil interests. In
his present post, however, the specific "recommendations" which he is authorized to make
are expected to be enforced. His first move in
his new office was to call an oil parley in
Washington to discuss plans for more effective utilization of the United States' petroleum
resources. Next he asked for the arrest of
"jackrabbit" starters and requested, successfully, the closing of Eastern gas stations
from 7 p.m. to 7 a.m. each day. Later, however, the oil shortage was found to be less
acute than he had believed, and by the end
of October gas stations were once more in
full-time operation.

In November 1941 Ickes was also appointed
Solid Fuels Coordinator for National Defense,
charged with assuring an adequate supply of
coal and coke.

Harold Le Claire Ickes was born on March
15, 1874 on a farm in Frankstown Township,
Blair County, near Hollidaysburg, Pennsylvania, the son of Jesse Boone and Martha
Ann (McEwen) Ickes. His family comes
from old stock. Its founder came to Pennsylvania with William Penn, and there exists
a city of Ickesville, named after another
ancestor who fought in the Revolution. When
young Ickes was 16 his mother died and he
went to live with his aunt in Chicago. There
he attended the Englewood High School and

the University of Chicago, getting his B. A.
degree in 1897. He had worked his way
through college by teaching in public evening
schools.

He worked as a reporter for a while and
covered the Democratic and Republican conventions in Chicago in 1900 for the Chicago
Record. Then he dropped his journalistic
career to return to the University of Chicago
to study law, from which he was graduated
cum laude in 1907. Soon after he was
admitted to the Bar. By 1911 he was fully
launched as a reformer and politician and had
married Anna Wilmarth Thompson, who had
gone to college with him and later married
and divorced Professor James Westfall
Thompson. Daughter of a wealthy manufacturer of gas fixtures, she had a distinguished
career of her own, was a trustee of the University of Illinois and subsequently was elected
several times to the state legislature. (She
died in 1935, victim of an automobile accident.)

Harold Ickes' career as a crusading politician had begun in his senior year at the
University of Chicago, when he campaigned
for John Maynard Harlan, an independent
Republican candidate for the office of Mayor
of Chicago. Though a novice who did not
"know a precinct from a ward," he made an
impressive showing, and in 1905, when he was
a sophomore in law school, was once again
invited to help with a campaign of Harlan's.
In 1911 he managed the unsuccessful campaign
of Charles E. Merriam for Republican Mayor
of Chicago. Although originally a Republican, Ickes did not mind reversing his affiliations, preferring to cleave to principles rather
than parties. In 1912 he backed Theodore
Roosevelt's Bull Moose campaign for President and after his defeat threw in his lot
definitely with the Progressives and supported
Hughes (see sketch this issue) in 1916. In
1920 he attended the Republican Party Convention as a delegate-at-large, helping to block
the attempt to nominate Harding unanimously
and then switching over to work for the
Democratic nominees. Until 1932 Ickes' candidates—at least to national office—uniformly
failed to be elected.

In-between his political activities, Ickes
divided his time between his residence in Winnetka (Thorncroft) and his law office in the
Chicago Loop. He took civil liberties cases
without pay, taught Americanization classes
at Hull House and waged a bitter fight against
the utilities and for municipal reform. Named
by his enemies "the gadfly of Cook County,"
he lived up to his name by sniping at Chicago's "Big Bill" Thompson, whom he was at
last instrumental in unseating, for a brief
while, and at Samuel Insull. The latter was
his special aversion and Ickes did everything
in his power to make things unpleasant, from
opposing Insull in his struggle to get a perpetual street railway franchise to blackballing
him out of the Chicago City Club. He became
known as a slightly embittered reformer, the
champion of the underdog.

In 1932, Ickes, at 58 "a futile worker for
civic betterment," finally hit the jackpot.
Roosevelt was elected, and Ickes had helped

by swinging the liberal Midwest Republicans to his side. In February 1933 he received an invitation from the President-elect to attend a conference on general economic problems. He came as an acknowledged student of conservation, with a strongly developed interest in Indian affairs. It was at this conference, held in the President's home in New York City on February 22, that Roosevelt saw him and "liked the cut of his jib." The result of their long and stimulating interview was the Secretaryship of the Interior. The liking was heartily reciprocated: ever since, Ickes has been the most loyal and uncompromising supporter that the President has had.

In 1933 it looked as though Ickes were going to make up with a vengeance for his years of "futile crusading." He was once again pleasantly surprised when to his already considerable responsibilities was added the monumental one of administering the Public Works Administration. For six years he had under his jurisdiction the expenditure of more than $5,000,000,000 on non-Federal and Federal public works projects, which included construction of public works of all kinds such as sewage systems, public buildings, highways and dams—public works which served the double purpose of answering public needs and giving work to the vast number of unemployed during America's worst depression. He owes his nickname of "Honest Harold" to the fact that billions of dollars were spent under his supervision without a breath of scandal. His detractors accuse him, however, of impairing departmental morale by suspicion and espionage. The fact remained that PWA contracts were graft-proof.

A particularly important part of PWA was the work it did in power and irrigation—among its projects were the gigantic Boulder Dam, Bonneville Power and the Grand Coulee Dam. Often the use of Federal money to build municipal projects brought Ickes into conflict with private utilities like Commonwealth and Southern. There was protest, for example, when Ickes offered 21 municipalities a total of over $9,000,000 to build power plants of their own when they were already served by private utilities. Ickes was charged with using his program as a "club" to drive down rates. His course of action was upheld by the Supreme Court in 1938, however, and the saving of millions of dollars of consumers' money, as a result of providing "yardsticks" through the Federal and Municipal power projects, has been called one of PWA's most important accomplishments. The first Federal low-cost housing program in America was another. Ickes himself, in his book *Back to Work* (1935), evaluates the PWA: "The Government embarked on the public works program because of the timidity of private capital and its refusal to come out from under the bed."

Ickes' fighting temperament has often brought him to the rostrum and microphone as a fervent apologist of the Administration, often, it is claimed, to say things that Roosevelt would like to but is not in a position to

HAROLD L. ICKES

say. From his mouth have come fiery diatribes against Big Business that have caused disgruntled opponents to call him "Roosevelt's hatchet man." He has been known to draw material for his attacks from such books as *America's 60 Families* by Ferdinand Lundberg. As early as 1934 he formulated the idea of the New Deal credo in his *The New Democracy*. This has been unsympathetically described as "the triumph of wishful thinking so dear to the savage, the child and the reformer." Another critic, however, says: "It is impossible not to feel drawn toward Mr. Ickes if you have ever met him; and it is equally hard not to admire the fine liberal spirit which animates his book. He wants everyone in this country to be prosperous and happy."

In 1938, Ickes, at that time "one of the few men around here who [was] not a candidate for President," toyed briefly with the idea of becoming Mayor of Chicago. The idea of smashing the Kelly-Nash machine in the city where he had spent most of his political life was an inviting one. But eventually he turned it down; he found sufficient excitement in his own department. For one thing, a debate over the air with Frank Gannett, owner of a chain of newspapers, started a controversy in 1939 that has shown no sign of ending in 1941. The subject was the freedom of the press and Ickes claimed that the press in the United States is subject to financial pressures which limit its freedom, cause improper slanting of news and editorials and make it unfair to certain groups of citizens. After Roosevelt's re-election in 1940 he continued his attack, pointing out that "we elected a President who was supported by less than 23 per cent of our daily press. . . This reveals a perilous situation requiring public consideration."

He pursued this thesis in two books: *America's House of Lords* (1939), and *Freedom of the Press Today* (1941), which assembles to-

ICKES, HAROLD L.—*Continued*

gether discussions on the subject by such newspapermen as Herbert Agar, Ralph Ingersoll, William Allen White and Raymond Clapper. On several occasions his sorties on columnists, or, as he indignantly calls them, "calumnists . . . ex-reporters who waste good white space to spread injurious gossip," made good copy. He found much pleasure in commenting on Walter Winchell's "obstetrical turn of mind," Dorothy Thompson's tendency to cover too much ground, Boake Carter's ability to "enter any intellectual goldfish swallowing contest." Sometimes his attacks took a poetical turn, as in this:

> *Who knowing scarce their ABC*
> *Rank doctors of philosophie?*
> *Who but the columnists?*
> *Who expound the Constitution*
> *Adding circum to locution?*
> *Why, the columnists.*
> *I'd like to strut and look profound*
> *And order Presidents around.*
> *I'd like to be a columnist.*

It has been rather unkindly suggested that the last remark is simon-pure truth.

Ickes played a most important part in the 1940 Presidential elections. It was General Hugh Johnson (about whom Ickes once ruefully moaned, "I would that he loved me much, much less than he does") who called him the "original triple termite" and claimed that he wrote the platform, uttered the keynote speech, mapped the whole strategy and prepared an outline for most of the campaign speeches. Though that is undoubtedly an exaggeration, it is true that Ickes, a veteran campaigner and properly inspired by having so much more promising a candidate than in the past, covered the country, lining up the votes. It was he, too, who answered the speeches of the Republican Party while the President was, in contrast to Willkie, resting his throat for the final spurt in the campaign. Ickes' gift for lethal invective came in handy. Before the nomination he had deflated candidate Dewey (after Dewey "had finally thrown his diaper into the ring"). The campaign for Willkie under way, he called the Republican nominee "a rich man's Roosevelt" and a "simple, barefoot Wall Street lawyer" (this last in deadly allusion to his emphasis on his clean, country-life antecedents). His activities during the campaign finally caused the *New Republic* to remark with some astonishment: "The Ik . . . is now one of the major political bosses of the country."

Ickes has been called a contentious and quarrelsome soul unable to live at peace with fellow New Dealers and possessor of "the worst temper between the Hatfield-McCoy country and La Guardia's office in City Hall, New York." Among people with whom he has tangled are Gifford Pinchot, Henry Wallace, whose Forest Service Ickes has coveted, Cissy Patterson, the publisher of the Washington *Times-Herald,* and Congressman Dies. He has more than once denounced "our native Fascists and appeasers," too—naming among

them Merwin K. Hart, Lawrence Dennis, Charles Lindbergh (see sketches this issue), Henry Ford, Father Coughlin, Major Al Williams. And he himself has been the recipient of some inspired name-calling, most of it, however, directed at his personality rather than his integrity or efficiency. He has been called "Harold the Meddler", "Donald Duck of the New Deal," a "professional rabble-rouser," a "common scold." The doughty secretary can take it, however, and give back as good as he gets. The worst press he ever got was on the pages of *Völkischer Beobachter* on the occasion of his refusing to permit the export of helium for the use of German dirigibles in 1939, and he welcomed it. Germany has continued to give him a bad press for his urging the United States to support Britain and Russia fully, to reject a "craven's truce."

Ickes is a rather thickset, bespectacled, vigorous man, with his gray hair growing thin on top. In 1938 he fluttered the Washington dovecots by marrying the 25-year-old Jane Dahlman (Smith '35, *cum laude*) sister of the widow of his late stepson, Wilmarth. With her and their two children, Harold McEwen, who was born September 4, 1939, and a daughter, Jane, born on May 26, 1941, he spends all the time he can on their estate at Headwaters Farm, Olney, Maryland. He has one child by his previous marriage, Raymond Wilmarth, a lawyer. He collects stamps. An ardent dahlia fan, he originated a peach-colored species which he patented and named Anna W. Ickes. He likes to garden without gloves, with his hands in the soil. Altogether he is a robust person and on occasion grows Whitmanesque, as in his 1940 Fourth of July speech, when he asked: "When are you going to laugh, Americans? When is the great, hard, angry, shouting, raspberry laugh of the American people going to yell down the west wind of this continent and out to sea and on out past the horizon?"

References

Bet Homes & Gard 13:9-11+ Ja '35 il por
Christian Sci Mon Mag p2+ Ag 26 '39 pors
Collier's 92:21+ S 30 '33 por
Good H 110:210 Ap '40
New Repub 74:331-3 My 3 '33
R of Rs 88:19-21 S '33 por
Sat Eve Post 212:5-7+ Jl 22 '39 il pors
Time 31:8-9 Je 6 '38 por; 33:34+ Ap 24 '39 il por; 38:14-16 S 15 '41
Babson, R. W. Washington and the Revolutionists p119-37 1934
Moley, R. After Seven Years p126-7 1939
Who's Who in America
Who's Who in Government
Who's Who in the Nation's Capital

IDLEMAN, FINIS SCHUYLER, REV. Sept. 12, 1875—Mar. 22, 1941 Pastor of the Central Church, Disciples of Christ, in New York City for 25 years; ordained in 1901;

assistant editor of the *Christian Union Quarterly;* administrative officer of the Federal Council of Churches of Christ in America; noted as liberal; wrote biography of Dr. Peter Ainslie, pastor of the Christian Temple of Baltimore.

References

Lit Digest 120:17 O 26 '35
Who's Who in America

Obituaries

Christian Cent 58:444 Ap 2 '41
N Y Times p45 Mr 23 '41 por

IMLAY, L(ORIN) E(VERETT) Nov. 2, 1864—June 9, 1941 Electrical engineer, associated with the Pioneer Tunnel Power Development at Niagara Falls; worked for the Westinghouse Electric Manufacturing Company, the Niagara Hudson Power system and the Buffalo, Niagara and Eastern Power Corporation, from which he retired in 1938; became director of statistics for the Niagara Hudson systems in 1930.

References

American Men of Science
Who's Who in America
Who's Who in Engineering 1925

Obituaries

N Y Times p23 Je 10 '41

INFELD, LEOPOLD (ĭn-fĕld) Aug. 20, 1898- Professor of applied mathematics, University of Toronto, Canada; physicist; author

Address: b. University of Toronto, 5, Ontario, Canada; h. 61 Austin Terrace, Toronto, Ontario, Canada

Leopold Infeld ("a tall, jovial man" with dark hair and gray eyes), professor of applied mathematics at the University of Toronto, author of more than thirty scientific papers printed in French, German, English and Polish, collaborator with Einstein on *The Evolution of Physics,* is the author of *Quest; The Evolution of a Scientist* (1941). It is an autobiography that has three subjects: "The Polish ghetto, from which Infeld originated; Leopold Infeld; and the discoveries of theoretical physics in which Infeld participated." And it is a fascinating and completely, sometimes painfully, honest book, more sensitively written than any but the rare novel.

Leopold Infeld was born on the principal street in Kraków's ghetto on August 20, 1898, the son of Salomon and Ernestine (Kahane) Infeld. Although his family was fairly prosperous, through his entire life he was to fight "the dark, narrow atmosphere" of the ghetto in which he was born. "To the ghetto Jew the Polish city was a strange and hostile world." At six, Leopold left his crowded, odorous Jewish school for the public school to which everyone went for four years by Franz Joseph's imperial decree. There he first learned Polish; there he got his first

LEOPOLD INFELD

real glimpse of the larger world. He was determined to go on to a Gymnasium and thence to a university, but his father closed this, the "easiest exit from the ghetto," by sending him to a citizen's school so that he might become a businessman like himself rather than a doctor or a lawyer.

Temporarily Leopold lost all interest in study, all ambition. Not until he was 13 did he discover the excitement of books and friends. It was then, too, that he lost his religious faith, began to commit all possible sins against the ritual. When his father found out, Leopold was beaten, but gradually his independence was accepted—and in more than religious matters. His father did not argue when Leopold bought three heavy volumes of physics, and after discovering that he needed a mathematics textbook in order to understand them, decided to study by himself in order to pass the University examination (the *matura*). Now his great ambition was to become a Gymnasium teacher, perhaps because he himself had been unable to attend. But his great passion was already for physics: "What I loved in physics was the rigorous character of its reasoning."

Young Infeld took his oral *matura* on May 9, 1916, passed with first honors—and on May 11 was drafted into army service. He found the War senseless and barrack life unbearable, but after a corruptible corporal helped him to desert he found himself in a more precarious situation than he had bargained for. Throughout most of the War he lived in constant fear of being discovered, until shortly before the Armistice he succeeded in getting himself classified as feeble-minded and returned safely to civilian life and the University of Kraków.

The defeat of the Central Powers brought independence to Poland; yet "in the fight for

INFELD, LEOPOLD—*Continued*

power in young Poland the reactionary forces won." It was not long before Infeld learned what real anti-Semitism meant. He left the University of Kraków for Berlin; there he found prejudice against the Poles. He enlisted Einstein's (see sketch this issue) help to gain admission to the University of Berlin and after much difficulty was allowed to enroll as a "special student," but his studies there brought him no credits toward a degree and he eventually returned to the inferior University of Kraków, where he obtained his Ph. D. in 1921.

In the Poland of 1921 no Jew could dream of becoming a teacher in any but a Jewish Gymnasium. For eight years the first doctor of theoretical physics in free Poland worked as a schoolteacher in small Polish provincial towns, although no university in Poland had a man able to teach theoretical physics. "Dependent on stupid, narrow, dull people who were the trustees of the school, constantly fighting with them for decent salaries, burdened with teaching, hating the streets, buildings and faces around me, I slowly lost all desire to open a scientific book and forgot what I had learned." Some interest returned when he joined the Polish Physical Society. Gradually he began doing scientific work again, publishing articles in German and French scientific journals.

It was at a meeting of the Physical Society in Wilno in 1928 that Dr. Infeld met and fell in love with a young woman scientist. Later he described that first meeting to her: "I behaved so badly, so noisily." "I know," she replied. "That kind of behavior comes from unfulfilled ambitions and an unhappy life." With his marriage to Halina, Infeld's life changed. But she was not well. He accompanied her to Vienna and to Italy for treatment. In the meanwhile his school was disqualified for an incident which had happened when he was in charge. He found a senior assistantship at the University of Lwów and in his second year there ("by an almost fantastic *coup* in which the anti-Semites canceled one another's arguments") was habilitated as a docent; but once more Halina became ill. It was in Leipzig that she died, in the last year of the Weimar Republic, and only the vision of a book "dedicated to Halina's memory" saved her husband from self-destruction. True, physics was all he knew; but even a book on physics might be written in a popular way. Eventually it appeared, with the dedication as he had envisioned it; its title was *New Pathways of Science,* later published in England as *The World in Modern Science* (1934).

Shortly afterward Dr. Infeld himself went to England, to Cambridge, on a Rockefeller scholarship. There he helped Max Born formulate a field theory which, according to *Time,* "bridges modern Quantum Mechanics and the nineteenth century electromagnetic wave equations of Scotland's brilliant James Clerk Maxwell." After England it was hard to return to Lwów, for all over Poland the tide of anti-Semitism was increasing, but Infeld still hoped to get a promotion to a professorship at his University. In the meanwhile he began writing articles against Fascism and against anti-Semitism for liberal papers. It was this, rather than the fact that he was a Jew, that was used as an excuse for his not receiving the promotion. When Infeld finally learned how foolish his hopes had been he once more turned to Einstein (now at Princeton) for help. Not long afterward he learned that the Institute for Advanced Study in Princeton had granted him a small fellowship for the academic year 1936 to 1937.

At "the most famous school of mathematics in the world," Fine Hall in Princeton, Infeld met Einstein, with whom he was to work on gravitational waves, for the second time in his life. Infeld's impressions of the great scientist form one of the most warm and interesting parts of his book, according to one reviewer, "an excellent condensed biography of Einstein, a biography of Einstein's spirit." Even when Infeld's fellowship was not renewed he was determined to remain in the United States. But at least $1,500 was needed in order to work for another year. How to get it? Once more the vision of a book appeared. He would write a popular book with Einstein! Einstein was enthusiastic; Simon and Schuster even more so; and the exciting work began. The remainder of the story of *The Evolution of Physics,* 1938 best seller, is well known. "To the end of my life I am stamped as the 'collaborator of Einstein,'" Infeld mourns; but "I no longer sat alone at teatime in the commons."

Soon, too, he was offered a year's lectureship at the University of Toronto, "a position very similar to the one in which I had begun my scientific career in Lwów 10 years before," and near the end of his academic year there accepted a professorship of applied mathematics. As soon as he finished his lectures (in April 1939) he left for New Jersey to marry Helen Schlauch, whom he had met in New York at the American Mathematical Society. (There is now one son, Eric.) Life, at last, was good.

But in August 1939, somewhere in the wilds of New England, he and Helen heard for the first time the news of Warsaw's bombardment, saw the ugly headlines. Infeld was torn between an unreasonable desire to return to die with his people and an unholy joy that he, at least, was safe. "Poland was beaten before the War began . . . by its own reactionary regime . . . by its own treatment of peasants, workers and Jews"; but he was a Pole. And was even America completely safe? "Am I witnessing here the beginning of a process of which anti-Semitism is an external sign, or are these only isolated insignificant cases and not characteristic of the greatest nation in the world?"

Something more than a physicist, Dr. Infeld's life even more than his words mark him as one who belongs to "the generation of scientists who were forced to view the world outside their island, who had to learn to ask: 'What are the forces which try to destroy science? How can we save our kingdom? How can we by our own efforts prevent or delay the decline of the world in which we live?'" "The scientist," he writes sadly, "tries to understand the origin of our solar system, the structure of the universe and the laws governing the atom. He has discovered X rays, the radioactive substances, and he has built cyclotrons. He has foreseen the existence of electromagnetic and electronic waves. Out of his thought has grown the technique of our century. But not until today has he begun to notice that the earth on which he moves is covered with sweat and with blood and that in the world in which he lives the *son of man has nowhere to lay his head.*"

References

Sat R Lit 23:12 Ap 5 '41
Time 31:39-44 Ap 4 '38 por
Infeld, L. Quest 1941
International Who's Who

INÖNÜ, ISMET (ē-nû-nü') Sept. 24, 1884- President of Turkey

Address: Ankara, Turkey

Ismet Inönü, whom John Gunther (see sketch this issue) calls "one of the best diplomats of modern times," has repeatedly announced that Turkey wants peace—although not at the price of her independence. For months during the Second World War he turned down the offers of Germany's Ambassador Von Papen (see sketch this issue) for a rapprochment between his country and the Nazis; he resisted the hints of Turkey's British ally that his country aid the Greeks; he maintained a friendly, if delicate, relation between Turkey and Russia. Until the signature of the Turkish-Bulgarian non-aggression pact of February 17, 1941 many observers believed that the use of Bulgaria for the passage of Nazi troops would cause Turkey, watchdog of the Dardanelles, to become actively belligerent, however, and when this did not prove to be the case they insisted that she would not be able to maintain her neutrality if Russia were involved. Yet the fall of 1941 found Turkey still not in the War, although in a position that could best be described as sitting on a powder-keg.

Ever since the Turkish Republic was founded by Kemal Ataturk in 1923 Ismet Inönü has been a leader of his people. He was born in 1884 in Izmir (then Smyrna), the son of Reshid and Djevriye, his father a judge on English Hill. At the age of twelve he entered the artillery school in Istanbul (then known as Constantinople) and then went on to the General Staff College, where he was two years behind Ataturk. He was graduated first in his class and immediately commissioned a captain. By the time he was 31 he had become a colonel in the Army.

During the First World War Inönü was sent to Palestine to fight the British and later, in 1917, was chief of staff to Ataturk in the fighting against the Russians in eastern Turkey. Then, after the War, when the national movement was formed, he joined forces with Ata-

Turkish Embassy

ISMET INÖNÜ

turk. When the Greek Army invaded Turkey "with the blessing of Britain and France," Inönü once again was Ataturk's chief of staff, his job the holding off of Greeks with guerrilla irregulars while the regular army was being organized. Twice he defeated the Greeks at the village of Inönü. Later, when Ataturk decreed that all Turks must have last names, he took his name of Inönü in memory of this victory.

When the Republic was proclaimed on October 29, 1923 Inönü became its first Premier, one of the triumvirate of Ataturk, Inönü and Fewzi Çakmak that directed its destinies. Ataturk was the President of the Republic and its creator and inspirer; Inönü was his right-hand man, the administrator and executor of the laws and reforms instituted. Under their leadership Turkey "passed from the Oriental middle ages to the twentieth century of the Occident." The hold of the Mohammedan Church was broken; progressive schools were started; clothes were westernized; women were given freedom; society as a whole was completely modernized and changed.

During the years that Ataturk was President, Inönü and Ataturk disagreed about many things, for Inönü's was a more moderate approach to reform than Ataturk's. Yet the two men never disagreed about Turkey's place in the modern world, and under them "the sick man of Europe" became a lusty one. In diplomacy, it was Inönü who did the guiding, aided by that greatest of all diplomatic blessings—deafness. It was he who had had the first and hardest job of making the peace with Greece legal at Lausanne in 1923 and he who faced down the annoyed Allied statesmen and won absolute sovereignty for the Turkish Republic. Later it was he who established friendly relations with all the contiguous states and most of the major powers in a long list of bi-lateral treaties. His was a policy founded on col-

INÖNÜ, ISMET—*Continued*

lective security which, he felt in 1937, was "in spite of everything the only possible remedy against the visionary aims of the peoples and the only basis on which one can reasonably hope to found a better world."

In 1937 Inönü resigned the Premiership after a period of fourteen years in office, except for a four months' interval from November 1924 to March 1925. The reasons for his resignation were the subject of much speculation. Some said he was forced out; others that he stepped out. Some said Ataturk had found him too pro-Russian; others that the cause was "probably mutual irritation despite mutual respect." Then in November 1938 Ataturk died, and 24 hours after his death the Grand National Assembly (parliament) unanimously chose Ismet Inönü as his successor for a four-year term.

Ismet took over, announcing: "It will be our task to see that Turkey falls neither into anarchy nor tyranny. The nation in the past has given ample proof of its heroism. With the support of its glorious army it will give further proof, if need be, in the future." Under Inönü the Turkish Republic continued much in the same form as under Ataturk, an authoritarian regime, but, most observers agree, not a Fascist one. Inönü, who believes in the Republic and modern reforms, still feels that the Turkish nation as a whole is not ready for the kind of political democracy which has been developed in western Europe. Yet, "though the Government directly or indirectly owns most of Turkey's new industry and controls everything," according to *Life* "Turkey is still a republic and Inönü still a President."

During Inönü's term as President, Turkey concluded a number of important negotiations and treaties, the most important the 1939 treaty of mutual assistance with England and France. This treaty stated that England and France would go to the aid of Turkey if it were attacked and in return Turkey would give help to the Allies if war spread to the Mediterranean area and if the Allies got into war by helping Romania or Greece (a promise that has not been kept). In any other war Turkey would remain benevolently neutral. But nothing, Inönü was careful to have inserted in the treaty, would compel Turkey "to take action having for its effect or involving as its consequence entry into armed conflict with the U. S. S. R."

It has been said that "the sober personality of Inönü is in itself an answer to the old charge that Turkey is a Fascist dictatorship." It is an explanation, too, of Turkey's diplomatic maneuvers. Unlike his roistering, lusty predecessor Inönü is "quiet, studious, monogamous, good-tempered, pious and conservative" —everything that Ataturk was not. He loves his shy wife, Mevhibe (whom he married in 1916), his sons, Omer and Erdel, and his daughter, Ozden; he likes to play bridge and billiards, ride fine horses, work out chess problems and listen to the Ankara Philharmonic Orchestra. And he looks the quiet sober man he is, with his small, frail body and small face, "dominated by a monumental nose" and topped by gray hair.

References

> Asia 36:606-10 S '36 por; 39:20-2 Ja '39 il por
> Gt Brit & East 52:120 F 2 '39
> Illustration 201:399 N 19 '38 por; 202: 501 Ap 22 '39 por
> Life 8:88-9 Ap 8 '40 pors
> Liv Age 355:434-5 Ja '39
> N Y Times VII p4 Ap 13 '41 il pors
> Newsweek 13:16-8 My 22 '39 il por (cover); 16:32 N 18 '40
> Scholastic 37:6+ D 16 '40 por
> Time 32:22+ N 21 '38 por; 34:25 S 4 '39 por
> International Who's Who

IRVINE, ALEXANDER FITZGERALD, REV. (ẽr'vĭn) 1863—Mar. 15, 1941 Congregational minister and author; lay preacher at the Episcopal Church of the Ascension, New York City from 1907 to 1910; caused stir in the congregation because of his liberal views and socialist tendencies; born in Ireland, he was self-educated and came to the United States in 1888, worked in a variety of lowly jobs until he became a missionary and then studied for the ministry; in recent years he had devoted himself to writing; his autobiography *From the Bottom Up* attracted much attention.

References

> Irvine, A. F. Fighting Parson 1930
> Irvine, A. F. From the Bottom Up 1914
> Who's Who in America

Obituaries

> N Y Times p45 Mr 16 '41

ISRAEL, EDWARD L., RABBI Aug. 30, 1896—Oct. 19, 1941 Rabbi; vice-president of the Synagogue Council of America; from 1923 until 1941, when he was about to become director of the Union of American Hebrew Congregations, served as rabbi of Har Sinai Congregation in Baltimore, Maryland; arbitration chairman of men's clothing industry in Baltimore; member of the 1939 White House Conference on Children in a Democracy and generally known as a liberal.

References

> Christian Cent 56:1580-1 D 20 '39
> Survey 76:45 F '40 por
> America's Young Men 1936-37
> Who's Who Among North American Authors
> Who's Who in America
> Who's Who in American Jewry

Obituaries

> N Y Times p17 O 20 '41

JACKSON, DANIEL DANA Aug. 1, 1870 —Sept. 1, 1941 Head of the Department of Chemical Engineering of Columbia University since 1918; authority on water supply and sanitation problems; joined the Brooklyn Water Supply Department in 1897; aided the Government during the First World War in technical matters relating to photography, explosives and water supply.

References

Who's Who in America
Who's Who in Engineering

Obituaries

N Y Times p17 S 2 '41 por
Sch & Soc 54:162 S 6 '41

JAMES, ARTHUR CURTISS June 1, 1867 —June 4, 1941 Financier; railroad builder; yachtsman; was one of the wealthiest men in the country and one of the least known to the public; a dominant factor in the control of 40,000 miles of American railroads, nearly one-seventh of the nation's total rail mileage; gave millions to charity; James W. Gerard named James as one of the 59 men who "ruled" America.

References

Newsweek 4:30 Ag 4 '34 por
Time 32:50 O 31 '38 por
Who's Who in America
Who's Who in Commerce and Industry
Who's Who in Railroading 1930

Obituaries

N Y Times p23 Je 5 '41 por

JAMIESON, LELAND (SHATTUCK) (jā′mĭ-sŭn) Jan. 10, 1904—July 9, 1941 Author; commercial aviation pilot; widely known for his aviation adventure stories in magazines and for two novels, *Attack* (1940) and *High Frontier* (1940); regularly piloted a plane between Miami and Jacksonville, doing his writing between runs; in 1939 received a medal for his "outstanding contributions to aviation outside the line of duty."

References

Who's Who Among North American Authors

Obituaries

N Y Times p19 Jl 10 '41 por
Pub W 140:252 Jl 26 '41

JANSSEN, CHARLES L. (jăn′sĕn) 1886— Jan. 22, 1941 Assistant professor of clinical surgery at the College of Physicians and Surgeons of Columbia University and associate attendant surgeon at Presbyterian Hospital; Belgian who served during the First World War and attended King Leopold, then Crown Prince; authority on abdominal surgery.

References

American Medical Directory
Directory of Medical Specialists 1939

Obituaries

N Y Times p21 Ja 23 '41

JEANS, SIR JAMES HOPWOOD Sept. 11, 1877- Astrophysicist; author

Address: Cleveland Lodge, Dorking, England

Few men of science have been showered with as many medals and honorary degrees as Sir James Jeans has won by his contributions to our knowledge of the solar system, the stars, radiation and related subjects. And probably no other scientist of like distinction has been the author of four best sellers in four successive years. Beginning as a teacher of applied mathematics, he has become a major figure in astronomy and cosmogony, and is today one of the two foremost popularizers of these subjects—the other being Sir Arthur Stanley Eddington (see sketch this issue).

Sir James received his title from the King, and not from his Scotch-descended father, W. T. Jeans. He was born in Lancashire on September 11, 1877, and although his family moved to London when he was three, a certain quiet solidity about him still gives the impression of a country rather than a city gentleman. After preparatory years at the Merchant Taylors' School he went to Trinity College, Cambridge, in the late '90s, expecting to make a study of the classics his life work. In this beginning, as well as in the final linking up of science and God, he resembles another scientist, Robert A. Millikan.

Before Jeans emerged from the famous "capital of the scientific world" he had transferred his attention to mathematics and had brilliantly distinguished himself. In 1900 he was Smith's Prizeman and in 1901 was made a Fellow of Trinity College. In 1904 he became university lecturer in mathematics. The following year he made his first trip to America, in response to an invitation from Woodrow Wilson, then president of Princeton University, to become professor of applied mathematics at that institution. During his five years in America the shy, handsome Britisher endeared himself to his colleagues, issued a number of important publications and married Charlotte Tiffany Mitchell of New London, Connecticut—a niece of "Ilk Marvel" renowned in the sentimental '80s as author of *Reveries of a Bachelor* and *Dream Life*.

Jeans' Alma Mater recalled him to England in 1910, and he taught applied mathematics at Cambridge. Four years later, when his brilliant *Radiation and the Quantum-Theory* was published, some of his American colleagues were "thrilled" to learn that this ardent disciple of the venerable Newtonian school had become "an inspired apostle of the new physics first inaugurated by Planck and Einstein in the beginning of this century." Einstein (see sketch this issue) himself was at this time still a clerk in the patent office of Switzerland

Continuing his researches and his emergence as a leading astrophysicist, Jeans in 1919—the year his *Problems of Cosmogony and Stellar Dynamics* was published—received the Medal of the Royal Society and became secretary of the Royal Astronomical Society.

(Continued next page)

SIR JAMES HOPWOOD JEANS

This position he held for 10 years, resigning then to devote himself entirely to his own scientific problems. In 1922 he received the Gold Medal of the Royal Astronomical Society. Since 1923 he has been research associate of the Mount Wilson Observatory, where, during his visits to this country, he has profited by the opportunity to examine the skies through the world's largest telescope.

Sir James was knighted by the King in 1928, in recognition of his contributions to science. This was the year his *Astronomy and Cosmogony* was published and also, in America, his first popular book, *Eos*. *The Universe Around Us* followed in 1929, and the next year *The Mysterious Universe*. Four other popular books have been published since then, all of them having sales unprecedented for scientific books. Seventeen thousand copies of *The Mysterious Universe* were sold the first week after its publication in England, and in 1934 it was announced that his last four books had sold 300,000 copies in England and America. Meanwhile he had become familiar to radio audiences through a series of talks, sponsored by the BBC, which formed the basis of his *The Stars in Their Courses*, published in 1931.

As popular author, Jeans is unanimously voted "a master of English and of mathematical physics" who, with his "incomparable gifts of lucid exposition, persuades even the non-mathematical mind that it can probe the secrets of inter-stellar space." When he begins, however, to discuss the "Great Architect of the Universe," whom he conceives as "a pure mathematician," to describe the cosmos as "his thoughts," and to dilate upon the philosophical implications of all this for mankind, opinion divides. From one school of critics we hear that *The Mysterious Universe* is "admirable for its mastery of its subject, its clarity and the philosophical soundness of

its conclusions," that "it would be difficult to find more real thought packed into such small compass" and that its "last chapter cannot possibly be ignored by anyone who wants to remain in touch with modern thought." The other side remarks that "doubtless some of [Jeans'] admirers will not applaud his present incursion into the domain of what Dr. David Starr Jordan calls 'sciosophy,'" that "we do not go to the most brilliant scientist of our time to hear things that might be excused in an Early Victorian," and, more excitedly, that "the public is being played upon and utterly misled by the dreamery of the rival mathematical astronomers and physicists."

The same type of comment has been passed on succeeding books. *New Backgrounds of Science* (1933) was termed "unrivaled as a broad outline of the most recent developments of theoretical physics" which could be "recommended with equal confidence to the physicist, the philosopher and the layman." But another critic commented: "Instead of disclosing the new backgrounds of science this book exhibits the new science against the background of an old philosophy. The dilemmas in which the author finds himself are the inevitable consequence of this incongruous setting."

His tremendous popular following did not come between Sir James and the scientific world. In 1931 he was awarded the Medal of the Franklin Institute for his "many fruitful contributions to mathematical physics, especially in the realms of the dynamical theory of gases and the theories of radiation, his challenging explanations of astronomical problems and his illuminating expositions of modern scientific ideas." When he came to this country to receive the medal he was honored at a dinner given jointly by the New York Museum of Science and Industry, the American Institute, the American Museum of Natural History, the Amateur Astronomers Association, the New York Academy of Sciences and the magazine *Scientific Monthly*. His speech to the guests was broadcast over the NBC network.

Still higher on his ample list of honors, degrees, medals, offices and memberships stands the Order of Merit, awarded to him in 1939. This is one of the greatest distinctions an Englishman can attain, and membership is limited to twenty-four. American newspapers, however, gave far more space that year to a controversy set off by his statement that "touch" in piano playing was merely a matter of how hard one hit the keys, and that a single tone struck by an umbrella would be no different from one made by the finger of Paderewski. The comment was made during a talk to the English Music Teachers' Association—no doubt a result of his book published in 1937, *Science and Music*.

In 1934 the beautiful Lady Jeans died, bequeathing to her husband the whole of her $500,000 estate. The following year Sir James was married to Susi Hock, a gifted young organist from Vienna whom he had met when she was playing in a Handel festival in Cambridge. About this time the Royal Institution won him back to teaching; he accepted their newly established chair in 1935. In 1936, at 59, he became the proud father of his first son, and later another boy was born. He has one daughter by his earlier marriage.

Rugged, handsome and quiet are the adjectives most often applied to Sir James, whose spacious home in Dorking, surrounded by huge rhododendrons, seems a more appropriate setting than a banquet chamber in a New York hotel. He likes to smoke an old briar pipe, with which he gestures as he talks, and to quote poetry in a deep voice. Very much the substantial Britisher, there is about him a simplicity and an air almost of boyishness—personal expression of the enthusiasm that has marked both his researches and his popular interpretations of them. It is the spirit that is apparent in his exclamation, (back in 1932) that "we of the present age know . . . almost nothing; we are pioneers setting out to explore . . . the glorious morning of the world."

References

Am Mercury 22:252-4 F '31
Contemp 139:8-13 Ja '31
Nation 131:653 D 10 '30; 137:81 Jl 19 '33
N Y Herald Tribune Books p3 N 16 '30
Newsweek 13:26 Ja 23 '39
Sci ns 74:187-95 Ag 21 '31
Sci Mo 32:567-8 Je '31 por; 33:5-11 Jl '31 por(p86)
Time 28:67 O 5 '36; 33:21 Ja 9 '39
Author's and Writer's Who's Who
Chesterton, G. K. As I Was Saying p49-54 1936
Leavis, F. R. ed. Determinations p281-312 1934
Phillpotts, E. Essays in Little p79-90 1931
Wallace, A. Religious Faith of Great Men p139-73 1934
Who's Who
Woolf, S. J. Drawn from Life p70-9 1932

JENKINS, LEW Dec. 4, 1916- Former world's lightweight champion

Address: c/o Twentieth Century Sporting Club, Inc, 1619 Broadway, New York City

Bulletin: Lew Jenkins lost the world's lightweight championship to Sammy Angott on December 19, 1941 at Madison Square Garden.

From January 1941 issue (revised):

Lew Jenkins leaped from obscurity to newspaper headlines and the lightweight championship of the world in one brief year. In May 1939, in New York City's Madison Square Garden, Jenkins scored a three-round technical knockout over the 135-pound champion, Lou Ambers, to annex the title. Barely a year before, Lew had arrived in New York an unknown, run-of-the-mill boxer who had barnstormed all over the country fighting wherever he could find a spot. Lew's climb

to the top has been the result of a lot of hard work, some lucky breaks and some particularly shrewd management. In his last 58 fights he has scored 31 knockouts.

Lew Jenkins was born of Irish stock in Brownwood, Texas on December 4, 1916, and when he was very young his parents moved

20th Century Sporting Club
LEW JENKINS

to nearby Sweetwater. There the "Sweet Swatter from Sweetwater" went to school intermittently, but mostly was apt to be on his hands and knees between two rows of West Texas long staple cotton, transferring the contents of the little green bolls to a 12-foot canvas sack tied around his neck. He was a "good" boy and the people of Sweetwater can't recall that he ever showed any of the traits which, later in the ring, made him one of the most relentless fighters the game has produced. Lew enjoyed all the sports that the average American boy likes, but horses and riding were (and still are) his favorites. So, in 1936, he went to El Paso, Texas to join the United States 8th Cavalry at Fort Bliss.

Private Jenkins was assigned to the task of fitting iron shoes to the feet of Uncle Sam's mules. While watching the inter-company boxing matches, he became interested and soon began fighting preliminaries in small town rings, receiving pay enough to buy his boxing gear. Lew once hitchhiked to Silver City, New Mexico, a distance of about 100 miles, for a match. He left Fort Bliss early in the morning and reached his destination just in time to enter the ring. Immediately after the bout he had to hike back to the

JENKINS, LEW—*Continued*

Fort to report for duty in the morning. His percentage of the gate receipts was $3.

On a furlough Lew went to Dallas to engage in his first real professional bout. His opponent, Kid Leva, was stiffened in short order. Although Lew received only $16 for this fight he aroused the interest of Fred Browning, well-to-do Dallas sportsman. After watching Jenkins train, Browning purchased his discharge from the Army. At the same time Lew met Katie Lucille Jenkins, midget auto-racer who invited him to see her in action. Lew accepted and saw the 100-pound Katie take the wheel of a stock car, miss a turn, catapult through the rail, turn over three times; then right the car, drive through the fence onto the track again and win the race. In less than four months he persuaded her to change the Miss to Mrs. and thereafter Katie was an important figure in Lew's management. She accompanies him to all his fights and is usually in his corner at bell time.

Lew and Katie traveled throughout most of Texas and made a trip to Mexico which was a "bust" financially. In some of the places where Lew fought, before his opponent climbed through the ropes, he didn't know whether he was going to fight a lightweight, middleweight or welterweight. There is no accurate check on just how many matches he engaged in during this period, and Jenkins himself doesn't know how many he won and lost. The important thing then wasn't the winning or losing, but getting enough money for hotels and meals and gasoline to the next town. In Los Angeles, Lew, who arranged his own fights, won a few bouts in the smaller arenas, but was unable to get suitable matches.

In the latter part of 1937 Lew and Katie drove to Chicago. There he began to fight regularly and in the better clubs. He won a lot of fights and lost some and, while most of the time the pay was small, he picked up valuable experience. Because Katie wanted to see the World's Fair, they came to New York. After a shaky start, Lew began piling up the imposing list of knockouts that brought him his title chance. When Lew first arrived in New York his affairs were handled by Frank Bachman, under agreement with Fred Browning. After a misunderstanding, Hymie Caplin, the Broadway legend, replaced Bachman. In Jenkins' first bout in Madison Square Garden he knocked out Primo Flores in five rounds; six weeks later kayoed Mike Belloise in seven rounds; and a month after stopped Billy Marquart in three rounds.

Jenkins has fought a number of times since he won the title from Ambers. The first was an overweight, non-title bout with the then welterweight champion, Henry Armstrong. It was generally agreed by sports writers that this was an overmatch for Jenkins, for Armstrong was considered one of boxing's all-time-greats: he held the featherweight, lightweight and welterweight titles at the same time. The

bout, however, was a natural from the spectators' point of view, with the hard-hitting Jenkins and the perpetual-motion Armstrong in the ring. Jenkins stopped a punch by the heavier Armstrong early in the fight and collapsed in his corner after the seventh round. He fought dusky Bob Montgomery in Philadelphia in his next fight, and although Jenkins was floored in the second round he went on to take a clean decision in 10 rounds. A 10-round non-title match with the world welterweight champion, Fritzie Zivic, resulted in a draw.

In his first defense of his title Lew gained sweet revenge over Pete Lello, who had knocked him out a few months before in Chicago. Of that fight Jenkins says that a cut eye forced the referee to stop the fight, but Lello says that he "knocked Jenkins colder than a herring." After the usual sparring first round, Jenkins went to work on Lello in the second and smacked his opponent to the canvas right after the bell. Although Lello gained his feet he had a "goofy" look on his face, and after three more trips to the deck, referee Arthur Donovan mercifully stopped the slaughter.

Bob Montgomery gave Lew a fine licking in a return match in May 1941, but since Montgomery exceeded lightweight limits, Jenkins retained the title. He was trounced again in October of the same year by Red Cochrane, but again in a non-title bout.

"Nobody," says Lew, "taught me to fight. Nobody teaches anybody to fight. They teach 'em to be smarter or carefuller, maybe, but you got to be a fighter right from the start, else you're never a fighter." Lew is cold, hard, merciless and has no nerves. His weatherbeaten face, with lumps of scar tissue over the eyes and the beginning of cauliflower on his ears, bears mute evidence that he has no high regard for the scientific end of the game—he just hits harder and oftener than his opponents. Someone once told him that if you batter at anything long enough something has to give, and that is just the way "this lad conducts his blitzkriegs" in the ring: a "hell-bent-for-leather, slam-bang fracas that never ebbs until the other half of the shindig starts sinking by the stern end."

Outside the ring Lew is a modest, unassuming young man with high cheekbones, a beak of a nose and tousled brown hair. He is five-feet-seven in height and the 135 lightweight limit bothers him not at all. He eats what he wants and his best fighting weight is around 131 pounds. He cares nothing for the extensive wardrobe that most boxers acquire, and is frequently seen in Broadway nightspots in polo shirt and slacks. When he retires he wants to buy a ranch in Texas and stock it with blooded cattle. With more than $50,000 from his last four fights he should be able to do this soon. But, with his dynamic punch, tremendous endurance and unquestioned courage, he may remain at the top for quite awhile. "Lew," says one sports commentator, "may not be the greatest champion his division has ever had, but he is certainly one of the most pleasing to watch in action."

References

Collier's 106:12+ Jl 20 '40 il por
N Y Herald Tribune X p7+ Jl 7 '40 por

JOHN, AUGUSTUS (EDWIN) Jan. 4, 1879- Welsh painter; etcher; lithographer; draughtsman

Address: h. 33 Tite St, Chelsea, London, S. W., England; Fryern Ct, Fordingbridge, Hampshire, England

Bearded, eccentric Augustus John, Britain's most famous living artist, possibly the most famous living portrait-painter in the world, and generally accepted as the original of Aldous Huxley's satyr-like John Bidlake in *Point Counter Point*, may or may not have Romany blood in him. It is known that he was born at Tenby, Wales on January 4, 1879, but further details are difficult to get. As T. W. Earp, art critic of the London *Daily Telegraph*, expressed it: "At a time when artists, along with other persons of repute, are inclined to meet willingly, if not even to induce, curiosity as to the non-professional side of their existence, John has been content to display himself through his work alone."

John was first heard of in 1894 as an art student at the Slade School, University College, London, where he studied under Professors Frederick Brown and Henry Tonks and in 1898 won a prize for composition against such competition as was furnished by fellow students like the late Sir John Lavery and the late Sir William Orpen. Even in those early days there was the wonderful "Old Masterish" quality about his drawing that later caused John Singer Sargent to say: "John's drawings are the best since the Renaissance"; and by 1899 this young man of 20 was having drawings accepted by the New English Art Club, then regarded as the *avant-garde* of British art. In 1901, the year he married Ida Nettleton, he was called up to Liverpool as instructor in drawing at University College. C. H. Reilly, the eminent teacher of architecture, gives some lively pictures of those early days. "Liverpool in 1904," he writes, "was still arguing about a caravan on its way there (North Wales) going down Bold Street at the fashionable hour with the Hon. Mrs. Dowdall, her one aristocrat, seated stockingless—a first-class event in those days— on the steps and behind her the Sampson and John families, with Dowdall, a rising young barrister now the County Court Judge, and [Augustus] John riding on nags behind." Under the tuition of Sampson and of the gypsies themselves John became expert in the difficult Romany language; and he learned to speak five other foreign tongues. "John as I knew him then," Reilly adds further, "was a glorious-looking young man of about twenty-five, tall and graceful with longish hair, big magnetic eyes, bearded like the pard, picturesquely dressed with big hat, sailor's jersey and earrings and with a fine springy walk."

AUGUSTUS JOHN

During his Liverpool days John started his portrait practice (not without causing considerable local controversy, hardly understandable in 1941), and earned a great deal of fame by such pictures as *Merekli* (1902) and *Dorelia* (1904) at the New English Art Club. The "John girl" has become well known since that time. She is a raven-haired, bold, vivid creature, loosely attired in flaming crimson or in some rich color combination of oranges and blues; and she has a certain dash and spirit hard to put in words. Once young John left a train at Marseille and went back to Spain to paint a girl he had seen from a train window.

It was also during this period that John began to etch; most of his etchings date between 1901 and 1910. They derive from the Rembrandt tradition, and their subjects are often types found in the slums of Liverpool, but his etching of W. B. Yeats as a young man is the one which is probably most famous. (Many of these early etchings were included in the comprehensive exhibition of his prints which was shown at the M. A. McDonald Gallery in New York City in December 1941 and was then presented to the Boston Public Library.) For a year or two John lived at Matching Green, Essex, a village which he left periodically to wander around in a caravan and make his first landscapes. He kept up his friendship and gypsy-lore studies with Sampson, who had a cottage in North Wales from which expeditions could conveniently be made.

John also lived for some time in Paris and on the Breton coast. His first one-man exhibition took place in 1908 at the Chenil Gallery, Chelsea, and in 1909 he settled in London. By the outbreak of the First World War he was well established, and by 1917 E. L. Allhusen was to call him "the most talked of artist in England today." During the War he served as an official artist with

JOHN, AUGUSTUS—*Continued*

the Canadians, holding the rank of major. He produced a big cartoon for the Canadian War Memorial and many portraits, including one of Premier Lloyd George; he was at the Peace Conference in 1919 and painted many of the participants; and he did some of the portraits for T. E. Lawrence's *Seven Pillars of Wisdom.* Lithography (which he started in 1917) had been added to his work with the brush, the pencil and the etching-needle.

In 1920 (the year when the practical British soap king Lord Leverhulme cut the head out of John's portrait of him so that he could get it into his safe and when nearly all the artists and dealers in London protested by a 24-hour strike) John had a show at the Alpine Club Gallery. He had always ignored the Royal Academy, but by 1921 the Academy could no longer ignore him, and he was elected an associate. In 1928 he became a full academician. Ten years later he resigned in a fit of temper because a portrait of T. S. Eliot by his friend Wyndham Lewis had been refused a place in the annual exhibit ("an inept act," John called it); but in February 1940, for the third time in its history, the Academy re-elected a resigned member.

It would have been quite simple for Augustus John to have become a fashionable portrait-painter and nothing more, for he has painted such eminent sitters as Lord Cecil, T. E. Lawrence, King Feisal, Herr Stresemann and, more recently, Britain's Queen Elizabeth for commissions ranging up to $15,000. But he has rejected the temptation. He need not paint a vulgar face because it has a good checkbook, and is at his best with a worthy subject—a weighty thinker like Thomas Hardy, or an enigmatic, provocative, anonymous figure like *The Smiling Woman*, or a fine interpretative artist, like Madame Suggia, the cellist. He is also capable of producing a whole show of, say, unknown West Indian sitters, as he did at Arthur Tooth's Bond Street gallery one year.

He is a great master of line whose actual brushwork in oil portraiture is loose, free and forceful and who as a draughtsman has done "work as precise and as punctilious and done with as much delicacy of skill as any by Ingres himself." The author of this last phrase, Arthur Symons, goes on to point out that John can at times be a satirist, "setting paint and pastel to play games of their own, burlesquing Rubens and Rembrandt and Millet as only one great painter could burlesque another"; but this is not a frequent mood, and John never makes fun of his portrait sitters, as Sargent so patently and constantly did.

Among John's figure compositions, both etched and in oil, there are some very notable ones of the gypsies, who are still his friends. They used to congregate on Epsom Downs some days prior to the Derby and all through the Epsom meeting, but were finally warned off one year, and John defended them. In

November 1931 he took a prominent part in the funeral ceremonies of Dr. John Sampson, ceremonies which were carried out in the Romany way. The ashes were carried up the Welsh mountain, Moel Coch, and Augustus John, cigaret in hand, recited from memory a Romany poem composed by Sampson and delivered an eloquent oration before seeing the ashes scattered from the mountain summit. In 1937 he served as president of the Gypsy Lore Society.

"Everything about Augustus John is picturesque," says Mary Cass Canfield, "—his name, his appearance, his point of view, his artistic career." *Time* credits him with dressing "like a Paris Bohemian of 1890" and possessing the remarkable trick of "looking fierce in one eye and hunted in the other." He is a man of wide culture with a taste for singing little French ballads and declaiming poetry. He lived for some time in Mallord Street, Chelsea, making frequent visits to Martigues, near Marseille, but in late years has been at Fordingbridge, Hampshire, where he owns an old stone manor and a bright pink studio.

John is a member of the New English Art Club, a Fellow of University College, London, president of the Society of Mural Painters, and has been a trustee of the Tate Gallery since 1933. That he is generous in his impulses is shown by his painting of Professor Oliver Elton on his retirement from Liverpool in 1926. The literature students wanted the portrait done, but they were not rich; so John accepted what they could raise, and produced a masterpiece.

Since the beginning of the Second World War he has been painting almost more than at any other time in his life. His sons are all fighting for England; a daughter, "Poppet," who can be described from his portrait of her as "a ravishing brunette whose hair cascades over her white shoulders," is divorced and living in London. There may or may not be another artist of talent in the family. Late in 1939, on seeing an exhibition of landscapes by his daughter Vivien, Augustus John gave his own frank opinion: "Rubbish!"

References

Amour Art 15:462 O '34 il
Arch R 77:65-8 F '35 il
Art Digest 9:19 Ja 1 '35 il; 14:12 Mr 1 '40; 14:7 S '40; 15:17 D 15 '40
Art News 36:21 My 7 '38
Newsweek 16:52 S 2 '40
Time 27:64 My 18 '36 por; 31:43-4 My 30 '38 por; 34:53 D 18 '39 por; 35:56 F 26 '40 por
Bertram, A. Augustus John 1923
Earp, T. W. Augustus John 1934
Harris, F. Contemporary Portraits 3rd ser. p181-9 nd
New Standard Encyclopedia of Art
Symons, A. Studies in Seven Arts p310-22 1925
Symons, A. Studies on Modern Painters p17-29 1925
Who's Who

JOHNSON, ALEXANDER Jan. 2, 1847
—May 17, 1941 American social worker of
international reputation; was instrumental in
developing modern social welfare and methods
of caring for the underprivileged; one of the
most influential of early social workers, who
worked for 59 years in correction field;
known to thousands of social workers in
America for his work as secretary and later
as consultant of the National Conference of
Charities and Corrections.

References
> Survey 72:162 Je '36 por; 74:146 My
> '38 por
> Who's Who in America 1922-23

Obituaries
> N Y Times p43 My 18 '41

JOHNSON, AMY 1903—Jan. 5, 1941
Noted English aviatrix; former wife of
James A. Mollison, noted pilot; killed while
on duty with the British Air Transport
Auxiliary; in 1930 made a solo flight from
England to Australia; in 1931 made a round-
trip flight from London to Tokyo; in 1933,
with her former husband, flew across the
Atlantic from England, landing in Bridgeport,
Connecticut.

References
> Lit Digest 105:32+ Je 28 '30 il pors;
> 116:31 Ag 5 '33 por
> Liv Age 339:212 O '30
> Outlook 155:178 Je 4 '30; 155:615 Ag
> 20 '30 por
> R of Rs 82:130 Jl '30 por
> Woman's J ns 15:4 Jl '30 por
> Banner, H. S. Amy Johnson pam 1933
> Who's Who

Obituaries
> N Y Times p1, 12 Ja 7 '41 por

JOHNSON, HIRAM (WARREN) Sept.
2, 1866- United States Senator from Cali-
fornia
Address: b. United States Senate, Washington,
D. C.; h. 1360 Montgomery St, San Francisco,
Calif.

In 1940 Senator Hiram Johnson ran for
his fifth term as Senator from California on
the Republican, Democratic and Progressive
tickets—"as happy as a clam at high tide"
at the triple nomination—and was sent back
to the Senate by 483,328 Democrats and
581,858 Republicans. "In 30 years of victory
Senator Johnson had never enjoyed such a vote
of confidence."
He enjoyed it despite the opposition of
Roosevelt, who once hailed him as the greatest
liberal of our time and later sadly commented
that no one in his wildest dreams could possibly consider Johnson a liberal or a progressive. He got these votes despite his own
strong and consistent opposition to Roosevelt
during the 1940 election campaign. Willkie
and McNary were eternally right, he said,
"upon the great issue, the all-important one

HIRAM JOHNSON

of a third term," and he warned the voters:
"Power is a heady wine. . . The gentleman
who seeks it now . . . has gathered unto himself more power than any ruler on earth has,
save in the totalitarian governments. . . All
of the forebodings of Washington, Jefferson
and Jackson are fulfilled and justified."
Johnson's platform for the 1940 campaign
was the platform that had been his almost all
his political life—a platform of complete isolationism for America. In his victory Senator
Rush Holt saw a victory for isolationism in
this country. Representative Joe Martin saw
in it a rebuke to Roosevelt; other Republicans
saw in it a happy omen for Republicanism in
general. But *Time's* summary of the general
reaction was: "When a state once acquires a
solid admiration for the gnarled, hickory character of an elder statesman, it often continues
to vote for him regardless of issues."
Senator Johnson, who is known less for the
statutes that bear his name than for those he
has stopped, is proud of his record of dissent
and particularly proud of the fight he has
waged against America's involvement in foreign affairs. It was Johnson who helped keep
us out of the League of Nations, out of the
Four-Power Pact; Johnson who opposed the
London Naval Treaty, the World Court, our
revised neutrality legislation; Johnson who
fought, mainly on the basis of the Johnson Act, which placed a Federal ban on loans
to governments in default of their war debts,
against the President's proposals to aid Great
Britain. Johnson is always fighting. "A man
must be a crank to do this sort of thing," he
admits. "I guess that's what I am. It always
seems that the unpleasant jobs fall to me."
Conservatives have fairly consistently dis-
trusted Hiram Johnson as too much of a
progressive and liberal. Liberals have called
him a reactionary. Both groups admit that
he is a complex mixture of revolutionary and

JOHNSON, HIRAM—*Continued*

standpatter. Both groups admit that he throws himself heart and soul, mind and body into any cause he believes in and against any cause he hates. Not all, however, will agree with the late Senator Borah's judgment of this: "The difference between me and Johnson," he once said, "is that I regard questions from the point of view of principles while he regards them from the point of view of personalities. When a man opposes me I do not become angry with him. On the next issue he may agree with me. When a man opposes Johnson, he hates him."

Hiram Johnson was born in Sacramento, California on September 2, 1886. His father, Grove Laurence Johnson, was a corporation lawyer, regarded as one of the cleverest members of the California Bar, a politician and a Congressman. It was of him that a native historian wrote: "The long continuance in the legislature of this adroit and malevolent man is one of the heaviest burdens carried by California today." Hiram Johnson's mother was Annie (DeMontfredy) Johnson.

Young Hiram went to public school in Sacramento and was graduated from the Sacramento High school when he was 17. He studied shorthand and then went into his father's office to study law and work as a stenographer. After a year of this, he left to enter the University of California, but stayed there only until his junior year, when he quit to marry Minnie L. McNeal. He was just 20.

In 1888 Johnson was admitted to the California Bar and began to practice in Sacramento with his father and his brother, Albert. He became a young and respected trial lawyer, "not particularly noted for the quality of his community service." His first fame came around the turn of the century, when he drove the gamblers out of the city; his next when he campaigned for a reform Mayor for the city. When the regular Republicans in this campaign tried to stop him by hiring every hall in the city, Johnson went out and hired a circus tent. His vituperative speeches attracted hundreds and his candidate was elected in a landslide.

In 1902 Johnson and his brother moved to San Francisco. Their partnership was soon dissolved, and Johnson proceeded by himself to build up a successful practice and to become one of the best jury lawyers on the Pacific Coast. But a storm was stirring in California. This state, long machine-ridden, began to bestir itself, and Johnson threw himself into the fight on the side of civic virtue. He became the spokesman of public protest and began to feel he was really working for something. As he put it: "My real life began when I was given an opportunity to quit working for myself and begin working for the people of the State." Johnson was a member of the staff of the prosecuting attorneys investigating the bribery cases which involved leading city officials and almost all public utility corporations in San Francisco, and he was selected in 1908 to take the place of the prosecuting attorney, Francis J. Heney, when the latter was shot down in court during a bribery prosecution.

In 1910 Johnson campaigned for Governor of California, touring the state in a little red automobile with one son driving the car and the other swinging a cowbell to tell the citizens he was going to speak. His platform was clean, reform government and a pledge to drive the Southern Pacific Railroad, of which his father was an attorney, out of politics. He won the fight and kept his pledges. First he assembled a cabinet and official family of young and idealistic reformers and then he proceeded to impress the state with "his simple direct manner and bulldog courage." He instituted a direct, non-partisan primary, a shorter ballot, prison reform, a workmen's compensation law, shorter hours for women—in brief, he made California "a laboratory of reform and advancement."

In 1912 Johnson emerged from local to national importance. In that year he ran for Vice-President with Theodore Roosevelt on the Bull Moose ticket and, though defeated, made an impact on the American political scene. Of him Theodore Roosevelt said to a friend: "Try to keep in touch with Hiram Johnson, for of all public men in this country he is one with whom I find myself in most complete sympathy. You are perfectly safe to follow his lead."

Johnson was re-elected to the Governorship of California in 1914 but served only until 1917, when he was elected United States Senator. It was during the 1916 campaign that he is supposed to have caused the defeat of Charles Evans Hughes (see sketch this issue), who, when he came to California, forgot to shake Johnson's hand, and "thus lost Johnson, California and the election." Once in the Senate, Johnson opposed our entry into the War and later Wilson's attempts at the League of Nations.

In 1920 Harding asked Johnson to be his Vice-President but Johnson, unsympathetic to Harding's political philosophy, refused, and in so doing lost himself the Presidency. Re-elected to the Senate in 1922 and 1928 after an unsuccessful campaign for the Presidency in 1924, Johnson in his third term bitterly opposed all of Hoover's policies and fought almost every major proposal Hoover advanced. He and Hoover hated each other.

The political atmosphere around Johnson calmed down a bit, however, when President Roosevelt took office in 1932, for the two men were, at that time, much in sympathy. Yet when Roosevelt offered Johnson a Cabinet post he refused, and he refused also a place on the 1933 Economic Conference. Johnson, staunch individualist, wanted to leave himself free to fight, if cause for fighting came up. It came in 1935, after Roosevelt endorsed him for his re-election in 1934 (which was won with the support of Hearst and the largest majority any Senator ever got), when Johnson blocked the World Court Plan. And fighting on foreign policy—on reciprocal trade treaties, on neutrality legislation, on international relations—continued long after that, stronger in 1941 than ever before. Johnson in that year sponsored the minority report of the Senate Foreign Relations Committee opposing the Aid-to-Britain Bill; he asserted in the Senate that Roosevelt "in violation of the Constitution" had entered into an "offensive and defensive" alliance with Churchill; he shouted against aid to Russia—"Good God! Did we ever sink so low before as to choose one cutthroat out of two?" Even on December 10, 1941, after he had voted along with all the rest of the Senate for a declaration of war, he attempted to hold up the passage of the bill authorizing the use of National Guard troops and selectees outside the Western Hemisphere.

This "baggy old man in a blue serge suit with white piping on his vest" is admired and respected for the real good he has done, for his tenacity and his fighting ability, but there are some who feel that from a vigorous crusader he has become a rather dour old man. They admit that "when Hiram Johnson is pleased to be genial there are few more winning men alive"; but insist that "when he is pleased to be cantankerous he steps out of competition."

In Washington his is the only Senator's office remaining in the Capitol Building itself, for he refused to move when the Senate Office Building opened. He was too fond of his old three-room suite there with its pictures of California and of himself in various stages of his career and its framed quotation from Lincoln which seems to dominate the room: "I must stand with anybody that stands right; stand with him while he is right and part with him when he goes wrong."

When he leaves his office Senator Johnson, known as a hard worker but a poor mixer, usually walks home (his only exercise now, though he once was a fine rider and swimmer) to spend his evenings with his wife and a detective story, or at the movies, or playing dominoes—"the best domino player in the world," his friends call him. In California the routine is much the same, with just about as much politics as in Washington. There he explains to his judge and lawyer friends that he has always voted as his conscience dictates, that he scorns party labels. "I'm a rotten politician," adds California's biggest vote-getter.

References

Lit Digest 119:13+ Mr 23 '35 por
Newsweek 5:15 Ja 26 '35 por; 16:64 S 9 '40
Time 27:15-16 F 24 '36 por; 36:17 S 9 '40 por; 36:13-14 O 28 '40
Gilbert, C. W. Mirrors of Washington p183-94 1921
Lowry, E. G. Washington Close-Ups p49-60 1921
Tucker, R. T. and Barkley, F. R. Sons of the Wild Jackass p96-122 1932
Who's Who in America
Who's Who in Law
Who's Who in the Nation's Capital

JOHNSON, HOWARD E. 1888(?)–May 1, 1941 Song writer who began career as pianist in theatres; wrote lyrics of *When the*

Moon Comes Over the Mountain, Ireland Must Be Heaven and wrote both music and lyrics for *M-o-t-h-e-r, Where Do We Go From Here?, There's a Broken Heart for Every Light on Broadway,* and *What Do You Want To Make Those Eyes At Me For?*; was author of lyrics for the musical comedy *Tangerine* (1924).

Obituaries

N Y Times p21 My 2 '41 por
Variety 142:78 My 7 '41

JOHNSON, MORDECAI WYATT Jan. 12, 1890- President of Howard University
Address: Howard University, Washington, D. C.

On March 1, 1941, the 74th annual Charter Day of Howard University, the students, faculty, employees, alumni and trustees of the University presented Mordecai Wyatt Johnson with a testimonial, paying tribute to his 15 years of service there. In it they cited the achievements of this "bald, spectacled, light-skinned" educator and clergyman who is the first Negro president of the largest Negro University in the country. They told how he had revolutionized the physical plant of the University, how he had placed its running on a sound financial basis, improved the quality and security of tenure of the teaching staff and insisted on high standards of scholarship.

Tributes to Mordecai Johnson, which include the Spingarn Medal, have been many during the years he has served his people—which means during all his adult life. He was born in Paris, Tennessee, the son of the Reverend Wyatt Johnson, a "silent and stern man, of unbending rectitude," and Carolyn (Freeman) Johnson, "emotional, energetic, inspiring." Mordecai went to public school in his home town and then in the fall of 1903 entered the high school department of Roger Williams University in Nashville. His career there was terminated a year later when the school burned down, and Mordecai moved on to Howe Institute in Memphis, Tennessee. In the fall of 1905 he entered Morehouse College in Atlanta, Georgia and in 1911 was graduated with a B. A.

Johnson received an appointment as a professor of English at Morehouse immediately after graduation. But teaching English wasn't what he wanted to do. That summer he attended the University of Chicago to study the social sciences, and in the fall of 1912 returned to Morehouse to teach economics and history, instead. Other summers of work at Chicago followed, and in 1913 he received a B. A. from this University.

Despite his second degree and his success at teaching, Johnson decided that he wanted to be a clergyman. He left his position at Morehouse in 1913 and entered Rochester Theological Seminary. While there he was pastor of the Second Baptist Church at Mumford, New York. He was graduated from Rochester in 1916—in 1921 he received his Bachelor of Divinity degree for a thesis entitled *The Rise of the Knights Templars*—and

Bachrach

MORDECAI WYATT JOHNSON

proceeded to take the position of student secretary for the Y. M. C. A. For one year he traveled around the Southwest, making a careful study of Negro schools and colleges, as a result of which he recommended the formation of the Southwestern Annual Student Conference. There was a future for Mordecai Johnson in Y. M. C. A. work, but he turned it down. He still wanted to preach. And with his wife—he had been married less than a year to Anna Ethelyn Gardner—he entered the pastorate of the First Baptist Church in Charleston, West Virginia. The Johnsons now have two daughters and three sons.

In Charleston, Dr. Johnson built up a strong church organization and became "the leading spirit in the social and economic life of the colored people" there. He threw himself into every forward movement—was active in the Negro Baptist Convention, became organizer of a cooperative society and a cooperative grocery, was founder of the Charleston branch of the National Association for the Advancement of Colored People. In 1921 he took a leave of absence to do graduate work at Harvard University and in 1922 was awarded a Master of Theology degree. He was one of the speakers at this commencement, and his address on *The Faith of the American Negro* has been called "the most notable one given by a representative of the Negro people since the speech of Booker T. Washington in Atlanta in 1895." This degree was followed by a D. D. from Howard in 1923 and from Gammon Theological Seminary in 1928.

After nine years in Charleston, Dr. Johnson was called to the presidency of Howard University despite his limited academic experience and lack of administrative training. His first address to the University was a call to duty, "simple, sincere, reassuring."

His activities were even more reassuring. Early in his administration the Twenty-Year Plan, a program of educational and physical development, was adopted, increased appropriations from the United States Government and private philanthropy were secured. During the years Dr. Johnson has headed Howard, there have been new academic buildings, new dormitories, new laboratories; the teaching staff has been doubled, teachers' salaries increased, teachers' tenure and security advanced; scholarly publications have been contributed by the faculty; academic standards have been raised to the point where the College of Dentistry, the Law School, the School of Religion and the College of Liberal Arts have all become accredited institutions. These are only steps forward, Dr. Johnson feels: his annual report for 1940 said that the University still needed more teachers, more books, more scholarship aid, more buildings. Under him, the more than 10,000 alumni and more than 200 students of the University feel this will be possible.

In his years at Howard, Dr. Johnson has occasionally been the subject of criticism, most notably in 1938, when a group of alumni charged him with the misuse of PWA money and unsympathetic behavior toward the Dean of Women. He denied these charges and said they were inspired by a group of Negro intellectuals close to the Government who hoped to get jobs in a shake-up. Most of the alumni agreed with him and in their Charter Day Tribute to him in 1941 cited not only the material achievements made during his administration but said to him: "You have instituted and developed democratic practices in the internal administration of the University and, in the face of criticism and pressure and at great personal sacrifice, you have at Howard University maintained academic freedom—the very life blood of a university in a democracy."

References

> Howard University Bul 20:3-5 Ja 1 '41
> Time 31:30+ Mr 28 '38 por
> Brawley, B. G. Negro Builders and Heroes p211-25 1937
> Bullock, R. W. In Spite of Handicaps p7-14 1927
> Leaders in Education 1941
> Ovington, M. W. Portraits in Color p43-52 1927
> Who's Who in America
> Who's Who in Colored America

JOHNSON, NUNNALLY Dec. 5, 1897- Scenarist; motion-picture producer

Address: b. c/o 20th Century-Fox Film Corp, Beverly Hills, Calif; h. 621 N. Maple Dr, Hollywood, Calif.

In February 1941, when the "Oscars" were being awarded at the banquet given by the Academy of Motion Picture Arts and Sciences, *The Grapes of Wrath* came into the limelight twice. Jane Darwell (see sketch this issue) was voted best supporting actress for her portrayal of Ma Joad, and John Ford (see sketch this issue) won an "Oscar" for his work as director of the picture. Behind the scenes was assistant producer Nunnally Johnson, who wrote the script for 20th Century-Fox, transcribing the Steinbeck novel more faithfully than most critics had thought possible. "The story line was clear," Johnson said with reportorial directness, "as old as the Bible—the migration of a people forced from their homes."

If Nunnally Johnson has a credo it might be expressed in the adage: "The story's the thing." This helps to make him a capable producer as well as a talented writer. But he is a writer first of all, aware of the seriousness of his craft. In 1935, when Darryl Zanuck (see sketch this issue) introduced him to the production end of the film business, Johnson took a script to Florida to mull over. He finally confessed that he wasn't getting anywhere. His fingers itched for a pencil or a typewriter. Zanuck gave in and said that he could, from then on, both write and produce.

"The nice thing about it," the thin, nervous, energetic writer-producer explained to critic Van Gelder, "is that since I'm hired as producer I can go out on a lot where a director is kicking my script around and say, 'Listen, what we want you to do is make this picture the way it's written heah on this papuh. Jus' you stick to this papuh.'"

The accent comes from Columbus, Georgia, where Nunnally Johnson was born in 1897, the son of James Nunnally and Pearl (Patrick) Johnson, and where he was educated. He got his first newspaper job there at the age of 16 and stayed in the newspaper business, off and on, until the late '20s, when magazine work occupied most of his time. He worked in the New York *Herald Tribune* city room, had as colleagues Ward Morehouse, Edward Hope, and a young bespectacled fellow named Richard Watts, Jr., who was Harriet Underhill's assistant. Newspaper work there, and on the New York *Post* and other papers, established him in that field. Humorous short stories, especially those for the *Saturday Evening Post,* made him known to a far wider public.

With the depression it became difficult, even for known talents like Nunnally Johnson's, to find markets. "Especially when you are writing humor," he expressed it, "a main thing you need is confidence—you must be sure that your little jokes are funny or you can't keep thinking up little jokes. My jokes hadn't sold, so how could I be sure of them? I was a real worried would-be humorist when I hit this town."

That, of course, was an exaggeration. He could even be humorous in a wry way about the Hollywood venture that dates from 1933: "They told me I could have a job at Paramount if I would pay my own fare from New York. It was humiliating to be so little wanted and—what was worse—I had to borrow the money to pay the railroad."

His first picture as scenarist was *A Bedtime Story.* He also did *Mama Loves Papa* for Paramount in 1933 and *Moulin Rouge* the fol-

NUNNALLY JOHNSON

lowing year. It was in that year, 1934, that he began to work with Darryl Zanuck, 20th Century-Fox producer. Three pictures on which he collaborated were good box office and identified him as a versatile and talented screen writer. The pictures were *The House of Rothschild, Bulldog Drummond Strikes Back* and the Eddie Cantor (see sketch this issue) film *Kid Millions.*

He credits much of the success of the latter to the ideas and dialogue of Arthur Sheekman and Nat Perrin, talks vaguely and humorously of how this comedy success was written. "They say, 'Well now, wouldn't it be funny to have Eddie in a palace?' So you write a big dramatic foundation for a comedy about a palace. Then they say, 'How would it be to have Eddie funny on a desert?' So you work on a desert sequence on the palace foundation. Then you get in something about a sheik and an ice cream factory. Well, I don't know just how it all gets written."

"I make faces when I write," Mr. Johnson admits candidly. "The most fun I have out of writing is imitating the characters. I act out all the parts as I write them. Eddie Cantor watched me one day for 10 minutes [unknown to Mr. Johnson, of course]." He rolled his blue eyes violently to demonstrate. But *Richelieu,* with George Arliss, gave him trouble. "It held me up, trying to get that lip right, like this, see. Very difficult, yes, but I finally got the technic."

Nunnally Johnson is of medium height, his hair thinning out at the part. If one were to type him it would probably be as a newspaperman. He has the keen look of the veteran reporter on the trail of a good story. "He looks like Lee Tracy," said Eileen Creelman, "a tall, lanky, blue-eyed Irish Lee Tracy from the deep South."

In 1935, after he had completed the scenario for *Thanks a Million,* producer Zanuck in-

JOHNSON, NUNNALLY—*Continued*

duced him to accept a contract as assistant producer. That year he did *The Man Who Broke the Bank at Monte Carlo,* a deft comedy with subtle undertones, starring Ronald Colman. In 1936 he worked on *The Prisoner of Shark Island, The Country Doctor* and *Banjo On My Knee.* As assistant producer for 20th Century-Fox he did five pictures the following year and his contract was renewed more favorably. (He is now writing and producing exclusively for 20th Century-Fox.)

Recent successes have been *The Grapes of Wrath; Chad Hanna; Wife, Husband and Friend; Rose of Washington Square; I Was an Adventuress;* and *Tobacco Road,* for which he went back to the Caldwell novel to find a good "story line" for picture purposes. *Roxy Hart* is his latest film. He works in a quiet office, dislikes telephones and probably has a pull with the operator, for his seldom rings. In completing a scenario and putting it on the screen Johnson fuses with his writing talent a capable executive sense. His varied experience has taught him to approach every writing job on its merits, with none of the lost motion that accrues when a writer tackles a new field insufficiently aware of its technical demands.

But Johnson's most valuable asset is his story sense. In writing *Jesse James* for the screen he wanted to recapture the narrative impact he felt when as a boy he first saw it dramatized. "When Jesse put down that gun and turned around, we used to scream at him, and yell, 'Look out, Jesse. Don't put down that gun.' It was a terrific moment. We all knew what was coming. I tried to get some of that in the picture. I wanted to get the feeling of that last scene."

In his work on scenarios, Johnson rewrites page by page, "until every word is the word I want." He has an understandable scorn for scenarists who take their work casually. "Writing is a profession, wherever you do it. And anyone who doesn't take his profession seriously is a fool." He believes that the days of the "idea" man are numbered and that respect for trained writers is on the increase in the cinema capital. This is all to the good, for, "like everybody else, we all want our names on stuff we are not ashamed of."

When Johnson departs from work in pictures it is usually to "relax" in some other field of writing. In 1939 he helped polish up the musical comedy *Nice Goin'* and in 1940 he did some feature work for the newspaper *PM,* in the form of humorous letters to the film editor. Rumor had it that these were terminated, (1) because the movie industry's feelings were being hurt by Johnson's sharp humor, and (2) because *PM* was willing to pay more money for Ben Hecht's column than for one by Johnson. Neither rumor has been confirmed.

Mr. Johnson's marriage on February 4, 1940 to Doris Bowdon of Memphis, Tennessee was his third. She is a 20th Century-Fox starlet who played Rosasharn in *The Grapes of Wrath.* He has two daughters: one of them, Marjorie

Johnson, the child of his first marriage, is a writer; the other, Nora, is by his second marriage in March 1927 which ended in divorce in February 1938.

One of the highest-paid writer-producers in Hollywood, Johnson probably enjoys his work for its own sake as sincerely as anyone in Hollywood. He likes Hollywood but takes it with a sense of humor, confesses that he "almost rented a house out there because the owner had invented a contraption to cool off the roof. Water poured down on it like rain. . . Did you know at picture openings they often applaud the sight of rain? At one Christmas week preview everyone cheered a snowstorm.

"Yes," he continued, "Hollywood is all right. I have a good time there. In fact, it's about the only place now where I can find my friends. A party looks like the old *Herald Tribune* city room. . . No, it looks more like a speakeasy."

References

N Y Herald Tribune p12 F 2 '40 por; p9 F 5 '40
N Y Times Book R p2 S 1 '40 por
Photoplay 53:22 N '39 por
International Motion Picture Almanac

JÓNASSON, HERMANN (yōn'á-sún)
1896- Premier of Iceland
Address: Reykjavik, Iceland

Since April 1940, when the *Althing* voted that "the situation now created makes it impossible for His Majesty, the King of Iceland, to execute his royal power" and vested it in the Icelandic Premier, Hermann Jónasson, and his Cabinet, Iceland has been an independent state, no longer under the sovereignty of King Christian of Denmark. And this actual independence, born of war, conquest and blockade, was legitimatized in May 1941 when the *Althing* moved to establish a republic.

Yet Iceland, a country without a navy, army or air force, strategically situated in the North Atlantic, has not been left to guard its independence unaided. Early in 1939 Germany sent warships and a "scientific expedition" there, but despite them the *Althing* refused Nazi demands for an air base on the island. Later, at the beginning of the War, a good many Germans were "touring" there, and shipwrecked Nazi crews frequently turned up. Aware of this and aware of Iceland's potentialities as an air and naval base for convoy work in the Atlantic, the British on May 10, 1940 occupied the island.

Premier Jónasson formally protested the landing of the expeditionary force, and it is rumored that the natives' reception of the troops was "anything but warm." Nevertheless, relations between the occupiers and the Icelanders soon became settled when it was demonstrated that the British had no intention of interfering in Iceland's internal affairs. It was little more than a year later, however, when the British suggested to Premier Jónasson that their Canadian and English troops there were needed elsewhere and that the United States was prepared to take over if "invited." He accepted the British suggestion and wrote President Roosevelt a letter stating the conditions under which occupation would be acceptable.

On July 7, 1941 President Roosevelt formally announced to Congress that American troops had landed in Iceland and that he had given the people of Iceland "the assurance that the American forces sent there would in no way interfere with the internal and domestic affairs of that country and that immediately upon the termination of the present international emergency all American forces will be at once withdrawn." The British hailed the occupation as "one of the most important events for some 'time past," and the Icelandic *Althing* voted its approval of it, 39 to 3.

Although American and possibly some British troops are in late 1941 busy in Iceland, providing aerial guardians for British-bound cargo ships clear up to the shores of England and erecting a dome of air power over the whole North Atlantic, the people of Iceland intend to continue their life in its ordinary, everyday way. The fishermen will continue to get their livelihood from the herring that swarm in island waters; the farmers will continue to till their bleak and unfertile land; the cows will be led out to pasture in the morning and brought home to milk at night. And the parliamentary form of government will prevail as it has prevailed in Iceland for more than a thousand years.

Under the Danish crown since 1381, and in 1918 declared an independent state with the Danish King as its monarch, Iceland has been governed during almost its entire history by its *Althing,* now an assembly of 42 popularly elected members, and in later years by its own Prime Minister as well, who must be an Icelander and live in Reykjavik. The man who has that position today is Hermann Jónasson, a powerfully built Icelander who was born in 1896 on a farm in northern Iceland.

Jónasson went to high school in the capital city of Reykjavik, and then to the University of Iceland, where he specialized in the study of law. After being graduated he became the assistant to the Reykjavik judge and continued in this position until 1928, when "the bulging Jónasson biceps and barrel chest filled the uniform" of police commissioner of Reykjavik. He held this position for six years, until 1934, when he entered politics.

In the spring of that year he was elected to the *Althing* as a member of the Progressive Party and by August of the same year had become Prime Minister. When in 1937 a coalition government was formed and the Cabinet, formerly composed of three members, was enlarged to five—two Progressives, two Conservatives and one Socialist were in it— Jónasson became Prime Minister of the new Cabinet. He continued to head it, without interruption, not faced, as were other Prime Ministers, by problems of unemployment, indebtedness or factionalism.

Keystone

HERMANN JÓNASSON

Nevertheless on October 22, 1941 the Iceland Government resigned. The reasons for Premier Jónasson's resignation were thought to be sharp rises in living costs and "unsettled difficulties" in connection with the joint occupation of Iceland. Although this first resignation was not accepted, on November 7 he resigned again. This time it was accepted. The Regent, as before, asked him and the Cabinet to remain in office until February 1942 when a new government could be formed.

In his youth Premier Jónasson, a rugged man with thick dark hair, square jaw and "a face that reflects determination and courage," was annually crowned king of the *Glima* and for many years kept winning this Icelandic wrestling championship in Norse games handed down through the centuries from the Vikings. He is still interested in this sport, and hopes to be able to enjoy it for a long time to come.

References

    Liv Age 360 :542-3 Ag '41
    Time 35 :28 Ap 22 '40 por

Europa

JONES, BILLY Mar. 15, 1889—Nov. 23, 1940 Early radio star, member of the team of Ernie Hare and Billy Jones, the Happiness Boys.

Obituaries

    N Y Herald Tribune p42 N 24 '40
    N Y Times p49 N 24 '40 por

JONES, CHESTER LLOYD Mar. 6, 1881—Jan. 13, 1941 Commercial expert and professor of economics at the University of Wisconsin; in 1918 was a director of the Bureau of Foreign Agents of the War Trade Board and during post-War years was a com-

JONES, CHESTER LLOYD—*Continued*
mercial attaché of the United States Department of Commerce in several foreign capitals; from 1929 to 1935 directed the Wisconsin School of Commerce; author of many books dealing with economics and American foreign interests.

References

Leaders in Education   1941
Who's Who in America
Who's Who in Government

Obituaries

N Y Herald Tribune p16 Ja 14 '41

BILLY JONES

JONES, NORMAN L. Sept. 19, 1870—Nov. 15, 1940 Justice of the Illinois State Supreme Court who served on the state bench for 25 years.

References

Who's Who in America
Who's Who in Law

Obituaries

N Y Herald Tribune p10 N 16 '40
N Y Times p17 N 16 '40

JONES, RUFUS M(ATTHEW) Jan. 25, 1863- Quaker leader; professor emeritus of Haverford College
Address: h. Haverford, Pa; South China, Me.

Dr. Rufus M. Jones, Quaker leader, preacher, author of almost 50 books, professor emeritus of philosophy, for many years has been "the nearest thing the Friends have to an international spokesman." In his late 70's, he is still active, still a vital part of that work

which, carried on without any distinctions of race, creed or political party, "has always been received with warm and tender love, answering the love that came to give." The Friends' Service Committee, which he helped to found and which he heads, is under his leadership bringing succor to war-racked Europe, to underprivileged America. Under his guidance camps have been established in this country for conscientious objectors so that they may "make a constructive contribution to national life." And with all this, Dr. Jones continues to preach at colleges and churches and to produce a book a year.

His latest published work (August 1941) is *A Small-town Boy*, in which he writes in fond and friendly fashion of life in China, Maine—of its town meeting, of Quaker meetings, of the old grocery store, the town's center of debate and culture, of local characters. A "genuine and genial" book, it reflects the spirit and the history of the man who wrote it. Together with *Finding the Trail of Life* (1926) it reveals the boyhood of Rufus Matthew Jones, who was born in the small Quaker village of South China, Maine on January 25, 1863. At his birth, his Aunt Peace, who was supposedly gifted with prophetic vision, announced: "This child will one day bear the message of the Gospel to distant lands and to peoples across the sea."

These words meant much in the Jones home, a home "where religion kept its fires always burning." Young Rufus' father, Edwin Jones, was a pious Quaker farmer; his mother, Mary G. (Hoxie) Jones, was the daughter of a Quaker cabinetmaker. At his mother's knee Rufus learned his Bible, and he learned its meaning and the meaning of his religion from the many itinerant Quaker preachers who came to stay with the Joneses. "I said 'thee' and 'thy' to everybody and I would fully as soon have used profane words as have said 'you' or 'yours' to any person," he remembers, and he grew up not only with a firm belief in the Quaker religion but with a certain conviction that he belonged to a chosen people.

Rufus Jones started his formal education at the age of four at the little country schoolhouse in South China and continued there until he transferred for three months to Oak Grove Seminary. Then, at the age of sixteen and one-half, he was granted a free scholarship in the famous Friends' School in Providence, Rhode Island—now the Moses Brown School. He set out for Providence, a lad who was, according to his own description, "very thin, nearly six feet tall, extremely green and awkward, but wide awake, keen, eager, and ambitious. I had never seen a real city. I had never been inside a railroad train. I had no idea what a steamboat was like."

The years there were "wonderful" years: Rufus was on the athletic teams, at the head of his classes, and his religious life was "steadily developing." Then Haverford College in Pennsylvania gave him a scholarship covering full tuition and living expenses. He entered this Quaker school in 1882 and three years later received his B. A. He had studied Greek, Latin, mathematics, philosophy; he had done research on American history and on "Mysticism and its Exponents"; he had been business manager and editor of *The Haverfordian*, president of the college Y. M. C. A., president of the political club; and he had been active among Friends and in Friends' work in Philadelphia and Germantown. One year after graduation he received a Master's Degree. He also holds D. D., Th. D., Litt. D., and LL. D. degrees.

Rufus Jones had intended, during his first undergraduate years, to study law, and a generous Quaker merchant offered him the necessary money. But Jones saw, "at first dimly and then more clearly," that he could not accept the offer. And as he worked on his thesis for graduation, on mysticism, he knew that "I had here found the field of my life work. Hereafter all my reading and thinking and research work bore directly or indirectly on some phase of mysticism." In later years he was to write many comprehensive volumes on the subject and to demonstrate in what H. H. Brinton calls his greatest contribution to Quaker history, that Quakerism "is not an isolated phenomenon but a movement which took shape and persisted as an integral part of the great current of mystical religion flowing out of a remote past."

The decision to study mysticism marked one turning point in Jones' career; the decision to teach at Oakwood Seminary, a Quaker boarding school at Union Springs, New York, instead of accepting a fellowship for graduate study in history at the University of Pennsylvania, marked another. He stayed there for a year and then went on the first of many trips abroad, studying in Paris and at the University of Heidelberg, meeting other Quakers. He returned to America to accept a position as teacher at the Friends' School in Providence, where he had formerly been a student. At the end of his first year of teaching he married Sarah Hawkshurst Coutant. "It was a beautiful union," he says, "and though destined to be short, it has through all the successive years colored and hallowed my life." After Mrs. Jones died, Dr. Jones was both mother and father to their son, Lowell Coutant, until he died in his eleventh year.

Two years in Providence were followed in 1899 by four years as principal of Oak Grove Seminary, a Quaker boarding school at Vassalboro, Maine, ten miles from his old home. This position, "full of responsibility and labor," was ended when "the call came to me" to become editor of the *Friends' Review* in Philadelphia, which later became *The American Friend*, and to be an instructor in philosophy at Haverford with an opportunity to do work in philosophy at the University of Pennsylvania. Rufus Jones began those 40 years of teaching (he became professor emeritus in 1934), which have associated him so inseparably with Haverford, and that Quaker work on a wider scale which has

Hans Roth

RUFUS M. JONES

made him perhaps the best known member of his faith.

In 1890 Rufus Jones had been "recorded" a minister in the Society of Friends, and in the years that followed he preached widely in colleges, churches, meetings and at one period as an "itinerant preacher" in the West. He had decided from the first, he says, "never to write a sermon, and I have always been resolved throughout my life not to preach in any case unless I felt profoundly impressed at the time that I had in my soul a living message for the particular occasion in hand." Along with his preaching, Rufus Jones was busy studying philosophy, at Harvard (M. A. 1901) and elsewhere, acting as trustee of Bryn Mawr College, teaching his classes, and traveling all over the world, especially in England. In this work, from 1902 on, he had the "rich cooperation" of his second wife, Elizabeth Bartram Cadbury of the Quaker Chocolate family. They have one daughter, Mary Hoxie.

In the winter of 1905 to 1906 Professor Jones set to work "seriously and systematically" on what was to be for many years his "magnum opus." When done, it covered the complete history of the Quaker movement from its birth to the year 1900 and further included a history of the mystical movements which preceded the rise of Quakerism. Six volumes, two of them by W. C. Braithwaite, presented these studies, the last of them, *The Later Periods of Quakerism*, published in 1921. He was doing this research and writing, along with other work which included the editing of *The American Friend*.

In 1912 Dr. Jones resigned the editorship of this paper. A year later he was editing an international monthly journal, *Present Day Papers*, which was forced to cease publication when the First World War broke out. This War brought Dr. Jones new duties and

JONES, RUFUS M.—*Continued*

new responsibilities. Like all Quakers a militant pacifist who believes that there is no good war or bad peace, Dr. Jones in 1917 organized the Friends' Service Committee to show that, while Quakers wouldn't accept military service, they were still ready to accept danger and hardship. He fought a long and eventually successful battle to have service with Friends' overseas units accepted as an alternative to service under arms.

These units, under Jones, went into the destroyed areas of northern France, rebuilt villages, including the whole destroyed Verdun section. When the Armistice was signed they bought up miscellaneous stores which the Army in Europe had left over and then sold them, using the profits to put up new buildings, to pay wages to German prisoners which their families got, for rehabilitation work in general. The Friends' Service Committee fed German children, put Polish refugees back on their farms, fought the famine in Russia. Later, during the Spanish Civil War, they fed both sides; and in 1941 they were still helping Spanish refugees in France. After the German anti-Jewish activities of November 1938, the Friends offered their services to the destitute thousands. When the Reich refused the offer, Jones himself with two associates went to Berlin and personally asked for permission to send relief workers. He told the heads of the Gestapo there: "We represent no governments, no international organizations, no sects, and we have no interest in propaganda in any form. . . We do not ask who is to blame for the trouble which may exist; we do not come to judge or criticize but to inquire whether there is anything we can do to promote human welfare and to relieve suffering." The request was granted, and Dr. Jones recalls that "when we left the room, they helped us on with our overcoats. And that," he adds with a grin, "is more than any one in Washington ever did for us." Two years later Dr. Jones was preparing to lead the Friends to the relief of Poland; after Poland to France; after France to other devastated countries. And at the same time he guided and guides their activities in the United States when they work with and for West Virginia miners or California Okies; when they build schools in Mexico or hostels for European refugees in Indiana.

Despite all the activity he leads and inspires, and despite illnesses that have plagued him much of his life, Dr. Jones today is a "tall, pink-cheeked, white-crested," erect man who looks taller than his six feet and walks with enormous strides at a fast pace. He still lives overlooking Haverford's cricket green and likes to watch from the window the sport he once played. But that's during school sessions only. Once spring comes he hastens up to South China, where he roams through the countryside and goes swimming (the doctors won't let him swing an ax as he used to love to do). He enjoys this sport "with loud whoops that startle his native Maine woods."

Many honors have come to Dr. Jones during his years of work. Ten colleges have given him honorary degrees; in 1938 he was the joint recipient of Philadelphia's Bok Award of $10,000 as that city's outstanding citizen; on his seventy-fifth birthday students of Quaker history presented him with a book in his honor, *Children of Light*, edited by H. H. Brinton. Probably the honor that has meant as much as any was accorded him in 1937 when he was made chairman of the Second World Conference of Friends, for as chairman he was able to address the world through an international radio hookup. To the world he gave the Quaker creed: "Quakerism as a way of life partakes of a universal spirit. . . Quakers are bound to keep humble and recognize their littleness. The Quaker philosophy of life sees in a human spirit something that of all things in the universe is most like that ultimate reality we call God, who is Spirit. Spirit like ours cannot come from anything else than Spirit."

References

Christian Cent 56:307 Mr 8 '39
Cur Hist 51:39 My '40 por
Fortune 22:70 D '40 por
N Y Herald Tribune X p14, 25+ Mr 10 '40 il por
Read Digest 36:115-18 Ap '40
Time 30:40 S 13 '37 por; 36:52 Jl 22 '40 por

Brinton, H. H. ed. Children of Light, in Honor of Rufus M. Jones 1938
Ferm, V. T. A. ed. Contemporary American Theology 1st ser. p191-215 2v 1932-33
Jones, R. M. Finding the Trail of Life 1926
Jones, R. M. Small-town Boy 1941
Jones, R. M. Trail of Life in College 1929
Jones, R. M. Trail of Life in the Middle Years 1934
Leaders in Education 1941
Twelve Modern Apostles and Their Creeds p110-25 1926
Who's Who Among North American Authors
Who's Who in America

JORDAN, FRANK C(RAIG) Sept. 24, 1865—Feb. 15, 1941 Nationally known astronomer and director of the Allegheny Observatory at the University of Pittsburgh who, with his wife, was burned to death in a fire at their home; was an expert on variable stars; represented the United States at the convention of the International Astronomical Union in Paris in 1935; taught at the University from 1910 until his death.

References

American Men of Science
Leaders in Education 1941
Who's Who in America

Obituaries

N Y Times p36 F 16 '41
Sch & Soc 53:243 F 22 '41
Sci ns 93:201 F 28 '41

JORDAN, JAMES EDWARD *See* Mc-Gee, F. and McGee, M.

JORDAN, MARIAN *See* McGee, F. and McGee, M.

JOWITT, SIR WILLIAM ALLEN (jou'-it) 1885- British Solicitor General

Address: b. Royal Courts of Justice, London, W. C. 2; h. 35, Upper Brook St, London, W. 1, England

When in 1929 Sir William Allen Jowitt was elected to Parliament on a Liberal ticket and within a week changed over to the Labor Party and accepted a remunerative office under it, there were many who questioned his motives. In 1941 he is England's Solicitor General, responsible with the Attorney General for all the legal business of the Crown. And none in England questions either his motives or his competence.

"A cool, self-possessed duelist with a mind as keen as a sword blade, wary and nimble-witted, thoroughly sure of his ground," Jowitt is never "truculent or overbearing" as he sustains the case of the Crown against individuals or companies in civil and criminal suits. "His strokes of wit leave no ugly wounds." In appearance he lacks completely the keen, eagle glance or strong features of the popular idea of a successful prosecuting lawyer, and an air of detachment and impartiality is characteristic. His voice is "easily produced; it has little volume, but carries well. Colorless and toneless and marvelously even, yet it is genuinely pleasant." In court and out, Sir William has a charming personality—even-tempered and patient.

This distinguished lawyer was the only boy in a family of 10 children. His father, the Reverend William Jowitt, Rector of Stevenage, Hertfordshire, sent him to Marlborough and then to New College, Oxford. After Oxford he read for the Bar and was called by the Middle Temple in 1909. Very shortly after, he began to prove the fine quality of his legal mind. He was a success as an advocate, his reputation and fortune grew, and he became a K. C.

It was in 1922 that Jowitt decided to go in for politics. He was elected to Parliament for the Hartlepools division, a shipbuilding and general industrial region in the Northeast, as a Liberal of radical tendencies. Two years later he was a member of the Royal Commission on the Lunacy Law and in that same year, at the division which wrecked the first Labor Administration, he voted not with his own party but for the Government. At the next election he lost his seat.

At the time of Labor's second victory, in 1929, Jowitt, who had been spending his time in private law practice, came back to Parliament, elected as a Liberal for Preston, Lancashire. The late Ramsay MacDonald at that time was forming his Administration and found himself faced with a dearth of learned advocates who held Labor views. MacDonald asked Jowitt to become Attorney General and

SIR WILLIAM ALLEN JOWITT

Jowitt accepted. "Those like myself," he wrote to MacDonald, "who have hitherto taken their stand as Radicals must now consider whether they ought not to render active support to your party as being today the only party which is an effective instrument to carry through those reforms which the country desires."

There was an immediate controversy over this shift, and arguments and brick-bats flew in the pages of the London *Times* and other journals. Jowitt's constituents didn't ask him to resign, but the Preston Reform Club passed a strongly-worded resolution against his action. Jowitt decided the only thing for him to do was to seek re-election as a Labor member, and on July 31, 1929 he got in without difficulty. Since Attorneys General are always knights, he became Sir William.

Jowitt's chief Parliamentary task in 1930 was the Trades Union Bill, and in the year following he brought in the Trades Disputes Bill to clarify the right to strike in a purely industrial cause. In 1931 he also became a Privy Councillor. This was the year of the financial crisis, and MacDonald took office as Prime Minister of a National Government. Jowitt went over with him and as a result was expelled from the Labor Party. He ran for election from the Combined Universities constituency, but the voters wouldn't have him. Several attempts were made to find him a seat in Parliament, but they all failed. As a result, in January 1932 he resigned his post as Attorney General and went back to private practice.

Private practice proved twice as lucrative as a Government post. (An Attorney General makes £10,000 a year, twice the salary of the Prime Minister.) He specialized in difficult and complicated commercial cases. In one of these, a suit between two radio companies in 1933, he spoke for 17 days running, and it

JOWITT, SIR WILLIAM ALLEN—*Cont.*
was estimated that his speeches totaled about half a million words.

In November 1936 Jowitt made his peace with the Labor Party and was elected for Ashton-under-Lyne, near Manchester, without opposition. He continued to serve in Parliament, "one of the most unpartisan speakers the House has known," and in May 1940 was made Solicitor General by Winston Churchill. In these years his principles have been made clear. He is a free trader and exponent of orthodox finance. In the days when peace seemed possible he was for arbitration in international affairs rather than for increased armaments. He believed then and he believes now in an active fight against unemployment, in the extension of social insurances, in the progressive improvement of working conditions.

Jowitt's London home is in aristocratic Brook Street and he has a country house at Wittersham in Kent. In 1913 he married Lesley, the second daughter of J. P. M'Intyre, and they have one daughter.

References

> Amalgamated Engineering Union Mo J p59-60 Ja '31 por
>
> Johnston, J. Hundred Commoners 1931
> Who's Who

JOYCE, JAMES   Feb. 2, 1882—Jan. 13, 1941   Irish author; first writing appeared in the *Fortnightly Review* and his first book, *Chamber Music,* a collection of poetry, was published in 1907; *Dubliners* (1914) and *The Portrait of the Artist as a Young Man* (1916) were followed by *Ulysses,* which was the center of a storm of controversy and wasn't legally admitted into the United States until 1933; latest work, interrupted often by his eye afflictions, was *Finnegan's Wake,* which appeared as *Work in Progress* in pamphlet form and in magazines and was published in the United States in 1939.

References

> Cur Hist 39:699-704 Mr '34
> Liv Age 346:362-3 Je '34
> New Repub 77:200-1 D 27 '33; 102:313 Mr 4 '40
> Pub W 124:2079 D 16 '33
> Time 33:78 My 8 '39 pors; 35:86 F 19 '40 por
> Author's and Writer's Who's Who
> Budgen, F. S. C. James Joyce and the Making of Ulysses 1934
> Chesterton, G. K. All I Survey p62-8 1933
> Golding, L. James Joyce 1933
> Gorman, H. S. James Joyce 1940
> Gorman, H. S. James Joyce; His First Forty Years 1924
> Griffin, G. Wild Geese p22-45 1938
> Kunitz, S. J. ed. Living Authors
> Magee, W. K. Irish Literary Portraits p131-50, p153-58 1935

> Rosenfeld, P. Men Seen p23-42 1925
> Verschoyle, D. ed. English Novelists p301-16 1936
> Who's Who

Obituaries

> N Y Herald Tribune p14 Ja 13 '41 pors
> N Y Herald Tribune Books p1+ Ja 26 '41 por
> Pub W 139:248 Ja 18 '41
> Sat R Lit 23:3-4+ Ja 25 '41 por
> Time 37:76 Ja 20 '41; 37:72+ F 10 '41 por
> Times [London] Lit Sup p45+ Ja 25 '41 por

KAGAWA, TOYOHIKO   (kä-gä'wä tō'-yô-hē'kô)   July 10, 1888-   Religious leader
Address: c/o Harper & Brothers, 49 E. 33rd St, New York City

Toyohiko Kagawa, it was once said, "is a prophet without a beard, a Mussolini without authority, a Gandhi without the local color of goat, loin cloth and loom." Evangelist, Christian leader, author, social worker, poet, pacifist, he has brought his message to millions in Japan and all over the world. It is a message of economic Christianity, through the cooperative movement. This to him is "the Christian way of economics," and "we cannot build a Christian world," he says, "until our economic life is Christian."

Kagawa has won millions of his countrymen to the cooperative plan—fishermen, weavers, doctors, farmers among them. He would like to win the world. Then, he feels, there would be peace. As he said some years ago: "The way to stop war is by cooperative movements, by cooperative international trade, by cooperative marketing. . . We must have the spirit of God incarnated in economic schemes and projects." He still believes this, despite his own country's conflict with China. An ardent pacifist who as late as 1936 was assuring the Western world that 99 per cent of his people wanted peace, he has become since the outbreak of war a thorn in the side of the Japanese militarists. His followers have been threatened, his public appearances met with resistance, and he himself in August 1940 was put in jail, charged with "violating the military code." He was freed after a month, prohibited from writing any article or book, preaching or giving out any interview on the subject of the War.

After that time he kept busy with his practical work among the poor and in the church. It was while occupied with this work that he came to the United States in January 1941—to confer with church and mission leaders here on the newly organized Church of Christ in Japan, created with his help from the merging of 42 denominations. He and Bishop Abe spent much time reassuring American churchmen that this merger was not the result of government domination or pressure, that it would not make the Japanese Church "a sycophantic instrument of empire." And

Kagawa also spent some time in beginning negotiations for a patent on a new game called "chemical chess" which he worked out in prison. Its purpose, he says, is to drive home to its players "the divine design in nature."

Half blind, his heart, kidneys and lungs weakened, a short, slight man with thick glasses who "looks more like a blind beggar than one of the most powerful forces among the masses of Japan," Kagawa has never ceased working for those things in which he believes. "Doctors gave me up years ago. It is faith in God that has kept me going," he says. From that faith he has launched and now supports in part or whole nineteen churches, seventeen kindergartens and schools, six cooperative societies, an ex-prisoners' home, an employment agency for girls, a social research bureau and two monthly periodicals, *Clouds* and *Columns*. With that faith he has converted thousands upon thousands.

He was not born with that faith. His father, Junichi Kagawa, was a Buddhist, a member of the Japanese Cabinet who served one term as secretary of the Privy Council. His mother was not a Christian either. His father left his wife for her, a Geisha girl in Kobe, where their son, Toyohiko, was born. Both parents died when he was only four, and he was brought up in Awa by his father's neglected wife. She hated this son of her errant husband. "You are the son of my enemy," she screamed at him day after day.

Toyohiko was sent regularly to the Buddhist Temple to study the Confucian classics and to be drilled in the fundamentals of the faith. He left Awa in his teens, however, to live with an uncle in the city of Tokushima, and there he entered the Boys' Middle School. At the same time he received permission to attend English Bible classes in order to learn the language. He learned more than just the language. The Bible opened up "vistas of a new and ever-enlarging life." Kagawa became a Christian. His uncle stormed and threatened and finally turned him out. But Kagawa prayed: "Oh, God, make me like Christ!"

Christian missionaries, impressed by his prayer, took him in and gave him a scholarship to the Presbyterian College in Tokyo. He entered this school in 1905 and for a while devoted himself avidly to the study in English of the works of Kant, Darwin, Ruskin, and especially Tolstoi, from whom he received his still-ardent belief in non-violence. His college studies were cut short when he became stricken with tuberculosis. He went to a fishing village not far from Kobe to recover, but the poverty and misery there wouldn't let him rest. Told by the doctors that he had only a short while to live, he replied: "If that is so I will make every day count."

In 1908 Kagawa settled down in the slums of Shinkawa, probably the worst of any in the world at that time. His home was a hut, six by six, surrounded by poverty and misery. For 14 years he lived there, visiting the sick, preaching to thieves and murderers and

Blackstone

TOYOHIKO KAGAWA

derelicts about the "God who cares," doing all he could to improve conditions. While there he finished his *Before the Dawn* (1924) and *The Psychology of Poverty*, both of which sold thousands of copies in Japan and brought the Japanese Government's attention to slum conditions. To these books and to Kagawa's work, almost directly, can be traced the Government's decision in 1921 to set aside 20,000,-000 yen to clean up the slums.

When Kagawa quit work in the slums, because "one individual working for individuals cannot change society," he had contracted trachoma (thirteen operations have not been able to cure it, and he has lost the sight of one eye altogether), four front teeth had been lost when a criminal attacked him, his health had been weakened. But he had gained a wife and helpmate. In 1914 Haru, daughter of Fusakichi Shiba, had married him and begun to assist him with his work. And he had laid a solid foundation for his views as a Christian radical.

After spending some time at Princeton University in the United States, Kagawa returned to Japan to organize the Labor Federation in 1918. This wasn't his first attempt at labor organization—in 1912 he had founded the first labor union in Japan among the shipyard workers—nor was it his last. He organized the Farmers' National Federation, the first laborers' school, the first laborers' newspaper. From 1919 on he took an active part in politics, speaking and writing for universal suffrage, for social reform in general, for the improvement of labor conditions. For this he was jailed during the rice riots of 1919 and again during the shipyard strikes of 1921. But the things he worked for were temporarily obtained: the Japanese won universal manhood suffrage, and in 1925 the law against trade-unionism was amended.

(Continued next page)

KAGAWA, TOYOHIKO—*Continued*

Even before then, however, the Japanese Government recognized the effectiveness of his work. In 1923 he was asked to help on the relief committees after the earthquake and fire that ravaged Kobe. One year later he became a member of the Imperial Economic Conference. Five years later, in 1929, the Government asked him to organize the social work in the city of Tokyo at a salary of $9,000 a year and the use of an auto. Kagawa took the job but not the money or auto and, working 10 days each month, brought about a complete reorganization of the Bureau of Social Welfare. When this was finished he resigned, for there was much else to be done.

There was his labor work: since 1923 he had been an active member of the Labor Exchange Committee. There was political work: never a candidate for Parliament himself, he had been organizing the masses to elect farmer and labor candidates to the national Diet. And there was, finally, his cooperative work, which, more than anything else, seemed to him the answer to Japan's and the world's needs. Kagawa revitalized the cooperatives which had existed for some years in Japan, built up new ones, remade the credit union movement, helped found cooperative schools. As part of all this there was the work of Christianizing Japan.

In 1931 Kagawa came to America to explain and to spread his ideas. He told of his program of social action, of its three foundation stones: first, the conversion of "individualists in whose conscience society is still unborn"; second, Christian fellowship on community lines, which meant approaching people "from their occupation, their daily work"; third, the relation of the converted individualist to the Christian community through "mutual aid" or "love in action." His tour was fairly successful, but caused no great excitement.

It was different when he came to America again at the end of 1935. The Federal immigration authorities refused him admission because of his trachoma, and it was only after church members throughout the country interceded in his behalf that President Roosevelt allowed him to enter on a seven months' visitors' permit and under the condition that he be constantly accompanied by a doctor and nurse and follow regulations laid down by the Public Health Service. His tour was sponsored by liberal evangelical churchmen, and there was wide interest wherever he spoke—among ministers whom he had scolded because they did nothing but "preach, preach, preach," among laymen who were eager to meet the man who had performed such practical miracles as marketing three-piece men's suits for $1.35. There was also strong opposition. A number of churchmen under the leadership of Dr. J. Frank Norris claimed that he was preaching "a sinister plan to advocate consumers' cooperatives and socialism under the cloak of the Christian Church." And there were businessmen who were alarmed at his doctrines and at his successful sponsorship and convincing

exposition of seven kinds of cooperative movements.

But antagonistic groups were unable to keep Kagawa from speaking. He answered their accusations in his reedy voice with its heavy Japanese accent. "Because I want the love of God to be applied in industry, in economics, in daily life, I am criticized as a Communist," he said. "What a joke!" And 750,000 people in 150 cities heard his message.

When Kagawa sailed from the United States for the annual convention of the World Sunday School Association in Norway, he left behind him a National Coordinating Advisory Committee to attempt to carry on his work and a committee to raise $300,000 in 10 years to build 1,000 rural churches in Japan. He also left a plea. "I ask your prayers," he told the American people, "for the maintenance of peace between this country and Japan."

He returned to his own country just before the beginning of the war with China, and when the war began found quite helpless the All-Japan Anti-War League which he had organized in 1928 with the Japanese Federation of Labor as its center. He remained silent for a while on the subject of the War, though his actions (he was the only one of the Japanese Christian leaders who refused to sign a statement saying that the fighting in China was a war of self defense) showed his uncompromising pacifism. Quietly he continued with his work, and in 1940 he headed an aggressive nationwide evangelistic movement which drew 86,485 people in 247 meetings.

After his prison term in 1940 he retired for recuperation, meditation and writing to an island in the Inland Sea. But he was shortly back in Osaka, Japan, revitalizing the evangelical work of the National Christian Council, teaching the Bible in the mornings and preaching the Gospel at public meetings in the evening of every day. This work, together with his leadership of the "Friends of Jesus," the Kingdom of God movement and the Kagawa Fellowship, as well as his continued efforts for cooperatives, became his concern again after his return to Japan in September 1941. In December 1941, with Japan and the United States at war, his American publishers could give no word of him.

Japan's most prolific writer, in his many years of activity Kagawa has written more than 100 works on economic, agrarian and devotional subjects, on history, philosophy, sociology. There are novels, poems, articles, too—among those available in English translations *A Grain of Wheat* (1933); *Christ and Japan* (1934); *Songs From the Slums* (1935); *Meditations on the Cross* (1935); *Brotherhood Economics* (1936); and *Behold the Man* (1941), a life of Jesus in the form of a novel, called "vivid, emotional, at times almost cinematic in its blood-and-thunders."

Despite the royalties from these works and the income from his magazines, Kagawa is a poor man. With his wife and their son and two daughters he lives simply and humbly in a modest home outside Tokyo.

The family budget is limited to $40 a month, and the rest of Kagawa's income is devoted to his work. His wife, whose special field is social work among women, still helps him, and his son is already a leader in Sunday School activities.

References

Atlan 157 :594-600 My '36
China W R 93 :58-60 Je 8 '40 il pors
Christian Cent 50 :1270-2 O 11 '33 ; 52 : 965-6 Jl 24 '35
Christian Sci Mon Mag p4+ Je 29 '38 il pors
Forum 95 :17-21 Ja '36 por (Same abr. Read Digest 28 :66-8 F '36)
Newsweek 6 :22 D 28 '35 ; 7 :42 Ap 25 '36 por
Pub W 128 :2319-21 D 28 '35 por
Time 26 :19 D 30 '35 por ; 28 :38 Jl 6 '36 por ; 36 :37 S 9 '40 por

Axling, W. Kagawa 1932
Baumann, M. Kagawa, an Apostle of Japan pam 1936
Ferguson, J. M. M. Kagawa the Fearless pam 1937
Heline, T. Kagawa, a Master Servant of the Savior Type pam nd
Hunter, A. A. Three Trumpets Sound 1939
Myers, H. W. Kagawa, Reverend Toyohiko, the Sensei of the Kobe Slums nd
Reid, T. W. Kagawa : Mystic and Man of Action pam 1937
Tiltman, M. H. God's Adventurers p166-82 1933
Van Baalen, J. K. Toyohiko Kagawa, the Christian pam 1936
Who's Who
Who's Who in Japan

KAHN, GUS(TAV GERSON) Nov. 6, 1886—Oct. 8, 1941 Popular song writer ; wrote many well known tunes, among them *Mammy, My Blue Heaven* and *Memories* ; collaborated with many famous composers but worked most consistently with Walter Donaldson ; went to Hollywood with Donaldson in 1933 and contributed lyrics to many screen musicals ; produced an average of six hits annually for twenty years.

References

Am Mag 103 :54-5 Je '27 por
International Motion Picture Almanac
Who's Who in American Jewry

Obituaries

N Y Times p23 O 9 '41

KAISER WILHELM II *See* Wilhelm II, Former German Kaiser

KALLIO, KYÖSTI (käl'yō kē-ŏs'tē) 1873—Dec. 19, 1940 Former President of Finland who resigned on November 28, 1940 because of ill health brought on by the hardships of his term of office during the Russian-Finnish War in 1939-40.

References

Am Scand R 28 :6 Mr '40 por
Christian Sci Mon Mag p4 Ap 21 '37 il pors
Lit Digest 124 (Digest 1) :15 O 23 '37 il pors
Newsweek 14 :N 13 '39 por (cover)
Scholastic 35 :8 O 30 '39 por
International Who's Who

Obituaries

N Y Times p5 D 20 '40 por
Newsweek 16 :19 D 30 '40 por
Time 36 :18 D 30 '40 por

KANIN, GARSON (kā'nĭn) Nov. 24, 1912- Motion-picture director

Address : b. c/o Training Film Laboratory, Fort Monmouth, N. J ; RKO Radio Studios, Inc, 780 Gower St, Los Angeles, Calif.

Hollywood is famous for boy wonders, most of whom flash brilliantly one week and are never heard of again. Garson Kanin is another of Hollywood's boy wonders, but one who has been doing spectacular feats for almost two years and seems likely to keep on doing them until long after the "boy" will have to be dropped before the "wonder." He has directed six pictures, and all of them have been remarkably good. In 1941 as Private Kanin he was working just as well for the Government at the Training Film Laboratory at Fort Monmouth, New Jersey. As technical adviser on war films, he was called frequently to Washington and various army camps before being mustered out of the Army and transferred to the Division of Information of the Office of Emergency Management. He started production of his first Government sponsored film in December.

Kanin was born in Rochester, New York, in a family that was poor but keenly conscious of music and the arts. By the time they had moved to New York, when he was 12, he could play the saxophone and clarinet well ; when, after a short term at James Madison High School, his father, a builder, went broke, he was able to support himself playing. His first job was in a small orchestra ; his next in vaudeville. The results of both, to quote Kanin, were "lousy." Then came burlesque, sessions as social director for summer camps and a short stretch as master of ceremonies in a night club. Finally he decided he needed training and enrolled in the American Academy of Dramatic Arts in New York.

Three days after graduation he landed a part in *Little Ol' Boy* and followed it up with small parts in a number of George Abbott plays, including *Boy Meets Girl* and *Three Men on a Horse.* "Then I went to Mr. Abbott to get a job," he says. There wasn't any, but "I got in the habit of coming up there every day and hanging around. One day there was an empty desk and by that time they had gotten used to me so I sat down and there I was." For George Abbott, Kanin read, acted, directed, painted scenery, everything.

(Continued next page)

GARSON KANIN

Then one day in 1937 Samuel Goldwyn came along and hired Kanin as a director. As Kanin tells it: "He brought me out to the coast and told me to familiarize myself with the studio. . . I kept asking Mr. Goldwyn what I was supposed to do, but all he would tell me was to take my time and learn the ropes. . . Finally I discovered what I was supposed to do. Whenever Mr. Goldwyn held a conference he loved to have a lot of men rush into the room and listen to him. I was just one of those men."

After Kanin had pleaded for any kind of work at all to do he stood up to Goldwyn. "Look," he said, "I'm a director. Give me some picture to do." Goldwyn scornfully asked: "Should I give you a million dollars to play around with?" When Kanin asked Goldwyn to give him a smaller picture, he was outraged. "I don't make smaller than million dollar pictures," he said. Kanin finally got a release from his contract and left, but not without having learned a good deal at Goldwyn's studio. "I spent nearly a year studying the mechanics of film-making before I got my first assignment," he says.

Kanin then signed with RKO and was given an obscure story, *A Man to Remember*, and only $100,000 (peanuts in Hollywood) to make a picture. What he made, made history. He followed it up with *Next Time I Marry*, also a limited budget picture, and *The Great Man Votes*, with John Barrymore in the leading role. From then on his budgets were not restricted, and he was given the job of directing Ginger Rogers in *Bachelor Mother*, a picture distinguished by its neat directorial touches.

The next picture Kanin was asked to make was *Anne of Windy Poplars*. Kanin refused and was suspended from the studio, but came back amicably enough to direct Irene Dunne

and Cary Grant (see sketch this issue) in a sprightly comedy hit called *My Favorite Wife*. His reputation was already well established, but critics did not hesitate to heap further laurels when *They Knew What They Wanted*, starring Charles Laughton and Carole Lombard, appeared. It was shortly after this last picture was shown in New York that Kanin was at a party. As he tells it: "Mr. Goldwyn was across the room. Suddenly he pointed at me and shouted: "You double-crosser, you. Why didn't you tell me you could direct?'"

Kanin is five-feet-seven inches tall and weighs 130 pounds, slender, nervous, "with a boy's face and a wide grin that leaps up toward each of his ears." In Hollywood he lives with his mother, father and his sister, Ruth, who for many months was considered by uninquiring Hollywood gossip scouts to be his "current" because he took her to dinner once in a while. A situation like this, or that with Goldwyn, amuses Kanin, who has a bright sense of humor. Toward his work, however, he is intensely serious and intensely earnest. Though acclaimed as the most inspired directing talent to come to Hollywood in years, he can say with complete sincerity: "I haven't yet made a picture that entirely pleases me. I haven't yet done anything that has come out on the screen just the way I saw it in my head. I guess I haven't quite got the technique yet."

References

Friday 1:19 My 24 '40 por
Life 7:27-8 Jl 3 '39
N Y World-Telegram p37 O 12 '40
Theatre Arts 25:225-6+ Mr '41; 25:
640-4 S '41

KARLOFF, BORIS Nov. 23, 1887- Stage and screen actor
Address: c/o Fulton Theatre, 210 W. 46th St, New York City; h. 45 E. 66th St, New York City

When the shadow of a sinister newcomer falls on the living room door in the peculiar household depicted in Joseph Kesselring's farcical murder mystery, *Arsenic and Old Lace*, there are squeals of delighted horror in the audiences which have filled the Fulton Theatre since the première of the play on January 13, 1941. They know that they are about to behold in the flesh the screen's most celebrated menace, none other than Boris Karloff, who has made Mary Wollstonecraft Shelley's *Frankenstein* a household word in America. It is just as likely that millions of film-goers are hazy in their minds as to the distinction between the monster and the scientist who invented him. "There goes Frankenstein," mutter people who see the actor on Manhattan streets, and nudge each other. The most famous misquotation in English literature is not easily corrected.

"Boris Karloff" is William Henry Pratt, an English gentleman who is tall, lanky and soft-voiced, with kind brown eyes and a disarming smile. In Baltimore on Christmas Day 1940 he dressed up as Santa Claus and handed out

BORIS KARLOFF

the presents at a Christmas party for about 300 crippled children, and in 1941 he played Santa Claus again.

He was born in London on November 23, 1887, the son of Eliza Sara (Millard) Pratt and a British Indian civil servant, Edward Pratt, who decided that this youngest son in a family of eight sons and a daughter should have a career in the British consular service. When he died all William's brothers had the same idea for him. As he tells it: "One after the other they went into the consular . . . and one after the other they would come back on leave and get after me. I would no sooner be rid of one than another would come along and speak to me sternly about my negligence in preparing for the consular." But William was not to be persuaded. After an education at Merchant Taylor's School, London, at Uppingham and King's College, he gathered together what funds he could and left for Canada in 1909.

His first work in Canada was on a farm in Ontario, followed by a day laborer's job at $2.50 a day. Then came a stab at selling real estate, another shift as a laborer and in 1910 he found himself in Vancouver still unsure of what he wanted to do. By the next year he had found out. He joined a theatrical company in Kamloops, British Columbia at $30 a week, playing the villain in his first part. He took the name of Karloff from ancestors of his mother's and added the appropriate Boris out of his head. The Kamloops troupe was stranded in Saskatchewan and before long Karloff was in the repertory company of an old actor, Harry St. Clair.

"St. Clair was absolutely honest," Karloff told Helen Ormsbee of the New York *Herald Tribune*. "If there was no money in the box office the ghost didn't walk, but whenever business was good he paid what he

owed us. In some towns we stayed a week, in others we settled down for a run. It was in Minot, North Dakota that we stayed 53 weeks and I played 106 parts. I was a quick study and the quickest study got the longest parts. So I played leads in *Paid in Full, Charley's Aunt, East Lynne, Way Down East, Bought and Paid For, Baby Mine, What Happened to Jones, Why Smith Left Home*—and many more. We all took turns at being stage manager and we never had a dress or prop rehearsal. We must have done some terrible acting, but let me say a word for the intelligence of our audiences. In towns where we did a different play each night we asked the audience to vote for the one they wanted us to repeat as our closing bill. You couldn't fool that public; it invariably put its finger on the best play. Today, when I hear people speak condescendingly of the sticks, I remember that."

He left St. Clair to join a road company of *The Virginian* in Chicago. With this troupe he toured the Western states for a year, winding up in Los Angeles in 1917. There the company disbanded. He found a place with a stock company in San Pedro, stayed a short time and then joined the Maude Amber Players of Vallejo because prospects looked brighter. The flu epidemic raised havoc with theatres and the Maud Amber Players disbanded for lack of funds.

Karloff again sought a job as laborer and subsequently worked long hours each day piling sacks of flour in a storeroom. Then, hearing that extras were being taken on at the Universal Studios, he applied for a job and was assigned to be a member of a mob in a picture being directed by Frank Borzage. Thereafter he was sometimes an extra, sometimes a player in small-time stock companies and sometimes a truck driver. He gradually obtained more important parts in pictures, but no real notice was taken of him until he was tested, with other candidates, for the monster in *Frankenstein*. He had meantime played in two British-Gaumont pictures in England.

During the filming of *Frankenstein*, Karloff's make-up required three hours to put on. An immense amount of nose putty had to be applied to his features, and his whole figure built up as well. The late Colin Clive played Frankenstein in the first picture of the series, released in 1931, but "it was the appalling creature called to life by Frankenstein that everybody talked about." That creature was, of course, Karloff. *The Bride of Frankenstein* was the first sequel; it was directed by James Whale, and John L. Balderston and Edmund Pearson worked on the scenario. Karloff was by this time married—to Dorothy Stine of Michigan, formerly a children's librarian,—and while *Son of Frankenstein*, the second sequel, was in production their first child, Sara, was born in 1938. (Another child has been born since then.) Karloff also played the title role in *The Mummy* and parts of varying importance in *The Mask of Fu Manchu, The Raven, Devil's Island, The Ghoul*, and most recently in

KARLOFF, BORIS—*Continued*

a picture based on the novel of psychical horror called *The Edge of Running Water*.

In *Arsenic and Old Lace*, "the comedy parts in the play are what float me along," Karloff has said. "If it weren't for the delightful acting of Josephine Hull, Jean Adair and Allyn Joslyn, my part would go for nothing. I'm content to be the villain in every piece, because I know it is expected of me. I've played a few straight parts in pictures, but the audiences were sure I was going to do something terrible and I think they were sorry I didn't. That is what it means to be typed."

"Playing to an audience is a great joy after years of acting for the camera," he states. "An audience's responses tell you everything, if you will listen. Sometimes they say: 'Yes, that's funny. We'll laugh if you'll give us a chance.' But if you hear coughing and rustling out in front, people are saying to you: 'Don't do that. It's no use. We aren't noticing.' The most beautiful thing of all is the complete stillness of an audience so intent that it scarcely breathes. I had almost forgotten these things. In pictures the director is your only audience."

Karloff also has had experience broadcasting, when he took a vacation from films in 1938 to play the lead in the NBC *Lights Out* dramas. Here he did not keep in character so far as to appear in his usual plaster, spirit gum, clay and paint.

References

> Bet Homes & Gard 17:22-3 My '39 il
> pors
> Collier's 108:60-1+ S 20 '41 il pors
> N Y Herald Tribune VI pl, 5 Ja 5 '41
> N Y Times IX p3 Ja 19 '41
> New Yorker 16:10-11 F 1 '41
> PM p14, 15 Ja 5 '41 pors
> International Motion Picture Almanac

KARNO, FRED 1865—Sept. 17, 1941 English music-hall star and producer; was the man who developed Charlie Chaplin into a starring music-hall comedian and brought him to the United States; as producer since 1900 presented other actors who became well known, including Stan Laurel; recently had been interested in motion pictures; real name John Westcott.

References

> Adeler, E. and West, C. Remember
> Fred Karno? 1939

Obituaries

> N Y Herald Tribune p18 S 19 '41

KARSNER, DAVID 1889—Feb. 20, 1941 Biographer and newspaperman; copyreader on the New York *Post*; Hollywood scenarist; former managing editor of the old New York *Call*; associated with many well known liberals; best known as author of *Silver Dollar* (1932), a book on the life of H. A. W. Tabor, Colorado millionaire, which was later made in-

to a motion picture starring Edward G. Robinson; also wrote two studies of his friend, Eugene V. Debs.

Obituaries

> N Y Times p15 F 22 '41
> Pub W 139:1133 Mr 8 '41

KAŠPAR, KARL, CARDINAL May 16, 1870—Apr. 21, 1941 Archbishop of Prague and Primate of Bohemia; gained international recognition for the fearless manner in which he opposed Nazi efforts to weaken the Roman Catholic Church in Bohemia after that part of Czechoslovakia was taken over by Germany in 1938; noted as expert on canon law and as a writer and theologian; elevated to the College of Cardinals in 1935.

References

> International Who's Who
> Who's Who in Central and East-Europe

Obituaries

> N Y Times p21 Ap 22 '41 por

KAST, LUDWIG W. (kăst) Mar. 2, 1877 —Aug. 14, 1941 President since 1928 of the Josiah Macy, Jr., Foundation for the support of medical research; consulting physician; member of the board of directors of the New York Post-Graduate Medical School and Hospital; contributed to many medical journals.

References

> American Medical Directory
> American Men of Science
> Leaders in Education 1941
> Who's Who in America
> Who's Who in American Medicine

Obituaries

> N Y Times p15 Ag 16 '41 por

KAUFMAN, GEORGE S. (kôf'măn) Nov. 16, 1889- Playwright; director

Address: b. c/o Random House, Inc, 20 E. 57th St, New York City; h. Holicong, Pa.

Despite the fact that he has been the biggest money maker in the contemporary theatre, George S. ("for nothing") Kaufman still is a picture of pale despair on first nights, looking "a little like the late Marie Antoinette in the tumbrel." And even when a play he was certain would flop proceeds to run for hundreds of performances, he starts working on another right away. The result has been at least one Kaufman play a year on the stage since 1921, and almost always one success a year.

In these years he has responded to nearly everything in American life, "from its pleasant private vagaries to political mismanagement and the serious threat of Fascism," and has almost consistently made sport of it. He is a satirist, though he refuses to concede the title, ("Satire is something that closes on Saturday night," he says), who has the gift of being able to make us laugh at ourselves. And yet he never gives offense.

To serious drama critics, this is a weakness. According to one: "He has amazing foresight in always taking the pulse of Broadway as the clue to its heart, a habit of always writing fashionable plays and never revolutionary ones." He will, they say sadly, sacrifice artistic integrity to stage demands, "let the least worthy of the drama's patrons establish its laws."

Kaufman shakes these criticisms off. There is little value, he feels, in talking about art in plays when all there actually is is good workmanship. He himself sticks to "dramatic construction which is seldom if ever really subtle or original but is always precisely right at the moment"; he concentrates on stretches of dialogue and touches of characterization which are amazingly shrewd and telling; he tosses off wisecracks, scornful observations, flippant repartee. He is, actually, a "really great practical theatre mind with no philosophy except that the theatre is entertainment and good entertainment pays."

This triumphantly successful writer and director of brightly studded plays, musical comedies and revues was born in Pittsburgh into a middle-class Jewish family whose members "managed to get in on every business as it was finishing and made a total of $4 among them." He went to public school in Pittsburgh and then moved north to Paterson, New Jersey with his father and mother, Joseph S. and Nettie (Schamberg) Myers Kaufman. He studied law for a while, three months to be exact, but still kept looking for his niche in life. A succession of jobs didn't seem to fill this, especially his job as wholesale agent for hatbands and pump ribbons—he was "almost spectacularly unsuccessful" at this, Alexander Woollcott (see sketch this issue) says.

He was doing better, though, outside his jobs, with his contributions to Franklin P. Adams' (see sketch this issue) column in the old *Evening Mail*. On the strength of them he eventually got an invitation to lunch; "F. P. A." took an interest in the lad and when the chance came recommended him for a position on the Washington *Times*. For a year, from 1912 to 1913, Kaufman conducted a column there called "This and That and a Little of the Other." Then, when he lost this job, F. P. A. helped him get his own on the *Evening Mail* (he had already gone on to other pastures). This column was called "Be That As It May" and appeared from 1914 to 1915.

Kaufman's next step up was to the New York *Herald Tribune*, where he served as drama reporter under the late Heywood Broun. It has been reported that Broun once lent Kaufman his job "in a burst of bad judgment" and rushed to take it back as soon as he read Kaufman's reviews. Kaufman got a chance to express his drama opinions, nevertheless. The New York *Times* took him on, and for 13 years Kaufman's criticism and editing brightened its pages. He threw out publicity handouts, dull recitals of plays and players and deftly waved his light touch over all. One of his light touch efforts has become

The New York Public Library
GEORGE S. KAUFMAN

legend. The *Times* used to run a drama information box which by means of asterisks, daggers and other signs dispensed information in voluminous footnotes. Deciding this had gone far enough, Kaufman one day found a new symbol in the composing room and placed it in front of *Strange Interlude*. The trail led to a footnote reading, "Does not carry dining car."

It was while he was on the *Times* that Kaufman wrote his first play, a farce called *Going Up*, which never saw an audience. Kaufman's agent, however, remembered its snappy dialogue when he was looking for somebody to fix up a comedy by the late Larry Evans. Kaufman came in as co-author with Evans and Walter Percival, and the play, *Someone in the House*, ran for 37 performances in 1918. That was the time of the influenza epidemic, which didn't help attendance much. Kaufman wanted to advertise: "Avoid crowds. See *Someone in the House*." His adaptation, *Jacques Duval*, did even worse in 1920.

Then came *Dulcy*, the great hit of the 1921 to 1922 theatre season, and Kaufman's first important collaboration. He and Marc Connelly borrowed the central character from F. P. A.'s column, where she appeared from time to time as a retailer of bromides, and proceeded to introduce something novel on the stage—satire from a point of view that was "smart" rather than popular. *Dulcy's* never-failing middle-class dullness was infinitely amusing, and the most famous playwrighting team of the '20s was launched.

They were more than just rising young playwrights, however. Kaufman and Connelly in those days were part of a group which "by virtue of talent, wit and hobnobbing together was coming to dominate the sophisticated Manhattan scene." It called itself the Thanatopsis Literary and Inside Straight Club and lunched at the Algonquin, while merry quips darted among its now-famous members— Dorothy Parker, the late Heywood Broun, Alexander Woollcott, F. P. A., the Marx Brothers and others.

Away from the club, Kaufman and Connelly kept working, and in 1922 their *To the Ladies* appeared, a warmly human play with its share of irony at the expense of masculine

KAUFMAN, GEORGE S.—*Continued*

complacency. It was followed in the same year by *The 49'ers* and *Merton of the Movies,* a sharp satire on Hollywood, from time to time revived by Hollywood itself. In 1923 Kaufman and Connelly had two more plays produced, *Helen of Troy, New York* and *The Deep Tangled Wildwood,* both failures. But they redeemed their reputations the next year with *Be Yourself* and *The Beggar on Horseback,* the latter an extremely effective play about a man who has a horrible dream that he has left the artistic life to enter big business.

This last play was the climax of their collaboration, and after it Kaufman and Connelly separated amicably. Kaufman immediately set to work on his own, and the result was *The Butter and Egg Man* (1924), a highly successful comedy which combined a terrific pace with realistic and minute detail, and *The Coconuts* (1925), a zany vehicle for the Marx Brothers. But Kaufman found he disliked working alone, and by 1926 was back to collaboration, this time with H. J. Mankiewicz on a not very profitable play named *The Good Fellow.*

Since then, with one exception, Kaufman has always been part of a two-man team. Joseph Wood Krutch explains it by saying that Kaufman is mainly a wit and skillful builder of character without much ability in creating plots, and Kaufman himself has said he doesn't think his work alone is particularly good. With someone else he is an ideal collaborator. "His adaptable, accommodating mind is geared to avoid collision. It is also geared to let the other fellow's personality rather than Kaufman's permeate the play." His work with Connelly has a kindliness and humanity evident in Connelly's own plays, and *The Beggar on Horseback*, particularly, is "obviously dominated by Connelly's delicate fantasy." In *The Royal Family* the tone "clearly results from the bravura touch of Miss Ferber"; the nostalgic sentimentality of *The Channel Road* is "pure Alexander Woollcott"; *Of Mice and Men,* which he staged, remains John Steinbeck's work.

Achieving the results of perfect collaboration with Kaufman, however, is no easy matter. Writing the play is always an evenly shared two-man job with long preliminary stretches for working out plot details before the dialogue is even started. And Kaufman is a perfectionist. Moss Hart (see sketch 1940 Annual) still calls their first job together "the Days of the Terror." From 10 a. m. "until exhausted" they worked and starved together, with Kaufman sometimes spending "two whole hours shaping one short sentence, a whole day discussing an exit." Kaufman prowls around and, according to Woollcott, "in the throes of composition seems to crawl up the walls of the apartment in the manner of the late Count Dracula." He picks up anything that catches his eye, looks it over, throws it down. This annoyed Edna Ferber, and once she placed a telegraph blank face down among the personal papers on her desk. Eventually Kaufman got

around to it, picked it up, and read: "George Kaufman is an old snoop." This sort of thing can go on for anything from five weeks to seven months, and has.

Back in 1924 Kaufman had written a sad venture, *Minick,* with Edna Ferber. Undiscouraged, he tried again with her in 1927 and this time clicked with *The Royal Family,* a history of the tumultuous vagaries of a theatrical family. With this play Kaufman had the added satisfaction of knowing that he was being taken seriously as a director as well as a playwright. It was, however, five years before he and Miss Ferber collaborated again, and in those years Kaufman's name appeared with those of five other theatrical lights.

In 1928 came another opus for the Marx Brothers, *Animal Crackers.* In 1929 came his first play with Woollcott, *The Channel Road,* a thoroughly panned venture. (His next, *The Dark Tower,* did even worse in 1933.) And in that same year *June Moon* was written with the late Ring Lardner. One year later Kaufman hitched up with Morrie Ryskind for a successful musical comedy called *Strike Up the Band,* and in that same year his first effort with Moss Hart, *Once in a Lifetime,* delighted audiences with its brilliant satire on Hollywood at the time talkies came in. Kaufman, who acted in this in the first dramatic appearance of his career, commented on his new collaborator, 15 years younger: "I have always been smart enough as I grew older to attach to myself the most promising lad that came along in the theatre."

The year 1931 was another big one for Kaufman. In it he and Howard Dietz presented *The Band Wagon,* "the wit, irony and beauty of whose sketches and musical numbers inaugurated a new era in musical revues," and in this year he and Ryskind gave the country the Pulitzer Prize-winning satire on American politics, *Of Thee I Sing.* The next year, which saw *Dinner At Eight* (Ferber and Kaufman) pulling in the audiences, wasn't a bad one either, and even 1933, in which *Let 'Em Eat Cake, Of Thee I Sing's* not quite so famous successor, appeared, can be considered good. The year 1934 actually had two hits: *Merrily We Roll Along,* a serious drama on disillusionment written with Moss Hart, and *Bring on the Girls,* a gay work by Kaufman and Ryskind; and in 1935 Washington society in national politics came in for satirization in *First Lady,* written with Katherine Dayton.

In 1936, though, Kaufman really hit the jackpot. *Stage Door,* with Ferber, was a hit; *You Can't Take It With You,* with Hart, was a wow (837 performances on Broadway) and a Pulitzer Prize winner. Then in 1937 came *I'd Rather Be Right,* with the book by Kaufman and Hart, music by Richard Rodgers and Lorenz Hart, acting by George M. Cohan and tickets for opening night selling for $165 a pair at a gentlemen's club. In 1938 *The Fabulous Invalid* and in 1939 *The American Way,* "that noble but glib paean to democracy" (both with Moss Hart), did pretty well for themselves, but it wasn't until Kaufman and

Hart's seventh collaboration that the bell rang loud again. *The Man Who Came to Dinner,* "an unexpurgated version of Alexander Woollcott," became one of the biggest smash hits of the past 10 years. It continued to run through July 12, 1941, long after *George Washington Slept Here,* their tenuous tale of life in the country promptly called by skeptics "George Kaufman slipped here," left the boards.

Kaufman broke away from successful writing for a while in 1941 to direct *Mr. Big* by Arthur Sheekman and Margaret Shane. The critics found his doing so a mistake; they bemoaned the play itself and looked sadly and futilely for "the usual Kaufman touch." Their only comfort came from reports of a new collaboration with Edna Ferber, *The Land Is Bright.* When it opened in October 1941, despite some misgivings on structure and theme, they conceded he had done it again. The play was a hit.

All these years of hits have meant that George S. Kaufman is the greatest success in the American theatre. Of his plays more than 15 have run close to 200 or more performances; 20 have been sold to the movies; and Kaufman, who usually has an interest in his productions, gets his share of the profits as well as royalties. But he shrugs his shoulders. "All I know is that I have earned a great deal of money and I haven't got any of it. If I don't get a hit each year I am in a darned bad way."

Kaufman, who is one of the best doctors in the theatre—on anyone's plays—does everything to see that his own will be hits, even after they are written—by directing the film versions and by directing and staging them in the theatre. It used to drive him crazy to see other directors mar his lines, twist his meanings, spot in laughs, and since 1925 he has not been giving them many chances to. One of the best directors in the business now, he usually starts with the last act and works backward, quiet, unobtrusive, listening in the back, "his head tilted a little to one side, his finger cocked in the corner of his mouth." Always he gives the impression that playwrighting and directing are part of the same thing, that gesture and movement are as much a part of the play as words. Because this is so, he rewrites as he goes along, shifting line, phrase, speech to suit the tempo and rhythm of movement he wants. But no one else dares shift them, and no actor ever ad libbed a syllable without his knowing it. Once during a performance he discovered that a star had made some changes in the script. "Your performance magnificent and improving every day," he wired. "Sorry I can't say same about the lines."

Kaufman is famous for quips like this, and his conversation off the stage is supposed to equal that of his plays. Puns are his forte, and some of them, like "One man's Mede is another man's Persian," will probably be quoted forever. He delivers them dead pan, and always there is a "look of utter mournfulness" on his face. Carelessly dressed, usually hatless, he sports a bushy pompadour, rimless glasses and heavy black eyebrows. Whether in his Manhattan town house or out on his Buck's County, Pennsylvania farm, he is bored by social rigmarole, fights innovation, and abhors athletics, except for an occasional fierce game of croquet. Poker and bridge are really his games, and Ely Culbertson calls him "the best amateur bridge player in the United States." He is the kind of player who detests dubs and says things like "I'd like a review of the bidding with the original inflections."

His dark-eyed, gray-haired wife, Beatrice Bakrow, whom he married in 1917 (they have one daughter), is gay and sociable, and it is she who keeps her husband in touch with friends like Robert Sherwood, Alexander Woollcott, Harpo Marx, Irving Berlin. He himself, according to *Time,* is "rangy and restless, hard to know, harder to understand, always blunt, always brusque, occasionally brutal, completely free from affectations, but bulging with quirks. He is frightened of growing old or being considered rich or losing his hair. He forms friendships slowly, feels he has few friends. He talks to himself, makes strange faces, nods his head."

References

Nation 137:156-8 Ag 9 '33 por; 150:192 F 10 '40
New Yorker 5:26-9 My 18 '29
No Am 237:76-83 Ja '34
Sat Eve Post 210:16-17+ Ja 1 '38 il pors
Sat R Lit 9:385-6 Ja 21 '33 por
Stage 15:27-30 Ag '38 il por
Theatre Arts 16:807-15 O '32; 23:788-98 N '39 il
Time 34:65-9 N 20 '39 il por
Flexner, E. American Playwrights: 1918-38 p198-282 1938
Gassner, J. W. Masters of the Drama p662-93 1940
Krutch, J. W. American Drama since 1918 p134-225 1939
Kunitz, S. J. ed. Living Authors 1937
Mersand, J. Traditions in American Literature p14-24 1939
Nathan, G. J. Passing Judgments p66-73 1935
Who's Who in America
Who's Who in American Jewry
Who's Who in the Theatre

KAYE, DANNY 1913- Comedian

Address: c/o Imperial Theatre, 249 W. 45th St, New York City

As the owner of "the most expressive mitts in the theatre," Danny Kaye might have expected to leap to top Broadway billing in the space of a few years. If so, he never admits it. This pleasant, rather shy youth with a gangling six-foot frame and an apologetic smile is still a bit dazed and bewildered by his success, but withal entirely pleased. Much of his time is spent thinking of his good fortune and plotting ways to make it a permanent state. He certainly hopes it keeps up at least until he can realize one

Marcus Blechman

DANNY KAYE

of his major ambitions: "to buy an apartment house in his old neighborhood and collect rents himself—and always, every time, say 'thank you' to the tenants—even if they can't pay anything."

Danny was born Danny Kominski, the youngest son of an East New York (Brooklyn) dress designer, in an environment where the rent was a pressing and everlasting problem. Neighborhood friends of his father's generation remember him as a bright social light, for even at the age of 10 he was able to make the most wonderful faces and could keep his audience (on the street corners or at the socials of East New York) convulsed whenever he felt like it. As a tender youth he made his first "professional" appearance as a pickaninny in a minstrel show given at P. S. 149, the set being an immense slice of watermelon with a pickaninny for every pit. Danny is somewhat dubious as to the success of this performance, for his hair at the moment was an uncompromising red and he had extremely white ears. (The ears are still white but the hair is now brown.)

For a time, after that, the theatre was neglected completely. At Thomas Jefferson High School, Danny became quite an athlete, devoting his time to handball, the breast stroke and the pole vault. Though he weighs only 150 pounds, he is still proud of his muscles and insists that interviewers poke them. In spite of the muscles, he was apparently shy even then, for he describes himself as "the kind of guy who stood behind the guy who whistled at the girls." At any rate, after three and one-half years of high school, Danny found his yearning for adventure more powerful than his zest for learning and departed abruptly for Florida with another boy. The pair started out with $1.50 and returned with $7—by virtue of Dan's singing and the

other boy's guitar playing—making hitchhiking a profitable pastime.

Danny's ventures were not always so successful, however. He got himself a soda-jerking job which he loathed and soon lost. After that, a job as an insurance clerk was given him which he held successfully for 10 months. Then, unfortunately, he was promoted to appraising cars. Made dizzy by lines of cars, he made his Big Mistake—one which cost the company $40,000. For this he was rewarded by being fired and, in addition, was shadowed by two Pinkerton men for months. The president of the company has apparently forgiven him now, for he wrote Danny a letter not long ago, saying: "I saw your act at the Riviera Club and enjoyed it very much. Back when you cost us that $40,000 I thought you were either a thief or a nitwit. It didn't occur to me that you were a comedian."

After his business fiasco, Danny started on his climb to stage fame by taking an entertainer's job at a summer camp in the Catskills, where he did anything remotely connected with the theatre. For this he was paid $200 for the first season and in several years worked up to a $1,000 salary. In the winter he lived on what he earned in the summer and tramped Broadway looking for an opening, but with no success. At the end of his fourth season at the camp, however, he joined two dancers to form a team called "The Three Terpsichoreans," and the act managed to get vaudeville bookings. At one point in their performance, Danny was to mince up to the girl and kiss her fingers gracefully. This he did very well until one night, just as he reached for her hand, he fell flat on his face and split his trousers. Shaken and bewildered, Danny had no choice but to obey the instructions the girl was hissing at him from the wings: "Wait for the laugh, Danny! Wait for the laugh." And the audience loved it. The incident became part of the routine and Danny received billing, choosing the name of Danny Kaye.

Eventually the act reached Detroit, where it was spotted by A. B. Marcus, proprietor and producer of an Oriental touring variety show which is an annual event, like the rainy season, in such cities as Peking, Tokyo, Penang and Singapore.

The ways of the East were mysterious to Danny. On one occasion when facing an audience in Tokyo composed chiefly of rigid-faced military men, who understood not a word of English, Danny struggled and sweated to promote a laugh. No response. Deciding that he was using the wrong tactics, he essayed a sad ballad. Still no response. As he tottered into the wings in desperation, he was met by the theatre manager who realized his despair—and explained that the Japanese were too polite to interrupt the lovely entertainment with noisy laughter and applause.

In spite of situations like this one, and Oriental stagehands who did their jobs of adjusting lighting and curtain ringing with true Eastern disregard of time and cues, Danny loved the East. In fact, he was just considering remaining there with a Dutch vaudeville group (A. B. Marcus, Inc., was about to sail for home) when the Japanese hurricane of 1936 arrived unexpectedly, bringing with it a loose brick which settled Danny's plans for him. When he woke up, he found himself on shipboard with A. B. Marcus.

He returned to America for a tour of the West, but finally decided he was getting nowhere and left the troupe for a job as Nick Long, Jr.'s, stooge at the Casa Mañana. After a season at another camp, he was eventually invited to Camp Tamiment, a summer spot for young professional people not far from Stroudsburg, Pennsylvania. It had been Max Liebman's custom for some seven years to put on a new revue at Tamiment every Saturday night for the ten weeks of the season, and it was with this that Danny was asked to assist. In this particular year, 1939, Max Liebman also had to assist him a young lady by the name of Sylvia Fine. She and Danny worked out some numbers together, Sylvia composing the lyrics and music. They found they had the same type of humor, and the acts were wonderful and much appreciated by the rural theatregoers. As a finale, on the last Saturday night of the season, the best numbers of all the revues were chosen and worked into one—and the *Straw Hat Revue* was born. By the end of September it was launched on Broadway by the Shuberts, and Danny had come into his own.

After the success of the *Straw Hat Revue,* Danny and Sylvia found they had much in common besides an ability to collaborate on sketches. They had lived as children on the same block in Brooklyn, and Danny had spent the summer of his thirteenth year running errands for her father. It seemed incredible that they hadn't met, but apparently they never had. They made up for their lack of earlier acquaintance by eloping to Florida and by being married at Fort Lauderdale on January 3, 1940. Danny still refers to his wife as Miss Sylvia Fine, and she still writes his sketches and helps him rehearse them, for which he gives her full credit, realizing that it is lack of good material which has kept many a good comedian in the "borscht circuit" rather than on Broadway.

Once Danny got a toe-hold on the ladder of success, he managed to keep climbing. As a result of his work in *Straw Hat Revue,* he was offered top billing at a cafe, La Martinique, and was there discovered by the swank set and the Broadway columnists. He even managed to convulse the waiters night after night, a much more difficult feat than amusing the customers. Other impressive engagements followed, among them one at the Chez Paris in Chicago and one at the Paramount Theatre in New York.

Then came the signing-up for *Lady in the Dark,* in which he played the part of Russell Paxton, doubling as chauffeur and magazine photographer. Critics acclaimed him. His most hilarious and best-remembered number was his Tschaikowsky number which is nothing more or less than the names of 50 genuine Russian composers strung together by Ira Gershwin simply for the tongue-twisting effect.

In 1941 Danny left *Lady in the Dark* for the featured lead in *Let's Face It,* a Broadway hit. The reviewers still agreed that both he and the audience appeared to be having the time of their playgoing lives, particularly when he went into his *Melody in F* number—a narrative of the career of a selectee, told in "triple-talk" and by means of pantomime, squeals, grunts and action. There's little doubt that in two years Danny Kaye has become one of the most important comics on the American stage.

The apartment in which he and Sylvia Fine live is on Central Park South—"right down the street from the Plaza." Danny loves to spend money. In fact, "because of Danny's idea that money should be scattered around like so much scrap paper, the Kaye finances have been put in the hands of a business manager. Danny still thinks that if he buys anything and sends the bill to his manager, he isn't spending money—because it doesn't come out of his weekly allowance."

References

Collier's 107:18+ Ap 12 '41 por
N Y Herald Tribune VI p5 N 9 '41
N Y Post p3 My 22 '41 por
N Y Sun p26 F 6 '41; p14 N 24 '41 por
N Y Times IX p1, 2 F 9 '41; VII p10+ N 16 '41 pors
N Y World-Telegram p5 N 8 '41
PM p51 Mr 23 '41 pors
Theatre Arts 25:435 Je '41 por

KEITH, DORA WHEELER Mar. 12, 1857—Dec. 27, 1940 Portrait painter and artist; did murals for the State Capitol Building at Albany, New York; won the Prang Prize two consecutive years, in 1885 and 1886; work is represented in the collections of many museums and private owners.

References

Variety Radio Directory 1940-41
Who's Who in America 1928-29
Who's Who in American Art

Obituaries

N Y Times p15 D 28 '40

KELLY, JUDITH Jan. 4, 1908- Author *Address:* b. c/o Harper and Brothers, 49 E. 33rd St, New York City; h. Beverly, Mass.

The author of the $10,000-Harper Prize novel for 1940 to 1941 is Judith Kelly, an attractive, fair-haired woman who is the mother of two children. Clifton Fadiman (see sketch this issue), one of the judges in the contest, called her novel "a warm, precise and searching study of the first few uncertain years of an American marriage." The story of a young couple who, "like all the other characters of her book, are blessed with education, social position and assured income," the particular contribution of *Marriage Is a Private Affair* (1941) is to illuminate a social class which (again in Fadiman's words) "has of late been neglected in our literature."

(Continued next page)

Royal Atelier

JUDITH KELLY

Other reviewers, for the most part, agreed with the *New Yorker* critic's appraisal, Sterling North finding the book completely deserving of the Harper Prize. And although Edith H. Walton, writing in the New York *Times Book Review*, thought the story that Judith Kelly had to tell conventional and familiar, she credited her with having "told it in terms which are so completely contemporary," with having "endowed it with so much freshness and sensitiveness and genuine intuition that it has the shock of truth and novelty." Her main weakness was "a tendency to dress up the obvious as portentous truth."

Born in Toronto, Canada on January 4, 1908, the daughter of Mr. and Mrs. Henry Grattan Kelly, Judith Kelly writes about people with a background similar to her own. Racially she is a mixture of "well-born, over-intellectualized New England, blended with immigrant Irish; and the two re-blended with impoverished Southern gentility." She attended Branksome Hall School until the age of 14, when her family moved to Boston; there she attended Miss Lee's School.

"During the early part of my life," she says, "we were what I guess you'd have to call rich. That is, the horses were ours, and good; and so were the dogs; and I had far too many clothes and too much pocket money. I was sent to Vassar [1927] and for three years had a perfectly heavenly time, which certainly had nothing to do with studying, but was entirely composed of boys, New Haven parties, special delivery letters (the more you got, of course, the more simply wonderful you were), clothes, telegrams, telephone calls and the absolute minimum of work.

"This might have gone on indefinitely if 1929 had not come along and, even worse,

1930. All at once we had no money at all, not even enough to see me through the last year of college. So a scholarship was necessary, and I was forced for the first time in my life to do a little real work; quite astonishingly it turned out to be fun. Even more important to me was the discovery of people's goodness, kindness and generosity in times of need."

"Well, after college" she goes on, [she was graduated in 1931], "there was still no money, so the next quest was jobs. People went on being wonderful—they got me jobs one after another, almost as fast as I lost them; they lent me money; they gave me needed clothes; and above everything they offered me the immense help of never doubting for one moment that I would some day pay them back." She worked in a bookshop and in a department store before her marriage, in the summer of 1933, to William D. English, a Boston lawyer. It was he who, as a wedding present, quietly paid off all her debts.

Regarding those first few years of her own marriage Judith Kelly is very modest. "Debts weren't my only drawback as a bride either. I wanted terribly to be a good cook but I was an abominable one; and over my housekeeping it is better to draw a veil. My husband, instead of justly resenting this, said straight off that if I could earn the money for a maid he would much rather have me doing something I liked and was qualified for than to see me struggling with burnt fingers and collapsible cakes. So after our marriage I kept on having jobs." There was a year on the Boston *Globe* and a year on the Boston *Transcript*. "Then unaccountably one day I remembered that my father had always said firmly I should be a writer, and just as unaccountably I heard myself saying to my husband: 'You know what I'd love to do? I'd love to stop working and write a novel.' To my terror my husband said: 'All right. Why don't you take a year off? I'll pay for the maid and you can have a little office somewhere and I'll get you a typewriter.' So there I was: committed."

Somehow Judith Kelly's first novel got itself written and published, though, as did a few short stories. *It Won't Be Flowers* (1936) made what she calls "the large noise of a feather falling on velvet." The story of a young woman, happily married and without any grave economic problems, who nevertheless acquires a social conscience, one reviewer found its handling "feebler and more rarefied than one could wish," the style "self-conscious," the adjectives "frequent and lush." Another, however, called it "lovely and moving, because it shines with youth and the never-to-be recaptured radiancy of the first venture." And most critics found it promising, at least.

"And then," Judith Kelly confesses, "our daughter was born and all mental equipment fled from me for over a year. I couldn't even write a grocery order. But somehow—after failures and false starts and mistakes that piled up on each other like mountains—this second book also got itself written, being finally completed only a month before our son was born." *Marriage Is a Private Affair* took two years to write, and the first draft seemed to her so bad that she hesitated even to show it to a publisher. When she finally did, he suggested that she enter it in the Harper contest, to which between 500 and 700 entries were submitted. The judges (Clifton Fadiman, Josephine Johnson, Louis Bromfield) cast their votes without knowing who the authors were.

There will, Judith Kelly hopes, be a third book, and a fourth, even though "now the whole cycle of brainlessness is starting all over again." She says: "I remember how, when I began writing, I promised myself that I would efficiently stagger babies and books—one of a kind on alternate years. Whenever I think of that neat, admirable plan I don't know whether to laugh or to burst into tears. Six years have passed and there are only two children and two books. My hope is to do much, much better in the next six."

References

Ind Woman 20:cover S '41 por
Ladies' H J 58:4 Mr '41 por
N Y Times p10 Ag 4 '41 por; p15 Ag 20 '41 por
N Y World-Telegram p7 Ag 4 '41 por
Pub W 140:317 Ag 2 '41 por
Sat R Lit 24:10 Ag 23 '41 por
Time 38:80 Ag 25 '41 por

KEMMERER, E(DWIN) W(ALTER) (kĕm′ẽr-ẽr) June 29, 1875- Economist; educator

Address: b. Princeton University, Princeton, N. J.; h. 161 Hodge Rd, Princeton, N. J.

Known the world over as the "Money Doctor," Professor Edwin Walter Kemmerer, expert economist, has successfully treated ailing currencies in more than a dozen different nations. Since 1928 he has been Walker Professor of International Finance at Princeton University, and from 1937 to 1940 was president of the Economists' National Committee on Monetary Policy. Following his first "doctoring" job in 1903, that of putting Philippine currency in a healthy condition, Dr. Kemmerer has performed similar services, heading committees of financial advisers, in Mexico, Guatemala, Colombia, the Union of South Africa, Chile, Poland, Ecuador, Bolivia and other countries. He was also instrumental in organizing the statistical department of the Federal Reserve Bank and is an authority on the Federal Reserve System. Among his more recent books which are standard as college texts and references are *Kemmerer on Money* (1934); *Money; The Principles of Money and their Exemplification in Outstanding Chapters of Monetary History* (1935); and *Inflation and Revolution; Mexico's Experience of 1912-1917* (1940).

Dr. Kemmerer's boyhood and early education provide a background story of handicaps, physical and financial, overcome by applying an early-developed theory of economics to living and earning a schooling. One of six

Orren Jack Turner

E. W. KEMMERER

children, Edwin Walter Kemmerer was born in Scranton, Pennsylvania on June 29, 1875, the son of Lorenzo Dow and Martha H. (Cortright) Kemmerer. His ancestors on both sides came to this country in Colonial days, fought in the War of Independence. His own father, after serving as a drummer boy in the Civil War, became train dispatcher and yardmaster at Scranton. Because of two severe attacks of diphtheria, Edwin could not go to school until after he was eight years old; he found himself a frail, "hot-house" product among rough, healthy boys. "I was a goody-goody boy," he confesses, "and I'm ashamed of it. I ran away from school only once, and then I am afraid it was because the other boys forced me."

Times were hard; and when the boy was 14 his family moved out to the little village of Factoryville because the father wanted his children to grow up in the country, and because an excellent school, the Keystone Academy, was located there. This school young Kemmerer was encouraged to enter, although he knew that because of the family's slim financial circumstances he must earn his own way. But he had from the start his parents' backing. "My father and I were chums when I was a boy," he says. "We used to enjoy particularly going fishing together. . . He was keenly interested in my ambitions and helped me in every way he could. My mother's influence was also very strong. She was always interested in what I was trying to do and no sacrifice was too great for her to make for her children."

Kemmerer decided that, since fishing was his recreation, he would also turn it to getting a much-needed income. The trout he caught in upland brooks he sold in Scranton; soon he was buying the catches made by other boys and re-selling them in town. Later he

KEMMERER, E. W.—*Continued*

added eels and bullheads to his fish business. In the summers he also spent hours in the hills picking huckleberries to be sold at three cents a quart. Soon realizing that he needed a year-round business, he developed an egg route. He called on farmers, bought their surplus eggs and resold them in Scranton. But he decided he could do better in the way of finances if he gave up school for a year and accumulated a certain amount of capital to go on with. So he took a job as train boy with the Union News Company, which he was able to continue along with his Saturday egg business. He saved enough to take up again, after a year, the purely scholastic side of education at the Academy.

For a short time young Kemmerer wanted to become a missionary; but this desire soon gave way to that of preparing himself for civil engineering. So he studied mathematics almost exclusively until he was 17, and even joined a Lackawanna Railway surveying corps. Then he decided that he didn't care overly much for mathematics. About this time he bought secondhand a book called *Getting on in the World, or Hints on Success in Life.* He thoroughly studied this book and underscored several passages in it. That which impressed him especially was a quotation from the historian Gibbons: "Every person has two educations—one which he receives from others, and one, more important, which he gives himself." To this Kemmerer added the proposition that in life, as in business, the return was proportionate to the amount of effort expended. Also, one must not specialize too soon. He decided a classical course would demand the most of him, and enrolled at Keystone Academy. Through sheer hard work he won the Latin and the Essay Prizes, and was graduated at the head of the school. His prize essay was called *Climbing the Industrial Ladder.* And the course in college which had interested him more than any other was the one in political economy. Then and there he determined he would devote his life to its study and become a professor of economics.

Which college for further study should he choose? He decided on Wesleyan University because its catalog contained the largest number of men with Ph. D.'s after their names. He hoped to give all his time to his studies during the college terms, so he worked summer vacations selling stereoscopes and stereoscopic views from house to house. In this he did so well that he organized groups of other college men to do it, and soon had a force of some 20 working for him, upon whose sales he received a commission. He read college alumni statistics and found that there was a close relation between scholarship in college and success in later life. So Kemmerer studied hard and was graduated in 1899 with Phi Beta Kappa honors and special distinction in economics.

His essay on the "Theory of Money" so impressed professors at Cornell that he was given $500 to continue his studies there. At the age of 26 he finished his graduate work at Cornell, receiving his Ph. D. in 1903. He had married Rachel Dickele in 1901. There were two positions open to him: one a $600-a-year instructorship at Purdue University; the other a managerial position at $3,000. The latter was a big temptation to a young married man; but Kemmerer stuck to his earlier decision to be a professor of economics.

Soon his first opportunity in applied economics came. William Howard Taft, then Governor of the Philippines, was having trouble over the currency question there and asked Kemmerer for an immediate report on the situation. He worked all of one night to get the report ready and, though the Secretary of War at first turned down his recommendations, they were later put into practice: Philippine currency was put on the gold standard in a healthy condition. Following this success he went on with his studies in the practice and theory of international banking while continuing teaching economics at Cornell and later at Princeton. He was financial adviser to the Government of Mexico in 1917, to Guatemala in 1919, and in 1923 chairman of the Committee of American Financial Advisers to Colombia.

In 1922 Kemmerer took his wife, his son Donald, then 17, and his daughter Ruth, 13, with him on his investigation of conditions in South America. It was a trip involving a dangerous adventure in which he and his family almost lost their lives. They had decided to visit the Iguassú Falls, probably the most beautiful in the world, and boarded a small river steamer for a three days' journey up Paraguay. The first night out they were awakened by a terrific explosion. All four had just time to jump into the water before it was covered with burning oil from a second explosion that killed the remaining passengers who had not escaped from the boat. One by one Kemmerer and his family succeeded in getting to shore, where they were given shelter until they could make the journey back to Buenos Aires.

To become a more competent "Money Doctor," Kemmerer studied the history of previous illnesses in each nation, and parallel cases. Hence when he was called upon to serve a particular government he already had the case in hand. As a result, he was able to reorganize the country's currency promptly and surely. This study contributed to his prompt and effective work with the Dawes Commission in 1924, the American Commission to China in 1929, and that to Turkey in 1934. During recent years several Latin-American countries have employed American financial advisers, prominent among them Dr. Kemmerer.

Kemmerer says there are two types of advisers: the general practitioner type, "which diagnoses the disease, prescribes the medicine, and then undertakes to take care of the patient until he has reasonably recovered," and the diagnostician or consultant type, "which merely diagnoses the difficulties, prescribes remedies, and then goes away."

Kemmerer says most of his advisory financial work has been of the second, or consultant, type. In making up a commission he is always careful to obtain "at least two men who can qualify as experts in each of the major fields of work."

Kemmerer's skill in choosing men to work with him has played no small part in his success. The sickly, "goody-goody" boy managed to overcome those psychological handicaps which other men retain in later life. "It is one of the triumphs of Kemmerer's self-education that it enabled him to disprove an almost invariable rule. He meets all sorts and conditions of men with that utter frankness and friendliness which is the hallmark of those who have finally achieved mastery of themselves." Fishing is still his favorite recreation, and he also enjoys a game of golf whenever he can.

References

Am Boy 1924
Sat Eve Post 206:35+ Ap 14 '34 il pors
Time 26:74 D 9 '35
Leaders in Education 1941
Who's Who Among North American Authors
Who's Who in America

KEMP, HAL Mar. 27, 1905—Dec. 21, 1940 Orchestra leader; killed in automobile crash; known in the United States and in Europe for his modern style of conducting; one of the most popular band leaders in the country; won the Keith Prize in a nation-wide contest; played before the Duke of Windsor, then Prince of Wales.

HAL KEMP

Obituaries

N Y Times p30 D 22 '40 por

KEMPER, JAMES S(COTT) Nov. 18, 1886- Former president of the United States Chamber of Commerce; insurance executive

Address: Mutual Insurance Bldg, Chicago, Ill; h. 945 Sheridan Rd, Winnetka, Ill.

In May 1940 "conservative yet liberal" James Scott Kemper was chosen president of the United States Chamber of Commerce. Most of the members were familiar with their "energetic, enthusiastic president" who "for 20 years out of the 54 of his hard-working life" has been associated with the United States Chamber of Commerce as officer, director and vice-president. As president of the organization until May 1941 he had followed in the conservative footsteps of his predecessors and had been the spokesman for business to the Federal government.

Since his election Kemper's pronouncements have frequently made news. *Life* Magazine (January 20, 1941) listed his name in an article called *The Ism of Appeasement*, quoting him as "doubting that the United States should trouble itself about anything except North America and the Panama Canal." On January 28 the committee of manufacture of the Chamber of Commerce announced that it believed "that anti-strike laws will prove ineffective and that they will deny fundamental rights to our citizens." It urged employers "to develop plans with their employees designed to promote the amicable and prompt adjustment of labor disputes which may arise." Speaking before the Senate Foreign Relations Committee on February 5 in opposition to the Lend-Lease Bill, Kemper said that the Chamber of Commerce believed in full defense for the United States but sought prevention of involvement in war. He emphasized that business not only did not embrace war as an opportunity for profit, but was definitely opposed to any profiteering on war materials. And at the twenty-ninth annual meeting of the Chamber of Commerce, in April 1941, at which the best business conditions since 1929 were reported, he spoke out against "hysterical derangement of our normal production" in order to speed up defense. In May 1941 Albert W. Hawk was elected president of the United States Chamber of Commerce.

A descendant in the sixth generation of John Peter Kemper of Germanna, Virginia, James Scott Kemper was born at Van Wert, Ohio, son of Hathaway and Mary Jane (Scott) Kemper. He comes of an old Virginia and Ohio family which from generation to generation produced Presbyterian clergymen. Apparently the blood of the circuit-riding parson still flows in the Kemper family, for Kemper is a past president of the Presbyterian Union of Chicago and a trustee of various theological and charitable organizations.

Although in 1941 he is president of a score of corporations, Kemper's career began modestly enough. After being graduated from high school in Van Wert, Ohio, he entered the employ of the Central Manufacturers Insurance Company of that city. In his early 20's he was made manager of the Western

JAMES S. KEMPER

department of the company with headquarters in Chicago. In 1912, when he was only 26 years old, the lumber interests of the nation sought his counsel in an effort to achieve lower insurance costs in operating under the then newly-enacted Workmen's Compensation Acts. His success in reducing insurance costs by removing the causes of accidents brought him nationwide recognition as an effective leader in the "Safety First" movement. After the First World War there was a strong need for insurance protection against loss of life and property caused by automobiles. Kemper was a pioneer in the cause of automobile accident prevention. He endowed the Kemper Foundation for Traffic Police Training at Northwestern University, which has since become an authority on traffic problems.

In 1912 Kemper became vice-president and general manager of the Lumbermen's Mutual Casualty Company. As president since 1916 of that organization (the largest writer of automobile casualty insurance in the country), he has devoted himself to the intricate problems of insurance underwriting. Since 1921 he has been president of James S. Kemper and Company, and at various other times has been made president of five other insurance companies, vice-president of another company and director of three other insurance companies. In addition he is now a member, formerly president, of a number of insurance organizations.

Although president of so many companies, he still finds time to be active in Republican politics—twice he was a delegate to Republican National Conventions. He is active in most local and state political campaigns and his advice to his 10,000 employees and representatives has always been: "Vote as you please but be sure to vote. Choose what party you prefer but keep your interest alive

in all that concerns your local and national government." He believes firmly that American businessmen in every community must take a more active part in politics if they want to see improvement in government.

Mr. Kemper's first wife (Mildred Estelle Hooper) died in 1927. He has two daughters and a son. In 1931 he married Mrs. Gertrude Ziesing Stout. He is "short, stocky," with a "slightly bald head and a rather mischievous mustache, with pearl stickpin and spectacles." Away from business Kemper is a lover and collector of great books and a keen yachtsman. He confesses that he is the world's worst golfer.

References

> Commerce (Chicago association of Commerce) 29:26-30 Jl '32
> N Y Times p9 O 8 '40
> U S News p37 My 10 '40 por
> Who's Who in America
> Who's Who in Commerce and Industry

KENDALL, WILLIAM MITCHELL Feb. 13, 1856—Aug. 8, 1941 Noted American architect; senior member of the New York architectural firm of McKim, Mead & White, designers of the Boston Public Library, several Harvard University buildings, New York's original Madison Square Garden, the Pennsylvania Railroad Station and Washington Square Arch; helped design structures in Europe in addition to many other buildings throughout the United States and Europe; joined the firm in 1882.

References

> American Art Annual 1924-25
> Who's Who in America

Obituaries

> N Y Times p15 Ag 9 '41
> Time 38:47 Ag 18 '41

KEYNES, JOHN MAYNARD (kānz) June 5, 1883- English economist; financial adviser to the British Treasury

Address: b. King's College, Cambridge, England; h. 46 Gordon Sq, W. C. 1, London, England

John Maynard Keynes, "the most gifted and provocative of contemporary economists," Fellow and Bursar of King's College, Cambridge, editor of the *Economic Journal*, former chairman of the National Mutual Life Insurance Company, secretary of the Royal Economic Society, member of the Economic Advisory Council, director of the Bank of England and financial adviser to the British Treasury, arrived in the United States in May 1941. He had been sent by Sir Kingsley Wood, Chancellor of the British Exchequer, to confer with the Washington Administration and the British Supply Council on the operation of the lease-lend law and other related matters.

To the United States he brought a warning that our economic life would be disrupted by a German victory and advice on the prevention of inflation. What Mr. Keynes has to say is heeded in Washington, for his influence there has been strong for many years. Back in 1933 he is said to have sold the pump-priming plan of government to Roosevelt (some still call him "the economic godfather of the New Deal"), and ever since then his disciples have played an important part in guiding government spending. He is, too, the author of a plan for England's financing of the War which has had an effect on government spending plans both in this country and in his own.

This plan was first presented in two articles to the London *Times* in November 1939 and in 1940 published in book form (*How to Pay for the War*) in a modified version. Its basic theory is that in wartime there is a scarcity of the goods ordinarily consumed by the civilian population. This, plus peak production for war, leads to a heavy demand for all goods, which in turn results in sharp increases in prices, or inflation. Keynes' proposal is to deflate while the War is going on by giving England less to spend.

Under his plan all earners would be allowed minimum incomes and from all earnings above them the Government would deduct a proportion as "deferred savings." These would be allowed to accumulate until after the War and then be paid out at such a time and in such a way as to avoid or restrict any post-War slump. The savings collected would be available for special emergencies and would be repaid through a capital levy after the War. At the same time that they were being collected the Government would provide a minimum ration of essential consumption goods at low prices for all and grant family allowances to the low income groups.

When the plan was first proposed, Britain was skeptical. The Labor Party objected to the element of compulsion; the Conservative Party didn't believe the liquidation of the "deferred savings" could be properly accomplished; other groups called it a slur on British patriotism. But as the War went on and threats of inflation became more and more apparent, large groups began to agree with the *Spectator's* verdict: "A reasoned scheme for avoiding the disaster of inflation." In April 1941 the deferred savings proposal and some of the least radical of Keynes' other suggestions were adopted in the new and heavy British budget.

Keynes himself emphasizes the fact that his aim in his plan was not only to solve the financial problem of England but "to snatch from the exigency of war positive social improvements." "The combination of universal family allowances in cash, the accumulation of working-class wealth under working-class control, a cheap ration of necessaries and a capital levy after the War," he says, "embodies an advance toward economic equality greater than any which we have made in recent times." This conception, like many of the implications of Keynes' general attitude on economic affairs, is closely allied to socialism, and his ideas on economic policy are

said to "exercise a greater influence on the Labor movement than those of probably any other single person." Yet Keynes is not a Socialist, nor a member of the Labor Party. Despite his perennial criticisms of laissez faire, his theory of peace and war debts, his attitude toward the gold standard, Keynes has been consistently allied with the Liberal Party and has occasionally written with some scorn about the Labor Party.

Planet News, London

JOHN MAYNARD KEYNES

His father's attitude was in some respects similar. John Neville Keynes is also a leading British economist, long prominent in the faculty and administration of Cambridge University. On his father's side and on that of his mother, Florence Ada (Brown) Keynes, John Maynard Keynes has also a heritage of non-conformism. His grandfather, John Keynes, was a famous non-conformist; his maternal grandfather, Dr. John Brown, preached in Bunyan's church at Bedford and was one of the great historians of non-conformity.

John Maynard Keynes was born in Cambridge, England and went to Eton College, where reports have it that the boys used to call him "Snout." (He still has a thin face and longish nose.) From Eton he went on to King's College, Cambridge. Here he was Twelfth Wrangler and president of the Cambridge Union Society, and was graduated in 1905 with highest honors and an M. A. Immediately he entered the India Office and spent two years there before he returned to Cambridge University as a lecturer in economics, a position he has continued to hold until today, though he has taken assignments from the government from time to time.

One of these came in 1913 and 1914, when he served as a member of the Royal Commission on Indian Finance and Currency;

KEYNES, JOHN MAYNARD—*Continued*
another in 1915, when for four years he was
associated with the British Treasury, for two
of these years as principal clerk. Because of
this position Keynes was made the Treasury's
representative at the Paris Peace Conference
and the British Chancellor of the Exchequer's
deputy on the Supreme Allied Economic Council. In 1919 he withdrew from the Conference
in disgust, certain that the people there were
merely sowing dragon's teeth that would
sprout new wars, and not long afterward he
published his *Economic Consequences of the
Peace* (1919), still called "the most important
study of the Treaty of Versailles that has
yet been published."

Much of the book is taken up with a
demonstration of the economic impossibility
of the reparations section of the Treaty, its
basic thesis that the peacemakers of 1919 concentrated on political and military considerations when they should have been thinking
of economic ones. It created a sensation. Its
argument was unpopular, its author damned
by the critics, and yet the book itself was
widely read and translated into every continental language.

From then on almost anything Keynes wrote
or stated in the many lectures and speeches
he made was bound to be significant to other
economists and to many who weren't
economists. He was soon recognized as the
challenger of the whole tradition of economic
orthodoxy. In 1920 appeared his *A Treatise
on Probability*, which, "according to some
commentators, only three men are capable of
understanding." In 1924 his tract *Monetary
Reform* was published. This investigated the
element of instability in England's economic
system due to its dependence upon a monetary
standard liable to great fluctuations in value,
and demonstrated the results of a situation
in which capitalism leaves savings and investment to the individual without imposing
a social control. After the publication of *A
Short View of Russia* in 1925 and *The End
of Laissez-Faire* in 1926, Keynes' well-known
Treatise on Money appeared in 1930, elaborating the view that the lack of coordination
between savings and investment is the main
cause of trade depression.

In the 1930's Keynes pleaded for a broad
credit base and denounced the gold standard
as a "barbaric relic." He also argued strongly
in lectures, in the many articles he contributed to economic journals, in speeches and in
his position as member of the Committee on
Finance and Industry from 1929 to 1931 for
the "gradual reconstruction of our social system with the object of providing everyone
with the means of maintaining a decent level
of consumption." During depression years he
diagnosed the cause of the depression as a
lack of mass purchasing power caused by a
severe deflation, and suggested, the first economist of international reputation to do so, wide
government spending to restore it and set industry in motion again. The British Government was largely unpersuaded, while the
American Government listened to his ideas

and carried many of them out. Many of his
views on a flexible money policy and the expansion of social service expenditures were
presented in *The General Theory of Employment, Interest and Money* (1936), which was
acclaimed in one quarter at least as "the most
important theoretical economic writing since
Marx's *Capital* or, if only classical economics
is to be considered as comparable, since Ricardo's *Principles*." It was preceded by *Essays
in Persuasion* (1931), "a record of his advice
and warnings on the economic issues of the
post-War years," and by *Essays in Biography*
(1933), a book whose first part contained
estimates of men in public life whom Keynes
knew, its second an account of a series of
notable economists. Like his other books it
is written in language that is both precise and
vivid. *The General Theory of Employment,
Interest and Money* was published in 1936.

During the War period Keynes' attitude
toward government spending changed from
that which influenced the New Deal. The
time is past, he believes, for the Government
to stimulate business activity; it should, instead,
devote its efforts to the contrary policy—to a
deliberate attempt to slow down the forces
threatening boom conditions. This meant, he
said, a cessation of public works, an increase
in taxes, a reduction of the public debt. He
also advocated strong rearmament and a policy
of "positive pacifism" involving a League reorganized really to enforce the decisions of
its members. For a time he hesitated to condemn completely the policies of the Government ("Herr Hitler, however disagreeable a
creature, is a queer one. National hysterias do
not last forever"), but by 1938, although he
had written that "Czechoslovakia should at
least attempt to negotiate with Germany a
reasonable solution of the problem of the
Sudeten Germans," he had become one of the
most bitter critics of Chamberlain's policies.
Munich was, to him, both dishonorable and
suicidal. Since July 1940 a member of the
Treasury Consultive Council and author of
plans for financing the War and the peace,
John Maynard Keynes is today doing all he
can to stop Hitler. It is also in this capacity
that he is able to see many of his economic
ideas put into effect, his activities far from
hampered by the position as director of the
Bank of England which he has held since
October 1941.

He is a "tall, heavily stooping figure, with
a pale face and hair growing very thin," and
has occasionally been as unconventional in his
living as in his economics. In 1925 he startled
a good part of two continents when he married Lydia Lopokova, a famous Russian
dancer. A member of the Bloomsbury group,
he continues to be interested in the ballet, in
art collecting. Frequently he has upset the
officials at the British Treasury. There was
the time, once, when he wanted to use a slang
word in a grave, semi-official document. Sir
Herbert Samuel admonished him: "There is
no such word in the English language." Unperturbed, Keynes replied: "But I wish to
extend the English language."

References

Time 37:30 F 10 '41 por; 37:86+ My 19 '41 por

Author's and Writer's Who's Who
Gardiner, A. G. Portraits and Portents p172-9 1926
Hodgson, S. Portraits and Reflections p152-7 1929
Who's Who

KILMER, ALINE Aug. 1, 1888—Oct. 1, 1941 Widow of Joyce Kilmer, the soldier-poet; author of six volumes of poems and essays which were published between 1919 and 1929; lectured frequently, until 1926, on literary topics; was vice-president of the Catholic Poetry Society of America.

References

Cath World 119:517-23 Jl '24
Poetry 36:102-3 My '30
Scholastic 26:6 Ap 27 '35 por

American Catholic Who's Who
American Women
Who's Who Among North American Authors
Who's Who in America

Obituaries

N Y Times p25 O 2 '41 por
Pub W 140:1576 O 18 '41

KILMER, MRS. JOYCE *See* Kilmer, A.

KIRKPATRICK, HELEN (PAULL) Oct. 18, 1909- Journalist

Address: c/o Chicago Daily News, Chicago, Ill.

Helen Kirkpatrick is the sole woman member of the Chicago *Daily News* foreign staff and one of the few American women correspondents in London. Though she is only in her early 30's, she is already being compared in journalistic circles with Dorothy Thompson and Anne O'Hare McCormick.

According to Ben Robertson of *PM,* she has been "in the thick and thin of everything since the Germans began raiding London. Long before the battle of London began she went to Dover, and that took courage as she never had been under fire before and Dover was not only being bombed, it was being shelled." By now she is used to it all, Helen Kirkpatrick says, and admits she has been able to sleep right through the biggest attacks. That is undoubtedly a necessary ability for a correspondent who files as many as three and four dispatches a day, most of them syndicated by the *Daily News* to twenty-four other leading American newspapers.

Much of her life, since the day she entered college, has been directed toward making Helen Kirkpatrick the successful foreign correspondent she is. She was born in Rochester, New York, the daughter of Lyman Bickford Kirkpatrick, a retired real estate broker and a direct descendant of the Colonel Joshua Fry who preceded George Washington as

HELEN KIRKPATRICK

the first commander of the Virginia forces, and Lyde (Paull) Kirkpatrick, and was educated at private schools in Rochester and at the Masters School at Dobbs Ferry, New York. In 1927 she entered Smith College. Here she did Special Honors work in history, was president of the International Relations Club in her senior year and in the spring of that same year won the $1,000 fellowship offered to Americans by the Students' International Union. She was graduated from Smith in 1931 and spent the following summer at the Zimmern School in Geneva and the winter at the Geneva Institute of International Relations. In 1932 the National Student Federation of America chose her as one of the two official student observers at the Disarmament Conference.

Back in America, Miss Kirkpatrick got herself a job at R. H. Macy & Company, the New York department store which is so often a temporary stopover for bright young college graduates. She started out as a salesclerk in the electrical appliance department and after a period of executive training was promoted to the position of assistant buyer in the lamp department. Later she was shifted to the same position in the handkerchief department—and this was the position from which she resigned in 1934 to go back to the field of international relations, only a short time after her marriage to Victor Polachek.

In November of that year Helen Kirkpatrick became executive secretary of the American Russian Institute for Cultural Relations with the Soviet Union. From here she went to Geneva for the Foreign Policy Association, to prepare reports on matters coming before the League of Nations for the Foreign Policy Association's *Research Bulletin.* In Geneva she addressed the League on several occasions as a representative of American students in-

KIRKPATRICK, HELEN—*Continued*

terested in promoting peace and world understanding. She tried to interpret events there to others. "One could wish," she wrote, "that the enthusiasm and challenge, combined with a dreadfully pessimistic facing of facts, that are felt here, could be felt in other places."

The more she was in Geneva, the more Helen Kirkpatrick wanted to write of her activities and discoveries. She was meeting important people like Anthony Eden, Pierre Laval, Litvinov (see sketch this issue), De Madariaga; she was becoming friends with the newspaper correspondents there. Occasionally she substituted for these correspondents when they were sick or vacationing and by 1937 was able to write: "I've finally got into the field I've always wanted, newspaper work. I started out by replacing the regular correspondent for the London *Daily Telegraph* and then got taken on during the League Assembly by the New York *Herald Tribune.*" That same year she obtained a divorce from her husband.

Other newspapers began to notice her work, and before long Helen Kirkpatrick was writing for many of the leading British newspapers and magazines, including the *Manchester Guardian* and the London *Daily Chronicle,* while acting as Geneva correspondent for the New York *Herald Tribune.* She was important enough in 1938 to give a radio talk from London on "Reaction in England Toward the Resignation of Anthony Eden."

By 1939 Miss Kirkpatrick had published her first book in London, *This Terrible Peace;* had lectured in America on "The Future of the British Empire", "Careers for American Women in Europe", "Behind the Scenes in London" and similar topics; and had founded and was editing the *Whitehall Letter,* a "highly influential" weekly digest of the news, published in London and distributed through the British Empire. To get material for this bulletin, read closely by Eden, Churchill, the King of Sweden and other statesmen, she commuted from one European trouble center to another. She was in Prague during the Sudetenland crisis; she covered Spain, the Balkans, Italy, Poland, Germany and France.

Then, in September 1939, she was asked to join the Chicago *Daily News* foreign staff, and proceeded to turn up "exclusives" that made her masculine competitors in such capitals as Prague, Madrid and Berlin green with envy. Time and again she filed world beats—on May 2, eight days before the Nazi invasion of Belgium, she cabled a message to the Chicago *Daily News,* which printed the following: "A private message from one of the best informed European correspondents of the *Daily News* says that the King of Belgium yesterday informed the United States Government that Belgium expects to be the next victim of Germany."

Helen Kirkpatrick continued to write books —her *Under the British Umbrella* was published at the end of 1939; and she lectured again in 1940 in the United States. Her topics this time were "Britain Looks at the Peace", "Behind the Barbed Wires of Europe", "A Foreign Correspondent Looks at Europe," and her audiences were enthusiastic. It was exciting to hear this tall, handsome, engagingly frank correspondent who looks like a typical American college girl tell of what she herself had seen and known in troubled Europe.

Back in London after this 1940 tour, Helen Kirkpatrick continued to win what are said to be among the best contacts of any American journalist resident in London by her forthrightness and sincerity, her perception and charm. And she continued to file those dispatches which are to many Americans, all over the United States, one of the best sources of information on Britain and the War.

References

Ind Woman 20:8 Ja '41
Smith Alumnae Q 31:259 My '40; 32:87 F '41

KIRKUS, VIRGINIA (kĕr'kŭs) Dec. 7, 1893- Bookshop and library consultant

Address: b. Virginia Kirkus' Bookshop Service, 439 E. 51st St, New York City; h. Redding Ridge, Conn.

Almost 300 booksellers and libraries subscribe to Virginia Kirkus' Bookshop Service. To them she and her two assistants give expert, unbiased information on new books and carefully considered opinions on their sales possibilities, in bulletins sent out every two weeks. Under heads like "Don't Overlook", "Must Books," and "Dark Horses," there are thumbnail descriptions of the plots and Miss Kirkus' recommendations, written in chatty, informal style.

Miss Kirkus pulls no punches. She is willing to "crack down on an author, however important, in spade-calling terms" if she doesn't think his latest work will sell. Once in a while she is wrong—Thomas Wolfe's *Of Time and the River* had only "snob appeal," and Mortimer Adler's *How to Read a Book* wouldn't sell, she said. But on the whole she manages to keep a batting average of about 85 per cent. She is also able to "discover" books published with little fanfare or by unknown authors. John Steinbeck's *Tortilla Flat* and Rachel Field's *Time Out of Mind* were enthusiastically hailed "Must promote."

In addition to the prepublication service, Miss Kirkus' office keeps its subscribers abreast of changing titles, prices, publication dates; it aids them in promotion ideas, prepares broadsides for their use among customers; it does holiday book lists, locates out-of-print books and answers all sorts of odd questions about books. And Miss Kirkus herself travels from coast to coast visiting booksellers and libraries, lecturing to women's clubs, discussing book problems.

Virginia Kirkus has been doing literary and related work for a good many years now. She was born in Meadville, Pennsylvania, the daughter of the Reverend Frederick Maurice Kirkus and Isabella (Clark) Kirkus. Her education was received first at the Misses Hebbs School in Wilmington, Delaware, then at Hannah More Academy in Reisterstown, Maryland and finally at Vassar College, from which she was graduated in 1916.

Out of college and fortified by teachers' training courses, Miss Kirkus settled down at the Greenhill School in Delaware (forerunner of the Tower Hill School), teaching English and history. At the end of three years she felt she had had enough teaching, even in a progressive school, and set out for New York and an editorial career.

Her first job was that of fashion editor for the Pictorial Review Company; her next, "back of the book" editor for *McCall's* Magazine. Meanwhile she was doing special freelance jobs for Doubleday, including the writing of *Everywoman's Guide to Health and Beauty* (1922). Before she did this book all she knew was that this publishing house wanted a book about something or other within five weeks. Miss Kirkus applied for the assignment, discussed terms and dates for half an hour and agreed to do the book. Then she discovered what it was to be about!

From *McCall's*, Miss Kirkus went to the children's book department of Harper & Brothers and stayed there as its head until 1932, responsible for the success of many new books and for the abridgments of many old ones, including *The Mill on the Floss* and *The White Company*. Then came the depression, which hit the children's book business between the eyes. "Publisher after publisher," Miss Kirkus says, "discontinued their departments, and my department at Harper's fell under the axe." This was the end of "the most responsible position I ever had."

Harper's gave Miss Kirkus six months to look for another position. "In the realization that perspective was needed to keep from being panicked into taking anything that was offered," she remembers, "I went ahead with plans to go abroad. On the homeward voyage the idea was born: that a service be established to act as liaison between publisher and bookseller, by providing the bookseller with prepublication information based on actual reading of advance material."

The service was launched in January 1933 with 20 publishers supplying material, and 10 subscribers ("optimists and progressives all of them"). Then when booksellers began finding how accurate Miss Kirkus' predictions were they began to sign up fast, and the publishers became even more cooperative. During the first year of the service 999 titles were reported; in 1940 almost 5,000 were covered.

During the years she has been heading her service, Miss Kirkus has found time to write a good many articles and, in collaboration with Frank Scully, two books for children, both published in 1935: *Fun in Bed for Children* and *Junior Fun in Bed*. "I'm bad at paper games myself," she explains, "so my mentality was probably just right for a sounding board for the audience for the books." She also found and still finds time for all those things a country place involves—old furniture, cooking, planning—in the home near Redding, Connecticut which she and her husband, Frank Glick, former football star at Princeton and

Werner Wolff

VIRGINIA KIRKUS

now a personnel executive, remodeled and landscaped. Her most recent book, *A House for the Week Ends* (1940) sets down her personal experiences with a Connecticut farmhouse and adds to it practical data, lists, costs "for the city dweller with a limited income, a yen for the country and limited time to enjoy it."

References

N Y Sun p32 D 13 '38 por
N Y World-Telegram p19 Ag 30 '40 por
American Women
Kirkus, V. A House for the Week Ends 1940
Who's Who in New York

KISEVALTER, GEORGE (kē-zâ-väl'tĕr) Apr. 4, 1883—Mar. 11, 1941 Aeronautical designer, bridge builder and engineer; born in Russia, he came to the United States during the First World War to inspect military material for his country; stayed and became a citizen; worked as aeronautical engineer and draftsman; helped to develop the *Bluebird* plane and helped design the system of bridges and parkways for the Belt Parkway and Bronx-Whitestone Bridge.

Obituaries

N Y Times p21 Mr 12 '41

KITTREDGE, GEORGE LYMAN Feb. 28, 1860—July 23, 1941 One of the world's greatest authorities on Shakespeare and early English literature; from 1894 until his retirement in 1936 was Gurney Professor of English Literature at Harvard University; known as "Kitty" to generations of students, his "English 2" course, which was a minute study of six of Shakespeare's plays, was a terror to ten thousand Harvard students; one

KITTREDGE, GEORGE LYMAN—*Cont.*
of the foremost teachers of his time, he
was the author of a number of books on
Shakespeare, Chaucer, English grammar,
Anglo-Saxon literature and English and Scottish popular ballads and folk songs.

References

Discussion 27:6+ Mr 2 '36
Nation 97:259-60 S 18 '13
Newsweek 7:28 My 9 '36
Sat R Lit 14:12 Jl 4 '36 por; 20:13 Ag
19 '39 por
Time 27:26 F 17 '36 por
Sherman, S. P. Shaping Men and
Women p65-86 1928
Who's Who in America

Obituaries

N Y Times p17 Jl 24 '41 por
Pub W 140:321 Ag 2 '41
Sch & Soc 54:76 Ag 2 '41
Time 38:34 Ag 4 '41 por

KOCH, THEODORE WESLEY Aug. 4,
1871—Mar. 23, 1941 Librarian of Northwestern University and author of more than
20 books on library science; had been librarian since 1919; had devoted his entire
career of 46 years to library work at Cornell
University, Library of Congress, University
of Michigan and Northwestern University.

References

Bul Bibliog 16:189 S '39 por
Leaders in Education 1941
Who's Who in America
Who's Who in Library Service

Obituaries

N Y Times p17 Mr 24 '41
Pub W 139:1559 Ap 12 '41
Sch & Soc 53:414 Mr 29 '41

**KOLB-DANVIN, MRS. CHARLES
LOUIS** *See* Radziwill, C., Princess

KOO, V(I) K(YUIN) WELLINGTON
(kōō) 1888(?)- Chinese Ambassador to the
Court of St. James's
Address: Chinese Embassy, London, England

Dr. V. K. Wellington Koo, who ever since
he left college "has moved suave and unruffled through a chaotic world of shifting
diplomatic scenes, wars and revolutions," has
been China's Ambassador to Great Britain
since April 1941. Cultured, polished and
tremendously educated politically, he is representing China with all the diplomatic understanding and finesse years of activity for his
country have given him.
Ku Wei-chun (V. K. Wellington Koo, as the
Western world knows him) was born in
Shanghai, the son of a wealthy father whose
hero was the Duke of Wellington. From 1899
to 1900 he studied at the Anglo-Chinese College in Shanghai and then spent a year at the
Yu Tsai School before entering St. John's

University. In 1904 he came to the United
States to enroll in Cook Academy in Ithaca,
New York in order to prepare himself for
an American college. His choice was Columbia University, which he entered in 1905. As
an undergraduate Koo took a liberal arts
course, distinguished himself for brilliancy in
his studies and rolled up a remarkable record
of extracurricular activities at the same time.
He was editor in chief of the *Spectator*, manager of the *Columbia* and *Columbia Monthly*,
winner of the Columbia-Cornell Debating
Medal (after a "suavely compelling, charmingly persuasive" speech defending America's
foreign policies), runner on the track team,
winner of the Philolescean Literary Prize and
member of Delta Epsilon Rho. After receiving his B. A. in 1908, he shifted from liberal
arts to political science and received an M. A.
in 1909 and in 1912 a Ph. D. for a thesis on
"The Status of Aliens in China." (Yale has
since given him an honorary LL. D., and his
own Government has honored him with many
decorations.)
Soon after he received his degree Koo returned to China to begin his political career.
His first position was that of secretary of the
Cabinet and to the President; his next that of
secretary to the Ministry of Foreign Affairs.
Later promoted to councilor and active as head
of the publicity office and as vice-chairman of
the commission to settle international claims
arising out of the Revolution, Koo continued
to deal with foreign affairs until July 1915,
when he was appointed Minister to Mexico.
Three months later he appeared in Washington
as Minister, the youngest diplomat of that rank
ever to come to this country.
At the Paris Peace Conference in 1919 Dr.
Koo was China's delegate, "spokesman for one-quarter of the human race," in his own words.
Here he presented China's claim for direct
restitution of the leased territory of Kiaochow,
the Tsingtao-Chinan Railroad and other German rights in Shantung Province, and when
these claims were turned down, he refused to
sign the Treaty of Versailles. He stayed in
Europe, however, as Chinese delegate to the
International Labor Conference in 1919 and in
August 1920 as chief Chinese delegate to the
League of Nations and a member of the Administrative Council, the man, according to
John Gunther (see sketch this issue), responsible for bringing China into the League.
By then he had become, in September 1920,
Envoy Extraordinary and Minister Plenipotentiary to the Court of St. James's. He had also
become the husband of Hui Lan, daughter of
Oei Tiong-han, one of the richest men in China.
The Koos spent their honeymoon in Geneva and
Mrs. Koo, 15 years younger than her husband,
began a life of shuttling back and forth over
the world and a career which has made her an
outstanding figure in international diplomacy.
Their elder son, Wellington, Jr., was born in
Washington, and after education in China entered Columbia; their younger, Freeman, born
in Peking, went from a Chinese school to
Harvard,

From London, Dr. Koo went to Washington in 1922 as one of the four Chinese delegates to the Conference on the Limitation of Naval Armaments and then returned to Peking to confer with his Government on the diplomatic questions raised by this conference. He stayed in China for many years, his first position that of president of the Commission for the Discussion of National Financial Questions. His next was that of Acting Minister of Foreign Affairs. In August 1922 he took this portfolio for the first of many times, was relieved of it in November of that same year and presented with it again in April 1923, after service as chief of the Preparations Bureau for the Special Tariff Conference.

In January 1924 Dr. Koo became Minister of Foreign Affairs for the third time and as such he signed the Sino-Russian Convention of 1924 which restored diplomatic relations with the Soviet Union. But when the Chihli Party was defeated by the Anfu-Fengtien faction in October 1924, his service ended and he fled from the capital, disguised, it is reported, in women's clothes. Before his next term as Foreign Minister, Dr. Koo served, in May 1926, as Minister of Finance, and set a precedent by publishing when he resigned a complete statement of the receipts and disbursements during his term in office.

In October 1926 Dr. Koo became Acting Prime Minister and president of the Customs Tariff Commission; in January 1927 he formed his second Cabinet. After a period as Prime Minister, Dr. Koo went into retirement which ended in 1931, when the Japanese began their invasion of Manchuria. Once again Minister of Foreign Affairs, Dr. Koo went to Geneva to represent China and became Chinese assessor to the Lytton Commission of the League which inquired into the situation. In playing that important role he was able to "make the members of the Commission appreciate fully the Chinese side of the problem," and though the Lytton report did not save Manchuria for China "it confirmed the condemnation of Japan as an international highway robber."

In 1932 Dr. Koo became Chinese Ambassador to France, a position he held until his transfer in April 1941 to the Embassy in London. Here he and Mrs. Koo entertained in a home decorated with Chinese furniture and furnishings, serving their guests famous Chinese dinners. But there was more work than entertaining for Dr. Koo. In 1933 he addressed the Assembly of the League of Nations, laying down the case against imperialism and militarism. In 1934 he was the chief delegate to the League and in that same year a member of the International Court of Arbitration at the Hague.

Although at one time some years ago there were rumors that Dr. Koo disapproved of the policies of the Nanking Government, he has never stopped working for it. When hostilities with Japan commenced, he was and has continued to be one of China's firmest fighters on the international front, representing China at League meetings, seeking China's inclu-

China Institute in America

V. K. WELLINGTON KOO

sion in an Anglo-French-Soviet accord, enlisting aid for his country from the democracies, warning the British not to make further concessions to Japan. "The recent history of both Europe and Asia," he said in 1939, "shows beyond a doubt the futility of trying to turn a tiger into a kitten by giving it a dish of cream." This is the policy he has maintained and the policy which, as Ambassador to England, he is undoubtedly urging the British to maintain.

References

N Y Times VII p9+ F 5 '39 por; p4 Ap 5 '41 por

Newsweek 1:18 Mr 4 '33 por

Who's Who

Who's Who in China

KORIZIS, ALEXANDER (kô-rē-zĭs') Apr. 15, 1885—Apr. 18, 1941 Late Premier of Greece

Bulletin: On April 18, 1941 the death of Premier Korizis was reported. It was known that a few hours before his death the supporters of a policy of further resistance against the Germans, who had finally moved in to help their Italian allies, had proposed the Government's immediate departure for Crete, and that he had opposed leaving Athens. The rumor that he had committed suicide remained unverified. General Tsalakoglou, who finally signed the Greek surrender and became head of the Axis-controlled Government, had been an old protégé of his.

From March 1941 issue:

Premier John Metaxas, Greece's strong man since 1936, died while his country was in the midst of a fierce struggle to preserve its independence. He was succeeded on January 29,

Greek War Relief Ass'n

ALEXANDER KORIZIS

1941 by Alexander Korizis, named by King George II to occupy not only the position of Premier but also the posts of Minister of Foreign Affairs, War, Aviation, Navy and Education.

The "complete antithesis of the man he succeeded in both background and appearance," this dignified, cultured, gray-haired banker was generally spoken of in the American press as a wise choice, despite his lack of military and even political experience. For years he has been a close friend of both King George and of Metaxas, "credited by the Greeks with knowing more about the affairs of his country than any other man living." Even more important, there are few groups in Greece likely to withhold their support from him at this critical time. Nevertheless there are some commentators who feel that there may be a weakening of Greek morale because of his lack of military knowledge; many others who see in his appointment merely a continuation of Metaxas' repressive dictatorship.

The Greeks themselves are not busy with speculation. They have the war with Italy to prosecute; they are faced by the added dangers that England's breaking off of diplomatic relations with Romania and Turkey's alliance with Bulgaria have brought. German troops are massed in Romania, and there are rumors of more German troops in Bulgaria; the fear of German assistance to Italy is a very real one. The Greeks are eager for encouragement, and this Korizis is giving them. As he said at Metaxas' funeral: "You have opened the road to victory. We shall march along inflexible and determined. We shall reach the end." Yet it is reported that he has refused to oust the Nazi military attaché from Greece.

Korizis has not often made ringing political speeches—most of his talking until now has been on national welfare work and on bank-

ing. Since 1903 he has devoted his life to banking, with the exception of two periods spent in the service of his Government. He was born in Poros, Greece, the son of George Korizis, a politician, and Catherine (Missirli) Korizis. His first ambition was to be a lawyer, and with this in view he attended the University of Athens to study law. He found he preferred finance and in 1903 started out in the banking world as a clerk in the National Bank of Greece.

Korizis' is the usual bank-clerk-to-bank-president story. He rose steadily—taking time out in 1912 to act as artillery captain in the Balkan War—until in 1928 he was made a vice-governor of the National Bank of Greece and in 1939 its governor. During these years Korizis was an active supporter of the farmers' cooperative movement and the originator of a branch bank of agricultural credit which was later succeeded by the Agricultural Bank of Greece, of whose board he became president.

It was in 1933 that Korizis first entered politics—as Minister of Finance. He kept this position only a short while, and it wasn't until 1936 that he again became associated with the Government. In this year, the year in which by a *coup* Metaxas established himself as dictator, Korizis became Minister of Public Assistance (Welfare), working closely with the man he succeeded but keeping himself clear of party politics. It was under Korizis that the first systematic social security plan in Greece was organized and got under way. In July 1939 he resigned his Cabinet position to take over his old duties as vice-governor of the National Bank of Greece and by August of that same year he was its governor.

Since the war with Italy began, Korizis' obvious role in it has been neither a military nor a political one. Mostly he has been doing national welfare work, both for the Government and as chairman of the Vanderbilt committee to aid civilian victims; mostly he has been urging the Greeks to "service." These affairs kept him busy—he used often to work the clock around. His new responsibilities will undoubtedly make his former activities seem almost like a vacation and leave him very little time for his wife, Elisabeth, his daughters and his son—and, of course, none at all for his hobby of yachting.

References

Liv Age 360:42-4 Mr '41 por
N Y Herald Tribune p1, 6 Ja 30 '41 por
Newsweek 17:20-1 F 10 '41
Time 37:29-30 F 10 '41 por
Who's Who in Central and East-Europe

Obituaries

N Y Times p1, 4 Ap 19 '41 por
Newsweek 17:24 Ap 28 '41

KOZLENKO, WILLIAM (kŏz-lĕng′kô) Oct. 1, 1908- Author; editor

Address: 3921 45th St, Long Island City, N. Y.

The revival and rejuvenation of the one-act play, usually credited to the radio and to Noel Coward (see sketch this issue), owe a good deal also to the efforts of William Kozlenko. Many a director of little theatres and settlement groups or radio programs would probably have even more gray hairs if it were not for the *One-Act Play Magazine* he founded in 1937, and his two boon books for amateur groups—*One Hundred Non-Royalty One-Act Plays* and *One Hundred Non-Royalty Radio Plays,* both published in 1940. The former volume "offers a well selected compilation of short dramatic vehicles which should prove helpful to amateur groups of all sorts." Beset with the problem of finding a suitable play for a special occasion or the needs of a particular group, a director need only consult a well-classified table of contents in order to find *the* play. Comedies, dramas, pageants; religious, holiday, historical plays, all are included. "Although designed to meet a definite need in the amateur play field, the plays may also be used by professional stage and commercial radio groups through payment of royalties and written permission from the publisher." Those which have been well recommended are: *And No Birds Sing, The Long Retreat, The Darkest Night, Who Stand and Wait* and *Saturday Supplement.*

The man who has made the one-act play his province was born in Philadelphia on October 1, 1908, the son of Jacob and Sara Kozlenko. When he was graduated from Central High School in Philadelphia he expected to be a musician, devoted himself assiduously to violin and piano, and even composed a little. Presently, however, he turned to literature and began writing about music, the theatre, fiction. In 1930 he published a monograph on George Jean Nathan which he signed Vladimar (a Russian equivalent of William). Presently, he became editor of the international publication, *Europa.* In 1937 he founded the *One-Act Play* Magazine, and he served as its editor until he resigned in 1940. Under his direction it became one of the few publications in America which offered an outlet to the gifted novice as well as to the established playwright. In selecting all types of plays for publication and including a number that are royalty free, as well as articles on all phases of theatrical endeavor, he made the magazine a valuable tool to various groups whose interest lies behind the footlights.

Kozlenko is author of a number of short plays published in various volumes: *This Earth Is Ours, Trumpets of Wrath, Not for Glory, The Street Attends a Funeral, Jacob Comes Home, The Devil Is a Good Man.* All have been produced in Europe and in America. (Two of his full-length plays were expected to see production in 1942, and in the fall of 1941 he was engaged on another.) His knowledge of craftsmanship has behind it the practical experience gained as organizer of the One Act Repertory Theatre in New York and consultant-director of the One Act Variety Theatre at the Provincetown Playhouse. He has been particularly interested in the social drama, and in 1939 he edited *The*

WILLIAM KOZLENKO

Best Short Plays of the Social Theatre. Each play in this volume "is a drama of protest, crying out against the insidious forces which tend, in a subtle or manifest way, to destroy freedom of thought and vitiate the right to live and work as free men in a free commonwealth." His most recent book, *American Scenes* (1941), gives "a panoramic study of America, seen through the eyes of the dramatists of the regions in which they live." Through the medium of the short plays represented in this book Kozlenko as editor presents "a document of contemporary democracy, with all its faults and virtues." He has been named editorial adviser to the John Day Company on the "Living Drama Series."

Music, displaced as a profession, has become Kozlenko's chief hobby, and he still hopes to finish a critical study of Beethoven which he began in 1939, as well as a novel. He has also been invited to write for motion pictures in Hollywood. His favorite sport is rowing. He and his wife Lenore, whom he married in 1931, have one son, Paul.

References

N Y Times IX p7 Ap 6 '41

KRAUS, RENÉ (krous) 1902- Author; journalist

Address: c/o J. B. Lippincott Co, 250 Park Ave, New York City

An eminent journalist and writer, René Kraus has gained considerable renown today as the biographer of one of the most fascinating and important personalities of our time, Winston Churchill. Particularly significant because of his personal acquaintance with "England's 11th-hour man," Kraus' book "commingles the well known facts of Churchill's career with intimate glances of the human being behind the legend." One critic writes

RENÉ KRAUS

about his *Winston Churchill* (1940): "Mr. Kraus is not, it seems to me, a great biographer; he is workmanlike, competent and not without a shrewd insight into his torrential subject, and the tremendous drive and brilliance of the extraordinary career which he describes supply the rest. Until the final accounts are cast up, the end is known and perspective is available, this is all one could reasonably ask. And it is quite enough."

The author has fought hard to achieve the detachment and the sense of perspective which are so difficult to attain in the midst of history in the making. André Maurois thinks that he has not altogether succeeded. "Coming events with him cast their shadows not before them but behind them. . . At times toward the end his book becomes a political pamphlet but . . . he is a good and reliable chronicler." The consensus of critical opinion is on the whole that René Kraus' book is "interesting, informative and bold" but that the author is completely overshadowed by the dynamic subject of his biography.

René Kraus, a tall handsome man with "flashing blue eyes and a cavalier manner," was born in Paris in 1902. His father was an Austrian and his mother a Frenchwoman. To complete his cosmopolitan background, he grew up in Vienna and in Berlin. He was graduated from the University of Vienna and worked for a time on a Paris newspaper. An interview with Chancellor Stresemann resulted in his getting a position with him as his Press Secretary. Later he became editor of Stresemann's *National Liberal Correspondence*, the official organ of the Liberal Party in Germany.

He left Germany a year after Hitler came to power. During that year he made himself very disagreeable indeed to the Nazis because of his secretly published diplomatic newsletter which was circulated all over Europe.

Eventually he got into hot water with the Gestapo: the intrepid journalist was imprisoned three times before he went to Austria in 1934. There he wrote for leading Austrian newspapers and was given the post of counselor to Chancellor Schuschnigg's Press Department. His last assignment before Hitler clamped down on Austria was as press attaché in the United States.

During his many years of diplomatic and journalistic activity in Europe he gained considerable personal knowledge of British public figures which he utilized in *The Men Around Churchill*, the book dealing with the important figures in England, that was published in the fall of 1941. This book, "chatty, generally well informed," presents studies of Lord Halifax, Anthony Eden, Ernest Bevin, Herbert Morrison (see sketches 1940 Annual), Sir John Dill (see sketch this issue), and many others of the men who are in charge of Britain's war effort. Kraus considers Churchill one of the really great men he has known—the only other one is Clemenceau.

Kraus used to spend a few months every year in London and still divides his time between that city and New York. Since coming to the United States, René Kraus has become an American citizen and has been a steady contributor to American national magazines. His work has appeared in *Redbook*, *Liberty*, *Cosmopolitan*, *Coronet* and the *Saturday Evening Post*, among others. The first interview with the late Lord Lothian to be given to any journalist, after his appointment as British Ambassador here, was given to René Kraus and appeared in *Liberty*. That magazine also published in serial form his Churchill biography before it was published by Lippincott.

Kraus' biography of Churchill and his sketches of the men around him represent a great stride in time from the subject of his former books. In 1938 his *Theodora, the Circus Empress* was published, a fictionized biography which the critics approved as a "fascinating . . . carefully done account of a most unusual woman and a decadent period." Of *The Private and Public Life of Socrates* (1940) a critic wrote: "First and last a clever book, [it] . . . manages to tell a familiar story with an air of strangeness and suspense, an ancient story with compellingly modern accent, a moral story with an unusual alternation of high seriousness and lighthearted sophistication."

KRAUSE, ALLEN K(RAMER) (krous) Feb. 13, 1881—May 12, 1941 Physician; prominent in the study of the pathology of tuberculosis; author of three books on disease and numerous articles for magazines and important encyclopedias; managing editor and editor of the *American Review of Tuberculosis* from 1916 to 1939; taught at Johns Hopkins and Stanford Universities; received the Trudeau Medal for Tuberculosis Research in 1931.

References

American Medical Directory
Leaders in Education 1941

Who's Who Among North American
Authors
Who's Who in America
Who's Who in American Medicine

Obituaries

N Y Times p23 My 13 '41
Sch & Soc 53:632 My 17 '41

KREBS, RICHARD JULIUS HERMAN
See Valtin, J.

KRIEBEL, HERMANN (krē'bl) Jan. 20,
1876—Feb. 17, 1941 Chief of the personnel
department of the German Foreign Office;
participant in Adolf Hitler's beer-hall *Putsch*
of 1923; in 1929 became chief military adviser
of Generalissimo Chiang Kai-shek; was member of Germany's 1919 Armistice Commission;
made his farewells to the Allied Commission
with the words: "See you again in 20 years."

References

Wer ist's?

Obituaries

N Y Times p24 F 18 '41
Time 37:50 Mr 3 '41

KRIVITSKY, WALTER G. 1900(?)—Feb.
10, 1941 Self-described former chief of the
Soviet Military Intelligence in Western Europe
who committed suicide; foe of Stalin who
testified before the Dies Committee, wrote
articles for the *Saturday Evening Post* and
published a book, *In Stalin's Secret Service*
(1939), to prove that the OGPU was a re-
morseless organization that always got its man,
that the American Communist Party was
directly connected with Moscow; entered the
United States on a visitor's visa in 1938 and
re-entered it in 1939 under the name of Walter
Poref; real name Samuel Ginsberg.

References

China W R 91:303 Ja 27 '40 por
Nation 149:32-3 Jl 8 '39
New Yorker 15:22 D 2 '39
Sat Eve Post 211:120 Ap 22 '39; 211:22
Je 24 '39
Krivitsky, W. G. In Stalin's Secret
Service 1939

Obituaries

Commonweal 33:435 F 21 '41
N Y Times p1+ F 11 '41 por
Newsweek 17:22 F 17 '41

KUBELIK, JAN (kōō'bĕ-lĭk) July 5,
1880—Dec. 5, 1940 Renowned Czech violinist
who won acclaim in concerts here and in music
centers all over the world by his brilliant
technique.

References

Lit Digest 116:11 N 18 '33 por; 116:48
D 2 '33
Pierre Key's Musical Who's Who
Thompson, O. ed. International Cyclo-
pedia of Music and Musicians 1939

Musical America

JAN KUBELIK

Who's Who
Wier, A. E. ed. Macmillan Encyclopedia of Music and Musicians 1938

Obituaries

N Y Times p23 D 6 '40 por

KUHLMANN, FREDERICK (kōōl'man)
Mar. 20, 1876—Apr. 19, 1941 Psychiatrist
whose development of mental tests and treatment of borderline mental cases won him national attention among psychiatrists; formerly
taught psychology at Clark University and the
Universities of Wisconsin, Illinois and Minnesota; had expected to retire on June 1, 1941
from his position as chief of the mental examination section of the Minnesota Division
of Social Welfare.

References

Leaders in Education 1941
Murchison, C. ed. Psychological Register 1932

Obituaries

N Y Herald Tribune p38 Ap 20 '41

KUNIYOSHI, YASUO (kŭn-nĭ-yōsh'ĭ
yä-sōō'ō) Sept. 1, 1893- Artist
Address: 118 Waverly Pl, New York City

Yasuo Kuniyoshi has been described as
"Japanese by birth but American by long
residence and conviction." Some of his best
paintings suggest the almost monochrome work
of the Chinese masters of landscape and yet,
though conditioned by his early Oriental background, Kuniyoshi's technique and mode of
expression are those of the Western World,

(Continued next page)

KUNIYOSHI, YASUO—*Continued*

His canvases, whether they are "socially conscious landscapes," wittily incongruous still lifes, or his characteristic pictures of women with drowsy slanted eyes and richly provocative mouths, have considerable influence on his contemporaries.

Kuniyoshi was born in Okayama, Japan, on September 1, 1893, the son of a small businessman, Ukichi Kuniyoshi, and his wife Itoko. When he was six years old he saw his first Western picture, a realistic battle scene, and was greatly impressed. But he did not intend to become an artist and willingly trained to become a weaver and dyer of fine fabrics. When he was sent to the United States in 1906, it was to study methods of industrial production, particularly in the textile field. Once in Seattle, however, he liked it so much that he decided to stay in America

Peter A. Juley & Son

YASUO KUNIYOSHI

forever, and with an heroic gesture he sent back the money his parents had given him for his stay. The immediate result was a period of semi-starvation, spent sitting by the Seattle harbor, watching the boats go in and out, munching peanuts (he has never eaten a peanut since). Finally he bestirred himself and went on to Los Angeles to earn a meager living as a houseboy and as a fruit picker in the Fresno and Imperial valleys. Evenings he spent at the Los Angeles School of Art and Design.

In 1910 Kuniyoshi came to New York to study art in earnest. He stayed with a friend of his father, a Mr. Kawabe, and attended the National Academy of Design from 1912 to 1914, when he changed to the Independent School of Art and studied under Homer Boss. He was poor, of course—odd jobs gave no kind of decent living, and it wasn't until his third winter in the East that he could

afford a winter coat—but he was cheerful, impressed by the art he was learning and discovering. The great Armory Show, particularly, left its mark on him. It was, in fact, too much of a mark, for it was only after he began to attend the Art Students League in 1916 and to study with Kenneth Hayes Miller that he began to develop a style of his own.

In the Art Students League, Kuniyoshi flourished. He made friends with other talented, up-and-coming artists like Alexander Brook, Reginald Marsh (see sketches this issue), Peggy Bacon, Henry Schnakenberg and Katherine Schmidt (whom he later married). He spent pleasant summers in Ogunquit. He was introduced into the famous Penguin Club and worshiped at the feet of Max Weber (see sketch this issue) and Jules Pascin. Soon he began timidly to exhibit— two paintings at the Daniel Gallery, a joint exhibition with Thomas Hart Benton in the first show of modern Americans organized by the Pennsylvania Academy of Fine Arts. *Fishing Village* was his first exhibited work.

Kuniyoshi's first one-man show in 1922 created a furore. But he came through unscathed, "except for the astonishing assumption that I was a humorist." It was an easy assumption to make, for the paintings abounded in grimacing brats, strangely foliated pastures with odd barns and geometric cows with triangular hips. The cows, especially, brought fame to the Kuniyoshi of this period. He objected. "I wasn't trying to be funny. I was painting cows because somehow I felt near to the cow." And he explained that he had been born in a "cow year" and that therefore, according to legend, his fate has been guided by bovine wisdom.

Recognition had come, but not prosperity, and until 1928 Kuniyoshi had to make a living by photographing the work of his fellow painters. He got to be quite an expert at it and once won first prize in the International Leica Exhibition. But he kept on painting and exhibiting steadily. In 1925 he went abroad and was so impressed by the work of Goya, Daumier and Renoir that he toyed seriously with the idea of remaining in Paris. He returned to America, however, and not long after became interested in lithography. It all started at the Whitney Studio Club when George Miller was demonstrating how lithographs were made. Kuniyoshi was asked to help Miller, and not long after saw possibilities for himself in this medium. He went to Paris again, in 1928, to work in black and white, and though his work was somewhat limited by his subjects (circus performers, his famous razor-backed cows, a few rocky landscapes and eccentric still lifes) it showed sure and lucid draughtsmanship and a permeating sense of color.

Not long after his return from this second trip to Paris, Kuniyoshi saw himself represented as one of 19 contemporary artists in an exhibition at the Museum of Modern Art in New York City. This was in 1929; two years later one of his works received an honorable mention at the Carnegie International Exhibition at Pittsburgh. Kuniyoshi, finally established as an artist, felt it was about time for him to return to Japan (it had been 25 years since he had seen his parents), and he managed to do this when sponsored by the paper *Mainichi* of Osaka. The trip was a mixture of triumph and disappointment. Although the great Japanese tycoon, Baron Mitsui, bought two of his pictures, Japanese artists and critics called his work typically European. Altogether Kuniyoshi felt strange and unnatural, and sailed back to America convinced that "my adopted home was really my home."

Recognitions, honors and sales continued to come to Kuniyoshi until today his place in American art is secure. He has maintained his record of winning a prize a year—among them the Temple Gold Medal of the Pennsylvania Academy of Fine Arts (1934) and the Los Angeles Museum Prize that same year; a Guggenheim Fellowship, on which he went to Mexico (1935); first prize in the American Section of the Golden Gate Exposition in San Francisco and second prize at the Carnegie International (1939). His works are represented in museums all over the country: in the Museum of Modern Art and the Whitney Museum, New York City; the Columbus Museum in Ohio; the Chicago Art Institute; and many others. Although he is considered an American artist, his not being a citizen (because of his Japanese birth) prevents his work from being bought by the Hearns Fund for the Metropolitan Museum. The Radio City Music Hall, though, boasts a brilliant mural by him, and his lithographs are owned by many museums. Kuniyoshi himself believes that "it's important for people, not just rich collectors and patrons, to buy pictures of their own. . . When I see people here buying pictures the way they buy radios and electric refrigerators, then I'll believe the American Renaissance is really at hand." He is proud that average people, rather than collectors, buy his work, and proud that he sells more pictures on the installment plan than any other American artist.

In the last decade Kuniyoshi has simplified his palette and subject matter and enlarged his canvas. His economy with paint has become more pointed: he tries to produce more color without using many colors. But his paintings are still flooded with an irridescent shimmer of color, with tender pinks, creamy flesh tones, opalescent silky greens. His nudes, particularly, have a special mother-of-pearl quality, a luminosity which he achieves by building a darker color on top of a lighter one. A theme upon which he particularly likes to elaborate is that of girls in attitudes of relaxation and contemplation—such paintings nearly all have the graphic titles of *All Alone, Waiting, I'm Tired, The Morning After.* As a rule overripe, sensuous, drowsy-eyed models dreamily looking at tabloids or listlessly leaning against a table are his favorite subjects and provide him with an opportunity for subtle and complicated tonal schemes. But there are sociological landscapes, too, tinged with mordant irony:

Cemetery and *Pie in the Sky* are pointed social comment.

Kuniyoshi never makes a small-scale preliminary composition, but draws straight onto the canvas. Usually he starts his paintings during the summer and keeps several of them going at the same time during the winter. The dealers complain that he never produces enough, and his shows, one every three years, have only about 15 canvases. Painting is a difficult and terribly important process for Kuniyoshi, one that is not to be hurried or slurred over. He starts "from reality, stating the facts before me. Then I paint without the object for a certain length of time, combining reality and imagination."

During the years Kuniyoshi has become identified with many organizations that aim to increase the dignity and standing of the American artist. He has been active in the Artists' Congress, in the American Society of Painters, Sculptors and Engravers, in the American Group, is a member of the American Printmakers and many other societies. He teaches at the Art Students League and has an evening class at the New School for Social Research in New York. After the outbreak of Japanese-American hostilities, Kuniyoshi's students gave him a "vote of confidence."

Kuniyoshi is a slender, comparatively tall man, with a thin line of mustache emphasizing his slightly sardonic grin, wears tortoise-shell glasses and is usually dressed in a sweatshirt, slacks and neat brogues. Summers are spent with his second wife, the former Sara Mazo, whom he married in 1935 (he was divorced from his first wife) in Woodstock, New York, that famous haunt of painters.

References

Art N 32:13 Mr 31 '34 por; 38-8+ Ja 28 '39 il
Creative Art 11:184-8 N '32 il por
Esquire 7:112-15 Ap '37 il
Liv Am Art Bul p1-3 Ap '39
Mag Art 33:72-83 F '40 il self pors
N Y World-Telegram p19 F 23 '40 il por
Parnassus 7:13 O '35 il; 12:17-22 F '40 il por
New Standard Encyclopedia of Art 1939
Who's Who in America
Who's Who in American Art

KUNZ, ALFRED A(UGUSTUS) (kōōns) May 21, 1893- Religious leader; camp director

Address: b. Pocket Testament League, 156 Fifth Ave, New York City; h. 17 S. Lyle Ave, Tenafly, N. J.

Just back from an exploratory 12-day, 3,000-mile tour of the United States military camps of the Middle West during which he conferred with chaplains in a dozen Army camps, held meetings in several, Alfred A. Kunz, executive secretary of the Pocket Testament League, is in 1941 and 1942 planning to accept invitations to "come back and stay longer" all along the way. He is encouraged in this plan by the consent and cooperation of the chief of

ALFRED A. KUNZ

chaplains, the Corps Area Commanders and the chaplains in the various camps, as well as by other Army and Government officials, many of whom have expressed their conviction that there is a vital spiritual need among the boys in the Army today.

The son of Alfred R. and Lena A. (Wolfe) Kunz, born in Brooklyn on May 21, 1893, Alfred Augustus Kunz feels that there is "a great deal of misunderstanding on the part of well meaning people today regarding God's requirements of man. Most people feel if we do the best we can, it is all that God can expect. The fact remains, however, that no one of us does really do the best he can, and even if he did, that would not be good enough because God requires perfection.

"As a boy of sixteen I joined the church, was active in church work, lived a respectable and moral life, only to discover after six years of church membership that I had no standing with God because the question of sin had never been settled in my life. At that time I held the belief that it doesn't make any difference what a man believes, as long as he is sincere. I have since discovered that it doesn't make any difference how sincere a man may be; if his trust is misplaced he is doomed to disaster. A sailor might have all the confidence possible in his ship, but if the vessel were leaking, his confidence would not keep it afloat.

"I was going my religious way to Hell, when at 22 I made the first great discovery a man must make in dealing with God—that I was a sinner and needed a Saviour. Shortly thereafter I made the second discovery necessary—that the Lord Jesus Christ . . . was the Saviour and Friend that I needed." Undoubtedly he was encouraged in this decision by Florence Palmer, whose spiritual life, even

before their marriage in May 1917, he says, "made me see she had something I lacked."

Alfred Kunz is not at all new to Army camps, having spent nine years as executive secretary of the YMCA, beginning back in 1917, first briefly at Camp Mills and Camp Merritt and then, until September 1926, at Fort Hancock. Tall, rangy, agile, his hobbies and favorite recreation including "all outdoor sports," the young "Y" secretary at first concentrated his efforts on athletics and educational service. Later he concluded that only spiritual work would have lasting values, and he decided to "put first things first" and devote his time exclusively to spiritual work.

As he had taken special courses to increase his speed and efficiency in his first business and advertising jobs (a short course at Cornell Agricultural College having persuaded him not to be a farmer), it was natural that later, when going into religious work, he felt he should study "so that my life in the Lord's work should be used as efficiently as possible for Him." The combination of part-time "Y" work at Fort Hancock and study at the Philadelphia School of the Bible proved exceedingly strenuous. This the Kunzes felt especially since they entered Bible school directly after the birth of their third daughter, Ruth Marianne (Carol Rae and Lois Hazel had come before; later came a son, Harvey Wadham). Nevertheless the young husband attended classes every day and "minded" the children at night while his wife took evening courses. When they completed their courses in 1926 Kunz "left a good salary to step out in faith, with nothing in view except serving the Lord in Christian work." But he soon found that "there is no waste in God's economy. When God has work in view for a man He fits him for it in advance."

Since 1926 he has been actively engaged in evangelistic and pastoral work and Bible teaching. He was for six years a teacher in the Hawthorne Evening Bible School, the Leader of the large Everyman's Bible Class of Hackensack, New Jersey for four years, and dean of the Elizabeth Evening Bible School since 1937.

Several men among the undenominational group known as "Plymouth Brethren," who were active in the YMCA, encouraged Kunz to center his activities in work with young people, which he has done with particular success. He likes to be with the younger generation, often seems to be one of them, with his disarming manner, his lively brown eyes quick to sober in understanding or crinkle with his ready smile, his love of the outdoors, his athletic leadership, his readiness for anything and suggestions for more.

His "vision" of a Christian camp for boys, "where, in addition to a healthy and happy vacation a lad could also secure a real and lasting spiritual benefit," became a reality with the opening of Deerfoot Lodge in the Adirondacks to 20 boy campers in 1930. By 1941 an enlarged camp was taxed to capacity with over 100 boys during the six weeks' season. In the meantime, so popular was Deerfoot Lodge that the boys' sisters begged for a camp, too, and in 1936 Kariwiyo Lodge was opened as a Christian camp for girls. Mrs. Kunz assists her founder-director husband as Camp Mother and nurse for both camps.

Early in 1941 Kunz was made executive secretary of the Pocket Testament League, which has had over a million voluntary members since its establishment in New York in 1916. Although the League is active in churches, schools, rural sections and prisons, Secretary Kunz is concentrating on work in CCC areas, where "Gospel Teams" of four or five young Christian businessmen conduct short services, distributing Gospels and Testaments, and in Army camps, supplying chaplains with Gospels and Testaments for free distribution, and holding services in the camps whenever possible.

A typical camp program includes organ music, a "chalk talk" and an illustrated lecture. One of a series of these talks is "America's Spiritual Foundation," in which Mr. Kunz quotes from the Presidents and great generals of America's early history, briefly outlines the history of the Bible through the days of the early martyrs and Pilgrims, emphasizing the place of the Bible in their lives, and picturing the "true torch of our Liberty" as the Statue of Liberty holding a Bible aloft. One of his slides is from the photograph of a New Testament that literally stopped a bullet, saving the life of the soldier who carried it in the First World War.

Copies of the Gospel of St. John are distributed free at the close of the meetings, with cards giving the Pocket Testament League membership pledge: "I hereby accept membership in the Pocket Testament League by making it the habit of my life to read a portion of the Bible each day (at least a chapter if possible), and to carry a Bible or New Testament with me." Any soldier signing the "pledge," either at the meeting or later, receives a special Army edition of the New Testament as a gift.

Most of the meetings will be held in the new Army chapels, of which a good many have already been completed at an average cost of $20,000 each. Planned so as to be quickly adaptable to any type of religious service whether Protestant, Catholic or Hebrew, these chapels each have a Hammond electric organ, accommodate about 400 and are placed conveniently in various parts of the camps, some camps having several—Fort Leonard Wood, for instance, has 12 of the new chapels. Although a very busy man, Mr. Kunz plans extensive tours to military camps in all parts of the country.

KYSER, KAY (kĭ′zĕr) June 18, 1906- Bandleader

Address: c/o Radio Features Service, Inc, 40 E. 49th St, New York City

Had he followed more than 100 years of family tradition Kay Kyser would have become a college professor. Almost every known relative of the popular bandleader has been associated with the field of education in

KAY KYSER

North Carolina. Kay Kyser chose instead to follow a musical career, building up his talent for genial comedy as an asset. In the 15 years since he left the campus at Chapel Hill, he has progressed to the point where, as "Professor" of the *College of Musical Knowledge,* his "classroom" consists of some millions of listeners, his gross income upwards of $10,000 weekly.

Recently at New York's Roxy Theatre a film featuring Kyser dominated the screen, his personality dominated the stage show and his followers filled the auditorium. Cecilia Ager, in reviewing the event, said: "It is hard to pinion Mr. Kyser's charm, examine and define it. He won't stay still long enough. On stage, he flits. On screen, he also flits. On screen there are close-ups, yet conscientious study of them still does not reveal Mr. Kyser's secret. . . Flash. I've got it. Mr. Kyser's allure is not so much physical as spiritual. He has a noble soul. He helps people in distress. He asks people questions, then answers them himself. He can't bear to see people tortured by doubts. He's humane. He's kind."

Kay Kyser comes by his Southern accent naturally—he was born in Rocky Mount, North Carolina, June 18, 1906. Nor is he a cultured hillbilly, as some writers have made out. The scholastic achievements of his forebears have been recorded by his 75-year-old mother (Kay's inspiration in his work), who was Emily Royster Howell before she became Mrs. Paul B. Kyser. First in line was Iowa Michigan Royster, elected to the Chapel Hill faculty almost a century ago. He was followed by other members of the family who became, respectively, professor of medicine, dean of the medical school and professor of surgery, dean of the graduate school and head of the Department of English, professor of Latin and Greek. And just prior to Kay's generation was Edward Vernon Howell,

KYSER, KAY—*Continued*

founder and dean of the present school of pharmacy.

With this background it was natural that his parents should anticipate a scholarly career for the boy whom they christened James King Kern Kyser, particularly since his mother had distinguished herself by becoming the first registered woman pharmacist in the state. Kay's father, also a pharmacist, passed the state examinations despite almost total blindness, with the help of his wife who read aloud the necessary textbooks. Their pharmacy in Rocky Mount had a statewide reputation and at one time they hoped that James might some day carry on the business. Kay's mother recalls looking at him for the first time and thinking: "You're a strange-looking baby—wonder what kind of druggist you'll make?"

Kay discarded his given names and settled down to his nickname at an early age, as well as to that flair for showmanship that went along with his more serious studies. It was during his high school years that his youthful energies began to find specific outlets. During his senior year he was cheerleader, class president, editor of the school's first Annual, member of various scholastic societies and coach of the junior football team. Lacking sufficient brawn to make high school varsity, he had formed the second-string team called the Tigers. Undefeated, they scored 261 points to their opponents' 23 in that single season. "Before entering the game," reported one observer, "they went into a huddle and James would lead them in prayer. It was selfish to pray for victory, so the prayer was for the strength to play the best game possible." Nor did his sense of sportsmanship stop there. On one occasion the opposing team had exhausted its reserves and Kay stepped in, playing against his own team. It is not recorded who won.

He entered the University of North Carolina in 1924 and it was not long before he had taken over most of the undergraduate events that called for a measure of showmanship. He was cheerleader, impresario of the University's three most pretentious musical shows and conductor of the proms, and when the late Hal Kemp, favorite bandleader of the campus, went North he bequeathed the campus musical rights to Kay and a band of six. Nor did it come as a surprise to his friends when in his junior year he gave up the study of law and turned to music as his main interest.

Kay's original idea had been to play clarinet but after a tryout the boys persuaded him to take the baton instead. Each of the boys in the group knew one tune, making a total of six to begin with. Kay filled in with showmanship. For their first out-of-town assignment they piled into an old Model-T jollopy—called *Passion* because it "het up" so quickly—and drove to Oxford, North Carolina, for a dance job that netted them $60. That was in 1926 and the boys who were with him on that date are still in the band. In 1927 George Duning joined on trumpet. A graduate of the Cincinnati Conservatory of Music, he soon forsook the trumpet to play piano and make arrangements for the band. Meanwhile Kay had pursued his study of theory, giving the band a solid musical foundation.

The theme chosen by Kyser in 1926 was Walter Donaldson's *Thinking Of You.* While still in college the group took dance jobs, many of which were far away from Chapel Hill. Forty colleges in the South, West and Midwest hired the orchestra for proms and hops.

Nor was Kay to be completely outdone scholastically by brother Edward (now associate professor of pharmacy at the University of North Carolina). In his senior year he was class president, editor of the college Annual, director of theatricals, conductor of a one-man tutoring system and "one of the best cheerleaders N. C. ever had." Membership in Sigma Nu and Alpha Kappa Psi didn't hurt the band business and the B. A. degree he got that year was a source of satisfaction to one who required not a sheepskin, but merely a baton and a band, to get ahead in life.

Never spectacular from an orchestral point of view, Kay Kyser's Orchestra has nevertheless been a favorite for many years in the "sweet" category of polls conducted by such musicians' magazines as *Down Beat.* As clowning and comedy featured the band's work it piled up votes in the "corn" division. Though a term of derision originally, the *corn band,* in today's musical parlance, may be either a novelty outfit or a band with specialized non-musical pretensions. About 1934 Kyser's Orchestra began to use musical devices that *set* them in the public mind. Numbers were announced by singing the song's title and the imminence of a vocal was announced by four bars from its theme. Another distinctive Kyser touch is a trill played by three muted trumpets, and known musically as a "bridge."

During his years in the band business Kay has broken scores of attendance records, starred in an RKO film, *That's Right, You're Wrong,* and was called back to mix music and showmanship with murder melodrama in *You'll Find Out.* *Playmates* was released in late December. For 1942 release he has appeared in *My Favorite Spy.* The most important single factor in his rise to fame was his elusive style of comedy that seemed hilariously funny in the aggregate, yet proved difficult of analysis. He was once described as "combining the snooping pantomime of Jimmy Durante, the mock seriousness of Eddie Cantor [see sketch this issue], the repartee of Fred Allen [see sketch this issue] and the shyness of Harold Lloyd." And while this is hyperbolic it suggests what is true, that Kay has in him a little of everything comic.

A few years ago the kidding that went on between Kay and his listeners crystallized in a radio program from the Blackhawk Hotel in Chicago. Presented as a sustaining feature over WOR, it was called *Kay Kyser's Kampus Klass.* It acquired a sponsor and became *Kay Kyser's College of Musical*

Knowledge. With quiz programs on the way up, this idea was the crowning touch to one already known as an incomparable showman.

Bespectacled, slender, average in height and with ash-blond hair, bachelor Kay often has a mildly surprised look in his blue eyes that fits perfectly into his role of "Professor." His nervous energy finds an outlet in his work, just as it did when he was high school cheerleader. "Dressed in a white flowing professor's robe, with a red hood and mortarboard," reported one visitor to a studio broadcast, "he jumps, cavorts, parades, mugs and waves his arms like a dervish with the tingling memies."

Known as one of radio's hardest workers, it is not unusual for Kyser to appear on the stage five times, hold a three-hour rehearsal for his broadcast, conduct the network show, then go off and play at a prom. As a fillip to such a day, he often bones up on the next week's script before turning in for the night. In November 1940 *Variety* reported that his earnings had gone so high that further bankroll pyramiding would be only for the benefit of the Government—in view of which he would "do nothing outside of one-nighters and his broadcasts until the first of the year!"

With Kay Kyser and his orchestra are such notables of sweet music as Ginny Simms, Harry Babbitt, Ish Kabibble and Sully Mason. In private life he has a Negro valet known as Mac, whose engraved calling cards list his six given names and the capacities in which he serves Kyser—"chef, chauffeur, personal secretary and chaperon to Mr. James K. Kyser, valet, the Man from the South."

Mustaches are Kyser's pet aversion and none of his musicians wears them. As for hobbies, he likes and finds time for swimming, horseback riding, movies and roller coasters—and always gets back in time to say familiarly, "Evenin', folks, how y'all?"

References

Christian Sci Mon p11 N 15 '40
Liberty 18:37-8 F 1 '41 por
N Y Times X p12 Mr 17 '40
PM p12 N 15 '40 por
Variety 140:1 N 20 '40
Variety Radio Directory

LA CAVA, GREGORY (lä kä'vä) Mar. 10, 1892- Film director

Address: b. Universal Pictures Corp, Universal City, Calif.

Gregory La Cava likes to think of himself as Hollywood's Neanderthal man, "a rebel, a throwback, a rugged individualist, a gay sprite, and an inveterate non-conformist." He has resisted all attempts to modernize his methods and has "sneered at Hollywood's phony caste system." His methods, he claims, are the same as they were in the early days of the cinema, and his cronies, today as then, are "newspapermen, ex-prize fighters, and W. C. Fields."

It was a long time before La Cava got the right to make pictures without studio interference, but his success has been so great

GREGORY LA CAVA

that today, it is said by Hollywood wags: "If La Cava suddenly decided that the sound stages should be painted a lurid green, an obscure clause in his contract would be found giving him the right to have the paint job launched at once at the studio's expense." His contracts are 60 pages long and provide for every imaginable contingency. It has been suggested to him that he throw away his script and shoot his contract instead.

Gregory La Cava was born in Towanda, Pennsylvania on March 10, 1892, the son of Pascal Nicholas and Eva (Wolz) La Cava. His father, musician and linguist, was the only Italian in that Irish town. Gregory attended the Towanda elementary school and the high school in Rochester, New York, where his family had moved. While in high school he worked for more than a year as a reporter on the Rochester *Evening Times.*

During his elementary and high school career, La Cava had shown promise in art work. He finally left his newspaper job to attend the Chicago Art Institute and later the Art Students League and the National Academy of Design in New York. Then La Cava opened his own studio in New York, but he "found art unremunerative." He managed to succeed moderately as a cartoonist for the American Press Association, the *Evening World,* and the *Sunday Herald.*

As a newspaper cartoonist, La Cava became interested in the problems and possibilities of animated cartoons for the screen. A pioneer in the field, he drew some of the early *Mutt and Jeff* cartoons. He organized and later headed the animated cartoon department of the William Randolph Hearst Enterprises. At this time he was a "hard-boiled, tough citizen who would fight any man in the house for $2 (and probably lose), and who never said 'No' when drinking unless someone asked,

LA CAVA, GREGORY—*Continued*

'Have you had enough?' He had more enemies than a centipede has legs."

In 1921, after four years of animated cartoon work, La Cava got his first job in the motion-picture industry which at that time was largely in and around New York. He wrote the *Torchy* stories for Johnny Hines, who was making two-reel comedies for Charles Burr. In 1922 La Cava began directing the Johnny Hines pictures, and it was in one of these La Cava two-reelers that Clara Bow made her screen debut. In 1924 he began writing and directing for Paramount. When the Company transferred the bulk of its activities to the West Coast in 1927, La Cava went to Hollywood. In 1929, after leaving Paramount, he accepted an offer from First National to direct Corinne Griffith in *Saturday's Children*.

The success of *Saturday's Children* induced him to abandon writing and drawing for directing. But his objection to supervision and the subsequent explosions and feuds caused him to move from studio to studio even though his work was generally conceded to be good. He went first to Pathe, where he directed *Big News* and *His First Command*, and then to RKO, for whom he directed *Laugh and Grow Rich*, *Smart Woman*, *Symphony of Six Million*, *Half-Naked Truth*, *Bed of Roses* and other pictures.

Among his successful pictures have been *Gabriel Over the White House* (1933); *Gallant Lady* (1933); *The Affairs of Cellini* (1934); *Private Worlds* and *What Every Woman Knows* (1935); *She Married Her Boss* and *My Man Godfrey* (1936); *Stage Door* (1937); *Fifth Avenue Girl* (1939); *Primrose Path* (1940); and *Unfinished Business* (1941). Almost every picture he has made has been a hit, and he has many imitators. His recent pictures strike a compromise between the "artistic" and the "commercial," and many critics believe that he and Frank Capra are the greatest directors in Hollywood. Although he makes only one picture a year, he is among the highest paid of the film capital's directors.

La Cava's unorthodox methods include his "cuff shooting" technique, a relic of the silent picture days when the director made up the story and dialogue as he went along. His "script" is merely a series of indexed notes in a loose-leaf notebook. It contains a description of the settings and also first-person narratives by the principal characters. La Cava has several alternate situations for each episode and he selects the one he wants the night before he is ready to film the scene. He often writes the dialogue right on the set. "A picture," he says, "is always in solution. It must be molded from day to day to suit the personalities of the people involved. It should crystallize only on the high point of any scene or action."

Another La Cava device which differs from the practices of other directors is that of shooting the picture in narrative sequence. Most directors shoot all the scenes that take place in one setting regardless of where they occur in the story. Their way saves money, but it is La Cava's contention that his way makes for better pictures. "The players get a better grasp of their characterization my way," he says. "They grow into the parts."

La Cava also used "mood music," another relic of silent picture days. He keeps a pianist playing on the set all the time except when a scene is actually being shot. He claims it improves both his and the actors' powers of concentration.

Because his script is never finished until the picture itself is completed, La Cava's performers never know what is going to happen next; nevertheless his policy is not to treat his actors as puppets, but to allow them reasonable freedom in the expression of their characterization and full freedom to suggest additions or changes in action and dialogue. He makes no retakes and "cuts and edits his film in the camera."

La Cava is interested in the operation of the human mind, and his admirers consider him a "truly distinguished psychologist, in an amateur way." In his pictures, he tends to place the emphasis upon people rather than events. He is said to love the "screwball type" both in life and on the screen, and it is reported that his idea of a "swell springboard" for a story is a situation involving a man who "ax murders" his wife after 40 years of married life and then explains that he "just got tired of her doing nothing for 40 years but smiling and rocking back and forth in a rocking chair." To "connoisseurs of movie craftsmanship" the earmarks of a La Cava picture are: mature and witty dialogue, sound psychology, and the "sure humanity with which it pries out the secret feelings of its gay but troubled characters."

Described as a "grizzled, bald, vigorous man with an irrepressible fund of humor, a fierce integrity, and an unholy belligerence that has kept him in hot water most of his life," La Cava is five feet nine inches tall, weighs 155 pounds, and has dark eyes and receding gray hair. He has been married twice. His present wife is Grace Garland, to whom he was married in March 1941. He has one son, Billy, by his first marriage.

La Cava's favorite recreations are playing golf and studying psychology. He also likes to sit around and drink or gossip with old friends, or "punch the bag with Grantland Rice (see sketch this issue), Damon Runyon, or Rube Goldberg."

References

Arts & Dec 51:24 D '39 por
Chicago Tribune Je 15 '41
Christian Sci Mon p12 Mr 21 '41
Collier's 101:18+ Mr 26 '38 por
Life 11:75 S 15 '41
N Y Herald Tribune VII p5 Mr 24 '40
Time 38:78 S 15 '41

International Motion Picture Almanac

LAFFOON, RUBY (lăf-fōon') Jan. 15, 1869—Mar. 1, 1941 Ex-Governor of Kentucky who during his term from 1931 to 1935 appointed 11,352 colonels, among whom were Mae West, Jean Harlow and Jack Dempsey; was center of a bitter fight involving state tax and the method of choosing the Democratic Party's candidate for Governor; before 1931 had been a judge for 10 years in Kentucky.

References

Am Mag 120:22-3+ O '35
Newsweek 6:7 N 16 '35 por

Who's Who in America
Who's Who in Government
Who's Who in Law

Obituaries

N Y Times p43 Mr 2 '41 por
Time 37:64 Mr 10 '41

LAHEY, FRANK H(OWARD) June 1, 1880- Surgeon; president of the American Medical Association

Address: b. 605 Commonwealth Ave, Boston, Mass; h. 118 Bay State Rd, Boston, Mass.

In June 1940 Dr. Frank Lahey was made president-elect of the American Medical Association and in June 1941 he took office in the Association. The unanimous election, which received an ovation from the House of Delegates of the A. M. A., was a fitting culmination to the years in which Dr. Lahey has been active in the Association as member of its Council on Scientific Assembly and its Council for Medical Education and Hospitals. It was also a recognition of the vastly important contributions which Dr. Lahey has made to surgery.

Dr. Lahey was also honored in 1940 when *Frank Howard Lahey: Birthday Volume* was published on his sixtieth birthday. In it there are medical articles by famous doctors, many of them inspired by his own work. As the dedication states: "We of the medical profession . . . offer to you this birthday volume in which you will find yourself reflected more often than we intend to confess."

Dr. Lahey's rise in the medical world has been steady ever since the day he left medical school. He was born in Haverhill, Massachusetts, the son of Thomas and Honora Frances (Towers) Lahey, and received his M. D. from Harvard in 1904. Then came two years of internship in the Long Island Hospital and the Boston City Hospital, followed by a position as resident surgeon of the Haymarket Square Relief Station in 1908 and an instructorship in surgery at the Harvard Medical School that same year. Dr. Lahey stayed at Harvard only for a year, until 1909, the year he was married to Alice Wilcox, but in 1912 returned to his old position there.

While acting as instructor at his Alma Mater, Dr. Lahey was also assistant professor and later professor of surgery in Tufts Medical School, from 1913 to 1917. (Ten years later Tufts gave him the honorary degree of Doctor of Science.) Then came the War;

DR. FRANK H. LAHEY

Dr. Lahey served as a major in the Army Medical Corps and also as the director of surgery in Evacuation Hospital Number 30, A. E. F., before returning to America to private practice.

It was in 1922 that Dr. Lahey first started his now famous Lahey Clinic, in a small building on Commonwealth Avenue. His own specialty was operating upon thyroids, and he developed a technique that has proved almost uniformly successful. Within 17 years he and his associates performed over 15,000 operations and lost only 100 patients. Under Dr. Lahey the clinic developed along other lines, too. Its doctors were able to contribute to knowledge of the treatment of peptic ulcer and cancer, the surgical treatment of thoracic diseases, techniques in surgery of the digestive tract. In 1941 the Lahey Clinic, a privately operated hospital, is housed in a large four-story building, staffed by 56 doctors who perform some 7,500 operations a year. "Its operating rooms presided over by Frank Lahey and his associates have long been a Mecca for surgeons seeking the most accepted and advanced methods in the surgical treatment of disease."

Dr. Lahey has spent the years since 1922 (with the exception of one year, in 1923 and 1924, which he spent as professor of clinical surgery in the Harvard Medical School) as an active, practicing surgeon in the Lahey Clinic and as chief surgeon of the Deaconess and Baptist Hospitals. He is famous for his discoveries of techniques and cures, and during these years he has made his presence and opinions and contributions felt in most of America's medical associations. He is a fellow and member of the board of governors of the American College of Surgeons, the American Association for the Study of Goiter, the American Surgical Society, the Massachusetts Medical Society, the International

LAHEY, FRANK H.—*Continued*

Surgical Society and many others. He is also the author of a number of articles and a member of the editorial boards of the *New England Journal of Medicine* and other medical publications. Despite his large practice and association activities, Dr. Lahey still finds time to talk widely on his failures and successes, illustrating his subject with colored films of operations. And he also finds time occasionally to play golf and indulge his ardent love of hunting.

References

> Time 35:57 Je 24 '40 il
> American Medical Directory
> Directory of Medical Specialists 1939
> Lahey Clinic. Frank Howard Lahey;
>   Birthday Volume 1940
> Who's Who in America

LAMBERT, SYLVESTER MAXWELL

Dec. 28, 1882- Physician; author

Address: b. c/o Little, Brown & Co, 34 Beacon St, Boston, Mass; h. Walnut Creek, Calif.

Bachrach

DR. SYLVESTER MAXWELL LAMBERT

"If any man should write a book it should be Lambert," Dr. Victor Heiser once said. It was Heiser (of *An American Doctor's Odyssey* fame), who many years before had sent Dr. Lambert to the South Sea Islands to fight hookworm—"to put the South Seas back 100 years, to the days when everybody was happy and well." And Lambert had done it. With "native assistants, hypodermic needles, microscopes and gallons of medicines," he had practically wiped out that disease, had cured more than a half million natives of hookworm, had made himself known and loved over "six million miles of island-sprinkled sea."

Eventually Dr. Sylvester Maxwell Lambert wrote that book, too. *Yankee Doctor in Paradise* (1941), produced after his retirement in 1939 because of failing eyesight, tells his remarkable story in a "candid and amusing" way and is called by Ralph Thompson "one of the better and brighter specimens" of the doctor-autobiography crop.

This amazing man was born on December 28, 1882 in Ellenville, New York, the son of William Walter and Harriet Celia (Taylor) Lambert. His mother's people had been small-town newspaper publishers for nearly a century; his father was a leather tanner and freethinker. Parental sacrifices sent him to Hamilton College in Clinton, New York. There he played football and was given his Ph.B. in 1903, and in 1904, although he had prepared for Johns Hopkins, he entered the Medical School of Syracuse University. Four years of "Spartan scholarship" brought him his M. D., and then there were four more years spent in practice in Rochester, New York before, in 1913, he took a position as medical director for the United Sugar Company in San Blas, Sinaloa, Mexico.

He had been in Mexico before. During his period in medical school he had taken a summer position as a nurse in a traveling hospital operated by a company constructing a railroad line through the states of Sonora and Sinaloa, and it was there that he had met Eloisa Tays, whom he married in October 1912. Now, from 1913 to 1916, he "practiced medicine between raids by Carranzistas, Villistas, Yaquis." Adventure pursued him. Finally, when one of Obrégon's most valued officers died after he had operated on him, he was jailed and sentenced to be shot. His case became an international affair; William Jennings Bryan sent down a cruiser; and eventually a gunboat deposited Dr. and Mrs. Lambert and their 10-months-old daughter safely in San Diego.

Next, from 1916 to 1918, he worked as a member of the staff of the United Fruit Company in their hospital in Limon, Costa Rica. Even then his eyesight was beginning to fail. In the First World War he was rejected as a doctor, and by 1918 his eyes had become so bad that he was unable to perform a major operation. He returned to the United States, believing himself finished as a medical practitioner.

Actually his real life as a medical practitioner was only beginning. Dr. Victor Heiser, then head of the Eastern Division of the Rockefeller Foundation, promptly offered him a position as the Foundation's representative in the South Pacific. He was to go to Papua (the southeast portion of New Zealand). Accepting even before he found out exactly where Papua was, he set out for Australia a few days later. There was a pause in North Queensland in order to cooperate with the Government in a health survey and to ballyhoo "a Yankee's message to Australasia—privies and more privies!" And then, in January 1919, two weeks after he had landed, he came down with the sprue. Doctors told him it was sure death unless he got out of the tropics. His weight went from 234 to 193 pounds, but he refused to return to the United States. "No man ever had the opportunity I've got," he insisted—"an untouched market to sell health in. With a little hard work, hundreds of thousands of lives can be saved. No blankety-blank disease can kill me!"

It didn't, either. Dr. Lambert, by some coincidence, read an article which contained a new remedy for the sprue. He had to guess at the dose, but he evidently guessed correctly, for in six months he was well. Leaving North Queensland soon after he had saved a little girl's life by a delicate operation performed without a license, he finally arrived in Papua in May 1920.

Dr. Lambert describes the Rockefeller Foundation's theory of economics: "Keep the native alive, restore his health, give him enough European knowledge to fend him against the evils of Europe, then he will go happily ahead cultivating the soil for the world and himself." In the South Seas he found much to be done. In some Pacific areas infections from hookworm ran as high as 98 per cent and leprosy, tuberculosis, malaria, yaws, dysentery and elephantiasis were also rampant. As he puts it: "Epidemics are the fruits of island hospitality."

There was much to be done, but superstition and, often, hostility toward the white man stood in the way of doing it. Dr. Lambert learned pidgin English. He learned to use the superstitions of the natives for his own purposes when he could not overcome them. He forgot dignity. Although his eyesight did not improve, eventually he was going around from island to island, lecturing, successfully treating 6,000 people a month for hookworm. "I've had natives faint in the middle of a hookworm lecture," he says. "I scared hell out of 'em." He did pioneer work in the mass treatment of intestinal parasites by carbon tetrachloride, treating practically the entire population of Fiji without an examination after his first experiments with it in 1922.

Said a British doctor in Fiji: "Only Lambert could have done this job. We British medical men are so overloaded with dignity we couldn't have unbent enough to get the confidence of the natives. Lambert plunged into villages and sold health as vigorously as though he were a peddler with a patent painkiller, cutting red tape and trampling on convention." Richard Crooks called him "the livest man in Fiji." In one part of Papua he was known as The Man Who Takes Off His Feet; in the Rennell Islands a chief tattooed on his left ankle a decoration consisting of two tiny fish, touching one another—a decoration which meant Lambert was to him as his own son.

But the treatment of hookworm was not all that Lambert did during his 20 years in the South Seas. He fought against "the hellish Mother Hubbard," which increased susceptibility to white men's diseases, and got the missionaries' and steamship companies' backing for his campaign. He was responsible for the building of thousands of latrines. And, perhaps most significant of all, he was the prime mover in founding the Central Medical School in Suva and in opening it to students from other islands as well as the Fiji Islands. Dr. Heiser hadn't wanted the school for native medical practitioners, hadn't believed the descendants of cannibals capable of becoming good doctors, but Dr. Lambert proved he was right. He is proud of his students who are now expert and conscientious surgeons and doctors; he has a great respect and admiration for the natives, particularly for the Fijians. He says: "The islander will survive to achieve great things in a brave new world. . . Utopia is always a long way off, but I'll risk a prophecy. Guide the native with sympathetic intelligence, and the time will come when he will cease to be our pupil. He will become our teacher. Not in the science of war, God deliver us, but in the more difficult art of living together in harmony and peace."

Bald, nearly six feet tall, rather plump, Dr. Lambert looks "like a popular country practitioner." Quick-tempered, he is capable of awe-inspiring profanity, hates formality—although in the South Seas he was quite willing to get dressed up when it was absolutely necessary and to go through interminable Government-demanded ceremonies, making flowery speeches to "British Big Shots." He wears heavy glasses which, in order to read, he takes off and holds three or four inches from his nose. In 1941 he, his wife and his two daughters, Harriette Rose and Sara Celia, live in Walnut Creek, California, where his hobbies are walking, contract bridge and weeding his garden. "Weeds stir my antagonism," the doctor confesses.

References

Am Mag 118:73+ N '34 por
Am Mercury 48:65-70 S '39 (Same abr. Harper 174:377-84 Mr '37
Read Digest 35:63-7 S '39)
American Medical Directory
Beatty, J. Americans All Over p397-407 1940
Heiser, V. G. American Doctor's Odyssey 1939
Lambert, S. M. Yankee Doctor in Paradise 1941

LAMBERTON, ROBERT ENEAS Sept. 14, 1886—Aug. 22, 1941 Mayor of Philadelphia since January 1940; had served as judge from 1931 to 1939; former sheriff; attorney; was mentioned as candidate for Governor of Pennsylvania in 1940.

References

Life 8:67 Je 24 '40 por
Time 35:17 Ja 8 '40; 37:19 My 26 '41
Who's Who in America

Obituaries

N Y Times p13 Ag 23 '41 por

LAND, EMORY S(COTT)   Jan. 9, 1879-
Chairman of the United States Maritime Commission

Address: b. United States Maritime Commission, Washington, D. C.; h. 2500 Massachusetts Ave, Washington, D. C.

EMORY S. LAND

According to Emory S. Land, chairman of the United States Maritime Commission, in 1941 "the need is for ships, ships and more ships."

To get these ships the Maritime Commission has been taking away everything from tankers to passenger ships such as the *America* from shipping lines operating under government subsidies; it has been building hundreds of new ones; it has been scraping together and repairing old vessels; and under a Congressional bill signed by the President in June 1941 it has requisitioned tons of idle alien ships which have been lying in American harbors. By September 1941 Land could announce that the construction program was not behind but ahead, and in December, with a war in the Pacific vastly increasing demands on American shipping facilities, he had confidence that it could eventually be doubled.

Admiral Emory Scott Land, on whom rests much of the responsibility for United States trade throughout the world with all that implies today, has been a Navy man all his life. But he was born far from the sea, in Canon City, Colorado, into a landlubber family. His parents were Scott E. and Jennie Taylor (Emory) Land, related to Charles A. Lindbergh's (see sketch this issue) family. Emory went to grammar, high school and college in the West and in 1898 was graduated from the University of Wyoming with B. S. and M. A. degrees. He went on to a distinguished career at Annapolis, marked by a last-minute winning touchdown in the Army-Navy game of 1900, by stellar activities in

track, baseball and swimming (they won him the Athletic Sword upon graduation) and by a scholastic record that placed him sixth in his class. The description of him in the class book of 1902 analyzes his personality: "Started right in the beginning and the rest was easy. Naturally of a timid, bashful disposition, he overcame it by strenuous effort. Has discovered that the best way to get what you want is to ask for it. Is not afraid of the good things of life."

Lieutenant Land was not long out of Annapolis when, in 1904, he was assigned to construction work in the Navy. A few years later he was sent to the Massachusetts Institute of Technology to take a postgraduate course in naval architecture; he left this college in 1907 with an M. S. degree and continued helping the Navy build right through the First World War, during which he was on duty in the Bureau of Construction and Repair. For his work here and for his comprehensive, technical study of German submarines he was awarded the Navy Cross for distinguished service. In 1919 he served with the Naval Armistice Commission—as Captain Land—and in 1920 he was for a short while Naval Attaché at the American Embassy in London.

The next 17 years, except for a year's leave of absence in 1928 and 1929 when he was vice-president and treasurer of the Guggenheim Fund for the Promotion of Aeronautics, were spent in the Navy in various capacities. In 1926 he was made assistant chief of the Bureau of Aeronautics of the Navy Department—he learned how to fly a plane in the 1920's—and continued in this position until 1928. In 1932 he was made head of the Navy's Bureau of Construction and Repair, in charge of building up the Navy to treaty strength. As though this job weren't enough, Rear Admiral Land regarded as part of his duties coaching, scouting and refereeing for Navy football teams.

Suddenly, in 1937, "the busiest guy in the Navy" announced he was going to retire. Fellow officers refused to believe it and quoted at the trim, wiry Admiral his own saying that "you can't keep a squirrel on the ground." He did resign, but he was out of the traces for only a few weeks, at the end of which President Roosevelt announced that he had been appointed a commissioner of the United States Maritime Commission. Less than a year later, when Joseph P. Kennedy, its first head, became Ambassador to England, Land was made chairman.

The Maritime Commission had been set up in 1936 when Congress finally realized the straits into which United States shipping had fallen. The fleet, most of which had been built during the First World War, was obsolescent and replacements weren't being made; operating costs were high and American shipping wasn't able to compete with foreign carriers; times were bad, business was bad; seamen were complaining about their wages and working conditions. The new Maritime Commission, replacing the "ineffectual, graft-ridden" Shipping Board, conducted a survey to decide what was to be done about all this, and when the survey was over orders started popping like bullets.

To meet the labor problem, higher wage scales and better conditions were instituted for the seamen, and the union question dealt with more reasonably. Land's own opinion on this was that "collective bargaining organizations provide a basic stabilizing influence and are therefore most desirable." At the same time, however, he attacked union hiring-and-firing control on government-owned ships.

The Maritime Commission's program called for the construction of 500 ships over a 10-year period, but Land, even in 1938, wasn't willing to go that slowly. He pushed things along so energetically that within two years the United States rose to second place among maritime powers, possessed of a merchant marine stronger than any since clipper ship days. Land introduced new ideas into their building. The new ships had special bulkheads, modern fire defense and navigation equipment. They were made with standard designs for the most part. Many of them were convertible ships which could be turned from liners or freighters into aircraft carriers, tankers, supply ships. Under his leadership the largest and costliest passenger ship ever built in the United States, the *America*, was launched; under him the first all-welded passenger liner in maritime history, the *African Comet*, took to the seas.

When built, these ships were either sold or chartered to private operating companies, and the difference between the cost of building them with American labor from American materials and the cost of building them abroad absorbed by the Commission. In return the operating company agreed to let the Government take over these ships if needed for defense. Land's contribution to this plan was a scheme which allows shipowners to turn in old vessels for credit against new ones.

Even after shipping line subsidies were reduced by the Neutrality Act and its restrictions, Land kept as busy as ever, finding new assignments for merchant ships, working out new routes, doubling his efforts to build the Merchant Marine. He also devoted his energies to building up personnel. New recruiting stations were set up; the system of maritime schools was expanded; the officer training system was standardized; competitive examinations for cadets were inaugurated.

Back in the summer of 1939, before the Second World War had begun, Admiral Land decided that an emergency was coming. In 41 days he let contracts for 67 ships, running the Commission into a deficit and scaring the daylights out of the red-tapers. He merely grinned at them: "See you in jail," and proceeded to get his ships built at pre-emergency prices. Then the War started, and by the end of 1940 the Commission had placed contracts for nearly 200 ocean-going vessels. By this time Land was warning the country: "We need at least a thousand good ships. Fifty ships a year multiplied by twenty years is a

thousand. But the legal life of a ship is only 20 years. Therefore, we are engaged on a program of 50 ships a year forever."

In July 1940 Land was made coordinator of shipbuilding activities for the National Defense Commission, in addition to his other duties. In February 1941 President Roosevelt added to them by assigning him the task of coordinating facilities for ocean transportation to see "that our shipping needs are cared for in an expeditious and effective manner." In March 1941 the Division of Emergency Shipping was created with Land at its head, and it was made his job to supervise the sale, charter, transfer and requisition of all emergency transportation tonnage and to exercise general control over American vessels transporting materials essential to national defense.

From time to time the duties of the Maritime Commission and Admiral Land continue to be extended. The bill authorizing the requisition of foreign merchant ships in American harbors was followed by an executive order empowering the Maritime Commission to take over these vessels and to operate or to dispose of them in the interests of national defense. And a bill put before Congress in July 1941 would give the Commission new and sweeping powers—the authority to control the movements, routes, services and cargoes of all merchant vessels.

There's "a touch of the mule skinner about Admiral Land when he's driving things through," and once in a while energetic activities lead to criticism. There has been criticism of his failure to utilize idle Great Lakes shipyards and to give shipbuilding orders to the small companies as well as to the large ones. In September 1941, after A F of L seamen along the East Coast struck for bigger bonuses, he seized several strike-stranded ships and had his Commission set up its own hiring hall in order to break the strike. Part of organized labor resented this, though much of the country-at-large had sympathized with his dictum on the San Francisco shipyard strike in the spring of 1941. He said there was "justification for every possible step the Government can take up to and including the use of United States forces to take those picket lines away so people who want to go to work can go to work."

Admiral Land doesn't always state his views in quite such dignified language and there are rumors current that he is the "casual dispenser" of the Maritime Commission's "most lurid and effective seagoing profanity." It is more than rumor that he is one of the best tennis players in it and better than middling in his poker and bridge. He sticks pretty much to walking these days, though, and can be seen almost any morning leaving his Massachusetts Avenue home, where he lives with Mrs. Land (she was Elizabeth C. Stiles of Newton Center, Massachusetts before their marriage in 1909), at a brisk trot. He arrives at the office in probably the best condition of all the Washington officials who get their exercise this way.

(Continued next page)

LAND, EMORY S.—*Continued*

References

> Am Mag 129:20-1+ Mr '40 il por
> Fortune 17:162 Ap '38 por; 24:36 Jl
>   '41 por
> Nation 152:631-2 My 31 '41
> N Y Herald Tribune X p4, 9 Ja 12 '41
>   por
> Newsweek 10:39 N 22 '37 por; 11:39
>   F 28 '38 por
> Time 31:13 F 28 '38 por; 34:65 S 11
>   '39 por; 37:12 Mr 31 '41
> U S News 9:41-2 D 20 '40
> Who's Who in America
> Who's Who in the Nation's Capital

LANE, GERTRUDE B(ATTLES) Died
Sept. 25, 1941 Editor of the *Woman's Home
Companion* since 1912 and a vice-president
and director of the Crowell-Collier Publishing Company; started as household editor of
her magazine and did much to improve health
of American women and children; in the
First World War was member of the Washington staff of the United States Food Administration; during her editorship circulation
jumped from 727,764 to more than 3,500,000
copies a month.

References

> Fortune 16:65 Ag '37 por
> N Y Herald Tribune p8 Je 17 '40
> Scholastic 30:11 My 15 '37 por; 33:7
>   N 19 '38 por
> Time 28:43-4 Jl 27 '36 por
> Who's Who in America
> Who's Who in Journalism

Obituaries

> N Y Times p23 S 26 '41 por

**LANG, COSMO GORDON, ARCH-
BISHOP OF CANTERBURY** Oct. 31,
1864-

Address: Lambeth Palace, London, S. E. 1,
England

The Right Honourable and Most Reverend
Cosmo Gordon Lang, D. D., D. C. L., LL.
D., D. Litt., Prelate of the Order of St. John
of Jerusalem, owner of the Grand Cross of
the Victorian Order, Lord Archbishop of
Canterbury, Primate of All England (and
known to irreverent Britishers as "Cosmo"
or "The Arch") once described his position as
"incredible, indefensible, inevitable." It is easy
to see why. The Church of England, with its
affiliates, includes many millions of members,
runs 13,500 churches and 8,500 schools in England alone, owns vast lands and has an income
of around £13,000,000 a year. Even during
peaceful times the Archbishop of Canterbury
has been burdened with the duties of being
on the right side every time a controversy
arises in this immensely powerful Church, of
representing the Church in legislation, of presiding at the Lambeth Conferences of Anglican
Bishops as well as at countless other conferences, of delivering thoroughly considered
public pronouncements on issues political, moral
and esthetic—and, incidentally, of blessing
"more masonry than any other churchman in
Christendom."

In 1941, with England embattled, the prestige
and responsibilities of Cosmo Cantuar (as he
signs himself) are perhaps greater than at
any time in his long career. At the very
beginning of the Second World War he announced: "The whole people of the United
Kingdom, as they enter upon the terrible
ordeal of war, may be able to join together
as one company in committing the national
life and cause to Almighty God." Early in
the War he requested that conscientious objectors be treated fairly, that the Government
stop spreading fear by exaggerated precautions,
that evacuated wives be enabled to join their
husbands. More recently he has had something
to say about British war aims: "Our task
is . . . to establish among nations the great
principles of justice and freedom. . . As for
the claim that in trying to establish justice
and freedom we are doing God's will, it lays
on us the responsibility at least of establishing
these principles in our own land." And in
July 1941 he set at rest the souls of Church
of England communicants who were bothered
by Britain's alliance with the Soviet Union.
"We must wish every success to the valiant
Russian armies and people," he said, "and be
ready to give them every possible help."

Cosmo Gordon Lang was the seventh son of
the Very Reverend John Marshall Lang, D. D.,
C. V. O., who was moderator of the Presbyterian Church of Scotland and principal of
Aberdeen University. He grew up in the
village of Fyvie, Aberdeenshire, the seat of
his father's country parish. After attending
Glasgow University, which gave him his M. A.
at the age of 18, he won a scholarship and
went to Balliol College, Oxford in 1882. There
he showed no symptoms of excessive piety.
He was elected to the presidency of the Oxford Union, that "nursery for British statesmen"; he wrote plays; he acted in amateur
theatricals given by the Oxford University
Dramatic Society. Of one of his performances
a critic wrote: "Mr. C. G. Lang delivered
his lines fairly well, although the reason he
had attired himself as a Doctor of Divinity
was scarcely apparent."

At this time Lang was studying law, preparing for a political career. Having taken a
Second in the classics in 1885 and a First in
modern history the next year, he continued his
studies at the Inner Temple, London, until
1889. The night before his Bar examinations,
according to one story, he was converted to the
Church, telegraphed his excuses to his law
examiners, and almost immediately departed
for a theological seminary. Only a year before he had been riding from Oxford to
Yorkshire to deliver a political speech. As
he himself put it: "The train was delayed
outside the station at Leeds. From the window
I looked down at slums, the like of which I
had never seen in East London. I saw a black-
coated figure and said to myself: 'There is a
poor devil of a parson spending his life in

hovels like these.' Within less than two years, I was myself the black-coated parson."

Ordained a minister of the Church of England in 1890, Lang was for three years a curate in Leeds, where he slept in a condemned tenement in a board bed two feet wide. But such a life was obviously not to be the permanent destiny of a young man with ambition and influential friends, a Fellow of All Souls College at Oxford. In 1893 Lang became a Fellow and a Dean of Divinity at Magdalen College, Oxford, where he was also the vicar of St. Mary's until in 1896, on the recommendation of Arthur Balfour, he was appointed vicar of the largest parish in England, Portsea. Portsea was just across from the Isle of Wight, where the late Queen Victoria spent her summers. She heard him preaching, thought him "so human," and from that time on they were good friends. He was until the Queen's death her Honorary Chaplain, and his rise in the Church was rapid. By 1901 he had become Bishop of Stepney, London's East End diocese, and Canon of St. Paul's; only seven years later he had the privilege of declining the Archbishopric of Montreal. A month after his refusal of that very important church post the Archbishop of York, Primate of England, died, and Lang received the appointment. He became the youngest archbishop in Europe.

As Archbishop of York (he was also appointed Privy Councillor in 1909), Cosmo Gordon Lang was said to have been a match for the "Edwardian liberals" who talked of disestablishment. In 1918, during the First World War, he visited the United States. In 1923 he was honored with the Royal Victorian Chain. And in August 1928 he was named to succeed Randall Thomas Davidson as Archbishop of Canterbury, a post of such shining importance that at State functions its incumbent ranks sixth after the King of England, England's Prime Minister ninth.

Nine years later Cosmo Cantuar played what was perhaps the most prominent and controversial role of his career, in the abdication of Edward VIII, the present Duke of Windsor. Personally very close to the late George V and Lord High Almoner to the King since 1933, the Archbishop delivered his finest oratory on the occasion of that sovereign's death. But his son seemed to him of an entirely different mold. In October 1936 Cosmo Cantuar and his colleague of York declined a dinner invitation at St. James's Palace at which Wallis Simpson would be present. Later, it is said, he threatened to withhold communion from Edward. The King replied: "Please remember that I am the head of your organization." On November 17 the Archbishop presided at a secret meeting of the House of Lords at which the *affaire Simpson* was thrashed out; by December 10 it was all over.

Even after Edward's abdication, however, Cosmo Cantuar did not relent. In a radio speech that same month he called for a return to religion, attacking Russia, birth control, and Mrs. Simpson, rebuking Edward "for hav-

The New York Public Library

COSMO GORDON LANG,
ARCHBISHOP OF CANTERBURY

ing sought his happiness in a manner inconsistent with the Christian principles of marriage and within a circle whose standards and ways of life are alien to all the best instincts and traditions of his people." It was also he who refused to allow any form of Church of England service at the Duke's wedding.

As a result, for months afterward the Archbishop was the subject of jibes and criticism, even from some who were not Edward's supporters. The Bishop of Durham announced: "I was always trained to believe that the Church of England is governed by the several bishops reigning in their several dioceses. I now find it is come to be some kind of novel body governed by the British Broadcasting Corporation and by two archbishops, Canterbury and York. I do not like it." A *New Statesman and Nation* correspondent was sarcastic: "The archbishops would call the nation back to Christianity with a couple of negatives. We are to hate Russia rather more and love women rather less." And one partciularly venomous poet contributed:

Milord Archbishop, what a scold you are.
And, when your man is down, how bold
*   you are.*
Of Christian charity how scant you are—
Ah, Auld Lang Swyne, how full of
*   cant-u-ar!*

At the coronation of George VI in May 1937 the Archbishop of Canterbury was, however, the most impressive figure present. It was he who stood on the dais as the King approached, who presented him to the four sides of the Abbey, who administered the oaths in an untrembling voice, placed the crown on his sovereign's head and anointed him with holy oil. He thoroughly approves of the present rulers of England, and it is said

LANG, COSMO GORDON—*Continued*

that King George, in turn, "looks to the Archbishop for political as well as spiritual advice."

A "ruddy, worldly wise, eloquent, opinionated" old man with a hawk nose, "pink, stern face . . . bald head fringed with a halo of delicate white fuzz . . . powerful stocky frame . . . imposing manner and . . . sonorous voice, which gives his best wisecracks a happy incongruity," Cosmo Cantuar looks his role. He is paid £15,000 a year, and is called one of the best-dressed clerics in England. He has a Lanchester limousine for town, an Armstrong-Siddeley for country trips. He is hardly on speaking terms with the "Red" Dean of Canterbury, but among his intimate friends are powerful political and financial figures, mainly ardent conservatives: Sir John Simon and J. P. Morgan, whose home he has visited and on whose yacht he has cruised the Mediterranean more than once.

Nevertheless in his own political pronouncements Cosmo Cantuar has not been found consistently in Tory ranks—although years ago he was burned in effigy in protest against the Church's refusal to lower rents on its Bayswater tenements, although in 1931 he offered public thanks when MacDonald made possible the formation of the National Government, and although in 1933 the farmers rioted against paying tithes to the Church of England. In 1934, for example, the Archbishop was advocating disarmament and support of the League of Nations and prodding the Government for its slow work in slum clearance, and early in 1939 he advocated an Anglo-Russian alliance in the House of Lords. (In 1938, however, when Jewish persecutions in Germany were at their height, he had been only wistful: "Would that the rulers of the Reich could realize that such excesses of hatred and malice put upon the friendship which we are ready to offer them an almost intolerable strain!")

The Archbishop has never married. Queen Victoria once suggested that he might be able to get along without so many curates if he did just that. Replied Cosmo Cantuar: "I can sack a curate, but I cannot sack a wife." In spite of his bachelor state and attitude toward divorce, the Archbishop is responsible for some singularly unprudish statements. But he cannot be called a feminist. He believes that "the best and greatest career for girls is that of making an English, Christian home." He gives women further advice: "Keep an eye on your husband but don't nag."

One of the things that few people know about him is that he is an author of a romance of the Scottish wars called *The Young Clanroy*, published in 1897. Only such titles as *The Miracles of Jesus, as Marks of the Way of Life* (1900); *The Parables of Jesus* (1906); and *The Opportunity of the Church of England* (1906) appear under his name in *Who's Who*, and perhaps there is a reason. That earlier effort has been described by one critic as follows: "It contains blood and thunder, an extraordinarily dewy heroine named Dorothy and a character called the Black Priest who

might interest students of Freudian psychology. . ."

Up until the War the Archbishop's normal day was busy, but fairly routinized: he would arise around 7, attend chapel at Lambeth Palace, have breakfast, spend most of his morning taking care of correspondence and callers, and then, after a light lunch, drive to the House of Lords, attend a public function or make a speech. Five o'clock would find him at tea; he would then write a few more letters before changing for dinner. Although a temperance crusader, he is no ascetic, enjoys port, claret, whisky, brandy and hock, and is numbered "among the town's five best after-dinner speakers." In those peaceful days he would nearly always go to the country during week ends, too, on Sundays preaching at small country churches in the diocese rather than at Canterbury Cathedral. Today his responsibilities are graver, his heart heavier.

References

Int Affairs 11:833-9 N '32
Life 7:48-53 D 25 '39 pors
New Statesman & Nation 12:968 D 12 '36; 12:1023-5+ D 19 '36; 13:9-10 Ja 2 '37
19th Cent 114:374-84 S '33
Spec 152:799 My 18 '34; 158:5-6 Ja 1 '37
Time 29:16-18 My 24 '37 il por (cover); 38:28 Ag 4 '41

Bennett, A. Things That Have Interested Me 1st ser p188-9 1921
Who's Who

LANGMUIR, ARTHUR COMINGS Feb. 7, 1872—May 14, 1941 Research chemist; world authority on shellac and glycerine; established international methods for shellac analysis; founded in 1931 the American Chemical Society's annual prize of $1,000 given to a young scientist for outstanding research; wrote many scientific papers; was brother of Irving Langmuir, who won the Nobel Prize for chemistry in 1932 (see sketch 1940 Annual).

References

American Men of Science
Chemical Who's Who
Who's Who in Engineering 1941
Who's Who in New York

Obituaries

N Y Times p23 My 15 '41 por

LANMAN, CHARLES ROCKWELL July 8, 1850—Feb. 20, 1941 Professor emeritus of Sanskrit at Harvard and ranking senior member of the officers of administration and instruction at the University (1880 to 1926); internationally recognized authority on Oriental literature and culture; member of many of the learned societies of the world; member of the original faculty at Johns Hopkins University when that institution was opened in 1876; his outstanding work was considered to be the 36-volume Harvard Oriental Series; recognized as one of the ablest scullers in the country, he had rowed up and down the Charles River for a total of nearly 12,000 miles.

References

Who's Who in America

Obituaries

N Y Times p19 F 21 '41
Sch & Soc 53:273 Mr 1 '41

LASKER, EMANUEL Dec. 24, 1868—
Jan. 11, 1941 Ex-chess champion who held the world's championship for 27 years, from 1894 to 1921; German who left Germany permanently after the Nazi regime came into power in 1933.

References

Reinfeld, F. and Fine, R. eds. Dr. Lasker's Chess Career 1935
Who's Who

Obituaries

N Y Times p45 Ja 12 '41 por

LASKI, HAROLD (JOSEPH) (lăs'kê)
June 30, 1893- Political scientist; author; historian

Address: h. Devon Lodge, Addison Bridge Pl, London, W. 14, England

Since the Second World War, Harold Laski has been the intellectual spokesman of the British Labor Party outside the Government, often criticizing the conduct of the War in its details, but always preaching that the first aim of the working class, to which all other aims must temporarily be subordinated, is the defeat of Hitler. A masterful pamphleteer, his book, *Where Do We Go From Here?* (1940), in which he made himself the apostle of "revolution by consent," has been perhaps the most lucid and widely read exposition of the views of those liberals and socialists who have supported the War wholeheartedly from its inception. And in 1941 he has produced several more short tracts, among them *Strategy of Freedom; an Open Letter to American Youth*, telling why the Axis powers must be defeated.

He was born in Manchester, England, on June 30, 1893, the second son of Nathan Laski. Brought up in an orthodox Jewish household, he attended Manchester Grammar School. Even before he went up to New College, Oxford, he had read the books of Beatrice and Sidney Webb and had been moved by Keir Hardie's tale of the bitter labor struggles of the Scottish miners. It was almost inevitable that he should join the Fabian Society at Oxford and engage in propaganda for the great social issue of the day: woman suffrage. Meetings with the late George Lansbury and H. W. Nevinson did much to confirm his convictions: from the first he learned the "meaning and importance of equality," from the latter the "meaning and importance of liberty." And when he was graduated in 1914, an Honorary Exhibi-

HAROLD LASKI

tioner who had received the Beit Essay Prize and a First Class in the School of Modern History, Lansbury asked him to write editorials for the *Daily Herald*.

His time with the *Herald* was brief. Within a few weeks the First World War broke out ("I should have liked to see a general strike proclaimed against the outbreak of war in 1914," he said, much later), and Laski volunteered. Rejected because of a weak heart, he accepted a position as lecturer in history at McGill University, Canada. He was there for two years, managed to get himself officially disliked by attacking Lloyd George's "bitter-endism," and in 1916 went on to Harvard to teach politics. While still at Harvard, he lectured at Amherst as Henry Ward Beecher lecturer in 1917 and at Yale as Harvard lecturer from 1919 to 1920. In the United States, too, he found his opinions disagreeable to university authorities. When the famous police strike broke out in Boston, Harvard offered its services to the city before finding out the reasons for the strike or the rights and wrongs of the city's position. Laski publicly doubted the wisdom of this attitude; he was "investigated," and although it was finally announced that he was "not to be dismissed," he quit Harvard in 1920 and went back to England.

In America, he says, he had seen, "more nakedly than I had seen in Europe, the significance of the struggle between capital and labor. I learned how little meaning there can be in an abstract political liberty which is subdued to the control of an economic plutocracy. . . I came back from America convinced that liberty has no meaning save in the context of equality, and I had begun to understand that equality also has no meaning unless the instruments of production are socially owned."

(Continued next page)

LASKI, HAROLD—*Continued*

Upon his return to England he joined both the Labor Party and the faculty of the London School of Economics and Political Science. He already realized that "to teach political science, it was not enough to read books; one had to learn politics from actual experience of their working." It remained only to put this knowledge into practice, while teaching, engaging in political journalism (he was for a time on the staff of the London *Nation*), and writing, on the average, a book a year.

In this he was remarkably successful. From 1921 to 1930 he served as vice-chairman of the British Institute of Adult Education; from 1922 to 1936 he was a member of the Fabian Society Executive. He "deviled" for ministers when Labor Governments were in power. He participated in industrial arbitration as a member of the Industrial Court after 1926; he helped the trade unions in every important strike, especially the general strike of 1926; he spent five years as alderman of a London borough. In 1929 he became a member of the Lord Chancellor's Committee on Delegated Legislation, in 1931 a member of the Departmental Committee on Local Government, in 1932 a member of the Departmental Committee on Legal Education and of the Council of the Institute of Public Administration. Almost the only thing he refused to do was to stand for the "surest Labor seat in England," and that seat was later conferred on Ramsay MacDonald.

At the same time Laski was gradually becoming a familiar figure at universities all over the world. Although retaining his professorship at the London School of Economics, from 1922 to 1925 he also lectured in political science at Magdalene College, Cambridge, and in 1926 he returned to teach political science in the University of London. From 1931 to 1933 he was at Yale as a visiting lecturer; in 1934 he gave a series of lectures at the Institute of Soviet Law in Moscow; in 1936 he was Donnellun Lecturer at Trinity College, Dublin. Students in France, Spain, Greece and pre-Hitler Germany knew him. And he returned constantly to America, where his friends included presidents and professors, writers and Supreme Court judges.

But it is as the author of works on political science that Laski has made his chief reputation. As Max Ascoli put it in 1935: "No other political scientist is giving such a stimulus to the development of political thought as is Harold Laski. No other has a greater capacity to open debates and at the same time to commit himself in a demonstration of responsible thinking by taking a definite stand." His "lucid dignity," his "admirable absence of passion," his "gift of terse epigrammatic statement and cogent argument," combining "theoretical acuteness with a feeling for practical politics," have caused him to be likened to Macaulay, to John Stuart Mill, to Bagehot.

What has always preoccupied him above all else is the problem of "combining individual freedom with social order" within the modern state. Known for many years as a

member of the Left-wing within the Labor Party, his varied attempts at solution of this problem have permitted him, at times, to be described as a near-Communist by Labor's Right-wing and as a Social Democrat by the Communists. In Laski's own words, up to 1920 his socialism "was above all the outcome of a sense of the injustice of things as they were. It had not yet become an insight into the processes of history." But by the late '30s he was writing, more bluntly: "I have been driven to the conclusion that no class voluntarily abdicates from the possession of power."

Although this last orthodox Marxist conclusion has presumably been abandoned in *Where Do We Go From Here?*, it is quite true that Laski's writings throughout the '20s and '30s were marked by an increasing pessimism at prospects of peaceful reform within the framework of present society, by increasing preoccupation with economic realities rather than abstract theories of the State. In *Studies in the Problem of Sovereignty* (1917); *Authority in the Modern State* (1919); and *Foundations of Sovereignty, and Other Essays* (1921), "an attempt at the reconstruction of political theory in terms of institutions more fitted to the needs we confront," Laski mainly confined himself to pleading the virtues of decentralization, of the pluralistic, as opposed to the monistic, State. In contrast, *A Grammar of Politics* (1925), while rejecting Marx's "prophecy of inevitable conflict" and complaining that the prospect he envisaged was "less a remedy than an unexplored formula," reflected Laski's own great concern with social injustice. Charles A. Beard (see sketch this issue), who had found his *Political Thought in England from Locke to Bentham* (1920) conventional and academic, announced: "Here is an author who quits hemming and hawing and asserts, declares and challenges."

Communism (1927) approached its subject with "intelligent and sympathetic skepticism." Laski continued to challenge both Marx and modern society, at that time seeing a possibility that "better industrial organization and the prospects of scientific discovery might easily make of capitalism a system able to satisfy the main wants of the workers." As late as 1930, writing in *Liberty in the Modern State*, he was optimistic about bringing about a permanent peace through the League of Nations. In November 1932, moreover, he was writing: "I think it is a safe prophecy that the Hitlerite movement has passed its apogee."

Perhaps, then, it was the depression that was responsible for the gloomier outlook of *Democracy in Crisis* (1933). (*Dangers of Obedience, and Other Essays* [1930]; *Politics* [1931]; and *Studies in Law and Politics* [1932] had appeared in the years between.) "Capitalism is doomed," Laski announced in this book, "and . . . the only alternative to revolution is the peaceful acceptance of socialism," the only alternative to war "the abrogation of the sovereign national state." By the next year, when a sequel, *The State in Theory and Practice*, appeared, Laski was speaking not of alternatives but of "the inevitability of revolution as the midwife of social change," the complete impossibility of creating an international order without that change. He ridiculed the argument that capitalism could enter on a new phase of economic well-being by extending the field of state-regulation, although continuing to write sporadically encouraging articles about the Roosevelt experiment. And in 1936 *The Rise of Liberalism* took the tone of an elegy.

The years immediately preceding the Second World War were stormy ones in the British Labor Party, as well as all over the world. In 1937, after a heated controversy, the Socialist League, of which Laski was a founder, was dissolved. Laski took no pains to hide his disapproval of the "defeatist" leadership of the British trade unions, particularly of Ernest Bevin (see sketch 1940 Annual) and Sir Walter Citrine (see sketch this issue), for their willingness to collaborate with Chamberlain's Government. He stressed the need for unity on the Left, castigated the timidity of the Labor Party, backed Sir Stafford Cripps' (see sketch 1940 Annual) proposal for a united front with the Communists and the Liberals, worked for an alliance with the Soviet Union.

In August 1939, when war seemed inevitable, Laski pleaded for a "Peace Conference Before the War"; otherwise, he predicted, its result could be nothing but "a Carthaginian peace . . . which will merely transfer the impact of Fascism from its present theatre of influence to a new stage." After Britain declared war he nevertheless remained hopeful enough about the future to contribute to the *New Statesman and Nation's* prompt discussion of what peace terms should include, although in October 1939 he wrote: "Until the specific aims of the British Government are known, the Labor Party must remain an opposition which purposes to become the Government of the country at the earliest moment." By May 1940, however, he was heralding the "birth of a new spirit in Britain with Mr. Churchill's Premiership and the entrance of the Labor Party as a 'full partner' in his Government." And by the time of the appearance of *Where Do We Go From Here?* Laski had returned to the implied hope of his pre-Marxist days: that it might be possible to conquer the "inherent tendencies of privilege to deny to democracy and freedom any power to expand which threatens its vested interests"; possible to form a "partnership between privilege and the masses" in England that would be "of a permanent character." With the British-Soviet alliance of June 1941 he became an eloquent spokesman for fuller understanding between the two nations, but remained distrustful of the British Communists.

In *The Danger of Being a Gentleman*, a collection of essays written, for the most part, in previous years but also published in 1940, the *Saturday Review of Literature* finds "not much trace of the militant Marxist Laski," either. In the eyes of most critics this is all to the good. *The American Presidency*, a third book published in that same year, has been placed alongside De Tocqueville and Bryce in importance, and the *New Statesman and Nation* called this analysis of the "traditions, conventions and laws in their relationship to the Cabinet and the Congress, and particularly to the people themselves," one of the best books ever written about the institutions of another country by a foreign observer. Laski has a particular faculty for wooing those who are in political disagreement with him into unwilling admiration by the urbanity of his style. As one critic puts it: "Like all courteous men, Laski gets away with murder."

Dark mustached, bespectacled, completely unmurderous looking, Laski was married to the former Frida Kerry of Acton Hall, Suffolk in 1911. There is one daughter, Diana.

References

Am R 7:507-15 O '36
Century 117:41-3 N '28
Christian Cent 52:787-9 Je 12 '35
Lit Digest 119:26 Ap 27 '35
Liv Age 339:267-70 N '30
Nation 148:59-61 Ja 14 '39
19th Cent 127:324-32 Mr '40; 129:209-29 Mr '41 (Same abr. Liv Age 360:354-61 Je '41)
Wilson Lib Bul 10:208 N '35 por; 15:360 Ja '41 por

Author's and Writer's Who's Who
Catlin, G. E. G. Story of the Political Philosophers p649-99 1939
Who's Who

LAUGHLIN, CLARA ELIZABETH (lŏk'lĭn) Aug. 3, 1873—Mar. 3, 1941 Author of a well-known series of travel books and founder of the Clara Laughlin Travel Services; known as novelist before the First World War, then turned her attention to travel and wrote her first book, *So You're Going to Paris* (1924), which was an immediate success and was followed by travel books on Italy, England, France, Germany, Austria, Spain, Ireland, Scotland, the Mediterranean and Scandinavia; when travel to Europe stopped, she wrote the first of a projected series on this country.

References

Author's and Writer's Who's Who
Laughlin, C. E. Traveling Through Life 1934
Who's Who Among North American Authors
Who's Who in America

Obituaries

N Y Times p23 Mr 4 '41

LAUGHLIN, IRWIN (BOYLE) (lŏk'lĭn) Apr. 26, 1871—Apr. 18, 1941 Former American Minister Plenipotentiary to Greece from 1924 to 1926 and Ambassador to Greece from 1929 to 1933; held many posts during his years as a career diplomat beginning in 1905;

LAUGHLIN, IRWIN—*Continued*
was grandson of James B. Laughlin, Pittsburgh steel manufacturer.

References

Who's Who in America
Who's Who in Government
Who's Who ·in the Nation's Capital

Obituaries

N Y Times p15 Ap 19 '41

LAURI, LORENZO, CARDINAL (lou'rê)
Oct. 15, 1865—Oct. 8, 1941 Chamberlain of
the Holy Roman Church since 1939; served
as a diplomatic representative of the Vatican
in Peru, Spain and Poland, and in Poland
negotiated a concordat between the United
States and the Vatican; made a cardinal in
1927; before he became chamberlain was
Grand Penitentiary of the church, in which
post he was confessor to Pope Pius XI on his
deathbed.

References

Time 33:30 F 20 '39 por
Chi è?

Obituaries

N Y Times p23 O 9 '41 por

LAVERY, SIR JOHN (lăv'ẽr-ĭ) 1856(?)
—Jan. 10, 1941 Irish artist whose works
hang in many European and American galleries; president of the Royal Society of
Portrait Painters since 1932; painted among
others George Bernard Shaw, Cardinal Hayes
and Shirley Temple; knighted in 1918; author
of *Life of a Painter,* published in 1940.

References

Atlan 165:28-34 Ja '40; 165:186-92 F
'40; 165:376-80 Mr '40
Nat R 114:621-3 My '40
Catholic Who's Who
Lavery, J. Life of a Painter 1940
Who's Who
Who's Who in Art

Obituaries

Christian Cent 58:200 F 5 '41
N Y Times p17 Ja 11 '41 por
Time 37:76 Ja 20 '41

LAWES, LEWIS E(DWARD) Sept. 13,
1883- Penologist
Address: h. Cloverly, Cold Spring-on-Hudson,
N. Y.

"Punishment never reforms. Prison administrations are in the nature of emergency governments, but prisoners should be allowed a
normal experience of life as far as possible."
In these words Lewis E. Lawes, probably
the best known prison warden in America,
expressed the principle which guided him
through 36 years of service in the Prison and
Correction Department of New York State.
On July 16, 1941 he said goodbye to Sing Sing,
where he had been warden since 1920. A tes-

timonial scroll was engraved and given him
by the prisoners, a silver service by the
civilian employees. In his letter of resignation he said he wanted to get out of harness
while he was still "vigorous, both physically
and mentally."

Warden Lawes, as probably he always will
be called even in his retirement, came up from
the ranks the hard way—just as did another
distinguished American penologist, August
Vollmer. Lewis Edward Lawes was born
in Elmira, New York, within a mile of the
New York State Reformatory. His father,
Harry Lewis Lawes, was a guard in the
prison; his mother was Sarah (Abbott)
Lawes. The salary of a guard did not provide any luxuries, and the young boy found
the drill team at the reformatory the most
interesting thing in town. He was told to
stay away from the "bad boys," but to him
they looked just like other boys, and he would
have given a lot to have been able to drill with
them.

Instead, when he was just 15, the big blond
boy turned up at a recruiting station and tried
to enlist in the Army for the Spanish-American War. The recruiting sergeant told him
to go back to school—Elmira Free Academy
—so, reluctantly, he did, for three years
more. In 1901 he finally succeeded in enlisting
in the Army, and he did a three-year stretch
in the Philippines. Then, back in Elmira,
he decided to get into that reformatory as a
guard if he couldn't do it any other way. He
took examinations and was appointed in 1905
—but not to Elmira Reformatory. Instead,
he was sent to Clinton Prison, called "the
Siberia of America" and located at Dannemora, New York. When he got off the train
on a rainy day and viewed the prospect, he
was so discouraged he wanted to go right
back. There was no train back, though, so
he decided to take a look, anyway. He stayed
at Clinton for six months, then was transferred to Auburn for six months more. Finally, in 1906, he was sent as a guard to
Elmira.

In those days, a guard had almost no chance
of advancement: politics stood in the way.
In 1912 Lawes nevertheless asked for leave
of absence and went to New York to study
sociology at the New York School of Social
Work. When he went back to Elmira it was
as chief guard and chief record clerk. In
1914 he became overseer of the New York
City Reformatory, and in 1915 its superintendent. Alfred E. Smith was at that time
Governor of New York, and he had been
watching Lewis Lawes' work. In 1919 he
sent for him and asked him (though Lawes
was a Republican) to become warden of Sing
Sing. Against his will, Lawes finally consented, knowing that Sing Sing had broken
practically every warden who served there.

On January 1, 1920, Lawes made his first
talk to the men in his charge at Sing Sing.
He quoted the old saw that "the easiest way
to get out of Sing Sing is to go in as
warden"—the average term for wardens had
been eleven months, and the one before him
had lasted six—and the men laughed. It was

his first step in winning their cooperation. Immensely interested in the pioneer prison reform work at Sing Sing of the late Thomas Mott Osborne, Lawes was yet more of a realist and less of a sentimentalist than Osborne had been. He kept many of Osborne's famous reforms, but he exempted from their benefits the eight per cent or so of the prisoners whom he considered incurable.

In his 21 years in Sing Sing, Warden Lawes had in his care 36,750 prisoners. (The average prison population is 2,500.) There were only two violent attempts at escape—there used to be twenty or more a year—and only two successful escapes, neither of them violent. He stressed athletics, entertainment, education. He went to bat for his men—as in the case of "Alabama" Pitts, the sensational outfielder developed in the prison, who was later denied a job on the Albany baseball team till Lawes went to Judge Kenesaw Mountain Landis about it. He directed the electrocution of two hundred ninety-nine men and four women but never saw one of them: he always turned his head when the current was switched on. He is strongly opposed to capital punishment on the ground that it is not a deterrent to murder. Among the notorious prisoners in Sing Sing during his service were Ruth Snyder, Judd Grey, Two-Gun Crowley, "Lucky" Luciano, Owney Madden, Charles E. Chapin (the New York editor who killed his wife, and who during his life-term built up the beautiful garden the prison now boasts), Fritz Kuhn (the Bundist), and Richard C. Whitney of the New York Stock Exchange.

The stories of many of the prisoners have been told by Warden Lawes in his books and over the radio. He has often been accused of publicity-seeking, because he will avail himself of any and every avenue of approach in order to put over his experiences and his penological beliefs. For several years, for example, he appeared as an actor in a series of radio plays built around Sing Sing stories. In 1935 he edited a magazine, *Prison Life Stories*. (That same year he went to London and was welcomed as a distinguished colleague by Scotland Yard.) He gave John Wexler the title for his famous play, *The Last Mile*, and he himself collaborated with Jonathan Finn in 1935 in a prison play called *Chalked Out*. It was pure melodrama, but critics remarked on its "chilling authenticity."

His books have never been dull treatises, but every one of them has carried a sermon as well as a story. They are: *Man's Judgment of Death* (1924); *Life and Death in Sing Sing* (1928); *Twenty Thousand Years in Sing Sing* (1932), an autobiographical account of Warden Lawes' life which was almost universally acclaimed by critics, became a choice of the Book-of-the-Month Club and sold 150,000 copies; *Cell 202, Sing Sing* (1935); *Invisible Stripes,* a book about the parole system, (1938); *Meet the Murderer*

LEWIS E. LAWES

(1940); and *Stone and Steel* (1941). *Twenty Thousand Years in Sing Sing* was made into a movie, but Warden Lawes didn't like it much; he says every suggestion he made in its filming was disregarded. His standing as a penologist is attested by the honorary D. Sc. degree which Colgate University gave him in 1934 and by the social service societies of which he has been an officer.

In 1905 Lawes married Kathryn Irene Stanley, an Elmira girl who was his best helper in the prison, especially with the women prisoners. They had three daughters, of whom the youngest, popularly known as "Cherie," was born in the prison and brought up by a series of "nurses" all of whom were husky convicts. She was the idol of the whole prison. Lawes' granddaughter is also prison-born. The first Mrs. Lawes died in 1937, and in 1939 Mr. Lawes married Elise Chisholm of Jackson, Mississippi.

His blond hair thinning, but his blue eyes still bright and his tall frame still sturdy, Lawes, said Henry F. Pringle, "looks a great deal like an able businessman, not a little like a priest, and something like a cop. He is well dressed and direct in his manner. He can be as sympathetic as any cleric . . . or he can be extraordinarily hard-boiled." He has, Mr. Pringle added, "done more than any other prison administrator in history to spread the gospel that vengeance is not a cure for crime, that rehabilitation is possible if convicts are treated like men instead of beasts." He himself says of his methods: "When you're mad at a man, make a boob of him and not a martyr." That is the way he tamed Two-Gun Crowley when that young desperado set fire to his cell and choked the plumbing: Lawes ordered him to be stripped naked—and his cellmates laughed at him instead of admiring his rebellion. He has the crusading spirit, but he is no long-faced re-

LAWES, LEWIS E.—*Continued*

former; to quote one commentator, his arc "the steady hand and the open heart."

For twenty-one years Warden Lawes was on duty or on call twenty-four hours a day, seven days a week. His highest salary has been $9,000 a year; he will retire on a pension of $6,000. He has already accepted a non-salaried post as president of the Boy Rangers of America. For a few months he played with his little granddaughter, dug potatoes, romped with the Labrador retriever, "Muffin," whom he bottle-fed as a puppy. In addition to the Boy Rangers' appointment he will probably take other positions—perhaps lecturing, perhaps acting as technical adviser in Hollywood, perhaps teaching, and almost certainly writing. Born crusaders like Lewis E. Lawes never quit crusading until they are brought home on their shields.

References

> Christian Cent 58:973 Ag 6 '41
> Collier's 108:58 Ag 16 '41
> Forum 99:52-5 Ja '38 (Same abr. Read Digest 32:104-7 Mr '38)
> Good H 95:30 S '32 por
> New Repub 71:266-7 Jl 20 '32
> N Y Herald Tribune p1, 9 Jl 7 '41 por
> N Y World-Telegram p3 Jl 7 '41 por
> New Yorker 2:15-17 Jl 10 '26
> Scholastic 25:25 O 6 '34 por

> American Historical Society, Inc. Lewis E. Lawes pam 1938
> Gillis, A. and Ketchum, R. Our America p99-117 1936
> Lawes, L. E. Twenty Thousand Years in Sing Sing 1932
> Who's Who Among North American Authors
> Who's Who in America

LAWFORD, ERNEST 1870—Dec. 27, 1940 Noted English actor who came to the United States in 1903; appeared on stage in a wide variety of character roles during the past 50 years; was original Charley in *Charley's Aunt*; played Polonius in modern-dress *Hamlet*.

References

> Stage 13:86 Ag '36 por; 14:67 D '36 por
> Who's Who in the Theatre

Obituaries

> N Y Times p15 D 28 '40
> Variety 141:46 Ja 1 '41

LAWSON, MARY Aug. 30, 1910—May(?), 1941. British film and stage star; killed in German air raid on Liverpool together with her film-producer husband, F. W. L. C. Beaumont; went on the stage when she was seven years old, later appearing in vaudeville and motion pictures.

References

> Play Pict 73:8 N '38 por
> Theatre World 30:252 D '38 por

International Motion Picture Almanac 1937-38
Who's Who in the Theatre

Obituaries

> N Y Times p4 My 10 '41 por

LAWSON, ROBERT Oct. 4, 1892- Artist; author

Address: b. c/o Viking Press, Inc, 18 E. 48th St, New York City; h. Rabbit Hill, Westport, Conn.

Ferdinand the Bull, smelling flowers; the Wee Men of Ballywooden; the first pictures for Carl Sandburg's *Rootabaga Stories* in *Designer* Magazine—these live with delight in the minds of grownups as well as children. Their creator, Robert Lawson, noted illustrator and etcher, was awarded the Caldecott Medal, 1941, for the most distinguished picture book for children. The book is *They Were Strong and Good* (1940), and Robert Lawson is responsible both for its pen-drawings and its simple running narrative concerning his ancestors: his grandfather, a sea captain; his mother, who as a little girl kept bees at a convent-school—all hard-working folk, not famous, but "strong and good."

Because he believes that today, in particular, it is important to give American children an interest and pride in their own backgrounds, Robert Lawson made this book. "He knew that all families tell children stories about their grandparents and sometimes about their great-grandparents and sometimes about their mothers and fathers, that children love these stories and get their own standards of conduct from them. He thought if he told just a few of the incidents that had impressed him as a child and gave them pictorially they would inspire other children to demand more stories about their fathers and mothers and their grandfathers and grandmothers." As a result, May Massee says, "we have had hundreds of letters from all over the country telling stories to show that the writers' ancestors too were 'strong and good.' They prove that this book is doing just what Mr. Lawson hoped it would."

American clear through—there were, of course, Scotch, Irish and Dutch among his ancestors—Robert Lawson was born in New York City on October 4, 1892, the son of William Bethel and Elma Cecilia (Bowman) Lawson. As his book tells us, his forefathers were people who did things: his grandfather fought Indians; his father, at 14, enlisted as a flag boy in the Confederate Army; his mother's father was a sea captain "who didn't run away from storms." Growing up in Montclair, New Jersey, "Rob" Lawson was also more interested in doing things than in being an artist. "As a child," he says, "I did not have any particular interest in drawing and did none until my last year in high school, when it was pointed out to me that I must prepare to do something in the world. I had always had a vague idea that I should like to be an engineer and build bridges, but, having managed to avoid every form of mathematics, this career did not seem very possible."

After high school in Montclair, New Jersey, Lawson entered, in 1911, the New York School of Fine and Applied Art, studying there three years under Howard Giles and Ray Sloan Bredin. From 1914 to 1917 he was in Greenwich Village doing odd scraps of illustration and designing scenery for the Washington Square Players. He worked there with Robert Edmond Jones, Lee Simonson and Joseph Platt, and began to "consider a career as a great scenic artist." The first drawings he sold were to *Harper's Weekly* (1914); he also illustrated for *Delineator* and *Vogue*. But the War stepped in between him and his career. He volunteered in the A. E. F., where he spent a year and a half in the Camouflage Section, 40th Engineers.

When he came back from France, Lawson worked for some 10 years at magazine illustration and commercial art. He made posters, advertisements, even greeting cards with "an imagination and technique that made his stand out far above the usual work in this field." Lawson believes that being forced to be practical as well as decorative in commercial work is excellent training for any artist.

In 1922 he married Marie Abrams, of Atlanta, Georgia, also an artist; and they settled in an old colonial house in Westport, Connecticut. Later they built their own home at Rabbit Hill, a few miles away, "where we hope to spend the rest of our days." In a successful effort to pay off the mortgage on the first house, they designed a Christmas card apiece a day for some two or three years.

Lawson's first offer of book illustration came in 1930, when he drew the dwarfs and gnomes for *The Wee Men of Ballywooden,* by Arthur Mason. At this time he also took up etching. In 1931 he was awarded the John Taylor Arms Prize given annually by the Society of American Etchers, and in the same year was included in the 20 leading American etchers commissioned to do a series of plates for the George Washington Memorial Association. In 1932 he was asked to do the annual members' plate for the S. A. E., and in that year he also had his first one-man show.

For a few years in New York he continued his commercial work, drew for the New York *Herald Tribune Magazine* section, and illustrated books for Ginn and Company. In 1937 he illustrated nine books—"my record for one year." Besides those already named, notable among books illustrated by him are Ella Young's *The Unicorn with Silver Shoes* (1932); Helen Dean Fish's *Four and Twenty Blackbirds* (1937); Elizabeth Coatsworth's *The Golden Horseshoe* (1935); Richard and F. H. C. Atwater's *Mr. Popper's Penguins* (1938); John Bunyan's *Pilgrim's Progress* (1939); Ruth Barnes' *I Hear America Singing* (1937); Samuel Clemens' *The Prince and the Pauper* (1937). He started writing his own books, in 1939, with *Ben and Me.* "Be-

Hansel Meith

ROBERT LAWSON

ing an author," he says, "isn't so bad. It's only one step lower than being an illustrator."

He does not consider himself a "children's illustrator." He believes, however, that children are much less limited in their tastes and understandings than adults are: they haven't been told what they ought to like, or what they ought to think. "Working for children pays much less money, much more in self-respect." When Lawson was doing the drawings for *The Story of Ferdinand* (1936) his elderly aunt said: "The idea of a bull smelling flowers; it just doesn't make sense." He explained that it was supposed to make nonsense, but she refused to be impressed: "Well, I guess I'm just not whimsical." To this Lawson adds: "If you knew my aunt Emma you'd realize what an understatement that was."

He sees much to admire in contemporary comic strips because they are covering fields of action interesting to children, and also show excellent draughtsmanship. Hence "thousands of children have the 'bad taste' to prefer them to children's books." His fear is lest the latter be "improved" too much. "We must not use children as guinea pigs for theories or as excuses for beautiful and unsalable editions. I would rather see 100,000 children writhing with glee over a small, dog-eared, cheaply printed book than to have had a hand in producing the most perfect specimen of the publisher's art, with 79 copies in circulation and 4,000 in the warehouse."

Helen Dean Fish says that, though he is a genial and delightful soul, there are two types of strangers who really irk him. "The first is the lady who greets him on introduction with a remark that shows she is quite unaware that he has even approached a drawing board except for the illustrating of *Ferdinand*. Secondly, he wearies of the would-be

LAWSON, ROBERT—*Continued*

writer of children's books—and these are legion—who sends him a manuscript (often without return postage) with the proposal that he illustrate the story, in which event the author is sure she can find a publisher and a huge popular success will result. These are the things that drive Robert Lawson out of his studio to work off steam in the lovely rose garden that he and Marie Lawson have made on Rabbit Hill. But before long he is back at work with pencils and brush, calling from his rich imagination drawings that stir emotions of humor, wonder and joy."

Lawson also collaborated with his good friend Munro Leaf, creator of *Ferdinand*, on a second book, *Simpson and Sampson*, which was published in the autumn of 1941 and was acclaimed by critics. Lawson also wrote and illustrated *I Discover Columbus* (1941), a tale of the voyages of Columbus as seen by his pet parrot. "My hobbies," he says, "are work, gardening, and disliking Mr. Roosevelt."

References

> Horn Book 16:16-26 Ja '40 il por; 17: 273-88 Jl '41 por
> Library J 66:591-2 Jl '41 il por
> N Y Times p32 Je 21 '41
> Pub W 139:2465-6 Je 21 '41 il por
> Who's Who in America
> Who's Who in American Art

LEAHY, FRANK (WILLIAM) Aug. 27, 1908- Football coach

Address: University of Notre Dame, South Bend, Ind.

No one will ever tackle the job of football coach at the University of Notre Dame without a sense of solemn obligation, for the spirit of Knute Rockne still hovers above the campus like a spectral overseer. Most of the educators and clerics still like to reminisce about the great genius of the gridiron, and his trail-blazing technique still dominates the Varsity team.

Rockne's numerous understudies still carry the torch of his tradition to other colleges where they serve as coaches. Some have even returned to the Alma Mater herself. Coaching at Notre Dame demands originality, audacity and experience. For all his mere 33 years, Frank Leahy, Notre Dame's newest coach, possesses these qualities in rich abundance. Close association with Rockne himself provided Leahy's extraordinary background.

Frank William Leahy was born in O'Neill, Nebraska in 1908, the son of Frank and Mary (Kane) Leahy. His father was a former Canadian, while his mother was a native of Pennsylvania. When Frank, Jr., was only a year old the Leahys moved to a town in South Dakota with the prophetic titles of Winner. Here Frank grew up in the buoyant atmosphere of the rural West and began, even as a boy, to show prowess as an athlete. He boxed, ran, wrestled and played baseball, football and basketball. Leahy came to the attention of the noted Notre Dame athlete, Earl

Walsh, when the latter assumed the job of football coach of Winner High School where Leahy was a student. It was Walsh who convinced Knute Rockne that Leahy deserved a grid scholarship to Notre Dame. In order to amass some necessary credits Leahy went to Omaha to attend Central High School, but scholarship wasn't his only concern. While in Omaha he boxed in amateur bouts, including one with Ace Hudkins, the Nebraska Wildcat, who was so impressed with Leahy that he advised him to become a professional fighter. The bout with Hudkins occurred when the fighter needed a sparring partner.

At Notre Dame Leahy began playing football as a freshman tackle, but the coaches soon saw that he had potentialities as a center. Aided by a classmate, he practiced snapping the ball indefatigably, even during study periods, and as a result won the Heving Medal in 1928 for being the most improved center. Then, after spring practice, he was again shifted to the backfield and made his mark as right tackle. He played on the National Championship team of 1929 and also began with the regular team the following year.

During the two seasons, Rockne's elevens went through 19 games without a defeat. Then, in the midst of the 1930 season, Leahy's football career was disrupted by a knee injury of serious proportions, and he had to undergo an operation. While waiting for his release from the hospital he turned from football action to theory, for it soon became evident that he would never be able to play again. His hospital sojourn had its compensations, though. Rockne himself was a frequent bedside companion and during these memorable visits poured a wealth of football knowledge into Leahy's eager ears. When Leahy came out of the hospital he knew more about football than when he had entered.

In spite of his disability Leahy insisted on appearing at scrimmage. Rockne decide to use him rather than risk the possibility of his entering into actual practice. Leahy was chosen coach for the tackles, told to put to use his knowledge gained on the field. Delighted, he decided to become a football coach, and on his graduation in 1931 accepted a position as line coach at Georgetown. In the two seasons he served there Leahy was able to experiment with many of his own ideas as well as with some handed down from the Old Master.

Leahy's next job was as assistant to Jim Crowley at Michigan State University, and when Crowley went to Fordham as head coach Leahy went along. Leahy served under Crowley for six seasons. His value was known to Crowley and to Fordham football analysts, but to the public at large he was a virtual unknown when he was offered the head coaching post at Boston College in 1939.

Leahy's position was not particularly exalted; Boston had dropped game after game with blithe abandon, and the sport was definitely in the "red." But what he did there is now football history. His energizing of one of the most uninspired football teams in the country was little short of miraculous.

The lackadaisical gridders appeared on the field during Leahy's first season as renovated men, filled with agility and driving forward with unwonted power, flashing startling plays with baffling frequency. Football interest was revived, and the sport boomed.

In Leahy's first season Boston won every game in its regular schedule except the one with Florida, but in his second season the Bostonians rode roughshod over every one of their ten regularly-scheduled opponents. To cap the climax they defeated Tennessee in the Sugar Bowl classic in New Orleans.

At the end of the 1940 season Boston tore up its previous contract with Leahy, although it had an additional year to run, and offered him another for a five-year term at a huge increase in salary. Leahy had already signed when news came that Elmer Layden had resigned as coach at Notre Dame to take the post of professional football commissioner. When he was sounded out as to the possibility of his taking Layden's vacated post, he asked for and received a release from his newly-signed contract with Boston.

"No other offer would have made me leave Boston," Leahy stated. "Practically every Notre Dame man wants to go back to his Alma Mater." Although his salary was not revealed it is known that his long-term contract with Notre Dame meant a drop in Leahy's earnings. He had, in addition, received offers from three other colleges and a professional team, one of which, he said, would have made him financially independent for life. But the lure of Notre Dame proved overpowering, and he spurned the other offers. His three assistants, Ed McKeever, John Druze and Joe McArdle, were retained on his staff when Leahy took his new post. McKeever is a Notre Dame alumnus, the others ex-stars from Fordham. Leahy lived up to expectations. In his first season Notre Dame was unbeaten, tied only by Army. For his achievement he received the New York *World Telegram's* Coach of the Year award, voted by 274 coaches throughout the country.

When he was appointed, Father O'Donnell of Notre Dame said: "Everywhere Frank has been he has exercised a fine influence on his associates." Leahy is a granite-jawed, blond, blue-eyed chap who looks even more youthful than his actual years. He has the knack of establishing perfect relationship with his men, and his metallic voice distributes football secrets and homilies on morals and behavior with impartiality. Like his unforgettable teacher, he likes to point out that there's a parallel between football and the even better known "game of life." As a coach he is noted for the unpredictable, tirelessly coming up with new plays and new twists to the old ones.

Leahy is known as a first-rate diplomat and an excellent after dinner speaker. In addition to his coaching he holds an important sales post with the United States Rubber Company. His chief hobbies are cards and golf, but during the football season he has little time for either.

FRANK LEAHY

Leahy is married to the former Florence Reilly of Brooklyn, whom he met in his Fordham days. They have three children: Sue, Frank, Jr., and Florence Victoria, who was born on the day before Boston's 1940 victory over Tulane.

References

Look 5:52-4 O 7 '41 pors
N Y Times p25 F 4 '41; p10 F 15 '41;
V p1-2 F 16 '41
N Y World-Telegram p17 F 15 '41 pors;
p14-15 N 29 '41 pors
Newsweek 17:54+ F 24 '41
Sat Eve Post 214:20-1+ O 18 '41 pors

LEAHY, WILLIAM D(ANIEL) (lā'hê) May 6, 1875- United States Ambassador to France

Address: b. Vichy, France; Department of State, Washington, D. C.

On November 23, 1940 President Roosevelt selected retired Admiral William D. Leahy, who was finishing his second term as Governor of Puerto Rico, as Ambassador to France to succeed William C. Bullitt. General John J. Pershing had previously refused the appointment on the grounds of ill health. The Senate unanimously confirmed Admiral Leahy's appointment on November 27. It was generally believed that, as Ambassador, Leahy would strengthen Pétain's hands in his negotiations with Germany by assuring him of the understanding and friendship of the United States. Further, the Vichy press praised President Roosevelt's selection. "The decision is considered as new proof of Mr. Roosevelt's sincere friendship for France," said the *Temps*. The French knew that, as admiral, Leahy had closely followed the situation at Martinique; and that his appointment was further expres-

WILLIAM D. LEAHY

sion of the Roosevelt Administration's interests in the problem of the West Indies.

In December Leahy sailed hopefully for France. But soon events were making it increasingly clear that his main task, the stiffening of Pétain's spine against collaboration, was an impossibly difficult one. And soon, too, there was a growing demand at home that the United States sever diplomatic relations with Vichy entirely and recognize De Gaulle.

Our Ambassador, who has probably played a larger part than any other man in shaping the policies of the United States Navy, is a native Iowan, born in Hampton, May 6, 1875, son of Michael Arthur and Rose (Hamilton) Leahy. He was graduated from the Ashland, Wisconsin High School in 1892 and from the United States Naval Academy in 1897. In 1904 he married Louise Tennent Harrington of San Francisco. They have one son, William Harrington. Leahy first saw service in the Spanish War during the Philippine Insurrection. In 1912 he was chief of staff of the Nicaraguan occupation and in 1916 held the same position in the Haitian campaign.

During the First World War Leahy attained the rank of captain, after being in command of the *U. S. S. Dolphin* in the Mexican Punitive Expedition of 1916. From 1927 to 1931 he was chief of the Bureau of Ordnance with the rank of rear admiral. In 1936 and 1937 he was promoted to admiral in command of the Battle Force, and he was chief of Naval Operations until he retired, at 65, in 1939. He is the only officer in naval history to have been chief of the two important bureaus of Ordnance and Navigation, as well as chief of Naval Operations. President Roosevelt awarded him the D. S. M. in 1939. He was appointed Governor of Puerto Rico in that year also.

It is said that, as Governor, Leahy liked the Puerto Ricans, and they liked him. The

only exception to his administration reported was that there was fear that he "might allow politicians to get away with practices that ought to be stopped." Radicals said: "He actually seems to believe in the Bill of Rights." Said to be an open-minded conservative, Leahy in general was considered "a straightforward, but businesslike and hardheaded person." To President Roosevelt he appealed "as a counselor on defense and as a man of superb, all-around ability." A tall man with a weatherbeaten face and bushy eyebrows, he is a strict disciplinarian, but easy and friendly when off duty. He plays a fair game of golf and likes bridge. His pet hobbies are his two grandchildren.

Prior to his Ambassadorial appointment, the Admiral in a White House conversation in June 1940 (according to *Newsweek*) "appeared intent upon shelving the Wage and Hour Act, outlawing strikes and other immediate moves to prohibit labor troubles in the defense program." He also advocated prompt purchase of British, French and Dutch possessions in the Caribbean. The Admiral said further that Puerto Rico was being turned into an American Gibraltar of such strength that no invader would be able to attack us without first reducing our island defenses in the Caribbean. "Bases capable of operating airplanes," he said, "could be prepared in the course of a few months." Puerto Rico had an allocation of some 20,000 relief workers, but at that time needed 10,000 more for the present defense program.

References

Cur Hist 52:9-10 D 24 '40
Lit Digest 122:10 N 21 '36
Nation 148:573 My 20 '39; 150:438 Ap 6 '40
N Y Herald Tribune p13 My 22 '40 por; p13 S 12 '40
N Y Times p8 O 8 '40; p1 N 23 '40 por; p19 N 24 '40
Newsweek 8:11-12 N 21 '36 por; 15:11 Je 17 '40
PM p6 N 24 '40
Scholastic 32:15S F 19 '38 por
Time 28:14 N 23 '36 por; 33:12 F 20 '39 por; 37:28-30 Ja 20 '41; 38:22 Ag 25 '41
Who's Who in America
Who's Who in the Nation's Capital

LEATHERS, FREDERICK JAMES, 1ST BARON 1881(?)- Head of the Ministry of War Transport and Shipping

Address: b. Ministry of War Transport, London, England; h. 3 Whitehall Court, London, S. W. 1, England

The first man ever to be put in control of all British shipping and transport services, from railroads to ports and highways, is "a tall, lanky man with a deeply creased, pleasant face, reminiscent of Viscount Halifax." The name of Frederick James Leathers does not appear in the British *Who's Who* for 1941, but there is no doubt that it will appear in the future: on May 1, 1941, when Lord

BARON LEATHERS

Beaverbrook became Minister of State, Winston Churchill announced that Leathers had been put in charge of the combined Ministries of Shipping and Transport and also named a member of the Privy Council.

Before he took over this post, critics in Britain had been complaining that lack of coordination between land and sea communications had caused damage from German bombers to valuable materials held at the ports. Now Leathers is the man responsible for "getting goods across the oceans and also for getting them unloaded, releasing the ships as quickly as possible." The measure of his success will be the success of Britain in the Battle of the Atlantic.

Leathers' career, while by no means so spectacular as that of Lord Beaverbrook, is the story of another poor boy who became wealthy and a peer. Frederick James Leathers was born in London's poor East End district the son of Robert and Emily (Seaman) Leathers and has lived all his life in the City of London; his father was a carpenter who died when his son was four months old. Frederick was only 14 when he began working as an office boy in the coal firm of William Cory & Sons, Limited, his weekly salary the extraordinary sum of seven shillings sixpence. Today he is not only the managing director of the firm with which he started, but also the director of 50 or 60 shipping, lighterage, cement, coal and transportation companies— British, Dutch and French. He married Emily Ethel Baxer in 1907 and has two sons and a daughter.

An expert on shipping, coaling and bunkering, soft-voiced Frederick Leathers had already made himself valuable to the British Government by serving as an adviser on coal in the Ministry of Shipping. In that capacity he met exigencies as they arose by directing

shipments of coal to ports all over the world. His first public appointment, however, was made in 1939, when he was appointed to the committee to advise the Lord Privy Seal on air raid shelter policy. Since he has never been elected to Parliament, and since before the appointment to his new post there was no time for an electoral contest that would put Leathers into the House of Commons, Churchill asked King George to raise him to the peerage as Baron Leathers of Pursfleet, Essex. Leathers' seat in the House of Lords will now permit him to sit in the Cabinet as well.

References

N Y Herald Tribune p1+ My 2 '41
N Y Times p1+ My 2 '41; p14 My 3 '41

LEBLANC, GEORGETTE 1875(?)—Oct. 26(?), 1941 Inspiration and associate of Maurice Maeterlinck, the Belgian poet, for 20 years; with him established a brilliant salon in Paris at which the great artists of the period were guests; acted in a number of Maeterlinck's works; published her memoirs, *Souvenirs: My Life with Maeterlinck* (1932).

References

Ann Pol et Litt 103:36 Jl 13 '34 por
Craftsman 21:410-11 Ja '12 il por
Harper's Bazaar 45:488-9 N '11 il
Musical Courier 87:13 Ag 30 '23 por;
    87:10 N 1 '23 por; 88:59 Ja 31 '24
    por; 88:27 F 21 '24 por
Theatre 14:128-31 O '11 pors; 33:174+
    Mr '21 por
Leblanc, G. Souvenirs 1932

Obituaries

N Y Herald Tribune p18 O 28 '41

LECKY, PRESCOTT (lĕk'ĭ) Nov. 1, 1892—May 30, 1941 Educator; consulting psychologist and lecturer on psychology in the extension division of Columbia University, New York City; had been member of the faculty since 1924; developed new theory of behavior, discarding the mechanistic viewpoint; his theory called "self-consistency" led to the formation of a new school of thought among educators and scientists.

References

Murchison, C. ed. Psychological Register 1932

Obituaries

N Y Times p11 My 31 '41

LEE, AURIOL Sept. 13, 1880(?)—July 2, 1941 English actress; director; producer; often called "the most versatile woman of the theatre"; after a long career as an actress, in which she established her name in many appearances in Europe and the United States, she turned to stage directing in the late 1920's, winning fame in this country and abroad with her productions; not only one of the most successful theatrical producers, but also one

LEE, AURIOL—*Continued*

of the theatre's few women directors; last production was the direction of *Old Acquaintance* in 1940.

References

> Am Mag 83:36 Je '17 por
> Theatre World 18:187 O '32; 19:33 Ja '33 por; 20:141 S '33; 28:113 S '37 por
> Town and Country 86:22 Ja 1 '32 por
> Vanity Fair 43:34 D '34 por
> Who's Who
> Who's Who in the Theatre

Obituaries

> N Y Times p16 Jl 4 '41 por
> Newsweek 18:6 Jl 14 '41 por
> Variety 143:54 Jl 9 '41

LEECH, PAUL NICHOLAS Aug. 12, 1889—Jan. 14, 1941 Chemist and author of many books on chemistry and pharmacy; chemist for the American Medical Association from 1913 to 1924; since 1924 director of the Association's chemical laboratory and since 1932 secretary of its Council on Pharmacy and Chemistry; at his death was director of the Division of Foods, Drugs and Physical Therapy for the Association.

References

> Time 28:50 S 21 '36 por
> American Men of Science
> Who's Who in America

Obituaries

> N Y Times p23 Ja 15 '41

LEHMANN, GEORGE July 31, 1865—Oct. 14, 1941 Violinist; composer; conductor; teacher; toured as soloist and leader of the Lehmann Quartet; conducted the Cleveland Symphony Orchestra from 1886 to 1889; in 1916 became director of the Lehmann Violin School; author of texts on violin playing.

References

> Baker's Biographical Dictionary of Musicians 1940
> Thompson, O. ed. International Cyclopedia of Music and Musicians 1939

Obituaries

> N Y Times p21 O 15 '41
> Variety 144:62 O 22 '41

LEHMANN, LOTTE (lä'män lŏt'tä) Opera singer

Address: Riverdale, N. Y.

Lotte Lehmann is a "musician's singer." Richard Strauss wrote an entire opera especially for her; Bruno Walter often stepped down from the conductor's podium to accompany her at the piano; her good friend Toscanini once joined in the *bravos* of the audience after her performance in *Fidelio*. She has been called "the singer who transcends mere singing, the artist with whom those of lesser vision could share exalted thought and feeling, and the woman of rare charm and warmth and human understanding. Her appeal as a public performer may derive from each or all of these compounds of her personality; but it is her chief glory that she can make the greatest part of her art the most simple, the most accessible and the first to capture the mind."

Born at Perleberg, near Hamburg, Germany, Lotte Lehmann was the daughter of Carl and Marie (Schuster) Lehmann. Her father was a small-town government official who wanted her to become a respectable stenographer or schoolteacher, and after the family moved to Berlin when Lotte was in her early teens she received the standard education for young ladies of good family at the local high school: music, languages, drawing. At first she thought she wanted to be a poet not of love, but of religion—and she still remembers the time she saw her first poem in print as one of the supreme moments of her life. But early in her adolescence she began to realize what she really wanted to do: to sing. This one thing she wanted desperately, in spite of her parents' puzzled and affectionate opposition. Even the suburban train sang to her, "I think I can—I knew I could," and she clung to her ambition stubbornly. Finally a neighbor's influence made it possible for her to enter the Royal Academy of Music.

She had little confidence in herself; she was shy, nervous. She worked hard to please her eminent teachers at the Academy, but could not. Finally they sent her home; she would never be a singer, never. Half-believing them, she still refused to turn to a "sensible" career. Finally a celebrated Wagnerian singer heard her sing, encouraged her, became her teacher—and young Lotte hounded the manager of the Hamburg Opera House into giving her a three-year contract, playing minor roles. Her debut as Freia in *Das Rheingold* brought the following comment: "A Fräulein Lehmann sang and played the part of Freia with touching awkwardness. As to the vocal qualities of the young lady, whose throat seemed constricted by excessive nervousness, we can as yet say nothing."

Her first success in Hamburg came when she substituted for a colleague as Elsa in *Lohengrin*. She has written about that experience: "The evening of the performance I did not see the audience. I did not even see the face of the director. I forgot everything—where I was, what the evening meant to me. I was Elsa, the Elsa that was first revealed to me by Klemperer, the Elsa that I now fully understood for the first time. Tears came to my eyes as the chorus sang *Heil dir Elsa*. And *Heil dir* my whole heart sings to the day of days which was the real beginning of my life."

Gradually more important parts came; she began to gain confidence, helped both by Gustav Breycha and by Otto Klemperer; and one evening after playing Micaela in *Carmen* she found the director of the Vienna State Opera waiting to give her a contract. He had been in the audience, hoping to find a tenor for his company.

It was in Vienna that Lotte Lehmann evolved her famous roles of Sieglinde in *Die Walküre*, of the Marschallin in *Der Rosenkavalier*, of Leonore in *Fidelio*—roles in which she was later to become so familiar to American audiences; it was there that she gave the first of her classic *Lieder* recitals. It was during one Vienna rehearsal that Richard Strauss heard her and selected her for the leading role in his *Ariadne auf Naxos*. She became the leading European interpreter of Strauss, once even staying with him and his wife in order to study for her role in *The Intermezzo* in which she took the part of his wife, and he wrote *Arabella* especially for her. And in Vienna, too, she met and in 1926 married an army colonel, Otto Krause. After her appearance in 1927 in the leading soprano role of Erich Korngold's *The Wonder of Heliane*, then having its première, the Vienna *Zeitung* wrote: "Lotte Lehmann is one of the greatest of the dramatic singers of our time." The Government conferred upon her the highest honor any artist could receive—the title of *Kammersängerin*—and she became an honorary member of the Vienna *Staatsoper* (State Opera).

But the Viennese were by no means alone in doing her honor. At the Paris Opéra in 1927 she sang the title role of *Fidelio*. It was the first time since the War that a German opera had been performed, and her triumph was such that she was offered the Légion d'Honneur for "distinguished artistic service." So moved was she at its presentation (she is one of the few women, and the only German woman to have been thus distinguished) that she didn't wait for the government official to kiss her on both cheeks, as was customary, but bent over and kissed him! In London she was made a member of the Covent Garden Opera, where she had won international fame in 1923; Sweden gave her its Medal of Art.

It was 1930 when Lotte Lehmann first came to the United States to sing with the Chicago Opera Company. She made her debut on October 28 as Sieglinde in *Die Walküre,* and more than one critic proclaimed her voice one of "heavenly beauty." At a recital debut in New York City not long afterward people were turned away from the doors, and at a second recital a month later the audience over flowed onto the stage. Wrote Olin Downes: "Some songs such as Schumann's *Der Nussbaum* and *Aufträge* had such effect that one is willing to go some time without hearing them sung by other singers."

On January 11, 1934 Lotte Lehmann made her debut on the Metropolitan stage, once more as Sieglinde. The next day the New York *Post* announced: "Never before in the history of the Metropolitan has there been such a scene . . . the instant the curtain fell the applause rang out spontaneously, and when Lotte Lehmann came before the footlights it rose in volume. Her confreres left her alone —something rare on the first curtain call—and

LOTTE LEHMANN

the whole audience broke into cheering which lasted a full 10 minutes."

Since that time her warmth, her vitality, her "unique manner of projecting her personality across the footlights, making of each individual in the auditorium a rapt audience of one" have made Lotte Lehmann one of the most beloved figures in the American musical world. She has sung in nearly every city in the United States. Of all her roles, the Marschallin in *Der Rosenkavalier* is the one with which she most identifies herself—and actually she has given more than two hundred-fifty performances in *Der Rosenkavalier,* in all three leading feminine roles, with fourteen different operatic organizations!

Today, however, she is even more interested in *Lieder* than in the opera. To her the *Lied* is like "a beautiful garden into which one goes, never wishing to open the gate and come back again into the world-glare." At first it was difficult for her to stay within the frame of a *Lied,* for she has the theatre in her blood; but with maturity she has learned constraint. In the future she plans to teach the art of *Lieder* to a few select pupils, in conjunction with her brother, Fritz Lehmann, who is at the David Mannes School. He and Bruno Walter, she says, are the two people who understand German *Lieder* as she does.

To these young pupils she will probably say: You must devote nearly every moment of your time to singing, to study. Languages and acting are almost as important as the development of the voice, and going to school is the least expensive way of acquiring them. A switch in teachers is good, however: it will broaden your viewpoint. Quick success is not good, so do not be discouraged. But the most crying need in America, where there is so

LEHMANN, LOTTE—*Continued*

much native talent, is for small opera troupes and companies to train you.

Lotte Lehmann herself still practices every day, still searches for new songs to increase her repertoire ("there is always something new to be learned"). But she also manages to read a great deal and to swim and ride horseback. According to *Time*, she resembles "the Viennese *Hausfrau* of tradition"; but audiences, more appreciative of her deep blue eyes fringed with dark lashes, her aristocratic small nose and her dimple, are inclined to disown the description.

Certainly Frau Lehmann isn't interested in home management; she can't cook, and has never tried to; she isn't in the least concerned with budgets, and is extravagant in her generosity toward her friends. And neither in taste nor in temperament is she anything but an artist—an artist of rather varied talents. She writes: her published works—a novel, *Eternal Flight* (1937), an autobiography, *Midway In My Song* (1938) and poems and articles in *Harper's Bazaar, Vogue* and other magazines —have earned praise from critics, and she has also written a book of poems, illustrated by herself. She paints. And she is one of the few opera stars who can act—critics call it acting, although she herself says: "When I play a part it must be an expression of something within myself; I must feel it." Speaking of her *Lieder* recitals, she says: "In this I cannot act; it is my sincerity which creates the bond between myself and my audience."

Formerly the "moving spirit" of Salzburg in the summers, today Lotte Lehmann's homeland lives for her mainly in her songs. In 1933, when the Nazi Government came to power in Germany, she renounced her fatherland and adopted Austria as her country. Then in 1938 the Nazi troops entered Austria, and in 1939, the year her husband died, Lotte Lehmann applied for her American citizenship papers. Her rambling residence in Riverdale, New York is her first permanent home in the United States, the country which must henceforth "keep peace, humanity and art treasures."

References

> Arts & Dec 48:16-18 Ap '38 pors
> Etude 53:701-2 D '35 por
> New Yorker 11:20-4 F 23 '35
> Newsweek 7:30 F 8 '36 por
> Theatre Arts Mo 21:285-92 Ap '37 pors
> Time 32:24 O 31 '38 por
> Vogue 93:73+ Ap 15 '39 por
> American Women
> Baker's Biographical Dictionary of Musicians 1940
> Eustis, M. Players at Work p118-27 1937
> Ewen, D. ed. Living Musicians 1940

> Ewen, D. Men and Women Who Make Music p143-61 1939
> Hope, C. Publicity Is Broccoli 1941
> Kaufmann, H. L. and Hansl, E. E. vom B. Artists in Music of Today p67 1933
> Lehmann, L. Midway In My Song 1938
> Who's Who in America

LEONARD, EDDIE 1871(?)—July 29, 1941 Greatest American minstrel of his day; always associated with his songs *Ida, Sweet as Apple Cider* and *Roly Boly Eyes* which he sang in blackface; his name famous for 45 years to vaudeville-goers; started first as baseball player, then turned to the stage while still a youngster and was a hit from the start until vaudeville "died" in the late '20s; appeared in motion pictures; composer of about 40 songs; real name Lemuel Gordon Toney.

References

> Motion Pict Mag 37:72 My '29 por; 38:33 Ag '29 por
> Theatre 38:29 S '23 por
> International Motion Picture Almanac 1936-37
> Leonard, E. What A Life, I'm Telling You 1934

Obituaries

> N Y Times p19 Jl 30 '41 por

LEONARD, EDWARD F., MGR. Mar. 4, 1870—Nov. 27, 1940 Pastor of St. Malachy's Roman Catholic Church in New York City; revered by Broadway stage folks for many of whom he was confessor.

MGR. EDWARD F. LEONARD

Obituaries

> N Y Times p23 N 28 '40 por

LEONIDOFF, LEON (lē′ŏn-ĭ-dŭf″ lē′ŏn)
Jan. 2, 1895- Senior producer and vice-president of the Radio City Music Hall
Address: Radio City Music Hall, Rockefeller Center, New York City

If one were to name America's leading director of spectacular stage productions and dance ensembles, it would probably be small, wiry, dark-eyed Leon Leonidoff. He is responsible for from 30 to 48 shows each year at Radio City's Music Hall, pride of New Yorkers and mecca for visitors from out of town.

On Friday at lunch—unless a show has been held over—department heads discuss the next show with Mr. Leonidoff. Monday the costume makers get to work. Material for a typical performance includes 90 ostrich boas, 1,700 yards featherbone, 4 gallons lacquer, 3 lbs. gold powder, 12 gross pompons, 775 yards red net, 2 gross great hooks and eyes, 35 yards velvet, 61 yards satin, 150 yards pattern cloth, etc. Promptly at 9 a. m. the photogenic Rockettes begin to master the intricacies of the new routines, rehearsing in shorts and blouses in their long mirrored hall. Precision is almost a god at Radio City, and they streamline their dances that way, under the watchful eyes of Rockette captain Emilia Sherman. The girls vary from five feet three inches to five feet seven inches in height, and when they face the audience in line formation—the taller girls placed near the center—the impression is created of a line of girls of even height.

During the week, while one show goes on for the Radio City audiences, another is being prepared backstage. Erno Rapee is in charge of music, Russell Markert and Gene Snyder direct the Rockettes, and Florence Rogge takes the kinks out of the Corps de Ballet. At 6 a. m. on Thursday the final rehearsal is called. An incredibly busy week behind him, the indefatigable Leonidoff sits down in the middle of the vast empty auditorium, armed with a script of the show, drawings of the scenes and portable microphone: "Then the whole spectacle, bit by bit, unfolds on the stage while he drones instructions, suggestions, criticisms through the microphone that carries his voice all over the theatre—never sharp or angry, always persuasive, almost gentle."

As a young man Leon Leonidoff was slated to become a doctor of medicine but he turned from this family choice of a profession to become, in turn, dancer, dance director and impresario. In moments of relaxation there comes to his features an expression that is puckish, alert, responsive, as though one part of his mind is occupied with the prescription for next week's audience. And, as one writer observed: "Like a wise doctor, he sugars his medicine with music and comedy. He takes a dash of opera, a bit of ballet, the colors of a desert sunset, then throws in clowns, chorus girls and a movie—and sells it four times a day to packed houses."

Leon Leonidoff was born January 2, 1895, the son of Jacob Leonidoff, a wealthy Bes-

Arthur Ermates

LEON LEONIDOFF

sarabian grain dealer, in the little Romanian village of Bender. The first "spectacle produced by Leonidoff" was put on in his father's back yard. With his young and enthusiastic colleagues, Leon managed to secure a quantity of his mother's fine linens and drapes to use as backdrops. And for the *opéra bouffe* atmosphere what could have been more appropriate than the bright buttons from elegant uniforms? Leon got his first "notice," too, in the form of a vigorous spanking from his father.

At the University of Geneva, where Leon studied chemistry, physics and did laboratory work in his medical course, he became a leading spirit in the dramatics club. They put on melancholy Russian dramas, light French farces, and, best of all, sprightly revues. The latter gave scope to Leon both as performer and as director, for he was a student of ballet. When the famous Russian director, George Pitoëff, came to Geneva, he invited Leonidoff to appear in several productions. Soon Pitoëff organized his own troupe, inviting the young medical student to join him as assistant producer and to dance leading roles with ballerina Ludmilla Pitoëff.

When the Pitoëff troupe moved to Lausanne, Leon gave up all pretense of studying medicine and went along with them. There wasn't much money in dance productions, but he liked the work. In collaboration with director Bonarell of the Lausanne Theatre of Drama and Opera, Leon helped to stage benefit performances with Russian students. Out of this grew the celebrated Isba Russe group. Their performances and their dances were of such verve and brilliance that they became known throughout Europe. Soon a wealthy broker sponsored them and brought the group to London, where their success encouraged them to try their luck in America.

LEONIDOFF, LEON—*Continued*

The Isba Russe dancers had their American debut January 25, 1920, at New York's Manhattan Opera House, where they put on *Dance of the Simpletons.* Leonidoff's success was almost immediate, for within a few months after his arrival in the United States he was made ballet director of the Capitol Theatre. Soon after that, Roxy (the late S. L. Rothafel) made him associate producer. At the Capitol, Leonidoff put on spectacles based on the music of Victor Herbert, and in 1923, on a Canadian tour, he worked with Victor Herbert on a production featuring his music. Before returning to the United States, Leonidoff ran a dancing school in Toronto for a brief period. Gradually, as he was called on to devote more attention to the production end of stagecraft, he found less and less time for dancing. From 1927 to 1932 he directed production at New York's Roxy Theatre and in the latter year (1932) Merlin H. Aylesworth, then president of NBC, invited him to become producer of spectacles at the world's newest and most elaborate of pleasure domes, Radio City Music Hall. Since 1934 Leonidoff has been senior producer and vice-president of the theatre.

At the Roxy, Leonidoff, who has a reputation for putting shows together on short notice, staged some 350 productions. On one occasion he did the seemingly impossible feat of starting from scratch and presenting an elaborate spectacle in two and one half days' time. At Radio City some six million persons each year come to see his creations. His Easter and Christmas shows have become national institutions, and ballets such as *Giselle* and *Scheherazade* have been highly praised as outstanding in that exacting field. An experiment in grand opera—one of the most difficult problems of staging that Leonidoff faced in his entire career—drew more than 250,000 people in two weeks. It was the famous *Madame Butterfly.*

In addition to giving his audiences the tried and true production numbers that they seem to expect, Leonidoff occasionally startles them with something different on the theory that "we've got to keep ahead of our audiences all the time." To this end he has brought to mass audiences the modernistically folksy *Petrushka* of Igor Stravinsky and Darius Milhaud's (see sketch this issue) *La Salade,* with scenery by the French painter Dérain and choreography by Serge Lifar. Said Leonidoff: "We must plan an entertainment that will satisfy many kinds of people. So if we have a heavy picture we try to put on a light show. If the picture is a comedy we use that chance for a more serious ballet, or perhaps an opera." As to the tremendous amount of work involved he says simply: "I have capable co-workers. We all do our best."

Called to Hollywood in 1937 to produce a dance sequence for the Grace Moore starring vehicle, *When You're in Love,* Leonidoff found a unique solution to the problem of placing ballet on the screen. First of all he recognized two objectives, only one of which was to express ballet forms on the

screen. The other was to fit this sequence to the rest of the film, much as a muralist adapts his work to its architectural setting. He consciously avoided showing movements that would be appropriate to stage choreography but might look awkward from a camera angle. Ballet shots alternated with close-ups of Miss Moore, and the former showed completed steps, not shifts from one position to another. "Thus," said Leonidoff, "the ballet is unique in showing not a single dance step, but only poses expressive of a mood."

Among Leonidoff's achievements is the Mickey Mouse extravaganza, staged in 1938, that pleased children, adults and even critics. In 1940 Leonidoff made all former glories pale with his *American Jubilee,* staged for the New York World's Fair, then promptly followed through with the spectacular *It Happens On Ice.* The former, said Brooks Atkinson of the New York *Times,* was "circus, show and copy-book lesson in Americanism." And of the latter he observed: "It is not much like the old frog pond where most of us awkwardly began with double-runners."

Leonidoff married St. Louis playwright Fannie Todd Mitchell at Mamaroneck, New York on October 6, 1930. The marriage ended in a Reno divorce, given Mrs. Leonidoff on October 26, 1932. After divorcing Leonidoff, Miss Mitchell married Seymour Woolner, who subsequently sued Leonidoff for alienation of affections. The Radio City producer retaliated with a countersuit, on the grounds that the Reno divorce was not legal in the state in which Woolner had been married. The tangle was resolved in September 1933 when in a higher court suits aggregating $1,125,000 were settled and discontinued.

Five feet five inches tall, Leonidoff appears to be super-charged with energy. Until 1940 he made annual trips abroad for study and rest. "The atmosphere about him," one learns, "is always tense. The small wiry Russian has an air of being about to spring frantically from his desk into the middle of one of his own extravaganzas. Quiet, courteous, attentive, his manner is still that of a man rushed to death and enjoying it."

LESCOT, ÉLIE (lĕs-kō' ȧ-lē') Dec. 9, 1883- President of Haiti

Address: b. Port-au-Prince, Haiti

On May 15, 1941 chubby Élie Lescot, former Haitian Minister to the United States and a member of the governing board of the Pan American Union, was inaugurated as the thirtieth President of the Republic of Haiti in the brilliantly decorated capital city of Port-au-Prince. M. Lescot had been elected President of Haiti a month before, although on April 9 United States newspapers had carried stories of crowds demonstrating in Port-au-Prince against his candidacy. At that time it was reported that thousands stormed the Legislature, smashed desks, shouted angrily. There seems to be some reason for believing that Lescot's predecessor, Stenio Vincent, was only too happy to give him the transfer of office at the National Palace after the inauguration ceremonies.

In the Black Republic, whose population is somewhere around 3,000,000, both Vincent and Lescot belong to the Élite—the comparatively small class which has from the beginning of its history been dominant both politically and socially. (A distinguished Haitian once said that 2,000 men from this class controlled Haiti absolutely.) Lightness of skin color, a predominantly European cultural pattern, a knowledge of French rather than Creole— these are among the features which distinguish Haiti's ruling class from the Noirs.

Lescot was born on December 9, 1883 in the village of Saint-Louis du Nord, where his parents always spent the summer. A member of an old family of Cap-Haïtien, he was educated there, and by the time he was 27 had become a member of the Legislative Assembly. After only three yèars in the Assembly he left to enter the judiciary, however, and was successively commissioner of the Court of the First Instance at Port-au-Prince, judge of the same court, examining magistrate at the capital, commissioner in the Court of Cassation.

At the same time he was taking an interest in politics. During the administration of President Borno, from 1922 to 1930, he served as Secretary of Public Education and of Agriculture; and when Vincent came into power in 1930 Lescot became Secretary of Justice and of the Interior. Vincent had been elected for a term of six years at a time when the United States was still occupying Haiti, but in 1935 he put through a plebiscite extending his term for five years more. According to *Time,* he "managed Haiti much as the late Huey Long managed Louisiana, sometimes sending to his Chamber of hand-picked deputies bills in sealed envelopes, which they passed without breaking the seal." He was hated by the Haitian exiles in Harlem, and the leader of the Party of Democratic Action, another exile in the United States, called his government "a pocket-sized version of Nazism."

Nevertheless Lescot and Vincent got along very well, and in recognition of Lescot's services as Secretary of the Interior, Vincent raised him to the rank of Grand Officer of the Order of Honor and Merit of Haiti and appointed him Haiti's Envoy Extraordinary and Minister Plenipotentiary at Ciudad Trujillo, capital of the Dominican Republic.

In the Dominican Republic, no stronghold of democracy either, Lescot apparently served his country well. For years a territorial dispute had been going on between the two republics: after less than two years in Ciudad Trujillo, Lescot worked out a formula acceptable to the Presidents of both countries whereby they would share the sovereignty of the West Indian island of Hispaniola. He was appointed chairman of the Haitian section of the Boundary Commission, and the Dominican Government conferred upon him the Cross of Grand Oficial del Orden de Mérito de Juan Pablo Duarte.

Albee

ÉLIE LESCOT

But Lescot's friendship with leaders of the Dominican Republic, particularly with President-dictator Rafael Trujillo (see sketch this issue), author of the 1937 Dominican invasion of Haitian territory in which several thousand border residents were massacred, did not add to his popularity in Haiti. And in the eyes of his political opponents the fact that he managed to secure indemnities for the victims did not make up for the fact that he accepted the grand cross of the same Dominican order of merit just before leaving the country to present to Franklin Delano Roosevelt his letters of credence as Envoy Extraordinary and Minister Plenipotentiary in the United States. That was on April 12, 1937. With him came his wife, the former Georgina Saint Aude.

Up to the last minute everyone expected that President Vincent would have himself re-elected for a third term by the members of the Senate and Chamber of Deputies when they convened as a National Assembly in April 1941. (There is no popular vote.) Vincent threw his support to his absent Minister, however, and on April 15 the vote in Lescot's favor was fifty-six to two. In a short speech issued from the United States, Haiti's President-elect then pledged himself to follow the policies of his predecessor; and on April 29, before departing for Haiti, he was entertained for the last time at the White House by a luncheon in his honor. A strong believer in cooperation with the United States, less than eight months later President Lescot followed President Roosevelt in declaring war on Japan, Germany and Italy.

References

Bul Pan Am Union 71:446-7 Je '37 por;
    75:325-8 Je '41
Friday 2:10-13 Mr 7 '41 il por

(Continued next page)

LESCOT, ÉLIE—*Continued*

Newsweek 17:32 My 26 '41
PM p8 Ap 10 '41 por
Time 37:39-40 Ap 28 '41 por
Who's Who in Latin America
Who's Who in the Nation's Capital

LEVINSON, SALMON OLIVER Dec. 29, 1865—Feb. 2, 1941 Attorney and philanthropist who sponsored the Kellogg-Briand Peace Pact; established the W. E. Borah Outlawry of War Foundation at the University of Idaho and gave the University of Chicago 50,000 documents showing the growth of the outlawry of war idea and telling of his dealings with famous statesmen; received Rosenberg Medal from the University of Chicago in 1931 for work in improving international relations, the Légion d'Honneur in 1934 and was proposed as a candidate for the Nobel Peace Prize in 1939.

References

Christian Cent 51:472 Ap 4 '34; 51:532 Ap 18 '34
Who's Who in America
Who's Who in American Jewry
Who's Who in Law

Obituaries

Christian Cent 58:264 F 19 '41
N Y Times p17 F 3 '41 por

LEVITZKI, MISCHA (lĕ-vĭt'skê mĭ'shä) May 25, 1898—Jan. 2, 1941 Noted concert pianist and composer; as child prodigy toured concert halls of Europe at the age of fourteen; born in Russia and was brought to the United States at the age of seven; won acclaim throughout the world, appearing in concerts and with leading symphony orchestras.

References

Musician 42:216 D '37 por
Baker's Biographical Dictionary of Musicians 1940
Ewen, D. ed. Living Musicians 1940
Pierre Key's Musical Who's Who
Thompson, O. ed. International Cyclopedia of Music and Musicians 1939
Vodarsky-Shiraeff, A. comp. Russian Composers and Musicians 1940
Who's Who in America
Who's Who in American Jewry

Obituaries

N Y Times p19 Ja 3 '41 por

LEWIS, DEAN (DE WITT) Aug. 11, 1874—Oct. 9, 1941 Surgeon; professor of surgery at the Johns Hopkins University from 1925 until his retirement in 1939; surgeon in chief at the Johns Hopkins Hospital; worked extensively in nerve, brain and abdominal surgery and made important discoveries in his field; ex-president of the American Medical Association.

References

American Medical Directory
American Men of Science

Directory of Medical Specialists 1939
Who's Who in America

Obituaries

N Y Times p23 O 10 '41

LEWIS, SIR WILLMOTT (HARSANT) June 18, 1877- Washington correspondent of the London *Times*
Address: h. 2356 Massachusetts Ave, Washington, D. C.

"On February 7, 1941, entranced listeners to the *Information Please* program were startled to hear an unbelievably British bass dispose with equal ease of questions dealing with *Alice in Wonderland* and the world situation, and efficiently exchange quips with Clifton Fadiman (see sketch this issue). The bass belonged to Sir Willmott ("Bill") Lewis, doing his best for England—as he had been doing it for the last 20 years in his official capacity as London *Times* correspondent in Washington and as unofficial liaison officer between the United States and the British Empire.

In Washington "Bill" Lewis reaps the mingled advantages of an impeccably British appearance and a thorough knowledge of American psychology. His appearance and speech are those of a stock Englishman—of the cocked eyebrow and stiff upper lip kind—and he plays this role with great enjoyment, to the delight of many Americans. But he has lived in the United States so long and studied life and customs here so thoroughly that his compatriots consider him an American with an invaluable knowledge of this country. (Even as early as 1914 some of them thought he was "a Harvard man putting on the dog.") He explains the Americans to the British and the British to the Americans. Few British visitors to Washington fail to avail themselves of the advice which Bill Lewis is always ready to dispense.

Sir Willmott Lewis was born in Cardiff, Wales, June 18, 1877, son of James Oliver and Marion Harsant (Butler) Lewis. His family was well-to-do and respected; his grandfather—incidentally, a fervent believer in the glorious destiny of the United States— was justice of peace and twice Mayor of his home town of Cardiff. Young Willmott Lewis had his preliminary schooling in Eastbourne and later went to Heidelberg and to the Sorbonne. He became proficient in languages and easily assimilated such culture as could be found in classrooms and cafes. One of the reasons for his later success was that chameleon-like ability to adapt himself to any environment. At the time, however, his accomplishments could get for him only a meager job writing wedding notices and obituaries on a Brighton newspaper. He taught himself shorthand, becoming as proficient in it as Billy Rose once was, and went to London to become a newspaperman in earnest.

His career underwent a slight detour when, for lack of anything else to do, he became an actor. This adventure lasted only for a short time, however, and after a brief so-

journ in the provinces Willmott came back to
London on the alert for another opportunity
to practice journalism. When the call came
he followed it to the other end of the world,
where he joined the staff of the North China
Herald in Shanghai as a combination assistant
editor and shorthand reporter. In Shanghai
he lived spectacularly, mostly on credit, owned
a stable of ponies and was the pride of
Shanghai society. Then he moved to Naga-
saki, Japan, to edit a small newspaper. While
there he married Lina Jessie Ringer.

In 1903 he talked James Gordon Bennett of
the New York *Herald* into giving him a job
covering the imminent disturbances in the Far
East. Then he went to Korea to wait for the
developments. His extreme popularity—he
was universally beloved as a good singer,
drinker and poker player—and his excellent
though unobtrusive knowledge of Japanese,
Chinese and Korean languages proved useful:
he was able to scoop the beginning of the
Russo-Japanese War and, as a matter of fact,
was in the midst of the first naval action.
Thereafter he covered the War, together with
aces like Richard Harding Davis and Martin
Egan.

After the War was over, Willmott Lewis
drifted to San Francisco. That first visit
to the United States was not so successful as
the subsequent one, and he led a none too
prosperous existence. At one time he opened
a gymnasium with a friend of his called Philadelphia Jack O'Brien. He returned to the
Orient, finally turning up in 1911 in the Philippines, where he was set to editing the Manila
Times under his friend and fellow correspondent Martin Egan. Incongruously enough,
his was the voice of militant Americanism in
the Philippines. He wrote the editorials and,
unable to afford the use of the Associated
Press, would substitute astonishingly correct
guesses about the news.

He got to Paris in 1917, after the United
States had entered the War, and was immediately put to work on the Paris headquarters
staff of George Creel's Committee on Public
Information, which was run by James Kerney,
editor of the Trenton, New Jersey, *Times*.
His personality and flawless knowledge of
French made him extremely valuable to that
organization and subsequently, when Kerney
went home, Willmott Lewis ran the whole
show, producing excellent propaganda for the
A. E. F. and finally winning a decoration, the
Légion d'Honneur. The Armistice left him
stranded in Paris in one of his occasional
periods of indigence. He even worked for a
time on the Paris *Herald,* that haven for temporarily embarrassed newspapermen.

He did not stay there long. He was soon
unearthed by Lord Northcliffe, the owner of
the London *Times,* who had been impressed
by his knowledge of American psychology and
his general efficiency. He offered him the post
of Washington correspondent of the London
Times, vacated by Sir Arthur Willert. Lewis
got to Washington in 1920 and has been there
ever since. As he himself says: "I have exhausted time in Washington. I am impinging

Harris & Ewing
SIR WILLMOTT LEWIS

upon eternity." The same social talents that
made him welcome in Shanghai, Manila and
Paris endeared him to Washington. He became known as a fashionable figure, a *bon
vivant,* a brilliant conversationalist. In 1926
he married Ethel Noyes, the daughter of
Frank Noyes, president of the Associated
Press (his first wife had died). One son
and two daughters were born to them. In
1931 he was made Knight Commander of the
Order of the British Empire.

Unofficially Sir Willmott Lewis has done
more to foster good relations between Great
Britain and the United States than any other
Englishman residing in Washington. He has
been the unofficial adviser and guide of all
the official ambassadors from England. His
unofficial cables to 10 Downing Street are read
perhaps more closely than his dispatches to his
paper. For important things to be done unofficially—from arranging private talks with
Stettinius and Knudsen to getting a daughter
of a Congressman presented to their Majesties
at the Court of St. James's—Bill Lewis is the
man to talk to. Besides, he influences American opinion in countless other ways—especially
by lecturing. Sir Willmott is an indefatigable
and ardent lecturer, although lately he has
somewhat abated his activity for fear of
being accused of propagandizing. His fees as
a lecturer are low; his speeches are ornate
and somewhat over the heads of the listeners
—which is a very subtle form of flattery. His
memory and erudition are fabulous, and he is
particularly fond of quoting from early American history. In March 1940 he began to put
out a weekly newsletter review of events
abroad, called *Foreign Correspondence*.

Sir Willmott has gained considerable renown in Washington as a witty and polished

LEWIS, SIR WILLMOTT—*Continued*

speaker. He likes to talk and does so with relish. The extent of his information is incredible, especially for a man who prefers talking to listening. He is the best-informed man in Washington even though he stays away from the traditional news sources such as press conferences and the State Department. The dispatches he sends to the London *Times* are thoughtful and well liked by his readers, although they naturally lack the sparkle and charm of his conversation. His style is generally somewhat heavy, weighted down by quotations from Santayana, Bacon, Tawney, Emerson, John Jay Chapman, Walter Bagehot, Arthur Twining Hadley, John Richard Green and countless others.

Sir Willmott is, of course, an ardent New Dealer—and not only since the War but from the earliest days of the New Deal. The results of the 1940 elections heartened him considerably. He has been, incidentally, not quite so farsighted about European as about American politics (in 1936 he predicted the size of Roosevelt's majority), and as late as March 1939 he refused to believe that Hitler would go to war. He himself has explained his pro-New Deal sympathies by saying ingenuously: "It is very much easier to be a liberal in your attitude to a country not your own than it is toward your own country." It may not be wrong to say that another good reason is that as a good Britisher he has always wanted the United States to abandon what he has politely preferred to call her policy of "unilateralism" and embark upon the policy of world-wide Anglo-American cooperation. But also he has often, though in terms veiled enough to be inoffensive to his listeners, deplored the "dangerous inequality of economic advantage; an inequality of contractual status as between industry highly integrated and labor still unorganized."

Sir Willmott is famous for his quips. Some of the wags in the National Press Club (where he spends a lot of time playing cards, talking steadily and absorbing information "through the pores") have said that his name should be Bonmott. It was he who said once, "I feel like a lion in a cage of Daniels." He remarked anent the London Naval Conference of 1930 that the American people insisted on "faith, hope, and parity." He characterized one politician as "Savonarola and soda," another as "a moralist in the worst sense of the word." His social activities have somewhat abated now from the frenzy that marked them in the first Washington years. He has been married for the third time—to the wealthy former Mrs. Norma (Bowler) Hull —and now lives a somewhat more sedate life in their beautiful house on Massachusetts Avenue in Washington, D. C., where there is a library of 7,500 books. Sir Willmott is an inveterate reader, particularly of American history.

References

Sat Eve Post 213:27+ Ja 25 '41 pors
Time 35:44 Ap 1 '40

Stearns, H. E. ed. America Now p573-80 1938
Who's Who
Who's Who in America

LEY, WILLY (lā vīl'ê) Oct. 2, 1906-
Author; scientist
Address: c/o Modern Age Books, Inc, 245 Fifth Ave, New York City

The May 1941 choice of the Scientific Book Club was "An Excursion into Romantic Zoology," or, as one reviewer describes it, a book "on the lunatic fringe of zoology" called *The Lungfish and the Unicorn* (1941). Willy Ley is the author. Says McCready Huston: "His clearing away the mists that hang over the twilight zones of knowledge is not only delightfully done but necessary. He is a master of the half-world where fact and fancy meet in the realm of beasts, birds, and fishes. He is never dull."

The Lungfish and the Unicorn deals with remarkable creatures: "those presumably mythological, those presumably extinct and those which ought to have become extinct but for various reasons didn't." The legendary dragon, basilisk, unicorn and sea serpent have probably never been honored with inclusion in a scientific volume before, but Willy Ley makes quite a case for some of them. The tatzelwurm, the geirfugl, the hoatzin, the okapi and the quagga have been more or less neglected, too. And it seems unlikely that many people know that the Cyclopes were elephants; that the last *real* penguin was killed in 1844; or that the horseshoe crab, found on Jones Beach and Cape May, is not only America's oldest inhabitant but actually a "freak hangover from Mesozoic times and earlier, a kind of antediluvian pre-scorpion or pre-spider," not really a crab at all. The New York *Times* reviewer, who presumably didn't know either, calls this "a good book all through."

Willy Ley was born on October 2, 1906 in Berlin, Germany, the son of Julius Ley, a business man, and Frida (May) Ley, the daughter of a government official. At intervals between 1920 and 1926 he attended the Universities of Berlin and Koenigsberg, where he specialized in zoology, paleontology and the history of science in general. His newspaper and literary career didn't begin, though, until he sent the correction of an error to a newspaper in Germany, saw it printed and actually received a small check besides. Encouraged, he began writing regularly about science for a number of magazines, and his first book, entitled *Trip Into Space* and concerning rocket ships, was published in Germany in 1926.

For a long time rockets remained Ley's chief preoccupation. In 1928 he published a treatise on the possibility of space travel which is said to have inspired the novel which was made into a movie by UFA and shown in the United States under the title *By Rocket to the Moon*; he then set to work on a history of rockets from the days of the ancient

Chinese and Greeks, of the fireworks-makers of Italy and of William Congreve to the present. (This was completed and published in 1931.) Nor did he limit himself to writing about rockets: he became the vice-president and secretary of the *Verein für Raumschiffahrt* and built it up from a small group of people interested in rockets to an organization which at one time had more than 1,000 members, a rocket-proving field on the outskirts of Berlin and a full-time staff of six engineers and mechanics. Ley, who spoke and wrote German, English, French, Latin, Dutch, Russian and Italian, kept up a correspondence with nearly every rocket experimenter in Europe and in America, and the *Verein für Raumschiffahrt* became the world center for news and information on rocketry. It also made the first really important contribution to the construction of liquid-fuel rockets in Europe, a subject on which Ley furnished some fundamental ideas. Finally, when the society was dissolved after the Hitler revolution, Ley became the moving spirit (officially, the vice-president) of its successor, which went under the name of the *E. V. Fortschrittliche Verkehrstechnik* and was located in Berlin.

In the meanwhile, though, Ley had not lost his interest in other phases of science. His studies formed the basis for a book on dragons which was published in 1928 and a biography of Konrad Gesner published the next year, and he continued to contribute steadily to magazines. Altogether there were eight books before *The Lungfish and the Unicorn,* and innumerable articles.

But there was no living in Hitler's Germany. On February 21, 1935 Willy Ley, like many a distinguished German refugee before him, arrived in New York City; one of his first acts was to travel down to Jones Beach to pay his respects to the horseshoe crab, to him a rare specimen previously glimpsed only in well-stocked European museums. His articles soon began to appear in *Esquire, Coronet, Natural History Magazine, Fauna, Frontiers* and *Zoo* as well as foreign periodicals. (The English titles, at least, show a talent for making a scientific study sound like a mystery story—particularly *The Fish That Made History, How the Moon Got Its Crater, Sad Story of the Lying Stones, Fire in the Anthill.*) Finally, in May 1940, Ley came to the newborn newspaper *PM* as one of three members of its department of scientific research. He has been there ever since, although he now constitutes the entire department. And through his editorship of the "New Weapons" page of that paper he was inspired to write another book, *Bombs and Bombing: What Every Civilian Should Know* (1941). In this the various types of bombs and methods of attack are described and information on how any attack can be countered by an equally well-prepared defense is given.

Willy Ley is described as tall, with "a mop of black hair and an intellectual, serious face." He will become a full-fledged United States citizen in 1942, having taken out his first

citizenship papers in June 1937. On Christmas Eve 1941 he married Olga Feldman, *PM's* writer on physical culture. His profession is his hobby, he says: at least he collects neither stamps, antiques nor matchboxes. *The Lungfish and the Unicorn* may be his first book in English, but it will not be his last. At present he is working on a book telling how the world was formed and developed and tentatively titled

WILLY LEY

Days of Creation, a book which Modern Age is expecting to issue early in 1942. If it is characterized by his usual "vigorous style" and "agreeable humor" there may be some danger that the weakhearted will find the past of our planet more attractive than its future.

References
New Outlook 164:28-9 O '34

LIEBLER, THEODORE A. (lĕb'lẽr) 1853(?)—Apr. 23, 1941 American theatrical producer; introduced Duse, Rejane, Arliss, Mrs. Patrick Campbell and the Irish Players to American audiences; from 1898 to 1912 presented 240 plays on Broadway, the majority of them hits; produced the first play by George Bernard Shaw to reach the United States.

Obituaries
N Y Times p21 Ap 24 '41

LINDBERGH, CHARLES A(UGUSTUS) Feb. 4, 1902- Aviator
Address: h. West Tisbury, Martha's Vineyard, Mass.

Bulletin: Upon the outbreak of the Japanese-United States hostilities Colonel Lindbergh issued the following statement: "We have been stepping closer to war for many months. Now it has come, and we must

CHARLES A. LINDBERGH

meet it as united Americans regardless of our attitude in the past toward the policy our Government has followed. Whether or not that policy has been wise, our country has been attacked by force of arms, and by force of arms we must retaliate." Later Lindbergh offered to help in the war effort and requested active Army air service. Secretary of War Stimson approved Lindbergh's offer.

From July 1941 issue (revised):

"The three most important groups who have been pressing this country toward war are the British, the Jewish and the Roosevelt administration. . . Their greatest danger to this country lies in their large ownership and influence in our motion pictures, our press, our radio and our government." "It is Roosevelt himself who advocates world dominion." "We in America have no reason to fear. . . We lack only a leadership that places America first —a leadership that tells what it means and means what it says." "I believe it is now too late for us to avoid going through in an American way what the nations of Europe have been going through in a European way. We are about to meet the greatest test since the Civil War."

It is Charles Lindbergh speaking in 1941— a new Lindbergh who frequently calls attention to the fact that during the First World War his father was also speaking on platforms against American intervention in Europe. His father was the late Charles Augustus Lindbergh, the son of a Swedish émigré who had been a member of his country's Parliament before coming to the United States. In the antitrust movement of 1906 he was elected to Congress, and there he raised his voice against the "money trust," against the "House of Morgan," against the maldistribution of wealth in the United States.

After the United States entered the War in 1917 his book, *Why Is Your Country at War?*, was suppressed by government agents; he himself was called seditious, pacifist, unpatriotic, Bolshevik, and was defeated when he ran for Governor of Minnesota in 1918. His argument was that a war economy further enriched the exploiting classes and impoverished the exploited. Critics of Colonel Lindbergh, however, have looked in vain in his speeches for the same preoccuption with the "little man"; the one thing he has yet to be called is Bolshevik.

Born in Detroit, Michigan on February 4, 1902, Charles Augustus Lindbergh grew up in Little Falls, Minnesota. His mother, the former Evangeline Lodge Land, a teacher of science, was of partially Irish descent. Of her son she said later: "He . . . lived a life more to himself than most boys. . . He does not take strikingly after one of his relatives. . . I would say that the out-of-door life was characteristic of his individuality, coupled with his love of being alone—with, first, animals, and then machines." On their Minnesota farm he "would spend entire days in the woods alone with his dog or some other animal." Then he designed and built a boat up there in the woods, and began to go boating with his dog. Next, for a while, his main preoccupation was "bronco busting," and when he went to the University of Wisconsin in 1920 to study mechanical engineering "he took his greatest interest in pistol shooting." "He finally left the University," she said, "because it was not teaching him what he liked to study, probably. Then he took to puttering about machinery. He had taken to motorcycles and automobiles, going on long tours over the country with them."

It was February 1922 when Charles Lindbergh left the University. On his motorcycle he headed for Lincoln, Nebraska, where he was already enrolled as a flying student with the Nebraska Aircraft Corporation. By summer of that year he was "barnstorming" with another aviator (he had had eight hours of actual instruction), and in April 1923 he bought his first plane—a wartime training plane—for $500. The next day he took his first flight alone, and in March 1924 he enrolled as a flying cadet in the United States Air Service Reserve at Brooks Field, San Antonio, Texas. In November 1925 he was commissioned a first lieutenant in the Missouri National Guard; for a while he was a test pilot at Lambert Field; and in April 1926 he made his first flight as a pilot in the United States Air Mail Service, a flight from Chicago to St. Louis. He was as fond of stunting as he was of practical jokes, and there are dozens of stories telling how, "when a certain St. Louis mail pilot came roaring in with capers which today would bring instant dismissal," the manager of the Chicago field would call: "Bellies to the ground! Here comes 'Slim'!"

For some time a prize of $25,000 had been posted for the aviator making the first flight between New York and Paris. Lindbergh was determined to win it. In February 1927, after finally acquiring the backing of a group of St. Louis businessmen who weren't averse to a little publicity for their city, he went to San Diego to order an airship made—*The Spirit of St. Louis.* It was May 10 when he took off from San Diego. He landed at Curtiss Field 21 hours and 20 minutes later, establishing a coast-to-coast record; and on May 20 he took off from Roosevelt Field alone, bound for Paris, with a few sandwiches in his pocket and some letters of introduction carefully tucked away.

All the world knows what happened after he landed in Paris the next day, remembers his touchingly naïve "I am Charles Lindbergh," the crowds gone mad, the joyful headlines, the receptions by heads of European governments, the special cruiser which President Coolidge ordered to bring the young flyer home. Before Lindbergh landed in Washington he had been promoted to a colonelcy in the Air Reserve, too, and a uniform was sent out to the cruiser, although he refused to wear it. On a triumphal tour of the United States 1,800 tons of paper were thrown on him in New York City alone; streets and even a town were named after him; his blond boyishness, his reticence, and even his apparent discomfort at so much public adulation captured the imagination of the people who cheered him in the streets almost as much as the daring thing he had done. He was "Lucky Lindy"—although even then some said it wasn't luck, that Lindbergh always planned everything very carefully in advance, that he was, in other words, as much a "good American businessman" as he was a great aviator. He was "the Lone Eagle." He was the young hero of whom *The Nation* wrote: "The happiest feature of the country's acclaim of Captain Lindbergh is that for once everybody, of every shade of opinion, can agree." He was a successful author: The New York *Times* syndicated his story of the flight and presented him with $250,000 in return, and his book, *We* (1927), was an immediate best seller. He was United States aviator No. 1: that year the Daniel Guggenheim Foundation for the Promotion of Aeronautics sponsored his air tour to 75 cities in the United States.

And, most of all, Lindbergh was America's "Ambassador of Good Will." In December 1927 he made a "good-will," non-stop flight to Mexico City, staying there a fortnight; "the good results . . . were even registered in the bond market, gains from fractions to as much as 1⅞ points being registered in Mexican bonds on the New York Stock Exchange on December 15." High government authorities next sponsored flights to Central America and the West Indies, including Havana, Cuba; and when in 1929 his engagement was announced to Anne Spencer Morrow (see sketch 1940 Annual), daughter of the late Dwight Morrow, former Morgan partner and at that time Ambassador to Mexico, the publicity attending their romance almost rivaled that of a Presidential election.

They were married on May 27, 1929. In 1930 the Lindberghs made their first transcontinental record together; and that same year a son, Charles Augustus, Jr., was born. Unlike many Americans who have leaped to fame, Lindbergh remained the public's darling. But by this time his feud with the press was well known. Most people blamed it on the callousness of reporters; even during the Lindberghs' honeymoon at sea, for instance, a photographer had pursued them in a motorboat. Others complained that their hero was more than a little inconsiderate, too: at a Cleveland air meet in 1929 he had made a dangerously low dive at a transport over the field (he was trying to warn the pilot to get out of the military zone, he explained); another time he sent a propeller blast of water into reporters' faces ("The trouble with those Washington men was that they simply did not know what to expect from an airplane in a wet field," remarked a friend of his); and puzzled newsreel audiences watched Lindbergh standing beside his plane while Anne struggled out of it with the luggage. All that seemed certain about his relationship to the press, however, was that although he was glad to have publicity for any aviation project at hand, personal publicity irritated him beyond measure, and he had a genius for making reporters his sworn enemies.

By the end of 1930, Lindbergh's personal fortune was estimated at over $1,500,000. Members of the New York Stock Exchange had at one time offered him $1,000,000 if he would not join a commercial aviation firm; he had refused and had accepted positions as technical adviser for both Transcontinental & Western Air Transport and Pan American Airways, with stock in both companies and a large annual salary from each. A domestic air route across the country was later initiated at his personal direction, and he did the official survey work, established operating policies and considered technical questions for a network of international lines. In 1931 the Lindberghs flew across the Pacific to act as "Ambassadors of American Good Will in the Orient." Not long after their return to the United States, in March 1932, the world was startled and shocked by the news of the kidnapping of their son. Lindbergh insisted upon supervising the search himself, even negotiated with the underworld for the child's return; but two months later his body was discovered near the couple's New Jersey estate. For a long time the case remained unsolved, while Lindbergh's antipathy for the press was intensified by its relentless pursuit of him, particularly after a second son, Jon Morrow, was born in August.

The Lindberghs continued to live in the United States for three years, however, although in June 1933 they gave their estate as a welfare project for children and that same year made a five months', 40,000-mile flight over five continents to survey transatlantic air routes, not returning until December. Then in 1934, after a United States Senate investigation headed by Senator Hugo Black (see sketch this issue) had turned up evidence of graft, the Government canceled air-mail contracts with all private lines. Lindbergh pro-

LINDBERGH, CHARLES A.—*Continued*

tested, and when called to testify was accused by Black of having received from the air lines money to which he was not entitled.

The episode was not pleasant; even less so was the ordeal of appearing in court after Richard Hauptmann was finally arrested that autumn as a suspect in the kidnapping of Charles Augustus, Jr., and the subsequent barrage of unpleasant publicity as the case dragged on through 1935. Finally, in December 1935, the Lindberghs set sail for England with their three-year-old son—in search of more protection against both kidnappers and Yellow Journalism than the United States could afford them. The Chicago *Tribune* announced: "No battle lost could bring the American People so great a humiliation"; Walter Winchell was "ashamed" of being an American citizen. Very few took the attitude of the Dayton *Daily News,* which proclaimed: "It is not a game thing the Lindberghs do. . ." There were rumors that Lindbergh would become a British citizen, but since he kept his commission as a reserve Army flyer as well as continuing as an unsalaried technical adviser for Pan American Airways, these were discounted.

In England the Lindberghs took up residence in the Weald, near Sevenoaks, where they lived in the "L-shaped 'hard-to-heat' house of Harold Nicholson, M. P., and of [his wife], novelist Victoria Sackville-West. . . The grim young man was hard to know, his smiling little wife more friendly but almost equally elusive, seldom seen." There, at least, they had privacy; for a very short time they almost dropped from the front pages. Then, in July 1936, Lindbergh received a letter from the United States military attaché in Berlin asking if he would accept an invitation from Hermann Goering (see sketch this issue) to visit Germany. He would. Once in Berlin, he made his first protracted tour of German aviation centers, was fêted everywhere. On his return to England, Lindbergh warned Prime Minister Baldwin of Germany's air power. He was ignored, as Churchill and others were being ignored at that time. It is reported that he emerged from the interview "in a cold rage."

The years 1936 and 1937 were spent in England, for the most part, although much time was spent on the continent. There was also a two months' trip to India in an airplane which the Lindberghs purchased and outfitted in England. In May 1937 another son, Land Morrow, was born; and October found them once more in Germany, receiving an ovation at the Munich Air Congress and being entertained by Goering again. When in December 1937 they left their children in England and returned to the United States, Lindbergh brought with him "probably more complete information on Europe's air plans, particularly those of Imperial Airways, than any individual on this side of the Atlantic." After three days of conferences with the Colonel, Pan American called for bids on plans for up to a dozen *Yankee Clippers* "of breath-taking size."

The visit to the United States was brief, however; in March 1938 the Lindberghs found a refuge on the Island of Illiec, near Port-Blanc, France, not far from the island laboratory of Lindbergh's friend Dr. Alexis Carrel (see sketch 1940 Annual), who in *Man the Unknown* openly expressed his contempt for democracy and for the "average man." While living in the United States, Lindbergh had worked for some time at the Rockefeller Institute as a biochemical assistant to the Nobel Prizeman, had designed a perfusion pump for Carrel's artificial heart, in which organs could be revived and made to function again; with him he later wrote *Culture of Organs,* published in 1938.

The Lindberghs were reported as frequent visitors to Lady Astor's Cliveden estate, too, and when the late Neville Chamberlain's visit to Berchtesgaden followed their visit to Russia in August that same year, the Soviet press was indignant. Said *Pravda*: "He had an order from English reactionary circles to prove the weakness of Soviet aviation and give Chamberlain the argument for capitulation at Munich in connection with Czechoslovakia." Although this was denied by his friends at the time (Lindbergh himself remained silent, as usual), in his own article in *Collier's* in 1941 the Colonel stated that at the time of Munich he "went to see one of the foremost leaders of England . . . at the request of other English leaders, to tell him my belief that the strength of German aviation was underestimated in England, and that the strength of Russian aviation was almost as much overestimated." He expressed the same opinion to an unnamed member of the French Cabinet.

The Lindberghs' third visit to Germany in October 1938, coming on the heels of Munich, was unfortunate. It was then that at a banquet (which Lindbergh attended at the request of Hugh Wilson [see sketch this issue], then United States Ambassador to Germany), that Goering presented the Colonel with the Service Cross of the Order of the German Eagle. It was a complete surprise to the State Department. In November the Lindberghs thanked Goering for his hospitality and made inquiries about leasing a house in Berlin; and by December public reaction in the United States had taken such a turn that Lindbergh's name had to be removed from the TWA slogan as no longer an asset to the sale of air travel. The Lindberghs, however, did not go through with their plans to live several months in Germany, but instead spent the winter in Paris. By April 1939 they were all back in the United States, planning to fly back in the spring of 1940 for a trip to Italy. In America the Colonel worked for the Air Corps and National Advisory Committee for Aeronautics, visiting practically all aircraft factories in the United States and maintaining his Army status on this basis. But this four month's tour of duty has been his only active service in the United States Army, and since that time he has not been in close touch with developments in military aviation in the United States.

In August 1939 Fulton Lewis, Jr., Washington commentator for the Mutual Broadcasting Company, invited Colonel Lindbergh to make a speech over that network giving his ideas on the tense international situation. Lindbergh refused at that time, but three weeks later accepted, and two days before his first speech pleading for strict American neutrality in the Second World War he terminated his four months' tour of duty as a reserve officer. (An article in the *Saturday Evening Post* claims that shortly before the speech he was visited by an emissary who offered him a future position as United States Secretary for Air if he would not criticize President Roosevelt's foreign policy, but that he refused.) It was the first of many such speeches. By the summer of 1940 when, after the fall of France, the Colonel predicted the demise of Great Britain within a few weeks, *Social Justice* was doing him the unsolicited honor of backing him for vice-president as running mate for Wendell Willkie.

The full storm of public criticism did not break over Lindbergh's head, however, until after his Chicago speech of August 1940, when he announced that "when the rich become too rich and the poor too poor, something happens." Widely quoted were a recommendation of cooperation with a victorious Germany—"never impossible when there is sufficient gain on both sides"—and an anxiety to "maintain the supremacy of our Western civilization" which reminded some people of an earlier plea for Anglo-American-German collaboration against the "pressing sea of Yellow, Black and Brown."

Of the many attacks which followed, perhaps Ralph Ingersoll's was the most immoderate: "I say very simply that Colonel Lindbergh in his speech in Chicago Sunday identified himself as Spokesman No. 1 for the fifth column." There were other editorials like that. But the *Commonweal* reproved him more mildly: "We may agree with you that America cannot solve Europe's problems, and yet disagree strongly with your solution of the general problem." And the *Christian Century*, which didn't agree with Lindbergh's views on a coming race conflict, still regretted the mud-slinging campaign against the Colonel and called him "America's war enemy No. 1."

In October 1940 came Lindbergh's first outspoken call for "new leadership"—in a radio speech that at the time was interpreted as a plea for the election of Wendell Willkie. Anne Lindbergh's *The Wave of the Future* had just been published, and their first daughter, Anne Spencer, born. In January 1941 the Colonel testified in Congress against the Lend-Lease Act, saying that Germany was producing 5,000 planes a month, that Britain could not win even with the help of the United States and that the United States itself would be in no danger of invasion if she would build up a force of 10,000 modern fighting planes and provide adequate bases for them. "I would prefer to see neither side win," he said; "I'd like to see a negotiated peace." In February, Senator Nye (see sketch this issue) suggested that Lindbergh seek a place in Congress. In

March *Collier's* published Lindbergh's *A Letter to Americans*, although the editors themselves were not in sympathy with his views. Finally, in the middle of April, the Colonel joined the America First Committee.

Since that time he has spoken to tremendous and enthusiastic crowds at America First rallies in many cities; he has been constantly attacked by interventionists as ambitious and Fascist-minded and by many non-interventionists as representing something greatly different from genuine American peace sentiments; some have called him "sincere" but "mistaken"; some suspect his motives but respect his information; and there are still others who think of him as a courageous American patriot who is being persecuted for his opinions (he has frequently been denied meeting places and, although he has been given much free time on the air, charges that there is a radio conspiracy against him, too). On April 28, 1941, offended by Roosevelt's reference to him as a "Copperhead," Lindbergh resigned his colonel's commission in the United States Army Air Corps Reserve. Stephen T. Early (see sketch this issue) wondered whether he was also returning his decoration to Hitler; but the New York *Times* found that neither Roosevelt nor Lindbergh was justified, called it an "Unhappy Incident." By May there were rumors that he was planning to run in Minnesota for his father's seat in order to make his voice felt in foreign policies and also that he might run for President in 1944.

It took Lindbergh nine days after the German invasion of Russia on June 22 to make any comment on the new turn in the War. Then he confided that he would rather be in alliance with Germany "or even England" than with Russia. His interpretation of the Second World War was that France and Britain brought it about in September 1939 by refusing to follow his advice and allow Hitler's expansion eastward.

In August, Lindbergh embroidered his theory further by suggesting that Great Britain might be against the United States before the War was over—her changed relations with Pétain's France and Mannerheim's Finland proved her fickleness. In September came the speech which caused charges of anti-Semitism to be leveled against Lindbergh and the America First Committee, though denied by both. And the ex-flyer's next speech, in October, discussed "the procedure" he believed should be followed if free speech ended in America and Roosevelt suspended the 1944 elections, both dangers which, he suggested, were imminent.

Lindbergh has often insisted that democracy no longer exists in the United States; his enemies, in turn, have challenged his devotion to the democratic principle. Harold Nicholson, British author and statesman, wrote as early as October 1939 that after the ordeal that the flyer was subjected to in his own country "he began to loathe democracy," to worship "virility." Such statements as "Racial strength is vital . . . politics a luxury" have also been quoted against him, and his close association with individuals like Law-

LINDBERGH, CHARLES A.—*Continued*

rence Dennis (see sketch this issue) and his acceptance of support from groups like Father Coughlin's have created further suspicion. Press comment in Rome and Berlin is uniformly laudatory of Lindbergh, and translations of his speeches turn up as Nazi propaganda in as out-of-the-way places as Ecuador. However, Lindbergh understandably resents reflections on his patriotism and has several times announced that he would welcome an investigation of his alleged Nazi connections.

Lindbergh is "still thin and young-looking, his wavy hair now receding a little." When he makes a speech his delivery is calm and unimpassioned—he is "calculating and cold," his enemies say, while his friends call him "undemonstrative, reserved, severe." James A. Mollison, the first man to fly from Britain to America, wrote in 1940 that when he met Lindbergh he would talk about nothing but aviation, that he wouldn't smoke, wouldn't drink—wasn't "one of us." Others say that he "seems content to have shut himself off completely from his life before his flight to sudden fame," has few personal friends, is no longer the young practical-joker who put kerosene in his roommate's water pitcher but rather "a very rich man with a very rich man's interests and, presumably, a very rich man's attitude toward life." One reporter, who says he knew him well, remarks: "He has figured everything out. He knows where the America First movement is going to take him." It seems certain, at any rate, that it will not take him away from the spotlight from which he had been retreating for so long.

References

Am Mag 127:16-17+ Ap '39 pors; 132: 106-9 Ag '41 pors
Liberty 18:16-17+ Je 7 '41 por; 18:18-19+ Je 14 '41 pors; 18:18-19+ Je 21 '41 por; 18:34-5+ Je 28 '41 pors
Life 11:65+ Ag 11 '41
Lit Digest 93:36-44 Je 11 '27 il pors map
New Repub 104:134-5 F 3 '41; 104:620-1 My 5 '41
New Yorker 6:26-9 S 20 '30; 6:30-3 S 27 '30
PM D 2, 3, 5, 6, 7, 8, 9, 10, 12, 13, 14 '41
Sat Eve Post 213:12-13+ D 28 '40 il pors; 213:27+ Je 21 '41 por
Time 27:34-6+ Ja 6 '36 il; 31:40+ Je 13 '38 il por (cover); 33:15-16 My 8 '39; 37:17-18 My 5 '41

America's Young Men
Bridges, T. C. and Tiltman, H. H. Heroes of Modern Adventure p268-77 1927
Clark, J. A. comp. College Book of Essays p543-7 1939
Fife, G. B. Lindbergh, the Lone Eagle 1927
Haines, L. and Haines, D. Lindberghs 1931
Lindbergh, C. A. We 1927

Lotz, P. H. ed. Vocations and Professions p85-96 1940
Mussey, V. T. H. Flying Adventures of Lindbergh 1933
Snyder, E. E. Biology in the Making p420-40 1940
Who's Who in America

LITVINOV, MAXIM (MAXIMOVITCH) (lĭt-vē′nôf) July 17, 1876- Soviet Ambassador to the United States; Deputy Commissar for Foreign Affairs

Address: Soviet Embassy, Washington, D. C.

"We always realized the danger which a Hitler victory in the West could constitute for us," said Maxim Litvinov in a radio broadcast to the United States and Great Britain on July 8, 1941. The "we," according to some American commentators, was Litvinov himself, and his statement, in the tactful language which underlings must apply to dictators, was tantamount to "I told you so." He reminded the Western powers that they, too, suffered by not taking his advice. As a matter of fact, if it had not been for the bloodshed and the burning cities, the occasion could have been considered a "great personal triumph for Litvinov."

After the Munich pact, symbol of Litvinov's failure in his campaign for collective security, the world at large wondered what the eventual reaction of Russia would be to the unequivocal snub by the Western powers. Those who were "informed," however, said: "Don't watch Russia; watch Litvinov." If he lost his job, Russia would be at best neutral in the inevitable conflict; at worst, an open ally of Germany. On May 1939, Litvinov was relieved of his post; in August, Stalin signed a non-aggression pact with Hitler. In June 1941, Germany invaded Russia; in November, Litvinov was designated Ambassador to Washington and appointed Deputy Commissar for Foreign Affairs.

Maxim Maximovitch Litvinov was born in Bialystok of a poor Jewish family on July 17, 1876. He is using one of his many *noms de révolution*, among which have been Papasha (dear papa) Felike, David Mordecai Finkelstein, M. G. Harrison and others. His real name is Meer Moiseëvich Vallakh, son of Moses and Anna (Perló) Vallakh.

At 17, after he had been graduated by the Bialystok Gymnasium, Maxim volunteered for service in the Russian Army and served five years as a common soldier. It was his army experiences, humiliating for a Jew in the Czar's Army, and his recollections of life in the ghetto at home which turned young Maxim into a revolutionary. In 1898 he joined the Social Democratic Party and in 1901 was arrested and sentenced to exile in Siberia. He never reached the Ural Mountains, but escaped to Switzerland, where he met Lenin, continued his revolutionary activities and edited a paper, *Iskra* (The Spark).

With a group of revolutionaries, he returned illegally to Russia and worked in the underground organization which precipitated the unsuccessful 1905 revolution. After "Bloody Sunday" and the collapse of the Party's plans, Litvinov was engaged in storing contraband arms in a secret depot on an island near Tallinn.

The following year found Maxim Litvinov quietly editing a legal newspaper, *New Life*, in St. Petersburg. On the side, however, he continued his revolutionary activities and in 1907 was sent abroad by Stalin to sell some bank notes seized in a bank raid at Tiflis, an action which the Czarist press characterized as a "holdup" rather than an act of revolution. In the course of his successful financial negotiations, Litvinov was arrested in Paris and expelled from France.

After a brief return to Russia, Litvinov went to London, where he worked for 10 years as salesman, clerk, teacher of languages and writer. In 1916 he married Ivy Low, an English radical writer, one of whose uncles was a former Lord Mayor of London, and another, Sir A. Maurice Low, the Washington correspondent of the London *Post*. It was during this period that Litvinov acquired his fluent English. His accent is irremediably tainted by years of association with London's East End slums, and came in for much ridicule during his early years as a diplomat.

When the First World War started, the underground revolutionary movement gained new momentum. Litvinov met Lenin and Bukharin in Zürich for a revolutionary conference and in 1917 Litvinov, under surveillance of the English secret police, became the Soviet Government's first representative to England. Since the British Government did not recognize the Soviet Government, it did not know what to do with him until August 1918 when the police arrested him and held him as a hostage for the British agent, Bruce Lockhart. When he was released, it was on condition that he leave England.

On his return to Russia, accompanied by his English wife and his son, Mischa, Litvinov became a member of the collegium of the *Narcomindel* (Foreign Office) and remained Assistant Commissar for Foreign Affairs under Tchicherin until 1930, when he replaced his superior as Commissar. His diplomatic career took him to Stockholm in 1918, Tallinn in 1919, Copenhagen in 1920 and Geneva in 1922. As a member of the Soviet delegation he made agreements with the American Relief Commission in 1922 and commercial treaties with Germany and Norway. In 1926 he began his annual "explosive" visits to disarmament *pourparlers*, where he "provoked the successive amusement, indignation, rage, and finally respect of the Western powers." In 1933 he came to the United States and successfully negotiated recognition of the U. S. S. R. In 1934 he piloted the Soviet Union into the League of Nations, and until 1939 he fought at Geneva for collective security.

At Geneva, Litvinov was responsible for one of the most dramatic moments in the history of mankind. The time was March 19, 1928; the scene, the meeting of the Preparatory Disarmament Committee of the

Sovfoto

MAXIM LITVINOV

League of Nations at Geneva; the protagonist, Maxim Litvinov, representative of a non-member country. "It seems to me," he said, "there has been more than enough discussion of disarmament. . . The Soviet Union declares it is ready to abolish all military forces as soon as a similar decision is passed and simultaneously carried out by other states. The Soviet Government asks the other Governments here if they are also ready."

Of course they were not ready and there is little doubt that Litvinov knew his bluff, if bluff it was, would not be called. The newspapers, however, made much of it, and peace-loving people all over the world saw a Utopian dream just miss reality.

The delegates of the other powers immediately rushed to their own defense. Litvinov was "sabotaging disarmament." By exposing the hypocritical motives governing the delegates, he rendered them ridiculous and thereby ineffective. They accused him of speaking over their heads to the proletariat of their countries, arousing hopes that neither he nor any other man or country could fulfill.

Early in 1935 Litvinov began his campaign to bring the Western democracies into a proposed "Eastern Locarno" to preserve the *status quo*. With the increasing strength of Fascism and the successive violations of the Versailles Treaty (to which Russia had not been a party), Litvinov increased his efforts to bind the Western democracies to a promise of mutual assistance. When Russia entered the League in 1934, Litvinov had promised the Western Powers that the Third International and political aggression would be put into the background. In May 1935 Laval signed a Franco-Soviet Pact, and two weeks later a Czecho-Soviet Pact was signed which provided for mutual assistance against aggression, provided France helped the victim.

(Continued next page)

LITVINOV, MAXIM—*Continued*

It was the Munich pact to bring "peace in our time" that defeated Litvinov and lowered his prestige in the Kremlin. After Chamberlain, Bonnet, the capitulation at Munich, the ill-dissimulated Franco-British hesitations, Stalin claimed that the international policy of his supposed allies was deceptive and vacillating, and that Russia would have to abandon hope for collective security and proceed to further her own interests.

Russia's most successful diplomat was not her most trusted Bolshevik. Within the Kremlin he was respected but neither a "dominant" figure nor a member of the powerful *Politburo*. As a Jew and the chief proponent of collective security against Fascism, Litvinov was unable to negotiate with Germany. In May 1939, therefore, Premier Molotov (see sketch 1940 Annual) relieved the Foreign Commissar of his portfolio and retained it with the premiership. In March 1941 Litvinov was dropped from the Central Committee of the Communist Party because of an "illness" from which he recovered as soon as Hitler invaded Russia. According to Walter Duranty, it was natural enough for him to withdraw when he ceased to be Foreign Commissar.

Until the German invasion of Russia, June 22, 1941, Litvinov was living in Russia. It was reported in the foreign press that he was exiled and perhaps executed. When Stalin took down his former plans for cooperation with Great Britain and the United States from the shelf and dusted them off for current use, he brought out Litvinov, alive and apparently as healthy as ever. The former Foreign Commissar's first job was to act as unofficial liaison officer between the Soviet Union and the United States and Britain. He was expected to become Joseph Stalin's "Colonel House" and visit London and Washington as the Soviet Ambassador at large. On November 6, 1941, however, it was announced that Russia's "ace diplomat" was named Ambassador to Washington to replace Oumansky (see sketch this issue), who had gone to Russia with the American supply mission and had not returned. Five days later his appointment as Deputy Commissar of Foreign Affairs was announced. The appointment of Litvinov to these important posts was taken as an indication not only of Russia's desire for close cooperation with the United States, but also of the fact that the Russians "do not expect indefinite developments in the near future to cut short this cooperation." He arrived in Washington, after a long and difficult trip, on December 7 and on December 11 was able to set at rest rumors that the U. S. S. R. might consider a separate peace. "We have a common cause and a common enemy," he said. A few days later Madame Litvinov, speaking to 10,000 at a Russian war relief rally in Boston, affirmed: "Our war is your war just as your war is our war."

Described as a salesman for the Soviets who "has the maddening persistence of a house-to-house oil burner vendor in a New Jersey suburb," Litvinov has been noted in international circles for his keen intelligence, his double-edged wit, and his lack of social graces. He wore the proper clothes of a diplomat but without the usual elegance. He failed to give diplomatic dinners and balls or to be properly impressed by the entertainment of his colleagues. He is "pudgy," and wears horn-rimmed spectacles to aid his gray-green eyes. His appearance is "far less like an international statesman than a New York cloak and suit salesman." His chief quality has been analyzed as an "inveterate stubbornness in argument which arises from his unvarying consistent point of view, plus an elasticity in negotiation that few statesmen can equal."

References

Christian Cent 56:628 My 17 '39
Collier's 97:34+ Ja 18 '36; p12+ Ja 3 '42 pors
Cur Hist 50:11-12 Je '39
Eur Nouv 22:477-9; 22:483-4; 22:500 My 6 '39
R of Rs 88:46 D '33
Sat R 160:208-9 S 21 '35 por; 162:424-5 O 3 '36 il; 162:501 O 17 '36
Time 33:22-3 My 15 '39 por; 36:20 Jl 15 '40 por
Gunther, J. Inside Europe p543-5 1940
Who's Who
Wolfe, H. C. The Imperial Soviets 1940

LLEWELLYN, SIR WILLIAM (loo-ĕl'ĭn) Dec. (?), 1863—Jan. 28, 1941 British portrait painter; numbered among his subjects members of the royal family; best-known works studies of King George V and Queen Mary; president of the Royal Academy for 10 years after 1928, when his election was considered in some circles as a "victory for the old school"; knighted in 1918.

References

Royal Soc Arts J 81:835-6 Jl 21 '33
Who's Who
Who's Who in Art

Obituaries

N Y Times p21 Ja 30 '41

LLOYD, GEORGE AMBROSE, 1ST BARON LLOYD OF DOLOBRAN *See* Lloyd of Dolobran, G. A. L., 1st Baron

LLOYD OF DOLOBRAN, GEORGE AMBROSE LLOYD, 1ST BARON Sept. 19, 1879—Feb. 5, 1941 Late British Secretary of State for the Colonies

Bulletin: On February 5, 1941 Lord Lloyd died in London of a recurrence of a type of poisoning contracted while he was campaigning in the desert with Lawrence of Arabia.

From January 1941 issue:

A picture of Lord Lloyd might well be called: "Portrait of an Imperialist," for the British Empire has been the inspiration of his career and he holds fast by all for which it stands. Compton Mackenzie once wrote to him: "I began for the first time in my life to appreciate that Imperialism could touch a man's soul as deeply as religion. . . If anyone could have converted me to Imperialism it would have been you with your passionate sincerity and high purpose and infinite seriousness."

Lloyd, in his full life, has done all the "right" things and been to all the "right" places. He has been by turns diplomat, army officer, bank director, Governor of an Indian province, Conservative Member of Parliament, High Commissioner, chairman of the British Council and Minister of the Crown. And in all these things he has shown himself a man of abundant energy, fearless, imaginative, fond of panoply and ceremony, a natural ruler of men, with the ruler's defects as well as his virtues.

George Lloyd was born at The Priory, Warwick, the son of S. S. Lloyd, member of the big banking house which runs Lloyds Bank. After schooling at Eton and university life at Cambridge, where he played a good deal of polo, George went into business in London. This didn't last long, for he already was smitten with wanderlust. At 15 he had been to Fez, Tangier and Gibraltar, and in 1899 he began to wander over Central Asia, India, the Persian Gulf, Syria and Turkey, and even went into Tibet over the Zogi La Pass. He wasn't traveling to see scenery or picturesque costumes: his interest was in studying political and social conditions, in learning the nature of the Oriental mind. To do this he became fluent in Turkish and Arabic.

In 1905, after his travels, Lloyd was appointed honorary attaché to the British Embassy at Constantinople, now Istanbul. One year later came his first big job: the working out of a trade route in Turkey, Mesopotamia and the Persian Gulf. He continued to study Turkish affairs and was in Constantinople in 1908 when the young Turks drove out Abdul Hamid. In the Balkan War of 1912, though British opinion was overwhelmingly with the Serbs and their allies, Lloyd was with Enver Pasha in the Tchataldja Lines.

Before this, however, Lloyd had returned to England and had entered Parliament in 1910 as Conservative Member for West Staffordshire. He held this seat until 1918, though all through the First World War he was engaged in military service with the Warwickshire Yeomanry—in Egypt, Gallipoli, Mesopotamia and the Hedjaz—and rose to captain, won the D. S. O. and was mentioned in dispatches six times. In 1917, after being present at the first Battle of Gaza, he was sent to the Hedjaz to assist T. E. Lawrence, who was fomenting the Arab revolt against the Turks. He proceeded with the advancing Arab forces as far as Jefer, but wasn't present at the fall of Damascus. Of him Lawrence wrote: "To him many things were needful; and so he did not stay very long

LORD LLOYD

with us. He did not see how much we liked him."

When the War was over Lloyd was offered the post of Governor of East Africa, but refused it. When he was offered the Governorship of Bombay, however, he accepted and was made a Knight of the Grand Cross of the Indian Empire. In Bombay Lloyd's regime was an iron-handed one—he even went so far as to have Gandhi arrested. Yet he is remembered there not only as the author of repressive measures and policies but also as the creative thinker who inspired fine housing schemes and the making of a great dam across the Indus at Sukkur, now called the Lloyd Barrage.

Lloyd's term as Governor expired in 1923 and he returned to Parliament in the following year as Conservative Member for Eastbourne. One of his associates in the House was the present Lord Halifax, with whom in 1919 he had collaborated on a book called The Great Opportunity. In 1923 Lloyd was made Privy Councillor and a Knight of the Grand Cross of the Star of India and in 1925 he was raised to the peerage as Baron Lloyd and sent out as High Commissioner for Egypt and the Sudan to succeed Lord Allenby.

Lloyd found Egypt, as he had previously found Bombay, in a highly disturbed political state following the assassination of the Sirdar, Sir Lee Stack. It was again, he felt, a case for the pressure of the iron hand. This lasted until 1929 when a Labor government came into power in England. This government wanted to push an arrangement for at least partial independence for Egypt through to completion, but "Lord Lloyd refused to grant the additional concessions to Egyptian

LLOYD OF DOLOBRAN, GEORGE AMBROSE LLOYD, 1ST BARON—*Cont.*

nationalist opinion to bring this about." His view was that the safety of Britain's vital trade route to India through the Mediterranean and the Suez Canal would be endangered; consequently he resigned.

Lloyd wasn't heard much of again until 1937, when he became chairman of the British Council, a newly formed organization created to promote British cultural ideas and ideals in foreign countries. Successful institutes and classes were formed in many countries, but the Government was far from generous in its contributions and in some quarters it was felt that Lloyd wasn't the right man to head this work.

In the Churchill Government, formed in May 1940, Lloyd is Secretary of State for the Colonies, a man who frankly supports the present British policy in Palestine, who is considered in the Cabinet to be a reinforcement on the Right, and most important, a man who is known to retain his stand for administrative efficiency, patriotism and energy, qualities much in demand in the present War crisis. He is also the author of *The British Case* (1940), a brief résumé of War issues from the British point of view. The London *Times* found it "as lofty, straightforward and succinct a presentation of the British case as could be wished"; the *Manchester Guardian*, however, while respecting him for "the sincerity and consistency of his Tory convictions," decided that it would be unfortunate if anyone got the impression that he was stating the opinions generally held in Great Britain, or that his book "represents the mind of the Government." His view of the Nazi-Soviet pact, for instance, was that Hitler had betrayed Western Europe—presumably in not going immediately ahead with his plans for eastward expansion.

In 1911 Lloyd married the Honorable Blanche Lascelles, who was Maid of Honour to the late Queen Alexandra. They have one son and heir, the Honorable Alexander David Frederick Lloyd, who was born on September 30, 1912.

References

> Christian Sci Mon p4 My 21 '40
> Strand Mag 96:516-24 Mr '39
> Lawrence, T. E. Seven Pillars of Wisdom 1935
> Mackenzie, C. Gallipoli Memories 1929
> Who's Who

Obituaries

> N Y Times p21 F 6 '41 por

LOEWY, RAYMOND (FERNAND) Nov. 5, 1893- Industrial designer

Address: b. 580 Fifth Ave, New York City; h. Sands Point, Long Island, N. Y.

America has no industrial designer with a work-career more dynamic than that of Raymond Loewy. During 1940 products manufactured from his design specifications, it is said, have aggregated more than one-half

billion dollars. Among his fifty clients Mr. Loewy includes five national railroads, three national automobile companies, four airplane manufacturers, two streetcar firms, three manufacturers of cosmetics, a bus company, six department and chain stores, and three steamship lines.

Early in 1940 Mr. Loewy made a trip from his Long Island home to Palm Springs, California, by auto, train and plane. All of these travel vehicles were personally styled by him. For Studebaker, Loewy designed the *Champion* passenger car; the *Broadway Limited* of the Pennsylvania Railway was once a blueprint in his drafting room; and for Transcontinental and Western Air, Incorporated, he designed the interiors of the Douglas and Boeing *Stratoliner* transports.

Whether he travels or stays at home, Loewy has right at hand his own designed products. In his kitchen he may have his own model of *Frigidaire*, or Sears Roebuck's *Coldspot* refrigerator. In his bathroom one may find Loewy-designed Pepsodent packages and toothbrushes or the Schick electric shaver; his wife may have her choice of perfume and toilet packages of Woodbury's, Jergen's, Elizabeth Arden's or Schiaparelli's products—all package-designed by her husband. And in the Loewy cellar there may even be Loewy-designed bottles of Seagram whiskey. If Loewy has his way, too, he will be safe from bombs in a place of his own designing—his latest idea is for a helicopter landing field in mid-town New York City, under which would be a great air-raid shelter.

The man whose ideas of design, present and future, are strictly streamlined Americana, was not born in this country. That event took place in Paris, France, on November 5, 1893; he was the son of Maximilian and Marie (Labalme) Loewy. Raymond Loewy was a student at the Chaptal College, Paris, from 1905 to 1910, and was graduated from L'École de Lanneau in 1919. During the First World War he was a captain in the French Army, winning the Légion d'Honneur and the Croix de Guerre.

After the Armistice, Loewy came to the United States to take up a career in engineering. Only an incident occurring on the voyage changed these plans and resulted in Loewy's American career's starting in the fashion field. On shipboard he was asked to make a charitable donation and could not afford it: he had just been discharged from the army with a brilliant record but with scarcely a *sou* to his name. But Loewy could draw, and as his contribution he made a sketch of one of the young women passengers. This was sold at auction to the British Consul General of New York at an exceptionally high price for an unknown artist—$100. As a result, young Loewy decided to go into fashion illustration. He began designing for *Vogue* and *Harper's Bazaar*—later did window displays for Saks Fifth Avenue, Macy's and other New York stores.

In 1926 Mr. Loewy decided to apply his taste for simple lines and his flair for fashion to industrial design. He designed an automobile for a national manufacturer; then, in rapid succession, office equipment, refrigerators, washing machines, stoves, heaters, etc. During the late '20s manufacturers became conscious of the trend toward well-styled and good-looking merchandise to increase sales-appeal. An example of what good design can do occurred in 1934 when Sears Roebuck consulted Loewy on engineering and styling their refrigerator. Loewy produced the now-famous *Coldspot* unit that was a complete departure from anything this company (or any other) had done before. From the first it was a notable sales success. In 1934 Sears Roebuck sold 140,000 units; in 1937 the number had jumped to 275,000. The design won first prize at the Paris International Exposition in 1937. Loewy is now also consultant stylist to the Frigidaire Corporation.

Raymond Loewy is probably the most important industrial designer in the field of transportation. In its September 1940 issue the magazine *Art and Industry* describes him as "perhaps the best-known in Europe. Raymond Loewy, whose organizations have been responsible for the design or redesign of products as wide apart in size and use as railway engines and saucepans, has during the past few years penetrated the British market to an unparalleled degree. Loewy himself can be classed as a public utility. Americans travel on his transcontinental buses, in his streamlined ships, his speed-conditioned automobiles, by the locomotives which are his special pride. Models in the Chrysler Motors Building at the New York World's Fair revealed him as a go-getter visionary of the Wellsian brand. The elliptical taxi, the sealed air liner, the streamlined, rear-engined car: these might have been lifted from Wells' *Things to Come*. The important difference is that many of Loewy's projects have already arrived."

Among notable Loewy creations are Greyhound bus terminals, Savarin bars, International Harvester equipment and the W. T. Grant stores. The fate of the *Morro Castle* set him to thinking of all-metal ships' interiors: accordingly chairs, closets, bureaus, tables, even lamp shades have been designed in metal by him for Pan-American ships such as the *Panama* and the *Cristobal*.

Loewy's own penthouse office and reception room are said to resemble "a Hollywood production." He employs some 75 designers: architects, engineers and artists, all busy in huge, beautifully lighted workrooms. "There is the pleasant sound of music from radios; Loewy thinks it stimulates the imagination." In his own personal apartment Loewy has used laminated plastic materials in the design of his furniture.

In a recent address to Harvard University students of the School of Business Administration, Loewy said that executives "must give major consideration to esthetics in industry." He believes that simple, esthetic lines are more pleasing than designs submerged under superfluous ornamentation. He attempts

RAYMOND LOEWY

to reduce a product to its absolute essentials without reaching the stage of aridity. He feels that the industrial designer must function as artist, engineer, silent salesman; and must coordinate his efforts so that, if possible, manufacturing costs may be lowered. The present design for taxis is his one big grievance. His idea of a taxi would be a light, short, three-wheeled affair, with doors opening automatically when the cab stops at the curb; the whole vehicle would be small enough to occupy very little parking space, and would be operated most economically.

Mr. Loewy is the recipient of many honors and prize awards. These include the degree of Royal Designer of Industry, conferred on him by the British Royal Society of Arts, which thus dignified an American for the first time in its 185-year history. In 1906 (at 13) he won the J. Gordon Bennett Medal for a model airplane that established a distance record; he owns the Branger Cup, given to him for the fastest speedboat ever built; and he was awarded the Gold Medal in the transportation field at the Paris Exposition in 1937, and first prize in the "All-American Package Competition" in 1939.

Soon after arriving in this country Loewy became a naturalized citizen, and in 1931 he married Virginia Thomson of Englewood, New Jersey. He lives in New York City, and often lectures at New York University and at the New School for Social Research. He says that his hobby is "deep sea diving," and of his future plans he states: "My future plans are to find a practical way to make plans for the future."

(Continued next page)

LOEWY, RAYMOND—*Continued*

References

Arch Forum 72:sup 11 My '40 por
Arts & Dec 43:29 Ja '36 por
Barron's 20:20 Jl 15 '40
Design 39:3-5 Ap '38 por
Mod Plastics 14:20-1 Jl '37 por
PM p29 S 14 '41
Who's Who in America

LOMAX, ALAN Jan. 15, 1915- Musical specialist; assistant in charge Archive of American Folk-song, Library of Congress

Address: Division of Music, Library of Congress, Washington, D. C.

Speaking before a group of librarians, Alan Lomax once said: "For the past five or six years, since graduating from college, I have been traveling the roads, smooth highways, the rough mountain tracks, the corduroy lumbering roads, the little muddy lanes and the wagon tracks, putting down on records what the people of America—the hardhanded and fey people of this country—have been singing and saying for the past hundred years and more. Having listened and recorded, I feel that these people have their own version of American history, their own literature, their own music . . . as worthy of being carefully guarded, stored up, used and studied as the accumulation of printed culture in libraries."

This young man whose main occupation in life is seeing to it that this folk art is recorded and studied was born on January 15, 1915 in Austin, Texas, the son of John A. and Bess (Brown) Lomax. His father came to Texas by oxcart soon after that state was admitted into the Union. Nine of the old cattle trails crisscrossed the state, and riders on the trails had their six-shooters ready for rustlers or rattlesnakes, whichever showed up first. In addition to songs of the trail the Lomaxes—there were two boys and two girls —heard songs of canebrake and cottonfield, Spanish settlers and shantymen of the Gulf ports, railroads and camp meetings, and, eastward in the Red River country, the deep bottom blues.

A Sheldon fellow of Harvard University in 1910, his father, John A. Lomax, soon completed a first folk-song collection, *Cowboy Songs and Other Frontier Ballads*. (In it was a song whose words and music had been given to him by a Negro camp cook; the song, *Home on the Range*, has since swept the country.) He then began the Library of Congress Archive that in 1941 comprises some 12,000 titles. Thus for Alan, and for his sister Bess (who has since sung with him on the radio), acquaintance with native music began in the home. There, and on long trips in the family car, they were never without music. They sang, and they sang all the time —the songs that document America more pertinently and often more accurately than the history books—songs of every phase of the country's rich development.

Alan went to Terrill Preparatory School, Dallas, to Choate School, had a year at Har-

vard and took his B. A. at the University of Texas. He then interrupted his studies at the latter University to go on his first recording trip with his father in 1933. In an old car and with a tent they headed for the Brazos bottoms and the prison camps. Alan's first experience in actual collecting is described by him in the following words: "That evening, when darkness had come up out of the bottom and settled over the whole plantation, we lighted a little kerosene lamp inside the schoolhouse and found that the room was full of Negroes—old men, peering at us out of dim eyes; young men, hats cocked at a rakish angle, red bandannas high about their throats, sitting off away from the women; women with babies; big-eyed children; young women with their backs to the men, giggling."

Another session was at a sharecropper's cabin, and "out in front lay the yard, deep with dust, turned silver by a full moon. . . Presently the guests began to arrive, some on horseback, some appearing suddenly on foot out of the tall weeds; rattling up in flivvers or driving their squeaking wagons. . .

> *De sun gonna shine in my back*
> *   door some day,*
> *De win' gonna rise an' blow*
> *   my blues away...*"

This trip was financed by a grant from the Carnegie Corporation, its results deposited in the newly constituted Archive of American Folk Song in the Library of Congress, and John A. Lomax made its first curator. In the years from 1933 to 1935 he and his son prepared and published their first collaborations, *American Ballads and Folk Songs* (1934) and *Negro Folk Songs as Sung by Lead Belly* (1936).

In 1935 Alan returned to college to his undergraduate passion, epistemology. In 1936 he wrote a paper on Saunders Pierce, founder of pragmatism and teacher of William James. Graduated that June, he spent a few months in Mexico, then came to Washington to assist his father in the Library, with the expectation of returning to epistemology after two years or so. It was December of that year when he revealed to librarian Putnam that he had had a letter from Zora Neal Hurston, well known Negro writer, concerning possibilities of folk-music collecting in Haiti. Putnam immediately arranged for his travel expenses and recording equipment, and finally young Lomax was off on his first solo jaunt.

His fiancée, Elizabeth Harold—pretty, blonde and young—followed him to Port au Prince, where they were married in February 1937. There the age of consent was 21 for the bride and 23 for the groom, and since the former was 19 and the latter 22 it was necessary for the President of Haiti to waive the bans before they could be married. It was done impressively, by parental consent and governmental decree, and the couple was presented with a long illuminated scroll in official French. They saved all the records made during the trip but lost the scroll, and to this day the precise date of their marriage is a matter of conjecture.

In Haiti the Lomaxes lived in a thatched hut, recorded native songs and voodoo dance rituals from 7 p. m. to anywhere between 2 and 5 a. m. each morning. They traveled about in a strictly native jollopy, painted yellow and trimmed in scarlet. "It was," said Alan, "like a great, square-cut, tropical fowl, a fantastic bird with an olive green beak and a black toupee, and it was named *Fleur d'Innocence.*" When they returned Alan helped his father to edit a new edition of *Cowboy Songs and Other Frontier Ballads* (1938). That was in May 1937. In June he was named assistant in charge of the Archive of American Folk Song under his father, its curator, and Dr. Harold Spivacke, who heads the music division; and both that year and the next he and his father carted their portable recording apparatus down the Library's quaint winding stairway and piled it into their car for further recording trips.

It seemed very unlikely, after all, that epistemology would turn out to be his profession. Even while taking a graduate course in anthropology at Columbia early in 1939 he continued his work in the folk-music field. In the spring of that year he supervised an album by Lead Belly (Huddie Ledbetter), the great folk singer who, "with his 12-string guitar, had sung his way out of both the Texas and Louisiana penitentiaries," and the success of this album of "Negro Sinful Songs" encouraged recording companies to bring to the public more and better examples of folk music. In the summer he did a documentary series of recordings by Ferdinand (Jelly Roll) Morton—pianist, composer, orchestra leader—one of the outstanding pioneers of jazz.

The early method of recording was to take a verse or two on the machine and write down additional verses. Gradually the idea of documentary records evolved. Some would begin with a dialogue between informant and collector. Others would continue the informal dialogue throughout the record. Finally as many as 75 records would be made to document the story, say, of Aunt Molly Jackson, "ballit" singer from the coal-veined hills of Kentucky. And funds for making some of these records available at cost to musicologists and others interested in grass-roots music were supplied by the Carnegie Corporation.

This folk music also reaches some 15,000,000 young listeners via Lomax's "Well-Springs of America" Series broadcast on *Columbia's School of the Air.* Begun in 1939, as the series continued it became more and more a survey of a state or an area, and radio listeners began paying tribute to this documentary approach by writing: "I like to listen to the songs about the unknown heroes of labor and the farms," or, regarding programs of Negro songs: "In them one sees courage and a rhythmic dignity." Folk singers are guests and contribute to material used in the script, but Lomax frequently sings too: he was good enough to entertain the King and Queen of England at the White House in 1939. He also collaborates with director

ALAN LOMAX

Nicholas Ray on the popular CBS feature, *Back Where I Come From,* featuring folk singers, tall tales and local lore; and in the summer of 1941, while off the air for the season, he was hard at work with his father and Ruth Seeger putting the finishing touches to *This Singing Country,* which was published by Macmillan.

In January 1941 he was appointed consultant on the Library of Congress Radio Project, set up by the Rockefeller Foundation to do experimental work in the field of educational radio. In 1942 he plans to travel in South America making more folk song records.

Slight of build, six feet tall, with dark brown eyes, wide forehead and black hair, Alan Lomax has a keen glance, a quick warm smile and a thoroughly democratic manner. He includes among his friends innumerable folk singers, many of them obscure and impoverished, others, like Woody Guthrie, well known. Such prominent American composers as Earl Robinson, Charles Seeger and Roy Harris are other friends of his. He works as long as 12 hours a day and when not working he is, like as not, playing his guitar and singing either for friends or for strange audiences. Sometimes, too, he finds time to go sailing, a favorite recreation, or to settle down with a good book for a few hours.

References

A. L. A. Bul 34:437-9+ S 1 '40
Christian Sci Mon Mag p9 Mr 8 '41 por
Etude 58:220 Ap '40 por
Southwest R 19:105 winter '34; 23:125 Ja '38

LONE RANGER See Graser, E. W.

LOSOVSKY, SOLOMON ABRAMOVICH See Lozovsky, S. A.

LOZOVSKY, S(OLOMON) A(BRAMO-VICH) (lô-zôf'skê) 1878- Vice-Commissar for Foreign Affairs, U. S. S. R.

Address: c/o Commissariat of Foreign Affairs, Moscow, U. S. S. R.

The New York Public Library

S. A. LOZOVSKY

"The blitzkrieg is a washout."

"The German claims of mighty victories remind me of the story of the hunter who shouted: 'I have caught a bear but he won't let me go!'"

With these attention-getting press dispatches, Vice-Commissar Lozovsky launched his new career as official press spokesman for the Soviet Union. A veteran Bolshevik, renowned for the number and variety of his speeches, writings and arrests, Lozovsky left the field of trade-union organization in 1939 to become Vice-Commissar for Foreign Affairs and in June 1941 added to his activities those of assistant director of the Soviet Information Bureau.

Like most of the Russian revolutionaries, Lozovsky has retained his party pseudonym, chosen originally to protect his real identity. The name is probably derived from Lozovaga, a small town where he began his revolutionary activities. He was born Solomon Abramovich Dridzo. His father was a Hebrew teacher whose earnings were not sufficient to support his family adequately, and Solomon's earliest recollections are of extreme poverty and privation. At the age of 11, young Dridzo left the classroom to help the family income and worked both as blacksmith and as butcher.

At the turn of the century, when he was 22, Lozovsky, the revolutionist, took the place of Dridzo, the hard-working son of the village "Malamud." In Panyutena and Lozovaga he organized Social Democratic Clubs among the railroad workers. Looking for broader fields of work, he left for the big city, St. Petersburg, where he very soon found himself in jail in the first of the many arrests which were to dot his colorful career. In 1904, after a year's imprisonment, he was expelled from the capital and sent to Kazan, where he found work as an agitator for the Kazan Committee of the Russian Social Democratic Revolutionary Party.

October 1905, date of the abortive October Revolution, when blood flowed in the streets of St. Petersburg and scattered riots and uprisings spread over Russia, found Lozovsky prominent in the Kazan agitations. As a result, he was tried and arrested several times.

He then moved the center of his activities to Kharkov, where in 1908 he was arrested and sentenced to exile in Siberia. He escaped on the way to his destination and went to Paris, where he remained from 1909 to 1917, an active member of the Paris division of the Russian Social Democratic Party.

During the First World War, Lozovsky was editor of several Russian publications in Paris, among them *Golos* (The Voice) and *Nasha Slovo* (Our Word). He was chosen secretary of the Hatters Trade Union and Bakers Cooperative in Paris and at the same time took active part in numerous international organizations, both political and trade union. As a result he was expelled from France.

In 1917 Lozovsky returned to Russia, where at the third All-Russian Conference of Trade Unions he was chosen secretary. In July of the same year he joined the radical Left wing of the Social Democratic Party, the new Russian Communist Party of the Bolsheviks. By the end of 1917 he was expelled from the ranks of the Party because he openly opposed Party policies, especially those dealing with trade unions, but in 1919 he made his peace with the orthodox and was readmitted.

From 1918 until 1939 Lozovsky was an executive member of most of the important trade-union organizations. In February 1918 he was chosen secretary of the Textile Workers Union and in July he became secretary of the Railroad Workers Union. He took part in the international trade-union organization which in 1921 became known as the Red International of Labor Unions. He was one of the founders of the *Profintern* (Trade Union International) and was chosen general secretary in April 1921.

As president of the Soviet delegation, Lozovsky attended the All-China Conference and the Pacific Trade Union Conference. He was candidate for membership in the praesidium of the Comintern and, during the election of deputies to the All-Russian Congress of the Soviets, he was elected deputy from Kurgizy, U. S. S. R., to the Soviet National assembly and a member of the council of the Communist Academy.

As one of the founders of the *Profintern,* Lozovsky was editor in chief (October 1928 to May 1933) of the official organ, *The Red International of Labor Unions Magazine,* published monthly in English, Russian, German, French and Spanish. His editorials cover a wide variety of topics from concrete methods of trade-union organization to more abstract discussions of internationalism. His style is direct, repetitious and full of slogans and catch phrases. His favorite expression is "self-criticism," and few of his articles fail to discuss the need for improvement from within. He continually preaches internationalism, singleness of purpose and revolutionary fervor. In his own life, although he has on occasion been at odds with the Party line, he has never wavered from following the correct procedure as he saw it.

In June 1939, three months before the Nazi-Soviet pact, Lozovsky was appointed Vice-Commissar for Foreign Affairs and exchanged the trade-union platform for the diplomatic banquet. In June 1941, at the outbreak of the Russo-German War, he was named assistant director of the Soviet Information Bureau, and most of the communiqués issued from Russia today are by Lozovsky. He is certain that "the farther east the Germans go the closer Hitler approaches the grave," and he has further described Nazi allegations of success to be "as much like the truth as Goebbels looks like Apollo."

His proven ability to hold several positions without neglecting the duties of any of them makes him especially well fitted to execute the exacting demands of the important offices he now holds. Described by *Time* as "rambunctious" and a "comedian," the new Soviet spokesman is a small, hirsute and energetic. Quentin Reynolds found "no trace of a peasant accent in his cultured speech. In addition to Russian, he speaks perfect French and German. He speaks English reluctantly but much better than he realizes, and his Spanish is good." Reynolds added that although the correspondents in Russia hate censorship, they "respect his because he does not lie."

References

Collier's 108:14+ D 13 '41 por
N Y Times p18 Je 29 '41; p1 Jl 28 '41; p3 Ag 10 '41
Red International of Labor Unions 1:2 N '28 por
Time 38:23 Jl 14 '41 por; 38:18 Ag 4 '41

International Who's Who

LUBIN, ISADOR (lū'bĭn) June 9, 1896-
Economist; assistant director of the Labor Division of OPM

Address: b. The White House, Washington, D. C.; h. 2737 Devonshire Pl, N. W., Washington, D. C.

Dr. Isador Lubin, economist and statistician, is a "progressive" with pro-labor leanings who has always shared the broad philosophy of the New Deal. It is easy to understand why he has filled increasingly important positions in Washington in recent years, climaxed by his appointment in June 1941 as aide to Harry Hopkins (see sketch this issue) in the organization and carrying out of the lease-lend program. Although this appointment,

ISADOR LUBIN

which necessitated Lubin's moving into the White House, was surrounded by secrecy, it was generally accepted that his special problem was to keep track of the nation's armament program—finding out where the money was going, how much material England was getting, the effect of the spending on domestic economy.

This sort of economic and statistical checkingup has been bald, spectacled Isador Lubin's specialty almost since he left college. He was born in Worcester, Massachusetts, the son of Harris and Hinda (Francke) Lubin, and after grammar and high school in Worcester attended Clark College there. After he received his B. A. in 1916 he went on to the University of Missouri for a year's graduate study which was followed by a year as economics instructor. With the First World War, Lubin entered government service, first as a statistician for the United States Food Administration, then, in 1918 and 1919, as a special expert on the United States War Industries Board.

His job here finished, Lubin returned to academic life and for a year continued his graduate studies, this time at the University of Michigan, where from 1920 to 1922 he was an assistant professor of economics. From here he went to the Brookings Institution in Washington, D. C., a research institution of wide repute which sometimes annoys New Dealers very much, and, with the exception of one year, in 1924, when he was associate professor of economics at the University of Missouri, he was associated with this organization for nine years. From its graduate school he received his Ph. D. in 1926; he was a member of its research staff specializing in labor's economic problems; he was a member of its teaching staff.

While still at Brookings, Dr. Lubin assisted the Government in 1928 and 1929 as

LUBIN, ISADOR—*Continued*

economic advisor to the Senate Committee on Education and Labor in its investigation into unemployment and in 1931 as adviser to the Committee on Manufacturers in its investigation into economic planning. Then, in 1933, he was made United States commissioner of labor statistics and took over the supervision of the Bureau's compilation of data on employment, pay rolls, labor turnover, wage and hour rates, cost of living, prices, industrial accidents and industrial agreements and its research into industry.and living conditions.

From the time he became commissioner of labor statistics, Dr. Lubin functioned as one of the Administration's high ranking advisers on wages and prices, working quietly behind the scenes year after year during the Roosevelt Administration. He also took on an impressive list of duties for the Government. He has been chairman of the Labor Advisory Board of the Federal Emergency Administration of Public Works; vice-chairman of the United States Central Statistical Board; a member of the Advisory Committee to the Federal Co-ordinator of Railroads; a member of the Technical Board of the President's Economic Security Committee; a member of the Cabinet sub-committee on the economic status of the cotton textile industry; a member of the Industrial Resources Committee; and, from 1938 to 1940, a member of the Temporary National Economic Committee.

When the TNEC conducted the most searching investigation of the internal economic and financial structure of industry made since the Pujo money trust investigation 29 years before, Lubin not only helped direct the general conduct of the investigation, but also appeared as witness before the Committee. Flanked by charts portraying the various aspects of the structure and performance of the economic system, he demonstrated the need for an adjustment to a better set of working principles made necessary by the weakening of the automatic force of competition. His testimony was impressive, and *Business Week* pointed out: "Lubin walks fast but he walks on the ground. Businessmen rely on his figures and respect his opinions."

It was inevitable that Dr. Isador Lubin should play a prominent part in the defense program from its very beginning. He served as consultant on many agencies set up, as administrative assistant to Sidney Hillman (on leave from the Bureau of Labor Statistics), assistant director of the Labor Division of OPM, as aide to the OPM Priorities Division. In most of these positions his main concern was with labor problems, and it was as a labor expert that he went out to the West Coast in April 1941 to make an agreement between the shipbuilders and the unions to prevent strikes. The agreement, the first overall zone-wide agreement of its kind, did not, however, prevent a long and difficult strike of machinists from breaking out almost immediately in violation of the orders of the Metal Trades Council which was a signatory to the contract in the shipyards. Still Lubin maintained consistently in reference to the defense program that the rights of labor must be safeguarded and argued frequently that strikes hadn't interfered with production as much as other factors under the control of management. He urged, too, the adoption of a nation-wide dismissal wage plan for persons working on defense orders in order to cushion the country against the effects of the wholesale layoffs expected to follow the completion of the defense program.

In all the years that Dr. Isador Lubin has been working for the Government, he has managed to find time to be an active member of the American Economic Association, of the American Statistical Association (vice-president in 1937 and 1938), of the International Association of Governmental Labor Officials, of the International Association of the Industrial Accident Board and Commissions. He is also the author of various monographs and reports, a frequent contributor to economic journals, and the author of a number of books on economic problems. In 1941 Clark University awarded him an honorable LL. D. degree and in that same year Lubin was made representative of the United States Government on the governing body of the International Labor Organization.

Dr. Lubin was married in 1923 to Alice E. Berliner of Washington, D. C. There is one daughter, Alice, of this marriage which ended in divorce in 1928. Dr. Lubin's second wife, Ann Shumaker, whom he married in 1932, died in 1935, leaving a daughter, Ann.

References

Business Week p16 Jl 2 '38 por; p13 D 3 '38 por; p23 D 21 '40 por
Newsweek 10:12 N 22 '37 por;12:38 D 12 '38 por
Sat Eve Post 211:6 O 29 '38 por; 212:11 Mr 30 '40 por
Time 37:89 Ap 21 '41 por
U S News 10:41 Je 13 '41 por
America's Young Men 1936-37
Who's Who in America
Who's Who in American Jewry
Who's Who in the Nation's Capital

LUCE, HENRY R(OBINSON) (lo͞os) Apr. 3, 1898- Editor; publisher

Address: b. Time & Life Bldg, 9 Rockefeller Plaza, New York City; h. Greenwich, Conn.

"Not since the time of S. S. McClure," says Quincy Howe, "has the United States seen a magazine genius who is Henry Luce's equal, and if his career follows his present course he is likely to become the most powerful American magazine editor of all time."

Howe might have called him an American publisher. But Henry R. Luce, co-founder, principal stockholder and chairman of the board of Time, Inc., remains primarily an editor. In 1941 his *Time, Life* and *Fortune* can boast a combined circulation of 4,232,000. The *March of Time* appears 13 times a year in 8,000 American, 3,000 foreign film houses. In 1940 alone Time, Inc., with 1,557 employees,

10 branch offices and 175 correspondents, made a net profit of $3,494,589.66—higher than any other United States magazine publisher. Time, Inc., has been called "the greatest success story of American journalism." And one of the secrets of its success is its major emphasis on its editorial department, presided over by Henry R. Luce, rather than on its advertising and circulation departments.

The key figure in this success was born on April 3, 1898 in Tengchow, China. The son of Dr. Henry Winters Luce, a well known Presbyterian missionary who died in December 1941, and of Elizabeth Middleton (Root) Luce, who was related to the late Elihu Root, Henry Robinson Luce spent most of his grade-school years in Shantung Province. He was 14 before he was sent to the United States to attend the Hotchkiss School at Lakeville, Connecticut, where he earned part of his board by waiting on table and working after school hours; there he met Briton Hadden, future co-founder of *Time*. They began their collaboration early— by editing the Hotchkiss school paper—and when that was over in 1916 they chose the same university: Yale.

At Yale young Luce edited the *Daily News*. As its editor he fought to double the hours of military training, and during 1918 he served for a short time as a second lieutenant (R. O. T. C.) of Field Artillery at Camp Jackson and Camp Zachary Taylor. A big man on the campus (Skull and Bones, Alpha Delta Phi, Phi Beta Kappa, Student Council), when he was graduated in 1920 he was voted "Most Brilliant" member of his senior class. Hadden was "Most Likely to Succeed."

After a year at Oxford, Luce worked for two months as a $16-a-week cub reporter on the Chicago *Daily News,* then joined his friend as reporter on the Baltimore *News*. While still at college they had cooperatively "reached the conclusion that most people were not well informed and that something should be done": what they now proposed to do was to start a news magazine. Within three months, working double time, they actually perfected their long-discussed invention, which they first thought of calling *Facts;* the next step was the announcement that they were quitting the *News*. That was in 1922.

The managing editor had been incredulous and pitying as he watched them depart—and so were others. But after nine hard months they succeeded in raising $86,000 to start their magazine, partially by canvassing their college friends for names of prospects, partially by peddling the stock from doorstep to doorstep. Offices were in a shabby brownstone house on New York's East Side; staff consisted of Luce, Hadden and three full-time writers, none of them with professional newspaper experience; equipment was a couple of secondhand desks, a used set of the *Encyclopaedia Britannica*, the daily papers. And the first issue of *Time* ("free from sensationalism . . . windy bias," boasted the final prospectus) not only came out as scheduled (March 3, 1923), but went to 12,000 readers.

HENRY R. LUCE

At this time Luce and Hadden were paying themselves $30 a week, working seven days a week, alternating each year as editor and business manager. S. J. Wolff comments: "Surely no stranger combination ever got together than these two young men." But intimates of the young men have quarreled with this statement by the noted artist-writer. As one of them puts it: "Hadden and Luce complemented each other to an amazing degree. In those early years Luce was much the quieter of the two, Hadden gayer, more ebullient. But fundamentally both were much the same. Luce was seeking out editorial ideas when acting as business manager, and conversely, Hadden was a very astute business manager when he was editor."

Certainly it was an extraordinarily fortunate combination. By the end of the first year what has since become known as *Time*-style was already beginning to evolve, and soon "backward the sentences rumbled in *Time*." Expressions like "tycoon" and "cine-maddict" made their appearance; in *Time's* pages people became "able", "potent", "nimble"—or "beady-eyed", "snaggle-toothed", "pig-faced." Emphasis was on personalities; to Luce: "People just aren't interesting in the mass. It's only individuals who are exciting." Circulation increased; *Time* moved its offices to Cleveland, and back to New York again. By 1927 the magazine was showing a profit ($3,860), and the next year circulation jumped from 171,600 to 219,000, while profits soared to $125,787. Luce was planning a deluxe, $1-a-copy business magazine called *Fortune* when Brit Hadden died of a streptococcus infection Deeply shaken, Luce confided to one of his writers: "With Brit gone, I frankly don't know how we'll come out of this. . ." Hadden's mother was paid almost a half million dollars in stock which he had

LUCE, HENRY R.—*Continued*

left her, so profitable had their project become by this time.

In spite of Hadden's tragic death, the first issue of *Fortune* appeared in January 1930, its contents ranging from articles on branch banking, hogs and glass blowing to advice on how to live in Chicago on a paltry $25,000 a year. Time, Inc., expanded rapidly: the *March of Time* broadcast its first news dramatization on March 6, 1931; in 1932 the *Architectural Forum* was purchased, the only one of its publications not based on an original journalistic concept, and its only unprofitable venture; the first *March of Time* newsreel was shown in February 1935.

In 1923 Luce had married Lila Ross Hotz of Chicago (there are two children: Henry III and Peter Paul), and in 1935 they were divorced. It was in November of that same year that Luce married Clare Boothe Brokaw, almost immediately after the inauspicious opening of her first Broadway play, *Abide With Me.* Her Broadway successes—*The Women, Kiss the Boys Good-Bye* and *Margin for Error*—came later.

In 1936, after several years of experiment, the first issue of *Life* appeared. A magazine aimed at "making of the unrespected photograph an instrument of significant journalism," it was one of the greatest sensations in publishing history but lost over $3,000,000 its first year because advertising rates had been figured on a circulation of only 250,000. Circulation quickly rose to 1,500,000; before long *Life* was turning in substantial profits and by 1941 had a circulation of over 3,250,000.

Now senior editor of all the publications, Luce keeps in close touch with the editorial activities of his staff, to whom he gives generous credit for the success of Time, Inc. He also credits the theory of "group journalism" —which in practice means that stories are worked out over the conference table rather than by any one writer. At editorial conferences he listens as intently to a cub as to a senior writer. Earlier to the office than they— writers arrive about 10:00—he crowds a prodigious amount of work into a long day, calls them together in his big penthouse office for a free airing of views, sends them memos which sometimes reiterate old dictums: "To keep men and women well-informed—that is the only axe *Time* has to grind. It is not the duty of the editorial department to win friends and influence people other than by putting out a fair and readable magazine."

Critics of his publications, however, have from time to time made light of what they call merely an illusion of objectivity. In 1937 Dwight MacDonald wrote a series in *The Nation* in which he attacked *Time, Life, Fortune:* "The Right object to Luce's journals because they indulge in 'personalities,' because

they make fun of stuffed-shirt dignity, because they are often 'sensational' and 'in bad taste.'.. What liberals object to is the habitual distortion or suppression of labor and radical news, the constant pooh-poohing of all movements for social progress." But, according to Quincy Howe, although for several years the foreign department of *Time* was left largely to an editor who "had a schoolgirl crush on Mussolini and who, after Hitler came into power, referred to Léon Blum as 'spidery Jew Blum,'" after that editor was eased out a much more liberal approach to news resulted. A third critic, Ferdinand Lundberg, in *America's Sixty Families* claimed that the editorial policies of Luce's journals were greatly influenced by the fact that Luce is a close friend of Thomas Lamont and that J. P. Morgan owns a large block of stock in Time, Inc., in his capacity as a trustee for the Davison family. To that Howe replies that actually Time, Inc., "owes less to Morgan money, brains and influence than it does to the ability of its own executives." Moreover, financial reports show that the Davison family owns only 5,000 shares of stock, while editors (including Luce himself) and employees of Time, Inc., and their families own 145,309 shares—some 60 per cent of the total shares of stock outstanding.

Howe says: "The unbroken success of Time, Inc., shows that it has always reacted spontaneously to new situations, and because Henry Luce is a great editor his publications have always reacted in the same way their readers have reacted." In the spring of 1936, for instance, it seemed to many commentators that Luce's publications were taking a pro-Landon, anti-labor slant; after the *Fortune* poll they became more friendly to Roosevelt and the CIO. And although it was an article by Willkie in *Fortune* and subsequent build-ups by *Time* and *Life* that brought the Republican candidate before the public eye in 1940, in June of that year Luce returned from a trip to Europe to announce that he would support Roosevelt's foreign policy vigorously.

After his return he contributed to the Committee to Defend America by Aiding the Allies; Clare Boothe Luce stayed in Europe, writing articles for *Life,* and later published a book, *Europe in the Spring* (1940). The première of a "full-length propaganda movie" about Americans in the First World War, *The Ramparts We Watch* (scheduled long before Luce left for Europe), a nationwide broadcast on the international situation by Luce and a new *Time* department, "National Defense," followed. Finally, in the spring of 1941, Luce's *American Century,* a short tract reprinted from his editorial in *Life* and containing his views on America's role in the Second World War, was published in book-form together with comments and criticism by men representing almost all shades of opinion.

"America is in the War," Luce announced, boldly. "We got in via defense." But "we are *not* in a war to defend American territory. We are in a war to defend and even to promote, encourage and incite so-called democratic principles throughout the world." He was confident that, as the senior partner of the British Empire, America would win this war; he saw "America as the dynamic center of ever-widening spheres of enterprise, America as the training center of the skillful servants of mankind, America as the Good Samaritan, really believing again that it is more blessed to give than to receive, and America as the powerhouse of the ideals of Freedom and Justice." But we must learn to think in larger terms. "For example, we think of Asia as being worth only a few hundred millions a year to us. Actually, in the decades to come Asia will be worth to us exactly zero —or else it will be worth to us four, five, ten billions of dollars a year. . ."

Returning in June 1941 from a six weeks' visit in China, where he has been a frequent traveler since his childhood there, he announced that Chiang Kai-shek is confident of ultimate victory if aid is received from the United States. Luce himself has contributed much to Chinese aid.

Henry Luce himself has no difficulty in thinking in large terms. His present income has been estimated by some outsiders at a million a year, although Mr. Luce's associates say it is large, but far less. He owns a 7,000-acre plantation outside of Charleston, South Carolina, and keeps a house in Greenwich, Connecticut. He has traveled extensively in Europe and Asia, has "observed many Great and Near Great," is listed in *Who's Who in America* and the *Social Register.*

He believes society must derive its leadership from men of ability, talent and capacity, and that a sense of obligation to society should accompany position and power: "Without the aristocratic principle no society can endure."

"Hard-working, puritanical," America's most famous editor wears conservatively undistinguished suits, white shirts, violent hued striped ties. One writer finds that "there is still something faintly Presbyterian about his shyness and his long, grave silences, in spite of the mildly satanic slant of his eyes under their wild and shaggy brows." Another confides: "The Luces have been called humorless, and it is true that in company their laughter is a fraction of a second slower than other people's and sometimes a little forced." Their conversation is sometimes strange; after long exposure to *Timestyle,* sentences like "No nitwit he" are likely to pop out. Luce smokes too much, disapproves of heavy drinking, plays a hard game of tennis, once announced: "I have no use for a man who lies in bed after 9 o'clock in the morning," and before the 1940 Presidential election informed the world that he con-

siders anybody who fails to vote a traitor and would never "knowingly sit down to a meal with such a person." He has "no fund of small social chatter . . . is fluent only when he can talk about a subject, preferably a big one," and his only hobby is "conversing with somebody who knows something." He says: "We, meaning Time, Inc., must keep our viewpoint national; I would rather talk to a man from Texas, for instance, than to a roomful of the brightest people in New York."

References

Christian Sci Mon Mag p3+ O 30 '35 il
Ladies' H J 55:25+ N '38 por
Nation 144:500-3 My 1 '37; 144:583-6 My 22 '37
New Yorker 12:20-5 N 28 '36; 16:21-6+ Ja 4 '41; 16:24+ Ja 11 '41
Scholastic 33:9-10+ N 19 '38 por
Time 31:37-8+, sup 1-28 F 28 '38 il por
America's Young Men
Balch, M. ed. Modern Short Biographies and Autobiographies p311-25 1940
Howe, Q. The News and How to Understand It p148-56 1940
New Yorker (periodical). Profiles From the New Yorker p297-311 1938
Who's Who in America
Who's Who in Commerce and Industry

LUCKSTONE, ISIDORE Jan. 29, 1861— Mar. 12, 1941 Vocal teacher, conductor, and at one time an internationally known accompanist; served as professor of education from 1925 to 1939 in the Music Department of New York University; had accompanied the late Enrico Caruso, Fritz Kreisler and Lillian Nordica.

References

Etude 56:433-4 Jl '38 por
Baker's Biographical Dictionary of Musicians 1940
Wier, A. E. ed. Macmillan Encyclopedia of Music and Musicians 1938

Obituaries

N Y Times p21 Mr 13 '41 por
Sch & Soc 53:368 Mr 22 '41

LUMPKIN, ALVA M(OORE) Nov. 13, 1886—Aug. 1, 1941 Democratic Senator from South Carolina; appointed July 20, 1941 to replace Senator James F. Byrnes, who was appointed to the Supreme Court; at time of appointment was a Federal district judge in South Carolina; served as a member of the General Assembly of that state from 1911 to 1915.

References

Who's Who in America
Who's Who in Law

Obituaries

N Y Times p15 Ag 2 '41 por

LUNT, ALFRED Aug. 19, 1893- Actor

FONTANNE, LYNN (fŏn'tän') Dec. 6, 1887(?)- Actress

Address: c/o Theatre Guild, 245 W. 52nd St, New York City; h. Genesee Depot, Wis.

When in May 1941 the Pulitzer Prize for the best play of 1940 went to Robert Sherwood (see sketch 1940 Annual) for *There Shall Be No Night*, the play's principals are taking a well-deserved vacation from a strenuous season. Since the play's Broadway opening in May 1940 Alfred Lunt and Lynn Fontanne had appeared as the Finnish scientist and his wife in half a hundred cities, nineteen states and two Canadian provinces, and had traveled some 12,000 miles with the rest of the cast. The 1940 to 1941 road tour was so successful that in November 1941 it was still on tour in the South and Southwest, even though by that time it might have been assumed that audiences had lost their first flush of sympathy for "little Finland," now an Axis satellite. It didn't close until the end of December of that year, when Robert Sherwood, its author, asked its recall since its plot, he felt, was opposed to America's war interests.

Vandamm

ALFRED LUNT

The Lunts almost didn't appear in this highly emotional play of the Russo-Finnish War. They were planning to take a 1940 vacation when Sherwood gave it to them to read while en route to their home in Genesee Depot, Wisconsin, a whistle stop in the beautiful lake country where Lunt spent his boyhood. As their train pulled into Harrisburg, Pennsylvania, Lynn Fontanne, who had read the script first, wired Sherwood: "This half of the combination returns in two weeks for rehearsals." Lunt thumbed through the typewritten pages, then settled down for a serious

reading. At Chicago he, too, wired the playwright, saying: "So does this half."

Three weeks after a brilliant opening *Variety* reported: "*Night* is topping all straight shows on Broadway, grosses since opening bettering some musicals and almost reaching the marks on the leaders in that division. Takings last week were $23,000, despite the continued slump, only variance being in standees." Usually sparing in curtain speeches, Lunt made more than a few for this play, and in July 1940 the Lunts broke a long-standing rule and made a radio broadcast for the first time—an excerpt from the play for a Red Cross benefit. "I wish you'd say for me," Lunt remarked of their part in it, "that giving these performances isn't just a generous gesture. It's something that we can't help doing." He, at least, was rewarded when the New York run extended into the summer and he shared with Barry Fitzgerald the New York drama critics' award for the best male performance of the 1939 to 1940 season.

Although Lunt could comment of their roles in *There Shall Be No Night*: "It's the first time in years that we've been respectably married," Alfred Lunt and Lynn Fontanne are in real life probably the most famous respectably married couple in the theatre. Miss Fontanne was born in the County of Essex, England, the daughter of Jules Pierre Antoine and Frances Ellen (Thornley) Fontanne. Her father was a brass type founder. The date of her birth is often given as December 6, 1887 (Mr. Lunt calls it "obviously ridiculous"), her given name as Lillie Louise. (*Time* and other sources agree with this—Miss Fontanne does not.) The only other clue to her age consists in the fact that she went to study under Ellen Terry at the age of 12, some say; at 15, according to others—and two years later (1905) played her first part on the road with Dame Terry in *Alice-Sit-by-the-Fire*.

Ellen Terry listened to the young actress recite, promised to coach her in Shakespearean and other roles for a year. Actually, she kept her for two, sending her off with a letter that read: "That's all I'm going to do for you, my dear. You must make your own career. The race is run by one and if I helped you any more it wouldn't be good for you. So run along now and don't ask me for any more letters or any more puffs. They'd hurt you more than they'd help you."

Lynn Fontanne got her first London part in 1909, in the Drury Lane Pantomime. She came to the United States for the first time in 1910, making her first New York appearance on November 7th of that year at Nazimova's 39th Street Theatre. The play in which she made her American debut failed so promptly that she was able to return to London the same year. There, in 1914, she was given her first important role, that of Gertrude in *Milestones*. In between plays the young actress volunteered for special war service and drove a military motor car through Devonshire. In 1916 she was back in London on the stage, where her work came to the attention of

Laurette Taylor and induced the latter to bring her back to America with her repertory company.

Besides working with Miss Taylor she had the experience, that first year of her second visit, of a short period in vaudeville. The company with which she appeared produced *The Minstrel Review of 1916*, and a critic remarked: "The interlocutor is a tall beauty with a beautiful face." Her work with Miss Taylor also brought her good notices. "A most aggressive and self-assertive young woman," the New York *Times* critic decided in 1916, the year when her work in *The Harp of Life* also "stood out as one of the bright spots." Said the New York *Sun*; "She was greeted with spontaneous applause in the middle of a scene in which she appeared."

She hadn't yet met Alfred Lunt, though. Born in Milwaukee, Wisconsin in 1893, he was the son of Alfred and Harriet Washborn (Briggs) Lunt. At the age of 12 he won an elocution contest but didn't think of acting as a career until long afterward. When he entered Carroll College at Waukesha, Wisconsin he was still intending to study architecture, and in 1913 he trekked to Harvard to continue his studies. He was sidetracked only by an offer to work with a repertory company at Castle Square Theatre, Boston at $5 weekly. At that theatre he made his stage debut in *The Gingerbread Man* and for a few years led a trouper's life, his work gaining the attention of critics more or less at the same time as that of his future wife. He toured with Margaret Anglin from 1914 to 1915, did a vaudeville turn with Mrs. Langtry (the "Jersey Lily"), appeared with Laura Hope Crews, and by 1916 was again with Miss Anglin's company. His first important New York role was as Claude Estabrook in *Romance and Arabella* (October 1917).

There, when Lynn Fontanne appeared in *The Wooing of Eve*, Alfred Lunt saw her for the first time. They met again in 1919 when both were trying out at New York's Hudson Theatre for summer stock in *A Young Man's Fancy*, Miss Fontanne fresh from a season of Shakespearean roles. When they were introduced Lunt was standing on a rickety staircase, and as he bent to take her hand his foot slipped and he toppled down the short flight of steps. They appeared in plays together that summer, after which Lynn Fontanne was given a part in O'Neill's unsuccessful *Chris* and Lunt appeared in the title role of *Clarence*, which opened to "rave" notices. In May 1920, when Lynn Fontanne went to England, his play was still running; road tours carried *Clarence* through 1921, when Lunt's future wife returned to star in *Dulcy*, a comedy about a talkative young woman.

Dulcy established Lynn Fontanne as one of the most capable actresses on the American stage and as one of the most attractive. A critic rhapsodized: "Starry-eyed, dark-haired, her features well defined, all luminous with a smile, which plays over them like sheet lightning across a summer sky." When she married the star of *Clarence* on May 26, 1922 they were already one of the theatre's famous couples, and photographers followed them to a picture-book honeymoon in the Wisconsin lake country.

As a theatre team, the careers of the Lunts coincided with their membership in the Theatre Guild. In 1924 they joined the Guild and on October 13, 1924, opened in *The Guardsman*.

Vandamm

LYNN FONTANNE

A critic wrote enthusiastically: "They have youth and great gifts and the unmistakable attitude of ascent, and those who saw them on opening night, bowing hand in hand for the first time, may well have been witnessing a moment in theatrical history. It is among the possibilities that we were seeing the first chapter in a partnership destined to be as distinguished as that of Henry Irving and Ellen Terry, and Sothern and Marlowe."

The critic was also a prophet. Except for a short interval in the 1920's, when Lynn Fontanne appeared in O'Neill's *Strange Interlude* and her husband in *Marco's Millions*, they have appeared together since that time, starring in a long cavalcade of successes: *Arms and the Man* (1925); *The Goat Song* (1926); *Pygmalion* (1926); *The Brothers Karamazov* (1927); *The Doctor's Dilemma* (1927); *Caprice* (London—Lunt's first appearance there, 1929); *Elizabeth the Queen* (1930); *Reunion in Vienna* (1931-32); *Design for Living* (1933); *Reunion in Vienna* (London 1934); *Point Valaine* (1935); *Taming of the Shrew* (1935); *Idiot's Delight* (1936); *The Sea Gull* (1938); *Amphitryon 38* (London 1938); *Amphitryon 38* (United States 1938-39); *Taming of the Shrew* (1940); and finally *There Shall Be No Night* (1940-41). Later in 1941 Alfred Lunt directed *Candle in the Wind*, with Helen Hayes.

LUNT, ALFRED and FONTANNE, LYNN—*Continued*

To those who have not witnessed the sophisticated acting of the Lunts it might be difficult to describe. The pacing is always extraordinarily effective and in the staging there is no superfluous action. But even more germane is the inflection of voice, a nuance of tone here, a sudden harshness there, and everyone in the audience waiting breathlessly on the next line.

Typical of critical comment on the Lunts is the statement that "they have carried on magnificently the great traditions of the theatre." What critical barbs have come their way have accused them of emphasizing style and *theatre* to the detriment of the play as such. When Miss Fontanne did *Pygmalion,* for example, George Jean Nathan remarked on "her habit of listening lovingly to the sound of her own voice."

Tall, dark, imperious, Lynn Fontanne insinuates herself into a part disarmingly, living it in her own mind. Once she found herself talking like "Dulcy" off stage, and in an interview during *Amphitryon 38* she was once found to be wearing the translucent nail polish that went with her part in that comedy. She recalled that Lunt had, on occasion, lived his parts too. "A long time ago," she said, "Alfred was considering a number of plays. He took the scripts to bed with him every night. And every morning I had breakfast, not with my actor-husband, but with his character of the moment."

Of her husband Alexander Woollcott (see sketch this issue) once said: "You can tell Alfred from the other actors. He's the one who works." Michel Mok describes him on one occasion: "With his pale, egg-shaped face, his weary brooding dark eyes, his light-brown hair meticulously brushed and parted in the center, he looked almost exactly as he did in the role of Harry Van, the hoofer, in Robert E. Sherwood's *Idiot's Delight.* From time to time there was in his voice that peculiar, boyish catch on a high note which you have heard so often from the stage." And, according to Lucius Beebe: "He gestures wildly with his hands, makes more faces than he does on stage, deprecates himself, his ability, his last performance. . . He has enormous pride in his success. His experienced eye can tell how good a house he is playing to, almost to a seat, and a few vacancies in the fifteenth row will drive him frantic." He worries, frets, despairs before every performance—"does much of the worrying for everyone in the cast."

Writing of them both, Charlotte Hughes had this to say: "There is more to their magnificent teamwork than a psychic ability to sense each other's moods and to time, to a split second, each other's reactions. When they get a new script, they start memorizing a set number of lines a day. They retire to their rooms and mumble, and their manager, Lawrence Farrell, sits in the living room between and dashes back and forth to each of them, hearing sections. They rehearse their own scenes over and over and over, argue about every gesture, every intonation."

The Lunts have long had an arrangement with the Theatre Guild whereby they get a percentage of the gross. They also have a company formed with Noel Coward (see sketch this issue), Transatlantic Productions, Incorporated, that came into being with *Design for Living* (1933). Percentage of the gross is good business for the Lunts, who have always been good box office, on the road as well as in New York. In fact, the Lunts—along with Katharine Cornell (see sketch this issue) and a few others—may be credited with giving the road what is asked for—good acting, good plays, good casts. On tour they have almost always grossed above $20,000 weekly, sometimes coming close to $40,000.

Generally shy of pictures, they have done only two: the seldom-mentioned *Second Youth* (1922) and *The Guardsman* (1932). For their work in the latter they were paid $75,000, but Alfred Lunt was reluctant to see it on the screen for fear it hadn't come off quite right. He let his wife see it first and bring back a report. Both were shocked when they first heard what their voices sounded like on a film track, but although they have since got over that to the extent of appearing on the radio and phonograph records, most informants believe they would refuse to consider another Hollywood offer unless it could be pretty much on their own terms. Turning down one fabulous proposition because the film story was uninteresting, Lunt remarked: "We can be bought but we can't be bored."

He doesn't think audiences should be bored, either, even in a Good Cause. For the Lunts' work in *Idiot's Delight* the Chicago Conference of Club Presidents (May 1937) gave them an award for their contribution and "effective service to peace." "The point to me," Lunt said of the famous Sherwood anti-war play, "is that it's enormously entertaining, and I think propaganda must be entertaining to be effective."

Away from the theatre, the Lunts have a Swedish-type farmhouse (gaily painted, with blue predominating) at Genesee Depot in Wisconsin. They both helped to make it over, just as they helped decorate their attractive New York apartment, with its sand-colored furniture, crystal chandeliers and cobalt-blue walls. It is in Wisconsin that they loaf between seasons, puttering about the garden and trying out their favorite recipes (both are gourmets and expert cooks). Before the War they enjoyed spending vacations abroad. In 1933 they had a firsthand glimpse at the progress of the theatre in the U. S. S. R., came home with glowing reports. Visits to Finland in 1934 and 1937 gave them a particular interest in *There Shall Be No Night.* In 1938 a clue to their itinerary lay in the miscellaneous packages that accompanied their extensive luggage. These included English marmalade, books on simplified French, and—on leash—four dachshunds.

The partnership of Lynn Fontanne and Alfred Lunt is taken for granted as much by the principals as by their public. Said Mr. Lunt: "I just love to play opposite Lynn, that's all. There's nobody else I want to play with." And Miss Fontanne echoed with: "I can't even give an explanation. Playing without Alfred is so fantastic I can't even think of it." Ring Lardner once wrote a humorous poem based on the idea that a certain play failed because Lynn Fontanne and Alfred Lunt were missing from the cast. Typical was this couplet:

It lacked two things, observed the man,
Just Alfred Lunt and Lynn Fontanne.

References

Ladies' H J 53:8+ Jl '36 pors; 57:14-15+ D '40 il pors
Life 3:106-9 N 1 '37 pors
New Repub 87:180 Je 17 '36
New Yorker 4:23-5 Ap 28 '28
Stage 13:36-9 My '36 il; 15:4-5 Je '38 por
Theatre Arts Mo 20:856-71 N '36 il pors; 23:414-18+ Je '39
Time 30:25-6 N 8 '37 por
Vogue 87:65+ Ap 1 '36
American Women
America's Young Men 1936-37
Brown, J. M. Upstage p110-14 1930
Eustis, M. Players at Work p29-46 1937
International Motion Picture Almanac
Moses, M. J. and Brown, J. M. eds. American Theatre as Seen by Its Critics p337-40 1934
Ormsbee, H. Backstage with Actors p230-65 1938
Who's Who in America
Who's Who in the Theatre

LYDENBERG, HARRY MILLER Nov. 18, 1874- Director of The Biblioteca Benjamin Franklin

Address: b. Biblioteca Benjamin Franklin, Mexico City, Mexico; h. 23 Park Rd, Scarsdale, N. Y.

Bulletin: Dr. Lydenberg, former director of the New York Public Library, in late 1941 became the director of The Biblioteca Benjamin Franklin. This library, similar to the former American Library in Paris, is not a government library but is sponsored by the Nelson Rockefeller (see sketch this issue) organization for better relations between the Americas, the American Library Association and other organizations.

From September 1941 issue:

The resignation of Dr. Harry Miller Lydenberg, director of The New York Public Library, to take effect on October 1, 1941, was announced July 21 by Mr. Frank L. Polk, president of the Library's Board of Trustees. Dr. Lydenberg had been on the staff of the Library since July 1, 1896, and had been director since November 1934.

"It is with profound regret," Mr. Polk said, "that the Board of Trustees makes this announcement. Dr. Lydenberg first indicated

The New York Public Library
HARRY MILLER LYDENBERG

his wish to retire more than a year and a half ago, on his sixty-fifth birthday, but until now we have been able to persuade him to remain. However, he has persisted in his determination, and the Board has most reluctantly bowed to his decision. His great knowledge, administrative ability and close association with his peers among the distinguished men of letters and book men of the world have been of tremendous advantage to the Library and, through it, to scholarship and research everywhere.

"Under his administration, in spite of the difficulties imposed by depression and war, the Library has grown in strength and influence. Although compelled to practice strict economy in the administration of the Circulation Department, he has kept the branches alive and the greatest needs of their readers have been cared for. Additions have been made to a number of the branch library buildings, and three new buildings, two in The Bronx and one for children and young people in Manhattan, have been added to the system. He was quick to meet the call for aid in the national defense program, and the Library is now giving special help to hundreds of young men in the several trade classes organized by the Board of Education.

"In addition to fostering the steady growth of the Reference Department collection in all the fields the Library attempts to cover, Dr. Lydenberg has been largely instrumental in securing, by gift or purchase, many single items and collections of outstanding importance.

"For his contribution to the world of letters as librarian, historian, bibliographer, editor, translator and author he has been honored by many professional and learned societies and by three universities. We, too, have appreciated his real ability as an administrator

LYDENBERG, HARRY MILLER—*Cont.*
and his professional and scholarly achievements, but, outstanding as they are, they are overshadowed by the man himself; kind, generous, self-effacing and wise. He has won the affection of all those who have had the privilege of association with him."

Harry Miller Lydenberg, the son of Wesley Braxton and Marianna (Miller) Lydenberg, was born in Dayton, Ohio, where he was educated in the public schools. He was graduated from Harvard University in 1897 and has received the degrees of Doctor of Letters from Tufts College and Columbia University and Doctor of Humane Letters from Union College. He was president of the American Library Association (1932-33), president of the Bibliographical Society of America (1929-31), and has for many years been secretary-treasurer of the American Council of Learned Societies. He is also a member of the American Philosophical Society and of the American Antiquarian Society.

In addition to his numerous articles for professional journals he is the author of the *History of The New York Public Library* (1923), *John Shaw Billings* (1924), *Paper or Sawdust, a Plea for Good Paper for Good Books* (1924), *The Care and Repair of Books* (with John Archer, 1931); editor of *Archibald Robertson, Lieutenant-General Royal Engineers, His Diaries and Sketches in America, 1762-1780* (1930). He is the translator, from the French of André Blum, of *On the Origin of Paper* (1934) and *The Origins of Printing and Engraving* (1940). The forthcoming volume of the proceedings of the American Antiquarian Society will carry his study of the Berkshire Republican Library at Stockbridge, Massachusetts.

Dr. Lydenberg has been an active member of the Committee on Conservation of Cultural Resources of the United States National Resources Planning Board since its formation.

Dr. Lydenberg's career with The New York Public Library began soon after the consolidation, in 1895, of the Lenox and Astor libraries and the Tilden Trust. He had completed his Harvard course in three years, so in 1896, although he was of the class of 1897, he joined the staff as a cataloger in the Lenox Branch. From 1896 to 1899 he was in charge of manuscripts and from 1899 to 1908 was assistant to the director. He was appointed chief reference librarian in 1908 and served in that position through 1927, after which he was, until 1934, assistant director. Since November 1934 he has been director.

Dr. Lydenberg, a short, slender, soft-spoken, shy scholar with an aversion to personal publicity, has little to say about his plans for the future except that he is going to do various pieces of writing, "nothing of any world-beating importance." One study will be of the life of George Philip Philes, a New York bookseller from 1857 until about 1890. "A very amusing, profane old cuss, who had to leave the state in the early '90s because— well, just because it was the best thing to do . . . he was very much of a character." The

second study will be of blind impressions, blank spaces in fifteenth century books where there are type impressions without any ink.

When Dr. Lydenberg retires to his Scarsdale home he and Mrs. Lydenberg (he married Madeliene Rogers Day of the Periodicals Division in 1912 and they have a son and a daughter) will have time to indulge in their many hobbies: everything pertaining to books —paper, printing, binding, gardening and walking. Dr. Lydenberg is a good walker and likes to tramp along country roads or through the woods.

References

> Library J 66:708 S 1 '41
> N Y Times p22 Jl 22 '41 por
> Pub W 131:494 Ja 30 '37 por; 140:243-4 Jl 26 '41 por; 140:301 Ag 2 '41
> Leaders in Education 1941
> Who's Who Among North American Authors
> Who's Who in America
> Who's Who in Library Service

LYNCH, WILLIAM J(OSEPH) 1888— June 24, 1941 Endocrinologist; regarded as a pioneer in this science, he had written numerous articles on the subject for medical journals and was a consultant to a number of Philadelphia hospitals and physicians.

References

> American Medical Directory

Obituaries

> N Y Herald Tribune p16 Je 25 '41

LYTTELTON, OLIVER 1893- British Minister of State in the Middle East
Address: 4 Connaught Pl, W. 2., London, England

In 1941, for the first time in Britain's history, a full ranking Cabinet Minister was assigned to an overseas headquarters. The Minister was Captain Right Honorable Oliver Lyttelton; the post the Middle East; his duties the carrying out on the War Cabinet's behalf of "measures necessary for the prosecution of the War in that theatre other than the conduct of military operations." He was to administer conquered territories and unravel the political snarls that have before burdened the Army there. This appointment, the Press Association of Great Britain commented in July 1941, might well "be the prelude to further strengthening the British position there and countering swiftly and effectively any pro-German influences." One of his first acts there was to try to lay the foundation for a federation of Arab states.

Captain Lyttelton has been associated with the Churchill Government since the fall of 1940, as president of the Board of Trade, and his activities there undoubtedly recommended him for his Middle Eastern post. When in January 1941 Prime Minister Churchill set up three new and small committees—the Import Executive, the Production Executive and an over-all executive committee—to obtain "more rapid and decisive action in the War," Lyttelton was made a member of the first two. As such, and as president of the Board of Trade, he broadcasted to the United States and Canada an appeal to "buy British," and announced to Commons Britain's need for more and more supplies of every kind from the United States. From time to time, too, he announced the Government's war industry plans. In March 1941 he said that the Government would concentrate the production of consumer goods in a few full-time "nucleus" factories, freeing other factories for war production or storage; a month later he presented in Commons a measure to impose a wider and more inflexible price control on consumer goods and a more thorough control of middleman profits. This, Lyttelton explained, was part of "a large design and extends over all the financial, industrial, commercial and social activities of the country."

It was probably for his activities in rationing clothes, however, that Lyttelton got the most publicity in his own country and this. He, one of the handsomest, wealthiest and, at that moment, best-dressed men in England, created the plan limiting the amount of clothes Englishmen and Englishwomen could buy and announced it to the public. He asked his countrymen to accept it with good grace. "Our sacrifice," he reminded them, "is little enough when others risk their lives for us."

Oliver Lyttelton was the only son of the late Alfred Lyttelton, who was Colonial Secretary under A. J. Balfour and famous as a cricketeer. At Eton and Cambridge he captained his teams and was one of the English eleven which played against Australia. His first wife was Laura Tennant, which made him a brother-in-law of the Countess of Oxford. Oliver followed his father to Eton and then went up to Trinity College, Cambridge. He also played cricket, though never in his father's class, and was on his university's golf team.

He was in the middle of his university career when the First World War began. Immediately he left his studies to enter the Army and in December 1914 was gazetted to the Guards. Early in 1915 he went out to France and from then until 1919 was continuously on active service, seeing heavy fighting but escaping wounds. Lyttelton was mentioned in dispatches three times and won both the M. C. and the D. S. O. From October 15, 1915 to 1918 he was adjutant to the 3rd Guards Battalion; in February 1918 he became brigade major to the 4th Guards Brigade and in September to the 2nd Brigade. He was a captain when demobilized.

He left the Army to enter business in the City of London as manager of the huge and powerful British Metal Corporation, Limited, and to begin a career which eventually brought him directorships in countless other corporations as well, plus a salary estimated at $80,000 a year. He became an expert in understanding and organizing the complicated economic ramifications of the non-ferrous metals, and it was this expert knowledge that led to his appoint-

OLIVER LYTTELTON

ment, early in September 1939, as controller of non-ferrous metals. This was the first time that Lyttelton, a power in industry, emerged as a public figure.

Lyttelton did well in that post. He entered the purchasing ring early and bought up enough non-ferrous metals for a three years' war before the prices began to skyrocket, saving British taxpayers many millions. Churchill must have been watching this youngish man carefully, for when Sir Andrew Rae Duncan (see sketch this issue) was moved from the Board of Trade to the Ministry of Supply on October 3, 1940, Lyttelton was appointed to succeed him. He plunged into work with what has been reported as a bold slashing of red tape. Later, under a wide extension of his powers, he was enabled to take over industry for defense purposes and to shift and re-allocate labor to any task he felt necessary. Some papers called him "the Czar of Industry" for this.

It was necessary to find a seat in Parliament for Lyttelton when he was elevated to the presidency of the Board of Trade. This was easily managed, for Viscount Wolmer had been granted a peerage in his own right, and Lyttelton was put up for the vacant seat at the military town of Aldershot. He was returned unopposed as a Conservative on November 26, 1940, and before the end of the year was sworn to the Privy Council (the King's advisory committee). He signalized his assumption of office by warning industry in general that it would have to submit to discipline as rigorous as that borne by the rest of the community.

Eight months after his appointment, when Britain was being stirred by the news that General Sir Claude John Eyre Auchinleck was replacing General Sir Archibald Percival Wavell (see sketch this issue) as commander in chief in the Middle East, the official

LYTTELTON, OLIVER—*Continued*

notice was also given out that a special service to deal with political and social problems on the spot there had been created. Its head was to be Captain Lyttelton, made a Minister of State and representative of the War Cabinet.

Captain Lyttelton was married in 1920 to Lady Moira Godolphin Osborne, fourth daughter of the tenth Duke of Leeds. They have three sons and one daughter.

References

N Y Sun p19 Je 3 '41
Newsweek 18:25 Jl 14 '41 por
Time 38:21 Jl 14 '41 por
Times [London] O 4 '40; Ja 7 '41
Who's Who
Who's Who in Commerce and Industry

MCADOO, WILLIAM GIBBS (măk′ă-dōō) Oct. 31, 1863—Feb. 1, 1941 Former Secretary of the Treasury and former Senator from California; came to New York in 1892 as lawyer and organized the Hudson and Manhattan Company which built the Hudson Tubes; Secretary of the Treasury from 1913 to 1918, financed America's participation in the First World War; also director-general of the railroads, director of the Federal Farm Loan Bank and manager of the United States Finance Corporation; unsuccessfully sought Democratic Presidential nomination in 1924; returned to California to practice law and led the California delegation which swung the nomination to Roosevelt in 1932; in 1933 was elected Senator from California but was defeated for the Senatorial nomination in 1939; retired from political life to become chairman of the board of the American President Steamship Lines.

References

Collier's 90:17 N 12 '32 il por
Lit Digest 114:7 S 17 '32
Time 26:14 S 23 '35 por; 32:4+ Ag 22 '38
Lippmann, W. Men of Destiny p112-19 1927
McAdoo, W. G. Crowded Years 1932
Synon, M. McAdoo, the Man and His Times 1924
Who's Who in America
Who's Who in the Nation's Capital 1934-35

Obituaries

N Y Times p1+ F 2 '41 por
Newsweek 17:6 F 10 '41
Time 37:16 F 10 '41

MACARTHUR, DOUGLAS Jan. 26, 1880- Commanding general of the United States Armed Forces in the Far East

Address: b. c/o War Dept, Washington, D. C.

General Douglas MacArthur, who in July 1941 was recalled to active duty as commander of the United States Army in the Far East, a command which became one of the most important in the world when the

Japanese attacked five months later, is a tall, slender, erect man with a brisk manner who comes of a celebrated Army family. He was born in Little Rock, Arkansas on January 26, 1880, the son of Lieutenant General Arthur and Mary P. (Hardy) MacArthur. His father helped to drive the Spaniards out of the Philippine Islands and himself served two years there as Governor General.

It was natural that young MacArthur should attend West Point. There he starred in baseball, playing right field and batting from the south side of the plate, and only sickness kept him from winning his letter four years in succession. When graduated in 1903, the No. 1 honor man of this class, he was commissioned a second lieutenant of engineers and sent to the Philippines. Promoted the following year to the rank of first lieutenant, he returned to the United States in October 1904 and spent several months (January to October 1905) with the California Debris Commission, also serving as chief engineering officer of the Pacific Division. Then followed a year in Japan as aide to his father, another year as Theodore Roosevelt's aide in Washington, and in 1908, after having been graduated from the Engineering School of Application, he joined Company K, 3rd Battalion of Engineers, at Fort Leavenworth, Kansas. He served at that station, at San Antonio, Texas and on detached service in the Canal Zone until August 1912 and until November 1912 was an instructor of engineering at Army Service Schools, Fort Leavenworth. In February 1911 he acquired the rank of captain.

It was 1912 when Captain MacArthur was ordered to Washington. There he was appointed to the General Staff Corps, and from April to September 1914 served with the Engineering Corps in the Vera Cruz Expedition. In December 1915 he was raised to the rank of major; finally, in September 1917, after the United States had entered the First World War, he was appointed chief of staff of the 42nd (Rainbow) Division with the rank of colonel of infantry.

In France the 37-year-old colonel participated in the Champagne-Marne and Aisne-Marne defensives; he was given the temporary rank of brigadier general in June 1918, placed in command of the 84th Infantry Brigade a few weeks later, and led it in the St. Mihiel, Essey, Pannes, Meuse-Argonne and Sedan offensives. He was twice wounded in action and he created a sensation by his insistence on going into battle with his men. The citation for "extraordinary heroism against an armed enemy" accompanying his Distinguished Service Cross read: "When Company D, 168th Infantry was under severe attack in the salient du Fays, France, he voluntarily joined it upon finding that he could do so without interfering with his normal duties, and by his coolness and conspicuous courage added materially to its success."

The Armistice in November 1918 found MacArthur temporarily commanding the 42nd Division once more before being put in command of the 84th Infantry Brigade, stationed with the Army of Occupation in Germany until April of the following year. Returning to the United States Military Academy (he was the youngest officer ever to head West Point), he immediately began to work toward the mechanization of the "horse and saber department." In January 1920 he was made a brigadier general in the regular army, and in 1922, before leaving for the Philippines again to serve for three years as commander of the District of Manila, the 23rd Infantry Brigade and Philippine Division, he married the former Mrs. Louise Cromwell Brooks in the Palm Beach home of her mother.

Promoted to the rank of major general in January 1925, MacArthur spent the next five years commanding the Fourth Corps Area in Atlanta, the Third Corps Area in Baltimore and, from 1928 to 1930, the Philippine Department. Finally, in November 1930, President Hoover made him chief of staff of the United States Army—the only chief of staff in United States history whose father had held the same post, and the youngest man to hold it since the First World War. At the same time the four-star insignia of a general was bestowed upon him (making him the youngest general since Grant), and the President announced: "It gives me great pleasure to promote so brilliant a soldier. He is the only one of the major generals having a sufficient period to serve in the Army before retirement to serve the full four-year term of chief of staff. There are several very eminent generals who rank above General MacArthur, but none of them could serve more than a year and a half of the full term."

The next few years, however, found the 52-year-old general the target of many shafts. In August 1932 he had directed the soldiers who "torched, bayonetted and bombed" the "Bonus Expeditionary Force" out of Anacostia Flats in the nation's capital, and the tender-hearted, while admitting that he had done, "technically, a swell job," criticized the action as both cruel and unnecessary. Friends said that MacArthur was only obeying orders, and MacArthur himself was quoted as having said that if Hoover had not given such orders "another week might have meant that the Government was in peril." Drew Pearson and Robert Allen (see sketch this issue), who had been among the most biting critics of his role in the "Bonus Battle," nevertheless continued blasting at him on other grounds. And the Senate munitions inquiry in 1934 brought forth charges that he had intervened in behalf of American plane builders seeking foreign contracts.

In 1935 General MacArthur, due to retire as chief of staff of the United States Army, became director of the organization of national defense of the Philippine Commonwealth. In May 1936 a bill made him military adviser to the Commonwealth at his regular salary, reputedly the highest paid to any military adviser in the world; and in August of that same year President Quezon

U. S. Army Signal Corps.

DOUGLAS MACARTHUR

(see sketch this issue) commissioned him field marshal of the Philippine Army. Mrs. Quezon handed him a golden baton.

Once more there was criticism from a few sources as well as praise. A writer in *The Nation* found it unsuitable that MacArthur should actually hold more power in the Philippines than any other representative of the United States, confessing fear that his military program (the Philippine Island Defense Act subjected Filipinos to military training from childhood up) would make economic independence from the United States impossible by 1946 and would help to maintain the present ruling clique in power by force. He wrote, bitterly: "General MacArthur now makes his contribution to our foreign relations by this unauthorized move to militarize the Filipino people."

General MacArthur, confident not only that the defenses of the Islands could in a few years be built up so effectively that conquest would cost an invader some half million men and between five and ten billion dollars but also that Japanese militarism would be a very real threat in the near future, nevertheless continued energetically with his program. On December 31, 1937 he retired from the Army at his own request but remained with the Philippine Army as field marshal, undiscouraged by hints in 1940 from Commissioner Francis B. Sayre and Quezon himself that the Islands were practically indefensible.

By 1941 relations between the United States and Japan were growing so tense that even former critics expressed little but gratification when, in July, President Roosevelt placed the land and sea forces of the Philippine Commonwealth under United States military and naval command for the duration of the emergency and appointed General MacArthur commander of the United States Army

MACARTHUR, DOUGLAS—*Continued*

in the Far East. Back in harness, MacArthur announced: "I am glad to be able to serve my country in this crucial time." Francis B. Sayre praised his appointment, saying. "General MacArthur is ideally equipped to integrate and to direct the joint defense measures of the United States and the Philippines." And his old friend President Quezon was the first to congratulate him.

After that there were frequent conferences with Quezon over the incorporation of the Philippine Army reservists into the United States Army, conferences with Sir Robert Brooke-Popham (see sketch this issue) over Anglo-United States military plans—and MacArthur's program of preparedness for any contingency reportedly began moving swiftly ahead. When the Japanese attack occurred, commentators praised the work he had done in the Philippines over a number of years and also the quality of the resistance which the Japanese met. On December 19, 1941 he became a full general in the Army of the United States for the second time.

The impeccably attired General has long been an outstanding advocate of preparedness for the United States as well as for the Philippines. He is also one of the United States' most thoroughly decorated commanders, having been honored for heroism or distinguished service not only by his own country and by Mexico, Ecuador and Italy but by the once-free nations of France, Belgium, Poland, Hungary, Czechoslovakia, Yugoslavia and Romania. Divorced from his first wife in 1929, he married the former Jean Faircloth in 1938, and has one son, Arthur.

References

Christian Sci Mon Mag p1-2+ N 2 '38 por
Collier's 93:17+ Ja 13 '34 il por; 98: 12-13+ S 5 '36 il por
Life 11:123+ D 8 '41 pors
Lit Digest 117:12 Je 2 '34 por
Nation 142:736-7 Je 10 '36
Nat Repub 23:1-2+ S '35 por
Newsweek 2:11 D 9 '33 por; 3:22 My 26 '34 por; 4:14 S 1 '34 por; 8:8-9 S 5 '36
Time 38:30 Ag 4 '41 il por
Who's Who in America
Who's Who in Government
Who's Who in the East
Who's Who in the Regular Army

MACBRIDE, ERNEST WILLIAM Dec. 12, 1866—Nov. 19, 1940 Emeritus professor of London University and former professor of zoology at McGill University in Montreal; in 1935 attacked the Darwinian theory of evolution.

References

Author's and Writer's Who's Who
Who's Who

Obituaries

N Y Herald Tribune p24 N 20 '40
N Y Times p21 N 20 '40

MCBRIDE, MARY MARGARET Nov. 16, 1899- Radio commentator; journalist

Address: National Broadcasting Co, 30 Rockefeller Plaza, New York City

In October of 1940, Mary Margaret McBride switched from a regional to a national hookup, from a 45 to a 15 minute broadcast, from 13 sponsors to an exclusive singleton, and from the pseudonym "Martha Deane" to her own name. Allowing for the increased circulation, the total area of her message-spread probably remained constant. Certainly her popularity suffered no decline, for shortly after the change she was voted the most popular woman on the air. Meanwhile a new and harried Martha Deane struggles to fill the voluminous mantle discarded by her predecessor.

Mary Margaret McBride became the most listened-to woman on the air by daily projecting over the microphone 45 minutes' worth of wide-eyed wonder at the universe. In a homey voice with a folksy twang she exclaimed to a host of invisible ladies over practically everything—from the way a musk deer sneezes to tablecloths at $9,000 apiece. Bobbing about in this geyser of human interest were pertinent items from the releases of her sponsors. It was whispered that important manufacturers stood in line waiting hopefully to be among those honored by mention—at a tidy figure. She has never tried to pass off advertising as self-started enthusiasm. At the same time, she has steadily refused to utter "even the teeniest white lie," or to recommend a product she could not genuinely believe in; and has gone to considerable lengths to test each one. The result is a ring of conviction that has a wonderfully tonic effect on sales.

Her facts also must come up to specification. Mere information is not enough; it must be unique, astounding, exciting, useful, or at any rate appealing. For example, just any tortoise, no matter how old he is, would not qualify for discussion on her program; but the tortoise of St. Helena who was alive when Napoleon was there rates as a tortoise with human interest. As Martha Deane she kept at least one reporter busy scouting and verifying for her, but she has always been her own best nose for news.

She was early celebrated as the only regular broadcaster who regularly spoke "ad lib," depending on a scant page of scribbled notes, the inspiration of the moment and the stimulus of the wares she nibbled so convincingly before the mike. She also depended, of course, upon Dick, the accomplished stooge who reminded her quite audibly which products she still had to mention, helped her draw the best out of her many interviewees, and generally contributed to the atmosphere of human warmth which helped her establish a new high in radio presentation.

The "sunbeam of CBS" began professional life as a sob sister. Private life she began somewhat earlier, in Paris, Missouri, on November 16, 1899. Her father, Thomas Walker McBride, had an unfortunate habit of moving on to a new farm just when the last one was really well broken in. On moving day her mother, Elizabeth (Craig) McBride, might sigh, "It's hardly worth while to have anything nice," but once they reached the new place she would settle down to her business as champion housekeeper and homemaker to a troupe of unbridled McBrides. She is the real heroine of Mary Margaret's warmly nostalgic *How Dear to My Heart,* published in 1940. The chief hero is Mama's kitchen stove. Her magnificent cooking, described with gusto and detail—not to mention recipes—seems to have conditioned her little daughter's future taste, career and silhouette.

A great-aunt who believed in higher education offered to put Mary Margaret through college, provided she would train herself to be a dean of women. But Mary Margaret had decided to be a newspaperwoman in New York, so she worked her way through the University of Missouri's School of Journalism. Later she was the first woman and the first radio commentator to be awarded her Alma Mater's medal for outstanding journalism.

She supported herself in college partly by looking after faculty children, but chiefly by working as reporter, part-time editor, advertising salesman and typesetter on a local newspaper. Her method of scooping rival society reporters was characteristic: she would telephone the local dairies, and if anyone had ordered extra ice cream she knew that a party was imminent. In spite of the extracurricular whirl in 1919 she completed the four-year course in three and a half years, and with the ink hardly dry on her diploma headed for Cleveland, where she forthwith became cub reporter on the *Cleveland Press.*

Her talent for highlighting the human values in any story soon won her feature assignments, and later a year as special correspondent in Washington. But New York was her goal, and before long her dream of being a newspaperwoman in the metropolis came true. When her first job in the big city petered out she took to heart the report that Frank A. Munsey of the *Evening Mail* melted at a woman's tears: she made straight for his office and wept her way onto his pay roll.

After the *Mail* was sold she turned to magazine writing, and eventually was contributing articles to a number of leading periodicals. Her writing has continued, even since the radio claimed her chief energies. In 1934 and 1935 she was woman's page editor for Newspaper Enterprise Association of New York City, and she has been joint author of several books. She collaborated with Prince Christopher of Greece on the history of his family and with Paul Whiteman on the story of his life, published under the title of *Jazz* (1926); with Alexander Williams on *Charm* (1927); and with Helen Josephy on four books: *Paris Is a Woman's Town* (1929); *London Is a Man's Town* (1930); *New York Is Everybody's Town* (1931); *Beer and Skittles* (a Friendly Modern Guide to Germany) (1932). As solo author she has had published, in addition to the recent autobiography,

The Story of Dwight W. Morrow (1930) and *Here's Martha Deane* (1936).

The jittery market of 1929 did such uncomfortable things to her savings and the literary market, both at the same time, that she again turned to job-hunting. Radio was not one of her chief thoughts but, hearing that a local station wanted a woman for a mid-afternoon spot, she casually auditioned along with 39 other applicants. Conscious of her Missouri twang and vast inexperience, she shrugged that attempt off without a second thought and proceeded to Washington on the trail of another job. The next morning a telegram informed her that her natural manner of voice had won the day.

The opening was for household-hinting, and she was to impersonate a helpful Grandmother. After three venerable days she unceremoniously amputated a couple of generations and came out under her true colors. The household hints soon went the way of Grandmother. Fascinated by the antics of a trained flea on Forty-Second Street, Mary Margaret told her audience about him the next day. Demands for more such tales came pouring in, and presently she was simply rattling on about whatever struck her fancy. For a while she gave three broadcasts weekly under her own name and five as Martha Deane.

MARY MARGARET MCBRIDE

Whatever the name and whatever the aegis, the technique remains the same: a simple, human, warm approach, a smile that carries right over the air. As Martha Deane she often interviewed people she felt her listeners would like to "meet"; and so cozy was the atmosphere of her broadcast, with appetizing samples to be nibbled, Mary Margaret and Dick at their respective mikes, and the stream of guess-whats rippling on and on, that even a novice soon forgot stage fright and the listening millions.

MCBRIDE, MARY MARGARET—*Cont.*

There is something babylike in the sweetness of Miss McBride's smile that fits well with the baby-smooth skin and the round, close-cropped head. The rest of her looks matronly enough, large and ample and soft—food is one of her hobbies as well as a professional interest. Other interests are books, the theatre and gardens. She loves flying, motoring and a great many people, including the 1,800 that write to her each week and the donors of the gifts that deluge the studio when her birthday comes around (an assortment that rivals her own topics for oddity and abundance).

In 1936 she was awarded a medal by the Woman's National Exposition of Arts and Industries for the year's greatest contribution to radio. The following year the Wall Paper Institute presented her with a medal for contributing to the stimulation of interest in the home. Her imitators are far more numerous than her medals, and at least as convincing a tribute to the *éclat* with which small-town girl brings Main Street to New York.

References

> Christian Sci Mon p1 O 22 '40 por
> N Y World-Telegram p9 Ja 27 '40
> Newsweek 12:22 N 21 '38
> Scholastic 37:21 D 16 '40 por
> Time 36:56-7 N 25 '40 por
> American Women
> McBride, M. M. Here's Martha Deane 1936
> McBride, M. M. How Dear To My Heart 1940
> Variety Radio Directory
> Who's Who in America

MCCARTHY, CLEM Sports commentator
Address: National Broadcasting Co, RCA Bldg, Radio City, New York City; h. 162 W. 56th St, New York City

Clem McCarthy, turf expert and sports commentator for the National Broadcasting Company, was born near Rochester, New York some 60 years ago, the son of an Irish horse dealer and auctioneer. The elder McCarthy's turf activities kept the family on the move all over the country, and Clem received his schooling in a dozen different cities.

It was natural that he should be interested in racing and just as natural that his first ambition should be to become a jockey. But the great Tod Sloan discouraged him—he pointed out that Clem was hardly streamlined enough for such a career. Clem resigned himself to his size and decided to try his luck as a handicapper. He did well enough to be hired as handicapper and reporter by a San Diego paper which had been looking for a long time for a man with McCarthy's knowledge of horses and wide acquaintance in the turf world. For many years McCarthy continued at this work, writing for both dailies and turf publications and occasionally contributing an article to popular magazines.

It was in 1928 that he made his debut before the microphone. He was in Chicago at the time a public address system was installed at Arlington Park to call the running of the races. Clem's experience as an auctioneer and extensive knowledge of racing made him an obvious choice for the announcer. As a result of his work here he was selected to handle the first broadcast of a Kentucky Derby, in 1928. Since that time he has handled all the Kentucky Derbies and many headline sports events, including several world championship bouts, for NBC.

During almost half a century's connection with turf events, McCarthy has acquired a wealth of memoirs. He has seen every Kentucky Derby since his first in 1896 and remembers sharply events like the famous "Jockeys' duel" there in 1933, when the boys on Brokers' Tip and Head Play fouled each other in the stretch and were striking each other with their bats when they thundered across the finish line. He remembers, too, that famous delay at the starting post of the $50,000 World's Fair Derby in Chicago in 1893 when 15 colts were an hour and one-half at the barrier. All these years of seeing and reporting have convinced him that Man o' War was the greatest of all American race horses and that the jockeys of today would be eating dust if the incomparable Sloan were still booting them down the stretch.

One of the theories Clem has developed over the years is that a horse may be able to do the Derby distance easily even though his sire lacked the stamina to negotiate a mile and three-sixteenths. For proof he cites McGee, a sprinter whose absolute limit in fast company was a mile; four of his sons were distance runners and two of them won the Derby. From his years' experience, too, Clem believes firmly in the efficacy of the photo-finish type of race judging—the camera, he feels, is much less likely to err than the human eye when two horses come down the stretch neck and neck.

McCarthy's command of words, the speed with which he follows the rapid developments of a race or prize fight, the years of training he has had handling sports events—all make him tops among those who work before the microphone at sports events. He has his opinions about contests away from the turf, too: Babe Ruth, to him, is still the most colorful baseball player of all time; Bob Fitzsimmons, the greatest heavyweight; Walter Johnson, 'way up in front among the pitching "great's" of history.

When McCarthy broadcasts, his voice has a vibrant quality which shares with the listener the color and thrills of the event he is reporting. He would like to use this talent (and this is one of his chief ambitions) in broadcasting the Grand National Steeplechase. Meanwhile he keeps energetically at the radio work he has now, at a lot of newsreel work, and at his sports column, which is syndicated in a number of papers.

He looks as energetic as he is. His small frame—Clem weighs 145 pounds and is five

CLEM MCCARTHY

feet nine—his iron-gray hair and light blue eyes all almost seem to give off sparks. His hobbies are good food, good music and good friends—among them many sports celebrities and many headliners in the show world. He is married and has no children.

References

International Motion Picture Almanac

MACDONALD, CORDELIA HOWARD

Feb. 1, 1848—Aug. 10, 1941 American actress who was the original Little Eva; thrilled thousands here and abroad by her portrayal of Harriet Beecher Stowe's character from *Uncle Tom's Cabin;* first played the part 88 years ago; called the "Shirley Temple of her day"; played other parts and concluded her stage career at the age of 12.

Obituaries

N Y Times p13 Ag 11 '41

MCGARRY, WILLIAM J(AMES), REV.

Mar. 14, 1894—Sept. 23, 1941 Editor of *Theological Studies,* a Catholic quarterly, since 1939; president of Boston College from 1937 to 1939; entered the Society of Jesus in 1911 and was ordained a priest in the Roman Catholic Church in 1925; professor of mathematics at Fordham University and of sacred Scripture at Weston College, where he was also dean of studies and dean of the theological faculty from 1934 to 1937; author of many books, the latest of which is *He Cometh,* published posthumously.

References

American Catholic Who's Who
Who's Who in America

Obituaries

N Y Times p23 S 24 '41 por

MCGEE, FIBBER Nov. 16, 1896- Radio actor

MCGEE, MOLLY Apr. 15, 1898- Radio actress

Address: b. National Broadcasting Co, Hollywood, Calif; h. 17121 Rancho, Encino, Calif.

Millions of Americans tune their radios each week to listen to one of the most consistently popular comic teams on the networks, that amiable braggart, Fibber McGee, and down-to-earth Molly. Ever since the Fibber McGee & Molly series was inaugurated in April 1935 it has ranked as one of the nation's top attractions, sometimes taking first place in the Crossley radio ratings and almost always among the first four favorites.

In real life James Edward Jordan and Marian (Driscoll) Jordan, they don't resemble their radio characters, but in many ways their story constitutes a saga equally interesting. "Fibber" was born on a farm five miles west of Peoria, the son of James W. and Mary (Tighe) Jordan. His youth was marked by two things that helped mold his career: an inordinate wanderlust and a love of singing. In Peoria he attended St. Mark's Grade School and later the Spaulding Institute, but in his spare time he studied voice and eagerly took every chance to display his talent. It was while he was singing in the choir of St. John's Church that he first met his future wife, the "Molly" of the duo.

The future Fibber studied singing for four years while engaged at various jobs. He was a wholesale drug clerk, a mail carrier, a washing-machine salesman and an insurance agent; but the desire for a stage career eventually proved irresistible. He was in love with Marian, but decided to realize his ambition before considering matrimony and went to Chicago, where he secured his first stage job. After that he returned to Peoria and Marian.

She was a native Peorian, the daughter of Daniel and Anna (Carroll) Driscoll, and had been drawn by the stage almost from infancy, despite strenuous parental objections. She studied at parochial schools and the Academy of Our Lady, Peoria, where she appeared in many amateur theatricals and concerts and dreamed of a career before the footlights. Later she studied voice, violin and piano at Runnell's School of Music in Peoria.

Marian's parents' distaste for things theatrical extended to her choice of a husband. They relented, however, when Jordan was called to the Army, and the marriage was planned for his return to civilian life. After serving at a Georgia training camp Jim was sent overseas to serve with the 122nd Engineers. He became violently ill at St. Nazaire. Refusing to leave France, he contributed his talents to the morale division of the overseas army, organizing a troupe of entertainers and touring the lines.

Once back in Peoria, Jordan got a job in a machine shop and married Marian, but the lure of the entertainment world haunted their domesticity. Finally it was Marian whose plans ripened to realization. As a musical couple, the Jordans embarked on a vaudeville

Maurice Seymour

FIBBER MCGEE

tour; then, on Marian's initiative, they organized a concert company. This lasted four years and brought the Jordans to hundreds of tank towns, opera houses and churches throughout the Middle West.

At the conclusion of their tours the company was disbanded and the Jordans drearily contemplated their next move. A cheerless odyssey of Middle Western mediocrity confronted them and they had little hope of breaking into the big time. In their discouragement the Jordans at this time even considered going to China. This was the result of a letter from Jordan's sister and brother-in-law, who were impresarios in China, urging them to revive the concert company and bring it across the seas, assuring them that it would prove a great hit. Just as the Jordans were on the verge of taking the advice, they received a second letter. It read: "Don't bring the kids. You'll be traveling in a land where it will be difficult to secure fresh milk." The Jordans looked at their two children. The Chinese tour was off.

Just when it seemed that the Jordans would have to seek another opening in vaudeville, radio came along. They were visiting friends at Rogers Park in Chicago and someone turned on the radio. Jordan listened thoughtfully for a while, then said: "Marian and I can do better than that." One of their friends challenged them to go on the radio, and Jordan, who has always been susceptible to a dare, accepted on the spot.

An audition over WIBO, Chicago, in 1925 proved satisfactory and the Jordans were hired for a song program over the air. After their initial performance they were engaged for one of the first sponsored programs in the Middle West. For this they received $10 a week. A portly, genial cartoonist, whose ability to think up gags rivaled his pen-and-

ink artistry, was the first to recognize the Jordans' potentialities as a radio dramatic team. He is Don Quinn, who still writes the Jordan shows and with whom the couple split three ways their weekly income of $6,000. Quinn's first sketch was called *Smack Out* and concerned a folksy grocery store proprietor who was always "smack out" of everything except gargantuan whoppers. The sketch proved a success and developed into a popular series. The Jordans played in this and other sketches over the National Broadcasting Company and also appeared on children's programs.

Not until the creation of *Fibber McGee & Molly*, however, did the Jordans reach radio heights. This was given its original network airing in April 1935 and has continued ever since, except during part of 1938 and 1939 when Mrs. Jordan's health caused its interruption for two seasons. The Fibber series was only moderately successful as a daytime feature, but when it was changed to one of the choicest night spots in the air, the 9:30 hour on Tuesday evenings, its popularity soared sensationally. Meanwhile the Jordan fortunes rose correspondingly; they built a home in Chicago which was the exact copy of one they had rented before their success.

In 1938 Marian, who plays not only Molly but several other characters, including Grandma, the dolorous Mrs. Wearybottom and the exasperating Teeny, a neighbor's child, suffered a nervous breakdown, and the Jordans moved to California. There they still live, in a modest, green-shuttered bungalow with a spacious workroom for Jim and rooms for the children. In 1937 they worked on their first motion picture, *This Way Please*. In December 1941 they are starred with their radio rivals Edgar Bergen and Charlie McCarthy in *Look Who's Laughing*.

MOLLY MCGEE

Fibber McGee & Molly is sponsored by S. C. Johnson and Son, Inc. Jordan seems to have been successful in augmenting his radio salary. he owns a factory which manufactures sand-blasting machinery and a Hires' Root Beer bottling plant in Kansas City.

In real life five-foot-six, one hundred seventy-three pound, shrewd, energetic Jim Jordan is the antithesis of the inept and braggadocio-loving Fibber. He runs a farm on his California property and spends much time in his tool shop. He likes to play ping-pong with the children, James Carroll and Kathryn. Marian, who is five-foot-four, spends her spare time reading mystery and love stories and collecting Chinese prints, of which she has already accumulated hundreds.

The popularity of the Fibber programs probably is explained by the fact that they combine bright, chuckle-invoking dialogue with sharply-delineated characterization etched by voice variations which range all the way from a faltering lisp to a deep growl. What's more, the programs have a distinctly American small-town tang. These are sure-fire radio ingredients and readily account for the almost astronomical weekly audience of the ex-vaudeville troupers from Peoria.

References

Newsweek 18:55 Ag 25 '41
Time 35:41 Ap 22 '40 pors
International Motion Picture Almanac
Variety Radio Directory

MCGEE, MOLLY See McGee, F. and McGee, M.

MCGINLEY, PHYLLIS 1905- Author
Address: b. c/o Duell, Sloane & Pearce, 270 Madison Ave, New York City; h. 12 Hazel Lane, Larchmont, N. Y.

Her two latest books of light verse, *A Pocketful of Wry* (1940) and *Husbands Are Difficult* (1941), establish Phyllis McGinley among the elect in a field that includes such notable rhyme-twisters as Ogden Nash and Margaret Fishback (see sketches this issue). The New York *Herald Tribune* says that Miss McGinley "tops the estimable number of our light versifiers from the point of view of both substance and craftsmanship," and the New York *Times* says that her "mastery of intricately cascading forms of light verse is pretty wonderful." Her poems have appeared in almost every type of periodical.

She has been praised in particular for her expert satire, including her "Complaint to the American Medical Association" concerning their members' unfair monopoly of best-selling autobiographies. She has a neat way of building poems from learned newspaper items. When the New York *Times* reports that scientists have discovered a rich source of vita-

PHYLLIS MCGINLEY

mins in grass, she writes of poor Nebuchad-nezzar, born too soon, lamenting:

I ranged the meadows beside the cattle
I fed on the fields to atone my sins
And no one knew I had found a subtle
Method of getting my vitamins.

Or, observing Mortimer Adler's dictum that "solitary reading is like drinking alone," considers the after-dinner book indulger who

A drunken fool, a literary sot,
Creeps to his lonely cot,
There to swig down and out of public view
Immoderate tankards of the Pierian brew.

There is an occasional poem that goes beyond light verse into another category, serious verse, such as the excellent psychological portrait, *The Old Woman With Four Sons.*

"I was born in Ontario, Oregon, in 1905," Miss McGinley writes us, "but since I left there at the tender age of three months I can scarcely lay claim to being a Native Daughter. I lived on a ranch in Eastern Colorado through my childhood, where the vanishing West had not quite vanished. I remember watching bronco-busting instead of baseball games on Sundays, for instance; and riding a buckskin pony three miles to school where my brother and I were the only pupils. And I remember blizzards and antelopes and coyotes and cattle being branded, although we shortly started raising wheat and sugar beets on our own place.

"After my father's death when I was 12 or 13 we went 'back home' to Ogden, Utah where my mother had been born and brought up and where her family had been pioneers. (But never Mormons.) Her name was Julia Kiesel, and her father and numerous brothers came from Germany—part of the exodus of Germans who left the country after Prussian-

MCGINLEY, PHYLLIS—*Continued*

ism first enveloped it. In fact, I like to boast to my husband, whose 'Connecticut Yankee ancestors have been hanging around these parts since the 1600's, that I am pure third-generation immigrant—German on one side and Irish on the other.

"After being graduated from college at the University of Utah, I taught a year at home and then reversed Horace Greeley by coming to New York. Found I wasn't suited to doing much of anything except teaching school or writing poetry, so I did both, one full time and the latter whenever I could. I'd always written verse, by the way, since at the age of six I went introspective and turned out this little stunner:

> *Sometimes in the evening*
> *When the sky is red and pink*
> *I love to lie in a hammock*
> *And think and think and think.*

Which must be the beginning of my lifelong preference for composing my stuff in a horizontal position.

"I quit teaching after four or five years of it, to free-lance for a short time and then (in a fit of free-lance jitters) to write copy in an advertising agency for five months and to help edit *Town and Country* for two. I was married then to Charles Hayden (1937) and have been pretty busy ever since with buying and furnishing and remodeling a house here in Larchmont Manor (an elderly house rather than an old one, since it was built around Civil War time); having a baby, Julie; and writing more verse than I ever had time for before."

Miss McGinley says that her interests are "old furniture, learning something about gardening, cooking on occasion and collecting recipes, which I wheedle the cook into experimenting with, and sticking pins into the smugger aspects of the social scene." Among her dislikes she lists: "getting up early, double-feature movies, most writers (and *all* literary parties), parsnips, people who froth at the mouth when you mention the New Deal, subways, advice and having my hair waved. I am passionately devoted, on the other hand, to breakfast in bed, the Cavalier poets, auctions, Utah scenery, kidneys-in-wine-sauce and Walt Disney.

"My eccentricities are few—putting sugar in my soup is the only one I can think of at the moment—and I'm what is known in the trade as a 'good, reliable worker.' That is, I always make a deadline. I am not very prolific and labor painstakingly over every piece I do. My burning ambition is to write a musical comedy in the Gilbert and Sullivan tradition but until some producer gets around to asking me directly to get to work, I'll probably be too busy to start it."

References

N Y Herald Tribune Books p28 D 8 '40
N Y Times p15 N 9 '40
Sat Eve Post 213:6 D 7 '40 por

MCGUIRE, DOROTHY   June 14, 1918-
Actress

Address: b. c/o Actors Equity Assn, 45 W. 47th St, New York City; h. 5 E. 54th St, New York City

"To put *Claudia* on Broadway," John Golden, the producer, told its author, Rose Franken (see sketch this issue), "it will be necessary to find an actress in her early 20's who can look 19, who has about 25 years' experience in show business, who is up to her knees in sawdust. She must be able to play comedy and tragedy. She must be able to play one of the longest parts ever written to my knowledge, 140 odd sides, and play the hell out of it. The odds are a thousand to one that there is no such actress."

There was. And her name is Dorothy McGuire. Two hundred and nine aspirants for the part of the sprightly young wife in the play had been interviewed when Miss McGuire, making the weary rounds, dropped into Golden's office. Rose Franken looked at her "almost childishly young face and figure, her soft, home-washed blondish hair and her large gray eyes," and approved. She listened to her read the part, and the search for Claudia was over. Dorothy McGuire had her first real Broadway part, and Broadway had a new actress.

It had taken Broadway four years to find it out. Miss McGuire had suspected it would be known someday ever since she was 12 and played the lead in *A Kiss for Cinderella* at the Omaha Little Theatre. She was born in Omaha, Nebraska and went to school there until her father, Thomas Johnson McGuire, died. Then her mother, Isabelle (Flaherty) McGuire, sent her to a convent in Indianapolis. Even here she managed to get theatre training by playing the role of the Virgin Mary in a religious play. After two years she went on to Pine Manor Junior College in Wellesley, Massachusetts.

With this preparation, Dorothy McGuire, at the age of 19, prepared to storm the citadels of Broadway. She heard that a man named Jed Harris was casting a play and went to see him. Her experience, she assured him, was good: directing plays at school with all-girl casts, acting in the Omaha Little Theatre. She didn't get the job. And she didn't get a lot of other jobs. She dined on tuna fish every night and spent lots of time living a generally gay life. It wasn't doing her much good: "You can't eat everything out of cans, forget to sleep and expect to be as healthy as Tarzan's Jane, now can you?" she asks. But she was getting around, asking for jobs and incidentally, she recalls, learning "how not to get along with agents. Every one of them thought I was a snip."

The general run of bad luck that had Dorothy McGuire calling herself a "failure" was stopped somewhat when she got a few radio jobs and even more when she became understudy to Martha Scott in *Our Town* in 1938. Then came what seemed like a real break: Martha Scott went to Hollywood and Dorothy McGuire took over the role. But it was toward the end of the play's run, the critics and the professional people who count had all seen the play, and she went pretty much unnoticed.

Sessions in summer stock followed this appearance and they in turn were followed by a part in the road company of *My Dear Children,* John Barrymore's vehicle. Things were picking up, and a part in *Swingin' the Dream* seemed to prove it. But *Swingin' the Dream* was a tremendous flop, and *Medicine Show* which followed it wasn't exactly a smash hit. The revival of *Kind Lady* was better, but not perfect. A really good role, in the Theatre Guild's *Liberty Jones,* was "practically promised" her, one for which she knew she was just made. Someone else got it. Miss McGuire had another egg in the basket, though, and when *The Time of Your Life* went on tour in 1940 she went along with it as Julie Haydon's understudy.

She came back to New York jobless, ready for the rounds, and she found Rose Franken and John Golden waiting for her (though they hadn't known it before she stepped into the office). Miss Franken immediately snatched her away for week-end coachings and general pepping up. Dorothy needed it. She was not, in fact, doing well at all during the first week of rehearsals, and she knew she wasn't. But then Miss Franken kindly said to her: "Don't worry if you hear talk about other people being tried out for your part. I still think you can do it," and she sailed right into it.

When the play opened in New York in February 1941, every critic in New York hailed Rose Franken's find. Dorothy McGuire's portrayal of the girlish young wife, given to introspection and eavesdropping, who outgrows in the three acts an exaggerated attachment for her mother, was called "enchanting", "beautifully played." Brooks Atkinson praised her for playing with "simplicity, casual frankness and personal charm" a part which he felt might easily have become "annoying or pixie," and he commented: "Although a little inexperienced as an actress, she is personally genuine; the charm she radiates across the play is not merely a theatre mannerism."

Dorothy McGuire herself will never forget the opening and her first solo curtain call after it: "It was out of this world, it was so wonderful. I couldn't see a person, the lights were so bright and so hazy at the same time. . . I was really beside myself. Nothing like that can ever happen again." Even the special award given her by the Drama League for the best performance by a young actor, much as it meant, was a pale thing after that first night's triumph.

Dorothy McGuire hugs closely all the praise and understanding she's getting these days, but despite new clothes, new furniture for her apartment on 54th Street, flying lessons, a coming tour of major cities and even the chance of acting Claudia in the Selznick film version, she keeps her feet right on the ground. "It's funny," she says. "You knock around for months, years sometimes, and all

Alfredo Valente

DOROTHY MCGUIRE

of a sudden you wind up in a hit and everybody makes a fuss over you. You keep reminding yourself that maybe next year you'll have to start all over again, or perhaps get into a flop or two. That's what keeps you balanced." She hasn't changed much. Her favorite costume is still a skirt and oversized sweater; one of her most prized possessions is still the old melodeon in her living-room; her friends still call her names like "McGoo" and "Frou"; and she's still embarrassed about the size of her feet.

This "pug-nosed, slightly blonde version of Greta Garbo" lives less riotously now than when she first came to New York. She still goes out a lot, but not with people who expect her to act like Claudia off stage. "I'm not that funny and snappy myself, and after the theatre I'm usually a little tired and like to sit back quietly and not make too much bright conversation." And that, she adds, "probably disappoints people."

References

Collier's 108:13+ Jl 19 '41 por
Life 11:118-22+ N 17 '41
N Y Herald Tribune VI p2 My 18 '41 por
N Y Times IX p3 Ap 20 '41
PM p50-1 F 23 '41 pors

MACKAY, SIR IVEN GIFFARD Apr. 7, 1882- Commander in chief of the Australian Army; educator

Commander in chief of the Australian Imperial Forces since August 1941, Major General Mackay's name became known to Americans in December 1940 as one of the commanders of the triumphant British Army of the Nile, which rolled up the Fascist forces in Egypt and Libya, Sidi Barrani, Bardia and Tobruk. For his work here he was knighted.

Australian Associated Press

SIR IVEN GIFFARD MACKAY

Tall, slim, and mild-mannered, Mackay's appearance belies the nickname "Ivan the Terrible" given him by Australian troops during the First World War, when, after serving as captain adjutant of the 4th Battalion at Gallipoli, he rose to the position of general officer commanding the 1st Infantry Brigade in France. In the process he collected at least one wound, several mentions in dispatches, the Distinguished Service Order and Bar, the Companion of St. Michael and St. George and the Croix de Guerre.

Son of a Presbyterian minister, the Rev. Isaac Mackay of Armadale, Scotland, and Emily Frances (King) Mackay of Lake Erie, Canada, he was born in Grafton, New South Wales and educated at Newington College, Sydney, and at St. Andrew's College, University of Sydney. In 1904, shortly after receiving his B. A., he became junior demonstrator in physics at the University of Sydney and later resident master and sportsmaster at Sydney Church of England Grammar School. In 1910 he returned to the University of Sydney as assistant demonstrator in physics; he remained there until the First World War broke out. After the War he returned to teaching, putting in a year's study at Emmanuel College, Cambridge, before returning to the University of Sydney. In 1933 he became headmaster of Cranbrook School, one of the fashionable schools in the suburbs of Sydney.

For eight years before the Second World War he had combined with his teaching duties the position of Commonwealth Film Appeal Censor, to whom producers dissatisfied with the rulings of film censorship boards carried their objections. In this position he reviewed thousands of feet of disputed American film.

A University "blue" in rugby and rowing, Major General Mackay has in later life confined his recreation to shooting, horseback riding and ocean surf bathing. In younger years he was expert at racing, tennis, football, cricket and rowing. He was married to Marjorie Eveline Meredith in 1914 and is the father of one son and two daughters.

Convinced, as were many Australian war veterans, that the First World War was only "Round 1," Mackay maintained his military connections and served as peace-time officer in the Commonwealth Military Forces, 2nd Division, from 1937 until the day the call came for what he characterized as "Round 2" in 1940. He then entered the conflict as Commander of the 6th Division.

References

Nature 147:52 Ja 11 '41
N Y Sun p22 Ja 8 '41
Who's Who

MCKENNEY, EILEEN   *See* West, N.

MCMEIN, NEYSA (măc-mēn' nē'så) Jan. 25, 1890- Artist
Address: h. 131 E. 66th St, New York City

"Just as the full quality of Heifetz's playing might not focus attention completely if he were eight feet tall, so there are plenty of folk in this country who can hardly keep their eyes on the mere work of so glamorous and eventful a lady as Neysa McMein. . . Because she has often allowed her pastels to be reproduced by thrifty processes that drain them of half their color and character; because she will cheerfully draw for a department store or a soapmaker; because of the newspaper reports of her judging beauties at Coney Island, or playing tunes or singing for wounded soldiers, or opening a new movie house in Toronto, or swimming impromptu in the Marne, she arouses suspicions either that she lacks the apocryphal virtue called dignity (which is quite true) or is a schemer for publicity (which is not true at all)—because of these things it is sometimes too hastily assumed that she can't be a serious and important artist."

Her good friend, Alexander Woollcott (see sketch this issue), has written this about Neysa McMein, whose soft-colored, glowing pastel portraits of women and children are familiar to and loved by many readers of leading women's magazines in this country. As a matter of fact, Miss McMein is one of the highest paid woman artists in America today. During 1937, while she was under exclusive contract to *McCall's,* she received, for instance, $2,500 per cover drawing. But, as Mr. Woollcott notes, she is generous to a degree, and readers of the New York *Times* will recall her vivid drawings of suffering, poverty-stricken women and babies donated for that paper's annual "One Hundred Neediest Cases" feature at Christmas time.

Neysa McMein was born in Quincy, Illinois, the daughter of Harry Moran and Isabelle Lee (Parker) McMein, January 25, 1890; and after her graduation from the local high school went to study at the Chicago Art Institute. She began her career by trying her hand at fashion drawings. During the First World War she made war posters, staged entertainments for the American soldiers and lectured in France. She came to New York as Marjorie Moran McMein, of Quincy, Illinois, but "docilely changed her name because some seeress had assured her in sibylline accents that it would bring her luck." During the First World War she was commissioned to make 14 war posters for France and the United States. She was a Y. M. C. A. entertainment lecturer in France in 1918.

In 1923 she married John Gordon Baragwanath, noted mining engineer and writer of adventure stories. The couple have one daughter, one English sheep dog and several cats—Miss McMein adores cats—one of which has seven toes on each foot.

The artist early in her career became well-known for her covers for the *Woman's Home Companion, Saturday Evening Post, McClure's* and other magazines. She was the first artist invited to the White House to paint portraits of President Harding and President Hoover. She has done portraits, in oil, of Ralph Barton, Janet Flanner, Dorothy Parker and other well-known personages, as well as a series of paintings of America's famous women, including Anne Lindbergh, Katharine Cornell (see sketch this issue), Edna St. Vincent Millay, Dorothy Thompson and Helen Hayes. She has never, however, been able to make a self-portrait.

But other artists have found her as lovely to look at as many of her own pastel drawings. The chief characteristics of her work, vitality and honesty, derive from her own personality. Her gifts of natural charm and sympathy draw to her studio in New York men and women prominent in the literary, artistic and social worlds. "She has made a small town of New York," one has said; and, "if you loiter in Neysa McMein's studio, the world will drift in and out."

It is a big, happy-go-lucky place, that studio, according to all descriptions. "The spot itself is a bleak, high-ceilinged room furnished by the processes of haphazard accumulation. Its decorations range from a Briggs strip, torn out of the morning paper and pinned askew on the wall, to a famous original, respectfully framed." There was a vivid shawl, a gift from the late David Belasco; or a stretch of gay tapestry bought in Paris. The "population" may consist of F. P. Adams, Bob Benchley (see sketches this issue), Irving Berlin, Marc Connelly, Edna Ferber or Charlie Chaplin, among others. Miss McMein works at her easel while they drift in and out, or play her piano, or hold heated discussions.

"She is beautiful, grave and slightly soiled. Her apron is a shabby, streaked remnant of a once neat garment. Her fair hair, all awry, is discolored from an endless drizzle of pastel dust. Her face is smooched with it. She

Hal Phyfe

NEYSA MCMEIN

itches to edge one of the pianists to the floor and join the concert herself. The poker game tempts her. But it is not until the daylight has dwindled to dusk that she comes wandering around the easel and drops into a chair, dog-tired but sociable. Indeed, she brings to a party the kind of wholehearted laughter for which your true comedian will work till he drops. Few persons can tell a story better, but unlike so many who have that gift, she can listen, too. She listens with all her might . . . which is half the art of acting, and almost the whole secret of good manners." Because of her hobbies, cats—and people—Miss McMein doesn't have much time, hard-working artist that she is, to do much with active games or sports. She is said, however, to be an expert croquet player, and has recently taken up bowling. In politics she is a Republican. She is one of those persons "to whom the most bizarre and nightmarish things are always happening." This is because, as Mr. Woollcott says of her, she has one secret: "an insatiable, childlike appetite for life."

References

Collier's 91 :24+ D 31 '32 por
Lit Digest 116 :11 O 14 '33 por
American Women
Birchman, W. Faces and Facts 1937
Who's Who in America
Who's Who in American Art
Woollcott, A. Enchanted Aisles p33-8
 1924

MCNAMARA, JAMES BARNABAS (măk'nǎ-mä'rȧ) 1882(?)—Mar. 8, 1941 Labor agent serving a life sentence for the 1910 bombing of the Los Angeles Times Building in which 21 persons were killed; died in prison; the crime was one of the most spectacular events in the history of labor troubles

MCNAMARA, JAMES BARNABAS—
Continued

in the United States; was arrested with his brother John, who served a 15-year sentence; they retained the late Clarence Darrow as defense counsel; both were befriended by the late Eugene V. Debs, the Socialist leader.

References

Cur Lit 50:569-75 Je '11
Lit Digest 44:3-4 Ja 6 '12
Survey 27:1339-40 D 9 '11

Obituaries

N Y Times p38 Mr 9 '41

MACVEAGH, LINCOLN (măk-vā′) Oct. 1, 1890- Diplomat; author

Address: b. American Legation, Reykjavik, Iceland; h. New Canaan, Conn.

When in August 1941 the nomination of lean, gray-haired, scholarly Lincoln MacVeagh as the first United States Minister to Iceland (the United States had been previously represented only by a consul) was approved by the Senate, someone commented that since Iceland was rich in sagas a scholar should be welcomed in Reykjavik. Mr. MacVeagh, who from 1933 to 1941 served as Envoy Extraordinary and Minister Plenipotentiary to Greece, is in any case likely to make himself welcome wherever he goes.

A member of the Society of Mayflower Descendants, he was born on October 1, 1890 in Narragansett Pier, Rhode Island, the son of the onetime Ambassador to Japan, Charles MacVeagh, and Fanny Davenport (Rogers) MacVeagh. When he was 13 he went to Groton, from which he was graduated in 1909, taking the Greek prize in his graduating year, and then went on to Harvard. There he first became acquainted with members of the Roosevelt family, was elected to Phi Beta Kappa,

LINCOLN MACVEAGH

and in 1913 was graduated *magna cum laude* in philosophy. For the next year he studied languages at the Sorbonne in Paris.

Young MacVeagh's first position had been as secretary to the director of the Boston Art Museum while he was still in college. Now, when he returned to the United States, he spent a year with the United States Steel Products Company before finding a job in publishing, the field in which he was interested. From 1915 to 1917, until America's entrance into the First World War interrupted his career, he was with Henry Holt and Company; then he enlisted in the Army, marrying Margaret Charlton Lewis of New York City in August 1917 before being sent to France. There he saw active service as a first lieutenant, later as a captain and major, and was cited by General Pershing "for exceptionally meritorious and conspicuous services." He returned to his position with Henry Holt and was with that firm until, in 1923, he set up his own publishing house, the Dial Press, Incorporated.

From 1923 to 1933, as president of the Dial Press, MacVeagh kept as his hobby the study of ancient and modern Greece. He was often seen commuting to his office from his Connecticut home, carrying a volume of Homer in the original Greek. No more suitable appointment could have been made than President Roosevelt's in 1933. When the United States' new Minister to Greece presented his credentials he immediately made himself *persona grata* to the Greek Government by speaking out informally in Greek.

Leaving his white legation office across the street from the cypress trees of the Royal Gardens in Athens, MacVeagh made frequent exploratory trips through the country during his eight years in Greece. It is reported that he gained knowledge of more parts of the country than any one of its inhabitants, covering mountain trails by donkey-back and on foot, passing at least one night in nearly every town. He also conducted archeological excavations beneath the eastern face of Acropolis Hill in Athens itself, discovering many missing fragments of pottery which he contributed to the Athens National Museum. He was made an honorary fellow of the Archeological Society of Athens.

A talented writer (his dispatches to Washington were classics in the State Department files because of their humor), the United States Minister to Greece eventually collaborated with his wife in writing a book. *Greek Journey* (1937) was a story for children telling about a trip through modern Greece in a Ford, with old Greek legends recounted all along the way. The New York *Times* reviewer commented: "This is a pleasant odyssey, lacking, perhaps, a certain spark in the narration, yet full of the color and beauty that is Greece."

When in 1940 war broke through the borders of his adopted country, it put an end to archeological expeditions and odysseys. Instead MacVeagh worked night and day to protect American lives and property. In April 1941 he followed the Greek Government to

Crete, but was called home by the State Department for "consultation" not long afterward. For five weeks he was forced by the Germans to stay in Athens while the attack on Crete was being prepared; then, on June 5, he, his wife and his daughter, Margaret Ewen, were finally permitted to leave Greece by way of Berlin. It was August before they stepped off a ship onto United States soil.

Interviewed immediately after landing, Mac-Veagh reported that the spirit of Greece was "magnificent." "I'm proud of that country," he said. "They are not whimpering a bit. They are defeated but unconquered." He told of a food situation verging on famine because of looting by the Germans, of remnants of the Greek Army wandering the country in beggary, of a total disruption of communications, but also of an anti-Nazi feeling so strong that the Greeks openly cheered the R. A. F. from streets and rooftops.

He is a man of average build, with a large, strong face, wavy hair and a cultivated New England voice. Lincoln MacVeagh is a Democrat and an Episcopalian, a member of the Stewart Society of Edinburgh and of the 80th Division Veterans Association, and a member of the Harvard, Century, University and P. E. N. Clubs.

References

N Y Post p3 Jl 21 '41 por
N Y Times p6 Ag 1 '41 por
N Y World-Telegram p1, 5 Jl 21 '41 por
Pub W 123:1956 Je 17 '33 por
U S News 9:36-7 N 8 '40 por
Who's Who in America

MAILHOUSE, MAX Feb. 5, 1857—Oct. 19, 1941 Neurologist; clinical professor of neurology at the Yale Medical School from 1907 to 1920; in 1930 chairman of a committee to study noise abatement in New Haven; had estimated that the effect of noises on nervous systems caused the nation a loss of $5,000,000 a week.

References

American Medical Directory
Who's Who in America
Who's Who in American Jewry

Obituaries

N Y Times p18 O 20 '41

MAISKY, IVAN (MIKHAILOVICH) (mĭs′kê) Jan. 19, 1884- Soviet Ambassador to Great Britain

Address: Embassy of the U. S. S. R., 13 Kensington Palace Gardens, London, W. 8, England

Soviet Ambassador to Great Britain since 1933, Ivan Mikhailovich Maisky is used to being a barometer for Anglo-Russian relations. Often a look around the ballroom of the Soviet Embassy during one of his receptions at which caviar and champagne are lavishly served has been sufficient to show how British officialdom feels toward his country. There

Sovfoto

IVAN MAISKY

have been times when the reception room was almost empty—and one knew that harsh words were being spoken elsewhere; there was the amazing occasion in 1939, with the possibility of an Anglo-Russian pact looming large in many minds and a British mission on its leisurely way to Moscow, when Prime Minister Neville Chamberlain himself came to partake graciously of the caviar. But perhaps never has the Soviet Embassy's stock stood so high as after June 22, 1941, and never has Maisky's role as the chief link "between these two great powers as they combine their military efforts against the common foe of Nazism" been so significant.

Comforting to the British as indicative of the Soviet Union's resolution to fight to the last was its Ambassador's pronouncement, shortly after the Nazis invaded his country: "Should Moscow fall, a catastrophe which I do not believe will occur, we will fight on, supplied by these factories and growing industries hidden in the Urals. The British have a song *It's a Long Way to Tipperary.* Well, it's a long way to the industries which will maintain the Red Army against Germany, a long hard way by air or land."

Quiet, soft-spoken Ambassador Maisky, with his grizzled Vandyke beard and smiling blue eyes, shows no external evidence of his revolutionary background. He was born in Kiriloff, Novgorod Province, Siberia, January 19, 1884, the son of an army doctor. His name at that time was Ivan Mikhailovich Lyakhovetsky; the one he now bears is assumed—a common practice among men engaged in revolutionary activities. Young Maisky became involved in these activities when he went to the University of St. Petersburg which, like many other universities of that time, was fertile ground for advanced ideas. They brought him jail and exile. In 1908, after having been expelled

MAISKY, IVAN—*Continued*

from the University and arrested, he left Russia and went to Germany. There he attended Munich University, specializing in economics.

It was while he was in Germany that he joined the Social Democratic movement. In 1912 he came to England. The story is current that he gained admission only with great difficulty. According to the immigration regulations of that time, he, as a third-class passenger, was supposed to have at least five pounds. Young Maisky had only three pounds, nineteen shillings and sixpence, and got by only because of a letter from George Tchicherin, later Russia's foreign commissar, which established him as a bona fide political refugee. For the next five years he made his living as a free-lance journalist in Fleet Street.

Came the Russian Revolution—and he went back to Russia, shed his Menshevik affiliations and became a Communist. His first post exploited his knowledge of the East—in 1919 he was made head of an expedition to explore Mongolia, and he was instrumental in helping to set up the Mongolian Republic. In 1921 he was made president of the State Planning Commission of his native Siberia. But by that time the Soviet regime was beginning to pay more attention to the impression it made abroad. It needed men like Maisky in key positions—men whose political reliability was supplemented by expert knowledge of foreign affairs and understanding of foreign mentality. In 1925, therefore, he was sent to London as counselor of the Soviet Embassy, staying there for two years. During the diplomatic career that ensued, Maisky also wrote several important books, among them *Contemporary Mongolia*, *Foreign Policy of RSFSR, 1917-1922* and *Trade Union Movement in the West*.

From 1927 to 1929 he was with the Soviet Embassy in Tokyo and from 1929 to 1932 Minister to Finland. Then he was sent back to England as Ambassador—a post that he has kept ever since. In that post he has lived through many difficult—and some disagreeable —moments, and even those who are opposed to him politically have admitted that he has handled them well. He was in Britain when the arrest of the Metro-Vickers engineers took place, precipitating an open breach between the Soviet and British Governments. He was there at the time of the Moscow trials, when a deputation sent by the General Council of the Trades Union Congress and the Executive Committee of the Labor Party visited him to register a protest. The Soviet Ambassador, while expressing his surprise at the unusual step, received the deputation with scrupulous politeness and gave explanations. And he was there throughout the period of icy coolness that descended after the signing of the Nazi-Soviet Non-Aggression Pact. During that period, devoted mainly to discussion of repatriation of some 400 Baltic seamen by the British Government, he allegedly sighed to his friends that he had adopted as his philosophy the Mongolian axiom: "This too shall pass."

Maisky has been called an "Anglophile" and has been described as belonging to the same "Western" group of leaders as Litvinov (see sketch this issue). He wholeheartedly supported Litvinov's dream of collective security and indivisible peace and in 1936 denounced the "modern philosophy of the mailed fist"; in March 1941, when Litvinov was dropped from the Central Committee, people were surprised to find Maisky one of the alternate appointees to his post. Between that time and the German invasion of Russia he also caused some mild speculation by his dickering for an Anglo-Russian trade agreement and his talks with Anthony Eden, and even before that he toured East End air raid shelters and received a hearty round of applause from the occupants. Now, with Russia in the War, he has had the pleasant but unusual experience of hearing his country toasted at a National Defense Committee luncheon.

Maisky's long stay in England has given him a profound knowledge of the British mentality, a knowledge which he has used to good advantage. He is "a good mixer," and manages to talk to people in their own language without modifying his own political attitudes. His personal relations with the Foreign Office have always been good. The Soviet Embassy in Kensington Palace Gardens, with its five-pointed star of red geraniums blazing in the center of the lawn, is efficiently run by his wife, the small, slim, fair-haired former Agnes Alexandrovna Skippin, who is a native of the village where he was born, and who gracefully performs her role of Doyenne of the Diplomatic Corps.

References

Christian Sci Mon p5 Jl 2 '41 por
Sat R 160:497 N 23 '35 por
Time 33:20 Ap 24 '39 por
Who's Who

MAKEMSON, MAUD W(ORCESTER) (măk′m-sŭn) Sept. 16, 1891- Astronomer

Address: b. Vassar College, Poughkeepsie, N. Y.

One of the Guggenheim fellowships in science for 1941 went to Maud Worcester Makemson, astronomer and chairman of the department of astronomy at Vassar College. Dr. Makemson's achievements in her particular field (culminating in a book, *The Morning Star Rises*, on Polynesian astronomy, to be published by the Yale University Press) are the more remarkable because she had little academic training and no knowledge of astronomy whatsoever prior to 1923. Before then her career had been that of a busy mother on a ranch in the Southwest who took whatever odd jobs she could find in order to help support her three growing children.

Maud Worcester was born at Center Harbor, New Hampshire on September 16, 1891, the daughter of Ira Eugene and Fannie Malvina (Davisson) Worcester. Her first introduction to astronomy, she tells us, actually came when she was a student at the Boston Girls' Latin School, but left little impression. "This was because I was extremely nearsighted and could

see only the moon and half a dozen or so
bright stars and planets. My parents had consulted an oculist when I was eight and had
been advised to postpone putting glasses on
me for as long as possible. That same winter, however, I was sent to an oculist and
the world was transformed. On the first clear
evening after the glasses were fitted my mother
took me out to look at the sky. I never look
at the starlit sky now without recapturing in
a degree at least the awe and wonder of that
first glimpse of the Milky Way glittering
across the sky brilliant with innumerable
stars."

But at the Latin School, from which she was
graduated in 1908, and during her year following at Radcliffe College, she took a classical course. "My mother wanted me to become
a novelist, and my own secret ambition, never
expressed of course, was to be married and
have children. If I had been a boy I should
have wanted to go to sea and follow in the line
of my Maine sea-faring ancestors on the
Worcester side of the family."

After her year at Radcliffe she taught
in a rural one-room school at Sharon, Connecticut. Also, before leaving the East, she
took an extension course in English composition at Boston University under Dallas Lore
Sharpe, but "experienced difficulty in finding
something interesting enough to write about."
Then, in the fall of 1911, she went with her
family to Pasadena, California.

She married Thomas Emmet Makemson of
Pasadena in 1912 (the couple are now divorced) "and commenced a career of raising
cows, chickens and children." A drought in
Southern California drove the young couple
first to the Imperial Valley, then to the Salt
River Valley of Arizona. There were no
books available to her during these first five
years except a copy of *The Winning of Barbara Worth* loaned by a neighbor; but Mrs.
Makemson managed to write two stories,
which were published in the *Arizona Magazine.*

In 1917 they moved to Tombstone Canyon
in Bisbee, an Arizona mining town. There
the necessity to augment the family income,
and the "urge to do something constructive in
the world," led Mrs. Makemson to find small
jobs she could do at home, such as tutoring
in Latin, making bread, crocheting lace and
hemming sheets for neighbors. "By the time
my third child was born in September 1917 I
had determined to get a regular job. My
mother had come to stay with me so that I
could leave the children. I was fortunate
enough to find something at once in the office
of the Bisbee *Review.* My duties were to
read proof, answer the telephone and look
after the office from 6 p. m. to 2 a. m.; but
in addition I was to take 'society' news over
the telephone and write up fashions one day a
week. For this I was to be paid space rates,
but the editor found it advisable to pay me
a straight salary when he saw the extent of
my first page."

When her husband joined the Marine Corps
in 1918 she began a regular reporting job on
the Arizona *Gazette* at Phoenix. Then, while

trying to find some way of earning a living
and yet being with the children, "an event
occurred which had a profound influence on
my life." This was in 1921, when she chanced
to see a remarkable display of the aurora
borealis in the desert north of Phoenix, coincidentally with a news report of a group of
large spots on the sun. Her scientific curiosity aroused, she began reading popular books
on astronomy. Next, ambitious to take an

Margaret DeM. Brown

MAUD W. MAKEMSON

extension course in astronomy at the University of California, she gave up her job in
Phoenix and joined her parents in Southern
California. There she taught fourth grade
for a while; and the following year she taught
also at Palmdale near her father's ranch,
taking a correspondence course in trigonometry.

In the summer of 1923, following a trip with
a Los Angeles astronomy class to Mt. Wilson
Observatory, her course was set. She arrived at Berkeley the moment morning classes
started, and plunged into work. In 1925 (at
the age of 34) she received her B. A. degree
at the University of California; and in 1930
she acquired her Ph. D., becoming an instructor in astronomy. After teaching mathematics and astronomy at Rollins College, Florida (1931-32), she became a professor of
astronomy at Vassar, where she now holds
her position as chairman of the department.

During the summer of 1935 Dr. Makemson
worked at the Bishop Museum in Honolulu,
investigating Polynesian astronomy. She has
also written a number of research articles
that have appeared in the *Astronomical Journal, Popular Astronomy, Sky, The American
Anthropologist,* etc. And in 1936 she and
her children excavated at the Pueblo of Ki-
nishba on the Apache Reservation with the

MAKEMSON, MAUD W.—*Continued*
expedition from the University of Arizona
under Dr. Byron Cummings.

Her daughter Lavon, educated in archeology
at the University of Arizona, is married and
the mother of two children. Her son Donald
teaches history at the University of California,
is the author of several articles on the Apaches
of the Southwest and an ensign in the Naval
Reserve. Harris, the younger son, is now a
California undergraduate and also interested
in writing.

Tall, energetic, blue-eyed, proud of, the
work of her children, whose interests she
shares, Dr. Makemson says her hobbies are
American Indians and exploring out-of-the-
way places in the Southwest and Mexico. In
politics she is a Socialist. She plans to spend
the year of her Guggenheim fellowship working at the Peabody Museum at Harvard University, "where all needed materials are close
at hand."

References

American Men of Science
American Women

MALINOWSKI, BRONISLAW (măl'ĭ-
nō'skê brô-nê'slàv) Apr. 7, 1884- Anthropologist

Address: b. Yale University, New Haven,
Conn; h. 6 Oppidans Rd, London, N. W. 3,
England; 261 Canner St, New Haven, Conn.

"Culture is nothing but the organized behavior of man." That is the central thesis of
the work of Dr. Bronislaw Malinowski, universally regarded as the father of the Functional School of anthropology. Malinowski,
who since 1927 has been professor of anthropology at the University of London, was in 1941
a visiting professor at Yale. He is a popular
lecturer. Famous for his wit, "brilliant, convincing and interesting even to a lay person,"
he puts particular emphasis on the application
of the most archaic experience of mankind to
the analysis of modern world problems. He
explores primitive magic to throw light on
modern totalitarian propaganda. He explores
savage society in order better to explain everything from nationalism and the persecution of
minorities to modern marriage, family and sex
relationships.

"Cultural anthropology can and must provide
the foundations of the social sciences," he
says, and at the same time "scientific anthropology . . . must work on the foundations laid
down by biology and physiology; it must work
hand in hand with the psychologist; and it
must learn as much as it can learn from the
student of environment, the geographer." It
must "approach primitive culture from the
angle of politics and economics, theory of religion and jurisprudence." These things may
be less "amusing to speak about or even to
listen to" than "head-hunting, juicy stories
about orgiastic ritual, somewhat shocking
forms of primitive marriage, obscene mutila-
tions and mysterious masked dances," but
they are scientifically more relevant.

In short, Malinowski regards as his real
contribution to anthropology and other social
and humanistic studies the attempt to develop
a scientific theory of culture. This he bases
on such principles: Science must study first
and foremost *what is* and later only concern
itself with *what might have been*. Science is
the cross-fertilization of experience and theory; the extraction from experiment, observation and experience of general rules with
a predictive value. In the science of man,
more particularly, it is necessary to realize
that human beings act either under the impulse
of animal drives or else strive for culturally
determined values guided by reason, ambition
and belief. Implements, customs and ideas survive or diffuse only because they are in some
way directly or indirectly useful, because they
satisfy some needs, physiological, social or
integrative. History is a sieve through which
only that which is vital and functioning, that
is, need-satisfying, passes and remains. What
is relevant in history can always be found
surviving in memory, in legends, in traditional
values and in mythologies. Malinowski thus
tries to build up an anthropology of live men
and women and not of marionettes playing
about with useless antiquities or non-function-
ally diffused "traits" and "trait complexes"
for the benefit of the reconstructing antiquarian. He does not deny either evolution or
diffusion. He fully accepts the concept of
survival and of borrowing. He maintains only
that first and foremost we must understand
why certain objects, customs, and ideas survive or diffuse, while others do not. Survival
and diffusion alike, he would argue, run always on lines of functional vitality.

The scientific principles, their application to
modern life, and the understanding of "the
savagery of modern civilization in the light
of the civilizations of savages," Malinowski has
embodied in his own field work and has also
tried to stimulate in the work of his numerous
pupils. The practical application of anthropology to colonial affairs he was able to implement through his association with the International Institute for the Study of African
Languages and Culture, established in London
in 1928. This institute organized extensive
field work in Africa, and developed a collaboration between administrators, missionaries, agricultural and medical experts and students
of native African education, jurisprudence, economics and religion.

Born in Poland on April 7, 1884, the parents
of Bronislaw Malinowski were *szlachta*—
landed gentry and nobility. (He has dropped
the use of his title of Count.) He attended
King Jan Sobieski Public School, then the
University at Kraków, where he took his
Ph. D. in physics and mathematics in 1908
with the highest honors in the Austrian Empire. He went then for two years to Leipsig,
where he engaged in original research in
Wilhelm Ostwald's laboratory of physical
chemistry, but also came under the influence
of the veteran psychologist Wundt, who at
that time was mostly interested in folk-psychol-
ogy, that is, anthropology. After having read

Frazer's *Golden Bough,* Malinowski decided to go to England. In 1914 he moved to London and worked at the British Museum and also at the London School of Economics, where he moved within the orbit of such famous scholars and thinkers as J. G. Frazer, Prince Kropotkin, Havelock Ellis, Hobhouse, E. Westermarck and Graham Wallas. In 1914 he set out on his first field expedition—with the Robert Mond Anthropological Expedition to New Guinea and North West Melanesia.

He didn't return to Europe until 1920. But when he returned to England it was with a wife—Elsie Rosaline Masson, daughter *of* the well known chemist and university professor Sir David Masson—whom he had married in 1919. (She died in 1935, leaving him three daughters. In June 1940 he married Anna Valetta Hayman-Joyce, sister of Brigadier Hayman-Joyce of the British General Staff. Mrs. A. V. Malinowska paints and exhibits—Paris, London, New York—under the nom de plume Valetta Swann.)

Studies which were published during these years of research in the field include *Primitive Religion and Social Differentiation* (in Polish, 1915); "The Natives of Mailu," in *Transactions of the Royal Society of South Australia* (1915); and "Baloma: the Spirits of the Dead in the Trobriand Islands," in the *Journal of the Royal Anthropological Institute* (1916). Since that time the Boston *Evening Transcript* has said of Dr. Malinowski: "His inquiry into the Kula system and his studies of the Trobrianders led to most that is significant in the modern development of social anthropology." For one thing, his experiences with primitive religion and magic convinced him that they both have highly useful psychological and social functions and that magic, particularly, is carried out on the principle that it "helps those who help themselves." As for religion, it is "the main integrative system of every civilization, primitive and developed alike; it constitutes the very foundation of culture."

It was 1924 when Dr. Malinowski became a Reader (a title which corresponds to that of associate professor in America) in social anthropology at the University of London; 1927 when he took the chair of anthropology, tenable at the London School of Economics. In the meanwhile, in 1926, he came for the first time to the United States as a guest of the Laura Spelman Memorial, traveled around the continent, visited Mexico, the Pueblo Indians of Arizona, and worked at the summer school of the University of California at Berkeley. In 1934 he made a trip to South and East Africa, doing survey work among the Bantu tribes with exotically colorful names— the Swazi, the Bemba, the Chagga, the Bantu Kavirondo. By the time he revisited the United States as Messenger lecturer at Cornell University in 1933 he was known not only as the author of books that have been translated into such diverse languages as Chinese, French, Spanish, Polish, Italian and German, the author of the *Encyclopaedia Britannica's* sec-

tion on marriage, kinship and social anthropology and of innumerable scientific monographs and articles, but as one of the greatest minds in the scientific world.

At the Harvard Tercentenary in 1936 delegates from 42 countries were present. It was Bronislaw Malinowski who represented the University of London and the Polish Academy, and President Conant (see sketch this issue) conferred an honorary D. Sc. degree upon him, citing him as "an anthropological explorer who initiated a new movement for the study of the gregarious habits of the

Esther Henderson

BRONISLAW MALINOWSKI

human race." Malinowski himself read a paper on culture in which he incidentally took his listeners on a world tour of primitive peoples—from the Masai to the Eskimos. He tried to show that there *can* be a genuine "science of culture"—that the chief task of anthropology is to search for determinism in the broadest and most fundamental principles of human behavior by reducing even the strangest customs and institutions to universally human and familiar elements. He heaped particular scorn on the concept of culture "as the self-revelation of an immanent Genius or Deity," a concept which, he said, reached its peak in Hegel's Historical Idealism and achieved its full practical application with the coming of "the latest incarnation of the Absolute"—Adolf Hitler. He felt that such distinguished anthropologists as Ruth Benedict (see sketch this issue), Franz Boas and Margaret Mead (see sketches 1940 Annual) exhibited certain dangerous tendencies toward mysticism or a concept of the "tribal genius," leaving no room for scientific analysis.

On that occasion Malinowski also delivered the oration at the Tercentenary Exercises of the Harvard Chapter of the Phi Beta Kappa Society. His oration, whose subject was war,

MALINOWSKI, BRONISLAW—*Cont.*

was later published in the *Atlantic Monthly* (December 1936), and some of the statements made in it are important even today when the Second World War is ravaging the world. Large audiences were attracted to his public lectures at the Symposium, and the press proclaimed him "one of the four greatest minds today."

The United States is only one of the many countries which have so honored him, however. In 1930 he became a corresponding member of the Polish Academy of Science (promoted in 1938 to full membership); in 1932 correspondent of the Italian Committee for the Study of Population Problems; in 1933 a member of the Royal Academy of Science of The Netherlands; in 1936 an honorary member of the Royal Society of New Zealand. In 1936, too, he lectured at the Oslo Institute for the Comparative Study of Cultures.

Malinowski crossed the Atlantic in the autumn of 1938 for the last time, not as an émigré, but by free choice, to spend his sabbatical year in this country. He insists, "I came here of my free volition not to teach but to learn, not to earn but to enjoy the climate, physical and spiritual, of this country which I had liked from my first visit in 1926." He naturally went to Arizona and spent the winter months of 1938-39 at Tucson, where he was studying incidentally the uprooted community of Yaqui Indians, whose larger settlements he visited on a trip to Sonora, Mexico. He spent part of the summer of 1939 and the two summer vacations of 1940 and 1941 in Mexico, where, late in 1941, he is engaged in systematic community studies in the state of Oaxaca. He also visited the Republic of Cuba several times, and he has a great many personal friends among the outstanding members of the Latin-American intelligentsia. His Spanish is good enough for lecturing and writing, several of his articles having appeared in Latin-American scientific journals and magazines.

When, in August 1939, Dr. Malinowski was preparing to return and resume his teaching duties in London, the War broke out, and he was advised from England to remain in the United States "for the duration." "I had already booked my cabin on the *Normandie* for September 13, an unlucky date (I have always been afraid of the number 13, and of sailing on a Friday). Since then the *Normandie* has been chained to her dock, and I have remained chained at Yale, a place which I greatly enjoy and maybe shall not leave for the rest of my natural existence. This is the reason why I have taken up my half-ethnographic, half-sociological study in Mexico, so as not to be a specialist in all ethnographies except that of the New World."

People who have never read *The Family Among Australian Aborigines* (1913); *Argonauts of the Western Pacific* (1922); *Crime and Custom in Savage Society* (1926); or *Coral Gardens and Their Magic* (1935) nevertheless regard Dr. Malinowski as an oracle

after listening to him for an hour. One of the most frequent questions they ask is: "Is primitive man an individualist or a communist?" Malinowski, who says that anthropology can give opinions as to the workings of institutions of property but not as to "that vague entity, human nature," is probably a little tired of answering that one. Other things he cannot repeat too often, however, particularly in these days: that it is "fallacious to regard war as a necessary result of man's biological nature"; yet that "peace is not a negative state, a mere absence of fighting." He says: "If we want to prevent war we must replace the part which it plays by a powerful and effective machinery which would take over some of its functions . . . an international superstate."

There are two distinctions which Malinowski values above all others. The first is a reference in the *New Yorker*—the phrase, "the great Malinowski." "This," says Malinowski, "is one of the *New Yorker's* best jokes." The other highly appreciated distinction is the extensive attack launched against him by the official Gauleiters of German ethnology. (Incidentally, Dr Malinowski has also been frontally attacked in a book published in the U. S. S. R., *The Intelligentsia of Great Britain*.)

A slender, scholarly-looking man, with an impressive dome of a forehead, Dr. Malinowski confesses that there are some customs and institutions he still can't understand. Although he has lived among semi-savage Carpathian mountaineers and among Baltic barons, has moved from Poland to North Africa and from the Canary Islands to North Germany and France, and is a sophisticate who finds nothing really mysterious about cannibalism, he is still both puzzled and repelled by golf, hara-kiri, the collecting of pickled heads and football.

References

Am Anthrop 35:401 '33; 39:275-90 Ap '37
N Y Times VII p7+ O 12 '41 por
Newsweek 8:20 S 19 '36
Author's and Writer's Who's Who
Cairns, H. Law and the Social Sciences 1935
Lowie, R. H. The History of Ethnological Theory p230-52 1937
Mirskiy, D. P. The Intelligentsia of Great Britain 1935
Who's Who
Who's Who in America
Who's Who in Central and East-Europe

MALLORY, F(RANK) B(URR) Nov. 12, 1862—Sept. 27, 1941 Pathologist; associated with the Harvard Medical School since 1890, first as assistant in histology, later as assistant, associate, and, from 1928 until his retirement in 1932, full professor of pathology; isolator and discoverer of the scarlet fever bacillus and contributor of knowledge about other infectious diseases; head of the Institute of Pathology at the Boston City Hospital from

1897 through 1932; established and edited for 15 years the *American Journal of Pathology* and was an organizer of the American Society of Pathologists and Bacteriologists.

References

> American Medical Directory
> American Men of Science
> Leaders in Education 1941
> Who's Who in America
> Who's Who in the East

Obituaries

> N Y Times p17 S 29 '41

MANN, TOM Apr. 15, 1856—Mar. 13, 1941 Veteran British labor leader who for more than 50 years was one of the most active Left-wing labor agitators in England; was frequently in trouble with the authorities; prominent in trade unionism, he gained a world-wide reputation in 1889 as one of the triumvirate staging a great dock strike; began as a Socialist in the '80s and ended as a Communist.

References

> Labour Mo 18:221-6 Ap '36
> Lit Digest 116:11 O 21 '33 por
> Newsweek 2:17 O 14 '33 por
> Author's and Writer's Who's Who
> Torr, D. Tom Mann pam 1936
> Who's Who

Obituaries

> N Y Times p21 Mr 14 '41

MARCIAL-DORADO, CAROLINA (mär-syäl′-dô-rä′dô) 1889—July 25, 1941 Professor of Spanish and head of the Spanish Department at Barnard College; had also taught at Bryn Mawr College, Wellesley and other colleges and universities; acted as Spanish editor for Ginn & Company from 1917 until 1924; was author of textbooks; twice decorated by the late King Alfonso of Spain for her efforts in behalf of that country.

References

> American Women
> Who's Who in America
> Who's Who in New York

Obituaries

> N Y Times p15 Jl 16 '41

MARGE *See* Damerel, D.

MARGESSON, DAVID (mär′jĕ-sŭn) 1890- British Secretary of State for War
Address: h. Boddington Manor, Byfield, Northants, England

The announcement (December 23, 1940) that tall, dark-skinned Captain David Margesson would occupy the post in the British War Office formerly filled by Anthony Eden came as a surprise to many, in spite of the fact that ambitious Captain Margesson had been men-

DAVID MARGESSON

tioned for Cabinet posts before. Since 1931 he had been chief Government whip, the martinet of the Conservative Party. It was he who took new Tory members of the House of Commons aside and gave them lectures on Party regularity, who always advised on and often vetoed appointments, who was supposed to have kept a black book of Conservative "rebels" who swerved even a little from the Party line. Churchill's name as well as Eden's must have occupied space in Captain Margesson's black book at times (even though since the spring of 1940 Margesson has been Churchill's "top sergeant," responsible for the discipline of the entire House of Commons), and it seemed probable that his appointment would be severely criticized by other members who still rated an entry there. One of them had attacked him openly in the House not so long before. It was also true, however, that Margesson's reputation for "reaction and autocracy" had never hurt his popularity with the rank and file of Conservatives in the House, who still held an overwhelming majority.

Born in 1890, Captain Margesson is the son of Sir Mortimer and the Lady Isabel Margesson, was educated at Harrow and at Cambridge, and then went to the United States. He was contemplating a business career there when the First World War broke out. Returning to England, he served from 1915 to 1918 as an adjutant with the 11th Hussars and earned the Military Cross. Years later he replied to a lady who wanted to know how he managed the supporters of the Government: "You must remember I was once adjutant of a cavalry regiment." It was 1922 when he was first elected to the House of Commons from the Upton Division of West Ham and until 1923 he also served as parliamentary private secretary to the Right Honorable Sir C. A. Montague Barlow, then Minister of Labor.

MARGESSON, DAVID—*Continued*

The following year Margesson was returned from Rugby, and in November of that year he became Conservative and assistant Government whip. From 1926 to 1929 and for a short period during 1931 he was junior lord of the Treasury; since 1931, when the first National Government was formed, he has been not only Government chief whip but parliamentary secretary to the Treasury; and in 1933 he became a Privy Councillor.

During Chamberlain's term as Prime Minister, Captain Margesson was known as his closest confidant, with all junior appointments under his control. The appointments were so widespread that critics claimed half the Tories in Parliament held Government positions! In March 1940 the London *Evening Standard* joined the *Manchester Guardian* in criticizing Margesson's control over the House: "Arguments are cut short by the crack of a whip. Like Disraeli, Captain Margesson believes that a majority is always the best repartee. . . It is intolerable that members should spend long hours debating the merits of, say, the appointment of an Economics Minister, only to discover at the end that the issue has been settled before the debate even began." The *Standard* also rejoiced over the fact that during wartime Captain Margesson could no longer create voting constituency trouble. "That weapon is now broken in Captain Margesson's hand. He is a Himmler [see sketch this issue] without his castor oil. This is the moment for revenge," it gloated, not many months before Captain Margesson received his present high Cabinet post.

As Secretary of State for War Captain Margesson received much favorable publicity when he cracked down on an Army officer for saying lower and middle class boys failed to make good officers. After the German invasion of the Soviet Union, however, some Laborites began to agitate for his removal on the grounds that he represented the forces of appeasement—or, at least, of anti-Soviet feeling—in the Government.

In 1916 Captain Margesson married Frances Leggett of New York; there are two daughters and a son. He is a member of London's swank Carlton and Turf Clubs. One of his daughters, Janet, of totally different political sympathies, was to have represented a British youth organization at the American Youth Congress in June 1941, but was unable to attend.

References

N Y Herald Tribune X p12+ F 23 '41
   il por
N Y Times p1, 4 D 23 '40 por
Time 35:21 Ap 8 '40 por
Who's Who

MARSH, REGINALD   Mar. 14, 1898-
American artist

Address: b. 1 Union Sq, New York City; h. 4 E. 12th St, New York City

Reginald Marsh likes the people on the wrong side of the track—burlesque girls, whom he paints with "sensual tenderness and deep appreciation"; Bowery bums; the crowds that throng Coney Island beaches; New York's working girls, swinging their husky legs, charging down the street in droves to the movies, pressing into the subways, togged out in 14th Street finery. Frequently critics call him "the Hogarth of Manhattan" and praise his observations of the thousands of typical metropolitan sights and sounds in which "you can hear the people jabber, hear the scuffling feet on the sidewalk, the clatter of passing vehicles." As Harry Salpeter says: "I venture the belief that should New York be razed to the ground at some future date and become a vast sheep meadow, the crowded tumultuous pictures of Marsh would tell our descendants more about the way in which their ancestor city dwellers lived, worked and played than lies in the power of any set of documents and newsprint that might be cracked open out of the ruined cornerstone of the Empire State Building."

In the summer heat, when the artists move en masse out to Connecticut or Maine, Marsh wanders around the city, sketchbook in hand, jotting down the materials for hundreds of pictures. Or he stands at the window of his studio on Union Square and looks down on its crowds through binoculars. There are some who say he looks through lenses distorted for satirical purposes and the result is caricature; others, that his feeling for Manhattan is neither over-sentimental nor over-sophisticated; still others, that there is "astonishing tenderness and understanding" in his depictions of the humbler class of New York shop girls. Marsh himself doesn't join the discussions, for he is the kind of man who doesn't talk much about his art or about anything else. "A quiet and self-contained monomaniac," his only concern is getting down what he sees and feels.

He sets it down mainly in large water colors and tempera because he likes to work rapidly. Once a sketch has been made, it is put into a projector and projected onto a large sheet of paper. With pencil Marsh then draws over the image the few guide lines desired as a layout for his painting. Sometimes the figure is modeled in Chinese ink or ivory black and the colors assembled over this underpainting. But whether Marsh is doing an etching, an oil, a water color or a tempera, the result comes out fast. There are some critics who feel that if he did half as much work he would do twice as well.

This artist who is said to look like a Swede not long off the boat and to talk, in his talkative moments, like a Hemingway character, actually is a product of some of America's better schools and the son of Fred Dana Marsh, exhibitor in the French Salon, painter of lovely ladies and associate member of the National Academy at 31. His mother, Alice (Randall) Marsh, was an artist, too, who studied under Frank Vincent Dumond in the early '90s and painted miniatures.

She and her husband were living in Paris when Reginald was born in an apartment house where the Café du Dôme now stands. Two years later, however, the family moved to Nutley, New Jersey, and it was there that Reginald, not yet three, produced his first drawing—a picture of a locomotive influenced, it is said, by his father's academic style. He kept drawing while attending various schools, including Lawrenceville, and he continued to draw after he entered Yale in the class of 1920. It was there that he painted his first, and last, still life. It was there, too, that he decided on a career.

His father had tried to discourage him from becoming an artist, but Reginald compromised on drawings for the Yale *Record*. Their reception encouraged him to take up illustrating as a profession, and he left Yale for New York and the magazines. Bit by bit he got a foothold in newspaper and magazine illustrating and cartooning (some people still scornfully call him an "illustrator"), and by 1921 he was doing work for *Vanity Fair* and soon after for *Harper's Bazaar*. Some of the people at *Harper's Bazaar* steered him to John Murray Anderson, producer of the *Greenwich Village Follies*, who hired him to design theatre curtains for several productions. Later he collaborated with Robert Edmond Jones and Cleon Throckmorton in designing curtains and settings for the hit *Fashion*, which the Provincetown Players presented in 1923 and 1924. He also did a curtain for Otis Skinner's *Sancho Panza*, another for John Murray Anderson's *Almanac,* and a number of curtains and settings for Paramount-Publix productions and Gluck-Sandor's Dance Center.

Meanwhile he had a steady position as well. In 1922 the New York *Daily News* gave him a three years' contract under the impression that they would be able to make him into another W. E. Hill. After four months in which they got nowhere with this ambition and couldn't find much for him to do, they set him to work reporting music halls and night clubs in cartoons. Marsh loved the work: he got around New York; he was drawing; and he even had time to try painting.

He had been studying art off and on at the Art Students League, for a while under John Sloan. It was there that he met his first wife, Betty Burroughs, a sculptor and daughter of the late Bryson Burroughs, painter and curator of painting at the Metropolitan Museum. (His present wife, Felicia Meyer, had a famous father, too: Herbert Meyer, the landscape painter.) In 1925 he continued his studies in Europe, where he concentrated on the Old Masters. He returned to the United States to take up sketching again, much of it for the *New Yorker*. At the same time, though, he did start painting the landscape around Flushing, Long Island and water colors of much of New York State. Some of the hundreds of pictures that resulted were shown at the Weyhe, Valentine and Marie Sterner Galleries.

In 1927 Kenneth Hayes Miller, who admired his water colors and drawings while at the same time deploring the fact that Marsh had never painted a picture, took him into his class

REGINALD MARSH

at the Art Students League for four or five months to study the principles of painting. With this as a basis Marsh in 1928 again went to Europe and spent months making copies of Rubens, Delacroix, Rembrandt, Titian and the other Masters. These are the ones that count, he feels, and impressionism, post-impressionism, abstractionism and modern streamlined experimentation have brought confusion into contemporary art.

Back in the United States again in 1929, Marsh rented a studio on Union Square and began to paint the New York scene. He experimented with various media, frequently under Miller's tutelage, and discovered that tempera was best suited to his painting temperament. In eight months he had prepared enough paintings to give his first full-sized exhibition at the Rehn Galleries, which included his first oils. The next year, in 1931, there was another exhibition of his work, and many others have been held at the Rehn Galleries since then.

During these years critical comment has, of course, been varied. In 1933 Henry McBride of the *Sun* ecstatically commented that he should be voted a Pulitzer Prize for "the best exhibition of the year," while of the same showing another critic said that his drawing, though skillful and spontaneous, was at times confused and negligent, and his color very often designed without intelligent organization. One year later the critics were praising Marsh's progress and Edward Alden Jewell commenting that "a previous tendency toward muddiness has largely disappeared. . . The colors appear cleaner; move with more ease in the rhythms they orchestrate." The adjectives "exciting", "turbulent", "dramatic" were frequently used.

Four years later, in 1938, the same adjectives were being used, but Jewell was disappointed and sharply critical. "Mr. Marsh," he

MARSH, REGINALD—*Continued*

said, "ought to do something drastic and at once in the way of cleaning up his palette and sharpening his draughtsmanship." In February 1939 the criticism shifted, however, when there was a large showing of nearly 50 of Marsh's etchings, engravings and drawings. Criticism then focused itself on the problem of presenting many figures in one scene, and the consensus was that in the early etchings there was frequently a confusion of values, a bewildering complexity which was absent in the later ones. *Girl Reading a Newspaper*, for instance, has "a rugged strength and simple incisiveness."

In 1940 the critics were discussing his "rhythmic power," his "freedom and galvanic sweep," the "vulgarity" or "life" of pictures like *The People's Follies No. 3* or *Grand Tier Box* or *Memories of the Stork Club* or of his drawings, most of which, according to Howard Devree, reveal Marsh's amazing mastery of technique free from the satirical touch of caricature which permeates with exaggeration his comment on social vulgarities. And in 1941 they were commenting that he had reached "the high-water mark of his career in easel painting," that he was painting, with more vigor, "single compositions and broader areas." According to critics, in this exhibition Marsh showed the results of his experimentation with a new oil technique; he showed, too, in *Easter on the I. R. T.* and *Coney Island Beach No. 3*, the influence of the technique of Jacques Maroger, former head of the laboratory of the Louvre and now teaching in New York, with whom he had recently studied. But the subjects remained the same as in his previous shows—everything from burlesque to the Bowery, from Coney Island to river-front scenes with a salty flavor. In addition to his painting Marsh has been making etchings and line engravings on copper.

For his work Reginald Marsh has received the Kohnstamm Prize from the Chicago Art Institute (1931), the first Wanamaker department store regional purchase prize (1934), the Thomas B. Clarke Prize from the National Academy of Design (1937) and the Watson F. Blair Prize from the Chicago Art Institute (1940). He is represented in the Metropolitan Museum of Art, in the Whitney Museum of American Art and elsewhere throughout the country, and there are murals by him in the Washington, D. C. Post Office and the New York City Custom House which have been called "some of the finest decorations that have been produced under Federal auspices."

References

Am Artist 5:4-10 Je '41 il pors
Am Mag Art 28:62 Ja '35; 29:848 D '36
Art Digest 11:10 D 1 '36; 13:25 F 15 '39 il; 15:17 Ja 1 '41 il
Creative Art 12:256-65 Ap '33 il por
Esquire 3:46-9+ Je '35 il
Forum 98:47 Jl '37 il
Life Ja 6 '39
Time 30:40 Ag 16 '37 por
Bower, W. ed. New Directions p303-20 1937
Who's Who in American Art

MARSHALL, VERNE Aug. 30, 1889- Chairman of defunct No Foreign War Committee; former publisher

Address: h. 532 Knollwood Dr, Cedar Rapids, Iowa

Bulletin: On April 29, 1941 Verne Marshall announced that the No Foreign War Committee would dissolve. It was organized, he said, "to provoke increased public discussion" of the danger of the United States going to war overseas. "These purposes have been served and all obligations of the committee met." In the annual election of officers on the Cedar Rapids (Iowa) *Gazette* in June 1941 he was supplanted as secretary, and since the termination of the No Foreign War Committee he has neither returned to the paper nor been conspicuous in public life.

From February 1941 issue:

On January 8, 1941 Verne Marshall resigned his active editorship (although still co-owner) of the Cedar Rapids *Gazette* in order to devote his full time to the direction of his month-old No Foreign War Committee, formed to counteract the "propaganda of the William Allen White Committee," which, according to Mr. Marshall, had developed "the same public psychology as that which was carefully created during the War period preceding our declaration of hostilities in April 1917."

After the first full-page advertisement of the Committee appeared in December 1940 in 52 newspapers all over the country (including Mr. White's Emporia *Gazette*), Mr. Marshall began getting himself, in many other newspapers, a barrage of publicity. His sensational story of peace "agenda" flown from Germany to the United States State Department in October 1939 by William Rhodes Davis (see sketch this issue), a New York oil operator —an "agenda" which, Marshall asserted, offered the opportunity for a just and honorable negotiated peace at that time—set people on both sides of the aid-to-the-Allies issue to questioning both Mr. Davis' and Mr. Marshall's connections and motives. Mr. Marshall claims that such a peace could be negotiated between Germany and Great Britain even now.

In spite of Mr. Marshall's warning, "Let no man accuse us of the No Foreign War Committee of being appeasers, Fifth Columnists, pro-Nazi, pro-British, pro-Fascist or of being anything save a group of determined pro-Americans," many individuals and groups have chosen to do just that. Among them was a sizable portion of the audience at a debate on, "Is a Hitler Defeat Essential to the United States?" sponsored by *America's Town Meeting of the Air*. Mr. Marshall took the negative, and met hostile response from many of his listeners.

L. M. Birkhead, national director of the Friends of Democracy, sent Marshall a telegram in which he charged: "Your organization can be properly classed with the haters of England, the defeatists and the anti-Semites. Your organization is no such bona fide keep-us-out-of-war movement as are the Quakers and similar high-minded and loyal American groups." Some of this controversy was due to the fact that "former leaders in the Christian Front movement and associates of Father Coughlin" were said to be sponsoring a meeting at which Mr. Marshall was planning to speak on January 12. By January 14 the field organizer of the Committee, O. K. Armstrong, had resigned, and some others whose names had been linked with the Committee seemed to be dropping away.

Mr. Marshall says: "We have built this campaign of ours from the grassroots upward." *The Nation* denies this, saying: "For all its homespun, small-town look, the financial and political roots of the new Committee strike into the same soil that nourishes the America First outfit; they may even be intertwined."

There is no doubt that Verne Marshall comes from the "grassroots" country. He was born in Cedar Rapids, Iowa on August 30, 1889, the son of Harry Lincoln and Emily (Kirkland) Marshall, and got his start in the newspaper business early—as a reporter on the Cedar Rapids *Republican* at the age of 19. The next year found him reporter and then city editor for the Sioux City *Journal;* in 1911 he was in Great Britain, doing special writing for the London *Chronicle;* and he came back to the United States to spend a year at Coe College in his home town and to become a reporter for the Minneapolis *Tribune* in 1913. It was 1914 when he became managing editor of the Cedar Rapids *Gazette,* after his father bought a part interest in the paper, and from then on his career was interrupted only by the First World War. That sent him to France in 1916 to drive an ambulance for the French Army, then to devote his time to Red Cross work, and when the United States entered the conflict he immediately enlisted as a private (he was later promoted to sergeant) in a machine gun battery. He was sent on a tour to sell Liberty Loan Bonds. Commissioned a second lieutenant, he "never was permitted to return to his division but was kept on special duty until the end of the War."

Marshall succeeded to the editorship of the *Gazette* after his father's death in 1932. He has been known not only as an old-line Republican but also as a "muckraker," although sometimes the results of his muckraking have been nebulous. In 1935 he made researches into a Woodbury County (Sioux City) illegal slot-machine ring which jogged a grand jury into indictments and convictions of 31 state officials for graft. For this exposure he was awarded the gold Pulitzer Plaque for the most meritorious public service by a newspaper in that year, but within 24 hours after the award the Iowa Supreme Court dissented, ruling that the special prosecutor had received a $700 special fee

VERNE MARSHALL

from the *Gazette* and that the convictions of the defendants were thereby invalidated. Marshall denied this, saying that "the court was misled by defense counsel," but the officials were nevertheless released. (There are still slot machines in Sioux City, too.) At another time Mr. Marshall campaigned for the elimination of prison labor in manufacturing; it is also still being used in Iowa.

Nevertheless Marshall remains a bumptious and energetic crusader. Most successful has been his campaign against the use in public schools of textbooks which he calls "subversive"—notably those of Harold Rugg (see sketch this issue). He has been hammering at this for a number of years, and the books are being gradually eliminated in Cedar Rapids itself.

The Second World War found him ready for another crusade. In June 1940 he wrote an article for *Scribner's Commentator,* a magazine which, he says, "fights for American independence and integrity." His article began: "There has never been a just war nor an honorable peace." Not until the middle of December 1940 did the No Foreign War Committee make its appearance, however. On October 20, 1940 a long distance telephone call summoned Marshall to New York; on November 4 a 2,500-word editorial in the *Gazette* said that there he was shown "secret documents" which made him "mentally drunk." He told of Mr. Davis' role in the Nazi peace plan without mentioning Davis by name, and also denounced President Roosevelt and asked for his defeat. Finally on December 17 the wires of the Associated Press, the United Press and Hearst's International News Service carried the story of the Committee's birth.

When on December 30 the "secret documents" mentioned in the editorial were revealed to 60 Washington correspondents dur-

MARSHALL, VERNE—*Continued*

ing a press conference arranged for by the *Gazette's* Washington correspondent the wires hummed even more loudly. Everyone wanted to know what Davis' connections with Germany have been (he is known to have sold oil to both Germany and Italy) and what his connections with the No Foreign War Committee might be (he denied being its "angel," as Marshall had intimated); everyone wondered who Marshall's financial backers were. Rumor connected Henry Ford as well as the heads of *Scribner's Commentator* with the formation of Marshall's Committee—and other names were discussed. In the meanwhile Marshall was speaking over the radio and into the newsreel microphone and holding daily press conferences that were always good for a headline. He said that his appeals for public support had been answered not only by a campaign of name-calling but by money, by thousands of signatures to telegrams to be sent to President Roosevelt, by promises of Congressional support.

The objectives of his committee, according to Mr. Marshall, are "few and simple. Our purpose is to prevent the United States from being sucked into the current chapter of Europe's interminable economic, political and ideological war. . . Also we intend to fight to the bitter end against any conspiracy or plan to eliminate the silly, fool dollar sign from consideration of aid to Britain." He doesn't want President Roosevelt to "give away our national defense" if the peril is "one-third as grave as you and Bill Knudsen say it is." But "there is absolutely nothing in the program or objectives of the No Foreign War Committee which would in the slightest degree hamper or seek withdrawal of full and legal help to our sister English-speaking nation."

It seems to be true, however, that his informal statements make more exciting reading. According to *PM*, he says things like: "I don't care who wins the War" and, "If Hitler comes to the U. S. A., I'll get myself back to Iowa, get on a piece of land and stay there." He has called radio commentators "idiots" and United States Senators "insane." He has announced a codicil to his will authorizing the use of any part of his estate needed for an investigation into the causes of death, injury or disappearance of any member of his family or household or any of his associates, special information that would facilitate such an investigation being in a strong box in Cedar Rapids.

In 1919 Mr. Marshall married Frances Durand Fiske of Cedar Rapids, and after her death married Clementine Robichaux of New Orleans, in 1932. There are four daughters by his first marriage and a daughter and son by his second. (One can hardly blame him if he once wrote the announcement of his fifth daughter's birth and misspelled her name!) He is a Presbyterian and a Mason and belongs to the Cedar Rapids Country Club and the National Press Club in Washington, D. C. Swarthy Mr. Marshall wears rimless spec-

tacles, chews cigars, punctuates his conversation with manly "damns" and "hells," and is fond of such words as "red-blooded" and "two-fisted." He can become belligerent. At *America's Town Meeting of the Air* he announced scowlingly, after provocation: "If anyone here says, I am not a true and loyal American, let him come up here and say it on this platform. I am 20 pounds underweight and I don't care how much he weighs."

References

> Nation 151:646-7 D 28 '40
> New Repub 104:50-1 Ja 13 '41
> New Yorker 16:14-15 Ja 11 '41
> Newsweek 7:13 Ja 11 '36 por
> PM p21 Ja 10 '41 por; p12 Ja 12 '41 por
> Time 27:49 My 18 '36 por; 37:51 Je 30 '41
> Who's Who in America

MARTIN, COLLIER FORD Jan. 22, 1873 —Mar. 22, 1941 Vice-dean of the Graduate School of Medicine of the University of Pennsylvania; taught medicine for 34 years at Temple University and the University of Pennsylvania; wrote a chapter in Cooke's *Rectal Surgery* and had written articles on his subject, proctology.

References

> American Medical Directory
> Who's Who in American Medicine

Obituaries

> N Y Times p23 Mr 25 '41

MARTIN, FRANK L(EE) July 7, 1881— July 18, 1941 Dean of the University of Missouri School of Journalism since 1935; started as an assistant professor in 1909 and helped develop the school, the first of its kind; from 1915 to 1916 served as news editor of the Japanese *Advertiser* in Tokyo and from 1931 to 1932 was exchange professor of journalism at Yenching University, Peiping, China.

References

> Sch & Soc 48:749 D 10 '38
> Leaders in Education 1941
> Who's Who in America

Obituaries

> N Y Times p13 Jl 19 '41 por

MASON, JOSEPH WARREN TEETS Jan. 3, 1879—May 13, 1941 Journalist; traveler; philosophy student; United Press war columnist and foreign correspondent; delved deeply into occidental and oriental philosophies and religions; wrote and lectured extensively on these subjects.

References

> Who's Who Among North American Authors
> Who's Who in America
> Who's Who in Japan

Obituaries

> N Y Times p21 My 14 '41 por

MATHEWS, SHAILER, REV. May 26, 1863—Oct. 23, 1941 Theologian; educator; dean of the University of Chicago Divinity School from 1908 to 1933, when he became professor emeritus; for more than 50 years a leading exponent of religion as "an aspect of the social process"; trustee of the Church Peace Union, 1914 to 1941; president of the Federal Council of Churches of Christ in America from 1912 to 1916; long identified with the Chautauqua Institution and associated with many other groups and activities; author of several scores of books, among them *Creative Christianity* (1935) and *New Faith for Old: an Autobiography* (1936).

References

Am Mag 109:50-1 Je '30
Christian Cent 49:1309 O 26 '32
Cur Hist 31:80-5 O '29 por
Lit Digest 105:22 Je 28 '30
System 51:291 Mr '27

Krumbine, M. H. ed. Process of Religion p1-12, 15-52 1933
Leaders in Education 1941
Mathews, S. New Faith for Old 1936
Who's Who Among North American Authors
Who's Who in America

Obituaries

N Y Times p23 O 24 '41 por

MATSUOKA, YÔSUKE (mät-sōō-ō′kä yō-sōō-kĕ) Mar. 1880- Former Foreign Minister of Japan

Address: Tokyo, 385 Nichome Sendaga, Shibuya-ku, Japan

Bulletin: In March 1941, at the invitation of Hitler, Yôsuke Matsuoka set out for Europe on a "grand tour of the Axis." He conferred with Stalin, Hitler and Mussolini; he was received by the Pope; and on his way back to Tokyo through Russia the Russo-Japanese pact, signed in April 1941, was born. It was only a few months later, however, in July 1941, when Matsuoka ceased to be Foreign Minister of Japan. Premier Konoye's new Cabinet, formed then, didn't include him, for his policies, based on the supposition that relations between Germany and Russia would continue peaceful, proved impractical once the invasion of Russia had begun.

From March 1941 issue:

"What is Japan fighting for?" once inquired Yôsuke Matsuoka, Japan's Foreign Minister. "For the fulfillment of her mission in Asia. That is the whole answer." This war which Japan is waging in China now, he says, is not "an imperialist war of greed and aggression. We are engaged in a moral crusade." The real reason for the present strained relations between the United States and Japan is "American misapprehension of Japan's aims and aspirations," he says.

Very often this self-confident, positive Foreign Minister is less urbane. In August 1940,

Japanese American News

YÔSUKE MATSUOKA

irked by United States' embargoes, he warned us: "The Japanese Government is through with toadying. From now on Japan will not make vain efforts to shake hands with countries who cannot be turned into friends." Three months later, after the trade agreement had not been renewed and United States' aid had been given to China, he was even more definite: "The United States is taking step after step in the wrong direction which might precipitate it into the vortex of armed conflict." And in the meantime he had "renovated" Japan's foreign policy in general.

"The most Westernized of Japanese leaders and the most dangerous to the West," Matsuoka's first move as Foreign Minister was to declare his intention of forging "a greater East Asia." An anti-American and anti-British campaign was inaugurated; mildly liberal Japanese diplomats in key positions all over the world were fired and replaced with reliable "positivists." Shortly after came the closing of the Burma Road and the signing of a new pact with Germany and Italy. For this pact Matsuoka has been called a thoroughgoing totalitarian; but there still are some commentators who feel he is "a levelheaded intellectual, not a hairbrained Fascist."

Whatever his label, Matsuoka has to be levelheaded, for his is "one of the toughest political assignments in the world," an assignment which involves staying on the right side of the Axis partners, conciliating the Russians, keeping the Americans from the actual boiling-over point and directing a country which has been fighting for four years and may have to fight a good many more.

Matsuoka has the qualifications for his job—diplomatic experience, the ability to get along with most foreigners, a thorough knowledge of the West and 17 years spent in the service of the South Manchurian Rail-

MATSUOKA, YÔSUKE—*Continued*

way. He was born in Yamaguchi-ken prefecture, the son of Sanjuro Matsuoka, into a family which had belonged to the Samurai class but had become poor. When he was 13 a cousin suggested that he come with him to America. In 1893 he arrived in Portland, Oregon.

In Portland, Matsuoka lived for a while at a Methodist Mission and attended the Atkinson Grammar School in Portland. Then the Pastor of the Mission found a home for him with William Dunbar and his sister Mrs. Isabelle Dunbar Beveridge, who treated him like a son and brought him up in the Christian religion. (Years later he stated: "While I am a Christian I am a Matsuoka Christian. I don't believe in a lot of things that they have attached to the regular sects in America and Europe.") After two and one-half years in high school in Oakland, California, Matsuoka returned to Portland to attend the law school of the University of Oregon. To pay his way through he sold coffee from door to door, worked as a bus boy, acted as an interpreter for a Japanese railroad labor contractor—and incidentally is supposed to have developed into a fine poker player—and was graduated in 1900.

Back in Japan, Matsuoka studied political science, read the classics and finally, in 1902, took the stiff foreign service examinations. By 1904 he was a vice-consul in Shanghai, and from then on his rise in the foreign service was fast. For 15 years he served as chief of the foreign section of the Kwantung Leased Territory, consul general at Mukden, secretary of the Embassy at Washington and secretary to the Foreign Minister. His command of English and his American manners made him a natural contact man between Japanese and Western· officials, and it was he who was largely responsible for organizing the vital Information Bureau of the Foreign Office.

In 1919 Matsuoka became secretary to Japan's Premier and attended the Versailles Peace Conference as interpreter for Prince Saionji, becoming friends there with Prince Konoye, Japan's present Premier. Shortly after, in 1920, Matsuoka resigned from the Foreign Office. He was tired of diplomacy and believed that a man couldn't get anywhere by staying in one place.

Five months later Matsuoka was a director of the South Manchurian Railway, "Japan's spearhead on the Asian continent." He remained in that position until 1926, when he retired "to meditate." One year later he was back, as vice-president. It was in 1929 that he first appeared as a political figure. In that year he attended the Pan-Pacific conference in Kyoto. When a Chinese delegate rose to attack Japan's Manchurian policy, Matsuoka delivered a fiery, unprepared speech which pointed the way toward Japan's later moves and created a furor.

Matsuoka was now definitely interested in politics. In 1930 he resigned his position with the South Manchurian Railway to run for a seat in the lower house and to win the election as a member of the Seiyukai Party. At the time of the Manchurian "incident" he was sent to Shanghai as the special envoy of the Foreign Minister and "played an important role behind the scenes in concluding a truce." Then, in 1932, Matsuoka was chosen to represent Japan in Geneva in connection with the League of Nations' recognition of conquered Manchuria (now Manchukuo). He put up a brilliant case for Japan's acting to insure her "lifeline" in speeches that were "unrehearsed, unconventional and eloquent" and, when the vote was forty-two to one against Japan, led the Japanese delegation out. He returned home a hero.

Immediately he resigned from Parliament and his position in the Seiyukai Party and announced that he no longer believed in political parties—"to wait for political parties to improve is like waiting for pigs to fly." He set up the League for the Dissolution of Political Parties, which aimed to abolish the parliamentary system and to establish an "imperialistic militarism sanctified by fanatical devotion to the Emperor as the Son of Heaven." By 1935, although he had declared only a year before that "in Japan dictatorship, Fascism or any similar system in which one man imposes a despotic will on the nation has absolutely no chance to thrive," *Time* was calling him an "arch-Fascist and patrioteer."

Matsuoka's "Showa Restoration" group made little headway but Matsuoka himself in 1935 was rewarded for his devotion to his country by the presidency of the South Manchurian Railway. This was more than just the leadership of a railroad. The South Manchurian Railway not only controls railroads, but also operates steamships, harbors, coal mines, oil plants, iron works, fertilizer plants, electric and gas plants, hotels and public works. The Japanese Government owns more than half its capital and entirely directs its policies. Matsuoka, as its head, was in charge of the economic reorganization of the area his country was "colonizing." He personally supervised the execution of the Railway's 10-year plan, which entailed the broadening of its rail net by 3,000 miles and the enlargement of the net of water-borne traffic. Under him 200 public schools and scores of libraries were founded; many hospitals were built. Even more important, Matsuoka was of great value as a liaison man between his company and the Army, although eventually it was because of Army interference that he resigned in 1939. "If they would just let a businessman run the country," he said regretfully, "I would put it on a paying basis in 10 years."

In 1937, when Konoye was Premier for the first time, Matsuoka had acted as his Cabinet advisory councilor. He was a logical Japanese choice for Foreign Minister when Konoye became Premier again in 1940, for it was felt that he had "gained the confidence of both civilians and soldiers, of big businessmen and gold-braided generals"; that his "quick understanding and salty wit" would make it difficult for even those who disagreed with his policies to dislike him. Americans like Roy Howard warned, however: "Matsuoka shows every sign of becoming the Japanese Führer."

In appearance Matsuoka is "urbane, roly poly," with a bristling cropped head. Personally he is supposed to be very affable and accessible, and Americans find his English, flavored with a Scotch accent which he inherited from the Dunbars with whom he lived in Portland, quite engaging. He loves to talk, whether to small or large groups. He will make an extemporaneous speech at the drop of a hat or talk along for hours on any subject. His enemies, in retaliation, once called him "the delegate from Oregon."

A typical Matsuoka day begins at five a. m., when he reads the papers and goes over documents. Then comes breakfast at seven followed by two or three hours receiving visitors. At ten Matsuoka goes to the office, where he stays until five or six before returning home with stuffed brief cases to spend part of the night working. He doesn't go out much socially but does entertain occasionally in the large European style house where he lives with his wife, Ryoku Shin, and his seven children. Mrs. Matsuoka is completely retiring. There was one foreigner who knew Matsuoka, who visited his house for 20 years and yet wasn't sure whether or not he had ever met her.

References

Am Mercury 51:322-8 N '40
Collier's 106:11+ D 28 '40 por
Cur Hist & Forum 52:17 O 22 '40
Life 9:28 O 14 '40 por
Liv Age 347:111-14 O '34; 359:337-40
    D '40
New Repub 103:865-6 D 23 '40
Newsweek 16:4 N 18 '40; 17:25 F 3
    '41
Time 26:20 Ag 12 '35 por; 36:27-8 Ag
    5 '40 por; 38:23-5 Jl 7 '41 por (cover)
Gunther, J. Inside Asia p78-9 1939
International Who's Who
Who's Who in Commerce and Industry
Who's Who in Japan

MAXTONE GRAHAM, JOYCE *See* Struther, J.

MAY, ANDREW JACKSON June 24, 1875- Chairman of House Military Affairs Committee

Address: b. House Office Bldg, Washington, D. C.; h. Prestonsburg, Kentucky; The Roosevelt Hotel, Washington, D. C.

"The Administration leader in whose hands are the new plans to strengthen the Army" is 170-pound Andrew Jackson May, chairman of the Military Affairs Committee of the United States House of Representatives, who has been known as a "millions-for-defense" man ever since his appearance on the Washington scene in 1931.

The Congressman from Kentucky was born in Langley, Kentucky on June 24, 1875, the

Harris & Ewing
ANDREW JACKSON MAY

son of John and Dorcus (Conley) May. He entered local politics rather early. For five years he taught in country schools in Floyd and Magoffin Counties in the Beaver Creek section of Kentucky; in 1896 he made his first political speech on behalf of the Presidential candidacy of William Jennings Bryan; two years later he acquired his degree from the Southern University Law School in Tennessee and was admitted to the Kentucky Bar. After 1900 he was in practice at Prestonburg, where he still makes his home.

It was in 1901 that Andrew Jackson May was appointed attorney for Floyd County. He held this office for eight years, and later became special judge in the Circuit Court for Johnson and Martin Counties. Law was only one side of his career, however. For two decades he had what he calls "an active and successful business career," and eventually he became president of the Beaver Valley Coal Corporation. But his political ambitions remained. In 1928 he finally ran for the United States House of Representatives on the Democratic ticket. He was completely flattened out, for the 10th (now the 7th) Congressional District of Kentucky was at that time a Republican stronghold. Two years changed that situation, however, and in 1931 Mr. May went to Washington as a member of the 72nd Congress. He has been there ever since, with one term as Congressman-at-Large from 1933 to 1935.

After his election Mr. May sold out his coal interests, but apparently maintained his concern for the coal industry. He has been a member of the House Military Affairs Committee ever since he first came to Congress, and it was while he was a member that the act creating the Tennessee Valley Authority was written and framed. At that time, Mr. May says, it was planned that the

MAY, ANDREW JACKSON—*Continued*

activities of TVA be limited to the development of interstate streams for navigation purposes. Since then he has found it competing with private industry, most particularly the Kentucky coal business, and has fought it tooth and nail. His Military Affairs Committee has charge of TVA requests for money, and in May 1939 Representative May sponsored a bill which drastically curbed its powers and which, he said, "would go a long way in restoring confidence of the public in the future of the electric-utility industry."

All in all, Mr. May has shown himself one of the staunchest Congressional defenders of private enterprise, a Democratic admirer of John Nance Garner rather than of Franklin Delano Roosevelt. In 1938 he stated: "In the last five years, there has been such wide expansion of Government agencies and activities both in and out of Washington that the Government now occupies in the states outside of Washington more office space than would be provided by 53 buildings of the size and capacity of the Empire State Building in New York."

Only since the War, then, has Mr. May found himself seeing eye to eye with the Administration in many respects. He has always been an enthusiastic advocate of army expansion, of "the strongest possible fortifications" for the coast, of a strong and highly centralized government authority in preparation for war. He has said: "I strictly adhere to the principles of George Washington, believing that national defense is the surest guarantee of peace."

Mr. May was a vociferous opponent of the Ludlow war referendum proposals. He asked for military training for the CCC boys. He was the author of the M-Day Bills passed in February 1938 providing for complete civilian and industrial mobilization in case of war, and he "sharply denied reports that his bills would forbid war profits." (According to Mr. May, the freeing of private enterprise is the most dependable stimulus to preparedness and victory in war, and he personally urged a $50,000,000 subsidy for American munitions makers rather than any legislative encroachments on their business.) As early as May 1940 he also proposed relaxing the cash-and-carry policy of sending war materials to the Allies and lifting the money ban against debt-defaulting nations, and it was the May bill passed in the summer of 1941 that permitted President Roosevelt to keep drafted men in the Army for the duration. May also sponsored an amendment to the bill which would have made "interference" with workers in defense a crime.

Andrew Jackson May is a Baptist, a Mason, and a member of the Rotary International. In July 1901 he was married to Julia Grace Mayo, and their three children (Olga May, Andrew Jackson, Jr., and Robert V.) are themselves all married now. The Kentucky Congressman likes eating and keeps his weight down to 170 pounds only by walking a mile every day. His is still president of the Greenbrier Mining Company, but when in January 1940 he learned that the firm had sold $500,000 worth of manganese to the United State Government he quickly called the deal off. His Congressional activities on behalf of national defense are entirely apart from his personal concerns, he says.

References

Business Week p7 Je 17 '39 por
N Y Sun p26 My 14 '40
N Y Times p1, 8 F 27 '41
Newsweek 13:39 Je 26 '39 por
Scholastic 34:20S F 25 '39 por
Time 33:10 F 6 '39 por
U S News 8:11 My 24 '40
Who's Who in America
Who's Who in the Nation's Capital

MAYNE, ETHEL C(OLBURN) (mān) Died Apr. 30, 1941   British writer; best known for her authoritative works on Lord and Lady Byron; wrote *Byron* (1912) and a second edition of the work in 1924; her *Life and Letters of Anne Isabella, Lady Byron* (1929) was one of the few studies of Lady Byron published; used pen name of Frances E. Huntly when writing in both the *Yellow Book* and *Chapman's Magazine;* wrote fiction and translated from French and German works.

References

Author's and Writer's Who's Who
Who's Who

Obituaries

N Y Herald Tribune p8 My 3 '41

MAYO, CHARLES W(ILLIAM) July 28, 1898-   Surgeon

Address: b. Mayo Clinic, Rochester, Minn; h. Ivy Cottage, Mayowood, Rochester, Minn.

A great tradition and the great responsibility which goes with it are the heritage of Dr. Charles W. Mayo, now the only surgeon left to carry on the family name at the world-famous Mayo Clinic. He is the son of the late Charles Horace Mayo and the nephew of the late William James Mayo, the two "country doctors" who made the little town of Rochester, Minnesota one of the world's most important medical centers. Rochester has been called America's "scientific Lourdes," not only because of the tremendous number of cures effected in the Mayo Clinic, but also because it is there that sufferers go whose health or lives have been despaired of by physicians elsewhere.

Charles William Mayo was born in Rochester, July 28, 1898, the son of Charles Horace Mayo, one of the directors of the then St. Mary's Clinic, and Edith (Graham) Mayo, a nurse graduated by the Woman's Hospital in Chicago. When his mother was chosen American Mother for 1940 by the American Mothers' Committee of the Golden Rule Foundation, she was described as "representative of the best there is in womanhood," Besides successfully raising ten children, eight of her own and two foster children, Edith Mayo was active in community affairs. She promoted the organization of the Civic League in Rochester, acting as its first president. She helped organize the local Y. W. C. A. to which she donated her town house in 1910. She was one of the founders of the Rochester Magazine Club and of the Mayo Clinic Women's Club.

Charles attended the Hill School, a preparatory school for boys at Pottstown, Pennsylvania, from 1912 to 1917, when he was admitted to Princeton University. During the first World War he served in the Students Army Training Corps and, in 1921, he was graduated with the degree of B. A. He received his M. D. from the University of Pennsylvania in 1926 and his M. S. in Surgery from the University of Minnesota in 1931. From 1926 to 1927 he was an interne at the Robert Packer Hospital at Sayre, Pennsylvania.

He married Alice Varney Plank in 1927, and they have five children. This next generation of Mayos includes two girls, Mildred and Edith, and three boys, Charles H., II, Edward and Joseph.

From 1927 to 1931 Charles W. Mayo was a Fellow in Surgery at the Mayo Clinic. Appointed an instructor in surgery at the Mayo Foundation Graduate School, now part of the University of Minnesota, in 1933, he was elevated to the rank of assistant professor in 1935.

As a member of the board of directors of the Mayo Clinic, Charles W. Mayo represents a family brilliant in science since the seventeenth century and unique in medicine since the middle of the nineteenth. The Mayo Clinic itself was founded after the cyclone of 1883, when the need for a hospital in Rochester inspired Dr. William Worral Mayo, Charles William's grandfather, in collaboration with the Mother Superior of the Sisters of the Order of St. Francis, to found a hospital. The Clinic of St. Mary's opened in 1889, modestly equipped with 45 beds. Continued by W. W. Mayo's two sons, William J. and Charles H., the Mayo Clinic grew in size and variety of its services until its reputation became international.

Doctors from all over the world gather at the clinic to observe the surgical procedures developed by the Mayos and their associates. "The history of the Mayo Clinic," says one eminent physician, "is the history of the development of modern surgery in medical practice." Not that the Mayos were daring innovators; sometimes they were criticized for their conservatism. The "secret of their success" lay rather in "doing the ordinary thing in the extraordinary way." They performed the "cleanest surgical work on record," and had "that transcendent capacity for taking trouble that Carlyle believed to be the distinguishing mark of a genius."

There are no streetcars in Rochester, because the whole town is a hospital quiet zone. The dominating structure is the main clinic building, known to local inhabitants as a

DR. CHARLES W. MAYO

"skyscraper," of 13 stories topped by a tower which houses the first set of carillon chimes heard west of Chicago. Rich and poor mix in the floating population and are equally well received at the clinic. No case is ever turned away. Fees are based on ability to pay. No "chiseling" is allowed, however, and the business department is famous for the accuracy of its estimates of patients' finances.

When his brother Joseph was killed in a train auto collision in 1936, Charles W. was left to carry on the tradition of the Mayo family alone. He is known as an especially capable surgeon in his own right and has contributed many articles to medical and scientific journals. He is a Fellow of the American College of Surgeons and a member of many medical associations. He was created a Commander in the Order of the Crown by the Italian Government in 1939 and holds honorary membership in the Societa Italiana di Chirurgia of Rome, Italy.

Dr. Mayo's fraternities are Sigma Xi and Nu Sigma Nu. He is an active Rotarian, having served as president from 1934 to 1935, a Mason (Knight Templar), a member of the American Legion, a member of the Izaak Walton League and a member and former president of the Riders' and Drivers' Club of Southern Minnesota. His hobbies are farming and riding; when he has the time for it, he enjoys fishing.

Charles W. Mayo is neither handsome nor homely. He has the high forehead, heavy eyebrows and dark eyes of his clan, but did not inherit the Mayo thin-lipped mouth. His expression is serious and so intent as to seem almost belligerent.

References

Newsweek 14:39 O 23 '39 por; 28:54+ D 8 '41 pors

(Continued next page)

MAYO, CHARLES W.—*Continued*

Sci N L 35:279 My 6 '39
Time 30:32-4 Ag 16 '37
American Medical Directory
America's Young Men
Clapsattle, H. B. The Doctors Mayo 1941
Who's Who in America

MEAD, CHARLES LAREW, BISHOP
July 20, 1868—May 17, 1941 Bishop of Kansas for the United Methodist Church until his retirement in 1940; was made a bishop in 1920; was host bishop at the historic uniting conference in 1939 when Northern and Southern Methodists and Methodist Protestants formed one church.

References

Who's Who in America

Obituaries

N Y Times p44 My 18 '41 por

MEAD, KATE CAMPBELL Apr. 6, 1867 —Jan. 1, 1941 Physician and author of books about women in medicine; was medical director at Bryn Mawr School in Baltimore from 1890 to 1893 and for the next 32 years practiced her profession in Middletown, Connecticut.

References

American Medical Directory
American Women
Who's Who Among North American Authors
Who's Who in America
Who's Who in American Medicine

Obituaries

N Y Herald Tribune p14 Ja 2 '41

MELCHIOR, LAURITZ (LEBRECHT HOMMEL) (měl'kǐ-ôr) Mar. 20, 1890-Metropolitan Opera tenor; concert and radio star
Address: h. Hotel Ansonia, New York City; The Viking, Beverly Hills, Calif.

For the sixteenth (1941-42) consecutive season the Metropolitan Opera has as its leading Wagnerian tenor Danish-born Lauritz Melchior, who has sung more performances of *Tristan, Siegfried* and *Tannhäuser* than any other artist alive or dead. By the beginning of the 1940-41 opera season he had rolled up this amazing Wagnerian record: 215 Siegfrieds, 171 Tristans, 146 Siegmunds, 109 Tannhäusers, 73 Lohengrins, 57 Parsifals; and he followed up this record with concert appearances all over the United States and in Hawaii.

Melchior, who with his massive tenor voice is known as a true Wagnerian *Heldentenor* —that is, heroic tenor—began his operatic career as a baritone. He was born in Copenhagen, Denmark, March 20, 1890, the son of Jörgen Conradt and Julie (Möller) Melchior. There, from 1896 to 1905, he attended the Melchior School, directed by his father and his grandfather. As a boy soprano in the

English church in Copenhagen he attracted the attention of Queen Alexandra, the Danish princess who had married Edward VII. He liked to sing and in 1908 he began to take singing lessons in earnest. When, four years later, he applied for admission to the Royal School of the Opera in Copenhagen, he was given an audition and his voice classified as a baritone.

Among the people who influenced the artist's career was his blind sister, Agnes, now teaching at the Royal School for the Blind in Copenhagen. As a girl she attended that school and with the other children was permitted to go to the Royal Opera, where there were boxes under the stage for the blind. She interested her brother in the performances, and after a while he became eyes for the blind children—he would sneak up and hide in the wings so that he could report what was taking place on the stage.

Another person whose influence was important was a housekeeper, Froeken Jensen, who came to take care of the Melchior children after Lauritz's mother died (he was only a month old). She encouraged the boy to become a singer and went every Sunday to the English church to hear him sing. Later she helped to pay for his singing lessons with proceeds from cookbooks that she began to publish after coming to the Melchior home.

He made his debut as a baritone April 2, 1913, at the Royal Opera House in Copenhagen, as Silvio in *Pagliacci*. Before he made his debut as a tenor five years later (October 8, 1918) he had sung thirty-five baritone roles. It was Mme. Charles Cahier, who had been in a traveling opera company with him, who convinced him that he was not a baritone. A "tenor with the lid on" is what she called him, and she urged the director to let him try a tenor role.

Hugh Walpole, the English novelist, had a great deal to do with Melchior's success. In 1919 the young singer had been invited to appear at a concert at Queen's Hall, London, with Sir Henry Wood conducting. Walpole chanced by and decided to go in. He was so impressed by the tenor's voice that he became immediately interested in him, and thereafter helped him with advice, encouragement and funds. The two men came to be very good friends, a friendship that has lasted until Walpole's death. Walpole dedicated several of his novels to Melchior and usually sent him the manuscript of a new book for criticism.

At Walpole's suggestion Melchior went to Germany to study Wagnerian roles under Frau Anna Bahr-Mildenburg. Later he studied with Siegfried and Cosima Wagner in Bayreuth, and in 1924 made his debut there, as Parsifal, also singing Siegmund that same year. His Metropolitan debut was in 1926, as Tannhäuser. Since then he has sung every important Wagnerian tenor role. Ten years after his debut Olin Downes in a review of his then current Siegfried wrote: "There is little new to be said of Melchior's singing of Siegfried's music, in which he seems to grow each season."

On the hundredth singing of Siegfried (1935) Melchior was presented with a hand-forged sword, made according to medieval tradition by Kenneth Lynch, metal craftsman of Long Island, New York, the presentation being made by Georg Bech, Danish Consul General to New York. This sword has been carried in subsequent performances of *Siegfried*. On the hundredth singing of Tristan (1936), the tenor received a wreath and a cup from the Metropolitan Opera Company. Up to that time he had sung Tristan in sixteen different opera houses all over the world and under twenty-two different conductors, including thirty-five times under Bodanzky, seventeen under Fürtwangler, five under Sir Thomas Beecham (see sketch this issue), four under Toscanini. When he reached his hundredth Tannhäuser it was recalled that the only other singer who had any record at all was Jean de Reszke, and during his whole lifetime he had sung the role less than 50 times.

Melchior's singing is not confined to the Metropolitan. He has appeared in many other opera houses, including Chicago and San Francisco, Covent Garden (London), the Paris Grand Opera, Copenhagen, Berlin State Opera, Teatro Colon in Buenos Aires, as well as at the Bayreuth and other festivals. As a concert and radio artist he has won wide recognition, during the course of a season making many appearances in addition to his opera performances. For the 1940-41 season 40 concerts were scheduled for before and during the Metropolitan season.

The six-foot-three tenor's manager is his blond, five-foot wife—whom he calls "Kleinchen" (Little One)—the former Maria Hacker, once a famous motion picture star of Germany, who met her husband by landing literally almost at his feet. She was rehearsing for a film role which required her to bail out of an airplane with a parachute. A kind wind blew her into Melchior's garden at Chossewitz, where he has a hunting estate. Since her marriage in 1925 Mrs. Melchior has been content to manage her husband's career. She goes with him on all his tours, makes his contracts, supervises his correspondence, relieves him of all business details, helps him entertain his guests and is on hand to wish him luck before each of his performances.

For young singers Melchior has this advice: "Don't be just a singer and nothing more, because if you are a one-track person you won't be a good singer! It is not enough to sing with technical skill. There must be feeling as well, and that can be expressed only if one has lived intensely and experienced joys and sorrows. That is why I tell younger singers to reach as many phases of life as they can."

Following his own advice, Lauritz Melchior is tremendously interested in life, in living. He is heroic not only in voice and stature, but also in his approach to life. His interests are many: he is famous for his cooking, especially his oxtail soup and his smörgåsbord; he spends much of his free time hunting, bringing home a deerskin for a Siegfried costume for himself or a panther for a coat

for his wife; he collects antique art objects, arranging them meticulously and harmoniously in his home; he is interested in people, and has many friends; he is not above a practical joke; he is capable of singing at a morning musicale in Washington, hopping a plane to make a *Siegfried* performance at the Metropolitan in New York and then singing a midnight broadcast the same evening. Perhaps one of the most unexpected phases of his career is his engagement by Columbia University's Teachers College, as a special lecturer on the therapeutic value of music to the

LAURITZ MELCHIOR

handicapped. It was through his blind sister that he acquired his interest in the physically handicapped, and before he lectured at Teachers College he had already done work at the New School for the Blind in New York.

On Melchior's Manhattan apartment door appears the sign, "Singer to the Royal Court of Denmark," a title which has been given to him by the Danish King. Denmark has also conferred upon him the Knighthood and Silver Cross of Dannebrog and the gold medal of "Ingenio et Arti." He is the only male singer who has received this latter decoration, which had previously been given only to women. France has conferred upon him the rosette of the Légion d'Honneur, Officier de l'Instruction Publique; Bulgaria the Cross for Service to Art; and Germany-Sachen-Coburg-Gotha the Carl Eduard Medal, First Class, for his services at the Bayreuth Festivals. He has also a Saxonian knighthood, and from Vassar College has received a gold medal for his services to art in the United States.

References

Am Mag 126:56 S '38 por
Am Scand R 23:152-60 Je '35 pors

(Continued next page)

MELCHIOR, LAURITZ—*Continued*

Arts & Dec 47:14-17+ N '37 il pors
Etude 55:429-30+ Jl '37 pors
N Y Post p10 Mr 21 '40
N Y Times VIII p7 F 28 '26 por; IX
    p6 S 8 '35; IX p10 Ja 22 '39 por; IX
    p5 Ag 27 '39
Time 35:51-4 Ja 22 '40 pors
Ewen, D. Men and Women Who Make
    Music p89-105 1939
Hope, C. Publicity Is Broccoli 1941
Thompson, O. ed. International Cyclo-
    pedia of Music and Musicians 1939
Who's Who
Who's Who in America

MENOCAL, MARIO GARCIA (mä'nô-
käl') Dec. 16(?), 1866—Sept. 7, 1941 One
of Cuba's most famous political figures;
President of Cuba from 1913 to 1921; was
head of the powerful Democratic-Republican
Party; was member of the coalition which
elected President Batista and was one of the
President's chief advisers.

References

Business Week p4 F 22 '33 por
Lit Digest 110:5 Ag 29 '31 por
Nation 110:230-1 F 21 '20
International Who's Who

Obituaries

N Y Times p7 S 8 '41 por

MENUHIN, YEHUDI (měn'ū-ĭn   yĕ-
hōō'dê) Apr. 22, 1916- Violinist
Address: b. c/o Evans and Salter, Steinway
Building, 113 W. 57th St, New York City;
h. Alma, Calif.

"It is easy to write the simple and final word
'perfection' against the performance of Yehudi
Menuhin," once wrote the London *Times,* and
critics and audiences all over the world have
unanimously hailed the magnificent technique,
the enchanting tone, the unerring taste of
this great violinist.

Yehudi Menuhin was a child prodigy; he
is now a genius. The growth of his musicianship has been steady since that day in 1923
when he first appeared as soloist in San Francisco. His parents, Moshe and Marutha Menuhin, weren't musicians, though relatives on
both sides were lovers of music. Moshe Menuhin, who was born in Russia and reared in
Palestine, was a Hebrew teacher in New York
when Yehudi was born; Mrs. Menuhin was a
teacher, too. When their son was nine months
old the Menuhins moved to San Francisco,
where Yehudi's father became superintendent
of the Jewish Educational Society.

It was in San Francisco that Yehudi heard
his first concert. He was less than a year old,
and he heard it because his parents were too
poor to afford to have someone take care of
him at home. He stayed quiet all through,
even seemed to be listening, and was taken to
others. When he was three he was given a
toy violin. Immediately he raised it to his
chin, drew the bow, and then threw it on the

floor when he heard the squeaky sound it
made. Instead of scolding him for breaking
the toy, his family bought him a real one.
On it he began taking lessons at the age of
four from Sigmund Anker. Later he was
taught by Louis Persinger, concertmaster of
the San Francisco Symphony Orchestra.

Three years from the time he took his
first lesson, pudgy little Yehudi appeared as
soloist with the San Francisco Orchestra,
playing the Mendelssohn violin concerto. One
year later he gave a recital at the Manhattan
Opera House in New York City and when he
was ten made his Carnegie Hall debut, playing
the Beethoven concerto with the New York
Symphony Orchestra. The critics looked at
the blue-eyed, pink-cheeked little boy in velvet
knee breeches and a white shirt and prepared
to listen with resignation. They left to write
paeans like that of Chotzinoff: "From the
fingers of this child of 10 the Beethoven concerto flowed in all its nobility, its repose, its
thoughtful and subjective beauty."

It was clear from the beginning of his
career that Menuhin was "a profound artist,
with integrity, taste and a high artistic
standard to which he clung tenaciously." He
never played the usual fireworks pieces that
show off technical ability, often at the expense of meaning; his encores were usually
the solo sonatas of Bach and his main pieces
the more profound in violin literature. At 11,
for instance, he played in one concert with
the Berlin Philharmonic Orchestra concerti
by Beethoven, Brahms and Bach. After this
concert a little man with bushy hair came
backstage, lifted him up and kissed him.
"Today, Yehudi," he said, "you have once
again proved to me that there is a God in
Heaven." The man was Albert Einstein (see
sketch this issue).

It was shortly after this concert that Menuhin began studying with Georges Enesco. He
went to him and said simply: "I want to
study with you." A great friendship was
started. Enesco advised his pupil to study
harmony and counterpoint, to read the biographies of great musicians and to learn the
history of music. He also advised Yehudi's
family to let their son appear in public
only 15 or 20 times a year and to devote the
rest of his time to quiet study and a quiet
way of life. His advice was accepted, and
the development of Menuhin "was achieved
in a perfect harmony of the various elements
concerned and without the feverish rush for
immediate maximum returns which has often
ruined youthful talents."

Yehudi and his two sisters, Hepzibah and
Yaltah, both enormously gifted pianists, never
went to school. Mrs. Menuhin taught her
children herself and had tutors for them
from time to time. They were never punished; they never went to the movies or
listened to the radio. They learned to speak
five languages fluently and grew up healthy
and well-informed, as well as extraordinarily
talented.

While he was growing up, Menuhin regularly appeared with the world's great symphony orchestras and in concerts. In Decem-

ber 1935 he completed his first around-the-world concert tour, in which he appeared in 63 cities in 13 countries, playing 110 engagements. Critics praised his tone—"one of the most enchanting sounds in violin history"; they talked and wrote of his magnificent technique, "capable of inexhaustible variations and unflagging in intrepid execution of trills, double stops and contrapuntal figurations"; they praised his understanding of the music, his ability to achieve what he believes is the meaning of violin playing: "to effect the most perfect realization humanly possible of one's own conception of the composer's message."

At the height of his success Menuhin retired for two years to his estate in the Santa Cruz mountains, near Los Gatos, California—two years which his mother had asked him to give her: "I wanted him to be a boy like other boys." Yehudi spent these years swimming, basking in the sun, driving, practicing, and emerged from them in 1937 a man, safely over that step from childhood to maturity so often fatal for prodigies.

Then he returned to the concert stage booked up for years to come. In 1940 he gave war-relief benefit concerts in Australia and one for the Palestine Conservatory of Music in New York; in 1941 he gave concerts in the United States and South America and gave many benefit performances for war victims. Since his return to the concert stage he has steadfastly refused to appear more than fifty times a season, though offered hundreds of engagements, for he believes that four or five months of concert work a year are enough: the rest of the time should be for study, rest and a quiet family life. With his Australian wife, Nola Ruby Nicholas, whom he married in May 1938, and his two children, Zamira and Krov, Menuhin spends long happy hours in California swimming, hiking or just relaxing in the sunshine. He was exempted from the first draft because of the family's dependency on him. Because of time spent this way he is broad-shouldered and well-built, muscular and robust, alive with health and vitality. He has also achieved throughout the years a "level calm and high poise."

This he applies to his study and to his playing. "I am always calm," he says. When he approaches a work for the first time, he goes over the score carefully before touching his violin. Then he plays and re-plays it and, as he says: "Each time I go over a piece of music I try to penetrate deeper into its meaning than I did the last time, and to bring up some new shade of sentiment, of color, of emphasis—or even of fingering—which never had occurred to me before." Always he uses the first edition of works (he has no use for arrangements), and he possesses an immense collection of original editions of violin literature. From his study he has made important restorations in performance of the original intentions of Mozart, Paganini and other composers, and it was he who performed for the first time the *Adelaide Concerto* of Mozart and the lost concerto of Schumann.

YEHUDI MENUHIN

Menuhin still continues to study with Enesco and to spend part of every year with him. Enesco denies that he actually teaches Menuhin. "When he plays," he says, "I sit in a big chair in a corner of the room and listen attentively. Sometimes Yehudi stops. He has caught in my eyes a glimpse of disapproval. I nod. I smile. I say, 'Ah there.' But I let him find out what, to my mind, is wrong. And he always finds out and makes the correction himself." Enesco and Menuhin's other teachers all feel they can teach him little or nothing: they feel he has an instinctive sixth sense which guides him in performing passages and interpreting phrases. Toscanini, for instance, listens to Menuhin frequently. Yehudi once complained: "You never correct me when I play. Why don't you tell me when I play badly?" "There's never anything wrong with your playing," Toscanini replied. "It's always perfect."

References

Etude 55:77-8 F '37; 56:285+ My '38 por
Mag Art 30:642 O '37 por
N Y Times IV p4 D 15 '40 pors
Newsweek 12:25 N 7 '38
Opera News 2:5+ O '37
Spec 160:584 Ap 1 '38

America's Young Men
Baker's Biographical Dictionary of Musicians
Bower, W. ed. New Directions p454-62 1937
Ewen, D. Men and Women Who Make Music p249-67 1939
Ewen, D. ed. Living Musicians 1940
Kaufmann, H. and Hansl, E. E. Artists in Music of Today 1933
Pierre Key's Musical Who's Who
Saleski, G. Famous Musicians of a Wandering Race 1927

(Continued next page)

MENUHIN, YEHUDI—*Continued*
Thompson, O. ed. International Cyclopedia of Music and Musicians 1939
Who's Who in America
Who's Who in American Jewry

MENZIES, ROBERT G(ORDON) (měn'-zĭs) Dec. 20, 1894- Former Prime Minister of Australia
Address: h. 10 Howard St, Kew, E. 4, Victoria, Australia

Bulletin: On August 29, 1941 Robert Gordon Menzies resigned as Prime Minister of Australia. His resignation was prompted by the Labor Party's rejection of his plea for a coalition government and this Party's indication that he ought to resign. In a public statement Menzies said that many colleagues felt he was unpopular with a large section of the press and people, and that this unpopularity had handicapped the effectiveness of his government. There had, for instance, been loud complaints when in February he went to England to sit in on meetings of the War Cabinet—a visit followed by a fact-seeking swing around the world which brought him to the United States in May.

Australian Associated Press
ROBERT G. MENZIES

From February 1941 issue:

Youngest Prime Minister ever to head Governmental administration in Australia, Robert Gordon Menzies was elected to that office, as head of the United Australia Party, in April 1939. Strongly opposed by members of the more conservative Country Party, particularly by Sir Earle Page, he achieved office by a narrow margin. The rift between the two parties has been an upsetting element in Australian politics for some years. Because of the seriousness of the War situation for the British Empire, however, Prime Minister Menzies realized the necessity of healing the breach as soon as possible.

In October 1940 his Cabinet had slightly more unity than before, owing to the inclusion of Sir Earle Page as Minister of Commerce. Currently Menzies heads a coalition government which, however, has only one vote more than the Labor Party, which has consistently refused to join it.

Yet although real unity behind Menzies is lacking, under him Australia's war production began to show results, and Labor completely approved of this effort. By the middle of 1941 Australia will have a munitions-making organization staffed by 80,000 workers. There has been steady expansion of stocks of raw materials such as jute, cotton, tinplate and industrial chemicals. The Government has guaranteed that no loss will be suffered through price swings in raw materials, but has ruled that "profits shall go to the State." It has also pledged to continue import control and price fixing for a "sufficient period" after the War to protect all parties.

Although some political observers say that Menzies "is not clever enough to hide his own cleverness," others are convinced that he is no man's fool. But his talents are not of a sort that necessarily make for popularity. He is said to be uncompromising in his adherence to a principle, and has more than once resigned office rather than yield ground. Moreover, he has a gift of repartee that often gives him an air of superiority and alienates mass sympathy. Even more important in a "country that was New Dealish long before the New Deal and where the labor movement is so tough that . . . Harry Bridges is just a pale expatriate compared to the kind they grow at home" is the fact that Menzies is a conservative who, Labor feels, represents Flinders Lane, Melbourne's Wall Street. It is nevertheless true that in his first broadcast after his election as Prime Minister Menzies himself said: "I am a singularly plain Australian, born in a little Victorian country town. I wasn't born to the purple. I've made my own way, such as it is. I hold the Prime Ministership not as an occasion for foolish vanity, but as a responsibility so great it might well deter a much better man than I can ever hope to be." It is said that, to those who best know Menzies, this self-portraiture is perfectly sincere.

The son of James Menzies, a storekeeper, he was educated in the state schools of Victoria, at Grenville College, Ballarat, and at Wesley College, Melbourne, from which he received his LL. M. He had gone through college on scholarships, consistently at the head of his class, and he left it with the Supreme Court Judges' Prize. He was called to the Bar May 2, 1918; was made K. C. in 1929. In 1927 he became arbitrator on salaries and conditions among the metropolitan daily papers of the Australian Journalists Association. By then he had built up a lucrative practice in which he earned as much as $100,000 a year. In 1929, with S. Kent Hughes, he founded the Young Nationalist Organization. He held his first important political position from 1928 to 1929: Minister without Portfolio in the McPherson Government. From 1932 to 1934 he was Attorney General, Minister of Railways and Deputy Premier. Since 1934 he has been Federal Attorney General and Minister for Industry; since 1936 deputy leader of the United Australia Party. He was so ambitious to become Prime Minister in the 1939 elections that (it is reported) he sprained his arm in his hurry to get to Parliament House in Canberra, and appeared at the meeting with his arm in a sling. When Sir Earle Page resigned in a huff, he accused Menzies of being "a stubborn mule, a back-stepper, a coward," and charged that he had resigned from the Army during the War instead of going overseas. The Laborites were incensed at this charge, and when Menzies rose in defense, the House cheered.

This son of an obscure country storekeeper who became Prime Minister is said to tower intellectually above most of his political contemporaries. He is one of the most able debaters and impressive public speakers Australia has ever produced, yet he says he has never made a big speech without suffering acute nervousness. He has been accused of personal ambition, yet in his early 30's surrendered one of Australia's richest legal practices for the much smaller financial rewards of political life. When elected leader of the United Australia Party he refused to solicit votes, saying that he would be elected on his merits or not at all.

Menzies is a formidable six-footer who weighs two hundred pounds. Cropped hair, stippled gray at the wide temples, curls in front over a well padded but fine featured face from which eyes look with an expression of detached, amused scrutiny. He is a voracious reader. Until the Second World War he read four or five books weekly, supplemented by detective yarns for train traveling. As an undergraduate he had something of a reputation as a verse-maker. He dislikes bridge, dancing, golf; likes tennis, squash rackets, and watching cricket matches. A witty and entertaining conversationalist, he prefers, above all things, good talk, and sometimes sharp talk. His quips, delivered in flat-toned, Australian-accented speech, are well known. Once, after he had been elected Prime Minister, a Left-winger baited him in public. "In your new office," he said, "I take it that you will consult the powerful interests who control you before you choose your Cabinet."

"Yes," said Menzies, "but, please, keep my wife's name out of this."

References

Christian Sci Mon p4 O 28 '40 por
Int Affairs 14:480-8 Jl '35
Liv Age 360:341-5 Je '41
N Y Times p6 S 5 '40; IV p5 N 24 '40 por; VII p7+ Ap 6 '41
Newsweek 18:22+ S 1 '41 por
Round Table 29:624-7 Je '39
Scholastic 37:14 O 7 '40 por
Time 33:29 My 1 '39 por; 37:16-17 My 19 '41
Who's Who
Who's Who in Australia

MERMAN, ETHEL Jan. 16, 1909- Musical comedy star

Address: b. c/o B. G. De Sylva, 551 Fifth Ave, New York City

When Ethel Merman was asked how she got to be a success, she thought it over for a while and then said: "I don't know. Except that I always gave 'em everything I had. It's pretty tough living up to that one rule—always giving them the old fire even when you feel like a squashed cake of ice. I mean, you know how it would be with any girl. There are plenty of headaches—and maybe heartaches too."

"A dynamic baggage with syncopation in every breath and gesture and a voice with the hard clarion forthrightness of a jazz trumpet," Ethel Merman has always succeeded in singing every song that comes her way so that it seems good. In every Broadway show she has graced since *Girl Crazy* in 1930, despite headaches or heartaches, she has shown "the kind of high spirits that suggest she is personally having the time of her life." And besides these she has "a sound knockabout comedy technique, the ability to stay on pitch while shouting at the top of her lungs, and above all, the air of being a hell of a nice girl, though possibly a bit on the violent side."

This singer whose "voice can hold a note as long as the Chase National Bank" admits, however, that she's lucky as well as good. "Why, I'm the gal that makes Cinderella a sob story," she says. She was born in Astoria, New York, the daughter of Edward Zimmerman, accountant, and Agnes Zimmerman, who used to be a choir singer, and brought up in a middle class home there. She went to Public School 4 in Long Island City and then to Bryant High School there.

She left high school trained to be a competent secretary and had little trouble getting herself a position as secretary to Caleb Bragg, president of the B. K. Vacuum Booster-Brake Company in Long Island City. But Ethel had been an ambitious girl ever since she was a youngster singing *How You Goin' To Keep 'Em Down on the Farm?* for the soldiers during the War. Now, when she wasn't taking dictation or typing, she sang at Astoria social affairs and office get-togethers. She never studied singing, though, and she never practiced. The way she did it was all right just as it was, she felt.

It was her secretarial position, strangely enough, that got Ethel Merman her start. She discovered one day that her boss knew George White, producer of the *Scandals,* and persuaded him to give her a note to him. Armed with it, she asked White for a spot in his next show. All she got was an offer of a part in the chorus. She turned it down, and went back to her typewriter. Neverthe-

ETHEL MERMAN

less, the interview had given her enough courage to persuade the owner of the Little Russia Restaurant on 57th Street in Manhattan to put her on the program for two weeks singing torch songs.

Lou Irwin, the theatrical agent, heard her there and began getting her other bookings. He even got her a movie contract with Warner Brothers for six months at $200 a week. Ethel Merman (she left the *zim* part of her name in Astoria with her typewriter) quit her job and sat around waiting for a chance to perform before the camera. All that happened was a weekly check, which looked good after $23 a week in Long Island City but did nothing to satisfy her ambitions. Ethel talked her agent into getting her released from the contract and booking her for less money in places where she could really sing.

After stopovers in small night clubs in New York and a larger one in Miami Beach, Florida, Ethel Merman finally landed in 1929 at Broadway's Les Ambassadeurs night club with the team of Jimmy Durante, Clayton and Jackson, and with this team she made the circuit of the theatres. It was while they were at the Paramount in Brooklyn in 1930 that an important producer, Vinton Freedley, saw her and immediately signed her for *Girl Crazy,* with music by George Gershwin. It opened in October 1930, and overnight Ethel Merman was a smash hit. She got the customers and the rest of the country with her rendition of *I Got Rhythm,* and the critics were soon saying that not since Marilyn Miller had there been a musical star of such unquestioned authority.

When *Girl Crazy* ended its run, George White dashed to get Ethel Merman into his *Scandals,* and not in the chorus either. From this play, after a tour of the Loew theatres in 1932, she went into *Take a Chance,* which

opened in November of that year. That was the musical comedy in which she sang *Eadie Was a Lady* and also the one that made the critics start talking about her "elemental magnificence," her "style," her "irresistible sense of humor."

Two years later, when she appeared in *Anything Goes,* they were still repeating these phrases, and one critic went so far as to rave that "to hear Miss Merman sing the word 'terrifically' in the show's best song, *I Get a Kick Out of You,* is to capture the most exciting esthetic experience in the theatre this season." It was after the opening of this play that its leading lady exclaimed: "I'm having a grand time. I'm just crazy about the kind of time I'm having. My life is full of clothes and interviews and posing for ads and radio offers and benefit performances and night club opportunities and marvelous things."

One of the radio offers was from Lysol, to do a 30-minute series over WABC during the summer of 1935. It was called *Rhythm at Eight,* and in it Ethel Merman picked out one of her past hit songs, built a slight story about it and then steamed off. In October 1936 she was back on Broadway in another hit, *Red, Hot, and Blue,* which John Mason Brown called an "inferior musical comedy" which would have been nothing without Ethel Merman and Jimmy Durante. These two were back together again in February 1939 in *Stars in Your Eyes,* with Ethel Merman "at the top of her form," playing her part with "enormous relish."

December 1939 brought *Dubarry Was a Lady,* which opened in time to catch the World's Fair crowds and delight them with Ethel Merman's ability to sing "high-brow lyrics with low-brow heartiness." And in October 1940 another comedy, *Panama Hattie,* started drawing in the people. Its scene a "canvas Canal Zone where morals are so loose as to be virtually detached," Miss Merman's part there was to save the canal locks and her boy friend from a fifth columnist's dynamiting attempt. It was after this show opened that Ethel Merman confessed what a lot of people had long suspected: "I guess I'm just typed for parts with across-the-railroad-tracks overtones, but I must admit they sit easily on me at that."

Long before *Panama Hattie,* which she left at the end of December 1941 because of ill health, motion picture audiences had been given a chance to judge for themselves. In 1934 Ethel Merman appeared in *We're Not Dressing* and *Kid Millions,* this last with Eddie Cantor (see sketch this issue); in 1935 she was seen in *The Big Broadcast*; in 1936, in *Strike Me Pink* (with Eddie Cantor again) and in the film version of *Anything Goes,* with Bing Crosby (see sketch this issue); in 1938 she was singing again before the camera in *Happy Landing* (with Sonja Henie and Don Ameche), in *Alexander's Ragtime Band,* in *Straight, Place and Show.*

In motion pictures this singer who Lucius Beebe thinks probably "takes vitamin B injections in quantities that would service a locomotive boiler," never made quite the hit she made on the stage. Though it was as easy to appreciate her pert, vivacious appearance, the big, round, dark eyes in her oval face, her dark flowing hair, some of the "bounce" was missing, perhaps due to Hays' Office regulations, perhaps due to the fact that most of the films she was in just didn't give her enough singing opportunities. Ethel Merman liked Hollywood all right but found it an "awful grind" and not very profitable. "You go out there and work your head off," she once said, "and then you find at the end of your picture that you'd have ended up with more money working for a smaller salary in New York."

Besides, Ethel Merman likes living in New York. Before she was married on November 16, 1940 to William B. Smith, a theatrical agent (she roared at the time: "Kid, love is wonderful," but was sued for divorce the following August for "cruelty" and divorced on October 2, 1941) she used to live with her family in a small, comfortable apartment on Central Park West. But she didn't stay at home much. Either she was going to prize fights, football and baseball games or making the rounds every night of the "breezier man-traps of the island." "Really, you know," she explains, "a girl's got to have some rest and relaxation and if she doesn't get it at El Morocco or Monte Carlo where can she find it?"

Despite the fact that jazz (she's an "un-rivaled projector" of it, according to John Mason Brown) brought her to the place where she could relax this way, Ethel Merman, who is now married to Robert D. Levitt, a Hearst promotion man in Manhattan, occasionally has yearnings for a legitimate role, "not exactly Lady Macbeth, you know," but something straight and dramatic. Whether she ever gets one or not she is determined, in her own words, to "make all the money I can, save what I can, and when I'm through I'll quit."

References

Collier's 95 :15+ F 16 '35 pors
Life 7 :58-60 D 11 '39 por
N Y Herald Tribune X p1-2 Ap 6 '41; p10 Ag 7 '41
Time 33 :55 F 20 '39 por ; 36 :65-7 O 28 '40 pors
Brown, J. M. Two on the Aisle p280-2 1938
International Motion Picture Almanac
Who's Who in the Theatre

MERRIAM, GEORGE ERNEST, REV.
1873—Mar. 10, 1941 Retired pastor of Homer Congregational Church; authority on George Washington; had served as a minister of both Presbyterian and Congregational churches; author of two books on religious subjects and a biography of George Washington.

Obituaries

N Y Times p23 Mr 11 '41

METAXAS, JOHN (mĕ-täks-äs') Apr. 12, 1871—Jan. 29, 1941 Premier of Greece; political career began in 1915 when opposed Greece's entry into the First World War on the Allies' side; after exile returned in 1920 but fled again in 1923 after heading a royalist counter-revolution in favor of King George II; returned in 1924 as Minister of Communications in republican government; when George II returned to the throne in 1935 entered the Cabinet and in 1936 was made Premier; shortly after established self as sole head of the Government by a *coup* and in 1938 was proclaimed "Premier for life" (see sketch 1940 Annual).

Obituaries

Christian Cent 58 :211 F 12 '41
N Y Times p1, 4 Ja 30 '41 por
Newsweek 17 :20-1 F 10 '41
Scholastic 38 :3 F 10 '41
Time 37 :29-30 F 10 '41

MEYER, EUGENE Oct. 31, 1875- Member of the National Defense Mediation Board; editor and publisher of the Washington Post

Address: b. Washington Post Bldg, Washington, D. C.; h. Mt. Kisco, N. Y.

EUGENE MEYER

Of Eugene Meyer, editor and publisher of the Washington *Post*, it has been said: "The world is directed by individuals and he is that directing individual wherever he happens to take an interest."

His career seems to have borne out that rather startling statement. Born in Los Angeles on October 31, 1875, Eugene Meyer is the son of an almost equally remarkable father: a Jewish merchant, Eugene Meyer, who emigrated from France by himself when he was 16, came to California "via the Isthmus and a mule's back," settled in Los Angeles when it was little more than a village, mar-

MEYER, EUGENE—*Continued*

ried Harriet Newmark, and finally engaged in commercial banking in San Francisco and New York as a representative of the French firm of Lazard Frères.

Young Eugene was educated in the public schools of San Francisco, spent a year (1892-93) at the University of California and then went on to Yale to take his B. A. in 1895. After Yale there were two years spent in the counting houses of his father's relatives in Paris, London, Berlin, Frankfurt, studying foreign banking, international finance and languages, learning the fundamentals of economics, learning, according to one writer, "to think, to analyze and to uncover the roots of the problems at hand. He developed a keen sense of self-reliance and a pragmatic philosophy of life."

None of this education was wasted. Upon his return he immediately entered his father's banking firm and worked for four years in the New York office of Lazard Frères as a clerk. By 1901 he felt that he was ready to open his own investment banking house, Eugene Meyer, Jr., and Company. Its success was amazingly prompt. By the promotion and distribution of securities "in enterprises which largely lay in new fields of business expansion" Meyer was able within a very few years to buy a seat on the Stock Exchange and to become director of an increasing number of corporations. "He was quite as hard and ruthless as any of his neighbors," said one critic. At least one of the Morgan partners was his associate in transactions from time to time, and Bernard Baruch (see sketch this issue), who had taken him under his financial wing when he first started out, gave him more than one helpful tip.

It was in 1917 that Meyer's career in the Government service began, a career which was to continue until 1933 with few interruptions. When the United States entered the First World War, Baruch brought him down to Washington to take charge of the division of non-ferrous metals of the War Industries Board. Meyer "dissolved his firm without having to worry about the size of his salary." Afterward he told the late Gutzon Borglum: "If you want to get ahead in politics, keep out until you have made your pile. That's what I did. Once you have money, everything opens to you."

He soon showed his talents as a dollar-a-year man. His first metals purchase saved the Government some $7,000,000, and while continuing to make such economies he also served as a member of the National War Savings Committee. In 1918 he was appointed a special assistant to the Secretary of War in connection with aircraft production, which was then causing great disappointment, and reorganization of the Department of Production followed his examination and report.

"Basically in temperament and in experience a deviser of ideas and an initiator and manager of projects," Meyer was so effective in all these jobs that in May 1918 President Wilson named him director of the War Fi-

nance Corporation of the United States, established to give financial support to industries whose operations were "necessary or contributory to the prosecution of the War" and to banking institutions that helped finance such industries. A few months later he became managing director, and remained such throughout the life of the Corporation.

After the War, until its activities were suspended in May 1920, the Corporation continued to function under new powers recommended by Meyer with the approval of the Secretary of the Treasury. Meyer, resigning as managing director that month, warned that reflation and falling prices would come on the heels of the War, and after the predicted collapse of commodity prices and markets actually began he urged the revival of the Corporation's activities before committees of Congress and others.

It was not long before a Congressional resolution, adopted in January 1921 over the veto of President Wilson, directed the Secretary of the Treasury to resume operations, and in March 1921 Meyer was recalled by newly-elected President Harding to serve again as managing director of the Corporation. By August its authority was extended to include work in the field of agricultural finance, and *Mirrors of Wall Street* recalls that he displayed as much political as financial acumen by "pegging up" weak spots in certain states which showed signs of going Democratic.

While pumping credit into agriculture, Meyer proved himself "as hard-boiled in Government service as he was in private business." Unprecedentedly, he insisted that borrowers should repay the money lent them by the Government, and when in 1925 the authority of the War Finance Corporation to make loans ceased forever, all its capital and a substantial profit were returned to the United States Treasury. A Congressional committee charged that Meyer had permitted his brokerage friends to make money out of the Corporation's transactions in government bonds, but the unproved charges did not prevent his appointment in 1926 as chairman of an emergency cotton commission of four. That year his commission was successful in preventing surplus cotton from the recent bumper crop from being dumped on the market, even if the basic problem of crop diversification in the South still remained.

One governmental attempt after another at stimulating production by extending increased credit to private industry or agriculture found Eugene Meyer at the helm. In 1927, at the request of President Coolidge, he undertook the task of reorganizing the Federal Farm Loan Board, the governmental agency which then regulated more than 70 banks engaged in making loans to or for the benefit of farmers. Meyer put them on a sound basis before he was through, but gained many enemies by his methods; before he resigned as Federal Farm Loan Commissioner in 1929 the late Huey Long was calling him "an ordinary tin-pot bucket-shop operator up in Wall Street . . . not even a legitimate banker."

For a while, then, Meyer waited, idle, for President Hoover to give him another job. But he was never idle long. In September 1930 he was recalled to public service as governor of the Federal Reserve Board. His appointment was fought by Iowa's Senator Brookhart, who called him "the Judas Iscariot to cooperation throughout the United States", "one who has worked the Shylock game for the interests of big business"; but Mark Sullivan of the New York *Herald Tribune* wrote: "There is not in the country a man better equipped to stand in the position which constitutes a bridge between the country's banking and currency system and, on the other hand, the country's structure of active business." And *Mirrors of Wall Street* phrased it: "His was the best financial mind in Washington, which had not seen his equal since Paul Warburg served on the Board." According to most reports, the Board, "previously belittled as a debating body and criticized for indecision, soon developed cohesion, independence, and a definite purpose."

In 1931, with the depression at its worst, Meyer prepared the bill creating the Reconstruction Finance Corporation, of which the War Finance Corporation had been the predecessor and prototype, and urged its enactment before committees of Congress in order to bring back prosperity to the United States. ("Virtually every financial emergency law proposed by President Hoover was suggested, in whole or in part, by Mr. Meyer.") It was February 1932 when the RFC was actually organized, trusted with the placing of a capital of $500,000,000 provided by the Government and with a large borrowing capacity, and no one was surprised to find Meyer, "enjoying the confidence of New York bankers and appointed chiefly for that reason," as its first chairman.

Promptly after the passage of the bill, Meyer began the task of setting up the necessary organization and machinery for the handling of its activities. Almost immediately the Corporation began making loans to railways, insurance companies, banks. After six months, however, Meyer resigned from the chairmanship, ostensibly to give full time to his duties as governor of the Federal Reserve Board, actually, according to Pearson and Allen (see sketch this issue), because of friction over the policies of Ogden Mills, Hoover's Secretary of the Treasury.

In May 1933, shortly after Roosevelt became President, Meyer resigned as governor of the Federal Reserve Board, too. But this did not mean retirement from public life. In June 1933 he bought the Washington *Post*, one of the five Washington dailies, for $825,000. For some time the paper had been losing $1,000,000 a year under unimaginative ownership. Rumors that Meyer's real interest was less in reviving Washington journalism than in the Republican Party brought a swift reply: "It will be my aim to improve the *Post*, and to make it an even better paper than it has been in the past. It will be conducted as an independent paper. . . I think I should . . .

make it clear that, in purchasing the *Post*, I acted entirely on my own behalf, without suggestions from or discussion with any person, group, or organization."

Meyer realized that the best way to gain circulation in competition with Washington's four other dailies was to concentrate on his editorial page and special columns. The correctness of his instincts can be measured by the fact that in eight years the *Post's* circulation went up 173 per cent, its advertising lineage 111 per cent, while its annual losses were reduced to $300,000. As for political slant, *Post* editorials forgot worries over the liberal turn in the New Deal to laud Roosevelt's foreign policy, particularly as expressed in the "quarantine the aggressor" speech at Chicago in 1937. Roosevelt returned the compliment by announcing publicly that one *Post* editorial perfectly expressed his own views—was very good, very clear, very honest. And in March 1941 he appointed Meyer to the National Defense Mediation Board.

"Butch" to his workers, a "tremendous hobnobber" who prowls around the *Post* building asking them every conceivable question, Meyer is a daily visitor to Washington's National Press Club—found lounging around there more often than at any of the eight swank New York and Washington clubs of which he is a member. With a fortune conservatively estimated at $30,000,000 in 1938, "the *Post* is for him—in a luxury sense—what steam yachts and strings of race horses may be for some other wealthy men." It is also true that "what he loses on the *Post* he can deduct from his income tax."

The happiness of the Meyer family is said to be something of a tradition in Washington society. Mrs. Eugene Meyer is the former Agnes Elizabeth Ernst, known at the time of her marriage in 1910 as one of the most beautiful women in New York, and there are five children: Florence (Mrs. Oscar Homolka), Elizabeth, Eugene III, Katharine (Mrs. Philip L. Graham) and Ruth. At their country seat in Mount Kisco, New York, everyone in the family can indulge in a fanatical devotion to riding, and Meyer himself can enjoy unusually good tennis with his son or daughters. Five feet eight, this Washington publisher's powerful shoulders and "opaque and glittering" dark eyes belie the impression given by receding hair and old-fashioned nose glasses. He smokes Corona-Coronas, reads avariciously, is fond of giving large dinner parties and occasional music recitals in his Washington home (he likes modern composers, too—some of them), and has an odd passion for dominoes, at which he is an expert. Felix Frankfurter (see sketch this issue) is one of his good friends. In conferences he likes to wisecrack, taking an "optimistic view of life and finance," but he wouldn't give an interview for publication even when in 1920 he witnessed the famous Wall Street bombing which killed 20 people. He is energetic, argumentative and at the same time secretive, "loves to answer questions by asking others in return," and once

MEYER, EUGENE—*Continued*

said: "Well, my father taught me to take care of myself. He hired Jim Corbett to teach me boxing. I haven't kept up that training but I retain a give-and-take attitude toward life."

References

Business Week p27-8 Jl 1 '31 por
Christian Sci Mon Mag p3+ My 20 '39 il por
Lit Digest 107:42 O 4 '30 por
Newsweek 1:23 Ap 22 '33; 1:27 Je 24 '33
R of Rs 82:54-6 N '30 por
Sat Eve Post 205:65-6 Jl 2 '32 il por
Time 31:35 Je 27 '38 por; 37:15 Mr ' 31 '41 por; 38:38 Jl 14 '41
World's Work 59:21 N '30; 60:49-53 F '31 il por
Allen, R. S. and Pearson, D. More Merry-Go-Round p114-54 1932
Mirrors of Wall Street p215-36 1933
Who's Who in America
Who's Who in American Jewry
Who's Who in Commerce and Industry
Who's Who in Government
Who's Who in the Nation's Capital

MILHAUD, DARIUS (mêl-ō′)   Sept. 4, 1892- Composer

Address: c/o Mills College, Oakland, Calif.

In the spring of 1940 music-loving Paris gathered at the Théâtre Nationale de l'Opéra to listen to the première of Darius Milhaud's opera *Medée*. It was something of an event, since it was the first opera shown since the War began and since it combined the talents of France's "most original and prolific composer" and of well known artists like Charles Dullin and André Masson. It was also the last opera to be produced by free France. By July the opera had been stopped, Paris had been taken and the composer had fled to the United States to teach composition at Mills College in Oakland, California.

On December 27, 1940 the corpulent, black-haired composer came to Manhattan to perform and to conduct at a one-day "festival" of his compositions (given by the League of Composers) which included excerpts from his operas, some symphonic poems, a string quartet and a cantata. Needless to say, this represented but a minute fraction of Milhaud's works. His output is enormous. Throughout his musical career, he has translated his experiences into music as naturally as thoughts into speech. He is interested in all the noises that human voices or instruments can make. He has set everything to music, from poetry by Francis Jammes to descriptions of agricultural machines and florists' catalogs. It has even been said that "he has composed too much music, relying on the prodigality of his genius rather than upon his sense of criticism." But his latest compositions, particularly the fateful militant *Cortège Funèbre*, a dirge for the fallen Netherlands, show that Darius Mil-

haud can "still turn expertly a phrase of hard-bitten counterpoint."

Darius Milhaud was born in Aix-en-Provence, France, on September 4, 1892. In 1910 he went to the Paris Conservatoire, where he studied violin under Berthélier, harmony under Xavier Leroux, counterpoint with Gédalge, and composition with Widor. During his years of study he won several prizes, among them the coveted *Prix de Composition Lepaulle* (in 1915), with his first work, a sonata for two violins and piano. He was preparing for the *Prix de Rome* when the War came, but in 1917 gave up music for a brief diplomatic career with the French legation at Rio de Janeiro.

Paradoxically this proved of considerable value to him in his musical career. His superior was Ambassador Paul Claudel, a well known poet, and there began a long collaboration from which came some of Milhaud's best works for the stage. Claudel wrote the librettos for Milhaud's *Protée* (1913-1919); *L'Homme et son Désir* (1918); and *Christophe Colomb* (1930), the last being the best known of his works. "Poet and composer were in thorough agreement on all points in their fondness for mingling the trite and the singular, the subtle and the coarse, realism and fantasy." In 1919 when Milhaud came back to Paris he brought with him a few experiments in South American rhythms, among them the well known *Saudades de Brazil* (1921).

Milhaud took up his musical career where the War had interrupted it and became the leader of the famous *Groupe des Six*, a group of young composers, fostered by Erik Satie and Jean Cocteau. The other five were Arthur Honegger (see sketch this issue), Francis Poulenc, Georges Auric, Louis Durey and Germaine Tailleferre. These gifted young enthusiasts, no longer satisfied with the esthetic theories of Debussy and Ravel, were mainly interested in breaking down the reign of impressionism in music. "Their inspiration was largely derived from the American jazz rhythms and popular music, which they parodied in a witty and sophisticated way." Undeniably, however, much of their work was motivated by the desire to *épater le bourgeois*.

Like the exponents of all the arts in the talky '20s, *Les Six* talked music as much as they composed it. One work they composed together was music for Cocteau's ballet *Les Mariés de la Tour Eiffel* (1921). Milhaud, however, soon freed himself from the group and began to compose music in his own unique style with his own personal vocabulary. His growth proved so rapid that in less than three years he was regarded as one of the most important musicians since Debussy. He was well known for his Wagnerophobia, his anti-impressionism, his interest in ragtime and jazz, his versatility and as a steadfast exponent of polytonality. To that period belong some of his sensational innovations, such as the use of cinema in grand opera (in *Christophe Colomb*) and the introduction of declamation performed in rhythm with accompaniment of percussion (*Les Choëphores*, 1919). His *Chris-*

tophe Colomb was hailed as the most sensational musical work of its time. The resurgence of ballet offered new possibilities for his music: his *La Création du Monde* (1923) for the Swedish ballet was the first jazz ballet to be performed, and later he wrote *Le Train Bleu* (1924) for Diaghilev.

Yet then, as now, it was hard to place Milhaud in any specific category. His versatility in music is Protean. His predilection for dissonance is undeniable; yet Aaron Copland could write of him: "Milhaud's gift is clearly that of lyricist. His musical nature impels him toward one end: a spontaneous outpouring of the emotion in terms of pure music. His music always sings." It is the dissonance used as a background to his ever-present melody that gives it its "modern" *cachet*. The truth is that Milhaud is a composer who strives for varied and original effects and gets them by various means, violent and poetic by turns, sometimes resorting to satire, even buffoonery.

Milhaud first came to the United States in the winter of 1923 to appear as soloist in his *Ballade* for the piano and orchestra and as conductor of his serenade with Dirk Foch's City Symphony Orchestra. He came back in the fall of 1926 to play his works under the direction of Damrosch and Willem Mengelberg, and on both occasions he made extensive lecture tours. (In France he has made his mark as a music critic, and he was awarded the Légion d'Honneur in 1934.)

Milhaud has written in practically every field of music. He has to his credit a symphony which was performed in New York on February 5, 1941 under the direction of Leopold Stokowski (see sketch this issue); 10 quartets; a great number of symphonic works; 12 theatrical pieces, most of them in one act (the best known are *La Brebis Egarée* [1923]; *Le Pauvre Matelot* [1927]; *Christophe Colomb* [1930]). He has written many ballets, among them *Le Boeuf sur le Toit* (1919) and *L'Homme et son Désir* (1921). The latest, *The Men from Midiam,* is expected to be performed by the Ballet Theatre of New York in 1942. Another important part of his creative activity is music for the films: his music for Jean Renoir's *Madame Bovary* has been played as a suite of short pieces. He has written numerous cantatas and accompaniments to poetry, too—best known are the *Voyage d'Été* and the *Cantate de la Mere et d'Enfant* to the text of Maurice Carême.

Darius Milhaud has retained from the old days his love for talking and theorizing. He was accompanied to the United States by his pretty, doe-eyed wife, Madeleine Milhaud, whom he had married in 1925. She is a well known actress and *diseuse* in her own right and has collaborated with Milhaud in his concerts. He has not been overly distressed by being uprooted from his native land. For one thing he finds the climate of California much like his native Provence. Then, too, he finds considerable "stimulus and invigoration in the dynamism and many challenges" of the American scene. Creative musicians, he says, are not silenced by political changes, however

DARIUS MILHAUD

drastic, and recalls that Verdi composed even under foreign domination.

References

Etude 59:589+ S '41 por
Liv Age 350:140-1 Ap '36
Modern Music 6:14 Ja '29
N Y Herald Tribune VI p6 D 22 '40 por
N Y Times IX p5 Jl 21 '40
Newsweek 17:43-4 Ja 6 '41 por
Revue Musicale 6:251 Mr '25
Time 36:39 Ag 12 '40 por
Baker's Biographical Dictionary of Musicians 1940
Ewen, D. ed. Composers of Today 1936
Qui Êtes-Vous?
Rosenfeld, P. Discoveries of a Music Critic p230-4 1936
Saleski, G. Famous Musicians of a Wandering Race 1927
Who's Who

MILLARD, BAILEY (mĭl'ûrd) Oct. 2, 1859—Mar. 20, 1941 Writer for the Los Angeles *Times* for past 17 years; former editor of metropolitan newspapers and of *Cosmopolitan* and *Munsey's* Magazine; as literary editor of the San Francisco *Examiner* first published Edwin Markham's *Man With the Hoe* (1899) and helped introduce the writings of Joaquin Miller; author of 11 books, some of them on history of the region about San Francisco.

References

Who's Who Among North American Authors
Who's Who in America

Obituaries

N Y Times p21 Mr 21 '41

MILLER, ALICE DUER July 28, 1874-
American poet, novelist and dramatist
Address: 450 E. 52nd St, New York City

"If only I'm not too muddle-headed . . ."
sighed Mrs. Miller while planning a narrative
poem based on American history.

Few self-criticisms could be wider of the
mark. "Muddle-headed" is probably the last
thing anyone who knows Mrs. Miller would
accuse her of being. The usual critical estimate of her novels is that they are "light and
expert." Her plays are first-class comedies.
Her sensational 1940 success, *The White
Cliffs*, which begins:

> I have loved England, dearly and
> deeply
> Since that first morning, shining and
> pure,
> The white cliffs of Dover I saw rising
> steeply
> Out of the sea that once made her
> secure

is undoubtedly one of the few poems which
sold 125,000 copies in its first ten months.
This is only the United States sale; it sold
25,000 in England and thousands more in
Central and South America during the same
period. It was abridged in *Life*, it was read
more than once over the radio by Lynn Fontanne (see sketch this issue), Mrs. Miller
herself read it many times for the benefit of
the British War Relief, and it was sold as a
film short.

Its author said modestly: "The success it
has had is due to British heroism rather than
to its own merits." But the National Poetry
Center, disagreeing with her, named her as
1941 winner of the Golden Scroll and Medal
of Honor it awards annually to the nation's
foremost poet, and Noel Coward (see sketch
this issue) wrote: "I should imagine that even

a Hottentot, providing he had a reasonable
knowledge of the English language, could not
fail to be impressed and touched by the
sincerity, quality and charm of this book, but
I am an Englishman and as such obviously
prejudiced, very prejudiced, indeed, and very
grateful." Even *Time*, which called it
doggerel, called it "grade-A doggerel."

This short novel in verse, the story of an
American girl married to an upper-class Englishman, who gives first her husband and then
her son to die for England, was Mrs. Miller's
second venture into narrative verse. The first
was *Forsaking All Others* (1931), a novel in
verse about divorce. Her most recent book
is *I Have Loved England* (1941), an historical
and literary text illustrated with 100 photographs of English scenes.

She is best known, however—or was, before
The White Cliffs—as a novelist. Among her
novels are *The Modern Obstacle* (1903);
Calderon's Prisoner (1903); *Less Than Kin*
(1909); *The Blue Arch* (1910); *Come Out of
the Kitchen* (1916) (a starring vehicle for
Ruth Chatterton and afterward a popular
film); *The Charm School* (made into a play
with Robert Milton in 1919); *The Beauty and
the Bolshevist* (1920); *Manslaughter* (1921);
The Priceless Pearl (1924); *The Reluctant
Duchess* (1925); *Gowns by Roberta* (as
Roberta, a highly successful musical comedy,
1933); *Come Out of the Pantry* (1934);
Death Sentence (1935); *Five Little Heiresses*
(1936); *The Rising Star* (1937); *Not For
Love* (1937); *And One Was Beautiful* (1938).

Besides this, she has written one play, *The
Springboard* (1928), and has collaborated in
the dramatization of three of her novels.
There have also been two non-fiction books, *Are
Women People?* (1915) and *Are Parents
People?* (1924). Her novels are usually
serialized before book publication in the *Saturday Evening Post*, the *Ladies' Home Journal*
or the *Woman's Home Companion*. Her
short stories have been collected into a volume under the title of *Taxi* (1931).

Mrs. Miller says that she started out in
life with the idea of becoming a "high brow"
novelist—Henry James was her model. She
had financed herself in college (she was
graduated from Barnard in 1899) by writing
stories for *Harper's* and *Scribner's* and short
essays for these and other literary magazines.
"After a time," she says, "I decided that I
was too ambitious in my writing attempts and
turned to lighter material." When she married Henry Wise Miller the fall after her
graduation from college, the young couple was
pretty hard up. Mrs. Miller decided to help
out by her writing. The *Saturday Evening
Post* accepted *Come Out of the Kitchen* "at
almost precisely the same time" that Mr.
Miller obtained a good position in Wall Street.
Neither of them has had to worry about finances since.

Mrs. Miller is a native New Yorker, born
July 28, 1874. Her parents were James G. K.
and Elizabeth (Meads) Duer—pronounced
"due-er." Her grandfather was Rufus King,
American Minister to England in 1844. In

ALICE DUER MILLER

her apartment on the East River, which is largely furnished with eighteenth century furniture, she has a console table that belonged to him, together with one that belonged to Edward Everett. The only sign of literary activity apparent to the visitor is the portable typewriter on an antique kneehole desk by the window. "I like to have lots of quiet when I work," she says.

She also still needs lots of encouragement. After every book she is sure it is her last, and that she will never be able to write another. After *And One Was Beautiful* she announced to her husband and son that she had reached the age of retirement and meant to stop writing, since all she could do in the future would be a mere rehash of the past. "Mother," said her son, "you've told me that in just the same way three times that I can remember. Why don't you stop it? You didn't mean it before and you don't mean it now." So instead of retiring she wrote *The White Cliffs*.

Though she has spent most of her life in New York, Mrs. Miller has lived for long periods in Costa Rica, on the French Riviera, in Scotland, and of course in London. She has visited Hollywood several times to help in filming her novels, but has never stayed there long. She is too attached to her family and to the beautiful apartment on the East River in which she has lived for the past 10 or 12 years.

In the teen years of the twentieth century, she was an active suffragist—as her book *Are Women People?* might suggest. She has always been rather socially minded. In 1916 she was one of the founders of the Women's City Club in New York, and was its first president. The anti-suffragists and feminine reactionaries in general shied away from the club—its sponsors advocated not only votes for women, but also such "radical" ideas as city planning, health education and crime prevention. Today the club has a membership of 1,067, including leaders among women in professional, business and social life.

Rather unexpectedly for so gentle and seemingly fragile a person, Mrs. Miller's favorite recreation is baseball. She is a long-time Giants fan, seldom misses a game and knows all the points and all the players. She is quite capable of conducting a technical discussion on a sport which interests few women of her generation.

Seen under less unconventional circumstances, Mrs. Miller is a slender, graceful woman, once blonde but now gray, with deepset blue eyes and a "feminine" taste in dress. She is thoroughly enjoying the excitement over *The White Cliffs*; though she has never cared for formal "society," she is entirely a woman of the world, one who likes to be in the forefront, doing things. No one to see her or hear her speak would think that she is in her late 60's. She has been indefatigable about flying out to Cleveland or Washington or Boston to autograph her books in the stores there. "I enjoy every minute of it," she told Robert Van Gelder, who interviewed her between trips. "All the cities seem so lively." The one thing Mrs. Miller does wish people would stop saying is that *The White Cliffs*, which grew out of her admiration for England in this hour of crisis, is in any way autobiographical. It is not; her husband is an American, and her son is alive and has never been a British soldier. Many of the minor incidents in the poem, however, are taken from real life. The only letter of complaint Mrs. Miller has received came from a man with a German name who accused her of "kowtowing to the British." "I certainly don't feel that that accusation is just," she says. "It is not wholly favorable, you know." As her poem ends:

> I am an American bred,
> I have seen much to hate here—
>   much to forgive
> But in a world where England is
>   finished and dead
> I do not wish to live.

References

Arts & Dec 38:10-13+ N '32 il
N Y Post p11 Mr 31 '41 por; p3 My 3 '41 por
N Y Times p19 Je 8 '41
New Yorker 3:24+ F 19 '27
Sat R Lit 13:1 Ap 11 '36 por
Scholastic 33:4 D 17 '38 por
Variety 141:2 Ja 1 '41
American Women
Overton, G. M. Women Who Make Our Novels p206-13 1929
Who's Who Among North American Authors
Who's Who in America

MILLER, DAYTON C(LARENCE) Mar. 13, 1866—Feb. 22, 1941 Internationally known physicist, who was best known for his experiments tending to prove the existence of the ether, experiments which challenged one of the basic hypotheses of Professor Albert Einstein's theory of relativity; leading authority on sound; had what is believed to be the world's largest collection of flutes; made one of gold which produces a curious rich tone that cannot be duplicated by any other instrument.

References

Sci Am 161:69 Ag '39 por
American Men of Science
Leaders in Education 1941
Who's Who in America
Who's Who in Engineering 1941

Obituaries

N Y Times p41 F 23 '41 por

MILLER, DOUGLAS (PHILLIPS) May 22, 1892- Economist; author; diplomat; assistant to William J. Donovan, United States coordinator of defense information

Address: c/o Little, Brown & Co, 34 Beacon St, Boston, Mass.

In 1941 one of the steady best sellers on non-fiction lists was Douglas Miller's *You*

DOUGLAS MILLER

Can't Do Business With Hitler (1941). There was nothing newsworthy about the book's title; the point was that Miller, who for 15 years had been in the service of businessmen at the United States Embassy in Berlin, was in a position to prove the case. President Roosevelt publicly praised the book, and William Shirer (see sketch this issue) of *Berlin Diary* fame announced: "It's a book that ought to be on the desk of every businessman in this country."

Reviewers found certain quotations particularly worth repeating. For instance: "There is no such thing as having purely economic relations with the totalitarian State. Every business deal carries with it political, military, social, propaganda implications." Or: "The Nazis believe in 100 per cent or nothing—and 100 per cent for them and nothing for us would be the usual arrangement." Or, again: "What the Nazis really would like: to unify Europe and divide America." Chapter headings were equally revealing: Hitler Is Our Enemy; Rule of Force Not Law; Leadership Principle; Militarism; Racial Superiority; Economic Sterility; Falsehood and Treaty Breaking.

Conservative, unsentimental, far from idealistic, Miller indicts Nazism not for its moral crimes but for the danger it holds to American business enterprise. He says: "I believe that what we do *now* will determine our economic history for years to come. And I believe that what affects the American businessman cannot help but affect every American." He also believes, though, that even if Hitler is defeated the world will never return to its old system of private trading and laissez-faire economy, an opinion which caused the New York *Herald Tribune* reviewer to call his own book "Nazi-minded."

"I make these statements," says Miller, "on the basis of my long residence in Berlin, my close association with Nazi leaders and their party, a detailed study of National Socialist books, pamphlets and newspapers from the very beginning of their movement when they were less cautious about discussing ultimate objectives. These convictions I formed slowly under the pressure of overwhelming evidence."

Born at Fayette, Iowa on May 22, 1892, Douglas Miller cast off his provincialism early. He was brought up in Minnesota, Vermont and Colorado and, after having been graduated from the East Denver High School in 1908 and from the University of Denver in 1913, earned his M. A. at the University and in 1915 was chosen from Colorado's scholars for a Rhodes Scholarship at Oxford University. In 1916 he went to Oxford. During vacations he did relief work with the British Army. In the spring of 1917 he went to India and became manager of the British Army canteens for Mesopotamia, and the period after the Armistice found him in Siberia, shipping relief supplies over the Trans-Siberian railroad. It was not until the fall of 1919 that he returned to Oxford. He obtained a degree in jurisprudence there in June 1920 and then was stationed in Stettin, Germany, in work consisting of the repatriation of Russian and German prisoners of war.

After he joined the United States Department of Commerce in October 1921 his rise was rapid. He became assistant chief of the Western European Division of the Bureau of Foreign and Domestic Commerce, also teaching in the Foreign Service School of Georgetown University. In May 1924 he began his 15 years' service with the American Embassy in Berlin, sent there as trade commissioner. In 1925 he became assistant commercial attaché, later commercial attaché.

From 1925 on, in his reports, he frequently noted the upward trend of German trade, growing business prosperity. This did not make him close his eyes to what was going on. As early as October 1931 he prepared a report to Washington on how the coming National Socialist State in Germany would operate, an account which "still stands substantially correct." But few others were worried; the next year Miller was attending a still-cheerful dinner in his honor given by the Board of Trade for German-American Commerce. An entry in Ambassador Dodd's diary in August 1933, not long after Hitler had come to power, is revealing: "Conferred with our commercial attaché here, Douglas Miller, who speaks German fluently and is married to a German wife. My first acquaintance with his work came only a day ago when his admirable survey of German conditions under the Hitler regime came to my desk, exceedingly well done." William Shirer wrote later: "Mr. Miller is not only a very able economist, but a student of history as well. In fact, in my time in Berlin he was undoubtedly the best informed man in our Embassy on all aspects of life under the Nazis."

The attitude of the commercial attaché toward most aspects of that life, after repeated visits to the Foreign Office to protest against the treatment of Americans attempting to do business in or with Germany, became so cynical that he framed on the wall of his office a motto taken from Hitler's newspaper: "Justice and good nature should be limited to one's own people." To one businessman, on the verge of ruin because of an arbitrary ruling by one Nazi official, he advised: (1) close up and clear out; (2) find out how much it would cost to persuade the official to change the ruling; (3) "a Nazi firm in similar circumstances might consider having the official assassinated."

Several years before the Second World War Douglas Miller was quite certain that it would come and that commercial relations between the United States and Germany would end; therefore in September 1938 he cabled a request to return to the United States, predicting war in the summer of 1939. In November of 1938 he was recalled, and in May 1939 he resigned his position as commercial attaché, planning to stay in the United States indefinitely.

In September 1939 Douglas Miller accepted a position as assistant professor of economics in the School of Commerce of the University of Denver. In June 1941, after having completed *You Can't Do Business With Hitler,* he was granted a year's leave of absence from the University to undertake a study of National Socialist economy under the auspices of the Rockefeller Foundation in New York City. Soon after that he was appointed assistant to Colonel William J. Donovan (see sketch this issue), coordinator of defense information. He was already the author of numerous published articles in Department of Commerce reports and trade information bulletins as well as the author of unpublished government reports, and since the publication of his book he has been much in demand as a writer of articles and as a speaker.

All of Miller's diplomatic experience has not been in Berlin. He has represented the United States in many international gatherings, having been on the staff of the American delegation to the Limitation of Armaments Conference in Washington in 1921, on the staff of the American delegation to the World Economic Conference in Geneva six years later and a delegate to a commission of the League of Nations for drawing up a draft for customs regulations in Geneva in 1935. He was also American delegate to the International Chamber of Commerce Convention in Berlin in 1937.

A balding, agreeable, full-faced man who looks like a successful American businessman himself and who smokes a pipe "big enough to 'bean' Hitler with," Douglas Miller is a member of the National Press Club in Washington, D. C. He has one son.

References

Pub W 140:392 Ag 9 '41 por
Sat R Lit 24:1 Jl 5 '41 por
Who's Who in Government

MILLION, J(OHN) W(ILSON) Mar. 6, 1863—Sept. 5, 1941 Educator; made president of Mardin College, Mexico, Missouri in 1897, after two years there as professor of history and political economy; from 1921 to 1926 was president of Des Moines University in Iowa; after his retirement was head of the Western Reference and Bond Association, a teachers' placement organization; active in Baptist church work.

References

Who's Who in America 1926-27

Obituaries

N Y Times p49 S 7 '41 por

MINOR, ROBERT July 15, 1884- Acting general secretary of the Communist Party
Address: Communist Party of the United States of America, 35 E. 12th St, New York City

On February 24, 1941, after the Supreme Court had upheld the four-year prison sentence against Earl Browder for passport fraud, it was announced that Robert Minor had been appointed acting general secretary of the Communist Party of the United States. For 20 years Minor, once a well known newspaper cartoonist, had been a member of the National Committee of the Party.

He was born on July 15, 1884 in San Antonio, Texas, the son of Robert Berkeley and Routez (Houston) Minor. His father was a schoolteacher and lawyer who later became a district judge—the great-grandson of General John Minor, who was active in the American Revolution. His mother was a member of General Sam Houston's family. Young Minor, however, attended public school for only four years: in his middle teens he "hit the road." His first job was as a messenger for the Western Union Telegraph Company, his second as a sign painter's apprentice. By the time he was 18 he was a working carpenter, and not long afterward he joined the Carpenters' Union of the American Federation of Labor.

After an unsuccessful carpenters' strike Minor found himself jobless once more, and once more began touring the country via freight train. He found a chance job as cartoonist for the San Antonio *Gazette,* contributed occasional drawings and cartoons to country weeklies and labor journals, and after a year or so of working at odd jobs in St. Louis he was rewarded with a job as sketch artist for the St. Louis *Post-Dispatch.* That was in 1906. Of these early drawings and cartoons Art Young says that they "looked as if they had been done with a blunt marking crayon on any kind of paper that was handy, and were never cluttered with detail—only an eyeful, and just a glance would give you the idea. His work was the forerunner of the crayon cartoons in the daily press of today."

Until 1913 Minor remained in St. Louis, dividing his time between cartooning and political activity. He had joined the Socialist Party in 1907, during the struggle for the

ROBERT MINOR

freedom of Bill Haywood, and became a member of the City Central Committee of St. Louis. Then, when he was 29, Joseph Pulitzer summoned him to New York to work for the old *World*—at a salary of $100 a week and a substantial bonus. (That same year Minor spent a short time in Paris, planning to study art, but instead interested himself in the French trade-union movement.) He drew anti-war cartoons for the *World* until the spring of 1915, when that newspaper changed its attitude toward the War; then he quit and went to work for the Socialist newspaper, the New York *Call.* He was sent to Europe to do sketches for the *Call* and for the Newspaper Enterprise Association, a syndicate of the Scripps newspapers, and soon was sending back dispatches, too, from France and from Italy. They pictured such discontent in those countries that eventually only the *Call* was printing them, however.

Back in the United States the next year, Minor was sent by the *Call* and by the NEA to the Mexican border, where war was expected to break out at any moment. The threat failed to materialize, though, and he went to Los Angeles. There he got a telegram telling him that five trade unionists had been arrested in connection with the Preparedness Day parade in San Francisco and urging him to help. For a year and a half he dropped everything else to become organizer for the International Workers' Defense League at a salary of $35 a week, managing publicity for the defense of Tom Mooney, who had been convicted and condemned to death.

In 1918 the *Liberator,* a Left-wing magazine endorsing the War aims set forth both by the Russians and by President Wilson, and somewhat less outspoken than the old *Masses,* was established. Minor was a contributing editor, and its first issue carried a cartoon

by him showing "the rope still around Mooney's neck." Mooney's sentence was commuted to life imprisonment, however, and by the spring of 1918 Minor was once more in Europe, this time as war correspondent for the Philadelphia *Daily Ledger.* While there he visited Russia, and sent articles back which were written from the viewpoint of an anarchist. Art Young says: "This was the philosophy that interested him most at the time: the doctrine that the individual should be free to live his own life unhampered by government restraints imposed against his will."

After the Armistice, Minor visited Germany and France. While in France he made a speech asking the workers not to ship munitions intended for use against Soviet Russia; he was arrested the next day and shipped to Coblenz, the headquarters of the American Army. He spent a month in an army prison, but the charges were finally dropped, and not long after his return to the United States Minor was elected to the Central Executive Committee (now the National Committee) of the Communist Party. At about the same time he began editing the *Liberator,* after Max Eastman resigned as its editor, and he remained at its helm until 1924, when it was submerged into the *Workers' Monthly.* He also drew for Art Young's *Good Morning.*

From 1924 to 1926 Minor lectured for the Communist Party, and in 1928 he became editor of the Communist organ, the *Daily Worker.* His editorship was interrupted when, on March 6, 1930, he was arrested with other Communist leaders for participating in an unemployed demonstration in Union Square. He was given an indeterminate sentence, and served six months in prison on Welfare Island and with a bridge-building gang on Riker's Island until released from prison in October 1930 to undergo an appendicitis operation.

In 1933 Minor polled 26,000 votes as Communist candidate for Mayor of New York City. He directed the work of the Communist Party on the behalf of the Scottsboro Boys and then, in 1935, went to New Mexico to organize the defense of 10 coal miners who were held on murder charges. While there he was kidnapped and seriously beaten up by vigilantes. The year 1936 found him once more running for political office, this time as Governor of New York State. The Communist Party supported Lehman against Dewey, however; Minor polled less than the required 50,000 votes and as a result the Communist Party was ruled off the ballot.

There followed two years in Spain as chief war correspondent of the *Daily Worker* and other associated American and Canadian daily newspapers. By the fall of 1939 Earl Browder was on trial for passport fraud and Minor became chairman of the Committee on Civil Rights for Communists. In November 1940 he was also a member of the committee of five that drew up the amendment to the Party's constitution dissociating the organization from the Communist International. As secretary of the Party, in June 1941 he led the "about-face" that made the European War, once condemned as "imperialist," the "business of the United States."

Minor is described as genial, a "tall, rugged man with a sharp nose and a bald pate fringed in white hair." Art Young once said of him in *Good Morning*: "When he talks, it is as if he thought a reporter for posterity were listening in, and his words and sentences are formed with precision, and are grammatical enough to suggest that a good college professor was lost to the world when Bob joined the proletarian movement." He has been married three times: in 1915 to Pearl Bazarie (they were divorced in 1919); in 1920 to Mary Heaton Vorse, the writer (divorced in 1922); later to ex-socialite Lydia Gibson, his present wife.

References

Daily Worker p1, 4 F 26 '41 por
N Y Herald Tribune p20 F 25 '41 por
N Y Post p3 F 25 '41
N Y Times p1, 16 F 25 '41 por
N Y World-Telegram p11 F 21 '41 il por
Time 37:24 Ap 7 '41 por
Young, A. H. Art Young: His Life and Times 1939

MINTON, SHERMAN Oct. 20, 1890-
Judge of the Seventh Circuit Court of Appeals
Address: h. New Albany, Ind.

Bulletin: On May 7, 1941 President Roosevelt nominated Sherman Minton to be a judge of the Seventh Circuit Court of Appeals, which includes the states of Indiana, Illinois and Wisconsin. The nomination was approved unanimously on May 15.

From March 1941 issue:

In January 1941 President Roosevelt announced that he had appointed Sherman Minton as one of his six White House administrative assistants: to be his legs, eyes and ears, especially on matters of defense. The ex-Senator, the President pointed out, has the requisite "passion for anonymity" for the job. He also has, it is agreed, the requisite sympathy with the President's aims.

Ever since he entered the Senate in 1935 Sherman Minton has been a firm supporter of the Administration. He was "one of the Administration's aces" in the Supreme Court fight; he fought against the Hatch Bill; he has repeatedly defended the New Deal spending and public debt policy; he has been strongly in favor of Roosevelt's defense measures. In fact, there have been only two times—when he voted for the soldiers' bonus and voted to override the Presidential veto on the measure to continue low interest rates to farmers—when he has publicly disagreed with the President.

To a good many people Sherman Minton's early New Deal stand in the Senate was somewhat unexpected, in the light of his conservative legal background. He was born in Georgetown, Indiana, the son of John Evan

and Emma (Lyvers) Minton. His family moved away from there when he was quite young, and Sherman was reared and educated in New Albany, Indiana. After being graduated from the New Albany high school in 1910 he went to Indiana University, received his letter in football and baseball, and left with an LL. B. in 1915. A year of graduate law work at Yale University followed, and Minton left New Haven with an LL. M. in 1916.

He went back to New Albany and started to practice law in his home town. Soon after he was in the swing of legal work there he married Gertrude Gurtz in 1917 (the Mintons now have three children) and soon after that found himself fighting in the First World War. From 1917 to 1919 he served as a captain in the United States Infantry, returning to his law practice when demobilized. At that time he was working for the firm of Stotsenburg and Weathers, which in 1922 became Stotsenburg, Weathers and Minton; he left it in 1925 to go to Miami, Florida to practice with the firm of Shutts and Bowen.

Harris & Ewing
SHERMAN MINTON

After three years in Florida, Minton returned to New Albany and his law practice there. When Paul V. McNutt became Governor of Minton's home state he appointed Minton public counselor of Indiana, his main job being to argue utility rates for the Indiana Public Service Commission. He was successful at this, and his efficiency in beating down the rates won him a reputation that extended even beyond his own state.

In 1934 Minton announced his candidacy for the Senate. McNutt gave him his backing; the Young Democrats put up posters saying "Sherman Minton's character and vision hold appeal to the Young Voter, likewise to both the Progressive and Conservative elements

MINTON, SHERMAN—*Continued*

of our citizenship. Conservatives know his principles are soundly founded. Progressives know he has foresight and stands for justice." Minton swept into office with the Democratic tide.

He first announced his arrival in the Senate when he called together a group of his colleagues for joint action to break a Huey Long filibuster. They broke it. Then he proceeded to make very clear his sympathies with the New Deal, despite his years of practice with law firms with large corporation accounts. Soon considered "one of the Administration's most capable men," he was offered the Senate's assistant Democratic leadership after the death of Joe Robinson, and there were many who kept bringing up his name for Supreme Court vacancies.

Senator Minton was most active on the Lobby Committee of the Senate, set up to investigate the whole business of lobbying in Washington. He was a member of the Committee in 1935 and its chairman in 1937, the subject of an infinite amount of controversy. It was also a position that gave rise to occasional humor. There was the time when a crate of celery went sent from Florida to each Senator who voted against the project to build a canal across the state's northern part. Minton got one, too. But he sent his back. In 1938 he received wide publicity when he introduced a bill, later defeated, making it a felony to publish a "known untruth," and also when he brought charges against *Rural Progress,* the farm journal edited by the late Glenn Frank of the Republican Committee.

The heavy-set Senator had a hard time when he ran for election in 1941 on the Democratic ticket in Willkie's home state. The Republican sweep sent Raymond E. Willis to the Senate and Sherman Minton to the "anonymity" he prizes. But it was short-lived. Two months later President Roosevelt had appointed him to his $10,000-a-year White House position.

References

Nation's Bus 25:17+ D '37
N Y Times p11 Ja 8 '41 por
Time 31:48 My 30 '38
Who's Who in America
Who's Who in Law
Who's Who in the Nation's Capital

MIRANDA, CARMEN (mê-rän'dä) 1913-
Singer; film actress
Address: c/o 20th Century-Fox Studios, Hollywood, Calif; h. Westwood, Hollywood, Calif.

Upon her arrival in the United States in the spring of 1939, Brazil's Carmen Miranda was hailed as "the best ambassador of good will that's come from those tropical shores." Since then Miss Miranda has gone before Technicolor cameras to sing and *samba* (a swing dance, according to *Time*) for American movie fans who understand no Portuguese

and would be surprised to learn that the songs were refined for their special benefit.

She is here to stay, according to news reports, and is already almost as well known here as in South America. In March 1941 the Roxy Theatre presented her in a stage show in conjunction with the New York première of *That Night in Rio,* in which she sings, dances and acts. It was the signal for more "ambassadorial" comments in the press, and, as usual, Miss Miranda was almost unreservedly praised by critics.

To Americans, Miss Miranda's style of dress is as intriguing as her presentation of songs *con moviemento.* Soon after her opening in New York in *The Streets of Paris,* the 1939 musical revue that took the New York World's Fair jinx off Broadway, her flamboyant costumes—suggesting the brash colors of tropical birds—attracted the attention of designers. Fashion pictures of Carmen Miranda appeared in profusion, featuring the heavy costume jewelry, the bold color contrasts of her flaring skirts and jaunty jackets, and modifications of the famous Miranda turban decorated with bananas, peaches, pears and other fruit.

Costumes and camera lend the illusion of height to Miss Miranda in her picture work. Flaring skirts and high turbans make it hard to believe that she is a mere five feet two inches tall, petite and vivacious. Similarly, the brilliant colors she wears have led critics to describe her eyes as gray, green or brown—in reality they are light brown flecked with gray and green. Set wide apart, below slanting brows, they add to the exotic note conveyed by the singer's halting but picturesque English. She has a large curly mouth and smiles often. She has a high, rounded forehead and dark reddish-brown hair, and her skin is dark enough to have been described as *café au lait.*

Born in Lisbon, Portugal in 1913, Miss Miranda's given name was Maria do Carmo da Cunha. Her parents were José Pinto Cunha and Maria Emilia (Miranda) da Cunha, and they took her at the age of three months to Rio de Janeiro, Brazil, where her father was in the wholesale produce business until his death a few years ago. Her parents were well off and disapproved of her wish to go on the stage. Well-brought up Brazilian girls didn't, ordinarily, grow up to sing in night clubs! At the age of 15, however, Carmen was set on a singing career and began making the rounds of local radio studios. After a number of unsuccessful auditions she finally had her radio debut over a Rio de Janeiro station.

By 1931 Carmen Miranda's talents were beginning to be recognized, and within a few years her fame in South America rivaled that of Raquel Meller. Her fame in the United States is inescapably bound up with her method of presenting songs, the dynamics of eyes, hands and hips that she sums up in the term *con moviemento,* but the keystone of her early success came from recordings. She had made more than 300 discs, nearly all of them best sellers in the South American market before the singer was known at all north of the equator. The success of these records was what led to night club and theatre engagements in her home city, sophisticated Rio de Janeiro, and elsewhere. She made three films and she toured the South American continent nine times, playing to packed houses.

With such a background, it is misleading to speak of her as a "discovery," as some writers have done. What happened was that Claiborne Foster, former actress and wife of Maxwell J. Rice, a Pan American Airways official stationed at Rio, saw Carmen Miranda at Rio's Casino Urca. This was a fashionable night club where she sang, it is said, for the equivalent of around $100 nightly. Miss Foster promptly wrote about her to Claude Greneker, Lee Shubert's press agent; on a South American cruise the veteran Broadway producer visited Rio, heard Miss Miranda and signed her to a three-year contract. Not everyone was made happy by his visit. When the singer's boat was about to sail, 500 woebegone swains were on hand to sing a favorite song, *Boneca de Pixe* (Tar Doll).

Brief notices heralded the impending arrival in New York of the Brazilian singing star, a situation that changed abruptly on her arrival. For with 20 words of English and something "different" about her that gave photographers a field day, she proved her own best press agent. "I say money, money, money!" she exclaimed. "I say money, money, money, and I say hot dog! I say yes, no, and I say money, money, money, and I say turkey sandwich and I say grape juice." Through her interpreter she added soberly: "This is the golden dream of my life to come here."

On her journey to America, Carmen brought her own *Bando da Lua* to play the rhythmic native tunes she sings, and its leader, Aloysio Oliveira, to act as her interpreter. The slack season had hit Broadway early in the spring of 1939, and critics went to the opening of *The Streets of Paris* curious to know what gave Lee Shubert the courage to compete with Grover Whalen and his wonder-world out at Flushing Meadows. The reviews were, to put it simply, raves. Critics were uncertain about her nationality, though enchanted with her personality. Brooks Atkinson wrote of her "Spanish singing"; a fellow critic spoke of "smothered dynamics and cool Spanish décor." Such technical errors were corrected hastily the next day and were, in any event, important only as indicating the kind of impression made.

In Miss Miranda's singing there is noticeable a subtle displacement of rhythmic accent, perhaps more often anticipatory than delayed in character, that gives her songs tremendous drive and that reminds one of the *swing* in jazz: Brazilian native music has African, as well as Indian, roots. None of her three songs was listed in the program. One told of a Madrid bullfight, another described her costume, and a third was "jost fast song." "She sings them mezza-voce," a critic observed, "with a quality that resembles the plunking, plangent tone of a guitar."

"Her face is too heavy to be beautiful," read one of her first press notices in New York, "her figure is nothing to write home about, and she sings in a foreign language. Yet she is the biggest theatrical sensation of the year." A reporter from the *New Yorker* was entranced by "slanting green eyes, brilliant, gently insinuating smile, the slow sinuous wiggling of her hips, the fluttering gestures of her hands." And an interviewer spoke of "volatile hands that flew together like a pair of lovebirds as she talked."

CARMEN MIRANDA

A few months after her arrival the South American star was doing night club shows as well as theatre work. In the fall of 1939 she appeared at the Waldorf-Astoria. Then came a role in *Down Argentine Way,* for which she was paid $20,000 minus the Shubert cut. This film was made while she was in New York, contractual obligations preventing her from making the trip to the Coast. 20th Century-Fox sent a director and a Technicolor crew to New York and the scenes featuring Miss Miranda were filmed at the Movietone Studio on Tenth Avenue.

For her second film, *That Night in Rio* (RKO 1941), the studio supplied Carmen with an English instructor. Her speech gradually became more intelligible but without loss of its charming inflections. The songs in this second film were disappointing, some of them a little too close to the more mundane products of our own Tin Pan Alley, and they failed to convey the full impact of Carmen Miranda's talents. Again, to some observers the dance sequences were not all they might have been. After the dance director Hermes Pan got through with the *samba,* it was a typical Hollywood production number. Her third film, *Weekend in Havana,* was well received. In December 1941 she made a fine

MIRANDA, CARMEN—*Continued*

impression in a leading role in *Sons O' Fun* with Olsen and Johnson.

Miss Miranda doesn't drink or smoke. She loves life, big cities, crowds and good food. For recreation she enjoys swimming, speed boating and motoring. She has been on the radio, and on "guest" spots her "torrid" charms are usually emphasized. Unmarried, she has made many tactful and complimentary remarks about American men.

She has four younger brothers and sisters, all of whom live in Brazil with her mother. One of the sisters, Aurora, is a singer who has been successful in New York night clubs. When Carmen went home for vacation in the summer of 1940, her family were at the boat to meet her, along with an estimated crowd of 35,000, and in honor of her visit President Vargas declared a legal holiday.

Her portrait was painted by Paul Meltzner, a fact that gave the artist much more publicity than his numerous paintings of the American scene. But by this time Carmen Miranda might be said to be part of it, in what she herself used naively to refer to as "that Souse American way."

References

Collier's 104:23+ Ag 12 '39 por
N Y Herald Tribune VI p4 Mr 9 '41
N Y Post Je 23 '39
New Yorker 15:15 O 28 '39
PM p55 S 7 '41 por
Vogue 94:50-1 Ag 1 '39 pors

MITROPOULOS, DIMITRI (mē-trō'-pōō-lŏs)   Feb. 18, 1896(?)-   Orchestra conductor

Address: c/o Minneapolis Symphony Orchestra, Minneapolis, Minn.

A Greek came bearing gifts to the 99-year-old Philharmonic-Symphony Society of New York in Carnegie Hall on Thursday evening, December 19, 1940. He came in the person of Dimitri Mitropoulos, conductor of the Minneapolis Symphony, who directed the Philharmonic-Symphony Orchestra in the first of 14 concerts. Ascetic in appearance, tall, bald, dynamic in action, and conducting without desk, baton or score, the newcomer stirred the audience to wild enthusiasm.

Mitropoulos was conducting the orchestra during John Barbirolli's winter vacation. It sounded "like an entirely different body from the one we have been listening to in late months," according to Olin Downes, music critic of the New York *Times*. "This is not said in malice, but as plain fact. The orchestra did not lead the conductor. The conductor led the orchestra, and there was pleasure in the adjusted relation." After Richard Strauss' *Symphonia Domestica*, which Mitropoulos made incredibly exciting, "the subscribers became so enthusiastic they did everything except steal the goalposts." Sometimes he gave the impression of being in the midst of the orchestra, pulling up an inner voice here, punching out an accent there, as the *New Yorker* music critic expressed it.

The other compositions played that evening included Beethoven's second *Leonore* overture and his Symphony Number 4 in B-flat major. The Strauss symphony reappeared on his second program, though not as well played, and was accompanied by three fugues from Bach's *Art of Fugue* and the first local performance of *The Coliseum at Night*. (This last composition is from *Two Impressions of Rome*, by Frederick Woltmann of Flushing, Long Island, who dedicated the score to the conductor and who was present to make his bow.) Mitropoulos returned to Minneapolis after his triumphant New York engagement, and has since been busy denying that he has been asked by the directors of the Philharmonic to become its permanent conductor. For one thing, John Barbirolli's contract has another year to run, as has his own. But he did return to New York to open the 1941-42 symphony season, conducting the NBC symphony orchestra at Radio City on October 7, 1941 and conducting the New York Philharmonic again in December of that year.

Dimitri Mitropoulos, who is the only Greek to have held a baton over the Philharmonic Orchestra in its long existence, was born in Athens, the son of Jean and Anagnostopoulou Mitropoulos. His father was the son of a priest; two of his father's brothers were monks; and the boy often visited his uncles at Mount Athos, where "he was inspired by the beauty and the unworldiness of the monasteries on the cliffs above the sea." At 14 he entered the Conservatory of Athens and studied there for six years, still intending to become a monk himself. But the Greek Orthodox religion forbids the use of any musical instruments in religious services, and Mitropoulos could not bear to be deprived of them.

"The reason I didn't become a monk," he explained to a New York *Times* interviewer, Ross Parmenter, "was because they didn't permit me to have a little harmonium." Relinquishing the religious life, he entered the Army, Greece then being at war with Bulgaria. Since he had played the percussion instruments in the conservatory orchestra, he was made a drummer in an army band. His carriage is still one of military erectness.

After the War and graduation from the University of Athens in 1919, the young musician went to study in Western Europe on scholarships, one of them arranged by Camille Saint-Saëns, the famous French composer. Saint-Saëns had heard and approved an opera which Mitropoulos had composed to the French text of Maurice Maeterlinck's *Soeur Béatrice* while still a student at the Athens Conservatory. The composer of *Samson et Delilah* not only wrote a newspaper article praising the opera, but arranged for Mitropoulos to study in Berlin under the eminent pianist-composer Ferruccio Busoni. (He spent 1920 in Brussels.)

It was in Berlin that Mitropoulos had his first experience in conducting an orchestra: he became assistant conductor at the German state opera house, the Berlin Staatsoper. In 1926 the Athens Conservatory called him back to make him permanent conductor of the

Symphony Orchestra in the place where he had once studied. In 1930 he appeared as guest conductor of the Berlin Philharmonic, and two years later he made his debut in Paris, conducting the Orchestre Symphonique de Paris. At this concert Mitropoulos played the solo part of Prokofiev's (see sketch this issue) Third Piano Sonata while conducting the orchestra. A fortnight later he was heard in England, and he then made a tour of the principal Italian cities. He visited Italy again in 1934, 1935 and 1939, and from 1934 through 1937 conducted an annual three months' orchestral season at Monte Carlo—all this while maintaining his connections with the Athens Conservatory.

Mitropoulos' American debut in 1936 was made as guest conductor of the Boston Symphony Orchestra, where he had come at the personal invitation of Serge Koussevitzky. Here also he played Strauss' *Symphonia Domestica* to great applause. His success was so outstanding that he was invited to return in a similar capacity the following year. That season he was invited to go to Minneapolis, where he has been ever since.

Minneapolis hostesses leave him in peace, since Mitropoulos asked them point blank whether they wanted a perfect musician or a society man, "if they wanted an agreeable entertaining conductor and bad music. They agreed with me and they never bother me." In the summers of 1938 and 1939 he went home to direct open-air concerts in ancient Greek theatres, but when another war seemed inevitable he hastened to return to the United States. He sailed from Athens on September 1, 1939, the day Hitler invaded Poland.

The question of nationalism does not trouble Mitropoulos when he is making up his programs. "I don't believe in making Russian music, in making German music," he told Parmenter. "I don't think Beethoven thought of German music. Music is almost universal. French, Italians, Germans never tried to take national themes. They composed as they did because they had French, Italian and German mentalities. Rachmaninoff still composes Russian music because it is in his blood. So why not compose here with an American mentality?"

A conductor's hardest task, Mitropoulos said, is deciding which kind of authority to use. "You can be a dictator or a president of a republic, and you can get good results both ways. I treat my musicians like colleagues." (At the first rehearsal he delighted the 101 members of the Philharmonic by naming most of them from memory.) It was plain from his intensity, however, remarked Parmenter, "that for all his gentleness, humor and democratic ideas, he could transfix an offending instrumentalist with a chilling and terrifying gaze."

"There is no conductor just like him," according to Olin Downes. "His scale of sonorities is a very wide one, from a barely audible pianissimo to a fortissimo next to deafening." Mitropoulos is obviously a great orchestral technician, remarked Virgil Thomson, the music critic of the New York *Herald*

DIMITRI MITROPOULOS

Tribune, who had begun his season with a bluntly unfavorable review of the Philharmonic's opening concert under the direction of John Barbirolli. "Mr. Mitropoulos conducts the wrong pieces magnificently, shows them a whale of a time. Maybe that is the right way to conduct second-class works. It will be interesting to hear what he does *with* or *to* Mozart, Schubert, Debussy." The *Christian Science Monitor* entered an exception to the "continual overstatement or understatement, whether of dynamics or of pace, that characterized his reading of the Beethoven numbers and impeded their natural flow."

A *New Yorker* interviewer found Mitropoulos "slender, peaceful-looking and bald. He has the solemnity of a monk." He allows himself practically no social life and never goes out after a concert. "His vigorous style, which involves great arm-waving and body action, so exhausts him that he merely staggers to his bed and falls into it. He violates an old occupational tradition by eating before his performances rather than afterward; he's almost a total vegetarian. He *is* a total vegetarian for fourteen days and then varies things on the fifteenth by adding chicken to his diet."

Mitropoulos knows the precise number and the contents of each measure in every piece he plays. "In rehearsals, he fascinates the orchestra by stopping it at a phrase and counting back rapidly to some earlier measure, sounding, in the process, a good deal like a professional American tobacco auctioneer." Besides his opera, Mitropoulos has composed various orchestral works and a *Concerto Grosso*. He is a Knight of Public Instruction in France.

References

Christian Sci Mon p6 D 28 '40
Lit Digest 123:28-9 Mr 20 '37
(Continued next page)

MITROPOULOS, DIMITRI—*Continued*

N Y Herald Tribune p18 D 20 '40 por
N Y Times p32 D 20 '40; IX p7 D 22
'40
New Yorker 16:48 D 28 '40; 16:14 Ja
11 '41; 16:73 Ja 18 '41
Newsweek 16:34 D 30 '40 por
Time 27:54 F 10 '36 por; 33:39 Ap 24
'39 por; 37:34-5 Ja 6 '41 por

Ewen, D. ed. Living Musicians 1940
Thompson, O. ed. International Cyclopedia of Music and Musicians 1939
Who's Who in America
Who's Who in Central and East-Europe
1933-34
Wier, A. E. ed. Macmillan Encyclopedia of Music and Musicians 1938

MOËN, LARS (mō'ĕn) Mar. 9, 1901-
Author; specialist on color photography
Address: b. Gevaert Co. of America, Inc,
Williamstown, Mass.

Under the Iron Heel is a book described as
"the first window through which daily life
in conquered Europe can be clearly glimpsed."
Its author, Lars Moën, was in conquered Belgium from the time the Nazis first captured
Antwerp until five months later, in October
1940, when he was told to "leave now or
remain until the end of the War." He left—
and returned to the United States to write
this, "the first full-length eyewitness account
of conditions within that country." *Under
the Iron Heel* also provides an invaluable insight into what is probably going on in other
countries under Nazi domination, particularly
occupied France and Holland.

In Belgium "the verb 'to eat' is conjugated
in every possible way whenever two people
meet." A whole population is near starvation.
Yet the Belgians, for the most part, do not approve of humanitarian plans to feed Europe:
they do not see any way by which the food
could be prevented from reaching Germany.
Some of them, particularly the Flemings, were
pro-German at the beginning of the War;
conditions in Belgium since the Nazis have
taken over have changed that attitude. Apparently there has even been some change
in the attitude of the Nazi armies of occupation, far from their homes and families, a little
bored, and disappointed in their faith that
the War would be over in the summer of 1940.

But as yet disaffection is slight: Hitler is
still a god, a hero, although the men around
him are openly criticized; and even the greater
part of those Germans who disapprove of
the Nazi regime is afraid not to win this
War. As for the Belgians, they seem to
feel that it will end not earlier than the
spring of 1942, not later than the spring of 1944,
with a German collapse—though not with a decisive British military victory. Even in 1940,
they believed that the United States would send
men, that Russia, too, would enter the War
when she felt that Germany was ready to collapse or revolt—and it is around the United
States and Russia, rather than Great Britain,
that are centered all of their hopes "of ultimate freedom and a new world order."

Some of the facts which Moën reports are
particularly interesting: that to the Belgians
King Leopold is neither a coward nor a traitor,
but a hero who has not played the Germans'
game and who has stayed with his people at
a time when London is filled with royal
refugees; that strong evidence exists to back
up the theory of an abortive invasion attempt
by the Nazis on England in September 1940.

Lars Moën has lived not only in Belgium,
but in France, England, Germany, Italy,
French Africa and the Soviet Union. As
he says, in most of these countries his work
brought him into direct contact with political
and military figures of importance, and he
was often in an advantageous position to observe what was going on behind the scenes.
He is an American, however. The son of
Adolph L. and Catherine M. Moën, he was
born in Bushnell, South Dakota, on March 9,
1901. Since his father's mercantile business
entailed frequent changes of address, his early
life was spent in the North and South Dakotas,
in Minnesota, Iowa and Wisconsin. He attended grade and high schools in three states
and was adopted by a tribe of Sioux Indians.

Moën was 16 when he completed high
school. During the next three years in Minneapolis his activities were varied. He worked
briefly as an actor; he worked on the Minneapolis *Journal,* for a photo finishing company,
for the Illinois Glass Company; he became
the editor of *Greater Amusements;* he joined
an advertising agency; he wrote scenarios
for a St. Paul industrial film company; he
became instructor in "an extremely dubious
school of motion picture acting." He was
publicity director of the St. Paul Community
Chest, entertainer for the War Camp Entertainment Service, conductor of dramatic activities at a settlement house. In 1920 he
spent a year in Fargo, North Dakota, where
he became motion picture editor and feature
writer on the Fargo *Forum,* wrote advertising
copy for local picture theatres, contributed
to fan magazines and "ran a short-lived newspaper syndicate aimed at newspapers too large
for boiler-plate but not big enough for the
regular syndicates." (He still thinks it was
a good idea.)

All this experience on the fringe of motion
pictures finally brought young Moën the
offer of a position as head of a motion picture
division of Babson's Statistical Organization
in 1921. He went to Massachusetts to take it.
In the East he arranged a publicity tie-up with
Pathe News, arranged for an economic survey
of the motion picture industry in collaboration with Columbia University and the *Motion
Picture News,* and as a result became a member of the editorial staff of *Motion Picture
News,* and as a result became a member
of the editorial staff of *Motion Picture
News.* He remained with that publication for
six years, also writing feature articles for magazines and New York Sunday newspapers and
occasionally editing films. He was co-author
and director of a series of Technicolor films,
too, and for several years was a member of the
publicity committee of the Society of Motion
Picture Engineers.

It was 1925 when Moën first visited all the principal European countries—on a survey of foreign motion picture production, distribution and exhibition. Two years later he moved to Paris. There he worked for some time as a fashion correspondent, then became technical adviser of the Cineromans studios, at that time the largest in Europe. When they were sold he was instrumental in forming the Gaumont-Franco Film-Aubert, a powerful rival group. Borrowed by Rex Ingram studios, he spent a year in Nice and then in Algiers and Morocco as technical director and scenarist.

While Moën was in London buying sound equipment his company inconveniently folded up, so he proceeded to become production editor of the first French-language talkie, then being produced at Elstree. He was briefly associated with an Elinor Glyn production, made four films with Monty Banks for Pathe, and was next engaged by the Asfi-Tobis studios as production editor of the first European out-of-door sound film. He remained with this studio until 1932, although farmed out for three MGM British productions, on one of which, *Diamond Cut Diamond,* he was co-author and editor.

In 1932 Moën was invited to work in the Soviet film industry, one of the few non-Russian and non-Communist engineers to hold an executive position there. He "went for three months out of curiosity," he says, and "stayed for nearly six years because I liked it." (He is now writing a book, *My Moscow Neighbors,* telling why.) It was in Russia that Moën suddenly became a scientist. He had expected to edit sound films, but found that a clerical error had resulted in his being invited to Russia instead of a scientist. He rectified the error by heading the physics division of the Scientific Research Institute of Motion Pictures and Photography, also becoming adviser to the State Gramophone Trust and consultant to the State X-ray Institute. He introduced standards into the manufacture of motion picture apparatus; he introduced dubbing of foreign language films into Russian, himself doing the Russian versions of *The Invisible Man* and *The Last Milliardaire*; he wrote feature articles and motion picture criticism for the Moscow *Daily News,* sometimes unmercifully panning the productions of his own studio; he was adviser on many Soviet productions, and made a few; and he was selected for the special brigade which made a film around Stalin's speech on the new constitution.

Finally, in 1937, Moën returned to England to concentrate solely on color reproduction, which had engaged a considerable amount of his attention since his first contact with Prizmacolor in 1916. There he became the research director of Truecolour Film, Limited, and spent at least half of each month in Paris. But it became increasingly difficult for him to carry on his experiments with a new color film process in London, and in the spring of 1939 he arranged the transfer of the laboratories to Antwerp, Belgium, although continuing to work in Paris during part of

Philip Halsman

LARS MOËN

each month. There were also frequent visits to England and Germany until war was declared.

Moën was in Paris when the general mobilization was ordered, and he left for Belgium at once, crossing the border just after Great Britain declared war on Germany. He arrived in Antwerp to learn that France had just followed suit. In Antwerp he lived in a small hotel, doing his research in a factory in the suburbs, and returned to Paris only once—in November 1939. Even after the German Army entered Belgium on May 18, 1940, he continued to work at his laboratory, sometimes spending most of the night there. He made efforts to get out of the country and back to America, but the Germans laughed at him. "What are you worrying about?" they asked. "The War will be over in 15 days."

The War was hardly over in 15 days. Around September, Moën moved into a working-class neighborhood near the factory, boarding with a baker's family. Six weeks later he was told he might leave (the Germans didn't know he was a former newspaperman), and on October 22 he left Belgium, paying 2,800 francs for a "conducted tour Brussels-Lisbon." After a journey across France and Spain and a stay in Lisbon under German auspices, he crossed to New York in a boat carrying 180 passengers, "chiefly refugees from all parts of Europe." In the United States he is engaged in photographic research with the Gevaert Company of America, Incorporated, at Williamstown, Massachusetts, and in independent research on color reproduction in New York.

Moën is described as "a slender man of medium height and with gray hair but a young face." Besides *Under the Iron Heel,*

MOËN, LARS—*Continued*

he has published "several million words for various newspapers and a vast amount of hack writing best forgotten." He is the author of *Are You Going to Russia?* (London 1934), *Looking Glass Land* and *Back from Looking Glass Land*, two series which appeared in *Passing Show* in 1933 and 1937, books in French and Russian on technical cinema questions, and is the co-author of the English libretto of the opera, *The Quiet Don* (Moscow 1937).

References

N Y World-Telegram p8 F 25 '41 il por

Moën, L.   Under the Iron Heel 1941

MOLLISON, AMY *See* Johnson, A.

MONSKY, HENRY (mŏn'skĭ) Feb. 4, 1890-   President of B'nai B'rith; lawyer

Address: b. 737 Omaha National Bank Bldg, Omaha, Neb; h. 90th and Dodge Sts, Omaha, Neb.

The oldest and largest national Jewish service and fraternal organization is B'nai B'rith. Its more than 150,000 members support youth work, carry out domestic and foreign relief, carry on activities for democracy, maintain hospitals and vocational service bureaus and issue frequent publications. At their head since 1938 has been Henry Monsky, lawyer and leader in civic and Jewish affairs.

HENRY MONSKY

A native son of Nebraska and Omaha, he is the first cornhusker to attain national stature in Jewish affairs and one of the very few Jewish leaders in America who live west of the Mississippi. He was born there on February 4, 1890, the son of Abraham and Betsy (Perisnev) Monsky, and went to school there, first to public schools and then to Creighton University, a Jesuit school. Monsky's father had wanted his son to become a rabbi, but Henry knew that law was what interested him, and it was with an LL. B. that he was graduated *cum laude* in 1912. He immediately began to practice law, rose rapidly in his profession, and for many years has been associated with the firm of Monsky, Grodinsky, Marer and Cohen in Omaha.

Almost all his life, social work and B'nai B'rith have been Monsky's chief interests, and to them in many years he has devoted more time than to the practice of law. He became interested in B'nai B'rith when he was very young, and in 1913, when he was but 23, he was elected president of the Omaha Lodge of B'nai B'rith. When he was 31 he was chosen president of District Grand Lodge No. 6 of B'nai B'rith, which includes the states of Nebraska, Iowa, Wisconsin, Minnesota, Michigan, Illinois and North and South Dakota, the largest of the seven districts. From this office he climbed to membership on the national executive committee, the organization's policy-making body between national conventions.

Two of B'nai B'rith's greatest achievements, the Hillel Foundations, which today serve nearly 15,000 Jewish students on 30 American campuses, and the Aleph Zadik Aleph junior order, which offers young boys a five-point program of religious, social service and cultural activities, originated in District No. 6, in which Monsky remained the principal figure for a decade and one-half. A. Z. A. was born right in Omaha, and Monsky was for long prominently identified with its development as a member of the supreme advisory council. His name is also inseparably associated with the organization of the Hillel Foundation and the expansion of the Anti-Defamation League, whose speakers' bureaus, discussion groups and publications aim to spread democracy.

His connection with all three of these B'nai B'rith agencies grew out of his leadership in the Wider Scope Campaign, for he was the chairman of a committee which recommended the establishment of this fund-raising plan which to this day is used to support all the major activities of the order. From 1927 to 1929 he served as national chairman of the Wider Scope Campaign which raised $2,000,000 for the establishment of the first group of Hillel Foundations and for the furtherance of the work of the Anti-Defamation League and the A. Z. A. His importance in B'nai B'rith was demonstrated, too, by his activities as the organization's representative on the Committee on Cooperation, which included the B'nai B'rith, the American Jewish Committee, the Jewish War Veterans and the American Jewish Congress.

In May 1938 Monsky, already hailed as "one of American Jewry's most forceful leaders," was elected president of B'nai B'rith, and in the spring of 1941 he was re-elected. Since he has taken office B'nai B'rith's working structure has been streamlined, membership has nearly doubled, and the organization's prestige has been **greatly** increased.   He is working constantly on its affairs, giving enormous amounts of time to the Anti-Defamation League, the Hillel Foundations, the A. Z. A., the *National Jewish Monthly* of which he is editor, the Vocational Service Bureau, emergency relief appeals, women's auxiliaries, membership drives and philanthropy. District secretaries, local leaders and other organization heads constantly consult him. He flies to all parts of the country to make speeches, attend conventions, confer with smaller groups. His correspondence is staggering.

Edward E. Grusd explains how he is able to do all this, in the *National Jewish Monthly* of March 1940. It is, he thinks, because Monsky "has the kind of a brain he has. It clicks! A problem that another would mull over for days before reaching a decision, Henry Monsky decides in a few minutes. His mistakes are amazingly few—and are mainly caused by his sentimental heart, not his head." And what he does is always well done. Few men in Jewish life, for instance, are able to match him in a conference or negotiations. "Again and again he has gone into important conferences where heated argument over policy or program has apparently wrecked all hope for agreement. Monsky's calm, dispassionate appraisal of relevant factors, his clear view of alternatives, his suaveness in moving over rough spots have often rescued a settlement."

Monsky's devotion to his people has not been demonstrated only in B'nai B'rith; he is prominently identified with most national Jewish organizations, including the United Jewish Appeal, the National Refugee Service, the National Conference of Christians and Jews and the Jewish Welfare Board. He has also been long active in many constructive civic causes. Founder of the Omaha Community Chest, he served as its first vice-president and later as president and chairman of the budget committee. He has been president of the Nebraska Conference of Social Work, a member of the Omaha Welfare Board, president of the Omaha Council of the Boy Scouts of America, member of the National Board of the Family Welfare Association of America, member of the National Board of Community Chests and Councils. He is now a member of the National Advisory Board of the American Forum for Democracy and for many years he has been a trustee of Father Flanagan's (see sketch this issue) famous Boys Town in Omaha. In July 1941 President Roosevelt appointed him to the National Volunteer Participation Committee which acts as an advisory and planning body in the organization of the Office of Civilian Defense headed by Mayor Fiorello LaGuardia of New York City.

Monsky is of medium height and weight, dark complected, with a thin, lined face. He speaks very well, but not as an orator who must rely on spellbinding for his effectiveness. He has no hobbies. Uninterested in golf or sailing or big game hunting, B'nai B'rith and social work are hobby and life enough for him. In 1915 he was married to Sadie Lesser,

and he has three children from this marriage: Joy, Hubert and Barbara. In 1937 he was married for the second time, to Mrs. Albert (Daisy) Rothschild, and he now has, besides his own children, a stepdaughter, Babette Rothschild.

References

Cur Hist 51:24 Ap '40 por
National Jewish Mo p197 Mr '40
Who's Who in America
Who's Who in American Jewry 1928

MOORE, R(OBERT) WALTON Feb. 26, 1859—Feb. 8, 1941 Counselor of the United States State Department and its third ranking official; served as Representative from Virginia from 1910 to 1931; was called to the State Department as Assistant Secretary by Cordell Hull, Secretary of State, in September 1933, to replace Raymond Moley who resigned; became Counselor in 1937.

References

Harper 174:229 F '37
New Outlook 163:35 My '34
Newsweek 2:9 S 30 '33
R of Rs 88:15 N '33; 94:19 D '36 pors
Time 29:16 My 31 '37 por
Who's Who in America
Who's Who in Law
Who's Who in the Nation's Capital

Obituaries

N Y Times p49 F 9 '41 por
Time 37:71 F 17 '41

MOORE-BRABAZON, J(OHN) C(UTH-BERT) T(HEODORE) (mōor-brä'bä-zŭn) Feb. 8, 1884- British Minister of Aircraft Production

Address: b. Ministry of Aircraft, London, England; h. 38 Eaton Sq, London, S. W. 1, England

Bulletin: On May 2, 1941 J. C. T. Moore-Brabazon was appointed to succeed Lord Beaverbrook as Minister of Aircraft Production. In July, answering criticism in the House of Commons, he promised that with the aid of American planes British raids on Berlin would soon make those on London look like "child's play." Not long afterward, critics, puzzled as to why England had not opened a second front, were wondering, in the words of *Time*, "about Arch-Tory Aircraft Production Minister Lieutenant Colonel J. C. T. Moore-Brabazon, who had been accused of expressing the wish that the Germans and the Russians would exterminate each other."

From May 1941 issue:

When Moore-Brabazon (his friends call him "Brab") was made Minister of Transport in May 1940, Prime Minister Churchill told him: "I am giving you a front-line job." Maintaining communications in spite of bombings is a difficult task that requires a level head and unusual organizing ability, and Moore-

J. C. T. MOORE-BRABAZON

Brabazon has done particularly well in keeping traffic moving in London. At the beginning of the War bus service was heavily reduced, and there was much crowding and waiting. "Brab" imported a large number of provincial buses, which still surprise London's little boys ("Daddy, I saw a Glasgow bus today!") He also introduced the "free lifts" system by which motorists receive an extra allowance of gasoline if they carry a label on their windshield offering rides to pedestrians at their own risk. Besides these, Moore-Brabazon is finding time and thought to devote to the improvement of railway meals and, even more important, he is responsible for the country's whole electrical system.

He is doing less well, however, in stopping road casualties. Unsympathetic pedestrians might point out that to put at the head of transportation a well known motorist who was once fined for dangerous driving and had his license suspended is like putting a burglar in charge of the police station. Auto accidents have been getting worse and worse since the days of Hore-Belisha (see sketch this issue), who was the only Transport Minister to do anything to stop them. By March 1941, 11,424 people had been killed on the roads since the War started—more than half as many as those killed by enemy bombing. Moore-Brabazon has admitted that these are "shaming figures," but has actually done little to change them.

He is the son of Lieutenant Colonel J. A. H. Moore-Brabazon of Tara Hall ("The Harp that once Through Tara's Halls"), County Meath, Eire and Emma Sophia, daughter of Alfred Richards of Forest Hill, London. Educated at Harrow and Trinity College, Cambridge, "Brab" became interested in automobiles in the days when to drive at all was an adventure. He was a personal friend of the late Honorable C. S. Rolls (the brains behind the Rolls-Royce

engine) and raced with him as his amateur mechanic. He raced a good deal by himself, too, in the early years of this century, and in 1907 won the Circuit des Ardennes by 27 seconds' margin in a thrilling contest, driving a Minerva under the Kaiserpreis formula. At the same meeting he ran second to Porliet in the Leiderkirke Cup.

By this time he had already begun to experiment with airplanes. Two models he constructed in 1907 did not amount to much, but in December 1908 he actually flew 450 yards in his own Voisin biplane at Issy-les-Moulineaux, France, the first Englishman to make such a flight. He intended to be, too, the first Englishman to fly the Channel, but Blériot beat him to it, largely because Moore-Brabazon was waiting for a British machine to fly. However, on the Isle of Sheppey in 1909 he won a prize of £1,000 offered by the London Daily Mail for flying a circular mile in an all-English plane. Later in that same year, at Eastchurch, he made the first flight ever accomplished by an Englishman in Great Britain proper. For this he was awarded the very first pilot's certificate ever issued by the Royal Aero Club and in commemoration he still uses FLY 1 for his car registration.

During the whole of the First World War, Moore-Brabazon served with the Royal Flying Corps (later R. A. F.) in France as equipment officer, winning the Military Cross and rising to the rank of lieutenant colonel. His main job was looking after aerial photography, but he did more than just look after it: he invented an air camera capable of many more exposures than any which had been made.

The War over, Moore-Brabazon stood for Parliament in the general election of 1918 and was returned as Conservative member for the Chatham Naval Station. He served on the first civil aviation committee and became chairman of the Air Mails Committee and of the Royal Aero Club. From 1923 until the defeat of the Conservative Government in 1924, he acted as parliamentary secretary to the Ministry of Transport. He returned to this same position when Labor rule ended after a few months and held it until 1927.

It was in this year that he resigned to enter business in London as chairman of a firm called Sensible Heat Distillation, Limited, which was set up to eliminate waste in coal. Fuel problems in general always occupied a good deal of his attention, and he has always strongly advocated a non-inflammable aviation fuel. Further business activities included directorships of Kodaks and of the Amalgamated Equipment Company, the firm that makes the London buses.

At the 1929 general election Moore-Brabazon, like many other Conservatives, lost his parliamentary seat to Labor, but with the formation of the National Government in 1931 he came back for Wallasey, Cheshire, a residential town known as "Liverpool's bedroom." He also served on the London County Council in 1931 and 1932. In the years that followed Moore-Brabazon was persistent on the subject of national defense, sharing the views of Churchill and Duff Cooper that all attempts at compromise with the dictatorships were in vain. "The snores of the Front Bench reverberate throughout the land," he warned in the days of the Baldwin administration. He got some chance to carry out his views during Sir Samuel Hoare's brief period as Secretary of State for Air early in 1940, when he was his parliamentary private secretary. He got even more when in May 1940 he attained Cabinet rank as Minister of Transport and a place on the Privy Council.

Moore-Brabazon is an all-round sportsman, particularly enthusiastic about bob-sleigh running. Until the War began he was known as one of the first dozen on the Cresta Run at St. Moritz, where in 1920, 1922 and 1927 he carried off the Curzon Cup. He plays a first-class game of golf and was president of the English Golf Union in 1938. His other interests include yachting and amateur cinematography and his first love, motoring—he is a founder-member of the Royal Automobile Club. "A sturdy, slow-moving man with an air of indolence that is very misleading," he showed a queer vein of humor in his early flying days by taking a pig up in a plane to show that "pigs could fly." In 1906 he married Hilda, daughter of the late Charles H. Krabbé of Buenos Aires, and they have two sons.

References

Autocar p362 O 11 '40 por
Morning Post Ja 14 '27
N Y Sun p17 My 5 '41
Times [London] F 16 '29
Who's Who

MORAN, LÉON (mô-răn') Oct. 4, 1864 —Aug. 4, 1941 American artist; frequent exhibitor at the National Academy of Design and at other national galleries; in 1904 won the gold medal prize awarded by the American Art Society in Philadelphia and another medal presented by the Philadelphia Art Club; full name John Léon Moran.

References

Who's Who in America
Who's Who in American Art

Obituaries

N Y Times p17 Ag 6 '41

MOREHOUSE, DANIEL WALTER Feb. 22, 1876—Jan. 21, 1941 President of Drake University in Iowa; astronomer; was awarded the Donahue Comet Medal for his discovery of the Morehouse Comet in 1908; associated with Drake University since 1900, first as professor of physics and astronomy, then as dean of men, as acting president, and as president since 1923.

References

American Men of Science
Leaders in Education 1932
Who's Who in America

Obituaries

N Y Times p21 Ja 22 '41
Sch & Soc 53:149 F 1 '41

MORRISON, ADRIENNE Mar. 1, 1889 —Nov. 20, 1940 Actress; literary agent; wife and partner of Eric Pinker, who was sentenced to prison for misappropriating money; was first wife of actor Richard Bennett and mother of Constance, Barbara and Joan Bennett.

References

Drama 21:16 My '31 por
N Y Dramatist 67:27 Ja 31 '12 por
Red Book 19:9 My '12
Who's Who in New York

Obituaries

N Y Herald Tribune p32 N 21 '40 pors
N Y Times p29 N 21 '40
Newsweek 16:6 D 2 '40 por
Pub W 138:2128 D 7 '40
Time 36:53 D 2 '40
Variety 140:54 N 27 '40

MORTON, JAMES F(ERDINAND) Oct. 18, 1870—Oct. 7, 1941 Curator of the Paterson, New Jersey, Museum since 1925; bibliophile and collector of rare minerals; champion of Esperanto, race equality, the study of genealogy and the single tax; author of many books on his interests and numerous poems.

References

Who's Who Among North American Authors
Who's Who in America

Obituaries

N Y Times p23 O 8 '41 por

MOSHER, GOUVERNEUR FRANK, BISHOP (mō'zhûr) Oct. 28, 1871—July 19, 1941 Former Protestant Episcopal Bishop of the Philippines who retired in 1940 after 21 years in the missionary field there; opened a mission in China where he served from 1896, the year of his ordination, until 1920; was active in teaching, hospital work and instructing natives in church work.

References

Stowe's Clerical Directory of the American Church 1932-33
Who's Who in America

Obituaries

N Y Times p31 Jl 20 '41 por

MOTT, FRANK LUTHER Apr. 4, 1886- Author; educator

Address: b. School of Journalism, University of Iowa, Iowa City, Iowa; h. Coralville, Route 1, Iowa City, Iowa

Of special interest at a time when world news is so important, and when that news

FRANK LUTHER MOTT

is suppressed or distorted in totalitarian nations, is the vital part newspapers can play in shaping and maintaining democracy in this country. The history of American journalism is largely the story of the establishment and growth of interdependent liberties: a free press and a democratic way of life. That is why most critics attached great importance to the appearance in 1941 of Frank Luther Mott's *American Journalism: A History of Newspapers in the United States Through 250 Years, 1690-1940.* Director of the School of Journalism at the University of Iowa, Dr. Mott won in 1939 the Pulitzer Prize in American history for his three-volume *History of American Magazines.* A worthy companion piece to this scholarly, highly praised survey, the later volume on the history of American journalism was likewise commended by critics as "easily the best in its field" and "a sure contender for another Pulitzer Prize."

A prodigious work of 750 pages, it covers, in nine divisions, everything from the appearance of *Publick Occurrences* in 1690 to the death of the Boston *Transcript* in 1941. In his review of Dr. Mott's book Ralph Thompson (New York *Times*) wrote: "He touches upon practically every conceivable phase of his subject: the colonial press, the contemporary press, yellow journalism, pink journalism, foreign-language newspapers, sporting and racing papers, Sunday editions, weekly editions, make-up, typography, circulation, advertising, paper stock, printing and ink, relations with the public and the State, comics, cartoons, consolidations and chains, reportorial techniques, editorial attitudes, syndicates, news associations, labor organizations and the principle of freedom of the press. The result, moreover, is not simply an informal hodgepodge of more or less relevant data, as this catalogue may suggest. It is an astutely ar-

ranged and carefully balanced survey, documented, illustrated, chronological in order and narrative in form."

The volume in particular is said to be "notable for its excellent treatment of the growth of American newspapers in the West and Midwest." Here firsthand experience underlies Dr. Mott's research authority. Born the son of an Iowa country editor, his earliest memory of newspapering was of standing knee-deep in water in his father's *Patriot* print shop when it was flooded by an overflowing creek. That was in What Cheer, Iowa. Frank Luther Mott was born on a nearby farm on April 4, 1886, the son of David Charles and Mary E. (Tipton) Mott. His parents were Quakers, and every Sunday the boy, after a week of hard work on his father's farm, trudged to the Quaker Church in the small Keokuk County community. Soon his father gave up farming and "audaciously set himself up as editor of the What Cheer *Patriot.*" When he became editor of the Tipton, Iowa *Advertiser* young Frank, at 10, learned to set type by hand in his father's shop, thus beginning his career as a practical printer.

By the time he was 16 and in high school, his father had moved his editorial chair to Audubon, Iowa, to the office of the Audubon *Republican.* In those days magazine publishers made it a practice to give local editors free subscriptions in return for publicity concerning a magazine article and, because Editor Mott was also an avid reader, there was an amazing collection of magazines on the bookshelves in the *Republican* office. Young Frank Luther set about arranging and indexing these magazines. Naturally he found himself reading them as he worked. This was the beginning of his lifelong interest in the magazines of America as they mirrored the growth of the nation—an interest culminating in the publication of his Pulitzer Prize-winning study.

From high school Mott entered Simpson College at Indianola, Iowa. After three years there he went to the University of Chicago, where he received his Ph. B. in 1907. In order to help earn his way through college he worked as a reporter on the El Reno (Oklahoma) *Daily American,* and assisted his father in editing the Marengo (Iowa) *Republican.* Soon Mott was editing by himself a weekly paper, the Grand Junction (Iowa) *Globe.*

In 1910 he married Vera H. Ingram, a Simpson College classmate. The couple have a daughter, Mildred Ingram, who is now carrying on the scholarly traditions of the family. Interested in archeology, she was recently awarded her Doctor's Degree at the University of Chicago.

After a few years of newspaper publishing, Mott decided to continue his education, so in 1918 he came East to study at Columbia University. He got a position teaching at a school for boys in Brooklyn and rode the subway back and forth to the Columbia campus, reading a pocket volume of Emerson as he rode. (His interest in Emerson still continues: he wants someday to write a study of Emerson's New England transcendentalism in imaginative literature.) In 1919 he received his M. A. degree at Columbia and that same year became professor of English at Simpson College.

It was in 1921 that he began his teaching career at the University of Iowa, when he became an assistant professor of English there. He went on with his studies toward his Doctor's Degree—his thesis was a magazine survey, a continuation of the work he had begun as a boy studying the magazines in his father's newspaper office. In 1927, when he had received an offer to become head of the Journalism Department at the University of Washington, the University of Iowa authorities decided that they needed Frank Luther Mott as director of their own growing School of Journalism. This position he currently holds at Iowa; and under his direction the University's Department of Journalism ranks among the best in the country.

During his years of teaching Dr. Mott had continued to write. His first publication, in 1917, was a critical work, *Six Prophets Out of the Middle West.* He also wrote short stories; and his story, *The Man with the Good Face,* originally published in *The Midland* (1921), was reprinted in O'Brien's *Best Short Stories* and attracted so much attention that it later appeared in various anthologies. It has been translated into several foreign languages, including Spanish for South American publication; and, as a classic of its kind, has been used in high school English classes throughout the United States. Always interested in creative writing, in poetry as well as fiction, Dr. Mott in 1925 became joint editor, with John T. Frederick (see sketch this issue), of *The Midland,* a national literary magazine founded by the latter. His *Rewards of Reading* appeared in 1926. Dr. Mott has edited special studies of the short story, and is co-editor of two collections for journalism students: *News Stories of 1933-1934,* two volumes (1934-35); and *Headlining America,* two volumes (1937-40).

The first volume of his *History of American Magazines* was published in 1930, covering the period from 1741 to 1850. It was for the second and third volumes (1938), covering the years between 1850 and 1885, that he received the Pulitzer Award in 1939. Critics concurred in praising the survey. One critic called it "a history which puts and will for decades continue to put all students of American history and literature greatly in his debt. But he has done more than that. In the processes of research, tabulation and analysis he has never forgotten that magazines, like books, are—if you will allow the syncopation—men." Two further volumes of this magazine history remain to be written; there should be five volumes when the work is completed.

An excellent teacher who wins the respect and friendship of his students, and who is held in high regard by editors and publishers throughout the country, Dr. Mott was honored with a banquet at the University of Iowa on the occasion of his Pulitzer Prize award. To this dinner came many of his former students, who make up a long list of active newspapermen in the United States. (The What Cheer, Iowa paper, where Dr. Mott had his own first experience in journalism, was by that time being edited by one of his former students.)

In the years since he was editor of the Grand Junction *Globe* genial Dr. Mott has grown stouter (he now weighs 190 pounds), and he admits to a coloring "moderately ruddy." He "wears bow ties, gardens in the back yard of his comfortable suburban home at Coralville, jams a cigar in his mouth and works at a typewriter for long hours in his book-lined study. He mixes freely with his fellow professors on the campus and with businessmen in Iowa City. . . He belongs to the Chamber of Commerce, reads detective novels for relaxation; he recites Negro poetry in dialect on occasion, and knows his quota of funny stories to tell at luncheon club meetings."

References

Des Moines Register My 15 '39
Des Moines Tribune p6 My 2 '39 pors
Pub W 135:1684-6 My 6 '39 por
Sat R Lit 20:6-8 My 6 '39 por
Leaders in Education 1941
Who's Who Among North American Authors
Who's Who in America

MOWAT, ROBERT B(ALMAIN) (mou'ăt) Sept. 26, 1883—Sept. 2, 1941 British historian; taught at Oxford University and had been professor of history at the University of Bristol since 1928; lectured in the United States at the University of Wisconsin in 1925 and 1926 and under the auspices of the Carnegie Foundation in 1941; author of many books on European and American history.

References

Author's and Writer's Who's Who
Who's Who

Obituaries

Pub W 140:1134 S 20 '41

MOWRER, EDGAR ANSEL Mar. 8, 1892- Journalist

Address: b. Chicago Daily News Bureau, Washington, D. C.

Edgar Ansel Mowrer, in 1941 Washington correspondent for the Chicago *Daily News* Foreign Service, has been called by Quincy Howe "a brilliant talker with a gift for exaggeration, a fanatical Hitler hater and a born crusader." But he has also been called one of the most able and well-informed journalists of his day. For a quarter of a century foreign correspondent for the Chicago *Daily News* in Paris, in Rome, in Berlin, he has covered two World Wars, he has had leisure to study the pattern of dictatorship as it gradually revealed itself in one European coun-

Harcourt

EDGAR ANSEL MOWRER

try after another, and he has numbered among his personal acquaintances Benito Mussolini and Hjalmar Schacht, Léon Blum and Chiang Kai-shek.

Born in Bloomington, Illinois on March 8, 1892, the son of Rufus and Nellie (Scott) Mowrer, as a young student at the University of Chicago he interrupted his university work in America in order to take special courses at the Sorbonne. It was during a brief visit to England during that period that he met his wife, Lilian Thomson (see sketch 1940 Annual), who in her book *Journalist's Wife* (1937) describes their first meeting in a railway carriage "without benefit of introduction." Before he began talking to her enthusiastically about Bergson and the *élan vital* she had thought that the man "with deep-set blue eyes behind very long lashes" was a Pole.

That same day young Mowrer wrote to his brother Paul, then Paris correspondent of the Chicago *Daily News*, to say that he had seen the girl he intended to marry. Actually the marriage did not take place until five years later. First he returned to the University of Michigan to take his B. A. in 1913, then returned to Paris that same year and settled on the Left Bank to study and to write. Philosophy and literature were his chief interests; he had no thought of becoming a newspaperman like his brother. His critical studies and essays were soon being published in the "more emancipated English reviews," and famous literary figures of the Latin Quarter gave him both criticism and encouragement.

It was in Paris that Mowrer watched a man post the first mobilization order of the First World War. A matter of a few months, he thought, along with the rest of the Parisians— and made comfortable plans to skate with Lilian through Holland the following January. Suddenly his brother Paul was sent to the Western Front as foreign correspondent. Edgar found himself pressed into the service of the *News*, in charge of the Paris office. For three weeks, until the victory of the Marne, he filed dispatches with the help of Paul's colleagues. Then Paul returned, read the carbons, doubled his younger brother's salary and sent him off on a bicycle to visit the battlefields around Meaux. From that time on his career was decided.

It was an adventurous career, right from the start. Mowrer's determination got him into trouble more than once. He scooped the world for a while, in Western Flanders, where he first saw action; in Ypres, where he was arrested on charges of espionage, he watched a bombardment from a prison; finally deported to England, he filed his dispatches, then set out for Belgium, where he was arrested once more before being allowed to proceed on his way.

As he traveled through Belgium a line from the poet Verhaeren began to haunt him: "Ruin installs itself and whistles at the four corners." He saw starvation, desolation, cruelty. He found out a great deal about conditions there—so much that one day he was suddenly asked to leave. Returning to Paris, he received an offer from the *News*: would he like a permanent position on the staff or his choice of Vienna or Rome as a resident post? He chose Rome, and departed at the beginning of May 1915, just a month before Italy was due to enter the War. It was while in Italy during this period that he made the acquaintance of one Benito Mussolini, a Socialist who had changed his position on the War and was making public speeches advocating Italy's entrance on the side of the Allies. Mowrer was told: "Come and see me whenever you are in Milan."

Not long afterward Mowrer wrote to Lilian to say that the War was going to last a long time and that they might as well get married immediately; in February 1916 he went to London to get her and bring her back to Rome. He himself was to be in Rome with her during most of the rest of the War, leaving for the Italian front only for short trips from time to time. He participated in the Italian defeat at Caporetto in 1917, watched and was amazed at the subsequent rallying of Italian martial spirit; he nearly died of Spanish influenza and, delirious in three languages, held long discussions on the origins of the War and its ultimate outcome; recuperating, while the Powers remade the map of Europe in Paris, he planned a series of articles on the "new society."

In 1939 Mowrer could comment that the Treaty of Versailles, with all its faults, had, after all, "created a far juster world" than before; that the real mistake on the part of the Allies was their failure to found and to establish a workable collective organization. In 1939 he could interpret the First World War as less a war for trade and empire than a crusade against the Germans, who "worshiped other gods than the children of liberalism." But whatever his views on the justice of that War and its settlement, he could not have remained very hopeful very long about his "new society" in Rome during those first post-War years, as Mussolini's young Fascists began rioting with increasing violence under the protection of the police. The march on Rome terminated the Mowrers' stay in the country he had celebrated in *Immortal Italy* (1922); there was no working under Fascist censorship, and in December 1923, seven months after the birth of a daughter, Diana Jane, he left for Berlin. His family followed a little later.

With the exception of short visits to Poland, Italy, France, London, Vienna and the United States, the Mowrers were to spend the next nine years in Germany. They were eventful, exciting, ominous years, as glimpsed in Mowrer's *Germany Puts the Clock Back* (1933; revised edition 1939). "These people are riding for a fall," he would say, looking up from the financial reports of Schacht and Gilbert during the period of greatest German prosperity. He saw that the Weimar Republic was committing suicide long before the day in January 1933 when he watched Hitler become Chancellor.

Yet the events of the next few months, in their full horror, could not have been anticipated by any newspaperman. When the foreign press learned what was actually taking place they accepted the common task of telling the world, putting aside all thoughts of personal competition; Mowrer, particularly, defied Nazi wrath and Nazi censorship. And although Germans who turned to foreign publications for information were informed by Goebbels (see sketch this issue) that they were reading lies, the people themselves continued to risk their lives in order to inform the "lying foreigners" about what was going on in Germany even beneath outward calm.

In November 1932 *Germany Puts the Clock Back*, tracing the disintegration of the Weimar Republic, was finished. It appeared in early January 1933, just a month before Hitler became Chancellor; and sales of the American edition were large in Germany until it was banned. During the first days of 1933 its author was elected president of the Foreign Press Association, and from the beginning he took an energetic attitude toward members threatened with expulsion from Germany. Soon the Nazis, who liked neither his book, his attitude, nor his press dispatches, suggested that he resign; the FPA refused to accept his resignation.

There followed a battle of nerves. After Mowrer received the Pulitzer Prize of $500 for the "best correspondence from abroad" during 1932 the Nazis changed their tactics from veiled threats of physical violence to friendly overtures, but hostilities were resumed when they discovered that he was not susceptible to flattery. In the meanwhile, although Nazi authorities were unaware of this, the *News* had decided that their Berlin correspondent was hardly working under the most favorable conditions, and had sent him word of a Tokyo assignment. Knowing that he was due to leave Germany in any case, when Mowrer heard that an Austrian newspaperman had been arrested he was shrewd enough to offer to resign from the presidency of the FPA in exchange for his friend's immediate release. His departure was hastened six days by the outwitted Nazis: a German Foreign Police official warned the American Government that unless he left Germany immediately they could not guarantee his physical safety. But British and American colleagues, as a farewell gift, presented him with a silver rose bowl inscribed to a "gallant fighter for the liberty of the Press."

After Germany, the Mowrers, still planning to go to Tokyo, had a brief vacation in the United States. The first "expelled" journalist to reach America, Mowrer gave a number of lectures there in an attempt to inform his countrymen about conditions in Germany. He found audiences rather incredulous—and so was Ambassador Dodd at first. Then, late in 1933, Mowrer and his family sailed once more—not for Tokyo but for Paris. Paul had just been made editor of his paper, and Edgar was replacing him as chief of the Paris bureau. They arrived on January 8, 1934, in the midst of the Stavisky riots, the Fascist demonstrations.

During the next years the European tragedy moved on relentlessly. In France it seemed that Fascism would triumph once more. "But Germans aren't Italians!" Mowrer had heard before; now he heard: "But Frenchmen aren't Germans!" In the field of international affairs the Nazis were also having everything their own way. In Saarbrücken in January 1935, Mowrer came to the conclusion that the plebiscite was a farce; at the Stresa Conference he heard Laval speaking tactfully about Italy's invasion of Abyssinia; in London in 1936 he listened to the English applauding like mad as the newsreels showed Hitler's march into the Rhineland.

Shortly after the Popular Front victory in France temporarily renewed hope for that country, Mowrer went as a war correspondent to Spain, where civil war had just broken out. There was also a brief visit to the United States and two months spent in the Soviet Union covering the adoption of the new Soviet Constitution before he returned to Paris to see his friend Blum's Government fall. He remained there until 1938, when he spent a few months in China gathering material for what is perhaps his most optimistic book, *The Dragon Wakes* (1939), also published as *Mowrer in China* in 1938; this time he returned to watch from France the events leading to Munich and finally culminating in the Second World War. With only a two months' visit to the United States in December 1939, he was in France all during the War until its fall in June 1940. His dispatches during that period may have erred in their optimism toward political conditions in France and French morale, but there were few newspapermen who did not make the same mistakes.

Edgar Ansel Mowrer returned to the United States in August 1940, filed his first story as Washington correspondent for the Chicago *Daily News* a few days later, and that same year published a series of articles on fifth-column activities in Europe, written in collaboration with William J. Donovan (see sketch this issue). In September 1941 he left for Singapore to report on conditions in this strategic naval base. A firm believer in the way of life in an America from which he has been largely absent during the past 30 years, the author of *This American World* (1928) (in which he argued that "Americanism is on the way to world empire") is convinced that unless smashing action is soon taken against Hitler the future of that way of life is very dark indeed.

John Gunther (see sketch this issue) describes Mowrer as "the most persistently engaging conversationalist I know . . . passionate, gloomy, explosive with biases (the right kind), overwrought, and very sweet when relaxed . . . the best educated American I ever met, Vincent Sheean [see sketch this issue] excepted. He is, unlike Sheean, a severe moralist. . . There is a touch of Lincoln in Edgar; and of Shelley; and of Mohammed. He believes in free speech so much that he would cheerfully slay any man who opposed it."

References

> Sat R Lit 10:52 Ag 19 '33
> Time 34:54 O 2 '39 por
>
> Mowrer, L. T. Journalist's Wife 1940
> Who's Who Among North American
>   Authors
> Who's Who in America

MUIR, RAMSAY 1872—May 4, 1941 One of the most prominent members of the British Liberal Party; succeeded Sir Herbert Samuel as party chairman in 1929; was Member of Parliament from 1923 to 1924; well known writer on history, politics and economics; made a lecture tour in the United States and then wrote America's impressions of England instead of the customary travel book.

References

> Author's and Writer's Who's Who
> Who's Who

Obituaries

> N Y Times p17 My 5 '41 por

MURPHY, FRANKLIN W(ILLIAM) Aug. 24, 1869—Nov. 22, 1940 Midwest farm leader and attorney who supported the campaign for the McNary-Haugen Bill.

References

> Who's Who in America
> Who's Who in Commerce and Industry

Obituaries

> N Y Herald Tribune p10 N 23 '40
> N Y Times p17 N 23 '40 por

MURRAY, CHARLIE July 22, 1872—July 29, 1941 American comedian who appeared on the stage and screen for 50 years; started career on the stage while a boy; left the theatre in 1912 to enter films; was one of the

FRANKLIN W. MURPHY

famous "Keystone Kops"; made notable series of film comedies, *The Cohens and Kellys*, with George Sidney.

References

> Motion Pict Classic 23:62 Ap '26 por;
> Motion Pict Mag 35:57+ F '28 por
> International Motion Picture Almanac

Obituaries

> N Y Times p17 Jl 30 '41

MURRAY, J. HAROLD Feb. 17, 1891— Dec. 11, 1940 Baritone; leading man in musical comedies in New York from 1921 to 1935; had starred in *Rio Rita, Castles in the Air, Captain Jinks* and *Face the Music;* left the stage in 1935 to become an executive and later president of the New England Brewing Company.

References

> Theatre 37:24 F '23 por
> Who's Who in the Theatre

Obituaries

> N Y Times p23 D 13 '40

MURRAY, PHILIP May 25, 1886- President of the Congress of Industrial Organizations

Address: b. CIO, 1106 Connecticut Ave, N.W., Washington, D. C.; h. 752 Berkshire Ave, Pittsburgh, Pa.

To both Capital and Labor the election of Philip Murray to the presidency of the CIO in November 1940 seemed the fitting climax, as the conservative New York *Herald Tribune* put it, to "36 years of progressive conciliatory activity among organized workers." Capital knows Philip Murray to be trustworthy; it knows him to be cautious and diplomatic, to have a thorough understanding of industrial detail; it knows that Philip Murray firmly believes that labor organizations should be stable and their contracts scrupulously observed. Labor knows that despite his soft-spoken manner and generous tact he is a hard-hitting fighter and a militant general in labor's fight for organization.

This man who has been recognized as "perhaps the most gifted triple-threat technician in the labor movement, as organizer, administrator and negotiator," was born in Blantyre, Lanarkshire, Scotland, the son of William and Rose Ann (Layden) Murray. His father was a coal miner, president of a large local of Scottish miners, who took his son to his first union meeting when he was six. When he was 10, Philip went to work in the mines after only a few years of school. Six years later, in 1902, his family emigrated to America and settled in Western Pennsylvania, where Philip immediately got himself a job in the coal mines.

His first labor dispute came two years later, when he was working for a mine in Westmoreland County near Irwin, Pennsylvania. He complained to the weighmaster that he was being short-weighted. The weighmaster denied it, and then, as Murray tells it, "a fight ensued. The weight boss took a shot at me with a balance weight from the scale. I hit him with a stool over the head. I happened to get the best of the argument, but I was discharged. Some 550 men went out in support of me. Mine guards were thrown around the place; my family was evicted from the company house. That was the beginning of these things that I am interested in." The strike was beaten, but in the meantime Murray had been elected president of his local union and had resolved to spend the rest of his life improving conditions for his fellow workers—as proof of his determination he was later to turn down good positions in private industry.

After his discharge from the coal mine, Murray began educating himself through correspondence courses; he became a United States citizen; he began to be more and more active in his union. In 1912 he was elected to the executive board of the United Mine Workers; in 1916 he was elected president of District No. 5 (the Pittsburgh area) of the Mine Workers; and in 1919 he was elected vice-president of the International Union of the Mine Workers, an office to which he was re-elected regularly every two years, until in 1940 he became president of the CIO.

During the First World War his ability as negotiator and pacifier was recognized by President Wilson, who made him a member of his War Labor Board. Harding, too, recognized this ability, when in 1921 he appointed him to sidetrack a civil war in the West Virginia mine fields, where 10,000 miners were in revolt. In 1935 Roosevelt, whom Murray has consistently if sometimes critically supported despite John L. Lewis, made him a member of the Labor and Industry Advisory

PHILIP MURRAY

Board of the NRA. During the first Roosevelt Administration Murray was also active in assisting in the preparation of various bills on bituminous coal mining, bills which eventually became the Guffy-Snyder Coal Act of 1934.

In 1935 Murray helped lead the movement of the CIO out of the A F of L, and in 1936 it was he who was put in charge of the CIO's Steel Workers' Organizing Committee, set up to organize steel. Directly or indirectly he is responsible for "carrying out one of the most elaborate, comprehensive and successful organizing campaigns in the history of unionism."

Murray continued as head of the SWOC (he remained its head while leading the CIO too), yet he was able to help outline the campaign to organize the automobile field in 1936, to settle the inter-union mess that arose in the Auto Workers' Union a few years later and to take on the duties of membership in the Petroleum Workers' Organizing Committee when it was formed in 1937. He also found time to become co-author of the book Organized Labor and Production (1940).

Philip Murray took office as president of the CIO in November 1940 at a time when his union was confronted by serious problems and important projects. John L. Lewis, leader of the CIO from its inception, had just resigned in a huff; a split in the union's ranks between the Left-wing group which had ardently followed Lewis and the more conservative group headed by the Amalgamated Clothing Workers of America seemed imminent. But Murray made clear his position and intentions from the beginning. First of all, he refused to accept the presidency except on his own terms—which meant a resolution passed by the CIO condemning Communism, Nazism and Fascism, and a clear understanding that he was to be nobody's yes-man. His terms were met.

It was immediately apparent that he wasn't Lewis' man Friday. It was immediately ap-

MURRAY, PHILIP—*Continued*

parent that he had his own methods of handling any threatened split. There was no "purge" of the Communists, though for years he had denied that a person "whose first allegiance is to a foreign government can be a good trade-union member, as he can't be a good citizen." And there was to be none, he said again and again, scotching in June 1941 "the great many speculative and often highly fantastic stories in the public press about splits, purges, Red-hunts . . . taking place in the CIO." There were, however, tactful dismissals here and there, until the issue became less urgent with the German invasion of Russia.

Murray scotched too, insinuations that the militant organizing plans laid down at the Convention at which he was elected president would mean a slowing-up of national defense. However, he insisted then and insisted later that Labor's rights were not to be revoked or destroyed, that "industry get on with the job by getting on with Labor." As head of the CIO he strongly opposed all anti-strike legislation and gave leadership to the organizing activities at Bethlehem Steel, at the Ford Motor Company and at United States Steel (as well as at non-defense spots, including the Transport Workers Union in New York City), but he did not support the unauthorized strike at North American Aviation, and he cleared up the big logger strike in Puget Sound.

He also supported national defense in a positive way. In December 1940 Murray presented to President Roosevelt a proposal to solve Labor problems and strengthen defense. There should be set up, he said, "industry councils" made up of an equal number of representatives from management and union labor, with a representative of the Government to act as chairman. The immediate objective of these councils would be to coordinate industries and Labor; the ultimate to coordinate the whole United States' economy. Murray backed, too, the Reuther (see sketch this issue) plan to increase plane production and himself made public a plan to achieve total steel output. He had made a survey of the steel industry, he said, and could, as a result, show steelmen how to increase production 30 per cent without expanding present facilities. As another step toward cooperation Murray agreed in March 1941 to serve as one of Labor's representatives on the new National Defense Mediation Board, though he had at first opposed the creation of such a Governmental agency.

Because of Murray's successful leadership in organization in 1940 and in 1941 (despite two months of illness), because of his interest in national defense, his determination to see that Labor maintained and furthered benefits it had won and his success in conciliating the warring factions in the CIO, he was unanimously supported by all sections of his union for re-election in November 1941. The large and enthusiastic following that had been his at the 1940 election was still his. Labor had continued to respond to his abilities as well as to a certain basic warmth and humanity of temperament which his predecessor never had.

At the CIO convention that month, in a strong speech, he emphasized the importance of maintaining production of war materials at its highest peak in order to defeat Hitler and assured President Roosevelt of labor's unqualified support for his foreign policies. At the same time, though, he supported the United Mine Workers' short-lived strike in protest at the NDMB decision refusing the union shop for the captive miners. He had been one of the CIO representatives who resigned from the Board after the decision, and he was also one of the most vociferous opponents of the Smith Bill which passed the House only a few days before the Japanese attack on Pearl Harbor. Murray and most friends of Labor urged, instead of repressive legislation, a conference of industry-labor representatives to work out plans to prevent stoppages and vastly increase production in defense industries.

The United States' declaration of war brought renewed assurances from Murray of Labor's patriotism and anxiety to participate more fully and directly in the war effort. It was not long before President Roosevelt called a conference similar to the one urged upon him. When it met in Washington in December 1941 Philip Murray was one of the CIO representatives present, empowered by his union to try to come to some agreement with representatives of industry.

In his middle 50's, Philip Murray's bearing is quiet and dignified, his manner of speech deliberate, sharpened by a droll humor and a soft Scottish accent. He is fairly tall and well set up (height five-feet-ten and one-half inches; weight, 178 pounds), with thin gray hair and a general resemblance to a small-town bank president. At home in Pittsburgh he lives in a square, plain, seven-room brick house which he built years ago, its rooms hung with pictures. ("The missus has a very good eye for such things.") He attends church regularly (he is a devout Catholic), is active as a member of the Knights of Columbus and the Elks, goes to the movies or prize fights very occasionally, and occasionally gets away from the hurly burly of Capital versus Labor to spend a quiet evening with his wife, Elizabeth Lavery, whom he married in 1910, and his son Joseph, a photographer. If he has a book on his lap, it's very likely to be a volume of O. Henry's short stories. Murray says he enjoys O. Henry "better than any fellow who ever wrote—he knew more about human beings."

References

Nation 151:172-3 Ag 31 '40
N Y Times p1, 15 N 22 '40; p1, 8 N 23 '40; p29 N 24 '40
Newsweek 16:33-4 D 2 '40 por
PM p19-21 N 22 '40 pors

Time 36:15-16 D 2 '40 por; 37:16-18 Ja
27 '41

American Catholic Who's Who
Brooks, R. R. R. As Steel Goes 1940
Who's Who in America
Who's Who in the Nation's Capital

MUSSOLINI, BRUNO Apr. 22, 1918—
Aug. 7, 1941 Son of Premier Mussolini; killed
while testing a bomber in Pisa, Italy; followed
his father's advice to "live dangerously";
fought in the Ethiopian and Spanish Civil
wars, as well as the Second World War.

References

New Statesman & Nation 14:639 O 23
'37
Read Digest 34:34-7 Mr '39

Obituaries

N Y Times p1, 3 Ag 8 '41 por
Time 38:16 Ag 18 '41 il

NARELLE, MARIE (nä-rĕl') 1874(?)—
Jan. 25, 1941 Concert singer; born Marie
Ryan in Australia but known professionally by
name of her first husband; made debut in
1904 at St. Louis World's Fair; toured in
1908 with John McCormack; after second
marriage to Harry A. Currie retired from
stage though sang occasionally for charity and
for experimental phonograph records made by
Edison; most recent appearance in England
in *Under Your Hat,* a musical show.

Obituaries

N Y Herald Tribune p14 Ja 29 '41
Variety 141:62 F 5 '41

NASH, OGDEN Aug. 19, 1902- Author
Address: b. c/o Little, Brown & Co, Boston,
Mass; h. 4300 Rugby Rd, Baltimore, Md.

Master of *bouffe rime,* adroit user of
Americana as spoken in subway and cocktail
conversation, Ogden Nash's most recent best
seller is *The Face Is Familiar* (October
1940). It is a selection of what he considers
the best of his light verse output to date;
among his seven previous books are *The
Primrose Path* (1935); the *Bad Parents' Garden of Verse* (1936); *I'm a Stranger Here
Myself* (1938). Mr. Nash has become well
known also through his guest appearances on
radio programs such as *Information Please*
and the Bing Crosby and Rudy Vallee hours.
Following each such appearance, it is said,
there has been a "healthy number" of re-
orders for his books.

Nash's work has been described as "a
mixed grill of fine pieces that have become
part of the folk sayings of the decade, as
well as some of those lamentably overblown
ventures in corded prose." The collected
Nash contains, for instance, along with succinct lines on the Phoenix and the Panther,
an exceptionally bad poem on Blake. He does
better with other literary observations:

*Let those who will read Alice B. Toklas
And I'll take the complete works of Shakespeare and a box of choclas*

and best, perhaps, on affairs of the heart:

*Affection leads to breach of promise
If you go around lavishing it on red hot
momise.*

OGDEN NASH

His work in general lacks the core of substance, the truly biting satire commanded by
other good light versifiers, and is best when
taken in small doses. Occasionally he produces a nutshell classic, such as his reflections
on the English:

*I think the English people are sweet
And we might as well get used to them
   because when they slip and fall they always
   land on their own or somebody else's feet.*

The English, as a matter of fact, find Nash's
work quite incomprehensible. Said the London
Times: "He writes humorous verse which
would be improved if the author took more
care with his rhymes. There are too many
false rhymes here, which give an impression
of laziness rather than smartness." At which
the *New Yorker* quipped a Nashian reply:

*Don't make a fetish
Of annoying the Bretish!*

Much of his wide popularity is due to the
fact that he "comes out against." As one
reviewer of *The Face Is Familiar* has said:
"Nash is no flash in the pan, no panderer to
the topical and transitory. His crusade is
ageless; his oriflamme beats in the winds of

NASH, OGDEN—*Continued*

every season; for he fights for every man the fight which every man is afraid to fight for himself. He comes right out against parsley, little boys, banquets, women's hats, salads, debt, bankers and the recent frightening epidemic of girl babies. He also comes out against time, athletics, people who are industrious, practical jokers, cocktail gadgets, the had-I-but-known type of detective story, the menace of the strange force of growing hair, rich people who let you buy them drinks while they tell you how poor they are."

Ogden Nash was born August 19, 1902 in Rye, New York. He comes from "a distinguished Southern ancestry including a revolutionary Governor of North Carolina and a revolutionary general who gave his name to Nashville, Tennessee." Nash has said further: "I have no private life and no personality." He grew up in various places up and down the East coast from Georgia to New England; and he admits that he is "a quarter-bred Harvard alumnus," having left Cambridge at the end of his freshman year. He has documents, he says, to prove that he left of his own free will.

For a year Nash taught at St. George's School, Newport, Rhode Island, where he lost his "entire nervous system carving lamb for a table of fourteen-year-olds." In the late '20s he came to New York City and got a job as a bond salesman; then one in advertising, writing car-cards. In 1925 he worked in the advertising department of Doubleday, Page & Company, after which he became a manuscript reader for another publishing company. Later he joined the staff of the *New Yorker* Magazine.

He likes good eating (what he doesn't like may be found listed *ad infinitum* as well as *ad absurdum* in his verses), he is married to Frances Rider Leonard, lives in Baltimore and has two children, "both of them she'ses."

Nash says that his reading of other people's illiterate manuscripts gave him the idea of writing his own. He did them in verse, because he believes you can say things in verse which if said in prose would result in tar and feathers. This is probably because nobody reads verse. Except perhaps Mr. Nash's kind, which, treading gently on all toes, individually on none, always makes the best-seller grade.

References

Christian Sci Mon Mag p12 N 30 '40
N Y Times p15 N 9 '40
Newsweek 11:31 Je '38 por
Sat R Lit 18:6 Je 4 '38 por; 20:3-4+
   Ap 29 '39 por
Scholastic 31:25E O 2 '37 por; 36:22+
   Mr 4 '40 por
America's Young Men
Who's Who in America

NATHAN, ROBERT R(OY)   Dec. 25, 1908- Economist

Address: National Defense Commission, Washington, D. C.

Robert R. Nathan, who was chosen one of the ten outstanding young men of 1940 by the United States Junior Chamber of Commerce, is the man responsible for surveying the defense requirements of both the United States and Great Britain. To do this, he has discovered, "one must vary from being an expert statistician and economist at one moment to being a commodity expert or industrial authority the next."

His position, he says, "entails the responsibility of determining what the military and non-military requirements of the nation and the British are going to be under the defense program, what is our capacity to meet these needs and, finally, pointing out the areas in which shortages will appear." This is a complicated task, since "the raw material data for these studies depend in a large measure on the data in the military services and in other government agencies. . . The work of bringing together the statistics is particularly difficult because so many of the items have no counterpart in peace time and specifications for raw material content are difficult to determine."

Robert Roy Nathan is eminently qualified to do this work—he has been doing important economic research since he was a college undergraduate. Born in Dayton, Ohio (one of a pair of twins, the other of whom, Lawrence M. Nathan, is now in the merchandising field), Robert attended grammar and high school in Dayton before he went on to the University of Pennsylvania's Wharton School of Commerce and Finance. He worked hard there— "selling and writing for newspapers and many other odd jobs: summer employment in factories, selling Real Silk hosiery, lots of retail selling, tutoring in several courses, part-time work with the Industrial Research Department of the University of Pennsylvania and many other types of work." Despite all these jobs and hard studying, Nathan was able to join the century-old Zelosophic Literary Society and take part in intramural boxing and wrestling. Looking at his six feet and one and one-half inches and two hundred pounds today, it is easy to surmise how effective he must have been in the ring and on the mat.

In June 1931 the Wharton School gave Nathan a B. S. degree in economics. He continued to study there and two years later received his M. A. He had already started working on a rather more permanent basis than that given him by his many jobs while an undergraduate—as research assistant at the University of Pennsylvania on Unemployment Surveys at Philadelphia—and in September 1933 he accepted the first of his government positions. For a year and one-half he worked on the original National Income Study of the United States Department of Commerce. He resigned in June 1934 to become assistant director of research of the Pennsylvania State Emergency Relief Board in Harrisburg, and after two months full time in that position spent the next three months "splitting a seven-day week between the Harrisburg position and the position as consultant on unemployment statistics for the President's

Harris & Ewing

ROBERT R. NATHAN

Committee on Economic Security, which established the background for the Social Security Act."

In December 1934 Nathan returned to the Department of Commerce and in June 1935 was made chief of the National Income Section in the Division of Economic Research. When that section was expanded into a division in 1939, he was made chief of the division. During much of this period he acted as state consultant on income for the National Resources Planning Board, made frequent field trips, working particularly with the State Planning Board of Wisconsin and the University of Wisconsin and with the State Resources Commission of Minnesota and the University of Minnesota. At the Department of Commerce, too, Nathan contributed a number of bulletins and articles on the subject of national income, the most ambitious of which was a report of some 300 pages published by the Government Printing Office titled *National Income in the United States 1929-1935*. Outside of his department he prepared a number of articles on income for the *Survey of Current Business*; contributed many articles to the *Encyclopedia Britannica* Year Book, to the *National Encyclopedia*, to the *International Labor Review*, to the volumes published by the National Bureau of Economic Research. All of these have been used widely.

Shortly after the Advisory Commission to the Council of National Defense was appointed in 1940, Nathan was given a leave of absence from the Department of Commerce, his first assignment the determination of military requirements. "At present," he said then, "I am responsible for coordinating studies on requirements and capacity," with "no particular formal title."

Mr. Nathan is a member of the American Statistical Association, the American Economic Association, the American Marketing Association, Pi Gamma Mu, the Executive Committee of the Conference on Research in National Income of Work. He is a past president of the Washington chapter of the American Statistical Association and nominee for vice-president of the Association for 1941. His main interest, it is easy to see, is economic research, but he does get away from charts, tables and statistical trends now and then for some deep-sea fishing.

References

Christian Sci Mon p2 Ja 10 '41 por

NEGHELLI, MARCHESE DI *See* Graziani, R.

NEHRU, JAWAHARLAL, PANDIT (nä'-rōō yä'wä-här-läl) Nov. 14, 1889- Indian Nationalist leader

Address: Anand Bhawan, Allahabad, India

Under the Defense of India Act "preaching pacifism" is forbidden. In the autumn of 1940 Gandhi, in seeking some method to campaign for Indian independence without embarrassing the British war effort, hit on the method of "token civil disobedience." Selected leaders in the Indian Nationalist movement were to brave arrest so that the people of India might remain aware that the movement had not been abandoned. Jawaharlal Nehru was one of the two men selected to start the campaign; both were immediately arrested and sentenced to prison. Nehru (known in India as "Jawaharlal," sometimes as "Pandit" or "wise man") received a jail term of four years, having refused to testify at his own trial. This sentence one British Laborite called "harsh in the extreme," and predicted it would have serious repercussions in India, Great Britain and the Americas. Parliamentary debates indicated that England was concerned with growing Indian unrest, and the *New Republic* announced: "British policy toward India seems without a spark of enlightenment, understanding or justice... Men like Mr. Churchill and Lord Halifax can apparently imagine no alternative to terrorization." In December 1941, however, the Pandit and 500 other members of the All-India Congress Party were released.

Prison is no novelty to Jawaharlal Nehru. According to John Gunther (see sketch this issue), he has spent seven terms in prison and has been previously sentenced to an aggregate of ten and one-half years, although he served only five and one-half years of them. His previous sentence was in 1934, after a "seditious" speech in Calcutta. It was in prison that political study led him to merge socialism with his nationalism; it was in prison that he wrote a history of the world in the form of letters to his daughter; and it was while serving a prison sentence that he wrote his autobiography, which was published in England in 1936 and hailed as the Indian "Education of Henry Adams." An American edition appeared early

PANDIT JAWAHARLAL NEHRU

in 1941 under the title *Toward Freedom,* with two new chapters added.

He was born in Allahabad November 14, 1889, the son of Motilal Nehru, a Kashmiri Brahman (equivalent to a Cabot or Lowell in the United States), a millionaire and one of India's most distinguished lawyers, yet a liberal who used to discuss with his son the conduct of the white man in India. In 1905 he took young Jawaharlal to England and put him in Harrow. There he stayed for three years, then went on to Cambridge, took his degree in 1910 and remained in London for two more years, studying law and passing his Bar examinations. At that time Nehru called himself a "Cyrenaic," read Pater and Wilde and tried, he said, "to ape the prosperous but somewhat empty-headed Englishman who is called a 'man about town.'"

It was 1912 before Jawaharlal returned to India with a vague desire to enter politics. His father was already active; it was at his house that in 1916 the coalition was made between the Moslem League and the Indian National Congress, a political mass organization of Indians at that time seeking Dominion status, later complete independence. Jawaharlal joined the Nationalist movement. During the First World War, he says, "there was little sympathy with the British in spite of loud professions of loyalty," and when the end of the War brought "intense repression, martial law in the Punjab and the famous Amritsar massacre" in place of the promised independence, Gandhi's doctrine of non-violent resistance found followers everywhere. During the non-cooperation campaign hundreds actually fought for the privilege of being arrested; in the month of December 1921, thirty thousand persons were imprisoned. Jawaharlal, who had become interested in the peasant movement, who was beginning to feel "shame at my own easy-going and comfortable life and our petty politics of the city . . . sorrow at the degradation and overwhelming poverty of India," followed Gandhi in spite of his father's disapproval. And within a year Motilal joined him, to work and fight with his son for nine years, devoting his fortune to the cause of India's independence, losing his health in British prisons. Even Jawaharlal's mother was to be beaten in demonstrations; his wife, Kamala, who died in 1936, was to follow her husband to jail; and in December 1940 his sister was arrested.

Making speeches, traveling all over the country and even to Ceylon investigating conditions, taking part in protest processions, agitating against the salt tax or other repressive measures, entering forbidden territory in defiance of the British, periodically imprisoned and released, Jawaharlal finally gave up his law practice to devote himself entirely to politics. He was elected to the headship of the Allahabad municipality and to Congress. Loyal to Gandhi and one of Gandhi's staunchest defenders, nevertheless Jawaharlal was by this time beginning to wonder if the "diapered saint" went far enough. He did not approve of Gandhi's glorification of poverty and renunciation; he himself was becoming convinced that India's problem was as much economic as political, that the land system must be changed and that the "vested interests"—brown as well as white—must be removed before this could come about.

In 1929 Gandhi pushed Jawaharlal forward for the presidency of Congress, and he was elected. His popularity with the masses and with Indian youth as well as with the intelligentsia reached such disturbing heights that after 1930 his playfully iconoclastic wife and daughter Indira began to address him: "Oh Jewel of India, what time is it?" "Oh Embodiment of Sacrifice, please pass the bread." For ten years Jawaharlal was either secretary or president of Congress; he was president three times. It was he who made Gandhi come out for complete independence; it was he who, in 1931, persuaded the Working Committee of Congress to accept a few planks that smacked a little of socialism. For a long time many of those in the Nationalist movement had been more radical than their leaders; Gandhi was accepted as a saint, but they did not all share the saint's patience. Now Jawaharlal, generally conceded to be Gandhi's successor, aroused India's 350 millions in a way that Gandhi never had. In the spring of 1936 he openly preached socialism to follow complete independence, and urged that his followers organize into workers' and peasants' unions. Reports that Gandhi had proclaimed his lifework ruined by this deviation were denied, and the two continued to work in close collaboration.

Before the elections to the Federal Legislature in February 1937 Jawaharlal, then chairman of the Congress Party executive committee, traveled 110,000 miles in 22 months, in one week made 150 speeches and brought 33,000,000 persons to the polls. The fighting slogan was one of political independence, of resistance to Sir Samuel Hoare's new Federal

Constitution of 1935, which Jawaharlal called a "charter of bondage" because it handed most of the control of the Chambers to Indian princes and landlords ("Britain's Fifth Column in India") and in addition gave Britain the power to veto any measures passed by the Indians. The Nationalists received an absolute majority in six key provinces and the largest single-party representation in the five remaining provinces, but in protest against the Constitution six Congress members refused to become cabinet ministers in their provinces. And although they came to terms within a few months, they pledged themselves to continue their opposition.

Early in 1939 Jawaharlal was faced with a dilemma. Bose, the Bengal Leftist leader, was elected to the presidency of Congress in spite of Gandhi's opposition. At that time Jawaharlal was a member of its Working Committee, and, although probably sympathetic to many of Bose's avowed aims his loyalty to Gandhi made him withdraw his support from the organization. The resignations of many others followed. Bose was out and Jawaharlal back on the Committee before the the year was out, however, and when in September 1939 Britain declared India belligerent without any formal reference or intimation to Indian representatives and rushed the Indian Constitution Amending Bill through Parliament, he was the author of a protest by the Working Committee. It asserted that war or peace was an issue that the Indians should be allowed to settle, that India's resources were not to be exploited for "imperialist ends," and that Britain must state her war and peace aims before she could expect cooperation. The answer to this protest, he said, "indicated sufficiently clearly that there was no intention and, so far as that government was concerned, no possibility of the ending of the imperialist structure in India." Therefore as intensely as the Indians detested Fascism and Nazism, they were not convinced that Britain was really fighting for any "new world order." And in the meanwhile the Congress governments in the provinces had resigned, parliamentary government had been suspended, and in India there was "full-blooded dictatorship and authoritarianism."

Jawaharlal concluded sadly: "The way of cooperation does not lie for us; the hundred-year-old hostility will remain and grow in future conflicts, and the breach, when it comes, as come it must, will also not be in friendship but in hostility." He would hope for a British victory in the present conflict, but he would not cooperate actively with India's rulers.

Nehru's release from prison found his position somewhat changed. "India," he said, "is prepared to go for an all-in aid in the war, if her political aspirations are satisfied." He told a group of students that India's warm regard for China, Russia and America justified war with Japan. But he also tried to make Britain aware that as long as the democratic aspirations of the Indian people remain unrealized ("the four freedoms" do not apply to India, Churchill has said), they cannot play their proper role in bringing about an Axis defeat.

John Gunther describes Jawaharlal as "an Indian who became a westerner; an aristocrat who became a socialist; an individualist who became a great mass leader." Unlike Gandhi, he emphasizes economics, believes in the industrialization and urbanization of India, advocates normal marriage and sex relationships, is a "devout rationalist" and, while not antireligious, has said "the spectacle of what is called religion, or at any rate organized religion, in India and elsewhere has filled me with horror." He is not concerned with Indian problems alone. During the Spanish War he visited and spoke for Loyalist Spain, and he has also visited and organized aid for China. He not only favors a classless, planned society but is convinced that anything that comes in its way "will have to be removed, gently if possible, forcibly if necessary." "Socialism is for me not merely an economic doctrine which I favor; it is a vital creed which I hold with all my head and heart." He is not a Communist chiefly because he resists "the Communist tendency to treat Communism as holy doctrine." He was in Moscow only once, with his father in 1927, to see the tenth anniversary festivities. Nor is he a member of the Congress Socialist Party. In Congress his position would probably be described as Left center, just as Gandhi's is Right center. The relationship between the two men is a very close one, if strange. Gandhi has said: "There is a heart-union between us which no intellectual differences can break," and Jawaharlal calls him "Bapu" (father). He has never underestimated what Gandhi has done for India: "Reactionary or revolutionary, he has changed the face of India, given pride and character to a cringing and demoralized people, built up strength and consciousness in the masses and made the Indian problem a world problem." Yet Nehru can also say of Gandhi: "What a problem and puzzle he has been!"

Jawaharlal is strikingly handsome: about five-feet-ten, with somber eyes, "adamant features" and a courtly, impressive bearing. Although moody and sometimes temperamental, both his writings and his speeches show all the understatement and the emotional restraint of "an Oxford lecturer." He is lonely: he speaks of being "at home nowhere," of "retreating into his shell," of an "inner hunger unsatisfied." Perhaps prison and solitary confinement have made him so. By nature he hates the "hurly-burly" of politics, loves winter sports, swimming, English poetry. Yet he has said: "I have not consciously renounced anything that I really valued." He is "more-or-less" a vegetarian, but no ascetic: sometimes smokes, and outside of India will take a little light wine. He hates British imperialism, but not the British: often has spent his holidays in England. He likes most "mountains, running water, children, glaciers, good conversation, all animals except bats and centipedes"; dislikes most "exploitation, cruelty and people who, in the

NEHRU, JAWAHARLAL—*Continued*

name of God, truth and the public good, are busy feathering their nests." John Gunther describes his autobiography as "subtle, complex, discriminating, infinitely cultivated, steeped in doubt, suffused with intellectual passion." He says: "Nehru the agnostic, Nehru the modern man, faces the colossal medievalism of India. He fights the British, but he fights the entrenched ritualism of his own people, too."

References

Asia 36:354-9 Je '36; 36:614 S '36; 36:626-30 O '36; 37:341 My '37; 39:92-6 F '39 il por; 39:252-5 My '39; 39:555-6 O '39; 39:662-3 N '39 il pors; 40:595-9 N '40

Christian Cent 53:1139 Ag 26 '36; 57:1404 N 13 '40

Christian Sci Mon Mag p3 Mr 2 '38 il por

Cur Hist 45:81-4 Mr '37 por; 54:44-6+ My '41

New Repub 103:677 N 18 '40; 104:538-9 Ap 21 '41

N Y Times p4 N 8 '40; IV p2 N 10 '40

Pacific Affairs 13:17-29 Mr '40

Read Digest 36:79-83 F '40

Survey G 26:481-4 S '37 il por

Time 30:18 Jl 19 '37 por; 33:23 Mr 6 '39 por; 37:102-4 F 24 '41

Bartlett, R. M. They Did Something About It p44-60 1939

Gunther, J. Inside Asia p408-25 1940

International Who's Who

Nehru, J. L. Autobiography 1936

Nehru, J. L. Eighteen Months in India, 1936-37: Being Further Essays and Writings 1938

Nehru, J. L. Toward Freedom 1941

Singh, A. Nehru: the Rising Star of India 1939

NELSON, DONALD M(ARR) Nov. 17, 1888- Executive director of the United States Supply, Priorities and Allocation Board

Address: b. Office of Production Management, Washington, D. C.; h. 595 Longwood Ave, Glencoe, Ill.

At the beginning of September 1941 the Supply, Priorities and Allocation Board was set up by the President as a possible solution to some of the troubles that had beset OPM and the defense effort. At its head was placed Donald Marr Nelson, who became simultaneously director of priorities for the Office of Production Management.

Nelson has had important responsibilities in the defense setup since June 1940, when he was made coordinating agent for all purchases under the old National Defense Advisory Board. "United States Shopper Number One," he immediately began to arrange for airplanes, tanks, battleships, foodstuffs, clothing, shoes. His approach to his problem was simple: "The housewife wants to buy to the best advantage.

We have the same objective," he said. By December 1940 Mr. Nelson had allotted almost all of the 10 billion dollars given him to spend, "constantly alert to the impact of the purchasing upon our whole social and economic system." He utilized the off-season productions of plants, split up the areas to manufacture commodities, spread out the production of woolen and cotton clothes. He thwarted profiteering—after the whole market of a certain kind of cotton had been cornered by one man, he had the specifications changed and saved the Government from paying prohibitive prices.

From this position Nelson, in 1941, was shifted to the head of the Division of Purchases in the Office of Production Management, his job still to plan purchasing, to assist in deliveries and to get the necessary materials at the lowest prices, at the right time and with the least possible effect on the consumer.

Always, under the Defense Commission, under the OPM and, later, in the SPAB, his policy has been to "unravel the kinks" before peak production and the delivery of defense material began, rather than to emphasize swift production at the expense of accuracy and and steadiness. I. F. Stone has called him "one of the ablest and most public-spirited of the dollar-a-year men," "the one leading businessman usually prepared to uphold the rights of Labor in the making of contracts" and "prepared to bargain as firmly in buying for his country as he would have in buying for his own company."

There is no doubt that Donald Nelson's efficiency in buying for the Government derives from his long years with Sears, Roebuck and Company. Today its executive vice-president and chairman of the executive committee, he has been connected with this mail-order house ever since he was graduated from college. He was born in Hannibal, Missouri, the son of Quincy Marr Nelson, a railroad man, and Mary Ann (MacDonald) Nelson, and he attended grade and high school in Hannibal. From high school he went to the University of Missouri, working his way through by the usual jobs of tending furnaces and waiting on tables, and the less usual ones of grading chemistry papers and even, in his last year, teaching chemistry to freshmen. In 1911 he was graduated with a Bachelor of Science degree and began to look ahead to a life spent teaching chemistry.

His first start was as an assistant at the University's Agricultural Experiment Station, but it lasted less than a year. The head of Sears, Roebuck's chemical laboratory had asked the chairman of the Missouri chemistry department to recommend a young man for an assistant's position. Nelson was picked and on April 1, 1912 started working for Sears, Roebuck and Company. He stayed in this and similar jobs until 1921, with time out for training at the Lowell Textile School and an apprenticeship at the American Woolen Mills, both arranged by the company. By the time of his next job he was also going

over the catalog copy to see that all its
advertisements were accurate as well as
catchy.

This next job, as manager of the men's
and boys' clothing department, was his first
big step up. It lasted for five years, at the
end of which Nelson became an assistant in
the general merchandising office. This was
in 1926, the year he married Helen Wishart
of Chicago. After a year's experience as
merchandising assistant, Nelson was promoted
to general merchandise manager. Then, in
1930, he was made vice-president in charge
of merchandising, a position he kept until
his further promotion in 1939 to executive
vice-president and chairman of the executive
committee.

At Sears, Roebuck, Nelson was the kind
of man you could set your watch by, according
to his associates. He was at his desk every
morning at 7:50 and most of his movements
from then on were just as regular. He built
up a reputation, too, for going after information "like a dentist after an ailing tooth,"
for catching trains to distant points on short
notice, for settling problems on the spot
whenever he could. And although a perfectionist about his work, he was still easy
to get along with. His subordinates, as
quoted in *Business Week,* used to say: "He
may not agree with you in what you think
ought to be done. But he can see why you
think as you do. And he never puts you on
the defensive."

During these years Nelson was always of
the opinion that government and business
should get along well together, even in
the period when other businessmen were
bitterly complaining of government interference. "Many businessmen think of the government as a place where men sit around a
table and devise plans for obstructing and
harassing businessmen," he once said, "and
many in Washington think of business as a
closely-knit conspiracy intent only on profit
and amassing wealth." Both points of view
are wrong, he feels. When he took a leave
of absence from his company to work with
the NRA, government, business and labor all
learned to respect him.

It was because of Nelson's successful NRA
activity and his reputation as a businessman
that rumors were current in 1938 that he
would be chosen to administer the Fair Labor
Standards Act. He didn't get this position,
but he was made chairman of the wage committee of the textile industry, the first to
tackle the problem of raising wages above
the 25 cent minimum. Two years later rumors
about him were again current—that he would
be appointed head of the National Defense
Commission. This didn't come true either,
but in June 1940 he was given the full-time
job of Treasury procurement chief, in charge
of the Government's ordinary purchasing and
chairman of the interdepartmental committee
coordinating foreign and domestic purchases.

Nelson's Treasury position lasted only a
month. His next was as coordinator of purchases for the Defense Commission. He said

DONALD M. NELSON

of it: "Confusion must be eliminated, procurement and delivery must be expedited...
The strength of the Army and Navy will depend upon having the required material at the
place where it is needed at the proper time."
To this task Nelson added responsibilities as
head of small business activities for the Defense Commission and, in October 1940, the
job of administrator of the priorities board,
set up within the Commission.

When the new over-all defense agency, the
Office of Production Management, was created
in January 1941, Nelson headed its Division
of Purchases. At the beginning of February
there were reports that he had handed in his
resignation, after a memorandum concerning
what he considered his duties had been
severely edited by the War and Navy Departments. At this point President Roosevelt
stepped in and gave Nelson the authority he
felt he should have—which meant the centralization, under him, of all defense buying,
although he was still left without authority
to pass on questions of expansion and priorities.
Nevertheless, he was again rumored on the
verge of resigning in May because of the slow
pace at which contracts were being let. He
himself pointed out that when he started working for the Government in the spring of 1940,
it was to be only "for two months." But he
did stay, and in September of the same year he
went on to even greater responsibilities. In
November 1941 he announced that the present
rate of defense expenditure was $3,500,000,000
a month.

Donald Nelson is a big, broad-shouldered
man, "about six feet, gray, with eyes sharp
as a fox's and a jaw that shuts like a breech-
bolt." He has "an appetite for hard work,
long hours, and a pipe that smells like an
unfrequented sulphur sink in Yellowstone
Park"; his public manner is "patient,

NELSON, DONALD M.—*Continued*

kindly, something like that of a railway information clerk." Away from the office he sometimes likes to play golf at the half dozen or so clubs he belongs to ("he is said to have the longest, most exasperating hook outside a Wodehouse story"), to fish, or, even more, just to sit quietly at the movies. That is better than exercise any time, he thinks. "The only exercise I take now," as quoted in *Time*, "is walking in the funeral processions of friends who died from too much of it."

References

> Business Week p15 Ag 27 '38 por; p18+ Ap 8 '39 por; p7 Jl 6 '40 por
> Cur Hist & Forum 52:18-19 Ja 10 '41 por
> Look 5:62-65 N 18 '41 pors
> N Y Post p10 S 19 '41 por
> N Y Times p8 F 5 '41; p10 F 6 '41; VII p8+ S 28 '41 il por
> Scholastic 33:20S O 1 '38 por; 39:15 S 29 '41 por
> Time 37:22 F 24 '41 por (cover)
> Who's Who in America
> Who's Who in Commerce and Industry

NEUMAN, LEO HANDEL (nū'măn) Sept. 12, 1868—Mar. 15, 1941 Specialist in internal medicine who was credited with originating the theory of the portable electrocardiograph to measure electrical currents of the heart; gave idea to the late Dr. Charles P. Steinmetz, who with other scientists in 1917 perfected the machine; taught medicine at the Albany Medical College and was author of many papers on gastro-intestinal and cardiac diseases.

References

> American Medical Directory

Obituaries

> N Y Times p45 Mr 16 '41

NEWBOLT, SIR FRANCIS GEORGE Nov. 21, 1863—Dec. 7, 1940 Attorney who was the first honorary professor of law of the Royal Academy; was also a lecturer on science and the author of several art books.

References

> Who's Who

Obituaries

> N Y Times p69 D 8 '40

NEWELL, EDWARD THEODORE Jan. 15, 1886—Feb. 18, 1941 Internationally recognized expert on coins and president of the American Numismatic Society since 1916; had devoted 30 years to coin study; was one of the foremost authorities in the field of Hellenistic coinages, and had an exceptionally thorough knowledge of the numismatics of the entire Greek and Roman world; had written many books and monographs on coins.

References

> Who's Who Among North American Authors
> Who's Who in America

Obituaries

> N Y Herald Tribune p18 F 20 '41

NEWLON, JESSE H(OMER) July 16, 1882—Sept. 1, 1941 Leader in experimental progressive education; director of the division of the foundations of education at Teachers College, Columbia University; faculty member since 1927; had taught in many schools and served as superintendent of schools in Lincoln, Nebraska and in Denver, Colorado; had served as president of the National Education Association; assailed United States high schools as being 30 years behind the times.

References

> Lit Digest 120:19 Jl 20 '35 por
> Nat Educ Assn J 14:201 Je '25 por; 24:59 F '35 por
> Time 36:48 Jl 22 '40
> Leaders in Education 1941
> Who's Who Among North American Authors
> Who's Who in America

Obituaries

> N Y Times p17 S 2 '41

NICE, HARRY (WHINNA) (nīs) Dec. 5, 1877—Feb. 25, 1941 Governor of Maryland from 1935 to 1939, one of three Republicans ever elected to that office; was mentioned for the Presidency; began his political career in 1903 as a member of the Baltimore City Council; had been judge and State's Attorney.

References

> Lit Digest 118:10 D 15 '34 por
> Sat Eve Post 207:17 D 29 '34 por
> State Gov 9:7 Ap '36 por
> Who's Who in America
> Who's Who in Law

Obituaries

> N Y Times p21 F 26 '41 por
> Time 37:64 Mr 10 '41

NICHOLS, DUDLEY Apr. 6, 1895- Screen writer

Address: Long Mountain Road, New Milford, Conn.

Dudley Nichols was born into an electrical age at a time when Edison was devising ways of getting electricity from dynamos into people's lives and homes. Though his father was bent on making him a surgeon, his first thoughts were of watts, ohms and amperes. His proudest achievement as a boy was the biggest Tesla coil anyone of his age had ever tried to construct, with millions of high frequency volts streaming out of its top electrode. For many years he paid annual birthday visits to Edison's New Jersey laboratory. And from the challenge of high voltages in the field of electrical engineering he went on to meet an analogous challenge in newspaper and magazine work and, later, in Hollywood.

Dudley Nichols was born in Wapakoneta, Ohio, on April 6, 1895, the son of Dr. Grant Byron and Mary (Means) Nichols. William McFee said of Dudley's father: "I have never forgotten that old chap, who resembled Henry Ford, saying he had 'brought over a thousand children into the world and never lost a mother.'"

Between periods of schooling Dudley worked at various jobs, including months with a line gang repairing high tension power lines. Boss of the gang was an Irishman named Cronin whose passion it was to "work the lines hot"—that is, to replace poles and insulators without shutting off the 33,000 volt current. This passion for voltage was shared by young Nichols, and he soon took up radio, which was then still being called "wireless."

In 1913, at the age of 18, he worked as a radio operator on ships plying the travel lanes of the Great Lakes. His first assignment was on the old wooden *S. S. Saronic.* One nightmare memory he has from that period is having to send out an SOS an hour after he had said "good night" to the lone operator on the *Huronic,* sister ship they had passed in mid-lake. Engine trouble had stalled the *Saronic,* and she was drifting on Point au Barques. Nichols had reason to be concerned, for there was no chance of "raising" the *Huronic* until his friend awakened next morning, nor would his transmitter reach anyone else. Fortunately a shift in wind saved them from being driven further inshore, and around daylight a shore station was contacted and help received.

While at the University of Michigan, which he entered in the fall of 1915, he was a paid student assistant in charge of the radio laboratory, and developed a new type of rotary discharger that was adapted by commercial wireless companies. Upon entry of the United States into the First World War, Mr. Nichols enlisted in the Navy. At the Great Lakes Training Station he set up a school of radio operators and by late summer, 1917, was in charge of a school of 900 men. He was too young to be promoted in rank and was offered the alternative of remaining as second in command or going overseas, joining Admiral Simms in London. Without hesitation, he chose London.

After a few months of staff work and contacts with leading Britishers, Nichols was transferred at his own request to mine laying work in the North Sea. At the close of the War he volunteered for mine sweeping and devised a method of electrical protection for mine sweepers, for which he was later awarded the Distinguished Service Medal (November 11, 1920). A newspaper colleague who interviewed him upon his return to America in 1919 wrote: "It was with the Nichols gadget that 50,000 mines were swept up in the North Sea by the Yankee Suicide Fleet without the loss of a man or ship. Before that the United States Suicide Squadron lost 18 trawlers—some of which the

Buxbaum

DUDLEY NICHOLS

British generously rented us at slightly above the usual trawler rate."

On his twenty-fourth birthday Nichols was promoted to junior lieutenant, No. 1 of that day, the highest rank that could be held by one of his age. But Nichols had had a brief experience in journalism when the New York *Times* published material on his North Sea experience, and he wanted to try his hand in this field. He turned down an offer by Managing Editor Van Anda of the *Times,* since Van Anda was a friend of the family and Nichols wanted to assure himself that he was getting a position on his own merits. He then tried every city room in New York, and at the last one, the old *Evening Post,* he was given a position. There, and on the New York *World,* Nichols worked for 10 years, covering important events in every field of that decade that began with the close of a war and ended with the beginning of a depression.

In his spare time he studied Latin and Greek in the Washington Square College of New York University, making a metrical translation of Ovid's *Metamorphoses.* During one vacation he worked his way through Central and South American waters, as wireless operator on the United Fruit boat *Turrialba,* of which William McFee was chief engineer. In 1924 he married Esta Varez Gooch-Collings, and in 1927 he went abroad, sending back items for the "opposite editorial" page. It was 1929 when he began to feel journalism a constraining influence. At three o'clock one afternoon he closed his desk and never went back.

His first intention was to go to Spain to write a book. A publisher offered an advance on it, and Nichols went to Winfield Sheehan, an old *World* man who was running the Fox Studio in Hollywood and who had many friends in Spain. Sheehan promised letters

NICHOLS, DUDLEY—*Continued*

for him to take along, and the next day, when Nichols called for them, his friend asked casually what his salary had been on the *World*. Nichols named his salary—it had been quite a good one, for newspaper work—and Sheehan offered him twice the money and a year's contract. But Nichols knew nothing about films. The theatre, yes. He had reviewed plays and had been a loyal friend of the old Provincetown Players group. To clinch the deal Mr. Sheehan blithely intimated that hardly anyone knew anything about motion pictures, anyway.

From the beginning of his Hollywood stay Dudley Nichols brought to his work a fresh and often iconoclastic point of view. Describing life as a choice of escape or pursuit, he found most of Hollywood's films escapist and compared filmdom's hacking to a farmer who works his field until it's sterile. "In the same way," said Mr. Nichols, "picture producers keep on fertilizing their fallow crops heavily with money and they are frightened when a shopworn product no longer will sell. They have revamped old stories and reproduced old pictures until the public is sated. Yet there is no limit to story material. They haven't begun to skim the surface of great stories already written, or waiting to be written."

He was given the Academy Award for the best adaptation of 1935 for his work on *The Informer* (1935), but refused it because of his connection with the Screen Writers' Guild, of which he was a member of the Board of Governors. "As one of the founders of the Screen Writers' Guild," he wrote in refusing the Award, "which was conceived in revolt against the Academy and was born out of disappointment with the way it functioned against the employed talent in any emergency, I deeply regret I am unable to accept the award. . . . To accept it would be to turn my back on nearly a thousand members of the Screen Writers' Guild."

Among his best adaptations are those on which he did the scenario and John Ford (see sketch this issue) acted as director. Many of their films were low-budget jobs, like *The Informer*, which cost $218,000. (In Hollywood, John Ford joked, that would be about the price of a good cigar.) *Stage Coach* (1939) cost only slightly more. Their pictures presented real characters in real life situations, avoided stilted formulas both in continuity and in casting. The firm structural unity of *The Long Voyage Home* (1940), which is made up of four plays by Eugene O'Neill, is as typical of Nichols' film writing as it is of Ford's direction.

Nichols wrote the script for Sean O'Casey's *The Plough And The Stars* in 1936, while cruising in Mexican waters aboard Ford's yacht. As Nichols recalled it, working on a yacht was no holiday, especially when his contract required that he turn in a completed script in a matter of a few weeks. Strict discipline was in order; so for three days he glared at the typewriter, meditating on throwing it overboard. He had trouble in

beginning each draft. At the third draft he found himself hating the script, the typewriter and the whole world. But he got over his hate in time to produce an excellent script and get in some fishing on the side.

In addition to his regular work, which includes more film successes than he can remember, Nichols did the narrative commentary for Joris Ivens' impressive documentary film on modern China, *The 400,000,000*. Then, in the spring of 1941, Nichols started out on a new venture with as much potential voltage for him as anything he has tackled in his long and colorful career. For he retired from screen writing to devote his whole time to free-lance work. One of his first jobs was revising *Somewhere in France*, a play by Carl Zuckmayer, for the Theatre Guild.

Tall, lean, with aquiline nose, brown eyes, and prematurely gray hair, Dudley Nichols is deliberate in speech and manner and, as one writer described him, "gives the impression of a man who would think his way through engineering or poetry, and all between." Quite unconscious of the significance of his metaphor, a colleague referred to him as "a dynamo of energy." He is six feet one and one-half inches tall, weighs one hundred ninety pounds.

When he lives on his Connecticut farm Dudley Nichols' favorite hobby is planting trees. For recreation he swims and plays croquet in summer, shovels snow in winter, and takes long walks the year round. Sometimes on summer nights, watching the cosmic voltage weave shimmering folds of aurora borealis across the sky, he is reminded of Jerry Cronin, whose passion it was to work the lines hot. And then, more likely than not, he looks ahead to what he will write the next day. "You extremists," William McFee once told him, "have all the fun."

References

N Y Herald Tribune Ag 9 '36
N Y Post Ja 24 '39 por
N Y Sun N 22 '39; N 25 '39; p18 O 10 '40
N Y Times p26 Mr 10 '36; IX p3 Jl 26 '36
Stage 13:59 S '36 por
International Motion Picture Almanac

NIEBUHR, REINHOLD, REV. (nē'boŏr) June 21, 1892-   Clergyman

Address: b. Union Theological Seminary, New York City; h. 99 Claremont Ave, New York City

For many years now Reverend Reinhold Niebuhr has been "a contradictory, conspicuous figure in the two worlds of religion and radical politics." In 1941, before the United States entered the War, he was, even more than usual, a center of controversy as leader of a group of eminent churchmen who believed that war could be a lesser evil than unchristian tyranny. He and his supporters had met and debated the issue; they had issued statements to the press denouncing pacifist isolation; and on February 7, 1941 they presented the first issue of *Christianity and Crisis,* an eight-page biweekly.

This magazine, intended mainly to oppose the staunchly pacifist tone of the existing interdenominational religious periodicals and particularly that of the *Christian Century,* was dedicated to the principle that "the halting of totalitarian aggression is a prerequisite to world peace and order." Backed by a number of influential sponsors, including Bishop Ivan Lee Holt, Bishop Francis J. McConnell, President Dodds of Princeton and William Allan Neilson, former president of Smith College, its editorial policy, guided by Reverend Niebuhr, was to be devoted to giving anti-pacifist churchmen a voice.

Niebuhr himself had said of his aims: "We think it dangerous to allow religious sensitivity to obscure the fact that Nazi tyranny intends to annihilate the Jewish race, to subject the nations of Europe to the domination of a 'master' race, to extirpate the Christian religion, to annul the liberties and legal standards which are the priceless heritage of ages of Christian and humanistic culture. . . The immediate task is the defeat of Nazi tyranny." This was not a new thesis for Reverend Niebuhr; it was one he had been preaching ever since 1933 in sermons, articles and even in one of his latest books, *Christianity and Power Politics* (1940). Those churchmen who remained pacifist, were, he felt, guilty of a "sentimentalized Christianity" which says that slavery is better than war.

Reinhold Niebuhr was born in Wright City, Missouri on June 21, 1892. His father, Gustave Niebuhr, was a scholarly German preacher who died when his children were young, and it was no easy task for his mother, Lydia (Hosto) Niebuhr, to bring them up. Both Reinhold and his brother Helmut Richard (now a professor in the Yale Divinity School) attended Elmhurst College in Illinois. Reinhold left in 1910 without a degree to enroll in the Eden Theological Seminary in St. Louis, Missouri. He stayed there until 1913 and then transferred to the Yale Divinity School, which gave him his Bachelor of Divinity degree in 1914 and his Master of Arts degree in 1915.

In 1915 Niebuhr was ordained in the ministry of the Evangelical Synod of North America and then took up pastoral duties in Detroit. His charge was the Bethel Evangelical Church, a "little working-class" congregation which consisted for the most part of auto workers. Under him the congregation grew; it acquired a new building and many new members. Forums were conducted, "sprightly, and occasionally distinguished by spectacular episodes"; intellectuals, radicals and liberals came to swell the original working-class membership.

It was in Detroit that Reverend Niebuhr gained his sympathies for the working people of this country. He began to champion their cause—he even went so far as to say at one time: "The lowliest peasant of the Dark Ages had more opportunity for self-expression than the highest paid employee in the Ford factory." It was inevitable that more conservative

THE REV. REINHOLD NIEBUHR

church circles should consider him dangerous; it was inevitable that there should be flare-ups between him and Detroit employers. In 1928 Niebuhr left Detroit for the "comparative calm of the Union Theological Seminary" in New York.

Reverend Niebuhr was no less of a radical there. His teachings as associate professor of the philosophy of religion and as professor of applied Christianity (since 1930) were based not only on the conservative traditions of the Lutheran and reformed churches but also on the political philosophy of John Dewey, the economic approach of Karl Marx, the everyday intricacies of the American labor movement. During the depression of the 1930's Niebuhr "rose to a position of commanding influence in the theological world." Americans had begun to wonder whether there might not be something wrong with the world, and Niebuhr tried to point out to them his views on its cure.

In *Moral Man and Immoral Society* (1932) he pointed out the impossibility of achieving any real social change except by some sort of force—a position, incidentally, far removed from the pacifism he ardently expressed in the 1920's. In *Reflections on the End of an Era* (1934) he stated that capitalistic civilization as it then existed was doomed. Others of his books and many articles presented similar theses. And Niebuhr visited strikers, talked to unions and was an active member of the Socialist Party and an editor of its paper, *The World Tomorrow.* In June 1940 he resigned from the Socialist Party, however, over the issue of the War and our relationship to it. In all these years Niebuhr was not only radical; he was also deeply religious. After listening to him talk, a fellow clergyman once said: "He can skin civilization, hang the hide up to dry and offer prayer over the carcass."

(Continued next page)

NIEBUHR, REINHOLD, REV.—*Cont.*

All Niebuhr's lectures—at the Union Theological Seminary and on the lecture platform—seem to affect his hearers in much the same way. This is particularly true of the Gifford Lectures, which he delivered at Edinburgh University in 1939 as the fifth American to be honored with this famous lectureship (his predecessors were William James, Josiah Royce, John Dewey and William E. Hocking). In these lectures, published in book form in 1941 under the title *The Nature and Destiny of Man,* as in almost all his lectures and writing, it is impossible not to be impressed by his sharp logic, his theological brilliance, the fresh quality of his mind. More often than not it is impossible not to be stirred to rebuttal and controversy by them. To some of his colleagues this is, perhaps, a shortcoming. As one put it: "He is almost too clever intellectually. A little more tenderness or downright compassion would help to balance his brilliance." There are others, however, particularly his students, who respond to the stimulation he gives them and find it almost without peer in the theological world.

Reverend Niebuhr is lecturing a good deal these days, especially on his viewpoint on the War. He heads the Union for Democractic Action, is chairman of the American Friends of German freedom and also continues to contribute articles to many journals. (He has been editor of the quarterly *Christianity and Society,* a contributing editor to the *Christian Century,* and now, of course, edits *Christianity and Crisis.*) Together with his teaching this gives the tall, bald, sharp-eyed professor little time for anything else but work and occasional afternoon walks along Riverside Drive with his English wife, Ursula Kellep-Compton, whom he married in 1931, and their two children.

References

> Am Scholar 7 no 1:3-11 [Ja] '38
> Christian Cent 57:1578-80 D 18 '40
> Newsweek 1:28 Ap 29 '33 por; 17:58-9 Ja 27 '41
> Time 37:35 F 3 '41 por; 37-38+ Mr 24 '41
>
> Jones, E. D. American Preachers of To-day p249-53 1933
> Who's Who in America

NOBLE, GLADWYN KINGSLEY Sept. 20, 1894—Dec. 9, 1940 Curator of Herpetology and Biology at the American Museum of Natural History, New York who was an authority on snakes and lizards.

References

> Time 34:31 S 4 '39 por
> American Men of Science
> Who's Who in America

Obituaries

> N Y Times p25 D 10 '40 por

C. H. Coles—American Museum of Natural History

GLADWYN KINGSLEY NOBLE

NOMURA, KICHISABURO (nō-mōō-rä' kĭ-chĭ-sä'bōō-rō) Dec. 1877- Former Japanese Ambassador to the United States

Address: c/o Homestead Hotel, Hot Springs, Va.

When Admiral Kichisaburo Nomura, Japan's Ambassador to the United States, presented his credentials to President Roosevelt on February 14, 1941, the President's reply to the diplomatic courtesies was: "There are developments in the relations between the United States and Japan which cause concern."

In less tactful terms the President might well have said that Japanese-American relations at this time were worse than they had ever been. Japan's "New Order" in Asia had been a source of concern for this Government and, in turn, Japan resented American embargoes on Japanese exports and American aid to China. Japan's alliance with Italy and Germany, and problems arising from the Sino-Japanese War (including claims for damages to American interests, exclusion of shipping from the Yangtze River and disputes over policing the International Settlement in Shanghai) had already led to an unprecedented state of tension between these two countries.

It was felt in many places in November 1940, when Nomura was appointed Ambassador, that he was the logical Japanese statesman to bring about a less delicate situation between his country and the United States. "I personally know of no issue impossible of peaceable solution," he said when appointed. Before leaving Japan he visited around and held conferences to win promises from the Army and Navy that their extremists would do nothing to embarrass him in his efforts. "In so far as he can control events, Admiral Nomura means that his assurances to the

United States Government can be accepted fully," was Hugh Byas' interpretation of this in the New York *Times.*

The optimism of American and Japanese commentators over Nomura's appointment was not entirely consistent, however. *Hochi,* the Japanese newspaper, warned that "sending an Ambassador to Washington is like ordering a man on horseback to charge a wall." American writers reminded the public that although Nomura knew the United States well and was "one of the United States' staunchest supporters in Japanese officialdom," he was still an important member of this officialdom, with aims substantially, if less radically, those of former Premier Matsuoka (see sketch this issue), who appointed him. His words on his appointment were evasive. "Let us in Japan and America guard the peace of the Pacific, the only bright light of hope now left to mankind."

Arrived in the United States—on a day of "strange stirrings in the Far East"—Admiral Nomura admitted that he found the "atmosphere" in the United States worse than he had expected. Uncertainty over Japanese intentions in the Far East and the United States freezing of Japanese credits here kept tension high, and the Admiral refused to give any concrete proposals for improving Japanese-American relations. By November war between the two countries seemed almost inevitable, but conversations continued, and on November 26 Secretary of State Hull (see sketch 1940 Annual) presented a memorandum for a general settlement of the Pacific's problems.

At 2:20 p.m. on December 7, 1941 Secretary of State Hull received Admiral Nomura and Japan's "peace" envoy, Saburo Kurusu. He read the Japanese answer to his memorandum rejecting American proposals a moment after news of the Japanese attack on Pearl Harbor had been received, and told the Japanese envoys: "In all my 50 years of public service I have never seen a document that was more crowded with infamous falsehoods and distortion. . . ." They walked out, "pale and quiet," having done their job. Until the American diplomatic corps could be returned to the United States Nomura was kept a virtual prisoner first in the Japanese Embassy and then at Hot Springs, Virginia.

Admiral Nomura has figured prominently in Japanese political life for many years. He started out as a humble cadet, however. Born in Wakayama-ken, the third son of Kisaburo Masuda, he was left fatherless and poor when still very young. He had to support himself through school by various jobs, one of them delivering fish for a peddler. About this time he was adopted by Masatane Nomura, whose name he took and with whom he lived while attending the Middle School.

In 1896 Nomura entered the Japanese Naval Academy and in 1898 was graduated with the Imperial Prize for scholarship. As a naval cadet he embarked on a training cruise in 1899 that took him over a good part of the world, and in 1901 followed this up with a commission to go with a number of other cadets to England to bring back the battleship

KICHISABURO NOMURA

Mikasa, which was built there. Shortly afterward the Russo-Japanese War broke out, and Nomura saw service on several ships before the end of the fighting. He was navigating officer on the *Saiyen* when she hit a mine. Nomura says of this: "Ship she go down; me I come up."

It was when this War ended that Nomura received his first diplomatic mission: in 1908 he was sent to Russia (next to Vienna) as naval attaché. Two years later he spent a year in Berlin, then returning to Japan to serve in the Bureau of Naval Affairs in the Japanese Naval Office. He was soon made an adjutant and given the position of secretary to the Navy Minister. The first World War found him in Washington, after the birth of his only son, Tadafhi—he had married Hideko Yamaguchi. Here he was "the popular card-playing naval attaché of a friendly second-rate power" and a student at Annapolis, as some point out rather sadly now. In 1918 he returned home to become captain of the cruiser *Yakumo.*

He was presently sent as part of the Japanese delegation to the signing of the Versailles Treaty. He later attended the 1921-to-1922 Washington Disarmament Conference, where he played an important part as technical adviser to the Japanese delegation in framing the treaty which suspended naval competition between the United States and Japan for 15 years. Then, back in Japan, he was appointed commander of the First Overseas fleet which patrolled the Yangtze River and the waters about Shanghai, and in 1926 he was made an admiral.

In 1929 Nomura was once again in the United States, this time as commander of a training squadron. His next important position was that of commander in chief of the Kuré Admiralty Port, followed by a position

NOMURA, KICHISABURO—*Continued*

as Supreme Commander of the Yokosuka Naval Base. It was while he was here that the "Shanghai Incident" of 1932 occurred, and he was ordered to proceed to the hostilities as the commander of the 3rd Fleet. He came through the fighting unscathed, but some weeks later, while on a reviewing stand in Shanghai, lost an eye when a Korean terrorist threw a bomb.

In 1937 Admiral Nomura resigned from active service, but he continued to serve his country as a member of the Supreme War Council, as adviser to many organizations and as president of the Peers' School. In September 1939, when Premier Nobuyuki Abe selected him for the post of Foreign Minister, he gave up his position at the Peers' School (despite entreaties such as that of one pupil: "Please remain and train us so that we may become worthy pillars of our country").

Nomura was chosen for this position for the same reasons that he was chosen for his Ambassador's position in 1940. It was believed that he would be able to improve relations with the United States, strained by the Panay incident and the abrogation of the 23-year-old commercial treaty. He made a sincere effort to do so. At the end of December 1939 he announced that Japan was going to open the Yangtze River to foreign trade. He tried, too, to establish a general policy for dealing with the United States—to settle all outstanding questions that had arisen during the Japanese Army's operations and so create an atmosphere that might make some sort of peace terms, probably with Wang Ching-wei, acceptable to Americans. But the cabinet of Premier Abe was short-lived, and Nomura's proposals possibly contributed to its downfall. After its crash Japan became a member of the Axis alliance and more totalitarian than ever.

The man whom Matsuoka sent to America in 1941 to have "heart-to-heart talks with President Roosevelt on means for improving the situation between our two countries" had the advantages of speaking English perfectly and of having known Roosevelt from the days when the President was in the Navy Department. Before this six-foot, 200-pound Japanese left for America he went around to see his doctor to get a new glass eye fitted. Then he decided to play safe and bought himself five extra ones. "I've a hunch my stay in the United States this time will be long," he explained.

References

> Contemporary Japan 8:1070-5 N '39
> Life 10:28-9 F 24 '41 il pors
> N Y Times p6 N 12 '40 por; p1, 7 N 26 '40; p10 N 27 '40; IV p2, p4 D 1 '40 por; p10 D 11 '40; VII p14, 29 F 9 '41 il pors; p1, 5 F 15 '41
> Newsweek 14:23-4 O 2 '39 por
> Time 38:24+ S 22 '41 por (cover)
> U S News 10:9-10 F 28 '41 por
> International Who's Who
> Who's Who in Japan

NOYES, WILLIAM A(LBERT) Nov. 6, 1857—Oct. 24, 1941 Chemist; first chief chemist of the National Bureau of Standards at Washington, 1903 to 1907; professor of chemistry at the University of Illinois until he became professor emeritus in 1926; his laboratory discovered illinium, a missing element; former president of the American Chemical Society and founder of *Chemical Abstracts*, the Society's world-wide reporting system; winner of many medals for distinguished service to chemistry; author of chemistry textbooks.

References

> Lit Digest 120:16 Ag 31 '35 por
> Sch & Soc 42:146-7 Ag 3 '35
> Sci ns 81:429 My 3 '35; 90:71-5 Jl 28 '39
> American Men of Science
> Chemical Who's Who
> Leaders in Education 1941
> Who's Who Among North American Authors
> Who's Who in America

Obituaries

> N Y Times p17 O 25 '41 por

NUFFIELD, WILLIAM RICHARD MORRIS, 1ST VISCOUNT Oct. 10, 1877- Director general of maintenance at British Air Ministry; automobile manufacturer

Address: Nuffield Place, Huntercombe, Henley-on-Thames, England

"I take off my hat to Morris," wrote a British journalist in *The Autocar*. "He is the only man who has ever got away with the assembled car proposition in this country." A multimillionaire who has been called "the British Ford," Morris' success is largely due to the fact that he designed a cheap family car of good and economical performance which was comfortable, roomy and had attractive lines. Before his day the Britisher of moderate means bought the old high-axle Ford.

Since he has become rich and a peer, Morris has made lavish gifts to good causes, which at the end of 1940 totaled more than $66,000,000. His chief beneficiaries have been his own employees, the medical profession, the University of Oxford, the unemployed in the Special Areas and the sports funds of the armed services. Typical of his attitude toward his money was the remark made when giving $4,000,000 to Oxford in 1936: "Giving is pleasant, but the worry which comes from giving is very great. In my own case, I have found this worry during the past few years beyond understanding. The idea that it is easy to give money away is the biggest fallacy in the world."

Morris was born at Worcester, the son of Frederick Morris, who had been a "public school" man, and of Emily Ann Pether, the daughter of a farmer. At the age of three he was taken to Wood Farm, Headington, just outside of Oxford, and since that time has always manifested a strong local patri-

otism for the city of Oxford and its great
university which poverty prevented him from
attending. After primary schooling at the
village school in Cowley—there were six
scholars in his class—he was apprenticed in a
bicycle shop at the age of 16.

Young Morris wanted to study medicine,
but that was out of the question, and after
nine months as an assistant he borrowed $20
and opened his own bicycle shop in Oxford.
From hiring and repairing he progressed to
selling and thence to manufacturing motorcycles. He proved to have real talent in
design: his "Morris machine" went well, and
by 1911 he had increased his capital to something around $16,000. (He had also acquired
innumerable championships for bicycle racing,
which he gave up in 1900.) Next he turned
to designing and manufacturing cars. In
1912 he set up a small factory at Cowley,
a village just outside Oxford, and inside of a
year his first cars were on the road. They
were named the "Morris Oxford."

The First World War came along just
as Morris was getting into his stride, but
he turned his works over to war production
and acted as supervisor at a nominal salary.
In 1919 he began again on cars. There were
two models—the "Morris Cowley" and the
slightly more expensive "Morris Oxford"—
and it wasn't long before they swept the
market. Morris believed in high wages and
low prices; when in 1921 there was general
talk of raising automobile prices he reduced
his. They called it business suicide, but in
1922 his sales were just under 7,000; in 1923
over 20,000; in 1925 more than 60,000. By
1926 he was employing 4,000 men and turning
out 1,000 cars a week. By this time he had
also reconstituted E. G. Wrigley, Limited,
of Birmingham, as Morris Commercial Cars,
Limited; had taken over the Léon Bollée
concern of Le Mans, France; had combined
with the Budd Manufacturing Company of
Philadelphia to make bodies; had started a
radiator factory. From the Morris Garages,
Limited, he began to turn out the M. G.
sports model, a smart little roadster. Morris'
days of poverty and struggle were over; and
he heralded his accession to the ranks of
big capital by a gift of $40,000 to complete
the endowment of the Department of Spanish
at the University of Oxford in 1926.

In 1927 the Wolseley motor company was
in a bad way financially, in spite of turning
out a high-class product. Morris bid for it
against American competition, bought it for
$2,920,000, and so went in for the luxury car
trade. Next came airplane work, with Wolseley Aero Engines, which he started in 1929;
and in that year he was made Sir William
(as a baronet, the rank higher than knight).
In 1930 he refused an American offer of
$44,000,000 for his total holdings. He was
raised to the peerage as Baron Nuffield in
1934 and advanced a grade to Viscount in
1938.

Nuffield is what is generally known as a
"rugged individualist." Although taking no
active part in politics, he is a conservative in
that he believes in private enterprise. He

VISCOUNT NUFFIELD

says: "When a man talks trade-unionism to
me I ask him to think again and talk to me
as a man. Everyone gets a square deal here.
I pay high wages and get good work. . . No,
my methods of production aren't anything like
Mr. Ford's. They are my own." He doesn't
like Governmental "interference" with his business, either. In 1936 he disagreed with the
Air Council on the question of "shadow factories," by which specific factories could be
turned over in wartime to the manufacture
of one specific machine part. He did
not think this the best or safest scheme,
said so and flatly refused to participate. Air
Minister Lord Swinton took more than three
months to make an appointment to discuss
matters, and Nuffield then announced: "This
is the first time in my life that I have been
turned down by a Cabinet Minister."

Early in 1937, however, Nuffield yielded and
established an armaments firm called Nuffield
Mechanisations, Limited, following this up in
June 1938 with an aircraft factory. He figured in a court case in that same month.
Two men were arrested in a charge of attempting to kidnap him for a ransom of
$400,000, and one of them was sent to seven
years' penal servitude. In September 1938 he
acquired Riley Motors. In May 1939 a luncheon was held at Grosvenor House, a big London hotel, to celebrate the completion and
dispatch of the millionth Morris vehicle. In
November 1939 Nuffield was appointed director general of maintenance at the Air
Ministry, his job to look after the repair of
aircraft and their equipment. (He is doing it
without any salary.) In May 1940 Lord Beaverbrook ordered him to submit to a merger
of his vast new aircraft works with the firm
of Vickers-Armstrong, Limited.

To summarize Nuffield's larger philanthropies: on six occasions he has given away

NUFFIELD, WILLIAM RICHARD MORRIS, 1ST VISCOUNT—*Continued*

$4,000,000 or more at one flick of the checkbook. The first was in 1936, when he presented the University of Oxford with $8,000,-000 for the establishment of a postgraduate medical school. In the same year he gave $8,500,000 in shares to his own employees, excepting those who were earning $4,000 a year or more, and established a fund of $8,000,000 for the Special Areas—that is, districts like South Wales and Northumberland in which large-scale unemployment had become chronic. In 1937 he actually founded a new college, Nuffield College, in the University of Oxford, with an endowment of $4,000,000; in 1939 he gave $6,000,000 to the improvement of recreational facilities for the armed forces and $5,000,000 for the coordination of hospital services in the provinces. Numerous specific hospitals have drawn enormous sums from him, and by his large-scale endowment plans for the linking up of clinical medicine and theoretical research he has given a tremendous push to the study of medicine in England. In 1938 he gave $2,000,000 to provide "iron lungs" for every hospital in the British Empire that could use one. And although medicine has been among his chief beneficiaries, many other causes have received great financial assistance from him: the Boy Scouts, the blind, numerous churches and educational institutions.

Nuffield once told an interviewer: "We have too many 'half time' directors in industry. Personally, I begin work at eight and don't leave until half-past seven." He is a very hard worker, and expects his men to be the same. For a long time he took no exercise or relaxation to speak of, but under medical advice he finally took up and now enjoys golf, squash and tennis. He has been described as "a small but very active man, strong and highly strung, with well-shaped hands." Another observer says that he is "so dark-complexioned that you might take him for one of Southern blood." He has hazel eyes, a large jaw and a strong chin, and is often given the adjective "bull-necked."

"Despite his wealth, his tastes remain simple. 'Shilling for twenty' cigarets are his favorite smoke. He waves away plutocratic cigars, and often finds a few shillings a day sufficient for pocket money." He doesn't like the legends of his "rising from the gutter," however, and in 1938 the London *Sunday Express* published an approved story saying "not a quarter of one per cent of the population can trace their ancestry back" as far as Nuffield. In 1904 he married Elizabeth Maud Anstey, daughter of an Oxford businessman. They live an unostentatious home life at Nuffield Place, Huntercombe, near Henley-on-Thames, and have no children.

References

Lit Digest 122:13 O 31 '36 por
Liv Age 354:42-6 Mr '38
Nature 140:697-8 O 23 '37
Newsweek 10:42 O 25 '37 por
Scholastic 30:21 Mr 13 '37
Spec Ag 21 '26

Time 31:16 Ja 24 '38 por; 31:36 Je 6 '38 por; 32:52 D 5 '38 por
Times [London] O 16 '36; O 29 '36; O 30 '36; N 25 '36; D 1 '36; D 22 '36; O 13 '37; O 14 '37; Je 10 '38; Je 14 '38; Jl 20 '38; Jl 21 '38; Jl 22 '38; Jl 23 '38; N 24 '38
Bridges, T. C. and Tiltman, H. H. Kings of Commerce p189-95 1928
British Parliament, Command Paper 5295 O 29 '36
Gardiner, A. G. Portraits and Portents 1927
Who's Who
Who's Who in Commerce and Industry

NUTTING, WALLACE, REV. Nov. 17, 1861—July 19, 1941 Antiquarian; author; illustrator; retired clergyman; one of the nation's foremost experts on American antiques, Dr. Nutting did not interest himself in that field until 1905, when ill health forced him to retire from the ministry; the first book which he illustrated with photographs and sketches was *Old New England Pictures* (1913), followed by the "States Beautiful Series" with books on Massachusetts, Connecticut, New Hampshire, Maine, Pennsylvania, New York and Virginia; he also wrote and illustrated books on England and Ireland; wrote his autobiography, *Wallace Nutting's Biography*, in 1936.

References

Am Mag 103:38-41 Ja '27 il por
National Mag 52:497 My '24 por
Nutting, W. Wallace Nutting's Biography 1936
Who's Who Among North American Authors
Who's Who in America

Obituaries

N Y Times p30 Jl 20 '41
Pub W 140:252 Jl 26 '41
Time 38:72 Jl 28 '41

NYE, GERALD P(RENTICE) Dec. 19, 1892- United States Senator from North Dakota

Address: b. Senate Office Bldg, Washington, D. C.; h. Cooperstown, N. D.; 3802 Gramercy St, Washington, D. C.

Bulletin: When Senator Nye heard the news of the Japanese attack on Pearl Harbor, he was scheduled to address an America First meeting in Pittsburgh. He gave his anti-war speech, and that evening declared that this was "just what Britain planned for us"; "we have been maneuvered into this by the President." The next day, however (December 8, 1941), he voted with the rest of the Senate for a declaration of war.

From November 1941 issue:

Since 1925, when a naïve country editor from North Dakota wearing "bulbous yellow shoes and an Old Oaken Bucket haircut" came to Washington to take his place in the Senate, Gerald P. Nye has been a center of controversy of one kind or another, but never of such nationwide scope as in 1941. At some times in his career he has been called a liberal, reformer and idealist, at others a reactionary and an opportunist, and at all times there have been some to call him a publicity seeker. Perhaps the only entirely consistent thread running through his career is the thread of isolationism. Since the Second World War began he has been damned as a dangerous appeaser and anti-Semite with personal ambitions, praised as an honest leader in the fight for peace, and apologized for as a misguided former liberal.

Gerald Prentice Nye was born in Hortonville, Wisconsin on December 19, 1892, the son of Irwin R. Nye, the crusading editor of country weeklies in that state and one of the original La Follette men, and of Phoebe Ella (Prentice) Nye. He spent most of his boyhood in Wittenberg, Wisconsin, where his family moved when he was two, but after having been graduated from high school he returned to Hortonville in 1911 to take over one of his father's papers, *The Review*. Thereafter, except for a few months spent on the Des Moines *Register*, he was to make his career in country journalism until 1925. He went first from Wisconsin to Iowa, and then, during the boom days of the First World War, journeyed to Fryburg, North Dakota.

In Fryburg, Nye started *The Pioneer*, a paper that was in those days the only privately-owned journal in the United States to support the rising Non-Partisan League. He was county food administrator and headed a couple of Liberty Loan drives but heard himself called "traitor" more than once. And he did a little name-calling himself. One of his wartime editorials on the late Senator La Follette announced that that gentleman had "made himself the most thorough anti-American on American shores and the most thorough ass of his time, Kaiser Wilhelm excluded perhaps." (Yet at a memorial service in 1925 for La Follette, Sr., Senator Gronna and William Jennings Bryan, he was to say: "Never once did their records permit successful attack. Their sincerity of purpose was never denied.")

In the year 1919 he and his wife, the former Anna Margaret Munch, whom he had married in 1916, settled down in Cooperstown, North Dakota. There Nye became editor and manager of the Griggs County *Sentinel Courier*, drafted for the job by a group of Non-Partisan farmers who had bought the paper. This "radical" activity caused him at first to be blackballed by the Masons and the Knights of Pythias. He has for many years now, however, been a member of both organizations. And it was not long before the despised Non-Partisan League had won control of the state, set it to building grain elevators and flour mills in an effort to defeat the "interests," and attained for itself a certain respectability.

Nye's backing helped La Follette and the Progressive Republican ticket in North Dakota

Haynes Inc.

GERALD P. NYE

in 1924. He was not a figure of any political importance himself, however, unless his presence on the Cooperstown school board made him that. After Senator Ladd died and Nye brought pressure through his paper to have the seat filled at once by gubernatorial appointment so that the many voters favoring measures to dispose of surplus farm products could be represented in the coming session, he was genuinely surprised when he received the appointment himself.

In December 1925 the "village Greeley" arrived in Washington. He waited outside the Capitol for a month while the Senate debated whether or not a Governor had the power to fill a Senatorial vacancy and while his daughter, Marjorie, hoped that sometime they would "give Papa a place to sit down." His friends finally sent him a milking stool. But Borah and Norris battled for the La Follette Republican; Nye himself rounded up laws and precedents; and a two-vote majority was finally convinced that he deserved his seat. "A bad day's work," scolded the New York *Times*. Nevertheless, when a few months later Nye ran for the balance of his term as an independent against a conservative Republican, he won, and was re-elected for a full term of six years.

With the shift of chairmanships following the elections, Nye had become head of the obscure Public Lands Committee. Soon he was presiding over his first investigation, the inquiry into the Continental Trading Company oil scandal which produced such sensational revelations concerning Harry F. Sinclair, Andrew Mellon and the Republican National Committee, finally forcing the revision of a government lease of a $100,000,000 oil field and the recovery of more than $7,000,000 in taxes and penalties. To Nye this whole affair demonstrated the "frightful influence of money upon our political and economic life as a nation."

(Continued next page)

NYE, GERALD P.—*Continued*

He soon became known as a stubborn fighter, whether it was for farm relief legislation or against the World Court ("no internationalist, he"), and that same year he proceeded to enhance his reputation by battling with President Coolidge over North Dakota patronage, Nye winning. The Baltimore *Sun* called him "Gerald, the·Giant-Killer," and the name persisted. So did Nye. He criticized Coolidge-Mellon taxation policies, attacked the war-debt settlement (the farmer's debts should be scaled down, too, he thought), accused the Coolidge Administration of domination by bankers and industrialists who didn't want to see agriculture on "an even footing with protected industries," supported all moves for higher inheritance and income taxes, spoke against monopoly, chain stores, branch banking. And although he finally swung over to Hoover, at the 1928 Republican Convention he opposed his nomination on the grounds that he didn't care about the farmer any more than Coolidge. Nye's was, in other words, the outlook of the old-fashioned agrarian rebel.

In April 1930 the voluble North Dakotan was appointed chairman of another investigating committee—to pry into Senate campaign expenditures. Once more the investigation was rich in revelations: the conspiracy against Nebraska's Senator Norris, the enormous expenditures in the Illinois and Pennsylvania campaigns, the Klan operations of the Republican Senatorial candidate in Kentucky. But there were even larger headlines when it was discovered that Ruth Hanna McCormick, whose affairs had been thoroughly publicized by the committee, was having her revenge by setting private detectives on Senator Nye's trail. His private life proved singularly uninteresting from her point of view.

In 1932 Nye was re-elected by a 3-1 majority despite the Democratic landslide. Now there was a "New Deal" President; but that wasn't what he wanted, either. To him the Blue Eagle was "a bird of prey on the masses"—fostering monopoly and price-fixing, suspending the anti-trust laws; and in December 1933 he declined Hugh Johnson's invitation to become a member of the NRA Board and "guard the interests of the small businessman." In 1934 he teamed up with Borah in vehement attacks on the NRA, although that same year he joined with the Democrats to elect a Democratic Governor in North Dakota.

By this time keeping the United States out of war at all costs had already begun to supplant agricultural reform as the main topic of Nye's speeches. In 1934 he slipped a rider into a revenue bill calling for tremendously increased wartime income taxes, volunteering to withdraw it only if the Senate would vote an investigation into the munitions industry. The Arms Inquiry began that year, with Nye presiding once more, and once more the facts brought out created a nationwide sensation, especially when J. P. Morgan was put on the carpet. Most liberals agreed that it "revealed the arms industry as a definite menace to world peace," and although some cast doubt on the importance of

Nye's role in the investigation (according to Kenneth Crawford it was thanks to the intelligence and industry of a staff headed by Stephen Raushenbush, Nye's counsel, that it was so fruitful) and others called him a headline hunter because of the "numerous and profitable" lecture engagements that followed, there were probably many more who felt, with Oswald Garrison Villard, that he was a "great leader in the fight for peace." In 1935 he won the Cardinal Newman Award.

In 1936 there was passed a permanent neutrality law drafted by Senators Nye, Clark (see sketch this issue) and Norris which forbade the shipment of arms to all belligerent countries. Since it contained no provision concerning civil wars, when Franco revolted in Spain an embargo on shipments of war materials to Spain was brought about by a special resolution. Nye did not vote against the resolution in the Senate in January 1937, and he favored the provision in the General Neutrality Act of May 1937 which added civil war to the conditions in a foreign country under which the President must establish an embargo. But it was soon evident that the effect of the embargo in this particular case was to prevent any help to one side while the other side was being aided by Germany and Italy, countries to which United States' arm shipments continued. In September 1935 Nye had spoken at a Detroit mass meeting of Father Coughlin's followers. Army Day in 1937 found him speaking at a dinner of the American League Against War and Fascism; and the next month the American Federation of Teachers charged that Yale had barred him from talking at the University because of his "liberal views." Finally, in May 1938, he introduced a Senate resolution proposing to end the embargo on Loyalist Spain. (It was shelved.)

To Nye, however, this was not a serious departure from isolationist principles. Nor did he court the favor of the Left for long. In July 1937, at a time when the National Labor Relations Board was considering a case against Tom Girdler and Little·Steel, he came out with a blast against the NLRB which, according to Kenneth Crawford, had emanated from the office of Girdler's press agent. Later, in January 1939, he was to back the WPA fund cut.

Nevertheless in 1938 Nye's campaign for the Senate was endorsed by Senators Borah, Norris, Wheeler, Capper and Shipstead; by William Green; by the National Non-Partisan Committee for the Re-election of Senator Nye, headed by Charles A. Beard and the *New Republic's* Bruce Bliven (see sketches this issue). The pacifist-minded Oswald Garrison Villard praised him for having "refused to allow himself to be bamboozled by the militarists or by the diplomats whose statesmanship has broken down," adding: "He votes not as he is told to vote but as his conscience dictates." Some Non-Partisan Leaguers in North Dakota were not so enthusiastic; one called him "a superficial liberal who has always flirted with the reactionaries and whose chief backers in the forthcoming election are the reactionary forces of the state." But not too many felt that way about him, and he was re-elected.

At this time Nazi propaganda in the United States was treated by Senator Nye as a danger at least as great as British propaganda. In May 1939 he asked public support for the film *Confessions of a Nazi Spy* (which he was later to list among films designed to bring the United States into war), calling it "a courageous effort to inform the American people about this great danger." His attitude toward the refugee problem created by Hitler, however, was that the United States should bar the entrance of Reich Jews, and in February 1939 he was cheered at a German-American Bund rally because of his attacks on Roosevelt's foreign policy. In July 1939 he was one of the group in Congress that defeated Roosevelt's attempt at repeal of the embargo. One of his first proposals after the final outbreak of the Second World War was that Roosevelt act as its mediator, and he continued to oppose any and all changes in neutrality legislation.

In February 1940, appointed to the Senate Foreign Relations Committee, Nye soon made himself one of Roosevelt's more powerful foes in the Senate. In speeches on the floor, before America First audiences and over the radio, he predicted the defeat in 1940 of Roosevelt. He opposed aid to Britain ("the greatest aggressor in modern history," whose impending doom "ought not to alarm us"), the draft bill, the sale of destroyers, the Lend-Lease Bill, the Great Lakes-St. Lawrence River development project, the occupation of Iceland, national daylight-saving time, the selective service extension plan and aid to Russia (populated by "thieves, human butchers and murderers of religion"). If Hitler should be victorious, there was no reason to think he would contemplate "retaliatory actions"; in any case, Nazism and Communism would destroy one another. When the *Robin Moor* was sunk, his first reaction was to suggest that the British might have done it—he "would be very much surprised if Germany had." He urged Charles Lindbergh's (see sketch this issue) candidacy for Congress.

But it was after an America First meeting on July 31, 1941, when Nye lashed out against anti-Hitler films, intoning the names of film producers who were predominantly Jewish, that a torrent of criticism of him began. As co-author of a resolution to investigate films and member of the Senate subcommittee appointed shortly afterward by Senator Wheeler to determine whether the investigation should actually be held, he made such statements as: "My objection to them [the film producers] is that they are foreign born and are in a position of power to control what 81,000,000 people a week see in our theatres." He listed such films as *The Great Dictator* and *Mortal Storm* as deliberate and dangerous war propaganda. He confirmed Lindbergh's statement that people of the Jewish faith were leaders in the movement toward war.

As a result, opponents accused him of anti-Semitism, intimidation and attempted censor-

ship; they asked how truthful movies could be otherwise than anti-Hitler, wondered why the investigation remained unconcerned about Fascist propaganda, pointed out that the movies are controlled by the banks rather than by the producers, anyway. Nye, in turn, accused the interventionists of having dragged in race prejudice to smear the non-interventionist cause and, in a speech at the annual dinner of the Steuben Society of America, called it "about the meanest thing that I have ever experienced in American politics." In the meanwhile a counter-investigation of the "Chinese control of laundries" was jokingly proposed.

Senator Nye long ago discarded his yellow shoes and high-water haircut, now wears, for the most part, "dark suits, white shirts, slightly flamboyant ties." His eyes have been variously described as pale blue and as hazel. He has a sharp nose, a strong, stubborn chin, a serious expression. His voice is low-pitched and quiet; he seldom makes frivolous remarks; he seldom laughs. But not all of his activities are as grim as his speeches in the Senate: he enjoys baseball (he was second baseman on his high school ball team), bass-fishing, rowing, reading Lincoln biographies and, according to *Newsweek* several years ago, the works of his favorite author, the late Harold Bell Wright. Nye is a Presbyterian. In March 1940 his first wife divorced him, and in December of that year he married Marguerite Johnson, an Illinois high school teacher whom he met in Estes Park, Colorado when he stepped out of his car to help her repair a tire. There are three children by his first wife: Marjorie Elleanor, Robert Gerald and James Prentice.

References

Am Mag 119:47+ My '35 por
Christian Cent 52:80-1 Ja 16 '35
Cur Hist 41:521-7 F '35
Lit Digest 87:13 D 5 '25 por; 88:12 Ja 30 '26 por; 90:5-6 Jl 17 '26; 106:5-7 S 20 '30 por; 118:12 S 22 '34 por; 121:5 Ja 4 '36 por (cover); 121:32 Ja 18 '36 por
Liv Age 347:309-14 D '34
Nation 138:154 F 7 '34; 146:245 F 26 '38; 146:543 My 7 '38; 147:89 Jl 23 '38
No Am 229:406-13 Ap '30
Scholastic 31:18S Mr 11 '39 por; 31:33 N 6 '37 por
Tucker, R. T. and Barkley, F. R. Sons of the Wild Jackass p292-315 1932
Unofficial Observer [pseud.] American Messiahs p134-54 1935
Who's Who in America
Who's Who in Government
Who's Who in the Nation's Capital

OBERON, MERLE Feb. 19, 1911- Motion-picture actress
Address: b. Alexander Korda Films, Inc, 1040 N. Las Palmas Ave, Hollywood, Calif.

From a cafe dance hostess who took her first job because she was hungry to a member of the histrionic aristocracy of Denham and Hollywood, Miss Oberon's career is a record of per-

MERLE OBERON

sistence, ingenuity, hard work and luck. A self-confessed poor business woman, Merle Oberon has succeeded in placing her name among those of the top-flight cinema actresses of today.

In Tasmania, a South Pacific island near Australia, the actress was born of Irish, French and Dutch descent and christened Estelle Merle O'Brien Thompson. Major Thompson, her father, had died before her birth, and the baby and her mother were left moderately well provided for, though not well enough for complete independence. When Merle was seven, therefore, her mother accepted the invitation of Lady Monteith, the child's godmother, to visit her in Bombay.

Soon after they were settled in Bombay, Mrs. Thompson, seeking to enlarge her small income, allowed herself to be persuaded to invest her small capital in a so-called American automobile agency. The agency did not exist except in the imagination of its promoter, who, having worked as much of Bombay as he could with safety, absconded with the entire Thompson fortune.

Now penniless, Merle and her mother moved to Calcutta to live with an uncle who accepted his new dependents with kindness and generosity. In Calcutta, in the Kiplingesque English colony of army officers and government officials, Merle grew up to be, at 16, a local beauty of whom all who met her said: "She ought to be in the movies." Gay and talented, she studied French and Hindustani as well as the regular curriculum at La Martinere College in Calcutta, and danced in the productions of the Calcutta Amateur Theatrical Society.

It was her uncle's leave of absence to go to England when his niece was 16 that turned the course of Merle's career. She might have continued to be one of the most beautiful girls in Calcutta and married a rising official who would one day make his name felt in the Colonial Office. London, however, to which she persuaded her uncle to let her accompany him, opened new vistas of opportunity, and when her uncle was ready to return to India, Merle was not at all willing to go with him. She had enrolled in a dancing school and the course was not yet completed. With his customary indulgence, her uncle let her remain for two months without him. She had £20, or $100, and a return ticket. When she had finished her dancing course she was to leave for Calcutta.

Merle had no intention whatsoever of returning. To burn her bridges most effectively, she cashed her return ticket voucher for $80 and bought a coat for $140. The $40 which remained dwindled away rapidly, and the ambitious girl, repeatedly turned away in her applications for screen tests, accepted a job as dance hostess at the Café de Paris. She felt that the position was beneath her. Army life in India made a great point of social distinctions, and Merle was too much inhibited by her early training to compromise without reluctance. The position paid two pounds ten a week and dinners. It was the dinners which constituted the deciding factor.

Her first screen test was ill-fated. Harry Lachman, to whom the would-be actress had applied time and again for a test, finally decided to test her for the role of a siren in a forthcoming picture. He neglected, however, to inform her that their interview was a test, so that when the actor began to hug and kiss her Merle struggled and screamed, arousing much amusement in bystanders, but unquestionably getting herself disqualified for the role of a vamp.

Mrs. Thompson, who was the only one in Calcutta who knew that Merle was not an outstanding success, came to London with the intention of persuading her daughter to return to India. It was the daughter, however, whose persuasion was successful, and the mother consented to remain. A later screen test proved luckier than the first, and Merle found herself playing bit parts at Wimbley for two pounds a day.

In 1932 London Film Productions offered her a five-year contract which she accepted. She played in *The Wedding Rehearsal, Men of Tomorrow, Dance of Witches* and *The Battle*, released in 1933 in America as *Thunder in the East*. It was not until she played the role of the luckless Anne Boleyn in Alexander Korda's *The Private Life of Henry VIII* that Merle Oberon's name became familiar to American audiences, however. The screen name which Merle had chosen for herself was O'Brien. Korda, who felt that O'Brien was too common, had promptly changed it to Auberon. This became Oberon only after his original choice had aroused the vehement protest of a prominent Bond Street hairdresser of the same name.

Since her first success, Miss Oberon has appeared in the following United Artists productions: *The Private Life of Don Juan*, with the late Douglas Fairbanks (1934); *The Scarlet Pimpernel*, with Leslie Howard (1934); *The Dark Angel*, "the first modern dress picture of its decade in which a feminine star has dared to appear in her own home-grown eyebrows" (1935); *These Three,* cinema dramatization of Lillian Hellman's (see sketch this issue) play, *The Children's Hour* (1936); *Beloved Enemy* (1936); *The Divorce of Lady X* (1938); and *The Cowboy and the Lady* (1938). She starred in *Broken Melody* for Olympic Pictures (1934); in *Folies Bergère* for Twentieth Century (1935); and in *I, Claudius* for London Films (1937).

In 1939 she elicited considerable critical acclaim with her portrayal of Cathy in Samuel Goldwyn's *Wuthering Heights.* As the passionate young Victorian in love with the brooding stableboy, Heathcliffe, but tempted by the love of worldly possessions and luxury to marry another, Miss Oberon's performance was generally conceded to be "mature", "fine," and "brilliant." According to the New York *Herald Tribune* her fine performance "seldom falters emotionally." *The Nation* found her interpretation of the role contained "legitimate modern overtones which stress the eternity of the conflict."

In 1940 she made two pictures for Warner Brothers, *Affectionately Yours* with Dennis Morgan, and *Till We Meet Again* with George Brent. In 1941 she starred in *That Certain Feeling,* a Lubitsch production.

Her latest vehicle, *Lydia,* was produced by her husband, Alexander Korda. This was the first production in which she had been interested financially, and her associates were treated to the unusual spectacle of a star's trying to avoid delays and cut down production costs. Her role in this picture, an American adaptation of the French film, *Carnet du Bal,* called for make-up and characterization stretching from that of a 16-year-old girl to that of an aged woman. Miss Oberon accepted unhesitatingly the realistic role which demanded a genuine aging and loss of glamor rather than the usual Hollywood characterizations which have been known to carry stars practically from the cradle to the grave without the semblance of a wrinkle, the loss of a tooth or the addition of more than a streak of gray hair.

Miss Oberon has been the featured actress in a number of radio plays. She performed in *I Love Thee* for the Columbia Broadcasting Company's Silver Theatre, and in *The Cowboy and the Lady* and *Till We Meet Again* for the Lux Radio Theatre. To the various patriotic organizations to which she has given freely of her time and effort, the use of her personality and reputation on the radio has brought considerable financial returns.

Although it is her present husband to whom, as her director, Miss Oberon gives full credit for teaching her to act, it was Samuel Goldwyn who saw her possibilities for roles other than that of an Eurasian siren. In any case, it must have been her knowledge of Hindustani, her life in India, or her birth in Tasmania which inspired those who applied the crayon to her eyes to make her appearance

exotic. Certainly her appearance off the screen did little to suggest her background. At a party where he first met her, Goldwyn decided to cast her in the chief role of *The Dark Angel.* Referring to her previous performance with Maurice Chevalier in *Folies Bergère,* Goldwyn's friends told him he had cut himself off "a nice slice of ham there." *The Dark Angel,* however, was a hit, and it was followed by *Wuthering Heights,* another success artistically as well as financially. The oriental vamp has become history, but Miss Oberon has become exceptionally good box office.

Rumor has linked Miss Oberon's name with almost every eligible celebrity in Europe and America. In the summer of 1939, however, Miss Oberon quietly married Alexander Korda, the director who discovered her possibilities and molded her career. Except for the time when she is traveling over the continent, broadcasting for the United Service Organizations and the British War Relief, or flying to England to make pictures with her husband, Miss Oberon enjoys a tranquil domesticity with her husband and her two young nephews, Michael and David Korda.

Among her associates in the screen world, as well as among her friends, Miss Oberon is noted for her friendly good nature, her radiant vitality and her capacity for enjoying herself. Hollywood is full of legends attesting to her impulsive generosity and her popularity. Miss Oberon is five feet two inches tall and weighs one hundred and twelve pounds. Her hair and eyes are brown without a suggestion of the oriental which used to be her trade-mark. At home in two hemispheres, Miss Oberon is as cool and competent with her knitting and portable radio during air raid alarms as on her Hollywood set between scenes.

References

Collier's 97:17-18 Mr 7 '36 pors; 108: 18+ S 13 '41 pors
Gt Brit & East 48:872 Je 17 '37 por
Life 1:46-9 D 21 '36 il pors
Motion Picture 51:42+ Je '36 il pors; 53:30-1 O '36 por; 53:34+ F '37 il por
Movie Classic 10:31+ My '36 por
N Y Herald Tribune X p14 F 25 '40 por
Photoplay 50:21+ Jl '36 por
Time 33:78 Je 12 '39
Windsor 87:227-33 Ja '38 il
International Motion Picture Almanac
Who's Who

O'BRIEN, EDWARD J(OSEPH HARRINGTON) Dec. 10, 1890—Feb. 25, 1941 Expatriate Boston poet, critic and noted short-story anthologist; editor since 1915 of the authoritative annual *Best Short Stories* and, since 1921, of the *Best British Short Stories;* was European story editor for MGM's British studios; spent greater part of his life in England; credited with having discovered many young authors and with having been

O'BRIEN, EDWARD J.—*Continued*

one of the first to recognize the merits of *Story* Magazine; short story series will be edited by Martha Foley (see sketch this issue); also used pseudonym Arthur Middleton for some of his writings.

References

>   Collier's 90:10+ O 22 '32 por
>   Lit Digest 123:24 My 29 '37 por
>   Sat R Lit 18:3-4+ Je 18 '38 por; 20:5
>   Jl 8 '39 por (pl)
>   Author's and Writer's Who's Who
>   Who's Who Among North American
>   Authors
>   Who's Who in America

Obituaries

>   N Y Times p21 F 26 '41
>   Pub W 139:1133 Mr 8 '41
>   Time 37:63 Mr 10 '41

O'CONNELL, WILLIAM (HENRY), CARDINAL Dec. 8, 1859- Archbishop of the See of Boston

Address: h. 2101 Commonwealth Ave, Brighton, Mass.

William Henry Cardinal O'Connell, Archbishop of the See of Boston, is dean of the Roman Catholic hierarchy in America. More than once he has been mentioned as a candidate for the Papacy. His pronouncements and sermons, delivered in a "slightly high-pitched Back Bay voice, reminiscent of Boston's famous novelist, Henry James," have for at least three decades made frequent headlines in the press. In his 80's now, he continues to make them. In March 1941 His Eminence was one of the three Archbishops of the Roman Catholic Church to sign a statement supporting Herbert Hoover's plan to send food to the small conquered nations of Europe. A few days later he announced that he sensed a feeling among people that secret maneuvers behind the scene of the Government were drawing the United States nearer to war—a state of affairs that "does not tally with democracy." And in April he was quoted as demanding that "strikes be outlawed for the preservation of the United States."

One of 11 sons of John and Bridget (Farley) O'Connell, poor Irish immigrants, William Henry O'Connell was born in Lowell, Massachusetts on the feast day of the Immaculate Conception, December 8, 1859. After attending public schools he entered St. Charles College in Maryland, and when illness caused him to return to Lowell he completed his baccalaureate course at Boston College. In 1881 Boston College gave him his B. A., *summa cum laude*.

Even aside from his scholarship young O'Connell left behind him a glittering reputation: he had composed hymns, taken a prominent part in debates and college plays, and in addition had been known as the best-dressed man and the owner of the most luxuriant crop of side whiskers on the campus. But from the first his intended vocation had been the Church. Archbishop Williams of Boston quite naturally took an interest in the brilliant young man, procured for him a scholarship to the American College at Rome, and in 1884 he was ordained a priest in Rome. Not long after his ordination he had to return to the United States, however, without having obtained his D. D. degree, and his prospects for advancement did not seem too good when he was appointed one of five curates of Saint Joseph's, in the West End of Boston.

Nevertheless in 1895, "without prior indication," Father O'Connell was made rector of the American College at Rome. In Rome he proved that the appointment had not been an error. He had a great gift for organization. He built up the College, interested Americans in it. Pope Leo XII, pleased, made him Chamberlain (with the title of Monsignor) and gave him ready access to the papal chambers. In 1897 he was named domestic prelate. And on April 22, 1901 he was appointed Bishop of Portland, Maine.

It was May when the "Bishop without a white hair on his head" was consecrated in Rome—July when he was installed in the Cathedral of Portland. There he strengthened the parishes, reduced the church debt, had the Cathedral remodeled by an excellent architect, and altogether put his diocese in the public eye to such an extent that the newspapers were soon asking for full transcripts of his sermons. Soon, too, Rome offered him the Archbishopric of Manila. He gave good reasons for not accepting that particular appointment. But he was not to remain in Portland long. In 1905, after the ending of the Russo-Japanese War, Pope Pius X named him assistant at the Pontifical Throne and selected him as Papal Envoy to Emperor Mutsuhito of Japan. It was an excellent choice, for Bishop O'Connell was a linguist who could speak Japanese as well as Latin, French, Italian, German, Spanish, Russian and Syrian. Upon his arrival in Japan he was immediately received by the Mikado and his Empress, and was so successful in his mission of restoring relations with that country that the Mikado decorated him with the Grand Cordon of the Sacred Treasure.

Only a year after having been sent to Japan, in March 1906, Bishop O'Connell was named Titular Archbishop of Constance and Coadjutor Archbishop of Boston, direct in line to the aged Archbishop Williams. The next year Williams died, and on August 30, 1907 O'Connell succeeded to the See of Boston, "second only in the American hierarchy to New York." The youngest Archbishop in the country, he was nevertheless already accustomed to wielding authority, and immediately told his parishioners: "When I ask you to do anything, trust me and do it." At the same time he was socially popular. That same year the Boston *Herald* announced: "He belongs to a leading Boston social club, one of the local golf clubs, and owns an automobile. He is reputed to be the best-dressed ecclesiastic in Boston."

In 1908 Archbishop O'Connell's name was put forward for the first time as a candidate for Cardinal, and although he was the youngest of all the candidates in years and service, he was elevated to the Cardinalate at Rome on November 27, 1911. When he returned to Boston in a driving snowstorm, the people lined the streets to welcome him and struggled to kiss his ring. "The desire to succeed is natural to the human heart," he said, that same year.

Since that time Cardinal O'Connell's reputation and authority have been even further enhanced. A familiar figure on the streets of Rome as well as of Boston, in 1913 Cardinal Rampolla spoke of him: "If the time ever comes to have an American Pope . . . I see nobody in the American hierarchy who can take the position except Cardinal O'Connell. He is a strong man. He is most popular at the Vatican. He has brought, as Peter's Pence, an enormous sum of money to Rome—more than any other Cardinal—in fact, almost more than any other state." In 1929 a journalist wrote: "His primacy is as well-organized and disciplined, even as prosperous, relatively, as a first class corporation."

A special law passed by the Massachusetts Legislature made Cardinal O'Connell the corporation sole of the Catholic Church of Boston: its president, its officers, its board of directors. Under his rule the Catholics of Irish blood have gained in power so tremendously that he himself has spoken of the change as a bloodless social and political revolution. Already existing Catholic societies were strengthened, new ones established; older charitable institutions were restaffed, new ones built; new parishes were created; Catholics were urged to enter public life.

At the same time the Cardinal's sermons became material for the front-page. Theological modernism, new scientific theories and changing moralities horrified him almost as much as Bolshevism, anarchism and atheism. He spoke bitterly of "apostles of modern thought" who class men "psychically as well as physically with the apes." In 1926 he called the New York American Museum of Natural History "an exhibition of what might justly be called the grotesque gullibility of the so-called scientists." In 1929 he derided Einstein (see sketch this issue) as one of a group of "petty, befogged professors . . . who have to set up some new standard to attract attention to themselves."

Although not participating in politics, Cardinal O'Connell also spoke out freely on issues of the day which he considered within the spiritual or moral domain of the Church. After the First World War he called on President Wilson to demand self-determination for Ireland at the Peace Conference, and later he praised President Harding for keeping the United States out of the League of Nations. In 1924 he publicly denounced the Child Labor Amendment (although he would have favored it if the word "gainful" had been inserted before the word "labor") ; in 1926 he announced that "compulsory prohibition is flatly opposed to Holy Scripture and to Catholic tradition"; and in 1932 he denounced Father Coughlin's "demagogic utterances to the poor."

Many Bostonians, moreover, suspect that the banning of books, plays, etc., in Boston is based very often on the Cardinal's judgment. Although there is no evidence to connect him directly with the censor, it is true that a few days after he spoke against J. P. Marquand's *H. M. Pulham, Esquire* the City Council called upon the police to ban the book for assailing "the character of Boston womanhood," and less recent examples could be

Harris & Ewing

WILLIAM CARDINAL O'CONNELL

listed. However, as the editor of one Boston newspaper once said: "If we have tried once we have tried a dozen times to identify the source of this censorship. Each time the search has ended in a dark alley. . . . We have been compelled to call it 'the system' and, because it is mysteriously powered, to bow to it."

Cardinal O'Connell has not only been honored by the Vatican but by the governments of many lands. He possesses the Lebanese Grand Medal of Merit, the Grand Crosses of the Order of Malta, of the Crown of Italy, of the Constantinian Order of St. George, of the Holy Sepulchre, and of the Légion d'Honneur. And in 1934, at his golden jubilee celebrating the fiftieth anniversary of his ordination to the priesthood, he was presented with a golden chalice by American bishops and honored by letters of praise from both Pope Pius XI and President Roosevelt. The President praised him particularly for his "consecrated service with a real and practical interest in good citizenship and inspiring patriotism." In that same year there appeared the Cardinal's autobiography, *Recollections of Seventy Years*, written in his usual "vigorous, sincere and richly virile style."

In 1918 A. Paul Keith bequeathed $4,000,000 to be divided equally between Harvard and Cardinal O'Connell as Archbishop of Boston.

(Continued next page)

O'CONNELL, WILLIAM, CARDINAL
—*Continued*
The Keith estate has been used to found schools and academies in Lowell, to erect added structures on the campus of St. John's Ecclesiastical Seminary and to build and equip modern additions to Saint Elizabeth's Hospital. In 1915 the Cardinal had announced that "the present age is an age of luxury, and luxury ought to have no place in any life"; but by 1926 he was confident that "the rich man and woman of the United States need have no fear of failing to enter the Heavenly Kingdom." His own Brighton home on the Seminary campus has an excellent private golf course, and although he spends many of his vacations in Florida he also owns a summer home at Marblehead, Massachusetts. There he built a fence to keep young lovers off the rocks, causing some irreverent wit to put up a sign: "The earth is the Lord's and the fullness thereof, but the rocks belong to the Cardinal."

References

Cath World 140:359 D '34
Commonweal 20:242 Je 29 '34; 20:430-1 Ag 31 '34
Newsweek 4:36 N 24 '34 por
Outlook 153:285-8 O 23 '29 por
Sat Eve Post 214:9-11+ O 4 '41 pors
Time 37:56 Ap 14 '41
American Catholic Who's Who
Dictionary of the American Hierarchy 1940
O'Connell, W. H. Recollections of Seventy Years 1934
Walsh, J. J. Our American Cardinals p170-221 1926
Whiting, E. E. William Cardinal O'-Connell 1932
Who's Who in America

O'CONNOR, ANDREW June 7, 1874—June 11, 1941 American sculptor, best known for his statue of Abraham Lincoln at Springfield, Illinois; started winning international prizes for sculpture early in the century and in 1928 was the first foreigner to win the prize for sculpture at the Beaux Arts Salon; among his works are *Mother of Sorrows,* in the Tate Gallery, London, and a monument to Governor John A. Johnson in St. Paul.

References

Lond Studio 14 (Studio 114):79-83 Ag '37 il
Cortissoz, R. American Artists p279-85 1923
Who's Who in America 1934-35

Obituaries

N Y Times p21 Je 11 '41

ODETS, CLIFFORD (ō-dĕts') July 18, 1906-   Playwright
Address: b. c/o Actors Equity, 45 W. 47th St, New York City; h. 327 E. 47th St, New York City

"In every Odets play, regardless of its theme or its worth," the drama critic of *Time* wrote some time ago, "at least once during the evening every spectator feels that a fire hose has been turned on his body, that a fist has connected with his chin." Ever since the day in 1935 when New York audiences saw his first drama and hailed him as "the foremost discovery of the '30s," audiences and critics have reacted that way. Many of them have not shared the frankly Leftish views of his earlier plays, many of them have even found his themes dull, his plotting inept, his structure uneven, but they have not been able to keep themselves from going along again and again with his "rich compassionate angry feeling for people, his tremendous dramatic punch, his dialogue, bracing as ozone."

In his youth no one ever expected Clifford Odets to become "the white hope of the American theatre." "This boy," he says in the third person in which he usually discusses himself, "was a very ordinary middle-class boy. . . He did typical things, for everything about him was typical, typical, so typical." His father, Louis J. Odets, worked in a print shop in Philadelphia, where his son was born on July 18, 1906. "I was a worker's son until the age of 12," the onetime idol of the proletariat recalls. But not long after, Odets Senior moved with his wife, Pearl (Geisinger) Odets, to New York in 1908 and there rose in the world. He acquired a print shop of his own, later became a direct mail advertising agent and by 1927, when he became vice-president and general sales manager of a Philadelphia boiler company, was a prosperous merchandising counselor.

Clifford grew up in The Bronx, a not too industrious student at Public School 52, and at Morris High School, which he attended from 1921 to 1923. He quit high school before graduation because it was a "waste of time," and took to writing poetry. His father, who had foreseen a prosperous career for his son as an advertising copywriter, smashed his typewriter, told him he was a good-for-nothing. Clifford stormed back. "You can't harness me to a truck—can't you see I'm not a truck horse?" "Believe me," he says now, "there were some very gloomy evenings."

Clifford's father believed that anything was better than having a poet for a son, and so there was little fuss made when Clifford announced that he was going to become an actor. He started out with a group of ardent amateurs known as the Drawing Room Players who put on one-act plays at the Heckscher Theatre, and then joined Harry Kemp's Poet's Theatre, a cooperative venture with headquarters in the basement of a church. From this Odets branched out with a group of his own, made up of former members of the Drawing Room Players. He offered it to various radio stations and from 1925 to 1927 there were performances off and on as a sustaining program. One of the performances was of an original play, *At the Waterline,* a "welter of coincidences" in which Odets starred.

At the same time that his group was shuffling along, Odets was functioning independently on the radio as the Roving Reciter, relying heavily on Robert W. Service and Rudyard Kipling for his stirring declamations. On the strength of these he was able to get a few weeks' work with stock companies around New York and finally found fairly regular employment with Mae Desmond's Stock Company which played around Philadelphia and Camden, New Jersey, with a tremendously varied repertoire. Hardly fit for juvenile roles because of his bushy hair and prominent features, Odets appeared as old men, middle-aged men, "characters." "A wig a day was my motto," he remembers. And it was good experience, too, he says. "It's possible to absorb a great deal of the playwright's method playing 32 different scripts in one stock season."

Clifford's family didn't realize their son was getting valuable training for playwriting. When Clifford wired home for money after the company broke up and then arrived penniless and jobless, they wondered seriously whether he would ever support himself. Clifford wondered, too. "Their son," he says, "was not industrious. He had temperament; he was moody. In a word he was artistic."

Nevertheless, their son was able not long afterward to get a job with the Theatre Guild, in 1928, and he appeared with the Guild in small parts now and again. He appeared, too, in *Roar China*, a production of the Guild Studio, a subsidiary of the Theatre Guild, made up of people interested in producing unusual plays, from which the Group Theatre eventually evolved. While the Group was being organized Odets sat in on the meetings and after them went home to a lonely furnished room on West 82nd Street and wrestled with his soul. But there was romance, too, in his life. There was a girl in Philadelphia who said: "Every girl should have one Clifford Odets in her life." In Springfield, Massachusetts there was a "horrible, exquisite love affair with something of the *Sorrows of Werther* about it."

In 1931 Odets went with the Group Theatre to Brookfield Center, Connecticut to rehearse his bit in *The House of Connelly*, the Group's first production; in 1932 he understudied Luther Adler in John Howard Lawson's *Success Story*. This was a period of Dostoevskian melancholy. Odets shaved off his hair, grew a beard, adopted turtle neck sweaters. He was oppressed by his belief that nobody thought very much of his acting and more oppressed by his own belief that it wasn't much good. "I was too tense. I just couldn't relax," he confesses.

He had begun, too, to work on a play, writing it in a cold-water flat on 57th Street, where he lived with some other Group members after the disastrous failure of Dawn Powell's *Big Night* in 1933. He finished the play in Warrensburg, New York, while rehearsing in *Men in White* which the Group put on in 1933, and called it *Awake and Sing*.

The Group Theatre was interested, but not interested enough to risk a production. Frank Merlin, the producer, took an option on it but dropped it after a year. Odets was in Boston at the time, acting with the Group company. He heard of a New Theatre League one-act play contest, locked himself in a hotel room for three days and came out with *Waiting for*

Alfredo Valente

CLIFFORD ODETS

Lefty. It won the prize and was presented at the New Theatre League Sunday nights. Everybody was excited about it; the Left acclaimed Odets as a revolutionary oracle, the critics hailed him as an infinitely promising playwright.

Based on the 1934 New York cab strike, this play was fiery, vigorous, compact, arousing soap-box propaganda in its portrayal of the hardships of the men on strike, in its indication of a way out for them. While the enthusiasm was strong, the Group decided to take a chance on *Awake and Sing*, and it was presented on February 19, 1935. Shortly after its opening the Group presented, too, *Waiting for Lefty* and *Till the Day I Die*. Within 35 days Odets had three plays running on Broadway and was "arousing more discussion in theatrical circles than any man since Eugene O'Neill." Nobody in New York could talk to even a subway guard without getting into a discussion about Odets.

Waiting for Lefty was a tremendous success and during the course of the year was acted all over the country by small theatre groups, was suppressed by local authorities more often than any other play in the history of the American Theatre, was awarded the Yale Drama Prize for 1935. Only George Jean Nathan was supercilious. He talked of "the short labor yell, *Waiting for Lefty*, and the short sis-boom-ah follow-up, *Till the Day I Die*." The critics fought him on his opinion of the first, but many of them were willing to agree about *Till the Day I Die*, a story of young Communists just after the beginning of the Hitler regime. It was based on a letter from Germany Odets had read in the *New Masses* and according to one critic, at least, it "sounded like it."

Awake and Sing was something else. Odets said he wrote it because "I was sore at my

ODETS, CLIFFORD—*Continued*

whole life. Getting nothing done." Because "I saw girls and boys were not getting a chance. . . I went over my boyhood and tabulated the people's lives which touched mine... I saw where my own experience was richest, where it hurt me most." The result was a study of a bewildered, frustrated, dreaming, rebellious Bronx family "caught in economic toils like wet fish in a net." In Odets' hands the language of The Bronx was turned into effective theatre speech and occasionally lifted into sheer poetry by the intensity of its emotion. The dialogue was pungent and evocative, the character creation sharp and sad and real. It has been, most critics agree, his best play, written, according to *Time,* before Odets "went honeymooning with the cosmos or confused himself with *Le Penseur* of Rodin."

During the long run of this play Odets was the darling of the Left, called by the Right, in the form of the London *Times,* "a fiery young Communist." He denied this. "A man making $1,000 a week," he said, "has no reason to be a Communist. I'm doing pretty well by myself and my fellow men. Everything that I've got I'll share with people who are not so fortunate. If that is Communism, then I'm a Communist." He tried to share with others in 1935, when he led a delegation of 15 liberals to Cuba to investigate conditions there. He was deported the day after his arrival and since then "his support of the proletariat has been mostly moral." He remains an active member of the League of American Writers.

The public waited in suspense for Odets' next play after *Awake and Sing* and was rewarded with *Paradise Lost* in December 1935. It was, most critics agreed, irrespective of their political opinions, a "muddy" play about the confused middle class. ("My interest is not in the presentation of an individual's problems but in those of a whole class.") A "pretentious, empty" play to others, to Clifford Odets it was, even years later, "my best and most mature play. By far! And without reservation." But nobody bought tickets to it, and Odets hopped off to Hollywood to the tune of $2,500 a week in order to keep it going.

Odets was in Hollywood for a year and one-half. The result of his labors there were two unproduced pictures, *Gettysburg* and *The River Is Blue,* and one produced by Paramount, *The General Died at Dawn.* Odets is felt to have spent his time writing dramatic fireworks into this film, and the critics sadly asked when they saw it on the screen: "Odets, where is thy sting?" Odets was busy in Hollywood, too, courting the actress and Academy winner, Luise Rainer, whom he married on January 8, 1937 after a suitable period of holding hands in public. Theirs was never a placid marriage. They were estranged that same year and Luise Rainer filed suit for a divorce; in November 1938 they were reconciled; in May 1940 they were finally divorced. Odets believed in a one-career marriage, Miss Rainer said by way of explanation.

Odets returned from Hollywood with the script of *Golden Boy* and some sage observations on life there. *Life* felt though, after *Golden Boy* was presented on November 4, 1937, that Hollywood had "matured his art, disciplined his style, taught him to tell a story." The story told of Joe Bonaparte who wanted to be on top, who was a good violinist and became a prize fighter. The first play that didn't depend for its appeal on Odets' economic opinions, it was admired for its mastery of stage technique and command of pungent dialogue; it was decried for the falseness of its ending, for its occasional strident melodrama, for its unevenness. "If every line in *Golden Boy* were as good as every third line is," one critic said, "it would be an unusual play." New York came to see it in droves; London admired it greatly; Hollywood bought it and produced it in 1939.

In 1938 Odets announced he was working on *The Silent Partner* and announced, too: "It will be the best labor play ever produced in this country or in any other country." But it was never produced and Broadway saw, instead, in December 1938, *Rocket to the Moon,* a play, according to Odets, about middle-class love. Joseph Wood Krutch thought it made "most other recent plays seem pallid indeed," but his confreres found it a "banal triangle whose originality goes no farther than a water cooler in a dentist's office," full of "pretentious earnestness."

Rocket to the Moon was no great success, and George Jean Nathan felt his lack of enthusiasm for Odets even more justified by *Night Music* (1940). "It shows once again," he said, "the dangers of critical overexuberance in the acceptance of early promise for full-fledged merit."

Odets' latest play, *Clash by Night,* with Tallulah Bankhead (see sketch this issue) opened on Broadway in December 1941. The New York *Times* said Odets "writes the first half of *Clash by Night* like a mature man of the theatre. Put that much of it down not only as his best work, but as some of the best literary work any one has done in the modern drama." *Time's* critic, however, found the play "the season's biggest disappointment."

"I am the most talented young playwright in the business," Odets once said. But he hastened to explain it was "because playwriting has reached a sad state." That's why he never goes to the theatre—"I have nothing to learn from American plays any more." He used to once, and in the first flush of his success he used to gad about with celebrities like Beatrice Lillie, Helen Hayes, Tallulah Bankhead. Today his companions are members of the Group Theatre, his favorite recreations going to concerts or listening to music in his New York apartment. His house is seldom empty of the music of Bach, Mozart, Beethoven coming from the phonograph or the sound of Odets' improvisations on his Hammond organ or lusty singing of an aria. "His love for music is ebullient, a little showy." "A good composer was lost when I took up writing," he says.

"At once shrewd and naïve, lusty and bookish, youthful and pompous," Clifford Odets used to be famous in the early days of his success for his sayings. "Mozart was a young genius, too," he once remarked to a friend who was listening to the phonograph. He still talks sometimes like one of the more lyrical characters in his own plays. According to John McCarten, it's not unusual for him to break into something like: "How sweet and nice to get up in the morning to see the glitter of the day—like when you were a kid." He never does get up in the morning, though, and does most of his work at night.

He is fairly tall and husky and proud of his looks, though it has been said that "in profile he vaguely resembles a pickerel." Bushy-haired, brown-eyed, dressed in diligently informal and sloppy clothes, in his abstracted moments "he could easily be mistaken for one of the more earnest students of New York University." He has these moments often. Sometimes he stands listening to the talk of people on the street, jotting down all they say. Sometimes he spends hours clipping everything interesting to him in the papers. Sometimes, any time, he has ideas and writes them down right away. All these jottings, clippings and ideas are carefully filed away by his secretary in huge filing cabinets in his apartment. With them, too, are duplicates of practically every letter he has ever written in his life. Altogether, he feels, he should have enough material to last him for at least the next 10 years of playwriting.

References

Am Mag 122:42-3+ O '36 por
Life 4:24-7 Ja 17 '38 il
New Yorker 13:21-7 Ja 22 '38
Players Mag 16:9-10+ My '40
Theatre Arts 23:257-65 Ap '39 por
Theatre World 30:84-5 Ag '38 por
Time 32:44-7 D 5 '38 il pors
Wilson Lib Bul 11:374 F '37 por
America's Young Men
Flexner, E. American Playwrights: 1918-1938 p283-309 1938
Mersand, J. Traditions in American Literature p32-50 1939
Millett, F. B. Contemporary American Authors 1940
Sobel, B. ed. Theatre Handbook 1940
Who's Who in America
Who's Who in American Jewry
Who's Who in the Theatre

ODLUM, FLOYD B(OSTWICK) (ŏd'lŭm) Mar. 30, 1892- Financier
Address: b. Office for Emergency Management, Washington, D. C.; h. Stamford, Conn.

On September 4, 1941 the slender, sandy-haired president of the Atlas Corporation, possibly the only man in the United States who made a great fortune out of the depression, was selected by President Roosevelt to head the new Defense Contracts Distribution Division of the Office of Production Management. The following day he announced that he was taking a leave of absence from Atlas in order to accept the position: "The President's request that I organize this division and get its work moving forward left me no choice

Underwood & Underwood
FLOYD B. ODLUM

as a matter of duty." The candidate of Leon Henderson and other New Dealers for the job of keeping small industries functioning by bringing them into the defense effort, Floyd B. Odlum was praised by that stern critic of "Knudsenism," I. F. Stone. "His resourcefulness, ingenuity and hospitality to new ideas in the operation of his own diverse business," wrote Stone at that time in *PM*, "promise success in his new assignment."

A few months later, however, disappointment in what had been actually accomplished was being expressed by more than one source. Odlum had been given a difficult job—one at which several men before him had failed—for the big defense plants, with three-fourths of all national defense contracts, were far from eager to pass on business to small manufacturers in the form of subcontracts.

Fortune once cataloged Odlum's various occupations, from the age of six on up. He has been all of these things in precisely this order, and still is a good many of them: "Methodist minister's son, berrypicker, vegetable sprayer, ditchdigger, celery tender, lumber piler, haberdasher's clerk, house-to-house canvasser, ostrich jockey, map salesman, assistant librarian, manager of dramatics and college periodicals, debater, boardinghouse entrepreneur, law clerk, utilities lawyer, first-class negotiator, amateur of investment companies, accumulator of same, underwriter, Utah enthusiast and Depression Phenomenon Class A."

He was born on March 30, 1892 in a Methodist parsonage at Union City, Michigan, the youngest of the five children of the Reverend George A. and Ellen (Anderson) Odlum. His father was a Canadian-born country preacher of Irish descent who kept moving around Michigan without ever reaching a parish that paid him much more than $800 a year. Floyd, like his brothers, did odd jobs. Graduated

ODLUM, FLOYD B.—*Continued*

from high school in Hillsdale at the age of 16, he went soon afterward with his mother and brothers to Boulder, Colorado, where she sought recovery from tuberculosis. The boys enrolled at the University there, Floyd planning to be an engineer but changing his mind at the moment of registration.

At college he studied journalism, working part time on Colorado newspapers, then prepared for the law. And, as the text under his graduation picture suggested, "Little Odd" managed "to get the running of everything to which there [was] a stipend attached." He ran a student laundry, managed the dramatic club, the Women's League Opera, the annual; he received a salary as student assistant librarian; in the summer he operated four fraternity houses as tourists' lodges. He was also four years on the debating team, won an oratorical prize, starred at pole-vaulting one year, was a member of the junior-prom committee and in 1915, when he was graduated with the degree of Bachelor of Laws, passed the State Bar examination at the top.

Once admitted to the Bar, young Odlum went to Salt Lake City (chosen because of a bargain offer in a train ticket!) to hang out his shingle. There he found a $50-a-month job in the legal department of Utah Power and Light, a subsidiary of the giant New York utility holding company, the Electric Bond and Share Corporation, and in 1915 married Hortense McQuarrie, daughter of a Mormon elder. A year later he was making $75 a month, and in 1917 there came the offer of a $100-a-month position as law clerk in Electric Bond and Share's Manhattan law shop, Simpson, Thacher & Bartlett. Mr. and Mrs. Odlum and their young son promptly packed up and arrived in New York City one June day, exhausted from three days of travel by coach and completely bewildered. For months they barely existed on his salary in a shabby apartment in Brooklyn. But Odlum's work on utilities contracts for Electric Bond and Share soon attracted the attention of Sidney Z. Mitchell, chairman of the company. When Mitchell grew tired of not having Odlum easily available he got him transferred to the offices of Electric Bond and Share, and in 1920 he was made a vice-president.

The "legal backbone of the company," Odlum also made himself an expert in accounting and electric power and worked so hard at domestic utilities consolidations that he developed nervous indigestion. It was 1926 when he became vice-chairman of Electric Bond and Share's foreign subsidiary, American and Foreign Power, and, with power of attorney from Mitchell, began buying up foreign electric and water-power companies—several hundred million dollars worth by 1931. During this period he made a record-breaking telephone call from London which lasted 95 minutes and cost $1,425.

In the meanwhile, in 1923, Odlum and a friend and their wives had started a private pool with a net capital of $39,600 for speculation in utilities and general securities. It was grandiosely named the United States Company, and paid a 65-per-cent dividend its very first year. By the end of 1925 net assets per common share were seventeen times what they had been two years before, and others were being rapidly admitted to the pool, which in 1928 became the Atlas Utilities and Investors Company, Ltd., of Montreal and the following year had its entire common stock taken over by the Atlas Utilities Company, newly incorporated in Delaware.

At that time total assets were about $6,000,-000. In the summer of 1929 Odlum sniffed the breeze, disposed of about half of Atlas' holdings, and, selling investors some $9,000,000 in new securities, kept the entire amount in cash and short-term notes. In the spring of 1930 Atlas, with $14,000,000 in assets, was therefore in a position to adopt Odlum's plan of buying up the less fortunate investment companies which were by that time lying all over Wall Street. The tactic was to buy enough stock to get control of a company at a price less than the asset value behind its stocks, preferably by an exchange of Atlas stocks; to sell the liquid items over which the company carried control; and then, with the part of the profits not going to minority stockholders (many of whom could be persuaded to exchange their stocks for Atlas stocks), to buy control of another investment company. Sometimes the process took three weeks, sometimes three years. But Wall Street's song became: "Little investment company, don't you cry: Atlas will get you by and by."

Just before Roosevelt's nomination, however, the Atlas Utilities Corporation became the plain Atlas Corporation, and soon after Roosevelt took office Odlum began selling utilities as fast as he could. Atlas was already managing many portfolio items that had not lent themselves to liquidation, and now Odlum began to specialize in large-scale financing rather than in buying up investment companies. He helped to reorganize the Greyhound Bus Lines, to put Madison Square Garden on a paying basis, to rebuild Bonwit Teller, New York's department store (he turned it over to his wife, who divorced him in 1935); and manufacturing companies, banks, real estate, motion picture and aviation companies all over the United States began to be more and more affected by Atlas. In February 1940 the corporation was split into two parts, one to stay in the financing business, the other to go to the United States Curtiss-Wright Corporation in a merger.

Odlum is still the largest holder in Atlas, with its assets of more than $100,000,000, as well as a director of American and Foreign Power, the United Fruit Company, the Italian Superpower Corporation and Madison Square Garden. As early as 1935 Arthur D. Howden Smith included him in a list of 30 men and families who "run America," and Congressman Adolph J. Sabath of Chicago once foresaw him and J. P. Morgan dividing control of all American industry. He himself, however, insists that he isn't really a Wall Street man. He says he doesn't know the symbols on a ticker ("I can't keep my balance if I watch prices"), wouldn't even know how to organize a stock-market pool, and that his business methods could be summed up by the slogan: "You buy when the other fellow sells, and sell when it looks rosiest." Convinced that capitalism and the "plutocratic demagogy" have a long lease on life, he nevertheless thinks of himself as a liberal and a "mild New Dealer." Roosevelt's Presidential campaign got $10,000 of his money in 1936, and he has never fought the Securities and Exchange Commission, although once in testimony before the Commission he said he thought Government regulation should not make "all companies conform to the same pattern simply because they invest in securities."

Sometimes pictured as ruthless but tactful, sometimes as warm-hearted but perspicacious, Odlum has acquired from his opponents the nickname "The Farmer" because of the rather careless Western look about him. The guilelessness of his features encourages the impression; but his smile can be complacent, and his blue eyes cold and sharp behind his horn-rimmed glasses. He "invariably moves fast, and as though he knew exactly where he was going"; his talk is orderly; and when he removes his glasses the "long, contained, confident face of an excellent trading strategist" is seen.

Odlum, who has two sons, Stanley Arnold and Bruce Wendell, by his first marriage, married Jacqueline Cochran (see sketch 1940 Annual), aviatrix and head of her own cosmetics company, on May 10, 1936. Just to make the record complete: he enjoys bad puns, squash, informal parties; he is a chain smoker but never touches alcohol, red meat or raw fruits; he lives unpretentiously, and bought his first boat—a houseboat—in 1936. He owns a small collection of nineteenth-century paintings, mainly of landscapes and beautiful women, and he himself is something of an artist. He relaxes by making copies of small bronzes in clay, but, with no illusions of immortal genius, invariably squeezes them back into lumps before going to bed!

References

Business Week p20 My 10 '33 por; p14 Ag 8 '36 por; p23 Mr 13 '37 por; p54 Jl 17 '37 por; p34-5 D 17 '38; p17 Ap 27 '40
Fortune 12:50-5+ S '35 il por
Look 5:16-19 D 2 '41 pors
Newsweek 3:25 My 5 '34; 15:57-9 Mr 18 '40 por
New Yorker 9:20-4 Ag 26 '33
R of Rs 88:48-9 N '33 por
Sat Eve Post 210:14-15+ Jl 10 '37 pors
Time 26:47 Ag 19 '35; 28:46+ Ag 10 '36 por; 32:37 Ag 1 '38 por; 35:59-60+ Ap 1 '40 por; 37:84 Mr 10 '41
International Motion Picture Almanac
New Yorker (periodical). Profiles from the New Yorker p268-78 1938
Who's Who in America
Who's Who in Commerce and Industry

O'DWYER, WILLIAM July 11, 1890- District Attorney of Brooklyn Borough, New York City

Address: b. Municipal Building, Brooklyn, New York

> Bulletin: On November 4, 1941, after a campaign marked by name-calling, by President Roosevelt's support of La Guardia and Governor Lehman's support of O'Dwyer, William O'Dwyer lost the New York City Mayoralty campaign by 133,841 votes. He sent a congratulatory wire to La Guardia and then announced to reporters, with a grin: "I've still got a job. That's a great advantage."

From September 1941 issue:

William O'Dwyer, Democratic candidate for Mayor of New York City in 1941 running against Fiorello La Guardia (see sketch 1940 Annual), is a "shrewd, scrappy" Irishman from County Mayo who just missed taking holy orders. He was born on July 11, 1890, the son of Patrick and Bridget O'Dwyer, who both taught in the local school where his sisters teach today. They sent him to the Jesuit University of Salamanca in Spain, and he might have stayed there if he had not been deficient in everything but languages. As it was, he was three years short of graduation when he picked up his things and shipped off to America. He landed in New York City in 1910. He had only $25.35 in his pocket, but after paying a month's rent in advance at a West Side boardinghouse he went right out and found a $20-a-week job as a laborer. He has lived in New York City ever since, even though he has traveled a long way from that boardinghouse.

At that time Bill O'Dwyer wanted to study medicine. "The best thing in the world I could think of doing was fixing up people's bodies. But I couldn't support myself for eight years in medical school. So I decided the next best thing would be fixing up people's legal troubles. I could study law and still draw my twenty bucks a week." That was how, while working as a longshoreman and later as a plasterer's helper (he helped build the Hotel McAlpin), he decided to start at the law school of Fordham University.

He was going to school evenings when he met Catherine ("Kitty") Lenihan, a telephone operator and a first-rate pianist. He married her in 1916, that same year became an American citizen, and in July 1917 joined New York City's police force at a salary of $1,000 a year as a patrolman on the toughest water-front beat in Brooklyn. Once he had to shoot a man—it wasn't a pleasant experience—and he still hates firearms. Finally, in 1923, he was admitted to the New York Bar. He quit the police force, and the next year opened an office on Court Street, with his first client a truckman accused of having stolen a hogshead of olives. A reporter friend had his headline all set—EX-COP WINS FIRST CASE—but it didn't work out quite that way.

(Continued next page)

WILLIAM O'DWYER

Nevertheless, in 1932 O'Dwyer's experience and legal ability brought him an appointment as New York City magistrate, and as a judge he became noted for his common sense as much as for his knowledge of law. Once he offered a habitual drunk the choice between jail and spending three hours alone with an unopened bottle of whiskey! Later designated to sit in Brooklyn's new experimental adolescent court, where all youths between the ages of 16 and 19 arrested in the borough were tried, he made a practice of consulting clergymen, welfare workers and probation officials before passing judgment. "You can always do something with the simple, misguided youngster," he said. "Very often you can make him a model man again just by threatening to send him away." He insisted, however, that some of the most confirmed criminals were young criminals, and that there were cases in which leniency was a mistake. That was a mistake which he didn't make, but it didn't mean that he was less interested in probation and crime prevention.

In 1938 O'Dwyer was appointed a County Court judge in Brooklyn by Governor Lehman, who had to fill a vacancy, and he was later elected to that post for a full 14-year term at a salary of $25,000 a year. When in 1939 he was elected District Attorney for Brooklyn Borough, he accepted a $5,000 cut in salary. He took office on January 1, 1940, and promptly began cleaning house and getting new men. Less than three months afterward, in his bleak office, reporters heard him announce the solution of fifty-six murders of the kind that are practically never solved—underworld murders, nearly all of them linked together. The trials, which began not long after that, were a press sensation. "Murder, Inc.," was the title popularly given to the ring of criminals involved, but O'Dwyer pointed

out that the appellation was really accurate only if it were read to mean "Murder, Incidental"—"incidental" to the various rackets in which the men were engaged.

There are difficulties unsuspected by the public in the way of getting convictions even for notorious gangsters and racketeers, O'Dwyer tells us. Men are always having to be released for lack of legal evidence. There was no more evidence than usual in the case of the "partners" in Murder, Inc., but "applied psychology" resulted in a chain of confessions. In April 1941 O'Dwyer declared that although crime was on the increase from coast to coast, there had been a reduction of 20 to 32 per cent in the number of crimes such as murder, manslaughter, robbery, burglary and felonious assault in Brooklyn in 1940. One of the reasons he is so eager to wage war on criminals may be that in 1924 his own brother was shot and killed by holdup men.

Ever since his election as District Attorney O'Dwyer had been mentioned as a possibility as Democratic candidate for Mayor. He, however, maintained that what he really wanted to do was go back on the County Court bench and stay there, and his friends said that he didn't know anything about being Mayor and wouldn't care to fulfill the obligations Tammany expects of any Mayor it puts in office, anyway. After he spoke at the annual Jefferson Day dinner in 1941 with the Democratic National Chairman acting as toastmaster his nomination was more seriously considered, though, and on July 16 New York Democratic leaders announced their agreement on the Mayoralty slate. According to the Brooklyn Democratic chief, O'Dwyer's distinguished public record would "make a strong appeal to the voters regardless of politics"—and some commentators insisted that he was not a "Tammany man," although owing allegiance to the Kelly organization in Brooklyn. Anti-Tammanyites, on the other hand, saw an attempt to use O'Dwyer's reputation for honesty and his respectability to bring back the "good old days" of Tammany rule.

"Bill-o" to his friends, Brooklyn's District Attorney is somewhere between five feet eight and five feet nine, and weighs around one hundred ninety pounds. "Quick to smile, ramrod-straight, with silky dark hair that keeps flopping over the forehead, he looks a young 45." His brogue becomes very apparent when he gets excited, and he does that often. He and his wife, both devout Catholics, live in the five-room half of an unpretentious two-family red-brick house in Brooklyn's Bay Ridge, a house distinguished by a substantial mortgage. Commissioner Valentine lent him two bodyguards and a 1930 Cadillac. O'Dwyer is "indifferent to liquor, friendly to pipes and cigars, ecstatic about stew, and flies into a mock rage over pistachio ice cream ('It's not Irish green!')"

He likes Dickens, especially *Dombey and Son*, likes Wagner's "noisier operas," Irish ballads, Irish history. His favorite radio programs—"Nothing highbrow, you understand" —are Jack Benny, Fibber McGee, Amos and Andy. He doesn't get much exercise. Of golf he says: "Confidentially, I'm a bum at the game." Of the Dodgers: "They'll cop the bunting this year sure." As for football, he once brought an Irish soccer team from his home county to prove that the game is tougher than American football.

Although O'Dwyer publicly proclaimed his support of Franco in the Spanish War early in 1939, in a speech in May 1941 he announced that when the time came to "count heads" the Irish would be found "side by side with those lined up against tyranny and aggression." Hints from Tammany that he would run on a platform of "peace" as well as opposition to administration, and the endorsement of his candidacy by the Hearst papers, did not prevent him from announcing later in the campaign that he supported President Roosevelt's foreign policies.

References

Life 8:96-9 Ap 15 '40 il
Lit Digest 119:18 Ja 12 '35 por
Look 4:28-9 Je 4 '40 pors
N Y Herald Tribune X p6, 9 Jl 21 '40 por
Newsweek 18:15 Jl 28 '41 por
PM p12-13 Je 30 '40 pors; p14 Jl 16 '41 por

O'HARA, JOHN (HENRY) Jan. 31, 1905-
Author; playwright

Address: b. c/o Duell, Sloan & Pearce, 270 Madison Ave, New York City; h. 1115 Fifth Ave, New York City

On Christmas Night 1940, a new musical comedy that became an instant Broadway hit, *Pal Joey*, opened at the Barrymore Theatre. Its producer was George Abbott; Rodgers and Hart were the creators of its music and lyrics; and the author was none other than young novelist John O'Hara, who put Pal Joey originally into a book (published in October 1940) made up from pieces about the night club crooner and hoofer he had "ben wreiting in the *New Yorkers* mag." The printed-page personality of this "poor man's Bing Crosby" expanded in popularity until O'Hara felt the urge to make him three-dimensional.

O'Hara, who is said to have "spent more time in night clubs than many men have in bed," was advised over a couple of highballs by his friend Dick Rodgers to make Joey the hero of a musical comedy. "He's a heel already; we'll make him the first hero of his kind," said Rodgers. So, with George Abbott immediately interested, the team got to work and wrote a play about Joey and his "mice" (pretty girls) and "moola" (money).

The musical comedy follows pretty much the fictional version, with some variations and several hit songs by Rodgers, and with Gene Kelly (later replaced by George Tapps) as Joey and Vivienne Segal playing the feminine lead. "For those who can park their morals in the lobby," says *Time's* theatre critic, "Pal Joey is a wow." Of Joey in the original book about him, Milton Rugoff (New York *Herald Tribune Books*) wrote: "He's as authentic as a radio commercial, a hot swing

JOHN O'HARA

band or a tabloid headline . . . a hot-spot song plugger, a Broadway trooper knocking around in the sticks, stuck with jobs m. c. ing [acting as master of ceremonies] in Windy City cribs for just enough 'moola' (dough to you) to keep him off the cake line. Down on his luck, Pal Joey pours out his petty larceny soul in 'missles' to his dear pal Ted who is doing all right by himself as a No. 1 band leader back on the main stem in good old N. Y. C."

O'Hara has often been called a second Ring Lardner; he has also been compared to Sinclair Lewis, and to Conrad and Hemingway. His first novel, *Appointment in Samarra* (1934), the story of three days in a man's life that ended in his suicide, was praised by critics for the hard, and hard-boiled, brilliance of his writing, and although some seemed to feel that he was "sliding over surfaces," they found him more than merely "promising." The material of *Butterfield 8* (1935) may not have been worthy of his talents, but it created a sensation. Said one critic of this story of a young girl who lived a fast life in New York City during the latter end of the speakeasy era: "Here is a cruel and ugly story that will make you sick and bitter, yet hold you till its last venomous line." That same year *The Doctor's Son and Other Stories*, many of which had been previously published in the *New Yorker*, showed O'Hara a "maestro of the literary cartoon" as well.

Hope of Heaven, his third novel, appeared in 1938. It concerned itself with the unhappy love affair of a Hollywood scenario writer

O'HARA, JOHN—*Continued*

and a bookshop clerk, was another "slick, tough, readable" piece of writing that most critics felt showed the brilliance but also the same limitations found in his earlier work. His most recent collection of short stories, *Files on Parade* (1939), was praised more highly. One critic, at least, rated him tops, writing: "No one, with the possible exception of Ring Lardner and Ernest Hemingway, has so well succeeded in summing up a lifetime in an instant, within the narrow frame of the classical unities."

Skeptical, ironical, with a kind of "inverted sentimentality," O'Hara's work has been called "degenerately morbid", "insufferably vulgar" —even "trash." Others find that the same qualities amount to honest realism. But no one denies the skill of his craftsmanship, nor the gift of his large, sensitive, canny ears for picking up the nuances of colloquial speech— the "New Yawkese" of night club, bar, theatre; the transcribed ideographic slang of *Variety*. Few writers can take such thoroughly worthless characters and make them not only shockingly recognizable but, many times, oddly sympathetic.

Pal Joey's creator was born in Pottsville, Pennsylvania January 31, 1905, the eldest of the seven children of a physician, Patrick Henry O'Hara, and Katharine Elizabeth (Delaney) O'Hara. The family is still puzzled by the Broadway slang he writes with such facility. O'Hara's environment as a boy has been described by him in *The Doctor's Son and Other Stories*. He says he "went through the motions" of getting an education at the Fordham Preparatory School, the Niagara Preparatory School, from which he was graduated in 1924, and the Keystone State Normal School. He then held jobs variously as reporter, engineer, boat steward, secretary in a briqueting plant, gas meter reader, freight clerk on the Pennsylvania Railroad, soda clerk and picture press agent. His break into the literary world came when Heywood Broun hired him as his secretary. He began writing criticism and features for newspapers (New York *Herald Tribune*, New York *Daily Mirror*, New York *Morning Telegraph*) and magazines (*Time* and *New Yorker*), and for a short time was editor in chief of the Pittsburgh *Bulletin-Index*. He also did some writing for Paramount Pictures (1924), Samuel Goldwyn (1937), RKO-Radio (1939) and Twentieth Century-Fox (1940), and even played a minor part in one picture, *The General Died at Dawn*. When his first novel, *Appointment in Samarra,* became a sensational success, he settled down solely to fiction production for a while, until, in July 1940, he also took over the authorship of a column, "Entertainment Week," in *Newsweek*.

Using the jargon of Joey and his pals, H. Allen Smith writes: "This John O. Hara is a big guy six foot over that writes books all the time he is not hitting the sauce in the 52nd st traps. . . I have always hear that this John O. Hara has got large ears and I find this true when I walk in his apt where he is bending over a small typewriter and the dog Ceser near bye, Joey, he has got a Pair of ears that Tommy and Bunny could use for mutes with enough left over to make a conga drumb other wise he is a handsome guy being big.

"Joey you have hear this guy on the radio that lisens to a party speak and says where they come from even the town some time. Well, this John O. Hara bens one of his big ears at me and after I have spoke a mear few wds he says, you come from a small town to and I says yes and he says Illinois, and I says I was born in Illinois and how the hell did he know it. Well Joey he is like this guy on the radio, he can lisen to a party and tell where they come from.

"This John O. Hara is a great guy for hitting the sauce and when he gets ready to write a book he goes out of town to some other city and locks himself up in a hotel room so he will not be bother with phones and vareous slugs that bother a man. So two years ago he goes to Philly to write a book and locks himself in this hotel room but dont stay there but gets to hitting the sauce and has his load on from morning to night and cant write even the word cat and rat. Then it comes time he should return back to N Y and he has got no wk. done and he is afraid his ever loving wife will pelt him with the elektric clock when he comes back empty hand it. So he sets down and writes a little article about you, Pal Joey, that he remembers from Waylin, and that is the first one.

"This John O. Hara is a very pleasant guy, Joey, and gets around and speaks of many big shots inametly . . . you wd be surprise to know that he is a student of le hotte jazz as the French say and has many hot contacts around, which is some thing you wd never be let to suspect when you first incounter him."

References

New Repub 103:665-6 N 11 '40
N Y Herald Tribune Books p4 N 3 '40
N Y World-Telegram p22 N 8 '40 por
Sat R Lit 17:10-12 F 19 '38 pors
Time 37:41 Ja 6 '41

America's Young Men
Who's Who in America

O'KEEFFE, GEORGIA (ō-kēf′) Nov. 15, 1887- Artist

Address: h. Lake George, N. Y.

The New York Tomorrow Committee of the now wrecked and dismantled New York World's Fair showed excellent judgment in designating Georgia O'Keeffe, painter of beautiful flower studies and stark but original landscapes, as one of the 12 most outstanding women in the past 50 years. So did the judges who chose one of her paintings, *Easthampton Dunes*, to represent New York State in the International Business Machines exhibition held there and later taken on tour. Her annual one-man exhibitions held since 1921 at the Intimate Gallery, which became "An American Place" in 1929, are attended by crowded groups of admirers. She has ceased to be the exclusive object of adoration of a cult which tried to read strange meanings into her beautiful and usually straightforward work. "An American Place," at 509 Madison Avenue, New York is presided over by her husband, Alfred Stieglitz, the eminent photographer (see sketch 1940 Annual), whom she married December 11, 1924. She has often served as his model.

"The reserve and controlled emotional intensity which are basic elements of Georgia O'Keeffe's character, together with her choice of subject, have led her critics to indulge in a flood of heavily ornate words, embellished with personal opinion and psychological conjectures, in evaluating her work. This has led to a confused impression of a painter whose art is singularly devoid of confusion," says the *Index of Twentieth Century Artists.* Her best-known and most highly regarded studies are studies of flowers, greatly enlarged, with startling use of contrasts and relationships—jack-in-the-pulpits, calla lilies and roses painted on narrow panels with beautiful feeling for design. When Miss O'Keeffe went to Taos, New Mexico to visit Mabel Dodge Luhan, she returned with bare unadorned landscapes of desert country, fine studies of twisted trees and bones of animals bleached white by the blazing sun. She has also painted many abstractions, attempting to express emotion in terms of paint.

Georgia O'Keeffe was born on November 15, 1887 at Sun Prairie, Wisconsin, not far from Madison, of Irish and Hungarian ancestry; her parents were Francis and Ida (Totto) O'Keeffe. Both her grandmothers, Isabel Dunham Wyckoff and Mary Catherine O'Keeffe, were artists, and two of her sisters, Catherine Kleinert O'Keeffe and Ida Ten Eyck O'Keeffe, exhibit today.

Georgia O'Keeffe attended the Chatham (Virginia) Episcopal Institute, and was graduated in 1904 after two years' study; her first school was the Sacred Heart Academy at Madison, which she attended from 1900 to 1901. She also spent a year (1901-02) at the Madison High School. She studied with Vanderpoel at the Art Institute of Chicago from 1904 to 1905 and later, from 1907 to 1908, at the Art Students League in New York City with Chase, Mora and Cox. Chase awarded her the prize for still life in his class. She worked in Chicago the rest of the year and also in 1909, making drawings for advertisements. Going to the summer school at the University of Virginia in 1912, O'Keeffe studied with Alon Bement, and at Teachers College, Columbia University, she studied with Bement and Dow from 1914 to 1916. In the latter year she became supervisor of public schools at Amarillo, Texas, and a year later taught at the West Texas State Normal College.

While in Texas she sent some drawings to a friend in New York to take the place of a letter; words did not come easily to her, and she preferred painting to writing. Without her permission, the friend showed the drawings to Alfred Stieglitz, who is said to

have ejaculated: "Finally a woman on paper !" So much impressed was he by their quality that he exhibited the drawings at "291," his famous gallery on Fifth Avenue. As a result, O'Keeffe abandoned teaching, came to New York again and rented a small room on 59th Street.

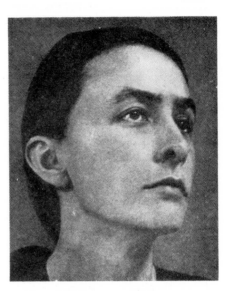

GEORGIA O'KEEFFE

On January 29, 1923 the first big exhibition of Georgia O'Keeffe's work was held at the Anderson Galleries, by courtesy of Mitchell Kennerley. Called "One Hundred Pictures," the exhibition had no catalog, and the pictures had no titles. In an announcement O'Keeffe stated that she had found first that though she was restrained from living where she wanted to, saying what she wanted to, doing what she wanted to, she could at least paint as she wanted to, and as she did so she found she could "say things with color and shapes that I couldn't say in any other way—things that I had no words for." The paintings were not signed because she believes that if there is any personal quality in a painting that will be signature enough. An O'Keeffe piece is usually quite unmistakable. Marsden Hartley calls them full of "utterly embedded femininity." "Her song is direct and affirmative, free of introspective agonies, devoid of feminine cringe and giggle," says Louis Kalonyme in *Creative Art,* January 1928. "An elemental freshness animates her painting. She lives openly in that feminine world furtively hidden by the Marie Laurencins."

Georgia O'Keeffe is forthright and simple, like her paintings, states Kalonyme. "A free smile curves on thin, large lips. Her face is colorless, the formation almost Chinese, painted by quietness and experience of life. Her white face is set off by the black garments she almost always wears." Dorothy Brett, one of D. H. Lawrence's disciples, describes

O'KEEFFE, GEORGIA—*Continued*

O'Keeffe as "sitting quietly, a half smile on her lips, a quizzical friendly look in her eyes, her beautiful long white hands folded in her lap, calm and quiet in her black-and-whiteness."

Georgia O'Keeffe spends much of the summer in New Mexico, though she spends part of it with her husband on a farm at Lake George, New York, where all the windows are usually uncurtained to afford an unobstructed view of the landscape. At first they lived on the lake shore, but the stench from the pigpens on the farm at the top of the hill obliged them to buy the place. This became the family home, and at one time Siteglitz and O'Keeffe lived there for months alone, she painting, he photographing.

The College of William and Mary awarded Georgia O'Keeffe an honorary doctorate in Fine Arts in 1938. She is represented by paintings in the Phillips Memorial Gallery, Washington, D. C.; the Museum of Art, Brooklyn, New York; the Cleveland Museum of Art; the Whitney Museum of American Art, the Museum of Modern Art and the Metropolitan Museum in New York City; the Tannahill Collection, in the Detroit Institute of Art; the Museum of Fine Arts, Springfield, Massachusetts; the Museum of the University of Minnesota at Minneapolis; and the Tate Gallery, London.

References

Art Digest 12:28 My 1 '38
Arts & Dec 44:19 Mr '36 por
Ind Woman 17:113 Ap '38
N Y Times II p2 F 4 '41 por
New Yorker 5:21-4 Jl 6 '29
Time 29:50+ F 22 '37 por; 35:42 F 12 '40 por
American Women
Bulliet, C. J. Apples and Madonnas 1927
Cheney, S. Primer of Modern Art 1924
Hartley, M. Adventures in the Arts p112-19 1921
Kootz, S. M. Modern American Painters 1930
Lane, J. W. Masters in Modern Art p95-101 1936
New Standard Encyclopedia of Art 1939
New Yorker (periodical). Profiles from the New Yorker p146-53 1938
Rosenfeld, P. Port of New York p199-210 1924
Who's Who in America
Who's Who in American Art

O'MELVENY, HENRY W(ILLIAM) Aug. 10, 1859—Apr. 14, 1941 Dean of the California Bar; played a prominent role in the legal, financial, business and cultural development of the State; his death ended a career of 59 years, which paralleled much of the growth of Los Angeles.

References

Who's Who in America
Whos' Who in Government
Who's Who in Law

Obituaries

N Y Times p23 Ap 15 '41

ORMANDY, EUGENE Nov. 18, 1899- Orchestra conductor

Address: b. Philadelphia Orchestra Assn, Girard Trust Co. Bldg, Philadelphia, Pa.

Since 1936 Eugene Ormandy has been a conductor of the Philadelphia Orchestra, one of the world's greatest orchestras, and since 1938 its musical director. To this orchestra he has brought his vital musicianship, his care for program making, his long years of musical experience.

Eugene Ormandy has been a musician all his life. Even before he was born in Budapest, Hungary his dentist father, Benjamin Ormandy, resolved that if he ever had a son he would be named after Jeno (Hungarian for Eugene) Hubay, the great violinist. His mother was Rosalie (Berger) Ormandy. At two Eugene could easily identify symphonies; almost before he could stand, he was playing on an eighth-size fiddle made especially for him. At four he interrupted a violin recital to announce loudly: "You played an F-sharp instead of an F," and at five he was admitted to the Royal Academy of Music. its youngest pupil.

Two years later Ormandy made his first public appearance and at eight entered the composition class of the well known composer, Leo Weiner, who shouted when he saw him: "Get out! This is a class for adults, not a kindergarten." Kodály, however, was not dismayed by Ormandy's youth and took him as a pupil, as did Jeno Hubay when he was 10. "My lessons with the great Hubay," he remembers, "filled my days with work and with dreams. My fingers were numb from the exercises of Kreutzer and Cramer, the showpieces of Vieuxtemps and Sarasate. I had tasted the intoxicating wine of being a 'Wunderkind,' and my whole ambition was to be a 'Wundermann' as well." At 14 he was awarded a Master's Degree from the Academy and an Artist's Diploma at 16. One year later he was made professor of music.

By this time Ormandy had already undertaken a series of tours in Germany and Austria as violin virtuoso and had studied composition, counterpoint and conducting with the outstanding Hungarian masters, Kodály, Weiner and Béla Bartók. Then came the First World War, and music was a precarious livelihood. Ormandy set out for the United States at the age of 21, lured by the promises of a too-persuasive manager who turned out to be completely untrustworthy. Ormandy found himself without a job, without money.

What he calls "difficult years" followed. Ormandy found himself a obscure violinist in a movie theatre, the Capitol, in New York

City. "It seemed," he says, "a bitter end to my young drama, but I know now that it was training of the most valuable kind." It wasn't long before he became concertmaster of this orchestra and a little later fourth assistant conductor. In a sudden emergency he was asked to conduct three movements of the Tschaikovsky *Fourth Symphony* with 15 minutes' notice. His wife, Steffy Goldner, harpist for many years with the New York Philharmonic and its only female member, heard the performance. She said later that the shock of seeing him conduct an orchestra of 85 men in a great masterpiece almost gave her heart failure. As for Ormandy himself, he says firmly that the performance "changed the course of my life." He had discovered a new instrument, "richer and more responsive than the violin."

For seven and one-half years, until 1929 when he was already a naturalized citizen, Ormandy remained at the Capitol Theatre, and during that period conducted a tremendous part of the symphonic repertoire, four or five performances a day. Conducting the same work 20 times a week was wonderful experience, he says. "It gives one opportunity to think, think, think, and to imagine new ways of bringing out the beauty of the work."

Ormandy began, too, to conduct many radio hours, work that he enjoyed, for, as he cautions musicians: "Don't be superior about the radio. Be thankful down on your knees that it has brought a whole new audience to music. People who might never have been touched by music through their whole lives, know now how much they need it, and they get it." Because of his success at the Capitol Theatre and over the radio, Ormandy was asked to conduct a New York Philharmonic Concert at the Lewisohn Stadium and in 1930 was engaged for two concerts at the Robin Hood Dell in Philadelphia. The following season he was engaged for a whole week.

In 1931 Ormandy had the honor of substituting with the Philadelphia Orchestra for Toscanini, who was ill. "The experience was unforgettable," Ormandy says. "It seemed even then like the climax of my career to lead (if only for two weeks) such an aggregation of musicians as the Philadelphia Orchestra, in the place of so distinguished a conductor as Stokowski [see sketch this issue] and as substitute for the great Toscanini."

After the Philadelphia engagement Ormandy was called to the Minneapolis Symphony Orchestra to take the place of its conductor, Willem Verbrughen (who was ill), and when it was known that Verbrughen would not be able to conduct again, Ormandy was given a four-year contract. In Minneapolis he "developed steadily and proved himself a serious, painstaking musician, a good judge of programs, with a simple, direct way of presenting them." Under him a "run-down orchestra" was made to sound "fresh and vital."

During his years in Minneapolis, Ormandy was guest conductor each year of the Philadelphia Orchestra. When Leopold Stokowski announced, in the spring of 1936, his intention of devoting a greater part of his time to

Emil Rhodes

EUGENE ORMANDY

research, Ormandy was appointed co-conductor with Stokowski for a three-year period. In 1938 the board of directors of the orchestra made him music director, which means that he is in charge of the orchestra's personnel, the content of the programs and the selection of guest artists and guest conductors.

It wasn't an easy job to take over from Stokowski, to hold audiences long accustomed to the excitement which Stokowski invariably provides, but Ormandy was able to do it, with his lyric gift and "meticulous care for detail and phrasing," with his ability as a program maker. Ormandy, who has presented many new composers on his programs and has done much to popularize Bruckner's works, firmly believes that "a program must be made up of important and significant music. . . But there has to be in every program something an audience can hum on its way home."

The meticulousness Ormandy always achieves is the result of long rehearsals, in which he is "as demanding as a drill-sergeant." He seems almost to look like one, too, when he conducts. Stiffly he marches up to the stand, clicks his heels with precision and plunges the orchestra into its performance. His rather pale face may register emotion and his blond hair may wave wildly, but his stance is rigid and his bow to the audience is a brisk bending at the waist. Almost always Ormandy conducts without a score, but deprecates this ability: "I don't think it makes any difference at all. It just happens to be very easy for me to memorize and so I do it. If it were any effort I should not bother with it at all, because I do not think it affects the performance in the slightest."

Off the podium Ormandy is just as energetic as he is on it. He plays a furious game of ping pong, at which Heifetz is the only musician who can beat him, and drives his car like a demon. He is energetic even in his photography, which he loves, and dashes all over as fast as he can to get as many pictures as possible of scenery and of people.

(Continued next page)

ORMANDY, EUGENE—*Continued*

References

Etude 56:357-8 Je '38 por
Mag Art 31:354-5 Je '38 por
N Y Times X p16 D 8 '40
Newsweek 7:21 F 1 '36 por
Time 27:38 Ja 13 '36; 28:45-6+ O 19
'36 por
America's Young Men
Ewen, D. Man With the Baton p270-8
1936
Ewen, D. Men and Women Who Make
Music p177-78 1939
Pierre Key's Musical Who's Who
Thompson, O. ed. International Cyclo-
pedia of Music and Musicians 1939
Who's Who in America
Who's Who in American Jewry

ORR, H(IRAM) WINNETT (ôr) Mar.
17, 1877- Orthopedic surgeon
Address: b. 308 Sharp Bldg, Lincoln, Neb;
h. 2701 Sheridan Blvd, Lincoln, Neb.

Anyone who ever has had a broken leg, or
thinks he might some day have one, has
reason to bless the name of Dr. H. Winnett
Orr. His plaster-cast technique means that
instead of weeks or even months of immobil-
ity, the injured person is walking a few hours
after the bone is set. The first steps in this
revolutionary technique were taken by Dr.
Orr when he was a military surgeon in France
during the First World War.

Hiram Winnett Orr was born in West
Newton, Pennsylvania, the son of Andrew
Wilson and Frances Josephine (Winnett)
Orr, but he was reared in Nebraska and may
be considered practically a Middle Westerner.
He attended the University of Nebraska from
1892 to 1895, but left after his junior year
and went to the medical school of the University of Michigan, where he received his
M. D. degree in 1899. He immediately began
practice in his home city of Lincoln, and
except for absence on war duty has been there
ever since.

Very early he began forging to the front of
his profession. Hardly out of medical college, he became editor of the *Western Medical
Review*, and remained its editor until 1906.
Since 1903 he has been lecturer on the history
of medicine at the medical school of the
University of Nebraska. In 1908 he was chief
medical inspector of the Lincoln public
schools, and in 1911 he became superintendent
of the Nebraska Orthopedic Hospital, holding
that post until 1917. When he returned to
Lincoln after the War it was as chief surgeon
of the hospital, a position he still holds. He
is also chief surgeon of the orthopedic department of the Lincoln General Hospital,
on the orthopedic staff of Bryan Memorial
Hospital (Lincoln was William Jennings
Bryan's home city), and consultant in
orthopedic surgery to the Veterans' Administration in Lincoln. He was editor of the
Journal of Orthopedic Surgery from 1919 to
1921.

It was therefore not as a narrowly experienced or unknown surgeon that he went
to France in 1918 as a major in the Medical
Corps of the A. E. F. He was not inexperienced as an officer, either, since he was a
captain in the Medical Reserve Corps in
1917. He was relieved from duty in 1919
with the rank of lieutenant colonel. He is now
a colonel in the Medical Corps of the Reserve,
and may be called back to active duty at any
time, despite his age; meanwhile he has a
special assignment as consultant in orthopedic
surgery. Before being sent to France he was
for more than a year on duty at the Welsh
Metropolitan War Hospital, near Cardiff.

It was in Wales, and later in France, that
Dr. Orr started his "revolution in surgery."
Perhaps the best known name in war surgery
at the time was that of Dr. Alexis Carrel
(see sketch 1940 Annual). Carrel's technique
in treating war wounds was based on the expectation that they would all be infected;
he treated them by frequent dressing, drainage
and irrigation with antiseptics, chiefly the so-
called Carrel-Dakin solution. Dr. Orr, whose
primary concern was with broken bones (so
frequently involved in war injuries), horrified
his colleagues by giving one thorough cleaning
to the wound, then packing it with gauze
(soaked in petroleum to avoid sticking) and
immobilizing it, together with the fracture, in
a plaster cast. The odor arising from the
pus-soaked casts was not reassuring. But in
nearly every case, when the casts were changed
after three or four weeks, infection had been
eliminated and healing had begun. During
the Spanish Civil War, 1,073 wounded in
Barcelona were treated by the Orr technique,
and only six died. Since the First World
War, Dr. Orr has been practicing and demonstrating his method in Lincoln, and if the
United States enters the Second World War,
there is no doubt that the Orr technique will
be widely applied. Even in osteomyelitis,
which involves infection of the bone, he
scrapes the infected bone and then immobi-
lizes it. In simple fractures he insures use of
the limb by the employment of traction pins
to hold the fracture set.

As a crusader for his technique, Dr. Orr
has written hundreds of articles and pamphlets. He has written books on the subject,
too: *The Treatment of Osteomyelitis and
Other Infected Wounds by Drainage and
Rest* (1927); *Osteomyelitis and Compound
Fractures* (1928), originally lectures given at
the Mayo Brothers' Clinic; *Osteomyelitis and
Compound Fractures and Other Infected
Wounds* (1929); *A New Era in the Treatment of Osteomyelitis and Other Infections*
(1930), first given as the Beaumont Lecture in
Detroit. He contributed the section on
osteomyelitis to the *Sajous Cyclopaedia* in
1931, and addressed the British Medical Association on the same subject in Dublin in 1933.

Where Dr. Orr finds the energy for all his
activities is a mystery, for he is one of the
busiest of surgeons. He is also a "joiner,"
and has held office in numerous professional
societies. He was librarian of the Nebraska
State Medical Association from 1900 to 1912,

DR. H. WINNETT ORR

its secretary in 1907 and its president in 1919; secretary of the American Orthopedic Association from 1915 to 1917 and its president in 1936; secretary of the Central States Orthopedic Society 1913 to 1917; chairman of the Orthopedic Section of the American Medical Association in 1921. He belongs to five other medical societies and three clubs. He has also written *History of the Nebraska State Medical Society* (1903); *The Rights of the Patient* (1920); and *A Civilian Surgeon's Story of the Great War* (1921).

On September 7, 1904, Dr. Orr married Grace Douglas, of Grinnell, Iowa, and they have two sons and three daughters. A slender, bespectacled man, now almost entirely bald, with a smooth-shaven, serious face, he lives very quietly, with little leisure for interests outside his profession. His hobby is the collecting of rare medical books, and he has one of the finest collections of these in existence. They fill the library of his Sheridan Boulevard home. Regularly, to the Nebraska Orthopedic Hospital, come visiting surgeons from all over the country (before the outbreak of the present War, from all over the world), to have Dr. Orr demonstrate to them his plaster-cast technique. Once confined to his own practice, it is now in wide use, and its proponents acclaim its simplicity and its prevention of dangerous complications. It is conceivable that thousands of American ex-soldiers may some day owe their normal health and lives, instead of long years of a crippled existence, to the theories and experiments of a modest yet far-seeing and aggressive surgeon from a small city in the Midwest.

References

Life 9:47-50 D 9 '40 il por

American Medical Directory
Directory of Medical Specialists 1939
Who's Who in America

ORTON, HELEN FULLER Nov. 1, 1872-
Author

Address: 37-05 88th St, Jackson Heights, Long Island, New York City

Helen Fuller Orton is the author of more than 20 books for children. Her two latest books are *Mystery at the Little Red Schoolhouse* (1941) and *The Brave Frontier* (1940) which is an "historical novel of Revolutionary times for younger readers, describing the defense of the Schoharie farmers in the New York Colony."

Many of Mrs Orton's books are founded on her memories of the farm 12 miles from Niagara Falls, New York, where she spent her childhood. She writes: "Our rambling farmhouse stood at the end of a long lane and was surrounded by apple orchards on three sides. In the village of Sanborn, a mile south, the family got the mail and the groceries, had the horses shod and took the train for the city. In the village of Pekin, a mile north, we went to church and to school." She was such a frail child that she was taught at home in her early years. Her favorite studies were Latin, literature and history. She also loved music. The family were not able to have many books, but those they had she read and reread—a few of poetry, Shakespeare in one volume, American history, some of the standard novels, volumes of old *Atlantic Monthly's* and *Ladies' Repository's* and the Bible. There were few children's books in the house, but there was fine reading in the *Youth's Companion* and *St. Nicholas*.

Both her father, Merritt Bond Fuller, and her mother, Lucy (Taylor) Fuller, had taught school before their marriage. Her father farmed in the summer and taught in winter. He was a firm believer in Latin as an essential part in education. Mrs. Orton had two brothers, younger than herself, and one older sister. Her ancestors, all English, were pioneers who stayed a generation or two in one locality and then moved westward, mostly by way of the Mohawk Valley. One, her great-great-grandfather, settled in the Wyoming Valley of Pennsylvania just in time to be caught in the Wyoming Massacre.

After her graduation from high school, Mrs. Orton taught for two years. She married Jesse F. Orton in 1895—he was at that time both teaching and studying at the University of Michigan. They lived in Ann Arbor for two years while he finished his law course. After living in Grand Rapids for several years they moved to New York in 1908. They have four sons: Malcolm, Lawrence, Douglas, Robert. Mrs. Orton is a Protestant, a member of several clubs and associations, is particularly interested in the early history of New York State, and gives occasional lectures on that subject and on the writing of children's books. It was at the suggestion of a young son, who loved to listen to her bedtime stories, that she wrote out her first stories and submitted them to a publisher. These stories were published in 1921 under the title *Prince and Rover of Cloverfield Farm*. Children at once took to the book. Since then she has been writing constantly, at the rate of about one book a

HELEN FULLER ORTON

year. Animal stories followed the Cloverfield Farm series; then came two whimsical tales. Since 1930 Mrs. Orton has written mostly stories with an historical background, such as *The Secret of the Rosewood Box* (1937); *The Treasure in the Little Trunk* (1932); *The Gold-Laced Coat* (1934); *Hoof-Beats of Freedom* (1936); and *A Lad of Old Williamsburg* (1938). Her first "modern" story was *Knights of the Snowstorm* (1939).

References

Brooklyn Daily Eagle Je 9 '24 por
Buffalo Times p3 S 2 '34 por
N Y Herald Tribune Books p10 N 13 '32
Wilson Lib Bul 8:320 Feb '34 por
American Women
Kunitz, S. J. and Haycraft, H. eds.
  Junior Book of Authors 1935
Who's Who in America

OSBORN, FREDERICK (HENRY) Mar. 21, 1889- Chief of the Morale Branch, United States Army

Address: b. War Department, Washington, D. C.; h. Garrison, N. Y.

The tallest general in the Army (six feet, eight inches) is Frederick Osborn, appointed chief of the Morale Branch of the War Department by President Roosevelt in September 1941 to meet the criticism that "Army morale has been impaired." He is also probably the general with the least fighting experience. A civilian who never actually served in the Army itself, Brigadier General (the rank is temporary) Osborn is the first to admit that he's no "military" man. There are a number of both military and non-military men who think that is a positive recommendation for the morale director of a largely drafted army.

Like President Roosevelt, to whom he has long been friend and neighbor, Frederick

Henry Osborn is a Hudson River squire whose family of lawyers, railroad magnates and philanthropists have lived on the Hudson for a hundred years. "If I have never been in the Army before," he says, "at least I was born in plain sight of West Point." As a matter of fact, Osborn was born in New York City on March 21, 1889, but the estate of his parents, William Church and Alice C. H. (Dodge) Osborn, on which his own house is now built, overlooks the Hudson just above Garrison.

His father, lawyer and president of the Metropolitan Museum of Art, has always been a champion of worthy causes, among them the valiant defense of Hudson River scenery from stoneblasting corporations. His uncle, the late Henry Fairfield Osborn, paleontologist, was noted in the scientific world, and Frederick as a boy often discussed problems of heredity with him. The nephew, however, in his book, *Preface to Eugenics* (1940), was to refute his uncle's belief that Anglo-Saxons are "God's special gift to earth" and that the "unfit" should be weeded out of society.

After attending the Browning School in New York City, Frederick Osborn entered Princeton, where he was graduated in 1910 with a Phi Beta Kappa key. A year with mining outfits in Alaska and Arizona followed, and then, during the college year 1911 to 1912 he did post-graduate work at Trinity College, Cambridge. In the fall of that same year his career in business management started, and in 1914, the year in which he was married to Margaret L. Schieffelin of New York City, he was made treasurer and vice-president in charge of traffic of the Detroit, Toledo and Ironton Railroad.

During the First World War, Osborn got some training for his present task, setting up field hospitals with the Red Cross. He returned from Europe, sold the railroad with which he had been associated to Henry Ford at a good profit, and busied himself in a number of enterprises. From 1921 until his retirement some 10 years later General Osborn was a partner of G. M. P. Murphy and Company, New York bankers. He has also been president of American Vitamins, Inc., chairman of the board of Colprovia Roads, Inc., and director of the Inter-continental Rubber Company, the Fifth Avenue Bank, the Panama Railroad and Steamship Company and Schieffelin and Company.

Through all his business career Frederick Osborn had been interested in the field of science. For many years—since his undergraduate days, in fact—he had studied the problems of heredity and environment, and after his retirement he began to devote himself to them full time. In 1933 he was editor of *Heredity and Environment,* in 1934 he was joint author with F. Lorimer of *The Dynamics of Population* and in 1940 his *Preface to Eugenics,* "a solid work packed with the results of painstaking inquiry and bristling with statistics," was published. In this book he took up the problem of genetic inheritance and stated his belief that voluntary population control is as much an earmark of sound eugenics as it is of democracy, while genetic plans in the hands of dictatorial power are dangerous and "not eugenic." He believes there should be freedom (with the aid of services to mothers and children by the state) for responsible parents to have children without having them an economic burden. He believes, too, from his studies of population decline, that it is highly necessary for "privileged" individuals to produce more children, and he has practiced what he preaches. The Frederick Osborns have a family of four daughters and two sons: Frederick, Margaret Louisa, John Jay, Alice Dodge, Virginia Sturges and Cynthia.

This eugenist, population expert, conservationist, business researcher, corporation executive, banker, art connoisseur and traffic expert came to Washington in 1940 as a dollar-a-year man: consultant on population with the division of statistical standards in the Bureau of the Budget. The day after he settled down in this job he was called by President Roosevelt to head the newly appointed civilian advisory committee to assist in the Selective Service Program. It then became his task to see to regulations covering deferments for men with dependents, men in vital occupations and conscientious objectors.

His next job came on January 9, 1941 when Secretary of War Stimson made him chairman of the Joint Army and Navy Committee for Welfare and Recreation. He served on it with two other very tall men, Robert E. Sherwood and Clarence A. Dykstra (see sketch this issue). When his present appointment came in September of that same year he simply moved across the hall in the War Department to carry on essentially the same work, this time "with a star on his shoulder."

He said of his appointment: "I am in charge of the Army Morale branch, but that doesn't really control army morale. That is determined primarily by the leadership offered by the officers and by the attitude of the country in general." He added: "My branch is in charge of morale in the sense that we are to provide for the leisure time and recreation of soldiers in camp. We are a policy-making group, to advise commanding officers who are in charge of recreation at posts." This means that General Osborn is in charge of Army post exchanges, "one of the country's largest retail businesses"; of the motion-picture service, Army hostesses, guest houses, athletic offices and recreational facilities; of correspondence courses and lectures. And he will give advice and formulate plans for recreation. As a scientist he is particularly interested in the research and analysis section of his branch and intends to get at "the facts which are basic in morale problems" and extract "from the knowledge thus assembled more effective methods of dealing with these problems as they arise"—the problems of "the individual man and the way his relations with other men in the group affect his behavior."

Osborn is a research associate in anthropology at the Museum of Natural History, New York, of which he is also a trustee. He is chairman of the Council on Population

FREDERICK OSBORN

Policy, a director in the American Population Association of the United States, the American Eugenics Society and the Association for Research in Human Heredity. He is, further, a member of the Palisades Interstate Park Commission, a trustee in the Carnegie Corporation, New York, director of the National Health Council and trustee of Lingnan University of Canton, China.

The tall, eye-arresting brigadier general is "very lean and dark, with a thatch of iron-gray hair becoming his 52 years and a little over. He wears his inches negligently and his manner is easy and reassuringly unassuming." He has not, as yet, put on his uniform. Mrs. Osborn does not dispute the assertion that it would take a lot of "tailor's fixin's" to turn him out a "complete soldier from tip to toe." But if "morale" begins at home, the six tall sons and daughters of General Osborn, as well as his wife, are willing to testify that, with the Osborn family at least, it is excellent. And Mrs. Osborn is witness to the fact that, although her husband is a mild mannered enough man, he believes firmly in what he is doing. "The other day in Washington," she said, "General Hershey [see sketch this issue] offered to give me a lift home. 'How about your husband,' he asked, 'will he come along?' I answered that my husband said he was going to walk. And General Hershey's reply was: 'If he says he's going to walk, he is going to walk.'"

References

N Y Sun p13 Ag 21 '41
N Y Times VII p12+ S 7 '41 por
Newsweek 18:28 S 1 '41 por
Scholastic 39:15 O 27 '41 por
Time 36:34 S 9 '40; 38:40 S 1 '41 por
U S News 9:36-7 N 1 '40 por

(Continued next page)

OSBORN, FREDERICK—*Continued*
American Men of Science
Who's Who in America
Who's Who in Commerce and Industry
Who's Who in Government

OSUMI, MINEO OSUMI, BARON (ō-sōō'mê mē-nā'ō)   May(?), 1876—Feb. 8, 1941(?) Japanese supreme war councilor; killed in crash of a naval plane in China; was Navy Minister of several Japanese cabinets between 1931 and 1936; as Japanese naval building program expanded in 1935, Admiral Baron Osumi said that it was the duty of every Japanese to eat only rice gruel or to starve, if necessary, in order to supply funds for naval appropriations.

References

Far East R 31:283 Ag '35 por
N Y Sun p18 Ja 13 '41
R of Rs 91:28 Ja '35
International Who's Who
Who's Who in Japan

Obituaries

N Y Times p4 F 8 '41
Time 37:27 F 17 '41

OTT, MEL(VIN THOMAS) Mar. 2, 1909- Baseball player; manager of New York Giants *Address*: b. New York Giants, Polo Grounds, New York City; h. Metairie, La.

Bulletin: On December 2, 1941 Mel Ott signed a 2-year contract as new manager of the New York Giants.

From July 1941 issue:

On May 22, 1941 Mel Ott of the New York Giants hit two home runs in a game at Cincinnati, the ninth and tenth such runs, respectively, of the 1941 baseball season; on June 15, in a game against the Cincinnati Reds, he exploded his sixteenth. These carried his record—a National League record for the most lifetime home runs—onward and upward past the 400 mark. Ott has also led the National League in homers five times. More remarkable still, the "Mighty Mite" has spent his entire career in big-time baseball, with no previous apprenticeship in minor leagues. He reported to Manager John McGraw back in 1925, and has been with the Giants ever since.

Besides being one of the greatest home-run hitters in the history of baseball, Ott has few peers as an outfielder. As a sports writer in *Scholastic* points out: "He is particularly famous for two tricks. On a long fly over his head, he can take one look at the ball, turn his back and run to the exact spot the ball will drop! He owns a buggy whip for an arm and can run a country mile for a fly. The other uncanny gift is for playing rebounds off the Polo Grounds' fences. He judges angles like an Einstein. Where other fielders go crazy playing caroms, Ott picks the hardest smashes off the wall on one or two bounces."

The highlights of Ott's career, as enumerated to sports writer Harold Kaese by the Mighty Mite himself, are: Hitting for the cycle (single, double, triple, homer) in Boston against the Braves on May 16, 1929, one of baseball's rarer feats. Hitting three home runs in a game against the Boston Braves at the Polo Grounds, New York, on August 31, 1930. Scoring six runs in a game on August 4, 1934. Being chosen on every National League All-Star Team except that of 1933 and setting a National League record for double plays (12) by an outfielder in 1929.

Ott was handed another and less desirable record in 1938 when he was hit three times by a pitched ball. He has also drawn more than 1,230 bases-on-balls or about one pass every seven times at bat, another National League record.

Exceptionally small as big-league sluggers go, Mel Ott has been called "the smallest fence buster the game has known." He stands five feet nine inches, and weighs 172 pounds. (Babe Ruth, Jimmy Foxx, Hack Wilson, Hank Greenberg, Rudy York, Johnny Mize and the late Lou Gehrig, other famous home-run kings, stood inches taller or were pounds heavier.) He has brown eyes, a square jaw, an uptilted nose, an equable disposition. He married Mildred Mattigny, a New Orleans girl, in 1930, and has two daughters, Lyn and Barbara Ann.

Like Mrs. Ott, Mel Ott is a product of Louisiana. He was born in Gretna, Louisiana, a small town just across the Mississippi River from New Orleans, on March 2, 1909. His father, Charles Ott, had been working for an oil refinery for some years; he and his brother were both good semi-professional ball players. Melvin Thomas was the second in a family of children which included Marguerite, the eldest, and a younger brother, Charles. He was taken out to the ball park before he could walk. At high school he played a little football and a lot of basketball, and also some semi-professional baseball around home and in Patterson, Louisiana. He toughened his muscles by fishing and hunting.

Finally, when Mel was 15, his boss, Harry P. Williams, a lumber man, sent him to New York to see "Jawn" McGraw, manager of the Giants. "The white-haired, fire-eating manager took one look at Mel squatting behind the plate and shook his head at the idea that Mel was a catcher. But, after watching him at bat, McGraw was sold." He probably wouldn't have been had he known Mel's real age, but the cagey recruit cheerfully lied about that. When Mel left Gretna for the Polo Grounds he weighed one hundred-sixty pounds, stood five feet seven inches, and had just celebrated his sixteenth birthday.

Ott reported to the Giants as a catcher, but it was not long before he was practicing in the outfield. In a few weeks McGraw stated: "Ott is the most natural hitter I ever saw. His style at the plate is perfect." The Giants finished second to the Pittsburgh Pirates in 1925, and Ott had not played in a single game, even to pinch-hit. Next year, when the team finished fifth, Ott had played 35 games and batted .383, but had not made a single home run. He spent the winter with rod and gun in Louisiana, and then McGraw took him to Hot Springs, Arkansas, to teach him to play second base. After a period of preparation McGraw announced that Ott was being carried as a reserve infielder. He got his chance at second base when he replaced Andy Cohen, and proved "steady but not sensational." McGraw decided that from then on Ott should play when right-handed pitchers were working against the Giants.

Ott batted only .282, his lowest average, in 1927, but the next year he drove home 77 runs and batted .322. Eighteen of these runs were homers. Ott says that his best season was in 1929, when he hit 42 home runs, his record total, and drove in 151 runs, also his best. The Giants finished third that season. In 1930 Mel batted .349. He fell under the significant .300 figure in 1931, 1933, 1937 and 1940; but for eight consecutive years, 1929 to 1936, he batted in over 100 runs for the Giants, and in 1937 fell short by only five. "I'd rather be a good hitter in the pinch than a high average hitter," is Ott's philosophy.

Bill Terry succeeded McGraw as manager in 1932. The next year came Ott's greatest thrill, when the Giants won from the Washington Senators. On his first time at bat, Ott "exploded a 400-foot home run into the lower right-field stands at the Polo Grounds with Joe Moore on base to send the Giants away to a 2-0 lead in the first inning." He hit homers on both his first and last times at bat, and the second one, a home run into the left center-field bleachers at Griffith Stadium, won the Series for the Giants (Ott's first World Series). In 1934 he batted in 135 runs to lead the National League. Though he hit home runs in both 1936 and 1937 World Series, his team was smothered by the Yankees. In 1936 Ott played 60 games at third base, where 10 errors brought his fielding average for the position down to .740. With his short, stocky frame he was not sufficiently nimble and agile to be an outstanding third baseman. In 1937, when the Giants won the pennant again, Ott played 113 games at "the hot corner" and brought up his fielding average to .971. In 1938 he was able once again to return to the outfield.

Ott is "probably the most unorthodox batter in baseball." The average slugger takes a low step toward the pitcher and swings right from the shoulder. Mel stands as close to the plate as the rules allow, with his toes no further than six inches away. A left-handed batsman, he gives a peculiar hitch, a sort of goose step, when he steps to meet the pitcher, and lifts his right foot stiffly, lowering his bat before stepping forward to bring the bat back to connect for another home run. For those unlucky wights who can't go to see this peculiar but effective performance, the National League has made a film, *Winning Baseball*. Mel thinks that this particular stance gives him more driving power.

New York Giants

MEL OTT

Ott's "pleasant disposition, fine competitive spirit, stability of character, and inherent versatility" make him popular with his teammates as well as with the fans.

References

Giants Jottings 6:2 My 16 '41 por
Scholastic 38:42 My 19 '41 il pors
Nason, J. and others. Famous American Athletes of Today 7th ser. p341-67 1940
Who's Who in Major League Baseball
Who's Who in the Major Leagues

OTTINGER, NATHAN (ö'ting'ĕr) 1874—Nov. 17, 1940 Former justice of the Supreme Court of New York, well known as a trial lawyer.

Obituaries

N Y Herald Tribune p16 N 18 '40 por
N Y Times p19 N 18 '40 por

OTTO OF AUSTRIA, ARCHDUKE Nov. 20, 1912- Pretender to Austro-Hungarian throne

Address: Essex House Hotel, 160 Central Park South, New York City

Among the royal exiles who have found a refuge and a welcome in the United States is an unusually good-looking young man, dark-haired, dapper, with a closely-trimmed mustache and a habit of looking over your head when he talks. Neither his memory nor his mother has ever allowed him to forget that he is Franz Joseph Otto Robert Maria Anton Karl Maximilian Heinrich Sixtus Xavier Renatus Ludwig Gaetan Pius Ignatius von Hapsburg-Lorraine, who (if the First World War had never happened) might today be Emperor of Austria and King of Hungary,

Weitzmann
ARCHDUKE OTTO OF AUSTRIA

Bohemia, Dalmatia, Croatia, Slavonia, Galicia, Illyria and other places which exist only on 1918 maps. Although "Archduke Otto" is a little simpler for Americans to remember, and the Nazis have maliciously dubbed him "Otto the Last," since the beginning of the Second World War there have been rumors that a British victory in Europe might mean a Hapsburg restoration. One writer says of this hopeful exile: "Otto is like a handsome young actor awaiting his cue in the wings of the European theatre."

It is true that he has been awaiting that cue for a long time. But it is also true that Otto's mother, Zita de Bourbon-Parma, a cousin of the late Alfonso of Spain, has been faithfully prompting him. It was 1911 when she married Archduke Karl of Hapsburg, nephew of Franz Josef, wartime Emperor of Austria. (Archduke Otto was born in Reichenau the next year.) It was November 21, 1916 when the elderly Franz Josef died and her husband succeeded to the throne as Charles IV. It was the latter part of 1918 when, on a visit to Hungary, the royal family received reports of a revolution in Fiume, following the rout and disintegration of the Austro-Hungarian Armies, and returned hastily to Vienna. The revolution soon spread to Austria, and in 1919 Charles was deposed and exiled with his family. Yet the Empress Zita has never lost hope of a triumphant return to Austria.

At first the royal family took refuge in Switzerland, shortly after a republican government was established in Austria. Charles made two attempts to regain his crown with the aid of monarchist groups, in 1921 reaching the suburbs of Budapest with an army. He was promptly banished with his family to

Funchal in the Portuguese island of Madeira, on the west coast of Africa, where they lived in poverty until Charles died. That was April 1, 1922, and on that date Otto became the legitimate ruler of Austria and Hungary.

He was a ruler whom no country would admit but Spain, but that didn't matter. He was offered a villa in the fishing village of Lequeitio on the Bay of Biscay, paid for by 200 Spanish grandees, and Zita brought her family there. There Otto was still addressed as "Your Majesty," and his imperial education continued under private tutors, including two monks. He learned to speak Hungarian, German, French, English, Spanish, Basque, Croation, Czech and "300 words of Finnish," and he prepared for the University.

After several years in Spain, the Hapsburgs finally left their pleasant villa for Castle Steenockerzeel in Belgium so that Otto could attend the University of Louvain in Brussels. There he specialized in political science, economics, financial and budgetary matters. He passed his examination for the degree of Doctor of Political and Social Sciences in 1935, writing a 358-page thesis on Customs and Successoral Rights of the Peasant Class and the Indivision of Rural Estates in Austria. It was full of tactful praise for the peasant class.

In the meanwhile things were looking more hopeful for the Hapsburgs in Austria in spite of the bitter opposition of Czechs, Serbs and Romanians to the mere thought of their restoration. Both before the murder of Dollfuss and after, there was talk of a *coup d'état.* In May 1934 the Austrian Constitution set up Roman Catholicism (the religion of the Hapsburgs) as the privileged church and provided for a President who would have powers as absolute as those Franz Josef had wielded over Austria-Hungary. In 1935 a law was enacted ordering some property returned to Otto and his family, including five Vienna apartment houses, thirteen castles, and estates whose combined rents had aided war cripples after the property was seized in 1919. At about the same time the "anti-Hapsburg" laws were abolished and the monument to the Republic on the Ringstrasse removed. Advocates of a Hapsburg restoration—and Otto himself—insisted that it was the only way to prevent forever an Austro-German *Anschluss.*

The time grew ripe, Otto thought. In June 1936 Otto's Monarchist organization published a letter from him in which he announced: "It is high time for decisive action. I am ready at any hour to return to the Fatherland." It was in 1936, too, that he said in an interview: "There are only two roads which are open: those to Monarchism, or to National Socialism. There is no room in my country for a liberal movement. . . Austria must be kept free of a discontented proletariat and the radical element which makes it so." There were also negotiations going on with foreign governments. A rumor that Otto would marry Princess Maria of Savoy, youngest daughter of the King of Italy, was considered a sign of Mussolini's approval of the restoration;

it was quickly quashed. And a mere unannounced visit by Otto to France would bring about the exchange of "a whole batch of agitated telegrams between Paris and other European capitals."

Nevertheless, as everyone knows, what happened was not a *coup d'état* by Otto, but a *coup d'état* by Hitler. The *Anschluss* of March 1938 entirely changed the picture for the young pretender. His estates were taken away again by the Nazis; a price was on his head throughout the Reich; and Hungary, his last hope, finally joined the Axis.

A mere King might have been disheartened; not an Emperor. In March 1940 when Otto arrived in the United States, traveling as "Otto de Bar," it was with a "tacit French blessing"; and it was reported that he hoped to enlist the support of American Catholics in another campaign for the Austrian throne. During his visit he lunched with Archbishop Francis Spellman, he had tea with the President and Mrs. Roosevelt; he chatted with J. P. Morgan; his retinue spoke of "meetings with Wall Street financiers, industrialists and others"; Alfred Duff Cooper intimated that conservative British opinion wouldn't be averse to a restored Hapsburg throne.

Yet Otto himself professed more enthusiasm for sight-seeing—the Statue of Liberty, New York City's La Guardia, and subway rides. He was here, he said, merely to study democracy, and advocated a federation of central European states after the War for which the Constitution of the United States should serve as a model—"a constitutional monarchy that will have democratic institutions." "I am sure that Austrian sentiment is with me," he said; though suspicious Czechs here remained openly unconvinced of the purity of his intentions and the vigor of his democratic faith. They were probably relieved when he left once more for Belgium in April. He was there until the Nazi invasion, when the imperial family fled to France.

Since the fall of France, Otto and his family have once more taken refuge in the United States. He predicts the present War will end with revolution in Austria, which will then spread to Bohemia-Moravia, Slovakia, Poland and the rest of Greater Germany. "Hitler will be beaten—the question is, when?" He expresses his desire to aid actively in plans for the resettlement of European Catholic refugees in the Dominican Republic. He continues to praise democracy. And he continues to talk of his Danubian Federation. He is popular in Washington, but doesn't stay in any one place very long. In March 1941 he slipped across the Mexican border, reportedly to confer with Austrian refugees there, and proceeded on a lecture tour of the Deep South and the West. (He had already lectured at Johns Hopkins, Fordham, Dartmouth and many other universities.) By June he was in Hollywood.

Otto gives the appearance of being a more than usually Eligible Young Man. He wears dark, conservative clothes, perfectly tailored; he speaks beautiful English; he never goes to night clubs, seldom to hotels and restaurants, attends only parties and receptions given by "persons of whose political and social standing he is sure"; he is a good golfer and tennis player, a "fair skier," refuses to dance simply because he is "out of practice"; he is a painstaking correspondent and reader of newspapers and books on politics; he prefers jazz to classical music, especially Wagner's, which is "too loud to sleep to"; he loves hunting, and was formerly addicted to auto racing and stamp collecting. But appearances are without doubt deceptive in the case of the author of *Letters from Exile*. The Empress Zita may or may not have said: "Even if my son is reduced to having only one servant, that one must call him 'Your Majesty.'" But surely she hopes that some day all the world will call him that.

References

Christian Cent 57:403 Mr 27 '40
Collier's 97:14+ Ap 18 '36 il pors
Cur Hist 44:32-7 Ag '36 il por
N Y World-Telegram p12 D 14 '40 pors
Newsweek 3:16-17 Ap 14 '34 il por; 6: 14-15 Jl 13 '30 por; 15:18 Mr 18 '40 por
Sat Eve Post 204:20-1+ Ap 9 '32 il pors
Spec 155:48-9 Jl 12 '35
Time 35:27 Mr 11 '40 por

Gunther, J. Inside Europe p320-9 1936
International Who's Who

OUMANSKY, CONSTANTINE (ALEX-ANDROVITCH) (o͞o-män′skĕ kŏn-stán-tēn′) May 14, 1902- Former Soviet Ambassador to the United States; director general of Tass, Soviet News Agency

Address: c/o Tass News Agency, Moscow, U. S. S. R.

On November 6, 1941 Constantine Oumansky was replaced by his former patron, Maxim Litvinov (see sketch this issue), as Soviet Ambassador to the United States. The man who had had the difficult job of representing his country in the United States during one of the coldest periods in the history of United States-Soviet relations, Oumansky was eminently qualified for his new position as director general of *Tass*, the Soviet news agency. On November 13 he was also appointed to the collegium of the Foreign Commissariat's governing board, the arm of the Soviet Foreign Office that acts in an advisory capacity on matters of foreign policies.

Few people doubted that the short, chubby, nearsighted Soviet official would continue to carry out efficiently the orders of his Government—as he has carried them out, unpurged, for the major part of his 39 years. Constantine Oumansky was born in Nikolaev, Russia, of obscure parents. While at high school his studies were interrupted by the 1917 Revolution and on its crest he landed in Moscow. There he attended the university and was graduated in 1921.

While still at the University of Moscow, Oumansky was doing journalistic work, and from 1918 on he worked for *Tass*, Soviet new agency, while spending his period of

CONSTANTINE OUMANSKY

military service as a diplomatic courier. In 1922, aided by his gift for languages, he became foreign editor of *Tass* and later its correspondent in Rome. From Rome he went to Paris, where he acted as manager of *Tass'* bureau.

In 1930 Oumansky was promoted to chief of the Press Division of the Commissariat of Foreign Affairs in Moscow, according to an unfriendly writer in the *American Mercury* "the least liked of the censors there," and the kind of ambitious young fellow who knows the right people, says the correct thing and holds correct, up-to-the-minute views. "Short garrulous, dapper he would smile ingratiatingly as he used his blue censor's pencil with abandon." In this position he frequently had the job of greeting distinguished foreigners, especially writers. In it, too, he was often attached to Soviet delegations in international conferences, particularly in Geneva, where he got to know Litvinov well.

In 1933 Oumansky accompanied Litvinov to the United States to help with the consideration of diplomatic relations between the United States and the Soviet Union. Three years later he became attached to the Soviet Embassy in Washington, and when former Ambassador A. A. Troyanovsky returned to Moscow in June 1938 Oumansky was made chargé d'affaires. On May 10, 1939, four days before his thirty-seventh birthday, he became Ambassador, the youngest envoy in Washington from a major power.

Three months later the Nazi-Soviet non-aggression pact complicated his task. Then came the Russo-Finnish War. The attitude of officials of the United States State Department (always free from excessive warmth) dropped below zero in friendliness toward Russia.

American public opinion was almost unanimously anti-Soviet. A "moral embargo" was placed on exports to Russia. Reporters kept questioning Oumansky about the late General Krivitsky's picture of him as a member of the Soviet secret police. After the Soviet Union absorbed Estonia, Latvia and Lithuania the United States, refusing to recognize the act, held Baltic ships in American ports. Protests were in vain.

Since the summer of 1940, however, Oumansky and Under-Secretary of State Sumner Welles had been repeatedly though interruptedly engaged in conferences, presumably in an effort to establish more harmonious relations between their countries. The conversations seemed to be bearing some fruit. In January 1941 the "moral embargo" was lifted. In March, Welles expressed his pleasure over assurances given by the Kremlin to Turkey. But the most reliable barometer of United States-Soviet relations had for some time been the quantity of machine tools released for export to Russia, and actually none were released during the first months of 1941. By April *PM's* Leonard Engel was writing: "Moscow and Washington now seem . . . to be on about as bad terms as possible without recall of an envoy." By May, Oumansky had almost given up hope, but was still lodging formal protests.

Only the German invasion of Russia a month later changed this situation, and changed it overnight. Where once the Soviet Ambassador, "tight-lipped and stern," had protested American restrictions and American policy, from June 1941 on he smilingly presented Russian requests on purchasing and aid and found them granted.

Oumansky, it is said, "has a keen mind, is inherently serious and inclined to miss humorous nuances." His favorite sport is horseback riding, and indoors it is contestable whether he prefers reading or playing Russian music over and over on his victrola. He has great confidence in his country. On June 23 his statement on the War read, in part: "Today ours is a nation of a moral and political unity and strength unknown in the past. . . Hitler's attack on my country will be crushed." This "enthusiasm for the Russian ideal" is, however, "blended with genuine admiration for American industry." He speaks excellent English, and during the earlier years of his stay in the United States traveled all over the country, speaking at many universities and in public forums.

During the period in which he was Ambassador, Oumansky's relations with the State Department were always very correct. So was his social life. Ambassador and Mrs. Oumansky (they have a daughter Nina) were well known for the respectable and fashionable entertainments they gave in the Soviet Embassy —badly attended in 1939, 1940 and the early part of 1941, well attended after June 1941. At them Mr. Oumansky's polished manners and his ready wit caused many a surprised guest to exclaim in an undertone: "But he doesn't seem like a Bolshevik."

References

Am Mercury 48:85-8 S '39
Newsweek 13:42 My 22 '39 por
Sat Eve Post 212:12 N 4 '39 por
U S News 11:47 Jl 11 '41 por
Who's Who in the Nation's Capital

OWENS, CLARENCE JULIAN July 4, 1877—Feb. 7, 1941 Attorney in international law and president for the last 30 years of the Southern Commercial Congress; expert on trade conditions; headed the International Trade Commission of the Southern Commercial Congress in 1922; urged a moratorium on war debts.

References

International Who's Who
Who's Who in the Nation's Capital

Obituaries

N Y Times p15 F 8 '41

OXENHAM, JOHN 1861(?)—Jan. 24, 1941 British novelist and poet; especially known for his First World War verse—his *Hymn for the Men at the Front* sold 8,000,000 copies; wrote almost 70 books; real name William Arthur Dunkerley.

References

Author's and Writer's Who's Who
Who's Who

Obituaries

Time 37:57 F 3 '41

PACE, CHARLES ASHFORD July 17, 1869—Dec. 12, 1940 Educator; attorney; banker; co-founder of Pace Institute and of Pace & Pace which conducts business schools in a number of cities; author of many law texts; organized bank in Suffern, New York.

Obituaries

N Y Times p23 D 13 '40 por

PACELLI, EUGENIO See Pius XII, Pope

PACKARD, ELEANOR Sept. 4, 1905- War correspondent
Address: b. United Press Assn, 220 E. 42nd St, New York City

The only ace woman war correspondent for the United Press, Eleanor Packard is said to have covered more warfare than any other newspaperwoman. After the outbreak of Italo-Greek hostilities she began cabling her dispatches from Rome. But this was not her first experience of the kind. When Mussolini's troops entered Albania (Good Friday 1939) Mrs. Packard flew to Tirana ahead of the Fascist invaders and watched the entire process of the Italian occupation of the Albanian capital. Her dispatches carried an eyewitness account of developments, and she made an international radio broadcast from the scene.

ELEANOR PACKARD

Concerning this important news event, following her landing at Tirana, she cabled: "I had been in Albania only two days when a messenger from the American Legation knocked on the door of the funny little Moslem hotel where the chambermaids wear harem trousers. It was just dawn. He said I must come to the Legation immediately for safety, as the Italians had just landed. Instead I went to the telegraph office, rounding up en route all the details I could. . . All that day I was busy automobiling everywhere . . . even got down toward Durazzo whence the Italians were marching toward Tirana. I returned to watch the Zog government depart at 5 p. m., as shooting broke out in the capital. During this firing I jumped, grasshopper fashion, down the streets and was nearly mowed down by one volley from an Albanian chimney-pot fortress as I was ducking into the post office to file another story. You get scared about things like that after they're over."

Mrs. Packard's remarkable career as a full-time war correspondent is the more amazing because she did not begin her work in journalism until 1930. In that year she went to Paris, where she met and married Reynolds Packard of the United Press Staff. Their honeymoon included an assignment in Vienna and a voyage to the South Seas. Since then her assignments have carried her around the world and onto four continents.

Although born in New York City, Eleanor Newell Cryan, daughter of A. N. Cryan, was brought up on a ranch near Yakima, Washington. She first attended the University of Washington, then came East to the Columbia School of Journalism, where she received her B. L. degree in 1927. During the early years of her marriage Mrs. Packard accompanied her husband on his round-the-world assignments and

PACKARD, ELEANOR—*Continued*

collaborated with him in getting stories, free-lancing a bit at the same time "on her own." Their "song-and-dance" act in international journalism became famous at the outbreak of the Sino-Japanese War, when the Packards were transferred to Shanghai. China is a big country to cover—far too big for two to do the job hand in hand. So there were several occasions when the Packards were hundreds of miles apart for weeks at a time. Often filing her stories quite independently of her husband, Mrs. Packard became a full-time war correspondent in her own right.

Eleanor Packard herself covered the bitter student riots in Cairo. And she was the only woman correspondent to cover the Ethiopian War. Then came the days of the tragic Spanish Civil War, when she went into the trenches and front lines there for vivid eyewitness copy. "It was a grim journalistic picnic when I covered the attacks on Madrid," she wrote. "I stayed at the hotel Talavera de la Reina and daily drove 90 miles to the front lines. With other correspondents I perched on top of windmills or behind chimneys, in deserted suburban villas surrounded by once-beautiful gardens now filled with the rubble of war, dead bodies, shrapnel-broken furniture and torn clothing. Every time we poked our heads out too far, the Madrid sharpshooters' bullets buzzed over us like wasps. Sometimes we all got together in the basement of some villa and munched Spanish omelets made into sandwiches and drank *vino* squirted into our mouths from goatskin *botas*. The best time of day, of course, was when we left for home. Even then we were afraid our way had been cut [off] or that we would be under fire."

In 1938 the Packards moved to Geneva. But when Hitler began making demands on Czechoslovakia Mrs. Packard was assigned to the Sudetan trouble zone. She filed brilliant exclusive stories on the Czech crisis and an eye-witness account of the German march into that country following the "peace" of Munich. After a brief interlude in Spain, Reynolds Packard became the U. P.'s bureau manager in Rome. Mrs. Packard was thus on the spot when Italy's Albanian invasion began.

Eleanor Packard has been described as "large, inclined toward stoutishness." She is much too busy as a war correspondent, she says, to pay attention to her figure. But she is capable of meeting rigorous physical exigencies on any occasion. If a story demands "shinnying down a drain pipe from a third floor window, Eleanor will shinny down the drain. If the story requires her to set out in a station wagon with bedding, food, water and equipment for a trip into the Egyptian desert, she'll go—even if she has to go alone. . . Eleanor Packard has made a success of a man's business because she asks and accepts no favors for her sex. She meets newsmen on their own ground, and her ability is thoroughly recognized and admired by the male press corps. She can take a beating on a story as well as any man in the business—and get a scoop as well as any man."

References

Ind Woman 20 :6-7 Ja '41 por

PADEREWSKI, IGNACE JAN (pà″dĕ-rĕf′skê ĭg′näts yän) Nov. 6, 1860—June 29, 1941 Polish pianist and statesman; made his first public appearance as pianist at the age of 12 and first concert tour in 1876, but period of real renown didn't begin until his concerts in Vienna in 1887 and Paris in 1888; in the years that followed he enjoyed repeated triumphs over the face of the globe; after the First World War he set up a Polish coalition cabinet in which he held the posts of Premier and Foreign Minister but submitted his resignation after the Supreme Council of the Allies refused to grant Poland its demands; in 1922 made his first post-War concert tour in America, and his last in 1939; after the outbreak of the war between Poland and Germany he consented to become a member of the Polish National Council and on January 22, 1940 accepted the Presidency of the new Polish Parliament in exile; in that same year he decided to settle in the United States and, once here, devoted himself to aid for Great Britain and Greece; composer of the well known *Minuet* and also of an opera, *Manru*, and a symphony in B-Minor; his memoirs, *My Story*, were published in 1937 in the *Saturday Evening Post* and later in book form.

References

Collier's 103 :16+ Ap 22 '39 por
Etude 48 :776 N '30; 49 :319-20+ My '31 por; 53 :571-2 O '35 il pors; 54 :209 Ap '36; 57 :442 Jl '39 por; 58-370 Je '40 por
N Y Herald Tribune p2 Ja 24 '40
N Y Times VII p11+ N 3 '40 il por; VII p9+ F16 '41 por; IX p7 Mr 30 '41 pors
New Yorker 6 :29-32 N 29 '30
Newsweek 11 :20-1 My 23 '38; 13 :31 F 27 '39 por; 15 :21 F 5 '40
Sat Eve Post 202 :37 Mr 15 '30; 209 : 5-7+ Ja 23 '37; 209 :16-17+ Ja 30 '37; 209 :18-19+ F 6 '37; 209 :26+ F 20 '37; 209 :26-7+ F 27 '37; 209 :20-1+ Mr 6 '37; 209 :28+ Mr 13 '37; 209 : 24-5+ Mr 30 '37 pors
Time 32 :32 O 24 '38; 33 :42+ F 27 '39 il pors; 35 :24 F 5 '40 por
Baker's Biographical Dictionary of Musicians 1940
Ewen, D. ed. Composers of Today 1936
Landau, R. Ignace Paderewski, Musician and Statesman 1934
Martens, F. H. Paderewski pam 1922
Men of Turmoil p231-39 1935
Paderewski, I. J. and Lawton, M. Memoirs 1938
Phillips, C. J. M. Paderewski, the Story of a Modern Immortal 1934
Who's Who in America
Who's Who in Central and East-Europe

Wier, A. E. ed. Macmillan Encyclopedia of Music and Musicians 1938
Woolf, S. J. Drawn from Life p151-58 1932

Obituaries

N Y Times p1+ Je 30 '41 por
Newsweek 18:4 Jl 7 '41 por
Time 38:33 Jl 7 '41 por

PALENCIA, ISABEL DE (pä-lĕnth′-ē-ä)
June 12, 1881- Spanish author; lecturer
Address: h. Avenida Mexico 113, Mexico City, Mexico

"No one who has not been an exile, or, worse still, a refugee, can have an adequate idea of what it means. The first strange impression is to find oneself adrift in the world with only one's clothes packed in a box or in a couple of suitcases—that is, if one has been lucky enough to have even them. . . House-owners are, as a rule, suspicious of refugees. . . Now they are considered outlaws of a sort when, as in the case of the Spanish refugees, they had to go into exile because they observed and defended the law of their land."

Those are the words of Isabel de Palencia, "a slight, graying woman with keenly intelligent eyes" who during the days of the Spanish War was her country's Minister Plenipotentiary to Sweden and to Finland. Today she is one of the 10,000 Loyalists who have made their new homes in Mexico City. In March 1941, during her tour of the United States, where she was currently lecturing, she predicted that the exiled members of the Spanish Loyalist Government may form a "free Spanish" force similar to the "free French" forces of De Gaulle. "Spaniards are a people one cannot drive," she says, proudly.

Isabel de Palencia has told her story in *I Must Have Liberty* (1940). The daughter of Juan Oyarzábal and Anne (Guthrie) de Oyarzábal, she was born in Málaga, Spain on June 12, 1881. Her father was a Spanish Catholic of semi-aristocratic family; her mother was a Scotch Protestant who joined the Spanish Church. Isabel, who herself preferred the Catholic services, was educated at the Convent of the Assumption in Málaga, where she found the life dreary and the instruction poor. She was, in fact, a born rebel. She read constantly by herself; when her grandmother died she revolted against wearing full mourning; she refused to wear corsets.

In all these youthful rebellions her rather modern father and mother backed her up, however. When it was time for Isabel Oyarzábal to take her place in society her refusal to do so was more serious. After a stay in London, where she was paid for teaching Spanish and where she met such celebrities as Ellen Terry and Pavlowa, the young Spanish girl decided that she too must have a career. In her world such a decision was almost unheard of ("there are many ways of being enslaved and not the least degrading is

ISABEL DE PALENCIA

the one that prevents us from using our own creative possibilities"). Yet she finally managed to persuade her mother to go with her to Madrid and to let her study for the stage.

The theatrical career of Isabel Oyarzábal was neither particularly long nor particularly brilliant—consisting for the most part of amateur acting in the art theatre of Pio Baroja. The main thing she accomplished there was to make the acquaintance of the penniless artist whom she married later, in 1909: Don Ceferino Palencia, the stepson of Madrid's leading actress. Isabel Oyarzábal gave up the theatre not for marriage, however, but in order to edit the first woman's magazine in Spain, *La Dama*. She also began to write, mainly news for the British press bureaus—she served on the staff of *El Sol* in Madrid (the only pro-Ally newspaper during the First World War), she was for six years Madrid correspondent for the London *Daily Mail*, and she did news coverage for the Laffan News Bureau and for the London *Standard*.

At that time Spain was a feudal country, its people 52 per cent illiterate. Only the rare Spanish woman was interested in progressive ideas, but such women existed. Isabel de Palencia was one of them, a pioneer. And, oddly enough, it was her husband's temporary desertion that turned her toward public life, toward the labor and woman suffrage movement. It was at least partially due to an attempt to find solace for her private sorrow that, in addition to her writing, she found herself lecturing for the Socialists; helping to found the first woman's club in Madrid; delivering a lecture before the Athenaeum, the first woman to do so; acting as a delegate to Carrie Chapman Catt's suffrage congresses. And during the '20s her face grew increasingly familiar to Paris and London audiences as she traveled about giving lectures on Spanish costume and folklore. In 1922, at the invitation

PALENCIA, ISABEL DE—*Continued*

of the Institute of International Education, she made the first of her many lecture tours of the United States.

Her husband, Don Ceferino, was working even more directly than she for the birth of the Spanish Republic. The Revolution of 1931 fulfilled their dreams, and under the Republic he became Civil Governor of three provinces. As for Isabel de Palencia, she acted as Spanish delegate to the League of Nations (the first woman to sign the convention for Spain), serving on the Committee of Experts on Slavery; she was the Spanish Government's delegate to the International Labor Conference, in charge of work for women and children; and she worked to help the Republic establish schools, to better the conditions of the peasants, to provide greater opportunities for children. There was a period of reaction from 1933 to 1936, but after the Republican victory in the elections of 1936 Don Ceferino became Minister to Latvia, Isabel de Palencia Plenipotentiary Minister to Sweden and later to Finland. She was the first Spanish woman to hold that rank.

Hers was a difficult job. She didn't know Swedish, although she knew several other languages; she had to dislodge the anti-Loyalist incumbent of her office; she had to learn the manners of the Swedish court. Says Marquis M. Childs: "I shall never forget the impression of this dark, quick-moving figure in the vast Spanish legation which had been the château of Prince Karl. With her ardent spirit, her dramatic intensity, she seemed strangely out of place in the big, cool rooms of a northern palace."

With Franco's rebellion Isabel de Palencia's job became even more difficult. It was a time when most women would have been unable to sleep for worry. She, too, was troubled by thoughts of her son Cefito, who was with the medical corps, of her aviator son-in-law, and of her husband and daughter Marissa, who were both in bombarded Barcelona and Valencia a large part of the time. But it was her duty not to be with them, but to try to win support for Loyalist Spain in other lands. For five weeks during the autumn of 1936 she toured the United States, making speeches; she appeared before the leading members of the British Parliament; she delivered an impassioned address before the British Labor Conference. She won innumerable friends for Spain in Sweden itself. Yet she was bitter against those governments, all of which continued to support the ironically named "nonintervention" pact.

When the Rightists finally marched triumphantly into Madrid, Isabel de Palencia and her family fled from Spain, leaving behind not only the family home outside Madrid but also a ceramics collection, valuables, even clothes. "It is not so terrible," she says. "At least you're free to begin life again as destiny tells you; not forced to live under a yoke." The Swedish Government offered them a permanent home; they chose Mexico. Today Don Ceferino Palencia and Isabel de Palencia,

Cefito, Marissa and Marissa's child are all living there.

It was after she left Spain that Isabel de Palencia wrote her autobiographical *I Must Have Liberty,* which was published late in 1940. It was by no means her first book. A member of the Academies of Arts and Letters in Cadiz and in Málaga, a playwright, a translator of Havelock Ellis and of Eugene O'Neill, Isabel de Palencia was also the author of *Study in Child Psychology;* a novel, *Sower Sowed His Seed;* and a novelette, *Hookie,* all written in Spanish; her authoritative *Regional Costumes of Spain* (1926) had already been translated into English; and two charming juveniles illustrated by her husband, *Saint Anthony's Pig* and *Juan, Son of the Fisherman.*

Critics compared *I Must Have Liberty* with books by Constancia de la Mora and by Alvarez del Vayo, books which, like hers, asserted that "the democracies lost their first great battle with the fall of Madrid," and at least one of them decided that the book of Isabel de Palencia was more mature than the former, more personal than the latter. True, many critics suggested that it was her abundant nature which gave "quality and stature" to a book "often commonplace in its writing and sometimes baldly factual in its record"; but Ralph Bates went further and called *I Must Have Liberty* "a book of deep passion and characteristic dignity, quite unmarred by grandiloquence." It is to be followed by a novel, *Masters of Hunger,* the story of a middle class family in Franco's Spain, which will be published in 1942.

Isabel de Palencia wears her "straight black hair streaked with gray" gathered into a simple knot at the back of her head. "Goyaesque in her middle age as in her youth," she "dresses in the deep, plain black that her countrywomen love." When she has time, she says, "I am going back to my hobby of long before the War"—the study of Spanish culture and folk art. (Her enthusiasm about Mexico is due not only to its resemblance to Spain, but also to its Indian influences.) She is continuing to write, too: one of her plays is now under consideration for production in the United States. And she will never stop working for the resurrection of Spain—"for democracy, the only political system under which the people can be happy."

References

Christian Sci Mon Mag p6+ Ag 26 '36 il por
N Y Herald Tribune p16 My 19 '41 por
N Y Post p3 D 6 '40 por
N Y World-Telegram p13 Mr 26 '41 por

International Who's Who
Palencia, I. de I Must Have Liberty 1940

PALMER, JAMES LYNWOOD 1865(?)—June 22, 1941 English painter of race horses; began his career in Canada, where he sketched in stables while working on a ranch; never went to art school and never showed his pic-

tures at an exhibition; painted the favorite
horses of King George V and those of a
majority of important owners in the United
States, Great Britain and France; wrote articles
on sporting subjects for English publications.

References

Apollo 17:175-80 My '33 il
Who's Who

Obituaries

N Y Times p19 Je 24 '41

PAPEN, FRANZ VON (pä'pĕn fränts fôn)
Oct. 29, 1879- German Ambassador to Turkey
Address: German Embassy, Ankara, Turkey

"A diplomatic smoothie, an international intriguer whom British Foreign Office wits call
'the German specialist for political dirty
work,'" since April 1939 Franz von Papen
has been German Ambassador to Turkey. In
Ankara he has been directing the activities of
the German colony, frankly calling upon its
members to attempt to influence Turkish public opinion, and on important occasions has
returned to Germany for consultation. The
spring of 1941 found him once more back
in Berlin, while the world awaited the results
of his return to Ankara. During his absence
a new tone had crept into the Turkish press.
Turkey, once firmly defiant of the Axis, had
become gradually "determinedly non-belliger-
ent, determined not to become an instrument
in the hands of others."

Finally, on May 12, Von Papen, traveling
with his daughter, was greeted at the Ankara
airport by diplomatic representatives of the
Axis. "I come as a dove of peace, bearing
an olive branch," he announced. "I assure
you you can all spend the summer pleasantly
at the beaches." The next day he began his
talks with the Turkish Government. Official
German sources said that Hitler did not intend
to make any political demands upon Turkey,
but Turkish sources believed that he would
try to negotiate an expanded commercial treaty
with their country, now largely cut off from
trade with Britain, and the British seemed to
expect that he would not limit himself to
economic demands. In any case, Hitler's envoy's description of himself as "a dove of
peace" had certain ironic overtones.

Nevertheless during the next few months no
news came out of Turkey of any Nazi diplomatic coup more important than the trade pact
between the two countries signed in June 1941.
Instead the "dove of peace" apparently was
busying himself with proposals, to British officials and middlemen, that Britain stop fighting and join Germany against the Soviet
Union.

Franz von Papen should be well remembered
in the United States. The descendant of a
noble family, he was born in Werl, Germany
on October 29, 1879. He attended military
schools and later commanded a battalion of
Uhlans in Berlin as a lieutenant of cavalry.
Then in 1905 he married Martha von Boch,
(by whom he has four daughters and a son),

FRANZ VON PAPEN Acme

the wealthy daughter of the owner of a Saar-
land ceramics firm, was soon transferred
to a better regiment, and at an early age
was promoted to the general staff. In 1914
he became German military attaché in the
German Embassy in Washington. There, in
collaboration with Captain Boy-Ed, the German naval attaché, he directed German espionage and sabotage. On December 28, 1915,
after a female British secret-service agent had
exposed their plots, he and Boy-Ed were expelled from the country. They returned to
Germany through the blockade with a British safeguard; en route Von Papen's luggage
was searched and confiscated, and 126 check
stubs were found showing payments to his
agents.

But this was not all that was discovered.
In April 1916, a few months later, a Federal
Grand Jury indicted Von Papen for a plot
to blow up the Welland Canal, an indictment
that was not quashed until 1932. It was also
revealed that one of his men had tried to
cause trouble in Mexico by persuading Pancho
Villa and Huerta to buy large quantities of
United States munitions; and a German spy
was caught bearing a letter from Von Papen
to his wife in which he had written, tactlessly:
"I always say to these idiotic Yankees that
they had better hold their tongues." Altogether,
it seemed at that time that Von Papen's practical talents for intrigue were not too impressive.

The German Government was not discouraged by his record. After a short period on
the Western Front during the Somme offensive,
Von Papen was sent to Palestine as chief
of staff of the Fourth Turkish Army. And
when Britain's late General Allenby ripped
the Turkish Army to pieces, Von Papen managed to get out of Nazareth with his Turks

PAPEN, FRANZ VON—*Continued*

just before the city was occupied by the British, once more leaving telltale papers behind. The British cabled London for instructions; one story says that they received the reply: "Forward papers. If Von Papen is captured, do not intern; send him to a lunatic asylum."

The post-War period found the careless conspirator not in a lunatic asylum, but in politics. Wealthy, a Catholic, a Prussian aristocrat without being a "Junker," an outspoken monarchist, he joined the Centrist (Catholic) Party and from 1921 to 1931 was a member of the Prussian Diet. Yet from the beginning he voted with the extreme Right wing which was opposed to the Christian Trade Unions, and after the Centrist leader Brüning came to power in March 1930 he was not above participating in a conspiracy to unseat him.

The year was 1932. The participants were mainly the "influential reactionary gentlemen" of the Herrenklub, under the leadership of General Kurt von Schleicher—Junkers, industrialists who had their own idea of a "new order." By promising the Nazis some concessions (the Storm Troopers had recently been banned), they thought they could secure Nazi support for a new Cabinet without letting National Socialism really gain power. President Von Hindenburg, re-elected in 1932, was a friend of Von Papen and himself of the Junker class; Von Papen therefore did not find it too difficult to persuade him to dismiss Brüning and name him Chancellor. It was May when the "Barons' Cabinet" thus came to power for the first time, with Von Papen as Chancellor, Von Schleicher as Reichswehr Minister and monocled Herrenklub members predominating. Von Papen had previously resigned from the Centrist Party, and on June 3 the Reichstag was dissolved by decree, after it became evident that the new government could not secure a majority there. New elections were called for July 31, 1932.

The history of the next few months is the history of how National Socialism came to power in Germany. Before the elections Von Papen negotiated the Lausanne Conference for the Abolishment of Reparations; he cut unemployment appropriations, the dole and pensions and introduced new consumers' taxes; in direct violation of the Constitution he got himself appointed Federal Commissioner to Prussia and ousted the unresisting Social Democrats from the Prussian Cabinet. In the July elections, however, the Nazis (who had meanwhile been permitted to wear uniforms, parade and resume their terrorist activities) won 37 per cent of the votes. Hitler threatened to withdraw his support from the Government unless he himself were appointed Chancellor. Von Hindenburg refused; the Nazis promptly launched a violent campaign against Von Papen's Cabinet. Once again Von Papen dissolved the Reichstag before his Government could be voted out of office. He was probably still hopeful of coming to an understanding with the Nazis. If so, his hopes were in vain; and, in any case, in the elections of

November 6 the Nazis polled only 32 per cent of the votes. Even Von Schleicher began to demand Von Papen's dismissal, and on November 17 he and his Cabinet finally resigned.

Von Schleicher, who became Chancellor on December 2, altered the Cabinet's personnel little, but planned to close the breach between Left and Right not by seeking Nazi support but by "a government of generals and trade-unionists." Von Papen, nursing his injured pride, began dropping dark hints of his friend's "agrarian Bolshevism" to the president of the Herrenklub, to the Junker Landbund and to the easily alarmed Von Hindenburg. Hugenberg (industrialist chairman of the National People's Party) and others joined him. On January 4, 1933 Von Papen performed the final treachery when he met Hitler, by this time thoroughly discouraged and depressed, at the home of the banker, Baron von Schroeder. The meeting resulted in four million new marks contributed by industrialists to the empty Nazi treasury. Von Schleicher, hearing rumors of a deal with the Nazis, reproached Von Papen, who reassured him. Said Von Schleicher, afterward: "He proved to be the kind of traitor beside whom Judas Iscariot is a saint."

It was January 28 when the aging and suggestible Junker President finally asked Von Schleicher to resign and asked Von Papen to form a new government. In return for their support, this time the Nazis had been promised representation. As the new Cabinet emerged on January 30, Hitler was Chancellor, Von Papen, Vice-Chancellor; but in it were nine non-Nazis, only three Nazis. Von Papen, Hugenberg & Company felt safe. But not for long. After Hindenburg had been persuaded to dissolve the Reichstag and call new elections for March 5, the Nazis, who had control of the police through Goering's (see sketch this issue) Cabinet position, struck out against rival parties, particularly the Communist Party. The Reichstag fire on February 27 was followed by fresh suppressions, terrorism, arrests. Fear of other alleged "Communist plots" brought new Nazi converts; and unlimited funds helped. Finally, when the March elections still did not give the Nazis a clear majority in the Reichstag, Hitler excluded the Communist deputies. The Enabling Act followed; the destruction of the trade unions and of all other political parties, agencies and institutions proceeded at a rapid pace. On April 11 Von Papen was forced to resign as Federal Commissioner to Prussia, Goering became Prussian Premier. Soon there were eight Nazis in the Cabinet, only six nervous non-Nazis, and Hindenburg had become completely dominated by Hitler.

Once more the master of intrigue had been overconfident of his own cleverness. Germany paid heavily for his mistake. But Von Papen himself, as Vice-Chancellor, hung on. In July 1933, even while Goering was suppressing all non-religious Catholic organizations in Prussia, Von Papen, who for years had been the Pope's German voice and who up to that year had gone to Rome as Papal Chamberlain, negotiated the Concordat with the Vatican. And shortly after the overwhelming *Ja* vote in November 1933 he became plenipotentiary of the Reich Government in questions relating to the Saar.

Still, criticism of the non-Nazi "reactionaries" in the Cabinet grew. Von Papen became increasingly uncomfortable. In June 1934, in an address at the University of Marburg ("a bit of courageous stupidity," F. L. Schuman called it), he criticized the lack of freedom of speech in the Third Reich, "in scarcely veiled terms" called for a restoration of the monarchy, an end to the one-party dictatorship, and attacked the party "radicals" who talked of a "Second Revolution" and of collectivization. The speech was suppressed in the press, the campaign against the "reactionaries" intensified. It was mainly the "radicals" who were purged on the Bloody Saturday that followed, but Von Papen was "assaulted, ejected from his office, closely questioned by Hitler's Élite Guard, and at last saved from death only by the intervention of Hindenburg and the Reichswehr." It was July 3 when he tendered his resignation as Vice-Chancellor. At that time Hitler refused to accept it, but in August, Von Papen was relieved of his post, sent as a "special envoy" to restore "friendly relations" with Austria. His appointment was one of the last documents signed by the dying Hindenburg, and before leaving he delivered Hindenburg's will to Hitler.

His work done in Germany, Von Papen now proceeded comfortably to the betrayal of Austria, where Dollfuss had just been murdered by the Nazis. In Vienna he was unwelcome, and the whole diplomatic corps practically ignored him. But he did his job. In 1936 he was made Ambassador to Austria ("with a special mission"); he negotiated the Austro-German agreement of July 1936; and two years later, with the help of Seyss-Inquart (see sketch this issue), he arranged the Hitler-Schuschnigg conference at Berchtesgaden at which the fate of Austrian independence was sealed. Two months after the *Anschluss* the body of his secretary was found floating in the Danube, but by that time Von Papen had returned to his estate in the Saar, where he could ride, fish and play tennis. In the winter of 1938 he went to Sweden to deliver "several innocuous lectures."

In mid-April 1939 Franz von Papen was made German Ambassador to Ankara. There, as "an inveterate intriguer who enjoys conspiracy as a pleasurable recreation" (Schuman), it can be assumed that he has spent delightful years. Socially, at least, he has all the equipment. A "fray-haired, thin-faced, thin-lipped man" who "dresses like a Bond Street manikin" and sports the decorations of Lazarus, Maritius and the Great Maltese Cross, he is known as the best ballroom dancer in Europe.

References

Am Mercury 52:475-82 Ap '41
Cath World 140:228-30 N '34
Dublin R 195:180-90 O '34

Fortnightly 156(ns 150):33-42 Jl '41
Nation 134:667 Je 15 '32
New Repub 71:256-8 Jl 20 '32; 79:196-7 Jl 4 '34
Newsweek 3:13 Je 30 '34 por
R of Rs 86:33-4 D '32 pors
Time 33:26+ My 1 '39

Blood-Ryan, H. W. Franz von Papen 1940.
Dutch, O. pseud. Errant Diplomat 1940
Gunther, J. Inside Europe p90-2 1940
International Who's Who
Koeves, T. Satan in a Top Hat 1941
Schuman, F. L. The Nazi Dictatorship 1935
Wer ist's?

PARDEE, GEORGE C(OOPER) (pär"-dē') July 25, 1857—Sept. 1, 1941 Former Governor of California 1903 to 1907; directed the relief work after the San Francisco earthquake and fire; had served as Mayor of Oakland; as physician was specialist in diseases of the eye and ear from 1885 to 1889.

References

American Medical Directory
Who's Who in America

Obituaries

N Y Times p17 S 2 '41

PARKE, WILLIAM 1873(?)—July 28, 1941 Veteran actor; stage and motion picture director; appeared with E. H. Sothern in *If I Were King*; was manager for Richard Mansfield; emerged from long retirement to play the part of Mr. Witherspoon in *Arsenic and Old Lace*.

References

N Y Dramatic Mirror 69:4 Mr 26 '13
Sci Am 144:32-3 Ja '31 il por

Obituaries

N Y Times p15 Jl 29 '41

PARKER, BARNETT 1889(?)—Aug. 5, 1941 Widely-known English stage and screen comedian; born in England and came to this country many years ago; among Broadway productions in which Mr. Parker had appeared were *Passing Show of 1923, Artists and Models* and *A Night in Paris*.

References

International Motion Picture Almanac

Obituaries

N Y Times p17 Ag 6 '41

PARMA, V. VALTA Mar. 31, 1878—Aug. 31, 1941 Former curator of the Rare Book Division of the Library of Congress; organized the program for collecting the Library's rare material into this division which he headed from 1927 to 1940.

(Continued next page)

PARMA, V. VALTA—*Continued*

References

    Lit Digest 123:26 Jl 10 '37 por

    Who's Who in Library Service

Obituaries

    Pub W 140:1134 S 20 '41

PARMOOR, CHARLES ALFRED CRIPPS, 1ST BARON Oct. 3, 1852—June 30, 1941 British statesman; father of Sir Stafford Cripps, England's Ambassador to Russia; began his public career as a lawyer, specializing in ecclesiastical law; in 1895 was made Attorney General to King Edward VII and continued in this position under Kings George V and Edward VIII; in Parliament from 1895 to 1914 as a Conservative, though with views that became increasingly progressive; strong pacifist who after the First World War was one of the architects of the Protocol to the League Covenant which provided for compulsory arbitration of international disputes and who continued to work for peace all his life; made Lord President of the Council when Labor came to power in 1929 and also served as leader of the House of Lords; knighted in 1908 and elevated to the peerage in 1914 on his appointment to the Judicial Committee of the Privy Council.

References

    Ann Pol et Litt 98:51 Ja 15 '32

    Sat R 151:717 My 16 '31

    Who's Who

Obituaries

    N Y Times p21 Jl 2 '41

PARSONS, HERBERT COLLINS Jan. 15, 1862—May 23, 1941 Pioneer in probation work; executive director of the Massachusetts Child Council; was instrumental in development of the probation system; wrote numerous articles and books on probation.

References

    Who's Who in Government

Obituaries

    N Y Herald Tribune p10 My 24 '41

PATTERSON, ROBERT P(ORTER) Feb. 12, 1891- United States Under-Secretary of War

Address: b. War Department, Washington, D. C.; h. Garrison, N. Y.; 1545 35th St, N. W., Washington, D. C.

One day, near the end of July 1940, a square-shouldered, upright, slender buck private was doing kitchen police duty at the Business and Professional Men's Training Camp in Plattsburg, New York. But he was interrupted; told to lay down his paring knife and assume the duties of Assistant Secretary of War. Five months later, on December 19, 1940, the Senate approved his promotion to Under-Secretary of War.

It was hardly a Cinderella story, however. Judge and Captain Patterson had become a rookie at Plattsburg only because he felt he was "out of date and wanted to get up-to-date information on army service." "My hope," he said, "was that I might be useful in case of emergency." This military service was just part of a distinguished military and judicial career. Robert Porter Patterson was born and brought up in Glens Falls, New York, the son of Charles R. and Lodice E. (Porter) Patterson. He received his education at Union College in Schenectady, New York, which gave him a B. A. degree in 1912, and at Harvard Law School, from which he received his Bachelor of Laws degree in 1915, after having served as chairman of the *Harvard Law Review* and marshal of his class in his third year.

Right after graduation Patterson was admitted to the New York Bar and, except for service in the Army, he practiced law in New York for the next 15 years. His first position was with the firm of Root, Clark, Buckner and Howland, but it lasted only until 1916, when Patterson resigned to go to the Mexican border with the 7th Infantry. On May 15, 1917 he was commissioned a second lieutenant, Infantry Section, Officers' Reserve Corps, and was placed on active duty at the Reserve Officers' Training Camp, Plattsburg Barracks, New York. Three months later he was commissioned a captain of infantry and assigned to the 152nd Depot Brigade at Camp Upton, New York.

On April 13, 1918 Captain Patterson left the United States for service in France with the 306th Infantry. Abroad he served in the Baccarat, Vesle and Forêt-d'Argonne defensive sectors and in the Oise-Aisne and Meuse-Argonne offensives. For gallant and meritorious action on the night of August 11, 1918 he was cited in General Orders; for "extraordinary heroism in action" on August 14 he was awarded the Distinguished Service Cross. Two days later he was wounded in action, and he was again cited in General Orders for gallantry on September 26. On March 26, 1919 Patterson was promoted to major of infantry and assigned to command the 2nd Battalion, 306th Infantry. A month later he returned to the United States and on May 27, 1919 was honorably discharged from the military service.

The War over, Captain Patterson returned to the practice of law as a member of the firm of Murray, Aldrich and Webb and continued with this firm until in 1930 President Hoover appointed him Judge of the United States District Court, Southern New York District. In his years on this court he established a record for non-reversals in the higher courts. At the same time he managed to make a success of raising chickens and flowers on his farm at Garrison on the Hudson, from which he commuted daily to New York City. And he managed to find time to spend with his wife, the former Margaret T. Winchester, whom he had married in 1920, and their four children, Robert P., Aileen W., Susan H. and Virginia.

Although Judge Patterson was a Republican, in March 1939 President Roosevelt elevated him to the position of Judge of the Circuit Court of Appeals for the Second Circuit, the second highest court in the land. One of his more prominent decisions here was the upholding of the conviction of Earl Browder for passport fraud. It was this life-time position, at $12,000 a year, that he gave up in July 1941 for a temporary post as Assistant Secretary of War at $10,000 a year. According to some commentators his appointment was requested by Secretary of War Stimson, whom Patterson had known slightly during the War, when they served in the same division, and had grown to know well when both were distinguished attorneys in New York; according to others, Patterson was President Roosevelt's choice, a selection in which Secretary Stimson concurred.

One of Judge Patterson's first actions after his nomination as Assistant Secretary of War was to urge the adoption of a system of compulsory military training. This, said he, was the only democratic way to raise an army for the United States—an Army which, he estimated, should stand at 1,300,000 men. Less than a year later, before a Senate committee, he was insisting that to demobilize any part of the Army at that time would be to "court disaster." At the same time he was urging that the Secretary of War be given authority "to vitalize the active list of the Army, removing therefrom those officers who are unable to stand up under the strain to which they must be subjected if we are to build up a modern army capable of meeting the demands of modern combat."

Frequently the spokesman for the War Department, more than once Patterson addressed industry, which he felt had "been doing its full share in the defense program." To assure industry that certification of new plant facilities requested by contractors to qualify for five-year tax amortization would be "impartially administered," he appointed in April 1941 a civilian board of review. And he continually reassured industry to "feel no anxiety whatever" over industrial conscription amendments. One of these he presented in June 1941 to the Military Affairs Committee of the Senate; when a Congressional uprising threatened he presented a substitute, which, however, was rejected by the Administration as "too tame." A third property seizure bill was presented by Wayne Coy in its place.

Frequently, too, Captain Patterson addressed labor, appealing for full cooperation: "The War Department will never ask of labor any sacrifice which it does not at the same time ask of management and of invested capital," he once said. He urged, particularly in the strike of building trades workers at Wright Field, that union members be "patriotic Americans," working hard in the defense effort. To his pleas labor leaders listened, although some of them objected to his statement in October 1940 that "disputes with the Labor Board" would not be "the determining element

U. S. Army Signal Corps.

ROBERT P. PATTERSON

in the award of contracts" and to a later statement that trivial labor cases would not be permitted to stop work on a defense contract or prevent the award of one. Probably most discussion on his attitude toward the labor problem, however, centered about his proposal in March 1941 for a revival of the National War Labor Board which functioned in 1918. Such a board, he felt, was more important than the setting up of "cooling off" legislation or punitive measures. "We need every man hour of production, and there should be no strikes or stoppages," he said.

The main job that Patterson was given in the War Department was that of taking charge of the Army's procurement division, the asking branch of the Army, responsible for about 7,000 different items. In this position and as a member of the Army and Navy Munitions Board he requested a reduction in auto production of as much as 50 per cent in order to release men, materials and management for turning out planes and tanks; he appealed to industry to extend its in-plant training and increase the number of shifts and refrain from "pirating" labor; he awarded contracts with "reasonable" profits in mind; he pleaded for more technicians. A while ago someone described Secretary Patterson as "fast-moving, concise, with the habit of command." These are qualities needed in an Under-Secretary of War of a nation arming for defense and victory.

References

Am Mag 132:67 S '41 por
Christian Sci Mon p6 Jl 26 '40 por
Nation's Bus 29:15 Mr '41 por
N Y Sun p14 Jl 24 '40
Time 36:11 Ag 5 '40 por; 36:75 D 9 '40 por; 37:22 F 24 '41 por

(Continued next page)

PATTERSON, ROBERT P.—*Continued*

Who's Who in America
Who's Who in Government
Who's Who in Law

PAUL, PRINCE OF YUGOSLAVIA

1893- Former First Regent of Yugoslavia

Under normal conditions the coronation ceremony of Peter II of Yugoslavia would have taken place in September 1941. Prince Paul, who since Alexander's assassination had ruled the country as First Regent, would have formally handed over the kingdom to Alexander's son on his eighteenth birthday. (Assuming, of course, that certain rumors as to Paul's own attachment to the crown had no basis in fact.) When in March 1941 Prince Paul's Ministers signified his Government's adherence to the Nazi three-power pact, however, conditions in Yugoslavia were no longer normal even for the eternally troubled Balkans. It was March 27, two days later, when a *coup d'état* by anti-Axis Yugoslavian Army leaders caused Peter II to come into his Balkan inheritance a little prematurely. Prince Paul fled the country, seeking refuge in Greece, where he remained as the guest of King George during the short-lived Yugoslavian resistance to the Nazis. Then in April, according to one report, he was caught sending a cable in code to the Croat leader Matchek, and asked to leave.

Prince Paul, who was always a bit ill at ease as a Balkan ruler, was born in 1893. His mother was Russian, a member of the House of Demidoff; his cousin, Alexander, was the Crown Prince of Yugoslavia. He was educated in Switzerland, at the Lycée at Belgrade, where he was the high-ranking student, and in 1910 he went to England to take his degree at Oxford. Three separate Balkan wars, and finally the First World War, interrupted his studies. Each time he came home to take an officer's commission; each time he returned to Oxford to study philosophy and literature. He did not take his degree until 1921, however, and his long residence in England has since led Serbs to call him "too English"—probably more because of his tailoring and tastes than his politics.

By this time Alexander was on the throne. Prince Paul's life was perhaps more enviable than that of his royal cousin, however: a scholar and an esthete, he spent much of his time traveling about among European art centers, and he built for himself a home of snow-white marble several miles south of Belgrade. Alexander had other problems. It was true that post-War treaties and plebiscites had doubled Serbian territory and tripled its population, but there was little unity among its peoples. The new kingdom of Serbs, Croats and Slovenes, called Yugoslavia, had been formed partly in order to weaken the new Austria and the new Hungary, partly in order to keep Italy off the Dalmatian coast which was to have been its reward for participation in the War on the side of the Allies. Woodrow Wilson's vaunted liberation and unity of the South Slav peoples existed more in word than in deed, for in Yugoslavia it was the Serbs who ruled, and a nominally democratic constitution appeased the Croatian autonomists hardly at all. After 1929 threats of revolution led Alexander to dispose almost entirely of parliamentary rule.

It was 1934 when Alexander was assassinated. His will provided that Prince Paul, as his nearest competent adult relative, should rule as First Regent until Alexander's young son, Peter, a shy, rather neglected boy, came into his majority. (Peter II's eighteenth birthday was in September 1941). Two other regents were also named. Prince Paul, who had previously no greater responsibility than that of pacifying the Croats as Viceroy of Croatia, was probably not too happy. Gossips say that he could not sleep without sedatives during the first months of his regency. Nevertheless he had ambitious plans. He promised to be a more liberal ruler than Alexander—during his first year, at least. He fought the old Serbs when they tried to hush up Alexander's testament. He conferred scrupulously with the Croatian leaders. He persuaded his first Premier to release the chief of the Croat opposition from jail. He made himself easily accessible, and people weren't afraid to tell him the truth.

This phase was soon over, however. Paul's consort was Princess Olga of Greece, a niece of the last Czar of Russia and the sister of the British Duchess of Kent. "The Duchess of Kent brought Balkan fashions to London, and Princess Olga brought Hitler's emissaries to the White Palace." Paul, after entering into secret negotiations with the Nazis, ousted his Prime Minister. Milan Stoyadinovitch, the Premier and Foreign Minister appointed in June 1935, was far from being either a democrat or a liberal. Soon the typical election was once more the kind in which the opposition gets the votes and the government the seats in Parliament. Although Yugoslavia had formerly been in the French political orbit, Prince Paul himself had no love at all for Bolshevism or anything which he considered kindred to it, such as the Popular Front Government in France; in 1936 the pact of mutual assistance offered by French Foreign Minister Delbos was rejected by the Little Entente (Czechoslovakia, Romania, Yugoslavia).

At the same time the shadow of Germany and Italy grew longer in Yugoslavia. Germany was an excellent potential customer for grain, and Stoyadinovitch argued for the restoration of the trade with Italy which had been lost when sanctions were imposed at the time of Ethiopia. There were friendly conferences with Hitler and other Nazi leaders, who had for some time been wooing the Yugoslavians passionately. In March 1937 a five-year political and economic pact with Italy was signed, and Count Ciano received from Prince Paul the Grand Cross of the Order of the White Eagle. At the same time Italy promised that she wouldn't occupy Albania (a promise kept for nearly all of two years, and in March 1939 it became known that Paul had agreed to the Italian invasion). That the Yugoslav Army and peoples are almost without exception opposed to this pro-Axis orientation seemed to make little difference.

Then came Munich. It destroyed the Little Entente, built up by France after the War in order to curb Germany, and it alarmed Prince Paul. In December 1938 he spent a week in London discussing foreign affairs with British statesmen and attempting to increase British trade with Yugoslavia, whose main exports are corn, fruit, iron and bauxite. Early in 1939 Premier Cvetkovitch and Foreign Minister Cincar-Markovitch took the place of Stoyadinovitch. In August 1939 it seemed even that Prince Paul might contrive a Balkan coalition to obstruct Germany's apparent drive toward the southeast. But he was hesitant. Careful neutrality, a policy of remaining friends with everyone, was his aim and that of his ministers. He had no wish to antagonize Germany. If he seemed pro-Axis, he had once explained, it was because "I bow to necessity. I am a realist."

The Moscow-Berlin non-aggression pact in August 1939 had immediate joyous repercussions in Yugoslavia, if not everywhere. Prospects for Balkan peace seemed better. An enlarged Croatia was suddenly given wide local autonomy and its own Parliament. A new government was formed which included six Croats. "Democratization" decrees paved the way for parliaments in seven other provinces, and freedom of the press and of assembly was restored. But little of this was permanent. And Yugoslavia moved further and further into the Axis orbit. In October 1940 Premier Cvetkovitch signed a new trade pact with Germany by which 60 per cent of Yugoslavia's exports would go to the Reich. "Our collaboration is not only economic but political," he said. By 1941 the Government's position was extremely delicate, the fact that popular sentiment was far from being pro-German being only a complicating factor. When Prince Paul said farewell to the United States' Colonel Donovan (see sketch this issue) with a "Good luck, until we meet again," the Yugoslav magazine that printed the remark was at first suppressed, although later permitted distribution.

By February 1941, with Germany pouring troops into Bulgaria, apparently in preparation for a Nazi *coup* in Greece, Premier Cvetkovitch and Foreign Minister Cincar-Markovitch sped to Austria to hold conversations with Hitler and Von Ribbentrop (see sketch this issue). Conversations between Prince Paul and the German Minister to Belgrade followed, and it was predicted that Yugoslavia would sign the three-power pact. Nothing happened immediately, however, except mobilization orders on March 4; and when the Soviet statement condemning Bulgaria's surrender to Hitler's demands was published, the public reaction was one of hopefulness.

There were also rumors of growing Croat, Bosnian and Herzegovinian separatist sentiments; rumors that during the delay Yugoslavia was attempting to break down Greece's refusal to submit to a German-dictated peace; rumors

Yugoslav Consulate General

PRINCE PAUL OF YUGOSLAVIA

that the Yugoslavian Government would sign a "compromise" treaty of non-aggression and friendship with the Reich, plus a friendship pact with the Soviet Union as a sop to public sentiment. Yet by mid-March, many observers believed that diplomatic pressure by Britain, Turkey (and even the United States), as well as threats of revolution in the provinces and in the Army, had brought about a reversal in official policy. It seemed that, aided by Britain and Turkey, Yugoslavia might possibly resist both diplomatic and military aggression by Germany. For some reason the British trusted Paul, and Anthony Eden thought of him as his friend.

This last hope temporarily vanished when, on March 25, 1941, in Vienna, representatives of the Belgrade Government signed a protocol of adherence to the three-power pact identical to those signed previously by Hungary, Romania, Slovakia and Bulgaria. (Nazi troops were pledged not to cross the nation, however.) In the meanwhile angry demonstrations and mass resignations from the Cvetkovitch Cabinet continued at home, while Prince Paul attempted to soothe the inflamed anti-German peasantry. He was unsuccessful. On March 27 Yugoslav Army leaders overthrew the Regency and Cabinet and made Peter II monarch in his own right. It was only a month later, however, that Peter followed Paul to Greece. Later Peter went to London, where he hoped to become an RAF pilot. Paul was reported to be in the Near East. His exact whereabouts remains a secret.

The unfortunate Prince Paul is tall and good-looking, with a "lofty forehead" and a "self-willed chin." He is said to have a pleasant personality. He loves books, music, pictures (he collects paintings), and the life of a

PAUL, PRINCE OF YUGOSLAVIA—
Continued

country gentleman, but apparently has a taste for authority and pomp and ceremony as well. His French and English are perfect. His one son was born in 1924. He is the founder of Prince Paul's Museum, a president of the Red Cross, and a General in the Royal Yugoslav Horse Guards. He would like to die in bed, but it doesn't seem likely: only one Karageorgeovitch ruler has succeeded in doing it. He, poor man, was insane.

References

Eur Nouv 22:455-6 Ap 29 '39
Liv Age 350:509-11 Ag '36
N Y Herald Tribune p1, 3 Mr 8 '41 por
N Y Sun p24 Mr 4 '41
N Y Times p3 Mr 28 '41
Newsweek 13:24 Je 19 '39 por; 14:21 S 4 '39 por
Scholastic 34:20 F 4 '39 por
Time 32:20-2 D 12 '38 il por; 38:31+ Ap 7 '41 por
Gunther, J. Inside Europe p457-8 1940
International Who's Who
Roucek, J. S. Politics of the Balkans p77-80 1939
Simone, A. Men of Europe p180-91 1941

PAXTON, WILLIAM MCGREGOR June 22, 1869—May 13, 1941 American artist called "court painter" of Philadelphia because he had painted so many portraits of distinguished natives of that city; painted portraits of Presidents Grover Cleveland and Calvin Coolidge; excelled at interiors; work often compared to that of the great Flemish masters, especially Vermeer; career spanned half a century of American art, during which he won many honors.

References

Who's Who in America
Who's Who in American Art

Obituaries

N Y Times p21 My 14 '41

PEARL, RAYMOND June 3, 1879—Nov. 17, 1940 Biologist, authority on population statistics and professor at Johns Hopkins University for many years; was author of many popular books on longevity, genetics and population.

References

Commonweal 23:12-13 N 1 '35
Sch & Soc 52:523 N 23 '40
American Men of Science
Leaders in Education 1932
Who's Who Among North American Authors
Who's Who in America

RAYMOND PEARL

Obituaries

N Y Herald Tribune p16 N 18 '40 por
N Y Times p19 N 18 '40 por
Newsweek 16:6 D 2 '40 por
Pub W 138:2128 D 7 '40

PEARSON, DREW (ANDREW RUSSELL) Dec. 13, 1896- Newspaper and radio columnist
Address: b. 1265 National Press Bldg, Washington, D. C.; h. 2820 Dumbarton Ave, Washington, D. C.

ALLEN, ROBERT (SHARON) July 14, 1900- Newspaper and radio columnist
Address: b. 1265 National Press Bldg, Washington, D. C.; h. 1525 28th St, N. W., Washington, D. C.

The *Washington Merry-Go-Round* is the most successful of the columns that come out of the nation's capital, read by more than 20 million people. It is also heard by millions over NBC. Its authors, Drew Pearson and Robert Allen, keep it popular by "sheer journalistic competence," by turning up "more exclusive stories than any other column." They get their information everywhere—from Cabinet members, friendly newspapermen who can't use in their own papers the juicy tidbits they discover, Senators, hired legmen, clerks, the President himself.

Pearson, generally, scours the State Department, the Army, Navy, the Department of Justice, the Treasury and the diplomatic corps; Allen concentrates on "The Hill"—on the Senate, House—on labor, the Supreme Court, agriculture. Pearson gets much of his material by going to the "right" places, giving parties where Administration high lights gather, conducting delicate telephone conversations. Allen, unlike him, bursts into offices, beats news "out of his victim with a club. He shouts, roars, blusters at Government officials, is profane and disrespectful until someone lets out something exclusive."

These two men, whose teamwork has made them "minor political powers around the capital" before whom bold Congressmen tremble, have been conducting their column since 1932 when they both were fired from their jobs for writing the book *Washington Merry-Go-Round*. Both are newspapermen of long experience. Drew Pearson was born in Evanston, Illinois, the son of Paul Martin Pearson, a Quaker professor who became Governor of the Virgin Islands and was unseated after a Senate investigation, and Edna (Wolfe) Pearson. He went to Phillips Exeter Academy in Exeter, New Hampshire, from which he was graduated in 1915, and then on to Swarthmore College, which he left in 1919 with a Bachelor of Arts degree and a Phi Beta Kappa key.

He set out for Europe to learn about diplomacy, but wound up as a director of post-War relief in the Balkans for the British Red Cross—there's a town in the Balkans now named Pearsonavatz in his honor. Back in the United States in 1921 Pearson became an instructor of industrial geography at the University of Pennsylvania. This lasted only a year; then he signed on the *S. S. President Madison* out of Seattle as a seaman and headed for the East.

ROBERT ALLEN

DREW PEARSON

The ship landed in Yokohama and Pearson left it to wander north to Saghalien and Nikolaevsk and back again to Vladivostok. He arrived there broke, but was able to persuade a girl in the passport office to give him a passport in return for a bar of chocolate. With it he went on to Japan and from there along the China coast to the Philippines. Pearson finally landed in Australia,

where he talked a lecture bureau into taking him under its wing, and he proceeded to lecture for six months in that country and in New Zealand. From there he went on to England, after a stopover in India to talk to Gandhi. He was writing up what he saw and did for Australian newspapers by this time and for the next 10 years continued to supply papers there, in India and in South Africa with news.

Europe opened up for Pearson as Asia had. With a newspaper syndicate contract he traveled up and down its length, stopping at intervals to interview "Europe's Twelve Greatest Men." And then, in an anti-climactic sort of way, he returned in 1924 to academic life—this time to Columbia University, where he taught commercial geography. A year of teaching was enough this time, too, and by 1925 Pearson was off again to the East, to Japan, to China (where he reported the anti-foreign strikes), to the Tibetan border.

In 1926 Pearson seemed to settle down for a bit. The year before, he had married the Countess Felicia Gizycka, daughter of Eleanor (Cissy) Patterson of Washington newspaper fame, and he now obtained a position on the staff of the *United States Daily*. But his was a job that kept him hopping around. In 1927 he was in Geneva covering the Naval Conference for the Tokyo *Jiji* and Japan *Advertiser;* in 1928 he accompanied Secretary of State Kellogg on trips to Paris and Dublin, and President Coolidge to Havana. Then in 1929 (he was concurrently employed by the *United States Daily*) Pearson joined the staff of the Baltimore *Sun* and shortly afterward went abroad to cover the London Naval Conference. A year later he was in Cuba, re-

PEARSON, DREW and ALLEN, ROBERT—*Continued*

porting the Revolution there, writing stories good enough to win honorable mention for the Pugsley Award for the best journalistic work of the year. He was also kept busy in Washington as head of the *Sun's* bureau there. He described himself anonymously in *Washington Merry-Go-Round* as follows: "Drew Pearson, the *Sun's* expert on foreign affairs, has the reputation of knowing more about the State Department than most of the people who run it, and to a considerable extent this is true."

It was in Washington that Pearson came to know Robert Allen well enough to collaborate with him. At that time Allen was head of the Washington Bureau of the *Christian Science Monitor,* a young man with a long newspaper history behind him. Born in Latonia, Kentucky, the son of Harry and Elizabeth (Sharon) Allen, "Bob" had been reporting local events while still in grade school. He gave this up at the age of 16 to enlist in the Pershing expedition to Mexico. After chasing Villa down by the border, he entered the University of Wisconsin.

Pearson's college career was far from a simple academic one. It was interrupted by the War, during which he went overseas with the cavalry, served with the Army of Occupation and returned home a second lieutenant. It was more or less interrupted by a job as cub police reporter on the Madison, Wisconsin *Capital Times.* Nevertheless he won his degree in 1922 and a year later, after a period of political reporting on the Wisconsin *State Journal* and the Milwaukee *Journal,* he went abroad on a scholarship from his university.

He spent the year from 1923 to 1924 at the University of Munich. How much he actually studied is still unknown; what is known is that while he was in Munich the Ludendorf-Hitler *putsch* took place, and he reported it for the *Christian Science Monitor.* This did little to further his academic career; it did set him well on the way to his newspaper one. Impressed by his coverage of the *putsch,* the *Monitor* gave him a roving assignment which took him through Central Europe and Italy.

Back in the United States, Allen worked for the United Press Association in New York for a while and then went to Washington as head of the *Monitor's* Washington bureau. Here he covered the 1928 and 1932 Presidential campaigns, went with Hoover on his good-will tour of Latin America, published a book called *Why Hoover Faces Defeat* (1932), wrote a series of articles on the political situation of every European capital. In Washington, too, in 1929, he married Ruth Finney, ace Scripps-Howard Washington correspondent and an authority on Federal power projects. They have no children.

In those days when Allen worked for the *Monitor* and Pearson for the *Sun* the two men used to get together and plot how they could use all the inside material on the Hoover Administration that they both had gathered.

Time and again they would make discoveries that their own papers refused to publish—and Pearson was convinced "that even the so-called liberal papers in the United States are increasingly controlled by their cash registers and that one of the few outlets to free journalism is through the medium of books." Allen agreed with him, and the result was the anonymous publication in 1931 of *Washington Merry-Go-Round,* full of "the gossip which the Capital loves to whisper but hates to see in print."

Both this book and its successor, *More Merry-Go-Round* (1932) (they sold 190,000 copies), were called "irreverent", "amusing", "stimulating", "shrewd," as well as "petty, malicious, inaccurate, biased" and dull. Speculation was wide and open as to its author—every Washington correspondent was mentioned for the honor and at one point there was an almost confirmed rumor that it had actually been written by a dozen different men. Enlightenment came to Washington and the public in 1932 and with it came dismissal notices to Pearson and Allen.

They weren't without friends, however. When they decided to keep on with the spade-work they had started in their books with a column by the same name, United Features took them on. It was far from a success at first—only a few newspapers would buy it when they started off at the end of 1932. By January 1933, though, 18 papers were taking it; by May 1934, 270 subscribed, and the number of papers which buy it stands at almost 350 in 1941. In February of that year Pearson and Allen branched out into a side line, a comic strip called "Hap Hazard," with a Washington correspondent of that name as its hero, and the unusual feature of using the names and pictures of real persons for background individuals. They also spent 13 weeks at the beginning of the year broadcasting *News for the Americas* over NBC.

Since 1932 Pearson and Allen have been amusing some people, surprising others and getting even more just plain mad. And the people who get most angry at them aren't always the victims of their disclosures; very often they are the other newspaper correspondents who have been soundly scooped, despite the fact that the *Washington Merry-Go-Round* column is written five days before publication and mailed to the subscribing papers. This means that for many years, and occasionally even now, its authors worked 19 hours a day and took no vacations. Pearson would go to bed at 1 and be up at 6; Allen would start sleeping at 3 and be up at 8.

Nevertheless they managed to do another book together, the *Nine Old Men* (1936) (its short sequel was *Nine Old Men at the Crossroads* [1937]), in which they "rip off the Supreme Court Justices' black robes and, with triumphant cynicism, find living, breathing mortals." To do this book, "buzzing with tittle tattle," they scouted all over for information and then settled down to the actual writing, with Pearson starting work at midnight and keeping on as long as he could and Allen jumping in at 6 in the morning and lasting until noon. To insure uniformity they traded the completed sections and partly rewrote them.

Their success together didn't keep these two men from writing apart from each other once in a while: there have been articles for important magazines and also a book called *The American Diplomatic Game* (1935), by Pearson in collaboration with Constantine Brown. Nor did it do anything to make "lithe, well-groomed," polished Pearson and "stubby, red-headed, carelessly dressed" Allen any more alike.

Pearson is one of the few columnists in Washington who receive society invitations and one of the few whose invitations are prized. The parties which he and his second wife, Luvie Moore (he was divorced from his first wife), give in their charming old colonial house in Georgetown are made bright by the presence of important and interesting people. Pearson enjoys himself at them and he also enjoys himself in the house's garden, one of the best in Washington, after the guests have gone. There are a cat, two black French poodles, a pond full of goldfish with names like Harry Hopkins and Harold Ickes, two children (a daughter of Pearson's by his first wife and a son of Mrs. Pearson's by her first husband). Pearson has a clipped mustache, brown hair that is growing less every day, and a slight tendency toward "Anthony Edenism."

Allen lives in Georgetown, too, and likes gardening as much as his collaborator does— he is said to get up early in summers to scrub the stalks of his dahlias with soap and water. Unlike Pearson, he rides horseback with the officers at Fort Myers, gives few parties and goes to few. He fumes, swears, chews gum incessantly. "An emotional, hard-boiled little man," he is so angry with Hitler now, according to Quincy Howe, "that he has his wife drilling with a gun." *Time* calls him "the Neanderthal type of liberal"; his partner "the parlor mauve type."

References

Collier's 103:11+ Ap 22 '39 pors
Lit Digest 118:13 Ag 25 '34
Time 33:34 F 13 '39 por

America's Young Men [R. Allen]
America's Young Men 1936-37 [D. Pearson]
Author's and Writer's Who's Who [D. Pearson]
Who's Who in America
Who's Who in the Nation's Capital

PEASE, CHARLES G(IFFIN) Dec. 4, 1854—Oct. 7, 1941 Founder and president of the Non-Smokers' Protective League of America; crusader against tobacco, coffee, tea, meat, liquor, condiments and chocolate; achieved passsage of ordnance forbidding smoking in the New York subways; was physician and dentist.

References

Outlook 135:141 S 26 '23 por

American Medical Directory
Who's Who in America

Obituaries

N Y Herald Tribune p18 O 9 '41 por
Time 38:22 O 20 '41

PEIRSE, SIR R(ICHARD) E(DMUND) C(HARLES) (pûrs) 1892- Air Chief Marshal of Britain's R. A. F., in charge of the Bomber Command

Address: b. Air Ministry, Berkeley Square House, London, W. 1; h. 29 The Vale, Chelsea, London, S. W. 3, England

As 1941 sped on, day by day, night by night, the British bombing offensive against Germany and German-occupied territory grew greater and greater. There had been a time when Britain's defensive action called for fighter planes that could vanquish enemy raids. But today operations were different. Britain's policy had become one of defending England along the French coast and in any part of Germany that bombers could reach effectively, a policy which called for long range bombers of heavy striking power.

British Press Service
SIR R. E. C. PEIRSE

The head of the men in Stirlings, Hampdens, Whitleys, Halifaxes and American-made Boeing Flying Fortresses is Sir R. E. C. Peirse, commanding Britain's bombing organization on the well built foundations of Sir Charles Portal (see sketch this issue). He is the son of an admiral, the late Sir Richard Peirse, K. C. B. Born at Croydon, he went to Monkton Combe School and then went on to the famous training ship *Conway*, moored in the Mersey in normal times, which as a rule prepares boys for officers' posts in the merchant service rather than for the Navy.

Peirse then spent a short time at King's College, London, and when in the early flying days the Admiralty called for air volunteers, he at once put his name down. He took his pilot's certificate (No. 460) at Brooklands in

PEIRSE, SIR R. E. C.—*Continued*

February 1913 when airplanes were really "crates." And when the First World War came, he was ready.

Early in 1914 he went to France with the famous squadron commanded by Commander Samson, and all through the War he saw distinguished service. In January 1915 he won the D. S. O. for a sustained and gallant series of attacks on U-boat bases at Zeebrugge, carried out in the teeth of heavy anti-aircraft fire, and successful even though his machine was hit. Later he served in Gallipoli and Italy and won the Air Force Cross.

During the War, in 1915, Peirse married Joyce, daughter of Armitage Ledgard of Thorner, Yorkshire. The War over, he remained in the R. A. F. as a professional officer and between 1929 and 1930 served in the Middle East. It was in 1930 that he first found himself in a post of great responsibility, becoming deputy director of Operations and Intelligence at the Air Ministry. In 1933 he was sent to Palestine and there formed for the first time a combined staff coordinating land, sea and air services. He stayed there for three years.

In 1939 Peirse became a member of the Air Council and in April 1940 vice-chief of the Air Staff. At this time he was knighted as K. C. B. (he had been made a Companion of the Bath in 1936). The position of vice-chief was a newly created one, inaugurated by Prime Minister Chamberlain in response to pressure from the British High Command for "stand-ins" for the heads of each of the fighting services. Actually, however, Peirse's promotion was a rise in title only, for he was already deputy chief of the Air Staff. In October of that same year, when Portal succeeded Newall as supreme chief of the R. A. F., Peirse took over the Bomber Command from Portal, his job the scientific planning of a campaign to wear down German industry. It was a job complicated by many problems: the enormous size of Germany, the variety of targets, the shortage of machines—but observers agreed that Peirse would be able to handle it.

He is proud of the length of time he himself has been flying. "I am still as good a pilot as I ever was, thank goodness!" he says. He gets a kick out of speeding his auto along, too, when the road is clear. Outside of this, he has a mild private interest in archeology. He is tall, broad-shouldered, efficient in a way that dates back to his nautical training days. And he believes in his work. "Those Elizabethans," he once said, "were men after my own heart, but I feel that to be part of the Royal Air Force in this century is the next best thing. I believe in the Service not only as a unit of defense, but as a school for character out of which the future will be built."

References

> Gt Brit & East 47:620 O 29 '36 por
> Ministry of Information Clip Sheet 26 Jl 3 '40
> Who's Who

PEIXOTTO, ERNEST (CLIFFORD) (pȧ-shō′tô) Oct. 15, 1869—Dec. 6, 1940 Mural painter and illustrator and former member of the New York Municipal Art Commission; his work was represented in the National Gallery at Washington and in public buildings in many parts of the country; was author of a number of travel books.

ERNEST PEIXOTTO

References

> Mag Art 32:372 Je '39
> Sat R Lit 9:613-15 My 27 '33
> Who's Who in America
> Who's Who in American Art
> Who's Who in American Jewry

Obituaries

> N Y Times p17 D 7 '40 por

PENN, ARTHUR A. Feb. 13, 1880—Feb. 6, 1941 Musician and composer; born in England and came to the United States in 1903; wrote more than 30 operettas of which the best known were *Yokohama Maid, Your Royal Highness, The Lass of Limerick Town* and *The China Shop*; the popular song *Smilin' Through* which he wrote in 20 minutes gained him greatest recognition; title of song was later used for a Jane Cowl play and two films.

References

> Baker's Biographical Dictionary of Musicians 1940
> Who's Who in America
> Wier, A. E. ed. Macmillan Encyclopedia of Music and Musicians 1938

Obituaries

> N Y Times p19 F 7 '41 por
> Variety 141:46 F 12 '41

PENNER, JOE Nov. 11, 1904—Jan. 10, 1941 Stage, radio and film comedian famous for his "Wanna Buy a Duck?" and "You Na-aasty Man"; born Josef Pinter in Hungary, he first started working in America in carnivals and graduated into vaudeville and musical shows; became widely known when he entered radio in 1933 as guest on Rudy Vallee's program; was playing in road company of *Yokel Boy* at time of his death.

References

Movie Classic 7:52+ D '34 por
Photoplay 46:71+ S '34 il por; 48:32-3+ N '35 il pors
Sat Eve Post 207:30+ N 10 '34
Time 24:46 D 3 '34
International Motion Picture Almanac
Variety Radio Directory

Obituaries

N Y Times Ja 11 '41
Newsweek 17:8 Ja 20 '41 por
Time 37:76 Ja 20 '41
Variety 141:24 Ja 15 '41

PENNIMAN, JOSIAH H(ARMAR) July 20, 1868—Apr. 10, 1941 Educator and author, who served both as provost and president of the University of Pennsylvania during his 43-year affiliation with the institution; retired as president of the University in 1926, but continued as provost.

References

Leaders in Education 1941
Who's Who in America
Who's Who in American Education

Obituaries

N Y Herald Tribune p18 Ap 11 '41
Sch & Soc 53:506 Ap 19 '41

PEPPER, CLAUDE (DENSON) Sept. 8, 1900- United States Senator from Florida *Address*: b. United States Senate, Washington, D. C.; h. Tallahassee, Fla.

Claude Pepper, United States Senator from Florida, is probably the most articulate and vociferous exponent in Congress of the urgency for aid to the Allies. An early assignment to the Senate Foreign Relations Committee, a trip to Europe and one look at Hitler gave birth in him to undying hatred of Nazism and an unconquerable belief that unless England is victorious America is doomed.

As early as May 1940 he was urging "aid short of war" to a more or less apathetic Senate. To them he said: "We can turn the scale of battle by goods and by money and by airplanes, and perhaps even more—by a straightforward manly declaration that we have enough self respect and enough affection for the institutions of democracy to tell Hitler and Hitlerism that we are his eternal and mortal enemy and that it is our will that as a political power he shall be destroyed from the face of the earth." By June he had evolved a definite program for America, a

CLAUDE PEPPER

seven-point program which involved conscription of industry and labor and giving the President power to suspend any law he felt might interfere with national defense. Later, it was Senator Pepper who presented the question of the transfer of over-age destroyers to England in the Senate and pioneered the compulsory military training bill.

Hardly a day went by in the summer and fall of 1940 in which Senator Pepper didn't tell the Senate that the United States must do everything possible to destroy Hitler. "If we are not willing to make up our minds that we are facing a new kind of a war and a new kind of a world, then I venture to predict, sadly, that we are going to lose that kind of a war and our kind of a world," was the gist of his message.

With the growth of pro-British sentiment in the nation Senator Pepper found that most of his program was being translated into action. He found, too, that some were vociferously opposed to his interventionist sentiments. At the end of August a group of women ("Mothers of the United States of America" and the "Congress of American Mothers") surrounded him in the Senate reception room, denounced his stand on conscription and strung up an effigy of him labeled "Claude (Benedict Arnold) Pepper" on Capitol Hill. The Senator was unperturbed. He told reporters that "their hanging of me in effigy is a splendid demonstration of what we all desire—freedom of speech and freedom of action." But the next day he warned the Senate: "Sometimes we do not know when we are being made the instrument of sinister forces, designed to accomplish not good but evil."

In 1941 he remained a firm supporter of President Roosevelt's foreign policy. He continued to urge America to "get tough"; he backed aid to Russia; he branded the film inquiry, a "witch hunt" and himself appeared

PEPPER, CLAUDE—*Continued*

in a propaganda motion picture short, *Victory From the West,* dealing with the question of whether the United States can produce enough military materials to help defeat Hitler. Attacks on him continued to be made, however, by those opposing intervention.

It has been generally believed that Senator Pepper, an ardent New Dealer and zealous supporter of the President, acts not only from personal conviction, but on the suggestion of the President. Senator Pepper's campaign in the spring of 1940 for the sale of war materials to the Allies came right after a long, confidential talk at the White House, and the New York *Herald Tribune* commented: "It has long been suspected that when the White House has an important balloon to send up it invites Senator Pepper to supply the necessary oratorical helium for the ascension."

Despite this impression, Senator Pepper is "generally credited with being earnest, sincere and honest," and has had that reputation ever since he started to practice law in 1925. He is one of those statesmen who have come up the hard, American way. His father, Joseph Wheeler Pepper, was a farmer near Dudleyville, Alabama, where he was born (his mother was Lena [Talbot] Pepper); and Claude, "probably the ugliest little squirt" around, had to start work when he was a boy. But he was ambitious, and it is told that the words, "Claude Pepper, United States Senator," were inscribed by him in the bark of a tree at Camp Hill, Alabama when he was 10.

After school in Alabama, young Pepper taught grammar and high school, emptied coal and ashes in a power plant and worked in a steel mill to support himself during his first semester at Alabama State University. Then came comparative comfort with a job running a dining hall, and though it took a good deal of time, he was able to make the track team and be graduated with honors and a Phi Beta Kappa key in 1921. Three years at Harvard Law School followed, with an LL. B. acquired in 1924.

After Harvard, Pepper taught law at the University of Arkansas for a year. Then he was admitted to the Florida Bar in 1925 and went into practice for himself at Perry. It wasn't long before he entered politics. In 1928 he became a member of the State Democratic Committee and stumped for Al Smith, and one year later he became a House member of the Florida State Legislature. After his term there he moved his practice to Tallahassee, became a member of the State Board of Public Welfare in 1931, and in 1933 of the State Board of Law Examiners.

In 1934 Pepper decided to capitalize on the name he had made for himself throughout the State and ran for United States Senator. He was defeated by 4,050 votes. In 1936, the year he was married to pretty Irene Mildred Webster, he ran without opposition for the unexpired term of Florida's Senator Duncan Fletcher and in 1938 he campaigned for a full six-year term. Endorsed by President Roosevelt through his son James, who said: "It is

our sincere hope that he will be returned to the Senate," his platform was a simple one. Pepper was for fair wages and reasonable hours, the old-age revolving-pension plan, for relief and WPA, and for the New Deal. He himself stated it even more simply: "It is time somebody in authority got in to do some fighting for the poor white man in the South. I have been up in Washington fighting and I will continue to do so."

Returned to the Senate, Pepper continued to support the New Deal, its borrowing and spending policy, its foreign policy, its relief policy. In 1938 the *New Republic* wrote of "his record of having gone down the line with the Administration on every issue," and stated that "his utterances in the Senate are for the most part simply the voice of Hyde Park in the drawling accents of northwest Florida."

In 1938 and 1939 Senator Pepper won a lot of attention and aroused much violent controversy with his bill (sponsored in the House by Representative Pepper) designed to incorporate all competent persons employed by the Federal Arts Project of the WPA into a permanent Federal Fine Arts Bureau. Immediately it won A F of L and CIO support and endorsement from the American Artists Congress, the Juilliard Graduate School, Actors Equity and other groups. Burgess Meredith, acting president of Equity, said of it: "Its fundamental purpose . . . is to establish a democratic art. . . No painter ever was helped by an empty stomach." It was opposed by people like Gutzon Borglum and Walter Damrosch, who summed up the objections by calling the bill "a relief measure on a huge scale instead of an effort to further art in its highest form," and by Otis Skinner who cried: "Good God, you can't legislate genius!" Reported favorably out of committee, the Pepper-Coffee bill was never passed. Pepper won cheers from liberals again in March 1941 when he introduced the Geyer anti-poll-tax bill in the Senate.

Whether he is supporting a fine arts bill or the sending of supplies abroad, Senator Pepper is "a most articulate person and a rough and ready debater," whose speeches are frequently punctuated by passionate passages. Mussolini, he warned, "will feel the sting of America's lash upon his body and he will crawl like a scourged slave to an ignoble dungeon" if Italy entered the European War. When he delivers his orations, his stocky figure and pock-marked face are full of energy, his black hair tosses about. According to *Time* he is "not well-liked in the Senate," yet there is no doubt of his influence on the voters back home in Florida, nor of the importance of his position as an exponent of President Roosevelt's policies, nor of the strength and honesty and effectiveness of his convictions.

References

Christian Sci Mon Mag p19 D 16 '36
New Repub 95:97-8 Je 1 '38; 102:822
    Je 17 '40
Newsweek 11:27 Mr 21 '38; 11:9-10 My
    16 '38 por; 15:33 Je 24 '40

PEW, JOSEPH N(EWTON), JR. Nov.
12, 1886- Vice-president of the Sun Oil Company

Address: b. 1608 Walnut St, Philadelphia, Pa;
h. Mill Creek Rd. & Dodd's Lane, Ardmore,
Pa.

Joseph N. Pew, Jr., one of the angels of the
Republican Party, has been called "the latest
model of political boss," with headquarters in
Philadelphia. According to *Time,* "all he
wants is a Republican United States Government." This hope flickered and went out like
a candle when Roosevelt was re-elected for the
third term, but Republican Governor James
(see sketch 1940 *Annual*) of Pennsylvania is
still there. According to *Fortune,* Pew has put
more than $2,000,000 into the Republican
Party. The money came from the oil wells
of the Sun Oil Company (Sunoco), of which
he is vice-president, and from the shipyards
of its affiliate, the Sun Shipbuilding & Dry
Dock Company, on whose board he serves as
a chairman.

Joseph Newton Pew, Jr., was born on
November 12, 1886, in Pittsburgh, the second
son of Joseph Newton and Mary Catherine
(Anderson) Pew. The Pews had always had
something to do with oil; his mother's family
pioneered in the oil fields, and in 1859 the
Pews were in Pennsylvania's first oil boom.
Joseph Pew, Sr., bought up properties right
and left and in 1901 founded the Sun Oil
Company with the idea of refining and distributing along the Eastern seaboard. In 1908
Joseph Pew, Jr., who had been educated at
Shadyside Academy and Cornell, came home
with the degree of mechanical engineer, and
began learning the oil business by laying pipes,
watching wells, building roads when necessary.
In 1912 Joseph Pew, Sr., died, leaving the
company to his sons, John Howard and Joseph,
and to his daughters.

The boys did well with the company their
father started. Brother John Howard piloted
it through the War. The founding of the
shipyard (Sun Shipbuilding & Dry Dock Company) belonged to that period when oil tankers
had to be built to ship lubricants to Europe.
Under the shrewd Pew management the company grew rich; by 1920 Sunoco grossed
$53,000,000 and netted $8,000,000, and the Pews
were able to get sole control of their company,
which they had up to then shared with the
United Gas Improvement Company. Since then
Sun Oil has been tightly held by the family
because of its policy of little outside financing.
In 1941, out of 2,435,000 shares of common
stock, the Pews own about 1,770,000; Joseph
Pew, as vice-president, owns 272,000. With
the company comfortably launched, he married
a pretty Philadelphia girl, Alberta C. Hensel,
settled down in fashionable Ardmore and began
leading a quietly social life along the Main
Line.

Acme

JOSEPH N. PEW, JR.

The Sun Oil Company continued expanding
during the '20s. They improved the quality
of their product by erecting the first mercury
vapor plant in the United States at Marcus
Hook. During that time, too, they initiated
their policy of putting only one grade of gasoline on the market—a policy that meant not
only a far more effective advertising appeal
but also considerable saving in labor and equipment.

Of even more far-reaching importance was
their decision to construct a series of gasoline
pipe lines from their refinery at Marcus Hook
to Newark, Cleveland, Syracuse. This decision was made during the depression, and it
took considerable courage to make it. It was
Joseph Pew who was responsible for persuading the company to take this step, which gave
Sunoco a low-cost distribution in the East
and Midwest. The profits made by the company in later years stemming back to this
step have caused Howard Pew to remark that
"the depression was in many ways the best
period we ever had." It was Joseph Pew who
was entrusted with the task of laying the pipes
—a task which necessitated considerable tact
and finesse. He had to secure over 1,000 permits to cross highways, 183 to cross railroads,
34 to cross rivers and canals and about 1,000
easements on property from landholders. Joseph
proved himself a skillful diplomat and obtained
a training which later proved useful in his
political career.

Today the earning emphasis of Sunoco has
shifted from refineries to pipe lines and
shipping. The Sun Shipbuilding & Dry Dock
Company earned for the Pews $3,500,000 during 1939 and 1940, and in 1941 the boom was
mounting. The labor problem, incidentally, is
much more acute in shipping than in the oil
enterprise, and in the summer of that year
there was a labor violation claim outstanding.
The four gasoline lines earn $1,000,000 yearly

PEW, JOSEPH N., JR.—*Continued*

for the Pews, as does a Texas line of crude
oil. And in 1941 Sunoco is the fifteenth largest
oil enterprise in the United States, a highly
integrated company used to adjusting itself
swiftly to economic conditions. An example
of this is its financing in 1936 of the Houdry
process. It became party, however, to a general suit against most integrated companies in
the oil industry charging monopolistic practices, and in 1941 it seemed possible that Thurman Arnold would bring those charges after
the Elkins Act suits were cleared away—although it also seemed possible that defense
pressure would prevent that. As a highly
individual enterprise Sunoco has been intransi-
gent toward the Government—an attitude reflected in Joseph Pew's political convictions—
and independent in its dealings with the rest
of the industry.

In 1932 Joseph Pew, although a staunch Republican all his life, was not inimical toward
Franklin Roosevelt. This attitude lasted until
the New Deal tried to insert a price-fixing
clause in the NRA Code. Joseph Pew, who
holds that "price-fixing is an evil, wicked
thing," was outraged. He sought recourse in
the Republican headquarters in Washington
and was horrified by the atmosphere of ruin
and desolation that prevailed there: "The office was deserted except for underlings and
one minor official who had dropped in to
answer his social correspondence." A disgruntled Republican in search of a party,
Joseph Pew, who had by this time become convinced that "the Government has become dangerously personalized" and that Roosevelt was
bent on stifling private enterprise, went back
to Pennsylvania. There, with a state machine
perfected by men like Penrose and Vare, he
expected to find some activity. There, too,
he was disappointed.

Pew decided that this sort of thing would
not do. "Democracy cannot attain its desired
end unless there is political opposition—co-
hesive, even if scattered; vocal, even if small;
active, even if not powerful," he claimed.
He put his convictions and his money to
work. As *Time* states: "He became Pennsylvania's G. O. P. boss by the simple but tremendous expedient of putting up the money."
He worked inconspicuously but with phenomenal success. In 1935 he bought the *Farm
Journal*, a rural publication with more than
1,000,000 circulation, to be used to swing the
rural vote into the Republican fold. He later
merged it with *The Farmer's Wife*, and together with other members of the Pew family
got control of the Chilton Press, which publishes *The Iron Age* and a string of other
trade magazines. And he preached to businessmen and joined forces with men like Colonel
Estes of Texas, whom he knew from the oil
business.

In 1935 Pew suffered a setback when a
Democratic candidate won the race for the
Mayoralty in Philadelphia while Pew was
"salmon fishing off Anacostia Island." Another setback followed when Alfred Landon
lost the Presidential election in 1936. But in

1938, with spirits lifted by rumors of the
G. O. P.'s resuscitation, he set about electing
Arthur H. James, with more success. The
State party spent close to $1,200,000 in the
James campaign, and, according to *Fortune*
(August 1939), the Pews had contributed 20
per cent of that sum.

A few days after the election Joseph Pew
sailed for Europe after making a statement
to the effect that he wanted no voice in
Cabinet making. Nevertheless his practice of
shoveling the money out to heelers and hench-
men ("You can't get votes by advertising for
them," he has remarked urbanely) has since
brought on his head many a charge of corrupt
politics. Mentioned as being behind James'
anti-New Deal legislation, perhaps he mis-
judged the effect of his backing, for in the
1940 election Pennsylvania went Democratic;
but whatever he failed to do, Pew helped to
bring to the forefront of the State party
many new faces: among them Jay Cooke, IV,
Philadelphia's Republican city chairman, whom
Pew headed toward the Senate; another of
them Moe Annenberg, the racing sheet publisher, later put in prison, who had once
ranged his Philadelphia *Inquirer* behind Pew.
In 1941 the Republicans once more emerged
triumphant in the Philadelphia municipal elections.

Pew, of course, has contributed heavily to
the national reorganization of the Republican
Party, working hand in hand with Old Guard
magnates like Ernest Weir (see sketch this
issue), Joe Grundy, etc. He contributed to the
vigorous shaking up all down the line, and
in 1940 went to the Republican Convention to
cast his own vote and, as *Time* had it, to
dictate 71 others. It was only with reluctance
that on the last ballot he released the Pennsylvania votes to Willkie, who had earlier declared
that he was "100 per cent against his policy of
turning the Republican Party back to the days
of Harding and Coolidge."

Joseph N. Pew's main interest is in politics
rather than in business. But he likes to spend
his spare time in his country estate in upper
Chester County, where he keeps a superb
stable of Percherons and a herd of cows. The
house is a broad, yellow stone, spacious Pennsylvania farmhouse surrounded by rolling green
acres. Six feet tall, with black, bushy eyebrows, a shrewd long upper lip and "a quick
humorless smile," Pew is, unlike his brother
John Howard, an expansive spender. Together
with his salary as vice-president he gets about
$300,000 yearly from the Sun Oil Company.
He has a son still in college and three
daughters.

References

> Fortune 23:50-9+ F '41 il pors
> Time 35:15-18 My 6 '40 pors
> Who's Who in Commerce and Industry

PHELAN, MICHAEL F(RANCIS)

(fā'lǎn) Oct. 22, 1875—Oct. 12, 1941 United
States Representative from Massachusetts
from 1913 to 1921; as chairman of the House
Banking and Currency Committee helped

frame the Federal Reserve Act; in 1937 appointed to Merrimac Valley Sewage Commission; later named chairman of the Massachusetts State Labor Relations Board.

References

American Catholic Who's Who
Who's Who in America 1928-29

Obituaries

N Y Herald Tribune p10 O 13 '41

PHILOFF, BOGDAN (DIMITROV) (fĕl-ŏf' bŏg-dän') Apr. 10, 1883- Prime Minister of Bulgaria

Address: Sofia, Bulgaria

Every mouthful of the Balkan pie that Hitler has swallowed has been watched with horrified fascination by the rest of the world. During much of 1941 this unflattering attention was focused on little Bulgaria, which for the second time in 25 years cast her lot with Germany. Her decision was particularly important because, besides being a buffer between Greece and Germany, Bulgaria had also long been considered the spearhead of a possible Pan-Slav movement in the Balkans.

The Bulgarian *Anschluss* took place when Bogdan Philoff, the scholarly, corpulent Premier of Bulgaria, went to Vienna to sign up with the Axis—a ceremony that had been performed by many statesmen before him. Bulgaria was the seventh nation to adhere to the Axis pact, which provides, mainly, that the signatories pledge mutual support to each other in the event any one of them is attacked.

Considerable diplomatic spadework was done around Premier Philoff in the months preceding Bulgaria's capitulation to the Nazi advance in the Balkans. During that time his itinerary was watched with great interest and anxiety. On January 1, 1941 Professor Philoff and his wife went to Vienna, ostensibly to consult Dr. Hans Eppinger, a Viennese specialist, about the Premier's stomach ulcers. But at the same time (although the Premier denied it) it is probable that another specialist was consulted—the German Foreign Minister Joachim von Ribbentrop (see sketch this issue). After Professor Philoff's return to Sofia, it was noticed that German military "experts and technicians" in civilian uniforms began to filter into Bulgaria.

The legitimate anxiety aroused by these ominous symptoms was somewhat assuaged by a speech Professor Philoff made on January 12, 1941, at Ruschuk. He stated uncompromisingly that Bulgaria stood for peace in the Balkans and he reaffirmed this statement of policy after Churchill's warning speech on February 9. On February 14, Turkey and Bulgaria signed a non-aggression pact which was deprecated by the British in view of the Bulgarians' growing Axis-ward tendency.

On March 3, after having finally signed his name to the pact with the Axis, Professor Philoff came back to his country to submit it to the Bulgarian single-chamber Parliament. Ironically enough he found Bulgaria celebrating its national Independence Day, and as thanks were being given in the domed Sofia cathedral

Bulgarian Legation

BOGDAN PHILOFF

for the deliverance from Turkish rule 63 years ago, the echoes of religious music mingled with the roar of German Army motorcycles streaming across Bulgaria to the Greek frontier. Professor Philoff explained to his Parliament the situation into which Bulgaria had been forced by the pressure of events, touched on Germany's aiming "temporarily . . . at safeguarding the peace of the Balkans." He also "warmly" thanked Germany for "the important place in the new order accorded little Bulgaria." As he spoke another piece of the Balkan jigsaw puzzle was added to the New Order.

Through all these months the harassed Professor Philoff has been brought to increasing prominence, unhappily riding the crest of the tidal wave of Nazi aggression in the Balkans. Right now he is the man whom history will hold responsible for Bulgarian adhesion to the German fortunes. This has been brought home to him in many ways—in Churchill's warning, in Ambassador George Rendel's chilly leave-taking. Yet this man, who must from now on watch the future with great anxiety, most of his life has been concerned solely with the past. Before he headed the Bulgarian Government he was best known as an archeologist, an authority on ancient Greece.

Bogdan Philoff was born on April 10, 1883, the son of Lieutenant Colonel Dimitri Philoff and his wife Elisabeth. His birthplace was Stara Zagora, a town in central Bulgaria. He studied in Germany, at the universities of Leipzig, Freiburg and Bonn. Soon he became an important name in archeology. In 1906 he was made conservator of the National Museum in Sofia and in 1910 its director. He taught archeology and the history of art in the University of Sofia. An outstanding personality in the educational field, he belonged to a number of archeological and scientific institutions in

PHILOFF, BOGDAN—*Continued*

Europe (among them the Greco-Bulgarian Society). His chief interest is in ancient Greece, a subject with which he deals in many monographs and books. He has also written a great deal about the history of Bulgarian art. His scientific works have brought him a post of honor: presidency of the Bulgarian Academy of Sciences. Among his published works are: *Die Altbulgarische Kunst* (1919); *Die Archaische Nekropole von Trebenischte* (1927); *Les Miniatures de la Chronique de Manassès* (1927); *Geschichte der Bulgarischen Kunst*, two volumes (1932, 1933); *Die Grabhügel Nekropole bei Duvanlij in Südbulgarien* (1934).

In November of 1938, during one of Premier Kiosseivanoff's periodical reshufflings of the Cabinet, Professor Philoff was given the portfolio of Public Instruction which he has kept to date, in conjunction with his other duties. Another member of that Cabinet was Ivan Bagryanoff, Minister of Agriculture, whose constant clashes with the Premier brought about another change of the Cabinet. On February 15, 1940 George Kiosseivanoff tendered to King Boris (see sketch this issue) the resignation of the eighth Cabinet he had formed. The cause of his resignation was supposed to be the King's refusal to drop the reputedly pro-German Minister of Agriculture. Professor Philoff was asked to take Kiosseivanoff's place as Premier and to choose his Cabinet.

Shrewd observers guessed that Philoff's Premiership was a temporary measure to save Kiosseivanoff's face, and that he would be soon replaced by the latter's enemy Bagryanoff. The plump, sedate professor, seemingly unaware of being the center of complicated political intrigues, in his acceptance speech promised to follow the policy of his predecessor in internal and foreign aspects. But this assurance failed to impress informed circles, who claimed that it was King Boris who ultimately dictated the policy of Bulgaria. And on the first anniversary of forming his Cabinet, Premier Philoff filled the Ministry of Agriculture with a notorious pro-German, Dimitri Kuscheff.

Professor Bogdan Philoff is a corpulent man, with a fat beak of a nose and scanty hair. His wife is the tall intellectual Eudoxie Pétéva, whom he married in 1932. There are no children. The Premier does not greatly relish his present post. The usual expression on his good-natured face is one of sadness and foreboding. Probably he appreciates only too well the irony inherent in the fact that Greece was brought to her knees through the offices of a man whose life's work had been the study of her antiquity.

References

Bulgarian British R 13:4 N-D '38 (por p3)
N Y Times p10 F 16 '40; p4 F 17 '40; p9 F 10 '41; pl, 37, pl, 38 Mr 2 '41; pl, 2 Mr 3 '41
Time 37:18 Ja 13 '41 por; 37:28-9 F 24 '41
International Who's Who
Who's Who in Central and East-Europe

PIERSON, WARREN LEE Aug. 29, 1896-
President of the United States Export-Import Bank

Address: Export-Import Bank, Washington, D. C.

Warren Lee Pierson, "a California lawyer with a sense of humor and a vast love of travel," is one of the key men today in Latin-American affairs, "official guardian of our enormous export trade." The Export-Import Bank which he heads lends money to exporters who wish to sell capital goods to foreigners who lack cash or are hampered by foreign exchange restrictions. It also lends money to foreign governments. In 1941 it is particularly active in making loans to help Latin America recover from the loss of European markets, in an attempt to thwart Germany and Italy, whose credit bureaus are particularly lenient.

Of the $700,000,000 provided by Congress to the Bank, almost $232,000,000 had been lent to Latin America by February 1941, Pierson announced. Brazil had received $20,-000,000 for a steel plant; the Dominican Republic had got $3,000,000 to build a slaughterhouse, community refrigerators and finish a large hotel; Venezuela received $3,000,000 for oil drilling machinery; Cuba was given a sum to develop its sugar industry; and other South American countries received similar loans. Pierson himself was active in the making of these loans: in the fall of 1940 he spent six months traveling through Latin America, straightening out details of the various credits, building up good will. And in March 1941 he sailed for Brazil on the first leg of a "general inspection tour," to "keep abreast of things in Central and South America," as Jesse Jones, Secretary of Commerce and Federal Loan Administrator, put it. He returned there again in August to look into new sources of war material and speed up production of material already contracted for, as well as to discuss credit operations.

These trips south are characteristic. Warren Lee Pierson has always been a man to solve problems in a practical way, by direct negotiations whenever possible. If he can't board a plane to where trouble exists, he finds out all about it by overseas telephone and gives advice over the wires. And in the same direct way diplomats, the heads of important national banks abroad, special representatives and industrialists coming to the United States to do business almost always call on Pierson after their more formal calls to the State Department.

This banker to much of the world was born in Princeton, Minnesota, the son of Louis W. and Hilda (Pearson) Pierson, but he was brought up and educated in California where his family moved when he was a boy. Here he attended the University of California and was graduated from it in 1917. He went right from college to France as an ambulance driver in the French Army and later enlisted in the A. E. F., which put him through an intensive course of training at the Saumur Artillery School. He served in the 101st

Regiment of Field Artillery and left the War a lieutenant.

Back in the United States, Pierson finished his interrupted education at Harvard Law School, which gave him an LL. B. in 1922. He immediately recrossed the country, passed his California Bar examination and settled down in Los Angeles as a lawyer, practicing successfully until 1933, when he was asked to come to Washington as counsel for the Re-

Underwood & Underwood
WARREN LEE PIERSON

construction Finance Corporation. He arrived there with his wife, Eleanor Shelton Mehnert, whom he had married in 1927, and has stayed there ever since. Since their marriage Mrs. Pierson has won independent fame as author of a mystery novel, *The Good Neighbor Murder*, (*The Defense Rests* is to be published in 1942) and as Mrs. Roosevelt's assistant at the Office of Civilian Defense.

In 1934 the Export-Import Bank was created to fill the need of providing credits for Russia. Pending the debt settlements between this country and the Soviet Union, the bank did nothing, and a second Export-Import Bank was set up to handle credits for Cuba. When the negotiations with Russia finally broke down, the two banks were merged with the power to lend to all nations. The new Export-Import Bank filled a longfelt need, for with almost every foreign nation in debt to the United States none had had money to buy United States products, and the country's banking system had possessed no machinery for providing foreign buyers with long-term credits.

When it was set up Pierson was made its general counsel and trustee. Two years later, in 1936, he became its president. Since then he has been active in financial negotiations all over the world, and particularly in the fertile field of South America. Today, more than

ever, his twinkling eyes and direct manner, his knowledge of South America and banking, are doing much to cement the Good Neighbor Policy.

References

Time 32:41 Ag 8 '38 por; 36:67 N 11 '40 por; 37:58+ F 10 '41 por
America's Young Men 1936-37
Who's Who in America
Who's Who in Commerce and Industry
Who's Who in the Nation's Capital

PILCHER, LEWIS F(REDERICK) May 1, 1871—June 15, 1941 Architect; state architect and commissioner of sites in New York, 1913 to 1923, when he became consulting architect to the United States Veterans' Bureau; among his works are the addition to Sing Sing Prison begun in 1919, the Terminal Dormitory at Vassar College and many projects completed for the War Department; taught at Vassar from 1900 to 1911, was vice-dean of the School of Fine Arts at the University of Pennsylvania from 1926 to 1929 and professor of architecture at Pennsylvania State College from 1929 to 1937; author of works on architecture.

References

American Art Annual 1924-25
Who's Who in America

Obituaries

N Y Times p15 Je 16 '41

PINZA, EZIO (pēn'tsä ĕts'ē-ō) May 18, 1892- Metropolitan basso and concert singer

Address: b. c/o Constance Hope Associates, Inc, 29 W. 57th St, New York City; h. 55 Central Park West, New York City

Ezio Pinza, one of the most popular bassos ever to appear in opera, began two entirely different careers before he became a singer. He was born in Rome, Italy, the son of Cesare and Clelia (Bulgarelli) Pinza. They hoped to make a civil engineer of him and for this purpose sent him to the University of Ravenna. But after a year he left, with some idea of studying singing. He did not, however, begin his musical career at once; first he made a try at professional bicycle riding to earn some quick money. For a year he took part in races, often riding for 12 hours at a stretch, a bag of food tied to his handle bars. "He covered a lot of ground, achieved a muscular figure and never won a race." His father then complained: "You must do something useful, you must go back to engineering."

By this time, however, Pinza had other plans. And it was his coming in second in a race that helped him to crystallize those plans. While taking a shower after the race he sang exuberantly over his near-victory. The other bicycle riders suggested that Pinza would make a better opera singer than bicycle rider. Though he listened to their advice he tried riding for a while longer, until his father decided to let him study singing instead of en-

EZIO PINZA

gineering and sent him to the Bologna Conservatory of Music. There he studied under Maestro Vezzani, and completed his studies in two years. Of this accomplishment he merely comments: "If you have money you study 10 years. If not, two. I study two."

"I was ready for my opera debut," the basso said, "when the War [the First World War] broke out. But that changed every plan again. I joined the Italian artillery, and kept my voice on ice for four years—four years of War in the Italian Alps, where the lowest altitude I got down to (except when on leave) was 6,000 feet above sea level."

Fortunately he came out of the War without even a scratch. His long postponed debut was made at the Teatro Reale dell' Opera, in Rome, as King Mark in Wagner's *Tristan und Isolde*. Two years later he was at La Scala in Milan, where for three years he sang under Toscanini. It was there that he was heard by Giulio Gatti-Casazza of the Metropolitan, and engaged.

His first New York role was in a revival of Spontini's *La Vestale*, during the 1926 season. His acting, as well as his singing, brought enthusiastic response from the audience, and from that time he has been one of the favorites of the Metropolitan Opera. Perhaps the role that he enjoys best is that of Figaro in *The Marriage of Figaro*, which was revived for him in 1940, the first time in 22 years that the Metropolitan had produced it. Other operas in which he has been particularly successful are *La Sonnambula, Louise, Nerone, Faust, Simon Boccanegra, Don Giovanni, The Barber of Seville* and *Boris Godunoff*. In Italy he sang all the Wagnerian operas and he hopes to sing them all in German in the United States. His voice and his style are adaptable to German, French and Italian singing. He appears not only with the Metropolitan Opera but also with the Chicago, the San Francisco and the St. Louis Opera Companies, and in Covent Garden, London. The 1941 season was his fourteenth with the Metropolitan.

In addition to his opera success Pinza has had a notable career on the concert stage, usually singing about 60 concerts a year, covering 50 cities in 25 states.

Pinza feels that a singer must study more than singing. "I study much harder now than when I was at the Conservatory," he has confessed. "I study not only singing, but acting, make-up, and background as well. In opera one must remember he is more than a singer. I feel that I must know all about the characters I am portraying—and as much about their times as I can find out."

Pinza has about 50 roles in his repertoire, and since he seeks out the smallest detail that will help him to interpret these rôles he has by now acquired a rich background of history and folklore. He considers it important to study not only his own part but his part in relation to the others, for only thus, he feels, can he give an adequate portrayal of his own role. Also he thinks the dramatic interpretation of a role as important as the musical. "Formerly," he has said, "artists gave thought to little else except singing. They just stood and sang, or at most made exaggerated and stereotyped gestures with their arms. Today this is not sufficient. After all, even if one sings beautifully, why be on the opera stage if that is all one does? No matter how marvelous the voice, an artist who fails through lack of acting ability to convey the character that the composer had in mind fails to give a good performance."

In make-up Pinza is an expert. He became interested in this art through frequent visits to the Pastel Room in the Louvre, Paris, where he noticed that in pastel drawings a single line could change facial features and character. Though he is one of the most handsome singers of the Metropolitan, six-feet-one with the athletic figure he acquired bicycling, his good looks are usually disguised under his clever make-up. For Mephistopheles he uses pointed effects—a pointed nose, chin, eyebrows, beard, and a peaked cap and feathers. As King Dodon in *Le Coq d'Or*, on the contrary, he looks a foot shorter than he is, by emphasizing roundness—with whiskers, hair, a broad putty nose and a pot belly. Basilio, in the *Barber of Seville*, he conceives as a "comic strip buffoon" and gets the effect he desires by a "long, downturned putty nose and lean, mask-like features, topped by a rectangular hat of grotesque proportions." As Don Giovanni, however, he retains his natural tall, stalwart, athletic figure.

Through his "leonine grace and magnificent voice"—a voice that ranges from bass to baritone—his skillful and imaginative make-up and his dramatic portrayals, Ezio Pinza has frequently stolen the spotlight from the tenor, though the latter is always the hero in the performance. His first singing (in 1938) of Boris Godunoff, a role in which he is considered the famous Chaliapin's successor, brought the audience to its feet. When he sang the role with the Chicago Opera Company the next year one critic wrote: "Ezio Pinza's Boris follows the tradition set by the great Chaliapin in action. Vocally, the Italian baritone put to shade memories of other Borises who have appeared on our lyric stage besides the Russian baritone." Some of his other portrayals have been acclaimed almost as enthusiastically.

It is reported, though, that the basso is indifferent to the opinions of the critics and that he never reads his press notices. He has said, "I do not mind what the critics say—so long as they sit in their chairs. If they learn to sing and come up on the stage, then maybe I listen to them. But the artistic conscience, that only the singer can trust."

Pinza married the former Doris Leak, of Larchmont, New York, a talented soloist of the Metropolitan ballet, in 1940. There are traces of his sporting past in his devotion to his 20-foot speed boat and his auto, rivaled only by his devotion to his young daughter, Clelia, born in August 1941.

References

Junior League Mag p38-9+ D '39 por
N Y Herald Tribune X p18 Mr 10 '40
N Y Times p10 F 7 '38; p23 S 30 '38 por; p31 S 24 '39 por
Theatre Arts 22:138-44 F '38 pors
Vogue 93:73+ Ap 15 '39 por

Baker's Biographical Dictionary of Musicians 1940
Ewen, D. Men and Women Who Make Music p239-48 1939
Ewen, D. ed. Living Musicians 1940
Thompson, O. ed. International Cyclopedia of Music and Musicians 1939
Who's Who in America

PITKIN, WALTER B(OUGHTON) Feb. 6, 1878- Author; psychologist; teacher

Address: b. 2960 Broadway, New York City; h. R. F. D. 1, Dover, N. J.

As the man who has made popular psychology pay to the tune of some 50 books of the career-uplift variety, including the 1932 bestselling *Life Begins at Forty* (second only to *Babbitt* as a household phrase book title), in 1940 Professor Walter B. Pitkin added *Art of Useful Writing* and *Escape From Fear* to his phenomenal list. With the latter title the energetically versatile, "omni-opinionated" Pitkin turned from careers to culture and world politics: "I aim at a cultural revolution about 10 times more profound than the petty political revolutions about which soapbox orators and old style campaigners chatter," he writes in *Escape From Fear.* "Most of the institutions and people to be destroyed must die off. We cannot shoot them at sunrise."

Revolutionist Pitkin is convinced that "Chaos engulfs all things human," that "everything is going to pieces." Nevertheless, as the author of *Careers After Forty* (1937), *Careers for Youth* (1936) and *Capitalism Carries On* (1935) has always assured us, there is still hope. Today man "can shape his destiny." How? "Impose your will on Chaos or perish. Like Cleopatra, be alive every minute. Don't live for somebody but for something."

Most critics dismissed this particular opus of Pitkin's with a brief, good-natured shrug;

WALTER B. PITKIN

but a reviewer in the Springfield (Massachusetts) *Republican* took it more seriously: "It is difficult to reconcile the various views expressed in this book. The many advantages of the totalitarian state are listed along with pronouncement of doom upon the democracies of the world. Among the things he seems to favor are restrictions of labor unions, suppression of 'squatting women' of the women's club variety, less freedom, more fighting, and the extermination of human beings of the type that psychologists and psychiatrists strive to save and reshape to useful citizenry."

Various interests and activities apart from teaching and book-writing have highlighted the career, before and after 40, of Columbia University's volatile professor. He was born in Ypsilanti, Michigan on February 6, 1878, the son of Caleb S. and Lucy T. (Boughton) Pitkin. After his graduation from the University of Michigan in 1900 he studied for five years at the Hartford (Connecticut) Theological Seminary. Some years of graduate study abroad followed: at the Sorbonne, Paris; at the University of Berlin, and at the University of Munich. In 1903 he married Mary B. Gray, of Hartford. The Pitkins have five sons: Richard, John, David, Robert and Walter.

From 1905 to 1909 Pitkin lectured on psychology at Columbia University, where he has been professor of journalism since 1912. He has also been on the editorial staff of the New York *Tribune* (1907-08) and of the *Evening Post* (1909-10); since 1927 he has been an editor of *Parents' Magazine* and from 1935 to 1938 an editorial director of the *Farm Journal*; he found time further to be, from 1927 to 1928, the American managing editor of the *Encyclopaedia Britannica* and, in 1929, story supervisor of Universal Pictures. In 1932 he founded the Institute of Life Planning, and he is in 1941 partner in a large-scale

PITKIN, WALTER B.—*Continued*

experimental farm in Centerville, Maryland. Among the Pitkiniana dashed off in more relaxed moments, besides the titles already mentioned, are *Art of Rapid Reading* (1929); *Take It Easy* (1935); *Making Good Before Forty* (1939); and *Seeing Our Country* (co-author) (1939).

One of Professor Pitkin's most unique extra-curricular activities was in June 1939 when, with the encouragement of Cleveland businessmen, he launched a new organization at Elyria, Ohio. This was called American Majority—a movement for the "betterment of America." It was also called by Pitkin a "League of the Middle Class in revolt against the predatory rich and the predatory poor." Elyria (a town in solidly Republican, prosperous territory) was chosen as headquarters because it "so thoroughly typifies the solidity, energy and patriotism of American life." Pitkin represented himself to the town as "an average American—farmer, city dweller, businessman, educator, sociologist, champion of the rights of the everyday citizen." Membership dues in the organization (whose exact aims seem to have been clothed in cloudy mystery) ranged from $100 for charter members to $1 for all young people under 25. Pitkin himself made a dynamic speech at the opening meeting. "Get up on your hind legs and bark," said he. "If you don't get results by barking, bite somebody."

Of Pitkin's part in this venture (which seems to have died after its initial flourish) Motier Harris Fisher (the *New Republic*, October 4, 1939) wrote, belligerently: "Pitkin has repeatedly warned industrialists that 'if capital doesn't speak up it is going to be defeated.' He is fond of saying: 'Heaven send us a Rabble Rouser of the Right.' . . His philosophy as set down in his books, his record of antagonism for the Newspaper Guild and labor organizations in general, and his condescending attitude toward democracy . . . leaves no doubt as to where his sympathies lie and which blind spots are largest. Convinced that men are too stupid to govern themselves, he has demonstrated his willingness to serve as a piper for big businessmen who have been humming a long time the tune to which he has found the words."

But Professor Pitkin, whose *Life Begins at Forty* had sold more than 350,000 copies, apparently did not feel overly in need of the backing of Big Business. A romanticist at heart, adventure in other forms beckoned him. For some years he had been carrying out the idea of a boat: one "with keels set on the principle of a catamaran, and with a square-rigged type of sail modernized by a welded steel mast and electric motors to operate the rig." This unique craft Pitkin called the *Experimenter*. Some $100,000 went into its construction. It was designed primarily to withstand typhoons in tropical waters. And it was toward the tropical waters of the Caribbean that the modern Ulysses headed

his ship from Newburgh, New York on New Year's Eve 1940.

The freeze-up in the Hudson River made the adventure-bound Professor rush his plans: the *Experimenter*, pushed by her twin Diesel engines, buzzed off amid the gathering ice cakes. A few hours out of Newburgh, ice cut a large gash in her planking, and in rushed the non-tropical Hudson. The captain and his crew of two hastily took to a row boat—only to find that the builders had forgotten to put in seats and oarlocks. Pitkin likewise abandoned the leaking row boat; and, like Eliza, jumped onto an ice cake floating downstream. He and his crew welcomed in the New Year atop their ice floe, munching sandwiches someone had thoughtfully brought along. His uninsured *Experimenter* a hopeless wreck, Pitkin the next day caught a plane to Florida. From there he wired friends in Manhattan: "Florida has chance of a lifetime and knows it. America faces south for next 50 years and the Caribbean must become American lake. Florida sits on the front steps of tomorrow's big business. That is why I am here."

As enthusiastic and irrepressible in his 60's as at 40, Professor Pitkin has set forth in the *Reader's Digest*, December 1940, some of the many things he wants to experience "Before I'm Eighty." His next two decades are to be brimful of things to do and places to go. He wants to "sit in an igloo of unbreakable glass on some West Indies peak to see hurricanes"; he wants to hear "a first class volcano in eruption; the drum concert of 500 baboons." He begs: "Let me whiff, many a time between the end and now, the lilacs of a New England spring, a still night of blossoms in a Florida orange grove. Let me breathe, over and over again, the lifting cleanliness of salt ocean air. For my palate, give me a thousand more dessert melons, picked as they fall from the stems and eaten before sunrise so that they are filled with the coolness of the night." Professor Pitkin would also like to be given the moon (astronomically speaking), the secrets of the ant and bee, and of the "creatures of the deep." But most of all he would like to "witness a thousand experiments with the chemicals that control character and help find the substances that clear befuddled minds."

References

Etude 55:624 S '37 por; 55:633-4 O '37 por
Lit Digest 123:26-7 Mr 27 '37
New Repub 100:240-1 O 4 '39
New Yorker 10:25-8 My 12 '34; 10:24-8 My 19 '34
Newsweek 14:14 Jl 10 '39 por
Read Digest 37:81-2 D '40
Sat R Lit 12:16 Je 22 '35 por
Time 34:17 Jl 10 '39 por; 35:17 Ja 15 '40 por
Leaders in Education 1941
Sarett, L. R. and Foster, W. T. comps. Modern Speeches on Basic Issues p37-9 1939
Who's Who in America

PIUS XII, POPE   Mar. 2, 1876-   The Pope

Address: The Vatican, Rome, Italy

The sixty-fifth birthday of Pius XII on March 2, 1941 was also the second anniversary of the swiftest election in papal history. Ten days later the second anniversary of his coronation was celebrated with solemn Masses and a public holiday for Vatican City. It had been two years since 200,000 people outside St. Peter's Cathedral had seen him receive the triple tiara, while 500,000,000 more, through the first broadcast of such a ceremony, had been able to hear the solemn words: "Receive the tiara adorned with three crowns, and know that thou art Father of princes and kings, Rector of the world, Vicar of our Saviour Jesus Christ."

The election of Cardinal Eugenio Pacelli on March 2, 1939 meant continuance of his predecessor's policy which, as Papal Secretary of State, he had helped to effect: a policy of opposition to race prejudice, religious persecution, wars of aggression. Cannons roared, the bells of Rome rang out, congratulations poured in. But there was small rejoicing in Germany, for the Reich had made it clear that of all candidates the "pro-Ally" Pacelli would be least acceptable.

His first message was a plea for peace, his chosen motto *Opus Justitiae Pax,* the coat of arms he selected showed a dove bearing an olive branch. And shortly after he was crowned, talk was heard of his efforts to convene a five-power conference for peaceful settlement of Europe's problems. These rumors the Vatican alternately fanned and smothered, for it stood committed by policy and also by Article 24 of the Lateran Treaty to remain outside all temporal disputes unless its services as peacemaker were requested. To be so pledged and to be at the same time champion of peace, foe of oppression and spiritual leader of 331,500,000 Catholics divided among contending nations, as well as the native of a fatherland which has become a dictatorship, is a position that easily gives rise to contradiction and speculation. Small wonder that Vatican diplomacy is more often guessed at than known.

It was known, however, that the Vatican would be available for a conference of powers, not including Russia. And no secret was made of His Holiness' great dread that Bolshevism and atheism might gain a foothold in Europe, of his brief hope that Franco's "desired Catholic victory" in Spain would end this threat, of his opposition to any alliance between Britain, Russia and France before the First World War. (Later, however, after Germany troops had invaded Russia, he refused to direct Catholics to take a pro-German stand. This war was not a religious crusade, in his view.)

As the War has gone on, pained but not daunted when his proposals are politely eluded, Pius has repeatedly renewed his peace efforts. Mundane diplomacy, offers of mediation and appeals to the dictators have been reinforced with orders for public Masses and Crusades of Prayer, for special appeals to the Blessed Virgin by little children bearing flowers. The

POPE PIUS XII

Pope himself has been deluged by appeals, private and public, from statesmen, churchmen and laymen, to take more active steps against war; he has been alternately and simultaneously applauded for vigor and denounced for weakness.

His relations with the Axis leaders have varied between friction and something resembling reconciliation. Rumors of accord with the Reich have been repeatedly smashed by new outbursts against Nazi persecutions from the Vatican radio or the semi-official Vatican newspaper, *Osservatore Romano.* In March of 1940, shortly after President Roosevelt broke a 70-year precedent and caused renewed talk of collaboration between the Holy See and the United States by sending Myron Taylor to the Vatican as his representative, an emissary from Hitler was also granted audience. Yet Foreign Minister Von Ribbentrop (see sketch this issue), it was said, took home nothing but "a delicate snubbing" and a nervous breakdown.

Ties with the Fascist government have similarly snapped and mended. After the papal rebuke called forth by Albania, the old breach between Vatican and Quirinal seemed on the way to healing. The King and the Pope actually exchanged visits for the first time since 1870, and it was informally hinted that the Papal Secretary of State and the new Italian Ambassador to the Holy See had reached a "gentleman's agreement" providing for parallel action against Communism, "the new menace of the West." When Belgium and Holland were invaded, however, the *Osservatore Romano* protested openly, sales were suppressed outside Vatican City, copies of the paper burned, readers of it thrown into the Trevi Fountain. After Italy entered the War, Fascists were forbidden to read it; Professor Gonella, its pro-Ally news columnist, mysteriously disappeared for two days; its editor

PIUS XII, POPE—*Continued*

went about with two bodyguards; war news was banned, and it became "as good as suppressed."

Rumor said that the columnist's return was due to the Pope's threat to broadcast the whole story; that the Nazis were going to force his resignation; that the Vatican was being held practically incommunicado; that haven had been offered in the United States. Then Pius announced his resolve to stay in the Vatican, and rumor subsided. A papal edict forbade political discussion in public places of Vatican City. Blackout was arranged, although the Allies had promised not to bomb Rome for fear of accidental injury to the Holy See. The Pope spent hours, possibly whole nights, on his knees in private prayer and from time to time there came reports of his ill health, caused by long prayers for peace and deep concern.

"Trimming his sails to the wind" was an unpleasant phrase bandied about during the next months, and uglier ones were shouted in England. From the distance of America, however, it was easier to appreciate the dilemma of a choice between "sharing the spoils of a Fascist-Nazi triumph" and alienating the countries to which two-thirds of the Pope's spiritual dependents owed temporal allegiance. Again in December the *Osservatore Romano* lashed out against Nazism, to the comfort of the Allies, who had "feared that silence meant tacit approval." They, however, soon were worrying again over the Pope's apparent sympathy for "quasi-Fascist France."

Both sides found some comfort in the Pope's outline for a post-War world, given in June 1941. In it he defended private property, asked for a more equitable distribution of the world's goods, for respect for the rights of workers, for respect for the integrity of the family and for less restrictions on immigration by large nations. And since then the Vatican has persisted in its attitude of strict neutrality. When Myron Taylor had audiences with the Pope again in the fall of 1941, reportedly to get him to declare the war against Germany a "just" war, nothing came of them.

If it were possible to speak of a Pope as a career man, the term would apply to Pius XII, whose whole training has shaped and equipped him for his present office despite his own wish to be a mere curate. His parents, Filippo and Virginia (Graziosi) Pacelli, had assumed that their second son, Eugenio, born on March 2, 1876, would follow the law like all the men of the aristocratic Pacelli family. Marcantonio Pacelli had served as the Papal State's Under-Secretary of the Interior from 1851 to 1870, and his son Filippo had been dean of the College of Consistorial Advocates (secular lawyers for the papacy). Filippo's first son, Francisco, did become an ecclesiastical lawyer, but Eugenio proved less interested in the family tradition than in the glory of God.

His religious inclination was evident even as a little boy attending a school conducted by nuns. The class cartoonist invariably represented Eugenio in prayer. Later he was sent to the Visconti Grammar School, a State rather than a parochial institution, where he headed his class, winning an Italy-wide essay contest on "Universal History" and distinguishing himself as a linguist. He delivered his first halting sermon to a Catholic boys' club of which he was a member. Later he was to preach fluently in Spanish, German, Hungarian, Portuguese, French, Italian and English, in great cathedrals throughout the world.

At Capranica College in Rome he earned his doctorate in theology, philosophy and law, and in 1899 was ordained a priest. His brilliant scholastic record attracted the attention of Monsignor Gasparri, Secretary of the Congregation for Extraordinary Ecclesiastical Affairs, and after a short term as professor of law at the Roman Seminary the quiet young man was transferred to Gasparri's department: first as junior clerk, later as principal copyist, and presently as Under-Secretary. He never again left the shadow of the Vatican. Twice he accepted professorships in Catholic institutions, but each time Monsignor Gasparri persuaded him to change his mind.

The first of his many trips abroad as papal emissary was in 1901, when he carried to London a personal letter of condolence from Pope Leo XIII to Edward VII on the death of Queen Victoria. In 1908 he returned for the London Eucharistic Congress. On his third visit, in 1911, for the coronation of King George V, he received the Coronation Medal, so that now he is the only Pope in history with a British decoration.

On the outbreak of the First World War, Pope Pius X died—of a broken heart, it was said. His successor, Benedict XV, promoted Gasparri to be his Secretary of State, while Pacelli took the latter's position in the Congregation for Extraordinary Ecclesiastical Affairs. Pope Benedict was highly pleased with his work in arranging the exchange of prisoners, the moving of the wounded, the relaying of information about the missing, and also with the codification of Canon Law which he completed in 1916. In May 1917, with a new title, Archbishop of Sardis, he was sent as papal nuncio to Munich, to initiate a peace movement.

He was still in Munich 15 months later when the War ended without benefit of clergy, and he remained there during the revolutionary outbreaks that followed. When armed looters broke into his home he received them in his ecclesiastical robes, reminded them that they were on extraterritorial soil and that it was never wise to kill a diplomat. With their revolvers leveled at his breast he lucidly and kindly analyzed their problem, while one by one the weapons dropped and the men silently made for the door. During his six years in Munich another future potentate named Adolf Hitler was in the city, at the head of a Nazi party numbering seven men; but apparently the two did not meet.

In 1925, after the Concordat between the Vatican and Bavaria had been signed, Pacelli was transferred to Berlin. There for four years he was "the doyen of the diplomatic corps, the first accredited diplomat to the Weimar Republic, and a spokesman for the chiefs of all foreign missions." When he left in 1929 President Hindenburg, deeply moved, assured him of Germany's undying gratitude, while thousands "Hoched" and "Heiled" him along the torchlit route to the railway station.

He had been recalled to succeed the aging Gasparri as Papal Secretary of State, an officer who "must know everything, understand everything, and say nothing." His has been called the best informed of all foreign offices, and the canniest. With the reports of 60 papal legates and 1,300 bishops pouring in from all over the world, and the bishops through their priests in touch with the people, in his new office "Pacelli probably had a better idea of what was going on in the world than anybody else in it."

The State of which he now became in effect Foreign Minister had changed character since his brother Francisco helped to draw up the Lateran Treaty of 1929 restoring to the Papal See the status of a temporal domain, whose ruler—the Pope—commands absolute sovereignty. It has 108 acres and in 1939 exchanged diplomatic representatives with 37 countries. And as Secretary of State, Pacelli put the Lateran Treaty into working order and did much toward making Vatican City as modern as New York, with its own electric power station, telephone and telegraph service, fleet of motorcars and radio designed by Marconi himself. (The Pope's own telephone is of solid gold and only the Secretary of State is privileged to call him on his private wire.)

Secretary Pacelli, in addition to being made a Cardinal, was appointed Archpriest of Saint Peter's, and in 1932 received the highest Order of the Italian Crown, conferring on the holder the right to address the King as "Cousin." In 1935 he succeeded Gasparri as Camerlengo (Chamberlain), who rules the Church during the period between the death of one Pope and the election of the next.

By employing Pacelli frequently as emissary abroad, Pope Pius XI carried on the education Gasparri had begun. When Pacelli first crossed the Atlantic in 1934 to attend the Eucharistic Congress in Buenos Aires, tens of thousands of pilgrims welcomed him. A much quoted instance of his self-discipline is that during a procession lasting over two hours he was drawn through Buenos Aires in a float, the whole time kneeling erect with hands pressed together in prayer before the exposed Host in the monstrance.

In 1936 he made an 8,000-mile tour of the United States by plane, swerving from his course to admire Niagara Falls, the Grand Canyon, Boulder Dam. During the flights he wrote letters on a portable typewriter and prepared countless speeches. The speed of the plane was all to his taste—both he and Pius XI

were suspected of starting late for appointments in order to make their chauffeurs drive really fast. His untiring readiness to meet the crowds that clamored for him was the marvel of hosts, as was his finesse with reporters. Asked to comment after lunching with President Roosevelt at Hyde Park, he answered cheerily, "I enjoyed lunching with a typical American family."

Nazi policy toward the Church brought repeated protests from Vatican City, which evoked answering protests from the Reich, so that this was a period of growing strain. The Vatican was by no means easy to gag. When Hitler banned Catholic literature, Pacelli had it flown in by plane. When Mussolini ordered the Italian Catholic Action group and the Catholic Boy Scouts disbanded, Pacelli realized that the Pope's answering encyclical would be suppressed in Rome. Therefore two priests flew with it to Paris and released it there; Mussolini learned its contents when the telegraph brought it to Rome and all the rest of the world.

On February 10, 1939, Cardinal Pacelli, as Camerlengo, announced to his fellow Cardinals: "The Pope is truly dead." Three weeks later he phoned his sisters Elisabetta and Giuseppina to tell them of his own election and to give them his blessing over the wire. Since that time his life has become increasingly strenuous. By December he was so worn with ceaseless activity and nightlong prayers for peace, by constant worry about persecutions and the menace of Communism, that for a week he had to cancel all engagements. Although still carrying his more than six-foot frame erect, he had become so emaciated that a visitor wrote: "The figure of the Pope in his simple white cassock and skullcap seems ascetic almost to the point of frailty." Surrounded by pomp and color—the crimson-damasked walls of the throne room, clerics in purple, the Swiss Guard in the vivid costumes designed for them by Michelangelo—he remained gentle yet austere, approachable yet remote. Those who were favored with an interview came away impressed with his patience, his voice and his eyes.

Today Pius XII keeps up his strenuous solitary walks in the Vatican Gardens, continues to rise early, to go through morning exercises in the completely equipped gymnasium adjoining his bedroom, to shave himself with an electric razor, to breakfast on black coffee and "dunked" bread. Most mornings he listens to radio news in eight languages; often he lunches lightly on nothing but an eggnog. Like St. Francis he greatly loves birds; and he keeps a flock of canaries that fly about him while he dines.

The smallest kingdom in the world, under his rule, is today a sanctuary-prison for diplomats of countries at war with Italy. Pius XII himself is neither pro-Ally nor pro-Axis. He is the Father of princes and kings, Rector of the World, Vicar of his Church, whose welfare he must place before all temporal matters. Yet, declares the *Osservatore Romano*, neither is he a neutral; "He should be considered a com-

PIUS XII, POPE—*Continued*

batant fighting for a just peace, based on the five points he has repeated twice."

References

> Cath World 149:108-10 Ap '39; 149:364-5 Je '39; 152:1-9 O '40; 152:491-3 Ja '41
> Christian Cent 56:342-3 Mr 15 '39
> Commonweal 29:677-9 Ap 14 '39
> Nation 148:285-8 Mr 11 '39
> New Repub 104:260 F 24 '41
> N Y Times p5 Ag 3 '40; p3 Ag 5 '40; p5 Ag 8 '40; p8 S 5 '40; IV p2 Mr 2 '41; p3 Mr 13 '41
> Newsweek 13:32 F 20 '39 por; 13:25-6 Mr 13 '39 il pors; 16:28 Jl 8 '40
> Time 33:30 F 20 '39 por; 33:36+ Mr 13 '39 por
>
> Catholic Who's Who
> Chi è?
> Dinneen, J. F. Pius XII, Pope of Peace 1939
> Roman Catholic Church. Pope Pius XII. Pope Speaks 1940
> Van Hoek, K. Pope Pius XII 1940
> Who's Who

PLASKETT, JOHN S(TANLEY) Nov. 17, 1865—Oct. 17, 1941 Astronomer; director of the Dominion of Canada's Astrophysical Observatory in Victoria, British Columbia, until 1935; gave the scientific world its most accurate information on the problem of rotation of the galaxy; discovered twin stars, named for him; scientific consultant for the firm of Warner and Swasey in Cleveland; recipient of many awards for his work.

References

> Cur Opinion 73:476 O '22 por
> Sci ns 81:415 My 3 '35
> Sci Mo 28:33 Ja '29 por; 41:183 Ag '35 por
>
> American Men of Science
> Who's Who

Obituaries

> N Y Times p19 O 18 '41 por

PONCINS, GONTRAN (JEAN-PIERRE DE MONTAIGNE), VICOMTE DE (pôN-săN' gôN-träN' zhäN pyâr' dĕ môN-tàn'y') Aug. 19, 1900- French author

Address: c/o Reynal & Hitchcock, 386 Fourth Ave, New York City

In the language of the Eskimo *Kabloona* means "white man." And when in 1940 Gontran de Poncins returned from 15 months in the Arctic wastes he brought back with him a diary and photographs which formed the basis of a best-selling book by that title—an April 1941 selection of the Book-of-the-Month Club. *Kabloona* is, according to Rockwell Kent, himself no stranger to the Eskimo, "a sensitive, an understanding and a loving record. It is a peaceful, beautiful and moving book. . . It is a book that possibly no Englishman, and no American of the English colonial and explora-

tory tradition, could have written." Irwin Edman calls it "a fascinating and sophisticated travel book . . . engrossing, simply as narrative . . . an essay in comparative morals . . . a collection of field notes . . . of an anthropologist without academic apparatus but with the alert sensibilities of a poetic man of the world . . . above all, the meditative journal of a highly bred Frenchman driven to re-examine himself and all the civilized values he had taken for granted."

Richard Finnie, reviewing the book for *Natural History*, struck a discordant note in this symphony of praise. Although admiring *Kabloona's* "high literary quality," its excellent "introspective and analytical writing," he announced that "it contains too many exaggerations, half-truths and misleading statements to be taken seriously for its Arctic lore" and that De Poncins' descriptions of Eskimo folkways, "although fascinating, are often shockingly distorted." He says, moreover, that the author was quite unjustified in fancying himself "as very nearly the first white man to hobnob with most of the Eskimos of that area."

Whatever the scientific accuracy of the book, there have been few stories stranger or more romantic than the life of its author—a Frenchman of aristocratic birth, a "child of civilization" who "wandered in the course of a few weeks into the stone age" and found himself oddly "relaxed, content, happy" there, completely at peace with himself for the first time in his life. Viscount Gontran Jean-Pierre de Montaigne de Poncins, born on an estate in southeast France on August 19, 1900, is a descendant of the famous French essayist whose name he bears. Until the age of 14 he remained at home, living with nature more closely than with his parents, and then prepared for a military academy. But the First World War was over by the time he finished his examinations. He joined the compulsory service as a private, and in 1920, after three months in the "Blue Devils," began serving as an interpreter with the French mission attached to the American Army of Occupation in the Rhineland. There a "mule-driving American sergeant" gave him the name "Mike," a name which he still enjoys hearing.

The next years account for the fact that today De Poncins speaks fluent and idiomatic German, English, Italian and Spanish. Interested in human psychology, in human adventure above all else, he left his *milieu* to mix with other people and try to understand them. He wanted to find out things by himself, without preconceived ideas. He wanted to know what people lived by, what helped them through life. He joined the cosmopolitan French Beaux Arts School and painted there for six years. He entered an Italian silk concern, as an apprentice in an Italian factory, eventually became director and in 1927 chairman of its London branch. It was 1929 when he quit: "His bones rejected the fat they were accumulating." He traveled restlessly everywhere between New Guinea and the Arctic Circle. He wrote about native life wherever he went, both for magazines and for the French newspapers for which he was correspondent, without ever thinking of writing a book. He gathered a variety of acquaintances ranging from royal families to Indian Brahmans, from workmen in factories to missionaries and natives in the South Pacific islands, from doctors to circus clowns.

Says Lewis Galantière, describing these years: "First he tried Cloudcuckooland, sailing a boat alone through the South Seas. Then he went into the sterner worlds of India, China and Arabia. In St. Jerome's time he would have gone into a cenoby; in our time, it turned out, he could go only to the Eskimos."

But it was not until one spring day in 1938 that De Poncins decided to go to the Eskimos. There was no particular reason for his decision—only "some time before that spring day the word 'Eskimo' had rung inside me and . . . the sound had begun to swell like the vibrations of a great bell and had eventually filled the whole of my subconscious being." He knew by hearsay of "a little handful of men calling themselves the Netsilikmiut (the Seal Eskimos)" who, "cut off from the surrounding world by ice-filled seas and trackless wastes . . . have been suffered to live their own life entirely untrammeled by outside influence, up to the present time." Without equipment, without much more money than baggage, without even plans, he made arrangements with Canada's "Bishop of the Wind" to fly with him from Fort McMurray, Canada part of the way to their land. It was June 11, 1938 when De Poncins left Paris, and not quite a month later when he climbed into the Bishop's plane. Sometime in the summer he reached the Hudson's Bay post on King William Land, an island north of the Arctic Circle, 10,000 miles square, with a population of 25 Eskimos. He had traveled by ship, railroad, airplane and Eskimo boat.

Thus began a year spent living the primitive life of the people of the Arctic, accompanying them on whaling trips, eating their food, following their customs, sometimes not seeing another white man for months on end. (At the same time scientific studies were made for the French Geographic Society and for the Museum of Natural History of France.) Says De Poncins, in Kabloona: "Hardest of all was not the severity of the climate, not the intensity of the cold, not the physical anguish which, often, I endured. The cold was a problem; but a very much more difficult problem was the Eskimo mentality. There was no getting on with the Eskimo except on his own terms; and I had to get on with him if I was to live with him. A good part of this book, therefore, is the story of the encounter of two mentalities, and of the gradual substitution of the Eskimo mentality for the European mentality within myself." The tale he has to tell is not an idyllic one, but gradually this Frenchman made the discovery "that the culture of the Stone Age could be as elaborate and often more satisfying than our own"—that the "arrogance of

the white man who thinks himself master wherever he goes" is an amusing but altogether stupid phenomenon.

Yet "for a Frenchman of our time the trail leads back to France." It was the War that brought De Poncins back—the War that would have been quite incomprehensible to

VICOMTE DE PONCINS

his Stone Age friends. He came back in a boat alone with two other men on a trip around Alaska and through Bering Strait, covering the 4,000 miles from the North Magnetic Pole to Vancouver in 57 days. In the Aleutian Islands he stopped to join the whalers in their whale hunt. Then, after a stay in Connecticut and in New York long enough to see the thousands of pages of his Arctic diary whipped into book-shape (Lewis Galantière was his collaborator, but the photographs and illustrations are entirely his own), De Poncins sailed from New York on the last eastbound voyage of the Champlain. He arrived in France three days before the fall of Paris.

Early in 1941 it was reported that he was living in occupied France and replenishing the larder on his family's country estate by using the primitive Eskimo tricks to trap pheasants. But on April 25, after patient efforts to facilitate his return to the United States, his publishers (Reynal & Hitchcock) received a cable from Lisbon: "Sailing today on Excalibur, Gontran de Poncins." When he arrived it was with permission to make another expedition into the Arctic, although he does not plan to go right away. "I like this writing," he says: "the excitement of it, the way for a little while the words spurt out, surprising me... I am having a wonderful time."

Galantière's description of the author is a vivid one: ". . . two features in his bony, aristocratic face are in perpetual contradiction with each other, so that, looking at him, you

PONCINS, GONTRAN, VICOMTE DE
—*Continued*

never can tell what he thinks of you. His eyes are alert, intelligent, and suspicious— what the French call *sauvage* when they mean untamed, unsociable; but his smile is so friendly and confiding that it belies the disquiet in his eyes."

References

Book-of-the-Month Club News p4 Mr '41 por
N Y Times Book R p2 My 25 '41 por
Sat R Lit 23:1 Mr 15 '41 por
Time 37:95 Mr 10 '41 por

Poncins, G. de M. de and Galantière, L. Kabloona 1941

POPE PIUS XII *See* Pius XII, Pope

POPHAM, SIR ROBERT (MOORE) BROOKE- *See* Brooke-Popham, Sir R. M.

PORTAL, SIR CHARLES (FREDERICK ALGERNON) (pôr'tăl) 1893- Chief of the British air staff

When Sir Charles Portal succeeded Sir Cyril Newall as chief of the air staff in October 1940, the British press in general hailed the new appointment as a sign that, having proved she could "take it," England was ready to show she could also "give it." In the months before his new appointment, during which Portal had been in charge of the Bomber Command, he had already shown a highly energetic and combative spirit. The British air offensive on German military objectives was pressed by him with the utmost vigor. Night after night heavy blows were delivered on oil storage tanks, docks, aircraft factories, munition works, canals, railways. Targets as distant as the Skoda works in Bohemia and the factories at Milan and Turin had been bombed. And while the night raids on England remained serious, the day raiders had been mastered by the Fighter Command. With the growing strength of the R. A. F. the time had come to plan ahead for the 1941 campaign; and Portal was evidently the man for the job. Portal's own words on hearing of his appointment were: "Good, now I'll bomb hell out of them."

A member of the War Cabinet is reported to have said once: "The War has produced only one man of genius. I mean Portal of the Bombers." Although his full stature is yet to be determined, Portal's past record promises well for it. He won his spurs in the First World War, where he gained a reputation for daring and courage. He has shown more than daring, however. He has the ability to plan. The targets selected by the R. A. F. in Germany and elsewhere are not chosen at random. They form part of a considered plan directed against German industry and communications, and that plan has been largely Portal's creation. No wonder the Nazi organization said: "The *Luftwaffe* will take notice of the new appointment."

There is a strain of Huguenot blood in the Portal family, which first came from France to England in 1695. Charles was born in Hungerford, Berkshire, the son of E. R. Portal, and lived during his youth in the Thames-side village of Pangbourne. He went to Winchester College, played cricket for his school and began to cultivate an antiquarian interest in falconry. By the time he was 16 he was writing about falconry in learned journals. At Christ Church, Oxford, he made no special impression as a scholar but became known as a young man who zoomed around the old city on a high-powered motorcycle. On it he won an important amateur race.

Portal was still an undergraduate when the First World War broke out. His first problem was how to get to the front—he solved it by riding his motorcycle. Immediately he enlisted as a dispatch rider in the Royal Engineers, was soon made a corporal, was in France during September and was named in Sir John French's very first dispatch from the field. A shellburst nearly put an end to his career before the year was out, but though five of his mates were killed by it Portal was only blown through the doorway. He pulled himself together quickly and was able to give first aid to some of the wounded before the ambulance arrived.

Early in 1915 Portal went home to England to train for a commission in the Royal Flying Corps (as the land air force was then called). After four months he got his single wing, as an observer. One of his first exploits was an almost successful pot shot with a Winchester automatic at Immelman, the German air ace who was flying low over the British lines. Portal hit his plane, but didn't down it. As an observer officer Portal worked carefully and methodically on "spotting" for the artillery, often ranging the guns himself and afterward flying over the target to note the results.

Eventually Portal passed from observing to piloting, and some of his fighting and bombing achievements are still remembered by those who were with him in France. One night he was over the enemy lines five times on bombing raids. Another time he tackled five German planes singlehanded, shot down three of them and returned safely to his base. During 1917 he won the D. S. O. and bar, and the M. C. He was a 25-year-old colonel when the War ended in 1918.

By this time the army and naval air services had been amalgamated as the Royal Air Force, and with the coming of peace Portal was granted a permanent commission in this arm of the service as squadron leader with the No. 59 Wing at Cranwell, Lincolnshire. In 1923 he was put through a course at the R. A. F. staff college and then went to the Air Ministry to serve on the air staff. In 1926 he took a senior officers' course at the Royal Naval College, and the year after took command of the No. 7 (Bomber) Squadron. It was here that he began that serious study of accurate bombing for which he has since become noted. In both the first and second

British Press Service

SIR CHARLES PORTAL

years of his new command he won the Laurence Minot Bombing Trophy, releasing the bombs himself each time.

After taking a course at the Imperial Defence College in 1928, Portal again went to the Air Ministry, doing staff work there from 1930 to 1934, when he was sent out to Aden, the youngest man ever entrusted with this command. From Aden he went to India for a time and from late 1935 until July 1937 acted as an instructor in the Imperial Defence College at home. It was in July 1937 that he was promoted to senior rank, as air vice-marshal, and in August he took over the important Air Ministry post of director of organization. In February 1939 he was made air member for personnel on the Air Council, and during that year became Companion of the Bath and rose to air marshal. The New Year's honors of 1940 created him a knight, as K. C. B. In March he took over the Bomber Command; on October 25 he became acting air chief marshal and chief of the air staff.

Charles Frederick Algernon Portal, more commonly known as Peter, is an inch short of six feet tall, "big-boned but slight, with a beakish nose and balding black hair." Two British army officers, seeing him for the first time when he arrived at Buckingham Palace to be knighted, gasped in one breath, according to Julian Bach, Jr., "Good God, he's fantastically ugly!" He is said to eat "with the parsimony of a sparrow and the regularity of a metronome."

Besides shooting, Portal's favorite recreations are sailing, fishing, taking photographs and, of course, flying. In 1909 he married Joan Margaret, youngest daughter of Sir Charles Glynn Welby, Baronet, and they have two daughters, Rosemary and Mavis. The Portals are living "for the duration" in a

London hotel bedroom, with suitcases piled in one corner, yachting manuals and a heavily thumbed copy of the *Oxford Book of English Verse* on a bedside shelf. Lady Portal says her husband is so busy that "once in a while he gets home—for breakfast."

References

Life 11:118-27 O 6 '41 il pors
N Y Herald Tribune X p4, 15 N 10 '40 por
Time 36:34 O 14 '40
Who's Who

PORTER, EDWIN S. 1870(?)—Apr. 30, 1941 Pioneer motion-picture producer who was associated with the late Thomas Alva Edison in the development and early use of motion-picture projectors; his career closely paralleled the development of the industry both technically and artistically; credited with making the first story film and the first Western thriller; in 1899 he photographed and produced *The Life of an American Fireman*; in 1903 he made *The Great Train Robbery*; purchased the American rights to Sarah Bernhardt's three-reel *Queen Elizabeth* and went into partnership with Adolph Zukor to form the Famous Players Company.

Obituaries

N Y Herald Tribune p18 My 1 '41
Variety 142:78 My 7 '41

PORTER, S(YLVIA) F(IELD) June 18, 1913- Financial columnist
Address: b. New York Post, 75 West St, New York City; h. 33 Fifth Ave, New York City

"My dear Mr. Porter." To the New York *Post's* financial column, "S. F. Porter Says," hundreds of letters have thus been addressed. It might amaze most of these letter writers—Wall Street operators, stock market speculators, or just plain subscribers bewildered by high finance—to learn that "Mr. Porter" is no dignified gray-beard, but an attractive, slim, dark-haired young woman who was born as recently as 1913.

Called "the girl wonder of Wall Street," Sylvia Porter holds the unique distinction of being the only woman writing a column on financial and allied subjects for a major city newspaper. She is the author of two books, *How To Make Money in Government Bonds* (1939), and *If War Comes to the American Home* (1941), besides numerous articles for national and financial magazines. Since July 1941 she has been the featured speaker on a weekly radio program over the National Broadcasting Company's network, talking to millions of women on the defense program and on financial and economic devolpements affecting the American family. It was the same "Mr. Porter" who in 1936, through an article in *Scribner's*, was instrumental in causing the Treasury Department to modify its policy in the matter of allotting oversubscribed issues of government bonds. This exposure of a neat little system of profiteering earned the high

Von Behr

S. F. PORTER

respect of a good many financial experts, including the Secretary of the Treasury. And it was S. F. Porter who, in a column in *The American Banker*, dared to call Secretary Morgenthau "obstinate and stupid" because of one of his early financial policies.

Sylvia Porter says that she deliberately signed the name S. F. Porter to her column because "I wanted to prevent any readers of the *Post* from knowing a girl was writing finance. I wanted the stuff to stand on its own and figured that unless someone happened to know me, the columns would stand or fall on their merits." The columns have stood. Now, even when it is generally known in Wall Street that the *Post's* financial columnist is a woman, there is "remarkably little prejudice."

Born in Patchogue, Long Island, New York on June 18, 1913, the daughter of Dr. Louis and Rose (Maisel) Feldman, young Sylvia Field Feldman started to be a writer at the tender age of six. Then, she says: "I wrote my first novel. (So help me. I discovered it in a cellar years ago.) It was about a girl who went over Niagara Falls in a barrel because her lover deserted her and it was written with the aid of *Saturday Evening Post* pictures pasted into a five-cent notebook. Quite an attractive job! And dedicated, if you please, to 'My Public.' "

After her graduation from high school she entered Hunter College, where she received a Phi Beta Kappa Key and her B. A. *magna cum laude* in 1932. In her junior year she switched from English literature to economics and finance. Reason: Mr. Reed Porter, "a tall blond who worked in a bank [they were married in 1931] and an overwhelming curiosity to know *why* everything was crashing around me and why people were losing their jobs." The depression was at its height

when she left college. "I knew I couldn't get a position in a newspaper office, so I went to Wall Street for my first real job. I got one—assistant to the president of an investment counsel house specializing in United States government bonds. He and I worked ten, twelve hours a day, learning about the government's bond market, about gold movements, about currency fluctuations." Meanwhile she took graduate work in her field at New York University's School of Business Administration.

During 1934 Miss Porter held odd jobs in various organizations specializing in different aspects of finance. She created and published in 1934 and 1935 the first service devoted exclusively to United States government bonds; and she began writing magazine articles. "In early spring 1935 I walked into the *Post* and suggested I write three columns a week on financial news. I got my chance." Soon she became that newspaper's regular finance writer covering a routine beat in Wall Street. It was in 1938 that she started a daily column, "Financial Post Marks," which subsequently became "S. F. Porter Says."

Miss Porter's book, *How To Make Money in Government Bonds*, was the first to be published covering all phases of government finance and the United States securities market. *If War Comes to the American Home* describes in simple language and by means of anecdotes the meaning of war and national defense to every American. The New York *Times* reviewer sums it up: "Facts, figures, broad word-pictures and succinct arguments are all presented with conversational ease. The book should be widely useful."

Besides her *Post* column, Sylvia Porter is also author of a weekly column on United States Government bond market trends, published in the *Commercial and Financial Chronicle*. Among the general magazines which have published her articles on financial subjects are the *American, Scribner's, Reader's Digest, Current History* and *Woman's Home Companion*. Her most noteworthy articles include "New Bait for Suckers," a story of investment counsel rackets; "A Woman and Her Money," investment hints for women; "Uncle Sam's Silver Scandal," on the United States silver policy; "The Tax Payer on the War Path"; "The Banker Takes Off His Top Hat." Her radio program, entitled *What Can I Do?* and done with June Hynd, assistant director of women's activities at NBC, is heard over station WJZ. She also makes occasional radio talks on her subject at other times and over other stations.

This formidable statistician and financial racket buster confesses that her one bona fide hobby is swimming. "I can go for a mile or so without stopping and without becoming fatigued. I also like to dance; like late parties with amusing, talkative people. (Dislike strong, 'silent' people known to have character and little else.) I like the theatre and am pretty partial to Scotch and soda as an aid to a party or an evening of talk. . . I like to eat oysters and chocolate cake, too; to read anything and everything. I go on detective story jags every few months, bring home three or four over a weekend and devour them at one sitting." Apparently her original ambition at the age of six to be a novelist still holds with Miss Porter. She is currently reported to be working hard on a novel, as yet unnamed.

"I'm a monumentally normal person," Miss Porter adds, "which, my mother says, just goes to show you. . ." Normal enough also to take her work seriously, Sylvia Porter is thoroughly convinced that there are "wonderful opportunities in this field. Women control more than 70 per cent of the wealth of this country, you know; 65 per cent of the savings accounts are in their names; women are the beneficiaries of most insurance policies. . . A woman financial writer can perform a real public service, I believe. In fact, if you are interested, that's my private crusade."

References

Am Mag 128:14-15+ Jl '39 por (p8)
Chicago Herald-American Ja 11 '41
New Yorker 14:12-13 F 4 '39
Time 33:51 Ap 3 '39 por

Shuler, M. and others. Lady Editor p34-6 1941

EMILY POST

POST, EMILY Oct. 3, 1873- Author; radio commentator; arbiter of etiquette

Address: c/o Funk & Wagnalls Co, 354 Fourth Ave, New York City

It seems incredible that as late as 1921 Emily Post was not part of our national vocabulary. What did people do, 20 years ago, when they wanted to talk about—or against—etiquette? She still is not in the dictionary, but she has already been compounded into "Emily-Posting." It is perhaps ironic that in this sense her name usually stands for an attitude she vigorously condemns.

Before she was elected by popular acclaim the American dictator of correct behavior, Emily Price Post indulged in a few gestures which were far from conventional. They followed a childhood and youth that were in every detail *comme il faut*. She was born in Baltimore, Maryland, on October 3, 1873—born to wealth, social position and a distinguished tradition. Her mother was Josephine (Lee) Price; her father Bruce Price, the architect who designed Quebec's Chateau Frontenac and many of the buildings in Tuxedo Park, New York. He was in addition a singularly handsome man of great charm and popularity, an intimate friend of the Duke of Connaught, who twitted him for looking every inch a peer. Bruce Price was also the sort of father whose only child loved to go with him to inspect the buildings he had under construction. Thus she became familiar with the skeletons of houses and with dizzy heights.

When Emily was five years old the family moved to New York City, where her life followed the approved pattern for childhood *à la mode*: summers in Bar Harbor, winters in the brownstone house on Tenth Street, with

lessons in the morning from her German governess, and a walk in the park every afternoon. Her later education naturally included gay trips abroad, where she became as intimate with titles as with joists and beams—inside information which later was to prove even more profitable.

When she made her debut in 1892 her loveliness created something of a furor. The Gibson girl formula might have been invented for her tall, willowy grace, dazzling complexion and rich crown of light brown hair. Sometimes after a ball it took four men to carry her cotillion favors to the carriage. (We may be sure none of them escorted her home, or dared to dream that she might "ask him in.") At the end of her first season she was married to the dashing Edwin M. Post, a banker who belonged to one of New York's pre-Vanderbilt families. Soon there were two sons, Edwin M. and Bruce, continuing the pleasant family custom of personal beauty and *savoir faire*.

The first sharp break in the smooth regularity of her life came when her husband lost his fortune after the panic of 1901. The second was her divorce, which left her with two young sons and no adequate means of support. She was the first divorcée, it is said, to combine her maiden name with that of her ex-husband. Mrs. Price Post, falling back on what she considered her chief talent, began to make little cardboard houses with windows of glazed paper, through which one might peer at tasteful furnishings and decorations of papier-mâché, sealing wax and paint. In those days, before the era of interior decoration, people were charmed—but this was hardly a substantial source of income.

Then someone said to her: "Why don't you write? Your letters are so marvelous!" Accordingly she exhumed some of her sprightly accounts of house parties in England, France

POST, EMILY—*Continued*

and Germany, worked into them a few fictional characters, and the result was *The Flight of a Moth,* published in 1904. To write for money was not quite "the thing" in her set, but she managed to accept about $3,000 without losing caste. From then on she rounded out a scanty income by writing, and her sprightly, frivolous novels, "confessions" and stories were remunerative enough to send her sons through Harvard. Her fiction always presented a European background, aswarm with titles and liveries, against which characters from the New World showed up to piquant—though always elegant—advantage.

She was living in a New York hotel when Richard Duffy, of Funk & Wagnalls, began to badger her about writing a book on etiquette. She scoffed. Etiquette was stupid and stuffy; she despised it and the people who took it seriously. Besides, she knew nothing about it. "But," he protested, "your books are full of nothing else!" Being to the manner born, she had never noticed that her novels were crammed with manners. Even so, it was too silly, and there were more than enough of such books. He said no more, but left with her the latest etiquette manual, published by a rival firm.

Coming home late one night after a dinner party, she dipped into it. When she came up for the third time, at two in the morning, she phoned him. "The woman doesn't know what she's writing about! It's a scandal!" Rather than see the great American public so gulled, she began work next morning at seven o'clock. She wrote 250,000 words in 10 months. Then, in 1922, the book was published—the first etiquette manual by a woman of high social position since Mrs. Sherwood (grandmother of the author Robert Sherwood) published hers in the '80s.

It was a best seller, and still is. Perhaps because of the author's own position, perhaps because it was so readable, perhaps because the increased mobility of our society had created a public already eager for this dose, if only it could be made palatable, her "blue book of social usage" went through edition after edition, each year increasing its sale. By early 1941 it had sold over half a million copies, at $4 each. None of her works has ever gone into a popular priced edition, although the newest has come down to $2.50.

Meanwhile, since 1931 she has been making radio broadcasts during the winter, and her columns, syndicated in about 135 newspapers with a circulation of some 6,500,000, bring in an average of over 250,000 letters each year. What she means to her correspondents is suggested by the response to Walter Winchell's announcement in his column that she was ill. Within an hour a hundred telegrams had arrived, and her room was overflowing with flowers from people she had never seen.

All the etiquette in America could not restrict its energetic autocrat to a single activity. She has found time to write testimonials at $3,000 for ginger ale, pamphlets at $5,000 for linen, silverware, glassware, even

to say a golden word for one of the cigarets nothing could induce her to smoke. After her architect son died in 1927, she sought consolation in remodeling old farmhouses into delightful country homes. House decoration she considers her true calling, and her *Personality of a House* (1930) is used as a textbook in many schools and colleges. People who want their homes designed by Emily Post are willing to pay handsomely for her services, or even for long-distance advice from New York.

Her own home is also her own product. With her son Bruce, who was just beginning to be a successful architect, she remodeled a building leased by herself and 17 friends in a cooperative revolt against the prevailing lack of closet space, large windows, and servants' dining rooms in New York. On the ground floor of this building her local secretaries cope with the daily avalanche of mail, while higher up where the view begins she inhabits a roomy apartment bright with her favorite chintzes and twittering with caged birds.

Until recently, when doctors' orders postponed her rising hour to six, she began each day at five-thirty, switching on the coffee percolator that stood ready by her bed and nibbling a bit of zwieback from the tray. Then she worked in bed, amid a flurry of pencils, papers and galley proofs, until half-past seven, when her servants began to stir. By eight the day was in full swing, and swung on steadily till bedtime, with mornings devoted to letters and the daily column, afternoons to appointments and talks. Most of the column mail is now handled by secretaries here and throughout the country; but special cases always receive special handling—the most special ones by Mrs. Post herself. She usually lunches at home, sometimes with her son Ned, her "beautiful black swan" who repays her careful teachings by giving her invaluable advice about what the correct gentleman will wear. Often she invites business associates for lunch; and when strong men lunch with Emily Post for the first time, they sometimes also wince. But they soon learn that the perfect lady is able to put a mutton chop at ease, even though it skid most greasily from its plate onto her daintiest doily.

Her first radio audition was in 1929. "I'm sure my voice isn't very good, so I really don't know why you bother," she fluted into the microphone while a group of potential sponsors listened in the next room. She was mistaken, however, and they all rushed in clamoring for her to name her price. A lady is never caught off guard. "How much do Amos and Andy get?" she inquired serenely. Being a true lady, she consented to close for $500 a broadcast—as a starter.

Neither radio nor any other engagement can keep her in town through the hot months which she regularly spends in Edgartown, Massachusetts, where she has converted a former farmhouse into an airy—though definitely not a streamlined—summer home. In the city her activity is professional rather than social, for she prefers a life of comparative retirement. Before her eyes began to trouble her she went frequently to the movies, often accompanied by her housekeeper. She likes to sew and on occasion has made her own clothes, which are of the feminine type, tending to the fluttery even in tailor-made hours.

That Mrs. Post's own views on etiquette have changed considerably was evident in the 1937 revision of her first book, and even more clear in her 1940 volume, *Children Are People*. The form she more and more minimizes, declaring, "nothing is less important than which fork you use." The spirit is all. Today, far from her first scornful attitude toward etiquette, she can proclaim: "Etiquette is the science of living. It embraces everything. It is honor. It is ethics."

References

Christian Sci Mon Mag p3 My 25 '38 pors
Ind Woman 20:103+ Ap '41 por
New Yorker 6:22-5 Ag 16 '30
Pict R 38:4+ O '36 por
Pub W 132:1101-2 S 18 '37
Sat Eve Post 209:18-19+ My 15 '37 pors
Time 30:46-8 S 20 '37 pors
Post, E. Flight of a Moth 1904
Who's Who in America

POUND, SIR (ALFRED) DUDLEY (PICKMAN ROGERS) Aug. 29, 1877- British Admiral of the Fleet; First Sea Lord

Address: Ravenswood, Gresham Rd, Staines, England

The administrative, political head of the British Admiralty is A. V. Alexander, its First Lord. Since 1939 Sir Dudley Pound, a practical sailor, has been his righthand man as First Sea Lord, bringing to the position varied experience both in big ships and in high executive posts ashore. Sir Dudley has the complete confidence of Winston Churchill, for during the First World War the two men worked together in the Admiralty, and Pound then and now shares the Churchillian pugnacity, is all for hitting the enemy when you can get at him.

Pound, whose book on the sea offensive is used as a text by the staff colleges of many countries, is an "all-arounder," a man "whose thoroughness is not pedantic, whose energy succumbs to neither red tape nor his chronic arthritis." For nearly 50 years he has served in the Navy—in a half-century which has seen great advances in the size, speed and armament of ships, substantial increases in the rapidity and range of gunfire, and the introduction of countless new mechanical devices. His alternating periods of service afloat and ashore have given him exceptional opportunities to coordinate strategy and tactics, and today, when many critics doubt the efficacy of capital ships, he remains deeply convinced that they are the backbone of a fleet. He is convinced, too, that the convoy system, organized during the First World War, continues and will successfully continue to keep losses from sub-

International

SIR DUDLEY POUND

marine action within bounds in the present War and to ensure the arrival of the food, oil and munitions on which the survival of Great Britain depends.

Like Sir Archibald Sinclair, Sir Dudley Pound is half American, for his father, Alfred John Pound, a barrister, married Elizabeth Pickman Rogers of Boston, Massachusetts. Dudley was born on the sea-lapped Isle of Wight and attended school at Fonthill at East Grinstead, Surrey and at The Limes, Greenwich, both rather small schools. Then, in 1891, at the usual age of 14, he entered the Navy as a cadet. Two years later he went out as a midshipman to the China Station in the *Royal Sovereign* and in 1896 received his first promotion, to sub-lieutenant. In these days he specialized in torpedo work and took a course qualifying him for torpedo lieutenant.

By 1909 Pound had risen to the rank of commander and seemed well set for advancement, though he had no special "pull." He was then transferred to the Torpedo Department at the Admiralty and remained there until 1911, when he went to sea again as second in command of the cruiser *Superb*, a crack ship. In it, writes Keble Chatterton, "not only did he acquit himself as a gifted organizer and overseer of men, but as an officer willing at any moment to lay down his life for them." He showed this when he made a gallant attempt to save three men from suffocation in a gas-filled hold, an act of courage for which he received the Royal Humane Society's Medal.

In January 1913 Pound was sent to the Naval War College at Portsmouth "for higher

POUND, SIR DUDLEY—*Continued*

studies as one marked out for staff work."
He remained there for one year and a half,
when he joined the cruiser *St. Vincent* as
second in command. At the end of 1914 he
was made a captain (a much higher rank
than the army captaincy and roughly equivalent
to colonel) and recalled to the Admiralty to
be naval assistant to Lord Fisher, then First
Sea Lord. He was only 37 years old.

His combination of sea experience and administrative work made Pound eminently
qualified for this position, yet he was moved
out of it for political reasons in the autumn
of 1915 when Fisher and Churchill resigned.
Immediately he took command of the 20,000
ton battleship *Colossus* and it wasn't long after
that when he saw action in the Battle of Jutland (May 31, 1916). In this fight the *Colossus*
sank a three funneled cruiser and beat off
two destroyers, after which she really got into
the thick of the danger. Then she sank the
cruiser *Lutzow*, sustained considerable damage
to her superstructure and narrowly averted
disaster by turning away from five torpedoes
traveling toward her. For his share in this
battle Pound was mentioned in dispatches.

July 1917 found him captain in the Admiralty once more, this time as director of
operations. In 1918 he was created a Companion of the Bath and received the American
D. S. M. Two years later he was in the
battleship *Hood* with Sir Roger Keyes and
later in that year commanded the *Repulse*.
Then back to the Admiralty again, as director
of plans and a naval A. D. C. to the King.
He left the Admiralty in 1925 and became
chief of staff to Keyes on the Mediterranean
Station after having been promoted to rear
admiral. Then came two years as chief of the
naval staff at the Admiralty, followed by two
years as commander of the battle cruiser
squadron. In 1930 he had been raised to vice-
admiral and in 1932 he became Second Sea
Lord and chief of naval personnel.

The years 1935 and 1936 must have been
among the most tense and anxious in Pound's
career, for he was promoted to admiral in
January 1935 and sent to fish in the very
troubled waters of the Mediterranean. He
was there all through the Abyssinian and
Spanish Wars, first as chief of staff to Sir
William Fisher and from March 1936 as
commander in chief of the Mediterranean
Fleet. His tactful and wary handling of a
most delicate naval and political situation
earned him a knighthood in 1937 as G. C. V. O.
The G. C. B. followed later.

On July 31, 1939 Sir Dudley Pound reached
the summit of his profession as First Sea
Lord and chief of the naval staff, with promotion to the rank of admiral of the fleet.
Under his general direction the Navy keeps
its watch over thousands of miles of sea,
and though depleted by losses, as the late
Lord Lothian announced in December 1940,
still guards Britain and British interests with
quiet efficiency.

The man who directs its movements with
A. V. Alexander is not a picturesque figure.
He is rarely in the news; his portrait is not
seen about in schools or clubs; he rarely
makes a public statement. Toward the navy
he is "a keen disciplinarian" whose "bark
is said to be worse than his bite." Solicitous
for the comfort of the lower deck, he started
at every home port an organization to look
after sailors' welfare and marriage allowances, "but the last thing that ever entered
his mind would be to become what is known
as a 'Popularity Jack.'"

In the troubled days of the Second World
War Pound takes only four or five hours'
sleep and has a bed in an office off his
chart-hung war room, in and out of which
he goes many times a night to confer with the
operations staff. He tries to keep fit, though,
by walking and shooting—he is "a first class
shot, and has been responsible for a catalog
showing the many kinds of game to be found
along the shores of the Mediterranean."
What with working and keeping fit for his
job Sir Dudley hasn't much time to spend
with Lady Pound, who runs the Knitted-
Garments-for-the-Navy. The War itself keeps
him from spending time with his two sons,
the elder a captain of the marines; the younger a Royal Navy lieutenant.

References

> Ministry of Information Clip-Sheet
> No 8 F 28 '40
> Time 35:22 Ap 22 '40 por (cover)
> Chatterton, E. K. Leaders of the Royal
> Navy pam 1940
> Tuohy, F. Twelve Lances for Liberty
> p181-4 1940
> Who's Who

POURTALÈS, GUY, COUNT DE (poor"-
tä"lĕs') Aug. 4, 1881—June 13, 1941 Novelist
and biographer; first novel, *Solitudes*, was
published in 1913; his *La Pêche Miraculeuse*,
published in America as *Shadows Around the
Lake* (1937), won the Grand Prix de Rome,
the Prix Gobert and the Heinemann Prize
in England; wrote biographies of Liszt,
Chopin and Wagner.

References

> Who's Who

Obituaries

> N Y Times p19 Je 13 '41 por
> Pub W 139:2478 Je 21 '41

**POWELL, ROBERT STEPHENSON
SMYTH BADEN-, 1ST BARON BADEN-
POWELL OF GILWELL** *See* Baden-
Powell of Gilwell, R. S. S. B.-P., 1st Baron

POWER, SIR D'ARCY Nov. 11, 1885—
May 18, 1941 Internationally known British
surgeon and author of medical works; was
visiting lecturer at Johns Hopkins University
from 1931 to 1932; made knight commander
of the Order of the British Empire; had been

member and former officer of most of Great Britain's leading medical societies.

References

Author's and Writers' Who's Who
Who's Who

Obituaries

N Y Herald Tribune p10 My 19 '41
Sch & Soc 53:666 My 24 '41

PRAJADHIPOK, FORMER KING OF SIAM (prà-chä'tĭ-pŏk) Nov. 8, 1893—May 30, 1941 Ascended the Siamese throne in 1925; for nearly 10 years until he abdicated in 1935 ruled more than 11 million people; abdicated because his Cabinet refused to accept his plans for reforms of the Constitution; visited the United States twice; died in England where he had made his home since his abdication.

References

Christian Sci Mon Mag p6 F 23 '38 por
Cur Hist 41:511-12 Ja '35; 42:111-12 Ap '35
Lit Digest 114:11 Jl 9 '32 por; 118:15, 118:33 N 10 '34 por
Newsweek 5:16 Mr 9 '35 por
No Am 239:82-8 Ja '35
R of Rs (Lond) 86:18-19 Ap '35
International Who's Who

Obituaries

N Y Times p26 My 31 '41 por
Time 37:63 Je 9 '41 por

PRÉVOST, MARCEL (prà'-vō') May 1, 1862—Apr. 8, 1941 Noted French novelist and playwright, one of the country's most prolific and most popular novelists; acquired his fame as "the ablest delineator of feminine character in fiction since Balzac"; elected to the French Academy in 1909 to fill the chair of Victorien Sardou; died in France at his home near Vianne.

References

Ann Pol et Litt 106:132-3 Ag 10 '35 por; 110:667-8 D 25 '37
Illustration 191:468 Ag 3 '35 por
International Who's Who
Qui Êtes-Vous?
Stephens, W. French Novelists of Today 1st ser. p45-81 1914-15

Obituaries

N Y Times p24 Ap 10 '41

PROKOFIEV, SERGE (SERGEYE-VICH) (prô-kô'fê-ĕf) Apr. 23, 1891- Composer; pianist; conductor

Address: Moscow, U. S. S. R.

The talent of Serge Prokofiev, prominent modern composer, has not always been understood or accepted. In his student days Prokofiev brought his first symphony to the composer Taneyev. The latter remarked that most of it was unoriginal, "tonic, dominant and subdominant." Deeply distressed to learn

SERGE PROKOFIEV

that his first important work contained nothing particularly his own, Prokofiev determined to study all the more seriously. This he did, under such instructors as Rimsky-Korsakoff and Liadov, meanwhile absorbing a less conventional musical viewpoint from Scriabin and Max Reger. A full decade passed before he again brought a score to Taneyev. "But, my dear boy," the old man exclaimed, "this is terrible!"

"Master," Prokofiev is said to have replied, "please remember what you said to me when I brought my G Major symphony."

Taneyev looked dazedly from the young composer to the score. "Good Lord," he asked, "am I responsible for this?"

Prokofiev weathered this shock, as he was to survive many another mishap in his career. He takes life in his stride, with indefatigable creative vigor and robust, if quiet, humor, and claims that he has no time for hobbies; though he wouldn't be completely groomed if there weren't a miniature chess set in his pocket. His new opera, Semyon Kotko, had its première in Moscow in June 1940. Meanwhile he was at work on a new score, a musical setting for Sheridan's The Duenna, and was converting themes from the opera into a symphonic suite that was scheduled for an early American production. "I burn my candle at three ends," he explained, "composing, conducting, and playing piano."

Born in Sontsovka, in the Ekaterinoslav district of South Russia on April 23, 1891, young Serge began his musical career at the age of five, composing Le Galop Hindou, which ignored the black keys of the piano. He first learned music from his mother, an excellent pianist who taught him to understand Beethoven and other composers. At the age of six he composed a march, a waltz and a rondo. At seven he was taken to Moscow

PROKOFIEV, SERGE—*Continued*

to hear *Prince Igor* and *Faust*. But his own opera, *The Giant,* written promptly upon his return home, had no libretto, having been modeled after the scores in his mother's library, which were for piano only. The libretto was coaxed along, however, and a grand première arranged at the home of an uncle, with Serge's cousins in the cast. "When your operas are played at the Imperial Theatre," his uncle said, "don't forget that the first performance of your first opera was given at my house." His second opera, *Desert Islands,* was left unfinished.

In 1901, at the age of ten, he studied with Glière, on the advice of Taneyev, and during three years managed to compose a symphony, two short operas and two piano sonatas. From Glière he went to the St. Petersburg Conservatory, where he remained for 10 years and was graduated in 1914. Besides his studies with Rimsky-Korsakoff and Liadov, he took conducting with Tcherepnin and piano lessons from Annette Essipova. He was awarded the Rubinstein Prize as pianist but failed to get the first award in composition. Aside from gaining a sound technical foundation at the Conservatory, he composed the *Symphony in E Minor,* two operas, six sonatas and about one hundred piano pieces. It was also during this period that he wrote *First Piano Concerto,* featuring the simultaneous use of two different tonalities, of which Boris de Schloezer wrote: "The form is always limpid, logical and perfectly natural."

Through all its various stages Prokofiev's music is characterized by firm structural qualities that De Schloezer had in mind when he described it as "a uniform terseness, continuous and almost mechanical. . . No shadows, no vagueness, but definite lines, sharp contours, clearly defined planes. The rhythms are always well-marked. . . He uses polytonality systematically. His form is clear and logical. In many respects his musical temperament comes near to that of the classics—especially of Scarlatti."

While Prokofiev was at the Conservatory, Glazounov, who could not approve the student's daring ways, nevertheless arranged a test performance of his symphony. Prokofiev found enthusiastic support from a society of contemporary music in St. Petersburg. Exempted from military service during the World War years as the only son of a widow, he composed the *Scythian Suite,* generally described as both *"primitivist"* and daring, but its story material was not thought by Diaghilev suitable for ballet. The composer then began work on *The Chout,* production of which was delayed until 1921, when Diaghilev put it on in Paris. (Diaghilev also produced his later ballets, *L'Enfant Prodigue* [1929] and *Surle Borysthène* [1930].) Another musical creation on which the young composer was at this time hard at work was an opera based on Dostoevsky's *The Gambler* (later produced by Meyerhold at the Leningrad Opera).

Granted a passport by the Russian Government in 1918, Prokofiev came to America, where he was promptly hailed by the *Musical Courier* as a "musical Bolshevik." His *Classical Symphony* had its American debut at Carnegie Hall in December 1918. One critic found it not distinguished and not classical. Another decided that the young Russian's music was "cold and cerebral." But although Olin Downes didn't feel that it quite out-Mozarted Mozart, he did agree that it was "witty and spirited." As a matter of fact, humor is often a component in Prokofiev's writing, though it has not always been recognized as such.

Considered almost since the beginning of his career a pianist of note, Prokofiev has toured the world several times, occasionally taking the baton to conduct one of his works or the work of other composers. In December 1921 something of a sensation was created by the world première of his opera, *The Love of Three Oranges,* at the Chicago Opera House. This, too, was a subject for controversy, but those who found it musically sound and effective burlesque were the confident majority. One critic wrote glowingly: "He strips grand opera of its glamor and makes it no longer grand. He makes opera safe for democracy, and that is the justification of all great burlesque—to humanize the object of its ridicule." A minority voice called it "a color marvel but enigmatic noise."

Prokofiev's ballet, *The Age of Steel (Le Pas d' Acier),* produced in Paris in 1927 and in America in 1931, was based upon the growing vigor of Soviet industry. It was unfavorably received in Paris by many critics and in America, strangely enough, it was produced as a satire on the machine age. Under these circumstances it was not strange that Gilman found it a "choregraphical what-not." Prokofiev's *Fourth Symphony* was composed for the fiftieth anniversary of the Boston Symphony Orchestra in 1930. It had a mixed reception, some listeners finding it difficult.

Among his numerous works are: the popular ballet, *Romeo and Juliet,* written for the Bolshoi Theatre in Moscow (1935), and the *Second Violin Concerto,* composed that same year. On his seventh visit to the United States in 1937 he conducted *Romeo and Juliet,* says *Time,* "with precise beat and knees that wobbled curiously but in accurate rhythm." As for the music, it was "a sly elusive projection of its subject, more lyric than early works but with less emphasis on 'new curves' than expected."

It may be arguable whether or not *Peter and the Wolf* takes a few program composers "for a ride" as one critic intimates, but there can be no doubt that the first American performance of this ballet was unlike its Russian première. *Peter and the Wolf* was created for the children's concert in Moscow on May 2, 1936. During the course of the ballet a voice declaimed the text, instructively and humorously assigning to each character its instrument of the appropriate timbre. In its entire artistic concept it was written for children. The first American performance, however, left out the voice of the narrator, which was properly restored for American listeners only when Koussevitzky recorded it with the Boston Symphony.

"Once a musical bad boy," reported *Time* in 1938, "he has today forsworn his 'smart' past, moved back to the Soviet Union and embarked on an expedition into what he describes as the 'deeper realms of music.'" Critics have found his recent works strikingly different from those of the early 1920's when Prokofiev lived in Paris. According to A. A. Fraser, "his style becomes much less fantastic and more intense, but this does not imply that it was formerly superficial. The discord used formerly rather as a sonority complete in itself now occurs logically at the meeting of different strands of melody and lines of thought, but polyphony is not a new feature of this composer."

Along somewhat similar lines, Prokofiev himself says: "There has been too much dissonance. Bach used dissonance as good salt for his music. Others applied pepper, seasoned the dishes more and more highly, till all healthy appetites were sick and until finally the music was nothing but pepper. Well, I think society has had enough of that." He also hints that changing audiences have affected his work. Today, he explains, there are many more people in the U. S. S. R. who like music, but a great deal of difficult music is inaccessible to them. Thus, while music should reach this new and larger audience it should not, in his opinion, sacrifice value. "I assure you," he concludes, "it is very difficult to find the language which will convey the new musical thought to the people, in terms they will understand, but I find the problem an inspiring one." Early in 1941 the composer was reported at work on a new opera based on Sheridan's play, *The Duenna,* and the music for a Russian film, *Ivan the Terrible.*

In appearance Prokofiev is above average height, thickly put together, with thin blond hair retreating from a bulging brow. His clothes "quietly praise a good tailor." His two sons have shown some talent for music but, says their father, "I have not encouraged them too much—with their mother a singer and me a pianist two more music-makers in the house would result in intolerable noise." His wife, Lina Llubera, the concert singer, has accompanied him during his visits to the United States and has often given concerts there. Both have always taken a keen, lively interest in things American and they have many American friends, among them Benny Goodman. Prokofiev's interest in jazz music is typical: "If one chooses what is best in rhythm, melody and instrumentation, one may come across great riches."

Prokofiev's special compositions for the Pushkin centenary (1936) included incidental music for Pushkin's drama *Eugene Onegin* and *Boris Godunov.* He also wrote a "gran-diose" cantata for the twentieth anniversary of the October Revolution, using authentic texts from speeches of Marx, Lenin and Stalin. It calls for four instrumental and two choral groups—about five hundred performers in all. Among the films for which Prokofiev has written music are *The Czar Wants To Sleep,* 1934 (from which came the orchestral suite *Lieutenant Kije*), and Eisenstein's *Alexander Nevsky,* shown in America in 1939. Prokofiev's most recent work, a sixth piano sonata, was introduced in America, in the winter of 1941, by the eminent pianist, Vladimir Horowitz.

References

Etude 47:583-4 Ag '29 por
Liv Age 357:89-90 S '39
Mercure de France 273:399-401 Ja 15 '37
Musical Courier D 19 '18
N Y Sun F 9 '38
N Y Times F 2 '30
Time 29:38 F 1 '37; 31:46-8 Ap 4 '38 por

Baker's Biographical Dictionary of Musicians 1940
Brower, H. M. Modern Masters of the Keyboard p223-38 1926
Ewen, D. Twentieth Century Composers p117-27 1937
Ewen, D. ed. Composers of Today 1936
Fraser, A. A. Essays on Music p112-21 1930
International Who's Who
Sabaneev, L. L. Modern Russian Composers p87-102 1927
Saminsky, L. Music of Our Day p194-201 1937
Thompson, O. ed. International Cyclopedia of Music and Musicians 1939

PYLE, ERNIE Aug. 3, 1900- Columnist; reporter

Address: b. Scripps-Howard Newspaper Alliance, Washington, D. C.; h. Albuquerque, N. Mex.

A roving reporter, "an inconspicuous little man with thinning reddish hair and a shy, pixy face," for the past few years has written so sensitively about small places, things and people that his itinerant column, *Ernie Pyle in London,* ran in 18 Scripps-Howard newspapers and 46 others. Ernie Pyle, who has covered some 200,000 miles in the Western Hemisphere, has written about almost everything—about the rain, old men with wooden legs, a Nebraska town on relief, zipper-pants difficulties. "In six years I've written on every subject from Mrs. Roosevelt to sore feet," he says. As his fellow-columnist Westbrook Pegler once commented: "Ernie Pyle writes his way along, keeps out of New York and other big cities that are over-covered by other reporters and writers, knows more small-town and dirt-road Americans than Jim Farley, and is better informed on the condition—or anyway the feeling—of the small people than Mrs. Roosevelt herself." And, as

ERNIE PYLE

a writer in *Time* puts it: "Whenever Ernie takes a vacation, editors are apt to reprint it."

In November 1940 Ernie Pyle flew via Lisbon to London and editors were more than glad to print and reprint what he saw there during the grim holiday season and after. His vivid, dramatic piece of January 1, 1941 on the London air bombardment excited so much attention that readers and critics have already made it their nomination as the "best column of the year." The "little fellow" hitherto content to write about little things has found himself almost over night topping the best that seasoned war correspondents in big cities have to offer.

"Some day when peace has returned again to this odd world," he wrote, "I want to come to London again and look down upon the peaceful silver curve of the Thames with its dark bridges. And I want to tell somebody who has never seen it how London looked on a certain night in the holiday season of the year 1940. It was a night when London was ringed and stabbed with fire. . . The closest fires were near enough for us to hear the crackling flames and the yells of firemen. Little fires grew into big ones even as we watched. . . The sky was red and angry, and overhead, making a ceiling in the vast heavens, there was a cloud of smoke. . . And now and then, through a hole in that pink shroud, there twinkled incongruously a permanent, genuine star—the old-fashioned kind that has always been there. . . These things all went together to make the most hateful, most beautiful single scene I have ever known."

Several of Ernie Pyle's cabled reports during February concerned London's public air-raid shelters. They remind him, he wrote, of nothing so much as "our own makeshift depression camps at home." But, like our camps,

they are gradually getting better, though "God knows there is plenty of room for better conditions in some of the shelters. The body heat of thousands of packed people makes some shelters stifling. In others, deep beneath stone arches and with concrete floors, the chill dampness is deadly. At one church in Stepney people were actually sleeping until recently in stone coffins that once held corpses." But the emptied crypts of St. Martin's Church have been fixed up "more like a club house. . . When you see a church with a bomb hole in its side and 500 pretty safe and happy people in its basement, and girls smoking cigarets inside the sacred walls without anybody yelling at them, then I say the church has found a real religion." A few months later his book, *Ernie Pyle in England*, was published, telling of all these things.

Since early boyhood Ernest Taylor (shortened to Ernie) Pyle has never been in one place long enough to have a home address. Not until 1940 did he finally buy a lot and build himself a house in Albuquerque, New Mexico ("I don't know what he'll use it for," remarked Scripps-Howard's Lee Miller), where he made his first brief visit in March 1941 after returning from London. He was born August 3, 1900 on a farm near Dana, Indiana; his father, William C. Pyle, still lives there. His mother, Maria Pyle, died early in 1941.

"I wasn't born in a log cabin," he wrote in one of his columns, "but I did start driving a team in the fields when I was nine years old, if that helps any." He attended Indiana University for three and a half years but quit without being graduated. Thereafter he worked for 12 years on various newspapers in Indiana, Washington, D. C., and New York.

While working for the Washington *Daily News* he met Geraldine Siebolds of Minnesota, who had a government job; in 1926 they were married. Fed up temporarily with the newspaper business, he drew out his savings, bought a Model-T Ford roadster. He and Mrs. Pyle then took the first of their many trips together, driving leisurely around the rim of the United States. "Jerry" Pyle, always referred to in her husband's column as "that girl who rides with me," has shared his highway adventures. Bob Fredericks in the Miami *Herald* writes of her: "To Ernie she is an inseparable part of a life venture and very much a partner in the business at hand of covering the world. . . It's always 'our column' and 'we' when the Pyles discuss things. And the Pyles don't talk for display purposes. They don't engage in little niceties [between] themselves to impress others. As said before, the Pyles have learned to report and describe facts and let the facts speak for themselves."

Ending this first trip in New York, Pyle went to work as a copyreader, then was called back to the Washington *News* again, where he was successively telegraph editor, aviation columnist and managing editor. He became the latter against his better judgment; and after he had "distinguished" himself by burying the arrest of Hauptmann, kidnapper of the Lindbergh baby, at the bottom of page one, he persuaded Scripps-Howard into letting him give up the managing editor's desk to experiment with a roving-reporter assignment. That was in 1935, and Ernie Pyle has been at it ever since.

"We have travelled by practically all forms of locomotion, including piggyback," he writes. "We have been in every country in the Western Hemisphere but two. We have stayed in more than eight hundred hotels, have crossed the continent exactly twenty-four times, flown in sixty-six different airplanes, ridden on twenty-nine different boats, walked two hundred miles, gone through five sets of tires and put out approximately $2,500 in tips. In the past six years, these columns have stretched out to the horrifying equivalent of twenty-two full-length books. Set in seven-point type they would make a newspaper column three-quarters of a mile long. The mere thought of it makes me sick at my stomach.

"Of all the places we've been, we'd rather pay another visit to Hawaii. In the States we are partial to New Mexico. My most interesting long trip was through Alaska, although I wasn't crazy about it at the time. . . We have worn out two cars, three typewriters, and pretty soon I'm going to have to have a new pair of shoes. I love to drive and never get tired of it, but on long days I do get to hurting on the bottom.

"The most serious predicament we've ever been in was when an airplane motor went dead as we were 10,000 feet over the Andes in northern Peru. But we flew for an hour on one motor, and it turned out just like all good short stories. Sure, we were scared. . . For four years straight we have got our last Christmas presents in April."

Ernie Pyle has visited the famous leper colony on Molokai Island in Hawaii; he has gone up the Yukon River by boat and flown to the Bering shore of Alaska; he drove from Texas to Mexico City before the new highway was finished; he has gone 2,800 feet down in a mine and 16,000 feet up in a Pan-American plane. "I weigh 108 pounds, eat left-handed, am 28 inches around the waist, and still have a little hair left," he says. Although Jerry, "that girl," didn't go with him on his London trip (from which he returned on March 22), she was still a contributing factor to "our" column while she waited for the husband's return to take the "vacation" that always makes news.

References

N Y World-Telegram p11 F 6 '41 por; p14 F 7 '41 por; p17 Mr 27 '41
Time 37:50+ Ja 13 '41 por
Pyle, E. Ernie Pyle in England 1941

QUEZON, MANUEL L(UIS) (kā'sŏn) Aug. 19, 1878- President of the Philippine Islands

Bulletin: On December 19, 1941 in an address broadcast from Manila, President Quezon announced: "We are fully pre-

Office of the President of the Philippines

MANUEL L. QUEZON

pared to defend the cause of liberty and democracy to the last drop of our blood." A week later Manila was formally declared an open city by General MacArthur (see sketch this issue) and Quezon fled with the armed forces and other heads of the Philippine Government. The capital was murderously bombed by the Japanese 30 hours later.

From August 1941 issue (revised):

"We owe our loyalty to America and we are bound to her by bonds of everlasting gratitude," said President Manuel L. Quezon on Loyalty Day (late in June 1941), a new holiday in the Philippine Islands. To the 100,000 demonstrating in Manila and to a curious world, he placed himself on record for the first time about where he stands on the Second World War. "Should the United States enter the War, she will find all of the people of this country, to the last man, on her side. Our stake in this War is our own future independence, and assurance that independence may endure."

This statement marked a radical and realistic change from an earlier attitude on the part of the Filipinos, inclined to appease Japan so as to avoid affronting a powerful neighbor whom they might one day be forced to face alone. In 1940 Quezon was openly expressing doubts about the country's ability to defend itself, and a slackening in the Philippine defense effort appeared in subsequent cuts in appropriations for munitions and equipment. But in April 1941, $50,000,000 was appropriated from funds owed to the Island Government, to be spent by the War, Navy and Interior Departments for defense of the Philippine Islands.

Now the 7,083 islands of the Philippine Archipelago, whose armed forces were incorporated into those of the United States

QUEZON, MANUEL L.—*Continued*

by President Roosevelt's order of July 26, 1941, are rapidly being transformed into the United States' first line of defense in the Orient. Key cities are being fortified and preparations have been made to evacuate the civilian populations of cities most exposed to attack. In a message to the National Assembly on February 1, President Quezon had maintained that it was up to the United States to provide air shelters and other civilian defense measures for the Islands until their independence became effective—in opposition to High Commissioner Francis B. Sayre, who held that the extent of the autonomy of the Philippine Government made it necessary for Philippine authorities to assume civilian defense responsibilities. However, on March 22, after the issue had been tossed back and forth, Quezon appointed a Civilian Emergency Administration.

Until 1941, President Quezon's most important problem was his attitude on the independence promised for July 4, 1946. Some people believe that he would like to see independence postponed indefinitely, perhaps in the form of a Dominion government. But reversing the political doctrine upon which he has based his whole meteoric career is no easy task, even for the supple President. He once told a graduating class at the normal school that he "prefers a government run like hell by Filipinos to one run like heaven by Americans." Strong factions in Manila, it is reported, particularly rich sugar men, have started a movement to request the United States to maintain some sort of tie with the Islands. Prime factors in this movement are the realization that the United States' withdrawal will smash up the Islands economically, open them wide to Japanese domination. The Philippine Government has offered to shut down exports of strategic materials—copra, iron ore, hemp—to all countries except the United States in the interest of American armament.

This political leader who has "more power than Franklin D. Roosevelt has yet dreamed of" was born Manuel Luis Quezon Antonio y Molina, in Baler, a desolate village on the eastern coast of the Island of Luzon, on August 19, 1878. His father, Lucio Quezon, was a Filipino and his mother, Maria (Molina) Quezon, was partly Spanish. Both schoolteachers, they taught Manuel his ABC's. The parish priest then carried on his education until he was 11. At school in Manila he was "bright but lazy" and nicknamed *gulerato*—"bluffer"—by his classmates. After having finished his work at the junior college at San Juan de Letran, he was appointed a lecturer at the University of Santo Tomas so that he could receive free board, lodging and tuition while studying law. His law studies were interrupted by the Spanish-American War.

"A fearless, quick-tempered, obstinate fighter," Manuel, who enlisted as Manuel Kison, was rapidly promoted from private to major, fighting first against the Spanish rulers and later against the American invaders. After the insurrection collapsed in 1899 he surrendered his sword, spent six months in jail, then returned to Manila. There he studied theology at the University until the Catholic fathers advised him to give up any idea of the priesthood and sent him to oversee one of their farms. He did not stay long: he returned to Manila to work in a Catholic savings bank. At the same time he resumed the study of law at the University of Santo Tomas and in 1903 passed the Bar examination. Sergio Osmeña, who was alternately to be his political ally and rival and who is now regarded as likely to succeed Quezon, was graduated at the same time.

At the death of his father Manuel Quezon returned to Baler and set up a law practice in Tayabas Province. In a few months he had more clients than he could handle. In answer to a call to public service, however, he gave up a lucrative private practice to take the post of provincial *fiscal*—prosecuting attorney—of Mindoro and later of Tayabas. He earned a national reputation almost at once for his prosecution of an American lawyer for fraud. In 1906 he resigned to start his political career. He was elected provincial Governor. "Demonstrating in the early elections characteristics of jumping from one side of an issue to another [he considers consistency a weakness], always picking the popular one," he showed that "he was obviously the potential Nationalist leader of the Islands." The following year he resigned from the Governorship to become a candidate for the Philippine Assembly on the Nacionalista Party platform. In the Assembly, Osmeña was elected Speaker of the House and Quezon floor leader.

As a reward for his ability to win over malcontents by his persuasive powers, in 1908 Quezon was sent as Philippine representative to an International Navigation Congress in St. Petersburg. The appointment was not made in time for him to attend the conference, but he visited and enjoyed Paris. Returning to the Islands, he decided that Washington, D.C., would be the best place to work for Philippine independence and next had himself appointed to the post of Resident Commissioner (with a voice in Congress, but no vote), a post which he held from 1909 to 1916. A Beau Brummell in Washington, "one of the world's best ballroom dancers" (among the best pupils Arthur Murray ever had, one night he took out 16 Murray instructresses all at once), he was rapidly becoming also one of the "world's supplest and hardest-boiled politicians." An effective lobbyist, he had the law revised so that Filipinos would form a majority on the Philippine Commission; in 1913 he helped arrange the appointment of pro-Filipino Francis Burton Harrison as Governor General; in 1916 he was the spiritual author of the Jones Bill.

In 1916 Quezon returned to the Islands, "the hero of his country," bringing with him the Jones Act, which gave the Filipinos power to legislate for themselves subject to a veto by the American Governor General, and which abolished the Philippine Commission. He was promptly elected to the Senate. At that time Osmeña and Quezon were almost of equal strength; but in the elections Quezon attacked Osmeña on the strength of the Wood-Forbes investigation and became President of the Nacionalista Party. In the Senate he was elected President.

There followed years of passionate struggle with General Wood, the Governor who had succeeded Harrison and reversed his pro-Filipino policy. Once, feeling slighted when he was made to wait in the Governor's office for an interview, Quezon stormed out, shouting: "Tell General Wood to go to hell!" As Senate President, Quezon fought to reduce the Governor Generalship position to a mere figurehead, "because we want a government of Filipinos, by the Filipinos and for the Filipinos." With other Governors "he ingratiated himself, cajoling, bluffing, threatening." He dodged back and forth to Washington; he had the 1925 Fairfield Law (for independence) shelved by insisting on instant, not eventual, complete independence for the Islands. In 1927, when he returned again to Washington to resume the struggle, he became ill. In his absence he was nevertheless elected Senator (1928) and re-elected President of the Senate. In 1931, after the Hawes-Cutting-Hare Law had been passed by the United States Senate, vetoed by President Hoover, and the veto overridden, Quezon opposed it. In Quezon's words, "America would still hold military and naval bases in the Philippines even after the latter's independence, and, moreover, export duties regulated in the law would destroy both industry and trade." Some say his opposition was based on a fear that Osmeña, who had accompanied him to Washington, might return to the Islands a national hero. In any case, the legislature supported Quezon and voted against the bill.

Quezon returned to the United States to lobby for a better law. In 1934 he secured the passage of the Tydings-McDuffie Bill, which, tentatively at least, won the fight. Complete independence was promised for 1946, and the bill also provided for duty-free importation of the principal Philippine products, sugar, coconut oil and cordage (Manila hemp) to the United States.

With the passage of this bill, Quezon's leadership was assured. In the election of 1935 he formed a Coalition Party (he believes in a one-party system, since "political parties are good only for evil things") reuniting the Nacionalistas, who had split over the Hawes Act, and with Osmeña as Vice-Presidential candidate he defeated General Aguinaldo for President by an overwhelming majority. His first act as chief executive, alarmed by aggressions in the Far East and in Europe, was to railroad a national defense bill through the rubber-stamp unicameral legislature. This made him chairman of the Council for National Defense, with the chief of staff directly subordinate to the President.

Some observers see in this national defense plan, which makes it almost impossible for any military clique to overthrow or dominate the President, "a strong Quezon personal defense plan." When he divested the speaker of the Philippine Assembly of his most important prerogative—the leadership of his party in that body—Quezon said: "The speaker of the legislative assembly presides over the deliberations of that body. That is his main and most important function. That is his only function." As for the President's functions: the purse strings of the nation are in his hands; he approves all bills before they are introduced into the legislature; and in 1940 the Constitution was amended so that he could run for re-election.

Another important step in the assumption of what his opponents call dictatorial powers was taken on August 10, 1940, when Quezon won "one of the hardest fights" of his colorful political career by jamming through the National Assembly the Emergency Powers Bill, which may change the social and economic structure of his country drastically. By a vote of 62 to 1 he was given authority to require civilians to give service to the Government, to outlaw strikes, to commandeer shipping and other transportation, to control food resources and to revise the educational system. President Quezon insisted that the measures, particularly the anti-spy restrictions, were necessary for the safety of the Islands, which contain large Japanese colonies and are almost surrounded by the expanding Japanese Empire. He also requested the extension of these powers until the new Assembly was elected in November. At that time he was re-elected President, for on August 16, 1941 his Nacionalista Party, taking advantage of the 1940 ruling although Quezon's health was reportedly "impaired from overwork," had nominated him as its candidate. At the time of nomination he said: "If the people elect me, I will serve."

Quezon can ordinarily count on about 75 or 85 per cent of the vote on any issue he puts up to the Filipinos. "By masterly handling of the patronage (he even appoints the village schoolteachers), by a passionate love of all things Filipino (except the opposition), and by a colorful personality that keeps him bounding into the limelight, he has kept first place among Island politicians." Perhaps John Gunther (see sketch this issue) revealed the secret of Quezon's phenomenal rise and his hold over his people when he wrote: "He is indisputably the best orator in the Islands, in any of the three languages, English [which he learned in six months], Spanish or Tagalog. His considerable charm, his patriotism, his executive capacity, his curious combination of American characteristics, like aggressive practicality, with a Latin heritage of suppleness and adroit facility in negotiation, all contributed to his career. But his knack of getting along well with both rich and poor, with the miserably fed peasants of the countryside as well as the Spanish millionaires in Manila, is probably his single most valuable characteristic. The masses adore him, because he gives them something. The rich eat out of his hand—when he isn't eating out of theirs—because he guarantees their survival. By using both he has built up an irresistible machine." Though according to Quezon any such report is "nonsensical,"

QUEZON, MANUEL L.—*Continued*

a movement is reported to be afoot to change the name of the Islands to Quezon; already there is a Quezon City; and students of the state-supported University of the Philippines have supposedly organized a "Quezon for King" Club.

On his way to the United States in 1918, when he was 40 years old, Quezon married his cousin, Aurora Aragon, then 29. They now have two daughters—Maria Aurora, "Baby"; Maria Zeneida, "Nini"; and a son, Manuel, Jr., "Nonong." Quezon's flair for living is both proverbial and prodigious. His Malacañan Palace outclasses the White House, and he, too, has a birthday ball, the proceeds of which go to a charity for the disease from which he once suffered—tuberculosis. His private office is large and richly furnished, and as he talks to visitors he teeters back and forth in a brocaded swivel chair. He makes frequent trips through the Islands on his swank white yacht, the *Casiana;* he still likes to dance and has lost none of his love for gaiety; his clothes are the wonder of the Islands. Short, slim, swarthy Don Manuel, as he is affectionately called by his people, looks much younger than his 63 years. Above his handsome face his hair is graying; bushy black eyebrows top penetrating eyes that even with pince-nez are sharp and bright. "Today, with a burnt-out look," says one commentator, "he still has the knack of charming, cajoling, trading or bullying his way to victory."

References

> Atlan 163:59-70 Ja '39 (Same abr. Read Digest 34:10-13 F '39)
> Christian Sci Mon Mag p1-2+ My 11 '38 il por
> Commonweal 24:259-60 Jl 3 '36
> Life 8:14+ Ap 1 '40 por
> Nation 144:320-2 Mr 20 '37
> Philippines-Japan 4:4-5+ D '39; 5:11-12+ Ja '40; 5:11-12+ F '40; 5:7-8+ Mr '40; 5:27-35 Ap '40; 5:23-34 My '40; 5:27-31 Je '40
> Time 30:11-12 S 20 '37 por; 36:16 S 2 '40 por
> American Catholic Who's Who
> Gunther, J. Inside Asia p287-304 1939
> Nolasco, T. D. de Filipino Case for American Retention 1940
> Quirino, C. Quezon, Man of Destiny 1935
> Rodriguez, E. B. President Quezon, his Biographical Sketch, Messages and Speeches 1940
> Who's Who in America 1916-17
> Who's Who in the Philippines
> Wise, J. H. and others, eds. Essays for Better Reading p129-43 1940

QUIDDE, LUDWIG (kvĭd'ĕ) Mar. 23, 1858—Mar. 4, 1941 German pacifist, exiled from Germany in 1913 for his pacifist activities, went to Switzerland, where he remained until after the First World War and then returned to Germany; collaborated with Strese-

mann, who with Briand won the Nobel Peace Prize in 1926; won the Nobel Prize in 1927 for his work for peace; after Hitler's advent to power he left Germany in 1933 and remained in Switzerland until his death.

References

> Wer ist's?
> Who's Who

Obituaries

> N Y Times p19 Mr 8 '41

QUILL, MICHAEL J(OSEPH) (kwĭl) Sept. 18, 1905- Labor leader; national president of the Transport Workers' Union
Address: b. 153 W. 64th St, New York City

In September 1941, at the third biennial convention of the Transport Workers' Union, Michael J. Quill was unanimously re-elected international president, and praise was given for the achievements of the union and its officers during the previous two years. They had engaged in more than one battle and made a rather phenomenal number of enemies in other quarters, however, for Michael Joseph Quill, labor's stormy petrel, feels right at home in the middle of a scrap. This thickset vehement Irishman was born and bred a rebel. He was born on September 18, 1905 "in the little mountain townland of Courtloughera, three miles from the village of Kilgarvan in County Kerry, Ireland." He went to National School there. His parents, John Daniel and Margaret (Lynch) Quill, were poor farmers. Like Kevin Barry, Mike Quill's entire family, including his three sisters and five brothers, "fought to free Ireland," and by the early '20s a large part of his family was in jail. Quill himself carried a rifle at 14, and when he landed in the United States in 1926 (appropriately enough he arrived in New York on St. Patrick's Day) he is reported to have carried a Black and Tan bullet in his hip.

Since his arrival Quill has handled pick and shovel in the Eighth Avenue subway construction and shoveled coal in the boiler room of the McAlpin Hotel. He went for a time to Pennsylvania, where he eked out a living by selling Roman Catholic religious art. At another time he worked as a handy man in a country club. In 1930 he returned to a gateman's job with a New York subway, the IRT, where he stayed for the next five years. In 1932 he became an American citizen.

In 1934 Quill and other IRT employees began to meet quietly in cafeterias, parks, saloons and furnished rooms to make plans to organize the IRT, then commonly considered a stronghold of company unionism. There was dissatisfaction because of long hours, bad conditions of work and exaggerated disciplinary measures. As a result something like 70 groups were formed after 17 months of furtive but steady organizing work.

In 1935 it was decided that Michael Quill would be more useful to his fellow employees as a full-time organizer than as a gateman, since the embryo union required most of his time. The immediate problem was to affiliate with a larger group, and the next two years were spent looking for a parent union. Quill's union was spurned by the Amalgamated Association of Street Electric, Railway and Motor Coach employees of America, and formed a brief and unsatisfactory association with the International Association of Machinists. In April 1937 the Transport Workers' Union became a part of the CIO, and in the next six months signed up 44,000 men and got closed-shop contracts with the major transit companies. Michael Quill claims that the following benefits have been won for most of the transit workers in New York within the past six years: a five- to six-day work week; two weeks' paid vacations and four paid holidays a year; restoration of all wage cuts made between 1930 and 1937 and some increases; and machinery for collective bargaining and for settling grievances. The union also possesses a voluntary health insurance program which was called "model" by *PM*.

In 1938 Michael Quill was elected to the City Council as a city councilman from The Bronx. That same year he went to Ireland with his bride, pretty, blond Maria Theresa O'Neill, who married him in December 1937 after seven years' courtship. (They now have a two-year-old son called John Daniel after Quill's father.) When Quill came back he was faced with an effort on the part of the Council's Tammany members to unseat him on a technicality. The attempt failed, and for the next two years Mike enlivened the proceedings with his vehement brogue. Among his pet subjects were the battle against the slums and for the institution of modern low-cost housing and public distribution of milk. In 1939, however, when Quill refused to endorse a resolution by the official committee of the American Labor Party in favor of the President's foreign policy and condemning the Russo-German Pact, he was repudiated by the Party. He ran for the Council on an independent ticket and was defeated.

In 1940 Quill was in the headlines because of a threatened city-wide tie up as a result of the Transportation Board's repudiation of the contract existing between the subway managements and the TWU. John L. Lewis' intervention averted the strike, and the city assumed the contracts until June 30, 1941. In March 1941 Michael Quill was again brought to the public eye when 3,500 Manhattan and Queens bus drivers walked out on a strike that lasted 11 days, disrupted the normal traveling habits of comfort-loving New Yorkers and brought about a great deal of angry recrimination. Not a single disorderly incident, nevertheless, took place. Arbitration was finally agreed upon when the arbitration issues were narrowed down to that of increased wages, and the Fifth Avenue Coach Company and the New York Omnibus Corporation abandoned their demands for reduction of wages and personnel.

MICHAEL J. QUILL

Next, on June 30, 1941, Transit Workers' Union's contracts with New York City, governing wages and conditions of work on the subway lines (which the city had taken over from the original managements in 1940 after the subway unification), expired. The Board of Transportation, backed by Mayor La Guardia, refused to renew them; Quill swore that no member of his union would work "one hour in the month of July without a signed contract." Notices were posted all over the subway system quoting the state's penal law on sabotage of railroad property with the Wicks Amendment providing stiff penalties for leaving any transit facility unattended. The tense situation was the culmination of weeks of furious campaigning on both sides, as two of the fiercest tempers in New York clashed. Quill called the Mayor a double-crosser and a swindler; the Mayor, who earlier had called Quill "pig-headed" and "obstinate," now countered with calling him a "dues collector" and an irresponsible labor leader. The Citizens Council deplored Quill's "provocative gestures" and chided the Board of Transportation for imitating them; and the Communist issue was brought up with considerable effect.

The issues, however, remained clearly defined: the city's stand was that it could not bargain collectively with any union or recognize a closed shop; the union claimed that the position of the city as an employer of labor was no different from that of any other employer and that it must therefore bargain collectively with the employees. It was a great relief to all sides when, 56 hours before the strike deadline and a few hours after the TWU voted to support Quill in a walkout, a temporary agreement was reached. The city agreed to continue the contracts pending final determination by the courts of its rights under the law and in the meanwhile to deal with the

QUILL, MICHAEL J.—*Continued*

TWU and provide an impartial grievance board to settle complaints. With both sides claiming victory, it was generally admitted that the atmosphere was considerably cleared, although TWU officials pronounced the raises voted in August unsatisfactory, and at the September convention Quill promised to continue his fight for a collective bargaining agreement.

Quill has often been accused of being a Communist. During the bus drivers' strike, the New York *Daily News* wrote: "One orthodox Red tactic is to hit a large community's key points in the hope of paralyzing the place and creating chaos so that a well-organized knot of Reds can then step in and take over." And during the preparations for the subway strike the *World-Telegram* in a series of articles accused the entire leadership of the TWU of Communist activities, as have, indirectly, the Mayor and David Dubinsky. Congressman Dies makes the same charge in his book *The Trojan Horse in America*. Michael Quill has often heatedly denied this, although he has remarked upon occasion that "he would rather be called a Red by rats than a rat by Reds." He had to be forcibly ejected from a turbulent but inconclusive session with the Dies Committee after having offered to show that the Committee was bent on sabotaging his union. His supporters have claimed that charges of Communism stem from a desire to "brand and remove from useful public life a militant and uncompromising trade-union leader," and a predominantly Irish Catholic membership is loyal to him. In September 1941 they were also overwhelming in their approval of a report calling for support of Roosevelt's foreign policy and the nation's fighting Hitlerism.

In his middle 30's, Michael Quill is one of the important labor leaders in the country. The Transport Workers' Union commands his services for $50 a week—a low among union leaders' salaries. For that salary he works hard, taking only a few days' vacation every year. He is a thickset shortish man, rather dapperly dressed. His Irish antecedents have survived in a brogue that in a moment of stress grows almost incomprehensible and in a black-briar stick that he has had for the last 23 years. As a veteran of the Irish fight for freedom, he hates the British Empire and keeps the portrait of James Connolly, Irish revolutionary fighter, together with those of Abraham Lincoln and John L. Lewis, on the walls of his office.

Quill is a spellbinder of the old school, vehement and fiery; his speeches, no accomplished orations, delight his followers and irritate his opponents to the boiling point. He is somewhat careless about his adjectives—one of the reasons for his quarrel with Mayor La Guardia; but occasionally his utterances assume an almost Biblical flavor and have a "history-is-being-made-tonight" ring. Such was his statement to the Board of Transportation before the agreement was reached: "We have, sir, broken negotiations. We will come back under different conditions and will negotiate

for our members." His hobbies are collecting union buttons, and mountain climbing—it is safe to assume that he finds it easier to indulge in the former than in the latter.

References

> Nation 149:479 O 28 '39
> New Repub 100:356 N 1 '39
> N Y World-Telegram p14 Mr 11 '41 por
> PM p14 Mr 13 '41
> Time 37:18 Mr 24 '41 por

RADZIWILL, CATHERINE, PRINCESS 1857(?)—May 11, 1941 Author and lecturer; daughter of a Czarist Russian Army officer; fled from her native land after the Bolshevik Revolution; during her youth had been a close friend of Russian royalty; credited with supplying direct evidence to prove that the anti-Semitic "Protocols of the Wise Men of Zion" were forgeries; wrote her autobiography, *It Really Happened* (1932), as well as numerous biographies of Russian and German members of royalty; used the pseudonym Count Paul Vassili for some of her writings; full name Mrs. Charles Louis Kolb-Danvin.

References

> Pict R 34:7+ Jl '33
> Radziwill, C. It Really Happened 1932
> Who's Who

Obituaries

> N Y Times p22 My 13 '41

RAEDER, ERICH (rä′dẽr) Mar. 24, 1876(?)- Commander in chief of the German Navy

Address: Berlin, W. 35, Tirpitzufer, Germany

In February 1941 German Grand Admiral Erich Raeder and Italian Admiral Arturo Riccardi had a conference (or rather "an exchange of opinions in a comradely spirit") which, according to reports, resulted in "complete agreement for waging a common sea war against England." The Nazi Grand Admiral has ever since the First World War been vehement in his insistence that the "fiction of British naval supremacy" must be dislodged by a resounding defeat. On January 28, 1941 he announced that "until the hour of decision" Britain would be reduced by a combination of blockade by sea and bombing attacks by air. After the War, he promised Bremen naval shipyard workers, Germany will build a huge fleet, maintaining "large overseas naval bases," which will "take the protection of German interests in the world into its strong hands and will carry the German flag and the German name, together with the German merchant fleet, over the space of the globe."

This "vest-pocket Admiral" was born in Wandsbek, Germany, the son of a minor government official. It was 1894 when he entered the Navy, but at first he was overlooked because of his small stature and put on the editorial staff of a German naval journal. He nevertheless rose from the rank of sub-lieutenant in 1897 to captain in 1905, and five years later was made a navigating officer on the imperial yacht *Hohenzollern.* He was an ardent monarchist then, and his personal flag still has the colors and emblems of the old Germany upon it rather than the swastika.

In 1911 Raeder acquired the rank of commander, and the following year became Vice-Admiral Hipper's chief of staff. He was on the German cruisers that shelled the British coast in 1914, and in May 1916 he was in the navigating room of the flagship *Liutzow* when the battle of Jutland began. The ship was battered to pieces, but the men were transferred by destroyer to a battle cruiser, and Raeder somehow escaped. In 1918, made captain of a vessel and commander of the *S. M. S. Cöln,* he was still discussing with other leaders the possibility of a naval replacement program when the Armistice came. A few months later, in June 1919, the remainder of the German High Seas Fleet was scuttled in fear of British confiscation. And although that same year Raeder became head of the Central Department of the Reich Naval Office, no post-War German Navy really existed.

After the War, Raeder wrote a book warning the Germans "never to take on the British fleet in a broadside battle." In 1922 he became rear admiral and inspector of Naval Education; in 1925 vice-admiral and commander of the Eastern Naval Station; and at last, in 1928, admiral and head of the Naval Command. He had long preached "raiding, hit-and-run harrying strategy." Now he began to build pocket battleships—ships that could "outrun anything that could defeat it and defeat anything that could overtake it." When Hitler came into power he obeyed him implicitly and was rewarded by being allowed to obtain steel for his warships in the face of the "greedy Goering-general staff combination."

He was rewarded by more than that. In 1935 Raeder became commander in chief of the Navy. In 1936 Hitler celebrated his own forty-seventh birthday anniversary by making Raeder an "admiral general," an invented title, and handing him a marshal's baton. In 1937 Raeder became an honorary member of the Nazi Party; in February 1938 he joined the Secret Cabinet Council. And in 1939 he became a grand admiral, the first since Von Tirpitz.

Long before this, at the Anglo-German Naval Agreement, Raeder had secured the exception of submarines and naval planes from tonnage quotas. He had been planning to build fast cruisers and submarines almost entirely. Hitler, however, insisted on some big ships with long guns, even two airplane carriers—and as a result Grand Admiral Raeder has not been able to employ his high-sea raiding technique in the present War as much as he had planned. Yet the German submarine fleet has been increasing much faster than Britain has been sinking it. Raeder announced in May 1941 that it would be used against United States ships if that country convoyed "contraband"—and proceeded to carry

ERICH RAEDER

out his threat in spite of protests of violation of international law.

Grand Admiral Raeder is about five feet six inches tall, "thin-lipped, taciturn," and wears a "wide-lapelled, heavily padded blue uniform" with an ornate gold dagger. He lives in a modest Charlottenburg villa near Berlin, keeps a dachshund, goes to concerts when music by Beethoven or Brahms is being played, is an enthusiastic yachtsman, and goes to every football game he can find. On shipboard, however, he is regarded as "fastidious and fussy . . . a strict disciplinarian who has the discomforting habit of poking about in galley's and crew's quarters of warships, and of making unexpected visits to outlying bases to check up on the tidiness of uniforms and the condition of the flower boxes in the barracks' windows." Once he inspected men just returned from the hardships of a six weeks' submarine cruise; he scolded them for slovenliness! His regulations against officers' and sailors' visiting saloons and bars in uniform, drinking alcohol before going on duty or smoking on an empty stomach don't make him particularly popular with his men, either.

Raeder is the author of many books on naval warfare, among them *Der Kreuzerkrieg in den Ausländischen Gewässern* (1922); *Das Krenzergeschwader* (1922); *Die Tätigkeit der Kleinen Kreuzer Emden und Karlsruhe* (1923); and *Der Krieg zur Zee.* In all of them he tries to explode what he considers the myth of British chivalry in warfare. Yet he himself has been accused by Germans of disgracing the tradition of the Navy—particularly when he sent ships to assist in the Fascist *coup* in Spain and ordered his men to shell defenseless Almeria.

(Continued next page)

RAEDER, ERICH—*Continued*

References

Life 8:86-8+ Ap 29 '40 il pors; 10:26
F 10 '41 por
N Y Sun p23 Mr 5 '40
N Y Times p5 F 18 '41
Scholastic 35:20S N 6 '39 por
International Who's Who
Wer ist's?

RATHBONE, JOSEPHINE ADAMS
1865(?)—May 17, 1941 Retired vice-director
of the Pratt Institute School of Library Science of Brooklyn, New York; president of the
American Library Association in 1931 to 1932;
joined the staff of the Pratt Institute in
1893 as an assistant cataloger; became instructor
three years later; in 1911 became vice-director
and retired from the position in 1938.

References

Bul Bibliog 15:81 S '34 por
Library J 62:32 Ja 1 '37; 63:288 Ap 1
'38 por; 63:591 Ag '38 por
Wilson Lib Bul 13:177 N '38 por
American Women
Leaders in Education 1941
Who's Who in America
Who's Who in Library Service

Obituaries

Library J 66:509 Je 1 '41
N Y Times p17 My 19 '41
Sch & Soc 53:666 My 24 '41

RAUSCHNING, HERMANN (roush'ning)
July 8, 1887- Author
Address: b. c/o Alliance Book Corp, 212 Fifth
Ave, New York City

"I know Hitler's intentions out of his own
mouth," Hermann Rauschning once said.
"Years ago he admitted with cynical frankness all those things which are now shaping
into reality." In three widely read books,
in articles, in personal interviews Dr.
Rauschning has told the world what Hitler
said, what Hitler plans, and, recently, how
a democratic world movement can destroy
Hitlerism. In a fourth book he has defended
himself for knowing these things.

The first of his books to hit the English-
speaking world was *The Revolution of Nihilism*, which appeared in Europe in 1938 and
in America in 1939 and went through 17 editions in a year. This analysis of the Hitler
regime by a former party member was full of
hair-raising revelations and remarkable predictions. It prophesied the Nazi conquest of
Czechoslovakia and a coming German-Russian
"alliance" (later Rauschning believed the non-
aggression pact "only a tactical expedient. In
due time [Hitler] will abandon his alliance
with Russia just as he dropped his pact with
Poland.") The Nazi theories, Rauschning disclosed, are merely window-dressing for be-
fuddling the masses, and Germany's real
rulers, a small Nazi inner circle, have one
program, power; one plan, plunder; one tactic,

terror. "The new [Nazi] social order will
consist of . . . blind obedience to an absolute
despotism . . . a progressive economic destruction of the middle class, and the all-pervading
atmosphere of barracks and prison . . . desolation, impoverishment, regimentation and the
collapse of civilized existence."

The Revolution of Nihilism was called "the
most searching analysis and truest account
of National Socialism in general and of Hitler
in particular that has yet been published,"
though many reviewers felt it was "too high-
pitched, shrill and vitriolic now and then." It
was followed in 1940 by *The Voice of Destruction*, a "report, most of it in quotation
marks, of Rauschning's confidential talks with
Hitler in 1932, 1933 and 1934, when democratic Europe still had no conception of what
was in store."

In the days when he was important in Nazi
circles, Rauschning used to jot down conversations soon after they were held, and from
these jottings emerges a "convincing, devastating impression of Der Führer and his
movement." There are skeptics, of course,
who wonder "how much these conversations
can be believed." But even skeptics agree
that as one reads along it is hard to preserve
a detached attitude, hard not to accept Rauschning's interpretations of Hitler, exaggerated
though they seem, hard not to be moved by
the book's "terrible warning."

Unlike this book and *The Revolution of
Nihilism*, the *Redemption of Democracy*
(1941), Rauschning's next book, was an attempt to show that "the nations that have
succumbed to Hitler had the germs of destruction already within them," that democracy must be re-evaluated. Rauschning believes that if England and America can produce a democratic world movement equal in
vigor and reality to the negative revolution
of Hitlerism, the Anglo-Saxon democracies
can destroy the very idea of a revolution of
nihilism. His book is, according to *Time*, a
"groping, fumbling, badly organized, passionately sincere effort to explain what many
people say glibly, few understand—that World
War II is a social revolution." To many,
Rauschning's ideas about "the coming Atlantic
Empire" are cogent; to others this book contains, in the words of the *New Yorker*, "high
theorizing (some of it brilliant) about the
'revolution of nihilism' and 'the termite
state' and 'the anarchy of the masses' but
suspiciously little of what committee chairmen
call constructive suggestions"; still others have
called his whole concept of democracy undemocratic.

Rauschning's latest book, *The Conservative
Revolution* (1941), is in part an *apologia*, a
defense of his motives in joining the Nazi
party, and it is also a statement of the political
and social views of a certain German school of
thought. In it he states that he would like to
see a "Christian" Fourth Reich built on a
"conservative", "traditional", "legitimist" base.
Malcolm Cowley points out that it "makes a
plea for common efforts in fighting Hitler and
in planning the new Europe that might follow
his defeat," but Franz Hoellering calls the

book "an involuntary portrait of the confused mind of persons of a certain type and level," and there have been other critics who have called its author "an anti-Nazi Nazi." He continues to insist that the Nazi movement was at first a great "regenerative force," only guided by the wrong people, in the wrong way. Some light may or may not have been thrown on his conception of the right people by his interpretation of Hess' (see sketch this issue) flight in May 1941. He called it the act of a patriot performed by a "man of good-will" who had broken with his Führer and sincerely sought peace.

The author of these revealing, startling, provocative books was born in East Prussia, in Thorn, which became Torun, Poland. His family was wealthy, military and landowning, and his father an army officer. Young Hermann was brought up in the family tradition. At an early age he was sent to Lichterfelde, a suburb of Berlin, to enroll in the Central Cadet School, and from here he went on to the military school in Potsdam.

Next came periods at the University of Munich, where he was a music student of Ludwig Thuille (in 1931 he published a book on the historical development of music in the Free City of Danzig), and years of study at the University of Berlin. In 1911 this University awarded him a Doctor of Philosophy degree in history. Rauschning returned to his family estates after he received his degree and stayed there until the First World War. During the War he fought and was wounded, and during the War he was married (in 1915) to Anna Schwarte. (They now have five children.)

After the War, Rauschning settled down in what had become the Free City of Danzig and spent much time considering what he felt to be injustices of the Versailles Treaty. Nothing, he felt, could go right in Germany until its terms had been corrected, and the solution, he felt, was a sort of peaceful pan-Germanism patterned along Bismarck's lines— "a sort of informal economic United States of Europe." When the Nazi Party came along he felt that at last some way out for Germany's plight had come. He saw in its program a help for farming problems—he himself had been busy farming and raising cattle on his Danzig estate; he saw in it the only possible way of achieving his own ideals for the future of Germany. Its "vulgar" anti-Semitism he did not take seriously.

Rauschning allied himself with the Nazis in 1931 and because of his position as the principal person in Danzig, one of Europe's crucial spots, soon became one of the leading figures of the Nazi Party. At first he was a little shocked by the excesses of the Party's leaders, but decided that they were the outpourings of a youthful revolutionary group which time and success would temper. In 1932 he was made president of the Landbund and in June 1933 was elected president of the Danzig Senate. During this period he came closer and closer to the inner circle of Hitler and Hitler's associates, his opportunities for learning the Führer's plans unlimited. Fre-

HERMANN RAUSCHNING

quently he dined at the Chancellery; he was Hitler's go-between in his off-stage talks with Poland's late President Pilsudski; he was present at important Party conferences.

This amity didn't last long, however. Early in 1934 Rauschning urged Hitler to make a peaceful and permanent alliance with the Poles. Hitler pointed out to him that such a pact might prevent the Reich from becoming a "great world-conquering entity. Only one can rule," he said. Rauschning was disturbed by this reasoning, and further differences of opinion between him and the Party leadership soon developed. When in 1934 he sent a congratulatory telegram to Von Papen (see sketch this issue), the hope of the counter-revolutionists, it was seized and he was placed under suspicion. Shortly after, he was charged with failing to secure a settlement of the Danzig controversy.

Rauschning offered to resign from the presidency of the Danzig Senate and take another post, but he was informed that Hitler didn't like voluntary resignations. "You must shake off all scruples," Hitler told him. "Only then will you understand the Party and the Party understand you." That understanding never came. Rauschning refused to arrest Catholic priests, disenfranchise the Jews and suppress rival parties on Nazi orders. In turn, when Danzig was faced with bankruptcy, the Reichsbank refused to give it money. Rauschning appealed to Hitler, but his communications were unanswered. He resigned his Danzig position. Then, when his active support of constitutionalism in the election of April 1935 got him even deeper into disfavor with the Nazi Party, he disposed of his lands and fled abroad.

Poland was his first place of refuge, and it was here that he wrote The Revolution of Nihilism. The activities of the Nazi machine he once ardently supported drove him from

RAUSCHNING, HERMANN—*Continued*

this country a few years later, and Rauschning continued his exile in London. In October 1941 he came to the United States, there
to settle and become a citizen. To this country
he offered his views on the present conflict
and its outcome. "The War can be won," he
said, "only by fighting."

References

Wilson Lib Bul 14:552 Ap '40 por
International Who's Who

RAVER, PAUL J(EROME) (rāv'ĕr) Apr.
27, 1894- Administrator of the Bonneville
Power Administration
Address: Route 11, Box 20, Waverly Heights,
Portland, Ore.

As the head of the Bonneville Power Administration, in 1941 Paul J. Raver is the
director of the greatest integrated hydroelectric
power system in the nation. With its two
titanic dams, Bonneville and the Grand Coulee,
designed ultimately to produce a total capacity
of 2,438,400 kilowatts, it bids fair to become
the biggest dispenser of electricity in the world.
Dr. Raver, a pioneer in the uncharted course
of Federal power administration, hopes eventually to "put every kilowatt in the Northwest
under public ownership." But to do this he
will have to break down the web of big
private systems that covers the Pacific Northwest, whose owners have long and successfully resisted the advance of socialized power.
In the meantime, the government-owned hydroelectric power in the Northwest is expected to
fulfill an important function within the framework of national defense: as early as August
1940, Dr. Raver, together with Alvin J. Wirtz,
Under-Secretary of the Interior, drafted a plan
whereby United States power could be used in
the manufacture of defense material in the

PAUL J. RAVER

Northwest, doing away with the necessity of
crosshauling Eastern supplies to the Pacific
coast.

Dr. Paul Jerome Raver's whole career as an
engineer seems to have been a preparation for
the vital post of public power administrator
which became his in 1939. He was born on
April 27, 1894 in Logansport, Indiana, the
son of Edward M. and Agnes R. (Henry)
Raver. He attended the University of Nebraska, and was graduated with a B. S. degree
in Civil Engineering in 1917. (He was later
to take his Master's Degree in Business Administration [1927] and his Ph. D. [1933] at
Northwestern University.) Immediately after
his graduation during the War he entered
the 18th Field Artillery, advancing to the rank
of lieutenant.

The War over, Lieutenant Raver took a job
as valuation engineer for the Chicago engineering firm of Hagenah and Erickson. He
spent four years in charge of field surveys,
pricing inventories and preparing valuation reports on various public utilities properties. In
1923 he became an estimating engineer for the
Chicago Surface Lines, where he got still more
specialized experience in his field. This experience in valuation and utility budget making
was to be useful when Raver found himself
faced with the preparation of mammoth budgets and construction plans at Bonneville.
During that period in Chicago—an era of
rugged individualism in business—Dr. Raver
gave but little thought to the philosophy of
public service, however. He was content with
getting to be a top-ranking technician in his
field.

In 1927 he was invited to give new vocational
courses in public utilities administration at
Northwestern University, where he was pro-
gressively instructor, assistant professor, associate professor and professor of public utilities.
He spent his summers making special field
surveys and so had opportunities to examine at
first hand, in a region where private operation
of utilities was developed to a high degree, the
weaknesses and strengths of private and state
utility administration.

He taught in the University until 1939, when
he took a leave of absence, but in 1933 he
also became supervisor of the Section of Rates
and Research of the Illinois Commerce Commission. This last job gave him his first opportunity to do creative work in the field of
utility regulation; among other things, he
supervised the handling of all rural electrification problems for the Commission and, as a
member of the Illinois Rural Electrification
Committee, took an active part in the development of the rural electric cooperatives throughout the state of Illinois. As a result of his
outstanding work for the Illinois Commerce
Commission he was appointed executive officer
in 1937 and its chairman in 1939. He had
hardly warmed the chair in his new office,
Dr. Raver says, when he was torn away by
the appointment to the post of Bonneville
Power Administrator.

Dr. Raver, with his family (his wife, the
former Loy Goss, whom he married in Chicago in 1922, and two daughters, Alice June

and Phyllis), went West. At Bonneville he found a construction program well developed: Bonneville Dam built and in operation, a project on the way for a $160,000,000-high-voltage transmission grid built to serve a section of the country comprising 13 per cent of the entire nation's land area. Yet no power had been sold. Dr. Raver's plans were somewhat hampered by the original BPA legislation which stipulated that while BPA could buy or build transmission lines and distribution equipment, it could not buy whole companies. Dr. Raver's predecessor, the late James Delmage Ross, had tried to work through Municipal and Public Utility Districts' (PUD's) local public power bodies, which were able to take over entire power companies. But not all of them decided to use Bonneville power, and worse blows came when the cities of Eugene, Portland and later Tacoma and Spokane also turned down Bonneville power.

Upon his appointment Dr. Raver therefore proceeded to streamline his organization: he tackled industrial customers, riding the crest of the defense expansion which found the BPA with plenty of power to spare; he tried to establish satisfactory procedures whereby Northwest farm organizations would get more abundant power service at reasonable rates. And after 19 months in office he was able to report to the Secretary of the Interior that the BPA now had contracts totaling well over $50,000,000 for nearly 300,000 kilowatts of Columbia-River-generated electricity.

With the Grand Coulee Dam adding more resources, Dr. Raver doggedly pursued his dream of total public power. The first large private company he tackled was Puget Sound Power & Light. Ten other Northwest private utilities would have to be bought out before Raver would get his public utility empire. But he is an indomitably patient man who knows his business, and he has the backing of the White House and the resources of the United States Treasury behind him.

A serious, bespectacled man, Dr. Raver probably knows more about the business of regulating public utilities than any other man in the country. He has been a regular contributor to technical magazines and has written numerous valuable monographs and reports on his subject. During his vacation in 1938, as a member of the Joint Committee on the Investigation of the Tennessee Valley Authority, he prepared the report on Appraisal of Rates and Power Policy of TVA. He has always been connected with and active in organizations allied to his field, and when he left Chicago he had to resign membership in such organizations as the Chicago Disciples Union, the Progress Committee of the National Association of Railroad and Utility Commissioners, etc. He has, however, retained his membership in the American Society of Civil Engineers, the National Power Committee, the editorial board of the *Journal of Land and Public Utility Economics* and the American Academy of Political and Social Science, among others.

With all that, he finds time to pamper his passion for fishing in the famous Oregon trout streams and occasionally to play a spectacular game of golf. His other hobbies are book collecting, making amateur films and music. He serves on the governing committee for the Portland Philharmonic Orchestra and, an accomplished pianist himself, he occasionally performs of an evening with Mrs. Raver and their two daughters as audience.

References

Business Week p5 Ag 26 '39 por
Time 37:65-7 Mr 31 '41 por

REED, JAMES, SR. Oct. 29, 1881—July 23, 1941 Bridge engineer; former commander in the Naval Construction Corps; builder of the Golden Gate Bridge at San Francisco; from 1915 to 1930 was superintendent of construction at Mare Island Navy Yard, where he was in charge of 8,000 workers and supervised the building of battleships, troopships and destroyers; established a record that has never been equaled when his men launched a destroyer only 17 days after the keel had been laid.

References

Who's Who in Engineering

Obituaries

N Y Times p17 Jl 24 '41

REEVE, SIDNEY A(RMOR) Mar. 27, 1866—June 12, 1941 Retired consulting engineer; for 10 years, from 1896 on, was professor of steam and hydraulic engineering at the Worcester Polytechnic Institute and also lectured on steam engineering at other institutions; was a consulting engineer with offices in New York from 1908 until his retirement several years ago; author of several books.

References

American Men of Science
Who's Who Among North American Authors
Who's Who in America 1922-23
Who's Who in Engineering 1925

Obituaries

N Y Times p19 Je 13 '41

REID, HELEN ROGERS (rēd) Nov. 23, 1882- Advertising manager and vice-president of the New York *Herald Tribune*

Address: New York Herald Tribune Bldg, 230 W. 41st St, New York City; h. 15 E. 84th St, New York City

"Pretty, gray-haired" Mrs. Ogden Mills Reid rules the advertising department of the New York *Herald Tribune*, probably the country's most important Republican newspaper, with a "small, sure hand." To her conferences she brings "all the intensity proclaimed by her thin lips and firm chin," and nobody can hold a job long on the sixth floor of the 41st Street building without learning that her pleasantly voiced "suggestions" are real orders. "Forty-

Alfred A. Knopf

HELEN ROGERS REID

eight hours a day," is what they say she works, and Mrs. Reid explains this by her love for work ("I have always worked") and her belief that "women have to work twice as hard as men to get the same recognition that men do."

Mrs. Reid's husband, Ogden Mills Reid, is the editor of the *Herald Tribune* and president of the New York Tribune, Incorporated. Although the editorial and advertising departments of many newspapers are known to disagree frequently on matters of policy, Mrs. Reid says that doesn't happen at the *Herald Tribune.* "We get along well," she says, "because we have a mutual regard for each other's abilities. I think, you see, that Ogden is a good editor. He seems to feel that I know the advertising and business ends." There was, however, an apocryphal story going the rounds that Mrs. Reid once came into her husband's office when he was reading proof on the next day's editorial leader and made some suggestions about it. "Helen," he is quoted as saying, "will you kindly get the dickens back to your office, attend to your work and let me do mine?" Mrs. Reid then left meekly. When questioned on the story's authenticity, she vigorously denied it. "Mr. Reid wouldn't talk like that," she said. "And besides I wouldn't walk out meekly."

Dynamic Mrs. Reid has come a long way from Appleton, Wisconsin, where she was born. Her parents, Benjamin Talbot Rogers and Sarah Louise (Johnson) Rogers, were well off, and she was their eleventh child. She studied at Grafton Hall in Wisconsin from the time she was 11 until she became 16 and then left Wisconsin to enter Barnard College in New York City. It was important for her to get through college, and when her money ran out at the end of her sophomore year, due to family complications, there was no thought of retreating to Appleton. She got herself

jobs and made enough money to be graduated with the class of 1903.

Shortly after commencement Helen Rogers became social secretary to Mrs. Whitelaw Reid and almost immediately after that Mr. Whitelaw Reid was appointed Ambassador to the Court of St. James. The Reids went to England, and Helen Rogers with them. Being secretary to the wife of an Ambassador with the responsibility of directing the work of several assistants was a hard job, she found. Once she had to study Burke's *Peerage* in one day so that she could seat Mrs. Whitelaw Reid's guests correctly.

Mrs. Reid's son, Ogden Mills, came to London on a vacation in 1910 and while there met his mother's pretty social secretary. They were married in March 1911 in Wisconsin, with Mrs. Whitelaw Reid having to cross the ocean to attend the ceremony. Then came six years in which Mrs. Ogden Reid devoted herself to family life—she has two sons, Whitelaw and Ogden Rogers and had a daughter, Elizabeth, who died. She also devoted herself to the suffrage movement, into which she plunged with fervor. In 1917 she collected $500,000 for the campaign in New York and says: "Winning the battle in New York in 1917 was winning the battle nationally two years later."

Her husband, meanwhile, had been working on the *Tribune,* which he joined in 1908 as a reporter and which he began to edit in 1913. In 1912 he had inherited it from his father. At that time it was a newspaper that was "stodgy, conservative," with a small circulation. But he never had time to be interested in the business side of the paper, and his wife persuaded him to let her join him on the paper. In 1918 she came on the staff without pay and began soliciting all kinds of advertisements. Within two years she took control of the advertising department and in 1922 was elected a vice-president.

By the time of the merger of the *Herald* and the *Tribune* in 1924 Mrs. Reid knew all the important and hundreds of unimportant advertising space buyers in New York and with the business she brought in was able to make her paper prosperous. Under her its advertising lineage increased from 4,170,812 lines in 1918 to 14,359,671 lines in 1939.

Today she continues as active as when she first started and for the past three years has directed the annual *Forum on Current Problems,* which the *Herald Tribune* sponsors, as well as a good deal of political (a Republican, Willkie was to her in 1940 "heaven's gift") and social activity. In 1935 the American Women's Association presented her with its annual Award for Eminent Attainment, the recipient of which must be not only a professional success but "successful as a woman." And Mrs. Reid, "as feminine as the scarlet polish on her fingernails," has gone on during these years with her career as a wife and mother. That doesn't mean that she has tied herself down to domestic affairs. She hasn't, for she believes that "the routine of running a home can be safely relegated to people trained and fitted for the task." That is why others manage the Reid's town house in New

York and their summer house in Purchase, New York, where Mrs. Reid gets a chance to satisfy her enthusiasm for flowers and swimming.

References

Fortune 12:88 S '35 por
Ind Woman 14:337+ O '35 por
Ladies' H J 53:50 Jl '36
Newsweek 6:19 N 23 '35 por; 7:19 Je 13 '36 por
American Women
Who's Who in America
Who's Who in Commerce and Industry

REID, MRS. OGDEN MILLS *See* Reid, H. R.

REINER, FRITZ (rī'nĕr) Dec. 19, 1888-
Conductor

Address: c/o Pittsburgh Symphony Orchestra, 913 Farmers Bank Bldg, Pittsburgh, Pa; h. Westport, Conn.

"You'd be an awful dope if you couldn't follow Reiner," a musician once said of the musical director of the Pittsburgh Symphony Orchestra. According to Oscar Levant, "he has evolved a personal sign language which leads an orchestra through the most complex scores . . . with the ease and sureness of a tightrope walker who performs a backward somersault blindfolded." Since 1931, as head of the Orchestra and Opera Department of the Curtis Institute in Philadelphia, he has also been imparting this skill to other musicians.

That Reiner himself is "a technician of uncommon adroitness and security," as Lawrence Gilman put it, all critics agree. There are some, however, who feel that he is an opera, rather than a symphony conductor, and that his talents for drilling singers, players and stagehands into a smooth organization are "alchemized into unnecessary nervousness when he concentrates on a symphony orchestra." Audiences refuse to quibble. Wherever Fritz Reiner conducts—Vienna, Rome, Barcelona, London, Milan, Buenos Aires, Stockholm, San Francisco, Rochester, New York, Hollywood, Philadelphia—halls are jammed.

He has been conducting for more than 30 years. Born in Budapest, Hungary on December 19, 1888, his parents, Ignatz and Vilma (Pollak) Reiner, allowed him to study music almost as soon as he could read and write. This was a concession on their part, since Fritz' father had decided to make him a lawyer. In high school he studied piano and composition, and was graduated from music school and public school at the same time. To please his father he enrolled in the University of Budapest as a law student and kept his musical studies for his spare hours. This division of interest ended after a short time, however, with the death of Ignatz Reiner. Fritz enrolled in the Royal Academy of Music in Budapest.

At the Royal Academy he played the timpani in the school orchestra. One day when the

FRITZ REINER

conductor was absent he was asked to fill in, and from then on his musical ambitions were crystallized. He knew he wanted to be a conductor. He was graduated in 1908 and after a short apprenticeship he became an assistant conductor at the Opéra Comique in Budapest. From there he went in 1910 to the National Theatre in Laibach, Yugoslavia; from there to Budapest's People's Opera House.

By 1914 Reiner was conductor of the Dresden Royal Opera House and "attracted the attention of the music world by the vitality and freshness of his interpretations." For eight years he conducted Wagner, Strauss and Italian opera until the post-War inflation in Germany played havoc with his post. In 1922 he left for the South to become conductor of the Teatro Costanzi in Rome and from there went on to Barcelona to conduct Wagner. It was while he was in Spain that he received a garbled wire from the second wife, Madame Berta (Gardini-Gerster) Reiner, mentioning something about the Cincinnati Symphony Orchestra. He wired her back telling her to use her own judgment and shortly after discovered that she had accepted the post of conductor in Cincinnati for him.

In September 1922 the Reiners arrived in the United States and headed for Cincinnati, where Fritz Reiner led the city's symphony orchestra through "nine distinguished years," crisscrossing America and Europe, at the same time, to make guest appearances with most of the world's leading musical bodies. After the 1930 to 1931 season Reiner resigned from the Cincinnati Symphony Orchestra to become head of the Orchestra and Opera Department of the Curtis Institute of Music, a position he held until May 3, 1941, when his resignation became effective. Here he told his pupils that the ultimate test of conducting "is the power to reach and convince other people in a harmonious way." Here the

REINER, FRITZ—*Continued*

results of his teaching were so successful that "when students have completed a course under my direction any one of them can stand up before an orchestra they have never seen before and conduct correctly a new piece at first sight, without verbal explanation and by means of only manual technic."

Reiner's next position came in 1934 when he organized a new opera company in Philadelphia under the management of the Philadelphia Orchestra Association. The company experimented in combining opera productions with symphonic concerts and in new presentations of old operas. Reiner believes firmly that "opera is not highbrow. A good opera," he says, "is a good show as well as an inspiring work of music." The public, he feels, will become more and more aware of this, and he sees the time coming "when all opera in America will be sung in English and when the vast majority of the singers will be native Americans."

In 1936 Fritz Reiner conducted more operas —in San Francisco and in Covent Garden, London. When he left San Francisco he left behind "an orchestra warm with his praises, a jubilant press, and an Opera Association beaming unanimously over San Francisco's most momentous season." In that same year he conducted the *Ford Sunday Evening Hour* over the radio in this country for the first time, as well as concerts for the BBC in England. The next year Reiner repeated his successes in San Francisco and London, and since then has won acclaim for his leadership of the New York Philharmonic Orchestra (both in its winter concerts and at Lewisohn Stadium summer concerts), of the Philadelphia Orchestra and of other leading symphonic and radio organizations.

In 1938 Reiner took up another permanent post, this time as conductor of the Pittsburgh Symphony Orchestra. He continues to conduct his programs of the world's great music both in Pittsburgh and in guest appearances. One of these appearances was in November and December 1940, when he conducted opera in Chicago for the first time, and the Chicago *Tribune's* critic hailed his conducting as "the eighth wonder of the world."

Reiner, who received the degree of Doctor of Music from the University of Pennsylvania in June 1940, rather inclines toward Wagner, on whose music he is an expert; he plays a good deal of Richard Strauss, whom he knew intimately in Dresden; he likes Bach; he thinks the moderns, especially American moderns, are fine. His are catholic musical tastes.

Whatever the performance, Fritz Reiner's rehearsals are strictly disciplined affairs. Held in a cold room whenever possible (Reiner hates heat), the conductor, whose ear "is so acute that he can detect a wrong bowing when his back is turned to the section from which it emanates," storms at any imperfections from the players. His command of English is far from perfect, but that doesn't inhibit him from telling any erring musician exactly what he thinks of him and his playing. As sharp-tongued Oscar Levant put it: "The reaction that he induces from the orchestras he has conducted runs the full gamut of all emotions but deep affection."

Otherwise, Fritz Reiner is a "plump, pleasant" man who likes to snap crack photographs and spend as much time as possible at Westport, Connecticut, where he and his present wife, Carlotta Irwin, have an unusually pleasant home. He has two children by his first marriage.

References

Etude 54:417-18 Jl '36 por
Time 28:28+ N 30 '36 por

Baker's Biographical Dictionary of Musicians 1940
Ewen, D. ed. Living Musicians 1940
Saleski, G. Famous Musicians of a Wandering Race 1927
Thompson, O. ed. International Cyclopedia of Music and Musicians 1939
Who's Who in America
Who's Who in American Jewry

REINHARDT, AURELIA HENRY (rĭn'-härt) Apr. 1, 1877- President of Mills College; moderator of the Unitarian Association
Address: Mills College, Oakland, Calif.

When the biographical publication *American Women* named her among the 10 outstanding women of 1940, Dr. Aurelia Reinhardt was genuinely surprised. "I've done nothing out of the ordinary," she exclaimed. "The reason I'm not interesting is that everything comes naturally to me."

One of the many honors that "came naturally" in May 1940 was her election as moderator of the Unitarian Association—the first woman to become titular head of this liberal denomination. The unpaid position is "no mere honorary title but a job that comes close to being that of a super-public-relations woman." Before her election Dr. Reinhardt had served the Association as vice-president, had been Western representative of its National Commission of Appraisal from 1935 to 1936, and had for 10 years been a member of the Board of Trustees of the Pacific Unitarian School for the Ministry, in Berkeley, California. Her record of outside activity is in keeping with the Unitarian tradition of outstanding and energetic women, including Susan B. Anthony, Lucy Stone, Julia Ward Howe, Dorothea Dix and Louisa May Alcott.

Dr. Reinhardt has been a Unitarian all her life, though her mother was a Quaker. She is of New England stock on both sides, but was born in San Francisco, to which one of her ancestors came by clipper ship around the Horn while others crossed the prairies in covered wagons. Her father, William Warner Henry of Bennington, Vermont, had sailed out of Boston Harbor in 1858 to seek his fortune in California, where he married Mary Rogers Merritt and on April 1, 1877 became the father of Aurelia Henry.

After preparing for college in a high school still called "The Boys' High" Aurelia Reinhardt received a B. L. degree at the University of California in 1898. Then she went to Yale, one of the first women to study in that University's rapidly developing Graduate School. She had always loved languages and at Yale specialized in them—classical, medieval and modern; her first printed studies were in this field. During 1901 and 1902 she held a scholarship in English at Yale, the following year received a fellowship, and in 1905 was granted her Ph. D. A year of study at Oxford followed, on a foreign fellowship from the American Association of University Women. Since her student days she has received many honorary degrees: from California in 1919, the University of Southern California in 1924, Colorado College in 1931, and from Mount Holyoke, Oberlin and Williams in 1937.

Dr. Reinhardt's teaching career had begun before she went to Yale, with three years of teaching English at the University of Idaho, from 1898 to 1901. After her year abroad she returned to Idaho and became instructor in English at the Lewiston State Normal School. There she remained until 1909, when she resigned to marry Dr. George Frederick Reinhardt, university physician and professor of hygiene at the University of California. In 1914 her husband died, leaving her with two sons to support. One of them, George Frederick, Jr., is in the diplomatic service and was stationed in Estonia; the other, Paul Henry, is a physician, like his father.

After her husband's death Dr. Aurelia Reinhardt returned at once to teaching. She was lecturer in English at the University of California from 1914 to 1916, when she became president of Mills College in Oakland, the second oldest women's college in the United States. It had been founded for the daughters of newly-rich gold miners in 1852, when California was at a frighteningly long distance from the Eastern schools (unless, as Dr. Reinhardt believes, the clipper ship captains were its real founders). Since 1916, under the guidance of the energetic scholar-administrator whom upperclasswomen address as "Pres," Mills has become one of the important women's colleges, especially strong in its departments of art, music, dramatics and literature.

Executive duties have never been allowed to fill all of Dr. Reinhardt's time. From 1923 to 1927 she was president of the American Association of University Women, whose fellowship years ago had helped to broaden her experience with and understanding of college organizations; from 1927 to 1933 she was chairman of its committee on international relations. She is on the council of the National Economic League, the board of trustees of the American Council of the Institute of Pacific Relations, the international relations committee of the National Education Association; is chairman of the department of education of the General Federation of Women's Clubs, and is active in many other organizations, ranging from the Daughters of the American Revolution and the

Associated News
AURELIA HENRY REINHARDT

Colonial Dames to the Dante Society; the Concordance Society and Philological Association of the Pacific Coast. She has been since 1933 a member of the National Committee on Mobilization for Human Needs. Keenly interested in politics, she served as an elector for the Republican Party in 1928, and as a member of the Committee on Policies in 1938. Strongly anti-New Deal, she has been active in the organization of Republican women known as Pro-America, devoting much of her time to speaking before branches throughout the country. She is chairman of the education committee of Pro-America for California.

With all this, Dr. Reinhardt has won a solid reputation as a scholar. She translated and edited the *De Monarchia of Dante Alighieri* in 1904; edited Ben Jonson's *Epicoene or The Silent Women* in 1906; was a contributor to *Selected Translations from Old English Poetry* in 1903; and writes occasional articles for the scholarly reviews. She is a member of Phi Beta Kappa. By way of recreation she collects books, and studies the birds and animals of the countryside about Mills College.

Dr. Reinhardt is tall, large-boned and deep-voiced, resembling a level-headed mother of a large family far more than an austere college president. Her energy is boundless; she is as untiring as she is modest. Extensive travels which have brought her into close contact with teachers and students of Europe and the Orient as well as those throughout our country have left her with a profound belief in the interdependence of religious faith and democracy. "As an educator, I find that the amazing objective triumphs of science are felt by the rising generation as not complete in their definition of life's problems and possibilities, and so on our

REINHARDT, AURELIA HENRY—*Cont.*

campuses we find interest in philosophy and religion on the increase. As a citizen I feel that our American democracy is rooted in religion."

References

> N Y Herald Tribune p11 My 20 '40 por
> Newsweek 15:41 Je 3 '40 por
> Time 35:48 Je 3 '40 por
> American Women
> Leaders in Education 1941
> Who's Who Among North American Authors
> Who's Who in America

RESNICK, LOUIS (rĕz'nĭk) May 1, 1891— Mar. 18, 1941 Public relations counsel and former newspaperman who had been industrial relations director of the National Society for the Prevention of Blindness for the past 15 years; had for many years been among the leaders of the movement to conserve human eyesight and had written on the subject; from 1925 to 1935 was director of public information and public education of the Welfare Council of New York; was public relations consultant for the International Labor Office in 1938 in Geneva, Switzerland.

References

> Newsweek 10:17 Ag 7 '37 por
> Who's Who in Journalism

Obituaries

> N Y Times p21 Mr 19 '41 por

REUTHER, WALTER (PHILIP) (rōōth-ēr) Sept. 1, 1907- Director of General Motors Department of the United Automobile Workers of America

Address: United Automobile Workers of America, 281 W. Grand Blvd, Detroit, Mich.

In February 1941 a statement by the Office of Production Management indicated that the Reuther plan to use the facilities of the automobile industry for mass production of defense planes had been shelved indefinitely because of "technical difficulties." Walter Reuther, one of the founders and national leaders of the United Automobile Workers of America (CIO) and by trade a highly skilled tool and diemaker, had made public his plan in December 1940 under the sponsorship of Philip Murray (see sketch this issue), president of the CIO. At that time he claimed that "if the idle men and the idle machines of the automotive industry were fully mobilized and private interests temporarily subordinated, we could turn out 500 modern fighting planes a day," and that in six months mass production could be a fact. His plan, he said, would also relieve unemployment and under-employment of skilled labor. Many believed that it was thoroughly practical, but it was opposed by most automobile manufacturer and therefore, according to I. F. Stone, never got the hearing it deserved.

By the end of 1941, with America at war and thousands of skilled auto workers jobless, all labor was demanding adoption of the plan.

Walter Philip Reuther was born in Wheeling, West Virginia, in the heart of the steel and mining industries, on September 1, 1907. The atmosphere of his home was one of intense interest in unions and labor problems. His father, Valentine Reuther, was, at the age of 23, president of the Ohio Valley Trades & Labor Assembly; his grandfather was for many years international organizer of the United Brewery Workers.

It was at the age of fifteen, after two years of high school, that Reuther went to work for the Wheeling Steel Corporation. There he served as an apprentice tool and diemaker. His connections with his first job were severed, prophetically, when he organized the workers in protest against Sunday and holiday work. Then, in 1927, Reuther went to Detroit, where the automobile industry seemed to beckon to young mechanics. There he worked for the Briggs Manufacturing Company, for General Motors, for the Coleman Tool and Die plant. Most of his shop experience was with the Ford Motor Company, where, after five years' employment at the Highland Park and Dearborn, Michigan plants, Reuther became foreman of some forty men in the tool and die room. His future as a Ford technician seemed assured, and while working nights he completed his education during the day, attending high school for two years and Wayne University for three.

But at the same time his interest in labor unions had grown. He organized and became president of the Social Problems Club at Wayne, specialized in labor and industrial problems, and took students to the picket line when strikes were in progress in Detroit. In the fall of 1932 he was discharged from Ford's, and after completing his school year he embarked with his brother Victor on a three-year trip around the world. They traveled on bicycles in Europe and visited England, Russia, Central Asia, China and Japan. They made a particular point of observing the operation of auto plants and machine shops wherever possible, working in shops and studying the labor movement. (*Time* says he "knows the automobile industry union-side out.")

In 1935 friends in Detroit wrote the Reuther brothers that their long-hoped-for opportunity to organize the auto workers appeared to be at hand; they hastened home. Walter Reuther organized and became president of the United Automobile Workers' West Side Local 174, Detroit, which rose from a membership of 78 to 30,000 in one year. (He is now its honorary president.) In 1936 he was elected to the executive board of the International Union, and he has been re-elected each year since. He was active in the sit-down strikes of 1937 and in every major strike in the automobile industry since that time.

Reuther led the first major strike in the Detroit auto industry, which broke out at Kelsey-Hayes Wheel in December 1936. The 10-day sit-down ended with a 75-cent beginning rate for both men and women, the best rate in

WALTER REUTHER

the industry. During this strike he was appointed international organizer and, soon afterward, West Side organization director. Reuther functioned in the Fisher No. 1 plant in Flint during the sit-down. In April 1937 he played an active part in what was then called the Ford Organization Committee, and he opened the Ford drive by the first broadcast of unionism—from an airplane over the River Rouge plant in Dearborn! He was in charge of the first union leaflet distribution at the Ford Rouge gates on May 26 of that year, when he, Richard T. Frankensteen and other unionists were attacked by Ford servicemen.

With the greater acceptance of unionism by the automobile corporations, Reuther worked on problems of making collective bargaining more efficient. He played a major part in negotiating an agreement with General Motors Corporation in 1937, when for the first time a joint impartial umpire was established to rule on disputes between workers and management. Since 1939 he has been the director of the General Motors Department of the UAW and, with his staff, which includes his wife (he married May Wolf in March 1936), handles the labor problems of some 160,000 workers in 70-odd General Motors plants. He and William Knudsen are therefore old acquaintances. Once, after a bout with a Detroit union committee headed by Reuther, President Knudsen announced: "Young man, I wish you were selling used cars for us." Reuther was puzzled. "*Used* cars!" "Yes," replied Knudsen, "*used* cars. Anybody can sell new cars." In the dispute with General Motors in the spring of 1941 Reuther was again chief union negotiator.

In the stormy internal life of the auto workers' union Reuther has taken what has been called a "middle of the road" position. He fought and helped eliminate from leadership Homer Martin, first president of the UAW, and, on the other hand, has been bitterly op-

posed to the Communists. He was a supporter of President Roosevelt in 1936 and again in 1940, and advocates a much greater participation of labor in national defense matters. He himself assisted Sidney Hillman on an advisory group dealing with the problem of training skilled workers in industry. Labor in the United States has a vital interest in the battle that Great Britain is fighting, he believes, and he advanced his program "in the belief that the need for planes is immediate and terrifying."

Red-haired, "pint-sized, pale" Reuther is still something of an athlete. In college he won several medals in both swimming and basketball.

References

Life 10:20 Ja 6 '41 por
Nation 152:2 Ja 4 '41
Newsweek 17:10 F 3 '41
Time 34:15 Jl 17 '39 por; 37:16 Ja 6 '41; 37:18 F 3 '41
U S News 10:9 Ja 3 '41; 10:28-9 Ja 10 '41 por

REYNOLDS, QUENTIN (JAMES) Apr. 11, 1902- Journalist; author

Address: b. c/o Crowell-Collier Publishing Co, 250 Park Ave, New York City

It was in January 1941 that Quentin Reynolds returned from Europe to stay for a while, and it was also in January 1941 that his book, *The Wounded Don't Cry*, was published. Soon a best seller, his account of his experiences in France and England was hailed as a "swift running eyewitness account, dramatic and enormously vivid." One reviewer went so far as to call it "at once a prose poem of human capacity to endure punishment for an ideal, a savage indictment of brute force and the chronicle of a brilliant reporter's experiences and reactions under fire." Only the *New Yorker* dissented mildly, with the suggestion that "the writing is just a touch on the Rover Boys' side."

The Wounded Don't Cry is a story of bombings and civilians and of a French General who apologized because the champagne wasn't iced. It is also a story of Reynold's personal experiences—his tricking the French into giving him a pass to the battle lines by a wire to "Uncle Franklin," care of the White House, that explained his difficulties and included "love to Aunt Eleanor"; his experiences driving an ambulance, siphoning gasoline from an Ambassador's car, doubletalking his way into England. In these stories, originally sent to *Collier's* Magazine, Quentin Reynolds' terse, racy writing is filled always with an understanding for the people of England. "I learn about England," he once wrote, "by spending my time at a Royal Air Force mess, spending my time on the beach at Dover with the army men, spending my time with the local volunteers in places like Seven Oaks in Kent, or a dozen places like it, spending my time in the pubs of rural England. In these places you hear England talking."

QUENTIN REYNOLDS

Back in America with two broken ribs from falling over a chair in a bombing raid and minus 50 of his usual 260 pounds, Quentin Reynolds proceeded to give in person his reactions to the War. He made a two weeks' personal appearance at the Strand Theatre in New York City and he announced his belief that there was too much talk of defense in America and not enough positive action. At the same time the two motion pictures he wrote and narrated, *London Can Take It* and *Christmas Under Fire*, were shown widely throughout the country. In these films, as Damon Runyon has pointed out, Reynolds' "voice produces an even greater effect than the film. His tones are low pitched. . . He uses few adjectives. He attempts no fancy stuff," and yet is able to make audiences understand what he feels the people of England are up against.

Before Reynolds returned to England in May 1941 the successor to *The Wounded Don't Cry, London Diary,* had been published, "the uncensored and unedited record of some hairraising and some hilarious experiences in streets and offices and hotels and countrysides that have become the War's main battlefield." In it Reynolds tried simply to put down stories about people he knows, what they are doing, how they are reacting. Once back in England to gather more material and send out more stories, he was soon working on another book, tentatively titled *Convoy.*

There is an impact in whatever Quentin Reynolds reports and talks about, an impact that is partly the result of his own Irish-American temperament, partly the result of his long years of reporting experience. Ever since he left college he has been turning news into readable material. He was born in New York City, the son of James Joseph Reynolds and Katherine (Mahoney) Reynolds. His father

was a public school principal in Brooklyn at that time and moved to the borough where he worked in 1905. Quentin went to public school in Brooklyn and then to the Brooklyn Manual Training High School. From there he went to Brown University.

A big lad, six-foot-one, it was almost inevitable that he should play football. He was a star at this and just as good at boxing (college heavyweight champion) and swimming. In 1924 Reynolds was graduated, quite certain that he was going to be a lawyer. He returned to Brooklyn, enrolled in the evening session of Brooklyn Law School and started looking around for daytime work. Most of it turned out to be on newspapers: first on the Brooklyn *Times* and then on the *Evening World*. By the time Reynolds got his Law Degree in 1930 he was a first-rate reporter.

Quentin Reynolds quietly tucked away his Law Degree and settled down on the *Evening World* as a reporter, rewrite man and finally sports writer. When the *World* ceased publication he went over to the *World-Telegram,* mostly as sports writer. It was in 1930 that Joseph V. Connolly started looking around for promising young writers for Hearst's newly taken over International News Service. He saw Reynolds' sports columns and liked them. When he asked Reynolds how he would like to be a general reporter for INS, Reynolds turned him down at first. That was until he heard the salary he would be getting. "Even then," as Damon Runyon puts it, "Reynolds was manifesting the tendency that was later to make him a somewhat celebrated figure around the Stork Club, 21, El Morocco, Club 18 and similar spots, and he had already discovered that a man-about-tables could always use a little more money."

Reynolds did reporting and rewrite for INS for a few years and then, in 1933, went to Germany as foreign correspondent. With H. R. Knickerbocker he saw Hitler and Goebbels (see sketch this issue) and the rest take over, and he didn't like it. He didn't hesitate to say so and as a result was "one of the first reporters tapped by Hitler for his little club, 'Deported Journalists and Exile Turnverein!'" Before he left Germany, however, the editors of *Collier's* had noticed his work and asked him to join their staff. Influenced by the fact that he would be able to do not only articles but fiction as well, Reynolds joined the staff in 1934 and has been with *Collier's* ever since, turning out about five short stories and about twenty-five articles a year on both the United States and Europe. In 1940 and 1941 it was *Collier's* that sent him to Europe—on a roving commission— and it is *Collier's* that the public has to thank for *The Wounded Don't Cry, London Diary* and some up to the minute stories from Russia in 1941.

Reynolds is "good-looking, convivial, a hearty eater, a free-handed spender, a natural born stayer-upper." The opening words of *The Wounded Don't Cry* are characteristic: "Hitler marched into Belgium just as I marched into the Ritz bar. The first thing I did was to order a drink. I don't know what Hitler did first." "A great conversationalist, a bachelor and usually most agreeable to a fight or a frolic, he could not help becoming a notable of New York night life." But despite nights out Reynolds always seems able to do a prodigious amount of work.

This red-headed, burly reporter for *Collier's* always has plans ahead for things to do. Sometime he intends to lecture all over on what he has seen abroad and what he believes the United States should do about it. Probably, he says, he will land in Hollywood, which has made him a number of offers, and stay there for a while. It won't be for long though, for he is most anxious to be in Europe and to report further all that has happened, is happening and seems likely to happen to "my neighbors: the people of London," and all the other people of Europe.

References

> Esquire 15:44+ Je '41
> N Y Daily Mirror p10 O 31 '40
> Newsweek 17:52 Ja 27 '41 por
> PM p16, 17 Ja 14 '41 por
> American Catholic Who's Who
> America's Young Men
> Reynolds, Q. J. The Wounded Don't Cry 1941

RHOADES, CORNELIA HARSEN (rōdz) Dec. 1, 1863—Nov. 28, 1940 Blind author of books for children who wrote the Brick House Series under the name of Nina Rhoades.

References

> Who's Who in America

Obituaries

> N Y Times p21 N 29 '40

RIBBENTROP, JOACHIM VON (rĭb'ĕn-trôp yō'ä-kĭm fôn) Apr. 30, 1893- Foreign Minister of Germany

Address: Ministry of Foreign Affairs, Berlin, Germany

Sir Nevile Henderson, who once called Ribbentrop "a friend of Great Britain," in the spring of 1941 was quoted as saying: "If I were given a gun and told to take two shots, I would shoot Himmler (see sketch this issue), then Ribbentrop, and brain Hitler with the butt of the rifle." Others might let Himmler wait. Joachim von Ribbentrop, Foreign Minister of the Third Reich, known in Germany as "the commercial traveler of National Socialism," is generally conceded to have had more influence on Hitler and on the policies of Nazi Germany than any other man. Says Oswald Dutch: "He knows accurately the market, his wares, and the demand; he has his representatives, scouts and informants everywhere. He knows the strength and the weaknesses of his competitors. And finally he knows, to a split second, the psychological moment for landing his catch." He is one of the few people who can see Hitler at any time, without an appointment. Jealous Nazi higher-

JOACHIM VON RIBBENTROP

ups—among them Goering, Hess, Rosenberg (see sketches this issue)—have nicknamed Von Ribbentrop "Iago." They say he won Hitler's favor by "poisoning his ear." They call him "the Wild Man of the Reich." Von Ribbentrop's $3,165,000 in foreign (including American) securities, in addition to his wealth in Germany itself, make him also one of the Reich's richest Nazi officials.

Joachim von Ribbentrop was born plain Joachim Ribbentrop. He was born on April 30, 1893, at Wesel on the Rhine, and was the son of Sophie (Hertwig) Ribbentrop and Richard Ribbentrop, a retired army officer. His travels began early. After attending the Imperial Lyceum in Metz young Joachim was sent by a wealthy aunt by marriage to school in Grenoble, France; to London, where he worked for a while as clerk in a German importing company; and finally to Switzerland. It was 1910 when he set out for America. He spent several months in New York and in Boston, part of the time as a free-lance journalist, and then went to Canada. His jobs there have been variously reported as draftsman, assistant engineer, bank clerk, wine salesman and railroad laborer. Whatever he was doing, he remained there until Germany declared war in August 1914, then managed somehow to get back to his own country— legend says he fled to America, then hid on a Dutch steamer that was searched on the high seas. He reached the German frontier in the autumn of 1914 and joined the 125th Regiment of Hussars.

He wasn't at the front long, although the Iron Cross, awarded for bravery in action, is prominent among his medals. His knowledge of English could be more valuable elsewhere. In 1915 there is some reason to believe that Ribbentrop was given a special position in a military mission at New York, working under Von Papen (see sketch this issue), the

RIBBENTROP, JOACHIM VON—*Cont.*

German military attaché who was finally recalled at the request of the United States after evidence that he had been directing German espionage and sabotage activities. Shortly after Von Papen's recall Ribbentrop, too, returned to Europe, and by early 1918 was with Von Papen once more. This time it was in Turkey, as adjutant to the plenipotentiary of the war office. And once more Von Papen's mission failed. Some say that Ribbentrop actually saved him from capture by the British.

As adjutant of the German delegation, Ribbentrop witnessed the signing of the Versailles "Dictate." (He had spent most of his time in Parisian salons trying to convince French capitalists that a strong Germany would be a bulwark against Bolshevism, an argument he was to use to better effect later.) After that there was no place for him among the officialdom of post-war Germany. But there were still opportunities to make money, and during the early years of the French occupation of the Rhineland, Ribbentrop speculated in inflated marks, imported French wines duty-free with the help of corruptible customs officials, and soon was engaged by the French firm of Pommery and Greno to act as their traveler and representative. His talents as traveling salesman were such that the German champagne firm of Henckel-Trocken offered him a position a few months later; and in 1920 Ribbentrop married Henckel's daughter, Annelies. (There are now two daughters and three sons, the youngest named "Adolf.") Ribbentrop was taken into his father-in-law's firm as a partner.

Up to this time Ribbentrop had been known as a socialist, a pacifist, a supporter of Stresemann. Now he was the joint owner of the Henckel cellars—a rich man with a country house in a suburb of Berlin. He was taken into the Herrenklub, where he kept in daily touch with big industrialists and bankers. He was intimate with prominent Jewish banking families, frequented their salons, and is reported to have become an Anglophile under the influence of Madame Rothschild, at whose house he played the part of an English gentleman in English society comedies. In his travels abroad he made the acquaintance of such figures as Mussolini, Barthou, Doumergue, Laval. In 1926 he added the "von" to his name by getting himself adopted by the same aunt who had been so helpful in his youth. (Some amended the name even further: to "Ribbensnob.") In 1927 he organized the Impegroma Importing Company with capital advanced by a wealthy Jewish banker. And in 1928, reputedly with hopes of putting Jewish competitors out of business, he was converted to National Socialism.

In the autumn of 1929 Von Ribbentrop met Hitler for the first time. One story says he was introduced to Hitler as "the man who gets as big a price for German champagne as others get for French champagne." Obviously such a man could be helpful, particularly if he also had Von Ribbentrop's connections with Von Papen and with the Herren-

klub. Although Von Ribbentrop didn't yet break his connections with Jewish high finance, he cooperated with Hitler. In 1933 he helped to bring about the famous meeting between Hitler and Von Papen at the home of the banker Von Schroeder—the meeting by which Von Papen was persuaded that if Hitler came to power he would leave the direction of foreign affairs in his hands, and Hitler acquired the necessary financial backing for his plans.

The plans succeeded—and Von Ribbentrop became sort of an "Anthony Eden of the Reich." He renewed acquaintanceships in foreign capitals. He mixed his blond, blue-eyed glamor with champagne, champagne with politics. He sold wine and ideology. Finally, in April 1934, at Hitler's behest, he was appointed Reichskommissar for Disarmament (in a government pledged to rearmament), and participated in the disarmament discussions at Geneva. More important, he organized the Ribbentrop Bureau, a private department of investigation and espionage with immense sums at its disposal whose services ranged from stirring up unrest in Africa to making Nazism popular among big business and high society circles in the democratic countries. And he continued to act as ambassador at large, "as Hitler's special plenipotentiary in particularly important affairs and also as a control on the ambassadors and envoys not yet entirely acquiescent to the system."

There seems to be little doubt that Von Ribbentrop had charm. In the fall of 1934 the easily impressed Jules Romains saw him as "a fairly tall, slender, spirited man, with amused eyes and thin, ironical lips, well dressed but without studied elegance, who spoke very good French in a clear voice, with a marked accent of the 'distinguished' kind. He liked to move around; he'd get up, sit in another chair, light cigarets. His conversation was animated, with quick shifts from one idea to another." Romains thought of him as "a Talleyrand or a Metternich"—one of those men "who are too subtle, too skeptical, and also too elegant, to have either partiality for the undertakings of imbeciles, madmen, and bloodthirsty rabble, or any wish to encourage them."

Yet Von Ribbentrop may have been able to describe himself to Romains as "a good European first and foremost" because no one as yet had had much opportunity to judge him by his acts. In 1935, after a foreign tour of Brussels, London and Paris for Hitler's information, he produced his first sample: the negotiation of the Anglo-German naval treaty. Soon afterward Belgium avowed her neutrality in the event of war; and in 1936, after the German occupation of the Rhineland, Von Ribbentrop was Germany's delegate at the London conference to decide exactly what to do about it. The answer was, of course, nothing.

After these impressive accomplishments for the Third Reich, Von Ribbentrop's appointment as German Ambassador to London in the summer of 1936 should have surprised no one, alarmed only the British. In London he wasn't as popular with everyone as he was at Cliveden, at Guilford, with the Marquis of Londonderry's set and with King Edward VIII, Mrs. Simpson and some of their friends. The staff of the German Embassy was considered "ridiculously numerous." Von Ribbentrop's ambitious plans for the building's remodeling brought clashes with the English Society for the Protection of National Monuments and with the Commissioner for Parks and Lawns. His son, it was rumored, was turned down by Eton, and contented himself by studying at Westminster in London. And Von Ribbentrop himself couldn't get into the most exclusive London clubs—in spite of his English valet, his English butler, the hint of an English accent in his German. Even his expert bridge and tennis and his accomplished violin playing couldn't sell the Third Reich to everyone. But he was making some powerful friends; and he was observing.

He was also not confining his activities to London. In November 1936 he dashed back to Berlin to sign the original anti-Comintern agreement with Japan, although it was Von Neurath who was German Secretary of State. The late Ambassador Dodd recorded in his diary his suspicion that Von Neurath did not wish to sign it, also that "Von Ribbentrop had worked out the matter long before he was sent to London. It was Hitler's way of popularizing Von Ribbentrop, who is not liked or respected very much here." Furthermore, Dodd suspected Von Ribbentrop of maneuvering the visit to Hitler of the late George Lansbury, British Laborite and No. 1 pacifist.

After the abdication of his friend Edward in December 1936 Von Ribbentrop attended the First Court of George VI, made headlines ("Nazi Insults King") and acquired a new nickname ("Brickendrop") by greeting the astonished and unresponsive King with a Nazi salute and a "Heil Hitler!", repeated three times. After that he spent more time working at the Ribbentrop Bureau in Berlin than in London, and it is claimed that his Anglophilia changed to Anglophobia because of his experience. He was not in England long. On February 4, 1938, Von Neurath was eased out of the German foreign ministry and Von Ribbentrop appointed to his post. "That commoner has always peddled his wares to the highest bidder," mourned Von Neurath, whose "von" was genuine. "May God have mercy on the Reich!"

He might have prayed for Europe, too. A little over a month later, when Von Ribbentrop took his final leave of London, Nazi troops were pouring into Austria. Von Ribbentrop had been closeted with Lord Halifax until the last minute, thereby preventing the Austrian Ambassador from making one last move with the British Government. Back in Berlin, Von Ribbentrop "attached himself firmly" to Heinrich Himmler, head of the Gestapo, built up a huge Foreign Office, and kept assuring Hitler that under no circumstances would the British fight. The Munich Pact of September 1938, followed by the December 1938 declaration of friendship with the French and the occupation of Czechoslovakia in March 1939, was the result and the triumph

of his monopoly of information, his diplomacy and his advice. When on August 23, 1939 he signed the non-aggression pact with the U. S. S. R. at Moscow, the names he was called were colorfully varied, but everyone agreed that it was a diplomatic *coup*. Only when Great Britain declared war on Germany a week later, with Nazi bombers darkening Polish skies, could anyone assert confidently that Von Ribbentrop was not infallible.

Since that time Von Ribbentrop has not stopped traveling. It was probably he who prodded Mussolini into entering the War and it was certainly he who sold the Three-Power Pact to Italy and to Japan and to more than one small nation. His already-excellent French and his passable Italian and Russian have improved, and the list of his uncomfortable diplomatic acquaintances has lengthened. His conferences with Mussolini, Matsuoka (see sketch this issue), Molotov, Philoff (see sketch this issue) and others have made millions of people hold their breaths with dread anticipation. As a prophet, however, he has not been completely successful. In March 1940 he expressed the opinion that the War should be over within a year; in March 1941 he expressed the same opinion.

References

Collier's 98 :15+ S 19 '36 por
Cur Hist 51 :23-5+ D '39 por
Engl R 62 .413-15 Ap '36
Life 8 :92+ Mr 11 '40 il pors (Same abr. Read Digest 36 :61-4 My '40)
Liv Age 350 :328 Je '36; 358 :548-51 Ag '40 por
N Y Herald Tribune X p7+ My 26 '40 pors
Sat Eve Post 213 :27+ N 16 '40 por
Time 29 :22-3 F 15 '37; 31 :19-20 Mr 21 '38 por

Bayles, W. D. Caesars in Goosestep p132-49 1941
Dutch, O. pseud. Hitler's Twelve Apostles p139-53 1940
Gunther, G. von. Von Ribbentrop 1939
Gunther, J. Inside Europe p88-9 1940
International Who's Who
Schuman, F. L. Night Over Europe p166-74 1941
Simone, A. Men of Europe p98-103 1941
Wer ist's?

RICE, GRANTLAND Nov. 1, 1880- Sports writer

Address: h. 1158 Fifth Ave, New York City

> *These are the rhymes from forty years*
> *Of service on a thousand fields,*

writes Grantland Rice, one of the best known and most affectionately regarded of American sports writers, in his book, *Only the Brave and Other Poems*, which was published in 1941. They are stirring, melodious, rather old-fashioned verses, an artful blend of *If*, *Invictus* and the poems of Eugene Field.

Most of the poems had appeared in his widely syndicated column, "The Sportlight," which he has been writing since 1930. Myriads

GRANTLAND RICE

of movie-goers, soothed and refreshed by the outdoor scenes of the Grantland Rice "Sportlights" short features shown at their neighborhood houses, are also familiar with his voice. Many of them are fans of his blonde actress-daughter Florence Rice, her father's pride and joy. She was born in 1910 and named Florence Davenport Rice. Her mother was Katharine Hollis of Americus, Georgia, whom Grantland Rice married on April 11, 1906.

Grantland Rice has seen thousands and thousands of sporting events in his many years of witnessing, participating in or writing about baseball, football, racing, golf, tennis, hunting, polo, rowing, field and track, and yacht racing. Once in 1923 he was called on to travel more than 16,000 miles and send back by telegraph and mail nearly a million words. He has wandered from Montana to Bermuda and all kinds of points in between.

"The drama of sport is a big part of the drama of life, and the scope of this drama is endless," wrote Rice in describing "My Greatest Thrill in Twenty-Two Years of Sport." "Sport has its triumphs and its tragedies, its great joys and its heavy sorrows, with more spectacular effect than most dramas may ever know. My life as a follower of sport has been one thrill after another; big thrills and little thrills—thrills of all descriptions marching by with the seasons. There has been the thrill of the new stars suddenly coming to fame on some great play, and the deeper thrill of the fading veteran coming back for another whack at glory after he was supposed to be down and out. The basis of the big thrill in sport is the uprising against heavy odds, the smaller man beating the larger one, the has-been coming back, the battered and broken rising to heights of glory."

Grantland Rice is a Tennessean, born at Murfreesboro on November 1, 1880, the son of Bolling H. and Beulah (Grantland) Rice. He received his preparatory education at the Nashville Military Academy and Wallace University School, Nashville, Tennessee, and obtained his B. A. degree from Vanderbilt University in 1901. At Vanderbilt he played both baseball and football, spending three years at shortstop and captaining the Vanderbilt baseball team in his senior year.

He is somewhat chary with details of his football career, but if casualties are to be counted Rice is there with a record, as a writer in *Outing* put it. In three years of play he managed to acquire a broken shoulder blade, a broken collarbone and four broken ribs, an average of two broken bones a year. From 1907 to 1911 he umpired and refereed throughout the South, learning something of how the game looks from the standpoint of the man with the official whistle. Rice was introduced to golf in 1910 at Nashville, and really plays, "not a medicinal 100 for the 18, but a scrappy game that will give even a champion his bad quarter hours."

But the role of a professional player was not for Rice. Immediately after graduation he got a job on the Nashville *News,* also writing for the *Forester Magazine* in 1901, and for the next three years (1902-04) he was on the staff of the Atlanta *Journal,* one of the great newspapers of the South. In 1905 Rice was a reporter on the Cleveland *News,* but he returned to his native state the next year to work for the Nashville *Tennessean* from 1906 to 1910. Then he came North. From 1911 to 1914 he worked on the New York *Mail,* whose columnist for two of those years was Franklin P. Adams (see sketch this issue).

In another year he followed "F. P. A." to the New York *Tribune* (now the *Herald Tribune*) and stayed there from 1914 to 1930, with a year off to serve in the First World War as first lieutenant in the 115th Regiment, Field Artillery, of the 30th Division (Tennessee National Guard) of the United States Army. He was in France with the American Expeditionary Forces in 1918 and 1919. "Incidentally, if you want some carefully assorted language with the emphasis properly placed, ask him his opinion of the fighters who wouldn't fight," wrote the *Outing* commentator the following year. "The name of an erstwhile champion is at the head of the list, and it includes all the heroes of the squared circle who preferred to stay at home and argue about the purses while the other fellows went to France and tossed their lives into the great ring over there."

Besides shooting 70 at golf (at Dunwoodie golf course, 72 at Scarsdale in medal play competition), Rice has shot quail, duck and wild turkey, and has caught salmon in New Brunswick, trout in Alberta. The only condition he specifies for enjoyable fishing is that the fish bite.

To swap yarns, Rice can find fellow sportsmen at the Players, Coffee House and Dutch Treat clubs in New York City. His golf clubs include the Englewood Golf Club, the National Golf Links and the Maidstone and

Deepdale Clubs. He is a Democrat and a Presbyterian; his college fraternity was Phi Delta Theta; Vanderbilt University made him an honorary member of Phi Beta Kappa in 1920; and he is a member of the Berzilius Society at Yale. Besides the new book of poems, *Only the Brave,* Rice has published *Songs of the Stalwart* (1917); *Sportlights of 1923* (1924); and *Songs of the Open* (1924).

He is president of Grantland Rice Sportlights, Incorporated, which makes fascinating, exciting and usually beautifully photographed moving-picture short features for which he supplies the vocal commentary. Besides keeping his column going, he is a frequent contributor to *Collier's* and other publications. His writing, it has been said, is for the good everyday sportsman and not for the hair-splitting expert, though he himself knows the techniques and fine points of practically every American sport.

References

Am Mag 97:41 My '24 por
Outing 75:323-4 Mr '20 por
International Motion Picture Almanac
Who's Who in America
Who's Who in Journalism

RICE, GREGORY Jan. 3, 1916- Long-distance runner
Address: h. 411 W. 115th St, New York City

Late in September 1941 fleet, wiry "Greg" Rice went into training again at the New York Athletic Club gymnasium, in the hope of surpassing his already extraordinary world-records in tearing off the three-mile run. He set one such record in February 1940, doing the course in the amazing time of 13.55 minutes, and a year later lowered records for both the two-mile and three-mile run, this time in the space of 13.51.

This young Montanan, who has out-streaked such famous European runners as Paavo Nurmi and Taisto Maki, is an accountant when not running his races, and spent several months in 1941 busily engaged in an office-building on lower Fifth Avenue in New York City, accumulating experience toward his final certification as a certified public accountant. Accounting was his major subject at Notre Dame University, where he received the degree of Bachelor of Science in commerce in 1939, and he spent a year and a half working at his new profession in South Bend, Indiana after graduation.

Greg Rice's mother, Mamie Mary (Bergman) Rice, was a native Montanan, and, says her son and only child, a broncho-breaker who could hold her own with any of the men. Joseph Matthew Rice, Greg's father, came from Arkansas, and has been a railroad mechanic all his life, except for doing a little farming. Joseph Gregory Rice was born January 3, 1916, in Deer Lodge, Montana. The family moved to Missoula when the boy was three and a half; and this town was his home until he matriculated at Notre Dame, except for one year spent in Burbank, California.

GREGORY RICE

Greg goes back home to see his family occasionally; the Missoula Chamber of Commerce brought him back by airplane in 1940 for an exhibition match, and the University of Montana, located in Missoula, followed suit the next year.

Greg Rice began running while in grammar school at Missoula, as a member of the local Boy Scout troop. Two newspaper routes also developed his leg muscles. He was a newsboy at 10, getting up at 4:30 a. m. to make his first delivery, and distributing out-of-town papers at noon. He had two separate paper routes and the agency for three out-of-state papers, keeping them all until his departure for Notre Dame in 1935, when he gave them to his three boy-assistants. In high school he competed each year in the Montana State Interscholastic Track and Field Meet. His best performances as a schoolboy were 2:01 in the half mile and 4:26.2 in the mile.

Until reaching the campus of Notre Dame, Rice had never run any farther than a mile and a half, which was part of his training schedule for the mile. At Notre Dame, however, he came under the tutelage of his "great friend and beloved coach," the late John P. Nicholson, who had seen him run in Chicago, and who immediately showed him the cross-country requirements of all his runners from the quarter mile up. At the end of the year's running, "Nick," as he was known to all his boys, told Rice that he could be a great two-miler if he put his heart into the task. This advice wasn't altogether pleasing to the young runner; he wished to be a miler. "I'm not kidding myself," he says, "I still hate cross-country. I've never enjoyed it, and I never will. But Nick taught me too clearly that a runner can't get along without it." "One couldn't be around 'Nick' long before he had you believing firmly in his ideas," and in 1937, Rice's sophomore year at Notre

RICE, GREGORY—*Continued*

Dame, he set a two-mile record (9:14 minutes) at the National Collegiate Athletic Association meet in Berkeley, California, a comeback after having previously placed fourth in the mile. (This setback had convinced him that he was not meant to be a miler.) At Los Angeles, in the 1939 meet, Rice won a two-mile victory in nine minutes, two seconds. He "wasn't satisfied with the time after the race, but coach and I were glad to have won from such a classy field."

In 1938 a European tour of six weeks with the American Athletic Union team under the direction of Peter Waters of Manhattan University gave Greg Rice an international reputation. The team landed at Southampton and went to London for an international meet on a bank holiday, competing with athletes from Poland, France, Esthonia, Sweden and Greece. They also appeared in Glasgow, Berlin, Dresden, Vienna and Budapest, flying from the Hungarian capital to Athens. In Berlin, Rice set a personal record for the 5,000-meter run of 14:54.

Rice amazed even himself during the two-mile run at the Knights of Columbus clubhouse in New York in March 1940. "I never felt that I could run that fast," he says. Undoubtedly his feat had much to do with his winning of the James E. Sullivan memorial trophy, presented him by the A. A. U. as the outstanding amateur athlete for 1940. In May 1941 he set a record for the 3,000-meter run. He won the National Cross Country Collegiate championship in 1938 and in November 1941 won the National A. A. U. Cross-Country championship at Yonkers, New York. Since Coach Nicholson's death on April 2, 1940, the end of some of Rice's longest runs has found him in tears, not from over-exertion but from emotion. "The saddest event in my running career was the loss of my coach, the late John P. Nicholson, to whom I owe all my success on the track. It was his inspiration and teachings, supplemented by my mother's and father's early training, that have enabled me to progress in track," wrote Rice.

At the toughest moments of his races—and Rice has passed out after some of them, notably in the intense heat of a Nebraska summer at Lincoln in 1939—the sense of Nicholson's actual presence seems very vivid, and Greg feels an added incentive to run his hardest. For that matter, "everyone has been extremely good to me, and this has made it much easier." "Gregory, the Great," as Charles Moran called him in the *Saturday Evening Post,* is a modest and unassuming young man. Described as "chunky," he stands only five feet four and a half inches, and weighs usually about 138 pounds. His dark brown hair is curly, and he has clear blue eyes. Accountancy and practice give him little time to himself, but he sees a movie a month and gets through the *Reader's Digest.* He also enjoyed *Panama Hattie.*

In his off-season from running, which lasts two months, Rice keeps in trim when away from his desk by playing tennis, handball and soft ball. He shares an apartment in the Columbia University section of Manhattan with a classmate from Notre Dame, and recently joined the huge New York Athletic Club on Central Park South. His real and original ambition was to be a major-league baseball star. Jimmy Foxx and Lefty Grove are his favorite players, and he states that he "is one of the many pulling for Ted Williams to win the batting championship with a better-than-400 average." So far he has found no time for romance.

"There is about him the simplicity of the Irish peasant and the fire of Brian Boru," comments Charles Moran, who also remarked once that Greg Rice looked like an altar boy without his cassock. And his well-beloved coach, John Patrick Nicholson, said, not long before his death, that Rice "has the confidence, the conviction, and the emotional stability to be the greatest three- and six-miler this country has ever developed."

References

> Look 5:17 My 6 '41 por
> N Y Sun p24 F 24 '41 por
> Sat Eve Post 212:27+ Je 29 '40 pors; 214:50+ N 8 '41

RICHARDS, C(HARLES) R(USS) Mar. 23, 1871—Apr. 17, 1941 President emeritus of Lehigh University; widely known educator; served as president of the University from 1922 to 1935; resigned his post because of ill health; revised the athletic system; increased the student body and faculty about 50 per cent and doubled the value of the plant.

References

> Sch & Soc 41:729 Je 1 '35
> Leaders In Education 1941
> Who's Who in America
> Who's Who in American Education

Obituaries

> N Y Times p21 Ap 18 '41

RICHARDS, JOHN G(ARDINER) Sept. 11, 1864—Oct. 9, 1941 Governor of South Carolina from 1927 to 1931; member of the State Tax Commission since 1935; as Governor unsuccessful in attempts to enforce State law against Sunday golf and gasoline sales.

References

> R of Rs 75:353 Ap '27 por
> Who's Who in America
> Who's Who in Government

Obituaries

> N Y Times p23 O 10 '41 por

RICHMAN, CHARLES J. Jan. 12, 1870—Dec. 1, 1940 Noted actor who was leading man for Ada Rehan and Lily Langtry on the stage and acted in many films.

References

Life 54:413 S 23 '09
Red Book 18:373+ D '11
Theatre 52:18 N '30 por
International Motion Picture Almanac 1937-38
Who's Who in the Theatre

Obituaries

N Y Times p23 D 2 '40 por
Variety 140:62 D 4 '40

RIDGE, LOLA 1883—May 19, 1941 One of the leading contemporary American poets; her longest poem, *Firehead,* dealing with the Crucifixion, was published in 1929 and won enthusiastic approval; much of her five books of poetry was taken up with the cause of labor and liberalism; worked as editor of *Others* and *Broom,* poetry magazines, and wrote popular fiction; received a Guggenheim fellowship in 1935.

References

Poetry 47:40-2 O '35
Aiken, C. P. Scepticisms p85-90 1919
Kunitz, S. J. ed. Living Authors 1937
Untermeyer, L. American Poetry Since 1900 p339-42 1923

Obituaries

N Y Times p23 My 21 '41
Sat R Lit 24:8 My 31 '41

RIGLING, ALFRED 1868—Dec. 8, 1940 Librarian of the Franklin Institute in Philadelphia where he collaborated with scientists and researchers and was assistant editor of the Institute's Journal.

Franklin Institute

ALFRED RIGLING

References

Special Libraries 24:133 Jl '33 por

Obituaries

N Y Times p25 D 10 '40

RING, BARBARA T(AYLOR) Apr. 2, 1879—Aug. 31, 1941 Psychiatrist; dramatist; administrator of the Ring Sanatorium at Arlington, Massachusetts; early works popular for amateur productions but later plays and pageants were presented on the legitimate stage and in films.

References

American Medical Directory
American Women

Obituaries

N Y Times p15 S 1 '41

RIPLEY, WILLIAM Z(EBINA) Oct. 13, 1867—Aug. 16, 1941 Professor emeritus of political economy at Harvard University; nationally known authority on railroad transportation; began a crusade against secrecy in the accounts of big corporations and trusts which greatly influenced legislation in behalf of the public interest; was Federal labor aide in the First World War; was author of numerous books.

References

Lit Digest 108:15 F 7 '31
Nation 136:190 F 22 '33
Newsweek 1:16 F 17 '33
R of Rs 74:341 O '26 por
Who's Who in America
Who's Who in Railroading

Obituaries

N Y Times p39 Ag 17 '41 por
Pub W 140:540 Ag 23 '41
Sch & Soc 54:122 Ag 23 '41
Time 38:44 Ag 25 '41

ROBERTS, ELIZABETH MADOX 1886 —Mar. 13, 1941 Kentucky novelist, poet and magazine writer; since publication of her first novel, *The Time of Man,* in 1926 Miss Roberts was recognized as one of the first-ranking novelists in America; critics acclaimed her *Black Is My Truelove's Hair* (1939) and *Song in the Meadow* (1940); *Not by Strange Gods* was called one of the ten outstanding books of the spring of 1941; her prose style and mastery of the poetic speech of Kentucky brought her wide acclaim as a writer's writer and several sought-after prizes—the John Reed Memorial Prize in 1928, a second prize in 1930 from the O. Henry Memorial Award Committee and a prize from the Poetry Society of South Carolina in 1931.

References

Scholastic 27:6 Ja 4 '36 por; 31:19E N 20 '37 por
Sewanee R 45:388-410 O '37
Va Q R 12:80-90 Ja '36
Wilson Lib Bul 4:418 My '30

(Continued next page)

ROBERTS, ELIZABETH MADOX—*Cont.*

American Women
Author's and Writer's Who's Who
Hatcher, H. H. Creating the Modern
　American Novel p247-61　1935
Kunitz, S. J. ed. Living Authors　1937
Millett, F. B. Contemporary American
　Authors　1940
Overton, G. M. Women Who Make
　Our Novels p286-90　1928
Who's Who in America

Obituaries

N Y Times p21 Mr 14 '41 por
Pub W 139 :1308 Mr 22 '41
Sat R Lit 23 :10 Mr 22 '41
Time 37 :67 Mr 24 '41
Wilson Lib Bul 15 :614 Ap '41

ROBERTS, GEORGE LUCAS　Nov. 19,
1860—Feb. 26, 1941　Founder and dean
emeritus of the Department of Education at
Purdue University; organized the department
in 1909 and retired in 1935; served as editor
of the *Educator-Journal*; was a frequent
lecturer before teachers' institutions.

References

Leaders in Education 1941
Who's Who in America　1936-37

Obituaries

N Y Times p19 F 27 '41
Sch & Soc 53 :309 Mr 8 '41

ROBERTS, KATE L(OUISE)　Died Aug.
12, 1941　Former reference librarian at the
Newark Free Public Library; had been on the
staff of The New York Public Library
previously; was author of a book of programs
for club women and reviser and editor for
various cyclopedias and dictionaries.

References

American Women
Who's Who Among North American
　Authors
Who's Who in America 1938-39

Obituaries

Pub W 140 :700 Ag 30 '41

ROBERTS, OWEN J(OSEPHUS)　May
2, 1875-　Supreme Court Justice
Address: b. Supreme Court Bldg, Washington,
D. C.; h. 1401 31st St., N. W., Washington,
D C.; Bryncoed Farm, Kimberton, Pa.

"Are toil and tears and blood itself too
much to sacrifice on the altar of freedom in
justification of our fathers' faith, in protection
of our own free lives, in perpetuation for
generations to come of the priceless liberties
for which the Stars and Stripes have always
stood?"
In these ringing words, spoken in Independence Hall in his native Philadelphia on Flag
Day of 1941, Owen J. Roberts, who has been
called "the great dissenter", "the hard-working
balance wheel" of the Supreme Court, pro-

claimed his stand in the national crisis. Later,
presiding at a national emergency rally in
New York's Madison Square Garden sponsored by the Council for Democracy, he took
the lead in urging full support of any measures adopted by the United States to "defeat
the dictatorships."
Justice Roberts was born into a prosperous,
conservative Philadelphia family, the son of
Josephus and Emma (Lafferty) Roberts, and
went no farther afield than his own city for
his education. He received his B. A. at the
University of Pennsylvania in 1895, then
attended the Law School of the University and
was awarded his LL. B. in 1898, immediately
being admitted to the Pennsylvania Bar. So
brilliant was his scholastic record, both in the
College of Liberal Arts and in the Law School,
that the year he was graduated he became
instructor in law at his Alma Mater. He
remained there for 20 years, resigning in 1918
as full professor.
At the same time his was far from a
cloistered professorial life. In spite of warnings from the then dominant political machine
in Philadelphia that he was a "goo-goo" and
a "reformer," the district attorney of Philadelphia County (co-terminus with the city)
made him his first assistant in 1901, and he
remained in that post until 1904. He engaged
actively in law practice as well, becoming
attorney for the Pennsylvania Railroad and for
other large trusts and corporations. Even so
early his economic bent, which may be
described as inherently conservative tinged by
a slight aristocratic liberalism, became apparent.
When, on the entry of the United States into
the First World War, he was appointed
prosecutor of espionage cases for the Eastern
District of Pennsylvania, the *Christian Science
Monitor* hailed him as a "vigorous, shrewd, and
tenacious" attorney who could be trusted not
to show leniency or weakness.
What made Owen J. Roberts a national
figure, however, was his appointment by
President Coolidge in 1924 as one of the two
prosecutors in the notorious Teapot Dome oil
case. It was in some ways a curious and
yet quite characteristic choice. Mr. Roberts
was then a director of several large corporations, including the American Telephone and
Telegraph Company; he had openly declared
himself against governmental investigation of
the Standard Oil Company; he was an avowed
enemy of the viewpoint which today we call
the New Deal. He was accused of deliberate
delay, and it is true that the net result of the
impressive case was merely the imprisonment
of the wretched Senator Fall of New Mexico.
But there seems no reason to doubt the complete integrity of the prosecuting attorneys.
Roberts was as thorough and unrelenting as
he was slow, and when the case drew to its
conclusion his name was familiar to every
literate American.
When, in May 1930, President Hoover
offered the name of Owen J. Roberts to fill
a vacancy in the United States Supreme Court,
the confirmation came to him almost by default. Hoover's first choice had been John
J. Parker of North Carolina, a judge hated

by organized labor because of his judicial approval of "yellow dog" labor contracts. By contrast, Roberts was highly acceptable. His appointment went through without a dissenting vote. But he proved a great disappointment to hopeful liberals. One of his very first acts as Supreme Court Justice was to cast the balance against the Railroad Retirement Act, and later it was his vote which killed the AAA.

At the time of this last decision Justice Roberts was the youngest member of the Court and appropriately energetic, writing more decisions than any other Justice. Before the complexion of the Court was changed by retirements, deaths and new appointments to its present prevailing liberalism, it was he who most often cast the decisive vote in the famous five to four decisions. Usually he was ranked as a conservative—occasionally as a reactionary; but he manifestly was doing his own thinking, and several times he made unexpectedly liberal decisions. The difficulty, as the *New Republic* once remarked, was that Roberts' liberal moments seldom coincided with those of the other occasional liberal, Charles Evans Hughes (see sketch this issue), so that in most cases the final vote was anti-New Deal.

In 1940 Roberts was strongly recommended as a possible Republican candidate for President, especially by opponents of Thomas E. Dewey. The candidacy died a-borning, partly because of the unexpected strength shown by the dark horse, Wendell Willkie, and partly because Justice Roberts gave it no encouragement. His ambitions have never been political, and, besides, he may have remembered what happened to Justice (not then Chief Justice) Hughes when he resigned from the Supreme Court in 1916 to run as Republican candidate for President in a Democratic year. (He did not return to the Court until three months before Roberts himself.)

To a certain extent Justice Roberts still retains his attitude of seesaw liberalism. In general, however, since the retirement of Justice McReynolds in February 1941, he has been considered the "conservative member" of the Court. Yet he is not a man on whom it is easy to pin labels. Perhaps the best estimate of his nature is the statement that he is "groping to preserve a humanitarian detachment." Meanwhile he is personally a most disarming man, whom no dignities or responsibilities can keep from remaining "human and approachable." He is probably the only one of the Supreme Court Justices who goes to work in the morning carrying his own lunch—a thermos bottle full of coffee, and one sandwich. Until the new Supreme Court Building was opened he had his office in the Capitol, and he used to drive himself to work in a not very new La Salle landau.

Quick-thinking, energetic, a facile speaker and writer, Justice Roberts actually enjoys working hard. His appearance when the Court meets has been described by such verbs as "leap and bound"—he hurries in, throws himself into his chair, immediately digs enthusiastically into the work before him.

OWEN J. ROBERTS

Usually a fastidious dresser, there was much surprise when, on the solemn occasion of his induction into the Court, he appeared attired in a bright red tie. When it was called to his attention he merely said carelessly that he had just happened to put it on that day.

Roberts is a large man, tall and upright, weighing 200 pounds, square-jawed and with deep-set eyes and an aggressive nose. He is by no means a formidable personality, however; *Fortune* remarked on his "ingratiating large-mouthed smile and pleasant manner." He is eminently gregarious, though he cares little for formal social events; he loves to tell jokes on himself, and likes to have company about him. One of his closest friends, in spite of their diametrically opposed views, is Secretary of Labor Frances Perkins. Mr. and Mrs. Roberts (the former Elizabeth Caldwell Rogers of Fairfield, Connecticut, whom he married in 1904) call her "Perkie," and see more of her when they are in Washington than of any other friend.

In his youth, studious as he was (he intended originally to be a teacher of Greek, and majored in Greek at college), Owen Roberts was also a good deal of an outdoors man, and he still retains a trace of his athletic past. He no longer hunts moose in Maine, and his riding has to be done on a very gentle horse since, years ago, another horse threw him and fractured his shoulder so badly that he still suffers pain from it; but when he is not in Washington he spends practically all his time on a farm at Kimberton, Pennsylvania, which he calls Bryncoed (Welsh for "wooded hill"). It is a real farm, 650 acres, and he is a practical farmer who raises blooded cattle, pigs, chickens, ducks and geese, grows vegetables for his family's own use, and has an active interest in the flower garden, which specializes in hollyhocks and madonna lilies. At the time when

ROBERTS, OWEN J.—*Continued*

he was most unpopular in labor circles, the rumor used to go about that he supervised his farm attired in plus fours. He does, but they are made of khaki and accompany a khaki shirt, woolen stockings and a battered old straw hat to which he is as attached as he is to his pipe.

As for the house itself, it is partly his own creation: a remodeled Colonial stone farmhouse which is furnished almost entirely with antique furniture belonging to its original period, and which has fifteen rooms and seven fireplaces. Justice Roberts is an enthusiastic remodeler, anyway: when his family lived in Georgetown, D. C., he remodeled the building which had been the slave quarters of the old house into a garage with a studio on its second floor for the use of his artist-daughter, Elizabeth Rogers.

While in college Justice Roberts was elected to Phi Beta Kappa, and he is a member of Psi Upsilon fraternity. In religion he is an Episcopalian, though not particularly active in church affairs. From 1921 to 1924 he was a trustee of Jefferson Medical College in Philadelphia, and an interest in public as well as private housing made him the representative of the United States Housing Corporation in that same city at the time of the First World War. He has received innumerable honors—including honorary doctorates from nine colleges, among them Princeton, Williams and his own University—but nothing yet has been able to make a stuffed shirt out of him.

Nor (though he may have to retire in 1945) is he anything but young and vigorous in mind and body. On December 18, 1941 Justice Roberts was appointed by President Roosevelt as head of a commission to report in early 1942 on the Pearl Harbor disaster of December 7. At 65, when he was mentioned as Republican candidate for President, *Time Magazine* called him "the so-called 'Swing Man' of the Supreme Court, relatively impervious alike to New Dealers or Conservatives, of greater physical and mental stamina than most United States leaders, with vast erudition, a natural oratorical voice trained to express sense rather than emotion, and an impressive presence."

References

Business Week p13 Ap 3 '37 por
Collier's 94:32 Jl 7 '34 por; 108:16 S 20 '41 por
Fortune 13:192+ My '36 por (p85)
Lit Digest 117:9+ Ap 7 '34 por; 120:6 S 7 '35 por
New Repub 85:303-5 Ja 22 '36; 87:232-5 Jl 1 '36
Newsweek 5:15 My 18 '35 por
Scholastic 26:21 My 25 '35 por
Time 35:21 Ap 15 '40 por
Pearson, D. and Allen, R. S. Nine Old Men p139-62 1936
Who's Who in America
Who's Who in Government
Who's Who in Law
Who's Who in the Nation's Capital

ROBESON, PAUL (BUSTILL) Apr. 9, 1898-   Baritone concert singer; actor

Address: 555 Edgecombe Ave, New York City

Paul Robeson says: "I have never been much interested in vocal virtuosity. I have never tried to sing an A-flat while the audience held on to the edge of its collective seat to see if I could make it." The distinguished Negro baritone, who has sung and acted around the world, was in the 1940 to 1941 season making a concert tour of the United States, his first in five years. Among his most popular numbers is the *Ballad for Americans,* which he introduced to the public in November 1939 on a Columbia *Pursuit of Happiness* program. He prefers folk songs to classical music, and his rendition of English, Hebrew, Mexican, Russian and German folk songs, often sung both in the original tongue and in English, shows the same understanding and deep sincerity that make him the most famous male singer of Negro spirituals of his day.

Paul Robeson was born in Princeton, New Jersey, the son of Anna Louisa (Bustill) Robeson, who was two-thirds Indian, and William Drew Robeson, a runaway slave who had put himself through Lincoln University and become a Methodist minister. The minister's son attended Rutgers College on a scholarship and made a remarkable record there: won the freshman prize in oratory and the sophomore and junior prizes in extemporaneous speaking, was a member of the glee club and the debating team, and a speaker at commencement. In addition he was a "four-letter" man —winning, in all, twelve letters in track, football, basketball and baseball—and was chosen All-American end by Walter Camp in 1917 and 1918. His academic record was equally good: one story says that when he received his first year's marks, consisting of seven *A*'s and one *B,* his father wanted him to account for the *B.* In his junior year he was elected to Phi Beta Kappa.

After having received his B. A. from Rutgers in 1919, Paul Robeson went on to Columbia to take his LL. B. He financed his law studies with week-end games of professional football, and even considered becoming a professional heavyweight boxer. It was during his four years at Columbia that he made the acquaintance of Alexander Woollcott (see sketch this issue), who wrote about him later: "I think I felt at the time that I had just crossed the path of someone touched by destiny. He was a young man on his way. He did not know where he was going, but I never in my life saw anyone so quietly sure, by some inner knowledge, that he was going somewhere."

When Robeson left Columbia he was taken into the office of Louis W. Stotesbury, a Rutgers man and a prominent New York lawyer. He hadn't considered becoming an actor. While at Columbia, however, he had taken part in an amateur play at the New York Y. M. C. A.; Eugene O'Neill, who had been in the audience, later wrote *Emperor*

Jones and offered the part to the young amateur who had impressed him so much. Robeson refused this role but soon afterward (1922) consented to play in *Taboo,* appearing with Margaret Wycherly in the United States and with Mrs. Patrick Campbell in London. He then appeared in *Emperor Jones* in New York and in London, and the English performance proved to be such an artistic triumph that he decided to give up law.

It was also in *Emperor Jones* that Robeson first made his reputation as a singer. One scene called for whistling. Robeson couldn't whistle, so he sang. Someone persuaded him to study voice seriously, and while waiting for another play to turn up he decided to give a concert, assisted by Lawrence Brown. A few nights before his debut in 1925 Heywood Broun heard the two men sing at the home of Walter White (Secretary of the National Association for the Advancement of Colored People). He wrote about them in his column with such enthusiasm that the concert—the first program of all-Negro music —was a great success.

Since that time Robeson's rich, communicative baritone voice has made itself heard and felt all over the world. He became even more popular as a singer of Negro spirituals than as an actor, and as well known in London and Moscow as in New York. During the Spanish Civil War he even visited Spain and sang *Water Boy, Ol' Man River* and *Road to Mandalay* to the Loyalist soldiers, for whose cause he continued to work. For a number of years he was completely absent from the legitimate stage in spite of the fact that *All God's Chillun,* the first play in which he appeared after *Emperor Jones,* had gained for him an international reputation, as did his performances in *Porgy, Stevedore* (in London only), *Show Boat, Othello* (in London only) and *The Hairy Ape.*

It was after an absence of eight years, however, that Robeson returned to Broadway early in 1940 in *John Henry.* The play was withdrawn after only five performances, but Brooks Atkinson, critic for the New York *Times,* wrote of it: "It serves chiefly to renew acquaintance with a man of magnificence who ought to be on the stage frequently in plays that suit him. For there is something heroic about this huge man with the deep voice and a great personal dignity. Count as one of the theatre's extravagances the fact that Paul Robeson is not an active figure in it."

Frequent appearances on the radio, more than 300 recordings, and roles in many films have made Robeson's voice and dramatic ability familiar to millions who have never attended his concert or theatre performances. Among the motion pictures in which he has had a starred or featured part are *Emperor Jones, Showboat, Sanders of the River, King Solomon's Mines, Dark Sands, Jericho, Song of Freedom.* He has made films for British as well as American producers, having for a long time made his home in England because he found less race prejudice there than in the United States.

PAUL ROBESON

The racial problem is one that Robeson has studied thoroughly. It was racial discrimination as much as his own acting ability that caused him to give up his career as a lawyer. He sent his son (in 1921 he married Eslanda Cardoza Goode) to school in the U. S. S. R. because he thought the boy could grow up normally there. And in January 1941 Robeson, with four other Negroes and five whites, was suing a San Francisco restaurant because, they asserted, they had been refused admission. Robeson also frequently speaks out on political issues in which he feels his race is deeply involved: in the summer of 1940 he was opposing conscription, speaking for peace—later, urging all Negroes in the industry to join the United Automobile Workers of America in their Ford organizing-drive—even later, speaking and singing at benefits for aid to Britain, China and the Soviet Union. He has been called a radical.

Robeson has been described as "massive, beautiful in physique, muscular, strong and handsome." He is said sometimes to reveal his Indian heritage "by locking himself in his room, the curtains drawn, and for days at a time escaping from all society of friends." For relaxation he studies languages: he knows Chinese, Russian, Spanish, Gaelic. Quite recently he turned to invention. Believing that he sings at his best only when he can hear himself, he began (with Professor Harold Burris-Meyer) to tackle the problem of providing a reflective surface for singers in acoustically imperfect halls. An "acoustical envelope" was evolved, and Robeson used it in October 1940 for the first time.

When the honorary degree of Doctor of Humane Letters was conferred upon Paul Robeson by Hamilton College in 1940, Dr. W. H. Cowley, the president, described him as a "student, athlete, lawyer, actor, singer

ROBESON, PAUL—*Continued*

and great American." He said: "In honoring you today, we do not, however, express our enthusiasm for your histrionic and musical achievements alone. We honor you chiefly as a man—a man of tremendous stature, energy and physical dexterity; a man of brilliant mind, a man whose sensitive spirit makes possible your penetrating interpretations; and a man who, above all else, travels across the world as an example of the humanity and the greatness of our democratic heritage."

References

Collier's 105:15+ Ja 13 '40 por
Key Reporter 5:1-2 spring '40 por
N Y Times p7 O 5 '28; p24 N 18 '28; p4 Ja 24 '38; IV p2 Ja 30 '38 por; p27 My 16 '39; p10 Ja 22 '40; IX p5 Je 23 '40 por
New Yorker 4:26-9 S 29 '28
Time 34:58-9 N 20 '39 por

Brawley, B. G. Negro Genius p269-96 1937
Ewen, D. ed. Living Musicians 1940
Hare, M. C. Negro Musicians and Their Music p352-85 1936
International Motion Picture Almanac
Johnson, J. W. Black Manhattan 1930
Kaufmann, H. L. and Hansl, E. E. vom B. Artists in Music of Today p87 1933
Ovington, M. W. Portraits in Color p205-17 1927
Robeson, E. C. Paul Robeson, Negro 1930
Sergeant, E. S. Fire Under the Andes p193-209 1927
Who's Who in America
Who's Who in Colored America
Wier, A. E. ed. Macmillan Encyclopedia of Music and Musicians 1938

ROBEY, RALPH W(EST) (rō′bê) Aug. 29, 1899- Economist; journalist

Address: b. Newsweek, 152 W. 42nd St, New York City; h. 450 Riverside Drive, New York City

Some time in 1940 the National Association of Manufacturers decided to find out whether there was any basis for "the growing apprehension about the contents of school textbooks." About social science textbooks they were particularly curious, and Ralph Robey was appointed to prepare abstracts of 563 textbooks in the fields of history, civics, sociology and economics so that no apprehensive school administrator or parent would have to spend too much energy in determining whether any one textbook gives "a fair and impartial presentation of our form of government and the private enterprise system."

It was February 1941 when the survey was finished. The New York *Times* promptly interviewed Mr. Robey to see what conclusions he had reached. Mr. Robey threw a bombshell. Few of the books he had been so busily abstracting were actually "communistic," he

found, but most were poorly written, unscholarly, and many of them belittled the accomplishments of democracy and held the private enterprise system up to ridicule. Discontent and skepticism were thus stirred up in immature pupils. "If you had an out-and-out Leftist slant, it would be much simpler to handle," he said. "What you get is a critical attitude that is destructive in its influence." Among others, the books of Harold Rugg (see sketch this issue) were quoted as examples.

The response was immediate. Twelve thousand delegates at the seventy-first annual convention of the American Association of School Administrators began tossing Mr. Robey's conclusions back and forth. Many decided the report was an attack on democratic education; others thought there should be further investigation. The Council for Democracy, which has for its chairman Raymond Gram Swing and which includes among its directors Colonel William Donovan, William Averell Harriman (see sketches this issue), Robert Sherwood and William Allen White, decided that Mr. Robey "deserves the censure of his colleagues" and that the N. A. M. survey has "given aid and comfort to those only too eager to impose an incompetent censorship on our schools." The American Committee for Democracy and Intellectual Freedom appointed a committee to "combat the censorship threat inherent in the textbook investigation" by testing the accuracy of the N. A. M. abstracts; the School Book Publishers National Association appointed another to "go into the matter of these charges specifically."

Merwin K. Hart (see sketch this issue), however, quickly moved to uphold Mr. Robey's charges, and in *Newsweek* Raymond Moley announced that he had "hoped for a long time that someone would point out the mistakes of fact and justified interpretation" with which some social science textbooks abound. He concluded: "The cleaning up to which both the Robey report and the New York legislative inquiry point must be done in the local communities." At the same time the National Association of Manufacturers itself proclaimed that Mr. Robey's conclusions were purely his own, and that "the abstracts themselves contain no opinions, are completely unprejudiced and can be used to advantage by any person sincerely eager to study the contents of our nation's textbooks." In April 1941 the N. A. M. offered to "co-operate with educators at any time" in order to prevent intolerant use of the abstracts.

Ralph West Robey, a "black-haired, handsome" man with a "lean, nervous face," is the writer of a weekly financial column for *Newsweek*, whose publisher is Malcolm Muir, a director of the National Association of Manufacturers. Since 1938 Mr. Robey has also been an assistant professor at Columbia University, but in 1941 is on a leave of absence: "I've been teaching for 17 years and it seemed to me it's time my students got a break." He was born in Masontown, West Virginia on August 29, 1899, the son of John Calvin and Joan (West) Robey, and took his B. A. from Indiana University in 1920.

of a youth. His diet includes four or five quarts of ice cream a day. His only sicknesses in 40 years have been three attacks of ptomaine poisoning.

In appearance Bill looks much younger than his 62 years. He has no wrinkles and there is only a touch of gray in his short-cropped, kinky hair. One writer says: "Time has walked across his face on soft cat feet. He might be 30 as he taps across the hardwood in a cascade of pure artistry." Robinson dresses showily, his favorite attire a plaid suit, check shirt and figured tie. He always dances in winter underwear.

Bill's conversation is largely "anecdotal" and his mode of verbal communication mostly "laconic." His favorite word is "copesetic," which he coined himself to mean "better than O.K." His singing has been described as "uninspired," and he plays no musical instrument. But his feet he manipulates with "ineffable grace and ease."

His sense of humor is well known. Once he went into a mid-town restaurant and seated himself at a table. The occupant of an adjoining booth objected and the manager advised Robinson that unpleasantness would be avoided by his speedy departure. The Negro dancer smiled. "Have you got a $10 bill?" he asked. "Sure," said the bewildered manager. "Here's one." Robinson took the bill, extracted six $10 notes from his own well-filled wallet and rolled them all in one ball. "Close your eyes for a moment," he directed. The other man complied. "Here," said Bill, extending the seven bills, "let's see you pick out the colored one." He was served.

References

Am Dancer p18+ Jl '39
Cue p6-7+ Ag 14 '37 por
Dance Mag 2:8-9 Ag '37 por
N Y Times X p2 Ap 9 '39
New Yorker 10:26-8 O 6 '34; 10:30-4 O 13 '34
PM p18 N 7 '40 pors
International Motion Picture Almanac
Who's Who in America
Who's Who in Colored America

ROBINSON, BOARDMAN Sept. 6, 1876-
Artist; teacher

Address: Colorado Springs Fine Arts Center, Colorado Springs, Colo.

Boardman Robinson is a tremendous, magnetic man. He has a careless gray beard that used to be a flaming red, and the eyes of a kind satyr peering out from under rude eyebrows. He is probably one of the few persons important in the world of art who makes as great a personal impression upon all who meet him as his work does upon critics.

This American artist was born on September 6, 1876, the son of John Henry and Lydia Jane (Parker) Robinson, in Somerset, Nova Scotia. (His father was a sea captain who sailed around the world six times.) After spending some years of his childhood in South Wales, he attended the Massachusetts Normal

BOARDMAN ROBINSON

Art School, then, like nearly all young artists of that particular period, went to Paris. There he attended L'Académie Colarossi and L'École des Beaux-Arts, acquired a great admiration for the work of Jean Louis Forain, failed completely in his effort to get his work exhibited and eventually returned to the United States. He spent a year in Boston, a year in San Francisco; then there were three more years in Paris before, in 1907, he came East and found himself a job in New York as illustrator and cartoonist for the *Morning Telegraph*.

Robinson's early drawings immediately attracted attention and admiration because of his ability to say exactly what he wanted to say powerfully yet gracefully, and in as few lines as possible. As one critic put it: "He was an exceptional draftsman even in those days. You always had a feeling that he drew very quickly with very little effort, with the least possible expenditure of time and energy— and there was buoyancy in his technique that seemed to reflect not so much the personality of the subject as his own vivacious delight in his work." By the time Robinson left the *Morning Telegraph* to work for the New York *Tribune* (1910-14) his cartoons were famous all over the country. Reedy of the St. Louis *Mirror* wrote: "Boardman Robinson has the finest, freest, swashing stroke, the greatest daring in massing his black and letting in his white." From the editor of *Cartoons* came a tribute of another kind: "His ideas are refreshing, the spirit of his work being attack on sham and on things, animate or not— customs, habits, individuals, corporations, and so forth—that obstruct the path of progress."

The early days of the First World War found Robinson in the Balkans and in Russia with the late John Reed. Many of his grim sketches of scenes in those war-torn countries appeared in *Metropolitan Magazine* in 1915,

ROBINSON, BOARDMAN—*Continued*

and his were the illustrations for Reed's *The War in Eastern Europe* (1916). His own *Cartoons of the War,* a devastating satire, was published the same year. By that time Robinson was on the staff of the old *Masses,* and during the famous *Masses* trial one of his cartoons, *Making the World Safe for Democracy,* was offered as an exhibit of a specific violation of the loosely interpreted Espionage Act. When in 1918 *The Liberator* was established, Robinson became a contributing editor to that publication, too. Soon it was the Peace Conference, rather than the War, that was being boldly satirized. Much later, a critic in the *Magazine of Art* remarked on "with what unerring comprehension he saw through the thin hypocritical shell of things to the essential core. The cartoons are prophetic; their content grows more significant with the years." Among the most famous are *God* and *The System Investigates Itself*—"the system" pictured in a luxurious bed, apparently searching for fleas and scratching like an ape.

In 1921 Charles Henry Meltzer, writing in *Arts and Decoration,* saw in Robinson "another Daumier." But Robinson himself was quoted in that same article: "I want to get back to the primitive. And chiefly to get back to Giotto. Rembrandt, of course, I love, and I love Daumier, but Giotto—" This was toward the end of his very productive cartooning period. There was no doubt that the content of his drawings kept them from as wide an audience as Robinson might otherwise have reached, although he was a staff member of the fairly conservative *Harper's Weekly* as well as of radical journals. One writer in the *Outlook* wanted more of his cartoons published even if the editors had to run them as "Cartoons by Boardman Robinson Which Do Not of Necessity Represent Our Views." In 1923 Robinson left the United States for England, where he drew cartoons for the London *Outlook.*

His stay in England was short. By 1925 he was back in the United States, an instructor at the Art Students League. Though he had said once: "I am esthetic, I suppose, but, though I understand the value of abstractions in my art, I am not satisfied unless I have a truth or an idea to build on," soon he was adding to his compassionate, impressionistic studies of such subjects as tramps, beggars and slum children more purely esthetic studies of dancers, nudes and landscapes.

By 1929 it was difficult to recognize the early Robinson in the mural panels painted for the Kaufman Department Store in Pittsburgh. (In 1921 there had been perhaps two paintings among all his work, which were, for the most part, charcoal or watercolor studies.) For these famous murals, portraying the *History of Commerce,* Robinson used a kind of specially treated automobile paint. One art critic, while acknowledging Robinson as an unequaled master of design, compared his work to that of another master, Pinturicchio, because he "stays picturesquely on the surface

and never hits out," is "never fiery." "His art does not yet transcend illustration," he commented. And Henry McBride came, saw, also remained unconquered, and went back to mourn (in the columns of the New York *Sun*) Robinson's desertion of caricature. "He could be, if he wished, the first satirical commentator upon American life."

Since 1930 Robinson has been art director at the Colorado Springs Fine Arts Center and, since 1934, also a teacher in the Fountain Valley School for Boys in Colorado Springs, Colorado. Among his most ambitious projects since then have been frescoes for the Colorado Springs Fine Arts Center; a mural, *Man And His Toys,* for the RCA Building in New York City's Rockefeller Center; 18 panels for the Department of Justice Building in Washington, D. C.; and a post-office mural for Englewood, Colorado. Versatile and tireless, he has done the illustrations for Random House editions of Dostoevsky's *The Brothers Karamazov* and *The Idiot* (powerful black-and-whites admirably keyed to the text) and of Edgar Lee Masters' *Spoon River Anthology.* Late in 1941 he was working on *Moby Dick* for the Limited Editions Club. He has made drawings and delicate water colors ranging in subject from dancers, dude ranches, "superbly sensuous" nudes and rodeos to a sorrowful and hungry Christ.

His landscapes are many, but the Rocky Mountains he finds hard to draw. "I have done perhaps 20 mountain pictures," he said in 1940, "and have destroyed just about all but . . . three. I cannot draw mountains. The minute I look at a mountain it seems to move both upward and toward me, and if I try to paint the thing in detail it gets static, like a post card. And the minute you get a range of mountains, you have something that is really going places. You have to be quick to catch it."

A monograph, *Boardman Robinson: Ninety Three Drawings* (1937), with an introduction by George Biddle, provides an excellent survey of Robinson's work, which is represented in the Harrison Gallery (Los Angeles Museum), the Metropolitan Museum, the Denver Art Museum and the Detroit Institute of Art. Biddle says: "I believe Robinson to be a great draftsman, a great *dessinateur* and consequently a great artist." Other critics, for the most part, seem to be divided between those who believe that as an artist Robinson has developed immeasurably in the past decade and those in whom anything signed "Boardman Robinson" inspires a nostalgia for his cartooning days. One critic, who thinks that it is as a draftsman that Robinson has most completely realized himself, finds his landscape drawing "almost disturbingly simple and complete," with "almost oriental comprehension and restraint." His nudes express "a maximum of force and organic movement with controlled energy." The variety and subtlety of his treatment of line is remarked on by nearly everyone. "In his recent work the more abstract element of design becomes a powerful governing influence on Robinson, especially in the water colors where line weaves a heavy black supporting pattern, like the leading in Gothic stained-glass windows—following and defining abstract form in rhythms that tumble with motion."

Married in 1903 to Sally Senter Whitney of San Francisco, herself a sculptor, Robinson has two sons, John Whitney and Bartlett Whitney. He is a member of the American Institute of Arts and Letters and, in 1941, chairman of the Jury for War Department Murals.

References

Art Digest 13:31 O 1 '38; 14:25 Mr 15 '40 il
Art N 38:19 Mr 9 '40 il
Arts & Dec 15:228-9 Ag '21 il por
Lit Digest 103:15-16 D 28 '29 il
Mag Art 30:150 Mr '37 self por; 34: 318-21 Je '41 il
Parnassus 12:29 O '40 il
Time 35:40 Mr 18 '40
Touchstone 6:207-11 Ja '20 il

Cheney, M. C. Modern Art in America p128-30 1939
New Standard Encyclopedia of Art
Robinson, B. Ninety Three Drawings 1937
Who's Who in America
Who's Who in American Art

ROBINSON, FREDERICK B(ERTRAND) Oct. 16, 1883—Oct. 19, 1941 Former president of the College of the City of New York; became a member of the College's faculty in 1906 and taught economics and public speaking; elected president in 1927 and resigned in 1939, after a career marked by a gift for organizing and numerous brushes with the student body; editor of many journals and author of *Effective. Public Speaking* and *Business Costs.*

References

Am Mag 95:12-13 Ja '23 por; 105:52-3 F '28 por; 107:22-3 F '29 il por
Lit Digest 118:10 Ag 18 '34 por
Nation 142:170 F 12 '36
New Yorker 9:28-31 N 18 '33
Newsweek 7:30 Je 20 '36
Sch & Soc 43:112-13 Ja 25 '36; 45:570 Ap 24 '37; 48:819 D 24 '38; 49:60 Ja 14 '39
Time 27:36 F 10 '36 por; 32:21 D 26 '38 por

Leaders in Education 1941
Who's Who Among North American Authors
Who's Who in America

Obituaries

N Y Times p17 O 20 '41 por

ROCHE, JOSEPHINE (ASPINWALL) (rōsh) Dec. 2, 1886- Director of the National Consumers' League; lecturer; industrialist
Address: b. Flatiron Bldg, Denver, Colo; h. 1615 Grant St, Denver, Colo.

JOSEPHINE ROCHE

For many years now Josephine Roche has received recognition for her accomplishments as a coal mine operator, a government official and a leader in the national movement toward health and social welfare. In 1935 Chi Omega gave her its national Achievement Award; in 1936 *American Women* named her as one of the 10 outstanding women in the United States; and in May 1941 the Federation of Women's Clubs chose her as one of those representing "the great strides made by women in the past 50 years."

Those social ideals for which Josephine Aspinwall Roche has fought long and hard—today she insists that the surest bulwark against encroachment by foreign ideologies lies in the wider application of democratic principles in American industry and life—are something she arrived at by herself. Her father, John J. Roche, was a leading coal operator and a conservative businessman. Her mother, Ella (Aspinwall) Roche, shared his ideas to a large extent. But Josephine, only 12 years after she was born in the town of Neligh, Nebraska, began to question social conditions as she found them. Her father had forbidden her to visit his mines because it was dangerous. Wide-eyed, she asked: "Then why is it safe enough for the miners?"

This questioning attitude persisted, and by the time Josephine Roche left Vassar College with a B. A. in 1908 she was deeply interested in all the problems of crime, child welfare and social advancement. She immediately devoted herself to their solution as a probation officer of the Denver, Colorado Juvenile Court (her family had moved there in 1906), but after a year's work she left Denver to study sociology at Columbia University. That was the year Frances Perkins was there, and the two women became fast friends, united by similar views on social and economic problems.

ROCHE, JOSEPHINE—*Continued*

Josephine Roche did settlement work for the New York Probation Society while studying, and after she received her Master's Degree in 1910 she continued the same sort of activity, branching out now and again to make social and industrial investigations for Columbia and the Russell Sage Foundation. Then in 1912 she returned to Denver to become the city's first policewoman, reported more successful in controlling crime and misdemeanors than the city's toughest male cops. The vice interests didn't like her, and she was ousted. Unperturbed, she devoted herself to the job of executive secretary of the Colorado Progressive Society.

This was interrupted in 1915 by an assignment in Europe and this country as special agent of England and the United States for the Commission for Relief in Belgium, **after** which she became director of the Girls Department in Denver's Juvenile Court under Judge Ben Lindsay. Before her passed most of the city's delinquent and underprivileged children, and each left an impression on a mind already sensitive to social injustice. Soon after America entered the War she left this court to serve, as an appointee of President Wilson, on the Committee on Public Information and as director of the Foreign Language Education Service.

Her work, which consisted of bringing together editors of foreign language newspapers and through them carrying information about America's aims and activities to the foreign population, was continued until 1923, when she became director of the editorial division of the United States Children's Bureau in Washington. By that time Miss Roche had been married and divorced. Edward Hale Bierstadt, a writer of continuity material for advertising broadcasts, became her husband on July 2, 1920 and her ex-husband two years later. Her work with the Children's Bureau ended in 1925 and was followed by two years as referee of Denver's Juvenile Court.

Then, in 1927, Miss Roche's father died and she inherited his holdings in the Rocky Mountain Fuel Company, the second largest coal mining company in Colorado. Shortly afterward there was a strike at one of the mines, and Miss Roche, who many years before had testified after the bloody Ludlow coal strike, told the State Industrial Commission that the strike was based on unbearable wrongs that were matters of common knowledge. This was a blow to her fellow stockholders, but a mild one compared to her proposal at a meeting that the United Mine Workers of America be asked to unionize the Rocky Mountain employees. Some of the stockholders threatened to sell their shares; immediately she took them up and within a short time had acquired a majority interest.

Her first move was to change the company's personnel: Edward P. Costigan, later Senator from Colorado and before then attorney for the United Mine Workers, was made counsel; John Lawson, former president of the Colorado State Federation of Labor, was made vice-president and director; she herself became a vice-president. Her second move was to announce to the miners that the company was ready to sign a union contract as soon as the miners were organized. By September 1928 the Rocky Mountain Fuel Company was operating under a contract which set a basic day wage of $7, the highest in Colorado, provided for arbitration, improved working conditions.

The other coal companies didn't like this, and they were upset again when Miss Roche, president of the company since 1929, decided that the existence of a "favored customer" class worked havoc with the coal industry and discontinued the practice at her mines. They didn't take it lying down. A price-cutting war was started. Things looked bad for Rocky Mountain, but the employees lent the company half their wages until the war was over, and it came through intact. Although the basic wage was reduced to $5.25 a day, still it was paying 25 cents more than its competitors. And it still was profitable. In 1933 the average daily production per miner in her company was 10.6 tons, while for all the mines in the state it was only 7.68 tons.

As the result of these experiences Miss Roche had much to do with the formation of the National Bituminous Coal Code during NRA days, and as a member of the Bituminous Coal Authority she worked untiringly. "The New Deal is not new to us," she told other coal operators. "We have been practicing it for six years." Her youthful features, softly waving gray hair and pleasant voice were conspicuous at the hearings. Once, during a tough session on the coal industry code, the deputy administrator, impressed by seeing her in an assembly of hard-bitten operators and miners, asked her to come to the platform. "This hearing needs some beauty," he wrote her in a note. But her reply, characteristically, was: "What this hearing needs is not beauty but guts."

It was a little later than this that Josephine Roche first entered politics for herself. She had stumped the West in 1912 for Theodore Roosevelt, but that experience was hardly preparation for the campaign for Colorado's Governorship which she undertook in 1934. The demand for her candidacy was first voiced by the editor of a newspaper in the southwestern part of the state; other editors took it up; and Josephine Roche bowed to the demand. In her ancient Buick she toured the state, her slogan "Roosevelt, Roche and Recovery," her platform an endorsement of the New Deal, the revision of the Colorado constitution along more liberal lines, a change in the state income tax. Liberals all over the country supported her, and Oswald Garrison Villard was voicing their sentiments when he declared: "Every woman in Colorado and every man there who believes in justice, in fair play, in a decent way of life for all who toil, in a square and new deal and in a decent economic world will vote . . . for Josephine Roche." Many of them did, but she lost the bitterly contested race. She had carried the cities but lost the country districts: the ranchers and mountaineers refused to believe that any woman could have as much ability as any man.

Washington believed it, though, and in November 1934 Roosevelt appointed Miss Roche Assistant Secretary of the Treasury in charge of the United States Health Service. As such she made a successful effort to coordinate the Federal Government's varied health work and inaugurated activities like the WPA's study of chronic disease and the nationwide rural sanitation program. She also served as the Treasury's representative on the President's Committee on Economic Security which drafted the recommendations on which the Social Security Act was based; and she served as chairman of the executive committee of the National Youth Administration when it was set up in 1935. Two years later Miss Roche became chairman of the Interdepartmental Committee to Coordinate Health and Welfare Activities which Roosevelt set up after the Social Security Act was passed—it was on the basis of studies by this committee and discussions by the National Health Conference, of which Miss Roche was chairman, that Senator Wagner (see sketch this issue) formulated his bill for a national health program.

In that same year, however, Miss Roche resigned her position as Assistant Secretary of the Treasury, to the regret of much of Washington. Everybody had liked her, respected her tact and efficiency—Senators, hard-boiled business men, workers. Postmaster General Farley's tribute was a heartfelt one. "She's the goods," he said. And Surgeon General Parran praised her "knowledge of public health and social problems," the "splendid and unique service" she had given.

She returned to her company and its active management, for her general manager had died and she was needed. Business was bad, due to competition from natural gas fields and oil; production was falling. Miss Roche asked the bondholders to take an interest cut, but they refused. Two years later, in July 1939, unable to effect a compromise that would keep the Rocky Mountain Fuel Company out of reorganization, she stepped out as its head. Once more she began devoting her time and energy to social problems, active as head of the Interdepartmental Committee, a position she had never resigned; in the National Health Conference; in the White House Conference on Children in a Democracy; in the National Consumers' League, of which she became president in 1939.

People who don't work directly with Miss Roche have come to know her and her ideas through the many lectures she has given all over the country. Dressed in what one commentator calls "what the well-dressed business woman should wear," her movements quick, nervous and feminine, the vitality of her personality quickly appealing, she has addressed audiences on "Our Stake in Industrial Democracy"; "Health Security—For Some or All?"; "Women and Industry"; "Youth in Today's Frontier"; and many other topics relevant to her experience with and feeling for social progress.

References

Collier's 95:14+ Je 15 '35 por
Forum 92:103-5 Ag '34
Ind Woman 13:394 D '34 por (p370);
  14:185+ Je '35
Lit Digest 118:8 S 1 '34 por
Nation 138:665 Je 13 '34
Newsweek 4:8 N 24 '34 por; 10:13
  N 8 '37 por
Time 30:13-14 N 8 '37 por; 34:51 Jl
  10 '39 por
American Women
Who's Who in America
Who's Who in Commerce and Industry

ROCKEFELLER, JOHN D(AVISON), JR.

Jan. 29, 1874- Industrialist; philanthropist

Address: h. 740 Park Ave, New York City

On April 27, 1941, in a letter to Arthur Hays Sulzberger, publisher of the New York *Times*, John D. Rockefeller, Jr., announced that the United States would have to deliver lend-lease materials safely to Britain in order to combat Hitlerism, and that although he had hated war all his life, "when all peaceful methods have failed and the issue was worth standing for at any price, even if it meant a fight, I have never hesitated to see it through on that basis." On June 9 it was announced that he had contributed $100,000 to the United Service Organizations for the program of Army and Navy recreation, and a month later he opened a house-to-house drive in New York to raise $3,500,000 for the U. S. O.

A man of whom it has been said that his "chief mission in life is giving away money," Mr. Rockefeller will no doubt be as busy fulfilling his mission during the Second World War as he was in the First, although already many of the responsibilities of administering the Rockefeller philanthropies have passed onto the shoulders of his sons, John D., III, Nelson A. (see sketch this issue), Laurance S., Winthrop and David. This is particularly true since Mr. Rockefeller resigned in 1939 as chairman of the Board of the General Education Board, a position which he had held since 1936, and in 1940 retired also as trustee and chairman of the Board of the Rockefeller Foundation. (He had been its president from 1913 to 1917 and its chairman from 1917 until his retirement.)

Born in Cleveland, Ohio on January 29, 1874, he was the only son of the richest man in the world, the late John Davison Rockefeller of Standard Oil fame, and of the late Laura C. (Spelman) Rockefeller. His was the kind of household where there were hymns in the evening, not even schoolwork permitted on Sundays, and Rockefeller, Jr., was "the model boy one reads about in story books," serious, pious and practical. His father believed in teaching his children the value of money and in consequence his heir practiced the violin at five cents an hour, worked on their Cleveland estate for fifteen cents an hour, and listened to his three sisters

Frank Ehrenford
JOHN D. ROCKEFELLER, JR.

mourn over the fact that their cousins were so much better off than the John D. Rockefellers.

When in 1893 it was time to choose a university, Rockefeller, Jr., chose Brown. There he took no business courses, didn't specialize, and saved half of his $100-a-month allowance. According to John K. Winkler, classmates remember him as "a pallid, earnest youth who did not smoke, drink, chew nor gamble, wore shiny suits, was faithful in his studies (particularly the cultivation of Orthodox Baptist Theology), and who sought to reform wilder students." He joined Alpha Delta Phi and in his third year made Phi Beta Kappa. But, Winkler continues, "as he looks back upon it, the chief event of his four years at Brown was his meeting with Abby [Greene] Aldrich [daughter of the late Senator Nelson W. Aldrich, wealthy merchant and public utilities magnate]. The Senator's daughter was a year younger and very like him in point of view. Though she had seen much of society in New York and Washington, she was serious-minded and cared little for frivolity. She and Junior often went buggy riding Sunday afternoons. They wrote chaste letters to each other after his graduation." It was not until four years after his graduation in 1897 that they were married. (Mrs. Rockefeller's brother, Winthrop Aldrich, is today president of the Rockefeller-controlled Chase National Bank.)

Immediately after his graduation John D. Rockefeller, Jr., entered his father's office at 26 Broadway, where he was given a perfectly free hand. ("Never in my business life did my father give me directions.") He studied books of accounts, read books on common law, sat in on conferences, business meetings, interviews—finally began signing various agreements and important papers for his father. His first important connection was as director of the Delaware, Lackawanna and Western Railroad. In the fall of 1899 he performed his first independent financial *coup,* clearing a considerable sum of money on the common stock of the United States Leather Company.

It was also in 1899 that young Rockefeller took over the direction of the men's Bible class of the Fifth Avenue Baptist Church, formerly led by Charles Evans Hughes (see sketch this issue). He was fond of little homilies—preached, for example, that the camel-needle parable no longer applied to the rich man: "Conditions now are different." He explained: "The growth of a large business is merely the survival of the fittest. It does the greatest good to the greatest number, although perhaps at the expense of the few. . . [It is] merely the working out of a law of God and nature." Rockefeller, Sr., came, listened, and pronounced: "I would rather see my son doing this work than see him a monarch on his throne." At that time both Rockefellers were old-fashioned Baptists, but around 1910 the younger Rockefeller began reading the "new" theology and "emerged a most ardent religious progressive and advocate of the Inter-Church Movement."

Before the First World War the philanthropic undertakings of the Rockefellers were not nearly so extensive as they later became. But already Rockefeller, Jr., had been associated with his father in the creation and development of the Rockefeller Institute for Medical Research in 1901 and of the General Education Board in 1902, and was a trustee of both; in 1910 he was made foreman of the Special Grand Jury in New York County which investigated the white slave traffic, and he developed and financed a now-defunct organization, the Bureau of Social Hygiene, which grew out of that investigation; in 1913 he had a role in the formation of the Rockefeller Foundation, serving as a trustee from its inception; both he and his father contributed liberally to the Anti-Saloon League.

In 1915 after the public had been stirred up by the shooting down of miners at the Rockefeller-controlled Colorado Fuel & Iron Company, and the Industrial Relations Commission headed by Senator Walsh began investigating the case, young Rockefeller emerged as the real head of his family, and a very capable one. Standard Oil borrowed the late Ivy Lee, "the most adroit accelerator of public opinion since P. T. Barnum," from the Pennsylvania Railroad. Rockefeller, Jr., made a most favorable impression on the stand. He pleaded ignorance of conditions, announced: "I am going to Colorado as soon as I can to learn for myself." Three days after the hearings, his father handed over to him a large enough block of shares in the company to give him control. Still under Ivy Lee's guidance, he did travel to Colorado, and the result was a plan for arbitration committees called "Republics of Labor" by which the men and the management would henceforward meet to settle disputes over the table, a plan which was later extended to many other Rockefeller properties. Rockefeller, Jr., has said: "In large part the difficulties that exist in our social state are due to nothing but misunderstanding."

Altogether, the entrance of Ivy Lee into the picture marked a turning point in Rockefeller history. In Winkler's words, Rockefeller, Jr., "became the Little Boy Blue of capitalism, the first Modern Money Magnate with Vision and Soul. Without dissipating by one jot the family's fortune or power, he induced the American people to stop attacking his father, and turned the attention of the critics to the great Rockefeller benefactions and to his efforts to bring about industrial rapprochement." His father also began to unload his fortune on him in great blocks; by 1921 he was to own most of the Rockefeller fortune and most of the real estate. Rockefeller philanthropies soon began to outweigh the origins of the Rockefeller fortune in the eyes of the public.

During the First World War, Rockefeller, Jr., served as chairman of the United War Work Campaign in New York City, which raised some $35,000,000, and the Rockefeller Foundation allotted $22,500,000 to war work between 1914 and 1918. In 1918, too, the Laura Spelman Rockefeller Memorial was founded. Between January 1917 and December 1940 an approximate $188,372,706 was actually spent by Rockefeller, Jr., for philanthropic purposes, and all of it carefully, with the utmost forethought. "A scientific Santa Claus," it is his contention that it is more difficult to give money away intelligently than to make it. In 1921 he founded the Institute of Social and Religious Research, contributed to it $3,000,000 until its demise in 1934. Although only about three per cent of his contributions have been devoted to charities, relief or labor, in 1922 he established an organization called Industrial Relations Counselors which at first made surveys of employer-employee relationships in numerous companies in which he had holdings, later for other concerns, and which eventually published many books on such subjects as unemployment insurance, profit sharing, etc.

In matters of religion he has worked consistently for interdenominationalism, among his many contributions to that cause being the building of the large Gothic Riverside Church for Dr. Harry Emerson Fosdick (see sketch 1940 Annual). Large sums of money have also been given to public parks, to the furtherance of better international relations (the International Education Board was founded in 1923), to scientific excavation and exploration, to experiments in private housing, to the restoration of historic monuments devastated in the First World War.

What is more, Mr. Rockefeller's business principles have impressed a suspicious world almost as much as his generosity. In 1928, when Senator Walsh and a Senate committee were investigating the Teapot Dome affair, he urged Colonel Stewart, chairman of the Indiana Company of Standard Oil in which he was a minority stockholder, to assist the committee in every way: "I want no profit derived from compromise with right." When Stewart's testimony was afterward almost completely reversed, Rockefeller moved to oust him, voting against him the proxies of the Rockefeller Foundation, the General Education Board and other Rockefeller endowments as well as those of the Harkness, Pratt and Whitney families, with which the Rockefellers are connected by marriage.

Only such writers as Ferdinand Lundberg, John T. Flynn and the anonymous author of *Mirrors of Wall Street* have remained suspicious of this present-day example of enlightened capitalism. They insist that control has actually been retained over funds "given away," while philanthropies make tax reductions possible; one says that extremely generous contributions to Republican war chests have been counted as philanthropies; the author of *Mirrors of Wall Street* alleges that Rockefeller's ousting of Colonel Stewart was due to the fact that he was competing with Standard Oil companies in which Rockefeller himself had much larger holdings, and that in any case Rockefeller was not too high-minded to vote his proxies in other companies in favor of Harry Sinclair, after that gentleman was released from prison.

As for Rockefeller's present relation to Standard Oil, it has been claimed that although the original Standard Oil combination was long ago dissolved by Supreme Court decree, after many mergers the Standard Oil Companies of New Jersey, of Indiana and of California (as well as Socony-Vacuum) have each become larger than the whole trust at the time of the dissolution order; and that although Rockefeller's individual shares in none of them now amount to 10 per cent of the companies' outstanding stock aggregates, there is little reason to believe that most of his former holdings have gone completely out of Rockefeller control. In the spring of 1941 Mr. Rockefeller felt called upon to deny responsibility for Standard Oil sales to Japan.

Not even the sternest of his critics, however, has ever denied that Mr. Rockefeller is one of the world's foremost exponents of what he calls "clean living," which he practices even more enthusiastically than he preaches. The wartime Ambassador from Austria-Hungary to the United States described him more than 20 years ago as: "Short, slight, and very pale, he did not find any pleasure or satisfaction in all his millions. When I asked him whether he ever went to dinners or balls he replied that he had to get up early and that even then he was only able to supervise a small number of the many undertakings dependent upon him. He seldom had time for parties or even entertainments, since he had to go to sleep early. He did, however, often dance at dinnertime to give himself a little exercise."

His are still the old-fashioned virtues. He strongly disapproves of individual charity, being an exponent of "self-help." He told S. J. Woolf years ago that the book which had influenced him more than any other he had ever read was Bruce Barton's *The Man Nobody Knows*. He has never smoked or taken a drink, although in 1932 he decided that prohibition had been a failure. Having learned the value of money early, Mr. Rockefeller sees to it that there are no out-of-season

ROCKEFELLER, JOHN D., JR.—Cont.

luxuries on the Rockefeller table, and roves around the house to make sure that lights are turned out when not in use. He wore ready-made clothes for years, and gave his first tip in 1908, after which he began to apply the 10 per cent rule "rigidly." His sons and his one daughter, now Mrs. David M. Milton, were simply brought up, too. Until 1924 or 1925 the younger boys were sent to school in an old-fashioned horse-drawn carriage; they never visited the theatre or even the movies until their mid-teens; and, according to one story, they were kept so unaware of their fabulous wealth that years ago, when a Maine playmate of David's asked why his father didn't buy him a bigger boat, he snapped back: "Who do you think we are, Vanderbilts?"

Among Mr. Rockefeller's recreations are riding and skating; in town he enjoys both squash and the electric horse. His father taught him to swim and to skate, but never taught him to play a passable game of golf. He still plays the violin occasionally, and he loves old architecture, tapestry and painting, although his wife, one of the chief supporters of the Museum of Modern Art, has never succeeded in converting him to Cézanne or Picasso. He also has a "passion for building—roads, houses, anything." Particularly dear to his heart was the restoration of colonial Williamsburg in Virginia—a dramatic contrast to the super-modernity of New York City's Rockefeller Center, in which "you can do almost anything . . . except sleep, worship, send your children to school and avoid paying rent to Mr. Rockefeller."

References

Am Mag 106:22-5 D '28 il por
Christian Cent 52:1511-13 N 27 '35
Fortune 12:69-73 Jl '35 il map; 14:38-46+ Jl '36 il pors tab
Lit Digest 120:7 N 23 '35 por
New Yorker 4:27-31 Je 2 '28; 4:20-4 Je 9 '28
Outlook 151:183 Ja 30 '29; 143:283 Je 23 '36 por
Sat Eve Post 211:8-9+ Jl 16 '38 pors (Same abr. Read Digest 33:88-92 S '38)
Time 26:34+ N 25 '35; 28:21-2 Jl 13 '36 por
Flynn, J. T. God's Gold 1932
Gillis, A. and Ketchum, R. Our America p313-28 1936
Lundberg, F. America's Sixty Families 1937
Mirrors of Wall Street p61-87 1933
Who's Who in America
Who's Who in Commerce and Industry
Winkler, J. K. John D. 1929
Woolf, S. J. Drawn From Life p263-71 1932

ROCKEFELLER, NELSON (ALDRICH) July 8, 1908- Coordinator of Inter-American Affairs

Address: Council of National Defense, Commerce Department Bldg, Washington, D. C.

"Welding the Americas" is the Presidential assignment for tall, genial Nelson Aldrich Rockefeller, second son of John D. Rockefeller, Jr. As "Coordinator of Commercial and Cultural Relations between the American Republics," young Rockefeller has been attempting to create better understanding between the two continents since his appointment in August 1940.

In order to devote all his time to his new position, he immediately resigned as director of several South American enterprises and obtained leave of absence as president of Rockefeller Center, Incorporated. In January 1941, it became evident that he would have to remain in Washington much of the time, and Rockefeller also gave up the presidency of the Museum of Modern Art, a position he had held since May 1939.

His background, experience and interests all qualify the young man for his position. Nelson Rockefeller was born in Bar Harbor, Maine, in 1908, one of the six children of Abby Greene (Aldrich) and John Davison Rockefeller, Jr., (see sketch this issue). From his maternal grandfather, Senator Nelson W. Aldrich of Rhode Island, he took his name. From his mother he inherited a genuine interest in all forms of artistic expression, and he is today particularly concerned about getting other people also to appreciate art.

At Dartmouth, which he entered in 1927, Nelson Rockefeller played on the soccer team for two years and edited a magazine called *The Five Lively Arts*. As a student he also distinguished himself sufficiently to get a Phi Beta Kappa key and a special fellowship enabling him to spend his senior year abroad studying music, painting, sculpture, and architecture. Much of his "wanderjahr" he spent in India, "where he had a long chat with Mahatma Gandhi and studied photography."

Upon graduation in 1930 with a B. A. degree, Rockefeller married Mary Todhunter Clark, daughter of a Philadelphia attorney, at the Clark home in Cynwyd, Pennsylvania, and set off on a world cruise that same year. (They have five children, including twins.) Until they left for Washington, the Nelson Rockefellers lived in Pocantico Hills near Tarrytown, New York.

For a year Nelson worked at the Chase National Bank, where his uncle, Winthrop Aldrich, is the president. Following this lesson in finance he became a director of Rockefeller Center in 1931 and in 1937 was elected president. When John D. Rockefeller, Jr., originally leased the land from Columbia University, it had been with the idea of using it for a new Metropolitan Opera House. This plan was suddenly and inexplicably abandoned, however, and the Standard Oil magnate found himself with a twenty-four-year lease and three renewal options to twelve acres of expensive Manhattan real estate. In the face of ridicule and condemnation, he spent $130,000,000 and built the Center.

It was during his early days at Rockefeller Center that Nelson Rockefeller had his first taste of international diplomacy. As president of the project, it became his unpleasant duty to inform the fiery Mexican muralist, Diego Rivera, that his portrait of Lenin did not fit into the scheme of things at the Center and would have to be removed from the murals Rivera was painting for the buildings. That Rockefeller was able to do this neatly and tactfully is much to his credit, for he was obliged to ignore a great deal of "thunder from the Left."

In addition to his New York interests Rockefeller has been director of several South American enterprises, among them the Creole Petroleum Corporation, a subsidiary of the Standard Oil Company of New Jersey, which has large holdings in Venezuela. Before taking a trip to South America in 1937 the young man mastered the Spanish language, a subject which he failed in college. It is his opinion that language is at the threshold of the barriers to good will between the Americas.

With his many business activities Nelson Rockefeller has since his college days combined a careful and diligent trusteeship at the Museum of Modern Art, of which his mother was a founder. As its treasurer in the early days of its organization, the "earnest, active young man" busied himself with the task of getting together the two million-odd dollars needed to pay for the construction and furnishing of a permanent building. In May 1939 he graduated to the Museum's presidency, the task he recently relinquished to John Hay Whitney, chairman of the Museum's Film Library.

Nelson Rockefeller's new position is much to his liking. The salary is not the attractive feature, since he joins the company of "dollar-a-year" men who receive only subsistence and other expense money for their labors. What appeals to Mr. Rockefeller is the chance to strengthen ties between this country and the Latin-American republics. It is a problem on which he has done some pioneering of his own.

To assist in the work ahead the "spark plug" of the committee appointed a board of experts, each with specific duties and responsibilities. With a relatively small initial government appropriation of 10 million dollars ($8,000,000 was appropriated for fiscal 1942) these men began an attempt to correlate governmental and private activities, working with the Office of Production Management. The job has been called "one of the biggest good will campaigns that ever captured the imagination of an advertising writer."

The immediate goal is to counteract the propaganda activities of the dictatorships in neighboring states below the Rio Grande. The program is both commercial and cultural, but "the dominating idea is to establish hemisphere solidarity in fact as well as theory." Necessity for speedy action became acutely apparent recently, when the committee's first survey of the Latin-American scene disclosed the fact that employees in some American firms there were actually "officials of anti-American powers" and were using United

NELSON ROCKEFELLER

States money to spread subversive propaganda in newspapers and over the radio. Some of the difficulties in the committee's task also became apparent when hundreds of these men, fired by their alarmed employers, promptly got jobs with competitors. By August 1941 Rockefeller was able to announce many steps had been taken to counteract Axis influence, however.

One of the most important aspects of the commercial program is the work of the Inter-American Development Commission, of which Rockefeller was appointed chairman October 17, 1940. This group was formed by representatives of 21 republics after their conference at Panama in June 1940. They hope to unify various programs and to fill the gap caused by loss of European markets. To put this plan into action, the Coordinator calls for immediate stimulation of imports from Latin America and recommends emergency loans by the United States to create employment and utilize United States machinery and supplies. The long-range commercial program of Rockefeller's committee will work on the development of new industries in Latin America, financed jointly by North and South American capital to absorb the region's surplus materials. With increasing internal prosperity, they will be able to provide an expanding market for American industrial products such as automobiles and machinery. Rockefeller has again and again asked for more ships and supplies for Latin-America.

Coupled with this economic program is a long-range cultural program including promotion of inter-American travel, exchange scholarships, art loans, concerts and hemispheric sports contests. Permanent settlement of United States citizens in Latin America will be encouraged. "Most visible progress" to date has been in the radio field, where

ROCKEFELLER, NELSON—*Continued*

eight American stations sending short waves to Latin America are being coordinated and CBS is completing the installation of more powerful equipment. Less successful was the placing of some $600,000 worth of advertising in Latin-American newspapers to stimulate tourist trade in the United States, for fat contracts were carelessly given to Axis-sympathizing newspapers while others friendly to the United States were ignored.

Rockefeller's committee has encountered many difficulties, and especially at the beginning of its existence was regarded with "chilly reserve" by the State Department for its occasional amateurishness and with astonishment for Mr. Rockefeller's "ability to pop in and out of a dozen committee meetings a day, to write innumerable memorandums, to argue lengthily with Congressmen, to send all over Latin America young men who astonished the natives with their apparent naïvete." And the problems that face it are very real. Long-term research and experimentation must be done and done efficiently. Secondly it must meet powerful and deep-rooted Nazi opposition. To do this, it is obliged to work without authority to overrule any government or private agency. If the staff does its work properly and is adequately backed, however, "Latin Americans and Anglo-Saxon Americans will understand each other well enough so that half the battle for Western Hemisphere defense is won, long before an enemy sets sail across either of the shielding oceans."

References

Cur Hist & Forum 52:130-1 D 10 '40
  52:17+ Ap '41
N Y Herald Tribune p1 Ag 17 '40 por
N Y Times p6 Ag 17 '40 por
Newsweek 17:45-6 Ja 20 '41
PM p8 N 10 '40 por
Scholastic 37:12 D 9 '40 por
Time 37:18 Ja 20 '41; 37:30+ Je 9 '41
  por
U S News 9:33 Ag 30 '40 por; 10:34-5
  Ja 17 '41 por
Who's Who in America

ROCKLEY, ALICIA-MARGARET AMHERST, BARONESS Died Sept. 13, 1941

Writer on gardening; wrote many books on this subject; during the First World War was honorary assistant director of horticulture of the food production department of the British Board of Trade; active in serving on London and Empire welfare committees.

References

Author's and Writer's Who's Who
Who's Who

Obituaries

N Y Times p17 S 15 '41

ROGERS, GINGER July 16, 1911- Film actress

Address: b. c/o RKO Studios, Hollywood, Calif; h. Beverly Hills, Calif.

After completing *Kitty Foyle* Ginger Rogers' studio gave her a few days off for a trip to New York. Radiantly white-collared, with diamond brooch, gold earrings and mink coat, Miss Rogers was greeted by a group of New York stenographers and presented with a scroll for her characterization of the white-collar girl. "Ginger," *Time* wrote glowingly, "with her shoulder-length tresses, her trim figure, her full lips, her prancing feet and honest-to-goodness manner, is the flesh-and-blood symbol of the United States working girl."

But the great triumph was still to come. In Hollywood the vivacious, red-haired star was given the coveted annual award of the Academy of Motion Picture Arts and Sciences for her performance in *Kitty Foyle.* Lynn Fontanne opened the envelope that contained the name of the winner, and her husband Alfred Lunt made the presentation of the "Oscar." "This," Ginger murmured between tears of excitement, "is the happiest moment of my life."

On July 16, 1911, in Independence, Missouri, a daughter was born to Eddins and Lela Emogene (Owens) McMath, christened Virginia Katherine. An enlarged photograph of mother and daughter, titled *Modern Madonna,* hangs in the State Building at Jefferson City, Missouri. Her parents separated when Ginger was still a baby, and she was twice "kidnapped" by her father, an electrical engineer. After a short period of white-collar typing for a Kansas City mail-order house at $9 weekly, Mrs. McMath worked in many parts of the country, taking her daughter with her. In Fort Worth, Texas, where Mrs. McMath managed the symphony orchestra and was a critic on the *Record,* they settled down. There in 1920, after the death of her first husband, Lela McMath became the wife of John Logan Rogers, and Ginger was formally adopted by her foster father.

By her own admission, competitiveness has always played a part in the career of Ginger Rogers. One of her first ambitions, to be a schoolteacher, may be understood in this light. She also wanted to be a pianist, but at the age of 11 she played MacDowell's *To A Wild Rose* in a local auditorium and her ambition was satisfied. She began acting as a child, playing leads in high school and PTA-sponsored plays. She was also fond of athletics and voted the leading all-round athlete of her class. The nickname "Ginger" dates from childhood and is variously attributed to a baby cousin's attempt to say Virginia, a schoolboy's kidding and a teacher's fraternal spirit.

Her professional career began when the Foys, well known vaudeville dance team, needed a substitute for one performance. Eddie Foy taught Ginger enough steps to fill in and also helped her to learn the Charleston, which was then the rage. With this as a wedge she got her mother's reluctant consent to enter a local Charleston contest in 1925, when she was 14. They stayed up late at night sewing hundreds of rhinestones on

Ginger's dress of white crepe romaine. She danced her way to first place, winning the chance to compete in the state-wide run-off held in Dallas three weeks later. The prize was a four weeks' vaudeville contract, won by Ginger against 120 contestants.

In vaudeville the tour of "Ginger Rogers and Her Red-Heads" was extended to 21 weeks. Mrs. Rogers traveled with her; Ginger got $100 a week but had to play as many as five shows a day. The company broke up in Chicago, and then Ginger was hustled back to Fort Worth and school. But not for long. The following summer she was doing a song-and-dance turn in a Galveston cafe, leaving it for another road tour that began with a show booked for 32 weeks in St. Louis, where Ginger was billed as "The Original John Held Jr. Girl." Playing in vaudeville for the next three years, she came into New York in 1929 to play a theatre date with Paul Ash's Orchestra. That year she was signed for her first musical comedy appearance, in *Top Speed.*

Breaking into musical comedy was a forward step for Ginger. It led to her inauspicious film debut, for one thing. Her first film was *Young Man of Manhattan* (Paramount 1929). This was made on Long Island, as were her next two Paramount films, *Queen High* and *Manhattan Mary,* both starring Ed Wynn. Her progress was rapid, if not yet spectacular from the Hollywood viewpoint. In 1930, at the age of 19, Ginger was being paid $1,000 a week to play the lead in the Gershwin musical comedy *Girl Crazy.*

Her first three Hollywood films were for Pathé, but musicals for other studios got more attention. In *Sitting Pretty* (Paramount 1933) she did a fan dance and in *Gold Diggers of 1933* (Warner) she wore a costume of glittering coins. Both were box-office hits, as was *Forty-Second Street* (Warner 1933). Her unusual singing voice of slightly husky timbre, her dancing ability and the naturalness of her acting all made her a favorite with film goers from the start. In 1933 she also did pictures for Fox, Universal, Monogram and RKO (*Flying Down to Rio*). Even after this latter film, the film that paired Fred Astaire and Ginger Rogers for the first time, her talents were farmed out—to Fox, Warner's and First National in 1934, in which year she also did three pictures for RKO.

Her first marriage, to vaudevillian Edward Culpepper in New Orleans in 1928, was not a success and terminated in divorce in 1931. In 1933, when she began to go out with Lew Ayres, the fan magazines played it up as a high-school girl's dream of a fine romance. On November 14, 1934, for her wedding to Lew Ayres, Ginger wore a gown of green chantilly lace with a short jacket, softly ruffled collar and tiny jeweled buttons. The Ayres separated in 1936, were finally divorced March 14, 1941. Most of Ginger's fans echoed *Time's* comment: "In spite of her two marriages (moderate for Hollywood), she represents the American girl—alert, friendly, energetic, elusive."

GINGER ROGERS

In 1933 Ginger was already making it known around RKO that she wanted dramatic roles as well as musical comedy parts. That the studio was mildly aware of this was shown by a press release asking fans to suggest a new name for "Ginger," since that hoydenish nickname might be undignified for "serious" billing. Partly to blame for this quasi-comedy were critics Alison Smith and Richard Watts, Jr., both of whom had deplored the nickname. The response must have been lukewarm, for Ginger was allowed to remain just that, with her gold-red hair and contrasting eyes of periwinkle blue (sometimes described as green).

A famous dancing team, Fred and Adele Astaire broke up when the latter became Lady Cavendish. His new partner would inevitably be compared to his lovely and talented sister. Ginger Rogers was chosen by the studio. That she proved a worthy successor is now a matter of record. *Flying Down to Rio* was the first of 10 Astaire-Rogers vehicles that grossed $18,000,000 for RKO. Ginger's determination to be known in her own right as well as having a reputation based upon these pictures was nothing more than self-protection. From their first film she and Fred Astaire have been close friends. That the friendship was press agentry, then or later, has been completely disproved in many statements by both.

For dance routines Ginger's weight, normally around one hundred fifteen pounds, went down to one hundred two pounds (she is five feet five inches tall). Routines were first worked out by Astaire and Hermes Pan, RKO dance director, who taught them to Ginger. Then Astaire and Ginger rehearsed together, adding whatever new ideas they got along the way. Of the pictures they made together, *Gay Divorcee, Top Hat* and *Roberta* were among the most successful,

ROGERS, GINGER—*Continued*

In April 1936 Ginger "had to try" something else. She stormed into the front office with demands for better working conditions—four pictures a year, of which one would be an Astaire-Rogers coupling—and a pay increase, which she received. Important dramatic roles came with *Stage Door* (1937); *Having Wonderful Time* (1938); and *Kitty Foyle* (1940). In all of these Ginger Rogers showed that she could act naturally and convincingly.

In 1940 Director Gregory LaCava said rather belatedly: "I have presented a new Ginger Rogers, a glamor-girl dancer turned actress." Not all critics agreed that *The Primrose Path* was the vehicle that turned the trick. Even *Kitty Foyle* has been criticized, though most reviewers agreed with *Time* that Ginger Rogers' part in it was "the prime performance of her new departure into drama." A dissenting voice as to the fitness of the story was John Mosher of the *New Yorker*. He found it a Hollywood view of white-collar girls and thought that Miss Rogers alone made it better than average.

Although critics differed, too, as to the appeal and humor of her next picture, a fantasy, *Tom, Dick and Harry* (1941), there were none who didn't find Ginger Rogers charming in it. She "plays the girl," said Bosley Crowther of the New York *Times,* "as no other actress we know could, with a perfect combination of skepticism and daffiness."

Ginger likes outdoor life, swims, plays tennis and tries her hand at skeet-shooting. Indoor hobbies include stamp-collecting, woodblock carving and dictionaries (words fascinate her). She likes to sketch, occasionally takes up sewing or reading but tires easily of both. She is an Honorary Admiral in the Texas Navy, and proud of it. Her house is on a high hill overlooking the cinema city. Behind mammoth retaining walls is a lavish estate which *Life* called a "high-school girl's dream house." Most amusing installation is a completely equipped soda fountain where she mixes chocolate sodas for guests.

Ginger has one hobby that comes in handy when she goes on shopping tours—a favorite form of relaxation. She browses around shops in disguise, and as a young girl was pleased to have been able to fool such shrewd gentlemen of Hollywood industry as Oscar Levant and director Mark Sandrich. She tried it once at a Hollywood preview, but the younger generation of autograph hunters caught on.

Expressing herself with unaffected naturalness and to the point, Ginger once summed up the benefits accruing from stardom. "You meet celebrities," she said, ". . . all the people you formerly only read about in newspapers. That is a thrill to me." And money brought security, as well as responsibility. A star, she pointed out, "has the finest advice and assistance in the care of her physical health." She even gets better service, as people pay

tribute to her position. "I enjoy it," Ginger admitted frankly. And, without egotism: "It's flattering."

As to the excitement of being famous: "We mustn't discount that, though it may wear off in time." And with her last word on the subject every psychologist would be prone to agree: "We might add to the advantages the self-confidence any success gives to the one who wins it."

References

Ind Woman 20:91 Ap 41 por (cover)
Life 10:28 Mr 10 '41 por
Look 4:34-5 Ap 9 '40 pors
N Y Post p9 Mr 29 '40; p5 Mr 1 '41
N Y Sun F 16 '36; p1 Mr 13 '40; p21 Ja 24 '41 por
N Y Times IX p4 F 16 '36; p17 F 28 '41
N Y World-Telegram p5 Mr 9 '40 por
Photoplay 54:18-19+ Je '40 por
Time 33:49-52 Ap 10 '39 il pors; 37:73 Ja 13 '41 por
American Women
International Motion Picture Almanac
Who's Who in America
Who's Who in the Theatre

ROGERS, MARK HOMER May 21, 1877—Oct. 5, 1941

Orthopedic surgeon at Massachusetts General Hospital from 1906 to 1924; assistant professor of orthopedic surgery at Tufts Medical School from 1915 to 1924, when he received a full professorship; held many positions in schools, hospitals and organizations.

References

American Medical Directory

Obituaries

N Y Times p17 O 6 '41

ROGERS, ROBERT EMMONS Apr. 12, 1888—May 13, 1941

Professor of English at the Massachusetts Institute of Technology; earned nationwide publicity in 1929 when he urged members of the graduating class "to be snobs and to marry the boss' daughter"; in 1934 he reversed himself and said that a young man should marry the stenographer in his office if she had a position; wrote many books; was columnist for the Boston *Evening American* and did radio broadcasting.

References

Fortune 14:111 N '36 por
Who's Who Among North American Authors
Who's Who in America

Obituaries

N Y Times p21 My 14 '41
Pub W 139:2077 My 24 '41
Time 37:71 My 26 '41

ROOSEVELT, SARA DELANO (rōz'-vĕlt) Sept. 21, 1855—Sept. 7, 1941

Mother of President Franklin D. Roosevelt; died at her home in Hyde Park, New York, following an acute circulatory collapse due to her advanced age; was matriarch of a family which, besides her only child, the President, included five grandchildren and ten great-grandchildren.

References

Good H 99:24-5+ S '34 il pors; 104: 29+ My '37 por
Ladies' H J 51:12-13+ Ap '34 il por
Life 8:30-1 Ap 29 '40 pors
Lit Digest 117:43-4 F 24 '34 por
Newsweek 4:16 Ag 18 '34; 4:10 S 29 '34 por; 6:39 S 28 '35 por; 7:37 My 30 '36 por; 10:12+ Jl 10 '37 pors
Time 27:73 My 11 '36
Halle, R. Gracious Lady 1935

Obituaries

N Y Times p1, 11 S 8 '41 por
Time 38:12-13 S 15 '41 pors

ROSE, MARY D. SWARTZ Oct. 31, 1874—Feb. 1, 1941 Professor of nutrition at Teachers College, Columbia University since 1921; during the First World War was a director of the Bureau of Conservation of the Federal Board and of the New York State Food Commission; member Nutrition Commission of the League and of the Council on Foods of the American Medical Association and president in 1937 and 1938 of the American Institute of Nutrition; author of many books on nutrition, including *Laboratory Handbook for Dietetics* (1912, fourth edition 1937), *Feeding the Family* (1916, fourth edition 1940), *Teaching Nutrition to Boys and Girls* (1932).

References

J Home Econ 32:35-6 Ja '40
American Men of Science
Who's Who Among North American Authors
Who's Who in America

Obituaries

N Y Times p46 F 2 '41

ROSENBERG, ALFRED (rō'-zĕn-bârg) Jan. 12, 1893- German political leader; Reichsminister for the East

Address: W. 35, Margaretenstr. 17, Berlin, Germany

Paradoxically, the man who has had the greatest influence on the direction of Adolf Hitler's foreign policy is one of the most unpopular men in Germany today. Dr. Alfred Rosenberg is said to have only one friend in the Third Reich, Adolf Hitler. But the Führer is friend enough for any one man. Concurrent with the attempted German "blitz" of Soviet Russia, the good Doctor was reported waiting impatiently to enter as *gauleiter* a new Eastern annex of the Nazi empire, the land of his birth whose destruction he had plotted for so long.

Called the Führer's "Father Confessor" and the "Grand Inquisitor" of the Third Reich, Rosenberg's main contribution to the Nazi

ALFRED ROSENBERG

Party has, of course, been his philosophy. The race-individuality of the Nordics, according to Rosenberg, accounts for all great cultures of the past, including the Greek and Roman; all decay and corruption are caused by the infusion through intermarriage of inferior blood strains. Man's full potentialities can be achieved, declares Rosenberg, only by recapturing the full Nordic racial purity of the ancient German tribes whose traditions and religion must once again inspire the German people. As director of the Nordic Faith movement Rosenberg has been the leading force behind the attack on Christianity by Hanns Kerrl, Hitler's administrator of church affairs; and his contribution to anti-Semitism on a world scale has been by no means inconsiderable. He was among the first to spread the notorious "Protocols of the Elders of Zion," long proved to be of Czarist origin, a document which he said was placed on his desk by a spiritual messenger.

Rosenberg has written on hundreds of subjects. His pamphlets and books include attacks on the Catholic Church, the Protestant Church, Free Masonry, Bolshevism, the Jews, Social Democracy and the Versailles Treaty. His *Der Mythos des Zwanzigsten Jahrhunderts* (1930)—"The Myth of the Twentieth Century"—is a fantastic 700-page compendium of the ideas of Houston Stewart Chamberlain, Gobineau, Spengler, Nietzsche, Bernhardi, Treitschke and LaGarde. It probably does much to justify the judgment of Dorothy Thompson that its author is a man of great intellect who is also a complete fool. Other books are: *Blood and Honor*; *The Character of National Socialism*; *Immortality in the Talmud*.

In spite of Rosenberg's fanatical Aryanism, some people think he does not look markedly Nordic. He is tall, thin and blond, with sharp features; yet the cast of his face is

ROSENBERG, ALFRED—*Continued*

heavy and Slavonic, betraying racial characteristics that might bar him from his own Aryan Valhalla. Neither rumors of possible Semitic antecedents nor a harsh Baltic accent which makes him an unimpressive speaker on the platform have proved insuperable drawbacks to his career, however.

Because he is both a German and a White Russian, Rosenberg has been Hitler's expert on Baltic and Russian affairs since 1919. On January 12, 1893, the same day his archenemy, Hermann Goering (see sketch this issue), was born in Bavaria, Rosenberg was born in Tallinn, Estonia, then Reval, Russia. Although he has admitted that his mother, Minna (Marcus) Rosenberg, was a Latvian and his father, Johann Rosenberg, an Estonian, his forebears came from the West. His father was an official in a German trading firm. German traditions and German patriotism typical of the *Auslandsdeutscher*, or "outland Germans," dominated the household. Among their Slavic neighbors many of the Baltic Germans regarded themselves as superior mortals, and it is evident that Rosenberg acquired this attitude early. Such convictions were also bolstered by his reading, for he was only 15 years old when he acquired a copy of Chamberlain's racial interpretation of history, *Foundations of the Nineteenth Century*, a book which later formed the basis for his own *Der Mythos des Zwanzigsten Jahrhunderts*.

Having attended Reval schools, from 1911 to 1915 Rosenberg was in Riga and Moscow continuing his studies. In spite of war and revolution he was able to carry on his course with scant interruption, for he was not conscripted for military service, and in 1917 he received from Moscow University his certificate as an engineer and architect. For a while he served as drawing master at Riga University, then, in 1918, made a trip to Paris. Never very communicative about his personal life, Rosenberg hints that he was on a counterrevolutionary mission; some of his enemies insist the trip was made on behalf of the Reds, others that he worked for the French Intelligence and left France only "after he saw no chance for a career." Hermann Goering publicly wondered at a party congress in 1925 "what kind of job that fellow had in Paris in 1918"; Chancellor Brüning accused him of having been "a patriotic Russian as late as 1918."

When Rosenberg returned to Reval later that year, his native city was occupied by German troops. Rosenberg says that he immediately offered his services to General Von Golz, the military authority in charge. The latter refused the offer because of Rosenberg's Russian citizenship. Undeterred, Rosenberg secured a job as a high school teacher and in his spare time blossomed as an anti-Bolshevik and anti-Semitic propagandist. Later, when the Red Army marched into the city, Rosenberg took to his heels. In December 1918 Rosenberg and his young wife, harassed and poverty-stricken, appeared in Munich. His

wife, who was gravely ill, died soon after of tuberculosis.

It was a gloomy period for Rosenberg, but at least he was among kindred souls. White Russian émigrés from all parts of Russia gravitated toward the German city, bearing with them a flaming hatred for Bolshevism. Anti-Semitism, a dividing tactic of the Czar, flourished everywhere. A letter from a Baltic noblewoman of his acquaintance gained Rosenberg an interview with Dietrich Eckart, the Nazi poet and journalist. According to Eckart, Rosenberg, despite his poverty, was "dandified" and "perfumed" and marked with the air of the supercilious intelligentsia. On entering Eckart's office, Rosenberg's first words were, "Can you use a fighter against the Jews?"; and Eckart replied coldly, "Certainly, if he can prove his capabilities."

Shortly after, Eckart is reported to have said, "I'd give ten Rosenbergs for one German with a fat wallet." Nevertheless, Eckart was unwillingly impressed by Rosenberg's voluminous writings, his intellectual scope and fanaticism, and in time lost his distaste for the Baltic émigré. Rosenberg was put to work writing pamphlets for the small German Workers Party, the forerunner of the Nazi movement. With Eckart he founded the Thule Society, devoted to the propagation of Aryan racial theories and the formation of a Nordic religion. Frequent tiffs with the Munich Soviet Government which then ruled the city, denunciation of the Versailles Treaty, the Jews and the Communist Party formed the Party's major activity. Rosenberg is also remembered for his 20-minute speech in the Marktplatz on April 8, 1919, when he ran just in time to avoid capture by the Red police.

Rosenberg first met Hitler in a small inn called The German Reich. The frenzied excorporal and the intense-eyed Balt were brought together by Eckart at a meeting that has been dubbed "the meeting between Faust and Mephistopheles." It is certain that this rendezvous was a fateful meeting of minds. Hitler himself was predisposed toward mysticism, and when this "nightmare dreamer" poured forth visions of a triumphant Germany where blond Nordics would practice the rites of their tribal forebears, Hitler listened wideeyed through the long hours of the night.

In the stormy days which followed, Rosenberg became a solid and unwavering supporter of Hitler. In 1921, when Julius Streicher and his inseparable companion, Hermann Esser, founders of the orgiastic Anti-Semitic Movement, attempted to seize control of the Party and shift its headquarters to Berlin, Rosenberg and Eckart sent word to Hitler to return at once. It was then that Hitler consolidated his power by starting a new party called the National Socialist German Workers Party and proclaiming himself Führer. To Rosenberg he entrusted the writing of a platform, and the Baltic writer complied with a document which contained for the first time the famous definition: "He is a German citizen who is a fellow-countryman. He is a fellow-countryman who is of German blood. Therefore no Jew can be a German."

Rosenberg's luck at sidestepping personal danger was proverbial. He took part in the huge Koburg riot in 1922 when 800 Storm Troopers battled on the streets with radical trade unionists. During the famous beer hall *putsch* on November 8, 1923, he was said to have been at Hitler's side, brandishing a revolver. However, unlike Hitler, Hess (see sketch this issue) and Strasser, he was not arrested, nor was he forced to make tracks over the border like Goering. And during Hitler's imprisonment in Landsberg Fortress his influence increased tremendously. He visited Hitler every day, and their exchange of ideas may account for the Rosenbergian racial dogma in *Mein Kampf*, written at this time. He also served as a link between Hitler and the other members who, because the party had been suppressed, now carried on their activities under cover of the legal Popular Liberty Movement.

By this time his career as a journalist was also well begun. Some time before, the budding anti-Semitic party had acquired title to a provincial weekly called *Völkischer Beobachter*, and when Eckart died in 1923 Rosenberg became sole editor of the paper, which had grown into a daily. Suppressed during Hitler's incarceration, it reappeared in 1925 with a new and more impressive format, and Rosenberg resumed editorship. With unconcealed contempt for the masses he deliberately spurned popular features and circulation-building dramatics and coolly devoted column after column to long-winded dialectics and racialism.

But by this time, too, the facade of harmony maintained by Hitler was beginning to crumble catastrophically. Gregor Strasser's North German following demanded an anti-capitalist program; the Rhineland industrialists and the Prussian nobility were equally insistent on suppressing working-class agitation. The latter bolstered their argument with heavy financial support; the division deepened, and Hitler leaned more and more to the Right Wing. Rosenberg, who also espoused the cause of the classes as opposed to the masses, became a target for the Strasser Leftists, who, among other things, deplored the way he edited the Party newspaper. Finally popular demand forced his retirement to the capacity of advisory editor, and it was not until the historic blood purge of June 1934 that prospects once again looked really bright for Alfred Rosenberg. (He was later restored to the editorship of the Party newspaper, and was also made an editor of the Party organ, the *Monthly Review*.)

The year 1930 found Rosenberg elected to the German Reichstag, however, and from 1931 to 1933, while Hitler was taking over in Germany, he served as a member of the Diplomatic Service with missions to England and Rome. Then, in 1933, came a striking display of the Führer's regard: he was appointed to make a good-will tour of England. The Baltic philosopher was pleased. His trip was commonly believed to be a prelude to the ambassadorship, a post he especially coveted. In Rosenberg's thesis Germany and England were destined to share the world, since the greatness of both countries lay in the Nordic blood flowing in the veins of their people. But Rosenberg's dream of translating political theory into action was frustrated when he committed one of the most monumental blunders in the history of a Nazi statesmanship extraordinarily rich in examples. He placed a swastika wreath on the tomb of the Unknown Soldier. The response was instantaneous. An enraged war veteran removed the swastika and threw the wreath in the Thames, for which he was fined 40 shillings; a series of workers' demonstrations demanded Rosenberg's ouster; the walls of London were covered with "Down with Rosenberg!" In high dudgeon Rosenberg summoned 100 British reporters to his hotel room and for half an hour lambasted them in German, a language none of them could understand. Then Rosenberg left hurriedly for Germany.

By way of sop Hitler appointed his faithful aide that same year to the post of Director of the Foreign Policy of the National Socialist Party, a sort of extra-curricular office. Here Rosenberg had an opportunity to mold many phases of Nazi policy: among other things, he ran a special secret school for Nazi "diplomacy." But his real specialty was the proposed invasion of Russia. His office became the headquarters for White Russian, Slavic, Romanian, Hungarian and Russo-German adventures of all kinds. Here the famous "Rosenberg Plan" was hatched. Its essential doctrine was that Germany would lure Poland into an alliance against Russia by promising to share with her the spoils of the Ukraine after a joint drive to the East. Once the goal was achieved, however, Poland and her newly-won possessions were to be seized by Germany, since Poland was, in Rosenberg's eyes, a "mongrel nation" of the biologically impure, unworthy of survival.

That the subsequent Russo-German Non-Aggression Pact was a stunning blow to Rosenberg was reported by many sources. He was depicted variously as a broken-hearted man, as a victim of nervous breakdown who had to retire to a sanitarium to recuperate and as a still-active propagandist compelled to operate on the sly. On the other hand, it was even more reliably reported that he never curbed his anti-Bolshevist diatribes at the monthly dinners which he gave for diplomats, and that after the fall of France his agents began circulating in that country and in Spain urging the collaboration of Catholicism in the anti-Bolshevist "crusade" to come. In the meanwhile he had acquired the important title of Director of Philosophic Outlook, a position which actually consists of inculcating with the Nazi philosophy all organizations associated with the Party.

Then Germany proceeded to invade Russia, and the dandified, scented "philosopher with the sour stomach" waited fretfully on the side-

ROSENBERG, ALFRED—*Continued*

lines for his triumphal re-entry into the land of his birth. But an unexpected hitch developed: the "inferior" Russians were smashing through Nazi siege lines around Moscow and Leningrad and sending the Rosenbergian "supermen" of the German Army in pell-mell retreat across the Don basin in the Ukraine. Although in November 1941 he had been made Reichsminister for the East, by December it looked as if Rosenberg might be denied realization of his hopes of ruling a Nazified Russia for some time to come.

References

> Cath World 148 :398-404 Ja '39; 153 :434-40 Jl '41
> Christian Cent 55 :1149 S 28 '38
> Contemp 159 :184-9 F '41
> Menorah J 24 :1-7 Ja '36
> New Outlook 165 :32-3 Je '35
> Newsweek 6 :16 N 9 '35 por; 7 :23 F 15 '36 por; 8 :22 Ag 8 '36 por
> R of Rs 93 :66 Ap '36
> Time 35 :33 Ja 22 '40 por; 36 :24 Jl 22 '40 por
>
> Bayles, W. D. Caesars in Goose Step p199-221 1940
> Dutch, O. pseud. Hitler's Twelve Apostles p81-96 1940
> Gunther, J. Inside Europe p92-4 1940
> International Who's Who
> Simone, A. Men of Europe p108-112 1941
> Wer ist's?

ROTHERMERE, HAROLD SIDNEY HARMSWORTH, 1ST VISCOUNT Apr. 26, 1868—Nov. 26, 1940 British author and publisher who, with his brother Alfred, Lord Northcliffe, owned the London *Daily Mail* and a chain of other newspapers and through them revolutionized journalism in Britain; was known as a backer of appeasement and an admirer of Hitler and Mussolini before the Second World War, but at its outbreak denounced them; always he and his papers believed in a strong hand in dealing with India and Egypt, low taxes and a large empire.

References

> China W R 78 :182-3 O 10 '36
> Sat R 157 :879-80 Jl 28 '34
> So Atlan Q 34 :419-43 O '35
>
> Author's and Writer's Who's Who
> Bridges, T. C. and Tiltman, H. H. Kings of Commerce p99-114 1928
> Gardiner, A. G. Portraits and Portents p283-91 1926
> Who's Who

Obituaries

> N Y Herald Tribune p26 N 27 '40 por
> N Y Times p8 N 27 '40 por

ROURKE, CONSTANCE MAYFIELD (rŏŏrk) Nov. 14, 1885—Mar. 23, 1941 Author and critic who gave up teaching at Vassar College for writing; traveled widely and mingled with all types of people to pre-

International

LORD ROTHERMERE

pare ballads, songs, stories and folk tales and made them a part of our written literary history; wrote a noted life of Audubon, a book on American humor and a life of the artist Charles Sheeler.

References

> Wilson Lib Bul 11 :458 Mr '37 por
> American Women
> Millett, F. B. Contemporary American Authors 1940
> Who's Who in America

Obituaries

> Nation 152 :368 Mr 29 '41
> N Y Times p17 Mr 24 '41
> Pub W 139 :1467 Ap 5 '41
> Sch & Soc 53 :414 Mr 29 '41

RUFFING, CHARLES H(ERBERT) May 5, 1905- Big-league baseball pitcher

Address: 8038 Marquette Ave, Chicago, Ill.

"The hotter the game the cooler the guy." This is a typical characterization of a 6-foot-2-inch, 220-pound red head who for over 10 seasons has been one of the main pillars of the New York Yankees, the plodding, iron-nerved Charles H. Ruffing, known variously as "Red" and "Chuck." Ruffing, a former coal miner, is, in 1941, 36 years old, a venerable baseball age. After a less-than-mediocre career in minor and major leagues and at an age when most players seek the sidelines, Ruffing was just beginning to get his second wind.

Charles Herbert Ruffing was born in the soft coal mining community of Granville, Illinois on May 5, 1905. His father was the

Mayor of Coaltown, a company community within the town of Nokomis, owned by the Reliance Coal Company where he was employed as foreman. Young Ruffing followed his father and brothers into the mines.

Almost inevitably baseball consumed his spare time; the miners were fanatical baseball fans and pitted their teams against those of other communities in a home-grown league. Among the natives who went on to big time baseball were Bill Barnes and Jim Bottomley of the St. Louis Cardinals, Andy Bender of the Pirates, the late George Vertol and Ruffing's own brother John, who was a Cardinals pitcher before he retired from baseball in 1924.

A potent fielder and batsman, Ruffing was offered his first baseball job in the old Kitty League when he was 16. His rejoicing was short-lived; six weeks later, in March 1921, while he was serving as a coupler hooking up empty freight cars, a co-worker misunderstood a signal. Brakes jammed agonizingly and as the long string of cars piled up, Ruffing's foot was caught beneath a wheel and was badly crushed. Blood poisoning set in and for weeks it was feared he would have to have his foot amputated. As it was, he had escaped annihilation by a hair's breadth.

Doctors finally succeeded in saving the foot, however, by amputating four toes. Although Ruffing was convinced his baseball days were over, he persisted in idling with a ball in his back yard. Doc Brennan, pool room owner and semi-pro baseball team manager, suggested that Ruffing concentrate on pitching and astounded him by offering him a job as semi-professional moundsman at $25 a week.

Brennan's advice bore fruit, and in the fall of 1922 Ruffing was hired by Danville in the Three-I League at $150 per month. No world-beater, Ruffing lost more games than he won, but scouts from the New York Giants, the Cleveland Indians and the Boston Red Sox evidently discerned certain potentialities. Although the Giants had offered $10,000, Danville manager Rudy Rulswith let Ruffing go to the Red Sox for a mere $4,000 because he thought the Boston manager would do a better job of breaking him in.

For six seasons Ruffing remained with Boston, a rather dubious distinction. During his first year, in 1924, the Red Sox painfully lifted themselves to the second-place-from-the-bottom niche of the American League; but in the succeeding years they languished in the bottom cubicle with monotonous regularity. If Ruffing wasn't responsible for this, at least he did little to improve matters, and once he was thrust back to the minors for a six weeks' period.

From 1924 to 1930 Ruffing lost 93 games to a total of 39 wins. In desperation the Boston manager placed him in the outfield, but here again Ruffing failed to shine. In 1928 he led the American League in defeats by losing 25 games; and he nearly equaled his record in the following year, when he dropped 22.

Part of the reason for Ruffing's retrogression was his admittedly atrocious support.

CHARLES H. RUFFING

Ruffing lost all incentive for self-improvement, allowed the fat to gather around his midriff. (His wife keeps him from getting that way now by judiciously managing his meals and seeing that he takes exercise in the open air during his off season.)

In a trade for Cedric Durst, an outfielder, Ruffing was finally acquired by the New York Yankees in 1930. There was an instantaneous change. "Nobody knows what a great team the Yankees are until he has played on a lousy ball club," Ruffing has said. "That first year I won fifteen games and lost three. Just a difference in teams." Incidentally, Jimmie Foxx, the baseball immortal, maintains that the advantage was mutual: "Watch Dickey and Ruffing. When they go the Yanks will collapse."

In 1936, at the age of 31, Ruffing pitched his first 20-game season. In each of the three following years he bettered his previous pitching average, despite the fact that in 1939 a sore arm (he throws and bats righthanded) had kept him benched for an entire month.

Ruffing was a holdout in 1932, when he unaccountably demanded $30,000 for the season instead of accepting the offered $15,000, which was $3,000 more than he had ever received before. Six weeks after the season began the real reason for his stubbornness came to light: he was irked because the Yankee management had failed to offer him a $1,000 bonus for his pinch-hitting prowess of the previous season. (Ruffing is the best hitting pitcher in baseball, possibly one of the best in the history of the game.) Finally, when the matter was straightened out, Ruffing returned to his team and started pitching against the pennant-avid Washington Senators after only 11 days of practice. Later that season, on September 23, he almost singlehandedly smashed the Philadelphia Athletics when he

RUFFING, CHARLES H.—*Continued*

allowed them only three hits in a ten-inning game and then proceeded to score a run in the last half of the tenth, a play which won the game for the Yankees.

This was the year that columnists linked his name with that of a Chicago show girl. The rumor was not scotched until 1934, when Ruffing announced that he was going to marry his childhood sweetheart, Pauline Mulholland, who worked in a Nokomis candy store. At the end of the season he returned to his home town for the ceremony. The entire community turned out in a two-day fiesta, and the Chamber of Commerce placed a sign on the highway designating Nokomis as the home of Ruffing, an act with which it had similarly honored Jim Bottomley.

"I got a burst of ambition the day I got married," Ruffing has said. "I figured I had to put out to get into the big money and I was sore the season was over." That he succeeded is evidenced from his earnings: $18,500 in 1933, $19,500 in 1934 and $20,000 in 1935. And his earnings have been mounting ever since. Once regarded by common consent as the dumbest pitcher in the league, Ruffing today is believed to be the smartest.

According to Bill Dickey, all this can be explained by the fact that Ruffing suddenly began to use his head. But it is also true that simultaneously he picked up a devastating "curve" ball. Credited with having won five World Series games for the Yankees (he pitched for his team through games in 10 successive pennant races), his duel with Brooklyn's Curt Davis in the opener of the 1941 Series at the Yankee Stadium climaxed another brilliant season.

Brown-eyed, sandy-haired Ruffing is taciturn and publicity-shy, which leads many to think he has an unpleasant personality. Others insist, however, that Ruffing "just doesn't talk when there's nothing to say." He has earned the title of the "Coolidge of baseball"—maybe because he is inarticulate, maybe because he is almost always master of every trying situation. He does not bear down hard until the pinches, and he pitches like a cool mechanism. Bowling is his principal hobby, also basketball and golf, but he is fond of watching football games and movies, too. Off season he divides his time between Nokomis and a Chicago apartment house which he owns.

References

> Am Mag 128:44-5+ Ag '39 il por
> N Y Herald Tribune p1, 27 O 2 '41
> Sat Eve Post 212:37 Mr 16 '40 il pors
> Spink, J. G. T. comp. Baseball Register 1941
> Who's Who in Major League Baseball
> Who's Who in the Major Leagues

RUGG, HAROLD (ORDWAY) Jan. 17, 1886- Professor of education; author

Address: b. 425 W. 123rd St, New York City; h. 600 West End Ave, New York City

Perhaps no one ever looked less like a dangerous radical than Harold Ordway Rugg,

"cherubic, gray-haired, balding." His social science textbooks have sold 2,000,000 copies and have been used in 4,000 schools, mainly in small towns; 10,000 teachers have used them, until quite recently, with little opposition from anyone. This seems surprising in view of the way they are often described today: "subversive"; "un-American"; "they twit the Founding Fathers"; "they have an alien ideology"; "they plan to substitute a new social order for our American Government"; "they debunk our great heroes of the past." At one public hearing a retired captain actually pointed his finger at mild-mannered Dr. Rugg and shouted: "There sits the ringmaster of the Fifth Columnists in America, financed by the Russian Government!"

Rugg himself, in his book, *That Men May Understand* (1941), says that these charges come mainly from people who have not read his books, or from self-interested minorities. John Dewey calls his books "conducive to unfettered thinking"; and teachers and pupils who have studied them have been quoted as saying: "they teach American life as it is actually lived"; "one who has studied under Rugg cannot fail to be impressed by his sincerity and vision of an ever greater and happier United States."

That Men May Understand is Harold Rugg's autobiography, the story of his "22-year battle to bring into the schools a full account of American life—its deficiencies and problems as well as its magnificent achievements." Here he answers his critics, and even presents a sample chapter from one of his volumes for junior high schools, "Citizenship and Civic Affairs." Lewis Gannett is a little peevish: "Mr. Rugg is passionately and profoundly American, but there is one characteristic which we like to think of as American that he seems to lack: a sense of humor." But books have more frequently been burned for the presence than for the absence of that. And in Mr. Gannett's eyes, Harold Rugg has made out an almost watertight case against the would-be book-burners.

Born in Fitchburg, Massachusetts on January 17, 1886, the author can trace his ancestry back nine generations and still find it rooted in New England soil. A cousin was the chief justice of the Massachusetts Supreme Court. Harold Ordway Rugg was the son of Edward Francis and Merion Abbie (Davidson) Rugg. He was brought up in the unimaginative atmosphere of a New England mill city, and in 1902, at the age of 16, left high school to earn a meager "living" for two years as a weaver in a textile mill. After this firsthand, and none too pleasant, study of industrialism, he managed to find his way to Dartmouth. There he took his B. S. in 1908, a year later took a Civil Engineering degree at Dartmouth's Thayer School of Civil Engineering, and then left his books "to spike rails and tamp ties on one of the great Middle Western railroad systems." Mathematical formulae worked out in practice, he was excited to discover; but theory interested him even more. Soon he was half the Civil Engineering Department of James Millikin University in Decatur, Illinois. He spent two years there, and then four at the University of Illinois, combining the teaching of engineering with the graduate study of education, psychology and sociology, and in 1915 taking his Ph. D. in education and sociology. By this time (1912) he had also married Bertha Miller of Franklin, Indiana (they have a son, Donald Alan, and a daughter, Dorothy Elizabeth).

Gradually it had become educational rather than engineering theory which interested him. But it was the era of "salvation through fact finding," and Rugg was busy proclaiming it— by surveys, by books on statistics and mathematics, by intelligence testing. In the winter of 1919 to 1920, the year he became professor of education at Columbia University's Teachers College, he measured and charted the abilities of every child in the Lincoln School there and built up the school's first system of records.

If in those first years Harold Rugg had known almost nothing of the "whole realm of the creative and appreciative processes," by the summer of 1920 that had become his great preoccupation. He had acquired the idea that American life could be presented to pupils in an integrated way rather than by the study of isolated fragments of history, economics and geography, and was busy at work preparing his "Social-Science Pamphlets": 1,000 mimeographed pages dealing with "immigration, town and city life, industries and trade, geographical factors in American life, conservation of natural resources, and the like." These were for the use of Lincoln School pupils only: he didn't know then that he was beginning what he now calls a "life sentence with a blank sheet of paper."

In 1922, with two research assistants, Rugg wrote and published privately the first printed edition of his pamphlets—ten of them. The next year, with more money and 16 research assistants, the second edition was cooperatively published, this time to be distributed to 375 school systems in 38 states. (The pamphlets then numbered 12, each containing some 300 pages.) They were still used under experimental conditions, however, and teachers and administrators gave suggestions for their improvement at round-table meetings all over the country before, in 1927, the pamphlets were scrapped for the first commercial edition put out by Ginn and Company. By 1931 Rugg knew his was a "life sentence." Six 600-page volumes for junior high schools under the general title *Man and His Changing Society,* six *Workbooks of Directed Study* and six *Teacher's Guides* had already appeared, and he was now making plans for the extension of the series "upward and downward."

It was during the depths of the depression that Rugg wrote the "long pamphlet" most frequently quoted against him by his detractors, *The Great Technology* (1933). Critics, however, seldom mention that this was written not for children, but for adult study groups. In Rugg's words, it was meant to serve as a synthesis of the "tangled economic

Mary Morris

HAROLD RUGG

and psychological factors which had caused the recurring 'jams' in our modern society." At about the same time Rugg was interesting himself in the now-defunct Technocracy movement and admittedly agreed with many of its concepts, although rejecting its "authoritarian" tendency. In February 1934 his report at a meeting of the National Education Association created a sensation in the press when he advocated a central planning agency for social science education, but it was a sensation which surprised him, particularly at a time when even conservatives were of the opinion that "something had to be done." In the meanwhile, with Louise Krueger, he had begun designing and writing his eight books for grades three to six, and boards of trustees were not yet worrying about whether or not his textbooks were "subversive."

As a matter of fact, Rugg's listing in Elizabeth Dilling's *Red Network* in 1934 (he had made a reference to the Russian youth movement in a 1933 *Herald Tribune* speech) probably set off the spark. A year or two later Rugg was branded "pro-Soviet" on the floor of Congress and someone denounced two of his books as Communistic, but the complaint was thrown out by educational officials. Early in 1938 he traveled 20,000 miles and found no "witch-hunt" going on anywhere. But in the next three years he was to spend almost as much time preparing statements as to his beliefs and defending himself at "heresy" trials and public debates as in bringing his junior high school series up to date and in preparing two new volumes.

In 1939 the campaign against Rugg began in all earnest, and by 1940 it had picked up momentum. Most energetically denunciatory were the Advertising Federation of America, the Hearst newspapers, Merwin K. Hart of the New York State Economic Council, O. K.

RUGG, HAROLD—*Continued*

Armstrong, George Sokolsky (see sketch this issue), Major A. G. Rudd, B. C. Forbes of *Forbes* Magazine and certain representatives of the American Legion. In February 1941 Ralph Robey (see sketch this issue) also quoted Rugg in his criticism of textbooks abstracted for the National Association of Manufacturers. By that time, as a result of the campaign, Rugg's books had been banned in Garden City and Manhasset, Long Island; in Hornell, Olean and Rome, New York; in Cedar Rapids, Iowa; in Mountain Lakes and Wayne Township, New Jersey. There had been fierce battles over them in the District of Columbia, Georgia and other states. Their public burning had been proposed in the Virginia State Legislature and in Binghamton, New York, where they were ordered off the library shelves; and in Bardner, Ohio the books were actually seized at a meeting of the school board and shoved into the furnace Some school administrators who themselves liked the books faced with pressure from their school boards, were deciding discretion was the better part of valor. And it seemed certain that all over the country other authors of other textbooks were frantically scanning them for dangerous thoughts.

On the other hand, in October 1940 Rugg's publishers announced that sales of his books had actually increased as another result of all this publicity. In more than one community the attempted censorship program has been discarded. Leading educators and former Rugg students and their parents (in Manhasset a good proportion wore Willkie buttons) as well as liberal organizations have loudly proclaimed the author's Americanism, some of them for the very reason for which a corresponding secretary of the Daughters of Colonial Wars wanted his books banned in Philadelphia: Rugg "tried to give the children an unbiased viewpoint." Among his better-known defenders are Bishop Francis J. McConnell, Charles Beard (see sketch this issue), Fannie Hurst and Franz Boas, the American Committee on Democracy and Intellectual Freedom and the American Civil Liberties Union.

According to Rugg himself, the cry of his critics is: "I haven't read the books, but," in essence, "they are bad!" Quotations out of context often create a totally erroneous impression, and in his new book he shows this by putting those statements most frequently quoted against him back into place. To the accusation that he advocates "the substitution of a cooperative commonwealth for the present system of American Government" and that he does not believe in "free enterprise" Rugg replies that he had advocated the development of a cooperative commonwealth, never its substitution, and that he believes in private enterprise and in social enterprise, too. To charges of Communism he states that he is not and never has been either a Communist or a Socialist, and that he has actually urged students and teachers not to devote too much time to the study of Marxian ideas. To those who believe children should not study the bad as well as the good features of American life he replies: "To keep issues out of the school is to keep life out of it!" Yet, he says, "I try to sell our democracy. I believe in it, and I make no bones about it."

"Spectacled, enthusiastic" Harold Rugg is now spending much time in his "book-lined, sculpture and watercolor-decorated study" preparing the first volume of a senior high school library to contain some half-dozen social science volumes. He is also continuing to write for *Scholastic,* in which he published more than a hundred articles between the years 1931 and 1941. And he can be heard almost any week in the month, on one public platform or another, defending the right of citizens of a democracy (including citizens in short pants) to be exposed to the viewpoint that the United States might tomorrow be an even more beautiful and prosperous country than it is today.

References

Inst Propaganda An Bul F 25 '41
Nation's Bus 28:27-8+ Ap '40
New Repub 104:327 Mr 10 '41
N Y Times p17 Ag 23 '40; p17 Ag 29
   '40; p6 F 22 '41; p38 Mr 16 '41
Newsweek 14:47 D 4 '39
PM p54-5 S 22 '40 il por
Pub W 138:1322-3 S 28 '40; 138:1492
   O 12 '40; 139:434 Ja 25 '41
Time 36:64-5 S 9 '40 por

Leaders in Education 1932
Rugg, H. That Men May Understand
   1941
Who's Who in America

RUNDSTEDT, GERD VON *See* Rundstedt, K. R. G. von

RUNDSTEDT, KARL (RUDOLF GERD) VON (fôn rōōnt'shtĕt gĕrt) Dec. 12, 1875- German Army officer

Address: Berlin, Chal.-2; Hardenbergstrasse 32, Germany

Perhaps future historians will record as Adolf Hitler's single greatest military achievement no conquest on the battlefield, but a conquest over the German Army tradition. Many believe that discord between the Army and the Nazi Party still stalks the Third Reich and will prove its undoing. No one, however, will try to confirm this by citing as example Field Marshal General Karl von Rundstedt.

The oldest member of the former High Command and the only present member of the Army who was an army corps Chief of Staff in the First World War, Rundstedt is one of Hitler's ablest generals. Fellow officers explaining the ineptitude of Chief of High Command Wilhelm Keitel (see sketch 1940 Annual), Hitler's plodding party hack who was so quickly elevated to his present position, say: "Keitel is such a fool he doesn't even take the advice of General Rundstedt."

To many Von Rundstedt, a thin-lipped, weathered, sharp-featured man with a mustache that looks like a contraction of Hitler's, symbolizes unity in Nazi Germany's military and political affairs. None can say for sure how firm is the basis for this unity, because Rundstedt can scarcely be regarded as an enthusiastic National Socialist. His background and training must cause him to consider Hitler an upstart. Nevertheless, it was at Hitler's orders that he was made a marshal of the Reich following his achievements in Poland and France. This may be regarded as a measure of the Führer's personal favor rather than a matter of military attainment alone, for Hitler has been known to withhold such honors from those deemed lacking in Nazi fervor, despite signal success on the battlefield (General Halder is a case in point). Moreover, Rundstedt's name appeared over a piece of strident nationalism in Hitler's own newspaper, the *Völkischer Beobachter*, during the Polish campaign. The article commemorated the war dead and exhorted the nation to greater sacrifice.

This is evidence, if not of Rundstedt's recent Nazi persuasion, then of his utter devotion to the German Army, regardless of the controlling political power. He demonstrated this devotion even under Social Democracy, which was anathema to the German militarists.

Karl Rudolf Gerd von Rundstedt was born in Aschersleben on December 12, 1875, the son of a general. His family is one of the oldest and most aristocratic in Prussia, and Rundstedt was dedicated to the German Army virtually from the cradle. He was sent to an officers' training school, launching his military career, like the great strategist Clausewitz, at the age of 12.

After receiving his commission, Rundstedt was chosen to attend the exclusive Cadet Academy at Potsdam. By the outbreak of the First World War he had reached the rank of major. It was, however, at the Alsace sector that Rundstedt, as commander of Infantry Regiment 171, first revealed extraordinary initiative under fire. Summoned by the General Staff to aid in formulating grand strategy, he remained with that body for the duration of the War.

Remaining with the Reichswehr, Rundstedt, with the rank of lieutenant colonel, was made commander of the Mark of Brandenburg, Third Military District, which included Berlin. This was a time of confusion during which many of Rundstedt's fellow officers abandoned their Prussian aloofness from political parties. Veteran and national groups, in opposition to nascent socialism, mushroomed everywhere.

Some army leaders, notably Goering (see sketch this issue), embraced the Nazi Party from the beginning and were active in Bavaria where it first took root; others planned to use it for their own ends, pending an eventual point of departure. Rundstedt seems to have been passive while his co-officers at the famous Herren Club in Berlin plotted to establish a "soldier-state" based on the theo-

KARL VON RUNDSTEDT

ries of Germany's great politico-militarists and ruled by the Prussian Army caste. An ardent monarchist, as were his fellow-Prussians, Rundstedt was personally antipathetic to Hitlerism and seems to have preferred even the Social Democrats to the bizarre followers of the Austrian ex-paper hanger. An anonymous army officer who kept a diary at the time wrote: "Rundstedt's opinion of the 'Leader' is exactly the same as my own; the two of them don't seem to be exactly the best of friends."

However, as the army authority of Berlin under a Social Democratic state government, Rundstedt found himself in an embarrassing position just before Hitler's ascension to power. This was in 1932 when the over-wily monarchist, Franz von Papen (see sketch this issue), was still making an effort to jockey both Socialism and National Socialism to oblivion. President von Hindenburg had made Von Papen chancellor, replacing Brüning. In a sudden and desperate show of strength Von Papen appointed himself national commissioner for Prussia and ordered the removal of the Social Democratic Prussian state government of Otto Braun, thereby stealing the Nazi thunder and attempting to outmaneuver Hitler in the latter's efforts to attain power.

It was Rundstedt's task to carry out the decree of martial law against Social Democrats with whom he had established friendly relations. For Rundstedt this was an unpleasant chore, and there are reports that he tried to have his army commission withdrawn. It is said that he was so gracious and sympathetic in arresting his unresisting friends that they harbored no resentment and were glad the job had been done by him rather than anyone else! Incidentally, Rundstedt's tact has gain-

RUNDSTEDT, KARL VON—*Continued*

ed him the title of "the first gentleman of the German Army."

Despite his personal animus, Rundstedt was not affected by Hitler's June 1934 blood purge which liquidated the chief source of army opposition nor by the "cold" purge notable for the sudden retirements of high-ranking military officials "for reasons of poor health." It is true that when Rundstedt retired in 1938 there were rumors of political discord, but he had reached the legal age for retirement. Moreover, he was recalled to the colors at the outbreak of the Second World War. This effectively dispelled the myth that he had been actively engaged in opposing Hitler, however he may have disapproved inwardly.

To date Rundstedt's performance in the Second World War has been brilliant. He has proven himself a master of the blitzkrieg technique, a "high priest of strategy," in recognition of which he was granted a marshal's baton on July 19, 1940. His name leaped to fame in 1939 in the opening phases of the War, when he commanded the armies which struck across southern Poland. Under his leadership the famous tank spearheads and *schnelltruppen* of General Guderian and General von Kleist stormed the Jablonica Pass and rolled into Galicia. He was in command at the fall of Kraków, Lódz and Przemyśl and at the battles at the San and the bend of the Vistula Rivers, which culminated in the entry of German troops into bomb-gutted Warsaw.

Rundstedt's role in the defeat of France is also significant. Analysts of the French campaign say it was the work of no one man; it was a blitzkrieg version of the famous "Shlieffen Plan" of 1914, with a few important variations, which took the French High Command completely off guard. General Rundstedt's armies were the first to break through at Sedan on May 14, stabbing the vital organ of the French defensive system and advancing through the Champagne district.

Rundstedt was dispatched to the southern front when Hitler's armies surged over the Russian border. For weeks his armies, for the first time during the current War, were unable to gain blitzkrieg tempo and seemed fated to engage in an agonizing war of attrition. But as General Budenny's (see sketch this issue) Russian forces were gradually pushed back across Bessarabia and over the Dneiper, Rundstedt's armies once again gained momentum, making deep thrusts into the Ukraine, occupying Kiev and entering upon vast encircling movements in conjunction with the armies of Marshal Bock.

But, after the most successful offensive in Hitler's entire Russian campaign, after his armies were smashing toward the oil wealth of the Caucasus, and down the Crimea toward the Black Sea naval base of Sevastopol, some-

thing happened to Rundstedt's troops. The tank spearhead group under Von Kleist suddenly found itself threatened at Rostov by a magnificent counter-offensive by Russian troops under Timoshenko (see sketch this issue). For the first time the amazed Nazi armies found themselves unable to hold an important objective. In order to escape a Russian pincers movement, Von Kleist's armies retreated hurriedly from Rostov, with the Russians in hot pursuit. In order to strengthen their position, Rundstedt withdrew troops from the Crimea to stem the Red tide along the Sea of Azov. But this weakened Rundstedt's Crimean offensive to such an extent that the besieged Russians there began to counter-attack, and the Nazis lost position after position, as the Russians demonstrated a skill and strength in counter-attack that had been completely unexpected.

Von Rundstedt could provide the key to the intricate entente between aristocratic Prussian militarism and brawling National Socialism, an entente that may yet disintegrate, but which, despite wishful thinking, shows little sign of doing so today.

In 1902 Rundstedt was married to Luise von Götz. They have one son, Hans-Gerd.

References

> N Y Sun pl, 10 Ag 27 '41 por
> Newsweek 18:21 Ag 18 '41 por
> Time 38:17 Ag 18 '41 por
> Bayles, W. D. Caesars in Goose Step p251-2 1940
> Wer ist's?

RUNKLE, ERWIN W(ILLIAM) May 20, 1869—Feb. 14, 1941 Faculty member of the Pennsylvania State College from 1893 until his retirement with the rank of professor emeritus in the Department of Philosophy in July 1938; served also as college librarian from 1904 to 1923; authority on the history of the college.

References

> Leaders in Education 1941
> Who's Who in America

Obituaries

> N Y Times p15 F 15 '41

RUSBY, HENRY H(URD) Apr. 26, 1855— Nov. 18, 1940 Former head of the Columbia University College of Pharmacy who was an expert on drugs and noted as a botanist and explorer.

References

> American Medical Directory
> American Men of Science
> Leaders in Education 1941
> Rusby, H. H. Jungle Memories 1933
> Who's Who Among North American Authors
> Who's Who in America

DR. HENRY H. RUSBY

Obituaries

> N Y Herald Tribune p26 N 19 '40 por
> N Y Times p23 N 19 '40 por
> Sch & Soc 52:523 N 23 '40

RUSSELL, CHARLES (EDWARD) Sept. 25, 1860—Apr. 23, 1941 Journalist, author and Socialist candidate for Governor, Mayor and Senator in New York; after 22 years as a successful newspaperman, in both the reportorial and executive branches of the business, he joined the ranks of the "muckrakers" and became a crusader against corrupt ownership of corporations; in later years concerned himself mainly with the Irish Republic and the plight of the Jews in Nazi Europe.

References

> Russell, C. E.   Bare Hands and Stone
>   Walls   1933
> Who's Who Among North American
>   Authors
> Who's Who in America

Obituaries

> N Y Times p21 Ap 24 '41 por

RUSSELL, MARY ANNETTE RUSSELL, COUNTESS 1867(?)—Feb. 9, 1941 English author who under the name of "Elizabeth" wrote *Elizabeth and Her German Garden* (1898), *The Enchanted April* (1923), *Mr. Skeffington* (1940) and other novels; first married to Count Henning August Arnim and then in 1916 to the second Earl Russell, a brother of Bertrand Russell.

References

> Delineator 108:7 My '26
> Mentor 15:49 Mr '27

N Y Post My 19 '31
Time 35:100+ Ap 15 '40 por
Wilson Lib Bul 6:390 F '32

> Cooper, A. P.   Authors and Others
>   1927
> Kunitz, S. J. ed.   Authors Today and
>   Yesterday 1933
> Lawrence, M.   School of Femininity
>   p281-310   1936
> Russell, M. A.   All the Dogs of My
>   Life   1936
> Ward, A. C.   The Nineteen-Twenties
>   1930
> Who's Who
> Williams, H.   Modern English Writers
>   1919

Obituaries

> N Y Times p17 F 10 '41

RYTI, RISTO (HEIKKI)   (rü-tĭ rĭs'tô) Feb. 3, 1889-   President of Finland

Address: Helsinki, Finland

Upon the resignation of the late Dr. Kallio as President of the Finnish Republic on November 29, 1940 it was Finland's wartime Prime Minister who was formally named Acting President. In actuality Prime Minister Risto Ryti had been filling the duties of the office since the beginning of Dr. Kallio's illness in the summer. It was therefore no great surprise to anyone when on December 4, 1940 Risto Ryti was elected President of Finland for Dr. Kallio's unexpired term, which ends in March 1943.

This banker-statesman who in 1940 was called "Finland's Alexander Hamilton" was the son of a farmer, Karl Evert Ryti, and of Ida Vivika (Juntilla) Ryti. He was born in 1889 in Huittinen, a small village in southwest Finland. In 1906 he began the study of law at Helsingfors University, was graduated in 1909, for four years practiced at the western seaport of Rauma, then in 1914 went to England for a year's further study at the University of London. He received his LL. B. from the University of Helsingfors the same year. Until 1919 he practiced law in the firm of Serlachius & Ryti in Helsinki, specializing in the laws governing waterways and water power. The Finns are not a talkative people, but the young lawyer must have been eloquent as well as resourceful. One story tells how during the Civil War of November 1917, when the Whites and the Reds were in arms against one another, he escaped from the house of a Finnish magnate, which had been attacked by the Reds. In a field he and his wife (he had married Gerda Paula Serlachius, daughter of the Councilor of Jurisprudence, the year before) were stopped by the bayonet of a Red soldier. Putting an expression of utter amazement on his face, Ryti pointed to something on the man's coat and asked him how in the world it happened that he had a button missing. The soldier looked; soon the two were discussing the mystery of the missing button in a friendly way; and they were still discussing it when the Finnish White Guards stole up on the soldier and disarmed him.

Finnish Information Center
RISTO RYTI

In 1919 Risto Ryti was elected to the Finnish Parliament as a deputy from the National Progressive Party. For a year after his election he was also manager of an export trade company, and from 1921 to 1924, when his term as deputy expired, he served as Minister of Finance as well. In 1923, before taking up new duties as Governor of the Bank of Finland, a state-owned institution chartered by Parliament but protected from governmental interference, he came to America to sign the Finnish debt agreement (not, by the way, a "war" debt but a debt incurred by the loan of food and grain during the civil war) and incidentally struck up a great friendship with Chief Justice Hughes (see sketch this issue).

When he returned to Finland he found necessary a policy of "easy money"—encouraging the Finns to borrow both at home and abroad. Between 1922 and 1930 the foreign debt rose by 25 per cent. It was under Risto Ryti's direction, however, that the capital of the Bank of Finland was built up until it was by far the most important bank in the country, universally respected; and it was Risto Ryti who was Finland's agent in "insisting upon paying, in paying, and in building up the country with debt-paying capacity" that has given the Finns a reputation for absolute honesty and dependability, so helpful to them in the Russo-Finnish War of 1939-40 that the pro-German sympathies of the Finnish Rightists were forgotten. From 1927 to 1929 Ryti again served as deputy as well as Governor of the Bank, and after 1928 as member of the Economic Advisory Council.

About this time the depression hit Finland, and hit it hard. Social and political turmoil culminated in the abortive Fascist *putsch* of 1931. Foreign trade (most of Finland's exports are to the British) sagged and collapsed.

It was up to Ryti to put the country back on a sound economic basis. He chose a policy of deflation. Imports were limited; costs were reduced; wages were cut tremendously; only minimum relief was given to the unemployed; public works almost ceased. But "out of the Finnish worker's abstinence," dictated by Ryti, "the foreign creditor was paid," and the country was also ready to get back its competitive position on the world market. By the time the Russo-Finnish War broke out 87 per cent of Finland's indebtedness had been paid. Ryti fostered internal development, too. Since four out of five Finns live on the land, he encouraged the diversification of agriculture and the development of water sites, around which new industrial cities could spring up.

In the meanwhile Ryti had served as delegate to the League of Nations in 1932, and in 1933 had been vice-chairman of Finland's delegation to the World Economic Conference. As one of the financial experts preparing the agenda for the Conference, it was his suggestion that France and the United States leave the gold standard simultaneously so that all countries could enter the parley on equal terms. Later events showed the wisdom of his suggestion. It was not heeded at the time, however, and the Conference was a failure. Again, in 1937, it was Ryti who warned the world of possible deflation. It is little wonder that Montagu Norman, Governor of the Bank of England, with whom Ryti often cooperated, ranked him second only to Germany's Dr. Schacht as a central banker.

On December 1, 1939, the day after the Russo-Finnish War began, the shake-up in the Finnish Cabinet brought Risto Ryti to the front as Prime Minister. It was a logical choice, for in 1938 he had been runner-up for the Presidency. All through the War and the subsequent peace negotiations he continued in office, remaining at his desk in the Bank even during air raids when the Bank itself was closed. He was the lone dissenter in the Cabinet when peace was made in March 1940. On March 27, 1940 he formed a new Cabinet to carry on Finland's vast reconstruction program. The things he verbally emphasized were the importance of a foreign policy of "peace and neutrality"; "friendly confidential relations with all nations"; defense; finding compensation for Finnish losses in industry, agriculture, communications and territory; rebuilding industry and export trade; increasing the exploitation of Finland's natural wealth; stabilizing the financial situation and currency, with the help of foreign loans. This last task he was particularly fitted to do, for it was generally conceded that he owned "the best Finnish voice for catching United States and British ears."

But as President of Finland, Ryti's was no easy task. Finland faced a serious food shortage. There was reconstruction to be done. There were refugees to be housed, clothed and fed. And the problem of relationships with her more powerful neighbors continued. Russia, interesting herself in Finland's recent election, had suggested that a "progressive" government, one friendly to the Soviet Union, would be welcome. Presumably Risto Ryti's election was a disappointment. Next German soldiers were given passage through Finland, the native Nazi movement was reported growing there, and, in the words of Finland's Minister of Supply, there were "malicious reports abroad" to the effect that Finland exported food to Germany. This friendliness toward the Nazis, before long, caused Finland's relations with Great Britain and the United States to become a little less warm than at the time of the Russo-Finnish conflict—and at a time when Finland was still seeking their help.

They became even less warm, and Ryti's problems were increased when, in June 1941, Finland went to war with Russia again, this time on the side of the Nazis. "The Kremlin," Ryti informed his people, "had decided on even more brutal measures against Finland than before." But, he added, "now we are not alone; great Germany, under her leader of genius, Reichsführer Hitler, had decided to wage war against the Soviet and other nations have joined Germany." When this "defensive" war "for the liberty of the fatherland" continued after Finland had recovered the territory lost the year before and Finnish strategy threatened allied shipments to Russia through the port of Murmansk, Stalin asked that England declare war on Finland and United States Secretary of State Hull sent a strongly-worded note to the Finnish Government. President Ryti, however, while refusing to consider a separate peace or to renounce claims to Russian territory that had never belonged to Finland, continued to insist that this was a war in the interest of Finnish "security" alone, without "political aims," that Finland was pursuing "an independent policy"; and this was his contention even after the Finnish Government signed the Anti-Comintern Pact.

Suave, "short, unobtrusive, looking older than his years but always neatly attired in conventional black coat and striped trousers," Risto Ryti is remarkable in many ways. His memory has been called "fantastic"—he never needs a note even when giving a budget message. He has a wide knowledge not only of ancient history but also of military history: when Finland began to prepare years ago it was he who took the chairmanship of a civilian committee on military affairs. One of his most unusual hobbies is reading horoscopes. And he is one of the few foreigners who has ever been knighted by the British Government, with which Finland is officially at war—as Knight Commander of the Royal Victorian Order!

References

Manchester Guardian p3 Mr 28 '40
N Y Herald Tribune p2 D 4 '39
N Y Sun p6 D 19 '40 por
N Y Times p6 Mr 28 '40 por
Elliston, H. B. Finland Fights p90-117 1940
International Who's Who
Who's Who in Central and East-Europe

SABATIER, PAUL (så″bå″tyå′ põl) Mar. 5, 1854—Aug. 15(?), 1941 Dean of the science faculty of Toulouse University, France, where he had taught since 1882; greatest claim to fame was his discovery of a commercially successful method of fat-hardening or hydrogenation; famed also for his experiments which led to the discovery of synthetic gasoline; shared the 1912 Noble Prize in chemistry; pursued his researches without thought of gain and lived on a French professor's salary—$1,700 a year.

References

Sci Mo 23:382 O '26 por
International Who's Who
Qui Êtes-Vous
Who's Who

Obituaries

N Y Times p15 Ag 16 '41
Sch & Soc 54:122 Ag 23 '41

SACKETT, FREDERIC M(OSELEY), JR. Dec. 17, 1868—May 18, 1941 Former United States Senator from Kentucky; American Ambassador to Germany from 1930 to 1933; served as Kentucky's Republican Senator from 1924 to 1930, when he accepted President Hoover's appointment as Ambassador to Germany.

References

Business Week p18 S 21 '32 por
Who's Who in America
Who's Who in Government
Who's Who in Law
Who's Who in the Nation's Capital 1934-35

Obituaries

N Y Herald Tribune p10 My 19 '41 por

SAINT-GAUDENS, HOMER (SCHIFF) (sånt gô′děnz) Sept. 28, 1880- Director of Fine Arts, Carnegie Institute, Pittsburgh, Pa. *Address*: b. Carnegie Institute, Pittsburgh, Pa; h. 701 St. James St, Pittsburgh, Pa; Windsor, Vt.

The attack made by Park Commissioner Robert Moses in March 1941 against the museums of New York City reminded some people once more that there are several enterprising and progressive museums in the hinterlands of the country. One such is the Carnegie Institute of Pittsburgh, over the destinies of whose department of Fine Arts Homer Saint-Gaudens, son of a famous father, has presided since 1921. One of the foremost authorities on camouflage methods in the United States, in 1941 Saint-Gaudens was on active military duty in Washington for one year as a lieutenant colonel in the Engineers Reserve Corps. His work in spreading knowledge and understanding of contemporary painting in the United States has won him honors from the governments of France, Hungary, Belgium and Italy.

HOMER SAINT-GAUDENS

Directly and collaterally on both sides of his house, Homer Saint-Gaudens comes of artistic stock. This inheritance he has enlarged and enriched by his own activities. He is the son of Augustus Saint-Gaudens, the great sculptor, and of Augusta Frederica Homer, a member of an old Boston family, who met her husband in Rome where she was a student of painting. Homer Saint-Gaudens' paternal uncle was Louis Saint-Gaudens, also a sculptor, who ranks not far below his greater brother. On the maternal side Homer Saint-Gaudens is a cousin of Sidney Homer, the composer (whose wife is Louise Homer, the opera singer), and is also related to the late Winslow Homer, the marine painter.

Homer Schiff Saint-Gaudens was born in Roxbury, Massachusetts on September 28, 1880, in the home of his maternal grandfather, Thomas Homer, a Boston merchant. He was educated at Lawrenceville School in New Jersey; at Cardwell's in Paris; at Hallam's in Dresden, Germany; and at Brown and Nichols, the college preparatory school in Cambridge, Massachusetts. All his life Saint-Gaudens has lived in an atmosphere of things artistic and among artists, and in boyhood and youth he passed most of his leisure time in his father's studio. Here and in his home he met and mingled with such outstanding artists as John La Farge, John Singer Sargent, Edwin Abbey, John W. Alexander, Frank Millet, Stanford White, Charles Follen McKim and Daniel Burnham. The artist's problems, purposes and point of view became as familiar to him as the technique of marbles or baseball to the ordinary American boy. More impressionable years were passed in Paris, where his father established himself to finish several important commissions.

On his parents' return to America from Europe he entered Harvard, where in extra-curricular activities he most distinguished himself in fencing, being captain and easily the best man on the University's team. One of his later associates in the theatre suggests that his skill was a gift from some Gascon ancestor. Saint-Gaudens took his Bachelor's degree in 1903. Writing to the secretary of his class 25 years later, Saint-Gaudens says (with a whimsicality perhaps derived from his relationship with J. M. Barrie, for whom he directed the first American production of *A Kiss for Cinderella*):

"My business or profession is dealing with temperament. Originally, it was solely my own. At present it is almost everybody else's. I started dealing with temperament on the New York *Evening Sun*, but when they made me real-estate editor I decided that temperament in The Bronx was too abstract and illusive and not sufficiently intense for me, so I got out. Next I went to *The Critic* Magazine where I dabbled my fingers in art temperament. Then my sardonic destiny led me to the *Metropolitan Magazine*, which was owned, at that time, by the Whitneys. Consequently, I learned about the temperament of horse racing. [Saint-Gaudens is keenly interested in horses and fox hunting. He owns two horses and is president of the Harts Run Hunt in Pittsburgh.] The editor, R. H. Russell, owned one-half of a race horse. We in the office always wondered which half. It would have guided us in nurturing his temperament. After that I went into the theatre, which is supposed to be to temperament what Harvard is to learning. Mostly I was under the aegis of Maude Adams, who, though she had much occasion to indulge in temperament herself, preferred to distract herself by experimenting with my temperament as an antidote to the troubled waters of other Thespian temperamentalities."

Through his father, who himself had been an ardent devotee of the stage from boyhood, Saint-Gaudens came to know and to love the theatre in Paris. Homer Saint-Gaudens was among the few critics who felt the charm of Barrie's *Peter Pan* when it was first done in New York, and his sympathetic and understanding comments on the fantasy brought him an offer to join the forces of Charles Frohman. He started at the bottom in the Frohman office, but in a few months was made stage director for Maude Adams. For her he directed the revivals of *Peter Pan, The Little Minister* and *What Every Woman Knows*, besides directing *A Kiss for Cinderella*. This work was varied by an association with Harley Granville-Barker in the presentation of *The Trojan Women* and other classical plays at Harvard and Princeton. Later Saint-Gaudens directed the productions of Brieux' *The Red Robe*, in which Lionel Barrymore was the star, and of *Beyond the Horizon*, the first full-length play by Eugene O'Neill and the first of that writer's works to receive a professional production on Broadway. Known as an excellent director in the theatre, Saint-Gaudens handled the pictorial side of the drama resourcefully and introduced several innovations into stage lighting.

Upon the entry of the United States into the First World War, Saint-Gaudens joined the first officers' camp at Plattsburg. He was commissioned first lieutenant and assigned to the work of organizing the first camouflage force in the United States. With this contingent he sailed to France in January 1918, and was soon promoted to captain. In command of Company A, 40th Engineers, he had charge of all the camouflage work of the 2nd Army, which held the line from Pont à Mousson to about 15 miles south of Verdun. "I found myself guiding the emotional destinies of 400 temperamentalities in the form of artists, plumbers, carpenters, and other eccentrics, who ultimately won the War by spreading scenery over the gory fields of the A. E. F." He was awarded the Order of the Purple Heart in the United States after he had been wounded in action.

Saint-Gaudens is now a lieutenant colonel in the Engineers Reserve Corps. Since 1922 he has spent some time each year, with two exceptions, in an army camp, in the interest of the camouflage service of the United States Army. In July 1921 he was made assistant director of Fine Arts at Carnegie Institute, and in 1922 director. He organized 16 of the series of annual international exhibitions of oil paintings, spending some months each year visiting the studios of American and European artists in his search for canvases. As Saint-Gaudens himself puts it: "Finally I came to Pittsburgh, where I am an art director, running an exhibition of modern painting that is supposed to be the news of all the pictorial temperament that's fit to print, carrying some sort of temperamental liquid on both shoulders and endeavoring at the same time to dodge the temperamental bricks hurled at me by advanced and academic temperamental paint jugglers." During his directorship, the Carnegie International, the only annual international exhibition of paintings in the world, grew in importance and was placed first among the exhibitions of paintings in the United States. Owing to world conditions the series was interrupted in 1940, but the hope was expressed of renewing it again at the earliest opportunity.

In his marriage to Carlota Dolley of Philadelphia, a painter of miniatures, Saint-Gaudens made another artistic alliance. They had two children, Augustus and Carlota. The first Mrs. Saint-Gaudens died in 1927. In 1929 he married Mary Louise McBride of Pittsburgh. Their summer home is at Cornish, New Hampshire (post office, Windsor, Vermont), near the Saint-Gaudens Memorial of which Saint-Gaudens is the director. This unique memorial consists of two studios of Augustus Saint-Gaudens and his home, Aspet, practically as he left them, and is visited every year by thousands of people from all parts of the country. The studios contain casts of almost everything the sculptor did. Homer Saint-Gaudens is the editor of *The Reminiscences of Augustus Saint-Gaudens,* published

in 1913, and the author of *The American Artist and His Times* (1941). The latter, a history "of American art from Colonial days to the present," has been called a "wise, mellow and altogether charming book."

A spectacled, keen-eyed, dapper man, with curling once-blond hair, Saint-Gaudens has other recreations besides hunting. In 1928 he wrote: "My recreation consists chiefly in alibi-ing my latest game of golf, and in endeavoring to drown myself sailing much-too-small a ketch through the Bahama Islands and catching fish that are never as good as those any one can see in the New York Aquarium." Recently he has given up both golf and vacationing in the Bahamas, however. He is a member of the Century, Harvard and Coffee House Clubs in New York City, and of the Pittsburgh Golf, Allegheny Country and Fox Chapel Clubs. To conclude his record of bouts with temperament, Saint-Gaudens records that he met "my hero, my temperamentless man," in the late Calvin Coolidge. Cornish is just across the Connecticut River from Windsor, Vermont, and Saint-Gaudens knows his Yankee types well.

References

Am Mag Art 29:670 O '36 por
Art Digest 8:12 O 15 '33 por; 9:7 O 15 '34 por; 10:7 O 15 '35 por
Carnegie Mag 12:131-43 O '38 pors; 13: 131-42 O '39 pors; 14:131-44 O '40 por
Christian Sci Mon Mag p6 Je 21 '41
Leaders in Education 1941
Who's Who in America

SAIONJI, KIMMOCHI, PRINCE (sī'ôn-jĕ kĭ-mō'chĕ) 1849—Nov. 24, 1940 The last of Japan's elder statesmen who aided the late Emperor in forming the modern Japanese state; had been advisor to many leaders in Japanese political life.

References

Asia 36:298-302 My '36 il por
Christian Sci Mon Mag p3+ Mr 25 '36 il por
Liv Age 354:229-31 My '38
Mercure Fr 287:84-98 O 1 '38
Trans-Pacific 22:15 My 24 '34; 22:5 Jl 12 '34; 22:4 Jl 19 '34; 22:5 S 27 '34
Omura, B. Last Genro 1938
Takekoshi, Y. Prince Saionji 1933
Who's Who .

Obituaries

N Y Herald Tribune p10 N 25 '40 por
N Y Times p8 N 25 '40 por
Newsweek 16:26 D 2 '40
Time 36:27 D 2 '40

SAKEL, MANFRED (săk'ĕl) June 6, 1906- Psychiatrist

Address: Murray Hill Hotel, 112 Park Ave, New York City

Dr. Manfred Sakel is the discoverer of "the greatest advance yet made in treating schizophrenia." In 1928, in Vienna, he was working

Blackstone

DR. MANFRED SAKEL

with morphine addicts just taken off their drug. He noted symptoms of high excitement, frenzy, mania and even brief insanity and from them developed a theory: that some physical or bodily change is suffered by the addict, as well as a mental change; that the cells of the brain attract to themselves more than usual quantities of exciting substances from the body's glands. Dr. Sakel decided to use insulin to pacify the drug addicts' excited nerve cells.

"The patients complained less and recovered more rapidly," he says. "The minds of these patients seemed to grow clearer." Then one day "I inadvertently gave a morphine patient an overdose of insulin." The man got insulin shock with convulsions and a coma, and to bring him out of the coma Dr. Sakel used glucose. "I was amazed at the result," he writes. "The patient's mind, until then completely befogged, was absolutely clear."

"This gave me an idea—to produce this effect in schizophrenics." Schizophrenics are people who suffer from a split personality, who live in a world of complete unreality, thinking themselves Napoleon or Cleopatra or haunted by visions of dire persecution. After several treatments these patients became more lucid and began to take an interest in their surroundings, and, of the first group Dr. Sakel treated, 17 per cent became well enough to return to their homes or jobs.

After working for five years Dr. Sakel announced his insulin shock cure before the Vienna Medical Society on November 3, 1933. The psychiatric world at first found the reports incredible, but, later, specialists came from all over the world to see the technique and its results for themselves. The method spread, and a high percentage of recoveries confirmed Dr. Sakel's own results. Of course the treatment is recognized to be dangerous, but Dr. Sakel feels that "when we consider

that patients . . . are generally looked on as lost, or very seriously ill in any case, I think there is justification for attempting a therapy, however dangerous, which gives some promise of success."

Probably Dr. Sakel's most famous patient is Vaslav Nijinsky, the famous ballet dancer who was stricken with schizophrenia. Through Dr. Sakel's shock treatments Nijinsky was able for the first time to leave the sanitarium where he had been confined since 1919. When Dr. Sakel, who with professional reticence refuses to discuss the chances of Nijinsky's recovery, came to America, Mme. Nijinsky tried to get an American visa for herself and Nijinsky in order to follow him and continue the cure. It was refused.

Dr. Sakel, who is still in his early 30's, was born in Nadworna, Austria, the son of Major S. and Golde S. Sakel. After attending the Gymnasium he spent four years at Bruenn College in Moravia (Austria) and left it in 1920 to enroll in the University of Vienna Medical School, where he stayed five years. In 1927 he was made head of the Hospital Lichterfelde, Berlin; later he became head of the Park Hospital in Vienna, and in 1933 research associate of the psychiatric clinic of the University of Vienna. In 1937 Dr. Sakel came to America, where he has been active as consultant and lecturer. He was the first to discover the possibilities of metrazol as well as insulin in the treatment of schizophrenia, but from the beginning warned doctors against its general use in preference to insulin shock.

When he can get away from patients and research, bachelor Dr. Sakel goes hiking and mountain climbing. He likes fishing, too.

References

Collier's 101:38-9+ F 12 '38 por
Sci Am 158:278-9 My '38
Time 29:26+ Ja 25 '37 por

Ratcliff, J. D.   Modern Miracle Men
    p125-36   1939

SALAZAR, ANTONIO DE OLIVEIRA
(sä-lä-zär') 1889- Premier of Portugal
Address: Lisbon, Portugal

Throughout the War Portugal has been the front door of Europe. From Lisbon, planes may no longer leave for New York and London, but it is most important for the United States and Britain that it remain neutral. President Roosevelt has announced that the United States cannot afford to see the Portuguese-held Azores in hostile hands. For Britain the defense of the Straits of Gibraltar depends on the use of her Atlantic neighbor's bases. Since the War began the eyes of the world have therefore been turned upon Portugal as well as upon Franco's Spain, wondering what Nazi designs might be, and in December 1941 Australian and Netherland troops found it necessary to occupy the island of Timor because of the presence of Japanese submarines off its shores.

Portugal has been connected with Great Britain by an alliance dating from 1386, and the

Portuguese propaganda department has called the British alliance "one of the cornerstones of Portuguese foreign policy," but this friendship is mainly, today especially, a matter of geographical and economic strategy. Britain's Atlantic neighbor is, like Britain, a small country with large colonial possessions: with an area of around 35,000 square miles and a population of some 7,000,000, she is still the world's fourth biggest colonial power. Her overseas possessions of 809,916 square miles she could not possibly protect by herself. And for a long time most of Portugal's exports—particularly port wine—went to Britain. Nevertheless, Portuguese trade with Germany now tops that with Britain, Nazi soldiers flood nearby Spain, visitors to Lisbon bring back tales of Nazi spies and Nazi propaganda, and it doesn't seem likely that Portugal's Army of 30,000 men and 126,000 reserves or its Navy of six destroyers and three submarines could strike terror into the hearts of any invader. Probably if Germany should move on land, however, the sea powers would quickly grab Portugal's colonies. This fact may keep Europe's front door open and Lisbon unblacked-out—or it may not.

Guiding Portugal's domestic and foreign policy is Dr. Antonio de Oliveira Salazar, an ascetic "little gray man," a Jesuit with a "deep-seated hatred of liberalism" but a genius for finance, for order and for efficiency. There is little question that Portugal is a dictatorship, but it has been called the mildest and least oppressive dictatorship in Europe.

Salazar was born in 1889, only a few weeks after Hitler, in the little town of Santa Comba. His parents were not wealthy, and he was educated by a man who gave private lessons in a cottage for about $1 a month. From earliest childhood he was deeply religious—he came near to being an ordained priest, they say—but he finally chose a lay profession and in 1916 became professor of economic sciences at Coimbra University, where he had been educated and taken his LL. D. Certainly he had no political ambitions then: he was once elected a deputy to the Chamber and did not even take his seat.

In those days Portugal was a republic, though scarcely a model one. A series of armed fights for power followed the revolution of 1910: from 1910 to 1926 there were 16 minor revolutions and 43 cabinets. A fierce anti-clericalism prevailed. No budget had been balanced since 1854. The League of Nations coined the word "Portugesé" to express the absolute low in national welfare.

Finally in 1926 the Army as a whole rose; on May 26 General Gomes da Costa stirred up the garrison at Braga and marched on Lisbon; General Carmona (now President of Portugal) joined him; and together they seized the Government. They found the treasury empty, and called on Dr. Salazar for aid. He spent two days examining the State finances, and his recommendations made the generals wince. Then, since they wouldn't give him full powers as Minister of Finance, he marched back to Coimbra to resume his professional duties.

Casa de Portugal

ANTONIO DE OLIVEIRA SALAZAR

Things went from bad to no better. By April 1928 the generals had reconsidered and were begging the professor to take full charge of the country's financial policy. He did. Salazar balanced his very first State budget—although at the price of great exactions from the country—and since then every budget has shown a surplus. The total public debt was reduced. Portuguese credit was rehabilitated. Portuguese exchange was stabilized at a par with the pound and state revenue enormously increased, partially by property taxes so huge that some peasants had to move off their land (there is no income tax in Portugal). State expenditure was considerably increased, too. A program of improving and building roads, harbors and hospitals began. Old monuments and buildings were restored. Unemployment was reduced. On the whole there is little doubt that Portugal's Minister of Finance did much to change the connotation of "Portugesé," although his adversaries claim that Salazar resembles the kings of the sixteenth century who made the state rich and the people poor.

Although in practice Salazar, rather than General Carmona, governed the country from the very first, he gradually absorbed nearly all the departments of state, too. In 1932 he became Prime Minister and the following year presented Portugal with an entirely new Constitution, one which provided that every trade should be organized on "corporative" lines and work under strictest Government supervision. Two Chambers were to approve all laws, but both were to be exclusively composed of partisans of the Government. Nominally the President was to have executive power, and he could choose his own Premier (provided it was Salazar); the President was also to be elected by plebiscite, but with only one candidate in the field. *The Catholic World* in 1938 called Portugal a

SALAZAR, ANTONIO DE OLIVEIRA—
Continued

"truly representative democracy," an example of the "model republic" suggested by Pope Pius XI in 1931 as the proper civil foundation for social reconstruction. Dollfuss in Austria, Vargas in Brazil and Franco in Spain were credited with having attempted similar experiments.

It was only a year or two after having become dictator that Salazar formed a political organization to back him—the "National Union" —became its president and dissolved all other parties, including the Catholic Center which he had organized. He retired nearly half of the Army officers and practically disarmed most of the Army, many of whose generals had opposed him. He did, however, furnish a few selected regiments (many of whose members had formerly been expelled from the Army for conspiring against the Republic) with green shirts and heavy arms. An espionage system was originated to keep watch over the officer personnel. Chiefs of the German Secret Service helped him form both his Portuguese Legion and his intelligence service. One commentator called this the transformation of a military dictatorship into a rule of civilians, while another wrote: "It appears indisputable that Dr. Salazar has deliberately disarmed Portugal to force it to follow a policy which can never be opposed to that of Spain."

Other features of Salazar's new State are familiar. Public discussion of politics was forbidden, although people could still criticize and discuss the regime in their homes and in cafes. A militant youth movement organized on Catholic lines sprang up. Religion (with a little arithmetic), was taught in all primary schools once more, and when Dr. Salazar slashed the education fund he announced: "One can be illiterate and very happy at the same time." (Almost 70 per cent of the Portuguese are, at least, illiterate.) Private banking was restricted to the advantage of a state-controlled bank. Strikes and lockouts were prohibited. Large Portugese landowners, however, were left in possession of their estates, and Portugal remained one of the few countries where free exchange still prevailed without currency restrictions.

Foreign policy became less dependent on Britain. Trade relations between France and Portugal were broken by Lisbon. In Portuguese schools German became an obligatory language. Privileges were given to Germans in the Portuguese African colony of Angola. Trade with Britain decreased; trade with Germany grew. Firmly anti-Bolshevist, too, Salazar exerted strong pressure on Chamberlain to prevent a Russo-British pact. During the Spanish War he broke off relations with Republican Spain; in the non-intervention discussions Portugal always sided with Germany and Italy; and Salazar's was the first country to sign a trade pact with Nationalist Spain. Franco simultaneously decorated the chief of the Gestapo, the chief of the Italian secret police and Dr. Salazar, and on March 18, 1939 signed a treaty promising to keep hands off Portugal. In that year, too, the Portuguese-British pact was amplified, Portugal being assured of the aid of the British fleet in the event of aggression and aid in the fortification of a few ports. But in the past few years there are numerous instances in which Britain went to unprecedented lengths to keep Portugal's good will and in which her advances were repeatedly snubbed.

Dr. Salazar is both a recluse and an ascetic. Legend says that he was spurned by his childhood sweetheart and took a vow of chastity; in any case, he is unmarried, although he has two small adopted daughters. He works 17 hours a day for $208 a month. His scholarly face, "not made for laughter," is lined with fatigue. He eats little; he sleeps badly. In eight years he has gone twice to the theatre and twice to the moving pictures, and in each case one visit was official. On his rare public appearances he wears a plain black suit and hat, without any medals or decorations. He insists that he be called, simply, "The Minister." He shuns publicity. He seldom lets himself be photographed. Even his style of speech is "terse and bare." He reads every newspaper he can, and says: "All that reading may be a vice, for what I learn from it does not make up for the time taken by it, but it confirms in me my ideas and brings me back to a prudent silence; if I had to speak every day I should soon have nothing left to say and would necessarily come to utter some stupidities." Dr. Salazar's appeal is too intellectual for him ever to be very popular with his people. Nor does he care for popularity; all he cares for is his work. He says, and means it: "I coldly do my duty."

References

Cath World 147:44-51 Ap '38
Christian Sci Mon Mag p1-2 F 9 '38 il por; p2 Ja 18 '41
Commonweal 26:317-19 Jl 23 '37
Contemp 158:320-4 S '40 (Same abr. Liv Age 359:131-4 O '40 por)
Life 9:66-7 Jl 29 '40 il por
Liv Age 356:435-9 Jl '39
Nation 152:495-6 Ap 26 '41
Newsweek 15:26+ Je 17 '40; 17:31 Ja 20 '41 por
Bainville, J. Dictators p233-9 1936
Carr, A. Juggernaut p415-32 1939
Derrick, M. Portugal of Salazar 1939
Ferro, A. Salazar: Portugal and Her Leader 1939
International Who's Who

SANBORN, (JOHN) PITTS

Oct. 19, 1879 —Mar. 7, 1941 Newspaperman; author and music critic; during the First World War was a correspondent in Europe; became music critic of the *Evening Mail* in 1923 and remained in the post when that newspaper was consolidated with the *Telegram* and later with the *Evening World* in New York City; wrote a musical novel, *Prima Donna* (1929), and a book about opera (1937); spoke over the radio as music commentator and was author of the program notes of the New York Philharmonic Symphony Society.

References

Scholastic 27:11-12 Ja 11 '36 por
Who's Who in America

Obituaries

Musical Am 61:28 Mr 10 '41 por
N Y Times p19 Mr 8 '41 por
Pub W 139:1308 Mr 22 '41

SARGENT, PORTER (EDWARD) June
6, 1872- Publisher; author
Address: b. 11 Beacon St, Boston, Mass; h.
26 Weybridge Rd, Brookline, Mass.

As described in the *Harvard Educational
Review,* Porter Sargent's *Handbook of Private Schools for American Boys and Girls,* the
twenty-fifth edition of which appeared in the
spring of 1941, is "published primarily for
the guidance of those who fancy their offspring misplaced except in schools for 'gentlemen's sons and daughters.'" But Mr. Sargent writes prefaces to these rather snobbish
directories—and his prefaces have probably
made him as famous as the fact that he
knows more about private schools than anyone in the United States. "In such surroundings Mr. Sargent's cocky criticisms of 99
and 44/100 per cent of all educational and
social institutions between the ages of fuzzy
chin and white beard is like finding a blob
of sweet cream in the center of a Roquefort
cheese. Finding comments as earnestly honest
and unafraid as those in the columns of such
a publication as *The Nation* would be stimulating. Finding them in a publication circulating primarily where special privilege is
rampant is also astonishing. The moral probably is that no one reads forewords. Or,
bone-chilling alternative, perhaps there is
loose in the private-school world a considerable number of individuals with forward-
looking social intelligence. It must be that
no one reads forewords."

Porter Sargent, "lively, lean-faced, high-
collared," is, according to his own definition,
a typical New Englander. (He claims that
"the first New Englanders became New Englanders because they were insurgents and
couldn't get along comfortably in old England"; that "the New Englander is an individualist; in his vigorous virility, a radical.") Nevertheless, although he may have
spent most of his life in Boston, he cannot
claim New England as a birthplace. He
was born in Brooklyn, New York on June
6, 1872, the son of Francis Porter and Roselyn
(Hitchcock) Sargent. It was 1893 when he
came to Harvard—in the days when bathtubs
were few and telephones fewer, when the
man who carried a football was the Great
American Hero, when the Boston Brahmins
were utterly secure in their domination over
all Harvard fraternities and class offices.

Young Sargent supposed it the greatest university in the world, sat on the bleachers at
football games all through his college years
and long after "with religious regularity,"
took his B. A. in 1896 and his M. A. the year
afterward, specializing in zoology and neu-

rology, and then "remained at Cambridge,
studying and teaching, for eight years after
his commencement." From 1896 to 1904 he
was a master of science at the Browne and
Nichols School there; from 1897 to 1901
he did research in comparative neurology at
Harvard, and from 1902 to 1904 worked
independently by means of grants from the
Carnegie Institute; altogether "Harvard practically ruined me," he says. "For 11 years
I lived in this atmosphere and I was rapidly
becoming academic-minded. I have since re-

Bachrach

PORTER SARGENT

garded my escape as the most fortunate event
in my life."

He escaped, after being employed from
1903 to 1904 as director of science for the
Nautical Preparatory School, by founding a
school of his own. It was called Sargent's
Travel School for Boys, and for 10 years
he divided his time between Europe and going
around and around the world with his pupils:
five times, to be exact. "In this way I got
my real education," he claims. He also
gained a rather extensive knowledge of
Europe, and prepared a handbook on Rome
which was to be the first in a series of
travel books. Then the First World War
discouraged traveling for pleasure. Nothing
daunted, for he had also been doing research
on schools, Mr. Sargent published the first
guide to American private schools in 1914.
It was so successful that he has been publishing them every year since that date.

In the way of furnishing information on
education, Mr. Sargent is much more than
a cataloger, however. He has published
guides to summer camps, biographies of private school teachers; he is the director of the
Sargent School Service, which offers advice
to parents of prospective students on where
to send a backward or precocious child or

SARGENT, PORTER—*Continued*

almost anything they happen to want to know, advice to schools on reorganization, on selection of personnel, on reasons for decreasing enrollment, or just plain advice.

In Sargent's early nineteenth-century Brookline house, on a knoll and surrounded by terraced gardens, his light can be seen burning until 2 a. m. He and his secretary start editing *Private Schools* in January, it usually comes out and is sent to the reviewers around May, and there's very little that it doesn't contain: details on the "history, age of admission, fees, courses, control, management and accrediting" of foreign and American schools and colleges . . . "how to choose schools, what to seek in them, how to fit a child to school, about the higher learning and those who purvey it, of the Angells and the Hutchins of this world, of the Roman Catholic and other churches and their effect upon the schools and upon education, of falling birth rates and what they signify. . . pitfalls for parents, the present educational chaos, gregarious learning, authority and the individual, what to do with children, damaged twigs, mystery or comedy, fetish and symbol, keeping teachers timid, the new economics, the academic mind, and the human comedy."

The prefaces themselves (sometimes published separately, in 1940 under the title *What Makes Lives*) may read more like "a random collection of provocative utterances than the presentation of a reasoned argument"—something like "a compilation of the daily outpourings of a newspaper columnist"—but, according to one reviewer, it is "a far more thoughtful and intelligent columnist than it is our privilege to have read." Mr. Sargent wants us to go back (or rather forward) "to the questing mind of the Greek before Plato, to our rightful heritage, the divine curiosity that man inherited from the Simian." He deplores the fact that so many young people sacrifice "their growing years to the prescribed forms of stultification," as perpetuated in too many educational institutions. He points out their financial control as explanation for what is taught in many of these institutions.

He talks about the "folklore" of education: commencement, the most fantastic and commercialized folkway; the elaborate code of caps and gowns; commencement speakers; history ("a lie agreed upon") ; college class groups; the British old school ties; the teaching of Latin. He finds Morgan influence over President Conant of Harvard and President Seymour (see sketch this issue) of Yale, semi-Fascist tendencies in the "medievalism" of Chicago's President Hutchins (see sketch 1940 Annual) ; he quotes James Harvey Robinson, "whom Butler [see sketch 1940 Annual] forced out of Columbia," as having said: "Any medieval monk would have agreed heartily with Dr. Butler." In 1940 he was insisting that Harvard and other universities had become subservient "to the fog that has blown in from Wall Street and Whitehall," and were leading a propaganda parade to war. In 1941 he was warning against book burnings, witch hunts, against "putting up mental shutters" under the pressure of war.

Indeed, until the Japanese attack on Pearl Harbor he was a rabid anti-interventionist, fond of sending out mimeographed bulletins exposing "British propaganda"; and in April 1941 Mr. Sargent published a 640-page volume titled *Getting Us Into War,* based on the 100 Sargent bulletins, which he promptly dispatched to the leaders of the Roosevelt Administration, to every member of Congress and to prominent educators, especially university presidents and students of the social sciences.

In 1907 Mr. Sargent was married to Margaret Upham of Boston at Rome, Italy. He is now a widower. Both of the Sargent boys were permitted to roam by themselves, without formal education. Upham died in 1934; for Porter, Jr., his father suggested Black Mountain College.

When questioned about his hobbies—aside from his "hobby of humans"—Mr. Sargent replies that he "does not distinguish between work and play." But Oriental art used to be his chief interest, gardening another, and most of his life, until the War, he has spent two months out of the year abroad. He has published numerous articles, and among his books not primarily concerned with the problems of education are *Spoils from a Crowded Life* (poems, 1935) ; *The New Immoralities* (1935) ; and *A Handbook of New England* (1916). In preparation is *Youth, Adventure and Revolt: the Story of a Boy's Life, 1913-1934; The Course of Human Events,* "reviewing what has led to the present sorry mess, is well along toward completion"; and Mr. Sargent hopes also to write some day a book of "Lives and What Made Them" and an "Alibiography," which will "establish alibis in every direction." In spite of all his writing and publishing he says: "Literary work I do not profess to do. My job is making books. I regard it as a kind of engineering; that is, putting words, sentences and paragraphs in such juxtaposition as to be useful. As an art it is merely a matter of selection and arrangement."

"Caustic without being bitter," blithely inconsistent, he can also say: "It's a good time for 'rugged individualism' of the right sort. It's a great time to live!"

References

Christian Sci Mon Mag p5 S 16 '36
Newsweek 7:18 My 30 '36
Private School News 9:10-11 Mr 20 '33
Scrib Com 9:58-63 F '41
Time 27:23-4+ My 25 '36 por; 31:35
　My 30 '38 por; 33:54 My 22 '39 por;
　34:34 D 25 '39

Leaders in Education 1941
Sargent, P. What Makes Lives 1940
Who's Who Among North American
　Authors
Who's Who in America 1938-39

SAVAGE, AUGUSTA (CHRISTINE)
Sculptor

Address: 143 W. 125th St, New York City

Visitors to the New York World's Fair during 1939 and 1940 no doubt noticed in front of the Contemporary Arts Building a piece of black statuary in the shape of a huge harp, an outstretched arm and hand forming the base, and the strings tapering down from the heads of singing Negroes. Kneeling in front of the harp, a Negro youth was holding out a placard with a few bars of music on it. The statue, 16 feet high and made in the semblance of black basalt, was designed to commemorate the Negro's contribution of music to the world.

Augusta Savage, the Negro sculptress who executed this work, was one of four women sculptors to be given commissions by the World's Fair, the others being Malvina Hoffman, Brenda Putnam and Gertrude Whitney (see sketch this issue). She explains that she took for her theme the so-called "Negro National Anthem," *Lift Every Voice and Sing*, by the well known poet, James Weldon Johnson, which begins

> *Lift every voice and sing*
> *Till earth and heaven ring*
> *Ring with the harmonies of liberty.*

The strings of the harp represent Negroes of every type and age, who are "lifting their voices and singing"; the sounding board is the hand and arm of the Creator. The kneeling youth offers the world the gift of song of his people, symbolized by the opening bars of *Lift Every Voice and Sing.*

Miss Savage was born in West Palm Beach, Florida, the daughter of Edward and Cornelia (Murphy) Fells. She attended public school and the State Normal School at Tallahassee. She was interested in sculpturing even as a child and used to model shapes from the red clay found near her home. At a local exhibit of her work she won a special $25 prize. Tourists who saw the exhibit contributed an additional $173, and some of them urged her to come to New York. In 1920 she managed to do so, and there entered Cooper Union, where she studied under George Brewster. What with her art studies, attending high school evenings to make up academic deficiencies and working to earn her board and room she was more than busy, yet managed to complete a four-year course in three years. In 1923 she won one of the one hundred scholarships offered by the French Government to the American Government to be given for study at Fontainbleau, which was retracted when it was learned that she was a Negro. Her compensation came when Herman McNeill offered to take her into his studio for the summer.

Later she did the head of a Negro boy, which she called *Gamin,* and this won for her a Julius Rosenwald scholarship for three successive years, 1929 to 1931. Thereupon she went to Paris for two and one-half years and studied with Felix Beuneteau and at the Grand-Chaumière. Through the aid of the Carnegie Foundation she also had eight months of travel and study in France, Belgium and Germany. She received citations for her work both at the Salon d'Automne and the Salon de Printemps at the Grand Palais, Paris.

AUGUSTA SAVAGE

Though Miss Savage is perhaps best known for her Negro heads, she has not confined her work to these. She has done work in stone, wood carving, painting, applied design and pottery. At an exhibit in the State Museum of New Jersey a carving of hers in wood, *The Chase,* received praise as one of the outstanding pieces of the show. One of her most recent exhibits was a one-man show for six weeks in the spring of 1939, at the Argent Galleries in New York City. Among her 15 works displayed were: *Woman of Martinique,* in Belgian marble; *Sisters in the Rain* (a small group of nuns), in bronze; *Martyr* (a Negro head), in plaster; *The Cat* (a "feline female"), in plaster; *Envy,* a carving in teakwood. Other galleries at which she has exhibited include the Salon d'Automne, Societé des Artistes Français and the Beaux Arts in Paris, the Anderson Galleries in New York City, the Architectural League, the National Association of Women Painters and Sculptors, and a gallery at the Philadelphia Sesquicentennial. She gave the first exhibit by a member of her race at the Douglass High School in Baltimore, Maryland.

Miss Savage has her own galleries, at 143 West 125th Street, New York City. There she not only carries on her creative work, but also gives art lessons. Her studies of African types have helped to stimulate some younger artists, and she has been effective in developing the talents of some of her pupils. She was married to the late Robert L. Poston.

References

Art Digest 9:19 Ap 15 '35 il
Art N 37:22 My 27 '39
Life 5:55 O 3 '38 il por
N Y Herald Tribune p17 F 15 '35 por
N Y Times p28 D 9 '37 por; II p5 D 25 '38; X p8 My 28 '39

(Continued next page)

SAVAGE, AUGUSTA—*Continued*

Locke, A. Negro Art: Past and Present p76-7 1936
Who's Who in American Art
Who's Who in Colored America

SCHECHTER, A(BEL) A(LAN) (shĕk'-tĕr) Aug. 10, 1907- Director of News and Special Events for the National Broadcasting Company

Address: National Broadcasting Co, RCA Bldg, Radio City, New York City; h. 112 Central Park South, New York City

A. A. Schechter is the short, stocky energetic bachelor who directs News and Special Events for the National Broadcasting Company. He has supervised the broadcasts of political conventions, prize fights, ball games, war news. He has arranged a singing mice contest and a talking parrot derby. Through his ingenuity radio listeners have heard the impressions of a deep-sea diver fathoms down, of a jockey streaking down the home stretch. They have heard Tony ("Two-Ton") Galento reading the part of Romeo, cobras hissing, voices from Cheops' tomb in the Great Pyramid. "I yip my head off for more and more good human-interest stories," Schechter explains.

A. A. SCHECHTER

These human-interest stories and much of the history of the early days of radio's newsgathering, together with highlights of Schechter's own saga with NBC, are presented in his book, *I Live on Air*, written with Edward Anthony and published in 1941. Charles Poore of the New York *Times* calls it "the most breezily uninhibited chronicle of alarms and excursions behind the dial's point I have read," and all the other critics call attention to the sense of humor and sense of the dramatic which enliven the book. Columbia Pictures

Corporation is said to be interested in its film rights as well as in the rights to Schechter's previous fictionalized book for boys, *Go Ahead, Garrison* (1940).

The man whose job makes him feel sometimes that he is "the city editor of the whole darn world," was born in Central Falls, Rhode Island, the son of George and Celia (Riven) Schechter, and went to high school there. While getting an education he started covering sports for the Providence *Journal*. This was in 1923, and after he had hung around the office for a while and made himself useful the paper finally hired him. Five years later, after commuting to the Boston University School of Journalism in his spare time, Schechter left the *Journal* for the Newark *Star-Eagle*. He was there only a few weeks, however, before he landed a job on the New York *World* and started covering stories like the Crater case and prohibition incidents.

It was while Schechter was working for the *World* that he engineered one of the first of his world-known scoops. The occasion was the marriage of the son of President Coolidge to the daughter of Governor Trumbull of Connecticut; the necessity was born of Coolidge's determination that reporters were not to be allowed in and were to be handed a printed release only after the ceremony was over. Schechter got the caterer to hire him as a waiter. As he tells it: "I spilled water on some of the guests, and the bride asked me for some water and I said, 'Yes, Ma'am,' and never did come back, but I got a lot of color for my story on the Coolidge wedding."

After the *World* folded, Schechter was with the Associated Press for a short time and then went to International News Service as city editor, the youngest in New York. Six months later, in 1932, he was in the publicity department of NBC, and shortly after was made responsible for the organization of news broadcasts. This was a hard job, for those were the days when the press services were withholding news from the radio. Armed with a telephone, tremendous energy and inability to take "no" for an answer, Schechter proceeded to get enough news to supply Lowell Thomas with adequate scripts. He was soon doing more. He was scooping the press services!

Since then the news department of NBC has grown to employ over 100 people, and Schechter as its head since 1938 has been in charge of broadcasts of Presidential inaugurations, American election coverages, the abdication of King Edward, the coronation of King George VI of England, the Sino-Japanese War, the Spanish War, the Austrian Anschluss, Munich, the Czechoslovakian crisis, the Second World War and all the major national and international events of our time. It was he who was responsible for the exclusive NBC broadcasts of the fall of Shanghai and Nanking and the bombing of the United States gunboat *Panay*; he who arranged the scoop by which James Bowen broadcast the scuttling of the *Graf Spee*. He has been in Addis Ababa, in Egypt, in England. He has informed the world of what is happening in every corner of the globe. And he has, besides, given Americans all those "human-interest stories" which, he feels, draw listeners. In October 1941 he began to share his experience with the Government when he was appointed civilian adviser to the Public Relations Division of the War Department.

All this means that Schechter's life is an enormously busy one, and the description of all he does, as told in the "My Day" chapter of *I Live on Air*, is enough to win admiration from the most hardened newspaperman. In the morning, he tells us, he reads his mail, discusses problems of various stations, answers important complaints. From then on he sees people all day long who have ideas for broadcasts; he sends men out on assignments; he answers questions on the material in scripts (is it incorrect? dangerous? in bad taste?); he talks to correspondents in London, Paris, Egypt, China through the batteries of phones on his desk; and after the day is over he frequently comes back at night for more of the same. "I find it necessary to keep in constant touch with my office," he says, "and never get out of telephone communication with the newsroom." This activity is more noticeable today during the War; but it has always gone on and will continue to go on, war or peace, for there are always special events to be thought up, special broadcasts to be given and special scoops to be made when one is director of News and Special Events for NBC.

References

Schechter, A. A. and Anthony, E. I Live on Air 1941

SCHERER, PAUL (EHRMAN), REV. (shĕr ĕr) June 22, 1892- Clergyman; radio broadcaster

Address: h. 3 W. 65th St, New York City

Describing the notable buildings on Central Park West in New York City, the Baedeker-like Rider's *New York City* (1924) remarks: "At the N. W. corner of 65th St. is the Evangelical Lutheran Church of Holy Trinity (estab. 1868). The present structure, erected in 1902, is in the French Gothic style, with a graceful copper *flêche*." When a reporter visited the church on Palm Sunday 1941 he also noted a bulletin board on the exterior which remarked in large letters that "The Cross Stands Where God Entered the Slums of the Human Heart." This was a sentence from the sermon preached that morning by Pastor Scherer, as he is called according to Lutheran custom.

Pastor Scherer, who in addition to his work in a large and important parish conducts a summer series of radio broadcasts which reaches a varied audience across the continent, has a magnetic personality. He is a man of medium stature but broad-shouldered, with thick iron-gray hair, mobile features which show wrinkles of laughter around his eyes, and a pleasant, resonant voice. During the course of his sermon he quoted from Thomas Hardy and from Eugene O'Neill's play, *Lazarus Laughed*, and enlivened it with a number of

THE REV. PAUL SCHERER

colloquial expressions. Unbelievers are trying to "turn God out neck and crop and leave him like a sucked orange by the wayside," the Pastor remarked, and inquired whether his hearers wanted to see God "go down a third time in a sea of things." Struggling human beings sometimes feel that they have been set down to live their lives on an abandoned farm, he said.

On the following Sunday, Pastor Scherer was the preacher at the United Easter Dawn service under the auspices of the Greater New York Federation of Churches, celebrated in a cathedral setting at the Radio City Music Hall in Rockefeller Center, and assisted by a childrens' choir of 200 voices from the Lutheran Church of the Good Shepherd in Brooklyn. His voice and presence were well adapted to these secular surroundings. He declared in his sermon that the first Easter took place in a world "very like our own today."

Paul Ehrman Scherer was born at Mount Holly Springs, Pennsylvania. His father had the imposing Lutheran name of Melanchthon Gideon Groseclose Scherer, and his mother was Alice Melvina Catherine (Ehrman) Scherer. At barely 19, Paul Scherer received his B. A. degree with first honors from the College of Charleston, South Carolina, and two years later obtained a Master's Degree (*magna cum laude*). By this time he had determined to become a minister, and consequently came back north to study at Mount Airy Theological Seminary, Philadelphia, Pennsylvania, which bestowed its Bachelor of Divinity degree on him in 1916.

Scherer remained at Mount Airy the next year on a research fellowship, and in 1918 went to Holy Trinity Lutheran Church, Buffalo, New York, as assistant pastor for a year. Before leaving Buffalo he married Lilie Fry Benbow of that city—on September 4, 1919. It

SCHERER, PAUL, REV.—*Continued*

was 1920 when he came to the Holy Trinity Lutheran Church as pastor, and he has remained there ever since except for numerous excursions into the field. Mrs. Scherer now sings alto in the choir, and two daughters, Barbara Benbow and Pamela Benbow, take part in the numerous activities of the parish. These include a Semper Fidelis Club, The Couple Club, the Intermediate Luther Leagues, the Men's Club and the Ladies' Aid Society. In April 1941 the younger element was hard at work on the rehearsal of "a most unusual and mysterious play" entitled *A Murder Has Been Arranged*, by E. Williams. After a recent rehearsal, according to *This Week*, the parish bulletin, "Miss Angela Jacobs, the beloved and very capable director of the [Senior Luther] League's many successes, explained: 'The cast is doing marvelously and will be prepared to present a production that everyone will enjoy seeing, one that will compare favorably with many a successful Broadway First-Nighter.'"

Dr. Scherer has lectured at Union Theological Seminary, New York City, where he has been a board member since 1937; at Union Theological Seminary, Richmond, Virginia; and at Gettysburg Seminary in Pennsylvania. He preached in England in the summer of 1930 and 1931, and in 1933 was not only Lutheran Day preacher at the Chicago Century of Progress but was also one of the foremost preachers on the occasion of the celebration of Luther's four-hundredth anniversary. He has given his "Great Preacher" series at Reading and Harrisburg, Pennsylvania and elsewhere, and is a familiar figure at various colleges and universities: Rhode Island State College, Vassar, Columbia, Hamilton, Duke, William and Mary.

His time and talent are also donated to the *Lutheran Laymen's Radio Hour* for the talks which he has delivered over the air from June to October ever since 1932. To make his broadcasts he comes to New York in the summer from the Northfield General Conference in Massachusetts, of which he has been general chairman since 1938, and from the Chautauqua Institute, New York, where he is chaplain.

Pastor Scherer has written extensively, from articles published in church publications, *McCall's, Journal of Religious Education, Record of Christian Work*, and the *Lutheran Quarterly Review*, to the two books in which some of his favorite sermons are collected. *When God Hides* (1934) was one of the most popular titles in "Harpers' Pulpit Series," and the publishers said of *Facts That Undergird Life* (1938) that "in content and presentation, each [of the 29 sermons included] is striking in its appeal to contemporary human beings who are striving to find a way of living that is satisfying to their spiritual needs."

Recognized as one of the foremost American preachers, Pastor Scherer has been the recipient of two honorary degrees: an LL. D. from the College of Charleston in 1935 and a Litt. D. from Wittenberg College, Springfield, Ohio, the next year. He was granted his D. D. degree from Roanoke College, Salem, Virginia, in 1923, three years after he began his career at Holy Trinity in New York City.

The atmosphere of Holy Trinity is far from austere, and Pastor Scherer is frequently found in the social rooms of the church enjoying a game of ping-pong. His only other diversion is playing a strictly amateur game of tennis.

References

> Church Directory of Greater New York
> Who's Who in America

SCHERTZINGER, VICTOR Apr. 8, 1889—Oct. 26, 1941 Film director; composer; said to be first man to write a musical score for a motion picture; directed the first Technicolor production; brought opera music to the films; helped establish screen musicals as popular entertainment; in recent years directed *Road to Zanzibar, Kiss the Boys Goodbye* and many others; composed long list of song hits, the most famous of them *Marcheta*.

References

> International Motion Picture Almanac

Obituaries

> N Y Times p17 O 27 '41 por

SCHILDER, PAUL FERDINAND (shil'dĕr) Feb. 15, 1886—Dec. 8, 1940 Psychiatrist at Bellevue Hospital, New York and research professor of psychiatry at the New York University College of Medicine.

References

> Forum 97:236-38 Ap '37 il
> American Medical Directory
> American Men of Science
> Directory of Medical Specialists 1939
> Who's Who in America
> Who's Who in American Jewry

Obituaries

> N Y Times p19 D 9 '40

SCHLINK, FREDERICK JOHN Oct. 26, 1891- Head of Consumers' Research; author

Address: h. Washington, N. J.

Once upon a time people read advertisements and went shopping in a random sort of way and didn't realize that they were "consumers." That was in the pre-Schlink period, though, the carefree days before everybody started looking for arsenic in the toothpaste and wondering if one brand of tomatoes really should cost twice as much as another. Now for some time at least two organizations have existed solely to tell you what to buy and what to avoid and why, and, more than anyone else, it is "lean, freckled, didactic" Frederick John Schlink who started this trend.

Frederick John Schlink was born in Peoria, Illinois on October 26, 1891, the son of Valentine Louis and Margaret (Brutcher) Schlink. He attended Peoria High School and then went on to the University of Illinois, where he was elected to Sigma Xi, received the degree of Bachelor of Science in 1912, and two years later acquired the degree of Mechanical Engineer, writing his thesis on scientific research for a laboratory instrument he himself invented. His first professional work was in machine design and plant control work, as associate physicist and technical assistant to the director of the United States Bureau of Standards in Washington, D. C. In that position a system of general control was introduced for coordinating and reporting the work going on in the numerous specialized laboratories of the Bureau, and also for facilitating the great volume of technical correspondence involved—especially in answering questions from the military and naval services and from other government departments. This was from 1913 to 1919.

The next year Mr. Schlink held the position of physicist in charge of the instruments-control department of the Firestone Tire and Rubber Company in Akron, Ohio, and here special new methods of test and adjustment were set up and original specifications written for purchase of some of the most widely used types of measuring instruments in the plant. Then in 1920 he accepted another position as mechanical engineer and physicist, doing the designing and testing of apparatus and measuring and testing equipment for the department of the Western Electric Company which later became the Bell Telephone Laboratories; and in 1922 he came to the American Standards Association as assistant secretary, where he worked on all sorts of specifications and methods-of-test questions until 1931.

It was not until 1927 that *Your Money's Worth* was published, written by Mr. Schlink with Stuart Chase. A summary of the "predicament in which competitive advertising and sales pressure place the consumer," it was a Book-of-the-Month Club selection, and immediately brought a stream of letters from readers who wanted help with their problems of selection and purchasing. The book told of the existence of a small local Consumers' Club at White Plains, New York, which Mr. Schlink directed and whose members were banded together to exchange information about various goods. Because of the nation-wide demand for such a service, it was decided to turn the local into a national, and by the end of a year there were 565 members. The organization grew until in 1929 it was issuing printed instead of mimeographed reports, and in December of that year it was incorporated under the name of Consumers' Research, Incorporated.

Consumer advice is one business that expanded with the depression. When people have very little money to spend they want to know exactly what they are spending it for. As the pioneer organization in the field, Consumers' Research, working on a nonprofit basis, aimed to apply impartial labora-

FREDERICK JOHN SCHLINK

tory tests to the advertised claims of trade-marked products and sell the results in printed bulletins. At the time of the stock market crash its membership was around 1,200. In 1930 an "angel" appeared with $10,000; by the autumn of that year there were some 5,200 subscribers; by 1931 there were 25,000; by early 1933, 45,000.

During this period a young man named Arthur Kallet had been on the board of directors, later working as secretary of the organization. He furnished a great deal of promotional advice, and, with Mr. Schlink, co-authored the best-selling *One Hundred Million Guinea Pigs* (1933). Soon after the appearance of this rather hair-raising book, which told the world that many extensively advertised products (from hair dyes to mouthwash) were either useless or dangerous, the long silent consumer became not only indignant but vocal. Nevertheless, in spite of Messrs. Schlink and Kallet's testimony and their lobbying in Washington, in spite of Senator Wagner's (see sketch this issue) support, the Copeland Bill, which was presently advanced in order to make shopping less adventurous, failed to pass Congress.

In 1933 Consumers' Research had moved its laboratories to a lovely hillside near Washington, New Jersey. One summer the country quiet was disturbed by a strike that was to have repercussions for the future—a strike of technicians and office workers in the Consumers' Research plant. There is more than one version of what it was about, but what is certain is that Mr. Kallet was on the strikers' side, Mr. Schlink on the other; that during the strike Mr. Kallet urged the strikers on and publicly attacked the labor policy of Consumers' Research and of Mr. Schlink; that when the National Labor Relations Board issued directions Consumers' Research ig-

SCHLINK, FREDERICK JOHN—*Cont.*

nored them; and that at the end Mr. Schlink retained control of Consumers' Research while Mr. Kallet, aided by other Consumers' Research experts who had been fired or quit, launched the rival Consumers' Union.

It seems also fairly certain that Mr. Schlink was embittered by the fight, convinced that there is a "conflict between the interests of the consumers and organized labor." He didn't object at all when adviser and vice-president J. B. Matthews later began assisting the Dies Committee. And Consumers' Research today makes a point of not reporting the labor conditions under which articles are made: "unbiased reports on such subject matter are not available from any quarter," they say.

Mr. Schlink's last book was *Eat, Drink and Be Wary* (1935), a discussion of food and diet and food adulteration, but the mass of material which Consumers' Research has assembled has also been the basis for books written by others: *Skin Deep*, by M. C. Phillips (who is married to Mr. Schlink); *Partners in Plunder*, by J. B. Matthews and R. E. Shallcross; and *Guinea Pigs No More*, by J. B. Matthews. Mr. Schlink himself has frequently contributed to technical, scientific and economic journals both in the United States and abroad, has written articles for various encyclopedias and has collaborated in many monographs, theses and school and college textbooks related to the technical testing and scientific investigation of goods and appliances used by "ultimate consumers." The special new field of economics known as "consumption economics" and now taught in many schools and colleges developed directly out of the book, *Your Money's Worth*, and the work begun by Consumers' Research.

In the work of Mr. Schlink's organization there is today "constant contact with several hundred scientific and technical workers in colleges, universities and government laboratories, in fields ranging from the testing and rating of scouring powders, hair dyes and nail polish to the testing of electric-motor-driven washing machines and automobile accessories." The work of these experts is carried on and brought to useful and practical form and conclusions by the organization, and so made available for information of the public and of the 60,000-odd subscribers of Consumers' Research. Technical advice and cooperation in the reporting of tests of consumer goods is also given to *Consumers' Digest*, which was originally developed under the auspices of Consumers' Research, but is now published by a separate organization.

Mr. Schlink, who lives with his wife and mother-in-law "in an old farmhouse heated by a kerosene floor burner" located in the beautiful western New Jersey hill country, has many hobbies: studying the new and second-hand markets for types of instruments prized by the mechanically-minded householder; designing and building radio sets and phonograph systems; inventing new and simplified methods of weighing and measuring that can be used by other home laboratory hobbyists

and researchers. He is licensed as a professional engineer, is a member or fellow of numerous professional and specialist societies, and is also a recipient (1919) of the Edward Longstreth Medal of the Franklin Institute, for the invention of a new type of measuring instrument. He and his family, as conscientiously wise and wary consumers, practice what they preach and "scrub their teeth with chalk, their laundry with soap mixed by 'Ma' Phillips," his mother-in-law.

References

Scrib Mag 102:21-6 N '37 por
Time 32:43-5 S 26 '38 por

American Men of Science
Who's Who Among North American Authors
Who's Who in America
Who's Who in Engineering

SCHNEIDER, HANNES (schnī'dẽr hän'-ĕs) 1890(?)- Ski master

Address: North Conway, N. H.

During recent years skiing has become a great American sport. The mountains of New England, the snowy reaches of Sun Valley, the peaks of the Pacific Coast all resound with cries of "track" as swiftly moving skiers negotiate their trails. To Hannes Schneider goes most of the credit for their ability to control their wooden runners and their speed in "schussing." His was the development of the "Arlberg" technique which is almost universally a characteristic of American skiing today.

Hannes Schneider skied almost as soon as he could walk. Born in Stuben, Austria, near the Tyrolean border, the son of a goat herder, his first runners were old barrel staves. On them he won a race for which the prize was his first pair of real skis. Then he was able to go faster, stop shorter, balance himself better. By the time he was 17, in 1907, he was hired as a ski instructor by St. Anton's Hotel Post.

In St. Anton am Arlberg, Schneider soon became aware that the Norwegian way of skiing current then was impractical for the long, steep, irregular Alpine slopes. The upright posture of the Norwegians, knees straight, body taut, lacked adaptability to terrain and, even more important, was difficult to do. Schneider began to ski in a crouch, his knees bent, his weight forward. And he taught the guests at St. Anton to do the same.

Then came the First World War and Schneider served with the Austrian Army, first in Russia and then in the Alps. Through officers he had taught at St. Anton he was able to get the job of teaching skiing to officers in all the Alpine regiments. Teaching them, he perfected his own technique, developing the Stem Christiana as its basic speed turn instead of the Norwegian-preferred Telemark. Hannes Schneider never claimed actually to have invented this technique; it had been used before. But without doubt he was the "first skier who tried to find out its principles, define them and understand them and

Bray

HANNES SCHNEIDER

reduce them to the simplest and most logical maneuvers for teaching purposes."

By 1920 Schneider was recognized as the best *Ski Meister* in the Alps. Hired as the leading man in the German film, *The Wonders of Skiing*, he was able through his magnificent performance to popularize skiing in Central Europe. Encouraged by its success, Hannes Schneider opened his Arlberg School in St. Anton and by 1925 it was the headquarters for most of Europe's skiers, would-be skiers and royalty. There were as many as 3,000 pupils a year, 400 a day, including King Alfonso of Spain, Prince Nicholas of Romania, King Albert of Belgium. There was a staff of 25 assistant teachers.

In 1930 Schneider was asked to visit Japan for one month to teach its royal family, army officers and students how to ski. In return the Japanese Government gave him the Sword of Honor, a fine silk kimono and $10,000. Hannes Schneider was prosperous. With the profits from his school and excursions to teach royalty he built the largest house in St. Anton—with thirteen rooms and two baths; he supported the village band, its school, its hospital, the village itself.

By then Schneider wasn't skiing much himself. His had been a career in which he never lost a downhill race or a slalom and had set marks in cross-country running and jumping. Schneider always ran carefully, avoiding acrobatics and trick stunts, but in 1926 he broke his hip and could no longer enter competitions. Still he continued to be one of skiing's greatest figures. At the indoor ski show at Madison Square Garden in New York in 1936 he was the main attraction; his films on skiing were enormously popular, particularly *The Ski Chase* (it was preceded by *Ski Rhythm*), first shown in the United States in 1938. *The Ski Chase* was called "the best skiing picture to reach these shores," and

Cue's reviewer warned its readers: "If you ski—or hope to—don't miss this."

Shortly after this film opened in New York, Hannes Schneider was arrested. The *Anschluss* between Germany and Austria had come and Schneider had refused to bow to it. Determinedly he tried to keep politics out of his ski school; he refused to fire a Jew; he turned out Nazi agents; he continued to be a devout Catholic. The Nazis, in answer, seized his school and exiled him to Germany under protective custody. He was released only through the protests of ski enthusiasts, and "after 10 months of negotiation on the part of Manhattan banker Harvey D. Gibson" arrived in the United States in February 1939 to continue his teaching at the new Hannes Schneider School at North Conway, New Hampshire.

References

Commonweal 27:708-9 Ap 22 '38
Time 28:31-2 D 21 '36 il por; 33:24+
    F 20 '39 por
Vogue 89:56-7+ Ja 1 '37 pors
Fanck, A. and Schneider, H. Wonders
    of Ski-ing 1933

SCHOFF, HANNAH KENT (shŭf) 1853 —Dec. 10, 1940 Child-aid leader; honorary president for 18 years of the National Congress of Parents and Teachers; editor; author; had devoted much of her time to the cause of underprivileged children; child-labor authority.

References

Who's Who in America
Who's Who Among North American
    Authors

Obituaries

N Y Times p27 D 12 '40

SCHRAM, EMIL (shräm) Nov. 23, 1893- President of the New York Stock Exchange *Address:* b. New York Stock Exchange, New York City

The selection of Emil Schram on May 6, 1941 for the "complicated, responsible and delicate post" of president of the New York Stock Exchange surprised Wall Street. Its first reaction was that the governors of the Exchange had "sold out" to the Administration, that they had, in the words of *Forbes* Magazine, "lost hope, that they have been so whipped that they have no fight left, that they have abjectly surrendered to Federal Bureaucracy." But much of the country at large, and even some of Wall Street, hailed this attempt to "bury the hatchet in a long feud with the Roosevelt Administration" and saw ahead a closer and more effective relationship between the Stock Exchange and the Government.

Emil Schram himself, who on July 1, 1941 took over his duties after a unanimous election and left more than half a dozen Government posts to do so, hastened to affirm this belief. He hoped, he told newspapermen, that there would be cordial relations

EMIL SCHRAM

between the Exchange and the Government and especially the Securities and Exchange Commission. He hastened, too, to allay the fears of those who felt him tarred with the New Deal brush. "I have never been a radical," he said. "Neither," he added, "do I consent to the name conservative—especially if conservative is defined as 'one who will not look at the new moon out of respect for that ancient and honorable institution, the old one.'" Even more reassuringly he announced: "I do not subscribe to the theory of government in business except as an emergency measure. Free markets are a proper and necessary adjunct of the democratic system." He praised "the constructive influence of speculation by informed people who can afford to assume risks."

The man who before his elevation to the presidency of the New York Stock Exchange had never been connected with the securities business was born in Peru, Indiana, the son of second generation German immigrants, Emil Alexander and Katharine (Graf) Schram. He was brought up in Peru and was graduated from high school there in 1911. Immediately he started working for the J. O. Cole Company, which ran a coal and lumberyard and had some farming interests in the state, first as general handy man and later as bookkeeper. But by the time 1915 came around he had acquired a wife, Mabel Miller of Anderson, Indiana, whom he married in 1914 (they now have three sons), and a much more responsible position.

He had become manager of a 5,000-acre tract of swampland in Illinois, in charge of draining, reclaiming and developing it. Within a few years it became profitable cornfields, and Schram himself acquired an interest in the project, now called the Hartwell Land Trust —an interest which he still keeps. Schram's activities spread out into grain elevators and

farming in general, but he remained tremendously interested in drainage, and by 1931 was head of the National Drainage Association. It was through this position that he first became associated with the Federal Government.

Drainage has always been one of the farmer's biggest concerns, and "drainage districts" which issue bonds and collect special taxes for amortization funds have been one solution. When the Reconstruction Finance Corporation was formed in 1932, it found these taxes and bonds a financial problem and set up a Drainage, Levee and Irrigation Division to handle it. In 1933 Schram was chosen to head it and moved to Washington. From handling loans to needy drainage and irrigation districts he was graduated to membership on the board of directors in 1936 and to the management of the RFC's business loan program. On the side, he became president of the Electric Home and Farm Authority and ran its program of financing the sale of electrical appliances.

When Jesse Jones was made Federal Loan Administrator in 1939 he chose Schram to succeed him as chairman of the RFC, and the New York *Times* commented that Schram was "probably the only man in the Government whose work is admired equally warmly by Jesse Jones and Thomas Corcoran"— certainly the only one whose career had been "jointly fostered by this ill-assorted pair." Schram took over the management of the RFC's multifold financial enterprises—supervising the making of loans to organizations as varied as railroads, cities, mink farms, reindeer ranches, mills and factories. Nevertheless he received little publicity, for although he was considered "one of the most capable members of the RFC" he was generally overshadowed by Jesse Jones, who was supposed to be operating the RFC in his capacities as Secretary of Commerce and Federal Loan Administrator. Yet it was he who made rulings as important as his order to retail credit men to work for stable prices and hold down consumer purchases on time.

Schram held a number of positions at the same time—director of the Federal National Mortgage Association, of Federal Prisons Industries, Inc., of the Export-Import Bank of Washington; member of the National Power Policy Commission, president of the Defense Plant Corporation, assistant priorities administrator in the OPM. And from time to time his name came up for still more jobs. One of these suggestions caused much controversy. When the presidency of the Federal Reserve Bank of Chicago became vacant in March 1941, Jesse Jones boosted Schram for the position. Chicago, however, revolted against Washington dictatorship, and after a good deal of publicity Schram lost out.

Jones is supposed to have boosted him again for the presidency of the Stock Exchange after William McChesney Martin, its first paid president, had been drafted into the Army. This time Schram won the $48,000-a-year post, after discussion which centered on his fitness, discussion which took into account both the insight into every type of business he had gained through his RFC position and the fact that he had had no Wall Street experience and had made no conspicuous mark in business, industry or finance. Schram himself accepted the nomination "subject to certain conditions having to do with steps that are now being taken in connection with improving the Administration organization." These conditions included a provision for more authority for the paid personnel and less control of the management by membership committees. And he added that "the presidency of the New York Stock Exchange appeals to me particularly because of the opportunity it affords for public service." Later he told Stock Exchange men that "the answer to [the Exchange's] problem lies in the operation of the Exchange not only as a business enterprise—but in the manner of a public utility as well."

This tall, baldish, blue-eyed, deep-voiced, affable Hoosier is a baseball fan who once had his aides comb New York City for two tickets for a Dodgers-Cardinals double-header. He is definitely not interested in politics: has never been a candidate for office nor boosted anyone else's candidacy. "Not built for it," he explains.

References

Business Week p62-3 My 10 '41 por
Cue 10:20 My 24 '41 por
N Y Herald Tribune p1, 31 My 7 '41 por
Newsweek 17:49 My 19 '41
Time 34:46 Jl 31 '39 por
Who's Who in America
Who's Who in the Nation's Capital

SCHROEDER, R(UDOLPH) W(IL-LIAM) (shrōd'ẽr) Aug. 14, 1886- Vice-president, in charge of safety, United Air Lines

Address: b. United Air Lines, 5959 S. Cicero Ave, Chicago, Ill; h. 2126 Thornwood Ave, Wilmette, Ill.

Ever since he began to fly, back around 1910, Major R. W. Schroeder, a tall lean man "with an expression like the attic window of a haunted house," has been making significant pronouncements. "One, thing aviation needs to be safer is two of everything"; "there is no place for heroes in flying"; "regular flights at higher altitudes make for safety, comfort and speed"—these are only some of them. To-day vice-president in charge of operations of the United Air Lines, for more than 30 years Major Schroeder has developed with the aviation industry.

Back in the days when early opera style horseless carriages were rumbling down Michigan Avenue in Chicago, Schroeder and his mechanic friend, Otto Brodie, began to fly out at the old Clearing field. Schroeder had been born in Chicago, the son of John August and Nora Ann (Reidy) Schroeder, and had attended Crane Technical School for two years. That was all the education he could afford, for his father had died and he had to work. He started in a garage and by 1904 was working as

United Air Lines

R. W. SCHROEDER

an airplane or auto mechanic whenever he got the chance.

After he met Otto Brodie, Schroeder spent many hours watching him coasting along in his Farman "pusher" about 50 feet above the ground. This "slow and low" flying made him shudder until one day he finally crawled into the plane and kidded his friend into flying 600 feet above the ground—the highest a plane had ever gone in Chicago until then. "I realized," Major Schroeder explains, "that the higher you go the more room you have and more time to adjust your plane in case of trouble before you reach the earth. After all, you can perform just about any sort of maneuver in the air without trouble, just as long as you get an even keel before you need to land. So then and there I became an apostle of high-altitude flying and I've never had reason to change." Brodie didn't listen to him, and one day his plane stalled at too low an altitude to recover. Chicago's first "regular" pilot was killed.

Schroeder flew more and more and studied more and more. And then in 1916 he enlisted in the aviation section of the United States Army's Signal Corps. Two years later he was chief test pilot for the Army at Dayton, Ohio, given every type and make of plane to test, making the first flight with oxygen up to 20,000 feet. By 1919 he was a major in the Army and chief of the air corps' field engineering staff. He was also busy making discoveries that have radically improved flying. He went up to 30,000 feet to test his theory of the possibility of higher speeds at higher altitudes —this was a world altitude record. He also interested C. F. Kettering of General Motors in the development of an anti-knock fuel for high compression engines; he conducted the first tests of a controllable pitch propeller and invented one which still pays him royalties;

SCHROEDER, R. W.—*Continued*

he developed and personally tested parachute flares for night landings; he made tests of the first turn indicator and out of that work recommended the same combination of blind flight instruments in use today; and in 1919 he made the first deliberately blind flight in aviation history over a plotted course.

Major Schroeder's experiments with high altitude flights almost cost him his life in 1920 when his oxygen tube failed, his eyeballs froze and his plane went into a dive of six miles in two minutes. His reaction was typical. This, he says, "taught me something. It taught me that sub-stratosphere high altitude flying will be done in a sealed cabin." It also confirmed his belief, despite everything, that "higher flying is safer flying."

In 1920 Major Schroeder left the Army and years later wrote to the Army chief of staff: "Any contributions I have made, any success that I have had in aviation are the result of the training, opportunities and experience given me by the United States Army Air Corps, and I owe my government a debt of gratitude." For a while after his discharge he did barnstorming and air racing, and then in 1921 he settled down as an aviation engineer for the Underwriters' Laboratories. A few years later he organized and operated for the Ford Motor Company the first large commercial airline in this country, carrying passengers, freight and mail, and by 1925 was its superintendent.

Major Schroeder's next position was that of manager of the Guggenheim Safe Aircraft Competition in 1928. One year later he was manager of the Curtiss Flying Service in Chicago, a position he held until 1931, when he became a partner in Sky Harbor Airport. In 1933 he left private industry temporarily to become chief airline inspector of the Department of Commerce, his job the investigation of accidents, particularly. "Orderly, patient and stubborn," aware from his own experience of the many things that might happen to a plane, his was an impressive record. In 1936 he became assistant director of the Bureau of Air Commerce.

In 1937 Major Schroeder left government service to become vice-president, in charge of safety, of the United Air Lines. At United Air Lines he has developed checks, schemes and regulations to make flying increasingly safe and he has continued to initiate and lead research into altitude flying. He has a pretty clear idea of what is coming in aviation. "The big cabins of future planes," he says, "will resemble good sized houses." And the big supercharged planes of this future will probably average 20,000 feet altitude across the country, their air content always the same, making one stop or flying non-stop, carrying from 30 to 40 passengers in lounge chairs or 20 sleeping. As he describes it: "The weather is always good way up there, the riding smooth, and a passenger can lunch in San Francisco and have dinner in New York, with, of course, tea on the plane."

Major Schroeder, known as "Shorty" wherever aviators are found, was married on July 29, 1934 to Janet T. Carr of Chicago, and they have one daughter. His answer to the question "Hobbies, favorite recreation or sport?" was one simple word, "Aviation." It has been rumored, however, that once in a while he dusts off his accordion, which he learned to play years ago. He knows seven pieces and can't learn any more, because when he learns an eighth he forgets the first. "It's just a blind spot in my psychology," he explains.

References

Collier's 100:21+ N 13 '37 pors

SCHULBERG, BUDD (WILSON) (shōōl'-bĕrg) Mar. 27, 1914- Author
Address: c/o Random House, 20 E. 57th St, New York City; h. 1225 Beverly Green, Beverly Hills, Calif.

Budd Schulberg's novel, *What Makes Sammy Run?*, was published on March 27, 1941, his twenty-seventh birthday. Immediately reviewers, even those reviewers who called attention to the book's unevenness, to the debt it owed to other writers, to occasional tendencies toward exaggeration, hailed it as "one of the most interesting and promising first novels to appear in several years."

It is the story of a "heel" in Hollywood, the story of Sammy Glick who gets to the top through cheating, lying, cadging, bullying. Nothing is left out. Sammy appears as copy boy, radio columnist, screen writer, budding genius, playwright and producer, and each step upward is at the expense of someone else. Sammy runs, and the author watches, wonders and finally understands. "I saw Sammy on a battlefield where every soldier was his own cause, his own army and his own flag, and I realized that I had singled him out not because he had been born into the world any more selfish, ruthless and cruel than anybody else, but because in the midst of a war that was selfish, ruthless and cruel Sammy was proving himself the fittest, the fiercest and the fastest."

Sammy's rise is in Hollywood, and everything in Hollywood is in the book, done "with understanding and grim tolerance": the serious artists, the night clubs, the trade paper racket where you buy good reviews; the bankers from New York who own the studios; the studio commissaries full of gossip; the little houses of the little people; the previews; the drinking; the rivalries. Budd Schulberg knows all these things. His mother is Adeline (Jaffe) Schulberg; his father is Benjamin Percival Schulberg, who has been a producer and top-flight executive in Hollywood for more than 20 years; and he himself has been working there off and on since he left college.

Budd Wilson Schulberg even grew up in Hollywood. He was born in New York City, however, and didn't get there until he was five and old enough to enter the kindergarten of the Wilton Place Grammar School. While still in grammar school he wrote a poem ("I'm afraid it was about Jehovah") that moved his mother to tears. "Terrible!" was his father's reaction. But Budd didn't care. From there he went to the Los Angeles High

School, from which he was graduated in 1931, to Deerfield Academy (Massachusetts) and to Dartmouth, which gave him a B. A. in 1936 in spite of the fact that he had "vexed the Tory alumni" by helping the Vermont quarry strikers. Most of the time in school and college Budd was editing his school papers: the *Blue and White Daily* (in which he wrote editorials about keeping the grounds clean), the *Deerfield Scroll* and *The Dartmouth*. And he knew when he left college exactly what he wanted to do.

BUDD SCHULBERG

First of all he married Virginia Ray, a dancer, in 1936. (They now have a daughter, Victoria.) Then he set out for Hollywood, where he had a job as a reader in the David O. Selznick (see sketch this issue) studio's story department and did "under-cover" work on *A Star Is Born* before getting a job as a junior writer. He finally resigned because he wasn't given enough to do. But he was writing stories, too, and eventually they came out in magazines like *Collier's, Liberty, Esquire* and *Story*. By 1940 he had the honor of being included in the late Edward J. O'Brien's Honor Roll for 1939. "I'm not one of those who think Hollywood can destroy you," he says firmly, "unless you are particularly intent on being destroyed. . . I even think it can improve your work, as long as you remember you have other work to do."

Schulberg remembered his other work in the fall of 1940 and set out to write the novel he wanted to write. He limited it to Hollywood, with the idea that if "we can figure out one slice of the world the rest may begin to make sense." He worked on it in Norwich, Connecticut, and when it was finished he returned to Hollywood, where RKO was already making *Passage from Bordeaux,* based

on a novelette he had written. There he plans to work on a new novel—probably one about a prize-fighter. And he will also have the job of dramatizing *Sammy* for Broadway production. A "big-shouldered, heavy-handed" young man who "talks shyly, introspectively, without flashy flourishes," Schulberg is rather proud of the fact that he was once Secretary of the Southern California Pigeon Racing Association "and on a good night can sing every libretto of Gilbert and Sullivan." He insists that his life in Hollywood is fairly simple. It has always been that way, he says. "I don't seem to have done any of those things that sound so exciting on the back flaps of books. I mean I have never harpooned whales off the coast of Alaska or sailed around the world in an open boat or put in a season as a sand hog under the Hudson River." If those are really the things that go with being a successful novelist, undoubtedly the answer most critics would give is: "You will, Budd, you will."

References

N Y Post p3 Jl 8 '41 por
N Y Times Book R p2+ Ag 10 '41 por
PM p47 Mr 30 '41 por; p14 Jl 9 '41 por
Pub W 139:1303-4 Mr 22 '41 por
International Motion Picture Almanac

SCHULTE, KARL JOSEPH, CARDINAL (shōōl'tĕ) Sept. 14, 1871—Mar. 11, 1941 Archbishop of Cologne; was one of the foremost negotiators of the Catholic Church with the National Socialists in Germany; interviewed Adolf Hitler many times but failed to arrive at an understanding and issued pastoral letters denouncing Nazi actions and trends.

References

Tablet 175:375 Ap 20 '40
International Who's Who

Obituaries

Cath World 153:108-9 Ap '41
N Y Times p22 Mr 12 '41

SCHUSTER, MAX LINCOLN *See* Simon, R. L. and Schuster, M. L.

SCOTT, RAYMOND Sept. 10, 1909- Composer; bandleader

Address: c/o Music Corporation of America, 745 Fifth Ave, New York City

"This Raymond Scott," wrote Carleton Smith, "is a press agent's natural. He suggests spoons in tones, does musical portraits of cows, fences, weeds, wrote a study on the feel of a thimble, a coin, a telephone." The latest creation of his fertile imagination is "silent" music in which, says *Time*, "the only sound from the stage is a rhythmic swish-swish from the drummer, a froggy slap-slap from the bull-fiddler, a soft plunk-plunk from the pianist. . . It was just

RAYMOND SCOTT

provocative enough to make listeners wonder whether the silence of other bands might sound better than Scott's. But the stunt showed that Mr. Scott still had his bid in as the most elfin of United States bandsters."

Ushering in his career with a "quintet" that contained six men, and a name out of the telephone directory—he was born Harry Warnow, brother of bandleader Mark Warnow of the *Hit Parade* show—Scott wrote brittle interpretative jazz pieces with titles like *Twilight in Turkey* and *Reckless Night on Board an Ocean Liner*. In the past year he has enlarged his band to 14 men, retaining the six-piece unit within the compass of the larger orchestra. The band plays dance music that often sounds "danceable" and even somewhat conventional, but it specializes in the descriptive effects, tone shadings and dynamics that made famous the music of the smaller group.

"Meeting Scott," Carleton Smith informs us, "you're surprised. Thickset, stubby, swarthy, his chief trait is his adolescence. At moments he's neither aware of himself nor of the world. He's no windbag. Nor does he act like a mad screwball. He doesn't smoke or drink. He smiles seldom and often runs his fingers through his shock of upstanding hair. Brooklyn-born, he gives off that same eerie, out-of-the-world charm found in the Dodgers." Scott is five feet ten inches tall, weighs one hundred-eighty pounds, has black hair and very dark brown eyes.

Scott's tendency to label things began during his boyhood. Given to experiments in sound techniques, he and his brother had all sorts of microphones and wires strung about their room, and Scott dubbed the hobby "creative acoustics." He was mood-conscious, as well, and arranged special lighting effects so that he might practice scales in blue, green and orange rooms. His musical likes ran to descriptive music such as Tschaikovsky's *1812 Overture*,

with its booming cannon, or the rolling sea of Debussy's *La Mer*.

His father, Joseph Warnow, had been a violinist in Russia (his mother was Sarah [Small] Warnow), and his older brother Mark was already prominent as a conductor-composer when Scott was graduated from Brooklyn Technical High School. At graduation exercises he played his own piano composition, *Metropolis*. The merits of it so impressed Mark that he sent his younger brother to the Institute of Musical Arts, New York City. The first public performance of the work of Raymond Scott took place in 1932, when brother Mark played *Xmas Night in Harlem*.

It was several years before what *Down Beat* called Scott's "huckleberry music" came into its own. Meanwhile he thought up curiously descriptive tunes to amusingly whacky titles because his mind ran that way. Somehow it seemed less dull than the standard dance music, innocuously titled. But Scott had only a limited circle of boosters, of whom CBS producer Phil Cohan was one. For such titles as Scott chose there was some slight precedent in the classical world (Prokofiev's [see sketch this issue] *Love of Three Oranges*) but in the jazz world one found them only as the exceptions (Forsythe's *Serenade to a Wealthy Widow;* Armstrong's *King of the Zulus at a Chitlin' Rag*).

In the 1930's Scott was a house pianist for CBS. He had the appearance of being shy and sensitive, and seemed a little moody at times. He played like a "blues" pianist, his fingers touching the keys lightly and his ear inclined to subtle nuances of tone. In June 1936 the group he played with on a 15-minute jazz spot moved, almost intact, into the band spot on the first network jazz program on the air, *Saturday Night Swing*. In the band, among others, were mustachioed Jerry Colonna, now a Hollywood film star (trombone), Bunny Berigan, now a bandleader, on trumpet, and the famous trap man, Johnny Williams, on drums. The "Quintet" as such was a nucleus of men from this band, and had its bow early in 1937 with *Twilight in Turkey*.

From then on the rise of Raymond Scott, his "Quintet" and his "huckleberry music," was phenomenal—in the best Broadway meaning of that term. In April his first records were waxed, and in August Darryl Zanuck (see sketch this issue) signed him for a year's work at 20th Century-Fox, Hollywood. *Toy Trumpet*, featured in a Shirley Temple picture, became the hit novelty tune of the year, and his adaptation of a Mozart theme, which he called *In An 18th Century Drawing Room*, had a prompt and—for Tin Pan Alley—surprisingly enduring prosperity. By August 1938, Scott and his men had worked in *Ali Baba Goes to Town; Sally, Irene and Mary; Happy Landing;* and *Rebecca of Sunnybrook Farm*. But he was temporarily off Hollywood, reportedly because he didn't approve the costumes in which a producer wished to dress the "Quintet." At any rate the East also had tempting offers, so Scott came back to New York and for the CBS network created a unique jazz laboratory, experimenting with toy trumpets, table tops, sea shells, wire whisks and even buckets of water.

"None of Scott's pieces," the composer said in an interview (he sometimes uses the third person in talking of himself) "are *written* by him. He doesn't compose notes—he composes sounds, tone variations." In creating numbers the band makes stacks of acetates (play-back records), and when a satisfactory one is made the number is transcribed from it. His instructions are not unlike his titles. "Play this loud," he might say, "as loud as you can play it, but no louder than you can play it soft." This is known in the Scott lexicon as "shock excitation."

"Crisp" is Raymond Scott's favorite adjective, and it describes his music. Succinct in statement and relatively free of the clichés that usually beset novelty dance music, it has attracted such discerning listeners as Stravinsky, Heifetz, Whiteman and Duke Ellington (see sketch this issue). Even when tinkering with the rhythm to suggest the waddle of a "Huckleberry Duck"—which turns out to be a duck that likes huckleberries—Scott keeps the crispness. Critic Carleton Smith thinks that he does so partly by driving his men like a drill sergeant and says he can be "unreasonable, demanding, petty about details," but the same has been said of many a conductor in what Mr. Scott's friends call the "longhair" division. The point seems to be that he wants his music a certain way, clearly expressed and technically solid, yet with real feeling, or, as he puts it, "spoiled, not perfect like Kostelanetz."

Scott's tunes are amusingly descriptive, sometimes a formidable task in view of the titles he gives them. Ten transcontinental air trips made him sensitive to the bumpy weather over Newark, New Jersey. Certain sounds and sensations accompanied this situation. The tone of the motor changed as the plane dropped and rose in the air pockets, and there was a definite rhythm to the hostess' repeated instruction, "Fasten your safety belts, please." Ergo, Mr. Scott composed a tune for the world's only six-man quintet, and it was appropriately called *Bumpy Weather Over Newark*.

War Dance for Wooden Indians was slightly more extreme. It was, he explained, "based on a real legend. It seems there's an old abandoned warehouse in a city in Oklahoma, full of wooden Indians. Once a year at midnight, they go into a war dance." And where, Mr. Scott was asked, had he heard the legend? Scott replied, unblinkingly: "I made it up."

Since his *Xmas Night in Harlem* Scott has turned out more than 25 successful numbers in like genre. In October 1939 his band was increased to standard name band dimensions and presented over CBS. In February 1940 the Ballet Theatre put on a six-scene operetta based on Scott's music, and late that year Scott discovered "silent" music.

In 1935 Scott married Pearl Stevens, a petite, pretty brunette. They have one daughter, Carolyn Scott Warnow. He met his wife as the result of a hunch. Friends described her, and Scott asked for her phone number. He phoned her the next day, making a recording

of the conversation. When she was about to hang up, he switched on the play-back. Soon after that they were married.

Raymond Scott, like his brother Mark Warnow, has a reputation for absent-minded and/or "whacky" deeds—lacing his shoes before he puts them on, refusing to sign a lease because a landlord won't let him park his limousine in the drawing room, etc. Whether these are fact or fiction, they fit into the public's idea of an almost normal home life for someone capable of writing a *Duet for Pistol and Piano* or *Dinner Music for a Pack of Hungry Cannibals*. Other stories tell of a more serious side, for Scott is more than a hobbyist in his sound experiments, some of his acoustical ideas having gone into practical usage. He is also conscientious in projecting his musical brain children. Mrs. Scott listens to them, and if one sounds even vaguely like another tune, it is discarded. Scott also shows his music to brother Mark, whose opinion is valued highly by the young composer and who grades it by percentage.

Surprising to music fans who might suppose his inventive and organizational talent to be channeled only into the field of composition is the knowledge that Scott is a business executive who operates a record company and a music publishing firm.

References

Am Mag 127:82 F '39 il por
Collier's 102:22+ Jl 23 '38 por
Liberty 18:54-5 Ja 8 '41 por
N Y World-Telegram D 22 '39
New Yorker 10:8 Ag 20 '38
Time 32:37 S 12 '38 por; 37:53 Mr 3 '41

SEABURY, DAVID Sept. 11, 1885- Psychologist

Address: b. 124 E. 40th St, New York City; h. 47 Narragansett Ave, Ossining, N. Y.

Perhaps the hardest man to see in New York is also one of the most approachable. If you want to consult David Seabury you must make an appointment months in advance. Yet he spends most of a long working day just seeing people.

The reason is that there are so many perfectly normal people with worries they want to talk over with "the normal man's psychologist." If you are a neurotic or a psychotic, it is easy to find a psychiatrist or a psychoanalyst who is interested in your case. If you want to be told a series of platitudes and merely ordered to cheer up, there are plenty of so-called psychologists to consult. But David Seabury is interested in the practical psychology of the normal human being, in the discovery and assembling of mental resources to create greater power and efficiency, in emotional education and the adjustment of personal and social relationships.

Not many people realize that David Seabury was originally David Dresser. His father was Julius Alphonsus Dresser, a pioneer of "mental healing"; his brother was Horatio W. Dresser, the founder of "New Thought"; his mother was the former Annetta Seabury. He himself

DAVID SEABURY

legally adopted his mother's name of Seabury as his surname, perhaps because his psychological theories were at variance with those of his father and brother, perhaps merely not to be confused with them.

David Seabury was born in Boston and grew up in a home where the names of William James, Josiah Royce and George Santayana were household words. Miss Alice Longfellow ("grave Alice" of her father's poem, *The Children's Hour*) was interested in him as a boy and encouraged him as a young man. His early education was in the historic Chauncey Hall School in Boston; then at 13 he was sent to the Scuola Bettini Recasoli in Florence, Italy, for a year. Returning to America, he studied under private tutors for four years, for two years was a special student at Harvard, then, at Miss Longfellow's suggestion, spent five more years in special study and research in Paris, London, Munich and Rome. He has no college degree, a rare thing for a consulting psychologist of his standing, but he is very far from a mere "popularizer" or a superficial adviser on psychological problems.

When Mr. Seabury finally returned to his native country for good, he settled in New York, where he began practice as a consulting psychologist in 1914. A year later he went to Indiana as consulting psychologist of the Culver Military Academy. In 1916 he was psychological examiner and lecturer for the R. O. T. C. at Fort Benjamin Harrison. He soon began to be known as a lecturer, and now gives up to 100 lectures a year. For many years he has given an annual course of lectures for the members of Town Hall, Incorporated, in New York City.

In 1923 Mr. Seabury was married to Florence Guy. Their home is in Ossining, New York, a beautiful country town. He has little time to enjoy its beauties, however, since he not only keeps long office hours full of interviews with clients but manages to get in several long lecture tours every year, and since 1924 has published 14 books. His lectures and books presented in non-technical language are solidly grounded on his clinical experience.

His first book, *Unmasking Our Minds* (1924), was very popular. It was four years later, however, in 1928, before he had leisure to publish another, *Growing Into Life*. In 1934. after another long interval, *What Makes Us Seem So Queer?* appeared. Since then the books have come faster: *Keep Your Wits* (1935); *How To Worry Successfully* (1936); *Help Yourself To Happiness* and *The Art of Selfishness* in 1937; *Build Your Own Future*, *Adventures in Self-Discovery* and *How To Get Things Done* (with Alfred M. Uhler) in 1938; *See Yourself As Others See You* and *Why We Love and Hate* in 1939; and *How Jesus Heals Our Minds Today* (1940). Many of these books were originally given as lectures and later worked out in book form.

Mr. Seabury calls his psychological system Centralism, and is the founder of the Centralist School of Psychology. "The only hope of civilization," he says, "lies in the application of psychology to everyday life, to business problems, to friendship, and to marriage." As consultant, as lecturer and as writer, he is chiefly concerned with making people realize things about themselves which they have never properly understood before, and then with getting them to apply this new knowledge to their day-to-day problems and relationships. As evidence of how closely he keeps in touch with the present, he has added a new lecture to his course on the psychology of peace and war. He has no children of his own, but he is keenly interested in young people, and has been particularly successful as a consulting psychologist in dealing with the problems of adolescent boys and girls.

Many of our troubles, he thinks, come from a misuse of the imagination, which should be our most useful servant. He himself is a lover of imaginative literature, especially of the drama, and one of his lectures is on modern drama from the psychological angle. The proper training of emotion, which may be our greatest strength or our greatest weakness, is another of his foundation stones. His whole work is oriented toward the establishment of self-critical judgment and self-administered mental hygiene, with the aim not only of making our lives pleasanter and more effective, but also of preventing the development of neuroses, "nervous breakdowns," and mental quirks.

In appearance, Mr. Seabury bears a striking resemblance to pictures of Shakespeare—as much so, almost, as did the late Sir Hall Caine. His hair has retreated from a high forehead, and he wears a full mustache and a Vandyke beard, both now well tinged with gray. His eyes are deep-set, with the horizontal bar across the top of the nose which so often marks the deep thinker. If one were to search for words to describe his personality the first to come to mind would be "informal", "direct", "practical" and "cheerful." There is nothing of the Pollyanna about David Seabury. Scholarly without being heavy, his books read like what they really are—talks with a man of keen mind and vast experience, who likes people and wants to help them.

Asked by an interviewer how he became first interested in psychology, Mr. Seabury looked bewildered. "Why," he finally said, "I grew up in it. Psychology is as native to me as my mother tongue, or as the customs we all learn as children. In our household, it was a custom we learned as children. The surprising thing would have been if I had become anything except a psychologist."

References

Time 28 :88 S 14 '36 por

Who's Who Among North American Authors

Who's Who in America

SELASSIE, HAILE, I *See* Haile Selassie I, Emperor of Ethiopia

SELDES, GEORGE (sĕl'dĕs) Nov. 16, 1890- Author; journalist
Address: b. 19 University Pl, New York City; h. Grist Mill Rd, Norwalk, Conn.

Nearly all his life George Seldes has been carrying on a battle for freedom of the press —freedom to print news as it happens without fear of censorship or distortion for the benefit of advertisers, or stockholders, or the fostering of any particular view in the minds of the public. More than 30 years' experience either trying to get the truth (as he sees it) into the newspapers or trying to get his books reviewed haven't made him any more resigned to the things a none-too-docile reporter finds himself up against. If anything, his indignation has increased with time, perhaps because he sees democracy as impossible without a truly free press, and Fascism as a danger more immediate than ever.

Born in Alliance, New Jersey on November 16, 1890, the son of George Sergius and Anna (Saphro) Seldes, George Seldes found himself in a Utopian colony started by his father, who acted as postmaster, teacher and justice of the peace. It didn't last long after his birth, however, and he went on to attend a perfectly non-Utopian high school in Vineland, New Jersey and the East Liberty Academy in Pittsburgh. He was 18 when he spent his first morning in a newspaper office—the office of the Pittsburgh *Leader*. "Timid, scared, but happy," he confided to the city editor: "My view of journalism is that it is the finest profession on earth. On the freedom of the press all our liberties are built." "Rats!" replied the city editor, who went on to tell him a thing or two. After the first day he didn't need much telling; his first story had been changed to please an advertiser. And after that he learned fast. He still remembers how a case involving the Mellons was so completely sup-

GEORGE SELDES

pressed that even the telegraph companies wouldn't send it over their wires.

After working as a reporter on the *Leader* and as copy desk and night editor on the Pittsburgh *Post* young Seldes decided to go on to college with $675 that he had saved. He picked Harvard (as did his brother Gilbert), spent a year from 1912 to 1913 as a special student—possibly the only pupil of George Pierce Baker who never wrote a play—and then went back to the *Post*. When the First World War began he was writing the headlines most of the time and putting the city edition to bed. In 1916 he became managing editor of *Pulitzer's Review* in New York City.

In October 1916 he went as a free-lance to England, covered the "front," became an assistant in the London office of the United Press, and when the United States finally declared war both he and his brother went to the Embassy and registered for war service. July 1917 found him serving as the entire reportorial staff of the Army edition of the Paris Chicago *Tribune* (of which he was later managing editor) and, one week later, as a member of the press section of the American Expeditionary Force. "We all more or less lied about the War," he says, and tells how "on Armistice Day four of us took an oath on the battlefield that we would tell the truth the rest of our lives, that we would begin telling the truth in time of preparation of war, that we would do what was humanly possible to prevent the recurrence of another such vast and useless horror. Then we all went back to prosaic reporting in America."

He didn't go back, however. He stayed in Europe as assistant to the London correspondent of the *Tribune* in 1919, and he was for nearly 10 years the nominal head of the Berlin Bureau of that paper. But the greater part of his time wasn't spent in Berlin. During the post-War period he investigated the Irish disturbances and interviewed all the Irish

SELDES, GEORGE—*Continued*

heroes, including Michael Collins and Figgis; he was in Italy in 1920 for the Fiume adventure and the so-called Red uprising (he was expelled); he was in Germany that same year for the Kapp *Putsch*. He smuggled news out of Moscow during the famine-days of 1922 and 1923 and was asked to leave the last year; he was expelled from Italy again in 1925 for being the first to report that Mussolini was "the military arm of the chambers of commerce and the manufacturing associations of Italy and that he personally was implicated in the assassination of the leading rival politician" (Matteotti).

Through 1925 and 1926 he was the only American correspondent with the French Army in Syria during the entire war, had a world scoop on the bombardment of Damascus, was accused by the French of starting a mutiny in the Foreign Legion when he interceded to save the life of a deserter, and was threatened with disembowelment by the Arabs on the charge that his dispatches were pro-French. He scooped the Vienna Revolution of 1927, too, and that same year investigated Mexico and discovered the falsity of the Avila documents.

During these years he had covered "wars, uprisings, peace conferences, assassinations and coronations of kings" and watched "the dictators on the march to power" in Europe and the Balkan and Baltic States. They were years of "continual struggle with censorship." He came out with a strong hatred of Fascism, only equalled by his hatred of war and its makers, and also the beginnings of an understanding of the forces in every country that threaten democracy. In 1929, the year after he resigned from the *Tribune,* he published *You Can't Print That.* Largely concerned with those European years, with suppressed stories about such figures as Lenin, Mussolini, Von Hindenberg, Von Ludendorff, Queen Marie, d'Annunzio, Bratianu, Masaryk, Beneš—most of whom he had interviewed—it touched only lightly on the status of freedom of the press in the democracies. It was favorably reviewed and widely read, and the same year saw the publication of the British edition of the book.

Then came the period that Seldes describes as characterized by depression and panic, the rise of the "public utility propaganda system," the NRA, the New Deal, new labor unrest, "new danger of dictatorship." And of growing nationalism and frantic preparation for war— in 1931 Seldes was already predicting world conflict for the early 1940's. *Can These Things Be!* (1931); *Sawdust Caesar* (written in 1932 and published in 1935), the inside story of Mussolini's rise to power, rejected by 24 publishers before printed; *World Panorama, 1918-1933* (1933); *The Vatican: Yesterday, Today, Tomorrow* (1934); *Iron, Blood and Profits* (1934), concerned with the "munitions racket"; and *Freedom of the Press* (1935) were published, each a little more toward the Left than the last in its point of view.

Seldes was listed as an editor of the now defunct magazine, *Ken,* when it started out with brave designs; he withdrew shortly afterward. Then, from December 1936 to May 1937, he was war correspondent in Spain for the New York *Post.* To his mind the things he had seen all tied up at last: he returned to write a book not so much about Spain and Franco as what he described as "a survey of the forces attempting, in the name of patriotism, to make a desert of the Bill of Rights" in the United States (*You Can't Do That,* 1937). This book the *Christian Century* and the *Churchman* found required reading, although the *Saturday Review of Literature* reviewer found it too exclusively preoccupied with the rights of labor.

In 1938 came *Lords of the Press.* Both more liberally documented and more sensational than *Freedom of the Press,* it attempted to find a relation between the interests (financial and otherwise) of the various publishers or owners of American newspapers, newspaper chains and press associations and the particular news-bias which Seldes found in their columns. His conclusions were generally unflattering; Roy Howard, the New York *Times,* the New York *Herald Tribune* came in for a large share of criticism. Most book reviewers ignored it, although various organizations sent letters asking those who had remained silent about their reasons and future intentions. Of those who did review it, Stanley Walker of the *Herald Tribune Books* found it filled with "hysteria, malice, innuendo and invective." On the other hand, the New York *Post* printed one-third of an "entirely favorable review"; William Allen White's son praised it in the *New Republic*; Charles Beard (see sketch this issue) and John Dewey sent letters of approval. And it has probably reached a wider audience than any of Seldes' other books except *You Can't Print That.*

Seldes' most recent books have been *The Catholic Crisis* (1939); and *Witch Hunt,* (1940). In May 1940 the first issue of his first publishing venture—a four-page weekly newsletter, *In Fact*—appeared. Seldes had said: "What I want to do is publish a magazine telling the truth. . . I would like to do what Lincoln Steffens did and I don't mind being called a muckraker." Among its purposes are, he says, to publish "the real inside news, the kind newspapers frequently get but dare not print"; to "fight Fascism." He says further: "The viewpoint of *In Fact* is simple: it is in favor of every idea, movement and organization that is for what we carelessly call liberalism, democracy, progress, but it intends to show up the frauds which hide behind these words; it is pro-labor, and especially pro-progressive labor. It believes in the 'general welfare' as written in the Constitution and challenges any publication feeding out of the hand of Big Business to prove by acts that its policy is the same." It is very definitely far to the Left of Center, and has not escaped charges of bias, however.

Mr. Seldes is married to Helen Larkin Wiesman of St. Louis, Missouri (whom he met in Paris). He has frequently contributed to various magazines: *Harper's, Scribner's, Saturday Evening Post* and *McCall's*, as well as to liberal and radical weeklies, *The Nation, New Republic* and *New Masses*. Only something world-shaking can make him speak on a public platform, however.

References

New Repub 98:33-4 F 15 '39
Wilson Lib Bul 13:366 F '39 por
Seldes, G. Freedom of the Press p19-38 1937
Who's Who in America
Who's Who in Journalism

SELFRIDGE, H(ARRY) GORDON Jan. 11, 1864(?)- English department store executive

Address: b. Selfridge and Co, 400 Oxford St, London, W. 1, England; h. Brook House, Park Lane, London, W. 1, England

The German *Blitzkrieg* against England did not spare Oxford Street, one of London's greatest shopping centers. One of the stores that "caught it" was the famous house of Selfridge and Company, though business has long since been going on there as usual. Selfridge's big pillared palace of commerce is one of the sights of London and one of the Capital's institutions. It has an information bureau that will tell you in two minutes what horse won the Derby in 1903, when Siam decided to call itself Thailand, what disease Henry VIII died of, and the location of the barber shop nearest to the place from which you are phoning. It has the biggest and highest roof garden in England; its services extend from safe deposits to silk stockings. And this store, the chief office of a big chain of general stores throughout England, is the creation of an American, Harry Gordon Selfridge.

At the age of 39 Selfridge had made some $1,500,000 in America and decided to retire. But he found retirement a bore and went back into business, this time in England. It was not until 1939 that he retired again to take the "inactive, empty post" of president of Selfridge's. And his retirement this time was a good deal less spectacular. Selfridge's, once an enormously profitable concern, has been showing only slight profits for the past few years, and Harry Selfridge left owing it £114,000. Although he had called Hitler a great patriot in 1937, he could blame him for part of his troubles. But there were other reasons, too, among them "an ill-timed expansion scheme" of eight years before. When in 1941 the company was reorganized he was retained as "consultant" at £2,000 a year, over the objections of a number of stockholders who felt the present financial condition of the firm was his fault.

Selfridge was unperturbed by this situation. He continued to work on his biography of the fifteenth-century Florentine trader Cosimo de Medici, and he continued to keep his faith in business as "a wonderful adventure, the greatest fun on earth." Always he has maintained: "I enjoy every minute of business," and this has been his consistent attitude throughout his whole career—throughout its ups and downs.

H. GORDON SELFRIDGE

If any one should suggest that a "business is fun" attitude is easy to understand in the boss of a big concern, Selfridge would probably answer, first, that he began as an employee and a humble one at that; second, that in his store everything is done to make life pleasant for the staff. Employees are given every help for diversion and encouraged, not driven, in their work. "Believe me," Selfridge once told an interviewer, "it is the worst policy to be too harsh with the young. . . Nothing pays worse than savaging employees. Rap a boy or girl over the knuckles unsympathetically and brutally in the morning and you get no more good out of him or her for the rest of the day." Selfridge is also credited with having said that if an employee does not win promotion in three years "there is something wrong with him—or with us." That the employees appreciate policies like these is evidenced by their presentation to Selfridge of a portrait bust of himself by Sir Thomas Brock, R. A., in 1914.

Selfridge is, in the words of the *Manchester Guardian*, "agreeable, unconventional and accessible, and clever in concealing his cleverness. He is also a man of the most ebullient optimism and tireless energy." There are those who like to believe this energy derives from his New England ancestry. Harry Gordon Selfridge was the only son of Robert O. Selfridge and Lois Frances (Baxter) Selfridge. His father was a New Englander who fought on the Northern side in the Civil War and died soon after the birth of his son in Ripon, Wisconsin.

When Harry was a year old his mother took him to Jackson, Michigan, where she

SELFRIDGE, H. GORDON—*Continued*

worked as a schoolteacher. Harry went to the public schools there and spent his vacations working at all sorts of odd jobs. His mother trained him carefully; she used to tell him stories which, "instead of beginning . . . with 'once upon a time' as a preface to a tale of bygone days . . . always looked to the future. 'Supposing, Harry,' she would say, 'that you were a man who had worked his way up and had made a fortune, let us suppose how you would live.'" Mrs. Selfridge lived long enough to find out.

Harry left school at fourteen to work in a bank and stayed there for two years as junior clerk. Then came a short spell as bookkeeper at a factory. By this time he had the necessary Congressman's nomination for Annapolis, but was turned down because he was a quarter of an inch too short. Finally in 1880 he made his real start—with the Chicago mail-order firm of Field, Leiter and Company, which later became the famous house of Marshall Field and Company. He began at $10 a week, mostly traveling. When, a year later, he was offered another job, Field gave him a salary increase and made him deputy manager of a department.

After he had been with Marshall Field almost six years—he was twenty-two then—Selfridge looked over the catalog of a Boston dry goods house and decided it had some good ideas in it for Marshall Field. He went to Boston, and from there to New York and Philadelphia, picking up suggestions, most of which were soon put to use in Chicago. It wasn't long before he had taken over the retail side of the firm, and, still in his middle 20's, was earning $5,000 a year. Journeys to Europe came next; and with them more new ideas—even the idea of starting his own business. Field, appalled at the idea, stepped his salary up to $20,000 at one stroke and in 1892 made him a junior partner in the firm. Then in 1903, when he was 39 and had made a fortune, Selfridge retired.

Selfridge traveled a little, looked after his fine collection of orchids and frequented the Chicago clubs. But he was bored: politics didn't interest him; he was still on the bright side of 40 and full of energy. Then he had a chance to acquire the Chicago firm of Schlesinger and Mayer. He took it, and after some months sold out again to Carson Pirie Scott & Company, having cleared a profit of $250,000. He says he is the only man ever to buy a business from five Jews and sell it to seven Scotchmen at a profit. It was 1906 when he went to London and, after thinking about it for a while, decided to start over again in business there.

The great Selfridge business was started at the west end of Oxford Street. For 10 months 1,500 workmen labored at the construction, which cost something like a million dollars, and finally in March 1909 the store was opened to a fanfare of advertising for its 130 departments. In the first year it sold some five million dollars' worth of goods and went right on from there. It was a social

center with reading rooms, rest rooms and a roof garden, as well as a place of commerce. Selfridge insisted that visitors shouldn't be pressed to buy but should be considered welcome guests even when they bought nothing. He attracted them to his store by skillful advertising and little semi-philosophical, beautifully written essays in the London *Times* signed "Callisthenes."

Then after the First World War a number of provincial and London suburban stores were taken under the Selfridge wing, though allowed to retain their distinctive characters. Selfridge himself had by that time written a book called *The Romance of Commerce* (1913) and he continued to live his belief in that romance. He also delivered himself in his years as head of his stores of a number of dicta: "Imagination is one of the very greatest secrets of success. I rank it almost as high as enthusiasm," is one. Another is, "The old homely adage about 'honesty being the best policy' sums up the wisdom of the world. Men sneer at copybook maxims, but if we all acted on them we would get along better than we do at present."

Selfridge lived first in Arlington Street and then in Portman Square, both "good addresses," not far from his business. Later he took the aristocratic Lansdowne House, and later still he moved to Carlton House Terrace. Today he has a flat in Park Lane, among the dukes. His speech, despite all his addresses and years spent as a popular host, still bears traces of America. In fact, it wasn't until May 6, 1937 that Selfridge became a British citizen.

In 1890 he married Rose Buckingham of Chicago, who died in 1918. There are three daughters and one son, H. Gordon Selfridge, Jr., now his father's successor at the head of the business.

References

Sat Eve Post 208:18-19+ Jl 27 '35;
  208:18-19+ Ag 10 '35; 208:26-7+ Ag
  24 '35; 208:30+ S 7 '35
Time 30:64+ O 18 '37 por; 34:73 N 13
  '39 por; 37:65 F 3 '41 por
Times [London] My 7 '37

Author's and Writer's Who's Who
Bridges, T. C. and Tiltman, H. H.
  Kings of Commerce p219-27 1928
Hodson, J. L. No Phantoms Here
  p221-7 1932
Who's Who
Who's Who Among North American
  Authors
Who's Who in America
Who's Who in Commerce and Industry

SELZNICK, DAVID O(LIVER) May 10, 1902- Motion-picture producer

Address: b. David O. Selznick Productions, Inc, Culver City, Calif; h. 9336 Washington Blvd, Beverly Hills, Calif.

David O. Selznick, second-generation producer, has made a long string of hits since he entered the film industry as a boy in 1921, but he may never get over the experience of making *Gone With the Wind*. He doesn't like to hear *Rebecca* preferred to the fabulous *GWTW*, though he got "Oscars" for producing both. "That makes me furious," Selznick once said (with a grin). "I really am furious—every time I hear that. And don't think I haven't heard it. At least 50 people have said it to me, and each time I go into a regular rage. There is nothing infuriates me so much. . . It was such a stupendous undertaking. Anything else, no matter what we'll ever make, will always seem insignificant after that."

During the last decade Selznick's successes have included: *Dinner at Eight, Dancing Lady* (MGM 1933); *David Copperfield* (MGM 1934); *Anna Karenina, A Tale of Two Cities* (MGM 1935); *Little Lord Fauntleroy, A Star Is Born* (Selznick-International 1936); *Prisoner of Zenda* (Selznick-International 1937); *Nothing Sacred* (United Artists 1937); *The Adventures of Tom Sawyer* (United Artists 1938); *Intermezzo* (United Artists-Selznick 1939); *GWTW* (Selznick-MGM 1940); and *Rebecca* (Selznick-International 1940). As prize getters Selznick pictures have always been successful, but the last-named picture established a record—it accounted for 10 of the 17 major "Oscars" in 1940.

"Mr. Selznick's big effort of 1941," predicts Duncan Underhill, "will be *Claudia, Jane Eyre* or an original by W. Somerset Maugham. The betting is that he will shoot the works on *Jane Eyre*." There is also the possibility that Selznick will produce a story on which Theodore Dreiser is now working, one that will serve as a vehicle to carry the tunes written by his brother Paul. Mr. Selznick is free to do any or none, renting out his high-priced stars to other studios while he makes up his mind. For he is now his own boss. Selznick-International, formed in 1935 with the backing of the wealthy John Hay (Jock) Whitney and a group of bankers, was dissolved in August 1940, "with profound regret . . . that the risks involved, due to world conditions, made it desirable for us to take this step."

As of that date *GWTW* had grossed $14,-000,000 (and has in 1941 gone over the $31,-000,000 mark!), and *Rebecca,* a box-office Cinderella in comparison, had earned $1,800,000. In a city where much was said to be colossal, one company had a happy, and colossal, ending. Selznick paced his office, explaining to reporters that Selznick-International had gone to the Hollywood Valhalla but that a new firm, David O. Selznick Productions, Incorporated, would assume its obligations. During the interview Selznick took nervous peeks at a gold wrist watch that bears the inscription, in Whitney's handwriting: "David—Xmas 1939. Praise de Lawd. Jack." In October he joined United Artists, buying a 25 per cent interest for $1,200,000 and agreeing to maintain constant production until he had finished $20,000,000 worth of pictures.

David O. Selznick was born in Pittsburgh, Pennsylvania, May 10, 1902, the son of Lewis Julius and Florence A. (Sachs) Selznick. He was educated at Hamilton Institute for Boys

and took special courses at Columbia University. But his real schooling began as office boy in his father's studio. An in-and-outer in early motion pictures, his father's slogan, "Selznick Pictures Make Happy Hours," was known to millions back in the days when a thumping upright piano compensated noisily for the lack of a sound track on the film. The elder Selznick's firm collapsed in 1923 but before that David was in the business himself,

DAVID O. SELZNICK

having produced and made a profit on his first picture in time to celebrate his twenty-first birthday.

In 1922, knocking around the hobo jungles of quickie moviedom in New York, Dave saw the possibility of a neat turnover in Luis Angel Firpo, the Wild Bull of the Pampas. The catch was that Firpo's fee was $1,000 a day. "So," relates Duncan Underhill, "Dave hired him at $500 for an afternoon, stuck him in front of a rented camera, and shot a six-reel picture. . . Territorial rights to this gripping drama sold for a net of $3,500 and Dave was on his way."

Opus 2 for the Selznick archives was a "Hollywood beauty contest" presided over by the late Valentino. The girls came by the thousands, but most of the footage in Dave's rented camera went to Valentino. This venture allowed him to pocket an additional profit of $1,500, and he deemed himself ready to storm the Hollywood citadel. Until 1925 he was with Select Pictures, working at publicity and advertising and tinkering with scenarios. In 1926 he went to Metro-Goldwyn-Mayer as junior story editor, bombarding the front office with little interoffice communications on production economies. Meanwhile, in private life he was observing the dictum of his father: "Live expensively. Live beyond your means if you have confidence in yourself. Money isn't

SELZNICK, DAVID O.—*Continued*

important." Dave's concession to this philosophy was an expensive car. The car got lost but the memos found their way to the executives of MGM and Dave was soon on his first production assignment. Sent out to make a Western, he made two. Said Selznick: "I went on location with two sets of stars and one supporting cast. I worked the cast twice."

In 1927 Selznick went to Paramount to head their writers' department but once more he made himself useful in production, and before he left in 1931 he was assistant producer and executive assistant to the general manager. From there he went to RKO Radio Pictures, staying with that firm until 1933 as executive vice-president in charge of production. His last job working for others was with MGM as vice-president in charge of production from 1933 to 1935. Then came the formation of Selznick-International, followed by the present firm that bears his own name. In 1936 MGM tried to tempt him with what is said to have been the largest salary ever offered to any living man for mere services. But Selznick refused. "At MGM I would be supervising the making of pictures," he explained. "I wouldn't be creating them. Here in my own company I create pictures. I have an active part in every phase of production. That's a lot of fun."

In transferring a book to the screen, Selznick likes to adhere as closely as possible to theme, mood, story line and characterizations. That's one reason why costs on *GWTW* were astronomical. And when he is not busy producing, he is an insatiable reader, as was his father. He thought of this in relation to his productions of Twain, Dickens and other authors: "I never realized before why I always wanted to make those pictures... Now I know it was because they were favorites of my father."

Mr. Selznick read *Gone With the Wind* before its publication in book form and immediately offered $50,000 for the story. A month after publication he turned down an offer of $350,000 for picture rights. Then began the process of filming it. Film tests alone cost $85,000. The search for a Scarlett O'Hara was far from a publicity stunt, though the newsworthiness of the event was proved by the fact that many of the girls who were film-tested for the part were helped to other jobs. Kyle Crichton tells the story of the meeting of Selznick and Vivien Leigh at a party given by Paulette Goddard, who had previously been tested for the part. He signed up Vivien Leigh almost immediately, and Miss Goddard, in a moment of pique, is alleged to have said: "Poor David! You really can't blame him. He was down to his last Whitney."

Selznick, a fellow producer commented, had "courage and the persistence to follow through. Courage is not worth much if you haven't the persistence to go through with your decisions." As illustration of this quality, writers have observed that in filming *Rebecca*, a story in which the leading character never appears,

and in choosing Joan Fontaine, a comparative newcomer, for the role of the fear-ridden girl, he was, from the Hollywood point of view, taking a long chance. Says Mr. Selznick: "I've had some luck in discovering newcomers and if I weren't honest with myself I might be pretty smug about it. But the real truth is that a producer can only find and put over new personalities when he has patience, and the money for overhead, and the authority to refuse to be rushed into making judgments."

In experiments in Technicolor—a field in which Whitney had investments—Selznick produced films in which the color was natural and realistic rather than "pretty" and obtrusive, as had so often been the case before. Among his Technicolor productions have been *A Star Is Born, Nothing Sacred*, and *GWTW*. In the first of these occurs a line that reflects Selznick's belief in his own judgment. He had given the leading role to Janet Gaynor, despite hints that she couldn't carry it off. Playing the role of a director in this film, Adolphe Menjou faces the camera and speaks a line supplied by Selznick: "Everyone will say I'm crazy, but I'll take a chance on her."

"If you work with the man," a writer said of Selznick, "you have to agree with him that he can handle your job better than you can. Everybody from cutter to director is reconciled to the voice of authority barking: 'Hey, lemme do that!'" When Director William Wellman received his Academy Award for *A Star Is Born*, he strode across the room and handed it to his boss with the remark: "Take it. You had more to do with winning it than I did." When the 1939 awards were handed out, director Victor Fleming (*GWTW*) was not there to get his. Said Duncan Underhill: "It was reported he was ill, but not with lovesickness for Dave Selznick. Dave dutifully accepted Fleming's 'Oscar.'"

Selznick is six-feet-one, muscular and energetic. He has dark hair, bushy brows and bespectacled brown eyes. In his attitude toward subject matter he has declared himself a believer in escapist pictures. At a Rochester University Round Table discussion he was asked whether he thought the movie industry would ever stop foisting trash on the public. Said Mr. Selznick: "If we don't give it to them, radio will."

His mother, Mrs. Lewis J. Selznick, according to Quentin Reynolds (see sketch this issue), "is known as one of the most charming women in Hollywood, proud of her sons, and only she knows how often both David and Myron come to her for advice." Although his brother, Myron Selznick, is Hollywood's most famous agent, their dealings within the industry are strictly business. Selznick was married on April 29, 1930, in Los Angeles, to Irene Gladys Mayer, and they have two sons. In 1940 he was made a member of the advisory board of the National Education Association's Committee on Motion Pictures, Department of Secondary Education. His studio has yet to count all the honors and awards showered upon him and the pictures he has produced.

References

Collier's 101 :11+ My 28 '38 il; 101 :19+
Je 4 '38 il pors; 107 :13+ Mr 8 '41
Life 7 :76-8+ D 18 '39 il pors
N Y Herald Tribune p6 Ag 24 '40
N Y Sun p24 Ap 16 '40; p24 Ag 24 '40
N Y World-Telegram p7 Mr 22 '41 por
Photoplay 51 :15-16 D '37 il por; 54 :13
Je '40
Time 26 :46-7 O 21 '35 por; 36 :31 S 2
'40 por

America's Young Men
International Motion Picture Almanac
Who's Who in America
Who's Who in American Jewry
Who's Who in Commerce and Industry

SEVERANCE, H(AROLD) CRAIG July 1, 1879—Sept. 2, 1941 Architect; among the many skyscrapers he designed were the Bank of the Manhattan Company Building, once the world's second tallest commercial structure, the Hotel Taft and the Ruppert Building; architect for the United States Navy on the $2,500,000 construction project at the Lakehurst, New Jersey, Naval Air Station.

Obituaries

N Y Times p23 S 3 '41 por

SEVERSKY, ALEXANDER PROCO-FIEFF DE *See* De Seversky, A. P.

SEYMOUR, CHARLES (sē'môr) Jan. 1, 1885- President of Yale University; historian *Address*: b. Yale University, New Haven, Conn; h. 43 Hillhouse Ave, New Haven, Conn.

Dr. Charles Seymour is president of one of America's great universities and what he has to say on current affairs is, consequently, important. In the past year he has told Yale students and the world at large that "our stake in the defense of Britain is almost as great as that of the British." He has advocated military training for undergraduates (though he feels this should be arranged so as not to interfere with their studies) and he has joined with other educational leaders in urging the universities of the nation to provide a moral and scientific background for a strong national defense.

To Seymour it is important that the colleges "clarify the issues which the citizens will face" and train their students "to think about those issues in reasonable terms." While he does not feel that colleges should "impose specific doctrines in the social, economic or political fields," he believes that they "must hold fast to a firm and definite creed: that there is a difference between right and wrong which cannot be destroyed by any negativist philosophy, that there is a distinction between the truth and the lie, between courage and cowardice, between the moral initiative and cynical irresponsibility. We believe that it is part of our university experience to make the distinction and to give effect to it." Although

Blackstone

CHARLES SEYMOUR

he voted for Willkie in 1940, he is a firm supporter of President Roosevelt's foreign policy.

"Ruddy, well-tailored, fond of rough tweed jackets and pipes," Dr. Seymour doesn't look much like the popular conception of a college president or of a distinguished historian. Nor is his hobby of collecting first editions of E. Phillips Oppenheim a conventional one for a man of his position. In his accomplishments as historian and Yale president, however, Dr. Seymour has lived up to all that was expected of a man of his background and training.

He is a Yale man through and through. His great-great-great-grandfather, Joseph Coit, was awarded an honorary degree at Yale's first commencement in 1702; his great-great-grandfather, Thomas Clap, was Yale's president from 1740 to 1776; his great-uncle, Jeremiah Day, was its president from 1817 to 1846; and his father, Thomas Day Seymour, was Hillhouse Professor of Greek language and literature at Yale for more than a quarter of a century. (His mother was Sarah M. [Hitchcock] Seymour.)

Charles Seymour was born in Yale's town, New Haven, Connecticut and was graduated from the Hillhouse High School there. He didn't enter Yale immediately, but went, instead, to King's College in Cambridge, England. With a Cambridge B. A. (1904), he entered Yale as a freshman and distinguished himself in the next four years not only as a scholar (he won a philosophical oration appointment, many prizes in English and the classics and a Phi Beta Kappa key) but as manager of the freshman and varsity crews and a member of Skull and Bones and Alpha Delta Phi. He left Yale with his second B. A. in 1908 for further study abroad—at the University of Paris—and returned after a year to Yale to work for his Ph. D. He received this degree in 1911, with a dissertation

SEYMOUR, CHARLES—*Continued*

entitled *The Development of Democracy in England Since 1832 as Shown in the Reform of the Representative System*. In that same year he married Gladys Marion Watkins. (There are now three Seymour children, and Mrs. Seymour is unanimously recognized as Yale's "most charming hostess.")

Dr. Seymour started his working career at Yale in the fall of 1911 as an instructor in history. By 1915 he was an assistant professor; by 1918, professor. He had already published *Electoral Reform in England and Wales* (1916) and, with D. P. Frary, *How the World Votes* (1918). It was his *The Diplomatic Background of the War* (1916) which brought him to the attention of Woodrow Wilson, however. Wilson appointed him chief of the Austro-Hungarian division of the American Commission to Negotiate Peace and later made him a delegate on the Romanian, Yugoslav and Czechoslovak territorial commissions at the Paris Peace Conference.

It was while he was serving in Europe that Seymour came to know Colonel House well, and the Colonel gave him his personal papers relating to the Peace Conference to form the World War documents collection at Yale, of which Seymour is still curator. Later, too, Seymour was to collect and edit the four volumes of *The Intimate Papers of Colonel House* (1926-28) and to write two books, *American Diplomacy During the World War* (1934) and *American Neutrality, 1914-1917* (1935), based on that association and his experiences. Only this latest one, called "a one-sided volume which certainly added nothing to his academic reputation," was not generally acclaimed. As an historian Seymour has usually "interpreted America's entrance into the War in legalistic rather than economic terms," and his view of the Versailles Treaty is that its mistakes are due not to the leaders at the Conference, but to "the masses in the victorious countries." "If," he says, "the last 20 years of world history reveal an appalling record of failure in the political, economic and social sense, it is not because of certain clauses written into the Versailles Treaty."

After the War and the peace negotiations Dr. Seymour returned to his history courses at Yale, very popular as a lecturer, for students flocked to hear about the negotiations at firsthand. In 1924 he left Yale for a year to become exchange professor at the Universities of Brussels, Ghent, Liège and Louvain. When he came back again in 1925 he was active not only as professor and historian but also in the administration of the University. In 1927 he became its provost, the chief link between Yale's faculty and administration. As provost he coordinated the school and departments, arranged budgetary appropriations and took some executive details off President Angell's hands. In the years before he became president of Yale, Dr. Seymour was active, too, in encouraging the college plan. He helped supervise the building of the colleges and in 1932

became master of one of them, Berkeley. He also was chairman of the Council of Masters.

It was because of these activities that it was felt, when the announcement of his appointment to the presidency of Yale by unanimous vote of the Yale Corporation was made in 1937, that he would continue Angell's principles. Angell himself said of the appointment: "The University is most fortunate in the choice of Provost Charles Seymour to be its next president. He will bring to the position a lifelong acquaintance with Yale and a sympathetic understanding of her traditions and ideals... He brings to his great office qualities of heart and mind which will, I am sure, instantly win the confidence and loyal support of the whole Yale family."

Only *The Nation* was a bit ironic: "He comes of the American intellectual elite, who have always supported the holders of economic power... Thorstein Veblen once wrote a brilliant book called *The Higher Learning in America: A Memorandum on the Conduct of the Universities by Business Men*. There is nothing in Provost Seymour's career which makes him from such a point of view an unsafe choice." But Yale undergraduates thought themselves fortunate at this choice of a Yale man for Yale—the Yale *News* wrote: "It is with the greatest confidence and happy anticipation that Yale can look forward to the administration of Charles Seymour."

References

Christian Cent 54:237 F 24 '37
Nation 144:199 F 20 '37
Newsweek 9:26 F 20 '37 por
Scholastic 30:16 Mr 6 '37 por
Sch & Soc 45:253 F 20 '37
Time 29:28+ F 22 '37 por

Leaders in Education 1941
Who's Who Among North American Authors
Who's Who in America
Who's Who in American Education

SEYSS-INQUART, ARTUR (zīs'ĭng'-kvärt är'tŏŏr) July 2, 1892- German High Commissioner of The Netherlands

Of all Nazi-occupied countries, The Netherlands is possibly giving its conquerors as unpleasant a time as any. The German High Commissioner there is Artur Seyss-Inquart, an intellectual-looking man whose disdainful expression may be due to the fact that he can hardly see without his spectacles. A decree of March 21, 1941 gives him authority "to set up machinery to execute summary justice—shooting for serious offenses—and to set aside Netherlands officials when necessary for 'public security.'" The Nazis are preparing for any possible future repetition of the riots, strikes and "conspiracies against German authority" that have worried them in the past: Nazi soldiers have been thrown into Dutch canals, among other things. On the other hand, the number of executions and mysterious murders of anti-Fascists that have taken place in Holland makes one wonder, a little, about the kind of "justice" dispensed prior to the decree.

Much water has gone under the bridge since the day in May 1940 when Seyss-Inquart was inducted as German High Commissioner of The Netherlands. Then he announced that: "Dutch laws hitherto observed shall remain in force as far as possible, Dutch officials are to be the instruments of power in the new administration. The independence of legal jurisdiction is to be preserved. . . The German Army would rather have entered this land with its arm raised in friendly salute than with weapons in hand. We did not come here to oppress the people and to deprive the nation of its freedom."

Since that time the economy of The Netherlands has been almost completely incorporated into that of the Reich. Dutch cattle, hogs, butter reserves, tobacco, oil and factory stocks have been fast disappearing, as have Dutch workmen conscripted for manual labor in Germany. Living costs are up, wages down, and although food rationing is apparently less drastic than in Belgium, Hollanders are not the rosy-cheeked, well-fed people they once were. Comprehensive restrictions on all Jewish activities have reduced Jews to the status of persons merely tolerated in the country; they are even forbidden to eat kosher meat.

High Commissioner Seyss-Inquart can remember one country that the Germany Army actually entered "with its arm raised in friendly salute"—although with weapons not completely forgotten. That country was Austria, a country which he himself helped betray to the Nazis. He is not an Austrian, however, but a Sudeten German, born on July 2, 1892 in Stannern near Iglau. Many of the associates of his youth later became leaders in the Czechoslovakian Nazi movement.

Seyss-Inquart was 16 when he first went to Vienna to study at the University of Vienna and take his law degree there. During those years, at least, he had liberal leanings—even toyed with the idea of joining the Social Democratic Party. His law practice interrupted by the World War, he served on the Izonzo front until discharged with a serious leg wound which still makes him limp a little. Another Catholic law student, Kurt Schuschnigg, had commanded the sector next to his; the two men continued their friendship. Schuschnigg, however, later joined the Christian Social Party, while Seyss-Inquart never openly belonged to any party until the days of the Fatherland Front.

Seyss-Inquart's history in the 1930's is an almost incredible Jekyll-and-Hyde story. One aspect is that of Schuschnigg's friend, a highly successful attorney with a large Jewish clientele, "a well-dressed man of aristocratic appearance and impeccable manners," popular in Viennese society, married, with two children and an apple orchard in which he takes great pride. He frankly favors union with Germany but certainly never sympathizes

ARTUR SEYSS-INQUART

openly with the Austrian National Socialist Party.

The other aspect is that of Hitler's secret Austrian representative (exactly when he had been converted to National Socialism is not certain). This man directs the agents of Nazi propaganda and terror in Austria, secures for them passports, residence permits, etc.; they meet at his home, they communicate with one another through him, in important matters they rely on his judgment. It seems impossible that for years no one should have discovered that the respectable attorney and the chief of the Nazi Fifth Column were one and the same person, even though Seyss-Inquart was a man with a brilliant mind and memory and a talent for "adjusting his face and manner to the person with whom he was talking."

Some of the facts are particularly hard to believe. When in March 1933 Chancellor Dollfuss made himself dictator of Austria and created the authoritarian Austrian State both Minister Schuschnigg and Artur Seyss-Inquart were made members of the Austrian Corporate Council. Yet shortly before the assassination of Dollfuss by Austrian National Socialists, when Germany sent 80 special agents into Austria to reorganize the outlawed National Socialist Party as an underground movement, the agents met safely at the home of Seyss-Inquart. After the death of Dollfuss, Schuschnigg became Chancellor; Seyss-Inquart's only speech from the floor was a protest against Schuschnigg's attack on pan-Germanism. Said Seyss-Inquart, mildly: "To me that I am a German is just as important as that I am an Austrian; the time is past when we can afford to be divided into national groups." Yet at about this time he was winning over to the cause of National Socialism the organization of Austrian hotel proprietors whose counsel he was—on the grounds that

SEYSS-INQUART, ARTUR—*Continued*

it would bring back their lost German tourist trade. And in 1935 he personally arranged to bring the Austrian Legion back across the border in small groups and hold it in readiness for a German invasion—a plan which later had to be abandoned.

After July 1936 a secret Committee of Seven was established at No. 4 Teinfaltstrasse, Vienna with the purpose of protecting the Austrian National Socialists and helping them infiltrate into Schuschnigg's Fatherland Front. Seyss-Inquart was a member. In January 1938 No. 4 was raided, a plot for revolution revealed and frustrated. Furthermore, when a Nazi terrorist was arrested Seyss-Inquart's address was found on him, as well as plans for an attack on the Chancellery. Nothing more happened to Seyss-Inquart than a cross-examination by the Prefect of Police. But the ominous discovery, with the attendant possibility of a purge by Schuschnigg, made Hitler decide to accelerate his plans.

By February 1938, with the Nazi threat to Austrian independence growing steadily worse, Schuschnigg's trusted adviser Seyss-Inquart (with the help of German Ambassador Von Papen [see sketch this issue]) managed to persuade him to go to Berchtesgaden and try to come to some kind of an understanding with Hitler. It turned out to be a peculiar sort of understanding. Hitler delivered an ultimatum whose terms Schuschnigg was forced to accept two days later. In it he demanded political amnesty and freedom for the Austrian National Socialists and a reconstructed Schuschnigg Cabinet, including Seyss-Inquart as Minister of the Interior with complete authority over the Austrian police apparatus. The alternative was—a German invasion.

Immediately upon receiving his new post from the bewildered Schuschnigg, Seyss-Inquart flew to Berlin to get further instructions from Hitler. Back in Vienna, one of his first moves was to grant the Nazis of Styria the right to wear swastikas and shout "Heil Hitler!" He also made plans to visit other provinces "to lay the foundation for an undisturbed organization of the Nazi movement throughout Austria." (A more surprising act was his order that 11 former Socialist members of the illegal Defense Corps be reinstated in Vienna's Fire Department!)

On March 9 Schuschnigg announced that a plebiscite would be held on March 13 by which the people of Austria would be permitted to vote for or against incorporation in the Reich. Hitler, outraged, presented a second ultimatum on March 11: the plebiscite must be called off, or the Nazis would march. That same evening, with all sorts of rumors going around the city, Schuschnigg's sad voice was heard over the loud-speaker: there would be no plebiscite. Immediately afterward Seyss-Inquart, not so saddened, spoke. He ordered the Austrian Army to make no resistance. What followed everyone knows. Schuschnigg resigned; for the moment Seyss-Inquart became Chancellor and Minister of Defense, and invited Hitler to send troops in to "preserve

order." "Austria is free. Austria is National Socialist. . . One People, One Reich, One Leader. Hail to our Leader. Heil Hitler!"

Hitler was more than prompt in accepting the invitation. On March 12 Austria was annexed. Schuschnigg saw his strange friend Seyss-Inquart next at the head of a band of Storm Troopers. Seyss-Inquart ordered the former Chancellor to remain in his apartment, stationed an armed guard there, and finally announced that he would be tried for treason. Yet, according to Oswald Dutch, Seyss-Inquart, too, was a "deceived deceiver." As soon as Hitler moved into Vienna he was given a position subordinate to *Gauleiter* Bürckel—named *Statthalter* of the *Ostmark*.

Seyss-Inquart remained in obscurity until, in March 1939, Bürckel and he began the Nazi campaign for Slovak "independence" with the aid of the Vienna radio station. In that same year he became Minister without Portfolio in the Reich Government, and after Germany took Poland in September 1939 he was honored with another post: Deputy Governor of the occupied territory. Now the man who wanted to govern Austria is governing the stubborn Dutch. According to Ludwig Lore, he says Holland must be brought to such a state of obedience that if the German Army should leave, the Dutch would actually ask it to return—no one must be left to oppose the Nazi rule.

References

> Liv Age 354:141-2 Ap '38
> Nation 146:502-4 Ap 30 '38
> Scholastic 32:15S Ap 2 '38 por
> International Who's Who

SHANNON, PEGGY Jan. 10, 1907(?)— May 11, 1941 Film actress and former *Ziegfeld Follies* girl; appeared in a long list of films; was a successor to Clara Bow, when that actress became ill, and took over some of her roles.

References

> Motion Pict 44:48-9 Ja '33 por; 45:52 Mr '33 por; 46:25 O '33 por; 47: 62-3 My '34 por
> Movie Classic 1:50+ S '31 por; 1:19+ Ja '32 por; 3:15 Ja '33 por; 5:34 S '33 por; 6:13 Je '34 por
> Photoplay 43:69, 108 D '32 il pors
> International Motion Picture Almanac
> Who's Who in the Theatre

Obituaries

> N Y Herald Tribune p10 My 12 '41 por
> Variety 142:54 My 14 '41

SHAPLEY, HARLOW (shăp'lē) Nov. 2, 1885- Astronomer

Address: b. Harvard College Observatory, Cambridge, Mass.

Harlow Shapley, "probably the country's best-known astronomer," has almost as many awards and medals as the stars he has discovered. The Draper Medal of the National Academy of Sciences, the Gold Medal of the English Royal Astronomical Society, the Janssen Prix of the Astronomical Society of France, the Pius XI Prize for Astronomy (awarded on November 30, 1941) are only a few of the decorations the learned world has given this alert, unruly-haired scientist who has "broken down the barriers of the skies."

Since 1921 Dr. Shapley has been director of the Harvard Observatory, and as Harvard director "has probably had a larger part in the many important recent advances in astronomical knowledge than any other one man." From his desk in Cambridge he is in close touch with the activities of scientists all over the earth who have telescopes in operation over every portion of the heavens. As one commentator put it: the astronomers gathered around him "have divided the heavens among them as if it were so much pie and made tremendous progress in exploring and charting it." At Harvard they have made the most complete collection of celestial photographs in the world and have made Harvard, too, one of the most important centers for astronomical news.

As head of the Harvard Observatory Dr. Shapley is incessantly called on to talk at scientific congresses, to attend meetings all over the world. In 1925, for instance, he was at Cambridge, England, heading the Commission on Variable Stars of the International Astronomical Union; the next year he was in Leyden; in 1933 he was in Mexico inspecting its National Observatory; in 1934 he visited 13 islands in the West Indies; in 1935 he was in Paris. Not infrequently, at these congresses, Dr. Shapley has been known to startle his fellow dignitaries. Once he woke them up sharply by comparing man to a plant louse embedded on a lilac bush.

Harlow Shapley's father, Willis Harlow Shapley, was a teacher who died when Harlow was a boy. His mother, Sarah (Stowell) Shapley, was a descendant of the Massachusetts Stowells who reached the United States in 1640. His parents were living in Nashville, Missouri when Harlow was born. There wasn't a lot of money for the education of Harlow and his younger brother John, former professor of art at the University of Chicago and now visiting professor at Johns Hopkins University, but they both managed well. Harlow went to Carthage Academy and then, after a year's work on a newspaper, entered the University of Missouri when he was 20. At Missouri his most important paper was on "Astronomy in Horace with 46 references to his works."

After a year's postgraduate work at the University of Missouri (he received his M. A. in 1911) Dr. Shapley went to Princeton University, from which he received his Ph. D. in 1913. Then, with his bride, Martha Betz of Kansas City, who became something of an astronomer herself and helped him with his papers, he went to the Mount Wilson Observatory in California. Here he spent seven busy and profitable years, "during which he

HARLOW SHAPLEY

emerged as one of the most brilliant and original of the younger astronomers."

His first astronomical work there was on variable stars and especially on the "enigmatical short-period variables known as Cepheids." In 1914 he put forward his "pulsation theory" of these stars. Then he made the discovery that variable stars held the key to stellar distances, a discovery which gave the world a new conception of the universe. Shapley was able to demonstrate that our universe is a thousand times bigger than the astronomers had previously supposed. At Mount Wilson, too, Dr. Shapley discovered a new center of the universe, a spot in the constellation Sagittarius, now called "Shapley Center." In 1918 he showed that our sun is a star of one of the star clusters in the heavens.

While he was measuring stellar distances, Dr. Shapley went off on a totally different line of scientific inquiry. He began to study ants. After he had noticed that the hotter an ant was the faster it would run along a track, he developed a theory about ant speed and temperature measurement on which he published papers. But he returned to investigating "such spectacular phenomena as the Great Gebula in Andromeda and forgot about the ants except for bottled specimens he keeps on his desk."

Since 1921 Dr. Shapley has been at the Harvard Observatory, doing significant research in astronomy and astrophysics and lecturing at various colleges and foundations throughout the world. One of the world's leading astronomers, he is still able to explain in simple language the complexities of the universe. In his writings and lectures he is particularly adept in making the layman see how the study of stars has personal meaning to him. He shows how navigation, keeping appointments, keeping time are all a part of astronomy. One of the "most human scientists

SHAPLEY, HARLOW—*Continued*

imaginable, he never dramatizes what he has done and insists that it is only as he and many others all over the world whittle away together that progress is made. He likes to insist that most of the advance in astronomical knowledge of recent years has been a matter of "girl-hours," the time of the young women who operate the photographic apparatus with which pictures of stars are taken.

Dr. Shapley is "a restless, pipe-smoking enthusiast . . . with a mind that darts from thought to thought so fast that his bristling conversation can hardly keep up with it." He likes people and he likes to discuss the universe with them in pungent talk. Sometimes he talks of religion: he believes "most astronomers are agnostics. Not atheists—that presumes more conviction than religion does. Scientists cannot have faith. Ours is a perpetual inquiry; any acceptance of faith—in a scientific or a metaphysical or an esthetic sense —brings inquiry to a halt." Most often he talks of the heavens, and sometimes, in talking, smiles at himself and other astronomers. "We make all this funny fury about things as old as the stars," he says. "Sometimes I suspect I know what they're twinkling at."

References

Am Mag 117:46 Je '34 por
N Y Herald Tribune X p8 Jl 7 '40 por
N Y World-Telegram p28 Ap 3 '41 por
Pop Sci 138:104-5 Ap '41 il
Time 26:28+ Jl 29 '35 por (cover)
American Men of Science
Leaders in Education 1941
Macpherson, H. C. Makers of Astronomy p212-40 1933
   p212-40 1933
Who's Who in America

SHAW, ARTIE May 26, 1910- Band leader
Address: c/o Andrew Weinberger, 67 W. 44th St, New York City

In March 1941 Artie Shaw completed a series of radio programs, coming East to New York for the last five broadcasts. Before him was the prospect of a vaudeville tour, but Artie turned it down and decided, instead, to refresh his musical point of view by a firsthand glimpse of the grass-roots of American music. Some columnists refused to believe that Artie was really on a grass-roots tour of native rhythms, since it detracted from the press picture of Shaw, the paradox. "Some people in the business think I'm either cracked or a poseur," said Shaw. "They refuse to believe that, with me, music is first."

It is nevertheless true that when Artie left his band in 1939—a year in which his income was close to a quarter of a million dollars—he said that he was fed up with the music business. Speculation as to his next move became so extravagant that one habitué of Lindy's, Broadway theatrical restaurant, said of the rumors: "You can take your pick but, as for me, there ain't no Artie Shaw."

In April 1941 Shaw announced that he would conduct an orchestra at the Lewisohn Stadium in New York City during the coming summer. From there he went on, with an enlarged and reorganized band, to barnstorm the country with a series of one-nighters.

Born in New York City in 1910, there was nothing in Artie Shaw's background to suggest a musical career. His father, Harry Shaw, was a photographer; his mother, Sarah, a seamstress. When Artie was seven the family moved to New Haven, Connecticut, where they established themselves in business.

Artie grew up in a period when at least one child to a city block played the saxophone. At the age of 13 he followed the trend, buying a saxophone with money earned as an errand boy. With it came five free lessons that Artie claimed he had to unlearn in order to play "hot" style later on. Meanwhile this minimum of formal training got him band jobs when he was still in his teens. He was not sure that he wanted to be a musician permanently, though. Once, when stranded with a barnstorming outfit in Lexington, Kentucky, he spent his spare time reading Jack London in the city library, and entertained some idea of being a writer.

But playing in bands was a ready means of earning a livelihood. When Shaw returned to New Haven he played with local bands and in 1925 took up clarinet so that he might get a job with a band in Florida. That, in a way, was the turning point. For the clarinet is Artie's instrument. It stimulated his interest in music and before he was 20 he was experimenting in composition and arrangement.

In 1929, while playing with a band in Cleveland, Ohio, Shaw won an essay contest sponsored by the Cleveland *Plain Dealer*. The prize was a round-trip plane ticket to California and he used it only one way—he joined Irving Aaronson's Orchestra in Los Angeles. Soon after the band came East Shaw left it to job around the radio stations. Playing saxophone more often than clarinet, he worked for many prominent band leaders on broadcasts, earning as much as $500 weekly.

In 1931 Leon (Bix) Beiderbecke, his friend and former roommate, died in comparative obscurity. From Bix (who inspired the novel *Young Man with a Horn*), Artie learned "hot" style. Another influence was that of the famous Negro drummer, the late Chick Webb. The handsome young clarinetist was a familiar figure at the Savoy and other places in Harlem where hot music could be heard.

But Artie hadn't given up the writing bug. In 1935 he bought a typewriter and a farm in Bucks County, Pennsylvania. He had hoped to do a book based on the life of Beiderbecke but, instead, found himself staring at blank pieces of white paper. Somehow he couldn't get the job under way. "It took a year for me to discover that a typewriter isn't a clarinet," said Mr. Shaw in recalling the episode.

On the day of his return from Bucks County he tried unsuccessfully to get work.

From 10 a. m. to 2 p. m. he toured the studios and booking agencies. Everywhere he met with the same reception—he "shouldn't have quit the business cold." From 2 p. m. to 4 p. m. he sat on a park bench, getting panicky. Then he telephoned his mother on the slim chance that there might be a message. There was. A swing concert was scheduled for May 1936, at the Imperial Theatre, and he was invited to participate.

This was Shaw's first appearance as a "hot" soloist, and he made the most of it. He convinced a string quartet that a quintet based on strings and clarinet would be musically effective. They appeared on the stage against a backdrop illustrating music manuscript, the strings striking an incongruous note amongst the "boogie woogie" and "barrelhouse" surrounding them. Reception from "hot" critics was mixed, but the next day Shaw had recording offers from three companies. An agency signed him for a larger band using the same basic instrumentation, with other instruments added. They opened cold in a New York hotel, and though other New York jobs followed, none served to establish the group. On the road they found themselves—as musicians say—working "strictly from hunger." The agency dropped them, and they were on their own once more.

This failure led Artie to junk his first big band. The Phoenix that rose from its ashes was a conventional 14-piece dance band. But even with the new outfit Shaw insisted upon his own musical values. He eschewed hits-of-the-week unless he considered them worthwhile vehicles. Apart from his own compositions, many of which have been popular, his choice of good but somewhat obscure numbers also helped to establish the band. (The recent popularity of *Frenesi* began with his Victor recording of the number.)

Using Tommy Dorsey's old truck, the band went on the road to "break in," sometimes making 600-mile jumps to play $250 dance jobs. They devised a unique system for saving hotel bills. Getting into a town in the morning, they would check in at a local hotel, sleep until it was time to work, then return after the job was over to sleep the night out.

In the spring of 1938 Shaw again broke precedent by taking on as girl vocalist the talented Negro singer, Billie Holiday. At this time Charlie Shribman of Boston saw possibilities in the band. He bought an interest and booked them into his Roseland State Ballroom, where they began the march to fame that led to such incidents as Shaw's having to interview en masse a group of college and school paper editors, playing for 20,000 shag enthusiasts on Boston Common, etc. By summer they had an enviable reputation throughout the country, due as much to their records as to their radio appearances. Working with arranger Jerry Grey, Shaw (whose musicianship has always been a factor in his success) produced solid, concerto-like arrangements of which *Begin The Beguine* was outstanding. (It was, in fact, one of the best-selling records of the 1930's.) Some

ARTIE SHAW

tunes, such as his own *Back Bay Shuffle,* depended less on the initial arrangement than on performance. The first New York hotel spot for the new band, in the fall of 1938, ran up a deficit but was worth it. After that came a deluge of radio and picture offers.

The year 1939 was a bonanza year, despite the loss of a few weeks during the spring through illness. In New York Shaw was stricken with *agranulocytopenia,* a usually fatal blood disease, and had to have several transfusions. Leaving his sickbed to fulfill a Hollywood contract, he caught pneumonia and was again laid up for days before he could get to work on his first feature-length picture, *Dancing Co-Ed,* starring Lana Turner. An Associated Press dispatch quoted Hollywood gossips as saying that they "quarreled endlessly throughout the only movie they had made together."

In November 1939 Mr. Shaw got off his famous blast against jitterbugs. Although he denied its sweeping character, a large part of the press quoted him as having said that jitterbugs were morons. He recently corrected this impression by stating: "It was the few rowdies who spoiled the whole thing for most of the kids who just wanted to listen or dance. . . . Anyway, I think that sort of music is on its way out."

That month he abruptly left his band and, on the advice of his physician, went to Mexico to rest. "Even before his recent illness," Alden Cook commented glumly, "he was a tense, moody young man." The musical world generally took the whole affair in its stride, regretting the inconvenience to musicians but in agreement with many of the criticisms Artie made of the music business at that time. It remained for the New York *Times* to see the incident in an heroic perspective. "Any commentary that might occur to us," the statement

SHAW, ARTIE—*Continued*

read, "would be lost in the Shakespearean sweep of Mr. Shaw's exodus: the kind of spectacularly irreverent farewell to his work and former associates that even the timidest soul must occasionally dream of, a beautifully incautious burning of all his bridges behind him."

Shaw was already on his way to Mexico when the *Saturday Evening Post* published an article on which he had collaborated. In this he threatened to leave the music business before it had another chance to lay him low, and talked frankly of the musician in America, who "hasn't only a financial and artistic problem with which to contend but must fight politics, corruption and a system of patronage."

Meanwhile, Shaw took time off to loaf and enjoy his two favorite sports, riding and swimming. Ironically, both got him into difficulties. He fractured a knee while rescuing from the Pacific undertow a Greenwich, Connecticut debutante. A few months later, in Hollywood, a fall from a horse laid him up for a few days. But he had returned from Mexico "with his equilibrium, his health and a hit tune called *Frenesi.*" With a new 23-man orchestra, he was signed up for the Burns-Allen show on NBC, the Paramount musical *Second Chorus* and many dance engagements.

It was after his return that Shaw started the dance band world by using a large orchestra that included several violins, violas and cellos. And although he maintained his place in the standard polls as a swing band he began to gain in the opposite, or "sweet," category, reflecting both his own versatility and the adaptability of his orchestral treatment. With *Concerto for Clarinet,* which he played in the Paramount film *Second Chorus,* his stock once more took an upward thrust. A little on the *tour de force* side, it brought to the public in a sort of omnibus package all the musical experiences of blues, "boogie woogie," and "hot" jazz that would have been less assimilable in more indigenous settings. In instrumentation, Shaw believes in flexibility and may employ anything from his "Gramercy Five" to an orchestra of concert proportions.

His marriage to movie actress Lana (Julia Jean) Turner—the red-headed "sweater girl" little more than a year out of high school—was Shaw's third. According to Sidney Skolsky, the night preceding their wedding was their first real date. Shaw phoned Lana, said Skolsky, and they went to the Cocoanut Grove (where Artie had played his first Hollywood band job in 1929). In the course of the evening they decided to get married, and flew to Yuma, Arizona, for that purpose. Enroute, the pilot learned that it would be impossible to land at Yuma, so he took them to Las Vegas, Nevada, instead. There they were married, on February 13, 1940. Separation came after only a few months of married life, and on September 12, 1940, Lana Turner was granted a divorce in a Los Angeles court.

Shaw is of medium height, and his dark brown eyes and handsome features have been an asset in Hollywood, though for years

Variety found his MC-ing stiff and unconvincing. Writing is still a hobby with him and he recalls how, as a youth, he read all he could of Lafcadio Hearn, then proceeded to read books mentioned by Hearn. Called "the intellectual of the swing band maestros," he enjoys fraternizing with writers Steinbeck, Saroyan and Donald Ogden Stewart (see sketch this issue), and he keeps a notebook in which he records his impressions. "I am using myself as a guinea pig," he admits. "My reactions to all this fame and excitement should be worth preserving."

References

> Esquire 12:94+ O '39 il
> N Y Post p3 Ag 4 '41 por
> N Y World-Telegram p16 F 14 '41 por
> Newsweek 18:74 S 8 '41
> Sat Eve Post 212:14-15+ D 2 '39 pors
> Victor Record R 3:13 Ap '40 pors; 10: 13-14+ F '41 pors
> Variety Radio Directory

SHAW, HENRY (LARNED KEITH) Aug. 8, 1873—Mar. 26, 1941 Pediatrician; founded (1913) the Child Hygiene Division of the New York State Department of Health; prolific writer on child health; editor of the "Happy Child Department" of *De-lineator* Magazine, advisory editor and writer for *Parent's Magazine* and contributor to the New York *Herald Tribune* Sunday Magazine.

References

> American Medical Directory
> Directory of Medical Specialists 1939
> Who's Who in America

Obituaries

> N Y Herald Tribune p20 Mr 27 '41

SHAWKEY, MORRIS PURDY Feb. 17, 1868—Feb. 6, 1941 President emeritus of Marshall College; had been president from 1923 to 1935; under his leadership the institution carried on an expansion program, increasing the registration from 1,000 to 2,000 students; public career began with service in the State Legislature of West Virginia in 1902; elected three times as state superintendent of schools, serving from 1908 to 1920.

References

> Leaders in Education 1932
> Who's Who Among North American Authors
> Who's Who in America

Obituaries

> N Y Times p15 F 8 '41

SHEARER, AUGUSTUS H(UNT) Feb. 21, 1878—May 31, 1941 One of the nation's foremost librarians; was in charge of the Buffalo Grosvenor Reference Library and its 350,000 volumes for nearly a quarter of a century; taught at Hamilton College; was a librarian at the Newberry Library until 1917, when he went to Buffalo; was founder and director of the Library Science Department of the University of Buffalo; author of historical writings.

References

Bul Bibliog 16:149-51 Ja '39 por
Leaders in Education 1941
Who's Who in America
Who's Who in Library Service

Obituaries

N Y Times p40 Je 1 '41

SHEEAN, VINCENT Dec. 5, 1899- Author; journalist

Address: c/o Doubleday, Doran & Co, Inc, 14 W. 49th St, New York City

Although—or perhaps because—his columnist friend Dorothy Thompson can describe him as a man who in another age would have been a great poet, Vincent Sheean represents to the American public the foreign correspondent *par excellence.* He is best known as the man who wrote *Personal History,* although since it appeared in 1935 he has been in the news for a number of books and exploits, not to mention an accident. He tried at least once to desert newspaper work and settle down as a novelist; but the pull of things happening in Europe and the push of newspaper editors were too much for a man with his knack of being where the news pops and picking it up hot—without gloves. Accordingly, he has been an articulate eyewitness of Europe's recent history. He was in Spain during most of its civil war, and witnessed the fall of Catalonia; he was in Czechoslovakia when the Nazis moved up their guns; he was in France when the Low Countries were invaded, and stayed until just before their collapse; he was in London through the intensive bombings and burnings of September 1940 and again in 1941.

Not Peace But a Sword gave his correspondent's-eye view of Europe between March 1938 and March 1939, and was the Book-of-the-Month Club selection for August 1939. Like *Personal History* (which had been a Literary Guild book), it is in the genre that has come to be known as "book journalism": "reporting in a literary style that goes beyond newspaper writing, presenting the temperament, the feelings and thoughts of the observer as he looks at worlds great and small. Within the limits of this genre Vincent Sheean is a master." Another critic hints at what those limits may be: "It is the sense of his living through great moments as quiveringly, as wonderingly, and sometimes as myopically as would you or I that gives to this book its human perspective and blunt reality."

This book may be accepted as a sequel to *Personal History,* which was the first, the most successful, and some critics say the best of the many volumes in which foreign correspondents during the last few years have combined history, autobiography and gossip about the great. It was generally hailed as a "rich, arresting and important piece of work," al-

VINCENT SHEEAN

though few guessed the impact and influence it was to have. Even the least enthusiastic conceded it to be one of the most vivid and forthright chronicles of the period that began with the Armistice in 1918 and ended with the crash in 1929. Nathaniel Peffer's comment about the earlier *An American Among the Riffi* (1926) is typical of the most adverse criticism brought against the author's journalistic books: "Mr. Sheean has all the qualities of the highest type of American newspaperman. He has a sense of the dramatic, he has courage, he can observe, he can write vividly, and he cannot understand the significance of what he sees." Opposite this may be set the exclamation of John Gunther (see sketch this issue) that Sheean "has muscles in his head. He thinks."

At the very beginning of his personal history James Vincent Sheean, in good newspaper style, came to earth just one jump ahead of the twentieth century. He was born in Pana, Illinois, on December 5, 1899, the son of William and Susan (MacDermot) Sheean. He has little to say about his early childhood except that it was "bookish," landing him at the University of Chicago with 17 years of inexperience and more knowledge of French, German and the literature of fiction than of the stodgier school subjects. He was "Jimmy" Sheean in those days, red-haired, freckled, and, rumor says, the darling of the campus. His first newspaper experience was acquired on the college daily, the *Maroon.*

His three and a half years of college life ended when the illness and death of his mother left him with neither the will nor the funds to continue at the University. He took a job with the Chicago *Daily News,* from which he was fired after two or three weeks. In an exit he describes as characteristic, he went straight from the editor's office to the train and proceeded to New York with no luggage

SHEEAN, VINCENT—*Continued*

and not much more money. There he worked on the New York *Daily News* (no relation to its Chicago namesake), then starting out on what was to prove a lucrative career as a tabloid. He "learned the formulas of the trade . . . sat at the feet of various 'radicals' . . . in Greenwich Village . . . got drunk in small bars," and labored valiantly to become sophisticated.

In the spring of 1922 he went to Paris and, after an autumn excursion to Italy, where Black Shirts and castor oil were just coming into vogue, he became foreign correspondent for the Chicago *Tribune*. From Lausanne and Geneva he went to the Rhineland in 1923 and 1924; then to Rome, Madrid, and the London of Ramsay MacDonald; finally, in December of 1924, to Morocco, where he reported the Rif rebellion and was the only foreign correspondent to secure an interview with Abd el-Krim. That adventure is fully described in *An American Among the Riffi*.

He was in China during the early days of the Communist revolution there and made the acquaintance of Madam Sun Yat-sen; in Russia he studied the effects of Bolshevism and underwent a series of social revelations (in later years somewhat modified, and after September 1939 rejected); he was in Jerusalem during the Arab-Jewish riots of 1929, in Europe when the Germany Army marched into the Ruhr Valley, in Ethiopia during the crisis there.

His short-lived determination to desert the newsfront for the ivory tower came in 1935, when he married blue-eyed, dark-haired Diana Forbes-Robertson, daughter of the great English actor Sir Johnston Forbes-Robertson and niece of the late Maxine Elliott. Mrs. Sheean has shared many of his recent adventures, including the London raids, and has made her own contribution to literature as co-editor, with Roger W. Straus, Jr., of *War Letters from Britain*, for which her husband wrote a foreword. She has also written *The Battle of Waterloo Road*, a graphic report on modern London which was published in December 1941. Both Mr. and Mrs. Sheean are active in finding American homes for English children, their natural energies and sympathies prodded to greater effort by remembrance of their own English experiences and concern for their innumerable English friends and connections.

Both had expected to return to England in March of 1941, but the return was delayed by danger they met in New York's peaceful Bronxville. In the middle of a freezing February night, the house they had rented from Dorothy Thompson burst into flame. The occupants were saved, as well as the manuscript of Vincent Sheean's forthcoming novel, *Bird of the Wilderness*; but thousands of dollars' worth of furniture and a formidable collection of mystery stories belonging to Sinclair Lewis perished in the flames.

Mrs. Sheean jumped from the second story holding the three-year-old Linda in her arms, while her husband—wakened by the shrieks of the nurse who had just dropped Linda's baby sister into the snow—jumped the equivalent of three and a half stories, alighting with a damaged leg, bad face burns, and a good deal of his prematurely gray hair singed off. He voted it "a closer call than I ever had in any war." The family moved to a New York hotel to recuperate, while father, before he left for England on an assignment for the *Saturday Evening Post,* finished his slightly scorched novel, perhaps hoping that baptism of fire would warm up its reception.

For his novels, while cordially received, have on the whole roused less spectacular response than the books of autobiographical history with which they have alternated. *The Anatomy of Virtue* in 1927 was greeted as "an interesting first novel" and one critic even called it "a relentless and pitiful story." *Gog and Magog*, a story of Communist Russia published in 1930, was recognized as having the inevitable Sheean verve and richness of political background, but was generally felt to be deficient in character building and story interest. *The Tide,* in 1933, was received with cordial calm as "a thought-provoking satire on the methods of modern journalism." "A newspaperman's novel," it was called, "witty, sometimes hilarious, engaging, realistic . . . somewhat shyly thoughtful and quite modest." As has often been the case with this author, adverse criticism took the form of qualified praise: one critic said *The Tide* "ultimately emerges as very good reading matter but nothing more. It could have been." *The Pieces of a Fan,* 14 short stories published in 1937, were "smooth, civilized, clever. . . For what they are they are capable, even brilliant. Coming from the author of *Personal History* they are grievously disappointing." The two historical novels, *Sanfelice* (1936) and *A Day of Battle* (1938) were praised for their "historic sweep" but not for their characterization. And when it was published in the fall of 1941 critics found *Bird of the Wilderness,* the story, most agreed, of Sheean's own life up to the time when *Personal History* began, a "sensitive study of adolescence" which, despite good writing, drama and insight, somehow "never seemed to come to grips with anything." Few critics attribute to any of the author's fiction so far the importance that is usually assumed for his more journalistic books—which include, besides those mentioned, *The New Persia* (1927). Perhaps Sheean was right when he wrote: "I must have been eminently fitted for a foreign correspondent."

The gray-haired Vincent Sheean who used to be red-haired "Jimmy" Sheean (he is still called that by his friends) is solid, six-foot-two and says he wears the map of Ireland on his face. He likes nothing better than a discussion, except an argument, and confesses that his gifts do not include a talent for leisure. His record and his bibliography—containing articles in most of our leading magazines—bear him out. It is said that his reputation for being always in the thick of things is not mere luck, since "his ardent sympathy for the downtrodden has led him where fire was hottest." Recently, in the summer of 1941, it led him to teach United

States history to schoolteachers in embattled Britain. Even more recently it sent him on a two months' trip to New Zealand, Australia, the Dutch East Indies, India and China to obtain material for articles for magazines and the New York *Herald Tribune* Syndicate on war conditions in the Pacific. His views on the War are not cheerful; or at least they were not in September 1941, when he stated his conviction that if England and America did not take more prompt and decisive action against the Germans they would probably lose the War.

References

Cur Hist 51:14 Ja '40 por
Life 8:15 Je 3 '40 por
Newsweek 7:33 Je 20 '36 por
Pub W 129:1949 My 16 '36 por; 139: 1935 My 10 '41 por
Sat Eve Post 208:120 Ap 18 '36 por; 209:108 N 7 '36 por; 213:9-11 D 21 '40 por (p6)
Scholastic 32:22E Ap 9 '38 por
Time 27:77 Je 22 '36 por; 32:53 Jl 25 '38 por; 34:51 Jl 31 '39 por; 34:22 N 13 '39 por; 36:75 O 14 '41 por; 37:44 F 17 '41
Wilson Lib Bul 9:464+ My '35 por
America's Young Men
Millett, F. B. Contemporary American Authors 1940
Sheean, V. Not Peace But a Sword 1939
Sheean, V. Personal History 1935
Who's Who in America

SHEEN, FULTON J(OHN), MGR. May 8, 1895- Roman Catholic priest; writer; educator

Address: Catholic University of America, Washington, D. C.

"Anything that I have comes from God. Glory be to God! Let that be my interview."

In these words Father Sheen answered a newspaperman who wished to interview him. To some they will sound like fanaticism, to others like humble and fervent faith. But they are thoroughly characteristic. Everything that Father Sheen does or says is founded on and inseparable from his church.

Fulton John Sheen was born in El Paso, Illinois, the son of Newton Morris Sheen, "an agriculturist and inventor, a farmer with a pronounced mechanical bent," and of Delia (Fulton) Sheen. A younger brother is a practicing physician in New York. Their uncle, Daniel Sheen, was a law partner of the great agnostic, Robert G. Ingersoll. The boys, however, were brought up strictly in the family faith, and were sent to parochial school in Peoria, where the parents moved while Father Sheen was still a small child. (His brother says: "I don't know where Fulton got his ability as a speaker, but I do know that my maternal grandfather used to pay me for making speeches in the house when I was four or five years old. On any topic at all.") Fulton went next to Spaulding

THE RT. REV. MGR. SHEEN

Institute, a secondary school conducted by the Christian Brothers, and at St. Viator College in Bourbonnais, Illinois he received his B. A. in 1917 and his M. A. in 1919. That same year he was ordained a priest.

After a year in a seminary in St. Paul, Minnesota, he went to the Catholic University of America, where he received the S. T. B. and J. C. B. degrees together in 1920. He studied next at Louvain University in Belgium, receiving its Ph. D. degree in 1923. The following year he became a D. D. of the University of Rome, and in 1925, while he was teaching at St. Edmund's College, Ware, England (and preaching in the summer at Westminster Cathedral, London), Louvain made him *Agrégé en Philosophie* and awarded him the Cardinal Mercier Prize. His education has been described as "a long and careful training in the rational principles enunciated by Aristotle at the peak of Greek thinking and reaffirmed by St. Thomas at the crest of Scholastic thinking." He has since had honorary LL. D. degrees conferred upon him by St. Viator, Loyola (Chicago) and St. Bonaventure (New York), and Marquette University gave him a Litt. D.

Returning to America with all these honors and achievements and an invitation to teach at the Catholic University of America, Father Sheen was nevertheless sent by his bishop to serve as parish priest in a poor Peoria parish. It was not until the end of 1926 that he joined the faculty of the Catholic University, where he is now a professor in the department of scholastic philosophy. Since that time he has made himself known as the foremost apologist and orator of the Catholic Church and as such has received many honors both from his church and from its educational institutions. From 1928 to 1931, inclusive, he again preached at the sum-

SHEEN, FULTON J., MGR.—*Continued*

mer conferences at Westminster Cathedral, and in 1930 and 1931 he lectured in the Catholic Summer School in Cambridge, England. For several Lenten seasons he was the Sunday evening preacher at the Church of the Paulist Fathers in New York, and since 1931 he has been Lenten orator at St. Patrick's Cathedral in that city. In 1934 he was appointed by Pope Pius XI Papal Chamberlain, with the title of Right Reverend Monsignor, and the next year Domestic Prelate. In 1936 he won the Cardinal Mazella Medal in philosophy.

To the general public, however, he is best known as preacher on the *Sunday Catholic Hour* of the National Broadcasting Company (sponsored by the National Council of Catholic Men). He began speaking on that hour in 1930, and since that time the National Council has distributed nearly 2,000,000 copies of his talks. Father Sheen himself receives from 3,000 to 6,000 letters a day asking him for copies of his talks, for explanations of Catholic doctrine, for marital advice; about a third of them come from non-Catholics. He personally dictates answers to about 200 of these letters every day, giving the rest to a staff of 20 clerks. He also fills some 150 speaking dates annually, in churches and at religious functions.

Father Sheen is not only a regular contributor to Catholic magazines (*Commonweal, America* and *New Scholasticism*), but has published nearly 30 books, among them *God and Intelligence* (1925); *Religion Without God* (1928); *Old Errors and New Labels* (1931); *The Eternal Galilea* (1934); *Philosophy of Science* (1934); *Calvary and the Mass* (1936); *The Moral Universe* (1936); *Communism the Opium of the People* (1937); *The Cross and the Crisis* (1928); *Liberty, Fraternity and Equality* (1938); *Victory Over Vice* (1939); *Freedom Under God* (1940); *Whence Come Wars* (1940); and *War and Guilt* (1941).

Many of his books are reprints of radio addresses on religious and moral topics; others are popular essays; still others are scholarly expositions of the fine points of Catholic doctrine. All of them teach that "the kingdom of God and his justice is the only important concern of life" and find the solution to the ills of the century in the restoration of the primacy of the spiritual in human affairs. Father Sheen attacks modern philosophy's conception of God, modern psychology's conception of man; he finds divorce as unholy a phenomenon as Hitler's breaking of treaties; he is, above all, appalled that "60 per cent of the children of the United States are today growing into manhood and womanhood without any formal moral or religious education." He is possibly most witty when discussing current affairs—when, for instance, ridiculing those who cried out for "academic freedom" during the Bertrand Russell controversy in 1940. However, as a reviewer in *Commonweal* put it: "The things he says are as old as the Catholic Church; it is the way he says them that is unique." His publishers have called him "the modern Chesterton" (he greatly admired Chesterton), and the *Christian Century* is almost alone in quarreling with this description. According to a writer in that magazine, his "style lacks the salty sparkle that preserves Chesterton's overfrequent paradoxes from growing stale. And he knocks down straw men until the battlefield is littered with them."

As for political and economic views, Father Sheen has on more than one occasion spoken out against "liberalism," against "monopolistic capitalism," against Fascism. But it is as the vitriolic opponent of Communism that he has made himself most felt. (In February 1928 he was called the "world's greatest authority" on Communism's technics by the Marquesa de Cienfuegos.) He says that there are but two complete philosophies of life: Communism and Christianity. To him Fascism is merely the reaction against Communism: "There would be no Mussolini or Hitler in the world today if there had been no Communism, just as there would be no rat-traps if there were no rats." In 1931 he agreed with Chesterton's praise of Mussolini, and during the Spanish War he supported Franco, taking his position, which coincided with the official view of the Catholic Church, in the name of religious liberty.

Shortly afterward E. S. Bates asked Father Sheen, in the columns of the *New Republic,* if his support of Franco's brand of religious liberty didn't expose his and other leading Catholic "liberals'" professed support of the separation of Church and State as merely a matter of strategy—if by "religious liberty" they didn't really mean "liberty for no one but Catholics." Michael Williams of *Commonweal,* however, took issue both with Bates' interpretation of the Spanish War and with Bates' use of the term "liberal" in connection with Father Sheen. What Father Sheen actually is, said Williams, is the "foremost American upholder of the great Scholastic tradition," an "ecclesiastical logician," a great apologist. Father Sheen still rejoices in "Christian Spain's" victory.

In the present War Father Sheen heatedly opposes aid to Russia unless the Soviet Union rejects atheism, restores church property— and he insists that if Russia remains communistic she should be barred from the peace council table. Altogether, his position has created some controversy. The America First Committee used a statement by him on lack of religious freedom in Russia in one of its advertisements; Fight for Freedom countered by quoting from leading Catholics who disagreed with him; the far-from-isolationist editor of the *Protestant Digest* called him a subtle "Fascist voice." Father Sheen opposed any alliance of the democracies with Russia long before the Second World War, and in a radio speech reprinted in *Scribner's Commentator* in May 1941 predicted that the "enemy of the world in the near future" was going to be Russia—even Germany was but a close second. In any case, wars are a form of chastisement for sin, he believes, and can be averted by a return to God. He has for some time been predicting that world peace could be achieved through the efforts of the Pope, "the only moral authority that is left in the world."

Affable but always serious, Father Sheen regards himself as a servant of the Church, to be worked to the limit of his strength in its service. He has long been noted as an instructor of Catholic converts, spending about 10 hours a week on their instruction, for each neophyte receives from 40 to 100 hours of training. His best-known convert, perhaps, was the late Heywood Broun, whose funeral sermon he preached about a year after his conversion. He also instructed Colonel Horace A. Mann, the man who was accused of having spread the anti-Catholic propaganda which contributed to the defeat of Alfred E. Smith in 1928; and Henry Ford, II, grandson of Henry Ford, who married a Roman Catholic girl. But the convert of whom he is proudest is his own Negro cook.

"Lean, black-a-vised, hollow-eyed," *Time* called this eloquent Catholic spokesman. But a friendlier commentator, in *PM*, described him in greater detail: "Monsignor Sheen is a slim, straight man in immaculately cut clerical robes who somehow looks taller than his less-than-medium height. His dark hair combs back from a high forehead like a disciplined wave. His gray eyes are deepset, his face long, his lips wide and mobile. He speaks, for the most part, quietly; in his accents is a note of tension, of restrained vigor. He gestures freely." He is busy every moment. In spite of ill health he travels constantly in his capacity as speaker and preacher; he used to make annual journeys to Lourdes; and he still lectures regularly to his university classes and gives part of every day to his writing on metaphysical, ethical and social themes. He is a member of the Catholic Philosophical Association, of which he was secretary-treasurer in 1928. In the fall of 1941 the March of Time presented *The Story of the Vatican,* the first complete motion picture ever made inside Vatican City, narrated by Father Sheen. It is little wonder that he says curtly that he "has no time for amusement."

References

Cath World 139:619 Ag '34; 147:737-8 S '38
Commonweal 29:435 F 10 '39
New Repub 97:371-2 F 1 '39
Newsweek 15:48 F '26 '40 por
Scrib Com 10:81-5 My '41 por(cover)
Time 35:60-1 Mr 11 '40 por
American Catholic Who's Who
America's Young Men 1936-37
Leaders in Education 1941
Who's Who in America
Who's Who in the Nation's Capital

SHEPPARD, MORRIS May 28, 1875— Apr. 9, 1941 Texas Senator; dean of Congress in length of service (1902-41); Democrat; best known as an ardent dry and as the sponsor of the national prohibition amendment to the Constitution; chairman of the Senate Military Affairs Committee; had written but not published a 35-volume index to Shakespeare titled *Selected Comments of Shakespeare on Over 4,000 Subjects,* which Shakespearean students have termed one of the most comprehensive and individualistic efforts yet completed.

References

Time 31:11 Je 27 '38 por; 35:17 Ja 29 '40 por
Who's Who in America
Who's Who in Government
Who's Who in Law
Who's Who in the Nation's Capital

Obituaries

N Y Times p23 Ap 10 '41 por
Newsweek 17:22 Ap 21 '41 por
Time 37:26 Ap 21 '41 por

SHERLEY, SWAGAR Nov. 28, 1871— Feb. 13, 1941 Washington attorney and for 16 years a Representative from Kentucky; was one of chief financial advisers to President Roosevelt in 1933 on the President's plans for reorganization of the Federal Government; elected to Congress in 1903 and served until 1919; acted as adviser to President Wilson during the First World War; represented the United States in 1935 in negotiations with Canada over damages involving the smelter of a mining company in British Columbia for which Canada agreed to pay the United States $350,-000.

References

Newsweek 1:16-17 F 17 '33
Who's Who in America
Who's Who in Law
Who's Who in the Nation's Capital

Obituaries

N Y Times p17 F 14 '41 por

SHINE, F(RANCIS) W(AYLES) June 25, 1874—Sept. 24, 1941 Ophthalmologist; became an assistant ophthalmic surgeon at the New York Eye and Ear Infirmary in 1907; had a large private practice in New York City and at time of death was a consulting ophthalmic surgeon on the staffs of the New York Eye and Ear Infirmary, the New York Hospital and Doctors Hospital.

References

American Medical Directory

Obituaries

N Y Times p25 S 25 '41 por

SHIRER, WILLIAM L(AWRENCE)
(shĭr'ẽr) Sept. 23, 1904- Foreign correspondent

Address: b. Columbia Broadcasting System, Inc, 485 Madison Ave, New York City; h. Arlington, Va.

WILLIAM L. SHIRER

"This is Berlin . . . " A voice well known to the American public in broadcasts from Berlin on the Columbia network's regular evening European news roundup was that of William L. Shirer, who returned to this country late in December 1940 and embarked on a lecture tour of the United States. Although listeners to his Berlin radio program were aware that "Bill" Shirer had to speak from a script previously passed upon by authorities and with a censor at his elbow, they were amazed at how much he managed to get across to his American audience. He made intellige...t use of a good speaking voice and an ironic sense of humor, knowing that German censors, trained only in academic English, could not catch word-meanings changed by a tone of voice nor get the implications of Shirer's "American" phrasing and slang.

During his stay in Germany, however, Shirer kept diaries and accumulated material which could never get past a censor. This inside, firsthand information about what he actually saw and heard was published in June 1941 in *Berlin Diary*, a July choice of the Book-of-the-Month Club and immediately a best seller. Its story covers all the crucial steps in Hitler's career of conquest which Shirer witnessed, from the 1934 Stavisky riots in Paris through the annexation of Austria in 1937, the signing of the Compiègne Armistice (Shirer had a scoop on this, for he learned that the French would accept the terms three hours before even the German

Government knew it) up to the British air raids on Berlin. Called by Joseph Barnes "the most important and the most exciting book written out of Germany since long before the War began,'' other critics have called attention to its "unusual interest and timeliness," to the completeness of the record of "the destruction of European civilization" observed "from the center of the whirlwind."

For his "consistently outstanding reporting" Shirer was awarded a silver medallion by the Headlines Club in July 1941.

William Lawrence Shirer has been a foreign correspondent since 1925. He was born in Chicago, September 23, 1904, the son of Seward Smith and Bessie Josephine (Tanner) Shirer. But he grew up in Iowa and attended Coe College at Cedar Rapids, from which he was graduated in 1925. He always wanted to be a newspaperman—his first job was a cub reporter's on the Cedar Rapids *Republican*—and when he got out of college he made up his mind that seeing something of the world beyond Iowa wouldn't be a bad idea for journalistic training. Accordingly young Shirer borrowed $200 from an uncle and from his college president, sailed for Europe via Montreal on a cattle boat, and spent $190 seeing England, Belgium and France.

He was down to his last $10, and in a few days due to take the cattle boat back home again. Instead, he got himself a job in the Paris office of the Chicago *Tribune*. His work was so good that in less than a year (1926) Shirer was transferred from the Paris office to the European staff. From then on until 1932 the whole continent became his "beat." He covered assignments not only in Paris, but in London, Rome, Geneva, Brussels, Amsterdam, Vienna and the Balkans. From 1929 to 1932 he was chief of the *Tribune's* Central European Bureau with headquarters in Vienna.

In Vienna in 1931 the young American correspondent met and married Theresa Stiberitz, a Viennese. She became his able assistant. They spent a honeymoon vacation year in 1932 "loafing" on the Catalan coast, swimming, fishing, reading, mountain-climbing.

Just before signing with the Universal News Service, Shirer spent what he calls his "most interesting years" in Afghanistan and India. The former Cedar Rapids cub reporter became a close friend and admirer of Mahatma Gandhi: "I spent much of my time traveling up and down the land with Gandhi," he writes, "and in my opinion he is the greatest man of our times. I studied Hindu philosophy but got badly stymied in the early stages. Still have a poke at it as an antidote for the ideas now popular in Central Europe."

In 1934 he joined the Universal News Service as Berlin correspondent, and three years later became continental representative of the Columbia Broadcasting System, with headquarters in Vienna. The broadcasting of crisis events direct from their source to the United States was in its pioneer stage, and Shirer—along with other foreign correspondents—had to learn while he worked. In an article, "Berlin Speaking," he has described his part and his experiences in developing this new technique. While in Prague during the Czech maneuvers of August 1938, Shirer gave a daily five-minute talk. Getting to the studio itself was often a real hazard; there were other backstage adventures. One day just before he went on the air, "while the troops and air force were rehearsing [their] show, a Skoda fighting plane, diving 10,000 feet, failed to come fully out of its dive and crashed a few feet from my microphone. As soon as we had extracted the pilot and observer from the debris of their plane—they were still alive, though mortally injured—we began our broadcast."

While his wife was in a Vienna hospital having her baby (Eileen Inga), Shirer—between hurried anxious efforts to see her—was trying to broadcast the Austrian *Anschluss*. The trouble was that the Nazis had taken over the radio. "I was a foreigner, unknown to the Nazis," he says. "Maybe I was a spy. Some youths with bayonets invited me to wait outside in the hall. I waited there. . . I was invited to leave. I have never been a man to argue with bayonets. I left. And I have never felt so licked in my life." It was his friend Ed Murrow, fellow CBS broadcaster in England, who came to the rescue by suggesting that he fly to London and give an uncensored broadcast of the Austrian proceedings from there. Shirer did, and that was how America got it.

After the annexation of Austria he transferred his office to Geneva, but went to Berlin at the start of total war in September 1939, where he remained until his return to the United States. In December 1940 *Life* Magazine asked him to write a series of articles on life in wartime Germany. In these, Shirer, using the same warm, informal note familiar to his listeners over 117 stations, told what the German people themselves experience, feel and think during Hitler's conquest regime. He described German life under the R. A. F. bombings, when the *Hauswirte* (air-raid concierges) are the real and feared dictators. He told of the inadequacies of the bombproof shelters for the people in general: the only good one in Berlin belongs to Hitler. "If Hitler has the best . . . the Jews have the worst. In many cases they have none at all." Where they are allowed to hover, "the force of the explosion is felt more and the greatest number of bomb splinters strike." He said that the British have not indiscriminately bombed Berlin in "terror" attacks. "They have too few planes and their bomb loads have been too light to wreak the kind of havoc which the *Luftwaffe* has been able to cause in London." He reported little hatred among the mass of the people against the British; none at all (thus far, because of strict foreign news censorship) against America. "But," he concluded, "were America to enter the War, the effect on German morale would be tremendous. The average German would think of it in very simple terms. 'America entered the War last time while we were still winning. We lost the War. America enters the War

now when we are again winning. We will probably lose it a second time.'"

In between work, Shirer tries to find a little time for his hobbies—walking, skiing (he lost an eye in a skiing accident), golf, symphony music, novel reading, and brushing up on history. In the fall of 1941, however, there was not much time for any of these things. Shirer was acting as consultant on a film being made in Hollywood, *Passage from Bordeaux* (at a fee of $20,000), and was also giving frequent lectures. His second daughter was born in December 1941.

References

Atlan 166:308-17 S '40; 167:265-83 Mr '41
Life 10:66-70+ F 3 '41; 10:56-8+ F 10 '41
N Y Times Book R p12 F 2 '41
Newsweek 14:43 S 11 '39 por
Time 38:43 S 1 '41
Who's Who in America

SHOSTAKOVICH, DMITRI (shŏs-tà-kô'-vich dmē'trē) Sept. 25, 1906- Composer
Address: Leningrad, Kirovsky pr. 14 KV4, U. S. S. R.

One of the first things Leopold Stokowski (see sketch this issue) did after his return from South America in November 1940 was to direct the first performance outside the Soviet Union of the Sixth Symphony by "the Mozart of modern Russia," Dmitri Shostakovich. The performance was arranged for by negotiations with the Amtorg Trading Corporation and the payment of a fee reputedly so large that it had to be specially approved by the directors of the Philadelphia Orchestra. As always, critics disagreed as to the merits and importance of this new but apparently not very unconventional symphonic work by one of the most controversial figures in modern music; the director enthusiastically defended it; and it seemed likely that the performance would be repeated until his audiences were "educated." Not long afterward Shostakovich received the Soviet Union's 100,000-ruble ($20,000) award for the highest achievement in arts and sciences for a piano quintet which received its American première on April 30, 1941.

According to Walter Duranty, "Shostakovich is regarded as Russia's most important contemporary musician." Born in St. Petersburg (now Leningrad) on September 25, 1906, the composer's entire life has been spent there. At the age of 13 he entered the Conservatory there, studied piano under Professor Nikolaiev, composition under Professor Steinberg and, according to one writer, advanced composition under Glazunov. While still there he composed works which (although they have been said to show the influence of Glazunov and one or two other contemporary Russian composers) gave evidence of "a very fine sensibility, flexibility and a very perceptible depth." Opus 1 consisted of three fantastic dances for the piano;

Soyuzphoto

DMITRI SHOSTAKOVITCH

the First Symphony, written when Shostakovich was in his early teens, was already
Opus 10. It has been described as "large
and brilliantly colored"—impish, with an undercurrent of seriousness and a long and
somber slow movement. It was 1925 when
Shostakovich left the Conservatory, and he
soon joined the Union of Soviet Composers.

Members of the Union of Soviet Composers were "pledged to support the socialist
program of construction with their art." An
early interview with the young composer
quoted him: "Music cannot help having a
political basis... The old composers, whether
they knew it or not, were upholding a political theory. Most of them, of course, were
bolstering the rule of the upper classes...
Lenin himself said that 'music is a means of
unifying broad masses of people.' Not a
leader of masses, perhaps, but certainly an
organizing force! For music has the power
of stirring specific emotions in those who
listen to it. Good music lifts and heartens
and lightens people for work and effort. It
may be tragic but it must be strong. It is
no longer an end in itself, but a vital weapon
in the struggle." He said elsewhere: "I am
a Soviet composer, and I see our epoch as
something heroic, spirited and joyous."

His Second and Third Symphonies seem
to bear out his words. Both use large choruses, "celebrating brotherhood, liberty and
revolution." The Second, known as the *October Symphony*, was completed in 1927 and
presented in Leningrad, Moscow, Kiev and
Karkov on the tenth anniversary of the
"fourteen days that shook the world." The
Third, dedicated to the May Day Festival,
completed in 1929 and first produced in 1930,
has been performed on every succeeding May
Day in the Soviet Union. A British critic,
while finding nothing particularly revolution-

ary in its mood, called it "the expression of
all the generous enthusiasms of young Russia." Then there was music for *The Golden
Age,* an "athletic ballet" completed in 1929
and produced at Leningrad in 1930; for *The
Bolt,* an "industrial ballet" also produced in
1930; and for Shostakovich's first opera, *The
Nose,* based on Gogol's novel and produced
for the first time in 1929. Most of these
did not attain any great popularity in Russia,
but the young composer was already known
as "a kind of composer-laureate to the Soviet
state" whose music broke away from old,
"bourgeois" forms and constituted a "repudiation of false romanticism."

Then, in December 1932, Shostakovich completed his second opera. It was titled *Lady
Macbeth of Mzensk,* was based on a novel
written in 1864 by Nikolai Leskov, and was
concerned with a neurotic woman who poi-
soned her father-in-law, persuaded her lover
to kill her husband and finally drowned herself, dragging down with her the woman
who had eventually lured her lover away.
Shostakovich said: "Leskov presents her simply as a cruel woman who 'wallows in fat'
and murders innocent people. But I have
conceived Katerina as a woman clever, gifted
and interesting. Set by fate in gloomy, miserable surroundings, belonging to a merchant
class which is hard, greedy and 'small,' her
life is sorrowful and pitiable." In other
words, the opera was directed against the
rich merchant class of Czarist days. Intended
as the first of four operas which would trace
the change in the position of Russian women
since 1840, it was given its world première
in Moscow in the summer of 1934 and greeted
with 35 minutes of "hysterical applause."

Soon it was being given all over the Soviet
Union. William Bullitt, at that time American Ambassador, heard it at Moscow and
Leningrad and announced that it "should convince all doubters that opera may indeed be
a great art." Dr. Rodzinski of the Cleveland
Symphony Orchestra heard it six times and
made arrangements to bring it to Cleveland.
Its American première on January 31, 1935
undoubtedly made Shostakovich more talked
about in the United States than any of his
previous works, although Stokowski had already given his First, Second and Third Symphonies their American premières and American audiences had also heard his Concerto
for Pianoforte and Orchestra, Opus 35.

Rodzinski himself hailed the opera as "one
of the most important contributions to contemporary music in the last 25 years"; Patrick
Hughes thought it second only to *Wozzeck*
as "the best opera of the post-War era";
the composer's sense of good theatre and
"the uncanny way the orchestra described
each character, each situation" were particularly praised. On the other hand, many
critics found it "vulgar", "imitative", "raucous", "melodramatic", "cheaply cynical." It
was performed only once in New York City,
but Virgil Thomson summed up the situation
by saying: "The New York audience loved
it. The New York critics hedged."

There seemed to be no doubt abroad that the opera was a typical expression of Soviet art, however. It was in the Soviet Union itself that controversy on that point shortly began to rage. Two articles that appeared in *Pravda* condemned Shostakovich for "deserting the classical path to which Soviet music should cling," called *Lady Macbeth,* "a muddle of sound . . . cacophony and lascivious naturalism" rather than "Socialist realism," even found in it certain "petty bourgeois Leftist" tendencies. At two conferences of the Union of Soviet Composers, filled with speechmaking and "self-criticism," the accusation was taken up. Shostakovich was condemned for pseudo-modernism and decadence, for "formalism, eccentricity, skepticism, straining for effect." Performances of *Lady Macbeth* were canceled at several theatres, and although the composer's ballet *Limpid Stream* was produced a month later, *Pravda* condemned that, too, for "stylization and vulgarization."

Nevertheless the controversy was not so much concerned with the music of one individual as with the entire trend of Soviet art at the time. As someone remarked, Shostakovich bore most of the brunt of the attack because he was considered Russia's most talented composer. At the same time negotiations for his next opera were being carried on, and *Lady Macbeth* continued to be performed at some theatres. And when his Fifth Symphony, "a thoughtful and tuneful glorification of the October Revolution," had its première in 1937 Moscow reviewers were almost unanimous in their approval. According to them it reflected his search for new paths in music creation, was "the expression of a psychological development as active as it is complex." (Previously Shostakovich had withdrawn his Fourth Symphony after a couple of rehearsals because, he said, he had not sufficiently learned his lesson.)

The Sixth Symphony, which was first performed in Moscow on December 3, 1939, was to be dedicated to the memory of Lenin, with a chorus. The chorus, however, was lacking when it was completed, and also lacking was "the universal approbation that greeted the Fifth Symphony." Among those American critics who damned it with faint praise were Virgil Thomson, who found it "clear, obvious, effective, old-fashioned. . . If it were signed by an American composer it would be classifiable as good, salable academicism." But Henry Simon called it "good music," designed to "stir the masses."

Shostakovich, who has worked in the Leningrad Conservatory since 1937, and who planned the world première of his reorchestration of Mussorgsky's *Boris Godunoff* for the end of December 1941 at the Bolshoi Theatre in Moscow, volunteered for service in the Peoples Army of Leningrad after the German attack on the Soviet Union. "I am ready and will spare neither life nor strength to fulfill any order," he said, also announcing: "I am writing my Seventh Symphony. I will attempt to depict the Battle of Leningrad and tell the story of the city's Home Guards." He

is described as looking like an incredibly shy schoolboy. Pale, solemn, cherubic, with "tremulous lips and hands", "thatched hair" and "wide eyes behind hornrimmed glasses," he doesn't often discuss his music. But in addition to the works already noted he has composed a great many piano and cello sonatas, pieces for the string octet and for the piano; music for stage productions of *Hamlet* and *King Lear* and for another ballet, *Don Quixote;* music for the sound films, *Golden Mountains, Alone, Maxim's Youth.* Critics have pointed out (many of them disapprovingly) that this music shows the various influences of Prokofieff, Hindemith (see sketches this issue), Stravinsky, Auric, Strauss, Chopin, Tschaikowsky, Mahler, Weber, Borodin, Mussorgsky, Liszt, Beethoven and Mozart—which surely makes it safe to classify him as an "eclectic." But, according to one writer, he is eclectic "in the good as well as the bad sense." Unlike many of his predecessors, Shostakovich seldom repeats a theme even in a transformed version, and tries to refrain from the repetition of *motifs.* "One gets the impression that he wants every bar of his composition to be different from the rest."

References

Modern Music p23-30 N-D '34; p123-6 Mr '35
Musical Courier 109:10 Jl 14 '31
N Y Times VIII p8 D 20 '31
Newsweek 3:29 Je 30 '34 il por; 5:22-3 F 9 '35
PM p54 Ap 27 '41 por
Spec 154:163 F 1 '35; 156:396 Mr 6 '36
Time 36:54 D 9 '40

Baker's Biographical Dictionary of Musicians 1940
Ewen, D. ed. Composers of Today 1936
International Who's Who
Rosenfeld, P. Discoveries of a Music Critic p237-50 1936
Thompson, O. ed. International Cyclopedia of Music and Musicians 1939
Vodarsky-Shiraeff, A. comp. Russian Composers and Musicians 1940

SHUMLIN, HERMAN (ELLIOTT) Dec. 6, 1898- Theatrical producer

Address: b. 229 W. 42nd St, New York City; h. 104 E. 40th St, New York City

While Ethel Barrymore (see sketch this issue), the star of Herman Shumlin's latest production, *The Corn Is Green,* was celebrating her fortieth anniversary as a star in February 1941, the producer and director of this play about an English schoolteacher and her young coal-miner protégé had reasons of his own for self-congratulation. The play had won practically unanimous critical acclaim, the theatregoing public was storming the box office and Miss Barrymore was giving the most luminous performance of her career.

It was also the third in an unbroken line of successes produced by Mr. Shumlin in recent seasons. *The Little Foxes* (1939),

Vandamm

HERMAN SHUMLIN

Lillian Hellman's bitter play of the new South, played almost a year and the picture rights were sold to Samuel Goldwyn for $100,000. The James Thurber-Elliott Nugent campus comedy, *The Male Animal*, ran several months in 1940 with a profit of $50,000 and was bought by Warner Brothers for $150,000. The fourth in line was Lillian Hellman's (see sketch this issue) *Watch on the Rhine*, which was the Critics' Circle choice for the best American play of 1941 and which settled down for a long run.

This producer who in 1941 had two enormously successful plays running on Broadway hasn't always been at the top. Before this there had been intervals between hits, and there had been failures and near-successes. The first four plays Mr. Shumlin produced, beginning with *Celebrity* in November 1927, were on view an aggregate of twelve weeks and one hundred eighteen performances. *Days to Come* ran one week in December 1936, and Thornton Wilder's *The Merchant of Yonkers* failed to amuse theatregoers for more than five weeks when produced in December 1938.

Herman Elliott Shumlin was born in Atwood, Colorado (George and Rebecca [Slavin] Shumlin were his parents), grew up in Newark, New Jersey and made his first and probably his last stage appearance in a school pageant as a Sioux warrior chanting an Ojibway ballad. That the play being performed was supposed to be *Alice in Wonderland* merely added to the confusion. He saw Sir Johnston Forbes-Robertson's *Hamlet* at the age of 10 in Newark's Broad Street Theatre, and it interested him in the theatre more than his own stage performance ever had.

Young Shumlin left the classroom in his second year of high school, for his family was not too prosperous. At 15 he was working in the offices of a Newark manufacturing plant, where he was dismissed and called a "Socialist" for asking why safety devices weren't demanded on the machines. Later he found a more interesting job—in the exploitation department of the New Jersey branch of Metro films. From this outpost of the picture industry he moved in on Broadway as reporter on the New York *Clipper*, a theatrical trade publication since defunct, and from there progressed to the *Billboard* as reporter and motion picture critic. Later he turned press agent for Schwab and Mandel, became general manager for Jed Harris during the Broadway runs of *Love 'Em and Leave 'Em, Broadway* (one of the greatest hits of all time) and *Spread Eagle*.

It was in 1927 that Shumlin presented his first production, Willard Keefe's *Celebrity*, with Paul Streger as partner. This lasted only 42 performances, but Shumlin kept on independently, presenting *The Command Performance, Tonight at 12* and *Button, Button* without any noticeable success. Then came *The Last Mile*, a harrowing play set in the death house of a prison, which won critical if not audience applause. Shumlin decided to go on producing what he liked instead of guessing about the public's taste.

It was not until the morning of November 14, 1930 that Shumlin found himself producer of a real hit. Vicki Baum's *Grand Hotel*, staged by Mr. Shumlin himself in his first attempt at direction, caught on immediately and played 257 performances on Broadway before it was made into a motion picture. Shumlin's next attempt, the Spewacks' *Clear All Wires*, did less well. Despite warm critical notices, this comedy about a high-pressure foreign correspondent ran only 12 weeks on Broadway. It later appeared as an MGM film success called *Comrade X*.

In 1934 Shumlin produced another success. Lillian Hellman, who had been his play reader for several years, brought him a play of her own based on one of the celebrated cases in William Roughead's *Bad Companions*. Ironically she called this work, which dealt with the ruin spread in a girls' school by a problem child who started a scandalous rumor about two of her teachers, *The Children's Hour*. Shumlin scoured the country to find suitable actors and found Florence McGee, Anne Revere, Katherine Emery and Robert Keith, who gave the play such a taut and vivid performance that it ran a year and one-half in New York. When it was banned in Boston he launched a campaign which resulted in revision of the State laws regarding censorial procedure. It was produced as a film by Samuel Goldwyn under the title of *These Three*—with a slight change of theme, however.

It was Miss Hellman again who presented Shumlin with his next big success, after two failures of his own productions (*Days to Come* and *The Merchant of Yonkers*) and one by the Theatre Guild (*Wine of Choice*) which he directed in 1938. Miss Hellman's *The Little Foxes*, the story of a family of predatory Southerners, starring temperamental Tallulah Bankhead, opened in 1939. It was followed by *The Corn Is Green,* which began its triumphant career on the evening of November 26, 1940, and in the spring of 1941 by *Watch on the Rhine.*

Herman Shumlin, who himself exhorts: "Establish the mood from the first moment of the play. Make the picture uniform and constant," has been called "a man of impulse and vagaries, who trusts implicitly his feeling for the dramatic and his ear for the authentic." His success has been attributed by a writer in *Theatre* "to his amazingly copious knowledge of useful facts and event and his tremendous energies for completing any undertaking upon which he may have engaged."

This bald, dynamic, intense producer is "a man who simply cannot make small talk," according to *Friday.* "Mention the weather and he launches into a furious discussion of it—the weather today, yesterday, tomorrow, last year, two years ago. He got to thinking about Russian once and before he knew it he was taking lessons. He got to thinking about photography recently and before his friends could stop him, he had a bathroom torn out and a darkroom installed. But this furious transmission of his thoughts into action seldom lasts long. His Russian lessons ended after two weeks. His darkroom has produced only one gray print of Maxwell Anderson's baby. And his campaign to reduce [the price of] theatre tickets lasted only a few weeks."

Shumlin is known as a man of strong convictions, not averse to a battle. (Early in 1940, for instance, he refused to play Finnish benefits, and at that time had the epithet "Communist" hurled at him.) The anti-Nazi hero of *Watch on the Rhine* expresses his own views on the necessity of fighting "again and again" for "our great human heritage." He says, too: "I do not want to die simply because there are many wrong things in the world. I want to live and do something about them."

Outside the theatre Shumlin has few hobbies. Five years ago he tried to master the piano but gave it up after a heroic struggle. He is divorced from the actress Rose Keane, whom he married in 1930, and since the prosperity of *The Children's Hour* he has had offices on the sixth floor of the Selwyn Theatre Building on West Forty-Second Street. One of the properties moved to his office at that time included a cigaret box used in *Tonight at 12* and labeled by its owner: "This cost $25,000."

References

Cue 3:3+ Ap 13 '35 por
Friday 2:8-9 Ja 10 '41 pors
N Y Times IX p1+ My 25 '41
Theatre 53:30+ Mr '31 por
Theatre Arts 24:373-4 My '40
Who's Who in American Jewry
Who's Who in the Theatre

SHUSTER, GEORGE N(AUMAN) Aug. 27, 1894- Author; educator
Address: Hunter College, 68th St. and Park Ave, New York City

Worldwide

GEORGE N. SHUSTER

George N. Shuster, who in 1940 became president of New York City's Hunter College, has sent us the following sketch of himself:

"I was born in Lancaster, Wisconsin, August 27, 1894, the son of Anthony and Elizabeth (Nauman) Shuster. My father's people were German Catholics, my great-grandfather having come to the United States with his children during 1848 because of the Revolution. My mother's people were German Lutherans, who had originally settled in Pennsylvania. The romance of my boyhood was the aftermath of the Civil War, Lancaster being a favorite place for G. A. R. conventions. Then the little town—a very pretty replica of New England villages—was literally fenced in with white tents, where the veterans bivouacked and (it must be confessed) drank copiously and long.

"My secondary education was received at St. Lawrence's College, Fond du Lac, Wisconsin, which was a German Gymnasium transplanted to the New World. We studied Latin and Greek incessantly, but we also learned modern languages, German and French. Notre Dame was my college—then a small institution, with a football team on the first rung of the ladder of fame. My dream was to enter West Point, but when the War came I turned instead to journalism and spent one hectic year trying to be a reporter. Then came 1917, military service, and thereupon 18 months of life with the A. E. F., first as a member of the Intelligence Section, G. H. Q., serving at the front during almost all the major battles in which the American Army was engaged, and then as an interpreter in the Army of Occupation. Subsequently I attended the University of Poitiers, France, emerging with a *Certificat d'Aptitude.*

SHUSTER, GEORGE N.—*Continued*

"Therewith began my deep interest in modern Europe. I had seen a good deal of post-War Germany—fighting in the streets, the first electoral campaign, hunger, the heavy pressure of the Armistice terms. And I had also seen a good deal of what went on round about the Peace Conference. But when I returned to the United States I had first of all to think of my health, which had been put to a severe strain. Quite accidentally a call came to teach English at Notre Dame, and I answered it thinking that the quiet life I had known on the campus would help me to recuperate. But the president of the University, the Rev. Father James Burns, and I became fast friends. I took my master's degree in French literature, became head of the department of English and remained at the University until my marriage to Doris Parks Cunningham in 1924. The principal literary product of those years was *The Catholic Spirit in Modern English Literature* (1922).

"Going to New York for graduate study at Columbia, I came into contact quite accidentally with the newly-formed *Commonweal* group, bent on starting a weekly magazine similar in character to *The Nation* and the *New Republic* but dedicated to religious principles. By the end of the year 1924 the magazine had begun publication, and I had started writing editorials for it. After six months I decided to sever my academic connections and to accept an editorial position first as associate editor and then as managing editor. The amount of work required by this periodical during the next 12 years was tremendous, but I retained some teaching connections, usually giving a course of lectures in some New York college. Books written during these years included one or two on Catholic subjects—*The Catholic Spirit in America* (1927); and *The Catholic Church and Current Literature* (1929). More and more, however, my thinking and reading were concerned with modern Germany, which I visited for long periods after 1929. This is reflected in such books as *The Germans* (1932); *Strong Man Rules* (1934); and *Like a Mighty Army* (1935). Translations from the German likewise followed in almost-too-rapid succession.

"During 1937 the Carnegie Corporation awarded me a very beguiling two-year fellowship in the study of the Weimar Republic and in particular of the Center Party. I spent most of the following two years abroad, witnessing among other things the taking over of Austria and the development of the Czechoslovak crisis. The book to be written is still in the writing, but I did manage to write the notes for the Reynal and Hitchcock edition of the English version of *Mein Kampf*. Meanwhile I had, largely for reasons of relaxation, turned to the writing of fiction. Here the most successful book was a novel, entitled *Look Away* (1939). The most recent publication, however, is once more in the field of English literature, *The English Ode from Milton to Keats* (1940).

"The Board of Higher Education of the City of New York invited me, in 1939, to become academic dean and acting president of Hunter College. After a year of service I became president. Meanwhile the degree of doctor of philosophy had been earned at Columbia University. I shall hope that the tasks, and they are many, of guiding an educational institution will not deflect me from the pursuits of rose-growing, carpentry and tennis in which I remain interested."

Dr. Shuster, according to *PM*, "often works at the college in the evening, takes only a sandwich for lunch, has never seen the color of his desk because of the papers piled on it. He drives a Buick, smokes Pall Malls, eats all kinds of breakfast foods, and buys his clothes at Altman's." He has one son, Robert.

References

> Commonweal 33:5 O 25 '40
> Newsweek 16:66 S 16 '40
> PM p20-1 O 29 '40 pors
> Time 36:60 S 16 '40
>
> American Catholic Who's Who
> America's Young Men 1936-37
> Leaders in Education 1941
> Who's Who in America

SILVER, ABBA HILLEL, RABBI (äb'ä hïl'ĕl) Jan. 28, 1893- Rabbi of Temple Tifereth Israel, Cleveland; author; social worker

Address: b. The Temple, E. 105th St. & Ansel Rd, Cleveland, Ohio; h. 246 E. 105th St, Cleveland, Ohio

"The church is a dynamic agency," wrote Rabbi Abba Hillel Silver in his book, *Religion in a Changing World*, published in 1930. Nobody can doubt this after glancing at the astronomical range of Rabbi Silver's own interests. At the top of the list is Zionism, and in this field he has, since Hitler's rise to power, been even more active than before, because he believes the Jewish homeland to be an even more crucial need today than in the past. Other interests, however, include many charities, unemployment relief, child welfare, Jewish education, civil liberties, birth control and the World Court.

Who's Who in America alone lists more than 30 organizational affiliations. This, probably, is no surprise to thousands, for Rabbi Silver's reputation is national in scope, and he is as well known in New York and San Francisco as in his adopted Cleveland. His radio broadcasts for Jewish holy days and other occasions over the national networks have brought his ringing voice to uncounted homes, while his personal appearances before various congregations have extended to many cities. He has traveled throughout the nation in behalf of overseas relief and is credited with having helped to raise millions of dollars for the relief of distressed Jews throughout the world.

Nevertheless Rabbi Silver has managed to find the time to write four books, at least three of which have definite contemporaneous interest and one of which will unquestionably

rank as a definitive reference work for Jewish
scholars. Recognized, with Rabbi Stephen
S. Wise (see sketch this issue) of New York,
as one of the major voices of Zionism, Rabbi
Silver has tried to synthesize Jewish tradition with American civilization, without, however, permitting the surrender of the former
in the fancied interests of the latter.

Rabbi Silver's scholarly thin face is topped
by pompadoured black hair edged with gray,
and his eyes, behind rimless spectacles, mirror
alert intensity. He was born in Neinstadt,
Schirwindt, Lithuania in 1893, the son of
Moses and Diana (Seamon) Silver. Brought
to America when he was nine years old, the
future Rabbi rapidly entered into the life
of the New World and proved especially
proficient in scholarship. Receiving a B. A.
from the University of Cincinnati in 1915, he
went on to the Hebrew Union College, from
which he was graduated as a qualified rabbi.
From the same college he received his D. D.
degree in 1925. (He also received an honorary Litt D. from Western Reserve, and
Hebrew Union College awarded him a
D. H. L. degree in 1941.) Following his induction as a clergyman Rabbi Silver served
from 1915 to 1917 in the Congregation L'Shem
Shamayim in Wheeling, West Virginia. Here
he met Virginia Horkheimer (the daughter
of Louis and Clementine Horkheimer), whom
he married in 1923.

Receiving a call from The Temple of
Cleveland (Tifereth Israel), Rabbi Silver returned to the state where he had attended
college. Since 1917 he has made his home
in Cleveland. Two children, both boys, were
born in that city. During the War he served
with the armed forces in France and was
decorated by the French Government with the
medal of the Officier de l'Instruction Publique. Later President Hoover placed him
on a national committee to alleviate unemployment.

Rabbi Silver's published works include: *The
Messianic Speculation in Israel* (1927); *The
Democratic Impulse in Jewish History* (1928);
Religion in a Changing World (1930); and
The World Crisis and Jewish Survival (1941).
The Messianic Speculation is an interesting com-
pilation of writings by Jewish prophets of
antiquity and the pseudo-prophets of Medie-
valism on the subject of the Messiah. It
is documented with references to the original
Hebrew sources, and traces references in the
Talmud as well as in the occult writings of
the medieval cabalists.

The Democratic Impulse is an historical
capitulation of Jewish social thought from
earliest times to the present and an examination of the strivings by the Jewish people for
a democratic order. In *Religion in a Changing World* Rabbi Silver squares political liberalism with modern religion, sees the
supposed "revolt" against religion as an ultra-
conservative and illiberal manifestation rather
than a daring innovation or a quest for freedom, and attempts to resolve the familiar
conflict between science and religion by cate-
gorizing the non-conflicting role of each in

Harry A. Cole

RABBI ABBA HILLEL SILVER

current civilization. In addition, Rabbi Silver
describes the necessity for an activist role
by the church in the social scheme and analyzes the relation of the Jew to his environment. Rejecting "assimilation," he states his
belief that this would only mean distorting
Jewish personality and renouncing its unique
qualities. He states that communion of minds,
which is the only basis for true fellowship
between Jew and non-Jew, does not decree
the surrender of Jewish distinctiveness, but
on the contrary means its careful survival.
The World Crisis deals with the subject
that is possibly Rabbi Silver's major concern:
the question of preserving Jewish culture and
Jewish life in a world of war and persecution.

Ohioans call Rabbi Silver the father of
the unemployment insurance movement in
that state. It was he who, as far back as
1928, persuaded the Consumers League of
Ohio to undertake a survey of unemployment
and unemployment insurance. As chairman
of the Committee on Unemployment Insurance, he helped to frame the state's pioneer
legislation on the subject, and he has been
appointed by Governor White as a member of
the state commission to study the problem.
He has also served as chairman of the Ohio
Committee on Unemployment Insurance. Widely known as a liberal, Rabbi Silver has been
chosen to help arbitrate many industrial disputes and is highly regarded by organized
labor.

Active in civic affairs, Rabbi Silver is often
called upon to assume a leading role in charitable or cultural activities from all sorts of
local groups. His interest in Cleveland is
attested to by his aid in the introduction of
the city-manager form of government and,
later on, in the fight to retain it from 1927

SILVER, ABBA HILLEL, RABBI—*Cont.*
to 1929 when the question of civic rule became a tremendous issue with the population.

References

N Y Times p15 D 27 '40; p2 S 15 '41
Recreation 31:10 Ap '37 por
Survey 76:190 Je '40 por
Who's Who in America
Who's Who in American Jewry

SIMON, RICHARD L(EO) (sī'mŏn) Mar. 6, 1899- Publisher
Address: b. Simon & Schuster, Inc, 1230 Sixth Ave, Rockefeller Center, New York City; h. 245 W. 11th St, New York City

SCHUSTER, M(AX) LINCOLN (shoo'-stĕr) Mar. 2, 1897- Publisher
Address: b. Simon & Schuster, Inc, 1230 Sixth Ave, Rockefeller Center, New York City; h. 11 E. 73rd St, New York City

The publishing house of Simon & Schuster is perhaps the most highly personalized in the United States. The tastes and personalities of its founders, Richard L. Simon and M. Lincoln Schuster, are reflected in everything, from the chatty Inner Sanctum ads to the comparatively small but varied list. Essandess, as the team is known to the trade,

RICHARD L. SIMON

has made its fortune mainly with financially profitable self-help books that teach the readers anything from *How To Become a Good Dancer* by Arthur Murray (1938) to *The Art of Thinking* by Abbé Dimnet (1928)— not to mention *How To Win Friends and Influence People* by Dale Carnegie (1938). (The latest venture of this sort is called *How To Do Practically Anything,* and the publishers believe that it will be a "how to" book to end all "how to" books.) It has also purveyed cul-

ture to the masses through a series of basic books such as *A Treasury of Art Masterpieces* (1939) and *A Treasury of the Theatre* (1940).

When Simon and Schuster joined forces in 1924, they immediately went counter to many staid publishing traditions: limiting themselves to a book list that was of necessity (and later by choice) comparatively small, they paid more attention to promotion than has ever been done before. They advertised on a hitherto unknown scale (about $150,000 was spent on advertising the Carnegie book in 1937), the first publishers to boost their wares in full-page newspaper advertisements. They were, too, pioneers in what Schuster prefers to call "planned publishing," which consists of assigning ideas to writers. This sort of publishing called for an extensive stock of ideas. Today Robert van Gelder, writing about Max Schuster, is amazed by the extent to which the ideas of his adolescence still shape his distinctly unusual career.

When they met neither of the future team of Essandess had had a particularly exciting career behind him. Richard Leo Simon was born in New York, March 6, 1899, the son of Leo Leopold Simon, a well-to-do wholesale milliner, and his wife, Anna (Mayer) Simon. He was the eldest of five children and, like the rest of the family, intensely musical, a taste that is reflected in a number of Essandess books on music: he used to write music for camp songs, pick up pocket money by accompanying the family's operatic friends, and lead glee clubs in high school and college. He attended Ethical Culture School and afterward went to Columbia University, from which he was graduated in 1920. In 1918 he stayed in Plattsburg, a second infantry lieutenant. His first job after he was graduated from college was in a sugar importing firm. In 1921 he sold pianos for the Aeolian Company. It was then that he met Schuster, who was recommended to him as a possible customer. Schuster did not buy a piano, but the two young men discovered a passion in common for Romain Rolland. From this sprang a friendship that has endured these 20 years. In 1921 Simon became a salesman for Boni and Liveright, where he learned a good deal about publishing, and two years later he was ready to start out on his own. From 1924 on his and Schuster's personal histories become submerged in that of Simon & Schuster, Incorporated.

Max Schuster, the more breathless half of Essandess, was born March 2, 1897, in Kalusz, Austria, the son of Barnet and Esther (Stieglitz) Schuster, and was brought to New York City when he was seven weeks old. His father ran a stationery and cigar store, and Max, who went to public school and De Witt Clinton High School, acquired an early taste for journalism by reading newspapers, which he helped his father sell. Another enthusiasm was for Abraham Lincoln: while in high school young Max adopted Lincoln as his middle name. After he was graduated from high school he went to see Charles Chapin, the celebrated city editor of the old New York *Evening World,* and by means of boyish bravado talked himself into his first full-time job as a copy boy at $5 a week. Joseph Pulitzer, publisher of the *World*, was his boyhood hero. His biography was to be one of the first Simon & Schuster books.

In 1913 he quit the *World*, and his parents, at a great personal sacrifice, sent him to Columbia University and the Pulitzer School of Journalism. At college Max was prominent in an unusually brilliant class and put out, together with Irwin Edman and George E. Sokolsky (see sketch this issue), a radical undergraduate magazine, *Challenge*. He partly earned his expenses in college by writing, selling magazine articles and acting as college correspondent for the Boston *Evening Transcript*. This journalistic experience helped him to get a job after graduation as Washington correspondent for the New Republic News Service, later the United Press. During the First World War he was chief of the publication service of the Bureau of War Risk Insurance of the Treasury Department and later director of publicity for the United States Navy Liberty Loan and Victory Loan campaigns. After he was demobilized he was assistant to Professor Walter B. Pitkin (see sketch this issue), and edited the trade journal of the Motor & Equipment Manufacturers Association. By 1924 he had saved up about $4,000 from his various activities. That sum and a like sum from Simon went into their publishing house, a project which he and Simon had been considering for a long time. They had, besides, "a mass of adolescent enthusiasm" and a lot of ideas, plans and projects, but no authors or contracts.

Although they found out that, contrary to popular belief, authors conspire to discourage new and unknown publishers, their venture was an immediate financial success—even if in a somewhat unorthodox manner. Their first book was a crossword puzzle series which they assigned to the puzzle editors of the Sunday *World*. Characteristically, it was the result of Richard Simon's having overheard his aunt say she wished there were a collection of crossword puzzles for her to give to a sick friend. (*Fun in Bed*, 1932, was another instance of profitable eavesdropping by Simon, who overheard people in stores ask for good books to send to sick friends.) The 47 various volumes have sold over 1,500,000 copies and netted for Simon and Schuster a profit of $100,000. Unfortunately, it also gave them a reputation for being trick publishers, undispelled for a while even by the biography of Pulitzer they put out the same year.

Their best seller of 1926 belonged to an entirely different category. In his undergraduate days Schuster, who studied philosophy under Professor Walter B. Pitkin, thought that a book on the lives of the philosophers would be a fine thing. Pitkin was too busy to write it. But Schuster never forgot the idea, and finally found what he wanted in Will Durant's books, which were being published and sold at a nickel apiece by E. Haldeman-Julius. *Story of Philosophy*, which sold over 500,000 copies and put Essandess definitely in the black, was, like

M. LINCOLN SCHUSTER

many another Simon and Schuster product, mainly an editing job. Another one was *The Bible Designed To Be Read as Living Literature* (1936), edited by the late Ernest Sutherland Bates and dubbed by Irwin Edman "the King Max Version of the Bible." The Essandess team is very proud of its popularity in England, the home of the King James' version.

The list of authors to whom Simon and Schuster have assigned ideas is long and impressive. They have, on occasion, called upon their friends, relatives and employees. *With Malice Toward Some*, a 1938 best seller, was written by Margaret Halsey, the wife of Richard Simon's brother Henry, on the occasion of her trip to England. Quincy Howe, the head of the editorial department, has written three books for Simon & Schuster: *England Expects Every American To Do His Duty* (1937), *Blood Is Cheaper Than Water* (1939) and *The News And How To Understand It* (1940). Among the alumni of the Columbia School of Journalism who have written books at the request of their classmate Schuster are Irwin Edman, Silas Seadler and Merryle Rukeyser. Simon even got his lawyer, René Wormser, to write *Your Will And What Not To Do About It* (1937). They try, however, to keep the emphasis off pure business and inspirational subjects and on culture and contemporary political scenes by such assignments as that of *Twelve Against the Gods* (1929) to William Bolitho; of *We Saw It Happen* (1938) to 13 foreign correspondents of the New York *Times*; or of *Men of Wealth* (1941) to John T. Flynn. That phenomenal money maker, Dale Carnegie's *How To Make Friends and Influence People* (which earned the author around a quarter of a million dollars and the staff a sizable year-end bonus), was the idea of the firm's business manager, who had attended the Carnegie course.

SIMON, RICHARD L. and SCHUSTER, M. LINCOLN—*Continued*

Graduating from the rather specialized interest in crossword puzzles, Simon and Schuster have acquired a list which includes Walter Pitkin, Eddie Cantor, Albert Einstein (see sketches this issue), Sidney Lenz, Robert Briffault, Cornelius Vanderbilt, Jr., Robert Ripley, Hendrik Willem Van Loon and Ferdinand Pecora. Although generally preferring to assign books, according to their "planned publishing" idea, Essandess has occasionally published manuscripts submitted to them—solely, it is said, upon the editorial recommendation. *Trader Horn,* a terrific best seller of 1927, was recommended by Clifton Fadiman (see sketch this issue). But this story of a picturesque tatterdemalion and his incredible adventures was given the full benefit of the Essandess promotional facilities to such an extent that it has been claimed that this and other Simon & Schuster best sellers owed their success solely to a high pressure advertising campaign, a statement with which Simon and Schuster disagree. By one method or another they have managed to produce a list of best sellers, so that their books have been selling at an impressive average of 20,000 (the average book sells approximately 1,200 copies).

Another literary triumph was John Cowper Powys' *Wolf Solent,* which was called a modern prose Hamlet by Percy Hutchison of the New York *Times,* to the great delight of the partners, who have always wanted to publish a classic. Generally, however, their fiction list has been rather weak. Clifton Fadiman, before leaving, did a lot to bolster it, being responsible for getting writers like Josephine Johnson, Christina Stead and Hans Fallada. But outside of Millen Brand's *The Outward Room* (1937), and Jerome Weidman's *I Can Get It For You Wholesale* (1939), few Essandess novels have reached the level of their other best sellers. The partners, who still learn as they run, have a small black book in which they record what they call their *flops d'éstime* and *succès de fiasco.* Not exactly in that category but still an unwelcome experience was their publication of Joan Lowell's *Cradle of the Deep* (1929), a roaring but unfortunately far from authentic sea story. Among the classical errors of omission they put their turning down of Grand Duchess Marie's *Education of a Princess,* which subsequently sold 200,000 copies for the Viking Press (1940). It was thereafter referred to in the office as "The Education of a Publisher" and, says Schuster earnestly, has taught them to pay more attention "to the inherent quality of the manuscript rather than to the field or classification in which it fell."

It was in 1927 that Essandess started its personal, chatty Inner Sanctum ads. The Inner Sanctum is the editorial conference room between the partners' offices where their brain children are born. In these ads, in the form of confidential letters to the trade and the public, the Essandess successes and failures are discussed with an amazing lack of inhibition. Occasionally they would chide the public for its lethargic attitude toward their favorite products ("It is simply incredible to your correspondents that a story so beautiful and with so obvious a popular appeal [as Alice Duer Miller's *Forsaking All Others*] can have been bought by so few people"), apologize for bad book jackets, discuss their love of music and admiration for the Philharmonic Symphony Orchestra and congratulate competitors on fortunate ventures.

Simon and Schuster have been too busy instigating books to write many of their own. In 1937 Simon, who is himself no mean photographer, wrote *Miniature Photography,* which was highly praised in an independent Inner Sanctum ad by Schuster, to his partner's great embarrassment. Schuster produced in 1935 *Eyes on the World,* a photographic history of 1934. That was not a great success, but Schuster's *A Treasury of the World's Great Letters* (1940), a lush and handsome job, was a best seller. Schuster had begun working on it about 25 years before, until his letter collection filled many mammoth volumes. A publisher as well as an editor, Schuster had planned the entire project as an integrated whole, always keeping in mind the trade promotion, and putting in it, as inducement to the reader, such facilitating devices as the classified table of contents, the grouping of letters by topics, the carefully thought out and effective headlines and background material. Simon, on his part, contributed an effective brochure to the members of the trade, which grateful Schuster called a "Treasury of Great Trade Letters." The second volume of *A Treasury of the World's Great Letters* came out in the fall of 1941, together with *A Treasury of Gilbert and Sullivan.*

Simon and Schuster function successfully as a team, with Simon on the sales and promotion end and Schuster principally an idea man. Simon, a tall, handsome, rangy man, who has been described as an amiable hedonist, makes frequent trips around the country, selling his firm's books and getting publishing ideas. It was his idea, for example, to enclose referendum cards in their books, asking readers for their opinion of the books. Many of the remarks that come back, besides providing a valuable gauge of public reaction, are quotable (though Simon admits that many others are unprintable) and have been used to good effect in advertisements. In 1934 Simon married Andrea Louise Heinemann, who once was the Simon & Schuster telephone girl, and they now have two daughters, Joanna and Lucy. His favorite recreations are bridge—he is an excellent player—tennis, golf and photography, the last of which he practices in the basement of his home in Greenwich Village. He also often plays the piano with a sure and skillful touch.

M. Lincoln Schuster (Max to his friends), who "looks like a merry young owl," was a confirmed bachelor until May 1940, when he married Ray Levison. Aside from his all-consuming passion for culture, his main characteristic is a maddening love for order. He has built up an elaborate filing system of colored slips of paper, duplicates, photostatic copies and abbreviations. Every morning his left-hand suit pocket is filled with batches of three-by-five colored slips which he covers with jotted notes during the course of the day. This bewildering stream of "M's" (maxims), "E. M.'s" (editorial memos), "M. A.'s" (maxim allusions), "G. A.'s" (good ads) and others flows from his left-hand to his right-hand pocket and is eventually typed and filed away to lie dormant in folders until it emerges in the form of books or advertising campaigns. He has been functioning for years at the speed of a dynamo, busy for 18 hours out of 24. Since his marriage, however, he has stepped down this tempo somewhat and has promised to bring home "my enthusiasms but not my manuscripts." Schuster is fond of gags and quips. In *Who's Who in America* he is listed as a member of Friends of Scripta Mathematica, Three Hours for Lunch Club, Society for Prevention of Cruelty to Newspaper Readers, Wednesday Culture Club That Meets on Fridays, and Downing Street Young Men's Marching Club.

Lately Simon & Schuster, Incorporated, have been installed in a fabulous glass penthouse which has been described as "not only the handsomest but probably the most compact and efficient publishing offices in the country." All the offices have an entire wall of glass (the publishers' offices have two) and are surrounded by a broad terrace with shrubs and flowers that the Radio City management changes every two weeks. Thus equipped for a lifetime of gracious publishing, the two partners are still as excited as ever about their profession. That Max Schuster actually came down with his wife to see his book in the press bespeaks a youthful and touching enthusiasm that more than 15 years in the publishing business might ordinarily be expected to dull.

References

N Y Times Book R p2 N 10 '40 por
New Yorker 15:22-8 S 30 '39; 15:24-30
  O 7 '39; 15:25-9 O 14 '39
Pub W 132:1832-6 N 6 '37 il; 138:24-7
  Jl 6 '40 il pors; 138:1588-90 O 19 '40 il
Read Digest 35:76-80 D '39
America's Young Men 1936-37 [M. L. Schuster]
Who's Who in America
Who's Who in American Jewry [M. L. Schuster]
Who's Who in Commerce and Industry

SIMONDS, FREDERIC W(ILLIAM) (sī'mŭnds) July 3, 1853—Mar. 27, 1941 Professor of geology at the University of Texas; oldest faculty member of the University where he has taught for 51 years; widely known among geologists as an authority on the stratigraphical geology of the Southwest and the physiography of North America; author of many scientific reports and papers and of two books of geology, which have had wide circulation.

References

American Men of Science
Who's Who in America

Obituaries

N Y Times p15 Mr 29 '41

SIMPSON, KENNETH F(ARRAND) May 4, 1895—Jan. 25, 1941 Republican Representative from New York and former president of the New York County Republican Committee; active in politics since 1922, two years after he received his law degree; Assistant United States Attorney, 1925 to 1927; important in New York State Republican Party as State Committeeman and since 1933 County Chairman until his resignation in December 1940 after his foe, Thomas Dewey, won control of the State Republican Party; was elected Congressman in 1940 and served only 23 days before his death.

References

Life 10:28 Ja 6 '41 por
N Y Times p1+ D 21 '40 por
New Yorker 15:21-7 O 28 '39
PM p13 N 10 '40 pors
Time 32:16 D 12 '38 por
Who's Who in America

Obituaries

N Y Times p1+ Ja 26 '41 por
Time 37:14 F 3 '41 por

SKILTON, CHARLES SANFORD Aug. 16, 1868—Mar. 12, 1941 Composer; professor of music at the University of Kansas since 1903; noted for his Indian melodies which have been widely played both in the United States and Europe; composer of three operas, several orchestral suites, chamber music and songs.

References

Baker's Biographical Dictionary of Musicians 1940
Leaders in Education 1941
Who's Who Among North American Authors
Who's Who in America
Who's Who in American Education
Wier, A. E. ed. Macmillan Encyclopedia of Music and Musicians 1938

Obituaries

N Y Times p21 Mr 13 '41
Sch & Soc 53:367 Mr 22 '41

SMEDLEY, CONSTANCE 1881—Mar. 9, 1941 Author and playwright; died in London; regained her eyesight after 6 years of blindness; lecturer at Columbia University and the University of California; prolific writer of books and plays which included *The April Princess, New Wine and Old Bottles* and *On the Fighting Line*.

References

Author's and Writer's Who's Who
Smedley, C. Crusaders 1929

Obituaries

N Y Times p21 Mr 13 '41

SMITH, HOWARD W(ORTH) Feb. 2, 1883- United States Representative from Virginia

Address: b. House Office Bldg, Washington, D. C.; h. 204 W. Walnut St, Alexandria, Va.

Acme

HOWARD W. SMITH

Mourns Congressman Howard W. Smith: "Labor fellows don't read my bills—they just say, 'Smith, he's anti-labor.'"

"A Virginia bank president, a church pillar and a dead ringer for Edward Everett Horton," late in 1940 Mr. Smith introduced a bill into Congress that Labor *did* read. It provided a 30-day "cooling period" before a strike could be declared in defense industries (plants manufacturing materials for land and naval forces, whether under Government contract or not); it made the closed shop illegal in defense territories; and it provided a sentence of life imprisonment for sabotage. Mr. Smith preferred it to Representative Hoffman's bill, which outlawed defense strikes outright: "I think we ought to try my bill first. You can't do this program by force, and I don't think you can go the whole way. If you told labor it can't strike, the next thing would be a demand that we conscript capital." He said further: "The only objection I got to the sabotage clause of my bill is that it provides life imprisonment—not death." He was "convinced that the public won't stand for monkey business," and that "sentiment is with us."

Nothing happened to this particular bill, and early in 1941 two amendments attached by Mr. Smith to the Lease-Lend Act were defeated in the House. But he didn't give up. Some months later he urged an amendment to the National Labor Relations Act to "restore the God-given right of every man to work without paying tribute to a labor union." He was one of the leaders of the anti-labor bloc in the House of Representatives which threatened to defeat legislation to change the Neutrality Act in November 1941 if anti-strike legislation were not passed, and the next month a drastic anti-strike bill which he introduced was actually passed by the House. Even this bill, however, lost support after Pearl Harbor, and Mr. Smith himself began devoting even more adjectives to the Japanese than to American labor unions.

Howard Worth Smith was born in Broad Run, Virginia on February 2, 1883, the son of William Worth and Lucinda (Lewis) Smith. He was graduated from the Bethel Military Academy in Warrenton, Virginia in 1901, and received his LL. B. from the University of Virginia two years later. In 1904 he hung up his shingle in Alexandria, and by 1917 was assistant general counsel to the Alien Property Custodian, by 1918 commonwealth's attorney of Alexandria. He held that office until 1922, when he became judge in Alexandria's Corporation Court, and a year later he married Anne Corcoran. A judgeship in the 16th Judicial Circuit of Virginia followed in 1928.

It was 1931 when Mr. Smith was first elected to the United States House of Representatives from the 8th Virginia District, and he has been re-elected to every succeeding Congress with the exception of a term as Congressman-at-large from 1933 to 1935. A Democrat, he didn't exactly make himself known as a New Dealer, even at first. He helped to prevent an investigation of silicosis deaths in West Virginia; he voted against appropriations to aid farm tenants; and when Senator Wagner's National Labor Relations Bill came up in 1935 he spoke and voted against it and later advised some employers to ignore it. He voted against every major relief bill. President Roosevelt called him "the greatest obstructionist in Congress" and tried unsuccessfully to "purge" him in 1938.

By 1939 the gentleman from Virginia was something of a leader among members of the anti-New Deal bloc in the House. He proposed a committee of five—the "Smith Committee"—to investigate the National Labor Relations Board, and became its chairman over the protest of Mary Norton, chairlady of the Labor Committee, who asserted: "Certainly he is the last man in the world to pass on labor legislation. I have taken the trouble to investigate his labor record and I have yet to find a single labor bill for the benefit of the workers of the country that he has ever voted for." After three months of study and investigation a set of drastic amendments to the National Labor Relations Act was introduced, approved by three of the five members of the Smith Committee. Senator Wagner (see sketch this issue) called the Smith amendments "a delusive remedy for the worker and a concrete weapon for the oppression of labor."

To Mr. Smith, on the other hand, they merely insured justice for the employer, for it was his opinion that "whatever may have been the sins or shortcomings of industry toward labor in the past, and they have been plenty, it has certainly been punished with sufficient severity in the last five years under the Wagner Act." As for the Act itself, he had decided that it "never intended to be either fair, impartial or judicial."

Congressman Smith is not a publicity seeker. Kenneth Crawford has described him rather as "a convinced, sincere, native American primitive who seems to believe, with Hamilton, that the populace is a beast. The beast must be caged." At that time Mr. Crawford was referring to another of Mr. Smith's bills, before Congress in 1939, which, among other things, recommended that aliens be confined in concentration camps for life if they belonged to any group which so much as "advised a change" in the American form of government. The bill providing for fingerprinting aliens, passed in 1940, is also Mr. Smith's brainchild.

Usually calm and courteous, Mr. Smith "wears a wing collar, fondles a pince-nez, resembles a slick, small town lawyer in the 1880's." He calls himself a "middle-of-the-road man," and is fond of talking of "labor's excesses" and "industry's responsibilities." "It's a question of give and take so that we may all do the same for the other fellow," he says. He blames nearly all strikes on the "Communistic labor board."

Back in Virginia Mr. Smith is not only the president of the Alexandria National Bank but is also engaged in farming and dairying. He is a member of the Maryland-Virginia Milk Producers Association, a Mason, an Odd Fellow, an Elk. An Episcopalian, he is also vice-president and a trustee of the National Crittenton Mission. He has two children: Howard Worth and Violett Adelaide.

References

Christian Sci Mon Mag p5+ Ap 27 '40
Nation 148:519-20 My 6 '39
PM p12 D 12 '40 por
Scholastic 36:10 Ap 8 '40 por
Time 34:10 Jl 31 '39 por; 34:8 D 25 '39 por
Who's Who in America
Who's Who in Law
Who's Who in the Nation's Capital

SMITH, ROY BURNETT Mar. 25, 1875 —Dec. 25, 1940 Professor emeritus of chemistry at Colgate University; member of the Colgate faculty for 41 years; began employment bureau for alumni of the University.

References

Chemical Who's Who

Obituaries

N Y Herald Tribune p12 D 26 '40

SMOOT, REED Jan. 10, 1862—Feb. 9, 1941 Former United States Senator from Utah; served five successive terms in the Senate from 1903 until he was defeated in the Roosevelt landslide of 1932, and distinguished himself as an expert on tariff, taxation and public finance; co-author of the Smoot-Hawley Bill, passed in 1930, which set high tariffs on commodities entering this country;

after retirement from politics was active in the affairs of the Mormon Church.

References

Collier's 90:14-15+ S 3 '32 por
Dennis, A. P. Gods and Little Fishes p207-27 1931
Twelve Modern Apostles and Their Creeds p175-88 1926
Who's Who in America
Who's Who in Government

Obituaries

N Y Times p17 F 10 '41 por

SMUTS, JAN CHRISTIAAN (smŭts) May 24, 1870- Prime Minister of the Union of South Africa

Address: Doornkloof, Irene, near Pretoria, South Africa

In his lifetime as a lawyer, a politician, a soldier, a rebel, a turncoat, a philosopher and a diplomat, Jan Christiaan Smuts—"Slim Jannie" or the "Ou' Baas" to his people—has gained more respect and attracted more hatred than any man in South Africa. One reason might be that Smuts, a stern disciple of duty, has not hesitated to ride roughshod over any obstacles in the way of his responsibilities—there have been many of these, since he has always done the work of three or four men.

In 1941 he conducted his third major war as Prime Minister of the Union of South Africa, officer commanding the Union Defense and a field marshal in the British Army. His activities in this War have been prolific. There has been talk of including him again in an Empire War Cabinet, not yet in existence. He was in Libya with General Wavell (see sketch this issue) when the latter unleashed his Somaliland offensive; it has been said that he was instrumental in carrying through the Ethiopian campaign; and one commentator has even suggested in that connection that he insisted on that campaign in order to insure a military success in Africa necessary to consolidate his precarious majority in the South African Parliament.

South Africa has long been divided into two political groups: one, headed by General James Barry Munnik Hertzog, hopes for a South Africa free of British influence under "reconstructed Afrikanderdom" (the Afrikanders are descendants of the old Dutch or Huguenot stock who were the first to settle in South Africa) and, if necessary, fitted into the totalitarian scheme of the "New Order for Africa." At the head of the other stands Smuts himself, with his program of Anglo-Boer cooperation. The outbreak of the Second World War found Hertzog and not Smuts at the helm of South African Government But on September 6, 1939, the day after Prime Minister Hertzog indicated that his policy would be "to continue as if no war were being waged," he was forced to surrender his office as an expert on tariff, taxation and thusiastic South Africa again climbed aboard the British war wagon. Since that time Smuts has on several occasions remarked that "South

JAN CHRISTIAAN SMUTS

Africa can have but one peace, and that is a peace through victory."

Jan Christiaan Smuts was born a British subject on a farm in the Cape of Good Hope on May 24, 1870, the year when the Kimberley diamond mines in South Africa were claimed by the British. He was the son of Jacobus Abraham Smuts, a Dutch farmer, and his wife, Catharina de Vries. Until he was 12, young Jan ran the farm as befits a younger son. Then, after his older brother died, he took over the business of family education and went to school in the village of Riebeek West, where he first learned to read and to write.

After four years young Smuts entered Victoria College, in Stellenbosch, where he learned Greek grammar by heart in a week, grew interested in philosophy, English and German poetry, and passed all his examinations at the head of the list. It was there that he met his future wife, Sybella Margaretha Krige, and, with sympathy and admiration, heard Cecil Rhodes speak in the imperial vein, predicting a United Africa. This was a concept which Smuts was to treasure for the rest of his life, even when his admiration for Rhodes was a thing of the past. In 1891 he won the Ebden Scholarship and went to read law at Cambridge. He did brilliantly there: won the George Long Prize, headed both parts of the Law Tripos and wrote *Walt Whitman: A Study in the Evolution of Personality.* This book, a remarkable piece of work for so young a man, though unpublished, was later hailed as an important work, anticipating the theory of psychoanalysis.

In 1895 Smuts returned to South Africa, where he was admitted to the Cape Bar. A successful career was ahead of him, a possibility of becoming one of "Cecil Rhodes' smart young men." This possibility vanished in a cloud of disillusionment when it was found that Rhodes was implicated in the scandalous Jameson Raid. Partly because of this disillusionment, partly to seek greater opportunities, Smuts went to Johannesburg, gave up his British nationality to become a second-class burgher in Paul Kruger's Transvaal. "Oom Paul," recognizing the young man's ability, made him State Attorney at 28. Smuts demonstrated his ability and his proverbial honesty by reforming the corrupt detective department.

At the time Smuts began to share in the fortunes of The Transvaal, South Africa was in the grip of a tension which was finally to resolve itself in the Boer War. The conflict was between the "old" Boers and the "Uitlanders," whose allegiance was to England and who, in spite of their considerable holdings and influence in The Transvaal, felt themselves to be unjustly treated. Smuts wanted to prevent the war. Together with Kruger he conferred with Lord Milner at the futile Bloemfontein meeting and personally negotiated with the British agent in The Transvaal. But when the war came he fought the British with all the cold obstinacy that was so characteristic of him.

After the first encouraging months of war, the weight of numbers began to tell, and Pretoria, The Transvaal capital, fell to the British—but not before Jan Smuts had robbed the Pretorian banks of Government funds and taken them along with him in order to be able to finance the Boer resistance for two more years. In 1901 he went to Cape Colony to become a commandant general and lead a guerrilla band against the English. In his saddle bag he carried a Greek testament and Kant's *Critique of Pure Reason.* For the next two years he carried on a continuous running fight with his ragged *commandos,* helped by Botha, De Wet, De la Rey. The end of the war in 1902 found him besieging the British in Ookiep. From there he traveled to assist in the Vereeniging peace negotiations.

For a while Smuts, who had refused to join Lord Milner's Legislative Council in what was now the Crown Colony of The Transvaal, was an embittered veteran. He spent the next two years tending his garden, like Candide. Then, in the year of Kruger's death, he formed with Botha a People's Party that called itself Het Volk and agitated for responsible government. It was this Party that sent Smuts to England in 1905, when the Liberal Party got into office. His task proved surprisingly easy: with the approval of Sir H. Campbell-Bannerman the British gave the Boers back self-government.

"They gave us back—in everything but name —our country. . . Has such a miracle of trust and magnanimity ever happened before? Only people like the English could do it. They may make mistakes, but they're a big people," wrote Smuts exultantly. This attitude henceforth characterized his relationship with the British and was to bring a great deal of censure on him and his colleague Botha on the part of the irreconcilables, who branded them turncoats and traitors.

In 1907 the first election under Responsible Government was won by the Het Volk Party led by Botha and Smuts. The popular Botha became Prime Minister, with Smuts under him holding the portfolios of Colonial Secretary and Minister of Education. Admittedly Smuts was the brains of the Administration; as such he had to bear the brunt of public criticism for many of his unpopular acts. He was the one to send Gandhi to jail over the question of Indian immigration, and he took the definite stand against Labor that ultimately was to unseat him. When his great dream of the Union of South Africa was finally achieved in 1910, largely due to his efforts, he still had to face distrust on the part of his people. (He took the portfolios of Interior, Mines and Defence, later exchanging the first two for that of Finance.) And it was Smuts who reaped the whole weight of popular discontent when he helped to break the Johannesburg miners' strike by calling out troops and illegally deporting labor leaders without trial, in 1914.

The outbreak of the First World War found many Boers willing to exploit the situation by attempting to wrest their lost independence from the now-occupied British. Smuts was against this policy. Under his direction the Parliament voted to join on Britain's side, but not without a short, angry rebellion led by General Maritz and some of Smuts' fellow campaigners in the Boer War. Smuts had to put this rebellion down before South Africa was able to pay attention to its German neighbor, Southwest Africa. His brilliant campaign in Southwest Africa was one of the first Allied successes.

Nevertheless, the residue of bitterness was left throughout the Union and bore bitter fruit for Jan Smuts in the election campaign of 1915. Smuts' life was threatened in Johannesburg; General Hertzog's Nationalist Party gained; and Smuts said that he "would like nothing better than to be out of this hell into which I have wandered and in which I have lived for the last two years." His wish was granted: in 1916, as a general of the British Army, he was billeted to carry on a successful campaign in German East Africa; in 1917 he went to England to take Premier Botha's place at an Imperial Conference which the Premiers of the different Dominions were to attend.

Sarah Gertrude Millin calls Smuts of that period "the Empire's Handy Man." Acclaimed and feted throughout the British Isles, he joined Lloyd George's War Cabinet of six. In 1917 he presided over the War Priorities Committee and the Air Organization Committee; the R. A. F. is the direct result of the work he did. Because of his immense popularity in Great Britain he was called upon to settle several strikes, notably a strike of Welsh miners. He was offered the Palestine command and the presidency of the Irish Convention, refusing both. He was sent out on missions to kings and called upon to report on the situation on various fronts. He, too, took part in planning war strategy, helping Allenby map out the Palestine campaign which ultimately took place in October of 1918. His

opinions were listened to with respect, particularly after his prediction of the breakthrough in the British line.

Then came the Armistice and the end of the War. On December 16, 1918 Smuts' resignation from the War Cabinet was announced. On that same day his plan for a League of Nations was published. "Europe," wrote Smuts, "is being liquidated and the League of Nations must be heir to this great estate." This concept was one of the causes that was nearest to his heart.

That his passion for the League brought him into close sympathy with Wilson was to be expected—the relationship was certainly a closer one than that with Lloyd George. Even in 1918 he had protested against the latter's theory of a "Knock-Down Blow," asking instead for a victory that would not jeopardize "the civilization we are out to save." These differences and Smuts' lonely attack on the Peace Treaty almost led to a quarrel. On the other hand it was Smuts' idea of reparations —with pensions and bonuses included among Germany's liabilities—that Wilson adopted.

The Peace Treaty was very different from what either Wilson or Smuts wanted. In a letter to Lloyd George, Smuts wrote: "This Treaty breathes a poisonous spirit of revenge which may yet scorch the fair face—not of a corner of Europe but of Europe." But Smuts was alone in what was probably the unhappiest time in his life, though with John Maynard Keynes (see sketch this issue) to share his misgivings. At first he refused to sign the Treaty, but was prevailed upon to do so by his friend and superior, Botha, and by Lloyd George. In the same afternoon his historic protest was published. His chief interest throughout the Peace Conference was still in the League of Nations. He drafted many clauses of the Covenant and drew up the celebrated Article XVI, under which sanctions were to be invoked against Italy in 1935.

The War and the making of the peace over, Smuts came back to a South Africa industrially depressed by the War. In August 1919 Botha died, leaving Smuts to assume the burden of Premiership and post-War depression. It was a heavy one, for Smuts' countrymen did not regard him with the wholehearted admiration accorded him in Europe. "Smuts' superlative achievement overseas, his acclaim there, crowned in their eyes his misdemeanors." One of these, in their opinion, was his use of troops to put down the Rand mines strike of 1922. General Hertzog, whose Nationalist Party had been steadily gaining adherents, remarked that "the Prime Minister's footsteps drip with blood," and recalled the "Butchery of Bullhoek" in 1920 when Government troops were sent against a native religious sect entrenched at Bullhoek. The culmination of these attacks came in 1924 when Smuts' Government went to defeat, which Smuts himself took, as was his wont, philosophically.

In spite of his preoccupation with the South African affairs, Jan Smuts' connections with Europe have never been severed. In 1921 he was helpful in bringing the Irish Free State

SMUTS, JAN CHRISTIAAN—*Continued*

into being. In 1923 he defended Wilson's policy and denounced the French policy on the Ruhr. And in 1930 Smuts, who calls it a justification of his life that he has stood unalterably by the Jews, opposed the Quota Law designed to keep Jewish immigrants out of his country, and was able to get some concessions. All during his life he struggled, wrote, spoke of his idea of the League of Nations. It was the greatest disappointment of his life that the United States rejected the League, which alone, he thought, "could save a tottering Europe."

During his years out of office Smuts' way of resting was, as usual, to do some other sort of work. He wrote *Holism and Evolution* (1926), in which he set out his philosophy, which consisted of seeing the world as "a rising series of wholes, from the simplest material patterns to the most advanced." He devoted his time to botany, to lone treks into the Kaffir country, and to farming. In 1929 he presided at the meeting of the British Association for the Advancement of Science. He accepted the Rhodes Memorial Lectureship at Oxford and in 1930 toured the United States and Canada in a series of lectures.

It was while he was in England presiding over the Centenary Meeting of the British Association that Britain went off the gold standard. He urgently recommended that South Africa follow suit, but his advice was derisively rejected by the Government. Nevertheless, it was on the cry of "Off Gold" that Smuts returned to office. The flight of capital from South Africa finally compelled the Government to change its mind. In 1933 coalition was the order of the day: for the good of the country Smuts submitted himself to General Hertzog, and a new Union Government was constituted. Smuts became Minister of Justice with wide powers—a post he kept until 1939, when the Second World War again brought him to the head of his Government.

Today Smuts is a slim, soldierly man with a trimmed gray beard and eyes that are "a cold clear blue, steely to hardness, brilliant, almost dazzling, almost affrighting." His manner is friendly but restrained. Freeman of 10 cities, possessor of 21 honorary degrees of universities in Great Britain, the United States, Canada and South America, he is "that rarity among Boers, a man of Europe." Instinctively he is a diplomat with a diplomat's humor and tastes. There is a great deal of the Puritan in him—"the things from which other people get enjoyment don't amuse him now and never did." Cultivated, erudite, with a good literary background and a colossal memory, he can talk well on any subject and movingly on a great one—but his earnestness sometimes makes it difficult to know whether he is "making an epigram or a cliché." He has never been an envious man and hates to believe that he has enemies. He has an inflexible—some say dangerous—sense of duty, which has often made him take law into his own hands. Like all Boers he is a farmer at heart: he has a model farm 10 miles from Pretoria. Its square,

single-storied house is usually full of people —his children (he has two sons and four daughters), grandchildren, relations, pilgrims and other guests invited by the hospitable Mrs. Smuts; but their noisy invasion stops at the door of Smuts' inner sanctum, his library.

References

Christian Sci Mon p7 N 6 '40 por
Christian Sci Mon Mag p3 S 30 '39 pors
Liv Age 360 :448-52 Jl '41 por
Nation 143 :163 Ag 8 '36
N Y Herald Tribune II p4 Mar 23 '41 por
Newsweek 14 :22 S 18 '39 por; 18 :25 S 1 '41 por
Sat R Lit 14 :5 My 23 '36 pors; 15 :5-8 D 5 '36 pors
Time 27 :87-9 My 25 '36 por; 34 :28 S 18 '39 por
Armstrong, H. C. Grey Steel 1937
Forbes, R. T. These Men I Knew p283-98 1940
Levi, N. ·Jan Smuts 1917
Men of Turmoil p287-96 1935
Millin, S. G. L. General Smuts 2v 1936
Riddell, G. A. R. More Things That Matter p161-5 1925
Slocombe, G. E. Mirror to Geneva p74-96 1938
South African Who's Who
Who's Who

SNELL, HENRY SNELL, 1ST BARON

Apr. 1, 1865- British statesman and municipal organizer

Address: Connaught Club, London, W. 2, England

Henry Snell's life is a Dick Whittington story. The 12-year-old boy who stood for hire in the market place at Newark-on-Trent 63 years ago became head of London's great County Council, a peer of the United Kingdom and in his old age captain of His Majesty's Gentlemen at Arms. Snell started life with every disadvantage, yet he rose slowly, quietly, overcoming all the handicaps of birth, lack of education and religious and political heresy. For 18 years now he has been in Parliament and in this period he has won widespread respect for his idealism, his skill in handling large issues in committee and the dignity and poise with which he has fulfilled his Parliamentary function. Today he is recognized as an authority on municipal and colonial affairs; his speeches and writings are informed with style; he is recognized as a scholar, though his only scholarly training was received at a few university extension lectures.

Henry Snell was born in the village of Sutton-on-Trent, Nottinghamshire, the son of farm workers, of a mother who could neither read nor write. His family was large, and Henry started to work at nine. His first job was scaring birds for local farmers. At 12 he was hired as an indoor servant to a farmer near Newark and from then on, through his adolescence, he was employed mainly as a pot-boy in various public houses and for a brief period as a French-polisher in Nottingham. His experiences in public houses left a deep mark on him. Never in his life has he used alcohol in any form or even smoked.

In his spare hours he began to read and Sundays attended a Unitarian chapel in Nottingham. The secretary to the Midland Institution for the Blind, also a chapel member, saw that young Snell was intelligent and made him his assistant, the first decent job he had had. He was still very poor, but his hours were shorter and the work congenial. He read more and more widely, and his interest in religion and politics grew stronger. In both he began to move rapidly to the Left. Soon even Unitarianism was not free enough for him. He became an agnostic and joined the National Secular Society. In politics he became a Socialist, joined the Social Democratic Federation, attended economics lectures by Professor J. E. Symes at University College, Nottingham, and took every opportunity to hear such speakers as William Morris, Charles Bradlaugh, George Jacob Holyoake and Annie Besant.

Early in 1890 Snell went to London as assistant-secretary to the Woolwich Charity Organization Society. All his leisure time, which meant from six or seven in the evenings and Sundays, was spent in ever deeper and deeper study and in open-air speaking for the causes of Rationalism and Socialism. In 1895 he took a big step up when he was appointed secretary to the director of the newly-founded London School of Economics. He was sent all over the country lecturing under the aegis of the Fabian Society (a gradualist Socialist group, of which the Webbs and George Bernard Shaw are famous members). But his health wasn't good and what with the constant traveling, late hours and hotel life, he had a breakdown in 1898.

Dr. Stanton Coit, a pillar of the Rationalist Press, came to the rescue. He offered Snell a three-year engagement as a lecturer which was accepted. Nevertheless, Snell began again to suffer from insomnia and nervous strain, and Coit sent him abroad to Switzerland for the summer of 1900. In 1902 he spent the spring and summer terms at the University of Heidelberg and afterward went on vacation to Grindelwald and to Venice, from which he was driven home by an attack of enteritis.

From 1902 to 1919 Snell continued his work for Socialism and Rationalism. In 1907 he was made secretary of the Secular Education League which worked for the removal of theological teaching from schools, and he conducted its propaganda until 1931. For 20 years he was a member of the executive council of the Fabian Society. When, in 1910, the Huddersfield Labor Party persuaded him to stand for Parliament, he was unsuccessful and he was unsuccessful again in 1918.

It is from 1919 on that Snell emerges as a public figure, for in that year he was elected to the London County Council for East Woolwich. He served there until 1925, and in 1934,

BARON SNELL

when Labor got its first majority on the Council, he was unanimously elected chairman and remained in the Chair until 1938. Meanwhile, in 1922, he had entered the wider sphere of national politics as Labor Member of Parliament for East Woolwich.

In Parliament Snell took a special interest in Dominion and Colonial matters, went to South Africa in 1924 as a delegate of the Empire Parliamentary Association and was one of two commissioners appointed in 1926 to report on the economic condition of British Guiana. In 1927 he served on a departmental committee to consider the question of pensions for colonial Governors; and in 1929 he was a member of the Commission of Inquiry into the riots in Palestine. That same year he received the honor of being selected to move the address to His Majesty on the opening of Parliament, a task which he carried out with conspicuous dignity and correctness.

In 1931 Snell was made Parliamentary Under-Secretary of State at the India Office and transferred to the House of Lords, with the chosen title of Baron Snell of Plumstead, in the County of Kent. Other honors he received include the order of the Companion of the British Empire (1930); an honorary LL. D. from London University (1936); and membership in the Privy Council (1937).

Snell's work at the India Office lasted only five months, after which the Labor Government went out of office, but he has continued to expound and maintain the principles of his Party in the House of Lords as one of a very small band of Labor peers. His present Royal Household office, as captain of the Gentlemen at Arms, is but a minor decorative one; but it should be remembered that Snell is 75 years old.

Few men in British public life have won so much affectionate respect from all parties as Henry Snell. He has never been an am-

SNELL, HENRY SNELL, 1ST BARON
—*Continued*

bitious man. Always he has been a quiet and persistent worker, profoundly concerned with problems of human character and freedom of thought, considering the highest task the betterment of the individual man. Sensitive and studious, he is known for his fair-mindedness. In the days when he had to fight elections, for instance, he would make no allusion at all to his opponent except to ask that he have a fair hearing. In 1936 Snell brought out his autobiography, *Men, Movements, and Myself,* having previously published *Daily Life in Parliament* (1930). He is unmarried.

References

    Snell, H. Daily Life in Parliament 1930
    Snell, H. Men, Movements, and Myself 1936
    Who's Who

SNOW, EDGAR (PARKS) July 19, 1905-
Foreign correspondent; author

Address: b. c/o Random House, 20 E. 57th St, New York City; h. Mungertown Rd, Madison, Conn.

EDGAR SNOW

For more than a decade Edgar Snow, "the most adventurous and enterprising newspaperman in China," has been wandering up and down the coast of Asia and penetrating far into the interior. From his wanderings have come newspaper reports, magazine articles and books, the latest of which is *The Battle for Asia* (1941). Called by Joseph Barnes, foreign editor of the New York *Herald Tribune,* "a newspaperman's book, in the best sense," it is a "serious, comprehensive and supremely authoritative job of reporting" made rich with vivid pictures of the fighting around Peiping

and Shanghai; weighted with facts and figures, social and political trends; dramatized by accounts of personal adventures, illuminating sketches of people in Asia and their work, tales of terror and sudden death. It was around the time of its publication that Snow returned to the United States for the first time in many months. (Not long afterward *Smash Hitler's International,* of which he was co-author, appeared.)

In *The Battle for Asia,* Edgar Snow draws a number of conclusions, not all of them acceptable to the critics who praise his brilliant and accurate writing. He still believes, as he believed when he wrote *Red Star Over China* (1938), that "political democracy and agrarian reform are China's great needs." As part of that, he states in *The Battle for Asia* that the struggle for China may well be lost if Chiang Kai-shek and the Communists fight each other. And he believes that American help should be sent, not to the Chinese bureaucracy, but to be administered jointly by a high committee representing all anti-Japanese groups in China in cooperation with United States advisers on the spot.

Edgar Parks Snow, who spent part of his youth as a harvest hand and later as a railway worker and seaman, was born a long way from China, in Kansas City, Missouri, the son of James Edgar and Anna Catherine (Edelman) Snow. After public school in Kansas City he spent 1923 and 1924 studying at Kansas City Junior College and from there went on to the University of Missouri. He left the University in 1926 for the Columbia School of Journalism and left Columbia, in 1927, for his first newspaper job—as a correspondent for the Kansas City *Star.*

This was followed by newspaper work in New York, interrupted one day later in 1927 when the thought suddenly occurred to him that one really should see Madagascar. His career as a traveling journalist, which has since taken him by steamer, junk, sampan, pony, camel, cart, palanquin and on foot through thousands of miles of the Orient, which has led him to know Indian saints and Annamite rebels, Chinese "Reds" and Japanese war barons, was under way.

Snow went first to Central America, then to Hawaii, supporting himself by writing for newspapers and magazines. By the end of 1928 he had wandered on to the Far East. He intended to stay there only six weeks and then to push on to Madagascar—he stayed there 12 years. For a while he lived in Shanghai, where he was assistant editor of the China *Weekly Review,* but this was merely his base. In 1929, at the invitation of Dr. Sun Fo (son of the deceased Dr. Sun Yat-sen), then Minister of Railways, he traveled over the entire system of government railways in China and Manchuria and toured Korea. A series of guide books on China was the result of these journeys.

During the Northwest famine, the worst in history, Snow visited Suiyuan, Shansi and Inner Mongolia and brought back for the New York *Herald Tribune* the first eyewitness accounts of that colossal tragedy in which more than 2,000,000 people met their death. Later, as correspondent for the Chicago *Tribune*, assisting J. B. Powell, the *Tribune's* veteran correspondent in the Far East, he covered the Sino-Russian hostilities in Manchuria during 1929 and 1930.

Shortly after this assignment, in 1930, Snow was appointed staff correspondent for the Consolidated Press Association and started off on assignments that took him to many of the known and some of the almost unknown places of the Middle and Far East. He organized a caravan and crossed southwestern China, through bandit-ridden, mountainous and little-traveled Yünnan, going by way of the Tali snow ranges down through the Shen States and Upper Burma into India. For months he lived almost entirely with Asiatics—often with people who had never seen a white man.

Other assignments took him to Formosa, where he narrowly missed death in a head-hunters' uprising in which more than 200 Japanese were massacred; to Indo-China, where he was the only American correspondent to report the serious agrarian revolt of 1930; to India, to follow the Satyagraha (non-resistance) movement; to Burma, where he was the only American correspondent to report the Tharawaddy uprisings against British rule; to the Dutch Indies, during the mutiny of the crew of the DeZeven Provincien; to milder adventures in Ceylon, Malay, Bali, the Celebes, Borneo and the Philippines.

During this time Snow was a special correspondent for the New York *Sun* and for the London *Daily Herald* and in 1934 he gave up his staff position with the Consolidated Press Association to devote his time to these two newspapers while continuing to write for many magazines, including the *Saturday Evening Post, Asia, Current History, Fortune* and *Look* Magazine. He had already published his first book, *The Far Eastern Front* (1933), which covered his experiences as a correspondent during the Sino-Japanese conflict from the outbreak of the Manchurian hostilities down to the Tangku armistice.

For a little while Edgar Snow and his wife, Helen Foster, who as "Nym Wales" has also written books and articles about the Far East (they were married in 1932), settled down in Peiping while Mr. Snow gave a series of lectures at Yenching University. Two years later, after varied newspaper reporting, he started off into the Communist part of China. Before he left he wrote: "In all these years the Reds have been in action no foreign newspaperman, practically no foreigner at all, in fact, has penetrated into these Red-controlled regions. If I get through it will be a world scoop."

Snow did get through Red territory, took pictures and came out again to score his world scoop with articles to the London *Daily Herald* and the *Saturday Evening Post*. His accounts of the Communist leaders, of the inside story of the kidnapping of Chiang Kai-shek, of the Red Army itself, of China's war tactics and objectives were published also, in 1938, in *Red Star Over China*. (*Living China*,

a collection of short stories by various Chinese, edited and translated by Snow, had been published the year before.) Immediately it became an international best seller, critics calling it "one of the most remarkable books ever written by a journalist about a foreign country," a "vitally important historical and political volume, rich in present significance and even more wealthy for future reference."

There were some critics, however, who felt that Snow's "interpretations of the course of the Chinese Revolution and his theorizing on the nature of the Chinese Communist movement" were "open to criticism." And there have been others, since the publication of his latest book, who deplore his sympathy for the Chinese Communists. Actually Edgar Snow belongs to no political group. He believes that the Communist movement in China is an attempt by the Chinese to rid themselves not only of foreign imperialistic designs but also of centuries of old oppression by bureaucratic officialdom, greedy bankers and others; that "the alleged Communism is largely a striving toward a democratic republic."

Still, it is in cooperatives that he sees the greatest hope for China. "The best thing I ever did," he says, "was to help draw up the plan for Chinese Industrial Cooperatives, of which I was co-founder, with Rewi Alley and my wife, Nym Wales. We conceived this form of 'productive relief' as a means of human rehabilitation, of quickly rebuilding industry lost during the present War, of fortifying the morale of the Chinese people, and of laying down an economic basis for protracted resistance—a kind of guerrilla industry to support China's guerrilla warfare. It was a huge success and has won international support. Unless it is suppressed by the Kuomintang (ruling party of China), Indusco (as Chinese Industrial Cooperatives are called) may provide for China an entirely new form in which to achieve industrialization."

References

Asia 37:74-5 F '37 il
Pub W 133:838-40 F 12 '38
Sat Eve Post 213:4 My 31 '41 por
Sat R Lit 17:22 Ja 1 '38 por (pl)
Who's Who in America

SOKOLSKY, GEORGE E(PHRAIM) (sô-kôl'skê) Sept. 5, 1893- Author; columnist; industrial consultant

Address: b. National Association of Manufacturers, New York City; h. 330 West End Ave, New York City

Called by *Time* Magazine "a star-spangled spieler for capitalism," and "a one-man intellectual front for conservative capital," George Sokolsky, author, lecturer, industrial consultant, has numerous outlets for his defense of the *status quo* in the "American way" of life. For several years a columnist for the New York *Herald Tribune,* he now conducts a similar column of comment, political and otherwise, for the New York *Sun;* he has done weekly broad-

GEORGE E. SOKOLSKY

casts for the National Association of Manufacturers since 1937; he is the author of six books and numerous magazine articles; he is well known to the general public through his appearances on such radio programs as the *Town Meeting of the Air.*

An ardent believer in the premise that "democracy and private enterprise are in practice inseparable," Sokolsky has been highly paid for his services as an industrial "consultant." In testimony before the La Follette Civil Liberties Committee it was disclosed that "Mr. Sokolsky received $28,599 from Hill and Knowlton, June 1936 to February 1938, for services to the American Iron and Steel Institute, for consultation and help in preparing booklets, as well as for some lectures and radio talks." According to Kenneth M. Lloyd, chairman of the Little Steel and Iron Institute, Sokolsky is the "outstanding advocate of the open shop in America."

In his writings Sokolsky has often frankly stated his own position and beliefs. "The right to win and use private wealth and to keep and use the benefits that derive from it is part of democracy," he asserts. "I am a conservative in the major ways of life, a capitalist in my economic thinking and a rigid constitutionalist in my political thinking. More than anything else, I fear the concentration of power in the hands of any one individual in government; no matter how benevolent he may be, no matter how sweet-tempered and kind-hearted, I fear the dictatorship of anybody."

The man who is capitalism's chief supporter began his adult life as a rabid young radical. Sokolsky explains his "conversion": two years in Russia during the Kerensky and early Lenin regimes completely "cured" him and placed him irrevocably in conservative ranks. "It was [my] firsthand acquaintance with Communists and the actual practice of Communism," he said

recently. "The Russian Revolution made me fearful of all revolutions, the brutality of the mob, the ruthlessness in the suppression of the individual . . . the utilization of all the machinery of despotisms to achieve an ideal . . . to me all this was distressing and disgusting."

George Ephraim Sokolsky was born in Utica, New York on September 5, 1893, the son of Solomon and Bertha (Rappaport) Sokolsky. They later moved to New York City. He writes that his people are "Polish Jews, mostly rabbis and musicians. On my mother's side there is a line that goes back to Italy several centuries ago—a line that moved over all of Europe, and is still moving. . . [I have] a red-headed aunt—might not that be attributable to the rape of Jewish women by Gustavus Adolphus's soldiers? My father came to this country in the 1880's to be a rabbi among struggling tailors, peddlers, and junk dealers. His was the task of keeping a poverty-stricken head high among the *nouveaux riches* who transferred their packs to shops and became department-store owners or manufacturers. His was a life of serving an ideal of faith, while the rewards went to the unholy and sometimes to the wicked."

From the New York City public schools Sokolsky went to Columbia University, where he studied journalism from 1913 to 1917. Following his graduation he went to Russia in 1917, filled with eager enthusiasm for what he felt was the dawn of a new era, not only for Russia but for the whole world. In Petrograd he edited the Russian *Daily News,* the only English-language newspaper there, and witnessed Kerensky's rise and fall and the beginning of the new Communist regime. His reactions soon became reflected in his paper; and in March 1918 he was ordered to leave the country and was placed on a Harbin-bound express train.

When he arrived in Harbin, China, Sokolsky possessed $1 in American money, but by various expedients managed to reach Peiping, where he obtained a position as an assistant editor of the newly established North China *Star.* A few months later he became adviser to the chief of police in the Province of Chihli. In 1919 he was a reporter for the Shanghai *Gazette,* owned by Dr. Sun Yat-sen. He became adviser to the Chinese Student Union and was employed by the Chinese to organize the Bureau of Public Information. From 1921 to 1924 he was president of the Shanghai *Journal of Commerce.* There followed 10 years of political reporting as a special correspondent in the Far East, during which time he represented such papers as the Philadelphia *Public Ledger,* the New York *Evening Post* and the London *Daily Express.* He was an intimate of Dr. Sun Yat-sen and other Chinese leaders and acquired a reputation as one of the best-informed American authorities on the Orient.

It was in 1922 that Sokolsky married a Chinese girl, Rosalind Phang. She was born in the West Indies and educated in England; they met in Shanghai. Of this marriage between a poor Polish-Jewish youth from New

York's East Side and a Chinese girl, Sokolsky has written (*Atlantic Monthly,* August 1933): "Mine is perhaps the most mixed of marriages. My wife is a Hakka. The Hakkas are the most vital of the aboriginal people of China; they are strong, independent, vigorous; excellent pirates, and splendid merchants. Their women never bound their feet; they carried short swords in their hair as a protection against rape by the conquering sons of Han." He says their marriage "did not fail" because "marriage is essentially a matter of readjustment—the more sensitive the individuals, the more delicate the readjustments. A mixed marriage is then, first of all, only a marriage; but should not be entered into by individuals who are not certain that they have transcended racial, national and religious affiliations." The couple had one son, Eric Solomon; Rosalind Phang died October 6, 1933. In 1935 Sokolsky married Dorothy Fiske of New York City; a son, George Ephraim, Jr., was born of this second marriage.

Back in the United States after 14 years in Asia, conditions here—even during depression years—struck Sokolsky with fresh impact and led him to "a keener appreciation of American traditions and principles." He became convinced that there was no place like America and no economic and political system as good as America's. These convictions he set down in the New York *Herald Tribune,* in articles for *Liberty,* etc. In 1928 he published *Outline of Universal History,* and in 1932 *The Tinder Box of Asia.* The latter was received with mixed reactions. According to *The Nation* (February 6, 1935): "If Mr. Sokolsky's book has not been written by the National Association of Manufacturers it should have been... It is sheer propaganda —crude, stupid and vicious." The Boston *Transcript* pointed out, however, that "the great amount of documentary evidence introduced in the various chapters adds much to the value of the book and strengthens its claim to a place among the permanent contributions to international history in these chaotic decades," and even the liberal *New Republic* called it "an unprejudiced factual study of the unique problem of China in world politics." Sokolsky's next book, *We Jews* (1935), received in general a consistently favorable press.

His most recent book, *The American Way of Life* (1939), consists of "a series of articles, originally published in *Liberty,* in which Mr. Sokolsky answers the authors of the 'guinea-pig' books and defends American advertising by showing how it has improved American ways of living." Of it the *Saturday Review of Literature* said: "This maladept attempt to whitewash the advertising game wholesale will create more critics of advertising than would any number of books about millions and millions of guinea pigs." George Watt, writing in *Consumers' Digest* (July 1939), says that "Sokolsky is delighted that modern women can get their meals out of packages and cans. He intimates that all we need do to live happily and energetically is to read the advertisements, turn the crank on

the cans, eat, drink and be merry—never wary. He assures us that 'you know what you're getting because you have read about it in advertisements.'" Mr. Watt says, however, that when he wrote Sokolsky telling him (with documented reports included) that some of the best-advertised foods contained all kinds of filth, animal and mineral, Mr. Sokolsky failed to acknowledge receipt of the reports sent him. One of the few favorable comments on the book came from the New York *Herald Tribune's* critic, who found it "a well-organized and interesting presentation of facts and conditions that have shown up piecemeal here and there in the various sham and real battles between politicians and businessmen."

The author of *The American Way of Life* lives on West End Avenue in New York City, in "a spacious apartment filled with antiques and rare Chinese art objects," and spends his summers on a farm near Otis, Massachusetts. Besides writing and lecturing, his favorite indoor sports include visits with like-minded neighbors. The late Heywood Broun reported in one of his columns (the *New Republic* June 22, 1938) how Sokolsky went often to see Isaac Don Levine, with whom he had "an affinity because he and I once believed in the Russian Revolution and we both now know what a shabby trick has been played upon the Russian people. So we can always spend a delightful day together swearing at the Communists, which is a splendid indoor sport. It might even be tried outdoors."

Up to the time of Pearl Harbor, Sokolsky opposed the Lend-Lease Bill, the transfer of great numbers of planes and ships to Great Britain, American aid to Russia, and preached the wisdom of remaining friends with Japan. He supports the war now, however.

In 1938 Sokolsky was awarded Columbia University's Medal for Distinction in Public Service, and he seems assured of his broadcast programs for the National Association of Manufacturers, and his place in the *Sun,* for as long as he continues his chosen career.

References

Atlan 152:137-46 Ag '33
China W R 85:412-15 Ag 27 '38; 86:70 S 17 '38
Consumers' Digest 6:44-7 Jl '39
New Repub 95:185 Je 22 '38; 97:339 Je 25 '39
Sat R Lit 20:31 Ap 29 '39
Time 32:22 Ag 1 '38

Cordell, W. H. ed. Molders of American Thought, 1933-34 p376-90 1934
Who's Who in America
Who's Who in American Jewry

SOONG, T. V. (sōōng) 1894- Foreign Minister of China

Address: Chungking, China

Bulletin: On December 23, 1941 T. V. Soong was made Foreign Minister of China. Political quarters interpreted his appointment as indicating new and intense cooperation among Generalissimo Chiang Kai-shek and his two brothers-in-law,

China Institute in America

T. V. SOONG

Soong and H. H. Kung, Finance Minister. Mr. Soong was in the United States at the time of his appointment. He replaces Dr. Quo Taichi, former Ambassador to Great Britain.

From March 1941 issue (revised):

T. V. Soong, China's former Finance Minister and now president of the Bank of China, is a "boyish, earnest, round-faced, spectacled" Chinese who is considered one of the shrewdest international financiers now on the world scene. Probably more than any one man he has kept China fairly good collateral against heavy odds; probably more than any one man he is responsible for English and American loans to his country. In 1939 the United States and England both lent $25,000,000 to finance Chinese purchases, and in 1940 Soong personally led a mission to the United States which brought forth in December a credit of $100,000,000. "Dr. Soong certainly knows how to sell the spirit of China," commented Secretary of Commerce Jesse Jones.

He was still selling it in 1941. In April he and United States Secretary of the Treasury Morgenthau signed a currency stabilization agreement involving the purchase of $50,000,000 of *yuan*, Chinese currency, by the American stabilization fund. In July this support was extended for another year.

This man who is supposed to have taught the Chinese "the art of central banking" is a member of the famous Soong family, the most influential in China. His father, Charles Jones Soong, came to America in his youth, became a Christian, took an American name, peddled hammocks in the Southern states, was graduated from Vanderbilt University and then went to China as a missionary. In China he helped found the Y. M. C. A. and established himself as a publisher of Bibles.

Eventually he entered politics and served Sun Yat-sen as secretary and treasurer. His wife, and T. V. Soong's mother, was a Miss Kwai Tsung Nie, "a strong, effective woman of unusual charm and perspicacity" who saw that her three sons and three daughters had the best education possible.

The parents' efforts with their children were successful: all grew up to achieve positions of importance in their country. Of the daughters, Mei-ling became the wife of Chiang Kai-shek and a leader of China; Ai-ling became the wife of H. H. Kung, China's Finance Minister; Ching-ling married Sun Yat-sen, the father of the Chinese Revolution. Of the sons, T. L. Soong has been manager of the Southwest Export and Import Bureau and of the Central Bank of China; T. A. Soong was a director of the salt tax; and T. V. Soong, the eldest of the sons, has been probably the most important factor in financing the Revolution and the present war against Japan.

T. V. Soong (Sung Tsu-wen) was born in Shanghai, China and received part of his high school education at St. John's in Shanghai, before his parents came to the United States to put their children in school. In this country Soong attended Vanderbilt University in Tennessee for a while and then shifted to Harvard, from which he was graduated in 1915. He went on to Columbia, where he was a brilliant student in economics. Then T. V. Soong went to work for a time in New York banking houses until he decided to return to China.

Back in his own country Soong started a business career, but he found the adjustment difficult and he was "impatient for the welfare of his country." In 1923 he went to Canton, where the Nationalist Government was established. He first became director of the Department of Commerce and then, in 1924, general manager of the Central Bank. Without adequate equipment or experience, almost overnight he "earned the reputation of a sound and competent financier." He introduced banking practices he had learned in the United States; he checked fraud and corruption, and caused the revenues to flow in. Yet, when he followed the Nationalist armies from Canton to Hankow, he was unable to repeat his success. A depression had set in.

In 1927, as *Life* tells it, it was Soong who ventured into Shanghai and persuaded the bankers in that city to support Chiang Kai-shek against the Communists, who had been up to that time eligible for membership in the Kuomintang but who, it was felt, were growing too strong; and shortly after his visit Chiang formed the new "Moderate" Government at Nanking which immediately broke with the Communists. (Strangely enough, it was also Soong who later, when Japan invaded the country, helped to persuade Chiang to fight the Japanese rather than the Reds.)

For a while at Nanking, where in 1928 he became Minister of Finance, all went well again. Soong was able to finance the Northern Expedition and secure the revenues necessary to consolidate the Nationalist Government. In the years in which he was Finance Minister, Chinese finances were put on a Western basis, the budget system was introduced, domestic tariff barriers were abolished, taxes were collected, a central banking system was established and the currency was unified.

In 1933, however, Soong resigned. His resignation was interpreted as a protest against the tremendous military expenditures of Chiang Kai-shek, leader of the Nationalist forces, and a protest, even more, against Chiang's early policy of conciliation toward Japan. Soong then formed the China Development and Finance Company, a banking discount and brokerage firm designed to hit Japan's capitalists in the pocketbook by developing competing factories and plants. And in 1936 he founded the Bank of China, of which he was and is the first chairman.

For some time after that, Soong and Chiang Kai-shek continued to be at odds. Soong tried to reduce military expenditures, while Chiang tried to increase them; by this time Soong's attitude toward the Communists and other groups was a friendly one, for he always felt that dissident elements should be united for defense; Chiang's was a less compromising one. Today, however, the two men are in agreement, for Chiang has met Soong halfway. As president of the Bank of China, Soong is now working closely with the military chief.

Those Americans who came to know Soong on his recent trip to the United States (he brought along his wife and three children) were impressed both by his fluent command of English and of American slang and by his Western appearance—"he can hardly be imagined wearing Chinese clothes," one commentator said. In his home in Shanghai can be seen as many evidences of his Western training as of his Eastern inheritance. His villa looks modern at first glance, but actually it is a treasure house of ancient jades and porcelains.

Americans were able to learn something of Soong's personality, too, when he was here. All have agreed that he is brilliant and hard-working; and most of them will concur with John Gunther's (see sketch this issue) estimate: "Stocky, glossy, with hair stiffly *en brosse*; diffident and direct by turn; not afraid to be rude, and intolerant of bores; enormously competent."

References

Atlan 159:185-8 F '37
China W R 72:177-8 Ap 6 '35; 84:99-100 Mr 26 '38
Life 10:90-7 Mr 24 '41 il pors
Lit Digest 116:14 D 23 '33 por

Gunther, J. Inside Asia p201-10 1939
Holcombe, A. H. The Spirit of the Chinese Revolution 1930
International Who's Who
Spencer, C. Three Sisters 1939
Who's Who in China
Who's Who in Commerce and Industry

SOYER, ISAAC Apr. 20, 1907- Artist
Address: 24 W. 96th St, New York City

SOYER, MOSES Dec. 25, 1899- Artist
Address: 308 W. 18th St, New York City

SOYER, RAPHAEL Dec. 25, 1899- Artist
Address: 403 W. 115th St, New York City

Midtown Galleries

ISAAC SOYER

Brother-combinations in the art world seem to hold a special attraction for critics and public alike. This is certainly true of the Soyers, whose "family style" in painting and lithography has been the subject of much speculation and some controversy. In early 1941 both Moses and Raphael were having one-man shows, and the old questions were again revived. Meanwhile the Soyers went on painting, each in his own way, pointing to such historic precedents as the brothers Van Eyck to those bewildered by prodigality of talent in one family.

The Soyers admit a fraternal relationship. Beyond that each claims to go his own way, painting the subject matter of his choice in his own manner. At an early age the brothers decided to avoid being in the same school together at the same time and never to share the same studio. The latter rule was broken only once, in 1939 when the Treasury Section of Fine Arts commissioned Moses and Raphael to do two panels on opposite walls of Kingsessing Postal Station in Philadelphia.

Their first intention had been to do the two panels separately, each signing one, but when they looked over the walls they decided this job would give admirable scope in which to test their ability to collaborate. As the mural got under way they discovered with amazement that each had his own painting habits, his own approach to the job at

Macbeth Gallery

MOSES SOYER

hand, and his own palette. This was a source of satisfaction, confirming their own ideas. Collaboration then became a serious creative effort in which dissimilar traits found expression.

The Soyer brothers bear a family resemblance to each other but are far from being peas in a pod. Even Raphael and Moses, who are twins, differ noticeably. This difference was more marked in the past, when Raphael's thin face contrasted with the chubby features of his brother. And though both had the same shade of brown eyes, those of Moses seemed brighter. Raphael and Moses are small-statured, their brother Isaac taller. Isaac is prematurely gray, and might appear older at first glance. The vigorous features of the younger brother are accented by dark brown, almost black, eyes beneath thick brows, and a great shock of hair.

The twins were born on December 25, 1899, Isaac on April 20, 1907—all three in the Tambov region of what was then Czarist Russia. From early childhood they looked to America as a land of promise. "Our favorite books," writes Moses, "were *Tom Sawyer, Uncle Tom's Cabin* and *Hiawatha,* and among the heroes of our childhood George Washington and Abraham Lincoln led all the rest. On week ends and holidays our mother would cover the large, round dining-room table with a shiny oilcloth, on which in barbaric red and green was pictured Brooklyn Bridge (Brooklynski Most), spanning the East River and joining the 'glass' skyscrapers of Manhattan with the slums of Brooklyn." And their father shared this enthusiasm. "'Who knows,' he would say wistfully, 'perhaps you too might one day be citizens of this great republic and contribute your talents and strength to its growth.'"

Their father had much to do with shaping the Soyer talent to productive maturity. The following description was written by Moses a year before his father's death in 1940: "Our father is a truly remarkable man. Self-taught and self-made, in the real American sense of the phrase, he toiled hard all his life, and has never deviated from the ideals he set for himself in his youth. At 70, presenting an appearance of a Rembrandtesque scholar, he is still full of life, tolerant to youth and vitally interested in world affairs."

The family name is an adaptation of the Hebrew *Schoar,* which means sentinel. Abraham Soyer came from a small Lithuanian village about which he wrote a two-volume book. He married Bella Schneyer and made a modest living teaching Hebrew and writing in Hebrew and Russian for newspapers in Odessa and elsewhere.

Life in Russia was not altogether happy for the Soyers. The shadow of racial persecution hung over the father, whose liberal ideas found little favor with the Governor of the province. Living, too, was a problem, though perhaps no more so than it was to be in America where Abraham Soyer had to start all over again in a strange land. Despite these difficulties Abraham and Bella Soyer made the home an island of warmth and sympathy for their children, from which they could view without rancor the realities of an oftentimes hostile world. Moses affords a glimpse of this family life when he writes of their mother, "We used to love to watch her embroider on towels and table spreads, illustrations of Russian fairy tales, in vivid, bright color schemes."

Their interest in art was stimulated by their father's drawings—primitive, yet alive—of people, birds and animals, often done to illustrate a point in scripture. Encouraged by their parents, the walls of the living room were always decorated with their childish efforts. Nor was academic training neglected. Both Raphael and Moses, the oldest of the children, knew some French, German and Hebrew, as well as their native Russian, and in the Gymnasium Raphael distinguished himself in drawing and writing. An adventure for the children came when three of them were bitten by a mad cat. Their father took them to Moscow for the Pasteur treatment, but there they saw only monuments, public buildings and stodgy pictorial art.

In 1912 the Governor of the province refused to renew the residence permit of Abraham Soyer. This was tantamount to exile. The Soyers packed hurriedly and took ship for America, settling finally in the East Bronx, not far from the "glass" skyscrapers but living in a world that harassed them with its poverty and bewildered them with its unfamiliar words. The language difficulty was so great that Moses and Raphael, who had been in advance of their age-group in Russia, did not enter high school until 1915.

The contrast between the home and the world outside was such that the children, and especially Raphael, tended to find a sanctuary within the narrow walls of the East Bronx apartment. There Raphael could brood and draw to his heart's content. He was less strong than Moses, though both suffered at one time from ill health. Some critics believe that through this background Raphael found a temperamental affinity with the weakly maladjusted. If this was so, however, it was because beneath his shyness was a core of strength, a stern and spiritual rightness. And while Moses had recourse to a similar inner balance he was more positive outwardly and could—as he did once—have it out with a bully who had been making life miserable for him and Raphael.

Writing for the Hebrew and Yiddish press and teaching private classes, the head of the Soyer family eked out a meager living that erased forever the dream he had had of sending his children to college. They still had their art, though, and kept at it despite all obstacles. A realization that they should help to support the family—now eight persons—forced Raphael and Moses to quit high school after a year. They had worked even before this, at part-time factory jobs and tending newsstands on Third Avenue. All three brothers had the experience of working at very low-paid jobs, for long hours, crowding their studies and their artistic ambitions in-between. Working for as little as $4 weekly, Raphael still managed to put aside nickels and dimes for art school tuition. Evenings he and Moses studied drawing at Cooper Union.

Both of the twins studied at the National Academy, beginning about 1918, and while there they decided on different studios and, in so far as was possible, different schools. However, the influences upon them were so often experiences made real through sharing, that their paths crossed frequently. Isaac followed his brothers to Cooper Union and while at the Academy Raphael and Moses went to sketch classes at the Beaux Arts Institute. Later Isaac, too, went to Beaux Arts.

While at the Academy Moses went to a Sunday art class at a club named after the Spanish labor leader Francisco Ferrer. There Henri and Bellows gave criticisms. "What a warm, generous, magnetic personality was Henri's!" Moses Soyer wrote, in recalling how Henri helped to show him the way he wanted to go, but began by looking at a drawing by Moses, taking it apart mercilessly, "pointing out its superficiality, its lack of character and its empty cleverness." Then the gaunt, lined, Lincolnian Henri showed Moses a Daumier reproduction from *The Liberator*. "Ignorant as I was," said Moses, "I could not help but be struck by the feeling of turbulence and movement, by the noble, unadorned simplicity of the drawing. I also felt the love and sympathy with which the artist drew this group of gaunt men and women and their sad-eyed, undernourished children."

A clue to what there may be of "family style" may be drawn from what followed. Moses bought a copy of *The Liberator,* rushed home with it and showed his brothers the

Daumier and reproductions of such Americans as Sloan, Henri, Minor and Luks. "What impressed us most," he recalled, "was their up-to-dateness, the contemporary spirit of the content." The influence of Degas upon the twins, and to possibly a lesser extent on Isaac, began at this time. It was inevitable that in a family so close what one liked the others liked in greater or lesser degree. Raphael admitted, for example, to an indebtedness to Rembrandt, Breughel, Goya, Eakins and Homer, and his brothers showed much the same likes.

Moses broke away from the Academy earlier than Raphael, going to the Educational Alliance, where he taught a life class from 1924 to 1926. In the same year that Moses began his teaching experience Raphael left the Academy to go to the Art Students League, where his teacher was Guy Pène du Bois. During these years art was only a part-time activity. All three brothers worked and all three, like their father, occasionally tutored youngsters in Hebrew. Among Moses' students was Ida Chassner, a tall angular girl with wide-set blue eyes and high cheekbones, who studied dancing at the Neighborhood Playhouse. They were married in 1926, when Moses was given a traveling fellowship, and went to Europe together, leaving the class at Educational Alliance for Isaac to take over.

Almost simultaneously, Raphael exhibited a painting called *Bronx Street Scene* in the Salons of America show. Through it he met Alexander Brook (see sketch this issue), who helped him to start selling his work both through the Whitney Studio Club and through the Daniel Gallery. In the early 1930's Valentine Dudensing sponsored him, buying four of the paintings in Raphael's one-man show for his own collection. Isaac and his pretty, exotic-looking wife had gone to Paris in 1928, the year Moses and Ida returned to America, but Raphael got a teaching job at the Art Students League in 1932 and didn't get abroad until three years later. On his trip he saw not only the galleries of Europe but went on to the U. S. S. R., where he was invited to speak before the International Society of Artists.

When critics speak of the "family style" they usually refer back to a period in the early 1930's when a group of painters—some, like Cikovsky and Berman, who had met the Soyers at the Educational Alliance or along the way—had similar traits in their work. There were impressionistic slashings of bright color that sometimes got on the fuzzy side and an undeniable similarity of subjects—even though the "languor and softness of the Soyer women" most often applied to the work of Raphael. This subject matter consisted of a frank identification with life, with young people—dancers, unemployed, shoppers and Left-wing groups—all the teeming life of a non-Park Avenue New York. Many critics objected to their continued emphasis on proletarian themes.

Edward Alden Jewell has said that the differences between the three brothers might easily be resolved by the simple expedient of

RAPHAEL SOYER

a group show. This would be especially enlightening if the paintings were chronological. In the early, somewhat primitive paintings by Raphael and Moses there are distinctions that point to their later development. Raphael's are intimate, with naively humorous touches, for, as Walter Gutman wrote: "He somehow feels into people as they see themselves, and into inanimate objects he reads a character that is humble and natural." And while in a comparable style, Moses' paintings of this period are more abstracted.

Sloan, Luks and Bellows—for all their differences—were harbingers of a new approach to realism. The Soyers stem from this influence. The model is never completely abstracted and is often a real personality like Walter Broe, the homeless wanderer (he died in 1940) who once suggested to Raphael that he include in a painting the sign from a Bowery Mission, "How Long Since You Wrote To Mother?" Discovered by Raphael, he became a favorite model of many prominent American artists, moved to the relative opulence of a Mills hotel and toward the end of his life learned to mouth wistfully such phrases as "the contemporary American scene."

Raphael's work found earlier and wider acceptance than that of his brothers. In 1932 he won the Kohnstamm Prize at the Chicago Art Institute, in 1934 his portrait of "Gitel" won him the PAFA Beck Gold Medal, and about the same time a painting of his was purchased by the Metropolitan Museum of Art. A rhythmic aptness of design and what might be called a distinctly impressionistic manner of painting mark his work. Like his brothers he "finds it futile to paint social content pictures consciously." All three have been categorized as belonging to the "social content" school, yet seldom has their work

been classed as outright propaganda. Each of the brothers distinguished himself in work done for governmental art projects.

Moses paints with a heavy outline and often with much impasto, using a palette knife more often than Raphael; Isaac works almost entirely with brushes, and his work is more thinly painted. Some of Moses' most effective work is in tight compact designs such as *Spanish Refugees* and *Mother and Children*. A type of dispersed composition, such as *Studio Rehearsal* and *The Green Room*, suggests a tendency toward the mural form and, indeed, his mural panels at Greenpoint Hospital in Brooklyn bear this out. Moses' work has vigor, a sturdy objective quality, and his remarkable knowledge of anatomy enables him to give spontaneity to what Margaret Bruening called "the give and take of muscular tension, the apparently careless but really practical control of posture."

Growing up with a younger generation than his brothers, Isaac's approach has in it more of the direct question and challenge that marked youth in the depression years. His ambitious compositional trend was noted by McBride, who found in his work "a classical feeling for balance and harmony." The familiar "spiral" design of the Old Masters may be noted in *Where Next?*, the study of the Spanish Civil War, in *School Girls* and in *Employment Agency* (the latter at the Whitney Museum). Isaac's palette might be said to follow Raphael's somewhat, though without such strongly accented grays and browns. One might hazard also the guess that Moses has more often used bright lemon yellows, oranges and reds, though lately Raphael has certainly used more "blonde" color. All three brothers, incidentally, are expert lithographers and have been honored for their graphic work.

Raphael most resembles his youthful self, and one could almost describe him just as Harry Salpeter did in 1938: "A fairly stiff wind might knock Raphael down, he looks that frail. Some years ago Alexander Brook did a full-length portrait of him, dressed in a sack of an overcoat and with as formless a hat pressing down upon his fawnlike ears. . . His body is as thin and small as it ever was, his eyes no less tired and his voice still the husky whisper."

The Soyers have little time for hobbies. Isaac still teaches Hebrew in The Bronx Y. M. H. A., all three teach at the New Art School that they founded two years ago and of which Moses was appointed director in March 1941, all three are married and each couple has one child. Like his younger brother Israel, Moses Soyer likes to write, and his wife Ida dances with Tamiris.

All three brothers are represented at the Whitney Museum of American Art; Moses and Raphael in the Phillips Memorial Gallery in Washington, D. C. and the Metropolitan Museum of Art (New York). Raphael's work is also in collections of the following museums: New York Public Library, Baltimore (Maryland) Museum of Art, Addison Museum

(Andover, Massachusetts), Columbus (Ohio) Gallery of Fine Arts. Moses is represented in the Toledo (Ohio) Museum of Art, Worcester (Massachusetts) Museum, New York Historical Society and Los Angeles (California) Museum. Their New York City galleries are: Raphael, Associated American Artists; Isaac, Midtown Galleries; Moses, Macbeth Gallery. Moses was given a one-man show in 1941 at the Little Gallery in Washington, D. C.

References

Art Digest 12:12 Mr 15 '38; 12:6 My 15 '38
Art N 36:13 Mr 12 '38
Esquire p59 My '38
Mag Art 32:201-7+ Ap '39 il
N Y Times X p8 S 23 '34; p17 Ja 30 '35; p17 F 20 '35; XI p7 Mr 31 '35; IX p9 My 19 '35; XI p9 Mr 6 '38 il; X p7 My 8 '38; X p10 My 7 '39; IX p9 F 4 '40
Who's Who in American Art
Who's Who in American Jewry [Soyer, Moses and Raphael]
Who's Who in New York [Soyer, Raphael]

V. Semler

ARMSTRONG SPERRY

SPERRY, ARMSTRONG Nov. (?), 1897- Author; artist

Address: b. The Macmillan Co, 60 Fifth Avenue, New York City; h. New Canaan, Conn.

The Newbery Medal for "the most distinguished contribution to American books for children in 1940" was awarded to Armstrong Sperry, author and illustrator of *Call It Courage* (1940), a story for boys about a Polynesian youth, Mafatu, who learned to overcome fear. The Medal was presented to Mr. Sperry in June 1941 at a meeting of the American Library Association in Boston, together with a presentation of the 1940 Caldecott Medal to illustrator Robert Lawson (see sketch this issue).

At least two special qualifications make Armstrong Sperry outstanding among the many notable writers of children's books. One is his unusual and authentic South Sea subject matter; another the fact that he is both writer and artist. Helen Follett, whose own juvenile books Sperry has illustrated, said to him: "The astonishing thing about you, 'Arm,' is not that you're a fine artist, or a fine writer, but that you are both!" At which "Arm" chuckled and remarked that being both was a "lot of hard work," but also "lots of fun." Since the appearance of his book he has had the opportunity of doing some more hard work that is "lots of fun": lecturing to groups of young students as well as to librarians and teachers.

The high standard of literary and artistic accomplishment in *Call It Courage* is the outgrowth of meticulous work in the juvenile book field, of careful and loving study of young readers' needs. In his Medal acceptance speech Sperry said: "*Call It Courage* meant a great deal to me in the writing but I had no idea that the response to the book would be so wide among children. I had feared that the concept of spiritual courage might be too adult for the age group such a book would reach, and that young people would find it less thrilling than the physical courage which battles pirates unconcerned or outstares the crouching lion. But it seems I was wrong— which only serves to prove that children have imagination enough to grasp any idea which you present to them with honesty and without patronage." Of the book's style Doris Patee has written: "In Armstrong Sperry's beautiful prose the tale moves smoothly and rapidly like a native chant, and its music rises and falls like the billows of the sea in its setting. Storytellers who have used the story often find children entranced not only by the story itself but by the cadence and rhythm of the language."

Connecticut-born, Armstrong Sperry's forebears were among the state's earliest settlers. On one side of his family the men followed the sea; on the other side they were farmers. "To this day Armstrong Sperry is aware of these two conflicting impulses with himself. He has a farm in the green hills of Vermont, and likes to make his acres yield a fine crop. Then he hankers for the sound of surf breaking, for the sight of tall ships. This hankering on a number of occasions has brought him down from the hills to the sea." As a boy young Sperry listened wide-eyed to the yarns of his great-grandfather, Captain Sereno Armstrong, who could tell of hair-raising adventures with pirates in the China Sea and among cannibals in lagoon-islands rich with pearls. In particular he spoke of a wonderful South Sea island, Bora Bora. Some day, the boy knew, he would have to find that island. Meantime, like other adventure-loving boys, he had to go to school. But at the Stamford

SPERRY, ARMSTRONG—*Continued*

Preparatory School he spent most of his time drawing pictures and scribbling stories. "His teachers shook their heads in gloomy doubt, certain that no good could come of any boy who preferred drawing cannibals to solving the knotty problems of algebra."

Sperry got his first formal training in art when he entered the Yale Art School. Then came the First World War, and he joined the Navy. But as soon as he was mustered out of service he headed for New York City and the Art Students League, where he studied for three years under George Bellows and Luis Mora. His practical career began when he answered an ad for "Help Wanted—Artist." He got the position—at $25 a week. A year followed during which he drew luscious pictures of vacuum cleaners, canned soup and beautiful blonde ladies who wore Venida hair nets. Somehow he found himself thinking more and more of old Captain Armstrong, the South Seas, and Bora Bora in particular. Sperry says that it was really Frederick O'Brien's *White Shadows in the South Seas*, which so enchanted him in his youth, that gave him the impetus to go there. "But this was before Hollywood discovered Tahiti, and before Miss Dorothy Lamour had made the sarong a national commodity." He wrote to O'Brien, however, concerning ways and means. "And that was how I came to be standing on the deck of a copra schooner, 16 years ago this month [June 1941], sailing from Tahiti to Bora Bora."

And his first sight of Bora Bora was all that he had ever dreamed: "I saw a single great peak that towered 2,000 feet, straight up from the plane of the sea. And the peak was buttressed like the walls of an ancient fortress, and it was made of basalt—volcanic rock—which glistened in the sun like amethyst. And there were waterfalls spilling from the clouds, and up in the mountains the wild goats were leaping from peak to peak. There was something so fresh about that island that it seemed as if it had just risen up from the floor of the sea that morning, and the spray was still shining on it."

He spent several months on this primitive enchanted island. He tells what happened there during a vanilla-bean boom, when a blight of the vanilla vine struck all the other islands except Bora Bora, which took on the aspect of a boom town in the Gold Rush days. The people found themselves millionaires over night: movie palaces sprang up, the men bought automobiles, the women Paris gowns. Murder and theft, too, came with these riches. As the old chief, Opu Nui, observed sadly, the people were losing their initiative, their good native customs and ways of living. Then suddenly the vanilla boom was over—new vines replaced the stricken ones in other islands. And the season of storms arrived. One afternoon a great hurricane struck. Their fine houses and possessions destroyed, the people fled to the mountains. They faced famine, and they had grown soft from easy living. Yet, led by the old chief, they rallied to win "a victory not so much over elemental disaster as a personal victory over themselves."

Sperry says: "The thing which remains with me most vividly from those months in Bora Bora, stronger than the manifold charm of the island, is the remembrance of the great courage with which that little band of Polynesians faced the destruction of their world and faced it down, and stooped, only to rebuild. And it is that courage which, in one form or another, I have tried to communicate to the readers of my books."

Children seemed the logical audience for the wealth of material in these South Sea experiences which he dually visualized in words and pictures. Sperry's first book, *One Day With Manu*, a tale of everyday life in Bora Bora, appeared in 1933. An immediate success, it was followed by *One Day With Jambi in Sumatra* (1934), with a Sumatran background. *One Day With Tuktu, an Eskimo Boy* (1935), telling of the life of an Eskimo boy, was based on research, not firsthand experience, and Sperry found such a book more difficult to do. There followed a sea story, *All Sail Set* (1935), a story of the clipper ship *Flying Cloud*. Then a land story, *Wagons Westward* (1936), based on his journey, by car, over the old Santa Fe Trail. The Southwest opened up a new field for him. Out of this came *Little Eagle, a Navajo Boy* (1938), a story of the Navajos. One more South Sea book, *Lost Lagoon* (1939), appeared just prior to *Call It Courage*, his eighth book for children. He illustrated Helen Follett's *Stars To Steer By* (1934).

Armstrong Sperry lives with his family in New Canaan, Connecticut. There is a daughter, Susan, who is the first audience and critic of her father's tales of high adventure. Young John Armstrong will be ready in a few years to lend her a hand. Sperry's first book was dedicated to his wife, Margaret, "who helped to make it grow." Of her Helen Follett writes: "She herself is an inspiring individual who understands and respects the needs of others. She realizes, of course, that a studio without a telephone is part of the working equipment for the daily routine her husband has established so definitely for himself. She understands the deep and insistent need of a creative artist for spiritual isolation, and that such a need for Armstrong Sperry is as essential as the air he breathes. . . To her, it is as if he sought the refuge of a banana tree on some tropical island, his typewriter and drawing board beside him. Sometimes, she says, you can almost hear the swish of encircling waters that make the isolation complete. Then, later on, you can almost hear them recede as he walks into the living room to become once again the head of the family, delightful host, and sterling friend."

References

A. L. A. Bul 35:422-3 Jl '41 il
Horn Book 17:269-72 Jl '41 por
Library J 66:589-90 Jl '41 il por
N Y Times p32 Je 21 '41 por
Pub W 139:2462-4 Je 21 '41 por

SPRING, HOWARD 1889- Author

Address: c/o The Viking Press, 18 E. 48th St, New York City; h. Hoopers Hill, Mylor, Falmouth, England

Author of the 1938 best seller, *My Son, My Son!*, Robert Howard Spring, noted British novelist equally admired in England and America, was able almost to equal his earlier achievement in his book, *Fame Is The Spur* (November 1940). Critics in general applaud this story of a man's rise to political power in England in our time. Hamer Shawcross, brought up in the slums of Manchester, becomes, through his leadership, ability and sincere ideals, chief of the British Labor Party. Mr. Spring presents a powerful character who impetuously pursues fame and wins that fame at the cost of personal disintegration. How the achievement of power corrupts a man who begins with the noblest intentions is the book's major theme: its whole background, however, is a vividly detailed panorama of England between 1890 and the present. Of it Mary Ross writes in the New York *Herald Tribune* Books: "The hold of this story and its glowing reality lie in the fact that Mr. Spring has not merely pictured a great man but has made you believe in him... *Fame Is the Spur* is a notable novel in its breadth and depth and in the fascination of the calvacade of pictures. Its theme, while immemorial, is of particular moment to our times."

In his autobiography, *Heaven Lies About Us* (1939), Howard Spring writes the poignant story of his boyhood of poverty, adventure and courage in Cardiff, Wales, where he was born in 1889. He was one of seven children brought up in a small crowded house in the "tough" part of town near the bars along the docks. His father was a day-laborer who never made enough to make ends meet and who died when young Howard was not yet in his teens. He and his brother Frank had to find jobs. Howard split kindling, ran errands as a butcher's boy, peddled rhubarb. He had to quit school at 12, but the brothers determined to get an education by studying evenings. Valiantly they slaved away at English, French, Latin and mathematics. "As I see it," Mr. Spring writes, "only the indefatigable realism of my mother kept us afloat. She worked her fingers to the bone, scrubbing and charring. It cost her much to bring up her sons."

Then, "blind chance took me to a newspaper office. I was happy there at once; and I have been happy in newspaper offices ever since." He was 22 when he joined the staff of the *Yorkshire Observer;* and in 1915 went to work on the *Manchester Guardian,* where he remained until 1931, when he joined the London *Evening Standard.* There he was book critic until he found it possible to give his time wholly to his own writing. During his newspaper career he married Marion Ursula Pye; the couple have two sons, David and Michael.

Mr. Spring began to be a writer, however, at a tender age. His first literary work, he says, was an *Ode on the Death of Mr. Glad-*

stone. "I was nine years old. I do not know why Mr. Gladstone's decease should have given birth to my muse, nor do I remember anything of the ode except the last line, 'The sun that sets in cloud shall rise in glory.'" This noble effort he hid in a tobacco tin in his bureau; and "from time to time I would sneak up to

F. W. Schmidt

HOWARD SPRING

the bedroom, unearth the ode, gloat sinfully upon it, and then bury it again."

In the sanctity of his bedroom he also produced his first novel. He shoved aside the time-honored but never-used basin and jug "set" on the washstand and got to work on a fine imitation of *David Copperfield.* This he sent to Dickens' publishers, thus giving them "the opportunity of keeping in the great tradition." It was a heavy blow to him when, alas, the manuscript came back. His first check (for £1, 12s. 6d.) came for a rollicking tale of public school life—no one had a more virginal knowledge of English public schools than poor young Howard. But it bought him a new overcoat, with a leftover "half crown in change to jingle in my pocket."

His first published book (1932) was *Darkie and Co.,* a tale for children, followed by another, *Sampson's Circus* (1936). In 1939 he wrote his third children's book, *Tumbledown Dick.* A work for adults was *Shabby Tiger* (1935), followed by its sequel, *Rachel Rosing* (1936), the story of a Jewish actress. Soon after this he began *My Son, My Son!* (published in England as *O Absalom!*), which achieved immediate and phenomenal success. It is the story of a boy who grew up in Manchester, but the author denies that it is autobiographical in any sense.

SPRING, HOWARD—*Continued*

In a letter (December 1939) to his publishers Mr. Spring wrote: "I am still doing no writing work. I'm busy with our local Defense Volunteers, which means patrolling the coast at dawn, looking out for invaders by air or water. One of these days, I suppose, they'll come; and then we'll see."

References

> Atlan 163:29-37 Ja '39; 163:211-18 F
> '39; 163:362-70 Mr '39
> N Y Herald Tribune Books p5 N 17 '40
> N Y Times Book R p5 N 17 '40 por
> Wilson Lib Bul 13:654 Je '39 por
> Author's and Writer's Who's Who
> Spring, H. Heaven Lies About Us 1939
> Who's Who

STAMP, JOSIAH CHARLES STAMP, 1ST BARON June 21, 1880—Apr. 16, 1941 Chief economic adviser to the British Government; chairman of the London, Midlands and Scottish Railway; director of the Bank of England; member of the 1924 Dawes Reparations Commission; leading pre-War advocate of German appeasement; often referred to as the busiest man in England; in *Who's Who* his biography takes up nearly two columns; killed together with Lady Stamp and their eldest son and heir, the Honorable Wilfred Carlyle Stamp, by German bombs which demolished their home.

References

> Christian Sci Mon Mag p3 Je 8 '40
> Author's and Writer's Who's Who
> Who's Who
> Who's Who in Broadcasting
> Who's Who in Commerce and Industry

Obituaries

> N Y Times p4 Ap 18 '41 por
> Time 37:71 Ap 28 '41

STEEL, JOHANNES Aug. 3, 1906-
Commentator for WMCA; writer; lecturer
Address: WMCA, 1657 Broadway, New York City

Perhaps more than any other commentator, Johannes Steel has reason to understand the psychology of the German mind, the mercilessly efficient working of the German machine. He himself was a small, reluctant cog in it at one time, working for Dr. Hjalmar Schacht. It is that special personal knowledge that has been responsible for many of his amazing scoops.

Johannes Herbert von Stahl (he had his name legally changed to Johannes Steel when he came to the United States in 1934) was born in Heidelberg in 1906, the son of Lieutenant Colonel Herman and Carolina (Norwood) von Stahl. His father was a nobly born staff officer with strong monarchist tendencies. His mother, an Englishwoman, lived in Germany through the War and suffered bitterly from social ostracism and the constant struggle to get enough to eat for her two sons in the midst of general famine. Johannes was educated at the Heidelberg Real Gymnasium and later went to the University of Heidelberg (his education was supplemented by studies at Oxford and Geneva). At that time student life at Heidelberg was entirely different from the operetta version, and the young German grew to maturity "in violently unstable social and political surroundings with nobody to help him understand the nature of the changes amid which he lived." His father's considerable fortune had disappeared, and the specter of inflation haunted his youth; young Steel therefore eked out the family fortunes by precarious speculation on the Black Bourse.

In the early '20s Steel was seeing many of his schoolmates join the National Socialist Party. He himself became a member of the Social Democratic Party and wielded considerable influence among his fellow students in the University of Berlin, to which he transferred. As he himself says, his activity at that time was largely political, not scholastic, and in 1928 he was rewarded by a seat in the Prussian Diet. His experience as a politician, however, proved short-lived: disinclined to follow rigid parliamentary discipline, he was soon relieved of his mandate. In the meantime he had been writing and had had his articles printed in provincial newspapers.

Later that same year Johannes Steel was given a post in the Commercial Intelligence Service connected with the Ministry of Economics. The purpose of the Service was to keep all branches of industry and commerce in Germany informed as to commercial possibilities in almost every part of the world, and to build up German products by almost any means. Afterward he was to call his work that "of a glorified traveling salesman on behalf of German industry and commerce." But at that time it gave him an opportunity to travel around the world, thus providing valuable background for his later work as a columnist and commentator. He went to Warsaw, Constantinople; he visited Greece, Egypt, Japan, the Far East. All kinds of strange and fascinating things, which he has described vividly in his biographical *Escape to the Present* (1937), happened to him. He rubbed elbows with armament kings and dope merchants; on his way to Baghdad, he was caught in a simoon; he rescued a captive Frenchwoman from the harem of the Arab sheik whose guest he was. The missions on which he was sent required tact, presence of mind and audacity, and that Steel possessed these qualifications was shown by his promotion in 1930 to the position of Foreign Economic Observer. In that capacity he made a tour of South America and stayed in Washington.

In 1932 Steel returned to Germany "as a private citizen, ready to do whatever I could to stop the Fascist onslaught." He found Von Papen (see sketch this issue) in power and the big industrialists maneuvering Hitler into position. He earned Nazi dislike by writing anti-Hitler editorials for the *Essener Nationale Zeitung* and by attacking other Nazi leaders elsewhere, but since he was a bright young man with valuable contacts outside of Germany, an attempt was made to win him over. He turned down an offer made personally by finance wizard Schacht. Finally, on February 8, 1933, a week after Hitler had been made Chancellor, he was arrested and thrown into a National Socialist *block-warte*. On the tenth day of his captivity he escaped by slugging his guard on the head with a poker and taking his uniform. A friend met him with clothes behind the statue of an emperor in the Sieges Allee, and the next day he arrived at the Gare du Nord in Paris. Like Heine, he had nothing to declare but his spirit: he had nothing on him except a few francs and a lottery ticket which he sent back to his family. (The ticket, by the way, won $600, and his family lived on it for the next six months.)

After a while Steel went on to London. There he got a part-time job on the *Sunday Chronicle* on the strength of an interview with the inaccessible film director Joseph von Sternberg. (Steel describes vividly his feelings on seeing that interview appear later under the quaint headline "Human Oyster Talks at Last But Not About Marlene's Legs.") He got another job with a curious publication called *New Britain*, run by a Serb named Mitrinović who was known in his leisure hours as "Cosmoi, the Spirit of the Earth." And during his stay in England he was also able to write and publish his book *Hitler as Frankenstein* (1933). These, however, were fairly lean days for Johannes Steel, colored by anxiety for his parents in Germany and grief for his brother Eric, who had been killed by the Nazis.

In January 1934 Steel finally decided to come to the United States. He arrived at that decision, he says, after reading the story of Carl Schurz, another German who had found refuge in America. His first few months here were spent in unadorned poverty, relieved by occasional articles published in *The Nation* and occasional lectures. It wasn't until June 1934 that he gained recognition—with a shrewd forecast of bloodletting in the Nazi ranks which he sold to Harry T. Saylor, the editor of the New York *Post*. Steel and the New York *Post*, which had gone out on the limb with this prediction, held their breaths until finally the blood purge of June 30 vindicated Steel's prophecy and assured his future as a journalist. Steel's valuable connections abroad finally bore fruit, and his record as a prophet was completed by his prediction of the assassinations of Dollfuss in Austria and of King Alexander in Marseilles. As a result of his *Putsch* scoop Steel became the foreign editor of the New York *Post*. In that same year appeared his *Second World War*, "a remarkably concise analysis of the European and Far Eastern situations and their potentialities for trouble."

From 1935 on, Johannes Steel covered Europe as correspondent for the *Post*, the Philadelphia *Record* and the Camden *Courier*.

In 1937 he became associated with WMCA and WOR as commentator and news analyst. His highly personalized, vital talks have since that time made him very popular with listeners, who like to hear his vivid diatribes against Hitler, his knowledgeable hints that bespeak a rich political background and limitless pipe lines from abroad. A colorful note is also injected into his broadcasts by his

Volpé

JOHANNES STEEL

accent, an odd mixture of German purr and Scotch burr. Like many another commentator, his reputation was considerably helped by his work during Munich, that commentators' Roman holiday, and in response to requests by his listeners a collection of his broadcasts entitled *Truth About Munich* was published in pamphlet form. Altogether, Johannes Steel is rather proud of the fact that his exploits in journalism and radio have made the Nazis uncomfortable enough to retaliate by depriving him of his German citizenship along with Thomas Mann, Arnold Zweig and others. There have been, he claims, several attempts to kidnap him across the German border during his trips abroad.

In September 1935 Johannes Steel married Rhys Caparn, a young sculptress in whose work he found "an expression of those things that Hitler and Mussolini were trying their best to destroy." Three years later he became an American citizen. A tall fair man with a round face and charming manners, he is also an excitable and voluble talker who gesticulates freely while broadcasting. Besides his work on the radio he is kept busy with lectures, with writing articles for such publications as *The Nation, Esquire, Current History* and *Liberty,* the last of which sent him abroad to interview British Cabinet ministers in May

STEEL, JOHANNES—*Continued*

1941, and with work on the executive board of the Overseas Press Club of America.

References

PM p13 S 23 '40 por

Steel, J. Escape to the Present 1937

STEELL, WILLIS 1859(?)—Jan. 31, 1941

Playwright, novelist and retired newspaperman; worked on the New York *Herald,* the old New York *Daily News* and the Chicago *Morning Telegraph* until 1903 when devoted himself to playwriting; among his plays were *Brother Dave* and *Girl of the Golden Horn*; his books include *Benjamin Franklin of Paris* and *The Prospector*; returned to newspaper work in 1916 on the New York *Sun* and worked for the Paris edition of the *Herald Tribune* from 1924 to 1932.

References

Who's Who in America   1930-31

Obituaries

N Y Herald Tribune p10 F 1 '41

STEELMAN, JOHN R(OY) June 23, 1900- Director of the United States Conciliation Service

Address: b. Department of Labor Bldg, Washington, D. C.

Bulletin: Heading the three-man board appointed by President Roosevelt in November 1941 to settle the crucial captive mines dispute, on December 2 Steelman cast an affirmative vote in the decision that granted the closed shop to the United Mine Workers.

From May 1941 issue:

In 1941 the question of industrial peace is one of the most important the United States has to settle. Strikes, lockouts, stoppages have been occurring widely in plants manufacturing defense materials; Congress has been debating compulsory legislation against these outbreaks; the public has been daily becoming more concerned. And the United States Conciliation Service has been working day and night to bring peace between employers and employees.

Its director, John R. Steelman, has spent days in conferences with the miners and the soft coal operators; he has flown out to the Allis-Chalmers plant in Milwaukee; he has discussed the strikes at the International Harvester Company's plants; he brought an end to the Vultee Aircraft Corporation strike; he has been hopping all over the country trying to settle the many small strikes that crop up in defense production. He has been doing all this without any authority or coercive powers. When he sits down with the owners or workers "he can only reason, plead—and maybe bluff."

The United States Conciliation Service, which employs 118 Commissioners of Conciliation distributed over the country, enters a controversy at the request of one or both of the parties involved. The conciliator assigned listens to both sides and tries to find where compromises can be made. As Steelman puts it: "The Service works on the theory that, if a dispute is settled by the parties themselves at the conference table, the resultant peace will be more enduring and leave less bitterness and rancor than if the dispute had been settled by authority of law or force." There must be no pressure of the government in the process on one side or the other. "The minute you make a cop of a conciliator," he says, "you have destroyed his usefulness. We do not want police authority. We believe it to be the very antithesis of the spirit in which really effective conciliation is carried on." He has been quoted: "Abolition of the right to strike was the entering wedge of Fascism in each of the countries it conquered."

That such a policy has been successful is evidenced by the record. In 1940 the Conciliation Service was called in on a total of 4,665 situations—strikes, threatened strikes, controversies, consultations, arbitrations, lockouts—and less than three per cent of these were listed as unable to adjust. It has been endorsed by groups as varied as the A F of L, the CIO, the National Association of Manufacturers, the United States Chamber of Commerce, all of whom expect it to maintain its record even during national defense. Only when there is a dispute which the Service cannot settle will the new National Defense Mediation Board be called in for action.

The "genial 200-pound six footer" who directs the Service was born in Thornton, Arkansas on a small farm from which his father and mother, Ples Cydney and Martha Ann (Richardson) Steelman, did their best to wrest a living. John went to grade school and high school near there and finished his secondary education just in time to get into the Army for the last few months of the First World War. By the time he was discharged from the Army he was a corporal and he was determined to get himself an education.

In the next ten years he attended four colleges and took four degrees, supporting himself during the summers as a logger and sawmill hand, in winters waiting on tables; peddling books and insurance, following wheat harvests, correcting papers for professors. By 1922 he had a B. A. degree from Henderson-Brown College in Arkadelphia, Arkansas; by 1924 an M. A., and by 1925 a Ph. B. from Vanderbilt University; by 1928, after a year's study at Harvard in 1926, a Ph. D. from the University of North Carolina.

Armed with this array of academic degrees, Steelman settled down in 1928 at Alabama College in Montevallo as a professor of sociology and economics. He stayed there until 1934, the year Secretary of Labor Perkins made a speech at Alabama College and met him. Before the year was out she had made him a Commissioner of Conciliation. Three years later, in 1937, he was named Director of the Conciliation Service.

Washington Press Photo Bureau
JOHN R. STEELMAN

Immediately he started working, spending from 10 to 15 hours a day in the office, seeing strings of people late into Saturday afternoon and Sunday. He patched up coal disputes, he helped settle the Washington, D. C. hotel strike, he kept miners, machinists and builders from striking and employers in major industries from lockouts. Each year his department has been handling between three and four thousand cases involving millions of workers, and each year the record of settlement has been a percentage high in the 90's.

There have been times when Steelman kept meetings between employers and employees going for 30 consecutive hours; times when he hasn't left the office for over 60 hours. And there is no time when his telephone isn't ringing. Mrs. Steelman, the former Emma Zimmerman, whom Steelman met at a union convention when she was secretary to the secretary of the Building and Construction Trades Council and married in 1939, says that the telephone starts at about 8 a. m. "Even breakfast is eaten to the ringing of the phone." When they are away on trips (Mrs. Steelman always goes with her husband to the large cities): "We snatch our meals in our hotel rooms because it's hard to be reached by phone in dining rooms or cafes." And this keeps up until 3:30 in the morning. It was because of his constant use of the telephone to discuss problems big and small that Steelman acquired a sort of paralytic cramp of the wrist and palm of his left hand which was relieved only by the installation of a special device that leaves his hands free.

Dr. Steelman doesn't mind the rush, the activity, the strain. He is a "husky vigorous man, with lively eyes and an enveloping warmth of personality," whom you'd be likely to size up "as a dock hand who had hoisted himself up in the world by his bootstraps," rather than as a Ph. D. former college pro-

fessor. In conferences with workers or management "his words tumble out with an almost juvenile eagerness when he talks, and his most academic discourses are punctuated by an effective choice of profanity which he never picked up in college." Time and again industrialists or powerful unions offer him jobs—at much more than the government pays him—but he turns them down every time. "Hell, this job is too much fun," he says.

References

Baltimore Sun Mag p1 D 1 '40 por
Cur Hist 50:8 Je '39
N Y Post p5 Ap 2 '41 por
N Y Times VII p11+ Mr 30 '41 por
Who's Who in America
Who's Who in the Nation's Capital

STEEN, MARGUERITE Author

Address: b. c/o Viking Press, Inc, 18 E. 48th St, New York City; h. 11 Apple Tree Yard, St. James', London, S. W. 1, England

One of the most prolific and gifted of modern English novelists, in *The Sun Is My Undoing* (1941), Marguerite Steen has written a lusty historical novel, this time more than 100 pages longer than *Gone with the Wind*. The violent chronicle of an eighteenth-century slave trader, his African mistress and his mulatto daughter, it is also the story of the "cause and progress of the slave trade and of the minority who, courageously and successfully, fought it out of existence." Its backgrounds range from the Bristol waterfront to the swamps and jungles of the African Gold Coast, from Cuban sugar plantations to Madrid palaces. Critics have been extravagant in their praise.

Miss Steen (she is unmarried) was born in Liverpool, England and started her educational career at the Belvedere Kindergarten in that city. Then, she says, her family left Liverpool and she was sent to a "horrible little private boarding school," whence she was finally removed at her own request to Kendal High School. There she did nothing for three years as a boarder "except have a good time and, within the limits of a strict minimum of work, imbibe a certain disposition to learn."

She had started to write at the age of about eight, and by the time she was fifteen had produced a three-volume prophecy in the form of a novel, containing an almost complete prediction of her own future career up to the age of about 30, with only one mistake—that her eventual career would be the stage, and writing only a sort of stepping stone. This early effort, she confesses, "shows no particular signs of literary talent, beyond a certain crude melodrama and a positively slushy sentiment; and no love affairs! Evidently at 15 my mind was slightly conventional."

During the First World War, at the age of 19, she was "booted unwillingly into schoolteaching." She loathed it, "loathed school environment and the absurd insincerities of the profession." After three years she flung herself into London with about 12

Mme. Yevonde, London

MARGUERITE STEEN

pounds in her pocket to try to get on the stage. (She had already published articles on stage décor.) She failed; spent all of her money and a bit more; pawned her few pawnable possessions and lived on a glass of Horlicks and a bun for 24 hours on end. Then by some chance she was offered a position as teacher of classic dancing and eurythmics in Halifax. She took it, and in three years had a big north country connection and was earning from £500 to £600 a year. But the stage had as great a lure as ever. Eventually she threw up security for £3 a week and an opportunity to tour with the Fred Terry-Julia Neilson Company.

She was with Fred Terry for three years. By 1926 matters were rather desperate. She had been six months out of work, and had only £50 a year of her own. Her "guide, monitor and dearest friend," Ellen Terry, impressed by letters that Marguerite Steen had written for her and by certain theatrical criticisms that she had done, had always insisted that she should write. The late W. J. Locke had also encouraged the idea: although he had read her first novel "and earned the gratitude of the publishers and public by gently but firmly suggesting its suppression," he thought that she had the "writing maggot" in her and would eventually produce something worthwhile. And she had taken their advice to the extent of scribbling away at a "society" novel in theatrical lodgings and scene docks.

That was how the stage became a stepping stone to a career as novelist for Marguerite Steen, directly contrary to her youthful prediction. The novel she had been working on was sold, and published in 1927 as *The Gilt Cage;* and although no critic hailed her as a genius, she continued to write, and to sell what she wrote. Many of her short stories

appeared even before the publication of her second novel, *Dark Duel* (1929) (published in England the year before as *Duel in the Dark*), which made use of her stage background in a story of psychological rivalry between an aging stage favorite and her granddaughter.

After that it was a strange year when American readers did not see the publication of at least one novel by Marguerite Steen. In 1930 *Reluctant Madonna* (London, 1929) appeared in the United States, and the next year saw the publication of *They That Go Down in Ships* (published in England the year before as *They That Go Down*). This last book, the story of the life of the daughter of a sailor's widow in the days of Lord Nelson, caused at least one American critic to greet Marguerite Steen as "a figure of individuality and definite promise" among the younger English novelists, and most of the others were equally enthusiastic. *The Wise and the Foolish Virgins* (1932), which, with "tenderness and a strongly controlled intensity, pointed at times with a biting irony," told the tragedy of a slum child who worshipped her very ordinary teacher, was also generally lauded.

Critics, however, differed rather more as to the merits of *Unicorn* (New York 1932; London 1931), the romance of an exiled archduchess who during the post-War years succeeded in rejecting her cold-storage upbringing and marrying a painter. They continued to disagree over *Stallion* (1932), an "earthy" novel with an English village background, and *Spider* (1933), the story of a magnificently unscrupulous widow of a great musical composer who builds a cult around his genius, with herself as high priestess.

The disagreement continued. *Matador* (1934), even though a choice of the Book Society in England and of the Book-of-the-Month Club in the United States, brought comments ranging all the way from the New York *Post's* awed "Only a very little short of being a masterpiece" to the *New Republic's* patronizing "Melodrama according to Hoyle." *One-Eyed Moon* (1935), the second book in a trilogy dealing with Spanish characters, earned high praise in the *Christian Science Monitor* but was rejected by the still patronizing *New Republic* with the suggestion that it "badly needs a breath of fresh air." And the third book of the trilogy, *The Tavern* (1936), which was called "a minor masterpiece" in the New York *Times,* was dismissed by its *Saturday Review of Literature* reviewer on the grounds that Miss Steen's treatment of human nature couldn't be taken seriously. Only the less ambitious *Return of a Heroine* (1936) apparently created the same reaction in them all. That was, it was generally agreed, a "psychological thriller," entertaining but not completely convincing.

All in all, if Marguerite Steen has been reading her clippings over a period of years, she must have occasionally been puzzled at learning that she has an immense talent for subtle character development and only a superficial understanding of people; that her work includes "nothing shopworn" and little but "theatrical episodes"; that her historical and foreign backgrounds are completely convincing and require a great deal more understanding and research; that she writes with absolute realism and with romantic flamboyance; that her novels are fundamentally serious, primarily works of entertainment, profoundly witty and morbidly humorless. She can, however, find something consistent in nearly all the criticism of her work: her novels, she is assured, are rich with dramatic action, and color, and appeal to the senses. Her experience on the stage has served her well, it seems.

Published in England but not in the United States have been *Ancestors* (1930), "a mental aberration" published under the name of Lennox Dryden; *When the Wind Blows* (1931); *Oakfield Plays* (1932); *Peepshow* (1933); *The Lost One, a Biography of Mary (Perdita) Robinson* (1937); *Who Would Have Daughters?* (1937); *The Marriage Will Not Take Place* (1938); *Family Ties* (1939); *Kind of Insolence, and Other Stories* (1940); and *French for Love* (1940) a play written with Derek Patmore. *Hugh Walpole: a Study* (1933), an enthusiastic appreciation of Walpole as the "great romantic" of modern English fiction, was Miss Steen's one published work of literary criticism.

Marguerite Steen's principal occupations, aside from her writing, have long been amateur play producing and painting. She had been drawing and painting since babyhood, and was destined for an artist by her family, but (owing partly to inefficient art instruction between the years of nine and eighteen) her interest lapsed for a while. Before the War her favorite subjects were Paris street scenes: houses give her "a feeling" which she tries to convey on canvas, she says. In peaceful days another hobby was motoring, in a small tourer model "with a gallant heart and an apparently inexhaustible capacity for climbing hills."

References

Wilson Lib Bul 11:366 F '37 por
Author's and Writer's Who's Who
Who's Who

STEINHARDT, LAURENCE A(DOLPH)

(stīn'härt) Oct. 6, 1892- United States Ambassador to Russia

Address: American Embassy, Moscow, U. S. S. R.; 30 Pine St, New York City

Bulletin: As the invading Germans approached Moscow, Ambassador Steinhardt, with the rest of the diplomatic corps, moved to the temporary Soviet capital of Kuibyshev. From there he traveled by plane to New York, arriving on November 26, 1941. There were indications that he would not return to Moscow, but would be given another strategic diplomatic post.

Associated Press
LAURENCE A. STEINHARDT

From July 1941 issue:

From August 1939 to June 1941, when the Nazi-Soviet pact was in effect, Laurence A. Steinhardt, the United States Ambassador to Russia, had the difficult task of trying to understand and interpret Russia's maneuverings while at the same time maintaining the necessary business relations between that country and his own. Since June 1941 his task has become even more complicated, for, with Russia at war with Germany, his are the manifold duties of a statesman in a belligerent country, bound to report to the United States not only the progress of the fighting, but the intricacies of Russia's policies.

This would be a hard job almost anywhere today. It has often been particularly difficult and delicate in the Soviet Union, for, as G. E. R. Gedye once explained: "In no other country are rulers at such pains to conceal their true policy from the diplomatic corps as in Russia. There is no other country which has so deliberately isolated its corps, so severely restricted intercourse between diplomats and Soviet Union political leaders and officials." Despite this, Ambassador Steinhardt has managed during the time he has been Ambassador to act as host to Russian Commissars, to entertain representatives of various foreign governments, Axis, Allied and neutral, and to report to Washington as much as possible of those actions and policies which bear on the world situation and the War.

Ambassador Steinhardt is doing this, and doing it with all the necessary qualities of both finesse and hardboiledness, after only seven years of diplomatic experience. These, however, were preceded by many years' experience as a lawyer, and he still believes that there is no training for a diplomat like work at the Bar. Laurence Adolph Steinhardt was born in New York City, the son of

STEINHARDT, LAURENCE A.—*Cont.*

Adolph M. and Addie (Untermyer) Steinhardt, and was educated in that city, first by private tutors, then by Columbia University, which gave him a B. A. in 1913 and an M. A. and an LL. B. in 1915.

Out of college, Steinhardt joined the accounting firm of Deloitte, Plender, Griffiths and Company and worked as an accountant until he was admitted to the Bar in 1916. That was the year when he acted as counsel to Waslaw Nijinsky in the first of the many cases he was to handle for internationally important people. For a while, however, his fast-moving career as a lawyer was halted, and Steinhardt entered the Army as a private. He moved ahead here, too, and soon was a sergeant in the 60th Field Artillery. Not much later he became associate counsel for the War Department; a member of the Provost Marshal General's staff; and an assistant in the Housing and Health Division of the War Department.

This last government position was his in 1919. A year later he became a member of the New York law firm of Guggenheimer, Untermyer & Marshall (the Untermyer part of it was his uncle) and was associated with it until 1933. For the economic background of his law practice, Steinhardt served as director of 10 corporations; he also wrote a number of books and articles on jurisprudence, finance and trade-unions; and he crossed the Atlantic scores of times to handle the affairs of the widely scattered clients of his firm.

Even though he was an important lawyer, Laurence Steinhardt didn't emerge as a political figure until 1932, the year in which he did "Trojan work" for Franklin Delano Roosevelt before the Chicago nominating convention, both as a member of the finance committee of the Democratic National Committee and as a firm supporter—which he has continued to be. Observers didn't hesitate to call Steinhardt's appointment as Minister to Sweden in 1933 a reward for this support, but at the same time they recognized his ability.

In July, Steinhardt set sail and, once in Sweden, helped negotiate the reciprocal trade agreement between the United States and that country. He also distinguished himself by his efficient handling of the aftermath of the Kreuger and Toll collapse and by his investigations into the feasibility of United States' recognition of the Soviet Union.

In 1937 Steinhardt moved to Peru and shortly afterward began diplomatically to prepare the ground for the eighth Pan-American Conference held in Lima in December 1938. It was his close cooperation, later, with Secretary of State Hull that did "much to achieve the eleventh hour success in the Declaration of Lima." After less than two years in this post, however, Steinhardt was recalled and transferred to Russia as the United States' Ambassador, the third to that country.

There was general satisfaction at the appointment because of the new Ambassador's knowledge of Russia and the Russian problem from his previous study of the question of recognition. There was satisfaction, too, because it was known then that the situation would be a difficult one which needed a man with Steinhardt's "tremendous capacity for detail and thoroughness." As Gedye describes him: "No trouble is too great for him, no detail too petty. He is the sort of man who will investigate a report on a given subject from 20 different angles, well knowing that only one stands a chance of being acted on, and is more than satisfied if eventually action is secured."

When Steinhardt left in May 1939 for Russia, accompanied by his wife, the former Dulcie Yates Hofmann whom he married in January 1923, and their daughter Dulcie Ann, his task wasn't an easy one. Yet it was felt by many at that time that the full-fledged military alliance between Britain and the Soviet Union for which Russia seemed anxious might still be negotiated before war broke out. This hope was shattered by the German-Russian non-aggression pact, and whatever other hope the situation still held seemed to be dissipated by the Soviet invasion of Poland, the invasion of Finland and the conclusion of forced pacts with the Baltic States. Steinhardt's job got more and more complicated and important. He not only reported, explained, enlightened his own government on the day to day happenings in Russia, but conferred long and earnestly with Premier-Foreign Commissar Molotov during the Finnish War, went to Tallinn, Estonia in what reporters felt was an attempt to bring about peace, though this was not confirmed in the United States; investigated the situation of the ship, *City of Flint*; gave information to newspapermen; reported in Washington for consultation in 1940; dealt with situations made important to the United States by the Axis conquest of the Balkans and the Russian pact with Japan; conferred with Japanese Foreign Minister Matsuoka (see sketch this issue) both before and after Matsuoka's visit to Berlin; tried to keep his country informed on the progress of the war between Russia and Germany when it finally broke out on June 22, 1941. And once war began he reported Russian progress and Russian needs to his country, later supervising the receipt and distribution of American war supplies.

Before war came to Moscow Ambassador and Mrs. Steinhardt often entertained Moscow's foreign colony and distinguished visitors at Spasso House. Part of this entertainment was made easy by Ambassador and Mrs. Steinhardt's fluency in languages (Russian is the only one he isn't at home in, though he has a working knowledge of it); part by the facilities for entertainment the Steinhardts were able to get together. Very often after a dinner party they would show an up-to-date American moving picture in a specially installed theatre; sometimes they would provide for informal dancing.

References

China W R 94:284 N 2 '40 por
N Y Times VII p21 Ap 21 '40 por
Newsweek 13:19 Mr 13 '39

U S News 9:57-8 O 18 '40 por; 11:39
Jl 4 '41 por
America's Young Men 1936-37
Who's Who in America
Who's Who in American Jewry

STEPHENSON, JAMES (stĕ'fĕn-sŭn)
Apr. 14, 1900—July 29, 1941 English-born
screen character actor; best known for his role
of the lawyer in *The Letter*, which starred
Bette Davis, he had also appeared in *Boy
Meets Girl, Cowboy From Brooklyn* and
Confessions of a Nazi Spy; had business career
before entering the theatre and subsequently
motion pictures; late in gaining recognition,
and died of a heart attack while he was on the
threshold of stardom in Hollywood.

References

International Motion Picture Almanac

Obituaries

N Y Times p17 Jl 30 '41

STERN, BILL July 1, 1907- NBC sports
announcer

Address: National Broadcasting Co, 30 Rockefeller Plaza, New York City

Bill Stern is NBC's sports announcer, with
an approach that is dramatic but a little more
scholarly than most. Adam hats, B. F. Goodrich tires, Colgate-Palmolive-Peet soap and
Twenty Grand cigarets have all had the
advantage of having their products mentioned
in his persuasive tones along with football
games and prize fights. And since 1938 he
has been doing sports comment for MGM's
News of the Day.

One of the younger radio commentators,
Bill Stern was born in Rochester, New York
on July 1, 1907, the son of a clothing manufacturer. After attending the Hackley School
in Tarrytown, New York and the Cascadilla
School in Ithaca he went on to Pennsylvania
Military College, in Chester, Pennsylvania.
There his enthusiasm about sports was more
active than vocal. He played football for
four years (three as varsity quarterback),
participated in tennis, basketball, boxing, crew,
and in 1930 came away with three letters as
well as a B. S. degree.

It seemed at first that Bill Stern would end
up in the theatre. He had led the college
orchestra in vaudeville, and after graduation
he got a humble start in the show business
by becoming an usher. Somewhat later a
stock company in Rochester took him on, and
next it was on to Hollywood. But it was
hard to get past the gate for an interview,
and Stern compromised by digging cement
postholes on the RKO lot for $5 a day.

For a long time he had annoyed his family
by pretending, usually in the shower, that he
was manning a "mike" at a big football game.
He hadn't considered football announcing as
a career, though, until in 1925 he got a job
announcing sports over WHAM in Rochester.
He continued in Austin, Birmingham, Cincinnati, New Orleans and many other cities

throughout the country before he returned to
theatre work in 1931 as assistant stage manager of the Roxy Theatre. A year later he
became stage manager of the Roxy; and the
Music Hall and the Center Theatre, both in
Radio City, opened that same year with Stern
as stage director.

After a couple of years of stage directing
he was anxious for a change. Nostalgic for
his mike, he appealed to an NBC executive
for permission to broadcast part of a football

Ray Lee Jackson

BILL STERN

game—and got it. Although still stage director for the Music Hall and Center Theatre,
he worked with Graham McNamee during the
1934 football season and won such wide popularity that he became guest announcer of the
Pontiac series that year. Finally, in June
1937, Bill Stern became a regular member of
the NBC Special Events staff.

Fight fans are particularly familiar with
his voice. For four years, until the contract
expired in June 1941, NBC and Adam Hat
Stores Inc. were sponsors of the big-time
bouts, and boxing enthusiasts grew used to
hearing the NBC team of Sam Taub and Bill
Stern "describing right hooks and Homburgs
with equal competency." Alton Cook of the
New York *World-Telegram* is only one of the
radio critics who consider him among the finest
sports commentators. He can tell a human
interest story, too. NBC people remember the
time Stern told a couple of million listeners
about a boy who saved his dog instead of his
new bicycle from a fire—and unwittingly
brought on a deluge of cash contributions
toward a new bicycle for the boy. (A bicycle
manufacturer finally took care of the situation himself.) And when, on the way to cover
a football game in Texas, an accident landed
him in the hospital for six months, the studio

STERN, BILL—*Continued*

received many anxious inquiries from his listeners.

Movie-goers know Bill Stern as the rather photogenic young man with the dark, intelligent face and the hat pulled down jauntily over one eye who appears for a brief moment before becoming merely the voice behind MGM's *News of the Day.* He is five-feet-ten, has brown hair and brown eyes, and weighs one hundred-fifty pounds. Although he lives in the country with his wife, Harriet May, because he finds the country more peaceful, there is nothing particularly rural about his diversions. His greatest extravagances are fast cars and speedboats; he likes music and the theatre; and he is another one of the growing army of Americans who believe they are experts on swing.

References

Schechter, A. A. and Anthony, E.
I Live on Air 1941
Variety Radio Directory

RISË STEVENS

STEVENS, RISË (rē'sá) June 11, 1913-
Opera singer

Address: c/o Metropolitan Opera Company, New York City

Risë Stevens is a tall, striking brunette who ever since her Metropolitan debut in 1938 has been delighting American audiences with her rich mezzo-soprano voice, her striking acting, her glamorous appearance. In *Mignon,* as the temptress in *Samson and Delilah,* in the title role of the *Rosenkavalier,* as Cherubino in the *Marriage of Figaro,* in many other operatic parts and in concert appearances, she has scored the sort of ovations for which every aspiring singer prays.

Her hopes and ambitions started many years ago, for it was clear from the time she was a child that she had a lovely voice. Her parents, Mr. and Mrs. Christian Steenbjorg, encouraged her, saw that she had lessons while she was going to school in New York City, where she was born, and were able to see their hopes for her on the way to fulfillment when Risë was only 10. It was then that she appeared, successfully, as a youthful prima donna on a children's radio program. By the time she had been graduated from Newtown High School in Long Island, at the age of 17, she was ready for operatic roles.

Her first opportunity was with the Opéra Comique Series at the Heckscher Theatre in New York, and for two intensive years Risë Stevens sang, two years in which she rose from chorus work to solo parts. It was while she was singing here that she was heard by the noted teacher Madame Anna Schoen-René, who immediately offered to teach her. She continued to teach her after Risë left the Opéra Comique Company to enter the Juilliard School of Music on a scholarship.

At the end of three years at this school, years in which she had been featured in several important student performances of *Orfeo* and *The Merry Wives of Windsor,* she was offered a Metropolitan Opera contract. She turned it down. She didn't have enough experience for the job, she explained. Then she went abroad to get it, working with Gutheil Schoder and Graf, singing in Salzburg and in Switzerland. It was in the spring of 1936 that she made her opera debut abroad —at the Prague Opera House, in *Mignon.* This was followed by appearances in *Carmen, Orfeo* and *Der Rosenkavalier.* Finally her successes in Prague brought her an invitation from the Vienna State Opera House to sing leading roles, and she accepted it.

The late Herbert F. Peyser heard her there as Octavian in *Der Rosenkavalier* and wrote the New York *Times:* "I heard, to begin with, a lovely blooming voice—a voice beautifully cultivated throughout its scale. Further, a skill and fastidiousness of taste in phrasing and nuance that betrayed artistry of a wholly exceptional order. And never have I seen in this opera the figure of Octavian played with such an exuberance paired with distinction or with such complete credibility of boyish verisimilitude." After two years of singing which earned her criticisms equally as flattering, Risë Stevens left Vienna for South America, there to make her debut at the Teatro Colon on September 2, 1938. Once again she appeared in *Der Rosenkavalier,* receiving, according to cable dispatches, "one of the most enthusiastic ovations ever given a newcomer."

By the time of her success here Risë Stevens was as sure that she wanted to perform for the Metropolitan as the Metropolitan was sure they wanted her. She signed a contract, and on November 22, 1938 made her first appearance with this august company, again in *Der Rosenkavalier,* in Philadelphia. She was a sensation. And when she made her New York debut on December 17 in *Mignon,* Olin Downes of the New York *Times* was moved to comment that here was "more than a voice for one or two lyrical roles, for it has unusual range, well adjusted registers, and there are colors in it. . . She gave the part of Mignon dramatic substance." "For her," *Time* summed up, "even the morosest critic prophesied an expansive future."

Mignon was followed by *Der Rosenkavalier* and by other operas, including the Wagner Ring dramas, in which she appeared in Erda and as Fricka. Then in the spring and summer of 1939 Risë Stevens sang at the world-famous Glyndebourne festival in England, the first American-born singer to appear there. She was re-engaged for 1940, when it was planned to feature her in *Carmen*, but the outbreak of war in Europe put an end to this project.

Risë Stevens returned to the Metropolitan Opera House triumphantly in 1939, and when she sang in the fall of 1940 in San Francisco she scored one of the greatest ovations in West Coast history. That same season the Metropolitan revived *Samson and Delilah* especially for her, making her the first American to sing the leading role in more than 22 years, and it was perfectly apparent to the enthralled audience why Samson fell. Meanwhile she continued during the summers to sing with the Teatro Colon in Buenos Aires and to appear in leading roles elsewhere. And there have been concert and radio engagements for this young singer all over this country.

In 1941 Metro-Goldwyn-Mayer, impressed equally by her voice and her unoperatic physical proportions, signed a long-term film contract with her and shortly after put her to work in *The Chocolate Soldier* opposite Nelson Eddy. This picture was released in the fall of 1941, and critics saluted a new movie star with "glamour as well as a voice."

This star who in 1941 was named one of the thirteen best-dressed women in the United States by the Fashion Academy admits that her handsome Hungarian husband, Walter Szurovy, whom she married in 1939, picks out all her hats. She admits, too, to a number of tastes, some usual, some completely unexpected in an opera singer: walking and swimming, collecting good luck mascots, going to the movies, getting up early, eating maraschino cherries, never sleeping on the same sheet twice, collecting Wedgewood china, cashmere sweaters, slim crystal glasses, tweeds, and taking out her dashing dachshund named "Wotan."

References

Musician 44:7+ Ja '39 pors; 45:13 D '40 por
Opera News 4:18 Mr 25 '40 por
Time 32:28 D 26 '38 por
Ewen, D. ed. Living Musicians 1940

STEWART, DONALD OGDEN Nov. 30, 1894- Motion picture scenarist; author
Address: h. Carmel, Calif.

Versatile and gifted Donald Ogden Stewart has to his credit seven books, all in a

DONALD OGDEN STEWART

humorous vein, and has edited another—this time a serious one—compiled of papers read before a Congress of the League of American Writers. His play *Rebound* starred talented Hope Williams in 1930. He has worked on numerous screen plays, often being called in to "doctor" a script or brighten up the dialogue. Among the pictures for which he has received writing credit either as writer or collaborator are: *Tarnished Lady*; *Smilin' Through*; *Dinner at Eight*; *Another Language*; *The White Sister*; *The Barretts of Wimpole Street*; *No More Ladies*; *The Prisoner of Zenda*; *Holiday*; *Marie Antoinette*; *Love Affair*; *Kitty Foyle*; *That Uncertain Feeling*; *A Woman's Face*.

Stewart was to do the book for a musical comedy based on Ludwig Bemelmans' (see sketch this issue) articles on hotel life that had appeared in the *New Yorker* Magazine, but by the end of 1941 plans for the show seemed to have fallen through. It would be his second Broadway musical show, the first having been a Joe Cook opus, *Fine and Dandy* (1930). After completing the latter book Mr. Stewart went to Hollywood and in the past 11 years there has rolled up a brilliant record of achievement as a screen writer. Early in 1941 he shared with Dalton Trumbo (see sketch this issue) the Academy of Motion Picture Arts and Sciences Award for the best screen play of 1940—*The Philadelphia Story*.

Born in Columbus, Ohio, November 30, 1894, Donald Ogden Stewart is the son of Gilbert Holland and Clara Landon (Ogden) Stewart. At 14 he was sent to Phillips Exeter, which usually turns out students for Harvard, and he entered Yale in the fall of 1912, taking his B. A. there in 1916. After graduation he worked for public service corporations and during the First World War served in the United States Navy as seaman, quartermaster and chief quartermaster, respectively. He then resumed his business

STEWART, DONALD OGDEN—*Cont.*

"career," but by that time was well on the way to being a writer.

His first book, *A Parody Outline of History*, published in 1921, lampooned the literary styles of William Lyon Phelps, Sinclair Lewis and others. It had an unusual success, as did his subsequent books—produced at the rate of one a year until 1926, a year in which on July 24th at Santa Barbara, California, he married Beatrice Ames. (His two sons, Ames Ogden and Donald Ogden, Jr., are children of this marriage, which ended in divorce on September 8, 1938. On March 4, 1939 Stewart married the former Ella Winter Steffens, widow of Lincoln Steffens. She is well known as a writer under her own name, Ella Winter.)

Described by Alexander Woollcott (see sketch this issue) as a "preposterously tall, blond man," he led the life of an émigré writer prior to his first marriage. While in Vienna in 1922 he "grew a splendid red beard and wrote *Perfect Behavior*." He shaved the beard before moving on to Budapest. In 1926, the year of *Mr. & Mrs. Haddock in Paris, France*, he was, wrote Grant Overton, "very near-sighted, fond of Beethoven, scotch, and Max Beerbohm." And although golf was listed as a hobby early in his career, the truth seems to have been that his favorite forms of relaxation were good books and good music. In the latter realm he progressed so far as an amateur that he could play some of Bach's pieces on the piano.

In 1928 Stewart took up acting, assuming the role of Nick Potter in Philip Barry's *Holiday*. He stayed with it through its long Broadway run that extended into June 1929, and also toured. In 1929 he published *Father William* and acted in his own play, *Rebound*, published in 1931.

In 1930 he went to Hollywood to live and to work, and in his more than 10 years there has become one of the cinema city's most famous screen writers. He has the professional writer's knack of doing the job at hand and doing it exceedingly well. He brought to life the pasteboard romance, *The Prisoner of Zenda*, by turning it into a comedy-romance, and the script of *The Barretts* he treated with the seriousness it deserved.

At a Town Hall (New York) symposium on films and national defense, Stewart quipped: "One man's propaganda can be another man's Zanuck." Hitting deeper than that, he insisted bluntly that people want to see themselves portrayed on the screen as they really are. "Films," he asserted, "must provide a deeper understanding of life than a guy gets out of a whiskey bottle and a sympathetic bartender."

President of the League of American Writers from 1937 to 1941, when Dashiell Hammett was elected, Mr. Stewart has defended it from attacks branding it as Left wing, asserting that its prime purpose has been and is the defense of literary freedom of speech. Quoting from the League's Call for a session opening in New York, June 6, 1941, he said: "Wherever the right to speak is lost we too are the losers."

President of the Hollywood Anti-Nazi League since its inception, Stewart has been the target of many vituperative attacks on the grounds that one or another of the groups he was connected with were Communist "front" organizations. None of these charges has been proved, and in some instances they may be attributed to a proclivity for name calling. What he stands for Stewart admits quite frankly. He is on the board of the Screen Writers' Guild, and his pro-labor bias has been shown in such things as his support of the Harry Bridges case. (He compared Dalton Trumbo's pamphlet on it to *J'Accuse*.)

Since 1940 Stewart has been president of the Hollywood branch of the League of American Writers as well as of the parent body. With a membership of several hundred, this branch has had a leading part in raising some $35,000 for exiled writers, and before that in collecting $25,000 for medical aid to Loyalist Spain. He quoted as his own firm conviction the League credo that: "Wherever civil liberties are abridged, our stories, poems, plays, essays, and books are abridged. The attacks on trade-unions, political minorities, and education are attacks on our basic convictions as writers and as citizens."

Six feet tall, weighing one hundred-eighty pounds, with grayish hair and blue eyes, he has a sobriety about him that makes his humorous asides doubly effective. Wearing rimless spectacles and speaking from the rostrum with little oratorical dash, the humor crops up in his serious speeches—he makes many of them—in sharply barbed phrases that drive home his points more surely than any dry-as-dust appraisal.

In discussing the possibility of a general cultural interchange between the peoples of the Americas, Stewart put forward the suggestion that documentary films replace the present tendency toward personal appearance tours of stars and pictures depicting only the music and gaiety of South America (as seen through the eyes of Hollywood production big-wigs).

While in Hollywood, Donald Ogden Stewart teaches at the League's school along with a faculty of other prominent Hollywood writers, in his spare time from picture work. He is one of the few writers whose part in films is stressed by critics. Dialogue or screen play by Stewart is a circumstance worthy of critical notice.

References

Hartford Times Mr 15 '41
Motion Picture Herald p22 Ap 22 '41
    por
N Y Herald Tribune My 4 '41
America's Young Men 1936-37
International Motion Picture Almanac
Overton, G. M. American Nights Entertainments p239-47 1923
Overton, G. M. Authors of the Day p131-7 1924
Overton, G. M. When Winter Comes to Main Street p88-101 1933
Who's Who Among North American Authors
Who's Who in America

STEWART, JAMES (MAITLAND) May 20, 1908(?)- Film actor

Address: c/o MGM Studios, Culver City, Calif.

James Stewart, winner of the Academy Award for 1940, has given up being the typical American youth. "I collected dogs and cats but I've stopped being overly extravagant in that fashion," the lanky Pennsylvanian insisted recently. Yet an inventory taken in 1940 of the Brentwood house shared by Stewart and John Swope disclosed: "two cats, a half dozen doves, unnumbered mice, and three dogs of questionable pedigree. Under the house are fifteen wild cats, the offspring of a pair of tame tabbies who took offense one day at Stewart, crawled under the house, multiplied, and have never come out. At night they howl."

Nevertheless, Stewart has stopped being what Kyle Crichton described as "the kid from Elm Street who rents the tux to go to the Junior Prom." He has insisted upon roles that would not exploit his personal qualities of quiet charm and droll humor. The result, in 1940, was his Academy-Award part in *The Philadelphia Story*. Had he been swayed by easy praise, he might long since have been type-casted out of popularity. "Hollywood," he admits frankly, "dishes out too much praise for small things, like my role in *Rose Marie*. I won't let it get me, but too much praise can turn a fellow's head if he doesn't watch his step." And he concludes: "If I hadn't been at some particular place at some particular time and some man hadn't happened to say so-and-so and I hadn't answered this-and-that, I'd still be hunting a job in an architect's office."

James Stewart is six feet two and one-half inches tall, has brown hair and gray eyes. His hair falls into his eyes, and he talks, says Miriam Teichner, "with an engaging little stumble that is almost a stutter. Going to see him, you had the feeling—that nice, sweet, gawky, shy boy stuff of his, with the underlip drooping, is probably just a line." But she discovered this was not so. He is self-conscious about his height, according to Dorothy Kilgallen, "and this makes him walk with a stoop, with his head bent as if he were always afraid of bumping it. He is unhappy about his lankiness, so he wears extra padding in the shoulders of his suits and will try any suggested diet to make him put on weight."

In early 1941 Stewart was still underweight (140 pounds) and deferred by the draft board because of it. MGM was relieved, but Jimmy's feelings were mixed. An added 10 pounds put on with a struggle finally got him accepted on March 21. He thereby became the first motion picture star to be drafted. Since he is an experienced aviator with a plane of his own, he was assigned to the Air Corps. According to news reports he took a pay cut of $11,979 monthly—the difference between his original Army renumeration of $21 monthly and his reported Hollywood income of $12,000 for the same period. Although he was eligible for release from the Army because of age he elected to remain as a soldier.

JAMES STEWART

His father had been in the Spanish-American War and had been a captain in the First World War. On a visit to France in 1939 Stewart searched out the ordnance shops his father had helped build for the A. E. F. in Bourges. None of the natives seemed to know where they were located. Finally he came upon someone able to direct him to "huge, empty buildings, hidden away in the woods." And when Stewart returned from his European holiday the Second World War was already in the air and his ship cut a path through the dark Atlantic, lights dimmed.

James Maitland Stewart was born in Indiana, Pennsylvania, the son of Alexander Maitland and Elizabeth Ruth (Jackson) Stewart. Stewarts had been in the hardware business there since 1840 and young Jimmy liked nothing better than to visit the store. As a child he was thin, wore glasses, and his two pet ambitions were to be a magician and a big game hunter. He dabbled in chemistry, radio and parlor tricks. While a member of a local Boy Scout troop he wrote, produced and acted in his first play, which was about the World War then going on. He even recruited his two younger sisters for parts in the historical production.

Acting in school plays at Model School, adjunct of the state teachers' college, and at Mercersburg Academy, from which he was graduated in 1928, James was still best-known as an accordion player when he entered Princeton. He wasn't quite certain what else he wanted to be. Starting out with a course in civil engineering, he switched to steam engineering but kept up the study of architecture that got him his B. S. in 1932. When not at his studies he was at his accordion or rehearsing for a Triangle Club play. The main inducement of the latter was a Christmas trip to New York—"being met at trains by Princeton alumni, the perfect hosts." In the fall of 1931 he was cheerleader, but the jinx was on Palmer Stadium that season and

STEWART, JAMES—Continued

the Tigers won few games. During vacations he and Bill Neff barnstormed in the home territory, combining accordion music with magic.

After graduation Jimmy went up to West Falmouth, Massachusetts, where his friend Josh Logan ran the summer theatre with a group called The University Players. Jobs for young architects were scarce and Stewart was glad to play the accordion for guests at the Old Silver Black Tea Room, also run by Logan. Jimmy had bit parts in *Whistling In The Dark* and in the tryout of *Goodbye Again*. His first New York play was the short-lived *Carrie Nation*. Then he went into the cast of *Goodbye Again* that began its Broadway run in the fall of 1932. "It seems apropos," said the New York *Sun* critic, "to say a few words about James Stewart, a player in this mad piece, who is on the stage for exactly three minutes and speaks no more than eight lines. Yet before this gentleman exits he makes a definite impression on audiences because he makes them laugh so hard."

In 1933 Stewart was stage manager for the Boston run of Jane Cowl's production of *Camille*. One night he rang down the curtain before Camille had had time to die. Reports vary as to what Miss Cowl said on that occasion. Nevertheless Blanche Yurka allowed him to stage-manage *Spring in Autumn,* and when it folded producer Arthur Beckhard found room for Stewart in his New York office, then a part for him in *All Good Americans*. In this play Jimmy was supposed to throw an accordion out the window once during each performance. He rebelled on the grounds that he was "an accordion player by nature," and was finally allowed to substitute a banjo.

There were several other stage parts for Jimmy before he packed his bags and headed West. In one he was supposed to be Viennese and succeeded, in the words of one critic, in being "as Viennese as a hamburger." In another, at the Red Barn Theatre on Long Island, the stage was so small that if Stewart fell prone in a scene when wounded, it would hardly leave room for the others to move about. He solved the problem by staggering blindly for 10 minutes—"literally dying by inches. . . It was," he recalled wryly, "the ham's dream of a great scene, and I was proud of it."

Jimmy and some of his friends—Henry Fonda, Burgess Meredith and others—organized the *Thursday Night Beer Club.* They often had such distinguished guests as Margaret Sullavan, whom Jimmy had dated when she visited Princeton, Helen Hayes and Katharine Cornell (see sketch this issue). Benny Goodman's clarinet often competed—successfully, according to Jimmy—with the battered accordion, and Benny, it was conceded by the group, was the club member "most likely to succeed."

Jimmy's first film was a two-reel comedy made by Warner Brothers in a Long Island studio. He was intrigued more by the $50 a day than by the prospect of a screen career.

However, in 1935, after a good year in several plays, he took a test at Fox. It was, he said, "one of those watch-the-horses-run affairs—you gravely turn your head from one side to the other, and assume that you're observing something intently." Nothing came of it, but his next, at MGM, got him a contract and a ticket to the coast. "I don't believe this happened," he drawled in one of his first West coast interviews. "All the while I'm wondering when they're going to change their minds about me."

His wonder became a state of alarm when he saw his first picture, *Murder Man.* "I murdered that part," he confesses. "I was all hands and feet and didn't seem to know what to do with either." It was also frightening to see oneself on the screen for the first time. Minor faults became glaringly obvious in the close-ups. He drew the proper moral and ever since has made a practice of viewing "rushes" of his films. He considers this important to "keep yourself from getting a bag of tricks."

Subsequent and much more successful pictures included *Wife Versus Secretary* (MGM, 1936); *Next Time We Love* (Universal, 1936); and *Seventh Heaven* (20th Century-Fox, 1937). In the following year he did *Shopworn Angel* for MGM, *Vivacious Lady* for RKO and *You Can't Take It With You* for Columbia. The latter was an outstanding comedy success. In a fast-paced Western, *Destry Rides Again* (1939), Stewart shared honors with Marlene Dietrich, and in 1940 in *The Shop Around the Corner* he had a chance to act again with Margaret Sullavan, with whom he had appeared in stage productions years before.

Mr. Smith Goes To Washington was one of the most talked-about pictures of 1939. His acting in the role of Mr. Smith got Jimmy the New York Critics' Award for the Best Male Performance of the year, and he was runner-up for first place in the Film Critics of America voting. The film, said *Theatre Arts*, was more fun than the Senate itself. "We like to remember the way his voice cracked when he got up to read his bill, and the way he dropped his hat when he met the senior Senator's daughter, and the way he whistled at the Senators when they turned their backs on him." The New York Film Critics' Award was presented by Mayor Fiorello La Guardia who, as a former Congressman, praised Stewart for the authenticity of his performance.

As the reporter in *The Philadelphia Story*, James Stewart did what was perhaps his finest acting job to date. It was, said the New York *Times*, a "brilliant performance," and almost all critics concurred in this judgment. His latest film (April 1941) is *Pot o' Gold,* in which he plays his beloved accordion. Unfortunately the producers felt his playing was not good enough and had a professional "dub" in the sound.

Indicative of the seriousness with which Jimmy takes his work is his praise of Director Capra (*You Can't Take It With You*): "Other directors sometimes let you do as you like and you can be so wrong. But Capra tells you, even though he never stops emphasizing the importance of 'keeping it natural.' And whatever he tells you is right. You know by the feel." He is interested in directing as well as acting and should like to be able, some day, both to write and to direct.

Henry Fonda and Josh Logan both shared the Brentwood house for a time. They married, leaving bachelors Swope and Stewart to carry on. Stewart is constantly put on the spot by gossip writers, as about to get serious with this or that glamorous star with whom he has been seen in public. He has a philosophy about marriage, which is: "Most successful marriages are those in which the people concerned are young enough to adapt their actions and thoughts to each other. When a fellow's been a bachelor quite a while he sort of gets in the habit of it." Despite this ominous statement, Jimmy seems in no danger of sinking into stuffiness.

His hobbies are few, if you discount the Brentwood "madhouse," the accordion and the magic. (He is professional on both counts, being an honorary member of the International Brotherhood of Magicians.) He builds model planes and has a pilot's license. He also takes "gag" pictures with a miniature camera. He is exactly the sort of conversationalist one might expect from some of his pictures, with a particular talent for involved allusion.

References

Brooklyn Daily Eagle Ja 9 '39
Collier's 100:26+ O 9 '37 pors
Friday 1:22 Je 28 '40 pors
Liberty 17:57-9 Je 15 '40 por
N Y Herald Tribune My 21 '39; VI p3 Je 30 '40
N Y Sun My 2 '33
N Y Times IX p4 Ag 21 '38; p25 F 2 '41; p6 Mr 8 '41
Time 37:22 F 17 '41 por
America's Young Men
International Motion Picture Almanac
Who's Who in America
Who's Who in the Theatre

STEWART, WILLIAM G(ODMAN) 1869—July 16, 1941 One of the best known American comic-opera baritones of his day; producer; manager; introduced tabloid operas in New York in the '20s; numbered some 70 operas in his repertoire with which he toured the country around the turn of the century.

Obituaries

N Y Herald Tribune p8 Jl 19 '41
Variety 143:62 Jl 23 '41

STILES, CHARLES WARDELL May 15, 1867—Jan. 24, 1941 Zoologist and retired surgeon of the United States Public Health Service who won wide acclaim for his discovery of the prevalence of hookworm disease in the South; lectured at the Johns Hopkins Medical School for 40 years and at the Navy Medical School from 1902 on; professor of zoology from 1902 to 1930, assistant surgeon general from 1910 to 1930 and medical director from 1930 to 1931 for the United States Public Health Service; author of many scientific works.

References

Hygeia 12:328-30 Ap '34 por
Lit Digest 115:18 Ap 15 '33 por
American Medical Directory
American Men of Science
Leaders in Education 1941
Who's Who Among North American Authors
Who's Who in America

Obituaries

N Y Times p15 Ja 24 '41
Time 37:57 F 3 '41

STILL, WILLIAM GRANT May 11, 1895-
Composer; conductor
Address: 3670 Cimarron St, Los Angeles, Calif.

The tone poem which accompanied each six-minute showing of Democracity in the Perisphere, at the New York World's Fair, was a composition of William Grant Still, an American Negro composer whose works range from songs for many Broadway shows, the radio and films to ballets and larger works for symphonic orchestras. The way in which he was chosen was interesting. Recordings of various works by many composers were played to the jury, without the names of the composers being disclosed. The jury liked best *Lenox Avenue* and *From a Deserted Plantation,* both works of Still, the first composed for the Columbia Broadcasting Company, the second for Paul Whiteman's Orchestra.

A musical exposition of the changing vision unfolded in Democracity—an expression in tone that was timed to the second with the action—was what Still presented in his tone poem. The work was orchestrated for a symphony orchestra, with a finale for chorus and orchestra, the chorus singing the theme song of the Fair. Within the six minutes episodes from a whole twenty-four hours were shown. To accompany scenes of the night life of the future Still used just a touch of jazz. The tone poem was played continuously, from recordings. Counting 12 hours to the Fair day there were 120 playings a day—a "multiplicity of presentation achieved by few composers living or dead."

William Grant Still was born in Woodville, Mississippi May 11, 1895, the son of William Grant and Carrie L. (Fambro) Still. He obtained his early training in Little Rock, Arkansas, where his mother taught literature in the high school. He attended Wilberforce University, and then Oberlin Conservatory of Music and the New England Conservatory. At Oberlin he received a scholarship in composition, completing a year's work in less than three months. Recently he has had two Guggenheim Fellowships and also a Rosenwald Fellowship to enable him to continue creative work. It was right after he left Wilberforce

Philadelphia Society for
Negro Records & Research

WILLIAM GRANT STILL

University that Still married Grave Bundy. There were three daughters and a son of this marriage, which ended in divorce. In 1939 Still was remarried—to Verna Arvey, pianist and journalist. They now have a son, Duncan Allan Still.

Though some of Still's early work was arranging popular music for jazz orchestras, he soon established himself as a serious composer who merely utilizes jazz idioms. Most of his compositions now are orchestral. He first attracted attention when the International Guild of Composers at one of their New York concerts (1926) presented four of his songs for solo voice and orchestra, in one of which, *Levee Land*, Florence Mills had the solo part and Eugene Goossens did the conducting. Some of Still's other works are: *Darker America,* a symphonic poem; *From the Land of Dreams; Log Cabin Ballads; From the Black Belt*; *Africa,* a symphonic poem; *Afro-American Symphony; New Symphony in G Minor*; three ballets, *Sahdji, La Guiablesse, The Sorcerer; Lenox Avenue,* for chorus and orchestra; and an opera, *Troubled Island,* for which Langston Hughes wrote the libretto, adapting it from his play, *Drums of Haiti.* He has also been the arranger for a number of successful musical shows, *Running Wild, Dixie to Broadway* and the fifth edition of Earl Carroll's *Vanities* among them.

Many of Still's works have been presented under the patronage of Howard Hanson (see sketch this issue) by the Eastman School of Music, Rochester, New York, one of his compositions usually appearing on the program of each annual festival. *Darker America* was first played by the Rochester Orchestra in 1927.

In the same year it was played also at the International Music Festival at Frankfurt, Germany. His *Afro-American Symphony* was given its première in Rochester, and was played in 1935 by the New York Philharmonic Orchestra (Hans Lange conducting), subsequently in Philadelphia (by the Philadelphia Symphony Orchestra, under Leopold Stokowski [see sketch this issue]), in Berlin, Leipzig and Stuttgart. The Philadelphia Orchestra, Stokowski conducting, in December 1937 presented his *New Symphony in G Minor,* based on jazz, blues and other American idioms. During the 1940 summer season at the Lewisohn Stadium, New York City, his ballad poem, *And They Lynched Him to a Tree,* words by Katherine Garrison Chapin, had its première under Artur Rodzinski. The poem was orchestrated for a double chorus, contralto solo and orchestra. And in 1941 Still put to music another of Miss Chapin's poems: *Plain Chant for America.*

When Still, in 1936, conducted the Hollywood Bowl Orchestra in his own compositions it was the first time that a Negro had conducted a major orchestra in the United States.

This composer is serious even in his pastimes —when asked his favorite diversion he replied: "The study of life with a view to learning that which will enable me to make my life more serviceable to mankind."

References

N Y Age p7 Ap 9 '38 por
N Y Times X p12 F 4 '37; XI p7 Ja 23 '38; IX p5 My 26 '40; p27 Je 26 '40
N Y World-Telegram p8 Je 8 '40
Time 30:44-5 D 20 '37 por
Arvey, V. William Grant Still pam 1939
Brawley, B. G. Negro Genius p297-316 1937
Hare, Mrs. M. C. Negro Musicians and Their Music p321-51 1936
Pierre Key's Musical Who's Who
Thompson, O. ed. International Cyclopedia of Music and Musicians 1939
Who's Who in Colored America

STILLWELL, LEWIS BUCKLEY Mar. 12, 1863—Jan. 19, 1941 Electrical engineer; was engineer for the Westinghouse Company from 1891 to 1897, and its electrical director from 1897 to 1900; since 1900 he has been a consultant on the electrification of many projects, including the New York Holland Tunnel; honored for his work with the Lamme Medal of the American Institute of Electrical Engineers, the medal of the American Society of Civil Engineers and the Edison Medal.

References

Sci Mo 42:284-5+ Mr '36 por
American Men of Science
Who's Who in America
Who's Who in Engineering

Obituaries

N Y Times Ja 20 '41 por

STOCKBERGER, W(ARNER) W. July
10, 1872- Botanist; special adviser to the
United States Secretary of Agriculture

Address: b. Department of Agriculture, Washington, D. C.; h. 529 Cedar St, N. W., Washington, D. C.

A pioneer in personnel administration in the
Federal Government, Dr. Warner W. Stockberger, who began his career as a botanist,
built up in the Department of Agriculture the
first central personnel agency, which became a
model for similar service in other departments.
He served as director of personnel for the
United States Department of Agriculture from
1923 until July 1, 1938, when he was appointed
special adviser to the Secretary of Agriculture
on problems of departmental administration.
Ex-Secretary Henry A. Wallace and other
officials have paid Dr. Stockberger the highest
of tributes for his ability as an organizer and
his humanitarian interests. He was in 1941
working on a history of personnel administration in the Department of Agriculture.

"I was born on a farm in Bennington Township, Licking County, Ohio, July 10, 1872,"
Dr. Stockberger writes us, "the son of George
Francis Stockberger and Frances Roena Warner, his wife. She was a granddaughter of
Daniel Poppleton, first settler in Hartford,
Licking County, Ohio, and great-granddaughter
of Samuel Poppleton, a Revolutionary soldier
who was with Ethan Allen at the capture of
Fort Ticonderoga." Young Warner, slight of
build, thin, never in robust health, was "not
built for a farmer," but became a studious
child who loved to read. The chief family
reading material was the exciting serials in the
New York *Ledger*, which the boy supplemented
on long winter evenings with the exploits of
Kit Carson and Robinson Crusoe.

In order to get money for a college education he alternately taught in the public schools
and attended the Utica, Ohio, Normal School
and Doane Academy at Granville, Ohio. His
work as a teacher was so satisfactory that he
was soon made high school teacher and superintendent of schools of Hanover, Ohio. In
1896 he married Maude N. Streeter of Croton,
Ohio (the couple have one daughter, Lucile),
and felt that he did not have the financial
means to continue his education. The president of Denison University made it possible
for him to do so by asking him to become a
student-instructor in history while going on
with his college work. On arriving at the
campus, however, Stockberger found that this
history instructorship no longer existed, but
that there was a similar vacancy in botany. It
was this fortuitous shift that took him into
the field of science, from which he did not turn
for 26 years, when, almost as abruptly, he
transferred to the business of personnel administration.

After five years of combined teaching and
education, in 1902 Stockberger received his
B. S. degree from Denison University. During his last year in college and the one following his graduation he held a full instructorship
in botany, entering also the Department of
Agriculture as an expert in histology, for

W. W. STOCKBERGER

which he received a salary far above the average for that day. He went on with his work
in science at George Washington University,
receiving his Ph. D. with majors in botany
and biology in 1907.

During the next 20 years the young scientist
published more than 60 articles in the biological
field in various professional and trade journals.
His works were summarized as "very productive both in scientific investigations along lines
of pharmacognosy, physiology and plant breeding, and in the practical application of the results of scientific investigations to problems of
crop production and utilization." Stockberger
was particularly interested in hop culture; his
researches in this took him abroad in 1911 to
study European methods of hop production
and utilization.

When in 1913 the Office of Drug, Poisonous,
and Oil Plant Investigations was formed, Dr.
Stockberger was placed in charge. He continued as the nominal head of this Division of
Drug and Related Plants (as it is now called)
until July 1, 1940. As office supervisor he was
in charge of a staff of 25 to 30 employees;
and he also held the responsibility for the administration of the Office of Plant Physiological Investigations, which carried another
staff of investigators.

Out of this arose his interest in problems
of management and human relations. He soon
became recognized as an efficient executive,
known not only for sound judgment but for
his ability to deal with men. He was an effective speaker, and diplomatically handled his
own department's relations with those of other
government departments. In an article on "The
Social Obligations of the Botanist" he early
gave evidence of a broad social consciousness.
Dr. Stockberger believes that science must take
into account "economic and social factors,"
and must have "a clear view of the readjust-

STOCKBERGER, W. W.—*Continued*

ments and changes which are constantly taking place in the domains of industry and education and in the fields of political and social affairs."

It was not surprising that a man of such beliefs should be chosen by Secretary of Agriculture Henry Wallace, Senior, to carry out the provisions of the Classification Act of 1923 as senior physiologist. The job soon entailed much more than that. Asked to devise a departmental promotion policy, he set up the Office of Personnel, which consolidated in one office many hitherto scattered functions. It was Dr. Stockberger's duty "to supervise and coordinate all departmental business activities, including personnel administration, budget, fiscal and accounting matters, purchasing of supplies and equipment, traffic, housing, etc." The creation of this office was a landmark in the history of personnel administration, both inside and outside the Department of Agriculture. It continued until 1934, when it was split into three parts, one of which retained the title of "Office of Personnel," a separate entity. This reorganization was approved by Dr. Stockberger because it was now possible "to give more consideration to the development of morale and the improvement of human relations within the service."

It is said that Dr. Stockberger's own major contribution is in the field of human relations and the stimulation of employee morale. He feels that administration becomes democratic only "when it is motivated by supreme respect for human personalities." These theories he turned into practicable working account. He did not hesitate to approve employee unions, and was himself a member of the National Federation of Federal Employees prior to becoming personnel director; thereafter he always defended employee unions, although they were quite unpopular in other quarters.

He is particularly proud of the Department of Agriculture Beneficial Association, formed in 1929 to provide economical group insurance for employees of the Department. Another result of his real interest in employee welfare has been the extension of personnel activities into the fields of safety and medical service. A Division of Safety was created in 1937 to study the accident problem, install a uniform system of recording injuries, a means of cooperating with other safety councils, and of conducting a program of safety education. Stockberger recommended also "early provision for the employment of a full-time medical officer and an adequate nursing staff."

A further interest of Dr. Stockberger's, although he feels that not much progress has as yet been made in its development, grew out of his desire to inaugurate supervisory training and career training for positions at the higher levels of personnel responsibility.

Because of his outstanding human interests and leadership Dr. Stockberger's counsel in Washington is always widely sought. William A. Jump, director of Agriculture's Finance Department, once said: "In a place with more

'doctors' to the square yard than probably any other place in the world, it is pretty generally understood when one says, 'Have you seen the Doctor?' he means, 'Have you seen Dr. Stockberger?'" And "the Doctor" is always ready to greet cheerfully every visitor who steps into Room 222 in the Administration Building of Agriculture. "His brow has become deeply furrowed. The wavy hair is turning gray. Deep, expressive lines on his face set off a smiling mouth; and penetrating, quizzical eyes play around the room or fix themselves intently on one spot as he launches into whatever subject the conversation may require. The burden of recent illness has slightly stooped his shoulders. He looks frail. Otherwise, he is the same man who turned to the personnel job in 1923."

He remains the botanist, too; and he retains his early love of history. It is said that history, genealogy and exploration in old graveyards are still his avocations. But liking people comes first. Possibly Dr. Stockberger's most prized possession is an inscribed gold medal given him by the Athletic and Recreational Association on the occasion of his election to honorary life membership in that organization. It shares honors on his watch chain only with his Phi Beta Kappa key.

References

Public Administration R 1:1 autumn '40
Survey G 25:93 F '36 por
American Men of Science
Who's Who in America
Who's Who in the Nation's Capital

STOCKBRIDGE, FRANK PARKER June 11, 1870—Dec. 7, 1940 Founder and editor of the *American Home Magazine*; also served in editorial positions on a number of New York newspapers; author of several books, the latest *Hedging Against Inflation* (1939).

FRANK PARKER STOCKBRIDGE

References

Cur Hist 50:64 My '39
Lit Digest 117:11 Mr 17 '34 por
Sat Eve Post 201:35-6 Ja 12 '29; 208:96
    F 29 '36
Who's Who Among North American
    Authors
Who's Who in America

Obituaries

N Y Times p69 D 8 '40 por

STOKOWSKI, LEOPOLD (ANTON STANISLAW) (stồ-kồf'skê) Apr. 18, 1882- Orchestra conductor

Address: h. New Milford, Conn.

"I would like to have been present, if I could have my choice of all moments in musical history, when Stokowski suddenly became conscious of his beautiful hands."

Those are Oscar Levant's words, but the sentiment is almost universal—or, at any rate, international. Leopold Stokowski ("Stoky" to his men) was in 1940 doing his bit for Pan-American solidarity by waving those same hands for the benefit of South American audiences. His "All-American Youth Orchestra," composed of twenty girls and sixty-odd boys, was acknowledged as sixth or seventh among the seventeen top-flight symphony orchestras of the United States after only three weeks of Maestro Stokowski's expert direction, and departed in July 1940 for a tour of South America, Cuba, Haiti, Puerto Rico and the Virgin Islands. They returned to give a New York concert on September 18, and after that his Philadelphians had him back for several of their regular concerts before he reorganized the group in 1941 for a tour of the United States, Canada and Mexico. In the meanwhile they were, no doubt, swarming to Walt Disney's *Fantasia*. Hollywood had been claiming more and more of their co-conductor's time and attention in recent years, anyway, and in March 1941 Stokowski finally resigned his leadership of the Philadelphia Symphony Orchestra.

Leopold Stokowski, "100 per cent American by training, instinct and absorption," was born in London, the son of a Polish father, Josef Boleslaw Kopernicus Stokowski. His mother was Irish. As a boy he spent a large part of his days studying the violin, playing Bach at night for recreation, and at the age of 16 began to study the organ. He attended Queen's College, Oxford, studying composition under Sir Humber Parry and the late Sir Edward Elgar, took his degree when he was 21, and after working as organist at St. James's Church in Piccadilly went on to study at the Paris Conservatoire and in Germany. It was 1905 when the blond, blue-eyed young man came to the United States and found a position as organist in New York's fashionable St. Bartholomew's Church.

Stokowski was there until 1908: in the summer of that year he conducted a series of concerts in London and "switched his allegiance from the console to the baton." The

Musical America

LEOPOLD STOKOWSKI

following year, when there was a movement to reorganize Cincinnati's Symphony Orchestra, he was offered the job. He was 27; "his eyes were blue and absurdly innocent, his hair golden, his mouth small and sensitive"; audiences found that when he moved his baton, music "became alive and spurted electric sparks. A nervous sensuousness informed allegros, staid wallowing adagios." In two years his fame spread. And when the Philadelphia Symphony Orchestra needed a new conductor its board of directors cabled an offer to him in Europe. It was 1912 when he returned to take command.

In staid Philadelphia, Stokowski blossomed as "a veritable Lucius Beebe, wearing his scores like so many changes of attire." In Levant's words: "A musical Lawrence of Arabia, one scarcely knew from whence the authentic Stokowski came, or what his background (prior to the Cincinnati Symphony days) was. Suddenly he emerged in full flower, bringing to orchestral conducting a quality which personalized it almost as completely as Diaghilev did the Russian ballet." It was after only two years in the Quaker city that he insisted on performing Mahler's *Symphony of a Thousand Voices* at an expense of $14,000. He was responsible for a great many of the American premières of Stravinsky, Schönberg, Edgar Varese; he "rewrote symphonic oomph" into Bach fugues; he was the first to add John Hays Hammond's tone-sustaining piano to his orchestra, the first to give a concert of quarter-tone music.

But that was not all. Stokowski conducted *Scheherazade* from behind a screen while the "mystic shapes of the Color Organ played on it"; he reseated his cellos to the right; he introduced Javanese gongs, Indian Temple bells and Chinese scales to the American orchestra; he did away with the institution of

STOKOWSKI, LEOPOLD—*Continued*

concertmaster. His great dream of an invisible orchestra he realized in peculiar fashion—by blotting his men from the audience's vision while beams of rose-colored light coming from three directions played on his own "tawny mane."

What is more, Stokowski tried to teach his audiences etiquette, chiding them for making noise during performances, praising them for being musically conscious enough to hiss new work but often insisting on their hearing music they didn't like, excluding late-comers from the concert hall until intermissions. He even satirized his audiences' behavior by a performance in which his men wandered about the stage during the musical ride of the *Valkyries*, and the flutes walked off, chatting, during four songs by Brahms!

Among his other habits, he not only dispensed with baton and score but made a practice of rushing out of the wings "like a high-powered executive on the way to a million-dollar conference," and once on the podium would give such a rapid-fire signal to start that even a docile audience hardly had time to hush. Said Levant: "It is quite possible that if he had not become bored with music, he eventually would have conducted the orchestra blindfolded, with his left arm tied behind his back."

Although some of these novelties doubtless came under the heading "stage tricks," enhancing his popularity with more people than they irritated and bringing him valuable publicity (it has been said that "the prudence of Mr. Koussevitzky and the humility of Mr. Toscanini were alike foreign to Mr. Stokowski"), a great many of Stokowski's experiments added something substantial to American music. In 1933 he started a series of "Concerts for Youth" at 75 cents top, let his audiences (ages 13 to 25) make up their own programs by vote, packed them in with "speeches, quips, unprogrammed surprises." (He once had them sing the *Internationale!*) He was a pioneer in making recordings, and later became expert in the science of acoustics; he not only introduced a great many modern composers but was one of the first symphony conductors to recognize the importance of jazz; he wasn't afraid to hire young men, and many of them went on to conduct their own orchestras.

And, of course, he made his men make music. That was most important. According to Levant, he created, "in the . . . mid-'20s, an instrument that demonstrated in its exquisitely sensual sound, its urbane virtuosity, how well a hundred men could be made to play together." He drilled them and drilled them until sometimes they detested him and until he himself emerged with hands trembling and clothes dripping with perspiration. The result was "incomparably polished and irridescent." Stokowski's all-Bach programs "scaled Parnassus," as did his men's rendition of Debussy and Stravinsky and the Russians in general. If some criticized him for the liberties he took with Beethoven and found his interpretation of

Brahms a little over-refined, that was a matter of taste. Only when Stokowski approached Tschaikowsky did the critics proclaim themselves almost unanimously embarrassed for him. Said one: "Here his penchant for exaggeration in dynamics and shifting of emphasis are given full rein, leaving the same impression one would get from reading a racy novel with the dirty passages underlined in red ink."

That there were many difficulties with Philadelphia's board of directors might have been expected: at one time Stokowski actually resigned in protest. But in the end he usually conquered. Even non-musical Philadelphians didn't underestimate their Maestro's importance to the city (commercially as well as culturally), and were in a constant state of fear that he would leave. So, by means of "a seasoned mixture of pious virtues and magnetic vices plus—very importantly plus—a rare deftness in attaining useful publicity," Leopold Stokowski, "an unwritten character out of Huxley's *Point Counterpoint*," became the first man to get the Bok Award as the "person who has done the most for Philadelphia." He became also the recipient of an honorary doctor's degree from the University of Pennsylvania, and one of the most famous orchestra conductors in the world.

It was not until 1937 that Hollywood seduced him—although he remained co-conductor of the Orchestra with Eugene Ormandy (see sketch this issue) until March 1941, when his resignation was given really firmly—and he made his initial screen appearance in *The Great Broadcast of 1937*. Those who missed seeing his famous hands then have had further opportunities in *One Hundred Men and a Girl* and *Fantasia*, which began as a short (*The Sorcerer's Apprentice*) and which Stokowski persuaded Walt Disney to turn into a full-length feature. The Army was given a chance, too, when he took over the band at Fort MacArthur, California for purposes of experimentation. But the largest audience he has at any one time doesn't see his hands at all—when he conducts the NBC Symphony Orchestra, of which he was made leader for the 1941-1942 season. On these radio concerts Stokowski does his own commentary, interpreting the music for the audience.

One of the conductor's friends once confided: "One week 'Stokie' is a Confucianist, the next week a Buddhist and the third an early Christian." Sometimes he is a vegetarian and sometimes he decides that a heavy meat diet is the thing. He is almost terrifyingly energetic, but his only recorded venture into politics was his orchestra's playing of Charles G. Dawes' *Melody* just before the 1924 Presidential election. He has been married twice: first to Olga Samaroff (a Texas pianist whose real name was Hickenlooper), whom he divorced in 1923; in 1926 to Evangeline Brewster Johnson, the daughter of I. W. Johnson of hospital-supply fame, whom he divorced in 1937. There are three daughters: one, Sonia Maria Noel, by his first marriage; two, Lyuba and Sadja, by his second. March

1938 found him, Garbo and a great many keyhole-peering newspapermen at the Villa Cimbrone in Ravello, Italy—but that was a mere interlude.

According to Stokowski, his most treasured dream is "to make the best possible music and to bring it to the greatest number of people anywhere."

References

Am Mercury 22:369-73 Mr '31
Collier's 104:11+ Ag 19 '39 il por
Harper 179:589-91 N '39
N Y Times VII p8+ N 16 '41
New Yorker 7:22-6 Mr 21 '31
Newsweek 4:16-17 D 15 '34 por; 4:30 D 22 '34; 15:32 Mr 4 '40
Read Digest 28:35-8 Je '36
Time 31:50-2 Mr 14 '38 por; 33:54 Ap 17 '39; 35:45 Je 10 '40 por; 36:39 Jl 29 '40; 36:72 S 30 '40
Baker's Biographical Dictionary of Musicians 1940
Ewen, D. Man With the Baton p197-226 1936
Ewen, D. ed. Living Musicians 1940
Parker, H. T. Eighth Notes p26-9 1922
Pierre Key's Musical Who's Who
Thompson, O. ed. International Cyclopedia of Music and Musicians 1939
Who's Who in America

STONE, HANNAH (MAYER) 1893(?)—July 10, 1941 Physician; birth-control pioneer; medical director of the Birth Control Clinical Research Bureau since its founding in 1923 by Margaret Sanger; co-author of books on marriage; won several court fights after arrests for her beliefs.

References

American Medical Directory
American Women

Obituaries

Nation 153:63 Jl 26 '41
N Y Times p15 Jl 11 '41 por

STONE, HARLAN FISKE Oct. 11, 1872—Chief Justice of the United States Supreme Court

Address: b. United States Supreme Court, Washington, D. C.; h. 2340 Wyoming Ave, Washington, D. C.

President Roosevelt's nomination of Associate Justice Harlan Fiske Stone to the position of Chief Justice of the United States Supreme Court on June 12, 1941 met with unanimous approval. "His experience, his record and his character make his choice obviously fitting," commented Attorney General Jackson, and others emphasized his "scholarship and application, his personal warmth and character." Justice Stone himself said modestly of the appointment: "It is a kind of recognition any man would appreciate. The responsibility is so great that it doesn't create any sense of elation. I should be happy if the thoroughness

Harris & Ewing

HARLAN FISKE STONE

and efficiency of the recent Chief Justice could be maintained."

Chief Justice Stone has had 16 years on the highest bench in the land and long years of legal experience and training before that to help him achieve that aim. He was born in Chesterfield, New Hampshire, where his mother, Ann Sophia (Butler) Stone, had taught school before her marriage and where his father, Frederick Lauson Stone, was a farmer. Two years after his birth his family moved to Amherst, Massachusetts so that Harlan's eldest brother could go to agricultural school there. Harlan himself went to public school in Amherst part of the time and the rest of the time lived the life of a typical farmer's son: he milked cows, plowed, reaped, pitched hay.

After two years of high school Harlan went to the agricultural school in town and distinguished himself "as the instigator of every ducking party, nightshirt parade and chapel rush which featured college life in those days." One of his escapades—stories differ about which one—proved his undoing, and Harlan was expelled. He decided to try another school and despite his record and despite his not having been graduated from high school was accepted by Amherst College in the class of 1894.

Harlan was a fireball there. He tutored other students, sold insurance and typewriters and still was able to manage the Amherst *Student,* win a Phi Beta Kappa key in his junior year, deliver the class oration, play right guard on the famous team of 1892 which defeated Williams 60 to 0, serve as class president for three years and be chosen "the man who would become most famous." And when his classmates voted on the greatest benefit the college had got from the town

STONE, HARLAN FISKE—*Continued*

of Amherst, the answer was unanimous: "Harlan Stone."

Stone knew he wanted to be a lawyer but knew, too, that it would cost money. Right out of college, therefore, he got a position teaching at the Newburyport High School. A former pupil remembers him as "a big, good-looking young man . . . determined and forceful in his manner without being anything but agreeable," who "gave the impression of physical, mental and moral power." From Newburyport, Stone went to the Columbia University School of Law, supporting himself by teaching history in Adelphi Academy in Brooklyn. In 1898 he received his law degree and was immediately admitted to the Bar.

The law firm of Sullivan and Cromwell got his services then, and later he transferred to the firm of Wilmer and Canfield. Law practice was in Stone's early career supplemented by teaching at Columbia, first as lecturer (1899-1902), then as professor (1902-1905). It wasn't until 1905 that he resigned to give all his time to his firm, which had by then become Satterlee, Canfield and Stone. Stone soon was busy making money, cultivating the connections that a partnership with a son-in-law of the elder J. P. Morgan brought within reach. It was felt that academic life was behind him forever. Yet in 1907, when Nicholas Murray Butler invited him to become dean of the Columbia Law School, Stone accepted—on the condition that Butler would make no appointments without first consulting the law faculty. Butler went over Stone's head almost immediately, and Stone resigned before he had even started. Three years later, in 1910, a group of professors and lawyers again asked Butler to draft Stone. Again Stone accepted, and this time Butler kept his word on professorial appointments.

Stone was popular at Columbia. Member of a downtown law firm, teacher of several classes, he not only found time to handle hundreds of details as dean and to write on legal subjects and institute reforms in the teaching and examining of law students, but he also managed to see any student who had problems and to try to advise him. In classes he stood twirling his glasses on a black silk ribbon, never opening a book, never razzing, never raising his voice above a conversational tone as he talked for an hour. "There was something about the kindliness of his manner, his desire to meet his class more than half way, the sense of fairness permeating everything he did," according to Pearson and Allen (see sketch this issue), "which made Stone loved and revered perhaps more than any other Columbia professor of that day."

There were many of Stone's actions during those years which marked him as something of a liberal. He objected when Professors J. McKeen Cattell and Henry Wadsworth Longfellow Dana were ousted for their pacifist utterances, and he acted as diplomatic go-between in getting a settlement for Cattell when he sued President Butler and the trustees of Co-

lumbia. He helped the Wilson Administration deal with conscientious objectors, traveling from camp to camp listening to their stories—a book on his experiences was published after the War. During Attorney General Palmer's "Red raids" he voiced active opposition. Yet to the more Leftish of his colleagues on the Columbia faculty Harlan Stone seemed in those years a complete conservative, for his own courses in personal property, mortgages and the law of equity were dryly legal, and his Wall Street connections and rich neighbors (Thomas W. Lamont and Dwight Morrow among them) in the fashionable suburb of Englewood, New Jersey were well known.

The impression of his conservatism seemed to be confirmed when in 1923 Stone resigned the deanship of the Columbia Law School to enter the law firm of Sullivan and Cromwell, which had a large corporation and estate practice. There he was considered a "hard-working, solid sort of person, willing on occasion to champion the rights of mankind, but safe nevertheless." His appointment by Calvin Coolidge to the Attorney Generalship in April 1924 was, consequently, well received. Coolidge and he had known each other for some time, ever since college, in fact, when Coolidge was a year ahead of Stone. They got to know each other better when Coolidge did some law work for Stone's father, who from a small-time farmer had become the biggest taxpayer in Amherst, thanks to horse swapping, cattle trading and farming. Once Stone was in the Cabinet, Coolidge and he became fairly intimate, and Stone is now reported to have the best stock of Coolidge anecdotes in Washington.

One of the first things Stone did as Attorney General was to rid the Bureau of Criminal Investigation of holdovers from Daugherty's "Red scare" reign. William J. Burns, its head, was ousted and J. Edgar Hoover selected in his place. Then Stone opened his guns against the Aluminum Corporation of America, controlled by the family of the late Andrew Mellon, who was at that time Secretary of the Treasury. He had barely started antitrust proceedings when, in March 1925, less than a year after he had become Attorney General, he was made by Coolidge an Associate Justice of the Supreme Court.

There were some misgivings about the appointment. Gossip had it that he had been "kicked upstairs" because of his antitrust activities. Some liberals attacked him for being a successful lawyer and counsel for great business enterprises. But there wasn't much opposition, actually, and Justice Stone took his place on the bench. At that time a liberal colleague wrote to the late Justice Brandeis: "For 10 years, Mr. Justice," it said, "I've been trying to educate him and have failed miserably. I wish you better luck."

At first it didn't look as though Brandeis would have better luck. Justice Stone moved slowly on the bench, scrupulously fair but still the kind of man whom President Hoover, with whom he used to play medicine ball, could seriously consider for the position of Chief

Justice when it became vacant in 1930. Yet people began to say of Stone that he was "always right the second time," that although his first reaction was often toward the conservatism of his Englewood-Wall Street days, his next was likely to be one of broad humanitarianism. Eventually, influenced somewhat by Oliver Wendell Holmes and by Brandeis, he came to be a pleader for a broader view of the Constitution to suit new needs. Time and again he stood with the liberals on the court against the conservatives, and "Brandeis, Holmes and Stone [later 'and Cardozo'] dissent" became a famous phrase.

Justice Stone's views, as expressed in his Supreme Court opinions, are that law itself is "a human institution for human needs"; that it is "not an end, but a means to an end—the adequate control and protection of those interests, social and economic, which are the special concern of government and hence of law—and that end is to be attained through reasonable accommodation of law to changing economic and social needs." It was part of this philosophy that caused him to crack down especially hard on his old Wall Street associates, on "the towering edifice of business and industry ... that seemed to be the impregnable fortress of a boasted civilization but which has developed unsuspected weaknesses." It was this philosophy, too, that led him, a Republican often mentioned for the Presidency, to uphold the New Deal—in voting for the abrogation of the gold clause contract in government bonds, the TVA, the National Labor Relations Act, the Wage and Hour Law; in dissenting from the decisions on the Guffey coal wage bill, on the New York Minimum Wage Law for women, and on the AAA. It was on this last that perhaps his most famous minority opinion was written; in it he accused the court of "sitting in judgment on the wisdom of legislative action" and contended that Congress' power to tax and spend "includes the right to relieve a nationwide economic maladjustment by conditional gifts of money." For this Alice Roosevelt Longworth shouted "Recreant!" at him.

Stone himself is supposed to have adopted something of the philosophy of Holmes, who said at the end of his long and full life: "About 75 years ago I learned that I was not God. And so when the people of the various states want to do something and I can't find anything in the Constitution expressly forbidding them to do it, I say, whether I like it or not, 'Goddam it, let 'em do it.'" Stone expressed much the same idea when he said: "I have nothing personally against the world in which I grew up. That world has always made me very comfortable. But I don't see why I should let my social predilections interfere with experimental legislation that is not prohibited in the Constitution."

On the bench Stone asks few questions, never heckles counsel, but he is a shrewd and canny fighter who "watches precedents like a hawk," sticks to the narrow issue. His opinions are cautiously phrased, for Stone says he has learned true humility toward the written word after having had his contributions to legal publications as a law professor quoted at him to prove both sides of cases argued before the Supreme Court. He writes them illegibly in outline on a pad with a thick pencil and then from his notes dictates facts and arguments to a stenographer. With this as a basis he and his secretary whip the opinion into shape, for Stone is not deft in expressing himself even though he always knows exactly what he wants to say. His secretary changes every year: he uses the position to launch new Columbia Law School graduates.

To his duties as Associate Justice are now added those of the Chief Justice. Justice Stone, as the Supreme Court's executive officer, now presides at its sessions and conferences and announces its orders. And there are many who feel that as he leans forward from the bench imposingly, his gray hair falling over his forehead, his figure solid, his face broad and clean-shaven, his manner benignly judicial, he is almost as impressive a figure of justice as were Taft and Hughes before him. On October 6, 1941 the nine Justices came together for the 1941 to 1942 term.

He is not a colorful figure, but he is a human one. He and Mrs. Stone, the former Agnes Harvey of Chesterfield, New Hampshire, whom he married in 1899, are very friendly people. They go out more than most of the justices and their wives, and Mr. Justice Stone makes any dinner or party he goes to lively with his stock of yarns. They attend all symphonies and concerts available in Washington, are great supporters of young musicians and artists and of the Washington Municipal Orchestra, and their Monday afternoon teas are jammed with people of all kinds. Summers they spend on Isle au Haut off the coast of Maine, where Mrs. Stone paints water colors and the Chief Justice mows the lawn, drives a dilapidated car and pulls his fishing dory to the mainland. Sometimes they're joined there by their two sons, Lauson, a lawyer and partner in the New York firm of Ignatius and Stone, and Marshall, a professor of mathematics at Harvard who, the Justice says, "writes books I can't understand."

References

Columbia Law R 36:351-81 Mr '36
Fortune 13:81-4 My '36 por
N Y County Law Assn Report 18:255-60 '26
N Y Law R 4:120-4 Mr '26
N Y Times VII p8 F 18 '40 por; VII p12+ Je 22 '41 por
Newsweek 7:31 F 15 '36 por; 17:18 Je 23 '41 por
Read Digest 39:22-7 Ag '41
Sat Eve Post 214:14-15+ S 20 '41 il pors
Time 37:15 Je 23 '41 por
Leaders in Education 1941
Who's Who in America
Who's Who in Law
Who's Who in the Nation's Capital

STONEHAVEN, JOHN LAWRENCE BAIRD, 1ST VISCOUNT Apr. 27, 1874—Aug. 19, 1941 Former Governor General of Australia; died in Scotland; elected to the House of Commons as a conservative in 1910; active in politics until his appointment in 1925 as Governor General of Australia; made a peer in 1925.

References

> Sat R 157:787 Jl 7 '34
> Who's Who

Obituaries

> N Y Times p17 Ag 21 '41 por
> Newsweek 18:41 S 1 '41 por
> Time 38:48 S 1 '41

STOUT, WESLEY WINANS Jan. 26, 1890- Editor of the Saturday Evening Post
Address: b. Saturday Evening Post, Independence Sq, Philadelphia, Pa; h. Ambler, Pa.

Since 1937 Wesley Winans Stout has edited the weekly with the largest gross advertising revenue and the largest circulation in the world. "Small, baldish," square-jawed, it is Stout whose penciled veto or acceptance determines what goes between the covers of the *Saturday Evening Post*. On Mondays the staff assembles in his office to "make up" the copy which will reach the public in four weeks—copy which usually includes three or four articles, a couple of serial installments, four or five pieces of fiction, and, of course, editorials, *Post Scripts, Keeping Posted*. In keeping with Curtis profits ($3,044,643.39 in 1940, an increase of 50.6 per cent over 1939), his salary is in figures that editors of smaller magazines must envy. In 1939 the Securities and Exchange Commission listed it as $46,422.76.

Stout became editor of the *Post* when the late George Horace Lorimer retired at the end of 1936. Before that he had been associate editor—for nearly 15 years. And, according to *Time*: "To the non-professional eye Mr. Lorimer trained Mr. Stout so thoroughly that Mr. Lorimer's last New Year's issue and Mr. Stout's first . . . seem to be cut from the same cloth. Each begins with a Leyendecker cherub and ends with a Dutch Cleanser ad, and what lies between is fairly homogeneous." Nor has the homogeneousness of what lies between been confined to that New Year's issue, and this is particularly uncanny in view of the fact that as a person Mr. Stout might have been expected to be remarkably dissimilar to his late employer.

For one thing, he has been an itinerant newspaperman for a good part of his life, rather than a solidly respectable citizen of Philadelphia. Born in Junction City, Kansas on January 26, 1890, the son of Francis Wellington Stout, a farm mortgage broker, and of Dora (Dougherty) Stout, Wesley Winans Stout spent only a year at the University of Kansas. Then, from 1907 to 1917, he kept moving all over the country. After getting his start on the Wichita *Beacon* he worked as a reporter and editor on newspapers from San Antonio and Mexico City to Seattle and San Francisco, seldom saving his money for any purpose but to pack up and go some place else. On the Kansas City *Star* he acquired a reputation as one of the best rewrite men and probably the very best poker player on which the city had ever laid eyes. His wildest adventure in Kansas City, however, was something that didn't really happen: he was reported dead in a pistol duel with Mexican bad men. (Two weeks before, he had lost his wallet on a border-bound train.)

It was 1916 before he got around to seeing New York while working for the New York *Globe*. He did not stay long with the *Globe*, either. In 1917 a friend recruiting for the Navy persuaded him to enlist. He applied for enlistment as a "fabric inspector," but it didn't matter: eventually he went overseas with the United States Naval Air Force. After the War two of the most pleasant years of his life were spent as the non-working "supercargo" of United States Shipping Board tramp steamers, and then in 1922, after another brief period on the *Globe*, he found his place on the *Saturday Evening Post*.

During those years under Mr. Lorimer's tutelage Stout wrote and ghostwrote innumerable articles—the back files of the *Saturday Evening Post* are full of them. They include much regional material on the United States, for Stout already knew remote corners of this country like his own back yard, and he hadn't stopped traveling. (A year after coming to the *Post*, in September 1923, he married an employee—Mary Lee Starr—and began carrying a second passenger in his car.) Stout was known as the only staff member who could say "No" to Lorimer. When he finally inherited Lorimer's desk and corner office on the sixth floor of the Curtis Building, his elderly predecessor was indignant when asked how long Stout had been groomed for the job. "A man makes his own place in this world," announced Lorimer, stiffly, "and Mr. Stout made his. We did not groom him for the post." Curtis' President Walter Dean Fuller (see sketch this issue) was happy to report, however, that Stout shared Lorimer's beliefs in "fundamental American doctrines." Other *Post* editors thought him "safe," too, but also thought that he might be "less rabidly anti-New Deal than his predecessor."

Actually under Stout's editorship the *Saturday Evening Post* seems to have moved hardly a millimeter to the Left, and many traditions have remained intact. Stout, who has a great admiration for his predecessor and who says of Lorimer: "In an age of tenors, he sang bass," still has everyone paid in cash, goes in for the same elaborate fire drills, has everything locked up in the same vault at night, and preserves the old Lorimer custom of having editors or associate editors reply personally to all communications from readers. The year 1937 did see certain other innovations, however: the first photographic covers, 15 new artists, "bleed" art work on inside pages, the publication of works of 147 new writers. Lorimer had never played handball

Photo-Crafters

WESLEY WINANS STOUT

with his staff, either, nor gone in 'for "convivial daily lunches," as Stout does.

As for Lorimer's stand on World War II, it is hard to say what it might have been. Until May 1941 Stout (or at least the *Post* editorial page) had been consistently isolationist, an editorial in the issue of April 26, 1941 summing up the magazine's position since the passage of the Lease-Lend Bill: ". . . for us the debate was closed when Congress enacted the bill that nobody wrote. . . We were then in the War to defeat Hitler by name. . . How to get through it and out of it all together must become the one shape of our thoughts; and to do it will require all the mind and character we possess." When this "scandalous isolationist policy" was criticized at a Curtis stockholders' meeting Walter Deane Fuller announced: "We believe in the freedom of the press in America. . . We're quite satisfied with the policy of the *Saturday Evening Post*." Nevertheless, an editorial in the May 24 issue finally announced that the *Saturday Evening Post* accepted the "American crusade" against Hitler; that although "everything we said on the losing side we still believe," for the United States to change its policy now would mean facing "the possibility of national death."

When they are not staying in a hotel room near the office, Mr. and Mrs. Stout live on a 10-acre estate outside Philadelphia. There the busy editor likes to tend his vegetable and flower gardens. Mrs. Stout has one son by a former marriage, but there are no other children. Mr. Stout does the great part of his copyreading at home evenings, but he still finds time to take frequent motor trips with Mrs. Stout and to attend an occasional horse race. Unlike the Lorimers, the Stouts take no part in Philadelphia's social life. Ac-

cording to *Time*, Wesley Winans Stout is "built like a bulldog, but . . . gives the impression of a man still unrooted to any one spot."

References

Newsweek 8:35-6 S 5 '36 por
PM p10 Ap 17 '41
Time 28:41 S 7 '36 por; 31:22-4 Ja 10 '38 pors
Who's Who in America

STOUT, WILLIAM BUSHNELL Mar. 16, 1880- Mechanical engineer; inventor; designer

Address: b. Stout Engineering Laboratories, Dearborn, Mich; h. 149 Lawrence Ave, Detroit, Mich.

When they call him "U. S. industry's most whimsical and unpredictable inventor," nobody argues; nor when they add that he turns out new mechanical devices "the way most men make doodles." Bill Stout, as he is known in the circles that control America's aeronautics and terranautics, is credited with "more technical innovations than any man since Edison." It is said that virtually every transport plane or bomber flying today is using some of his developments.

He has to his credit a substantial list of "firsts" in vehicles for road and rail, as well as for air. Among his minor "doodles" are a brick-conveyor which saved one firm $10,000 a year; a streamlined motorbus two tons lighter than previous models, able to carry 24 passengers at 70 miles an hour; an improved theatre seat; an air-conditioned bed; and a staggering number of mechanical toys. For all his reputation of eccentric genius, hardheaded businessmen have voted him a wizard of salesmanship; and it was he who organized America's first successful all-passenger plane service.

To do that much means starting early, and Bill Stout began when he was a scrawny little boy whose eyes were so bad he couldn't catch a ball. His father, the Reverend James Frank Stout, was a semi-itinerant Methodist preacher who was saving souls in Quincy, Illinois when his wife, Mary C. (Bushnell) Stout, on March 16, 1880, gave birth to William Bushnell Stout.

While the other boys were playing ball young William took refuge in the workshop, where he soon became an expert at devising and whittling out toys which he later taught his friends to make. From that time dates the nickname of "Jack Knife," which he later signed to his syndicated toy columns in Midwestern papers. His tinkering was in the family tradition, for an ancestor, David Bushnell, had produced during the American Revolution a tiny submarine known as "Bushnell's Turtle."

High school was hard on Jack Knife, but things went better after he transferred to the Mechanical Arts High School in St. Paul, where he boarded with friends while his father preached in another town. At the University of Minnesota, after supporting himself by

Society of Automotive Engineers

WILLIAM BUSHNELL STOUT

keeping (and losing) a laundry, waiting on table and teaching manual training, he began to write about the mechanical toys he used to make. His articles brought in enough to finish paying his way through college and later to finance a trip to Europe. As a side line he wrote fiction, which he illustrated himself. The toy columns telling boys how to make strange and wonderful contraptions out of a rubber band, a hairpin and two tooth-picks, continued for years, eventually helping to finance aeronautical experiments in a day when the airplane itself was considered a toy—and a daft one at that.

In 1906 Stout married Alma E. Raymond, and they honeymooned through Europe on a motorcycle and shavings from the Jack Knife. Funds were eked out, though almost imperceptibly, by a series of articles on aviation. When the bridal pair returned the groom himself built their St. Paul home and every stick of furniture—no doubt from rubber bands and match boxes. He was then editing a boy's page in the St. Paul *Dispatch*. (His experience with girls' toys has apparently been confined to those for his daughter, Wilma Frances.) From then on, however, the technical engineering articles increased in number and importance.

By 1912 he was writing so authoritatively about various types of motor engines that he was appointed aviation and technical editor of the Chicago *Tribune*. Presently he joined the staff of *Motor Age* and *Automobile*. In Chicago he founded a magazine, *Aerial Age,* and organized some high school boys into a club for building scientifically toy gliders and planes. Two of those boys are today important airplane manufacturers.

In a sense Stout rode to Detroit on his honeymoon horse, for he was called there by

Scripps-Booth in 1914 to redesign their motor-cycle. The result was the first Scripps-Booth automobile, which the designer was a bit timid about demonstrating—because he had never driven a motorcar before! After several years, in 1917, he left Scripps-Booth to manage the newly formed aircraft division of Packard.

When the First World War came the Government enlisted his knowledge for the Aircraft Production Board, and as technical adviser he exasperated the Army experts by his unorthodox notions about airplane construction. With disapproving frowns they did consent to construction of a trial model, the sight of which gave them technological colic. But when they called in Orville Wright to test it, this dean of the air pronounced it "the next step in aviation." Stout likes to recall that Orville Wright got his first idea for the heavier-than-air machine from the same diagram that gave Stout his first airward impulse: an illustration in a boys' weekly, with directions for making a toy plane of bamboo, tissue paper and a rubber band.

On the strength of the Government experiment, he was able to establish the Stout Engineering Laboratories, where in 1919 he built the first American commercial monoplane, the famous Batwing. This was followed in 1920 by the first all-metal plane designed in America, a torpedo plane for the Navy. The Laboratories' test flights were successful, but the Navy pilot, unfamiliar with the mechanism, wrecked the plane with a crash that spared the flier but was fatal to the builder's solvency.

He still had a typewriter, however, and at once instituted a campaign unprecedented in method and result. He sternly refused to accept money from anyone who expected to profit by the investment or who was not genuinely interested in the project. "Invest with me and lose your shirt" was his theme song; and with an expenditure of less than $100 he raised $128,000, in the process winning fame as "the man who sold the airplane to Henry Ford." His sales letters were actually a correspondence course in aeronautics; every man who received them read every letter, and some still keep them on file. Among those who subscribed $1,000 apiece were Edsel Ford, Walter Chrysler, Edward Budd, William Knudsen, Fred Fisher and Robert Stranahan, who had lost with him on his last two ventures.

Henry Ford, who for years had been declining invitations to take to the air, finally offered two to one for all holdings in the Stout Metal Airplane Company. The enthusiastic stockholders refused to sell, however, until Stout made it possible for them to convert their unpromised profits into an even bolder enterprise, the Stout Air Services.

When Ford bought the Stout Metal Airplane Company he persuaded Stout to come along as vice-president and general manager. Thus it was that Bill Stout became designer of the Ford trimotor plane, which Army experts promptly denounced as a "tin goose," fit only for roasting. Today every Army bomber incorporates the most revolutionary features of that "tin goose."

Having proved the solid worth of another airy notion, Stout was ready for the next round in his highly profitable "one-man dog-fight with the past." Again at a two-to-one profit, Stout Air Services was sold in 1929 to a company that was later taken over by United Air Lines, and the Stout Engineering Laboratories were revived for research and development work in aeronautics. In 1941 they are still developing, though work has not been confined to aircraft. Two that fly by earth are the Pullman Railplane, America's first gasoline-driven railroad car, and our first Diesel-electric engine, designed for the Union Pacific. And in 1936 Stout returned to the motorcar with his startling *Scarab*, which is already influential in motorcar design, and is likely to be more so when people accept his idea that "the current automobile is as obsolete . . . as the horse-drawn vehicle."

Streamlined into a beetle, with rear engine, no running boards, and an interior modeled on the cozy living-room plan, the *Scarab* ran from California to Detroit with an unspilled glass of water on its dashboard, to show how it could take the bumps. It gave as many shocks as it absorbed, but the prophecy begins to be fulfilled. However, "by the time they get around to copy us we'll be on to something else." Already he is "on to" a convertible Sky Car that turns into an auto to drive home from the airport, and an all-metal collapsible super-trailer, which its creator believes is in line with prefabricated shelter for the masses and solution of the housing problem. Meanwhile, the market for small planes has opened up, and the second Sky Car will be a stainless steel flier which should sell for about $1,000. The millenium itself, Stout believes, might be manufactured in the right sort of laboratories, for he holds that engineering is the hope of humanity and mass production the only instrument for social betterment.

This is the day when poets look like bond salesmen, and scientists like artists. Stout has the true thatch of genius, a wild mop of hair which he pushes around when he gets excited. He has been described as the least affected and most amiable of men, looking like "a cross between Groucho Marx and Fritz Kreisler," carrying about him the tang of the country store and a large aura of leisure—perhaps made up of the time his speed engines have saved. He, too, preaches a gospel, though not his father's. It is printed in large letters on the wall of his drafting room: SIMPLICATE AND ADD MORE LIGHTNESS.

References

Fortune 15:105 Mr '37 por; 23:46-51+ Ja '41 il pors
Mag of Business 52:560-1 N '27
Newsweek 5:30 F 2 '35 il
Sat Eve Post 213:21+ D 7 '40 il pors
Sci Am 140:231 Mr '29 por; 153:319 D '35 por

Time 34:44 S 25 '39 por
World's Work 50:423-8 Ag '25 il pors
Who's Who in America
Who's Who in Commerce and Industry
Who's Who in Engineering

STOWELL, CLARENCE WARNER (stō'ĕl) 1878—Nov. 26, 1940 Teacher, lecturer and sales executive who played a leading role, his first acting effort, in *The Ramparts We Watch.*

CLARENCE WARNER STOWELL

Obituaries

N Y Herald Tribune p25 N 27 '40 por
N Y Times p23 N 27 '40 por

STRAWBRIDGE, ANNE WEST Mar. 20, 1883—Sept. 9, 1941 Flier; author; made her first flight in 1936 but became rapidly known as a pilot; in 1938 published a book dealing with her flying experiences, *Above the Rainbow;* also known as an artist; had exhibited her paintings in many cities in this country.

References

American Women
Who's Who in American Art

Obituaries

N Y Times p23 S 10 '41

STRÖMBERG, LEONARD, REV. 1871— July 3, 1941 Clergyman; writer of Swedish novels; pastor of the Swedish Methodist Church in Oakland, Nebraska for 29 years; after more than 40 best sellers in his homeland, Gustav V, King of Sweden, awarded him a

STRÖMBERG, LEONARD, REV.—*Cont.*
royal decoration; full name Oscar Leonard
Strömberg.

Obituaries
N Y Times p16 Jl 4 '41

STRONG, LEE A(BRAM) June 17, 1886—
June 2, 1941 Chief of the United States
Bureau of Entomology and Plant Quarantine
since 1934; devoted 30 years to fighting the
pests that destroy plants and cause annual
losses of many millions of dollars in the
United States; chief concern was the Japanese
beetle; cooperated with state and municipal
officials, the Work Projects Administration
and agricultural experts, nurserymen, produce
growers and representatives of gardening organizations in trying to exterminate this pest;
worked in the California State Department of
Agriculture and the Federal Horticultural
Board of the Department of Agriculture
before taking his last position.

References
Lit Digest 116:13 O 28 '33 por
Sci ns 78:305 O 6 '33
Sci Am 150:3 Ja '34 por
Who's Who in America
Who's Who in the Nation's Capital

Obituaries
N Y Times p21 Je 3 '41 por

STRONG, WILLIAM MCCREERY
1899(?)—Mar. 26, 1941 Vice-president and
director of Batten, Barton, Durstine & Osborn, advertising agency; originated or collaborated on many notable advertising campaigns, among them campaigns for the
Saturday Evening Post, New York *Herald
Tribune* and the Harvard Classics; from two
of his hobbies came two books, *Photography
for Fun* (1934) and *How to Travel Without
Being Rich* (1937).

Obituaries
N Y Times p23 Mr 27 '41 por

STRUTHER, JAN June 6, 1901- Author
Address: c/o Harcourt, Brace & Co, Inc, 383
Madison Ave, New York City

Mrs. Miniver, that pleasantly beguiling English lady whose book about herself and her
family (published July 1940) became so popular in this country, is Jan Struther, whose
real name in turn is Mrs. Maxtone Graham.
Miss Struther, shortly after her book's publication in the United States, came to New
York to live, bringing two of her children,
Janet and Robert. The eldest, 16-year-old
James, is in school at home. He happens to
be pretty near enlistment age, and, she says,
"an excellent shot." She and the younger
children came by ship to Canada, along with
many other English mothers and children;
then on to New York City, where they expect
to stay "for the duration."

The reflections of Miss Struther's Mrs.
Miniver are revealed through a series of little
sketches (previously printed in the London
Times) on the ordinary, day-by-day incidents
in a typical English middle-class household
just before the War came in 1939. The
majority of reviewers, particularly in America,
has found the book, *Mrs. Miniver,* an unqualified delight. Her creator has been compared to
—and to the slight disadvantage of—the "Provincial Lady," Virginia Woolf, Charles Lamb
and Shakespeare. No one can help quoting
from her, Lewis Gannett remarks. "Much of
the fun of reading *Mrs. Miniver* lies in the delight of sudden recognition. Mrs. Miniver is
beautifully aware of the profundity and uni-
versality of trivialities." Among these
trivialities are jottings on Christmas for the
three children, shopping, going to the dentist,
and having "honey sandwiches, brandy-snaps
and small ratafia biscuits" for tea in a well-
ordered household staffed by four well-
trained servants. Other American critics have
been impressed by Mrs. Miniver's culture as
represented by her love for John Donne and
the *New Yorker* Magazine.

The dissenting opinion comes from English
reviewers. Rosamond Lehmann writes: "It is
not so much that we are irritated by her being
pleased with herself . . . it is in her humility
that we suspect her most." And E. M. Forster
(writing in the *New Statesman and Nation*)
says that *Mrs. Miniver* invites a reaction similar
to that of a Gloucester parson who was "a
kindly, friendly fellow who had the right word
for every occasion. But when the right word
was spoken and he passed out of earshot,
swinging his stick and looking right and left at
the sky, the villagers came into their own for
a moment and used foul language about him.
To preserve their manhood and their self-
respect, they had to splutter a little smut."
He continues: "She thinks she is in the top
drawer of all, and that her good behavior is
the best kind of behavior," that she hankers
after the feudal stronghold already "condemned
as uninhabitable." It may be that Miss Struther
created her Mrs. Miniver as an indictment
of this typical British middle-class attitude; if
so, the Miniver-adoring readers of the London
Times failed to see this, along with 90 per cent
of the book critics. In her interviews with
two New York writers, Robert Van Gelder
and Stephen Benét, Jan Struther's reflections
on her home, her children and her impressions
of this country resemble those of her own
Mrs. Miniver.

"She is so exactly what her wide reading
public expects her delightful Mrs. Miniver to
be," write Stephen and Rosemary Benét, "that
they not only accept her, but they refuse to
separate the two ladies, or allow that there may
be any difference between them." Miss Struther
says that this leads to unexpected complications,
even for her family: she too has a businessman
husband and three children of the same ages as
Mrs. Miniver's. Miss Struther protests against
this adulation on the part of the public for her
Mrs. Miniver. "The time came when finally
I was heartily sick of the woman. She was

so popular that I had to stick to it, but when one of our papers offered a prize for the best parody on *Mrs. Miniver* I wrote much the cruelest parody, sent it in under a pen name, and won the prize." She asked the paper to give the money award to the second-best entry; but they let her keep her winnings, which she

Shelburne

JAN STRUTHER

sent to "an organization for distressed gentle-women."

Jan Struther was born in England June 6, 1901 as Joyce Anstruther. Hence her pen-name, Jan Struther. Her father was Henry Torrens Anstruther; her mother was the Honorable Dame Eva Anstruther, made a Dame because of her service to England in the First World War. She also wrote—under the name Eva Struther. Miss Struther's mother-in-law, too, was a writer. Her husband, Anthony Maxtone Graham, to whom she was married in 1923, is Scotch, and her father-in-law is the senior partner of Maxtone Graham & Sime, of Edinburgh, London and Canada. Miss Struther was educated privately in London and began to publish stories and poems when she was 15.

"In appearance Miss Struther is small, dark-haired and very attractive. Like Elizabeth Barrett she has 'a pair of fine eyes' in an expressive face. She is intelligent, outgiving and pleasant. . . It may annoy her to be told that she has many qualities that we consider American: the quick response, the adaptability which we think

of, probably quite mistakenly, as peculiarly our own." In her appearances on *Information Please* radio programs, Miss Struther appealed to listeners by her ready response to the quiz questions, her fine sense of humor, her intelligence. The Benéts say further that what she likes best to write is poetry. She is the author of one volume of serious poems, *The Glass-Blower* (1941), and several collections of light verse. Prior to her present book she published a collection of essays and sketches, *Try Anything Twice* (1938). Of her essays in general it has been said: "These essays are beautifully written, with form, with style and a deceptive simplicity. They may look easy to do. So does Mr. Houseman's poetry look simple to a beginner. In both cases, every word is in place, like the flowers in a pruned and tended garden."

Since coming to New York Miss Struther has spent much time roaming over the city, taking elevated rides, looking in shop windows, visiting the parks and watching the people. She says: "My children are delighted when they hear taxi drivers say 'foist' and 'thoid,' just as in the films. They say, 'Gosh, aren't the cops tough!' with the very greatest admiration. It is good, too, to hear European languages freely spoken without people making notes and whispering, 'Fifth Columnists.'"

References

N Y Herald Tribune p15 Jl 25 '40 por
N Y Herald Tribune Books p7 O 13 '40
N Y Times Book R p2 Ag 25 '40 por; X p36 N 17 '40
Time 36:68 Ag 5 '40 por

Author's and Writer's Who's Who
Who's Who

STUART, DUANE REED Sept. 27, 1873—Aug. 29, 1941 Professor of Latin language and Latin literature at Princeton University; chairman of the Princeton Department of Classics; had taught at Bryn Mawr College, Yale University and many other schools; was author and editor of various books.

References

Leaders in Education 1941
Who's Who in America

Obituaries

N Y Herald Tribune p8 Ag 30 '41
Sch & Soc 54:161 S 6 '41

STUART, JAMES EVERETT Mar. 24. 1852—Jan. 2, 1941 American artist whose paintings have been exhibited throughout the world and are permanently in the White House, various American universities and many museums; favorite subjects were Western landscapes; grandson of Gilbert Stuart, the famous painter of George Washington.

References

Who's Who in America
Who's Who in American Art

Obituaries

N Y Times p13 Ja 4 '41

STURGES, PRESTON (stûr'jĕs) Aug.
29, 1898- Author; film director; producer
Address: b. 322 Directors' Bldg, Paramount
Pictures, Inc, 5451 Marathon St, Hollywood,
Calif.

PRESTON STURGES

The Great McGinty, a picture that brought
Preston Sturges an "Oscar" in 1941 as the best
screen play of 1940, was known to the trade
as a "sleeper." Its small budget ($325,000)
marked it as Paramount's noble experiment
on behalf of its author-director, Preston
Sturges. In turn, and as a gesture of good
will, Sturges sold the script to Paramount for
$10. But when the large neon "Oscar" was
turned on outside Hollywood's Biltmore on
February 27, 1941, and Darryl Zanuck distributed technical awards, the "sleeper" came
to life with a bang. And it seemed something
like a parable of Sturges' life, which had
"slept" in indecision and unprofitable ventures
until an illness in 1927 seemed somehow to
put the house in order.

Sturges, Idwal Jones tells us, is "genially
extrovert. . . He swings across the lot with
rattan cane, sweater looped about his neck,
and a straw hat." And his appearance seems
to bear out this impression. He has been
aptly described as "a big chesty party with
a mop of black hair and a black, bristly
mustache." Still, the observation that "he has
been immune to surprise since the age of
three or thereabouts" is possibly surface judgment. An expression, sometimes of worldli-
ness but occasionally of boyish wonder or sly
youthfulness, suggests a more dynamic personality.

Born in Chicago, the son of Edmund and
Mary (Dempsey) Biden, Preston was adopted
by Solomon Sturges, whom his mother married after divorcing her first husband. Preston's foster father was a stockbroker, a sportsman—champion cyclist of Illinois. Little

Preston's psyche was to be buffeted about on
the one hand by the winds of commerce, whose
keen velocity he found refreshing, and the
swirling of robes in a Grecian dance. For a
peculiarity of the marriage was his parents'
agreement that the late Mary Desti—the name
by which his mother was best known—should
spend six months of each year in Paris. There
young Preston Sturges was all but overwhelmed by celebrities, all but smothered in
culture. Isadora Duncan was a close friend
of his mother and Preston was being
groomed to scale Olympus. Often as a small
child he was put to bed in the afternoon so
that he could be fresh and wide awake for
the opera at night. He had his first taste
of champagne in his infancy, when Isadora
spoon-fed him on it to cure a pulmonary complaint. It was little wonder that when Preston first went to the Coulter School in Chicago
he cycled there—but in flowing Greek robes!

"He came out of this life," said Alva Johnston, "hating art and music, burning with zeal
to become a stockbroker like his foster father."
Sturges learned to draw and paint but the only
effective use he made of this talent was in designing advertising posters for his mother's
cosmetics shop in Paris. He was taught piano
but had to learn all over again to write scores
for his musical shows—the scores were not
highly successful—and today he plays piano by
ear, does not read a note of music! According
to Johnston some of his literary "hates"—
Shakespeare, Molière—are merely prejudices of
this nature.

When he was 11 his parents decided to separate and, asked to choose between them, he
chose his father. It was then he learned for
the first time that he had been adopted. At
about this time Solomon Sturges was seriously
injured in an automobile accident. His wife
spent a year nursing him back to health, then
went to Paris, taking her son with her. She got
a divorce from Sturges and was married to
Vely Bey, scion of a distinguished Turkish
family. Using her husband's family formulas in
cosmetics as a basis, Mary Desti in 1911 opened
the first modern beauty shop in Paris. While
in his teens Preston managed the Deauville
branch, and later the one in New York.

Besides studying at the Coulter School, Pres-
ton attended at various times the Lycée Janson,
Paris; l'Ecole des Roches in Northern France;
La Villa Lausanne in Switzerland; a Berlin
Gymnasium; and, finally, a school in
Dresden.

In 1914, at the age of 16, Preston got a job
as runner for a Wall Street brokerage house.
His pay was $7 a week but it was raised to $10
before he left the following year. Previous to
this experience he had had a short-lived contact
with the stage. In 1914, through Isadora Duncan, he was given the job of assistant stage
manager for the New York presentation of
Oedipus Rex. He muffed the signals one night
and turned thunder on before lightning, drown-
ing out a speech by one of the principals. It
was after this that he embraced Wall Street
temporarily.

During the War, Sturges wanted to join the Air Corps but was rejected because of bad eyesight. After official Washington learned that his eyes were good enough for the British Air Corps they relented. He became a member of the 63rd Air Squadron and went to the School of Military Aeronautics at Austin, Texas, where he remained until the Armistice. There he made his first sortie into literature, writing *300 Words of Humor* for the school paper, *Park Field Gnat*.

Returning to New York, Sturges went into the cosmetics business, inventing the kissproof lipstick. He looked toward a future in this growing industry, but the business had to be turned over to his mother, who had had bad luck with her shops in Paris and London. From then until 1927 Sturges tried his hand at various jobs and was a miscellaneous, if not always successful, inventor. In 1927 he and Estelle (Mudge) Sturges, whom he married in 1923, separated, most of his ventures had fizzled or failed entirely, and he was about to be staked jointly to a shop, Maison Desti, by his mother and Solomon Sturges, his foster father. Then came his illness, an appendectomy, and during convalescence an amazing crystallization of his personality. Armed with Brander Matthews' *A Study of The Drama*, he seems to have reached the decision that one did not have to be a social freak in order to be a writer.

An attempt to dramatize his period of hospitalization failed before it was completely written, but *The Guinea Pig* opened in Provincetown in 1929 and had 16 weeks on Broadway. Then came *Strictly Dishonorable*, the comedy about which he might have made his quip that "dialogue consists of the bright things you would like to have said except that you didn't think of them in time." It was a success from the day of its opening, September 18, 1929, but as he watched the action unfold Sturges was so sure he had written a failure that he went off and had a few drinks. His mother awakened him early the next morning with comments such as "the cleverest comedy in town" (John Anderson); "occasionally wobbly in its writing, particularly in its motivations . . . but at all times high-spirited and gay" (John Mason Brown); and "a well-nigh perfect comedy" (J. Brooks Atkinson).

The two plays that followed did not go over well, but the third, *Child of Manhattan* (1931) did, despite Atkinson's comment that it was "tawdry" and "a sophomoric romance." It was later filmed by Columbia (1933), and for its screen rights Sturges was paid $40,000. Meanwhile, in 1931, Universal filmed *Strictly Dishonorable*. An operetta, *The Well of Romance*, was poorly received. The New York *Times'* critic said that the music was not endowed with any great originality but that it was superior to the libretto. In 1932 Sturges moved to Hollywood to do a script of Wells' *The Invisible Man* for Universal. The script was shelved but Sturges stayed on to do a long string of successful scenarios and many original screen plays.

Although the picturization of *Strictly Dishonorable* was his first screen success, so far as the public was concerned, he had had his first contact with films while the play was running on Broadway. In 1929 he did two scenarios for Paramount that were filmed in the company's Eastern studio and starred Miriam Hopkins. He began his Hollywood career at $1,000 a week, climbed rapidly to what Alva Johnston calls the "subsistence level of $2,500." With *The Power and the Glory* (Universal, 1933) he established a precedent by getting a percentage of the gross as well as $17,500 outright. Among the many other successful films he has written are: *30-Day Princess, We Live Again, Diamond Jim, Imitation of Life, Next Time We Love, One Rainy Afternoon, If I Were King, Twentieth Century* and *Sullivan's Travels*.

"If I have any success," Sturges once was quoted as saying, "it is an act of God." A close scrutiny of his life, however, reveals that there was at least some collaboration. It was Sturges who insisted upon directing his own pictures. He finally had the chance when Paramount let him take the script of *McGinty*, which had been kicking around Hollywood for years without any takers, and direct it himself. "When a picture gets good notices," he said, "everyone but the writer is the prince. So I decided I was going to be one of the princes." Then he got his "Oscar" as a writer.

"*McGinty*," said Archer Winston, "you could dismiss as a lucky inspiration. *Christmas in July* was harder to explain away. Its advertising satire was sharp. But with *The Lady Eve* Sturges performs the impossible of the sow's ear into silk purse." Another critic thought the dialogue somewhat padded in the latter film, and the camera work at times static. Up to this point, according to this observer, he had been "more showman than artist." He suggested that Sturges could handle "more dimensional material than he had in his last two pictures."

Sturges' first marriage ended in divorce in 1928. On April 12, 1930 he married Eleanor Post Hutton, who subsequently inherited more than a million dollars from her grandfather C. W. Post, the cereal king. This marriage was annulled November 3, 1932 on the grounds that the previous (Mexican) divorce was not valid. His third marriage was to Mrs. Louise Sargeant Tevis at Reno, Nevada.

Writing and directing for Paramount, Sturges' income is said to be $2,750 weekly. He also derives an income from his restaurant, The Players, and keeps a hand in business with his concern, the Sturges Engineering Company, manufacturers of vibrationless Diesel engines. He likes sports and good food, has a house that was built according to his ideas, and has a collection of ships' models as well as a yacht and a power launch.

References

Friday 1:20-1 N 8 '40 pors
N Y Herald Tribune VI p1, 4 Mr 2 '41
N Y Times IX p4 Ag 4 '40; IX p5 Mr 2 '41
N Y World-Telegram Jl 16 '38
Newsweek 16:44+ Ag 19 '40

(Continued next page)

STURGES, PRESTON—*Continued*

Sat Eve Post 213:9-11+ Mr 8 '41 il
pors; 213:25+ Mr 15 '41 il pors
Time 36:91-2 O 21 '40 por

International Motion Picture Almanac
Who's Who in the Theatre

SUNG TSU-WEN *See* Soong, T. V.

SUYDAM, EDWARD HOWARD (si'-dŭm) Feb. 22, 1885—Dec. 23, 1940 Noted book illustrator; artist; his pencil drawings, etchings and block prints are widely known and are included in museums, libraries and private collections; in 1940 completed two series of sketches of Virginia to illustrate books.

References
Who's Who in American Art

Obituaries
N Y Times p15 D 24 '40

SWANN, W(ILLIAM) F(RANCIS) G(RAY) Aug. 29, 1884- Physicist; director of the Bartol Research Foundation of the Franklin Institute

Address: b. c/o Bartol Research Foundation, Whittier Pl, Swarthmore, Pa; h. 609 Ogden Ave, Swarthmore, Pa.

It was in 1935 that Dr. W. F. G. Swann "went down into a deep bank vault, picked up the murmuring of a cosmic ray . . . and put it on the radio." This is not what bank vaults are ordinarily used for, but the usual is not Dr. Swann's forte. He was making another of his daring and original experiments. That he was also making scientific history was by this time hardly news to a man who has been characterized as "one of the most brilliant physicists in the world." He is one of those twentieth century wizards who deal in quantities and forces too large or too small for the human eye to glimpse or the ordinary mind to grasp. He has been peculiarly successful in working out mechanisms to trap, record and measure such elusive entities as atoms and cosmic rays. He had charge, for example, of the recording machinery that went up in the stratosphere flight sponsored by the United States Army Air Corps and the National Geographic Society in 1935. Incidentally, he was the one who harnessed that "very eminent cosmic ray" that inaugurated the festive illumination of the New York World's Fair in 1939.

Dr. Swann's ray on the radio was described as "a low, noncommittal hill-billy humming which might have been Woodie Guthrie goin' down the road and feelin' bad." The Professor himself had covered a good deal of road before reaching that point. He had traveled all the way from Shropshire, England, where he was born at Ironbridge on August 29, 1884; and from the field of medicine, which he first chose because "it was thought to be a profession in which it was possible to make a living."

His father was William Francis and his mother Anne (Evans) Swann, and he himself a Shropshire lad with a "bad memory and a natural antipathy to physics and mathematics." Rather than learn by heart a proposition from Euclid, he bluffed it through when he was called on and ended by producing a proof that was quite correct—though definitely not Euclid's. In later years he continued to find his own solutions to problems others had solved differently, as well as solutions to some no one had yet answered.

In order to earn money for the microscope indispensable to medical studies, he substituted for a friend who played the cello in a theatre orchestra. The orchestra conductor offered to hire the substitute and fire the regular, but Swann did not fancy either the tactics or the job. Having earned the microscope, he discovered that medicine with all its tongue-twisting terms was very hard on the memory. He also discovered in a bookshop a very old volume, price four cents, which contained an amazing array of mathematical subjects, including calculus, astronomy, dynamics and geodesy. Perhaps that tuppence paid his way into the Hall of Fame. At any rate, there ended his medical career.

Soon he was the happy possessor of a scholarship to the Royal College of London, where he became a junior instructor after graduation, in 1905. Before long his research in physics had gained wide recognition, and in 1907 he was invited to accept a lecturing position at the University of Sheffield. Here, as in a number of posts, he did extracurricular duty as conductor of the University Orchestra. He was a highly individualistic conductor always, one who on one occasion composed the last-act music for a college play during the first intermission. More important to his extracurricular life at Sheffield was his marriage in 1909 to Sarah Frances Mabel Thompson, of Preston Park, Sussex. Mrs. Swann had studied violin at Brussels Conservatory and is today an enthusiastic chamber music player on viola and violin.

The Swanns have been residents of America since 1913, when the Carnegie Institute of Washington called Dr. Swann to be chief of the Physics Division of the Department of Terrestrial Magnetism. In this capacity he designed and saw installed atmospheric electric equipment on the yacht *Carnegie*; and he also superintended the installing of elaborate automatic atmospheric electric equipment in Washington. He found time, however, to deliver a series of lectures for the Bureau of Standards; and the story goes that when he heard they were scheduled for eight in the morning he protested: "An Englishman seldom stays up that late!"

Repartee was perhaps not the chief reason why in 1917 he was made consultant at the Bureau of Standards, where he again became conductor of an orchestra—this time one that included a number of physicists who are now world-famous. During the War he assisted in directing research work on the problem of submarine detection.

He went West in 1918 to be professor of physics at the University of Minnesota. Four years later he accepted a professorship at the University of Chicago, leaving there in 1924 to become professor of physics at Yale University and director of the Sloane Physics Laboratory. In 1927 he became director of the Bartol Research Foundation of the Franklin Institute, and has been since 1923 associate editor of the *Journal of the Franklin Institute.* He has published about one hundred seventy-five scientific papers in various journals, and two books—*The Architecture of the Universe* (1934) and, as part author, *The Story of Human Error* (1936); has contributed to the *Encyclopedia Britannica;* and has been in constant demand for public lectures, as well as for private or public musical performances.

At present he is conductor of the Swarthmore Symphony Orchestra, which he founded and which comprises about 72 players. Because nobody in the group could handle a French horn or a bass clarinet, he and his assistant, Dr. William E. Danforth, devised an electrical "oscillion" so ingenious that it can be made to sound like either instrument, so simple that a child can master it. Dr. Swann himself still plays the cello when his duties as conductor and researcher permit. His three children share the interests of their parents: William Francis, graduated from Harvard University in 1937, is in 1941 in the research laboratories of the Eastman Kodak Company; Charles Paul is at Harvard studying to be an engineer; Sylvia, a student at Wellesley College, has already played piano concerti in public with her father's orchestra in Swarthmore.

1941 finds Dr. Swann's investigations centered chiefly about cosmic radiation; but he is also recognized as an authority in thermal measurements, electromagnetic theory, electroconductivity, relativity, terrestrial magnetism, atmospheric electricity and atomic structure. That formidable array would hardly suggest that one of his great talents is his ability to make abstract theories comprehensible and vivid for the layman. "Think of a fuel," he tells us, "such that a tenth of an ounce would heat a good-sized house for a year . . . an ounce would drive a forty-horsepower automobile eight hours a day for four years, a quarter of an ounce would run a large airplane around the world." This, he goes on, was a fabulous dream of yesterday, and is a potential reality of tomorrow. "It is atomic energy." And from that point he continues to describe, simply and graphically as a radio announcer, the drama that has made cause-and-effect into a crude, outworn concept and has reduced reality itself to a dream, "no more than the reflection of your own thoughts shining upon the face of nature."

This pioneer of our expanding cosmos is a tall man, whose wind-blown gray hair is apt to overtop the heads of those about him. His rugged face shows more lines of laughter than of thought, although both exercises seem to be habitual and effortless with him. His hands are practiced with the golf club as well as with

W. F. G. SWANN

the cello bow and the even more delicate instruments of his laboratory.

His honors have been in proportion to his activities, and like them too many to list in full. He was given an honorary M. A. degree by Yale in 1924, and an honorary D. Sc. by Swarthmore College in 1929. (His original D. Sc. was received in 1910 in London.) He is Honorary Fellow of Trinity College, London, member of many honorary societies, past president of the American Physical Society, and secretary and councilor of the American Philosophical Society.

References

Nat Hist 36:255-61 O '35 por
N Y Herald Tribune XI p14, 52 O 27
 '40 por; II p7 N 10 '40 por
N Y Sun p14 O 31 '40
Sci Am 157:3 Jl '37 por
Sci Mo 41:430-3 N '35
Time 29:58 My 3 '37 por

American Men of Science
Leaders in Education 1941
Who's Who in America
Who's Who in Engineering

SWENSON, ALFRED G. 1883(?)—Mar. 28, 1941 Stage and radio actor; began his stage career at the age of 21; had appeared on most of the leading network programs since entering that field in 1929; had roles in a number of sketches including *Big Sister, Hilltop House* and *Pretty Kitty Kelly.*

References

N Y Dram 70:12 D 31 '13 por; 76:13
 D 30 '16 por

Variety Radio Directory

Obituaries

N Y Times p15 Mr 29 '41
Variety 142:48 Ap 2 '41

SWIFT, ERNEST JOHN Jan. 8, 1883—
Oct. 19, 1941 Vice-chairman in charge of
insular and foreign operations of the American Red Cross since 1935; had worked with
the Red Cross since the First World War,
both abroad and in the United States, where
he served as manager for the Eastern area,
directing operations in states east of the
Mississippi River.

References

Who's Who in America
Who's Who in the Nation's Capital

Obituaries

N Y Times p17 O 20 '41 por

SWOPE, GERARD Dec. 1, 1872- Chairman of the New York City Housing Authority; honorary president of the General Electric Company; member of National Defense
Mediation Board
Address: b. 570 Lexington Ave, New York
City; 122 E. 42nd St; h. "The Croft," Ossining, N. Y.

GERARD SWOPE

Henry Ford once called Gerard Swope "the
world's best salesman." For 20 years he
sold the General Electric Company and its
products to the world; in 1941, as head of
New York City's Housing Authority, he is
selling the public his ideas on low-rent public
housing. He believes that, financed "by a
partnership of the Federal government, the
State government and the local government,"
and with "further work on simplification of
financing, standardization of building . . .
and generally with steadier work at higher
earning . . . we will be nearer to a solution
of this serious and difficult problem of providing low-cost housing for the low income
groups."

All his life Gerard Swope has been recognized as a successful businessman. "Many
call him the finest corporation executive officer that ever struck a balance sheet, precise,
exacting, a man of almost frightening purposefulness." He is also a man of broad
social outlook, "a New Dealer before the
New Deal," who introduced many employee
welfare projects into General Electric and
was generally active in government projects.
His present housing work and his service on
the National Defense Mediation Board, to
which he was appointed in the spring of 1941,
are other manifestations of his social-minded
activities.

Gerard Swope was born in St. Louis, Missouri, the son of Jewish parents, Isaac and
Ida Swope, and brought up there. His first
job was as a helper at $1 a day in the Chicago
service shop of the General Electric Company in 1893—he had gone there to see the
World's Fair. His next was with the Western
Electric Company in 1895. In the meanwhile,
however, he had graduated from the
Massachusetts Institute of Technology in 1895
with a degree in electrical engineering. (Since
then five colleges have given him honorary
degrees.)

From the shops of Western Electric, Swope
worked himself up to a manager's position in
St. Louis in 1899, and to general sales manager in New York in 1908. By this time he
had married Mary Dayton Hill of New
Brunswick, New Jersey in 1901. They have
five children. In 1913 he rose to vice-president
and director. Then came the First World
War, and Mr. Swope won the Distinguished
Service Medal for his work on the General
Staff's Board of Purchase, Storage and Traffic. The War over, he was offered the job of
organizing and heading International General
Electric, the foreign department of the General Electric Company, and he accepted it.
This wasn't the first time General Electric had
offered him a position. Back in 1909, when
Western Electric sold out its power apparatus
business, General Electric Company had
offered to take him along with it. But Swope
refused: "I'm no chattel," he said. "I'll stay
where I am."

As the first president of the International
General Electric Company, Swope was able
in three years of incessant travel from Japan
to England to "build I. G. E. from nothing
into a General Electric subsidiary owning or
having an interest in practically all of the important electric plants outside the United
States from Europe to the Orient." Then, in
1922, when Charles Coffin retired from the
presidency of the General Electric Company,
Swope was elected its president after only
three years with the company. He held this
position until his retirement on January 1,
1940, when he became honorary president.

When Mr. Swope took over in 1922, the
General Electric Company was hardly a factor
in the electric appliance business of this country. The only product it sold widely was the
incandescent electric lamp. Today its business
has become a business in consumer goods, in
refrigerators, vacuum cleaners, washing ma-

chines, radios. During his leadership General Electric ceased to be both an engineering firm and a utility operator. In 1924 it cut apart Electric Bond and Share and later other utility holdings; in 1932 it cut loose RCA.

In these years of changing enterprises Mr. Swope was supreme in the realm of production and technology, his ever-present motto the General Electric slogan: "We must keep everlastingly at the job of creating More Goods for More People at Less Cost." It was a profitable motto, for in those years General Electric stockholders never missed a dividend. And at the same time the welfare of the employees was a major consideration—there has never been a strike at the General Electric Company.

In 1936 the employees joined the CIO and have since been working under a contract. They have been given more than just those things a union contract provides, however. The 67,000 or so employees under Swope's leadership have had a profit-sharing plan, cost-of-living wage adjustments and a form of unemployment insurance. They also came to know Mr. Swope through his meetings in the shops with the men and through his answering of any questions put to him there. They have learned his preciseness as well as his understanding. Men who casually suggested, "A fine day," would as often as not have him snap back: "What's fine about it?"

During many of his years at the General Electric Company, Gerard Swope was active in social and economic activities on an even broader scale. As early as 1931 he presented the Swope Plan on Stabilization of Industry, the basic idea of which was that industry be allowed to work out its own problems through an organization of industrial or trade associations. When the NRA came into being under Roosevelt, Swope was a member of its Industrial Advisory Board. Then, when his term of service closed, he announced a plan by which business would keep its self-government, even under the NRA. It provided for a panel of eminent businessmen to act as a board of appeals on any questions that might arise in the interpretation and enforcement of national code provisions. By most businessmen it was welcomed; but *The Nation* called it a plan "for a big business dictatorship of the country," and Roosevelt opposed it.

From the NRA, Swope went to the Department of Commerce in 1933 as the first chairman of its Business Advisory and Planning Council, and in that same year acted as chairman of the Coal Arbitration Board and as a member of the first National Labor Board. In 1934 he was a member of the President's Advisory Council on Economic Security and in 1937 a member of the Advisory Council on Social Security. It was while he served on this last Council that he advanced his plan to provide old-age pensions for the 21,000,000 workers of the country —domestics, farm hands, employees of nonprofit organizations—excluded from the Federal scheme. Then in 1938 Mr. Swope served as chairman of the Industrial Relations Commission to Great Britain and Sweden.

In both his activities for his country and his activities for his company Mr. Swope, it is generally agreed, more than justifies the description in the tribute paid to him by the General Electric Company when he retired—"a man who was well ahead of other business heads in vision and sympathy for the welfare of the most humble worker."

References

Business Week p11 N 4 '33
Fortune 21:68-9+ Ja '40 por
N Y Times p1, 33 Ja 26 '41
Newsweek 9:39 My 22 '37
Hall, J. R. Tomorrow's Route pam 1932
Unofficial Observer [pseud.] New Dealers p28-73 1934
White, T. M. Famous Leaders of Industry 3d ser. p273-82 1931
Who's Who in America
Who's Who in American Jewry
Who's Who in Commerce and Industry
Who's Who in Engineering

SZOSTAKOVITCH, DIMITRI *See* Shostakovich, D.

TAGORE, SIR RABINDRANATH (tägōr' rȧ-bēn'drȧ-nȧt-h') May 6, 1861—Aug. 7, 1941 One of India's greatest poets who was famous also as playwright, philosopher, historian, musician, painter and actor; wrote about 50 dramas, nearly 100 books of verse containing more than 3,000 poems, about 40 works of fiction, innumerable songs, about 15 books of literary, political and religious essays and scores of other books; visited the United States several times on lectures tours; received the Nobel Prize in Literature in 1913; was knighted by George V in 1915; established an International University in India in 1901.

References

Asia 33:230-5 Ap '33 il pors; 34:555-7 S '34; 36:764 D '36 por; 40:304 Je '40 por
Christian Sci Mon Mag p2 My 31 '41 por
Cur Opinion 70:209-10 F '21
Liv Age 309:361-5 My 7 '21; 310:155-9 Jl 16 '21; 316:735-6 Mr 24 '23; 318: 477-8 S 8 '23; 322:95 Jl 12 '24; 329: 148-51 Ap 17 '26; 338:559-60 Jl 1 '30; 339:260-2 N '30
Mentor 9:29-30 My '21 il por
New Repub 61:199 Ja 8 '30
R of Rs 71:657-8 Je '25
Sch & Soc 34:681-6 N 21 '31
Author's and Writer's Who's Who
Bake, A. A. Indian Music and Rabindranath Tagore pam 1932
Chislett, W. Moderns and Near-Moderns p216-19 1928
Hind, C. L. More Authors and I p285-91 1922
Kunitz, S. J. ed. Living Authors 1937
Russell, G. W. Living Torch p166-7 1938

TAGORE, SIR RABINDRANATH—*Cont.*

Scudder, V. D. Privilege of Age p60-5 1939

Shanks, E. B. First Essays on Literature p251-7 1923-27

Who's Who

Obituaries

Commonweal 34:462-5 S 5 '41
Nation 153:205 S 6 '41
N Y Times p15 Ag 8 '41 por
Poetry 58:348-9 S '41
Pub W 140:469 Ag 16 '41
Sch & Soc 54:105 Ag 16 '41
Time 38:47 Ag 18 '41

TALLEY, JAMES (ELY) July 22, 1864—July 3, 1941 Heart specialist; served as professor of cardiology at the University of Pennsylvania Graduate School for 17 years; founded a hospital for babies and helped to open the Navy Base Hospital at Brest, France; acted as consultant to many hospitals; contributed to many medical journals.

References

American Medical Directory
Who's Who in the East

Obituaries

N Y Times p11 Jl 5 '41

TALMADGE, EUGENE Sept. 23, 1884- Governor of Georgia

Address: b. State Capitol, Atlanta, Ga; h. McRae, Ga.

Eugene Talmadge, Governor of Georgia, often talks against "foreign-born professors" —meaning those born out of the state of Georgia. It is undeniable that he himself was born there, the son of Thomas Romalgus and Carrie (Roberts) Talmadge, in the little town of Forsyth. He was educated at the University of Georgia, where he took his law degree in 1907; the next year he was admitted to the Georgia Bar and set up practice in the town of McRae; and in 1909 he married a moderately wealthy widow, Mattie Thurmond, who shortly afterward inherited 1,500 acres of farm land (still in Georgia). From 1912 on Talmadge farmed it and helped neighbors with legal advice to such effect that by 1918 he was solicitor of the McRae City Court, and in 1920 became attorney for Telfair County for a term of three years. In 1927 he ran for his first state office: as Commissioner of Agriculture.

Eugene Talmadge was "just a plain ol' dirt farmer." He said so, and rural voters knew it when they saw him pull up to a courthouse's steps in his horse and buggy, flicking a fly off his horse's ear with a squirt of tobacco juice, snapping his red galluses before climbing down. As Commissioner of Agriculture from 1927 to 1933 his gestures were memorable, too: the dropping of great numbers of people from the payroll for economy's sake; attacks on the "Fertilizer Trust," on Armour-Swift "control" of hog-raisers; the shipment

of several carloads of Georgia hogs to Chicago with the guarantee that they would "kill hard." Due to the peculiarities of Georgia hogs this last act apparently cost the State around $20,000, and impeachment loomed, but Talmadge not only managed to get a petition signed demanding that the proceedings be dropped but actually turned the notoriety into valuable publicity. Charged with having stolen $20,000, he assured the farmers: "Sure I stole it. But I stole it for you."

Shortly afterward, in 1932, the dirt farmers' candidate won the Democratic gubernatorial nomination from a field of six—a feat equivalent to election in the solid South. His nomination was due partly to Georgia's "rotten borough" system (three counties, with less than 1,000 voters each, cast as many votes in the primaries as the entire city of Atlanta, and Talmadge is fond of saying, "I can carry any county that ain't got street cars"), but his talents as a campaigner and the varied appeals in his platform also had something to do with it. He would reduce property taxes; he would lower license fees for automobiles; he would compel the public utilities to reduce their rates; he would take the highway department "out of the hands of the politicians and return it to the people."

Before Talmadge came to office in 1933 practically the only appointment the Governor of Georgia controlled was that of his private secretary. But this Governor had learned from his friend Huey Long. He promptly fired everyone who didn't agree with him and replaced them with his own appointees. In order to remove the Highway Commission he had to call out the State militia, so he invoked a clause in the State constitution giving him the right to "quell insurrections." He cut the payrolls of the various State services, thus reducing their operating expenses; he slashed effectually at school appropriations, according to most sources, though he himself says he actually increased them; and he reduced the cost of administering the penal system by pardoning or paroling prisoners by the hundreds. He vetoed any number of bills passed by the State Legislature.

All in all, though, Talmadge kept the first three of his promises, and cut Georgia's debt besides. When his methods were called "crooked, high-handed, unconstitutional, dictatorial and tyrannical" he had his answer ready: "A lot of people say they like what I did, but don't like the way I did it. I don't either, but if a bunch of hogs get into your fields or your garden or your flowers and won't come out when you say 'sooey sooey, sooey,' then you have to use the language and methods that hogs and pigs understand." An article in the *American Mercury* for June 1934 was titled: *Georgia At Last Has a Good Governor*. George Creel, writing in *Collier's* in December 1935, said: ". . . there is general admission that the Wild Man from Sugar Creek, honest, efficient and economical, has made one of the best Governors in the history of the state."

Labor, however, neither liked what he did nor the way he did it. In September 1934 (reportedly after a conference with leading textile manufacturers, who contributed $20,000 to his next campaign fund), the Governor decided to do something about the textile strikes in Georgia. He called out 3,700 National Guardsmen; they seized pickets and put them into an open concentration camp without trial; and for long after that martial law made it a crime in Georgia to picket within "a radius of 500 feet" of any National Guardsman. According to one writer, Talmadge's was an alliance of the small property-owner, the farmer who himself hires a few sharecroppers, with the road contractor and millowner "against factory labor, farm labor and the wretched sharecropper." According to Benjamin Stolberg, even as Commissioner of Agriculture, Talmadge had been "in covert intimacy with the Black Shirts, the 'American Fascisti'" who specialized in night riding among Negro sharecroppers. He himself has admitted that he once helped to flog a Negro.

In 1934, when Talmadge was renominated and re-elected, he nevertheless carried 156 out of 159 counties on a platform that had not a single New Deal plank. It was not until Harry Hopkins' (see sketch this issue) action the next year, when he refused to let Talmadge's staff administer relief any longer and put a female Federal agent in control, that the Governor's enmity toward the Roosevelt Administration became open, however. He assailed AAA's "scarcity program," although as Commissioner of Agriculture he himself had advocated a "cotton holiday." He wanted no relief at all—"let 'em starve!" He didn't want skilled labor to have more than 10 cents an hour or unskilled more than 5 cents under the State Relief Administration. He wanted to abolish TVA, NRA, PWA, WPA, social security, old-age pensions. According to Washington's version he had obtained everything he could from Federal agencies for his State and had reduced State expenditures until the Federal Government was carrying almost the entire relief and school burden of Georgia, and was now busying himself with unfair comparisons between Federal "extravagance" and his own economy. According to his own version he was a Jeffersonian Democrat—"I believe the less guv'ment the better"—who was defending the American Constitution and the private enterprise system and who would never forgive Roosevelt for having "killed religion in the hearts of the American people."

With Huey Long he planned to "stop Roosevelt" in 1936, and at the beginning of that year he called a "Grass Roots Convention of Southern Democrats" at Macon, Georgia for that purpose. John Raskob, Pierre du Pont and other heavy contributors apparently hoped that if a third Presidential candidate ran, a Republican might be able to step into the White House. The scantily attended convention, at which literature was distributed showing Mrs. Roosevelt with two Negroes, endorsed Talmadge "as a candidate to lead this country out of the morass of Communism"; and the next day he announced plans for a country-wide speaking tour against the Administration.

Keystone

EUGENE TALMADGE

As it turned out, however, Huey Long was assassinated not long afterward. Talmadge's Presidential boom was a failure, and since he couldn't succeed himself for a third term as Governor he ran for the seat of Georgia's junior Senator. He even took back some of the things he had said about Roosevelt, announcing, in July 1936: "I'll support the President as long as I think he's right... I want to protect him from bureaucrats like Wallace and Hopkins." His platform, which included the abolition of tax-exempt government bonds, a Federal budget of less than $1,000,000 a year, 2 cent postage and the abolition of the Federal income tax, didn't get him the Democratic nomination, but he remained undiscouraged, going back to practicing law as a member of the firm of Talmadge, Fraser & Camp and keeping his name before the public eye.

In 1938 an excellent opportunity arose. Roosevelt was favoring a New Deal candidate against senior Senator Walter F. George, and Talmadge was quick to take advantage of the situation by entering the race. This time Big Business was the target of his campaign: "Senator George is very smart... Whenever the rights of the people are violated, our senior Senator spoke on one side and voted on the other..." But Talmadge's own program would "lead us to the Promised Land," he assured Georgia. "I will provide a homestake and a grubstake for the unemployed. I will protect the farmer and the worker with high tariffs. I will expand the CCC camps. Why, fellow Georgians, I will make America another Garden of Eden!" When the polls closed election night Talmadge was far in the lead, but when he woke up George was ahead. Crying that he had been "counted out in 30 counties," he filed protest, but the election boards ruled against him.

TALMADGE, EUGENE—*Continued*

During the next months, it is reported, Talmadge came to an understanding with Georgia's Governor Rivers, and Talmadge men began getting positions in Rivers' administration. In 1940 Talmadge ran for Governor for the third time with increased support. "I'm going to stick to Georgia this time," he promised. In the elections 162,916 votes gave him the Governorship once more (there were more than 1,500,000 adults in Georgia according to the 1940 census, but there is also a poll tax). And a few hours after his inauguration in January 1941, according to the New York *Times*, he once more turned the Governorship into a "practical dictatorship." During one session of the legislature he obtained the passage of a bill authorizing him to handle all state funds and "maneuvered a resolution extending the Governor's term to four years and specifically extending his own present term."

After that date the "Wild Man from Sugar Creek"—with his eye on the United States Senate, according to many commentators—began earning more nationwide publicity than during any of his previous administrations. Accusing two prominent Georgian educators ("furriners") of advocating the equality of Negroes and Whites, a charge which they denied, he first tried unsuccessfully to get them dismissed by the Board of Regents of Georgia University; then, in July 1941, he revised the Board of Regents and tried again with a board which gave him personal control of the State university system. They were dismissed by a vote of ten to five, but a storm of protest arose both within Georgia and without. Some even recalled that in 1936 Talmadge had been responsible for such statements as: "Hitler is a mighty fine man. . . The man must be helping his people or they'd put him out. Ain't it so?" "What you need in New York is not La Guardia but Mussolini. A little castor oil would go a long way toward starting the wheels of industry goin' again." In August the Governor advocated burning all books favoring racial co-education. In October the Southern University Conference dropped the University of Georgia from its ranks because of "political interference," and students on its campus burned the Governor in effigy; in December the Southern Association of Colleges and Secondary Schools dropped 10 state colleges of Georgia from its accredited list for the same reason.

In spite of his easily caricatured "Harold Lloyd glasses" and "Napoleonic haircut," Talmadge is a "dynamic and powerful stump speaker," a man of "strength and driving force" who, in George Creel's words, is "utterly without doubt as to the justice and wisdom of his own judgment, decisions and actions." Nor is he without charm. He sometimes dresses up in Wild West clothes for photographic purposes; his "How you all?" is "constant and hearty"; he enjoys wrestling,

fox hunting and deer shooting with the men; he says he has never been tired in his life and that he knows three-fourths of the citizens of Georgia by their first names. It is rumored that he makes political capital out of being a dirt farmer (he still has a 1,100-acre farm in Monroe County), but can really be grammatical when he tries. He is a good Baptist who refused to consider prohibition repeal in 1933, a member of Sigma Nu and Phi Kappa Phi, a Mason, an Odd Fellow, a Woodman of the World, the father of two sons and two daughters, and the owner and editor of *The Statesman*, a strongly anti-Negro newspaper.

References

Am Mercury 32:241-5 Je '34
Collier's 96:31+ D 21 '35 por; 97:12-13+ My 2 '36 il; 108:17+ D 6 '41 por
Lit Digest 116:9 Jl 15 '33 por; 116:30 S 2 '33 por; 118:5 S 22 '34 por; 120:150 N 9 '35 por; 121:5 F 1 '36 por; 121:9 Mr 7 '36
Nation 142:269-71 Mr 4 '36; 142:316-18 Mr 11 '36; 153:93-4 Ag 2 '41
New Repub 86:35-7 F 19 '36
N Y Times IV p10 Ja 9 '41 por; IV p8 Jl 27 '41 por
Newsweek 1:8+ Jl 1 '33 por; 3:10+ Mr 31 '34 por; 5:14 Je 15 '35 por; 7:12-13 F 8 '36 pors; 8:11-12 S 19 '36 il por; 18:50 Jl 28 '41
Time 28:10-11 S 7 '36 por (cover); 37:55 Je 30 '41
Michie, A. A. and Ryhlick, F. Dixie Demagogues p182-201 1939
Unofficial Observer [pseud.] American Messiahs p172-92 1935
Who's Who in America
Who's Who in Government
Who's Who in Law

TAYLOR, EDWARD T(HOMAS) June 19, 1858—Sept. 3, 1941

Democratic Representative from Colorado; oldest member of the House of Representatives; first elected in 1909; chairman of the important House Appropriations Committee; one of nine Representatives in the history of the Chamber to sit in 15 consecutive terms.

References

Who's Who in America
Who's Who in Government
Who's Who in Law
Who's Who in the Nation's Capital

Obituaries

N Y Times p21 S 4 '41 por

TAYLOR, HENRY O(SBORN) Dec. 5, 1856—Apr. 13, 1941

Author and philosopher; one of the world's foremost authorities on the history of civilization; delivered the Lowell lectures at Harvard University in 1917 and the West lectures at Stanford in 1920; devoted ten years to preparing his masterpiece, *The Medieval Mind,* which went into five editions by 1938.

References

Who's Who in America

Obituaries

N Y Times p17 Ap 14 '41 por
Pub W 139:1749 Ap 26 '41

TAYLOR, RICHARD Sept. 18, 1902- Cartoonist; artist
Address: Putnam Park Rd, Bethel, Conn.

"Everything I ever attempted in the way of serious art seemed to me to have a humorous streak in it," says cartoonist Richard Taylor. "I've served my time at playing second fiddle to Picasso and the Paris Boys of the Modern Movement, turning out very bad abstractions in the best Post-Cubist manner. When I stick to humor I think I at least do something with a degree of originality, however small, and that what I do has some power. I came to the conclusion that I would rather be a good buffoon than a mediocre serious artist."

This artist who is famous for his "bug-eyed characters" is finding, after making this decision, that more and more people are taking his buffoonery seriously. His first exhibition of his "unpublished" humorous pictures at the Walker Galleries in New York City in December 1940 inspired enthusiastic comments. "The exhibition provides a happy hour backstage with a deft draftsman whose eye for humanity's foibles is sure and keen," said the *Art Digest.* "His pen, dipped in just enough acid, pierces the very core of fatuousness, pomposity and other frailties of our characters." The *Journal-American's* critic commented: "These drawings, both in black and white and water color, have such fecundity of invention, such beguiling incongruity, such variations of unexpectedness . . . that one might lose sight of the amazing skill of the draftsmanship and the charming color patterns of the papers."

Since this first exhibition there have been others—at Hudson's Gallery in Detroit, at the Albright Art Gallery in Buffalo; shows were given in June 1941 at the Addison Gallery in Andover, Massachusetts and at the Valentine Gallery, New York in December 1941; and the directors of the Whitney Museum, the Museum of Modern Art, and the Metropolitan Museum of Art in New York City, the Museum of Fine Arts in Boston and several private galleries have bought some of his pictures. The art world finds Richard Taylor a far from mediocre artist. And a delighted public continues to grin at the fantasies he continues to publish in the *New Yorker, Collier's* and the *Saturday Evening Post.*

Richard Taylor's "bad dreams about snipe-nosed, chocolate-eyed ladies" have been said to be inspired by "visions of crumpetlike forms which visit him after a heavy meal." He himself admits to having "little visions." But, he hastens to explain: "I don't mean

that I go into a trance or anything like that, but I do see, more or less completely, whatever I draw before it is drawn. I never have any trouble getting ideas; all I have to do is get into a corner somewhere where it is reasonably quiet and let my mind wander. At

RICHARD TAYLOR

once my imagination becomes filled with the people I draw."

Some come out purely funny, as in the scene of a shoe salesman addressing himself to the sizable foot of a well-set-up woman and asking her: "Now which is the bad little piggie-wiggie?" Sometimes they are satirical—one is the picture of the sculptor starting to attack a monumental block of granite and calling down to the model: "Smile." There are others which "have to do with a kind of eerie and oozy world wherein women hover like vultures over men who rarely escape." And there are others even more sinister—as in *Scourge,* which reveals the horrors of country living.

The artist who is responsible for all these was born in Fort William, Ontario, Canada, of English descent on his father's side; Scottish-Dutch on his mother's. As a child he was always drawing, and at 12 he began his formal art education "under a conservative landscape and figure painter, an associate member of the Royal Canadian Academy." Later Taylor studied at the Ontario College of Art and the Los Angeles School of Art and Design. "No university education. No degrees. No honors." Throughout school, he confesses, he was very dull in everything but history and literary composition, in which he got high marks; "had no mind whatever for mathematics or problems of any sort." He still doesn't, and he seldom guesses the right culprit in the many mystery stories he reads.

TAYLOR, RICHARD—*Continued*

Taylor first began drawing cartoons in 1927 for the *Goblin* Magazine, a Toronto University publication which by that time had become a professional journal. He drew for it until it folded and then "lived precariously doing all sorts of commercial art in Toronto." He painted in his spare time, successfully enough to exhibit with the Ontario Society of Artists and once with the Royal Canadian Academy, though he was never elected to membership in either body.

In 1935 Taylor came to New York with illustrations for a book. When he submitted them to Simon & Schuster, the editors liked the drawings but not the book, and turned it down. Clifton Fadiman (see sketch this issue) suggested, though, that Taylor try the *New Yorker* Magazine and helped him to introduce his work there. Shortly after, his first drawing appeared in this magazine, and since then his work has appeared there regularly, as well as in *Collier's* and the *Saturday Evening Post*. He has also livened various advertising campaigns while continuing to work on the humorous fantasies he first began to draw in 1940.

Richard Taylor does most of his work in Bethel, Connecticut, where he lives in a forest beside a pond full of bull frogs. He is fond of "beer, faded wallpaper and rain," uninterested in sports of any kind except tennis ("plays poorly") and swimming ("after a fashion").

References

Collier's 106:66 S 28 '40 self por
Who's Who in American Art

TEIXEIRA-GOMES, MANUEL (tä-shä′rà gō′mǐsh) May 27, 1862—Oct. 18, 1941 President of Portugal from 1923 to 1925, when he resigned; was the first Portuguese Ambassador to London; represented his country at the Versailles Peace Conference and meetings of the League of Nations; first Minister Plenipotentiary of the Portuguese Republic to the Court of St. James.

Obituaries

N Y Herald Tribune p42 O 19 '41

TELEKI, PAUL, COUNT (tä′lä-kē) Nov. 1, 1879—Apr. 3, 1941 Premier of Hungary who committed suicide, according to a report, rather than submit to Hungary's entry into the Second World War; called the "great tightrope walker" because of his trying to balance the difficult feat of aligning Hungary with the Axis and yet keeping her from falling under complete German domination; public career was dominated chiefly by a desire to restore to Hungary the lands lost by the Trianon treaties at the end of the First World War; expert geographer who taught at Budapest University; was made Foreign Minister in 1920; in 1938 was made Minister of Education; became Premier in 1939.

References

Geog R 30:684 O '40
Time 33:24 Je 26 '39 por
International Who's Who
Who's Who in Central and East-
Europe

Obituaries

N Y Times p1+ Ap 4 '41 por

TENNENT, DAVID HILT May 28, 1873—Jan. 14, 1941 Biologist and professor at Bryn Mawr College; member of the Bryn Mawr faculty for 38 years; conducted investigations in marine biology and was engaged in active research on the photodynamic effects of vital dyes; president of the American Society of Zoologists in 1916 and of the American Society of Naturalists in 1937.

References

American Men of Science
Leaders in Education 1932
Who's Who in America

Obituaries

Sci ns 93:103 Ja 31 '41
N Y Times p23 Ja 15 '41 por
Sch & Soc 53:115 Ja 25 '41

TERBOVEN, JOSEF (tĕr-bō′vĕn) May 23, 1898- Reich Commissioner for Norway

Address: Essen, Bädekerstrasse 23, Germany

One of Nazi Germany's most vociferous proponents of the *herrenvolk*, or rule by a superior caste of Aryan mental and physical giants, is a little man with a mild, negative face behind spectacles. He is Josef Terboven, Reich Commissioner for Norway, who was once a bank clerk and who—despite the lofty honors heaped on him by a grateful Führer—still looks like one.

In spite of his insignificant appearance, Terboven's position is by no means insignificant. As administrator of German rule in a country which, even by Nazi admission, is seething with rebellion, Terboven's efforts have not been crowned with the success that marked his earlier assignments for the Nazi Party; and at times it appears that momentous events threaten to overwhelm this little troubleshooter of the Third Reich.

Josef Terboven was born in Essen, Germany on May 23, 1898 and came of age during the bleak post-War period. It is possible that his first contact with Hitlerism was made at Munich when the struggling Nazi Party was trying to get a foothold in that city. Terboven was attending the university there, after prior study at the University of Freiberg. At a time when thousands of declassed and disillusioned German youth were unemployed and desperately seeking a way out through the various political parties arising in Germany, Terboven managed to get a job in a bank. It is obvious that he did not regard this position as equal to his talents, for in 1925 he became active in the National Socialist Party of Essen.

Terboven's role in the growth of the Party can best be explained by the ground swell that, almost from the first, threatened to rend it apart. Gregor Strasser, an ex-Communist, originally gave Hitlerism its "mass base" by luring to neo-Leftist slogans the industrial proletariat of the Ruhr. On the other hand, Hitler, no anti-capitalist, wished to convince the iron and steel magnates that the real program of the Nazi Party was actually to crush radicalism and trade-union agitation.

In this impending schism Hitler found Terboven an invaluable ally. The young party activist had already proved his worth to National Socialism by his envenomed speech making. His flair for invective, rivaled only by Hitler's, was hated and feared by the political opposition, and had attracted considerable attention. He was made *Gauleiter* of the Essen branch of the Party, in Strasser's Rhineland stronghold.

Terboven denounced the radical faction and proceeded to cajole and bully the Rhine millionaires into financial support of the Nazi Party. In this he was spectacularly successful. Even municipal government officials were soon eating out of his hand. When Hermann Goering (see sketch this issue), himself no amateur in the art of prying open pocketbooks, took a trip to Essen, he was awe-struck at Terboven's feat in having persuaded Franz Bracht, the Mayor of Essen, to open in Terboven's name a secret account of funds from the local treasury. This was the time when Terboven purchased the first of a series of eight-cylinder Mercèdes cars. A psychiatric study of Terboven's love for display—he is inordinately ostentatious—might find it a compensation for his unimpressive physique.

One of the Essen *Gauleiter's* major accomplishments was to persuade the Ruhr magnates to purchase the *Essener National Zeitung* in order to launch an anti-Communist crusade. Terboven was made publisher, and the paper was transformed into an organ of National Socialism. His career was temporarily clouded when a fellow party member brought him up on morals charges involving the former's daughter, but the case was quashed by a friendly judge.

Although Terboven's part in linking the Party with the financial sources of industrial Germany is clear, his aid in liquidating the Strasser opposition is not. In June 1934 Terboven's marriage was celebrated with great pomp at his luxurious villa in Essen. High officials from the entire province came laden with gifts; Hitler and Goering arrived to serve as witnesses. No one dreamed that only two days later, on June 30th, there would occur the famous purge of Strasser, together with a heterogeneous following of Reichswehr and Storm Troop leaders. In all, 700 Nazis were killed in cold blood. Hitler's presence at the wedding was apparently premeditated as a means of throwing the opposition off guard.

On another occasion Terboven figured in important Nazi plans when he was the subject of a testimonial dinner attended by 32 consuls and consuls general. The French Consul

JOSEF TERBOVEN

General Dobler waxed lyrical in his praise of Terboven and the Führer. The spirit of good will flowed with the champagne, and diplomats regarded the gathering as an omen of international fealty. Two days later the world was stunned by the news that German troops had marched into the demilitarized Rhineland.

In 1941 Terboven is still Governor of the Rhine Province and district leader of Essen. He is reported to have been a practitioner of "the strategy of terror" long before he was sent to Norway; this is undoubtedly the reason he was selected to subdue the Norwegians. During the Munich crisis and after, Terboven's threats against the Czechs and other peoples were freely offered.

Terboven reached Norway on April 23, 1940. Apparently he was the personal representative of Heinrich Himmler (see sketch this issue), head of the Gestapo, the organization of secret police entrusted with the task of bringing the recalcitrant Northerners to heel. At first the Nazis promised, however, that his role would be temporary, that he would act merely as intermediary between Germany and the Norwegian Administration.

But under Nazi domination of Norway conflict immediately piled on conflict. Major Vidkun Quisling (see sketch 1940 Annual), leader of the Norwegian Nazi Party, the *Nasjonal Samling,* failed completely to gain the backing of the Norwegian people. Prominent churchmen protested Quisling's meddling with the Church. Members of the Supreme Court resigned in a body over interference with the administration of justice. Workers went on strike because of the arrest of their trade-union leaders. Terboven abolished the Norwegian monarchy and the country's parliamentary party, with the exception of the *Samling* (Quisling's Party). But even the puppet parliament was unable to garner the

TERBOVEN, JOSEF—*Continued*

legal two-thirds vote necessary to make official the deposal of King Haakon, who had fled to England.

Silent opposition was shown the invaders by the open display of patriotic symbols and through forms of non-cooperation. General von Falkenhorst, the military occupation official, is believed to have held Terboven somewhat in check for a time, but he was eventually sent to Finland to command German troops there in the war against Russia.

And not all Norwegian opposition was passive. Food trains bound for Germany were derailed; unexplained landslides engulfed Nazi lines; road signs were removed, and secret anti-Quisling newspapers appeared. Quisling had to bear the brunt of National Socialism's unpopularity, and his position became uncertain. In May 1941 he was requested by Terboven to turn back 500,000 *kröner* in state money which he had allegedly taken from the Oslo Finance Ministry for needs of the Party.

As popular unrest mounted, particularly after Germany declared war on Russia, the puppet parliament gave Terboven the power to declare a national state emergency. A state of civil siege was finally declared in the area around Oslo in August 1941. Radios in the coastal areas of Skagerrak and the North Sea, and in five cities on the Swedish border, were confiscated, and a few days later three Norwegians were shot by German firing squads, the first cases of capital punishment in the history of modern Norway. When, on September 9, 1941, British troops suddenly swooped on Spitzbergen, rescuing a group of French soldiers and Norwegian and Russian coal miners and leaving the famed Spitzbergen coal mines in flames, the Nazis had their strongest intimation to date that trouble threatened Norway from without as well as from within.

Since the German High Command indicated it would be tied up in the Russian campaign throughout the winter, Terboven issued orders for Norwegian families to turn in a major portion of their blankets for use by the Nazi troops on the Eastern front, a measure which scarcely served to increase the popularity of the occupying forces. This, however, did not disturb Terboven, who declared in a public statement: "It is a matter of indifference to Germany if several thousand persons, perhaps several hundred thousand Norwegian men, women and children, die of hunger or cold this winter as the result of war."

Meanwhile negotiations were under way to lay the basis for Norway's future role in Hitler's "New Order." It was reported that at the conclusion of the War Terboven planned to withdraw, leaving the regime in charge of a Quislingite, with Quisling himself assuming an important state position (providing the Quisling Party had gained popular roots). In the meantime troops were to be retained "for security of the state" and the future Norway was to cede its most vital harbors to Germany as naval bases.

Yet the continued failure of Germany's efforts to pacify Norway can be prophesied from the ever-growing signs of open and secret opposition, and the ever more violent reprisals by the Nazis. With Quisling's adherents, according to his own figures, estimated at no more than 40,000, or less than one per cent of the total population, and with the future fraught with uncertainty, the position of the little ex-bank clerk from Essen becomes increasingly unenviable.

References

> Life 11:26 S 22 '41 por
> N Y Sun p24 Ap 26 '40; p29 S 12 '41
> Newsweek 17:30+ My 12 '41
> Time 35:34 My 6 '40
> Wer ist's?

TERZIAN, HARUTYUN G. (tĕr'zhän härū'tĭ-ŭn) 1888(?)—Sept. 2, 1941 Outstanding authority on the production of carbureted and blue water gas; spent nearly thirty years in operation and development work in the gas industry; born in Turkish Armenia; taught at the American University at Beirut for three years; associate of United Engineers and Constructors, Inc.; formerly worked for the Syracuse (New York) Lighting Company.

Obituaries

> N Y Times p21 S 4 '41

THOMAS, FREEMAN FREEMAN-, 1ST MARQUESS OF WILLINGDON *See* Willingdon, F. F.-T., 1st Marquess of

THOMPSON, GEORGE L. Nov. 22, 1864 —Sept. 1, 1941 New York State Senator; senior member of the New York Legislature in years of service; chairman of the Senate Finance Committee; served in the State Senate for 33 years.

References

> Who's Who in Government
> Who's Who in New York

Obituaries

> N Y Times p18 S 2 '41

THOMPSON, JAMES WESTFALL June 3, 1869—Sept. 30, 1941 Historian; professor of history at the University of Chicago, 1895 to 1932; from 1932 to 1939 Sidney Hellman Ehrman professor of European history at the University of California; internationally known scholar in the field of medieval history; author of many books, the latest of which, *History of Historical Writing,* he regarded as the culmination of his life work; former vice-president of the American Historical Association.

References

> Sat Eve Post 197:44 My 23 '25
> Leaders in Education 1941
> Who's Who in America

Obituaries

> N Y Times p21 O 1 '41

THOMPSON, REGINALD CAMPBELL

Aug. 21, 1876—May (?), 1941 World-famous English archeologist and Assyriologist; worked in the British Museum and University of Chicago; conducted excavations at Nineveh, Carchemish, Abu Shahrain and Wadi Sarga; wrote extensively on archeology and Assyriology for scientific publications.

References

Author's and Writer's Who's Who
Who's Who

Obituaries

N Y Times p23 My 27 '41

THORE, WENDELL PHILLIPS

1879(?) —Mar. 13, 1941 Leading advocate of the Townsend plan in Massachusetts; devoted a quarter of a century to sponsoring old-age assistance legislation; former State leader of the old Progressive Party; well known in local and State politics; ran for Governor in 1914 and also for the United States Senate.

Obituaries

N Y Times p17 Mr 15 '41

THORNDIKE, EDWARD L(EE) Aug. 31, 1874- Educator

Address: h. Montrose, N. Y.

Dr. Edward L. Thorndike, educational psychologist and author of the intelligence test bearing his name, became an emeritus professor at Columbia University in July 1940. He has been kept busy since then. In 1941 he lectured at the California Institute of Technology. In 1942 he will be William James lecturer at Harvard University. He has also continued his studies of the social scene begun in 1935 with a large grant from the Carnegie Foundation— studies on a far vaster scale than even he had dreamed of when he was a young student testing the responses and intelligence of fish, baby chicks and primates.

When Dr. Thorndike's researches make headlines, as they did on the publication of his study of newspapers from 28 cities, it is because the startling and oftentimes controversial conclusions result from principles of scientific measurement. In a recent study, published January 1941 in the *Scientific Monthly*, he describes as slanderous the claim that today's newspapers are purely commercial enterprises. "The newspaper of today," says Dr. Thorndike, "with considerable disregard for the cravings of the populace, provides a conventional mixture of facts about what has happened during the past 24 hours at home and abroad, descriptions of athletic contests, statistics about prices, fiction and humor in words and pictures, and notes about women's styles, housekeeping, politics, personal health and happiness, and occasionally about the impersonal world of truth and beauty."

A teacher since 1898, Dr. Thorndike is well known for his work in educational psychology and educational statistics. His first papers,

bearing such curious titles as *The Psychology of Fishes* and *The Mental Life of Monkeys*, brought him to the attention of leaders in the field of education, who admired his scholarship and his ability to tackle learning problems scientifically. This work was to have a significance far beyond the limits of his original field. In the 441 items listed in a recent

EDWARD L. THORNDIKE

bibliography—from an issue of the *Teachers College Record* commemorating his 40 years at Columbia—many reflect his contributions to social science. Even the profit motive has been fair game for this educator's probing. In 1936 he published his opinion that within specific fields, even cultural ones, the profit motive acted as a fair measure of value and therefore "in our civilization pecuniary profit or loss is regarded as proof and a measure of competence and achievement."

Born in Williamsburg, Massachusetts, August 31, 1874, Edward Lee Thorndike was the son of the Reverend Edward R. and Abby B. (Ladd) Thorndike. He took his first B. A. in 1895 at Wesleyan University, Middletown, Connecticut, and a second at Harvard the following year, staying to work for his M. A. (1897). At Harvard, William James recognized the promise of the young graduate student, and at Columbia, where he took his Doctor's Degree in 1898, Cattell and Boas initiated him into what was then a novelty in psychology, the statistical treatment of test results.

In that year he accepted an instructorship in teaching at the College for Women, Western Reserve University. Dean James E. Russell of Teachers College knew of his experimental studies of the behavior of monkeys and thought of it, with scholarly equanimity, as "a pretty good steppingstone to a study of the nature and behavior of children." He came to see

THORNDIKE, EDWARD L.—*Continued*

Thorndike at Western Reserve. Said Russell: "At that time neither the term nor the subject of educational psychology had been created; but I had a notion that a field of study so obviously fundamental to educational theory and practice should have both a name and a sponsor in the kind of teachers' college which I was planning. After listening to one class exercise, I was satisfied that I had found the right man for the job. I promptly offered him an instructorship and he as characteristically accepted it at once."

As a result of this interview Thorndike came to Teachers College in 1899 as instructor in genetic psychology. His studies in animal psychology were already well known to educators and had even received some attention in the press. A typical experiment, conducted with monkeys, had to do with food placed in boxes that could be easily opened. It was found that monkeys learned from their own impulses when these brought the desired results, while they learned little, if anything, from being taught. Monkeys, Thorndike stated, "occupy an intermediate position in every main psychological feature between mammals in general and the human species."

Thorndike chose measurement as a key to scientific progress in education. To critics who point to the fluidity of action he says: "Everything that exists exists in quantity." Even the mind "is a host of highly particularized and independent faculties." In the course of his work he devised scales for measuring excellence of reading, English composition, handwriting and drawing, and intelligence tests for various grade levels. He has applied exact quantitative methods to the study of human nature, behavior and education, produced measurements of mental fatigue, correlation between various abilities, inheritability of intellect and character and the rate and conditions of effective learning. "His service to pedagogical procedure," says Dean Russell, "has revolutionized educational administration." A recent example of his applications of psychology is given by the definitions and illustrative sentences in the Thorndike Century dictionaries (*Junior Dictionary* 1935; *Senior Dictionary* 1941).

For years there were three Thorndike brothers on the Columbia faculty. According to a jingle circulated among Columbia students:

English, history and psych,
Each one has its own Thorndike.

They were Ashley, the literary scholar and an authority on Shakespeare who died in 1933, Lynn, the historian, and Edward, who got his adjunct professorship in 1901 and the chair of educational psychology in 1904. From 1900 to 1902 he also headed the Department of Comparative Psychology at Woods Hole. On August 29, 1900 he married Elizabeth Moulton of Lynn, Massachusetts. Of the five children born of this marriage, four are living.

A holder of numerous degrees from American and European universities, Dr. Thorndike is the author of several standard psychology texts, one of the first of which was *Educational Psychology* (1903). The next year he published *Mental and Social Measurements* and in 1911 *Animal Intelligence*. In-between were numerous texts and monographs that often anticipated more elaborate works. He has done research on the psychology of arithmetic, the psychology of algebra, and many other curricular questions. One of his best-known works, *A Teacher's Word Book* (1921), is a pioneering effort in the vocabulary field.

From 1917 to 1918 Dr. Thorndike was chairman of a committee on the classification of personnel for the United States Army. He has worked several times on grants from the Carnegie Corporation, through whose help in 1927 he launched a series of investigations into the psychology of learning.

At first glance it might seem ironical that the author of the CAVD intelligence test and of such learned works as *Your City* (1939) and *Human Nature and the Social Order* (1940) should be best known to the general public because of the psychological experiments with animals and fish. In these studies, however, the major objective was to trace the evolution of the intellect. Thorndike's Law of Effect, a law that had its origin in the early tests, was ultimately placed on a stronger basis by ingenious experiments in human learning. And as these researches developed Dr. Thorndike came to the conclusion that repetition and reward were important factors in learning. In 1932 he reported on a series of six experiments with baby chicks: "Rewarding a connection strengthened it; punishing weakened it little or not at all."

A colleague at Teachers College remarked that Thorndike has always been a center of controversy. This has been true not merely of his conclusions based on measurable factors but of his writings in the social science field, where generalities have been inevitable. *Human Nature and the Social Order* starts with original human nature (the genes) as a basis and works down to acquired and environmental additions. It is in studies of this nature that his theories run counter to those of many prominent thinkers. As his writings bear upon the sociological it is not surprising, therefore, that he is thought of as a defender of "capitalism or the system of private enterprise," even though such a designation side-steps the issue of his positive contributions to social science.

Thorndike's eyes are keen and clear, his expression one of quiet concentration. One gets the impression that he has lived seriously, but has enjoyed life. This is testified to by Dean Russell, who writes both of Thorndike, the educator, whose contributions to educational psychology would perhaps resist even his own talents at measuring, and Thorndike, the man, "whose open-mindedness, native honesty, sympathetic understanding, good judgment, readiness to spend himself for others, abounding good will and genial cooperation have given him the place he holds in the affection of all who have had the good fortune to come under his influence."

"In developing the subject of educational psychology and in making it a fit study for students in all departments," said Dean Russell, "Professor Thorndike has shaped the character of the college in its youth. Quick to size up a problem, clear and direct in his thinking about it, almost uncanny in his methods of approach to a solution of it, prompt and positive in giving his conclusions once he had worked his way through it—these traits were as characteristic of him at the beginning of his career as they have come to be peculiarly his own in later years. His mental equipment and his methods of work would have made for success in almost any field of human endeavor."

A member of many learned societies, Dr. Thorndike was president of the American Association for the Advancement of Science in 1934. He is also a past president of the New York Academy of Sciences and of the American Psychological Association.

References

N Y Times p25 Ap 12 '40
Sch & Soc 39 :87-8 Ja 20 '34
Sci ns 79 :88-9 F 23 '41
Sci Mo 38 :187-9 F '34 por
Teachers Col Rec 41 :696-8 My '40 por
(frontispiece)
Curti, M. E. Social Ideas of American Educators p459-98 1935
Leaders in Education 1941
Murchison, C. ed. Psychological Register 1932
Who's Who Among North American Authors
Who's Who in America
Winkler, J. K. and Bromberg, W. Mind Explorers p251-84 1939

TIMBERLAKE, CHARLES B(ATEMAN) Sept. 25, 1854—May 31, 1941 Republican Representative from the Second Colorado Congressional District in the House of Representatives from 1915 to 1933; one of his main objectives, which he was never able to carry out completely, was the levying of a high tariff and restrictions on the import of sugar from the Philippine Islands; fought for equitable freight rates for the Rocky Mountain region.

References

Who's Who in America
Who's Who in Government

Obituaries

N Y Times p41 Je 1 '41 por

TIMOSHENKO, SEMYON (KONSTANTINOVICH) (tĭ-mŏ-shĕn'kŏ sĕ-myôn') 1895-Marshal of the Red Army

With the Soviet Union and Germany locked in a death struggle, the attention of the world has been focused on Red Army leaders. The

Sovfoto

SEMYON TIMOSHENKO

attack on the Soviet Union showed Hitler's religious adherence to the program laid out in *Mein Kampf*. Although the Russians may not have expected the Blitzkrieg to strike at the precise moment it did, there is no doubt that they had visualized its possibility and had prepared to meet it. The man who on July 11, 1941 was placed in command of the main Russian line on the central front directly west of Moscow was Marshal Timoshenko, who is a member of the Supreme Military Council headed by Stalin and who until Stalin took charge had been People's Commissar of Defense. In October of that same year he was shifted from heavily beleaguered Moscow to a command in the South where at that time Germans were threatening to cut Russia off from its oil and greatest remaining industrial centers.

A veteran of the Civil War, schooled in Soviet military academies, Semyon Konstantinovich Timoshenko is a typical product of the Russian military caste. He was born in 1895, in a small poverty-stricken Bessarabian village of Furmanka. At that time Bessarabia was a part of Russia; it was taken over by her neighbor Romania during the Civil War and was reoccupied by the Soviet Union in 1940. Son of a poor peasant, Konstantine Timoshenko by name, young Semyon attended the village school and later worked as a farmhand for the well-to-do peasants ("kulaks" in the later Soviet terminology). According to a Welsh schoolmaster, he is the son of Charles Jenkins, a Welsh technician who married a Russian girl; but the Russians take this story no more seriously than the old joke that he is an Irishman named Tim O'Shenko. He wanted to become a village schoolmaster, but his parents couldn't afford to send him to the city for schooling.

TIMOSHENKO, SEMYON—Continued

In 1915 he was conscripted into the Imperial Army and sent to the Western Front, where he was trained in the use of machine guns, the first shipment of which had then come into Russia from the United States.

The regime of the Czarist Army did not seem to agree with the young soldier. His service came to an abrupt end in 1917, when he was court-martialed and jailed for striking an officer, but the Revolution of 1917 set him free. The War went on under the Provisional Government; when that Government was overthrown, Timoshenko's regiment, which had early shown revolutionary tendencies, killed its officers and joined the Red Army. In the years that followed Timoshenko fought White Russians, foreign intervention troops and occasional bandits on many fronts—and invariably on horseback. He was sent with his brigade to put down a restoration movement among the Don Cossacks. In 1918 he joined a Black Sea partisan detachment, in which he was elected, as was the custom, platoon and later squadron commander.

In 1919, after Budenny's (see sketch this issue) famous First Mounted Army was formed, he was given the command of the 6th and 4th Cavalry Divisions. His was a guerrilla brand of warfare. With his highly mobile regiment he moved and struck swiftly, constantly harrying the unsuspecting foe. The story is still alive of his unexpected appearance in Rostov, where he surrounded the hotel in which the White officers were having their supper and came in to tell them, coolly: "Finish your supper and follow me into the basement; I am Timoshenko of the 4th Cavalry Division of the Red Army."

In 1919 he was entrenched in Tsaritsyn (now Stalingrad), which was being besieged by a formidable White Army force. It was then that he met Stalin and Voroshilov (see sketch this issue), who were commanding the Red Army defense forces. He became very friendly with Stalin; their friendship was to last for 22 years with excellent results for Timoshenko. Stalin later stated that it was Timoshenko who was responsible for "the foundation of the Red Army as a formidable force." However that may be, his exploits made him something of a legendary figure in the lore of the Russian Civil War. In 1920 he participated in the spectacular dash to the gates of Warsaw, was wounded five times while fighting Baron Wrangel at Perekop, in the Crimea. That year, too, he met Lenin for the first time, when the First Mounted Army sent him as its delegate to the Eighth Congress of the Soviets.

The Civil War over and the Soviet regime entrenched, Timoshenko began his training in Russian military schools learning military technique and Marxist political doctrine and incidentally his three R's: like many of the partisan commanders who distinguished themselves in the Civil War, he was virtually illiterate. He attended the special Frunze Higher Military Academy, where his undeniable military experience was supplemented by the formal study of military sci-

ence; he was graduated in 1922, completed the courses for the higher command in 1927 and those for commander-commissars in 1930. In the meantime he had been given various Red Army commands. In 1925 he was made commander-commissar of the 3rd Cavalry Corps and in 1933 assistant commander of the troops of the White Russian Military Area. By 1935 he had completed his military education by extensive trips abroad to study "capitalistic" armies.

Although a veteran Communist (he joined the party in 1919 and is now a member of the Central Committee of the Communist Party of the Soviet Union), he was strictly an army man, steering clear of politics. Perhaps it was to that fact that he owed his rapid rise to the top at the time when many of his superiors were removed. In September 1935 he became assistant commander of the Kiev Military Area. After the execution of Marshal Tukhachevski and several other top Red Army generals, Timoshenko was given commands in important areas. In June 1937 he was transferred to the North Caucasian Military Area—a vital spot, the site of large oil fields. In February 1938 he returned to Kiev as full commander and member of the Military Council of the Kiev Special Military Area.

His post being next door to Poland, it was Timoshenko who in September 1939 headed the march of the Red Army into Poland after Germany had occupied its western half. It was not precisely a military exploit of high order. The Russian dispatches covering the advance of the Army into Poland featured mainly the mileage it covered daily and the "lofty character" of the Soviet soldier: one of the Soviet papers used as an example the fact that not a single apple hanging over the orchard walls in the line of the Army's march was picked. Of an entirely different caliber was the task which faced him in the winter of 1939, when he was sent with supplementary troops to spur the lagging campaign in Finland. He was placed in command of the operations which ultimately smashed the Mannerheim Line.

The extent of his participation in the Finnish War was, however, not made clear until a few weeks later. On the night of May 7, the centenary of the birth of Peter Ilyitch Tschaikowsky, Semyon Timoshenko appeared in a box of Moscow's Bolshoi Opera House in the illustrious company of three Kremlin big shots—Stalin, Voroshilov and Molotov—and it was apparent to the cheering audience that a new star had risen. The next day the Soviet papers carried the story of the honors heaped on the rugged cavalryman. Together with two other generals active in the Finnish War he was made a marshal of the Red Army. He was also awarded the Order of Lenin, one of Russia's highest honors, and designated a Hero of the Soviet Union for his leadership of the Polish and Finnish campaigns. In this way Stalin gave his old friend most of the credit for bringing the Finnish War to its victorious conclusion. Even more important was his appointment as the People's Commissar of Defense, in the place of Marshal Voroshilov, who was moved up to the post of assistant chairman of the Council of People's Commissars and made a Vice-Premier.

A fit culmination to this success story was the new Marshal's visit in October 1940 to his native village of Furmanka, a trip made possible by the Soviet Union's re-annexation of Bessarabia. This memorable occasion is preserved for posterity in a documentary film called *Soviet Frontiers on the Danube,* which was shown in New York soon after the Soviet-German War was declared. It shows Timoshenko in his resplendent white uniform getting a local-boy-makes-good reception from the villagers and everybody getting quite emotional about it, including himself. After more than 20 years' separation he met his brother Efrem and with old friends participated in an all-night celebration in his honor.

Aside from this lighter aspect of his activities, as a Defense Commissar, Timoshenko had his job of whipping the Red Army into shape for the test that was bound to come. Several public statements on his part indicated that he saw war not far ahead, although diplomatically he avoided mentioning from what direction it would come. On October 5, 1940, in his address to the graduating class of a Russian military academy, he said: "You are entering the ranks when the flames of the second imperialist war are enveloping the West and the East. The Soviet Union . . . stands outside the orbit of war, but this does not mean that we are safe from any provocations that may threaten our borders. Under those conditions we must be ready for any emergency and further strengthen the Red Army's fighting capacity."

In the process of tightening up the Army, Timoshenko used to good effect the lessons he learned in Finland. One was the necessity for the rapid mechanization of the Army. According to Walter Duranty, he felt that there was too much stress on techniques and not enough field training. To remedy this he instituted an elaborate combat training service. In a speech he made to the officer corps in the beginning of the vast military maneuvers that took place last year, Marshal Timoshenko stressed his intention to "check up on the fitness of our small units. . . If each such particle attains real efficiency and imbues genuine military culture in all of our larger units, our troops, should they be called on to fight, will carry on their operations without sustaining heavy losses."

Timoshenko's appointment was a signal for other significant reforms. To his influence was ascribed the temporary eclipse of the political commissars when the military commanders were given full control of military operations. Much of the Red Army's camaraderie vanished with other tightening-up decrees. Regular titles for top officers came back; common soldiers were required to salute their superiors; absolute obedience became the order of the day, although Timoshenko claimed that his idea was to "develop the initiative

and energy of the junior ranks without losing the authority of the higher."

Timoshenko, who is a powerfully built man with craggy features and not a hair on his flat-topped head, is about as young a marshal at 46 as a great nation ever had. He is known as a disciplinarian and a hard taskmaster. A song written in his honor by a Ukrainian poet entitled *After the Beloved Commander* claims, however, that "he treats his soldiers like sons," and that they in turn "are ready to follow the beloved commander into any battlefield." He has been copiously decorated. Besides the diamond-studded, gold and platinum star indicating his rank of a Soviet marshal, he has three orders of the Red Banner and an honorary sword for his Civil War exploits and an Order of Lenin for peacetime work. His military slogan today is the same one he used during the Civil War: "Don't ask what the numerical strength of the enemy is but ask *where* it is; then find and destroy it." With the smashing Russian counter-offensive against the Nazis which began in December 1941, he put this slogan to good use.

References

Am R Soviet Union 4:52-4 Ag '41
Liv Age 360:539-42 Ag '41
N Y Sun p17 Je 24 '41
N Y Times p10 Ja 28 '41; p14 My 9 '40 por
Newsweek 17:14 Je 30 '41 por
Sci Mo 50:564 Je '40 por
Time 35:39 My 20 '40 por; 36:26 O 21 '40 por; 37:24+ Je 30 '41 por (cover)
Voks Special Bul 5:5-8 Mr '41

TINNEY, FRANK 1878—Nov. 28, 1940 Former musical comedy star and headliner on Broadway, known for blackface roles.

References

Am Mag 91:34-5+ F '21 pors
Graphic 112:192 Ag 1 '25 por
Green Book 14:1090-1 D '15 pors
Theatre 16:59 Ag '12 por; 20:281 D '14 por; 32:270 N '20 por; 38:29 S '23 por
Who's Who in America 1926-27
Who's Who in the Theatre

Obituaries

Variety 140:56 D 4 '40

TITULESCU, NICOLAS (tē-tōō-lĕs'kōō nē'kō-läs) 1883—Mar. 17, 1941 Former Foreign Minister of Romania who served for six terms; noted for his verbal tilts during the League of Nations sessions in Geneva; with Edward Beneš was a leader in the late Little Entente; was called Foreign Minister at Large of France because of his pro-French tendencies.

References

Eur Nouv 19:917-18 S 12 '36
Lit Digest 117:10 Mr 31 '34 por; 122:13-14 S 12 '36 por
Liv Age 347:315-17 D '34

(Continued next page)

TITULESCU, NICOLAS—*Continued*

New Statesman & Nation 12:700-1 N 7 '36

Who's Who

Who's Who in Central and East-Europe

Obituaries

N Y Times p23 Mr 18 '41 por
Time 37:67 Mr 24 '41

TOBEY, CHARLES W(ILLIAM) (tō'bê)
July 22, 1880- United States Senator from
New Hampshire

Address: b. Senate Office Bldg, Washington,
D. C.; h. Temple, N. H.

Senator Charles William Tobey is a Republican from New Hampshire with "a hound-keen nose for trouble—a word indissolubly connected in his mind with Franklin Roosevelt." He has smelt trouble in the "encroachment of government upon the liberty and inherent rights of a free people"; in the "camouflage" and "duplicity" and "snooping" of the 1940 census; and, until Pearl Harbor, in the Administration's foreign policy, a "gigantic conspiracy "to drive the American people to war.

Ever since the Lease-Lend Bill was proposed, the spare, partially bald Senator has been on his toes. Back in February 1941 he demanded from Roosevelt a "candid statement" of his intention in the future disposition of units of the American Navy. And once the Bill was passed, he rushed in to battle. On March 31, 1941 he offered a resolution in the Senate against the use of convoys. The action on this, said he, would show the nation whether Administration forces "mean business" in their protestations that they want to keep this country out of the War. It was significant, he felt, when the Senate Foreign Relations Committee put the resolution into a quiet pigeonhole.

Senator Tobey looked into the matter further and a few weeks later announced that he had reports to prove that the American ships were "escorting" British ships to rendezvous in mid-ocean designated by the British Admiralty. His proof, printed boldly in the Washington *Times-Herald* under an eight-column headline, was two letters from unnamed persons: one a relative of a boy in the Navy who said he had been on convoy duty; another, a man who knew a young girl whose fiancé had told her he was leaving on convoy duty. The response to the announcement was tremendous, and the Administration quickly issued a firm denial through Senator Barkley (see sketch this issue), who said that Secretary of the Navy Franklin Knox and Admiral Harold Stark had authorized him to say that "not a single ship, American or foreign, carrying any war materials from any place to any other place had been convoyed or was being convoyed from any place to any other place and that no orders had been received from anybody in authority to give such orders for con-

voying any ship of any kind from any place to any other place anywhere in the world."

Senator Tobey was not completely convinced and asked Roosevelt, by wire, for "a frank and unequivocal and complete statement" on the "vital matter of convoys." At the same time he continued to line up support in Congress for his anti-convoy resolution. In the beginning of May, however, the Senate Foreign Relations Committee voted down convoy resolutions and voted down, too, holding hearings on them. Tobey said the Committee was so thorough it reminded him of the old Yankee who was asked by the undertaker what should be done with the body of a far-from-favorite relative. The Yankee wired back: "Embalm, bury, cremate and freeze—take no chances." Despite this, Senator Tobey continued the fight in and out of the Senate (speaking at America First Committee meetings and over the radio), and by the fall of 1941, when the Neutrality Act was revised, his indignation had become even more righteous and raucous than before. Events of December 7 changed all this, however.

None of this is going to mellow Senator Tobey's attitude toward the Roosevelt Administration. He is a "New England Yankee farmer," he says, and proud of it. Actually he was born in Roxbury, Massachusetts, the son of William H., and Ellen Hall (Parker) Tobey, and didn't get to the New Hampshire countryside until 1904. Before then he had attended the Roxbury Latin School and spent a good many years earning his living. When he started, at 16, there were jobs for him in insurance, banking and farming until he finally settled down with the F. M. Hoyt Shoe Company in New Hampshire and started the steady, American rise to the company's presidency.

By this time he was living in Temple, New Hampshire on his 100-acre farm and had married (in 1902) Francelia M. Lovett of Boston. He had already made his start in politics by being elected to head the Temple Board of Selectmen. From this position he went on to the New Hampshire House of Representatives in 1915 and 1916, again in 1919 and 1920 (this term he served as Speaker) and once more in 1923 to 1924. A year later he ran for State Senator and was successful both in getting to the Senate and after, for his fellow Senators elected him their president and New Hampshire's Lieutenant Governor.

From there it was only one step to the Governorship itself, and Tobey took it in 1929. His term was made memorable to some by the stir created when he visited the State's asylum for delinquent girls and discovered miserable conditions. Things were soon changed. But from 1930, when he left the Governor's seat, until 1933, when he entered the United States Congress as Representative from the Second New Hampshire District, Senator Tobey was not a widely known figure on the national political front.

This was remedied somewhat when as one of his first actions in Congress he asked what Sol Bloom, head of the United States Constitution Sesquicentennial Commission, was up to. He was active in expressing his opinions and proposing legislation, but it wasn't until 1939 when he transferred from the House of Representatives to the Senate that he cut a really nation wide swath. A year later he presented the Tobey Resolution to strike out the income questions in the census questionnaire and objected to most of the questions being asked. "There is a growing suspicion," he warned, "that the Government has ulterior motives in inquiring into the salary income of the low income groups for the first time." He spoke in forums, in meetings, over the radio, assisted in his work by Charles Tobey, Jr., his son and secretary. (He has another son and two daughters.) He asked the people to start local "anti-snooping clubs" to put an end to "this sort of snooping into your personal affairs." "I may be old-fashioned," he said, "but I am one of those who honestly believes that the rights of the people are fundamental," and he warned legislators that "the American people will cry out with shame and like Macbeth cry, 'Hold, enough!'" They didn't. Roosevelt openly rebuked Tobey for advising the American people to violate the law; the resolution never came to the Senate floor; the American people answered the questions; and, as one commentator put it, this "fast-talking, old-fashioned, nightshirt-wearing, God-fearing New Hampshire gent . . . has done more to advertise this year's census than if Harry Hopkins [see sketch this issue] had hired Billy Rose to do it."

Between his census and convoy fights Senator Tobey was active in the investigation into the settlement of the 1932 radio patent pool monopoly case and as a member of a subcommittee of the Senate Committee on Campaign Expenditures conducting a voting inquiry in New Jersey. His 1932 interest in radio was seen again in 1941 when as a member of the Senate Interstate Commerce Committee he heard the White resolution to investigate the Federal Communications Commission. He also suggested the compilation of records of stations on their broadcasts of speeches on the war issue. In the hearings he was "in rare form—he had everybody on the ropes." He stormed, questioned, rattled every skeleton he could.

He has been generally active on the floor, too—the kind of Senator who frequently gets to shouting during debate. The official shorthand reporters say he talks faster than any other Senator; other Senators say he often talks more to the point than most. Once during Senate hearings he told a railroad executive to "cut out the bunk," and at another hearing involving a Federal judge he insisted: "I don't give a damn for dignity."

In the midst of the hurly-burly that surrounds his Senate career, Senator Tobey, who never drinks ("I've been dry since birth") and whose favorite dish is New England apple pie, confesses that his ambition is "to go back full time to rural life." "I have a country place at Temple, New Hampshire," he once told a reporter, "and I can say to you because of its

Acme

CHARLES W. TOBEY

natural scenery it's the original Garden of Eden without the Original Sin."

References

Boston Transcript p8 Mr 7 '40
N Y Post p12 Ap 6 '40 por
Time 37:14 Ap 28 '41 por
Who's Who in America
Who's Who in Government
Who's Who in the Nation's Capital

TOJO, EIKI See Tojo, H. (tō'yô ā'ê-kê)

TOJO, HIDEKI (tō'yô hê-dā'kê) Dec. 1884-Japanese statesman and general
Address: Kwantung Army Headquarters, Hsinking, Japan

Since 1931 the Japanese Government has been largely dominated by the Japanese Army and the Army has been ruled by a small clique within it known as the Kwantung Army, the army of occupation in Manchukuo. It is this *corps d'élite* to which Tojo, the Prime Minister of Japan, belongs and in which he rose from an ambitious young officer to Chief of Staff. Known throughout his military career as Eiki Tojo, upon his ascension to the Premiership Tojo announced that he preferred Hideki as a first name.

Tojo is often referred to as *Kamiseri* (razor blade) by his military colleagues because of his sharp temperament. He is expected to come "closer to the role of dictator than any man since General Sadao Araki in 1932." Although this is not the first Japanese Cabinet headed by a military person, this is the first time that the Kwantung Army, hitherto content to exert its power more or less indirectly, has come out into the open. By special act of the Emperor, Tojo is permitted to keep his Army post as well as his Premiership, though under Japanese law he

Japanese American News

HIDEKI TOJO

should have resigned from the Army before accepting a political post. Even before the Japanese attack on Pearl Harbor the new Tojo Cabinet, therefore, was generally regarded as "the most military and potentially belligerent government that has come to power in Japan."

Hideki Tojo was born in Tokyo, December 1884, the son of Lieutenant General Eikyo Tojo. Destined as a youth to follow in the military tradition of his family, he entered the Military Staff College and was graduated in 1915. Entering the Army immediately after graduation, he served as aide-de-camp in the War Office and then was sent to Germany in 1919 as resident officer. In 1922 he returned to his Alma Mater, the Military Staff College, to teach.

Finding the career of military instructor too limited for his ambitions, Tojo became the chief mobilization section commander of the 1st Infantry Regiment, the sectional chief of the General Staff Office and commander of the 24th Infantry Brigade. In the Kwantung Bureau he was commander of the Gendarmerie headquarters and chief of police affairs, and in 1937 he became lieutenant general and chief of staff in the Japanese Army in China. For a time he organized a military inquiry which checked Japanese Army loyalty in China. His "red brick headquarters bulged with dossiers on every Kwantung officer, and he was known as Manchukuo's bogey man."

Until 1938 Tojo had concerned himself chiefly with rising in the military hierarchy. When he came near the top, he turned his attention to the acquisition of civil power and accepted the office of Vice-Minister of War under General Seishiro Itagaki, a position which he held from May to December 1938. His insistence upon regimentation of every phase of Japanese life made him so many enemies among influential business groups that in December he was taken out of the ministry and made director of Military Aviation for Japan. In July 1940 he returned to the Cabinet as War Minister, one of the youngest War Ministers in Japanese history. When Premier Konoye's (see sketch 1940 Annual) Cabinet fell in October 1941, Tojo was chosen to form a new Cabinet, and on October 20, 1941 the new Premier made a pilgrimage to the Ise shrine, where he announced his new office to the Sun Goddess. Then he returned by airplane to Tokyo, where he announced his new responsibilities at the shrine of the Emperor Meiji and at the Yasakuni shrine for the war dead.

In 1937 Tojo had said that Japan must be able to fight Russia and China at the same time. In 1940, when Japan joined the Axis, Tojo said he was "overwhelmed with a mingled feeling of austerity and joy" and rejoiced that his nation would go "with renewed strength toward Japan's fixed goal in world affairs." His designation as Premier, however, was regarded by part of the American press as indicative of the victory of "moderate" nationalism. In his very first radio broadcast as Premier, Tojo said that Japan was determined to settle the "China affair" and to fulfill her ultimate object "to contribute to world peace." He continued the Washington conversations and called for November 1941 the first session of the Japanese Diet to be held since 1937.

According to Japanese writers, Tojo's aim was to build Japan into a "high degree defense state . . . a government established on a military economy." "In Tojo's opinion," a Japanese magazine wrote, "the entire nation should move as one cannon ball of fiery resolution." He was known as violently anti-Russian and as the author of some stinging remarks against Britain and the United States. Although he kept the most important portfolios for himself, those of war and home ministries, he chose as Foreign Minister, Shigenori Togo, the former Ambassador to Moscow, who is married to a German woman. In a speech at Osaka, October 26, 1941, Tojo declared that "Japan must go on and develop in everexpanding progress—there is no retreat! . . If Japan's hundred millions merge and go forward, nothing can stop us. . . Wars can be fought with ease."

On December 16, 1941, a week after the outbreak of Japanese-American hostilities, Premier Tojo, addressing an extraordinary session of the Japanese Diet, asserted that Japan had declared war on the United States only after trying all means of peaceful settlement. On the last day of December he warned the Japanese people to expect a long war despite early successes because the United States had "just begun to mobilize its potential war power."

Tojo is a member of the *samurai* class, the lesser nobility of feudal Japan, now generally characterized as the "headstrong army caste." Described as "smart, hard-boiled, resourceful and contemptuous of theories, sentiments, and negotiations," Tojo speaks "incisively" and is "known by the Japanese people for his quick intellect."

Tojo's rapidity of speech, as well as the quick, jerky puffs of his ever-present cigar, indicates to the observer a great deal of nervous energy. Bald, but young as Japanese Premiers go, he looks out at the world through horn-rimmed spectacles and above a sprawling mustache. He is married to Katsui, eldest daughter of Mantaro Ito.

References

Life 11 :34 O 27 '41 por
N Y Herald Tribune p19 O 19 '41 ; p3 O 27 '41
N Y Sun p6 Jl 19 '40
N Y Times p5 O 18 '41 por ; p1, 9 O 19 '41 ; p3 O 20 '41
PM p5 O 19 '41
Time 38 :23 N 3 '41 por (cover)
Who's Who in Japan

TOLAND, GREGG (tō'lănd) May 29, 1904- Film photographer
Address: b. Samuel Goldwyn Studios, Hollywood, Calif ; h. 1718 Ambassador Ave, Beverly Hills, Calif

In the spring of 1941 a picture appeared which most critics agreed in calling the most sensational product to date of the United States film industry, with important new techniques in picture making and story telling. The picture was *Citizen Kane*, and the two men largely responsible for it were Orson Welles (see sketch this issue), who directed and played the lead in it, and Gregg Toland, who photographed it. Toland worked on every camera setup and lighting arrangement with the youthful director.

They experimented for new camera angles, new compositions and light effects, tried to achieve power and economy. One of the innovations was the use of low ceilings to intensify the mood and to give the impression of depth. Some of the scenes that were played covered two 100-foot sound stages, and one scene was shot through a hole in the floor. By means of his new method of movie photography called "pan focus" Toland was able to get the whole scene into every shot with foreground, middleground and background equally sharp, and thus to make interesting use of details: a good example of this is a shot of Susan Kane's attempted suicide, with the medicine bottle, glass and spoon in foreground and two frantic figures looming in the back. It shows Toland's fondness for realistic detail (which he has in common with Alfred Hitchcock [see sketch this issue]) and his capacity for consistently achieving fine composition.

The ordinary spectator who sees the picture without understanding the technical angles is merely impressed by the splendid vitality of the picture, the smooth, beautiful and exciting way in which it tells its story, with the camera always deftly pointing up the narrative. But people in the profession appreciate the extraordinary technical novelties that Toland offers: the aged and streaked documentary shots which the *March of Time* runs

GREGG TOLAND

off after Kane's death; the Opera House sequence where Toland does something which Hollywood has always said you couldn't do— shoot straight into bright lights—and the camera climbs high up into the flies to show the two stagehands' robust reaction to Susan's bad singing; or the scene that takes the spectator from the interior of a house right out into the exterior of a snow scene without a break—a bit that gave Toland and Welles four days of infinite trouble. A rumor had started in Hollywood, where Welles is not too popular, that much of the credit given to Welles by right belongs to Toland. Toland's comment to this was: "I worked out every shot in the picture with Welles. I even sat in on the polishing of the scenario with him. He is one of the greatest directors I ever worked with."

Toland ought to know, for he has worked with the best of them. A director's rather than a star's cameraman, he shot pictures for William Wyler and John Ford (see sketch this issue). After 20 years on the job he is commonly conceded to be one of the half dozen top men. Gregg Toland was born in Charleston, Illinois on May 29, 1904, the son of Frank and Genieve (Turman) Toland. At a very early age he already knew more or less what he wanted: after a perfunctory trot through intermediate grade school he enrolled in a technical school to study electrical engineering. At 15, after having mastered trigonometry and become unusually proficient in mechanical drawing, he dropped school altogether and went to work in the Fox Studios as an office boy. There he discovered that what he really wanted to do was camera work. He served a year's apprenticeship before becoming an assistant cameraman in 1920.

The apprenticeship in camera work is an arduous and exacting one, and the progression from one step to another slow, with the acolyte

TOLAND, GREGG—*Continued*

having to prove himself every inch of the way. Gregg Toland was an assistant cameraman for six years. His duties were at first purely mechanical, involving tasks like changing the focus, gauging the distance between the player and the camera, loading the camera, etc. Then he was promoted to the status of the operating cameraman, whose function is actually to work the camera. He worked for a number of years under George Barnes, the ace cameraman who got the 1941 annual Academy Award for his photography of *Rebecca,* and followed him into the employ of Samuel Goldwyn in 1922. It is said that when he was working on Gloria Swanson's picture, *The Trespasser,* Laura Hope Crews told Goldwyn: "That young man should be a cameraman. He's got the makings of a great one." At any rate it was Goldwyn who gave him his first chance in 1929 by letting him photograph an Eddie Cantor (see sketch this issue) picture as the director of photography. He has since been under contract to Goldwyn.

Among cameramen Toland's reputation is that of an artist. He has been known for many innovations, for doing "mad, radical" things with his camera, which nevertheless turn out to be remarkably effective. Thus, when shooting *Les Miserables* (which received a nomination for the motion picture Academy Award in 1935), he used the smallest number of lights ever used on a picture, lighting some scenes with only two or three lights and shooting into the shadows. But this departure from time-honored usage succeeded in giving an impression of depth and density to the gloomy picture, and Toland was once more credited with "daring, initiative and imagination." He, too, was responsible for the excellent photography of such varied fare as *Dark Angel* (1935); *Dead End* (another candidate for the motion picture Academy Award in 1937); and *Goldwyn Follies* (1938).

In 1939 his weird windswept effects in *Wuthering Heights,* directed by William Wyler, got him the coveted "Oscar." In 1940 he helped produce other winners: such masterpieces of exceptional photography as *The Grapes of Wrath* (that gained John Ford 1940's directorial award), *The Long Voyage Home* and others. Presumably *Citizen Kane* will bring in more kudos when its turn to be considered as part of the filmland's achievement for 1941 comes up. At any rate it has already brought the man behind the camera more direct praise than it has ever been any cameraman's fortune to receive.

When Toland is assigned to a picture he reads the scenario carefully. Then come numerous conferences with the art director about color and design of the sets, the costumes, the make-up. Numerous make-up tests take place, particularly in the case of new actors, of whom there were so many in *Citizen Kane.* Lights are tried out on sets and on individual actors. Everything is welded into the atmosphere and mood of the story being filmed. Toland is constantly experimenting with new means of achieving realism. A favorite device of his is

to conceal an electric bulb inside a candlestick to intensify light.

Toland receives a salary that compares favorably with those of highly paid stars—his contract with Samuel Goldwyn pays him $62,000 a year. On this he lives a quiet, modest life without fanfare, one of a "skilled, unpublicized, tight little fraternity," member of a union as exclusive as a Boston club. One of his major interests is the United States Naval Reserve in which he was commissioned a lieutenant in 1941. He was married to the former Helene Haskin in 1934 and has a daughter, Lothian. Lean, youthful, with a small mustache, Toland reportedly wants to be a director—an ambition which the studios will make every effort to frustrate, for a cameraman of his caliber is even rarer than a good director.

References

    Life 10:110-16 My 26 '41 pors
    N Y Post p6 Ap 29 '41
    Theatre Arts 25:646-54 S '41 por
    Time 36:76 D 2 '40

    International Motion Picture Almanac

TOMASI, MARI (tô-mä′sē mä′rĭ) Feb. 1, 1910- Author

Address: b. c/o Vermont Writers Project, Post Office Bldg, Montpelier, Vt; h. 63 Barre St, Montpelier, Vt.

Deep Grow the Roots, a first novel by Mari Tomasi, was selected by the American Booksellers' Association and the New York *Herald Tribune* as "one of the 10 most outstanding first novels of the year 1940." The locale of Miss Tomasi's novel is the Piedmont hill country of northern Italy at the time of the Ethiopian War. Two young lovers strive to understand their part in the approaching war. "What is it all about?" asks Luigi, owner of a chestnut grove. "Why must I, Luigi, go to fight in this Ethiopia, give up Nina, leave my trees?" His efforts to escape Mussolini's dream of empire bring him tragedy.

Called by one critic "as delightful a first story as a reviewer can happen upon," and by another "a story of poignant earthy simplicity and beauty, written from tender insight and with exquisite restraint," *Deep Grow the Roots* has also been taken to task for its unrelieved lyricism "drenched in an atmosphere of sunshine and poetic writing."

Miss Tomasi, petite, with gray eyes and brown hair, writes us from her Vermont home: "Most of my first eight years were spent in a wheelchair. Shortly after a successful operation, I visited the Piedmont country of northern Italy with my father. I could never forget the lovely, peaceful atmosphere of that hill country and last year [1940] I employed the Piedmont setting for my first novel—*Deep Grow the Roots.*

"My father, Bartholomew Tomasi, and my mother, Margherita (Contratto) Tomasi, were born in Turin, Italy. After a tour of Central and South America and the States, my father settled in Vermont, feeling that the Green

MARI TOMASI

Mountain State was most like the hill-and-lake country of his Italian home. Here in Vermont, too, he met his childhood friend, Margherita Contratto, and married her.

"I was the third child, born in the apartment over my father's Main Street store—a combination fruit store and cigar manufacturing plant [in Montpelier]. It was difficult to follow the sports of the more active members of the family. One of my favorite pastimes was hiding and curling up behind a showcase, listening to any and all conversations between my father and his customers. I struggled, too, in those early days with a very childish dictionary containing such entries as—Sun: what comes out when it don't rain.

"I was taught by the Sisters of Mercy in St. Michael's parochial grade school. After graduating from the local high school, I had two years of college, one at Wheaton (Norton, Massachusetts, 1926-27); the second at Trinity (Burlington, Vermont). My father's sudden death put an end to my college course. I have taught country school, done private tutoring, and have had short stories published. At present I am employed on the Vermont Writers Project. In my spare time I am working on a new novel which revolves around Italian-American stonecutters in Vermont.

"I am not married. I live with my mother, three brothers, and a sister in a little house just a stone's throw from Montpelier's business section. In spite of the nearness to Main Street, we have a good-size vegetable garden where we grow—for our own use—almost everything from grapes to Chinese cabbage. My special pet is a small flower garden."

References

Hill Trails F '41
N Y Times p21 O 23 '40; N 27 '40

TOWERS, J(OHN) H(ENRY) Jan. 30, 1885- Chief of the United States Navy Department Bureau of Aeronautics

Address: b. Navy Department, Bureau of Aeronautics, Washington, D. C.

"An outline of Admiral Towers' naval career," a commentator once wrote, "is almost a synopsis of the history of American naval aviation." Ever since he first flew a plane in 1911 he has fought to develop the Navy's air arm, and since his promotion to chief of the Navy's Bureau of Aeronautics in 1939 he has been fighting harder than ever. Admiral Towers isn't one of those, however, who demand an independent air command. To him "the aircraft program is part of the naval expansion as a whole"; to him the question is not one of planes versus ships but of planes plus ships.

This blond, spare Navy chief who still gets in about 100 flying hours a year was born in Rome, Georgia, the son of William Magee and Mary (Norton) Towers. He went to grammar and high school in Rome and then, in 1901, entered the Georgia School of Technology to take a civil engineering course. Less than a year later he received an appointment to the United States Naval Academy and in 1906 was graduated.

At Annapolis he had begun his Navy career by training on old square-riggers based there. He continued it after graduation, on the *U. S. S. Kentucky,* where for three years he did engineering duty. His next assignment was to the *U. S. S. Michigan,* on which he was made fire control officer and spotter. When in the spring of 1911 this ship won the Gunnery Trophy and Battle Efficiency Pennant, Lieutenant Towers received letters of commendation for the performance of his duties from the President and the Secretary of the Navy. Throughout the days of steam Towers advanced, serving on many ships that were scrapped long before the First World War.

Ensign Towers applied for aviation duty in November 1910 and was ordered to this duty in the spring of 1911. In August 1911, after instruction under Glenn H. Curtiss, he became the third man to qualify as a United States Naval aviator. The next two years were spent serving at the Navy's first air station at Annapolis, where he was in charge of the Naval Aviation Camp. Here he piloted test flights (in October 1912 he set a world record for endurance in a seaplane and an American record for endurance in any type plane) that helped develop the Navy's earliest seaplanes, catapult launchings, night flying and bomb dropping.

Towers didn't escape without accidents. On June 20, 1912, while flying as a passenger in a Wright seaplane at an altitude of 1,700 feet, both he and the pilot were thrown from the plane by a sudden atmospheric disturbance. The pilot fell clear and was killed, but Lieutenant Towers managed to grasp a forward projection on the plane and to fall with it. The injuries he suffered left him with a damaged left eye which has meant that ever since

U. S. Navy

J. H. TOWERS

he has had to have a co-pilot along when he flies. As a result of this accident safety belts were adopted by the Navy.

In January 1914 Lieutenant Towers was transferred to Pensacola, Florida as executive officer; during the Mexican disturbance that summer he was in command of aviation units established on shore at Vera Cruz. Then, when the European War broke out, he was ordered to duty as an aviation observer in Europe and was attached to the American Embassy in London for more than two years. He married Lily Carstairs of that city in October 1915; there are two children of this marriage, which later ended in a divorce.

In the autumn of 1916 Towers was recalled from Europe, assigned to duty in Operations in charge of naval aviation under that office and also made a supervisor of the Naval Aviation Flying Corps, which at that time was just beginning. When the Division of Aviation in Operations was established he was made assistant director of naval aviation, a position he kept until February 1919.

During the First World War the science of aviation advanced tremendously, and in its advance the soundness of many of Towers' ideas was demonstrated. Convinced that long-distance flights were entirely practicable, he applied for and was given duty in connection with a proposed transatlantic flight, and it was he who organized and commanded a unit of flying boats of the "NC" type which in May 1919 made the first transatlantic flight in the world's history. When his own NC-3 was forced down onto a rough sea short of the Azores, he and the crew rigged sails and sailed it for three days until they reached Ponta Delgada.

His next assignment was that of executive officer of the *U. S. S. Aroostook* and senior aide to Commander Aircraft Squadrons of the Pacific Fleet. He continued in that organization in various capacities, among them as commander of the destroyer *U. S. S. Mugford,* until in November 1921 he was ordered to the Naval Air Station at Pensacola as executive officer. Two years later he was again sent abroad, this time as assistant attaché for aviation at the Embassies in England, France, Italy, Germany and The Netherlands.

When Commander Towers returned to the United States in September 1925 he immediately became a member of the board of inquiry on the loss of the *U. S. S. Shenandoah,* and then was assigned as executive officer of the *U. S. S. Langley,* the first aircraft carrier of the United States Navy. Two years later he was placed in command of this vessel. When an explosion of a main gasoline storage tank took place he fought the fire so effectively that some years later Secretary of the Navy Swanson awarded him a letter of commendation which said: "Your coolness and courage in the face of danger, combined with vigorous action in suppressing the fire, are responsible to a large degree for the prevention of a catastrophe."

In August 1928 Commander Towers was ordered to the Bureau of Aeronautics as head of the Plans Division and in April 1929 was made assistant chief of the Bureau. Commissioned a captain, he not only carried out his Bureau duty under an appointment by President Hoover but served as a member of the National Advisory Committee for Aeronautics, the government organization with jurisdiction over the scientific study of and research into fundamental problems in aeronautics. In August 1930 he was married for the second time, to Pierrette Anne Chauvin de Grandmont.

He left these positions in June 1931 to become chief of staff, commander aircraft, battle force, stationed on the *U. S. S. Saratoga.* Two years later he spent one year at the Naval War College at Newport, Rhode Island and after the completion of his course was ordered to duty as commanding officer at the Naval Air Station at San Diego, California. Here he was in close touch with the fleet, for it is from this station that the majority of aircraft operates and it is also this station which meets the problems of repairing, overhauling and maintaining the fleet squadrons.

After two years here he was again appointed chief of staff, commander aircraft, battle force, and he kept this duty until June 1937, when he was ordered to command the *U. S. S. Saratoga.* This ship, with the *U. S. S. Lexington,* is not only the largest aircraft carrier afloat but the largest ship of any type in the United States Navy. His next shift in June 1938 to the position of assistant chief of the Bureau of Aeronautics made him the only person ever to have held this position twice. And when, one year later, he was appointed by the President to his position of chief of the Bureau of Aeronautics and made a rear admiral, the appointment was widely hailed: most commentators felt it was about time that the Navy air arm have as chief a man who had spent the greater part of his professional career as an airman; and some of them felt that President Roosevelt himself had had a hand in making it.

Since his appointment Admiral Towers has frequently written, talked and reported to governmental bodies on the progress of his department. He has told about progress in the building program for combat planes, carriers, flying boats and torpedo planes with every modern device; he has revealed plans for a naval pilot training program; he has told of the present and given his hopes for the future state of Navy aviation. And always he has urged more planes, not only for ourselves but for Britain. "The British," he says, "are fighting our battle."

References

Aviation 39:38-9+ Ag '40 por
Newsweek 13:51 Mr 27 '39
Time 35:14 Je 3 '40 por; 37:20-1 Je 23 '41 por (cover)
Who's Who in America
Who's Who in Government
Who's Who in the East

TOWNSEND, HARRY E(VERETT) Mar. 10, 1879—July 25, 1941 American painter, illustrator and etcher; was one of the eight official artists for the United States Army in France in the First World War; painted murals for Connecticut public buildings; won several prizes for his paintings.

References

Who's Who in American Art

Obituaries

N Y Herald Tribune p14 Ag 6 '41

TRUEX, ERNEST 1890- (trū′ĕx) Actor
Address: c/o Actors Equity Assn, 45 W. 47th St, New York City

Ernest Truex, the diminutive actor, grew up in the country town of Rich Hill, Missouri. He was born in St. Louis, Missouri in 1890, but moved to Rich Hill when his father, Dr. J. L. Truex, was appointed by local coal operators as physician to the miners.

The actor's career began "by default." To repay a doctor's bill to Ernest's father, an impoverished Shakespearean actor took Ernest as a pupil. The five-year-old child made his first public appearance at the town opera house as Hamlet in the ghost scene. Introduced as "the youngest and smallest actor on any stage, in costume," he was an immediate success. He says that now he is content to be a comedian: he has played his Hamlet.

An article in the Rich Hill *Clarion* the next day commented enthusiastically upon his performance. "The star of the company was little Ernest Truex, five years old. . . Master Truex is an artist, and was warmly encored earlier in the evening when he recited The

Vandamm

ERNEST TRUEX

Fire Fiend and responded with a burlesque on *Beautiful Snow.* This mere tot came on the stage with the ease of a veteran and, with a voice that would have filled a house twice as large, and with an interpretation far beyond his years, rendered his difficult numbers in a splendid manner."

For two years the young prodigy continued his studies with the Shakespearean tutor, acquiring in that time an extensive repertoire. When he was eight, he toured the Midwest in company with a little girl from the same school. In Kansas City, he went to see O. D. Woodward, manager of the local stock company, who was amused by the child but interested in his talent. As a result of the interview, Truex was hired to play the part of Aulus in *Quo Vadis* in 1899, and remained with the company to take such juvenile roles as Cedric in *Little Lord Fauntleroy* and Willie in *East Lynne.*

There followed a 10-year association with the Illytch Garden Stock Company in Denver, during which Truex played with the greatest stars of the day. In *Alice-Sit-by-the-Fire* he toured the country with Mary Shaw and again with Ezra Kendall in *The Land of the Dollars.*

During high school days in Denver, Truex was a classmate of Douglas Fairbanks and Harold Lloyd. After graduation he set out to conquer New York. Unfortunately, however, no one on Broadway had heard of his remarkable career. While he looked for a part, he took a job making change in Adolph Zukor's penny arcade on Fourteenth Street.

TRUEX, ERNEST—*Continued*

The road to Broadway began in Toronto. At the races he was introduced to Lillian Russell, who asked him if he was riding. When Truex said that he was an actor and not a jockey, she mentioned a jockey role in her next play and took his name. In the autumn of 1908, a telegram offering him the part in *Wildfire* launched Truex's New York career. Three decades later he played the part of Lillian Russell's father on the screen.

The actor recalls his disillusionment, while playing opposite the famous star, in discovering that she smoked cigars. "She liked only those with little yellow spots on them and the others she gave to me," he relates.

When *Wildfire* closed Truex appeared in seven plays in London, the first of which was *The Fall Guy*. *The First Year, Five O'Clock Girl* and others followed. While appearing in the original production of *Havana* he married Julia Mills, a dancer. Their two sons, Philip and James, were graduated recently from Haverford College in Pennsylvania.

The first Mrs. Truex died in Atlantic City November 15, 1930. The next year Truex married 21-year-old Mary Jane Barrett, a co-player in the *Third Little Show*. She is the mother of Barrett Truex, who, at six, is the only Truex not currently engaged in stage work. James is a member of a road company of *The Man Who Came to Dinner,* while his brother Philip is in a New York production. On October 25, 1938 Mrs. Truex was granted a divorce because she claimed that her husband "spied on her and was unreasonably jealous." In March 1941 Truex was married for the third time—to Sylvia Field, the actress.

The screen version of *Whistling in the Dark,* produced in 1933, was Ernest Truex's first movie. "His acting," wrote a newspaper critic, "is just as effective in the picture as it was on the stage. In fact, he fills the part so well that it is difficult to imagine anybody who could compete with him." Other film successes included *Warrior's Husband* (1933); *The Adventures of Marco Polo* (1938); and, in 1940, *His Girl Friday* and *Slightly Honorable.*

But the stage is his first love and he returned to it in 1940, after four years' absence, in Kaufman and Hart's (see sketches this issue) *George Washington Slept Here,* which is his forty-seventh on Broadway. In this play the comedian encountered all the difficulties of rural existence, not the least of which was an insect plague. The dilapidated house, which Fuller buys for its historical significance, presented one problem after another to the enthusiastic husband and his skeptical wife. His last show before the Hollywood sojourn was *Frederika.*

Ernest Truex has been described as "that endlessly praised actor" and "one of the most artful clowners in the theatre. He has a blissful knack of stirring wistfulness into every pun, pity into every tumble." He is only slightly over five feet tall, has all his clothes made especially for him in New York City.

"Just the same height as Napoleon," he says by way of describing his build.

Truex says that his leading ambition is to play in "something that's really fine and real." His conception of acting is incorporated in part of an open letter to his son, written in June 1933: "Consider the willow tree whose dainty branches sway in the greatest breeze, but whose roots go deep and whose trunk is tough and hard to break."

References

Green Book 18:988-9 D '17 il por
Illustrated London News 169:1126 D 18 '26 pors
Motion Picture Classic 8:32-3+ Je '19 il por
N Y Herald Tribune VI p1+ O 13 '40; VI p5 N 17 '40 pors
Strand (N. Y.) 48:113-15 Ag '40 por
International Motion Picture Almanac 1937-38
Who's Who in the East
Who's Who in the Theatre

TRUJILLO MOLINA, RAFAEL L(ÉONIDAS) (troo-hē'lyō) Oct. 24, 1891-
Generalissimo of the Dominican Army

Address: Estancia Ramfis, Ciudad Trujillo, Dominican Republic

In July 1938, when President Roosevelt called the Evian Conference to consider the problems of refugees, one of the few offers of tangible assistance came from Generalissimo Rafael L. Trujillo, at that time President of the Dominican Republic, who donated more than 26,000 acres in Sosua Province, which he bought from the United Fruit Company, for the settlement of refugees. They were guaranteed citizenship, freedom from molestation, discrimination or persecution; the only restriction was that they must be white, for the General wishes to increase the proportion of whites among his people. By January 1941 around 700 families were already settled there, and Trujillo, pleased by the success of his experiment, donated another 50,000 acres. The eventual goal is 100,000 refugees, both Jewish and non-Jewish.

Few democracies have done so much to solve the refugee problem. Oddly enough, the Dominican Republic, which occupies some two-thirds of the island of Haiti, has a population of approximately 1,500,000 and has been ruled by Trujillo since 1930, is not a democracy. There is only one political party in the country. And although there are no records on imprisonments, Trujillo's political enemies say that he is responsible for thousands imprisoned, tortured and murdered —among them writers and editors who refused to praise him, officials of past administrations who wouldn't enter his government (and some who did), plantation owners and peasants who protested confiscation of their land, dissident students and professors.

Under the tight Dominican censorship anyone spreading "information of subversive character, injurious to the authorities or defamatory of the government" is tried as a common criminal; even foreigners have reason to be afraid. The labor movement has practically been destroyed, with labor leaders arrested and imprisoned and striking workers forced back to work by soldiers, although some social legislation, such as an eight-hour day, has been instituted. Trujillo and his near relatives live luxuriously and have gradually acquired a "totalitarian trade monopoly" over salt production, cattle, milk, butter and other products; the Generalissimo has also acquired a large financial interest in an insurance company, a shoe factory and a tobacco farm as well as a 3,000-acre rancho and many large holdings where rice is grown.

This does not mean that there is no one to speak a good word for the "Caribbean Caesar." He himself boasts that there is neither crime nor unemployment in the Dominican capital and that his government has balanced its budget every year during the depression. Oswald Garrison Villard, writing in 1937, listed among the dictator's accomplishments the introduction of compulsory education (although school enrollment was then below the 1920 average!), the building of modern roads, bridges, telegraph and telephone lines. Villard also asserted that Trujillo had distributed parts of the public domain to needy families, had been generous in his charities, had encouraged agriculture and small holdings of land rather than large plantations, and that although there was no doubt at all that he made himself a millionaire, he had also given "pretty honest public service," raising public revenue solely by import and export duties. "One feels that his own spirit of virility and vitality has penetrated the whole nation. . . Foreigners who know the situation declare that he has done more for Santo Domingo than all his predecessors for 50 years back."

Nearly everyone, too, has pointed out that the Dominican Army (which in 1936 got 16 per cent of the budget's attention) is a "very efficient body"—so efficient, according to Helen Lombard, writing in *PM*, that, "outwardly at least, his country is calm and peaceful." She calls the Generalissimo "one of the most colorful 'head guys' in the whole Western Hemisphere."

The facts about the early life of Generalissimo Rafael Léonidas Trujillo Molina—officially Benefactor of the Fatherland, Savior, Hero, Titan, Admiral, Doctor Honoris Causa in the Economic Political Sciences—have not been too well established. It seems to be settled that he was born October 24, 1891 in San Cristóbal, but his father, José Trujillo Valdez, has been variously described as a humble mountain peasant and a storekeeper and a cattle dealer in San Cristóbal. His mother was Julia Molina Chevalier. Carleton Beals (see sketch this issue), who gives the Generalissimo the benefit of few doubts, says that young Rafael was a cattle rustler and forger before joining the National Guard after the United States occupied the country in 1916; another writer says, simply, that young Rafael rose from the post of telegraph operator. According to official biographers, he quit that

Dominican Legation

RAFAEL L. TRUJILLO MOLINA

position to attend a military academy, and was graduated as a second lieutenant.

In any case, it is certain that by 1922 he had become a captain in the National Guard; that under Vásquez, who became President in 1924, he was promoted until he became commander of the entire National Guard, which he renamed the "National Army", "recreating the sort of militarism American occupation had attempted to abolish"; and that today he can speak of the United States Marines as his "Alma Mater."

What happened in 1930 and afterward is not so misty. In February of that year there was a revolt against Vásquez, who had been prolonging his four-year Presidential term through changes in the laws governing elections. The Army, under Trujillo's command, did not defend the Government; it is claimed that they had a previous agreement with the revolutionaries. A provisional President was put in immediately, but another Presidential election was to be held in May, and the Confederation of Parties named Trujillo as their candidate. Their terroristic tactics made the opposing ticket of the National Progressive Alliance withdraw, and in the ensuing election Trujillo apparently received more votes than there were registered voters in Santo Domingo. A Supreme Court judge who declared the elections fraudulent had to flee; so did the opposition's candidates, and, eventually, the former provisional President himself, who had been elected Vice-President.

At 37 the world's youngest ruler of a sovereign state, on inauguration day (August 16) Trujillo wore a gold-braided uniform placarded "God and Trujillo." Three weeks after he took office a cyclone almost completely destroyed Santo Domingo, and, according to Villard, he was given an immediate opportunity to show what he could do. With the help of

TRUJILLO MOLINA, RAFAEL L.—
Continued

the American Red Cross he rebuilt "a new and handsome city, clean and well policed," with "new streets . . . well planned and well paved", "modern buses and good water"; he also spent $2,500,000 "in improving the docks and dredging the channel into the Ozanna River." He announced: "I'm no Marc Antony. I aspire to be a Julius Caesar in deeds. If I were Nero I would burn down Santo Domingo to rebuild it more beautifully."

It was August 1931 when the Dominican Party, with Trujillo at its head, was organized; government employees were required to contribute 10 per cent of their salary to the treasury. In 1932 the Cuban Minister wrote of a "reign of terror, perpetuated by clandestine assassinations"; later the Cuban Government broke off relations with Santo Domingo because of the treatment of its citizens. In 1934 Trujillo was re-elected by "civic reviews"—masses of peasants herded together to shout adherence to his regime. Although no Dominicans except members of the Army and police were allowed to have weapons, there were sporadic revolutionary plots—that year, for example, government buildings in Santiago were bombed. Other conspiracies, it has been claimed, were "trumped up" to suit Trujillo's purposes. But the outside world knew little of the details of his dictatorship until in October 1937 the Dominican Army and police murdered Haitian border residents—men, women and children, all civilians, all defenseless. Their number was estimated as at least 10,000 by Quentin Reynolds (see sketch this issue), writing in *Collier's* not long afterward. He concluded that the affair had been planned by Trujillo and executed at his orders, although excused as a bandit skirmish at the time. More than one observer decided forthwith that the Dominican dictator was "attempting to allay domestic dissension by cooking up a foreign difficulty," and expected war with Haiti to break out, but apologies and a financial settlement were eventually made.

At the same time Trujillo was proclaiming his popularity far and wide. He had an entirely new province and the main city of the country named after him (the city of Santo Domingo became Ciudad Trujillo in 1936), as well as many of the bridges and other public works. He had himself recommended for the Nobel Peace Prize. Across the front page of every newspaper was a large black banner praising him. An electric sign in red, white and blue, with letters a foot high, celebrated "God and Trujillo." "Viva Trujillo!" shouted Dominican automobile license plates, too. In 1938 he refused a third term as President, "following United States precedent," and began to rule instead as Generalissimo of the Army, a title which he had received in 1932. "I voluntarily, and against the wishes of my people, refused re-election to that high office," he announced.

At the same time, too, the "Napoleon of the West Indies" was boasting that the Dominican Republic bases its institutions "on the fundamental principles expressed in the Constitution of the United States." He has often reaffirmed a policy of continental unity and solidarity with the United States, a willingness to cooperate with any defense plans. When running for his second term as President he secured a photograph from President Roosevelt inscribed "To Rafael Trujillo from his good friend Franklin D. Roosevelt," and thousands of copies were nailed to Santo Domingo tree trunks. In the summer of 1939 he visited the United States before sailing for Europe and was fêted in Washington and in New York City. During his second visit in September 1940 the United States agreed to relinquish control of the Dominican customs. Here again in December 1940, he was entertained by General Marshall, Chief of Staff, and by President and Mrs. Roosevelt, and secured a loan of $3,000,000 from the Export-Import Bank. A year later, after the Pearl Harbor disaster, the Dominican Republic declared war on the Axis powers.

The Generalissimo is described as "of medium height and brown complexion," with a "fine figure" and a "close-cropped, fast-graying mustache." Villard says he is "very attractive when he laughs." He "discarded his first wife, a peasant like himself, mother of two daughters, and married a pale aristocratic beauty, Bienvenida Ricardo y Roman." He next divorced Bienvenida and married María de los Angeles Martinez Alba, by whom he had a son nicknamed "Ramfis" and titled "Illustrious Child," a military genius who was born in 1930 and by 1933 was drawing $150 a month as colonel in the Army. (Maria herself has been allowed to run the country's hardware and laundry monopolies.)

Trujillo "guzzles gallons of champagne, unchilled"; it is said that he has not read more than a dozen serious books in his life, although his political thought can be obtained in three volumes, printed in Spanish; he has a great passion for horseback riding; he once imported to his capital a French cabaret complete with dancing girls, waiters, chefs and liquor. But his life is not altogether lighthearted. When he receives visitors four gunmen train sub-machine guns on them, and his guests walk timorously and respectfully backward out of his presence.

References

Bul Pan Am Union 73:506-9 S '39 por
Cur Hist 48:31-4 Ja '38 il (Same abr. Read Digest 32:20-2 Ap '38)
Foreign Policy Rep 12:30-4 Ap 15 '36
Lit Digest 122:13 Jl 4 '36 por; 122:47 S 5 '36
Nation 144:323-4 Mr 20 '37
N Y Sun p15 F 1 '41
Newsweek 10:13 Jl 31 '37 il
PM p8 N 29 '40; p13 Ja 10 '41 por; p7 Ja 14 '41

Ariza, S. Trujillo: the Man and His Country 1939
De Besault, L. President Trujillo, His Work and the Dominican Republic 1936

Gunther, J. Inside Latin America p440-5
1941
International Who's Who
Who's Who in Latin America

TRUMBO, DALTON 1905- Novelist;
screen writer
Address: b. c/o J. B. Lippincott Co, Philadelphia, Pa.

This young novelist and screen writer who
brought General Andrew Jackson back to life
in *The Remarkable Andrew* (January 1941)
is already known to readers for his horrify-
ing anti-war novel, *Johnny Got His Gun*
(1939) and to movie-goers for his adaptations of such screen plays as *Kitty Foyle*
and *A Man to Remember*. The remarkable
thing about Dalton Trumbo is his versatility
and fecundity as a writer, plus a genuine—
and so far unshakable—integrity. He takes
writing for films as seriously as he does his
novel writing: "He believes it's a great job
and you can make fine pictures in Hollywood
if you fight for them."

The Remarkable Andrew is to be released
by Paramount in early 1942. As a novel
it is a biting, satirical allegory, something on
the order of *Candide*. It concerns a poor
but honest young bookkeeper, Andrew Long,
whose hobby is reading the biographies of
America's historically great. One day when
young Andrew's books won't balance and he
gets into a jam with the town's crooked politicians, to the rescue comes his particular
American hero, good old whiskey-drinking
General Jackson. The pages in which Jackson talks with his protégé about the War
are full of witty, "satiric shafts at New
Deal economy and philosophy" and at the
Administration's foreign policy. "By Jupiter,
it just shows what can happen when a Whig
gets into the White House!" growls the
General. When told that Roosevelt isn't a
Whig, but "the greatest Democratic President
since Andrew Jackson," the ghost of Jackson
nearly passes out. Major critical opinion
lauded the book, in spite of its controversial
content, because it was clever, funny, readable
—and timely. "It is an important book if
only because a man dared to write it with the
times so out of joint."

Like the doughty Jackson, Dalton Trumbo
is himself a fighter: he fought to get into
print exactly what he wanted to say in *The
Remarkable Andrew* and in *Johnny Got His
Gun*. He has fought Hollywood censorship
boards in defending his belief that people want
better films. "The American people should be
able to exercise their democratic right to approve or disapprove the pictures Hollywood
gives them." He has fought for trade union
rights, and in 1941 was the author of a pamphlet on the Harry Bridges case, likened by
Donald Ogden Stewart (see sketch this issue)
to *J'Accuse*.

For Dalton Trumbo comes of fighting American stock. His first ancestor of whom he
has direct knowledge was Jacob Trumbo, a
mixture of French and Swiss, who settled in

Baskerville

DALTON TRUMBO

Virginia in 1730. His mother's family, the
Tillerys, arrived a little later, swung down into
Missouri. Both branches fought in the Revolution and the Indian Wars, and on opposite
sides during the Civil War. After the Civil
War, Trumbo's maternal grandfather moved
to Colorado and was a frontier sheriff during
the battles between cattlemen and sheepherders.
Grandpa was a straight shooter: he died a
natural death just before Dalton's first book
was published. He always maintained that his
grandson was "a damnsight better writer than
O. O. McIntyre."

Dalton Trumbo was born in 1905 in Colorado in an apartment his parents occupied
back of a small-town library. The family
moved to Grand Junction, where Dalton went
to high school and worked as a cub reporter
on the local paper. The westward trek begun
by the family 200 years earlier was then completed when they moved on to California.
Dalton was in his first year at the University
of Colorado; but at the death of his father he
joined his family and went to work as a night
bread-wrapper in the largest bakery in Los
Angeles. There he worked nearly 10 years.
During that time he wrote eighty-eight short
stories and six novels, all rejected; attended
the University of Southern California for almost two years, reviewed movies for a trade
magazine and did various other jobs.

Finally he began selling stories and essays to
Vanity Fair, *The Forum* and other magazines,
and quit his bakery job. In 1934 he became
managing editor of the Hollywood *Spectator*,
then went to Warner Brothers as a reader in
the story department. His first books, *Eclipse*
(1935) and *Washington Jitters* (1936, later
produced as a stage play by the Theatre Guild)
were published. While at Warner's he also
sold stories to the *Saturday Evening Post*
and *Liberty*.

TRUMBO, DALTON—*Continued*

For his third novel, *Johnny Got His Gun* (1939), Trumbo got the idea from reading about a British officer who was a World War "basket case"—a living thing from which war had taken arms, legs, sight, hearing, speech. How such a pitiable victim felt, thought, finally communicated, told in the stream-of-consciousness method, made "a book that can never be forgotten by anyone who reads it." On his radio program Arch Oboler presented a dramatic monologue of it, played by James Cagney.

Dalton Trumbo has tried to dispel the popular assumption that "all Hollywood writers are hacks." He believes that the position of a script writer should not be that of a hired employee who must carry out orders. He himself once got a 20-day payroll suspension for refusal to accept writing assignments because of the poor quality of the material handed to him. Screen plays, like stage plays, should be written on a free-lance basis, he thinks, so that producers will respect a writer's work. This Trumbo proved feasible by writing three original screen plays in one year and selling each of them. Among his screen plays are *A Bill of Divorcement*, *We Who Are Young* and *The Man with the Shovel*. He considers *A Man to Remember* his best screen work to date.

Trumbo lives on a mile-high ranch 85 miles from Hollywood with his beautiful wife, Cleo, and their baby daughter. He met his wife when she was working at a roadside hamburger stand, and enjoys telling stuffed shirts that "Cleo was a waitress." He has been East only once. At that time he took pictures with a movie camera of scenes which he felt were relics of the past and which he wants to show his young daughter when she grows up. Trumbo has no other hobbies; he almost never exercises; and he belongs to no organization except the Screen Writers' Guild.

References

Friday 1:25 D 13 '40 por
N Y Times p21 My 23 '40
Variety 138:5 My 8 '40
International Motion Picture Almanac

TRYON, GEORGE CLEMENT TRYON, 1ST BARON May 15, 1871—Nov. 24, 1940 British Commissioner of Public Works since May 1940 after five years as Postmaster General.

References

Who's Who

Obituaries

N Y Times p17 N 25 '40 por

TUGWELL, REX(FORD GUY) July 10, 1891- Governor of Puerto Rico

Address: b. Government House, San Juan, Puerto Rico

Rexford Guy Tugwell, the debonair ex-Brain Truster who on August 25, 1941 was confirmed by the Senate as Governor of Puerto

REX TUGWELL

Rico, was born on July 10, 1891 in Sinclairville, New York. The son of Dessie (Rexford) and Charles Henry Tugwell, a prosperous farmer, he attended high school in Buffalo, worked during his last year as reporter on the *Courier*, then in 1911 went on to the Wharton School of Finance and Commerce of the University of Pennsylvania to major in economics.

Four years later he took his B. S. in economics—having been managing editor of the college newspaper, a member of the prom committee and a credit to Delta Upsilon. In 1914 he had married Florence E. Arnold, and for two years after graduation stayed at the University of Pennsylvania as instructor in economics, in 1916 taking his Master's Degree. His ambitions were already apparent; a poem written in 1915 announces:

> I am sick of a Nation's stenches;
> I am sick of propertied Czars;
> I have dreamed my great dream
>   of their passing.
> I have gathered my tools and my
>   charts;
> My plans are fashioned and
>   practical:
> I shall roll up my sleeves—make
>   America over!

In 1917, when Professor Scott Nearing was dismissed, he rolled up his sleeves and went to the University of Washington as assistant professor of economics. In Paris managing the American University Union during the last months of the First World War, he returned to an instructorship in economics at Columbia University. He was to remain there for many years, one of the most popular lecturers on the campus: assistant professor from 1922 to 1926; associate professor from 1926 to 1931; professor from 1931 to 1937, during his period of Government service in Washington.

That he was already impatient with orthodox economics, convinced that industry should be regulated to serve social ends, was evident from his earliest writings: his doctorate thesis, *The Economic Basis of Public Interest*, published in 1922, when he exchanged his Mister for a Doctor; articles in academic quarterlies and in the *New Republic*, of which he was a contributing editor; an untextbook-like textbook called *American Economic Life and the Means of Its Improvement* (1925), written with two equally experimental colleagues and liberally illustrated with pictures of the contemporary world; *Industry's Coming of Age* (1927), with its prefatory indictment of the way his subject was ordinarily taught.

Tugwell mingled freely with the Socialists of the League for Industrial Democracy and the Civil Liberties Union, and in the summer of 1927 took advantage of an opportunity to spend two months in the Soviet Union with a delegation of 13 trade-unionists and intellectuals which also included Stuart Chase, today one of his most articulate admirers. The result was a critical survey, *Soviet Russia in the Second Decade* (1928), which Tugwell edited and to which he contributed a chapter on Russian agriculture. He came back impressed, convinced that "the Russians and ourselves have much to learn from one another," but completely unsympathetic with revolutionary tactics: "Force never solves anything," he is fond of saying.

That same year, too, Tugwell spent six months making a survey of the American agricultural problem for New York's Governor, and in 1928 he was working for Al Smith's election to the Presidency. Intensely critical of the Harding, Coolidge and Hoover regimes, convinced long before the stock market crash of 1929 that the American economic system was due to collapse if its abuses were not corrected, in December 1931 he made a speech before the American Economic Association of Washington in which he announced that a planned economy would necessarily imply the death of *laissez faire,* the virtual abolition of business.

His approach to economic problems, in other words, prefigured the New Deal to a certain extent (though in Paul W. Ward's words, he spoke things "that neither Marx or Winchell knew till now"). And when in 1932 Roosevelt was campaigning for the Democratic Presidential nomination, Raymond Moley, who had known Tugwell at Columbia, suggested that he might be a valuable counselor. Tugwell joined Moley and A. A. Berle as one of Roosevelt's close pre-election advisers, particularly on agricultural problems; later he urged Moley to recommend Henry Wallace as Secretary of Agriculture; he, in turn, was asked by Wallace to be Assistant Secretary; and that was how, in 1933, the aloof professor came to the New Deal in an official capacity.

With "brooding eyes and molded features enframed by wavy hair," Tugwell was generally conceded to be the handsomest of the New Deal figures, and by the time the "brain trust" had become little more than a journalist's handle he was generally acknowledged as its spokesman. A widely publicized interview with the Scripps-Howard newspapers on January 26, 1933, in which he had advocated a $5,000,-000,000 fund to be used partly for relief, mainly to redistribute purchasing power, and "drastically higher" income and inheritance taxes, may have had something to do with this, even though he was obviously far from having his advice taken on all matters. He opposed internationalism as a foreign policy but urged international agreements to control production; he argued for extremely rapid expenditure of public works money so that its effect might be felt immediately, fought for provisions for consumer-protection in the National Recovery Act—and was defeated on all scores. Within the AAA itself Wallace and Tugwell, who advocated crop reduction rather than the dumping of farm surpluses, were eventually victorious, however, and Tugwell fathered currency legislation, the processing tax, the CCC. In 1934 he was a member of the Housing Board, the Surplus Relief Administration, the Commercial Policy Committee, the Public Works Board.

But he made enemies. His friends called him "too honest to keep his views to himself," his enemies called him a "Socialist" and a "Red." *The Industrial Discipline and the Government Arts* (1933) provided ammunition, although few book critics found it more than "ambitious for a good life for all"; so did *The Battle for Democracy* (1935), mainly a collection of his Washington speeches in favor of economic democracy and in defense of the New Deal; so did his plea for a farmer-labor alliance in Los Angeles that year; and the pure food and drugs law whose drafting he supervised at for nine months.

He was called both "the Administration's No. 1 embarrassment" and "Roosevelt's whipping-boy." As early as 1933 Mark Sullivan began dropping dire hints that Tugwell had entrapped a fundamentally conservative President into sponsoring a radical policy which would quietly revolutionize America; in June 1934, when he was nominated as Under-Secretary of Agriculture, the Senate Agricultural Committee which confirmed his appointment held a session in which similar suspicions were voiced; a certain Dr. William A. Wirt "discovered" a plot to overthrow the Government and establish a Red dictatorship with Tugwell as the Lenin or Stalin of the movement. To the *American Mercury* he was "the sweetheart of the regimenters," with a "grand-ducal manner"; to the *Saturday Evening Post* his literary style was best described as "Yours for the Revolution; Constitution, I love you." Tugwell, who called himself a conservative bent on saving capitalism from itself, gave up hope "that people who don't know me or anything about me will ever stop talking unknowingly about me." More than once he offered to resign. But there were too many to whom he was a symbol of Washington

TUGWELL, REX—*Continued*

progressivism and who, like Stuart Chase, were grateful that a man "so aware of the major currents in modern life" was "close to the wheel of the ship of state."

Although well in the background by the time of the 1936 elections, Tugwell was put in charge of the land-use part of the $4,800,000 work-relief fund, to be used for soil erosion, rural rehabilitation and electrification. His Resettlement Administration, later absorbed by the Agriculture Department and renamed the Farm Security Administration, also inherited from other departments certain subsistence-homestead projects. Government loans started needy farming families on new land, with new equipment. His controversial green-belt "Tug-welltowns" have since been used by both private enterprise and government as models for low-income suburban housing projects. His work in this Administration was, as always, both praised and attacked. Even one writer in *The Nation* called him a "fumbler" as a man of action, but in November 1936, when he resigned to become an executive vice-president of the American Molasses Company, Henry Wallace told newsmen: "You know, Rex has been one of the most vigorous fighters for the capitalist system that I know of. . . Men of Tugwell's courage and insight are rare. We shall all regret that he is no longer in the Government."

Tugwell did not completely quit politics, however. He continued to write articles urging the continuation of New Deal policies and finally giving regretful reasons for their virtual abandonment, and in April 1938 he was chosen by New York's La Guardia to succeed A. A. Berle as chairman of the City Planning Commission. That year he worked out the first annual capital budget for New York City ever used by any American Government—and he wrote the budget again in November 1940.

Finally, in May 1941, he sailed to Puerto Rico as special adviser to Secretary of the Interior Ickes (see sketch this issue), there holding hearings on the methods for enforcement of the law forbidding corporate ownership of more than 500 acres of land (ignored by the large sugar plantations) and on proposals for implementing the Puerto Rican Land Authority. Barely a month after his return in June he was selected as chancellor of the University of Puerto Rico with the backing of Luis Muñoz Marin, head of the Popular Party; and a few days later he was nominated as Governor of the "small and hungry" Island, rapidly being transformed by the United States into the key link for Caribbean and Canal Zone defense. The Senate Committee on Territories and Insular Affairs approved the nomination on August 18, 1941 and the Senate itself a week later. On September 19 Tugwell took the oath of office, simultaneously resigning as chancellor of the University. In his address he called for cooperation to combat the Island's "chief problem" of poverty.

Tugwell was divorced from his wife in 1938. There are two daughters, Tanis and Marcia. That same year he married Grace Falke. They have a son, Tyler. Tugwell himself is a gourmet, particularly expert in the preparation of rare salads; he scorns contract bridge; he likes to go canoeing around the island his parents own on Lake Ontario; he likes good talk. Raymond Moley once said: "Rex was like a cocktail: his conversation picked you up and made your brain race along." Books by him not previously mentioned are *Our Economic Society and Its Problems* (with Howard Copeland Hill, 1934), an "exceptionally realistic, practical and illuminating exposition," and *Redirecting Education* (with L. H. Keyserling, 1935), which includes his essay titled "Social Objectives in Education."

References

Am Mercury 39:77-86 S '36
Nation 138:61-2 Ja 17 '34; 143:623 N 28 '36
New Outlook 161:13-17 Mr '33
New Yorker 11:20+ Mr 23 '35; 11: 22+ Mr 30 '35
Newsweek 1:16-17 Ap 8 '33 por; 3:9-10 My 5 '34 por; 8:16-17 N 28 '36 il por
Sat Eve Post 209:8-9+ Ag 1 '36 il pors
Scrib Mag 94:257-66 N '33 por
Time 28:12-13 N 30 '36 por; 36:86-8 N 25 '40 por
America's Young Men 1936-37
Gillis, A. and Ketchum, R. Our America p357-72 1936
Lindley, E. K. Roosevelt Revolution p304-8 1933
Moley, R. After Seven Years 1939
Unofficial Observer [pseud.] New Dealers p85-92 1934
Who's Who in America
Who's Who in Commerce and Industry
Who's Who in the Nation's Capital 1934-35

ULRICH, CHARLES (KENMORE) 1859(?)—July 5, 1941 Playwright, journalist, novelist and publicist; one of the leading playwrights for amateurs who wrote more than 40 plays and sketches; had been on staff of the Chicago *Tribune* and the New York *Herald*; in 1918 became a member of the publicity staff of Paramount Pictures and later was with Pathe and the Code Authority of the motion picture industry; while with Paramount developed the "pressbook."

Obituaries

N Y Times p27 Jl 6 '41
Variety 143:54 Jl 9 '41

UPHAM, FRANCIS BOURNE, REV. Nov. 21, 1862—Mar. 19, 1941 Methodist minister for 53 years, former pastor of the John Street Church, Manhattan, oldest Methodist church in the United States; one of the leaders of his denomination, he had been former superintendent of the Brooklyn district of his church from 1911 to 1917; author of many religious books.

References
Who's Who Among North American
    Authors
Who's Who in America

Obituaries
N Y Times p22 Mr 20 '41 por

UREY, HAROLD C(LAYTON) (ü'rĭ)
Apr. 29, 1893- Chemist; head of the Department of Chemistry, Columbia University, New York City

Address: b. Columbia University, New York City; h. 355 Highwood Ave, Leonia, N. J.

Harold C. Urey was the youngest man ever to receive the Willard Gibbs Medal of the Chicago Section of the American Chemical Society, one of the highest awards in the chemical world. He was among the youngest to be awarded a still higher honor—the highest, in fact, that a scientist can attain: the Nobel Prize in science. Both came to him in 1934 (he was 41 then), as a result of his work in discovering and isolating that "excessively rare atomic freak known as 'heavy' hydrogen." In the fall of 1940 Professor Urey again was in the news, with sulphur the latest in his now substantial list of heavy atoms.

So rare is the heavy hydrogen atom that it represents only one in every 5,000 atoms of ordinary hydrogen. So costly was it that the "heavy" water manufactured from it was valued at $75,000 a gallon. And cheap at the price; for by the method formerly tried, it would have required an amount of water equal to the weight of the entire universe to produce one cubic centimeter of the precious liquid. So important was the achievement that it started new lines of research in three major scientific fields: chemistry, physics, biology. The entire research staffs of several leading universities, after Dr. Urey's first announcement in 1931 that he had isolated the heavy hydrogen atom, devoted their study to "deuterium," as it was called. The scientific world seemed to agree that no other recent accomplishment had exerted so profound an influence.

While a large number of his colleagues busied themselves digesting the results of his researches, Dr. Urey went on inquiring into the nature of what he had produced. The heavy hydrogen atom itself made possible horizon-shattering experiments with heavy water. But he added new elements to the heavy list in rapid succession, so that by 1938 he was able to announce: "We now have [the heavy isotopes of] hydrogen, oxygen, nitrogen and carbon; atoms from which 75 per cent of all substances are formed." Producing the carbon atom required the use of two deadly poisons, and canaries were kept near the apparatus to give warning by their death if any of the fatal gas was escaping. Aside from labor and apparatus, the new material cost $400 an ounce to produce. It was pointed out that if the carbon in coal came at that price, it would set the householder back $12,800,000 a ton.

HAROLD C. UREY

In the fall of 1940, sulphur joined the heavyweight atoms, its heavy isotope being produced in a tube 150 feet long. Appropriately enough, this new addition, like heavy carbon, was of particular importance to research in biology and medicine; for when Dr. Urey first entered college he intended to make biology his field, and even today he declares that nothing is more fun for him than talking to "a bunch of biologists."

Columbia's "Nobleman" is a product of the Midwest and our rural schools. He was born in Walkerton, Indiana, on April 29, 1893, the son of Samuel Clayton and Cora Rebecca (Reinoehl) Urey. When he was only six his father died, and his early education was due to heroic efforts by his mother, later aided by his stepfather. Rural schools contributed twice to his training, for he taught in them from 1911 to 1914, after his family had moved to Montana.

In 1917 he emerged from the University of Montana with a B. Sc. in zoology, ready to take his place as a biologist delving into the secrets of life. But during the War the country needed chemists, and for the next two years he served the Barrett Chemical Company of Philadelphia in this capacity. He has been serving as a chemist ever since. In 1919 he returned to the University of Montana as instructor in chemistry, but left to take his doctor's degree at the University of California. After receiving this in 1923 he spent a year in Copenhagen, as American-Scandinavian Foundation Fellow, studying under the noted atomic physicist, Professor Nils Bohr.

On his return to America he became associate in chemistry at Johns Hopkins University, where he remained until he joined the Columbia University faculty as associate professor in 1929. In 1930 he added to an extensive bibliography of papers and articles a book, written with A. E. Ruark: *Atoms, Mole-*

UREY, HAROLD C.—*Continued*

cules and Quanta. The year (1934) that brought him the Willard Gibbs Medal and the Nobel Prize also saw him promoted to full professorship at Columbia, where in 1941 he still teaches. In 1939 he was appointed executive officer of the Department of Chemistry.

While teaching at Johns Hopkins, in 1926 he married Frieda Daum, who has passed with honors the course for which there should be a matron of science degree. She has won campus plaudits if not a diploma for gentle firmness toward a husband not always able to resist the lure of a three-story nitrogen machine wrapped in tinfoil. More than once, unable to tear himself away, he has pitched a cot in the laboratory and camped there for the night.

It is whispered, too, that Mrs. Urey is responsible for the fact that her husband has not a wider reputation as an absent-minded professor. Campus reporters claim that he takes endless ribbing about it from those who know, and is generous about sharing the laughs when he walks into a class and begins lecturing, only to discover that he is in the wrong room. The favorite tale is about the day he hurried to his office wearing mismated shoes. They felt so strange he thought they must need shining, but after deep concentration discovered that they were just different shapes. At noon he went home for lunch, delighted at the chance to set his feet right—and returned in the afternoon wearing the same shoes, only this time one of them was shined!

Home is not easy to lunch at now, because he lives in Leonia, New Jersey, in the academic colony of educators from Columbia and other city institutions. As the father of four children (Gertrude Elizabeth, Frieda Rebecca, Mary Alice and John Clayton), his interest in education extends to the public schools, and in 1938 he was elected a member of the Leonia school board. He probably ranks this honor high among the many he has received—and their name is legion. He has honorary degrees from three universities, was editor from 1933 to 1940 of the *Journal of Chemical Physics*, is member of enough illustrious academies and societies to fill a modest telephone book and was awarded the Davy Medal in 1940.

The recipient of all these honors—and in 1935 of the very first bronze "Columbia Lion" awarded by the affiliated Columbia Alumni Clubs of New Jersey—is of medium height, with square shoulders, round face, alert brown eyes and graying brown hair. He periodically breaks himself of smoking two packages of cigarets a day by chewing gum with the vigor that marks all his undertakings. When his jaws have had a six months' workout, he breaks himself of gum-chewing by reverting to cigarets. In addition to being an expert in the structure of atoms and molecules, thermodynamic properties of gases, absorption spectra, Raman spectra and the separation of isotopes, he has other interests.

Professor Urey feels himself as much a citizen as a scientist. Former chairman of the

University Federation for Democracy and Intellectual Freedom, champion of Loyalist Spain, one of the scientists actively organized to further the objectives of the Committee for Defending America by Aiding the Allies, ardent in behalf of refugees from Fascist countries, he has never, in his efforts to widen the boundaries of knowledge, lost sight of the fellow humans whose domain he sought to increase. There is no hiatus between his convictions and his work. "A scientist can work best," he declares, "only when he is free to follow up what interests him. No dictator knows enough to tell scientists what to do. . . Only in democratic nations can science flourish."

He himself realizes that the scholar and researcher does not invariably share his emphasis. At the dedication of the New York Museum of Science and Industry in its new Radio City quarters, he voiced a direct challenge to economists and social scientists to secure a proper distribution of the products of science and industry. "It is one of the outstanding disappointments of scientific men that in spite of the accomplishments which I have briefly indicated, people still go cold, and they live in miserable tenements or shacks. . . We challenge our colleagues in other fields of work to undertake the task of bringing these things to the many who need them, and thus bring to them a more abundant life." A more abundant life: those words may be accepted as the goal, the gift, or the self-portrait of the speaker.

References

Christian Sci Mon N 17 '34; F 12 '36
Columbia Spec N 16 '34; N 19 '34; N 29 '34; Ap 9 '35; O 4 '35; D 5 '35; F 11 '36; D 13 '37; D 7 '38
La Nature 63 pt 1:236 Mr 1 '35 por
Lit Digest 117:11 Mr 10 '34 por
N Y Herald Tribune F 11 '34; Ap 28 '34; X Ap 29 '34; N 16 '34; Je 8 '38; D 6 '38; S 15 '39; S 9 '40
N Y Times p17 Ap 28 '34 por; p5 N 16 '34 por; p23 D 5 '35; VIII p11 O 10 '37 il por; p34 F 12 '39; p20 S 15 '39; p13 Jl 5 '40
Newsweek 4:38 N 24 '34 por
Sci Am 152:102-3 F '35
Sci Mo 38:387-90 Ap '34 por

American Men of Science
America's Young Men 1936-37
Chemical Who's Who
Hylander, C. J. American Scientists p169-70 1935
Ratcliff, J. D. Modern Miracle Men p111-24 1939
Who's Who in America

VALTIN, JAN (väl-tăN' yän) Dec. 17, 1905- Author

Address: c/o Alliance Book Corp, 212 Fifth Ave, New York City

Perhaps no book in recent years has received so much publicity as Jan Valtin's *Out of the Night.* Originally published in November 1940 as the anonymous autobiography of a former German secret agent of the Communist International, in February 1941 it was published in a revised edition as the selection of the Book-of-the-Month Club. By March 1941 it had sold some 347,000 copies, and was far ahead of any other non-fiction title in popularity. Critics called it "as vast in background, as moving, illuminating and humanly significant as a great novel", "an historical document of the first rank," a story that "casts a flood of light on the international underworld that has grown up in the shadow of the totalitarian dictatorships." It was condensed in two consecutive issues of *Life* (February 24 and March 3, 1941) and in *Reader's Digest* (March 1941) ; it was plugged on the radio ; the New York *Times* wrote an editorial about it.

At the same time the publisher's claims to absolute authenticity had not completely convinced even some of the critics who praised it. The Communists, of course, were vehement in their denunciations. But even Lewis Gannett complained that "such a witness as 'Valtin' is suspect as any story-telling spy . . . it sometimes suggests the anti-Soviet researches of Isaac Don Levine." A few other critics had similar doubts, although most decided, with Vincent Sheean (see sketch this issue), that the harrowing story was, "in the main, true." On the other hand, Freda Utley, Bertram D. Wolfe and *Time* made no such reservations, and W. H. Chamberlin called it "the most valuable work of its kind since the publication of the reminiscences of the fugitive Soviet intelligence officer Krivitzky." Valtin himself admitted some time after its publication that he "put into the story some things that happened to other people, not in order to make them appear my life," but as "typical of the totalitarian way."

Valtin's real identity has by this time been officially established both by records and by his own admission, although at one time he insisted that his life would be endangered if his name were known. He is Richard Julius Herman Krebs and, according to San Quentin prison records, was born in Darmstadt, Germany on December 17, 1905. (In *Out of the Night*, however, Valtin says he was born in 1904, near Mainz, and at another time he mentions that he was 11 by the time of the outbreak of the First World War.) From that point until his arrival in New York his autobiography is almost all that is available for information about him.

In that he tells us that he was the oldest of six children, the son of a traveling employee of the North German Lloyd, and spent his childhood in China, Malaya, Italy and other foreign lands. The First World War came, and left a Germany that was starving and disrupted. Valtin's father, a Social Democrat, was a leader in the Kaiser's fleet in November 1918. The boy himself became a cyclist for the revolutionary sailors' committee in the Weser shipyards in Hamburg, and was with the Young Spartacists throughout the disturbances of the winter. When the movement in Hamburg and in Bremen

JAN VALTIN

was crushed, he escaped to sea. By 1923, after varied hardships and humiliations, he returned to Germany, and in May he joined the Communist Party as an "activist" in the maritime unions. During the next two years he traveled all over the world for the Comintern (the Communist International), distributing propaganda, fomenting strikes, engaging in sabotage; and in 1925 he spent a year at the Communist university in Leningrad.

The year 1926 found him in California, where he was ordered by the Comintern to execute a "traitor." Neither willing to do it nor willing to disobey orders, he fumbled the job, and was sentenced to San Quentin for three years. (In the book, Valtin was arrested for striking a man "off a crowded street in broad daylight"; prison records, however, show that he was arrested for slugging a Los Angeles shopkeeper, Maurice L. Goodstein, a registered Republican who had lived in the United States since 1889, in an argument over the price of some shirts. There are also serious discrepancies in the two records of the trial.) His first year in San Quentin was spent in the prison jute mill. But life there was not entirely bad. He had not read a book since his fourteenth birthday; now he read Jack London, Conrad, studied English, French, Spanish, navigation, journalism, map making. (A great deal of this, at least, can be verified, for people at the University of California remember him as a promising former student.) By his second year he was prison librarian, by his third year a teacher of languages and mathematics. At the same time he had 30 articles published in the San Quentin *Bulletin*. Yet, he says, he managed to organize secret Marxist schooling circles, a library of revolutionary literature and an atheist league, and to maintain contact with the Comintern network outside. In the first days of December 1929 he left San Quentin, and

VALTIN, JAN—*Continued*

three days later boarded a steamer bound for Europe.

Back in Germany, Valtin was given steadily more important assignments; by 1931 he had been taken into the "inner circles of the Comintern" and was directing water-front operations in Western Europe. By the next year, at the time of the most violent struggles against the Nazis, he was working in Germany directly under Dimitrov (now General Secretary of the Executive Committee of the Communist International). It was February 1933 when Valtin was captured by the German secret police, the Gestapo; after four years of almost incredible horror in Nazi concentration camps he received orders from the Comintern to get himself accepted as a Gestapo agent. He was successful in his deception and was sent to do espionage in the Soviet Union, but his young son and his wife, Firelei, who years before had joined the Communist Party out of devotion to him, were left as hostages with the Nazis. Moreover, by this time he was thoroughly disillusioned with the Comintern, wanted above all to rescue his wife, and when he returned to working with the OGPU (the Russian secret service), his independent attitude made his comrades suspicious. Valtin escaped, fled. Soon he found himself denounced in the Party press as a Gestapo agent; as a direct result, in July 1938 Firelei was seized by the Gestapo. The book closes after Valtin has received word of his wife's death in prison, in July 1938.

Many critics have described Valtin's book as showing the gradual degradation of the Communist International from an idealistic instrument of world revolution into a tool of the Russian state, of the OGPU; but the picture which Valtin paints shows little but betrayal, deception and errors from the very beginning. On none of his visits to the Soviet Union did Valtin see anything but misery. Furthermore, "the professional revolutionists are, with one or two brief and minor exceptions, represented as lascivious, greedy and cynical men." Even Dimitrov, almost universally remembered as the hero of the Reichstag fire trial, was in Valtin's eyes a "large, soft, flabby-faced individual . . . dressed like a dandy and smelling of heavy perfume," a small-minded tyrant who had secretly collaborated with Nazi leaders in destroying the last shreds of Social Democracy and the trade unions, who at the trial itself had been promised acquittal in advance and merely put up a show of defiance to Goering (see sketch this issue). There is hardly a chapter in which Valtin does not mention his own doubts, his sudden urges to "get free" in order to go back to the sea, to earn his living by writing, or simply to lead a normal life with Firelei. Yet this is the alleged record of 20 years of fanatical devotion to a cause. The book takes its title from William Ernest Henley's *Invictus*:

> Out of the night that covers me,
>   Black as the Pit from pole to pole,
> I thank whatever gods may be
>   For my unconquerable soul.

A story published in *PM* makes Krebs seem even more mysterious than Valtin. Among other things, it quotes a friend of his, Robert Bek-Gran, as saying that he was merely one of seven Hamburg boys who became waterfront terrorists, ran errands for various revolutionary societies, at times shipped out as sailors and finally became professional revolutionists. According to Bek-Gran, Krebs was never the "important Communist" that the book portrays, never on any "inner circle of the Comintern." One by one, he says, the seven youths escaped from Nazi prisons or were released and came to the United States; Krebs was the last. Early in 1938 he jumped ship at Norfolk and came to New York to get in touch with the others (Krebs himself at first denied both of these statements, but later said frankly that he "skipped ship" at Norfolk and came up the highways to New York); Bek-Gran helped feed him, and when in the fall of 1939 Krebs contracted pleurisy, Bek-Gran arranged for his hospitalization. Later, Bek-Gran says, he took him to his Connecticut home, where Krebs stayed until 1940 while working on the first draft of his novel, originally a novel of the sea, with neither an anti-Fascist nor an anti-Communist aim.

It is known that Krebs had already had two articles published in *Ken* under the name of Jan Valtin, and that in 1939 Eugene Lyons of the *American Mercury* accepted an article entitled *Communist Agent*. Finally Isaac Don Levine "discovered" Krebs, took him to his place in Danbury, Connecticut, staked him to $10 a week while working, and later did the "cutting" on *Out of the Night*.

There have been mysterious rumors as to Krebs' connections with the FBI, too. Said Leonard Lyons, in his (New York *Post*) gossip column: "Krebs, now being guarded by Federal men, has received permission to remain in this country in return for the assistance he is rendering the government." The reporter from *PM* who interviewed Valtin said he "mentioned the FBI frequently . . . made it clear that he had powerful friends here now." Evidently the Book-of-the Month Club's acceptance of *Out of the Night* was clinched only after A. A. Berle of the State Department had read it. On the other hand, Kenneth Crawford of *PM* announced "with complete assurance" that Krebs had received no immunity from deportation from any branch of the Government, and said he was deportable on five counts, the most important of which was the California conviction for assault in 1926. On March 13 it was reported that the Justice Department had actually begun action to deport him, although obviously there would be difficulty in finding a place to which to send him. On March 28 he was arrested and released on bond after questioning. In the meanwhile, subpoenaed by the Dies subcommittee, Krebs testified that "it is impossible for anyone to be released from a Nazi concentration camp unless he takes a pledge to serve the Gestapo," a generalization which brought protests from groups trying to aid refugees. Deportation hearings continued all this time, but nothing was settled. In August Krebs tried to secure a pardon from the State Advisory Board at San Francisco and William Allen White begged Governor Olson to pardon him, a request which was not granted until November 30.

Two published interviews with Krebs provide a fairly good description of him. His right ear isn't much good; he was slugged with a loaded club, he says. The upper teeth on the right side of his jaw are missing, too. But he is more than six feet tall, with wavy medium brown hair, "a good straight nose, a high forehead and, in general, excellent features," and shows no scars in spite of re-counted whippings across the face with wet leather. "His almost childlike Teutonic face is placid, but every once in a while it clouds up and you see violence and turbulence underneath. His voice, too, is by turns quiet and stormy." He is said to show, in conversation, "something of the same remarkable memory that the book implies." Since his arrival in the United States he has been married—to 17-year old Abigail Harris. A son was born to them on July 26, 1941.

Krebs proclaims that he is high on the OGPU's list for assassination, and at his home in the country keeps not only a rifle but also a 200-pound Great Dane, trained "to bark at strangers and to go for the throat at a word." He also religiously hid his face from all photographers until March 1941; what made him change his mind about it all is not known. As for the Gestapo: "I am not so sure they want me—enough, that is, to do anything about it." A new book of short stories is due in February 1942 called *Bird in the River*. *Out of the Night* is all the "politics" that he is of a mind to write, although an article about the OGPU signed by Jan Valtin and entitled *Why Krivitzky Died* appeared in Hearst's New York *Journal-American* not long after the suicide. In other publications similar articles, as well as articles praising the United States and American democracy, have appeared since then, and their author has been in great demand as a lecturer and radio speaker.

References

Book-of-the-Month Club News p1-4 Ja '41 il
Ken Ag 3 '39
N Y Times Book R p2, 20 F 9 '41 il
New Yorker 17:14-15 Mr 15 '41
Newsweek 17:534 Ja 20 '41; 17:14 F 24 '41
PM p12-15 Mr 3 '41 il por; p7 Mr 5 '41; p10 Mr 7 '41; p15-16 Mr 30 '41 por
Pub W 139:1124-5 Mr 8 '41
Wilson Lib Bul 16:213-19+ N '41
Valtin, J. Out of the Night 1941

VAN DEVANTER, WILLIS (văn' dê-văn'-tẽr) Apr. 17, 1859—Feb. 8, 1941 Former associate justice of the United States Supreme Court; started practice of law in 1881; Wyoming State Supreme Court Chief Justice 1889; returned to private practice to serve as counsel for most of the Wyoming powerful

interests after only one year on the bench; in 1897 was made United States Assistant Attorney General and stayed in this post until 1903 when Theodore Roosevelt made him judge of the Eighth Circuit Court of Appeals; named to Supreme Court in 1910 by President Taft and served there until his retirement in 1937, winning a reputation as a consistent conservative, an uncomprising dry and a foe of all major New Deal legislation.

References

Fortune 13:178+ My '36 por (p83)
Lit Digest 117:9+ Ap 7 '34 por (cover)
Nation's Bus 25:17-18+ Jl '37 por
New Repub 87:166-9 Je 17 '36
Time 29:17-18 My 31 '37 por
Pearson, D. and Allen, R. S. Nine Old Men p186-97 1936
Who's Who in America
Who's Who in Government
Who's Who in Law
Who's Who in the Nation's Capital

Obituaries

N Y Times p47 F 9 '41 por

VAN DOREN, IRITA Mar. 16, 1891- Editor

Address: b. Books, New York Herald Tribune, 230 W. 41st St, New York City; h. 6 W. 77th St, New York City

Editor since 1926 of the New York *Herald Tribune's* weekly review section, *Books*, Irita Van Doren holds the high respect of the book trade and book-reading public throughout the country. Her skilled editorial judgment, her efficiency and punctuality in getting news and reviews of the latest books to readers, and her genuinely democratic policy of selecting not only books but reviewers to represent all shades of tastes and opinions, have made *Books* invaluable to authors, publisher, librarians and booksellers, as well as to readers in general.

"Since *Books* is published as part of a large newspaper," Mrs. Van Doren says with regard to her editorial policy, "it must count among its potential readers people of every variety, taste and opinion (not all readers of the *Herald Tribune* are Republicans!)" And, since all kinds of books are published, "it seems only fair to review them from the point of view from which they are written, so that they will ultimately find the audience for whom they are intended. . . We try not to editorialize on book reviews, though our record in this matter is not always 100 per cent good, as it is often difficult to steer a clear course between an editorial attitude and a frank expression of opinion. However, we firmly believe that reviews should be signed, and have followed that policy from the beginning."

Annually *Books* sponsors, together with the American Booksellers' Association, a Book and Author luncheon series held in New York City. Mrs. Van Doren is in charge of selecting the speakers for these luncheons. Among the writers who have spoken at the series

Ben Pinchot

IRITA VAN DOREN

are Vincent Sheean, John Gunther, Jan Struther (see sketches this issue), Ève Curie, Carl Sandburg, Edna Ferber, André Maurois, Dorothy Thompson and Lin Yutang. When she became editor of *Books* Mrs. Van Doren inaugurated a staff of visiting critics as front-page features, which ran for five years. Since then the outstanding book of the week is usually front-page news. Another feature running currently is a weekly biographical-critical study, by Stephen and Rosemary Benét, of some well known contemporary writer. Also of special interest to readers is the chart of best sellers compiled from statistics sent in by booksellers from all over the country. *Books* reviews annually upward of 2,500 books, and nearly 300 reviewers write for the section each year. Each fall and each spring there is a special Children's Book Number, and three other special seasonal numbers annually.

An early interest in and love for books shaped Irita Van Doren's career from the beginning. She was born in Birmingham, Alabama on March 16, 1891, the daughter of John Taylor and Ida (Brooks) Bradford. Her mother's family was from Alabama, her father's lived in Florida; and when she was four the Bradfords moved to Tallahassee. Her father died when she was nine; and her mother was left with the problem of bringing up and educating four children: Irita, the eldest, her sister and two younger brothers. Mrs. Bradford turned her amateur skills to practical use. An accomplished musician, she gave music lessons. She was also a good cook, and the children helped her in putting up the many jars of preserves and jellies which were exchanged at the local stores for staple groceries. They made this work fun: all

loved books and they took turns reading aloud on the big shady veranda while guavas and figs were prepared for the boiling kettles.

Irita Bradford attended the Florida State College for Women at Tallahassee, from which she was graduated in 1908—at the precocious age of 17—and in recent years, after the chapter was instituted there, given Phi Beta Kappa honors. She was editor of the college literary magazine, and became interested in going North to study through the influence of S. Marion Tucker, a professor at the college who was a Ph. D. of Columbia University. Accordingly she came in 1909 to Columbia to take her Doctor's Degree. While studying at Columbia she tried all kinds of jobs to earn her tuition, including a year as substitute teacher at Hunter College. Her special interests, in addition to English, were Latin and mathematics.

At Columbia she met Carl Van Doren, well known biographer and critic, who was then also a graduate student there. In August 1912 they were married. He was by this time a young instructor, and during the early years of their marriage Mrs. Van Doren helped him with the research on his first books. The young couple bought an old farm in West Cornwall, Connecticut, where they spent the long summer vacations. Three children were born: Anne (1915), Margaret (1917) and Barbara (1920). The marriage was dissolved by divorce in 1935.

From 1919 to 1922 Mrs. Van Doren was on the editorial staff of *The Nation*, from 1922 to 1923 advertising manager of that weekly, then in 1923 succeeded John Macy as its literary editor. When Stuart P. Sherman was made editor in 1924 of the *Herald Tribune Books*, he came on condition that she become his assistant; since he was interested chiefly in critical writing, he did not want to be responsible for all the details involved in getting out a publication. Under this arrangement Mr. Sherman confined his activities to a weekly critical article and left the running of *Books* largely to Mrs. Van Doren. On his death in 1926 she succeeded him as editor.

Irita Van Doren's unusually vivid, warmly engaging manner and her ready wit make many friends; her real interest in people, her generosity, her tolerant, liberal viewpoint, hold them. With a personality suggesting light over water quickened by a fresh breeze (there is deep water beneath, and the obtuse may well be wary), one is not surprised to learn that Mrs. Van Doren's hobby is sailing. As a girl she spent her summers on the Gulf of Mexico and learned to sail and fish. Now her idea of a real vacation is to sail with friends, cruising preferably along the ragged Maine coast.

References

Pub W 133:1841 My 7 '38 por; 136: 1338-47 S 30 '39 pors; 137:1733 My 4 '40 por
Scholastic 32:25E My 7 '38 por; 36:24 My 6 '40 por

American Women
Who's Who in America

VANSITTART, ROBERT (GILBERT), 1ST BARON (văn-sĭt'ärt) June 25, 1881- British diplomat

Address: 44 Park St, Grosvenor Sq, W. 1, London, England

On June 25, 1941, having reached the age of 60, Baron Robert Vansittart of Denham ("Machiavelli-and-Soda") retired from his post as chief diplomatic adviser to the British Foreign Secretary. Since his appointment to that newly-created office in January 1938 the "magnificent anonymity" of the man who shaped British foreign policy throughout the '30s (and at whose house Cabinet Ministers and kings were happy to dine) had been more magnificent than ever. Between his visit to the United States in the autumn of 1938 and the announcement of his retirement one of the few references to his activities had been a note in *Newsweek* reporting that he was heading a new department entitled the British Council for Publicity Abroad and was attempting to combat Nazi and Fascist propaganda in other countries. After the Second World War his name was mentioned even less frequently, at least until the publication of his *Black Record* early in 1941. It was not until after his retirement that Baron Vansittart of Denham (he was included on King George VI's June honors list) announced that he could "speak plainly."

Eugene C. Young, long-time foreign editor of the New York *Times*, commented on this comparative lack of publicity while Vansittart was still permanent Under-Secretary of State for the Foreign Office. Going through the *Times* morgue, Young found fat envelopes on Simon, Hoare, Eden (see sketches 1940 Annual), Baldwin, almost nothing on Vansittart— "no speeches, no interviews, no exploitation." "Yet," he continued, "I knew this person, in the time under review, had been the real stabilizing power in the London Foreign Office, the one who always had to be consulted when great decisions were to be taken."

The bare facts of Vansittart's life are available enough. He was the eldest son of the late Captain Robert Arnold Vansittart, master of the estate of Huxley and North Cray, himself without a title but with ancestors and close relatives who held high positions in the British Army and Government. Young Robert was educated at Eton and entered the diplomatic service as an attaché in 1902, when he was only 21, after having presented satisfactory references and passed a rigorous examination. The next year he was in Paris, training at the Paris Embassy at a time when France and Britain were quarreling over Africa. A French writer who knew him at the time described him as a good companion, sportsman, linguist who already gave the impression of knowing everyone and everything and of having read every book written. To all appearances the young diplomat was chiefly interested in poetry (particularly that of Henri de Régnier) and the theatre—he himself had written a French play, *Les Pariahs*, which had had a 100-night run at the Théâtre Molière—and yet there was a suggestion of reserve about him.

The New York Public Library

LORD VANSITTART

He was popular with the French. And he rose quickly in the diplomatic service: in 1905 became third secretary, in 1906 earned the decoration of the Royal Victorian Order for unrecorded reasons, and a year later left Paris to spend seven years in the Orient. He was in Teheran in 1907 when Britain was struggling with Russia for control of Persia; the following year he was appointed second secretary; and in 1909, when Britain was trying to get a firm grip on Egypt, he was sent to Cairo. The First World War found him assistant clerk in the Foreign Office, and in 1915 he turned up in Stockholm to try to block Swedish cooperation with the Germans in letting them get supplies from the outside.

After becoming first secretary in 1919 and returning to Paris to collaborate with Sir Eyre Crowe in the peace negotiations and the adjustment of Anglo-French relations, he came to the attention of the newly-appointed British Foreign Secretary, "mammoth, crusty" Lord Curzon, "ardent imperialist and nationalist." Appointed a counselor, he served as Lord Curzon's private secretary until his retirement—from 1920 to 1924—and then became head of Whitehall's American department. In 1928 Prime Minister Stanley Baldwin took him as his principal private secretary (his diplomatic rank by this time was Assistant Under-Secretary of State); Ramsay MacDonald kept him as his own secretary; he accompanied the Prime Minister to the United States and Canada.

It was 1930 when Vansittart was appointed permanent Under-Secretary of State for Foreign Affairs. As one writer phrases it, the man who holds this position must have proved that he is "sound" —"no idealist and no internationalist . . . one who has dedicated his life and career to the country and the Empire and therefore one who will always think in terms

VANSITTART, ROBERT, 1ST BARON
—*Continued*

of their interests. These men are hard-headed, practical, and, because of their long experience in dealing with diplomatic maneuvering, at least gently cynical realists."

Indeed, Vansittart's was a position far more important than most Cabinet posts, for "no party government could remove him if he personally behaved himself and then it could act only with the consent of the King. He was above party, the acknowledged guardian of the policy and security of Britain and the British Empire . . . the shepherd of Prime Ministers and secretaries." The files of the permanent organization, full of carefully collected facts on every imaginable subject (the permanent Under-Secretary has the British Secret Service under his direct control, and disburses thousands of pounds of the Foreign Office's "secret funds") are consulted whenever any important international issue arises; the King, who must be consulted on all such affairs and give his approval to every Cabinet decision, every important note to an ambassador or minister, also depends chiefly on the permanent office for his decisions.

It was said that Sir Robert was one of the three men who really ruled Britain, and even Karl Abshagen wrote: "It would be difficult to exaggerate the influence this highly intelligent, finely cultured, versatile man has had on his Parliamentary chiefs, particularly those who, like MacDonald and Henderson, were never quite up to his social assurance and his Eton manners, but also on Mr. Baldwin, whose complaisance and irresolution in international affairs he easily parried with his acknowledged superiority in expert knowledge and detailed information! He had, indeed, and probably still has, fuller and more intimate information (though colored and one-sided) in every field of international policy than any other man in England."

When MacDonald visited President Roosevelt in 1933 to arrange for American participation in the World Economic Conference, Vansittart, who in 1931 had been knighted as commander of St. Michael and St. George, was by his side in all important negotiations. He was present at the Stresa Conference; in 1935 he drafted the Anglo-German naval treaty (at which the French cried "Treason!") ; at the time of the Ethiopian crisis he initiated the policy by which the Government agreed to sanctions in order to win an electoral victory, afterward made them ineffective and dropped them; and at the Anglo-French Conference on Ethiopia in December 1935 he was constantly with Sir Samuel Hoare while the latter was outlining to Laval (see sketch 1940 Annual) the scheme by which Italy would get more than half of Abyssinia.

When the terms of this last plan were prematurely revealed and public indignation aroused, a great part of the press felt that Hoare was "taking the rap" for Vansittart. Vansittart even offered to resign, and for a while the general impression was that he had retired, but the winter of 1936 found him in Berlin, attending the Olympic games and incidentally persuading Germany that she must not demand territorial concessions from Spain for aiding Franco. Then in July 1937 *Newsweek* reported that he was negotiating with the Royalists among Franco's forces, evidently hoping through them to wean Franco away from both Mussolini and Hitler, and at the same time was wooing the Nazis with an eye to having them help Mussolini less and less. Apparently this was all part of a general plan: "Britain . . . wants Franco to win, but cannot openly support him; and wants Mussolini to lose, but cannot afford to see him withdraw from Spain."

At about the same time the late Robert Dell was writing indignantly in *The Nation* that Anthony Eden, then Foreign Secretary, was being allowed "to say things that he himself believes, or at least half believes," only in order "to deceive people about the real nature and aims of British policy." Dell also accused the permanent Under-Secretary of having tried to break up the Little Entente and the Balkan Entente and of wanting to "reform" the League of Nations into a debating society without coercive powers against an aggressor. According to this writer, Vansittart's aim was to keep Britain aloof from all pacts of mutual assistance east of the Rhine and to disengage France from any such commitments, under the illusion that by the time Hitler had "gone east" England would be strong enough to make an alliance with the Nazis on her own terms and to force France to come into the Anglo-German combination as a second-class power. To back up this interpretation Dell produced evidence that Vansittart had been hostile to the Franco-Russian alliance, had supported Belgium when she broke her British and French alliance, and had encouraged the Henlein Party in Czechoslovakia and Yugoslavia's rapprochement with Italy and Germany. Others have been equally certain that Vansittart's views were by that time strongly anti-German, however, and that he was merely unable to convince the appeasers of the dangers inherent in their policies.

After Chamberlain became Prime Minister in 1937 it was given out that Vansittart had retired, although it was also hinted once more that he might become next Ambassador to the United States. Then in January 1938, after Chamberlain had sent Lord Halifax (see sketch 1940 Annual) to Berlin against Vansittart's will and the mission had failed, the "temporary eclipse of his influence" apparently came to an end. He was elevated to the title of Knight Grand Cross of the Most Honorable Order of the Bath, and a special post was created for him: "chief diplomatic adviser to the Foreign Office," with the duties of "advising the Secretary of State [still Anthony Eden] upon all major questions of policy concerning foreign affairs . . . representing the Foreign Office on any occasions, whether at home or abroad."

He remained in his quarters and kept the same salary (3,000 pounds a year), and although the intimate direction of the experts of the permanent office passed out of his hands to Sir Alexander Cadogan, Robert Dell once again mourned: "In practice he will be a permanent Foreign Secretary responsible only to his nominal superior, who will be obliged to cover him and take the responsibility for his policy . . . more than ever . . . withdrawn from the control of Parliament and public opinion. . . The policy of an understanding with the Fascist powers is likely to be pursued more consistently and perhaps more openly than hitherto."

Nevertheless *Fortune* suggested that Chamberlain "politely kicked Sir Robert Vansittart into an upstairs job that effectively prevents him from raising awkward questions about foreign policy." Circumstances seemed to show that he was in conflict with both Eden and the appeasers, and it seems certain, at least, that his disillusionment with the Nazis considerably preceded Chamberlain's. Others since then have indicated that his chief function was the direction and coordination of British propaganda abroad, but no one seems to have known the exact extent and nature of his activities from that time until his retirement in June 1941. Earlier that year, however, he had published a tract called *Black Record* which caused violent controversy in Britain because of his insistence that the British were fighting not only Hitlerism, but the entire German people, who had always been bloodthirsty.

In 1921 Vansittart married Mrs. Gladys Robinson Duff, an American, the daughter of General William C. Heppenheimer. She died in 1928, leaving one daughter, and in 1931 he married Lady Colville—"Cricket"—Baker, the daughter of the late Herbert Ward. He is tall, broad-shouldered, today "as nervously active . . . as at 36," still an expert tennis player. His face, which "is inclined to look rather gloomy until he smiles," seems "to hide his real feelings at times and leads his enemies to say he is 'faintly sinister.'" He speaks and writes nearly every language, among them Arabic, French and German; three novels and four volumes of his verse have been published; one of his many published plays in English, *The Cap and Bells,* has been produced; and he was the author of much of the dialogue and lyrics of Alexander Korda's *The Thief of Bagdad* and of most of the second half of the film, *Sixty Glorious years.*

References

Christian Sci Mon Mag p3 O 13 '37 pors; p6 Je 28 '41
Commonweal 23:397-8 F 7 '36
N Y Herald Tribune p4 My 22 '41 por
N Y Sun p15 Jl 17 '41
Nation 145:93-5 Jl 24 '37; 146:97-8 Ja 22 '38
Newsweek 10:11-12 Jl 31 '37 por
R Deux Mondes s8 43:580-8 F 1 '38
Time 27:26 Mr 23 '36 por; 28:20 Ag 10 '36 por; 31:18 Ja 10 '38 por; 37:28 Je 2 '41 por; 38:19 Ag 18 '41
Sargent, P. What Makes Lives 1940
Who's Who
Young, E. J. Looking Behind the Censorships 1938

VAN WAGONER, MURRAY D(ELOS)

(văn wăg′ŏn-ēr) Mar. 18, 1898- Governor of Michigan

Address: b. Executive Office, Lansing, Mich.

MURRAY D. VAN WAGONER

The burly, decisive Governor who has piloted the storm-tossed relations between Michigan capital and labor in 1941 has yet to be classified by either side as a conservative or a radical. Murray D. Van Wagoner heads an industrial state whose chief executives almost invariably become labeled one way or the other when they attempt to referee labor differences among most laborites. Thus Frank Murphy became the bane of Big Business, while his successor, Bible-spouting Luren D. Dickinson, gained the reputation of an unmitigated reactionary.

Perhaps the difficulty in classifying him is because Van Wagoner has used the big stick with cool impartiality. However, this has not been his only weapon in adjusting industrial differences. He has employed cajolery, persuasion and Jovian calm, and has even resorted to bluster and wrathful threats when the occasion seemed to warrant. Whether because of or in spite of these methods, Van Wagoner's popularity is unrivaled with trade-union leaders and corporation heads alike, a fact that augurs well for the Governor's political future. Today his has achieved amazing success.

Van Wagoner, a heavy-set, broad-shouldered, ex-collegiate gridiron star, impresses people with his blunt energy and robust laughter. He was born March 18, 1898 on a farm near Kingston, Michigan, of English and Dutch ancestry. His father was James Van Wagoner and his mother Florence (Loomis) Van Wagoner. In 1900 his family moved to Pontiac, where Van Wagoner attended the public schools and early displayed indications of aggressiveness and leadership. At the University of Michigan,

VAN WAGONER, MURRAY D(ELOS)
—Continued

which he entered in 1917, he took a civil engineering course, specializing in highway engineering and highway transport because the family car always got stuck in the mud when he went riding with the girl he later married. She was Helen Jossman, who had been in his third-grade class at Baldwin School. Young Van Wagoner, smitten from the outset, bribed a fellow-pupil to exchange seats with him so that he could be near her. They were married in 1924; their two children, both girls, are Ellen Louise and Jo Ann.

Van Wagoner's college schedule was rather crowded: he worked after classes until midnight in a garage and played on the football team during his freshman and part of his sophomore year, until a knee injury put an end to this part of his career. He spent the summers working at the Pontiac Motor Company in order to earn his way through the University. He was vice-president of his engineering class, president of a university club and a member of three engineering clubs. After receiving his degree in 1921 he secured a position with the State Highway Commission as resident construction engineer and division bridge engineer.

For a while after he was married Van Wagoner worked with a Pontiac engineering firm and then hung out his shingle for his own engineering company, which existed for seven years. His first political venture occurred in 1928 when he ran for county surveyor on the Democratic ticket, following the precedent of his father, James Van Wagoner, who had served as county treasurer for a single term. His father's accomplishment had been no mean feat for an active Democrat in rock-ribbed Republican Oakland County. But Murray Van Wagoner didn't fare so well: he was defeated.

Active in Pontiac civic affairs, Van Wagoner was persuaded to run for county drain commissioner in 1930. Success crowned his campaign, the major plank of which was a promise not to build drains on tax-delinquent property, thus saving money for the taxpayers. He was the first Democrat in 20 years to win the post and was re-elected by a considerable majority two years later. His achievement in cracking the iron Republican façade earned him the unanimous nomination of the 1933 Democratic State Convention for the position of state highway commissioner. In the April election he defeated the Republican nominee, carrying his own county by 15,000 votes. He was the first Democrat to hold this post, and when his term expired four years later in 1937 he was re-elected.

In 1940 Van Wagoner entered the primaries for Governor. A favorable situation had developed for the Democrats because of a split in the opposition party. The aged, eccentric Governor Dickinson, seeking re-election, was not a popular choice even in his own party and was opposed by seven aspirants. He suddenly strengthened his position with a show of boldness, however: he broke with Frank McKay, state Republican boss. The defeat of

Dickinson by 131,391 votes in the general election was a personal tribute to Van Wagoner, since the results showed voters had cut a swath across party lines to place him in office. The Republican Party won the Michigan electoral college votes, and Republican Senator Arthur H. Vandenberg defeated his Democratic opponent by a comfortable margin. There were Democrats in some minor offices, but the new Democratic Governor found himself confronted by Republican control of both houses of the State legislature.

On retiring, Governor Dickinson sent a list of 58 appointments to the Senate for confirmation. Van Wagoner, hearing of it, sent his own list so that it reached the Senate floor simultaneously with the Dickinson list, He thus forestalled a last-minute Republican coup. Making an appeal for unity, Van Wagoner received unexpectedly gratifying cooperation from the GOP legislature. His program for reducing the state deficit, for Civil Service, for state salary adjustments and for social legislation was approved to a great degree by the opposition.

Van Wagoner's tenure was crowded with exciting events from the start. He had scarcely been inaugurated when one of the most momentous strikes in the history of the state threatened to tie up all gas and electric power in southern Michigan. This was when members of the International Brotherhood of Electrical Workers, an A F of L affiliate, demanded higher wages and preferential shops in the 900 Southern companies of the Consumers' Power Company. Van Wagoner warned that he would not tolerate a stoppage of power, saying, "If you stop it, I'll throw a switch and start it again. Remember, boys, I'm an engineer." Threatening that if the strike occurred he would declare a state of emergency, the Governor requested the legislature to remain beyond its regular session for the possible declaration of such emergency. Meanwhile the Michigan 30-day "cooling off" law was invoked to delay the walkout, and a special three-man mediation board labored to settle the dispute.

Having weathered one storm, the new Governor faced a troublesome future. Militant labor had made the greatest strides in years and was making itself heard. The next month the Ford Motor Company, long regarded as the bastion of the open shop, flared into industrial conflict. Earlier, a strike had been averted temporarily when the three-man mediation board, certifying that the plant had defense orders, succeeded in invoking the 30-day delay. At the expiration of this period mass picket lines ringed the vast auto empire, and there were reports of violence almost hourly. Van Wagoner spent 36 hours on the telephone urging, imploring and bullying both sides to adjust their differences. He asked Washington to withhold attempts to have the dispute handled by the Defense Labor Mediation Board until all local conciliation facilities were exhausted. Finally, on April 8, Philip Murray (see sketch this issue), president of the CIO, flew to Detroit to confer with Harry Bennett, Ford Personnel Manager, and on April 10 United Auto Workers Union president R. J. Thomas on behalf of his union accepted as a basis for settling the strike a three-point formula presented by Van Wagoner. The proposal included reinstatement of discharged members and arbitration of the grievances of others; mutual consultation before a labor board election to decide which union would represent the workers; and the promise that both labor and management would do the utmost to expedite the election. Thomas declared to Van Wagoner, "I think you have done as fine a job as anyone in the country could" and, in appreciation, withdrew the picket lines from the River Rouge, Highland Park and Detroit Lincoln plants.

After some additional negotiations a CIO victory followed, and auto workers of the sprawling plants in Michigan and of the 34 assembly plants throughout the country returned to work. This was the first time in 38 years of Ford history that the company had dealt with a trade union.

On the heels of the Ford settlement, however, trouble developed at the General Motors Michigan plants, affecting virtually all the company's units throughout the country. As the Governor once again prepared to swing into action, he was checkmated by the Republican-dominated State Mediation Board which invoked the "cooling-off" law without consulting the Governor. Summoning the board before him, Van Wagoner castigated what he called the "hostility and obstructionism" of the two Republican members of the three-man board and demanded their immediate resignation. The two Republicans refused to resign, but Van Wagoner nevertheless appointed two other members in their stead. The new board was successful in staving off a strike.

The next problem which confronted Michigan's Governor was that of putting to work in defense jobs thousands of Detroit factory workers left idle when their plants began the belated switch to all-out defense production. He asked that Army schedules be advanced on items that could be made right away, so that defense orders might flood Michigan during the first half of 1942. He also made plans for a program of post-War building, while vetoing immediate appropriations for the same purpose.

With all his achievement in the field of labor relations Van Wagoner is still the genial, popular, chain-cigar-smoking executive who first confounded the Republicans in Oakland County. He lives with his family in a moderately-large house in Lansing (Michigan boasts no executive mansion), and his close friends call him "Pat." He likes a friendly game of poker and golf, likes to play with the children and to go bowling with his wife. One of his major interests remains highway construction and transportation. He was formerly president of the American Road Builders' Association, was an official delegate to the International Road Congress at The Hague in 1938 as an appointee of President Roosevelt, and is now a member of a national committee on street and highway improvements.

References

> Life 10:17-19 Ja 20 '41 il pors
> Michigan Historical Mag 25 no 1:5-13 '41 por
> N Y Sun p28 Ap 23 '41 por
> Scholastic 38:16 Ap 21 '41 por
> Who's Who in Government
> Who's Who in Michigan

VINCENT, GEORGE EDGAR Mar. 21, 1864—Feb. 1, 1941 Former president of the Rockefeller Foundation and former president of the University of Minnesota; started academic career as member of University of Chicago faculty, where he was appointed professor of sociology, dean of the junior college in 1904 and dean of the College of Arts, Literature and Science in 1907; president of the University of Minnesota from 1911 until 1917 when he became president of the Rockefeller Foundation; retired in 1929 and became a lecturer and social service worker; awarded a gold medal from the National Institute of Social Science in 1935; in 1940 was appointed the first James Humphrey Hoyt Memorial lecturer at Yale University.

References

> Rotarian 56:8-11 Ja '40
> Leaders in Education 1932
> Who's Who in America

Obituaries

> N Y Herald Tribune p38 F 2 '41 por
> Time 37:68 F 10 '41

VINCENT, LEON H(ENRY) Jan. 1, 1859 —Feb. 10, 1941 Author and lecturer who gave annual courses for many years in schools and colleges throughout the country on English and American literature; author of many books of which the best-known is *American Literary Masters,* which is used as a textbook in many colleges.

References

> Who's Who in America 1938-39

Obituaries

> N Y Times p21 F 12 '41

VON PAPEN, FRANZ *See* Papen, F. von

VON RIBBENTROP, JOACHIM *See* Ribbentrop, J. von

VON RUNDSTEDT, GERD *See* Rundstedt, K. R. G. von

VON RUNDSTEDT, KARL RUDOLF GERD *See* Rundstedt. K. R. G. von

VOORHIS, HORACE JERRY *See* Voorhis, J.

VOORHIS, JERRY (voor-ēz) Apr. 6, 1901- United States Representative from California

Address: b. 138 House Office Bldg, Washington, D. C.; h. R. F. D. #1, San Dimas, Calif.

Jerry Voorhis, who wears old clothes, is usually pictured smoking a straight-stem pipe and looks even younger than his not-very many years, would never be chosen to sit for Portrait of a Typical Congressman. His career hasn't followed a typical pattern, either.

Washington Press

JERRY VOORHIS

Horace Jeremiah Voorhis was born in Ottawa, Kansas on April 6, 1901, the son of Charles Brown and Ella Ward (Smith) Voorhis. His father was a very wealthy man, but Jerry was educated in the public schools of Kansas and Michigan until he went to Yale, where he received his B. A. in 1923. He is a member of Phi Delta Kappa and of Phi Beta Kappa. Following his graduation, he traveled in Germany on a good-will tour as a representative of the Y. M. C. A., and then returned to the United States to work as a cowboy in Wyoming, to handle freight on the railroads, and to work in a Ford assembly plant in Charlotte, North Carolina until 1925. In November 1924 he married Alice Louise Livingston of Washington.

From 1925 to 1926 Mr. Voorhis taught at the Allendale Farm School in Lake Villa, Illinois, and during the following year served as director of Dray Cottage at the Home for Boys in Laramie, Wyoming. It was 1928 when he became headmaster and trustee of the Voorhis School for Boys in San Dimas, California—where, in Mr. Voorhis' words, 60 underprivileged boys "make their home, learn farming, printing, mechanics and a number of other vocations; go to school; publish a newspaper; organize athletic teams; and learn from living the fundamentals of Christian

citizenship." That same year he received his M. A. degree from Claremont College, California.

In the days before the New Deal, Mr. Voorhis was a registered Socialist, and he lectured on labor problems at California's Pomona College from 1930 until he resigned in 1935, also contributing to *The World Tomorrow* and similar publications. In those days he advocated nationalization of both industry and land—although not the organization of collective farms or anything of the sort. It was 1934 when he first ventured into politics as the Democratic candidate for the California State Assembly, but he was not elected to public office until 1936, when he ran for Congress on the Democratic ticket and was elected by a majority of 8,589. Mr. Voorhis explained his former Socialism by saying: "That was the only way I could vote my protest against the reactionary leadership of both major parties. I was never a full-fledged Socialist, and now Mr. Roosevelt has made it possible for me to be a Democrat with a clear conscience."

He seemed to be a full-fledged New Dealer, at any rate. In Washington he soon became known as a member of the group of Congressmen, most of them young and many of them new to the House of Representatives, who fought against relief cuts, insisted that the problem of unemployment be faced, eschewed "Red-baiting." He called one action of the Dies Committee "reprehensible," and after his re-election in 1938 by a much more substantial majority than before, urged that the Committee be discontinued and its work be carried on by one of the regular committees of the House. Even at that time, however, he gave it as his opinion that the business of every recognized political party or group in the country should be required to be an "open book"—the names of its members known—and advocated the deportation of aliens who preached giving fealty to any foreign government. In February 1939 the late Speaker Bankhead appointed him to the vacancy on the committee which he had so frequently criticized.

The only results could be either a change in the methods and purposes of the Dies Committee or in those of Mr. Voorhis. Most people seem to think that there has been a little of both. According to *Time*: "Having come to check and scoff, the new member remained to respect the work if not the chairman of the Committee." In 1939 he refrained from voting on the much-criticized action of the Committee in publishing the membership list (mailing list, according to some sources) of the American League for Peace and Democracy. On the other hand, there is reason to believe that the unusually temperate tone of the report of the activities of the Dies Committee published in January 1940 was partially his work.

In November 1940 Jerry Voorhis was re-elected to the Seventy-Seventh Congress with a majority of 44,000. There he is a member of the Flood Control, the World War Veterans'

Legislation and the Public Lands and Rivers and Harbors Committees. He is also a lay reader in the Episcopal Church—he takes his religion seriously—and a member of the Democratic State Committee and of the American Federation of Teachers. He "talks more like Harvard than Yale." As for hobbies, his, he says, are boys (he has two of his own, Jerry Livingston and Charles Brown, as well as a daughter, Alice Nell), baseball and American history. In 1938 the plant of the Voorhis School for Boys was given to the State of California as an outright gift by the Voorhis family, and it is now used as a vocational school and branch of the state university.

References

Sat Eve Post 209:11 My 22 '37 por
Survey G 27:231 Ap '38 por
Time 33:11 F 20 '39 por; 34:14 N 6 '39 por
America's Young Men
Who's Who in America
Who's Who in the Nation's Capital

VORONOFF, SERGE (vô'rȯ-nŏf sĕr-gē')
1866- Surgeon; specialist in surgical grafting procedures
Address: b. c/o Alliance Book Corp, 212 Fifth Ave, New York City

The Russian-born surgeon who back in the '20s captured the popular imagination by his use of grafted animal glands for human rejuvenation was, in the autumn of 1940, a refugee to the United States from occupied France. Dr. Serge Voronoff arrived with his wife (he married a pretty nineteen-year-old Viennese girl, Fraulein Gertrude Schwetz, in 1934), planning to lecture here on his theory of grafting monkey thyroid glands on backward children and hoping to secure a laboratory and monkeys so that he could carry on the research in cancer serum which was interrupted by World War II. "The monkey," according to him, "is a warehouse of spare parts for the whole human body."

No shy, cloistered savant, Dr. Voronoff seems more at home in a *salon* than in the laboratory. Erect, impeccably groomed, looking 10 or 15 years younger than his 70-odd years, he kisses women's hands upon introduction, smokes expensive Turkish cigarets and rents hotel rooms by the suite. When asked whether he has subjected himself to his rejuvenation treatment he replies: "This is my professional secret. If you think I don't look too bad, then you must reach your own conclusions." Seeing him, there can be no doubt that he is a wizard, that he is, in fact, Mephistopheles in person: only the forked chin-beard is necessary to complete the resemblance. "I have produced the supersheep... Some day I may be able to produce the super-man," he said years ago. One believes him.

He began his gland-grafting experiments in 1919. A graduate of the University of Paris, a Doctor in Medicine of the Faculty of Paris and surgeon in chief of the Russian Hospital,

DR. SERGE VORONOFF

during the First World War he was also made surgeon in chief of Military Hospital 197. He was able to carry on his experiments without cash by means of the cooperation of the French Minister of Agriculture. At first he used rams instead of human beings, grafting the sex glands of apes and chimpanzees into their bodies in an attempt to stimulate the flow of sex hormones, checking the blood groups of donor and recipient. Afterward he felt safe in using human "guinea pigs." He began to make sensational claims. The normal life span of man was 140 years, according to this distinguished surgeon, and the Elixir of Life might not prove such a fantastic dream after all. Although conservatives deplored this extravagance, he received signal honors from the French medical profession: in recognition of his success the destructive hunting of monkeys was actually forbidden in French colonial possessions, and he was presented with the Légion d'Honneur.

Because of the wide publicity given to his rejuvenation experiments some years ago, particularly by Gertrude Atherton, few people in the United States connect him with anything else. This particular operation took place before the age of 60, and resulted, it was claimed, in increased brain power and increased physiological vigor for a period of five or six years. (In the case of a woman, however, this was a major rather than a minor operation.) It was flippantly rumored that four San Quentin convicts who were subjected to it, goat rather than monkey glands being used, demonstrated the potency of their new tissues by vaulting their prison walls and escaping! But animals as well as human beings could be rejuvenated. According to Voronoff, "one of my most discussed experiments of this kind was the rejuvenation of a race horse, named

VORONOFF, SERGE—*Continued*

Don Zuniga, which a few years ago, after being rejuvenated, came in first in the Autuil steeplechase." The Italian Government utilized his discoveries in horse-breeding, and in Algeria Voronoff has improved a stock of sheep.

But the grafting of animal glands was not limited to purposes of rejuvenation. Grafting opened up wide possibilities for curing the innumerable ills to which mankind is subject, and Voronoff's most recent work has been concerned with remedying thyroid deficiency— particularly in children—by the grafting of monkey thyroid glands. He has toured all over the world, giving demonstrations for innumerable medical institutions. Once during a visit to the Far East he was agreeably surprised to find on the shelves of the bookshops in the principal Hindu towns a Hindu translation of his books (treatises on surgery, gynecology, the grafting of skin, bones, ovaries, thyroid and interstitial glands, etc.). "Hindu doctors," he said, "had a perfect knowledge of my operative methods. They had themselves discovered several interesting improvements which they explained to me in a most learned fashion."

In France Voronoff was director of the biology laboratory at L'École des Hautes Etudes, and director of experimental surgery of the Station Physiologique of the College de France at Nice. His wife worked with him as laboratory assistant. He came with her to the United States in May 1939 on his way to lectures and conferences in South America and Mexico, but returned to France in December of that year to become an executive in the medical service of the French Army, in charge of a special section on bone and skin grafting at the chief military hospital in Cannes. At Menton he also had a laboratory and a monkey farm with 120 monkeys, where he most recently had been carrying on research in cancer serum. This project was one of the casualties of World War II, for in the French-Italian fighting his laboratory was destroyed, and the Italians took his monkeys into the cold mountains, where he feared they met an uncomfortable death. Shortly afterward Voronoff and his wife fled to Portugal, and thence to the United States, and in January 1941 the Italian Government seized all his property in Italy.

Among Voronoff's books which have been translated into English are: *Rejuvenation by Grafting* (1925); *Conquest of Life* (1928); *Love and Thought in Animals and Men* (1937). He is also co-author of *Testicular Grafting from Ape to Man* (1933), and one of the contributors to *Sidelights from the Surgery* (1938). *From Cretin to Genius* was published in the United States in November 1941.

References

Forum 71:639-46 My '24
Lit Digest 123:17-18 Ja 2 '37 il por
N Y Herald Tribune D 28 '39 por
N Y Post p11 Ja 29 '41
N Y Times p7 Jl 27 '40
Sci Am 133:226-7 O '25 il por

Forbát, S. and Voronoff, S. Sidelights from the Surgery 1938
Haire, N. Rejuvenation, the Work of Steinach, Voronoff, and Others 1924
Ojetti, U. As They Seemed to Me p57-60 1927
Viereck, G. S. Glimpses of the Great p268-84 1940
Who's Who

VOROSHILOV, KLEMENTII (EFREMOVICH) (vō-rŏ-shē'lŭf clä-měn-tē yf-rām'-ŏ-vĭtch) Feb. 3, 1881- First Marshal of the Union of Soviet Socialist Republics

Address: The Kremlin, Moscow, Russia

Marshal Klementii Efremovich Voroshilov, called "Clim" by the Russians, has often been mentioned as Stalin's possible successor. On May 8, 1940 he was relieved of his duties as People's Commissar of Defense and appointed assistant chairman of the Council of People's Commissars, of which he was already a member, and also chairman of the Defense Committee under the Council. Stalin himself assumed direct administrative control of the Red Army after the War with Germany began, and Voroshilov was sent to the fighting front. He organized the defense of Leningrad, then, after Stalin reorganized Russia's western front command, was set to forming great new armies from raw conscripts to take their stand beyond Moscow. In December 1941 it was reported that he had been appointed commander of Soviet forces in the Far East; the Russians "wanted the front well-protected."

Klementii Voroshilov was born in Verkhnii, the District of Yekaterinoslav, in the Ukraine. His father, Efrem, was a railroad watchman; his mother did housework by the day. Until he was 12 years old Klementii was completely illiterate. He was only seven when he began to work in a coal mine twelve hours a day for ten *kopecks* a day, from time to time also assisting in pasturing the village herd and sometimes even going begging with his sister —a more or less respectable profession in Czarist Russia. When he was 12 he attended an agrarian lower school and, after learning to read and write and not much more, joined the workers at a metallurgical plant in Lugansk in 1896. He was a born revolutionary, although he wasn't yet a member of the Social Democratic Party: when only a boy he was arrested for refusing to take his hat off to an officer. Soon he was reading and circulating pamphlets among the workers.

There followed years of political involvement. He organized his first strike in a steel factory in 1899, and was arrested. Later that year he led another, and was blacklisted. He had to leave Lugansk. For the next three years he was "on the run," using aliases— among them "Plakhov" and "Volodka." Finally in 1903, the year he joined the Social-Democratic Party, he returned to Lugansk. He organized fighting units among the workers of the Hartmann Works there in order to defend their meetings against the raids of the Cossacks, and was elected president of the group of Workers' Deputies. Once more he was arrested, but the threat of a general strike forced the police to free him. He ran a revolutionary printing plant and smuggled out papers in the sleeves of his sheepskin coat.

When the Social-Democratic Party split into two factions—the Bolsheviks and the Mensheviks—Voroshilov was on the Bolshevik side. All through 1905 Russia saw "a succession of strikes, street-battles, peasant risings and military mutinies." Some of the most violent fighting took place in Lugansk, where Voroshilov had organized his fighting squads. When the revolt was crushed he supervised the burying of arms and ammunition there, thinking they would be wanted again, and in 1906 went to his Party's conference in Stockholm, where he saw Lenin for the first time. "That remains the most vivid impression of my whole life," he said later. He remained Lenin's supporter, and at the same conference met another of his supporters—the 27-year-old Stalin. He saw both of them again the next year, at the conference in London.

This was the period of the Duma, and trade unions had been legalized. Voroshilov, as chairman of his union, had reorganized his fighting squads into the Red Guard. His arrest was ordered, and finally he was captured and sentenced to three years in Archangel. He escaped, went to Baku, where he was to remain for several years, and immediately made contact with Stalin. When the First World War broke out Voroshilov forged some documents in order to avoid military service, found a job in a St. Petersburg munitions factory and began spreading sedition. He helped to bring the munition-workers out on strike in 1917 to force the abdication of the Czar, was one of a reception committee which welcomed Lenin when he arrived there on April 3, and shortly afterward returned to his old position in Lugansk in order to secure a Bolshevik majority in the Soviet there and overthrow the Provisional Government. It was November 7 when the Bolsheviks seized power in St. Petersburg, and he was sent there as a delegate from his Soviet. He was put in charge of the Defense Committee and became police prefect of the city, working with the Cheka, until the Germans began invading the Ukraine. Then he went back once more.

By 1918 Russia was being invaded not only by the Germans but also by the Allied Armies. As commander of the 5th (then the 10th) Ukranian Army Voroshilov was "successively —and sometimes almost simultaneously— general, political propagandist, engineer and traffic controller." He was appointed commander in chief of the Red forces at Tsaritsin (today Stalingrad), with Stalin his Political Commissar, and held the city against Krasnov's forces. After quarrels with Trotsky, then Minister of War, Voroshilov was transferred to the Ukraine. He became, early in 1919, People's Commissar for the Interior, commander of the military region of Kharkov, and commander of the 14th Army. He created and commanded the First Cavalry Army whose advance through the Ukraine did

Sovfoto

KLEMENTII VOROSHILOV

so much to drive out the invaders then, and, in 1920, the Poles. Although the Russians were eventually defeated by Pilsudski, he brought his army back intact. Voroshilov served again in the Ukraine when General Wrangel was driven into the sea, in 1921 suppressed a mutiny at Kronstadt, and later that year served against the Chinese in Manchuria. It was also in 1921 that he became a member of the Executive Committee of the Communist Party.

From 1924 to 1925 Voroshilov was commander of the Moscow military district, in 1925 was appointed People's Commissar for Defense and President of the Revolutionary Military Council of the U. S. S. R. Since 1926 he has been one of the regular members of the Politburo, central directorate of the Soviet Union. In his military capacity (until recently his department was responsible for the Navy and air force as well as the Army), he organized the general staff, mechanized the forces of the Red Army, built up a large air arm, encouraged such novelties as a parachute infantry, and set up two separate and entirely self-sufficient Far Eastern armies.

Voroshilov is supposed to have a genius for strategy and tactics and an intellectual grasp of military problems as well as great physical energy. His avowed aim was to make the Soviet Union so strong that it could resist military attack from any combination of powers, and he always said that no war against the Soviet Union would be fought on Soviet territory. He believes in education, including political education, for the men of the Red Army. According to John Gunther (see sketch this issue), he was "not a very strict disciplinarian, but his men respect him because he allows no cliques or favoritism; he is the guardian of fair play." His only writings have been on military subjects.

VOROSHILOV, KLEMENTII—*Cont.*

According to Gunther, too, Voroshilov is the "most popular leader in the Soviet Union . . . not ambitious, not a politician, and his personality is pleasing. . . He is not an intriguer, not a wirepuller; neither a fanatic nor an arid intellectual, he is easily the most personable of the commissars." In appearance Voroshilov is blue-eyed, pug-nosed, short in the waist, "looks almost like a cherub." Rosita Forbes describes him as a "prodigiously vital" man, one who drinks, swears, storms into a room and shouts, loves noise, food, laughter, vodka, horses, guns, dancing.

Voroshilov had a "whirlwind romance with the exquisite Jadwiga, daughter of his adjutant, whom he married within an hour of an equally impetuous divorce." His heroes are Sweden's Gustavus Adolphus and Alexander the Great. He is one of Stalin's closest friends, although he reputedly disagreed with him several years ago on the question of collectivization of agriculture and, unlike Stalin, believed in arousing the Russian national spirit. Several years ago he said his greatest ambition was "to see my country acknowledged the United States of Europe," and, for himself, to have "great fortifications called after me." The last ambition at least has been realized. The Russian fortifications along the Finnish border were called the Voroshilov line. (And Lugansk is now Voroshilovgrad.)

References

Am Mercury 32:320-1 Jl '34
Christian Sci Mon Mag p6 Jl 20 '40 il por
Cur Hist 45:112-13 D '36
Eur Nouv 22:871-2 Ag 12 '39 por (cover)
Lit Digest 116:15 S 30 '33 por
Newsweek 15:33 My 20 '40
Time 35:38 My 20 '40
Forbes, R. These Men I Knew p81-94 1940
Gunther, J. Inside Europe p541-2 1940
Trease, G. Clem Voroshilov, the Red Marshal pam 1940
Wheatley, D. Red Eagle 1937

WADHAMS, ROBERT PELTON Jan. 10, 1879—Dec. 16, 1940 Professor of clinical surgery at the New York University College of Medicine since 1933; a member of the faculty for past 31 years; in 1938 received the Alumni Meritorious Service Award for "distinguished service to the University."

References

American Medical Directory
Who's Who in America
Who's Who in American Medicine

Obituaries

N Y Times p25 D 18 '40 por

WAGNER, ROBERT F(ERDINAND) June 8, 1877- United States Senator from New York

Address: b. Senate Office Bldg, Washington, D. C.; h. 530 E. 86th St, New York City

Senator Robert F. Wagner is chairman of the Senate Committee on Banking and Currency and a member of the Senate's Interstate Commerce, Foreign Relations, Expenditures in the Executive Departments, and Public Lands and Surveys Committees. It is not for his membership on these committees that his name is known to millions of Americans, however, but rather for those bills he has sponsored and supported. The NIRA, the Social Security Act, the Railway Pension Law, the United States Housing Act, the highly controversial National Labor Relations Act, anti-lynching bills, bills for Federal aid to the crippled, blind and dependent—these are only some of the measures for which he has been responsible since he first entered the Senate in 1927.

This "small, stocky, inconspicuous, gray-haired" Senator who has placed on the books "legislation more important and more far-reaching than any American in history," was born in Germany, in the town of Nastatten, in Hesse-Nassau. For many years his ancestors had been farmers, teachers and Lutheran ministers in the Rhineland; his father, Reinhardt Wagner, was a farmer; his mother a teacher. Then, like many of their neighbors, the Wagners decided to go to America. They arrived in New York in 1885, when Robert was eight years old, and were met at the pier by Robert's elder brother August, who supported the family until Reinhardt Wagner got a job as janitor of a tenement house on East 106th Street.

Robert grew up in this slum neighborhood, helping his family by selling newspapers on a route that got him up at three in the morning. "My boyhood was a pretty rough passage," the Senator says now, and "impelled me to work for the passage of every measure that I thought would ameliorate the conditions I saw." To those who suggest today that his life is proof that it is possible to rise from and above the slums, Wagner answers furiously: "That is the most god-awful bunk. I came through it, yes. That was luck, luck, luck. Think of the others." Something of his creed and of his feeling toward the United States is found in his testament published in *I Am An American* (1941), a collection.

With his brother's help, and with the help of work as a bellhop at the New York Athletic Club and occasional tutoring jobs, Robert Wagner was graduated from the College of the City of New York in 1898, with a Phi Beta Kappa key and a reputation as a star quarterback. Immediately he got his teacher's certificate and spent the summer after graduation teaching. There was a professor at City College, however, who felt Wagner would be wasting his time as a teacher. He urged him to study law, and with borrowed money Wagner went ahead. By 1900 he had a law degree from the New York Law School.

Even before then he had started his political career. One day, while he was still in law school, Wagner walked into the Algonquin Democratic Club in Yorkville and, fortified by his record as a debater at college, asked to be allowed to make a short speech in the current campaign. "I apparently did all right," he says, "for they asked me to make another speech later." One speech led to another and by 1904 Wagner was a member of the New York Assembly and a staunch Tammany Democrat.

Wagner's first move in the Assembly was to introduce a bill reducing the fare on the Brooklyn elevated from ten to five cents—it was vetoed by the Governor. Soon he was recognized as a rising young Democrat and by 1908 had been elevated to the State Senate, where he served until 1918, floor leader in 1911 and acting lieutenant-governor for a few months in 1914. It was in 1911 that Wagner first became active in proposing the sort of social legislation with which his name is to-day identified. That was the year of the great fire at the Triangle Shirtwaist Company. Wagner immediately demanded an investigation in the State Senate; a committee was appointed and he was made its chairman. For many months he went all over New York State investigating factory conditions, and from his investigations came a series of 56 laws which have since become a model for other states. Wagner also advocated unemployment insurance as early as 1911 and brought in, later, the first Workmen's Compensation Law.

During these years in New York State politics Wagner was able to build up a successful law practice of his own and won some of the most important cases giving recognition to the rights of labor, including a case which virtually outlawed the "yellow dog" contract in New York State. But he gave up this practice, and his political activities as well, in 1919 when he was elected justice of the Supreme Court of New York.

Wagner served on the bench until 1926, designated in 1924 to the Appellate Division of the First Department. He was regarded as "a sound and able judge" and many of his decisions, especially those concerned with labor law, are still cited in the courts. He upheld the constitutionality of the home rule amendment for New York City and of the wartime emergency rent laws. He sustained the right of employees to engage in collective bargaining and granted the first injunction in favor of a labor union.

Then in 1926 Tammany asked him to run for United States Senator, and due to a split in the ranks for the Republican candidate he won by a narrow margin; he repeated his success in 1932 and 1938 by a much wider one. In the Senate, Wagner immediately established himself as a champion of the underdog. In Coolidge's day he warned: "We are facing a change in industrial organization as revolutionary as that which occurred in the beginning of the last century." He begged for action to control unemployment—"We must tear down the house of misery in which dwell the unemployed." Again and again he submitted bills to obtain reliable unemployment statistics, to remedy unemployment, and again and again he was voted down.

Harris & Ewing

ROBERT F. WAGNER

No holy reformer, he plodded steadfastly for these things.

When Hoover came in, Senator Wagner kept up the battle and his bill authorizing the Department of Labor to collect and publish labor statistics was made law in 1930. His bill giving Federal aid to the unemployed— the Garner-Wagner Bill—was vetoed by Hoover, however. In this first term in Congress Senator Wagner advocated more relief, a commission to study unemployment, a stabilization board to plan a public construction program; he was successful in getting passed the Relief and Construction Act of 1932 ("the first clear acceptance of Federal responsibility for the unemployed") and a bill advocating the establishment of a Federal employment agency. He was also active in the creation of the Reconstruction Finance Corporation.

Year after year Senator Wagner called for job insurance, old-age pensions, labor laws, aid for the unemployed. They called him a Socialist, and he countered: "A good Tammany Democrat like me turning Socialist? What's socialistic in limiting hours of labor to give the workers more leisure and to raise their standard of living?" Then came Roosevelt, and Senator Wagner came into his own, "the legislative pilot of the New Deal." One of his first acts was to sponsor the amendment to the Relief Act of 1932 which increased the amount of Federal funds for relief. His next was to get passed the bill for a Federal employment agency which he had proposed, without success, before. And in 1933 he helped draft and put through the Senate the recovery measures of 1933—the NIRA, the $500,000,000 Federal Emergency Relief Administration, the emergency farm mortgage refinancing system, the Federal Employment Stabilization Board for

WAGNER, ROBERT F.—*Continued*

public works planning, the laws setting up the CCC. When the NIRA ran into labor troubles in the summer of 1933 Wagner was made chairman of the National Labor Board.

That was in 1933. In 1934 he introduced the unemployment insurance bill which became the basis for the unemployment insurance features of the Social Security Act of 1936—it was a happy day for him when this measure, for which he had agitated since his first days in the Senate, was finally passed. In 1934, too, he sponsored the Railway Retirement Act of 1934 and subsequent amendments. In the next years there came, through his untiring activities, the Social Security Act and the National Labor Relations Act—which almost everybody calls the Wagner Act.

None of the measures he sponsored aroused as much controversy as this act, eagerly awaited by labor and liberal groups and considered by them labor's "Magna Carta." Employers have charged that it is biased in favor of employees, and even some labor groups have accused it of giving rise to favoritism of one kind or another. Yet, three years after it was passed, Wagner affirmed: "I am more than ever convinced of its essential wisdom, its essential justice and its significant accomplishments." He strongly opposed the suggestions of the House Committee headed by Representative Howard Smith (see sketch this issue) which investigated the Labor Board. These, he insisted, would alter the law so as to make it "a delusive remedy for the worker and a concrete weapon for the oppression of labor." Nevertheless, Wagner has stated again and again that he believes the law is far from perfect, that it believes it should be "perfected in the light of sufficient experience."

After Wagner had had his NLRA passed he turned the greater part of his attention to the problem of housing. In 1935 he had introduced his first housing bill in the Senate after an investigation of public housing in Europe, and in 1936 he pushed it again. Finally, in 1937, the United States Housing Plan was passed, not quite in the form Wagner wanted it, but passed nevertheless, and a year later came the National Housing Act of 1938 which greatly enlarged and expanded the powers of the Federal Housing Administration.

In 1939 Wagner introduced a bill to provide for a national health program, and one of the anti-lynching bills he has perennially introduced into the Senate ever since he became a member. In 1940 he sponsored, among other legislation, a bill to extend the benefits of the Social Security Act, the national hospital bill, a bill for loans to Latin America, another authorizing the freezing of funds and credits in foreign-owned accounts. And in 1941 he not only continued to push these measures, but also introduced a resolution to establish a Post-Emergency Economic Advisory Commission. A serious illness kept him away from his Senatorial duties during much of the year, but he remained a firm supporter of President Roosevelt's foreign policies.

Senator Wagner's history in the Senate is almost a history of progressive legislation during the past years. Some of his proposals have become law; for some of them he is still fighting. And around most of them there has been controversy and criticism. Yet little of this criticism or attack has been leveled against Senator Wagner himself. Even his opponents have recognized his "steadfastness, sentiment, endurance, zest for facts, untiring purpose and fearlessness." They know that he has neither the desire nor the talent to exploit himself; that his speeches are sober, his purpose high-minded.

They know this partly because Senator Wagner never puts on a "good show." He is seldom eloquent, seldom tricky in strategy, avoids personalities, invective and flippancy, and his most impressive appearances are made in committee rooms, where he is "affable, intent, persuasive. . . He never tires of answering questions, never impugns the motives of his opponents. At the same time, as fast as the committee's digestion permits, he pours in the facts." He is a stocky figure, under medium height, with a firm mouth, strong chin and blue eyes.

To some it has seemed an anomaly that this fighter for New Deal causes should still be a supporter of Tammany Hall, one who drops around to chat with the "boys" in his old clubhouse when he is in New York. During the fight between Tammany and Roosevelt in 1932 he was a neutral; when La Guardia was running for Mayor of New York in 1933 and in 1941 he gave nominal support to the Tammany candidate; and Tammany tried to draft him for this job in 1937—a draft he declined. When questioned about his stand on Tammany, Wagner replies that he originally joined Tammany Hall because it was the Democratic organization in New York and because he still thinks of it as "the cradle of modern liberalism."

A man as active as Senator Wagner finds little time for recreation, and a swim in the pool of the Shoreham Hotel where he lives in Washington is about all he has been able to manage lately. But he doesn't feel he's losing out: he is fighting for what he believes in and that is life and work and recreation enough. And he has his son Robert F., Jr., who, after Yale and Harvard, was, in his 20's, in the New York State Legislature and already fighting his father's fight for the underprivileged until his resignation in December 1941 to join the Army.

References

　Am Mag 128:42-3+ D '39 por
　Collier's 93:18+ Je 2 '34 por
　Forum 96:124-8 S '36 por
　Lit Digest 116:5-6 D 16 '33 por; 124
　　(Digest 1):12 Jl 24 '37
　Nation 145:29 Jl 10 '37
　New Yorker 3:24-6 Mr 5 '27
　Newsweek 1:18 Je 3 '33 por; 5:21 F 2
　　'35 por

Salter, J. T. ed. American Politician
p109-23 1938
Unofficial Observer [pseud.] New Deal-
ers p28-73 1934
Who's Who in America
Who's Who in Government
Who's Who in Law
Who's Who in the Nation's Capital

**WAKEFIELD, CHARLES CHEERS
WAKEFIELD, 1ST VISCOUNT** 1859—
Jan. 15, 1941 English businessman, philanthropist and former Lord Mayor of London;
headed own oil firm of C. C. Wakefield and
Company, Limited, and was chairman of the
North British and Mercantile Insurance Company; donated more than £1,000,000 to
hospitals, gave freely to art galleries and backed
the development of land, sea and air speed,
founding the Wakefield Gold Trophy.

References

Author's and Writer's Who's Who
Who's Who
Who's Who in Commerce and Industry

Obituaries

N Y Times p21 Ja 16 '41 por

WALKER, STUART Mar. 4, 1888—Mar.
13, 1941 Producer, actor and playwright;
founded the Portmanteau Theatre; directed
repertory companies in the Midwest; since
1931 had been a film director and producer
and directed *Tonight Is Ours, Great Expectations* and *The Mystery of Edwin Drood.*

References

Drama 8:1-8 F '18
Theatre 27:76 Mr '18 por; 34:323 N '21
por
International Motion Picture Almanac
Who's Who Among North American
Authors
Who's Who in America
Who's Who in the Theatre

Obituaries

N Y Times p21 Mr 14 '41 por

WALLACE, (DAVID) EUAN 1892—
Feb. 9, 1941 Former Minister of Transport
(1939) in England; chief of Air Raid Protection services in London since 1940; Conservative Member of Parliament; had held many
government posts in England and Canada after
serving in France during the First World
War, in which he was wounded and won the
Military Cross; in 1919 served as assistant
military attaché in Washington, D. C.

References

Gt Brit & East 45:718 D 5 '35 por; 46:
219 F 13 '36 por
Who's Who

Obituaries

N Y Times p23 F 11 '41 por

WALPOLE, SIR HUGH (SEYMOUR)
1884—June 1, 1941 One of England's most
prolific and popular contemporary novelists;
died in England; was engaged in talks to
America and the Empire for the British
Broadcasting Corporation shortly before his
death; averaged more than a book a year
from the appearance of his first novel in 1909
to the end of his life; wrote novels, short
stories, children's tales, fantasies, dramatiza-
tions, adaptations, plays and innumerable prefaces; his novels were "lusty, full-blooded, old-
fashioned, painted on a canvas as big as the
side of a barn, with a cast of characters large
enough to fill a Ziegfeld stage"; was knighted
in 1937 for his services to literature.

References

Bookm 76:254 Mr '33
Christian Sci Mon Mag p3 O 23 '35 il
por
Golden Bk 18:24a D '33 por; 22:176 Ag
'35
N Y Herald Tribune X p4, 23-4 Ap 13
'41 por
Sat R Lit 16:23 O 23 '37
Scholastic 25:5 O 27 '34 por
Time 35:99 My 13 '40 por
Adcock, A. St. J. Gods of Modern Grub
Street p293-9 1923
Author's and Writer's Who's Who
Dane, D. Tradition and Hugh Walpole
1929
Goldring, D. Reputations p37-63 1920
Hind, C. L. Authors and I p283-88 1921
Johnson, R. B. Some Contemporary
Novelists: Men p53-78 1922
Kunitz, S. J. ed. Living Authors 1937
Overton, G. M. Authors of the Day
p227-42 1924
Schreiber, G. ed. Portraits and Self-
Portraits p155-7 1936
Steen, M. Hugh Walpole: a Study 1922
Swinnerton, F. A. Georgian Scene p279-
315 1934
Who's Who

Obituaries

N Y Times p17 Je 2 '41 por

WALSH, GEORGE ETHELBERT Mar.
12, 1865—Feb. 7, 1941 Author whose first
book, *The Mysterious Burglar,* was published
in 1901; he estimated that during his years
as an author he had written 500 serials and
1,000 short stories; first joined the staff of
the New York *Tribune* in 1890; started one
of the first technical newspaper syndicates in
1893 and served as newspaper correspondent
for many papers.

References

Who's Who in America

Obituaries

N Y Herald Tribune p38 F 9 '41

WALSH, WILLIAM HENRY Mar. 8,
1882—Mar. 28, 1941 Hospital expert; one
of the country's leading consulting experts
on hospital planning and organization; since

WALSH, WILLIAM HENRY—*Cont.*
1928 Dr. Walsh had specialized in studies and surveys to determine the hospital needs of communities in connection with hospital construction, a field in which he pioneered; institutions planned by him had total value of $250,000,000; was former surgeon in the United States Health Service.

References

American Medical Directory
Who's Who in America

Obituaries

N Y Times p15 Mr 29 '41 por

WALSH, WILLIAM THOMAS (wôlch)
Sept. 11, 1891- Author; university professor
Address: b. Manhattanville College of the Sacred Heart, Convent Ave, and 133rd St, New York City; h. 110 Beach Ave, Larchmont, N. Y.

On May 20, 1941, before an audience of 1,000, Dr. William Thomas Walsh was presented with the Laetare Medal. Conferred annually since 1883 on an outstanding member of the Catholic laity by the University of Notre Dame and regarded as the highest honor a Catholic layman can receive in the United States, this award went to a professor of English literature who has published novels, plays and lyric poems as well as historical and biographical studies, but at the ceremony Dr. Walsh's historical findings on Spain came in for particular praise. According to the citation they had "brought Isabella and Ferdinand, the Catholics, out of the dark closets to which pharisaical history has confined them, into the warming light of truth."

Dr. Walsh, acknowledging the tribute and thanking the University, said that the medal "is not so much a tribute to myself but to the truth I have attempted to tell." This truth mainly concerns the past of Catholic Spain, whose history, he found, "had been corrupted and perverted," while the Spanish people had been "misrepresented in a most despicable fashion" as part of a movement against the church. His motive in writing *Isabella of Spain* (1930) was therefore a chivalrous one: "The life of Columbus' patron and America's godmother has never been told completely and coherently in our language. Prescott could never wholly forget the prejudices of an early nineteenth century Bostonian. Condescension is the worst possible attitude for a historian, for condescension is not a window, but a wall." A second biography with a similar aim, *Philip II*, was a choice of the Catholic Book Club in 1937; and in 1940 Dr. Walsh's *Characters of the Inquisition* appeared. In spite of his preoccupation with Catholic themes, Protestant critics have found much to praise in his historical books.

He was born in Waterbury, Connecticut on September 11, 1891. All his ancestors were Irish, his grandfather, Michael Walsh, having come to this country in the years following the potato famine of 1848. Michael Walsh hated slavery. Just before the Civil War he had a small farm in Maryland, not far from Baltimore, and he would sometimes hide runaway Negroes in the attic of his house. When war came he enlisted in the Union Army, was taken prisoner and sent to a Confederate camp; he returned home, shattered in health, to die.

Michael Walsh's widow, unable to run the farm, took her three young children to Connecticut. One of them, William Thomas Walsh, the historian's father, went to work in a factory when he was 11 and continued to work in factories for more than half a century. For a long time after his marriage to Elizabeth Josephine Bligh (who is still living), and the birth of William Thomas, Jr., in Waterbury in 1891, he was a foreman in a watch factory. Hard working, never very far from financial anxiety, he was nevertheless "a contented and happy man, a devout Catholic, loved by a great many people." His son says feelingly, "I think he was one of the greatest men I have ever known," and when a newspaper friend met his father the year before he died he exclaimed: "Walsh, your father is a personage!"

"I think I became a writer instead of a musician because one day I went down a different street (why, I don't remember) and met a man who told me of a job for a high school boy (I was then 16) on the Waterbury *American*," writes Dr. Walsh. "I had previously peddled newspapers and worked for two miserable summers in a factory. Through newspaper work I was able to go to Yale [where he took his B. A. degree in 1913]. There I was correspondent for the Associated Press and also conductor of the Yale University Symphony Orchestra.

"One night I got so interested in a concert at which we played Schubert's *Unfinished Symphony* that I forgot to file my report on the football team, and dear old Bill Myers of the A. P. fired me pronto, and very properly—though he afterward recommended me to several New York editors, after graduation. I was sorry to hear that the following year the University Orchestra gave up serious music, and went back to the balderdash that we did away with in 1912 and 1913. Nobody paid much attention to our reform, which we took very seriously. We had a lot of fun, but I'm rather glad no records were made of our performances of the *Unfinished Symphony* and Haydn's Eleventh, for I don't imagine they would sound so good now."

After graduation Walsh continued newspaper work on Waterbury, New Haven and Hartford papers in Connecticut, and was copy reader and feature writer for the Philadelphia *Public Ledger*. He wrote editorials for the Hartford *Times* and was its correspondent on the Mexican border. Shortly before the outbreak of the First World War he married Helen Gerard Sherwood of Waterbury, Connecticut, in May 1914, and after the United States entered the War he kept the home fires burning in the most practical fashion, as chief of Anthracite Distribution of the Connecticut State Fuel Administration.

From newspaper reporting and coal distribution Walsh went into the teaching field, his first position that of instructor at the Hartford, Connecticut Public High School in 1918. The year following he became head of the English Department at the Roxbury School; he remained there until 1933 (the year he received his Doctor of Literature degree from Fordham University), when he was made professor of English at the Manhattanville College of the Sacred Heart in New York. Dr. Walsh is still teaching there today, and has found time between his duties to write and publish a novel of New England life, *Out of the Whirlwind* (1935); a play in blank verse, *Shekels* (1938); and a volume of poetry, *Lyric Poems* (1939).

Many of the most poignant poems in the latter are addressed to his son and namesake, William Thomas Walsh III, who lived only from February 4, 1921 to September 23, 1922. There is, however, an eighteen-year-old son, Peter Walsh, for whom his father wrote *Legacy For Peter*; and there are four daughters, Betsy Purves, Jane, Grace Sherwood (Sister M. Concepta) and Helen Teresa. The eldest, Betsy, has taught history at Ravenhill Academy, Germantown, Pennsylvania since her graduation from Manhattanville College in 1936, and has recently finished her first novel. Sister M. Concepta lives at the Sacred Heart Convent of the Sisters of Mercy, Belmont, North Carolina.

This is Dr. Walsh's own testimony concerning his devotion to music: "I still get my chief recreation and relaxation out of music. No matter how busy I am, I try to spend a few minutes a day playing on the violin. Eduard Herrmann, from whom I took some lessons in 1924, taught me how to keep in practice with about 15 minutes of intensive work every day—certain exercises, some scales with different bowings, and a few minutes on some concerto. At the MacDowell Colony [in Peterboro, New Hampshire] in 1929 and 1931 I used to do sonatas with Charles Haubeil and Harold Morris and others, and now and then I played with a string quartet.

"Ensemble work of course is the greatest delight. Every evening after dinner I used to play a game of cowboy pool with Edwin Arlington Robinson, after which he would go to his room with an armful of detective stories to read himself to sleep. Robinson's friendship is one of my happiest memories. My play *Shekels* gave him the idea for his poem *Nicodemus,* which he read to me one evening in lieu of the pool game, before sending it to the *Yale Review,* where it was first published."

Dr. Walsh is a powerfully-built man, a six-footer weighing two hundred and ten pounds, and has blue eyes and receding dark hair. He walks, swims and plays tennis, besides playing Bach partitas on his violin (or the sonatas of Bach, Beethoven, Mozart, Brahms and César Franck, if there is a pianist handy.) He doesn't smoke, but enjoys drinking with friends—"or without friends, for that matter." At present he is at work on a life of St. Teresa of Avila, to be published in 1942.

Blackstone

WILLIAM THOMAS WALSH

References

Cath World 153:234-5 My '41
N Y Times p42 Mr 23 '41 por; p18 My 21 '41 por
American Catholic Who's Who
Who's Who in America

WALTER, EUGENE Nov. 27, 1874—Sept. 26, 1941 Playwright and motion picture scenarist; started career as newspaperman; plays include *Homeward Bound* (1910), *The Trail of the Lonesome Pine,* in which his first wife, Charlotte Walker, had the leading role (1911), *The Little Shepherd of Kingdom Come* (1916), *Thieves in Clover* (1927) and *Different Women* (1927); wrote Fox Movietone productions; in 1936 joined Radio Pictures, collaborating on the screenplay *Women Friends* for Paramount.

References

Am Playwright 2:37 F '13
Arts & Dec 14:13 N '20 por
Drama no. 21:110-21 F '16
Theatre 17:75 Mr '13; 21:235-7 My '15 por
Who's Who in America 1928-29
Who's Who in the Theatre

Obituaries

N Y Times p17 S 27 '41

WALTER, WILMER Feb. 9, 1884—Aug. 23, 1941 Radio and stage actor; played David Harum in the radio sketch of that name for more than five years; had been a radio performer for twelve years; was leading man with various stock companies previously.

References

Variety Radio Directory

Obituaries

N Y Times p15 Ag 25 '41
Variety 143:54 Ag 27 '41

WARNER, MILO J(OSEPH) Nov. 11, 1891- Former National Commander of the American Legion

Address: 3443 Darlington Rd, Toledo, O.

Bretzman

MILO J. WARNER

Those who were associated with Milo J. Warner as he administered the affairs of the office of National Commander of the American Legion know that he is thorough in seeking advice and information before reaching any decision. Throughout his term as Commander which expired September 18, 1941 he used the conference method almost continuously to determine the opinion of the Legion in all sections of the United States. His associates will also testify that, once he reaches a decision, he drives straight through with a plan of action.

Although the basic principles and program of the American Legion have changed very little in a war-torn world, the more than one million members of the organization, now headed by Lynn U. Stambaugh, do have many varying opinions about how their program shall be administered and conducted. The present national emergency has brought many new problems to the Legion, and in interpreting the veterans' viewpoint Commander Warner has had many policy decisions to make. He has urged repeatedly that the United States convoy goods to England and has insisted that there be increased aid of all kinds given to this country, especially since the invasion of Russia, which, however, he believes "does not call for a change in attitude toward the Communist Party in the United States." He has pleaded for continued opposition to Communism as well as Fascism and Nazism and urged the country "as a united nation" to give full support to the President's program of national defense and aid to the

allies "free of any selfish, personal or partisan interests."

This heavy-set, ruddy-faced man whom everybody calls "Mike" was born in Lime City, Ohio and spent his early years as a country boy, educated in the traditional little red schoolhouse. His father, Smith Warner, had operated a country store and wind-jamming coal vessel on the Great Lakes before he retired from active work and moved with his wife, Mary Ellen (Brownsberger) Warner, and children into Toledo. It was in Toledo that young Milo Warner received his high school training, ran errands and did chores to earn money. After high school Warner went to Ohio State University, where he was president of the Student Council in his senior year. From this university he received a B. A. in 1913 and three years later his law degree.

As an undergraduate Warner took as much of the military course as he could and found it good basic training for his service with the Ohio National Guard on the Mexican border that followed soon after he left law school. There were months then of dreary service, riding and roaming over the sand dunes in the Rio Grande Valley. But life in the Army on the border had its compensations for Warner, since it was there that he met and married Dorothy Casad Bennett on June 1, 1917. Two days after his wedding he was commissioned a second lieutenant in the regular United States Army and assigned to the 18th Cavalry. Later he was detailed to the third Provisional Officers Training School at Fort Leavenworth.

Two promotions within a few months brought him a captaincy and the command of Battery B of the 76th Field Artillery of the Third Division. With this Battery he arrived in France in April 1918. Not long afterward, near Le Charmel, a lone German plane appeared from out a low-hanging cloud one morning and dropped a bomb that landed in one of the gun emplacements of Battery B. Several men were killed outright, and Captain Warner was one of those critically injured. A splinter of the bomb ripped through the femoral artery of his left leg, another through a shin, and a finger was badly mangled.

Today there are no signs of the wounds Captain Warner suffered, but in 1918 there were many months of hospitalization to be undergone. It was while he was in the hospital in France that he received the news of the birth of his first child, Milo Joseph, Jr. Later two more children were born, Donald Wesley and Carolyn Bennett.

His wounds prevented Captain Warner from continuing his career in the regular Army, and he returned to Toledo to practice law. Here he became associated with the firm of Doyle and Lewis, specialists in insurance, railroad and corporation law. And here he immediately became active in the American Legion, first as post adjutant and service officer of Vernon McCune Post No. 132 at Toledo, then as post commander. In 1924, after serving as chairman of the Lucas County Council of the Legion, he became the State Department Commander of the Legion in Ohio. He served also as national executive committeeman for Ohio, as National Vice-Commander and as chairman of the National Rehabilitation Committee before his landslide election as National Commander on September 26, 1940.

Warner was able, too, to be active in Toledo civic affairs, and has been a member of the Toledo Industrial Peace Board which has won national recognition for its part in maintaining "a better than average industry-labor record" there. He served as trustee of the Toledo Chamber of Commerce and headed the National and State Affairs Committee of that body. He has been president of the Toledo Exchange Club, the Anthony Wayne Chapter of Sons of the American Revolution and the Toledo Memorial Association. And as a lawyer he has served as president of the Toledo Bar Association and chairman of the Committee on Unauthorized Practice of Law for both the Toledo and Ohio Bar Associations. With this record and his Legion record, it is small wonder that Commander Warner is "without a hobby."

The American Legion, under Commander Warner and under his successor, has been intensively engaged in charting a course that will provide the greatest help for the nation in reaching through to a total, all-out defense on land, at sea and in the air. It was this demand for service on the part of the Legion that led Commander Warner to head a mission to Great Britain "to study the manner in which civilian defense efforts have been conducted." In January 1941, with two other Legion heads, he flew the Atlantic and returned to this country after a month abroad with material to evolve the Legion's program for establishing civilian defenses in the United States. Not long afterward he offered Lieutenant General Emmons, commanding the General Headquarters Air Force, the complete facilities of the National Legion organization and its 11,766 posts throughout the country to assist the Air Corps in organizing air raid precautionary services. He hopes, along with every other citizen, that no enemy bomb will ever fall on American soil. But if it does he is determined that, so far as the Legion can prevent it, there will be no civilian unpreparedness.

References

Am Legion Mag p20-1+ D '40 pors
Nat Educ Assn J 29:248 N '40 por
Scholastic 39:11 S 22 '41 por

Who's Who in Law
Who's Who in the Regular Army

WARREN, HARRY MARSH, REV. Apr. 19, 1867—Dec. 21, 1940 Baptist minister; president of the Save-a-Life League for prevention of suicide; founded the organization 34 years ago after a sermon in which he invited people who contemplated suicide to visit him; said it had kept 30,000 persons from self-destruction.

References

Lit Digest 122:27 Ag 8 '36 por
Who's Who in America

Obituaries

N Y Times p19 D 23 '40

WASON, EDWARD H(ILL) (wô'sŭn) Sept. 2, 1865—Feb. 6, 1941 Ex-Congressman who served as Representative from New Hampshire from 1914 to 1932 and was for years secretary of the National Republican Congressional Committee; upon his retirement from Congress after nine successive terms, was ranking Republican member of the Appropriations Committee and of the Committee on Agriculture; had a varied career in local politics; president of the New Boston Railroad Company and a director of banks.

References

Who's Who in America
Who's Who in Government

Obituaries

N Y Times p19 F 7 '41

WATERS, ETHEL Oct. 31, 1900- Singer; actress

Address: h. 352 W. 115th St, New York City

Ethel Waters, the unforgettable singer of *Stormy Weather* and *Dinah*, of *Havin' A Heat Wave* and *Supper Time*, the first Negro of her sex to star alone on Broadway (in *Mamba's Daughters* in 1938 and 1939), in March 1941 completed an eminently successful Broadway run of the musical fable called *Cabin in the Sky* and then took it on tour.

Cabin in the Sky is a Negro fantasy craftily designed to display all of Miss Waters' talents to best advantage—a sort of combination of *Liliom* and *Green Pastures*. The book is by Lynn Root, the lyrics by John Latouche; Vernon Duke (see sketch this issue) wrote the stirring music, which begins with an aria entitled *Taking a Chance on Love* which Miss Waters sings "with elation and ecstacy as though it were a song in praise of all creation"; the Russian choreographer George Balanchine staged the dances, including one by Miss Waters herself, "the most massive cancan of the season." ("You call those few steps I take dancing," she snorts disdainfully. "Why, I've been dancing all my life, only nobody'd let me do any before on the stage.")

There was a large part of Ethel Waters' life during which she didn't have much to dance about. She was born October 31, 1900 in Chester, Pennsylvania, the daughter of John Wesley Waters and Louisa Tar (Anderson) Waters. The Waters family, which was a large one, moved to Philadelphia. There they lived in great poverty. Miss Waters says: "I've stolen food to live on when I was a child. . . I was a tough child. I was too large and too poor to fit, and I fought back." Occasionally the Sisters in the nuns' school which she attended invented errands for the

Bob Golby

ETHEL WATERS

overgrown, sensitive child and asked her to have lunch or dinner with them in return.

Her first employment was in a second-class Philadelphia hotel, where she worked as chambermaid and laundress for $4.75 a week. On her night out, which happened to be Halloween and her birthday, she went to a night club on Juniper Street. There, protected by a mask, she was persuaded to sing two songs. Two neighborhood boys, much excited, urged her to turn professional, and at 17 she appeared on the stage of the Lincoln Theatre in Baltimore. She was charmed with the $9 paid her until she discovered that her two impresarios were receiving $25 a week from the management.

Other engagements followed, chiefly in the theatres and cabarets of the South. "When I was a honkytonk entertainer," Miss Waters recently told Earl Wilson, "I used to work from nine until unconscious. I was just a young girl and when I tried to sing anything but the double-meaning songs they'd say: "Oh, my God, Ethel, get hot!" At home she sang Negro spirituals.

"Every time they'd write a serious or sweet song," she said to another New York *Post* interviewer two years ago, "they'd give it to Florence Mills, Minto Cato or somebody else." But from an obscure Harlem night club, a cellar cafe at 132nd Street, Ethel Waters finally came downtown to the Plantation Club to substitute for Florence Mills. She created a sensation by singing *Dinah*. Once, as their star, she was invited to sing in Paris. Not really wanting to travel, she asked $500 a week; they took Josephine Baker, an end girl, instead. "But she went great, with my stuff," Miss Waters says.

Her first Broadway appearance was in *Africana,* a Negro revue which "swirled and stomped" at Daly's West Sixty-Third Street

Theatre in 1927. In 1930 Lew Leslie placed her in his *Blackbirds,* and the next year in *Rhapsody in Black.* Another *Rhapsody* was produced in 1932, and in 1933 Ethel Waters was starred in Irving Berlin's *As Thousands Cheer* at the Music Box Theatre, with Clifton Webb, Helen Broderick and the late Marilyn Miller. In that musical comedy she did an imitation of Josephine Baker. Berlin and his collaborator, Moss Hart, gave weekly parties for the cast and their friends and repeatedly invited Miss Waters. She never attended, although she offered to come and sing for the company if she might leave immediately afterward.

At Home Abroad (1935), in which she was co-starred with Beatrice Lillie, was the last musical revue in which Ethel Waters appeared. Since 1934 she had been singing on the radio; a recital at Carnegie Hall in 1938 was a new departure for her. But it was in *Mamba's Daughters,* produced in December 1938, that she scored her real personal triumph. She brought it back to Broadway several months later for an engagement at $1.65 top, and "when it was over I just wanted to put myself away and retire," she told one interviewer. "I didn't want nothing to spoil it." In her mind *Cabin in the Sky* can't compare with *Mamba's Daughters.* "Don't mention anything I've ever done on the musical comedy stage in the same breath with Hagar," she cautioned. "It's easy to go along a song. You pick up the lyrics or some special strain in the music and it carries you on. But this straight acting is different. You're out there on your own. You've got to *be* that character—no matter what kind it is—and *stay* that character." Miss Waters has also been featured in one talking picture, *On with the Show.*

This "tawny Yvette Guilbert" and "bronzed Raquel Meller" has earned more than a million dollars since the days when she "went through Swarthmore College in two weeks—as a charwoman." Every Friday night, after receiving her pay check of $2,000, she is in the habit of putting on wedgies (kind to her weak ankles), calling her chauffeur, and riding in her new Lincoln-Zephyr up to 115th Street and Morningside Avenue in Harlem, where she owns two apartment houses. There she ascends to the 10-room suite which she shares with her second husband, Eddie Mallory, a handsome Negro musician who operates a restaurant called Fat Man's Place. (Three or four of her dozen godchildren are usually living with her, too; they call her "Mummy.") One room in her apartment is entirely devoted to religious purposes. Miss Waters, very devout, says laughingly: "I keep praising the Lord so much I don't have any other hobbies. I keep asking Him for some original ideas for me. I ask Him for so much, I guess I keep Him scufflin'!" But she is also the kind of a person who can fight and "loves to fight." In fact, "I used to have such a temper I had to start controlling myself."

There is race prejudice in the theatrical profession as well as in any other. An enthusias-

tic theatregoer, Miss Waters usually gets a
seat in the last row of the orchestra. "One
woman gave me a corsage once when she recognized me, but some of them have a way of
hurting you." Yet, "I don't lament the prejudice," she told Oliver Claxton. "You can read
Native Son and there is one statement of the
Negro's case, and you can then read *Grapes
of Wrath* and realize that white holds down
white. It's all a struggle for supremacy."

Ethel Waters is a "tall, solid woman—
'monolithic,' a reviewer once called her
—with a look of quiet, serenely confident dignity about her." Her favorite dresses are
plain black, adorned by some one of her remarkable collection of necklaces, assembled
from all over the world. Asked if it were
true that she weighs 160 pounds, Miss Waters
chortled: "Honey, if you say 185, we'll call
it a deal!" She is that kind of person.

References

Cue 9:19 N 30 '40 pors
Life 9:63+ D 9 '40 il pors
N Y Post p6 D 6 '40 pors
N Y Times IX p1, 3 N 10 '40
International Motion Picture Almanac
Who's Who in America
Who's Who in the Theatre

**WAVELL, SIR ARCHIBALD (PER-
CIVAL)** (wā'vĕl) May 5, 1883- British
general; commander in chief in India
Address: b. c/o British War Office, London,
England

Bulletin: On July 1, 1941 the British High
Command announced that General Sir
Archibald Wavell and General Sir Claude
Auchinleck were exchanging positions.
Wavell was to be general officer commanding in chief in India, and Auchinleck
was to assume Wavell's former position
as general officer commanding in chief in
the Middle East. Newspaper opinion was
divided between belief that the change
marked a demotion for Wavell and belief
that it was an indication of England's
desire to have its best general in India in
case of a Nazi thrust there.

From March 1941 issue:

On September 12, 1940 the Italians under
General Graziani invaded Egypt. Within a
short time they had advanced as far as Sidi
Barrani, where they were reported to be
consolidating a strong position preparatory ·to
a further thrust toward Mersa Matruh. But
the British Army of the Middle East was also
making its preparations. Highly mechanized
and strongly reinforced, plans for the cooperation of the Navy and the R. A. F. had been
carefully laid. On December 8 Sir Archibald
Wavell struck hard and swiftly, running up
tanks to the coast to cut off Sidi Barrani,
while the navy and the R. A. F. pounded such
Italian forces as were able to retreat westward. Within a fortnight there were no more
Italians in Egypt except prisoners. Then, by
Christmas, the British had invested Bardia in

SIR ARCHIBALD WAVELL

Italian Libya; by January 1941 they had won
the battle for Tobruk; by February advanced
units had reached El Agheila.

"It is not the victory alone," wrote the
London *Times* after Sidi Barrani, "which will
hearten and inspire the whole Empire and all
our friends outside it; there will also be
universal delight in the boldness of Sir Archibald Wavell's conception, the masterly skill
of the planning, the dash of the execution
and the cooperation of the R. A. F., which
blinded the enemy in the skies and prevented
him from attempting to retrieve the situation
by his favourite dive-bombing tactics." For
the first time in the annals of battle, land,
air and sea forces had been combined against
an enemy who thought himself safe behind
his defences, and though credit must go to
Cunningham of the navy and Longmore of the
R. A. F., these operations definitely marked
out Sir Archibald Wavell as a general of the
first order. His later successes throughout
Libya confirmed this.

Wavell, known to 90 per cent of his army
as "Archie," had an orthodox British education, but emerged from "public school" and
military college with most unconventional
ideas. Some of his public statements make
that clear. Once he said: "My ideal infantry-
man has the qualities of a successful poacher,
a cat burglar and a gunman." Lecturing to
a Royal United Services Institute, he announced: "There is too much stress on 'spit
and polish,' on details of the regulations and
of dress, at the expense of mental liveliness
and independence of thought." His requirements for leadership—which he himself meets
—are these. "A leader must have personality,
which is really simply knowing your own
mind and being perfectly determined to get it.
He must have a genuine interest in, and
knowledge of, humanity—the raw material of

WAVELL, SIR ARCHIBALD—*Continued*
his trade. If I had to take one quality as the
mark of a really great commander, I should
call it the spirit of adventure. He must have
at least a touch of the gambler."

Wavell is the grandson of a soldier and the
son of a soldier, the late Major General
Archibald Graham Wavell, C. B. He was
educated at Winchester College, at the Royal
Military College, Sandhurst, and at the Staff
College, Camberley. In 1901 he passed into
the Black Watch as a subaltern, in time to
serve in the later stages of the South African
War, in which he won a medal with four
clasps. He was next heard of in 1908, on
the northwest frontier of India, fighting
against the Zakka Khel tribesmen; here once
more he won a medal with clasp.

Wavell's next and characteristically unconventional step was to obtain leave for the
whole of 1910 in order to live with a family
in Moscow and learn Russian. He acquired
a thorough command of this difficult language
and in 1911 (now a junior captain) was sent
to Russia to attend the Army maneuvers.
With him he took his instructions written in
Russian in an envelope marked "Secret."
When the police examined him at the
frontier, they arrested him for possessing a
Russian secret document and threw him in
prison. Wavell was able to explain everything, however, and was released the next
morning with profuse apologies and a gold
watch by way of compensation.

When the First World War came along
Wavell went to France and served there from
August 1914 to 1916, taking time out in 1915
to marry Eugenie Marie Quirk. (They now
have one son and three daughters.) In 1916
he was badly wounded at Le Cateau and was
invalided home with the Military Cross and
one eye lost. On recovery he was sent in
October to use his Russian again as liaison
officer with the Army of the Caucasus.
Wavell remained in Russia until June 1917
and returned to England with the Orders of
St. Vladimir and St. Stanislas. He had made
a friend of the Grand Duke Nicholas, too.

Next came three years in the Near East
under General Allenby. As fighting officer
and as a member of the staff, Wavell followed
through the campaign of the Egyptian Expeditionary Force which resulted in the defeat of
the Turks in Palestine. He went out there
as brevet lieutenant colonel; in 1918 was made
a brigadier general of the 20th corps; and
during 1919 and 1920 occupied the same position on the staff of the Egyptian Expeditionary
Force. He was then transferred for a time
to the army of occupation on the Rhine and
in 1921 reached the rank of colonel.

From July 1923 to January 1926 Wavell was
at the War Office as general staff officer,
grade I. Then, after further War Office
work, he was appointed commander of the
6th Infantry Brigade at Aldershot in 1930
and served there until 1934. Meanwhile he
had been, from 1932 to 1933, A. D. C. to the
King, and in 1933 he reached the rank of
major general. From 1935 until August 1937

he was in command of the 2nd division at
Aldershot. Then he was sent to Palestine
to deal with the situation between Jews and
Arabs. According to *Time,* he "participated
in such ruthless suppression of native revolts
that his enemies called him 'the greatest bloodhound' ever sent to put down the Arabs."

After serving in Palestine and Trans-Jordan
until April 1938, Wavell returned to England
as general officer commanding the Southern
Command with the rank of lieutenant general.
On the outbreak of the present War he was
given the command in the Middle East and on
October 25, 1940 was raised to the rank of
full general, although during Britain's darkest
days in the autumn of 1940 there was great
pressure to relieve him of his command.
Wavell, however, refuses to move faster than
military knowledge tells him is wise, refuses
to attack before he is ready, and then believes
in attacking suddenly. In the Middle East he
has been demonstrating his own dictum, made
in 1935, that "the commander of the future
must be able to handle air forces with the
same knowledge as forces on land. . . It is
this combination which will bring success in
future wars." And it was General Wavell
who in February 1941 dropped "a handful of
British parachutists in doubtful uniforms" into
Italy.

During these years of service Wavell has
become known not only as a successful commander in the field but as a military writer
of distinction. His manual on desert fighting
is a text in the Staff College, and his book
on *The Palestine Campaigns,* begun after his
return from Egypt and Palestine in 1920 and
published in 1928, is recognized as authoritative. In 1940 he published *Allenby: a Study
in Greatness,* an eloquent book on his former
commanding officer.

Wavell is a sturdy, quiet, keen, likable man
who talks easily and well and who wears a
monocle to shield his blind eye. His favorite
sport is skiing, but since there hasn't been
much opportunity for "schussing" on the desert
sands he has compromised on golf. He was
made Companion of the Order of St. Michael
and St. George in 1919, Companion of the
Bath in 1935 and Knight Commander of the
Bath in 1939. He also holds the order of
Commander of the Légion d'Honneur and
those of El Nahda and of the Nile. He is
variously called "The Fox", "The Wizard",
"The Mediterranean Magician" and "The
Bloodhound." Even Germany's General Keitel
called Wavell the only one of Britain's full
generals who is any good and said: "He is
very, very good."

References

Life 10:63-4+ Mr 3 '41 pors
N Y Times VII p6, 21 F 9 '41 por
Newsweek 17:27 Ja 20 '41; 17:24 F 3
    '41
PM p4 F 17 '41 por
Time 36:34+ O 14 '40 il por (cover);
    37:21-4 Mr 3 '41 por

Author's and Writer's Who's Who
Who's Who

WEAVER, AFFIE 1855—Nov. 18, 1940 Actress who was leading lady for Edwin Booth and who toured the United States widely in a number of roles.

Obituaries

N Y Herald Tribune p26 N 19 '40 por
N Y Times p24 N 19 '40

WEBB, WALTER LORING June 25, 1863—Jan. 24, 1941 Civil engineer who taught at Cornell University and the University of Pennsylvania; author of *Railroad Construction* (1931), and other books on engineering as well as many articles; awarded the Fuertes Graduate Gold Medal in 1932 by Cornell University.

References

American Men of Science
Who's Who Among North American Authors
Who's Who in America
Who's Who in Engineering

Obituaries

N Y Times p36 Ja 26 '41

WEBER, MAX (wĕb'ēr) Apr. **18,** 1881- Artist

Address: 10 Hartley Rd, Great Neck, L. I., N. Y.

For over 30 years Max Weber, "one of America's outstanding painters," has been giving exhibitions of his work, exhibitions which "have left their mark on the history of American painting." In 1941 full recognition of this was finally given him. In the beginning of February he received the Temple Gold Medal at the annual exhibition of the Pennsylvania Academy; in that same month the Associated American Artists gave the largest exhibition of his paintings ever held; in March he was awarded the W. A. Clark Prize of $1,000 from the Corcoran Gallery of Art for his canvas *Poor Fishing*; and in October he won first prize of $750 at the Chicago Art Institute with *Winter Twilight*.

His A. A. A. show, which drew 22,000 people and was kept three weeks longer than scheduled, was called by the critics both "warm and stimulating" and "disappointingly vague." Its 58 canvases were diversified— figure themes, landscapes, still lifes, "sweating workmen struggling with structural steel, bearded rabbis wailing in bare-floored synagogues, blimpy Picasso-like nudes." To many observers the Ghetto scenes were the most impressive. To them, works like *The Night Class, Students of the Torah, Chassidic Dance* had "a blend of sadness and gaiety, gentlest irony and profound understanding that makes them stand out as truly distinctive performances." Max Weber's own comment on these paintings was: "I thank God I'm here in America and can have this exhibition and show these bearded rabbis. Only, Hitler should see this!"

"Weber," it was once said, is "the most unpredictable painter in America. He refuses to stand still long enough to be labeled. To the art critic this is perhaps his most exasperating vice; to his art, a sign of undiminishing vitality." He has studied and knows the movements of art, but what he paints is distinguishingly his own. Often he is a symbolist, "one of the few American artists who has sufficient philosophic depth to be able successfully to cloak his symbols in strong pigment garments without being either descriptive or literary." He is "a religious painter who looks upon life from a deeply religious point of view." He is a man who "lives deeply in the spirit and yet, as in *Mexican Pot with Flowers* and *After Bathing,* can make statements for the undiluted joy of making them." He is a still life painter of "massive simplicity." He has a "particular talent for sensitive and richly subdued flower studies." But whatever the inspiration, whatever the theme, "in nearly all of Weber's pictures there are wonderfully rich texture, vigorous line, deep and resonant color and powerful pictorial architecture."

Colten

MAX WEBER

This artist who did so much to introduce modern art to America was born in Bialystok, Russia, the son of Morris and Julia (Getz) Weber. Ten years after his birth in 1881 he came with his family to America and with them settled down in Brooklyn, New York. There he attended the Boys' High School, from which he was graduated in 1898; there he attended Pratt Institute. For three years he studied drawing and art at Pratt under Arthur Wesley Dow (one of these three years on a scholarship), and in 1900 he was graduated.

Weber started out as an art teacher, first in the public schools of Lynchburg, Virginia,

WEBER, MAX—*Continued*

where he taught drawing and manual training; second at the State Normal School in Duluth, Minnesota, where for two years he headed the drawing department. During these teaching years Weber had been saving money, and in 1905 he went to Europe to study, enrolling first under Jean Paul Laurens at the Académie Julien in Paris. After four months there he injured his hand and while it was healing haunted the museums, studying Persian and Chinese art, the Europeans, the Spanish and Italian primitives—"with the true post-impressionist's insatiable interest in art's remoter and more obscure pasts."

In 1906 Weber visited Spain and Italy; in 1907 he spent five months studying the Italian primitives and Renaissance painters. "I can remember," he tells us, "when I arrived in Florence. It was four in the morning in that hour just before dawn when everything is still. . . I left my bags in the station and went immediately to look at the Duomo and Giotto's Tower. . . There it is, I said, and I opened my arms to it as to a dear friend who had come back after years of absence." After this trip, Weber returned to Paris to study at the Académie de la Grande Chaumière and the Académie Colarossi in Paris and to get to know the art of the French modernists. He saw pictures by Cézanne—"as soon as I saw them they gripped me at once and forever"; he studied the work of Matisse and Picasso; he became a good friend of Henri Rousseau. And after studying the art of the Low Countries as well he returned to America in 1908, a foe of the academic formula and all its labeled sources.

This "pioneer for modernism" found America unreceptive. In 1909, at a time when hardly anyone in America had seen the work of Cézanne and other Frenchmen, he gave the first exhibition of his paintings at the Haas Gallery which was located in a basement on Madison Avenue. His work showed the "plastic design or organization of form, space and color which at that time was practically unknown," and it amused the critics, who advised him to forget the odd notions he had picked up in Paris. Weber was almost discouraged, and he was broke. He applied for a job as art instructor in the New York City schools, only to be told, after a test, that he couldn't draw well enough to teach art.

He continued to draw and paint, nevertheless, and to study the art of the American Indian and the works of their ancestors in Central and South America. This he made his own, and this, together with everything in America—skyscrapers, bridges, trains—he put into the pictures of that period: *Chinese Restaurant, Rush Hour, New York at Night.* Some of these works were exhibited by Alfred Stieglitz in 1910 at "291" with the canvases of other artists. In that same year, too, Weber arranged the first Rousseau exhibition in America—his enthusiasm for this painter merely proved to the critics how misguided an artist Weber was.

Weber's first one-man show was held at "291" in 1911. It drew great crowds and bitter attacks. One critic called it "a brutal, vulgar and unnecessary display of art license"; another said it was "difficult to write of these atrocities with moderation, for they are positively an insult to ordinary intelligence." Yet by the time of Weber's next show in 1912 there were a few people who began to see that he could draw and was a fine colorist, among them Robert Henri and Arthur B. Davies. The circle of admirers of the early Webers—the oils, water colors, black and whites, gouaches showing "massed and interblent figures emerging, as if reluctantly, from backgrounds which hold them, in geometric designs or in the indistinctly defined shapes of amorphous earth masses"— began to grow, and by 1913 he was distinguished enough for the Newark Museum to invite him to hold a one-man exhibition. That same year he showed nine of his paintings with the Grafton Group in England on the invitation of Roger Fry. This English art critic admired his works. "I wish to tell you . . ." he wrote, "how greatly struck I was by the extraordinary power that they seemed to me to indicate."

From 1915 to 1923 Weber was in virtual retirement, exhibiting rarely. He continued to work, however, and in the gradual development of his art was seen a turning away from cubism and futurism to a "style of his own." Before 1920 symbolic figure groups began to appear, suggesting, as in *The Musicians* and *The Women,* Old Testament characters or the personifications of anciently meaningful, almost forgotten proverbs. "It was with the entrance of this Hebraic quality into his art," one critic comments, "that his destiny as a great modern religious painter began to show fulfillment."

In 1920 and 1921 Weber taught at the Art Students League in New York and returned there again in 1926 and 1927. Before his second period as teacher, though, he had had, in 1924, two one-man shows. The first museum purchase of his work had also been made, by the Phillips Memorial Gallery in 1926. Soon after, the Metropolitan and then the Whitney followed suit. (In 1941 Weber is represented in the Los Angeles Museum, the Newark Museum, the Museum of Modern Art in New York City, in the Brooklyn Museum, which in March 1941 bought his *Music,* and in many other places.) In 1928, almost 20 years after his first exhibition, the Chicago Art Institute awarded him its Potter Palmer Gold Medal and $1,000.

By 1930 Weber was famous enough to be selected by the Museum of Modern Art as one of the first and few living Americans to whom it gave a retrospective exhibition. There were other exhibitions of his work, the last before the recent Associated American Artists show, in 1937. No longer did the critics scoff or scold; no longer did they fail to understand what he had done and was doing. Weber himself was little impressed by their praise: he received it as calmly as he had received their censure, which he attributed to "bigoted intolerance."

"At 60 Max Weber is painting with augmented power and with intensified eloquence." He remains "as aspiring, as eager, as questioning as a young man." A genial "roundheaded bird-like little man," he lives in Great Neck, Long Island with his wife, Frances Abrams, whom he married in 1916, and their two children, Maynard Jay and Judith Sarah, in a rambling stucco house filled with a vast collection of French moderns. "I never saw a family more at peace and quietly devoted or more natural and happy together," Forbes Watson comments on their home life.

Here Max Weber writes poems and essays (his *Cubist Poems* was published in 1914, *Essays on Art* in 1916, *Primitives* in 1927); occasionally does some sculpture (he intends to do more of it in the future); and mostly paints. He is modest about what he has done. "If after a lifetime of living your art," he says, "you can add just a little bit to art, that is something."

References

Am Mag Art 29:41-2 Ja '36 il
Amour Art 15:468 O '34 il
Art Digest 10:13 D 15 '35 il
Art N 34:18 N 30 '35; 36:19 N 13 '37
Forum 103:96 F '40 il
Friday 2:18-20 My 2 '41 il pors
Jewish Survey 1:18-19 My '41 il por
Mag Art 34:78-83 F '41 il
Newsweek 12:21-2 D 12 '38 il

Cheney, M. C. Modern Art in America
    p58-60 1939
New York City. Museum of Modern
    Art. Max Weber pam 1930
Who's Who in America
Who's Who in American Art
Who's Who in American Jewry

WEILL, KURT (wîl) Mar. 2, 1900- Composer

Address: Brook House, South Mountain Rd, New City, N. Y.

Kurt Weill is a composer who has "something of Mozart and the better moments of Cole Porter." He has written symphonic music, opera, songs, arias, popular hits. He has written for the theatre, the radio, the films and will write for any other medium "which can reach the public which wants to listen to music." "I have never acknowledged the difference between 'serious' and 'light' music," he says. "There is only good music and bad music."

Music of every kind has been Kurt Weill's interest all his life. He was born in Dessau, Germany and raised in a home where music was a part of everyday living. His father, Albert Weill, was a Jewish cantor and composer; his mother, Emma (Ackermann) Weill, loved music, too. As a child he studied the piano and by the time he was 17 was almost supporting his family with his earnings

Hermann-Pix

KURT WEILL

as a performer and accompanist. He was also composing seriously—songs, operas, symphonic works.

In 1918 Weill entered the Berlin Hochschule to study music under Professors Krasselt and Humperdinck, but he was made restless by the academic teaching and restless by the stodgy music he heard around him. He left after less than a year to take various positions in the German provinces. For a while in 1919 he was coach at the Dessau Theatre; in 1920 he was director of the Ludenscheid Opera House. But a year of directing productions, coaching singers, orchestrating music and conducting operas taught him how little he really knew about music. He returned to Berlin in 1921 to study theory and harmony under the famous Busoni.

Weill remained with Busoni until 1924. He was composing as well as studying, and in 1923 his highly complicated *Fantasy, Passacaglia and Hymn* was finished. Its style was not to remain characteristic of Weill's work, and when he was assigned to do a children's ballet for a Russian company visiting Berlin, it became simple and direct. As one critic was later to comment: "He has everywhere striven for clearness of structure and in his process of simplification has arrived at a style that is adroit in treatment except for the occasional whimsy of a lilting rhythm."

In 1925 Weill was called to Dresden to conduct a performance of Busoni's *Dr. Faust*. Weill told Fritz Busch, the conductor there, that the dramatist Georg Kaiser was writing a play with operatic possibilities. Weill approached Kaiser, persuaded him to make it into an opera, and in 1926 *The Protagonist* had its first appearance at the Dresden State Opera House under Busch. It was Weill's first opera and a great success. The Berlin State Opera was impressed and commissioned Weill to write another with Ivan Goll. This was called *The*

WEILL, KURT—Continued

Royal Palace, and because it had "the dullest opera book in existence" it was a failure. Still, in it was an unusual mixture of play, pantomime and opera assisted by films, and in it were evidences of Weill's growing interest in jazz.

After its performance, Weill returned to his first collaborator, Georg Kaiser, and with him turned out a charming *opéra bouffe, The Czar Has Himself Photographed,* which delighted audiences in 80 theatres throughout Germany. While they were enjoying it, Weill was busy with Bert Brecht working on the *Three Penny Opera,* a very free, squalid and savage modernization of Gay's *Beggar's Opera.* When finished it was sent around to all the Berlin producers and turned down by all of them. But Weill finally got a backer, and the opera was produced in 1928 and immediately became a sensation on the whole continent. European critics were ecstatic about this work, in which Weill's wife, Lotte Lenya Blamauer, a singer and *diseuse* of "most extraordinary personality" whom he had married in 1928, starred. They called attention to its combination of short scenes, airs, duets, trios, chorus; to its use of the canon, the rhythms of the tango, the "shimmy," the "blues," marches; to the full harmony, the "merry and devilishly earnest" melodies, the sonorous orchestration; to the effectiveness of the whole. However, when it was produced in the United States in April 1933, most critics snorted. They found the translation inept, the production confused, the whole "highbrow musical comedy stuff" that was a travesty on the original.

With the *Three Penny Opera,* Weill and Brecht settled down as a team, and with its production Weill was convinced of the kind of music he wanted to write. He decided that it was the theatre with music, rather than opera, in which he was interested, a middle ground where all the best techniques of drama, musical comedy, ballet and opera could meet. He was tired of composing for a limited audience, "limited," he felt, "not only numerically but emotionally and intellectually." "I wanted," he said later, "to reach the real people, a more representative public than any opera house attracts." Convinced that "many modern composers have a feeling of superiority toward their audiences," he insisted: "I write for today. I don't give a damn about writing for posterity." The serious music critics made a name for this kind of composing—*Gebrauchsmusik*—music for practical purposes, composed with prospective audiences in mind. They didn't hesitate to label Weill one of its foremost exponents.

However, labels and pigeonholes were far from their minds when they heard the next musical play done by Weill and Brecht. The nucleus of this play had been presented at Baden in 1927 as "a clever and savage skit on the degeneration of society, the triumph of sensualism, the decay of art" based on five poems of Bert Brecht. When it was reworked and presented in 1930 at Leipzig

as a full musical play, this tale of three jailbirds who founded a utopian town pandering to man's lowest instincts, *The Rise and Fall of the City of Mahagonny,* provoked "the most tumultous riot in the history of the German stage." During one performance half of the audience threw stink bombs at the other enthusiastic half; police were called in; the lights were kept on throughout all its acts. But even those who loathed its obscenity and its biting iconoclasm agreed that the music was ever vivacious in its rhythms, that there were moments of lyrical force, that jazz had been skillfully used.

In that same year Brecht and Weill were able to edify the school children in over 500 schools throughout Germany. Their *Der Jasager,* presented by the German Government, was a musical play stressing the necessity of sacrifice by the weaker individuals for the good of humanity. Its music showed, it was agreed, "contrapuntal skill and fertility of invention." "It was music that was effective, strongly rhythmed, plain, clearly outlined and unornate in structure."

In 1930, too, Brecht and Weill presented *Lindbergh's Flight,* a classical cantata composed especially for radio performance and intended to be sung, afterward, as a school piece. Weill had originally written it in 1929 with some collaboration with Hindemith (see sketch this issue), but he wrote it in its present form with Brecht alone. Called "one of the few important choral works produced by contemporary music and surely one of the finest," which revealed Weill as "one of the most gifted of Germany's young composers," it was also labeled "over-refined and polished," "lacking in inspiration." This piece and the plays of 1930 were the last produced by the Weill-Brecht collaboration. Brecht had become deeply involved in political activity, and Weill had to seek out another partner.

He found Caspar Nehar and with him wrote *Die Bürgshaft* (The Pledge) for the Berlin Municipal Opera. Like his other works, it inspired divided criticism. There were those to call it "the first operatic work of distinctly modern hue that has met with approval from all quarters of the local musical camp"; others to find it a "long-winded farrago of didactic moralizing and proletarian propaganda" which "mercilessly exposes Weill's inferiority as a writer of straight tune."

Liked or disliked, it was the last of Weill's plays to enjoy a run in Germany. His *Silver Lake,* written with Georg Kaiser, opened simultaneously in 11 large cities in Germany in February 1933 and was hailed the morning after its opening by the majority of the critics. That was what the drama page of the newspapers said; on the front page there was a story saying that henceforth all works by Kurt Weill, that *Kultur Bolshevist,* were banned from Germany forever. There were no second performances, and Weill fled to Paris.

He was received there with open arms and immediately commissioned to write a ballet for Tilly Losch, *The Seven Deadly Sins.* Then Weill, who always sought out original playwrights and persuaded them his music would enrich their dramatic texts, interested Jacques Deval, the author of *Tovarisch,* in writing a musical play. Its title was *Marie Galante,* and it was a fair success in 1934. Later its songs became very famous in Paris. But Weill left Paris for London, where in 1935 with Vambéry he wrote *A Kingdom for a Cow.* London didn't like it, and Weill was easily persuaded to accompany Max Reinhardt to the United States to prepare for the production of *The Eternal Road.* Shortly after his arrival he took out his first citizenship papers.

He, Reinhardt and Franz Werfel had long discussed the creation of the play. "Our common task," he says, "was to bind speech and music into a perfect fusion. I sought to make the musical score an integral part of the action." With the inspiration of the Hebraic melodies he had learned from childhood on, he says, "I tried to create music that would communicate naturally and inevitably the stories of the Old Testament." Before American audiences heard his spiritual, poetic and mystical score for this unwieldy production in 1937 they had been treated to other examples of his work. In 1933 they had heard the *Three Penny Opera* and *Der Jasager,* and in 1934 the New York Philharmonic had presented his symphonic fantasy, *Three Night Scenes.* New York critics found the latter "disappointing", "banal", "prolix," and wondered whether his reasons for writing anything but theatre music were valid. He said: "I consider myself a theatre composer... I write absolute music in order to control my own style. You must turn away from your own habitual way occasionally. So then I write symphonic works."

The critics were much happier about his efforts for *Johnny Johnson,* a play by Paul Green which the Group Theatre produced in 1936. They found his score for this sardonic fable of the First World War "delectable," "roguishly satirical, spiced with a whippy jazz technique, perfectly and admirably suited to its purpose." And the general comment on Broadway was: "From now on all of the boys are going to have to watch their step. We won't be able to get away with the old musical comedy formula very much longer." Hollywood was impressed, too, and gave him a contract under which he produced the musical accompaniment for Fritz Lang's *You and Me.*

He was busy after his return to Broadway from Hollywood. First there was the music for Maxwell Anderson's *Knickerbocker Holiday* in 1938, which to most audiences was clever, rich-sounding, witty and almost good enough to make up for the play's flat book. Then there was the score for *Railroads on Parade* at the New York World's Fair, which backed up the spectacle with effective sequences. There was music for novachord as a part of Elmer Rice's play, *Two on an Island.* There was, in 1940, the music for the Ballet Theatre's performance of *The Judgment of Paris,* and the performance on the *Pursuit of Happiness* program of *Magna Carta* which he wrote with Maxwell Anderson as a "ballad history." Most recently there has been the score for *Lady in the Dark.*

He and Moss Hart (see sketch 1940 Annual) planned this last popular stage work as something different from the usual musical comedy, as a "musical play" in which music, lyrics (by Ira Gershwin) and book were to be welded by a new process. The play went over big, but critics disagreed about Weill's contribution to it. Brooks Atkinson called Weill "the best writer of theatre music in the country. . . Without Mr. Weill's beautifully integrated music it would be difficult to evoke the strange imagery that distinguishes [*Lady in the Dark*] from the ordinary run of musical comedy." Stark Young found the music "very successful," but there were others to say that "Mr. Gershwin's original talent deserves songs less reminiscent than Mr. Weill's." This accusation of a lack of originality in jazz composition has often been hurled at Weill and has often been explained away by referring to his musical background, of which jazz was never a hereditary or integral part, as it was of George Gershwin's, for instance.

It will probably be an integral part of his everyday life from now on, though. This soft-spoken composer, who has thinning dark hair and an oval smooth-shaven face fronted by eye-glasses, has settled down with his wife in an old remodeled house on a farm near Suffern, New York, where he intends to live for many, many years. He never thinks of himself as other than an "American" composer now.

References

    Anbruch 14:135 S '32
    Christian Sci Mon Mag p8 Ap 27 '38 por
    Ménestral 92:417 O 10 '30
    Modern Music 11:42 N-D '33
    N Y Sun p26 F 3 '40
    N Y Times IX p1, 3 Ap 13 '41; IX p1 S 7 '41

    Baker's Biographical Dictionary of Musicians 1940
    Ewen, D. ed. Composers of Today 1936
    International Who's Who
    Rosenfeld, P. Discoveries of a Music Critic p250-6 1936
    Saleski, G. Famous Musicians of a Wandering Race 1927
    Who's Who in American Jewry
    Who's Who in the Theatre

WEIR, ERNEST T(ENER) (wēr) Aug. 1, 1875- Industrialist; chairman of the board of the National Steel Corporation

Address: b. Grant Bldg, Pittsburgh, Pa; h. Schenley Apts, Pittsburgh, Pa.

Ernest T. Weir, chairman of the board and director of the National Steel Corporation, the Weirton Steel Company, the Hanna Iron Ore Corporation, the Bank of Weirton and countless other corporations, looks like a

ERNEST T. WEIR

"genial, kindly and prosperous pastor," with "his healthy pink complexion, soft blue eyes and benevolent expression." Instead, he is one of the fightingest industrialists of this country, firm in his belief that the New Deal leads to business perdition, firm in his determination that his companies will not be organized by the CIO or any other outside union.

These convictions are part of Ernest Weir's philosophy, a philosophy which is based on his belief in free competition, for capital as well as labor. And this philosophy is the result of his own life. "Every dollar I have today," he says, "has come from [the first plant I started] and the large company that grew from it. No one ever gave me anything." Since he was 15 Ernest Weir has been working. That was the year his father, James Weir, died. Ernest left public school in Pittsburgh, the city where he was born, and got himself a job with the Braddock Wire Company as office boy. Every week he brought home to his mother, Margaret (Manson) Weir, the $3 he earned. He had to do this "if there was to be food on the table," he says.

A year later, in 1892, Weir became connected with the Oliver Wire Company. He wasn't an office boy long, and by 1901 had advanced sufficiently to take the position of chief clerk at the Monongahela Tin Plate Mills and marry Mary Kline. (There are twin sons and one daughter of this marriage. His second marriage, to Mrs. Aeola Dickson Siebert, took place in 1926, and after a divorce he married Mary Hayward of New York City on December 11, 1941.) In 1903 he was superintendent of the Monessen Mills of the United States Steel Corporation, and when he left this company in 1905 to form his own, he was manager.

With his brother and J. R. Phillips he bought an old tin plate mill at Clarksburg, West Vir-

ginia and scraped together enough capital to put life into it. "We had to fight every inch of the way," Weir recalls. "We had to meet our pay rolls and pay for our materials C. O. D.; the wages we took home to our families often were less than those paid to many of our employees... With my associates I worked long hard hours and made financial sacrifices in which my family shared, in the hope that I could help build the company into a strongly founded, successful enterprise. That happened."

This company, the Phillips Sheet and Tin Plate Company, prospered with Weir as its president from 1908 on, and by 1916 it had added several other plants and formed the Weirton Steel Company, a recognized power in the industry. With this company and others like the Hanna Iron Ore Company and the Great Lakes Steel Corporation, Weir formed the National Steel Corporation in 1929. When the depression settled down on the other steel companies, Weir's showed a profit every year —in 1931 National made more than all other steel companies put together; in 1932 it was the only company that showed a profit; and every year after, its books were written in black.

The other steel companies were distrustful. They said Weir made his profits by cutting prices to get business away from others. Some of Weir's employees claimed he made them at their expense. But Weir himself "kept his mouth shut, fought everybody that got in his way and forged ahead," concentrating, unlike the others, on much tonnage in sheet strip and tin plate and little in the heavier forms of steel. In 1941 the National Steel Company continues to be one of the most profitable, and the New York *Times*, in May of that year, reported Weir's salary as $345,000.

From the beginning of his company, Weir says: "We paid a fair wage to workmen," and he has continuously preached high wages. At the same time, "a stubborn, hard-hitting individualist," he has fought any union that tried to secure them for his employees, and has, according to *The Nation*, kept his employees "under strict control" in the city of Weirton, West Virginia, which has grown up around the mills. Weir himself calls the town "a community that is American in principle and spirit."

Most of the controversy between Weir and the unions began in 1933, when the NRA provided the right of employees to collective bargaining and a National Labor Board was set up. Weir made his own arrangements for an employee election in Weirton, and the Amalgamated Association of Iron, Steel and Tin Workers immediately responded with a strike. They lost the strike, and the Labor Board lost the case it brought against Weir for "coercion, intimidation and interference" against Weirton employees.

Soon after the National Labor Relations Act was passed, the Weirton Company was accused of anti-union activity; of flagrant violation of the Wagner Act"; of "conducting a campaign of terrorism"; and after years of litigation was ordered in 1940 to disestablish the union to which it "contributed financial and other support" and to stop "terrorizing" the CIO. During these years the CIO's Steel Workers Organizing Company never got to first base at Weirton, and even in 1937, when it was calling strikes all over Little Steel, "did not dare to strike against Weir." Some observers attribute this to Weir's policy of giving the employees increases before they get to the point of demanding them. This happened in 1937 when, only a few hours before the United States Steel Corporation and the SWOC signed a union contract, he announced he was going to boost the wages of the 21,000 employees in National's mills to $5 a day. This happened again in April 1941 when he granted a 10-cents-an-hour wage increase to his employees while the SWOC was negotiating for the same amount with United States Steel. Of this latter increase Weir said: "There was an improvement in the industry and we felt the workers should share in it."

Weir's most recent battle with the CIO was in the fall of 1941, when his refusal to consider a union shop in the captive mines was followed by the National Defense Mediation's Board decision that precipitated the United Mine Workers' strike. The final decision was against him, however.

Weir's war against the Roosevelt Administration has not been directed against its labor policies only. With some of its aims he has been in sympathy: "The factories, stores and railroads that turn out goods and services have got to turn out income with which their goods and services may be bought," he once said. "What's more they have got to be sure that income is distributed among the workers in such a way that they will be able to buy." He has, too, declared himself "heartily in favor" of unemployment insurance and old-age pensions. With most of its aims, however, and all of the means it has used to achieve them, he is in disagreement.

This man, who wrote in 1936 that "the American business system today represents the highest reach so far attained in man's eternal fight to wrest a better, easier living from nature," has fought bitterly against the restraints that the New Deal has imposed on that system. He has said that the "Federal Administration regards itself as the enemy of [the productive system of the country] and uses the power of government to shackle it on every side." Last year, in his position as president of the Iron and Steel Institute, he criticized the Administration for neglecting our defenses, for permitting excessive exports of scrap steel and failing to build up adequate reserves of strategic raw materials, for pouring billions of dollars down "ratholes of political waste"; and in his position as chairman of the finance committee of the Republican National Committee (he resigned from this in April 1941) urged the defeat of Roosevelt. He was said also to have been one of the heaviest contributors to the America First Committee. In the light of this background there was widespread surprise and no little indignation when Weir announced in April 1941 that he supported the policy of Leon Henderson, price administrator, in "freezing" the steel industry's prices. He said then: "There are no facts available today on which . . . to determine the necessity of a price change now. . . It won't hurt the industry to take three months to produce facts." After the wage boost and this statement there was no explanation needed when the National Steel Corporation in June 1941 withdrew from the American Iron and Steel Institute of which Weir had once been president.

Ernest Weir belongs to almost a score of clubs and enjoys himself at the sports they provide. But his real hobby, he says, is to try to find out what makes our economic system tick, and the extracurricular organization in which he is most interested is the Maurice Falk Foundation, which has $5,000,-000,000 to spend for "the encouragement, improvement and betterment of mankind."

References

Am Mag 116:59 Ag '33 por
Fortune 14:118-23+ O '36
Nation 143:237-9 Ag 29 '36
Newsweek 2:4-5 D 23 '33 por; 5:8 Mr 9 '35 por; 7:42 Ap 4 '36 por; 10:12 Ag 28 '37
Who's Who in America
Who's Who in Commerce and Industry

WELCH, WILLIAM A(DDAMS) Aug. 20, 1868—May 4, 1941 General manager and chief engineer of the Palisades Interstate Park Commission of New York and New Jersey who resigned in 1940 after 40 years of work; 1,000,000 campers used the 103 camps he built; known as the father of the state park movement; planned parks for many states; in his cabin on Bear Mountain, New York he was consulted by park experts from all over the United States and Europe; there he was host to President Theodore Roosevelt, President Harding, President Hoover and President Franklin D. Roosevelt as well as many famous explorers and public-spirited citizens.

References

Who's Who in America

Obituaries

N Y Times p17 My 5 '41 por

WELLES, ORSON May 6, 1915- Producer, actor and director of the theatre, motion pictures and radio

Address: 1430 Broadway, New York City

Ever since Orson Welles burst upon the American stage with the erratic refulgence of a meteor, his great problem has been to keep up with the legend of Orson Welles that has dogged him since the age of two. He has been regarded with mingled alarm and disbelief as a sort of theatrical baby

ORSON WELLES

Gargantua; he has been hailed as the white hope of the American theatre; he has also occasionally been called a ham and a faker. But in view of his achievements this last conclusion has had to be abandoned: "Orson Welles," said one critic after watching him romp through a rehearsal of *Native Son,* with which he returned to the theatre after two years in Hollywood, is "a very noisy young man, but he is no phony."

It is characteristic of Orson Welles to have picked out as his first play since Hollywood the dramatization of *Native Son* by Richard Wright, one of 1940's most controversial and hard-hitting books, the most biting story ever written about a Negro in America. The consensus of opinion was that Orson Welles measured up to the book. Brooks Atkinson wrote about him: "Mr. Welles has come back to the theatre with all the originality and imagination he had when he was setting off firecrackers in the *Mercury.* . . Mr. Welles is a young man with a lot of flaring ideas, and when he is standing on the director's podium, he renews the youth of the theatre."

George Orson Welles was born in Kenosha, Wisconsin, on May 6, 1915, son of Richard Head and Beatrice (Ives) Welles. His father was an inventor and promoter, his mother a talented musician. From an early age Orson moved in a welter of talented personalities: he met painters, musicians, actors, cartoonists, who treated him as if he were an adult. His greatest admirer (later, his guardian) was Dr. Maurice Bernstein, who was impressed by Orson when the latter was a toddler of two, dropping pearls of wisdom from baby lips. Dr. Bernstein was the first to introduce Orson to drama by presenting him with a puppet theatre. At the same time Orson was exposed to other arts, in which he did very

well, becoming a proficient cartoonist at the age of 10. As a side line he learned magic from Houdini—this came in handy later when he eloped at the age of nine with a fascinating contemporary, intending to support her by practicing his sleight-of-hand tricks on street corners. During his childhood Orson was at his most glorious. His friends who knew him then tend to disparage his present accomplishments: Orson at twenty-six is overshadowed by the glorious memory of Orson at six.

Young Welles had no education except this informal kind when he was finally sent to school at 10. He had read all of Shakespeare, was proficient in belles lettres, amused himself by a critical analysis of *Thus Spake Zarathustra;* but he didn't know how to add or subtract. When this lack was pointed out to him, "there will always be," he said, "people around to add and subtract for me." He still doesn't know how to add simple figures—though he does considerably better with the astronomic ones that prevail in the motion picture and theatre industry. He finally went to Todd High School, in Woodstock, Illinois, largely because it specialized in dramatics.

Contrary to expectations he enjoyed his stay at Todd's. For one thing he was allowed to revolutionize the place; the school was made into a progressive school to keep up with Orson. Also the Todd dramatics began to include Shakespeare and obscure Elizabethans. He also contracted a friendship with the headmaster, Roger Hill, with whom he was later to cooperate in 1933 in editing Shakespeare for reading and staging by students.

Orson was graduated from high school in 1930, decided against going to college and in a brash advertisement offered his services to the theatre. He was talked by his guardian (his father had died when Orson was 13) into postponing his thespian ambitions and going on a sketching tour in Ireland. Young Orson traveled by donkey cart until fate caught up with him in Dublin when he attended a performance of the Gate Players at the Abbey Theatre. Orson talked the Gate director, Hilton Edwards, into giving him the part of Duke Alexander in *Jew Suss.* His performance, after the mannerisms of an aged Shakespearian actor had been ruthlessly sloughed off, was enthusiastically praised, as were his other performances of the season. He was asked to be a guest star at the Abbey Theatre. He was then only 16—a fact that nobody guessed, Orson having played an adult since he was 10. Later only his American citizenship prevented him from getting juicy roles in London.

In 1932 Orson came back to New York. Nobody raised the customary fuss over him and a supercilious office boy at the Shubert Theatre called him "kiddie." Orson retired to Chicago—and later to Morocco—to sulk Achilles-like in his tent. It was a sad little interim: his first attempt to write a serious play, *Marching Song,* was rejected; but his stories were accepted by a pulp magazine. Orson was crushed. Clouds lifted very soon, however. Thorton Wilder, meeting Orson at a cocktail party, brought glad tidings of Orson's Dublin fame having penetrated to New York, and gave the young man an introduction to Alexander Woollcott (see sketch this issue). Presently young Welles was touring with Katharine Cornell (see sketch this issue), playing Mercutio and Tybalt in Shakespeare and Marchbanks in *Candida*. In 1934 he met John Houseman, the producer of Gertrude Stein's *Four Saints in Three Acts*, and played in MacLeish's *Panic*, which Houseman produced. During the summer of 1935 he participated in the Woodstock Dramatic Festival, acting and directing. He also married the pretty, 18-year-old Virginia Nicholson, who played in the Woodstock Company. Orson Welles is now the father of a little girl named Christopher, but the Welleses were divorced in 1940. (In 1941 it was rumored that Dolores Del Rio would become the next Mrs. Welles.)

In 1935 Orson Welles was back in New York trying to work out a scheme whereby he and John Houseman would enrich the theatre independently. They could not raise enough money. Welles' father, horrified by young Orson's light-hearted way of flinging money around, had left him money which he could not touch until he was 25. Accordingly Orson bestirred himself and began to make money on the radio. He was in great demand, particularly in his characterization of "The Shadow," whose sinister voice sent cold chills down the backs of countless potential criminals.

That year Welles and Houseman were asked by the Government to help launch the Federal Theatre in New York. Young Welles began to do weird and wonderful things to Shakespeare. His first attempt was *Macbeth*, staged in Haiti, with an all-Negro cast, and a generous sprinkling of voodoo-doctors to take the place of three witches. Then followed Marlowe's *Dr. Faustus*. Welles, his face made up grotesquely, his voice mellow as an organ, wandered like a lost soul among gigantic shadows and shifting shafts of light. Critics hailed the revolutionary technique. But it was expensive: Welles had to dip into his own pocket in order to defray the expenses and to cut through the red tape.

The association with the WPA came to a spectacular end after the production of Marc Blitzstein's *The Cradle Will Rock*, when Welles, the production held up by a last minute order from Washington, wandered over New York in search of a theatre, followed by his audience. *The Cradle* became a landmark in the history of the Federal Theatre; Welles and Houseman left WPA and founded the Mercury Theatre, with *Julius Caesar* as its first production. It was played in modern dress, against the background of bare red-brick theatre walls. Caesar strutted in Fascist uniform; Welles as Brutus wore the conservative suit and wide shabby coat of an intellectual. In 1938, the Mercury

Theatre presented *Shoemakers' Holiday, Heartbreak House* and *Danton's Death*.

It was in 1938, too, that the **Mercury Theatre of the Air** went on Columbia Broadcasting System, with Welles writing, editing and directing the sketches and often playing in them. On Halloween of that year he broadcasted the script of H. G. Wells' *War of the Worlds*. He had thought the script a bit dull, and enlivened it by setting the invasion of the Martians at Grover's Mill, New Jersey. An appreciable part of the New Jersey population, upon tuning in on the broadcast, took to the hills. The Wonder Boy's interplanetary high jinks had started a serious panic. Welles and CBS were deluged with threats, statistics of minor injuries and calls from people who wanted personally to swear at Welles. The incident provided some valuable material for a Princeton treatise on mass psychology: *The Invasion from Mars* (1940), by Hadley Cantril.

Meanwhile the Mercury Theatre became tarnished by the possession of several flops. *Danton's Death* (1938) was followed by the *Five Kings* (1939)—Welles' pet project since his school days, a combination of five Shakespearian chronicle plays. It proved too ambitious an undertaking even for Orson Welles. Soon thereafter Welles signed a four-way contract with RKO, as writer, actor, director and producer. His first venture was to be Conrad's *Heart of Darkness*. Orson Welles flew to Hollywood in August 1940, with the members of the Mercury Theatre and a beard that he grew in preparation for his work as an actor.

Shrieks of rage arose in Hollywood, provoked as much by the incredible contract as by the beard. Welles got a poor press in Hollywood; he was misquoted, branded a phony, a failure. People sat back and waited for the balloon to collapse. Gene Lockhart contributed a bit of doggerel:

> *Little Orson Annie's come to our*
> *house to play,*
> *An' josh the motion pitchurs up an'*
> *skeer the stars away*
> *An' shoo the Laughtons off the lot an'*
> *build the sets an' sweep*
> *An' wind the film an' write the talk*
> *an' earn her board-an'-keep;*
> *An' all us other acters, when our*
> *pitchur work is done,*
> *We set around the Derby bar an'*
> *has the mostest fun,*
> *A-list'nin' to the me-tales 'at Annie*
> *tells about,*
> *An' the Gobblewelles'll git YOU*
> *Ef you DON'T WATCH OUT!*

But Welles was busy writing two scripts, the *Heart of Darkness* and the *Smiler With a Knife*, both of which were turned down. When his third attempt, *Citizen Kane*, in which Welles himself played the lead, was approved and shot in 10 furious weeks, Hollywood jeers were answered and young Mr. Welles found himself in the headlines again.

Citizen Kane, which was finished in the beginning of 1941, has been hailed by those

WELLES, ORSON—*Continued*

who saw it as "the most sensational product of the U. S. movie industry," full of subtleties, smashing new techniques, extraordinary technical novelties. It is the story of a egomaniac newspaper tycoon, the tragedy of a modern Midas who changes all he touches into gold and dies hungry for humanity. The story presented a certain parallel to the life of William Randolph Hearst, who was said to have objected vociferously, threatening reprisals in form of publicity boycott, sizzling exposés, etc. For a while it looked as if RKO, for whom Welles made his picture, would withhold it from circulation. Welles, who has a 25 per cent interest in the film, on his side threatened legal action. The picture was released in early May in New York City. It was selected as the best film of the year by the National Board of Review of Motion Pictures and by the New York Film Critics' Circle. In June 1941 Welles signed a new contract with RKO to produce and direct three pictures a year.

At 26, Orson Welles is tall and chubby, weighing about 200 pounds. He eats a great deal and exudes energy. Richard Wright says about him: "One Orson Welles on earth is enough. Two of them would no doubt bring civilization itself to an end. If there were 10,000 Orson Welles, society would fly apart like an exploding bomb." He is a noisy, expansive, jovial young man who calls everybody "loveboat," and has kept his love for mugging, for grotesque make-up.

References

Collier's 101:14+ Ja 29 '38 pors
Life 10:108-16 My 26 '41 il pors
New Republic 104:760-1, 824-5 Je 2, 16 '41
N Y World-Telegram p8 F 10 '40 por; p11 F 12 '40 por
New Yorker 14:22-7 O 8 '38
Newsweek 17:62 Ja 20 '41
Sat Eve Post 212:9-11+ Ja 20 '40 pors; 212:24-5+ Ja 27 '40; 212:27+ F 3 '40 por
Scholastic 33:21E Ja 14 '39 por
America's Young Men
Brown, J. M. Two on the Aisle p38-44 1938
Maloney, R. Essay Annual, 1939 p51-62 1939
Variety Radio Directory
Who's Who in America
Who's Who in the Theatre

WELSH, HERBERT Dec. 4, 1851—June 28, 1941 One of the founders of the Indian Rights Association; acted as its president for 11 years and secretary for 34 years; interested in many other public welfare movements; a vigorous fighter for the rights of the American Indian; gave up his art career to continue his work for the Indian; lecturer and con-

tributor to magazines on the Indian question, civil service reform and problems of municipal government; author of numerous books.

References

Who's Who Among North American Authors
Who's Who in America

Obituaries

N Y Times p17 Je 30 '41

WEST, ANNIE BLYTHE Feb. 25, 1860—Mar. 13, 1941 Missionary who for more than 40 years served in Japan; her work for the Presbyterian Board of Foreign Missions was mainly evangelistic, first among women and children and later also among nurses and patients in the Red Cross Hospital and the Home for Disabled Soldiers in Tokyo; in honor of her service the Japanese Government conferred upon her the Sixth Degree of the Order of the Crown.

Obituaries

N Y Times p44 Mr 16 '41

WEST, NATHANAEL 1906—Dec. 22, 1940 Novelist and screen writer killed in an automobile accident; author of *Miss Lonelyhearts* (1933), *Cool Million* (1934) and *The Day of the Locust* (1939); his wife, Eileen McKenney, was also fatally injured; she was one of the leading characters in two books by her sister, Ruth McKenney, and the subject of a play, *My Sister Eileen*.

References

International Motion Picture Almanac

Obituaries

N Y Times p23 D 23 '40

WEYMOUTH, FRANK E(LWIN) June 2, 1874—July 22, 1941 Renowned hydraulic engineer who was in charge of the government investigations of the Boulder Dam project; as surveyor of the project he is credited by engineers with having furnished the basis of facts and figures for that enterprise; general manager and chief engineer of the metropolitan water district of Southern California; served as chief of the United States Reclamation Bureau from 1920 to 1924.

References

Who's Who in America
Who's Who in Engineering

Obituaries

N Y Times p19 Jl 23 '41

WHIPPLE, MAURINE Jan. 20, 1906- Author

Address: c/o Houghton Mifflin Co, 2 Park St, Boston, Mass.

The Giant Joshua is a first novel that Maurine Whipple, its dark, vivacious, youthful-looking author, calls the only true story about the Mormons ever written. Published in 1941, it has inevitably had to meet comparison with Vardis Fisher's recent *Children of God,* although Fisher's book was primarily an epic of the Mormon migration and Miss Whipple's the story of a particular Mormon settlement—the Dixie Mission in St. George, Utah. Her novel is also unusual in that it discusses the institution of polygamy from a woman's point of view, that of its heroine, Clory, who at 17 becomes the third wife of her guardian.

The story of the Dixie Mission begins in 1861 and covers 26 years of a people's struggle against economic hardship, social disapproval and political persecution. Clory's own life is one of work, poverty, sorrow; of battle against her own lurking doubts of the Mormon faith, against a short-lived love for her husband's eldest son, against the jealousy of Bathseba, her husband's first wife. Nowhere are the Mormons idealized; Miss Whipple calls them "human beings by birth and only saints by adoption." Yet she says, too: "The Mormons were the happiest people that ever lived. They sang their way across the continent and they idolized Brother Brigham." Critics have found her exhaustively detailed book "rich, robust and oddly exciting"; some have criticized its great length, its style or its handling of material, but even one of its sternest critics, Clifton Fadiman (see sketch this issue), remarks that as a piece of reconstruction *The Giant Joshua* is "vigorous, animated and perceptive, even humorous at times."

Few writers are as well equipped as Miss Whipple to write about the Mormons. They are her people; this is her faith; St. George is where she was born on January 20, 1906, the daughter of Charles and Anne (MacAllister) Whipple. It was from her own mother that she learned of the "polygamy raids" by United States marshals that took place after polygamy was outlawed in the '80s. Children were captured and made to give evidence against their parents, and Miss Whipple's mother was forced many times to hide in the sagebrush on freezing nights in order to avoid them.

The story of Clory, too, might be the story of Maurine Whipple's own grandmother, who was only ten years old when she set out from Philadelphia with her father, one of a group chosen by Brigham Young to settle the Dixie Mission. It took her six months to get to Utah, pushing a handcart. She was sixteen when she became the bride of the fifty-year-old missionary who had led her and her father across the plains, and she, like Clory, was one of the Mormon women who were unhappy in polygamy. The other wives were older and resented her; later, when her husband was transferred to another temple, he discarded her for an even younger wife. Yet there were good reasons for the Mormon institution of polygamy, however much it may have warped individual lives. Says Miss Whipple: "When the Mormons arrived in Utah they had been raided and murdered to such an extent that they had five women to every man. Brigham Young

saw he had these alternatives: A colony of women who would likely break up into a section of spinsters and prostitutes. Polygamy was the only answer. Each woman would be better off with a fifth of a man than none."

Maurine Whipple herself had a girlhood that was normal enough. She studied first at Dixie Junior College in St. George, then attended the University of Utah. There she lived in a basement, sometimes went without meals, did washing for other students, worked in a store, and in-between times somehow managed to pile up enough credits to get her B. A. in 1926. She also joined Chi Delta Phi. After doing postgraduate work during the summer at the University of California in Los Angeles she proceeded to teach country high schools (although she had majored in English composition, she found herself teaching dramatics and tap dancing); she worked on public playgrounds; and she organized and managed her own private schools in towns throughout Utah, Idaho, Nevada and California. In her spare time she continued to write.

MAURINE WHIPPLE

It was not until 1937, however, that a friend persuaded her to send a story called *Beaver Dam Wash,* written some time before, to the Writers' Conference which was meeting in Boulder, Colorado. She did; members of the Conference—particularly the late Ford Madox Ford—were impressed; and Maurine Whipple received a telegram asking her to come to Colorado at once. She got there by hitchhiking, stayed there by borrowing $100, and the next summer went to the Conference again as a teaching fellow.

The year 1938 was really memorable for other reasons, though. *Beaver Dam Wash* was not sold—hasn't been sold yet, as a matter of fact—but the publishing firm of Houghton, Mifflin awarded Maurine Whipple a $1,000 fellowship in order to write *The*

WHIPPLE, MAURINE—*Continued*

Giant Joshua. At last all the hours she had spent among her people listening with passionate interest to their stories, and all the "burning zeal" which she feels for the Mormons as a group could find their place in a book.

In the summer of 1940 Miss Whipple taught and lectured at the University of Colorado, and after the publication of *The Giant Joshua* she paid a round of visits in Boston, New York and Washington and completed plans for a season's lecture tour. But soon she was hard at work on her second novel. She has no intentions of being a "one book" author, enjoys her work even though she has to bribe herself to get down to it of a morning, and when she gets going sometimes works fifteen hours at a stretch.

As for her tastes—Miss Whipple tells us: "I love children, even unmanageable children. Dogs, cats, books, magazines, flowers—growing them, etc.—and people. Mainly people. Mountain climbing is a favorite diversion, also dancing—tap and ballroom—and swimming." She is not married but has a number of men friends, and says that she is planning one of these days "to settle down with somebody on the top of a rocky mountain and write stories and observe all the goings-on of the neighbors." She tells us further: "I know what it is to be hungry and I also know what it is to be too well-fed. My philosophy is that nothing can get you down as long as you remember to keep laughing—mostly at yourself."

References

Boston Transcript Jl 1 '38
N Y World-Telegram p5 Ja 3 '41 por
Pub W 133:2360 Je 18 '38 por

WHITFORD, HARRY NICHOLS 1871(?)—May 16, 1941 Internationally-known authority on crude rubber production; manager for past 16 years of the crude rubber department of the Rubber Manufacturers Association; professor of tropical forestry at Yale University from 1917 to 1923; made world-wide survey of crude rubber production for the United States Department of Agriculture.

Obituaries

N Y Herald Tribune p36 My 18 '41

WHITNEY, GERTRUDE (VANDERBILT) Sculptor

Address: 871 Fifth Ave, New York City

In an article devoted to America's wealthiest women *Fortune* said, "There is possibly something symbolic about Gertrude Vanderbilt Whitney's leaning toward marble, for she has all of its strong-mindedness and authority. There is assurance in whatever she undertakes, from running the Whitney Museum to fighting for the custody of her niece Gloria Vanderbilt."

From the same source comes this statement: "The Whitney women have always been as active, as prominent, as newsworthy as the Whitney men. They have had backgrounds, interests, minds of their own." This probably would have been true whether or not Gertrude Vanderbilt had married Harry Payne Whitney. It was this marriage that made the great-granddaughter of Cornelius Vanderbilt one of the richest women in the land. Her husband's net estate, at his death in 1930, was valued at $62,808,000.

Born in New York City in the last century, the daughter of Cornelius and Alice (Gwynne) Vanderbilt, Gertrude Vanderbilt attended Brearley School and began to study art at an early age. Perhaps the prestige of great-grandfather Cornelius, who made his first money rowing market-garden produce from Staten Island to Manhattan, was a challenge to the slight, delicate-featured girl. She studied sculpture under Hendrik C. Andersen and James E. Fraser, took a course at the Art Students League, and later studied under Andrew O'Connor in Paris.

On August 25, 1896, she married Harry Payne Whitney, whose traditional pattern was cut out for him in business and in sports. A director of the Guaranty Trust Company, he was also interested in many other business ventures, and was known as the premier sportsman of his day. Mrs. Whitney took time off from her consuming devotion to art to become familiar with her husband's hobbies and to bring up her children on the lovely 600-acre estate at Old Westbury, Long Island. Her three children are Cornelius Vanderbilt Whitney, Mrs. G. Maccullough Miller and Mrs. Barklie McKee Henry. Though by no means a typical society woman, Mrs. Whitney's scale of living is impressive. In addition to the Long Island estate and a studio in Greenwich Village, she maintains a town house at 871 Fifth Avenue and a box at the Metropolitan Opera House.

Mrs. Whitney first met Juliana Force (see sketch this issue) when she required the assistance of a secretary to help edit a novel she had written. It was a relationship that was to prove immensely valuable to both women, and the novel was all but forgotten as more significant events began to take shape. The younger woman, with her sharp perception and executive ability, helped give direction to Mrs. Whitney's interest in American art and artists. In 1908 the Whitney Studio was opened at 8 West 8th Street with Mrs. Force as director. Two years later Mrs. Whitney discarded the anonymity that had cloaked her own creative efforts, allowing her name to be used when her sculpture, *Paganism Immortal,* won a distinguished rating at a National Academy show.

From then on Mrs. Whitney's artistic life had two facets, to create in her own right and to encourage American artists of talent to create. To a great extent this phase of her life is also the story of Juliana Force, and one need emphasize here only that Mrs. Whitney, who has carved so many and such massive memorials, can claim two monuments to her own interest in art. First, there is the living trend of a native art that she helped to encourage and, second, its embodiment in the Whitney Museum of American Art.

That her participation in this development was never a mere sideline or hobby is testified to in her description of her four passions: that talent be encouraged in youth; that the young artists be given a lay audience that will buy as well as a critical audience that will appraise; that the public know the art of its people; finally, that the development of a characteristic, vigorously American art that has taken place within the last 50 years become part of the country's artistic consciousness. "Mrs. Whitney's interest," says *Fortune,* "has often helped young American artists to get a hearing, it has disproved the theory that American millionaires never buy anything but European Old Masters."

Working in a wide variety of sculptural media, Mrs. Whitney has executed commissioned works for many countries abroad as well as for many parts of her native land. A kind of romantic grandeur distinguishes many of these creations, such as the World's Fair commissioned work, *To the Morrow,* an immense bird in flight, the nude figures of a man and woman where the head would be. But *Peter Stuyvesant,* also done for the World's Fair, had more of Dutch dignity about him, only the largeness of concept marking it as by the same artist. "The great Cornelius," wrote J. T. McGovern, "dealt only in marine and railroad consolidation. Gertrude Vanderbilt Whitney worked in art in the grand manner. Her subjects were lofty in spirit and she executed them on a heroic scale. Consider the *Columbus* statue erected at Palos, 70 feet high; the bronze *Buffalo Bill* on top of Lookout Mountain, said to be the tallest figure in bronze which had up to then been designed by a woman; the A. E. F. *Memorial,* 60 feet high, erected upon a rocky eminence over the harbor of St. Nazaire, where the first troops of the American Expeditionary Force landed in France; and the great group and background *El Dorado* done for the Panama Exposition."

In her commissioned works, where she has usually to deal with specifically historical subject matter, Mrs. Whitney handles with complete equanimity the most realistic materials. In her salon sculpture one might almost be permitted to make a sharp distinction and to say that here we are being shown more intimate aspects of the artist's talent. Most critics agree substantially with Edward Alden Jewell's appraisal of Mrs. Whitney's sculpture, written after he had seen an exhibit of her work in 1936. "The approach in most of this work," said Jewell, "is essentially romantic, often decorative. Sometimes, however, there are graver passages, as in the tragic severed head of *John the Baptist,* held aloft by Salome—her figure treated with a contrasting lightness of touch that would be appropriate in a piece of innocent ornamental sculpture for the garden."

Henry McBride noted in this exhibit of her work the absence of a "feeling for time," and suggested that "she not only escaped the present tempestuous era but escaped as well the domination of the terrible Old Masters." That this statement could not apply to the bulk of her commissioned works is fairly obvious. And one may assume that it was partly because of them that she was one of four women sculptors

GERTRUDE WHITNEY

invited to depict on Flushing Meadows the World of Tomorrow. Authentic detail has always featured Mrs. Whitney's treatment of historical subjects. For the equestrian statue of *Buffalo Bill,* for example, she used a cow pony for a model. Even so, over-zealous newsmen printed a story hinting that the model had been one of her husband's polo ponies!

Along with her own creative work, Mrs. Whitney's partisanship of American art and artists has occupied much of her time and absorbed a great deal of her money. Hers was never patronage, however. From the beginning she made it plain that philanthropy could only encourage bad art if it were confused with art appreciation. Mrs. Whitney's philanthropy, therefore, was something distinct from her attitude toward art and artists *per se.* If during the years when the Whitney Studio Club and Gallery existed "many were provided with the absolute necessities of life by Mrs. Whitney," this did not mean that paintings for the Whitney collection were accepted on the basis of the artist's economic need. On the contrary, they were accepted only on artistic merit. And critics might quarrel as to the relative merits of this or that artist, yet agree that in a period of little more than two decades Juliana Force and Gertrude Whitney managed to assemble the most representative collection of modern American art in the country.

Nor was Mrs. Whitney the only buyer during these years. Through Mrs. Force's attractively furnished apartment passed many of the country's most promising younger artists, some of its neglected oldsters, while through Mrs. Whitney's drawing room passed collectors or potential collectors, many of whom made that inevitable visit downtown to the gallery to buy their first Sloan, Luke or Bellows. Thin, unusually tall, Mrs. Whitney's green gowns and brownish hair were a familiar sight at museum and gallery openings. In 1931 the Whitney

WHITNEY, GERTRUDE—*Continued*
Museum of American Art opened its doors with Juliana Force as director and Mrs. Whitney on its board of trustees but otherwise disavowing other than fraternal contact with the modern yet typically American façade built up from three old houses on West 8th Street. This was not discreet self-effacement, and it implied no departure from Mrs. Whitney's lifelong concern for the present and future of native art. It was simply a statement of fact and in this sense a generous tribute to the executive genius and the good judgment of Mrs. Force.

Since its opening there have been two attempts to involve the Whitney Museum in controversy. In 1933 when Juliana Force was named regional head of the Public Works of Art Project she felt compelled to explain to the press that there was, in fact, no connection between the Government and the Museum, that she had received her appointment as a qualified individual. In the year that followed there developed in the State Supreme Court a prolonged legal case as Mrs. Whitney sought to gain custody of her niece, Gloria Laura Morgan Vanderbilt. This case was finally settled in 1936 by Gloria's mother being given custody during summers and vacations, Mrs. Whitney the rest of the time, but not before it had been revealed that $4,000 monthly was required to care for Gloria Vanderbilt. The Museum entered into the picture very briefly when Nathan Burke, counsel for Gloria's mother, wished to photograph some of the nude sculptures, a request denied by the Court.

Mrs. Whitney belongs to numerous art societies and clubs and has been awarded many honorable mentions and medals. "In art" Mrs. Whitney said, "man has always found the comfort and joy, relaxation and aspiration which help to take away heartache. It is music, rhythm of line, color, words, drama, which bring refreshment and which keep alive our trust in human nature and our belief in the future."

References
>Art Digest 14:3 O 1 '39
>Arts & Dec 50:34 Je '39 por
>Fortune 14:116-18 N '36 por
>Mag Art 32:558-67+ O '39 il
>American Women
>McGovern, J. T. Diogenes Discovers Us p257-74 1933
>Who's Who in America
>Who's Who in American Art

WHITTLESEY, CHARLES F. 1868— Jan. 1, 1941 American architect; one of the first architects in this country to make use of reinforced concrete, using exposed concrete surfaces with ornamentation cast in place; built the Philharmonic Auditorium in Los Angeles and the Huntington Hotel in Pasadena, California.

Obituaries
>N Y Times p23 Ja 2 '41

WICK, FRANCES G(ERTRUDE) Oct. 2, 1875—June 15, 1941 Chairman of the Department of Physics of Vassar College; internationally recognized for her work in the field of luminescence or cold light; taught at Vassar since 1910 with leaves of absence to carry on research at other institutions.

References
>American Men of Science
>American Women

Obituaries
>N Y Herald Tribune p10 Je 16 '41
>Sch & Soc 54:10 Jl 5 '41

WILE, FREDERIC WILLIAM (wīl) Nov. 30, 1873—Apr. 7, 1941 Newspaper correspondent; author and columnist; for many years he had been a contributor of editorials and signed columns in the Washington *Post;* pioneer radio reporter; sued Germans for his arrest in 1914 as suspected spy and collected $6,000; wrote autobiography *News Is Where You Find It* in 1939.

References
>Lit Digest 121:36 Ap 18 '36 por
>Author's and Writer's Who's Who
>Who's Who in America
>Who's Who in American Jewry
>Who's Who in Journalism
>Wile, F. W. News Is Where You Find It 1939

Obituaries
>N Y Times p25 Ap 8 '41 por
>Pub W 139:1853 My 3 '41

WILHELM II, FORMER GERMAN KAISER (vĭl'hĕlm) Jan. 27, 1859—June 4, 1941 Friedrich Wilhelm Victor Albert Hohenzollern, former Emperor of Germany and King of Prussia; died in exile at his estate in Doorn, The Netherlands, to which he had fled after the defeat of Germany in the First World War; outlived fame, glory, defeat and even violent hatred, becoming a forgotten legend to the millions who had seen him as an ogre during the First World War; ascended the throne in 1888; first 25 years of his reign were marked by peace; after his exile wrote thousands of words to prove his innocence of the charge that he alone caused the First World War.

References
>Am Hist R 45:834-41 Jl '40
>Am Mercury 50:155-61 Je '40
>China W R 89:413-16 Ag 26 '39
>Christian Cent 55:756-8 Je 15 '38
>Newsweek 3:17+ Mr 24 '34; 10:18 N 15 '37; 15:26 F 12 '40 por; 15:29 My 27 '40 por
>19th Cent 128:174-81 Ag '40
>Sat Eve Post 210:5-7+ O 23 '37 il por (Same abr. Read Digest 31:34-8 D '37)
>Time 35:22 F 12 '40 por
>Baumont, M. Fall of the Kaiser 1931
>Chesterton, G. K. Varied Types p237-45 1903

Churchill, W. L. S. Great Contempo-
    raries p21-31 1937
Dombrowski, E. German Leaders of
    Yesterday and Today p79-91 1920
International Who's Who
Ludwig, E. Wilhelm Hohenzollern, the
    Last of Kaisers 1932
Martin, W. Statesmen of the War in
    Retrospect, 1918-1928 p3-17 1928
Nowak, K. F. Kaiser and Chancellor
    1930
Viereck, G. S. Kaiser on Trial 1937
Viviani, R. As We See It 1923
Waters, W. H. H. Potsdam and Doorn
    1935
Zedlitz-Trützchler, R. Twelve Years at
    the Imperial German Court 1924

Obituaries

N Y Times p1, 8, 9 Je 5 '41 pors

WILKINS, T(HOMAS) RUSSELL June
6, 1891—Dec. 10, 1940 Professor of physics
at the University of Rochester; internationally
known in the field of science; famed for his
studies of the atom; in the fall of 1940 perfected a special camera to study the nuclei of
chemical elements; also widely known for his
pioneer studies of cosmic rays.

References

Newsweek 7:44 Je 27 '36 por
American Men of Science
Who's Who in America

Obituaries

N Y Times p27 D 11 '40 por

WILKINSON, ELLEN (CICELY) 1891-
Parliamentary Secretary to the British Ministry
of Home Security
Address: 18 Guilford St, London, W. C. 1,
England

Ellen Wilkinson, trade-union leader, Laborite,
Leftist critic of the British Government, is in
1941 working closely with the Churchill Administration, her job that of Parliamentary Secretary to the Ministry of Home Security. She
is still as much of a feminist as she ever was,
and has been urging greater utilization of
women in Britain's war efforts. Women, she
thinks, are needed in every sort of work, and
when women are properly trained England will
be better prepared for that time when "Hitler
throws everything at us, including the kitchen
stove."

Almost all her life Ellen Wilkinson has been
absorbed in political problems. "I should say,"
writes Ethel Mannin, "that Ellen Wilkinson
cares about politics as most women care about
clothes and love, that for her those things will
always be unimportant incidentals in the business
of living." In spite of that this "stumpy, bright-
eyed little person with a permanently quizzical
expression and a shock of red hair" is not, the
same observer hastens to add, "the de-humanized
mass of politics devoid of natural feeling which
that statement suggests." She radiates enthusiasm and energy, she is "real."

ELLEN WILKINSON

Ellen Cicely Wilkinson was born in the cotton city of Manchester, where her father,
Richard Wilkinson, was an operative in one of
the mills. Later he became an insurance agent,
but not until Ellen was almost grown up. She
was brought up in "one of those dreary little
houses which make up many of the streets of
Manchester," and attended a State primary
school. From there she won a scholarship to
the Stretford Road Secondary School in Manchester and after that she went on to the University of Manchester, which gave her a Master
of Arts degree.

For a while after graduation Ellen worked
as a teacher. Her heart, though, was in politics.
As early as 1912 she joined the Independent
Labor Party, then a powerful force in the labor
movement, and in that same year started agitating for woman suffrage. A year later,
when the suffragettes were causing great embarrassment to the Liberal Government, she
became organizer to the National Union of
Women's Suffrage Societies, a post she kept
for two years. Then, with the War on, she
threw herself into the trade-union movement;
by 1915 she was national organizer for the National Union of Distributive and Allied Workers. She remembers those War years well.
Compared with them, she says, life as a member
of the House is child's play. This must have
been particularly true since she was at the
time a member of the Women's International
League, opposed to the War.

Always a Leftist within her trade-union,
Miss Wilkinson joined the Communist Party
of Great Britain when it was founded in 1920,
and from 1923 to 1926 sat on the Manchester
City Council as a Communist. She was also
one of the founders of the University Socialist
Federation, one of the first members of the
British Bureau of the Red International of
Labor Unions (later called the National Minor-
ity Movement) and a leader of the Plebs

WILKINSON, ELLEN—*Continued*

League and the Labor Research Department. During the Irish "troubles" she was in Ireland as a member of the Labor Commission on Ireland, dashing in and out of those places where the shooting was fiercest. Later she went to Washington to give evidence on what she saw before the American Commission on Ireland.

In 1923 Miss Wilkinson contested Ashton-under-Lyne as official Labor candidate. She lost the election. The next year she switched from the Communist to the Labor Party, for she saw by then that if she were to do practical work for the laboring people it would have to be under the auspices of the official Labor Party. The switch proved successful, and she was returned for Middlesborough. Once in Parliament, Ellen Wilkinson distinguished herself by asking many and embarrassing questions, by arguing vehemently ("she's a born arguer," her colleagues say) for those things in which she believes. She also made herself conspicuous by her "intrepid spirit and irrepressible perkiness." There was one debate in 1926 when she was being a bit of a nuisance to her opponents. The Conservative Member for Dulwich quietly admonished her: "Be quiet, Miss Perky!" Laughter began to spread around the House, and Ellen herself got only as far as saying: "Mr. Speaker, is it in order for an Honorable Member to describe another . . ?" when she broke down and joined in.

In 1926 Miss Wilkinson played an active part in the General Strike, touring the country up and down, speaking in Parliament, in meeting halls, from soapboxes. As in all her speeches, her strong voice was badly managed; her appearance was unimpressive. But audiences all over England recognized her "clear understanding and assertive will." It was partly as a result of these excursions that she collapsed in the House in 1927 and had to spend some weeks in the country recuperating from a nervous breakdown. She came back ready to continue the fight and stayed in Parliament until the 1931 election, when she was ousted.

During all these years in politics Miss Wilkinson was a prolific journalist and writer whose contributions appeared in many labor and other papers. One of them, an article published in the *New Leader* in 1929, cast doubts on the impartiality of the chairman of the Committee of Ways and Means and got her into trouble. She was censured for breach of privilege. In that same year she brought out a first novel, *Clash*, built upon political issues.

During the four years she was out of Parliament, Ellen Wilkinson continued to write. Her *The Division Bell Mystery* appeared in 1933; *Why War?* and *Why Fascism?* (in collaboration with Dr. E. Conze) in 1934. She did much more than just writing in those years. She was busy with trade-union work; she made a visit to India in 1933 and returned to criticize the Government's administration there; she visited Russia; she was in Germany

during the terror which followed the Reichstag fire; she was in Detroit and other United States auto centers in 1935, reporting on the conditions of work, employee organization and the management policy she found there. And always she was an indefatigable worker against Fascism, her flat a center of organization, her services at the disposal of thousands of meetings. She traveled all over Europe and her own country, combating Fascism, reporting what she found in Spain in 1935, in Germany, in England.

She continued this work after she was returned to Parliament in 1935 as Labor Member for Jarrow, a northeastern shipbuilding town which for many years has existed in a state of industrial depression. She fought for Jarrow in Parliament, and when the Jarrow men sent a band of marchers to London to impress the Government with the need of doing something for this town, she marched at their head, despite her frail health. In 1939, too, she published a book on Jarrow, *Town That Was Murdered*, and in it laid the blame for its misfortunes on capitalist greed and mismanagement.

As a member of the National Executive Committee on the Labor Party she was one of the three who in 1938 voted for Sir Stafford Cripps' (see sketch 1940 Annual) proposal for a Popular Front against the Conservatives. But, as Patricia Strauss puts it, "she always managed adroitly not to wander too far from the hearth of orthodox Labor domesticity."

In the House itself she continued to be the question-asking, "perky", "Socialist spitfire" of her previous terms. She initiated there an important piece of legislation in 1938, the Hire-Purchase Act. The issues involved were complicated, and the measure had to be carefully nursed. She did this with such skill that when the bill became law (without a dissenting voice at its third reading) she was congratulated by the attorney general on "her patient and skillful handling of the prolonged negotiations with the various interests concerned."

Her hard work in Parliament definitely put her in line for a position in the all-party Government which Churchill formed in May 1940, and the job of Parliamentary Secretary to the Ministry of Pensions fitted in well with the work for social betterment she had been doing. In October 1940 she left the Ministry of Pensions to help Herbert Morrison, Home Security Minister, provide food and shelter for bombed Londoners. She is known as the "Shelter Queen."

Opinions of her have somewhat changed since the days when she was known in England as "Red Nell." In 1941 there were some on Britain's Left who called her a hireling of the capitalists; there were others who yelled, "Take her away," when in October she made a speech urging "cool strategy" rather than emotion in Britain's attitude toward aid to Russia (Communists blamed the discourtesy on provocateurs); there were some former associates who deplored her belief that England could not open up a second front at that time. But there were also many who were still sure that Ellen Wilkinson "has never forgotten her working-class origin or lost contact with the rank and file of the movement."

References

Christian Sci Mon Mag p12 Jl 27 '40 por
Liv Age 359:41-3 S '40 por
N Y Sun p17 O 28 '41
Newsweek 16:23 O 21 '40
PM p5 Ag 4 '40 por
Johnston, J. A Hundred Commoners p112-14 1931
Mannin, E. Confessions and Impressions p173-8 1937
Strauss, P. Bevin and Co. p131-48 1941
Who's Who

WILLIAM II, EMPEROR *See* Wilhelm II, Former German Kaiser

WILLIAMS, EMLYN Nov. 26, 1905-
Playwright; actor
Address: 15 Pelham Crescent, London, S. W. 7, England

At the age of 36 Emlyn Williams is London's reigning playwright and bids fair to become New York's, too. In a dull and dreary theatre season his *The Corn Is Green* opened in November 1940 to give the New York City stage something of its usual glory. A play which, according to Brooks Atkinson of the *Times,* "comes as close to being a masterpiece as a journeyman theatregoer can reasonably expect," it is the story of a woman who turns a surly-mannered, smutty-faced Welsh miner into an educated man. But it wasn't the bare plot that mattered to the wildly enthusiastic critics; it was Emlyn Williams' ability to show depth and integrity of character, to create a "stirring, high-minded drama that . . . illuminated something precious in the long story of man's blind struggle in the network of the stars." Joseph Wood Krutch, writing in *The Nation,* and George Jean Nathan were almost alone in dissenting from the general verdict.

The background of *The Corn Is Green* is very much the background of Emlyn Williams' own life. The son of a Welsh iron-maker, Richard Williams, and his hard-working wife, Mary Williams, he was born in the tiny Welsh hamlet of Mostyn in Flintshire and was eight before he could speak a word of English, nineteen before he ever saw a play. But he was always interested in the theatre—"I'm Welsh and the theatre is one of the fundamental instincts of my people." Almost before he could talk he would dress himself up in sheets and perilously and solitarily act on the edge of his bed dramas he made up himself. Later, as he tells it, "I read a great deal . . . *Pilgrim's Progress* and the Bible; and always as I read I saw the characters between imaginary footlights and back cloths, as people in a play."

Emlyn was sent to the Holywell County School and there trained by interested teachers to become a schoolmaster. He won a scholarship in French to Christ Church, Oxford, spent four brilliant years there and went down with an M. A. But he was sure by then that he

EMLYN WILLIAMS

would never be a schoolteacher, for at Oxford he had seen his first real play, Somerset Maugham's *The Camel's Back.* "I was caught in a spell that has enthralled me ever since. . . I felt, too, I must create such characters and such situations. So I went home and wrote a play."

The play was *Full Moon,* a rather Chekhovian sort of thing in which everything happened, but life went on. It was acted by the Oxford University Dramatic Society, of which Williams became an active member. But it was not easy to get parts on the stage after he left Oxford and there was a period of standing in long queues at agents' offices and tiresome waiting. Finally in 1927 came a part in *And So to Bed,* a very small one, but a part. Then followed a role in his second play, *Glamour,* called a "youthfully crude but promising effort," which didn't exactly set the Thames on fire and left Williams looking for another acting part. He got a number of them in the next few years, in none of which he achieved fame.

Then, in 1930, came Williams' first success as a playwright. His *A Murder Has Been Arranged* was presented in a Sunday night show and after the first performance managers fought to produce it. The story went around then that Williams invited five managers to his flat, threw the manuscript at them and said, "Bid, Gentlemen, Bid,"—so successfully that he got an advance of £1,000. When he was asked if this were true Williams said: "All but one thing. There were seven managers."

In 1931 came his *Port Said,* in which Williams acted, and then Edgar Wallace's *The Case of the Frightened Lady,* in which Williams was a tremendous success as Lord Lebanon. After a season in other plays in London, Williams came with the Wallace "shocker" to New York in 1933—its name was changed to

WILLIAMS, EMLYN—*Continued*

Criminal at Large—and was praised for "one of the exceptional characterizations of the current season." In that year and the next there were many London plays in which Williams appeared, and his own *Vessels Departing* and *Spring 1600* were produced, as well as his adaptations of *The Late Christopher Bean* and *Josephine.* Then, in 1935, came his *Night Must Fall,* a great hit which ran in London with him in the leading role, for over a year.

This "taut, slick study in psychopathic homicide" is the story of Dan, who murders a woman at the hotel where he is bus boy, plans throughout the play to murder another woman, and finally does. The latter's niece, Olivia, is meanwhile the victim of both terror and fascination. It is a play of "extraordinary tension," called by every critic "first-rate theatre." It has been told that so skillful was Williams' own part in it that an old lady once refused to ride up in an elevator with him. Williams, however, insisted that "my interest in murder is purely objective."

When *Night Must Fall* was brought to the United States in 1936 it flopped despite its success in London, despite Alexander Woollcott's (see sketch this issue) statement that Williams was "one of the half dozen actors left in the world whom I would want to see no matter what the play," despite his and others' praise of the play. A few months later when Williams was describing the hectic life of New York he didn't hesitate to say that "the only quiet place in it was the auditorium of the Ethel Barrymore Theatre," where it played. Later his play was made into a film with Robert Montgomery and Rosalind Russell, a critics' if not a box-office success.

After he returned to England, Williams, together with John Gielgud, acted in another of his own plays, *He Was Born Gay,* but it lasted only 10 days. Then he went to the Old Vic Repertory Theatre and for one year appeared in a number of plays, including Shakespeare's *Richard III* and *Measure for Measure,* and Ibsen's *Ghosts.* In 1938 came his own *The Corn Is Green,* in which he acted the part of Morgan Evans, taken in the American performance by Richard Waring. In 1940 it was still playing in London and in the spring of that year was joined by *The Light of Heart,* the story of a drunken, down-at-the-heels actor who gets his last chance to stage a comeback in a production of *King Lear.* Critics hailed this play, too (though iconoclast George Jean Nathan read it and wondered why), and it was planned for Broadway production.

During these years as playwright and actor, Emlyn Williams has also turned his attention to the films. It was in 1932 that he first appeared on the screen—in the adaptation of *The Case of the Frightened Lady*—and from then on he has appeared in a number of motion pictures, including *Night Alone, The Citadel* and *They Drive by Night.* He has also adapted a number of films.

Emlyn Williams is a round-faced, boyish-looking, not very tall man with a mop of hair streaked with gray, an attractive Oxford slur and a habit of lolling around in slightly disheveled suits. Lucius Beebe can "recall few more amiable, approachable or persuasively articulate persons," and there are friends who say he is these even when he's working on a play. According to them he can be interrupted at his work without growling and depends on his powers of concentration to keep him up to schedule. It has been said that he wrote the last scene of *Night Must Fall* during a party. During one of its rowdiest moments he suddenly stood up from the typewriter and exclaimed: "I've finished it!"

For many years Emlyn Williams was a bachelor. But now he is married to Molly O'Shann and they have two children, whom Mrs. Williams brought to the United States in the fall of 1940. Not allowed to bring out money for their support, she arranged for a job as "technical adviser" to Herman Shumlin (see sketch this issue), producer of *The Corn Is Green,* in order to collect enough to provide for them until the royalties came rolling in. In April 1941 she returned to London, however.

References

Esquire 16:88+ N '41
N Y Times X p1 D 1 '40
Theatre Arts 20:824-5 O '36
Theatre World 19:218 My '33 por; 24: 34-5 Jl '35 por; 24:125 S '35 por; 27: 34 Ja '37 por; 30:179 O '38 por
Time 28:52 O 12 '36 por; 35:71 My 6 '40
International Motion Picture Almanac
Who's Who
Who's Who in the Theatre

WILLIAMS, JOHN D. 1886(?)—Mar. 22, 1941 Former stage director and producer who had produced many famous American plays, including *Rain* with Jeanne Eagels, *The Copperhead* with Lionel Barrymore, *Justice* with John Barrymore and *Zack* with Richard Bennett; produced plays by Pinero, Maugham and Shaw; credited with being the first to discover Eugene O'Neill as a playwright and produced the first Broadway production of O'Neill's *Beyond the Horizon.*

Obituaries

N Y Times p23 Mr 25 '41

WILLIAMS, PAUL R. Feb. 18, 1894- Architect

Address: 3839 Wilshire Blvd, Los Angeles, Calif; 1271 W. 35th St, Los Angeles, Calif.

Shortly before the New York World's Fair closed in 1940 there was held at the Court of Peace on the Fair grounds a Diamond Jubilee celebration of the enactment of the 13th Amendment (which outlawed slavery). A special commemorative stamp had been issued by the United States Post Office Department, and a sheet of 100 of these and a certificate of merit were presented to each of several Negroes in recognition of their achievements.

Among the recipients was Paul R. Williams, Los Angeles architect, one of the leading architects of the West, a member of the Los Angeles Municipal Housing Commission and an associate architect on government jobs in Washington, with offices in both that city and Los Angeles. Mr. Williams has designed homes for a number of film people, including Will Hays, Grace Moore, Bill Robinson (see sketch this issue), Lon Chaney, Corinne Griffith, Zasu Pitts, as well as for many other prominent residents of California and elsewhere. He was architect for other types of buildings also: a Hollywood Y. M. C. A., fraternity and sorority houses for the University of California, the West Coast Company Theatre and the Sunset Plaza Apartments in Hollywood, California. A recent issue of *Life* showed pictures of William Paley's Beverly Hills home, the Saks Fifth Avenue Beverly Hills store, and the Music Corporation of America Building (Beverly Hills), all designed by Williams. One of his latest designs was for the $100,000 home that Charles Cottrell (Andy of "Amos 'n' Andy") has built in Los Angeles.

When Paul Williams was in Polytechnic High School he decided that he wanted to be an architect. He was living in Los Angeles, where he was born, the son of Chester Stanley and Lila (Wright) Williams, and where as a child he had played with other children without being made aware that he was "different." It was not until as a schoolboy he applied for a job that he encountered prejudice: he learned that he was not taken because he was a Negro.

"I passed," he said, "through successive stages of bewilderment, inarticulate resentment and, finally, reconciliation to the status of my race. Eventually, however, as I grew older and thought more clearly, I found in my condition an incentive to personal accomplishment, an inspiring challenge. Without having the wish to 'show them,' I developed a fierce desire to 'show myself.' I wanted to vindicate every ability I had. I wanted to acquire new abilities. I wanted to prove that I, *as an individual,* deserved a place in the world."

Therefore when his instructor tried to have him face reality, by asking him, "Who ever heard of a Negro architect?" he decided that if at this point he allowed the fact that he was a Negro to checkmate his ambition he would be starting a habit of "defeatism"; that he owed it to himself and to his people to accept this challenge—feeling as he did that white people would be fair-minded enough to give him an opportunity to prove his worth as an individual.

He worked his way through the University of California and then attended the Beaux Arts Institute of Design, winning the Beaux Arts Medal. After graduation he got a Los Angeles telephone book and took down the names of all the architects in the city. One by one he went to them, until he found one willing to take a Negro draftsman. He began as general utility man, but gradually worked his way up to chief draftsman, acquiring experience in all branches. The Society of Architects of Los Angeles took him in. By this

time he felt that he was ready to open his own office.

A theory that he had about the cause of prejudice helped him to become established: he had decided that most prejudice was unreasoned; that the average American generalized about Negroes as he generalized about many other things, without much thought; that if he could somehow shock some people into looking upon him as an "individual" Negro he might be able to sell his ability. He, therefore, developed several tricks as "attention-getters." Often a person would come into his office not knowing that he was a Negro and would then try to withdraw graciously. Perhaps he would say that he was "just shopping around," that he was thinking of spending about $8,000 but that he was not ready to make a decision. Williams would then say, "I am sorry but I have been forced to make it a rule never to do houses costing less than $10,000—but won't you sit down a moment. Perhaps I may be able to give you some ideas . . ." Frequently in this way he got a hearing, and sometimes a client.

Another device he had of attracting attention was drawing upside-down—right-side-up for the prospective client who was sitting opposite him. As he talked, consulting the client about details, he would make a rough sketch of the plans. This trick, he says, invariably aroused interest.

PAUL R. WILLIAMS

During this time he was forced to accept small commissions—in spite of his trying to give the impression that he handled only large ones. And because they *were* small he acquired what he regards as invaluable experience, for he had to figure costs very rigidly.

When he was first consulted on a residence costing more than $100,000 he tried another trick. The automobile manufacturer who wanted the house built told him that he had already discussed plans with some other ar-

WILLIAMS, PAUL R.—*Continued*

chitects, and asked him how soon he could have preliminary drawings ready. When Williams said by four the next day the manufacturer thought that impossible, since the other architects had all wanted two or three weeks, and was impressed enough to let Williams go ahead. The latter presented the plans at four the next day—by working for twenty-two hours without eating or sleeping.

Mr. Williams is a member of the American Institute of Architects. He has been a registered architect since 1915, and was listed in *Who's Who in Architecture* (of the *American Art Annual*) published in 1924. He has won several western and national competitions. For years now he has had to refuse about 25 per cent of the commissions offered him, commissions that come from other sections of the country as well as from his own state. He has had as many as 13 draftsmen working under him at one time, several of them white. Not long ago he reported that he was planning 33 buildings—business buildings, homes, apartment houses. When he plans private houses he thinks of building *homes* for individuals, and studies the economic problems, the habits and tastes of each client. Designs and descriptions of his buildings are found frequently in *Arts and Decoration, Architectural Forum, California Arts and Decoration* and other journals.

Mr. Williams married Della Givens on June 27, 1917. They have two children.

References

> Am Mag 124:59+ Jl '37 por
> Arch & Eng 141:18-42+ Je '40 il por (p12)
> Arts & Dec 41:10-15 Ag '34 il
> Life 5:54 por (p58) O 3 '38
> N Y Amsterdam News p17 O 26 '40
> Opportunity (National Urban League) 16:81 Mr '38 il
>
> American Art Annual 1924-25
> Who's Who in Colored America

WILLIAMS, WILLIAM ROBERT June 13, 1867—Nov. 17, 1940 Former professor of clinical medicine at the College of Physicians and Surgeons, Columbia University and an authority on hygiene, therapeutics and pharmacology.

References

> American Medical Directory
> Who's Who in America

Obituaries

> N Y Times p19 N 18 '40 por

WILLINGDON, FREEMAN FREEMAN-THOMAS, 1ST MARQUESS OF Sept. 12, 1866—Aug. 12, 1941 Former Governor General of Canada and Viceroy of India; had the reputation of being one of the shrewdest negotiators and ablest trouble shooters in the British Empire for more than 40 years; was one of few commoners ever created a marquess.

References

> Business Week p14 S 17 '30 por
> Fortune 135:488-500 Ap '31
> Gt Brit & East 46:511 Ap 16 '36; '46:545-6 Ap 23 '36; 51:69 Jl 21 '38
> Lit Digest 108:14 F 7 '31 por
> Near East 44:406-8 Ap 4 '35
> 19th Cent 119:592-603 My '36
> Sat Eve Post 200:3 F 25 '28 por
> Spec 156:783 My 1 '36
> Who's Who

Obituaries

> N Y Times p17 Ag 31 '41

WILLS, C. HAROLD June 1, 1878—Dec. 30, 1940 Auto engineer; chief engineer and manufacturing manager of the Ford Motor Company from 1903 to 1919; one of the automobile industry's leading metallurgists and chemical engineers; developed the use of vanadium steel for commercial purposes and of molybdenum steel in automobile construction; designed the Model-T Ford.

Obituaries

> N Y Times p15 D 31 '40

WILSON, CHARLES E(RWIN) July 18, 1890- President of General Motors Corporation

Address: b. c/o General Motors Corp, Detroit, Mich; h. Bloomfield Hills, Mich.

When William Knudsen was called to Washington in the spring of 1940 to work on the Defense Commission, his place as president of the General Motors Corporation was taken by Charles E. Wilson, "a soft-faced, hard-headed engineer and production man." Since he has headed this large and important company Wilson himself has had a good deal to say on the defense program. Surveying the country as a whole, he has stated that defense can be "successfully completed only by improving efficiency . . . and by sacrifice." And he has given it as his opinion that "unless engineers, technicians, highly skilled mechanics and managers work more than 40 hours a week the program will never be completed on time."

Charles E. Wilson has also informed the public on the part that General Motors is playing in preparedness. In February 1941 he announced that arrangements had been completed for the production of parts and sub-assemblies for 200 twin-engine bombers monthly and that in its Buick and Allison division airplane engine production was being boosted from 500 to 1,500 units a month. The full aviation program that General Motors is undertaking, he estimates, will probably mean the employment of 40,000 additional men.

Production in great quantity, however, was not expected to get under way until the third quarter of 1941. Although backlog defense orders were large, in 1940 only three and one-third per cent of General Motors' output had been for defense, less than eight per cent in the first quarter of 1941, and there was still a boom in the production of private motor cars, the greatest in years.

For more than 20 years Charles Erwin Wilson has been an executive of the General Motors Corporation; he came to that company with years of engineering experience behind him. He was born in Minerva, Ohio, where his father, Thomas Erwin Wilson, was principal of the Minerva School and where his mother, Rosalind (Unkefer) Wilson, had also been a teacher. A few years later the Wilsons moved to Mineral, Ohio, and Charles went to public school there. He finished his pre-college education in Bellevue High School in Pittsburgh, Pennsylvania and then attended the Carnegie Institute of Technology, from which he was graduated in 1909 as an electrical engineer.

Shortly after graduation Charles Wilson joined the engineering staff of the Westinghouse Electric and Manufacturing Company in the Pittsburgh district as a student apprentice. He stayed in the employ of this company for 10 years, and it was here that he received his first real training in the practical application of engineering knowledge. He learned more, too: he learned the importance of costs and of volume manufacturing.

At Westinghouse, Wilson came into contact with automobile manufacturers and grew more and more interested in their problems. In 1912—a year also made important by his marriage to Jessie Ann Curtis—he designed the first automobile starting motors made by the Westinghouse Company. By 1916 he was in charge of all automobile electrical engineering equipment there. When the First World War came along, Wilson was put in charge of design and development of Westinghouse radio generators and dynamotors for the Army and Navy.

In April 1919, after the War was over, Wilson joined the General Motors Corporation as chief engineer and sales manager of the automobile division of the Remy Electric Company, a General Motors subsidiary with headquarters in Detroit. Later he was transferred to Anderson, Indiana as chief engineer of the company. Here he initiated a redesigning program that materially helped to put the Remy Electric Company's operations on a sound financial basis. By December 1921 Wilson was factory manager and four years later became general manager. Then, in 1926, when the Dayton Engineering Laboratories Company was added to the Remy Electric Company, he became president and general manager of the newly organized Delco Remy Corporation.

During the next two years the Delco Remy Corporation, which employed about 12,000 people, developed under his direction the Lovejoy shock absorbers, industrial motors for refrigeration and washing machines, automobile lamps and Delco batteries. By the end of 1928 the Delco Remy Division had spread out from Anderson, Indiana to three other cities, and Mr. Wilson himself had been made a vice-president of the General Motors Corporation and transferred to Detroit.

CHARLES E. WILSON

Wilson's main duties after his promotion were to acquire properties to expand the Corporation's activities (he assisted in arranging for the purchase of minority interests in the Bendix Aviation Corporation and the North American Aviation Corporation as well as for the purchase of many properties and businesses) and to develop its parts and accessory business. His activities spread out from here, and by the time of his promotion to executive vice-president on May 1, 1939 he was interested not only in the operation of the parts and accessory companies, but also in labor relations problems and the business planning of production. On June 6, 1940, when Knudsen left for Washington, Wilson became acting president of the Corporation, and that same month held a press conference in Detroit in which he put the damper on the practicability of the Reuther (see sketch this issue) plan for defense production; in January 1941 he became its president, and in June of that year the Corporation distributed to him as a bonus 3,782 shares of common stock.

When Mr. Wilson can get away from the multitude of duties and responsibilities involved in the leadership of a great corporation, he spends time with his six children (three boys and three girls) and sometimes snatches an hour or two for a game at the Bloomfield, Michigan Golf Club or a meet at the Bloomfield Open Hunt Club.

References

Am Mag 131:11 My '41 por
Business Week p17 D 25 '37 por
Fortune 18:45 D '38 por
Newsweek 17:41+ Ja 20 '41 por
Time 36:20 D 9 '40 por

Who's Who in America
Who's Who in Commerce and Industry

WILSON, GEORGE ARTHUR Mar. 17, 1864—Oct. 4, 1941 Teacher of philosophy; taught at Dickinson College and at Syracuse University from 1899 until 1937, when he became professor emeritus; contributor of articles and book reviews to philosophical and religious journals; author of *The Self and Its World* (1926); in early years held Methodist pastorates.

References

> Leaders in Education 1941
> Who's Who Among North American Authors
> Who's Who in America 1934-35
> Who's Who in the East

Obituaries

> N Y Times p17 O 6 '41

WILSON, H(ALSEY) W(ILLIAM) May 12, 1868- Publisher

Address: b. The H. W. Wilson Co, 950-972 University Ave, New York City; h. "Greenehold" at Croton Heights, Yorktown Heights, N. Y.

When the members of the American Library Association gathered in Boston in June 1941 for their annual conference, no face was more familiar to the librarians than that of H. W. Wilson, founder and president of The H. W. Wilson Company. In terms of statistics the Boston conference was Mr. Wilson's thirty-fourth, and Association files show that only five living members have exceeded his attendance record. Further, to thousands of other librarians the world over who have never laid eyes on him, the name of H. W. Wilson is as inseparably associated with bibliographical publications as that of Webster with dictionaries or Bartlett with quotations. "We couldn't keep house without the Wilson indexes" is a phrase that has become a byword in the profession.

Halsey William Wilson was born at Wilmington, Vermont, the son of John Thompson and Althea (Dunnell) Wilson. He is a descendant of the great Baptist, Roger Williams, Mary Dyer, the Quaker martyr, and Anne Hutchinson. By the time he was two and a half years old both parents had died, and he lived with his maternal grandparents until he was twelve. At that time he went with an aunt to Iowa and later to Minnesota. He was educated at Beloit College and the University of Minnesota; in 1939 Brown University made him a Doctor of Letters. He married Justina Leavitt of Minneapolis in 1895.

Although the history of what was later to become The H. W. Wilson Company began, strictly speaking, with the first issue of the *Cumulative Book Index* in 1898, the ten years previous paved the way. In December 1889 two students at the University of Minnesota, Henry S. Morris and Halsey W. Wilson, formed a partnership to deal in student textbooks and supplies. The University authorities saw in the enterprise a good thing for the University and granted the use of a nine-by-twelve room in the "Old Main" building on the campus. It was in this tiny space that a corporation which now measures its sales at more than three-quarters of a million dollars annually had its real beginning.

Two years later, after the graduation of Henry Morris, Halsey Wilson carried on alone. At this time an idea took shape for greater efficiency in the book business. Every book dealer or librarian knows the problem posed by the patron who wants information about a new book and who can give the author, or the title, or the general subject classification, but never all three. Unless an up-to-date catalog is at hand the search becomes exasperating. At that time there was no such catalog to consult and H. W. Wilson's idea was to provide a cumulative monthly list of books which should include in one alphabet the author's name, the title and general subject heading. It would be experimental. It would require money. Several years passed. Then in 1898 the project was launched. Estimating the cost of a cumulative list at $500 a year for printing—he expected to do the compiling, copymaking, proofreading, bookkeeping and mailing at home evenings with the assistance of his enthusiastic wife, whose labor was equally cheap—Halsey Wilson was emboldened to risk publication on his own account, in the optimistic hope that 500 subscribers might be found among booksellers and librarians who would pay $1 a year for the service. The first year, as Mr. Wilson recalls it, "was memorable for some heartening endorsements, nearly 300 subscriptions and a rapidly growing deficit." Nevertheless, the undertaking kept going ahead, and, when a change of residence was made, the publishing office occupied a wing with an outside entrance and Marion E. Potter became the first paid editor and started her notable career with The H. W. Wilson Company.

In 1900 Mr. Wilson negotiated the erection of a two-story building just off the campus which housed the book shop and the publishing department. Before long, outside rooms had to be rented to permit expansion. Here the *United States Catalog* saw the light of day and the universally known *Readers' Guide to Periodical Literature* was "born." The *Book Review Digest* appeared in 1905. Shortly afterward a three-story building was erected and the Company moved into its third home. Other publications and a rapidly growing staff marked progress. In 1913 the need of nearness to publishing centers in the East became apparent and Mr. Wilson transplanted his Company, with 13 carloads of equipment to White Plains, New York. Here again quarters were quickly outgrown and a final move was made in 1917 to the present light, airy location on the east bank of the Harlem River, in The Bronx, New York City. The five-story building which housed the Company comfortably in 1917 was supplemented in 1929 by an eight-story modern structure on the south, and in 1938 by a six-story building on the north. The Company, it may be said, is one of the few contemporary publishing houses which do all of their own typesetting, printing and binding.

Today the venture started by a young bookseller and his wife in 1898 employs a staff of 340 people who receive an annual payroll of nearly half a million dollars. Sales for the fiscal year of 1940 were just under $800,000. The Company's activities now comprise some 15 major publications of a subscription or semi-subscription nature and a list of miscellaneous works of bibliography and reference. A department, begun in Minneapolis, stocks more than 2,000,000 copies and sets of back number periodicals for purchase by libraries and individuals who wish to complete sets of magazines.

Cooperation is a favorite word in the Wilson vocabulary, as the following instances will show. Subscribers are asked to vote on material for indexes and matters of editorial policy. Mr. Wilson has invited the American Library Association and the Special Libraries Association to have representatives sit *ex officio* with the Company's board of directors. Shares of dividend-bearing, participating stock in the Company are distributed periodically to the Company's staff. Almost from the beginning the Company's work schedule has been consistently more liberal than required by law. Today there is a uniform five-day week of thirty-six and a half hours, with two weeks' vacation each year with pay. The Company maintains a no-cost hospital plan and participates equally with interested staff members in an annuity retirement benefit.

It is the belief of the staff who know Mr. Wilson well that he might have been an inventor if he had not turned to the "ordered life of bibliography." Countless mechanical processes and short cuts used in the involved business of cumulative indexing and publishing are the product of his never-idle mind. Aside from the cumulative method and its intricate ramifications, perhaps his most revolutionary contribution to the business of bibliographical publishing is his "service basis" method of charge, whereby the cost to each library is in proportion to the use made of the service.

The H. W. Wilson Company has been not only Halsey W. Wilson's career but virtually his whole life, his recreation as well as his work—evenings, Sundays and holidays. His vacations have been few. The longest was a trip to Europe in 1920. There have been many business absences; but motor jaunts with Mrs. Wilson, for week ends or a little longer, have sufficed for vacations. The major outside interest in his life is a 250-acre tract of land near Yorktown Heights, in historic upper Westchester County, New York. Known as Croton Heights, it has direct rail connection with The Wilson Company offices, which are just across the avenue from the terminal of the Putnam Division of the New York Central Railroad. Today some 46 families, including several of The Wilson Company staff, have summer or year around homes at Croton Heights. In the center of the community stands Mr. and Mrs. Wilson's sturdy colonial house, built in 1740. They

Kaiden-Keystone

H. W. WILSON

call it "Greenehold" because it served as Colonel Christopher Greene's headquarters in the darkest hour in Westchester during the Revolutionary War. Close by is Croton Heights Inn, which until 1941 was Mrs. Wilson's summer hobby.

When living in the City, Mr. Wilson habitually walks to work, and he is usually the first in the building in the morning and the last to leave at night. He modestly boasts that he has never known a day's illness. He has recently made a tryout of commuting and likes it so well that the City apartment has been given up. Punctuality being almost a fetish, it matters little to him that in order to reach his desk in good season he must rise at six o'clock and walk to the station for a seven-twenty-six train. He prefers the train to driving, as the extra hour morning and evening gives him time to read and work on new publishing projects. Mrs. Wilson shares her husband's energy and capacity for unselfish effort. An ardent worker for suffrage, she became a member of the National Suffrage Board and was appointed by Mrs. Carrie Chapman Catt to write the textbook and conduct suffrage schools throughout the country. Later she did state educational work for the Democratic Party. In 1941 she supervised the publication of a memorial volume entitled *Victory: How Women Won It*, commemorating the centennial anniversary of the woman's rights movement. Several years after her marriage to Halsey Wilson, she returned to the University of Minnesota to complete her college course and today wears a Phi Beta Kappa key. For several years she did editorial work for the *Book Review Digest*.

A "Profile" by Creighton Peet in the *New Yorker* of October 29, 1938 describes Halsey W. Wilson as "a slight, quiet, baldish man

WILSON, H. W.—*Continued*

who wears spectacles and probably looks just as a bibliographer ought to look. . . In spite of the fact that his business has expanded to such enormous proportions, he has never allowed himself any ostentatious gestures. He hasn't even a private office or a personal secretary, and he works in one corner of a large floor filled with editorial employees. He has, however, indulged himself in two minor fancies: the dummy lighthouse on the roof of the building (symbolic of indexes enlightening the world); and a ten-cent mousetrap, unbaited, which stands on one of the bookcases in the editorial room, signifying that the H. W. Wilson indexes are *better* indexes."

Despite his predominant devotion to his Company, Mr. Wilson is by no means antisocial. His college fraternity is Phi Kappa Psi, he is a Scottish Rite Mason and a life member of the American Library Association. He is the author of a concise manual called *The Bookman's Reading and Tools* which has gone through several editions. Also it is an open secret that he is the "Harold Workman Williams" who collaborated in compiling the first of the three *Toaster's Handbooks* published by the Company. He does not smoke, though he does not object to the habit in others. His views on liquor are stronger. He learned to play the pipe organ and piano in his youth and frequently for relaxation spends a half hour at the piano with old classical favorites. Solitaire, motion pictures and clipping and filing jokes are other occasional pastimes. He is accustomed to grasp both sides of a controversial question before reaching conclusions. *The Handbook Series* and *The Reference Shelf* are outgrowths of this deep-seated trait. There is a whimsical quality in his turn of a phrase which is a constant delight to his friends. He loves children and animals. He takes lively interest in young musicians who have talent and the necessary qualifications for developing it. His library shows an increasing number of volumes on the persecution of human beings for their beliefs, on the modern fight for the freedoms and on education for the free man. He is also a modest collector of rare books. Since coming to The Bronx Mr. Wilson has taken active part in civic affairs and has been instrumental in obtaining certain municipal improvements. At the present time he is busily engaged in organizing sentiment and support for a much needed subway extension to serve The West Bronx.

It is a testimonial both to Halsey W. Wilson's gift of vision and practical business ability that his is virtually the only bibliographical venture of any size which has ever succeeded without the aid of subsidies or subventions. But of these faculties, say his fellow-workers, vision has always played the greater part. "Money has never come first with Mr. Wilson," writes a colleague of many years. "That quality (with unfailing patience and hard work) is the key to his success. It is business sense applied to giving libraries, and especially the users of libraries,

what his vision tells him they want. That spirit of unselfish service symbolizes the man and the company he founded and has guided for so many years."

References

A. L. A. Bul 33:731 D '39
Fort Worth Star-Telegram N 2 '41 (Same Hartford Times N 2 '41; Indianapolis Star N 2 '41; San Diego Union N 2 '41)
New Yorker 14:25-8 O 29 '38; 14:80 N 12 '38
Wilson Lib Bul 13:250-1 D '38; 14:80 S '39

Leaders in Education 1941
Who's Who in America
Who's Who in Commerce and Industry
Who's Who in Library Service
Who's Who in New York
Who's Who in the East
Wilson, H. W., Co. A Quarter Century of Cumulative Bibliography pam 1923

WILSON, HUGH (ROBERT)   Jan. 29, 1885-   Lecturer; former diplomat

Address: Yale University, New Haven, Conn.

"We do not love, we do not hate, we do not judge, we do not condemn; we observe, we reflect, we report." That is the motto of the United States diplomatic service as Hugh Wilson would have it, and it effectively sums up his own career for more than a quarter of a century. Recalled as Ambassador to Germany in November 1938, he was one of Secretary of State Cordell Hull's closest advisers in Washington until his formal resignation in December 1940, and he has since been named to the Lamont Lectureship in Government at Yale University. In March 1941 appeared the second volume of his autobiography, *Diplomat Between Wars*.

Hugh Robert Wilson was born in Evanston, Illinois on January 29, 1885, the son of Hugh Robert Wilson, a Chicago shirt manufacturer, and Alice (Tousey) Wilson. He was educated at the Hill School in Pottstown, Pennsylvania, went on to Yale to take his B. A. in 1906, and the next year entered the family business. "More unhappy than the majority" during his three years of business experience, he still didn't decide to follow his own desires and enter the Foreign Service until 1910, when his mother died. He had inherited an income, his brother Oliver encouraged him to do as he pleased, and he thereupon departed for Paris to enter L'École Libre des Sciences Politiques, one of the best training schools for diplomats-to-be.

Life in Paris was "one of the few things that are better in realization than anticipation." Hugh Wilson was almost sorry when in 1911 the Minister to Lisbon cabled him the offer of a position as his private secretary. "A few months of revolution, old-fashioned border raids, color and bull fights" preceded a visit to Washington late in the autumn of the same year, when Hugh Wilson took his examinations and was accepted as a member of the Foreign Service; and January 1912 found him in Guatemala as United States chargé d'affaires. He had no chief: "in those days of 'dollar diplomacy' and in those regions the voice of the United States was the voice of Jove"; and for nearly two years the young man felt as important as he probably ever did again.

But those untroubled years before the First World War were brief. During a leave of absence in Paris, Katherine Bogle agreed to marry him. They were married on April 25, 1914, and in August set sail for Buenos Aires, where Wilson had been assigned. During the sea voyage war was declared (even at the time of Sarajevo the young diplomat had not been apprehensive, since he had "no real conception of the political commitments of Europe and their ramifications"), and after only a year and a half in Buenos Aires and a vacation in the United States he was ordered to Berlin. That was 1916, and it was as a junior member of the Embassy staff in Berlin that Wilson saw the United States drawn into the First World War.

Upon the breaking of diplomatic relations with Germany, Hugh Wilson crossed the frontier with Gerard and the staff of the Embassy. His next assignment was in Vienna; it was brief, for the United States presently declared war on Austria-Hungary. From Vienna he went to Berne, Switzerland, "perhaps the best international observation post in the world," and for the remainder of the War he was there as chargé d'affaires. Hugh Robert Wilson, III, was born on March 12, 1918.

An attack of influenza brought another leave of absence to Mr. Wilson early in 1919, but by 1921 he was back in Germany as counselor of the Embassy, the highest competitive post in the Foreign Service. In spite of personal bitterness regarding the Treaty of Versailles, he negotiated the Peace Treaty with Germany that year. An assignment in Tokyo followed—peaceful after Germany's post-War chaos—and in 1924 he was back in Washington as chief of the Bureau of Current Information of the State Department and as chief of the Executive Committee of the Foreign Service Personnel Board.

Robert Allen and Drew Pearson (see sketch this issue) wrote of Hugh Wilson that he was at that time among the little group of career diplomats who "appointed themselves and their own tried and trusted friends as members of the Personnel Board to pass upon promotions," who "picked their friends for the best foreign posts and saw to it that the amenable Mr. Kellogg got them approved at the White House." In 1927, they said, "everything that possibly could break against the controlling career clique did break," and the ringleaders, seeing "the handwriting on the wall," appointed themselves to diplomatic posts abroad just before the "smash" occurred. There is little indication of any of this in Mr. Wilson's memoirs, but it is true that in 1927 he was appointed Envoy Extraordinary and Minister Plenipotentiary to Switzerland, a country for which he had always had a par-

HUGH WILSON

ticular admiration. He was to spend 10 years there.

During those 10 years Mr. Wilson had a perfect attendance record at the European conferences to which the United States sent delegations. He devoted most of his attention to the League of Nations, sending valuable reports to the State Department; he negotiated numerous treaties under the League, including the only one which is being observed by the belligerent powers today—the treaty on the treatment of war prisoners; he served as delegate to the General Disarmament Conference in Geneva from 1932 to 1935.

On the whole, however, Mr. Wilson believes that it is better for both Europe and the United States that his country stayed out of the League of Nations. He spoke of his doubts and his grave concern as he watched from Geneva the application of the nonrecognition policy to Manchukuo, as he listened to condemnation of Germany "which, like that of Japan, was not backed up by a show of force but remained in the realm of phrases," as he observed the application of sanctions to Italy even after Addis Ababa had fallen. He believed that if such measures could not be applied ruthlessly they should not be applied at all. But he made few claims to prophecy.

It was the summer of 1937, after the role of Geneva in world affairs had almost vanished and the affairs of the Spanish War were in the hands of the "Non-Intervention" Committee in London, that Hugh Wilson was summoned home to serve as Assistant Secretary of State under Cordell Hull. In December of the same year he was appointed Ambassador to Germany to succeed the late William E. Dodd, with the endorsement of the Nazis. And in November of the next year he was recalled, following the Grynszpan shooting in Paris and the subsequent pogroms. Supposedly he was recalled

WILSON, HUGH—*Continued*

merely in order to give a "firsthand picture" of the situation; actually no diplomat took his place after that, and in December 1940 Mr. Wilson formally resigned, having acted for two years as special adviser for Secretary of State Cordell Hull.

Education of a Diplomat, the first chapter of his autobiography, published in 1938, was described by Oswald Garrison Villard as "a delightful little volume, one certain to make every reader eager to meet him and to know the attractive personality he reveals. It has great charm, excellent description, much understanding of men and manners, and a great deal of humor." Martha Dodd was more critical: "The author fulfills all the requirements he thinks a diplomat should have: he is suave, discreet, non-partisan. He makes no attempt to get at the essence of a nation or a race; he skims the surface of life and history wherever he goes; social, cultural and political backgrounds hold no interest for him." The same comments might be equally applicable to the more recently published *Diplomat Between Wars,* which brings his history up to the summer of 1937. Hugh Wilson says: "When and if the third chapter will be written, I am not sure. Certainly the present does not seem to me to be the time for an account of that nature."

Hugh Wilson is described as "mild-mannered and genial," with "keen blue eyes, a broad brow, precise speech, and a distinguished bearing." His own urbanity he finds sadly lacking in most modern diplomacy. The diplomacy characteristic of our era, he finds, is one of "vituperation by radio, of international mudslinging." He says further: "If a choice between sincerity and manners were necessary, I should unhesitatingly choose manners for 99 per cent of the people with whom I come in contact." It may be this emphasis that makes nearly all his characterizations so polite: Goebbels (see sketch this issue) was "an interesting and stimulating conversationalist," Mussolini "courtesy itself." It may also account for his rather extraordinary idea for a coalition government: the Conservatives to run internal affairs, the Socialists to handle foreign relations!

References

Deutsch Rundsch 257:1-5 O '38
Time 30:10 D 20 '37 por; 32:10 N 28 '38 por
Who's Who in America
Who's Who in Government
Who's Who in the Nation's Capital
Wilson, H. R. Diplomat Between Wars 1941
Wilson, H. R. Education of a Diplomat 1938

WINANT, JOHN G(ILBERT) (wĭn'ănt) Feb. 23, 1889- United States Ambassador to England

Address: b. American Embassy, London, England; h. 274 Pleasant St, Concord, N. H.

After Joseph Kennedy resigned his post as Ambassador to Great Britain in late 1940, newspapers and commentators began saying that John G. Winant would be his successor. Twice before they were wrong in predicting positions for him—in 1933, when they announced that he was to be the 1936 Republican Presidential nominee, and in July 1940, when they were sure he would be named chairman of the National Labor Relations Board. This time, though, they were right. On February 6, 1941 President Roosevelt announced his appointment to the Court of St. James.

A scholar and a "social-doer," three times Governor of a state that traditionally never re-elects a Governor, a leader in the fight for social security and director of the International Labor Office in Geneva, John Gilbert Winant was born in New York City, the son of Frederick and Jeanette L. (Gilbert) Winant. From a very well-to-do home he went to St. Paul's School in Concord, New Hampshire and from there to Princeton, which years later, in 1925, awarded him an M. A. for graduate study on government problems. In 1912 Winant left Princeton to return to St. Paul's as a teacher of English and assistant rector. He bought land in Concord and proceeded to make himself a citizen of New Hampshire. The First World War interrupted his teaching, however, and in 1917 Winant enlisted in the Army as an aviation private. He rose to be a crack flier, captain and commander of the Eighth Observation Squadron on the French Front.

Back from the War, Winant entered New Hampshire Republican politics. First he ran for the Legislature and served his first term, from 1917 on, in the House of Representatives. In 1921 he shifted to the State Senate and then in 1923 back to the House again. It was in these years that Winant began working for better social conditions: he campaigned in the Legislature for a 48-hour week for women and the abolition of child labor.

Encouraged by his success, Winant ran for Governor of New Hampshire in 1925. His opponents warned the voters against him. He was, they said, a New Yorker; he was rich, bookish; he was a schoolmaster and no politician. Nevertheless, Winant became at 36 the youngest Governor in the country, and proceeded to attack the employers of child labor, the power-trusters, the entrenched interests that were invading public rights, and also Republican Senator George Higgins Moses, who had warned: "That young cock of a schoolmaster had better watch out or he's going to have his wings clipped."

Winant ran for a second term as Governor in 1926, but those were boom years when the people didn't need a champion. He was defeated. When times got hard, the people voted him back, and from 1931 to 1934 he served two terms in the State Capitol, one of the few Republicans who escaped the guillotine of November 1932. A Boston newspaperman once explained his re-election: "The reason probably lies in Winant himself. He seems to be as clean as a blade. He's an idealist but not one of these 'holier than thou' guys. When the situation requires it he fights hard and cleanly. . . He's got common sense, a sincerity you can't laugh off and a beautiful kind of neighborliness." Winant himself partly explains it, too, when he says: "I have never bargained or bartered for public office."

Under Winant, New Hampshire's administrative machinery was overhauled, reorganized and modernized. It was under him that New Hampshire made a notable contribution toward relieving unemployment. Long before the NRA his "New Hampshire Plan" for re-employment by reducing hours, sharing work and making capital and labor equally accountable was helping to relieve the depression for his state.

In 1934 President Roosevelt, whom Winant has always supported despite his Republican allegiances (he came out for his election in 1940), appointed him chairman of a three-man board to mediate the big textile strike. Then in 1935 Winant, who already was president of the National Consumers' League, vice-president of the American Association for Labor Legislation and a trustee of the International Y. M. C. A., was made the United States' delegate to the International Labor Office in Geneva. He accepted the appointment, he says, because "I felt that peace was the prime issue before the peoples of the world." Shortly afterward he was elected an assistant director of the I. L. O., which meant that for the first time the I. L. O. was directed by a citizen of a country which was not a member of the League of Nations.

The I. L. O., it should be explained, was set up by the Treaty of Versailles, one part of which stated that the failure of any nation to adopt humane labor standards "is an obstacle in the way of other nations which desire to improve the conditions in their own countries." Its functions are to collect and distribute labor data, conduct investigations, publish a periodical and to adopt "conventions" under which the ratifying countries establish employment agencies, bar child labor, set minimum work weeks, etc. It wasn't until 1934 that the United States joined the I. L. O.

Winant represented his country there until world conditions forced the removal of I. L. O. headquarters from Geneva to Montreal. He returned from Geneva in 1935 for a period "to help organize social security in this country because I believed that if democracy in the United States was to continue to function it must rest on a fairer social base." As the first chairman of the Social Security Board, in 1935 and 1936, Winant "achieved a reputation as an administrator that was virtually unequaled in any of the New Deal agencies." In his resignation, made in order to answer his own party's attacks on the President's social security program, were clearly stated his social beliefs: "Having seen the tragedy of war, I have been consistently interested in the ways of peace. Having seen some of the cruelties of the depression, I have wanted to help with others in lessening the hardships, the suffering and the humiliations forced upon

American citizens because of our previous failure as a nation to provide effective social machinery for meeting the problems of dependency and unemployment." For a while after his resignation Winant continued to write and speak on the subject of social security and then returned to Geneva, to the I. L. O. In 1939 he became its director.

Because of his past record, his appointment as Ambassador to Great Britain was felt to be significant. Not only was he already well acquainted with Anthony Eden, Ernest Bevin and other British leaders, but his concern with social problems, it was believed, would have value both during the War and later. Winant gave evidences of his social beliefs when in a nationwide broadcast, shortly after his appointment, he warned the victors, whom he predicted would be the British, to build a "democratic world of tomorrow" based on social justice and economic security as a prerequisite to a "real and lasting peace."

Once in England, he proceeded to carry out the usual duties of ambassadorship plus the extraordinary ones demanded by the United States' entrance into the War and its program of aid to Great Britain. He learned about conditions there, signed the agreement

Underwood & Underwood
JOHN G. WINANT

leasing sites for naval and air bases from Britain, conferred with British leaders and reported to President Roosevelt what he knew about the state of affairs. Back in America in June for a short while, he warned this country that the British position was "extremely grave," though England did not face "any immediate or impending disaster." And from time to time he made similar statements.

Tall, dark, with high cheekbones, deep-set eyes and jutting features, Winant has always had something of a Lincolnesque look, and his opponents say he carefully cultivates this by wearing unpressed shiny suits, despite his

WINANT, JOHN G.—*Continued*

income from inherited money and oil wells in the Southwest. Actually he has no pretentions at all, and Mrs. Winant, the former Constance Rivington Russell of New York, whom he married in 1919 (they have three children, John, Jr., Rivington Russell and Constance, who in February 1941 eloped with Peruvian Carlos Valando), has as few as he. Interested in breeding West Highland White Terriers, she placed a sign, "Puppies for Sale," on the Executive Mansion in Concord when her husband, the Governor, moved in.

References

> Am Mag 115:58-9+ Ap '33 por
> Collier's 94:14-15+ Jl 14 '34 pors
> Cur Hist & Forum 53:22-4+ Je '41
> Lit Digest 120:27 S 7 '35 por
> Nation 151:387-8 O 26 '40
> N Y Times p1, 9 Ja 21 '41 por; VII p6+ F 16 '41 por
> Newsweek 2:15 D 23 '33 por
> Scholastic 27:25 S 21 '35 por
> Survey 74:248 Jl '38
>
> Who's Who in America
> Who's Who in Government

WINSOR, FREDERICK Mar. 29, 1872— Nov. 26, 1940 Headmaster of the Middlesex School for many years and a leader in secondary school education; author of *The Art of Human Behavior*.

References

> Leaders in Education 1932
> Who's Who in America

Obituaries

> N Y Times p23 N 27 '40

WISE, STEPHEN S(AMUEL), RABBI Mar. 17, 1874- Rabbi of the Free Synagogue of New York; president of the American Jewish Congress

Address: b. 40 W. 68th St, New York City; h. 340 W. 57th St, New York City

On March 17, 1940 the Free Synagogue of New York City celebrated the 66th birthday of its founder, Dr. Stephen S. Wise, and his 33rd year as its head. The gifts which he received on that occasion were singularly symbolic and appropriate. The members of his congregation presented him with a gold seal ring worn by the late Theodore Herzl, the pioneer of Zionism, and with plans for a new $500,000 synagogue to be built next door to the present temple, with a huge social hall, a 1,250-seat auditorium, a film projection room and other improvements. The presentation of Herzl's ring was most appropriate because Dr. Wise has been one of the most ardent advocates of Zionism in America and has fought tirelessly for this cause during his 45 years of service in the rabbinate.

The new synagogue, besides being a monument to his lifelong services to liberal Judaism, is a most necessary improvement, for Dr. Wise's drawing power as a preacher had long

ago proved greater than the auditorium's 600-seat capacity in the old synagogue; his Sunday services had long ago been moved downtown to Carnegie Hall. A less solemn note was struck when the Friendly Sons of St. Patrick of Bridgeport, Connecticut contributed its bit by making Dr. Wise an honorary member of its society.

Dr. Stephen Samuel Wise thinks he has the distinction of being the only rabbi to have been born on St. Patrick's Day. He was born in 1874, in Budapest, Hungary, the son of Dr. Aaron and Sabine de Fischer (Farkashasy) Wise. His father was a rabbi, too—Dr. Wise is the seventh rabbi in direct succession in his family—and his parents brought him to New York when he was one year old. His education followed family tradition in preparing him for the rabbinate: it included public schools; classics and languages at the College of the City of New York, Semitics and philosophy at Columbia. He received his B. A. degree from Columbia in 1892, his Ph. D. in 1901, and at 19 became an assistant to Dr. Henry S. Jacobs at the Madison Avenue Synagogue. Within a year he was its head. Handsome, earnest, with good stage presence, he was a great success as pastor and greatly in demand as lecturer. In 1900, after a lecture on Zionism in Portland, Oregon, he accepted an offer to become rabbi of the Temple Beth Israel there for the next six years. He gained attention by his sermons on political and social matters, "often descending from the temple to the market place to expose civic wrongs."

At the end of six years he left his Portland congregation and came to New York, which as the biggest Jewish community in the United States provided a better field for his endeavors, to "inject some vitality into American Judaism." For a while there was a strong possibility that he would preach from the conservative pulpit of Temple Emanu-El. But Dr. Wise's independence and unwillingness to compromise his freedom of speech prevented this arrangement. He decided to have a synagogue of his own, and his powerful and persuasive personality got him the backing of such men as Henry Morgenthau, Adolph Lewisohn, Oscar Straus and Isaac N. Seligman. By 1907 he had his Free Synagogue, so named because it was to have a free pulpit and a democratic organization, with no pew rents or regular dues, and the rabbi was to have complete freedom in his religious and social work. He has been its rabbi ever since.

In 1898 Dr. Wise, a fervent Zionist from the beginning of his career, had founded the Zionist Organization of America, another manifestation of his lifelong struggle to establish an unrestricted Jewish national home in Palestine. With the end of the First World War imminent, he saw the possibility of his dream coming true. Although for many years he had been an outspoken, uncompromising pacifist, with the coming of the War he had embraced the Allied cause and had made many patriotic and virulently anti-German statements. In 1917 he, together with Supreme Court Justice Louis Brandeis, Felix Frankfurter (see sketch this issue) and others, founded the

American Jewish Congress, whose purpose was to represent Jews "as a group and not solely as individuals." He was present as representative of that Congress at the Versailles Peace Conference in 1919 (he was decorated by the Légion d'Honneur for his activities), and since 1924 he has been alternately its president and honorary president.

As the most ardent spokesman of Zionism in the United States, Dr. Wise has since that time found himself pledged to an existence full of controversy and strife. The conception of a Jewish National Home in Palestine, in conjunction with the sacrifices it requires even from those Jews who have no desire to inhabit it themselves, was not a universally popular one. Conservative Jewry, represented by the American Jewish Committee, was not as willing to engage in demonstrations and mass protests as was the more articulate American Jewish Congress. It feared that to the Gentile mind the Zionist aims would mean that the Jews were plotting a "world superstate." Others believed that Jewish nationalism was an escapist concept which solved no fundamental problems. Dr. Wise is uncompromising in his attitude toward Jewish opponents of Zionism, however. In 1938, speaking in Cleveland in favor of a referendum for a united front for United States Jewry, he was bitter. "In 1933," he said, "we offered German-Jewish groups an opportunity to unite. . . They said they were Germans first, Germans who happened to be Jews. I am a Jew who is an American. I was a Jew before I was an American. I have been an American all my life, but I've been a Jew for 4,000 years."

Dr. Wise also waged a bitter battle against the British Government's attempts to hedge from the promises contained in the Balfour Declaration. "Great Britain," he said on many occasions, "must not fail the Jewish people. American Jews dare not fail Palestine." His dynamic personality made itself felt at most of the international conferences, where the future of the Jewish national home and the interests of Jewry in general were at stake. His voice was ever raised against any compromise, and he has always been the most violent foe of partition. In 1941 he broke into print with a dramatic plea to Britain to arm and equip a Jewish army in Palestine. This plea was made on behalf of the Emergency Committee for Zionist affairs, one of the numerous organizations which Dr. Wise runs (he is co-chairman). "If the Jews in Palestine are murdered by the Arabs and the Axis powers, without a chance to defend themselves, it will be one of the blackest pages in British history. They are wards of Great Britain under a mandate and they should not be permitted to die like rabbits." In September 1941 he presented a declaration, endorsed by the Zionist organization of America, calling upon Great Britain "to proclaim establishment of the Jewish Commonwealth of Palestine as an integral and essential part of a democratic world order" when peace is restored.

Zionism is not the only issue on which Dr. Wise has been vocal. Orthodox Jews, it is said, consider him much too politically minded.

American Hebrew

RABBI STEPHEN S. WISE

Ideas, persons and institutions which he has attacked include "drinking, prohibition, smoking, Henry Ford, war, pacifism, sex forums, suggestive plays, censorship, John Erskine, powder, lipstick, Felix M. Warburg," and, of course, Hitler. Witty, dramatic, "a quick rather than a deep thinker," he has thundered from many pulpits, and has not minded antagonizing important people in the process of "serving his people." He claims, proudly, that he was the "first of the Americans to call attention to the dangers of Nazism."

A reformer with a flair for organization, most of his ventures and the institutions which he has founded have fared well, in the financial as well as spiritual sense. For the past 20-odd years of his association with the American Jewish Congress he has raised and distributed a vast amount of money for support of various activities. In 1922 he founded the Jewish Institute of Religion, a rabbinical school which has been called "a sincere, scholarly attempt to place liberal Judaism on a well-organized basis." One of his more recent activities was the establishment of the Congress House, a non-sectarian home for refugees from European dictatorship. He was also instrumental in opening in March 1941 a research institute with the twofold task of dealing with war conditions affecting Jews and with proposals to settle Jewish questions at any forthcoming peace conference. Under the auspices of this institute, to be known as the Institute of Jewish Affairs, Contemporary and Post-War, the first All-American Jewish Conference in Montevideo, Uruguay took place in July 1941. One of its purposes was to identify Jews in the Western Hemisphere more closely with American life, said Dr. Wise.

With his leonine, rugged head, his burning eyes, his cello-like voice, Dr. Wise has always

WISE, STEPHEN S., RABBI—*Continued*
been an impressive figure, off as well as on
the pulpit. He has wit, charm, vitality,
generosity. Even his enemies admit that,
while accusing him of a certain amount of
smugness and fondness for limelight. He
lives simply, giving much of his income and
most of his time to the causes he espouses.
He has a passion for allying himself sensationally with large issues and is perhaps the
only rabbi in this country who is well known
to non-Jews as well as to Jews. In private
life Dr. Wise loses something of his Jehovian
aspect and becomes "playful, informal, boister-
ous, an incessant tease and practical joker."
His wife, the former Louise Waterman, whom
he married in 1900, has worked side by side
with him and is now president of the Women's
Division of the American Jewish Congress.
She is at present also active in another of Dr.
Wise's works: the Congress House. They
have two children, Mrs. Justine Wise Polier,
a judge in New York City, and James Waterman Wise, author and lecturer, and in June
1941 they adopted a six-year-old British boy,
Dennie Edward Mitchell.

In spite of all his other activities, Dr. Wise
has found time to write several books, among
them *How To See Life* (1917); *Child Versus
Parent* (1922); *The Great Betrayal* (with
Jacob de Haas, 1930). He edited *Opinion*, a
magazine of Jewish life and letters, and his
sermons have been published in 10 volumes,
under the title *Free Synagogue Pulpit.*

The present war has been enlisting even
more of Dr. Wise's inexhaustible energy on
behalf of the United States and its Allies. At
least one statement was an optimistic one. On
March 17, 1941, in celebration of the 45th anniversary of his service in the rabbinate, he stated
that he had never been as confident as he is
today about the future of civilization. The
world, he feels, is beginning to understand that
"anti-Jewishness is anti-justice, anti-freedom,
anti-democracy, anti-decency and anti-civiliza-
tion. . . There will be no real Jewish emancipation until there is human emancipation. I believe
that after the War, after Hitlerism shall have
been crushed forever, the Jewish people will
be dealt with justly at the peace table." If so
Dr. Wise will certainly be present to see
that they get their rights.

References

Christian Cent 51:525-7 Ap 18 '34; 51:
    666 My 16 '34
N Y World-Telegram p17 Mr 16 '40
New Yorker 7:22-5 N 7 '31
Newsweek 15:52 Mr 25 '40 il por
Time 28:37-8 Jl 20 '36 por; 31:24 Je 20
    '38 por
Jones, E. D. American Preachers of
    Today p63-71 1933
Leaders in Education 1941
Who's Who in America
Who's Who in American Jewry
Wise, J. W. Jews Are Like That! p83-
    103 1928

WOLFF, MARITTA M. Dec. 25, 1918-
Author
Address: c/o Random House, Inc, 20 E. 57th
St, New York City

One of the most important first novels that
appeared in 1941 was Maritta M. Wolff's
Whistle Stop, which was the 1940 winner of
the major prize in the Avery and Jule
Hopwood Awards given at the University of
Michigan. Attractive young Miss Wolff wrote
the book during her senior year there, and less
than a year after her graduation in 1940
Random House was announcing that it had
gone into its fifth printing, with 20,000 copies
already published.

Whistle Stop, which numbers Sinclair Lewis
and Franklin P. Adams (see sketch this issue)
among its more fervent admirers, is "a
fiercely honest, tough, bare-knuckled excursion
into the seamy side of American small-town
life." One critic calls the young author "a
sort of female James Farrell," another likens
her to John Steinbeck and Erskine Caldwell,
a third speaks of "the lush vitality of Thomas
Wolfe, the concentration on the unusual among
the lowly that characterized Carson McCullers'
first novel and the rich and casual bawdiness
which made Victoria Lincoln's *February Hill*
a joyous tale"; the only thing on which they
all seem to agree is that she is a realistic
writer of unusual talent. Her novel tells the
story of the Veeches, "a large, tumultuous
and poverty-stricken tribe" who live in a small
Michigan town on the outskirts of a city called
Ashbury and who have been described by
Clifton Fadiman (see sketch this issue) as
"the most unpleasant family since *Tobacco
Road*," by Edith H. Walton as "people who
suffer and struggle and blunder and are
intolerably real." According to the former,
if Miss Wolff "can write this way at 22, she
should be good for a banning in Boston before
she's 25."

This controversial new author was born on
Christmas Day 1918 at her grandparents' farm
in Michigan, when her father was still in
France with the A. E. F. She says: "I was
a very lonely child, and seldom played with
other children. I attended a one-room rural
school, after the best American tradition. It
would be nice if I could say that I walked two
miles to school every day, but if I remember
correctly, it was only a half a mile that I
walked. I apparently began to write as soon
as I grasped the essentials of penmanship,
plays, poems, short stories. . . My one hobby,
if you like to call it that, was developing, as
far back as I can remember, even under the
handicap of my somewhat isolated life in the
country, an inordinate interest in people and
anything and everything happening to them."

After attending high school in Grass Lake,
Michigan—a town with a population of some
800—Miss Wolff moved to Ann Arbor. There
she entered the university in order to study
journalism, "but somehow got sidetracked into
the English Department." After receiving two
minor Hopwood Awards for short stories
which helped pay college expenses, she wrote
Whistle Stop in her senior year. ("I simply

MARITTA M. WOLFF

wrote down all that I had picked up here and there about life and people in various small towns in Michigan.") All that she had picked up here and there turned out to be quite a lot—two or three times the present length of her novel—and, as Clifton Fadiman said, showed "she did not learn her trade in the college classroom." It was 1940 when she not only received the major Hopwood Award but a Bachelor's Degree in English composition and a Phi Beta Kappa key which she has since refused to wear.

Harry Maule of Random House was enthusiastic when he read Miss Wolff's manuscript, and *Whistle Stop* was soon scheduled for publication in the spring of 1941. Says her editor: "I hope I am not exaggerating too much when I say that there is justification for feeling the same excitement on reading her first book as there was when people read the first books of Scott Fitzgerald, Thomas Wolfe, Ernest Hemingway, etc. I don't mean to compare her to any of these. I merely mean that her first book reveals a tremendous writing talent, and that by any standards whatsoever, *Whistle Stop* is a big and an important novel."

According to its author, her interest in reading began to wane in high school, and she now reads mostly newspapers, poetry and drama rather than novels. She is, however, addicted to jazz (New Orleans style) and boogie-woogie piano playing, and, she says: "My favorite occupation of some long standing is hanging around the places where people congregate, hamburger stands, coffee joints, bars. I have never been able to get interested in much of anything else but people." The *New Yorker* critic announces that she "has no right to be so ruthless and so mature at 22."

References

Pub W 139:1205-6 Mr 15 '41 por

WOOD, ROBERT E(LKINGTON) June 13, 1879- Chairman of board, Sears, Roebuck & Company; former acting chairman, America First Committee

Address: b. Sears, Roebuck & Co, Arthington & Homan Aves, Chicago, Ill; h. 162 Laurel Ave, Highland Park, Ill.

Acting chairman of the America First Committee until its formal dissolution in December 1941, for 12 years General Robert E. Wood has also been president of Sears, Roebuck & Company and since 1939 chairman of its board.

Robert Elkington Wood was born in Kansas City, Missouri on June 13, 1879, the son of Robert Whitney and Lillie (Collins) Wood. His father had been with John Brown's raiders, had been a captain in the Union Army, a Kansas homesteader, a Colorado gold prospector, a coal and ice merchant. Young Wood went to West Point as much because he could get a free education there as because the military life appealed to him. He was graduated in 1900, thirteenth in a class of 54 and probably the only cadet with the distinction of having saved money on his government pay of $45 monthly. That same year he was posted to the Philippines (it was at the time of the Philippine Insurrection), and in two years there he was promoted from second to first lieutenant in the 3rd cavalry. For a brief period in 1902 he was posted in Montana; for two years he taught French and Spanish at West Point; and the year 1905 found him in Panama.

He was to spend 10 years there. Promoted from assistant chief quartermaster to chief quartermaster and director of the Panama Railroad Company, during the construction of the Panama Canal he hired thousands of employees, ordered and distributed millions of dollars worth of supplies a year. (" 'You're fired,' are the only words many a man ever remembers his saying.") Before the United States entered the First World War, however, Wood retired from the Army. He spent two years, from 1915 to 1917, with Du Pont and as assistant to the president of General Asphalt Company, but in 1918 donned his uniform once more. A colonel and a brigadier general, he acted as quartermaster general for the entire United States until 1919, buying and distributing food, clothing and matériel for 4,000,000 soldiers. Perhaps no one has ever had Army experience so helpful as General Wood's in the operation of a mail-order business.

His first mail-order house was Montgomery Ward, and until 1924 General Wood was vice-president of that company. By the time he left to become vice-president of Sears, Roebuck (*Fortune* has intimated that he was fired), Montgomery Ward was really beginning to show the other firm a contest. But not for long. Both Wood and President Kittle of Sears believed that the next great national growth would come from the South; they opened a string of Southern mail-order houses, then a retail chain in the larger cities. When Kittle died in 1928 General Wood suc-

ROBERT E. WOOD

ceeded to his position, and he began the practice of establishing several medium-sized neighborhood department stores in big cities rather than one mammoth store downtown. As a result, a citified chain store system has been added to the original Chicago mail-order house, which itself sold $200,000,000 worth of merchandise annually.

There are now around 500 Sears Roebuck department stores in nearly every state in the Union, and by themselves they gross from $350,000,000 to $375,000,000 a year. Sears sells 50,000 different things, from auto casualty insurance to mousetraps, and owns a seat on the New York Commodity Exchange. The original Chicago plant now handles 20 per cent (instead of the former 85 per cent) of the mail-order business. In 1938 Sears' gross income was close to $575,000,000, and the company has lost money only one year—in 1932. It was 1939 when, in deference to the Sears' retirement rule, General Wood moved up from president to chairman of the board, but he has remained "in the driver's seat."

In 1938, at least, the editors of *Fortune* looked upon General Wood as a man with an enlightened social philosophy. He himself once said: "I am a firm believer in the capitalistic system. Nevertheless I do not see that the charge of socialism, communism, or regimentation should be hurled at every new proposal or reform. . . A lot of businessmen won't look at the facts. . . Their reasoning is based on their dislikes. When you know the average current income and trend for tenant farmers and sharecroppers in some states, for example, you can't dismiss the problem by saying they are shiftless. Instead, you know something has to be done to protect society against such a focus of trouble, and you lose your horror of

the fellow who is willing to try to clear up the mess."

Until his disagreement on foreign policy Wood therefore remained on comparatively friendly terms with New Dealers. He voted for Roosevelt in 1932 and in 1936; he applauded AAA, SEC, Social Security, the housing program; he has been called to Washington dozens of times either to advise or to testify or to serve on committees, and early in 1939 Harry Hopkins (see sketch this issue) appointed him to a temporary post as official adviser on business relations, without title or administrative duties. But he has not been in complete agreement with the Administration's domestic program. During its first years he called for the desterilization of sterilized gold, described the modification of capital gains and undistributed profits taxes as "burning the house down to get roast pig," begged for an end to "hate talks." He had some misgivings about his 1936 vote, and by 1940 had returned to the Republican fold: at one time he himself was mentioned as a possible Republican Presidential candidate.

As for his attitude toward Sears' employees, he believes that Sears' Savings and Profit Sharing Pension Plan "helps to avoid labor unrest and strikes, and gives the employee a feeling of greater security and unity of interest with the employer." A constant-wage plan for seasonal workers and sickness and vacation allowances are other features of Sears' policy.

General Wood is a director in the Atlas Corporation, the United Fruit Company, the Illinois Central Railroad and the National Life Insurance Company; he is department chairman of the Federal Reserve Bank of Chicago; and in September 1938 he became one of the three "public" governors of the New York Stock Exchange by appointment of President Martin. He resigned his post as chairman of the Economic Policy Committee of the National Association of Manufacturers in July 1941.

The General's America First activities brought him under public fire more than once. Secretary of the Interior Ickes (see sketch this issue) once called him "apparently a fellow traveler" of the Nazis. But many interventionists spared him while attacking other prominent isolationists, and although he never showed any signs of open disagreement with Colonel Lindbergh (see sketch this issue) or others, it was frequently rumored that he planned to resign or dissolve the America First Committee if the international situation should grow so critical that disunity placed the country in actual danger. This he apparently did not consider necessary until the Japanese attack on Pearl Harbor. On December 1, 1941 he announced that America First would "go into the 1942 national elections" with support for candidates opposing the Administration's foreign policy, which was condemned as a "trend toward Fascism in America." On December 8 he was quoted: "We opposed participation in this War in good faith, but now that we are in it, we shall support it."

In April 1908 General Wood married Mary Butler Hardwick of Augusta, Georgia. He is a great believer in big families, and they have four daughters and a son. (Grandchildren get 200 shares of Sears common stock when born.) Wood is usually up at 6, full of "storming, gregarious exuberance," and in bed before 11. Clothes don't matter to him; he is sometimes so impatient that he eats caramels with their paper on; he is a "restrained doodler"; his favorite expression is "let's charge," and his company has sometimes been called the "Old Soldiers' Home" because there is more than one retired military man in it. He has a remarkable memory, even more for figures than for people, so inaccuracy makes him lose his temper more quickly than anything else. In Panama they say that he used to turn down parties in order to stay home and study census figures, and today the United States Census reports and the *Statistical Abstract* still comprise his *Book of Revelations!* His life is not entirely a matter of statistics, however. He is a good horseman and dancer, a great reader of biography and history, an enthusiastic shot and fly-fisherman.

References

Business Week p17 Mr 11 '39 por; p17 O 8 '38 por; p13 D 17 '38 por
Fortune 17:66-9+ My '38 il pors
Time 31:56 Ja 17 '38 por; 32:56 O 10 '38 por; 38:18-20 O 6 '41 por
Who's Who in America
Who's Who in Commerce and Industry

WOOLF, VIRGINIA (1883(?)—Mar. (?), 1941 British author who wrote her first novel, *The Voyage Out,* in 1915 and continued to write until her death, by suicide, at her home in Lewes, Sussex, England; critics call her novel, *The Years* (1937), her masterpiece; together with writing, her great interest was fine printing; with her husband she founded the Hogarth Press, a commercial venture where they brought out meritorious works by young authors; critics have placed Mrs. Woolf in the rank of pioneer as a novelist; Hugh Walpole wrote that she and Rebecca West divide the feminine crown of modern English letters between them.

References

19th Cent 115:112-25 Ja '34
Sat R Lit 15:3-4+ F 6 '37 por
Sewanee R 47:235-41 Ap '39
Time 29:93-6 Ap 12 '37 por (cover)
Va Q R 10:587-602 O '34
Wilson Lib Bul 3:516 Mr '29
Brewster, D. and Burrell, A. Adventure or Experience p77-116 1930
Holtby, W. Virginia Woolf 1932
Johnson, R. B. Some Contemporary Novelists: Women p147-60 1920
Kunitz, S. J. ed. Living Authors 1937
Lawrence, M. School of Femininity p339-82 1936

Verschoyle, D. ed. English Novelists p281-97 1936
Who's Who

Obituaries

N Y Herald Tribune p1, 23 Ap 3 '41 por
Pub W 139:1559 Ap 12 '41
Sat R Lit 23:12 Ap 12 '41

WOOLLCOTT, ALEXANDER (wŏŏl'-kŭt) Jan. 19, 1887- Lecturer; critic; actor
Address: h. Bomoseen, Vt.

The hero of Kaufman and Hart's play, *The Man Who Came to Dinner,* is "an unexpurgated version of Alexander Woollcott." "Taking their good friend and boon companion by the seat of his ample pants, the authors have landed him in a wheel chair in the wilds of a Middle Western town disguised as Sheridan Whiteside, radio speaker, writer and friend of the great." As though this weren't enough, for a long while Woollcott impersonated himself in the road companies of the play, taking a disarming pleasure in acting as crusty, crotchety, selfish and mischief-making as he really is. "It's all Woollcott and a yard wide," the critics agreed.

There are some of his "800 intimate friends," of course, who deny this. They've become used to having him address them as "Hello, repulsive," used to having him tactfully say good-by in choice phrases like "I find you are beginning to disgust me. How about getting the hell out of here?" And they insist that though he likes to give the impression of being a nail-eater, actually he has "a heart modeled after Louisa M. Alcott and Florence Nightingale."

This radio star, playwright, critic, author, actor, lecturer and anthologist, who has a general resemblance to an owl and an anatomy like St. Nicholas, was born in Phalanx, New Jersey, where his grandfather had helped found a socialistic community. It was no longer this by the time Alexander entered it and all that was left was the 85-room building where his mother, Frances Grey (Bucklin) Woollcott, gave birth to him on January 19, 1887. His father, Walter Woollcott, was an Englishman and a good deal of a rolling stone—lawyer, accountant, government clerk, stock exchange operator.

In 1899 he moved his family to Kansas City, Missouri and stayed there long enough to enroll his son in school and let him start his education. Alexander's teacher there, when interviewed much later, remembered him as a frail, delicate lad and a constant reader. "He thirsted for knowledge," she recalls, "and I realized even then that he would go far." In 1895 he went back to Phalanx with his three brothers and sister to continue his schooling and from there went on to Central High School in Philadelphia. He spent his high school days living alone (his father had wandered off again), supporting himself by doing book reviewing and odd jobs for the *Evening Telegraph* and *Record.*

Richard Carver Wood

ALEXANDER WOOLLCOTT

From Philadelphia, Alexander set out for Hamilton College at Clinton, New York and, once there, proceeded to put his finger into every campus pie—except athletics, of course. He distinguished himself as editor of the college magazine; founder, director and actor of the drama club; winner of a Phi Beta Kappa key in his junior year; and wearer of corduroy trousers and a turtle-neck sweater topped off by a red fez. When he was graduated in 1909 there were many sighs of regret. The Woollcott legend was already taking form.

But Woollcott himself entered the Chemical National Bank in New York as a $15-a-week clerk. Fortunately he got a job on the New York *Times* not too long afterward, through the auspices of Samuel Hopkins Adams, a trustee of Hamilton College. Woollcott, according to Wolcott Gibbs, wasn't much of a reporter, "not exactly hostile to facts, but apathetic about them," and definitely disinclined to chase around. After he had been beaten on numberless scoops and worn himself out to the point of a nervous breakdown, the *Times* in 1914 made him its dramatic critic. It wasn't much of a job—the *Times* was somewhat haughty on the subject of the drama—but Woollcott knew he had come into his own.

For three years Woollcott held forth on the *Times.* Already he "gushed one day like a Southern belle, the next flogged like Simon Legree." And he wrote the first of his books, *Mrs. Fiske—Her Views on Actors, Acting and the Problems of Production* (1917), a book which "fairly barks with the joyous shouts of a fox terrier hearing his master's voice on the victrola." All this was interrupted by the First World War, which saw Woollcott

in 1917 as a private serving at Base Hospital No. 9 with the Medical Corps. From here he was transferred to Paris as a reporter for the A. E. F. magazine, *The Stars and Stripes,* and given a roving commission. He visited the front lines and came through action "unperforated," to write about men in the trenches "with the same romantic intensity he had once reserved for Mrs. Fiske." Although no one who knew Alexander Woollcott ever believed he really was a soldier even when he appeared in uniform, he left the Army a sergeant.

Woollcott went back to the *Times* and proceeded to indulge wild enthusiasms and deepest hates—a strolling player of not much importance, he once said, was so matchless a genius that "some of us would crawl on our hands and knees" to see him perform. George Jean Nathan remembered this and other extravagances when in 1921 he wrote an article about Woollcott called *The Seidlitz Powder of Times Square.* On the good side, it has been said, his *Times* pieces gave "an excitement, a quality of having been there and seen it yourself which you couldn't get from anyone else."

This same sort of drama criticism persisted when Woollcott went over to the New York *Herald* in 1922 and from there in 1925 to New York *World,* where he stayed until 1928. Never was he a sober critic searching for the eternal verities of his profession, but a partisan reviewer writing in a style that "combined treacle and pure black bile." Wolcott Gibbs sums up the general impression of Woollcott as a drama reviewer in the *New Yorker.* He had, he says, "enthusiasm, an honest love for the theatre and a gift for the neat and deadly phrase. On the other hand, he was sentimental, partisan and maddeningly positive about everything. . . His style, which could be lucid and witty, could also be muddled and frantic." And these characteristics were even more apparent in his books: in *The Command Is Forward* (1919); *Shouts and Murmurs* (1922); *Enchanted Aisles* (1924); *The Story of Irving Berlin* (1925); *Going to Pieces* (1928); and *Two Gentlemen and a Lady* (1928).

Woollcott's drama columns and his books often showed their author "hot on the scene of personalities and people; gossip, tidbits he can relish, news fictionalized into importance and narrated with a skill which is as uncommon as its zest." Many of them revealed his own expansive social life. It was and continued to be one "that might have seemed exhausting to Catherine of Russia." From the 1920's on, Woollcott emerged as a metropolitan character and an early member of that group which took charge of humor in America. The Thanatopsis Literary and Inside Straight Club, made up of George Kaufman, F. P. Adams (see sketches this issue), the late Heywood Broun, Dorothy Parker, Robert Sherwood, the Marx Brothers and other lights, was its name; the Algonquin Hotel its meeting place; and Woollcott its "spiritual focus." He used to entertain its members and other important people all day long on Sundays, "dressed in rumpled pajamas and an ancient, rather horrible dressing gown," receiving them in his apartment "from a throne in one corner with an air that would have done credit to Queen Victoria." When success started to break up the group, Woollcott managed to keep them together by taking over with others a wooded retreat at Lake Bomoseen, Vermont, at first a cooperative venture, now half-owned and "almost wholly buffaloed by Mr. Woollcott." There Woollcott spends his summers, playing croquet, exchanging quips with people like Marc Connelly, Neysa McMein (see sketch this issue), Dorothy Parker, Harpo Marx, and mostly just talking.

Woollcott resigned from the *World* in 1928 because he was worn out writing theatre criticism and because he was not so thin as he had been—"the after-the-theatre congestion in Times Square was driving him crazy." He began to write intensively for the magazines: on the theatre, on the books he liked and hated, on the restaurants at which he ate, on murder and gruesome Americana. His style was "a heavenly compound of Dickens and Chesterton with perhaps a little earthly leaven of Booth Tarkington and even hellish prophecies here and there of Lucius Beebe."

But the stock market crash upset this pleasant way of earning a living. Woollcott lost heavily, and what with obligations to his family, to his New York apartment and to his place at Bomoseen, money became important. He wrote advertising copy, lectured, wrote, and went on the air. His first radio appearance was in October 1929 in a 15-minute sustaining program called *The Town Crier*; later he took over a sustaining program in which he reviewed books as *The Early Bookworm*. He left radio in March 1931, returned again in September 1933, and was off and on again until 1939, when a 39-week contract seemed too much to commit himself to. "I had other things in mind," he said. As the Town Crier he charmed listeners with anecdotes and plugged the books he liked. "The most influential salesman of books in the United States," those were the days when he "loomed larger on the American cultural scene than Dr. Eliot's five-foot shelf." He had only to mention he had gone "quietly mad" over a book to have the stores and libraries deluged with requests for it. Among those he plugged especially hard were Hilton's *Good-bye, Mr. Chips* and Woollcott's *While Rome Burns* (1934).

This book of his was a collection of his writings, many of them from his "Shouts and Murmurs" column in the *New Yorker*, full of odd, unexpected facts, full of the japes and witticisms of his friends. It sold 290,000 copies. It was followed in 1935 by the *Woollcott Reader* and in 1937 by *Woollcott's Second Reader*, best-selling collections of the writings Woollcott liked best. Only the critics were captious. One pointed out that the *Readers* reveal "Woollcott's chief reasons for reading: a good laugh or a good cry," and Louis Kronenberger called them "second-rate taste at its most formidable and deceptive, tricked out in its Sunday best, beckoning and easy to take." He objected, especially, to Woollcott's critical dicta, to phrases as overwhelming as "the most moving and uplifting tale ever told in the English language," or "as simple and modest and perfect as a Vermeer." To others these judgments were merely characteristic of Woollcott's greatest glory—his refusal to hedge, a refusal he once expressed in what John Mason Brown feels will be his rightful epitaph. "Whenever wishing to say that *Ethan Frome* was the best short story ever written by an American or that *The Greek Commonwealth* was the best historical work ever written anywhere, he never sneaked in a 'probably' or a 'perhaps' under the delusion that in some way it would give him a judicious air or a suggestion of profundity." And there was public recognition of the success of this technique when Archibald MacLeish, Librarian of Congress, appointed Woollcott special counselor to the library to recommend titles for the fiction shelves outside the door of the President's study.

During the days of radio and editing Woollcott hadn't forsaken the stage. His first play, *The Channel Road*, based on De Maupassant and written in collaboration with George S. Kaufman, had been staged in 1929. The critics gleefully fell upon it and tore it to shreds—the kindest thing they said was that it had "fine writing, the sort of fine writing that turns into lead in the theatre." This ran about four weeks, and that was about the length of the run of his second play, *The Dark Tower* (1933), also written with Kaufman. Woollcott likewise graced the stage in these years as an actor. In November 1931 he appeared in S. M. Behrman's *Brief Moment*, and spent his evenings lolling around on a sofa and insulting people. Everybody loved it, and they loved it when he did much the same sort of thing again in Behrman's *Wine of Choice* in 1938. They still loved it when he did it again in *The Man Who Came to Dinner*, a role which he quit in the fall of 1941 to go to England, "crossing the perilous seas at the age of 55, carrying a box of chocolates for Lady Astor." Once there, he returned to the air for CBS, broadcasting to America "tales of humble guts," tales of human interest "with the familiar Woollcott graces, the cheerfully dry eye, the careful throb." He came back to the United States in November, after talking to most of England, with plans for a book and a quotation from himself that had charmed the British: "There'll always be an England, now that Averell's here."

Each stage appearance meant that Woollcott's very elaborate schedule of living became even more complicated. Usually he lays out his engagements at least a month in advance, and when he is in New York his calendar "is as precisely calculated as a dentist's." His hundreds of friends drop in whenever he sends for them, to be treated to splendid luncheons (Woollcott himself had to leave the Coast

WOOLLCOTT, ALEXANDER—*Cont.*

company of *The Man Who Came to Dinner* after a meal of snails, rice balls, bisque of clam, baby squid with sauce à la Genoise, saddle of lamb, fondue of truffles, cress salad) and splendid talk and/or' invective. A bachelor who never even came close to getting married, he is a terrific matchmaker who does his best to inveigle his friends into matrimony. When he is not receiving, as often as not he is indulging in his voluminous correspondence, writing letters like that he sent to the headmistress of a school who had received his name as a recommendation for a prospective pupil: "I implore you to accept this unfortunate child and remove her from her shocking environment." And wherever he is, this littérateur—who, with his beaked nose, tight mouth, negligible mustache and thick glasses all closely grouped together, reminds Wolcott Gibbs of Tarkington's description of someone else: "Her face is sort of small but the other parts of her head terribly wide"—always makes himself completely at home. In March 1941, when *The Man Who Came to Dinner* was being performed in Washington, Woollcott stayed at the White House and nearly took over the place. When Mrs. Roosevelt returned there after a trip, he greeted her affably enough, however. "Come right in, Mrs. Roosevelt," he said.

References

Cosmopolitan 102:8+ Ja '37 por
Life 7:86-7 O 30 '39 il pors
Liv Age 348:186-7 Ap '35
N Y Herald Tribune VII p4 Ap 7 '35 por
New Yorker 15:24-9 Mr 18 '39; 15:24-9 Mr 25 '39; 15:22-7 Ap 1 '39
Newsweek 4:25-6 O 13 '34 por
Stage 12:18-19 Ja '35 por
Time 25:48 Ja 28 '35 por; 31:52-3 Mr 7 '38 por

Brown, J. M. Upstage p225-32 1930
Who's Who in America
Who's Who in the Theatre

WRIGHT, BERLIN H(ART) 1851—Nov. 26, 1940 Astronomer, surveyor and geologist who furnished weather and stellar information to almanacs.

Obituaries

N Y Times p23 N 28 '40

WRIGHT, FRANK LLOYD June 8, 1869- Architect

Address: h. "Taliesin," Spring Green, Wis.

Frank Lloyd Wright is "regarded by many as the greatest architect of the twentieth century and is conceded even by skeptics to have one of the most restless and imaginative minds the art of architecture has ever known." Countries as remote as Holland and Japan count him a major force in the development of their contemporary styles; 31 states in this country contain his work; and there is no state which

doesn't have buildings dominated by his influence. At 71 Frank Lloyd Wright is a living "old master."

From November 13, 1940 to January 5, 1941 the Museum of Modern Art in New York presented *Frank Lloyd Wright, American Architect,* a comprehensive exhibition of his work which, according to *Time,* "recorded as exciting a body of architectural thinking as has come from the brain of anyone since Michelangelo." In the exhibition, the first in this country to attempt to show the entire range of his career, were shown 18 models of skyscrapers, factory buildings, houses; of a farm, a bridge, a filling station, all made with the utmost attention to detail. Drawings and architectural plans, large black and white photographs and color transparencies, together with the models, demonstrated the remarkable diversity of Wright's work.

There were shown "Fallingwater," the house built over a waterfall at Bear Run, Pennsylvania; the great hotel Wright built in Tokyo in 1916; a permanent desert camp built of stone, wood and canvas; concrete block houses in California; the Johnson Wax factory at Racine, Wisconsin; and his model of "Broadacres," Wright's answer to the problem of living in a machine and city age, based on his belief that "concentration of population is murder—whether in peace time or war." From all of these emerge the basic ideas of his architecture—modern, functional, often startling, designed to fit into its surroundings and answer the purpose for which it is built. For Frank Lloyd Wright any materials are right: "Stick, stone, steel. Pottery, concrete, glass. Yes, pulp, too, as well as pigment." Any design is right if it fills its purpose. "Consistency? It is seldom the word for the imaginative mind in action."

Frank Lloyd Wright is the grandson of a Welsh hatter and preacher who settled in Spring Valley, Wisconsin and raised a big family of farmers, preachers and schoolteachers. His father, William Russell Cary Wright, was a New England preacher who studied medicine, preached in a Baptist Church in Connecticut and a Unitarian one in the Midwest, taught music, read Sanscrit and finally walked out on his family. His mother, Anna Lloyd (Jones) Wright, brought him up, encouraged him in his work and taught him that "simplicity of heart is just as necessary for an architect as for a farmer or a minister, if the architect is going to build great buildings."

After a youth spent in Richland Center, Wisconsin, where he was born on June 8, 1869 and in Madison, where his uncle had a farm, Frank Lloyd Wright entered the University of Wisconsin in 1884. He wanted to study architecture, but there was no school of architecture. The nearest thing to it the University had was engineering, and for three years, three years of work and poverty, he kept at engineering. In 1887 he gave it up and set out for Chicago with $7 in his pocket.

In Chicago he got himself a job as a draftsman in an architect's office for $8 a week. One year later he was working for

Adler and Sullivan, one of the largest architectural firms in Chicago and the best place in the world to learn architecture as a modern practical progression. Louis Sullivan hated sham; he hated the falsity of the architecture then popular; and in his office Wright learned much. Since Sullivan was interested mainly in building skyscrapers he gave Wright most of the domestic work which came to the firm, and Wright built many houses. By this time he was married to Catherine Lee. His family was growing and, never very provident, his debts began to mount up. On the side he started to execute a few small commissions for houses. When Sullivan discovered this he broke their contract and Wright was on his own. In 1894 he opened his office.

Immediately Wright began to develop a new kind of residence instead of the gloomy ill-proportioned and badly planned Victorian house then in vogue. His compositions, known as "Prairie houses," were low and extended, without attics, with their roofs low-pitched and gardens and terraces made part of the composition. The first dwellings to "break the hold on American builders' minds of centuries of pastward routine," they weren't liked at first—conservatives shuddered at them—but it wasn't long before the attractiveness of their spaciousness was recognized. In 20 years after he left Sullivan, Wright designed and built in the Midwest nearly 100 houses "for which no precedent existed anywhere."

In 1905 Wright designed the first office building in the United States (in Buffalo, New York) to use metal-bound, plate glass doors and windows, all metal furniture, air conditioning, magnesite as an architectural material. The next year he went on a trip to Japan and on his return asked his wife for a divorce. She refused to grant it (there were six children), and Wright left her to go to Tuscany to live.

In 1911 Wright was back in the United States, his first job the building of "Taliesin" ("shining brow" in Welsh), a large farm home in Spring Green, Wisconsin. Two years later this was burned to the ground, but Wright had rebuilt it by 1915. Shortly after, he left for Japan with a commission to build the Imperial Hotel in Tokyo, a difficult engineering problem, for the building had to be made to withstand earthquakes. Wright built a flexible building with structurally independent parts on a cushion of soft mud, and when the great earthquake of 1923 demolished most of the city the Imperial Hotel was still standing.

Back in America, Miriam Noel, the second Mrs. Wright, left him, and in 1928 he was married again to Olga Lazovich of Montenegro after a bitter period of law suits, publicity and poverty and, after "Taliesin" had burned down again and been rebuilt. When the hue and cry died down Wright began to do more and more teaching, writing and lecturing and less building, for although the Paris Exposition of 1925 had given his work a great world impetus, he was not yet fashionable throughout this country. In 1930 he was still ignored by conventional architects, not invited to take part in

FRANK LLOYD WRIGHT

the Chicago World's Fair, though he had clients.

In 1931, however, with the publication of a series of lectures he had delivered at Princeton, entitled *Modern Architecture,* Wright's influence began to be more widely felt, until in 1938 an entire issue of the *Architectural Forum* was devoted to his work and in 1941 King George of England awarded him the Royal Gold Medal for Architecture. Meanwhile he had set up "Taliesin" as a workshop, farm and studio for apprentices, where some 50 disciples now work in the fields, do construction work and engage in musical and theatrical activities in buildings that seem to grow naturally and inevitably out of their surroundings.

In his autobiography published in 1932 Frank Lloyd Wright told of his years of work and living—in it he "combined magnificent self-revelation with the most stimulating discussion of architecture ever heard in the United States." From it one learns that Wright is not only responsible for engineering feats such as new concrete blocks, mushroom pillars, cantilevers, new lighting facilities, but that he believes that the spirit behind what is built is what matters. To him architecture is "the Idea of the thing—made to sing to heaven." In him is the belief that "man takes a positive hand in creation whenever he puts a building upon the earth beneath the sun."

At 71 Wright is still in the vanguard. At 71 he continues to make significant designs, secure in his knowledge that though his work has been called "crack-brained, impractical, expensive," no building of his has ever cracked or buckled through faulty engineering. His latest designs, like his earliest, have caused consternation. In 1940 he produced a revolutionary plan for what he called the "first completely functional church," in Kansas City, air conditioned, with pillars of light

WRIGHT, FRANK LLOYD—*Continued*

instead of a tower, and a triple-decker parking space as an integral part—"it is immoral and unethical to build a structure without providing for the traffic it will attract," he convinced the church board. He is also working on a commission for a 25-towered copper and crystal streamlined apartment development in Washington which will cost about $15,000,000 and fill 10 acres with apartment houses, a hotel, a garage and a motion picture theatre.

Frank Lloyd Wright is a small, white-haired, dapper man, immaculate in appearance. Today, as always, he is vocally and unbashfully proud of his work, proud of his books—*Modern Architecture,* (1930); *Disappearing City,* (1932); *Organic Architecture,* (1940); *Frank Lloyd Wright on Architecture* (1941). Yet when one sees his buildings or the Museum of Modern Art show, it doesn't sound like boasting to hear him say, "I have been told that I am the only American who has contributed to the culture of Europe," or to hear him describe the Imperial Hotel in the Tokyo earthquake "somewhat as an angler might describe a very large fish."

References

Arch Forum 68:sup 1-102 Ja '38 il pors
Design 37:2-5+ D '35
New Repub 87:94-5 Je 3 '36
New Yorker 6:22-5 Jl 19 '30
No Am 246 no 1:48-64 [S] '38
Pencil Points 19:137-44 Mr '38 il
Scholastic 32:21E+ F 12 '38 por
Time 31:29-32 Ja 17 '38 il por (cover) (Discussion 31:2+ Ja 31 '38); 36:58 N 23 '40; 36:38-40 D 2 '40 il

Cahill, H. and Barr, A. H. eds. Art in America in Modern Times p70-2 1934
Craven, T. Modern Art p273-89 1934
Mumford, L. Brown Decades p107-81 1931
Stearns, H. E. ed. Amèrica Now p104-6 1938
Who's Who in America
Wijdeveld, H. T. ed. Life-Work of the American Architect, Frank Lloyd Wright 1925
Wright, F. L. Autobiography 1932

WRIGHT, HUNTLEY Aug. 7, 1869—July 10, 1941

Veteran British musical comedy actor who was on the stage for 48 years and made appearances in the United States; long career included radio broadcasting and motion pictures.

References

Illustrated London News 135:396 S 18 '09 por
Theatre 7:281 O '07 por
Who's Who
Who's Who in the Theatre

Obituaries

N Y Times p13 Jl 12 '41
Variety 143:54 Jl 16 '41

WYATT, JOHN WHITLOW (wī'ăt) Sept. 27, 1908- Major-league baseball pitcher

Address: 615 Gibson St, Cedartown, Ga.

European war and national politics took a back seat in the borough of Brooklyn in September 1941. For the first time in some 20 years the Brooklyn Dodgers, after a season-long nip-and-tuck with the St. Louis Cardinals, finally came home with a National League pennant. Brooklyn went berserk, the clamor lasting for days; newspapers rhapsodized and educators solemnly talked of a Brooklyn cultural renaissance.

Next month the bottom dropped out of the borough's brief delirium when "Dem Bums," to use the affectionate Brooklynese, lost the World Series to the New York Yankees. Solace to their defeat, however, was the fact that the Dodgers had been the only team to snatch a World Series game from the well-nigh invincible Yankees since 1927. The man who deserves much of the credit for this lone victory is tall, rangy, partially-bald John Whitlow Wyatt, whom most Brooklynites call "Whit."

"A Southern soldier of misfortune," Wyatt, who throws and bats righthanded, served a fantastically checkered apprenticeship in baseball, shuttling back and forth between the big leagues and the minor leagues for 14 years, stalked by a series of accidents disheartening enough to destroy a dozen careers. Not until he suddenly began to register marked pitching control did he stabilize his position in the big leagues. This was when he had reached his 30's, an age when most players have retired or have passed their peak.

The son of an engineer, Wyatt was born on September 27, 1908 at Kensington, Georgia, near the Civil War battlefield of Chickamauga Creek. His family tree boasts of many who fought the Yankees, namesakes of Wyatt's non-military adversaries. He was no baseball wizard in his youth, yet his style caught the eye of a Detroit American League scout named Ed Goosetree, who had come to look over one of Whit's classmates at the Cedartown High School. Basketball and football were Wyatt's games and his prowess earned him a grid scholarship to the Georgia School of Technology. Fearing the loss of baseball material, Goosetree offered Wyatt a contract whereby the Detroit team would pay for his tuition, provided he refrained from playing football. Whit accepted, but in two months he left college to devote himself to baseball.

In the summer of 1927 Wyatt pitched for a hosiery mill team in Tennessee and the next year Detroit assigned him to Evansville in the Three-I League, where he won 14 games and lost 12 during his first season. During his second he won 22 and lost six, giving up a total of only 86 earned runs in 255 innings. Convinced he was ready for his big-time debut, the Detroit manager placed him on the pitching staff in 1929. In his new berth Wyatt was surprisingly unimpressive. After serving through 1930 and part of 1931, he was demoted to Beaumont in the Texas League.

Back in the minors, Wyatt reverted to type by promptly winning 11 games and dropping three and gaining a run average of only 1.53 a game. He was reclaimed by the Tigers in the following year and exchanged in May 1933 for Vic Frasier, a pitcher, of the Chicago White Sox.

On June 13, 1933 Wyatt was robbed of baseball immortality in the last moments of a game against the St. Louis Browns. Ted Gullic singled in the ninth inning, simultaneously breaking his bat and Wyatt's no-hit record for the game. This happened again in 1941 when Phil Masi of the Boston Braves also singled in the ninth inning to deprive Wyatt of a hitless record.

Wyatt's occupational mishaps are legion; one of the most serious occurred while he was with Chicago. He was forced to undergo an operation in which 14 bone chips were removed from his elbow. Although he remained with the club for two seasons, his efficiency was far below par and eventually he was sent to Kansas City. Here Whit caught his stride again, winning twelve games and sustaining seven defeats and, incidentally, attracting the attention of the Cleveland Indians' scout. His tenure with Cleveland, following the usual pattern, was brief. Some say wildness accounted for this; others, that Cleveland was anxious to take back Ken Keltner, an ex-Indian who was now serving with Milwaukee.

Another factor accounting for the trade was a spell of typical Wyatt hard luck. Hailed from the bull pen in the eighth inning of a tied game with the Yankees, Wyatt was required to smother a sudden rally which had filled two bases. While Wyatt was in the midst of a windup, Ben Chapman of the Yankees stole home from third, scoring the decisive run. Infuriated, Manager Steve O'Neill was doubly receptive to a deal exiling Wyatt to the minors.

Unaccountably, Harry Bendinger, the Milwaukee manager, had an idea that Wyatt, notwithstanding his ups and downs, would yet yield "pay dirt." Wyatt himself didn't think so and in 1928 he was so thoroughly discouraged that he had already written a figurative "finis" on his baseball career and had retired to his 700-acre cotton plantation near Buchanan, Georgia. Earlier, his pitching arm had suddenly gone numb while he was on the mound facing Babe Ruth, and the ball had slithered off to an impotent angle. Bendinger's long-distance call, however, brought an offer of a contract whereby Whit would get 15 per cent of his purchase price if a major-league team bought him at the end of the year.

"I've already been turned down by two major leagues," snorted the embittered Whit. "Who'd buy me? I'm through. I'll sign, but I want a straight contract." This reply eventually cost Whit $5,500, for it turned out he had underestimated himself. Every time Wyatt hit the minor leagues he seemed to bounce back with renewed confidence, and his season with Milwaukee was no exception; he won twenty-three games, lost seven, led the

JOHN WHITLOW WYATT

American Association for strike-outs and hurled 10 shutouts. This qualified him as the outstanding pitcher in the minor leagues. As a result his fame spread to Larry MacPhail, shrewd president of the Brooklyn Dodgers. MacPhail, no gambler, watched Wyatt in action, then decided to buy him.

This was one of MacPhail's few flyers, for Wyatt was still a highly uncertain commodity. He reportedly paid something like $30,000. The investment brought gratifying dividends. Wyatt's comeback was assured but his troubles were far from over. In his first year as a Dodger he collided with Lonnie Frey of Cincinnati and suffered a shattered knee cap. An operation was followed by a 42-day hospital sojourn during which his leg was bundled in a cast.

Returning to the mound, Wyatt hobbled through the following season, still bothered by the pain. Meanwhile he developed one of his most valuable assets, a "slider" ball that is virtually unbuntable. He won 15 games and lost 14. In 1941 he garnered 22 and dropped 11. He is a cagey and persevering moundsman whose armory contains a baffling slow ball, a speed curve and a cool head in a crisis. During a game he seems to get better as he goes along, apparently withholding great reserves of power until the final innings.

Wyatt winters on his Georgia farm. Here he first met Edna Elizabeth White, whom he married on February 4, 1933. There are two young children, Barbara Jane and Whitlow, Jr. For exercise Whit likes to work on the farm, go hunting and fishing and play golf. He is one of the most likable players in any ball club, popular alike with players and fans.

References

Spink, J. G. T. comp. Baseball Register 1941

Who's Who in Major League Baseball Who's Who in the Major Leagues

YARROW, WILLIAM (yăr'ō) Sept. 24, 1891—Apr. 21, 1941 American mural painter; for Princeton University he painted the largest mural series ever commissioned for an American college; his paintings are found in many museums; received the silver medal in 1915 at the Panama Pacific Exposition and the gold medal of the Art Club of Philadelphia; vice-president of the British-American Ambulance Corps which he helped found in 1940; originated the idea of "Thumbs Up Cavalcade," a group of five ambulances which toured the country on a fund-raising drive; organization had raised almost $2,000,000 for Britain by April 1941.

References

Who's Who in American Art

Obituaries

N Y Times p21 Ap 22 '41 por

YOUNG, ROSE (EMMET) 1869—July 6, 1941 Author; editor; leader in the movement for woman suffrage; inaugurated feature articles which were designed to show that women were adaptable for work other than in the home; wrote many novels and magazine articles.

References

Who's Who Among North American Authors 1933-35
Who's Who in America

Obituaries

N Y Times p19 Jl 8 '41 por
Woman's J ns 14:12-13 Je '29

ZANUCK, DARRYL F(RANCIS) (zăn'-ŭk) Sept. 5, 1902- Motion picture producer
Address: b. 20th Century-Fox Film Corp, Beverly Hills, Calif; h. 546 Ocean Front, Santa Monica, Calif.

Hollywood is divided into two camps on the subject of Darryl Zanuck: "those who think he is a genius and those who think he is a menace." The year 1941 gave both sides a chance to revise or confirm their convictions, for that was the year in which new policies were inaugurated at 20th Century-Fox, of which Zanuck is vice-president in charge of production.

In January 1941 the company finished its most disastrous year since it was started, with a net loss of more than one-half million dollars. Part of this was due to the loss of European markets; part to flops like *Brigham Young, The Blue Bird, Little Old New York*. And this last, some whispered, could be traced to Zanuck's strongly centralized hold over 20th Century-Fox. True or not, after April 1941 drastic moves toward decentralization were made: there were to be three new producers who would pick and cast their own stories; Zanuck himself, whose contract has been renewed until 1943, was to concentrate on only eight out of twenty-four pictures that year.

This may have meant a change in opinion about Zanuck's genius. It certainly meant a change from the "kind of combination army post and metropolitan newspaper office" that Zanuck has perfected at 20th Century-Fox. Up to this time he has been producing 25 class-A pictures a year, and as much as 90 per cent of each picture as it appears on the screen is usually Zanuck's own work. When he produces a film, he works on the story, holding as many as two conferences a day, in them ad libbing dialogue, acting out parts, directing scenes, producing whole sequences at top speed; then he okays the casting, supervises the costuming and scenery, looks over the daily rushes, cuts the finished film foot by foot—does everything but act in it himself. People under him are consulted (he is the producer who once told an executive, "For God's sake don't say yes until I finish talking"), and they are given details to carry out. But the initiative and responsibility for the entire output of 20th Century-Fox have, until now, been Zanuck's.

This producer, who has been a "wonder boy" for so many years, started his career in the motion pictures much younger than most. He was born in Wahoo, Nebraska, where his father, Frank Zanuck, owned and operated the Grand Hotel. At eight he was taken by his mother, Louise (Torpin) Zanuck, to Los Angeles and placed in the Page Military Academy while she tried to regain her health. He did go to school occasionally; much of the time he was playing hooky to work as an extra on the old Essanay lot in Glendale. When his mother discovered his film career she determinedly cut it short by shipping him back to Nebraska and warning him to study faithfully.

He heeded her warning only until he reached the eighth grade, and fellow workers now nod understandingly when they hear him saying things like "more time for betterment and correctment" or uttering Goldwynisms without the accent. At the age of 14, prompted by "a love of firearms and itch to travel," he enlisted in the Sixth Nebraska Infantry and went down to the Mexican border. From Mexico he went to France, where he served with the 163rd Division of the A. E. F., acted as runner, saw front-line service for nearly a year and boxed in the bantam class. He was mustered out in 1920, still a private. He had, however, already determined on his career. Some letters to his grandfather in Nebraska about life in the A. E. F. had been printed in the local papers and some of them had even been reprinted in the *Stars and Stripes*. Zanuck knew he was going to be a writer.

He began to write furiously—two stories a week. And after a year of this, success came when he sold *Mad Desire* to *Physical Culture* Magazine. He immediately set out for Hollywood, "a slender youth with buck teeth, a hope-chest mustache and a Nebraska accent," sent in a card to William Russell, then acting for Fox Films, and sold him an original story. When he learned that the man who adapted his story got almost three times as much money as he had, he became an adapter and filled in his next opus with technical terms like close-up and fade-in. For the next couple of years he did a brisk business in both originals and adaptations.

Then, in 1923, the tide receded. The studios decided that big names were necessary, proceeded to corner all the important authors they could line up and let the unimportant ones go. Zanuck found himself catching rivets in a San Pedro shipyard, organizing the Darryl Poster Service and selling hair tonic. It was this last occupation that got him back into the motion picture business, for he persuaded the manufacturer to pay for the printing of his book, *Habit and Other Short Stories* (1923). It contained one short story, two rejected scenarios and a one hundred-page hair tonic testimonial, more or less disguised. It was an impressive work in which "Zanuck's characters never looked at things when they might as well rivet jet orbs on them. They never walked through doors when they might as well stride through portals."

And Zanuck sold it, piece by piece, to the film studios: the story, the two rejected scenarios and the hair tonic ad. He got $11,000 for the lot. He also got himself a job. A steady income was useful now that he was married to Virginia Fox, whom he had met on a blind date. She gave up her career as leading lady for Buster Keaton to settle down, raise a family of three children and act as guinea pig for her husband's work. "She has the attitude of a typical movie fan from Omaha," Zanuck says proudly.

For a while Zanuck was scenario editor to Mack Sennett until he was hired by the Fox Film Corporation. After a year in which he wrote almost one picture a week, he was taken over in 1924 by Warners at $150 a week to do scripts for *Rin Tin Tin*. He soon established himself as "the greatest dog-script writer in history." At the same time he was learning how to cut, direct and produce pictures, so thoroughly that by 1927 he had been given his own production unit with a share of the profits. That was the year in which he made the *Jazz Singer* with Al Jolson, the first full-length talkie, and *Noah's Ark*, the first and biggest catastrophe of his career. By 1929 he was Warner's general production chief; by 1931 chief executive in charge of all the productions of the combined Warner and First National Companies.

He had already made a reputation for plucking sensational drama out of the day's news. First there was gang warfare pure and simple—*Doorway to Hell, Little Caesar* and others. Then, when the trend he started was beginning to fade out, there came gang warfare enlivened and heightened by the magnificent stroke of having a man sock a woman—*Public Enemy*. "Every other underworld picture has had a thug with a little bit of good in him," Zanuck explained. "He reforms before the fade-out. This guy is no good at all. It'll go big." It did. So did his *I Am a Fugitive from a Chain Gang*, another example of moving picture journal-

DARRYL F. ZANUCK

ism in which every box-office rule was violated: the boy didn't get the girl, the fugitive remained a fugitive, the ending was tragic.

It was a success and, like most of the other films he produced, it had been cheap to make. Zanuck wasn't content, though, merely to stick to the day's news. He started the musical film cycle with *42nd Street* and a series on the problems of the working girl with *The Office Wife*. And then, after he had made hundreds of pictures for them, he quit Warner Brothers in 1933 on 24 hours' notice, tearing up a $5,000-a-week contract. His reason was that the company had failed to restore a 50 per cent pay cut to the employees two weeks after the date it had been promised.

He went over to United Artists, where independent producers work independently and market their pictures through a cooperative sales organization, and with the help of Joseph Schenck he set up 20th Century Pictures. Schenck, the president of United Artists, became president of the new company and Zanuck its vice-president. Zanuck's first picture was *The Bowery;* shortly after, announcing that the front-page news was dead as a source for films, he started the biographical cycle with *The House of Rothschild,* starring George Arliss. He had taken Arliss over from his former employers along with Constance Bennett, Loretta Young and other stars.

This success was followed by *Lloyds of London* and other historical films, as well as by pictures which retained much of his former melodramatic verve. By May 1935 Zanuck had completed eighteen pictures, of which only one, *Born To Be Bad,* was a failure. His company was flourishing. One month later it had been withdrawn from United Artists and merged with debt-laden Fox Films. Schenck, who had resigned from the head of United

ZANUCK, DARRYL F.—*Continued*

Artists, was to be chairman; Zanuck was to be a vice-president at $260,000 a year. Hollywood was skeptical. Yet after Zanuck had thrown out most of the Fox scripts, stopped shooting on others, installed his own production manager, re-inventoried studio properties, cut down the payroll ten thousand dollars a week and really set to work, the company of 20th Century-Fox showed a profit of three and one-half millions the first year, sixteen million the next two.

Zanuck continued in the new firm his old attitude toward the making of films. "I believe in gearing up a studio to produce pictures for today's audience and not for the Smithsonian Institution," he once said. "A motion picture lives three months at most. There is no use pretending we are making pictures for the ages." Polish to him is unimportant; if the entertainment is strong enough the flaws won't be noticed. And four weeks, he feels, is shooting time enough for an average picture. That this policy works seems to be demonstrated by hits like *Alexander's Ragtime Band, In Old Chicago, Jesse James* and *The Great American Broadcast* and by his winning the Irving G. Thalberg Memorial Award for "the most consistent high quality of production achievement for 1937." (Later it was his company which produced the honest, realistic *Grapes of Wrath*, which won the New York Film Critics' Award as an outstanding production of 1940.) Even the United States Government was impressed by the record. In the beginning of 1941 he was commissioned a lieutenant colonel of the Signal Corps Reserve with the assignment to produce educational shorts which the War Department is circulating throughout the Army camps. That same year he produced *A Yank in the R. A. F.*

The record, however, hasn't been completely perfect. Although Zanuck has made box-office sensations out of a long list of male actors—Tyrone Power, James Cagney, Henry Fonda, Edward G. Robinson, to mention only a few—his history with women actresses has been less spectacular. Sonja Henie and Alice Faye are his only real triumphs. Shirley Temple, too, is considered a Zanuck failure, for he took her out of cheap pictures to star her in expensive ones, at a loss. In general there have been objections to his handling of stars, accusations that he "puts his brand on them in much the same manner that he put his initials in neon tubing on his former Beverly Hills home."

Also on the debit side, to some, is his complete control over his company's outfit; to even more, there is the evidence of the state of his company's finances as of January 1941. This last may be changed under the new organization. What was more certainly changed were Zanuck's work habits. Until then he had been working from 16 to 18 hours a day, up at 8, at the studio at 10.30, work until 7 p. m.; home for dinner; then back at 8.30 to keep at it until 2 or 3 in the morning. In his lush inner office, decorated with large

stuffed heads on the wall, a zebra-skin bench and screen and a dead lion on the floor, and in his home, there are dictaphones all over—and Zanuck dictates into them "on any pretext." With more leisure it is expected that he will spend more time riding, boxing, skiing, playing polo (he is an enthusiast at this sport, in which he has a two-goal rating) and swimming in the small basement pool at the studio, in which lumps of ice are kept floating. Many of the people who know this small, thin, light-haired "jumping jack executive" are skeptical, however. Energy like his, they feel, can never be sublimated in chasing polo balls or shooting tigers, or even in teaching soldiers the fine points of hygiene and warfare. After 20 years in the film business, they warn, Zanuck is still a "wonder boy."

References

Collier's 93:20+ Ja 6 '34 por
Fortune 12:85-93+ D '35 il pors
Life 2:26-31 F 15 '37 il pors; 10:96-100+ Ap 14 '41 il pors
Motion Picture 51:55+ F '36 por
New Yorker 10:24-8 N 10 '34; 10:24-9 N 17 '34
Newsweek 6:27 Jl 27 '35 por
Sat Eve Post 212:16-17+ Jl 1 '39 pors
Time 26:47-8 N 25 '35 por

International Motion Picture Almanac
New Yorker (periodical). Profiles from the New Yorker p362-80 1938
Who's Who in America
Who's Who in Commerce and Industry

ZILBOORG, GREGORY (zĭl'bōorg) Dec. 25, 1890- Psychiatrist

Address: b. 14 E. 75th St, New York City; h. 885 Park Ave, New York City

One of the best known (and one of the most versatile) practicing psychiatrists in the United States today is Dr. Gregory Zilboorg. Some of the world's most famous personalities have come to his quietly sumptuous office to be turned inside out. There are few dark corners of the human mind that he hasn't pried into: the meaning of loneliness, the real reasons for suicide, the apparently inexplicable impulses behind certain types of murder. His conclusions on such subjects have not only gone into reports before medical and psychiatric associations and into journals of the profession but also into such magazines as *Harper's,* and they have a way of provoking interest and disagreement. Goebbels (see sketch this issue), for instance, could never read this docilely: "True war spirit cannot be created by propaganda. . . War propaganda is somehow helplessly inefficient when people have enough to eat and when they are not afraid and when they are permitted to be socially angry."

Born in Kiev, Russia on December 25, 1890 (Christmas to the Western world), Gregory Zilboorg was the son of Moses and Anne (Braun) Zilboorg. He was graduated from the Gymnasia in Kiev in 1911 and six years later took his M. D. from the Psychoneurological Institute in what was then St. Petersburg. Even before receiving his degree, however, he had served with the Russian Army from 1915 to 1916 as a physician in a base hospital, and had participated in the first revolution in Russia's capital. When the short-lived Lvov Government came into power in 1917 he became secretary to the Minister of Labor, and he continued in that position under the unfortunate Kerensky. He once called himself an "intellectual revolutionist."

A revolution brings out unexpected talents. From medicine and statesmanship Zilboorg turned effortlessly to journalism, in 1918, and edited a daily paper (*Kiev*) until the Germans occupied South Russia. Forced to leave Russia shortly afterward, he came to the United States in 1919, and in December of that year married Ray Leibow of New York. (There are two children, Gregory and Nancy.) "Lecturing, journalism and the theatre" were his preoccupations for the next seven years. He wrote *The Passing of the Old Order in Europe* (1920); he did translations from the Russian, among them *He Who Gets Slapped*, by Andreev (1921) and *We*, by Zamiatin (1924). But he had never lost his interest in his old love, psychiatry, and by 1926 (the year after he became a United States citizen) he had taken his M. D. from Columbia's College of Physicians and Surgeons and joined the staff of the Bloomingdale Hospital. He remained there for five years, with an interval between 1929 and 1930 as assistant at the Psychoanalytic Institute in Berlin.

Since 1931 Dr. Zilboorg has engaged in private practice in psychiatry and psychoanalysis in New York City. During that time, however, the range of his activities has multiplied, if anything. In 1931 his translation from the German of *The Criminal, the Judge and the Public,* by Alexander and Staub, was published; his translation of *Outline of Clinical Psychoanalysis,* by Fenichel, followed in 1934; in 1935 his own *The Medical Man and the Witch During the Renaissance* appeared. (In that same year he had been Noguchi lecturer on the history of medicine at Johns Hopkins University, and this was a collection of his lectures.)

Articles in his own field published in medical journals around this time reveal a great clinical interest in psychiatric history, in the problems of the parent-child relationship, in the treatment of schizophrenia, in the mentality of the criminal. But an even greater percentage of his writings concerned the problem of suicide: what were the reasons for suicidal tendencies in primitive as well as in modern man, particularly among the young? At the meeting of the American Orthopsychiatric Association in February 1937 Dr. Zilboorg presented some of his conclusions and strongly advocated that a completely new concept of suicide be adopted by his profession. And by 1938 funds had actually been made available (reputedly with the assistance of a wealthy former patient) for setting up a Committee for the Study of Suicide in New York City. Dr. Zilboorg became its secretary and director, and it is expected that the findings of the Committee will be ready for publication soon.

A speech before another annual meeting of the American Orthopsychiatric Association, in February 1939, has not yet produced such concrete results, but may have repercussions in the future. Dr. Zilboorg complained that legal technicalities prevented psychiatrists from studying criminals, and announced that in many cases a murderer might be more socially useful alive than dead; he cited one case in which if the murderer hadn't been executed "he would have presented invaluable material to the psychiatrist" and thus to the courts, which in the future would have to deal with many similar cases.

Dr. Zilboorg is a Freudian who places great emphasis on "instinctual drives" and whose language varies between the smoothly turned, witty phrase and sudden questions like: "What are the creative and what are the disintegrating combinations of this triad: narcissism, megalomania, hostility?" Small, dark, mustached, with thick-lens glasses that lend him a rather enigmatic expression, he looks quite capable of answering them. He is a "minor darling of Manhattan's intellectual cocktail set," which delights in his "waspish wit and

Newspictures
DR. GREGORY ZILBOORG

fluent conversation." Zilboorg "is rated very highly in his field, but some of his medical colleagues have worked up an intense dislike for him, mainly on two counts: he is unorthodox, and he is phenomenally successful. He has a Whistlerian aptitude in the gentle art of making enemies, evidenced by a bluntness of speech and an outspoken criticism of the work of certain colleagues."

The medical associations of which he is a member occupy several lines in *Who's Who in America*: among those in which he has held office are the New York Society for Medical History and the Psychoanalytic Society. On

ZILBOORG, GREGORY—*Continued*

November 10, 1941 his *History of Medical Psychology*, written in collaboration with George W. Henry, was brought out by the W. W. Norton Company. It was called by a critic "the best of its kind to appear in English."

References

Sat Eve Post 214:14-15+ D 6 '41 pors
Time 33:45 Mr 6 '39 por
American Medical Directory
Directory of Medical Specialists 1939
Who's Who Among North American
    Authors
Who's Who in America

ZORINA, VERA (zō-rē'nä) Jan. 2, 1917-
Dancer

Address: b. c/o Louis Shurr, 1501 Broadway, New York City; h. 120 East End Ave, New York City

"You'll have to change your name," Colonel de Basil casually remarked.

"No," answered the girl.

"Yes," said the owner of the Ballet Russe. "Everybody changes the name when joining the Russian Ballet."

The girl ran her finger down the column of suggestions and stopped at the last name. "All right," she said, "this one is the least annoying."

And that's how Vera Zorina was born.

Originally, the 17-year-old ballerina had been Eva Brigitta Hartwig. Born in Berlin, Germany on January 2, 1917, the daughter of Fritz and Bille Wimpel (Mann) Hartwig, she was educated in Paris, London and Venice —wherever she happened to be dancing. But Kristiansund, Norway, where her family came from and where she spent her summers as a child, is still her "home town."

On her sixth birthday Brigitta was presented with her first pair of ballet slippers. These she wore constantly in the daytime and was discovered taking them to bed with her. At the age of eight she arranged her first contract—to dance every afternoon in the amusement park of a German spa. As a pupil of Edourdova's, Brigitta went to school in the morning, danced in the afternoon and did her homework in the evening.

After her father's swift and tragic death, the 11-year-old girl turned her whole attention to her career. In Paris she studied under Preobrajeuska and danced publicly whenever she could find an opportunity. From France Brigitta and her mother went to London, where Nicholas Légat became her coach —the same Légat who trained Pavlowa and Nijinsky.

Kristiansund was the scene of her first stage appearance—as a butterfly in a Flower Ballet in December 1923. When she was only 14, Brigitta became the partner of Anton Dolin. With him she danced in Max Reinhardt's *Midsummer Night's Dream* (1929) and *Tales of Hoffman* (1931). A tour of

Europe followed during which she was given a chance to dance with Serge Lifar in Venice.

It was during her engagement in *Ballerina* at the Gaiety Theatre, London, in October 1933 that Brigitta was "discovered" by Colonel de Basil and Léonide Massine of the Ballet Russe. After the dancing equivalent of an audition, Brigitta joined the Russian Ballet and, much against her will, became Vera Zorina.

She hoped that the name might be only temporary, but there was much comment in the papers, and "Zorina" stuck. With the company the ballerina appeared at the Metropolitan Opera House in 1934 and at Covent Garden in 1935 and 1936.

Zorina claims that it wasn't until Massine taught her how to interpret painting in terms of dancing and vice versa that she began to get what she had been reaching for. It was then she realized that she must understand painting, music, good writing and dancing in order to get anywhere in any one of them.

After a transcontinental tour of the United States, Zorina returned to England with the Ballet Russe, fully intending to remain in the company. It was there that she met Dwight Deere Wiman, who was producing the English version of *On Your Toes*. Given an audition, Zorina amazed the producer by reading lines from a seduction scene with "level directness and an instinct for humor." Nothing of the usual ballet-actress technique was present in Zorina's interpretation. She got the part of Vera Baranova, which she played at the Palace Theatre, London, in February 1937 and at the Coliseum in April of the same year.

While the dancer was still in London, Sam Goldwyn, Hollywood producer, gave her a part in his new *Follies* without first taking any screen tests of her. Afterward he cabled for shots of "what he had bought." The result was that the small dancing bit Zorina was first scheduled to do was changed to a starred acting role running through the whole picture. Later she had the lead in the movie version of *On Your Toes*.

Director of her dances in the *Goldwyn Follies* was talented George Balanchine, whom Zorina married at Staten Island, New York on Christmas Eve 1938. Today Balanchine keeps her limber with daily lessons and insists that she practice at least one hour before each performance.

New Yorkers got their first glimpse of the Norwegian star on the stage of the Shubert Theatre, where she opened May 11, 1938 as Angel in *I Married An Angel*. In the fall of 1940 *Louisiana Purchase* opened. In it the 23-year-old star was able to "burn them up with a torch dance that combines trucking, ballet turns and conga steps." In the fall of 1941 the musical comedy was taken on tour.

Zorina's face has been described as "the one most of our illustrators have been looking for—oval, pale ivory, framed in a long bob of dark blond hair; slightly humorous, long, gray eyes; high cheekbones; a practically perfect nose and a generous, well-shaped mouth." Her appearance is enhanced by her carefully chosen clothes which made her, in 1941, according to the Fashion Academy, one of America's 13 best-dressed women.

When she isn't dancing, Zorina likes drawing, driving, reading and sleeping. She skis and swims beautifully but does not care for games like golf and tennis. Her pet hates include Brussels sprouts, cigars, small rooms, starched white collars, shopping and bluish lipstick. To keep her ankles slim, Vera Zorina usually wears low-heeled shoes. She never diets, but she likes to breakfast on grapefruit and coffee, lunch on salad, grapefruit and an occasional hamburger. Her main superstition is rain: she insists that it brings good luck on the opening night of a new show. But a checkered horse is good luck, too. Late in 1941 she was looking around for one, because she wanted to be chosen as Maria in the film version of *For Whom The Bell Tolls,* a part for which she had just been tested.

The ballerina has been described as "the hottest musical comedy hit in a decade" and credited with "shaking the mothballs out of the ballet and dancing it back to nationwide popularity. From the old fashioned leaps, pirouettes, and toe stands which used to delight czars and princesses, Zorina has developed a style of hot ballet that thrills Americans."

References

Am Mag 130:86-7 N '40
Collier's 101:15+ Mr 12 '38

VERA ZORINA

Life 4:48-9 My 30 '38 pors
N Y Post p15 My 2 '40 por; p13 S 19
'41 por; p3 O 9 '41 por
Stage 1:74 N '40
American Women
Newnham, J. K. Dancing Times p138-9;
148-50 1939
Who's Who in the Theatre

BIOGRAPHICAL DICTIONARIES CONSULTED

The publication dates listed are those of volumes in CURRENT BIOGRAPHY's reference collection. When no date appears for biographical dictionaries in the list of references at end of sketches, latest edition has been used.

American Catholic Who's Who 1940-41

American Medical Directory 1938
American Men of Science 1938
American Women 1939-40
America's Young Men 1938-39
Australian Biographical Dictionary 1934
Author's and Writer's Who's Who 1934

Baker's Biographical Dictionary of Musicians 1940
Blue Book of American Aviation 1940
Bolton, T. American Book Illustrators 1938

Catholic Who's Who 1936
Chambers's Biographical Dictionary 1938
Chemical Who's Who 1937
Chi è? 1936
China Year Book 1935

Dictionary of the American Hierarchy 1940
Dictionnaire National des Contemporains 1936
Directory of Medical Specialists 1939

Europa v2
Ewen, D. ed. Composers of Today 1936
Ewen, D. ed. Living Musicians 1940

Film Daily Year Book 1939

International Motion Picture Almanac 1939-40
International Press Who's Who; New Zealand 1938
International Who's Who 1940

Japan-Manchoukuo Year Book 1940

Keesing's Contemporary Archives 1937-40; 1940-43
Kunitz, S. J. ed. Authors Today and Yesterday 1933

Kunitz, S. J. ed. Living Authors 1937
Kunitz, S. J., and Haycraft, H. eds. American Authors 1600-1900 1938
Kunitz, S. J., and Haycraft, H. eds. Junior Book of Authors 1935

Leaders in Education 1941

Mantle, B. Contemporary American Playwrights 1938
Millett, F. B. Contemporary American Authors 1940
Murchison, C. ed. Psychological Register 1932

New Standard Encyclopedia of Art 1939
New York City. Museum of Modern Art Twenty Centuries of Mexican Art 1940

Pierre Key's Musical Who's Who 1931

Qui Êtes-Vous? 1924

Ringel, F. J. ed. America as Americans See It 1932
Rus 1930

Saleski, G. Famous Musicians of a Wandering Race 1927
Sobel, B. ed. Theatre Handbook 1940

Texian Who's Who 1937
Thompson, O. ed. International Cyclopedia of Music and Musicians 1939

Variety Radio Directory 1940-41
Vodarsky-Shiraeff, A. comp. Russian Composers and Musicians 1940

Wer ist Wer 1937
Wer ist's? 1935
Who's Who 1941
Who's Who Among North American Authors 1936-39
Who's Who in America 1940-41

Who's Who in American Art 1940-41
Who's Who in American Education 1933-34
Who's Who in American Jewry 1938-39
Who's Who in Art 1934
Who's Who in Australia 1938
Who's Who in Broadcasting 1933
Who's Who in Canada 1936-37
Who's Who in Central and East-Europe 1935-36
Who's Who in China 1936
Who's Who in Colored America 1938-40
Who's Who in Commerce and Industry 1940-41
Who's Who in Engineering 1941
Who's Who in Finance, Banking and Insurance 1925-26
Who's Who in Government 1932
Who's Who in Japan 1937
Who's Who in Journalism 1928
Who's Who in Jurisprudence 1925
Who's Who in Latin America 1940
Who's Who in Law 1937
Who's Who in Library Service 1933
Who's Who in Major League Baseball 1933
Who's Who in Music Education 1925
Who's Who in New York 1938
Who's Who in New Zealand and the Western Pacific 1932
Who's Who in Railroading 1940
Who's Who in the East 1930
Who's Who in the Major Leagues 1937
Who's Who in the Nation's Capital 1938-39
Who's Who in the Regular Army 1925
Who's Who in the Theatre 1939
Wier, A. E. ed. Macmillan Encyclopedia of Music and Musicians 1938

PERIODICALS AND NEWSPAPERS CONSULTED

A. L. A. Bul—American Library Association Bulletin $3; free to members. American Library Assn, 520 N Michigan Ave, Chicago

Adv & Selling—Advertising and Selling $2. Robbins Pub Co, Inc, 9 E 38th St, New York

Am Artist—American Artist $3. Watson-Guptill Publications, Inc, 330 W 42nd St, New York
Formerly Art Instruction

Am Assn Univ Women J—American Association of University Women Journal $1. American Assn of University Women, 1634 I St, N. W., Washington, D. C.

Am Hist R—American Historical Review $5; free to members of the American Historical Assn. Macmillan Co, 60 Fifth Ave, New York

Am Home—American Home $1. American Home Magazine Corp, 251 Fourth Ave, New York

Am Mag—American Magazine $2.50. Crowell-Collier Pub Co, Springfield, Ohio

Am Mag Art See Mag Art

Am Mercury—American Mercury $3. American Mercury, Inc, 570 Lexington Ave, New York

Am Phot—American Photography $2.50. American Photographic Pub Co, 353 Newbury St, Boston

Am Scand R—American Scandinavian Review $2; free to members. American Scandinavian Foundation, 116 E 64th St, New York

Am Scholar—American Scholar $2. United Chapters of the Phi Beta Kappa, 12 E 44th St, New York

Amerasia—Amerasia $2.50. Amerasia, 125 E 52nd St, New York

Amour Art—L'Amour de l'Art 170fr; foreign postage 40fr and 60fr. Editions Hypérion, 21 rue de Berri, Paris (8e)
Name changed to Prométhée, L'Amour de l'Art January 1939

Ann Am Acad—Annals of the American Academy of Political and Social Science $5; free to members. 3457 Walnut St, Philadelphia

Apollo—Apollo 35s. Field Press, Ltd, Field House, Bream's Bldgs, Chancery Lane, London, EC 4 ($7.50. 18 E 48th St, New York)
Temporary Address: 16 Whittington Court, London, N 2

Art Digest—Art Digest $3. Art Digest, Inc, 116 E 59th St, New York

Art N—Art News $7. Art News, Inc, 136 E 57th St, New York

Arts & Dec—Arts and Decoration; The Spur $3.50. Artspur Publications, Inc, 34 N Crystal St, East Stroudsburg, Pa.
Spur combined with Arts and Decoration August 1940

Asia—Asia $4. Editorial Publications, Inc, 40 E 49th St, New York

Asiatic R—Asiatic Review £1 5s. East and West, Ltd, 3 Victoria St, London, SW 1

Assn Am Col Bul—Association of American Colleges Bulletin $3. Assn of American Colleges, 19 W 44th St, New York

Atlan—Atlantic Monthly $5. Atlantic Monthly Co, 8 Arlington St, Boston

Beaux Arts—Beaux-Arts. Chronique des Arts et de la Curiosité 40fr; foreign postage 20fr and 30fr. La Gazette des Beaux Arts, 140 faubourg Saint Honoré, Paris (VIIIe)

Bet Homes & Gard—Better Homes & Gardens $1. Meredith Pub Co, 1714 Locust St, Des Moines, Iowa

Bookm—Bookman (discontinued)

Bookm (London) See Life & Letters To-day

Books (N Y Herald Tribune See N Y Herald Tribune Books

Books (N Y Times) See N Y Times Book R

Bul Museum Modern Art See New York City. Museum of Modern Art Bul

Bul Pan Am Union See Pan Am Union Bul

Business Week—Business Week $5. McGraw-Hill Pub Co, Inc, 330 W 42nd St, New York

Cahiers Art—Cahiers d'Art 170fr; foreign postage 50fr and 100fr. Éditions Cahiers d'Art, 14 rue du Dragon, Paris (VIe)

Canad Forum—Canadian Forum $2. Canadian Forum, Ltd, 28 Wellington St, W, Toronto 5, Canada

Canad Hist R—Canadian Historical Review $2. University of Toronto Press, Toronto

Cath School J—Catholic School Journal $2. Bruce Pub Co, 540 N Milwaukee St, Milwaukee, Wis.

Cath World—Catholic World $4. Catholic World, 401 W 59th St, New York

China W R—China Weekly Review $8. Millard Pub Co, 160 Ave Edward VII, Shanghai

Christian Cent—Christian Century $4. Christian Century Press, 407 S Dearborn St, Chicago

Christian Sci Mon—Christian Science Monitor (Atlantic edition) $9. Christian Science Pub Society, 1 Norway St, Boston

Christian Sci Mon Mag—Christian Science Monitor Weekly Magazine Section $2.60. Christian Science Pub Society, 1 Norway St, Boston

Churchman—The Churchman $4. Churchman Co, 425 Fourth Ave, New York

Col Engl—College English $3. University of Chicago Press, 5750 Ellis Ave, Chicago
Formerly English Journal (College Edition)

Collier's—Collier's $2. Crowell-Collier Pub Co, Springfield, Ohio

Commonweal—Commonweal $5. Commonweal Pub Co, Inc, 386 Fourth Ave, New York

Cong Digest—Congressional Digest $5. Congressional Digest, 2131 LeRoy Place, Washington, D. C.

Connoisseur—Connoisseur 30s. Connoisseur, Ltd, 28 & 30 Grosvenor Gardens, London, SW 1 ($7.50. Connoisseur and International Studio, 572 Madison Ave, New York)

Contemp—Contemporary Review $9.50. Contemporary Review Co, Ltd, 19, 19a Cursitor St, London, EC 4

Country Life—Country Life $5. Polo Magazine, Inc, 1270 Sixth Ave, New York

Cue—Cue (Manhattan edition) $3. Cue Publishing Co, Inc, 6 E 39th St, New York

Cur Hist See Cur Hist ns

Cur Hist & Forum See Cur Hist ns

Cur Hist ns—Current History $2. Current History, 225 Varick St, New York
Forum and Century combined with Current History May 23, 1940 as Current History and Forum.
Current History and Forum combined with Events July 21, 1941 and the name Current History restored.

Design—Design $3. Design Pub Co, Box 267, Columbus, Ohio

Deutsch Rundsch—Deutsche Rundschau 12m. Kurfürstenstr 42, Berlin, W 35

Dublin R—Dublin Review 15s. Burns Oates & Washbourne, Ltd, 28 Ashley Pl, London, SW 1

Eccl R—Ecclesiastical Review $4. American Ecclesiastical Review, 1722 Archer St, Philadelphia

Educa—Education $4. Palmer Co, 370 Atlantic Ave, Boston

El Engl R—Elementary English Review $2.50. Elementary English Review, Box 67, North End Station, Detroit

Engl J—English Journal $3. University of Chicago Press, 5750 Ellis Ave, Chicago
Formerly English Journal (High School edition)

Engl R See Nat R

Esquire—Esquire $5. Esquire, Inc, 919 N Michigan Ave, Chicago

Etude—Etude $2.50. Theodore Presser Co, 1712 Chestnut St, Philadelphia

Eur Nouv—L'Europe Nouvelle 150fr. 73bis quai d'Orsay, Paris (VIIe)

Far East R—Far Eastern Review $5. 24 The Bund, Shanghai
Foreign Affairs—Foreign Affairs $5. Council on Foreign Relations, Inc, 45 E 65th St, New York
Foreign Policy Rep—Foreign Policy Reports $5. (to libraries subscription includes Foreign Policy Bulletins and 6 headline books); $3 to F. P. A. members. Foreign Policy Assn, Inc, 22 E 38th St, New York
Fortnightly—Fortnightly $8.50. Fortnightly Review, Ltd, 13 Buckingham St, London, WC 2
Fortune—Fortune $10. Time, Inc, 330 E 22d St, Chicago
Forum See Cur Hist ns
Friday—Friday (discontinued)

Good H—Good Housekeeping $2.50. Hearst Magazines, Inc, 57th St & Eighth Ave, New York

Harper—Harper's Magazine $4. Harper & Bros, 49 E 33rd St, New York
Harper's Bazaar—Harper's Bazaar $5. Hearst Magazines, Inc, 572 Madison Ave, New York
Home & F See House B
Horn Book—Horn Book $2.50. Horn Book, Inc, 264 Boylston St, Boston
House & Gard—House and Garden $3. Condé Nast Publications, Inc, Graybar Bldg, 420 Lexington Ave, New York
House B—House Beautiful combined with Home and Field $2.50. Hearst Magazines, Inc, 572 Madison Ave, New York
Combined with Home and Field

Illustration—L'Illustration 490fr. 13 rue Saint-Georges, Paris (IXᵉ) ($13. French and European Publications, Inc, 610 Fifth Ave, New York)
Ind Woman—Independent Woman $1.50. National Federation of Business and Professional Women's Clubs, Inc, 1819 Broadway, New York
Int Concil—International Conciliation 25c a year. Carnegie Endowment for International Peace, 405 W 117th St, New York

J Adult Ed—Journal of Adult Education 75c single copy. American Assn for Adult Education, 60 E 42nd St, New York

Ladies' H J—Ladies' Home Journal $1. Curtis Pub Co, Independence Sq, Philadelphia
Liberty—Liberty $2. Macfadden Publications, Inc, 205 E 42nd St, New York
Library J—Library Journal $5. R. R. Bowker Co, 62 W 45th St, New York
Life—Life $4.50. Time, Inc, 330 E 22nd St, Chicago
Life & Letters To-day—Life and Letters To-day 14s. 41 Upper Town Rd, Greenford, Middlesex, Eng. ($3.50. International News Co, 131 Varick St, New York)
London Mercury absorbed Bookman January 1935
Life and Letters To-day absorbed London Mercury and Bookman May 1939
Lit Digest—Literary Digest (discontinued)
Liv Age—Living Age $5. Living Age Co, Inc, 25 W 45th St, New York
London Mercury—London Mercury and Bookman See Life & Letters To-day
London Studio (Studio)—London Studio, American edition of the Studio $6. Studio Publications, Inc, 381 Fourth Ave, New York (28s; foreign postage 2s; The Studio, Ltd, 44 Leicester Sq, London, WC 2)
Look—Look $2. Look, Inc, 715 Locust St, Des Moines, Iowa

Mag Art—Magazine of Art $5; free to members. American Federation of Arts, Barr Bldg, Farragut Sq, Washington, D. C.
Formerly American Magazine of Art

Mercure Fr—Mercure de France 140fr. 26 rue de Condé, Paris (VIᵉ)
Mis R—Missionary Review of the World (discontinued)
Mo Labor R—Monthly Labor Review $3.50. Superintendent of Documents, Washington, D. C.
Musical Am—Musical America $3. Musical American Corp, 113 W 57th St, New York
Musical Courier—Musical Courier $3. Music Periodicals Corp, 119 W 57th St, New York
Musical Q—Musical Quarterly $3. G. Schirmer, Inc, 3 E 43rd St, New York
Musician—Musician $3. Eugene Belier, 113 W 57th St, New York

N Y Herald Tribune—New York Herald Tribune $17, including Sunday edition. New York Tribune, Inc, 230 W 41st St, New York
N Y Herald Tribune Books—New York Herald Tribune Books $1. New York Tribune, Inc, 230 W 41st St, New York
N Y Post—New York Post $10. New York Post, Inc, 75 West St, New York
N Y Sun—New York Sun $12. New York Sun, Inc, 280 Broadway. New York
N Y Times—New York Times $17, including Sunday edition. The New York Times Co, 229 W 43rd St, New York
N Y Times Book R—New York Times Book Review $2. The New York Times Co, 229 W 43rd St, New York
N Y World-Telegram—New York World-Telegram $12. New York World-Telegram Corp, 125 Barclay St, New York
Nat Bd of R Mag—National Board of Review Magazine $2; free to members. National Board of Review of Motion Pictures, Inc, 70 Fifth Ave, New York
Nat Educ Assn J—National Education Association Journal $2; free to members. National Education Assn, 1201 16th St, N W, Washington, D. C.
Nat R—National Review 30s. Rolls House, 2 Bream's Bldg, London, E
Absorbed English Review August 1937
Nation—The Nation $5. The Nation, Inc, 55 Fifth Ave, New York
Nation's Bus—Nation's Business $3. Chamber of Commerce of the United States, 1615 H St, N W, Washington, D. C.
Nature—Nature Magazine $3. American Nature Assn, 1214 16th St, N W, Washington, D.C.
New Outlook—New Outlook (discontinued)
New Repub—New Republic $5. Editorial Publications, Inc, 40 E 49th St, New York
New Statesman & Nation—New Statesman and Nation—Week-end Review 32s. 6d. 10 Great Turnstile, London, WC 1
New York City. Museum of Modern Art Bul—Bulletin of the Museum of Modern Art. Membership. Museum of Modern Art, 11 W 53rd St, New York
New Yorker—New Yorker $5. F-R. Pub Corp, W 53rd St, New York
Newsdom—Newsdom $2. Newsdom, Inc, Pub, 63 Park Row, New York
Newsweek—Newsweek $4. Newsweek 152 W 42nd St, New York
19th Cent—Nineteenth Century and After $8.75. Constable & Co, Ltd, 10 & 12 Orange St, London, WC 2
No Am R—North American Review $4. North American Review Corp, 123 William St, New York
Nuova Antol—Nuova Antologia 180 l. Via del Collegio Romano 10, Rome

Opera News—Opera News $3; free to members. Metropolitan Opera Guild, Inc, 654 Madison Ave, New York
Outlook—Outlook (discontinued)

Pan Am Union Bul—Bulletin of the Pan American Union $1.50. Pan American Union, 17th St and Constitution Ave, N W, Washington, D. C.
Parnassus—Parnassus (discontinued)
Photoplay—Photoplay $1. Macfadden Publications, Inc, 122 E 42nd St, New York
Combined with Movie Mirror

Pictures on Exhibit—Pictures on Exhibit $1. Pictures Pub Co, 724 Fifth Ave, New York
PM—PM $14, including Sunday edition. Harry C. Holden, Subscription Manager, P.O. Box 81, Times Square Station, New York
Poetry—Poetry $3. 232 E Erie St, Chicago
Pol Sci Q—Political Science Quarterly $5; free to members. Academy of Political Science, Columbia University, New York
Pop Mech—Popular Mechanics Magazine $2.50. Popular Mechanics Co, 200 E Ontario St, Chicago
Progressive Educ—Progressive Education $3. Progressive Education Assn, 221 W 57th St, New York
Pub W—Publishers' Weekly $5. R. R. Bowker Co, 62 W 45th St, New York

Queen's Q—Queen's Quarterly $2. Queen's University, Kingston, Canada

R Deux Mondes—Revue des Deux Mondes 230fr. Royat (Puy-de-Dôme (Boîte postale n° 11
R of Rs—Review of Reviews (discontinued)
Read Digest—Reader's Digest $3. Reader's Digest Assn, Inc, Pleasantville, New York
Recreation—Recreation $2. National Recreation Assn, 315 Fourth Ave, New York
Ref Shelf—Reference Shelf $6 per volume of ten bound numbers, published irregularly. The H. W. Wilson Co, 950-972 University Ave, New York
Rotarian—Rotarian $1.50. Rotary International, 35 E Wacker Drive, Chicago
Royal Inst Brit Arch J—Royal Institute of British Architects Journal £1 16s postpaid. The Institute, 66 Portland Pl, London, W 1

San Francisco Chronicle—San Francisco Chronicle $15.60. Chronicle Publishing Co, 901 Mission St, San Francisco
Sat Eve Post—Saturday Evening Post $2. The Curtis Pub Co, Independence Sq, Philadelphia
Sat R Lit—Saturday Review of Literature $4. Saturday Review Co, Inc, 25 W. 45th St, New York
Sch & Soc—School and Society $5; free to members of the Society for the Advancement of Education. Science Press, Grand Central Terminal, New York
Sch Arts—School Arts $3. School Arts, Printers Bldg, Worcester, Mass.
Scholastic—Scholastic (high school teacher edition) $2. (combined, or teacher edition only); school group rate (two or more subscriptions to one address) $1 for special editions. $1.30 for combined edition. Scholastic Corp, 430 Kinnard Ave, Dayton, Ohio
Sci Am—Scientific American $4. Munn & Co, Inc, 24 W 40th St, New York
Sci Mo—Scientific Monthly $5. Science Press, Grand Central Terminal, New York

Sci N L—Science News Letter $5. Science Service, Inc, 1719 N St, N W, Washington, D. C.
Sci ns—Science $6. Science Press, Grand Central Terminal, New York
Scrib Com—Scribner's Commentator $3. P. & S. Pub, Inc, Lake Geneva, Wis.
Scrib Mag—Scribner's Magazine (discontinued)
So Atlan Q—South Atlantic Quarterly $3. Duke University Press, Durham, N. C.
Spec—Spectator 30s. 99 Gower St, London, WC 1
Satge—Stage (discontinued)
Studio (Am edition) See London Studio
Survey—Survey $3. Survey Associates, Inc, 112 E 19th St, New York
Survey G—Survey Graphic $3. Survey Associates, Inc, 112 E 19th St, New York

Theatre Arts—Theatre Arts $3.50. Theatre Arts, Inc, 40 E 49th St, New York
Formerly Theatre Arts Monthly
Time—Time $5. Time, Inc, 330 E 22nd St, Chicago
Travel—Travel $4. Robert M. McBride & Co, Inc, 116 E 16th St, New York

U S Bur Labor—Monthly Labor R See Mo Labor R
U S Bur Labor Bul—United States Bureau of Labor Statistics. Bulletins. Free to libraries. Bureau of Labor Statistics, Washington, D. C. Purchase orders, Superintendent of Documents, Washington, D. C.
U S News—United States News $2. United States News Bldg, 22nd and M Sts, N W, Washington, D. C.
U S Office Educ Bul—United States Office of Education. Bulletins. Free to libraries. Office of Education, Washington, D. C. Purchase orders, Superintendent of Documents, Washington, D. C.

Va Q R—Virginia Quarterly Review $3. University of Virginia, Charlottesville, Virginia
Variety—Variety $10. Variety, Inc, 154 W 46th St, New York
Vital Speeches—Vital Speeches of the Day $3. City News Pub Co, 33 W 42nd St, New York

Wilson Lib Bul—Wilson Library Bulletin $1. The H. W. Wilson Co, 950-972 University Ave, New York
Formerly Wilson Bulletin
Woman's H C—Woman's Home Companion $1. Crowell-Collier Pub Co, Springfield, Ohio
Writer—The Writer $3. The Writer, Inc, 8 Arlington St, Boston

Yale R ns—Yale Review $3. Yale University Press, 143 Elm St, New Haven

NECROLOGY—1941

(See 1940 annual volume for 1940 necrology)

Abbott, Edwin Milton
Acheson, Albert R(obert)
Adams, Joseph H(enry)
Adkins, Charles
Adler, Guido
Aguirre Cerda, Pedro
Aked, Charles F(rederic), Rev.
Aldrich, Chester Holmes
Alexander, Harry Held
Alfonso XIII, Former King of Spain
Amherst, Alicia-Margaret, Baroness Rockley   See Rockley, A.-M. A, Baroness
Amsden, Charles (Avery)
Andersen, Hendrik Christian
Anderson, Sherwood
Argeseanu, George
Armfield, Anne Constance   See Smedley, C.
Armour, Allison V(incent)
Arsonval, Jacques Arsène d'
Atwell, Wayne J(ason)
Aughinbaugh, William (Edmund)
Austin, F(rederick) Britten
Austin, Herbert Austin, 1st Baron
Ayres, Agnes

Baca-Flor, Carlos
Bach, Reginald
Bacon, George P(reston)
Bada, Angelo
Baden-Powell of Gilwell, Robert Stephenson Smyth Baden-Powell, 1st Baron
Baer, William J(acob)
Baird, John Lawrence, 1st Viscount Stonehaven   See Stonehaven, J. L. B., 1st Viscount
Baker, Charles Whiting
Banting, Sir Frederick Grant
Barnard, James Lynn
Barringer, Paul Brandon
Beard, Daniel Carter
Beauchamp, Mary Annette   See Russell, M. A. R., Countess
Beck, Martin
Begg, Colin Luke
Bell, Thomas M(ontgomery)
Benson, Francis Colgate, Jr.
Berg, Ernst J(ulius)
Berg, Irving H(usted)
Bergson, Henri (Louis)
Bernard, Émile
Bickel, George L.
Bigelow, William (Pingry)
Birdseye, Claude Hale
Blackton, J(ames) Stuart
Blatch, Harriot Stanton
Bliss, A(ndrew) Richard, Jr.
Block, Paul
Blumenthal, George
Bodansky, Meyer

Bolles, Stephen
Bonham, Milledge Louis, Jr.
Bonine, Frederick N.
Borglum, Gutzon
Bowman, George E(rnest)
Brandeis, Louis D(embitz)
Brewster, Benjamin, Bishop
Brewster, Chauncey Bunce, Bishop
Bridge, Frank
Bridges, Robert
Brooks, Robert C(larkson)
Brown, Carleton (Fairchild)
Brown, Helen Dawes
Browne, Dame Sidney Jane
Brush, George de Forest
Buckner, Emory R(oy)
Buffum, Charles A(lbert)
Burke, Edmund J., Father
Burr, Henry
Burwash, Lachlin Taylor
Bush, Wendell T.
Byron, William D(evereux)

Calfee, John Edward
Calverton, V(ictor) F(rancis)
Cammerer, Arno B(erthold)
Campbell, Philip P(itt)
Campbell, Willis C(ohoon)
Campinchi, César
Candler, Warren A(kin), Bishop
Cannon, Annie J(ump)
Carey, Charles Henry
Carle, Richard
Cauldwell, Leslie Giffen
Cecil, Mary
Cerda, Pedro Aguirre   See Aguirre Cerda, P.
Chadourne, Marc
Chapin, Charles Value
Chapman, Blanche
Chevrolet, Louis
Chiappe, Jean
Claussen, Julia
Clay, Laura
Clemensen, Erik Christian
Coates, John
Coffin, Haskell
Colby, Charles DeWitt
Collison, Wilson
Condon, Frank
Connah, Douglas John
Connell, Karl
Connery, Lawrence J(oseph)
Conness, Robert
Copeland, Benjamin, Rev.
Coxe, Howard (Cleveland)
Craigavon, James Craig, 1st Viscount
Cripps, Charles Alfred, 1st Baron Parmoor   See Parmoor, C. A. C., 1st Baron

Csáky, István, Count   See Csáky, S., Count
Csáky, Stephen, Count
Cubberley, Ellwood P(atterson)
Cunningham, William Francis
Curran, Pearl Gildersleeve
Cushing, Charles C(yprian) S(trong)
Cushing, Tom   See Cushing, C. C. S.

Daly, Thomas A., Father
Damerel, Donna
Danforth, William
Danvin, Mme. Charles   See Radziwill, C., Princess
Dargan, E(dwin) Preston
D'Arsonval, Jacques Arsène   See Arsonval, J. A. d'
Daugherty, Harry M(icajah)
Davenport, Eugene
Davies, Sir (Henry) Walford
Davis, William Rhodes
De Long, Emma J. Wotton
De Pourtalès, Guy, Count   See Pourtalès, G., Count de
Devaney, John Patrick
Devereaux, William Charles
De Vry, Herman A.
Dinsmore, Charles Allen, Rev.
Divine, Frank H(enry), Rev.
Dolly, Jenny
Douglas, Walter J.
Driesch, Hans (Adolf Eduard)
Droch, pseud.   See Bridges, R.
Dubois, Eugène
Du Bose, Horace Mellard, Bishop
Dunkerley, William Arthur   See Oxenham, J.
Dunn, J(oseph) Allan (Elphinstone)
Du Puy, William Atherton

Eggleston, Edward Mason
Eidmann, Frank Lewis
Eldridge, Edward H(enry)
Elizabeth, pseud.   See Russell, M. A. R., Countess
Ellis, Carleton
Eltinge, Julian
Emerson, Victor Lee
Emmerson, Louis Lincoln
Emmet, William L(eRoy)
Esch, John J(acob)
Ettl, John
Evans, Anne
Evans, Sir Arthur (John)
Eves, Reginald Grenville

Fagnani, Charles P(rospero), Rev.
Falkner, Roland Post
Farny, George W(imbor)

Morehouse, Daniel Walter
Morrison, Adrienne
Morton, James F(erdinand)
Mosher, Gouverneur Frank, Bishop
Mowat, Robert B(almain)
Muir, Ramsay
Murphy, Franklin W(illiam)
Murray, Charlie
Murray, J. Harold
Mussolini, Bruno

Narelle, Marie
Neuman, Leo Handel
Newbolt, Sir Francis George
Newell, Edward Theodore
Newlon, Jesse H(omer)
Nice, Harry (Whinna)
Noble, Gladwyn Kingsley
Noyes, William A(lbert)
Nutting, Wallace, Rev.

O'Brien, Edward J(oseph Harrington)
O'Connor, Andrew
O'Melveny, Henry W(illiam)
Osumi, Mineo Osumi, Baron
Ottinger, Nathan
Owens, Clarence Julian
Oxenham, John

Pace, Charles Ashford
Paderewski, Ignace Jan
Palmer, James Lynwood
Pardee, George C(ooper)
Parke, William
Parker, Barnett
Parma, V. Valta
Parmoor, Charles Alfred Cripps, 1st Baron
Parsons, Herbert Collins
Paxton, William McGregor
Pearl, Raymond
Pease, Charles G(iffin)
Peixotto, Ernest (Clifford)
Penn, Arthur A.
Penner, Joe
Penniman, Josiah H(armar)
Phelan, Michael F(rancis)
Pilcher, Lewis F(rederick)
Plaskett, John S(tanley)
Porter, Edwin S.
Pourtalès, Guy, Count de
Powell, Robert Stephenson Smyth Baden-, 1st Baron Baden-Powell of Gilwell   See Baden-Powell of Gilwell, R. S. S. B.-P., 1st Baron
Power, Sir D'Arcy
Prajadhipok, Former King of Siam
Prévost, Marcel

Quidde, Ludwig

Radziwill, Catherine, Princess
Rathbone, Josephine Adams
Reed, James, Sr.
Reeve, Sidney A(rmor)
Resnick, Louis
Rhoades, Cornelia Harsen
Richards, C(harles) R(uss)
Richards, John G(ardiner)

Richman, Charles J.
Ridge, Lola
Rigling, Alfred
Ring, Barbara T(aylor)
Ripley, William Z(ebina)
Roberts, Elizabeth Madox
Roberts, George Lucas
Roberts, Kate L(ouise)
Robinson, Frederick B(ertrand)
Rockley, Alicia-Margaret Amherst, Baroness
Rogers, Mark Homer
Rogers, Robert Emmons
Roosevelt, Sara Delano
Rose, Mary D. Swartz
Rothermere,   Harold   Sidney Harmsworth, 1st Viscount
Rourke, Constance Mayfield
Runkle, Erwin W(illiam)
Rusby, Henry H(urd)
Russell, Charles (Edward)
Russell, Mary Annette Russell, Countess

Sabatier, Paul
Sackett, Frederic M(oseley), Jr.
Saionji, Kimmochi, Prince
Sanborn, (John) Pitts
Schertzinger, Victor
Schilder, Paul Ferdinand
Schoff, Hannah Kent
Schulte, Karl Joseph, Cardinal
Severance, H(arold) Craig
Shannon, Peggy
Shaw, Henry (Larned Keith)
Shawkey, Morris Purdy
Shearer, Augustus H(unt)
Sheppard, Morris
Sherley, Swagar
Shine, F(rancis) W(ayles)
Simonds, Frederic W(illiam)
Simpson, Kenneth F(arrand)
Skilton, Charles Sanford
Smedley, Constance
Smith, Roy Burnett
Smoot, Reed
Stamp, Josiah Charles Stamp, 1st Baron
Steell, Willis
Stephenson, James
Stewart, William G(odman)
Stiles, Charles Wardell
Stillwell, Lewis Buckley
Stockbridge, Frank Parker
Stone, Hannah (Mayer)
Stonehaven, John Lawrence Baird, 1st Viscount
Stowell, Clarence Warner
Strawbridge, Anne West
Strömberg, Leonard, Rev.
Strong, Lee A(bram)
Strong, William McCreery
Stuart, Duane Reed
Stuart, James Everett
Suydam, Edward Howard
Swenson, Alfred G.
Swift, Ernest John

Tagore, Sir Rabindranath
Talley, James (Ely)

Taylor, Edward T(homas)
Taylor, Henry O(sborn)
Teixeira-Gomes, Manuel
Teleki, Paul, Count
Tennent, David Hilt
Terzian, Harutyun G.
Thomas, Freeman Freeman-, 1st Marquess of Willingdon   See Willingdon, F. F.-T., 1st Marquess of
Thompson, George L.
Thompson, James Westfall
Thompson, Reginald Campbell
Thore, Wendell Phillips
Timberlake, Charles B(ateman)
Tinney, Frank
Titulescu, Nicolas
Townsend, Harry E(verett)
Tryon, George Clement Tryon, 1st Baron

Ulrich, Charles (Kenmore)
Upham, Francis Bourne, Rev.

Van Devanter, Willis
Vincent, George Edgar
Vincent, Leon H(enry)

Wadhams, Robert Pelton
Wakefield, Charles Cheers Wakefield, 1st Viscount
Walker, Stuart
Wallace, (David) Euan
Walpole, Sir Hugh (Seymour)
Walsh, George Ethelbert
Walsh, William Henry
Walter, Eugene
Walter, Wilmer
Warren, Harry Marsh, Rev.
Wason, Edward H(ill)
Weaver, Affie
Webb, Walter Loring
Welch, William A(ddams)
Welsh, Herbert
West, Annie Blythe
West, Nathanael
Weymouth, Frank E(lwin)
Whitford, Harry Nichols
Whittlesey, Charles F.
Wick, Frances G(ertrude)
Wile, Frederic William
Wilhelm   II,   Former   German Kaiser
Wilkins, T(homas) Russell
William II, Emperor   See Wilhelm II, Former German Kaiser
Williams, John D.
Williams, William Robert
Willingdon, Freeman Freeman-Thomas, 1st Marquess of
Wills, C. Harold
Wilson, George Arthur
Winsor, Frederick
Woolf, Virginia
Wright, Berlin H(art)
Wright, Huntley

Yarrow, William
Young, Rose (Emmet)

BY PROFESSION—1941

Architecture

Aldrich, Chester Holmes obit
Breuer, Marcel
Fielding, Mantle obit
Greenough, Carroll obit
Gropius, Walter (Adolf Georg)
Hackett, Horatio B(alch) obit
Hewlett, J(ames) Monroe obit
Hopkins, Alfred obit
Kendall, William Mitchell obit
Pilcher, Lewis F(rederick) obit
Severance, H(arold) Craig obit
Whittlesey, Charles F. obit
Williams, Paul R.
Wright, Frank Lloyd

Art

Adrian, (Gilbert)
Alain, (Daniel A.)
Andersen, Hendrik Christian obit
Baca-Flor, Carlos obit
Baer, William J(acob) obit
Bernard, Émile obit
Blumenthal, George obit
Borglum, Gutzon obit
Brook, Alexander
Brush, George de Forest obit
Campbell, E. Simms
Cauldwell, Leslie Giffen obit
Coffin, Haskell obit
Connah, Douglas John obit
Curry, John Steuart
Czettel, Ladislas
Dehn, Adolf (Arthur)
Eggleston, Edward Mason obit
Ettl, John obit
Eves, Reginald Grenville obit
Fiene, Ernest
Fitzpatrick, D(aniel) R(obert)
Force, Juliana
Ganso, Emil obit
Gill, Eric obit
Gross, Chaim
Hinckley, Robert obit
Horgan, Stephen H(enry) obit
Hughes, Toni
John, Augustus (Edwin)
Keith, Dora Wheeler obit
Kuniyoshi, Yasuo
Lavery, Sir John obit
Lawson, Robert
Llewellyn, Sir William obit
McMein, Neysa
Marsh, Reginald
Moran, Léon obit
O'Connor, Andrew obit
O'Keeffe, Georgia
Palmer, James Lynwood obit
Paxton, William McGregor obit

Peixotto, Ernest (Clifford) obit
Robinson, Boardman
Saint-Gaudens, Homer (Schiff)
Savage, Augusta (Christine)
Soyer, Isaac; Soyer, Moses; and Soyer, Raphael
Stuart, James Everett obit
Suydam, Edward Howard obit
Taylor, Richard
Townsend, Harry E(verett) obit
Weber, Max
Whitney, Gertrude (Vanderbilt)
Yarrow, William obit

Aviation

Bishop, William Avery
De Seversky, Alexander P(rocofieff)
Douglas, Donald W(ills)
Grizodubova, Valentina (Stepanovna)
Hughes, Howard (Robard)
Jamieson, Leland (Shattuck) obit
Johnson, Amy obit
Kisevalter, George obit
Lindbergh, Charles A(ugustus)
Mussolini, Bruno obit
Schroeder, R(udolph) W(illiam)

Diplomacy

Abetz, Otto
Biddle, Anthony J(oseph) Drexel, Jr.
Bowers, Claude G(ernade)
Butler, Nevile (Montagu)
Campbell, Sir Gerald
Csáky, Stephen, Count obit
Dawson, William
Gauss, Clarence E(dward)
Grew, Joseph Clark
Henry, Jules obit
Houghton, Alanson B(igelow) obit
Koo, V(i) K(yuin) Wellington
Laughlin, Irwin (Boyle) obit
Leahy, William D(aniel)
Litvinov, Maxim (Maximovitch)
MacVeagh, Lincoln
Maisky, Ivan (Mikhailovich)
Nomura, Kichisaburo
Sackett, Frederic M(oseley), Jr. obit
Steinhardt, Laurence A(dolph)
Wilson, Hugh (Robert)
Winant, John G(ilbert)

Education

Aydelotte, Frank
Bacon, George P(reston) obit
Barnard, James Lynn obit
Barringer, Paul Brandon obit
Beard, Charles A(ustin) and Beard, Mary
Beard, Mary See Beard, C. A. and Beard, M.
Berg, Irving H(usted) obit
Bergson, Henri (Louis) obit
Bonham, Milledge Louis, Jr. obit
Brooks, Robert C(larkson) obit
Brown, Carleton (Fairchild) obit
Brown, Charles H(arvey)
Buffum, Charles A(lbert) obit
Burke, Edmund J., Father obit
Burnham, James
Bush, Wendell T. obit
Calfee, John Edward obit
Carnegie, Dale
Conant, James B(ryant)
Counts, George S(ylvester)
Cubberley, Ellwood P(atterson) obit
Dargan, E(dwin) Preston obit
Davenport, Eugene obit
Downs, Robert B(ingham)
Driesch, Hans (Adolf Eduard) obit
Dykstra, Clarence A(ddison)
Eldridge, Edward H(enry) obit
Flexner, Abraham
Florinsky, Michael T.
Ford, Worthington C(hauncey) obit
Forsythe, Robert S(tanley) obit
Gildersleeve, Virginia C(rocheron)
Gillespie, Louis John obit
Graham, Frank P(orter)
Harris, James Rendel obit
Hazard, Paul
Hazen, Charles D(owner) obit
Hill, Frank Pierce obit
Howe, Samuel B(urnett) obit
Hyvernat, Henry, Mgr. obit
Jackson, Daniel Dana obit
Johnson, Mordecai Wyatt
Jones, Chester Lloyd obit
Kemmerer, E(dwin) W(alter)
Kittredge, George Lyman obit
Koch, Theodore Wesley obit
Lanman, Charles Rockwell obit
Laski, Harold (Joseph)
Lecky, Prescott obit
Lydenberg, Harry Miller
MacBride, Ernest William obit
McGarry, William J(ames), Rev. obit
Marcial-Dorado, Carolina obit

Martin, Frank L(ee) obit
Mathews, Shailer, Rev. obit
Million, J(ohn) W(ilson) obit
Morehouse, Daniel Walter obit
Mott, Frank Luther
Muir, Ramsay obit
Newell, Edward Theodore obit
Newlon, Jesse H(omer) obit
Parma, V. Valta obit
Penniman, Josiah H(armar) obit
Pitkin, Walter B(oughton)
Rathbone, Josephine Adams obit
Reinhardt, Aurelia Henry
Richards, C(harles) R(uss) obit
Rigling, Alfred obit
Ripley, William Z(ebina) obit
Roberts, George Lucas obit
Roberts, Kate L(ouise) obit
Robinson, Frederick B(ertrand) obit
Rogers, Robert Emmons obit
Rose, Mary D. Swartz obit
Rugg, Harold (Ordway)
Runkle, Erwin W(illiam) obit
Sargent, Porter (Edward)
Seabury, David
Seymour, Charles
Shawkey, Morris Purdy obit
Shearer, Augustus H(unt) obit
Shuster, George N(auman)
Smith, Roy Burnett obit
Stuart, Duane Reed obit
Thompson, James Westfall obit
Thorndike, Edward L(ee)
Vincent, George Edgar obit
Wilson, George Arthur obit
Wilson, H(alsey) W(illiam)
Winsor, Frederick obit

Engineering

Acheson, Albert R(obert) obit
Adams, Joseph H(enry) obit
Alexander, Harry Held obit
Baker, Charles Whiting obit
Berg, Ernst J(ulius) obit
De Forest, Lee
Dennis, Olive Wetzel
Douglas, Walter J. obit
Eidmann, Frank Lewis obit
Emerson, Victor Lee obit
Emmet, William L(eRoy) obit
Farny, George W(imbor) obit
French, Hollis obit
Goldmark, Henry obit
Gresley, Sir (Herbert) Nigel obit
Grimshaw, Robert obit
Hovey, Otis Ellis obit
Imlay, L(orin) E(verett) obit
Raver, Paul J(erome)
Reed, James, Sr. obit
Reeve, Sidney A(rmor) obit
Stillwell, Lewis Buckley obit
Stout, William Bushnell
Terzian, Harutyun G. obit
Webb, Walter Loring obit
Welch, William A(ddams) obit

Weymouth, Frank E(lwin) obit
Wills, C. Harold obit

Government— International

(See also Diplomacy)

Aguirre Cerda, Pedro biog and obit
Alfonso XIII, Former King of Spain obit
Anderson, Sir John
Argeseanu, George obit
Arias, Arnulfo
Boris III, King of Bulgaria
Bracken, Brendan
Campinchi, César obit
Castillo, Ramón S.
Cecil of Essendon, Robert Arthur James Cecil, 1st Baron
Chiappe, Jean obit
Craigavon, James Craig, 1st Viscount obit
Cross, Ronald H(ibbert), 1st Baronet
Curtin, John
Darlan, Jean (Louis Xavier François)
Darré, R(ichard) Walther (Oskar)
Duncan, Sir Andrew Rae
Evans, Sir Edward R(atcliffe) G(arth) R(ussell)
Flandin, Pierre-Étienne
Frank, Hans
Goebbels, Joseph
Goering, Hermann (Wilhelm)
Guertner, Franz obit
Haile Selassie I, Emperor of Ethiopia
Hepburn, Mitchell F(rederick)
Hess, Rudolf
Himmler, Heinrich
Hore-Belisha, Leslie
Huntziger, Charles (Léon Clément) biog and obit
Hymans, Paul obit
Inönü, Ismet
Jónasson, Hermann
Jowitt, Sir William Allen
Kallio, Kyösti obit
Keynes, John Maynard
Korizis, Alexander biog and obit
Leathers, Frederick James, 1st Baron
Lescot, Élie
Lloyd of Dolobran, George Ambrose Lloyd, 1st Baron biog and obit
Lozovsky, S(olomon) A(bramovich)
Lyttelton, Oliver
Margesson, David
Matsuoka, Yôsuke
Menocal, Mario Garcia obit
Menzies, Robert G(ordon)
Metaxas, John obit
Moore-Brabazon, J(ohn) C(uthbert) T(heodore)

Nehru, Jawaharlal, Pandit
Otto of Austria, Archduke
Oumansky, Constantine (Alexandrovitch)
Papen, Franz von
Parmoor, Charles Alfred Cripps, 1st Baron obit
Paul, Prince of Yugoslavia
Philoff, Bogdan (Dimitrov)
Prajadhipok, Former King of Siam obit
Quezon, Manuel L(uis)
Ribbentrop, Joachim von
Rosenberg, Alfred
Ryti, Risto (Heikki)
Saionji, Kimmochi, Prince obit
Salazar, Antonio de Oliveira
Seyss-Inquart, Artur
Smuts, Jan Christiaan
Snell, Henry Snell, 1st Baron
Soong, T. V.
Stamp, Josiah Charles Stamp, 1st Baron obit
Stonehaven, John Lawrence Baird, 1st Viscount obit
Teixeira-Gomes, Manuel obit
Teleki, Paul, Count obit
Terboven, Josef
Titulescu, Nicolas obit
Tojo, Hideki
Tryon, George Clement Tryon, 1st Baron obit
Vansittart, Robert (Gilbert), 1st Baron
Wallace, (David) Euan obit
Wilhelm II, Former German Kaiser obit
Wilkinson, Ellen (Cicely)
Willingdon, Freeman Freeman-Thomas, 1st Marquess of obit

Government— United States

(See also Diplomacy)

Acheson, Dean (Gooderham)
Adkins, Charles obit
Allen, Florence (Ellinwood)
Barkley, Alben W(illiam)
Bell, Thomas M(ontgomery) obit
Biddle, Francis (Beverley)
Birdseye, Claude Hale obit
Black, Hugo (La Fayette)
Bolles, Stephen obit
Brandeis, Louis D(embitz) obit
Byrnes, James F(rancis)
Byron, William D(evereux) obit
Cammerer, Arno B(erthold) obit
Campbell, Philip P(itt) obit
Clark, Bennett Champ
Cohen, Benjamin V(ictor)
Collier, John
Connally, Tom
Connery, Lawrence J(oseph) obit
Coudert, Frederic René, Jr.

Currie, Lauchlin (Bernard)
Daugherty, Harry M(icajah) obit
Davis, William H(ammatt) obit
Devereaux, William Charles obit
Dirksen, Everett M(cKinley)
Donovan, William J(oseph)
Douglas, William O(rville)
Early, Stephen T.
Eccles, Marriner S(toddard)
Eicher, Edward C(layton)
Emmerson, Louis Lincoln obit
Esch, John J(acob) obit
Falkner, Roland Post obit
Fish, Hamilton
Fitzgibbons, John obit
Folger, A(lonzo) D(illard) obit
Frank, Jerome N(ew)
Frankfurter, Felix
Glass, Carter
Harriman, W(illiam) Averell
Harrison, Pat obit
Hawley, Willis C(hatman) obit
Hill, J(ohn) B(oynton) P(hilip) Clayton obit
Hopkins, Harry L(loyd)
Houston, Andrew Jackson obit
Hughes, Charles Evans
Ickes, Harold L(e Claire)
Johnson, Hiram (Warren)
Jones, Norman L. obit
Laffoon, Ruby obit
Lamberton, Robert Eneas obit
Land, Emory S(cott)
Lubin, Isador
Lumpkin, Alva M(oore) obit
McAdoo, William Gibbs obit
May, Andrew Jackson
Miller, Douglas (Phillips)
Minton, Sherman
Moore, R(obert) Walton obit
Nathan, Robert R(oy)
Nelson, Donald M(arr)
Nice, Harry (Whinna) obit
Nye, Gerald P(rentice)
O'Dwyer, William
Pardee, George C(ooper) obit
Patterson, Robert P(orter)
Pepper, Claude (Denson)
Phelan, Michael F(rancis) obit
Pierson, Warren Lee
Richards, John G(ardiner) obit
Roberts, Owen J(osephus)
Rockefeller, Nelson (Aldrich)
Sheppard, Morris obit
Simpson, Kenneth F(arrand) obit
Smith, Howard W(orth)
Smoot, Reed obit
Steelman, John R(oy)
Stockberger, W(arner) W.
Stone, Harlan Fiske
Strong, Lee A(bram) obit
Talmadge, Eugene
Taylor, Edward T(homas) obit
Thompson, George L. obit
Timberlake, Charles B(ateman) obit

Tobey, Charles W(illiam)
Tugwell, Rex(ford Guy)
Van Devanter, Willis obit
Van Wagoner, Murray D(elos)
Voorhis, Jerry
Wagner, Robert F(erdinand)
Wason, Edward H(ill) obit

Industry

Austin, Herbert Austin, 1st Baron obit
Baruch, Bernard M(annes)
Biggers, John D(avid)
Block, Paul obit
Camrose, William Ewert Berry, 1st Viscount
Chevrolet, Louis obit
Daché, Lilly
Davis, William Rhodes biog and obit
Draper, Dorothy (Tuckerman)
Field, Marshall, III
Fuller, S(amuel) R(ichard), Jr.
Fuller, Walter Deane
Goudy, Frederic W(illiam)
Grace, Eugene Gifford
Hart, Merwin K(imball)
Heckscher, August· obit
Hirst, Hugo Hirst, 1st Baron
James, Arthur Curtiss obit
Kemper, James S(cott)
Kirkus, Virginia
Loewy, Raymond (Fernand)
Meyer, Eugene
Nuffield, William Richard Morris, 1st Viscount
Odlum, Floyd B(ostwick)
Pew, Joseph N(ewton), Jr.
Rockefeller, John D(avison), Jr.
Schram, Emil
Selfridge, H(arry) Gordon
Strong, William McCreery obit
Swope, Gerard
Weir, Ernest T(ener)
Wilson, Charles E(rwin)
Wood, Robert E(lkington)

Journalism

Allen, Jay (Cooke, Jr.)
Allen, Robert Sharon See Pearson, D. A. R. and Allen, R. S.
Blake, Doris
Bliven, Bruce
Bridges, Robert obit
Byers, Margaretta
Dennis, Lawrence
Du Puy, William Atherton obit
Fougner, G. Selmer obit
Franklin, Jay
Gannett, Lewis (Stiles)
Gunther, John
Howard, Bart B. obit
Karsner, David obit
Kirkpatrick, Helen (Paull)
Lane, Gertrude B(attles) obit
Lewis, Sir Willmott (Harsant)

Luce, Henry R(obinson)
Mason, Joseph Warren Teets obit
Mowrer, Edgar Ansel
Packard, Eleanor
Pearson, Drew (Andrew Russell) and Allen, Robert (Sharon)
Porter, S(ylvia F(ield)
Post, Emily
Pyle, Ernie
Reid, Helen Rogers
Reynolds, Quentin (James)
Rice, Grantland
Robey, Ralph (West)
Rothermere, Harold Sidney Harmsworth, 1st Viscount obit
Russell, Charles (Edward) obit
Sanborn, (John) Pitts obit
Sheean, Vincent
Shirer, William L(awrence)
Snow, Edgar (Parks)
Sokolsky, George E(phraim)
Steell, Willis obit
Stockbridge, Frank Parker obit
Stout, Wesley Winans
Van Doren, Irita
Wile, Frederic William obit

Labor

Carey, James B(arron)
Citrine, Sir Walter (McLennan)
McNamara, James Barnabas obit
Mann, Tom obit
Murray, Philip
Quill, Michael J(oseph)
Reuther, Walter (Philip)

Law

Abbott, Edwin Milton obit
Buckner, Emory R(oy) obit
Carey, Charles Henry obit
Devaney, John Patrick obit
Heydt, Herman A(ugust) obit
Levinson, Salmon Oliver obit
Murphy, Franklin W(illiam) obit
Newbolt, Sir Francis George obit
O'Melveny, Henry W(illiam) obit
Ottinger, Nathan obit
Owens, Clarence Julian obit
Pace, Charles Ashford obit
Sherley, Swagar obit

Literature

Adams, James Truslow
Alegría, Ciro
Anderson, Sherwood obit
Attaway, William (Alexander)
Austin, F(rederick) Britten obit
Bacon, Leonard
Beals, Carleton
Becker, May Lamberton
Bemelmans, Ludwig

Benchley, Robert (Charles)
Benson, Sally
Brooks, Van Wyck
Brown, Helen Dawes obit
Burnett, Whit   See Foley, M. and Burnett, W.
Calverton, V(ictor) F(rancis) obit
Cerf, Bennett A(lfred)
Chadourne, Marc obit
Condon, Frank obit
Coxe, Howard (Cleveland) obit
Crow, Carl
De Long, Emma J. Wotton obit
Dunn, J(oseph) Allan (Elphinstone) obit
Estes, Harlow
Finger, Charles Joseph obit
Fishback, Margaret
Fitzgerald, F(rancis) Scott (Key) obit
Foley, Martha and Burnett, Whit
Gogarty, Oliver (St. John)
Goodrich, Arthur (Frederick) obit
Goodrich, Marcus (Aurelius)
Greenbie, Sydney
Gruber, Frank
Guest, Edgar A(lbert)
Haycraft, Howard
Higgins, Frederick Robert obit
Joyce, James obit
Kelly, Judith
Kilmer, Aline obit
Kraus, René
Laughlin, Clara Elizabeth obit
McGinley, Phyllis
McKenney, Eileen obit See West, N. obit
Mayne, Ethel C(olburn) obit
Millard, Bailey obit
Miller, Alice Duer
Mowat, Robert B(almain) obit
Nash, Ogden
Nutting, Wallace, Rev. obit
O'Brien, Edward J(oseph Harrington) obit
O'Hara, John (Henry)
Orton, Helen Fuller
Oxenham, John obit
Palencia, Isabel de
Poncins, Gontran (Jean-Pierre de Montaigne), Vicomte de
Pourtalès, Guy, Count de obit
Prévost, Marcel obit
Radziwill, Catherine, Princess obit
Rauschning, Hermann
Rhoades, Cornelia Harsen obit
Ridge, Lola obit
Roberts, Elizabeth Madox obit
Rockley, Alicia-Margaret Amherst, Baroness obit
Rourke, Constance Mayfield obit
Russell, Mary Annette Russell, Countess obit

Schulberg, Budd (Wilson)
Schuster, M(ax) Lincoln. See Simon, R. L. and Schuster, M. L.
Seldes, George
Simon, Richard L(eo) and Schuster, M(ax) Lincoln
Smedley, Constance obit
Sperry, Armstrong
Spring, Howard
Steen, Marguerite
Strawbridge, Anne West obit
Struther, Jan
Tagore, Sir Rabindranath obit
Taylor, Henry O(sborn) obit
Tomasi, Mari
Valtin, Jan
Vincent, Leon H(enry) obit
Walpole, Sir Hugh (Seymour) obit
Walsh, George Ethelbert obit
Walsh, William Thomas
West, Nathanael obit
Whipple, Maurine
Wolff, Maritta M.
Woolf, Virginia obit
Woollcott, Alexander

Medicine

Aughinbaugh, William (Edmund) obit
Banting, Sir Frederick Grant obit
Begg, Colin Luke obit
Benson, Francis Colgate, Jr. obit
Bliss, A(ndrew) Richard, Jr. obit
Bonine, Frederick N. obit
Browne, Dame Sidney Jane obit
Campbell, Willis C(ohoon) obit
Chapin, Charles Value obit
Colby, Charles DeWitt obit
Connell, Karl obit
Cunningham, William Francis obit
DeKleine, William
Fiske, James Porter obit
Ford, W(illiam) W(ebber) obit
Frank, Louis obit
Greenfield, Abraham Lincoln obit
Griffith, J(ohn) P(rice) Crozer obit
Hall, George W(ashington) obit
Hartwell, John A(ugustus) obit
Holland, Charles Thurstan obit
Horney, Karen
Horsfall, Frank L(appin), Jr.
Janssen, Charles L. obit
Kast, Ludwig W. obit
Krause, Allen K(ramer) obit
Kuhlmann, Frederick obit
Lahey, Frank H(oward)
Lambert, Sylvester Maxwell

Lewis, Dean (De Witt) obit
Lynch, William J(oseph) obit
Mailhouse, Max obit
Mallory, F(rank) B(urr) obit
Martin, Collier Ford obit
Mayo, Charles W(illiam)
Mead, Kate Campbell obit
Neuman, Leo Handel obit
Orr, H(iram) Winnett
Pease, Charles G(iffin) obit
Power, Sir D'Arcy obit
Ring, Barbara T(aylor) obit
Rogers, Mark Homer obit
Sakel, Manfred
Schilder, Paul Ferdinand obit
Shaw, Henry (Larned Keith) obit
Shine, F(rancis) W(ayles) obit
Stiles, Charles Wardell obit
Stone, Hannah (Mayer) obit
Talley, James (Ely) obit
Voronoff, Serge
Wadhams, Robert Pelton obit
Walsh, William Henry obit
Williams, William Robert obit
Zilboorg, Gregory

Military

Barratt, Sir Arthur Sheridan
Brooke, Sir Alan (Francis)
Brooke-Popham, Sir Robert (Moore)
Budenny, Semyon M(ikhailovich)
Chen Cheng
Cunningham, Sir Andrew Browne
Dill, Sir John G(reer)
Drum, Hugh A(loysius)
Graziani, Rodolfo
Hershey, Lewis B(laine)
Hodges, Courtney H.
Kriebel, Hermann obit
MacArthur, Douglas
Mackay, Sir Iven Giffard
Osborn, Frederick (Henry)
Osumi, Mineo Osumi, Baron obit
Peirse, Sir R(ichard) E(dmund) C(harles)
Portal, Sir Charles (Frederick Algernon)
Pound, Sir (Alfred) Dudley (Pickman Rogers)
Raeder, Erich
Rundstedt, Karl (Rudolf Gerd) von
Timoshenko, Semyon (Konstantinovich)
Towers, J(ohn) H(enry)
Trujillo Molina, Rafael L(éonidas)
Voroshilov, Klementii (Efremovich)
Wavell, Sir Archibald (Percival)

Motion Pictures

Abbott, Bud and Costello, Lou
Ayres, Agnes obit

Blackton, J(ames) Stuart   obit
Brennan, Walter (Andrew)
Cecil, Mary   obit
Clair, René
Collison, Wilson   obit
Cooper, Gary
Costello, Lou   See Abbott, B.
   and Costello, L.
Crosby, Bing
Darwell, Jane
Davis, Bette
De Vry, Herman A.   obit
Durbin, Deanna
Fairbanks, Douglas (Elton), Jr.
Fields, Stanley   obit
Ford, John
Forrest, Allan   obit
Gabin, Jean
Garland, Judy
Gordon, C(harles) Henry   obit
Grant, Cary
Hiller, Wendy
Hitchcock, Alfred (Joseph)
Johnson, Nunnally
Kanin, Garson
Karloff, Boris
La Cava, Gregory
Lawson, Mary   obit
Miranda, Carmen
Murray, Charlie   obit
Nichols, Dudley
Oberon, Merle
Parker, Barnett   obit
Porter, Edwin S.   obit
Richman, Charles J.   obit
Rogers, Ginger
Schertzinger, Victor   obit
Selznick, David O(liver)
Shannon, Peggy   obit
Stephenson, James   obit
Stewart, Donald Ogden
Stewart, James (Maitland)
Stowell, Clarence Warner   obit
Sturges, Preston
Toland, Gregg
Trumbo, Dalton
Walker, Stuart   obit
Zanuck, Darryl F(rancis)

Music

Adler, Guido   obit
Bada, Angelo   obit
Beecham, Sir Thomas, 2nd
   Baronet
Bigelow, William (Pingry)   obit
Bridge, Frank   obit
Buck, Gene
Burleigh, Harry T(hacker)
Burr, Henry   obit
Carmichael, Hoagy
Claussen, Julia   obit
Coates, John   obit
Coolidge, Elizabeth Sprague
Curran, Pearl Gildersleeve   obit
Danforth, William   obit
Davies, Sir (Henry) Walford
   obit
Duke, Vernon
Ellington, Duke
Grey, Clifford   obit

Handy, William C(hristopher)
Hanson, Howard (Harold)
Harty, Sir (Herbert) Hamilton
   obit
Hawkins, Erskine
Hill, Billy   obit
Hindemith, Paul
Honegger, Arthur
Huberman, Bronislaw
Johnson, Howard E.   obit
Kahn, Gus(tav Gerson)   obit
Kemp, Hal   obit
Kubelik, Jan   obit
Kyser, Kay
Lehmann, George   obit
Lehmann, Lotte
Levitzki, Mischa   obit
Lomax, Alan
Luckstone, Isidore   obit
Menuhin, Yehudi
Milhaud, Darius
Mitropoulos, Dimitri
Narelle, Marie   obit
Ormandy, Eugene
Paderewski, Ignace Jan   obit
Penn, Arthur A.   obit
Pinza, Ezio
Prokofiev, Serge (Sergeyevich)
Reiner, Fritz
Robeson, Paul (Bustill)
Scott, Raymond
Shaw, Artie
Shostakovich, Dmitri
Skilton, Charles Sanford   obit
Stevens, Risë
Stewart, William G(odman)
   obit
Still, William Grant
Stokowski, Leopold (Anton
   Stanislaw)
Weill, Kurt

Radio

Adams, Franklin P(ierce)
Allen, Fred
Benny, Jack
Berg, Gertrude
Bernie, Ben
Bowes, Edward
Cantor, Eddie
Chester, Edmund
Crossley, Archibald M(addock)
Damerel, Donna   obit
Fadiman, Clifton
Frederick, John T(owner)
Graser, Earle W.   obit
Grauer, Ben(nett Franklin)
Heatter, Gabriel
Hope, Bob
Jones, Billy   obit
McBride, Mary Margaret
McGee, Fibber and McGee,
   Molly
McGee, Molly   See McGee, F.
   and McGee, M.
Penner, Joe   obit
Schechter, A(bel) A(lan)
Steel, Johannes
Stern, Bill
Walter, Wilmer   obit

Religion

Aked, Charles F(rederic), Rev.
   obit
Booth, Evangeline (Cory)
Brewster, Benjamin, Bishop   obit
Brewster, Chauncey Bunce,
   Bishop   obit
Candler, Warren A(kin), Bishop
   obit
Clinchy, Everett R(oss), Rev.
Copeland, Benjamin, Rev.   obit
Daly, Thomas A., Father   obit
Dinsmore, Charles Allen, Rev.
   obit
Divine, Frank H(enry), Rev.
   obit
Du Bose, Horace Mellard,
   Bishop   obit
Fagnani, Charles P(rospero),
   Rev.   obit
Fitzpatrick, George L., Mgr.
   obit
Flanagan, E(dward) J(oseph),
   Mgr.
Fredman, Samuel, Rabbi   obit
Greenway, Walter Burton, Rev.
   obit
Grieff, Joseph Nicholas, Mgr.
   obit
Hall, Frank Oliver, Rev.   obit
Hickey, Thomas F., Archbishop
   obit
Holmes, John Haynes, Rev.
Idleman, Finis Schuyler, Rev.
   obit
Irvine, Alexander Fitzgerald,
   Rev.   obit
Israel, Edward L., Rabbi   obit
Jones, Rufus M(atthew)
Kagawa, Toyohiko
Kašpar, Karl, Cardinal   obit
Kunz, Alfred A(ugustus)
Lang, Cosmo Gordon, Arch-
   bishop of Canterbury
Lauri, Lorenzo, Cardinal   obit
Leonard, Edward F., Mgr.   obit
Mead, Charles Larew, Bishop
   obit
Merriam, George Ernest, Rev.
   obit
Mosher, Gouverneur Frank,
   Bishop   obit
Niebuhr, Reinhold, Rev.
O'Connell, William (Henry),
   Cardinal
Pius XII, Pope
Scherer, Paul (Ehrman), Rev.
Schulte, Karl Joseph, Cardinal
   obit
Sheen, Fulton J(ohn), Mgr.
Silver, Abba Hillel, Rabbi
Strömberg, Leonard, Rev.   obit
Upham, Francis Bourne, Rev.
   obit
Warren, Harry Marsh, Rev.
   obit
West, Annie Blythe   obit
Wise, Stephen S(amuel),
   Rabbi

Science

Amsden, Charles (Avery) obit
Andrews, Roy Chapman
Armour, Allison V(incent) obit
Arsonval, Jacques Arsène d' obit
Atwell, Wayne J(ason) obit
Barber, Mary I(sabel)
Beebe, William
Benedict, Ruth
Blakeslee, A(lbert) F(rancis)
Bodansky, Meyer obit
Brooks, Matilda M(oldenhauer)
Burwash, Lachlin Taylor obit
Cannon, Annie J(ump) obit
Clemensen, Erik Christian obit
Compton, Karl T(aylor)
Dubois, Eugène obit
Eddington, Sir Arthur (Stanley)
Einstein, Albert
Ellis, Carleton obit
Evans, Sir Arthur (John) obit
Fish, Marie Poland
Fisher, Clarence S(tanley) obit
Frazer, Sir James (George) obit
Freundlich, Herbert (Max Finlay) obit
Granger, Walter obit
Haas, Arthur E(rich) obit
Hill, Justina Hamilton
Hill, Robert (Thomas) obit
Hogben, Lancelot (Thomas)
Hoxie, Charles A. obit
Hrdlička, Aleš
Infeld, Leopold
Jeans, Sir James Hopwood
Jordan, Frank C(raig) obit
Langmuir, Arthur Comings obit
Leech, Paul Nicholas obit
Ley, Willy
Makemson, Maud W(orcester)
Malinowski, Bronislaw
Miller, Dayton C(larence) obit
Moën, Lars
Morton, James F(erdinand) obit
Noble, Gladwyn Kingsley obit
Noyes, William A(lbert) obit
Pearl, Raymond obit
Plaskett, John S(tanley) obit
Rusby, Henry H(urd) obit
Sabatier, Paul obit
Schlink, Frederick John
Shapley, Harlow
Simonds, Frederic W(illiam) obit
Swann, W(illiam) F(rancis) G(ray)
Tennent, David Hilt obit
Thompson, Reginald Campbell obit

Urey, Harold C(layton)
Whitford, Harry Nichols obit
Wick, Frances G(ertrude) obit
Wilkins, T(homas) Russell obit
Wright, Berlin H(art) obit

Social Service

Abbott, Edith
Baden-Powell of Gilwell, Robert Stephenson Smyth Baden-Powell, 1st Baron obit
Barnett, Eugene E(pperson)
Beard, Daniel Carter obit
Blatch, Harriot Stanton obit
Clay, Laura obit
Evans, Anne obit
Geer, Alpheus obit
Hall, George A(lbert) obit
Hesselgren, Kerstin
Johnson, Alexander obit
Lawes, Lewis E(dward)
Monsky, Henry
Parsons, Herbert Collins obit
Resnick, Louis obit
Roche, Josephine (Aspinwall)
Schoff, Hannah Kent obit
Swift, Ernest John obit
Wakefield, Charles Cheers Wakefield, 1st Viscount obit
Welsh, Herbert obit
Young, Rose (Emmet) obit

Sports

Budge, Donald
Conn, Billy
DiMaggio, Joe
Feller, Bob
Gehrig, Lou obit
Jenkins, Lew
Lasker, Emanuel obit
Leahy, Frank (William)
McCarthy, Clem
Ott, Mel(vin Thomas)
Rice, Gregory
Ruffing, Charles H(erbert)
Schneider, Hannes
Wyatt, John Whitlow

Theatre

Anderson, Judith
Bach, Reginald obit
Bankhead, Tallulah (Brockman)
Barrymore, Ethel
Beck, Martin obit
Bickel, George L. obit
Carle, Richard obit
Chapman, Blanche obit
Conness, Robert obit
Cornell, Katharine

Coward, Noel (Pierce)
Crouse, Russel
Cushing, Charles C(yprian) S(trong) obit
Dolly, Jenny obit
Dunham, Katherine
Eltinge, Julian obit
Fields, Gracie
Fields, Lew obit
Fitzgerald, Cissy obit
Fontanne, Lynn See Lunt, A. and Fontanne, L.
Franken, Rose
Franklin, Irene obit
Frohman, Daniel obit
Harris, Sam H(enry) obit
Hartwig, Walter obit
Hawley, H. Dudley obit
Hellman, Lillian
Hurok, S(olomon)
Karno, Fred obit
Kaufman, George S.
Kaye, Danny
Kozlenko, William
Lawford, Ernest obit
Leblanc, Georgette obit
Lee, Auriol obit
Leonard, Eddie obit
Leonidoff, Leon
Liebler, Theodore A. obit
Lunt, Alfred and Fontanne, Lynn
MacDonald, Cordelia Howard obit
McGuire, Dorothy
Merman, Ethel
Morrison, Adrienne obit
Murray, J. Harold obit
Odets, Clifford
Parke, William obit
Robinson, Bill
Shumlin, Herman (Elliott)
Swenson, Alfred G. obit
Tinney, Frank obit
Truex, Ernest
Ulrich, Charles (Kenmore) obit
Walter, Eugene obit
Waters, Ethel
Weaver, Affie obit
Welles, Orson
Williams, Emlyn
Williams, John D. obit
Wright, Huntley obit
Zorina, Vera

Other Professions

Bowman, George E(rnest) obit
Krivitsky, Walter G. obit
Marshall, Verne
Minor, Robert
Quidde, Ludwig obit
Roosevelt, Sara Delano obit
Thore, Wendell Phillips obit
Warner, Milo J(oseph)

CUMULATED INDEX—1940 AND 1941

This is a cumulation of all names which have appeared in the monthly issues of CURRENT BIOGRAPHY during 1940 and 1941.

All names marked 1940 appeared in the 1940 CURRENT BIOGRAPHY annual volume.

All names marked obit are obituary notices.

Abbott, Bud and Costello, Lou 1941
Abbott, Edith 1941
Abbott, Edwin Milton obit 1941
Abbott, George 1940
Abbott, Robert Sengstacke obit 1940
Abetz, Otto 1941
Acheson, Albert R(obert) obit 1941
Acheson, Dean (Gooderham) 1941
Adamic, Louis 1940
Adams, Franklin P(ierce) 1941
Adams, James Truslow 1941
Adams, Joseph H(enry) obit 1941
Adams, Thomas obit 1940
Addington, Sarah obit 1940
Addis Ababa, Pietro Badoglio, Duca d' 1940
Additon, Henrietta Silvis 1940
Adkins, Charles obit 1941
Adler, Cyrus obit 1940
Adler, Guido obit 1941
Adler, Harry Clay obit 1940
Adler, Mortimer Jerome 1940
Adrian, (Gilbert) 1941
Aguirre Cerda, Pedro biog and obit 1941
Aitken, William Maxwell, 1st Baron Beaverbrook See Beaverbrook, W. M. A., 1st Baron
Aked, Charles F(rederic), Rev. obit 1941
Alain, (Daniel A.) 1941
Aldrich, Chester Holmes obit 1941
Aldrich, Winthrop Williams 1940
Alegría, Ciro 1941
Alexander, Albert Victor 1940
Alexander, Harry Held obit 1941
Alfonso XIII, Former King of Spain obit 1941
Allen, Florence (Ellinwood) 1941
Allen, Fred 1941
Allen, Gracie 1940
Allen, Jay (Cooke, Jr.) 1941
Allen, Joel Nott obit 1940
Allen, Robert Sharon See Pearson, D. A. R. and Allen, R. S.
Allyn, Lewis B. obit 1940
Almazán, Juan Andreu 1940
Alsberg, Carl Lucas obit 1940
Altenburg, Alexander obit 1940
Alter, George Elias obit 1940

Amherst, Alicia-Margaret, Baroness Rockley See Rockley, A.-M. A., Baroness obit
Amsden, Charles (Avery) obit 1941
Amsterdam, Birdie 1940
Andersen, Hendrik Christian obit 1941
Anderson, Abraham Archibald obit 1940
Anderson, George Everett obit 1940
Anderson, Sir John 1941
Anderson, John Crawford obit 1940
Anderson, Judith 1941
Anderson, Marian 1940
Anderson, Mary 1940
Anderson, Mary See Navarro, M. de obit
Anderson, Sherwood obit 1941
Andrews, Roy Chapman 1941
Angell, James Rowland 1940
Antonescu, Ion 1940
Archbishop of Canterbury See Lang, C. G., Archbishop of Canterbury
Arco, Georg Wilhelm Alexander Hans, Graf von obit 1940
Argeseanu, George obit 1941
Arias, Arnulfo 1941
Armfield, Anne Constance See Smedley, C. obit
Armour, Allison V(incent) obit 1941
Armstrong, Edwin Howard 1940
Arnold, Thurman Wesley 1940
Aronson, Louis V. obit 1940
Arsonval, Jacques Arsène d' obit 1941
Ashmun, Margaret Eliza obit 1940
Astor, Nancy Witcher, Viscountess 1940
Atalena, pseud. See Jabotinsky, V. E. obit
Atherton, Gertrude 1940
Attaway, William (Alexander) 1941
Attlee, Clement Richard 1940
Atwell, Wayne J(ason) obit 1941
Aughinbaugh, William (Edmund) obit 1941
Aulaire, Ingri d' and Aulaire, Edgar, Parin d' 1940
Austin, F(rederick) Britten obit 1941
Austin, Herbert Austin, 1st Baron obit 1941
Austin, William Lane 1940

Avenol, Joseph Louis Anne 1940
Aydelotte, Frank 1941
Ayres, Agnes obit 1941
Ayres, Leonard Porter 1940
Azaña, Manuel obit 1940

Baca-Flor, Carlos obit 1941
Bach, Reginald obit 1941
Bachrach, Elise Wald obit 1940
Bacon, George P(reston) obit 1941
Bacon, Leonard 1941
Bacon, Peggy 1940
Bada, Angelo obit 1941
Baden-Powell of Gilwell, Robert Stephenson Smyth Baden-Powell, 1st Baron obit 1941
Badoglio, Pietro See Addis Ababa, P. B., Duca d'
Baer, William J(acob) obit 1941
Bailey, Sir Abe, 1st Baronet obit 1940
Bailey, Guy Winfred obit 1940
Baird, John Lawrence, 1st Viscount Stonehaven See Stonehaven, J. L. B., 1st Viscount obit
Baker, Asa George obit 1940
Baker, Charles Whiting obit 1941
Baker, Ray Stannard [David Grayson, pseud.] 1940
Balbo, Italo obit 1940
Baldwin, Roger Nash 1940
Bampton, Rose 1940
Bankhead, Tallulah (Brockman) 1941
Bankhead, William Brockman biog and obit 1940
Banning, Margaret Culkin 1940
Banting, Sir Frederick Grant obit 1941
Barber, Mary I(sabel) 1941
Barbirolli, John 1940
Barclay, McClelland 1940
Barkley, Alben W(illiam) 1941
Barlow, Howard 1940
Barnard, James Lynn obit 1941
Barnett, Eugene E(pperson) 1941
Barney, Samuel E. obit 1940
Barnouw, Erik 1940
Barr, Frank Stringfellow 1940
Barratt, Sir Arthur Sheridan 1941
Barrère, Camille Eugène Pierre obit 1940
Barrett, Wilton Agnew biog and obit 1940
Barringer, Emily Dunning 1940
Barringer, Paul Brandon obit 1941

Barrow, Joseph Louis　See Louis J.

Barry, Patrick Frank, Bishop obit 1940

Barrymore, Ethel 1941

Barthé, Richmond 1940

Bartók, Béla 1940

Bartol, William Cyrus obit 1940

Barton, George obit 1940

Baruch, Bernard M(annes) 1941

Bates, Ernest Sutherland biog and obit 1940

Bates, Granville obit 1940

Batista Y Zaldivar, Fulgencio 1940

Baur, Bertha obit 1940

Beals, Carleton 1941

Beard, Charles A(ustin) and Beard, Mary 1941

Beard, Daniel Carter obit 1941

Beard, Mary See Beard, C. A. and Beard, M.

Beauchamp, Mary Annette See Russell, M. A. R., Countess obit

Beaverbrook, William Maxwell Aitken, 1st Baron 1940

Beck, Martin obit 1941

Becker, May Lamberton 1941

Bedford, Herbrand Arthur Russell, 11th Duke of　obit 1940

Beebe, Lucius 1940

Beebe, William 1941

Beecham, Sir Thomas, 2nd Baronet 1941

Beer, Thomas obit 1940

Begg, Alexander Swanson obit 1940

Begg, Colin Luke obit 1941

Bel Geddes, Norman　See Geddes, N. B.

Bell, Thomas M(ontgomery) obit 1941

Bemelmans, Ludwig 1941

Benchley, Belle Jennings 1940

Benchley, Robert (Charles) 1941

Benedict, Ruth 1941

Benjamin, William Evarts obit 1940

Bennett, James O'Donnell biog and obit 1940

Benny, Jack 1941

Benson, Allan Louis obit 1940

Benson, Edward Frederic biog and obit 1940

Benson, Francis Colgate, Jr. obit 1941

Benson, John 1940

Benson, Sally 1941

Bentley, Irene obit 1940

Benton, Thomas Hart 1940

Berg, Ernst J(ulius) obit 1941

Berg, Gertrude 1941

Berg, Irving H(usted) obit 1941

Berg, Patricia Jane 1940

Bergman, Ingrid 1940

Bergson, Henri (Louis) obit 1941

Berle, Adolf Augustus, Jr. 1940

Bernard, Émile obit 1941

Bernie, Ben 1941

Berry, Martha McChesney 1940

Berry, William Ewert, 1st Viscount Camrose　See Camrose, W. E. B., 1st Viscount

Besteiro Y Fernandez, Julian obit 1940

Bethe, Hans Albrecht 1940

Bevin, Ernest 1940

Bevis, Howard Landis 1940

Bickel, George L. obit 1941

Biddle, Anthony J(oseph) Drexel, Jr. 1941

Biddle, Francis (Beverley) 1941

Bigelow, William (Pingry) obit 1941

Biggers, John D(avid) 1941

Binet-Valmer, Jean obit 1940

Binkley, Robert Cedric obit 1940

Birdseye, Claude Hale obit 1941

Birge, Raymond Thayer 1940

Bishop, William Avery 1941

Black, Alexander obit 1940

Black, Hugo (La Fayette) 1941

Blackton, J(ames) Stuart obit 1941

Blake, Doris 1941

Blake, Nicholas, pseud.　See Day-Lewis, C.

Blaker, Richard obit 1940

Blakeslee, A(lbert) F(rancis) 1941

Blanch, Arnold 1940

Blatch, Harriot Stanton obit 1941

Blatchley, Willis Stanley obit 1940

Blau, Bela obit 1940

Bliss, A(ndrew) Richard, Jr. obit 1941

Blitzstein, Marc 1940

Bliven, Bruce 1941

Bloch, Charles Edward obit 1940

Block, Paul obit 1941

Block, Rudolph　See Lessing, B., pseud. obit

Blodgett, Katharine Burr 1940

Blum, Léon 1940

Blumenthal, George obit 1941

Blumer, George Alder obit 1940

Boas, Franz 1940

Bodansky, Meyer obit 1941

Bodanzky, Artur obit 1940

Boggs, Charles Reid obit 1940

Bolles, Stephen obit 1941

Bolton, Frances Payne 1940

Bonci, Alessandro obit 1940

Bonham, Milledge Louis, Jr. obit 1941

Bonine, Frederick N. obit 1941

Booker, Edna Lee 1940

Booth, Ballington obit 1940

Booth, Evangeline (Cory) 1941

Borah, William Edgar biog and obit 1940

Borglum, Gutzon obit 1941

Boris III, King of Bulgaria 1941

Bosch, Carl obit 1940

Bourke-White, Margaret　See White, M. B.

Bourne, Jonathan, Jr.　obit 1940

Bower, Bertha Muzzy, pseud. of Bertha Muzzy Sinclair-Cowan obit 1940

Bowers, Claude G(ernade) 1941

Bowes, Edward 1941

Bowes, Major　See Bowes, E.

Bowman, George E(rnest) obit 1941

Bracken, Brendan 1941

Bradbury, James H. obit 1940

Brainerd, Norman, pseud.　See Fuller, S. R., Jr.

Brandeis, Louis D(embitz) obit 1941

Brandenburg, William A. obit 1940

Branly, Edouard obit 1940

Brauchitsch, Heinrich Alfred Hermann Walther von 1940

Breckenridge, Lester Paige obit 1940

Brennan, Walter (Andrew) 1941

Breuer, Marcel 1941

Brewster, Benjamin, Bishop obit 1941

Brewster, Chauncey Bunce, Bishop obit 1941

Bridge, Frank obit 1941

Bridges, Alfred Bryant Renton　See Bridges, H.

Bridges, Harry 1940

Bridges, Robert obit 1941

Bristow, Gwen 1940

Bronshtein, Lev Davidovich　See Trotsky, L. obit

Brook, Alexander 1941

Brooke, Sir Alan (Francis) 1941

Brooke-Popham, Sir Robert (Moore) 1941

Brookes, George S., Rev. 1940

Brooks, Matilda M(oldenhauer) 1941

Brooks, Robert C(larkson) obit 1941

Brooks, Van Wyck 1941

Broun, Heywood　obit 1940

Brown, A. Ten Eyck obit 1940

Brown, Carleton (Fairchild) obit 1941

Brown, Charles H(arvey) 1941

Brown, Francis Shunk obit 1940

Brown, Helen Dawes obit 1941

Brown, John Franklin obit 1940

Browne, Dame Sidney Jane obit 1941

Brownson, Josephine 1940

Brush, George de Forest obit 1941

Bryan, Julien Hequembourg 1940

Bryce, Elizabeth Marion, Viscountess obit 1940

Bryson, Lyman 1940

Buchan, John, 1st Baron Tweedsmuir biog and obit 1940

Buchanan, Thomas Drysdale obit 1940

Buchman, Frank Nathan Daniel, Rev. 1940

Buck, Gene 1941

Buckner, Emory R(oy) obit 1941

Budd, Ralph 1940

Budenny, Semyon M(ikhailovich) 1941

Budge, Donald 1941

Buffum, Charles A(lbert) obit 1941

Bulgakov, Michael Afanasievich biog and obit 1940

Bullitt, William Christian 1940

Bunau-Varilla, Philippe obit 1940

Burdick, Charles Kellogg obit 1940

Burke, Edmund J., Father obit 1941

Burke, Edward Raymond 1940

Burleigh, George William obit 1940

Burleigh, Harry T(hacker) 1941

Burliuk, David 1940

Burnett, Whit See Foley, M. and Burnett, W.

Burnham, James 1941

Burns, George See Allen, G.

Burns, James Aloysius, Father obit 1940

Burr, Henry obit 1941

Burton, Charles Emerson, Rev. obit 1940

Burton, Lewis William, Bishop obit 1940

Burton, Richard obit 1940

Burwash, Lachlin Taylor obit 1941

Bush, Vannevar 1940

Bush, Wendell T. obit 1941

Butler, Nevile (Montagu) 1941

Butler, Nicholas Murray 1940

Butler, Smedley Darlington obit 1940

Byers, Margaretta 1941

Byrnes, James F(rancis) 1941

Byron, William D(evereux) obit 1941

Cahill, Michael Harrison obit 1940

Cairns, Huntington 1940

Caldwell, Erskine 1940

Caldwell, Mrs. Erskine See White, M. B.

Caldwell, Taylor 1940

Calfee, John Edward obit 1941

Callow, John Michael obit 1940

Calverton, V(ictor) F(rancis) obit 1941

Camac, Charles Nicoll Bancker obit 1940

Camacho, Manuel Avila 1940

Cammerer, Arno B(erthold) obit 1941

Campbell, E. Simms 1941

Campbell, Sir Gerald 1941

Campbell, Mrs. Patrick obit 1940

Campbell, Philip P(itt) obit 1941

Campbell, Willis C(ohoon) obit 1941

Campinchi, César obit 1941

Camrose, William Ewert Berry, 1st Viscount 1941

Canavan, Joseph J. obit 1940

Canby, Al H. obit 1940

Candler, Warren A(kin), Bishop obit 1941

Cannon, Annie J(ump) obit 1941

Canterbury, Archbishop of See Lang, C. G., Archbishop of Canterbury

Canton, Allen A. obit 1940

Cantor, Eddie 1941

Cantu, Giuseppe obit 1940

Carewe, Edwin obit 1940

Carey, Charles Henry obit 1941

Carey, James B(arron) 1941

Carle, Richard obit 1941

Carmichael, Hoagy 1941

Carmody, John Michael 1940

Carnegie, Dale 1941

Carol II 1940

Carpenter, Sir Henry Cort Harold obit 1940

Carpenter, Lewis Van obit 1940

Carrel, Alexis 1940

Carson, John Renshaw obit 1940

Carter, John Franklin, Jr. See Franklin, J.

Carton de Wiart, Adrian 1940

Carver, George Washington 1940

Casey, Edward Pearce obit 1940

Casey, Richard Gardiner 1940

Castillo, Ramón S. 1941

Catt, Carrie Chapman 1940

Caturáni, Michele Gaëtano obit 1940

Cauldwell, Leslie Giffen obit 1941

Cavero, Salvador obit 1940

Cecil, Mary obit 1941

Cecil, Robert Arthur James, 1st Baron Cecil of Essendon See Cecil of Essendon, R. A. J. C., 1st Baron

Cecil of Essendon, Robert Arthur James Cecil, 1st Baron 1941

Cerda, Pedro Aguirre See Aguirre Cerda, P.

Cerf, Bennett A(lfred) 1941

Chaddock, Robert Emmet obit 1940

Chadourne, Marc obit 1941

Chadwick, Helene obit 1940

Chamberlain, John Rensselaer 1940

Chamberlain, Neville obit 1940

Chamberlain, Paul Mellen obit 1940

Chang Shan-tze obit 1940

Chapin, Charles Value obit 1941

Chapin, James 1940

Chaplin, Charlie 1940

Chapman, Blanche obit 1941

Chappedelaine, Louis de obit 1940

Chase, Charley obit 1940

Chase, Edna Woolman 1940

Chase, Mary Ellen 1940

Chase, Stuart 1940

Chase, William Sheafe, Rev. obit 1940

Chen Cheng 1941

Cherne, Leo M. 1940

Chesser, Elizabeth Sloan obit 1940

Chester, Edmund 1941

Chevrolet, Louis obit 1941

Chiang Kai-shek 1940

Chiang Kai-shek, Mme. See Chiang M.

Chiang Mei-ling [Mme. Chiang Kai-shek] 1940

Chiappe, Jean obit 1941

Chotzinoff, Samuel 1940

Christie, Agatha 1940

Chrysler, Walter Percy obit 1940

Churchill, Berton obit 1940

Churchill, Winston Leonard Spencer 1940

Ciano, Galeazzo, Conte 1940

Citrine, Sir Walter (McLennan) 1941

Clair, René 1941

Clapper, Raymond 1940

Clark, Bennett Champ 1941

Clark, Marguerite obit 1940

Claussen, Julia obit 1941

Clay, Laura obit 1941

Clemensen, Erik Christian obit 1941

Clinchy, Everett R(oss), Rev. 1941

Clive, Edward E. obit 1940

Coates, John obit 1941

Cochran, Charles Blake 1940

Cochran, Jacqueline 1940

Coffin, Haskell obit 1941

Cohen, Benjamin V(ictor) 1941

Colby, Charles DeWitt obit 1941

Cole, Jessie Duncan Savage obit 1940

Coleman, Georgia obit 1940

Collier, John 1941

Collins, Eddie obit 1940

Collins, Edward Day obit 1940

Collins, George Lewis obit 1940

Collins, Lorin Cone obit 1940

Collison, Wilson obit 1941

Colquitt, Oscar Branch obit 1940

Companys, Luis obit 1940

Compton, Arthur Holly 1940

Compton, Karl T(aylor) 1941

Conant, James B(ryant) 1941

Condon, Frank obit 1941

Conley, William Gustavus obit 1940

Conn, Billy 1941

Connah, Douglas John obit 1941

Connally, Thomas Terry See Connally, T.

Connally, Tom 1941

Connell, Karl obit 1941

Connery, Lawrence J(oseph) obit 1941

Conness, Robert obit 1941

Connolly, Walter obit 1940

Converse, Frederick Shepherd obit 1940

Cook, Frederick Albert obit 1940

Coolidge, Dane obit 1940

Coolidge, Elizabeth Sprague 1941

Cooper, Alfred Duff 1940

Cooper, Courtney Ryley obit 1940

Cooper, Gary 1941

Copeland, Benjamin, Rev. obit 1941

Copland, Aaron 1940

Corcoran, Thomas Gardiner 1940

Cordier, Constant obit 1940

Corey, Paul 1940

Cornell, Katharine 1941

Cortelyou, George Bruce obit 1940

Corwin, Norman 1940

Garland, Judy 1941
Garvey, Marcus obit 1940
Gates, William obit 1940
Gatti-Casazza, Giulio obit 1940
Gaulle, Charles de   See De Gaulle, C.
Gauss, Clarence E(dward) 1941
Gauthier, Joseph Alexandre George, Archbishop obit 1940
Gayda, Virginio 1940
Geddes, Norman Bel 1940
Geer, Alpheus obit 1941
Gehrig, Lou biog 1940 obit 1941
George, Albert Bailey obit 1940
Géraud, André [Pertinax, pseud.] 1940
Gesell, Arnold 1940
Gibbs, George obit 1940
Gibson, Ernest Willard obit 1940
Gideonse, Harry David 1940
Gilbreth, Lillian Evelyn 1940
Gilder, Robert Fletcher obit 1940
Gildersleeve, Virginia C(rocheron) 1941
Gill, Eric obit 1941
Gillespie, Louis John obit 1941
Gilmer, Elizabeth Meriwether See Dix, D., pseud.
Gilmore, Melvin Randolph obit 1940
Gilmour, Sir John obit 1940
Ginsberg, Samuel See Krivitsky, W. G. obit
Glass, Carter 1941
Glenn, Mary Wilcox obit 1940
Goebbels, Joseph 1941
Goering, Hermann (Wilhelm) 1941
Goetz, George See Calverton, V. F. obit
Gogarty, Oliver (St. John) 1941
Goldenweiser, Alexander A. obit 1940
Goldman, Emma obit 1940
Goldmark, Henry obit 1941
Goldmark, Peter Carl 1940
Goldsmith, Lester Morris 1940
Goler, George Washington obit 1940
Gomá Y Tomás, Isidoro, Cardinal obit 1940
Goodrich, Arthur (Frederick) obit 1941
Goodrich, James Putnam obit 1940
Goodrich, Marcus (Aurelius) 1941
Gordon, C(harles) Henry obit 1941
Gordon, John Sloan obit 1940
Göring, Hermann Wilhelm See Goering, H. W.
Gorman, Herbert Sherman 1940
Gort, John Standish Surtees Prendergast Vereker, 6th Viscount 1940
Goudge, Elizabeth 1940
Goudy, Frederic W(illiam) 1941
Grace, Eugene Gifford 1941
Grafton, Samuel 1940
Graham, Frank P(orter) 1941
Granger, Walter obit 1941

Grant, Cary 1941
Grant, Ethel Watts Mumford See Mumford, E. W. obit
Grant, Robert obit 1940
Graser, Earle W. obit 1941
Grauer, Ben(nett Franklin) 1941
Graves, Frederick Rogers, Bishop obit 1940
Graves, William Sidney obit 1940
Grayson, David, pseud. See Baker, R. S.
Graziani, Rodolfo 1941
Green, Julian 1940
Greenbie, Sydney 1941
Greene, Frank Russell obit 1940
Greenfield, Abraham Lincoln obit 1941
Greenough, Carroll obit 1941
Greenway, Walter Burton, Rev. obit 1941
Greenwood, Arthur 1940
Grenfell, Sir Wilfred Thomason obit 1940
Gresley, Sir (Herbert) Nigel obit 1941
Grew, Joseph Clark 1941
Grey, Clifford obit 1941
Grieff, Joseph Nicholas, Mgr. obit 1941
Griffith, J(ohn) P(rice) Crozer obit 1941
Grimshaw, Robert obit 1941
Griswold, Augustus H. obit 1940
Grizodubova, Valentina (Stepanovna) 1941
Grofé, Ferde 1940
Gropius, Walter (Adolf Georg) 1941
Gropper, William 1940
Gross, Chaim 1941
Gruber, Frank 1941
Gruenberg, Sidonie Matsner 1940
Gruppe, Charles Paul obit 1940
Guertner, Franz obit 1941
Guest, Edgar A(lbert) 1941
Guillaumat, Marie Louis Adolphe obit 1940
Guise, Jean Pierre Clément Marie, Duc de obit 1940
Gunter, Julius Caldeen obit 1940
Gunther, John 1941
Guthrie, Charles Ellsworth, Rev. obit 1940
Guthrie, William Buck obit 1940

Haakon VII, King of Norway 1940
Haas, Arthur E(rich) obit 1941
Hackett, Horatio B(alch) obit 1941
Haddon, Alfred Cort obit 1940
Hadfield, Sir Robert Abbott, 1st Baronet obit 1940
Haggard, William David obit 1940
Haile Selassie I, Emperor of Ethiopia 1941
Hainisch, Michael obit 1940
Haldane, John Burdon Sanderson 1940
Hale, Arthur, Rev. obit 1940
Halifax, Edward Frederick Lindley Wood, 3rd Viscount 1940

Hall, Frank O(liver), Rev. obit 1941
Hall, George A(lbert) obit 1941
Hall, George W(ashington) obit 1941
Hall, James obit 1940
Hambro, Carl Joachim 1940
Hamilton, George Livingston obit 1940
Hamlin, Clarence Clark obit 1940
Hammond, Aubrey Lindsay obit 1940
Handy, William C(hristopher) 1941
Hanson, Howard (Harold) 1941
Hanson, Ole obit 1940
Harada, Tasuku, Rev. obit 1940
Harden, Sir Arthur obit 1940
Hardy, Ashley Kingsley obit 1940
Harington, Sir Charles obit 1940
Harkness, Edward Stephen biog and obit 1940
Harlan, Otis obit 1940
Harmsworth, Harold Sidney, 1st Viscount Rothermere See Rothermere, H. S. H., 1st Viscount obit
Harper, Alexander James obit 1940
Harriman, Florence Jaffray Hurst 1940
Harriman, W(illiam) Averell 1941
Harrington, Francis Clark obit 1940
Harris, James Rendel obit 1941
Harris, Roy 1940
Harris, Sam H(enry) obit 1941
Harrison, Pat obit 1941
Hart, Basil Henry Liddell- See Liddell Hart, B. H.
Hart, Lorenz See Rodgers, R. and Hart, L.
Hart, Merwin K(imball) 1941
Hart, Moss 1940
Hartwell, John A(ugustus) obit 1941
Hartwig, Walter obit 1941
Harty, Sir (Herbert) Hamilton obit 1941
Hawes, Elizabeth 1940
Hawkins, Erskine 1941
Hawley, H. Dudley obit 1941
Hawley, Willis C(hatman) obit 1941
Haycraft, Howard 1941
Haynes, Roy Asa obit 1940
Hazard, Paul 1941
Hazen, Charles D(owner) obit 1941
Head, Sir Henry obit 1940
Heath, S. Burton 1940
Heatter, Gabriel 1941
Heckscher, August obit 1941
Hedin, Sven Anders 1940
Heidenstam, Verner von obit 1940
Hellman, Lillian 1941
Heming, Arthur Henry Howard obit 1940
Henderson, Leon 1940

Severance, H(arold) Craig obit 1941

Seversky, Alexander Procofieff de See De Seversky, A. P.

Sevier, Henry Hulme obit 1940

Seymour, Charles 1941

Seyss-Inquart, Artur 1941

Shambaugh, Benjamin Franklin obit 1940

Shannon, Peggy obit 1941

Shapley, Harlow 1941

Sharp, Harry Clay obit 1940

Shaw, Artie 1941

Shaw, Henry (Larned Keith) obit 1941

Shaw, Louis Agassiz obit 1940

Shawkey, Morris Purdy obit 1941

Shearer, Augustus H(unt) obit 1941

Sheean, Vincent 1941

Sheen, Fulton J(ohn), Mgr. 1941

Sheppard, Morris obit 1941

Sherley, Swagar obit 1941

Sherman, Frederic Fairchild obit 1940

Sherwood, Robert 1940

Shine, F(rancis) W(ayles) obit 1941

Shinn, Florence Scovel obit 1940

Shinn, Milicent Washburn obit 1940

Shirer, William L(awrence) 1941

Shostakovich, Dmitri 1941

Shoup, Oliver Henry obit 1940

Shumlin, Herman (Elliott) 1941

Shuster, George N(auman) 1941

Sigerist, Henry Ernest 1940

Sikorski, Wladyslaw 1940

Sikorsky, Igor Ivan 1940

Sillanpää, Frans Eemil 1940

Silver, Abba Hillel, Rabbi 1941

Silzer, George Sebastian obit 1940

Simmons, Furnifold McLendell obit 1940

Simon, John Allsebrook, 1st Viscount 1940

Simon, Richard L(eo) and Schuster, M(ax) Lincoln 1941

Simonds, Frederic W(illiam) obit 1941

Simpson, Kenneth F(arrand) obit 1941

Simpson, Helen de Guerry obit 1940

Sinclair, Sir Archibald, 4th Baronet 1940

Sinclair-Cowan, Bertha Muzzy See Bower, B. M., pseud. obit

Singer, Richard obit 1940

Skilton, Charles Sanford obit 1941

Sloan, Alfred Pritchard, Jr. 1940

Slye, Maud 1940

Smedley, Constance obit 1941

Smith, Clyde Harold obit 1940

Smith, Howard W(orth) 1941

Smith, Kate 1940

Smith, Roy Burnett obit 1941

Smith, Wilbur Fisk obit 1940

Smoot, Reed obit 1941

Smuts, Jan Christiaan 1941

Snell, Henry Snell, 1st Baron 1941

Snow, Edgar (Parks) 1941

Soglow, Otto 1940

Sokolsky, George E(phraim) 1941

Soong, T. V. 1941

Soukup, Frantisek obit 1940

Soyer, Isaac; Soyer, Moses; and Soyer, Raphael 1941

Spellman, Francis Joseph, Archbishop 1940

Spender, Stephen 1940

Sperry, Armstrong 1941

Sperti, George Speri 1940

Spiller, William Gibson obit 1940

Spitalny, Phil 1940

Spottswood, James obit 1940

Sprague, Embert Hiram obit 1940

Spring, Howard 1941

Spry, Constance 1940

Squires, Richard Anderson obit 1940

Stamp, Josiah Charles Stamp, 1st Baron obit 1941

Stanley, Freelan O. obit 1940

Stark, Harold Raynsford 1940

Stassen, Harold Edward 1940

Steel, Johannes 1941

Steell, Willis obit 1941

Steelman, John R(oy) 1941

Steen, Marguerite 1941

Steinbeck, John 1940

Steinberg, Hans Wilhelm 1940

Steinberg, Milton, Rabbi 1940

Steinhardt, Laurence A(dolph) 1941

Stekel, Wilhelm [Willy Bojan, Dr. Serenus, pseuds.] obit 1940

Stephens, Ward obit 1940

Stephenson, James obit 1941

Stern, Bill 1941

Stettinius, Edward Reilly, Jr. 1940

Steuer, Max David obit 1940

Stevens, Risë 1941

Stevenson, E. Robert 1940

Stewart, Donald Ogden 1941

Stewart, George Craig, Bishop obit 1940

Stewart, James (Maitland) 1941

Stewart, William G(odman) obit 1941

Stieglitz, Alfred 1940

Stiles, Charles Wardell obit 1941

Still, William Grant 1941

Stillwell, Lewis Buckley obit 1941

Stimson, Henry Lewis 1940

Stimson, Julia Catherine 1940

Stine, Charles Milton Altland 1940

Stockberger, W(arner) W. 1941

Stockbridge, Frank Parker obit 1941

Stoddard, Frederick Lincoln biog and obit 1940

Stokowski, Leopold (Anton Stanislaw) 1941

Stone, Hannah (Mayer) obit 1941

Stone, Harlan Fiske 1941

Stone, John Charles obit 1940

Stonehaven, John Lawrence Baird, 1st Viscount obit 1941

Stookey, Charley 1940

Storr, Vernon Faithfull, Rev. obit 1940

Stout, Wesley Winans 1941

Stout, William Bushnell 1941

Stowe, Leland 1940

Stowell, Clarence Warner obit 1941

Strasser, Otto 1940

Stravinsky, Igor 1940

Strawbridge, Anne West obit 1941

Streit, Clarence 1940

Strömberg, Leonard, Rev. obit 1941

Strong, Lee A(bram) obit 1941

Strong, William McCreery obit 1941

Struther, Jan 1941

Stuart, Duane Reed obit 1941

Stuart, James Everett obit 1941

Stuart, Jesse 1940

Sturges, Preston 1941

Suesse, Dana 1940

Suñer, Ramón Serrano See Serrano Suñer, R.

Sung, Tsu-wen See Soong, T. V.

Suydam, Edward Howard obit 1941

Swann, W(illiam) F(rancis) G(ray) 1941

Swenson, Alfred G. obit 1941

Swift, Ernest John obit 1941

Swing, Raymond Gram 1940

Switzer, George obit 1940

Swope, Gerard 1941

Szigeti, Joseph 1940

Szold, Henrietta 1940

Szostakovitch, Dimitri See Shostakovich, D.

Tabouis, Geneviève 1940

Taft, Robert Alphonso 1940

Tagore, Sir Rabindranath obit 1941

Tainter, Charles Sumner obit 1940

Talley, James (Ely) obit 1941

Talmadge, Eugene 1941

Tanner, John Henry obit 1940

Tate, Allen 1941

Taussig, Frank William obit 1940

Taylor, Deems 1940

Taylor, Edward T(homas) obit 1941

Taylor, Francis Henry 1940

Taylor, Henry O(sborn) obit 1941

Taylor, Myron Charles 1940

Taylor, Richard 1941

Teixeira-Gomes, Manuel obit 1941

Teleki, Paul, Count obit 1941

Templeton, Alec 1940

Tennent, David Hilt obit 1941

Terboven, Josef 1941

Terzian, Harutyun G. obit 1941

Tetrazzini, Luisa obit 1940

Thayer, Ernest Lawrence obit 1940

Thomas, Freeman Freeman-, 1st Marquess of Willingdon See Willingdon, F. F.-T., 1st Marquess of obit